TH
AMERICAN EPHEMERIS

for the

21st Century

2000-2050

at Noon

Revised & Expanded Third Edition

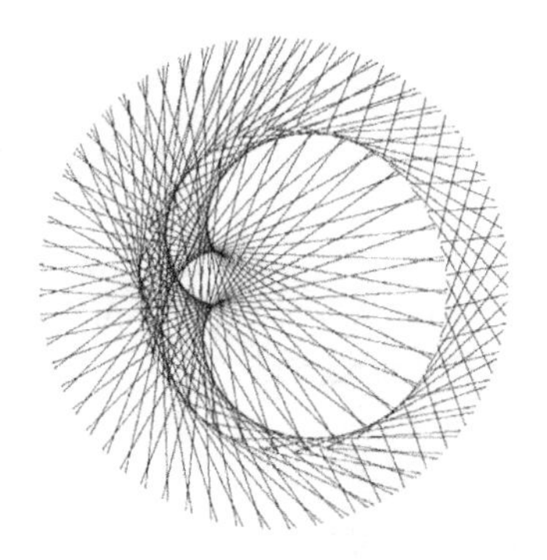

compiled and programmed by

Neil F. Michelsen

and

Rique Pottenger

ACS Publications
an imprint of Starcrafts LLC
New Hampshire

The American Ephemeris for the 21st Century
2000-2050 at Noon

Revised & Expanded Third Edition
First printing 2010

Expanded Second Edition
First printing 1997

First Edition 1982

Compiled and programmed by Neil F. Michelsen and Rique Pottenger

Cover design by Maria Kay Simms
The mandala used on the cover is Earth Mars, as computer plotted by Neil F. Michelsen for his book Tables of Planetary Phenomena

Introductory text by Maria Kay Simms
with technical assistance by Rique Pottenger

ISBN 978-1-934976-14-2

Published by ACS Publications, an imprint of Starcrafts LLC
PO Box 466, Exeter, NH 03833
334-A Calef Hwy, Epping, NH 03042
http://www.acspublications.com
http://www.starcraftspublishing.com
http://www.astrocom.com

Printed in the United States of America

Introduction to this Revised and Expanded Third Edition of *The American Ephemeris*

Technically, the new millennium began on January 1, 2001. Because the Gregorian calendar counts years from 1, the year 2000 was the final year of the 20sth century. The 21st century runs from 2001-2100. However, we are including the "bonus" year 2000 within this ephemeris, as well as in its prior incarnations, because that has consistently been the expressed preference of users since Neil F. Michelsen's first publication of his 21st Century ephemeris in 1982.

A Brief History of Publication of *The American Ephemeris*

Since the 1976 first edition of *The American Ephemeris, 1931-1980, The American Ephemeris for the 20th Century, 1900 to 2000* has been published in successive Midnight and Noon editions, each with revisions according to the latest and most accurate orbital data available. Since 1988, files and algorithms from Jet Propulsion Laboratory export ephemeris files have been used. Specialty versions have included *The American Heliocentric Ephemeris* and *The American Sidereal Ephemeris.*

In 1982 Neil F. Michelsen published his first 21st Century ephemeris. *The American Ephemeris for the 21st Century at Midnight.* This first edition included the entire century in a relatively small first printing, but at that time many users were not just quite ready to look so very far into the future and expressed to Neil their preference for a lighter and less costly option. In response, Neil programmed this 2000-2050 ephemeris, in both midnight and noon versions. Several years after Neil's 1990 passing, newer data called for an update, so the Expanded Second Edition was published in 1997, with revisions by Rique Pottenger.

The New American Ephemeris

In 2005, Maria Kay Simms, Trustee of The Michelsen-Simms Family Trust, proposed to ACS that a new revision of *The American Ephemeris for the 21st Century* should be published, and that it was time to once again expand it to the entire century. ACS declined to publish the full century, but provided a letter of permission for the Trust and Rique Pottenger to produce and publish a new full 21st century ephemeris, using Michelsen's programming routines, and the name *American Ephemeris* within its title. Subsequently, ***The New American Ephemeris for the 21st Century, 2000-2100 at Midnight, Michelsen Memorial Edition***, compiled and programmed by Rique Pottenger, based on the earlier work of Neil F. Michelsen, was published in 2006 by Starcrafts Publishing, the imprint of Starcrafts LLC, a business Simms had formed in New Hampshire.

This 2006 *New American Ephemeris* edition also includes a text section, partially in Michelsen's own writing and partially in the testimonials of others, that traces the earlier development of computer technology for astrologers and Michelsen's contribution to it.

Pottenger obtained the most current Jet Propulsion Laboratory data for this new ephemeris, utilized programming refinements not yet available during Michelsen's lifetime, and added several new features, most notably obvious the inclusion of Ceres and Eris, in response to the 2006 decisions of the International Astronomical Union in regard to the planets in our solar system.

Several of Michelsen's other ephemerides have since been republished by Starcrafts LLC, until only the two most popular 2000-2050 midnight and noon versions remained unrevised since 1997. Now, with the recent full return of all rights of Michelsen's work to the Michelsen-Simms Family Trust, and our recent acquistion of assets of the former Astro Communications

Services, Inc., Starcrafts LLC is pleased to present this new ***Revised and Expanded Third Edition*** of ***The American Ephemeris 2000-2050*** in both midnight and noon versions, under our ACS Publications imprint. All of the new refinements and features of the "New American" series are included, but because we are now entirely free to do so, we are publishing these volumes with their original titles and author, with Rique added as co-author for his substantial updates.

New in the Revised and Expanded Third Edition

The Status and Positions of Pluto, Eris and Ceres

In 2006, the IAU announced a redefinition of planet, that is basically:

- a body that orbits around the Sun (or a star)
- has sufficient mass for its self-gravity to overcome rigid body forces so that it assumes an equilibrium (or put more simply, a nearly round shape),
- "has cleared the neighborhood" around its orbit.

By that definition, IAU decided that Pluto could no longer be called a planet—and likely nothing else beyond Neptune would qualify either. Pluto occupies a region of the Universe called the Kuiper Belt that is apparently rife with icy rocks.

A new category of "dwarf planet" was created to include Pluto and a new planet beyond Pluto that is larger than Pluto and was initially heralded a new planet after discovery by by astronomer Michael Brown of California Institute of Technology in July of 2005. The newcomer, at first nicknamed Xena by Brown, was on September 13, 2006, officially named for Eris, the Greek Goddess of Discord. Brown was quoted as saying the name was "too perfect to resist." It fit well the discord among astronomers that led to this decision (and reportedly still exists, particularly among some who were not present at the IAU meeting).

Then, during that 2006 IAU meeting, it was decided to promote Ceres, the largest of the asteroids orbiting between Mars and Jupiter, to the new dwarf planet category. Ceres had briefly been thought a planet upon her discovery in 1801, until so many more bodies were also found orbiting nearby that the new category of asteroid was devised for them, thus the "asteroid belt."

We waited for IAU decisions in the summer of 2006, along with anxious school textbook publishers. We knew full well that astrologers would **never** demote Pluto, no matter what the astronomers termed him to be, so we decided that the thing to do was to leave Pluto in his usual column of daily longitude positions, and to add Ceres in her own column between Mars and Jupiter.

In order to avoid further expanding of the book size or reducing the type size, Eris, orbiting so far beyond Pluto that her positions vary at most only a very few minutes from one month to the next, is listed with her monthly positions in the Astro Data box at lower right of each page.

Since 2006, more "dwarfs" have been discovered in the Kuiper Belt, and it is to be expected that more will be, perhaps many more. The astronomers have decided on a new term to define the subset of dwarf planets beyond Neptune. These are now called Plutoids, in honor of Pluto (or perhaps we might also think of this as some sort of consolation prize for him—an apology for his demotion). But the page size of the ephemeris is limited, so it seems best at this time to include bodies such as Chiron and the asteroids that are in wide general use, rather than newly discovered Plutoids. When more decisive data and demand emerges, a Plutoid ephemeris is possible.

Other New Features

Rique has rewritten the computer generating program to a great extent. The program is now Windows based, making it considerably easier to use. One advantage to this new version is that it enables checking for double ingresses on the same day. One was found in December 2007. The Node crosses from Pisces to Aquarius, goes direct, and crosses back into Pisces on the same day. The old ephemeris generating program did not check for this detail, so the prior edition only shows the next ingress into Aquarius, which comes three days later.

Some station times will also be shown as slightly different from prior versions of the ephemeris, due to the new program's improvements in calculation.

A significantly more accurate formula has been obtained for the Galactic Center (shown in the Astro Data box at lower right of each page), so it, too, will show as slightly different from the prior edition.

Also included in the Astro Data box are the monthly positions for astrology's now "major three" of the formerly four major asteroids: Pallas, Juno and Vesta.

Phenomena in the far left Astro Data column is sorted by time as well as date. In the previous ACS publication, they were not sorted by time, so if two events occurred on the same day, the later one might be higher in the column.

Planetary Ingress data includes R after the sign if the planet is retrograde when it ingresses.

General Information

This noon ephemeris is based on ET (ephemeris time). *The American Ephemeris for the 20th Century* is based on UT (Universal Time). A uniform measurement of time is required for the calculation of planetary positions because the Earth's rotation is too irregular to be used for this purpose, even though our clocks are synchronized to that rotation. Various disturbances such as tidal coupling with the Moon or earthquakes cause Earth to either speed up or slow down. Our clocks are adjusted to the changing speed of the Earth by the addition of a "leap second" such as was done on June 30, 1982. We are now adding leap seconds, rather than subtracting, since Earth's rotation is slowing slightly, causing the civil day to become very slightly longer.

The difference between ET and UT is called Delta T. In order to calculate the most accurate horoscopes, primarily for solar and lunar returns, the time of the chart must be adjusted by adding Delta T to the UT of the chart before interpolating to find the planetary positions. It is not feasible to predict so far in advance into the 21st century what the Delta T values will be. This is why this ephemeris, like nearly all ephemerides currently used by astrologers, is based on ET.

Accuracy of Planetary Positions

Successive editions of the ephemeris differ slightly from earlier versions because of increased accuracy of data available from the Jet Propulsion Laboratory (JPL). Since 1984, JPL data has been used in *The Astronomical Almanac,* a joint publication of the US Naval Observatory and the Royal Greenwich Observatory. Differences are so small that they will show up mainly in the times of aspects, sign ingresses, 0 declinations and stations that appear in the phenomena section at the bottom of each page. The most dramatic changes are seen in a few void-of-course Moon times where an aspect time that previously started the void period shifts to just after the Moon enters a new sign, so that an earlier aspect becomes the determining time for the beginning of the void Moon.

Positions of Chiron are determined by numerical integration using elements from the *Soviet Asteroid Ephemeris.* The integration program is an adaptation of the A.P.A.E. Volume XXII procedure as implemented by Mark Pottenger.

All positions are apparent, meaning they are corrected for light time. For example, the light from the Sun takes 8-1/2 minutes to reach the Earth, and in that time the Sun moves about 20.5" (seconds of arc). So the Sun's apparent position is 20.5" less than the geometric one.

Finally, the planet positions are transformed to the ecliptic of date, which means that precession and nutation (the wobble of the Earth on its axis) are applied.

Eclipses

The solar and lunar eclipses were recalculated by using JPL data. Because of the accuracy of this data, it was justifiable to list the duration of the geocentric maximum of total and annular solar eclipses to the second of time. This edition identifies six different types of solar eclipses. Since the method of calculation is improved over editions published prior to 1997, solar eclipse times may be up to several minutes more accurate. See **Key to the Phenomena Section** for further explanation.

Additional Features

Sun and Moon positions are given to the nearest second of arc; all other positions to the nearest tenth of a minute. Because of its irregular movement, the True Node of Moon is listed daily. The Mean Node of Moon is listed once each month.

Direct/Retrograde indicators are given on the day that the planet goes direct or retrograde. Look in the far left Astro Data section at the bottom of the page for the exact ET time of the station. If the planet's station is marked D, those persons born prior to that time have the planet retrograde; after that time, direct.

Phenomena sections for each month give all lunar phases, solar and lunar eclipses, stations, ingresses, outer planet aspects, planetary crossings of the celestial equator and void-of-course Moon data. See **Key to the Phenomena Section** for details.

Summary of Differences from editions of the 20th Century ephemerides:

- The 21st is in ET; the 20th is in UT.
- No Delta T values are given in the Astro Data section for the reasons discussed above.
- The position of the Galactic Center is given in place of Delta T.

Summary of Differences from the prior edition of *The American Ephemeris for the 21st Century 2000-2050 at Noon*

- Improvements to the ephemeris generating program enable finding double ingresses in a single day and more accurate station times.
- Daily positions for Ceres have been inserted between Mars and Jupiter
- A new formula more accurately determines the position of Galactic Center.
- Monthly positions of Eris, plus asteroids Pallas, Juno and Vesta are added to the far right Astro Data box, along with the monthly position of Chiron.
- Planetary Ingress Astro Data includes R after the sign if planet is retrograde at ingress.
- Phenomena in the far left Astro Data column is sorted by time as well as date.

Key to the Phenomena Section

The phenomena data at the bottom of each page is listed in six sections, counting from left to right. Within sections 1, 2, 5 and 6, the first month is normally separated from the second month by a blank line, unless there are too many lines of phenomena, in which case, the blank line is removed, and users must look at the day numbers to see when one month ends and another starts (see Sep-Oct 2009). Also, overflow from the leftmost section appears in the bottom of the next to the leftmost section (see Jul-Aug 2010). All sections except Section 6 list the astrological events by day, hour and minute of occurrence, with the headings of these three columns shown as Dy Hr Mn. Illustrated examples of each section follow:

Section 1, Astro Data, provides three types of information:

- **Stations** are indicated by a planet glyph followed by D or R, indicating whether the planet is direct or retrograde.
- Planets at 0° **Declination** are indicated by a planet glyph, a zero and or S indicating whether the planet is moving North or South as it crosses the celestial equator.
- **Aspects** between the **Outer** planets, Jupiter through Pluto.

Astro Data	Dy Hr Mn
☽0S	5 11:10
♄ R	13 15:58
☿ D	15 16:53
☽0N	19 21:43
♄□♇	31 21:28
☽0S	1 20:40
♃⚻♄	5 8:15
♃✶♇	6 17:52
☽0N	16 3:59

Section 1

Section 2: Planetary Ingress Table

This table shows the day and time each planet enters a new sign of the zodiac.

Planet Ingress	Dy Hr Mn
♃ ♓	18 2:11
♀ ♒	18 14:36
☉ ♒	20 4:29
☿ ♒	10 9:07
♀ ♓	11 12:11
☉ ♓	18 18:37

Section 2

Sections 3–4: Void ☽

Void of Course ☽ data for the first month is shown in Section 3, and the second month is shown in **Section 4**. The Void period starts with the last major aspect (☌✶□△☍) to ☽ whose day, hour and minute are given, and ends when ☽ enters the next sign indicated by the sign glyph plus the day, hour and minute of entry. The Void period may begin in the preceding month. Ceres has not been added to the Void-of-Course data. Pluto remains, as before.

Section 3

Last Aspect Dy Hr Mn			☽ Ingress	Dy Hr Mn
1 15:44	♅	△	♌	2 2:42
3 21:56	♃	☍	♍	4 2:54
5 17:26	♅	☍	♎	6 4:59
8 6:08	♃	△	♏	8 10:01
10 15:03	♃	□	♐	10 18:11
13 2:44	♃	✶	♑	13 4:55
15 9:04	♀	☌	♒	15 17:18
17 20:24	♆	☌	♓	18 6:18
20 6:07	♅	☌	♈	20 18:37
22 19:47	♆	✶	♉	23 4:41
25 3:04	♆	□	♊	25 11:12
27 6:33	♆	△	♋	27 14:02
29 4:50	♅	△	♌	29 14:11
31 6:28	♆	☍	♍	31 13:24

Section 4

Last Aspect Dy Hr Mn			☽ Ingress	Dy Hr Mn
2 4:18	♅	☍	♎	2 13:43
4 9:28	♆	△	♏	4 16:57
6 16:12	♆	□	♐	7 0:05
9 4:59	♀	✶	♑	9 10:45
11 12:40	♅	✶	♒	11 23:25
14 4:34	♆	☌	♓	14 12:24
16 14:33	♅	☌	♈	17 0:31
19 3:53	♆	✶	♉	19 10:56
21 12:16	♆	□	♊	21 18:48
23 17:30	♆	△	♋	23 23:30
25 17:49	♅	△	♌	26 1:09
27 20:16	☿	☍	♍	28 0:53

Section 5

☽ Phases & Eclipses Dy Hr Mn		
7 10:41	☾	17♎01
15 7:12	●	25♑01
15 7:07:40	●	A 11'07"
23 10:54	☽	3♉20
30 6:19	○	10♌15
5 23:50	☾	17♏04
14 2:52	●	25♒18
22 0:43	☽	3♊17
28 16:39	○	9♍59

Section 5: Moon Phases and Eclipses

This box contains **Moon Phases** and **Eclipse** data. The day, hour, minute and zodiacal position of the Moon is given for each.

● New Moon
☽ First Quarter Moon
○ Full Moon
☾ Third Quarter Moon

Shown at left is the Section 5 data box showing Moon phases and Eclipses for both months on an ephemeris page. Note the extra symbols included in the upper month. An eclipse symbol following a phase symbol means an eclipse occurred on the day of that phase. The time and type of eclipse are on the line below the Moon phase.

● indicates a **Lunar Eclipse**. The three types of lunar eclipses are indicated as follows:

A = an Appulse, a penumbral eclipse where Moon enters only the penumbra of Earth.

P = a Partial eclipse, where Moon enters the umbra without being totally immersed in it.

T = a Total eclipse, where Moon is entirely immersed within the umbra.

The time of greatest obscuration is given. This, in general, is not the exact time of the opposition in longitude. The magnitude of the lunar eclipse, which is the fraction of Moon's diameter obscured by the shadow of Earth at the greatest phase, is also given.

● = a **Solar Eclipse**. The six types are:

P = a **Partial** eclipse where Moon does not completely cover the solar disk.

T = a **Total** eclipse where Moon completely covers the solar disk, as seen from a shadow path on Earth's surface.

A = an **Annular** eclipse is "total," but Moon is too far from Earth for the apex of its shadow to reach Earth's surface. Thus Moon will not entirely hide the Sun, and a narrow ring of light will surround the dark New Moon.

AT = an **Annular-Total** eclipse, total for part of the path, annular for the rest.

A non-C = a rare **Annular** eclipse where the central line does not touch Earth's surface.

T non-C = a rare **Total** eclipse where the central line does not touch Earth's surface.

The time of greatest eclipse is given to the second, which, in general, is not the exact time of conjunction in longitude. For perfect eclipses the magnitude is given; for total and annular ones, the duration in minutes and seconds is given.

Section 6: Monthly Positions

This box contains six items of Astro Data for each of the two months on the page, with a blank line separating the two months.

Astro Data
1 January 2010
Julian Day # 40178
SVP 5♓06'56"
GC 26♐58.7 ⚴ 7♏57.4
Eris 20♈55.4R ⚵ 4♈37.6
⚷ 23♒08.6 ⚶ 6♍38.3
☽ Mean ☊ 21♑36.5

1 February 2010
Julian Day # 40209
SVP 5♓06'50"
GC 26♐58.8 ⚴ 17♏24.5
Eris 20♈58.4 ⚵ 18♈36.0
⚷ 25♒08.4 ⚶ 3♍32.6R
☽ Mean ☊ 19♑58.0

Section 6

Beginning with the first line of the top month, a numbered identification of each line follows:

1. First day of the month for the phenomena given.

2. **The Julian Day** is the count of the number of days elapsed since December 31, 1899, at Greenwich Noon. January 1, 1900, is Julian Day 1; January 1, 1901, is Julian Day 366, etc. This information can be used to calculate the midpoint in time between two events. For the astronomical Julian Day number counted from January 1, 4713 BC, add 2,415,020 to the number given for noon on the first day of the month.

3. **SVP** (the **Synetic Vernal Point)** is the tropical 0° point in the sidereal zodiac, as defined by Cyril Fagan. The tropical and sidereal zodiacs coincided in AD 231 and have diverged at the rate of one degree every 71-1/2 years as the tropical zodiac's starting point continues its retrograde movement on the ecliptic because of the precession of the equinoxes. Tropical positions are converted to sidereal by adding the degree, minutes and seconds of the SVP to the tropical longitude and subtracting one sign.

4. The **monthly position** of the **Galactic Center** is given, using the longitude of Sagittarius A. As was explained earlier, the position will differ somewhat from prior editions due to a significantly more accurate formula for its calculation.

5. **Monthly positions** are given for **Eris**, listed by her name, **Chiron** ⚷ and the 3 major asteroids in general use by astrologers, **Pallas** ⚴, **Vesta** ⚶, and **Juno** ⚵. Originally, **Ceres** ⚳ was also to be here. She has been moved into the planetary order of columns showing daily positions.

☽ Mean ☊ Interpolation			
2	3.2'	17	50.8'
3	6.4'	18	54.0'
4	9.5'	19	57.2'
5	12.7'	20	1° 0.4'
6	15.9'	21	1° 3.5'
7	19.1'	22	1° 7.7'
8	22.2'	23	1° 9.9'
9	25.4'	23	1°13.1'
10	28.6'	25	1°16.2'
11	31.8'	26	1°19.4'
12	34.9'	27	1°22°6'
13	38.1'	28	1°25.8'
14	41.3'	29	1°29.9'
15	44.5'	30	1°32.1'
16	47.7'	31	1°35.3'

6. The mean position for Moon's North Node is given. Explanation follows:

The **Mean Lunar Node** (☽ Mean ☊) is so regular in its motion that it can be accurately calculated for any day in the month for noon from the position given in this section for the first day of the month.

Mean Node Interpolation Table

Use the Moon Mean Node interpolation table shown at left to correct the monthly position given in Section 6 to be accurate for the current day. Enter the table using the day of the month for which you want the mean Node. The minutes, or degrees and minutes, obtained must then be subtracted from the first of the month position.

Example: birthday of February 16, 2001: Moon's Mean Node position on that date (as given at the bottom right of the ephemeris page) is 14 ♋ 02.6. Entering the Mean ☊ Interpolation table at 16 gives 47.7'. So, 14° ♋ 1.0' –47.7 = 13° ♋ 13.3'.

Key to the Glyphs

☉	Sun
☽	Moon
☿	Mercury
♀	Venus
♂	Mars
⚳	Ceres
♃	Jupiter
♄	Saturn
♅	Uranus
♆	Neptune
♇	Pluto
☊	Moon's Node
	Eris
⚷	Chiron
⚴	Pallas
⚵	Juno
⚶	Vesta

♈	Aries
♉	Taurus
♊	Gemini
♋	Cancer
♌	Leo
♍	Virgo
♎	Libra
♏	Scorpio
♐	Sagittarius
♑	Capricorn
♒	Aquarius
♓	Pisces

●	New Moon
☽	First Quarter Moon
○	Full Moon
☾	Third Quarter Moon
	Solar Eclipse
	Lunar Eclipse

Glyph	Angle	Aspect
☌	0°	conjunction
⚺	30°	semisextile
∠	45°	semisquare (or octile)
⚹	60°	sextile
□	90°	square
△	120°	trine
⚼	135°	sesquisquare (or tri-octile)
⚻	150°	quincunx
☍	180°	opposition

LONGITUDE — January 2000

Day	Sid.Time	☉	0 hr ☽	Noon ☽	True ☊	☿	♀	♂	⚳	♃	♄	♅	♆	♇
1 Sa	18 41 50	10♑22 05	7♏17 04	13♏18 54	3♌57.0	1♑53.3	1♐33.9	27♒57.8	4♎27.2	25♈15.2	10♉23.7	14♒48.6	3♒11.6	11♐27.3
2 Su	18 45 46	11 23 16	19 18 30	25 16 20	3R 53.4	3 26.8	2 46.5	28 44.3	4 40.2	25 17.7	10R 22.6	14 51.6	3 13.7	11 29.4
3 M	18 49 43	12 24 26	1♐12 47	7♐08 16	3 49.5	5 00.7	3 59.1	29 30.8	4 52.9	25 20.5	10 21.6	14 54.6	3 15.9	11 31.5
4 Tu	18 53 39	13 25 37	13 03 06	18 57 38	3 45.8	6 34.9	5 11.8	0♓17.4	5 05.4	25 23.4	10 20.6	14 57.7	3 18.0	11 33.5
5 W	18 57 36	14 26 47	24 52 08	0♑46 55	3 42.7	8 09.4	6 24.6	1 03.9	5 17.5	25 26.6	10 19.8	15 00.8	3 20.2	11 35.6
6 Th	19 01 32	15 27 58	6♑42 11	12 38 13	3 40.5	9 44.3	7 37.4	1 50.5	5 29.3	25 29.9	10 19.1	15 04.0	3 22.4	11 37.6
7 F	19 05 29	16 29 09	18 35 14	24 33 28	3D 39.2	11 19.6	8 50.3	2 37.0	5 40.8	25 33.5	10 18.6	15 07.1	3 24.6	11 39.7
8 Sa	19 09 26	17 30 19	0♒33 08	6♒34 29	3 39.0	12 55.3	10 03.2	3 23.5	5 52.0	25 37.2	10 18.1	15 10.3	3 26.8	11 41.7
9 Su	19 13 22	18 31 29	12 37 46	18 43 14	3 39.6	14 31.4	11 16.2	4 10.0	6 02.8	25 41.1	10 17.7	15 13.5	3 29.0	11 43.6
10 M	19 17 19	19 32 39	24 51 10	1♓01 53	3 40.7	16 07.9	12 29.2	4 56.6	6 13.3	25 45.3	10 17.5	15 16.7	3 31.2	11 45.6
11 Tu	19 21 15	20 33 48	7♓15 42	13 32 55	3 42.0	17 44.8	13 42.3	5 43.1	6 23.5	25 49.6	10D 17.3	15 20.0	3 33.5	11 47.5
12 W	19 25 12	21 34 57	19 53 55	26 19 02	3 43.1	19 22.2	14 55.4	6 29.5	6 33.3	25 54.1	10 17.3	15 23.2	3 35.7	11 49.4
13 Th	19 29 08	22 36 05	2♈48 37	9♈22 59	3 43.9	21 00.0	16 08.5	7 16.0	6 42.8	25 58.8	10 17.4	15 26.5	3 37.9	11 51.3
14 F	19 33 05	23 37 13	16 02 27	22 47 17	3R 44.2	22 38.4	17 21.7	8 02.5	6 51.9	26 03.6	10 17.6	15 29.8	3 40.2	11 53.2
15 Sa	19 37 01	24 38 19	29 37 40	6♉33 42	3 44.0	24 17.2	18 35.0	8 48.9	7 00.7	26 08.7	10 17.9	15 33.1	3 42.4	11 55.1
16 Su	19 40 58	25 39 26	13♉35 26	20 42 42	3 43.4	25 56.5	19 48.3	9 35.4	7 09.1	26 13.9	10 18.3	15 36.4	3 44.7	11 56.9
17 M	19 44 55	26 40 31	27 55 19	5♊12 50	3 42.6	27 36.3	21 01.6	10 21.8	7 17.2	26 19.3	10 18.9	15 39.7	3 47.0	11 58.7
18 Tu	19 48 51	27 41 36	12♊34 45	20 00 21	3 41.9	29 16.6	22 14.9	11 08.2	7 24.9	26 24.9	10 19.5	15 43.1	3 49.2	12 00.5
19 W	19 52 48	28 42 40	27 28 48	4♋59 09	3 41.3	0♒57.4	23 28.3	11 54.6	7 32.2	26 30.7	10 20.3	15 46.5	3 51.5	12 02.3
20 Th	19 56 44	29 43 43	12♋30 22	20 01 21	3D 41.0	2 38.8	24 41.7	12 40.9	7 39.1	26 36.7	10 21.2	15 49.8	3 53.8	12 04.0
21 F	20 00 41	0♒44 46	27 30 58	4♌58 11	3 40.9	4 20.6	25 55.2	13 27.3	7 45.7	26 42.8	10 22.2	15 53.2	3 56.1	12 05.7
22 Sa	20 04 37	1 45 47	12♌21 58	19 41 24	3 41.0	6 03.0	27 08.7	14 13.6	7 51.9	26 49.1	10 23.3	15 56.6	3 58.3	12 07.4
23 Su	20 08 34	2 46 49	26 55 43	4♍04 18	3R 41.1	7 45.8	28 22.2	14 59.9	7 57.6	26 55.5	10 24.5	16 00.1	4 00.6	12 09.1
24 M	20 12 30	3 47 49	11♍06 41	18 02 33	3 41.1	9 29.1	29 35.8	15 46.1	8 03.0	27 02.1	10 25.8	16 03.5	4 02.9	12 10.7
25 Tu	20 16 27	4 48 49	24 51 46	1♎34 21	3 41.0	11 12.8	0♑49.4	16 32.4	8 08.0	27 08.9	10 27.3	16 06.9	4 05.2	12 12.4
26 W	20 20 24	5 49 49	8♎10 25	14 40 15	3 40.9	12 56.9	2 03.0	17 18.6	8 12.6	27 15.8	10 28.8	16 10.4	4 07.4	12 13.9
27 Th	20 24 20	6 50 48	21 04 11	27 22 40	3D 40.7	14 41.3	3 16.7	18 04.8	8 16.8	27 22.9	10 30.4	16 13.8	4 09.7	12 15.5
28 F	20 28 17	7 51 46	3♏36 10	9♏45 14	3 40.7	16 26.0	4 30.4	18 51.0	8 20.5	27 30.2	10 32.2	16 17.3	4 12.0	12 17.0
29 Sa	20 32 13	8 52 44	15 50 26	21 52 21	3 40.8	18 10.8	5 44.1	19 37.2	8 23.9	27 37.6	10 34.1	16 20.7	4 14.3	12 18.6
30 Su	20 36 10	9 53 41	27 51 34	3♐48 40	3 41.3	19 55.7	6 57.9	20 23.3	8 26.8	27 45.2	10 36.0	16 24.2	4 16.5	12 20.0
31 M	20 40 06	10 54 38	9♐44 13	15 38 47	3 42.0	21 40.5	8 11.6	21 09.5	8 29.3	27 52.9	10 38.1	16 27.7	4 18.8	12 21.5

LONGITUDE — February 2000

Day	Sid.Time	☉	0 hr ☽	Noon ☽	True ☊	☿	♀	♂	⚳	♃	♄	♅	♆	♇
1 Tu	20 44 03	11♒55 33	21♐32 52	27♐27 00	3♌42.9	23♒25.0	9♑25.4	21♓55.6	8♎31.4	28♈00.8	10♉40.3	16♒31.2	4♒21.1	12♐22.9
2 W	20 47 59	12 56 28	3♑21 37	9♑17 09	3 43.8	25 09.1	10 39.3	22 41.6	8 33.0	28 08.8	10 42.6	16 34.6	4 23.3	12 24.3
3 Th	20 51 56	13 57 22	15 14 00	21 12 30	3 44.5	26 52.5	11 53.1	23 27.7	8 34.2	28 17.0	10 45.0	16 38.1	4 25.6	12 25.7
4 F	20 55 53	14 58 15	27 12 59	3♒15 43	3R 44.8	28 34.9	13 07.0	24 13.7	8 35.0	28 25.3	10 47.5	16 41.6	4 27.9	12 27.0
5 Sa	20 59 49	15 59 07	9♒20 56	15 28 49	3 44.5	0♓16.1	14 20.8	24 59.7	8R 35.3	28 33.8	10 50.2	16 45.1	4 30.1	12 28.3
6 Su	21 03 46	16 59 57	21 39 34	27 53 18	3 43.5	1 55.6	15 34.7	25 45.7	8 35.2	28 42.4	10 52.9	16 48.6	4 32.3	12 29.6
7 M	21 07 42	18 00 47	4♓10 07	10♓30 08	3 41.9	3 33.2	16 48.6	26 31.6	8 34.7	28 51.1	10 55.7	16 52.1	4 34.6	12 30.9
8 Tu	21 11 39	19 01 35	16 53 25	23 20 01	3 39.7	5 08.2	18 02.6	27 17.5	8 33.7	29 00.0	10 58.6	16 55.6	4 36.8	12 32.1
9 W	21 15 35	20 02 21	29 50 00	6♈23 24	3 37.2	6 40.1	19 16.5	28 03.4	8 32.3	29 09.0	11 01.6	16 59.1	4 39.0	12 33.3
10 Th	21 19 32	21 03 06	13♈00 14	19 40 35	3 35.0	8 08.5	20 30.4	28 49.2	8 30.4	29 18.2	11 04.8	17 02.6	4 41.2	12 34.4
11 F	21 23 28	22 03 50	26 24 26	3♉11 49	3 33.2	9 32.6	21 44.4	29 35.0	8 28.1	29 27.5	11 08.0	17 06.0	4 43.4	12 35.6
12 Sa	21 27 25	23 04 32	10♉02 45	16 57 13	3D 32.3	10 51.8	22 58.4	0♈20.8	8 25.4	29 36.9	11 11.3	17 09.5	4 45.6	12 36.7
13 Su	21 31 22	24 05 12	23 55 09	0♊56 29	3 32.4	12 05.4	24 12.4	1 06.6	8 22.2	29 46.4	11 14.7	17 13.0	4 47.8	12 37.7
14 M	21 35 18	25 05 51	8♊01 06	15 08 47	3 33.2	13 12.6	25 26.3	1 52.3	8 18.6	29 56.1	11 18.3	17 16.5	4 50.0	12 38.7
15 Tu	21 39 15	26 06 28	22 19 17	29 32 16	3 34.6	14 12.8	26 40.3	2 37.9	8 14.5	0♉05.9	11 21.9	17 19.9	4 52.1	12 39.8
16 W	21 43 11	27 07 03	6♋47 20	14♋03 58	3 36.0	15 05.3	27 54.3	3 23.6	8 10.0	0 15.8	11 25.6	17 23.4	4 54.3	12 40.7
17 Th	21 47 08	28 07 36	21 21 35	28 39 32	3R 36.9	15 49.3	29 08.4	4 09.2	8 05.1	0 25.8	11 29.4	17 26.8	4 56.4	12 41.7
18 F	21 51 04	29 08 08	5♌57 07	13♌13 35	3 36.7	16 24.3	0♒22.4	4 54.7	7 59.8	0 35.9	11 33.3	17 30.3	4 58.6	12 42.6
19 Sa	21 55 01	0♓08 38	20 28 10	27 40 06	3 35.1	16 49.7	1 36.4	5 40.2	7 54.1	0 46.2	11 37.3	17 33.7	5 00.7	12 43.4
20 Su	21 58 57	1 09 07	4♍48 39	11♍53 10	3 32.1	17 05.3	2 50.5	6 25.7	7 47.9	0 56.5	11 41.3	17 37.1	5 02.8	12 44.3
21 M	22 02 54	2 09 34	18 53 03	25 47 50	3 28.0	17R 10.7	4 04.5	7 11.1	7 41.3	1 07.0	11 45.5	17 40.5	5 04.9	12 45.1
22 Tu	22 06 51	3 09 59	2♎37 09	9♎20 45	3 23.2	17 06.0	5 18.6	7 56.5	7 34.4	1 17.6	11 49.8	17 43.9	5 06.9	12 45.8
23 W	22 10 47	4 10 23	15 58 31	22 30 29	3 18.3	16 51.2	6 32.7	8 41.9	7 27.0	1 28.3	11 54.1	17 47.3	5 09.0	12 46.6
24 Th	22 14 44	5 10 46	28 56 46	5♏17 37	3 14.1	16 26.9	7 46.8	9 27.2	7 19.2	1 39.1	11 58.5	17 50.7	5 11.0	12 47.3
25 F	22 18 40	6 11 07	11♏33 21	17 44 25	3 10.9	15 53.5	9 00.9	10 12.5	7 11.0	1 50.0	12 03.0	17 54.1	5 13.1	12 47.9
26 Sa	22 22 37	7 11 27	23 51 17	29 54 30	3D 09.2	15 12.0	10 15.0	10 57.7	7 02.5	2 01.0	12 07.6	17 57.4	5 15.1	12 48.6
27 Su	22 26 33	8 11 46	5♐54 40	11♐52 23	3 09.0	14 23.5	11 29.1	11 43.0	6 53.6	2 12.1	12 12.3	18 00.8	5 17.1	12 49.2
28 M	22 30 30	9 12 03	17 48 18	23 43 03	3 10.0	13 29.1	12 43.2	12 28.1	6 44.3	2 23.3	12 17.1	18 04.1	5 19.1	12 49.7
29 Tu	22 34 26	10 12 18	29 37 17	5♑31 39	3 11.6	12 30.4	13 57.3	13 13.3	6 34.7	2 34.6	12 21.9	18 07.4	5 21.0	12 50.3

Astro Data	Planet Ingress	Last Aspect	☽ Ingress	Last Aspect	☽ Ingress	☽ Phases & Eclipses	Astro Data
Dy Hr Mn	Dy Hr Mn	Dy Hr Mn	Dy Hr Mn	Dy Hr Mn	Dy Hr Mn	Dy Hr Mn	
♄ D 12 5:00	♂ ♓ 4 3:02	2 19:29 ♂ □	♐ 2 21:33	1 13:09 ♃ △	♑ 1 17:11	6 18:15 ● 15♑44	1 January 2000
☽0N 13 15:38	☿ ♒ 18 22:21	5 1:07 ♃ △	♑ 5 10:25	4 2:17 ♃ □	♒ 4 5:32	14 13:35 ☽ 23♈41	Julian Day # 36525
♃□♇ 26 3:37	☉ ♒ 20 18:24	7 14:01 ♃ □	♒ 7 22:54	6 13:35 ♃ ⚹	♓ 6 16:03	21 4:42 ○ 0♌26	SVP 5♓15'49"
☽0S 26 5:58	♀ ♑ 24 19:54	10 1:42 ♃ ⚹	♓ 10 10:00	8 19:47 ♂ ☌	♈ 9 0:18	21 4:45 ● T 1.325	GC 26♐50.4 ⚴ 14♌02.6R
		12 2:24 ☉ ⚹	♈ 12 18:49	11 5:20 ♃ ☌	♉ 11 6:22	28 7:58 ☾ 7♏42	Eris 18♈35.5R ⚵ 7♑59.8
⚳ R 5 18:12	☿ ♓ 5 8:10	14 17:48 ♃ ☌	♉ 15 0:39	12 23:23 ♀ △	♊ 13 10:24		⚷ 11♐37.0 ⚶ 5♐58.3
☽0N 9 21:00	♂ ♈ 12 1:05	16 21:51 ☿ △	♊ 17 3:26	15 5:52 ☉ △	♋ 15 12:46		☽Mean ☊ 5♌02.4
♂0N 13 14:04	♃ ♉ 14 21:41	18 22:22 ♃ ⚹	♋ 19 4:02	17 12:52 ♀ ☍	♌ 17 14:12	5 13:04 ● 16♒02	
☿ R 21 12:48	♀ ♒ 18 4:44	20 22:37 ♃ □	♌ 21 3:59	18 19:07 ♅ ☍	♍ 19 15:54	5 12:50:26 ● P 0.580	1 February 2000
☽0S 22 15:26	☉ ♓ 19 8:34	23 1:31 ♀ △	♍ 23 5:08	20 21:00 ☿ ☍	♎ 21 19:22	12 23:22 ☽ 23♉33	Julian Day # 36556
		24 7:49 ♂ ☍	♎ 25 9:10	23 3:17 ♅ △	♏ 24 1:59	19 16:28 ○ 0♍20	SVP 5♓15'44"
		27 12:01 ♃ ☍	♏ 27 17:02	25 12:19 ♅ □	♐ 26 12:11	27 3:55 ☾ 7♐51	GC 26♐50.4 ⚴ 4♌41.0R
		29 7:12 ♂ △	♐ 30 4:19	28 0:29 ♅ ⚹	♑ 29 0:46		Eris 18♈39.0 ⚵ 19♑34.1
							⚷ 14♐45.3 ⚶ 21♐43.8
							☽Mean ☊ 3♌23.9

March 2000 — LONGITUDE

Day	Sid.Time	☉	0 hr ☽	Noon ☽	True ☊	☿	♀	♂	⚳	♃	♄	♅	♆	♇
1 W	22 38 23	11♓12 32	11♑26 44	17♑23 09	3♌13.4	11♓28.9	15♒11.5	13♈58.4	6♎24.7	2♉46.0	12♉26.9	18♒10.7	5♒23.0	12♐50.8
2 Th	22 42 20	12 12 45	23 21 26	29 22 06	3R 14.4	10R 26.0	16 25.6	14 43.4	6R 14.4	2 57.5	12 31.9	18 13.9	5 24.9	12 51.2
3 F	22 46 16	13 12 56	5♒25 38	11♒32 24	3 14.1	9 23.3	17 39.8	15 28.4	6 03.7	3 09.1	12 37.0	18 17.2	5 26.8	12 51.7
4 Sa	22 50 13	14 13 05	17 42 46	23 57 00	3 12.0	8 22.2	18 53.9	16 13.4	5 52.8	3 20.8	12 42.1	18 20.4	5 28.7	12 52.1
5 Su	22 54 09	15 13 12	0♓15 18	6♓37 47	3 07.8	7 24.0	20 08.0	16 58.3	5 41.5	3 32.5	12 47.4	18 23.6	5 30.5	12 52.4
6 M	22 58 06	16 13 18	13 04 30	19 35 24	3 01.8	6 29.7	21 22.2	17 43.2	5 30.0	3 44.4	12 52.7	18 26.8	5 32.4	12 52.8
7 Tu	23 02 02	17 13 21	26 10 25	2♈49 20	2 54.4	5 40.3	22 36.3	18 28.1	5 18.2	3 56.3	12 58.1	18 30.0	5 34.2	12 53.0
8 W	23 05 59	18 13 23	9♈31 56	16 17 57	2 46.4	4 56.5	23 50.5	19 12.9	5 06.2	4 08.3	13 03.6	18 33.2	5 36.0	12 53.3
9 Th	23 09 55	19 13 23	23 07 03	29 58 56	2 38.8	4 18.7	25 04.6	19 57.6	4 53.9	4 20.4	13 09.1	18 36.3	5 37.8	12 53.5
10 F	23 13 52	20 13 20	6♉53 15	13♉49 40	2 32.4	3 47.3	26 18.8	20 42.3	4 41.4	4 32.6	13 14.7	18 39.4	5 39.6	12 53.7
11 Sa	23 17 48	21 13 16	20 47 52	27 47 36	2 27.9	3 22.4	27 32.9	21 27.0	4 28.6	4 44.9	13 20.4	18 42.5	5 41.3	12 53.9
12 Su	23 21 45	22 13 09	4♊48 36	11♊50 39	2D 25.5	3 04.2	28 47.0	22 11.6	4 15.7	4 57.2	13 26.1	18 45.5	5 43.0	12 54.0
13 M	23 25 42	23 13 00	18 53 34	25 57 11	2 25.1	2 52.5	0♓01.2	22 56.2	4 02.7	5 09.6	13 31.9	18 48.6	5 44.7	12 54.1
14 Tu	23 29 38	24 12 49	3♋01 20	10♋05 52	2 25.8	2D 47.1	1 15.3	23 40.8	3 49.4	5 22.1	13 37.8	18 51.6	5 46.4	12R 54.1
15 W	23 33 35	25 12 35	17 10 38	24 15 27	2R 26.8	2 48.0	2 29.4	24 25.2	3 36.1	5 34.6	13 43.7	18 54.6	5 48.0	12 54.1
16 Th	23 37 31	26 12 20	1♌20 06	8♌24 19	2 26.9	2 54.7	3 43.6	25 09.7	3 22.6	5 47.3	13 49.8	18 57.5	5 49.7	12 54.1
17 F	23 41 28	27 12 02	15 27 48	22 30 13	2 25.1	3 07.1	4 57.7	25 54.1	3 09.0	5 59.9	13 55.8	19 00.4	5 51.3	12 54.1
18 Sa	23 45 24	28 11 41	29 31 08	6♍30 09	2 20.9	3 24.9	6 11.8	26 38.4	2 55.4	6 12.7	14 01.9	19 03.3	5 52.8	12 54.0
19 Su	23 49 21	29 11 19	13♍26 48	20 20 37	2 14.2	3 47.8	7 25.9	27 22.7	2 41.6	6 25.5	14 08.1	19 06.2	5 54.4	12 53.8
20 M	23 53 17	0♈10 55	27 11 11	3♎58 03	2 05.3	4 15.5	8 40.0	28 06.9	2 27.8	6 38.4	14 14.4	19 09.1	5 55.9	12 53.7
21 Tu	23 57 14	1 10 28	10♎40 51	17 19 18	1 55.0	4 47.7	9 54.1	28 51.1	2 14.0	6 51.3	14 20.7	19 11.9	5 57.4	12 53.5
22 W	0 01 11	2 10 00	23 53 10	0♏22 19	1 44.4	5 24.2	11 08.2	29 35.3	2 00.2	7 04.3	14 27.0	19 14.7	5 58.9	12 53.3
23 Th	0 05 07	3 09 30	6♏46 43	13 06 26	1 34.5	6 04.6	12 22.3	0♉19.4	1 46.4	7 17.4	14 33.4	19 17.4	6 00.3	12 53.0
24 F	0 09 04	4 08 58	19 21 38	25 32 34	1 26.2	6 48.9	13 36.4	1 03.5	1 32.6	7 30.5	14 39.9	19 20.1	6 01.8	12 52.7
25 Sa	0 13 00	5 08 24	1♐39 35	7♐43 06	1 20.1	7 36.7	14 50.5	1 47.5	1 18.8	7 43.6	14 46.4	19 22.8	6 03.1	12 52.4
26 Su	0 16 57	6 07 48	13 43 36	19 41 38	1 16.4	8 27.8	16 04.6	2 31.4	1 05.1	7 56.9	14 53.0	19 25.5	6 04.5	12 52.1
27 M	0 20 53	7 07 11	25 37 48	1♑32 43	1D 14.9	9 22.0	17 18.7	3 15.4	0 51.5	8 10.1	14 59.6	19 28.1	6 05.9	12 51.7
28 Tu	0 24 50	8 06 32	7♑27 04	13 21 31	1 14.8	10 19.3	18 32.8	3 59.2	0 37.9	8 23.5	15 06.3	19 30.7	6 07.2	12 51.3
29 W	0 28 46	9 05 51	19 16 45	25 13 27	1R 15.3	11 19.3	19 46.9	4 43.1	0 24.5	8 36.8	15 13.0	19 33.3	6 08.5	12 50.8
30 Th	0 32 43	10 05 08	1♒12 18	7♒13 56	1 15.3	12 22.0	21 01.0	5 26.9	0 11.2	8 50.3	15 19.8	19 35.8	6 09.7	12 50.3
31 F	0 36 40	11 04 24	13 18 57	19 27 55	1 13.7	13 27.2	22 15.1	6 10.6	29♍58.1	9 03.7	15 26.6	19 38.3	6 10.9	12 49.8

April 2000 — LONGITUDE

Day	Sid.Time	☉	0 hr ☽	Noon ☽	True ☊	☿	♀	♂	⚳	♃	♄	♅	♆	♇
1 Sa	0 40 36	12♈03 37	25♒41 21	1♓59 38	1♌09.9	14♓34.9	23♓29.2	6♉54.3	29♍45.1	9♉17.3	15♉33.5	19♒40.7	6♒12.1	12♐49.3
2 Su	0 44 33	13 02 49	8♓23 06	14 52 00	1R 03.4	15 44.8	24 43.3	7 37.9	29R 32.3	9 30.8	15 40.4	19 43.1	6 13.3	12R 48.7
3 M	0 48 29	14 01 59	21 26 24	28 06 19	0 54.4	16 56.9	25 57.3	8 21.5	29 19.6	9 44.4	15 47.3	19 45.5	6 14.4	12 48.1
4 Tu	0 52 26	15 01 06	4♈51 35	11♈41 56	0 43.5	18 11.2	27 11.4	9 05.1	29 07.2	9 58.1	15 54.3	19 47.9	6 15.5	12 47.5
5 W	0 56 22	16 00 12	18 36 57	25 36 09	0 31.6	19 27.5	28 25.5	9 48.6	28 55.1	10 11.8	16 01.3	19 50.2	6 16.6	12 46.8
6 Th	1 00 19	16 59 16	2♉38 55	9♉44 36	0 20.1	20 45.7	29 39.5	10 32.1	28 43.1	10 25.5	16 08.4	19 52.4	6 17.7	12 46.1
7 F	1 04 15	17 58 18	16 52 30	24 01 55	0 10.2	22 05.9	0♈53.6	11 15.5	28 31.4	10 39.3	16 15.5	19 54.7	6 18.7	12 45.4
8 Sa	1 08 12	18 57 17	1♊12 09	8♊22 36	0 02.7	23 27.9	2 07.6	11 58.8	28 20.0	10 53.1	16 22.6	19 56.9	6 19.7	12 44.6
9 Su	1 12 08	19 56 14	15 32 42	22 41 57	29♋58.0	24 51.8	3 21.6	12 42.2	28 08.9	11 06.9	16 29.8	19 59.0	6 20.6	12 43.8
10 M	1 16 05	20 55 10	29 49 59	6♋56 30	29 55.9	26 17.3	4 35.6	13 25.4	27 58.1	11 20.8	16 37.0	20 01.1	6 21.6	12 43.0
11 Tu	1 20 02	21 54 02	14♋01 18	21 04 13	29 55.4	27 44.7	5 49.6	14 08.6	27 47.6	11 34.7	16 44.3	20 03.2	6 22.5	12 42.2
12 W	1 23 58	22 52 53	28 05 11	5♌04 09	29 55.4	29 13.7	7 03.6	14 51.8	27 37.4	11 48.6	16 51.6	20 05.2	6 23.3	12 41.3
13 Th	1 27 55	23 51 41	12♌01 06	18 56 01	29 54.5	0♈44.4	8 17.6	15 34.9	27 27.6	12 02.6	16 58.9	20 07.2	6 24.1	12 40.4
14 F	1 31 51	24 50 26	25 48 53	2♍39 38	29 51.6	2 16.8	9 31.6	16 18.0	27 18.0	12 16.5	17 06.2	20 09.2	6 24.9	12 39.5
15 Sa	1 35 48	25 49 10	9♍28 12	16 14 29	29 46.0	3 50.8	10 45.6	17 01.0	27 08.9	12 30.5	17 13.6	20 11.1	6 25.7	12 38.5
16 Su	1 39 44	26 47 51	22 58 21	29 39 38	29 37.4	5 26.5	11 59.5	17 44.0	27 00.0	12 44.6	17 21.0	20 12.9	6 26.4	12 37.6
17 M	1 43 41	27 46 30	6♎18 09	12♎53 42	29 26.3	7 03.8	13 13.5	18 26.9	26 51.6	12 58.6	17 28.4	20 14.7	6 27.1	12 36.6
18 Tu	1 47 37	28 45 07	19 26 06	25 55 09	29 13.5	8 42.8	14 27.4	19 09.7	26 43.5	13 12.7	17 35.8	20 16.5	6 27.8	12 35.5
19 W	1 51 34	29 43 42	2♏20 45	8♏42 45	29 00.2	10 23.4	15 41.4	19 52.6	26 35.8	13 26.8	17 43.3	20 18.2	6 28.5	12 34.5
20 Th	1 55 31	0♉42 16	15 01 07	21 15 52	28 47.5	12 05.7	16 55.3	20 35.3	26 28.4	13 40.9	17 50.8	20 19.9	6 29.1	12 33.4
21 F	1 59 27	1 40 47	27 27 04	3♐34 52	28 36.6	13 49.6	18 09.2	21 18.1	26 21.5	13 55.1	17 58.3	20 21.6	6 29.6	12 32.3
22 Sa	2 03 24	2 39 17	9♐39 29	15 41 13	28 28.2	15 35.2	19 23.1	22 00.7	26 14.9	14 09.2	18 05.8	20 23.2	6 30.2	12 31.2
23 Su	2 07 20	3 37 46	21 40 26	27 37 33	28 22.5	17 22.4	20 37.1	22 43.4	26 08.8	14 23.4	18 13.4	20 24.7	6 30.7	12 30.0
24 M	2 11 17	4 36 12	3♑33 04	9♑27 30	28 19.4	19 11.4	21 51.0	23 25.9	26 03.0	14 37.6	18 21.0	20 26.3	6 31.2	12 28.9
25 Tu	2 15 13	5 34 37	15 21 28	21 15 35	28D 18.3	21 02.0	23 04.9	24 08.5	25 57.6	14 51.8	18 28.6	20 27.7	6 31.6	12 27.7
26 W	2 19 10	6 33 00	27 10 31	3♒06 55	28R 18.2	22 54.3	24 18.8	24 51.0	25 52.7	15 06.0	18 36.2	20 29.1	6 32.0	12 26.5
27 Th	2 23 06	7 31 22	9♒05 30	15 06 57	28 18.1	24 48.3	25 32.7	25 33.4	25 48.1	15 20.3	18 43.8	20 30.5	6 32.4	12 25.2
28 F	2 27 03	8 29 42	21 11 56	27 21 08	28 16.8	26 44.0	26 46.6	26 15.8	25 44.0	15 34.5	18 51.4	20 31.8	6 32.8	12 24.0
29 Sa	2 31 00	9 28 01	3♓35 08	9♓54 30	28 13.6	28 41.3	28 00.5	26 58.2	25 40.3	15 48.8	18 59.1	20 33.1	6 33.1	12 22.7
30 Su	2 34 56	10 26 18	16 19 43	22 51 08	28 07.8	0♉40.3	29 14.3	27 40.5	25 37.0	16 03.0	19 06.7	20 34.4	6 33.3	12 21.4

Astro Data

	Dy Hr Mn
♄⚻♇	6 12:15
☽0N	8 2:48
☿D	14 20:41
♇R	15 11:52
♃□♆	16 17:15
☉0N	20 7:36
☽0S	21 0:38
☽0N	4 10:47
♀0N	9 14:18
♃⚻♇	16 0:48
☿0N	16 18:12
☽0S	17 8:38

Planet Ingress

	Dy Hr Mn
♀ ♓	13 11:37
☉ ♈	20 7:36
♂ ♉	23 1:26
⚳ ♍R	31 8:26
♀ ♈	6 18:38
☊ ♋R	9 0:12
☿ ♈	13 0:18
☉ ♉	19 18:41
☿ ♉	30 3:54

Last Aspect / ☽ Ingress

Last Aspect Dy Hr Mn		☽ Ingress Dy Hr Mn
1 4:39	♂ □	♒ 2 13:15
4 1:13	♀ ☌	♓ 4 23:31
6 5:18	☉ ☌	♈ 7 6:55
9 2:35	♀ ✶	♉ 9 12:02
11 11:32	♀ □	♊ 11 15:47
13 7:00	☉ □	♋ 13 18:52
15 13:44	☉ △	♌ 15 21:44
17 18:08	♂ △	♍ 18 0:49
20 4:45	☉ ☍	♎ 20 4:58
22 10:27	♂ ☍	♏ 22 11:18
23 23:54	♅ □	♐ 24 20:44
26 11:27	♅ ✶	♑ 27 8:52
28 23:44	♀ ✶	♒ 29 21:35

Last Aspect / ☽ Ingress

Last Aspect Dy Hr Mn		☽ Ingress Dy Hr Mn
31 12:20	♅ ☌	♓ 1 8:13
3 7:45	♀ ☌	♈ 3 15:23
5 2:05	♅ ✶	♉ 5 19:30
7 8:25	☿ ✶	♊ 7 21:59
9 16:02	☿ □	♋ 10 0:17
12 0:46	☿ △	♌ 12 3:17
13 21:15	☉ △	♍ 14 7:20
15 13:46	♄ △	♎ 16 12:37
18 17:43	☉ ☍	♏ 18 19:36
20 10:37	♂ ☍	♐ 21 4:59
22 21:26	♅ ✶	♑ 23 16:48
25 18:13	♂ △	♒ 26 5:43
28 10:46	♀ ✶	♓ 28 17:07

☽ Phases & Eclipses

Dy Hr Mn	
6 5:18	● 15♓57
13 7:00	☽ 23♊01
20 4:45	○ 29♍53
28 0:22	☾ 7♑38
4 18:13	● 15♈16
11 13:31	☽ 21♋58
18 17:43	○ 28♎59
26 19:31	☾ 6♒51

Astro Data

1 March 2000
Julian Day # 36585
SVP 5♓15'41"
GC 26♐50.5 ⚴ 28♋42.3R
Eris 18♈51.0 ⚵ 0♒09.0
⚷ 16♐39.2 ⚶ 5♑26.4
☽ Mean ☊ 1♌51.7

1 April 2000
Julian Day # 36616
SVP 5♓15'38"
GC 26♐50.6 ⚴ 1♌06.6
Eris 19♈09.8 ⚵ 10♒38.6
⚷ 17♐13.2R ⚶ 18♑09.6
☽ Mean ☊ 0♌13.2

LONGITUDE — May 2000

Day	Sid.Time	☉	0 hr ☽	Noon ☽	True ☊	☿	♀	♂	⚳	♃	♄	♅	♆	♇
1 M	2 38 53	11♉24 33	29♓29 00	6♈13 28	27♋59.6	2♉40.9	0♉28.2	28♉22.7	25♍34.1	16♉17.3	19♉14.4	20♒35.5	6♒33.6	12♐20.1
2 Tu	2 42 49	12 22 47	13♈04 27	20 01 46	27R49.5	4 43.1	1 42.1	29 05.0	25R31.6	16 31.6	19 22.1	20 36.7	6 33.8	12R18.7
3 W	2 46 46	13 20 59	27 05 01	4♉13 40	27 38.3	6 46.8	2 55.9	29 47.1	25 29.6	16 45.8	19 29.8	20 37.8	6 34.0	12 17.4
4 Th	2 50 42	14 19 10	11♉27 00	18 44 10	27 27.4	8 51.9	4 09.8	0♊29.3	25 27.9	17 00.1	19 37.5	20 38.8	6 34.1	12 16.0
5 F	2 54 39	15 17 19	26 04 16	3♊26 17	27 17.9	10 58.3	5 23.7	1 11.4	25 26.7	17 14.4	19 45.2	20 39.8	6 34.2	12 14.6
6 Sa	2 58 35	16 15 26	10♊49 12	18 12 05	27 10.7	13 05.9	6 37.5	1 53.4	25 25.9	17 28.7	19 53.0	20 40.8	6 34.3	12 13.2
7 Su	3 02 32	17 13 31	25 33 59	2♋54 07	27 06.2	15 14.6	7 51.3	2 35.4	25D25.5	17 43.0	20 00.7	20 41.7	6 34.4	12 11.8
8 M	3 06 29	18 11 35	10♋11 47	17 26 27	27D04.2	17 24.0	9 05.2	3 17.3	25 25.6	17 57.3	20 08.4	20 42.5	6R34.4	12 10.4
9 Tu	3 10 25	19 09 37	24 37 41	1♌45 12	27 04.0	19 34.2	10 19.0	3 59.2	25 26.0	18 11.6	20 16.1	20 43.3	6 34.4	12 08.9
10 W	3 14 22	20 07 36	8♌48 50	15 48 30	27R04.4	21 44.7	11 32.8	4 41.1	25 26.9	18 25.8	20 23.9	20 44.1	6 34.3	12 07.5
11 Th	3 18 18	21 05 34	22 44 14	29 36 04	27 04.2	23 55.5	12 46.6	5 22.9	25 28.1	18 40.1	20 31.6	20 44.8	6 34.2	12 06.0
12 F	3 22 15	22 03 30	6♍24 07	13♍08 32	27 02.3	26 06.1	14 00.4	6 04.6	25 29.8	18 54.4	20 39.3	20 45.4	6 34.1	12 04.5
13 Sa	3 26 11	23 01 24	19 49 26	26 26 57	26 58.1	28 16.3	15 14.2	6 46.3	25 31.9	19 08.6	20 47.0	20 46.0	6 34.0	12 03.0
14 Su	3 30 08	23 59 16	3♎01 12	9♎32 18	26 51.4	0♊25.9	16 27.9	7 28.0	25 34.3	19 22.9	20 54.8	20 46.6	6 33.8	12 01.5
15 M	3 34 04	24 57 07	16 00 20	22 25 20	26 42.5	2 34.5	17 41.7	8 09.6	25 37.2	19 37.1	21 02.5	20 47.1	6 33.6	11 59.9
16 Tu	3 38 01	25 54 56	28 47 23	5♏06 31	26 32.1	4 41.9	18 55.5	8 51.2	25 40.4	19 51.4	21 10.2	20 47.5	6 33.3	11 58.4
17 W	3 41 58	26 52 43	11♏22 46	17 36 10	26 21.3	6 47.8	20 09.2	9 32.7	25 44.1	20 05.6	21 17.9	20 48.0	6 33.1	11 56.9
18 Th	3 45 54	27 50 29	23 46 48	29 54 44	26 11.0	8 51.9	21 23.0	10 14.2	25 48.1	20 19.8	21 25.6	20 48.3	6 32.8	11 55.3
19 F	3 49 51	28 48 14	6♐00 04	12♐02 57	26 02.1	10 54.1	22 36.7	10 55.6	25 52.4	20 34.0	21 33.3	20 48.6	6 32.4	11 53.7
20 Sa	3 53 47	29 45 57	18 03 34	24 02 09	25 55.3	12 54.2	23 50.5	11 37.0	25 57.2	20 48.1	21 41.0	20 48.9	6 32.1	11 52.2
21 Su	3 57 44	0♊43 39	29 58 58	5♑54 22	25 50.9	14 51.9	25 04.2	12 18.4	26 02.3	21 02.3	21 48.6	20 49.1	6 31.7	11 50.6
22 M	4 01 40	1 41 20	11♑48 41	17 42 23	25D48.7	16 47.1	26 18.0	12 59.7	26 07.8	21 16.4	21 56.3	20 49.3	6 31.2	11 49.0
23 Tu	4 05 37	2 39 00	23 35 56	29 29 49	25 48.4	18 39.7	27 31.7	13 40.9	26 13.6	21 30.6	22 04.0	20 49.4	6 30.8	11 47.4
24 W	4 09 33	3 36 39	5♒24 38	11♒20 56	25 49.3	20 29.6	28 45.4	14 22.2	26 19.8	21 44.7	22 11.6	20R49.5	6 30.3	11 45.8
25 Th	4 13 30	4 34 17	17 19 21	23 20 32	25 50.4	22 16.8	29 59.2	15 03.4	26 26.4	21 58.8	22 19.2	20 49.5	6 29.8	11 44.2
26 F	4 17 27	5 31 54	29 25 07	5♓33 45	25R51.0	24 01.0	1♊12.9	15 44.5	26 33.3	22 12.8	22 26.8	20 49.4	6 29.2	11 42.6
27 Sa	4 21 23	6 29 29	11♓47 04	18 05 39	25 50.2	25 42.4	2 26.6	16 25.6	26 40.5	22 26.9	22 34.4	20 49.4	6 28.6	11 41.0
28 Su	4 25 20	7 27 04	24 30 04	1♈00 47	25 47.7	27 20.8	3 40.4	17 06.6	26 48.1	22 40.9	22 42.0	20 49.2	6 28.0	11 39.3
29 M	4 29 16	8 24 38	7♈38 11	14 22 33	25 43.3	28 56.3	4 54.1	17 47.7	26 56.0	22 54.9	22 49.6	20 49.0	6 27.4	11 37.7
30 Tu	4 33 13	9 22 12	21 13 59	28 12 27	25 37.4	0♋28.7	6 07.8	18 28.6	27 04.2	23 08.9	22 57.1	20 48.8	6 26.7	11 36.1
31 W	4 37 09	10 19 44	5♉17 45	12♉29 28	25 30.6	1 58.0	7 21.6	19 09.6	27 12.8	23 22.8	23 04.6	20 48.5	6 26.0	11 34.5

LONGITUDE — June 2000

Day	Sid.Time	☉	0 hr ☽	Noon ☽	True ☊	☿	♀	♂	⚳	♃	♄	♅	♆	♇
1 Th	4 41 06	11♊17 15	19♉47 00	27♉09 34	25♋23.8	3♋24.2	8♊35.3	19♊50.5	27♍21.7	23♉36.7	23♉12.1	20♒48.2	6♒25.3	11♐32.8
2 F	4 45 02	12 14 46	4♊36 15	12♊05 58	25R17.9	4 47.4	9 49.1	20 31.4	27 30.9	23 50.6	23 19.6	20R47.8	6R24.5	11R31.2
3 Sa	4 48 59	13 12 16	19 37 35	27 09 55	25 13.5	6 07.3	11 02.8	21 12.2	27 40.4	24 04.5	23 27.0	20 47.4	6 23.7	11 29.6
4 Su	4 52 56	14 09 44	4♋41 48	12♋12 09	25D11.1	7 24.1	12 16.5	21 53.0	27 50.3	24 18.3	23 34.5	20 47.0	6 22.9	11 28.0
5 M	4 56 52	15 07 12	19 39 57	27 04 19	25 10.5	8 37.5	13 30.2	22 33.7	28 00.4	24 32.1	23 41.9	20 46.4	6 22.1	11 26.4
6 Tu	5 00 49	16 04 38	4♌24 33	11♌40 05	25 11.2	9 47.7	14 44.0	23 14.4	28 10.8	24 45.8	23 49.2	20 45.9	6 21.2	11 24.7
7 W	5 04 45	17 02 03	18 50 32	25 55 37	25 12.6	10 54.5	15 57.7	23 55.1	28 21.6	24 59.5	23 56.6	20 45.3	6 20.3	11 23.1
8 Th	5 08 42	17 59 27	2♍55 14	9♍49 23	25R13.7	11 57.9	17 11.4	24 35.7	28 32.6	25 13.2	24 03.9	20 44.6	6 19.4	11 21.5
9 F	5 12 38	18 56 50	16 38 08	23 21 41	25 13.8	12 57.7	18 25.1	25 16.2	28 43.9	25 26.9	24 11.2	20 43.9	6 18.4	11 19.9
10 Sa	5 16 35	19 54 12	0♎00 13	6♎34 02	25 12.6	13 54.0	19 38.8	25 56.8	28 55.5	25 40.5	24 18.4	20 43.2	6 17.5	11 18.3
11 Su	5 20 31	20 51 32	13 03 23	19 28 35	25 09.8	14 46.6	20 52.5	26 37.3	29 07.3	25 54.0	24 25.6	20 42.4	6 16.5	11 16.7
12 M	5 24 28	21 48 52	25 49 54	2♏07 39	25 05.7	15 35.4	22 06.3	27 17.7	29 19.5	26 07.5	24 32.8	20 41.5	6 15.4	11 15.1
13 Tu	5 28 25	22 46 11	8♏22 06	14 33 31	25 00.6	16 20.4	23 20.0	27 58.1	29 31.9	26 21.0	24 40.0	20 40.6	6 14.4	11 13.5
14 W	5 32 21	23 43 28	20 42 09	26 48 15	24 55.2	17 01.4	24 33.7	28 38.5	29 44.5	26 34.4	24 47.1	20 39.7	6 13.3	11 11.9
15 Th	5 36 18	24 40 46	2♐52 01	8♐53 43	24 50.1	17 38.3	25 47.4	29 18.8	29 57.4	26 47.8	24 54.2	20 38.8	6 12.2	11 10.3
16 F	5 40 14	25 38 02	14 53 32	20 51 43	24 45.8	18 11.2	27 01.1	29 59.1	0♎10.6	27 01.1	25 01.2	20 37.7	6 11.1	11 08.8
17 Sa	5 44 11	26 35 18	26 48 29	2♑44 04	24 42.7	18 39.7	28 14.8	0♋39.4	0 24.0	27 14.4	25 08.2	20 36.7	6 10.0	11 07.2
18 Su	5 48 07	27 32 34	8♑38 45	14 32 47	24D40.9	19 03.9	29 28.5	1 19.6	0 37.6	27 27.7	25 15.2	20 35.6	6 08.8	11 05.7
19 M	5 52 04	28 29 49	20 26 30	26 20 13	24 40.5	19 23.7	0♋42.2	1 59.8	0 51.5	27 40.9	25 22.1	20 34.4	6 07.6	11 04.2
20 Tu	5 56 00	29 27 03	2♒14 17	8♒09 06	24 41.2	19 39.1	1 55.9	2 40.0	1 05.7	27 54.0	25 29.0	20 33.3	6 06.4	11 02.6
21 W	5 59 57	0♋24 18	14 05 06	20 02 43	24 42.5	19 49.8	3 09.6	3 20.1	1 20.0	28 07.1	25 35.8	20 32.0	6 05.2	11 01.1
22 Th	6 03 54	1 21 32	26 02 27	2♓04 47	24 44.2	19R56.0	4 23.3	4 00.2	1 34.6	28 20.1	25 42.6	20 30.8	6 04.0	10 59.6
23 F	6 07 50	2 18 46	8♓10 15	14 19 24	24 45.6	19 57.7	5 37.0	4 40.2	1 49.4	28 33.1	25 49.4	20 29.5	6 02.7	10 58.1
24 Sa	6 11 47	3 15 59	20 32 45	26 50 52	24R46.5	19 54.7	6 50.8	5 20.2	2 04.4	28 46.0	25 56.1	20 28.1	6 01.4	10 56.6
25 Su	6 15 43	4 13 13	3♈14 14	9♈43 19	24 46.5	19 47.3	8 04.5	6 00.2	2 19.7	28 58.9	26 02.8	20 26.7	6 00.1	10 55.2
26 M	6 19 40	5 10 27	16 18 34	23 00 17	24 45.7	19 35.6	9 18.2	6 40.1	2 35.1	29 11.7	26 09.4	20 25.3	5 58.8	10 53.7
27 Tu	6 23 36	6 07 40	29 48 45	6♉44 04	24 44.1	19 19.6	10 32.0	7 20.1	2 50.8	29 24.4	26 15.9	20 23.8	5 57.4	10 52.3
28 W	6 27 33	7 04 54	13♉46 12	20 54 59	24 42.0	18 59.6	11 45.7	7 59.9	3 06.7	29 37.1	26 22.5	20 22.3	5 56.1	10 50.9
29 Th	6 31 29	8 02 08	28 10 03	5♊30 51	24 39.9	18 36.0	12 59.5	8 39.8	3 22.7	29 49.7	26 28.9	20 20.8	5 54.7	10 49.5
30 F	6 35 26	8 59 22	12♊56 42	20 26 41	24 38.0	18 08.9	14 13.2	9 19.6	3 39.0	0♊02.3	26 35.3	20 19.2	5 53.3	10 48.1

Astro Data	Dy Hr Mn
☽ 0N	1 20:45
⚳ D	7 21:53
♆ R	8 12:31
♄□♅	13 8:35
☽ 0S	14 15:23
♃□♅	20 13:17
♅ R	25 8:21
♃☌♄	28 16:05
☽ 0N	29 7:07
☽ 0S	10 21:38
☿ R	23 8:33
☽ 0N	25 16:06

Planet Ingress		Dy Hr Mn
♀	♉	1 2:50
♂	♊	3 19:19
☿	♊	14 7:11
☉	♊	20 17:50
♀	♊	25 12:16
☿	♋	30 4:28
⚳	♎	15 16:43
♂	♋	16 12:31
♀	♋	18 22:16
☉	♋	21 1:49
♃	♊	30 7:36

Last Aspect Dy Hr Mn		☽ Ingress	Dy Hr Mn
30 21:14	♂ ⚹	♈	1 0:56
2 13:00	♅ ⚹	♉	3 4:55
4 15:08	♅ □	♊	5 6:24
6 16:02	♅ △	♋	7 7:15
8 16:32	♄ ⚹	♌	9 9:02
11 0:12	☿ □	♍	11 12:42
13 15:58	☿ △	♎	13 18:28
15 8:56	♅ △	♏	16 2:17
18 7:36	☉ ☍	♐	18 12:10
20 5:31	♅ ⚹	♑	21 0:02
23 7:32	♀ △	♒	23 13:01
25 9:57	♄ □	♓	26 1:08
28 4:19	☿ □	♈	28 10:09
29 23:17	♅ ⚹	♉	30 15:03

Last Aspect Dy Hr Mn		☽ Ingress	Dy Hr Mn
1 6:09	♃ ☌	♊	1 16:35
3 2:04	♂ ☌	♋	3 16:31
5 7:49	♃ ⚹	♌	5 16:46
7 10:23	♃ □	♍	7 18:58
9 15:49	♃ △	♎	9 24:00
12 2:16	♂ △	♏	12 7:56
14 11:32	♃ ☍	♐	14 18:19
17 1:52	♀ ☍	♑	17 6:28
19 14:47	♃ △	♒	19 19:27
22 4:26	♃ □	♓	22 7:53
24 15:41	♃ ⚹	♈	24 17:57
26 7:24	♅ ⚹	♉	27 0:20
29 2:35	♃ ☌	♊	29 3:00

☽ Phases & Eclipses Dy Hr Mn		
4 4:13	●	14♉00
10 20:02	☽	20♌27
18 7:36	○	27♏40
26 11:56	☾	5♓32
2 12:15	●	12♊15
9 3:30	☽	18♍37
16 22:28	○	26♐03
25 1:01	☾	3♈47

Astro Data

1 May 2000
Julian Day # 36646
SVP 5♓15'35"
GC 26♐50.6 ⚴ 9♌08.1
Eris 19♈29.3 ⚵ 19♒15.0
⚷ 16♐18.3R ⚶ 27♑15.5
☽ Mean ☊ 28♋37.9

1 June 2000
Julian Day # 36677
SVP 5♓15'31"
GC 26♐50.7 ⚴ 20♌20.1
Eris 19♈45.9 ⚵ 25♒20.3
⚷ 14♐20.2R ⚶ 1♒12.4
☽ Mean ☊ 26♋59.4

July 2000 — LONGITUDE

Day	Sid.Time	☉	0 hr ☽	Noon ☽	True ☊	☿	♀	♂	⚳	♃	♄	♅	♆	♇
1 Sa	6 39 23	9♋56 36	27♊59 48	5♋34 54	24♋36.8	17♋38.8	15♋27.0	9♋59.4	3♎55.5	0♊14.8	26♉41.7	20♒17.6	5♒51.9	10♐46.7
2 Su	6 43 19	10 53 50	13♋10 49	20 46 19	24D 36.2	17R 06.2	16 40.7	10 39.2	4 12.2	0 27.2	26 48.0	20R 16.0	5R 50.5	10R 45.4
3 M	6 47 16	11 51 03	28 20 13	5♌51 25	24 36.4	16 31.6	17 54.5	11 18.9	4 29.0	0 39.6	26 54.3	20 14.3	5 49.0	10 44.0
4 Tu	6 51 12	12 48 17	13♌18 54	20 41 49	24 37.0	15 55.4	19 08.3	11 58.6	4 46.1	0 51.9	27 00.5	20 12.6	5 47.6	10 42.7
5 W	6 55 09	13 45 30	27 59 28	5♍11 18	24 37.9	15 18.4	20 22.0	12 38.2	5 03.3	1 04.1	27 06.6	20 10.8	5 46.1	10 41.4
6 Th	6 59 05	14 42 43	12♍16 57	19 16 13	24 38.8	14 41.1	21 35.8	13 17.8	5 20.7	1 16.2	27 12.7	20 09.0	5 44.6	10 40.2
7 F	7 03 02	15 39 56	26 09 03	2♎55 29	24 39.3	14 04.2	22 49.6	13 57.4	5 38.3	1 28.3	27 18.7	20 07.2	5 43.1	10 38.9
8 Sa	7 06 59	16 37 08	9♎35 43	16 10 01	24R 39.5	13 28.3	24 03.3	14 37.0	5 56.1	1 40.3	27 24.7	20 05.4	5 41.6	10 37.7
9 Su	7 10 55	17 34 20	22 38 43	29 02 11	24 39.4	12 54.1	25 17.1	15 16.5	6 14.0	1 52.2	27 30.6	20 03.5	5 40.1	10 36.4
10 M	7 14 52	18 31 33	5♏20 52	11♏35 12	24 38.9	12 22.1	26 30.8	15 55.9	6 32.1	2 04.0	27 36.4	20 01.6	5 38.6	10 35.2
11 Tu	7 18 48	19 28 45	17 45 38	23 52 37	24 38.3	11 52.9	27 44.6	16 35.4	6 50.4	2 15.8	27 42.2	19 59.7	5 37.0	10 34.1
12 W	7 22 45	20 25 57	29 56 37	5♐58 01	24 37.8	11 27.1	28 58.4	17 14.8	7 08.8	2 27.4	27 47.9	19 57.7	5 35.5	10 32.9
13 Th	7 26 41	21 23 09	11♐57 16	17 54 46	24 37.3	11 05.1	0♌12.1	17 54.2	7 27.3	2 39.0	27 53.6	19 55.7	5 33.9	10 31.8
14 F	7 30 38	22 20 22	23 50 51	29 45 54	24 37.0	10 47.4	1 25.9	18 33.6	7 46.1	2 50.5	27 59.1	19 53.7	5 32.4	10 30.7
15 Sa	7 34 34	23 17 35	5♑40 15	11♑34 13	24 36.9	10 34.3	2 39.7	19 12.9	8 05.0	3 01.9	28 04.7	19 51.7	5 30.8	10 29.6
16 Su	7 38 31	24 14 48	17 28 06	23 22 11	24 36.8	10 26.2	3 53.4	19 52.2	8 24.0	3 13.3	28 10.1	19 49.6	5 29.2	10 28.6
17 M	7 42 28	25 12 01	29 16 46	5♒12 08	24 36.8	10D 23.2	5 07.2	20 31.4	8 43.1	3 24.5	28 15.5	19 47.5	5 27.6	10 27.5
18 Tu	7 46 24	26 09 15	11♒08 33	17 06 19	24 36.8	10 25.6	6 21.0	21 10.7	9 02.5	3 35.7	28 20.8	19 45.4	5 26.0	10 26.5
19 W	7 50 21	27 06 29	23 05 43	29 07 04	24 36.6	10 33.6	7 34.7	21 49.9	9 21.9	3 46.7	28 26.0	19 43.3	5 24.4	10 25.5
20 Th	7 54 17	28 03 44	5♓10 41	11♓16 54	24 36.2	10 47.2	8 48.5	22 29.1	9 41.5	3 57.7	28 31.2	19 41.1	5 22.8	10 24.6
21 F	7 58 14	29 00 59	17 26 02	23 38 28	24 35.7	11 06.5	10 02.3	23 08.2	10 01.2	4 08.6	28 36.3	19 38.9	5 21.2	10 23.6
22 Sa	8 02 10	29 58 16	29 54 33	6♈14 39	24 35.2	11 31.6	11 16.0	23 47.3	10 21.1	4 19.3	28 41.3	19 36.7	5 19.6	10 22.7
23 Su	8 06 07	0♌55 33	12♈39 09	19 08 23	24D 34.8	12 02.5	12 29.8	24 26.4	10 41.1	4 30.0	28 46.3	19 34.5	5 18.0	10 21.8
24 M	8 10 03	1 52 51	25 42 41	2♉22 21	24 34.7	12 39.1	13 43.6	25 05.5	11 01.2	4 40.6	28 51.1	19 32.3	5 16.3	10 21.0
25 Tu	8 14 00	2 50 10	9♉07 38	15 58 43	24 34.9	13 21.4	14 57.4	25 44.6	11 21.5	4 51.1	28 55.9	19 30.0	5 14.7	10 20.2
26 W	8 17 57	3 47 29	22 55 40	29 58 30	24 35.4	14 09.5	16 11.2	26 23.6	11 41.8	5 01.5	29 00.6	19 27.8	5 13.1	10 19.4
27 Th	8 21 53	4 44 50	7♊07 04	14♊21 06	24 36.2	15 03.2	17 25.0	27 02.6	12 02.3	5 11.8	29 05.3	19 25.5	5 11.5	10 18.6
28 F	8 25 50	5 42 12	21 40 12	29 03 47	24 37.0	16 02.4	18 38.8	27 41.6	12 23.0	5 21.9	29 09.8	19 23.2	5 09.8	10 17.8
29 Sa	8 29 46	6 39 35	6♋31 09	14♋01 26	24R 37.6	17 07.0	19 52.6	28 20.5	12 43.7	5 32.0	29 14.3	19 20.9	5 08.2	10 17.1
30 Su	8 33 43	7 36 59	21 33 40	29 06 47	24 37.7	18 17.0	21 06.4	28 59.5	13 04.6	5 42.0	29 18.7	19 18.6	5 06.6	10 16.5
31 M	8 37 39	8 34 24	6♌39 41	14♌11 12	24 37.2	19 32.2	22 20.2	29 38.4	13 25.6	5 51.8	29 23.0	19 16.3	5 04.9	10 15.8

August 2000 — LONGITUDE

Day	Sid.Time	☉	0 hr ☽	Noon ☽	True ☊	☿	♀	♂	⚳	♃	♄	♅	♆	♇
1 Tu	8 41 36	9♌31 49	21♌40 15	29♌05 47	24♋35.9	20♋52.4	23♌34.0	0♌17.2	13♎46.7	6♊01.5	29♉27.3	19♒13.9	5♒03.3	10♐15.2
2 W	8 45 32	10 29 15	6♍26 53	13♍42 44	24R 34.1	22 17.5	24 47.8	0 56.1	14 07.9	6 11.1	29 31.4	19R 11.6	5R 01.7	10R 14.6
3 Th	8 49 29	11 26 42	20 52 43	27 56 21	24 32.0	23 47.2	26 01.6	1 34.9	14 29.2	6 20.6	29 35.4	19 09.2	5 00.1	10 14.0
4 F	8 53 26	12 24 10	4♎53 19	11♎43 31	24 30.0	25 21.4	27 15.3	2 13.7	14 50.6	6 30.0	29 39.4	19 06.8	4 58.5	10 13.5
5 Sa	8 57 22	13 21 38	18 26 56	25 03 44	24 28.4	26 59.8	28 29.1	2 52.4	15 12.1	6 39.3	29 43.3	19 04.4	4 56.8	10 13.0
6 Su	9 01 19	14 19 07	1♏34 11	7♏58 40	24D 27.5	28 42.1	29 42.9	3 31.2	15 33.7	6 48.4	29 47.1	19 02.1	4 55.2	10 12.5
7 M	9 05 15	15 16 37	14 17 36	20 31 31	24 27.4	0♌28.0	0♍56.7	4 09.9	15 55.5	6 57.4	29 50.8	18 59.7	4 53.6	10 12.0
8 Tu	9 09 12	16 14 07	26 40 56	2♐46 25	24 28.2	2 17.2	2 10.5	4 48.6	16 17.3	7 06.3	29 54.4	18 57.3	4 52.1	10 11.6
9 W	9 13 08	17 11 38	8♐48 34	14 47 57	24 29.6	4 09.3	3 24.2	5 27.2	16 39.2	7 15.1	29 57.9	18 54.9	4 50.5	10 11.2
10 Th	9 17 05	18 09 11	20 45 08	26 40 39	24 31.3	6 03.8	4 38.0	6 05.9	17 01.2	7 23.7	0♊01.4	18 52.5	4 48.9	10 10.9
11 F	9 21 01	19 06 44	2♑35 04	8♑28 51	24 32.8	8 00.6	5 51.7	6 44.5	17 23.4	7 32.2	0 04.7	18 50.1	4 47.3	10 10.6
12 Sa	9 24 58	20 04 18	14 22 30	20 16 25	24R 33.6	9 59.0	7 05.5	7 23.1	17 45.6	7 40.6	0 07.9	18 47.7	4 45.8	10 10.3
13 Su	9 28 55	21 01 53	26 11 01	2♒06 41	24 33.5	11 58.9	8 19.2	8 01.6	18 07.8	7 48.8	0 11.1	18 45.3	4 44.2	10 10.0
14 M	9 32 51	21 59 30	8♒03 43	14 02 25	24 32.0	13 59.8	9 33.0	8 40.2	18 30.2	7 56.9	0 14.2	18 42.9	4 42.7	10 09.8
15 Tu	9 36 48	22 57 07	20 03 04	26 05 52	24 29.2	16 01.4	10 46.7	9 18.7	18 52.7	8 04.9	0 17.1	18 40.6	4 41.1	10 09.6
16 W	9 40 44	23 54 46	2♓11 01	8♓18 44	24 25.2	18 03.3	12 00.4	9 57.2	19 15.2	8 12.7	0 20.0	18 38.2	4 39.6	10 09.5
17 Th	9 44 41	24 52 26	14 29 09	20 42 25	24 20.4	20 05.3	13 14.2	10 35.7	19 37.8	8 20.4	0 22.7	18 35.8	4 38.1	10 09.3
18 F	9 48 37	25 50 07	26 58 41	3♈18 05	24 15.2	22 07.2	14 27.9	11 14.1	20 00.6	8 27.9	0 25.4	18 33.4	4 36.6	10 09.2
19 Sa	9 52 34	26 47 50	9♈40 44	16 06 46	24 10.3	24 08.6	15 41.6	11 52.5	20 23.3	8 35.3	0 28.0	18 31.1	4 35.1	10 09.2
20 Su	9 56 30	27 45 35	22 36 19	29 09 32	24 06.3	26 09.5	16 55.3	12 30.9	20 46.2	8 42.6	0 30.5	18 28.7	4 33.7	10D 09.1
21 M	10 00 27	28 43 21	5♉46 33	12♉27 31	24 03.6	28 09.7	18 09.0	13 09.3	21 09.2	8 49.7	0 32.8	18 26.3	4 32.2	10 09.1
22 Tu	10 04 23	29 41 09	19 12 33	26 01 45	24D 02.5	0♍08.9	19 22.7	13 47.7	21 32.2	8 56.7	0 35.1	18 24.0	4 30.8	10 09.2
23 W	10 08 20	0♍38 58	2♊55 13	9♊53 00	24 02.8	2 07.2	20 36.4	14 26.1	21 55.3	9 03.5	0 37.3	18 21.7	4 29.3	10 09.2
24 Th	10 12 17	1 36 50	16 55 04	24 01 19	24 03.9	4 04.4	21 50.1	15 04.4	22 18.5	9 10.2	0 39.4	18 19.4	4 27.9	10 09.3
25 F	10 16 13	2 34 43	1♋11 37	8♋25 41	24 05.2	6 00.5	23 03.8	15 42.7	22 41.7	9 16.7	0 41.3	18 17.1	4 26.5	10 09.5
26 Sa	10 20 10	3 32 38	15 43 06	23 03 24	24R 05.9	7 55.4	24 17.4	16 21.0	23 05.0	9 23.0	0 43.2	18 14.8	4 25.2	10 09.6
27 Su	10 24 06	4 30 35	0♌25 56	7♌49 58	24 05.2	9 49.1	25 31.1	16 59.3	23 28.4	9 29.2	0 45.0	18 12.5	4 23.8	10 09.8
28 M	10 28 03	5 28 34	15 14 40	22 39 07	24 02.7	11 41.6	26 44.8	17 37.6	23 51.9	9 35.2	0 46.6	18 10.3	4 22.5	10 10.1
29 Tu	10 31 59	6 26 34	0♍02 22	7♍23 25	23 58.2	13 32.7	27 58.4	18 15.8	24 15.4	9 41.1	0 48.2	18 08.0	4 21.1	10 10.4
30 W	10 35 56	7 24 35	14 41 21	21 55 16	23 52.0	15 22.7	29 12.1	18 54.0	24 39.0	9 46.8	0 49.6	18 05.8	4 19.8	10 10.7
31 Th	10 39 52	8 22 39	29 04 23	6♎08 04	23 45.0	17 11.3	0♎25.8	19 32.2	25 02.7	9 52.3	0 51.0	18 03.6	4 18.5	10 11.0

Astro Data Dy Hr Mn	Planet Ingress Dy Hr Mn
☽0S 8 4:26	♀ ♌ 13 8:03
☿D 17 13:22	☉ ♌ 22 12:44
☽0N 22 22:51	
♃△♆ 27 11:23	♂ ♌ 1 1:22
	♀ ♍ 6 17:33
☽0S 4 12:28	☿ ♌ 7 5:43
⚳0S 6 20:12	♄ ♊ 10 2:28
☽0N 19 4:02	☿ ♍ 22 10:12
♇D 20 22:44	☉ ♍ 22 19:50
☽0S 31 21:38	♀ ♎ 31 3:36

Last Aspect Dy Hr Mn	☽ Ingress Dy Hr Mn	Last Aspect Dy Hr Mn	☽ Ingress Dy Hr Mn
30 11:48 ♅ △	♋ 1 3:10	1 12:35 ♄ □	♍ 1 13:28
2 21:37 ♄ ⚹	♌ 3 2:39	3 14:51 ♄ △	♎ 3 15:32
4 22:27 ♄ □	♍ 5 3:20	5 18:57 ♀ ⚹	♏ 5 21:05
7 1:58 ♄ △	♎ 7 6:48	8 6:19 ♄ ☍	♐ 8 6:31
9 4:11 ♀ □	♏ 9 13:49	9 20:16 ♅ ⚹	♑ 10 18:45
11 20:30 ♀ △	♐ 12 0:07	11 6:03 ♀ △	♒ 13 7:44
13 16:04 ♅ ⚹	♑ 14 12:29	15 5:14 ☉ ☍	♓ 15 19:42
16 21:49 ♄ △	♒ 17 1:28	16 19:59 ♀ ☍	♈ 18 5:45
19 10:38 ♄ □	♓ 19 13:45	20 9:15 ☉ △	♉ 20 13:32
21 23:09 ☉ △	♈ 22 0:10	22 18:52 ☉ □	♊ 22 18:56
23 22:12 ♂ □	♉ 24 7:45	24 7:58 ♀ □	♋ 24 22:01
26 10:21 ♄ ☌	♊ 26 12:03	26 14:12 ♄ ⚹	♌ 26 23:18
27 20:19 ♅ △	♋ 28 13:31	28 4:45 ♅ ☍	♍ 28 23:56
30 12:19 ♄ ⚹	♌ 30 13:25	31 1:22 ♀ ☌	♎ 31 1:34

☽ Phases & Eclipses Dy Hr Mn	Astro Data
1 19:21 ● 10♋14	1 July 2000
1 19:33:36 ✔ P 0.477	Julian Day # 36707
8 12:54 ☽ 16♎39	SVP 5♓15'25"
16 13:56 ○ 24♑19	GC 26♐50.8 ⚴ 2♍33.3
16 13:57 • T 1.768	Eris 19♈54.9 ⚵ 26♒48.9R
24 11:03 ☾ 1♉51	⚷ 12♐20.6R ⚶ 28♑02.2R
31 2:26 ● 8♌12	☽ Mean ☊ 25♋24.1
31 2:14:06 ✔ P 0.603	
	1 August 2000
7 1:03 ☽ 14♏50	Julian Day # 36738
15 5:14 ○ 22♒41	SVP 5♓15'20"
22 18:52 ☾ 29♉58	GC 26♐50.8 ⚴ 15♍54.8
29 10:20 ● 6♍23	Eris 19♈54.6R ⚵ 22♒29.1R
	⚷ 11♐08.5R ⚶ 20♑54.8R
	☽ Mean ☊ 23♋45.6

LONGITUDE September 2000

Day	Sid.Time	☉	0 hr ☽	Noon ☽	True ☊	☿	♀	♂	⚳	♃	♄	♅	♆	♇
1 F	10 43 49	9♍20 43	13♎05 48	19♎57 13	23♋37.9	18♍58.7	1♎39.4	20♌10.4	25♎26.4	9♊57.7	0♊52.2	18♒01.4	4♒17.3	10♐11.3
2 Sa	10 47 46	10 18 49	26 42 10	3♏20 35	23R31.7	20 44.8	2 53.0	20 48.5	25 50.2	10 02.9	0 53.3	17R59.2	4R16.0	10 11.7
3 Su	10 51 42	11 16 57	9♏52 36	16 18 27	23 26.9	22 29.7	4 06.6	21 26.7	26 14.0	10 07.9	0 54.4	17 57.1	4 14.8	10 12.2
4 M	10 55 39	12 15 06	22 38 31	28 53 13	23 24.0	24 13.3	5 20.2	22 04.8	26 38.0	10 12.8	0 55.3	17 55.0	4 13.6	10 12.7
5 Tu	10 59 35	13 13 16	5♐03 06	11♐08 45	23D23.0	25 55.8	6 33.8	22 42.9	27 01.9	10 17.5	0 56.1	17 52.9	4 12.4	10 13.2
6 W	11 03 32	14 11 28	17 10 47	23 09 51	23 23.3	27 37.0	7 47.4	23 20.9	27 26.0	10 22.0	0 56.8	17 50.8	4 11.2	10 13.7
7 Th	11 07 28	15 09 42	29 06 36	5♑01 43	23 24.5	29 17.0	9 01.0	23 59.0	27 50.0	10 26.3	0 57.4	17 48.8	4 10.1	10 14.3
8 F	11 11 25	16 07 57	10♑55 49	16 49 33	23R25.5	0♎55.9	10 14.5	24 37.0	28 14.2	10 30.4	0 57.9	17 46.7	4 09.0	10 14.9
9 Sa	11 15 21	17 06 13	22 43 31	28 38 17	23 25.5	2 33.7	11 28.1	25 15.0	28 38.4	10 34.4	0 58.2	17 44.7	4 07.9	10 15.5
10 Su	11 19 18	18 04 32	4♒34 22	10♒32 16	23 23.9	4 10.3	12 41.6	25 53.0	29 02.6	10 38.2	0 58.5	17 42.8	4 06.8	10 16.2
11 M	11 23 15	19 02 51	16 32 24	22 35 09	23 20.0	5 45.7	13 55.1	26 31.0	29 26.9	10 41.8	0R58.7	17 40.8	4 05.8	10 16.8
12 Tu	11 27 11	20 01 13	28 40 48	4♓49 38	23 13.7	7 20.1	15 08.6	27 08.9	29 51.2	10 45.2	0 58.7	17 38.9	4 04.8	10 17.6
13 W	11 31 08	20 59 36	11♓01 48	17 17 26	23 05.3	8 53.3	16 22.1	27 46.8	0♏15.6	10 48.5	0 58.7	17 37.0	4 03.8	10 18.3
14 Th	11 35 04	21 58 01	23 36 37	29 59 19	22 55.3	10 25.4	17 35.5	28 24.8	0 40.0	10 51.5	0 58.5	17 35.2	4 02.8	10 19.1
15 F	11 39 01	22 56 28	6♈25 31	12♈55 07	22 44.8	11 56.5	18 49.0	29 02.7	1 04.5	10 54.4	0 58.2	17 33.4	4 01.9	10 19.9
16 Sa	11 42 57	23 54 57	19 28 01	26 04 05	22 34.6	13 26.4	20 02.4	29 40.5	1 29.0	10 57.1	0 57.8	17 31.6	4 01.0	10 20.8
17 Su	11 46 54	24 53 28	2♉43 09	9♉25 05	22 25.9	14 55.3	21 15.8	0♍18.4	1 53.6	10 59.6	0 57.4	17 29.8	4 00.1	10 21.7
18 M	11 50 50	25 52 01	16 09 44	22 57 01	22 19.3	16 23.0	22 29.2	0 56.2	2 18.2	11 01.8	0 56.8	17 28.1	3 59.2	10 22.6
19 Tu	11 54 47	26 50 36	29 46 49	6♊39 03	22 15.3	17 49.7	23 42.6	1 34.1	2 42.9	11 03.9	0 56.1	17 26.4	3 58.4	10 23.6
20 W	11 58 44	27 49 14	13♊33 41	20 30 40	22D13.6	19 15.2	24 56.0	2 11.9	3 07.6	11 05.9	0 55.3	17 24.8	3 57.6	10 24.5
21 Th	12 02 40	28 47 54	27 29 58	4♋31 32	22 13.5	20 39.6	26 09.4	2 49.7	3 32.3	11 07.6	0 54.3	17 23.2	3 56.8	10 25.6
22 F	12 06 37	29 46 36	11♋35 19	18 41 12	22R13.9	22 02.8	27 22.8	3 27.5	3 57.1	11 09.1	0 53.3	17 21.6	3 56.1	10 26.6
23 Sa	12 10 33	0♎45 20	25 49 01	2♌58 34	22 13.5	23 24.8	28 36.1	4 05.3	4 22.0	11 10.4	0 52.2	17 20.1	3 55.4	10 27.7
24 Su	12 14 30	1 44 07	10♌09 30	17 21 28	22 11.3	24 45.6	29 49.5	4 43.0	4 46.8	11 11.5	0 50.9	17 18.6	3 54.7	10 28.8
25 M	12 18 26	2 42 56	24 33 56	1♍46 21	22 06.5	26 05.1	1♏02.8	5 20.8	5 11.7	11 12.4	0 49.6	17 17.1	3 54.0	10 29.9
26 Tu	12 22 23	3 41 47	8♍58 05	16 08 24	21 58.9	27 23.3	2 16.1	5 58.5	5 36.7	11 13.2	0 48.2	17 15.7	3 53.4	10 31.1
27 W	12 26 19	4 40 40	23 16 35	0♎21 56	21 48.8	28 40.1	3 29.4	6 36.2	6 01.7	11 13.7	0 46.6	17 14.3	3 52.8	10 32.3
28 Th	12 30 16	5 39 35	7♎23 42	14 21 18	21 37.3	29 55.4	4 42.7	7 13.9	6 26.7	11 14.0	0 44.9	17 12.9	3 52.2	10 33.5
29 F	12 34 13	6 38 32	21 14 09	28 01 49	21 25.5	1♏09.2	5 56.0	7 51.5	6 51.7	11R14.1	0 43.2	17 11.6	3 51.7	10 34.7
30 Sa	12 38 09	7 37 31	4♏44 00	11♏20 31	21 14.5	2 21.4	7 09.2	8 29.2	7 16.8	11 14.0	0 41.3	17 10.4	3 51.2	10 36.0

LONGITUDE October 2000

Day	Sid.Time	☉	0 hr ☽	Noon ☽	True ☊	☿	♀	♂	⚳	♃	♄	♅	♆	♇
1 Su	12 42 06	8♎36 31	17♏51 19	24♏16 29	21♋05.5	3♏31.9	8♏22.5	9♍06.8	7♏42.0	11♊13.7	0♊39.3	17♒09.1	3♒50.7	10♐37.3
2 M	12 46 02	9 35 34	0♐36 13	6♐50 52	20R59.0	4 40.5	9 35.7	9 44.4	8 07.1	11R13.2	0R37.3	17R08.0	3R50.2	10 38.7
3 Tu	12 49 59	10 34 39	13 00 50	19 06 37	20 55.1	5 47.2	10 48.9	10 22.0	8 32.3	11 12.5	0 35.1	17 06.8	3 49.8	10 40.0
4 W	12 53 55	11 33 45	25 08 46	1♑07 55	20D53.3	6 51.7	12 02.1	10 59.6	8 57.5	11 11.6	0 32.8	17 05.8	3 49.4	10 41.4
5 Th	12 57 52	12 32 53	7♑04 43	12 59 51	20R53.0	7 54.0	13 15.3	11 37.1	9 22.7	11 10.5	0 30.5	17 04.7	3 49.1	10 42.9
6 F	13 01 48	13 32 03	18 54 00	24 47 54	20 53.0	8 53.7	14 28.4	12 14.6	9 48.0	11 09.2	0 28.0	17 03.7	3 48.8	10 44.3
7 Sa	13 05 45	14 31 15	0♒42 12	6♒37 35	20 52.2	9 50.8	15 41.5	12 52.2	10 13.3	11 07.7	0 25.5	17 02.8	3 48.5	10 45.8
8 Su	13 09 41	15 30 28	12 34 42	18 34 09	20 49.7	10 44.9	16 54.6	13 29.7	10 38.6	11 06.0	0 22.8	17 01.9	3 48.3	10 47.3
9 M	13 13 38	16 29 43	24 36 30	0♓42 14	20 44.7	11 35.8	18 07.7	14 07.1	11 04.0	11 04.1	0 20.1	17 01.0	3 48.0	10 48.8
10 Tu	13 17 35	17 29 00	6♓51 48	13 05 31	20 36.9	12 23.2	19 20.8	14 44.6	11 29.3	11 02.0	0 17.3	17 00.2	3 47.8	10 50.4
11 W	13 21 31	18 28 19	19 23 40	25 46 25	20 26.6	13 06.7	20 33.8	15 22.0	11 54.7	10 59.7	0 14.3	16 59.4	3 47.7	10 52.0
12 Th	13 25 28	19 27 40	2♈13 50	8♈45 54	20 14.4	13 46.0	21 46.8	15 59.4	12 20.1	10 57.2	0 11.3	16 58.7	3 47.6	10 53.6
13 F	13 29 24	20 27 03	15 22 27	22 03 18	20 01.3	14 20.6	22 59.8	16 36.9	12 45.5	10 54.5	0 08.2	16 58.0	3 47.5	10 55.2
14 Sa	13 33 21	21 26 28	28 48 09	5♉36 36	19 48.7	14 50.2	24 12.8	17 14.2	13 11.0	10 51.6	0 05.0	16 57.4	3 47.4	10 56.9
15 Su	13 37 17	22 25 55	12♉28 15	19 22 40	19 37.7	15 14.3	25 25.7	17 51.6	13 36.5	10 48.5	0 01.8	16 56.8	3D47.4	10 58.5
16 M	13 41 14	23 25 24	26 19 22	3♊17 57	19 29.3	15 32.2	26 38.6	18 29.0	14 02.0	10 45.2	29♉58.4	16 56.3	3 47.4	11 00.2
17 Tu	13 45 10	24 24 56	10♊17 58	17 19 05	19 23.9	15 43.6	27 51.5	19 06.3	14 27.5	10 41.8	29 55.0	16 55.8	3 47.5	11 02.0
18 W	13 49 07	25 24 30	24 20 58	1♋23 22	19 21.1	15R47.9	29 04.4	19 43.6	14 53.0	10 38.1	29 51.5	16 55.4	3 47.6	11 03.7
19 Th	13 53 04	26 24 06	8♋26 04	15 28 55	19 20.4	15 44.6	0♐17.2	20 21.0	15 18.5	10 34.3	29 47.9	16 55.0	3 47.7	11 05.5
20 F	13 57 00	27 23 44	22 31 49	29 34 39	19 20.4	15 33.1	1 30.1	20 58.3	15 44.1	10 30.2	29 44.2	16 54.6	3 47.8	11 07.3
21 Sa	14 00 57	28 23 25	6♌37 20	13♌39 47	19 19.8	15 13.0	2 42.9	21 35.5	16 09.7	10 26.0	29 40.5	16 54.4	3 48.0	11 09.1
22 Su	14 04 53	29 23 08	20 41 52	27 43 26	19 17.3	14 44.2	3 55.7	22 12.8	16 35.3	10 21.6	29 36.7	16 54.1	3 48.2	11 10.9
23 M	14 08 50	0♏22 53	4♍44 18	11♍44 12	19 12.2	14 06.4	5 08.4	22 50.0	17 00.9	10 17.1	29 32.8	16 53.9	3 48.5	11 12.8
24 Tu	14 12 46	1 22 41	18 42 51	25 39 52	19 04.3	13 19.8	6 21.2	23 27.3	17 26.5	10 12.3	29 28.8	16 53.8	3 48.7	11 14.7
25 W	14 16 43	2 22 30	2♎34 52	9♎27 27	18 53.7	12 24.9	7 33.9	24 04.5	17 52.2	10 07.4	29 24.8	16 53.7	3 49.1	11 16.6
26 Th	14 20 39	3 22 22	16 17 10	23 03 37	18 41.6	11 22.4	8 46.6	24 41.6	18 17.8	10 02.3	29 20.7	16D53.7	3 49.4	11 18.5
27 F	14 24 36	4 22 16	29 46 25	6♏25 13	18 29.0	10 13.4	9 59.2	25 18.8	18 43.5	9 57.0	29 16.6	16 53.7	3 49.8	11 20.4
28 Sa	14 28 33	5 22 11	12♏59 45	19 29 50	18 17.2	8 59.7	11 11.9	25 56.0	19 09.2	9 51.5	29 12.3	16 53.8	3 50.2	11 22.4
29 Su	14 32 29	6 22 09	25 55 22	2♐16 20	18 07.3	7 43.2	12 24.5	26 33.1	19 34.9	9 45.9	29 08.1	16 53.9	3 50.7	11 24.4
30 M	14 36 26	7 22 08	8♐32 49	14 45 01	18 00.0	6 26.0	13 37.1	27 10.2	20 00.6	9 40.2	29 03.8	16 54.1	3 51.2	11 26.4
31 Tu	14 40 22	8 22 09	20 53 11	26 57 42	17 55.4	5 10.6	14 49.6	27 47.3	20 26.3	9 34.3	28 59.4	16 54.3	3 51.7	11 28.4

Astro Data	Dy Hr Mn
♀0S	2 3:35
♃☍♇	4 11:15
☿0S	8 13:45
♄R	12 11:35
☽0N	15 9:31
☉0S	22 17:29
☽0S	28 7:06
♃R	29 12:53
☽0N	12 17:01
♃☍♇	13 8:05
♆D	15 14:13
☿R	18 13:42
☽0S	25 15:45
♅D	26 15:25

Planet Ingress	Dy Hr Mn
☿ ♎	7 22:23
⚳ ♏	12 20:39
♂ ♍	17 0:20
☉ ♎	22 17:29
♀ ♏	24 15:27
☿ ♏	28 13:29
♄ ♉R	16 0:45
♀ ♐	19 6:19
☉ ♏	23 2:49

Last Aspect Dy Hr Mn		☽ Ingress Dy Hr Mn
1 12:24 ♂ ⚹	♏	2 5:56
4 1:36 ☿ ⚹	♐	4 14:09
6 22:27 ☿ □	♑	7 1:48
8 10:28 ☉ △	♒	9 14:46
11 20:10 ♂ ☍	♓	12 2:35
13 19:38 ☉ ☍	♈	14 12:01
16 18:51 ☉ △	♉	16 19:06
18 17:32 ☉ △	♊	19 0:23
21 1:29 ☉ □	♋	21 4:17
23 3:59 ♀ □	♌	23 7:01
25 1:34 ☿ ⚹	♍	25 9:03
26 3:45 ♃ □	♎	27 11:23
28 16:58 ♅ △	♏	29 15:31

Last Aspect Dy Hr Mn		☽ Ingress Dy Hr Mn
30 22:43 ♅ □	♐	1 22:51
3 8:04 ♅ ⚹	♑	4 9:43
5 12:35 ♀ ⚹	♒	6 22:34
8 8:56 ♅ ☌	♓	9 10:37
11 1:10 ♀ △	♈	11 19:52
13 8:54 ☉ ☍	♉	14 2:07
16 6:19 ♄ ☌	♊	16 6:20
18 1:02 ☉ △	♋	18 9:38
20 12:16 ♄ ⚹	♌	20 12:43
22 15:13 ♄ □	♍	22 15:53
24 18:35 ♄ △	♎	24 19:31
26 1:04 ♅ △	♏	27 0:24
29 6:05 ♄ ☍	♐	29 7:41
31 13:44 ♂ □	♑	31 18:03

☽ Phases & Eclipses Dy Hr Mn	
5 16:28	☽ 13♐24
13 19:38	○ 21♓18
21 1:29	☾ 28♊22
27 19:54	● 5♎00
5 11:00	☽ 12♑30
13 8:54	○ 20♈19
20 8:00	☾ 27♋14
27 7:59	● 4♏12

Astro Data

1 September 2000
Julian Day # 36769
SVP 5♓15'17"
GC 26♐50.9 ⚴ 29♍39.7
Eris 19♈44.8R ⚵ 15♒12.8R
⚷ 11♐21.2 ⚶ 18♑08.4
☽ Mean ☊ 22♋07.1

1 October 2000
Julian Day # 36799
SVP 5♓15'14"
GC 26♐51.0 ⚴ 13♎07.5
Eris 19♈29.0R ⚵ 12♒00.0
⚷ 12♐56.1 ⚶ 22♑10.3
☽ Mean ☊ 20♋31.8

November 2000 — LONGITUDE

Day	Sid.Time	☉	0 hr ☽	Noon☽	True☊	☿	♀	♂	⚳	♃	♄	♅	♆	♇
1 W	14 44 19	9♏22 12	2♑59 00	8♑57 34	17♋53.2	3♏59.4	16♐02.2	28♍24.3	20♏52.0	9♊28.2	28♉55.0	16♒54.6	3♒52.2	11♐30.4
2 Th	14 48 15	10 22 16	14 53 57	20 48 46	17D 52.9	2R 54.6	17 14.6	29 01.4	21 17.7	9R 22.0	28R 50.5	16 54.9	3 52.8	11 32.5
3 F	14 52 12	11 22 23	26 42 40	2♒36 18	17R 53.4	1 58.0	18 27.1	29 38.4	21 43.4	9 15.7	28 46.0	16 55.3	3 53.4	11 34.5
4 Sa	14 56 08	12 22 30	8♒30 22	14 25 32	17 53.6	1 11.3	19 39.5	0♎15.4	22 09.1	9 09.2	28 41.4	16 55.7	3 54.1	11 36.6
5 Su	15 00 05	13 22 39	20 22 32	26 22 01	17 52.6	0 35.5	20 51.9	0 52.3	22 34.8	9 02.6	28 36.8	16 56.2	3 54.8	11 38.7
6 M	15 04 02	14 22 50	2♓24 38	8♓31 01	17 49.6	0 11.2	22 04.2	1 29.3	23 00.6	8 55.8	28 32.2	16 56.7	3 55.5	11 40.8
7 Tu	15 07 58	15 23 02	14 41 43	20 57 13	17 44.3	29♎58.5	23 16.5	2 06.2	23 26.3	8 49.0	28 27.5	16 57.3	3 56.3	11 42.9
8 W	15 11 55	16 23 16	27 17 57	3♈44 14	17 36.6	29D 57.3	24 28.7	2 43.1	23 52.0	8 42.0	28 22.8	16 58.0	3 57.0	11 45.1
9 Th	15 15 51	17 23 31	10♈16 16	16 54 07	17 27.2	0♏07.1	25 40.9	3 20.0	24 17.7	8 34.9	28 18.0	16 58.6	3 57.9	11 47.2
10 F	15 19 48	18 23 48	23 37 45	0♉26 59	17 16.9	0 27.3	26 53.1	3 56.9	24 43.4	8 27.7	28 13.3	16 59.4	3 58.7	11 49.4
11 Sa	15 23 44	19 24 06	7♉21 29	14 20 48	17 06.9	0 57.0	28 05.2	4 33.7	25 09.2	8 20.4	28 08.5	17 00.2	3 59.6	11 51.6
12 Su	15 27 41	20 24 26	21 24 24	28 31 36	16 58.1	1 35.4	29 17.2	5 10.5	25 34.9	8 13.0	28 03.7	17 01.0	4 00.5	11 53.7
13 M	15 31 37	21 24 48	5♊41 42	12♊53 57	16 51.6	2 21.5	0♑29.2	5 47.3	26 00.6	8 05.5	27 58.8	17 01.9	4 01.5	11 55.9
14 Tu	15 35 34	22 25 12	20 07 36	27 21 55	16 47.5	3 14.5	1 41.2	6 24.1	26 26.3	7 57.9	27 54.0	17 02.8	4 02.4	11 58.2
15 W	15 39 31	23 25 38	4♋36 13	11♋49 54	16D 45.9	4 13.6	2 53.1	7 00.8	26 52.0	7 50.2	27 49.1	17 03.8	4 03.5	12 00.4
16 Th	15 43 27	24 26 05	19 02 27	26 13 25	16 46.1	5 17.9	4 04.9	7 37.6	27 17.7	7 42.5	27 44.2	17 04.8	4 04.5	12 02.6
17 F	15 47 24	25 26 35	3♌22 28	10♌29 19	16 47.1	6 26.8	5 16.8	8 14.3	27 43.4	7 34.7	27 39.4	17 05.9	4 05.6	12 04.9
18 Sa	15 51 20	26 27 06	17 33 47	24 35 45	16R 47.8	7 39.6	6 28.5	8 51.0	28 09.1	7 26.8	27 34.5	17 07.1	4 06.7	12 07.1
19 Su	15 55 17	27 27 39	1♍35 08	8♍31 51	16 47.2	8 55.8	7 40.2	9 27.6	28 34.8	7 18.9	27 29.6	17 08.3	4 07.8	12 09.4
20 M	15 59 13	28 28 13	15 25 53	22 17 12	16 44.7	10 14.9	8 51.9	10 04.3	29 00.5	7 10.9	27 24.7	17 09.5	4 09.0	12 11.6
21 Tu	16 03 10	29 28 50	29 05 46	5♎51 32	16 40.0	11 36.4	10 03.4	10 40.9	29 26.2	7 02.8	27 19.8	17 10.8	4 10.2	12 13.9
22 W	16 07 06	0♐29 28	12♎34 26	19 14 24	16 33.3	12 59.9	11 15.0	11 17.5	29 51.8	6 54.7	27 14.9	17 12.1	4 11.4	12 16.2
23 Th	16 11 03	1 30 07	25 51 21	2♏25 10	16 25.4	14 25.2	12 26.4	11 54.1	0♐17.5	6 46.6	27 10.0	17 13.5	4 12.6	12 18.5
24 F	16 15 00	2 30 49	8♏55 47	15 23 06	16 17.1	15 51.9	13 37.8	12 30.6	0 43.1	6 38.5	27 05.1	17 14.9	4 13.9	12 20.8
25 Sa	16 18 56	3 31 32	21 47 03	28 07 36	16 09.3	17 19.8	14 49.2	13 07.1	1 08.8	6 30.3	27 00.3	17 16.4	4 15.2	12 23.1
26 Su	16 22 53	4 32 16	4♐24 44	10♐38 28	16 02.8	18 48.7	16 00.5	13 43.6	1 34.4	6 22.1	26 55.4	17 17.9	4 16.6	12 25.4
27 M	16 26 49	5 33 01	16 48 55	22 56 11	15 58.2	20 18.4	17 11.7	14 20.0	2 00.0	6 13.9	26 50.6	17 19.5	4 17.9	12 27.7
28 Tu	16 30 46	6 33 48	29 00 28	5♑02 00	15D 55.6	21 48.8	18 22.8	14 56.5	2 25.6	6 05.7	26 45.8	17 21.1	4 19.3	12 30.0
29 W	16 34 42	7 34 36	11♑01 06	16 58 07	15 54.9	23 19.8	19 33.9	15 32.8	2 51.2	5 57.5	26 41.1	17 22.7	4 20.7	12 32.3
30 Th	16 38 39	8 35 25	22 53 27	28 47 34	15 55.7	24 51.2	20 44.8	16 09.2	3 16.7	5 49.3	26 36.3	17 24.5	4 22.2	12 34.7

December 2000 — LONGITUDE

Day	Sid.Time	☉	0 hr ☽	Noon☽	True☊	☿	♀	♂	⚳	♃	♄	♅	♆	♇
1 F	16 42 35	9♐36 15	4♒40 58	10♒34 12	15♋57.3	26♏23.0	21♑55.7	16♎45.5	3♐42.2	5♊41.2	26♉31.6	17♒26.2	4♒23.7	12♐37.0
2 Sa	16 46 32	10 37 06	16 27 50	22 22 29	15 59.2	27 55.1	23 06.5	17 21.8	4 07.8	5R 33.0	26R 26.9	17 28.0	4 25.2	12 39.3
3 Su	16 50 29	11 37 58	28 18 47	4♓17 23	16R 00.4	29 27.4	24 17.2	17 58.1	4 33.3	5 24.9	26 22.3	17 29.9	4 26.7	12 41.6
4 M	16 54 25	12 38 50	10♓18 55	16 24 02	16 00.6	1♐00.0	25 27.9	18 34.3	4 58.7	5 16.9	26 17.7	17 31.7	4 28.3	12 43.9
5 Tu	16 58 22	13 39 43	22 33 21	28 47 28	15 59.4	2 32.7	26 38.4	19 10.5	5 24.2	5 08.9	26 13.1	17 33.7	4 29.9	12 46.3
6 W	17 02 18	14 40 37	5♈06 55	11♈32 11	15 56.8	4 05.5	27 48.8	19 46.7	5 49.6	5 00.9	26 08.6	17 35.6	4 31.5	12 48.6
7 Th	17 06 15	15 41 32	18 03 39	24 41 35	15 53.0	5 38.4	28 59.1	20 22.8	6 15.0	4 53.0	26 04.1	17 37.7	4 33.1	12 50.9
8 F	17 10 11	16 42 28	1♉26 11	8♉17 26	15 48.4	7 11.5	0♒09.3	20 58.9	6 40.4	4 45.1	25 59.7	17 39.7	4 34.7	12 53.2
9 Sa	17 14 08	17 43 24	15 15 14	22 19 16	15 43.9	8 44.6	1 19.4	21 34.9	7 05.7	4 37.3	25 55.3	17 41.8	4 36.4	12 55.6
10 Su	17 18 04	18 44 21	29 29 06	6♊44 06	15 39.9	10 17.8	2 29.3	22 11.0	7 31.1	4 29.6	25 51.0	17 44.0	4 38.1	12 57.9
11 M	17 22 01	19 45 19	14♊03 32	21 26 30	15 37.1	11 51.1	3 39.2	22 47.0	7 56.4	4 22.0	25 46.8	17 46.1	4 39.9	13 00.2
12 Tu	17 25 58	20 46 18	28 52 04	6♋19 12	15D 35.6	13 24.4	4 48.9	23 22.9	8 21.6	4 14.4	25 42.6	17 48.4	4 41.6	13 02.5
13 W	17 29 54	21 47 18	13♋46 53	21 14 07	15 35.4	14 57.9	5 58.5	23 58.9	8 46.9	4 07.0	25 38.4	17 50.6	4 43.4	13 04.8
14 Th	17 33 51	22 48 19	28 39 57	6♌03 34	15 36.3	16 31.4	7 08.0	24 34.8	9 12.1	3 59.6	25 34.4	17 52.9	4 45.2	13 07.1
15 F	17 37 47	23 49 21	13♌24 11	20 41 12	15 37.7	18 05.1	8 17.3	25 10.6	9 37.3	3 52.3	25 30.4	17 55.3	4 47.0	13 09.4
16 Sa	17 41 44	24 50 23	27 54 09	5♍02 38	15 39.1	19 38.8	9 26.5	25 46.4	10 02.4	3 45.2	25 26.4	17 57.7	4 48.8	13 11.7
17 Su	17 45 40	25 51 27	12♍06 27	19 05 26	15R 39.9	21 12.7	10 35.5	26 22.2	10 27.6	3 38.1	25 22.5	18 00.1	4 50.7	13 14.0
18 M	17 49 37	26 52 31	25 59 33	2♎48 52	15 40.0	22 46.7	11 44.4	26 58.0	10 52.6	3 31.2	25 18.7	18 02.5	4 52.5	13 16.3
19 Tu	17 53 33	27 53 36	9♎33 28	16 13 31	15 39.1	24 20.9	12 53.2	27 33.7	11 17.7	3 24.4	25 15.0	18 05.0	4 54.4	13 18.5
20 W	17 57 30	28 54 42	22 49 10	29 20 39	15 37.4	25 55.2	14 01.8	28 09.3	11 42.7	3 17.7	25 11.4	18 07.5	4 56.4	13 20.8
21 Th	18 01 27	29 55 49	5♏48 11	12♏11 58	15 35.2	27 29.7	15 10.3	28 45.0	12 07.7	3 11.1	25 07.8	18 10.1	4 58.3	13 23.0
22 F	18 05 23	0♑56 57	18 32 14	24 49 12	15 32.8	29 04.4	16 18.5	29 20.6	12 32.7	3 04.7	25 04.3	18 12.7	5 00.2	13 25.3
23 Sa	18 09 20	1 58 05	1♐03 04	7♐14 02	15 30.7	0♑39.3	17 26.7	29 56.1	12 57.6	2 58.5	25 00.9	18 15.3	5 02.2	13 27.5
24 Su	18 13 16	2 59 14	13 22 17	19 28 02	15 29.0	2 14.4	18 34.6	0♏31.6	13 22.5	2 52.3	24 57.6	18 18.0	5 04.2	13 29.8
25 M	18 17 13	4 00 23	25 31 28	1♑32 47	15 27.9	3 49.8	19 42.4	1 07.0	13 47.3	2 46.3	24 54.3	18 20.7	5 06.2	13 32.0
26 Tu	18 21 09	5 01 33	7♑32 12	13 29 55	15D 27.5	5 25.4	20 50.0	1 42.4	14 12.1	2 40.5	24 51.2	18 23.4	5 08.2	13 34.2
27 W	18 25 06	6 02 43	19 26 12	25 21 18	15 27.7	7 01.3	21 57.3	2 17.8	14 36.9	2 34.9	24 48.1	18 26.2	5 10.3	13 36.4
28 Th	18 29 03	7 03 53	1♒15 31	7♒09 09	15 28.3	8 37.4	23 04.5	2 53.1	15 01.6	2 29.4	24 45.1	18 29.0	5 12.3	13 38.6
29 F	18 32 59	8 05 03	13 02 34	18 56 08	15 29.1	10 13.8	24 11.5	3 28.3	15 26.2	2 24.0	24 42.2	18 31.8	5 14.4	13 40.7
30 Sa	18 36 56	9 06 13	24 50 16	0♓45 24	15 29.9	11 50.6	25 18.3	4 03.5	15 50.8	2 18.8	24 39.5	18 34.7	5 16.5	13 42.9
31 Su	18 40 52	10 07 23	6♓42 02	12 40 40	15 30.6	13 27.6	26 24.8	4 38.7	16 15.4	2 13.8	24 36.8	18 37.5	5 18.6	13 45.0

Astro Data (Dy Hr Mn)

	Dy Hr Mn
☿D	8 2:27
♂0S	8 23:24
☽0N	9 2:43
☽0S	21 22:50
☽0N	6 13:07
♃△♆	9 14:17
☽0S	19 4:51

Planet Ingress (Dy Hr Mn)

	Dy Hr Mn
♂ ♎	4 2:01
☿ ♎R	7 7:29
♀ ♑	13 2:15
☉ ♐	22 0:20
⚳ ♐	22 19:38
☿ ♐	3 20:27
♀ ♒	8 8:49
☉ ♑	21 13:38
☿ ♑	23 2:04
♂ ♏	23 14:38

Last Aspect / ☽ Ingress (November)

Last Aspect Dy Hr Mn		☽ Ingress Dy Hr Mn
3 5:38	♂△	♒ 3 6:42
5 16:27	♄□	♓ 5 19:14
8 2:05	♄✶	♈ 8 5:03
10 5:08	♀△	♉ 10 11:13
12 11:13	♄☌	♊ 12 14:28
13 18:52	♅△	♋ 14 16:22
16 14:31	♄✶	♌ 16 18:20
18 17:05	♄□	♍ 18 21:16
20 23:46	☉✶	♎ 21 1:36
22 8:19	♅△	♏ 23 7:34
25 9:53	♄☍	♐ 25 15:34
27 0:58	♅✶	♑ 28 1:58
30 7:35	♄△	♒ 30 14:27

Last Aspect / ☽ Ingress (December)

Last Aspect Dy Hr Mn		☽ Ingress Dy Hr Mn
3 0:52	☿□	♓ 3 3:24
5 7:27	♀✶	♈ 5 14:18
7 20:23	♀□	♉ 7 21:28
9 18:01	♄☌	♊ 10 0:51
11 14:16	♂△	♋ 12 1:50
13 19:05	♄✶	♌ 14 2:10
15 19:58	♄□	♍ 16 3:31
18 0:42	☉□	♎ 18 7:02
20 11:08	☉✶	♏ 20 13:13
22 12:29	♄☍	♐ 22 21:58
24 10:04	♀✶	♑ 25 8:55
27 10:53	♄△	♒ 27 21:26
29 23:48	♀☌	♓ 30 10:28

☽ Phases & Eclipses (Dy Hr Mn)

Dy Hr Mn	
4 7:28	☽ 12♒11
11 21:16	○ 19♉47
18 15:26	☾ 26♌36
25 23:12	● 4♐00
4 3:56	☽ 12♓18
11 9:04	○ 19♊38
18 0:42	☾ 26♍24
25 17:23	● 4♑14
25 17:35:59	● P 0.723

Astro Data

1 November 2000
Julian Day # 36830
SVP 5♓15'11"
GC 26♐51.1 ⚴ 26♎59.3
Eris 19♈10.6R ⚵ 15♒25.6
⚷ 15♐41.7 ⚶ 1♒17.5
☽ Mean ☊ 18♋53.2

1 December 2000
Julian Day # 36860
SVP 5♓15'06"
GC 26♐51.1 ⚴ 10♏04.5
Eris 18♈56.3R ⚵ 23♒57.5
⚷ 19♐00.7 ⚶ 12♒56.3
☽ Mean ☊ 17♋17.9

LONGITUDE — January 2001

Day	Sid.Time	☉	0 hr ☽	Noon ☽	True ☊	☿	♀	♂	⚳	♃	♄	♅	♆	♇
1 M	18 44 49	11♑08 32	18♓41 48	24♓46 01	15♋31.0	15♑04.9	27♒31.1	5♏13.8	16♐39.9	2♊09.0	24♉34.2	18♒40.5	5♒20.7	13♐47.1
2 Tu	18 48 45	12 09 42	0♈53 50	7♈05 50	15R31.2	16 42.6	28 37.1	5 48.8	17 04.4	2R04.4	24R31.7	18 43.4	5 22.8	13 49.3
3 W	18 52 42	13 10 51	13 22 34	19 44 32	15 31.2	18 20.5	29 42.9	6 23.8	17 28.8	1 59.9	24 29.3	18 46.4	5 24.9	13 51.4
4 Th	18 56 38	14 12 00	26 12 15	2♉46 08	15 31.1	19 58.8	0♓48.5	6 58.7	17 53.2	1 55.6	24 27.0	18 49.4	5 27.1	13 53.4
5 F	19 00 35	15 13 09	9♉26 33	16 13 45	15D31.0	21 37.4	1 53.7	7 33.6	18 17.5	1 51.6	24 24.8	18 52.4	5 29.3	13 55.5
6 Sa	19 04 32	16 14 17	23 07 52	0♊08 55	15 31.0	23 16.2	2 58.7	8 08.4	18 41.7	1 47.7	24 22.7	18 55.4	5 31.4	13 57.5
7 Su	19 08 28	17 15 25	7♊16 43	14 30 59	15 31.2	24 55.3	4 03.4	8 43.2	19 05.9	1 44.0	24 20.7	18 58.5	5 33.6	13 59.6
8 M	19 12 25	18 16 33	21 51 10	29 16 35	15 31.4	26 34.7	5 07.8	9 17.9	19 30.1	1 40.4	24 18.9	19 01.6	5 35.8	14 01.6
9 Tu	19 16 21	19 17 41	6♋46 23	14♋19 34	15R31.5	28 14.3	6 11.9	9 52.6	19 54.2	1 37.1	24 17.1	19 04.7	5 38.0	14 03.6
10 W	19 20 18	20 18 48	21 55 00	29 31 28	15 31.4	29 54.0	7 15.6	10 27.2	20 18.2	1 34.0	24 15.4	19 07.9	5 40.2	14 05.6
11 Th	19 24 14	21 19 55	7♌07 44	14♌42 35	15 31.0	1♒33.8	8 19.1	11 01.7	20 42.2	1 31.1	24 13.9	19 11.0	5 42.4	14 07.5
12 F	19 28 11	22 21 02	22 14 51	29 43 30	15 30.3	3 13.6	9 22.2	11 36.2	21 06.1	1 28.3	24 12.4	19 14.2	5 44.7	14 09.5
13 Sa	19 32 07	23 22 08	7♍07 35	14♍26 22	15 29.4	4 53.4	10 24.9	12 10.6	21 30.0	1 25.8	24 11.1	19 17.4	5 46.9	14 11.4
14 Su	19 36 04	24 23 14	21 39 16	28 45 53	15 28.5	6 33.0	11 27.3	12 44.9	21 53.7	1 23.5	24 09.8	19 20.6	5 49.1	14 13.3
15 M	19 40 01	25 24 21	5♎46 00	12♎39 32	15 27.8	8 12.2	12 29.3	13 19.2	22 17.5	1 21.3	24 08.7	19 23.9	5 51.4	14 15.2
16 Tu	19 43 57	26 25 27	19 26 33	26 07 16	15D27.5	9 51.0	13 30.9	13 53.4	22 41.1	1 19.4	24 07.7	19 27.1	5 53.6	14 17.0
17 W	19 47 54	27 26 32	2♏41 56	9♏10 56	15 27.8	11 29.1	14 32.1	14 27.6	23 04.7	1 17.7	24 06.8	19 30.4	5 55.9	14 18.9
18 Th	19 51 50	28 27 38	15 34 39	21 53 34	15 28.6	13 06.3	15 32.9	15 01.7	23 28.3	1 16.1	24 06.0	19 33.7	5 58.1	14 20.7
19 F	19 55 47	29 28 43	28 08 07	4♐18 46	15 29.8	14 42.3	16 33.3	15 35.7	23 51.7	1 14.8	24 05.3	19 37.0	6 00.4	14 22.5
20 Sa	19 59 43	0♒29 48	10♐26 01	16 30 16	15 31.2	16 16.9	17 33.3	16 09.7	24 15.1	1 13.7	24 04.7	19 40.3	6 02.7	14 24.2
21 Su	20 03 40	1 30 53	22 31 59	28 31 33	15 32.5	17 49.6	18 32.8	16 43.5	24 38.5	1 12.8	24 04.3	19 43.7	6 04.9	14 26.0
22 M	20 07 36	2 31 57	4♑29 22	10♑25 47	15R33.2	19 20.0	19 31.8	17 17.3	25 01.7	1 12.1	24 03.9	19 47.0	6 07.2	14 27.7
23 Tu	20 11 33	3 33 00	16 21 06	22 15 39	15 33.2	20 47.7	20 30.3	17 51.0	25 24.9	1 11.6	24 03.7	19 50.4	6 09.5	14 29.4
24 W	20 15 30	4 34 03	28 09 43	4♒03 33	15 32.1	22 12.1	21 28.4	18 24.7	25 48.0	1D11.3	24D03.6	19 53.8	6 11.8	14 31.1
25 Th	20 19 26	5 35 04	9♒57 25	15 51 34	15 29.9	23 32.6	22 25.9	18 58.2	26 11.0	1 11.3	24 03.6	19 57.2	6 14.1	14 32.7
26 F	20 23 23	6 36 05	21 46 14	27 41 41	15 26.8	24 48.6	23 22.8	19 31.7	26 34.0	1 11.4	24 03.7	20 00.6	6 16.3	14 34.3
27 Sa	20 27 19	7 37 05	3♓38 09	9♓35 55	15 23.0	25 59.3	24 19.2	20 05.0	26 56.8	1 11.7	24 03.9	20 04.0	6 18.6	14 35.9
28 Su	20 31 16	8 38 04	15 35 17	21 36 33	15 19.0	27 03.9	25 15.0	20 38.3	27 19.6	1 12.3	24 04.3	20 07.4	6 20.9	14 37.5
29 M	20 35 12	9 39 02	27 40 03	3♈46 08	15 15.1	28 01.7	26 10.2	21 11.5	27 42.3	1 13.0	24 04.7	20 10.9	6 23.2	14 39.0
30 Tu	20 39 09	10 39 58	9♈55 11	16 07 37	15 12.0	28 51.8	27 04.7	21 44.6	28 04.9	1 14.0	24 05.3	20 14.3	6 25.4	14 40.6
31 W	20 43 05	11 40 54	22 23 50	28 44 17	15 10.0	29 33.3	27 58.6	22 17.6	28 27.4	1 15.1	24 06.0	20 17.7	6 27.7	14 42.0

LONGITUDE — February 2001

Day	Sid.Time	☉	0 hr ☽	Noon ☽	True ☊	☿	♀	♂	⚳	♃	♄	♅	♆	♇
1 Th	20 47 02	12♒41 48	5♉09 23	11♉39 34	15♋09.3	0♓05.6	28♓51.8	22♏50.5	28♐49.8	1♊16.5	24♉06.7	20♒21.2	6♒30.0	14♐43.5
2 F	20 50 59	13 42 40	18 15 14	24 56 45	15D09.7	0 28.0	29 44.3	23 23.4	29 12.2	1 18.1	24 07.7	20 24.7	6 32.3	14 44.9
3 Sa	20 54 55	14 43 32	1♊44 25	8♊38 27	15 11.1	0R39.8	0♈36.0	23 56.1	29 34.4	1 19.8	24 08.7	20 28.1	6 34.5	14 46.3
4 Su	20 58 52	15 44 22	15 38 58	22 45 58	15 12.6	0 40.7	1 27.0	24 28.7	29 56.6	1 21.8	24 09.8	20 31.6	6 36.8	14 47.7
5 M	21 02 48	16 45 10	29 59 16	7♋18 33	15R13.8	0 30.6	2 17.1	25 01.3	0♑18.7	1 24.0	24 11.1	20 35.1	6 39.0	14 49.1
6 Tu	21 06 45	17 45 57	14♋43 18	22 12 47	15 13.8	0 09.4	3 06.4	25 33.7	0 40.6	1 26.4	24 12.4	20 38.6	6 41.3	14 50.4
7 W	21 10 41	18 46 43	29 46 08	7♌22 16	15 12.3	29♒37.7	3 54.9	26 06.0	1 02.5	1 28.9	24 13.9	20 42.0	6 43.5	14 51.7
8 Th	21 14 38	19 47 28	15♌00 01	22 38 03	15 09.0	28 56.1	4 42.4	26 38.3	1 24.3	1 31.7	24 15.4	20 45.5	6 45.8	14 52.9
9 F	21 18 34	20 48 11	0♍15 04	7♍49 45	15 04.2	28 05.7	5 29.0	27 10.4	1 46.0	1 34.6	24 17.1	20 49.0	6 48.0	14 54.2
10 Sa	21 22 31	21 48 52	15 20 50	22 47 14	14 58.6	27 07.9	6 14.6	27 42.4	2 07.5	1 37.8	24 18.9	20 52.5	6 50.2	14 55.4
11 Su	21 26 28	22 49 33	0♎07 59	7♎22 19	14 52.8	26 04.4	6 59.2	28 14.3	2 29.0	1 41.1	24 20.8	20 55.9	6 52.4	14 56.5
12 M	21 30 24	23 50 13	14 29 42	21 29 48	14 47.8	24 56.8	7 42.7	28 46.1	2 50.4	1 44.6	24 22.8	20 59.4	6 54.6	14 57.7
13 Tu	21 34 21	24 50 51	28 22 28	5♏07 46	14 44.2	23 47.2	8 25.2	29 17.8	3 11.6	1 48.3	24 24.9	21 02.9	6 56.8	14 58.8
14 W	21 38 17	25 51 28	11♏45 53	18 17 11	14D42.3	22 37.4	9 06.5	29 49.4	3 32.8	1 52.2	24 27.2	21 06.4	6 59.0	14 59.8
15 Th	21 42 14	26 52 05	24 42 06	1♐01 09	14 42.1	21 29.2	9 46.7	0♐20.8	3 53.8	1 56.3	24 29.5	21 09.8	7 01.2	15 00.9
16 F	21 46 10	27 52 40	7♐14 56	13 24 02	14 43.1	20 24.2	10 25.6	0 52.1	4 14.8	2 00.5	24 31.9	21 13.3	7 03.4	15 01.9
17 Sa	21 50 07	28 53 13	19 29 06	25 30 45	14 44.7	19 23.8	11 03.3	1 23.3	4 35.6	2 05.0	24 34.5	21 16.8	7 05.5	15 02.9
18 Su	21 54 03	29 53 46	1♑29 37	7♑26 16	14R45.9	18 29.0	11 39.7	1 54.4	4 56.3	2 09.6	24 37.1	21 20.2	7 07.7	15 03.8
19 M	21 58 00	0♓54 17	13 21 17	19 15 11	14 46.1	17 40.8	12 14.7	2 25.3	5 16.9	2 14.4	24 39.8	21 23.7	7 09.8	15 04.8
20 Tu	22 01 57	1 54 47	25 08 27	1♒01 33	14 44.4	16 59.6	12 48.3	2 56.1	5 37.4	2 19.4	24 42.7	21 27.1	7 11.9	15 05.6
21 W	22 05 53	2 55 15	6♒54 52	12 48 46	14 40.6	16 25.8	13 20.4	3 26.7	5 57.7	2 24.5	24 45.7	21 30.6	7 14.0	15 06.5
22 Th	22 09 50	3 55 42	18 43 32	24 39 29	14 34.3	15 59.5	13 51.0	3 57.2	6 17.9	2 29.9	24 48.7	21 34.0	7 16.1	15 07.3
23 F	22 13 46	4 56 07	0♓36 49	6♓35 45	14 26.0	15 40.7	14 20.0	4 27.6	6 38.0	2 35.4	24 51.9	21 37.4	7 18.2	15 08.1
24 Sa	22 17 43	5 56 31	12 36 28	18 39 06	14 16.1	15 29.2	14 47.4	4 57.7	6 58.0	2 41.1	24 55.1	21 40.8	7 20.3	15 08.8
25 Su	22 21 39	6 56 52	24 43 48	0♈50 43	14 05.7	15D24.7	15 13.0	5 27.8	7 17.8	2 46.9	24 58.5	21 44.2	7 22.3	15 09.5
26 M	22 25 36	7 57 12	6♈59 58	13 11 43	13 55.5	15 27.0	15 36.9	5 57.7	7 37.5	2 52.9	25 01.9	21 47.6	7 24.4	15 10.2
27 Tu	22 29 32	8 57 30	19 26 06	25 43 20	13 46.7	15 35.6	15 58.9	6 27.4	7 57.1	2 59.1	25 05.5	21 50.9	7 26.4	15 10.9
28 W	22 33 29	9 57 46	2♉03 36	8♉27 08	13 40.0	15 50.3	16 19.0	6 56.9	8 16.5	3 05.4	25 09.1	21 54.3	7 28.4	15 11.5

Astro Data

	Dy Hr Mn
☽ 0N	2 22:02
☽ 0S	15 11:25
♄ D	25 0:25
♃ D	25 8:39
☽ 0N	30 4:24
♀ 0N	30 12:19
☿ R	4 1:57
☽ 0S	11 19:54
☿ D	25 15:43
☽ 0N	26 9:25

Planet Ingress

	Dy Hr Mn
♀ ♓	3 18:15
☿ ♒	10 13:27
☉ ♒	20 0:17
☿ ♓	1 7:14
♀ ♈	2 19:15
⚳ ♑	4 15:42
☿ ♒R	6 19:58
♂ ♐	14 20:07
☉ ♓	18 14:28

Last Aspect / ☽ Ingress (January)

Last Aspect Dy Hr Mn		☽ Ingress Dy Hr Mn
1 11:37	♄ ⚹	♈ 1 22:15
3 10:11	♅ ⚹	♉ 4 6:58
6 2:10	♄ ☌	♊ 6 11:45
7 19:20	♅ △	♋ 8 13:10
10 12:40	☿ ☍	♌ 10 12:45
12 3:09	♄ □	♍ 12 12:27
14 4:14	♄ △	♎ 14 14:06
16 12:36	☉ □	♏ 16 19:03
19 1:45	☉ ⚹	♐ 19 3:37
20 18:19	♅ ⚹	♑ 21 14:58
23 15:40	♄ △	♒ 24 3:44
26 5:29	☿ ☌	♓ 26 16:40
28 19:49	♀ ☌	♈ 29 4:36
31 13:37	☿ ⚹	♉ 31 14:22

Last Aspect / ☽ Ingress (February)

Last Aspect Dy Hr Mn		☽ Ingress Dy Hr Mn
2 10:32	♄ ☌	♊ 2 20:57
4 8:14	♅ △	♋ 5 0:01
6 17:32	♂ △	♌ 7 0:22
8 21:26	☿ ☍	♍ 8 23:36
10 20:19	♂ ⚹	♎ 10 23:47
12 17:32	☿ △	♏ 13 2:52
15 3:25	☉ □	♐ 15 10:03
17 19:23	☉ ⚹	♑ 17 21:00
19 23:04	♄ △	♒ 20 9:55
22 12:19	♄ □	♓ 22 22:46
25 0:26	♄ ⚹	♈ 25 10:21
27 4:35	♅ ⚹	♉ 27 20:07

☽ Phases & Eclipses

Dy Hr Mn	
2 22:33	☽ 12♈37
9 20:25	○ 19♋39
9 20:22	T 1.189
16 12:36	☾ 26♎27
24 13:08	● 4♒37
1 14:03	☽ 12♉47
8 7:13	○ 19♌35
15 3:25	☾ 26♏30
23 8:22	● 4♓47

Astro Data

1 January 2001
Julian Day # 36891
SVP 5♓15'01"
GC 26♐51.2 ⚴ 22♏48.4
Eris 18♈49.5R ⚵ 6♓21.0
⚷ 22♐35.3 ⚶ 26♒35.2
☽ Mean ☊ 15♋39.5

1 February 2001
Julian Day # 36922
SVP 5♓14'56"
GC 26♐51.3 ⚴ 3♐59.4
Eris 18♈53.2 ⚵ 21♓07.6
⚷ 25♐45.8 ⚶ 11♓04.0
☽ Mean ☊ 14♋01.0

March 2001 — LONGITUDE

Day	Sid.Time	☉	0 hr ☽	Noon ☽	True ☊	☿	♀	♂	⚳	♃	♄	♅	♆	♇
1 Th	22 37 26	10♓58 00	14♉54 11	21♉25 02	13♋35.7	16♒10.6	16♈37.1	7♐26.3	8♑35.8	3♊11.9	25♉12.8	21♒57.6	7♒30.4	15♐12.1
2 F	22 41 22	11 58 12	27 59 58	4♊39 17	13D 33.8	16 36.2	16 53.2	7 55.5	8 55.0	3 18.6	25 16.7	22 01.0	7 32.3	15 12.6
3 Sa	22 45 19	12 58 22	11♊23 16	18 12 10	13 33.7	17 06.7	17 07.2	8 24.6	9 14.0	3 25.4	25 20.6	22 04.3	7 34.3	15 13.1
4 Su	22 49 15	13 58 30	25 06 12	2♋05 31	13R 34.3	17 41.8	17 19.0	8 53.4	9 32.8	3 32.4	25 24.6	22 07.6	7 36.2	15 13.6
5 M	22 53 12	14 58 36	9♋10 09	16 20 03	13 34.6	18 21.1	17 28.6	9 22.1	9 51.5	3 39.5	25 28.7	22 10.9	7 38.1	15 14.1
6 Tu	22 57 08	15 58 40	23 35 01	0♌54 41	13 33.4	19 04.3	17 35.9	9 50.6	10 10.1	3 46.7	25 32.9	22 14.1	7 40.0	15 14.5
7 W	23 01 05	16 58 41	8♌18 30	15 45 47	13 29.9	19 51.3	17 40.8	10 19.0	10 28.5	3 54.2	25 37.2	22 17.4	7 41.9	15 14.9
8 Th	23 05 01	17 58 41	23 15 37	0♍47 00	13 23.7	20 41.7	17R 43.4	10 47.1	10 46.8	4 01.7	25 41.6	22 20.6	7 43.8	15 15.2
9 F	23 08 58	18 58 38	8♍18 46	15 49 43	13 15.1	21 35.3	17 43.5	11 15.0	11 04.9	4 09.4	25 46.1	22 23.8	7 45.6	15 15.5
10 Sa	23 12 55	19 58 33	23 18 37	0♎44 15	13 04.9	22 31.9	17 41.2	11 42.8	11 22.8	4 17.3	25 50.6	22 27.0	7 47.4	15 15.8
11 Su	23 16 51	20 58 27	8♎05 34	15 21 33	12 54.3	23 31.3	17 36.3	12 10.3	11 40.6	4 25.3	25 55.2	22 30.2	7 49.2	15 16.0
12 M	23 20 48	21 58 19	22 31 27	29 34 39	12 44.5	24 33.3	17 29.0	12 37.6	11 58.2	4 33.4	25 59.9	22 33.3	7 51.0	15 16.2
13 Tu	23 24 44	22 58 09	6♏30 47	13♏19 39	12 36.6	25 37.9	17 19.1	13 04.7	12 15.7	4 41.6	26 04.7	22 36.4	7 52.7	15 16.4
14 W	23 28 41	23 57 57	20 01 16	26 35 49	12 31.0	26 44.7	17 06.8	13 31.6	12 33.0	4 50.0	26 09.6	22 39.5	7 54.4	15 16.5
15 Th	23 32 37	24 57 44	3♐03 37	9♐25 07	12 27.9	27 53.8	16 52.0	13 58.3	12 50.1	4 58.6	26 14.6	22 42.6	7 56.1	15 16.6
16 F	23 36 34	25 57 29	15 40 50	21 51 23	12D 26.9	29 05.0	16 34.7	14 24.8	13 07.1	5 07.2	26 19.6	22 45.7	7 57.8	15 16.7
17 Sa	23 40 30	26 57 12	27 57 25	3♑59 38	12R 26.9	0♓18.2	16 15.1	14 51.0	13 23.8	5 16.0	26 24.7	22 48.7	7 59.5	15R 16.8
18 Su	23 44 27	27 56 54	9♑58 42	15 55 20	12 27.0	1 33.3	15 53.2	15 16.9	13 40.4	5 24.9	26 29.9	22 51.7	8 01.1	15 16.8
19 M	23 48 23	28 56 34	21 50 13	27 43 59	12 26.0	2 50.2	15 29.0	15 42.7	13 56.8	5 34.0	26 35.2	22 54.7	8 02.7	15 16.7
20 Tu	23 52 20	29 56 12	3♒37 15	9♒30 37	12 23.0	4 08.9	15 02.7	16 08.1	14 13.1	5 43.2	26 40.5	22 57.7	8 04.3	15 16.7
21 W	23 56 17	0♈55 48	15 24 37	21 19 43	12 17.3	5 29.3	14 34.5	16 33.3	14 29.1	5 52.4	26 45.9	23 00.6	8 05.9	15 16.6
22 Th	0 00 13	1 55 23	27 16 22	3♓14 55	12 08.8	6 51.4	14 04.3	16 58.2	14 45.0	6 01.9	26 51.4	23 03.5	8 07.4	15 16.4
23 F	0 04 10	2 54 55	9♓15 41	15 18 55	11 57.6	8 15.0	13 32.5	17 22.9	15 00.6	6 11.4	26 57.0	23 06.4	8 08.9	15 16.3
24 Sa	0 08 06	3 54 26	21 24 48	27 33 28	11 44.5	9 40.2	12 59.2	17 47.2	15 16.1	6 21.0	27 02.6	23 09.2	8 10.4	15 16.1
25 Su	0 12 03	4 53 54	3♈45 01	9♈59 29	11 30.5	11 06.9	12 24.6	18 11.3	15 31.3	6 30.8	27 08.3	23 12.0	8 11.9	15 15.8
26 M	0 15 59	5 53 20	16 16 53	22 37 11	11 16.9	12 35.2	11 48.9	18 35.1	15 46.4	6 40.6	27 14.1	23 14.8	8 13.3	15 15.6
27 Tu	0 19 56	6 52 45	29 00 22	5♉26 23	11 04.9	14 04.9	11 12.3	18 58.6	16 01.2	6 50.6	27 19.9	23 17.6	8 14.7	15 15.3
28 W	0 23 52	7 52 07	11♉55 12	18 26 50	10 55.4	15 36.0	10 35.0	19 21.7	16 15.8	7 00.7	27 25.8	23 20.3	8 16.1	15 14.9
29 Th	0 27 49	8 51 27	25 01 15	1♊38 31	10 48.8	17 08.6	9 57.4	19 44.6	16 30.3	7 10.9	27 31.8	23 23.0	8 17.4	15 14.6
30 F	0 31 46	9 50 45	8♊18 41	15 01 51	10 45.1	18 42.7	9 19.6	20 07.1	16 44.5	7 21.2	27 37.8	23 25.7	8 18.8	15 14.2
31 Sa	0 35 42	10 50 00	21 48 08	28 37 38	10 43.8	20 18.1	8 41.9	20 29.3	16 58.4	7 31.6	27 43.9	23 28.3	8 20.1	15 13.7

April 2001 — LONGITUDE

Day	Sid.Time	☉	0 hr ☽	Noon ☽	True ☊	☿	♀	♂	⚳	♃	♄	♅	♆	♇
1 Su	0 39 39	11♈49 14	5♋30 30	12♋26 48	10♋43.6	21♓55.0	8♈04.5	20♐51.2	17♑12.2	7♊42.1	27♉50.1	23♒30.9	8♒21.3	15♐13.3
2 M	0 43 35	12 48 24	19 26 39	26 30 01	10R 43.3	23 33.3	7R 27.8	21 12.7	17 25.7	7 52.7	27 56.3	23 33.4	8 22.6	15R 12.8
3 Tu	0 47 32	13 47 33	3♌36 51	10♌47 00	10 41.6	25 13.0	6 51.9	21 33.9	17 39.1	8 03.4	28 02.6	23 36.0	8 23.8	15 12.3
4 W	0 51 28	14 46 39	18 00 09	25 15 55	10 37.5	26 54.1	6 17.1	21 54.7	17 52.1	8 14.2	28 08.9	23 38.5	8 25.0	15 11.7
5 Th	0 55 25	15 45 43	2♍33 44	9♍52 57	10 30.7	28 36.7	5 43.5	22 15.1	18 05.0	8 25.1	28 15.3	23 40.9	8 26.1	15 11.1
6 F	0 59 21	16 44 44	17 12 47	24 32 21	10 21.2	0♈20.7	5 11.4	22 35.2	18 17.6	8 36.1	28 21.7	23 43.3	8 27.2	15 10.5
7 Sa	1 03 18	17 43 43	1♎50 44	9♎06 57	10 10.0	2 06.2	4 41.0	22 54.9	18 30.0	8 47.2	28 28.2	23 45.7	8 28.3	15 09.9
8 Su	1 07 15	18 42 41	16 20 06	23 29 19	9 58.2	3 53.2	4 12.5	23 14.2	18 42.1	8 58.3	28 34.8	23 48.1	8 29.4	15 09.2
9 M	1 11 11	19 41 36	0♏33 50	7♏33 00	9 47.1	5 41.6	3 45.9	23 33.2	18 54.0	9 09.6	28 41.4	23 50.4	8 30.4	15 08.5
10 Tu	1 15 08	20 40 29	14 26 20	21 13 31	9 37.8	7 31.5	3 21.5	23 51.7	19 05.6	9 20.9	28 48.0	23 52.6	8 31.4	15 07.8
11 W	1 19 04	21 39 21	27 54 24	4♐28 58	9 31.0	9 22.9	2 59.3	24 09.8	19 17.0	9 32.3	28 54.7	23 54.9	8 32.4	15 07.0
12 Th	1 23 01	22 38 11	10♐57 21	17 19 51	9 26.8	11 15.9	2 39.4	24 27.4	19 28.1	9 43.8	29 01.5	23 57.1	8 33.3	15 06.2
13 F	1 26 57	23 36 59	23 36 50	29 48 47	9D 25.0	13 10.3	2 21.8	24 44.6	19 39.0	9 55.4	29 08.2	23 59.2	8 34.2	15 05.4
14 Sa	1 30 54	24 35 45	5♑56 16	11♑59 52	9 24.7	15 06.2	2 06.7	25 01.4	19 49.6	10 07.1	29 15.1	24 01.3	8 35.1	15 04.5
15 Su	1 34 50	25 34 30	18 00 15	23 58 06	9R 24.9	17 03.6	1 54.0	25 17.7	20 00.0	10 18.8	29 22.0	24 03.4	8 36.0	15 03.7
16 M	1 38 47	26 33 13	29 54 04	5♒48 53	9 24.5	19 02.5	1 43.8	25 33.6	20 10.0	10 30.6	29 28.9	24 05.5	8 36.8	15 02.8
17 Tu	1 42 44	27 31 54	11♒43 12	17 37 40	9 22.6	21 02.8	1 36.1	25 48.9	20 19.8	10 42.5	29 35.9	24 07.5	8 37.6	15 01.8
18 W	1 46 40	28 30 34	23 32 56	29 29 34	9 18.5	23 04.5	1 30.8	26 03.7	20 29.3	10 54.4	29 42.9	24 09.4	8 38.3	15 00.9
19 Th	1 50 37	29 29 12	5♓28 06	11♓29 03	9 11.8	25 07.5	1D 28.0	26 18.1	20 38.6	11 06.5	29 49.9	24 11.3	8 39.1	14 59.9
20 F	1 54 33	0♉27 48	17 32 49	23 39 47	9 02.7	27 11.8	1 27.5	26 31.9	20 47.5	11 18.6	29 57.0	24 13.2	8 39.7	14 58.9
21 Sa	1 58 30	1 26 22	29 50 13	6♈04 20	8 51.8	29 17.2	1 29.4	26 45.2	20 56.2	11 30.7	0♊04.2	24 15.0	8 40.4	14 57.9
22 Su	2 02 26	2 24 54	12♈22 17	18 44 07	8 40.0	1♉23.6	1 33.6	26 57.9	21 04.5	11 43.0	0 11.3	24 16.8	8 41.0	14 56.8
23 M	2 06 23	3 23 25	25 09 49	1♉39 19	8 28.5	3 30.8	1 40.1	27 10.1	21 12.6	11 55.3	0 18.5	24 18.6	8 41.6	14 55.7
24 Tu	2 10 19	4 21 54	8♉12 29	14 49 07	8 18.3	5 38.8	1 48.8	27 21.7	21 20.3	12 07.6	0 25.8	24 20.3	8 42.2	14 54.6
25 W	2 14 16	5 20 21	21 29 01	28 11 56	8 10.3	7 47.2	1 59.6	27 32.7	21 27.8	12 20.1	0 33.1	24 21.9	8 42.7	14 53.5
26 Th	2 18 12	6 18 46	4♊57 39	11♊45 55	8 04.9	9 55.9	2 12.5	27 43.2	21 34.9	12 32.6	0 40.4	24 23.5	8 43.2	14 52.4
27 F	2 22 09	7 17 09	18 36 30	25 29 15	8D 02.2	12 04.5	2 27.5	27 53.0	21 41.7	12 45.1	0 47.7	24 25.1	8 43.6	14 51.2
28 Sa	2 26 06	8 15 30	2♋23 57	9♋20 30	8 01.5	14 12.9	2 44.4	28 02.3	21 48.3	12 57.7	0 55.1	24 26.6	8 44.1	14 50.0
29 Su	2 30 02	9 13 49	16 18 45	23 18 38	8 02.0	16 20.7	3 03.2	28 10.9	21 54.5	13 10.4	1 02.5	24 28.1	8 44.5	14 48.8
30 M	2 33 59	10 12 06	0♌20 03	7♌22 55	8R 02.6	18 27.6	3 23.8	28 18.9	22 00.3	13 23.1	1 09.9	24 29.5	8 44.8	14 47.5

Astro Data	Dy Hr Mn
♀ R	9 1:07
☽ 0S	11 6:02
♇ R	18 2:39
☉ 0N	20 13:32
☽ 0N	25 15:09
♃△♆	5 14:25
☽ 0S	7 16:13
☿ 0N	9 2:44
♀ D	20 4:35
☽ 0N	21 22:46

Planet Ingress		Dy Hr Mn
☿	♓	17 6:06
☉	♈	20 13:32
☿	♈	6 7:15
☉	♉	20 0:37
♄	♊	20 22:00
☿	♉	21 20:09

Last Aspect Dy Hr Mn		☽ Ingress	Dy Hr Mn
1 18:58	♄ ☌	♊	2 3:37
3 18:46	♅ △	♋	4 8:25
6 3:11	♄ ⚹	♌	6 10:31
8 3:51	♄ □	♍	8 10:45
10 4:02	♄ △	♎	10 10:48
12 2:45	☿ △	♏	12 12:44
14 12:18	☿ □	♐	14 18:18
17 3:49	☿ ⚹	♑	17 4:03
19 14:42	☉ ⚹	♒	19 16:37
21 23:04	♄ □	♓	22 5:29
24 10:59	♄ ⚹	♈	24 16:45
26 13:11	♅ ⚹	♉	27 1:52
29 4:30	♄ ☌	♊	29 9:02
31 2:55	♅ △	♋	31 14:24

Last Aspect Dy Hr Mn		☽ Ingress	Dy Hr Mn
2 14:27	♄ ⚹	♌	2 17:55
4 16:47	♄ □	♍	4 19:48
6 18:19	♄ △	♎	6 20:58
8 12:32	♅ △	♏	8 23:02
11 1:44	♄ ☍	♐	11 3:48
13 1:57	♂ ☌	♑	13 12:22
15 23:01	♄ △	♒	16 0:12
18 12:27	♄ □	♓	18 13:01
20 17:42	♂ □	♈	21 0:19
23 3:35	♂ △	♉	23 8:57
25 5:09	♅ □	♊	25 15:12
27 16:13	♂ ☍	♋	27 19:50
28 21:55	☿ ⚹	♌	29 23:26

☽ Phases & Eclipses Dy Hr Mn	
3 2:04	☽ 12♊33
9 17:24	○ 19♍12
16 20:46	☾ 26♐19
25 1:22	● 4♈28
1 10:50	☽ 11♋46
8 3:23	○ 18♎22
15 15:32	☾ 25♑43
23 15:27	● 3♉32
30 17:09	☽ 10♌25

Astro Data

1 March 2001
Julian Day # 36950
SVP 5♓14'53"
GC 26♐51.3 ⚴ 11♐44.6
Eris 19♈04.8 ⚵ 5♈51.2
⚷ 27♐50.7 ⚶ 24♓24.6
☽ Mean ☊ 12♋32.0

1 April 2001
Julian Day # 36981
SVP 5♓14'50"
GC 26♐51.4 ⚴ 15♐55.1
Eris 19♈23.5 ⚵ 23♈11.6
⚷ 28♐53.6 ⚶ 9♈07.3
☽ Mean ☊ 10♋53.5

LONGITUDE May 2001

Day	Sid.Time	☉	0 hr ☽	Noon ☽	True ☊	☿	♀	♂	⚳	♃	♄	♅	♆	♇
1 Tu	2 37 55	11♉10 21	14♌27 05	21♌32 26	8♋02.2	20♉33.3	3♈46.2	28♐26.2	22♑05.9	13♊35.9	1♊17.4	24♒30.9	8♒45.2	14♐46.3
2 W	2 41 52	12 08 33	28 38 45	5♍45 48	7R 59.9	22 37.5	4 10.3	28 33.0	22 11.1	13 48.7	1 24.8	24 32.2	8 45.4	14R 45.0
3 Th	2 45 48	13 06 44	12♍53 14	20 00 42	7 55.4	24 40.0	4 36.1	28 39.0	22 16.0	14 01.5	1 32.3	24 33.5	8 45.7	14 43.7
4 F	2 49 45	14 04 53	27 07 43	4♎13 49	7 48.9	26 40.3	5 03.5	28 44.4	22 20.6	14 14.5	1 39.9	24 34.8	8 45.9	14 42.4
5 Sa	2 53 41	15 02 59	11♎18 25	18 20 58	7 40.9	28 38.4	5 32.4	28 49.2	22 24.8	14 27.4	1 47.4	24 36.0	8 46.1	14 41.1
6 Su	2 57 38	16 01 04	25 20 53	2♏17 38	7 32.4	0♊33.9	6 02.8	28 53.2	22 28.7	14 40.4	1 55.0	24 37.1	8 46.3	14 39.7
7 M	3 01 35	16 59 08	9♏10 41	15 59 35	7 24.3	2 26.6	6 34.7	28 56.6	22 32.2	14 53.5	2 02.6	24 38.2	8 46.4	14 38.3
8 Tu	3 05 31	17 57 09	22 44 00	29 23 37	7 17.6	4 16.4	7 07.9	28 59.3	22 35.5	15 06.6	2 10.2	24 39.3	8 46.5	14 36.9
9 W	3 09 28	18 55 09	5♐58 18	12♐27 58	7 12.8	6 03.2	7 42.4	29 01.2	22 38.3	15 19.7	2 17.8	24 40.3	8 46.6	14 35.5
10 Th	3 13 24	19 53 08	18 52 39	25 12 30	7D 10.1	7 46.7	8 18.3	29 02.4	22 40.8	15 32.9	2 25.4	24 41.2	8R 46.6	14 34.1
11 F	3 17 21	20 51 05	1♑27 46	7♑38 45	7 09.3	9 26.8	8 55.3	29R 02.9	22 43.0	15 46.1	2 33.1	24 42.2	8 46.6	14 32.7
12 Sa	3 21 17	21 49 01	13 45 52	19 49 35	7 10.0	11 03.6	9 33.6	29 02.7	22 44.8	15 59.4	2 40.8	24 43.0	8 46.6	14 31.3
13 Su	3 25 14	22 46 56	25 50 24	1♒48 54	7 11.4	12 36.8	10 13.0	29 01.7	22 46.3	16 12.7	2 48.5	24 43.8	8 46.5	14 29.8
14 M	3 29 10	23 44 49	7♒45 39	13 41 18	7R 12.7	14 06.5	10 53.4	29 00.0	22 47.4	16 26.0	2 56.2	24 44.6	8 46.4	14 28.3
15 Tu	3 33 07	24 42 41	19 36 29	25 31 50	7 13.2	15 32.5	11 34.9	28 57.4	22 48.1	16 39.4	3 03.9	24 45.3	8 46.3	14 26.8
16 W	3 37 04	25 40 32	1♓27 59	7♓25 33	7 12.4	16 54.8	12 17.5	28 54.2	22R 48.5	16 52.8	3 11.6	24 46.0	8 46.1	14 25.3
17 Th	3 41 00	26 38 21	13 25 10	19 27 23	7 09.9	18 13.4	13 00.9	28 50.1	22 48.5	17 06.2	3 19.3	24 46.6	8 45.9	14 23.8
18 F	3 44 57	27 36 10	25 32 43	1♈41 40	7 05.7	19 28.1	13 45.3	28 45.3	22 48.1	17 19.7	3 27.1	24 47.2	8 45.7	14 22.3
19 Sa	3 48 53	28 33 57	7♈54 39	14 12 00	7 00.3	20 39.0	14 30.6	28 39.8	22 47.4	17 33.1	3 34.8	24 47.7	8 45.5	14 20.8
20 Su	3 52 50	29 31 43	20 34 00	27 00 49	6 54.2	21 46.0	15 16.8	28 33.4	22 46.3	17 46.7	3 42.6	24 48.2	8 45.2	14 19.2
21 M	3 56 46	0♊29 28	3♉32 32	10♉09 09	6 48.0	22 49.0	16 03.7	28 26.3	22 44.9	18 00.2	3 50.3	24 48.6	8 44.8	14 17.7
22 Tu	4 00 43	1 27 11	16 50 34	23 36 36	6 42.6	23 48.0	16 51.5	28 18.5	22 43.0	18 13.8	3 58.1	24 49.0	8 44.5	14 16.1
23 W	4 04 39	2 24 54	0♊26 56	7♊21 14	6 38.5	24 42.9	17 40.0	28 09.9	22 40.8	18 27.4	4 05.9	24 49.3	8 44.1	14 14.5
24 Th	4 08 36	3 22 35	14 19 05	21 20 00	6 36.0	25 33.6	18 29.2	28 00.5	22 38.2	18 41.0	4 13.7	24 49.6	8 43.7	14 13.0
25 F	4 12 33	4 20 15	28 23 32	5♋29 08	6D 35.1	26 20.1	19 19.1	27 50.5	22 35.3	18 54.7	4 21.4	24 49.8	8 43.2	14 11.4
26 Sa	4 16 29	5 17 54	12♋36 20	19 44 38	6 35.6	27 02.3	20 09.7	27 39.7	22 32.0	19 08.4	4 29.2	24 50.0	8 42.8	14 09.8
27 Su	4 20 26	6 15 31	26 53 35	4♌02 46	6 36.9	27 40.0	21 00.9	27 28.2	22 28.3	19 22.1	4 37.0	24 50.1	8 42.3	14 08.2
28 M	4 24 22	7 13 06	11♌11 47	18 20 17	6 38.3	28 13.3	21 52.7	27 16.1	22 24.3	19 35.8	4 44.8	24 50.2	8 41.7	14 06.6
29 Tu	4 28 19	8 10 41	25 27 59	2♍34 34	6R 39.2	28 42.1	22 45.1	27 03.3	22 19.9	19 49.5	4 52.5	24R 50.3	8 41.2	14 05.0
30 W	4 32 15	9 08 13	9♍39 49	16 43 28	6 39.1	29 06.3	23 38.1	26 49.8	22 15.1	20 03.2	5 00.3	24 50.2	8 40.6	14 03.4
31 Th	4 36 12	10 05 44	23 45 18	0♎45 07	6 37.8	29 25.9	24 31.7	26 35.8	22 10.0	20 17.0	5 08.0	24 50.2	8 39.9	14 01.8

LONGITUDE June 2001

Day	Sid.Time	☉	0 hr ☽	Noon ☽	True ☊	☿	♀	♂	⚳	♃	♄	♅	♆	♇
1 F	4 40 09	11♊03 14	7♎42 41	14♎37 48	6♋35.4	29♊40.8	25♈25.8	26♐21.2	22♑04.5	20♊30.7	5♊15.8	24♒50.1	8♒39.3	14♐00.1
2 Sa	4 44 05	12 00 43	21 30 15	28 19 50	6R 32.2	29 51.0	26 20.4	26R 06.0	21R 58.7	20 44.5	5 23.5	24R 49.9	8R 38.6	13R 58.5
3 Su	4 48 02	12 58 10	5♏06 22	11♏49 38	6 28.7	29R 56.7	27 15.5	25 50.2	21 52.5	20 58.3	5 31.3	24 49.7	8 37.9	13 56.9
4 M	4 51 58	13 55 37	18 29 30	25 05 47	6 25.4	29 57.7	28 11.1	25 34.0	21 46.0	21 12.1	5 39.0	24 49.4	8 37.1	13 55.3
5 Tu	4 55 55	14 53 02	1♐38 24	8♐07 16	6 22.8	29 54.2	29 07.2	25 17.3	21 39.2	21 25.9	5 46.7	24 49.1	8 36.3	13 53.7
6 W	4 59 51	15 50 27	14 32 21	20 53 39	6 21.1	29 46.3	0♉03.7	25 00.1	21 32.0	21 39.7	5 54.4	24 48.8	8 35.6	13 52.1
7 Th	5 03 48	16 47 50	27 11 15	3♑25 15	6D 20.4	29 34.3	1 00.7	24 42.5	21 24.5	21 53.6	6 02.1	24 48.4	8 34.7	13 50.5
8 F	5 07 44	17 45 13	9♑35 50	15 43 14	6 20.6	29 18.2	1 58.1	24 24.6	21 16.6	22 07.4	6 09.8	24 47.9	8 33.9	13 48.8
9 Sa	5 11 41	18 42 35	21 47 42	27 49 35	6 21.5	28 58.4	2 55.9	24 06.3	21 08.5	22 21.2	6 17.4	24 47.4	8 33.0	13 47.2
10 Su	5 15 38	19 39 57	3♒49 14	9♒47 06	6 22.9	28 35.2	3 54.1	23 47.7	21 00.0	22 35.1	6 25.1	24 46.9	8 32.1	13 45.6
11 M	5 19 34	20 37 18	15 43 37	21 39 17	6 24.3	28 09.1	4 52.7	23 28.8	20 51.2	22 48.9	6 32.7	24 46.3	8 31.2	13 44.0
12 Tu	5 23 31	21 34 38	27 34 37	3♓30 11	6 25.4	27 40.3	5 51.7	23 09.7	20 42.1	23 02.8	6 40.3	24 45.7	8 30.2	13 42.4
13 W	5 27 27	22 31 58	9♓26 32	15 24 15	6R 26.1	27 09.4	6 51.0	22 50.4	20 32.7	23 16.6	6 47.9	24 45.0	8 29.2	13 40.8
14 Th	5 31 24	23 29 17	21 23 56	27 26 08	6 26.2	26 36.9	7 50.7	22 31.0	20 23.1	23 30.5	6 55.5	24 44.2	8 28.2	13 39.2
15 F	5 35 20	24 26 36	3♈31 27	9♈40 25	6 25.7	26 03.4	8 50.7	22 11.5	20 13.1	23 44.3	7 03.1	24 43.5	8 27.2	13 37.6
16 Sa	5 39 17	25 23 55	15 53 33	22 11 20	6 24.8	25 29.4	9 51.0	21 52.0	20 02.9	23 58.1	7 10.6	24 42.6	8 26.1	13 36.1
17 Su	5 43 13	26 21 13	28 34 11	5♉02 25	6 23.6	24 55.5	10 51.7	21 32.4	19 52.4	24 12.0	7 18.1	24 41.8	8 25.0	13 34.5
18 M	5 47 10	27 18 31	11♉36 19	18 16 02	6 22.4	24 22.4	11 52.6	21 12.9	19 41.7	24 25.8	7 25.6	24 40.9	8 23.9	13 32.9
19 Tu	5 51 07	28 15 49	25 01 38	1♊53 02	6 21.4	23 50.4	12 53.9	20 53.5	19 30.7	24 39.7	7 33.1	24 39.9	8 22.8	13 31.4
20 W	5 55 03	29 13 06	8♊50 03	15 52 23	6 20.7	23 20.3	13 55.4	20 34.2	19 19.5	24 53.5	7 40.5	24 38.9	8 21.7	13 29.8
21 Th	5 59 00	0♋10 23	22 59 34	0♋11 03	6D 20.4	22 52.5	14 57.2	20 15.2	19 08.0	25 07.3	7 47.9	24 37.9	8 20.5	13 28.3
22 F	6 02 56	1 07 40	7♋26 12	14 44 15	6 20.4	22 27.4	15 59.3	19 56.3	18 56.4	25 21.1	7 55.3	24 36.8	8 19.3	13 26.8
23 Sa	6 06 53	2 04 56	22 04 24	29 25 51	6 20.7	22 05.6	17 01.6	19 37.8	18 44.6	25 34.9	8 02.7	24 35.7	8 18.1	13 25.3
24 Su	6 10 49	3 02 12	6♌47 43	14♌09 13	6 21.0	21 47.4	18 04.2	19 19.6	18 32.5	25 48.7	8 10.0	24 34.5	8 16.8	13 23.8
25 M	6 14 46	3 59 27	21 29 33	28 48 01	6 21.3	21 33.1	19 07.0	19 01.8	18 20.3	26 02.4	8 17.3	24 33.3	8 15.6	13 22.3
26 Tu	6 18 42	4 56 42	6♍04 00	13♍16 57	6 21.4	21 22.9	20 10.1	18 44.4	18 08.0	26 16.2	8 24.5	24 32.0	8 14.3	13 20.8
27 W	6 22 39	5 53 55	20 26 27	27 32 08	6 21.5	21D 17.2	21 13.3	18 27.5	17 55.5	26 29.9	8 31.7	24 30.7	8 13.0	13 19.3
28 Th	6 26 36	6 51 09	4♎33 47	11♎31 13	6 21.5	21 16.1	22 16.8	18 11.1	17 42.8	26 43.6	8 38.9	24 29.4	8 11.7	13 17.9
29 F	6 30 32	7 48 21	18 24 23	25 13 15	6 21.5	21 19.7	23 20.5	17 55.3	17 30.1	26 57.3	8 46.1	24 28.0	8 10.4	13 16.4
30 Sa	6 34 29	8 45 34	1♏57 51	8♏38 17	6 21.7	21 28.1	24 24.5	17 40.0	17 17.2	27 11.0	8 53.2	24 26.6	8 09.0	13 15.0

Astro Data	Dy Hr Mn
☽0S	5 0:55
♃☍♇	6 10:48
♆ R	11 1:14
♂ R	11 16:09
⚳ R	17 0:30
☽0N	19 7:49
♅ R	29 15:12
☽0S	1 7:39
☿ R	4 5:22
♃⚼♆	14 8:22
☽0N	15 16:57
♃△♅	19 12:26
♄△♆	25 7:16
☿ D	28 5:50
☽0S	28 13:17

Planet Ingress		Dy Hr Mn
☿	♊	6 4:54
☉	♊	20 23:45
♀	♉	6 10:26
☉	♋	21 7:39

Last Aspect Dy Hr Mn			☽ Ingress	Dy Hr Mn
1 23:45	♂	△	♍	2 2:17
4 2:40	♂	□	♎	4 4:51
6 6:05	♂	⚹	♏	6 8:02
8 3:26	♅	□	♐	8 13:06
10 19:21	♂	☌	♑	10 21:11
12 16:18	☉	△	♒	13 8:21
15 18:54	♂	⚹	♓	15 21:02
18 6:19	♂	□	♈	18 8:42
20 14:50	♂	△	♉	20 17:30
22 14:08	♅	□	♊	22 23:13
24 23:13	♂	☍	♋	25 2:43
26 12:45	♀	□	♌	27 5:13
29 5:14	☿	⚹	♍	29 7:39
31 9:41	☿	□	♎	31 10:42

Last Aspect Dy Hr Mn			☽ Ingress	Dy Hr Mn
2 14:43	☿	△	♏	2 14:57
4 11:30	♅	□	♐	4 20:59
7 4:42	☿	☍	♑	7 5:24
7 6:58	♀	△	♒	9 16:21
12 0:40	☿	△	♓	12 4:55
14 10:27	☿	□	♈	14 17:04
16 18:33	☉	⚹	♉	17 2:40
18 23:23	♅	□	♊	19 8:43
21 3:26	♃	☌	♋	21 11:42
22 14:12	♀	⚹	♌	23 12:56
25 7:23	♃	⚹	♍	25 13:59
27 10:13	♃	□	♎	27 16:12
29 15:08	♃	△	♏	29 20:30

☽ Phases & Eclipses Dy Hr Mn		
7 13:54	○	17♏04
15 10:12	☾	24♒38
23 2:47	●	2♊03
29 22:10	☽	8♍35
6 1:40	○	15♐26
14 3:29	☾	23♓09
21 11:59	●	0♋10
21 12:04:47	●	T 04'56"
28 3:21	☽	6♎31

Astro Data

1 May 2001
Julian Day # 37011
SVP 5♓14'46"
GC 26♐51.5 ⚴ 13♐27.1R
Eris 19♈43.0 ⚵ 10♉38.1
⚷ 28♐29.9R ⚶ 23♈01.1
☽ Mean ☊ 9♋18.2

1 June 2001
Julian Day # 37042
SVP 5♓14'42"
GC 26♐51.5 ⚴ 5♐04.4R
Eris 19♈59.7 ⚵ 28♉59.2
⚷ 26♐54.0R ⚶ 6♉44.5
☽ Mean ☊ 7♋39.7

July 2001 LONGITUDE

Day	Sid.Time	☉	0 hr ☽	Noon ☽	True ☊	☿	♀	♂	⚳	♃	♄	♅	♆	♇
1 Su	6 38 25	9♋42 46	15♏14 39	21♏47 06	6♋22.0	21♊41.4	25♉28.6	17♐25.3	17♑04.3	27♊24.7	9♊00.3	24♒25.2	8♒07.6	13♐13.6
2 M	6 42 22	10 39 57	28 15 46	4♐40 50	6 22.4	21 59.6	26 32.9	17R 11.2	16R 51.3	27 38.3	9 07.3	24R 23.7	8R 06.2	13R 12.2
3 Tu	6 46 18	11 37 09	11♐02 27	17 20 48	6 22.8	22 22.8	27 37.5	16 57.8	16 38.2	27 51.9	9 14.3	24 22.2	8 04.8	13 10.8
4 W	6 50 15	12 34 20	23 36 03	29 48 23	6R 23.0	22 50.9	28 42.2	16 45.1	16 25.0	28 05.5	9 21.3	24 20.6	8 03.4	13 09.5
5 Th	6 54 11	13 31 32	5♑57 59	12♑05 01	6 23.0	23 23.9	29 47.1	16 33.0	16 11.8	28 19.1	9 28.2	24 19.0	8 02.0	13 08.1
6 F	6 58 08	14 28 43	18 09 43	24 12 17	6 22.7	24 01.8	0♊52.2	16 21.7	15 58.6	28 32.6	9 35.1	24 17.4	8 00.6	13 06.8
7 Sa	7 02 05	15 25 54	0♒12 56	6♒11 55	6 21.9	24 44.5	1 57.5	16 11.2	15 45.4	28 46.2	9 41.9	24 15.7	7 59.1	13 05.5
8 Su	7 06 01	16 23 06	12 09 30	18 05 59	6 20.7	25 32.0	3 03.0	16 01.4	15 32.2	28 59.6	9 48.7	24 14.0	7 57.6	13 04.2
9 M	7 09 58	17 20 17	24 01 42	29 57 00	6 19.2	26 24.3	4 08.7	15 52.3	15 19.0	29 13.1	9 55.4	24 12.3	7 56.1	13 03.0
10 Tu	7 13 54	18 17 29	5♓52 15	11♓47 53	6 17.6	27 21.2	5 14.5	15 44.1	15 05.8	29 26.5	10 02.1	24 10.5	7 54.6	13 01.7
11 W	7 17 51	19 14 42	17 44 19	23 42 03	6 16.1	28 22.7	6 20.5	15 36.6	14 52.7	29 39.9	10 08.8	24 08.7	7 53.1	13 00.5
12 Th	7 21 47	20 11 55	29 41 33	5♈43 21	6 15.0	29 28.8	7 26.7	15 29.9	14 39.6	29 53.3	10 15.4	24 06.9	7 51.6	12 59.3
13 F	7 25 44	21 09 08	11♈47 58	17 55 58	6D 14.5	0♋39.4	8 33.0	15 24.1	14 26.6	0♋06.6	10 21.9	24 05.0	7 50.1	12 58.1
14 Sa	7 29 40	22 06 22	24 07 51	0♉24 10	6 14.6	1 54.4	9 39.4	15 19.1	14 13.6	0 19.9	10 28.4	24 03.1	7 48.5	12 56.9
15 Su	7 33 37	23 03 36	6♉45 25	13 12 05	6 15.4	3 13.7	10 46.1	15 14.9	14 00.8	0 33.2	10 34.9	24 01.2	7 46.9	12 55.8
16 M	7 37 34	24 00 51	19 44 35	26 23 15	6 16.6	4 37.4	11 52.9	15 11.5	13 48.1	0 46.4	10 41.3	23 59.3	7 45.4	12 54.7
17 Tu	7 41 30	24 58 07	3♊08 20	10♊00 01	6 17.9	6 05.2	12 59.8	15 09.0	13 35.5	0 59.6	10 47.6	23 57.3	7 43.8	12 53.6
18 W	7 45 27	25 55 24	16 58 17	24 03 01	6R 18.9	7 37.1	14 06.9	15 07.4	13 23.1	1 12.8	10 53.9	23 55.3	7 42.2	12 52.5
19 Th	7 49 23	26 52 41	1♋13 56	8♋30 34	6 19.2	9 12.9	15 14.1	15D 06.6	13 10.8	1 25.9	11 00.1	23 53.3	7 40.6	12 51.5
20 F	7 53 20	27 49 58	15 52 17	23 18 18	6 18.5	10 52.6	16 21.4	15 06.6	12 58.6	1 38.9	11 06.3	23 51.2	7 39.0	12 50.4
21 Sa	7 57 16	28 47 17	0♌47 40	8♌19 20	6 16.8	12 35.9	17 28.9	15 07.5	12 46.7	1 52.0	11 12.4	23 49.1	7 37.4	12 49.4
22 Su	8 01 13	29 44 35	15 52 09	23 24 57	6 14.2	14 22.6	18 36.5	15 09.3	12 34.9	2 04.9	11 18.5	23 47.0	7 35.8	12 48.5
23 M	8 05 10	0♌41 54	0♍56 35	8♍25 56	6 11.0	16 12.6	19 44.2	15 11.8	12 23.4	2 17.9	11 24.5	23 44.9	7 34.2	12 47.5
24 Tu	8 09 06	1 39 13	15 52 00	23 13 53	6 07.9	18 05.5	20 52.1	15 15.3	12 12.0	2 30.8	11 30.4	23 42.8	7 32.6	12 46.6
25 W	8 13 03	2 36 33	0♎30 53	7♎42 27	6 05.2	20 01.1	22 00.0	15 19.5	12 00.9	2 43.6	11 36.3	23 40.6	7 31.0	12 45.7
26 Th	8 16 59	3 33 53	14 48 12	21 47 55	6D 03.6	21 59.1	23 08.1	15 24.6	11 50.0	2 56.4	11 42.1	23 38.4	7 29.4	12 44.8
27 F	8 20 56	4 31 13	28 41 32	5♏29 08	6 03.1	23 59.3	24 16.3	15 30.5	11 39.4	3 09.1	11 47.8	23 36.2	7 27.7	12 44.0
28 Sa	8 24 52	5 28 34	12♏10 52	18 47 01	6 03.7	26 01.1	25 24.7	15 37.2	11 29.0	3 21.8	11 53.5	23 34.0	7 26.1	12 43.2
29 Su	8 28 49	6 25 55	25 17 54	1♐43 53	6 05.1	28 04.4	26 33.1	15 44.7	11 18.9	3 34.4	11 59.1	23 31.7	7 24.5	12 42.4
30 M	8 32 45	7 23 17	8♐05 24	14 22 50	6 06.7	0♌08.8	27 41.6	15 53.0	11 09.0	3 47.0	12 04.6	23 29.5	7 22.8	12 41.6
31 Tu	8 36 42	8 20 40	20 36 37	26 47 08	6R 08.0	2 13.9	28 50.3	16 02.0	10 59.4	3 59.5	12 10.1	23 27.2	7 21.2	12 40.9

August 2001 LONGITUDE

Day	Sid.Time	☉	0 hr ☽	Noon ☽	True ☊	☿	♀	♂	⚳	♃	♄	♅	♆	♇
1 W	8 40 38	9♌18 03	2♑54 46	8♑59 55	6♋08.3	4♌19.4	29♊59.1	16♐11.8	10♑50.2	4♋11.9	12♊15.5	23♒24.9	7♒19.6	12♐40.2
2 Th	8 44 35	10 15 27	15 02 53	21 04 00	6R 07.2	6 25.1	1♋08.0	16 22.4	10R 41.2	4 24.3	12 20.8	23R 22.6	7R 18.0	12R 39.5
3 F	8 48 32	11 12 52	27 03 34	3♒01 51	6 04.5	8 30.6	2 17.0	16 33.6	10 32.5	4 36.7	12 26.1	23 20.3	7 16.3	12 38.9
4 Sa	8 52 28	12 10 17	8♒59 05	14 55 31	6 00.0	10 35.8	3 26.1	16 45.6	10 24.1	4 48.9	12 31.3	23 18.0	7 14.7	12 38.3
5 Su	8 56 25	13 07 44	20 51 23	26 46 54	5 54.2	12 40.3	4 35.3	16 58.3	10 16.0	5 01.1	12 36.4	23 15.6	7 13.1	12 37.7
6 M	9 00 21	14 05 11	2♓42 19	8♓37 52	5 47.4	14 44.1	5 44.6	17 11.7	10 08.3	5 13.3	12 41.4	23 13.3	7 11.5	12 37.1
7 Tu	9 04 18	15 02 39	14 33 47	20 30 22	5 40.3	16 47.0	6 54.1	17 25.8	10 00.8	5 25.4	12 46.4	23 10.9	7 09.9	12 36.6
8 W	9 08 14	16 00 09	26 27 54	2♈26 43	5 33.6	18 48.8	8 03.6	17 40.5	9 53.7	5 37.4	12 51.3	23 08.6	7 08.2	12 36.1
9 Th	9 12 11	16 57 40	8♈27 10	14 29 39	5 28.0	20 49.4	9 13.3	17 55.9	9 47.0	5 49.3	12 56.1	23 06.2	7 06.6	12 35.6
10 F	9 16 07	17 55 12	20 34 34	26 42 23	5 24.0	22 48.8	10 23.0	18 12.0	9 40.5	6 01.2	13 00.8	23 03.8	7 05.0	12 35.2
11 Sa	9 20 04	18 52 46	2♉53 34	9♉08 36	5D 21.8	24 46.8	11 32.9	18 28.7	9 34.4	6 13.0	13 05.5	23 01.4	7 03.5	12 34.8
12 Su	9 24 01	19 50 21	15 28 00	21 52 16	5 21.3	26 43.5	12 42.8	18 46.0	9 28.7	6 24.7	13 10.0	22 59.0	7 01.9	12 34.4
13 M	9 27 57	20 47 58	28 21 52	4♊57 17	5 22.1	28 38.8	13 52.9	19 03.9	9 23.3	6 36.4	13 14.5	22 56.6	7 00.3	12 34.0
14 Tu	9 31 54	21 45 36	11♊38 54	18 27 04	5 23.3	0♍32.7	15 03.0	19 22.4	9 18.2	6 48.0	13 18.9	22 54.2	6 58.7	12 33.7
15 W	9 35 50	22 43 16	25 22 00	2♋23 47	5R 24.1	2 25.1	16 13.3	19 41.6	9 13.5	6 59.5	13 23.3	22 51.9	6 57.2	12 33.5
16 Th	9 39 47	23 40 57	9♋32 24	16 47 36	5 23.6	4 16.1	17 23.6	20 01.3	9 09.2	7 10.9	13 27.5	22 49.5	6 55.6	12 33.2
17 F	9 43 43	24 38 39	24 08 56	1♌35 48	5 21.2	6 05.6	18 34.1	20 21.6	9 05.2	7 22.3	13 31.7	22 47.1	6 54.1	12 33.0
18 Sa	9 47 40	25 36 24	9♌07 20	16 42 29	5 16.7	7 53.7	19 44.6	20 42.5	9 01.5	7 33.5	13 35.7	22 44.7	6 52.6	12 32.8
19 Su	9 51 36	26 34 09	24 20 03	1♍58 43	5 10.2	9 40.4	20 55.2	21 03.9	8 58.3	7 44.7	13 39.7	22 42.3	6 51.0	12 32.7
20 M	9 55 33	27 31 56	9♍37 06	17 13 49	5 02.5	11 25.6	22 05.9	21 25.9	8 55.4	7 55.8	13 43.6	22 39.9	6 49.5	12 32.5
21 Tu	9 59 30	28 29 43	24 47 31	2♎17 02	4 54.7	13 09.5	23 16.7	21 48.4	8 52.8	8 06.8	13 47.4	22 37.5	6 48.0	12 32.5
22 W	10 03 26	29 27 32	9♎41 18	16 59 31	4 47.6	14 51.9	24 27.5	22 11.4	8 50.6	8 17.7	13 51.1	22 35.1	6 46.6	12 32.4
23 Th	10 07 23	0♍25 23	24 11 03	1♏15 31	4 42.3	16 33.0	25 38.5	22 34.9	8 48.8	8 28.6	13 54.7	22 32.8	6 45.1	12D 32.4
24 F	10 11 19	1 23 14	8♏12 44	15 02 44	4 39.0	18 12.7	26 49.5	22 59.0	8 47.4	8 39.3	13 58.2	22 30.4	6 43.6	12 32.4
25 Sa	10 15 16	2 21 07	21 45 41	28 21 53	4D 37.7	19 51.0	28 00.6	23 23.5	8 46.3	8 50.0	14 01.7	22 28.1	6 42.2	12 32.4
26 Su	10 19 12	3 19 01	4♐51 45	11♐15 48	4 37.9	21 28.0	29 11.8	23 48.6	8 45.5	9 00.5	14 05.0	22 25.7	6 40.8	12 32.5
27 M	10 23 09	4 16 56	17 34 34	23 48 37	4R 38.7	23 03.6	0♌23.1	24 14.1	8D 45.2	9 11.0	14 08.2	22 23.4	6 39.4	12 32.6
28 Tu	10 27 05	5 14 53	29 58 32	6♑04 54	4 39.0	24 38.0	1 34.5	24 40.0	8 45.2	9 21.3	14 11.4	22 21.1	6 38.0	12 32.8
29 W	10 31 02	6 12 50	12♑08 17	18 09 12	4 38.1	26 11.0	2 45.9	25 06.4	8 45.5	9 31.6	14 14.4	22 18.8	6 36.6	12 32.9
30 Th	10 34 59	7 10 50	24 08 10	0♒05 38	4 35.0	27 42.6	3 57.4	25 33.2	8 46.2	9 41.7	14 17.4	22 16.5	6 35.3	12 33.2
31 F	10 38 55	8 08 50	6♒02 01	11 57 42	4 29.3	29 13.0	5 09.0	26 00.5	8 47.3	9 51.8	14 20.3	22 14.2	6 33.9	12 33.4

Astro Data

	Dy Hr Mn
☽0N	13 0:49
♂ D	19 22:46
☽0S	25 19:27
♄☍♇	5 17:21
☽0N	9 6:55
♃⚻♆	15 7:42
♃⚼♅	19 7:40
☽0S	22 3:27
♇ D	23 16:09
⚳ D	28 0:43
☿0S	31 17:12

Planet Ingress

	Dy Hr Mn
♀ ♊	5 16:45
☿ ♋	12 22:48
♃ ♋	13 0:04
☉ ♌	22 18:27
☿ ♌	30 10:19
♀ ♋	1 12:19
☿ ♍	14 5:05
☉ ♍	23 1:28
♀ ♌	27 4:13

Last Aspect / ☽ Ingress (July)

Last Aspect Dy Hr Mn		☽ Ingress Dy Hr Mn
1 19:26	♀ ☍	♐ 2 3:14
4 8:37	♃ ☍	♑ 4 12:23
5 15:05	☉ ☍	♒ 6 23:34
9 10:29	♃ △	♓ 9 12:06
12 0:10	♃ □	♈ 12 0:37
13 23:53	♅ ⚹	♉ 14 11:14
16 7:42	♅ □	♊ 16 18:27
18 11:47	♅ △	♋ 18 21:57
20 19:45	☉ ☌	♌ 20 22:44
22 12:35	♅ ☍	♍ 22 22:30
24 7:49	♀ □	♎ 24 23:09
26 15:11	♅ △	♏ 27 2:18
29 3:51	☿ △	♐ 29 8:45
31 16:25	♀ ☍	♑ 31 18:17

Last Aspect / ☽ Ingress (August)

Last Aspect Dy Hr Mn		☽ Ingress Dy Hr Mn
1 2:22	♃ ☍	♒ 3 5:54
5 4:53	♅ ☌	♓ 5 18:31
7 5:40	♂ □	♈ 8 7:06
10 4:54	♅ ⚹	♉ 10 18:24
12 22:33	☿ □	♊ 13 3:00
14 19:44	♅ △	♋ 15 7:56
16 13:04	♀ ☌	♌ 17 9:26
19 2:56	☉ ☌	♍ 19 8:54
20 20:22	♀ ⚹	♎ 21 8:20
23 1:35	♀ □	♏ 23 9:51
25 11:17	♀ △	♐ 25 15:00
27 12:51	♂ ☌	♑ 28 0:03
30 6:29	☿ △	♒ 30 11:49

☽ Phases & Eclipses

Dy Hr Mn	
5 15:05	○ 13♑39
5 14:56	☍ P 0.495
13 18:46	☾ 21♈25
20 19:45	● 28♋08
27 10:09	☽ 4♏27
4 5:57	○ 11♒56
12 7:54	☾ 19♉41
19 2:56	● 26♌12
25 19:56	☽ 2♐40

Astro Data

1 July 2001
Julian Day # 37072
SVP 5♓14'37"
GC 26♐51.6 ⚴ 28♏18.4R
Eris 20♈08.8 ⚵ 16♊42.8
⚷ 24♐54.1R ⚶ 19♉04.1
☽ Mean ☊ 6♋04.4

1 August 2001
Julian Day # 37103
SVP 5♓14'31"
GC 26♐51.7 ⚴ 27♏54.0
Eris 20♈08.7R ⚵ 4♋35.5
⚷ 23♐18.3R ⚶ 0♊16.1
☽ Mean ☊ 4♋25.9

LONGITUDE — September 2001

Day	Sid.Time	☉	0 hr ☽	Noon ☽	True ☊	☿	♀	♂	⚳	♃	♄	♅	♆	♇
1 Sa	10 42 52	9♍06 52	17♒53 00	23♒48 13	4♋21.0	0♎42.0	6♌20.7	26♐28.1	8♑48.7	10♋01.7	14♊23.0	22♒11.9	6♒32.6	12♐33.7
2 Su	10 46 48	10 04 56	29 43 37	5♓39 25	4R 10.5	2 09.7	7 32.4	26 56.2	8 50.4	10 11.5	14 25.7	22R 09.7	6R 31.3	12 34.0
3 M	10 50 45	11 03 01	11♓35 49	17 33 01	3 58.5	3 36.0	8 44.3	27 24.6	8 52.5	10 21.3	14 28.2	22 07.5	6 30.0	12 34.3
4 Tu	10 54 41	12 01 08	23 31 10	29 30 26	3 45.9	5 00.9	9 56.2	27 53.5	8 54.9	10 30.9	14 30.7	22 05.2	6 28.8	12 34.7
5 W	10 58 38	12 59 17	5♈31 00	11♈33 04	3 33.8	6 24.5	11 08.2	28 22.7	8 57.7	10 40.4	14 33.0	22 03.0	6 27.6	12 35.1
6 Th	11 02 34	13 57 27	17 36 49	23 42 29	3 23.3	7 46.7	12 20.2	28 52.3	9 00.8	10 49.8	14 35.3	22 00.9	6 26.3	12 35.5
7 F	11 06 31	14 55 40	29 50 20	6♉00 40	3 15.1	9 07.4	13 32.4	29 22.2	9 04.2	10 59.1	14 37.5	21 58.7	6 25.1	12 36.0
8 Sa	11 10 28	15 53 54	12♉13 49	18 30 08	3 09.6	10 26.6	14 44.6	29 52.5	9 08.0	11 08.3	14 39.5	21 56.6	6 24.0	12 36.5
9 Su	11 14 24	16 52 11	24 50 02	1♊13 56	3 06.6	11 44.3	15 56.9	0♑23.2	9 12.1	11 17.3	14 41.4	21 54.5	6 22.8	12 37.0
10 M	11 18 21	17 50 29	7♊42 15	14 15 26	3D 05.6	13 00.4	17 09.3	0 54.2	9 16.5	11 26.3	14 43.3	21 52.4	6 21.7	12 37.6
11 Tu	11 22 17	18 48 50	20 53 54	27 38 03	3R 05.7	14 14.9	18 21.7	1 25.5	9 21.2	11 35.1	14 45.0	21 50.3	6 20.6	12 38.2
12 W	11 26 14	19 47 13	4♋28 12	11♋24 36	3 05.6	15 27.6	19 34.2	1 57.2	9 26.3	11 43.8	14 46.7	21 48.3	6 19.5	12 38.9
13 Th	11 30 10	20 45 38	18 27 23	25 36 32	3 04.1	16 38.6	20 46.8	2 29.2	9 31.7	11 52.3	14 48.2	21 46.3	6 18.5	12 39.5
14 F	11 34 07	21 44 05	2♌51 51	10♌12 57	3 00.2	17 47.6	21 59.5	3 01.5	9 37.4	12 00.8	14 49.6	21 44.3	6 17.4	12 40.2
15 Sa	11 38 03	22 42 35	17 39 15	25 09 56	2 53.7	18 54.7	23 12.2	3 34.1	9 43.4	12 09.1	14 50.9	21 42.4	6 16.4	12 41.0
16 Su	11 42 00	23 41 06	2♍43 59	10♍20 13	2 44.6	19 59.6	24 25.0	4 07.0	9 49.7	12 17.3	14 52.1	21 40.5	6 15.4	12 41.7
17 M	11 45 57	24 39 39	17 57 20	25 33 55	2 33.9	21 02.3	25 37.9	4 40.3	9 56.3	12 25.3	14 53.2	21 38.6	6 14.5	12 42.5
18 Tu	11 49 53	25 38 14	3♎08 36	10♎40 01	2 22.7	22 02.6	26 50.8	5 13.8	10 03.2	12 33.2	14 54.2	21 36.7	6 13.6	12 43.3
19 W	11 53 50	26 36 51	18 06 59	25 28 25	2 12.4	23 00.4	28 03.8	5 47.6	10 10.5	12 41.0	14 55.1	21 34.9	6 12.7	12 44.2
20 Th	11 57 46	27 35 29	2♏43 31	9♏51 40	2 04.0	23 55.4	29 16.8	6 21.7	10 18.0	12 48.6	14 55.9	21 33.1	6 11.8	12 45.1
21 F	12 01 43	28 34 09	16 52 28	23 45 46	1 58.2	24 47.4	0♍29.9	6 56.1	10 25.8	12 56.1	14 56.5	21 31.3	6 10.9	12 46.0
22 Sa	12 05 39	29 32 52	0♐31 37	7♐10 14	1 55.0	25 36.2	1 43.1	7 30.7	10 33.9	13 03.5	14 57.1	21 29.6	6 10.1	12 47.0
23 Su	12 09 36	0♎31 35	13 41 57	20 07 15	1 53.8	26 21.5	2 56.3	8 05.6	10 42.3	13 10.7	14 57.5	21 27.9	6 09.3	12 48.0
24 M	12 13 32	1 30 21	26 26 41	2♑40 52	1 53.6	27 03.2	4 09.6	8 40.8	10 50.9	13 17.7	14 57.8	21 26.2	6 08.6	12 49.0
25 Tu	12 17 29	2 29 08	8♑50 26	14 56 03	1 53.4	27 40.8	5 22.9	9 16.2	10 59.9	13 24.6	14 58.1	21 24.6	6 07.8	12 50.0
26 W	12 21 26	3 27 57	20 58 23	26 58 04	1 51.9	28 14.0	6 36.3	9 51.8	11 09.1	13 31.4	14R 58.2	21 23.0	6 07.1	12 51.1
27 Th	12 25 22	4 26 48	2♒55 43	8♒51 56	1 48.2	28 42.4	7 49.8	10 27.7	11 18.6	13 38.0	14 58.2	21 21.4	6 06.5	12 52.2
28 F	12 29 19	5 25 40	14 47 15	20 42 10	1 41.8	29 05.7	9 03.3	11 03.8	11 28.3	13 44.5	14 58.1	21 19.9	6 05.8	12 53.4
29 Sa	12 33 15	6 24 34	26 37 08	2♓32 33	1 32.5	29 23.5	10 16.9	11 40.1	11 38.3	13 50.8	14 57.8	21 18.5	6 05.2	12 54.5
30 Su	12 37 12	7 23 30	8♓28 45	14 26 02	1 20.8	29 35.4	11 30.5	12 16.7	11 48.5	13 56.9	14 57.5	21 17.0	6 04.6	12 55.7

LONGITUDE — October 2001

Day	Sid.Time	☉	0 hr ☽	Noon ☽	True ☊	☿	♀	♂	⚳	♃	♄	♅	♆	♇
1 M	12 41 08	8♎22 28	20♓24 39	26♓24 48	1♋07.4	29♎40.8	12♍44.1	12♑53.4	11♑59.0	14♋02.9	14♊57.1	21♒15.6	6♒04.1	12♐56.9
2 Tu	12 45 05	9 21 28	2♈26 38	8♈30 18	0R 53.3	29R 39.5	13 57.8	13 30.4	12 09.8	14 08.7	14R 56.5	21R 14.3	6R 03.5	12 58.2
3 W	12 49 01	10 20 30	14 35 54	20 43 31	0 39.8	29 30.9	15 11.6	14 07.6	12 20.8	14 14.4	14 55.9	21 12.9	6 03.0	12 59.5
4 Th	12 52 58	11 19 34	26 53 15	3♉05 10	0 27.9	29 14.9	16 25.4	14 44.9	12 32.0	14 19.9	14 55.1	21 11.7	6 02.6	13 00.8
5 F	12 56 54	12 18 40	9♉19 22	15 35 59	0 18.5	28 51.0	17 39.3	15 22.5	12 43.5	14 25.2	14 54.2	21 10.4	6 02.2	13 02.1
6 Sa	13 00 51	13 17 48	21 55 09	28 17 02	0 12.1	28 19.2	18 53.3	16 00.2	12 55.2	14 30.4	14 53.2	21 09.2	6 01.8	13 03.5
7 Su	13 04 48	14 16 59	4♊41 51	11♊09 50	0 08.5	27 39.5	20 07.2	16 38.2	13 07.2	14 35.4	14 52.1	21 08.1	6 01.4	13 04.9
8 M	13 08 44	15 16 12	17 41 15	24 16 22	0D 07.2	26 52.1	21 21.3	17 16.3	13 19.4	14 40.3	14 51.0	21 07.0	6 01.1	13 06.3
9 Tu	13 12 41	16 15 27	0♋55 30	7♋38 56	0R 07.1	25 57.6	22 35.4	17 54.6	13 31.8	14 45.0	14 49.7	21 05.9	6 00.8	13 07.8
10 W	13 16 37	17 14 45	14 26 56	21 19 44	0 07.2	24 56.7	23 49.5	18 33.1	13 44.4	14 49.5	14 48.2	21 04.9	6 00.5	13 09.2
11 Th	13 20 34	18 14 05	28 17 28	5♌20 14	0 06.2	23 50.5	25 03.7	19 11.7	13 57.2	14 53.8	14 46.7	21 03.9	6 00.3	13 10.7
12 F	13 24 30	19 13 27	12♌27 57	19 40 26	0 03.0	22 40.5	26 17.9	19 50.5	14 10.3	14 57.9	14 45.1	21 03.0	6 00.1	13 12.3
13 Sa	13 28 27	20 12 52	26 57 22	4♍18 11	29♊57.2	21 28.3	27 32.2	20 29.5	14 23.6	15 01.9	14 43.4	21 02.1	5 59.9	13 13.8
14 Su	13 32 23	21 12 19	11♍42 13	19 08 36	29 49.1	20 16.0	28 46.5	21 08.6	14 37.1	15 05.7	14 41.5	21 01.3	5 59.8	13 15.4
15 M	13 36 20	22 11 48	26 36 20	4♎04 21	29 39.2	19 05.5	0♎00.9	21 47.9	14 50.8	15 09.3	14 39.6	21 00.5	5 59.6	13 17.0
16 Tu	13 40 17	23 11 19	11♎31 28	18 56 31	29 28.7	17 59.0	1 15.3	22 27.4	15 04.7	15 12.7	14 37.6	20 59.8	5 59.6	13 18.6
17 W	13 44 13	24 10 52	26 18 24	3♏36 05	29 18.9	16 58.3	2 29.7	23 07.0	15 18.8	15 15.9	14 35.4	20 59.1	5D 59.5	13 20.3
18 Th	13 48 10	25 10 27	10♏48 41	17 55 29	29 10.9	16 05.3	3 44.2	23 46.8	15 33.1	15 18.9	14 33.2	20 58.4	5 59.5	13 22.0
19 F	13 52 06	26 10 04	24 55 57	1♐49 45	29 05.3	15 21.5	4 58.7	24 26.7	15 47.6	15 21.8	14 30.8	20 57.8	5 59.6	13 23.7
20 Sa	13 56 03	27 09 43	8♐36 42	15 16 51	29 02.2	14 47.8	6 13.2	25 06.8	16 02.3	15 24.5	14 28.4	20 57.3	5 59.6	13 25.4
21 Su	13 59 59	28 09 24	21 50 23	28 17 35	29D 01.3	14 25.1	7 27.8	25 47.0	16 17.2	15 26.9	14 25.8	20 56.8	5 59.7	13 27.1
22 M	14 03 56	29 09 07	4♑38 53	10♑54 47	29 01.8	14D 13.6	8 42.4	26 27.3	16 32.2	15 29.2	14 23.2	20 56.4	5 59.9	13 28.9
23 Tu	14 07 52	0♏08 51	17 05 53	23 12 46	29R 02.6	14 13.4	9 57.1	27 07.8	16 47.5	15 31.3	14 20.5	20 56.0	6 00.0	13 30.7
24 W	14 11 49	1 08 37	29 16 07	5♒16 34	29 02.7	14 24.2	11 11.8	27 48.4	17 02.9	15 33.2	14 17.7	20 55.6	6 00.2	13 32.5
25 Th	14 15 46	2 08 25	11♒14 47	17 11 25	29 01.2	14 45.5	12 26.5	28 29.1	17 18.5	15 34.9	14 14.7	20 55.3	6 00.5	13 34.3
26 F	14 19 42	3 08 14	23 07 06	29 02 25	28 57.7	15 16.6	13 41.2	29 09.9	17 34.3	15 36.4	14 11.7	20 55.1	6 00.7	13 36.2
27 Sa	14 23 39	4 08 05	4♓57 56	10♓54 10	28 51.8	15 56.8	14 56.0	29 50.9	17 50.3	15 37.8	14 08.6	20 54.9	6 01.0	13 38.1
28 Su	14 27 35	5 07 58	16 51 35	22 50 36	28 43.9	16 45.1	16 10.8	0♒31.9	18 06.4	15 38.9	14 05.5	20 54.7	6 01.4	13 40.0
29 M	14 31 32	6 07 52	28 51 35	4♈54 49	28 34.5	17 40.8	17 25.6	1 13.1	18 22.7	15 39.8	14 02.2	20 54.6	6 01.8	13 41.9
30 Tu	14 35 28	7 07 48	11♈00 35	17 09 02	28 24.5	18 43.0	18 40.4	1 54.4	18 39.1	15 40.5	13 58.8	20D 54.6	6 02.2	13 43.8
31 W	14 39 25	8 07 46	23 20 20	29 34 33	28 14.8	19 50.9	19 55.3	2 35.7	18 55.7	15 41.0	13 55.4	20 54.6	6 02.6	13 45.8

Astro Data

	Dy Hr Mn
☽0N	5 12:05
☽0S	18 13:22
♃⊼♇	19 23:24
⊙0S	22 23:06
♄R	27 0:05
☿R	1 19:25
☽0N	2 17:46
♃⊼♄	10 7:04
☽0S	15 23:56
♆D	18 1:49
♀0S	18 8:12
☿D	23 0:22
☽0N	30 1:04
♅D	30 22:56

Planet Ingress

	Dy Hr Mn
☿ ♎	1 0:38
♂ ♑	8 17:52
♀ ♍	21 2:10
⊙ ♎	22 23:06
☊ ♊R	13 1:47
♀ ♎	15 11:43
⊙ ♏	23 8:27
♂ ♒	27 17:20

Last Aspect / ☽ Ingress (September)

Last Aspect Dy Hr Mn		☽ Ingress Dy Hr Mn
1 17:37	♂ ⚹	♓ 2 0:33
4 8:38	♂ □	♈ 4 12:59
6 22:32	♂ △	♉ 7 0:19
8 18:31	♅ □	♊ 9 9:42
11 1:43	♅ △	♋ 11 16:10
13 3:17	⊙ ⚹	♌ 13 19:17
15 8:36	♀ ☌	♍ 15 19:40
17 10:28	⊙ ☌	♎ 17 19:01
19 16:39	♀ ⚹	♏ 19 19:28
21 21:10	⊙ ⚹	♐ 21 23:03
24 0:33	♅ ⚹	♑ 24 6:49
26 14:39	♅ □	♒ 26 18:06
29 5:29	☿ △	♓ 29 6:51

Last Aspect / ☽ Ingress (October)

Last Aspect Dy Hr Mn		☽ Ingress Dy Hr Mn
30 13:03	♄ □	♈ 1 19:09
4 4:46	☿ ☍	♉ 4 6:02
5 22:34	♅ □	♊ 6 15:13
8 16:25	☿ △	♋ 8 22:20
10 17:48	☿ □	♌ 11 2:55
12 16:35	☿ ⚹	♍ 13 4:59
15 4:53	♀ ☌	♎ 15 5:27
16 19:24	⊙ ☌	♏ 17 6:04
18 22:31	♂ ⚹	♐ 19 8:48
21 11:43	⊙ ⚹	♑ 21 15:12
23 20:13	♂ ☌	♒ 24 1:27
25 19:33	♅ ☌	♓ 26 13:57
27 21:32	♃ △	♈ 29 2:16
30 19:18	♅ ⚹	♉ 31 12:49

☽ Phases & Eclipses

Dy Hr Mn		
2 21:44	○	10♓28
10 19:01	☾	18♊08
17 10:28	●	24♍36
24 9:32	☽	1♑24
2 13:50	○	9♈26
10 4:21	☾	16♋56
16 19:24	●	23♎30
24 2:59	☽	0♒46

Astro Data

1 September 2001
Julian Day # 37134
SVP 5♓14'27"
GC 26♐51.8 ⚴ 3♐13.5
Eris 19♈59.1R ⚵ 21♋31.5
⚷ 22♐53.0 ⚶ 8♊55.2
☽ Mean ☊ 2♋47.4

1 October 2001
Julian Day # 37164
SVP 5♓14'25"
GC 26♐51.8 ⚴ 11♐42.0
Eris 19♈43.3R ⚵ 6♌23.3
⚷ 23♐48.7 ⚶ 13♊15.7
☽ Mean ☊ 1♋12.1

November 2001 LONGITUDE

Day	Sid.Time	☉	0 hr ☽	Noon ☽	True ☊	☿	♀	♂	⚳	♃	♄	♅	♆	♇
1 Th	14 43 21	9♏07 46	5♉51 45	12♉11 56	28♊06.4	21♎03.7	21♎10.2	3♒17.2	19♑12.5	15♋41.4	13♊51.9	20♒54.6	6♒03.1	13♐47.7
2 F	14 47 18	10 07 48	18 35 05	25 01 11	27R 59.9	22 20.8	22 25.2	3 58.8	19 29.4	15R 41.5	13R 48.3	20 54.7	6 03.6	13 49.7
3 Sa	14 51 15	11 07 52	1♊30 10	8♊02 00	27 55.7	23 41.5	23 40.1	4 40.4	19 46.5	15 41.4	13 44.6	20 54.9	6 04.1	13 51.7
4 Su	14 55 11	12 07 57	14 36 39	21 14 06	27D 53.8	25 05.2	24 55.1	5 22.2	20 03.7	15 41.2	13 40.9	20 55.1	6 04.7	13 53.8
5 M	14 59 08	13 08 05	27 54 21	4♋37 24	27 53.8	26 31.5	26 10.1	6 04.0	20 21.1	15 40.7	13 37.0	20 55.4	6 05.3	13 55.8
6 Tu	15 03 04	14 08 15	11♋23 18	18 12 04	27 54.9	27 59.9	27 25.2	6 45.9	20 38.6	15 40.0	13 33.2	20 55.7	6 05.9	13 57.9
7 W	15 07 01	15 08 27	25 03 45	1♌58 24	27 56.2	29 30.0	28 40.3	7 28.0	20 56.2	15 39.1	13 29.2	20 56.0	6 06.6	13 59.9
8 Th	15 10 57	16 08 41	8♌56 00	15 56 32	27R 56.8	1♏01.6	29 55.4	8 10.0	21 14.0	15 38.1	13 25.2	20 56.4	6 07.3	14 02.0
9 F	15 14 54	17 08 57	22 59 55	0♍06 00	27 56.1	2 34.3	1♏10.5	8 52.2	21 32.0	15 36.8	13 21.1	20 56.9	6 08.0	14 04.1
10 Sa	15 18 50	18 09 15	7♍14 33	14 25 16	27 53.5	4 07.9	2 25.6	9 34.5	21 50.1	15 35.3	13 16.9	20 57.4	6 08.8	14 06.2
11 Su	15 22 47	19 09 35	21 37 42	28 51 22	27 49.3	5 42.3	3 40.8	10 16.8	22 08.3	15 33.6	13 12.7	20 58.0	6 09.6	14 08.4
12 M	15 26 44	20 09 57	6♎05 38	13♎19 51	27 43.8	7 17.1	4 56.0	10 59.2	22 26.6	15 31.8	13 08.4	20 58.6	6 10.4	14 10.5
13 Tu	15 30 40	21 10 20	20 33 17	27 45 10	27 37.8	8 52.4	6 11.2	11 41.7	22 45.1	15 29.7	13 04.0	20 59.3	6 11.3	14 12.7
14 W	15 34 37	22 10 46	4♏54 45	12♏01 17	27 32.2	10 27.9	7 26.4	12 24.3	23 03.7	15 27.4	12 59.6	21 00.0	6 12.2	14 14.8
15 Th	15 38 33	23 11 13	19 04 08	26 02 40	27 27.6	12 03.7	8 41.6	13 06.9	23 22.4	15 24.9	12 55.2	21 00.7	6 13.1	14 17.0
16 F	15 42 30	24 11 42	2♐56 26	9♐45 02	27 24.6	13 39.5	9 56.9	13 49.6	23 41.2	15 22.3	12 50.7	21 01.6	6 14.1	14 19.2
17 Sa	15 46 26	25 12 13	16 28 14	23 05 54	27D 23.3	15 15.4	11 12.2	14 32.4	24 00.2	15 19.4	12 46.1	21 02.4	6 15.1	14 21.4
18 Su	15 50 23	26 12 45	29 38 02	6♑04 45	27 23.5	16 51.3	12 27.4	15 15.3	24 19.3	15 16.3	12 41.6	21 03.4	6 16.1	14 23.6
19 M	15 54 19	27 13 18	12♑26 16	18 42 54	27 24.8	18 27.1	13 42.7	15 58.2	24 38.5	15 13.1	12 36.9	21 04.3	6 17.2	14 25.8
20 Tu	15 58 16	28 13 53	24 55 03	1♒03 10	27 26.6	20 02.8	14 58.0	16 41.2	24 57.9	15 09.7	12 32.3	21 05.4	6 18.3	14 28.1
21 W	16 02 13	29 14 29	7♒07 47	13 09 26	27 28.3	21 38.5	16 13.4	17 24.2	25 17.3	15 06.0	12 27.6	21 06.4	6 19.4	14 30.3
22 Th	16 06 09	0♐15 06	19 08 44	25 06 17	27R 29.3	23 14.0	17 28.7	18 07.3	25 36.8	15 02.2	12 22.8	21 07.6	6 20.6	14 32.6
23 F	16 10 06	1 15 44	1♓02 41	6♓58 35	27 29.3	24 49.4	18 44.0	18 50.4	25 56.5	14 58.2	12 18.0	21 08.7	6 21.7	14 34.8
24 Sa	16 14 02	2 16 23	12 54 34	18 51 15	27 28.0	26 24.6	19 59.4	19 33.6	26 16.3	14 54.0	12 13.2	21 09.9	6 23.0	14 37.1
25 Su	16 17 59	3 17 03	24 49 12	0♈48 58	27 25.6	27 59.7	21 14.7	20 16.8	26 36.1	14 49.7	12 08.4	21 11.2	6 24.2	14 39.4
26 M	16 21 55	4 17 44	6♈51 02	12 55 51	27 22.4	29 34.7	22 30.1	21 00.0	26 56.1	14 45.1	12 03.6	21 12.5	6 25.5	14 41.6
27 Tu	16 25 52	5 18 27	19 03 51	25 15 21	27 18.8	1♐09.5	23 45.5	21 43.4	27 16.1	14 40.4	11 58.7	21 13.9	6 26.8	14 43.9
28 W	16 29 48	6 19 11	1♉30 39	7♉49 57	27 15.2	2 44.2	25 00.9	22 26.7	27 36.3	14 35.5	11 53.8	21 15.3	6 28.1	14 46.2
29 Th	16 33 45	7 19 56	14 13 24	20 41 03	27 12.1	4 18.8	26 16.2	23 10.1	27 56.6	14 30.5	11 48.9	21 16.8	6 29.4	14 48.5
30 F	16 37 42	8 20 42	27 12 55	3♊48 56	27 09.9	5 53.3	27 31.7	23 53.5	28 16.9	14 25.3	11 44.0	21 18.3	6 30.8	14 50.8

December 2001 LONGITUDE

Day	Sid.Time	☉	0 hr ☽	Noon ☽	True ☊	☿	♀	♂	⚳	♃	♄	♅	♆	♇
1 Sa	16 41 38	9♐21 29	10♊28 57	17♊12 46	27♊08.7	7♐27.7	28♏47.1	24♒37.0	28♑37.4	14♋19.9	11♊39.1	21♒19.8	6♒32.2	14♐53.1
2 Su	16 45 35	10 22 18	24 00 09	0♋50 50	27D 08.5	9 02.1	0♐02.5	25 20.5	28 57.9	14R 14.4	11R 34.2	21 21.4	6 33.7	14 55.4
3 M	16 49 31	11 23 07	7♋44 30	14 40 49	27 09.1	10 36.4	1 17.9	26 04.0	29 18.5	14 08.7	11 29.3	21 23.1	6 35.1	14 57.7
4 Tu	16 53 28	12 23 58	21 39 26	28 40 02	27 10.1	12 10.6	2 33.4	26 47.5	29 39.3	14 02.8	11 24.3	21 24.8	6 36.6	15 00.0
5 W	16 57 24	13 24 51	5♌42 16	12♌45 49	27 11.3	13 44.8	3 48.8	27 31.1	0♒00.1	13 56.8	11 19.4	21 26.5	6 38.2	15 02.3
6 Th	17 01 21	14 25 44	19 50 22	26 55 37	27 12.3	15 19.0	5 04.3	28 14.7	0 21.0	13 50.7	11 14.5	21 28.3	6 39.7	15 04.6
7 F	17 05 17	15 26 39	4♍01 18	11♍07 07	27R 12.8	16 53.2	6 19.7	28 58.3	0 41.9	13 44.4	11 09.6	21 30.1	6 41.3	15 06.9
8 Sa	17 09 14	16 27 35	18 12 49	25 18 06	27 12.7	18 27.5	7 35.2	29 42.0	1 03.0	13 38.0	11 04.7	21 32.0	6 42.9	15 09.2
9 Su	17 13 11	17 28 33	2♎22 44	9♎26 26	27 12.1	20 01.7	8 50.7	0♓25.7	1 24.1	13 31.4	10 59.8	21 33.9	6 44.5	15 11.6
10 M	17 17 07	18 29 32	16 28 53	23 29 49	27 11.2	21 36.0	10 06.2	1 09.4	1 45.3	13 24.7	10 54.9	21 35.8	6 46.1	15 13.9
11 Tu	17 21 04	19 30 31	0♏28 55	7♏25 53	27 10.1	23 10.4	11 21.7	1 53.1	2 06.6	13 17.9	10 50.1	21 37.8	6 47.8	15 16.2
12 W	17 25 00	20 31 32	14 20 24	21 12 10	27 09.2	24 44.8	12 37.2	2 36.9	2 28.0	13 11.0	10 45.2	21 39.9	6 49.5	15 18.5
13 Th	17 28 57	21 32 34	28 00 53	4♐46 18	27 08.6	26 19.3	13 52.7	3 20.7	2 49.5	13 04.0	10 40.4	21 42.0	6 51.2	15 20.8
14 F	17 32 53	22 33 37	11♐28 10	18 06 18	27D 08.3	27 54.0	15 08.2	4 04.5	3 11.0	12 56.8	10 35.6	21 44.1	6 53.0	15 23.1
15 Sa	17 36 50	23 34 41	24 40 31	1♑10 44	27 08.2	29 28.7	16 23.7	4 48.3	3 32.6	12 49.6	10 30.9	21 46.3	6 54.7	15 25.4
16 Su	17 40 46	24 35 45	7♑36 53	13 59 02	27 08.3	1♑03.5	17 39.2	5 32.2	3 54.2	12 42.2	10 26.2	21 48.5	6 56.5	15 27.7
17 M	17 44 43	25 36 50	20 17 13	26 31 35	27 08.5	2 38.4	18 54.7	6 16.0	4 16.0	12 34.8	10 21.5	21 50.7	6 58.3	15 30.0
18 Tu	17 48 40	26 37 55	2♒42 22	8♒49 49	27R 08.7	4 13.5	20 10.3	6 59.9	4 37.8	12 27.2	10 16.9	21 53.0	7 00.1	15 32.2
19 W	17 52 36	27 39 01	14 54 15	20 56 04	27 08.7	5 48.6	21 25.8	7 43.8	4 59.7	12 19.6	10 12.3	21 55.4	7 02.0	15 34.5
20 Th	17 56 33	28 40 07	26 55 41	2♓53 35	27 08.5	7 23.9	22 41.3	8 27.7	5 21.6	12 11.9	10 07.7	21 57.7	7 03.9	15 36.8
21 F	18 00 29	29 41 13	8♓50 15	14 46 15	27 08.4	8 59.2	23 56.8	9 11.6	5 43.6	12 04.2	10 03.2	22 00.1	7 05.8	15 39.0
22 Sa	18 04 26	0♑42 20	20 42 07	26 38 28	27D 08.2	10 34.6	25 12.3	9 55.6	6 05.6	11 56.3	9 58.8	22 02.6	7 07.7	15 41.3
23 Su	18 08 22	1 43 26	2♈35 52	8♈34 55	27 08.3	12 10.0	26 27.8	10 39.5	6 27.7	11 48.5	9 54.4	22 05.0	7 09.6	15 43.5
24 M	18 12 19	2 44 33	14 36 14	20 40 21	27 08.6	13 45.4	27 43.3	11 23.4	6 49.9	11 40.5	9 50.0	22 07.6	7 11.5	15 45.8
25 Tu	18 16 16	3 45 40	26 47 52	2♉59 16	27 09.1	15 20.8	28 58.9	12 07.3	7 12.1	11 32.5	9 45.7	22 10.1	7 13.5	15 48.0
26 W	18 20 12	4 46 47	9♉15 02	15 35 36	27 09.9	16 56.1	0♑14.4	12 51.3	7 34.4	11 24.5	9 41.5	22 12.7	7 15.5	15 50.2
27 Th	18 24 09	5 47 54	22 01 18	28 32 24	27 10.7	18 31.3	1 29.9	13 35.2	7 56.7	11 16.5	9 37.3	22 15.3	7 17.5	15 52.4
28 F	18 28 05	6 49 02	5♊09 05	11♊51 23	27 11.4	20 06.2	2 45.4	14 19.1	8 19.1	11 08.4	9 33.2	22 18.0	7 19.5	15 54.6
29 Sa	18 32 02	7 50 09	18 39 17	25 32 37	27R 11.7	21 40.8	4 00.9	15 03.1	8 41.6	11 00.3	9 29.2	22 20.6	7 21.5	15 56.8
30 Su	18 35 58	8 51 17	2♋31 04	9♋34 14	27 11.5	23 14.9	5 16.4	15 47.0	9 04.0	10 52.2	9 25.3	22 23.4	7 23.6	15 59.0
31 M	18 39 55	9 52 25	16 41 37	23 52 34	27 10.6	24 48.5	6 31.9	16 30.9	9 26.6	10 44.1	9 21.4	22 26.1	7 25.6	16 01.1

Astro Data

	Dy Hr Mn
♄☍♇	2 5:51
♃R	2 15:36
☽0S	12 9:16
☽0N	26 9:47
♃⚻♇	27 0:03
☽0S	9 16:10
☽0N	23 18:38

Planet Ingress

	Dy Hr Mn
☿ ♏	7 19:54
♀ ♏	8 13:29
☉ ♐	22 6:02
☿ ♐	26 18:25
♀ ♐	2 11:13
⚳ ♒	5 11:55
♂ ♓	8 21:53
☿ ♑	15 19:56
☉ ♑	21 19:23
♀ ♑	26 7:26

Last Aspect / ☽ Ingress

Last Aspect Dy Hr Mn	☽ Ingress Dy Hr Mn
2 4:21 ♅ □	♊ 2 21:14
4 19:46 ☿ △	♋ 5 3:45
7 7:11 ☿ □	♌ 7 8:35
8 20:31 ♅ ☍	♍ 9 11:50
10 18:41 ☉ ⚹	♎ 11 13:54
13 0:43 ♅ △	♏ 13 15:46
15 6:41 ☉ ☌	♐ 15 18:52
17 8:15 ♅ ⚹	♑ 18 0:41
20 5:58 ☉ ⚹	♒ 20 9:56
22 7:39 ☿ □	♓ 22 21:53
25 5:30 ☿ △	♈ 25 10:27
27 4:45 ♂ ⚹	♉ 27 21:07
29 23:22 ♀ ☍	♊ 30 5:05

Last Aspect / ☽ Ingress

Last Aspect Dy Hr Mn	☽ Ingress Dy Hr Mn
2 1:49 ♂ △	♋ 2 10:31
3 11:05 ♃ ☌	♌ 4 14:17
6 14:21 ♂ ☍	♍ 6 17:12
7 22:58 ☿ □	♎ 8 19:58
10 8:44 ♅ □	♏ 10 23:10
12 12:49 ♅ □	♐ 13 3:31
15 8:25 ☿ ☌	♑ 15 9:49
16 9:36 ♃ ☍	♒ 17 18:44
20 2:42 ☉ ⚹	♓ 20 6:10
22 8:46 ♀ □	♈ 22 18:46
25 3:22 ♀ △	♉ 25 6:13
27 0:24 ♅ △	♊ 27 14:40
29 6:26 ♅ △	♋ 29 19:41
31 13:44 ☿ ☍	♌ 31 22:10

☽ Phases & Eclipses

Dy Hr Mn	
1 5:42	○ 8♉52
8 12:22	☾ 16♌10
15 6:41	● 22♏58
22 23:22	☽ 0♓44
30 20:50	○ 8♊43
7 19:53	☾ 15♍47
14 20:48	● 22♐56
14 20:53:02	● A 03'53"
22 20:57	☽ 1♈05
30 10:42	○ 8♋48
30 10:30	● A 0.893

Astro Data

1 November 2001
Julian Day # 37195
SVP 5♓14'22"
GC 26♐51.9 ⚴ 22♐21.9
Eris 19♈24.9R ⚵ 19♌12.2
⚷ 25♐59.2 ⚶ 11♊32.2R
☽ Mean ☊ 29♊33.5

1 December 2001
Julian Day # 37225
SVP 5♓14'17"
GC 26♐52.0 ⚴ 3♑37.7
Eris 19♈10.5R ⚵ 27♌37.0
⚷ 28♐53.2 ⚶ 4♊31.2R
☽ Mean ☊ 27♊58.2

LONGITUDE — January 2002

Day	Sid.Time	☉	0 hr ☽	Noon ☽	True ☊	☿	♀	♂	⚳	♃	♄	♅	♆	♇
1 Tu	18 43 51	10♑53 33	1♌06 24	8♌22 21	27♊09.1	26♑21.3	7♑47.4	17♓14.8	9♒49.2	10♋35.9	9♊17.5	22♒28.9	7♒27.7	16♐03.3
2 W	18 47 48	11 54 41	15 39 37	22 57 26	27R 07.2	27 53.2	9 02.9	17 58.7	10 11.8	10R 27.8	9R 13.8	22 31.7	7 29.8	16 05.4
3 Th	18 51 45	12 55 49	0♍15 01	7♍31 38	27 05.2	29 23.9	10 18.4	18 42.6	10 34.5	10 19.7	9 10.1	22 34.5	7 31.9	16 07.5
4 F	18 55 41	13 56 58	14 46 39	21 59 29	27 03.6	0♒53.2	11 33.9	19 26.5	10 57.2	10 11.6	9 06.5	22 37.4	7 34.0	16 09.6
5 Sa	18 59 38	14 58 06	29 09 40	6♎16 49	27D 02.6	2 20.7	12 49.4	20 10.4	11 19.9	10 03.5	9 03.0	22 40.3	7 36.2	16 11.7
6 Su	19 03 34	15 59 15	13♎20 39	20 21 00	27 02.4	3 46.1	14 04.9	20 54.3	11 42.7	9 55.5	8 59.6	22 43.2	7 38.3	16 13.8
7 M	19 07 31	17 00 25	27 17 43	4♏10 46	27 03.1	5 08.9	15 20.3	21 38.1	12 05.6	9 47.4	8 56.2	22 46.2	7 40.4	16 15.9
8 Tu	19 11 27	18 01 34	11♏00 11	17 45 59	27 04.5	6 28.7	16 35.8	22 22.0	12 28.5	9 39.5	8 53.0	22 49.2	7 42.6	16 17.9
9 W	19 15 24	19 02 44	24 28 14	1♐07 04	27 06.1	7 45.0	17 51.3	23 05.9	12 51.4	9 31.5	8 49.8	22 52.2	7 44.8	16 20.0
10 Th	19 19 20	20 03 53	7♐42 32	14 14 46	27R 07.4	8 57.0	19 06.8	23 49.7	13 14.4	9 23.6	8 46.7	22 55.2	7 47.0	16 22.0
11 F	19 23 17	21 05 03	20 43 51	27 09 51	27 07.9	10 04.1	20 22.3	24 33.6	13 37.4	9 15.8	8 43.7	22 58.3	7 49.2	16 24.0
12 Sa	19 27 14	22 06 12	3♑32 52	9♑52 58	27 07.2	11 05.6	21 37.8	25 17.4	14 00.4	9 08.0	8 40.8	23 01.4	7 51.4	16 25.9
13 Su	19 31 10	23 07 21	16 10 14	22 24 43	27 05.2	12 00.6	22 53.3	26 01.2	14 23.5	9 00.3	8 38.0	23 04.5	7 53.6	16 27.9
14 M	19 35 07	24 08 30	28 36 31	4♒45 44	27 01.7	12 48.3	24 08.8	26 45.0	14 46.6	8 52.7	8 35.3	23 07.6	7 55.8	16 29.8
15 Tu	19 39 03	25 09 38	10♒52 29	16 56 54	26 57.1	13 27.8	25 24.2	27 28.8	15 09.7	8 45.2	8 32.7	23 10.7	7 58.1	16 31.8
16 W	19 43 00	26 10 45	22 59 12	28 59 34	26 51.6	13 58.2	26 39.7	28 12.6	15 32.9	8 37.7	8 30.2	23 13.9	8 00.3	16 33.7
17 Th	19 46 56	27 11 52	4♓58 16	10♓55 35	26 46.1	14 18.6	27 55.1	28 56.4	15 56.1	8 30.4	8 27.8	23 17.1	8 02.5	16 35.5
18 F	19 50 53	28 12 58	16 51 54	22 47 34	26 41.0	14R 28.3	29 10.6	29 40.1	16 19.3	8 23.1	8 25.5	23 20.3	8 04.8	16 37.4
19 Sa	19 54 49	29 14 04	28 43 01	4♈38 45	26 36.9	14 26.8	0♒26.0	0♈23.9	16 42.5	8 16.0	8 23.3	23 23.6	8 07.0	16 39.2
20 Su	19 58 46	0♒15 08	10♈35 15	16 33 04	26 34.2	14 13.7	1 41.5	1 07.6	17 05.8	8 08.9	8 21.2	23 26.8	8 09.3	16 41.0
21 M	20 02 43	1 16 12	22 32 47	28 35 00	26D 33.1	13 48.9	2 56.9	1 51.3	17 29.1	8 02.0	8 19.2	23 30.1	8 11.6	16 42.8
22 Tu	20 06 39	2 17 14	4♉40 19	10♉49 20	26 33.4	13 12.8	4 12.3	2 34.9	17 52.4	7 55.2	8 17.3	23 33.3	8 13.8	16 44.6
23 W	20 10 36	3 18 16	17 02 40	23 20 54	26 34.8	12 26.1	5 27.7	3 18.6	18 15.8	7 48.5	8 15.5	23 36.6	8 16.1	16 46.3
24 Th	20 14 32	4 19 17	29 44 35	6♊14 13	26 36.4	11 29.9	6 43.1	4 02.2	18 39.1	7 41.9	8 13.8	23 40.0	8 18.4	16 48.1
25 F	20 18 29	5 20 17	12♊50 11	19 32 48	26R 37.6	10 25.8	7 58.4	4 45.8	19 02.5	7 35.5	8 12.2	23 43.3	8 20.7	16 49.7
26 Sa	20 22 25	6 21 15	26 22 17	3♋18 39	26 37.7	9 15.6	9 13.8	5 29.4	19 25.9	7 29.2	8 10.8	23 46.6	8 22.9	16 51.4
27 Su	20 26 22	7 22 13	10♋21 48	17 31 25	26 35.9	8 01.6	10 29.2	6 13.0	19 49.3	7 23.1	8 09.4	23 50.0	8 25.2	16 53.1
28 M	20 30 18	8 23 10	24 47 01	2♌07 54	26 32.1	6 46.0	11 44.5	6 56.5	20 12.8	7 17.0	8 08.2	23 53.4	8 27.5	16 54.7
29 Tu	20 34 15	9 24 06	9♌33 14	17 01 57	26 26.5	5 30.9	12 59.9	7 40.0	20 36.2	7 11.2	8 07.1	23 56.8	8 29.8	16 56.3
30 W	20 38 12	10 25 00	24 32 57	2♍05 00	26 19.7	4 18.6	14 15.2	8 23.5	20 59.7	7 05.5	8 06.0	24 00.1	8 32.0	16 57.9
31 Th	20 42 08	11 25 54	9♍36 52	17 07 21	26 12.6	3 10.7	15 30.5	9 06.9	21 23.2	6 59.9	8 05.1	24 03.5	8 34.3	16 59.4

LONGITUDE — February 2002

Day	Sid.Time	☉	0 hr ☽	Noon ☽	True ☊	☿	♀	♂	⚳	♃	♄	♅	♆	♇
1 F	20 46 05	12♒26 47	24♍35 20	1♎59 50	26♊06.2	2♒08.8	16♒45.8	9♈50.3	21♒46.6	6♋54.5	8♊04.3	24♒07.0	8♒36.6	17♐00.9
2 Sa	20 50 01	13 27 39	9♎20 01	16 35 14	26R 01.3	1R 14.0	18 01.1	10 33.7	22 10.2	6R 49.3	8R 03.6	24 10.4	8 38.9	17 02.4
3 Su	20 53 58	14 28 31	23 45 01	0♏49 06	25 58.4	0 27.2	19 16.4	11 17.1	22 33.7	6 44.2	8 03.1	24 13.8	8 41.1	17 03.9
4 M	20 57 54	15 29 21	7♏47 22	14 39 51	25D 57.4	29♑48.6	20 31.6	12 00.4	22 57.2	6 39.3	8 02.6	24 17.2	8 43.4	17 05.3
5 Tu	21 01 51	16 30 11	21 26 41	28 08 07	25 57.9	29 18.5	21 46.9	12 43.7	23 20.7	6 34.6	8 02.3	24 20.7	8 45.7	17 06.7
6 W	21 05 47	17 31 00	4♐44 29	11♐16 07	25 59.1	28 56.9	23 02.2	13 27.0	23 44.3	6 30.0	8 02.0	24 24.1	8 47.9	17 08.1
7 Th	21 09 44	18 31 48	17 43 25	24 06 45	25R 59.8	28 43.5	24 17.4	14 10.3	24 07.9	6 25.6	8D 01.9	24 27.6	8 50.2	17 09.5
8 F	21 13 41	19 32 36	0♑26 32	6♑43 06	25 59.2	28D 38.0	25 32.7	14 53.5	24 31.4	6 21.4	8 01.9	24 31.1	8 52.5	17 10.8
9 Sa	21 17 37	20 33 22	12 56 47	19 07 55	25 56.4	28 40.0	26 47.9	15 36.8	24 55.0	6 17.4	8 02.0	24 34.5	8 54.7	17 12.1
10 Su	21 21 34	21 34 06	25 16 44	1♒23 29	25 51.0	28 49.0	28 03.1	16 20.0	25 18.6	6 13.6	8 02.2	24 38.0	8 56.9	17 13.4
11 M	21 25 30	22 34 50	7♒28 23	13 31 37	25 43.0	29 04.5	29 18.3	17 03.1	25 42.2	6 09.9	8 02.6	24 41.5	8 59.2	17 14.6
12 Tu	21 29 27	23 35 32	19 33 19	25 33 39	25 32.7	29 26.1	0♓33.5	17 46.2	26 05.7	6 06.4	8 03.0	24 45.0	9 01.4	17 15.8
13 W	21 33 23	24 36 13	1♓32 46	7♓30 48	25 20.9	29 53.2	1 48.6	18 29.3	26 29.3	6 03.2	8 03.6	24 48.4	9 03.6	17 17.0
14 Th	21 37 20	25 36 52	13 27 56	19 24 18	25 08.6	0♒25.5	3 03.8	19 12.4	26 52.9	6 00.1	8 04.2	24 51.9	9 05.8	17 18.2
15 F	21 41 16	26 37 30	25 20 09	1♈15 43	24 56.9	1 02.6	4 18.9	19 55.5	27 16.5	5 57.2	8 05.0	24 55.4	9 08.0	17 19.3
16 Sa	21 45 13	27 38 06	7♈11 16	13 07 08	24 46.7	1 44.1	5 34.0	20 38.5	27 40.1	5 54.5	8 05.9	24 58.8	9 10.2	17 20.3
17 Su	21 49 10	28 38 40	19 03 41	25 01 20	24 38.9	2 29.5	6 49.1	21 21.4	28 03.7	5 52.0	8 06.9	25 02.3	9 12.4	17 21.4
18 M	21 53 06	29 39 13	1♉00 32	7♉01 48	24 33.7	3 18.6	8 04.2	22 04.4	28 27.2	5 49.7	8 08.1	25 05.8	9 14.6	17 22.4
19 Tu	21 57 03	0♓39 44	13 05 41	19 12 45	24D 31.1	4 11.2	9 19.3	22 47.3	28 50.8	5 47.6	8 09.3	25 09.2	9 16.7	17 23.4
20 W	22 00 59	1 40 13	25 23 36	1♊38 52	24 30.4	5 06.8	10 34.3	23 30.2	29 14.4	5 45.7	8 10.6	25 12.7	9 18.9	17 24.4
21 Th	22 04 56	2 40 41	7♊59 10	14 25 05	24R 30.8	6 05.4	11 49.3	24 13.0	29 38.0	5 43.9	8 12.1	25 16.1	9 21.0	17 25.3
22 F	22 08 52	3 41 06	20 57 11	27 35 59	24 30.9	7 06.7	13 04.3	24 55.9	0♓01.5	5 42.4	8 13.7	25 19.6	9 23.2	17 26.2
23 Sa	22 12 49	4 41 30	4♋21 52	11♋15 08	24 29.8	8 10.4	14 19.3	25 38.6	0 25.1	5 41.1	8 15.4	25 23.0	9 25.3	17 27.1
24 Su	22 16 45	5 41 52	18 15 55	25 24 11	24 26.5	9 16.5	15 34.3	26 21.4	0 48.6	5 40.0	8 17.2	25 26.5	9 27.4	17 27.9
25 M	22 20 42	6 42 11	2♌39 39	10♌01 49	24 20.5	10 24.8	16 49.2	27 04.1	1 12.1	5 39.1	8 19.1	25 29.9	9 29.5	17 28.7
26 Tu	22 24 39	7 42 29	17 29 59	25 03 09	24 11.9	11 35.1	18 04.1	27 46.7	1 35.6	5 38.4	8 21.1	25 33.3	9 31.5	17 29.4
27 W	22 28 35	8 42 45	2♍40 10	10♍19 39	24 01.5	12 47.3	19 19.0	28 29.4	1 59.1	5 37.9	8 23.2	25 36.7	9 33.6	17 30.2
28 Th	22 32 32	9 43 00	18 00 10	25 40 13	23 50.5	14 01.3	20 33.9	29 12.0	2 22.6	5 37.5	8 25.4	25 40.1	9 35.6	17 30.9

Astro Data

	Dy Hr Mn
☽0S	5 21:27
♃⊻♄	18 0:34
♃□♅	18 18:26
☿R	18 20:53
♂0N	20 1:12
☽0N	20 2:13
♃⊼♆	20 10:59
♄△♆	23 8:20
☽0S	2 3:36
♄D	8 1:33
☿D	8 17:29
☽0N	16 8:17

Planet Ingress

	Dy Hr Mn
☿ ♒	3 21:39
♂ ♈	18 22:54
♀ ♒	19 3:43
☉ ♒	20 6:03
☿ ♑R	4 4:20
♀ ♓	12 1:19
☿ ♒	13 17:21
☉ ♓	18 20:14
⚳ ♓	22 10:28

Last Aspect / ☽ Ingress

Last Aspect Dy Hr Mn		☽ Ingress Dy Hr Mn
2 11:18	♅ ☍	♍ 2 23:35
4 7:31	♂ ☍	♎ 5 1:25
6 16:06	♅ △	♏ 7 4:42
8 21:04	♅ □	♐ 9 9:59
11 6:50	♂ □	♑ 11 17:19
13 19:25	♂ ✶	♒ 14 2:42
16 0:26	♅ ☌	♓ 16 14:01
19 2:28	♀ ✶	♈ 19 2:36
21 1:51	♅ ✶	♉ 21 14:48
23 12:30	♅ □	♊ 24 0:29
25 19:24	♅ △	♋ 26 6:18
26 19:05	♃ ☌	♌ 28 8:32
29 23:05	♅ ☍	♍ 30 8:41

Last Aspect / ☽ Ingress

Last Aspect Dy Hr Mn		☽ Ingress Dy Hr Mn
31 11:47	♇ □	♎ 1 8:45
3 0:46	♅ △	♏ 3 10:36
5 14:03	♅ ✶	♐ 5 15:22
7 12:40	♅ ✶	♑ 7 23:09
10 6:51	☿ ☌	♒ 10 9:16
12 10:22	♅ ☌	♓ 12 20:54
14 7:45	♇ □	♈ 15 9:27
17 19:56	☉ ✶	♉ 17 21:59
19 23:35	♅ □	♊ 20 8:51
22 7:54	♅ △	♋ 22 16:17
24 13:40	♂ □	♌ 24 19:37
26 16:31	♂ △	♍ 26 19:48
28 3:18	♀ ☍	♎ 28 18:48

☽ Phases & Eclipses

Dy Hr Mn		
6 3:56	☾	15♎39
13 13:30	●	23♑11
21 17:48	☽	1♉31
28 22:52	○	8♌51
4 13:34	☾	15♏33
12 7:42	●	23♒25
20 12:03	☽	1♊40
27 9:18	○	8♍36

Astro Data

1 January 2002
Julian Day # 37256
SVP 5♓14'11"
GC 26♐52.0 ⚴ 15♑35.4
Eris 19♈03.6R ⚵ 29♌52.3R
⚷ 2♑13.1 ⚶ 28♉27.2R
☽ Mean ☊ 26♊19.8

1 February 2002
Julian Day # 37287
SVP 5♓14'06"
GC 26♐52.1 ⚴ 27♑19.9
Eris 19♈07.1 ⚵ 24♌34.5R
⚷ 5♑21.1 ⚶ 28♉52.2
☽ Mean ☊ 24♊41.3

March 2002 LONGITUDE

Day	Sid.Time	☉	0 hr ☽	Noon ☽	True ☊	☿	♀	♂	⚳	♃	♄	♅	♆	♇
1 F	22 36 28	10♓43 12	3♎18 18	10♎53 05	23♊40.2	15♒17.1	21♓48.7	29♈54.5	2♓46.1	5♋37.4	8♊27.7	25♒43.5	9♒37.6	17♐31.5
2 Sa	22 40 25	11 43 23	18 23 21	25 48 05	23R 31.7	16 34.5	23 03.5	0♉37.0	3 09.6	5D 37.5	8 30.1	25 46.9	9 39.6	17 32.2
3 Su	22 44 21	12 43 33	3♏06 33	10♏18 12	23 25.8	17 53.5	24 18.3	1 19.5	3 33.0	5 37.8	8 32.7	25 50.2	9 41.6	17 32.8
4 M	22 48 18	13 43 40	17 22 44	24 20 04	23 22.6	19 14.1	25 33.1	2 02.0	3 56.4	5 38.2	8 35.3	25 53.6	9 43.6	17 33.3
5 Tu	22 52 14	14 43 47	1♐10 18	7♐53 42	23D 21.4	20 36.0	26 47.9	2 44.4	4 19.9	5 38.9	8 38.1	25 56.9	9 45.6	17 33.9
6 W	22 56 11	15 43 52	14 30 37	21 01 30	23R 21.4	21 59.4	28 02.6	3 26.8	4 43.3	5 39.7	8 40.9	26 00.3	9 47.5	17 34.4
7 Th	23 00 08	16 43 55	27 26 53	3♑47 18	23 21.1	23 24.2	29 17.3	4 09.1	5 06.6	5 40.8	8 43.9	26 03.6	9 49.4	17 34.8
8 F	23 04 04	17 43 57	10♑03 18	16 15 26	23 19.5	24 50.2	0♈32.0	4 51.4	5 30.0	5 42.1	8 46.9	26 06.9	9 51.3	17 35.2
9 Sa	23 08 01	18 43 57	22 24 14	28 30 12	23 15.5	26 17.6	1 46.7	5 33.7	5 53.4	5 43.5	8 50.1	26 10.1	9 53.2	17 35.6
10 Su	23 11 57	19 43 56	4♒33 47	10♒35 24	23 08.5	27 46.3	3 01.3	6 15.9	6 16.7	5 45.1	8 53.3	26 13.4	9 55.1	17 36.0
11 M	23 15 54	20 43 53	16 35 25	22 34 10	22 58.6	29 16.2	4 16.0	6 58.2	6 40.0	5 47.0	8 56.7	26 16.6	9 56.9	17 36.3
12 Tu	23 19 50	21 43 47	28 31 56	4♓28 58	22 46.0	0♓47.3	5 30.6	7 40.3	7 03.3	5 49.0	9 00.1	26 19.9	9 58.8	17 36.6
13 W	23 23 47	22 43 40	10♓25 28	16 21 38	22 31.6	2 19.7	6 45.1	8 22.5	7 26.5	5 51.2	9 03.6	26 23.1	10 00.6	17 36.9
14 Th	23 27 43	23 43 31	22 17 38	28 13 37	22 16.6	3 53.3	7 59.7	9 04.6	7 49.8	5 53.6	9 07.3	26 26.3	10 02.4	17 37.1
15 F	23 31 40	24 43 20	4♈09 44	10♈06 10	22 02.1	5 28.2	9 14.2	9 46.6	8 13.0	5 56.2	9 11.0	26 29.4	10 04.1	17 37.3
16 Sa	23 35 37	25 43 07	16 03 05	22 00 41	21 49.4	7 04.2	10 28.7	10 28.7	8 36.2	5 59.0	9 14.8	26 32.6	10 05.9	17 37.4
17 Su	23 39 33	26 42 52	27 59 13	3♉58 57	21 39.2	8 41.5	11 43.2	11 10.7	8 59.3	6 02.0	9 18.7	26 35.7	10 07.6	17 37.6
18 M	23 43 30	27 42 35	10♉00 11	16 03 18	21 32.1	10 20.0	12 57.6	11 52.6	9 22.4	6 05.1	9 22.8	26 38.8	10 09.3	17 37.7
19 Tu	23 47 26	28 42 16	22 08 41	28 16 48	21 27.9	11 59.7	14 12.0	12 34.6	9 45.5	6 08.4	9 26.9	26 41.9	10 10.9	17 37.7
20 W	23 51 23	29 41 54	4♊28 06	10♊43 08	21D 26.1	13 40.7	15 26.4	13 16.5	10 08.6	6 12.0	9 31.1	26 44.9	10 12.6	17R 37.7
21 Th	23 55 19	0♈41 30	17 02 26	23 26 32	21R 25.8	15 22.9	16 40.8	13 58.3	10 31.6	6 15.7	9 35.3	26 48.0	10 14.2	17 37.7
22 F	23 59 16	1 41 04	29 56 00	6♋31 19	21 25.8	17 06.4	17 55.1	14 40.1	10 54.6	6 19.5	9 39.7	26 51.0	10 15.8	17 37.7
23 Sa	0 03 12	2 40 36	13♋13 00	20 01 24	21 24.9	18 51.1	19 09.4	15 21.9	11 17.5	6 23.6	9 44.2	26 53.9	10 17.4	17 37.6
24 Su	0 07 09	3 40 05	26 56 48	3♌59 21	21 21.9	20 37.2	20 23.6	16 03.6	11 40.5	6 27.8	9 48.7	26 56.9	10 18.9	17 37.5
25 M	0 11 06	4 39 32	11♌09 01	18 25 32	21 16.5	22 24.5	21 37.8	16 45.3	12 03.4	6 32.2	9 53.3	26 59.8	10 20.4	17 37.3
26 Tu	0 15 02	5 38 57	25 48 28	3♍17 06	21 08.5	24 13.1	22 52.0	17 27.0	12 26.2	6 36.8	9 58.0	27 02.7	10 21.9	17 37.2
27 W	0 18 59	6 38 19	10♍50 29	18 27 30	20 58.6	26 03.1	24 06.2	18 08.6	12 49.0	6 41.5	10 02.8	27 05.6	10 23.4	17 36.9
28 Th	0 22 55	7 37 39	26 06 50	3♎47 01	20 47.9	27 54.4	25 20.3	18 50.2	13 11.8	6 46.4	10 07.7	27 08.4	10 24.9	17 36.7
29 F	0 26 52	8 36 57	11♎26 36	19 04 07	20 37.8	29 47.0	26 34.4	19 31.7	13 34.5	6 51.5	10 12.7	27 11.3	10 26.3	17 36.4
30 Sa	0 30 48	9 36 13	26 38 11	4♏07 35	20 29.4	1♈40.9	27 48.4	20 13.2	13 57.2	6 56.7	10 17.7	27 14.0	10 27.7	17 36.1
31 Su	0 34 45	10 35 28	11♏31 19	18 48 35	20 23.4	3 36.2	29 02.4	20 54.7	14 19.8	7 02.1	10 22.8	27 16.8	10 29.0	17 35.8

April 2002 LONGITUDE

Day	Sid.Time	☉	0 hr ☽	Noon ☽	True ☊	☿	♀	♂	⚳	♃	♄	♅	♆	♇
1 M	0 38 41	11♈34 40	25♏58 50	3♐01 44	20♊20.0	5♈32.8	0♉16.4	21♉36.1	14♓42.5	7♋07.7	10♊28.0	27♒19.5	10♒30.4	17♐35.4
2 Tu	0 42 38	12 33 51	9♐57 10	16 45 14	20D 18.8	7 30.6	1 30.4	22 17.5	15 05.0	7 13.4	10 33.2	27 22.2	10 31.7	17R 35.0
3 W	0 46 34	13 33 00	23 26 09	0♑00 19	20 19.0	9 29.8	2 44.3	22 58.8	15 27.6	7 19.3	10 38.6	27 24.9	10 33.0	17 34.5
4 Th	0 50 31	14 32 07	6♑28 10	12 50 15	20R 19.4	11 30.1	3 58.2	23 40.1	15 50.0	7 25.3	10 44.0	27 27.5	10 34.2	17 34.1
5 F	0 54 28	15 31 13	19 07 09	25 19 28	20 18.9	13 31.6	5 12.0	24 21.4	16 12.5	7 31.5	10 49.5	27 30.1	10 35.4	17 33.6
6 Sa	0 58 24	16 30 16	1♒27 48	7♒32 46	20 16.7	15 34.1	6 25.9	25 02.7	16 34.9	7 37.8	10 55.0	27 32.7	10 36.6	17 33.0
7 Su	1 02 21	17 29 18	13 34 55	19 34 49	20 12.0	17 37.6	7 39.7	25 43.9	16 57.2	7 44.3	11 00.6	27 35.2	10 37.8	17 32.5
8 M	1 06 17	18 28 18	25 32 58	1♓29 50	20 04.8	19 41.9	8 53.4	26 25.0	17 19.5	7 51.0	11 06.3	27 37.7	10 38.9	17 31.9
9 Tu	1 10 14	19 27 17	7♓25 52	13 21 26	19 55.5	21 46.9	10 07.2	27 06.2	17 41.7	7 57.7	11 12.1	27 40.2	10 40.0	17 31.3
10 W	1 14 10	20 26 13	19 16 51	25 12 27	19 44.5	23 52.4	11 20.9	27 47.3	18 03.9	8 04.7	11 17.9	27 42.6	10 41.1	17 30.6
11 Th	1 18 07	21 25 07	1♈08 29	7♈05 10	19 33.0	25 58.1	12 34.5	28 28.4	18 26.1	8 11.7	11 23.8	27 45.0	10 42.2	17 29.9
12 F	1 22 03	22 24 00	13 02 42	19 01 16	19 21.8	28 03.9	13 48.2	29 09.4	18 48.1	8 19.0	11 29.8	27 47.3	10 43.2	17 29.2
13 Sa	1 26 00	23 22 50	25 01 01	1♉02 08	19 12.1	0♉09.4	15 01.8	29 50.4	19 10.2	8 26.3	11 35.8	27 49.7	10 44.2	17 28.5
14 Su	1 29 57	24 21 39	7♉04 46	13 09 06	19 04.4	2 14.5	16 15.3	0♊31.4	19 32.1	8 33.8	11 41.9	27 51.9	10 45.1	17 27.7
15 M	1 33 53	25 20 25	19 15 18	25 23 36	18 59.2	4 18.7	17 28.8	1 12.3	19 54.1	8 41.4	11 48.0	27 54.2	10 46.0	17 26.9
16 Tu	1 37 50	26 19 10	1♊34 14	7♊47 28	18D 56.4	6 21.7	18 42.3	1 53.2	20 15.9	8 49.2	11 54.2	27 56.4	10 46.9	17 26.1
17 W	1 41 46	27 17 52	14 03 37	20 23 00	18 55.8	8 23.3	19 55.8	2 34.1	20 37.7	8 57.1	12 00.5	27 58.5	10 47.8	17 25.2
18 Th	1 45 43	28 16 32	26 45 59	3♋12 55	18 56.5	10 23.0	21 09.2	3 14.9	20 59.4	9 05.1	12 06.8	28 00.7	10 48.6	17 24.3
19 F	1 49 39	29 15 10	9♋44 12	16 20 12	18 57.6	12 20.6	22 22.5	3 55.7	21 21.1	9 13.3	12 13.2	28 02.7	10 49.4	17 23.4
20 Sa	1 53 36	0♉13 46	23 01 16	29 47 42	18R 58.2	14 15.6	23 35.9	4 36.5	21 42.7	9 21.6	12 19.6	28 04.8	10 50.2	17 22.5
21 Su	1 57 32	1 12 20	6♌39 44	13♌37 31	18 57.5	16 07.9	24 49.2	5 17.2	22 04.2	9 30.0	12 26.1	28 06.8	10 50.9	17 21.5
22 M	2 01 29	2 10 51	20 41 05	27 50 19	18 54.9	17 57.1	26 02.4	5 57.8	22 25.7	9 38.5	12 32.7	28 08.8	10 51.6	17 20.6
23 Tu	2 05 26	3 09 20	5♍04 57	12♍24 32	18 50.5	19 43.0	27 15.6	6 38.5	22 47.1	9 47.1	12 39.3	28 10.7	10 52.3	17 19.6
24 W	2 09 22	4 07 47	19 48 26	27 15 52	18 44.6	21 25.3	28 28.7	7 19.1	23 08.4	9 55.9	12 45.9	28 12.5	10 52.9	17 18.5
25 Th	2 13 19	5 06 12	4♎45 52	12♎17 20	18 38.1	23 03.9	29 41.8	7 59.7	23 29.7	10 04.8	12 52.6	28 14.4	10 53.5	17 17.5
26 F	2 17 15	6 04 34	19 49 07	27 19 59	18 31.7	24 38.5	0♊54.9	8 40.2	23 50.9	10 13.8	12 59.3	28 16.2	10 54.1	17 16.4
27 Sa	2 21 12	7 02 55	4♏48 45	12♏14 17	18 26.5	26 09.0	2 07.9	9 20.7	24 12.0	10 22.9	13 06.1	28 17.9	10 54.7	17 15.3
28 Su	2 25 08	8 01 15	19 35 35	26 51 47	18 22.9	27 35.4	3 20.9	10 01.1	24 33.1	10 32.1	13 13.0	28 19.6	10 55.2	17 14.1
29 M	2 29 05	8 59 32	4♐02 11	11♐06 16	18D 21.2	28 57.4	4 33.9	10 41.6	24 54.0	10 41.4	13 19.9	28 21.3	10 55.6	17 13.0
30 Tu	2 33 01	9 57 48	18 03 44	24 54 25	18 21.1	0♊14.9	5 46.8	11 22.0	25 15.0	10 50.9	13 26.8	28 22.9	10 56.1	17 11.8

Astro Data	Planet Ingress	Last Aspect	☽ Ingress	Last Aspect	☽ Ingress	☽ Phases & Eclipses	Astro Data
Dy Hr Mn	Dy Hr Mn	Dy Hr Mn	Dy Hr Mn	Dy Hr Mn	Dy Hr Mn	Dy Hr Mn	
☽0S 1 12:24	♂ ♉ 1 15:06	2 11:58 ♅ △	♏ 2 18:52	1 2:15 ♅ □	♐ 1 6:49	6 1:26 ☾ 15♐17	1 March 2002
♃D 1 15:16	♀ ♈ 8 1:43	4 14:44 ♅ □	♐ 4 21:56	3 7:14 ♅ ✶	♑ 3 11:59	14 2:04 ● 23♓19	Julian Day # 37315
♀0N 10 8:18	☿ ♓ 11 23:35	7 2:33 ♀ □	♑ 7 4:49	5 10:01 ♂ △	♒ 5 21:08	22 2:29 ☽ 1♋17	SVP 5♓14'02"
☽0N 15 13:46	☉ ♈ 20 19:17	8 15:07 ☉ ✶	♒ 9 14:57	8 4:10 ♅ ☌	♓ 8 8:59	28 18:26 ○ 7♎54	GC 26♐52.2 ⚴ 7♒18.0
♇R 20 14:56	☿ ♈ 29 14:45	11 19:30 ♅ ☌	♓ 12 2:57	10 17:32 ♂ ✶	♈ 10 21:42		Eris 19♈18.6 ⚵ 17♌49.1R
☉0N 20 19:17		14 2:04 ☉ ☌	♈ 14 15:35	13 9:53 ☿ ☌	♉ 13 9:56	4 15:30 ☾ 14♑41	⚷ 7♑34.7 ⚶ 4♊15.3
☽0S 28 23:15	♀ ♉ 1 6:41	16 21:09 ♅ ✶	♉ 17 4:02	15 16:54 ♅ □	♊ 15 20:57	12 19:22 ● 22♈42	☽ Mean ☊ 23♊12.3
☿0N 31 16:54	☿ ♉ 13 10:12	19 12:54 ☉ ✶	♊ 19 15:21	18 2:18 ♅ △	♋ 18 6:02	20 12:49 ☽ 0♌16	
	♂ ♊ 13 17:37	21 18:15 ♅ △	♋ 22 0:07	19 23:56 ♀ ✶	♌ 20 12:22	27 3:01 ○ 6♏41	1 April 2002
♄△♆ 2 2:38	☉ ♉ 20 6:22	23 10:20 ♀ □	♌ 24 5:14	22 12:31 ♅ ☍	♍ 22 15:36		Julian Day # 37346
☽0N 11 19:48	♀ ♊ 25 17:58	26 1:58 ♅ ☍	♍ 26 6:45	24 14:07 ♀ △	♎ 24 16:23		SVP 5♓13'59"
☽0S 25 10:02	☿ ♊ 30 7:17	28 1:32 ♅ ☍	♎ 28 6:05	26 13:30 ♅ △	♏ 26 16:16		GC 26♐52.2 ⚴ 17♒03.1
		30 0:58 ♀ ☍	♏ 30 5:22	28 14:27 ♅ □	♐ 28 17:14		Eris 19♈37.2 ⚵ 15♌19.4
				30 18:11 ♅ ✶	♑ 30 21:04		⚷ 8♑57.9 ⚶ 13♊41.8
							☽ Mean ☊ 21♊33.8

LONGITUDE — May 2002

Day	Sid.Time	☉	0 hr ☽	Noon ☽	True ☊	☿	♀	♂	⚳	♃	♄	♅	♆	♇
1 W	2 36 58	10♉56 03	1♑38 20	8♑15 40	18♊22.2	1♊27.9	6♊59.6	12♊02.3	25♓35.8	11♋00.4	13♊33.8	28♒24.5	10♒56.5	17♐10.6
2 Th	2 40 55	11 54 16	14 46 40	21 11 46	18 23.8	2 36.3	8 12.4	12 42.7	25 56.5	11 10.1	13 40.8	28 26.0	10 56.9	17R 09.4
3 F	2 44 51	12 52 27	27 31 23	3♒46 03	18R 25.1	3 40.1	9 25.2	13 23.0	26 17.2	11 19.8	13 47.8	28 27.5	10 57.2	17 08.2
4 Sa	2 48 48	13 50 37	9♒56 19	16 02 47	18 25.4	4 39.0	10 37.9	14 03.2	26 37.8	11 29.7	13 54.9	28 29.0	10 57.5	17 06.9
5 Su	2 52 44	14 48 46	22 06 03	28 06 40	18 24.5	5 33.2	11 50.6	14 43.5	26 58.3	11 39.6	14 02.0	28 30.4	10 57.8	17 05.6
6 M	2 56 41	15 46 53	4♓05 15	10♓02 20	18 22.0	6 22.4	13 03.3	15 23.7	27 18.7	11 49.7	14 09.2	28 31.7	10 58.1	17 04.3
7 Tu	3 00 37	16 44 58	15 58 28	21 54 10	18 18.3	7 06.7	14 15.9	16 03.8	27 39.1	11 59.9	14 16.4	28 33.0	10 58.3	17 03.0
8 W	3 04 34	17 43 03	27 49 52	3♈46 02	18 13.6	7 46.0	15 28.4	16 44.0	27 59.3	12 10.1	14 23.6	28 34.3	10 58.5	17 01.7
9 Th	3 08 30	18 41 05	9♈43 01	15 41 13	18 08.4	8 20.2	16 41.0	17 24.1	28 19.5	12 20.4	14 30.9	28 35.5	10 58.6	17 00.3
10 F	3 12 27	19 39 07	21 40 54	27 42 22	18 03.3	8 49.4	17 53.4	18 04.2	28 39.6	12 30.9	14 38.2	28 36.6	10 58.7	16 59.0
11 Sa	3 16 24	20 37 06	3♉45 51	9♉51 33	17 58.9	9 13.5	19 05.9	18 44.2	28 59.6	12 41.4	14 45.6	28 37.8	10 58.8	16 57.6
12 Su	3 20 20	21 35 05	15 59 37	22 10 14	17 55.7	9 32.4	20 18.3	19 24.2	29 19.5	12 52.0	14 52.9	28 38.8	10 58.9	16 56.2
13 M	3 24 17	22 33 02	28 23 31	4♊39 36	17 53.7	9 46.3	21 30.6	20 04.2	29 39.3	13 02.7	15 00.4	28 39.8	10R 58.9	16 54.8
14 Tu	3 28 13	23 30 57	10♊58 33	17 20 31	17D 53.0	9 55.1	22 42.9	20 44.2	29 59.0	13 13.5	15 07.8	28 40.8	10 58.9	16 53.3
15 W	3 32 10	24 28 51	23 45 35	0♋13 52	17 53.5	9R 59.0	23 55.1	21 24.1	0♈18.6	13 24.4	15 15.2	28 41.7	10 58.8	16 51.9
16 Th	3 36 06	25 26 43	6♋45 28	13 20 30	17 54.7	9 58.0	25 07.3	22 04.0	0 38.1	13 35.3	15 22.7	28 42.6	10 58.7	16 50.4
17 F	3 40 03	26 24 33	19 59 04	26 41 18	17 56.2	9 52.2	26 19.5	22 43.9	0 57.5	13 46.4	15 30.2	28 43.5	10 58.6	16 49.0
18 Sa	3 43 59	27 22 22	3♌27 16	10♌17 04	17 57.4	9 41.9	27 31.6	23 23.7	1 16.7	13 57.5	15 37.8	28 44.2	10 58.5	16 47.5
19 Su	3 47 56	28 20 09	17 10 42	24 08 11	17R 58.1	9 27.4	28 43.6	24 03.6	1 35.9	14 08.7	15 45.3	28 45.0	10 58.3	16 46.0
20 M	3 51 53	29 17 54	1♍09 26	8♍14 20	17 57.9	9 08.8	29 55.6	24 43.3	1 55.0	14 19.9	15 52.9	28 45.7	10 58.1	16 44.5
21 Tu	3 55 49	0♊15 37	15 22 37	22 34 00	17 56.9	8 46.6	1♋07.5	25 23.1	2 14.0	14 31.3	16 00.5	28 46.3	10 57.8	16 43.0
22 W	3 59 46	1 13 19	29 48 04	7♎04 17	17 55.3	8 21.2	2 19.4	26 02.8	2 32.8	14 42.7	16 08.1	28 46.9	10 57.6	16 41.4
23 Th	4 03 42	2 11 00	14♎22 04	21 40 44	17 53.4	7 53.0	3 31.2	26 42.5	2 51.6	14 54.2	16 15.8	28 47.4	10 57.2	16 39.9
24 F	4 07 39	3 08 39	28 59 32	6♏17 41	17 51.5	7 22.6	4 43.0	27 22.1	3 10.2	15 05.7	16 23.4	28 47.9	10 56.9	16 38.3
25 Sa	4 11 35	4 06 16	13♏34 23	20 48 51	17 50.0	6 50.4	5 54.6	28 01.7	3 28.7	15 17.3	16 31.1	28 48.3	10 56.5	16 36.8
26 Su	4 15 32	5 03 52	28 00 19	5♐08 06	17D 49.1	6 17.0	7 06.3	28 41.3	3 47.1	15 29.0	16 38.8	28 48.7	10 56.1	16 35.2
27 M	4 19 28	6 01 27	12♐11 37	19 10 21	17 48.9	5 43.0	8 17.9	29 20.9	4 05.4	15 40.8	16 46.5	28 49.1	10 55.7	16 33.7
28 Tu	4 23 25	6 59 01	26 03 55	2♑52 03	17 49.2	5 09.1	9 29.4	0♋00.4	4 23.6	15 52.6	16 54.2	28 49.4	10 55.2	16 32.1
29 W	4 27 22	7 56 35	9♑34 36	16 11 32	17 49.9	4 35.8	10 40.8	0 40.0	4 41.6	16 04.5	17 01.9	28 49.6	10 54.8	16 30.5
30 Th	4 31 18	8 54 07	22 42 57	29 09 01	17 50.8	4 03.6	11 52.2	1 19.4	4 59.5	16 16.4	17 09.7	28 49.8	10 54.2	16 28.9
31 F	4 35 15	9 51 38	5♒29 59	11♒46 14	17 51.6	3 33.1	13 03.6	1 58.9	5 17.3	16 28.4	17 17.4	28 50.0	10 53.7	16 27.3

LONGITUDE — June 2002

Day	Sid.Time	☉	0 hr ☽	Noon ☽	True ☊	☿	♀	♂	⚳	♃	♄	♅	♆	♇
1 Sa	4 39 11	10♊49 08	17♒58 10	24♒06 14	17♊52.1	3♊04.9	14♋14.9	2♋38.3	5♈35.0	16♋40.5	17♊25.2	28♒50.1	10♒53.1	16♐25.7
2 Su	4 43 08	11 46 37	0♓10 57	6♓12 52	17R 52.4	2R 39.3	15 26.1	3 17.7	5 52.5	16 52.6	17 33.0	28R 50.1	10R 52.5	16R 24.1
3 M	4 47 04	12 44 06	12 12 32	18 10 30	17 52.5	2 16.8	16 37.2	3 57.1	6 09.9	17 04.7	17 40.7	28 50.1	10 51.9	16 22.5
4 Tu	4 51 01	13 41 34	24 07 23	0♈03 43	17 52.2	1 57.8	17 48.3	4 36.5	6 27.2	17 17.0	17 48.5	28 50.1	10 51.2	16 20.9
5 W	4 54 57	14 39 01	6♈00 05	11 57 00	17 51.9	1 42.5	18 59.4	5 15.8	6 44.3	17 29.2	17 56.3	28 50.0	10 50.5	16 19.3
6 Th	4 58 54	15 36 28	17 55 00	23 54 34	17 51.6	1 31.2	20 10.3	5 55.1	7 01.3	17 41.6	18 04.1	28 49.8	10 49.7	16 17.7
7 F	5 02 51	16 33 54	29 56 09	6♉00 10	17 51.4	1 24.1	21 21.2	6 34.4	7 18.1	17 54.0	18 11.9	28 49.6	10 49.0	16 16.1
8 Sa	5 06 47	17 31 19	12♉07 00	18 16 56	17D 51.3	1D 21.3	22 32.1	7 13.7	7 34.8	18 06.4	18 19.7	28 49.4	10 48.2	16 14.5
9 Su	5 10 44	18 28 44	24 30 17	0♊47 13	17 51.3	1 22.9	23 42.9	7 52.9	7 51.4	18 18.9	18 27.5	28 49.1	10 47.4	16 12.9
10 M	5 14 40	19 26 08	7♊07 56	13 32 32	17R 51.4	1 29.1	24 53.6	8 32.1	8 07.7	18 31.4	18 35.3	28 48.8	10 46.6	16 11.3
11 Tu	5 18 37	20 23 31	20 01 03	26 33 30	17 51.4	1 39.7	26 04.2	9 11.3	8 24.0	18 44.0	18 43.1	28 48.4	10 45.7	16 09.7
12 W	5 22 33	21 20 53	3♋09 49	9♋49 54	17 51.2	1 54.9	27 14.8	9 50.5	8 40.1	18 56.6	18 50.9	28 47.9	10 44.8	16 08.1
13 Th	5 26 30	22 18 15	16 33 37	23 20 47	17 50.8	2 14.6	28 25.3	10 29.7	8 56.0	19 09.3	18 58.7	28 47.5	10 43.9	16 06.5
14 F	5 30 26	23 15 36	0♌11 10	7♌04 34	17 50.3	2 38.7	29 35.7	11 08.8	9 11.8	19 22.0	19 06.5	28 46.9	10 42.9	16 04.9
15 Sa	5 34 23	24 12 56	14 00 42	20 59 19	17 49.6	3 07.3	0♌46.0	11 47.9	9 27.4	19 34.7	19 14.3	28 46.4	10 42.0	16 03.3
16 Su	5 38 20	25 10 14	28 00 07	5♍02 49	17 49.0	3 40.2	1 56.3	12 27.0	9 42.8	19 47.5	19 22.1	28 45.7	10 41.0	16 01.7
17 M	5 42 16	26 07 32	12♍07 08	19 12 46	17D 48.7	4 17.5	3 06.5	13 06.0	9 58.0	20 00.3	19 29.8	28 45.1	10 39.9	16 00.1
18 Tu	5 46 13	27 04 50	26 19 23	3♎26 43	17 48.7	4 58.9	4 16.6	13 45.1	10 13.1	20 13.2	19 37.6	28 44.4	10 38.9	15 58.5
19 W	5 50 09	28 02 06	10♎34 25	17 42 11	17 49.1	5 44.5	5 26.6	14 24.1	10 28.0	20 26.1	19 45.4	28 43.6	10 37.8	15 57.0
20 Th	5 54 06	28 59 21	24 49 39	1♏56 28	17 49.8	6 34.1	6 36.5	15 03.1	10 42.8	20 39.0	19 53.1	28 42.8	10 36.7	15 55.4
21 F	5 58 02	29 56 36	9♏02 17	16 06 43	17 50.8	7 27.8	7 46.3	15 42.0	10 57.3	20 51.9	20 00.8	28 41.9	10 35.6	15 53.8
22 Sa	6 01 59	0♋53 50	23 09 24	0♐09 56	17 51.6	8 25.4	8 56.1	16 21.0	11 11.7	21 04.9	20 08.5	28 41.1	10 34.5	15 52.3
23 Su	6 05 56	1 51 04	7♐07 57	14 03 05	17R 52.1	9 26.8	10 05.7	16 59.9	11 25.9	21 18.0	20 16.2	28 40.1	10 33.3	15 50.8
24 M	6 09 52	2 48 17	20 54 59	27 43 21	17 51.9	10 32.1	11 15.3	17 38.8	11 39.9	21 31.0	20 23.9	28 39.1	10 32.1	15 49.2
25 Tu	6 13 49	3 45 30	4♑27 54	11♑08 26	17 51.0	11 41.2	12 24.7	18 17.7	11 53.7	21 44.1	20 31.6	28 38.1	10 30.9	15 47.7
26 W	6 17 45	4 42 43	17 44 45	24 16 46	17 49.3	12 54.0	13 34.1	18 56.5	12 07.4	21 57.2	20 39.3	28 37.1	10 29.7	15 46.2
27 Th	6 21 42	5 39 55	0♒44 27	7♒07 49	17 46.9	14 10.4	14 43.3	19 35.4	12 20.8	22 10.3	20 46.9	28 35.9	10 28.5	15 44.7
28 F	6 25 38	6 37 08	13 27 00	19 42 10	17 44.2	15 30.5	15 52.5	20 14.2	12 34.0	22 23.4	20 54.5	28 34.8	10 27.2	15 43.3
29 Sa	6 29 35	7 34 20	25 53 34	2♓01 29	17 41.5	16 54.2	17 01.6	20 53.0	12 47.1	22 36.6	21 02.1	28 33.6	10 25.9	15 41.8
30 Su	6 33 31	8 31 32	8♓06 19	14 08 28	17 39.1	18 21.4	18 10.5	21 31.8	12 59.9	22 49.8	21 09.7	28 32.4	10 24.6	15 40.3

Astro Data

Aspect	Dy Hr Mn
♃⚻♆	1 1:45
☽0N	9 2:52
♆R	13 12:11
☿R	15 18:52
♃⚼♅	17 5:12
☽0S	22 18:51
♄☍♇	26 2:45
♃⚻♇	31 10:06
♅R	3 0:12
☽0N	5 10:39
☿D	8 15:13
♃⚺♄	11 7:37
☽0S	19 1:10

Planet Ingress

Planet	Dy Hr Mn
⚳ ♈	14 13:17
♀ ♋	20 13:28
☉ ♊	21 5:30
♂ ♋	28 11:44
♀ ♌	14 20:17
☉ ♋	21 13:25

Last Aspect / ☽ Ingress (May)

Last Aspect Dy Hr Mn		☽ Ingress Dy Hr Mn
1 17:18	☉ △	♒ 3 4:45
5 12:48	♅ ☌	♓ 5 15:47
7 2:12	♇ □	♈ 8 4:23
10 13:48	♅ ⚹	♉ 10 16:33
13 0:30	♅ □	♊ 13 3:05
15 9:10	♅ △	♋ 15 11:34
17 11:28	☉ ⚹	♌ 17 17:53
19 20:35	♀ ⚹	♍ 19 22:02
21 16:54	♂ □	♎ 22 0:20
23 23:40	♅ △	♏ 24 1:39
26 1:21	♅ □	♐ 26 3:21
28 6:41	♂ ☍	♑ 28 6:55
29 11:47	♃ ☍	♒ 30 13:36

Last Aspect / ☽ Ingress (June)

Last Aspect Dy Hr Mn		☽ Ingress Dy Hr Mn
1 21:20	♅ ☌	♓ 1 23:38
3 10:59	♄ □	♈ 4 11:52
6 21:48	♅ ⚹	♉ 7 0:08
9 8:15	♅ □	♊ 9 10:30
11 16:06	♅ △	♋ 11 18:16
13 21:45	♀ ☌	♌ 13 23:40
16 1:18	♅ ☍	♍ 16 3:25
18 0:30	☉ □	♎ 18 6:12
20 6:40	☉ △	♏ 20 8:43
22 9:28	♅ □	♐ 22 11:43
24 13:39	♅ ⚹	♑ 24 16:02
26 7:38	♃ ☍	♒ 26 22:37
29 5:13	♅ ☌	♓ 29 8:02

☽ Phases & Eclipses

Dy Hr Mn	
4 7:17	☾ 13♒39
12 10:46	● 21♉32
19 19:43	☽ 28♌39
26 11:52	○ 5♐04
26 12:04	A 0.689
3 0:06	☾ 12♓16
10 23:48	● 19♊54
10 23:45:22	A 00'22"
18 0:30	☽ 26♍37
24 21:43	○ 3♑11
24 21:28	A 0.209

Astro Data

1 May 2002
Julian Day # 37376
SVP 5♓13'56"
GC 26♐52.3 ⚵ 24♒25.5
Eris 19♈56.7 ⚴ 18♌51.5
⚷ 9♑00.2R ⚶ 24♊51.9
☽ Mean ☊ 19♊58.5

1 June 2002
Julian Day # 37407
SVP 5♓13'51"
GC 26♐52.4 ⚵ 28♒42.9
Eris 20♈13.5 ⚴ 26♌28.9
⚷ 7♑47.6R ⚶ 7♋36.3
☽ Mean ☊ 18♊20.0

July 2002 — LONGITUDE

Day	Sid.Time	☉	0 hr ☽	Noon ☽	True ☊	☿	♀	♂	⚳	♃	♄	♅	♆	♇
1 M	6 37 28	9♋28 44	20♓08 23	26♓06 37	17♊37.5	19♊52.1	19♌19.4	22♋10.5	13♈12.5	23♋03.0	21♊17.3	28♒31.1	10♒23.3	15♐38.9
2 Tu	6 41 25	10 25 57	2♈03 40	8♈00 07	17D 36.8	21 26.3	20 28.1	22 49.3	13 24.9	23 16.3	21 24.8	28R 29.8	10R 21.9	15R 37.5
3 W	6 45 21	11 23 09	13 56 33	19 53 32	17 37.1	23 03.9	21 36.8	23 28.0	13 37.1	23 29.5	21 32.3	28 28.4	10 20.6	15 36.1
4 Th	6 49 18	12 20 22	25 51 42	1♉51 36	17 38.1	24 44.8	22 45.3	24 06.7	13 49.1	23 42.8	21 39.8	28 27.0	10 19.2	15 34.7
5 F	6 53 14	13 17 35	7♉53 51	13 58 58	17 39.7	26 28.9	23 53.7	24 45.4	14 00.8	23 56.1	21 47.3	28 25.6	10 17.8	15 33.3
6 Sa	6 57 11	14 14 48	20 07 30	26 19 55	17 41.3	28 16.2	25 02.0	25 24.1	14 12.3	24 09.4	21 54.7	28 24.1	10 16.4	15 31.9
7 Su	7 01 07	15 12 02	2♊36 38	8♊58 00	17R 42.4	0♋06.5	26 10.2	26 02.8	14 23.6	24 22.7	22 02.1	28 22.6	10 15.0	15 30.6
8 M	7 05 04	16 09 16	15 24 20	21 55 48	17 42.6	1 59.6	27 18.3	26 41.5	14 34.6	24 36.1	22 09.5	28 21.1	10 13.5	15 29.2
9 Tu	7 09 00	17 06 30	28 32 30	5♋14 27	17 41.5	3 55.5	28 26.3	27 20.1	14 45.5	24 49.4	22 16.8	28 19.5	10 12.1	15 27.9
10 W	7 12 57	18 03 44	12♋01 31	18 53 28	17 39.1	5 53.8	29 34.1	27 58.7	14 56.0	25 02.8	22 24.2	28 17.9	10 10.6	15 26.6
11 Th	7 16 54	19 00 59	25 49 59	2♌50 37	17 35.3	7 54.5	0♍41.9	28 37.3	15 06.3	25 16.2	22 31.5	28 16.2	10 09.1	15 25.4
12 F	7 20 50	19 58 14	9♌54 51	17 02 06	17 30.7	9 57.1	1 49.4	29 15.9	15 16.4	25 29.5	22 38.7	28 14.5	10 07.6	15 24.1
13 Sa	7 24 47	20 55 28	24 11 41	1♍22 58	17 25.9	12 01.5	2 56.9	29 54.5	15 26.2	25 42.9	22 45.9	28 12.8	10 06.1	15 22.9
14 Su	7 28 43	21 52 43	8♍35 15	15 47 54	17 21.6	14 07.3	4 04.2	0♌33.1	15 35.8	25 56.3	22 53.1	28 11.0	10 04.6	15 21.7
15 M	7 32 40	22 49 57	23 00 17	0♎11 51	17 18.4	16 14.2	5 11.4	1 11.6	15 45.1	26 09.7	23 00.2	28 09.2	10 03.1	15 20.5
16 Tu	7 36 36	23 47 12	7♎22 07	14 30 40	17D 16.6	18 22.0	6 18.4	1 50.2	15 54.1	26 23.1	23 07.4	28 07.4	10 01.5	15 19.3
17 W	7 40 33	24 44 27	21 37 12	28 41 26	17 16.3	20 30.4	7 25.3	2 28.7	16 02.9	26 36.5	23 14.4	28 05.6	10 00.0	15 18.1
18 Th	7 44 29	25 41 42	5♏43 11	12♏42 20	17 17.2	22 38.9	8 32.0	3 07.2	16 11.4	26 49.9	23 21.4	28 03.7	9 58.4	15 17.0
19 F	7 48 26	26 38 57	19 38 47	26 32 28	17 18.6	24 47.4	9 38.5	3 45.7	16 19.6	27 03.3	23 28.4	28 01.8	9 56.8	15 15.9
20 Sa	7 52 23	27 36 12	3♐23 22	10♐11 26	17R 19.6	26 55.6	10 44.9	4 24.2	16 27.6	27 16.7	23 35.4	27 59.8	9 55.3	15 14.8
21 Su	7 56 19	28 33 28	16 56 40	23 39 00	17 19.7	29 03.3	11 51.2	5 02.6	16 35.2	27 30.1	23 42.3	27 57.9	9 53.7	15 13.8
22 M	8 00 16	29 30 44	0♑18 26	6♑54 53	17 18.0	1♌10.2	12 57.2	5 41.1	16 42.6	27 43.5	23 49.1	27 55.9	9 52.1	15 12.7
23 Tu	8 04 12	0♌28 00	13 28 18	19 58 38	17 14.4	3 16.1	14 03.1	6 19.5	16 49.7	27 56.9	23 56.0	27 53.9	9 50.5	15 11.7
24 W	8 08 09	1 25 17	26 25 50	2♒49 51	17 08.7	5 21.0	15 08.8	6 57.9	16 56.5	28 10.3	24 02.7	27 51.8	9 48.9	15 10.8
25 Th	8 12 05	2 22 35	9♒10 40	15 28 16	17 01.5	7 24.6	16 14.3	7 36.4	17 03.0	28 23.6	24 09.4	27 49.8	9 47.3	15 09.8
26 F	8 16 02	3 19 53	21 42 43	27 54 04	16 53.4	9 26.8	17 19.6	8 14.8	17 09.3	28 37.0	24 16.1	27 47.7	9 45.7	15 08.9
27 Sa	8 19 58	4 17 12	4♓02 28	10♓08 05	16 45.0	11 27.6	18 24.8	8 53.1	17 15.2	28 50.4	24 22.7	27 45.6	9 44.0	15 07.9
28 Su	8 23 55	5 14 32	16 11 09	22 11 58	16 37.3	13 27.0	19 29.7	9 31.5	17 20.8	29 03.7	24 29.3	27 43.4	9 42.4	15 07.1
29 M	8 27 52	6 11 52	28 10 51	4♈08 14	16 31.1	15 24.8	20 34.5	10 09.9	17 26.1	29 17.1	24 35.8	27 41.3	9 40.8	15 06.2
30 Tu	8 31 48	7 09 14	10♈04 32	16 00 15	16 26.6	17 21.0	21 39.0	10 48.2	17 31.1	29 30.4	24 42.3	27 39.1	9 39.2	15 05.4
31 W	8 35 45	8 06 36	21 55 56	27 52 09	16D 24.2	19 15.6	22 43.3	11 26.6	17 35.7	29 43.7	24 48.7	27 36.9	9 37.5	15 04.6

August 2002 — LONGITUDE

Day	Sid.Time	☉	0 hr ☽	Noon ☽	True ☊	☿	♀	♂	⚳	♃	♄	♅	♆	♇
1 Th	8 39 41	9♌04 00	3♉49 29	9♉48 35	16♊23.5	21♌08.6	23♍47.5	12♌04.9	17♈40.1	29♋57.0	24♊55.1	27♒34.7	9♒35.9	15♐03.8
2 F	8 43 38	10 01 25	15 50 04	21 54 35	16 24.1	22 59.9	24 51.4	12 43.3	17 44.1	0♌10.3	25 01.4	27R 32.4	9R 34.3	15R 03.0
3 Sa	8 47 34	10 58 51	28 02 46	4♊15 13	16R 25.1	24 49.7	25 55.0	13 21.6	17 47.8	0 23.6	25 07.6	27 30.2	9 32.6	15 02.3
4 Su	8 51 31	11 56 19	10♊32 32	16 55 13	16 25.6	26 37.8	26 58.5	13 59.9	17 51.1	0 36.9	25 13.8	27 27.9	9 31.0	15 01.6
5 M	8 55 27	12 53 47	23 23 44	29 58 26	16 24.7	28 24.3	28 01.7	14 38.3	17 54.2	0 50.1	25 20.0	27 25.6	9 29.4	15 01.0
6 Tu	8 59 24	13 51 17	6♋39 33	13♋27 13	16 21.8	0♍09.3	29 04.7	15 16.6	17 56.8	1 03.3	25 26.1	27 23.3	9 27.7	15 00.3
7 W	9 03 21	14 48 48	20 21 22	27 21 49	16 16.6	1 52.6	0♎07.4	15 54.9	17 59.2	1 16.5	25 32.1	27 21.0	9 26.1	14 59.7
8 Th	9 07 17	15 46 20	4♌28 11	11♌39 53	16 09.2	3 34.3	1 09.9	16 33.2	18 01.2	1 29.7	25 38.0	27 18.7	9 24.5	14 59.1
9 F	9 11 14	16 43 53	18 56 13	26 16 19	16 00.4	5 14.5	2 12.1	17 11.5	18 02.8	1 42.9	25 43.9	27 16.4	9 22.9	14 58.6
10 Sa	9 15 10	17 41 27	3♍39 13	11♍03 50	15 51.1	6 53.1	3 14.0	17 49.7	18 04.1	1 56.0	25 49.7	27 14.0	9 21.3	14 58.1
11 Su	9 19 07	18 39 02	18 29 07	25 54 01	15 42.4	8 30.1	4 15.7	18 28.0	18 05.0	2 09.1	25 55.5	27 11.7	9 19.7	14 57.6
12 M	9 23 03	19 36 38	3♎17 31	10♎38 46	15 35.5	10 05.6	5 17.0	19 06.3	18 05.6	2 22.2	26 01.2	27 09.3	9 18.1	14 57.1
13 Tu	9 27 00	20 34 14	17 56 59	25 11 34	15 30.8	11 39.5	6 18.1	19 44.5	18R 05.8	2 35.2	26 06.8	27 06.9	9 16.5	14 56.7
14 W	9 30 56	21 31 52	2♏22 04	9♏28 11	15D 28.4	13 11.9	7 18.8	20 22.8	18 05.7	2 48.2	26 12.4	27 04.5	9 14.9	14 56.3
15 Th	9 34 53	22 29 31	16 29 45	23 26 43	15 27.9	14 42.7	8 19.2	21 01.0	18 05.2	3 01.2	26 17.9	27 02.2	9 13.3	14 55.9
16 F	9 38 50	23 27 11	0♐19 10	7♐07 13	15R 28.2	16 11.9	9 19.3	21 39.2	18 04.4	3 14.2	26 23.3	26 59.8	9 11.7	14 55.6
17 Sa	9 42 46	24 24 51	13 51 04	20 30 56	15 28.3	17 39.6	10 19.1	22 17.5	18 03.1	3 27.1	26 28.6	26 57.4	9 10.1	14 55.3
18 Su	9 46 43	25 22 33	27 07 03	3♑39 40	15 26.9	19 05.6	11 18.4	22 55.7	18 01.6	3 40.0	26 33.9	26 55.0	9 08.6	14 55.0
19 M	9 50 39	26 20 16	10♑08 59	16 35 14	15 23.3	20 30.1	12 17.5	23 33.9	17 59.6	3 52.8	26 39.1	26 52.6	9 07.1	14 54.8
20 Tu	9 54 36	27 18 00	22 58 35	29 19 11	15 17.0	21 52.9	13 16.1	24 12.1	17 57.3	4 05.6	26 44.2	26 50.2	9 05.5	14 54.6
21 W	9 58 32	28 15 45	5♒37 09	11♒52 35	15 07.9	23 14.0	14 14.3	24 50.3	17 54.7	4 18.4	26 49.3	26 47.8	9 04.0	14 54.4
22 Th	10 02 29	29 13 31	18 05 35	24 16 14	14 56.5	24 33.4	15 12.1	25 28.5	17 51.6	4 31.1	26 54.2	26 45.4	9 02.5	14 54.3
23 F	10 06 25	0♍11 19	0♓24 35	6♓30 43	14 43.7	25 51.1	16 09.5	26 06.7	17 48.2	4 43.8	26 59.1	26 43.0	9 01.0	14 54.2
24 Sa	10 10 22	1 09 08	12 34 44	18 36 46	14 30.6	27 06.9	17 06.5	26 44.9	17 44.5	4 56.5	27 04.0	26 40.7	8 59.5	14 54.1
25 Su	10 14 19	2 06 59	24 36 57	0♈35 29	14 18.2	28 20.9	18 03.0	27 23.1	17 40.4	5 09.1	27 08.7	26 38.3	8 58.0	14D 54.1
26 M	10 18 15	3 04 51	6♈32 37	12 28 37	14 07.5	29 33.0	18 59.1	28 01.3	17 35.9	5 21.6	27 13.3	26 35.9	8 56.6	14 54.0
27 Tu	10 22 12	4 02 45	18 23 50	24 18 39	13 59.3	0♎43.0	19 54.6	28 39.4	17 31.0	5 34.1	27 17.9	26 33.5	8 55.1	14 54.1
28 W	10 26 08	5 00 41	0♉13 30	6♉08 53	13 53.8	1 50.9	20 49.7	29 17.6	17 25.8	5 46.6	27 22.4	26 31.2	8 53.7	14 54.1
29 Th	10 30 05	5 58 39	12 05 19	18 03 23	13 50.8	2 56.7	21 44.3	29 55.8	17 20.2	5 59.0	27 26.8	26 28.8	8 52.3	14 54.2
30 F	10 34 01	6 56 38	24 03 43	0♊06 55	13D 49.8	4 00.2	22 38.3	0♍34.0	17 14.3	6 11.4	27 31.1	26 26.5	8 50.9	14 54.3
31 Sa	10 37 58	7 54 40	6♊13 41	12 24 38	13R 49.7	5 01.2	23 31.9	1 12.2	17 08.0	6 23.7	27 35.4	26 24.1	8 49.5	14 54.5

Astro Data (Dy Hr Mn)

	Dy Hr Mn
☽0N	2 18:26
☽0S	16 6:10
♃⚻♅	23 7:19
☽0N	30 1:34
♄⚼♆	30 2:40
♃⚼♇	1 23:31
♀0S	6 18:39
☽0S	12 12:02
⚳R	13 15:00
♄△♅	21 7:19
☿0S	24 16:51
☽0N	26 7:54
♇D	26 11:02

Planet Ingress (Dy Hr Mn)

		Dy Hr Mn
☿	♋	7 10:37
♀	♍	10 21:10
♂	♌	13 15:24
☿	♌	21 22:42
☉	♌	23 0:16
♃	♌	1 17:21
☿	♍	6 9:52
♀	♎	7 9:10
☉	♍	23 7:18
☿	♎	26 21:11
♂	♍	29 14:39

Last Aspect / ☽ Ingress (July)

Last Aspect Dy Hr Mn		☽ Ingress	Dy Hr Mn
1 5:44	♃ △	♈	1 19:50
4 5:12	♅ ⚹	♉	4 8:17
6 15:58	♅ □	♊	6 19:02
8 23:38	♅ △	♋	9 2:38
11 4:26	♂ ☌	♌	11 7:09
13 6:43	♅ ☍	♍	13 9:42
15 5:09	♃ ⚹	♎	15 11:40
17 10:59	♅ △	♏	17 14:14
19 14:36	♅ □	♐	19 18:03
21 19:45	♅ ⚹	♑	21 23:27
24 3:06	♃ ☍	♒	24 6:41
26 11:48	♅ ☌	♓	26 16:05
29 2:02	♃ △	♈	29 3:40
31 15:49	♃ □	♉	31 16:18

Last Aspect / ☽ Ingress (August)

Last Aspect Dy Hr Mn		☽ Ingress	Dy Hr Mn
2 22:59	♅ □	♊	3 3:48
5 8:43	♅ ⚹	♋	5 12:03
5 8:43	♅ ⚹	♌	7 16:28
9 13:38	♅ ☍	♍	9 18:04
11 12:02	♄ □	♎	11 18:39
13 15:12	♅ △	♏	13 20:02
15 18:14	♅ □	♐	15 23:26
17 23:40	♅ ⚹	♑	18 5:16
19 20:14	♅ △	♒	20 13:18
22 22:30	☉ ☍	♓	22 23:12
25 6:59	♅ ☌	♈	25 10:49
27 21:19	♂ △	♉	27 23:33
30 4:45	♅ □	♊	30 11:46

☽ Phases & Eclipses (Dy Hr Mn)

Dy Hr Mn		
2 17:20	☾	10♈39
10 10:27	●	18♋00
17 4:48	☽	24♎27
24 9:08	○	1♒18
1 10:23	☾	9♉00
8 19:16	●	16♌04
15 10:13	☽	22♏25
22 22:30	○	29♒39
31 2:32	☾	7♊32

Astro Data

1 July 2002
Julian Day # 37437
SVP 5♓13'46"
GC 26♐52.4 ⚴ 28♒12.2R
Eris 20♈22.7 ⚵ 5♍58.4
⚷ 5♑55.9R ⚶ 20♋36.3
☽ Mean ☊ 16♊44.7

1 August 2002
Julian Day # 37468
SVP 5♓13'41"
GC 26♐52.5 ⚴ 22♒24.7R
Eris 20♈22.7R ⚵ 16♍54.8
⚷ 4♑08.1R ⚶ 4♌25.0
☽ Mean ☊ 15♊06.2

LONGITUDE — September 2002

Day	Sid.Time	☉	0 hr ☽	Noon ☽	True ☊	☿	♀	♂	⚳	♃	♄	♅	♆	♇
1 Su	10 41 54	8♍52 43	18♊40 28	25♊01 47	13♊49.4	5♎59.7	24♎24.8	1♍50.3	17♈01.4	6♌36.0	27♊39.5	26♒21.8	8♒48.1	14♐54.6
2 M	10 45 51	9 50 48	1♋29 11	8♋03 10	13R47.9	6 55.4	25 17.2	2 28.5	16R54.4	6 48.2	27 43.6	26R19.5	8R46.8	14 54.9
3 Tu	10 49 48	10 48 55	14 44 08	21 32 24	13 44.2	7 48.3	26 08.9	3 06.7	16 47.1	7 00.4	27 47.6	26 17.2	8 45.5	14 55.1
4 W	10 53 44	11 47 05	28 28 04	5♌31 05	13 37.9	8 38.2	27 00.1	3 44.9	16 39.4	7 12.5	27 51.5	26 14.9	8 44.2	14 55.4
5 Th	10 57 41	12 45 15	12♌41 12	19 57 57	13 29.1	9 24.8	27 50.6	4 23.0	16 31.4	7 24.5	27 55.3	26 12.6	8 42.9	14 55.7
6 F	11 01 37	13 43 28	27 20 36	4♍48 15	13 18.5	10 07.8	28 40.4	5 01.2	16 23.0	7 36.5	27 59.0	26 10.4	8 41.6	14 56.1
7 Sa	11 05 34	14 41 43	12♍19 48	19 54 00	13 07.2	10 47.2	29 29.5	5 39.4	16 14.4	7 48.4	28 02.6	26 08.1	8 40.3	14 56.4
8 Su	11 09 30	15 39 59	27 29 30	5♎04 57	12 56.5	11 22.6	0♏17.9	6 17.6	16 05.4	8 00.3	28 06.1	26 05.9	8 39.1	14 56.8
9 M	11 13 27	16 38 16	12♎39 01	20 10 30	12 47.7	11 53.7	1 05.5	6 55.7	15 56.1	8 12.1	28 09.5	26 03.7	8 37.9	14 57.3
10 Tu	11 17 23	17 36 36	27 38 17	5♏01 29	12 41.5	12 20.3	1 52.3	7 33.9	15 46.5	8 23.8	28 12.9	26 01.5	8 36.7	14 57.8
11 W	11 21 20	18 34 57	12♏19 26	19 31 37	12 38.0	12 41.9	2 38.3	8 12.1	15 36.6	8 35.5	28 16.1	25 59.4	8 35.6	14 58.3
12 Th	11 25 17	19 33 19	26 37 47	3♐37 48	12D36.7	12 58.4	3 23.5	8 50.3	15 26.4	8 47.1	28 19.2	25 57.2	8 34.4	14 58.8
13 F	11 29 13	20 31 44	10♐31 44	17 19 44	12R36.6	13 09.3	4 07.8	9 28.4	15 16.0	8 58.6	28 22.3	25 55.1	8 33.3	14 59.4
14 Sa	11 33 10	21 30 09	24 02 07	0♑39 11	12 36.4	13R14.3	4 51.1	10 06.6	15 05.2	9 10.1	28 25.2	25 53.0	8 32.2	15 00.0
15 Su	11 37 06	22 28 37	7♑11 20	13 38 59	12 35.0	13 13.2	5 33.4	10 44.8	14 54.3	9 21.4	28 28.1	25 51.0	8 31.1	15 00.7
16 M	11 41 03	23 27 05	20 02 32	26 22 23	12 31.3	13 05.5	6 14.8	11 22.9	14 43.0	9 32.7	28 30.8	25 48.9	8 30.1	15 01.3
17 Tu	11 44 59	24 25 36	2♒38 54	8♒52 28	12 24.8	12 51.1	6 55.1	12 01.1	14 31.6	9 44.0	28 33.4	25 46.9	8 29.1	15 02.0
18 W	11 48 56	25 24 08	15 03 22	21 11 53	12 15.5	12 29.8	7 34.2	12 39.3	14 19.9	9 55.1	28 36.0	25 44.9	8 28.1	15 02.8
19 Th	11 52 52	26 22 42	27 18 17	3♓22 45	12 03.9	12 01.5	8 12.3	13 17.4	14 08.0	10 06.2	28 38.4	25 43.0	8 27.1	15 03.6
20 F	11 56 49	27 21 18	9♓25 30	15 26 42	11 50.9	11 26.2	8 49.2	13 55.6	13 55.8	10 17.2	28 40.8	25 41.0	8 26.2	15 04.4
21 Sa	12 00 46	28 19 55	21 26 29	27 25 01	11 37.4	10 44.1	9 24.8	14 33.8	13 43.5	10 28.1	28 43.0	25 39.1	8 25.3	15 05.2
22 Su	12 04 42	29 18 35	3♈22 26	9♈18 56	11 24.7	9 55.7	9 59.1	15 11.9	13 31.0	10 38.9	28 45.1	25 37.3	8 24.4	15 06.0
23 M	12 08 39	0♎17 16	15 14 40	21 09 51	11 13.7	9 01.4	10 32.2	15 50.1	13 18.4	10 49.7	28 47.1	25 35.4	8 23.5	15 06.9
24 Tu	12 12 35	1 15 59	27 04 45	2♉59 38	11 05.1	8 02.2	11 03.8	16 28.3	13 05.6	11 00.3	28 49.1	25 33.6	8 22.7	15 07.9
25 W	12 16 32	2 14 45	8♉54 50	14 50 43	10 59.4	6 59.1	11 34.0	17 06.5	12 52.6	11 10.9	28 50.9	25 31.8	8 21.9	15 08.8
26 Th	12 20 28	3 13 33	20 47 41	26 46 13	10 56.2	5 53.4	12 02.7	17 44.6	12 39.5	11 21.3	28 52.6	25 30.1	8 21.1	15 09.8
27 F	12 24 25	4 12 23	2♊46 49	8♊50 01	10D55.2	4 46.6	12 29.9	18 22.8	12 26.3	11 31.7	28 54.2	25 28.4	8 20.4	15 10.8
28 Sa	12 28 21	5 11 15	14 56 24	21 06 34	10 55.5	3 40.4	12 55.5	19 01.0	12 13.0	11 42.0	28 55.7	25 26.7	8 19.6	15 11.9
29 Su	12 32 18	6 10 10	27 21 08	3♋40 43	10R56.0	2 36.5	13 19.4	19 39.2	11 59.6	11 52.2	28 57.1	25 25.1	8 18.9	15 13.0
30 M	12 36 14	7 09 07	10♋05 55	16 37 17	10 55.6	1 36.6	13 41.7	20 17.4	11 46.1	12 02.3	28 58.3	25 23.5	8 18.3	15 14.1

LONGITUDE — October 2002

Day	Sid.Time	☉	0 hr ☽	Noon ☽	True ☊	☿	♀	♂	⚳	♃	♄	♅	♆	♇
1 Tu	12 40 11	8♎08 06	23♋15 18	0♌00 23	10♊53.5	0♎42.4	14♏02.1	20♍55.6	11♈32.6	12♌12.3	28♊59.5	25♒21.9	8♒17.7	15♐15.2
2 W	12 44 08	9 07 08	6♌52 48	13 52 42	10R49.1	29♍55.4	14 20.7	21 33.9	11R19.0	12 22.2	29 00.6	25R20.4	8R17.1	15 16.4
3 Th	12 48 04	10 06 12	21 00 00	28 14 26	10 42.5	29R16.7	14 37.5	22 12.1	11 05.3	12 32.0	29 01.5	25 18.9	8 16.5	15 17.6
4 F	12 52 01	11 05 18	5♍35 32	13♍02 34	10 34.2	28 47.5	14 52.2	22 50.3	10 51.7	12 41.7	29 02.4	25 17.4	8 16.0	15 18.8
5 Sa	12 55 57	12 04 26	20 34 35	28 10 25	10 25.1	28 28.4	15 05.0	23 28.5	10 38.1	12 51.3	29 03.1	25 16.0	8 15.4	15 20.1
6 Su	12 59 54	13 03 36	5♎48 48	13♎28 18	10 16.4	28D19.7	15 15.7	24 06.8	10 24.4	13 00.8	29 03.7	25 14.6	8 15.0	15 21.3
7 M	13 03 50	14 02 48	21 07 30	28 45 00	10 09.2	28 21.7	15 24.2	24 45.0	10 10.9	13 10.2	29 04.2	25 13.3	8 14.5	15 22.7
8 Tu	13 07 47	15 02 03	6♏19 28	13♏49 46	10 04.3	28 34.3	15 30.6	25 23.2	9 57.3	13 19.4	29 04.6	25 12.0	8 14.1	15 24.0
9 W	13 11 43	16 01 19	21 14 54	28 34 09	10D01.7	28 57.1	15 34.7	26 01.5	9 43.8	13 28.6	29 04.9	25 10.8	8 13.7	15 25.4
10 Th	13 15 40	17 00 37	5♐46 56	12♐52 57	10 01.2	29 29.6	15R36.5	26 39.7	9 30.4	13 37.6	29 05.1	25 09.5	8 13.4	15 26.8
11 F	13 19 37	17 59 57	19 52 04	26 44 19	10 02.0	0♎11.3	15 36.0	27 18.0	9 17.1	13 46.5	29R05.1	25 08.4	8 13.1	15 28.2
12 Sa	13 23 33	18 59 18	3♑29 53	10♑09 04	10R03.0	1 01.4	15 33.0	27 56.2	9 03.9	13 55.3	29 05.1	25 07.3	8 12.8	15 29.6
13 Su	13 27 30	19 58 42	16 42 15	23 09 52	10 03.2	1 59.2	15 27.7	28 34.5	8 50.9	14 04.0	29 04.9	25 06.2	8 12.5	15 31.1
14 M	13 31 26	20 58 07	29 32 24	5♒50 22	10 02.0	3 03.9	15 20.0	29 12.7	8 37.9	14 12.6	29 04.6	25 05.2	8 12.3	15 32.6
15 Tu	13 35 23	21 57 34	12♒04 16	18 14 34	9 58.6	4 14.6	15 09.8	29 51.0	8 25.2	14 21.0	29 04.2	25 04.2	8 12.1	15 34.1
16 W	13 39 19	22 57 02	24 21 47	0♓26 19	9 53.2	5 30.7	14 57.2	0♎29.3	8 12.5	14 29.3	29 03.7	25 03.2	8 12.0	15 35.7
17 Th	13 43 16	23 56 32	6♓28 37	12 29 04	9 46.0	6 51.5	14 42.2	1 07.5	8 00.1	14 37.5	29 03.1	25 02.4	8 11.9	15 37.3
18 F	13 47 12	24 56 05	18 27 59	24 25 42	9 37.7	8 16.2	14 24.8	1 45.8	7 47.9	14 45.5	29 02.4	25 01.5	8 11.8	15 38.9
19 Sa	13 51 09	25 55 39	0♈22 31	6♈18 39	9 29.0	9 44.2	14 05.1	2 24.1	7 35.8	14 53.4	29 01.6	25 00.7	8 11.7	15 40.5
20 Su	13 55 06	26 55 15	12 14 23	18 09 54	9 20.8	11 15.1	13 43.2	3 02.3	7 24.0	15 01.2	29 00.7	25 00.0	8D11.7	15 42.2
21 M	13 59 02	27 54 52	24 05 25	0♉01 09	9 13.7	12 48.2	13 19.1	3 40.6	7 12.4	15 08.9	28 59.6	24 59.2	8 11.7	15 43.8
22 Tu	14 02 59	28 54 32	5♉57 19	11 54 07	9 08.5	14 23.3	12 53.0	4 18.9	7 01.0	15 16.4	28 58.5	24 58.6	8 11.8	15 45.5
23 W	14 06 55	29 54 14	17 51 47	23 50 36	9 05.2	15 59.8	12 24.9	4 57.2	6 49.9	15 23.8	28 57.2	24 58.0	8 11.9	15 47.2
24 Th	14 10 52	0♏53 59	29 50 50	5♊52 49	9D03.9	17 37.5	11 55.1	5 35.5	6 39.0	15 31.0	28 55.8	24 57.4	8 12.0	15 49.0
25 F	14 14 48	1 53 45	11♊56 52	18 03 22	9 04.3	19 16.1	11 23.8	6 13.9	6 28.4	15 38.1	28 54.3	24 56.9	8 12.1	15 50.8
26 Sa	14 18 45	2 53 33	24 12 44	0♋25 24	9 05.6	20 55.3	10 51.0	6 52.2	6 18.1	15 45.1	28 52.8	24 56.4	8 12.3	15 52.5
27 Su	14 22 41	3 53 24	6♋41 49	13 02 26	9 07.3	22 35.0	10 17.0	7 30.5	6 08.0	15 51.9	28 51.1	24 56.0	8 12.5	15 54.4
28 M	14 26 38	4 53 17	19 27 45	25 58 11	9R08.6	24 14.9	9 42.0	8 08.9	5 58.3	15 58.6	28 49.3	24 55.7	8 12.8	15 56.2
29 Tu	14 30 35	5 53 12	2♌34 10	9♌16 05	9 08.9	25 55.1	9 06.3	8 47.2	5 48.9	16 05.1	28 47.4	24 55.3	8 13.1	15 58.0
30 W	14 34 31	6 53 09	16 04 12	22 58 45	9 07.8	27 35.2	8 30.1	9 25.6	5 39.7	16 11.5	28 45.4	24 55.1	8 13.4	15 59.9
31 Th	14 38 28	7 53 09	29 59 46	7♍07 12	9 05.3	29 15.3	7 53.6	10 03.9	5 30.9	16 17.7	28 43.3	24 54.9	8 13.7	16 01.8

Astro Data

	Dy Hr Mn
☽0S	8 20:19
♃☍♆	11 12:07
☿R	14 19:40
☽0N	22 13:50
☉0S	23 4:56
☿0N	4 6:00
☽0S	6 6:56
☿D	6 19:29
♀R	10 18:36
♄R	11 13:02
♃∠♄	13 14:25
☿0S	15 13:37
♂0S	19 14:01
☽0N	19 19:59
♆D	20 13:54

Planet Ingress

	Dy Hr Mn
♀ ♏	8 3:06
☉ ♎	23 4:56
☿ ♍R	2 9:27
☿ ♎	11 5:57
♂ ♎	15 17:39
☉ ♏	23 14:19
☿ ♏	31 22:44
♃△△	28 0:03

Last Aspect / ☽ Ingress (September)

Last Aspect Dy Hr Mn		☽ Ingress	Dy Hr Mn
1 16:56	♄☌	♋	1 21:15
3 20:32	♀□	♌	4 2:38
6 1:34	♀✶	♍	6 4:17
8 0:55	♄□	♎	8 3:58
10 0:53	♄△	♏	10 3:49
11 22:53	♅□	♐	12 5:45
14 7:55	♄☍	♑	14 10:49
16 5:59	☉△	♒	16 18:55
19 2:36	♄△	♓	19 5:19
21 14:37	♄□	♈	21 17:12
24 3:30	♄✶	♉	24 5:56
26 9:28	♅□	♊	26 18:28
29 3:02	♄☌	♋	29 5:03

Last Aspect / ☽ Ingress (October)

Last Aspect Dy Hr Mn		☽ Ingress	Dy Hr Mn
30 19:00	♂✶	♌	1 11:59
3 13:17	♄✶	♍	3 14:53
5 13:23	♄□	♎	5 14:52
7 12:30	♄△	♏	7 13:58
9 12:39	☿✶	♐	9 14:22
11 16:09	♄☍	♑	11 17:46
13 22:43	♂△	♒	14 0:52
16 9:17	♄△	♓	16 11:08
18 21:18	♄□	♈	18 23:15
21 9:56	♄✶	♉	21 11:58
23 14:15	♅□	♊	24 0:18
26 9:02	♄☌	♋	26 11:11
28 8:23	☿□	♌	28 19:21
30 21:52	♄✶	♍	31 0:00

☽ Phases & Eclipses

Dy Hr Mn		
7 3:11	●	14♍20
13 18:09	☽	20♐47
21 14:00	○	28♓25
29 17:04	☾	6♋23
6 11:19	●	13♎02
13 5:34	☽	19♑43
21 7:21	○	27♈43
29 5:29	☾	5♌37

Astro Data

1 September 2002
Julian Day # 37499
SVP 5♓13'37"
GC 26♐52.6 ⚴ 14♒45.5R
Eris 20♈13.3R ⚵ 28♍23.4
⚷ 3♑14.8R ⚶ 18♌22.0
☽ Mean ☊ 13♊27.7

1 October 2002
Julian Day # 37529
SVP 5♓13'33"
GC 26♐52.7 ⚴ 10♒48.5R
Eris 19♈57.5R ⚵ 9♎36.3
⚷ 3♑37.6 ⚶ 1♍44.4
☽ Mean ☊ 11♊52.4

November 2002 LONGITUDE

Day	Sid.Time	☉	0 hr ☽	Noon☽	True☊	☿	♀	♂	⚳	♃	♄	♅	♆	♇
1 F	14 42 24	8♏53 10	14♍20 48	21♍40 07	9♊01.6	0♏55.2	7♏17.1	10♎42.3	5♈22.4	16♌23.7	28♊41.0	24♒54.7	8♒14.1	16♐03.7
2 Sa	14 46 21	9 53 14	29 04 34	6♎33 18	8R57.4	2 35.0	6R40.8	11 20.7	5R14.3	16 29.6	28R38.7	24R54.6	8 14.5	16 05.6
3 Su	14 50 17	10 53 20	14♎05 23	21 39 41	8 53.3	4 14.4	6 05.0	11 59.0	5 06.5	16 35.4	28 36.3	24D54.5	8 15.0	16 07.6
4 M	14 54 14	11 53 27	29 14 59	6♏50 02	8 49.9	5 53.6	5 29.8	12 37.4	4 59.0	16 41.0	28 33.8	24 54.5	8 15.5	16 09.5
5 Tu	14 58 10	12 53 37	14♏23 34	21 54 25	8 47.7	7 32.5	4 55.6	13 15.8	4 51.9	16 46.4	28 31.2	24 54.5	8 16.0	16 11.5
6 W	15 02 07	13 53 48	29 21 27	6♐43 44	8D46.9	9 11.1	4 22.6	13 54.2	4 45.2	16 51.6	28 28.5	24 54.6	8 16.6	16 13.5
7 Th	15 06 04	14 54 01	14♐00 29	21 11 06	8 47.3	10 49.3	3 50.9	14 32.6	4 38.8	16 56.7	28 25.7	24 54.8	8 17.2	16 15.6
8 F	15 10 00	15 54 16	28 15 10	5♑12 27	8 48.5	12 27.1	3 20.7	15 11.1	4 32.8	17 01.6	28 22.8	24 55.0	8 17.8	16 17.6
9 Sa	15 13 57	16 54 32	12♑02 53	18 46 33	8 50.0	14 04.6	2 52.2	15 49.5	4 27.2	17 06.4	28 19.8	24 55.2	8 18.5	16 19.6
10 Su	15 17 53	17 54 50	25 23 41	1♒54 36	8 51.4	15 41.8	2 25.6	16 27.9	4 22.0	17 11.0	28 16.7	24 55.5	8 19.1	16 21.7
11 M	15 21 50	18 55 09	8♒19 41	14 39 25	8R52.1	17 18.6	2 01.0	17 06.3	4 17.1	17 15.4	28 13.5	24 55.9	8 19.9	16 23.8
12 Tu	15 25 46	19 55 30	20 54 19	27 04 54	8 52.0	18 55.1	1 38.6	17 44.7	4 12.6	17 19.6	28 10.3	24 56.3	8 20.6	16 25.9
13 W	15 29 43	20 55 52	3♓11 44	9♓15 21	8 51.0	20 31.2	1 18.3	18 23.2	4 08.5	17 23.7	28 06.9	24 56.7	8 21.4	16 28.0
14 Th	15 33 39	21 56 15	15 16 19	21 15 10	8 49.2	22 07.0	1 00.4	19 01.6	4 04.8	17 27.6	28 03.5	24 57.2	8 22.2	16 30.1
15 F	15 37 36	22 56 39	27 12 23	3♈08 27	8 46.9	23 42.6	0 44.9	19 40.0	4 01.4	17 31.3	28 00.0	24 57.7	8 23.1	16 32.2
16 Sa	15 41 33	23 57 06	9♈03 50	14 58 55	8 44.4	25 17.8	0 31.7	20 18.5	3 58.5	17 34.8	27 56.4	24 58.4	8 24.0	16 34.4
17 Su	15 45 29	24 57 33	20 54 07	26 49 46	8 42.1	26 52.8	0 21.1	20 56.9	3 55.9	17 38.1	27 52.7	24 59.0	8 24.9	16 36.6
18 M	15 49 26	25 58 02	2♉46 11	8♉43 40	8 40.2	28 27.5	0 12.9	21 35.4	3 53.7	17 41.3	27 49.0	24 59.7	8 25.8	16 38.7
19 Tu	15 53 22	26 58 32	14 42 29	20 42 51	8 39.0	0♐01.9	0 07.2	22 13.9	3 51.9	17 44.3	27 45.2	25 00.5	8 26.8	16 40.9
20 W	15 57 19	27 59 04	26 45 00	2♊49 07	8D38.4	1 36.2	0D04.0	22 52.3	3 50.5	17 47.1	27 41.3	25 01.3	8 27.8	16 43.1
21 Th	16 01 15	28 59 38	8♊55 26	15 04 06	8 38.4	3 10.2	0 03.3	23 30.8	3 49.4	17 49.7	27 37.3	25 02.1	8 28.9	16 45.3
22 F	16 05 12	0♐00 13	21 15 19	27 29 16	8 38.8	4 44.1	0 05.0	24 09.3	3 48.8	17 52.1	27 33.3	25 03.0	8 30.0	16 47.5
23 Sa	16 09 08	1 00 50	3♋46 09	10♋06 08	8 39.6	6 17.8	0 09.1	24 47.8	3D48.5	17 54.4	27 29.2	25 04.0	8 31.1	16 49.7
24 Su	16 13 05	2 01 28	16 29 27	22 56 16	8 40.3	7 51.3	0 15.5	25 26.3	3 48.6	17 56.4	27 25.0	25 05.0	8 32.2	16 52.0
25 M	16 17 02	3 02 08	29 26 50	6♌01 19	8 40.9	9 24.7	0 24.3	26 04.8	3 49.1	17 58.3	27 20.8	25 06.0	8 33.4	16 54.2
26 Tu	16 20 58	4 02 50	12♌39 56	19 22 51	8 41.3	10 57.9	0 35.4	26 43.3	3 49.9	18 00.0	27 16.5	25 07.2	8 34.6	16 56.4
27 W	16 24 55	5 03 33	26 10 12	3♍02 06	8R41.5	12 31.0	0 48.6	27 21.9	3 51.2	18 01.4	27 12.2	25 08.3	8 35.8	16 58.7
28 Th	16 28 51	6 04 17	9♍58 33	16 59 34	8 41.4	14 04.0	1 04.0	28 00.4	3 52.8	18 02.7	27 07.8	25 09.5	8 37.1	17 01.0
29 F	16 32 48	7 05 04	24 04 59	1♎14 37	8 41.3	15 36.9	1 21.4	28 38.9	3 54.7	18 03.8	27 03.3	25 10.8	8 38.3	17 03.2
30 Sa	16 36 44	8 05 51	8♎28 07	15 45 03	8D41.2	17 09.8	1 40.9	29 17.5	3 57.1	18 04.7	26 58.8	25 12.1	8 39.7	17 05.5

December 2002 LONGITUDE

Day	Sid.Time	☉	0 hr ☽	Noon☽	True☊	☿	♀	♂	⚳	♃	♄	♅	♆	♇
1 Su	16 40 41	9♐06 41	23♎04 51	0♏26 52	8♊41.2	18♐42.5	2♏02.3	29♎56.1	3♈59.8	18♌05.4	26♊54.3	25♒13.4	8♒41.0	17♐07.8
2 M	16 44 37	10 07 31	7♏50 19	15 14 22	8 41.3	20 15.1	2 25.6	0♏34.6	4 02.9	18 05.9	26R49.7	25 14.8	8 42.4	17 10.0
3 Tu	16 48 34	11 08 23	22 38 07	0♐00 38	8R41.4	21 47.6	2 50.7	1 13.2	4 06.3	18 06.2	26 45.0	25 16.2	8 43.8	17 12.3
4 W	16 52 31	12 09 17	7♐21 02	14 38 24	8 41.4	23 20.0	3 17.5	1 51.8	4 10.1	18R06.3	26 40.3	25 17.7	8 45.2	17 14.6
5 Th	16 56 27	13 10 11	21 51 58	29 01 00	8 41.2	24 52.2	3 46.1	2 30.3	4 14.2	18 06.2	26 35.6	25 19.3	8 46.7	17 16.9
6 F	17 00 24	14 11 07	6♑04 54	13♑03 13	8 40.7	26 24.4	4 16.2	3 08.9	4 18.8	18 05.9	26 30.9	25 20.9	8 48.2	17 19.2
7 Sa	17 04 20	15 12 03	19 55 37	26 41 56	8 40.0	27 56.3	4 47.9	3 47.5	4 23.6	18 05.4	26 26.1	25 22.5	8 49.7	17 21.5
8 Su	17 08 17	16 13 00	3♒22 05	9♒56 09	8 39.1	29 28.1	5 21.1	4 26.1	4 28.8	18 04.7	26 21.3	25 24.2	8 51.2	17 23.8
9 M	17 12 13	17 13 58	16 24 21	22 46 57	8 38.1	0♑59.6	5 55.7	5 04.7	4 34.4	18 03.8	26 16.4	25 25.9	8 52.8	17 26.1
10 Tu	17 16 10	18 14 56	29 04 21	5♓16 58	8 37.4	2 30.8	6 31.7	5 43.3	4 40.2	18 02.7	26 11.5	25 27.7	8 54.3	17 28.4
11 W	17 20 07	19 15 55	11♓25 21	17 30 01	8D37.1	4 01.7	7 09.1	6 21.9	4 46.4	18 01.4	26 06.7	25 29.5	8 56.0	17 30.7
12 Th	17 24 03	20 16 55	23 31 34	29 30 35	8 37.3	5 32.2	7 47.7	7 00.5	4 53.0	17 59.9	26 01.8	25 31.4	8 57.6	17 33.0
13 F	17 28 00	21 17 55	5♈27 39	11♈23 24	8 38.0	7 02.1	8 27.6	7 39.1	4 59.9	17 58.3	25 56.8	25 33.3	8 59.3	17 35.3
14 Sa	17 31 56	22 18 55	17 18 24	23 13 15	8 39.2	8 31.5	9 08.7	8 17.7	5 07.1	17 56.4	25 51.9	25 35.2	9 00.9	17 37.6
15 Su	17 35 53	23 19 56	29 08 28	5♉04 35	8 40.6	10 00.1	9 50.9	8 56.3	5 14.6	17 54.3	25 47.0	25 37.2	9 02.6	17 39.8
16 M	17 39 49	24 20 58	11♉02 05	17 01 25	8 42.0	11 27.9	10 34.3	9 34.9	5 22.4	17 52.1	25 42.0	25 39.2	9 04.4	17 42.1
17 Tu	17 43 46	25 22 00	23 02 59	29 07 08	8R42.9	12 54.6	11 18.7	10 13.5	5 30.5	17 49.6	25 37.1	25 41.3	9 06.1	17 44.4
18 W	17 47 42	26 23 03	5♊14 10	11♊24 21	8 43.1	14 20.0	12 04.1	10 52.1	5 38.9	17 47.0	25 32.1	25 43.4	9 07.9	17 46.7
19 Th	17 51 39	27 24 07	17 37 52	23 54 53	8 42.4	15 44.0	12 50.5	11 30.8	5 47.7	17 44.1	25 27.2	25 45.6	9 09.7	17 49.0
20 F	17 55 36	28 25 11	0♋15 28	6♋39 41	8 40.7	17 06.2	13 37.9	12 09.4	5 56.7	17 41.1	25 22.2	25 47.8	9 11.5	17 51.2
21 Sa	17 59 32	29 26 15	13 07 32	19 38 57	8 38.1	18 26.3	14 26.2	12 48.0	6 06.0	17 37.9	25 17.3	25 50.0	9 13.4	17 53.5
22 Su	18 03 29	0♑27 21	26 13 52	2♌52 11	8 34.8	19 44.0	15 15.3	13 26.7	6 15.6	17 34.5	25 12.4	25 52.3	9 15.2	17 55.8
23 M	18 07 25	1 28 26	9♌33 45	16 18 26	8 31.2	20 58.8	16 05.3	14 05.3	6 25.5	17 30.9	25 07.5	25 54.6	9 17.1	17 58.0
24 Tu	18 11 22	2 29 33	23 06 04	29 56 29	8 28.0	22 10.2	16 56.1	14 44.0	6 35.7	17 27.2	25 02.6	25 56.9	9 19.0	18 00.2
25 W	18 15 18	3 30 40	6♍49 33	13♍45 04	8 25.6	23 17.7	17 47.8	15 22.6	6 46.2	17 23.2	24 57.7	25 59.3	9 20.9	18 02.5
26 Th	18 19 15	4 31 47	20 42 54	27 42 54	8D24.3	24 20.6	18 40.1	16 01.3	6 56.9	17 19.1	24 52.9	26 01.8	9 22.9	18 04.7
27 F	18 23 11	5 32 56	4♎44 53	11♎48 41	8 24.3	25 18.3	19 33.2	16 40.0	7 07.9	17 14.8	24 48.0	26 04.2	9 24.8	18 06.9
28 Sa	18 27 08	6 34 05	18 54 06	26 00 56	8 25.3	26 09.9	20 26.9	17 18.7	7 19.1	17 10.3	24 43.2	26 06.7	9 26.8	18 09.1
29 Su	18 31 05	7 35 14	3♏08 56	10♏17 48	8 26.8	26 54.7	21 21.4	17 57.3	7 30.7	17 05.7	24 38.5	26 09.3	9 28.8	18 11.3
30 M	18 35 01	8 36 24	17 27 11	24 36 43	8R28.2	27 31.7	22 16.5	18 36.0	7 42.4	17 00.9	24 33.7	26 11.8	9 30.8	18 13.5
31 Tu	18 38 58	9 37 34	1♐45 56	8♐54 23	8 28.8	28 00.1	23 12.1	19 14.7	7 54.5	16 55.9	24 29.0	26 14.4	9 32.8	18 15.7

Astro Data	Dy Hr Mn
☽ 0S	2 18:03
♅ D	4 6:28
☽ 0N	16 2:45
♀ D	21 7:13
⚳ D	23 17:26
☽ 0S	30 3:18
♃ R	4 12:23
☽ 0N	13 10:05
♄△♅	16 21:36
♃△♇	18 13:21
☽ 0S	27 9:30
♄⚻♆	30 22:31

Planet Ingress	Dy Hr Mn
☿ ♐	19 11:30
☉ ♐	22 11:55
♂ ♏	1 14:27
☿ ♑	8 20:22
☉ ♑	22 1:15

Last Aspect Dy Hr Mn		☽ Ingress	Dy Hr Mn
1 23:20	♄ □	♎	2 1:29
3 22:57	♄ △	♏	4 1:11
5 16:49	♅ □	♐	6 1:02
8 0:15	♄ ☍	♑	8 3:00
9 8:23	☉ ⚹	♒	10 8:28
12 14:07	♄ △	♓	12 17:43
15 1:39	♄ □	♈	15 5:39
17 14:07	♄ ⚹	♉	17 18:25
20 1:35	☉ ☍	♊	20 6:26
22 12:08	♄ ☌	♋	22 16:49
24 16:52	♂ □	♌	25 1:01
27 1:52	♄ ⚹	♍	27 6:43
29 5:02	♄ □	♎	29 9:55

Last Aspect Dy Hr Mn		☽ Ingress	Dy Hr Mn
1 11:08	♂ ☌	♏	1 11:16
3 4:16	♅ □	♐	3 11:59
5 7:57	♄ ☍	♑	5 13:40
5 20:21	♀ ⚹	♒	7 17:55
9 18:36	♄ △	♓	10 1:47
12 5:04	♄ □	♈	12 12:59
14 17:20	♄ ⚹	♉	15 1:44
17 5:12	♅ □	♊	17 13:44
19 19:11	☉ ☍	♋	19 23:31
21 9:32	☿ ☍	♌	22 6:49
24 4:59	♅ ☍	♍	24 12:06
26 7:11	♄ □	♎	26 15:54
28 12:16	☿ □	♏	28 18:42
30 17:05	☿ ⚹	♐	30 21:02

☽ Phases & Eclipses Dy Hr Mn	
4 20:36	● 12♏15
11 20:53	☽ 19♒17
20 1:35	○ 27♉33
20 1:48	☍ A 0.860
27 15:47	☾ 5♍13
4 7:35	● 11♐58
4 7:32:15	☌ T 02'04"
11 15:50	☽ 19♓26
19 19:11	○ 27♊42
27 0:32	☾ 5♎04

Astro Data

1 November 2002
Julian Day # 37560
SVP 5♓13'30"
GC 26♐52.7 ⚴ 12♒03.2
Eris 19♈39.2R ⚵ 20♎55.8
⚷ 5♑15.8 ⚶ 15♍02.5
☽ Mean ☊ 10♊13.9

1 December 2002
Julian Day # 37590
SVP 5♓13'25"
GC 26♐52.8 ⚴ 17♒16.3
Eris 19♈24.6R ⚵ 1♏11.9
⚷ 7♑45.1 ⚶ 26♍47.6
☽ Mean ☊ 8♊38.6

LONGITUDE — January 2003

Day	Sid.Time	☉	0 hr ☽	Noon ☽	True ☊	☿	♀	♂	⚳	♃	♄	♅	♆	♇
1 W	18 42 54	10♑38 45	16♐01 31	23♐06 47	8♊28.0	28♑18.9	24♏08.4	19♏53.4	8♈06.8	16♌50.7	24♊24.4	26♒17.1	9♒34.9	18♐17.9
2 Th	18 46 51	11 39 56	0♑09 38	7♑09 32	8R 25.4	28R 27.4	25 05.3	20 32.1	8 19.3	16R 45.4	24R 19.8	26 19.7	9 36.9	18 20.0
3 F	18 50 47	12 41 07	14 05 55	20 58 21	8 21.1	28 24.7	26 02.6	21 10.8	8 32.1	16 40.0	24 15.2	26 22.5	9 39.0	18 22.2
4 Sa	18 54 44	13 42 18	27 46 25	4♒29 46	8 15.4	28 10.3	27 00.5	21 49.5	8 45.1	16 34.4	24 10.7	26 25.2	9 41.1	18 24.3
5 Su	18 58 40	14 43 29	11♒08 10	17 41 30	8 08.9	27 44.1	27 58.9	22 28.1	8 58.4	16 28.6	24 06.2	26 28.0	9 43.2	18 26.4
6 M	19 02 37	15 44 39	24 09 43	0♓32 53	8 02.4	27 06.1	28 57.8	23 06.8	9 11.9	16 22.7	24 01.8	26 30.8	9 45.3	18 28.5
7 Tu	19 06 34	16 45 50	6♓51 12	13 04 55	7 56.6	26 17.0	29 57.2	23 45.5	9 25.6	16 16.6	23 57.4	26 33.6	9 47.4	18 30.6
8 W	19 10 30	17 46 59	19 14 23	25 20 03	7 52.2	25 17.8	0♐57.0	24 24.2	9 39.5	16 10.4	23 53.1	26 36.5	9 49.6	18 32.7
9 Th	19 14 27	18 48 09	1♈22 22	7♈21 56	7 49.6	24 10.1	1 57.2	25 02.9	9 53.7	16 04.1	23 48.8	26 39.3	9 51.7	18 34.7
10 F	19 18 23	19 49 18	13 19 17	19 15 05	7D 48.7	22 56.0	2 57.8	25 41.5	10 08.1	15 57.7	23 44.6	26 42.3	9 53.9	18 36.7
11 Sa	19 22 20	20 50 26	25 09 58	1♉04 35	7 49.3	21 37.7	3 58.9	26 20.2	10 22.7	15 51.1	23 40.5	26 45.2	9 56.0	18 38.8
12 Su	19 26 16	21 51 34	6♉59 35	12 55 39	7 50.8	20 17.8	5 00.3	26 58.9	10 37.5	15 44.4	23 36.4	26 48.2	9 58.2	18 40.8
13 M	19 30 13	22 52 41	18 53 23	24 53 25	7 52.3	18 58.9	6 02.1	27 37.6	10 52.5	15 37.6	23 32.4	26 51.2	10 00.4	18 42.8
14 Tu	19 34 09	23 53 48	0♊56 19	7♊02 37	7R 53.1	17 43.4	7 04.3	28 16.2	11 07.7	15 30.7	23 28.5	26 54.2	10 02.6	18 44.7
15 W	19 38 06	24 54 54	13 12 47	19 27 14	7 52.3	16 33.2	8 06.8	28 54.9	11 23.1	15 23.6	23 24.7	26 57.2	10 04.8	18 46.7
16 Th	19 42 03	25 56 00	25 46 17	2♋10 10	7 49.4	15 30.0	9 09.7	29 33.6	11 38.7	15 16.5	23 20.9	27 00.3	10 07.1	18 48.6
17 F	19 45 59	26 57 05	8♋39 01	15 12 54	7 44.3	14 35.1	10 12.9	0♐12.3	11 54.5	15 09.3	23 17.2	27 03.4	10 09.3	18 50.5
18 Sa	19 49 56	27 58 09	21 51 43	28 35 17	7 37.1	13 49.2	11 16.4	0 50.9	12 10.5	15 02.0	23 13.6	27 06.5	10 11.5	18 52.4
19 Su	19 53 52	28 59 13	5♌23 21	12♌15 30	7 28.4	13 12.6	12 20.2	1 29.6	12 26.6	14 54.6	23 10.1	27 09.7	10 13.8	18 54.3
20 M	19 57 49	0♒00 16	19 11 19	26 10 17	7 19.2	12 45.6	13 24.3	2 08.3	12 43.0	14 47.1	23 06.6	27 12.8	10 16.0	18 56.2
21 Tu	20 01 45	1 01 19	3♍11 49	10♍15 21	7 10.5	12 27.8	14 28.7	2 47.0	12 59.5	14 39.6	23 03.2	27 16.0	10 18.3	18 58.0
22 W	20 05 42	2 02 21	17 20 20	24 26 14	7 03.4	12D 19.0	15 33.4	3 25.6	13 16.2	14 32.0	23 00.0	27 19.2	10 20.5	18 59.8
23 Th	20 09 38	3 03 23	1♎32 32	8♎38 50	6 58.4	12 18.5	16 38.4	4 04.3	13 33.1	14 24.3	22 56.8	27 22.4	10 22.8	19 01.6
24 F	20 13 35	4 04 24	15 44 44	22 49 58	6D 55.8	12 26.0	17 43.6	4 43.0	13 50.1	14 16.5	22 53.7	27 25.7	10 25.0	19 03.4
25 Sa	20 17 32	5 05 25	29 54 18	6♏57 33	6 55.2	12 40.8	18 49.1	5 21.7	14 07.3	14 08.7	22 50.6	27 28.9	10 27.3	19 05.1
26 Su	20 21 28	6 06 26	13♏59 37	21 00 24	6 55.8	13 02.3	19 54.8	6 00.3	14 24.7	14 00.9	22 47.7	27 32.2	10 29.6	19 06.8
27 M	20 25 25	7 07 26	27 59 49	4♐57 49	6R 56.4	13 29.9	21 00.8	6 39.0	14 42.3	13 53.0	22 44.9	27 35.5	10 31.9	19 08.5
28 Tu	20 29 21	8 08 25	11♐54 18	18 49 11	6 55.8	14 03.1	22 07.0	7 17.7	15 00.0	13 45.1	22 42.2	27 38.8	10 34.1	19 10.2
29 W	20 33 18	9 09 24	25 42 19	2♑33 33	6 53.0	14 41.4	23 13.4	7 56.3	15 17.8	13 37.1	22 39.5	27 42.1	10 36.4	19 11.9
30 Th	20 37 14	10 10 22	9♑22 40	16 09 26	6 47.4	15 24.3	24 20.0	8 35.0	15 35.9	13 29.2	22 37.0	27 45.4	10 38.7	19 13.5
31 F	20 41 11	11 11 19	22 53 36	29 34 53	6 39.0	16 11.5	25 26.8	9 13.6	15 54.0	13 21.2	22 34.6	27 48.8	10 41.0	19 15.1

LONGITUDE — February 2003

Day	Sid.Time	☉	0 hr ☽	Noon ☽	True ☊	☿	♀	♂	⚳	♃	♄	♅	♆	♇
1 Sa	20 45 08	12♒12 15	6♒13 02	12♒47 47	6♊28.2	17♑02.4	26♐33.8	9♐52.3	16♈12.4	13♌13.2	22♊32.2	27♒52.2	10♒43.3	19♐16.7
2 Su	20 49 04	13 13 10	19 18 56	25 46 17	6R 15.9	17 56.8	27 41.0	10 30.9	16 30.8	13R 05.2	22R 30.0	27 55.5	10 45.5	19 18.2
3 M	20 53 01	14 14 04	2♓09 44	8♓29 13	6 03.3	18 54.4	28 48.3	11 09.5	16 49.4	12 57.2	22 27.9	27 58.9	10 47.8	19 19.8
4 Tu	20 56 57	15 14 57	14 44 46	20 56 31	5 51.6	19 54.8	29 55.9	11 48.1	17 08.2	12 49.2	22 25.8	28 02.3	10 50.1	19 21.2
5 W	21 00 54	16 15 48	27 04 37	3♈09 21	5 41.8	20 57.9	1♑03.6	12 26.7	17 27.1	12 41.2	22 23.9	28 05.7	10 52.4	19 22.7
6 Th	21 04 50	17 16 38	9♈11 04	15 10 11	5 34.5	22 03.4	2 11.4	13 05.3	17 46.1	12 33.2	22 22.1	28 09.1	10 54.6	19 24.2
7 F	21 08 47	18 17 27	21 07 10	27 02 33	5 29.9	23 11.1	3 19.4	13 43.9	18 05.3	12 25.3	22 20.4	28 12.5	10 56.9	19 25.6
8 Sa	21 12 43	19 18 14	2♉56 57	8♉50 59	5D 27.7	24 20.9	4 27.6	14 22.5	18 24.6	12 17.4	22 18.8	28 16.0	10 59.2	19 27.0
9 Su	21 16 40	20 18 59	14 45 18	20 40 35	5 27.2	25 32.6	5 35.9	15 01.1	18 44.0	12 09.5	22 17.3	28 19.4	11 01.4	19 28.3
10 M	21 20 36	21 19 43	26 37 33	2♊36 54	5R 27.4	26 46.0	6 44.4	15 39.6	19 03.5	12 01.7	22 15.9	28 22.9	11 03.7	19 29.7
11 Tu	21 24 33	22 20 26	8♊39 18	14 45 27	5 27.1	28 01.1	7 52.9	16 18.2	19 23.2	11 53.9	22 14.7	28 26.3	11 05.9	19 31.0
12 W	21 28 30	23 21 07	20 55 57	27 11 24	5 25.3	29 17.8	9 01.7	16 56.7	19 43.0	11 46.2	22 13.5	28 29.8	11 08.2	19 32.2
13 Th	21 32 26	24 21 46	3♋32 18	9♋59 03	5 21.1	0♒35.9	10 10.5	17 35.2	20 02.9	11 38.5	22 12.5	28 33.2	11 10.4	19 33.5
14 F	21 36 23	25 22 24	16 31 58	23 11 14	5 14.1	1 55.4	11 19.5	18 13.8	20 22.9	11 30.9	22 11.6	28 36.7	11 12.6	19 34.7
15 Sa	21 40 19	26 23 00	29 56 53	6♌48 46	5 04.5	3 16.3	12 28.6	18 52.3	20 43.1	11 23.4	22 10.7	28 40.1	11 14.9	19 35.9
16 Su	21 44 16	27 23 35	13♌46 37	20 49 57	4 53.0	4 38.4	13 37.8	19 30.8	21 03.3	11 16.0	22 10.0	28 43.6	11 17.1	19 37.0
17 M	21 48 12	28 24 08	27 58 10	5♍10 31	4 40.7	6 01.7	14 47.2	20 09.3	21 23.7	11 08.6	22 09.4	28 47.1	11 19.3	19 38.2
18 Tu	21 52 09	29 24 39	12♍26 08	19 44 06	4 28.8	7 26.2	15 56.6	20 47.7	21 44.1	11 01.3	22 08.9	28 50.5	11 21.5	19 39.2
19 W	21 56 06	0♓25 09	27 03 26	4♎23 13	4 18.8	8 51.9	17 06.2	21 26.2	22 04.7	10 54.1	22 08.6	28 54.0	11 23.7	19 40.3
20 Th	22 00 02	1 25 38	11♎42 33	19 00 36	4 11.4	10 18.6	18 15.9	22 04.7	22 25.3	10 47.0	22 08.3	28 57.4	11 25.8	19 41.3
21 F	22 03 59	2 26 05	26 16 41	3♏30 15	4 06.9	11 46.4	19 25.7	22 43.1	22 46.1	10 40.0	22D 08.1	29 00.9	11 28.0	19 42.3
22 Sa	22 07 55	3 26 31	10♏40 51	17 48 11	4 05.0	13 15.3	20 35.6	23 21.6	23 07.0	10 33.2	22 08.1	29 04.4	11 30.2	19 43.3
23 Su	22 11 52	4 26 56	24 52 03	1♐52 25	4 04.6	14 45.3	21 45.6	24 00.0	23 28.0	10 26.4	22 08.2	29 07.8	11 32.3	19 44.2
24 M	22 15 48	5 27 19	8♐49 15	15 42 37	4 04.5	16 16.3	22 55.6	24 38.4	23 49.0	10 19.7	22 08.4	29 11.3	11 34.4	19 45.2
25 Tu	22 19 45	6 27 42	22 32 39	29 19 28	4 03.3	17 48.3	24 05.8	25 16.8	24 10.2	10 13.2	22 08.7	29 14.7	11 36.6	19 46.0
26 W	22 23 41	7 28 02	6♑03 11	12♑43 56	3 59.8	19 21.4	25 16.1	25 55.2	24 31.5	10 06.8	22 09.1	29 18.2	11 38.7	19 46.9
27 Th	22 27 38	8 28 22	19 21 49	25 56 54	3 53.3	20 55.4	26 26.5	26 33.6	24 52.8	10 00.5	22 09.6	29 21.6	11 40.8	19 47.7
28 F	22 31 35	9 28 39	2♒29 14	8♒58 50	3 43.9	22 30.5	27 36.9	27 12.0	25 14.3	9 54.3	22 10.3	29 25.0	11 42.8	19 48.5

Astro Data

	Dy Hr Mn
☿ R	2 18:22
☽ 0N	9 17:39
☿ D	23 1:09
☽ 0S	23 14:12
♆ R	30 17:15
♆ D	31 6:45
⚳ 0N	1 21:19
☽ 0N	6 1:03
♃☍♆	16 9:13
☽ 0S	19 20:24
♄ D	22 7:42

Planet Ingress

	Dy Hr Mn
♀ ♐	7 13:08
♂ ♐	17 4:23
☉ ♒	20 11:54
♀ ♑	4 13:28
☿ ♒	13 1:01
☉ ♓	19 2:01

Last Aspect / ☽ Ingress (January)

Last Aspect Dy Hr Mn		☽ Ingress	Dy Hr Mn
1 17:24	♅ ⚹	♑	1 23:44
4 0:57	☿ ☌	♒	4 3:58
6 8:46	♀ □	♓	6 10:58
8 11:56	☿ ⚹	♈	8 21:16
11 3:11	♅ ⚹	♉	11 9:49
13 17:45	♂ ☍	♊	13 22:09
16 2:17	♅ △	♋	16 7:57
18 10:49	☉ ☍	♌	18 14:30
20 13:47	♅ ☍	♍	20 18:33
22 9:35	♄ □	♎	22 21:24
24 19:49	♅ △	♏	25 0:10
26 23:15	♅ □	♐	27 3:27
29 3:27	♅ ⚹	♑	29 7:31
30 10:35	☿ ☌	♒	31 12:45

Last Aspect / ☽ Ingress (February)

Last Aspect Dy Hr Mn		☽ Ingress	Dy Hr Mn
2 16:03	♅ ☌	♓	2 19:56
4 14:54	♄ □	♈	5 5:45
7 14:23	♅ ⚹	♉	7 18:00
10 3:29	♅ □	♊	10 6:46
12 14:30	♅ △	♋	12 17:20
13 12:23	♀ ☍	♌	15 0:05
17 1:19	♅ ☍	♍	17 3:24
18 15:57	♄ □	♎	19 4:49
21 4:30	♅ △	♏	21 6:10
23 7:16	♅ □	♐	23 8:47
25 11:52	♅ ⚹	♑	25 13:12
27 12:59	♀ ☌	♒	27 19:26

☽ Phases & Eclipses

Dy Hr Mn		
2 20:24	●	12♑01
10 13:16	☽	19♈53
18 10:49	○	27♋55
25 8:34	☾	4♏57
1 10:49	●	12♒09
9 11:12	☽	20♉17
16 23:52	○	27♌54
23 16:47	☾	4♐39

Astro Data

1 January 2003
Julian Day # 37621
SVP 5♓13'19"
GC 26♐52.9 ⚴ 25♒17.0
Eris 19♈17.6R ✱ 10♏26.9
⚷ 10♑48.3 ⚶ 6♎38.2
☽ Mean ☊ 7♊00.1

1 February 2003
Julian Day # 37652
SVP 5♓13'14"
GC 26♐52.9 ⚴ 4♓49.6
Eris 19♈21.0 ✱ 17♏19.7
⚷ 13♑50.2 ⚶ 12♎10.0
☽ Mean ☊ 5♊21.6

March 2003 LONGITUDE

Day	Sid.Time	☉	0 hr ☽	Noon ☽	True ☊	☿	♀	♂	⚳	♃	♄	♅	♆	♇
1 Sa	22 35 31	10♓28 55	15♒25 41	21♒49 44	3♊31.9	24♒06.7	28♑47.4	27♐50.3	25♈35.8	9♌48.3	22♊11.0	29♒28.5	11♒44.9	19♐49.2
2 Su	22 39 28	11 29 10	28 10 58	4♓29 20	3R 18.2	25 43.8	29 58.0	28 28.6	25 57.4	9R 42.4	22 11.9	29 31.9	11 46.9	19 49.9
3 M	22 43 24	12 29 22	10♓44 48	16 57 22	3 04.1	27 22.0	1♒08.7	29 06.9	26 19.1	9 36.7	22 12.9	29 35.3	11 49.0	19 50.6
4 Tu	22 47 21	13 29 33	23 07 03	29 13 55	2 50.7	29 01.3	2 19.4	29 45.2	26 40.9	9 31.1	22 14.0	29 38.7	11 51.0	19 51.2
5 W	22 51 17	14 29 41	5♈18 05	11♈19 44	2 39.3	0♓41.6	3 30.2	0♑23.4	27 02.8	9 25.6	22 15.2	29 42.0	11 53.0	19 51.8
6 Th	22 55 14	15 29 48	17 19 04	23 16 24	2 30.5	2 22.9	4 41.0	1 01.6	27 24.8	9 20.4	22 16.5	29 45.4	11 55.0	19 52.4
7 F	22 59 10	16 29 53	29 12 04	5♉06 29	2 24.6	4 05.4	5 52.0	1 39.8	27 46.8	9 15.2	22 17.9	29 48.8	11 56.9	19 53.0
8 Sa	23 03 07	17 29 56	11♉00 07	16 53 28	2 21.4	5 49.0	7 02.9	2 18.0	28 08.9	9 10.3	22 19.5	29 52.1	11 58.9	19 53.5
9 Su	23 07 03	18 29 56	22 47 08	28 41 42	2D 20.3	7 33.6	8 14.0	2 56.2	28 31.1	9 05.5	22 21.1	29 55.5	12 00.8	19 53.9
10 M	23 11 00	19 29 55	4♊37 49	10♊36 09	2R 20.4	9 19.4	9 25.1	3 34.3	28 53.3	9 00.8	22 22.9	29 58.8	12 02.7	19 54.4
11 Tu	23 14 57	20 29 52	16 37 25	22 42 16	2 20.6	11 06.3	10 36.2	4 12.4	29 15.7	8 56.4	22 24.7	0♓02.1	12 04.6	19 54.8
12 W	23 18 53	21 29 46	28 51 26	5♋05 33	2 19.7	12 54.4	11 47.4	4 50.5	29 38.1	8 52.1	22 26.7	0 05.4	12 06.5	19 55.2
13 Th	23 22 50	22 29 38	11♋25 14	17 51 04	2 16.9	14 43.6	12 58.7	5 28.5	0♉00.5	8 47.9	22 28.8	0 08.6	12 08.4	19 55.5
14 F	23 26 46	23 29 28	24 23 30	1♌02 54	2 11.7	16 34.0	14 10.0	6 06.5	0 23.0	8 44.0	22 31.0	0 11.9	12 10.2	19 55.8
15 Sa	23 30 43	24 29 15	7♌49 28	14 43 18	2 04.1	18 25.6	15 21.3	6 44.5	0 45.6	8 40.2	22 33.3	0 15.1	12 12.0	19 56.1
16 Su	23 34 39	25 29 01	21 44 14	28 51 59	1 54.7	20 18.3	16 32.7	7 22.5	1 08.3	8 36.6	22 35.7	0 18.4	12 13.8	19 56.3
17 M	23 38 36	26 28 44	6♍05 59	13♍25 33	1 44.4	22 12.2	17 44.2	8 00.4	1 31.0	8 33.2	22 38.2	0 21.6	12 15.6	19 56.5
18 Tu	23 42 32	27 28 25	20 49 45	28 17 32	1 34.3	24 07.1	18 55.7	8 38.4	1 53.8	8 30.0	22 40.8	0 24.7	12 17.3	19 56.7
19 W	23 46 29	28 28 04	5♎47 45	13♎19 10	1 25.8	26 03.3	20 07.3	9 16.3	2 16.6	8 26.9	22 43.5	0 27.9	12 19.0	19 56.8
20 Th	23 50 26	29 27 41	20 50 36	28 20 51	1 19.5	28 00.4	21 18.8	9 54.1	2 39.5	8 24.1	22 46.3	0 31.0	12 20.7	19 56.9
21 F	23 54 22	0♈27 16	5♏48 53	13♏13 46	1 15.9	29 58.6	22 30.5	10 32.0	3 02.5	8 21.4	22 49.2	0 34.2	12 22.4	19 57.0
22 Sa	23 58 19	1 26 50	20 34 45	27 51 13	1D 14.6	1♈57.8	23 42.2	11 09.8	3 25.5	8 18.9	22 52.2	0 37.3	12 24.1	19R 57.1
23 Su	0 02 15	2 26 22	5♐02 46	12♐09 09	1 14.8	3 57.8	24 53.9	11 47.5	3 48.5	8 16.6	22 55.3	0 40.3	12 25.7	19 57.1
24 M	0 06 12	3 25 52	19 10 15	26 06 03	1R 15.6	5 58.5	26 05.7	12 25.3	4 11.7	8 14.5	22 58.5	0 43.4	12 27.3	19 57.0
25 Tu	0 10 08	4 25 21	2♑56 42	9♑42 22	1 15.7	7 59.9	27 17.5	13 03.0	4 34.9	8 12.5	23 01.9	0 46.4	12 28.9	19 57.0
26 W	0 14 05	5 24 48	16 23 17	22 59 43	1 14.1	10 01.7	28 29.4	13 40.7	4 58.1	8 10.8	23 05.3	0 49.4	12 30.5	19 56.9
27 Th	0 18 01	6 24 13	29 31 57	6♒00 17	1 10.3	12 03.8	29 41.3	14 18.3	5 21.4	8 09.2	23 08.8	0 52.4	12 32.0	19 56.8
28 F	0 21 58	7 23 36	12♒24 58	18 46 16	1 04.1	14 05.9	0♓53.2	14 55.9	5 44.7	8 07.9	23 12.4	0 55.4	12 33.5	19 56.6
29 Sa	0 25 55	8 22 57	25 04 26	1♓19 40	0 56.0	16 07.8	2 05.2	15 33.4	6 08.1	8 06.7	23 16.0	0 58.3	12 35.0	19 56.4
30 Su	0 29 51	9 22 16	7♓32 10	13 42 06	0 46.5	18 09.2	3 17.2	16 10.9	6 31.5	8 05.7	23 19.8	1 01.2	12 36.5	19 56.2
31 M	0 33 48	10 21 34	19 49 37	25 54 53	0 36.6	20 09.8	4 29.2	16 48.4	6 55.0	8 04.9	23 23.7	1 04.1	12 37.9	19 55.9

April 2003 LONGITUDE

Day	Sid.Time	☉	0 hr ☽	Noon ☽	True ☊	☿	♀	♂	⚳	♃	♄	♅	♆	♇
1 Tu	0 37 44	11♈20 49	1♈58 02	7♈59 12	0♊27.2	22♈09.2	5♓41.2	17♑25.8	7♉18.5	8♌04.3	23♊27.7	1♓06.9	12♒39.3	19♐55.6
2 W	0 41 41	12 20 03	13 58 34	19 56 19	0R 19.3	24 07.1	6 53.3	18 03.2	7 42.1	8R 03.9	23 31.7	1 09.7	12 40.7	19R 55.3
3 Th	0 45 37	13 19 14	25 52 37	1♉47 45	0 13.3	26 03.1	8 05.4	18 40.5	8 05.7	8D 03.7	23 35.9	1 12.5	12 42.0	19 54.9
4 F	0 49 34	14 18 23	7♉41 57	13 35 32	0 09.5	27 56.9	9 17.6	19 17.7	8 29.3	8 03.7	23 40.1	1 15.3	12 43.3	19 54.6
5 Sa	0 53 30	15 17 30	19 28 51	25 22 17	0D 07.9	29 48.0	10 29.7	19 54.9	8 53.0	8 03.8	23 44.5	1 18.0	12 44.6	19 54.1
6 Su	0 57 27	16 16 35	1♊16 17	7♊11 19	0 08.0	1♉36.0	11 41.9	20 32.1	9 16.8	8 04.2	23 48.9	1 20.7	12 45.9	19 53.7
7 M	1 01 24	17 15 38	13 07 54	19 06 35	0 09.2	3 20.6	12 54.1	21 09.2	9 40.5	8 04.7	23 53.4	1 23.4	12 47.1	19 53.2
8 Tu	1 05 20	18 14 38	25 07 56	1♋12 34	0 10.7	5 01.5	14 06.3	21 46.2	10 04.4	8 05.5	23 58.0	1 26.0	12 48.3	19 52.7
9 W	1 09 17	19 13 37	7♋21 05	13 34 06	0R 11.8	6 38.3	15 18.6	22 23.2	10 28.2	8 06.4	24 02.6	1 28.6	12 49.5	19 52.2
10 Th	1 13 13	20 12 32	19 52 14	26 16 02	0 11.8	8 10.7	16 30.8	23 00.1	10 52.1	8 07.5	24 07.4	1 31.2	12 50.7	19 51.6
11 F	1 17 10	21 11 26	2♌46 02	9♌22 41	0 10.2	9 38.4	17 43.1	23 37.0	11 16.0	8 08.8	24 12.2	1 33.7	12 51.8	19 51.0
12 Sa	1 21 06	22 10 17	16 06 19	22 57 11	0 07.0	11 01.3	18 55.4	24 13.8	11 40.0	8 10.3	24 17.1	1 36.2	12 52.9	19 50.3
13 Su	1 25 03	23 09 06	29 55 21	7♍00 43	0 02.5	12 19.1	20 07.7	24 50.5	12 03.9	8 12.0	24 22.1	1 38.7	12 54.0	19 49.7
14 M	1 28 59	24 07 53	14♍13 00	21 31 41	29♉57.3	13 31.7	21 20.1	25 27.2	12 27.9	8 13.8	24 27.2	1 41.1	12 55.0	19 49.0
15 Tu	1 32 56	25 06 37	28 56 07	6♎25 23	29 52.0	14 38.7	22 32.4	26 03.8	12 52.0	8 15.9	24 32.3	1 43.5	12 56.0	19 48.3
16 W	1 36 52	26 05 20	13♎58 26	21 34 05	29 47.5	15 40.3	23 44.8	26 40.4	13 16.0	8 18.1	24 37.6	1 45.8	12 56.9	19 47.5
17 Th	1 40 49	27 04 00	29 11 06	6♏48 09	29 44.4	16 36.1	24 57.2	27 16.9	13 40.1	8 20.5	24 42.9	1 48.2	12 57.9	19 46.7
18 F	1 44 46	28 02 39	14♏23 58	21 57 24	29D 42.9	17 26.1	26 09.6	27 53.3	14 04.3	8 23.0	24 48.2	1 50.4	12 58.8	19 45.9
19 Sa	1 48 42	29 01 15	29 27 20	6♐52 53	29 42.8	18 10.3	27 22.0	28 29.7	14 28.4	8 25.8	24 53.7	1 52.7	12 59.7	19 45.1
20 Su	1 52 39	29 59 51	14♐13 17	21 27 59	29 43.9	18 48.5	28 34.5	29 06.0	14 52.6	8 28.7	24 59.2	1 54.9	13 00.5	19 44.3
21 M	1 56 35	0♉58 24	28 36 35	5♑38 53	29 45.4	19 20.8	29 47.0	29 42.2	15 16.8	8 31.8	25 04.8	1 57.1	13 01.3	19 43.4
22 Tu	2 00 32	1 56 56	12♑34 49	19 24 26	29 46.7	19 47.1	0♈59.5	0♒18.3	15 41.0	8 35.1	25 10.4	1 59.2	13 02.1	19 42.5
23 W	2 04 28	2 55 26	26 07 56	2♒45 34	29R 47.2	20 07.4	2 12.0	0 54.4	16 05.3	8 38.6	25 16.1	2 01.3	13 02.9	19 41.5
24 Th	2 08 25	3 53 55	9♒17 39	15 44 33	29 46.6	20 21.8	3 24.5	1 30.4	16 29.6	8 42.2	25 21.9	2 03.4	13 03.6	19 40.6
25 F	2 12 22	4 52 22	22 06 41	28 24 28	29 44.9	20 30.4	4 37.1	2 06.3	16 53.9	8 46.0	25 27.8	2 05.4	13 04.3	19 39.6
26 Sa	2 16 18	5 50 47	4♓38 18	10♓48 35	29 42.1	20R 33.2	5 49.6	2 42.1	17 18.2	8 49.9	25 33.7	2 07.3	13 04.9	19 38.6
27 Su	2 20 15	6 49 11	16 55 45	23 00 09	29 38.7	20 30.5	7 02.2	3 17.8	17 42.6	8 54.1	25 39.7	2 09.3	13 05.6	19 37.5
28 M	2 24 11	7 47 33	29 02 09	5♈02 05	29 35.0	20 22.4	8 14.8	3 53.4	18 06.9	8 58.3	25 45.7	2 11.1	13 06.2	19 36.5
29 Tu	2 28 08	8 45 53	11♈00 18	16 57 04	29 31.5	20 09.2	9 27.4	4 28.9	18 31.3	9 02.8	25 51.8	2 13.0	13 06.7	19 35.4
30 W	2 32 04	9 44 12	22 52 41	28 47 25	29 28.6	19 51.3	10 40.0	5 04.3	18 55.7	9 07.4	25 58.0	2 14.8	13 07.2	19 34.3

Astro Data

	Dy Hr Mn
☽ 0N	5 8:03
☽ 0S	19 5:34
☉ 0N	21 1:00
☿ 0N	22 22:41
♇ R	23 5:14
♃∠♄	27 14:15
☽ 0N	1 14:32
♃ D	4 3:05
☽ 0S	15 16:36
♀ 0N	24 16:47
☿ R	26 12:00
☽ 0N	28 20:41

Planet Ingress

		Dy Hr Mn
♀	♒	2 12:41
♂	♑	4 21:18
☿	♓	5 2:05
♅	♓	10 20:54
⚳	♉	13 11:27
☉	♈	21 1:01
☿	♈	21 12:17
♀	♓	27 18:15
☿	♉	5 14:38
☊	♉R	13 23:44
☉	♉	20 12:04
♀	♈	21 16:19
♂	♒	21 23:49

Last Aspect / ☽ Ingress (March)

Last Aspect Dy Hr Mn			☽ Ingress	Dy Hr Mn
2 2:31	♅	☌	♓	2 3:27
4 13:05	♂	□	♈	4 13:31
7 1:11	♅	⚹	♉	7 1:37
9 14:30	♅	□	♊	9 14:39
11 11:25	♄	☌	♋	12 2:13
13 21:14	☉	△	♌	14 10:07
16 1:25	♄	⚹	♍	16 13:54
18 10:36	☉	☍	♎	18 14:44
20 3:03	♄	△	♏	20 14:39
22 4:31	♀	□	♐	22 15:34
24 11:59	♀	⚹	♑	24 18:49
25 18:17	♂	☌	♒	27 0:52
28 20:28	♄	△	♓	29 9:27
31 7:00	♄	□	♈	31 20:06

Last Aspect / ☽ Ingress (April)

Last Aspect Dy Hr Mn			☽ Ingress	Dy Hr Mn
2 22:06	☿	☌	♉	3 8:21
5 0:16	♂	△	♊	5 21:25
7 21:36	♄	☌	♋	8 9:37
10 5:35	♂	☍	♌	10 18:55
12 14:19	♄	⚹	♍	13 0:08
14 18:39	♂	△	♎	15 1:43
16 20:23	♂	□	♏	17 1:17
18 21:53	♂	⚹	♐	19 0:53
21 1:03	♀	□	♑	21 2:21
22 12:41	☿	△	♒	23 6:59
25 6:20	♄	△	♓	25 15:03
27 17:19	♄	□	♈	28 1:55
30 6:13	♄	⚹	♉	30 14:27

☽ Phases & Eclipses

Dy Hr Mn		
3 2:36	●	12♓06
11 7:16	☽	20♊18
18 10:36	○	27♍25
25 1:52	☾	4♑00
1 19:20	●	11♈39
9 23:41	☽	19♋42
16 19:37	○	26♎24
23 12:19	☾	2♒56

Astro Data

1 March 2003
Julian Day # 37680
SVP 5♓13'10"
GC 26♐53.0 ⚴ 14♓06.5
Eris 19♈32.3 ⚵ 20♏20.5
⚷ 16♑07.4 ⚶ 11♎20.3R
☽ Mean ☊ 3♊52.7

1 April 2003
Julian Day # 37711
SVP 5♓13'07"
GC 26♐53.1 ⚴ 24♓35.6
Eris 19♈50.9 ⚵ 18♏51.0R
⚷ 17♑44.6 ⚶ 4♎27.5R
☽ Mean ☊ 2♊14.2

LONGITUDE — May 2003

Day	Sid.Time	☉	0 hr ☽	Noon ☽	True ☊	☿	♀	♂	⚳	♃	♄	♅	♆	♇
1 Th	2 36 01	10♉42 28	4♉41 32	10♉35 19	29♉26.6	19♉29.0	11♈52.6	5♒39.6	19♉20.2	9♌12.2	26♊04.2	2♓16.6	13♒07.7	19♐33.1
2 F	2 39 57	11 40 44	16 29 01	22 22 55	29D 25.6	19R 02.8	13 05.3	6 14.7	19 44.6	9 17.1	26 10.5	2 18.3	13 08.2	19R 32.0
3 Sa	2 43 54	12 38 57	28 17 16	4♊12 25	29 25.5	18 33.3	14 17.9	6 49.8	20 09.1	9 22.2	26 16.9	2 19.9	13 08.6	19 30.8
4 Su	2 47 50	13 37 09	10♊08 38	16 06 17	29 26.2	18 00.9	15 30.6	7 24.8	20 33.6	9 27.5	26 23.3	2 21.6	13 09.0	19 29.6
5 M	2 51 47	14 35 18	22 05 44	28 07 21	29 27.3	17 26.3	16 43.2	7 59.6	20 58.1	9 32.9	26 29.7	2 23.2	13 09.4	19 28.4
6 Tu	2 55 44	15 33 26	4♋11 34	10♋18 47	29 28.6	16 50.2	17 55.9	8 34.3	21 22.6	9 38.5	26 36.2	2 24.7	13 09.7	19 27.1
7 W	2 59 40	16 31 32	16 29 28	22 44 04	29 29.7	16 13.1	19 08.6	9 08.9	21 47.1	9 44.2	26 42.8	2 26.2	13 10.0	19 25.9
8 Th	3 03 37	17 29 37	29 03 02	5♌26 49	29R 30.5	15 35.8	20 21.3	9 43.4	22 11.6	9 50.1	26 49.4	2 27.7	13 10.3	19 24.6
9 F	3 07 33	18 27 39	11♌55 52	18 30 34	29 30.8	14 58.9	21 34.0	10 17.8	22 36.2	9 56.1	26 56.1	2 29.1	13 10.5	19 23.3
10 Sa	3 11 30	19 25 39	25 11 15	1♍58 11	29 30.5	14 23.0	22 46.7	10 52.0	23 00.7	10 02.3	27 02.8	2 30.4	13 10.7	19 22.0
11 Su	3 15 26	20 23 37	8♍51 33	15 51 23	29 29.9	13 48.8	23 59.4	11 26.1	23 25.3	10 08.6	27 09.5	2 31.7	13 10.8	19 20.7
12 M	3 19 23	21 21 34	22 57 38	0♎10 02	29 29.0	13 16.7	25 12.1	12 00.0	23 49.9	10 15.0	27 16.3	2 33.0	13 11.0	19 19.3
13 Tu	3 23 19	22 19 28	7♎28 12	14 51 33	29 28.2	12 47.4	26 24.8	12 33.8	24 14.4	10 21.6	27 23.2	2 34.2	13 11.1	19 17.9
14 W	3 27 16	23 17 21	22 19 22	29 50 46	29 27.5	12 21.3	27 37.6	13 07.5	24 39.0	10 28.3	27 30.1	2 35.4	13 11.1	19 16.6
15 Th	3 31 13	24 15 12	7♏24 42	15♏00 03	29D 27.1	11 58.7	28 50.3	13 41.0	25 03.6	10 35.2	27 37.0	2 36.5	13R 11.2	19 15.2
16 F	3 35 09	25 13 02	22 35 38	0♐10 17	29 27.0	11 39.9	0♉03.1	14 14.4	25 28.2	10 42.2	27 44.0	2 37.6	13 11.2	19 13.7
17 Sa	3 39 06	26 10 51	7♐42 48	15 12 07	29 27.1	11 25.2	1 15.8	14 47.6	25 52.8	10 49.3	27 51.0	2 38.6	13 11.1	19 12.3
18 Su	3 43 02	27 08 38	22 37 14	29 57 19	29 27.3	11 14.9	2 28.6	15 20.7	26 17.4	10 56.6	27 58.1	2 39.6	13 11.1	19 10.9
19 M	3 46 59	28 06 24	7♑11 41	14♑19 49	29 27.5	11D 08.9	3 41.4	15 53.6	26 42.1	11 04.0	28 05.2	2 40.6	13 11.0	19 09.4
20 Tu	3 50 55	29 04 08	21 21 24	28 16 15	29R 27.6	11 07.5	4 54.2	16 26.4	27 06.7	11 11.5	28 12.3	2 41.5	13 10.9	19 08.0
21 W	3 54 52	0♊01 52	5♒04 20	11♒45 46	29 27.6	11 10.6	6 07.1	16 59.0	27 31.3	11 19.1	28 19.5	2 42.3	13 10.7	19 06.5
22 Th	3 58 49	0 59 34	18 20 47	24 49 42	29D 27.5	11 18.3	7 19.9	17 31.4	27 56.0	11 26.9	28 26.7	2 43.1	13 10.5	19 05.0
23 F	4 02 45	1 57 16	1♓12 55	7♓30 53	29 27.5	11 30.5	8 32.7	18 03.6	28 20.6	11 34.8	28 34.0	2 43.9	13 10.3	19 03.5
24 Sa	4 06 42	2 54 56	13 44 07	19 53 06	29 27.7	11 47.2	9 45.6	18 35.6	28 45.2	11 42.8	28 41.3	2 44.6	13 10.0	19 02.0
25 Su	4 10 38	3 52 35	25 58 24	2♈00 32	29 28.0	12 08.2	10 58.5	19 07.4	29 09.9	11 51.0	28 48.6	2 45.2	13 09.7	19 00.5
26 M	4 14 35	4 50 14	8♈00 01	13 57 22	29 28.5	12 33.6	12 11.3	19 39.0	29 34.5	11 59.2	28 55.9	2 45.8	13 09.4	18 58.9
27 Tu	4 18 31	5 47 51	19 53 05	25 47 37	29 29.1	13 03.2	13 24.2	20 10.4	29 59.2	12 07.6	29 03.3	2 46.4	13 09.0	18 57.4
28 W	4 22 28	6 45 27	1♉41 25	7♉34 54	29 29.8	13 37.0	14 37.1	20 41.6	0♊23.8	12 16.1	29 10.7	2 46.9	13 08.7	18 55.8
29 Th	4 26 24	7 43 02	13 28 27	19 22 25	29R 30.3	14 14.7	15 50.0	21 12.6	0 48.5	12 24.7	29 18.1	2 47.3	13 08.2	18 54.3
30 F	4 30 21	8 40 37	25 17 07	1♊12 54	29 30.4	14 56.3	17 03.0	21 43.3	1 13.1	12 33.4	29 25.6	2 47.7	13 07.8	18 52.7
31 Sa	4 34 18	9 38 10	7♊10 01	13 08 44	29 30.1	15 41.7	18 15.9	22 13.8	1 37.7	12 42.2	29 33.1	2 48.1	13 07.3	18 51.1

LONGITUDE — June 2003

Day	Sid.Time	☉	0 hr ☽	Noon ☽	True ☊	☿	♀	♂	⚳	♃	♄	♅	♆	♇
1 Su	4 38 14	10♊35 42	19♊09 19	25♊12 00	29♉29.2	16♉30.8	19♉28.8	22♒44.0	2♊02.4	12♌51.2	29♊40.6	2♓48.4	13♒06.8	18♐49.6
2 M	4 42 11	11 33 13	1♋17 01	7♋24 36	29R 27.9	17 23.5	20 41.8	23 14.0	2 27.0	13 00.2	29 48.2	2 48.7	13R 06.3	18R 48.0
3 Tu	4 46 07	12 30 43	13 34 57	19 48 20	29 26.1	18 19.7	21 54.8	23 43.8	2 51.6	13 09.4	29 55.7	2 48.9	13 05.7	18 46.4
4 W	4 50 04	13 28 12	26 04 57	2♌25 02	29 24.3	19 19.3	23 07.7	24 13.3	3 16.2	13 18.7	0♋03.3	2 49.0	13 05.1	18 44.8
5 Th	4 54 00	14 25 40	8♌48 50	15 16 34	29 22.5	20 22.2	24 20.7	24 42.5	3 40.9	13 28.0	0 10.9	2 49.1	13 04.5	18 43.2
6 F	4 57 57	15 23 06	21 48 28	28 24 46	29 21.2	21 28.4	25 33.7	25 11.5	4 05.5	13 37.5	0 18.6	2R 49.2	13 03.8	18 41.6
7 Sa	5 01 53	16 20 31	5♍05 38	11♍51 15	29D 20.5	22 37.7	26 46.7	25 40.1	4 30.1	13 47.0	0 26.2	2 49.2	13 03.1	18 40.0
8 Su	5 05 50	17 17 55	18 41 46	25 37 13	29 20.7	23 50.3	27 59.7	26 08.5	4 54.6	13 56.7	0 33.9	2 49.2	13 02.4	18 38.4
9 M	5 09 47	18 15 18	2♎37 37	9♎42 53	29 21.4	25 05.9	29 12.7	26 36.6	5 19.2	14 06.5	0 41.5	2 49.1	13 01.7	18 36.8
10 Tu	5 13 43	19 12 40	16 52 51	24 07 12	29 22.7	26 24.5	0♊25.7	27 04.4	5 43.8	14 16.3	0 49.2	2 49.0	13 00.9	18 35.2
11 W	5 17 40	20 10 00	1♏25 33	8♏47 20	29 23.9	27 46.2	1 38.7	27 31.9	6 08.3	14 26.2	0 57.0	2 48.8	13 00.1	18 33.6
12 Th	5 21 36	21 07 20	16 11 56	23 38 32	29R 24.6	29 10.8	2 51.8	27 59.1	6 32.9	14 36.3	1 04.7	2 48.6	12 59.3	18 32.0
13 F	5 25 33	22 04 39	1♐06 17	8♐34 14	29 24.5	0♊38.4	4 04.8	28 26.0	6 57.4	14 46.4	1 12.4	2 48.3	12 58.4	18 30.4
14 Sa	5 29 29	23 01 57	16 01 24	23 26 47	29 23.3	2 08.9	5 17.9	28 52.5	7 21.9	14 56.6	1 20.2	2 48.0	12 57.6	18 28.8
15 Su	5 33 26	23 59 15	0♑49 23	8♑08 17	29 20.9	3 42.4	6 31.0	29 18.7	7 46.4	15 06.9	1 27.9	2 47.6	12 56.7	18 27.2
16 M	5 37 22	24 56 32	15 22 40	22 31 50	29 17.6	5 18.7	7 44.1	29 44.6	8 10.9	15 17.3	1 35.7	2 47.2	12 55.7	18 25.7
17 Tu	5 41 19	25 53 48	29 35 12	6♒32 22	29 13.9	6 57.9	8 57.2	0♓10.1	8 35.4	15 27.7	1 43.5	2 46.7	12 54.8	18 24.1
18 W	5 45 16	26 51 04	13♒23 04	20 07 12	29 10.2	8 39.9	10 10.3	0 35.3	8 59.8	15 38.3	1 51.2	2 46.2	12 53.8	18 22.5
19 Th	5 49 12	27 48 20	26 44 49	3♓16 05	29 07.2	10 24.8	11 23.5	1 00.0	9 24.3	15 48.9	1 59.0	2 45.7	12 52.8	18 20.9
20 F	5 53 09	28 45 35	9♓41 18	16 00 50	29 05.2	12 12.4	12 36.6	1 24.4	9 48.7	15 59.6	2 06.8	2 45.1	12 51.8	18 19.3
21 Sa	5 57 05	29 42 51	22 15 10	28 24 48	29D 04.4	14 02.7	13 49.8	1 48.4	10 13.1	16 10.4	2 14.6	2 44.4	12 50.7	18 17.8
22 Su	6 01 02	0♋40 06	4♈30 19	10♈32 20	29 04.9	15 55.6	15 03.0	2 11.9	10 37.5	16 21.2	2 22.4	2 43.7	12 49.6	18 16.2
23 M	6 04 58	1 37 20	16 31 26	22 28 15	29 06.2	17 51.1	16 16.2	2 35.1	11 01.9	16 32.2	2 30.2	2 43.0	12 48.5	18 14.7
24 Tu	6 08 55	2 34 35	28 23 24	4♉17 29	29 07.9	19 49.0	17 29.5	2 57.8	11 26.3	16 43.2	2 38.0	2 42.2	12 47.4	18 13.1
25 W	6 12 51	3 31 50	10♉11 04	16 04 44	29 09.4	21 49.1	18 42.7	3 20.0	11 50.6	16 54.3	2 45.8	2 41.4	12 46.2	18 11.6
26 Th	6 16 48	4 29 04	21 59 00	27 54 19	29R 10.1	23 51.4	19 56.0	3 41.8	12 15.0	17 05.4	2 53.6	2 40.5	12 45.1	18 10.1
27 F	6 20 45	5 26 19	3♊51 09	9♊49 54	29 09.5	25 55.7	21 09.3	4 03.1	12 39.3	17 16.6	3 01.4	2 39.6	12 43.9	18 08.6
28 Sa	6 24 41	6 23 33	15 50 54	21 54 28	29 07.3	28 01.6	22 22.6	4 23.9	13 03.6	17 27.9	3 09.3	2 38.6	12 42.7	18 07.1
29 Su	6 28 38	7 20 47	28 00 50	4♋10 14	29 03.3	0♋09.1	23 35.9	4 44.3	13 27.8	17 39.3	3 17.1	2 37.6	12 41.4	18 05.6
30 M	6 32 34	8 18 02	10♋22 48	16 38 39	28 57.8	2 17.7	24 49.2	5 04.1	13 52.0	17 50.7	3 24.8	2 36.5	12 40.2	18 04.1

Astro Data

	Dy Hr Mn
☽ 0S	13 3:11
♆ R	16 0:49
♄ ▭ ♆	20 7:07
☿ D	20 7:33
☽ 0N	26 2:53
♃ ☍ ♆	3 2:56
♅ R	7 6:59
☽ 0S	9 11:25
☽ 0N	22 9:29
♄ △ ♅	24 23:35

Planet Ingress

	Dy Hr Mn
♀ ♉	16 10:59
☉ ♊	21 11:13
⚳ ♊	27 12:49
♄ ♋	4 1:29
♀ ♊	10 3:33
☿ ♊	13 1:35
♂ ♓	17 2:27
☉ ♋	21 19:12
☿ ♋	29 10:18

Last Aspect / ☽ Ingress (May)

Last Aspect Dy Hr Mn		☽ Ingress Dy Hr Mn
2 5:28	☿ ☌	♊ 3 3:28
5 8:44	♄ ☌	♋ 5 15:43
7 4:22	♀ □	♌ 8 1:47
10 3:14	♄ ⚹	♍ 10 8:32
12 7:10	♄ □	♎ 12 11:43
14 8:14	♄ △	♏ 14 12:15
16 3:37	☉ ☍	♐ 16 11:44
18 8:43	♄ ☍	♑ 18 12:04
20 13:30	☉ △	♒ 20 15:02
22 18:50	♄ △	♓ 22 21:42
25 5:34	♄ □	♈ 25 8:00
27 18:42	♄ ⚹	♉ 27 20:33
29 15:54	♂ □	♊ 30 9:33

Last Aspect / ☽ Ingress (June)

Last Aspect Dy Hr Mn		☽ Ingress Dy Hr Mn
1 20:56	♄ ☌	♋ 1 21:28
3 16:28	♀ ⚹	♌ 4 7:26
6 6:19	♀ □	♍ 6 14:52
8 16:28	♀ △	♎ 8 19:31
10 17:01	♂ △	♏ 10 21:40
12 21:52	☿ ☍	♐ 12 22:13
14 21:06	♂ ⚹	♑ 14 22:39
15 3:14	♅ ⚹	♒ 17 0:42
19 1:09	☉ △	♓ 19 5:58
21 14:46	☉ □	♈ 21 15:07
23 3:29	♇ △	♉ 24 3:16
25 13:42	♃ □	♊ 26 16:14
29 2:32	☿ ☌	♋ 29 3:53

☽ Phases & Eclipses

Dy Hr Mn	
1 12:16	● 10♉43
9 11:54	☽ 18♌27
16 3:37	○ 24♏53
16 3:41	T 1.128
23 0:32	☾ 1♓30
31 4:21	● 9♊20
31 4:09:21	A 03'37"
7 20:29	☽ 16♍41
14 11:17	○ 23♐00
21 14:46	☾ 29♓49
29 18:40	● 7♋37

Astro Data

1 May 2003
Julian Day # 37741
SVP 5♓13'04"
GC 26♐53.1 ⚴ 4♈30.7
Eris 20♈10.4 ⚵ 13♏03.8R
⚷ 18♑07.4R ⚶ 28♍55.3R
☽ Mean ☊ 0♊38.8

1 June 2003
Julian Day # 37772
SVP 5♓12'59"
GC 26♐53.2 ⚴ 14♈01.5
Eris 20♈27.3 ⚵ 6♏49.3R
⚷ 17♑16.5R ⚶ 0♎16.8
☽ Mean ☊ 29♉00.3

July 2003 LONGITUDE

Day	Sid.Time	☉	0 hr ☽	Noon ☽	True☊	☿	♀	♂	⚳	♃	♄	♅	♆	♇
1 Tu	6 36 31	9♋15 15	22♋57 51	29♋20 27	28♉51.2	4♋27.3	26♊02.6	5♓23.4	14♊16.3	18♌02.2	3♋32.6	2♓35.4	12♒38.9	18♐02.6
2 W	6 40 27	10 12 29	5♌46 28	12♌15 51	28R 44.2	6 37.5	27 15.9	5 42.1	14 40.4	18 13.7	3 40.4	2R 34.3	12R 37.6	18R 01.2
3 Th	6 44 24	11 09 42	18 48 36	25 24 40	28 37.7	8 48.1	28 29.3	6 00.4	15 04.6	18 25.4	3 48.2	2 33.1	12 36.3	17 59.7
4 F	6 48 21	12 06 55	2♍04 01	8♍46 35	28 32.3	10 58.7	29 42.7	6 18.1	15 28.7	18 37.0	3 55.9	2 31.9	12 34.9	17 58.3
5 Sa	6 52 17	13 04 08	15 32 20	22 21 15	28 28.6	13 09.1	0♋56.1	6 35.2	15 52.8	18 48.8	4 03.7	2 30.6	12 33.6	17 56.9
6 Su	6 56 14	14 01 20	29 13 17	6♎08 24	28D 26.8	15 19.1	2 09.5	6 51.7	16 16.9	19 00.5	4 11.4	2 29.3	12 32.2	17 55.5
7 M	7 00 10	14 58 32	13♎06 33	20 07 40	28 26.6	17 28.4	3 22.9	7 07.7	16 40.9	19 12.4	4 19.2	2 28.0	12 30.8	17 54.1
8 Tu	7 04 07	15 55 44	27 11 41	4♏18 25	28 27.5	19 36.7	4 36.4	7 23.0	17 04.9	19 24.3	4 26.9	2 26.6	12 29.4	17 52.7
9 W	7 08 03	16 52 56	11♏27 42	18 39 16	28R 28.5	21 44.0	5 49.9	7 37.8	17 28.9	19 36.2	4 34.6	2 25.2	12 28.0	17 51.4
10 Th	7 12 00	17 50 08	25 52 47	3♐07 49	28 28.7	23 50.0	7 03.3	7 52.0	17 52.9	19 48.2	4 42.2	2 23.7	12 26.6	17 50.1
11 F	7 15 56	18 47 20	10♐23 51	17 40 17	28 27.3	25 54.6	8 16.8	8 05.5	18 16.8	20 00.3	4 49.9	2 22.2	12 25.1	17 48.7
12 Sa	7 19 53	19 44 31	24 56 28	2♑11 40	28 23.7	27 57.6	9 30.4	8 18.4	18 40.6	20 12.4	4 57.6	2 20.7	12 23.7	17 47.4
13 Su	7 23 50	20 41 43	9♑25 07	16 36 03	28 17.9	29 59.1	10 43.9	8 30.7	19 04.5	20 24.5	5 05.2	2 19.1	12 22.2	17 46.2
14 M	7 27 46	21 38 55	23 43 43	0♒47 26	28 10.3	1♌58.9	11 57.5	8 42.2	19 28.3	20 36.7	5 12.8	2 17.5	12 20.7	17 44.9
15 Tu	7 31 43	22 36 08	7♒46 35	14 40 40	28 01.6	3 57.0	13 11.0	8 53.1	19 52.1	20 48.9	5 20.4	2 15.9	12 19.2	17 43.7
16 W	7 35 39	23 33 20	21 29 15	28 12 07	27 52.8	5 53.3	14 24.6	9 03.4	20 15.8	21 01.2	5 28.0	2 14.2	12 17.7	17 42.4
17 Th	7 39 36	24 30 34	4♓49 06	11♓20 14	27 45.0	7 47.8	15 38.2	9 12.9	20 39.5	21 13.5	5 35.5	2 12.5	12 16.2	17 41.2
18 F	7 43 32	25 27 47	17 45 38	24 05 33	27 38.8	9 40.5	16 51.9	9 21.7	21 03.2	21 25.9	5 43.0	2 10.8	12 14.6	17 40.1
19 Sa	7 47 29	26 25 02	0♈20 21	6♈30 28	27 34.6	11 31.4	18 05.5	9 29.7	21 26.8	21 38.3	5 50.5	2 09.0	12 13.1	17 38.9
20 Su	7 51 25	27 22 17	12 36 24	18 38 44	27D 32.5	13 20.5	19 19.2	9 37.1	21 50.4	21 50.8	5 58.0	2 07.2	12 11.5	17 37.8
21 M	7 55 22	28 19 33	24 38 04	0♉35 04	27 32.1	15 07.8	20 32.9	9 43.6	22 13.9	22 03.2	6 05.4	2 05.4	12 10.0	17 36.6
22 Tu	7 59 19	29 16 49	6♉30 24	12 24 43	27 32.7	16 53.2	21 46.6	9 49.4	22 37.4	22 15.8	6 12.8	2 03.5	12 08.4	17 35.6
23 W	8 03 15	0♌14 07	18 18 42	24 13 00	27R 33.3	18 36.9	23 00.4	9 54.5	23 00.8	22 28.3	6 20.2	2 01.6	12 06.8	17 34.5
24 Th	8 07 12	1 11 25	0♊08 15	6♊05 05	27 32.9	20 18.7	24 14.1	9 58.7	23 24.3	22 40.9	6 27.6	1 59.7	12 05.2	17 33.4
25 F	8 11 08	2 08 45	12 04 02	18 05 37	27 30.9	21 58.8	25 27.9	10 02.2	23 47.6	22 53.5	6 34.9	1 57.7	12 03.6	17 32.4
26 Sa	8 15 05	3 06 05	24 10 19	0♋18 31	27 26.5	23 37.0	26 41.7	10 04.8	24 10.9	23 06.2	6 42.2	1 55.7	12 02.0	17 31.4
27 Su	8 19 01	4 03 26	6♋30 32	12 46 37	27 19.6	25 13.5	27 55.6	10 06.7	24 34.2	23 18.9	6 49.5	1 53.7	12 00.4	17 30.4
28 M	8 22 58	5 00 47	19 06 57	25 31 35	27 10.4	26 48.2	29 09.4	10R 07.8	24 57.4	23 31.6	6 56.7	1 51.7	11 58.8	17 29.5
29 Tu	8 26 54	5 58 10	2♌00 31	8♌33 40	26 59.7	28 21.0	0♌23.3	10 08.0	25 20.6	23 44.4	7 03.9	1 49.6	11 57.2	17 28.6
30 W	8 30 51	6 55 33	15 10 53	21 51 54	26 48.3	29 52.1	1 37.2	10 07.5	25 43.7	23 57.2	7 11.0	1 47.5	11 55.5	17 27.7
31 Th	8 34 48	7 52 57	28 36 28	5♍24 14	26 37.4	1♍21.3	2 51.1	10 06.1	26 06.8	24 10.0	7 18.2	1 45.4	11 53.9	17 26.8

August 2003 LONGITUDE

Day	Sid.Time	☉	0 hr ☽	Noon ☽	True☊	☿	♀	♂	⚳	♃	♄	♅	♆	♇
1 F	8 38 44	8♌50 21	12♍14 52	19♍08 01	26♉28.2	2♍48.8	4♌05.0	10♓04.0	26♊29.8	24♌22.8	7♋25.2	1♓43.3	11♒52.3	17♐26.0
2 Sa	8 42 41	9 47 47	26 03 20	3♎00 30	26R 21.3	4 14.3	5 18.9	10R 01.0	26 52.7	24 35.7	7 32.3	1R 41.1	11R 50.7	17R 25.1
3 Su	8 46 37	10 45 12	9♎59 14	16 59 17	26 17.1	5 38.0	6 32.9	9 57.3	27 15.6	24 48.5	7 39.3	1 39.0	11 49.0	17 24.3
4 M	8 50 34	11 42 39	24 00 26	1♏02 31	26D 15.2	6 59.8	7 46.9	9 52.8	27 38.5	25 01.4	7 46.2	1 36.8	11 47.4	17 23.6
5 Tu	8 54 30	12 40 06	8♏05 24	15 08 58	26R 14.9	8 19.6	9 00.8	9 47.6	28 01.2	25 14.4	7 53.1	1 34.6	11 45.7	17 22.8
6 W	8 58 27	13 37 34	22 13 05	29 17 38	26 15.0	9 37.4	10 14.8	9 41.6	28 23.9	25 27.3	8 00.0	1 32.3	11 44.1	17 22.1
7 Th	9 02 23	14 35 02	6♐22 28	13♐27 25	26 14.2	10 53.2	11 28.9	9 34.9	28 46.6	25 40.2	8 06.8	1 30.1	11 42.5	17 21.5
8 F	9 06 20	15 32 31	20 32 14	27 36 39	26 11.4	12 06.8	12 42.9	9 27.5	29 09.2	25 53.2	8 13.6	1 27.8	11 40.9	17 20.8
9 Sa	9 10 17	16 30 02	4♑40 20	11♑42 51	26 05.9	13 18.3	13 57.0	9 19.3	29 31.7	26 06.2	8 20.3	1 25.6	11 39.2	17 20.2
10 Su	9 14 13	17 27 33	18 43 47	25 42 39	25 57.7	14 27.6	15 11.0	9 10.5	29 54.2	26 19.2	8 27.0	1 23.3	11 37.6	17 19.6
11 M	9 18 10	18 25 05	2♒38 57	9♒32 11	25 47.1	15 34.5	16 25.1	9 01.0	0♋16.5	26 32.2	8 33.6	1 21.0	11 36.0	17 19.0
12 Tu	9 22 06	19 22 38	16 21 53	23 07 38	25 35.1	16 39.0	17 39.2	8 50.9	0 38.9	26 45.3	8 40.2	1 18.6	11 34.4	17 18.5
13 W	9 26 03	20 20 12	29 49 03	6♓25 52	25 22.9	17 41.0	18 53.3	8 40.1	1 01.1	26 58.3	8 46.7	1 16.3	11 32.8	17 18.0
14 Th	9 29 59	21 17 47	12♓57 53	19 25 02	25 11.6	18 40.4	20 07.5	8 28.8	1 23.3	27 11.3	8 53.2	1 14.0	11 31.2	17 17.5
15 F	9 33 56	22 15 24	25 47 19	2♈04 52	25 02.2	19 37.0	21 21.6	8 16.9	1 45.4	27 24.4	8 59.6	1 11.6	11 29.6	17 17.1
16 Sa	9 37 52	23 13 02	8♈17 55	14 26 46	24 55.3	20 30.6	22 35.8	8 04.4	2 07.4	27 37.4	9 06.0	1 09.3	11 28.0	17 16.7
17 Su	9 41 49	24 10 42	20 31 49	26 33 33	24 51.0	21 21.2	23 50.0	7 51.4	2 29.4	27 50.5	9 12.3	1 06.9	11 26.4	17 16.3
18 M	9 45 46	25 08 23	2♉32 30	8♉29 14	24 48.9	22 08.6	25 04.2	7 37.9	2 51.3	28 03.6	9 18.6	1 04.5	11 24.8	17 15.9
19 Tu	9 49 42	26 06 05	14 24 25	20 18 40	24 48.4	22 52.6	26 18.4	7 24.0	3 13.1	28 16.7	9 24.8	1 02.1	11 23.2	17 15.6
20 W	9 53 39	27 03 50	26 12 42	2♊07 11	24 48.3	23 33.0	27 32.7	7 09.6	3 34.8	28 29.8	9 30.9	0 59.8	11 21.7	17 15.3
21 Th	9 57 35	28 01 36	8♊02 50	14 00 18	24 47.7	24 09.6	28 46.9	6 54.9	3 56.5	28 42.9	9 37.0	0 57.4	11 20.1	17 15.0
22 F	10 01 32	28 59 24	20 00 16	26 03 20	24 45.5	24 42.2	0♍01.2	6 39.9	4 18.1	28 55.9	9 43.0	0 55.0	11 18.6	17 14.8
23 Sa	10 05 28	29 57 13	2♋10 06	8♋21 05	24 41.0	25 10.5	1 15.5	6 24.5	4 39.5	29 09.0	9 49.0	0 52.6	11 17.0	17 14.6
24 Su	10 09 25	0♍55 04	14 36 43	20 57 22	24 33.9	25 34.3	2 29.8	6 09.0	5 00.9	29 22.1	9 54.9	0 50.2	11 15.5	17 14.5
25 M	10 13 21	1 52 57	27 23 18	3♌54 40	24 24.3	25 53.4	3 44.2	5 53.2	5 22.2	29 35.2	10 00.7	0 47.8	11 14.0	17 14.3
26 Tu	10 17 18	2 50 51	10♌31 28	17 13 39	24 12.9	26 07.4	4 58.5	5 37.3	5 43.5	29 48.3	10 06.4	0 45.4	11 12.5	17 14.2
27 W	10 21 15	3 48 47	24 00 58	0♍53 05	24 00.8	26 16.2	6 12.9	5 21.3	6 04.6	0♍01.4	10 12.1	0 43.0	11 11.0	17 14.2
28 Th	10 25 11	4 46 44	7♍49 33	14 49 49	23 49.2	26R 19.4	7 27.2	5 05.2	6 25.6	0 14.5	10 17.8	0 40.6	11 09.6	17D 14.1
29 F	10 29 08	5 44 43	21 53 18	28 59 21	23 39.3	26 16.9	8 41.6	4 49.2	6 46.5	0 27.5	10 23.3	0 38.2	11 08.1	17 14.1
30 Sa	10 33 04	6 42 43	6♎07 17	13♎16 27	23 31.9	26 08.5	9 56.0	4 33.2	7 07.3	0 40.6	10 28.8	0 35.8	11 06.7	17 14.1
31 Su	10 37 01	7 40 45	20 26 16	27 36 09	23 27.3	25 53.9	11 10.4	4 17.4	7 28.1	0 53.6	10 34.2	0 33.5	11 05.3	17 14.2

Astro Data

	Dy Hr Mn
♃△♇	1 12:48
☽0S	6 17:05
♃∠♄	9 2:43
☽0N	19 16:42
♂R	29 7:37
☽0S	2 21:43
☽0N	16 0:19
☿0S	20 8:58
☿R	28 13:43
♇D	29 3:36
☽0S	30 3:39
♃☍♅	30 4:38

Planet Ingress

	Dy Hr Mn
♀ ♋	4 17:40
☿ ♌	13 12:11
☉ ♌	23 6:05
♀ ♌	29 4:26
☿ ♍	30 14:06
⚳ ♋	10 18:16
♀ ♍	22 11:37
☉ ♍	23 13:09
♃ ♍	27 9:27

Last Aspect / ☽ Ingress

Last Aspect Dy Hr Mn	☽ Ingress Dy Hr Mn
29 18:40 ☉☌	♌ 1 13:14
3 18:07 ♀✶	♍ 3 20:17
5 4:16 ♇□	♎ 6 1:21
7 10:24 ♃✶	♏ 8 4:45
9 18:00 ☿△	♐ 10 6:49
11 15:54 ♃△	♑ 12 8:22
13 19:22 ☉☍	♒ 14 10:39
15 22:58 ♃☍	♓ 16 15:15
18 14:50 ☉△	♈ 18 23:21
21 7:02 ☉□	♉ 21 10:49
23 9:15 ♀✶	♊ 23 23:43
25 21:39 ♃✶	♋ 26 11:24
28 19:27 ♀☌	♌ 28 20:18
30 15:47 ♃☌	♍ 31 2:28

Last Aspect / ☽ Ingress

Last Aspect Dy Hr Mn	☽ Ingress Dy Hr Mn
1 9:03 ♇□	♎ 2 6:49
4 1:35 ♃✶	♏ 4 10:13
6 5:23 ♃□	♐ 6 13:12
8 9:02 ♃△	♑ 8 16:03
9 14:58 ☿△	♒ 10 19:25
12 18:36 ♃☍	♓ 13 0:20
14 10:30 ☿☍	♈ 15 8:01
17 14:37 ♃△	♉ 17 18:54
20 4:30 ♃□	♊ 20 7:42
22 18:16 ☉✶	♋ 22 19:45
24 20:52 ☿✶	♌ 25 4:49
26 12:01 ♇△	♍ 27 10:28
29 7:27 ☿☌	♎ 29 13:42
30 18:38 ♇✶	♏ 31 16:01

☽ Phases & Eclipses

Dy Hr Mn	
7 2:33	☽ 14♎36
13 19:22	○ 20♑59
21 7:02	☾ 28♈08
29 6:54	● 5♌46
5 7:29	☽ 12♏29
12 4:49	○ 19♒05
20 0:49	☾ 26♉37
27 17:27	● 4♍02

Astro Data

1 July 2003
Julian Day # 37802
SVP 5♓12'53"
GC 26♐53.3 ⚴ 21♈51.5
Eris 20♈36.6 ✱ 4♏43.2
⚷ 15♑37.0R ⚵ 7♎37.4
☽ Mean ☊ 27♉25.1

1 August 2003
Julian Day # 37833
SVP 5♓12'48"
GC 26♐53.4 ⚴ 27♈23.3
Eris 20♈36.8R ✱ 7♏18.8
⚷ 13♑45.6R ⚵ 19♎05.6
☽ Mean ☊ 25♉46.6

LONGITUDE — September 2003

Day	Sid.Time	☉	0 hr ☽	Noon ☽	True ☊	☿	♀	♂	⚳	♃	♄	♅	♆	♇
1 M	10 40 57	8♍38 48	4♏45 39	11♏54 20	23♉25.2	25♍33.3	12♍24.9	4♓01.7	7♋48.7	1♍06.7	10♋39.6	0♓31.1	11♒03.8	17♐14.3
2 Tu	10 44 54	9 36 53	19 01 55	26 08 07	23D 24.9	25R 06.4	13 39.3	3R 46.2	8 09.2	1 19.7	10 44.8	0R 28.7	11R 02.5	17 14.4
3 W	10 48 50	10 34 59	3♐12 47	10♐15 47	23R 25.0	24 33.4	14 53.7	3 30.9	8 29.6	1 32.7	10 50.0	0 26.4	11 01.1	17 14.6
4 Th	10 52 47	11 33 06	17 17 01	24 16 25	23 24.5	23 54.6	16 08.2	3 16.0	8 49.9	1 45.7	10 55.2	0 24.1	10 59.7	17 14.8
5 F	10 56 44	12 31 15	1♑13 55	8♑09 27	23 22.1	23 10.3	17 22.6	3 01.4	9 10.0	1 58.7	11 00.2	0 21.7	10 58.4	17 15.0
6 Sa	11 00 40	13 29 25	15 02 56	21 54 13	23 17.2	22 21.1	18 37.1	2 47.2	9 30.1	2 11.6	11 05.2	0 19.4	10 57.1	17 15.3
7 Su	11 04 37	14 27 36	28 43 12	5♒29 42	23 09.8	21 27.6	19 51.6	2 33.4	9 50.1	2 24.6	11 10.1	0 17.1	10 55.8	17 15.6
8 M	11 08 33	15 25 50	12♒13 31	18 54 27	23 00.1	20 30.7	21 06.0	2 20.1	10 09.9	2 37.5	11 14.9	0 14.8	10 54.5	17 15.9
9 Tu	11 12 30	16 24 04	25 32 18	2♓06 50	22 49.0	19 31.6	22 20.5	2 07.2	10 29.6	2 50.4	11 19.6	0 12.6	10 53.2	17 16.2
10 W	11 16 26	17 22 21	8♓37 54	15 05 20	22 37.6	18 31.3	23 35.0	1 54.9	10 49.2	3 03.3	11 24.2	0 10.3	10 52.0	17 16.6
11 Th	11 20 23	18 20 39	21 29 02	27 48 56	22 27.1	17 31.3	24 49.5	1 43.1	11 08.7	3 16.1	11 28.8	0 08.1	10 50.8	17 17.1
12 F	11 24 19	19 18 59	4♈05 04	10♈17 30	22 18.3	16 32.8	26 04.0	1 31.9	11 28.0	3 29.0	11 33.3	0 05.8	10 49.6	17 17.5
13 Sa	11 28 16	20 17 21	16 26 22	22 31 54	22 11.8	15 37.4	27 18.6	1 21.3	11 47.2	3 41.8	11 37.7	0 03.6	10 48.4	17 18.0
14 Su	11 32 12	21 15 44	28 34 23	4♉34 09	22 07.9	14 46.3	28 33.1	1 11.3	12 06.3	3 54.5	11 42.0	0 01.4	10 47.3	17 18.5
15 M	11 36 09	22 14 10	10♉31 39	16 27 20	22D 06.2	14 00.8	29 47.6	1 02.0	12 25.2	4 07.3	11 46.2	29♒59.3	10 46.1	17 19.1
16 Tu	11 40 06	23 12 39	22 21 43	28 15 24	22 06.2	13 22.2	1♎02.2	0 53.3	12 44.1	4 20.0	11 50.3	29 57.1	10 45.0	17 19.6
17 W	11 44 02	24 11 09	4♊08 58	10♊03 04	22 07.0	12 51.3	2 16.7	0 45.3	13 02.7	4 32.7	11 54.4	29 55.0	10 43.9	17 20.3
18 Th	11 47 59	25 09 41	15 58 21	21 55 30	22R 07.7	12 29.0	3 31.3	0 38.1	13 21.3	4 45.4	11 58.4	29 52.9	10 42.9	17 20.9
19 F	11 51 55	26 08 16	27 55 10	3♋58 03	22 07.4	12D 15.9	4 45.9	0 31.6	13 39.6	4 58.0	12 02.2	29 50.8	10 41.9	17 21.6
20 Sa	11 55 52	27 06 53	10♋04 46	16 15 57	22 05.4	12 12.3	6 00.5	0 25.8	13 57.9	5 10.6	12 06.0	29 48.8	10 40.8	17 22.3
21 Su	11 59 48	28 05 32	22 32 09	28 53 51	22 01.4	12 18.5	7 15.1	0 20.8	14 16.0	5 23.2	12 09.7	29 46.7	10 39.9	17 23.0
22 M	12 03 45	29 04 13	5♌21 28	11♌55 18	21 55.3	12 34.3	8 29.7	0 16.5	14 33.9	5 35.7	12 13.3	29 44.7	10 38.9	17 23.8
23 Tu	12 07 41	0♎02 57	18 35 31	25 22 10	21 47.6	12 59.8	9 44.3	0 13.0	14 51.6	5 48.2	12 16.8	29 42.8	10 38.0	17 24.6
24 W	12 11 38	1 01 42	2♍15 08	9♍14 08	21 39.2	13 34.5	10 58.9	0 10.4	15 09.3	6 00.6	12 20.2	29 40.8	10 37.1	17 25.5
25 Th	12 15 35	2 00 29	16 18 45	23 28 24	21 31.0	14 18.0	12 13.5	0 08.5	15 26.7	6 13.0	12 23.5	29 38.9	10 36.2	17 26.3
26 F	12 19 31	2 59 19	0♎42 22	7♎59 51	21 24.0	15 09.8	13 28.1	0D 07.4	15 44.0	6 25.4	12 26.7	29 37.0	10 35.3	17 27.2
27 Sa	12 23 28	3 58 10	15 19 56	22 41 41	21 19.0	16 09.4	14 42.7	0 07.1	16 01.0	6 37.7	12 29.8	29 35.2	10 34.5	17 28.2
28 Su	12 27 24	4 57 04	0♏04 12	7♏26 33	21D 16.2	17 16.0	15 57.4	0 07.7	16 18.0	6 50.0	12 32.8	29 33.3	10 33.7	17 29.1
29 M	12 31 21	5 55 59	14 47 55	22 07 33	21 15.4	18 29.0	17 12.0	0 09.0	16 34.7	7 02.2	12 35.7	29 31.6	10 33.0	17 30.1
30 Tu	12 35 17	6 54 56	29 24 49	6♐39 12	21 16.1	19 47.7	18 26.7	0 11.2	16 51.3	7 14.4	12 38.5	29 29.8	10 32.2	17 31.1

LONGITUDE — October 2003

Day	Sid.Time	☉	0 hr ☽	Noon ☽	True ☊	☿	♀	♂	⚳	♃	♄	♅	♆	♇
1 W	12 39 14	7♎53 55	13♐50 19	20♐57 50	21♉17.3	21♍11.4	19♎41.3	0♓14.2	17♋07.6	7♍26.5	12♋41.3	29♒28.1	10♒31.5	17♐32.2
2 Th	12 43 10	8 52 56	28 01 36	5♑01 28	21R 18.2	22 39.4	20 55.9	0 18.0	17 23.8	7 38.6	12 43.9	29R 26.4	10R 30.9	17 33.3
3 F	12 47 07	9 51 58	11♑57 25	18 49 28	21 17.9	24 11.2	22 10.6	0 22.6	17 39.8	7 50.6	12 46.4	29 24.8	10 30.2	17 34.4
4 Sa	12 51 04	10 51 02	25 37 40	2♒22 06	21 15.9	25 46.1	23 25.2	0 27.9	17 55.6	8 02.6	12 48.8	29 23.1	10 29.6	17 35.5
5 Su	12 55 00	11 50 08	9♒02 50	15 39 58	21 12.1	27 23.6	24 39.9	0 34.0	18 11.2	8 14.5	12 51.1	29 21.6	10 29.0	17 36.7
6 M	12 58 57	12 49 16	22 13 37	28 43 51	21 06.7	29 03.2	25 54.5	0 40.9	18 26.6	8 26.3	12 53.3	29 20.0	10 28.5	17 37.9
7 Tu	13 02 53	13 48 25	5♓10 46	11♓34 26	21 00.4	0♎44.6	27 09.1	0 48.6	18 41.8	8 38.1	12 55.4	29 18.5	10 28.0	17 39.1
8 W	13 06 50	14 47 36	17 54 54	24 12 17	20 53.8	2 27.2	28 23.8	0 57.0	18 56.7	8 49.9	12 57.3	29 17.1	10 27.5	17 40.4
9 Th	13 10 46	15 46 49	0♈26 38	6♈38 03	20 47.8	4 10.8	29 38.4	1 06.1	19 11.5	9 01.5	12 59.2	29 15.6	10 27.0	17 41.7
10 F	13 14 43	16 46 04	12 46 38	18 52 32	20 42.8	5 55.1	0♏53.0	1 15.9	19 26.0	9 13.2	13 01.0	29 14.2	10 26.6	17 43.0
11 Sa	13 18 39	17 45 21	24 55 55	0♉56 57	20 39.4	7 39.8	2 07.6	1 26.5	19 40.4	9 24.7	13 02.6	29 12.9	10 26.2	17 44.3
12 Su	13 22 36	18 44 41	6♉55 52	12 52 57	20D 37.6	9 24.8	3 22.3	1 37.7	19 54.5	9 36.2	13 04.2	29 11.6	10 25.8	17 45.7
13 M	13 26 33	19 44 02	18 48 30	24 42 52	20 37.4	11 09.8	4 36.9	1 49.6	20 08.3	9 47.6	13 05.6	29 10.3	10 25.5	17 47.1
14 Tu	13 30 29	20 43 26	0♊36 27	6♊29 41	20 38.4	12 54.7	5 51.6	2 02.2	20 22.0	9 59.0	13 07.0	29 09.1	10 25.2	17 48.5
15 W	13 34 26	21 42 52	12 23 02	18 17 00	20 40.1	14 39.5	7 06.2	2 15.4	20 35.4	10 10.2	13 08.2	29 07.9	10 24.9	17 50.0
16 Th	13 38 22	22 42 20	24 12 09	0♋09 02	20 41.9	16 23.9	8 20.8	2 29.3	20 48.5	10 21.4	13 09.3	29 06.8	10 24.7	17 51.4
17 F	13 42 19	23 41 51	6♋08 16	12 10 25	20 43.3	18 08.0	9 35.5	2 43.8	21 01.4	10 32.6	13 10.3	29 05.7	10 24.5	17 52.9
18 Sa	13 46 15	24 41 23	18 16 08	24 26 00	20R 43.9	19 51.7	10 50.1	2 58.9	21 14.1	10 43.7	13 11.2	29 04.7	10 24.3	17 54.5
19 Su	13 50 12	25 40 59	0♌40 37	7♌00 32	20 43.3	21 34.9	12 04.8	3 14.6	21 26.5	10 54.6	13 12.0	29 03.7	10 24.2	17 56.0
20 M	13 54 08	26 40 36	13 26 16	19 58 15	20 41.7	23 17.5	13 19.4	3 31.0	21 38.6	11 05.5	13 12.7	29 02.7	10 24.1	17 57.6
21 Tu	13 58 05	27 40 15	26 36 48	3♍22 12	20 39.1	24 59.7	14 34.1	3 47.9	21 50.5	11 16.4	13 13.3	29 01.8	10 24.0	17 59.2
22 W	14 02 02	28 39 57	10♍14 31	17 13 42	20 36.0	26 41.2	15 48.7	4 05.4	22 02.1	11 27.1	13 13.7	29 00.9	10D 24.0	18 00.8
23 Th	14 05 58	29 39 41	24 19 34	1♎31 41	20 33.0	28 22.3	17 03.4	4 23.5	22 13.4	11 37.8	13 14.0	29 00.1	10 24.0	18 02.5
24 F	14 09 55	0♏39 27	8♎49 31	16 12 20	20 30.3	0♏02.7	18 18.0	4 42.1	22 24.5	11 48.4	13 14.3	28 59.4	10 24.0	18 04.1
25 Sa	14 13 51	1 39 15	23 39 13	1♏09 12	20 28.6	1 42.6	19 32.7	5 01.2	22 35.2	11 58.9	13R 14.4	28 58.6	10 24.1	18 05.8
26 Su	14 17 48	2 39 06	8♏41 09	16 13 57	20D 27.8	3 21.9	20 47.3	5 21.0	22 45.7	12 09.3	13 14.4	28 58.0	10 24.2	18 07.6
27 M	14 21 44	3 38 58	23 46 27	1♐17 34	20 28.0	5 00.7	22 02.0	5 41.2	22 55.8	12 19.6	13 14.3	28 57.3	10 24.3	18 09.3
28 Tu	14 25 41	4 38 52	8♐46 16	16 11 39	20 28.9	6 39.0	23 16.6	6 02.0	23 05.7	12 29.8	13 14.0	28 56.8	10 24.5	18 11.1
29 W	14 29 37	5 38 48	23 32 57	0♑49 32	20 30.0	8 16.7	24 31.3	6 23.2	23 15.3	12 39.9	13 13.7	28 56.2	10 24.7	18 12.9
30 Th	14 33 34	6 38 45	8♑00 57	15 06 51	20 31.1	9 53.9	25 45.9	6 45.0	23 24.5	12 50.0	13 13.3	28 55.8	10 24.9	18 14.7
31 F	14 37 31	7 38 44	22 07 05	29 01 34	20R 31.8	11 30.6	27 00.5	7 07.2	23 33.4	12 59.9	13 12.7	28 55.3	10 25.2	18 16.5

Astro Data

	Dy Hr Mn
♄⚻♆	5 5:11
☿0N	8 9:51
☽0N	12 7:55
♀0S	18 0:45
☿D	20 8:53
☉0S	23 10:48
☽0S	26 12:16
♂D	27 7:53
☿0S	9 14:42
☽0N	9 14:58
♃⚻♆	16 18:49
♆D	23 1:55
☽0S	23 23:00
♄R	25 23:43

Planet Ingress

		Dy Hr Mn
♅	♒R	15 3:48
♀	♎	15 15:59
☉	♎	23 10:48
☿	♎	7 1:29
♀	♏	9 18:57
☉	♏	23 20:10
☿	♏	24 11:21

Last Aspect / ☽ Ingress (September)

Last Aspect Dy Hr Mn			☽ Ingress	Dy Hr Mn
2 10:19	☿	⚹	♐	2 18:33
4 11:24	☿	□	♑	4 21:52
6 12:44	☿	△	♒	7 2:16
8 9:02	♇	⚹	♓	9 8:08
11 5:42	♀	☍	♈	11 16:10
13 1:41	♇	△	♉	14 2:51
16 15:27	♅	□	♊	16 15:33
19 3:52	♅	△	♋	19 4:08
21 10:22	☉	⚹	♌	21 14:04
23 19:34	♅	☍	♍	23 20:06
25 1:53	♇	□	♎	25 22:50
27 23:11	♅	△	♏	27 23:53
30 0:10	♅	□	♐	30 0:58

Last Aspect / ☽ Ingress (October)

Last Aspect Dy Hr Mn			☽ Ingress	Dy Hr Mn
2 2:26	♅	⚹	♑	2 3:22
3 22:41	☿	△	♒	4 7:46
6 13:07	♅	☌	♓	6 14:21
7 23:31	♇	□	♈	8 23:09
11 8:32	♅	⚹	♉	11 10:06
13 21:04	♅	□	♊	13 22:46
16 9:55	♅	△	♋	16 11:42
18 12:32	☉	□	♌	18 22:42
21 4:19	♅	☍	♍	21 6:02
22 13:20	♇	□	♎	23 9:28
25 8:32	♅	△	♏	25 10:10
27 8:16	♅	□	♐	27 9:56
29 8:53	♅	⚹	♑	29 10:38
31 8:08	♀	⚹	♒	31 13:42

☽ Phases & Eclipses

Dy Hr Mn		
3 12:35	☽	10♐36
10 16:37	○	17♓34
18 19:04	☾	25♊27
26 3:10	●	2♎38
2 19:10	☽	9♑11
10 7:29	○	16♈35
18 12:32	☾	24♋43
25 12:51	●	1♏41

Astro Data

1 September 2003
Julian Day # 37864
SVP 5♓12'44"
GC 26♐53.4 ⚴ 28♈24.4R
Eris 20♈27.4R ⚵ 13♏29.5
⚷ 12♑33.2R ⚶ 2♏55.0
☽ Mean ☊ 24♉08.1

1 October 2003
Julian Day # 37894
SVP 5♓12'41"
GC 26♐53.5 ⚴ 23♈20.3R
Eris 20♈11.8R ⚵ 21♏40.1
⚷ 12♑29.2 ⚶ 17♏39.6
☽ Mean ☊ 22♉32.7

November 2003 LONGITUDE

Day	Sid.Time	☉	0 hr ☽	Noon ☽	True ☊	☿	♀	♂	⚳	♃	♄	♅	♆	♇
1 Sa	14 41 27	8♏38 45	5♒50 23	12♒33 39	20♉31.9	13♏06.8	28♏15.2	7♓29.9	23♋42.1	13♍09.7	13♋12.0	28♒55.0	10♒25.5	18♐18.3
2 Su	14 45 24	9 38 47	19 11 35	25 44 27	20R31.4	14 42.6	29 29.8	7 53.0	23 50.4	13 19.5	13R11.2	28R54.6	10 25.8	18 20.2
3 M	14 49 20	10 38 50	2♓12 33	8♓36 13	20 30.5	16 17.9	0♐44.4	8 16.6	23 58.3	13 29.1	13 10.3	28 54.3	10 26.2	18 22.1
4 Tu	14 53 17	11 38 55	14 55 47	21 11 35	20 29.3	17 52.7	1 59.0	8 40.6	24 05.9	13 38.6	13 09.3	28 54.1	10 26.6	18 24.0
5 W	14 57 13	12 39 02	27 23 57	3♈33 14	20 28.1	19 27.2	3 13.6	9 05.0	24 13.2	13 48.0	13 08.2	28 53.9	10 27.1	18 25.9
6 Th	15 01 10	13 39 10	9♈39 43	15 43 43	20 27.1	21 01.2	4 28.2	9 29.8	24 20.2	13 57.4	13 07.0	28 53.8	10 27.5	18 27.9
7 F	15 05 06	14 39 20	21 45 31	27 45 23	20 26.4	22 34.9	5 42.8	9 55.0	24 26.8	14 06.6	13 05.7	28 53.7	10 28.0	18 29.8
8 Sa	15 09 03	15 39 32	3♉43 35	9♉40 24	20D26.0	24 08.1	6 57.4	10 20.6	24 33.1	14 15.7	13 04.2	28D53.7	10 28.6	18 31.8
9 Su	15 13 00	16 39 46	15 36 03	21 30 49	20 25.9	25 41.1	8 12.0	10 46.5	24 39.0	14 24.7	13 02.7	28 53.7	10 29.2	18 33.8
10 M	15 16 56	17 40 01	27 24 57	3♊18 44	20 26.0	27 13.7	9 26.5	11 12.8	24 44.5	14 33.5	13 01.0	28 53.8	10 29.8	18 35.8
11 Tu	15 20 53	18 40 19	9♊12 27	15 06 24	20 26.2	28 45.9	10 41.1	11 39.5	24 49.7	14 42.3	12 59.2	28 53.9	10 30.4	18 37.8
12 W	15 24 49	19 40 38	21 00 55	26 56 21	20R26.3	0♐17.8	11 55.7	12 06.5	24 54.5	14 50.9	12 57.4	28 54.1	10 31.1	18 39.9
13 Th	15 28 46	20 40 59	2♋53 04	8♋51 28	20 26.4	1 49.4	13 10.3	12 33.8	24 59.0	14 59.5	12 55.4	28 54.3	10 31.8	18 41.9
14 F	15 32 42	21 41 21	14 51 58	20 55 03	20 26.3	3 20.7	14 24.8	13 01.5	25 03.0	15 07.9	12 53.3	28 54.6	10 32.5	18 44.0
15 Sa	15 36 39	22 41 46	27 01 10	3♌10 47	20 26.1	4 51.7	15 39.4	13 29.4	25 06.7	15 16.1	12 51.1	28 55.0	10 33.3	18 46.1
16 Su	15 40 35	23 42 13	9♌24 25	15 42 34	20D26.0	6 22.4	16 53.9	13 57.7	25 10.0	15 24.3	12 48.9	28 55.3	10 34.1	18 48.2
17 M	15 44 32	24 42 41	22 05 42	28 34 16	20 25.9	7 52.7	18 08.5	14 26.3	25 12.9	15 32.3	12 46.5	28 55.8	10 35.0	18 50.3
18 Tu	15 48 29	25 43 11	5♍08 42	11♍49 22	20 26.1	9 22.8	19 23.0	14 55.2	25 15.4	15 40.2	12 44.0	28 56.3	10 35.8	18 52.4
19 W	15 52 25	26 43 43	18 36 32	25 30 23	20 26.6	10 52.5	20 37.6	15 24.3	25 17.5	15 48.0	12 41.4	28 56.8	10 36.7	18 54.6
20 Th	15 56 22	27 44 17	2♎30 58	9♎38 11	20 27.2	12 21.8	21 52.1	15 53.8	25 19.2	15 55.6	12 38.7	28 57.4	10 37.7	18 56.7
21 F	16 00 18	28 44 53	16 51 49	24 11 25	20 27.9	13 50.8	23 06.6	16 23.5	25 20.5	16 03.1	12 35.9	28 58.0	10 38.6	18 58.9
22 Sa	16 04 15	29 45 30	1♏36 24	9♏05 58	20R28.4	15 19.3	24 21.1	16 53.5	25 21.3	16 10.5	12 33.1	28 58.7	10 39.6	19 01.1
23 Su	16 08 11	0♐46 09	16 39 10	24 14 56	20 28.6	16 47.4	25 35.7	17 23.7	25R21.8	16 17.7	12 30.1	28 59.4	10 40.7	19 03.2
24 M	16 12 08	1 46 49	1♐52 03	9♐29 18	20 28.1	18 15.0	26 50.2	17 54.3	25 21.8	16 24.8	12 27.0	29 00.2	10 41.7	19 05.4
25 Tu	16 16 04	2 47 31	17 05 24	24 39 07	20 27.1	19 42.1	28 04.7	18 25.0	25 21.5	16 31.7	12 23.9	29 01.1	10 42.8	19 07.6
26 W	16 20 01	3 48 14	2♑09 20	9♑35 01	20 25.5	21 08.5	29 19.2	18 56.1	25 20.7	16 38.5	12 20.7	29 02.0	10 44.0	19 09.9
27 Th	16 23 58	4 48 58	16 55 19	24 09 24	20 23.7	22 34.2	0♑33.7	19 27.3	25 19.5	16 45.2	12 17.3	29 02.9	10 45.1	19 12.1
28 F	16 27 54	5 49 44	1♒17 18	8♒18 11	20 21.9	23 59.2	1 48.2	19 58.8	25 17.8	16 51.7	12 13.9	29 03.9	10 46.3	19 14.3
29 Sa	16 31 51	6 50 30	15 12 07	21 59 08	20 20.6	25 23.2	3 02.7	20 30.5	25 15.8	16 58.0	12 10.4	29 05.0	10 47.5	19 16.5
30 Su	16 35 47	7 51 17	28 39 23	5♓13 12	20D20.0	26 46.2	4 17.1	21 02.5	25 13.3	17 04.2	12 06.8	29 06.0	10 48.8	19 18.8

December 2003 LONGITUDE

Day	Sid.Time	☉	0 hr ☽	Noon ☽	True ☊	☿	♀	♂	⚳	♃	♄	♅	♆	♇
1 M	16 39 44	8♐52 05	11♓40 56	18♓03 03	20♉20.3	28♐07.9	5♑31.5	21♓34.6	25♋10.4	17♍10.3	12♋03.2	29♒07.2	10♒50.1	19♐21.0
2 Tu	16 43 40	9 52 54	24 20 03	0♈32 26	20 21.3	29 28.3	6 46.0	22 07.0	25R07.0	17 16.2	11R59.5	29 08.4	10 51.4	19 23.3
3 W	16 47 37	10 53 44	6♈40 46	12 45 34	20 22.8	0♑47.1	8 00.4	22 39.5	25 03.3	17 21.9	11 55.6	29 09.6	10 52.7	19 25.5
4 Th	16 51 33	11 54 34	18 47 24	24 46 44	20 24.6	2 04.1	9 14.8	23 12.2	24 59.1	17 27.5	11 51.8	29 10.9	10 54.0	19 27.8
5 F	16 55 30	12 55 26	0♉44 06	6♉39 55	20 26.0	3 18.9	10 29.2	23 45.2	24 54.5	17 32.9	11 47.8	29 12.2	10 55.4	19 30.1
6 Sa	16 59 27	13 56 18	12 34 39	18 28 41	20R26.7	4 31.3	11 43.5	24 18.3	24 49.5	17 38.2	11 43.8	29 13.6	10 56.9	19 32.3
7 Su	17 03 23	14 57 12	24 22 22	0♊16 03	20 26.3	5 40.9	12 57.9	24 51.5	24 44.1	17 43.3	11 39.7	29 15.1	10 58.3	19 34.6
8 M	17 07 20	15 58 06	6♊10 01	12 04 34	20 24.5	6 47.2	14 12.2	25 25.0	24 38.3	17 48.2	11 35.5	29 16.5	10 59.8	19 36.9
9 Tu	17 11 16	16 59 02	17 59 56	23 56 21	20 21.4	7 49.7	15 26.5	25 58.6	24 32.1	17 53.0	11 31.3	29 18.1	11 01.3	19 39.1
10 W	17 15 13	17 59 58	29 54 04	5♋53 16	20 17.1	8 47.9	16 40.8	26 32.3	24 25.4	17 57.6	11 27.0	29 19.6	11 02.8	19 41.4
11 Th	17 19 09	19 00 56	11♋54 12	17 57 03	20 12.0	9 41.2	17 55.1	27 06.2	24 18.4	18 02.0	11 22.7	29 21.3	11 04.3	19 43.7
12 F	17 23 06	20 01 54	24 02 04	0♌09 29	20 06.6	10 28.8	19 09.3	27 40.3	24 10.9	18 06.3	11 18.3	29 22.9	11 05.9	19 46.0
13 Sa	17 27 03	21 02 54	6♌19 33	12 32 33	20 01.5	11 10.0	20 23.6	28 14.5	24 03.1	18 10.4	11 13.9	29 24.6	11 07.5	19 48.3
14 Su	17 30 59	22 03 54	18 48 45	25 08 30	19 57.4	11 43.9	21 37.8	28 48.8	23 54.9	18 14.3	11 09.4	29 26.4	11 09.1	19 50.5
15 M	17 34 56	23 04 56	1♍32 06	7♍59 53	19 54.7	12 09.8	22 52.0	29 23.3	23 46.3	18 18.1	11 04.8	29 28.2	11 10.8	19 52.8
16 Tu	17 38 52	24 05 58	14 32 13	21 09 23	19D53.6	12 26.6	24 06.2	29 58.0	23 37.3	18 21.6	11 00.2	29 30.0	11 12.5	19 55.1
17 W	17 42 49	25 07 01	27 51 43	4♎39 29	19 53.9	12R33.6	25 20.3	0♈32.7	23 28.0	18 25.0	10 55.6	29 31.9	11 14.2	19 57.4
18 Th	17 46 45	26 08 06	11♎32 53	18 32 03	19 55.2	12 30.0	26 34.5	1 07.6	23 18.3	18 28.2	10 50.9	29 33.9	11 15.9	19 59.6
19 F	17 50 42	27 09 11	25 36 59	2♏47 37	19 56.7	12 15.1	27 48.6	1 42.6	23 08.2	18 31.3	10 46.2	29 35.8	11 17.6	20 01.9
20 Sa	17 54 38	28 10 17	10♏03 41	17 24 47	19R57.6	11 48.5	29 02.7	2 17.7	22 57.8	18 34.1	10 41.4	29 37.8	11 19.4	20 04.2
21 Su	17 58 35	29 11 24	24 50 21	2♐19 37	19 57.0	11 10.3	0♒16.8	2 53.0	22 47.1	18 36.8	10 36.6	29 39.9	11 21.2	20 06.4
22 M	18 02 32	0♑12 32	9♐51 40	17 25 26	19 54.5	10 20.8	1 30.9	3 28.4	22 36.0	18 39.3	10 31.8	29 42.0	11 23.0	20 08.7
23 Tu	18 06 28	1 13 40	24 59 47	2♑33 26	19 50.0	9 21.0	2 44.9	4 03.9	22 24.7	18 41.5	10 27.0	29 44.2	11 24.8	20 11.0
24 W	18 10 25	2 14 49	10♑05 10	17 33 45	19 43.7	8 12.1	3 58.9	4 39.5	22 13.0	18 43.7	10 22.1	29 46.3	11 26.7	20 13.2
25 Th	18 14 21	3 15 58	24 58 05	2♒17 11	19 36.6	6 56.3	5 12.9	5 15.3	22 01.1	18 45.6	10 17.2	29 48.6	11 28.6	20 15.4
26 F	18 18 18	4 17 07	9♒30 14	16 36 37	19 29.5	5 36.0	6 26.8	5 51.1	21 48.9	18 47.3	10 12.3	29 50.8	11 30.5	20 17.7
27 Sa	18 22 14	5 18 16	23 35 56	0♓27 57	19 23.3	4 13.7	7 40.8	6 27.0	21 36.5	18 48.8	10 07.4	29 53.1	11 32.4	20 19.9
28 Su	18 26 11	6 19 26	7♓12 40	13 50 14	19 18.7	2 52.2	8 54.6	7 03.1	21 23.8	18 50.2	10 02.5	29 55.5	11 34.3	20 22.1
29 M	18 30 07	7 20 35	20 20 56	26 45 10	19D16.2	1 34.3	10 08.5	7 39.2	21 10.9	18 51.3	9 57.5	29 57.9	11 36.3	20 24.3
30 Tu	18 34 04	8 21 44	3♈03 27	9♈16 22	19 15.5	0 22.1	11 22.3	8 15.4	20 57.8	18 52.3	9 52.6	0♓00.3	11 38.2	20 26.5
31 W	18 38 01	9 22 53	15 24 33	21 28 37	19 16.2	29♐17.6	12 36.0	8 51.8	20 44.5	18 53.0	9 47.6	0 02.7	11 40.2	20 28.7

Astro Data (Dy Hr Mn)

♃✶♄ 1 17:14
☽0N 5 21:13
♅D 8 12:45
☽0S 20 9:41
⚳R 24 2:34

☽0N 3 3:01
♄⊼♆ 14 12:49
☿R 17 16:03
☽0S 17 17:57
♂0N 17 19:19
☽0N 30 9:21

Planet Ingress (Dy Hr Mn)

♀ ♐ 2 21:43
☿ ♐ 12 7:20
☉ ♐ 22 17:44
♀ ♑ 27 1:08

☿ ♑ 2 21:35
♂ ♈ 16 13:25
♀ ♒ 21 6:33
☉ ♑ 22 7:05
♅ ♓ 30 9:15
☿ ♐R 30 19:54

Last Aspect Dy Hr Mn	☽ Ingress Dy Hr Mn	Last Aspect Dy Hr Mn	☽ Ingress Dy Hr Mn
2 19:41 ♀ □	♓ 2 19:53	2 9:40 ☿ □	♈ 2 10:57
4 6:37 ♇ □	♈ 5 5:04	4 20:53 ♅ ✶	♉ 4 22:31
7 14:17 ♅ ✶	♉ 7 16:30	7 9:56 ♅ □	♊ 7 11:27
10 3:01 ♅ □	♊ 10 5:15	9 22:49 ♅ △	♋ 10 0:12
12 15:58 ♅ △	♋ 12 18:11	12 6:54 ♂ △	♌ 12 11:41
14 13:40 ☉ △	♌ 15 5:49	14 20:06 ♅ ☍	♍ 14 21:08
17 12:40 ♅ ☍	♍ 17 14:37	16 17:50 ♀ △	♎ 17 3:48
19 14:16 ☉ ✶	♎ 19 19:43	19 6:40 ♅ △	♏ 19 7:21
21 19:46 ♅ △	♏ 21 21:25	21 7:44 ♅ □	♐ 21 8:17
23 19:29 ♅ □	♐ 23 21:04	23 7:30 ♅ ✶	♑ 23 7:56
25 18:59 ♅ ✶	♑ 25 20:32	24 13:53 ♃ △	♒ 25 8:14
27 3:53 ♂ ✶	♒ 27 21:49	27 10:59 ♅ ☌	♓ 27 11:11
30 0:47 ♅ ☌	♓ 30 2:26	29 0:04 ♇ □	♈ 29 18:09

☽ Phases & Eclipses (Dy Hr Mn)

1 4:26 ☽ 8♒20
9 1:14 ○ 16♉13
9 1:20 • T 1.018
17 4:16 ☾ 24♌23
23 23:00 ● 1♐14
23 22:50:20 • T 01'58"
30 17:17 ☽ 8♓05

8 20:38 ○ 16♊20
16 17:43 ☾ 24♍21
23 9:44 ● 1♑08
30 10:04 ☽ 8♈17

Astro Data

1 November 2003
Julian Day # 37925
SVP 5♓12'37"
GC 26♐53.6 ⚴ 14♈19.1R
Eris 19♈53.4R ⚵ 1♐30.0
⚷ 13♑39.0 ⚶ 3♐45.6
☽ Mean ☊ 20♉54.2

1 December 2003
Julian Day # 37955
SVP 5♓12'32"
GC 26♐53.6 ⚴ 9♈25.3R
Eris 19♈38.8R ⚵ 11♐44.4
⚷ 15♑45.0 ⚶ 19♐48.0
☽ Mean ☊ 19♉18.9

LONGITUDE — January 2004

Day	Sid.Time	☉	0 hr ☽	Noon☽	True☊	☿	♀	♂	⚳	♃	♄	♅	♆	♇
1 Th	18 41 57	10♑24 02	27♈29 17	3♉27 10	19♉17.5	28♐22.2	13♒49.8	9♈28.2	20♋31.0	18♍53.6	9♋42.6	0♓05.2	11♒42.2	20♐30.9
2 F	18 45 54	11 25 10	9♉22 57	15 17 14	19R 18.5	27R 36.6	15 03.5	10 04.6	20R 17.4	18 54.0	9R 37.7	0 07.7	11 44.2	20 33.0
3 Sa	18 49 50	12 26 19	21 10 39	27 03 43	19 18.2	27 01.3	16 17.1	10 41.2	20 03.6	18R 54.2	9 32.7	0 10.3	11 46.3	20 35.2
4 Su	18 53 47	13 27 28	2♊56 58	8♊50 52	19 15.9	26 36.3	17 30.7	11 17.8	19 49.7	18 54.2	9 27.8	0 12.9	11 48.3	20 37.3
5 M	18 57 43	14 28 36	14 45 50	20 42 14	19 11.2	26 21.5	18 44.2	11 54.6	19 35.7	18 54.0	9 22.9	0 15.5	11 50.4	20 39.5
6 Tu	19 01 40	15 29 44	26 40 23	2♋40 32	19 03.9	26D 16.2	19 57.8	12 31.3	19 21.6	18 53.6	9 18.0	0 18.2	11 52.5	20 41.6
7 W	19 05 36	16 30 52	8♋42 55	14 47 41	18 54.3	26 19.9	21 11.2	13 08.2	19 07.5	18 53.0	9 13.1	0 20.9	11 54.6	20 43.7
8 Th	19 09 33	17 32 00	20 54 57	27 04 51	18 43.2	26 32.0	22 24.6	13 45.1	18 53.3	18 52.3	9 08.2	0 23.6	11 56.7	20 45.8
9 F	19 13 30	18 33 08	3♌17 24	9♌32 40	18 31.5	26 51.7	23 38.0	14 22.1	18 39.0	18 51.3	9 03.3	0 26.4	11 58.8	20 47.9
10 Sa	19 17 26	19 34 16	15 50 41	22 11 30	18 20.3	27 18.4	24 51.3	14 59.1	18 24.8	18 50.1	8 58.5	0 29.2	12 00.9	20 49.9
11 Su	19 21 23	20 35 23	28 35 08	5♍01 39	18 10.6	27 51.4	26 04.5	15 36.2	18 10.5	18 48.8	8 53.7	0 32.0	12 03.1	20 52.0
12 M	19 25 19	21 36 30	11♍31 07	18 03 39	18 03.3	28 30.0	27 17.7	16 13.4	17 56.3	18 47.2	8 48.9	0 34.8	12 05.2	20 54.0
13 Tu	19 29 16	22 37 38	24 39 21	1♎18 23	17 58.7	29 13.7	28 30.8	16 50.6	17 42.1	18 45.5	8 44.2	0 37.7	12 07.4	20 56.0
14 W	19 33 12	23 38 45	8♎00 54	14 47 05	17D 56.6	0♑02.0	29 43.9	17 27.8	17 28.0	18 43.6	8 39.4	0 40.6	12 09.6	20 58.0
15 Th	19 37 09	24 39 52	21 37 07	28 31 07	17 56.3	0 54.4	0♓57.0	18 05.2	17 13.9	18 41.5	8 34.8	0 43.5	12 11.8	21 00.0
16 F	19 41 05	25 40 59	5♏29 13	12♏31 28	17R 56.7	1 50.4	2 09.9	18 42.5	16 59.9	18 39.2	8 30.1	0 46.5	12 14.0	21 02.0
17 Sa	19 45 02	26 42 06	19 37 51	26 48 14	17 56.5	2 49.8	3 22.8	19 20.0	16 46.1	18 36.7	8 25.6	0 49.5	12 16.2	21 03.9
18 Su	19 48 59	27 43 13	4♐02 23	11♐19 52	17 54.5	3 52.1	4 35.7	19 57.5	16 32.4	18 34.0	8 21.0	0 52.5	12 18.4	21 05.9
19 M	19 52 55	28 44 19	18 40 12	26 02 41	17 49.8	4 57.1	5 48.5	20 35.0	16 18.8	18 31.1	8 16.5	0 55.5	12 20.6	21 07.8
20 Tu	19 56 52	29 45 26	3♑26 30	10♑50 44	17 42.3	6 04.5	7 01.2	21 12.6	16 05.4	18 28.1	8 12.1	0 58.6	12 22.8	21 09.7
21 W	20 00 48	0♒46 31	18 14 21	25 36 18	17 32.2	7 14.1	8 13.9	21 50.2	15 52.1	18 24.8	8 07.7	1 01.7	12 25.1	21 11.6
22 Th	20 04 45	1 47 36	2♒55 33	10♒11 05	17 20.5	8 25.7	9 26.5	22 27.9	15 39.1	18 21.4	8 03.4	1 04.8	12 27.3	21 13.4
23 F	20 08 41	2 48 40	17 22 00	24 27 32	17 08.5	9 39.1	10 39.0	23 05.6	15 26.3	18 17.8	7 59.1	1 07.9	12 29.6	21 15.2
24 Sa	20 12 38	3 49 44	1♓27 04	8♓20 09	16 57.5	10 54.1	11 51.4	23 43.4	15 13.7	18 14.0	7 54.9	1 11.1	12 31.8	21 17.1
25 Su	20 16 35	4 50 46	15 06 33	21 46 11	16 48.6	12 10.7	13 03.8	24 21.2	15 01.4	18 10.0	7 50.7	1 14.2	12 34.1	21 18.8
26 M	20 20 31	5 51 47	28 19 09	4♈45 40	16 42.4	13 28.7	14 16.1	24 59.1	14 49.3	18 05.9	7 46.7	1 17.4	12 36.4	21 20.6
27 Tu	20 24 28	6 52 47	11♈06 08	17 20 59	16 38.8	14 47.9	15 28.3	25 37.0	14 37.5	18 01.6	7 42.6	1 20.6	12 38.6	21 22.3
28 W	20 28 24	7 53 47	23 30 49	29 36 14	16D 37.4	16 08.5	16 40.4	26 14.9	14 26.0	17 57.1	7 38.7	1 23.9	12 40.9	21 24.1
29 Th	20 32 21	8 54 44	5♉37 54	11♉36 31	16R 37.2	17 30.1	17 52.4	26 52.8	14 14.8	17 52.5	7 34.8	1 27.1	12 43.2	21 25.8
30 F	20 36 17	9 55 41	17 32 47	23 27 26	16 37.1	18 52.8	19 04.3	27 30.8	14 03.9	17 47.7	7 31.1	1 30.4	12 45.5	21 27.4
31 Sa	20 40 14	10 56 37	29 21 08	5♊14 34	16 36.0	20 16.6	20 16.2	28 08.8	13 53.4	17 42.7	7 27.3	1 33.7	12 47.7	21 29.1

LONGITUDE — February 2004

Day	Sid.Time	☉	0 hr ☽	Noon☽	True☊	☿	♀	♂	⚳	♃	♄	♅	♆	♇
1 Su	20 44 10	11♒57 31	11♊08 23	17♊03 11	16♉32.8	21♑41.4	21♓27.9	28♈46.9	13♋43.2	17♍37.6	7♋23.7	1♓37.0	12♒50.0	21♐30.7
2 M	20 48 07	12 58 24	22 59 32	28 57 55	16R 26.9	23 07.1	22 39.5	29 24.9	13R 33.3	17R 32.4	7R 20.2	1 40.3	12 52.2	21 32.3
3 Tu	20 52 04	13 59 16	4♋58 46	11♋02 29	16 18.0	24 33.7	23 51.1	0♉03.0	13 23.8	17 27.0	7 16.7	1 43.6	12 54.6	21 33.9
4 W	20 56 00	15 00 07	17 09 22	23 19 38	16 06.6	26 01.2	25 02.5	0 41.1	13 14.7	17 21.4	7 13.3	1 46.9	12 56.9	21 35.5
5 Th	20 59 57	16 00 56	29 33 26	5♌50 52	15 53.3	27 29.5	26 13.8	1 19.3	13 05.9	17 15.7	7 10.0	1 50.3	12 59.1	21 37.0
6 F	21 03 53	17 01 44	12♌11 55	18 36 34	15 39.2	28 58.7	27 25.0	1 57.4	12 57.5	17 09.9	7 06.8	1 53.7	13 01.4	21 38.5
7 Sa	21 07 50	18 02 31	25 04 41	1♍36 07	15 25.6	0♒28.8	28 36.1	2 35.6	12 49.5	17 03.9	7 03.7	1 57.0	13 03.7	21 40.0
8 Su	21 11 46	19 03 17	8♍10 41	14 48 13	15 13.7	1 59.7	29 47.1	3 13.8	12 41.9	16 57.8	7 00.6	2 00.4	13 06.0	21 41.4
9 M	21 15 43	20 04 02	21 28 28	28 11 17	15 04.5	3 31.4	0♈58.0	3 52.0	12 34.7	16 51.5	6 57.7	2 03.8	13 08.2	21 42.8
10 Tu	21 19 39	21 04 45	4♎56 30	11♎43 57	14 58.3	5 03.9	2 08.7	4 30.2	12 27.9	16 45.2	6 54.8	2 07.2	13 10.5	21 44.2
11 W	21 23 36	22 05 28	18 33 32	25 25 12	14 55.1	6 37.3	3 19.4	5 08.5	12 21.6	16 38.7	6 52.1	2 10.6	13 12.7	21 45.6
12 Th	21 27 33	23 06 09	2♏18 55	9♏14 39	14D 54.1	8 11.5	4 29.9	5 46.7	12 15.6	16 32.1	6 49.4	2 14.0	13 15.0	21 46.9
13 F	21 31 29	24 06 49	16 12 25	23 12 14	14R 54.1	9 46.5	5 40.2	6 25.0	12 10.0	16 25.4	6 46.8	2 17.5	13 17.3	21 48.2
14 Sa	21 35 26	25 07 29	0♐14 03	7♐17 50	14 53.7	11 22.4	6 50.5	7 03.3	12 04.9	16 18.6	6 44.4	2 20.9	13 19.5	21 49.5
15 Su	21 39 22	26 08 07	14 23 29	21 30 48	14 51.7	12 59.1	8 00.6	7 41.6	12 00.2	16 11.6	6 42.0	2 24.3	13 21.7	21 50.7
16 M	21 43 19	27 08 44	28 39 32	5♑49 20	14 47.1	14 36.7	9 10.6	8 20.0	11 56.0	16 04.6	6 39.8	2 27.8	13 24.0	21 52.0
17 Tu	21 47 15	28 09 20	12♑59 45	20 10 13	14 39.6	16 15.1	10 20.4	8 58.3	11 52.1	15 57.5	6 37.6	2 31.2	13 26.2	21 53.2
18 W	21 51 12	29 09 55	27 20 09	4♒28 51	14 29.6	17 54.4	11 30.2	9 36.7	11 48.7	15 50.3	6 35.6	2 34.7	13 28.4	21 54.3
19 Th	21 55 08	0♓10 28	11♒35 36	18 39 41	14 17.9	19 34.7	12 39.7	10 15.0	11 45.8	15 43.0	6 33.6	2 38.2	13 30.6	21 55.5
20 F	21 59 05	1 11 00	25 40 26	2♓37 10	14 05.8	21 15.8	13 49.1	10 53.4	11 43.2	15 35.7	6 31.8	2 41.6	13 32.8	21 56.6
21 Sa	22 03 02	2 11 30	9♓29 22	16 16 34	13 54.5	22 57.9	14 58.4	11 31.8	11 41.2	15 28.2	6 30.0	2 45.1	13 35.0	21 57.6
22 Su	22 06 58	3 11 58	22 58 28	29 34 50	13 45.1	24 40.9	16 07.5	12 10.3	11 39.5	15 20.7	6 28.4	2 48.5	13 37.2	21 58.7
23 M	22 10 55	4 12 24	6♈05 39	12♈30 56	13 38.3	26 24.8	17 16.5	12 48.7	11 38.3	15 13.2	6 26.9	2 52.0	13 39.4	21 59.7
24 Tu	22 14 51	5 12 49	18 50 55	25 05 52	13 34.3	28 09.7	18 25.3	13 27.1	11 37.5	15 05.6	6 25.5	2 55.4	13 41.5	22 00.7
25 W	22 18 48	6 13 12	1♉16 12	7♉22 23	13D 32.6	29 55.6	19 33.9	14 05.5	11D 37.2	14 57.9	6 24.2	2 58.9	13 43.7	22 01.6
26 Th	22 22 44	7 13 33	13 24 57	19 24 31	13 32.6	1♓42.5	20 42.3	14 44.0	11 37.3	14 50.2	6 23.0	3 02.3	13 45.8	22 02.5
27 F	22 26 41	8 13 52	25 21 43	1♊17 13	13R 33.1	3 30.4	21 50.5	15 22.4	11 37.8	14 42.5	6 21.9	3 05.8	13 47.9	22 03.4
28 Sa	22 30 37	9 14 09	7♊11 43	13 05 52	13 33.2	5 19.2	22 58.6	16 00.9	11 38.8	14 34.7	6 20.9	3 09.2	13 50.1	22 04.2
29 Su	22 34 34	10 14 24	19 00 24	24 55 57	13 31.9	7 09.1	24 06.5	16 39.4	11 40.2	14 26.9	6 20.0	3 12.7	13 52.2	22 05.1

Astro Data

	Dy Hr Mn
♃ R	3 23:58
☿ D	6 13:45
☽ 0S	13 23:18
☽ 0N	26 16:59
♀ 0N	9 14:46
☽ 0S	10 3:54
☽ 0N	23 1:40
⚳ D	25 18:39

Planet Ingress

		Dy Hr Mn
☿	♑	14 11:03
♀	♓	14 17:17
☉	♒	20 17:43
♂	♉	3 10:05
☿	♒	7 4:21
♀	♈	8 16:22
☉	♓	19 7:51
☿	♓	25 12:59

Last Aspect / ☽ Ingress (January)

Last Aspect Dy Hr Mn			☽ Ingress	Dy Hr Mn
1 2:28	☿	△	♉	1 5:03
2 19:22	♃	△	♊	3 17:59
5 23:15	☿	☍	♋	6 6:40
7 20:01	♃	⚹	♌	8 17:39
10 22:01	☿	△	♍	11 2:39
13 8:02	☿	□	♎	13 9:39
15 4:47	☉	□	♏	15 14:34
17 11:49	☉	⚹	♐	17 17:19
19 3:59	♇	☌	♑	19 18:25
21 5:35	♂	□	♒	21 19:12
23 9:34	♂	⚹	♓	23 21:30
25 11:10	♇	□	♈	26 3:07
28 5:01	♂	☌	♉	28 12:47
30 2:05	♀	⚹	♊	31 1:19

Last Aspect / ☽ Ingress (February)

Last Aspect Dy Hr Mn			☽ Ingress	Dy Hr Mn
2 12:57	♂	⚹	♋	2 14:04
4 17:54	☿	☍	♌	5 0:51
6 17:39	♇	△	♍	7 9:04
9 0:24	♇	□	♎	9 15:14
11 5:43	☉	△	♏	11 19:59
13 13:41	☉	□	♐	13 23:36
15 20:21	☉	⚹	♑	16 2:15
17 5:01	♃	△	♒	18 4:28
19 17:35	♇	⚹	♓	20 7:28
21 22:11	♇	□	♈	22 12:46
24 18:56	☿	⚹	♉	24 21:31
26 2:56	♃	△	♊	27 9:23
29 10:09	♀	⚹	♋	29 22:13

☽ Phases & Eclipses

Dy Hr Mn		
7 15:41	○	16♋40
15 4:47	☾	24♎21
21 21:06	●	1♒10
29 6:04	☽	8♉40
6 8:48	○	16♌54
13 13:41	☾	24♏11
20 9:19	●	1♓04
28 3:25	☽	8♊53

Astro Data

1 January 2004
Julian Day # 37986
SVP 5♓12'26"
GC 26♐53.7 ⚴ 11♈56.4
Eris 19♈31.6R ⚵ 22♐31.8
⚷ 18♑31.2 ⚶ 6♑31.0
☽ Mean ☊ 17♉40.5

1 February 2004
Julian Day # 38017
SVP 5♓12'21"
GC 26♐53.8 ⚴ 20♈34.7
Eris 19♈34.8 ⚵ 2♑59.1
⚷ 21♑24.7 ⚶ 23♑03.0
☽ Mean ☊ 16♉02.0

March 2004 LONGITUDE

Day	Sid.Time	☉	0 hr ☽	Noon ☽	True ☊	☿	♀	♂	⚳	♃	♄	♅	♆	♇
1 M	22 38 31	11♓14 37	0♋53 11	6♋52 41	13♉28.5	8♓59.9	25♈14.1	17♉17.8	11♋42.0	14♍19.1	6♋19.3	3♓16.1	13♒54.2	22♐05.9
2 Tu	22 42 27	12 14 48	12 55 03	19 00 47	13R 22.7	10 51.7	26 21.6	17 56.3	11 44.2	14R 11.2	6R 18.7	3 19.5	13 56.3	22 06.6
3 W	22 46 24	13 14 57	25 10 18	1♌24 00	13 14.7	12 44.4	27 28.9	18 34.8	11 46.8	14 03.4	6 18.1	3 23.0	13 58.4	22 07.3
4 Th	22 50 20	14 15 04	7♌42 09	14 04 57	13 04.9	14 38.1	28 35.9	19 13.2	11 49.9	13 55.6	6 17.7	3 26.4	14 00.4	22 08.0
5 F	22 54 17	15 15 09	20 32 30	27 04 47	12 54.4	16 32.6	29 42.7	19 51.7	11 53.3	13 47.7	6 17.4	3 29.8	14 02.4	22 08.7
6 Sa	22 58 13	16 15 12	3♍41 43	10♍23 05	12 44.2	18 27.9	0♉49.3	20 30.2	11 57.2	13 39.9	6 17.2	3 33.2	14 04.4	22 09.3
7 Su	23 02 10	17 15 13	17 08 37	23 57 59	12 35.3	20 24.0	1 55.7	21 08.6	12 01.5	13 32.0	6D 17.2	3 36.6	14 06.4	22 09.9
8 M	23 06 06	18 15 13	0♎50 47	7♎46 33	12 28.5	22 20.7	3 01.8	21 47.1	12 06.1	13 24.2	6 17.2	3 39.9	14 08.4	22 10.4
9 Tu	23 10 03	19 15 10	14 44 51	21 45 13	12 24.2	24 17.9	4 07.7	22 25.5	12 11.2	13 16.5	6 17.3	3 43.3	14 10.4	22 11.0
10 W	23 13 59	20 15 06	28 47 14	5♏50 27	12D 22.3	26 15.5	5 13.3	23 04.0	12 16.6	13 08.7	6 17.6	3 46.7	14 12.3	22 11.4
11 Th	23 17 56	21 15 00	12♏54 33	19 59 11	12 22.4	28 13.2	6 18.6	23 42.4	12 22.4	13 01.0	6 18.0	3 50.0	14 14.2	22 11.9
12 F	23 21 53	22 14 52	27 04 04	4♐09 00	12 23.3	0♈11.0	7 23.8	24 20.9	12 28.6	12 53.3	6 18.5	3 53.3	14 16.1	22 12.3
13 Sa	23 25 49	23 14 43	11♐13 46	18 18 11	12R 24.2	2 08.5	8 28.6	24 59.3	12 35.2	12 45.7	6 19.1	3 56.6	14 18.0	22 12.7
14 Su	23 29 46	24 14 32	25 22 06	2♑25 23	12 24.0	4 05.5	9 33.2	25 37.8	12 42.1	12 38.1	6 19.8	4 00.0	14 19.9	22 13.1
15 M	23 33 42	25 14 20	9♑27 49	16 29 16	12 22.0	6 01.6	10 37.5	26 16.2	12 49.4	12 30.5	6 20.6	4 03.2	14 21.7	22 13.4
16 Tu	23 37 39	26 14 06	23 29 29	0♒28 14	12 18.0	7 56.5	11 41.5	26 54.7	12 57.1	12 23.1	6 21.5	4 06.5	14 23.5	22 13.7
17 W	23 41 35	27 13 50	7♒25 14	14 20 13	12 12.1	9 49.9	12 45.2	27 33.1	13 05.1	12 15.7	6 22.5	4 09.8	14 25.3	22 14.0
18 Th	23 45 32	28 13 32	21 12 50	28 02 46	12 04.9	11 41.3	13 48.6	28 11.6	13 13.5	12 08.3	6 23.7	4 13.0	14 27.1	22 14.2
19 F	23 49 28	29 13 13	4♓49 41	11♓33 16	11 57.3	13 30.3	14 51.7	28 50.0	13 22.2	12 01.1	6 25.0	4 16.2	14 28.9	22 14.4
20 Sa	23 53 25	0♈12 51	18 13 15	24 49 23	11 50.2	15 16.4	15 54.5	29 28.5	13 31.3	11 53.9	6 26.3	4 19.4	14 30.6	22 14.5
21 Su	23 57 22	1 12 27	1♈21 30	7♈49 27	11 44.4	16 59.2	16 57.0	0♊06.9	13 40.7	11 46.8	6 27.8	4 22.6	14 32.3	22 14.6
22 M	0 01 18	2 12 02	14 13 12	20 32 46	11 40.4	18 38.3	17 59.1	0 45.4	13 50.4	11 39.8	6 29.4	4 25.8	14 34.0	22 14.7
23 Tu	0 05 15	3 11 34	26 48 16	2♉59 51	11D 38.3	20 13.1	19 00.8	1 23.8	14 00.5	11 32.9	6 31.1	4 28.9	14 35.7	22 14.8
24 W	0 09 11	4 11 04	9♉07 48	15 12 25	11 38.0	21 43.3	20 02.2	2 02.2	14 10.9	11 26.2	6 32.9	4 32.0	14 37.3	22R 14.8
25 Th	0 13 08	5 10 32	21 14 06	27 13 17	11 38.9	23 08.4	21 03.2	2 40.7	14 21.6	11 19.5	6 34.8	4 35.1	14 39.0	22 14.8
26 F	0 17 04	6 09 58	3♊10 27	9♊06 09	11 40.6	24 28.1	22 03.8	3 19.1	14 32.6	11 12.9	6 36.9	4 38.2	14 40.6	22 14.7
27 Sa	0 21 01	7 09 21	15 00 58	20 55 28	11 42.3	25 42.1	23 04.0	3 57.5	14 44.0	11 06.4	6 39.0	4 41.3	14 42.1	22 14.7
28 Su	0 24 57	8 08 42	26 50 17	2♋46 03	11R 43.4	26 49.9	24 03.8	4 35.9	14 55.6	11 00.1	6 41.2	4 44.3	14 43.7	22 14.6
29 M	0 28 54	9 08 01	8♋43 25	14 43 00	11 43.4	27 51.4	25 03.2	5 14.3	15 07.6	10 53.9	6 43.6	4 47.3	14 45.2	22 14.4
30 Tu	0 32 51	10 07 18	20 45 25	26 51 16	11 42.0	28 46.3	26 02.1	5 52.7	15 19.8	10 47.8	6 46.0	4 50.3	14 46.7	22 14.2
31 W	0 36 47	11 06 32	3♌01 05	9♌15 22	11 39.3	29 34.3	27 00.6	6 31.1	15 32.4	10 41.9	6 48.6	4 53.2	14 48.2	22 14.0

April 2004 LONGITUDE

Day	Sid.Time	☉	0 hr ☽	Noon ☽	True ☊	☿	♀	♂	⚳	♃	♄	♅	♆	♇
1 Th	0 40 44	12♈05 44	15♌34 34	21♌59 01	11♉35.4	0♉15.5	27♉58.6	7♊09.5	15♋45.2	10♍36.0	6♋51.2	4♓56.2	14♒49.6	22♐13.8
2 F	0 44 40	13 04 54	28 29 01	5♍04 43	11R 31.0	0 49.6	28 56.0	7 47.8	15 58.3	10R 30.3	6 54.0	4 59.1	14 51.0	22R 13.5
3 Sa	0 48 37	14 04 01	11♍46 11	18 33 20	11 26.6	1 16.6	29 53.0	8 26.2	16 11.6	10 24.8	6 56.8	5 01.9	14 52.4	22 13.2
4 Su	0 52 33	15 03 06	25 25 59	2♎23 50	11 22.8	1 36.5	0♊49.4	9 04.5	16 25.3	10 19.4	6 59.8	5 04.8	14 53.8	22 12.9
5 M	0 56 30	16 02 09	9♎26 27	16 33 17	11 20.0	1 49.3	1 45.3	9 42.9	16 39.2	10 14.1	7 02.8	5 07.6	14 55.1	22 12.5
6 Tu	1 00 26	17 01 10	23 43 45	0♏57 08	11D 18.5	1R 55.1	2 40.6	10 21.2	16 53.3	10 09.0	7 05.9	5 10.4	14 56.4	22 12.1
7 W	1 04 23	18 00 09	8♏12 43	15 29 45	11 18.2	1 54.1	3 35.4	10 59.5	17 07.7	10 04.1	7 09.2	5 13.1	14 57.7	22 11.7
8 Th	1 08 20	18 59 07	22 47 29	0♐05 13	11 18.9	1 46.6	4 29.5	11 37.8	17 22.4	9 59.3	7 12.5	5 15.9	14 58.9	22 11.2
9 F	1 12 16	19 58 02	7♐22 16	14 38 02	11 20.2	1 32.8	5 23.1	12 16.1	17 37.3	9 54.6	7 16.0	5 18.6	15 00.2	22 10.7
10 Sa	1 16 13	20 56 56	21 52 00	29 03 42	11 21.5	1 13.2	6 15.9	12 54.4	17 52.5	9 50.2	7 19.5	5 21.2	15 01.4	22 10.2
11 Su	1 20 09	21 55 48	6♑12 45	13♑18 51	11R 22.4	0 48.2	7 08.2	13 32.7	18 07.9	9 45.8	7 23.1	5 23.9	15 02.5	22 09.7
12 M	1 24 06	22 54 39	20 21 47	27 21 22	11 22.6	0 18.5	7 59.7	14 10.9	18 23.5	9 41.7	7 26.9	5 26.5	15 03.7	22 09.1
13 Tu	1 28 02	23 53 27	4♒17 29	11♒10 03	11 21.9	29♈44.6	8 50.5	14 49.2	18 39.4	9 37.7	7 30.7	5 29.1	15 04.8	22 08.5
14 W	1 31 59	24 52 14	17 59 02	24 44 26	11 20.4	29 07.2	9 40.6	15 27.5	18 55.5	9 33.9	7 34.6	5 31.6	15 05.9	22 07.8
15 Th	1 35 55	25 50 59	1♓26 13	8♓04 26	11 18.4	28 27.1	10 30.0	16 05.7	19 11.8	9 30.2	7 38.6	5 34.1	15 06.9	22 07.1
16 F	1 39 52	26 49 43	14 39 06	21 10 15	11 16.3	27 45.2	11 18.5	16 44.0	19 28.4	9 26.7	7 42.6	5 36.6	15 07.9	22 06.4
17 Sa	1 43 49	27 48 24	27 37 56	4♈02 12	11 14.4	27 02.1	12 06.3	17 22.2	19 45.2	9 23.4	7 46.8	5 39.0	15 08.9	22 05.7
18 Su	1 47 45	28 47 04	10♈23 08	16 40 48	11 12.9	26 18.8	12 53.2	18 00.4	20 02.1	9 20.3	7 51.1	5 41.4	15 09.9	22 05.0
19 M	1 51 42	29 45 42	22 55 19	29 06 47	11D 12.0	25 36.0	13 39.2	18 38.7	20 19.3	9 17.3	7 55.4	5 43.8	15 10.8	22 04.2
20 Tu	1 55 38	0♉44 18	5♉15 22	11♉21 14	11 11.7	24 54.5	14 24.3	19 16.9	20 36.7	9 14.6	7 59.9	5 46.1	15 11.7	22 03.4
21 W	1 59 35	1 42 52	17 24 35	23 25 40	11 11.9	24 15.0	15 08.4	19 55.1	20 54.3	9 12.0	8 04.4	5 48.4	15 12.5	22 02.5
22 Th	2 03 31	2 41 24	29 24 45	5♊22 09	11 12.6	23 38.1	15 51.6	20 33.3	21 12.2	9 09.6	8 09.0	5 50.6	15 13.4	22 01.7
23 F	2 07 28	3 39 54	11♊18 13	17 13 20	11 13.4	23 04.4	16 33.7	21 11.5	21 30.2	9 07.3	8 13.7	5 52.8	15 14.2	22 00.8
24 Sa	2 11 24	4 38 22	23 07 55	29 02 26	11 14.1	22 34.3	17 14.8	21 49.7	21 48.4	9 05.3	8 18.4	5 55.0	15 14.9	21 59.8
25 Su	2 15 21	5 36 48	4♋57 21	10♋53 11	11 14.8	22 08.3	17 54.8	22 27.9	22 06.8	9 03.4	8 23.3	5 57.2	15 15.7	21 58.9
26 M	2 19 18	6 35 11	16 50 29	22 49 48	11 15.2	21 46.6	18 33.5	23 06.0	22 25.3	9 01.7	8 28.2	5 59.3	15 16.4	21 57.9
27 Tu	2 23 14	7 33 33	28 51 42	4♌56 44	11R 15.3	21 29.5	19 11.1	23 44.2	22 44.1	9 00.2	8 33.2	6 01.3	15 17.0	21 56.9
28 W	2 27 11	8 31 53	11♌05 30	17 18 31	11 15.3	21 17.2	19 47.5	24 22.3	23 03.0	8 58.9	8 38.3	6 03.3	15 17.7	21 55.9
29 Th	2 31 07	9 30 10	23 36 19	29 59 24	11 15.1	21 09.6	20 22.5	25 00.5	23 22.1	8 57.8	8 43.4	6 05.3	15 18.3	21 54.9
30 F	2 35 04	10 28 26	6♍28 10	13♍02 58	11D 15.0	21D 07.0	20 56.2	25 38.6	23 41.4	8 56.9	8 48.7	6 07.3	15 18.9	21 53.8

Astro Data	Planet Ingress	Last Aspect	☽ Ingress	Last Aspect	☽ Ingress	☽ Phases & Eclipses
Dy Hr Mn	Dy Hr Mn	Dy Hr Mn	Dy Hr Mn	Dy Hr Mn	Dy Hr Mn	Dy Hr Mn
♃⊼♆ 4 0:13	♀ ♉ 5 18:13	3 3:43 ♀ □	♌ 3 9:19	1 23:57 ♀ □	♍ 2 2:46	6 23:15 ○ 16♍43
♄ D 7 16:52	☿ ♈ 12 9:45	5 17:14 ♀ △	♍ 5 17:19	3 18:25 ♇ □	♎ 4 7:53	13 21:02 ☾ 23♐37
☽0S 8 10:27	☉ ♈ 20 6:50	7 8:50 ♇ □	♎ 7 22:32	5 21:28 ♇ ⚹	♏ 6 10:25	20 22:42 ● 0♈39
☿0N 13 3:14	♂ ♊ 21 7:40	9 12:44 ♇ ⚹	♏ 10 2:04	7 11:07 ♆ □	♐ 8 11:51	28 23:49 ☽ 8♋38
☉0N 20 6:50		12 4:12 ☿ △	♐ 12 4:58	10 0:31 ♇ ☌	♑ 10 13:34	
☽0N 21 10:11	☿ ♉ 1 2:29	13 21:02 ☉ □	♑ 14 7:53	12 3:47 ☉ □	♒ 12 16:34	5 11:04 ○ 16♎00
♇ R 24 15:10	♀ ♊ 3 14:58	16 5:35 ♂ △	♒ 16 11:11	14 19:28 ☿ ⚹	♓ 14 21:25	12 3:47 ☾ 22♑35
	☿ ♈R 13 1:24	18 12:16 ♂ □	♓ 18 15:27	16 13:44 ♇ □	♈ 17 4:25	19 13:22 ● 29♈49
☽0S 4 19:38	☉ ♉ 19 17:51	20 20:58 ♂ ⚹	♈ 20 21:30	19 13:22 ☉ ☌	♉ 19 13:44	19 13:35:06 ● P 0.737
☿ R 6 20:29		22 15:15 ♇ △	♉ 23 6:11	20 19:37 ♆ □	♊ 22 1:11	27 17:34 ☽ 7♌47
☽0N 17 17:23		24 22:30 ♀ ☌	♊ 25 17:36	23 23:23 ☿ ⚹	♋ 24 13:57	
☿ D 30 13:06		27 22:45 ☿ ⚹	♋ 28 6:24	26 9:57 ☿ □	♌ 27 2:15	
		30 16:01 ☿ □	♌ 30 18:08	29 2:09 ♂ ⚹	♍ 29 12:01	

Astro Data

1 March 2004
Julian Day # 38046
SVP 5♓12'17"
GC 26♐53.8 ⚴ 2♉19.0
Eris 19♈46.6 ⚵ 11♑52.3
⚷ 23♑46.7 ⚶ 8♒02.6
☽ Mean ☊ 14♉29.9

1 April 2004
Julian Day # 38077
SVP 5♓12'13"
GC 26♐53.9 ⚴ 17♉27.2
Eris 20♈05.2 ⚵ 19♑34.3
⚷ 25♑31.3 ⚶ 23♒11.2
☽ Mean ☊ 12♉51.3

LONGITUDE May 2004

Day	Sid.Time	☉	0 hr ☽	Noon ☽	True ☊	☿	♀	♂	⚳	♃	♄	♅	♆	♇
1 Sa	2 39 00	11♉26 39	19♍44 05	26♍31 38	11♉15.0	21♈09.2	21♊28.5	26♊16.7	24♋00.8	8♍56.1	8♋54.0	6♓09.1	15♒19.4	21♐52.7
2 Su	2 42 57	12 24 50	3♎25 41	10♎26 06	11 15.1	21 16.2	21 59.3	26 54.8	24 20.5	8R55.5	8 59.3	6 11.0	15 19.9	21R51.6
3 M	2 46 53	13 23 00	17 32 37	24 44 50	11 15.2	21 27.9	22 28.6	27 32.9	24 40.2	8 55.1	9 04.8	6 12.8	15 20.4	21 50.5
4 Tu	2 50 50	14 21 07	2♏02 11	9♏23 57	11R15.3	21 44.3	22 56.3	28 10.9	25 00.2	8D54.9	9 10.3	6 14.6	15 20.8	21 49.3
5 W	2 54 47	15 19 13	16 49 18	24 17 15	11 15.2	22 05.2	23 22.4	28 49.0	25 20.2	8 54.9	9 15.9	6 16.3	15 21.2	21 48.1
6 Th	2 58 43	16 17 18	1♐46 50	9♐16 57	11 14.9	22 30.5	23 46.8	29 27.1	25 40.5	8 55.1	9 21.5	6 18.0	15 21.6	21 46.9
7 F	3 02 40	17 15 21	16 46 33	24 14 38	11 14.3	23 00.0	24 09.5	0♋05.1	26 00.9	8 55.4	9 27.3	6 19.6	15 22.0	21 45.7
8 Sa	3 06 36	18 13 22	1♑40 14	9♑02 32	11 13.6	23 33.6	24 30.4	0 43.1	26 21.4	8 55.9	9 33.1	6 21.2	15 22.3	21 44.5
9 Su	3 10 33	19 11 22	16 20 48	23 34 27	11 12.9	24 11.2	24 49.4	1 21.2	26 42.1	8 56.6	9 38.9	6 22.8	15 22.6	21 43.2
10 M	3 14 29	20 09 21	0♒43 03	7♒46 19	11D12.4	24 52.5	25 06.5	1 59.2	27 02.9	8 57.5	9 44.8	6 24.3	15 22.8	21 42.0
11 Tu	3 18 26	21 07 19	14 44 05	21 36 19	11 12.2	25 37.6	25 21.7	2 37.2	27 23.9	8 58.6	9 50.8	6 25.8	15 23.0	21 40.7
12 W	3 22 22	22 05 15	28 23 03	5♓04 28	11 12.4	26 26.1	25 34.8	3 15.2	27 45.0	8 59.8	9 56.8	6 27.2	15 23.2	21 39.3
13 Th	3 26 19	23 03 10	11♓40 45	18 12 11	11 13.1	27 18.1	25 45.8	3 53.2	28 06.3	9 01.2	10 02.9	6 28.5	15 23.4	21 38.0
14 F	3 30 16	24 01 03	24 39 04	1♈01 42	11 14.2	28 13.3	25 54.7	4 31.2	28 27.6	9 02.8	10 09.1	6 29.9	15 23.5	21 36.7
15 Sa	3 34 12	24 58 55	7♈20 27	13 35 37	11 15.3	29 11.8	26 01.4	5 09.2	28 49.2	9 04.6	10 15.3	6 31.2	15 23.5	21 35.3
16 Su	3 38 09	25 56 46	19 47 32	25 56 31	11 16.3	0♉13.3	26 05.9	5 47.2	29 10.8	9 06.6	10 21.6	6 32.4	15 23.6	21 33.9
17 M	3 42 05	26 54 36	2♉02 52	8♉06 52	11R16.8	1 17.7	26R08.1	6 25.2	29 32.6	9 08.7	10 27.9	6 33.6	15R23.6	21 32.5
18 Tu	3 46 02	27 52 25	14 08 49	20 08 57	11 16.6	2 25.1	26 07.9	7 03.1	29 54.5	9 11.0	10 34.3	6 34.7	15 23.6	21 31.1
19 W	3 49 58	28 50 12	26 07 31	2♊04 48	11 15.6	3 35.2	26 05.4	7 41.1	0♌16.5	9 13.5	10 40.8	6 35.8	15 23.5	21 29.7
20 Th	3 53 55	29 47 57	8♊01 02	13 56 27	11 13.6	4 48.1	26 00.5	8 19.1	0 38.7	9 16.2	10 47.3	6 36.9	15 23.5	21 28.2
21 F	3 57 51	0♊45 42	19 51 20	25 45 57	11 10.9	6 03.7	25 53.2	8 57.0	1 01.0	9 19.0	10 53.8	6 37.9	15 23.4	21 26.8
22 Sa	4 01 48	1 43 25	1♋40 36	7♋35 35	11 07.6	7 21.8	25 43.4	9 35.0	1 23.3	9 22.0	11 00.4	6 38.8	15 23.2	21 25.3
23 Su	4 05 45	2 41 06	13 31 14	19 27 55	11 04.2	8 42.6	25 31.3	10 12.9	1 45.8	9 25.2	11 07.1	6 39.7	15 23.0	21 23.9
24 M	4 09 41	3 38 46	25 26 02	1♌25 59	11 01.1	10 05.9	25 16.7	10 50.8	2 08.5	9 28.5	11 13.8	6 40.6	15 22.8	21 22.4
25 Tu	4 13 38	4 36 25	7♌28 13	13 33 12	10 58.7	11 31.7	24 59.7	11 28.8	2 31.2	9 32.1	11 20.5	6 41.4	15 22.6	21 20.9
26 W	4 17 34	5 34 02	19 41 25	25 53 22	10D57.2	13 00.0	24 40.4	12 06.7	2 54.0	9 35.7	11 27.3	6 42.2	15 22.3	21 19.4
27 Th	4 21 31	6 31 37	2♍09 34	8♍30 30	10 56.9	14 30.7	24 18.8	12 44.6	3 17.0	9 39.6	11 34.2	6 42.9	15 22.0	21 17.8
28 F	4 25 27	7 29 11	14 56 39	21 28 28	10 57.5	16 03.9	23 54.9	13 22.5	3 40.0	9 43.6	11 41.1	6 43.5	15 21.7	21 16.3
29 Sa	4 29 24	8 26 44	28 06 22	4♎50 41	10 58.8	17 39.5	23 29.0	14 00.4	4 03.2	9 47.7	11 48.0	6 44.1	15 21.3	21 14.8
30 Su	4 33 20	9 24 15	11♎41 38	18 39 22	11 00.3	19 17.5	23 01.1	14 38.2	4 26.4	9 52.1	11 55.0	6 44.7	15 20.9	21 13.2
31 M	4 37 17	10 21 45	25 43 51	2♏54 55	11R01.4	20 58.0	22 31.3	15 16.1	4 49.7	9 56.5	12 02.0	6 45.2	15 20.5	21 11.7

LONGITUDE June 2004

Day	Sid.Time	☉	0 hr ☽	Noon ☽	True ☊	☿	♀	♂	⚳	♃	♄	♅	♆	♇
1 Tu	4 41 14	11♊19 14	10♏12 15	17♏35 17	11♉01.4	22♉40.9	21♊59.8	15♋54.0	5♌13.2	10♍01.2	12♋09.0	6♓45.7	15♒20.0	21♐10.1
2 W	4 45 10	12 16 41	25 03 18	2♐35 25	11R00.1	24 26.1	21R26.8	16 31.8	5 36.7	10 06.0	12 16.1	6 46.1	15R19.5	21R08.6
3 Th	4 49 07	13 14 08	10♐10 32	17 47 29	10 57.3	26 13.8	20 52.4	17 09.7	6 00.3	10 10.9	12 23.2	6 46.5	15 19.0	21 07.0
4 F	4 53 03	14 11 34	25 24 59	3♑01 44	10 53.3	28 03.8	20 16.9	17 47.5	6 24.1	10 16.0	12 30.4	6 46.8	15 18.4	21 05.4
5 Sa	4 57 00	15 08 59	10♑36 26	18 07 53	10 48.5	29 56.2	19 40.5	18 25.4	6 47.9	10 21.3	12 37.6	6 47.1	15 17.9	21 03.9
6 Su	5 00 56	16 06 23	25 35 01	2♒56 55	10 43.8	1♊50.8	19 03.4	19 03.2	7 11.8	10 26.7	12 44.8	6 47.3	15 17.3	21 02.3
7 M	5 04 53	17 03 46	10♒12 52	17 22 19	10 39.8	3 47.8	18 25.9	19 41.1	7 35.7	10 32.2	12 52.1	6 47.5	15 16.6	21 00.7
8 Tu	5 08 50	18 01 09	24 24 58	1♓20 39	10 37.1	5 46.9	17 48.2	20 18.9	7 59.8	10 37.9	12 59.4	6 47.6	15 16.0	20 59.1
9 W	5 12 46	18 58 31	8♓09 26	14 51 28	10D35.9	7 48.0	17 10.6	20 56.7	8 24.0	10 43.7	13 06.7	6 47.7	15 15.3	20 57.5
10 Th	5 16 43	19 55 53	21 27 04	27 56 36	10 36.0	9 51.2	16 33.2	21 34.5	8 48.2	10 49.7	13 14.1	6R47.8	15 14.5	20 55.9
11 F	5 20 39	20 53 14	4♈20 32	10♈39 21	10 37.2	11 56.1	15 56.4	22 12.3	9 12.5	10 55.8	13 21.5	6 47.7	15 13.8	20 54.3
12 Sa	5 24 36	21 50 35	16 53 36	23 03 48	10 38.7	14 02.8	15 20.4	22 50.2	9 36.9	11 02.1	13 28.9	6 47.7	15 13.0	20 52.7
13 Su	5 28 32	22 47 55	29 10 28	5♉14 09	10R39.8	16 10.9	14 45.4	23 28.0	10 01.4	11 08.5	13 36.4	6 47.6	15 12.2	20 51.1
14 M	5 32 29	23 45 15	11♉15 18	17 14 24	10 39.7	18 20.3	14 11.5	24 05.8	10 26.0	11 15.0	13 43.8	6 47.4	15 11.3	20 49.6
15 Tu	5 36 25	24 42 34	23 11 51	29 08 05	10 37.8	20 30.6	13 39.1	24 43.6	10 50.6	11 21.7	13 51.3	6 47.2	15 10.5	20 48.0
16 W	5 40 22	25 39 53	5♊03 25	10♊58 12	10 34.0	22 41.8	13 08.2	25 21.4	11 15.3	11 28.5	13 58.9	6 46.9	15 09.6	20 46.4
17 Th	5 44 19	26 37 11	16 52 42	22 47 13	10 28.1	24 53.4	12 39.0	25 59.2	11 40.1	11 35.5	14 06.4	6 46.6	15 08.7	20 44.8
18 F	5 48 15	27 34 29	28 41 58	4♋37 11	10 20.4	27 05.2	12 11.8	26 37.0	12 05.0	11 42.5	14 14.0	6 46.3	15 07.7	20 43.2
19 Sa	5 52 12	28 31 47	10♋33 04	16 29 52	10 11.6	29 17.0	11 46.4	27 14.8	12 29.9	11 49.7	14 21.6	6 45.9	15 06.8	20 41.6
20 Su	5 56 08	29 29 04	22 27 46	28 27 00	10 02.4	1♋28.4	11 23.2	27 52.6	12 54.9	11 57.1	14 29.2	6 45.4	15 05.8	20 40.1
21 M	6 00 05	0♋26 20	4♌27 49	10♌30 28	9 53.7	3 39.3	11 02.2	28 30.4	13 20.0	12 04.5	14 36.8	6 44.9	15 04.7	20 38.5
22 Tu	6 04 01	1 23 35	16 35 14	22 42 26	9 46.4	5 49.2	10 43.4	29 08.3	13 45.1	12 12.1	14 44.5	6 44.4	15 03.7	20 37.0
23 W	6 07 58	2 20 50	28 52 24	5♍05 31	9 40.9	7 58.2	10 27.0	29 46.0	14 10.3	12 19.8	14 52.1	6 43.8	15 02.6	20 35.4
24 Th	6 11 54	3 18 05	11♍22 11	17 42 47	9 37.6	10 05.8	10 12.8	0♌23.8	14 35.6	12 27.6	14 59.8	6 43.2	15 01.5	20 33.9
25 F	6 15 51	4 15 18	24 07 47	0♎37 36	9D36.3	12 12.0	10 01.1	1 01.6	15 00.9	12 35.6	15 07.5	6 42.5	15 00.4	20 32.3
26 Sa	6 19 48	5 12 31	7♎12 40	13 53 21	9 36.6	14 16.7	9 51.7	1 39.4	15 26.3	12 43.7	15 15.2	6 41.8	14 59.3	20 30.8
27 Su	6 23 44	6 09 44	20 40 01	27 32 56	9R37.4	16 19.7	9 44.7	2 17.2	15 51.8	12 51.8	15 22.9	6 41.0	14 58.1	20 29.3
28 M	6 27 41	7 06 56	4♏32 16	11♏38 05	9 37.7	18 20.8	9 40.1	2 55.0	16 17.3	13 00.1	15 30.7	6 40.2	14 56.9	20 27.8
29 Tu	6 31 37	8 04 08	18 50 16	26 08 32	9 36.7	20 20.1	9D37.8	3 32.8	16 42.8	13 08.5	15 38.4	6 39.3	14 55.7	20 26.3
30 W	6 35 34	9 01 19	3♐32 24	11♐01 13	9 33.5	22 17.5	9 37.9	4 10.6	17 08.5	13 17.0	15 46.2	6 38.4	14 54.5	20 24.8

Astro Data	Dy Hr Mn
♃⚹♄	1 20:32
☽0S	2 6:00
♃ D	5 3:07
☽0N	14 23:10
♆ R	17 12:14
♀ R	17 22:30
☽0S	29 15:28
♅ R	10 15:48
☽0N	11 4:29
♄⊼♆	24 16:41
☽0S	25 22:40
♀ D	29 23:17

Planet Ingress	Dy Hr Mn
♂ ♋	7 8:47
☿ ♉	16 6:55
⚳ ♌	18 18:01
☉ ♊	20 17:00
☿ ♊	5 12:49
☿ ♋	19 19:51
☉ ♋	21 0:58
♂ ♌	23 20:52

Last Aspect Dy Hr Mn		☽ Ingress Dy Hr Mn	
1 11:32	♂□	♎	1 18:04
3 16:50	♂△	♏	3 20:40
4 21:38	♆□	♐	5 21:09
7 11:52	☿☍	♑	7 21:18
9 13:04	☿□	♒	9 22:47
11 19:32	☿⚹	♓	12 2:53
14 2:15	♀⚹	♈	14 10:03
16 12:18	♀⚹	♉	16 19:58
19 4:53	☉☌	♊	19 7:48
21 12:15	♀☌	♋	21 20:36
22 18:59	♄☌	♌	24 9:08
26 9:43	♀⚹	♍	26 19:53
28 16:18	♀□	♎	29 3:24
30 19:10	♀△	♏	31 7:09

Last Aspect Dy Hr Mn		☽ Ingress Dy Hr Mn	
1 21:17	☿☍	♐	2 7:53
3 17:13	♇☌	♑	4 7:13
5 12:29	♂☍	♒	6 7:11
7 18:10	♇⚹	♓	8 9:39
9 23:38	♂△	♈	10 15:50
12 11:32	♂□	♉	13 1:38
15 2:35	♂⚹	♊	15 13:45
17 20:28	☉☌	♋	18 2:38
20 10:47	♂☌	♌	20 15:06
22 7:55	♇△	♍	23 2:11
24 17:20	♇□	♎	25 10:51
26 23:42	♇⚹	♏	27 16:14
29 0:58	☿△	♐	29 18:17

☽ Phases & Eclipses Dy Hr Mn	
4 20:34	○ 14♏42
4 20:31	• T 1.303
11 11:05	☾ 21♒05
19 4:53	● 28♉33
27 7:58	☽ 6♍22
3 4:21	○ 12♐56
9 20:03	☾ 19♓18
17 20:28	● 26♊57
25 19:09	☽ 4♎32

Astro Data

1 May 2004
Julian Day # 38107
SVP 5♓12'10"
GC 26♐54.0 ⚴ 3♊49.2
Eris 20♈24.7 ⚵ 24♑03.7
⚷ 26♑07.9 ⚶ 6♓29.1
☽ Mean ☊ 11♉16.0

1 June 2004
Julian Day # 38138
SVP 5♓12'05"
GC 26♐54.1 ⚴ 21♊50.2
Eris 20♈41.4 ⚵ 24♑04.3R
⚷ 25♑33.9R ⚶ 18♓02.1
☽ Mean ☊ 9♉37.5

July 2004 LONGITUDE

Day	Sid.Time	☉	0 hr ☽	Noon ☽	True ☊	☿	♀	♂	⚳	♃	♄	♅	♆	♇
1 Th	6 39 30	9♋58 30	18♐34 04	26♐09 54	9♉27.9	24♋12.9	9♊40.2	4♌48.3	17♌34.1	13♍25.7	15♋53.9	6♓37.5	14♒53.3	20♐23.3
2 F	6 43 27	10 55 41	3♑47 30	11♑25 30	9R 20.3	26 06.3	9 44.9	5 26.1	17 59.9	13 34.4	16 01.7	6R 36.5	14R 52.0	20R 21.8
3 Sa	6 47 23	11 52 52	19 02 34	26 37 18	9 11.4	27 57.7	9 51.7	6 03.9	18 25.7	13 43.3	16 09.5	6 35.4	14 50.7	20 20.4
4 Su	6 51 20	12 50 03	4♒08 25	11♒34 46	9 02.3	29 47.0	10 00.7	6 41.7	18 51.5	13 52.2	16 17.2	6 34.4	14 49.4	20 18.9
5 M	6 55 17	13 47 14	18 55 23	26 09 28	8 54.2	1♌34.3	10 11.9	7 19.5	19 17.4	14 01.2	16 25.0	6 33.2	14 48.1	20 17.5
6 Tu	6 59 13	14 44 25	3♓16 30	10♓16 08	8 47.8	3 19.5	10 25.0	7 57.3	19 43.4	14 10.4	16 32.8	6 32.1	14 46.7	20 16.1
7 W	7 03 10	15 41 37	17 08 17	23 53 01	8 43.6	5 02.7	10 40.2	8 35.0	20 09.4	14 19.6	16 40.6	6 30.9	14 45.4	20 14.7
8 Th	7 07 06	16 38 48	0♈30 34	7♈01 19	8D 41.7	6 43.8	10 57.3	9 12.8	20 35.4	14 29.0	16 48.4	6 29.6	14 44.0	20 13.3
9 F	7 11 03	17 36 01	13 25 44	19 44 23	8 41.3	8 22.9	11 16.3	9 50.6	21 01.5	14 38.4	16 56.2	6 28.3	14 42.6	20 11.9
10 Sa	7 14 59	18 33 13	25 57 51	2♉06 47	8R 41.6	9 59.9	11 37.1	10 28.4	21 27.6	14 48.0	17 03.9	6 27.0	14 41.2	20 10.6
11 Su	7 18 56	19 30 26	8♉11 49	14 13 36	8 41.6	11 34.9	11 59.7	11 06.2	21 53.8	14 57.6	17 11.7	6 25.6	14 39.8	20 09.2
12 M	7 22 52	20 27 40	20 12 44	26 09 50	8 40.2	13 07.8	12 23.9	11 44.0	22 20.1	15 07.3	17 19.5	6 24.2	14 38.3	20 07.9
13 Tu	7 26 49	21 24 54	2♊05 28	8♊00 08	8 36.7	14 38.6	12 49.8	12 21.8	22 46.4	15 17.2	17 27.3	6 22.8	14 36.9	20 06.6
14 W	7 30 46	22 22 09	13 54 18	19 48 26	8 30.5	16 07.3	13 17.3	12 59.7	23 12.7	15 27.1	17 35.1	6 21.3	14 35.4	20 05.3
15 Th	7 34 42	23 19 24	25 42 53	1♋37 59	8 21.6	17 34.0	13 46.2	13 37.5	23 39.1	15 37.1	17 42.9	6 19.8	14 33.9	20 04.1
16 F	7 38 39	24 16 40	7♋34 03	13 31 17	8 10.4	18 58.4	14 16.6	14 15.3	24 05.5	15 47.2	17 50.6	6 18.2	14 32.4	20 02.8
17 Sa	7 42 35	25 13 56	19 29 56	25 30 09	7 57.6	20 20.7	14 48.4	14 53.1	24 32.0	15 57.4	17 58.4	6 16.6	14 30.9	20 01.6
18 Su	7 46 32	26 11 12	1♌32 06	7♌35 54	7 44.3	21 40.8	15 21.6	15 31.0	24 58.5	16 07.6	18 06.1	6 15.0	14 29.4	20 00.4
19 M	7 50 28	27 08 29	13 41 42	19 49 35	7 31.6	22 58.6	15 56.0	16 08.8	25 25.0	16 18.0	18 13.9	6 13.4	14 27.9	19 59.2
20 Tu	7 54 25	28 05 46	25 59 43	2♍12 14	7 20.5	24 14.2	16 31.7	16 46.7	25 51.6	16 28.4	18 21.6	6 11.7	14 26.3	19 58.0
21 W	7 58 21	29 03 03	8♍27 17	14 45 06	7 11.9	25 27.3	17 08.5	17 24.5	26 18.3	16 38.9	18 29.3	6 09.9	14 24.8	19 56.9
22 Th	8 02 18	0♌00 21	21 05 52	27 29 52	7 06.0	26 38.1	17 46.6	18 02.4	26 44.9	16 49.5	18 37.0	6 08.2	14 23.2	19 55.8
23 F	8 06 15	0 57 39	3♎57 22	10♎28 41	7 02.9	27 46.3	18 25.7	18 40.2	27 11.6	17 00.2	18 44.7	6 06.4	14 21.6	19 54.7
24 Sa	8 10 11	1 54 57	17 04 07	23 44 01	7 01.8	28 51.9	19 05.9	19 18.1	27 38.3	17 10.9	18 52.4	6 04.5	14 20.0	19 53.6
25 Su	8 14 08	2 52 16	0♏28 39	7♏18 20	7 01.7	29 54.9	19 47.1	19 56.0	28 05.1	17 21.8	19 00.0	6 02.7	14 18.5	19 52.5
26 M	8 18 04	3 49 35	14 13 15	21 13 33	7 01.4	0♍55.1	20 29.4	20 33.8	28 31.9	17 32.6	19 07.6	6 00.8	14 16.9	19 51.5
27 Tu	8 22 01	4 46 55	28 19 17	5♐30 20	6 59.6	1 52.4	21 12.5	21 11.7	28 58.8	17 43.6	19 15.3	5 58.9	14 15.3	19 50.5
28 W	8 25 57	5 44 15	12♐46 26	20 07 10	6 55.5	2 46.7	21 56.6	21 49.6	29 25.6	17 54.6	19 22.9	5 56.9	14 13.7	19 49.5
29 Th	8 29 54	6 41 36	27 31 55	4♑59 52	6 48.8	3 37.8	22 41.6	22 27.5	29 52.5	18 05.7	19 30.4	5 55.0	14 12.1	19 48.5
30 F	8 33 51	7 38 57	12♑30 06	20 01 29	6 39.7	4 25.6	23 27.5	23 05.4	0♍19.4	18 16.9	19 38.0	5 53.0	14 10.4	19 47.6
31 Sa	8 37 47	8 36 19	27 32 49	5♒02 52	6 29.0	5 10.1	24 14.2	23 43.3	0 46.4	18 28.2	19 45.5	5 50.9	14 08.8	19 46.7

August 2004 LONGITUDE

Day	Sid.Time	☉	0 hr ☽	Noon ☽	True ☊	☿	♀	♂	⚳	♃	♄	♅	♆	♇
1 Su	8 41 44	9♌33 42	12♒30 25	19♒54 17	6♉17.9	5♍50.9	25♊01.7	24♌21.2	1♍13.4	18♍39.5	19♋53.0	5♓48.9	14♒07.2	19♐45.8
2 M	8 45 40	10 31 06	27 13 26	4♓26 59	6R 07.8	6 27.9	25 50.0	24 59.1	1 40.4	18 50.8	20 00.5	5R 46.8	14R 05.6	19R 45.0
3 Tu	8 49 37	11 28 30	11♓34 14	18 34 43	5 59.6	7 01.0	26 39.0	25 37.0	2 07.4	19 02.2	20 08.0	5 44.7	14 03.9	19 44.1
4 W	8 53 33	12 25 56	25 28 08	2♈14 23	5 53.8	7 29.9	27 28.7	26 14.9	2 34.5	19 13.7	20 15.4	5 42.6	14 02.3	19 43.3
5 Th	8 57 30	13 23 23	8♈53 36	15 25 59	5 50.6	7 54.5	28 19.2	26 52.9	3 01.6	19 25.3	20 22.8	5 40.5	14 00.7	19 42.5
6 F	9 01 26	14 20 51	21 51 55	28 11 54	5D 49.4	8 14.6	29 10.3	27 30.8	3 28.7	19 36.9	20 30.2	5 38.3	13 59.0	19 41.8
7 Sa	9 05 23	15 18 20	4♉26 29	10♉36 16	5R 49.3	8 29.9	0♋02.1	28 08.8	3 55.9	19 48.5	20 37.5	5 36.1	13 57.4	19 41.1
8 Su	9 09 19	16 15 51	16 41 55	22 44 05	5 49.2	8 40.4	0 54.5	28 46.8	4 23.1	20 00.2	20 44.8	5 33.9	13 55.8	19 40.4
9 M	9 13 16	17 13 24	28 43 38	4♊40 43	5 48.1	8R 45.7	1 47.5	29 24.8	4 50.3	20 12.0	20 52.1	5 31.7	13 54.1	19 39.7
10 Tu	9 17 13	18 10 57	10♊36 28	16 31 21	5 45.0	8 45.9	2 41.0	0♍02.8	5 17.5	20 23.8	20 59.3	5 29.4	13 52.5	19 39.1
11 W	9 21 09	19 08 32	22 25 56	28 20 45	5 39.3	8 40.6	3 35.2	0 40.8	5 44.7	20 35.7	21 06.6	5 27.2	13 50.9	19 38.4
12 Th	9 25 06	20 06 09	4♋16 17	10♋12 58	5 31.1	8 29.9	4 29.9	1 18.8	6 12.0	20 47.7	21 13.7	5 24.9	13 49.3	19 37.9
13 F	9 29 02	21 03 46	16 11 12	22 11 18	5 20.5	8 13.7	5 25.1	1 56.8	6 39.3	20 59.7	21 20.9	5 22.6	13 47.6	19 37.3
14 Sa	9 32 59	22 01 25	28 13 31	4♌18 05	5 08.4	7 52.0	6 20.8	2 34.9	7 06.7	21 11.7	21 28.0	5 20.3	13 46.0	19 36.8
15 Su	9 36 55	22 59 06	10♌25 09	16 34 50	4 55.6	7 24.9	7 17.0	3 12.9	7 34.0	21 23.8	21 35.1	5 18.0	13 44.4	19 36.3
16 M	9 40 52	23 56 47	22 47 13	29 02 20	4 43.4	6 52.7	8 13.7	3 51.0	8 01.4	21 35.9	21 42.1	5 15.7	13 42.8	19 35.8
17 Tu	9 44 49	24 54 30	5♍20 13	11♍40 52	4 32.8	6 15.6	9 10.9	4 29.1	8 28.7	21 48.1	21 49.1	5 13.3	13 41.2	19 35.4
18 W	9 48 45	25 52 14	18 04 17	24 30 29	4 24.6	5 34.0	10 08.5	5 07.2	8 56.1	22 00.3	21 56.0	5 11.0	13 39.6	19 35.0
19 Th	9 52 42	26 49 59	0♎59 28	7♎31 17	4 19.1	4 48.4	11 06.5	5 45.3	9 23.6	22 12.5	22 02.9	5 08.6	13 38.0	19 34.6
20 F	9 56 38	27 47 45	14 06 00	20 43 43	4 16.3	3 59.7	12 04.9	6 23.4	9 51.0	22 24.8	22 09.7	5 06.3	13 36.5	19 34.3
21 Sa	10 00 35	28 45 33	27 24 31	4♏08 32	4D 15.6	3 08.4	13 03.8	7 01.5	10 18.4	22 37.2	22 16.6	5 03.9	13 34.9	19 34.0
22 Su	10 04 31	29 43 22	10♏55 54	17 46 45	4R 15.9	2 15.6	14 03.0	7 39.7	10 45.9	22 49.5	22 23.3	5 01.5	13 33.3	19 33.7
23 M	10 08 28	0♍41 12	24 41 12	1♐39 19	4 16.2	1 22.2	15 02.6	8 17.8	11 13.4	23 02.0	22 30.0	4 59.1	13 31.8	19 33.4
24 Tu	10 12 24	1 39 03	8♐41 07	15 46 32	4 15.4	0 29.3	16 02.6	8 56.0	11 40.9	23 14.4	22 36.7	4 56.7	13 30.2	19 33.2
25 W	10 16 21	2 36 55	22 55 24	0♑07 27	4 12.6	29♌38.0	17 02.9	9 34.2	12 08.4	23 26.9	22 43.3	4 54.3	13 28.7	19 33.1
26 Th	10 20 18	3 34 49	7♑22 18	14 39 25	4 07.5	28 49.3	18 03.6	10 12.4	12 35.9	23 39.4	22 49.9	4 51.9	13 27.2	19 32.9
27 F	10 24 14	4 32 44	21 58 11	29 17 48	4 00.3	28 04.5	19 04.7	10 50.6	13 03.4	23 52.0	22 56.4	4 49.6	13 25.7	19 32.8
28 Sa	10 28 11	5 30 40	6♒37 27	13♒56 13	3 51.6	27 24.4	20 06.1	11 28.8	13 30.9	24 04.5	23 02.8	4 47.2	13 24.2	19 32.7
29 Su	10 32 07	6 28 37	21 13 12	28 27 27	3 42.6	26 50.0	21 07.8	12 07.0	13 58.5	24 17.1	23 09.2	4 44.8	13 22.7	19 32.6
30 M	10 36 04	7 26 37	5♓38 08	12♓44 29	3 34.3	26 22.2	22 09.8	12 45.2	14 26.0	24 29.8	23 15.6	4 42.4	13 21.3	19D 32.6
31 Tu	10 40 00	8 24 37	19 45 51	26 41 42	3 27.5	26 01.6	23 12.2	13 23.5	14 53.6	24 42.4	23 21.9	4 40.0	13 19.8	19 32.6

Astro Data	Planet Ingress	Last Aspect	☽ Ingress	Last Aspect	☽ Ingress	☽ Phases & Eclipses	Astro Data
Dy Hr Mn	Dy Hr Mn	Dy Hr Mn	Dy Hr Mn	Dy Hr Mn	Dy Hr Mn	Dy Hr Mn	
☽ 0N 8 10:40	☿ ♌ 4 14:53	1 2:54 ♇ ☌	♑ 1 18:02	1 20:52 ♀ △	♓ 2 4:35	2 11:10 ○ 10♑54	1 July 2004
♃⚻♆ 9 21:11	☉ ♌ 22 11:51	3 14:26 ☿ ☍	♒ 3 17:23	4 2:59 ♀ □	♈ 4 8:00	9 7:35 ☾ 17♈25	Julian Day # 38168
☽ 0S 23 3:48	☿ ♍ 25 13:59	5 2:16 ♇ ⚹	♓ 5 18:27	6 14:00 ♀ ⚹	♉ 6 15:27	17 11:25 ● 25♋13	SVP 5♓11'59"
♄⚻♇ 31 15:21	⚳ ♍ 29 18:40	7 5:31 ♇ □	♈ 7 23:04	9 0:47 ♂ □	♊ 9 2:34	25 3:38 ☽ 2♏32	GC 26♐54.1 ⚵ 9♋44.7
		9 12:53 ♇ △	♉ 10 7:52	10 20:00 ♃ □	♋ 11 15:21	31 18:06 ○ 8♒51	Eris 20♈50.6 ⚴ 19♑04.7R
☽ 0N 4 18:28	♀ ♋ 7 11:03	11 23:30 ☉ ⚹	♊ 12 19:46	13 10:18 ♄ ☌	♌ 14 3:31		⚷ 24♑06.6R ⚶ 25♓49.2
♃□♇ 6 21:32	♂ ♍ 10 10:15	14 12:34 ♇ ☍	♋ 15 8:41	16 1:25 ☉ ☌	♍ 16 13:50	7 22:02 ☾ 15♉42	☽ Mean ☊ 8♉02.2
♄⚼♅ 7 8:27	☉ ♍ 22 18:54	17 11:25 ☉ ☌	♌ 17 20:57	18 7:16 ♃ ☌	♎ 18 22:10	16 1:25 ● 23♌31	
☿ R 10 0:33	☿ ♌R 25 1:34	19 18:51 ☿ ☌	♍ 20 7:45	21 1:40 ☉ ⚹	♏ 21 4:38	23 10:13 ☽ 0♐37	1 August 2004
♃⚹♄ 17 16:34		21 21:49 ♇ □	♎ 22 16:40	22 20:55 ♃ ⚹	♐ 23 9:10	30 2:23 ○ 7♓03	Julian Day # 38199
☽ 0S 19 8:31		24 21:55 ☿ ⚹	♏ 24 23:09	25 11:14 ☿ △	♑ 25 11:48		SVP 5♓11'53"
♇ D 30 19:39		26 10:49 ♂ □	♐ 27 2:49	27 2:59 ♃ △	♒ 27 13:09		GC 26♐54.2 ⚵ 28♋09.1
		28 15:07 ♀ ☍	♑ 29 3:59	29 9:24 ☿ ☍	♓ 29 14:34		Eris 20♈50.6R ⚴ 12♑10.1R
		30 11:22 ♄ ☍	♒ 31 3:55	31 8:29 ♃ ☍	♈ 31 17:47		⚷ 22♑17.1R ⚶ 28♓18.5R
							☽ Mean ☊ 6♉23.8

LONGITUDE — September 2004

Day	Sid.Time	☉	0 hr ☽	Noon☽	True☊	☿	♀	♂	⚳	♃	♄	♅	♆	♇
1 W	10 43 57	9♍22 40	3♈31 42	10♈15 38	3♉22.9	25♌48.8	24♋14.8	14♍01.8	15♍21.2	24♍55.1	23♋28.1	4♓37.6	13♒18.4	19♐32.7
2 Th	10 47 53	10 20 44	16 53 26	23 25 12	3D 20.5	25D 44.2	25 17.8	14 40.0	15 48.7	25 07.8	23 34.3	4R 35.2	13R 17.0	19 32.7
3 F	10 51 50	11 18 50	29 51 08	6♉11 33	3 20.1	25 48.0	26 21.0	15 18.3	16 16.3	25 20.6	23 40.4	4 32.8	13 15.6	19 32.8
4 Sa	10 55 46	12 16 58	12♉26 53	18 37 36	3 20.9	26 00.5	27 24.6	15 56.7	16 43.9	25 33.3	23 46.4	4 30.5	13 14.2	19 33.0
5 Su	10 59 43	13 15 08	24 44 16	0♊47 29	3 22.1	26 21.7	28 28.4	16 35.0	17 11.5	25 46.1	23 52.4	4 28.1	13 12.8	19 33.1
6 M	11 03 40	14 13 20	6♊47 52	12 46 03	3R 22.8	26 51.5	29 32.5	17 13.4	17 39.2	25 58.9	23 58.4	4 25.8	13 11.5	19 33.3
7 Tu	11 07 36	15 11 34	18 42 41	24 38 25	3 22.2	27 29.7	0♌36.8	17 51.7	18 06.8	26 11.8	24 04.3	4 23.4	13 10.2	19 33.6
8 W	11 11 33	16 09 50	0♋33 52	6♋29 39	3 19.9	28 16.0	1 41.4	18 30.1	18 34.4	26 24.6	24 10.1	4 21.1	13 08.9	19 33.8
9 Th	11 15 29	17 08 09	12 26 19	18 24 26	3 15.7	29 10.1	2 46.3	19 08.6	19 02.0	26 37.5	24 15.8	4 18.8	13 07.6	19 34.1
10 F	11 19 26	18 06 29	24 24 29	0♌26 54	3 09.7	0♍11.7	3 51.4	19 47.0	19 29.7	26 50.4	24 21.5	4 16.4	13 06.3	19 34.5
11 Sa	11 23 22	19 04 51	6♌32 05	12 40 20	3 02.4	1 20.1	4 56.8	20 25.4	19 57.3	27 03.3	24 27.1	4 14.1	13 05.0	19 34.8
12 Su	11 27 19	20 03 15	18 51 56	25 07 04	2 54.6	2 34.9	6 02.3	21 03.9	20 25.0	27 16.2	24 32.6	4 11.9	13 03.8	19 35.2
13 M	11 31 15	21 01 41	1♍25 51	7♍48 21	2 47.0	3 55.6	7 08.1	21 42.4	20 52.6	27 29.1	24 38.1	4 09.6	13 02.6	19 35.7
14 Tu	11 35 12	22 00 09	14 14 35	20 44 30	2 40.5	5 21.5	8 14.1	22 20.9	21 20.2	27 42.0	24 43.5	4 07.3	13 01.4	19 36.1
15 W	11 39 09	22 58 39	27 17 59	3♎54 54	2 35.6	6 52.1	9 20.4	22 59.4	21 47.9	27 55.0	24 48.8	4 05.1	13 00.2	19 36.6
16 Th	11 43 05	23 57 10	10♎35 05	17 18 21	2 32.7	8 26.7	10 26.8	23 38.0	22 15.5	28 07.9	24 54.0	4 02.9	12 59.1	19 37.1
17 F	11 47 02	24 55 44	24 04 31	0♏53 23	2D 31.7	10 04.9	11 33.5	24 16.5	22 43.2	28 20.9	24 59.2	4 00.7	12 58.0	19 37.7
18 Sa	11 50 58	25 54 19	7♏44 46	14 38 29	2 32.2	11 46.1	12 40.3	24 55.1	23 10.8	28 33.8	25 04.3	3 58.5	12 56.9	19 38.3
19 Su	11 54 55	26 52 56	21 34 23	28 32 18	2 33.5	13 29.8	13 47.3	25 33.7	23 38.4	28 46.8	25 09.3	3 56.4	12 55.8	19 38.9
20 M	11 58 51	27 51 35	5♐32 05	12♐33 37	2 34.9	15 15.4	14 54.6	26 12.3	24 06.1	28 59.8	25 14.2	3 54.2	12 54.8	19 39.6
21 Tu	12 02 48	28 50 15	19 36 42	26 41 12	2R 35.7	17 02.6	16 02.0	26 51.0	24 33.7	29 12.8	25 19.1	3 52.1	12 53.8	19 40.3
22 W	12 06 44	29 48 57	3♑46 53	10♑53 32	2 35.2	18 51.0	17 09.6	27 29.6	25 01.3	29 25.7	25 23.8	3 50.1	12 52.8	19 41.0
23 Th	12 10 41	0♎47 41	18 00 52	25 08 32	2 33.3	20 40.2	18 17.3	28 08.3	25 28.9	29 38.7	25 28.5	3 48.0	12 51.8	19 41.7
24 F	12 14 38	1 46 26	2♒16 10	9♒23 21	2 30.1	22 29.9	19 25.3	28 47.0	25 56.5	29 51.7	25 33.1	3 46.0	12 50.9	19 42.5
25 Sa	12 18 34	2 45 13	16 29 35	23 34 23	2 25.9	24 20.0	20 33.4	29 25.7	26 24.1	0♎04.6	25 37.7	3 44.0	12 49.9	19 43.3
26 Su	12 22 31	3 44 02	0♓37 14	7♓37 38	2 21.5	26 10.1	21 41.7	0♎04.4	26 51.7	0 17.6	25 42.1	3 42.0	12 49.1	19 44.2
27 M	12 26 27	4 42 52	14 35 04	21 29 04	2 17.4	28 00.1	22 50.2	0 43.1	27 19.2	0 30.6	25 46.5	3 40.0	12 48.2	19 45.1
28 Tu	12 30 24	5 41 45	28 19 13	5♈05 11	2 14.3	29 49.8	23 58.8	1 21.9	27 46.8	0 43.5	25 50.7	3 38.1	12 47.4	19 46.0
29 W	12 34 20	6 40 39	11♈46 42	18 23 34	2 12.3	1♎39.1	25 07.7	2 00.7	28 14.3	0 56.5	25 54.9	3 36.2	12 46.5	19 46.9
30 Th	12 38 17	7 39 36	24 55 41	1♉23 03	2D 11.6	3 28.0	26 16.6	2 39.5	28 41.9	1 09.4	25 59.0	3 34.3	12 45.8	19 47.9

LONGITUDE — October 2004

Day	Sid.Time	☉	0 hr ☽	Noon☽	True☊	☿	♀	♂	⚳	♃	♄	♅	♆	♇
1 F	12 42 13	8♎38 35	7♉45 46	14♉03 58	2♉12.0	5♎16.2	27♌25.8	3♎18.3	29♍09.4	1♎22.3	26♋03.0	3♓32.5	12♒45.0	19♐48.9
2 Sa	12 46 10	9 37 36	20 17 56	26 27 58	2 13.3	7 03.8	28 35.0	3 57.2	29 36.9	1 35.2	26 06.9	3R 30.7	12R 44.3	19 49.9
3 Su	12 50 07	10 36 39	2♊34 27	8♊37 50	2 14.9	8 50.8	29 44.5	4 36.1	0♎04.4	1 48.2	26 10.7	3 28.9	12 43.6	19 50.9
4 M	12 54 03	11 35 44	14 38 36	20 37 17	2 16.5	10 37.0	0♍54.1	5 15.0	0 31.9	2 01.1	26 14.5	3 27.2	12 43.0	19 52.0
5 Tu	12 58 00	12 34 52	26 34 27	2♋30 40	2R 17.6	12 22.5	2 03.8	5 53.9	0 59.4	2 13.9	26 18.1	3 25.5	12 42.3	19 53.1
6 W	13 01 56	13 34 02	8♋26 32	14 22 39	2 18.0	14 07.2	3 13.7	6 32.8	1 26.9	2 26.8	26 21.7	3 23.9	12 41.7	19 54.3
7 Th	13 05 53	14 33 15	20 19 37	26 18 03	2 17.5	15 51.1	4 23.8	7 11.8	1 54.3	2 39.6	26 25.1	3 22.2	12 41.2	19 55.5
8 F	13 09 49	15 32 30	2♌18 30	8♌21 31	2 16.2	17 34.3	5 33.9	7 50.8	2 21.8	2 52.5	26 28.5	3 20.6	12 40.6	19 56.7
9 Sa	13 13 46	16 31 46	14 27 37	20 37 16	2 14.4	19 16.7	6 44.2	8 29.8	2 49.2	3 05.3	26 31.7	3 19.1	12 40.1	19 57.9
10 Su	13 17 42	17 31 06	26 50 53	3♍08 50	2 12.2	20 58.3	7 54.7	9 08.9	3 16.6	3 18.1	26 34.9	3 17.6	12 39.6	19 59.2
11 M	13 21 39	18 30 27	9♍31 24	15 58 45	2 10.2	22 39.2	9 05.2	9 48.0	3 44.0	3 30.9	26 37.9	3 16.1	12 39.2	20 00.4
12 Tu	13 25 36	19 29 51	22 31 03	29 08 17	2 08.4	24 19.3	10 15.9	10 27.1	4 11.3	3 43.6	26 40.9	3 14.6	12 38.8	20 01.8
13 W	13 29 32	20 29 16	5♎50 25	12♎37 17	2 07.2	25 58.7	11 26.7	11 06.2	4 38.7	3 56.3	26 43.8	3 13.2	12 38.4	20 03.1
14 Th	13 33 29	21 28 44	19 28 38	26 24 08	2D 06.7	27 37.4	12 37.7	11 45.3	5 06.0	4 09.0	26 46.5	3 11.9	12 38.0	20 04.5
15 F	13 37 25	22 28 14	3♏23 24	10♏25 56	2 06.7	29 15.4	13 48.7	12 24.5	5 33.3	4 21.7	26 49.2	3 10.6	12 37.7	20 05.9
16 Sa	13 41 22	23 27 46	17 31 16	24 38 50	2 07.2	0♏52.8	14 59.9	13 03.7	6 00.6	4 34.3	26 51.7	3 09.3	12 37.5	20 07.3
17 Su	13 45 18	24 27 20	1♐48 06	8♐58 29	2 07.9	2 29.4	16 11.1	13 42.9	6 27.8	4 46.9	26 54.2	3 08.1	12 37.2	20 08.7
18 M	13 49 15	25 26 55	16 09 28	23 20 32	2 08.5	4 05.5	17 22.5	14 22.1	6 55.0	4 59.5	26 56.5	3 06.9	12 37.0	20 10.2
19 Tu	13 53 11	26 26 33	0♑31 12	7♑41 02	2 09.0	5 40.9	18 34.0	15 01.4	7 22.2	5 12.0	26 58.7	3 05.7	12 36.8	20 11.7
20 W	13 57 08	27 26 12	14 49 40	21 56 43	2R 09.3	7 15.6	19 45.6	15 40.7	7 49.4	5 24.5	27 00.9	3 04.6	12 36.7	20 13.3
21 Th	14 01 05	28 25 52	29 01 55	6♒05 00	2 09.3	8 49.8	20 57.3	16 20.0	8 16.5	5 37.0	27 02.9	3 03.6	12 36.5	20 14.8
22 F	14 05 01	29 25 35	13♒05 45	20 03 58	2 09.1	10 23.4	22 09.0	16 59.3	8 43.6	5 49.4	27 04.8	3 02.6	12 36.5	20 16.4
23 Sa	14 08 58	0♏25 19	26 59 30	3♓52 12	2 08.9	11 56.5	23 20.9	17 38.7	9 10.7	6 01.8	27 06.6	3 01.6	12D 36.4	20 18.0
24 Su	14 12 54	1 25 04	10♓41 56	17 28 37	2D 08.7	13 28.9	24 32.9	18 18.0	9 37.7	6 14.2	27 08.3	3 00.7	12 36.4	20 19.6
25 M	14 16 51	2 24 52	24 12 07	0♈52 21	2 08.7	15 00.8	25 45.0	18 57.4	10 04.7	6 26.5	27 09.9	2 59.8	12 36.4	20 21.3
26 Tu	14 20 47	3 24 41	7♈29 15	14 02 46	2 08.8	16 32.2	26 57.1	19 36.8	10 31.7	6 38.7	27 11.4	2 59.0	12 36.5	20 22.9
27 W	14 24 44	4 24 32	20 32 50	26 59 26	2R 08.9	18 03.0	28 09.4	20 16.3	10 58.6	6 50.9	27 12.8	2 58.2	12 36.6	20 24.6
28 Th	14 28 40	5 24 25	3♉22 35	9♉42 19	2 08.8	19 33.4	29 21.8	20 55.8	11 25.5	7 03.1	27 14.0	2 57.5	12 36.7	20 26.3
29 F	14 32 37	6 24 20	15 58 42	22 11 49	2 08.6	21 03.1	0♎34.2	21 35.3	11 52.4	7 15.2	27 15.2	2 56.8	12 36.8	20 28.1
30 Sa	14 36 33	7 24 17	28 21 51	4♊28 58	2 08.1	22 32.4	1 46.8	22 14.8	12 19.2	7 27.3	27 16.2	2 56.1	12 37.0	20 29.8
31 Su	14 40 30	8 24 16	10♊33 23	16 35 25	2 07.3	24 01.1	2 59.4	22 54.3	12 46.0	7 39.4	27 17.2	2 55.6	12 37.2	20 31.6

Astro Data

	Dy Hr Mn
☽0N	1 3:33
☿D	2 13:11
☽0S	15 14:47
♃⚼♆	15 21:00
☉0S	22 16:30
☽0N	28 12:39
♂0S	29 13:28
☿0S	30 14:54
♃0S	6 19:14
♃⚻♅	10 11:08
☽0S	12 23:21
♆D	24 11:57
☽0N	25 20:22

Planet Ingress

		Dy Hr Mn
♀	♌	6 22:17
☿	♍	10 7:39
☉	♎	22 16:31
♃	♎	25 3:24
♂	♎	26 9:17
☿	♎	28 14:14
⚳	♎	3 8:07
♀	♍	3 17:21
☿	♏	15 22:58
☉	♏	23 1:50
♀	♎	29 0:40

Last Aspect / ☽ Ingress (September)

Last Aspect Dy Hr Mn		☽ Ingress	Dy Hr Mn
2 16:18	☿ △	♉	3 0:17
5 6:57	♀ ⚹	♊	5 10:26
7 18:09	☿ ⚹	♋	7 22:51
10 4:43	♃ ⚹	♌	10 11:07
12 1:23	♇ △	♍	12 21:17
15 0:56	♃ ☌	♎	15 4:55
17 1:33	♄ □	♏	17 10:26
19 12:25	♃ ⚹	♐	19 14:31
21 16:20	♃ □	♑	21 17:36
23 19:42	♃ △	♒	23 20:11
25 6:26	♀ ☍	♓	25 22:56
28 1:13	☿ ☍	♈	28 2:58
30 1:54	♄ □	♉	30 9:25

Last Aspect / ☽ Ingress (October)

Last Aspect Dy Hr Mn		☽ Ingress	Dy Hr Mn
2 16:35	♀ □	♊	2 18:56
4 10:29	♇ ☍	♋	5 6:55
7 12:14	♄ ☌	♌	7 19:24
9 10:44	♇ △	♍	10 6:01
12 7:33	♄ ⚹	♎	12 13:33
14 14:23	☿ ☌	♏	14 18:11
16 15:44	♄ △	♐	16 20:59
18 15:47	☉ ⚹	♑	18 23:08
20 22:00	☉ □	♒	21 1:39
22 12:22	♇ ⚹	♓	23 5:14
25 5:18	♄ △	♈	25 10:25
27 12:25	♄ □	♉	27 17:39
29 21:51	♄ ⚹	♊	30 3:12

☽ Phases & Eclipses

Dy Hr Mn		
6 15:12	☾	14♊21
14 14:30	●	22♍06
21 15:55	☽	29♐00
28 13:10	○	5♈45
6 10:13	☾	13♋30
14 2:49	●	21♎06
14 3:00:23	•	P 0.928
20 22:00	☽	27♑51
28 3:08	○	5♉02
28 3:05	•	T 1.308

Astro Data

1 September 2004
Julian Day # 38230
SVP 5♓11'49"
GC 26♐54.3 ⚴ 15♌54.8
Eris 20♈41.1R ⚵ 9♑09.7R
⚷ 20♑53.9R ⚶ 23♓46.0R
☽ Mean ☊ 4♉45.3

1 October 2004
Julian Day # 38260
SVP 5♓11'46"
GC 26♐54.3 ⚴ 2♍02.4
Eris 20♈25.4R ⚵ 11♑47.7
⚷ 20♑31.0 ⚶ 16♓35.3R
☽ Mean ☊ 3♉09.9

November 2004 LONGITUDE

Day	Sid.Time	☉	0 hr ☽	Noon ☽	True☊	☿	♀	♂	⚳	♃	♄	♅	♆	♇
1 M	14 44 27	9♏24 17	22♊35 22	28♊33 35	2♉06.4	25♏29.3	4♎12.1	23♎33.9	13♎12.8	7♎51.3	27♋18.0	2♓55.0	12♒37.5	20♐33.4
2 Tu	14 48 23	10 24 20	4♋30 30	10♋26 32	2R 05.3	26 56.9	5 24.9	24 13.5	13 39.5	8 03.3	27 18.7	2R 54.5	12 37.8	20 35.3
3 W	14 52 20	11 24 25	16 22 12	22 17 59	2 04.4	28 23.9	6 37.8	24 53.2	14 06.1	8 15.1	27 19.3	2 54.1	12 38.1	20 37.1
4 Th	14 56 16	12 24 33	28 14 26	4♌12 07	2D 03.8	29 50.4	7 50.7	25 32.9	14 32.8	8 27.0	27 19.8	2 53.7	12 38.5	20 39.0
5 F	15 00 13	13 24 42	10♌11 36	16 13 28	2 03.7	1♐16.2	9 03.8	26 12.5	14 59.4	8 38.7	27 20.2	2 53.3	12 38.9	20 40.8
6 Sa	15 04 09	14 24 53	22 18 19	28 26 42	2 04.1	2 41.3	10 16.9	26 52.3	15 25.9	8 50.4	27 20.4	2 53.0	12 39.3	20 42.7
7 Su	15 08 06	15 25 07	4♍39 12	10♍56 19	2 05.0	4 05.7	11 30.1	27 32.0	15 52.4	9 02.1	27R 20.6	2 52.8	12 39.7	20 44.7
8 M	15 12 03	16 25 22	17 18 32	23 46 16	2 06.2	5 29.4	12 43.3	28 11.8	16 18.9	9 13.6	27 20.6	2 52.6	12 40.2	20 46.6
9 Tu	15 15 59	17 25 40	0♎19 51	6♎59 30	2 07.5	6 52.2	13 56.7	28 51.6	16 45.3	9 25.1	27 20.5	2 52.5	12 40.8	20 48.5
10 W	15 19 56	18 25 59	13 45 22	20 37 28	2R 08.4	8 14.1	15 10.1	29 31.4	17 11.7	9 36.6	27 20.3	2 52.4	12 41.3	20 50.5
11 Th	15 23 52	19 26 20	27 35 38	4♏39 36	2 08.6	9 35.0	16 23.5	0♏11.3	17 38.0	9 48.0	27 20.0	2D 52.3	12 41.9	20 52.5
12 F	15 27 49	20 26 43	11♏48 55	19 03 01	2 08.0	10 54.7	17 37.0	0 51.2	18 04.2	9 59.3	27 19.6	2 52.3	12 42.5	20 54.5
13 Sa	15 31 45	21 27 08	26 21 11	3♐42 35	2 06.4	12 13.3	18 50.6	1 31.1	18 30.4	10 10.5	27 19.1	2 52.4	12 43.2	20 56.5
14 Su	15 35 42	22 27 34	11♐06 16	18 31 17	2 03.9	13 30.4	20 04.3	2 11.1	18 56.6	10 21.7	27 18.4	2 52.5	12 43.9	20 58.6
15 M	15 39 38	23 28 02	25 56 37	3♑21 18	2 01.0	14 46.0	21 18.0	2 51.0	19 22.7	10 32.8	27 17.7	2 52.7	12 44.6	21 00.6
16 Tu	15 43 35	24 28 31	10♑44 23	18 05 03	1 58.1	15 59.9	22 31.7	3 31.0	19 48.7	10 43.8	27 16.8	2 52.9	12 45.4	21 02.7
17 W	15 47 32	25 29 02	25 22 34	2♒36 21	1 55.7	17 11.8	23 45.5	4 11.1	20 14.7	10 54.8	27 15.8	2 53.2	12 46.2	21 04.8
18 Th	15 51 28	26 29 34	9♒45 54	16 50 55	1D 54.3	18 21.5	24 59.4	4 51.1	20 40.6	11 05.6	27 14.7	2 53.5	12 47.0	21 06.9
19 F	15 55 25	27 30 07	23 51 13	0♓46 41	1 54.0	19 28.6	26 13.3	5 31.2	21 06.5	11 16.4	27 13.5	2 53.9	12 47.9	21 09.0
20 Sa	15 59 21	28 30 41	7♓37 22	14 23 21	1 54.8	20 32.9	27 27.2	6 11.3	21 32.3	11 27.1	27 12.2	2 54.3	12 48.8	21 11.1
21 Su	16 03 18	29 31 16	21 04 48	27 41 55	1 56.3	21 33.9	28 41.2	6 51.4	21 58.0	11 37.7	27 10.8	2 54.8	12 49.7	21 13.2
22 M	16 07 14	0♐31 52	4♈14 57	10♈44 08	1 58.0	22 31.2	29 55.2	7 31.6	22 23.7	11 48.3	27 09.3	2 55.3	12 50.7	21 15.4
23 Tu	16 11 11	1 32 30	17 09 44	23 32 01	1R 59.2	23 24.4	1♏09.3	8 11.7	22 49.3	11 58.7	27 07.6	2 55.9	12 51.6	21 17.5
24 W	16 15 07	2 33 09	29 51 11	6♉07 28	1 59.4	24 12.7	2 23.5	8 52.0	23 14.8	12 09.1	27 05.9	2 56.5	12 52.7	21 19.7
25 Th	16 19 04	3 33 49	12♉21 04	18 32 10	1 58.2	24 55.8	3 37.6	9 32.2	23 40.2	12 19.4	27 04.0	2 57.2	12 53.7	21 21.8
26 F	16 23 01	4 34 31	24 40 58	0♊47 35	1 55.2	25 32.7	4 51.9	10 12.5	24 05.6	12 29.5	27 02.1	2 57.9	12 54.8	21 24.0
27 Sa	16 26 57	5 35 13	6♊52 12	12 54 59	1 50.5	26 02.9	6 06.1	10 52.8	24 31.0	12 39.6	27 00.0	2 58.7	12 55.9	21 26.2
28 Su	16 30 54	6 35 58	18 56 03	24 55 37	1 44.4	26 25.5	7 20.4	11 33.1	24 56.2	12 49.6	26 57.9	2 59.5	12 57.0	21 28.4
29 M	16 34 50	7 36 43	0♋53 52	6♋51 02	1 37.6	26 39.7	8 34.8	12 13.4	25 21.4	12 59.5	26 55.6	3 00.4	12 58.2	21 30.6
30 Tu	16 38 47	8 37 30	12 47 20	18 43 05	1 30.5	26R 44.6	9 49.2	12 53.8	25 46.5	13 09.3	26 53.3	3 01.3	12 59.4	21 32.8

December 2004 LONGITUDE

Day	Sid.Time	☉	0 hr ☽	Noon ☽	True☊	☿	♀	♂	⚳	♃	♄	♅	♆	♇
1 W	16 42 43	9♐38 18	24♋38 35	0♌34 13	1♉24.0	26♐39.7	11♏03.6	13♏34.2	26♎11.5	13♎19.0	26♋50.8	3♓02.3	13♒00.7	21♐35.1
2 Th	16 46 40	10 39 08	6♌30 23	12 27 30	1R 18.7	26R 24.1	12 18.1	14 14.7	26 36.5	13 28.6	26R 48.2	3 03.3	13 01.9	21 37.3
3 F	16 50 36	11 39 59	18 26 05	24 26 39	1 15.1	25 57.5	13 32.6	14 55.2	27 01.3	13 38.1	26 45.6	3 04.4	13 03.2	21 39.5
4 Sa	16 54 33	12 40 51	0♍29 43	6♍35 54	1D 13.4	25 19.7	14 47.1	15 35.7	27 26.1	13 47.5	26 42.8	3 05.5	13 04.5	21 41.8
5 Su	16 58 30	13 41 44	12 45 46	18 59 54	1 13.3	24 30.8	16 01.7	16 16.2	27 50.8	13 56.8	26 40.0	3 06.7	13 05.9	21 44.0
6 M	17 02 26	14 42 39	25 18 55	1♎43 23	1 14.3	23 31.7	17 16.3	16 56.8	28 15.5	14 05.9	26 37.0	3 07.9	13 07.3	21 46.2
7 Tu	17 06 23	15 43 35	8♎13 49	14 50 40	1 15.8	22 23.6	18 30.9	17 37.4	28 40.0	14 15.0	26 34.0	3 09.2	13 08.7	21 48.5
8 W	17 10 19	16 44 33	21 34 20	28 25 04	1R 16.7	21 08.1	19 45.6	18 18.0	29 04.4	14 23.9	26 30.8	3 10.5	13 10.1	21 50.8
9 Th	17 14 16	17 45 31	5♏22 59	12♏28 03	1 16.1	19 47.6	21 00.3	18 58.7	29 28.8	14 32.8	26 27.6	3 11.9	13 11.5	21 53.0
10 F	17 18 12	18 46 30	19 40 02	26 58 28	1 13.6	18 24.7	22 15.0	19 39.3	29 53.1	14 41.5	26 24.3	3 13.3	13 13.0	21 55.3
11 Sa	17 22 09	19 47 32	4♐22 43	11♐51 54	1 08.7	17 02.3	23 29.8	20 20.1	0♏17.2	14 50.1	26 20.9	3 14.8	13 14.6	21 57.5
12 Su	17 26 05	20 48 34	19 24 57	27 00 40	1 01.9	15 43.1	24 44.5	21 00.8	0 41.3	14 58.6	26 17.4	3 16.3	13 16.1	21 59.8
13 M	17 30 02	21 49 36	4♑37 42	12♑14 40	0 53.8	14 29.6	25 59.3	21 41.6	1 05.3	15 06.9	26 13.9	3 17.9	13 17.7	22 02.1
14 Tu	17 33 59	22 50 39	19 50 14	27 23 05	0 45.6	13 23.9	27 14.2	22 22.4	1 29.2	15 15.2	26 10.2	3 19.5	13 19.3	22 04.3
15 W	17 37 55	23 51 43	4♒52 04	12♒16 12	0 38.3	12 27.6	28 29.0	23 03.2	1 52.9	15 23.3	26 06.5	3 21.1	13 20.9	22 06.6
16 Th	17 41 52	24 52 47	19 34 43	26 47 03	0 32.8	11 41.8	29 43.8	23 44.1	2 16.6	15 31.2	26 02.7	3 22.8	13 22.5	22 08.9
17 F	17 45 48	25 53 51	3♓52 50	10♓51 55	0 29.6	11 06.9	0♐58.7	24 25.0	2 40.2	15 39.1	25 58.9	3 24.6	13 24.2	22 11.1
18 Sa	17 49 45	26 54 56	17 44 21	24 30 17	0D 28.4	10 43.1	2 13.6	25 05.9	3 03.6	15 46.8	25 54.9	3 26.4	13 25.9	22 13.4
19 Su	17 53 41	27 56 01	1♈10 01	7♈43 56	0 28.7	10D 30.1	3 28.5	25 46.8	3 26.9	15 54.4	25 50.9	3 28.2	13 27.6	22 15.6
20 M	17 57 38	28 57 06	14 12 28	20 36 07	0R 29.6	10 27.4	4 43.4	26 27.8	3 50.2	16 01.8	25 46.8	3 30.1	13 29.3	22 17.9
21 Tu	18 01 35	29 58 11	26 55 22	3♉10 43	0 29.9	10 34.3	5 58.3	27 08.7	4 13.3	16 09.1	25 42.7	3 32.0	13 31.1	22 20.2
22 W	18 05 31	0♑59 17	9♉22 39	15 31 36	0 28.7	10 50.1	7 13.3	27 49.8	4 36.3	16 16.3	25 38.5	3 34.0	13 32.9	22 22.4
23 Th	18 09 28	2 00 23	21 38 01	27 42 16	0 25.0	11 13.9	8 28.2	28 30.8	4 59.1	16 23.3	25 34.2	3 36.0	13 34.7	22 24.6
24 F	18 13 24	3 01 29	3♊44 42	9♊45 36	0 18.5	11 45.1	9 43.2	29 11.9	5 21.9	16 30.2	25 29.9	3 38.0	13 36.5	22 26.9
25 Sa	18 17 21	4 02 36	15 45 15	21 43 52	0 09.3	12 22.8	10 58.2	29 53.0	5 44.5	16 37.0	25 25.5	3 40.1	13 38.3	22 29.1
26 Su	18 21 17	5 03 43	27 41 39	3♋38 48	29♈57.7	13 06.3	12 13.2	0♐34.1	6 07.0	16 43.6	25 21.1	3 42.3	13 40.2	22 31.3
27 M	18 25 14	6 04 50	9♋35 27	15 31 46	29 44.6	13 55.0	13 28.2	1 15.3	6 29.4	16 50.0	25 16.6	3 44.4	13 42.1	22 33.6
28 Tu	18 29 10	7 05 57	21 27 56	27 24 05	29 31.1	14 48.3	14 43.3	1 56.5	6 51.7	16 56.4	25 12.0	3 46.6	13 44.0	22 35.8
29 W	18 33 07	8 07 05	3♌20 26	9♌17 11	29 18.3	15 45.7	15 58.3	2 37.7	7 13.8	17 02.5	25 07.5	3 48.9	13 45.9	22 38.0
30 Th	18 37 04	9 08 13	15 14 35	21 12 55	29 07.2	16 46.7	17 13.3	3 19.0	7 35.8	17 08.5	25 02.8	3 51.2	13 47.9	22 40.2
31 F	18 41 00	10 09 21	27 12 32	3♍13 48	28 58.7	17 50.9	18 28.4	4 00.3	7 57.7	17 14.4	24 58.2	3 53.5	13 49.8	22 42.3

Astro Data

	Dy Hr Mn
♀0S	1 1:21
♄ R	8 6:55
☽0S	9 9:17
♅ D	11 19:13
⚳0S	13 13:11
☽0N	22 2:09
♃△♆	29 8:27
☿ R	30 12:18
☽0S	6 18:31
☽0N	19 7:07
☿ D	20 6:30

Planet Ingress

		Dy Hr Mn
☿	♐	4 14:41
♂	♏	11 5:12
☉	♐	21 23:23
♀	♏	22 13:32
⚳	♏	10 18:53
♀	♐	16 17:11
☉	♑	21 12:43
♂	♐	25 16:05
☊	♈R	26 7:30

Last Aspect / ☽ Ingress (November)

Last Aspect Dy Hr Mn		☽ Ingress Dy Hr Mn
1 1:22	♂ △	♋ 1 14:54
4 2:01	☿ △	♌ 4 3:33
6 8:46	♂ ✶	♍ 6 15:01
8 18:33	♄ ✶	♎ 8 23:24
11 4:03	♂ ☌	♏ 11 4:06
13 1:35	♄ △	♐ 13 5:57
14 15:59	♇ ☌	♑ 15 6:34
17 3:08	♄ ☍	♒ 17 7:40
19 5:51	☉ □	♓ 19 10:39
21 15:36	☉ △	♈ 21 16:12
23 18:48	♄ □	♉ 24 0:17
26 4:38	♄ ✶	♊ 26 10:26
28 15:05	☿ ☍	♋ 28 22:12

Last Aspect / ☽ Ingress (December)

Last Aspect Dy Hr Mn		☽ Ingress Dy Hr Mn
1 4:29	♄ ☌	♌ 1 10:51
3 14:53	☿ △	♍ 3 23:01
6 2:29	♄ ✶	♎ 6 8:47
8 8:42	♄ □	♏ 8 14:45
10 11:04	♄ △	♐ 10 16:55
12 4:04	♇ ☌	♑ 12 16:43
14 11:45	♀ ✶	♒ 14 16:11
16 8:34	☉ ✶	♓ 16 17:25
18 16:41	☉ □	♈ 18 21:53
21 5:17	☉ △	♉ 21 5:53
23 13:42	♂ ☍	♊ 23 16:33
25 13:31	♇ ☍	♋ 26 4:39
28 7:35	♄ ☌	♌ 28 17:15
30 14:55	♇ △	♍ 31 5:34

☽ Phases & Eclipses

Dy Hr Mn	
5 5:54	☾ 13♌09
12 14:28	● 20♏33
19 5:51	☽ 27♒15
26 20:08	○ 4♊55
5 0:54	☾ 13♍14
12 1:30	● 20♐22
18 16:41	☽ 27♓07
26 15:07	○ 5♋12

Astro Data

1 November 2004
Julian Day # 38291
SVP 5♓11'42"
GC 26♐54.4 ⚴ 17♍07.4
Eris 20♈07.1R ⚵ 19♑04.4
⚷ 21♑18.6 ⚶ 13♓57.4
☽ Mean ☊ 1♉31.4

1 December 2004
Julian Day # 38321
SVP 5♓11'37"
GC 26♐54.5 ⚴ 29♍32.1
Eris 19♈52.6R ⚵ 29♑06.0
⚷ 23♑04.9 ⚶ 17♓52.8
☽ Mean ☊ 29♈56.1

LONGITUDE — January 2005

Day	Sid.Time	☉	0 hr ☽	Noon ☽	True ☊	☿	♀	♂	⚳	♃	♄	♅	♆	♇
1 Sa	18 44 57	11♑10 30	9♍17 07	15♍22 57	28♈53.0	18♐57.9	19♐43.5	4♐41.6	8♏19.4	17♎20.1	24♋53.5	3♓55.9	13♒51.8	22♐44.5
2 Su	18 48 53	12 11 39	21 31 49	27 44 15	28R50.0	20 07.4	20 58.6	5 23.0	8 41.0	17 25.6	24R48.7	3 58.3	13 53.8	22 46.7
3 M	18 52 50	13 12 48	4♎00 49	10♎22 04	28D49.0	21 19.1	22 13.7	6 04.3	9 02.5	17 31.0	24 44.0	4 00.7	13 55.8	22 48.8
4 Tu	18 56 46	14 13 57	16 48 36	23 20 57	28R49.1	22 32.8	23 28.8	6 45.8	9 23.8	17 36.3	24 39.2	4 03.2	13 57.8	22 51.0
5 W	19 00 43	15 15 07	29 59 38	6♏45 06	28 49.0	23 48.3	24 43.9	7 27.2	9 44.9	17 41.3	24 34.3	4 05.7	13 59.9	22 53.1
6 Th	19 04 39	16 16 17	13♏37 41	20 37 34	28 47.4	25 05.4	25 59.1	8 08.7	10 05.9	17 46.2	24 29.5	4 08.3	14 01.9	22 55.3
7 F	19 08 36	17 17 27	27 44 49	4♐59 15	28 43.4	26 24.0	27 14.2	8 50.2	10 26.8	17 51.0	24 24.6	4 10.9	14 04.0	22 57.4
8 Sa	19 12 33	18 18 38	12♐20 30	19 47 55	28 36.6	27 43.8	28 29.4	9 31.7	10 47.5	17 55.5	24 19.7	4 13.5	14 06.1	22 59.5
9 Su	19 16 29	19 19 48	27 20 38	4♑57 34	28 27.0	29 04.8	29 44.5	10 13.3	11 08.0	17 59.9	24 14.8	4 16.1	14 08.2	23 01.6
10 M	19 20 26	20 20 58	12♑37 22	20 18 38	28 15.8	0♑26.9	0♑59.7	10 54.9	11 28.4	18 04.2	24 09.9	4 18.8	14 10.3	23 03.6
11 Tu	19 24 22	21 22 08	27 59 50	5♒39 24	28 04.0	1 50.0	2 14.8	11 36.5	11 48.6	18 08.2	24 04.9	4 21.5	14 12.5	23 05.7
12 W	19 28 19	22 23 17	13♒15 55	20 48 03	27 53.2	3 14.0	3 30.0	12 18.2	12 08.6	18 12.1	24 00.0	4 24.3	14 14.6	23 07.7
13 Th	19 32 15	23 24 26	28 14 41	5♓34 56	27 44.5	4 38.9	4 45.2	12 59.9	12 28.5	18 15.8	23 55.0	4 27.1	14 16.7	23 09.8
14 F	19 36 12	24 25 34	12♓48 08	19 53 54	27 38.5	6 04.5	6 00.3	13 41.6	12 48.2	18 19.3	23 50.1	4 29.9	14 18.9	23 11.8
15 Sa	19 40 08	25 26 41	26 52 05	3♈42 44	27 35.3	7 30.9	7 15.5	14 23.3	13 07.7	18 22.7	23 45.1	4 32.7	14 21.1	23 13.8
16 Su	19 44 05	26 27 48	10♈26 02	17 02 23	27 34.1	8 58.1	8 30.7	15 05.0	13 27.0	18 25.9	23 40.2	4 35.6	14 23.3	23 15.7
17 M	19 48 02	27 28 54	23 32 15	29 56 09	27 34.0	10 25.9	9 45.8	15 46.8	13 46.1	18 28.9	23 35.3	4 38.5	14 25.5	23 17.7
18 Tu	19 51 58	28 29 59	6♉14 42	12♉28 31	27 33.7	11 54.4	11 01.0	16 28.6	14 05.1	18 31.7	23 30.3	4 41.4	14 27.7	23 19.6
19 W	19 55 55	29 31 03	18 38 13	24 44 24	27 31.8	13 23.5	12 16.1	17 10.5	14 23.9	18 34.3	23 25.4	4 44.4	14 29.9	23 21.6
20 Th	19 59 51	0♒32 07	0♊47 40	6♊48 34	27 27.5	14 53.3	13 31.3	17 52.3	14 42.5	18 36.8	23 20.5	4 47.3	14 32.1	23 23.5
21 F	20 03 48	1 33 09	12 47 37	18 45 16	27 20.3	16 23.7	14 46.5	18 34.2	15 00.8	18 39.0	23 15.7	4 50.3	14 34.3	23 25.4
22 Sa	20 07 44	2 34 11	24 41 56	0♋38 00	27 10.0	17 54.8	16 01.6	19 16.1	15 19.0	18 41.1	23 10.8	4 53.4	14 36.6	23 27.2
23 Su	20 11 41	3 35 12	6♋33 46	12 29 32	26 57.2	19 26.4	17 16.8	19 58.1	15 37.0	18 43.0	23 06.0	4 56.4	14 38.8	23 29.1
24 M	20 15 38	4 36 12	18 25 30	24 21 53	26 42.8	20 58.7	18 31.9	20 40.1	15 54.8	18 44.7	23 01.2	4 59.5	14 41.1	23 30.9
25 Tu	20 19 34	5 37 11	0♌18 52	6♌16 35	26 27.8	22 31.6	19 47.1	21 22.1	16 12.4	18 46.3	22 56.4	5 02.6	14 43.3	23 32.7
26 W	20 23 31	6 38 09	12 15 10	18 14 46	26 13.5	24 05.1	21 02.3	22 04.1	16 29.8	18 47.6	22 51.7	5 05.7	14 45.6	23 34.5
27 Th	20 27 27	7 39 07	24 15 31	0♍17 34	26 01.0	25 39.2	22 17.4	22 46.2	16 46.9	18 48.8	22 47.0	5 08.8	14 47.8	23 36.3
28 F	20 31 24	8 40 04	6♍21 08	12 26 23	25 51.2	27 14.0	23 32.6	23 28.3	17 03.8	18 49.7	22 42.3	5 12.0	14 50.1	23 38.0
29 Sa	20 35 20	9 40 59	18 33 36	24 43 03	25 44.4	28 49.5	24 47.7	24 10.4	17 20.6	18 50.5	22 37.7	5 15.2	14 52.4	23 39.7
30 Su	20 39 17	10 41 54	0♎55 04	7♎10 02	25 40.6	0♒25.6	26 02.9	24 52.5	17 37.0	18 51.1	22 33.1	5 18.4	14 54.7	23 41.4
31 M	20 43 13	11 42 49	13 28 20	19 50 24	25D39.2	2 02.4	27 18.0	25 34.7	17 53.3	18 51.5	22 28.6	5 21.6	14 56.9	23 43.1

LONGITUDE — February 2005

Day	Sid.Time	☉	0 hr ☽	Noon ☽	True ☊	☿	♀	♂	⚳	♃	♄	♅	♆	♇
1 Tu	20 47 10	12♒43 42	26♎16 43	2♏47 43	25♈39.2	3♒39.8	28♑33.2	26♐16.9	18♏09.3	18♎51.7	22♋24.1	5♓24.8	14♒59.2	23♐44.7
2 W	20 51 06	13 44 35	9♏23 52	16 05 35	25R39.4	5 18.0	29 48.3	26 59.2	18 25.1	18R51.7	22R19.6	5 28.1	15 01.5	23 46.4
3 Th	20 55 03	14 45 27	22 53 14	29 47 06	25 38.5	6 56.9	1♒03.5	27 41.4	18 40.7	18 51.6	22 15.3	5 31.4	15 03.8	23 48.0
4 F	20 59 00	15 46 19	6♐47 22	13♐54 04	25 35.5	8 36.6	2 18.6	28 23.8	18 56.0	18 51.2	22 10.9	5 34.6	15 06.0	23 49.6
5 Sa	21 02 56	16 47 09	21 07 01	28 25 55	25 30.0	10 17.0	3 33.8	29 06.1	19 11.1	18 50.7	22 06.7	5 38.0	15 08.3	23 51.1
6 Su	21 06 53	17 47 58	5♑50 12	13♑19 06	25 22.0	11 58.1	4 48.9	29 48.4	19 25.9	18 49.9	22 02.4	5 41.3	15 10.6	23 52.6
7 M	21 10 49	18 48 45	20 51 38	28 26 39	25 12.2	13 40.1	6 04.1	0♑30.8	19 40.4	18 49.0	21 58.3	5 44.6	15 12.9	23 54.1
8 Tu	21 14 46	19 49 35	6♒02 51	13♒38 54	25 01.8	15 22.8	7 19.2	1 13.2	19 54.7	18 47.8	21 54.2	5 48.0	15 15.2	23 55.6
9 W	21 18 42	20 50 21	21 13 22	28 44 57	24 52.0	17 06.3	8 34.4	1 55.7	20 08.7	18 46.5	21 50.2	5 51.3	15 17.4	23 57.1
10 Th	21 22 39	21 51 06	6♓12 25	13♓34 43	24 44.0	18 50.7	9 49.5	2 38.1	20 22.5	18 45.0	21 46.3	5 54.7	15 19.7	23 58.5
11 F	21 26 36	22 51 49	20 50 58	28 00 31	24 38.5	20 35.8	11 04.6	3 20.6	20 36.0	18 43.3	21 42.4	5 58.1	15 22.0	23 59.9
12 Sa	21 30 32	23 52 31	5♈02 58	11♈58 06	24D35.7	22 21.8	12 19.7	4 03.1	20 49.1	18 41.4	21 38.6	6 01.4	15 24.2	24 01.2
13 Su	21 34 29	24 53 11	18 45 55	25 26 34	24 34.9	24 08.5	13 34.8	4 45.6	21 02.1	18 39.4	21 34.9	6 04.8	15 26.5	24 02.6
14 M	21 38 25	25 53 49	2♉00 23	8♉27 45	24 35.5	25 56.1	14 49.9	5 28.2	21 14.7	18 37.1	21 31.2	6 08.2	15 28.8	24 03.9
15 Tu	21 42 22	26 54 26	14 49 12	21 05 19	24R36.3	27 44.5	16 05.0	6 10.8	21 27.0	18 34.6	21 27.6	6 11.7	15 31.0	24 05.2
16 W	21 46 18	27 55 01	27 16 41	3♊23 58	24 36.3	29 33.6	17 20.1	6 53.4	21 39.1	18 32.0	21 24.2	6 15.1	15 33.3	24 06.4
17 Th	21 50 15	28 55 34	9♊27 48	15 28 48	24 34.6	1♓23.5	18 35.1	7 36.0	21 50.8	18 29.2	21 20.8	6 18.5	15 35.5	24 07.7
18 F	21 54 11	29 56 06	21 27 35	27 24 44	24 30.6	3 14.1	19 50.2	8 18.7	22 02.3	18 26.2	21 17.4	6 21.9	15 37.7	24 08.9
19 Sa	21 58 08	0♓56 35	3♋20 49	9♋16 18	24 24.4	5 05.3	21 05.2	9 01.3	22 13.4	18 23.1	21 14.2	6 25.4	15 39.9	24 10.0
20 Su	22 02 05	1 57 03	15 11 41	21 07 21	24 16.1	6 57.1	22 20.2	9 44.0	22 24.2	18 19.7	21 11.1	6 28.8	15 42.2	24 11.2
21 M	22 06 01	2 57 29	27 03 41	3♌01 00	24 06.5	8 49.3	23 35.3	10 26.7	22 34.8	18 16.2	21 08.0	6 32.3	15 44.4	24 12.3
22 Tu	22 09 58	3 57 54	8♌59 34	14 59 38	23 56.3	10 42.0	24 50.3	11 09.5	22 45.0	18 12.5	21 05.1	6 35.7	15 46.6	24 13.3
23 W	22 13 54	4 58 16	21 01 23	27 04 58	23 46.6	12 34.9	26 05.3	11 52.3	22 54.8	18 08.7	21 02.2	6 39.2	15 48.7	24 14.4
24 Th	22 17 51	5 58 37	3♍10 32	9♍18 11	23 38.2	14 27.8	27 20.3	12 35.1	23 04.4	18 04.6	20 59.4	6 42.6	15 50.9	24 15.4
25 F	22 21 47	6 58 56	15 28 02	21 40 11	23 31.7	16 20.6	28 35.2	13 17.9	23 13.6	18 00.4	20 56.8	6 46.1	15 53.1	24 16.4
26 Sa	22 25 44	7 59 14	27 54 44	4♎11 49	23 27.6	18 13.1	29 50.2	14 00.7	23 22.5	17 56.1	20 54.2	6 49.5	15 55.2	24 17.3
27 Su	22 29 40	8 59 30	10♎31 32	16 54 04	23D25.7	20 05.0	1♓05.2	14 43.6	23 31.1	17 51.5	20 51.7	6 52.9	15 57.4	24 18.3
28 M	22 33 37	9 59 44	23 19 35	29 48 16	23 25.6	21 55.9	2 20.1	15 26.5	23 39.3	17 46.9	20 49.3	6 56.4	15 59.5	24 19.2

Astro Data

	Dy Hr Mn
☽0S	3 1:25
☽0N	15 13:30
♄⚻♇	20 1:38
☽0S	30 6:26
♃R	2 2:27
☽0N	11 22:24
♄⚼♅	17 20:00
☽0S	26 11:34

Planet Ingress

	Dy Hr Mn
♀ ♑	9 16:57
☿ ♑	10 4:10
☉ ♒	19 23:23
☿ ♒	30 5:38
♀ ♒	2 15:43
♂ ♑	6 18:33
☿ ♓	16 17:47
☉ ♓	18 13:33
♀ ♓	26 15:08

Last Aspect / ☽ Ingress (January)

Last Aspect Dy Hr Mn		☽ Ingress	Dy Hr Mn
2 6:24	♄ ⚹	♎	2 16:21
4 14:21	♄ □	♏	5 0:01
6 18:30	♄ △	♐	7 3:45
9 3:03	♀ ☌	♑	9 4:12
10 17:59	♄ ☍	♒	11 3:08
12 15:45	♇ ⚹	♓	13 2:51
14 20:23	☉ ⚹	♈	15 5:28
17 6:59	☉ □	♉	17 12:07
19 22:20	☉ △	♊	19 22:25
21 21:27	♇ ☍	♋	22 10:43
24 9:18	♄ ☌	♌	24 23:22
26 22:40	♇ △	♍	27 11:25
29 21:08	☿ △	♎	29 22:14

Last Aspect / ☽ Ingress (February)

Last Aspect Dy Hr Mn		☽ Ingress	Dy Hr Mn
1 3:22	♀ □	♏	1 6:52
2 22:58	♄ △	♐	3 12:22
5 13:09	♂ ☌	♑	5 14:33
7 1:48	♄ ☍	♒	7 14:27
9 4:20	♇ ⚹	♓	9 14:00
11 5:15	♇ □	♈	11 15:22
13 10:55	☉ ⚹	♉	13 20:19
16 3:09	☿ □	♊	16 5:19
18 5:24	♇ ☍	♋	18 17:14
20 12:07	♄ ☌	♌	21 5:56
23 9:48	♀ ☍	♍	23 17:45
25 17:01	♇ □	♎	26 4:00
28 1:50	♇ ⚹	♏	28 12:22

☽ Phases & Eclipses

Dy Hr Mn		
3 17:47	☾	13♎28
10 12:04	●	20♑21
17 6:59	☽	27♈16
25 10:33	○	5♌34
2 7:28	☾	13♏33
8 22:29	●	20♒16
16 0:17	☽	27♉25
24 4:55	○	5♍41

Astro Data

1 January 2005
Julian Day # 38352
SVP 5♓11'31"
GC 26♐54.5 ⚴ 8♎53.7
Eris 19♈45.5R ⚵ 11♒29.7
⚷ 25♑35.5 ⚶ 26♓34.7
☽ Mean ☊ 28♈17.7

1 February 2005
Julian Day # 38383
SVP 5♓11'26"
GC 26♐54.6 ⚴ 12♎36.5R
Eris 19♈48.9 ⚵ 25♒15.9
⚷ 28♑19.6 ⚶ 7♈58.9
☽ Mean ☊ 26♈39.2

March 2005 LONGITUDE

Day	Sid.Time	☉	0 hr ☽	Noon ☽	True☊	☿	♀	♂	⚳	♃	♄	♅	♆	♇
1 Tu	22 37 33	10♓59 57	6♏20 22	12♏56 04	23♈26.7	23♓45.6	3♓35.1	16♑09.4	23♏47.1	17♎42.0	20♋47.0	6♓59.8	16♒01.6	24♐20.0
2 W	22 41 30	12 00 09	19 35 38	26 19 17	23 28.2	25 33.6	4 50.0	16 52.4	23 54.7	17R37.0	20R44.9	7 03.3	16 03.7	24 20.8
3 Th	22 45 27	13 00 19	3♐07 12	9♐59 33	23R29.1	27 19.5	6 04.9	17 35.4	24 01.8	17 31.9	20 42.8	7 06.7	16 05.8	24 21.6
4 F	22 49 23	14 00 27	16 56 26	23 57 52	23 28.7	29 02.8	7 19.9	18 18.4	24 08.6	17 26.6	20 40.8	7 10.2	16 07.9	24 22.4
5 Sa	22 53 20	15 00 34	1♑03 46	8♑13 56	23 26.6	0♈43.1	8 34.8	19 01.4	24 15.1	17 21.2	20 38.9	7 13.6	16 09.9	24 23.1
6 Su	22 57 16	16 00 40	15 28 01	22 45 33	23 22.9	2 19.8	9 49.7	19 44.5	24 21.1	17 15.6	20 37.2	7 17.0	16 12.0	24 23.8
7 M	23 01 13	17 00 44	0♒05 56	7♒28 25	23 17.9	3 52.4	11 04.6	20 27.5	24 26.8	17 09.9	20 35.5	7 20.4	16 14.0	24 24.5
8 Tu	23 05 09	18 00 46	14 52 07	22 16 08	23 12.4	5 20.3	12 19.4	21 10.6	24 32.1	17 04.0	20 33.9	7 23.9	16 16.0	24 25.1
9 W	23 09 06	19 00 46	29 39 26	7♓01 02	23 07.2	6 43.0	13 34.3	21 53.7	24 37.1	16 58.0	20 32.5	7 27.3	16 18.0	24 25.7
10 Th	23 13 03	20 00 45	14♓19 57	21 35 17	23 02.9	7 59.9	14 49.2	22 36.9	24 41.6	16 51.9	20 31.1	7 30.7	16 20.0	24 26.3
11 F	23 16 59	21 00 41	28 46 14	5♈52 06	23 00.2	9 10.6	16 04.0	23 20.0	24 45.8	16 45.7	20 29.9	7 34.0	16 22.0	24 26.8
12 Sa	23 20 56	22 00 36	12♈52 23	19 46 43	22D59.1	10 14.5	17 18.8	24 03.2	24 49.5	16 39.3	20 28.8	7 37.4	16 23.9	24 27.3
13 Su	23 24 52	23 00 28	26 34 51	3♉16 44	22 59.4	11 11.2	18 33.6	24 46.4	24 52.9	16 32.9	20 27.8	7 40.8	16 25.9	24 27.8
14 M	23 28 49	24 00 19	9♉52 27	16 22 12	23 00.7	12 00.4	19 48.4	25 29.6	24 55.9	16 26.3	20 26.9	7 44.1	16 27.8	24 28.2
15 Tu	23 32 45	25 00 07	22 46 16	29 05 03	23 02.4	12 41.8	21 03.2	26 12.8	24 58.5	16 19.6	20 26.1	7 47.5	16 29.7	24 28.6
16 W	23 36 42	25 59 53	5♊19 01	11♊28 41	23 04.0	13 15.0	22 18.0	26 56.0	25 00.7	16 12.8	20 25.4	7 50.8	16 31.5	24 29.0
17 Th	23 40 38	26 59 37	17 34 37	23 37 24	23R04.8	13 40.0	23 32.7	27 39.3	25 02.4	16 06.0	20 24.8	7 54.1	16 33.4	24 29.4
18 F	23 44 35	27 59 18	29 37 37	5♋35 54	23 04.5	13 56.7	24 47.5	28 22.5	25 03.8	15 59.0	20 24.4	7 57.4	16 35.2	24 29.7
19 Sa	23 48 31	28 58 57	11♋32 49	17 28 59	23 03.2	14R05.0	26 02.2	29 05.8	25 04.8	15 51.9	20 24.0	8 00.7	16 37.0	24 29.9
20 Su	23 52 28	29 58 34	23 24 56	29 21 13	23 00.8	14 05.1	27 16.9	29 49.1	25R05.4	15 44.8	20 23.8	8 04.0	16 38.8	24 30.2
21 M	23 56 25	0♈58 09	5♌18 19	11♌16 43	22 57.6	13 57.2	28 31.6	0♒32.4	25 05.5	15 37.6	20D23.7	8 07.2	16 40.6	24 30.4
22 Tu	0 00 21	1 57 42	17 16 51	23 19 03	22 54.1	13 41.6	29 46.2	1 15.7	25 05.3	15 30.3	20 23.7	8 10.4	16 42.3	24 30.5
23 W	0 04 18	2 57 12	29 23 41	5♍31 02	22 50.8	13 18.9	1♈00.9	1 59.1	25 04.6	15 23.0	20 23.8	8 13.7	16 44.1	24 30.7
24 Th	0 08 14	3 56 40	11♍41 18	17 54 42	22 47.9	12 49.6	2 15.5	2 42.4	25 03.6	15 15.6	20 24.0	8 16.8	16 45.8	24 30.8
25 F	0 12 11	4 56 06	24 11 21	0♎31 21	22 45.8	12 14.5	3 30.1	3 25.8	25 02.1	15 08.1	20 24.3	8 20.0	16 47.4	24 30.8
26 Sa	0 16 07	5 55 30	6♎54 45	13 21 34	22D44.7	11 34.2	4 44.7	4 09.2	25 00.2	15 00.6	20 24.7	8 23.2	16 49.1	24R30.9
27 Su	0 20 04	6 54 51	19 51 47	26 25 23	22 44.5	10 49.9	5 59.3	4 52.6	24 57.9	14 53.1	20 25.2	8 26.3	16 50.7	24 30.9
28 M	0 24 00	7 54 11	3♏02 17	9♏42 26	22 45.1	10 02.3	7 13.8	5 36.0	24 55.2	14 45.5	20 25.9	8 29.4	16 52.3	24 30.9
29 Tu	0 27 57	8 53 30	16 25 43	23 12 05	22 46.1	9 12.7	8 28.4	6 19.5	24 52.1	14 37.8	20 26.7	8 32.5	16 53.9	24 30.8
30 W	0 31 54	9 52 46	0♐01 23	6♐53 33	22 47.2	8 22.0	9 42.9	7 02.9	24 48.6	14 30.2	20 27.5	8 35.6	16 55.5	24 30.7
31 Th	0 35 50	10 52 01	13 48 28	20 45 58	22 48.1	7 31.2	10 57.4	7 46.4	24 44.6	14 22.5	20 28.5	8 38.7	16 57.0	24 30.6

April 2005 LONGITUDE

Day	Sid.Time	☉	0 hr ☽	Noon ☽	True☊	☿	♀	♂	⚳	♃	♄	♅	♆	♇
1 F	0 39 47	11♈51 14	27♐45 56	4♑48 11	22♈48.7	6♈41.5	12♈11.9	8♒29.9	24♏40.3	14♎14.8	20♋29.6	8♓41.7	16♒58.5	24♐30.4
2 Sa	0 43 43	12 50 25	11♑52 31	18 58 42	22R48.7	5R53.6	13 26.4	9 13.4	24R35.6	14R07.1	20 30.8	8 44.7	17 00.0	24R30.2
3 Su	0 47 40	13 49 34	26 06 27	3♒15 26	22 48.3	5 08.4	14 40.9	9 56.9	24 30.4	13 59.4	20 32.1	8 47.7	17 01.5	24 30.0
4 M	0 51 36	14 48 42	10♒25 16	17 35 33	22 47.5	4 26.6	15 55.4	10 40.4	24 24.9	13 51.6	20 33.5	8 50.7	17 02.9	24 29.8
5 Tu	0 55 33	15 47 48	24 45 48	1♓55 30	22 46.7	3 48.8	17 09.8	11 24.0	24 19.0	13 43.9	20 35.0	8 53.6	17 04.3	24 29.5
6 W	0 59 29	16 46 52	9♓04 08	16 11 09	22 45.9	3 15.6	18 24.2	12 07.5	24 12.6	13 36.2	20 36.7	8 56.5	17 05.7	24 29.2
7 Th	1 03 26	17 45 54	23 16 00	0♈18 09	22 45.4	2 47.2	19 38.6	12 51.1	24 05.9	13 28.5	20 38.4	8 59.4	17 07.0	24 28.8
8 F	1 07 23	18 44 54	7♈17 06	14 12 24	22D45.1	2 24.0	20 53.0	13 34.6	23 58.8	13 20.8	20 40.3	9 02.2	17 08.4	24 28.4
9 Sa	1 11 19	19 43 52	21 03 40	27 50 33	22 45.1	2 06.1	22 07.4	14 18.2	23 51.4	13 13.2	20 42.2	9 05.0	17 09.7	24 28.0
10 Su	1 15 16	20 42 48	4♉32 50	11♉10 21	22 45.2	1 53.6	23 21.8	15 01.7	23 43.6	13 05.5	20 44.3	9 07.8	17 10.9	24 27.6
11 M	1 19 12	21 41 42	17 43 02	24 10 54	22 45.3	1D46.5	24 36.1	15 45.3	23 35.4	12 57.9	20 46.4	9 10.6	17 12.2	24 27.1
12 Tu	1 23 09	22 40 34	0♊34 05	6♊52 44	22R45.4	1 44.8	25 50.4	16 28.8	23 26.8	12 50.4	20 48.7	9 13.3	17 13.4	24 26.6
13 W	1 27 05	23 39 24	13 07 09	19 17 39	22 45.3	1 48.4	27 04.7	17 12.4	23 18.0	12 42.9	20 51.1	9 16.0	17 14.5	24 26.1
14 Th	1 31 02	24 38 11	25 24 38	1♋28 32	22 45.2	1 57.1	28 19.0	17 56.0	23 08.7	12 35.4	20 53.5	9 18.7	17 15.7	24 25.5
15 F	1 34 58	25 36 57	7♋29 51	13 29 06	22 45.0	2 10.7	29 33.3	18 39.5	22 59.2	12 28.1	20 56.1	9 21.3	17 16.8	24 24.9
16 Sa	1 38 55	26 35 40	19 26 50	25 23 38	22D45.0	2 29.2	0♉47.5	19 23.1	22 49.4	12 20.7	20 58.8	9 23.9	17 17.9	24 24.3
17 Su	1 42 52	27 34 21	1♌20 03	7♌16 42	22 45.0	2 52.3	2 01.8	20 06.7	22 39.2	12 13.5	21 01.6	9 26.5	17 19.0	24 23.6
18 M	1 46 48	28 32 59	13 14 08	19 12 57	22 45.4	3 19.9	3 16.0	20 50.2	22 28.8	12 06.3	21 04.4	9 29.1	17 20.0	24 22.9
19 Tu	1 50 45	29 31 36	25 13 40	1♍16 50	22 45.9	3 51.7	4 30.1	21 33.8	22 18.0	11 59.2	21 07.4	9 31.6	17 21.0	24 22.2
20 W	1 54 41	0♉30 10	7♍22 55	13 32 23	22 46.7	4 27.6	5 44.3	22 17.3	22 07.1	11 52.1	21 10.5	9 34.0	17 22.0	24 21.5
21 Th	1 58 38	1 28 42	19 45 36	26 02 56	22 47.5	5 07.3	6 58.4	23 00.9	21 55.8	11 45.2	21 13.7	9 36.5	17 22.9	24 20.7
22 F	2 02 34	2 27 12	2♎24 39	8♎50 57	22 48.1	5 50.8	8 12.6	23 44.5	21 44.3	11 38.4	21 16.9	9 38.9	17 23.8	24 19.9
23 Sa	2 06 31	3 25 40	15 21 56	21 57 40	22R48.4	6 37.8	9 26.7	24 28.0	21 32.6	11 31.6	21 20.3	9 41.2	17 24.7	24 19.1
24 Su	2 10 27	4 24 06	28 38 06	5♏23 05	22 48.2	7 28.2	10 40.7	25 11.6	21 20.6	11 24.9	21 23.7	9 43.6	17 25.5	24 18.3
25 M	2 14 24	5 22 30	12♏12 24	19 05 47	22 47.3	8 21.8	11 54.8	25 55.1	21 08.4	11 18.4	21 27.3	9 45.9	17 26.3	24 17.4
26 Tu	2 18 21	6 20 53	26 02 51	3♐03 10	22 45.9	9 18.5	13 08.8	26 38.7	20 56.1	11 11.9	21 30.9	9 48.1	17 27.1	24 16.5
27 W	2 22 17	7 19 13	10♐06 16	17 11 39	22 44.1	10 18.2	14 22.9	27 22.2	20 43.5	11 05.6	21 34.6	9 50.4	17 27.9	24 15.6
28 Th	2 26 14	8 17 33	24 18 47	1♑27 09	22 42.2	11 20.8	15 36.9	28 05.8	20 30.8	10 59.4	21 38.5	9 52.5	17 28.6	24 14.6
29 F	2 30 10	9 15 51	8♑36 15	15 45 34	22 40.6	12 26.1	16 50.9	28 49.3	20 18.0	10 53.3	21 42.4	9 54.7	17 29.3	24 13.6
30 Sa	2 34 07	10 14 07	22 54 39	0♒03 08	22D39.6	13 34.0	18 04.9	29 32.8	20 05.0	10 47.3	21 46.4	9 56.8	17 30.0	24 12.7

Astro Data

	Dy Hr Mn
☿0N	4 17:05
☽0N	11 8:43
♃△♆	14 7:48
☿ R	20 0:14
☉0N	20 12:34
⚳ R	21 9:30
♄ D	22 2:55
♀0N	25 6:10
☽0S	25 18:24
♇ R	27 2:30
☽0N	7 18:14
☿ D	12 7:46
☿0S	14 4:23
☿0N	21 0:02
☽0S	22 2:52

Planet Ingress

		Dy Hr Mn
☿	♈	5 1:35
☉	♈	20 12:34
♂	♒	20 18:03
♀	♈	22 16:26
♀	♉	15 20:38
☉	♉	19 23:38

Last Aspect / ☽ Ingress

Last Aspect Dy Hr Mn			☽ Ingress	Dy Hr Mn
2 10:26	☿	△	♐	2 18:31
4 21:46	☿	□	♑	4 22:13
6 8:30	♄	☍	♒	6 23:50
8 15:29	♇	⚹	♓	9 0:33
10 16:45	♇	□	♈	11 2:04
12 20:14	♇	△	♉	13 6:06
15 6:11	♂	△	♊	15 13:45
17 19:20	☉	□	♋	18 0:45
20 13:00	♂	☍	♌	20 13:18
22 14:22	♇	△	♍	23 1:11
25 0:37	♇	□	♎	25 11:01
27 8:31	♇	⚹	♏	27 18:30
29 7:07	♄	△	♐	29 23:58

Last Aspect / ☽ Ingress

Last Aspect Dy Hr Mn			☽ Ingress	Dy Hr Mn
31 18:26	♇	☌	♑	1 3:49
2 14:35	♄	☍	♒	3 6:32
4 23:33	♇	⚹	♓	5 8:46
7 2:04	♇	□	♈	7 11:29
9 6:01	♇	△	♉	9 15:51
11 5:38	♄	⚹	♊	11 22:56
14 5:02	♀	⚹	♋	14 9:04
16 14:39	☉	□	♌	16 21:18
19 8:14	☉	△	♍	19 9:28
21 8:46	♇	□	♎	21 19:28
23 16:47	♂	△	♏	24 2:26
26 0:25	♂	□	♐	26 6:47
28 6:04	♂	⚹	♑	28 9:34
29 22:01	♄	☍	♒	30 11:55

☽ Phases & Eclipses

Dy Hr Mn		
3 17:37	☾	13♐14
10 9:12	●	19♓54
17 19:20	☽	27♊18
25 21:00	○	5♎18
2 0:51	☾	12♑23
8 20:33	●	19♈06
8 20:36:51	•	AT00'42"
16 14:39	☽	26♋42
24 10:07	○	4♏20
24 9:56	•	A 0.865

Astro Data

1 March 2005
Julian Day # 38411
SVP 5♓11'22"
GC 26♐54.7 ⚴ 9♎08.4R
Eris 20♈00.2 ⚵ 8♓29.7
⚷ 0♒35.0 ⚶ 19♈32.3
☽ Mean ☊ 25♈10.2

1 April 2005
Julian Day # 38442
SVP 5♓11'18"
GC 26♐54.8 ⚴ 29♍53.2R
Eris 20♈18.8 ⚵ 23♓43.6
⚷ 2♒25.9 ⚶ 3♉00.6
☽ Mean ☊ 23♈31.7

LONGITUDE May 2005

Day	Sid.Time	☉	0 hr ☽	Noon☽	True☊	☿	♀	♂	⚳	♃	♄	♅	♆	♇
1 Su	2 38 03	11♉12 22	7♒10 36	14♒16 46	22♈39.4	14♈44.5	19♉18.8	0♓16.4	19♏51.8	10♎41.5	21♋50.5	9♓58.9	17♒30.6	24♐11.6
2 M	2 42 00	12 10 35	21 21 21	28 24 06	22 40.0	15 57.5	20 32.8	0 59.9	19R 38.6	10R 35.7	21 54.6	10 00.9	17 31.2	24R 10.6
3 Tu	2 45 56	13 08 46	5♓24 50	12♓23 21	22 41.1	17 12.9	21 46.7	1 43.4	19 25.3	10 30.2	21 58.9	10 02.9	17 31.7	24 09.5
4 W	2 49 53	14 06 57	19 19 30	26 13 08	22 42.5	18 30.6	23 00.6	2 26.8	19 11.8	10 24.7	22 03.2	10 04.8	17 32.3	24 08.4
5 Th	2 53 50	15 05 05	3♈04 07	9♈52 18	22R 43.7	19 50.5	24 14.5	3 10.3	18 58.4	10 19.4	22 07.7	10 06.7	17 32.7	24 07.3
6 F	2 57 46	16 03 13	16 37 33	23 19 46	22 44.1	21 12.8	25 28.4	3 53.7	18 44.8	10 14.2	22 12.2	10 08.6	17 33.2	24 06.2
7 Sa	3 01 43	17 01 18	29 58 47	6♉34 31	22 43.5	22 37.2	26 42.3	4 37.1	18 31.3	10 09.2	22 16.8	10 10.4	17 33.6	24 05.0
8 Su	3 05 39	17 59 23	13♉06 51	19 35 44	22 41.6	24 03.7	27 56.2	5 20.5	18 17.8	10 04.3	22 21.4	10 12.2	17 34.0	24 03.8
9 M	3 09 36	18 57 25	26 01 06	2♊22 57	22 38.4	25 32.4	29 10.0	6 03.9	18 04.2	9 59.6	22 26.2	10 13.9	17 34.4	24 02.6
10 Tu	3 13 32	19 55 26	8♊41 18	14 56 14	22 34.2	27 03.2	0♊23.8	6 47.3	17 50.7	9 55.0	22 31.0	10 15.6	17 34.7	24 01.4
11 W	3 17 29	20 53 25	21 07 53	27 16 24	22 29.5	28 36.1	1 37.6	7 30.6	17 37.2	9 50.6	22 36.0	10 17.3	17 35.0	24 00.2
12 Th	3 21 25	21 51 23	3♋22 03	9♋25 07	22 24.8	0♉11.0	2 51.4	8 13.9	17 23.8	9 46.4	22 41.0	10 18.9	17 35.3	23 58.9
13 F	3 25 22	22 49 19	15 25 55	21 24 51	22 20.6	1 48.0	4 05.2	8 57.2	17 10.5	9 42.3	22 46.0	10 20.5	17 35.5	23 57.6
14 Sa	3 29 19	23 47 13	27 22 21	3♌18 55	22 17.4	3 27.1	5 18.9	9 40.4	16 57.2	9 38.3	22 51.2	10 22.0	17 35.7	23 56.3
15 Su	3 33 15	24 45 05	9♌15 03	15 11 18	22D 15.6	5 08.2	6 32.6	10 23.6	16 44.0	9 34.6	22 56.4	10 23.4	17 35.9	23 55.0
16 M	3 37 12	25 42 56	21 08 15	27 06 29	22 15.1	6 51.4	7 46.3	11 06.8	16 31.0	9 31.0	23 01.7	10 24.9	17 36.0	23 53.7
17 Tu	3 41 08	26 40 44	3♍06 37	9♍09 16	22 15.8	8 36.7	9 00.0	11 50.0	16 18.1	9 27.6	23 07.0	10 26.3	17 36.1	23 52.3
18 W	3 45 05	27 38 32	15 15 01	21 24 28	22 17.2	10 24.0	10 13.7	12 33.1	16 05.4	9 24.3	23 12.5	10 27.6	17 36.2	23 51.0
19 Th	3 49 01	28 36 17	27 38 09	3♎56 36	22 18.8	12 13.4	11 27.3	13 16.2	15 52.8	9 21.2	23 18.0	10 28.9	17R 36.2	23 49.6
20 F	3 52 58	29 34 01	10♎20 16	16 49 30	22R 19.9	14 04.8	12 41.0	13 59.2	15 40.4	9 18.3	23 23.6	10 30.1	17 36.2	23 48.2
21 Sa	3 56 54	0♊31 43	23 24 37	0♏05 46	22 19.7	15 58.3	13 54.6	14 42.2	15 28.2	9 15.6	23 29.2	10 31.3	17 36.2	23 46.8
22 Su	4 00 51	1 29 24	6♏53 02	13 46 18	22 18.0	17 53.8	15 08.1	15 25.2	15 16.2	9 13.0	23 34.9	10 32.5	17 36.1	23 45.4
23 M	4 04 48	2 27 03	20 45 22	27 49 50	22 14.4	19 51.3	16 21.7	16 08.1	15 04.4	9 10.6	23 40.7	10 33.6	17 36.0	23 43.9
24 Tu	4 08 44	3 24 41	4♐59 10	12♐12 42	22 09.3	21 50.8	17 35.3	16 51.0	14 52.9	9 08.4	23 46.5	10 34.7	17 35.9	23 42.5
25 W	4 12 41	4 22 19	19 29 40	26 49 10	22 03.1	23 52.1	18 48.8	17 33.9	14 41.6	9 06.4	23 52.4	10 35.7	17 35.7	23 41.0
26 Th	4 16 37	5 19 55	4♑10 18	11♑32 06	21 56.7	25 55.3	20 02.3	18 16.8	14 30.5	9 04.5	23 58.3	10 36.6	17 35.5	23 39.6
27 F	4 20 34	6 17 30	18 53 37	26 14 00	21 51.0	28 00.1	21 15.8	18 59.5	14 19.7	9 02.9	24 04.4	10 37.6	17 35.3	23 38.1
28 Sa	4 24 30	7 15 04	3♒32 28	10♒48 19	21 46.7	0♊06.6	22 29.3	19 42.3	14 09.1	9 01.4	24 10.4	10 38.4	17 35.1	23 36.6
29 Su	4 28 27	8 12 37	18 01 00	25 10 05	21D 44.1	2 14.5	23 42.8	20 25.0	13 58.9	9 00.0	24 16.6	10 39.3	17 34.8	23 35.1
30 M	4 32 23	9 10 09	2♓15 18	9♓16 26	21 43.4	4 23.7	24 56.2	21 07.6	13 48.9	8 58.9	24 22.8	10 40.0	17 34.5	23 33.6
31 Tu	4 36 20	10 07 40	16 13 26	23 06 19	21 43.9	6 34.0	26 09.6	21 50.2	13 39.2	8 57.9	24 29.0	10 40.8	17 34.1	23 32.0

LONGITUDE June 2005

Day	Sid.Time	☉	0 hr ☽	Noon☽	True☊	☿	♀	♂	⚳	♃	♄	♅	♆	♇
1 W	4 40 17	11♊05 11	29♓55 08	6♈40 02	21♈45.0	8♊45.1	27♊23.1	22♓32.8	13♏29.9	8♎57.2	24♋35.3	10♓41.4	17♒33.7	23♐30.5
2 Th	4 44 13	12 02 41	13♈21 11	19 58 44	21R 45.7	10 56.8	28 36.5	23 15.3	13R 20.8	8R 56.6	24 41.7	10 42.1	17R 33.3	23R 29.0
3 F	4 48 10	13 00 10	26 32 53	3♉03 48	21 45.1	13 08.8	29 49.9	23 57.7	13 12.1	8 56.1	24 48.1	10 42.7	17 32.9	23 27.4
4 Sa	4 52 06	13 57 38	9♉31 37	15 56 29	21 42.5	15 21.0	1♋03.2	24 40.1	13 03.7	8D 55.9	24 54.6	10 43.2	17 32.4	23 25.9
5 Su	4 56 03	14 55 06	22 18 31	28 37 49	21 37.5	17 32.9	2 16.6	25 22.4	12 55.7	8 55.8	25 01.1	10 43.7	17 31.9	23 24.3
6 M	4 59 59	15 52 32	4♊54 27	11♊08 30	21 30.2	19 44.3	3 30.0	26 04.6	12 48.0	8 56.0	25 07.7	10 44.1	17 31.4	23 22.8
7 Tu	5 03 56	16 49 58	17 20 03	23 29 09	21 21.0	21 55.0	4 43.3	26 46.8	12 40.6	8 56.3	25 14.3	10 44.5	17 30.8	23 21.2
8 W	5 07 52	17 47 23	29 35 56	5♋40 29	21 10.7	24 04.7	5 56.6	27 28.9	12 33.6	8 56.8	25 21.0	10 44.9	17 30.2	23 19.6
9 Th	5 11 49	18 44 48	11♋42 57	17 43 32	21 00.1	26 13.2	7 09.9	28 10.9	12 27.0	8 57.4	25 27.7	10 45.1	17 29.6	23 18.1
10 F	5 15 46	19 42 11	23 42 26	29 39 55	20 50.3	28 20.2	8 23.2	28 52.8	12 20.7	8 58.3	25 34.5	10 45.4	17 28.9	23 16.5
11 Sa	5 19 42	20 39 33	5♌36 18	11♌31 58	20 42.1	0♋25.7	9 36.4	29 34.7	12 14.9	8 59.3	25 41.3	10 45.6	17 28.2	23 14.9
12 Su	5 23 39	21 36 54	17 27 18	23 22 46	20 36.0	2 29.3	10 49.7	0♈16.5	12 09.3	9 00.5	25 48.1	10 45.7	17 27.5	23 13.3
13 M	5 27 35	22 34 15	29 18 53	5♍16 10	20 32.3	4 31.1	12 02.9	0 58.2	12 04.2	9 01.9	25 55.0	10 45.8	17 26.8	23 11.7
14 Tu	5 31 32	23 31 34	11♍15 14	17 16 41	20D 30.7	6 30.8	13 16.1	1 39.8	11 59.4	9 03.5	26 02.0	10R 45.9	17 26.0	23 10.2
15 W	5 35 28	24 28 52	23 21 08	29 29 14	20 30.6	8 28.4	14 29.2	2 21.4	11 55.1	9 05.2	26 09.0	10 45.9	17 25.2	23 08.6
16 Th	5 39 25	25 26 10	5♎41 37	11♎58 55	20R 31.1	10 23.9	15 42.4	3 02.8	11 51.1	9 07.1	26 16.0	10 45.8	17 24.4	23 07.0
17 F	5 43 22	26 23 26	18 21 43	24 50 33	20 31.3	12 17.1	16 55.5	3 44.2	11 47.4	9 09.2	26 23.0	10 45.7	17 23.5	23 05.4
18 Sa	5 47 18	27 20 42	1♏25 52	8♏08 03	20 30.0	14 08.1	18 08.6	4 25.5	11 44.2	9 11.4	26 30.1	10 45.6	17 22.7	23 03.8
19 Su	5 51 15	28 17 57	14 57 17	21 53 41	20 26.6	15 56.7	19 21.7	5 06.7	11 41.4	9 13.9	26 37.3	10 45.4	17 21.8	23 02.3
20 M	5 55 11	29 15 12	28 57 07	6♐07 18	20 20.7	17 43.0	20 34.8	5 47.8	11 38.9	9 16.5	26 44.4	10 45.1	17 20.8	23 00.7
21 Tu	5 59 08	0♋12 26	13♐23 43	20 45 39	20 12.6	19 27.0	21 47.8	6 28.8	11 36.8	9 19.2	26 51.6	10 44.9	17 19.9	22 59.1
22 W	6 03 04	1 09 40	28 12 11	5♑42 14	20 03.0	21 08.7	23 00.8	7 09.7	11 35.1	9 22.2	26 58.9	10 44.5	17 18.9	22 57.6
23 Th	6 07 01	2 06 53	13♑14 37	20 48 03	19 52.9	22 48.0	24 13.8	7 50.5	11 33.8	9 25.3	27 06.1	10 44.1	17 17.9	22 56.0
24 F	6 10 57	3 04 06	28 21 13	5♒52 54	19 43.6	24 24.9	25 26.8	8 31.2	11 32.9	9 28.6	27 13.4	10 43.7	17 16.9	22 54.5
25 Sa	6 14 54	4 01 18	13♒21 56	20 47 19	19 36.1	25 59.5	26 39.8	9 11.9	11 32.3	9 32.0	27 20.8	10 43.2	17 15.8	22 52.9
26 Su	6 18 51	4 58 31	28 08 14	5♓24 02	19 31.0	27 31.6	27 52.7	9 52.4	11D 32.1	9 35.6	27 28.1	10 42.7	17 14.7	22 51.4
27 M	6 22 47	5 55 43	12♓34 18	19 38 46	19 28.4	29 01.4	29 05.6	10 32.8	11 32.3	9 39.3	27 35.5	10 42.1	17 13.6	22 49.8
28 Tu	6 26 44	6 52 56	26 37 20	3♈30 06	19D 27.5	0♌28.7	0♌18.5	11 13.0	11 32.8	9 43.3	27 42.9	10 41.5	17 12.5	22 48.3
29 W	6 30 40	7 50 08	10♈17 13	16 58 57	19R 27.6	1 53.6	1 31.4	11 53.2	11 33.8	9 47.3	27 50.3	10 40.9	17 11.3	22 46.8
30 Th	6 34 37	8 47 21	23 35 38	0♉07 38	19 27.3	3 16.0	2 44.2	12 33.3	11 35.0	9 51.6	27 57.8	10 40.1	17 10.2	22 45.3

Astro Data	Dy Hr Mn
☽ 0N	5 1:29
♃⚻♅	7 7:38
☽ 0S	19 11:45
♆ R	19 23:37
♄⚻♇	23 22:48
☽ 0N	1 6:41
♃ D	5 7:21
♄⚼♅	12 3:25
♅ R	14 22:39
☽ 0S	15 19:41
♂ 0N	20 3:22
⚳ D	26 12:28
☽ 0N	28 11:35

Planet Ingress		Dy Hr Mn
♂	♓	1 2:59
♀	♊	10 4:15
☿	♉	12 9:15
☉	♊	20 22:48
☿	♊	28 10:45
♀	♋	3 15:19
☿	♋	11 7:04
♂	♈	12 2:31
☉	♋	21 6:47
☿	♌	28 4:02
♀	♌	28 5:54

Last Aspect Dy Hr Mn			☽ Ingress	Dy Hr Mn
2 4:48	♇	⚹	♓	2 14:44
4 8:23	♇	□	♈	4 18:37
6 13:23	♇	△	♉	7 0:02
9 5:16	♀	☌	♊	9 7:30
11 14:59	☿	⚹	♋	11 17:21
13 15:05	☉	⚹	♌	14 5:18
16 8:58	☉	□	♍	16 17:47
19 1:01	☉	△	♎	19 4:31
21 0:41	♇	⚹	♏	21 11:50
23 4:55	♄	△	♐	23 15:39
25 6:53	♇	☌	♑	25 17:12
27 15:23	☿	△	♒	27 18:11
29 9:20	♇	⚹	♓	29 20:10

Last Aspect Dy Hr Mn			☽ Ingress	Dy Hr Mn
31 17:54	♀	□	♈	1 0:09
3 5:25	♀	⚹	♉	3 6:21
5 5:26	♂	⚹	♊	5 14:37
7 18:51	♂	□	♋	8 0:47
10 10:19	♂	△	♌	10 12:41
12 11:41	♇	△	♍	13 1:23
15 5:25	♄	⚹	♎	15 13:00
17 15:04	☉	△	♏	17 21:25
19 20:08	♄	△	♐	20 1:46
21 15:35	♇	☌	♑	22 2:53
23 22:05	♄	☍	♒	24 2:37
25 15:24	♇	⚹	♓	26 3:04
28 5:52	♀	△	♈	28 5:52
30 7:58	♄	□	♉	30 11:46

☽ Phases & Eclipses Dy Hr Mn		
1 6:25	☾	10♒59
8 8:47	●	17♉52
16 8:58	☽	25♌36
23 20:19	○	2♐47
30 11:48	☾	9♓10
6 21:56	●	16♊16
15 1:23	☽	24♍04
22 4:15	○	0♑51
28 18:25	☾	7♈08

Astro Data

1 May 2005
Julian Day # 38472
SVP 5♓11'14"
GC 26♐54.8 ⚴ 23♍50.0R
Eris 20♈38.3 ⚵ 8♈50.0
⚷ 3♒15.3 ⚶ 16♉17.0
☽ Mean ☊ 21♈56.4

1 June 2005
Julian Day # 38503
SVP 5♓11'09"
GC 26♐54.9 ⚴ 24♍51.8
Eris 20♈55.2 ⚵ 24♈36.6
⚷ 2♒57.7R ⚶ 29♉55.1
☽ Mean ☊ 20♈17.9

July 2005 LONGITUDE

Day	Sid.Time	☉	0 hr ☽	Noon ☽	True ☊	☿	♀	♂	⚳	♃	♄	♅	♆	♇
1 F	6 38 33	9♋44 34	6♉35 20	12♉59 06	19♈25.5	4♌35.8	3♌57.1	13♈13.2	11♏36.7	9♎56.0	28♋05.3	10♓39.4	17♒09.0	22♐43.8
2 Sa	6 42 30	10 41 47	19 19 20	25 36 23	19R 21.4	5 53.1	5 09.9	13 53.0	11 38.7	10 00.5	28 12.8	10R 38.6	17R 07.8	22R 42.3
3 Su	6 46 26	11 39 01	1♊50 32	8♊02 06	19 14.5	7 07.8	6 22.7	14 32.6	11 41.1	10 05.2	28 20.3	10 37.7	17 06.5	22 40.8
4 M	6 50 23	12 36 14	14 11 19	20 18 25	19 04.7	8 19.9	7 35.5	15 12.1	11 43.9	10 10.1	28 27.9	10 36.9	17 05.3	22 39.3
5 Tu	6 54 20	13 33 28	26 23 34	2♋26 58	18 52.6	9 29.2	8 48.2	15 51.5	11 47.0	10 15.1	28 35.5	10 35.9	17 04.0	22 37.9
6 W	6 58 16	14 30 41	8♋28 44	14 29 03	18 39.1	10 35.7	10 01.0	16 30.7	11 50.4	10 20.3	28 43.1	10 34.9	17 02.7	22 36.5
7 Th	7 02 13	15 27 55	20 28 01	26 25 48	18 25.3	11 39.3	11 13.7	17 09.8	11 54.3	10 25.6	28 50.7	10 33.9	17 01.4	22 35.0
8 F	7 06 09	16 25 08	2♌22 35	8♌18 33	18 12.3	12 39.9	12 26.3	17 48.7	11 58.4	10 31.1	28 58.3	10 32.9	17 00.1	22 33.6
9 Sa	7 10 06	17 22 22	14 13 56	20 08 58	18 01.0	13 37.4	13 39.0	18 27.5	12 02.9	10 36.7	29 06.0	10 31.8	16 58.7	22 32.2
10 Su	7 14 02	18 19 36	26 03 59	1♍59 20	17 52.3	14 31.8	14 51.6	19 06.1	12 07.8	10 42.5	29 13.6	10 30.6	16 57.3	22 30.8
11 M	7 17 59	19 16 49	7♍55 25	13 52 39	17 46.4	15 22.8	16 04.2	19 44.5	12 13.0	10 48.4	29 21.3	10 29.4	16 56.0	22 29.4
12 Tu	7 21 55	20 14 03	19 51 33	25 52 38	17 43.2	16 10.5	17 16.8	20 22.8	12 18.5	10 54.4	29 29.0	10 28.2	16 54.5	22 28.1
13 W	7 25 52	21 11 16	1♎56 29	8♎03 42	17D 41.9	16 54.6	18 29.3	21 00.9	12 24.3	11 00.6	29 36.7	10 26.9	16 53.1	22 26.7
14 Th	7 29 49	22 08 30	14 14 53	20 30 41	17R 41.8	17 34.9	19 41.8	21 38.8	12 30.5	11 07.0	29 44.4	10 25.6	16 51.7	22 25.4
15 F	7 33 45	23 05 43	26 51 43	3♏18 35	17 41.6	18 11.5	20 54.3	22 16.6	12 37.0	11 13.4	29 52.1	10 24.2	16 50.2	22 24.1
16 Sa	7 37 42	24 02 57	9♏51 49	16 31 54	17 40.2	18 44.0	22 06.8	22 54.2	12 43.8	11 20.0	29 59.8	10 22.8	16 48.8	22 22.8
17 Su	7 41 38	25 00 11	23 19 13	0♐13 59	17 36.8	19 12.4	23 19.2	23 31.6	12 50.9	11 26.8	0♌07.6	10 21.4	16 47.3	22 21.6
18 M	7 45 35	25 57 25	7♐16 16	14 25 57	17 30.9	19 36.5	24 31.6	24 08.8	12 58.4	11 33.6	0 15.3	10 19.9	16 45.8	22 20.3
19 Tu	7 49 31	26 54 39	21 42 42	29 05 55	17 22.7	19 56.2	25 43.9	24 45.8	13 06.1	11 40.6	0 23.0	10 18.4	16 44.3	22 19.1
20 W	7 53 28	27 51 54	6♑34 49	14♑08 20	17 12.8	20 11.3	26 56.2	25 22.7	13 14.1	11 47.8	0 30.8	10 16.9	16 42.8	22 17.9
21 Th	7 57 25	28 49 09	21 45 17	29 24 16	17 02.3	20 21.7	28 08.5	25 59.3	13 22.5	11 55.0	0 38.6	10 15.3	16 41.3	22 16.7
22 F	8 01 21	29 46 25	7♒03 52	14♒42 37	16 52.5	20R 27.2	29 20.8	26 35.7	13 31.1	12 02.4	0 46.3	10 13.7	16 39.7	22 15.5
23 Sa	8 05 18	0♌43 41	22 19 09	29 52 10	16 44.5	20 27.8	0♍33.0	27 12.0	13 40.0	12 09.9	0 54.1	10 12.1	16 38.2	22 14.4
24 Su	8 09 14	1 40 57	7♓20 36	14♓43 32	16 38.9	20 23.5	1 45.2	27 48.0	13 49.2	12 17.6	1 01.8	10 10.4	16 36.6	22 13.2
25 M	8 13 11	2 38 15	22 00 19	29 10 29	16 35.9	20 14.1	2 57.3	28 23.8	13 58.6	12 25.3	1 09.6	10 08.7	16 35.1	22 12.1
26 Tu	8 17 07	3 35 34	6♈13 50	13♈10 18	16D 34.9	19 59.8	4 09.4	28 59.4	14 08.4	12 33.2	1 17.3	10 06.9	16 33.5	22 11.0
27 W	8 21 04	4 32 53	20 00 01	26 43 13	16R 35.1	19 40.6	5 21.5	29 34.8	14 18.4	12 41.2	1 25.1	10 05.1	16 31.9	22 10.0
28 Th	8 25 00	5 30 14	3♉20 16	9♉51 35	16 35.1	19 16.7	6 33.5	0♉09.9	14 28.6	12 49.3	1 32.8	10 03.3	16 30.3	22 08.9
29 F	8 28 57	6 27 35	16 17 37	22 38 54	16 34.0	18 48.2	7 45.6	0 44.8	14 39.2	12 57.5	1 40.5	10 01.5	16 28.7	22 07.9
30 Sa	8 32 54	7 24 58	28 55 54	5♊09 07	16 30.8	18 15.6	8 57.5	1 19.4	14 50.0	13 05.9	1 48.3	9 59.6	16 27.1	22 06.9
31 Su	8 36 50	8 22 22	11♊19 02	17 26 04	16 25.1	17 39.1	10 09.5	1 53.8	15 01.0	13 14.3	1 56.0	9 57.7	16 25.5	22 05.9

August 2005 LONGITUDE

Day	Sid.Time	☉	0 hr ☽	Noon ☽	True ☊	☿	♀	♂	⚳	♃	♄	♅	♆	♇
1 M	8 40 47	9♌19 47	23♊30 40	29♊33 10	16♈16.8	16♌59.3	11♍21.4	2♉27.9	15♏12.4	13♎22.9	2♌03.7	9♓55.7	16♒23.9	22♐05.0
2 Tu	8 44 43	10 17 13	5♋33 56	11♋33 14	16R 06.5	16R 16.8	12 33.3	3 01.8	15 23.9	13 31.6	2 11.4	9R 53.8	16R 22.3	22R 04.1
3 W	8 48 40	11 14 40	17 31 22	23 28 33	15 54.8	15 32.3	13 45.1	3 35.4	15 35.7	13 40.4	2 19.2	9 51.8	16 20.7	22 03.2
4 Th	8 52 36	12 12 08	29 25 01	5♌20 57	15 42.7	14 46.3	14 56.9	4 08.6	15 47.8	13 49.3	2 26.8	9 49.8	16 19.0	22 02.3
5 F	8 56 33	13 09 36	11♌16 32	17 11 59	15 31.3	13 59.9	16 08.7	4 41.6	16 00.1	13 58.3	2 34.5	9 47.7	16 17.4	22 01.4
6 Sa	9 00 29	14 07 06	23 07 28	29 03 13	15 21.6	13 13.7	17 20.4	5 14.4	16 12.6	14 07.4	2 42.2	9 45.7	16 15.8	22 00.6
7 Su	9 04 26	15 04 37	4♍59 26	10♍56 24	15 14.1	12 28.7	18 32.1	5 46.8	16 25.4	14 16.6	2 49.8	9 43.6	16 14.1	21 59.8
8 M	9 08 23	16 02 09	16 54 24	22 53 45	15 09.2	11 45.8	19 43.7	6 18.9	16 38.4	14 25.9	2 57.5	9 41.4	16 12.5	21 59.1
9 Tu	9 12 19	16 59 41	28 54 49	4♎58 00	15D 06.7	11 05.7	20 55.3	6 50.6	16 51.6	14 35.3	3 05.1	9 39.3	16 10.9	21 58.3
10 W	9 16 16	17 57 14	11♎03 44	17 12 31	15 06.2	10 29.3	22 06.9	7 22.1	17 05.0	14 44.9	3 12.7	9 37.1	16 09.2	21 57.6
11 Th	9 20 12	18 54 49	23 24 49	29 41 11	15 06.8	9 57.4	23 18.4	7 53.2	17 18.7	14 54.5	3 20.3	9 35.0	16 07.6	21 56.9
12 F	9 24 09	19 52 24	6♏02 09	12♏28 14	15R 07.7	9 30.7	24 29.9	8 24.0	17 32.5	15 04.2	3 27.8	9 32.8	16 06.0	21 56.3
13 Sa	9 28 05	20 50 00	18 59 56	25 37 44	15 07.8	9 09.6	25 41.3	8 54.5	17 46.6	15 14.0	3 35.4	9 30.6	16 04.3	21 55.7
14 Su	9 32 02	21 47 37	2♐22 00	9♐13 04	15 06.3	8 54.8	26 52.6	9 24.6	18 00.9	15 23.9	3 42.9	9 28.3	16 02.7	21 55.1
15 M	9 35 58	22 45 15	16 11 05	23 16 04	15 03.0	8D 46.7	28 03.9	9 54.4	18 15.4	15 33.9	3 50.4	9 26.1	16 01.1	21 54.5
16 Tu	9 39 55	23 42 55	0♑27 52	7♑46 07	14 57.7	8 45.6	29 15.2	10 23.8	18 30.1	15 43.9	3 57.9	9 23.8	15 59.5	21 54.0
17 W	9 43 52	24 40 35	15 10 16	22 39 29	14 50.9	8 51.7	0♎26.4	10 52.8	18 45.0	15 54.1	4 05.3	9 21.5	15 57.9	21 53.5
18 Th	9 47 48	25 38 16	0♒12 48	7♒49 04	14 43.6	9 05.2	1 37.6	11 21.5	19 00.0	16 04.3	4 12.7	9 19.2	15 56.2	21 53.0
19 F	9 51 45	26 35 59	15 26 58	23 05 10	14 36.7	9 26.2	2 48.7	11 49.7	19 15.3	16 14.7	4 20.1	9 16.9	15 54.6	21 52.5
20 Sa	9 55 41	27 33 42	0♓42 16	8♓16 57	14 31.1	9 54.6	3 59.7	12 17.6	19 30.8	16 25.1	4 27.5	9 14.6	15 53.1	21 52.1
21 Su	9 59 38	28 31 27	15 48 00	23 14 23	14 27.3	10 30.6	5 10.7	12 45.1	19 46.4	16 35.6	4 34.8	9 12.3	15 51.5	21 51.7
22 M	10 03 34	29 29 14	0♈35 11	7♈49 45	14D 25.7	11 13.9	6 21.6	13 12.2	20 02.2	16 46.2	4 42.1	9 09.9	15 49.9	21 51.4
23 Tu	10 07 31	0♍27 02	14 57 38	21 58 34	14 25.7	12 04.4	7 32.5	13 38.9	20 18.2	16 56.8	4 49.4	9 07.6	15 48.3	21 51.0
24 W	10 11 27	1 24 52	28 52 28	5♉39 25	14 26.8	13 01.9	8 43.3	14 05.1	20 34.3	17 07.5	4 56.6	9 05.2	15 46.7	21 50.7
25 Th	10 15 24	2 22 44	12♉19 39	18 53 31	14 28.1	14 06.2	9 54.0	14 30.9	20 50.6	17 18.4	5 03.8	9 02.8	15 45.2	21 50.5
26 F	10 19 21	3 20 38	25 21 24	1♊43 47	14R 28.8	15 16.8	11 04.8	14 56.2	21 07.1	17 29.2	5 11.0	9 00.4	15 43.6	21 50.2
27 Sa	10 23 17	4 18 33	8♊01 12	14 14 10	14 28.3	16 33.5	12 15.4	15 21.0	21 23.8	17 40.2	5 18.1	8 58.1	15 42.1	21 50.0
28 Su	10 27 14	5 16 31	20 23 16	26 29 00	14 26.1	17 55.9	13 26.0	15 45.4	21 40.6	17 51.3	5 25.2	8 55.7	15 40.6	21 49.9
29 M	10 31 10	6 14 30	2♋31 54	8♋32 29	14 22.3	19 23.5	14 36.5	16 09.3	21 57.6	18 02.4	5 32.3	8 53.3	15 39.1	21 49.7
30 Tu	10 35 07	7 12 31	14 31 14	20 28 33	14 17.0	20 55.9	15 47.0	16 32.6	22 14.8	18 13.5	5 39.3	8 50.9	15 37.6	21 49.6
31 W	10 39 03	8 10 33	26 24 53	2♌20 34	14 10.7	22 32.7	16 57.4	16 55.5	22 32.1	18 24.8	5 46.3	8 48.5	15 36.1	21 49.5

Astro Data Dy Hr Mn	Planet Ingress Dy Hr Mn
♃⚻♅ 8 18:22	♄ ♌ 16 12:32
☽0S 13 2:01	☉ ♌ 22 17:42
☿R 23 3:00	♀ ♍ 23 1:02
☽0N 25 18:07	♂ ♉ 28 5:13
☽0S 9 7:15	♀ ♎ 17 3:06
☿D 16 3:51	☉ ♍ 23 0:47
♃△♆ 17 19:37	
♀0S 18 10:57	
☽0N 22 3:06	

Last Aspect Dy Hr Mn	☽ Ingress Dy Hr Mn
2 17:03 ♄ ⚹	♊ 2 20:27
4 16:37 ♇ ☍	♋ 5 7:08
7 16:55 ♄ ☌	♌ 7 19:12
9 16:50 ♇ △	♍ 10 7:58
12 19:13 ♄ ⚹	♎ 12 20:10
15 5:33 ♄ □	♏ 15 5:52
17 2:16 ☉ △	♐ 17 11:36
19 6:04 ♀ △	♑ 19 13:27
21 11:01 ☉ ☍	♒ 21 12:56
23 7:34 ♂ ⚹	♓ 23 12:13
25 0:20 ♇ □	♈ 25 13:24
27 17:24 ♂ ☌	♉ 27 17:55
29 5:00 ☿ □	♊ 30 2:03

Last Aspect Dy Hr Mn	☽ Ingress Dy Hr Mn
31 21:12 ♇ ☍	♋ 1 12:53
2 16:01 ♃ □	♌ 4 1:11
5 21:46 ♇ △	♍ 6 13:55
8 10:11 ♇ □	♎ 9 2:10
10 21:12 ♇ ⚹	♏ 11 12:36
13 12:07 ♀ ⚹	♐ 13 19:48
15 20:44 ♀ □	♑ 15 23:14
17 1:03 ♃ □	♒ 17 23:40
19 17:54 ☉ ☍	♓ 19 22:53
21 9:46 ♇ □	♈ 21 23:02
23 11:47 ♇ △	♉ 24 1:59
25 6:15 ♆ □	♊ 26 8:44
28 2:50 ♇ ☍	♋ 28 18:58
30 7:23 ♃ □	♌ 31 7:15

☽ Phases & Eclipses Dy Hr Mn	
6 12:04	● 14♋31
14 15:21	☽ 22♎16
21 11:01	○ 28♑47
28 3:20	☾ 5♉10
5 3:06	● 12♌48
13 2:40	☽ 20♏28
19 17:54	○ 26♒50
26 15:19	☾ 3♊29

Astro Data

1 July 2005
Julian Day # 38533
SVP 5♓11'04"
GC 26♐55.0 ⚴ 1♎12.0
Eris 21♈04.5 ⚵ 9♉46.5
⚷ 1♒43.8R ⚶ 12♊46.6
☽ Mean ☊ 18♈42.6

1 August 2005
Julian Day # 38564
SVP 5♓10'58"
GC 26♐55.0 ⚴ 11♎00.6
Eris 21♈04.6R ⚵ 24♉52.2
⚷ 29♑58.8R ⚶ 25♊24.3
☽ Mean ☊ 17♈04.2

LONGITUDE — September 2005

Day	Sid.Time	☉	0 hr ☽	Noon ☽	True ☊	☿	♀	♂	⚳	♃	♄	♅	♆	♇
1 Th	10 43 00	9♍08 38	8♌15 59	14♌11 25	14♈04.2	24♌13.2	18♎07.8	17♉17.8	22♏49.6	18♎36.1	5♌53.3	8♓46.1	15♒34.6	21♐49.5
2 F	10 46 56	10 06 44	20 07 08	26 03 26	13R58.0	25 57.1	19 18.1	17 39.6	23 07.2	18 47.5	6 00.2	8R43.7	15R33.2	21D49.5
3 Sa	10 50 53	11 04 52	2♍00 30	7♍58 35	13 52.8	27 43.8	20 28.3	18 00.8	23 24.9	18 58.9	6 07.0	8 41.3	15 31.7	21 49.5
4 Su	10 54 50	12 03 01	13 57 53	19 58 38	13 49.0	29 32.9	21 38.5	18 21.5	23 42.9	19 10.5	6 13.8	8 38.9	15 30.3	21 49.5
5 M	10 58 46	13 01 13	26 01 01	2♎05 16	13D46.8	1♍23.9	22 48.6	18 41.6	24 00.9	19 22.0	6 20.6	8 36.5	15 28.9	21 49.6
6 Tu	11 02 43	13 59 25	8♎11 37	14 20 18	13 46.2	3 16.5	23 58.6	19 01.1	24 19.1	19 33.7	6 27.3	8 34.1	15 27.5	21 49.7
7 W	11 06 39	14 57 40	20 31 37	26 45 51	13 46.8	5 10.1	25 08.6	19 20.0	24 37.4	19 45.4	6 34.0	8 31.7	15 26.1	21 49.9
8 Th	11 10 36	15 55 56	3♏03 17	9♏24 16	13 48.2	7 04.5	26 18.5	19 38.3	24 55.9	19 57.1	6 40.6	8 29.4	15 24.8	21 50.1
9 F	11 14 32	16 54 14	15 49 07	22 18 11	13 49.8	8 59.4	27 28.3	19 55.9	25 14.5	20 08.9	6 47.2	8 27.0	15 23.4	21 50.3
10 Sa	11 18 29	17 52 33	28 51 48	5♐30 15	13R51.1	10 54.5	28 38.0	20 13.0	25 33.3	20 20.8	6 53.7	8 24.7	15 22.1	21 50.5
11 Su	11 22 25	18 50 54	12♐13 49	19 02 44	13 51.6	12 49.5	29 47.7	20 29.3	25 52.2	20 32.7	7 00.1	8 22.3	15 20.8	21 50.8
12 M	11 26 22	19 49 16	25 57 06	2♑57 00	13 51.0	14 44.3	0♏57.2	20 45.1	26 11.2	20 44.7	7 06.5	8 20.0	15 19.5	21 51.1
13 Tu	11 30 19	20 47 40	10♑02 20	17 12 55	13 49.4	16 38.6	2 06.7	21 00.1	26 30.3	20 56.7	7 12.9	8 17.6	15 18.3	21 51.5
14 W	11 34 15	21 46 06	24 28 24	1♒48 16	13 47.0	18 32.5	3 16.1	21 14.5	26 49.5	21 08.8	7 19.2	8 15.3	15 17.0	21 51.8
15 Th	11 38 12	22 44 33	9♒11 53	16 38 26	13 44.2	20 25.6	4 25.4	21 28.2	27 08.9	21 20.9	7 25.4	8 13.0	15 15.8	21 52.2
16 F	11 42 08	23 43 01	24 07 00	1♓36 34	13 41.6	22 18.0	5 34.6	21 41.2	27 28.4	21 33.1	7 31.6	8 10.8	15 14.6	21 52.7
17 Sa	11 46 05	24 41 32	9♓06 05	16 34 25	13 39.5	24 09.6	6 43.8	21 53.5	27 48.0	21 45.3	7 37.8	8 08.5	15 13.4	21 53.1
18 Su	11 50 01	25 40 04	24 00 32	1♈23 26	13D38.3	26 00.3	7 52.8	22 05.0	28 07.7	21 57.6	7 43.8	8 06.2	15 12.3	21 53.6
19 M	11 53 58	26 38 38	8♈42 11	15 56 03	13 38.0	27 50.1	9 01.7	22 15.8	28 27.5	22 09.9	7 49.8	8 04.0	15 11.2	21 54.2
20 Tu	11 57 54	27 37 14	23 04 22	0♉06 43	13 38.5	29 38.9	10 10.5	22 25.8	28 47.4	22 22.2	7 55.8	8 01.8	15 10.0	21 54.7
21 W	12 01 51	28 35 53	7♉02 45	13 52 21	13 39.5	1♎26.8	11 19.3	22 35.1	29 07.5	22 34.6	8 01.6	7 59.6	15 09.0	21 55.3
22 Th	12 05 47	29 34 33	20 35 29	27 12 19	13 40.7	3 13.7	12 27.9	22 43.6	29 27.6	22 47.1	8 07.4	7 57.4	15 07.9	21 56.0
23 F	12 09 44	0♎33 16	3♊43 02	10♊08 01	13 41.7	4 59.6	13 36.4	22 51.2	29 47.9	22 59.5	8 13.2	7 55.2	15 06.9	21 56.6
24 Sa	12 13 41	1 32 01	16 27 38	22 42 24	13R42.4	6 44.6	14 44.8	22 58.1	0♐08.2	23 12.0	8 18.9	7 53.1	15 05.9	21 57.3
25 Su	12 17 37	2 30 48	28 52 47	4♋59 22	13 42.6	8 28.6	15 53.2	23 04.1	0 28.7	23 24.6	8 24.5	7 51.0	15 04.9	21 58.1
26 M	12 21 34	3 29 38	11♋02 42	17 03 20	13 42.2	10 11.7	17 01.4	23 09.3	0 49.2	23 37.2	8 30.0	7 48.9	15 03.9	21 58.8
27 Tu	12 25 30	4 28 30	23 01 51	28 58 48	13 41.4	11 53.8	18 09.5	23 13.7	1 09.9	23 49.8	8 35.5	7 46.8	15 03.0	21 59.6
28 W	12 29 27	5 27 24	4♌54 44	10♌50 08	13 40.4	13 35.0	19 17.5	23 17.1	1 30.6	24 02.4	8 40.9	7 44.8	15 02.1	22 00.4
29 Th	12 33 23	6 26 20	16 45 30	22 41 18	13 39.3	15 15.3	20 25.4	23 19.7	1 51.5	24 15.1	8 46.2	7 42.7	15 01.2	22 01.3
30 F	12 37 20	7 25 19	28 37 57	4♍35 49	13 38.4	16 54.7	21 33.1	23 21.4	2 12.4	24 27.8	8 51.5	7 40.8	15 00.4	22 02.2

LONGITUDE — October 2005

Day	Sid.Time	☉	0 hr ☽	Noon ☽	True ☊	☿	♀	♂	⚳	♃	♄	♅	♆	♇
1 Sa	12 41 16	8♎24 19	10♍35 16	16♍36 36	13♈37.7	18♎33.2	22♏40.7	23♉22.3	2♐33.5	24♎40.6	8♌56.7	7♓38.8	14♒59.5	22♐03.1
2 Su	12 45 13	9 23 22	22 40 07	28 46 01	13R37.3	20 10.9	23 48.3	23R22.2	2 54.6	24 53.4	9 01.8	7R36.9	14R58.8	22 04.0
3 M	12 49 10	10 22 27	4♎54 31	11♎05 49	13D37.1	21 47.7	24 55.6	23 21.2	3 15.8	25 06.2	9 06.8	7 34.9	14 58.0	22 05.0
4 Tu	12 53 06	11 21 33	17 20 03	23 37 19	13 37.2	23 23.7	26 02.9	23 19.3	3 37.1	25 19.0	9 11.8	7 33.1	14 57.3	22 06.0
5 W	12 57 03	12 20 42	29 57 46	6♏21 27	13 37.3	24 58.9	27 10.0	23 16.6	3 58.5	25 31.8	9 16.6	7 31.2	14 56.5	22 07.0
6 Th	13 00 59	13 19 53	12♏48 28	19 18 51	13R37.3	26 33.3	28 17.0	23 12.9	4 20.0	25 44.7	9 21.4	7 29.4	14 55.9	22 08.1
7 F	13 04 56	14 19 06	25 52 40	2♐29 58	13 37.3	28 06.9	29 23.8	23 08.3	4 41.6	25 57.6	9 26.1	7 27.6	14 55.2	22 09.2
8 Sa	13 08 52	15 18 20	9♐10 46	15 55 07	13 37.2	29 39.7	0♐30.5	23 02.9	5 03.2	26 10.5	9 30.7	7 25.9	14 54.6	22 10.3
9 Su	13 12 49	16 17 37	22 43 00	29 34 25	13 37.0	1♏11.8	1 37.0	22 56.5	5 24.9	26 23.4	9 35.3	7 24.2	14 54.0	22 11.4
10 M	13 16 45	17 16 55	6♑29 19	13♑27 38	13D36.9	2 43.2	2 43.4	22 49.3	5 46.7	26 36.4	9 39.7	7 22.5	14 53.5	22 12.6
11 Tu	13 20 42	18 16 15	20 29 15	27 33 59	13 37.0	4 13.7	3 49.5	22 41.2	6 08.6	26 49.4	9 44.1	7 20.9	14 53.0	22 13.8
12 W	13 24 39	19 15 36	4♒41 37	11♒51 51	13 37.2	5 43.6	4 55.5	22 32.2	6 30.6	27 02.3	9 48.4	7 19.3	14 52.5	22 15.1
13 Th	13 28 35	20 14 59	19 04 18	26 18 33	13 37.8	7 12.6	6 01.4	22 22.4	6 52.6	27 15.3	9 52.6	7 17.7	14 52.0	22 16.3
14 F	13 32 32	21 14 24	3♓34 04	10♓50 16	13 38.4	8 41.0	7 07.0	22 11.7	7 14.7	27 28.3	9 56.7	7 16.2	14 51.6	22 17.6
15 Sa	13 36 28	22 13 51	18 06 33	25 22 12	13 39.0	10 08.5	8 12.4	22 00.3	7 36.8	27 41.4	10 00.7	7 14.7	14 51.2	22 18.9
16 Su	13 40 25	23 13 20	2♈36 33	9♈48 52	13R39.3	11 35.3	9 17.7	21 48.0	7 59.0	27 54.4	10 04.6	7 13.3	14 50.8	22 20.3
17 M	13 44 21	24 12 50	16 58 30	24 04 46	13 39.2	13 01.3	10 22.7	21 35.0	8 21.3	28 07.4	10 08.5	7 11.9	14 50.5	22 21.7
18 Tu	13 48 18	25 12 23	1♉07 07	8♉05 01	13 38.5	14 26.5	11 27.5	21 21.2	8 43.7	28 20.5	10 12.2	7 10.5	14 50.2	22 23.1
19 W	13 52 14	26 11 58	14 58 04	21 45 56	13 37.2	15 50.9	12 32.1	21 06.6	9 06.1	28 33.5	10 15.9	7 09.2	14 49.9	22 24.5
20 Th	13 56 11	27 11 35	28 28 25	5♊05 26	13 35.4	17 14.4	13 36.5	20 51.4	9 28.6	28 46.6	10 19.4	7 07.9	14 49.7	22 25.9
21 F	14 00 08	28 11 14	11♊36 59	18 03 12	13 33.4	18 37.0	14 40.6	20 35.4	9 51.1	28 59.6	10 22.9	7 06.6	14 49.5	22 27.4
22 Sa	14 04 04	29 10 55	24 24 17	0♋40 33	13 31.4	19 58.6	15 44.5	20 18.8	10 13.8	29 12.7	10 26.2	7 05.4	14 49.3	22 28.9
23 Su	14 08 01	0♏10 39	6♋52 23	13 00 12	13 29.9	21 19.3	16 48.2	20 01.6	10 36.4	29 25.8	10 29.5	7 04.3	14 49.2	22 30.4
24 M	14 11 57	1 10 25	19 04 32	25 05 54	13D29.0	22 38.9	17 51.6	19 43.8	10 59.2	29 38.8	10 32.7	7 03.2	14 49.1	22 32.0
25 Tu	14 15 54	2 10 13	1♌04 52	7♌02 03	13 29.0	23 57.3	18 54.7	19 25.4	11 22.0	29 51.9	10 35.8	7 02.1	14 49.0	22 33.6
26 W	14 19 50	3 10 03	12 58 02	18 53 26	13 29.7	25 14.5	19 57.6	19 06.5	11 44.8	0♏05.0	10 38.7	7 01.1	14D49.0	22 35.2
27 Th	14 23 47	4 09 55	24 48 52	0♍44 54	13 31.1	26 30.4	21 00.2	18 47.1	12 07.7	0 18.0	10 41.6	7 00.1	14 49.0	22 36.8
28 F	14 27 43	5 09 50	6♍42 07	12 41 04	13 32.8	27 44.8	22 02.5	18 27.3	12 30.7	0 31.1	10 44.4	6 59.1	14 49.1	22 38.4
29 Sa	14 31 40	6 09 46	18 42 16	24 46 09	13 34.4	28 57.6	23 04.5	18 07.2	12 53.7	0 44.1	10 47.0	6 58.3	14 49.1	22 40.1
30 Su	14 35 37	7 09 45	0♎53 10	7♎03 40	13R35.4	0♐08.6	24 06.3	17 46.6	13 16.7	0 57.2	10 49.6	6 57.4	14 49.2	22 41.8
31 M	14 39 33	8 09 46	13 17 58	19 36 17	13 35.4	1 17.7	25 07.7	17 25.9	13 39.9	1 10.2	10 52.0	6 56.6	14 49.4	22 43.5

Astro Data

Astro Data	Dy Hr Mn
♇ D	2 10:53
☽ 0S	5 12:35
♄□♇	9 23:54
♃✶♇	18 3:58
☽ 0N	18 13:37
♄⊼♅	21 5:50
☿ 0S	22 6:21
☉ 0S	22 22:25
♃□♅	23 4:56
♂ R	1 22:05
☽ 0S	2 19:04
☽ 0N	15 23:38
♆ D	26 23:25
☽ 0S	30 2:53

Planet Ingress

Planet Ingress	Dy Hr Mn
☿ ♍	4 17:54
♀ ♏	11 16:15
☿ ♎	20 16:41
☉ ♎	22 22:24
⚳ ♐	24 2:20
♀ ♐	8 1:01
☿ ♏	8 17:16
☉ ♏	23 7:43
♃ ♏	26 2:53
☿ ♐	30 9:03

Last Aspect / ☽ Ingress (September)

Last Aspect Dy Hr Mn		☽ Ingress	Dy Hr Mn
2 11:45	☿ ☌	♍	2 19:57
4 15:41	♇ □	♎	5 7:53
7 8:34	♀ ☌	♏	7 18:11
9 7:32	♂ ☍	♐	10 2:04
11 16:53	♇ ☌	♑	12 6:58
13 18:23	♂ △	♒	14 9:03
15 20:24	♇ ✶	♓	16 9:25
18 2:02	☉ ☍	♈	18 9:44
19 22:37	♃ ☍	♉	20 11:48
22 16:42	☉ △	♊	22 17:08
24 12:58	♃ △	♋	25 2:11
27 1:25	♃ □	♌	27 14:04
29 15:13	♃ ✶	♍	30 2:45

Last Aspect / ☽ Ingress (October)

Last Aspect Dy Hr Mn		☽ Ingress	Dy Hr Mn
2 1:23	♂ △	♎	2 14:25
4 15:16	♃ ☌	♏	5 0:04
7 5:53	♀ ☌	♐	7 7:29
9 6:21	♃ ✶	♑	9 12:45
11 10:43	♃ □	♒	11 16:06
13 13:35	♃ △	♓	13 18:06
15 6:56	♇ □	♈	15 19:40
17 18:59	♃ ☍	♉	17 22:05
19 10:52	♂ ☌	♊	20 2:45
22 9:08	♃ △	♋	22 10:42
24 21:17	♃ □	♌	24 21:50
27 2:24	☿ □	♍	27 10:29
29 21:07	☿ ✶	♎	29 22:16

☽ Phases & Eclipses

Dy Hr Mn		
3 18:46	●	11♍21
11 11:38	☽	18♐50
18 2:02	○	25♓16
25 6:42	☾	2♋18
3 10:29	●	10♎19
3 10:32:47	✔	A 04'31"
10 19:02	☽	17♑34
17 12:15	○	24♈13
17 12:04	•	P 0.062
25 1:18	☾	1♌44

Astro Data

1 September 2005
Julian Day # 38595
SVP 5♓10'54"
GC 26♐55.1 ⚴ 22♎44.5
Eris 20♈55.3R ✱ 8♊28.4
⚷ 28♑27.9R ⚵ 6♋52.7
☽ Mean ☊ 15♈25.7

1 October 2005
Julian Day # 38625
SVP 5♓10'50"
GC 26♐55.2 ⚴ 5♏09.5
Eris 20♈39.6R ✱ 18♊33.4
⚷ 27♑48.6R ⚵ 16♋04.8
☽ Mean ☊ 13♈50.3

November 2005 — LONGITUDE

Day	Sid.Time	☉	0 hr ☽	Noon ☽	True ☊	☿	♀	♂	⚳	♃	♄	♅	♆	♇
1 Tu	14 43 30	9♏09 49	25♎58 46	2♏25 33	13♈34.1	2♐24.7	26♐08.7	17♉04.8	14♐03.0	1♏23.2	10♌54.4	6♓55.9	14♒49.5	22♐45.2
2 W	14 47 26	10 09 53	8♏56 36	15 31 53	13R31.6	3 29.3	27 09.4	16R43.7	14 26.2	1 36.3	10 56.6	6R55.2	14 49.7	22 47.0
3 Th	14 51 23	11 10 00	22 11 16	28 54 32	13 27.8	4 31.3	28 09.8	16 22.4	14 49.5	1 49.3	10 58.8	6 54.5	14 50.0	22 48.8
4 F	14 55 19	12 10 08	5♐41 27	12♐31 41	13 23.3	5 30.2	29 09.8	16 01.0	15 12.8	2 02.3	11 00.8	6 53.9	14 50.3	22 50.6
5 Sa	14 59 16	13 10 19	19 24 56	26 20 49	13 18.7	6 25.9	0♑09.4	15 39.6	15 36.2	2 15.2	11 02.8	6 53.4	14 50.6	22 52.4
6 Su	15 03 12	14 10 30	3♑18 58	10♑19 02	13 14.6	7 17.8	1 08.6	15 18.3	15 59.6	2 28.2	11 04.6	6 52.9	14 50.9	22 54.3
7 M	15 07 09	15 10 44	17 20 38	24 23 28	13 11.5	8 05.6	2 07.4	14 57.1	16 23.1	2 41.1	11 06.3	6 52.4	14 51.3	22 56.1
8 Tu	15 11 06	16 10 58	1♒27 12	8♒31 35	13D10.0	8 48.8	3 05.8	14 36.0	16 46.5	2 54.1	11 07.9	6 52.0	14 51.7	22 58.0
9 W	15 15 02	17 11 14	15 36 20	22 41 15	13 09.8	9 26.7	4 03.7	14 15.1	17 10.1	3 07.0	11 09.4	6 51.7	14 52.1	22 59.9
10 Th	15 18 59	18 11 32	29 46 06	6♓50 41	13 10.8	9 58.9	5 01.1	13 54.5	17 33.6	3 19.8	11 10.8	6 51.4	14 52.6	23 01.8
11 F	15 22 55	19 11 51	13♓54 49	20 58 15	13 12.4	10 24.6	5 58.0	13 34.2	17 57.2	3 32.7	11 12.0	6 51.1	14 53.1	23 03.7
12 Sa	15 26 52	20 12 11	28 00 48	5♈02 10	13R13.6	10 43.1	6 54.4	13 14.2	18 20.9	3 45.5	11 13.2	6 50.9	14 53.7	23 05.7
13 Su	15 30 48	21 12 33	12♈02 06	19 00 17	13 13.7	10R53.8	7 50.3	12 54.6	18 44.5	3 58.3	11 14.2	6 50.7	14 54.3	23 07.7
14 M	15 34 45	22 12 56	25 56 24	2♉50 06	13 12.0	10 55.9	8 45.6	12 35.5	19 08.2	4 11.1	11 15.2	6 50.6	14 54.9	23 09.6
15 Tu	15 38 41	23 13 21	9♉41 03	16 28 52	13 08.4	10 48.8	9 40.4	12 16.8	19 32.0	4 23.8	11 16.0	6D50.6	14 55.5	23 11.6
16 W	15 42 38	24 13 47	23 13 15	29 53 55	13 02.8	10 31.8	10 34.5	11 58.6	19 55.8	4 36.5	11 16.7	6 50.6	14 56.2	23 13.6
17 Th	15 46 35	25 14 15	6♊30 35	13♊03 05	12 55.6	10 04.6	11 28.0	11 40.9	20 19.6	4 49.2	11 17.3	6 50.6	14 56.9	23 15.7
18 F	15 50 31	26 14 45	19 31 18	25 55 10	12 47.7	9 27.0	12 20.9	11 23.9	20 43.4	5 01.8	11 17.8	6 50.7	14 57.7	23 17.7
19 Sa	15 54 28	27 15 16	2♋14 44	8♋30 07	12 39.7	8 39.0	13 13.1	11 07.4	21 07.3	5 14.5	11 18.2	6 50.9	14 58.5	23 19.8
20 Su	15 58 24	28 15 49	14 41 31	20 49 13	12 32.7	7 41.3	14 04.6	10 51.5	21 31.2	5 27.0	11 18.5	6 51.1	14 59.3	23 21.8
21 M	16 02 21	29 16 24	26 53 33	2♌54 57	12 27.2	6 34.8	14 55.4	10 36.3	21 55.1	5 39.6	11R18.6	6 51.3	15 00.1	23 23.9
22 Tu	16 06 17	0♐17 00	8♌53 55	14 50 57	12 23.6	5 21.1	15 45.4	10 21.8	22 19.1	5 52.1	11 18.7	6 51.7	15 01.0	23 26.0
23 W	16 10 14	1 17 38	20 46 39	26 41 37	12D22.0	4 02.2	16 34.6	10 08.0	22 43.0	6 04.5	11 18.6	6 52.0	15 01.9	23 28.1
24 Th	16 14 10	2 18 18	2♍36 31	8♍31 59	12 22.1	2 40.5	17 23.1	9 54.9	23 07.0	6 17.0	11 18.4	6 52.4	15 02.8	23 30.3
25 F	16 18 07	3 18 59	14 28 41	20 27 18	12 23.1	1 18.8	18 10.6	9 42.6	23 31.1	6 29.3	11 18.1	6 52.9	15 03.8	23 32.4
26 Sa	16 22 04	4 19 42	26 28 28	2♎32 49	12R24.3	29♏59.7	18 57.3	9 31.0	23 55.1	6 41.7	11 17.7	6 53.4	15 04.8	23 34.5
27 Su	16 26 00	5 20 27	8♎40 57	14 53 23	12 24.7	28 45.9	19 43.1	9 20.2	24 19.2	6 54.0	11 17.2	6 53.9	15 05.9	23 36.7
28 M	16 29 57	6 21 13	21 10 38	27 33 04	12 23.4	27 39.7	20 27.9	9 10.2	24 43.3	7 06.2	11 16.5	6 54.6	15 06.9	23 38.8
29 Tu	16 33 53	7 22 00	4♏01 00	10♏34 38	12 19.9	26 42.8	21 11.8	9 00.9	25 07.5	7 18.4	11 15.8	6 55.2	15 08.0	23 41.0
30 W	16 37 50	8 22 49	17 14 01	23 59 07	12 13.8	25 56.6	21 54.6	8 52.5	25 31.6	7 30.5	11 14.9	6 55.9	15 09.1	23 43.2

December 2005 — LONGITUDE

Day	Sid.Time	☉	0 hr ☽	Noon ☽	True ☊	☿	♀	♂	⚳	♃	♄	♅	♆	♇
1 Th	16 41 46	9♐23 39	0♐49 43	7♐45 29	12♈05.6	25♏21.6	22♑36.3	8♉45.0	25♐55.8	7♏42.6	11♌14.0	6♓56.7	15♒10.3	23♐45.4
2 F	16 45 43	10 24 31	14 45 56	21 50 31	11R55.9	24R58.2	23 16.9	8R38.2	26 20.0	7 54.7	11R12.9	6 57.5	15 11.5	23 47.6
3 Sa	16 49 39	11 25 23	28 58 30	6♑09 10	11 45.8	24D46.2	23 56.3	8 32.3	26 44.2	8 06.7	11 11.7	6 58.4	15 12.7	23 49.8
4 Su	16 53 36	12 26 17	13♑21 42	20 35 19	11 36.4	24 45.1	24 34.5	8 27.2	27 08.4	8 18.6	11 10.4	6 59.3	15 14.0	23 52.0
5 M	16 57 33	13 27 11	27 49 13	5♒02 44	11 28.9	24 54.3	25 11.4	8 23.0	27 32.6	8 30.4	11 09.0	7 00.3	15 15.3	23 54.2
6 Tu	17 01 29	14 28 06	12♒15 13	19 26 08	11 23.8	25 12.9	25 46.9	8 19.6	27 56.9	8 42.3	11 07.5	7 01.3	15 16.6	23 56.4
7 W	17 05 26	15 29 02	26 35 03	3♓41 41	11D21.2	25 40.1	26 21.1	8 17.0	28 21.1	8 54.0	11 05.8	7 02.4	15 17.9	23 58.7
8 Th	17 09 22	16 29 59	10♓45 47	17 47 14	11 20.7	26 15.0	26 53.8	8 15.3	28 45.4	9 05.7	11 04.1	7 03.5	15 19.3	24 00.9
9 F	17 13 19	17 30 56	24 45 59	1♈42 02	11R21.1	26 56.9	27 25.0	8D14.3	29 09.7	9 17.3	11 02.2	7 04.7	15 20.7	24 03.1
10 Sa	17 17 15	18 31 53	8♈35 24	15 26 09	11 21.2	27 44.8	27 54.6	8 14.2	29 34.0	9 28.8	11 00.3	7 05.9	15 22.1	24 05.4
11 Su	17 21 12	19 32 52	22 14 21	29 00 01	11 19.9	28 38.2	28 22.6	8 14.8	29 58.3	9 40.3	10 58.2	7 07.1	15 23.5	24 07.6
12 M	17 25 09	20 33 50	5♉43 12	12♉23 53	11 16.1	29 36.3	28 48.8	8 16.3	0♑22.6	9 51.7	10 56.1	7 08.5	15 25.0	24 09.8
13 Tu	17 29 05	21 34 50	19 02 01	25 37 32	11 09.4	0♐38.5	29 13.3	8 18.5	0 46.9	10 03.0	10 53.8	7 09.8	15 26.5	24 12.1
14 W	17 33 02	22 35 50	2♊10 22	8♊40 24	10 59.7	1 44.3	29 36.0	8 21.5	1 11.2	10 14.3	10 51.5	7 11.2	15 28.0	24 14.3
15 Th	17 36 58	23 36 51	15 07 30	21 31 35	10 47.7	2 53.3	29 56.7	8 25.2	1 35.5	10 25.5	10 49.0	7 12.7	15 29.6	24 16.6
16 F	17 40 55	24 37 53	27 52 33	4♋10 19	10 34.3	4 05.0	0♒15.5	8 29.7	1 59.9	10 36.6	10 46.5	7 14.2	15 31.2	24 18.8
17 Sa	17 44 51	25 38 55	10♋24 52	16 36 14	10 20.7	5 19.2	0 32.3	8 34.9	2 24.2	10 47.7	10 43.8	7 15.7	15 32.8	24 21.1
18 Su	17 48 48	26 39 58	22 44 30	28 49 47	10 08.1	6 35.4	0 47.0	8 40.8	2 48.5	10 58.6	10 41.1	7 17.3	15 34.4	24 23.3
19 M	17 52 44	27 41 02	4♌52 19	10♌52 22	9 57.5	7 53.4	0 59.5	8 47.5	3 12.9	11 09.5	10 38.2	7 19.0	15 36.1	24 25.6
20 Tu	17 56 41	28 42 07	16 50 16	22 46 26	9 49.6	9 13.1	1 09.8	8 54.8	3 37.2	11 20.3	10 35.3	7 20.7	15 37.8	24 27.8
21 W	18 00 38	29 43 12	28 41 20	4♍35 29	9 44.4	10 34.1	1 17.9	9 02.7	4 01.5	11 31.0	10 32.3	7 22.4	15 39.5	24 30.1
22 Th	18 04 34	0♑44 18	10♍29 27	16 23 53	9 41.9	11 56.4	1 23.6	9 11.4	4 25.9	11 41.7	10 29.2	7 24.2	15 41.2	24 32.3
23 F	18 08 31	1 45 24	22 19 24	28 16 41	9 41.1	13 19.8	1R27.0	9 20.7	4 50.2	11 52.2	10 26.0	7 26.0	15 42.9	24 34.5
24 Sa	18 12 27	2 46 32	4♎16 27	10♎19 24	9 41.1	14 44.2	1 28.0	9 30.6	5 14.6	12 02.7	10 22.7	7 27.9	15 44.7	24 36.8
25 Su	18 16 24	3 47 40	16 26 14	22 37 37	9 40.7	16 09.4	1 26.5	9 41.2	5 38.9	12 13.0	10 19.3	7 29.8	15 46.5	24 39.0
26 M	18 20 20	4 48 48	28 54 11	5♏16 31	9 38.6	17 35.4	1 22.6	9 52.4	6 03.2	12 23.3	10 15.8	7 31.7	15 48.3	24 41.2
27 Tu	18 24 17	5 49 57	11♏45 07	18 20 21	9 34.2	19 02.1	1 16.2	10 04.2	6 27.6	12 33.5	10 12.3	7 33.7	15 50.1	24 43.4
28 W	18 28 13	6 51 07	25 02 31	1♐51 42	9 26.9	20 29.4	1 07.3	10 16.6	6 51.9	12 43.6	10 08.6	7 35.8	15 52.0	24 45.6
29 Th	18 32 10	7 52 17	8♐47 51	15 50 41	9 17.0	21 57.3	0 55.9	10 29.6	7 16.2	12 53.5	10 04.9	7 37.9	15 53.9	24 47.9
30 F	18 36 07	8 53 28	22 59 46	0♑14 27	9 05.1	23 25.7	0 42.0	10 43.1	7 40.5	13 03.4	10 01.2	7 40.0	15 55.8	24 50.1
31 Sa	18 40 03	9 54 39	7♑33 53	14 57 05	8 52.7	24 54.7	0 25.7	10 57.3	8 04.8	13 13.2	9 57.3	7 42.1	15 57.7	24 52.2

Astro Data Dy Hr Mn	Planet Ingress Dy Hr Mn	Last Aspect Dy Hr Mn	☽ Ingress Dy Hr Mn	Last Aspect Dy Hr Mn	☽ Ingress Dy Hr Mn	☽ Phases & Eclipses Dy Hr Mn
☽0N 12 7:17	♀ ♑ 5 8:12	31 23:18 ♀ ⚹	♏ 1 7:30	2 15:18 ♇ ☌	♑ 3 1:43	2 1:26 ● 9♏43
☿R 14 5:43	☉ ♐ 22 5:16	2 14:07 ♂ ☍	♐ 3 13:56	4 18:57 ☿ ⚹	♒ 5 3:37	9 1:58 ☽ 16♒46
♅D 16 0:08	☿ ♏R 26 11:55	5 5:59 ♇ ☌	♑ 5 18:18	6 21:59 ☿ □	♓ 7 5:45	16 0:59 ○ 23♉46
♄R 22 9:02		6 20:19 ♂ △	♒ 7 21:32	9 4:18 ♀ ⚹	♈ 9 9:03	23 22:12 ☾ 1♍43
☽0S 26 11:09	⚳ ♑ 11 13:42	9 12:32 ♇ ⚹	♓ 10 0:24	11 10:51 ♀ □	♉ 11 13:47	
♃△♅ 27 11:57	☿ ♐ 12 21:20	11 15:34 ♇ □	♈ 12 3:23	13 18:47 ♀ △	♊ 13 20:00	1 15:02 ● 9♐31
	♀ ♒ 15 15:59	13 19:09 ♇ △	♉ 14 7:03	15 17:12 ♇ ☍	♋ 16 4:02	8 9:37 ☽ 16♓24
☿D 4 2:23	☉ ♑ 21 18:36	16 0:59 ☉ ☍	♊ 16 12:11	17 0:34 ♃ △	♌ 18 14:19	15 16:17 ○ 23♊48
♃∠♇ 7 23:50		18 7:03 ♇ ☍	♋ 18 19:43	21 1:10 ☉ △	♍ 21 2:40	23 19:37 ☾ 2♎05
☽0N 9 12:23		21 4:04 ☉ △	♌ 21 6:11	23 4:31 ♇ □	♎ 23 15:27	31 3:13 ● 9♑32
♂D 10 4:04		23 5:26 ♇ △	♍ 23 18:43	25 15:54 ♇ ⚹	♏ 26 2:05	
♃□♄ 17 5:17		25 18:11 ♇ □	♎ 26 6:59	27 7:27 ♆ □	♐ 28 8:45	
☽0S 23 18:44		28 4:39 ♇ ⚹	♏ 28 16:34	30 3:02 ♇ ☌	♑ 30 11:36	
♀R 24 9:37		30 15:17 ☿ ☌	♐ 30 22:33			

Astro Data

1 November 2005
Julian Day # 38656
SVP 5♓10'47"
GC 26♐55.2 ⚴ 18♏34.2
Eris 20♈21.3R ⚵ 22♊52.8
⚷ 28♑15.3 ⚶ 22♋09.0
☽ Mean ☊ 12♈11.8

1 December 2005
Julian Day # 38686
SVP 5♓10'42"
GC 26♐55.3 ⚴ 1♐41.9
Eris 20♈06.7R ⚵ 19♊08.9R
⚷ 29♑42.5 ⚶ 22♋37.0R
☽ Mean ☊ 10♈36.5

LONGITUDE — January 2006

Day	Sid.Time	☉	0 hr ☽	Noon ☽	True☊	☿	♀	♂	⚳	♃	♄	♅	♆	♇
1 Su	18 44 00	10♑55 49	22♑22 58	29♑50 22	8♈40.9	26♐24.1	0♒07.0	11♉11.9	8♑29.1	13♏22.9	9♌53.4	7♓44.4	15♒59.6	24♐54.4
2 M	18 47 56	11 57 00	7♒18 07	14♒45 06	8R 31.2	27 54.0	29♑46.0	11 27.1	8 53.4	13 32.5	9R 49.4	7 46.6	16 01.6	24 56.6
3 Tu	18 51 53	12 58 10	22 10 16	29 32 42	8 24.3	29 24.3	29R 22.7	11 42.9	9 17.7	13 42.0	9 45.3	7 48.9	16 03.6	24 58.8
4 W	18 55 49	13 59 21	6♓51 41	14♓06 38	8 20.4	0♑55.0	28 57.3	11 59.1	9 41.9	13 51.3	9 41.2	7 51.2	16 05.6	25 00.9
5 Th	18 59 46	15 00 30	21 17 07	28 22 55	8D 18.8	2 26.2	28 29.8	12 15.8	10 06.2	14 00.6	9 37.0	7 53.6	16 07.6	25 03.1
6 F	19 03 42	16 01 40	5♈23 55	12♈20 09	8R 18.7	3 57.7	28 00.5	12 33.1	10 30.4	14 09.7	9 32.7	7 56.0	16 09.6	25 05.2
7 Sa	19 07 39	17 02 49	19 11 43	25 58 48	8 18.5	5 29.7	27 29.4	12 50.8	10 54.6	14 18.7	9 28.4	7 58.4	16 11.6	25 07.3
8 Su	19 11 36	18 03 57	2♉41 39	9♉20 31	8 17.0	7 02.1	26 56.8	13 08.9	11 18.8	14 27.6	9 24.1	8 00.9	16 13.7	25 09.4
9 M	19 15 32	19 05 06	15 55 40	22 27 21	8 13.1	8 34.9	26 22.9	13 27.6	11 42.9	14 36.4	9 19.7	8 03.4	16 15.7	25 11.5
10 Tu	19 19 29	20 06 13	28 55 48	5♊21 14	8 06.2	10 08.1	25 47.9	13 46.6	12 07.1	14 45.1	9 15.2	8 05.9	16 17.8	25 13.6
11 W	19 23 25	21 07 21	11♊43 49	18 03 42	7 56.4	11 41.7	25 12.0	14 06.1	12 31.2	14 53.6	9 10.7	8 08.5	16 19.9	25 15.7
12 Th	19 27 22	22 08 28	24 21 00	0♋35 48	7 44.2	13 15.8	24 35.5	14 26.0	12 55.3	15 02.1	9 06.1	8 11.1	16 22.0	25 17.8
13 F	19 31 18	23 09 34	6♋48 10	12 58 11	7 30.5	14 50.3	23 58.6	14 46.3	13 19.4	15 10.4	9 01.5	8 13.7	16 24.2	25 19.8
14 Sa	19 35 15	24 10 40	19 05 53	25 11 21	7 16.6	16 25.3	23 21.6	15 06.9	13 43.5	15 18.6	8 56.9	8 16.4	16 26.3	25 21.9
15 Su	19 39 12	25 11 46	1♌14 39	7♌15 55	7 03.5	18 00.8	22 44.8	15 28.0	14 07.5	15 26.6	8 52.2	8 19.1	16 28.5	25 23.9
16 M	19 43 08	26 12 51	13 15 17	19 12 56	6 52.4	19 36.8	22 08.5	15 49.4	14 31.5	15 34.5	8 47.5	8 21.9	16 30.6	25 25.9
17 Tu	19 47 05	27 13 55	25 09 06	1♍04 05	6 44.0	21 13.3	21 32.8	16 11.2	14 55.5	15 42.3	8 42.7	8 24.6	16 32.8	25 27.9
18 W	19 51 01	28 14 59	6♍58 12	12 51 51	6 38.4	22 50.3	20 58.0	16 33.4	15 19.5	15 50.0	8 37.9	8 27.4	16 35.0	25 29.8
19 Th	19 54 58	29 16 03	18 45 28	24 39 32	6 35.5	24 27.8	20 24.4	16 55.9	15 43.5	15 57.5	8 33.1	8 30.2	16 37.2	25 31.8
20 F	19 58 54	0♒17 07	0♎34 37	6♎31 18	6D 34.8	26 05.9	19 52.2	17 18.7	16 07.4	16 04.9	8 28.3	8 33.1	16 39.4	25 33.7
21 Sa	20 02 51	1 18 10	12 30 11	18 31 55	6 35.2	27 44.6	19 21.5	17 41.8	16 31.3	16 12.2	8 23.5	8 36.0	16 41.6	25 35.6
22 Su	20 06 47	2 19 13	24 37 11	0♏46 40	6R 35.7	29 23.8	18 52.7	18 05.3	16 55.1	16 19.3	8 18.6	8 38.9	16 43.8	25 37.5
23 M	20 10 44	3 20 15	7♏01 01	13 20 53	6 35.1	1♒03.7	18 25.7	18 29.1	17 18.9	16 26.3	8 13.7	8 41.8	16 46.0	25 39.4
24 Tu	20 14 41	4 21 17	19 46 53	26 19 32	6 32.8	2 44.1	18 00.8	18 53.2	17 42.7	16 33.1	8 08.8	8 44.8	16 48.2	25 41.3
25 W	20 18 37	5 22 18	2♐59 16	9♐46 24	6 28.1	4 25.2	17 38.1	19 17.6	18 06.5	16 39.8	8 03.9	8 47.8	16 50.5	25 43.1
26 Th	20 22 34	6 23 19	16 41 04	23 43 16	6 21.0	6 06.9	17 17.6	19 42.3	18 30.2	16 46.3	7 59.0	8 50.8	16 52.7	25 45.0
27 F	20 26 30	7 24 19	0♑52 45	8♑09 04	6 12.3	7 49.2	16 59.5	20 07.3	18 54.0	16 52.7	7 54.1	8 53.9	16 55.0	25 46.8
28 Sa	20 30 27	8 25 19	15 31 33	22 59 17	6 02.7	9 32.2	16 43.8	20 32.5	19 17.6	16 59.0	7 49.1	8 56.9	16 57.2	25 48.6
29 Su	20 34 23	9 26 18	0♒31 12	8♒06 05	5 53.6	11 15.8	16 30.6	20 58.1	19 41.2	17 05.1	7 44.2	9 00.0	16 59.5	25 50.3
30 M	20 38 20	10 27 16	15 42 35	23 19 21	5 46.0	13 00.0	16 19.8	21 23.9	20 04.8	17 11.0	7 39.3	9 03.1	17 01.8	25 52.1
31 Tu	20 42 16	11 28 12	0♓55 03	8♓28 25	5 40.7	14 44.8	16 11.5	21 49.9	20 28.4	17 16.8	7 34.4	9 06.3	17 04.1	25 53.8

LONGITUDE — February 2006

Day	Sid.Time	☉	0 hr ☽	Noon ☽	True☊	☿	♀	♂	⚳	♃	♄	♅	♆	♇
1 W	20 46 13	12♒29 08	15♓58 23	23♓23 58	5♈37.9	16♒30.2	16♑05.6	22♉16.3	20♑51.9	17♏22.4	7♌29.5	9♓09.4	17♒06.3	25♐55.5
2 Th	20 50 10	13 30 02	0♈44 26	7♈59 15	5D 37.3	18 16.1	16D 02.3	22 42.8	21 15.4	17 27.9	7R 24.6	9 12.6	17 08.6	25 57.1
3 F	20 54 06	14 30 54	15 08 04	22 10 41	5 38.1	20 02.5	16 01.3	23 09.6	21 38.8	17 33.2	7 19.7	9 15.8	17 10.9	25 58.8
4 Sa	20 58 03	15 31 46	29 07 07	5♉57 28	5R 39.1	21 49.4	16 02.8	23 36.7	22 02.1	17 38.3	7 14.9	9 19.0	17 13.2	26 00.4
5 Su	21 01 59	16 32 36	12♉41 58	19 20 53	5 39.4	23 36.7	16 06.6	24 03.9	22 25.5	17 43.3	7 10.0	9 22.2	17 15.4	26 02.0
6 M	21 05 56	17 33 24	25 54 35	2♊23 27	5 38.2	25 24.3	16 12.8	24 31.4	22 48.8	17 48.1	7 05.2	9 25.5	17 17.7	26 03.6
7 Tu	21 09 52	18 34 11	8♊47 52	15 08 16	5 34.8	27 12.1	16 21.2	24 59.2	23 12.0	17 52.8	7 00.4	9 28.7	17 20.0	26 05.1
8 W	21 13 49	19 34 57	21 24 59	27 38 26	5 29.4	28 59.9	16 31.9	25 27.1	23 35.2	17 57.2	6 55.7	9 32.0	17 22.3	26 06.7
9 Th	21 17 45	20 35 41	3♋48 55	9♋56 46	5 22.2	0♓47.7	16 44.7	25 55.2	23 58.3	18 01.6	6 51.0	9 35.3	17 24.6	26 08.2
10 F	21 21 42	21 36 24	16 02 17	22 05 42	5 13.8	2 35.1	16 59.7	26 23.5	24 21.4	18 05.7	6 46.3	9 38.6	17 26.8	26 09.6
11 Sa	21 25 39	22 37 05	28 07 16	4♌07 12	5 05.2	4 22.1	17 16.7	26 52.0	24 44.5	18 09.7	6 41.7	9 42.0	17 29.1	26 11.1
12 Su	21 29 35	23 37 45	10♌05 41	16 02 57	4 57.2	6 08.3	17 35.7	27 20.7	25 07.4	18 13.5	6 37.1	9 45.3	17 31.4	26 12.5
13 M	21 33 32	24 38 23	21 59 10	27 54 33	4 50.4	7 53.5	17 56.6	27 49.5	25 30.4	18 17.1	6 32.5	9 48.6	17 33.7	26 13.9
14 Tu	21 37 28	25 39 00	3♍49 18	9♍43 39	4 45.5	9 37.2	18 19.3	28 18.6	25 53.3	18 20.6	6 28.0	9 52.0	17 35.9	26 15.3
15 W	21 41 25	26 39 36	15 37 52	21 32 13	4 42.5	11 19.1	18 43.9	28 47.8	26 16.1	18 23.8	6 23.5	9 55.4	17 38.2	26 16.6
16 Th	21 45 21	27 40 10	27 27 02	3♎22 39	4D 41.5	12 58.8	19 10.2	29 17.2	26 38.8	18 26.9	6 19.1	9 58.7	17 40.4	26 17.9
17 F	21 49 18	28 40 42	9♎19 27	15 17 54	4 42.0	14 35.7	19 38.2	29 46.7	27 01.5	18 29.9	6 14.7	10 02.1	17 42.7	26 19.2
18 Sa	21 53 14	29 41 14	21 18 25	27 21 31	4 43.5	16 09.4	20 07.8	0♊16.4	27 24.2	18 32.6	6 10.4	10 05.5	17 44.9	26 20.5
19 Su	21 57 11	0♓41 44	3♏27 43	9♏37 34	4 45.3	17 39.2	20 38.9	0 46.3	27 46.8	18 35.2	6 06.2	10 08.9	17 47.2	26 21.7
20 M	22 01 08	1 42 13	15 51 36	22 10 24	4R 46.7	19 04.5	21 11.5	1 16.3	28 09.3	18 37.6	6 02.0	10 12.3	17 49.4	26 22.9
21 Tu	22 05 04	2 42 41	28 34 29	5♐04 23	4 47.0	20 24.6	21 45.6	1 46.5	28 31.8	18 39.8	5 57.8	10 15.8	17 51.6	26 24.1
22 W	22 09 01	3 43 07	11♐40 32	18 23 19	4 46.1	21 39.0	22 21.0	2 16.8	28 54.2	18 41.8	5 53.8	10 19.2	17 53.8	26 25.2
23 Th	22 12 57	4 43 32	25 13 01	2♑09 47	4 43.8	22 46.9	22 57.8	2 47.2	29 16.6	18 43.6	5 49.8	10 22.6	17 56.0	26 26.3
24 F	22 16 54	5 43 56	9♑13 36	16 24 18	4 40.3	23 47.8	23 35.8	3 17.8	29 38.8	18 45.3	5 45.8	10 26.1	17 58.3	26 27.4
25 Sa	22 20 50	6 44 19	23 41 30	1♒04 38	4 36.3	24 40.9	24 15.0	3 48.6	0♒01.1	18 46.7	5 42.0	10 29.5	18 00.4	26 28.5
26 Su	22 24 47	7 44 39	8♒32 54	16 05 22	4 32.3	25 25.8	24 55.4	4 19.4	0 23.2	18 48.0	5 38.2	10 33.0	18 02.6	26 29.5
27 M	22 28 43	8 44 58	23 40 55	1♓18 17	4 29.0	26 02.0	25 36.8	4 50.5	0 45.3	18 49.1	5 34.5	10 36.4	18 04.8	26 30.5
28 Tu	22 32 40	9 45 16	8♓56 12	16 33 21	4 26.8	26 29.0	26 19.4	5 21.6	1 07.3	18 50.0	5 30.8	10 39.8	18 07.0	26 31.5

Astro Data

	Dy Hr Mn
♄♇♇ (♄⚻♇)	1 7:54
☽0N	5 17:09
♄⚻♅	19 21:03
☽0S	20 1:06
♃□♆	28 1:26
☽0N	2 0:22
♀D	3 9:20
☽0S	16 6:49
☿0N	26 13:13

Planet Ingress

	Dy Hr Mn
♀ ♑R	1 20:19
☿ ♑	3 21:27
☉ ♒	20 5:16
☿ ♒	22 20:43
☿ ♓	9 1:23
♂ ♊	17 22:45
☉ ♓	18 19:27
⚳ ♒	25 10:51

Last Aspect / ☽ Ingress (January)

Last Aspect Dy Hr Mn		☽ Ingress Dy Hr Mn
31 9:10	♃ ⚹	♒ 1 12:15
3 11:45	☿ ⚹	♓ 3 12:45
5 12:11	♀ ⚹	♈ 5 14:45
7 14:35	♀ □	♉ 7 19:10
9 18:57	♀ △	♊ 10 2:00
12 1:47	♇ ☍	♋ 12 10:51
14 9:49	☉ ☍	♌ 14 21:32
17 0:36	♇ △	♍ 17 9:50
19 22:14	☉ △	♎ 19 22:50
22 8:54	☿ □	♏ 22 10:30
23 21:54	♂ ☍	♐ 24 18:39
26 15:26	♇ ☌	♑ 26 22:32
28 7:58	♂ △	♒ 28 23:10
30 16:01	♇ ⚹	♓ 30 22:33

Last Aspect / ☽ Ingress (February)

Last Aspect Dy Hr Mn		☽ Ingress Dy Hr Mn
1 16:07	♇ □	♈ 1 22:47
3 18:34	♇ △	♉ 4 1:32
5 21:01	☿ □	♊ 6 7:33
8 15:05	☿ △	♋ 8 16:34
10 20:54	♂ ⚹	♌ 11 3:45
13 11:49	♂ □	♍ 13 16:14
16 3:22	♂ △	♎ 16 5:10
18 17:00	☉ △	♏ 18 17:12
20 10:04	♀ ⚹	♐ 21 2:39
23 2:07	♇ ☌	♑ 23 8:17
25 0:59	☿ ⚹	♒ 25 10:16
27 4:27	♇ ⚹	♓ 27 9:57

☽ Phases & Eclipses

Dy Hr Mn	
6 18:58	☽ 16♈19
14 9:49	○ 24♋05
22 15:15	☾ 2♏27
29 14:16	● 9♒32
5 6:30	☽ 16♉19
13 4:45	○ 24♌20
21 7:18	☾ 2♐31
28 0:32	● 9♓16

Astro Data

1 January 2006
Julian Day # 38717
SVP 5♓10'35"
GC 26♐55.4 ⚴ 14♐58.3
Eris 19♈59.5R ⚵ 12♊59.0R
⚷ 1♒57.6 ⚶ 16♋38.9R
☽ Mean ☊ 8♈58.1

1 February 2006
Julian Day # 38748
SVP 5♓10'30"
GC 26♐55.5 ⚴ 27♐23.3
Eris 20♈02.7 ⚵ 13♊37.8
⚷ 4♒32.3 ⚶ 9♋21.0R
☽ Mean ☊ 7♈19.6

March 2006 LONGITUDE

Day	Sid.Time	☉	0 hr ☽	Noon ☽	True ☊	☿	♀	♂	⚳	♃	♄	♅	♆	♇
1 W	22 36 37	10♓45 31	24♓08 27	1♈40 19	4♈25.9	26♓46.7	27♑03.0	5♊52.9	1♒29.2	18♏50.7	5♌27.2	10♓43.3	18♒09.1	26♐32.4
2 Th	22 40 33	11 45 45	9♈07 57	16 30 27	4D 26.3	26R 54.9	27 47.5	6 24.2	1 51.1	18 51.2	5R 23.8	10 46.7	18 11.2	26 33.3
3 F	22 44 30	12 45 57	23 47 08	0♉57 29	4 27.4	26 53.5	28 33.0	6 55.8	2 12.8	18 51.6	5 20.4	10 50.2	18 13.4	26 34.1
4 Sa	22 48 26	13 46 07	8♉01 13	14 58 10	4 28.9	26 42.8	29 19.4	7 27.4	2 34.5	18R 51.7	5 17.1	10 53.6	18 15.5	26 35.0
5 Su	22 52 23	14 46 14	21 48 22	28 31 57	4 30.1	26 23.1	0♒06.6	7 59.1	2 56.1	18 51.6	5 13.8	10 57.1	18 17.6	26 35.8
6 M	22 56 19	15 46 20	5♊09 11	11♊40 23	4R 30.8	25 54.9	0 54.7	8 31.0	3 17.7	18 51.4	5 10.7	11 00.5	18 19.6	26 36.6
7 Tu	23 00 16	16 46 23	18 05 59	24 26 26	4 30.7	25 19.0	1 43.6	9 02.9	3 39.1	18 51.0	5 07.6	11 03.9	18 21.7	26 37.3
8 W	23 04 12	17 46 25	0♋42 12	6♋53 47	4 29.7	24 36.3	2 33.2	9 35.0	4 00.5	18 50.4	5 04.7	11 07.4	18 23.8	26 38.0
9 Th	23 08 09	18 46 24	13 01 42	19 06 24	4 28.0	23 47.9	3 23.6	10 07.2	4 21.8	18 49.6	5 01.8	11 10.8	18 25.8	26 38.7
10 F	23 12 06	19 46 21	25 08 24	1♌08 08	4 25.9	22 54.9	4 14.7	10 39.4	4 43.0	18 48.6	4 59.0	11 14.2	18 27.8	26 39.3
11 Sa	23 16 02	20 46 16	7♌06 01	13 02 29	4 23.7	21 58.6	5 06.5	11 11.8	5 04.1	18 47.4	4 56.3	11 17.6	18 29.8	26 39.9
12 Su	23 19 59	21 46 09	18 57 54	24 52 36	4 21.6	21 00.5	5 59.0	11 44.2	5 25.1	18 46.1	4 53.8	11 21.0	18 31.8	26 40.5
13 M	23 23 55	22 45 59	0♍46 56	6♍41 12	4 20.0	20 01.8	6 52.1	12 16.8	5 46.0	18 44.5	4 51.3	11 24.4	18 33.8	26 41.1
14 Tu	23 27 52	23 45 48	12 35 40	18 30 38	4 19.0	19 03.8	7 45.8	12 49.4	6 06.9	18 42.8	4 48.9	11 27.8	18 35.8	26 41.6
15 W	23 31 48	24 45 35	24 26 20	0♎23 02	4D 18.5	18 07.8	8 40.1	13 22.1	6 27.6	18 40.9	4 46.6	11 31.2	18 37.7	26 42.0
16 Th	23 35 45	25 45 19	6♎21 00	12 20 27	4 18.6	17 14.7	9 35.0	13 54.9	6 48.3	18 38.8	4 44.4	11 34.6	18 39.6	26 42.5
17 F	23 39 41	26 45 02	18 21 41	24 24 57	4 19.0	16 25.5	10 30.4	14 27.8	7 08.9	18 36.5	4 42.3	11 37.9	18 41.5	26 42.9
18 Sa	23 43 38	27 44 43	0♏30 33	6♏38 46	4 19.7	15 41.0	11 26.3	15 00.7	7 29.3	18 34.0	4 40.3	11 41.3	18 43.4	26 43.3
19 Su	23 47 35	28 44 22	12 49 55	19 04 19	4 20.3	15 01.8	12 22.8	15 33.7	7 49.7	18 31.4	4 38.4	11 44.6	18 45.3	26 43.6
20 M	23 51 31	29 44 00	25 22 20	1♐44 16	4 20.9	14 28.2	13 19.8	16 06.8	8 10.0	18 28.6	4 36.6	11 47.9	18 47.1	26 43.9
21 Tu	23 55 28	0♈43 36	8♐10 30	14 41 20	4 21.2	14 00.5	14 17.2	16 40.0	8 30.1	18 25.6	4 34.9	11 51.2	18 48.9	26 44.2
22 W	23 59 24	1 43 10	21 17 06	27 58 04	4R 21.3	13 39.0	15 15.1	17 13.3	8 50.2	18 22.4	4 33.3	11 54.5	18 50.7	26 44.5
23 Th	0 03 21	2 42 42	4♑44 28	11♑36 27	4 21.3	13 23.6	16 13.5	17 46.6	9 10.2	18 19.1	4 31.9	11 57.8	18 52.5	26 44.7
24 F	0 07 17	3 42 13	18 34 05	25 37 22	4D 21.3	13 14.2	17 12.2	18 20.0	9 30.0	18 15.6	4 30.5	12 01.1	18 54.3	26 44.9
25 Sa	0 11 14	4 41 42	2♒46 08	10♒00 06	4 21.3	13D 10.9	18 11.4	18 53.5	9 49.8	18 11.9	4 29.2	12 04.3	18 56.0	26 45.0
26 Su	0 15 10	5 41 09	17 18 50	24 41 46	4 21.3	13 13.3	19 11.0	19 27.0	10 09.4	18 08.0	4 28.1	12 07.6	18 57.7	26 45.2
27 M	0 19 07	6 40 34	2♓08 12	9♓37 15	4 21.5	13 21.4	20 10.9	20 00.7	10 28.9	18 04.0	4 27.0	12 10.8	18 59.4	26 45.2
28 Tu	0 23 04	7 39 57	17 07 58	24 39 20	4R 21.7	13 34.8	21 11.2	20 34.3	10 48.3	17 59.8	4 26.1	12 14.0	19 01.1	26 45.3
29 W	0 27 00	8 39 18	2♈10 14	9♈39 36	4 21.7	13 53.4	22 11.8	21 08.1	11 07.6	17 55.4	4 25.3	12 17.2	19 02.7	26R 45.3
30 Th	0 30 57	9 38 37	17 06 21	24 29 31	4 21.5	14 16.8	23 12.8	21 41.9	11 26.8	17 50.9	4 24.5	12 20.3	19 04.3	26 45.3
31 F	0 34 53	10 37 55	1♉48 12	9♉01 40	4 20.9	14 44.9	24 14.1	22 15.8	11 45.8	17 46.2	4 23.9	12 23.5	19 05.9	26 45.3

April 2006 LONGITUDE

Day	Sid.Time	☉	0 hr ☽	Noon ☽	True ☊	☿	♀	♂	⚳	♃	♄	♅	♆	♇
1 Sa	0 38 50	11♈37 10	16♉09 19	23♉10 42	4♈20.1	15♓17.3	25♒15.7	22♊49.7	12♒04.7	17♏41.4	4♌23.4	12♓26.6	19♒07.5	26♐45.2
2 Su	0 42 46	12 36 23	0♊05 33	6♊53 45	4R 19.2	15 53.9	26 17.6	23 23.8	12 23.5	17R 36.4	4R 23.0	12 29.7	19 09.0	26R 45.1
3 M	0 46 43	13 35 33	13 35 20	20 10 27	4 18.3	16 34.4	27 19.8	23 57.8	12 42.2	17 31.3	4 22.8	12 32.8	19 10.6	26 44.9
4 Tu	0 50 39	14 34 41	26 39 22	3♋02 27	4D 17.6	17 18.6	28 22.2	24 31.9	13 00.7	17 26.0	4 22.6	12 35.8	19 12.1	26 44.7
5 W	0 54 36	15 33 47	9♋20 09	15 32 58	4 17.3	18 06.3	29 25.0	25 06.1	13 19.1	17 20.6	4D 22.5	12 38.9	19 13.5	26 44.5
6 Th	0 58 33	16 32 51	21 41 25	27 46 05	4 17.6	18 57.4	0♓28.0	25 40.3	13 37.4	17 15.0	4 22.6	12 41.9	19 15.0	26 44.3
7 F	1 02 29	17 31 52	3♌47 32	9♌46 21	4 18.4	19 51.6	1 31.2	26 14.6	13 55.5	17 09.4	4 22.7	12 44.8	19 16.4	26 44.0
8 Sa	1 06 26	18 30 51	15 43 08	21 38 25	4 19.6	20 48.8	2 34.7	26 48.9	14 13.5	17 03.5	4 23.0	12 47.8	19 17.8	26 43.7
9 Su	1 10 22	19 29 48	27 32 45	3♍26 39	4 21.0	21 48.8	3 38.4	27 23.3	14 31.4	16 57.6	4 23.4	12 50.7	19 19.1	26 43.4
10 M	1 14 19	20 28 43	9♍20 37	15 15 05	4 22.3	22 51.5	4 42.4	27 57.7	14 49.1	16 51.5	4 23.9	12 53.6	19 20.5	26 43.0
11 Tu	1 18 15	21 27 35	21 10 28	27 07 10	4R 23.1	23 56.9	5 46.6	28 32.2	15 06.7	16 45.4	4 24.5	12 56.5	19 21.8	26 42.6
12 W	1 22 12	22 26 25	3♎05 32	9♎05 51	4 23.2	25 04.7	6 51.0	29 06.7	15 24.1	16 39.1	4 25.2	12 59.4	19 23.1	26 42.2
13 Th	1 26 08	23 25 13	15 08 24	21 13 25	4 22.3	26 14.9	7 55.6	29 41.3	15 41.4	16 32.6	4 26.0	13 02.2	19 24.3	26 41.7
14 F	1 30 05	24 23 59	27 21 07	3♏31 39	4 20.5	27 27.4	9 00.5	0♋15.9	15 58.6	16 26.1	4 26.9	13 05.0	19 25.5	26 41.3
15 Sa	1 34 01	25 22 44	9♏45 11	16 01 49	4 17.8	28 42.0	10 05.5	0 50.5	16 15.5	16 19.5	4 27.9	13 07.7	19 26.7	26 40.7
16 Su	1 37 58	26 21 26	22 21 40	28 44 50	4 14.5	29 58.9	11 10.7	1 25.2	16 32.4	16 12.8	4 29.1	13 10.5	19 27.9	26 40.2
17 M	1 41 55	27 20 07	5♐11 22	11♐41 22	4 11.0	1♈17.8	12 16.2	1 59.9	16 49.1	16 06.0	4 30.3	13 13.2	19 29.0	26 39.6
18 Tu	1 45 51	28 18 46	18 14 51	24 51 55	4 07.8	2 38.7	13 21.8	2 34.7	17 05.6	15 59.1	4 31.7	13 15.9	19 30.1	26 39.0
19 W	1 49 48	29 17 23	1♑32 36	8♑16 57	4 05.3	4 01.6	14 27.6	3 09.5	17 21.9	15 52.1	4 33.1	13 18.5	19 31.2	26 38.4
20 Th	1 53 44	0♉15 59	15 04 59	21 56 44	4D 04.0	5 26.4	15 33.6	3 44.3	17 38.1	15 45.1	4 34.7	13 21.1	19 32.3	26 37.7
21 F	1 57 41	1 14 33	28 52 12	5♒51 19	4 03.8	6 53.1	16 39.7	4 19.2	17 54.2	15 37.9	4 36.3	13 23.7	19 33.3	26 37.0
22 Sa	2 01 37	2 13 05	12♒54 02	20 00 10	4 04.6	8 21.6	17 46.0	4 54.1	18 10.0	15 30.7	4 38.1	13 26.3	19 34.3	26 36.3
23 Su	2 05 34	3 11 36	27 09 33	4♓21 52	4 06.0	9 52.0	18 52.4	5 29.1	18 25.7	15 23.4	4 40.0	13 28.8	19 35.2	26 35.6
24 M	2 09 30	4 10 05	11♓36 47	18 53 48	4 07.4	11 24.2	19 59.0	6 04.1	18 41.3	15 16.1	4 42.0	13 31.2	19 36.2	26 34.8
25 Tu	2 13 27	5 08 33	26 12 23	3♈31 55	4R 08.0	12 58.2	21 05.8	6 39.2	18 56.6	15 08.7	4 44.1	13 33.7	19 37.0	26 34.0
26 W	2 17 24	6 06 58	10♈51 40	18 10 52	4 07.3	14 34.0	22 12.7	7 14.2	19 11.7	15 01.2	4 46.2	13 36.1	19 37.9	26 33.2
27 Th	2 21 20	7 05 22	25 28 43	2♉44 24	4 05.0	16 11.6	23 19.7	7 49.4	19 26.7	14 53.7	4 48.5	13 38.5	19 38.7	26 32.3
28 F	2 25 17	8 03 45	9♉57 06	17 06 06	4 01.2	17 50.9	24 26.9	8 24.5	19 41.5	14 46.2	4 50.9	13 40.8	19 39.5	26 31.4
29 Sa	2 29 13	9 02 05	24 10 41	1♊10 19	3 56.1	19 32.1	25 34.1	8 59.7	19 56.1	14 38.6	4 53.4	13 43.1	19 40.3	26 30.5
30 Su	2 33 10	10 00 24	8♊04 30	14 52 56	3 50.3	21 15.0	26 41.5	9 35.0	20 10.5	14 31.0	4 56.0	13 45.4	19 41.0	26 29.6

Astro Data

	Dy Hr Mn
☽ 0N	1 10:34
☿ R	2 20:32
♃ R	4 18:03
☿0S	11 18:51
☽ 0S	15 12:45
♃□♆	16 7:06
☉0N	20 18:27
☿ D	25 13:43
☽ 0N	28 21:45
♇ R	29 12:41
♄ D	5 12:55
☽ 0S	11 19:20
☿0N	21 1:11
☽ 0N	25 7:24

Planet Ingress

	Dy Hr Mn
♀ ♒	5 8:40
☉ ♈	20 18:27
♀ ♓	6 1:22
♂ ♋	14 1:00
☿ ♈	16 12:21
☉ ♉	20 5:27

Last Aspect / ☽ Ingress

Last Aspect Dy Hr Mn		☽ Ingress Dy Hr Mn
1 4:15 ♀ ⚹	♈	1 9:20
3 7:43 ♀ □	♉	3 10:23
5 8:15 ☿ ⚹	♊	5 14:39
7 16:10 ♇ ☍	♋	7 22:39
9 20:42 ☿ △	♌	10 9:43
12 15:39 ♇ △	♍	12 22:25
15 4:34 ♇ □	♎	15 11:14
17 16:32 ♇ ⚹	♏	17 23:00
20 7:55 ☉ △	♐	20 8:44
22 9:49 ♇ ☌	♑	22 15:37
23 23:31 ♃ ⚹	♒	24 19:22
26 15:19 ♇ ⚹	♓	26 20:34
28 15:21 ♇ □	♈	28 20:32
30 15:42 ♇ △	♉	30 21:02

Last Aspect / ☽ Ingress

Last Aspect Dy Hr Mn		☽ Ingress Dy Hr Mn
1 15:53 ♀ □	♊	1 23:50
4 2:26 ♀ △	♋	4 6:16
5 17:20 ☿ △	♌	6 16:26
8 23:03 ♂ ⚹	♍	9 5:00
11 15:00 ♂ □	♎	11 17:48
13 22:43 ♇ ⚹	♏	14 5:09
15 18:30 ♆ □	♐	16 14:21
18 18:42 ☉ △	♑	18 21:14
20 1:16 ♃ ⚹	♒	21 1:57
22 23:04 ♇ ⚹	♓	23 4:44
25 0:36 ♇ □	♈	25 6:13
27 1:45 ♇ △	♉	27 7:28
29 1:32 ♀ ⚹	♊	29 9:59

☽ Phases & Eclipses

Dy Hr Mn	
6 20:17	☽ 16♊07
14 23:37	○ 24♍15
14 23:49	A 1.030
22 19:12	☾ 2♑01
29 10:16	● 8♈35
29 10:12:23	● T 04'07"
5 12:02	☽ 15♋34
13 16:41	○ 23♎37
21 3:30	☾ 0♒54
27 19:45	● 7♉24

Astro Data

1 March 2006
Julian Day # 38776
SVP 5♓10'26"
GC 26♐55.5 ⚴ 7♑13.8
Eris 20♈13.9 ⚵ 20♊19.8
⚷ 6♒45.2 ⚶ 7♋38.7
☽ Mean ☊ 5♈50.6

1 April 2006
Julian Day # 38807
SVP 5♓10'23"
GC 26♐55.6 ⚴ 15♑33.5
Eris 20♈32.4 ⚵ 1♋35.7
⚷ 8♒40.1 ⚶ 12♋01.8
☽ Mean ☊ 4♈12.1

LONGITUDE — May 2006

Day	Sid.Time	☉	0 hr ☽	Noon ☽	True ☊	☿	♀	♂	⚳	♃	♄	♅	♆	♇
1 M	2 37 06	10♉58 40	21♊35 24	28♊11 52	3♈44.7	22♈59.7	27♓49.1	10♋10.2	20♒24.7	14♏23.4	4♌58.7	13♓47.6	19♒41.7	26♐28.6
2 Tu	2 41 03	11 56 55	4♋42 23	11♋07 09	3R39.9	24 46.2	28 56.7	10 45.5	20 38.7	14R15.8	5 01.5	13 49.8	19 42.4	26R27.7
3 W	2 44 59	12 55 08	17 26 27	23 40 42	3 36.4	26 34.5	0♈04.4	11 20.9	20 52.5	14 08.2	5 04.4	13 52.0	19 43.1	26 26.7
4 Th	2 48 56	13 53 19	29 50 21	5♌55 57	3D34.5	28 24.6	1 12.3	11 56.3	21 06.1	14 00.5	5 07.4	13 54.1	19 43.7	26 25.6
5 F	2 52 53	14 51 27	11♌58 02	17 57 16	3 34.2	0♉16.5	2 20.2	12 31.6	21 19.5	13 52.8	5 10.5	13 56.2	19 44.2	26 24.6
6 Sa	2 56 49	15 49 34	23 54 14	29 49 37	3 35.1	2 10.2	3 28.3	13 07.1	21 32.7	13 45.2	5 13.7	13 58.2	19 44.8	26 23.5
7 Su	3 00 46	16 47 39	5♍44 03	11♍38 09	3 36.6	4 05.7	4 36.5	13 42.5	21 45.7	13 37.6	5 16.9	14 00.2	19 45.3	26 22.4
8 M	3 04 42	17 45 41	17 32 34	23 27 52	3R37.9	6 03.0	5 44.7	14 18.0	21 58.4	13 29.9	5 20.3	14 02.1	19 45.8	26 21.3
9 Tu	3 08 39	18 43 42	29 24 37	5♎23 21	3 38.4	8 02.0	6 53.1	14 53.5	22 11.0	13 22.3	5 23.8	14 04.0	19 46.2	26 20.1
10 W	3 12 35	19 41 42	11♎24 32	17 28 35	3 37.3	10 02.8	8 01.5	15 29.0	22 23.3	13 14.7	5 27.3	14 05.9	19 46.6	26 19.0
11 Th	3 16 32	20 39 39	23 35 53	29 46 42	3 34.3	12 05.2	9 10.1	16 04.6	22 35.4	13 07.2	5 30.9	14 07.7	19 47.0	26 17.8
12 F	3 20 28	21 37 35	6♏01 17	12♏19 48	3 29.1	14 09.2	10 18.7	16 40.2	22 47.3	12 59.7	5 34.7	14 09.5	19 47.3	26 16.6
13 Sa	3 24 25	22 35 29	18 42 20	25 08 53	3 22.1	16 14.7	11 27.4	17 15.8	22 58.9	12 52.2	5 38.5	14 11.3	19 47.7	26 15.4
14 Su	3 28 22	23 33 22	1♐39 26	8♐13 50	3 13.9	18 21.6	12 36.3	17 51.5	23 10.3	12 44.8	5 42.4	14 13.0	19 47.9	26 14.1
15 M	3 32 18	24 31 13	14 51 57	21 33 33	3 05.2	20 29.8	13 45.2	18 27.1	23 21.5	12 37.4	5 46.4	14 14.7	19 48.2	26 12.9
16 Tu	3 36 15	25 29 04	28 18 25	5♑06 16	2 57.1	22 39.0	14 54.2	19 02.8	23 32.5	12 30.1	5 50.5	14 16.3	19 48.4	26 11.6
17 W	3 40 11	26 26 52	11♑56 51	18 49 52	2 50.4	24 49.2	16 03.2	19 38.5	23 43.2	12 22.8	5 54.7	14 17.9	19 48.6	26 10.3
18 Th	3 44 08	27 24 40	25 45 07	2♒44 19	2 45.7	27 00.0	17 12.4	20 14.3	23 53.6	12 15.6	5 58.9	14 19.4	19 48.8	26 09.0
19 F	3 48 04	28 22 27	9♒41 17	16 41 50	2D43.2	29 11.3	18 21.6	20 50.1	24 03.8	12 08.5	6 03.3	14 20.9	19 48.9	26 07.6
20 Sa	3 52 01	29 20 12	23 43 48	0♓47 03	2 42.6	1♊22.8	19 31.0	21 25.9	24 13.8	12 01.4	6 07.7	14 22.3	19 49.0	26 06.3
21 Su	3 55 58	0♊17 56	7♓51 25	14 56 45	2 43.1	3 34.2	20 40.4	22 01.7	24 23.4	11 54.4	6 12.2	14 23.7	19 49.0	26 04.9
22 M	3 59 54	1 15 39	22 02 55	29 09 41	2R43.8	5 45.3	21 49.8	22 37.5	24 32.9	11 47.5	6 16.8	14 25.1	19R49.0	26 03.6
23 Tu	4 03 51	2 13 21	6♈16 49	13♈24 01	2 43.4	7 55.7	22 59.4	23 13.4	24 42.0	11 40.7	6 21.4	14 26.4	19 49.0	26 02.2
24 W	4 07 47	3 11 03	20 30 58	27 37 13	2 41.0	10 05.3	24 09.0	23 49.3	24 50.9	11 34.0	6 26.2	14 27.6	19 49.0	26 00.8
25 Th	4 11 44	4 08 43	4♉42 19	11♉45 47	2 36.2	12 13.6	25 18.6	24 25.3	24 59.5	11 27.4	6 31.0	14 28.8	19 48.9	25 59.3
26 F	4 15 40	5 06 22	18 47 05	25 45 40	2 28.8	14 20.5	26 28.4	25 01.2	25 07.9	11 20.9	6 35.9	14 30.0	19 48.8	25 57.9
27 Sa	4 19 37	6 04 00	2♊41 00	9♊32 36	2 19.3	16 25.8	27 38.2	25 37.2	25 15.9	11 14.5	6 40.8	14 31.1	19 48.6	25 56.5
28 Su	4 23 33	7 01 36	16 20 02	23 02 55	2 08.7	18 29.3	28 48.0	26 13.2	25 23.7	11 08.2	6 45.9	14 32.2	19 48.5	25 55.0
29 M	4 27 30	7 59 12	29 40 59	6♋14 05	1 58.0	20 30.7	29 57.9	26 49.3	25 31.2	11 02.0	6 51.0	14 33.2	19 48.3	25 53.5
30 Tu	4 31 27	8 56 46	12♋42 06	19 05 07	1 48.3	22 29.9	1♉07.9	27 25.3	25 38.4	10 55.9	6 56.2	14 34.2	19 48.0	25 52.1
31 W	4 35 23	9 54 19	25 23 16	1♌36 48	1 40.4	24 26.8	2 17.9	28 01.4	25 45.3	10 50.0	7 01.5	14 35.2	19 47.7	25 50.6

LONGITUDE — June 2006

Day	Sid.Time	☉	0 hr ☽	Noon ☽	True ☊	☿	♀	♂	⚳	♃	♄	♅	♆	♇
1 Th	4 39 20	10♊51 51	7♌46 03	13♌51 26	1♈34.8	26♊21.4	3♉28.0	28♋37.6	25♒51.9	10♏44.1	7♌06.8	14♓36.0	19♒47.4	25♐49.1
2 F	4 43 16	11 49 21	19 53 28	25 52 41	1R31.6	28 13.4	4 38.2	29 13.7	25 58.2	10R38.5	7 12.2	14 36.9	19R47.1	25R47.6
3 Sa	4 47 13	12 46 50	1♍49 41	7♍45 06	1D30.4	0♋02.8	5 48.4	29 49.8	26 04.2	10 32.9	7 17.7	14 37.7	19 46.7	25 46.0
4 Su	4 51 09	13 44 18	13 39 36	19 33 52	1 30.4	1 49.7	6 58.6	0♌26.0	26 09.9	10 27.5	7 23.3	14 38.4	19 46.3	25 44.5
5 M	4 55 06	14 41 44	25 28 34	1♎24 24	1R30.6	3 33.9	8 08.9	1 02.2	26 15.3	10 22.2	7 28.9	14 39.1	19 45.9	25 43.0
6 Tu	4 59 02	15 39 09	7♎22 00	13 22 01	1 30.1	5 15.4	9 19.2	1 38.5	26 20.3	10 17.0	7 34.6	14 39.7	19 45.4	25 41.4
7 W	5 02 59	16 36 33	19 25 03	25 31 39	1 27.8	6 54.1	10 29.6	2 14.7	26 25.1	10 12.1	7 40.3	14 40.3	19 45.0	25 39.9
8 Th	5 06 56	17 33 56	1♏42 19	7♏57 27	1 23.2	8 30.1	11 40.1	2 51.0	26 29.5	10 07.2	7 46.1	14 40.9	19 44.4	25 38.4
9 F	5 10 52	18 31 19	14 17 23	20 42 22	1 16.0	10 03.4	12 50.6	3 27.2	26 33.7	10 02.5	7 52.0	14 41.4	19 43.9	25 36.8
10 Sa	5 14 49	19 28 40	27 12 32	3♐47 54	1 06.4	11 33.8	14 01.1	4 03.6	26 37.5	9 58.0	7 57.9	14 41.8	19 43.3	25 35.2
11 Su	5 18 45	20 26 00	10♐28 21	17 13 42	0 55.3	13 01.5	15 11.7	4 39.9	26 40.9	9 53.6	8 03.9	14 42.3	19 42.7	25 33.7
12 M	5 22 42	21 23 20	24 03 37	0♑57 41	0 43.5	14 26.2	16 22.4	5 16.2	26 44.1	9 49.3	8 09.9	14 42.6	19 42.1	25 32.1
13 Tu	5 26 38	22 20 39	7♑55 25	14 56 14	0 32.4	15 48.1	17 33.1	5 52.6	26 46.9	9 45.3	8 16.0	14 42.9	19 41.4	25 30.6
14 W	5 30 35	23 17 57	21 59 34	29 04 49	0 22.9	17 07.1	18 43.8	6 29.0	26 49.4	9 41.3	8 22.2	14 43.2	19 40.7	25 29.0
15 Th	5 34 31	24 15 15	6♒11 23	13♒18 43	0 16.0	18 23.2	19 54.6	7 05.4	26 51.5	9 37.6	8 28.4	14 43.4	19 40.0	25 27.4
16 F	5 38 28	25 12 33	20 26 20	27 33 48	0 11.8	19 36.2	21 05.5	7 41.9	26 53.3	9 34.0	8 34.7	14 43.6	19 39.2	25 25.8
17 Sa	5 42 25	26 09 50	4♓40 47	11♓46 58	0 10.0	20 46.2	22 16.4	8 18.3	26 54.8	9 30.6	8 41.0	14 43.7	19 38.5	25 24.3
18 Su	5 46 21	27 07 07	18 52 10	25 56 12	0 09.6	21 53.0	23 27.3	8 54.8	26 55.9	9 27.3	8 47.4	14R43.7	19 37.6	25 22.7
19 M	5 50 18	28 04 23	2♈58 58	10♈00 22	0 09.5	22 56.6	24 38.3	9 31.3	26 56.7	9 24.2	8 53.8	14 43.8	19 36.8	25 21.1
20 Tu	5 54 14	29 01 40	17 00 20	23 58 47	0 08.3	23 57.0	25 49.4	10 07.8	26R57.1	9 21.3	9 00.3	14 43.7	19 35.9	25 19.6
21 W	5 58 11	29 58 56	0♉55 37	7♉50 42	0 05.1	24 54.0	27 00.5	10 44.4	26 57.1	9 18.5	9 06.8	14 43.6	19 35.1	25 18.0
22 Th	6 02 07	0♋56 12	14 43 53	21 34 59	29♓59.1	25 47.6	28 11.6	11 21.0	26 56.9	9 16.0	9 13.4	14 43.5	19 34.1	25 16.4
23 F	6 06 04	1 53 28	28 23 46	5♊10 00	29 50.4	26 37.6	29 22.8	11 57.6	26 56.2	9 13.6	9 20.0	14 43.3	19 33.2	25 14.9
24 Sa	6 10 00	2 50 43	11♊53 24	18 33 43	29 39.3	27 24.0	0♊34.0	12 34.2	26 55.2	9 11.3	9 26.7	14 43.1	19 32.2	25 13.3
25 Su	6 13 57	3 47 59	25 10 40	1♋44 02	29 26.8	28 06.6	1 45.3	13 10.9	26 53.8	9 09.3	9 33.4	14 42.8	19 31.2	25 11.8
26 M	6 17 54	4 45 14	8♋13 38	14 39 19	29 14.2	28 45.4	2 56.6	13 47.6	26 52.1	9 07.4	9 40.2	14 42.5	19 30.2	25 10.2
27 Tu	6 21 50	5 42 29	21 01 00	27 18 42	29 02.5	29 20.1	4 08.0	14 24.3	26 50.0	9 05.7	9 47.0	14 42.2	19 29.2	25 08.7
28 W	6 25 47	6 39 43	3♌32 29	9♌42 29	28 52.7	29 50.8	5 19.4	15 01.0	26 47.6	9 04.2	9 53.9	14 41.7	19 28.1	25 07.1
29 Th	6 29 43	7 36 57	15 48 57	21 52 11	28 45.5	0♌17.2	6 30.8	15 37.8	26 44.8	9 02.9	10 00.8	14 41.3	19 27.0	25 05.6
30 F	6 33 40	8 34 10	27 52 34	3♍50 32	28 41.0	0 39.2	7 42.3	16 14.5	26 41.6	9 01.8	10 07.7	14 40.8	19 25.9	25 04.1

Astro Data

	Dy Hr Mn
♃△♅	5 3:49
♀0N	6 11:53
☽0S	9 2:27
♆ R	22 13:07
☽0N	22 14:12
♃∠♇	31 8:43
☽0S	5 9:41
☽0N	18 18:58
♅ R	19 7:41
⚳ R	21 4:08
♃□♄	22 18:45
♄⚼♇	30 1:40

Planet Ingress

		Dy Hr Mn
♀	♈	3 10:26
☿	♉	5 8:29
☿	♊	19 20:53
☉	♊	21 4:33
♀	♉	29 12:42
☿	♋	3 11:22
♂	♌	3 18:44
☉	♋	21 12:27
☊	♓R	22 9:04
♀	♊	24 0:32
☿	♌	28 19:58

Last Aspect / ☽ Ingress (May)

Last Aspect Dy Hr Mn			☽ Ingress	Dy Hr Mn
1 11:14	♀	□	♋	1 15:18
3 18:36	☿	□	♌	4 0:19
6 5:03	♇	△	♍	6 12:21
8 17:50	♇	□	♎	9 1:11
11 5:16	♇	⚹	♏	11 12:26
13 6:52	☉	☍	♐	13 20:57
15 20:17	♇	☌	♑	16 3:00
18 2:11	☉	△	♒	18 7:20
20 9:22	☉	□	♓	20 10:40
22 6:47	♇	□	♈	22 13:25
24 9:17	♇	△	♉	24 16:02
26 10:40	♂	⚹	♊	26 19:20
28 23:24	♀	⚹	♋	29 0:35
31 4:43	♂	☌	♌	31 8:53

Last Aspect / ☽ Ingress (June)

Last Aspect Dy Hr Mn			☽ Ingress	Dy Hr Mn
2 17:35	☿	⚹	♍	2 20:18
5 0:31	♇	□	♎	5 9:10
7 12:16	♇	⚹	♏	7 20:42
9 10:11	♆	□	♐	10 5:06
12 2:36	♇	☌	♑	12 10:20
13 16:52	♀	△	♒	14 13:33
16 8:25	♇	⚹	♓	16 16:06
18 14:09	☉	□	♈	18 18:55
20 21:21	☉	⚹	♉	20 22:24
23 0:45	♀	☌	♊	23 2:50
25 0:03	♇	☍	♋	25 8:49
27 16:04	☿	☌	♌	27 17:10
29 18:25	♇	△	♍	30 4:16

☽ Phases & Eclipses

Dy Hr Mn		
5 5:14	☽	14♌35
13 6:52	○	22♏23
20 9:22	☾	29♒14
27 5:27	●	5♊48
3 23:07	☽	13♍13
11 18:04	○	20♐41
18 14:09	☾	27♓12
25 16:06	●	3♋58

Astro Data

1 May 2006
Julian Day # 38837
SVP 5♓10'19"
GC 26♐55.7 ⚴ 19♑29.3
Eris 20♈51.9 ⚵ 14♋19.7
⚷ 9♒39.4 ⚶ 20♋33.2
☽ Mean ☊ 2♈36.8

1 June 2006
Julian Day # 38868
SVP 5♓10'13"
GC 26♐55.7 ⚴ 17♑23.0R
Eris 21♈08.9 ⚵ 28♋13.9
⚷ 9♒35.9R ⚶ 2♌00.1
☽ Mean ☊ 0♈58.3

July 2006 LONGITUDE

Day	Sid.Time	☉	0 hr ☽	Noon ☽	True ☊	☿	♀	♂	⚳	♃	♄	♅	♆	♇
1 Sa	6 37 36	9♋31 24	9♍46 36	15♍41 19	28♓38.7	0♌56.8	8♊53.8	16♌51.3	26♒38.1	9♏00.8	10♌14.7	14♓40.2	19♒24.8	25♐02.6
2 Su	6 41 33	10 28 36	21 35 17	27 29 08	28D 38.2	1 09.9	10 05.3	17 28.1	26R 34.2	9R 00.0	10 21.7	14R 39.6	19R 23.6	25R 01.1
3 M	6 45 30	11 25 49	3♎23 32	9♎19 09	28R 38.3	1 18.4	11 16.9	18 05.0	26 30.0	8 59.4	10 28.8	14 39.0	19 22.4	24 59.6
4 Tu	6 49 26	12 23 01	15 16 42	21 16 50	28 38.0	1R 22.2	12 28.6	18 41.8	26 25.4	8 59.0	10 35.8	14 38.3	19 21.2	24 58.1
5 W	6 53 23	13 20 13	27 20 13	3♏27 32	28 36.4	1 21.3	13 40.2	19 18.7	26 20.5	8D 58.8	10 43.0	14 37.5	19 20.0	24 56.6
6 Th	6 57 19	14 17 24	9♏39 20	15 56 11	28 32.7	1 15.8	14 51.9	19 55.6	26 15.2	8 58.7	10 50.1	14 36.7	19 18.7	24 55.1
7 F	7 01 16	15 14 36	22 18 32	28 46 44	28 26.6	1 05.7	16 03.7	20 32.6	26 09.6	8 58.8	10 57.3	14 35.9	19 17.5	24 53.7
8 Sa	7 05 12	16 11 47	5♐21 05	12♐01 40	28 18.2	0 51.0	17 15.5	21 09.5	26 03.7	8 59.1	11 04.5	14 35.0	19 16.2	24 52.2
9 Su	7 09 09	17 08 58	18 48 30	25 41 23	28 08.2	0 32.0	18 27.3	21 46.5	25 57.4	8 59.6	11 11.8	14 34.1	19 14.9	24 50.8
10 M	7 13 05	18 06 10	2♑40 01	9♑43 55	27 57.6	0 08.9	19 39.2	22 23.5	25 50.7	9 00.3	11 19.1	14 33.1	19 13.6	24 49.4
11 Tu	7 17 02	19 03 21	16 52 28	24 04 56	27 47.4	29♋42.0	20 51.1	23 00.5	25 43.8	9 01.2	11 26.4	14 32.1	19 12.2	24 48.0
12 W	7 20 59	20 00 33	1♒20 31	8♒38 18	27 38.9	29 11.5	22 03.1	23 37.5	25 36.5	9 02.2	11 33.7	14 31.1	19 10.9	24 46.6
13 Th	7 24 55	20 57 45	15 57 26	23 17 01	27 32.6	28 38.1	23 15.1	24 14.6	25 28.9	9 03.4	11 41.1	14 30.0	19 09.5	24 45.2
14 F	7 28 52	21 54 57	0♓36 14	7♓54 20	27 29.0	28 02.0	24 27.1	24 51.7	25 21.0	9 04.7	11 48.5	14 28.9	19 08.1	24 43.9
15 Sa	7 32 48	22 52 10	15 10 41	22 24 46	27D 27.6	27 24.0	25 39.2	25 28.8	25 12.7	9 06.3	11 55.9	14 27.7	19 06.7	24 42.5
16 Su	7 36 45	23 49 23	29 36 08	6♈44 30	27 27.7	26 44.5	26 51.3	26 05.9	25 04.1	9 08.0	12 03.3	14 26.5	19 05.3	24 41.2
17 M	7 40 41	24 46 37	13♈49 39	20 51 27	27R 28.2	26 04.4	28 03.5	26 43.1	24 55.3	9 09.9	12 10.8	14 25.2	19 03.8	24 39.9
18 Tu	7 44 38	25 43 52	27 49 52	4♉44 54	27 27.9	25 24.2	29 15.7	27 20.3	24 46.1	9 12.0	12 18.3	14 23.9	19 02.4	24 38.6
19 W	7 48 34	26 41 08	11♉36 33	18 24 53	27 25.9	24 44.6	0♋28.0	27 57.5	24 36.7	9 14.3	12 25.8	14 22.6	19 00.9	24 37.3
20 Th	7 52 31	27 38 24	25 09 57	1♊51 49	27 21.7	24 06.4	1 40.3	28 34.7	24 26.9	9 16.7	12 33.3	14 21.2	18 59.4	24 36.1
21 F	7 56 28	28 35 41	8♊30 30	15 06 02	27 15.0	23 30.3	2 52.7	29 12.0	24 16.9	9 19.3	12 40.9	14 19.8	18 57.9	24 34.8
22 Sa	8 00 24	29 32 59	21 38 26	28 07 42	27 06.5	22 56.9	4 05.1	29 49.3	24 06.7	9 22.1	12 48.4	14 18.3	18 56.4	24 33.6
23 Su	8 04 21	0♌30 18	4♋33 50	10♋56 47	26 56.7	22 26.9	5 17.5	0♍26.6	23 56.1	9 25.0	12 56.0	14 16.8	18 54.9	24 32.4
24 M	8 08 17	1 27 37	17 16 36	23 33 15	26 46.7	22 00.7	6 30.0	1 04.0	23 45.3	9 28.1	13 03.6	14 15.3	18 53.4	24 31.3
25 Tu	8 12 14	2 24 57	29 46 48	5♌57 17	26 37.5	21 39.0	7 42.5	1 41.3	23 34.3	9 31.4	13 11.2	14 13.7	18 51.8	24 30.1
26 W	8 16 10	3 22 17	12♌04 49	18 09 32	26 29.9	21 22.2	8 55.1	2 18.7	23 23.1	9 34.9	13 18.8	14 12.1	18 50.3	24 29.0
27 Th	8 20 07	4 19 38	24 11 37	0♍11 20	26 24.3	21 10.6	10 07.7	2 56.2	23 11.6	9 38.5	13 26.5	14 10.5	18 48.7	24 27.8
28 F	8 24 03	5 17 00	6♍08 57	12 04 49	26 21.1	21D 04.6	11 20.3	3 33.6	22 59.9	9 42.3	13 34.1	14 08.8	18 47.1	24 26.7
29 Sa	8 28 00	6 14 22	17 59 20	23 52 56	26D 19.9	21 04.4	12 33.0	4 11.1	22 48.1	9 46.2	13 41.8	14 07.1	18 45.6	24 25.7
30 Su	8 31 57	7 11 44	29 46 07	5♎39 24	26 20.2	21 10.3	13 45.7	4 48.6	22 36.0	9 50.3	13 49.4	14 05.4	18 44.0	24 24.6
31 M	8 35 53	8 09 08	11♎33 21	17 28 35	26 21.4	21 22.4	14 58.4	5 26.1	22 23.8	9 54.6	13 57.1	14 03.6	18 42.4	24 23.6

August 2006 LONGITUDE

Day	Sid.Time	☉	0 hr ☽	Noon ☽	True ☊	☿	♀	♂	⚳	♃	♄	♅	♆	♇
1 Tu	8 39 50	9♌06 31	23♎25 43	29♎25 24	26♓22.6	21♋40.7	16♋11.2	6♍03.7	22♒11.4	9♏59.1	14♌04.8	14♓01.8	18♒40.8	24♐22.6
2 W	8 43 46	10 03 56	5♏28 17	11♏35 01	26R 23.0	22 05.4	17 24.0	6 41.3	21R 58.9	10 03.7	14 12.5	13R 59.9	18R 39.2	24R 21.6
3 Th	8 47 43	11 01 21	17 46 12	24 02 28	26 22.1	22 36.5	18 36.9	7 18.9	21 46.2	10 08.4	14 20.2	13 58.1	18 37.5	24 20.6
4 F	8 51 39	11 58 47	0♐24 20	6♐52 18	26 19.4	23 13.9	19 49.8	7 56.5	21 33.5	10 13.3	14 27.9	13 56.2	18 35.9	24 19.7
5 Sa	8 55 36	12 56 13	13 26 45	20 07 58	26 15.0	23 57.6	21 02.8	8 34.2	21 20.6	10 18.4	14 35.6	13 54.3	18 34.3	24 18.8
6 Su	8 59 32	13 53 41	26 56 04	3♑51 05	26 09.4	24 47.6	22 15.7	9 11.9	21 07.6	10 23.6	14 43.3	13 52.3	18 32.7	24 17.9
7 M	9 03 29	14 51 09	10♑52 48	18 00 54	26 03.1	25 43.7	23 28.8	9 49.6	20 54.5	10 29.0	14 51.0	13 50.3	18 31.1	24 17.1
8 Tu	9 07 26	15 48 38	25 14 50	2♒33 54	25 57.0	26 45.8	24 41.8	10 27.3	20 41.4	10 34.5	14 58.7	13 48.3	18 29.4	24 16.3
9 W	9 11 22	16 46 07	9♒57 15	17 23 56	25 51.9	27 53.7	25 54.9	11 05.1	20 28.3	10 40.2	15 06.4	13 46.3	18 27.8	24 15.5
10 Th	9 15 19	17 43 38	24 52 51	2♓22 56	25 48.4	29 07.3	27 08.1	11 42.9	20 15.0	10 46.0	15 14.1	13 44.2	18 26.2	24 14.7
11 F	9 19 15	18 41 10	9♓53 05	17 22 13	25D 46.6	0♌26.4	28 21.2	12 20.7	20 01.8	10 52.0	15 21.8	13 42.1	18 24.5	24 13.9
12 Sa	9 23 12	19 38 44	24 49 24	2♈13 45	25 46.5	1 50.6	29 34.5	12 58.6	19 48.5	10 58.1	15 29.5	13 40.0	18 22.9	24 13.2
13 Su	9 27 08	20 36 18	9♈34 33	16 51 11	25 47.5	3 19.9	0♌47.7	13 36.5	19 35.3	11 04.3	15 37.1	13 37.9	18 21.3	24 12.5
14 M	9 31 05	21 33 54	24 03 15	1♉10 25	25 48.9	4 53.7	2 01.1	14 14.4	19 22.0	11 10.7	15 44.8	13 35.8	18 19.6	24 11.8
15 Tu	9 35 01	22 31 32	8♉12 31	15 09 29	25R 50.0	6 31.9	3 14.4	14 52.3	19 08.8	11 17.2	15 52.5	13 33.6	18 18.0	24 11.2
16 W	9 38 58	23 29 11	22 01 19	28 48 09	25 50.0	8 14.0	4 27.8	15 30.3	18 55.6	11 23.9	16 00.2	13 31.4	18 16.4	24 10.6
17 Th	9 42 55	24 26 52	5♊30 06	12♊07 25	25 48.8	9 59.6	5 41.2	16 08.3	18 42.5	11 30.7	16 07.8	13 29.2	18 14.7	24 10.0
18 F	9 46 51	25 24 35	18 40 17	25 08 57	25 46.2	11 48.4	6 54.7	16 46.3	18 29.4	11 37.7	16 15.5	13 27.0	18 13.1	24 09.4
19 Sa	9 50 48	26 22 19	1♋33 40	7♋54 40	25 42.4	13 39.8	8 08.2	17 24.4	18 16.5	11 44.8	16 23.1	13 24.7	18 11.5	24 08.9
20 Su	9 54 44	27 20 05	14 12 13	20 26 32	25 37.9	15 33.6	9 21.8	18 02.5	18 03.6	11 52.0	16 30.7	13 22.4	18 09.9	24 08.4
21 M	9 58 41	28 17 52	26 37 50	2♌46 20	25 33.2	17 29.3	10 35.4	18 40.6	17 50.8	11 59.3	16 38.3	13 20.2	18 08.3	24 08.0
22 Tu	10 02 37	29 15 41	8♌52 16	14 55 48	25 28.9	19 26.5	11 49.0	19 18.8	17 38.2	12 06.8	16 45.9	13 17.9	18 06.7	24 07.5
23 W	10 06 34	0♍13 31	20 57 10	26 56 35	25 25.5	21 24.8	13 02.7	19 57.0	17 25.7	12 14.4	16 53.5	13 15.6	18 05.1	24 07.1
24 Th	10 10 30	1 11 22	2♍54 16	8♍50 28	25 23.2	23 23.8	14 16.4	20 35.2	17 13.3	12 22.2	17 01.1	13 13.2	18 03.5	24 06.7
25 F	10 14 27	2 09 15	14 45 25	20 39 26	25D 22.2	25 23.3	15 30.2	21 13.5	17 01.1	12 30.0	17 08.6	13 10.9	18 01.9	24 06.4
26 Sa	10 18 24	3 07 09	26 32 49	2♎25 54	25 22.3	27 23.0	16 43.9	21 51.8	16 49.1	12 38.0	17 16.1	13 08.6	18 00.4	24 06.1
27 Su	10 22 20	4 05 05	8♎19 03	14 12 40	25 23.2	29 22.6	17 57.8	22 30.1	16 37.3	12 46.1	17 23.6	13 06.2	17 58.8	24 05.8
28 M	10 26 17	5 03 02	20 07 12	26 03 06	25 24.7	1♍21.8	19 11.6	23 08.4	16 25.6	12 54.4	17 31.1	13 03.8	17 57.2	24 05.5
29 Tu	10 30 13	6 01 00	2♏00 52	8♏01 01	25 26.3	3 20.6	20 25.5	23 46.8	16 14.2	13 02.7	17 38.6	13 01.5	17 55.7	24 05.3
30 W	10 34 10	6 59 00	14 04 06	20 10 39	25 27.6	5 18.7	21 39.4	24 25.2	16 03.0	13 11.2	17 46.0	12 59.1	17 54.2	24 05.1
31 Th	10 38 06	7 57 02	26 21 14	2♐36 25	25R 28.3	7 16.0	22 53.4	25 03.7	15 52.1	13 19.8	17 53.4	12 56.7	17 52.7	24 05.0

Astro Data

	Dy Hr Mn
☽0S	2 16:38
☿R	4 19:35
♃D	6 7:19
☽0N	15 23:56
♃∠♇	25 4:55
☿D	29 0:40
☽0S	29 23:11
♄⚻♅	1 4:23
☽0N	12 7:12
☽0S	26 5:23
♃△♅	29 9:14
♄☍♆	31 9:55

Planet Ingress

	Dy Hr Mn
☿ ♋R	10 20:19
♀ ♋	19 2:42
♂ ♍	22 18:54
☉ ♌	22 23:19
☿ ♌	11 4:11
♀ ♌	12 20:22
☉ ♍	23 6:24
☿ ♍	27 19:32

Last Aspect / ☽ Ingress

Last Aspect Dy Hr Mn		☽ Ingress Dy Hr Mn
2 6:59	♇ □	♎ 2 17:07
4 19:18	♇ ⚹	♏ 5 5:14
6 19:55	♂ □	♐ 7 14:15
9 10:32	♇ ☌	♑ 9 19:26
11 20:59	☿ ☍	♒ 11 21:47
13 14:24	♇ ⚹	♓ 13 23:01
15 19:57	☿ △	♈ 16 0:40
18 1:34	♀ ⚹	♉ 18 3:45
20 5:49	♂ □	♊ 20 8:39
22 15:18	♂ ⚹	♋ 22 15:29
24 9:08	☿ ☌	♌ 25 0:26
27 0:33	♇ △	♍ 27 11:37
29 13:07	♇ □	♎ 30 0:28

Last Aspect / ☽ Ingress

Last Aspect Dy Hr Mn		☽ Ingress Dy Hr Mn
1 1:55	♇ ⚹	♏ 1 13:09
3 9:09	☿ △	♐ 3 23:14
5 19:23	♇ ☌	♑ 6 5:21
8 1:45	☿ ☍	♒ 8 7:48
9 23:00	♇ ⚹	♓ 10 8:11
12 7:18	♀ △	♈ 12 8:23
14 0:15	♇ △	♉ 14 10:01
16 1:52	☉ □	♊ 16 14:08
18 12:31	☉ ⚹	♋ 18 21:04
20 7:07	♂ ⚹	♌ 21 6:34
23 6:20	♇ □	♍ 23 18:09
25 19:01	♇ □	♎ 26 7:02
28 8:03	♇ ⚹	♏ 28 19:57
30 20:43	♂ ⚹	♐ 31 7:01

☽ Phases & Eclipses

Dy Hr Mn	
3 16:38	☽ 11♎37
11 3:03	○ 18♑42
17 19:14	☾ 25♈04
25 4:32	● 2♌07
2 8:47	☽ 9♏56
9 10:55	○ 16♒44
16 1:52	☾ 23♉05
23 19:11	● 0♍31
31 22:58	☽ 8♐24

Astro Data

1 July 2006
Julian Day # 38898
SVP 5♓10'08"
GC 26♐55.8 ⚴ 9♑54.8R
Eris 21♈18.3 ⚵ 11♌50.8
⚷ 8♒34.6R ⚶ 14♌38.3
☽ Mean ☊ 29♓23.0

1 August 2006
Julian Day # 38929
SVP 5♓10'03"
GC 26♐55.9 ⚴ 2♑36.0R
Eris 21♈18.6R ⚵ 25♌46.1
⚷ 6♒56.1R ⚶ 28♌43.7
☽ Mean ☊ 27♓44.6

LONGITUDE — September 2006

Day	Sid.Time	☉	0 hr ☽	Noon☽	True☊	☿	♀	♂	⚳	♃	♄	♅	♆	♇
1 F	10 42 03	8♍55 04	8♐56 42	15♐22 37	25♓28.2	9♍12.4	24♌07.3	25♍42.2	15♒41.4	13♏28.5	18♌00.8	12♓54.3	17♒51.2	24♐04.8
2 Sa	10 45 59	9 53 08	21 54 37	28 33 03	25R27.5	11 07.8	25 21.4	26 20.7	15R30.9	13 37.3	18 08.2	12R51.9	17R49.7	24R04.8
3 Su	10 49 56	10 51 14	5♑18 13	12♑10 17	25 26.1	13 02.2	26 35.4	26 59.2	15 20.7	13 46.2	18 15.5	12 49.5	17 48.2	24 04.7
4 M	10 53 53	11 49 20	19 09 18	26 15 08	25 24.5	14 55.5	27 49.5	27 37.8	15 10.8	13 55.3	18 22.8	12 47.1	17 46.7	24D04.7
5 Tu	10 57 49	12 47 29	3♒27 30	10♒45 56	25 22.9	16 47.7	29 03.6	28 16.4	15 01.1	14 04.4	18 30.1	12 44.8	17 45.3	24 04.7
6 W	11 01 46	13 45 38	18 09 47	25 38 13	25 21.6	18 38.7	0♍17.7	28 55.0	14 51.8	14 13.7	18 37.3	12 42.4	17 43.8	24 04.7
7 Th	11 05 42	14 43 50	3♓10 18	10♓44 54	25D20.8	20 28.6	1 31.9	29 33.7	14 42.7	14 23.0	18 44.5	12 40.0	17 42.4	24 04.8
8 F	11 09 39	15 42 03	18 20 53	25 57 01	25 20.5	22 17.3	2 46.1	0♎12.4	14 33.9	14 32.5	18 51.7	12 37.6	17 41.0	24 04.8
9 Sa	11 13 35	16 40 17	3♈32 06	11♈05 00	25 20.8	24 04.9	4 00.3	0 51.1	14 25.5	14 42.1	18 58.8	12 35.2	17 39.6	24 05.0
10 Su	11 17 32	17 38 34	18 34 39	26 00 08	25 21.3	25 51.3	5 14.6	1 29.9	14 17.3	14 51.7	19 05.9	12 32.8	17 38.3	24 05.1
11 M	11 21 28	18 36 53	3♉20 39	10♉35 36	25 21.9	27 36.5	6 28.9	2 08.7	14 09.5	15 01.5	19 13.0	12 30.4	17 36.9	24 05.3
12 Tu	11 25 25	19 35 14	17 44 32	24 47 10	25 22.5	29 20.6	7 43.2	2 47.5	14 01.9	15 11.4	19 20.0	12 28.0	17 35.6	24 05.5
13 W	11 29 22	20 33 37	1♊43 23	8♊33 11	25R22.8	1♎03.6	8 57.6	3 26.4	13 54.8	15 21.3	19 27.0	12 25.7	17 34.3	24 05.8
14 Th	11 33 18	21 32 02	15 16 42	21 54 09	25 22.9	2 45.5	10 12.0	4 05.3	13 47.9	15 31.4	19 34.0	12 23.3	17 33.0	24 06.1
15 F	11 37 15	22 30 30	28 25 51	4♋52 09	25 22.8	4 26.3	11 26.4	4 44.3	13 41.4	15 41.5	19 40.9	12 21.0	17 31.7	24 06.4
16 Sa	11 41 11	23 28 59	11♋13 27	17 30 11	25 22.7	6 06.1	12 40.9	5 23.2	13 35.2	15 51.8	19 47.8	12 18.6	17 30.5	24 06.8
17 Su	11 45 08	24 27 31	23 42 48	29 51 45	25D22.5	7 44.8	13 55.4	6 02.3	13 29.4	16 02.1	19 54.6	12 16.3	17 29.2	24 07.1
18 M	11 49 04	25 26 05	5♌57 27	12♌00 19	25 22.5	9 22.4	15 09.9	6 41.3	13 23.9	16 12.6	20 01.4	12 14.0	17 28.0	24 07.6
19 Tu	11 53 01	26 24 41	18 00 48	23 59 15	25 22.5	10 59.0	16 24.5	7 20.4	13 18.8	16 23.1	20 08.1	12 11.7	17 26.8	24 08.0
20 W	11 56 57	27 23 18	29 56 04	5♍51 34	25 22.7	12 34.6	17 39.0	7 59.6	13 14.0	16 33.7	20 14.8	12 09.4	17 25.7	24 08.5
21 Th	12 00 54	28 21 58	11♍46 06	17 39 59	25R22.8	14 09.3	18 53.6	8 38.7	13 09.6	16 44.4	20 21.5	12 07.1	17 24.5	24 09.0
22 F	12 04 51	29 20 40	23 33 29	29 26 54	25 22.8	15 42.9	20 08.3	9 17.9	13 05.5	16 55.1	20 28.1	12 04.8	17 23.4	24 09.5
23 Sa	12 08 47	0♎19 24	5♎20 32	11♎14 38	25 22.6	17 15.6	21 22.9	9 57.2	13 01.9	17 06.0	20 34.6	12 02.6	17 22.3	24 10.1
24 Su	12 12 44	1 18 10	17 09 30	23 05 25	25 22.1	18 47.2	22 37.6	10 36.5	12 58.5	17 16.9	20 41.1	12 00.3	17 21.2	24 10.7
25 M	12 16 40	2 16 57	29 02 39	5♏01 32	25 21.3	20 18.0	23 52.3	11 15.8	12 55.6	17 28.0	20 47.5	11 58.1	17 20.2	24 11.4
26 Tu	12 20 37	3 15 47	11♏02 23	17 05 33	25 20.3	21 47.7	25 07.0	11 55.1	12 53.0	17 39.1	20 53.9	11 55.9	17 19.2	24 12.0
27 W	12 24 33	4 14 38	23 11 23	29 20 15	25 19.1	23 16.5	26 21.7	12 34.5	12 50.8	17 50.2	21 00.3	11 53.8	17 18.2	24 12.7
28 Th	12 28 30	5 13 31	5♐32 33	11♐48 42	25 18.1	24 44.3	27 36.5	13 14.0	12 48.9	18 01.5	21 06.5	11 51.6	17 17.2	24 13.5
29 F	12 32 26	6 12 26	18 09 04	24 34 05	25D17.4	26 11.1	28 51.3	13 53.4	12 47.4	18 12.8	21 12.8	11 49.5	17 16.3	24 14.2
30 Sa	12 36 23	7 11 23	1♑04 08	7♑39 34	25 17.1	27 37.0	0♎06.1	14 32.9	12 46.3	18 24.2	21 18.9	11 47.4	17 15.3	24 15.0

LONGITUDE — October 2006

Day	Sid.Time	☉	0 hr ☽	Noon☽	True☊	☿	♀	♂	⚳	♃	♄	♅	♆	♇
1 Su	12 40 20	8♎10 22	14♑20 43	21♑07 50	25♓17.4	29♎01.8	1♎20.9	15♎12.5	12♒45.6	18♏35.7	21♌25.0	11♓45.3	17♒14.5	24♐15.9
2 M	12 44 16	9 09 22	28 01 05	5♒00 34	25 18.2	0♏25.5	2 35.7	15 52.0	12D45.2	18 47.3	21 31.1	11R43.3	17R13.6	24 16.7
3 Tu	12 48 13	10 08 24	12♒06 15	19 17 57	25 19.3	1 48.2	3 50.6	16 31.7	12 45.1	18 58.9	21 37.0	11 41.3	17 12.8	24 17.6
4 W	12 52 09	11 07 27	26 35 20	3♓57 55	25 20.4	3 09.8	5 05.5	17 11.3	12 45.5	19 10.5	21 43.0	11 39.3	17 12.0	24 18.5
5 Th	12 56 06	12 06 33	11♓25 03	18 55 53	25R21.1	4 30.3	6 20.3	17 51.0	12 46.1	19 22.3	21 48.8	11 37.3	17 11.2	24 19.5
6 F	13 00 02	13 05 40	26 29 29	4♈04 46	25 21.0	5 49.5	7 35.2	18 30.7	12 47.2	19 34.1	21 54.6	11 35.3	17 10.4	24 20.5
7 Sa	13 03 59	14 04 49	11♈40 32	19 15 35	25 20.0	7 07.5	8 50.2	19 10.5	12 48.6	19 45.9	22 00.3	11 33.4	17 09.7	24 21.5
8 Su	13 07 55	15 04 01	26 48 43	4♉18 47	25 18.0	8 24.2	10 05.1	19 50.2	12 50.3	19 57.9	22 06.0	11 31.5	17 09.0	24 22.5
9 M	13 11 52	16 03 14	11♉44 41	19 05 32	25 15.4	9 39.5	11 20.1	20 30.1	12 52.4	20 09.9	22 11.6	11 29.7	17 08.4	24 23.6
10 Tu	13 15 48	17 02 30	26 20 33	3♊29 08	25 12.4	10 53.3	12 35.0	21 10.0	12 54.8	20 21.9	22 17.1	11 27.9	17 07.7	24 24.7
11 W	13 19 45	18 01 48	10♊30 55	17 25 40	25 09.7	12 05.6	13 50.0	21 49.9	12 57.6	20 34.0	22 22.5	11 26.1	17 07.1	24 25.8
12 Th	13 23 42	19 01 09	24 13 20	0♋54 02	25 07.6	13 16.1	15 05.0	22 29.8	13 00.8	20 46.2	22 27.9	11 24.3	17 06.6	24 26.9
13 F	13 27 38	20 00 32	7♋28 01	13 55 37	25D06.4	14 24.8	16 20.1	23 09.9	13 04.2	20 58.4	22 33.2	11 22.6	17 06.0	24 28.1
14 Sa	13 31 35	20 59 57	20 17 18	26 33 34	25 06.4	15 31.5	17 35.1	23 49.9	13 08.0	21 10.7	22 38.5	11 20.9	17 05.5	24 29.3
15 Su	13 35 31	21 59 24	2♌44 58	8♌52 04	25 07.4	16 36.0	18 50.2	24 30.0	13 12.1	21 23.0	22 43.6	11 19.3	17 05.1	24 30.6
16 M	13 39 28	22 58 54	14 55 29	20 55 49	25 09.0	17 38.2	20 05.2	25 10.1	13 16.6	21 35.4	22 48.7	11 17.7	17 04.6	24 31.9
17 Tu	13 43 24	23 58 26	26 53 37	2♍49 29	25 10.8	18 37.8	21 20.3	25 50.3	13 21.4	21 47.8	22 53.7	11 16.1	17 04.2	24 33.1
18 W	13 47 21	24 58 00	8♍43 56	14 37 30	25R12.2	19 34.5	22 35.4	26 30.5	13 26.5	22 00.3	22 58.6	11 14.6	17 03.8	24 34.5
19 Th	13 51 17	25 57 36	20 30 38	26 23 47	25 12.7	20 28.2	23 50.6	27 10.7	13 31.9	22 12.8	23 03.5	11 13.1	17 03.5	24 35.8
20 F	13 55 14	26 57 14	2♎17 20	8♎11 40	25 11.8	21 18.3	25 05.7	27 51.0	13 37.7	22 25.4	23 08.2	11 11.6	17 03.2	24 37.2
21 Sa	13 59 11	27 56 55	14 07 06	20 03 55	25 09.3	22 04.7	26 20.8	28 31.4	13 43.8	22 38.0	23 12.9	11 10.2	17 02.9	24 38.6
22 Su	14 03 07	28 56 37	26 02 22	2♏02 41	25 05.1	22 46.9	27 36.0	29 11.8	13 50.2	22 50.6	23 17.5	11 08.8	17 02.6	24 40.0
23 M	14 07 04	29 56 22	8♏05 02	14 09 38	24 59.5	23 24.4	28 51.2	29 52.2	13 56.9	23 03.3	23 22.0	11 07.5	17 02.4	24 41.5
24 Tu	14 11 00	0♏56 09	20 16 37	26 26 09	24 53.0	23 56.9	0♏06.3	0♏32.6	14 03.9	23 16.1	23 26.5	11 06.2	17 02.2	24 42.9
25 W	14 14 57	1 55 57	2♐38 23	8♐53 28	24 46.3	24 23.6	1 21.5	1 13.1	14 11.2	23 28.9	23 30.8	11 04.9	17 02.1	24 44.4
26 Th	14 18 53	2 55 47	15 11 32	21 32 47	24 40.0	24 44.2	2 36.7	1 53.7	14 18.8	23 41.7	23 35.1	11 03.7	17 02.0	24 46.0
27 F	14 22 50	3 55 39	27 57 23	4♑25 32	24 35.0	24 57.9	3 51.9	2 34.3	14 26.7	23 54.6	23 39.2	11 02.5	17 01.9	24 47.5
28 Sa	14 26 46	4 55 33	10♑57 25	17 33 16	24 31.7	25R04.3	5 07.1	3 14.9	14 34.9	24 07.5	23 43.3	11 01.4	17D01.8	24 49.1
29 Su	14 30 43	5 55 28	24 13 18	0♒57 42	24D30.3	25 02.7	6 22.3	3 55.5	14 43.4	24 20.4	23 47.3	11 00.3	17 01.8	24 50.7
30 M	14 34 40	6 55 25	7♒46 39	14 40 19	24 30.4	24 52.5	7 37.6	4 36.2	14 52.2	24 33.3	23 51.2	10 59.3	17 01.9	24 52.3
31 Tu	14 38 36	7 55 24	21 38 46	28 42 03	24 31.5	24 33.2	8 52.8	5 17.0	15 01.2	24 46.3	23 55.0	10 58.3	17 01.9	24 54.0

Astro Data

	Dy Hr Mn
♇ D	4 23:22
☽ 0N	8 17:06
♂0S	10 19:54
☿0S	13 21:57
☽ 0S	22 11:28
☉0S	23 4:04
♃□♆	24 20:32
♀0S	3 1:07
⚳ D	3 2:03
☽ 0N	6 4:16
☽ 0S	19 17:39
♃□♄	25 17:27
☿ R	28 19:17
♆ D	29 7:57

Planet Ingress

		Dy Hr Mn
♀	♍	6 6:16
♂	♎	8 4:19
☿	♎	12 21:09
☉	♎	23 4:04
♀	♎	30 10:03
☿	♏	2 4:39
☉	♏	23 13:28
♂	♏	23 16:39
♀	♏	24 9:59

Last Aspect / ☽ Ingress (September)

Last Aspect Dy Hr Mn			☽ Ingress	Dy Hr Mn
2 7:50	♂	□	♑	2 14:36
4 14:25	♂	△	♒	4 18:16
6 9:30	♇	✶	♓	6 18:58
8 9:03	♇	□	♈	8 18:24
10 8:53	♇	△	♉	10 18:31
12 20:59	☿	△	♊	12 21:00
14 16:02	♇	☍	♋	15 2:55
17 0:33	☉	✶	♌	17 12:16
19 12:18	♇	△	♍	20 0:08
22 11:46	☉	☌	♎	22 13:07
24 14:12	♇	✶	♏	25 1:55
27 5:33	♀	✶	♐	27 13:17
29 20:46	♀	□	♑	29 22:02

Last Aspect / ☽ Ingress (October)

Last Aspect Dy Hr Mn			☽ Ingress	Dy Hr Mn
2 3:17	☿	□	♒	2 3:25
3 20:15	♇	✶	♓	4 5:34
5 20:35	♇	□	♈	6 5:33
7 20:06	♇	△	♉	8 5:05
9 17:09	♄	□	♊	10 6:07
12 0:23	♇	☍	♋	12 10:22
14 6:28	♂	□	♌	14 18:39
16 21:02	♂	✶	♍	17 6:17
19 8:19	♇	□	♎	19 19:20
22 5:59	♂	☌	♏	22 7:55
24 6:57	☿	☌	♐	24 18:54
26 18:03	♇	☌	♑	27 3:48
29 1:31	☿	✶	♒	29 10:18
31 5:32	♇	✶	♓	31 14:12

☽ Phases & Eclipses

Dy Hr Mn		
7 18:43	○	15♓00
7 18:52	•	P 0.184
14 11:16	☾	21♊30
22 11:46	●	29♍20
22 11:41:16	•	A 07'09"
30 11:05	☽	7♑09
7 3:14	○	13♈43
14 0:27	☾	20♋31
22 5:15	●	28♎40
29 21:26	☽	6♒19

Astro Data

1 September 2006
Julian Day # 38960
SVP 5♓09'58"
GC 26♐55.9 ⚴ 1♑00.7
Eris 21♈09.4R ⚵ 9♍19.1
⚷ 5♒21.3R ⚶ 13♍31.2
☽ Mean ☊ 26♓06.1

1 October 2006
Julian Day # 38990
SVP 5♓09'55"
GC 26♐56.0 ⚴ 4♑45.4
Eris 20♈53.8R ⚵ 21♍52.1
⚷ 4♒29.5R ⚶ 28♍15.8
☽ Mean ☊ 24♓30.8

November 2006 LONGITUDE

Day	Sid.Time	☉	0 hr ☽	Noon ☽	True ☊	☿	♀	♂	⚳	♃	♄	♅	♆	♇
1 W	14 42 33	8♏55 24	5♓50 05	13♓02 40	24♓32.7	24♏04.6	10♏08.0	5♏57.8	15♒10.5	24♏59.3	23♌58.7	10♓57.4	17♒02.0	24♐55.7
2 Th	14 46 29	9 55 25	20 19 31	27 40 10	24R 33.1	23R 26.5	11 23.2	6 38.6	15 20.1	25 12.4	24 02.4	10R 56.5	17 02.1	24 57.3
3 F	14 50 26	10 55 29	5♈04 01	12♈30 21	24 31.8	22 38.9	12 38.5	7 19.4	15 30.0	25 25.4	24 05.9	10 55.6	17 02.3	24 59.1
4 Sa	14 54 22	11 55 34	19 58 17	27 26 49	24 28.3	21 42.5	13 53.7	8 00.4	15 40.1	25 38.5	24 09.3	10 54.8	17 02.5	25 00.8
5 Su	14 58 19	12 55 40	4♉54 54	12♉21 27	24 22.6	20 38.0	15 09.0	8 41.3	15 50.5	25 51.7	24 12.7	10 54.0	17 02.7	25 02.5
6 M	15 02 15	13 55 49	19 45 21	27 05 33	24 15.2	19 26.8	16 24.2	9 22.3	16 01.2	26 04.8	24 15.9	10 53.3	17 03.0	25 04.3
7 Tu	15 06 12	14 55 59	4♊21 09	11♊31 18	24 06.8	18 10.6	17 39.5	10 03.3	16 12.1	26 18.0	24 19.0	10 52.7	17 03.2	25 06.1
8 W	15 10 09	15 56 12	18 35 23	25 32 54	23 58.5	16 51.7	18 54.7	10 44.4	16 23.2	26 31.2	24 22.1	10 52.1	17 03.6	25 07.9
9 Th	15 14 05	16 56 26	2♋23 34	9♋07 18	23 51.3	15 32.4	20 10.0	11 25.5	16 34.6	26 44.4	24 25.0	10 51.5	17 03.9	25 09.8
10 F	15 18 02	17 56 43	15 44 08	22 14 18	23 46.0	14 15.3	21 25.3	12 06.7	16 46.2	26 57.6	24 27.9	10 51.0	17 04.3	25 11.6
11 Sa	15 21 58	18 57 01	28 38 07	4♌56 02	23 42.7	13 02.9	22 40.6	12 47.9	16 58.1	27 10.9	24 30.6	10 50.5	17 04.8	25 13.5
12 Su	15 25 55	19 57 22	11♌08 36	17 16 25	23D 41.5	11 57.6	23 55.9	13 29.2	17 10.2	27 24.1	24 33.3	10 50.1	17 05.2	25 15.4
13 M	15 29 51	20 57 44	23 20 06	29 20 21	23 41.8	11 01.1	25 11.1	14 10.5	17 22.6	27 37.4	24 35.8	10 49.7	17 05.7	25 17.3
14 Tu	15 33 48	21 58 08	5♍17 50	11♍13 14	23 42.7	10 14.9	26 26.4	14 51.8	17 35.1	27 50.7	24 38.2	10 49.4	17 06.3	25 19.2
15 W	15 37 45	22 58 34	17 07 13	23 00 27	23R 43.3	9 40.0	27 41.8	15 33.2	17 47.9	28 04.0	24 40.6	10 49.1	17 06.8	25 21.2
16 Th	15 41 41	23 59 02	28 53 33	4♎47 06	23 42.6	9 16.7	28 57.1	16 14.6	18 00.9	28 17.3	24 42.8	10 48.9	17 07.4	25 23.1
17 F	15 45 38	24 59 31	10♎41 38	16 37 39	23 39.7	9D 05.1	0♐12.4	16 56.1	18 14.2	28 30.6	24 44.9	10 48.7	17 08.1	25 25.1
18 Sa	15 49 34	26 00 03	22 35 34	28 35 47	23 34.3	9 04.9	1 27.7	17 37.6	18 27.6	28 44.0	24 46.9	10 48.6	17 08.7	25 27.1
19 Su	15 53 31	27 00 36	4♏38 36	10♏44 16	23 26.1	9 15.4	2 43.0	18 19.2	18 41.3	28 57.3	24 48.8	10D 48.6	17 09.4	25 29.1
20 M	15 57 27	28 01 10	16 52 59	23 04 52	23 15.7	9 36.0	3 58.4	19 00.8	18 55.2	29 10.6	24 50.6	10 48.6	17 10.1	25 31.1
21 Tu	16 01 24	29 01 47	29 20 00	5♐38 24	23 03.7	10 05.7	5 13.7	19 42.5	19 09.3	29 24.0	24 52.3	10 48.6	17 10.9	25 33.2
22 W	16 05 20	0♐02 24	12♐00 02	18 24 51	22 51.2	10 43.7	6 29.0	20 24.2	19 23.6	29 37.3	24 53.9	10 48.7	17 11.7	25 35.2
23 Th	16 09 17	1 03 04	24 52 46	1♑23 41	22 39.4	11 29.0	7 44.4	21 05.9	19 38.1	29 50.7	24 55.3	10 48.8	17 12.5	25 37.3
24 F	16 13 14	2 03 44	7♑57 30	14 34 08	22 29.4	12 20.8	8 59.7	21 47.7	19 52.8	0♐04.0	24 56.7	10 49.0	17 13.4	25 39.4
25 Sa	16 17 10	3 04 26	21 13 30	27 55 34	22 22.0	13 18.4	10 15.0	22 29.5	20 07.7	0 17.4	24 57.9	10 49.3	17 14.3	25 41.4
26 Su	16 21 07	4 05 08	4♒40 18	11♒27 40	22 17.4	14 20.9	11 30.4	23 11.4	20 22.8	0 30.7	24 59.1	10 49.6	17 15.2	25 43.5
27 M	16 25 03	5 05 52	18 17 48	25 10 40	22D 15.4	15 27.8	12 45.7	23 53.3	20 38.1	0 44.1	25 00.1	10 49.9	17 16.2	25 45.7
28 Tu	16 29 00	6 06 37	2♓06 19	9♓04 49	22R 15.1	16 38.4	14 01.0	24 35.2	20 53.5	0 57.4	25 01.0	10 50.3	17 17.2	25 47.8
29 W	16 32 56	7 07 22	16 06 11	23 10 22	22 15.3	17 52.2	15 16.4	25 17.2	21 09.2	1 10.7	25 01.8	10 50.8	17 18.2	25 49.9
30 Th	16 36 53	8 08 09	0♈17 16	7♈26 45	22 14.5	19 08.8	16 31.7	25 59.3	21 25.0	1 24.1	25 02.5	10 51.3	17 19.3	25 52.0

December 2006 LONGITUDE

Day	Sid.Time	☉	0 hr ☽	Noon ☽	True ☊	☿	♀	♂	⚳	♃	♄	♅	♆	♇
1 F	16 40 49	9♐08 56	14♈38 30	21♈52 09	22♓11.8	20♏27.7	17♐47.0	26♏41.3	21♒41.0	1♐37.4	25♌03.0	10♓51.8	17♒20.4	25♐54.2
2 Sa	16 44 46	10 09 45	29 07 13	6♉23 05	22R 06.2	21 48.6	19 02.3	27 23.4	21 57.1	1 50.7	25 03.5	10 52.4	17 21.5	25 56.4
3 Su	16 48 43	11 10 34	13♉39 02	20 54 18	21 57.6	23 11.2	20 17.7	28 05.6	22 13.4	2 04.0	25 03.9	10 53.1	17 22.6	25 58.5
4 M	16 52 39	12 11 25	28 08 03	5♊19 26	21 46.6	24 35.3	21 33.0	28 47.8	22 29.9	2 17.2	25 04.1	10 53.8	17 23.8	26 00.7
5 Tu	16 56 36	13 12 16	12♊27 36	19 31 47	21 34.2	26 00.7	22 48.3	29 30.1	22 46.6	2 30.5	25R 04.2	10 54.5	17 25.0	26 02.9
6 W	17 00 32	14 13 09	26 31 17	3♋25 34	21 21.7	27 27.1	24 03.6	0♐12.4	23 03.4	2 43.7	25 04.3	10 55.3	17 26.3	26 05.1
7 Th	17 04 29	15 14 03	10♋14 09	16 56 48	21 10.3	28 54.4	25 18.9	0 54.7	23 20.4	2 57.0	25 04.2	10 56.2	17 27.5	26 07.3
8 F	17 08 25	16 14 58	23 33 20	0♌03 48	21 01.1	0♐22.5	26 34.2	1 37.1	23 37.5	3 10.2	25 04.0	10 57.1	17 28.8	26 09.5
9 Sa	17 12 22	17 15 54	6♌28 22	12 47 17	20 54.6	1 51.3	27 49.6	2 19.5	23 54.8	3 23.3	25 03.6	10 58.1	17 30.1	26 11.7
10 Su	17 16 18	18 16 51	19 00 57	25 09 52	20 50.9	3 20.6	29 04.9	3 02.0	24 12.3	3 36.5	25 03.2	10 59.1	17 31.5	26 13.9
11 M	17 20 15	19 17 49	1♍14 36	7♍15 44	20 49.3	4 50.4	0♑20.2	3 44.5	24 29.8	3 49.7	25 02.7	11 00.1	17 32.9	26 16.1
12 Tu	17 24 12	20 18 49	13 13 58	19 09 58	20 49.0	6 20.6	1 35.5	4 27.1	24 47.6	4 02.8	25 02.0	11 01.2	17 34.3	26 18.3
13 W	17 28 08	21 19 49	25 04 28	0♎58 09	20 48.9	7 51.2	2 50.8	5 09.7	25 05.4	4 15.9	25 01.2	11 02.4	17 35.7	26 20.6
14 Th	17 32 05	22 20 51	6♎51 44	12 45 54	20 47.7	9 22.1	4 06.1	5 52.3	25 23.5	4 28.9	25 00.4	11 03.6	17 37.2	26 22.8
15 F	17 36 01	23 21 53	18 41 18	24 38 35	20 44.5	10 53.3	5 21.4	6 35.0	25 41.6	4 42.0	24 59.4	11 04.8	17 38.7	26 25.0
16 Sa	17 39 58	24 22 57	0♏38 18	6♏40 57	20 38.7	12 24.8	6 36.7	7 17.8	25 59.9	4 55.0	24 58.3	11 06.1	17 40.2	26 27.2
17 Su	17 43 54	25 24 01	12 47 01	18 56 52	20 29.9	13 56.5	7 52.0	8 00.6	26 18.3	5 08.0	24 57.1	11 07.5	17 41.7	26 29.5
18 M	17 47 51	26 25 07	25 10 47	1♐28 57	20 18.6	15 28.4	9 07.3	8 43.4	26 36.9	5 20.9	24 55.7	11 08.9	17 43.3	26 31.7
19 Tu	17 51 47	27 26 13	7♐51 31	14 18 28	20 05.4	17 00.5	10 22.6	9 26.3	26 55.6	5 33.8	24 54.3	11 10.3	17 44.9	26 33.9
20 W	17 55 44	28 27 20	20 49 45	27 25 11	19 51.7	18 32.9	11 37.9	10 09.2	27 14.4	5 46.7	24 52.8	11 11.8	17 46.5	26 36.2
21 Th	17 59 41	29 28 27	4♑04 32	10♑47 30	19 38.6	20 05.4	12 53.2	10 52.1	27 33.4	5 59.5	24 51.1	11 13.4	17 48.2	26 38.4
22 F	18 03 37	0♑29 35	17 33 45	24 22 53	19 27.4	21 38.1	14 08.5	11 35.2	27 52.4	6 12.3	24 49.4	11 15.0	17 49.9	26 40.6
23 Sa	18 07 34	1 30 43	1♒14 33	8♒08 21	19 19.0	23 11.1	15 23.8	12 18.2	28 11.6	6 25.1	24 47.5	11 16.6	17 51.5	26 42.9
24 Su	18 11 30	2 31 51	15 03 57	22 01 03	19 13.6	24 44.2	16 39.1	13 01.3	28 30.9	6 37.8	24 45.6	11 18.3	17 53.3	26 45.1
25 M	18 15 27	3 33 00	28 59 22	5♓58 41	19D 11.1	26 17.6	17 54.4	13 44.4	28 50.4	6 50.5	24 43.5	11 20.0	17 55.0	26 47.3
26 Tu	18 19 23	4 34 08	12♓58 52	19 59 45	19 10.6	27 51.2	19 09.6	14 27.6	29 09.9	7 03.1	24 41.3	11 21.8	17 56.8	26 49.5
27 W	18 23 20	5 35 16	27 01 17	4♈03 22	19R 10.8	29 25.0	20 24.9	15 10.8	29 29.5	7 15.7	24 39.1	11 23.6	17 58.6	26 51.7
28 Th	18 27 17	6 36 25	11♈05 57	18 08 55	19 10.3	0♑59.1	21 40.1	15 54.0	29 49.3	7 28.2	24 36.7	11 25.5	18 00.4	26 53.9
29 F	18 31 13	7 37 33	25 12 11	2♉15 34	19 08.0	2 33.4	22 55.3	16 37.3	0♓09.2	7 40.7	24 34.2	11 27.4	18 02.2	26 56.1
30 Sa	18 35 10	8 38 41	9♉18 52	16 21 47	19 03.1	4 08.1	24 10.6	17 20.6	0 29.1	7 53.1	24 31.7	11 29.3	18 04.0	26 58.3
31 Su	18 39 06	9 39 50	23 24 00	0♊25 07	18 55.4	5 43.0	25 25.8	18 04.0	0 49.2	8 05.5	24 29.0	11 31.3	18 05.9	27 00.5

Astro Data	Dy Hr Mn
♃⚻♇	1 4:13
☽0N	2 14:16
☽0S	16 0:04
☿D	18 0:24
♅D	20 6:09
☽0N	29 21:19
♄R	6 4:08
☽0S	13 6:52
☽0N	27 1:58

Planet Ingress	Dy Hr Mn
♀ ♐	17 8:03
☉ ♐	22 11:03
♃ ♐	24 4:44
♂ ♐	6 4:59
☿ ♐	8 5:53
♀ ♑	11 5:34
☉ ♑	22 0:23
☿ ♑	27 20:56
⚳ ♓	29 0:56

Last Aspect Dy Hr Mn		☽ Ingress Dy Hr Mn
2 7:55	♃ △	♈ 2 15:47
4 8:05	♇ △	♉ 4 16:06
6 10:19	♃ ☍	♊ 6 16:47
8 11:17	♇ ☍	♋ 8 19:47
10 21:00	♃ △	♌ 11 2:35
13 8:30	♃ □	♍ 13 13:20
15 22:42	♀ ⚹	♎ 16 2:15
18 5:42	♇ ⚹	♏ 18 14:48
20 23:55	♃ ☌	♐ 21 1:16
23 1:21	♇ ☌	♑ 23 9:26
25 1:44	♂ ⚹	♒ 25 15:42
27 13:01	♇ ⚹	♓ 27 20:22
29 16:30	♇ □	♈ 29 23:31

Last Aspect Dy Hr Mn		☽ Ingress Dy Hr Mn
1 18:42	♇ △	♉ 2 1:27
4 0:33	♂ ☍	♊ 4 3:06
5 23:13	♇ ☍	♋ 6 6:02
7 1:14	♅ △	♌ 8 11:53
10 20:36	♀ △	♍ 10 21:32
13 2:33	♇ □	♎ 13 10:02
15 15:34	♇ ⚹	♏ 15 22:44
17 23:33	♄ □	♐ 18 9:11
20 14:02	☉ ☌	♑ 20 16:40
21 16:06	♀ ☌	♒ 22 21:50
24 20:10	♇ ⚹	♓ 25 1:44
27 3:06	☿ □	♈ 27 5:05
29 2:55	♇ △	♉ 29 8:09
31 2:38	♀ △	♊ 31 11:17

☽ Phases & Eclipses Dy Hr Mn	
5 12:59	○ 12♉58
12 17:46	☾ 20♌12
20 22:19	● 28♏27
28 6:30	☽ 5♓53
5 0:26	○ 12♊43
12 14:33	☾ 20♍25
20 14:02	● 28♐32
27 14:49	☽ 5♈42

Astro Data

1 November 2006
Julian Day # 39021
SVP 5♓09'51"
GC 26♐56.1 ⚴ 12♑09.2
Eris 20♈35.5R ⚵ 3♎56.3
⚷ 4♒38.5 ⚶ 13♎41.8
☽ Mean ☊ 22♓52.3

1 December 2006
Julian Day # 39051
SVP 5♓09'46"
GC 26♐56.2 ⚴ 21♑16.3
Eris 20♈20.8R ⚵ 14♎15.4
⚷ 5♒48.5 ⚶ 28♎31.6
☽ Mean ☊ 21♓16.9

LONGITUDE — January 2007

Day	Sid.Time	☉	0 hr ☽	Noon☽	True☊	☿	♀	♂	⚳	♃	♄	♅	♆	♇
1 M	18 43 03	10♑40 58	7♊24 41	14♊22 13	18♓45.4	7♑18.2	26♑41.0	18♐47.4	1♓09.4	8♐17.8	24♌26.3	11♓33.3	18♒07.8	27♐02.7
2 Tu	18 46 59	11 42 06	21 17 12	28 09 09	18R 33.9	8 53.7	27 56.2	19 30.9	1 29.7	8 30.1	24R 23.4	11 35.4	18 09.7	27 04.9
3 W	18 50 56	12 43 14	4♋57 36	11♋42 07	18 22.2	10 29.6	29 11.3	20 14.4	1 50.0	8 42.3	24 20.5	11 37.5	18 11.6	27 07.1
4 Th	18 54 52	13 44 23	18 22 21	24 58 03	18 11.5	12 05.8	0♒26.5	20 57.9	2 10.5	8 54.4	24 17.5	11 39.7	18 13.6	27 09.2
5 F	18 58 49	14 45 31	1♌29 00	7♌55 09	18 02.7	13 42.4	1 41.7	21 41.5	2 31.1	9 06.5	24 14.3	11 41.9	18 15.6	27 11.4
6 Sa	19 02 46	15 46 39	14 16 31	20 33 14	17 56.5	15 19.4	2 56.8	22 25.1	2 51.7	9 18.6	24 11.1	11 44.1	18 17.5	27 13.5
7 Su	19 06 42	16 47 47	26 45 32	2♍53 43	17 52.9	16 56.7	4 11.9	23 08.8	3 12.4	9 30.5	24 07.8	11 46.4	18 19.5	27 15.7
8 M	19 10 39	17 48 55	8♍58 12	14 59 27	17D 51.6	18 34.5	5 27.0	23 52.5	3 33.3	9 42.4	24 04.5	11 48.7	18 21.5	27 17.8
9 Tu	19 14 35	18 50 03	20 58 00	26 54 25	17 51.9	20 12.7	6 42.1	24 36.2	3 54.2	9 54.3	24 01.0	11 51.0	18 23.6	27 19.9
10 W	19 18 32	19 51 12	2♎49 20	8♎43 25	17 52.8	21 51.3	7 57.2	25 20.0	4 15.2	10 06.1	23 57.5	11 53.4	18 25.6	27 22.0
11 Th	19 22 28	20 52 20	14 37 20	20 31 45	17R 53.3	23 30.3	9 12.3	26 03.8	4 36.3	10 17.8	23 53.8	11 55.8	18 27.7	27 24.1
12 F	19 26 25	21 53 28	26 27 23	2♏24 54	17 52.6	25 09.8	10 27.4	26 47.7	4 57.4	10 29.4	23 50.1	11 58.3	18 29.8	27 26.2
13 Sa	19 30 21	22 54 37	8♏24 56	14 28 08	17 49.9	26 49.7	11 42.5	27 31.6	5 18.7	10 41.0	23 46.4	12 00.8	18 31.9	27 28.2
14 Su	19 34 18	23 55 45	20 35 05	26 46 16	17 45.0	28 30.1	12 57.5	28 15.6	5 40.0	10 52.5	23 42.5	12 03.3	18 34.0	27 30.3
15 M	19 38 15	24 56 53	3♐02 10	9♐23 09	17 38.0	0♒10.8	14 12.5	28 59.6	6 01.4	11 03.9	23 38.6	12 05.9	18 36.1	27 32.3
16 Tu	19 42 11	25 58 01	15 49 28	22 21 16	17 29.4	1 52.0	15 27.6	29 43.6	6 22.9	11 15.2	23 34.6	12 08.5	18 38.2	27 34.4
17 W	19 46 08	26 59 08	28 58 37	5♑41 26	17 20.1	3 33.5	16 42.6	0♑27.7	6 44.5	11 26.5	23 30.6	12 11.1	18 40.4	27 36.4
18 Th	19 50 04	28 00 15	12♑29 30	19 22 29	17 11.2	5 15.4	17 57.6	1 11.8	7 06.1	11 37.7	23 26.5	12 13.8	18 42.5	27 38.4
19 F	19 54 01	29 01 22	26 19 58	3♒21 24	17 03.6	6 57.6	19 12.5	1 56.0	7 27.8	11 48.8	23 22.3	12 16.5	18 44.7	27 40.3
20 Sa	19 57 57	0♒02 28	10♒26 13	17 33 44	16 58.0	8 40.0	20 27.5	2 40.2	7 49.6	11 59.8	23 18.1	12 19.2	18 46.9	27 42.3
21 Su	20 01 54	1 03 33	24 43 19	1♓54 16	16 54.8	10 22.6	21 42.4	3 24.4	8 11.4	12 10.7	23 13.8	12 22.0	18 49.1	27 44.3
22 M	20 05 50	2 04 37	9♓05 57	16 17 48	16D 53.7	12 05.3	22 57.3	4 08.7	8 33.3	12 21.6	23 09.4	12 24.8	18 51.3	27 46.2
23 Tu	20 09 47	3 05 41	23 29 16	0♈39 54	16 54.4	13 48.0	24 12.2	4 53.0	8 55.3	12 32.3	23 05.0	12 27.6	18 53.5	27 48.1
24 W	20 13 44	4 06 45	7♈49 19	14 57 11	16 55.7	15 30.6	25 27.1	5 37.3	9 17.3	12 43.0	23 00.6	12 30.4	18 55.7	27 50.0
25 Th	20 17 40	5 07 44	22 03 17	29 07 25	16R 56.7	17 12.8	26 41.9	6 21.7	9 39.4	12 53.5	22 56.1	12 33.3	18 57.9	27 51.9
26 F	20 21 37	6 08 44	6♉09 25	13♉09 11	16 56.6	18 54.6	27 56.8	7 06.1	10 01.6	13 04.0	22 51.5	12 36.2	19 00.1	27 53.7
27 Sa	20 25 33	7 09 44	20 06 37	27 01 38	16 54.9	20 35.6	29 11.5	7 50.5	10 23.8	13 14.4	22 47.0	12 39.2	19 02.4	27 55.6
28 Su	20 29 30	8 10 42	3♊54 08	10♊44 02	16 51.2	22 15.7	0♓26.3	8 35.0	10 46.1	13 24.7	22 42.3	12 42.1	19 04.6	27 57.4
29 M	20 33 26	9 11 38	17 31 14	24 15 36	16 46.0	23 54.6	1 41.0	9 19.5	11 08.4	13 34.8	22 37.7	12 45.1	19 06.9	27 59.2
30 Tu	20 37 23	10 12 34	0♋57 02	7♋35 23	16 39.9	25 31.9	2 55.8	10 04.1	11 30.8	13 44.9	22 33.0	12 48.1	19 09.1	28 01.0
31 W	20 41 20	11 13 29	14 10 33	20 42 23	16 33.4	27 07.1	4 10.4	10 48.7	11 53.2	13 54.9	22 28.3	12 51.2	19 11.4	28 02.7

LONGITUDE — February 2007

Day	Sid.Time	☉	0 hr ☽	Noon☽	True☊	☿	♀	♂	⚳	♃	♄	♅	♆	♇
1 Th	20 45 16	12♒14 22	27♋10 49	3♌35 47	16♓27.6	28♒39.9	5♓25.1	11♑33.3	12♓15.7	14♐04.8	22♌23.5	12♓54.2	19♒13.7	28♐04.4
2 F	20 49 13	13 15 14	9♌57 12	16 15 07	16R 22.8	0♓09.8	6 39.7	12 18.0	12 38.2	14 14.6	22R 18.8	12 57.3	19 15.9	28 06.2
3 Sa	20 53 09	14 16 06	22 29 33	28 40 36	16 19.7	1 36.0	7 54.3	13 02.6	13 00.8	14 24.2	22 14.0	13 00.4	19 18.2	28 07.9
4 Su	20 57 06	15 16 56	4♍48 26	10♍53 16	16D 18.2	2 58.2	9 08.8	13 47.4	13 23.5	14 33.8	22 09.1	13 03.5	19 20.5	28 09.5
5 M	21 01 02	16 17 45	16 55 21	22 55 00	16 18.3	4 15.5	10 23.4	14 32.1	13 46.1	14 43.2	22 04.3	13 06.7	19 22.7	28 11.2
6 Tu	21 04 59	17 18 33	28 52 36	4♎48 34	16 19.5	5 27.2	11 37.8	15 16.9	14 08.9	14 52.6	21 59.5	13 09.8	19 25.0	28 12.8
7 W	21 08 55	18 19 20	10♎43 22	16 37 30	16 21.3	6 32.6	12 52.3	16 01.8	14 31.6	15 01.8	21 54.6	13 13.0	19 27.3	28 14.4
8 Th	21 12 52	19 20 06	22 31 32	28 26 01	16 23.1	7 30.9	14 06.7	16 46.6	14 54.4	15 10.9	21 49.7	13 16.2	19 29.6	28 16.0
9 F	21 16 48	20 20 51	4♏21 34	10♏18 48	16R 24.5	8 21.3	15 21.1	17 31.6	15 17.3	15 19.9	21 44.8	13 19.4	19 31.8	28 17.5
10 Sa	21 20 45	21 21 35	16 18 20	22 20 48	16 24.9	9 03.2	16 35.5	18 16.5	15 40.2	15 28.8	21 39.9	13 22.7	19 34.1	28 19.0
11 Su	21 24 42	22 22 18	28 26 48	4♐36 57	16 24.3	9 35.8	17 49.8	19 01.5	16 03.1	15 37.5	21 35.1	13 25.9	19 36.4	28 20.5
12 M	21 28 38	23 23 00	10♐51 47	17 11 49	16 22.5	9 58.6	19 04.1	19 46.5	16 26.1	15 46.1	21 30.2	13 29.2	19 38.7	28 22.0
13 Tu	21 32 35	24 23 41	23 37 29	0♑09 08	16 19.9	10R 11.2	20 18.4	20 31.5	16 49.1	15 54.7	21 25.3	13 32.5	19 41.0	28 23.5
14 W	21 36 31	25 24 21	6♑47 02	13 31 19	16 16.8	10 13.2	21 32.6	21 16.6	17 12.2	16 03.0	21 20.4	13 35.8	19 43.3	28 24.9
15 Th	21 40 28	26 25 00	20 21 58	27 18 52	16 13.7	10 04.7	22 46.8	22 01.7	17 35.3	16 11.3	21 15.6	13 39.1	19 45.5	28 26.3
16 F	21 44 24	27 25 37	4♒21 43	11♒30 05	16 11.2	9 45.8	24 01.0	22 46.9	17 58.4	16 19.4	21 10.7	13 42.5	19 47.8	28 27.7
17 Sa	21 48 21	28 26 13	18 43 23	26 00 54	16 09.4	9 16.9	25 15.1	23 32.0	18 21.6	16 27.4	21 05.9	13 45.8	19 50.1	28 29.0
18 Su	21 52 18	29 26 47	3♓21 49	10♓45 15	16D 08.6	8 38.7	26 29.2	24 17.2	18 44.8	16 35.3	21 01.1	13 49.1	19 52.3	28 30.3
19 M	21 56 14	0♓27 19	18 10 15	25 35 51	16 08.7	7 52.3	27 43.2	25 02.5	19 08.0	16 43.0	20 56.3	13 52.5	19 54.6	28 31.6
20 Tu	22 00 11	1 27 50	3♈01 07	10♈25 09	16 09.4	6 58.8	28 57.2	25 47.7	19 31.2	16 50.6	20 51.5	13 55.9	19 56.8	28 32.9
21 W	22 04 07	2 28 20	17 47 09	25 06 25	16 10.5	5 59.7	0♈11.2	26 33.0	19 54.5	16 58.0	20 46.8	13 59.3	19 59.1	28 34.1
22 Th	22 08 04	3 28 47	2♉22 20	9♉34 25	16 11.6	4 56.6	1 25.1	27 18.3	20 17.8	17 05.3	20 42.0	14 02.7	20 01.3	28 35.3
23 F	22 12 00	4 29 12	16 42 18	23 45 44	16R 12.2	3 51.2	2 38.9	28 03.6	20 41.2	17 12.5	20 37.4	14 06.1	20 03.5	28 36.5
24 Sa	22 15 57	5 29 36	0♊44 34	7♊38 45	16 12.4	2 45.1	3 52.7	28 49.0	21 04.5	17 19.5	20 32.7	14 09.5	20 05.7	28 37.6
25 Su	22 19 53	6 29 58	14 28 16	21 13 12	16 12.1	1 40.0	5 06.5	29 34.4	21 27.9	17 26.4	20 28.1	14 12.9	20 08.0	28 38.7
26 M	22 23 50	7 30 17	27 53 41	4♋29 53	16 11.3	0 37.4	6 20.2	0♒19.8	21 51.3	17 33.1	20 23.6	14 16.3	20 10.2	28 39.8
27 Tu	22 27 47	8 30 35	11♋01 58	17 30 07	16 10.4	29♒38.5	7 33.8	1 05.2	22 14.7	17 39.7	20 19.0	14 19.7	20 12.4	28 40.9
28 W	22 31 43	9 30 51	23 54 34	0♌15 30	16 09.4	28 44.4	8 47.4	1 50.6	22 38.2	17 46.2	20 14.6	14 23.2	20 14.5	28 41.9

Astro Data Dy Hr Mn	Planet Ingress Dy Hr Mn	Last Aspect Dy Hr Mn	☽ Ingress Dy Hr Mn	Last Aspect Dy Hr Mn	☽ Ingress Dy Hr Mn	☽ Phases & Eclipses Dy Hr Mn
☽0S 9 14:05	♀ ♒ 4 3:32	2 10:07 ♇ ☍	♋ 2 15:15	30 21:32 ♅ △	♌ 1 5:16	3 13:59 ○ 12♋48
♃□♅ 22 21:43	☿ ♒ 15 9:26	3 13:59 ☉ ☍	♌ 4 21:15	3 10:56 ♇ △	♍ 3 14:35	11 12:46 ☾ 20♎54
☽0N 23 7:07	♂ ♑ 16 20:55	7 0:57 ♇ △	♍ 7 6:19	5 22:38 ♇ □	♎ 6 2:16	19 4:02 ● 28♑41
	☉ ♒ 20 11:02	9 12:52 ♇ □	♎ 9 18:16	8 11:40 ♇ ⚹	♏ 8 15:11	25 23:03 ☽ 5♉36
☽0S 5 21:28	♀ ♓ 28 3:33	12 1:57 ♇ ⚹	♏ 12 7:09	10 10:40 ♄ □	♐ 11 3:02	
☿R 14 4:37		14 15:51 ☿ ⚹	♐ 14 18:12	13 8:46 ♇ ☌	♑ 13 11:43	2 5:46 ○ 12♌59
☽0N 19 15:12	☿ ♓ 2 9:21	16 21:30 ♇ ☌	♑ 17 1:50	15 3:25 ♀ ⚹	♒ 15 16:36	10 9:52 ☾ 21♏16
♀0N 23 4:07	☉ ♓ 19 1:10	19 4:02 ☉ ☌	♒ 19 6:17	17 16:15 ☉ ☌	♓ 17 18:31	17 16:15 ● 28♒37
♄☍♆ 28 12:02	♀ ♈ 21 8:22	21 5:02 ♇ ⚹	♓ 21 8:49	19 16:44 ♇ □	♈ 19 19:07	24 7:57 ☽ 5♊19
	♂ ♒ 26 1:33	23 7:12 ♇ □	♈ 23 10:53	21 17:43 ♇ △	♉ 21 20:04	
	☿ ♒R 27 3:02	25 9:51 ♇ △	♉ 25 13:30	23 19:48 ♂ △	♊ 23 22:43	
		27 16:09 ♀ □	♊ 27 17:11	26 1:23 ♇ ☍	♋ 26 3:49	
		29 18:41 ♇ ☍	♋ 29 22:17	27 6:04 ♅ △	♌ 28 11:31	

Astro Data

1 January 2007
Julian Day # 39082
SVP 5♓09'40"
GC 26♐56.2 ⚴ 1♒43.7
Eris 20♈13.5R ⚵ 22♎39.3
⚷ 7♒49.1 ⚶ 13♏17.3
☽ Mean ☊ 19♓38.5

1 February 2007
Julian Day # 39113
SVP 5♓09'34"
GC 26♐56.3 ⚴ 12♒31.9
Eris 20♈16.5 ⚵ 27♎24.0
⚷ 10♒14.5 ⚶ 26♏45.6
☽ Mean ☊ 18♓00.0

March 2007 LONGITUDE

Day	Sid.Time	☉	0 hr ☽	Noon ☽	True ☊	☿	♀	♂	⚳	♃	♄	♅	♆	♇
1 Th	22 35 40	10♓31 04	6♌33 09	12♌47 41	16♓08.6	27♒56.0	10♈01.0	2♒36.1	23♓01.6	17♐52.5	20♌10.1	14♓26.6	20♒16.7	28♐42.9
2 F	22 39 36	11 31 16	18 59 18	25 08 14	16R 08.1	27R 13.9	11 14.5	3 21.6	23 25.1	17 58.6	20R 05.7	14 30.0	20 18.9	28 43.9
3 Sa	22 43 33	12 31 26	1♍14 38	7♍18 44	16D 07.8	26 38.5	12 27.9	4 07.2	23 48.6	18 04.6	20 01.4	14 33.5	20 21.0	28 44.8
4 Su	22 47 29	13 31 34	13 20 43	19 20 49	16 07.7	26 10.1	13 41.3	4 52.7	24 12.1	18 10.4	19 57.1	14 36.9	20 23.2	28 45.7
5 M	22 51 26	14 31 40	25 19 14	1♎16 15	16 07.8	25 48.6	14 54.6	5 38.3	24 35.7	18 16.1	19 52.9	14 40.3	20 25.3	28 46.6
6 Tu	22 55 22	15 31 44	7♎12 07	13 07 08	16R 07.9	25 34.0	16 07.8	6 23.9	24 59.2	18 21.6	19 48.8	14 43.8	20 27.4	28 47.4
7 W	22 59 19	16 31 47	19 01 37	24 55 55	16 07.9	25D 26.2	17 21.0	7 09.5	25 22.8	18 26.9	19 44.7	14 47.2	20 29.5	28 48.2
8 Th	23 03 15	17 31 48	0♏50 25	6♏45 32	16 07.8	25 24.9	18 34.2	7 55.2	25 46.4	18 32.1	19 40.6	14 50.7	20 31.6	28 49.0
9 F	23 07 12	18 31 48	12 41 42	18 39 23	16 07.6	25 29.9	19 47.2	8 40.9	26 10.0	18 37.1	19 36.7	14 54.1	20 33.7	28 49.7
10 Sa	23 11 09	19 31 45	24 39 06	0♐41 20	16 07.3	25 40.8	21 00.3	9 26.5	26 33.6	18 42.0	19 32.7	14 57.5	20 35.7	28 50.5
11 Su	23 15 05	20 31 42	6♐46 38	12 55 32	16D 07.0	25 57.4	22 13.2	10 12.3	26 57.2	18 46.7	19 28.9	15 01.0	20 37.8	28 51.1
12 M	23 19 02	21 31 36	19 08 35	25 26 19	16 07.0	26 19.3	23 26.1	10 58.0	27 20.8	18 51.2	19 25.2	15 04.4	20 39.8	28 51.8
13 Tu	23 22 58	22 31 29	1♑49 14	8♑17 47	16 07.3	26 46.1	24 39.0	11 43.8	27 44.5	18 55.6	19 21.5	15 07.8	20 41.8	28 52.4
14 W	23 26 55	23 31 20	14 52 25	21 33 26	16 07.8	27 17.7	25 51.7	12 29.6	28 08.1	18 59.8	19 17.8	15 11.2	20 43.8	28 53.0
15 Th	23 30 51	24 31 10	28 21 05	5♒15 30	16 08.5	27 53.6	27 04.5	13 15.4	28 31.8	19 03.8	19 14.3	15 14.6	20 45.8	28 53.6
16 F	23 34 48	25 30 58	12♒16 40	19 24 24	16 09.3	28 33.6	28 17.1	14 01.2	28 55.4	19 07.7	19 10.9	15 18.0	20 47.8	28 54.1
17 Sa	23 38 44	26 30 44	26 38 24	3♓58 07	16R 09.9	29 17.5	29 29.7	14 47.0	29 19.1	19 11.3	19 07.5	15 21.4	20 49.7	28 54.6
18 Su	23 42 41	27 30 28	11♓22 52	18 51 50	16 10.1	0♓04.9	0♉42.2	15 32.9	29 42.8	19 14.8	19 04.2	15 24.8	20 51.7	28 55.0
19 M	23 46 38	28 30 10	26 24 00	3♈58 15	16 09.6	0 55.7	1 54.7	16 18.7	0♈06.4	19 18.2	19 01.0	15 28.2	20 53.6	28 55.5
20 Tu	23 50 34	29 29 50	11♈33 24	19 08 15	16 08.5	1 49.7	3 07.0	17 04.6	0 30.1	19 21.3	18 57.8	15 31.6	20 55.5	28 55.9
21 W	23 54 31	0♈29 28	26 41 36	4♉12 18	16 06.9	2 46.6	4 19.4	17 50.5	0 53.8	19 24.3	18 54.8	15 34.9	20 57.3	28 56.2
22 Th	23 58 27	1 29 03	11♉39 21	19 01 51	16 05.0	3 46.3	5 31.6	18 36.4	1 17.5	19 27.0	18 51.8	15 38.3	20 59.2	28 56.5
23 F	0 02 24	2 28 37	26 19 05	3♊30 29	16 03.2	4 48.7	6 43.8	19 22.3	1 41.2	19 29.6	18 49.0	15 41.6	21 01.0	28 56.8
24 Sa	0 06 20	3 28 08	10♊35 42	17 34 32	16 01.8	5 53.5	7 55.8	20 08.3	2 04.9	19 32.1	18 46.2	15 44.9	21 02.8	28 57.1
25 Su	0 10 17	4 27 37	24 26 55	1♋12 57	16D 01.2	7 00.8	9 07.8	20 54.2	2 28.5	19 34.3	18 43.5	15 48.2	21 04.6	28 57.3
26 M	0 14 13	5 27 04	7♋52 50	14 26 51	16 01.4	8 10.2	10 19.8	21 40.1	2 52.2	19 36.3	18 41.0	15 51.5	21 06.4	28 57.5
27 Tu	0 18 10	6 26 29	20 55 22	27 18 47	16 02.4	9 21.9	11 31.6	22 26.1	3 15.9	19 38.2	18 38.5	15 54.8	21 08.1	28 57.7
28 W	0 22 07	7 25 51	3♌37 34	9♌52 08	16 03.9	10 35.6	12 43.3	23 12.1	3 39.6	19 39.9	18 36.1	15 58.1	21 09.9	28 57.8
29 Th	0 26 03	8 25 10	16 02 58	22 10 30	16 05.5	11 51.3	13 55.0	23 58.0	4 03.2	19 41.4	18 33.8	16 01.3	21 11.6	28 57.9
30 F	0 30 00	9 24 28	28 15 10	4♍17 24	16R 06.8	13 08.9	15 06.6	24 44.0	4 26.9	19 42.7	18 31.6	16 04.6	21 13.2	28 58.0
31 Sa	0 33 56	10 23 43	10♍17 35	16 16 03	16 07.3	14 28.3	16 18.1	25 30.0	4 50.5	19 43.8	18 29.5	16 07.8	21 14.9	28R 58.0

April 2007 LONGITUDE

Day	Sid.Time	☉	0 hr ☽	Noon ☽	True ☊	☿	♀	♂	⚳	♃	♄	♅	♆	♇
1 Su	0 37 53	11♈22 56	22♍13 11	28♍09 15	16♓06.6	15♓49.5	17♉29.5	26♒16.0	5♈14.1	19♐44.8	18♌27.5	16♓11.0	21♒16.5	28♐58.0
2 M	0 41 49	12 22 07	4♎04 34	9♎59 24	16R 04.7	17 12.5	18 40.8	27 02.0	5 37.8	19 45.5	18R 25.6	16 14.2	21 18.1	28R 58.0
3 Tu	0 45 46	13 21 15	15 54 00	21 48 37	16 01.4	18 37.1	19 52.0	27 48.0	6 01.4	19 46.1	18 23.8	16 17.3	21 19.7	28 57.9
4 W	0 49 42	14 20 22	27 43 30	3♏38 53	15 56.9	20 03.5	21 03.1	28 34.0	6 25.0	19 46.5	18 22.1	16 20.5	21 21.3	28 57.8
5 Th	0 53 39	15 19 27	9♏35 01	15 32 09	15 51.8	21 31.4	22 14.1	29 20.0	6 48.6	19R 46.7	18 20.5	16 23.6	21 22.8	28 57.7
6 F	0 57 36	16 18 30	21 30 36	27 30 37	15 46.4	23 01.0	23 25.0	0♓06.1	7 12.2	19 46.7	18 19.0	16 26.7	21 24.3	28 57.5
7 Sa	1 01 32	17 17 32	3♐32 33	9♐36 45	15 41.5	24 32.1	24 35.9	0 52.1	7 35.8	19 46.5	18 17.7	16 29.7	21 25.8	28 57.3
8 Su	1 05 29	18 16 31	15 43 33	21 53 23	15 37.5	26 04.9	25 46.6	1 38.1	7 59.3	19 46.2	18 16.4	16 32.8	21 27.2	28 57.1
9 M	1 09 25	19 15 29	28 06 40	4♑23 48	15 34.9	27 39.2	26 57.2	2 24.2	8 22.9	19 45.6	18 15.2	16 35.8	21 28.7	28 56.9
10 Tu	1 13 22	20 14 25	10♑45 15	17 11 28	15D 33.8	29 15.0	28 07.8	3 10.2	8 46.4	19 44.9	18 14.2	16 38.9	21 30.1	28 56.6
11 W	1 17 18	21 13 19	23 42 52	0♒19 52	15 34.1	0♈52.4	29 18.2	3 56.3	9 09.9	19 44.0	18 13.2	16 41.8	21 31.5	28 56.3
12 Th	1 21 15	22 12 12	7♒02 49	13 52 01	15 35.3	2 31.3	0♊28.5	4 42.3	9 33.5	19 42.8	18 12.3	16 44.8	21 32.8	28 55.9
13 F	1 25 11	23 11 03	20 47 40	27 49 52	15 36.7	4 11.8	1 38.7	5 28.4	9 56.9	19 41.5	18 11.6	16 47.7	21 34.1	28 55.5
14 Sa	1 29 08	24 09 52	4♓58 32	12♓13 30	15R 37.6	5 53.9	2 48.9	6 14.4	10 20.4	19 40.0	18 10.9	16 50.6	21 35.4	28 55.1
15 Su	1 33 05	25 08 39	19 34 20	27 00 28	15 37.2	7 37.5	3 58.9	7 00.5	10 43.9	19 38.4	18 10.4	16 53.5	21 36.7	28 54.7
16 M	1 37 01	26 07 24	4♈31 07	12♈05 19	15 34.9	9 22.7	5 08.8	7 46.5	11 07.3	19 36.5	18 10.0	16 56.4	21 37.9	28 54.2
17 Tu	1 40 58	27 06 08	19 41 57	27 19 46	15 30.8	11 09.4	6 18.6	8 32.5	11 30.7	19 34.4	18 09.7	16 59.2	21 39.1	28 53.7
18 W	1 44 54	28 04 49	4♉57 25	12♉33 35	15 25.0	12 57.8	7 28.2	9 18.6	11 54.1	19 32.2	18 09.5	17 02.0	21 40.3	28 53.2
19 Th	1 48 51	29 03 29	20 06 58	27 36 20	15 18.4	14 47.7	8 37.8	10 04.6	12 17.5	19 29.8	18D 09.4	17 04.8	21 41.5	28 52.6
20 F	1 52 47	0♉02 07	5♊00 39	12♊19 02	15 11.9	16 39.2	9 47.2	10 50.6	12 40.8	19 27.2	18 09.4	17 07.5	21 42.6	28 52.0
21 Sa	1 56 44	1 00 42	19 30 50	26 35 34	15 06.3	18 32.3	10 56.5	11 36.6	13 04.2	19 24.4	18 09.5	17 10.2	21 43.7	28 51.4
22 Su	2 00 40	1 59 16	3♋33 00	10♋23 06	15 02.3	20 27.1	12 05.7	12 22.6	13 27.5	19 21.5	18 09.7	17 12.9	21 44.7	28 50.8
23 M	2 04 37	2 57 47	17 05 59	23 41 55	15D 00.1	22 23.4	13 14.8	13 08.6	13 50.7	19 18.4	18 10.1	17 15.6	21 45.8	28 50.1
24 Tu	2 08 34	3 56 16	0♌11 17	6♌34 34	14 59.7	24 21.3	14 23.7	13 54.5	14 14.0	19 15.1	18 10.5	17 18.2	21 46.8	28 49.4
25 W	2 12 30	4 54 42	12 52 19	19 05 06	15 00.5	26 20.8	15 32.5	14 40.5	14 37.2	19 11.6	18 11.1	17 20.8	21 47.8	28 48.7
26 Th	2 16 27	5 53 07	25 13 33	1♍18 15	15 01.7	28 21.7	16 41.1	15 26.4	15 00.4	19 08.0	18 11.7	17 23.3	21 48.7	28 47.9
27 F	2 20 23	6 51 29	7♍19 49	13 18 51	15R 02.5	0♉24.2	17 49.6	16 12.3	15 23.5	19 04.1	18 12.5	17 25.8	21 49.6	28 47.1
28 Sa	2 24 20	7 49 50	19 15 54	25 11 29	15 01.9	2 28.0	18 57.9	16 58.2	15 46.6	19 00.2	18 13.3	17 28.3	21 50.5	28 46.3
29 Su	2 28 16	8 48 08	1♎06 05	7♎00 10	14 59.3	4 33.2	20 06.1	17 44.1	16 09.7	18 56.0	18 14.3	17 30.8	21 51.3	28 45.5
30 M	2 32 13	9 46 24	12 54 06	18 48 16	14 54.4	6 39.5	21 14.2	18 30.0	16 32.8	18 51.7	18 15.4	17 33.2	21 52.1	28 44.6

Astro Data Dy Hr Mn	Planet Ingress Dy Hr Mn	Last Aspect Dy Hr Mn	☽ Ingress Dy Hr Mn	Last Aspect Dy Hr Mn	☽ Ingress Dy Hr Mn	☽ Phases & Eclipses Dy Hr Mn	Astro Data
☽0S 5 4:32	♀ ♉ 17 22:02	2 19:04 ♇ △	♍ 2 21:33	1 13:39 ♇ □	♎ 1 15:44	3 23:18 ○ 13♍00	1 March 2007
☿D 8 4:45	☿ ♓ 18 9:36	5 6:57 ♇ □	♎ 5 9:26	4 2:31 ♇ ⚹	♏ 4 4:37	3 23:22 • T 1.233	Julian Day # 39141
♃△♄ 16 22:43	⚳ ♈ 19 5:28	7 19:52 ♇ ⚹	♏ 7 22:18	6 2:56 ♀ ☍	♐ 6 16:58	12 3:55 ☾ 21♐11	SVP 5♓09'30"
☽0N 19 1:53	☉ ♈ 21 0:08	10 1:52 ☿ □	♐ 10 10:38	9 1:37 ♇ ☌	♑ 9 3:37	19 2:44 ● 28♓07	GC 26♐56.4 ⚴ 22♒06.3
☉0N 21 0:08		12 18:28 ♇ ☌	♑ 12 20:36	11 9:58 ♀ △	♒ 11 11:24	19 2:32:57 ◖ P 0.876	Eris 20♈27.6 ⚵ 27♎11.4R
♇R 31 22:46	♂ ♓ 6 8:51	14 20:22 ♀ □	♒ 15 2:53	13 13:51 ♇ ⚹	♓ 13 15:40	25 18:17 ☽ 4♋43	⚷ 12♒24.1 ⚶ 6♐50.7
	☿ ♈ 10 23:08	17 4:02 ♀ ⚹	♓ 17 5:31	15 15:03 ♇ □	♈ 15 16:48		☽ Mean ☊ 16♓31.1
☽0S 1 10:51	♀ ♊ 12 2:16	19 4:00 ♇ □	♈ 19 5:43	17 14:28 ♇ △	♉ 17 16:12	2 17:16 ○ 12♎35	1 April 2007
♃R 6 1:24	☉ ♉ 20 11:08	21 3:34 ♇ △	♉ 21 5:16	19 2:30 ♆ □	♊ 19 15:52	10 18:05 ☾ 20♑29	Julian Day # 39172
☿0N 14 6:39	☿ ♉ 27 7:17	22 15:13 ♆ □	♊ 23 6:07	21 15:53 ♇ ☍	♋ 21 17:51	17 11:37 ● 27♈05	SVP 5♓09'27"
☽0N 15 12:50		25 7:58 ♇ ☍	♋ 25 9:50	23 9:11 ☿ □	♌ 23 23:39	24 6:37 ☽ 3♌43	GC 26♐56.4 ⚴ 1♓59.5
♄D 19 21:25		26 14:37 ♅ △	♌ 27 17:05	26 7:03 ♇ △	♍ 26 9:25		Eris 20♈46.0 ⚵ 21♎50.2R
☽0S 28 16:35		30 1:25 ♇ △	♍ 30 3:28	28 19:15 ♇ □	♎ 28 21:46		⚷ 14♒21.3 ⚶ 13♐56.3
							☽ Mean ☊ 14♓52.5

LONGITUDE — May 2007

Day	Sid.Time	☉	0 hr ☽	Noon ☽	True ☊	☿	♀	♂	⚳	♃	♄	♅	♆	♇
1 Tu	2 36 09	10♉44 39	24♎42 58	0♏38 30	14♓47.1	8♉47.0	22♊22.0	19♓15.9	16♈55.8	18♐47.3	18♌16.6	17♓35.6	21♒52.9	28♐43.7
2 W	2 40 06	11 42 52	6♏35 05	12 32 57	14R 37.7	10 55.3	23 29.8	20 01.7	17 18.8	18R 42.7	18 17.9	17 37.9	21 53.7	28R 42.8
3 Th	2 44 03	12 41 03	18 32 17	24 33 15	14 27.1	13 04.4	24 37.3	20 47.5	17 41.8	18 37.9	18 19.3	17 40.2	21 54.4	28 41.9
4 F	2 47 59	13 39 13	0♐36 00	6♐40 41	14 16.0	15 14.1	25 44.7	21 33.4	18 04.7	18 33.0	18 20.8	17 42.5	21 55.1	28 40.9
5 Sa	2 51 56	14 37 20	12 47 29	18 56 34	14 05.6	17 24.0	26 51.9	22 19.2	18 27.6	18 27.9	18 22.4	17 44.7	21 55.7	28 39.9
6 Su	2 55 52	15 35 27	25 08 05	1♑22 17	13 56.6	19 33.9	27 59.0	23 04.9	18 50.4	18 22.7	18 24.1	17 47.0	21 56.4	28 38.9
7 M	2 59 49	16 33 32	7♑39 23	13 59 38	13 49.9	21 43.6	29 05.8	23 50.7	19 13.2	18 17.4	18 25.9	17 49.1	21 57.0	28 37.9
8 Tu	3 03 45	17 31 35	20 23 21	26 50 48	13 45.6	23 52.7	0♋12.5	24 36.4	19 36.0	18 11.9	18 27.8	17 51.2	21 57.5	28 36.8
9 W	3 07 42	18 29 37	3♒22 20	9♒58 16	13D 43.7	26 01.1	1 19.0	25 22.2	19 58.8	18 06.2	18 29.9	17 53.3	21 58.0	28 35.7
10 Th	3 11 38	19 27 38	16 38 57	23 24 40	13 43.4	28 08.3	2 25.4	26 07.9	20 21.5	18 00.5	18 32.0	17 55.4	21 58.5	28 34.6
11 F	3 15 35	20 25 37	0♓15 42	7♓12 13	13R 43.8	0♊14.1	3 31.5	26 53.5	20 44.1	17 54.6	18 34.2	17 57.4	21 59.0	28 33.5
12 Sa	3 19 32	21 23 35	14 14 21	21 22 06	13 43.7	2 18.2	4 37.4	27 39.2	21 06.7	17 48.6	18 36.5	17 59.3	21 59.4	28 32.4
13 Su	3 23 28	22 21 32	28 35 17	5♈53 38	13 42.0	4 20.4	5 43.2	28 24.8	21 29.3	17 42.4	18 38.9	18 01.3	21 59.8	28 31.2
14 M	3 27 25	23 19 28	13♈16 38	20 43 37	13 37.9	6 20.5	6 48.7	29 10.4	21 51.8	17 36.2	18 41.4	18 03.2	22 00.2	28 30.0
15 Tu	3 31 21	24 17 22	28 13 43	5♉45 56	13 31.2	8 18.2	7 54.1	29 56.0	22 14.3	17 29.8	18 44.1	18 05.0	22 00.5	28 28.8
16 W	3 35 18	25 15 15	13♉19 06	20 51 59	13 22.2	10 13.4	8 59.2	0♈41.5	22 36.7	17 23.3	18 46.8	18 06.8	22 00.8	28 27.6
17 Th	3 39 14	26 13 06	28 23 18	5♊51 48	13 11.8	12 05.9	10 04.1	1 27.0	22 59.1	17 16.7	18 49.6	18 08.6	22 01.1	28 26.3
18 F	3 43 11	27 10 57	13♊16 19	20 35 50	13 01.3	13 55.5	11 08.8	2 12.5	23 21.5	17 10.1	18 52.5	18 10.3	22 01.3	28 25.1
19 Sa	3 47 07	28 08 45	27 49 27	4♋56 31	12 51.8	15 42.2	12 13.2	2 57.9	23 43.8	17 03.3	18 55.5	18 12.0	22 01.5	28 23.8
20 Su	3 51 04	29 06 32	11♋56 36	18 49 25	12 44.3	17 25.9	13 17.5	3 43.3	24 06.0	16 56.4	18 58.6	18 13.6	22 01.7	28 22.5
21 M	3 55 01	0♊04 17	25 34 57	2♌13 20	12 39.3	19 06.5	14 21.4	4 28.7	24 28.2	16 49.4	19 01.8	18 15.2	22 01.8	28 21.2
22 Tu	3 58 57	1 02 01	8♌44 49	15 09 50	12 36.6	20 44.0	15 25.1	5 14.0	24 50.3	16 42.4	19 05.1	18 16.7	22 01.9	28 19.9
23 W	4 02 54	1 59 43	21 28 53	27 42 33	12D 35.8	22 18.2	16 28.6	5 59.3	25 12.4	16 35.3	19 08.5	18 18.2	22 02.0	28 18.5
24 Th	4 06 50	2 57 24	3♍51 28	9♍56 18	12R 35.8	23 49.2	17 31.7	6 44.5	25 34.4	16 28.1	19 11.9	18 19.7	22R 02.0	28 17.1
25 F	4 10 47	3 55 02	15 57 42	21 56 23	12 35.6	25 16.9	18 34.6	7 29.7	25 56.3	16 20.9	19 15.5	18 21.1	22 02.0	28 15.8
26 Sa	4 14 43	4 52 40	27 52 58	3♎48 07	12 34.0	26 41.2	19 37.2	8 14.8	26 18.2	16 13.6	19 19.2	18 22.4	22 02.0	28 14.4
27 Su	4 18 40	5 50 16	9♎42 26	15 36 27	12 30.4	28 02.1	20 39.5	9 00.0	26 40.1	16 06.2	19 22.9	18 23.7	22 02.0	28 13.0
28 M	4 22 36	6 47 50	21 30 43	27 25 42	12 24.1	29 19.6	21 41.5	9 45.0	27 01.8	15 58.8	19 26.7	18 25.0	22 01.9	28 11.6
29 Tu	4 26 33	7 45 23	3♏21 47	9♏19 22	12 15.1	0♋33.7	22 43.2	10 30.1	27 23.6	15 51.3	19 30.6	18 26.2	22 01.7	28 10.1
30 W	4 30 30	8 42 56	15 18 45	21 20 10	12 03.7	1 44.2	23 44.5	11 15.0	27 45.2	15 43.8	19 34.6	18 27.4	22 01.6	28 08.7
31 Th	4 34 26	9 40 26	27 23 50	3♐29 55	11 50.7	2 51.1	24 45.5	12 00.0	28 06.8	15 36.3	19 38.7	18 28.6	22 01.4	28 07.2

LONGITUDE — June 2007

Day	Sid.Time	☉	0 hr ☽	Noon ☽	True ☊	☿	♀	♂	⚳	♃	♄	♅	♆	♇
1 F	4 38 23	10♊37 56	9♐38 30	15♐49 41	11♓37.3	3♋54.4	25♋46.2	12♈44.9	28♈28.3	15♐28.7	19♌42.9	18♓29.7	22♒01.2	28♐05.8
2 Sa	4 42 19	11 35 25	22 03 31	28 20 01	11R 24.4	4 53.9	26 46.5	13 29.8	28 49.8	15R 21.1	19 47.1	18 30.7	22R 00.9	28R 04.3
3 Su	4 46 16	12 32 53	4♑39 14	11♑01 10	11 13.3	5 49.7	27 46.5	14 14.6	29 11.2	15 13.5	19 51.5	18 31.7	22 00.6	28 02.8
4 M	4 50 12	13 30 20	17 25 52	23 53 23	11 04.7	6 41.6	28 46.1	14 59.3	29 32.5	15 05.9	19 55.9	18 32.6	22 00.3	28 01.3
5 Tu	4 54 09	14 27 46	0♒23 48	6♒57 12	10 59.0	7 29.6	29 45.3	15 44.1	29 53.8	14 58.2	20 00.4	18 33.5	22 00.0	27 59.8
6 W	4 58 05	15 25 12	13 33 44	20 13 31	10 56.0	8 13.6	0♌44.1	16 28.7	0♉15.0	14 50.6	20 04.9	18 34.4	21 59.6	27 58.3
7 Th	5 02 02	16 22 36	26 56 45	3♓43 36	10 54.9	8 53.4	1 42.4	17 13.4	0 36.1	14 42.9	20 09.6	18 35.2	21 59.2	27 56.8
8 F	5 05 59	17 20 01	10♓34 13	17 28 46	10 54.9	9 29.1	2 40.4	17 57.9	0 57.2	14 35.3	20 14.3	18 36.0	21 58.7	27 55.3
9 Sa	5 09 55	18 17 24	24 27 20	1♈29 57	10 54.5	10 00.5	3 38.0	18 42.5	1 18.2	14 27.6	20 19.1	18 36.7	21 58.3	27 53.7
10 Su	5 13 52	19 14 47	8♈36 34	15 47 02	10 52.6	10 27.5	4 35.1	19 26.9	1 39.1	14 20.0	20 24.0	18 37.3	21 57.8	27 52.2
11 M	5 17 48	20 12 10	23 01 03	0♉18 12	10 48.4	10 50.1	5 31.7	20 11.3	1 59.9	14 12.4	20 28.9	18 38.0	21 57.2	27 50.6
12 Tu	5 21 45	21 09 32	7♉37 55	14 59 29	10 41.6	11 08.3	6 27.9	20 55.7	2 20.6	14 04.9	20 34.0	18 38.5	21 56.7	27 49.1
13 W	5 25 41	22 06 54	22 22 05	29 44 47	10 32.4	11 21.9	7 23.6	21 40.0	2 41.3	13 57.3	20 39.1	18 39.0	21 56.1	27 47.5
14 Th	5 29 38	23 04 15	7♊06 34	14♊26 27	10 21.7	11 30.9	8 18.8	22 24.2	3 01.9	13 49.8	20 44.2	18 39.5	21 55.4	27 46.0
15 F	5 33 35	24 01 35	21 43 24	28 56 30	10 10.8	11R 35.4	9 13.5	23 08.4	3 22.4	13 42.4	20 49.5	18 39.9	21 54.8	27 44.4
16 Sa	5 37 31	24 58 55	6♋04 56	13♋08 00	10 00.8	11 35.3	10 07.6	23 52.5	3 42.8	13 35.0	20 54.8	18 40.3	21 54.1	27 42.9
17 Su	5 41 28	25 56 15	20 05 11	26 56 05	9 52.7	11 30.8	11 01.1	24 36.5	4 03.2	13 27.6	21 00.2	18 40.6	21 53.4	27 41.3
18 M	5 45 24	26 53 33	3♌40 33	10♌18 32	9 47.0	11 21.9	11 54.1	25 20.5	4 23.4	13 20.3	21 05.6	18 40.9	21 52.7	27 39.8
19 Tu	5 49 21	27 50 50	16 50 11	23 15 43	9 43.9	11 08.8	12 46.5	26 04.4	4 43.5	13 13.1	21 11.2	18 41.1	21 51.9	27 38.2
20 W	5 53 17	28 48 07	29 35 34	5♍50 09	9D 42.8	10 51.6	13 38.2	26 48.2	5 03.6	13 06.0	21 16.7	18 41.3	21 51.1	27 36.6
21 Th	5 57 14	29 45 23	12♍00 03	18 05 50	9 42.9	10 30.7	14 29.3	27 32.0	5 23.6	12 58.9	21 22.4	18 41.4	21 50.3	27 35.1
22 F	6 01 10	0♋42 38	24 08 10	0♎07 41	9R 43.2	10 06.3	15 19.7	28 15.7	5 43.4	12 51.9	21 28.1	18 41.5	21 49.4	27 33.5
23 Sa	6 05 07	1 39 53	6♎05 04	12 00 59	9 42.7	9 38.9	16 09.4	28 59.3	6 03.2	12 45.0	21 33.9	18R 41.5	21 48.6	27 31.9
24 Su	6 09 04	2 37 07	17 56 06	23 51 02	9 40.4	9 08.7	16 58.4	29 42.8	6 22.9	12 38.1	21 39.7	18 41.5	21 47.7	27 30.4
25 M	6 13 00	3 34 20	29 46 26	5♏42 43	9 36.0	8 36.4	17 46.6	0♉26.3	6 42.4	12 31.4	21 45.6	18 41.5	21 46.7	27 28.8
26 Tu	6 16 57	4 31 33	11♏40 33	17 40 22	9 29.2	8 02.4	18 34.0	1 09.7	7 01.9	12 24.8	21 51.6	18 41.3	21 45.8	27 27.3
27 W	6 20 53	5 28 46	23 42 33	29 47 28	9 20.3	7 27.4	19 20.6	1 53.1	7 21.3	12 18.2	21 57.6	18 41.2	21 44.8	27 25.7
28 Th	6 24 50	6 25 58	5♐55 24	12♐06 34	9 09.9	6 51.8	20 06.4	2 36.3	7 40.5	12 11.8	22 03.6	18 41.0	21 43.8	27 24.2
29 F	6 28 46	7 23 10	18 21 07	24 39 09	8 59.1	6 16.3	20 51.2	3 19.5	7 59.7	12 05.5	22 09.8	18 40.7	21 42.8	27 22.7
30 Sa	6 32 43	8 20 21	1♑00 41	7♑25 41	8 48.7	5 41.5	21 35.2	4 02.6	8 18.7	11 59.3	22 15.9	18 40.4	21 41.7	27 21.1

Astro Data

Astro Data	Dy Hr Mn
⚳0N	4 22:14
♃△♄	6 7:12
♃□♅	11 3:33
☽0N	12 21:48
♂0N	20 4:37
♆R	25 1:09
☽0S	25 22:22
☽0N	9 4:01
☿R	15 23:42
☽0S	22 4:55
♅R	23 14:44
♄☍♆	25 15:55

Planet Ingress

Planet Ingress	Dy Hr Mn
♀ ♋	8 7:29
☿ ♊	11 9:18
♂ ♈	15 14:07
☉ ♊	21 10:13
☿ ♋	29 0:57
♀ ♌	5 18:00
⚳ ♉	5 19:00
☉ ♋	21 18:08
♂ ♉	24 21:28

Last Aspect / ☽ Ingress

Last Aspect Dy Hr Mn		☽ Ingress Dy Hr Mn
1 8:08	♇ ⚹	♏ 1 10:42
3 6:43	♆ □	♐ 3 22:49
6 6:47	♇ ☌	♑ 6 9:22
8 7:36	♂ ⚹	♒ 8 17:49
10 21:48	☿ □	♓ 10 23:33
12 23:54	♇ □	♈ 13 2:20
15 0:25	♇ △	♉ 15 2:49
16 19:28	☉ ☌	♊ 17 2:35
19 0:58	♇ ☍	♋ 19 3:39
21 7:47	☉ ⚹	♌ 21 7:58
23 13:10	♇ △	♍ 23 16:27
26 0:45	♇ □	♎ 26 4:17
28 16:18	☿ △	♏ 28 17:12
30 17:13	♀ △	♐ 31 5:08

Last Aspect Dy Hr Mn		☽ Ingress Dy Hr Mn
2 11:30	♇ ☌	♑ 2 15:10
4 21:45	♀ ☍	♒ 4 23:16
7 1:48	♇ ⚹	♓ 7 5:25
9 5:53	♇ □	♈ 9 9:27
11 7:58	♇ △	♉ 11 11:30
12 23:18	♆ □	♊ 13 12:25
15 10:00	♇ ☍	♋ 15 13:46
17 7:40	♂ □	♌ 17 17:26
19 21:23	☉ ⚹	♍ 20 0:47
22 6:51	♇ □	♎ 22 11:45
24 19:24	♇ ⚹	♏ 25 0:28
26 20:24	♄ □	♐ 27 12:25
29 17:09	♇ ☌	♑ 29 22:06

☽ Phases & Eclipses

Dy Hr Mn		
2 10:10	○	11♏38
10 4:28	☾	19♒09
16 19:28	●	25♉33
23 21:04	☽	2♍21
1 1:05	○	10♐12
8 11:44	☾	17♓19
15 3:14	●	23♊41
22 13:16	☽	0♎46
30 13:50	○	8♑25

Astro Data

1 May 2007
Julian Day # 39202
SVP 5♓09'23"
GC 26♐56.5 ⚴ 10♓15.4
Eris 21♈05.6 ⚵ 15♎12.4R
⚷ 15♒28.4 ⚶ 14♐25.4R
☽ Mean ☊ 13♓17.2

1 June 2007
Julian Day # 39233
SVP 5♓09'18"
GC 26♐56.6 ⚴ 16♓34.9
Eris 21♈22.6 ⚵ 12♎04.4R
⚷ 15♒37.0R ⚶ 8♐20.3R
☽ Mean ☊ 11♓38.7

July 2007 — LONGITUDE

Day	Sid.Time	☉	0 hr ☽	Noon ☽	True ☊	☿	♀	♂	⚳	♃	♄	♅	♆	♇
1 Su	6 36 39	9♋17 32	13♑54 07	20♑25 51	8♓39.8	5♋08.1	22♌18.2	4♉45.6	8♉37.7	11♐53.2	22♌22.2	18♓40.1	21♒40.6	27♐19.6
2 M	6 40 36	10 14 44	27 00 46	3♒38 43	8R 33.0	4R 36.5	23 00.2	5 28.6	8 56.5	11R 47.2	22 28.5	18R 39.7	21R 39.5	27R 18.1
3 Tu	6 44 33	11 11 55	10♒19 34	17 03 09	8 28.7	4 07.4	23 41.2	6 11.5	9 15.2	11 41.4	22 34.8	18 39.2	21 38.4	27 16.6
4 W	6 48 29	12 09 06	23 49 21	0♓38 04	8D 26.7	3 41.2	24 21.1	6 54.3	9 33.8	11 35.7	22 41.2	18 38.7	21 37.3	27 15.1
5 Th	6 52 26	13 06 17	7♓29 12	14 22 42	8 26.6	3 18.5	25 00.0	7 37.0	9 52.3	11 30.1	22 47.6	18 38.2	21 36.1	27 13.6
6 F	6 56 22	14 03 29	21 18 28	28 16 29	8 27.4	2 59.6	25 37.7	8 19.6	10 10.7	11 24.6	22 54.1	18 37.6	21 34.9	27 12.1
7 Sa	7 00 19	15 00 41	5♈16 41	12♈18 58	8R 28.0	2 44.9	26 14.2	9 02.1	10 28.9	11 19.3	23 00.7	18 37.0	21 33.7	27 10.6
8 Su	7 04 15	15 57 53	19 23 14	26 29 20	8 27.6	2 34.7	26 49.5	9 44.6	10 47.1	11 14.1	23 07.2	18 36.3	21 32.5	27 09.2
9 M	7 08 12	16 55 06	3♉37 02	10♉46 03	8 25.4	2D 29.3	27 23.6	10 27.0	11 05.1	11 09.1	23 13.9	18 35.6	21 31.2	27 07.7
10 Tu	7 12 08	17 52 19	17 56 02	25 06 30	8 21.1	2 28.8	27 56.3	11 09.2	11 22.9	11 04.2	23 20.6	18 34.8	21 29.9	27 06.3
11 W	7 16 05	18 49 33	2♊16 59	9♊26 53	8 15.0	2 33.5	28 27.7	11 51.4	11 40.7	10 59.5	23 27.3	18 34.0	21 28.6	27 04.9
12 Th	7 20 02	19 46 47	16 35 34	23 42 24	8 07.7	2 43.3	28 57.6	12 33.5	11 58.3	10 54.9	23 34.1	18 33.1	21 27.3	27 03.4
13 F	7 23 58	20 44 02	0♋46 44	7♋47 56	8 00.1	2 58.5	29 26.1	13 15.5	12 15.7	10 50.5	23 40.9	18 32.2	21 26.0	27 02.0
14 Sa	7 27 55	21 41 17	14 45 25	21 38 41	7 53.1	3 19.0	29 53.1	13 57.4	12 33.1	10 46.2	23 47.7	18 31.3	21 24.6	27 00.7
15 Su	7 31 51	22 38 32	28 27 20	5♌11 01	7 47.6	3 44.8	0♍18.4	14 39.2	12 50.3	10 42.1	23 54.6	18 30.3	21 23.3	26 59.3
16 M	7 35 48	23 35 47	11♌49 33	18 22 50	7 43.9	4 16.1	0 42.2	15 20.9	13 07.3	10 38.1	24 01.5	18 29.3	21 21.9	26 57.9
17 Tu	7 39 44	24 33 02	24 50 54	1♍13 53	7D 42.2	4 52.7	1 04.2	16 02.5	13 24.2	10 34.4	24 08.5	18 28.2	21 20.5	26 56.6
18 W	7 43 41	25 30 18	7♍32 00	13 45 34	7 42.1	5 34.6	1 24.5	16 44.0	13 40.9	10 30.8	24 15.5	18 27.1	21 19.1	26 55.2
19 Th	7 47 37	26 27 34	19 54 59	26 00 44	7 43.2	6 21.7	1 42.9	17 25.3	13 57.5	10 27.3	24 22.5	18 25.9	21 17.6	26 53.9
20 F	7 51 34	27 24 50	2♎03 19	8♎03 17	7 44.8	7 14.1	1 59.4	18 06.6	14 13.9	10 24.0	24 29.6	18 24.7	21 16.2	26 52.6
21 Sa	7 55 31	28 22 06	14 01 14	19 57 47	7R 46.0	8 11.7	2 14.0	18 47.8	14 30.2	10 21.0	24 36.7	18 23.4	21 14.7	26 51.4
22 Su	7 59 27	29 19 23	25 53 33	1♏49 11	7 46.3	9 14.3	2 26.6	19 28.8	14 46.3	10 18.0	24 43.9	18 22.1	21 13.2	26 50.1
23 M	8 03 24	0♌16 39	7♏45 17	13 42 27	7 45.3	10 22.0	2 37.1	20 09.7	15 02.3	10 15.3	24 51.0	18 20.8	21 11.8	26 48.9
24 Tu	8 07 20	1 13 57	19 41 18	25 42 21	7 42.7	11 34.5	2 45.5	20 50.6	15 18.1	10 12.7	24 58.2	18 19.5	21 10.2	26 47.6
25 W	8 11 17	2 11 14	1♐46 09	7♐53 08	7 38.7	12 51.9	2 51.7	21 31.3	15 33.7	10 10.3	25 05.5	18 18.1	21 08.7	26 46.4
26 Th	8 15 13	3 08 32	14 03 44	20 18 16	7 33.7	14 14.0	2 55.6	22 11.9	15 49.2	10 08.1	25 12.7	18 16.6	21 07.2	26 45.2
27 F	8 19 10	4 05 51	26 37 02	3♑00 13	7 28.2	15 40.7	2R 57.3	22 52.4	16 04.4	10 06.1	25 20.0	18 15.1	21 05.7	26 44.1
28 Sa	8 23 07	5 03 10	9♑27 55	16 00 11	7 22.9	17 11.8	2 56.7	23 32.7	16 19.6	10 04.3	25 27.3	18 13.6	21 04.1	26 42.9
29 Su	8 27 03	6 00 30	22 36 58	29 18 08	7 18.4	18 47.1	2 53.7	24 13.0	16 34.5	10 02.6	25 34.7	18 12.1	21 02.6	26 41.8
30 M	8 31 00	6 57 50	6♒03 28	12♒52 43	7 15.2	20 26.4	2 48.3	24 53.1	16 49.2	10 01.1	25 42.0	18 10.5	21 01.0	26 40.7
31 Tu	8 34 56	7 55 11	19 45 33	26 41 37	7D 13.4	22 09.6	2 40.6	25 33.1	17 03.8	9 59.8	25 49.4	18 08.8	20 59.4	26 39.6

August 2007 — LONGITUDE

Day	Sid.Time	☉	0 hr ☽	Noon ☽	True ☊	☿	♀	♂	⚳	♃	♄	♅	♆	♇
1 W	8 38 53	8♌52 33	3♓40 30	10♓41 49	7♓13.1	23♋56.2	2♍30.5	26♉13.0	17♉18.2	9♐58.7	25♌56.8	18♓07.2	20♒57.8	26♐38.6
2 Th	8 42 49	9 49 56	17 45 07	24 50 02	7 13.9	25 46.1	2R 17.9	26 52.8	17 32.4	9R 57.8	26 04.2	18R 05.5	20R 56.3	26R 37.5
3 F	8 46 46	10 47 20	1♈56 10	9♈03 07	7 15.2	27 38.9	2 03.1	27 32.4	17 46.4	9 57.0	26 11.7	18 03.8	20 54.7	26 36.5
4 Sa	8 50 42	11 44 45	16 10 33	23 18 08	7 16.6	29 34.4	1 45.9	28 11.9	18 00.2	9 56.4	26 19.1	18 02.0	20 53.0	26 35.5
5 Su	8 54 39	12 42 12	0♉25 33	7♉32 32	7R 17.4	1♌32.0	1 26.4	28 51.3	18 13.8	9 56.0	26 26.6	18 00.2	20 51.4	26 34.6
6 M	8 58 35	13 39 40	14 38 48	21 44 03	7 17.3	3 31.5	1 04.7	29 30.6	18 27.2	9D 55.8	26 34.1	17 58.4	20 49.8	26 33.6
7 Tu	9 02 32	14 37 09	28 48 03	5♊50 31	7 16.1	5 32.6	0 40.9	0♊09.7	18 40.4	9 55.8	26 41.6	17 56.5	20 48.2	26 32.7
8 W	9 06 29	15 34 39	12♊51 10	19 49 45	7 14.0	7 34.8	0 15.0	0 48.7	18 53.3	9 56.0	26 49.2	17 54.6	20 46.6	26 31.8
9 Th	9 10 25	16 32 11	26 46 00	3♋39 36	7 11.4	9 37.8	29♌47.3	1 27.5	19 06.1	9 56.3	26 56.7	17 52.7	20 45.0	26 31.0
10 F	9 14 22	17 29 44	10♋30 20	17 17 55	7 08.5	11 41.3	29 17.7	2 06.2	19 18.6	9 56.9	27 04.3	17 50.8	20 43.3	26 30.1
11 Sa	9 18 18	18 27 19	24 02 09	0♌42 47	7 06.0	13 45.0	28 46.5	2 44.8	19 31.0	9 57.6	27 11.9	17 48.8	20 41.7	26 29.3
12 Su	9 22 15	19 24 54	7♌19 41	13 52 42	7 04.0	15 48.6	28 13.9	3 23.2	19 43.0	9 58.5	27 19.5	17 46.8	20 40.1	26 28.5
13 M	9 26 11	20 22 31	20 21 47	26 46 53	7D 02.9	17 51.9	27 39.9	4 01.4	19 54.9	9 59.6	27 27.1	17 44.8	20 38.4	26 27.8
14 Tu	9 30 08	21 20 09	3♍08 02	9♍25 20	7 02.7	19 54.6	27 04.9	4 39.5	20 06.5	10 00.9	27 34.7	17 42.7	20 36.8	26 27.0
15 W	9 34 05	22 17 47	15 38 55	21 49 01	7 03.2	21 56.6	26 28.9	5 17.4	20 17.9	10 02.3	27 42.3	17 40.6	20 35.1	26 26.3
16 Th	9 38 01	23 15 27	27 55 52	3♎59 48	7 04.1	23 57.8	25 52.3	5 55.2	20 29.0	10 04.0	27 49.9	17 38.5	20 33.5	26 25.6
17 F	9 41 58	24 13 08	10♎01 11	16 00 25	7 05.3	25 58.0	25 15.2	6 32.8	20 39.9	10 05.8	27 57.5	17 36.4	20 31.9	26 25.0
18 Sa	9 45 54	25 10 50	21 57 59	27 54 21	7 06.5	27 57.1	24 38.0	7 10.2	20 50.6	10 07.8	28 05.2	17 34.3	20 30.2	26 24.4
19 Su	9 49 51	26 08 34	3♏50 02	9♏45 37	7 07.4	29 55.0	24 00.7	7 47.5	21 00.9	10 10.0	28 12.8	17 32.1	20 28.6	26 23.8
20 M	9 53 47	27 06 18	15 41 38	21 38 41	7R 07.8	1♍51.6	23 23.8	8 24.6	21 11.1	10 12.4	28 20.4	17 29.9	20 27.0	26 23.2
21 Tu	9 57 44	28 04 04	27 37 20	3♐38 21	7 07.8	3 47.0	22 47.3	9 01.5	21 20.9	10 14.9	28 28.1	17 27.7	20 25.4	26 22.7
22 W	10 01 40	29 01 50	9♐41 48	15 48 43	7 07.4	5 41.1	22 11.6	9 38.3	21 30.5	10 17.6	28 35.7	17 25.5	20 23.8	26 22.1
23 Th	10 05 37	29 59 38	21 59 29	28 14 33	7 06.8	7 33.9	21 36.8	10 14.9	21 39.9	10 20.6	28 43.3	17 23.2	20 22.1	26 21.7
24 F	10 09 34	0♍57 27	4♑34 22	10♑59 17	7 06.0	9 25.3	21 03.3	10 51.3	21 48.9	10 23.6	28 51.0	17 21.0	20 20.5	26 21.2
25 Sa	10 13 30	1 55 18	17 29 36	24 05 29	7 05.3	11 15.3	20 31.0	11 27.5	21 57.7	10 26.9	28 58.6	17 18.7	20 18.9	26 20.8
26 Su	10 17 27	2 53 09	0♒47 04	7♒34 18	7 04.8	13 04.0	20 00.4	12 03.6	22 06.2	10 30.3	29 06.2	17 16.4	20 17.4	26 20.4
27 M	10 21 23	3 51 02	14 27 04	21 25 08	7 04.5	14 51.4	19 31.4	12 39.5	22 14.5	10 33.9	29 13.9	17 14.1	20 15.8	26 20.1
28 Tu	10 25 20	4 48 56	28 28 07	5♓35 32	7D 04.4	16 37.5	19 04.4	13 15.1	22 22.4	10 37.7	29 21.5	17 11.8	20 14.2	26 19.7
29 W	10 29 16	5 46 52	12♓46 50	20 01 19	7 04.5	18 22.2	18 39.3	13 50.6	22 30.0	10 41.6	29 29.1	17 09.5	20 12.6	26 19.4
30 Th	10 33 13	6 44 50	27 18 17	4♈36 56	7R 04.5	20 05.6	18 16.4	14 25.9	22 37.4	10 45.7	29 36.7	17 07.1	20 11.1	26 19.1
31 F	10 37 09	7 42 49	11♈56 30	19 16 11	7 04.5	21 47.8	17 55.7	15 01.0	22 44.4	10 50.0	29 44.3	17 04.8	20 09.5	26 18.9

Astro Data

	Dy Hr Mn
☽ 0N	6 8:42
☿ D	10 2:15
☽ 0S	19 12:22
♀ R	27 17:29
☽ 0N	2 14:07
♄ △ ♇	6 10:36
♃ D	7 2:05
☽ 0S	15 20:16
☽ 0N	29 21:54

Planet Ingress

	Dy Hr Mn
♀ ♍	14 18:25
☉ ♌	23 5:01
☿ ♌	4 17:16
♂ ♊	7 6:02
♀ ♌R	9 1:11
☿ ♍	19 13:02
☉ ♍	23 12:09

Last Aspect / ☽ Ingress (July)

Last Aspect Dy Hr Mn		☽ Ingress Dy Hr Mn
1 8:46	♅ ⚹	♒ 2 5:25
4 6:04	♇ ⚹	♓ 4 10:53
6 10:10	♇ □	♈ 6 14:58
8 13:07	♇ △	♉ 8 17:55
10 16:55	♀ □	♊ 10 20:11
12 21:13	♀ ⚹	♋ 12 22:40
14 12:05	☉ ☌	♌ 15 2:44
17 3:56	♇ △	♍ 17 9:40
19 13:45	♇ □	♎ 19 19:54
22 6:30	☉ □	♏ 22 8:19
24 10:31	♄ □	♐ 24 20:31
27 0:14	♇ ☌	♑ 27 6:22
29 2:24	♂ △	♒ 29 13:15
31 11:57	♇ ⚹	♓ 31 17:42

Last Aspect / ☽ Ingress (August)

Last Aspect Dy Hr Mn		☽ Ingress Dy Hr Mn
2 15:38	♂ ⚹	♈ 2 20:44
4 17:32	♇ △	♉ 4 23:17
7 1:51	♂ ☌	♊ 7 2:02
9 5:28	♀ ⚹	♋ 9 5:37
10 12:58	♅ △	♌ 11 10:43
13 13:35	♀ ☌	♍ 13 18:04
15 21:03	♇ □	♎ 16 4:05
18 12:22	♄ ⚹	♏ 18 16:14
21 1:35	♄ □	♐ 21 4:45
23 12:55	♄ △	♑ 23 15:21
24 23:42	♅ ⚹	♒ 25 22:36
28 1:25	♄ ☍	♓ 28 2:35
29 22:23	♇ □	♈ 30 4:26

☽ Phases & Eclipses

Dy Hr Mn	
7 16:55	☾ 15♈12
14 12:05	● 21♋41
22 6:30	☽ 29♎06
30 0:49	○ 6♒31
5 21:21	☾ 13♉05
12 23:04	● 19♌51
20 23:55	☽ 27♏35
28 10:36	○ 4♓46
28 10:38	☍ T 1.476

Astro Data

1 July 2007
Julian Day # 39263
SVP 5♓09'12"
GC 26♐56.6 ⚳ 19♓20.8
Eris 21♈32.1 ⚵ 13♎55.1
⚷ 14♒47.5R ⚶ 2♐50.3R
☽ Mean ☊ 10♓03.5

1 August 2007
Julian Day # 39294
SVP 5♓09'06"
GC 26♐56.7 ⚳ 17♓18.4R
Eris 21♈32.6R ⚵ 19♎36.9
⚷ 13♒16.4R ⚶ 3♐56.9
☽ Mean ☊ 8♓25.0

LONGITUDE — September 2007

Day	Sid.Time	☉	0 hr ☽	Noon ☽	True ☊	☿	♀	♂	⚳	♃	♄	♅	♆	♇
1 Sa	10 41 06	8♍40 50	26♈35 14	3♉52 57	7♓04.4	23♍28.6	17♌37.3	15♊36.0	22♉51.2	10♐54.4	29♌51.9	17♓02.4	20♒08.0	26♐18.7
2 Su	10 45 02	9 38 53	11♉08 43	18 21 58	7R 04.2	25 08.3	17R 21.2	16 10.7	22 57.6	10 59.0	29 59.4	17R 00.0	20R 06.5	26R 18.5
3 M	10 48 59	10 36 58	25 32 14	2♊39 10	7D 04.0	26 46.7	17 07.5	16 45.2	23 03.8	11 03.8	0♍07.0	16 57.7	20 05.0	26 18.4
4 Tu	10 52 56	11 35 05	9♊42 29	16 41 58	7 04.0	28 23.8	16 56.3	17 19.5	23 09.6	11 08.7	0 14.5	16 55.3	20 03.5	26 18.3
5 W	10 56 52	12 33 14	23 37 32	0♋29 06	7 04.2	29 59.8	16 47.5	17 53.5	23 15.1	11 13.8	0 22.1	16 52.9	20 02.0	26 18.2
6 Th	11 00 49	13 31 26	7♋16 40	14 00 17	7 04.7	1♎34.5	16 41.1	18 27.4	23 20.2	11 19.0	0 29.6	16 50.5	20 00.5	26 18.1
7 F	11 04 45	14 29 39	20 40 00	27 15 56	7 05.4	3 08.1	16 37.1	19 01.0	23 25.0	11 24.5	0 37.1	16 48.1	19 59.1	26D 18.1
8 Sa	11 08 42	15 27 54	3♌48 12	10♌16 53	7 06.1	4 40.4	16D 35.5	19 34.4	23 29.5	11 30.0	0 44.6	16 45.7	19 57.6	26 18.1
9 Su	11 12 38	16 26 10	16 42 08	23 04 05	7 06.7	6 11.6	16 36.2	20 07.5	23 33.7	11 35.7	0 52.0	16 43.3	19 56.2	26 18.2
10 M	11 16 35	17 24 29	29 22 51	5♍38 34	7R 07.0	7 41.6	16 39.3	20 40.5	23 37.5	11 41.6	0 59.5	16 40.9	19 54.8	26 18.2
11 Tu	11 20 31	18 22 50	11♍51 23	18 01 28	7 06.8	9 10.4	16 44.7	21 13.1	23 40.9	11 47.7	1 06.9	16 38.5	19 53.4	26 18.3
12 W	11 24 28	19 21 12	24 08 56	0♎14 00	7 06.0	10 38.0	16 52.2	21 45.5	23 44.0	11 53.8	1 14.3	16 36.1	19 52.0	26 18.5
13 Th	11 28 25	20 19 36	6♎16 51	12 17 42	7 04.5	12 04.4	17 02.0	22 17.7	23 46.8	12 00.2	1 21.7	16 33.7	19 50.6	26 18.6
14 F	11 32 21	21 18 02	18 16 49	24 14 27	7 02.5	13 29.5	17 13.8	22 49.6	23 49.2	12 06.7	1 29.1	16 31.3	19 49.3	26 18.9
15 Sa	11 36 18	22 16 30	0♏10 55	6♏06 35	7 00.2	14 53.4	17 27.7	23 21.2	23 51.2	12 13.3	1 36.4	16 28.9	19 48.0	26 19.1
16 Su	11 40 14	23 14 59	12 01 48	17 57 01	6 57.8	16 16.0	17 43.7	23 52.6	23 52.9	12 20.1	1 43.7	16 26.6	19 46.7	26 19.4
17 M	11 44 11	24 13 30	23 52 38	29 49 10	6 55.8	17 37.3	18 01.5	24 23.7	23 54.2	12 27.0	1 51.0	16 24.2	19 45.4	26 19.7
18 Tu	11 48 07	25 12 03	5♐47 06	11♐46 58	6 54.4	18 57.3	18 21.3	24 54.5	23 55.2	12 34.1	1 58.2	16 21.8	19 44.1	26 20.0
19 W	11 52 04	26 10 38	17 49 19	23 54 44	6D 53.8	20 15.9	18 42.9	25 25.0	23 55.7	12 41.3	2 05.4	16 19.5	19 42.9	26 20.4
20 Th	11 56 00	27 09 14	0♑03 45	6♑16 57	6 54.1	21 33.0	19 06.2	25 55.3	23R 55.9	12 48.6	2 12.6	16 17.1	19 41.7	26 20.7
21 F	11 59 57	28 07 52	12 34 52	18 58 00	6 55.1	22 48.6	19 31.3	26 25.2	23 55.8	12 56.1	2 19.8	16 14.8	19 40.5	26 21.2
22 Sa	12 03 54	29 06 31	25 26 50	2♒01 45	6 56.5	24 02.7	19 58.0	26 54.9	23 55.2	13 03.7	2 26.9	16 12.5	19 39.3	26 21.6
23 Su	12 07 50	0♎05 12	8♒43 04	15 30 59	6 58.0	25 15.1	20 26.3	27 24.3	23 54.3	13 11.5	2 34.0	16 10.2	19 38.1	26 22.1
24 M	12 11 47	1 03 55	22 25 36	29 26 50	6R 58.9	26 25.7	20 56.2	27 53.3	23 53.0	13 19.4	2 41.0	16 07.9	19 37.0	26 22.7
25 Tu	12 15 43	2 02 40	6♓34 29	13♓48 08	6 58.9	27 34.5	21 27.5	28 22.0	23 51.3	13 27.4	2 48.0	16 05.6	19 35.9	26 23.2
26 W	12 19 40	3 01 26	21 07 14	28 31 01	6 57.7	28 41.3	22 00.4	28 50.5	23 49.3	13 35.5	2 55.0	16 03.3	19 34.8	26 23.8
27 Th	12 23 36	4 00 15	5♈58 36	13♈28 57	6 55.2	29 46.0	22 34.6	29 18.6	23 46.8	13 43.8	3 01.9	16 01.1	19 33.7	26 24.4
28 F	12 27 33	4 59 05	21 00 57	28 33 25	6 51.7	0♏48.4	23 10.1	29 46.3	23 44.0	13 52.2	3 08.8	15 58.8	19 32.7	26 25.1
29 Sa	12 31 29	5 57 58	6♉05 10	13♉35 04	6 47.6	1 48.4	23 47.0	0♋13.8	23 40.8	14 00.7	3 15.7	15 56.6	19 31.7	26 25.7
30 Su	12 35 26	6 56 53	21 02 05	28 25 16	6 43.7	2 45.8	24 25.1	0 40.8	23 37.2	14 09.4	3 22.5	15 54.4	19 30.7	26 26.4

LONGITUDE — October 2007

Day	Sid.Time	☉	0 hr ☽	Noon ☽	True ☊	☿	♀	♂	⚳	♃	♄	♅	♆	♇
1 M	12 39 23	7♎55 50	5♊43 53	12♊57 18	6♓40.5	3♏40.4	25♌04.4	1♋07.6	23♉33.2	14♐18.1	3♍29.3	15♓52.2	19♒29.8	26♐27.2
2 Tu	12 43 19	8 54 50	20 05 08	27 07 07	6D 38.5	4 31.9	25 44.9	1 34.0	23R 28.9	14 27.0	3 36.0	15R 50.1	19R 28.8	26 28.0
3 W	12 47 16	9 53 52	4♋03 08	10♋53 14	6 37.9	5 20.1	26 26.5	2 00.0	23 24.1	14 36.1	3 42.7	15 48.0	19 27.9	26 28.8
4 Th	12 51 12	10 52 57	17 37 35	24 16 24	6 38.6	6 04.6	27 09.2	2 25.6	23 19.0	14 45.2	3 49.3	15 45.9	19 27.1	26 29.6
5 F	12 55 09	11 52 03	0♌50 00	7♌18 45	6 40.1	6 45.2	27 53.0	2 50.8	23 13.5	14 54.4	3 55.9	15 43.8	19 26.2	26 30.5
6 Sa	12 59 05	12 51 12	13 43 02	20 03 14	6 41.7	7 21.4	28 37.7	3 15.6	23 07.6	15 03.8	4 02.5	15 41.7	19 25.4	26 31.4
7 Su	13 03 02	13 50 23	26 19 46	2♍32 59	6R 42.7	7 52.9	29 23.4	3 40.1	23 01.4	15 13.3	4 09.0	15 39.7	19 24.6	26 32.3
8 M	13 06 58	14 49 37	8♍43 15	14 50 56	6 42.4	8 19.4	0♍10.0	4 04.1	22 54.7	15 22.8	4 15.4	15 37.7	19 23.8	26 33.2
9 Tu	13 10 55	15 48 52	20 56 19	26 59 41	6 40.3	8 40.2	0 57.5	4 27.7	22 47.7	15 32.5	4 21.8	15 35.7	19 23.1	26 34.2
10 W	13 14 52	16 48 10	3♎01 18	9♎01 25	6 36.3	8 55.0	1 45.8	4 50.8	22 40.4	15 42.3	4 28.1	15 33.7	19 22.4	26 35.2
11 Th	13 18 48	17 47 29	15 00 13	20 57 55	6 30.3	9R 03.2	2 35.0	5 13.5	22 32.6	15 52.3	4 34.4	15 31.8	19 21.7	26 36.3
12 F	13 22 45	18 46 51	26 54 44	2♏50 51	6 22.8	9 04.4	3 25.0	5 35.8	22 24.5	16 02.3	4 40.6	15 29.9	19 21.1	26 37.3
13 Sa	13 26 41	19 46 15	8♏46 28	14 41 50	6 14.3	8 58.1	4 15.7	5 57.5	22 16.1	16 12.4	4 46.8	15 28.0	19 20.5	26 38.5
14 Su	13 30 38	20 45 41	20 37 09	26 32 42	6 05.7	8 43.9	5 07.2	6 18.8	22 07.3	16 22.6	4 52.9	15 26.2	19 19.9	26 39.6
15 M	13 34 34	21 45 08	2♐28 47	8♐25 44	5 57.8	8 21.4	5 59.4	6 39.7	21 58.2	16 33.0	4 58.9	15 24.4	19 19.3	26 40.7
16 Tu	13 38 31	22 44 38	14 23 55	20 23 44	5 51.3	7 50.5	6 52.2	7 00.0	21 48.8	16 43.4	5 04.9	15 22.7	19 18.8	26 41.9
17 W	13 42 27	23 44 09	26 25 37	2♑30 04	5 46.8	7 11.1	7 45.8	7 19.9	21 39.0	16 53.9	5 10.8	15 20.9	19 18.3	26 43.2
18 Th	13 46 24	24 43 43	8♑37 35	14 48 43	5D 44.4	6 23.3	8 39.9	7 39.2	21 29.0	17 04.5	5 16.7	15 19.2	19 17.9	26 44.4
19 F	13 50 21	25 43 17	21 03 59	27 23 58	5 43.8	5 27.7	9 34.7	7 58.0	21 18.6	17 15.2	5 22.5	15 17.6	19 17.4	26 45.7
20 Sa	13 54 17	26 42 54	3♒49 13	10♒20 15	5 44.5	4 25.2	10 30.1	8 16.3	21 08.0	17 26.0	5 28.2	15 16.0	19 17.0	26 47.0
21 Su	13 58 14	27 42 32	16 57 33	23 41 32	5R 45.6	3 16.8	11 26.1	8 34.0	20 57.0	17 36.9	5 33.9	15 14.4	19 16.7	26 48.3
22 M	14 02 10	28 42 12	0♓32 31	7♓30 40	5 46.1	2 04.1	12 22.7	8 51.2	20 45.8	17 47.9	5 39.5	15 12.8	19 16.4	26 49.6
23 Tu	14 06 07	29 41 54	14 36 03	21 48 30	5 44.9	0 49.1	13 19.7	9 07.9	20 34.3	17 59.0	5 45.0	15 11.3	19 16.1	26 51.0
24 W	14 10 03	0♏41 37	29 07 39	6♈32 58	5 41.6	29♎33.9	14 17.4	9 23.9	20 22.6	18 10.1	5 50.5	15 09.8	19 15.8	26 52.4
25 Th	14 14 00	1 41 23	14♈03 36	21 38 34	5 35.9	28 20.6	15 15.5	9 39.4	20 10.6	18 21.4	5 55.9	15 08.4	19 15.6	26 53.9
26 F	14 17 56	2 41 10	29 16 39	6♉56 31	5 28.1	27 11.7	16 14.1	9 54.3	19 58.4	18 32.7	6 01.2	15 07.0	19 15.4	26 55.3
27 Sa	14 21 53	3 40 59	14♉36 42	22 15 45	5 19.2	26 09.1	17 13.3	10 08.6	19 46.0	18 44.1	6 06.4	15 05.7	19 15.2	26 56.8
28 Su	14 25 50	4 40 51	29 52 17	7♊24 57	5 10.3	25 14.8	18 12.9	10 22.2	19 33.4	18 55.6	6 11.6	15 04.4	19 15.1	26 58.3
29 M	14 29 46	5 40 45	14♊52 40	22 14 29	5 02.4	24 30.1	19 12.9	10 35.3	19 20.6	19 07.2	6 16.7	15 03.1	19 15.0	26 59.8
30 Tu	14 33 43	6 40 40	29 29 42	6♋37 52	4 56.6	23 56.2	20 13.4	10 47.7	19 07.6	19 18.8	6 21.7	15 01.9	19 14.9	27 01.4
31 W	14 37 39	7 40 38	13♋38 45	20 32 18	4 53.0	23 33.7	21 14.4	10 59.4	18 54.4	19 30.5	6 26.7	15 00.7	19D 14.9	27 03.0

Astro Data

	Dy Hr Mn
☿0S	5 19:16
♇ D	7 14:56
♀ D	8 16:15
☽0S	12 3:44
⚳ R	20 13:06
☉0S	23 9:52
☽0N	26 8:00
☽0S	9 10:06
♃□♅	9 18:25
☿ R	12 4:00
☽0N	23 18:46
♃✶♆	30 4:00
♆ D	31 20:07

Planet Ingress

	Dy Hr Mn
♄ ♍	2 13:50
☿ ♎	5 12:03
☉ ♎	23 9:52
☿ ♏	27 17:19
♂ ♋	28 23:56
♀ ♍	8 6:54
☉ ♏	23 19:16
☿ ♎R	24 3:38

Last Aspect / ☽ Ingress (September)

Last Aspect Dy Hr Mn		☽ Ingress Dy Hr Mn
1 5:20 ♄ △	♉	1 5:36
3 0:48 ☿ △	♊	3 7:31
5 11:02 ☿ □	♋	5 11:09
6 17:05 ♅ △	♌	7 17:00
9 18:08 ♇ △	♍	10 1:11
12 4:15 ♇ □	♎	12 11:32
14 16:11 ♇ ✶	♏	14 23:38
16 23:42 ☉ ✶	♐	17 12:22
19 16:49 ☉ □	♑	19 23:53
22 6:16 ☉ △	♒	22 8:19
24 9:15 ♂ △	♓	24 12:56
26 12:32 ♂ □	♈	26 14:24
28 14:00 ♂ ✶	♉	28 14:18
30 5:11 ♀ □	♊	30 14:35

Last Aspect / ☽ Ingress (October)

Last Aspect Dy Hr Mn		☽ Ingress Dy Hr Mn
2 10:53 ♇ ☍	♋	2 16:58
3 20:42 ♅ △	♌	4 22:28
7 5:29 ♀ ☌	♍	7 7:04
9 11:09 ♇ □	♎	9 17:59
11 23:24 ♇ ✶	♏	12 6:14
13 21:24 ♆ □	♐	14 18:59
17 0:34 ♇ ☌	♑	17 7:04
19 8:34 ☉ □	♒	19 16:53
21 19:37 ☉ △	♓	21 23:03
23 20:18 ♇ □	♈	24 1:25
25 21:47 ♇ △	♉	26 1:08
27 7:17 ♆ □	♊	28 0:12
29 19:52 ♇ ☍	♋	30 0:51

☽ Phases & Eclipses

Dy Hr Mn	
4 2:33	☾ 11♊12
11 12:45	● 18♍25
11 12:32:24	✔ P 0.751
19 16:49	☽ 26♐22
26 19:46	○ 3♈20
3 10:07	☾ 9♋49
11 5:02	● 17♎30
19 8:34	☽ 25♑35
26 4:53	○ 2♉23

Astro Data

1 September 2007
Julian Day # 39325
SVP 5♓09'02"
GC 26♐56.8 ⚴ 10♓31.2R
Eris 21♈23.5R ⚵ 27♎44.6
⚷ 11♒40.3R ⚶ 11♐24.5
☽ Mean ☊ 6♓46.5

1 October 2007
Julian Day # 39355
SVP 5♓08'59"
GC 26♐56.9 ⚴ 3♓34.0R
Eris 21♈08.0R ⚵ 6♏59.3
⚷ 10♒39.0R ⚶ 22♐23.4
☽ Mean ☊ 5♓11.2

November 2007 LONGITUDE

Day	Sid.Time	☉	0 hr ☽	Noon ☽	True ☊	☿	♀	♂	⚳	♃	♄	♅	♆	♇
1 Th	14 41 36	8♏40 38	27♋18 41	3♌58 09	4♓51.6	23♎22.7	22♍15.7	11♋10.5	18♉41.1	19♐42.3	6♍31.5	14♓59.6	19♒14.9	27♐04.6
2 F	14 45 32	9 40 41	10♌31 09	16 58 08	4D 51.7	23D 23.2	23 17.5	11 20.8	18R 27.7	19 54.2	6 36.3	14R 58.5	19 14.9	27 06.2
3 Sa	14 49 29	10 40 45	23 19 39	29 36 16	4R 52.2	23 34.6	24 19.6	11 30.5	18 14.1	20 06.2	6 41.0	14 57.4	19 15.0	27 07.8
4 Su	14 53 25	11 40 52	5♍48 35	11♍57 09	4 52.1	23 56.5	25 22.1	11 39.4	18 00.4	20 18.2	6 45.6	14 56.4	19 15.1	27 09.5
5 M	14 57 22	12 41 00	18 02 33	24 05 18	4 50.2	24 27.9	26 25.0	11 47.6	17 46.7	20 30.2	6 50.2	14 55.5	19 15.2	27 11.2
6 Tu	15 01 19	13 41 11	0♎05 54	6♎04 46	4 45.8	25 08.1	27 28.2	11 55.1	17 32.8	20 42.4	6 54.6	14 54.5	19 15.4	27 12.9
7 W	15 05 15	14 41 23	12 02 20	17 58 56	4 38.6	25 56.1	28 31.8	12 01.8	17 18.9	20 54.6	6 59.0	14 53.7	19 15.6	27 14.6
8 Th	15 09 12	15 41 37	23 54 54	29 50 30	4 28.4	26 51.2	29 35.7	12 07.8	17 05.0	21 06.9	7 03.3	14 52.9	19 15.9	27 16.4
9 F	15 13 08	16 41 54	5♏45 58	11♏41 31	4 15.9	27 52.3	0♎39.9	12 12.9	16 51.0	21 19.2	7 07.5	14 52.1	19 16.1	27 18.1
10 Sa	15 17 05	17 42 12	17 37 19	23 33 31	4 02.0	28 58.9	1 44.4	12 17.3	16 37.0	21 31.7	7 11.6	14 51.4	19 16.5	27 19.9
11 Su	15 21 01	18 42 32	29 30 19	5♐27 50	3 47.7	0♏10.0	2 49.2	12 20.9	16 23.1	21 44.1	7 15.6	14 50.7	19 16.8	27 21.8
12 M	15 24 58	19 42 53	11♐26 16	17 25 47	3 34.4	1 25.2	3 54.3	12 23.7	16 09.1	21 56.7	7 19.5	14 50.1	19 17.2	27 23.6
13 Tu	15 28 54	20 43 16	23 26 36	29 28 58	3 22.9	2 43.7	4 59.7	12 25.6	15 55.2	22 09.3	7 23.4	14 49.5	19 17.6	27 25.4
14 W	15 32 51	21 43 41	5♑33 09	11♑39 30	3 14.1	4 05.1	6 05.4	12R 26.7	15 41.4	22 21.9	7 27.1	14 49.0	19 18.1	27 27.3
15 Th	15 36 48	22 44 07	17 48 21	24 00 08	3 08.3	5 28.9	7 11.3	12 27.0	15 27.6	22 34.6	7 30.8	14 48.5	19 18.5	27 29.2
16 F	15 40 44	23 44 35	0♒15 16	6♒34 14	3 05.3	6 54.7	8 17.5	12 26.5	15 13.9	22 47.4	7 34.3	14 48.1	19 19.1	27 31.1
17 Sa	15 44 41	24 45 03	12 57 32	19 25 41	3D 04.3	8 22.2	9 23.9	12 25.1	15 00.4	23 00.2	7 37.8	14 47.7	19 19.6	27 33.0
18 Su	15 48 37	25 45 33	25 59 10	2♓38 27	3R 04.3	9 51.1	10 30.6	12 22.9	14 46.9	23 13.0	7 41.2	14 47.4	19 20.2	27 35.0
19 M	15 52 34	26 46 04	9♓23 57	16 16 02	3 03.9	11 21.1	11 37.5	12 19.8	14 33.6	23 25.9	7 44.4	14 47.1	19 20.8	27 36.9
20 Tu	15 56 30	27 46 37	23 14 55	0♈20 41	3 01.9	12 52.0	12 44.6	12 15.8	14 20.5	23 38.9	7 47.6	14 46.8	19 21.5	27 38.9
21 W	16 00 27	28 47 10	7♈33 14	14 52 19	2 57.4	14 23.7	13 51.9	12 11.0	14 07.5	23 51.9	7 50.7	14 46.7	19 22.1	27 40.9
22 Th	16 04 23	29 47 45	22 17 23	29 47 41	2 50.1	15 56.0	14 59.5	12 05.3	13 54.7	24 04.9	7 53.6	14 46.5	19 22.9	27 42.9
23 F	16 08 20	0♐48 22	7♉22 16	14♉59 57	2 40.3	17 28.8	16 07.3	11 58.8	13 42.1	24 18.0	7 56.5	14D 46.5	19 23.6	27 44.9
24 Sa	16 12 17	1 48 59	22 39 22	0♊19 05	2 28.9	19 01.9	17 15.3	11 51.4	13 29.7	24 31.1	7 59.3	14 46.4	19 24.4	27 46.9
25 Su	16 16 13	2 49 38	7♊57 37	15 33 30	2 17.2	20 35.3	18 23.5	11 43.1	13 17.6	24 44.3	8 02.0	14 46.5	19 25.2	27 49.0
26 M	16 20 10	3 50 19	23 05 24	0♋32 07	2 06.6	22 08.9	19 31.9	11 34.0	13 05.6	24 57.5	8 04.5	14 46.6	19 26.1	27 51.0
27 Tu	16 24 06	4 51 01	7♋52 42	15 06 23	1 58.2	23 42.7	20 40.5	11 24.0	12 54.0	25 10.7	8 07.0	14 46.7	19 27.0	27 53.1
28 W	16 28 03	5 51 45	22 12 42	29 11 23	1 52.6	25 16.6	21 49.3	11 13.2	12 42.5	25 24.0	8 09.4	14 46.9	19 27.9	27 55.2
29 Th	16 31 59	6 52 30	6♌02 24	12♌45 53	1 49.7	26 50.5	22 58.3	11 01.5	12 31.4	25 37.3	8 11.6	14 47.1	19 28.8	27 57.3
30 F	16 35 56	7 53 16	19 22 09	25 51 38	1D 48.7	28 24.6	24 07.4	10 49.0	12 20.5	25 50.7	8 13.8	14 47.4	19 29.8	27 59.4

December 2007 LONGITUDE

Day	Sid.Time	☉	0 hr ☽	Noon ☽	True ☊	☿	♀	♂	⚳	♃	♄	♅	♆	♇
1 Sa	16 39 52	8♐54 04	2♍14 53	8♍32 29	1♓48.6	29♏58.6	25♎16.7	10♋35.7	12♉09.9	26♐04.0	8♍15.9	14♓47.7	19♒30.8	28♐01.5
2 Su	16 43 49	9 54 54	14 45 04	20 53 18	1R 48.3	1♐32.6	26 26.2	10R 21.5	11R 59.6	26 17.5	8 17.8	14 48.1	19 31.8	28 03.6
3 M	16 47 46	10 55 45	26 57 51	2♎59 22	1 46.5	3 06.6	27 35.9	10 06.6	11 49.7	26 30.9	8 19.6	14 48.5	19 32.9	28 05.7
4 Tu	16 51 42	11 56 37	8♎58 27	14 55 43	1 42.2	4 40.7	28 45.7	9 50.9	11 40.0	26 44.4	8 21.4	14 49.0	19 34.0	28 07.9
5 W	16 55 39	12 57 30	20 51 42	26 46 54	1 35.1	6 14.7	29 55.6	9 34.4	11 30.7	26 57.9	8 23.0	14 49.6	19 35.1	28 10.0
6 Th	16 59 35	13 58 25	2♏41 46	8♏36 42	1 25.0	7 48.7	1♏05.7	9 17.2	11 21.7	27 11.4	8 24.5	14 50.2	19 36.3	28 12.2
7 F	17 03 32	14 59 21	14 32 04	20 28 08	1 12.6	9 22.7	2 16.0	8 59.3	11 13.1	27 25.0	8 25.9	14 50.8	19 37.5	28 14.3
8 Sa	17 07 28	16 00 19	26 25 10	2♐23 23	0 58.6	10 56.7	3 26.3	8 40.7	11 04.8	27 38.5	8 27.2	14 51.5	19 38.7	28 16.5
9 Su	17 11 25	17 01 17	8♐22 56	14 23 58	0 44.1	12 30.7	4 36.9	8 21.5	10 56.9	27 52.1	8 28.4	14 52.2	19 40.0	28 18.7
10 M	17 15 21	18 02 17	20 26 35	26 30 55	0 30.5	14 04.7	5 47.5	8 01.7	10 49.4	28 05.8	8 29.4	14 53.0	19 41.3	28 20.9
11 Tu	17 19 18	19 03 17	2♑37 02	8♑45 04	0 18.8	15 38.8	6 58.3	7 41.3	10 42.2	28 19.4	8 30.4	14 53.9	19 42.6	28 23.0
12 W	17 23 15	20 04 18	14 55 09	21 07 23	0 09.8	17 12.9	8 09.1	7 20.4	10 35.4	28 33.1	8 31.3	14 54.8	19 43.9	28 25.2
13 Th	17 27 11	21 05 19	27 21 58	3♒39 07	0 03.9	18 47.1	9 20.1	6 59.0	10 29.0	28 46.7	8 32.0	14 55.7	19 45.3	28 27.4
14 F	17 31 08	22 06 22	9♒59 03	16 22 04	0 00.8	20 21.4	10 31.2	6 37.1	10 23.0	29 00.4	8 32.6	14 56.7	19 46.7	28 29.6
15 Sa	17 35 04	23 07 24	22 48 27	29 18 34	29♒59.9	21 55.7	11 42.4	6 14.9	10 17.4	29 14.1	8 33.1	14 57.8	19 48.1	28 31.9
16 Su	17 39 01	24 08 28	5♓52 44	12♓31 19	0♓00.3	23 30.1	12 53.7	5 52.3	10 12.2	29 27.8	8 33.5	14 58.9	19 49.6	28 34.1
17 M	17 42 57	25 09 31	19 14 39	26 03 03	0 00.6	25 04.7	14 05.1	5 29.4	10 07.4	29 41.6	8 33.8	15 00.0	19 51.1	28 36.3
18 Tu	17 46 54	26 10 35	2♈56 43	9♈55 50	29♒59.7	26 39.4	15 16.6	5 06.2	10 02.9	29 55.3	8 34.0	15 01.2	19 52.6	28 38.5
19 W	17 50 51	27 11 39	17 00 26	24 10 24	29 56.8	28 14.2	16 28.2	4 42.9	9 58.9	0♑09.0	8R 34.1	15 02.5	19 54.1	28 40.7
20 Th	17 54 47	28 12 44	1♉25 29	8♉45 15	29 51.4	29 49.2	17 39.9	4 19.3	9 55.3	0 22.8	8 34.0	15 03.8	19 55.7	28 42.9
21 F	17 58 44	29 13 48	16 09 04	23 36 07	29 43.7	1♑24.4	18 51.7	3 55.7	9 52.1	0 36.5	8 33.9	15 05.1	19 57.3	28 45.1
22 Sa	18 02 40	0♑14 54	1♊05 27	8♊35 57	29 34.5	2 59.7	20 03.6	3 32.0	9 49.3	0 50.3	8 33.6	15 06.5	19 58.9	28 47.3
23 Su	18 06 37	1 15 59	16 06 26	23 35 39	29 24.9	4 35.3	21 15.6	3 08.3	9 46.9	1 04.0	8 33.2	15 07.9	20 00.5	28 49.6
24 M	18 10 33	2 17 06	1♋02 24	8♋25 34	29 16.1	6 11.0	22 27.7	2 44.6	9 44.9	1 17.8	8 32.7	15 09.4	20 02.2	28 51.8
25 Tu	18 14 30	3 18 12	15 44 06	22 57 10	29 09.1	7 47.0	23 39.8	2 21.0	9 43.3	1 31.6	8 32.1	15 11.0	20 03.9	28 54.0
26 W	18 18 26	4 19 19	0♌04 05	7♌04 23	29 04.5	9 23.2	24 52.0	1 57.5	9 42.2	1 45.3	8 31.4	15 12.5	20 05.6	28 56.2
27 Th	18 22 23	5 20 26	13 57 48	20 44 13	29D 02.2	10 59.7	26 04.3	1 34.2	9 41.4	1 59.1	8 30.6	15 14.2	20 07.3	28 58.4
28 F	18 26 20	6 21 34	27 23 44	3♍56 34	29 02.0	12 36.4	27 16.7	1 11.2	9D 41.0	2 12.8	8 29.7	15 15.8	20 09.0	29 00.6
29 Sa	18 30 16	7 22 42	10♍23 06	16 43 46	29 03.0	14 13.3	28 29.2	0 48.3	9 41.0	2 26.6	8 28.6	15 17.5	20 10.8	29 02.8
30 Su	18 34 13	8 23 51	22 59 06	29 09 42	29R 04.1	15 50.4	29 41.7	0 25.8	9 41.4	2 40.3	8 27.5	15 19.3	20 12.6	29 05.0
31 M	18 38 09	9 25 00	5♎16 11	11♎19 12	29 04.5	17 27.7	0♐54.3	0 03.7	9 42.2	2 54.1	8 26.2	15 21.1	20 14.4	29 07.2

Astro Data	Planet Ingress	Last Aspect	☽ Ingress	Last Aspect	☽ Ingress	☽ Phases & Eclipses	Astro Data
Dy Hr Mn	Dy Hr Mn	Dy Hr Mn	Dy Hr Mn	Dy Hr Mn	Dy Hr Mn	Dy Hr Mn	
☿D 1 23:02	♀ ♎ 8 21:06	31 17:14 ☿ □	♌ 1 4:49	3 2:13 ♇ □	♎ 3 6:02	1 21:19 ☾ 9♌04	1 November 2007
☽0S 5 15:26	☿ ♏ 11 8:42	3 7:15 ♇ △	♍ 3 12:46	5 14:49 ♇ ⚹	♏ 5 18:32	9 23:04 ● 17♏10	Julian Day # 39386
♀0S 11 15:20	☉ ♐ 22 16:51	5 18:12 ♇ □	♎ 5 23:48	7 10:18 ♆ □	♐ 8 7:12	17 22:34 ☽ 25♒12	SVP 5♓08'55"
♂R 15 8:26		8 6:47 ♇ ⚹	♏ 8 12:19	10 15:37 ♇ ☌	♑ 10 18:52	24 14:31 ○ 1♊55	GC 26♐56.9 ⚴ 0♓52.1
☽0N 20 3:54	☿ ♐ 1 12:22	10 3:20 ♆ □	♐ 11 1:00	11 23:58 ♅ ⚹	♒ 13 5:02		Eris 20♈49.7R ⚵ 17♏18.3
♅D 24 10:16	♀ ♏ 5 13:30	13 7:54 ♇ ☌	♑ 13 13:02	15 11:52 ♃ ⚹	♓ 15 13:16	1 12:45 ☾ 8♍56	⚷ 10♒33.1 ⚶ 5♑59.0
	☊ ♒R 15 6:02	15 9:20 ☉ ⚹	♒ 15 23:31	17 18:28 ♃ □	♈ 17 18:54	9 17:41 ● 17♐16	☽ Mean ☊ 3♓32.7
☽0S 2 20:47	☊ ♓ 15 21:29	18 2:52 ♇ ⚹	♓ 18 7:16	19 19:34 ☿ △	♉ 19 21:39	17 10:19 ☽ 25♓05	
♃☌♇ 11 19:37	☊ ♒R 18 8:06	20 7:27 ♇ □	♈ 20 11:25	21 6:07 ♆ □	♊ 21 22:15	24 1:17 ○ 1♋50	1 December 2007
☽0N 17 10:12	♃ ♑ 18 20:12	22 8:41 ♇ △	♉ 22 12:20	23 20:27 ♇ ☍	♋ 23 22:19	31 7:52 ☾ 9♎14	Julian Day # 39416
♄R 19 14:11	☿ ♑ 20 14:44	23 18:54 ♆ □	♊ 24 11:30	25 13:18 ♀ △	♌ 25 23:53		SVP 5♓08'50"
⚳D 28 23:25	☉ ♑ 22 6:09	26 7:39 ♇ ☍	♋ 26 11:08	28 2:55 ♇ △	♍ 28 4:45		GC 26♐57.0 ⚴ 3♓24.9
☽0S 30 3:35	♀ ♐ 30 18:03	28 4:24 ☿ △	♌ 28 13:24	30 13:09 ♀ ⚹	♎ 30 13:38		Eris 20♈34.9R ⚵ 27♏31.3
	♂ ♊R 31 16:01	30 17:26 ☿ □	♍ 30 19:45				⚷ 11♒27.9 ⚶ 20♑22.5
							☽ Mean ☊ 1♓57.4

LONGITUDE — January 2008

Day	Sid.Time	☉	0 hr ☽	Noon ☽	True ☊	☿	♀	♂	⚳	♃	♄	♅	♆	♇
1 Tu	18 42 06	10♑26 10	17♎19 24	23♎17 27	29♒03.4	19♑05.2	2♐07.0	29♊41.9	9♉43.4	3♑07.8	8♍24.9	15♓23.0	20♒16.3	29♐09.4
2 W	18 46 02	11 27 20	29 13 56	5♏09 30	29R 00.3	20 42.8	3 19.7	29R 20.6	9 45.0	3 21.5	8R 23.4	15 24.8	20 18.1	29 11.5
3 Th	18 49 59	12 28 30	11♏04 42	17 00 03	28 55.0	22 20.6	4 32.5	28 59.8	9 47.0	3 35.2	8 21.8	15 26.8	20 20.0	29 13.7
4 F	18 53 55	13 29 41	22 56 04	28 53 10	28 48.0	23 58.5	5 45.4	28 39.4	9 49.3	3 48.9	8 20.1	15 28.8	20 21.9	29 15.9
5 Sa	18 57 52	14 30 51	4♐51 44	10♐52 07	28 39.6	25 36.4	6 58.3	28 19.7	9 52.1	4 02.6	8 18.4	15 30.8	20 23.8	29 18.0
6 Su	19 01 49	15 32 02	16 54 36	22 59 25	28 30.9	27 14.2	8 11.3	28 00.5	9 55.2	4 16.3	8 16.5	15 32.8	20 25.8	29 20.2
7 M	19 05 45	16 33 13	29 06 44	5♑16 41	28 22.6	28 51.9	9 24.3	27 42.0	9 58.8	4 29.9	8 14.5	15 35.0	20 27.7	29 22.3
8 Tu	19 09 42	17 34 24	11♑29 22	17 44 52	28 15.5	0♒29.3	10 37.4	27 24.0	10 02.7	4 43.5	8 12.4	15 37.1	20 29.7	29 24.5
9 W	19 13 38	18 35 35	24 03 11	0♒24 21	28 10.3	2 06.3	11 50.5	27 06.8	10 06.9	4 57.1	8 10.2	15 39.3	20 31.7	29 26.6
10 Th	19 17 35	19 36 45	6♒48 23	13 15 17	28 07.1	3 42.8	13 03.7	26 50.3	10 11.6	5 10.7	8 07.9	15 41.5	20 33.7	29 28.7
11 F	19 21 31	20 37 55	19 45 03	26 17 43	28D 06.0	5 18.6	14 16.9	26 34.5	10 16.6	5 24.3	8 05.5	15 43.8	20 35.7	29 30.8
12 Sa	19 25 28	21 39 05	2♓53 19	9♓31 54	28 06.5	6 53.5	15 30.1	26 19.4	10 21.9	5 37.8	8 03.0	15 46.1	20 37.8	29 32.9
13 Su	19 29 24	22 40 13	16 13 31	22 58 15	28 08.0	8 27.1	16 43.4	26 05.1	10 27.7	5 51.3	8 00.4	15 48.4	20 39.8	29 35.0
14 M	19 33 21	23 41 22	29 46 11	6♈37 23	28 09.5	9 59.3	17 56.7	25 51.6	10 33.8	6 04.8	7 57.7	15 50.8	20 41.9	29 37.0
15 Tu	19 37 18	24 42 29	13♈31 52	20 29 41	28R 10.5	11 29.6	19 10.1	25 38.9	10 40.2	6 18.3	7 54.9	15 53.2	20 44.0	29 39.1
16 W	19 41 14	25 43 36	27 30 46	4♉35 01	28 10.2	12 57.6	20 23.5	25 26.9	10 47.0	6 31.7	7 52.0	15 55.7	20 46.1	29 41.1
17 Th	19 45 11	26 44 42	11♉42 15	18 52 12	28 08.5	14 23.0	21 36.9	25 15.8	10 54.1	6 45.1	7 49.1	15 58.2	20 48.2	29 43.2
18 F	19 49 07	27 45 47	26 04 30	3♊18 39	28 05.4	15 45.1	22 50.4	25 05.5	11 01.5	6 58.4	7 46.0	16 00.7	20 50.3	29 45.2
19 Sa	19 53 04	28 46 52	10♊34 07	17 50 13	28 01.3	17 03.4	24 03.9	24 56.0	11 09.3	7 11.7	7 42.9	16 03.2	20 52.5	29 47.2
20 Su	19 57 00	29 47 56	25 06 14	2♋21 23	27 56.9	18 17.2	25 17.4	24 47.3	11 17.4	7 25.0	7 39.7	16 05.8	20 54.6	29 49.2
21 M	20 00 57	0♒48 59	9♋34 54	16 45 59	27 52.8	19 25.8	26 31.0	24 39.5	11 25.9	7 38.3	7 36.4	16 08.5	20 56.8	29 51.1
22 Tu	20 04 54	1 50 01	23 53 55	0♌57 59	27 49.6	20 28.4	27 44.6	24 32.4	11 34.6	7 51.5	7 33.0	16 11.1	20 59.0	29 53.1
23 W	20 08 50	2 51 03	7♌57 39	14 52 23	27D 47.7	21 24.2	28 58.3	24 26.2	11 43.7	8 04.7	7 29.5	16 13.8	21 01.2	29 55.0
24 Th	20 12 47	3 52 04	21 41 52	28 25 52	27 47.2	22 12.4	0♑11.9	24 20.7	11 53.1	8 17.8	7 26.0	16 16.5	21 03.4	29 56.9
25 F	20 16 43	4 53 04	5♍04 15	11♍37 03	27 47.7	22 52.0	1 25.6	24 16.1	12 02.7	8 30.9	7 22.4	16 19.3	21 05.6	29 58.8
26 Sa	20 20 40	5 54 03	18 04 23	24 26 29	27 49.1	23 22.3	2 39.3	24 12.3	12 12.7	8 43.9	7 18.7	16 22.1	21 07.8	0♑00.7
27 Su	20 24 36	6 55 02	0♎43 41	6♎56 21	27 50.8	23 42.5	3 53.1	24 09.2	12 23.0	8 56.9	7 14.9	16 24.9	21 10.0	0 02.6
28 M	20 28 33	7 56 00	13 04 58	19 10 02	27 52.3	23R 52.0	5 06.9	24 06.9	12 33.5	9 09.9	7 11.1	16 27.7	21 12.2	0 04.4
29 Tu	20 32 29	8 56 58	25 12 07	1♏11 46	27R 53.3	23 50.4	6 20.7	24 05.5	12 44.4	9 22.8	7 07.1	16 30.6	21 14.4	0 06.3
30 W	20 36 26	9 57 55	7♏09 37	13 06 16	27 53.5	23 37.4	7 34.5	24D 04.7	12 55.5	9 35.6	7 03.2	16 33.5	21 16.7	0 08.1
31 Th	20 40 23	10 58 51	19 02 18	24 58 20	27 52.8	23 13.1	8 48.4	24 04.8	13 06.9	9 48.4	6 59.1	16 36.4	21 18.9	0 09.9

LONGITUDE — February 2008

Day	Sid.Time	☉	0 hr ☽	Noon ☽	True ☊	☿	♀	♂	⚳	♃	♄	♅	♆	♇
1 F	20 44 19	11♒59 47	0♐54 56	6♐52 41	27♒51.4	22♒38.0	10♑02.3	24♊05.6	13♉18.6	10♑01.2	6♍55.0	16♓39.4	21♒21.2	0♑11.7
2 Sa	20 48 16	13 00 41	12 52 05	18 53 39	27R 49.4	21R 52.8	11 16.2	24 07.1	13 30.6	10 13.9	6R 50.9	16 42.3	21 23.5	0 13.4
3 Su	20 52 12	14 01 35	24 57 48	1♑04 57	27 47.3	20 58.7	12 30.1	24 09.4	13 42.8	10 26.5	6 46.6	16 45.3	21 25.7	0 15.1
4 M	20 56 09	15 02 28	7♑15 27	13 29 34	27 45.2	19 57.2	13 44.0	24 12.4	13 55.3	10 39.1	6 42.4	16 48.4	21 28.0	0 16.9
5 Tu	21 00 05	16 03 20	19 47 31	26 09 28	27 43.5	18 50.1	14 58.0	24 16.1	14 08.1	10 51.6	6 38.0	16 51.4	21 30.3	0 18.5
6 W	21 04 02	17 04 11	2♒35 29	9♒05 37	27 42.4	17 39.3	16 12.0	24 20.6	14 21.1	11 04.1	6 33.7	16 54.5	21 32.5	0 20.2
7 Th	21 07 58	18 05 01	15 39 48	22 17 57	27D 41.9	16 26.9	17 26.0	24 25.7	14 34.3	11 16.5	6 29.2	16 57.6	21 34.8	0 21.9
8 F	21 11 55	19 05 50	28 59 53	5♓45 25	27 41.9	15 14.9	18 40.0	24 31.5	14 47.9	11 28.9	6 24.8	17 00.7	21 37.1	0 23.5
9 Sa	21 15 52	20 06 37	12♓34 18	19 26 16	27 42.4	14 05.1	19 54.0	24 38.0	15 01.6	11 41.1	6 20.2	17 03.9	21 39.4	0 25.1
10 Su	21 19 48	21 07 22	26 21 01	3♈18 14	27 43.0	12 59.4	21 08.0	24 45.1	15 15.6	11 53.3	6 15.7	17 07.0	21 41.7	0 26.6
11 M	21 23 45	22 08 06	10♈17 36	17 18 50	27 43.6	11 59.0	22 22.1	24 52.9	15 29.8	12 05.5	6 11.1	17 10.2	21 43.9	0 28.2
12 Tu	21 27 41	23 08 49	24 21 35	1♉25 33	27 44.0	11 05.0	23 36.1	25 01.3	15 44.3	12 17.5	6 06.5	17 13.4	21 46.2	0 29.7
13 W	21 31 38	24 09 30	8♉30 28	15 36 01	27R 44.3	10 18.2	24 50.2	25 10.3	15 59.0	12 29.5	6 01.8	17 16.6	21 48.5	0 31.2
14 Th	21 35 34	25 10 09	22 41 55	29 47 54	27 44.3	9 39.0	26 04.2	25 20.0	16 13.9	12 41.5	5 57.1	17 19.8	21 50.8	0 32.7
15 F	21 39 31	26 10 47	6♊53 40	13♊58 56	27 44.2	9 07.7	27 18.3	25 30.2	16 29.1	12 53.3	5 52.4	17 23.1	21 53.1	0 34.1
16 Sa	21 43 27	27 11 23	21 03 25	28 06 48	27D 44.1	8 44.3	28 32.4	25 41.1	16 44.4	13 05.1	5 47.7	17 26.4	21 55.3	0 35.5
17 Su	21 47 24	28 11 57	5♋08 46	12♋09 00	27 44.1	8 28.7	29 46.5	25 52.4	17 00.0	13 16.8	5 42.9	17 29.6	21 57.6	0 36.9
18 M	21 51 21	29 12 29	19 07 12	26 03 00	27 44.2	8D 20.6	1♒00.5	26 04.4	17 15.8	13 28.4	5 38.1	17 32.9	21 59.9	0 38.3
19 Tu	21 55 17	0♓13 00	2♌56 07	9♌46 14	27 44.4	8 19.7	2 14.7	26 16.9	17 31.7	13 39.9	5 33.3	17 36.3	22 02.1	0 39.7
20 W	21 59 14	1 13 29	16 33 04	23 16 21	27R 44.5	8 25.7	3 28.8	26 29.9	17 47.9	13 51.4	5 28.5	17 39.6	22 04.4	0 41.0
21 Th	22 03 10	2 13 56	29 55 54	6♍31 33	27 44.5	8 38.0	4 42.9	26 43.4	18 04.3	14 02.8	5 23.7	17 42.9	22 06.7	0 42.3
22 F	22 07 07	3 14 22	13♍03 09	19 30 41	27 44.2	8 56.4	5 57.0	26 57.4	18 20.9	14 14.1	5 18.9	17 46.3	22 08.9	0 43.5
23 Sa	22 11 03	4 14 46	25 54 08	2♎13 35	27 43.5	9 20.3	7 11.1	27 11.9	18 37.6	14 25.3	5 14.0	17 49.6	22 11.2	0 44.7
24 Su	22 15 00	5 15 08	8♎29 09	14 41 04	27 42.6	9 49.4	8 25.3	27 26.9	18 54.5	14 36.4	5 09.2	17 53.0	22 13.4	0 45.9
25 M	22 18 56	6 15 29	20 49 33	26 54 58	27 41.4	10 23.3	9 39.4	27 42.3	19 11.7	14 47.4	5 04.4	17 56.3	22 15.6	0 47.1
26 Tu	22 22 53	7 15 49	2♏57 39	8♏58 03	27 40.2	11 01.7	10 53.6	27 58.2	19 29.0	14 58.3	4 59.5	17 59.7	22 17.8	0 48.3
27 W	22 26 50	8 16 07	14 56 37	20 53 53	27 39.2	11 44.2	12 07.7	28 14.6	19 46.5	15 09.2	4 54.7	18 03.1	22 20.1	0 49.4
28 Th	22 30 46	9 16 24	26 50 21	2♐46 36	27D 38.6	12 30.5	13 21.9	28 31.3	20 04.1	15 19.9	4 49.9	18 06.5	22 22.3	0 50.5
29 F	22 34 43	10 16 39	8♐43 13	14 40 47	27 38.6	13 20.3	14 36.1	28 48.6	20 22.0	15 30.6	4 45.1	18 09.9	22 24.5	0 51.5

Astro Data

Aspect	Dy Hr Mn
♃∠♆	12 11:56
☽0N	13 14:56
♃△♄	21 9:15
☽0S	26 12:11
☿R	28 20:34
♂D	30 22:35
☽0N	9 20:47
☿D	19 2:58
☽0S	22 21:21

Planet Ingress

Planet	Dy Hr Mn
☿ ♒	8 4:47
☉ ♒	20 16:45
♀ ♑	24 8:07
♇ ♑	26 2:38
♀ ♒	17 16:23
☉ ♓	19 6:51

Last Aspect / ☽ Ingress (January)

Last Aspect Dy Hr Mn		☽ Ingress Dy Hr Mn
2 0:34	♂△	♏ 2 1:33
4 0:32	☿✶	♐ 4 14:14
7 0:28	♇☌	♑ 7 1:44
8 11:38	☉☌	♒ 9 11:14
11 17:53	♇✶	♓ 11 18:45
13 23:42	♇□	♈ 14 0:24
16 3:41	♇△	♉ 16 4:14
18 2:06	☉△	♊ 18 6:31
20 7:47	♇☍	♋ 20 8:06
21 10:57	♅△	♌ 22 10:21
24 14:44	♇△	♍ 24 14:49
26 11:33	♂□	♎ 26 22:36
28 21:49	♂△	♏ 29 9:36
31 8:36	☿□	♐ 31 22:09

Last Aspect / ☽ Ingress (February)

Last Aspect Dy Hr Mn		☽ Ingress Dy Hr Mn
2 22:22	♂☍	♑ 3 9:53
4 18:21	♅✶	♒ 5 19:11
7 15:51	♂△	♓ 8 1:47
9 21:06	♂□	♈ 10 6:18
12 1:01	♂✶	♉ 12 9:35
14 5:06	♀△	♊ 14 12:20
16 10:18	☉△	♋ 16 15:13
17 21:14	♅△	♌ 18 18:52
20 17:54	♂✶	♍ 21 0:07
23 2:16	♂□	♎ 23 7:46
25 13:36	♂△	♏ 25 18:07
27 14:55	♆□	♐ 28 6:23

☽ Phases & Eclipses

Dy Hr Mn	
8 11:38	● 17♑33
15 19:47	☽ 25♈02
22 13:36	○ 1♌54
30 5:04	☾ 9♏40
7 3:46	● 17♒44
7 3:56:08	• A 02'12"
14 3:35	☽ 24♉49
21 3:32	○ 1♍53
21 3:27	• T 1.106
29 2:19	☾ 9♐52

Astro Data

1 January 2008
Julian Day # 39447
SVP 5♓08'44"
GC 26♐57.1 ⚴ 9♓58.8
Eris 20♈27.5R ⚵ 7♐47.3
⚷ 13♒15.0 ⚶ 5♒54.6
☽ Mean ☊ 0♓18.9

1 February 2008
Julian Day # 39478
SVP 5♓08'39"
GC 26♐57.1 ⚴ 19♓06.0
Eris 20♈30.4 ⚵ 17♐07.1
⚷ 15♒31.2 ⚶ 21♒40.4
☽ Mean ☊ 28♒40.4

March 2008 — LONGITUDE

Day	Sid.Time	☉	0 hr ☽	Noon ☽	True ☊	☿	♀	♂	⚳	♃	♄	♅	♆	♇
1 Sa	22 38 39	11♓16 53	20♐39 54	26♐41 09	27♒39.1	14♒13.5	15♒50.3	29♊06.2	20♉40.0	15♑41.1	4♍40.3	18♓13.4	22♒26.7	0♑52.6
2 Su	22 42 36	12 17 05	2♑45 07	8♑52 21	27 40.1	15 09.6	17 04.5	29 24.3	20 58.1	15 51.6	4R 35.5	18 16.8	22 28.8	0 53.6
3 M	22 46 32	13 17 16	15 03 22	21 18 39	27 41.5	16 08.7	18 18.7	29 42.7	21 16.5	16 02.0	4 30.7	18 20.2	22 31.0	0 54.5
4 Tu	22 50 29	14 17 25	27 38 36	4♒03 34	27 42.8	17 10.3	19 32.9	0♋01.6	21 35.0	16 12.2	4 26.0	18 23.6	22 33.2	0 55.5
5 W	22 54 25	15 17 32	10♒33 50	17 09 33	27R 43.8	18 14.5	20 47.1	0 20.8	21 53.7	16 22.4	4 21.3	18 27.1	22 35.3	0 56.4
6 Th	22 58 22	16 17 38	23 50 48	0♓37 33	27 44.1	19 20.9	22 01.3	0 40.4	22 12.5	16 32.4	4 16.6	18 30.5	22 37.5	0 57.3
7 F	23 02 19	17 17 42	7♓29 36	14 26 42	27 43.3	20 29.6	23 15.5	1 00.4	22 31.4	16 42.4	4 11.9	18 33.9	22 39.6	0 58.1
8 Sa	23 06 15	18 17 44	21 28 25	28 34 17	27 41.6	21 40.3	24 29.6	1 20.7	22 50.6	16 52.2	4 07.3	18 37.4	22 41.7	0 58.9
9 Su	23 10 12	19 17 44	5♈43 39	12♈55 51	27 38.9	22 53.0	25 43.8	1 41.4	23 09.8	17 01.9	4 02.7	18 40.8	22 43.8	0 59.7
10 M	23 14 08	20 17 41	20 10 08	27 25 45	27 35.8	24 07.6	26 58.0	2 02.4	23 29.2	17 11.5	3 58.1	18 44.2	22 45.9	1 00.5
11 Tu	23 18 05	21 17 37	4♉41 56	11♉57 56	27 32.6	25 24.0	28 12.2	2 23.8	23 48.8	17 21.0	3 53.6	18 47.7	22 47.9	1 01.2
12 W	23 22 01	22 17 31	19 13 04	26 26 43	27 29.9	26 42.0	29 26.4	2 45.5	24 08.5	17 30.4	3 49.2	18 51.1	22 50.0	1 01.9
13 Th	23 25 58	23 17 23	3♊38 20	10♊47 30	27D 28.2	28 01.7	0♓40.6	3 07.5	24 28.4	17 39.6	3 44.7	18 54.5	22 52.0	1 02.5
14 F	23 29 54	24 17 12	17 53 51	24 57 07	27 27.6	29 23.0	1 54.8	3 29.8	24 48.3	17 48.7	3 40.4	18 58.0	22 54.0	1 03.2
15 Sa	23 33 51	25 16 59	1♋57 09	8♋53 50	27 28.2	0♓45.8	3 08.9	3 52.4	25 08.4	17 57.8	3 36.0	19 01.4	22 56.1	1 03.8
16 Su	23 37 48	26 16 44	15 47 08	22 37 02	27 29.6	2 10.1	4 23.1	4 15.4	25 28.7	18 06.7	3 31.8	19 04.8	22 58.0	1 04.3
17 M	23 41 44	27 16 26	29 23 36	6♌06 52	27 31.2	3 35.8	5 37.3	4 38.6	25 49.0	18 15.4	3 27.5	19 08.2	23 00.0	1 04.9
18 Tu	23 45 41	28 16 06	12♌46 54	19 23 46	27R 32.4	5 03.0	6 51.4	5 02.0	26 09.5	18 24.1	3 23.4	19 11.6	23 02.0	1 05.4
19 W	23 49 37	29 15 44	25 57 32	2♍28 16	27 32.5	6 31.6	8 05.6	5 25.8	26 30.1	18 32.6	3 19.3	19 15.0	23 03.9	1 05.8
20 Th	23 53 34	0♈15 20	8♍56 00	15 20 46	27 31.2	8 01.5	9 19.7	5 49.8	26 50.8	18 41.0	3 15.2	19 18.4	23 05.8	1 06.3
21 F	23 57 30	1 14 54	21 42 38	28 01 37	27 28.1	9 32.9	10 33.9	6 14.1	27 11.7	18 49.2	3 11.2	19 21.8	23 07.7	1 06.7
22 Sa	0 01 27	2 14 25	4♎17 46	10♎31 08	27 23.4	11 05.5	11 48.0	6 38.6	27 32.6	18 57.3	3 07.3	19 25.2	23 09.6	1 07.0
23 Su	0 05 23	3 13 55	16 41 49	22 49 54	27 17.3	12 39.5	13 02.1	7 03.4	27 53.7	19 05.3	3 03.5	19 28.6	23 11.5	1 07.4
24 M	0 09 20	4 13 23	28 55 33	4♏58 54	27 10.5	14 14.9	14 16.3	7 28.4	28 14.9	19 13.2	2 59.7	19 31.9	23 13.3	1 07.7
25 Tu	0 13 16	5 12 48	11♏00 13	16 59 44	27 03.6	15 51.6	15 30.4	7 53.6	28 36.1	19 20.9	2 56.0	19 35.3	23 15.1	1 07.9
26 W	0 17 13	6 12 13	22 57 47	28 54 42	26 57.4	17 29.6	16 44.5	8 19.1	28 57.5	19 28.5	2 52.3	19 38.6	23 16.9	1 08.2
27 Th	0 21 10	7 11 35	4♐50 54	10♐46 50	26 52.4	19 09.0	17 58.7	8 44.8	29 19.0	19 35.9	2 48.7	19 41.9	23 18.7	1 08.4
28 F	0 25 06	8 10 55	16 43 00	22 39 55	26 49.2	20 49.7	19 12.8	9 10.7	29 40.7	19 43.2	2 45.3	19 45.2	23 20.5	1 08.6
29 Sa	0 29 03	9 10 14	28 38 09	4♑38 18	26D 47.7	22 31.8	20 26.9	9 36.8	0♊02.4	19 50.4	2 41.8	19 48.5	23 22.2	1 08.7
30 Su	0 32 59	10 09 31	10♑40 58	16 46 46	26 47.8	24 15.3	21 41.0	10 03.2	0 24.2	19 57.4	2 38.5	19 51.8	23 23.9	1 08.8
31 M	0 36 56	11 08 46	22 56 20	29 10 15	26 48.9	26 00.1	22 55.1	10 29.7	0 46.1	20 04.3	2 35.2	19 55.1	23 25.6	1 08.9

April 2008 — LONGITUDE

Day	Sid.Time	☉	0 hr ☽	Noon ☽	True ☊	☿	♀	♂	⚳	♃	♄	♅	♆	♇
1 Tu	0 40 52	12♈07 59	5♒29 07	11♒53 27	26♒50.3	27♓46.3	24♓09.3	10♋56.5	1♊08.1	20♑11.0	2♍32.1	19♓58.3	23♒27.3	1♑08.9
2 W	0 44 49	13 07 11	18 23 44	25 00 21	26R 51.1	29 34.0	25 23.4	11 23.4	1 30.2	20 17.5	2R 29.0	20 01.5	23 28.9	1R 09.0
3 Th	0 48 45	14 06 20	1♓43 34	8♓33 32	26 50.5	1♈23.0	26 37.5	11 50.6	1 52.4	20 24.0	2 26.0	20 04.8	23 30.5	1 08.9
4 F	0 52 42	15 05 28	15 30 15	22 33 33	26 47.9	3 13.4	27 51.6	12 17.9	2 14.7	20 30.2	2 23.1	20 08.0	23 32.1	1 08.9
5 Sa	0 56 39	16 04 33	29 43 04	6♈58 14	26 43.1	5 05.3	29 05.7	12 45.5	2 37.1	20 36.3	2 20.2	20 11.1	23 33.7	1 08.8
6 Su	1 00 35	17 03 37	14♈18 22	21 42 32	26 36.4	6 58.6	0♈19.7	13 13.2	2 59.6	20 42.3	2 17.5	20 14.3	23 35.2	1 08.7
7 M	1 04 32	18 02 39	29 09 43	6♉38 47	26 28.5	8 53.3	1 33.8	13 41.1	3 22.1	20 48.0	2 14.8	20 17.4	23 36.8	1 08.5
8 Tu	1 08 28	19 01 39	14♉08 33	21 37 51	26 20.4	10 49.5	2 47.9	14 09.2	3 44.8	20 53.7	2 12.3	20 20.6	23 38.3	1 08.4
9 W	1 12 25	20 00 36	29 05 33	6♊30 38	26 13.3	12 47.0	4 01.9	14 37.4	4 07.5	20 59.1	2 09.8	20 23.7	23 39.7	1 08.1
10 Th	1 16 21	20 59 32	13♊52 13	21 09 34	26 07.8	14 45.9	5 16.0	15 05.8	4 30.4	21 04.4	2 07.5	20 26.8	23 41.2	1 07.9
11 F	1 20 18	21 58 25	28 22 08	5♋29 33	26 04.5	16 46.2	6 30.0	15 34.4	4 53.3	21 09.6	2 05.2	20 29.8	23 42.6	1 07.6
12 Sa	1 24 14	22 57 16	12♋31 36	19 28 15	26D 03.2	18 47.7	7 44.1	16 03.2	5 16.2	21 14.6	2 03.0	20 32.9	23 44.0	1 07.3
13 Su	1 28 11	23 56 04	26 19 32	3♌05 38	26 03.5	20 50.5	8 58.1	16 32.1	5 39.3	21 19.4	2 00.9	20 35.9	23 45.3	1 07.0
14 M	1 32 08	24 54 50	9♌46 48	16 23 19	26R 04.2	22 54.4	10 12.1	17 01.1	6 02.4	21 24.0	1 59.0	20 38.9	23 46.7	1 06.6
15 Tu	1 36 04	25 53 34	22 55 30	29 23 43	26 04.5	24 59.3	11 26.1	17 30.3	6 25.6	21 28.5	1 57.1	20 41.8	23 48.0	1 06.2
16 W	1 40 01	26 52 15	5♍48 18	12♍09 33	26 03.2	27 05.1	12 40.1	17 59.7	6 48.9	21 32.8	1 55.3	20 44.8	23 49.3	1 05.8
17 Th	1 43 57	27 50 55	18 27 47	24 43 16	25 59.6	29 11.7	13 54.0	18 29.2	7 12.2	21 36.9	1 53.6	20 47.7	23 50.5	1 05.4
18 F	1 47 54	28 49 32	0♎56 14	7♎06 54	25 53.3	1♉18.8	15 08.0	18 58.8	7 35.7	21 40.8	1 52.0	20 50.5	23 51.7	1 04.9
19 Sa	1 51 50	29 48 07	13 15 28	19 22 04	25 44.5	3 26.2	16 22.0	19 28.5	7 59.1	21 44.6	1 50.6	20 53.4	23 52.9	1 04.3
20 Su	1 55 47	0♉46 40	25 26 51	1♏29 57	25 33.5	5 33.7	17 35.9	19 58.4	8 22.7	21 48.2	1 49.2	20 56.2	23 54.1	1 03.8
21 M	1 59 43	1 45 12	7♏31 29	13 31 36	25 21.3	7 41.1	18 49.9	20 28.4	8 46.3	21 51.7	1 47.9	20 59.0	23 55.2	1 03.2
22 Tu	2 03 40	2 43 41	19 30 27	25 28 12	25 08.8	9 48.0	20 03.8	20 58.6	9 10.0	21 54.9	1 46.8	21 01.8	23 56.3	1 02.6
23 W	2 07 37	3 42 09	1♐25 03	7♐21 14	24 57.1	11 54.2	21 17.7	21 28.9	9 33.7	21 58.0	1 45.7	21 04.6	23 57.4	1 02.0
24 Th	2 11 33	4 40 35	13 17 03	19 12 47	24 47.2	13 59.2	22 31.7	21 59.3	9 57.6	22 00.9	1 44.7	21 07.3	23 58.5	1 01.3
25 F	2 15 30	5 38 59	25 08 50	1♑05 36	24 39.6	16 02.9	23 45.6	22 29.8	10 21.4	22 03.6	1 43.9	21 10.0	23 59.5	1 00.7
26 Sa	2 19 26	6 37 22	7♑03 34	13 03 12	24 34.8	18 04.9	24 59.5	23 00.4	10 45.4	22 06.1	1 43.1	21 12.6	24 00.5	1 00.0
27 Su	2 23 23	7 35 43	19 05 05	25 09 47	24 32.3	20 04.9	26 13.4	23 31.2	11 09.4	22 08.5	1 42.5	21 15.2	24 01.4	0 59.2
28 M	2 27 19	8 34 03	1♒17 54	7♒30 05	24D 31.6	22 02.6	27 27.3	24 02.0	11 33.4	22 10.6	1 41.9	21 17.8	24 02.3	0 58.4
29 Tu	2 31 16	9 32 21	13 46 55	20 09 04	24R 31.8	23 57.7	28 41.2	24 33.0	11 57.5	22 12.6	1 41.5	21 20.4	24 03.2	0 57.7
30 W	2 35 12	10 30 38	26 37 04	3♓11 29	24 31.6	25 50.0	29 55.1	25 04.1	12 21.7	22 14.4	1 41.2	21 22.9	24 04.1	0 56.8

Astro Data Dy Hr Mn	Planet Ingress Dy Hr Mn	Last Aspect Dy Hr Mn	☽ Ingress Dy Hr Mn	Last Aspect Dy Hr Mn	☽ Ingress Dy Hr Mn	☽ Phases & Eclipses Dy Hr Mn	Astro Data
☽0N 8 5:10	♂ ♋ 4 10:02	1 16:55 ♂ ☍	♑ 1 18:34	2 9:15 ♆ ☌	♓ 2 20:56	7 17:15 ● 17♓31	1 March 2008
♃⚼♄ 18 10:43	♀ ♓ 12 22:52	3 6:17 ♅ ⚹	♒ 4 4:26	4 21:44 ♀ ☌	♈ 5 0:28	14 10:47 ☽ 24♊14	Julian Day # 39507
☉0N 20 5:50	☿ ♓ 14 22:47	5 21:47 ♆ ☌	♓ 6 10:54	6 15:02 ♆ ⚹	♉ 7 1:21	21 18:41 ○ 1♎31	SVP 5♓08'34"
☽0S 21 5:21	☉ ♈ 20 5:49	7 19:05 ♅ ☌	♈ 8 14:24	8 15:14 ♆ □	♊ 9 1:28	29 21:48 ☾ 9♑34	GC 26♐57.2 ⚴ 29♓03.6
♃⚹♅ 29 0:18	⚳ ♊ 29 9:23	10 11:10 ♀ ⚹	♉ 10 16:15	10 16:12 ♆ △	♋ 11 2:44		Eris 20♈41.9 ⚵ 24♐13.2
		12 17:27 ♀ □	♊ 12 17:55	12 18:33 ☉ □	♌ 13 6:30	6 3:56 ● 16♈44	⚷ 17♒41.4 ⚶ 6♓18.6
♇ R 2 9:24	☿ ♈ 2 17:46	14 20:25 ☿ △	♋ 14 20:39	15 4:57 ☉ △	♍ 15 13:08	12 18:33 ☽ 23♋13	☽ Mean ☊ 27♒08.3
☽0N 4 15:14	♀ ♈ 6 5:36	16 18:59 ☉ △	♌ 17 1:05	17 6:00 ♃ △	♎ 17 22:11	20 10:26 ○ 0♏43	
☿0N 5 5:40	☿ ♉ 17 21:08	18 18:39 ♆ ☍	♍ 19 7:26	19 20:55 ♆ △	♏ 20 9:01	28 14:13 ☾ 8♒39	1 April 2008
♀0N 9 1:03	☉ ♉ 19 16:52	20 19:29 ♅ ☍	♎ 21 15:46	22 8:55 ♆ □	♐ 22 21:08		Julian Day # 39538
☽0S 17 11:24	♀ ♉ 30 13:35	23 12:42 ♆ △	♏ 24 2:07	24 21:39 ♆ ⚹	♑ 25 9:48		SVP 5♓08'31"
		26 0:37 ♆ □	♐ 26 14:12	27 14:19 ♀ □	♒ 27 21:28		GC 26♐57.3 ⚴ 10♈38.0
		28 13:22 ♆ ⚹	♑ 29 2:44	30 5:26 ♀ ⚹	♓ 30 6:12		Eris 21♈00.3 ⚵ 28♐54.5
		31 4:55 ☿ ⚹	♒ 31 13:35				⚷ 19♒38.8 ⚶ 21♓32.6
							☽ Mean ☊ 25♒29.8

LONGITUDE — May 2008

Day	Sid.Time	☉	0 hr ☽	Noon ☽	True ☊	☿	♀	♂	⚳	♃	♄	♅	♆	♇
1 Th	2 39 09	11♉28 53	9♓52 44	16♓41 11	24♒30.0	27♉39.2	1♉09.0	25♋35.3	12♊45.9	22♑16.0	1♍40.9	21♓25.4	24♒04.9	0♑56.0
2 F	2 43 06	12 27 06	23 37 01	0♈40 15	24R 26.1	29 25.3	2 22.9	26 06.6	13 10.2	22 17.5	1D 40.8	21 27.9	24 05.7	0R 55.1
3 Sa	2 47 02	13 25 18	7♈50 44	15 08 04	24 19.6	1♊08.0	3 36.8	26 38.1	13 34.6	22 18.7	1 40.8	21 30.3	24 06.5	0 54.2
4 Su	2 50 59	14 23 28	22 31 38	0♉00 34	24 10.6	2 47.1	4 50.6	27 09.6	13 59.0	22 19.7	1 40.9	21 32.7	24 07.2	0 53.3
5 M	2 54 55	15 21 37	7♉33 49	15 10 08	24 00.1	4 22.6	6 04.5	27 41.2	14 23.4	22 20.6	1 41.1	21 35.1	24 08.0	0 52.3
6 Tu	2 58 52	16 19 44	22 48 09	0♊26 26	23 49.2	5 54.4	7 18.4	28 13.0	14 47.9	22 21.2	1 41.4	21 37.4	24 08.6	0 51.4
7 W	3 02 48	17 17 50	8♊03 34	15 38 11	23 39.1	7 22.2	8 32.2	28 44.8	15 12.5	22 21.7	1 41.8	21 39.7	24 09.3	0 50.4
8 Th	3 06 45	18 15 54	23 09 05	0♋35 12	23 31.1	8 46.2	9 46.1	29 16.8	15 37.0	22 22.0	1 42.3	21 41.9	24 09.9	0 49.4
9 F	3 10 41	19 13 56	7♋55 44	15 10 03	23 25.7	10 06.1	10 59.9	29 48.8	16 01.7	22R 22.1	1 43.0	21 44.1	24 10.5	0 48.3
10 Sa	3 14 38	20 11 56	22 17 49	29 18 49	23 22.8	11 22.0	12 13.7	0♌21.0	16 26.4	22 22.0	1 43.7	21 46.3	24 11.0	0 47.3
11 Su	3 18 35	21 09 54	6♌13 05	13♌00 46	23 21.9	12 33.7	13 27.6	0 53.2	16 51.1	22 21.7	1 44.6	21 48.4	24 11.5	0 46.2
12 M	3 22 31	22 07 50	19 42 11	26 17 40	23 21.8	13 41.3	14 41.4	1 25.5	17 15.9	22 21.3	1 45.5	21 50.5	24 12.0	0 45.1
13 Tu	3 26 28	23 05 45	2♍47 42	9♍12 44	23 21.4	14 44.5	15 55.2	1 57.9	17 40.7	22 20.6	1 46.5	21 52.6	24 12.4	0 43.9
14 W	3 30 24	24 03 37	15 33 17	21 49 49	23 19.4	15 43.5	17 09.0	2 30.4	18 05.6	22 19.7	1 47.7	21 54.6	24 12.9	0 42.8
15 Th	3 34 21	25 01 28	28 02 51	4♎12 48	23 15.1	16 38.0	18 22.7	3 03.0	18 30.5	22 18.7	1 48.9	21 56.6	24 13.2	0 41.6
16 F	3 38 17	25 59 17	10♎20 07	16 25 09	23 08.0	17 28.1	19 36.5	3 35.6	18 55.4	22 17.5	1 50.3	21 58.5	24 13.6	0 40.4
17 Sa	3 42 14	26 57 04	22 28 16	28 29 46	22 58.1	18 13.6	20 50.3	4 08.4	19 20.4	22 16.1	1 51.8	22 00.4	24 13.9	0 39.2
18 Su	3 46 10	27 54 50	4♏29 54	10♏28 55	22 45.9	18 54.6	22 04.0	4 41.2	19 45.4	22 14.5	1 53.3	22 02.2	24 14.2	0 38.0
19 M	3 50 07	28 52 35	16 27 01	22 24 22	22 32.3	19 30.9	23 17.8	5 14.1	20 10.5	22 12.7	1 55.0	22 04.1	24 14.4	0 36.7
20 Tu	3 54 04	29 50 18	28 21 10	4♐17 33	22 18.4	20 02.6	24 31.6	5 47.1	20 35.5	22 10.7	1 56.8	22 05.8	24 14.6	0 35.5
21 W	3 58 00	0♊48 00	10♐13 43	16 09 50	22 05.3	20 29.5	25 45.3	6 20.1	21 00.7	22 08.6	1 58.6	22 07.6	24 14.8	0 34.2
22 Th	4 01 57	1 45 41	22 06 06	28 02 45	21 54.1	20 51.6	26 59.1	6 53.3	21 25.8	22 06.2	2 00.6	22 09.2	24 15.0	0 32.9
23 F	4 05 53	2 43 20	4♑00 01	9♑58 14	21 45.4	21 08.9	28 12.8	7 26.5	21 51.0	22 03.7	2 02.7	22 10.9	24 15.1	0 31.6
24 Sa	4 09 50	3 40 59	15 57 44	21 58 53	21 39.5	21 21.4	29 26.6	7 59.8	22 16.3	22 01.0	2 04.8	22 12.5	24 15.2	0 30.3
25 Su	4 13 46	4 38 36	28 02 07	4♒07 53	21 36.3	21 29.2	0♊40.3	8 33.1	22 41.5	21 58.1	2 07.1	22 14.0	24 15.3	0 28.9
26 M	4 17 43	5 36 12	10♒16 42	16 29 07	21D 35.2	21R 32.3	1 54.0	9 06.6	23 06.9	21 55.1	2 09.5	22 15.6	24R 15.3	0 27.6
27 Tu	4 21 39	6 33 48	22 45 40	29 06 55	21R 35.2	21 30.7	3 07.8	9 40.1	23 32.2	21 51.9	2 11.9	22 17.0	24 15.3	0 26.2
28 W	4 25 36	7 31 22	5♓33 26	12♓05 45	21 35.2	21 24.7	4 21.5	10 13.6	23 57.6	21 48.4	2 14.5	22 18.4	24 15.2	0 24.8
29 Th	4 29 33	8 28 55	18 44 20	25 29 37	21 34.2	21 14.3	5 35.3	10 47.3	24 23.0	21 44.9	2 17.1	22 19.8	24 15.1	0 23.4
30 F	4 33 29	9 26 28	2♈21 55	9♈21 22	21 31.2	20 59.8	6 49.0	11 21.0	24 48.4	21 41.1	2 19.9	22 21.2	24 15.0	0 22.0
31 Sa	4 37 26	10 24 00	16 27 59	23 41 35	21 25.8	20 41.5	8 02.7	11 54.8	25 13.9	21 37.2	2 22.7	22 22.4	24 14.9	0 20.5

LONGITUDE — June 2008

Day	Sid.Time	☉	0 hr ☽	Noon ☽	True ☊	☿	♀	♂	⚳	♃	♄	♅	♆	♇
1 Su	4 41 22	11♊21 31	1♉01 45	8♉27 51	21♒18.1	20♊19.8	9♊16.5	12♌28.7	25♊39.3	21♑33.1	2♍25.6	22♓23.7	24♒14.7	0♑19.1
2 M	4 45 19	12 19 02	15 59 00	23 34 09	21R 08.8	19R 54.8	10 30.2	13 02.6	26 04.9	21R 28.8	2 28.7	22 24.9	24R 14.5	0R 17.6
3 Tu	4 49 15	13 16 35	1♊12 00	8♊51 13	20 59.0	19 27.2	11 43.9	13 36.6	26 30.4	21 24.4	2 31.8	22 26.0	24 14.3	0 16.2
4 W	4 53 12	14 14 00	16 30 20	24 07 56	20 49.9	18 57.3	12 57.7	14 10.7	26 56.0	21 19.8	2 35.0	22 27.1	24 14.0	0 14.7
5 Th	4 57 08	15 11 28	1♋42 39	9♋13 15	20 42.6	18 25.7	14 11.4	14 44.8	27 21.6	21 15.1	2 38.3	22 28.2	24 13.7	0 13.2
6 F	5 01 05	16 08 54	16 38 42	23 58 09	20 37.6	17 52.9	15 25.2	15 19.0	27 47.2	21 10.2	2 41.7	22 29.2	24 13.4	0 11.7
7 Sa	5 05 02	17 06 20	1♌11 02	8♌16 56	20D 35.1	17 19.5	16 38.9	15 53.3	28 12.9	21 05.1	2 45.2	22 30.2	24 13.0	0 10.2
8 Su	5 08 58	18 03 44	15 15 41	22 07 18	20 34.6	16 45.9	17 52.6	16 27.7	28 38.6	20 59.9	2 48.8	22 31.1	24 12.6	0 08.7
9 M	5 12 55	19 01 07	28 51 58	5♍29 58	20 35.0	16 13.0	19 06.4	17 02.1	29 04.3	20 54.6	2 52.5	22 32.0	24 12.2	0 07.2
10 Tu	5 16 51	19 58 29	12♍01 43	18 27 42	20R 35.5	15 41.0	20 20.1	17 36.5	29 30.0	20 49.1	2 56.2	22 32.8	24 11.8	0 05.7
11 W	5 20 48	20 55 50	24 48 25	1♎04 26	20 35.0	15 10.7	21 33.8	18 11.0	29 55.7	20 43.5	3 00.1	22 33.6	24 11.3	0 04.2
12 Th	5 24 44	21 53 10	7♎16 18	13 24 35	20 32.7	14 42.6	22 47.5	18 45.6	0♋21.5	20 37.7	3 04.0	22 34.3	24 10.7	0 02.6
13 F	5 28 41	22 50 29	19 29 47	25 32 27	20 28.1	14 17.0	24 01.2	19 20.3	0 47.3	20 31.9	3 08.0	22 35.0	24 10.2	0 01.1
14 Sa	5 32 38	23 47 47	1♏33 02	7♏31 58	20 21.3	13 54.5	25 14.9	19 55.0	1 13.1	20 25.8	3 12.1	22 35.6	24 09.6	29♐59.6
15 Su	5 36 34	24 45 04	13 29 41	19 26 31	20 12.6	13 35.4	26 28.6	20 29.7	1 38.9	20 19.7	3 16.3	22 36.2	24 09.0	29 58.0
16 M	5 40 31	25 42 21	25 22 49	1♐18 51	20 02.8	13 20.0	27 42.3	21 04.5	2 04.7	20 13.5	3 20.5	22 36.7	24 08.4	29 56.5
17 Tu	5 44 27	26 39 37	7♐14 53	13 11 09	19 52.6	13 08.7	28 56.0	21 39.4	2 30.6	20 07.1	3 24.9	22 37.2	24 07.7	29 54.9
18 W	5 48 24	27 36 53	19 07 52	25 05 13	19 43.1	13 01.5	0♋09.7	22 14.3	2 56.4	20 00.6	3 29.3	22 37.6	24 07.0	29 53.4
19 Th	5 52 20	28 34 07	1♑03 25	7♑02 38	19 35.0	12D 58.8	1 23.5	22 49.3	3 22.3	19 54.0	3 33.8	22 38.0	24 06.3	29 51.8
20 F	5 56 17	29 31 22	13 03 05	19 04 58	19 28.9	13 00.6	2 37.2	23 24.4	3 48.2	19 47.3	3 38.3	22 38.4	24 05.6	29 50.3
21 Sa	6 00 13	0♋28 36	25 08 30	1♒13 59	19 25.0	13 07.0	3 50.9	23 59.5	4 14.1	19 40.5	3 43.0	22 38.6	24 04.8	29 48.7
22 Su	6 04 10	1 25 50	7♒21 40	13 31 52	19D 23.3	13 18.1	5 04.6	24 34.6	4 40.1	19 33.7	3 47.7	22 38.9	24 04.0	29 47.2
23 M	6 08 07	2 23 03	19 44 55	26 01 12	19 23.3	13 34.0	6 18.3	25 09.8	5 06.0	19 26.7	3 52.5	22 39.1	24 03.1	29 45.6
24 Tu	6 12 03	3 20 16	2♓21 07	8♓45 03	19 24.4	13 54.5	7 32.0	25 45.1	5 32.0	19 19.6	3 57.4	22 39.2	24 02.3	29 44.1
25 W	6 16 00	4 17 30	15 13 25	21 46 37	19 25.6	14 19.8	8 45.7	26 20.4	5 58.0	19 12.5	4 02.3	22 39.3	24 01.4	29 42.5
26 Th	6 19 56	5 14 43	28 25 02	5♈09 00	19R 26.2	14 49.7	9 59.5	26 55.8	6 24.0	19 05.3	4 07.3	22R 39.4	24 00.5	29 41.0
27 F	6 23 53	6 11 56	11♈58 46	18 54 31	19 25.5	15 24.2	11 13.2	27 31.2	6 50.0	18 58.0	4 12.4	22 39.4	23 59.5	29 39.4
28 Sa	6 27 49	7 09 09	25 56 17	3♉04 01	19 23.1	16 03.3	12 26.9	28 06.7	7 16.0	18 50.6	4 17.6	22 39.3	23 58.6	29 37.9
29 Su	6 31 46	8 06 23	10♉17 27	17 36 10	19 19.0	16 47.0	13 40.7	28 42.2	7 42.0	18 43.2	4 22.8	22 39.2	23 57.6	29 36.3
30 M	6 35 42	9 03 36	24 59 35	2♊26 53	19 13.8	17 35.0	14 54.4	29 17.8	8 08.1	18 35.7	4 28.1	22 39.1	23 56.6	29 34.8

Astro Data (Dy Hr Mn)

Astro Data	Dy Hr Mn
☽0N	2 1:01
♄D	3 3:08
♃R	9 12:12
☽0S	14 16:17
♃✶♅	21 18:06
☿R	26 15:49
♆R	26 16:16
☽0N	29 8:56
☽0S	10 21:40
☿D	19 14:32
☽0N	25 14:49
♃⚼♄	26 7:58
♅R	27 0:02

Planet Ingress (Dy Hr Mn)

Planet Ingress	Dy Hr Mn
☿ ♊	2 20:01
♂ ♌	9 20:21
☉ ♊	20 16:02
♀ ♊	24 22:53
⚳ ♋	11 15:59
♇ ♐R	14 5:14
♀ ♋	18 8:50
☉ ♋	21 0:00

Last Aspect / ☽ Ingress (May)

Last Aspect Dy Hr Mn		☽ Ingress	Dy Hr Mn
2 9:36	♆ ✶	♈	2 10:52
4 7:17	♂ □	♉	4 11:59
6 8:23	♂ ✶	♊	6 11:18
8 1:37	♆ △	♋	8 11:03
10 0:07	♃ ☍	♌	10 13:11
12 8:10	♆ ☍	♍	12 18:49
14 16:39	☉ △	♎	15 3:47
17 3:30	♆ △	♏	17 15:00
20 2:12	☉ ☍	♐	20 3:20
22 4:20	♆ ✶	♑	22 15:56
24 12:27	♅ ✶	♒	25 3:53
27 2:50	♆ ☌	♓	27 13:39
29 6:24	♅ ☌	♈	29 19:54
31 12:55	♆ ✶	♉	31 22:20

Last Aspect / ☽ Ingress (June)

Last Aspect Dy Hr Mn		☽ Ingress	Dy Hr Mn
2 13:04	♆ □	♊	2 22:07
4 12:10	♆ △	♋	4 21:17
6 9:33	♅ △	♌	6 22:01
8 15:42	♆ ☍	♍	9 2:02
10 19:43	♅ ☍	♎	11 9:56
13 9:16	♆ △	♏	13 20:54
15 21:30	♅ △	♐	16 9:21
18 21:38	♇ ☌	♑	18 21:53
20 19:03	♅ ✶	♒	21 9:35
23 19:05	♇ ✶	♓	23 19:33
26 2:17	♇ □	♈	26 2:50
28 6:15	♇ △	♉	28 6:51
30 6:44	♂ □	♊	30 8:04

☽ Phases & Eclipses (Dy Hr Mn)

Dy Hr Mn	Phase
5 12:19	● 15♉22
12 3:48	☽ 21♌48
20 2:12	○ 29♏27
28 2:58	☾ 7♓10
3 19:24	● 13♊34
10 15:05	☽ 20♍06
18 17:32	○ 27♐50
26 12:11	☾ 5♈15

Astro Data

1 May 2008
Julian Day # 39568
SVP 5♓08'27"
GC 26♐57.3 ⚵ 22♈22.5
Eris 21♈19.8 ❋ 29♐12.2R
⚷ 20♒50.6 ⚴ 5♈35.5
☽ Mean ☊ 23♒54.4

1 June 2008
Julian Day # 39599
SVP 5♓08'23"
GC 26♐57.4 ⚵ 4♉47.6
Eris 21♈36.7 ❋ 24♐33.1R
⚷ 21♒07.4R ⚴ 19♈01.6
☽ Mean ☊ 22♒16.0

July 2008 LONGITUDE

Day	Sid.Time	☉	0 hr ☽	Noon ☽	True ☊	☿	♀	♂	⚳	♃	♄	♅	♆	♇
1 Tu	6 39 39	10♋00 50	9♊57 08	17♊29 17	19♒08.1	18♊27.5	16♋08.2	29♌53.5	8♋34.1	18♑28.2	4♍33.5	22♓38.9	23♒55.5	29♐33.3
2 W	6 43 36	10 58 04	25 02 08	2♋34 29	19R 02.7	19 24.3	17 21.9	0♍29.2	9 00.2	18R 20.6	4 38.9	22R 38.7	23R 54.5	29R 31.8
3 Th	6 47 32	11 55 18	10♋05 07	17 32 52	18 58.5	20 25.4	18 35.7	1 05.0	9 26.3	18 13.0	4 44.4	22 38.4	23 53.4	29 30.3
4 F	6 51 29	12 52 31	24 56 43	2♌15 44	18 55.8	21 30.8	19 49.5	1 40.8	9 52.3	18 05.4	4 50.0	22 38.0	23 52.3	29 28.8
5 Sa	6 55 25	13 49 45	9♌29 12	16 36 32	18D 54.8	22 40.2	21 03.2	2 16.7	10 18.4	17 57.7	4 55.6	22 37.7	23 51.1	29 27.3
6 Su	6 59 22	14 46 58	23 37 22	0♍31 31	18 55.2	23 53.8	22 17.0	2 52.6	10 44.5	17 50.0	5 01.3	22 37.2	23 50.0	29 25.8
7 M	7 03 18	15 44 11	7♍18 57	13 59 46	18 56.5	25 11.5	23 30.7	3 28.6	11 10.6	17 42.3	5 07.0	22 36.7	23 48.8	29 24.3
8 Tu	7 07 15	16 41 24	20 34 13	27 02 39	18 58.0	26 33.1	24 44.5	4 04.6	11 36.7	17 34.6	5 12.9	22 36.2	23 47.6	29 22.8
9 W	7 11 11	17 38 37	3♎25 28	9♎43 11	18R 59.2	27 58.7	25 58.2	4 40.7	12 02.8	17 26.9	5 18.7	22 35.6	23 46.4	29 21.4
10 Th	7 15 08	18 35 49	15 56 17	22 05 21	18 59.4	29 28.2	27 12.0	5 16.8	12 28.9	17 19.2	5 24.6	22 35.0	23 45.1	29 19.9
11 F	7 19 05	19 33 02	28 10 56	4♏13 36	18 58.4	1♋01.4	28 25.8	5 53.0	12 55.0	17 11.5	5 30.6	22 34.4	23 43.8	29 18.5
12 Sa	7 23 01	20 30 15	10♏13 54	16 12 23	18 56.1	2 38.4	29 39.5	6 29.3	13 21.2	17 03.8	5 36.7	22 33.7	23 42.6	29 17.0
13 Su	7 26 58	21 27 27	22 09 32	28 05 52	18 52.7	4 18.9	0♌53.3	7 05.5	13 47.3	16 56.1	5 42.8	22 32.9	23 41.3	29 15.6
14 M	7 30 54	22 24 40	4♐01 50	9♐57 50	18 48.6	6 02.9	2 07.0	7 41.9	14 13.4	16 48.4	5 48.9	22 32.1	23 39.9	29 14.2
15 Tu	7 34 51	23 21 53	15 54 16	21 51 29	18 44.3	7 50.2	3 20.8	8 18.3	14 39.5	16 40.8	5 55.1	22 31.3	23 38.6	29 12.8
16 W	7 38 47	24 19 06	27 49 48	3♑49 29	18 40.3	9 40.7	4 34.5	8 54.7	15 05.6	16 33.2	6 01.4	22 30.4	23 37.2	29 11.5
17 Th	7 42 44	25 16 19	9♑50 48	15 53 59	18 37.0	11 34.0	5 48.3	9 31.2	15 31.7	16 25.6	6 07.7	22 29.4	23 35.9	29 10.1
18 F	7 46 41	26 13 33	21 59 13	28 06 41	18 34.6	13 30.1	7 02.0	10 07.7	15 57.9	16 18.1	6 14.0	22 28.5	23 34.5	29 08.8
19 Sa	7 50 37	27 10 47	4♒16 35	10♒29 03	18D 33.4	15 28.6	8 15.8	10 44.3	16 24.0	16 10.6	6 20.5	22 27.4	23 33.1	29 07.4
20 Su	7 54 34	28 08 02	16 44 14	23 02 19	18 33.2	17 29.3	9 29.5	11 20.9	16 50.1	16 03.2	6 26.9	22 26.4	23 31.6	29 06.1
21 M	7 58 30	29 05 17	29 23 27	5♓47 47	18 33.9	19 31.8	10 43.3	11 57.6	17 16.2	15 55.9	6 33.4	22 25.3	23 30.2	29 04.8
22 Tu	8 02 27	0♌02 33	12♓15 29	18 46 43	18 35.2	21 35.8	11 57.0	12 34.3	17 42.3	15 48.6	6 40.0	22 24.1	23 28.7	29 03.6
23 W	8 06 23	0 59 50	25 21 38	2♈00 24	18 36.5	23 41.1	13 10.8	13 11.1	18 08.4	15 41.3	6 46.5	22 22.9	23 27.3	29 02.3
24 Th	8 10 20	1 57 07	8♈43 10	15 30 03	18 37.5	25 47.2	14 24.6	13 47.9	18 34.5	15 34.2	6 53.2	22 21.7	23 25.8	29 01.0
25 F	8 14 16	2 54 26	22 21 06	29 16 23	18R 38.1	27 53.9	15 38.3	14 24.8	19 00.7	15 27.1	6 59.9	22 20.4	23 24.3	28 59.8
26 Sa	8 18 13	3 51 45	6♉15 51	13♉19 24	18 37.9	0♌00.9	16 52.1	15 01.7	19 26.8	15 20.1	7 06.6	22 19.1	23 22.8	28 58.6
27 Su	8 22 09	4 49 06	20 26 50	27 37 53	18 37.1	2 07.9	18 05.8	15 38.7	19 52.9	15 13.2	7 13.3	22 17.8	23 21.3	28 57.4
28 M	8 26 06	5 46 27	4♊52 07	12♊09 03	18 35.9	4 14.6	19 19.6	16 15.7	20 18.9	15 06.4	7 20.1	22 16.4	23 19.7	28 56.2
29 Tu	8 30 03	6 43 50	19 28 05	26 48 31	18 34.5	6 20.8	20 33.4	16 52.8	20 45.0	14 59.7	7 27.0	22 15.0	23 18.2	28 55.1
30 W	8 33 59	7 41 14	4♋09 35	11♋30 27	18 33.2	8 26.3	21 47.2	17 29.9	21 11.1	14 53.1	7 33.9	22 13.5	23 16.6	28 54.0
31 Th	8 37 56	8 38 38	18 50 18	26 08 16	18 32.2	10 30.8	23 00.9	18 07.1	21 37.2	14 46.6	7 40.8	22 12.0	23 15.1	28 52.9

August 2008 LONGITUDE

Day	Sid.Time	☉	0 hr ☽	Noon ☽	True ☊	☿	♀	♂	⚳	♃	♄	♅	♆	♇
1 F	8 41 52	9♌36 04	3♌23 32	10♌35 22	18♒31.8	12♌34.4	24♌14.7	18♍44.4	22♋03.3	14♑40.2	7♍47.8	22♓10.4	23♒13.5	28♐51.8
2 Sa	8 45 49	10 33 30	17 43 03	24 46 03	18D 31.7	14 36.7	25 28.5	19 21.6	22 29.3	14R 33.9	7 54.7	22R 08.9	23R 11.9	28R 50.7
3 Su	8 49 45	11 30 57	1♍43 53	8♍36 15	18 32.1	16 37.8	26 42.2	19 59.0	22 55.3	14 27.8	8 01.8	22 07.2	23 10.3	28 49.7
4 M	8 53 42	12 28 25	15 22 54	22 03 47	18 32.6	18 37.6	27 56.0	20 36.4	23 21.4	14 21.8	8 08.8	22 05.6	23 08.7	28 48.7
5 Tu	8 57 39	13 25 53	28 38 56	5♎08 29	18 33.1	20 35.9	29 09.8	21 13.8	23 47.4	14 15.9	8 15.9	22 03.9	23 07.1	28 47.7
6 W	9 01 35	14 23 22	11♎32 41	17 51 51	18 33.6	22 32.8	0♍23.5	21 51.3	24 13.4	14 10.1	8 23.0	22 02.2	23 05.5	28 46.7
7 Th	9 05 32	15 20 53	24 06 23	0♏16 43	18 33.9	24 28.2	1 37.3	22 28.8	24 39.4	14 04.5	8 30.2	22 00.4	23 03.9	28 45.7
8 F	9 09 28	16 18 23	6♏23 23	12 26 53	18R 34.0	26 22.0	2 51.0	23 06.4	25 05.3	13 59.0	8 37.4	21 58.6	23 02.3	28 44.8
9 Sa	9 13 25	17 15 55	18 27 47	24 26 40	18 34.0	28 14.4	4 04.8	23 44.1	25 31.3	13 53.6	8 44.6	21 56.8	23 00.7	28 43.9
10 Su	9 17 21	18 13 28	0♐24 04	6♐20 34	18D 33.9	0♍05.2	5 18.5	24 21.7	25 57.2	13 48.4	8 51.8	21 55.0	22 59.0	28 43.0
11 M	9 21 18	19 11 01	12 16 44	18 13 06	18 34.0	1 54.5	6 32.2	24 59.5	26 23.2	13 43.4	8 59.1	21 53.1	22 57.4	28 42.2
12 Tu	9 25 14	20 08 36	24 10 11	0♑08 28	18 34.1	3 42.3	7 45.9	25 37.3	26 49.1	13 38.5	9 06.4	21 51.2	22 55.8	28 41.4
13 W	9 29 11	21 06 11	6♑08 25	12 10 26	18 34.3	5 28.6	8 59.6	26 15.1	27 15.0	13 33.8	9 13.7	21 49.2	22 54.1	28 40.6
14 Th	9 33 08	22 03 48	18 14 54	24 22 09	18 34.6	7 13.4	10 13.3	26 53.0	27 40.8	13 29.2	9 21.0	21 47.3	22 52.5	28 39.8
15 F	9 37 04	23 01 25	0♒32 29	6♒46 07	18R 34.9	8 56.7	11 27.0	27 30.9	28 06.7	13 24.8	9 28.3	21 45.3	22 50.9	28 39.1
16 Sa	9 41 01	23 59 04	13 03 14	19 24 00	18 35.0	10 38.5	12 40.7	28 08.9	28 32.5	13 20.5	9 35.7	21 43.3	22 49.2	28 38.3
17 Su	9 44 57	24 56 44	25 48 28	2♓16 41	18 34.8	12 18.8	13 54.4	28 46.9	28 58.3	13 16.5	9 43.1	21 41.2	22 47.6	28 37.6
18 M	9 48 54	25 54 25	8♓48 40	15 24 20	18 34.3	13 57.8	15 08.1	29 24.9	29 24.1	13 12.5	9 50.5	21 39.2	22 46.0	28 37.0
19 Tu	9 52 50	26 52 08	22 03 37	28 46 23	18 33.5	15 35.2	16 21.7	0♎03.1	29 49.9	13 08.8	9 57.9	21 37.1	22 44.3	28 36.3
20 W	9 56 47	27 49 52	5♈32 29	12♈21 45	18 32.4	17 11.3	17 35.4	0 41.2	0♌15.6	13 05.2	10 05.4	21 34.9	22 42.7	28 35.7
21 Th	10 00 43	28 47 37	19 13 59	26 08 59	18 31.2	18 45.9	18 49.1	1 19.4	0 41.3	13 01.8	10 12.8	21 32.8	22 41.1	28 35.1
22 F	10 04 40	29 45 25	3♉06 31	10♉06 22	18 30.3	20 19.1	20 02.7	1 57.7	1 07.0	12 58.6	10 20.3	21 30.6	22 39.5	28 34.6
23 Sa	10 08 36	0♍43 14	17 08 17	24 12 02	18D 29.7	21 50.9	21 16.3	2 36.0	1 32.7	12 55.5	10 27.8	21 28.5	22 37.8	28 34.1
24 Su	10 12 33	1 41 05	1♊17 19	8♊23 54	18 29.7	23 21.3	22 30.0	3 14.4	1 58.3	12 52.6	10 35.3	21 26.3	22 36.2	28 33.6
25 M	10 16 30	2 38 58	15 31 28	22 39 43	18 30.3	24 50.2	23 43.6	3 52.9	2 24.0	12 50.0	10 42.8	21 24.0	22 34.6	28 33.1
26 Tu	10 20 26	3 36 53	29 48 19	6♋56 53	18 31.3	26 17.7	24 57.3	4 31.3	2 49.6	12 47.4	10 50.3	21 21.8	22 33.0	28 32.7
27 W	10 24 23	4 34 49	14♋05 04	21 12 26	18 32.5	27 43.8	26 10.9	5 09.9	3 15.1	12 45.1	10 57.8	21 19.6	22 31.4	28 32.3
28 Th	10 28 19	5 32 48	28 18 34	5♌23 01	18R 33.4	29 08.4	27 24.5	5 48.5	3 40.7	12 43.0	11 05.4	21 17.3	22 29.8	28 31.9
29 F	10 32 16	6 30 47	12♌25 20	19 25 05	18 33.7	0♎31.5	28 38.1	6 27.1	4 06.2	12 41.0	11 12.9	21 15.0	22 28.3	28 31.5
30 Sa	10 36 12	7 28 49	26 21 49	3♍15 09	18 33.2	1 53.1	29 51.7	7 05.8	4 31.6	12 39.3	11 20.5	21 12.7	22 26.7	28 31.2
31 Su	10 40 09	8 26 52	10♍04 42	16 50 10	18 31.7	3 13.1	1♎05.3	7 44.5	4 57.1	12 37.7	11 28.0	21 10.4	22 25.1	28 30.9

Astro Data	Dy Hr Mn
☽ 0S	8 4:52
☽ 0N	22 19:52
☽ 0S	4 13:49
☽ 0N	19 1:49
♂ 0S	21 14:31
☿ 0S	28 5:14
☽ 0S	31 23:14

Planet Ingress	Dy Hr Mn
♂ ♍	1 16:22
☿ ♋	10 20:18
♀ ♌	12 18:40
☉ ♌	22 10:56
☿ ♌	26 11:49
♀ ♍	6 4:21
☿ ♍	10 10:52
♂ ♎	19 10:04
⚳ ♌	19 21:28
☉ ♍	22 18:03
☿ ♎	29 2:51
♀ ♎	30 14:42

Last Aspect Dy Hr Mn		☽ Ingress	Dy Hr Mn
2 7:09	♇ ☍	♋	2 7:54
3 20:15	♅ △	♌	4 8:16
6 10:05	♇ △	♍	6 11:05
8 16:22	♇ □	♎	8 17:32
11 2:15	♇ ⚹	♏	11 3:36
13 3:06	♆ □	♐	13 15:51
16 2:45	♇ ☌	♑	16 4:21
18 8:00	☉ ☍	♒	18 15:41
20 23:26	♇ ⚹	♓	21 1:09
23 6:40	♇ □	♈	23 8:23
25 11:31	♇ △	♉	25 13:15
27 4:53	♆ □	♊	27 15:56
29 15:26	♇ ☍	♋	29 17:13
31 5:32	♅ △	♌	31 18:23

Last Aspect Dy Hr Mn		☽ Ingress	Dy Hr Mn
2 19:00	♇ △	♍	2 21:00
5 0:17	♇ □	♎	5 2:29
7 9:03	♇ ⚹	♏	7 11:27
9 21:03	☿ □	♐	9 23:11
12 9:05	♇ ☌	♑	12 11:43
14 17:10	♂ △	♒	14 22:57
17 5:15	♇ ⚹	♓	17 7:47
19 11:42	♇ □	♈	19 14:11
21 16:54	☉ △	♉	21 18:39
23 9:20	♆ □	♊	23 21:49
25 21:53	♇ ☍	♋	26 0:20
28 0:15	☿ ⚹	♌	28 2:52
30 3:45	♇ △	♍	30 6:19

☽ Phases & Eclipses Dy Hr Mn	
3 2:20	● 11♋32
10 4:36	☽ 18♎18
18 8:00	○ 26♑04
25 18:43	☾ 3♉10
1 10:14	● 9♌32
1 10:22:10	● T 02'27"
8 20:21	☽ 16♏38
16 21:18	○ 24♒21
16 21:11	○ P 0.807
23 23:51	☾ 1♊12
30 19:59	● 7♍48

Astro Data

1 July 2008
Julian Day # 39629
SVP 5♓08'17"
GC 26♐57.5 ⚴ 16♉50.3
Eris 21♈46.2 ⚵ 17♐57.9R
⚷ 20♒27.1R ⚶ 0♉27.0
☽ Mean ☊ 20♒40.7

1 August 2008
Julian Day # 39660
SVP 5♓08'11"
GC 26♐57.6 ⚴ 28♉56.4
Eris 21♈46.5R ⚵ 14♐07.8R
⚷ 19♒02.7R ⚶ 9♉40.8
☽ Mean ☊ 19♒02.2

LONGITUDE — September 2008

Day	Sid.Time	☉	0 hr ☽	Noon ☽	True ☊	☿	♀	♂	⚳	♃	♄	♅	♆	♇
1 M	10 44 06	9♍24 57	23♍31 18	0♎07 56	18♒29.2	4♎31.5	2♎18.9	8♎23.3	5♌22.5	12♑36.3	11♍35.6	21♓08.0	22♒23.6	28♐30.7
2 Tu	10 48 02	10 23 03	6♎39 57	13 07 21	18R 26.0	5 48.3	3 32.4	9 02.2	5 47.8	12R 35.1	11 43.1	21R 05.7	22R 22.0	28R 30.5
3 W	10 51 59	11 21 10	19 30 10	25 48 35	18 22.5	7 03.4	4 46.0	9 41.1	6 13.2	12 34.1	11 50.7	21 03.3	22 20.5	28 30.3
4 Th	10 55 55	12 19 20	2♏02 47	8♏13 06	18 19.1	8 16.7	5 59.6	10 20.0	6 38.4	12 33.3	11 58.3	21 01.0	22 19.0	28 30.1
5 F	10 59 52	13 17 31	14 19 52	20 23 32	18 16.4	9 28.1	7 13.1	10 59.0	7 03.7	12 32.7	12 05.8	20 58.6	22 17.5	28 30.0
6 Sa	11 03 48	14 15 43	26 24 33	2♐23 27	18 14.6	10 37.6	8 26.6	11 38.1	7 28.9	12 32.3	12 13.4	20 56.2	22 16.0	28 29.9
7 Su	11 07 45	15 13 57	8♐20 46	14 17 06	18D 13.9	11 45.1	9 40.1	12 17.2	7 54.1	12D 32.1	12 21.0	20 53.9	22 14.5	28 29.8
8 M	11 11 41	16 12 12	20 13 03	26 09 12	18 14.4	12 50.4	10 53.6	12 56.3	8 19.2	12 32.0	12 28.5	20 51.5	22 13.0	28D 29.8
9 Tu	11 15 38	17 10 29	2♑06 11	8♑04 35	18 15.7	13 53.4	12 07.1	13 35.5	8 44.3	12 32.2	12 36.1	20 49.1	22 11.6	28 29.8
10 W	11 19 34	18 08 47	14 05 00	20 08 01	18 17.4	14 54.1	13 20.6	14 14.8	9 09.3	12 32.5	12 43.6	20 46.7	22 10.1	28 29.8
11 Th	11 23 31	19 07 07	26 14 08	2♒23 52	18 19.0	15 52.2	14 34.0	14 54.1	9 34.3	12 33.1	12 51.1	20 44.3	22 08.7	28 29.8
12 F	11 27 28	20 05 29	8♒37 38	14 55 50	18R 19.9	16 47.6	15 47.4	15 33.4	9 59.3	12 33.8	12 58.7	20 41.9	22 07.3	28 29.9
13 Sa	11 31 24	21 03 52	21 18 44	27 46 35	18 19.5	17 40.1	17 00.9	16 12.8	10 24.2	12 34.7	13 06.2	20 39.5	22 05.9	28 30.1
14 Su	11 35 21	22 02 17	4♓19 28	10♓57 26	18 17.7	18 29.4	18 14.3	16 52.3	10 49.0	12 35.8	13 13.7	20 37.1	22 04.6	28 30.2
15 M	11 39 17	23 00 44	17 40 24	24 28 10	18 14.2	19 15.4	19 27.6	17 31.8	11 13.8	12 37.1	13 21.2	20 34.7	22 03.2	28 30.4
16 Tu	11 43 14	23 59 12	1♈20 26	8♈16 51	18 09.3	19 57.8	20 41.0	18 11.3	11 38.5	12 38.6	13 28.7	20 32.3	22 01.9	28 30.6
17 W	11 47 10	24 57 43	15 16 55	22 20 06	18 03.7	20 36.3	21 54.4	18 50.9	12 03.2	12 40.3	13 36.1	20 29.9	22 00.6	28 30.8
18 Th	11 51 07	25 56 15	29 25 49	6♉33 28	17 57.9	21 10.7	23 07.7	19 30.6	12 27.9	12 42.2	13 43.6	20 27.5	21 59.3	28 31.1
19 F	11 55 03	26 54 50	13♉42 25	20 52 05	17 52.9	21 40.6	24 21.0	20 10.3	12 52.5	12 44.2	13 51.0	20 25.1	21 58.0	28 31.4
20 Sa	11 59 00	27 53 27	28 01 55	5♊11 23	17 49.2	22 05.6	25 34.3	20 50.1	13 17.0	12 46.5	13 58.5	20 22.7	21 56.7	28 31.8
21 Su	12 02 57	28 52 07	12♊20 05	19 27 36	17D 47.2	22 25.5	26 47.6	21 29.9	13 41.5	12 48.9	14 05.9	20 20.4	21 55.5	28 32.2
22 M	12 06 53	29 50 48	26 33 40	3♋38 01	17 46.9	22 39.7	28 00.9	22 09.8	14 05.9	12 51.5	14 13.3	20 18.0	21 54.3	28 32.6
23 Tu	12 10 50	0♎49 32	10♋40 30	17 40 57	17 47.8	22R 48.1	29 14.2	22 49.7	14 30.3	12 54.3	14 20.7	20 15.7	21 53.1	28 33.0
24 W	12 14 46	1 48 18	24 39 17	1♌35 25	17 49.1	22 50.0	0♏27.5	23 29.7	14 54.6	12 57.3	14 28.0	20 13.3	21 51.9	28 33.5
25 Th	12 18 43	2 47 07	8♌29 16	15 20 47	17R 49.9	22 45.3	1 40.7	24 09.7	15 18.9	13 00.5	14 35.3	20 11.0	21 50.8	28 34.0
26 F	12 22 39	3 45 57	22 09 51	28 56 24	17 49.3	22 33.6	2 53.9	24 49.8	15 43.0	13 03.8	14 42.6	20 08.7	21 49.7	28 34.5
27 Sa	12 26 36	4 44 50	5♍40 18	12♍21 25	17 46.8	22 14.5	4 07.2	25 30.0	16 07.1	13 07.4	14 49.9	20 06.4	21 48.6	28 35.1
28 Su	12 30 32	5 43 44	18 59 38	25 34 48	17 41.9	21 48.0	5 20.4	26 10.2	16 31.2	13 11.1	14 57.2	20 04.1	21 47.5	28 35.7
29 M	12 34 29	6 42 41	2♎06 45	8♎35 23	17 34.9	21 14.0	6 33.6	26 50.4	16 55.1	13 15.0	15 04.4	20 01.8	21 46.4	28 36.3
30 Tu	12 38 26	7 41 40	15 00 36	21 22 19	17 26.2	20 32.5	7 46.7	27 30.7	17 19.0	13 19.1	15 11.6	19 59.5	21 45.4	28 36.9

LONGITUDE — October 2008

Day	Sid.Time	☉	0 hr ☽	Noon ☽	True ☊	☿	♀	♂	⚳	♃	♄	♅	♆	♇
1 W	12 42 22	8♎40 41	27♎40 32	3♏55 16	17♒16.6	19♎44.0	8♏59.9	28♎11.1	17♌42.9	13♑23.3	15♍18.8	19♓57.3	21♒44.4	28♐37.6
2 Th	12 46 19	9 39 43	10♏06 37	16 14 43	17R 07.2	18R 48.9	10 13.0	28 51.5	18 06.6	13 27.7	15 25.9	19R 55.1	21R 43.5	28 38.4
3 F	12 50 15	10 38 48	22 19 48	28 22 08	16 58.7	17 48.1	11 26.1	29 32.0	18 30.3	13 32.4	15 33.0	19 52.9	21 42.5	28 39.1
4 Sa	12 54 12	11 37 55	4♐22 05	10♐20 02	16 51.9	16 42.8	12 39.2	0♏12.5	18 53.9	13 37.1	15 40.1	19 50.7	21 41.6	28 39.9
5 Su	12 58 08	12 37 03	16 16 28	22 11 53	16 47.3	15 34.3	13 52.3	0 53.1	19 17.4	13 42.1	15 47.2	19 48.5	21 40.7	28 40.7
6 M	13 02 05	13 36 13	28 06 51	4♑01 56	16D 44.9	14 24.2	15 05.4	1 33.7	19 40.8	13 47.2	15 54.2	19 46.4	21 39.8	28 41.6
7 Tu	13 06 01	14 35 25	9♑57 48	15 55 05	16 44.4	13 14.4	16 18.4	2 14.4	20 04.2	13 52.5	16 01.1	19 44.3	21 39.0	28 42.4
8 W	13 09 58	15 34 39	21 54 27	27 56 34	16 44.9	12 06.8	17 31.4	2 55.2	20 27.4	13 58.0	16 08.1	19 42.2	21 38.2	28 43.3
9 Th	13 13 55	16 33 54	4♒02 04	10♒11 38	16R 45.7	11 03.4	18 44.4	3 36.0	20 50.6	14 03.6	16 15.0	19 40.1	21 37.4	28 44.3
10 F	13 17 51	17 33 12	16 25 49	22 45 12	16 45.7	10 05.9	19 57.4	4 16.8	21 13.7	14 09.4	16 21.8	19 38.1	21 36.7	28 45.2
11 Sa	13 21 48	18 32 31	29 10 15	5♓41 21	16 44.0	9 16.1	21 10.3	4 57.7	21 36.7	14 15.3	16 28.6	19 36.1	21 36.0	28 46.2
12 Su	13 25 44	19 31 51	12♓18 47	19 02 41	16 40.0	8 35.1	22 23.2	5 38.6	21 59.5	14 21.4	16 35.4	19 34.1	21 35.3	28 47.2
13 M	13 29 41	20 31 14	25 53 03	2♈49 42	16 33.4	8 04.2	23 36.1	6 19.6	22 22.3	14 27.7	16 42.2	19 32.1	21 34.6	28 48.3
14 Tu	13 33 37	21 30 39	9♈52 19	17 00 23	16 24.7	7 43.9	24 49.0	7 00.7	22 45.1	14 34.1	16 48.8	19 30.2	21 34.0	28 49.4
15 W	13 37 34	22 30 05	24 13 14	1♉30 02	16 14.5	7D 34.6	26 01.8	7 41.8	23 07.7	14 40.7	16 55.5	19 28.3	21 33.4	28 50.5
16 Th	13 41 30	23 29 34	8♉49 52	16 11 45	16 04.1	7 36.4	27 14.7	8 23.0	23 30.2	14 47.4	17 02.1	19 26.4	21 32.8	28 51.6
17 F	13 45 27	24 29 05	23 34 38	0♊57 30	15 54.6	7 49.0	28 27.4	9 04.2	23 52.6	14 54.3	17 08.6	19 24.6	21 32.3	28 52.8
18 Sa	13 49 24	25 28 38	8♊19 23	15 39 27	15 47.1	8 12.0	29 40.2	9 45.4	24 14.9	15 01.3	17 15.1	19 22.8	21 31.8	28 54.0
19 Su	13 53 20	26 28 14	22 56 56	0♋11 14	15 42.1	8 44.7	0♐52.9	10 26.8	24 37.1	15 08.5	17 21.6	19 21.0	21 31.3	28 55.2
20 M	13 57 17	27 27 52	7♋21 56	14 28 41	15 39.6	9 26.5	2 05.7	11 08.2	24 59.2	15 15.9	17 28.0	19 19.2	21 30.9	28 56.4
21 Tu	14 01 13	28 27 32	21 31 20	28 29 50	15D 39.0	10 16.6	3 18.4	11 49.6	25 21.2	15 23.4	17 34.4	19 17.5	21 30.5	28 57.7
22 W	14 05 10	29 27 14	5♌24 12	12♌14 34	15R 39.2	11 14.1	4 31.0	12 31.1	25 43.0	15 31.0	17 40.7	19 15.9	21 30.1	28 59.0
23 Th	14 09 06	0♏26 59	19 01 04	25 43 54	15 38.9	12 18.2	5 43.7	13 12.7	26 04.8	15 38.8	17 46.9	19 14.2	21 29.7	29 00.3
24 F	14 13 03	1 26 46	2♍23 17	8♍59 23	15 36.9	13 28.0	6 56.3	13 54.3	26 26.4	15 46.7	17 53.1	19 12.6	21 29.4	29 01.7
25 Sa	14 16 59	2 26 35	15 32 23	22 02 27	15 32.4	14 42.9	8 08.9	14 35.9	26 47.9	15 54.7	17 59.2	19 11.1	21 29.1	29 03.1
26 Su	14 20 56	3 26 26	28 29 42	4♎54 13	15 24.7	16 02.1	9 21.4	15 17.6	27 09.3	16 02.9	18 05.3	19 09.6	21 28.9	29 04.5
27 M	14 24 53	4 26 19	11♎16 04	17 35 18	15 14.2	17 25.0	10 34.0	15 59.4	27 30.5	16 11.3	18 11.3	19 08.1	21 28.7	29 05.9
28 Tu	14 28 49	5 26 15	23 51 57	0♏06 01	15 01.3	18 51.0	11 46.5	16 41.3	27 51.6	16 19.7	18 17.3	19 06.6	21 28.5	29 07.4
29 W	14 32 46	6 26 12	6♏17 31	12 26 30	14 47.2	20 19.6	12 59.0	17 23.1	28 12.6	16 28.3	18 23.2	19 05.2	21 28.3	29 08.8
30 Th	14 36 42	7 26 11	18 33 01	24 37 08	14 33.0	21 50.3	14 11.4	18 05.1	28 33.5	16 37.1	18 29.0	19 03.9	21 28.2	29 10.4
31 F	14 40 39	8 26 12	0♐39 01	6♐38 48	14 19.9	23 22.8	15 23.9	18 47.1	28 54.2	16 45.9	18 34.8	19 02.5	21 28.1	29 11.9

Astro Data

	Dy Hr Mn
♀0S	1 14:23
♃ D	8 4:17
♃△♄	8 23:19
♇ D	9 3:15
☽0N	15 9:38
☉0S	22 15:46
☿ R	24 7:18
☽0S	28 7:31
☽0N	12 19:01
☿ D	15 20:09
☽0S	25 13:38

Planet Ingress

	Dy Hr Mn
☉ ♎	22 15:46
♀ ♏	24 3:00
♂ ♏	4 4:35
♀ ♐	18 18:32
☉ ♏	23 1:10

Last Aspect / ☽ Ingress (September)

Last Aspect Dy Hr Mn		☽ Ingress	Dy Hr Mn
1 9:03	♇ □	♎	1 11:46
3 17:10	♇ ⚹	♏	3 20:03
5 15:46	♆ □	♐	6 7:12
8 16:44	♇ ☌	♑	8 19:46
10 13:16	♅ ⚹	♒	11 7:21
13 13:20	♇ ⚹	♓	13 16:06
15 19:04	♇ □	♈	15 21:40
17 22:27	♇ △	♉	18 0:58
19 22:52	☉ △	♊	20 3:18
22 5:05	☉ □	♋	22 5:50
23 21:18	♂ □	♌	24 9:15
26 11:21	♇ △	♍	26 13:53
28 17:32	♇ □	♎	28 20:07

Last Aspect / ☽ Ingress (October)

Last Aspect Dy Hr Mn		☽ Ingress	Dy Hr Mn
1 1:49	♇ ⚹	♏	1 4:27
2 22:47	♆ □	♐	3 15:15
6 1:10	♇ ☌	♑	6 3:50
7 19:38	♅ ⚹	♒	8 16:04
10 23:14	♇ ⚹	♓	11 1:32
13 5:04	♇ □	♈	13 7:08
15 7:37	♇ △	♉	15 9:32
17 7:34	♀ ☍	♊	17 10:26
19 9:53	♇ ☍	♋	19 11:41
21 11:56	☉ □	♌	21 14:36
23 17:54	♇ △	♍	23 19:41
26 1:04	♇ □	♎	26 2:49
28 10:07	♇ ⚹	♏	28 11:48
30 5:46	♆ □	♐	30 22:42

☽ Phases & Eclipses

Dy Hr Mn		
7 14:05	☽	15♐19
15 9:14	○	22♓54
22 5:05	☾	29♊34
29 8:13	●	6♎33
7 9:05	☽	14♑28
14 20:03	○	21♈51
21 11:56	☾	28♋27
28 23:15	●	5♏54

Astro Data

1 September 2008
Julian Day # 39691
SVP 5♓08'07"
GC 26♐57.6 ⚵ 9♊56.4
Eris 21♈37.3R ⚴ 15♐32.7
⚷ 17♒27.4R ⚶ 14♉38.8
☽ Mean ☊ 17♒23.7

1 October 2008
Julian Day # 39721
SVP 5♓08'04"
GC 26♐57.7 ⚵ 17♊59.9
Eris 21♈21.7R ⚴ 21♐06.8
⚷ 16♒20.3R ⚶ 13♉24.1R
☽ Mean ☊ 15♒48.4

November 2008 LONGITUDE

Day	Sid.Time	☉	0 hr ☽	Noon☽	True☊	☿	♀	♂	⚳	♃	♄	♅	♆	♇
1 Sa	14 44 35	9♏26 15	12♐36 44	18♐33 05	14♒08.9	24♎56.6	16♐36.2	19♏29.1	29♌14.7	16♑54.9	18♍40.5	19♓01.3	21♒28.1	29♐13.4
2 Su	14 48 32	10 26 20	24 28 12	0♑22 28	14R 00.7	26 31.5	17 48.6	20 11.3	29 35.2	17 04.1	18 46.2	19R 00.0	21D 28.1	29 15.0
3 M	14 52 28	11 26 26	6♑16 21	12 10 20	13 55.4	28 07.4	19 00.9	20 53.4	29 55.4	17 13.3	18 51.7	18 58.8	21 28.1	29 16.6
4 Tu	14 56 25	12 26 34	18 04 59	24 00 54	13 52.7	29 43.8	20 13.2	21 35.6	0♍15.6	17 22.7	18 57.3	18 57.7	21 28.2	29 18.3
5 W	15 00 22	13 26 43	29 58 43	5♒59 05	13 51.9	1♏20.7	21 25.4	22 17.9	0 35.5	17 32.2	19 02.7	18 56.6	21 28.3	29 19.9
6 Th	15 04 18	14 26 54	12♒02 42	18 10 16	13 51.8	2 58.0	22 37.6	23 00.2	0 55.3	17 41.8	19 08.1	18 55.5	21 28.4	29 21.6
7 F	15 08 15	15 27 07	24 22 27	0♓39 55	13 51.3	4 35.4	23 49.7	23 42.6	1 15.0	17 51.6	19 13.3	18 54.5	21 28.6	29 23.3
8 Sa	15 12 11	16 27 20	7♓03 18	13 33 08	13 49.3	6 13.0	25 01.8	24 25.0	1 34.4	18 01.4	19 18.6	18 53.5	21 28.7	29 25.0
9 Su	15 16 08	17 27 36	20 09 55	26 53 56	13 44.9	7 50.5	26 13.9	25 07.5	1 53.8	18 11.4	19 23.7	18 52.6	21 29.0	29 26.7
10 M	15 20 04	18 27 53	3♈45 26	10♈44 23	13 37.8	9 28.0	27 25.9	25 50.0	2 12.9	18 21.4	19 28.8	18 51.8	21 29.2	29 28.4
11 Tu	15 24 01	19 28 11	17 50 38	25 03 46	13 28.2	11 05.4	28 37.8	26 32.6	2 31.9	18 31.6	19 33.8	18 50.9	21 29.5	29 30.2
12 W	15 27 57	20 28 31	2♉23 09	9♉47 57	13 17.0	12 42.7	29 49.7	27 15.2	2 50.7	18 41.9	19 38.7	18 50.1	21 29.9	29 32.0
13 Th	15 31 54	21 28 53	17 17 07	24 49 29	13 05.2	14 19.8	1♑01.6	27 57.9	3 09.3	18 52.3	19 43.5	18 49.4	21 30.2	29 33.8
14 F	15 35 51	22 29 16	2♊23 44	9♊58 31	12 54.4	15 56.7	2 13.4	28 40.7	3 27.8	19 02.9	19 48.3	18 48.7	21 30.6	29 35.6
15 Sa	15 39 47	23 29 41	17 32 32	25 04 31	12 45.7	17 33.4	3 25.1	29 23.5	3 46.0	19 13.5	19 53.0	18 48.1	21 31.1	29 37.5
16 Su	15 43 44	24 30 08	2♋33 23	9♋58 09	12 39.7	19 09.9	4 36.8	0♐06.3	4 04.1	19 24.2	19 57.6	18 47.5	21 31.5	29 39.4
17 M	15 47 40	25 30 37	17 18 07	24 32 42	12 36.5	20 46.1	5 48.4	0 49.2	4 22.0	19 35.0	20 02.1	18 47.0	21 32.0	29 41.2
18 Tu	15 51 37	26 31 08	1♌41 34	8♌44 34	12D 35.5	22 22.2	7 00.0	1 32.2	4 39.7	19 46.0	20 06.6	18 46.5	21 32.6	29 43.1
19 W	15 55 33	27 31 40	15 41 40	22 33 00	12R 35.6	23 58.0	8 11.5	2 15.2	4 57.2	19 57.0	20 10.9	18 46.0	21 33.1	29 45.1
20 Th	15 59 30	28 32 14	29 18 47	5♍59 20	12 35.5	25 33.6	9 22.9	2 58.3	5 14.4	20 08.1	20 15.2	18 45.6	21 33.7	29 47.0
21 F	16 03 26	29 32 50	12♍34 58	19 06 05	12 33.9	27 08.9	10 34.3	3 41.4	5 31.5	20 19.3	20 19.4	18 45.3	21 34.4	29 48.9
22 Sa	16 07 23	0♐33 27	25 33 03	1♎56 14	12 29.9	28 44.1	11 45.6	4 24.6	5 48.3	20 30.6	20 23.5	18 45.0	21 35.0	29 50.9
23 Su	16 11 20	1 34 07	8♎15 59	14 32 38	12 23.1	0♐19.1	12 56.9	5 07.8	6 05.0	20 42.0	20 27.5	18 44.8	21 35.7	29 52.9
24 M	16 15 16	2 34 48	20 46 28	26 57 44	12 13.4	1 53.9	14 08.1	5 51.1	6 21.4	20 53.5	20 31.4	18 44.6	21 36.5	29 54.9
25 Tu	16 19 13	3 35 30	3♏06 40	9♏13 27	12 01.6	3 28.6	15 19.2	6 34.5	6 37.6	21 05.1	20 35.2	18 44.4	21 37.2	29 56.9
26 W	16 23 09	4 36 14	15 18 15	21 21 13	11 48.5	5 03.1	16 30.3	7 17.9	6 53.5	21 16.8	20 39.0	18 44.4	21 38.1	29 58.9
27 Th	16 27 06	5 36 59	27 22 29	3♐22 11	11 35.2	6 37.5	17 41.2	8 01.4	7 09.2	21 28.6	20 42.6	18D 44.3	21 38.9	0♑00.9
28 F	16 31 02	6 37 46	9♐20 27	15 17 26	11 22.9	8 11.8	18 52.1	8 44.9	7 24.7	21 40.4	20 46.2	18 44.3	21 39.8	0 03.0
29 Sa	16 34 59	7 38 34	21 13 19	27 08 17	11 12.6	9 46.0	20 02.9	9 28.4	7 39.9	21 52.3	20 49.6	18 44.4	21 40.7	0 05.0
30 Su	16 38 55	8 39 23	3♑02 36	8♑56 32	11 04.9	11 20.1	21 13.7	10 12.0	7 54.9	22 04.3	20 53.0	18 44.5	21 41.6	0 07.1

December 2008 LONGITUDE

Day	Sid.Time	☉	0 hr ☽	Noon☽	True☊	☿	♀	♂	⚳	♃	♄	♅	♆	♇
1 M	16 42 52	9♐40 13	14♑50 25	20♑44 35	11♒00.0	12♐54.1	22♑24.3	10♐55.7	8♍09.6	22♑16.4	20♍56.2	18♓44.7	21♒42.6	0♑09.2
2 Tu	16 46 49	10 41 05	26 39 30	2♒35 37	10D 57.6	14 28.0	23 34.9	11 39.4	8 24.1	22 28.6	20 59.4	18 44.9	21 43.6	0 11.3
3 W	16 50 45	11 41 57	8♒33 26	14 33 30	10 57.3	16 01.9	24 45.3	12 23.2	8 38.3	22 40.9	21 02.5	18 45.2	21 44.6	0 13.4
4 Th	16 54 42	12 42 50	20 36 26	26 42 50	10 58.0	17 35.8	25 55.7	13 07.0	8 52.2	22 53.2	21 05.4	18 45.5	21 45.6	0 15.5
5 F	16 58 38	13 43 43	2♓53 20	9♓08 35	10R 58.8	19 09.7	27 05.9	13 50.9	9 05.9	23 05.6	21 08.3	18 45.9	21 46.7	0 17.6
6 Sa	17 02 35	14 44 38	15 29 12	21 55 48	10 58.6	20 43.6	28 16.1	14 34.8	9 19.3	23 18.0	21 11.1	18 46.3	21 47.9	0 19.7
7 Su	17 06 31	15 45 33	28 28 54	5♈09 00	10 56.7	22 17.4	29 26.1	15 18.7	9 32.4	23 30.6	21 13.7	18 46.8	21 49.0	0 21.9
8 M	17 10 28	16 46 29	11♈56 25	18 51 24	10 52.6	23 51.3	0♒36.0	16 02.7	9 45.2	23 43.2	21 16.3	18 47.3	21 50.2	0 24.0
9 Tu	17 14 24	17 47 25	25 53 59	3♉04 01	10 46.4	25 25.2	1 45.8	16 46.8	9 57.7	23 55.8	21 18.8	18 47.9	21 51.4	0 26.2
10 W	17 18 21	18 48 23	10♉21 08	17 44 44	10 38.6	26 59.1	2 55.5	17 30.9	10 10.0	24 08.6	21 21.1	18 48.5	21 52.6	0 28.3
11 Th	17 22 18	19 49 21	25 13 59	2♊47 50	10 30.4	28 33.0	4 05.0	18 15.1	10 21.9	24 21.4	21 23.4	18 49.2	21 53.9	0 30.5
12 F	17 26 14	20 50 20	10♊25 05	18 04 23	10 22.6	0♑06.9	5 14.4	18 59.3	10 33.5	24 34.2	21 25.5	18 50.0	21 55.2	0 32.7
13 Sa	17 30 11	21 51 19	25 44 17	3♋23 24	10 16.3	1 40.9	6 23.7	19 43.5	10 44.9	24 47.1	21 27.6	18 50.8	21 56.6	0 34.8
14 Su	17 34 07	22 52 20	11♋00 20	18 33 52	10 12.2	3 14.8	7 32.8	20 27.9	10 55.9	25 00.1	21 29.5	18 51.6	21 57.9	0 37.0
15 M	17 38 04	23 53 21	26 02 54	3♌26 34	10D 10.4	4 48.7	8 41.8	21 12.2	11 06.6	25 13.2	21 31.4	18 52.5	21 59.3	0 39.2
16 Tu	17 42 00	24 54 23	10♌44 11	17 55 18	10 10.4	6 22.6	9 50.6	21 56.6	11 17.0	25 26.2	21 33.1	18 53.4	22 00.7	0 41.4
17 W	17 45 57	25 55 27	24 59 40	1♍57 11	10 11.6	7 56.4	10 59.3	22 41.1	11 27.0	25 39.4	21 34.7	18 54.4	22 02.2	0 43.6
18 Th	17 49 54	26 56 31	8♍47 57	15 32 11	10R 12.9	9 30.0	12 07.8	23 25.6	11 36.7	25 52.6	21 36.3	18 55.5	22 03.6	0 45.8
19 F	17 53 50	27 57 35	22 10 10	28 42 19	10 13.4	11 03.5	13 16.2	24 10.2	11 46.1	26 05.8	21 37.7	18 56.5	22 05.1	0 48.0
20 Sa	17 57 47	28 58 41	5♎09 03	11♎30 52	10 12.5	12 36.8	14 24.4	24 54.8	11 55.1	26 19.1	21 39.0	18 57.7	22 06.6	0 50.2
21 Su	18 01 43	29 59 48	17 48 13	24 01 35	10 09.7	14 09.7	15 32.4	25 39.4	12 03.7	26 32.5	21 40.2	18 58.9	22 08.2	0 52.4
22 M	18 05 40	1♑00 55	0♏11 28	6♏18 16	10 05.1	15 42.3	16 40.2	26 24.1	12 12.0	26 45.9	21 41.2	19 00.1	22 09.8	0 54.6
23 Tu	18 09 36	2 02 03	12 22 27	18 24 23	9 59.0	17 14.3	17 47.9	27 08.9	12 20.0	26 59.4	21 42.2	19 01.4	22 11.4	0 56.8
24 W	18 13 33	3 03 12	24 24 25	0♐22 54	9 51.9	18 45.7	18 55.4	27 53.7	12 27.5	27 12.9	21 43.1	19 02.7	22 13.0	0 59.0
25 Th	18 17 29	4 04 21	6♐20 07	12 16 21	9 44.6	20 16.2	20 02.7	28 38.5	12 34.7	27 26.4	21 43.8	19 04.1	22 14.6	1 01.2
26 F	18 21 26	5 05 31	18 11 50	24 06 48	9 37.9	21 45.8	21 09.8	29 23.4	12 41.6	27 40.0	21 44.5	19 05.5	22 16.3	1 03.3
27 Sa	18 25 23	6 06 41	0♑01 30	5♑56 06	9 32.4	23 14.1	22 16.7	0♑08.4	12 48.0	27 53.6	21 45.0	19 07.0	22 18.0	1 05.5
28 Su	18 29 19	7 07 51	11 50 52	17 46 00	9 28.5	24 41.0	23 23.3	0 53.4	12 54.1	28 07.3	21 45.4	19 08.5	22 19.7	1 07.7
29 M	18 33 16	8 09 01	23 41 46	29 38 23	9D 26.3	26 06.0	24 29.8	1 38.4	12 59.7	28 21.0	21 45.7	19 10.1	22 21.5	1 09.9
30 Tu	18 37 12	9 10 12	5♒36 10	11♒35 26	9 25.9	27 29.0	25 36.0	2 23.5	13 05.0	28 34.7	21 45.9	19 11.7	22 23.3	1 12.1
31 W	18 41 09	10 11 22	17 36 30	23 39 46	9 26.7	28 49.4	26 42.0	3 08.6	13 09.8	28 48.5	21R 46.0	19 13.4	22 25.0	1 14.3

Astro Data (Dy Hr Mn)

♆ D 2 6:40
♄☍♅ 4 13:37
☽ 0N 9 4:30
♃⚹♅ 13 5:41
♃△♄ 21 12:14
☽ 0S 21 18:17
♅ D 27 16:10
♃⚺♆ 28 10:36

☽ 0N 6 12:27
☽ 0S 18 23:42
♄ R 31 18:09

Planet Ingress (Dy Hr Mn)

⚳ ♍ 3 17:26
☿ ♏ 4 16:01
♀ ♑ 12 15:26
♂ ♐ 16 8:28
☉ ♐ 21 22:45
☿ ♐ 23 7:10
♇ ♑ 27 1:04

♀ ♒ 7 23:38
☿ ♑ 12 10:14
☉ ♑ 21 12:05
♂ ♑ 27 7:31

Last Aspect / ☽ Ingress (November)

Last Aspect Dy Hr Mn			☽ Ingress	Dy Hr Mn
2 9:43	♇	☌	♑	2 11:14
4 6:48	♂	⚹	♒	5 0:03
7 9:34	♇	⚹	♓	7 10:44
9 16:29	♇	□	♈	9 17:27
11 19:19	♇	△	♉	11 20:06
13 17:14	♂	☍	♊	13 20:12
15 19:18	♇	☍	♋	15 19:53
17 13:44	☉	△	♌	17 21:09
20 0:49	♇	△	♍	20 1:14
22 8:03	♇	□	♎	22 8:21
24 17:46	♇	⚹	♏	24 17:55
26 12:34	♆	□	♐	27 5:15
29 0:55	♆	⚹	♑	29 17:49

Last Aspect / ☽ Ingress (December)

Last Aspect Dy Hr Mn			☽ Ingress	Dy Hr Mn
1 15:45	♀	☌	♒	2 6:46
4 2:16	♆	☌	♓	4 18:24
7 0:44	♀	⚹	♈	7 2:45
8 21:36	☿	△	♉	9 6:53
10 22:24	♃	△	♊	11 7:34
12 18:02	♆	△	♋	13 6:41
14 22:28	♃	☍	♌	15 6:24
17 0:47	☉	△	♍	17 8:37
19 10:30	☉	□	♎	19 14:24
21 16:58	♃	□	♏	21 23:38
24 5:31	♃	⚹	♐	24 11:14
26 23:26	♂	☌	♑	26 23:57
29 9:21	♃	☌	♒	29 12:44

☽ Phases & Eclipses (Dy Hr Mn)

6 4:04 ☽ 14♒07
13 6:18 ○ 21♉15
19 21:32 ☾ 27♌56
27 16:56 ● 5♐49

5 21:27 ☽ 14♓08
12 16:38 ○ 21♊02
19 10:30 ☾ 27♍54
27 12:23 ● 6♑08

Astro Data

1 November 2008
Julian Day # 39752
SVP 5♓08'00"
GC 26♐57.8 ⚴ 20♊27.0R
Eris 21♈03.4R ⚵ 29♐49.8
⚷ 16♒03.9 ⚶ 6♉22.4R
☽ Mean ☊ 14♒09.9

1 December 2008
Julian Day # 39782
SVP 5♓07'55"
GC 26♐57.8 ⚴ 14♊00.9R
Eris 20♈48.7R ⚵ 10♑07.7
⚷ 16♒46.9 ⚶ 0♉21.3R
☽ Mean ☊ 12♒34.6

LONGITUDE — January 2009

Day	Sid.Time	☉	0 hr ☽	Noon ☽	True ☊	☿	♀	♂	⚳	♃	♄	♅	♆	♇
1 Th	18 45 05	11♑12 32	29♒45 37	5♓54 30	9♒28.3	0♒06.7	27♒47.7	3♑53.8	13♍14.3	29♑02.3	21♍46.0	19♓15.1	22♒26.9	1♑16.5
2 F	18 49 02	12 13 43	12♓06 52	18 23 11	9 30.1	1 20.6	28 53.2	4 39.0	13 18.3	29 16.2	21R 45.8	19 16.8	22 28.7	1 18.6
3 Sa	18 52 58	13 14 52	24 43 56	1♈09 35	9R 31.5	2 30.2	29 58.3	5 24.2	13 21.9	29 30.0	21 45.6	19 18.6	22 30.5	1 20.8
4 Su	18 56 55	14 16 02	7♈40 37	14 17 24	9 32.0	3 35.1	1♓03.3	6 09.5	13 25.2	29 43.9	21 45.2	19 20.5	22 32.4	1 22.9
5 M	19 00 52	15 17 11	21 00 21	27 49 41	9 31.5	4 34.3	2 07.9	6 54.8	13 28.0	29 57.8	21 44.8	19 22.3	22 34.3	1 25.1
6 Tu	19 04 48	16 18 20	4♉45 36	11♉48 08	9 29.8	5 27.2	3 12.2	7 40.2	13 30.3	0♒11.8	21 44.2	19 24.3	22 36.2	1 27.2
7 W	19 08 45	17 19 29	18 57 10	26 12 24	9 27.2	6 12.9	4 16.2	8 25.6	13 32.3	0 25.8	21 43.5	19 26.2	22 38.1	1 29.4
8 Th	19 12 41	18 20 37	3♊33 22	10♊59 23	9 24.3	6 50.4	5 19.9	9 11.1	13 33.8	0 39.8	21 42.7	19 28.3	22 40.1	1 31.5
9 F	19 16 38	19 21 45	18 29 37	26 03 04	9 21.4	7 18.8	6 23.2	9 56.6	13 34.9	0 53.8	21 41.8	19 30.3	22 42.1	1 33.6
10 Sa	19 20 34	20 22 53	3♋38 35	11♋13 57	9 19.2	7 37.3	7 26.3	10 42.1	13 35.6	1 07.8	21 40.8	19 32.4	22 44.1	1 35.7
11 Su	19 24 31	21 24 00	18 50 53	26 25 10	9D 17.9	7R 45.2	8 28.9	11 27.7	13R 35.8	1 21.9	21 39.7	19 34.6	22 46.1	1 37.8
12 M	19 28 27	22 25 07	3♌56 34	11♌24 03	9 17.5	7 41.7	9 31.2	12 13.3	13 35.6	1 36.0	21 38.5	19 36.7	22 48.1	1 39.9
13 Tu	19 32 24	23 26 13	18 46 39	26 03 36	9 18.0	7 26.5	10 33.1	12 58.9	13 35.0	1 50.1	21 37.1	19 38.9	22 50.1	1 42.0
14 W	19 36 21	24 27 20	3♍14 19	10♍18 24	9 19.1	6 59.5	11 34.6	13 44.6	13 33.9	2 04.2	21 35.7	19 41.2	22 52.2	1 44.1
15 Th	19 40 17	25 28 26	17 15 38	24 05 58	9 20.3	6 21.0	12 35.6	14 30.3	13 32.4	2 18.3	21 34.2	19 43.5	22 54.2	1 46.1
16 F	19 44 14	26 29 31	0♎49 28	7♎26 22	9 21.4	5 31.7	13 36.3	15 16.1	13 30.4	2 32.5	21 32.5	19 45.8	22 56.3	1 48.2
17 Sa	19 48 10	27 30 37	13 57 00	20 21 44	9R 22.0	4 32.9	14 36.6	16 01.9	13 28.0	2 46.6	21 30.8	19 48.2	22 58.4	1 50.2
18 Su	19 52 07	28 31 42	26 41 04	2♏55 30	9 22.1	3 26.1	15 36.4	16 47.7	13 25.2	3 00.8	21 28.9	19 50.6	23 00.5	1 52.2
19 M	19 56 03	29 32 48	9♏05 34	15 11 49	9 21.6	2 13.4	16 35.7	17 33.6	13 21.9	3 15.0	21 27.0	19 53.0	23 02.6	1 54.2
20 Tu	20 00 00	0♒33 52	21 14 49	27 15 06	9 20.8	0 57.0	17 34.6	18 19.6	13 18.1	3 29.1	21 24.9	19 55.5	23 04.8	1 56.2
21 W	20 03 56	1 34 57	3♐13 11	9♐09 36	9 19.7	29♑39.4	18 32.9	19 05.5	13 14.0	3 43.3	21 22.8	19 58.0	23 06.9	1 58.2
22 Th	20 07 53	2 36 01	15 04 50	20 59 18	9 18.6	28 22.8	19 30.8	19 51.5	13 09.3	3 57.5	21 20.5	20 00.6	23 09.1	2 00.1
23 F	20 11 50	3 37 04	26 53 27	2♑47 40	9 17.7	27 09.6	20 28.1	20 37.6	13 04.3	4 11.7	21 18.2	20 03.2	23 11.2	2 02.1
24 Sa	20 15 46	4 38 07	8♑42 18	14 37 41	9 17.1	26 01.4	21 24.9	21 23.6	12 58.8	4 25.9	21 15.7	20 05.8	23 13.4	2 04.0
25 Su	20 19 43	5 39 09	20 34 07	26 31 51	9 16.7	24 59.9	22 21.1	22 09.7	12 52.9	4 40.1	21 13.2	20 08.4	23 15.6	2 05.9
26 M	20 23 39	6 40 11	2♒31 09	8♒32 15	9D 16.6	24 06.1	23 16.7	22 55.9	12 46.5	4 54.3	21 10.5	20 11.1	23 17.8	2 07.8
27 Tu	20 27 36	7 41 11	14 35 21	20 40 39	9 16.7	23 20.7	24 11.7	23 42.0	12 39.8	5 08.5	21 07.8	20 13.8	23 20.0	2 09.7
28 W	20 31 32	8 42 10	26 48 22	2♓58 40	9R 16.8	22 44.2	25 06.0	24 28.2	12 32.6	5 22.7	21 05.0	20 16.6	23 22.2	2 11.6
29 Th	20 35 29	9 43 09	9♓11 47	15 27 53	9 16.8	22 16.5	25 59.7	25 14.4	12 25.0	5 36.9	21 02.1	20 19.4	23 24.5	2 13.4
30 F	20 39 25	10 44 06	21 47 12	28 09 55	9 16.6	21 57.7	26 52.7	26 00.7	12 17.0	5 51.1	20 59.1	20 22.2	23 26.7	2 15.2
31 Sa	20 43 22	11 45 02	4♈36 15	11♈06 26	9 16.4	21D 47.3	27 45.0	26 47.0	12 08.7	6 05.3	20 56.0	20 25.0	23 28.9	2 17.0

LONGITUDE — February 2009

Day	Sid.Time	☉	0 hr ☽	Noon ☽	True ☊	☿	♀	♂	⚳	♃	♄	♅	♆	♇
1 Su	20 47 19	12♒45 57	17♈40 40	24♈19 09	9♒16.1	21♑44.9	28♓36.5	27♑33.3	11♍59.9	6♒19.5	20♍52.8	20♓27.9	23♒31.2	2♑18.8
2 M	20 51 15	13 46 50	1♉02 04	7♉49 32	9D 15.9	21 50.2	29 27.2	28 19.6	11R 50.8	6 33.6	20R 49.5	20 30.8	23 33.4	2 20.6
3 Tu	20 55 12	14 47 42	14 41 42	21 38 34	9 16.0	22 02.5	0♈17.2	29 06.0	11 41.3	6 47.8	20 46.2	20 33.7	23 35.7	2 22.3
4 W	20 59 08	15 48 33	28 40 07	5♊46 14	9 16.3	22 21.3	1 06.2	29 52.4	11 31.4	7 01.9	20 42.8	20 36.6	23 38.0	2 24.1
5 Th	21 03 05	16 49 22	12♊56 41	20 11 10	9 16.8	22 46.2	1 54.4	0♒38.8	11 21.3	7 16.0	20 39.3	20 39.6	23 40.2	2 25.8
6 F	21 07 01	17 50 10	27 29 12	4♋50 14	9 17.6	23 16.5	2 41.7	1 25.2	11 10.7	7 30.1	20 35.8	20 42.6	23 42.5	2 27.4
7 Sa	21 10 58	18 50 57	12♋13 36	19 38 30	9 18.3	23 52.0	3 28.0	2 11.7	10 59.9	7 44.2	20 32.1	20 45.6	23 44.8	2 29.1
8 Su	21 14 55	19 51 42	27 04 04	4♌29 23	9R 18.7	24 32.1	4 13.4	2 58.2	10 48.8	7 58.3	20 28.4	20 48.7	23 47.0	2 30.7
9 M	21 18 51	20 52 25	11♌53 31	19 15 30	9 18.6	25 16.5	4 57.7	3 44.7	10 37.3	8 12.3	20 24.6	20 51.7	23 49.3	2 32.4
10 Tu	21 22 48	21 53 08	26 34 36	3♍49 28	9 17.8	26 04.7	5 40.9	4 31.3	10 25.6	8 26.4	20 20.8	20 54.8	23 51.6	2 33.9
11 W	21 26 44	22 53 48	10♍59 53	18 05 01	9 16.4	26 56.5	6 23.0	5 17.8	10 13.6	8 40.4	20 16.9	20 57.9	23 53.9	2 35.5
12 Th	21 30 41	23 54 28	25 04 26	1♎57 45	9 14.4	27 51.6	7 04.0	6 04.4	10 01.4	8 54.3	20 12.9	21 01.1	23 56.2	2 37.1
13 F	21 34 37	24 55 06	8♎44 47	15 25 29	9 12.3	28 49.6	7 43.7	6 51.0	9 48.9	9 08.3	20 08.8	21 04.2	23 58.4	2 38.6
14 Sa	21 38 34	25 55 44	21 59 55	28 28 17	9 10.2	29 50.5	8 22.3	7 37.7	9 36.2	9 22.2	20 04.7	21 07.4	24 00.7	2 40.1
15 Su	21 42 30	26 56 20	4♏50 54	11♏08 09	9 08.7	0♒53.9	8 59.5	8 24.3	9 23.3	9 36.1	20 00.6	21 10.6	24 03.0	2 41.5
16 M	21 46 27	27 56 55	17 20 30	23 28 29	9D 07.9	1 59.6	9 35.4	9 11.0	9 10.2	9 50.0	19 56.4	21 13.8	24 05.3	2 43.0
17 Tu	21 50 23	28 57 28	29 32 39	5♐33 36	9 08.0	3 07.6	10 09.9	9 57.7	8 56.9	10 03.9	19 52.1	21 17.0	24 07.6	2 44.4
18 W	21 54 20	29 58 01	11♐31 57	17 28 19	9 08.9	4 17.6	10 43.0	10 44.5	8 43.5	10 17.7	19 47.8	21 20.2	24 09.8	2 45.8
19 Th	21 58 17	0♓58 32	23 23 19	29 17 32	9 10.4	5 29.5	11 14.6	11 31.2	8 29.9	10 31.5	19 43.4	21 23.5	24 12.1	2 47.2
20 F	22 02 13	1 59 02	5♑11 34	11♑05 57	9 12.2	6 43.2	11 44.6	12 18.0	8 16.2	10 45.2	19 39.0	21 26.8	24 14.4	2 48.5
21 Sa	22 06 10	2 59 31	17 01 14	22 57 54	9 13.8	7 58.6	12 13.0	13 04.8	8 02.4	10 59.0	19 34.6	21 30.1	24 16.6	2 49.8
22 Su	22 10 06	3 59 58	28 56 23	4♒57 06	9R 14.7	9 15.6	12 39.8	13 51.6	7 48.5	11 12.6	19 30.1	21 33.4	24 18.9	2 51.1
23 M	22 14 03	5 00 23	11♒00 23	17 06 33	9 14.5	10 34.2	13 04.8	14 38.4	7 34.5	11 26.3	19 25.6	21 36.7	24 21.1	2 52.4
24 Tu	22 17 59	6 00 47	23 15 51	29 28 27	9 13.0	11 54.1	13 28.1	15 25.3	7 20.5	11 39.9	19 21.0	21 40.0	24 23.4	2 53.6
25 W	22 21 56	7 01 09	5♓44 30	12♓04 07	9 10.0	13 15.5	13 49.4	16 12.1	7 06.5	11 53.5	19 16.4	21 43.4	24 25.6	2 54.8
26 Th	22 25 52	8 01 30	18 27 18	24 54 05	9 05.9	14 38.3	14 08.9	16 59.0	6 52.4	12 07.0	19 11.8	21 46.7	24 27.9	2 56.0
27 F	22 29 49	9 01 48	1♈24 24	7♈58 11	9 00.9	16 02.3	14 26.3	17 45.8	6 38.4	12 20.5	19 07.1	21 50.1	24 30.1	2 57.1
28 Sa	22 33 46	10 02 05	14 35 20	21 15 45	8 55.8	17 27.6	14 41.7	18 32.7	6 24.4	12 33.9	19 02.4	21 53.5	24 32.3	2 58.3

Astro Data

	Dy Hr Mn
☽0N	2 18:29
⚳R	11 13:05
☿R	11 16:46
♃⚺♇	12 19:52
☽0S	15 7:50
♃∠♅	27 23:06
☽0N	29 23:51
♀0N	30 9:32
♃⚼♄	30 23:04
☿D	1 7:11
♄☍♅	5 10:57
☽0S	11 18:15
☽0N	26 6:14

Planet Ingress

	Dy Hr Mn
☿ ♒	1 9:52
♀ ♓	3 12:37
♃ ♒	5 15:42
☉ ♒	19 22:41
☿ ♑R	21 5:37
♀ ♈	3 3:42
♂ ♒	4 15:56
☿ ♒	14 15:40
☉ ♓	18 12:47

Last Aspect / ☽ Ingress (January)

Last Aspect Dy Hr Mn		☽ Ingress Dy Hr Mn
31 18:35	♀ ☌	♓ 1 0:28
3 8:52	♃ ⚹	♈ 3 9:51
5 2:45	♆ ⚹	♉ 5 15:47
7 6:06	♆ □	♊ 7 18:13
9 6:41	♆ △	♋ 9 18:15
11 4:28	♄ ⚹	♌ 11 17:42
13 6:39	♆ ☍	♍ 13 18:34
15 14:38	☉ △	♎ 15 22:31
18 2:47	☉ □	♏ 18 6:21
20 3:38	♆ □	♐ 20 17:31
22 16:25	♆ ⚹	♑ 23 6:19
25 9:09	☿ ☌	♒ 25 18:58
27 17:14	♆ ☌	♓ 28 6:13
30 9:25	♀ ☌	♈ 30 15:26

Last Aspect / ☽ Ingress (February)

Last Aspect Dy Hr Mn		☽ Ingress Dy Hr Mn
1 18:09	♂ □	♉ 1 22:10
4 1:28	♂ △	♊ 4 2:16
5 17:45	♆ △	♋ 6 4:07
7 19:08	☿ ☍	♌ 8 4:44
9 19:30	♆ ☍	♍ 10 5:39
12 4:19	☿ △	♎ 12 8:34
14 14:47	☿ □	♏ 14 14:52
16 21:38	☉ □	♐ 17 0:54
19 1:37	♆ ⚹	♑ 19 13:26
21 9:02	♅ ⚹	♒ 22 2:07
24 2:09	♆ ☌	♓ 24 13:01
26 6:11	♅ ☌	♈ 26 21:25

☽ Phases & Eclipses

Dy Hr Mn	
4 11:57	☽ 14♈16
11 3:28	○ 21♋02
18 2:47	☾ 28♎08
26 7:56	● 6♒30
26 7:59:44	A 07'54"
2 23:14	☽ 14♉15
9 14:50	○ 21♌00
9 14:39	A 0.900
16 21:38	☾ 28♏21
25 1:36	● 6♓35

Astro Data

1 January 2009
Julian Day # 39813
SVP 5♓07'49"
GC 26♐57.9 ⚴ 5♊05.0R
Eris 20♈41.4R ⚵ 21♑58.2
⚷ 18♒23.0 ⚶ 0♉29.1
☽ Mean ☊ 10♒56.1

1 February 2009
Julian Day # 39844
SVP 5♓07'44"
GC 26♐58.0 ⚴ 5♊45.5
Eris 20♈44.5 ⚵ 4♒29.7
⚷ 20♒31.0 ⚶ 6♉30.2
☽ Mean ☊ 9♒17.6

March 2009 LONGITUDE

Day	Sid.Time	☉	0 hr ☽	Noon ☽	True ☊	☿	♀	♂	⚳	♃	♄	♅	♆	♇
1 Su	22 37 42	11♓02 20	27♈59 17	4♉45 48	8♒51.2	18♒54.1	14♈55.0	19♒19.6	6♍10.5	12♒47.3	18♍57.7	21♓56.8	24♒34.5	2♑59.3
2 M	22 41 39	12 02 33	11♉35 12	18 27 20	8R47.7	20 21.8	15 06.1	20 06.5	5R56.6	13 00.6	18R53.0	22 00.2	24 36.7	3 00.4
3 Tu	22 45 35	13 02 43	25 22 05	2♊19 20	8D45.6	21 50.7	15 14.9	20 53.5	5 42.8	13 13.9	18 48.3	22 03.6	24 38.9	3 01.4
4 W	22 49 32	14 02 52	9♊18 58	16 20 50	8 45.2	23 20.7	15 21.5	21 40.4	5 29.2	13 27.2	18 43.5	22 07.0	24 41.1	3 02.4
5 Th	22 53 28	15 02 59	23 24 49	0♋30 43	8 46.0	24 51.9	15 25.6	22 27.3	5 15.6	13 40.3	18 38.7	22 10.5	24 43.3	3 03.4
6 F	22 57 25	16 03 03	7♋38 21	14 47 28	8 47.4	26 24.3	15R27.4	23 14.3	5 02.2	13 53.5	18 34.0	22 13.9	24 45.5	3 04.4
7 Sa	23 01 21	17 03 05	21 57 46	29 08 52	8R48.6	27 57.8	15 26.7	24 01.2	4 49.0	14 06.6	18 29.2	22 17.3	24 47.6	3 05.3
8 Su	23 05 18	18 03 06	6♌20 21	13♌31 44	8 48.9	29 32.4	15 23.5	24 48.1	4 36.0	14 19.6	18 24.4	22 20.7	24 49.7	3 06.2
9 M	23 09 15	19 03 04	20 42 29	27 51 59	8 47.4	1♓08.1	15 17.8	25 35.1	4 23.1	14 32.5	18 19.6	22 24.1	24 51.9	3 07.0
10 Tu	23 13 11	20 02 59	4♍59 38	12♍04 49	8 43.9	2 45.0	15 09.6	26 22.1	4 10.5	14 45.4	18 14.9	22 27.6	24 54.0	3 07.8
11 W	23 17 08	21 02 53	19 06 54	26 05 20	8 38.4	4 23.1	14 58.9	27 09.0	3 58.1	14 58.3	18 10.1	22 31.0	24 56.1	3 08.6
12 Th	23 21 04	22 02 45	2♎59 33	9♎49 09	8 31.4	6 02.2	14 45.7	27 56.0	3 45.9	15 11.1	18 05.3	22 34.4	24 58.2	3 09.4
13 F	23 25 01	23 02 35	16 33 46	23 13 10	8 23.7	7 42.6	14 30.0	28 43.0	3 34.0	15 23.8	18 00.5	22 37.9	25 00.2	3 10.1
14 Sa	23 28 57	24 02 24	29 47 12	6♏15 53	8 16.0	9 24.1	14 11.8	29 29.9	3 22.4	15 36.4	17 55.8	22 41.3	25 02.3	3 10.8
15 Su	23 32 54	25 02 10	12♏39 17	18 57 37	8 09.3	11 06.8	13 51.3	0♓16.9	3 11.0	15 49.0	17 51.1	22 44.7	25 04.4	3 11.5
16 M	23 36 50	26 01 55	25 11 11	1♐20 24	8 04.2	12 50.7	13 28.5	1 03.9	2 59.9	16 01.6	17 46.4	22 48.2	25 06.4	3 12.1
17 Tu	23 40 47	27 01 39	7♐25 41	13 27 36	8 01.1	14 35.9	13 03.5	1 50.9	2 49.2	16 14.0	17 41.7	22 51.6	25 08.4	3 12.7
18 W	23 44 44	28 01 20	19 26 42	25 23 38	7D59.9	16 22.2	12 36.4	2 37.9	2 38.7	16 26.4	17 37.0	22 55.0	25 10.4	3 13.3
19 Th	23 48 40	29 01 00	1♑19 01	7♑13 31	8 00.2	18 09.8	12 07.4	3 24.9	2 28.6	16 38.7	17 32.3	22 58.4	25 12.4	3 13.8
20 F	23 52 37	0♈00 38	13 07 48	19 02 33	8 01.3	19 58.6	11 36.6	4 11.9	2 18.8	16 51.0	17 27.7	23 01.9	25 14.3	3 14.3
21 Sa	23 56 33	1 00 14	24 58 23	0♒55 58	8R02.4	21 48.7	11 04.2	4 58.9	2 09.4	17 03.2	17 23.1	23 05.3	25 16.3	3 14.8
22 Su	0 00 30	1 59 49	6♒55 53	12 58 42	8 02.5	23 40.1	10 30.3	5 45.9	2 00.3	17 15.3	17 18.6	23 08.7	25 18.2	3 15.2
23 M	0 04 26	2 59 21	19 04 54	25 14 56	8 00.8	25 32.7	9 55.2	6 32.9	1 51.7	17 27.3	17 14.0	23 12.1	25 20.1	3 15.6
24 Tu	0 08 23	3 58 52	1♓29 11	7♓47 56	7 56.9	27 26.5	9 19.1	7 19.8	1 43.3	17 39.2	17 09.6	23 15.5	25 22.0	3 16.0
25 W	0 12 19	4 58 21	14 11 23	20 39 38	7 50.5	29 21.6	8 42.3	8 06.8	1 35.4	17 51.1	17 05.1	23 18.8	25 23.9	3 16.4
26 Th	0 16 16	5 57 47	27 12 42	3♈50 28	7 42.0	1♈18.0	8 04.9	8 53.8	1 27.9	18 02.9	17 00.7	23 22.2	25 25.7	3 16.7
27 F	0 20 13	6 57 12	10♈32 44	17 19 14	7 32.0	3 15.5	7 27.2	9 40.7	1 20.8	18 14.5	16 56.3	23 25.6	25 27.6	3 16.9
28 Sa	0 24 09	7 56 35	24 09 36	1♉03 23	7 21.7	5 14.3	6 49.5	10 27.7	1 14.0	18 26.2	16 52.0	23 28.9	25 29.4	3 17.2
29 Su	0 28 06	8 55 55	8♉00 07	14 59 19	7 12.1	7 14.1	6 12.0	11 14.6	1 07.7	18 37.7	16 47.8	23 32.3	25 31.2	3 17.4
30 M	0 32 02	9 55 14	22 00 28	29 03 05	7 04.3	9 14.9	5 34.9	12 01.6	1 01.8	18 49.1	16 43.6	23 35.6	25 32.9	3 17.6
31 Tu	0 35 59	10 54 30	6♊06 44	13♊11 00	6 58.8	11 16.7	4 58.5	12 48.5	0 56.4	19 00.4	16 39.4	23 38.9	25 34.7	3 17.7

April 2009 LONGITUDE

Day	Sid.Time	☉	0 hr ☽	Noon ☽	True ☊	☿	♀	♂	⚳	♃	♄	♅	♆	♇
1 W	0 39 55	11♈53 44	20♊15 32	27♊20 04	6♒55.9	13♈19.4	4♈23.1	13♓35.4	0♍51.3	19♒11.7	16♍35.3	23♓42.3	25♒36.4	3♑17.9
2 Th	0 43 52	12 52 55	4♋24 21	11♋28 13	6D55.0	15 22.7	3R48.8	14 22.3	0R46.7	19 22.9	16R31.3	23 45.6	25 38.1	3 18.0
3 F	0 47 48	13 52 04	18 31 31	25 34 09	6R55.3	17 26.5	3 15.9	15 09.2	0 42.6	19 33.9	16 27.3	23 48.8	25 39.8	3 18.0
4 Sa	0 51 45	14 51 11	2♌36 01	9♌36 59	6 55.5	19 30.7	2 44.5	15 56.0	0 38.8	19 44.9	16 23.4	23 52.1	25 41.4	3R18.0
5 Su	0 55 42	15 50 15	16 36 58	23 35 48	6 54.4	21 35.1	2 14.8	16 42.9	0 35.5	19 55.8	16 19.5	23 55.4	25 43.1	3 18.0
6 M	0 59 38	16 49 17	0♍33 18	7♍29 15	6 51.1	23 39.2	1 47.0	17 29.7	0 32.6	20 06.5	16 15.7	23 58.6	25 44.7	3 18.0
7 Tu	1 03 35	17 48 17	14 23 23	21 15 24	6 45.0	25 43.0	1 21.2	18 16.5	0 30.1	20 17.2	16 12.0	24 01.8	25 46.3	3 17.9
8 W	1 07 31	18 47 15	28 04 58	4♎51 45	6 36.2	27 46.0	0 57.6	19 03.3	0 28.1	20 27.7	16 08.4	24 05.0	25 47.8	3 17.8
9 Th	1 11 28	19 46 10	11♎35 24	18 15 38	6 25.1	29 48.0	0 36.2	19 50.1	0 26.5	20 38.2	16 04.8	24 08.2	25 49.3	3 17.7
10 F	1 15 24	20 45 04	24 52 07	1♏24 39	6 12.8	1♉48.6	0 17.2	20 36.9	0 25.4	20 48.6	16 01.3	24 11.3	25 50.9	3 17.5
11 Sa	1 19 21	21 43 55	7♏53 02	14 17 11	6 00.4	3 47.4	0 00.5	21 23.6	0 24.6	20 58.8	15 57.9	24 14.5	25 52.3	3 17.3
12 Su	1 23 17	22 42 45	20 37 05	26 52 48	5 49.1	5 44.2	29♓46.3	22 10.4	0D24.3	21 09.0	15 54.5	24 17.6	25 53.8	3 17.1
13 M	1 27 14	23 41 33	3♐04 29	9♐12 24	5 39.8	7 38.5	29 34.5	22 57.1	0 24.4	21 19.0	15 51.2	24 20.7	25 55.2	3 16.8
14 Tu	1 31 11	24 40 19	15 16 51	21 18 15	5 33.0	9 30.0	29 25.2	23 43.8	0 25.0	21 28.9	15 48.0	24 23.8	25 56.6	3 16.5
15 W	1 35 07	25 39 03	27 17 03	3♑13 48	5 28.9	11 18.4	29 18.4	24 30.5	0 25.9	21 38.8	15 44.9	24 26.9	25 58.0	3 16.2
16 Th	1 39 04	26 37 46	9♑09 04	15 03 28	5 27.0	13 03.4	29 14.0	25 17.1	0 27.3	21 48.5	15 41.9	24 29.9	25 59.4	3 15.9
17 F	1 43 00	27 36 27	20 57 40	26 52 20	5 26.5	14 44.6	29D12.1	26 03.8	0 29.1	21 58.0	15 38.9	24 32.9	26 00.7	3 15.5
18 Sa	1 46 57	28 35 06	2♒48 10	8♒45 51	5 26.6	16 22.0	29 12.5	26 50.4	0 31.3	22 07.5	15 36.1	24 35.9	26 02.0	3 15.1
19 Su	1 50 53	29 33 44	14 46 04	20 49 30	5 25.9	17 55.2	29 15.3	27 37.0	0 33.9	22 16.9	15 33.3	24 38.9	26 03.2	3 14.6
20 M	1 54 50	0♉32 20	26 56 45	3♓08 26	5 23.5	19 24.1	29 20.4	28 23.5	0 36.9	22 26.1	15 30.6	24 41.8	26 04.5	3 14.2
21 Tu	1 58 46	1 30 54	9♓25 03	15 47 02	5 18.8	20 48.4	29 27.8	29 10.1	0 40.3	22 35.2	15 28.0	24 44.7	26 05.7	3 13.7
22 W	2 02 43	2 29 26	22 14 44	28 48 21	5 11.4	22 08.1	29 37.4	29 56.6	0 44.1	22 44.2	15 25.5	24 47.6	26 06.9	3 13.1
23 Th	2 06 39	3 27 57	5♈28 01	12♈13 40	5 01.5	23 23.0	29 49.1	0♈43.1	0 48.3	22 53.0	15 23.1	24 50.5	26 08.0	3 12.6
24 F	2 10 36	4 26 26	19 05 06	26 01 58	4 49.9	24 33.0	0♈02.8	1 29.5	0 52.9	23 01.7	15 20.8	24 53.3	26 09.1	3 12.0
25 Sa	2 14 33	5 24 53	3♉03 48	10♉09 57	4 37.8	25 37.9	0 18.6	2 16.0	0 57.9	23 10.3	15 18.5	24 56.1	26 10.2	3 11.4
26 Su	2 18 29	6 23 18	17 19 43	24 32 19	4 26.3	26 37.8	0 36.3	3 02.4	1 03.3	23 18.8	15 16.4	24 58.9	26 11.3	3 10.7
27 M	2 22 26	7 21 42	1♊46 53	9♊02 35	4 16.8	27 32.5	0 55.9	3 48.8	1 09.1	23 27.1	15 14.4	25 01.7	26 12.3	3 10.1
28 Tu	2 26 22	8 20 03	16 18 37	23 34 14	4 10.0	28 21.9	1 17.4	4 35.1	1 15.2	23 35.3	15 12.4	25 04.4	26 13.3	3 09.4
29 W	2 30 19	9 18 23	0♋48 45	8♋01 38	4 06.0	29 06.0	1 40.5	5 21.4	1 21.7	23 43.4	15 10.6	25 07.1	26 14.3	3 08.6
30 Th	2 34 15	10 16 40	15 12 26	22 20 48	4D04.3	29 44.8	2 05.4	6 07.7	1 28.6	23 51.3	15 08.8	25 09.8	26 15.3	3 07.9

Astro Data

	Dy Hr Mn
♀ R	6 17:18
☽ 0S	11 4:38
☉ 0N	20 11:45
♃⚻♄	22 16:47
☽ 0N	25 14:06
☿ 0N	27 15:29
♃∠♇	27 17:04
♇ R	4 17:37
☽ 0S	7 12:50
⚳ D	12 17:41
♀ D	17 19:25
☽ 0N	21 22:45
♂ 0N	25 23:30

Planet Ingress

		Dy Hr Mn
☿	♓	8 18:57
♂	♓	15 3:21
☉	♈	20 11:45
☿	♈	25 19:56
☿	♉	9 14:22
♀	♓R	11 12:48
☉	♉	19 22:45
♂	♈	22 13:45
♀	♈	24 7:19
☿	♊	30 22:30

Last Aspect / ☽ Ingress (March)

Last Aspect Dy Hr Mn			☽ Ingress	Dy Hr Mn
28 17:52	♆	⚹	♉	1 3:34
2 22:43	♆	□	♊	3 8:00
5 2:11	♆	△	♋	5 11:08
7 0:30	♅	△	♌	7 13:25
9 7:57	♂	☍	♍	9 15:35
11 5:49	♅	☍	♎	11 18:47
13 22:40	♂	△	♏	14 0:24
16 0:44	☉	△	♐	16 9:23
18 17:48	☉	□	♑	18 21:20
20 20:07	♅	⚹	♒	21 10:08
23 12:10	♆	☌	♓	23 21:09
25 16:54	♅	☌	♈	26 5:04
28 2:18	♆	⚹	♉	28 10:10
30 6:02	♆	□	♊	30 13:37

Last Aspect / ☽ Ingress (April)

Last Aspect Dy Hr Mn			☽ Ingress	Dy Hr Mn
1 9:04	♆	△	♋	1 16:31
3 9:00	♅	△	♌	3 19:34
5 15:40	♆	☍	♍	5 23:02
7 16:53	♅	☍	♎	8 3:23
10 1:46	♆	△	♏	10 9:24
12 17:30	♀	△	♐	12 18:02
15 4:08	♀	□	♑	15 5:28
17 16:43	♀	⚹	♒	17 18:20
19 22:17	♆	☌	♓	20 5:56
22 13:30	♀	☌	♈	22 14:10
24 12:12	♆	⚹	♉	24 18:47
26 15:43	☿	☌	♊	26 21:03
28 16:24	♆	△	♋	28 22:39

☽ Phases & Eclipses

Dy Hr Mn		
4 7:47	☽	13♊52
11 2:39	○	20♍40
18 17:48	☾	28♐16
26 16:07	●	6♈08
2 14:35	☽	12♋59
9 14:57	○	19♎53
17 13:37	☾	27♑40
25 3:24	●	5♉04

Astro Data

1 March 2009
Julian Day # 39872
SVP 5♓07'40"
GC 26♐58.0 ⚵ 14♊05.4
Eris 20♈55.6 ⚴ 16♒01.7
⚷ 22♒32.8 ⚶ 15♉06.5
☽ Mean ☊ 7♒48.7

1 April 2009
Julian Day # 39903
SVP 5♓07'37"
GC 26♐58.1 ⚵ 27♊41.5
Eris 21♈14.0 ⚴ 28♒40.0
⚷ 24♒30.8 ⚶ 26♉37.4
☽ Mean ☊ 6♒10.1

LONGITUDE — May 2009

Day	Sid.Time	☉	0 hr ☽	Noon ☽	True ☊	☿	♀	♂	⚳	♃	♄	♅	♆	♇
1 F	2 38 12	11♉14 55	29♋26 30	6♌29 25	4♒04.1	0♊18.1	2♈31.8	6♈53.9	1♍35.9	23♒59.1	15♍07.2	25♓12.4	26♒16.2	3♑07.1
2 Sa	2 42 09	12 13 08	13♌29 27	20 26 36	4R 04.0	0 45.9	2 59.9	7 40.1	1 43.5	24 06.7	15R 05.7	25 15.0	26 17.0	3R 06.3
3 Su	2 46 05	13 11 19	27 20 53	4♍12 22	4 02.7	1 08.4	3 29.4	8 26.3	1 51.4	24 14.2	15 04.2	25 17.6	26 17.9	3 05.5
4 M	2 50 02	14 09 28	11♍01 04	17 47 02	3 59.3	1 25.4	4 00.4	9 12.4	1 59.7	24 21.6	15 02.9	25 20.1	26 18.7	3 04.6
5 Tu	2 53 58	15 07 35	24 30 17	1♎10 48	3 53.1	1 37.0	4 32.8	9 58.5	2 08.3	24 28.8	15 01.6	25 22.6	26 19.5	3 03.7
6 W	2 57 55	16 05 40	7♎48 34	14 23 32	3 44.2	1R 43.2	5 06.6	10 44.6	2 17.3	24 35.8	15 00.5	25 25.1	26 20.2	3 02.8
7 Th	3 01 51	17 03 44	20 55 36	27 24 42	3 33.1	1 44.3	5 41.6	11 30.6	2 26.6	24 42.8	14 59.4	25 27.5	26 21.0	3 01.9
8 F	3 05 48	18 01 45	3♏50 45	10♏13 39	3 20.7	1 40.3	6 18.0	12 16.5	2 36.2	24 49.5	14 58.5	25 29.9	26 21.6	3 00.9
9 Sa	3 09 44	18 59 46	16 33 22	22 49 50	3 08.1	1 31.5	6 55.5	13 02.5	2 46.2	24 56.1	14 57.7	25 32.3	26 22.3	3 00.0
10 Su	3 13 41	19 57 44	29 03 06	5♐13 12	2 56.6	1 18.1	7 34.2	13 48.4	2 56.4	25 02.6	14 56.9	25 34.6	26 22.9	2 59.0
11 M	3 17 37	20 55 41	11♐20 16	17 24 26	2 46.9	1 00.4	8 14.0	14 34.3	3 07.0	25 08.9	14 56.3	25 36.9	26 23.5	2 57.9
12 Tu	3 21 34	21 53 37	23 25 57	29 25 07	2 39.8	0 38.8	8 54.9	15 20.1	3 17.9	25 15.0	14 55.8	25 39.1	26 24.1	2 56.9
13 W	3 25 31	22 51 31	5♑22 16	11♑17 49	2 35.3	0 13.6	9 36.8	16 05.9	3 29.1	25 21.0	14 55.4	25 41.4	26 24.6	2 55.8
14 Th	3 29 27	23 49 24	17 12 15	23 06 04	2D 33.2	29♉45.4	10 19.7	16 51.6	3 40.5	25 26.9	14 55.0	25 43.5	26 25.1	2 54.7
15 F	3 33 24	24 47 15	28 59 50	4♒54 09	2 32.8	29 14.7	11 03.5	17 37.4	3 52.3	25 32.5	14 54.8	25 45.7	26 25.6	2 53.6
16 Sa	3 37 20	25 45 06	10♒49 40	16 47 01	2R 33.2	28 42.1	11 48.3	18 23.0	4 04.3	25 38.1	14D 54.7	25 47.8	26 26.0	2 52.5
17 Su	3 41 17	26 42 55	22 46 54	28 49 59	2 33.5	28 08.0	12 34.0	19 08.7	4 16.7	25 43.4	14 54.7	25 49.9	26 26.4	2 51.3
18 M	3 45 13	27 40 43	4♓56 56	11♓08 23	2 32.5	27 33.2	13 20.4	19 54.2	4 29.3	25 48.6	14 54.8	25 51.9	26 26.8	2 50.1
19 Tu	3 49 10	28 38 29	17 24 58	23 47 14	2 29.7	26 58.2	14 07.7	20 39.8	4 42.2	25 53.6	14 55.0	25 53.9	26 27.1	2 49.0
20 W	3 53 06	29 36 15	0♈15 37	6♈50 32	2 24.7	26 23.7	14 55.8	21 25.3	4 55.3	25 58.4	14 55.3	25 55.8	26 27.4	2 47.7
21 Th	3 57 03	0♊33 59	13 32 12	20 20 43	2 17.5	25 50.2	15 44.7	22 10.7	5 08.7	26 03.1	14 55.7	25 57.7	26 27.7	2 46.5
22 F	4 01 00	1 31 43	27 16 03	4♉17 56	2 08.7	25 18.3	16 34.2	22 56.1	5 22.4	26 07.6	14 56.2	25 59.6	26 27.9	2 45.3
23 Sa	4 04 56	2 29 25	11♉25 58	18 39 33	1 59.4	24 48.5	17 24.4	23 41.5	5 36.3	26 11.9	14 56.8	26 01.4	26 28.1	2 44.0
24 Su	4 08 53	3 27 06	25 57 54	3♊20 08	1 50.5	24 21.4	18 15.3	24 26.8	5 50.5	26 16.1	14 57.6	26 03.2	26 28.3	2 42.7
25 M	4 12 49	4 24 46	10♊45 14	18 12 07	1 43.1	23 57.2	19 06.9	25 12.1	6 05.0	26 20.0	14 58.4	26 05.0	26 28.4	2 41.4
26 Tu	4 16 46	5 22 25	25 39 41	3♋06 54	1 37.9	23 36.5	19 59.0	25 57.3	6 19.7	26 23.8	14 59.3	26 06.7	26 28.5	2 40.1
27 W	4 20 42	6 20 03	10♋32 46	17 56 23	1D 35.1	23 19.5	20 51.7	26 42.5	6 34.6	26 27.5	15 00.3	26 08.3	26 28.6	2 38.8
28 Th	4 24 39	7 17 39	25 17 01	2♌34 02	1 34.4	23 06.4	21 45.0	27 27.6	6 49.8	26 30.9	15 01.5	26 09.9	26R 28.7	2 37.4
29 F	4 28 36	8 15 13	9♌46 59	16 55 32	1 35.0	22 57.4	22 38.8	28 12.6	7 05.2	26 34.1	15 02.7	26 11.5	26 28.7	2 36.1
30 Sa	4 32 32	9 12 46	23 59 30	0♍58 47	1R 35.8	22D 52.8	23 33.2	28 57.6	7 20.8	26 37.2	15 04.1	26 13.0	26 28.6	2 34.7
31 Su	4 36 29	10 10 18	7♍53 25	14 43 28	1 36.0	22 52.5	24 28.0	29 42.6	7 36.6	26 40.1	15 05.5	26 14.5	26 28.6	2 33.3

LONGITUDE — June 2009

Day	Sid.Time	☉	0 hr ☽	Noon ☽	True ☊	☿	♀	♂	⚳	♃	♄	♅	♆	♇
1 M	4 40 25	11♊07 48	21♍29 05	28♍10 25	1♒34.6	22♉56.7	25♈23.4	0♉27.4	7♍52.7	26♒42.8	15♍07.0	26♓15.9	26♒28.5	2♑31.9
2 Tu	4 44 22	12 05 17	4♎47 42	11♎21 05	1R 31.1	23 05.4	26 19.2	1 12.3	8 09.0	26 45.3	15 08.7	26 17.3	26R 28.4	2R 30.5
3 W	4 48 18	13 02 44	17 50 48	24 17 01	1 25.7	23 18.6	27 15.4	1 57.1	8 25.5	26 47.7	15 10.4	26 18.7	26 28.2	2 29.0
4 Th	4 52 15	14 00 11	0♏39 56	6♏59 41	1 18.6	23 36.2	28 12.2	2 41.8	8 42.2	26 49.8	15 12.3	26 20.0	26 28.0	2 27.6
5 F	4 56 11	14 57 36	13 16 25	19 30 18	1 10.5	23 58.3	29 09.3	3 26.4	8 59.1	26 51.8	15 14.2	26 21.2	26 27.8	2 26.2
6 Sa	5 00 08	15 55 01	25 41 26	1♐49 58	1 02.3	24 24.7	0♉06.9	4 11.1	9 16.2	26 53.6	15 16.2	26 22.4	26 27.5	2 24.7
7 Su	5 04 05	16 52 24	7♐56 02	13 59 46	0 54.7	24 55.3	1 04.9	4 55.6	9 33.5	26 55.2	15 18.4	26 23.6	26 27.3	2 23.2
8 M	5 08 01	17 49 47	20 01 20	26 00 56	0 48.5	25 30.2	2 03.2	5 40.1	9 50.9	26 56.6	15 20.6	26 24.7	26 27.0	2 21.8
9 Tu	5 11 58	18 47 09	1♑58 47	7♑55 07	0 44.1	26 09.2	3 02.0	6 24.6	10 08.6	26 57.8	15 22.9	26 25.8	26 26.6	2 20.3
10 W	5 15 54	19 44 30	13 50 12	19 44 24	0D 41.6	26 52.2	4 01.1	7 09.0	10 26.5	26 58.8	15 25.4	26 26.8	26 26.2	2 18.8
11 Th	5 19 51	20 41 50	25 38 03	1♒31 33	0 41.0	27 39.1	5 00.6	7 53.3	10 44.5	26 59.6	15 27.9	26 27.8	26 25.8	2 17.3
12 F	5 23 47	21 39 10	7♒25 21	13 19 55	0 41.7	28 29.9	6 00.4	8 37.6	11 02.7	27 00.3	15 30.5	26 28.7	26 25.4	2 15.8
13 Sa	5 27 44	22 36 29	19 15 48	25 13 31	0 43.2	29 24.5	7 00.5	9 21.8	11 21.1	27 00.7	15 33.2	26 29.6	26 24.9	2 14.3
14 Su	5 31 40	23 33 48	1♓13 39	7♓16 48	0 44.7	0♊22.8	8 01.0	10 06.0	11 39.6	27R 01.0	15 36.0	26 30.5	26 24.4	2 12.7
15 M	5 35 37	24 31 06	13 23 35	19 34 34	0R 45.7	1 24.6	9 01.8	10 50.1	11 58.4	27 01.0	15 38.9	26 31.3	26 23.9	2 11.2
16 Tu	5 39 34	25 28 25	25 50 22	2♈11 33	0 45.6	2 30.1	10 02.9	11 34.1	12 17.3	27 00.9	15 41.9	26 32.0	26 23.3	2 09.7
17 W	5 43 30	26 25 42	8♈38 37	15 12 02	0 44.2	3 39.1	11 04.3	12 18.1	12 36.3	27 00.6	15 45.0	26 32.7	26 22.7	2 08.1
18 Th	5 47 27	27 23 00	21 52 08	28 39 11	0 41.3	4 51.5	12 05.9	13 02.0	12 55.6	27 00.1	15 48.1	26 33.3	26 22.1	2 06.6
19 F	5 51 23	28 20 17	5♉33 17	12♉34 24	0 37.4	6 07.3	13 07.9	13 45.9	13 14.9	26 59.4	15 51.4	26 33.9	26 21.5	2 05.1
20 Sa	5 55 20	29 17 34	19 42 17	26 56 33	0 32.9	7 26.6	14 10.1	14 29.7	13 34.5	26 58.5	15 54.8	26 34.5	26 20.8	2 03.5
21 Su	5 59 16	0♋14 51	4♊16 36	11♊41 38	0 28.6	8 49.1	15 12.5	15 13.4	13 54.2	26 57.4	15 58.2	26 35.0	26 20.1	2 02.0
22 M	6 03 13	1 12 08	19 10 45	26 42 52	0 25.1	10 14.9	16 15.2	15 57.1	14 14.0	26 56.1	16 01.7	26 35.4	26 19.4	2 00.4
23 Tu	6 07 09	2 09 24	4♋16 49	11♋51 24	0 22.7	11 44.0	17 18.2	16 40.7	14 34.0	26 54.6	16 05.3	26 35.9	26 18.6	1 58.9
24 W	6 11 06	3 06 40	19 25 27	26 57 47	0D 21.8	13 16.3	18 21.4	17 24.3	14 54.2	26 52.9	16 09.0	26 36.2	26 17.8	1 57.3
25 Th	6 15 03	4 03 55	4♌27 23	11♌53 19	0 22.1	14 51.8	19 24.7	18 07.7	15 14.4	26 51.1	16 12.8	26 36.5	26 17.0	1 55.8
26 F	6 18 59	5 01 10	19 14 48	26 31 13	0 23.2	16 30.5	20 28.4	18 51.1	15 34.9	26 49.0	16 16.7	26 36.8	26 16.1	1 54.3
27 Sa	6 22 56	5 58 24	3♍42 08	10♍47 15	0 24.6	18 12.2	21 32.2	19 34.5	15 55.4	26 46.8	16 20.6	26 37.0	26 15.3	1 52.7
28 Su	6 26 52	6 55 37	17 46 24	24 39 36	0R 25.8	19 57.0	22 36.2	20 17.7	16 16.1	26 44.3	16 24.7	26 37.1	26 14.4	1 51.2
29 M	6 30 49	7 52 50	1♎26 55	8♎08 31	0 26.2	21 44.8	23 40.4	21 00.9	16 36.9	26 41.7	16 28.8	26 37.3	26 13.4	1 49.6
30 Tu	6 34 45	8 50 03	14 44 40	21 15 40	0 25.7	23 35.4	24 44.9	21 44.0	16 57.9	26 38.9	16 33.0	26R 37.3	26 12.5	1 48.1

Astro Data

	Dy Hr Mn
☽0S	4 18:27
☿R	7 5:01
♄D	17 2:08
☽0N	19 7:02
♃⊻♅	19 14:26
♃☌♆	27 20:07
♆R	29 4:30
☿D	31 1:22
☽0S	31 23:03
♅⊻♆	10 1:45
♃R	15 7:51
☽0N	15 14:13
☽0S	28 4:57

Planet Ingress

		Dy Hr Mn
☿	♉R	13 23:54
☉	♊	20 21:52
♂	♉	31 21:19
♀	♉	6 9:08
☿	♊	14 2:48
☉	♋	21 5:47

Last Aspect / ☽ Ingress (May)

Last Aspect Dy Hr Mn			☽ Ingress	Dy Hr Mn
30 16:46	♅	△	♌	1 0:57
2 22:09	♆	☍	♍	3 4:38
5 1:32	♅	☍	♎	5 9:52
7 10:02	♆	△	♏	7 16:49
9 18:49	♆	□	♐	10 1:50
12 5:56	♆	⚹	♑	12 13:10
15 1:00	☿	△	♒	15 2:02
17 10:41	☿	□	♓	17 14:18
19 21:44	☉	⚹	♈	19 23:31
21 22:37	♆	⚹	♉	22 4:41
24 0:50	♆	□	♊	24 6:35
26 1:19	♆	△	♋	26 6:59
28 3:07	♂	□	♌	28 7:45
30 8:19	♂	△	♍	30 10:19

Last Aspect / ☽ Ingress (June)

Last Aspect Dy Hr Mn			☽ Ingress	Dy Hr Mn
1 8:33	♅	☍	♎	1 15:18
3 18:01	♀	☍	♏	3 22:45
6 2:19	♃	□	♐	6 8:25
8 13:52	♃	⚹	♑	8 20:01
11 3:32	☿	△	♒	11 8:54
13 21:06	☿	□	♓	13 21:33
16 1:19	♅	☌	♈	16 7:53
18 9:36	☉	⚹	♉	18 14:21
20 12:03	♃	□	♊	20 17:01
22 12:21	♃	△	♋	22 17:13
24 11:26	♅	△	♌	24 16:51
26 12:30	♃	☍	♍	26 17:48
28 15:27	♅	☍	♎	28 21:26

☽ Phases & Eclipses

Dy Hr Mn		
1 20:45	☽	11♌36
9 4:03	○	18♏41
17 7:27	☾	26♒32
24 12:12	●	3♊28
31 3:23	☽	9♍50
7 18:13	○	17♐07
15 22:16	☾	24♓56
22 19:36	●	1♋30
29 11:30	☽	7♎52

Astro Data

1 May 2009
Julian Day # 39933
SVP 5♓07'33"
GC 26♐58.2 ⚵ 12♋40.0
Eris 21♈33.5 ⚴ 10♓21.1
⚷ 25♒47.8 ⚶ 8♊51.8
☽ Mean ☊ 4♒34.8

1 June 2009
Julian Day # 39964
SVP 5♓07'28"
GC 26♐58.2 ⚵ 28♋39.4
Eris 21♈50.5 ⚴ 21♓14.5
⚷ 26♒13.7R ⚶ 22♊05.1
☽ Mean ☊ 2♒56.3

July 2009 LONGITUDE

Day	Sid.Time	☉	0 hr ☽	Noon ☽	True ☊	☿	♀	♂	⚳	♃	♄	♅	♆	♇
1 W	6 38 42	9♋47 15	27♎41 51	4♏03 34	0♒24.2	25♊28.8	25♉49.5	22♉27.1	17♍19.0	26♒36.0	16♍37.3	26♓37.3	26♒11.5	1♑46.6
2 Th	6 42 38	10 44 27	10♏21 11	16 35 04	0R 22.0	27 24.8	26 54.3	23 10.1	17 40.2	26R 32.8	16 41.6	26R 37.3	26R 10.5	1R 45.0
3 F	6 46 35	11 41 39	22 45 34	28 53 04	0 19.3	29 23.3	27 59.3	23 53.0	18 01.5	26 29.5	16 46.1	26 37.2	26 09.5	1 43.5
4 Sa	6 50 32	12 38 50	4♐57 51	11♐00 17	0 16.5	1♋24.0	29 04.5	24 35.8	18 22.9	26 25.9	16 50.6	26 37.1	26 08.4	1 42.0
5 Su	6 54 28	13 36 01	17 00 40	22 59 16	0 14.0	3 26.8	0♊09.8	25 18.6	18 44.5	26 22.2	16 55.2	26 36.9	26 07.3	1 40.5
6 M	6 58 25	14 33 13	28 56 23	4♑52 18	0 12.1	5 31.4	1 15.4	26 01.3	19 06.2	26 18.4	16 59.8	26 36.7	26 06.2	1 39.0
7 Tu	7 02 21	15 30 24	10♑47 17	16 41 36	0 10.9	7 37.6	2 21.1	26 43.9	19 28.0	26 14.3	17 04.6	26 36.4	26 05.1	1 37.5
8 W	7 06 18	16 27 35	22 35 31	28 29 20	0D 10.4	9 45.0	3 26.9	27 26.4	19 49.9	26 10.1	17 09.4	26 36.1	26 04.0	1 36.0
9 Th	7 10 14	17 24 47	4♒23 21	10♒17 51	0 10.6	11 53.4	4 33.0	28 08.9	20 11.9	26 05.8	17 14.3	26 35.7	26 02.8	1 34.6
10 F	7 14 11	18 21 58	16 13 12	22 09 44	0 11.4	14 02.5	5 39.2	28 51.3	20 34.0	26 01.2	17 19.2	26 35.3	26 01.6	1 33.1
11 Sa	7 18 08	19 19 10	28 07 49	4♓07 52	0 12.3	16 12.0	6 45.5	29 33.7	20 56.2	25 56.5	17 24.2	26 34.9	26 00.4	1 31.6
12 Su	7 22 04	20 16 22	10♓10 17	16 15 32	0 13.3	18 21.5	7 52.0	0♊15.9	21 18.5	25 51.7	17 29.3	26 34.4	25 59.2	1 30.2
13 M	7 26 01	21 13 35	22 24 02	28 36 17	0 14.2	20 30.9	8 58.7	0 58.1	21 40.9	25 46.6	17 34.5	26 33.8	25 57.9	1 28.8
14 Tu	7 29 57	22 10 48	4♈52 44	11♈13 52	0R 14.7	22 39.8	10 05.5	1 40.2	22 03.4	25 41.4	17 39.7	26 33.2	25 56.6	1 27.3
15 W	7 33 54	23 08 02	17 40 06	24 11 53	0 14.8	24 48.0	11 12.5	2 22.3	22 26.0	25 36.1	17 45.0	26 32.6	25 55.3	1 25.9
16 Th	7 37 50	24 05 17	0♉49 32	7♉33 23	0 14.7	26 55.4	12 19.6	3 04.2	22 48.8	25 30.6	17 50.4	26 31.9	25 54.0	1 24.5
17 F	7 41 47	25 02 32	14 23 38	21 20 23	0 14.3	29 01.7	13 26.8	3 46.1	23 11.6	25 25.0	17 55.8	26 31.1	25 52.7	1 23.1
18 Sa	7 45 43	25 59 48	28 23 37	5♊33 09	0 13.8	1♌06.9	14 34.2	4 27.9	23 34.5	25 19.2	18 01.3	26 30.3	25 51.4	1 21.8
19 Su	7 49 40	26 57 05	12♊48 38	20 09 36	0 13.4	3 10.7	15 41.8	5 09.7	23 57.5	25 13.3	18 06.9	26 29.5	25 50.0	1 20.4
20 M	7 53 37	27 54 22	27 35 23	5♋05 07	0 13.2	5 13.0	16 49.4	5 51.3	24 20.6	25 07.3	18 12.5	26 28.6	25 48.6	1 19.1
21 Tu	7 57 33	28 51 40	12♋37 53	20 12 34	0D 13.1	7 13.9	17 57.2	6 32.9	24 43.7	25 01.1	18 18.2	26 27.7	25 47.2	1 17.7
22 W	8 01 30	29 48 59	27 48 02	5♌23 06	0R 13.1	9 13.1	19 05.1	7 14.4	25 07.0	24 54.8	18 23.9	26 26.8	25 45.8	1 16.4
23 Th	8 05 26	0♌46 18	12♌56 34	20 27 20	0 13.1	11 10.7	20 13.1	7 55.8	25 30.4	24 48.4	18 29.7	26 25.8	25 44.4	1 15.1
24 F	8 09 23	1 43 37	27 54 22	5♍16 46	0 13.0	13 06.7	21 21.2	8 37.1	25 53.8	24 41.9	18 35.6	26 24.7	25 42.9	1 13.8
25 Sa	8 13 19	2 40 57	12♍33 47	19 44 50	0 12.8	15 00.9	22 29.5	9 18.4	26 17.3	24 35.2	18 41.5	26 23.6	25 41.4	1 12.6
26 Su	8 17 16	3 38 18	26 49 32	3♎47 37	0 12.5	16 53.5	23 37.8	9 59.5	26 40.9	24 28.4	18 47.5	26 22.5	25 40.0	1 11.3
27 M	8 21 12	4 35 38	10♎39 00	17 23 45	0 12.2	18 44.4	24 46.3	10 40.6	27 04.6	24 21.6	18 53.5	26 21.3	25 38.5	1 10.1
28 Tu	8 25 09	5 32 59	24 02 02	0♏34 09	0D 12.0	20 33.5	25 54.9	11 21.5	27 28.3	24 14.6	18 59.6	26 20.1	25 37.0	1 08.9
29 W	8 29 06	6 30 21	7♏00 27	13 21 21	0 12.0	22 21.0	27 03.5	12 02.4	27 52.2	24 07.6	19 05.7	26 18.8	25 35.5	1 07.7
30 Th	8 33 02	7 27 43	19 37 19	25 48 52	0 12.3	24 06.7	28 12.3	12 43.2	28 16.1	24 00.4	19 11.9	26 17.5	25 33.9	1 06.5
31 F	8 36 59	8 25 06	1♐56 31	8♐00 45	0 13.0	25 50.8	29 21.2	13 23.9	28 40.0	23 53.2	19 18.1	26 16.2	25 32.4	1 05.4

August 2009 LONGITUDE

Day	Sid.Time	☉	0 hr ☽	Noon ☽	True ☊	☿	♀	♂	⚳	♃	♄	♅	♆	♇
1 Sa	8 40 55	9♌22 29	14♐02 06	20♐01 04	0♒13.9	27♌33.1	0♋30.3	14♊04.5	29♍04.1	23♒45.9	19♍24.4	26♓14.8	25♒30.8	1♑04.2
2 Su	8 44 52	10 19 53	25 58 08	1♑53 45	0 14.8	29 13.8	1 39.4	14 45.1	29 28.2	23R 38.5	19 30.7	26R 13.4	25R 29.3	1R 03.1
3 M	8 48 48	11 17 18	7♑48 20	13 42 19	0 15.6	0♍52.9	2 48.6	15 25.5	29 52.4	23 31.1	19 37.1	26 11.9	25 27.7	1 02.0
4 Tu	8 52 45	12 14 44	19 36 03	25 29 55	0R 16.1	2 30.3	3 57.9	16 05.9	0♎16.6	23 23.5	19 43.6	26 10.4	25 26.1	1 01.0
5 W	8 56 41	13 12 10	1♒24 14	7♒19 17	0 16.0	4 06.0	5 07.4	16 46.2	0 40.9	23 16.0	19 50.0	26 08.9	25 24.6	0 59.9
6 Th	9 00 38	14 09 37	13 15 24	19 12 48	0 15.3	5 40.0	6 16.9	17 26.3	1 05.3	23 08.3	19 56.6	26 07.3	25 23.0	0 58.9
7 F	9 04 35	15 07 06	25 11 47	1♓12 35	0 13.9	7 12.4	7 26.5	18 06.4	1 29.7	23 00.7	20 03.1	26 05.7	25 21.4	0 57.9
8 Sa	9 08 31	16 04 35	7♓15 25	13 20 34	0 11.8	8 43.2	8 36.3	18 46.4	1 54.2	22 53.0	20 09.7	26 04.1	25 19.8	0 56.9
9 Su	9 12 28	17 02 06	19 28 15	25 38 44	0 09.4	10 12.2	9 46.1	19 26.3	2 18.8	22 45.2	20 16.4	26 02.4	25 18.1	0 55.9
10 M	9 16 24	17 59 37	1♈52 15	8♈09 04	0 06.9	11 39.6	10 56.0	20 06.1	2 43.4	22 37.4	20 23.1	26 00.7	25 16.5	0 55.0
11 Tu	9 20 21	18 57 11	14 29 26	20 53 40	0 04.7	13 05.3	12 06.1	20 45.9	3 08.0	22 29.6	20 29.8	25 59.0	25 14.9	0 54.1
12 W	9 24 17	19 54 45	27 21 59	3♉54 41	0 03.1	14 29.2	13 16.2	21 25.5	3 32.8	22 21.8	20 36.6	25 57.2	25 13.3	0 53.2
13 Th	9 28 14	20 52 21	10♉32 01	17 14 11	0D 02.3	15 51.4	14 26.4	22 05.0	3 57.6	22 13.9	20 43.4	25 55.4	25 11.6	0 52.4
14 F	9 32 10	21 49 59	24 01 24	0♊53 48	0 02.5	17 11.8	15 36.7	22 44.5	4 22.4	22 06.1	20 50.2	25 53.5	25 10.0	0 51.5
15 Sa	9 36 07	22 47 38	7♊51 26	14 54 19	0 03.5	18 30.4	16 47.2	23 23.8	4 47.3	21 58.2	20 57.1	25 51.7	25 08.4	0 50.7
16 Su	9 40 04	23 45 19	22 02 20	29 15 14	0 04.8	19 47.1	17 57.7	24 03.1	5 12.3	21 50.4	21 04.0	25 49.8	25 06.7	0 49.9
17 M	9 44 00	24 43 01	6♋32 41	13♋54 11	0 06.1	21 01.9	19 08.3	24 42.2	5 37.3	21 42.5	21 11.0	25 47.8	25 05.1	0 49.2
18 Tu	9 47 57	25 40 45	21 19 05	28 46 39	0R 06.7	22 14.7	20 19.0	25 21.3	6 02.4	21 34.7	21 17.9	25 45.9	25 03.5	0 48.4
19 W	9 51 53	26 38 30	6♌16 00	13♌46 07	0 06.2	23 25.4	21 29.8	26 00.2	6 27.5	21 26.9	21 25.0	25 43.9	25 01.8	0 47.7
20 Th	9 55 50	27 36 17	21 15 59	28 44 31	0 04.3	24 34.0	22 40.6	26 39.1	6 52.6	21 19.1	21 32.0	25 41.9	25 00.2	0 47.1
21 F	9 59 46	28 34 05	6♍10 38	13♍33 20	0 01.2	25 40.4	23 51.6	27 17.8	7 17.9	21 11.4	21 39.1	25 39.8	24 58.6	0 46.4
22 Sa	10 03 43	29 31 54	20 51 42	28 04 54	29♑57.1	26 44.4	25 02.6	27 56.4	7 43.1	21 03.6	21 46.2	25 37.8	24 56.9	0 45.8
23 Su	10 07 39	0♍29 44	5♎12 18	12♎13 24	29 52.7	27 45.9	26 13.7	28 34.9	8 08.4	20 56.0	21 53.3	25 35.7	24 55.3	0 45.2
24 M	10 11 36	1 27 36	19 07 54	25 55 38	29 48.5	28 44.9	27 24.9	29 13.3	8 33.8	20 48.4	22 00.5	25 33.6	24 53.7	0 44.6
25 Tu	10 15 33	2 25 29	2♏36 37	9♏10 59	29 45.2	29 41.2	28 36.1	29 51.6	8 59.2	20 40.8	22 07.7	25 31.4	24 52.0	0 44.1
26 W	10 19 29	3 23 23	15 39 01	22 01 06	29D 43.1	0♎34.5	29 47.5	0♋29.8	9 24.6	20 33.3	22 14.9	25 29.3	24 50.4	0 43.6
27 Th	10 23 26	4 21 19	28 17 41	4♐29 19	29 42.5	1 24.9	0♌58.9	1 07.8	9 50.1	20 25.9	22 22.1	25 27.1	24 48.8	0 43.1
28 F	10 27 22	5 19 16	10♐36 34	16 40 02	29 43.1	2 12.0	2 10.4	1 45.8	10 15.6	20 18.5	22 29.4	25 24.9	24 47.2	0 42.7
29 Sa	10 31 19	6 17 14	22 40 20	28 38 06	29 44.5	2 55.6	3 22.0	2 23.6	10 41.2	20 11.3	22 36.6	25 22.7	24 45.6	0 42.3
30 Su	10 35 15	7 15 14	4♑33 57	10♑28 29	29 46.2	3 35.7	4 33.6	3 01.4	11 06.8	20 04.1	22 43.9	25 20.4	24 44.0	0 41.9
31 M	10 39 12	8 13 14	16 22 17	22 15 53	29R 47.5	4 11.8	5 45.3	3 39.0	11 32.4	19 57.0	22 51.3	25 18.2	24 42.4	0 41.5

Astro Data

	Dy Hr Mn
♃⊻♅	1 1:05
♅ R	1 7:39
♃☌♆	10 9:14
☽0N	12 20:22
☽0S	25 13:20
☽0N	9 2:09
♃⊼♄	19 15:08
☿0S	21 21:07
☽0S	21 23:36

Planet Ingress

		Dy Hr Mn
☿	♋	3 19:21
♀	♊	5 8:24
♂	♊	12 2:57
☿	♌	17 23:09
☉	♌	22 16:37
♀	♋	1 1:29
☿	♍	2 23:08
⚳	♎	3 19:34
☊	♑R	21 19:27
☉	♍	22 23:40
♂	♋	25 17:17
☿	♎	25 20:19
♀	♌	26 16:13

Last Aspect / ☽ Ingress

Last Aspect Dy Hr Mn			☽ Ingress	Dy Hr Mn
30 22:00	♃	△	♏	1 4:20
3 10:04	♀	☍	♐	3 14:12
5 19:18	♅	□	♑	6 2:09
8 9:44	♂	△	♒	8 15:04
11 2:18	♂	□	♓	11 3:45
13 8:04	♅	☌	♈	13 14:41
15 15:08	♆	⚹	♉	15 22:31
17 20:49	♅	⚹	♊	18 2:42
19 22:13	♅	□	♋	20 3:52
22 2:36	☉	☌	♌	22 3:29
23 20:29	♆	☍	♍	24 3:24
25 23:15	♅	☍	♎	26 5:27
28 2:54	♆	△	♏	28 10:57
30 12:56	♅	△	♐	30 20:11

Last Aspect Dy Hr Mn			☽ Ingress	Dy Hr Mn
2 5:43	☿	△	♑	2 8:09
4 13:22	♅	⚹	♒	4 21:09
7 0:21	♆	☌	♓	7 9:35
9 12:46	♅	☌	♈	9 20:24
11 20:04	♆	⚹	♉	12 4:51
14 3:18	♅	⚹	♊	14 10:27
16 6:20	♅	□	♋	16 13:14
18 7:10	♅	△	♌	18 13:58
20 10:03	☉	☌	♍	20 14:02
22 11:45	♂	□	♎	22 15:13
24 18:11	♂	△	♏	24 19:17
26 18:36	♅	△	♐	27 3:17
29 5:27	♅	□	♑	29 14:45

☽ Phases & Eclipses

Dy Hr Mn	
7 9:23	○ 15♑24
7 9:40	A 0.156
15 9:54	☾ 23♈03
22 2:36	● 29♋27
22 2:36:24	T 06'39"
28 22:01	☽ 5♏57
6 0:56	○ 13♒43
6 0:40	A 0.402
13 18:56	☾ 21♉09
20 10:03	● 27♌32
27 11:43	☽ 4♐21

Astro Data

1 July 2009
Julian Day # 39994
SVP 5♓07'23"
GC 26♐58.3 ⚴ 14♌03.0
Eris 22♈00.1 ⚵ 29♓38.7
⚷ 25♒43.2R ⚶ 5♋06.4
☽ Mean ☊ 1♒21.0

1 August 2009
Julian Day # 40025
SVP 5♓07'17"
GC 26♐58.4 ⚴ 29♌38.3
Eris 22♈00.5R ⚵ 4♈20.7
⚷ 24♒26.5R ⚶ 18♋31.9
☽ Mean ☊ 29♑42.6

LONGITUDE — September 2009

Day	Sid.Time	☉	0 hr ☽	Noon☽	True☊	☿	♀	♂	⚳	♃	♄	♅	♆	♇
1 Tu	10 43 08	9♍11 17	28♑09 48	4♒04 32	29♑47.7	4♎43.8	6♌57.1	4♋16.5	11♎58.1	19♒49.9	22♍58.6	25♓15.9	24♒40.9	0♑41.2
2 W	10 47 05	10 09 20	10♒00 29	15 58 03	29R 46.2	5 11.3	8 09.0	4 53.8	12 23.8	19R 43.0	23 05.9	25R 13.6	24R 39.3	0R 40.9
3 Th	10 51 02	11 07 26	21 57 34	27 59 20	29 42.9	5 34.2	9 21.0	5 31.1	12 49.5	19 36.2	23 13.3	25 11.3	24 37.7	0 40.6
4 F	10 54 58	12 05 32	4♓03 35	10♓10 32	29 37.7	5 52.1	10 33.0	6 08.2	13 15.3	19 29.5	23 20.7	25 09.0	24 36.2	0 40.4
5 Sa	10 58 55	13 03 41	16 20 20	22 33 07	29 31.0	6 04.7	11 45.1	6 45.3	13 41.1	19 22.9	23 28.1	25 06.7	24 34.6	0 40.2
6 Su	11 02 51	14 01 51	28 48 56	5♈07 53	29 23.2	6R 11.8	12 57.3	7 22.2	14 07.0	19 16.5	23 35.5	25 04.4	24 33.1	0 40.0
7 M	11 06 48	15 00 03	11♈29 58	17 55 13	29 15.2	6 13.0	14 09.5	7 58.9	14 32.8	19 10.1	23 42.9	25 02.0	24 31.6	0 39.8
8 Tu	11 10 44	15 58 17	24 23 40	0♉55 18	29 07.9	6 08.0	15 21.9	8 35.6	14 58.7	19 03.9	23 50.3	24 59.6	24 30.1	0 39.7
9 W	11 14 41	16 56 33	7♉30 09	14 08 15	29 02.0	5 56.7	16 34.3	9 12.1	15 24.7	18 57.8	23 57.8	24 57.3	24 28.6	0 39.6
10 Th	11 18 37	17 54 51	20 49 37	27 34 17	28 58.0	5 38.9	17 46.7	9 48.5	15 50.6	18 51.8	24 05.2	24 54.9	24 27.1	0 39.6
11 F	11 22 34	18 53 12	4♊22 20	11♊13 47	28D 56.1	5 14.5	18 59.3	10 24.8	16 16.6	18 46.0	24 12.7	24 52.5	24 25.7	0D 39.5
12 Sa	11 26 31	19 51 34	18 08 41	25 07 03	28 56.0	4 43.4	20 11.9	11 01.0	16 42.7	18 40.3	24 20.2	24 50.1	24 24.2	0 39.5
13 Su	11 30 27	20 49 59	2♋08 52	9♋14 03	28 56.8	4 05.9	21 24.6	11 37.0	17 08.7	18 34.7	24 27.6	24 47.7	24 22.8	0 39.6
14 M	11 34 24	21 48 25	16 22 29	23 33 57	28R 57.6	3 22.2	22 37.4	12 12.9	17 34.8	18 29.4	24 35.1	24 45.3	24 21.4	0 39.7
15 Tu	11 38 20	22 46 54	0♌48 07	8♌04 34	28 57.4	2 32.7	23 50.2	12 48.6	18 00.9	18 24.1	24 42.6	24 42.9	24 20.0	0 39.8
16 W	11 42 17	23 45 25	15 22 47	22 42 07	28 55.2	1 38.2	25 03.1	13 24.2	18 27.0	18 19.0	24 50.1	24 40.5	24 18.6	0 39.9
17 Th	11 46 13	24 43 58	0♍01 50	7♍21 07	28 50.7	0 39.5	26 16.0	13 59.7	18 53.2	18 14.1	24 57.6	24 38.1	24 17.2	0 40.1
18 F	11 50 10	25 42 33	14 39 07	21 54 56	28 43.7	29♍37.7	27 29.1	14 35.0	19 19.4	18 09.3	25 05.0	24 35.7	24 15.9	0 40.3
19 Sa	11 54 06	26 41 09	29 07 42	6♎16 36	28 34.9	28 34.1	28 42.1	15 10.1	19 45.6	18 04.7	25 12.5	24 33.3	24 14.6	0 40.5
20 Su	11 58 03	27 39 48	13♎20 55	20 20 01	28 25.2	27 30.1	29 55.3	15 45.1	20 11.8	18 00.3	25 20.0	24 30.9	24 13.3	0 40.7
21 M	12 01 59	28 38 28	27 13 25	4♏00 47	28 15.6	26 27.2	1♍08.5	16 20.0	20 38.1	17 56.1	25 27.5	24 28.5	24 12.0	0 41.0
22 Tu	12 05 56	29 37 11	10♏41 56	17 16 50	28 07.3	25 27.1	2 21.7	16 54.7	21 04.4	17 52.0	25 35.0	24 26.1	24 10.7	0 41.4
23 W	12 09 53	0♎35 55	23 45 36	0♐08 29	28 01.0	24 31.3	3 35.0	17 29.2	21 30.7	17 48.1	25 42.4	24 23.7	24 09.5	0 41.7
24 Th	12 13 49	1 34 40	6♐25 50	12 38 06	27 56.9	23 41.3	4 48.4	18 03.6	21 57.0	17 44.4	25 49.9	24 21.4	24 08.2	0 42.1
25 F	12 17 46	2 33 28	18 45 49	24 49 34	27D 55.1	22 58.4	6 01.8	18 37.8	22 23.3	17 40.8	25 57.4	24 19.0	24 07.0	0 42.5
26 Sa	12 21 42	3 32 17	0♑49 59	6♑47 44	27 54.8	22 23.7	7 15.3	19 11.9	22 49.6	17 37.5	26 04.8	24 16.6	24 05.9	0 43.0
27 Su	12 25 39	4 31 08	12 43 30	18 37 58	27R 55.3	21 58.1	8 28.8	19 45.8	23 16.0	17 34.3	26 12.2	24 14.3	24 04.7	0 43.5
28 M	12 29 35	5 30 01	24 31 50	0♒25 43	27 55.5	21 42.3	9 42.4	20 19.5	23 42.4	17 31.3	26 19.7	24 11.9	24 03.6	0 44.0
29 Tu	12 33 32	6 28 55	6♒20 18	12 16 10	27 54.5	21D 36.6	10 56.0	20 53.1	24 08.8	17 28.6	26 27.1	24 09.6	24 02.5	0 44.5
30 W	12 37 28	7 27 51	18 13 52	24 13 56	27 51.3	21 41.3	12 09.7	21 26.5	24 35.2	17 26.0	26 34.5	24 07.3	24 01.4	0 45.1

LONGITUDE — October 2009

Day	Sid.Time	☉	0 hr ☽	Noon☽	True☊	☿	♀	♂	⚳	♃	♄	♅	♆	♇
1 Th	12 41 25	8♎26 49	0♓16 48	6♓22 52	27♑45.6	21♍56.1	13♍23.5	21♋59.7	25♎01.6	17♒23.6	26♍41.9	24♓04.9	24♒00.3	0♑45.7
2 F	12 45 22	9 25 49	12 32 26	18 45 45	27R 37.3	22 20.9	14 37.2	22 32.8	25 28.0	17R 21.3	26 49.3	24R 02.6	23R 59.3	0 46.3
3 Sa	12 49 18	10 24 51	25 02 59	1♈24 12	27 26.6	22 55.2	15 51.1	23 05.6	25 54.4	17 19.3	26 56.6	24 00.4	23 58.3	0 47.0
4 Su	12 53 15	11 23 55	7♈49 25	14 18 34	27 14.5	23 38.6	17 05.0	23 38.3	26 20.9	17 17.5	27 03.9	23 58.1	23 57.3	0 47.7
5 M	12 57 11	12 23 00	20 51 30	27 28 02	27 02.0	24 30.2	18 18.9	24 10.8	26 47.3	17 15.9	27 11.3	23 55.9	23 56.3	0 48.4
6 Tu	13 01 08	13 22 08	4♉07 55	10♉50 55	26 50.4	25 29.6	19 32.9	24 43.2	27 13.8	17 14.4	27 18.6	23 53.6	23 55.4	0 49.2
7 W	13 05 04	14 21 18	17 36 43	24 25 04	26 40.7	26 35.9	20 46.9	25 15.3	27 40.3	17 13.2	27 25.8	23 51.4	23 54.5	0 50.0
8 Th	13 09 01	15 20 31	1♊15 42	8♊08 21	26 33.6	27 48.3	22 01.0	25 47.3	28 06.8	17 12.2	27 33.1	23 49.2	23 53.6	0 50.8
9 F	13 12 57	16 19 46	15 02 51	21 59 01	26 29.4	29 06.2	23 15.2	26 19.0	28 33.3	17 11.3	27 40.3	23 47.1	23 52.8	0 51.7
10 Sa	13 16 54	17 19 03	28 56 44	5♋55 52	26D 27.6	0♎28.8	24 29.3	26 50.6	28 59.8	17 10.7	27 47.6	23 44.9	23 51.9	0 52.5
11 Su	13 20 51	18 18 22	12♋56 23	19 58 12	26R 27.3	1 55.5	25 43.6	27 22.0	29 26.3	17 10.3	27 54.8	23 42.8	23 51.2	0 53.5
12 M	13 24 47	19 17 44	27 01 16	4♌05 28	26 27.2	3 25.6	26 57.9	27 53.1	29 52.8	17D 10.0	28 01.9	23 40.7	23 50.4	0 54.4
13 Tu	13 28 44	20 17 08	11♌10 42	18 16 46	26 26.0	4 58.6	28 12.2	28 24.0	0♏19.3	17 10.0	28 09.1	23 38.6	23 49.7	0 55.4
14 W	13 32 40	21 16 34	25 23 28	2♍30 27	26 22.6	6 33.9	29 26.6	28 54.8	0 45.8	17 10.1	28 16.2	23 36.5	23 49.0	0 56.4
15 Th	13 36 37	22 16 02	9♍37 20	16 43 41	26 16.3	8 11.2	0♎41.0	29 25.3	1 12.4	17 10.5	28 23.3	23 34.5	23 48.3	0 57.4
16 F	13 40 33	23 15 34	23 48 56	0♎52 33	26 07.1	9 50.0	1 55.4	29 55.5	1 38.9	17 11.1	28 30.3	23 32.5	23 47.6	0 58.4
17 Sa	13 44 30	24 15 06	7♎53 53	14 52 22	25 55.6	11 29.9	3 09.9	0♌25.6	2 05.5	17 11.8	28 37.3	23 30.5	23 47.0	0 59.5
18 Su	13 48 26	25 14 41	21 47 24	28 38 28	25 42.8	13 10.8	4 24.4	0 55.4	2 32.0	17 12.8	28 44.3	23 28.6	23 46.4	1 00.6
19 M	13 52 23	26 14 18	5♏25 04	12♏06 52	25 30.0	14 52.2	5 39.0	1 25.0	2 58.5	17 14.0	28 51.2	23 26.7	23 45.9	1 01.8
20 Tu	13 56 20	27 13 57	18 43 36	25 15 07	25 18.5	16 34.1	6 53.6	1 54.3	3 25.1	17 15.3	28 58.2	23 24.8	23 45.4	1 03.0
21 W	14 00 16	28 13 38	1♐41 23	8♐02 29	25 09.3	18 16.2	8 08.2	2 23.4	3 51.6	17 16.9	29 05.0	23 23.0	23 44.9	1 04.2
22 Th	14 04 13	29 13 21	14 18 39	20 30 11	25 02.8	19 58.4	9 22.9	2 52.2	4 18.2	17 18.7	29 11.9	23 21.1	23 44.4	1 05.4
23 F	14 08 09	0♏13 05	26 37 29	2♑41 01	24 59.0	21 40.5	10 37.5	3 20.8	4 44.7	17 20.7	29 18.7	23 19.4	23 44.0	1 06.6
24 Sa	14 12 06	1 12 52	8♑41 20	14 39 02	24D 57.4	23 22.5	11 52.3	3 49.1	5 11.2	17 22.8	29 25.4	23 17.6	23 43.6	1 07.9
25 Su	14 16 02	2 12 39	20 34 47	26 29 14	24R 57.1	25 04.3	13 07.0	4 17.1	5 37.8	17 25.2	29 32.2	23 15.9	23 43.2	1 09.2
26 M	14 19 59	3 12 29	2♒23 05	8♒17 02	24 57.1	26 45.8	14 21.8	4 44.9	6 04.3	17 27.7	29 38.8	23 14.2	23 42.9	1 10.6
27 Tu	14 23 55	4 12 20	14 11 47	20 08 01	24 56.1	28 26.9	15 36.6	5 12.4	6 30.8	17 30.5	29 45.5	23 12.6	23 42.6	1 11.9
28 W	14 27 52	5 12 13	26 06 25	2♓07 35	24 53.3	0♏07.7	16 51.4	5 39.6	6 57.3	17 33.4	29 52.1	23 11.0	23 42.3	1 13.3
29 Th	14 31 49	6 12 07	8♓12 07	14 20 32	24 48.1	1 48.1	18 06.3	6 06.5	7 23.8	17 36.6	29 58.6	23 09.4	23 42.1	1 14.7
30 F	14 35 45	7 12 04	20 33 17	26 50 45	24 40.1	3 28.0	19 21.2	6 33.2	7 50.3	17 39.9	0♎05.1	23 07.9	23 41.9	1 16.1
31 Sa	14 39 42	8 12 02	3♈13 11	9♈40 45	24 29.7	5 07.5	20 36.1	6 59.5	8 16.7	17 43.4	0 11.5	23 06.4	23 41.8	1 17.6

Astro Data	Dy Hr Mn
☽0N	5 8:25
☿R	7 4:45
⚳0S	9 9:23
♇D	11 16:59
♄⊼♆	12 22:59
♄☍♅	15 12:52
☽0S	18 9:58
☉0S	22 21:19
☿0N	23 2:04
☿D	29 13:15
☽0N	2 15:37
♅⊻♆	5 3:09
♃D	13 4:36
☿0S	13 5:45
☽0S	15 18:27

Planet Ingress	Dy Hr Mn
☿ ♍R	18 3:27
♀ ♍	20 13:33
☉ ♎	22 21:20
☿ ♎	10 3:47
⚳ ♏	12 18:31
♀ ♎	14 22:47
♂ ♌	16 15:33
☉ ♏	23 6:45
☿ ♏	28 10:10
♄ ♎	29 17:10
♀0S	17 19:05
☽0N	29 23:36

Last Aspect Dy Hr Mn		☽ Ingress	Dy Hr Mn
31 18:10	♅ ⚹	♒	1 3:44
3 5:20	♆ ☌	♓	3 15:59
5 16:54	♅ ☌	♈	6 2:15
8 0:13	♆ ⚹	♉	8 10:19
10 7:18	♅ ⚹	♊	10 16:18
12 11:31	♅ □	♋	12 20:21
14 13:58	♅ △	♌	14 22:40
16 16:12	♀ ☌	♍	16 23:57
18 23:57	☿ ☌	♎	19 1:27
20 18:44	♆ △	♏	21 4:53
23 3:34	♄ ⚹	♐	23 11:44
25 14:16	♄ □	♑	25 22:20
28 3:34	♄ △	♒	28 11:08
30 11:35	♆ ☌	♓	30 23:27

Last Aspect Dy Hr Mn		☽ Ingress	Dy Hr Mn
3 3:30	♄ ☍	♈	3 9:22
5 5:47	♂ □	♉	5 16:34
7 17:20	♄ △	♊	7 21:48
10 1:36	☿ □	♋	10 1:49
12 1:38	♄ ⚹	♌	12 5:04
13 21:21	♆ ☍	♍	14 7:46
16 10:19	♂ ⚹	♎	16 10:31
18 5:34	☉ ☌	♏	18 14:24
20 18:58	♄ ⚹	♐	20 20:50
23 6:40	☉ ⚹	♑	23 6:40
25 18:16	♄ △	♒	25 19:09
28 7:23	☿ △	♓	28 7:46
30 4:57	♅ ☌	♈	30 17:57

☽ Phases & Eclipses Dy Hr Mn	
4 16:04	○ 12♓15
12 2:17	☾ 19♊28
18 18:45	● 25♍59
26 4:51	☽ 3♑15
4 6:11	○ 11♈10
11 8:57	☾ 18♋11
18 5:34	● 24♎59
26 0:43	☽ 2♒44

Astro Data

1 September 2009
Julian Day # 40056
SVP 5♓07'13"
GC 26♐58.5 ⚴ 14♍49.2
Eris 21♈51.4R ⚵ 2♈42.8R
⚷ 22♒52.7R ⚶ 1♌38.9
☽ Mean ☊ 28♑04.1

1 October 2009
Julian Day # 40086
SVP 5♓07'10"
GC 26♐58.5 ⚴ 29♍04.3
Eris 21♈35.9R ⚵ 26♓00.5R
⚷ 21♒40.3R ⚶ 13♌39.6
☽ Mean ☊ 26♑28.7

November 2009 LONGITUDE

Day	Sid.Time	☉	0 hr ☽	Noon ☽	True ☊	☿	♀	♂	⚳	♃	♄	♅	♆	♇
1 Su	14 43 38	9♏12 01	16♈13 31	22♈51 26	24♑17.8	6♏46.5	21♎51.0	7♌25.6	8♏43.2	17♒47.1	0♎17.9	23♓04.9	23♒41.6	1♑19.1
2 M	14 47 35	10 12 03	29 34 18	6♉21 51	24R 05.4	8 25.2	23 06.0	7 51.4	9 09.7	17 51.0	0 24.3	23R 03.5	23R 41.5	1 20.6
3 Tu	14 51 31	11 12 06	13♉13 41	20 09 19	23 53.8	10 03.3	24 21.0	8 16.8	9 36.1	17 55.1	0 30.6	23 02.1	23 41.5	1 22.1
4 W	14 55 28	12 12 11	27 08 15	4♊09 53	23 44.1	11 41.1	25 36.0	8 41.9	10 02.5	17 59.4	0 36.8	23 00.8	23D 41.4	1 23.7
5 Th	14 59 24	13 12 19	11♊13 38	18 18 56	23 37.0	13 18.4	26 51.0	9 06.7	10 29.0	18 03.8	0 43.0	22 59.5	23 41.5	1 25.3
6 F	15 03 21	14 12 28	25 25 14	2♋32 02	23 32.9	14 55.3	28 06.1	9 31.2	10 55.4	18 08.4	0 49.1	22 58.3	23 41.5	1 26.9
7 Sa	15 07 18	15 12 39	9♋38 54	16 45 29	23D 31.2	16 31.8	29 21.2	9 55.3	11 21.8	18 13.2	0 55.2	22 57.1	23 41.6	1 28.5
8 Su	15 11 14	16 12 53	23 51 30	0♌56 42	23 31.2	18 07.9	0♏36.3	10 19.1	11 48.2	18 18.2	1 01.2	22 55.9	23 41.7	1 30.1
9 M	15 15 11	17 13 08	8♌00 56	15 04 05	23R 31.6	19 43.7	1 51.4	10 42.6	12 14.5	18 23.4	1 07.2	22 54.8	23 41.8	1 31.8
10 Tu	15 19 07	18 13 25	22 06 01	29 06 40	23 31.1	21 19.1	3 06.6	11 05.6	12 40.9	18 28.7	1 13.1	22 53.7	23 42.0	1 33.5
11 W	15 23 04	19 13 45	6♍05 58	13♍03 47	23 28.7	22 54.1	4 21.8	11 28.3	13 07.2	18 34.3	1 19.0	22 52.7	23 42.2	1 35.2
12 Th	15 27 00	20 14 06	20 00 01	26 54 29	23 23.8	24 28.8	5 37.0	11 50.6	13 33.5	18 39.9	1 24.7	22 51.7	23 42.5	1 36.9
13 F	15 30 57	21 14 29	3♎47 01	10♎37 23	23 16.3	26 03.3	6 52.2	12 12.6	13 59.8	18 45.8	1 30.5	22 50.8	23 42.7	1 38.7
14 Sa	15 34 53	22 14 54	17 25 20	24 10 36	23 06.7	27 37.4	8 07.4	12 34.1	14 26.1	18 51.8	1 36.1	22 49.9	23 43.0	1 40.4
15 Su	15 38 50	23 15 21	0♏52 53	7♏31 56	22 55.9	29 11.3	9 22.7	12 55.2	14 52.4	18 58.0	1 41.7	22 49.0	23 43.4	1 42.2
16 M	15 42 47	24 15 50	14 07 29	20 39 19	22 45.1	0♐44.9	10 37.9	13 15.9	15 18.6	19 04.4	1 47.2	22 48.2	23 43.8	1 44.0
17 Tu	15 46 43	25 16 20	27 07 17	3♐31 16	22 35.2	2 18.2	11 53.2	13 36.2	15 44.8	19 11.0	1 52.7	22 47.5	23 44.2	1 45.9
18 W	15 50 40	26 16 52	9♐51 13	16 07 10	22 27.3	3 51.4	13 08.5	13 56.0	16 11.0	19 17.7	1 58.1	22 46.8	23 44.6	1 47.7
19 Th	15 54 36	27 17 25	22 19 14	28 27 36	22 21.8	5 24.3	14 23.8	14 15.4	16 37.2	19 24.5	2 03.4	22 46.2	23 45.1	1 49.6
20 F	15 58 33	28 18 00	4♑32 32	10♑34 22	22D 18.8	6 56.9	15 39.2	14 34.4	17 03.4	19 31.6	2 08.6	22 45.6	23 45.7	1 51.5
21 Sa	16 02 29	29 18 36	16 33 31	22 30 25	22 18.0	8 29.4	16 54.5	14 52.8	17 29.5	19 38.7	2 13.8	22 45.0	23 46.2	1 53.3
22 Su	16 06 26	0♐19 13	28 25 35	4♒19 37	22 18.6	10 01.7	18 09.9	15 10.8	17 55.6	19 46.1	2 18.9	22 44.5	23 46.8	1 55.3
23 M	16 10 22	1 19 51	10♒13 06	16 06 41	22 19.9	11 33.8	19 25.2	15 28.4	18 21.6	19 53.6	2 23.9	22 44.1	23 47.4	1 57.2
24 Tu	16 14 19	2 20 31	22 01 00	27 56 44	22R 20.8	13 05.7	20 40.6	15 45.4	18 47.6	20 01.2	2 28.9	22 43.7	23 48.1	1 59.1
25 W	16 18 16	3 21 11	3♓54 34	9♓55 10	22 20.7	14 37.4	21 55.9	16 02.0	19 13.6	20 09.0	2 33.7	22 43.3	23 48.8	2 01.1
26 Th	16 22 12	4 21 53	15 59 12	22 07 16	22 18.8	16 08.8	23 11.3	16 18.0	19 39.6	20 17.0	2 38.5	22 43.0	23 49.5	2 03.1
27 F	16 26 09	5 22 35	28 19 58	4♈37 47	22 14.9	17 40.1	24 26.7	16 33.5	20 05.5	20 25.1	2 43.2	22 42.8	23 50.2	2 05.0
28 Sa	16 30 05	6 23 19	11♈01 11	17 30 30	22 09.1	19 11.2	25 42.1	16 48.5	20 31.4	20 33.3	2 47.9	22 42.6	23 51.0	2 07.0
29 Su	16 34 02	7 24 04	24 05 58	0♉47 41	22 02.0	20 42.0	26 57.5	17 03.0	20 57.3	20 41.7	2 52.4	22 42.4	23 51.8	2 09.1
30 M	16 37 58	8 24 50	7♉35 36	14 29 34	21 54.4	22 12.6	28 12.9	17 16.9	21 23.1	20 50.2	2 56.9	22 42.3	23 52.7	2 11.1

December 2009 LONGITUDE

Day	Sid.Time	☉	0 hr ☽	Noon ☽	True ☊	☿	♀	♂	⚳	♃	♄	♅	♆	♇
1 Tu	16 41 55	9♐25 37	21♉29 14	28♉34 08	21♑47.2	23♐42.8	29♏28.3	17♌30.3	21♏48.9	20♒58.9	3♎01.3	22♓42.3	23♒53.6	2♑13.1
2 W	16 45 51	10 26 25	5♊43 40	12♊57 05	21R 41.2	25 12.8	0♐43.8	17 43.1	22 14.7	21 07.7	3 05.6	22D 42.3	23 54.5	2 15.2
3 Th	16 49 48	11 27 14	20 13 37	27 32 23	21 37.0	26 42.3	1 59.2	17 55.3	22 40.4	21 16.7	3 09.8	22 42.3	23 55.5	2 17.2
4 F	16 53 45	12 28 05	4♋52 31	12♋13 09	21D 34.9	28 11.5	3 14.6	18 06.9	23 06.1	21 25.8	3 13.9	22 42.5	23 56.4	2 19.3
5 Sa	16 57 41	13 28 57	19 33 28	26 52 42	21 34.7	29 40.1	4 30.1	18 17.9	23 31.8	21 35.0	3 18.0	22 42.6	23 57.5	2 21.4
6 Su	17 01 38	14 29 50	4♌10 13	11♌25 25	21 35.7	1♑08.1	5 45.5	18 28.3	23 57.4	21 44.3	3 21.9	22 42.8	23 58.5	2 23.5
7 M	17 05 34	15 30 44	18 37 52	25 47 12	21 37.2	2 35.4	7 01.0	18 38.0	24 23.0	21 53.8	3 25.8	22 43.1	23 59.6	2 25.6
8 Tu	17 09 31	16 31 40	2♍53 11	9♍55 36	21R 38.3	4 01.9	8 16.5	18 47.2	24 48.5	22 03.4	3 29.6	22 43.4	24 00.7	2 27.7
9 W	17 13 27	17 32 37	16 54 23	23 49 29	21 38.3	5 27.4	9 32.0	18 55.6	25 14.0	22 13.1	3 33.3	22 43.8	24 01.8	2 29.8
10 Th	17 17 24	18 33 35	0♎40 54	7♎28 40	21 36.8	6 51.9	10 47.4	19 03.4	25 39.4	22 23.0	3 36.9	22 44.2	24 03.0	2 31.9
11 F	17 21 20	19 34 34	14 12 49	20 53 26	21 33.8	8 15.0	12 02.9	19 10.5	26 04.8	22 32.9	3 40.4	22 44.6	24 04.2	2 34.0
12 Sa	17 25 17	20 35 34	27 30 35	4♏04 19	21 29.4	9 36.5	13 18.4	19 16.9	26 30.2	22 43.0	3 43.8	22 45.2	24 05.4	2 36.2
13 Su	17 29 14	21 36 36	10♏34 42	17 01 46	21 24.3	10 56.3	14 33.9	19 22.6	26 55.5	22 53.2	3 47.1	22 45.7	24 06.7	2 38.3
14 M	17 33 10	22 37 38	23 25 36	29 46 15	21 19.1	12 13.9	15 49.5	19 27.6	27 20.7	23 03.6	3 50.3	22 46.4	24 08.0	2 40.5
15 Tu	17 37 07	23 38 41	6♐03 45	12♐18 12	21 14.4	13 29.1	17 05.0	19 31.8	27 46.0	23 14.0	3 53.5	22 47.0	24 09.3	2 42.6
16 W	17 41 03	24 39 45	18 29 40	24 38 16	21 10.8	14 41.3	18 20.5	19 35.3	28 11.1	23 24.6	3 56.5	22 47.8	24 10.6	2 44.8
17 Th	17 45 00	25 40 50	0♑44 08	6♑47 25	21 08.5	15 50.2	19 36.0	19 38.1	28 36.2	23 35.3	3 59.4	22 48.5	24 12.0	2 47.0
18 F	17 48 56	26 41 56	12 48 21	18 47 10	21D 07.6	16 55.2	20 51.5	19 40.1	29 01.3	23 46.1	4 02.2	22 49.4	24 13.4	2 49.1
19 Sa	17 52 53	27 43 01	24 44 07	0♒39 34	21 07.9	17 55.7	22 07.1	19 41.3	29 26.3	23 56.9	4 05.0	22 50.2	24 14.8	2 51.3
20 Su	17 56 50	28 44 08	6♒33 52	12 27 25	21 09.1	18 50.9	23 22.6	19R 41.7	29 51.2	24 07.9	4 07.6	22 51.2	24 16.3	2 53.5
21 M	18 00 46	29 45 14	18 20 40	24 14 07	21 10.9	19 40.2	24 38.1	19 41.4	0♐16.1	24 19.1	4 10.1	22 52.2	24 17.8	2 55.7
22 Tu	18 04 43	0♑46 21	0♓08 17	6♓03 43	21 12.6	20 22.8	25 53.6	19 40.2	0 40.9	24 30.3	4 12.5	22 53.2	24 19.3	2 57.8
23 W	18 08 39	1 47 28	12 01 00	18 00 43	21 13.9	20 57.7	27 09.1	19 38.3	1 05.7	24 41.6	4 14.9	22 54.3	24 20.8	3 00.0
24 Th	18 12 36	2 48 35	24 03 30	0♈09 55	21R 14.6	21 24.1	28 24.7	19 35.5	1 30.4	24 53.0	4 17.1	22 55.4	24 22.4	3 02.2
25 F	18 16 32	3 49 42	6♈20 37	12 36 08	21 14.3	21 41.0	29 40.2	19 32.0	1 55.0	25 04.5	4 19.2	22 56.6	24 24.0	3 04.4
26 Sa	18 20 29	4 50 50	18 57 02	25 23 48	21 13.3	21R 47.7	0♑55.7	19 27.6	2 19.6	25 16.1	4 21.2	22 57.8	24 25.6	3 06.6
27 Su	18 24 25	5 51 57	1♉56 50	8♉36 27	21 11.6	21 43.3	2 11.2	19 22.5	2 44.1	25 27.8	4 23.1	22 59.1	24 27.2	3 08.7
28 M	18 28 22	6 53 05	15 22 52	22 16 09	21 09.7	21 27.3	3 26.7	19 16.5	3 08.6	25 39.6	4 24.9	23 00.4	24 28.9	3 10.9
29 Tu	18 32 19	7 54 12	29 16 14	6♊22 51	21 07.8	20 59.4	4 42.2	19 09.7	3 33.0	25 51.4	4 26.6	23 01.8	24 30.6	3 13.1
30 W	18 36 15	8 55 20	13♊35 36	20 53 54	21 06.3	20 19.8	5 57.7	19 02.0	3 57.3	26 03.4	4 28.2	23 03.2	24 32.3	3 15.3
31 Th	18 40 12	9 56 28	28 17 01	5♋44 02	21 05.3	19 29.1	7 13.2	18 53.6	4 21.5	26 15.5	4 29.7	23 04.7	24 34.0	3 17.4

Astro Data

Dy Hr Mn
♆ D 4 18:11
☽ 0S 12 0:15
♄□♇ 15 15:21
☽ 0N 26 7:39

♅ D 1 20:29
☽ 0S 9 4:52
♃⚺♅ 12 17:21
♂ R 20 13:27
♃☌♆ 21 8:52
☽ 0N 23 15:04
☿ R 26 14:40

Planet Ingress

Dy Hr Mn
♀ ♏ 8 0:24
☿ ♐ 16 0:29
☉ ♐ 22 4:24

♀ ♐ 1 22:05
☿ ♑ 5 17:25
⚳ ♐ 20 20:27
☉ ♑ 21 17:48
♀ ♑ 25 18:18

Last Aspect / ☽ Ingress (November)

Last Aspect Dy Hr Mn			☽ Ingress	Dy Hr Mn
1 13:30	♆	⚹	♉	2 0:46
3 18:05	♆	□	♊	4 4:54
6 3:48	♀	△	♋	6 7:44
7 22:27	♅	△	♌	8 10:24
10 2:44	♆	☍	♍	10 13:31
12 7:14	☿	⚹	♎	12 17:23
14 11:11	♆	△	♏	14 22:25
16 19:15	☉	☌	♐	17 5:23
19 2:47	♆	⚹	♑	19 15:02
22 3:05	☉	⚹	♒	22 3:12
24 3:37	♆	☌	♓	24 16:09
26 14:18	♀	△	♈	27 3:12
28 23:34	♆	⚹	♉	29 10:35

Last Aspect / ☽ Ingress (December)

Last Aspect Dy Hr Mn			☽ Ingress	Dy Hr Mn
1 13:40	♀	☍	♊	1 14:25
3 10:29	☿	☍	♋	3 16:02
5 5:10	♅	△	♌	5 17:08
7 8:59	♆	☍	♍	7 19:07
9 10:06	♅	☍	♎	9 22:48
11 17:46	♆	△	♏	12 4:33
14 1:19	♆	□	♐	14 12:26
16 12:03	☉	☌	♑	16 22:33
18 20:09	♅	⚹	♒	19 10:40
21 12:55	♀	⚹	♓	21 23:43
24 8:10	♀	□	♈	24 11:41
26 11:45	♃	⚹	♉	26 20:27
28 17:55	♃	□	♊	29 1:14
30 20:31	♃	△	♋	31 2:46

☽ Phases & Eclipses

Dy Hr Mn
2 19:15 ○ 10♉30
9 15:57 ☾ 17♌23
16 19:15 ● 24♏34
24 21:40 ☽ 2♓45

2 7:32 ○ 10♊15
9 0:14 ☾ 17♍03
16 12:03 ● 24♐40
24 17:37 ☽ 3♈03
31 19:14 ○ 10♋15
31 19:24 ☍ P 0.076

Astro Data

1 November 2009
Julian Day # 40117
SVP 5♓07'07"
GC 26♐58.6 ⚴ 13♎13.0
Eris 21♈17.6R ⚵ 21♓33.8R
⚷ 21♒13.1 ⚶ 24♌41.0
☽ Mean ☊ 24♑50.2

1 December 2009
Julian Day # 40147
SVP 5♓07'02"
GC 26♐58.7 ⚴ 26♎04.4
Eris 21♈02.9R ⚵ 24♓46.4
⚷ 21♒43.9 ⚶ 2♍50.5
☽ Mean ☊ 23♑14.9

LONGITUDE — January 2010

Day	Sid.Time	☉	0 hr ☽	Noon ☽	True ☊	☿	♀	♂	⚳	♃	♄	♅	♆	♇
1 F	18 44 08	10♑57 35	13♋13 58	20♋45 44	21♑05.0	18♑28.2	8♑28.7	18♌44.3	4♐45.7	26♒27.6	4♎31.1	23♓06.2	24♒35.8	3♑19.6
2 Sa	18 48 05	11 58 43	28 18 12	5♌50 14	21D 05.3	17R 18.8	9 44.2	18R 34.2	5 09.8	26 39.8	4 32.3	23 07.7	24 37.6	3 21.8
3 Su	18 52 01	12 59 51	13♌20 46	20 48 48	21 05.9	16 03.0	10 59.7	18 23.4	5 33.8	26 52.1	4 33.5	23 09.3	24 39.4	3 23.9
4 M	18 55 58	14 00 59	28 13 26	5♍33 54	21 06.6	14 43.2	12 15.2	18 11.7	5 57.8	27 04.5	4 34.6	23 11.0	24 41.2	3 26.1
5 Tu	18 59 54	15 02 08	12♍49 37	20 00 07	21 07.2	13 22.0	13 30.7	17 59.2	6 21.7	27 17.0	4 35.5	23 12.7	24 43.0	3 28.2
6 W	19 03 51	16 03 16	27 05 06	4♎04 22	21R 07.5	12 02.1	14 46.1	17 45.9	6 45.5	27 29.5	4 36.3	23 14.4	24 44.9	3 30.4
7 Th	19 07 48	17 04 25	10♎57 54	17 45 46	21 07.6	10 46.0	16 01.6	17 31.8	7 09.2	27 42.1	4 37.1	23 16.2	24 46.8	3 32.5
8 F	19 11 44	18 05 34	24 28 06	1♏05 08	21 07.5	9 35.7	17 17.1	17 16.9	7 32.9	27 54.8	4 37.7	23 18.0	24 48.7	3 34.6
9 Sa	19 15 41	19 06 43	7♏37 08	14 04 25	21 07.3	8 32.9	18 32.6	17 01.4	7 56.5	28 07.6	4 38.2	23 19.9	24 50.6	3 36.8
10 Su	19 19 37	20 07 52	20 27 20	26 46 12	21D 07.2	7 38.9	19 48.1	16 45.0	8 20.0	28 20.4	4 38.6	23 21.8	24 52.6	3 38.9
11 M	19 23 34	21 09 01	3♐01 22	9♐13 11	21 07.1	6 54.4	21 03.6	16 28.0	8 43.4	28 33.3	4 38.9	23 23.8	24 54.5	3 41.0
12 Tu	19 27 30	22 10 11	15 21 58	21 28 03	21 07.2	6 19.7	22 19.1	16 10.2	9 06.7	28 46.3	4 39.1	23 25.8	24 56.5	3 43.1
13 W	19 31 27	23 11 19	27 31 42	3♑33 14	21 07.4	5 54.8	23 34.5	15 51.8	9 29.9	28 59.3	4R 39.2	23 27.8	24 58.5	3 45.2
14 Th	19 35 23	24 12 28	9♑32 54	15 30 58	21R 07.5	5 39.6	24 50.0	15 32.8	9 53.1	29 12.4	4 39.1	23 29.9	25 00.5	3 47.2
15 F	19 39 20	25 13 36	21 27 41	27 23 18	21 07.5	5D 33.4	26 05.5	15 13.2	10 16.1	29 25.6	4 39.0	23 32.1	25 02.5	3 49.3
16 Sa	19 43 17	26 14 44	3♒18 03	9♒12 13	21 07.2	5 35.9	27 20.9	14 52.9	10 39.1	29 38.8	4 38.7	23 34.2	25 04.6	3 51.4
17 Su	19 47 13	27 15 51	15 06 03	20 59 49	21 06.6	5 46.3	28 36.4	14 32.2	11 02.0	29 52.1	4 38.3	23 36.4	25 06.6	3 53.4
18 M	19 51 10	28 16 58	26 53 51	2♓48 27	21 05.7	6 04.1	29 51.8	14 10.9	11 24.7	0♓05.5	4 37.9	23 38.7	25 08.7	3 55.4
19 Tu	19 55 06	29 18 03	8♓43 58	14 40 46	21 04.5	6 28.7	1♒07.3	13 49.2	11 47.4	0 18.9	4 37.3	23 41.0	25 10.8	3 57.5
20 W	19 59 03	0♒19 08	20 39 16	26 39 53	21 03.3	6 59.3	2 22.7	13 27.0	12 10.0	0 32.3	4 36.6	23 43.3	25 12.9	3 59.5
21 Th	20 02 59	1 20 12	2♈43 04	8♈49 18	21 02.1	7 35.5	3 38.1	13 04.4	12 32.4	0 45.8	4 35.8	23 45.7	25 15.0	4 01.5
22 F	20 06 56	2 21 16	14 59 04	21 12 53	21D 01.3	8 16.6	4 53.5	12 41.6	12 54.8	0 59.4	4 34.9	23 48.1	25 17.2	4 03.4
23 Sa	20 10 52	3 22 18	27 31 14	3♉54 38	21 01.1	9 02.4	6 08.9	12 18.4	13 17.1	1 13.0	4 33.9	23 50.5	25 19.3	4 05.4
24 Su	20 14 49	4 23 19	10♉23 31	16 58 20	21 01.4	9 52.2	7 24.3	11 54.9	13 39.2	1 26.7	4 32.7	23 53.0	25 21.5	4 07.3
25 M	20 18 46	5 24 19	23 39 27	0♊27 09	21 02.3	10 45.7	8 39.7	11 31.3	14 01.3	1 40.4	4 31.5	23 55.5	25 23.6	4 09.3
26 Tu	20 22 42	6 25 19	7♊21 37	14 22 54	21 03.5	11 42.6	9 55.1	11 07.5	14 23.2	1 54.2	4 30.2	23 58.0	25 25.8	4 11.2
27 W	20 26 39	7 26 17	21 30 56	28 45 28	21 04.7	12 42.4	11 10.4	10 43.6	14 45.0	2 08.0	4 28.8	24 00.6	25 28.0	4 13.1
28 Th	20 30 35	8 27 14	6♋06 02	13♋32 03	21R 05.5	13 45.1	12 25.8	10 19.6	15 06.7	2 21.8	4 27.2	24 03.2	25 30.2	4 15.0
29 F	20 34 32	9 28 10	21 02 41	28 36 58	21 05.5	14 50.3	13 41.1	9 55.5	15 28.3	2 35.7	4 25.6	24 05.9	25 32.4	4 16.9
30 Sa	20 38 28	10 29 05	6♌13 47	13♌51 53	21 04.4	15 57.7	14 56.4	9 31.5	15 49.8	2 49.6	4 23.9	24 08.5	25 34.6	4 18.7
31 Su	20 42 25	11 29 59	21 30 01	29 06 50	21 02.4	17 07.3	16 11.7	9 07.6	16 11.2	3 03.6	4 22.0	24 11.2	25 36.8	4 20.5

LONGITUDE — February 2010

Day	Sid.Time	☉	0 hr ☽	Noon ☽	True ☊	☿	♀	♂	⚳	♃	♄	♅	♆	♇
1 M	20 46 22	12♒30 52	6♍41 06	14♍11 38	20♑59.6	18♑18.8	17♒27.0	8♌43.8	16♐32.4	3♓17.6	4♎20.1	24♓14.0	25♒39.0	4♑22.4
2 Tu	20 50 18	13 31 44	21 37 26	28 57 37	20R 56.5	19 32.1	18 42.3	8R 20.1	16 53.5	3 31.6	4R 18.0	24 16.8	25 41.3	4 24.2
3 W	20 54 15	14 32 35	6♎11 32	13♎18 42	20 53.6	20 47.0	19 57.6	7 56.6	17 14.5	3 45.7	4 15.9	24 19.5	25 43.5	4 25.9
4 Th	20 58 11	15 33 25	20 18 52	27 11 55	20 51.3	22 03.5	21 12.9	7 33.4	17 35.4	3 59.8	4 13.7	24 22.4	25 45.8	4 27.7
5 F	21 02 08	16 34 15	3♏57 57	10♏37 10	20D 50.1	23 21.5	22 28.1	7 10.4	17 56.2	4 13.9	4 11.3	24 25.2	25 48.0	4 29.4
6 Sa	21 06 04	17 35 04	17 09 53	23 36 31	20 50.1	24 40.8	23 43.4	6 47.8	18 16.8	4 28.1	4 08.9	24 28.1	25 50.3	4 31.1
7 Su	21 10 01	18 35 52	29 57 34	6♐13 32	20 51.2	26 01.3	24 58.6	6 25.5	18 37.3	4 42.3	4 06.4	24 31.0	25 52.5	4 32.8
8 M	21 13 57	19 36 38	12♐24 59	18 32 28	20 52.9	27 23.1	26 13.8	6 03.6	18 57.6	4 56.5	4 03.8	24 34.0	25 54.8	4 34.5
9 Tu	21 17 54	20 37 24	24 36 31	0♑37 42	20 54.7	28 46.1	27 29.0	5 42.2	19 17.8	5 10.8	4 01.1	24 36.9	25 57.1	4 36.2
10 W	21 21 51	21 38 09	6♑36 31	12 33 27	20R 56.0	0♒10.2	28 44.2	5 21.3	19 37.9	5 25.1	3 58.3	24 39.9	25 59.4	4 37.8
11 Th	21 25 47	22 38 53	18 28 57	24 23 26	20 56.3	1 35.3	29 59.4	5 00.9	19 57.9	5 39.4	3 55.4	24 42.9	26 01.6	4 39.4
12 F	21 29 44	23 39 35	0♒17 17	6♒10 52	20 55.1	3 01.5	1♓14.6	4 41.0	20 17.6	5 53.7	3 52.5	24 46.0	26 03.9	4 41.0
13 Sa	21 33 40	24 40 16	12 04 28	17 58 23	20 52.1	4 28.7	2 29.8	4 21.7	20 37.3	6 08.0	3 49.4	24 49.0	26 06.2	4 42.6
14 Su	21 37 37	25 40 56	23 52 52	29 48 10	20 47.3	5 56.9	3 44.9	4 03.1	20 56.8	6 22.4	3 46.3	24 52.1	26 08.5	4 44.1
15 M	21 41 33	26 41 34	5♓44 29	11♓42 02	20 41.1	7 26.0	5 00.0	3 45.1	21 16.1	6 36.8	3 43.0	24 55.2	26 10.8	4 45.6
16 Tu	21 45 30	27 42 11	17 41 02	23 41 40	20 34.1	8 56.1	6 15.2	3 27.7	21 35.3	6 51.2	3 39.7	24 58.3	26 13.0	4 47.1
17 W	21 49 26	28 42 46	29 44 10	5♈48 46	20 26.8	10 27.1	7 30.2	3 11.0	21 54.3	7 05.6	3 36.4	25 01.5	26 15.3	4 48.6
18 Th	21 53 23	29 43 19	11♈55 43	18 05 17	20 20.0	11 59.1	8 45.3	2 55.1	22 13.2	7 20.0	3 32.9	25 04.7	26 17.6	4 50.0
19 F	21 57 19	0♓43 51	24 17 45	0♉33 27	20 14.6	13 32.0	10 00.4	2 39.8	22 31.9	7 34.5	3 29.4	25 07.8	26 19.9	4 51.4
20 Sa	22 01 16	1 44 21	6♉52 42	13 15 53	20 10.9	15 05.9	11 15.4	2 25.3	22 50.4	7 48.9	3 25.8	25 11.1	26 22.2	4 52.8
21 Su	22 05 13	2 44 49	19 43 22	26 15 32	20D 09.2	16 40.7	12 30.4	2 11.6	23 08.8	8 03.4	3 22.1	25 14.3	26 24.4	4 54.2
22 M	22 09 09	3 45 15	2♊52 43	9♊35 16	20 09.1	18 16.4	13 45.4	1 58.7	23 27.0	8 17.9	3 18.4	25 17.5	26 26.7	4 55.5
23 Tu	22 13 06	4 45 40	16 23 29	23 17 37	20 10.1	19 53.1	15 00.4	1 46.5	23 45.0	8 32.4	3 14.6	25 20.8	26 29.0	4 56.8
24 W	22 17 02	5 46 02	0♋17 46	7♋23 58	20R 11.4	21 30.7	16 15.3	1 35.1	24 02.9	8 46.9	3 10.7	25 24.0	26 31.2	4 58.1
25 Th	22 20 59	6 46 23	14 36 08	21 53 59	20 11.9	23 09.3	17 30.3	1 24.5	24 20.6	9 01.4	3 06.8	25 27.3	26 33.5	4 59.4
26 F	22 24 55	7 46 41	29 17 03	6♌44 43	20 10.8	24 48.9	18 45.2	1 14.6	24 38.1	9 15.8	3 02.8	25 30.6	26 35.7	5 00.6
27 Sa	22 28 52	8 46 58	14♌16 08	21 50 19	20 07.5	26 29.5	20 00.0	1 05.6	24 55.4	9 30.3	2 58.8	25 33.9	26 38.0	5 01.8
28 Su	22 32 48	9 47 12	29 26 08	7♍02 18	20 01.9	28 11.0	21 14.9	0 57.3	25 12.5	9 44.8	2 54.6	25 37.3	26 40.2	5 03.0

Astro Data (Dy Hr Mn)

☽0S 5 11:10
♄ R 13 15:58
☿ D 15 16:53
☽0N 19 21:43
♄□♇ 31 21:28

☽0S 1 20:40
♃⊼♄ 5 8:15
♃✱♇ 6 17:52
☽0N 16 3:59

Planet Ingress (Dy Hr Mn)

♃ ♓ 18 2:11
♀ ♒ 18 14:36
☉ ♒ 20 4:29

☿ ♒ 10 9:07
♀ ♓ 11 12:11
☉ ♓ 18 18:37

Last Aspect Dy Hr Mn		☽ Ingress Dy Hr Mn	
1 15:44	♅ △	♌	2 2:42
3 21:56	♃ ☍	♍	4 2:54
5 17:26	♅ ☍	♎	6 4:59
8 6:08	♃ △	♏	8 10:01
10 15:03	♃ □	♐	10 18:11
13 2:44	♃ ✱	♑	13 4:55
15 9:04	♀ ☌	♒	15 17:05
17 20:24	♆ ☌	♓	18 6:18
20 6:07	♅ ☌	♈	20 18:37
22 19:47	♆ ✱	♉	23 4:41
25 3:04	♆ □	♊	25 11:12
27 6:33	♆ △	♋	27 14:02
29 4:50	♅ △	♌	29 14:11
31 6:28	♆ ☍	♍	31 13:24

Last Aspect Dy Hr Mn		☽ Ingress Dy Hr Mn	
2 4:18	♅ ☍	♎	2 13:43
4 9:28	♆ △	♏	4 16:57
6 16:12	♆ □	♐	7 0:05
9 4:59	♀ ✱	♑	9 10:45
11 12:40	♅ ✱	♒	11 23:25
14 4:34	♆ ☌	♓	14 12:24
16 14:33	♅ ☌	♈	17 0:31
19 3:53	♆ ✱	♉	19 10:56
21 12:16	♆ □	♊	21 18:48
23 17:30	♆ △	♋	23 23:30
25 17:49	♅ △	♌	26 1:09
27 20:16	♅ ☍	♍	28 0:53

☽ Phases & Eclipses (Dy Hr Mn)

7 10:41 ☾ 17♎01
15 7:12 ● 25♑01
15 7:07:40 ● A 11'07"
23 10:54 ☽ 3♉20
30 6:19 ○ 10♌15

5 23:50 ☾ 17♏04
14 2:52 ● 25♒18
22 0:43 ☽ 3♊17
28 16:39 ○ 9♍59

Astro Data

1 January 2010
Julian Day # 40178
SVP 5♓06'56"
GC 26♐58.7 ⚴ 7♏57.4
Eris 20♈55.4R ⚵ 4♈37.6
⚷ 23♒08.6 ⚶ 6♍38.3
☽ Mean ☊ 21♑36.5

1 February 2010
Julian Day # 40209
SVP 5♓06'50"
GC 26♐58.8 ⚴ 17♏24.5
Eris 20♈58.4 ⚵ 18♈36.0
⚷ 25♒08.4 ⚶ 3♍32.6R
☽ Mean ☊ 19♑58.0

March 2010 LONGITUDE

Day	Sid.Time	☉	0 hr ☽	Noon☽	True☊	☿	♀	♂	⚳	♃	♄	♅	♆	♇
1 M	22 36 45	10♓47 25	14♍37 32	22♍10 30	19♑54.6	29♒53.6	22♓29.7	0♌49.9	25♐29.5	9♓59.3	2♎50.5	25♓40.6	26♒42.5	5♑04.1
2 Tu	22 40 42	11 47 36	29 39 58	7♎04 47	19R 46.2	1♓37.3	23 44.5	0R 43.2	25 46.2	10 13.8	2R 46.3	25 43.9	26 44.7	5 05.2
3 W	22 44 38	12 47 46	14♎23 59	21 36 47	19 38.0	3 22.0	24 59.3	0 37.3	26 02.8	10 28.3	2 42.0	25 47.3	26 46.9	5 06.3
4 Th	22 48 35	13 47 54	28 42 37	5♏41 07	19 31.0	5 07.7	26 14.1	0 32.2	26 19.2	10 42.8	2 37.7	25 50.7	26 49.1	5 07.4
5 F	22 52 31	14 48 00	12♏32 08	19 15 43	19 25.8	6 54.5	27 28.8	0 27.9	26 35.3	10 57.3	2 33.4	25 54.0	26 51.3	5 08.4
6 Sa	22 56 28	15 48 05	25 52 04	2♐21 32	19 22.7	8 42.5	28 43.5	0 24.3	26 51.3	11 11.8	2 29.0	25 57.4	26 53.5	5 09.4
7 Su	23 00 24	16 48 09	8♐44 35	15 01 46	19D 21.7	10 31.5	29 58.2	0 21.5	27 07.1	11 26.2	2 24.5	26 00.8	26 55.7	5 10.4
8 M	23 04 21	17 48 10	21 13 41	27 20 59	19 22.0	12 21.6	1♈12.9	0 19.5	27 22.6	11 40.7	2 20.1	26 04.2	26 57.8	5 11.4
9 Tu	23 08 17	18 48 11	3♑24 20	9♑24 25	19R 22.9	14 12.8	2 27.5	0 18.2	27 38.0	11 55.2	2 15.6	26 07.6	27 00.0	5 12.3
10 W	23 12 14	19 48 09	15 21 52	21 17 20	19 23.2	16 05.1	3 42.2	0D 17.7	27 53.1	12 09.6	2 11.0	26 11.1	27 02.1	5 13.2
11 Th	23 16 11	20 48 06	27 11 26	3♒04 45	19 22.1	17 58.4	4 56.8	0 17.9	28 08.0	12 24.0	2 06.5	26 14.5	27 04.3	5 14.0
12 F	23 20 07	21 48 01	8♒57 47	14 51 03	19 18.8	19 52.8	6 11.4	0 18.9	28 22.7	12 38.4	2 01.9	26 17.9	27 06.4	5 14.8
13 Sa	23 24 04	22 47 54	20 44 58	26 39 56	19 12.8	21 48.3	7 25.9	0 20.5	28 37.2	12 52.8	1 57.2	26 21.3	27 08.5	5 15.6
14 Su	23 28 00	23 47 45	2♓36 16	8♓34 15	19 04.1	23 44.7	8 40.4	0 22.9	28 51.4	13 07.2	1 52.6	26 24.7	27 10.6	5 16.4
15 M	23 31 57	24 47 35	14 34 07	20 36 04	18 53.1	25 42.0	9 54.9	0 26.0	29 05.4	13 21.6	1 47.9	26 28.2	27 12.7	5 17.1
16 Tu	23 35 53	25 47 22	26 40 15	2♈46 46	18 40.7	27 40.2	11 09.4	0 29.7	29 19.2	13 35.9	1 43.3	26 31.6	27 14.7	5 17.8
17 W	23 39 50	26 47 08	8♈55 43	15 07 10	18 27.9	29 39.1	12 23.9	0 34.2	29 32.7	13 50.3	1 38.6	26 35.0	27 16.8	5 18.5
18 Th	23 43 46	27 46 51	21 21 12	27 37 51	18 15.8	1♈38.6	13 38.3	0 39.3	29 46.0	14 04.6	1 33.8	26 38.5	27 18.8	5 19.1
19 F	23 47 43	28 46 33	3♉57 14	10♉19 24	18 05.5	3 38.6	14 52.7	0 45.1	29 59.0	14 18.9	1 29.1	26 41.9	27 20.8	5 19.7
20 Sa	23 51 40	29 46 12	16 44 29	23 12 37	17 57.8	5 38.8	16 07.0	0 51.6	0♑11.8	14 33.1	1 24.4	26 45.3	27 22.9	5 20.3
21 Su	23 55 36	0♈45 49	29 43 59	6♊18 44	17 52.9	7 39.2	17 21.3	0 58.7	0 24.3	14 47.3	1 19.7	26 48.8	27 24.8	5 20.9
22 M	23 59 33	1 45 24	12♊57 07	19 39 21	17D 50.6	9 39.4	18 35.6	1 06.4	0 36.6	15 01.6	1 15.0	26 52.2	27 26.8	5 21.4
23 Tu	0 03 29	2 44 56	26 25 39	3♋16 13	17 50.1	11 39.2	19 49.9	1 14.7	0 48.6	15 15.7	1 10.2	26 55.6	27 28.8	5 21.8
24 W	0 07 26	3 44 26	10♋11 14	17 10 49	17R 50.3	13 38.3	21 04.1	1 23.6	1 00.4	15 29.9	1 05.5	26 59.0	27 30.7	5 22.3
25 Th	0 11 22	4 43 54	24 15 01	1♌23 45	17 49.8	15 36.3	22 18.3	1 33.1	1 11.9	15 44.0	1 00.8	27 02.4	27 32.6	5 22.7
26 F	0 15 19	5 43 19	8♌36 51	15 53 59	17 47.4	17 32.9	23 32.5	1 43.2	1 23.1	15 58.1	0 56.1	27 05.8	27 34.5	5 23.1
27 Sa	0 19 15	6 42 43	23 14 38	0♍38 11	17 42.4	19 27.7	24 46.6	1 53.9	1 34.0	16 12.1	0 51.4	27 09.2	27 36.4	5 23.4
28 Su	0 23 12	7 42 03	8♍03 49	15 30 36	17 34.7	21 20.2	26 00.7	2 05.1	1 44.7	16 26.1	0 46.7	27 12.6	27 38.3	5 23.8
29 M	0 27 09	8 41 22	22 57 29	0♎23 21	17 24.5	23 10.2	27 14.7	2 16.8	1 55.1	16 40.1	0 42.1	27 16.0	27 40.1	5 24.1
30 Tu	0 31 05	9 40 38	7♎47 06	15 07 37	17 13.0	24 57.1	28 28.8	2 29.1	2 05.2	16 54.0	0 37.4	27 19.4	27 41.9	5 24.3
31 W	0 35 02	10 39 53	22 23 53	29 35 03	17 01.4	26 40.6	29 42.7	2 41.8	2 15.0	17 07.9	0 32.8	27 22.7	27 43.7	5 24.5

April 2010 LONGITUDE

Day	Sid.Time	☉	0 hr ☽	Noon☽	True☊	☿	♀	♂	⚳	♃	♄	♅	♆	♇
1 Th	0 38 58	11♈39 05	6♏40 22	13♏39 17	16♑50.9	28♈20.2	0♉56.7	2♌55.1	2♑24.5	17♓21.8	0♎28.2	27♓26.1	27♒45.5	5♑24.7
2 F	0 42 55	12 38 16	20 31 28	27 16 44	16R 42.6	29 55.7	2 10.6	3 08.9	2 33.7	17 35.6	0R 23.6	27 29.4	27 47.3	5 24.9
3 Sa	0 46 51	13 37 25	3♐55 07	10♐26 46	16 37.0	1♉26.6	3 24.5	3 23.1	2 42.7	17 49.4	0 19.1	27 32.8	27 49.0	5 25.0
4 Su	0 50 48	14 36 33	16 52 00	23 11 16	16 33.8	2 52.6	4 38.4	3 37.8	2 51.3	18 03.2	0 14.6	27 36.1	27 50.7	5 25.1
5 M	0 54 44	15 35 38	29 25 04	5♑34 00	16 32.7	4 13.4	5 52.2	3 53.0	2 59.6	18 16.9	0 10.1	27 39.4	27 52.4	5 25.2
6 Tu	0 58 41	16 34 42	11♑38 43	17 39 54	16 32.5	5 28.9	7 06.0	4 08.6	3 07.7	18 30.5	0 05.7	27 42.7	27 54.1	5R 25.2
7 W	1 02 38	17 33 44	23 38 13	29 34 24	16 32.3	6 38.7	8 19.7	4 24.7	3 15.4	18 44.1	0 01.3	27 46.0	27 55.7	5 25.2
8 Th	1 06 34	18 32 44	5♒29 07	11♒23 03	16 30.8	7 42.6	9 33.4	4 41.2	3 22.7	18 57.7	29♍56.9	27 49.3	27 57.3	5 25.2
9 F	1 10 31	19 31 42	17 16 49	23 11 01	16 27.2	8 40.5	10 47.1	4 58.2	3 29.8	19 11.2	29 52.6	27 52.5	27 58.9	5 25.1
10 Sa	1 14 27	20 30 38	29 06 14	5♓02 57	16 20.9	9 32.3	12 00.8	5 15.5	3 36.5	19 24.6	29 48.3	27 55.7	28 00.5	5 25.0
11 Su	1 18 24	21 29 33	11♓01 37	17 02 38	16 11.9	10 17.8	13 14.4	5 33.3	3 42.9	19 38.0	29 44.1	27 59.0	28 02.0	5 24.9
12 M	1 22 20	22 28 26	23 06 19	29 12 55	16 00.4	10 57.0	14 28.0	5 51.4	3 49.0	19 51.4	29 39.9	28 02.2	28 03.6	5 24.8
13 Tu	1 26 17	23 27 16	5♈22 38	11♈35 36	15 47.4	11 29.7	15 41.5	6 10.0	3 54.7	20 04.7	29 35.7	28 05.4	28 05.1	5 24.6
14 W	1 30 13	24 26 05	17 51 51	24 11 25	15 33.8	11 56.0	16 55.0	6 29.0	4 00.1	20 17.9	29 31.7	28 08.5	28 06.5	5 24.4
15 Th	1 34 10	25 24 52	0♉34 16	7♉00 18	15 21.0	12 15.9	18 08.5	6 48.3	4 05.1	20 31.1	29 27.7	28 11.7	28 08.0	5 24.1
16 F	1 38 06	26 23 37	13 29 26	20 01 34	15 10.0	12 29.3	19 21.9	7 08.0	4 09.8	20 44.2	29 23.7	28 14.8	28 09.4	5 23.8
17 Sa	1 42 03	27 22 20	26 36 33	3♊14 18	15 01.7	12R 36.5	20 35.3	7 28.0	4 14.2	20 57.3	29 19.8	28 17.9	28 10.8	5 23.5
18 Su	1 46 00	28 21 01	9♊54 42	16 37 43	14 56.3	12 37.6	21 48.7	7 48.4	4 18.2	21 10.3	29 16.0	28 21.0	28 12.1	5 23.2
19 M	1 49 56	29 19 40	23 23 17	0♋11 25	14 53.6	12 32.7	23 02.0	8 09.2	4 21.8	21 23.2	29 12.2	28 24.1	28 13.5	5 22.8
20 Tu	1 53 53	0♉18 16	7♋02 06	13 55 23	14D 52.9	12 22.1	24 15.3	8 30.3	4 25.1	21 36.1	29 08.5	28 27.1	28 14.8	5 22.4
21 W	1 57 49	1 16 51	20 51 17	27 49 51	14R 53.1	12 06.1	25 28.5	8 51.7	4 28.0	21 48.9	29 04.9	28 30.1	28 16.1	5 22.0
22 Th	2 01 46	2 15 23	4♌51 04	11♌54 52	14 52.8	11 45.2	26 41.7	9 13.5	4 30.6	22 01.6	29 01.3	28 33.1	28 17.3	5 21.5
23 F	2 05 42	3 13 53	19 01 11	26 09 47	14 51.0	11 19.7	27 54.8	9 35.5	4 32.8	22 14.3	28 57.8	28 36.1	28 18.5	5 21.0
24 Sa	2 09 39	4 12 20	3♍20 25	10♍32 42	14 46.8	10 50.3	29 07.9	9 57.9	4 34.6	22 26.9	28 54.4	28 39.1	28 19.7	5 20.5
25 Su	2 13 35	5 10 45	17 46 07	25 00 07	14 40.0	10 17.4	0♊21.0	10 20.5	4 36.1	22 39.4	28 51.0	28 42.0	28 20.9	5 20.0
26 M	2 17 32	6 09 09	2♎14 00	9♎27 03	14 31.0	9 41.9	1 34.0	10 43.5	4 37.2	22 51.9	28 47.8	28 44.9	28 22.0	5 19.4
27 Tu	2 21 29	7 07 30	16 38 28	23 47 27	14 20.7	9 04.2	2 47.0	11 06.7	4 37.9	23 04.3	28 44.6	28 47.7	28 23.1	5 18.8
28 W	2 25 25	8 05 50	0♏53 17	7♏55 13	14 10.2	8 25.2	3 59.9	11 30.2	4R 38.3	23 16.6	28 41.5	28 50.6	28 24.2	5 18.2
29 Th	2 29 22	9 04 07	14 52 39	21 45 04	14 00.7	7 45.5	5 12.7	11 54.0	4 38.2	23 28.8	28 38.4	28 53.4	28 25.3	5 17.5
30 F	2 33 18	10 02 23	28 32 06	5♐13 29	13 53.1	7 06.0	6 25.6	12 18.1	4 37.8	23 40.9	28 35.5	28 56.2	28 26.3	5 16.8

Astro Data	Dy Hr Mn
☽0S	1 8:05
♀0N	9 18:57
♂ D	10 17:10
☽0N	15 10:20
☿0N	18 19:58
☉0N	20 17:33
☽0S	28 18:43
♇ R	7 2:35
☽0N	11 17:02
♅⚺♆	13 7:44
☿ R	18 4:06
☽0S	25 2:42
♄☍♅	26 23:24
⚳ R	28 23:02

Planet Ingress		Dy Hr Mn
☿	♓	1 13:29
♀	♈	7 12:34
☿	♈	17 16:13
⚳	♑	19 13:48
☉	♈	20 17:33
♀	♉	31 17:36
☿	♉	2 13:07
♄	♍R	7 18:52
☉	♉	20 4:31
♀	♊	25 5:06

Last Aspect Dy Hr Mn			☽ Ingress	Dy Hr Mn
1 17:37	♅	☍	♎	2 0:32
3 20:45	♆	△	♏	4 2:12
6 4:33	♀	△	♐	6 7:37
8 11:14	♆	⚹	♑	8 17:14
10 22:00	♅	⚹	♒	11 5:43
13 12:58	♆	☌	♓	13 18:45
16 0:02	☿	☌	♈	16 6:33
18 11:24	♆	⚹	♉	18 16:30
20 19:42	♆	□	♊	21 0:29
23 1:50	♆	△	♋	23 6:17
25 4:40	♅	△	♌	25 9:40
27 7:05	♆	☍	♍	27 10:58
29 6:56	♅	☍	♎	29 11:22
31 12:14	♀	☍	♏	31 12:42

Last Aspect Dy Hr Mn			☽ Ingress	Dy Hr Mn
2 12:55	♆	□	♐	2 16:54
4 20:59	♆	⚹	♑	5 1:08
7 8:19	♅	⚹	♒	7 12:52
9 21:45	♆	☌	♓	10 1:49
12 12:52	♄	☍	♈	12 13:32
14 19:24	♆	⚹	♉	14 22:56
17 4:58	♄	△	♊	17 6:09
19 10:22	☉	⚹	♋	19 11:40
21 14:08	♄	⚹	♌	21 15:43
23 15:36	♆	☍	♍	23 18:25
25 18:22	♄	☌	♎	25 20:18
27 19:46	♆	△	♏	27 22:30
30 0:41	♅	△	♐	30 2:37

☽ Phases & Eclipses Dy Hr Mn		
7 15:43	☾	16♐57
15 21:02	●	25♓10
23 11:01	☽	2♋43
30 2:27	○	9♎17
6 9:38	☾	16♑29
14 12:30	●	24♈27
21 18:21	☽	1♌32
28 12:20	○	8♏07

Astro Data

1 March 2010
Julian Day # 40237
SVP 5♓06'47"
GC 26♐58.9 ⚴ 22♏23.6
Eris 21♈09.3 ⚵ 3♉15.4
⚷ 27♒06.2 ⚶ 26♌31.8R
☽ Mean ☊ 18♑29.0

1 April 2010
Julian Day # 40268
SVP 5♓06'44"
GC 26♐58.9 ⚴ 21♏43.7R
Eris 21♈27.7 ⚵ 20♉39.9
⚷ 29♒04.2 ⚶ 21♌42.8R
☽ Mean ☊ 16♑50.5

LONGITUDE — May 2010

Day	Sid.Time	☉	0 hr ☽	Noon ☽	True ☊	☿	♀	♂	⚳	♃	♄	♅	♆	♇
1 Sa	2 37 15	11♉00 38	11♐49 07	18♐19 01	13♑47.8	6♉27.2	7♊38.4	12♌42.4	4♑37.1	23♓53.0	28♍32.6	28♓58.9	28♒27.3	5♑16.1
2 Su	2 41 11	11 58 51	24 43 21	1♑02 22	13R45.0	5R49.9	8 51.1	13 06.9	4R35.9	24 05.0	28R29.8	29 01.7	28 28.2	5R15.4
3 M	2 45 08	12 57 02	7♑16 27	13 26 03	13D44.2	5 14.7	10 03.8	13 31.7	4 34.4	24 16.9	28 27.1	29 04.4	28 29.2	5 14.6
4 Tu	2 49 04	13 55 12	19 31 39	25 33 53	13 44.6	4 42.1	11 16.5	13 56.8	4 32.5	24 28.7	28 24.5	29 07.1	28 30.1	5 13.8
5 W	2 53 01	14 53 20	1♒33 19	7♒30 37	13R45.4	4 12.6	12 29.1	14 22.1	4 30.2	24 40.5	28 22.0	29 09.7	28 30.9	5 13.0
6 Th	2 56 58	15 51 27	13 26 26	19 21 27	13 45.6	3 46.7	13 41.6	14 47.6	4 27.6	24 52.1	28 19.5	29 12.3	28 31.8	5 12.2
7 F	3 00 54	16 49 32	25 16 19	1♓11 41	13 44.3	3 24.7	14 54.2	15 13.4	4 24.5	25 03.7	28 17.2	29 14.9	28 32.6	5 11.3
8 Sa	3 04 51	17 47 36	7♓08 10	13 06 22	13 41.1	3 06.8	16 06.6	15 39.4	4 21.1	25 15.2	28 14.9	29 17.4	28 33.3	5 10.4
9 Su	3 08 47	18 45 39	19 06 51	25 10 05	13 35.7	2 53.3	17 19.1	16 05.6	4 17.3	25 26.6	28 12.8	29 19.9	28 34.1	5 09.5
10 M	3 12 44	19 43 40	1♈16 32	7♈26 34	13 28.3	2 44.4	18 31.4	16 32.1	4 13.1	25 37.9	28 10.7	29 22.4	28 34.8	5 08.6
11 Tu	3 16 40	20 41 40	13 40 30	19 58 33	13 19.6	2D40.0	19 43.8	16 58.7	4 08.6	25 49.1	28 08.7	29 24.9	28 35.4	5 07.6
12 W	3 20 37	21 39 38	26 20 51	2♉47 29	13 10.4	2 40.3	20 56.1	17 25.6	4 03.7	26 00.2	28 06.8	29 27.3	28 36.1	5 06.6
13 Th	3 24 33	22 37 35	9♉18 24	15 53 32	13 01.6	2 45.3	22 08.3	17 52.7	3 58.4	26 11.2	28 05.1	29 29.6	28 36.7	5 05.6
14 F	3 28 30	23 35 31	22 32 41	29 15 38	12 54.2	2 54.8	23 20.5	18 20.0	3 52.7	26 22.1	28 03.4	29 32.0	28 37.3	5 04.6
15 Sa	3 32 27	24 33 25	6♊02 06	12♊51 47	12 48.7	3 09.0	24 32.7	18 47.5	3 46.7	26 32.9	28 01.8	29 34.3	28 37.8	5 03.5
16 Su	3 36 23	25 31 17	19 44 19	26 39 23	12 45.4	3 27.6	25 44.8	19 15.2	3 40.3	26 43.6	28 00.3	29 36.6	28 38.3	5 02.4
17 M	3 40 20	26 29 08	3♋36 38	10♋35 46	12D44.3	3 50.5	26 56.8	19 43.1	3 33.6	26 54.2	27 58.9	29 38.8	28 38.8	5 01.3
18 Tu	3 44 16	27 26 57	17 36 28	24 38 28	12 44.7	4 17.7	28 08.8	20 11.2	3 26.5	27 04.7	27 57.6	29 41.0	28 39.3	5 00.2
19 W	3 48 13	28 24 45	1♌41 33	8♌45 28	12 45.9	4 49.1	29 20.8	20 39.5	3 19.1	27 15.0	27 56.4	29 43.1	28 39.7	4 59.1
20 Th	3 52 09	29 22 31	15 50 02	22 55 03	12R46.9	5 24.5	0♋32.6	21 07.9	3 11.4	27 25.3	27 55.3	29 45.3	28 40.1	4 57.9
21 F	3 56 06	0♊20 15	0♍00 19	7♍05 39	12 46.8	6 03.8	1 44.5	21 36.6	3 03.3	27 35.5	27 54.3	29 47.3	28 40.4	4 56.7
22 Sa	4 00 02	1 17 57	14 10 49	21 15 33	12 45.2	6 46.8	2 56.2	22 05.4	2 54.9	27 45.5	27 53.4	29 49.4	28 40.7	4 55.5
23 Su	4 03 59	2 15 38	28 19 34	5♎22 33	12 41.8	7 33.6	4 07.9	22 34.4	2 46.2	27 55.5	27 52.6	29 51.4	28 41.0	4 54.3
24 M	4 07 56	3 13 17	12♎24 10	19 24 00	12 36.9	8 23.9	5 19.6	23 03.5	2 37.2	28 05.3	27 51.9	29 53.3	28 41.3	4 53.1
25 Tu	4 11 52	4 10 55	26 21 41	3♏16 48	12 31.1	9 17.6	6 31.2	23 32.8	2 27.8	28 15.0	27 51.4	29 55.2	28 41.5	4 51.8
26 W	4 15 49	5 08 31	10♏08 57	16 57 46	12 25.1	10 14.6	7 42.7	24 02.3	2 18.2	28 24.6	27 50.9	29 57.1	28 41.7	4 50.5
27 Th	4 19 45	6 06 06	23 42 55	0♐24 07	12 19.7	11 15.0	8 54.1	24 31.9	2 08.3	28 34.1	27 50.5	29 59.0	28 41.8	4 49.3
28 F	4 23 42	7 03 40	7♐01 08	13 33 48	12 15.4	12 18.4	10 05.5	25 01.7	1 58.1	28 43.4	27 50.2	0♈00.8	28 42.0	4 48.0
29 Sa	4 27 38	8 01 13	20 02 04	26 25 55	12 12.7	13 25.0	11 16.9	25 31.6	1 47.7	28 52.6	27 50.0	0 02.5	28 42.1	4 46.6
30 Su	4 31 35	8 58 45	2♑45 26	9♑00 47	12D11.6	14 34.6	12 28.1	26 01.7	1 37.0	29 01.7	27D50.0	0 04.2	28 42.1	4 45.3
31 M	4 35 32	9 56 16	15 12 12	21 19 59	12 11.9	15 47.2	13 39.3	26 31.9	1 26.1	29 10.7	27 50.0	0 05.9	28R42.1	4 44.0

LONGITUDE — June 2010

Day	Sid.Time	☉	0 hr ☽	Noon ☽	True ☊	☿	♀	♂	⚳	♃	♄	♅	♆	♇
1 Tu	4 39 28	10♊53 46	27♑24 31	3♒26 13	12♑13.2	17♉02.6	14♋50.5	27♌02.3	1♑14.9	29♓19.6	27♍50.1	0♈07.5	28♒42.1	4♑42.6
2 W	4 43 25	11 51 15	9♒25 34	15 23 05	12 14.9	18 20.9	16 01.6	27 32.8	1R03.4	29 28.3	27 50.3	0 09.1	28R42.1	4R41.2
3 Th	4 47 21	12 48 43	21 19 19	27 14 50	12 16.5	19 42.1	17 12.6	28 03.5	0 51.8	29 36.9	27 50.7	0 10.7	28 42.0	4 39.8
4 F	4 51 18	13 46 11	3♓10 16	9♓06 11	12R17.4	21 06.0	18 23.5	28 34.3	0 40.0	29 45.4	27 51.1	0 12.2	28 41.9	4 38.4
5 Sa	4 55 14	14 43 38	15 03 14	21 02 00	12 17.3	22 32.6	19 34.4	29 05.2	0 27.9	29 53.7	27 51.6	0 13.6	28 41.8	4 37.0
6 Su	4 59 11	15 41 04	27 03 05	3♈07 04	12 16.1	24 02.0	20 45.2	29 36.3	0 15.7	0♈01.9	27 52.3	0 15.0	28 41.6	4 35.6
7 M	5 03 07	16 38 29	9♈14 27	15 25 45	12 13.8	25 34.1	21 56.0	0♍07.5	0 03.3	0 09.9	27 53.0	0 16.4	28 41.4	4 34.2
8 Tu	5 07 04	17 35 54	21 41 25	28 01 47	12 10.6	27 08.9	23 06.6	0 38.9	29♐50.8	0 17.8	27 53.8	0 17.7	28 41.2	4 32.7
9 W	5 11 00	18 33 18	4♉27 10	10♉57 45	12 07.1	28 46.4	24 17.2	1 10.4	29 38.1	0 25.6	27 54.8	0 19.0	28 40.9	4 31.3
10 Th	5 14 57	19 30 42	17 33 41	24 14 56	12 03.7	0♊26.5	25 27.8	1 42.0	29 25.3	0 33.2	27 55.8	0 20.2	28 40.6	4 29.8
11 F	5 18 54	20 28 05	1♊01 25	7♊52 55	12 00.9	2 09.3	26 38.3	2 13.8	29 12.4	0 40.7	27 57.0	0 21.4	28 40.3	4 28.3
12 Sa	5 22 50	21 25 28	14 49 09	21 49 42	11 58.9	3 54.7	27 48.7	2 45.6	28 59.4	0 48.1	27 58.2	0 22.5	28 39.9	4 26.8
13 Su	5 26 47	22 22 49	28 54 04	6♋01 43	11D58.0	5 42.7	28 59.0	3 17.7	28 46.3	0 55.3	27 59.6	0 23.6	28 39.5	4 25.4
14 M	5 30 43	23 20 10	13♋12 02	20 24 24	11 58.1	7 33.2	0♌09.2	3 49.8	28 33.1	1 02.3	28 01.0	0 24.6	28 39.1	4 23.9
15 Tu	5 34 40	24 17 30	27 38 09	4♌52 40	11 58.9	9 26.3	1 19.4	4 22.0	28 19.8	1 09.2	28 02.6	0 25.6	28 38.7	4 22.4
16 W	5 38 36	25 14 50	12♌07 19	19 21 32	12 00.0	11 21.7	2 29.5	4 54.4	28 06.6	1 15.9	28 04.2	0 26.6	28 38.2	4 20.8
17 Th	5 42 33	26 12 08	26 34 47	3♍46 37	12 01.1	13 19.5	3 39.4	5 26.9	27 53.3	1 22.5	28 05.9	0 27.5	28 37.7	4 19.3
18 F	5 46 30	27 09 25	10♍56 36	18 04 23	12R01.8	15 19.6	4 49.4	5 59.5	27 40.0	1 28.9	28 07.8	0 28.3	28 37.1	4 17.8
19 Sa	5 50 26	28 06 42	25 09 41	2♎12 15	12 01.9	17 21.7	5 59.2	6 32.2	27 26.7	1 35.2	28 09.7	0 29.1	28 36.5	4 16.3
20 Su	5 54 23	29 03 58	9♎11 52	16 08 24	12 01.4	19 25.8	7 08.9	7 05.1	27 13.4	1 41.3	28 11.8	0 29.9	28 35.9	4 14.8
21 M	5 58 19	0♋01 13	23 01 42	29 51 41	12 00.4	21 31.6	8 18.5	7 38.0	27 00.1	1 47.2	28 13.9	0 30.6	28 35.3	4 13.2
22 Tu	6 02 16	0 58 27	6♏38 17	13♏21 25	11 59.1	23 39.0	9 28.0	8 11.1	26 46.9	1 53.0	28 16.1	0 31.3	28 34.6	4 11.7
23 W	6 06 12	1 55 41	20 01 05	26 37 13	11 57.8	25 47.7	10 37.5	8 44.2	26 33.8	1 58.6	28 18.4	0 31.9	28 33.9	4 10.2
24 Th	6 10 09	2 52 54	3♐09 50	9♐38 56	11 56.6	27 57.4	11 46.8	9 17.5	26 20.8	2 04.1	28 20.9	0 32.5	28 33.2	4 08.6
25 F	6 14 05	3 50 07	16 04 32	22 26 42	11 55.8	0♋07.9	12 56.0	9 50.9	26 07.8	2 09.4	28 23.4	0 33.0	28 32.5	4 07.1
26 Sa	6 18 02	4 47 20	28 45 30	5♑01 01	11D55.4	2 18.9	14 05.2	10 24.3	25 54.9	2 14.5	28 26.0	0 33.4	28 31.7	4 05.6
27 Su	6 21 59	5 44 32	11♑13 23	17 22 45	11 55.4	4 30.2	15 14.2	10 57.9	25 42.2	2 19.4	28 28.7	0 33.9	28 30.9	4 04.0
28 M	6 25 55	6 41 44	23 29 18	29 33 18	11 55.7	6 41.3	16 23.1	11 31.6	25 29.6	2 24.2	28 31.5	0 34.2	28 30.1	4 02.5
29 Tu	6 29 52	7 38 56	5♒34 58	11♒34 38	11 56.1	8 52.2	17 31.9	12 05.3	25 17.1	2 28.8	28 34.4	0 34.6	28 29.2	4 00.9
30 W	6 33 48	8 36 07	17 32 37	23 29 19	11 56.5	11 02.4	18 40.6	12 39.2	25 04.8	2 33.3	28 37.3	0 34.8	28 28.3	3 59.4

Astro Data

	Dy Hr Mn
♄⚻♆	2 22:23
☽0N	9 0:09
☿ D	11 22:29
☽0S	22 8:10
♃☍♄	23 5:38
♃⚺♆	28 8:15
♄ D	30 18:09
♆ R	31 18:49
☽0N	5 7:35
♃☌♅	8 11:28
☽0S	18 13:07
♄⚻♆	28 2:47

Planet Ingress

		Dy Hr Mn
♀	♋	20 1:06
☉	♊	21 3:35
♅	♈	28 1:45
♃	♈	6 6:29
♂	♍	7 6:12
⚳	♐R	7 18:25
☿	♊	10 5:42
♀	♌	14 8:51
☉	♋	21 11:30
☿	♋	25 10:33

Last Aspect / ☽ Ingress (May)

Last Aspect Dy Hr Mn			☽ Ingress	Dy Hr Mn
2 8:09	♅	□	♑	2 10:01
4 19:08	♅	⚹	♒	4 20:53
7 6:37	♆	☌	♓	7 9:35
9 20:13	♅	☌	♈	9 21:30
12 4:12	♆	⚹	♉	12 6:49
14 12:29	♅	⚹	♊	14 13:19
16 17:07	♅	□	♋	16 17:47
18 20:36	♅	△	♌	18 21:07
20 23:44	☉	□	♍	20 23:59
23 2:35	♅	☍	♎	23 2:51
25 4:02	♆	△	♏	25 6:18
27 11:15	♅	△	♐	27 11:17
29 16:41	♃	□	♑	29 18:45

Last Aspect / ☽ Ingress (June)

Last Aspect Dy Hr Mn			☽ Ingress	Dy Hr Mn
1 3:42	♃	⚹	♒	1 5:09
3 14:57	♆	☌	♓	3 17:35
6 5:50	♃	☌	♈	6 5:51
8 13:14	♆	⚹	♉	8 15:42
10 19:51	♆	□	♊	10 22:12
12 23:36	♆	△	♋	13 1:51
15 0:39	♄	⚹	♌	15 3:55
17 3:25	♆	☍	♍	17 5:42
19 5:05	♄	☌	♎	19 8:14
21 9:46	♆	△	♏	21 12:15
23 15:33	♆	□	♐	23 18:11
25 23:34	♆	⚹	♑	26 2:22
28 9:57	♄	△	♒	28 12:53

☽ Phases & Eclipses

Dy Hr Mn		
6 4:16	☾	15♒33
14 1:05	●	23♉09
20 23:44	☽	29♌51
27 23:08	○	6♐33
4 22:14	☾	14♓11
12 11:16	●	21♊24
19 4:31	☽	27♍49
26 11:31	○	4♑46
26 11:40		P 0.537

Astro Data

1 May 2010
Julian Day # 40298
SVP 5♓06'40"
GC 26♐59.0 ⚴ 14♏25.8R
Eris 21♈47.2 ⚵ 7♊58.5
⚷ 0♓25.4 ⚶ 23♌55.2
☽ Mean ☊ 15♑15.2

1 June 2010
Julian Day # 40329
SVP 5♓06'35"
GC 26♐59.1 ⚴ 6♏13.3R
Eris 22♈04.3 ⚵ 25♊48.4
⚷ 0♓59.2 ⚶ 1♍49.7
☽ Mean ☊ 13♑36.7

July 2010 — LONGITUDE

Day	Sid.Time	☉	0 hr ☽	Noon ☽	True ☊	☿	♀	♂	⚳	♃	♄	♅	♆	♇
1 Th	6 37 45	9♋33 19	29♒25 07	5♓20 30	11♑56.8	13♋11.9	19♌49.2	13♍13.2	24♐52.6	2♈37.5	28♍40.4	0♈35.1	28♒27.4	3♑57.9
2 F	6 41 41	10 30 31	11♓15 54	17 11 51	11 57.0	15 20.3	20 57.7	13 47.3	24R40.7	2 41.6	28 43.5	0 35.2	28R 26.5	3R 56.4
3 Sa	6 45 38	11 27 43	23 08 51	29 07 29	11R 57.1	17 27.5	22 06.1	14 21.4	24 28.9	2 45.5	28 46.8	0 35.4	28 25.5	3 54.8
4 Su	6 49 34	12 24 55	5♈08 16	11♈11 47	11D 57.1	19 33.3	23 14.3	14 55.7	24 17.3	2 49.2	28 50.1	0 35.5	28 24.5	3 53.3
5 M	6 53 31	13 22 07	17 18 35	23 29 13	11 57.1	21 37.7	24 22.4	15 30.1	24 05.9	2 52.8	28 53.5	0R 35.5	28 23.5	3 51.8
6 Tu	6 57 28	14 19 20	29 44 13	6♉04 04	11 57.2	23 40.4	25 30.5	16 04.5	23 54.8	2 56.1	28 57.0	0 35.5	28 22.5	3 50.3
7 W	7 01 24	15 16 33	12♉29 11	18 59 58	11 57.5	25 41.4	26 38.4	16 39.1	23 43.9	2 59.3	29 00.6	0 35.4	28 21.4	3 48.8
8 Th	7 05 21	16 13 46	25 36 43	2♊19 36	11 57.9	27 40.7	27 46.1	17 13.7	23 33.2	3 02.3	29 04.3	0 35.3	28 20.3	3 47.3
9 F	7 09 17	17 11 00	9♊08 44	16 04 03	11 58.3	29 38.2	28 53.8	17 48.5	23 22.8	3 05.1	29 08.0	0 35.2	28 19.2	3 45.8
10 Sa	7 13 14	18 08 14	23 05 24	0♋12 27	11R 58.7	1♌33.8	0♍01.3	18 23.3	23 12.6	3 07.7	29 11.9	0 34.9	28 18.1	3 44.3
11 Su	7 17 10	19 05 29	7♋24 44	14 41 39	11 58.8	3 27.5	1 08.7	18 58.3	23 02.8	3 10.1	29 15.8	0 34.7	28 16.9	3 42.9
12 M	7 21 07	20 02 43	22 02 27	29 26 18	11 58.5	5 19.3	2 15.9	19 33.3	22 53.2	3 12.3	29 19.8	0 34.4	28 15.7	3 41.4
13 Tu	7 25 04	20 59 58	6♌52 16	14♌19 22	11 57.8	7 09.2	3 23.0	20 08.4	22 43.9	3 14.4	29 23.9	0 34.0	28 14.5	3 39.9
14 W	7 29 00	21 57 13	21 46 36	29 12 59	11 56.8	8 57.3	4 30.0	20 43.7	22 34.9	3 16.2	29 28.0	0 33.6	28 13.3	3 38.5
15 Th	7 32 57	22 54 28	6♍37 36	13♍59 35	11 55.6	10 43.3	5 36.8	21 19.0	22 26.2	3 17.9	29 32.3	0 33.2	28 12.1	3 37.1
16 F	7 36 53	23 51 42	21 18 13	28 32 53	11 54.5	12 27.5	6 43.4	21 54.4	22 17.9	3 19.3	29 36.6	0 32.7	28 10.8	3 35.6
17 Sa	7 40 50	24 48 57	5♎43 05	12♎48 28	11D 53.7	14 09.8	7 49.9	22 29.8	22 09.8	3 20.6	29 41.0	0 32.2	28 09.5	3 34.2
18 Su	7 44 46	25 46 13	19 48 50	26 44 03	11 53.5	15 50.2	8 56.3	23 05.4	22 02.1	3 21.7	29 45.5	0 31.6	28 08.2	3 32.8
19 M	7 48 43	26 43 28	3♏34 08	10♏19 10	11 53.8	17 28.6	10 02.4	23 41.0	21 54.7	3 22.6	29 50.0	0 30.9	28 06.9	3 31.4
20 Tu	7 52 39	27 40 43	16 59 17	23 34 42	11 54.7	19 05.2	11 08.4	24 16.8	21 47.7	3 23.2	29 54.7	0 30.3	28 05.5	3 30.1
21 W	7 56 36	28 37 59	0♐05 40	6♐32 27	11 56.0	20 39.8	12 14.2	24 52.6	21 41.0	3 23.7	29 59.4	0 29.5	28 04.2	3 28.7
22 Th	8 00 32	29 35 15	12 55 20	19 14 35	11 57.3	22 12.5	13 19.8	25 28.5	21 34.6	3 24.0	0♎04.1	0 28.8	28 02.8	3 27.4
23 F	8 04 29	0♌32 31	25 30 31	1♑43 23	11R 58.2	23 43.3	14 25.3	26 04.5	21 28.6	3R 24.1	0 09.0	0 27.9	28 01.4	3 26.0
24 Sa	8 08 26	1 29 48	7♑53 27	14 00 59	11 58.5	25 12.2	15 30.5	26 40.5	21 22.9	3 24.0	0 13.9	0 27.1	28 00.0	3 24.7
25 Su	8 12 22	2 27 06	20 06 14	26 09 24	11 57.9	26 39.1	16 35.6	27 16.7	21 17.6	3 23.7	0 18.9	0 26.2	27 58.6	3 23.4
26 M	8 16 19	3 24 24	2♒10 45	8♒10 29	11 56.2	28 04.0	17 40.4	27 52.9	21 12.6	3 23.2	0 23.9	0 25.2	27 57.2	3 22.1
27 Tu	8 20 15	4 21 42	14 08 51	20 06 05	11 53.4	29 27.0	18 45.1	28 29.2	21 08.0	3 22.5	0 29.1	0 24.2	27 55.7	3 20.9
28 W	8 24 12	5 19 02	26 02 25	1♓58 07	11 49.9	0♍47.8	19 49.5	29 05.6	21 03.8	3 21.7	0 34.2	0 23.2	27 54.2	3 19.6
29 Th	8 28 08	6 16 22	7♓53 29	13 48 49	11 45.9	2 06.6	20 53.7	29 42.1	20 59.9	3 20.6	0 39.5	0 22.1	27 52.7	3 18.4
30 F	8 32 05	7 13 43	19 44 26	25 40 43	11 41.9	3 23.3	21 57.7	0♎18.6	20 56.3	3 19.3	0 44.8	0 21.0	27 51.2	3 17.2
31 Sa	8 36 01	8 11 05	1♈38 04	7♈36 53	11 38.3	4 37.8	23 01.5	0 55.2	20 53.2	3 17.8	0 50.2	0 19.8	27 49.7	3 16.0

August 2010 — LONGITUDE

Day	Sid.Time	☉	0 hr ☽	Noon ☽	True ☊	☿	♀	♂	⚳	♃	♄	♅	♆	♇
1 Su	8 39 58	9♌08 28	13♈37 38	19♈40 47	11♑35.7	5♍50.1	24♍05.0	1♎31.9	20♐50.4	3♈16.2	0♎55.6	0♈18.6	27♒48.2	3♑14.8
2 M	8 43 55	10 05 52	25 46 51	1♉56 20	11D 34.2	7 00.0	25 08.3	2 08.7	20R 47.9	3R 14.3	1 01.1	0R 17.4	27R 46.7	3R 13.6
3 Tu	8 47 51	11 03 18	8♉09 47	14 27 42	11 33.9	8 07.6	26 11.4	2 45.6	20 45.8	3 12.2	1 06.7	0 16.1	27 45.1	3 12.5
4 W	8 51 48	12 00 44	20 50 37	27 19 00	11 34.7	9 12.7	27 14.2	3 22.5	20 44.1	3 10.0	1 12.3	0 14.8	27 43.6	3 11.4
5 Th	8 55 44	12 58 12	3♊53 19	10♊33 55	11 36.2	10 15.2	28 16.8	3 59.5	20 42.7	3 07.6	1 18.0	0 13.4	27 42.0	3 10.3
6 F	8 59 41	13 55 42	17 21 06	24 15 04	11 37.6	11 15.1	29 19.1	4 36.7	20 41.7	3 04.9	1 23.8	0 12.0	27 40.4	3 09.2
7 Sa	9 03 37	14 53 12	1♋15 50	8♋23 20	11R 38.4	12 12.1	0♎21.1	5 13.8	20 41.1	3 02.1	1 29.6	0 10.6	27 38.9	3 08.2
8 Su	9 07 34	15 50 44	15 37 15	22 57 09	11 38.0	13 06.2	1 22.9	5 51.1	20D 40.8	2 59.1	1 35.5	0 09.1	27 37.3	3 07.1
9 M	9 11 31	16 48 17	0♌22 21	7♌52 00	11 36.1	13 57.3	2 24.4	6 28.5	20 40.9	2 55.9	1 41.4	0 07.6	27 35.7	3 06.1
10 Tu	9 15 27	17 45 50	15 25 06	23 00 28	11 32.5	14 45.1	3 25.6	7 05.9	20 41.3	2 52.5	1 47.4	0 06.0	27 34.1	3 05.1
11 W	9 19 24	18 43 25	0♍36 52	8♍13 00	11 27.6	15 29.5	4 26.5	7 43.4	20 42.1	2 48.9	1 53.4	0 04.4	27 32.5	3 04.2
12 Th	9 23 20	19 41 01	15 47 35	23 19 23	11 22.1	16 10.4	5 27.0	8 21.0	20 43.3	2 45.1	1 59.5	0 02.8	27 30.8	3 03.2
13 F	9 27 17	20 38 38	0♎47 17	8♎10 22	11 16.8	16 47.4	6 27.3	8 58.6	20 44.8	2 41.2	2 05.6	0 01.1	27 29.2	3 02.3
14 Sa	9 31 13	21 36 16	15 27 51	22 39 10	11 12.5	17 20.5	7 27.2	9 36.4	20 46.6	2 37.1	2 11.8	29♓59.4	27 27.6	3 01.4
15 Su	9 35 10	22 33 55	29 43 57	6♏42 02	11 09.7	17 49.4	8 26.8	10 14.2	20 48.9	2 32.8	2 18.0	29 57.7	27 26.0	3 00.6
16 M	9 39 06	23 31 35	13♏33 25	20 18 13	11D 08.5	18 13.9	9 25.9	10 52.0	20 51.4	2 28.3	2 24.3	29 55.9	27 24.3	2 59.7
17 Tu	9 43 03	24 29 16	26 56 42	3♐29 14	11 08.8	18 33.8	10 24.8	11 30.0	20 54.3	2 23.7	2 30.6	29 54.1	27 22.7	2 58.9
18 W	9 47 00	25 26 58	9♐56 13	16 18 09	11 10.0	18 48.8	11 23.2	12 08.0	20 57.5	2 18.9	2 37.0	29 52.3	27 21.1	2 58.1
19 Th	9 50 56	26 24 41	22 35 31	28 48 48	11 11.4	18 58.7	12 21.2	12 46.1	21 01.1	2 13.9	2 43.4	29 50.4	27 19.4	2 57.4
20 F	9 54 53	27 22 25	4♑58 31	11♑05 08	11R 12.0	19R 03.2	13 18.9	13 24.3	21 05.0	2 08.8	2 49.9	29 48.5	27 17.8	2 56.6
21 Sa	9 58 49	28 20 10	17 09 08	23 10 55	11 11.2	19 02.3	14 16.1	14 02.6	21 09.3	2 03.5	2 56.4	29 46.6	27 16.1	2 55.9
22 Su	10 02 46	29 17 56	29 10 53	5♒09 23	11 08.4	18 55.7	15 12.8	14 40.9	21 13.8	1 58.0	3 03.0	29 44.6	27 14.5	2 55.2
23 M	10 06 42	0♍15 44	11♒06 46	17 03 18	11 03.3	18 43.2	16 09.1	15 19.3	21 18.7	1 52.4	3 09.6	29 42.7	27 12.9	2 54.6
24 Tu	10 10 39	1 13 33	22 59 16	28 54 54	10 56.2	18 25.0	17 04.9	15 57.7	21 23.9	1 46.7	3 16.2	29 40.7	27 11.2	2 53.9
25 W	10 14 35	2 11 24	4♓50 24	10♓46 01	10 47.3	18 00.8	18 00.2	16 36.3	21 29.4	1 40.8	3 22.9	29 38.6	27 09.6	2 53.3
26 Th	10 18 32	3 09 16	16 41 55	22 38 19	10 37.4	17 30.8	18 55.0	17 14.9	21 35.2	1 34.8	3 29.6	29 36.6	27 08.0	2 52.8
27 F	10 22 28	4 07 09	28 35 26	4♈33 29	10 27.4	16 55.3	19 49.3	17 53.5	21 41.3	1 28.6	3 36.3	29 34.5	27 06.3	2 52.2
28 Sa	10 26 25	5 05 04	10♈32 43	16 33 26	10 18.2	16 14.5	20 43.1	18 32.3	21 47.8	1 22.3	3 43.1	29 32.4	27 04.7	2 51.7
29 Su	10 30 22	6 03 01	22 35 54	28 40 30	10 10.6	15 29.0	21 36.3	19 11.1	21 54.5	1 15.8	3 49.9	29 30.2	27 03.1	2 51.2
30 M	10 34 18	7 01 00	4♉47 34	10♉57 31	10 05.1	14 39.3	22 28.9	19 50.0	22 01.5	1 09.3	3 56.8	29 28.1	27 01.5	2 50.7
31 Tu	10 38 15	7 59 01	17 10 48	23 27 51	10 01.9	13 46.1	23 20.9	20 29.0	22 08.9	1 02.6	4 03.7	29 25.9	26 59.9	2 50.3

Astro Data	Dy Hr Mn
☽ 0N	2 15:01
♅ R	5 16:50
♃ 0N	8 17:52
☽ 0S	15 19:44
♃ R	23 12:04
♃□♇	25 4:21
♄☍♅	26 17:08
☽ 0N	29 22:06
♃ 0S	31 2:24
♂ 0S	31 17:46
♃□♇	3 5:34
♀ 0S	6 10:16
⚳ D	8 18:32
☽ 0S	12 4:54
♃☍♄	16 20:46

Planet Ingress	Dy Hr Mn
☿ ♌	9 16:30
♀ ♍	10 11:33
♄ ♎	21 15:11
☉ ♌	22 22:22
☿ ♍	27 21:44
♂ ♎	29 23:47
♀ ♎	7 3:49
♅ ♓R	14 3:37
☉ ♍	23 5:28
☿ R	20 20:00
♄□□	21 10:17
☽ 0N	26 4:38

Last Aspect Dy Hr Mn		☽ Ingress	Dy Hr Mn
30 22:04	♆ ☌	♓	1 1:11
3 11:18	♄ ☍	♈	3 13:45
5 21:25	♆ ⚹	♉	6 0:30
8 6:11	♄ △	♊	8 7:52
10 10:18	♄ □	♋	10 11:39
12 11:49	♄ ⚹	♌	12 12:55
14 10:24	♆ ☍	♍	14 13:16
16 13:47	♄ ☌	♎	16 14:25
18 14:27	♆ △	♏	18 17:43
20 23:44	♄ ⚹	♐	20 23:50
23 4:52	♆ ⚹	♑	23 8:40
25 14:21	♂ △	♒	25 19:39
28 3:47	♆ ☌	♓	28 8:01
30 3:45	♀ ☍	♈	30 20:43

Last Aspect Dy Hr Mn		☽ Ingress	Dy Hr Mn
2 3:55	♆ ⚹	♉	2 8:14
4 12:45	♆ □	♊	4 16:55
6 21:23	♀ □	♋	6 21:51
7 18:47	☿ ⚹	♌	8 23:24
10 19:11	♆ ☍	♍	10 23:02
12 0:05	☿ ☌	♎	12 22:44
14 20:07	♆ △	♏	15 0:27
17 5:25	♅ △	♐	17 5:35
19 13:59	♅ □	♑	19 14:18
22 1:09	♅ ⚹	♒	22 1:38
24 8:31	♆ ☌	♓	24 14:12
27 2:01	♅ ☌	♈	27 2:50
29 8:49	♆ ⚹	♉	29 14:36

☽ Phases & Eclipses Dy Hr Mn	
4 14:36	☾ 12♈31
11 19:42	● 19♋24
11 19:34:39	● T 05'20"
18 10:12	☽ 25♎42
26 1:38	○ 3♒00
3 5:00	☾ 10♉47
10 3:09	● 17♌25
16 18:15	☽ 23♏47
24 17:06	○ 1♓26

Astro Data

1 July 2010
Julian Day # 40359
SVP 5♓06'30"
GC 26♐59.2 ⚴ 4♏18.8
Eris 22♈13.9 ⚵ 12♋39.2
⚷ 0♓37.8R ⚶ 12♍51.5
☽ Mean ☊ 12♑01.4

1 August 2010
Julian Day # 40390
SVP 5♓06'25"
GC 26♐59.2 ⚴ 8♏42.7
Eris 22♈14.6R ⚵ 29♋21.9
⚷ 29♒28.6R ⚶ 26♍22.7
☽ Mean ☊ 10♑22.9

LONGITUDE September 2010

Day	Sid.Time	☉	0 hr ☽	Noon ☽	True ☊	☿	♀	♂	⚳	♃	♄	♅	♆	♇
1 W	10 42 11	8♍57 04	29♉49 11	6♊15 16	10♑00.7	12♍50.5	24♎12.3	21♎08.0	22♐16.5	0♈55.8	4♎10.6	29♓23.7	26♒58.3	2♑49.9
2 Th	10 46 08	9 55 08	12♊46 35	19 23 36	10D 01.0	11R 53.5	25 03.1	21 47.1	22 24.4	0R 48.9	4 17.5	29R 21.5	26R 56.7	2R 49.5
3 F	10 50 04	10 53 15	26 06 42	2♋56 14	10R 01.7	10 56.1	25 53.2	22 26.3	22 32.6	0 41.9	4 24.5	29 19.3	26 55.1	2 49.2
4 Sa	10 54 01	11 51 24	9♋52 27	16 55 28	10 01.6	9 59.7	26 42.6	23 05.6	22 41.1	0 34.7	4 31.5	29 17.0	26 53.5	2 48.9
5 Su	10 57 57	12 49 34	24 05 14	1♌21 31	9 59.9	9 05.6	27 31.3	23 44.9	22 49.8	0 27.5	4 38.6	29 14.8	26 52.0	2 48.6
6 M	11 01 54	13 47 46	8♌43 54	16 11 45	9 55.8	8 14.9	28 19.2	24 24.3	22 58.8	0 20.2	4 45.7	29 12.5	26 50.4	2 48.3
7 Tu	11 05 51	14 46 01	23 44 10	1♍20 07	9 49.2	7 28.8	29 06.4	25 03.8	23 08.1	0 12.8	4 52.8	29 10.2	26 48.9	2 48.1
8 W	11 09 47	15 44 17	8♍58 20	16 37 29	9 40.5	6 48.6	29 52.8	25 43.4	23 17.7	0 05.3	4 59.9	29 07.9	26 47.3	2 47.9
9 Th	11 13 44	16 42 34	24 16 06	1♎52 47	9 30.7	6 15.2	0♏38.4	26 23.0	23 27.5	29♓57.7	5 07.0	29 05.5	26 45.8	2 47.7
10 F	11 17 40	17 40 54	9♎26 10	16 55 02	9 21.0	5 49.3	1 23.0	27 02.7	23 37.6	29 50.1	5 14.2	29 03.2	26 44.3	2 47.6
11 Sa	11 21 37	18 39 15	24 18 20	1♏35 14	9 12.5	5 31.7	2 06.8	27 42.5	23 48.0	29 42.4	5 21.4	29 00.8	26 42.8	2 47.5
12 Su	11 25 33	19 37 38	8♏45 09	15 47 43	9 06.1	5D 23.0	2 49.7	28 22.3	23 58.6	29 34.6	5 28.6	28 58.5	26 41.3	2 47.4
13 M	11 29 30	20 36 02	22 42 47	29 30 24	9 02.1	5 23.3	3 31.5	29 02.3	24 09.4	29 26.8	5 35.8	28 56.1	26 39.8	2D 47.4
14 Tu	11 33 26	21 34 28	6♐10 48	12♐44 20	9D 00.4	5 32.9	4 12.4	29 42.2	24 20.6	29 19.0	5 43.1	28 53.7	26 38.4	2 47.4
15 W	11 37 23	22 32 56	19 11 27	25 32 43	9 00.1	5 51.8	4 52.1	0♏22.3	24 31.9	29 11.1	5 50.3	28 51.3	26 37.0	2 47.4
16 Th	11 41 20	23 31 25	1♑48 44	8♑00 06	9R 00.3	6 19.8	5 30.8	1 02.4	24 43.5	29 03.2	5 57.6	28 49.0	26 35.5	2 47.5
17 F	11 45 16	24 29 56	14 07 27	20 11 24	8 59.9	6 56.7	6 08.3	1 42.6	24 55.3	28 55.2	6 04.9	28 46.6	26 34.1	2 47.6
18 Sa	11 49 13	25 28 28	26 12 35	2♒11 33	8 57.7	7 42.2	6 44.5	2 22.9	25 07.4	28 47.2	6 12.2	28 44.2	26 32.7	2 47.7
19 Su	11 53 09	26 27 02	8♒08 51	14 04 58	8 53.1	8 35.7	7 19.6	3 03.2	25 19.6	28 39.2	6 19.6	28 41.8	26 31.4	2 47.8
20 M	11 57 06	27 25 38	20 00 22	25 55 26	8 45.6	9 36.8	7 53.3	3 43.6	25 32.1	28 31.2	6 26.9	28 39.4	26 30.0	2 48.0
21 Tu	12 01 02	28 24 15	1♓50 31	7♓45 57	8 35.4	10 44.9	8 25.6	4 24.1	25 44.8	28 23.2	6 34.2	28 36.9	26 28.7	2 48.2
22 W	12 04 59	29 22 55	13 41 59	19 38 50	8 22.9	11 59.4	8 56.6	5 04.6	25 57.8	28 15.2	6 41.6	28 34.5	26 27.4	2 48.5
23 Th	12 08 55	0♎21 36	25 36 42	1♈35 45	8 09.1	13 19.5	9 26.1	5 45.2	26 10.9	28 07.2	6 49.0	28 32.1	26 26.1	2 48.7
24 F	12 12 52	1 20 19	7♈36 07	13 37 57	7 55.0	14 44.7	9 54.0	6 25.9	26 24.3	27 59.2	6 56.3	28 29.7	26 24.8	2 49.0
25 Sa	12 16 49	2 19 04	19 41 22	25 46 30	7 41.9	16 14.4	10 20.4	7 06.6	26 37.8	27 51.2	7 03.7	28 27.3	26 23.5	2 49.4
26 Su	12 20 45	3 17 52	1♉53 32	8♉02 38	7 30.8	17 47.9	10 45.2	7 47.4	26 51.6	27 43.2	7 11.1	28 24.9	26 22.3	2 49.7
27 M	12 24 42	4 16 41	14 13 59	20 27 50	7 22.3	19 24.7	11 08.3	8 28.3	27 05.6	27 35.3	7 18.5	28 22.5	26 21.1	2 50.1
28 Tu	12 28 38	5 15 33	26 44 27	3♊04 09	7 16.8	21 04.1	11 29.6	9 09.2	27 19.7	27 27.4	7 25.9	28 20.1	26 19.9	2 50.6
29 W	12 32 35	6 14 27	9♊27 17	15 54 12	7 14.0	22 45.8	11 49.1	9 50.2	27 34.1	27 19.6	7 33.3	28 17.8	26 18.7	2 51.0
30 Th	12 36 31	7 13 24	22 25 17	29 00 57	7 13.1	24 29.2	12 06.8	10 31.3	27 48.7	27 11.8	7 40.7	28 15.4	26 17.6	2 51.5

LONGITUDE October 2010

Day	Sid.Time	☉	0 hr ☽	Noon ☽	True ☊	☿	♀	♂	⚳	♃	♄	♅	♆	♇
1 F	12 40 28	8♎12 22	5♋41 33	12♋27 27	7♑13.0	26♍14.0	12♏22.5	11♏12.5	28♐03.4	27♓04.1	7♎48.1	28♓13.0	26♒16.4	2♑52.1
2 Sa	12 44 24	9 11 23	19 18 56	26 16 14	7R 12.5	27 59.8	12 36.2	11 53.7	28 18.3	26R 56.4	7 55.5	28R 10.7	26R 15.3	2 52.6
3 Su	12 48 21	10 10 27	3♌19 27	10♌28 32	7 10.3	29 46.3	12 47.9	12 35.0	28 33.5	26 48.8	8 02.9	28 08.3	26 14.3	2 53.2
4 M	12 52 18	11 09 32	17 43 18	25 03 22	7 05.6	1♎33.2	12 57.5	13 16.4	28 48.8	26 41.2	8 10.3	28 06.0	26 13.2	2 53.8
5 Tu	12 56 14	12 08 40	2♍28 08	9♍56 50	6 58.1	3 20.4	13 05.0	13 57.8	29 04.2	26 33.8	8 17.7	28 03.7	26 12.2	2 54.5
6 W	13 00 11	13 07 50	17 28 29	25 01 57	6 48.3	5 07.6	13 10.2	14 39.3	29 19.9	26 26.4	8 25.1	28 01.4	26 11.2	2 55.1
7 Th	13 04 07	14 07 02	2♎35 58	10♎09 14	6 37.0	6 54.7	13R 13.2	15 20.9	29 35.7	26 19.1	8 32.5	27 59.1	26 10.2	2 55.8
8 F	13 08 04	15 06 16	17 40 24	25 08 14	6 25.7	8 41.5	13 13.9	16 02.5	29 51.7	26 11.9	8 39.9	27 56.8	26 09.3	2 56.6
9 Sa	13 12 00	16 05 33	2♏31 34	9♏49 25	6 15.6	10 28.0	13 12.3	16 44.2	0♑07.9	26 04.8	8 47.3	27 54.5	26 08.3	2 57.4
10 Su	13 15 57	17 04 51	17 01 02	24 05 49	6 07.7	12 14.0	13 08.2	17 26.0	0 24.2	25 57.8	8 54.6	27 52.3	26 07.5	2 58.2
11 M	13 19 53	18 04 11	1♐03 25	7♐53 43	6 02.4	13 59.5	13 01.8	18 07.9	0 40.7	25 51.0	9 02.0	27 50.1	26 06.6	2 59.0
12 Tu	13 23 50	19 03 33	14 36 46	21 12 46	5 59.8	15 44.5	12 53.0	18 49.8	0 57.4	25 44.2	9 09.3	27 47.9	26 05.8	2 59.9
13 W	13 27 46	20 02 56	27 42 05	4♑05 10	5D 59.0	17 28.9	12 41.7	19 31.8	1 14.2	25 37.6	9 16.7	27 45.7	26 05.0	3 00.8
14 Th	13 31 43	21 02 22	10♑22 36	16 34 58	5R 59.2	19 12.6	12 28.0	20 13.8	1 31.2	25 31.1	9 24.0	27 43.6	26 04.2	3 01.7
15 F	13 35 40	22 01 49	22 42 55	28 47 08	5 59.0	20 55.7	12 11.9	20 56.0	1 48.3	25 24.7	9 31.3	27 41.4	26 03.4	3 02.6
16 Sa	13 39 36	23 01 18	4♒48 16	10♒47 00	5 57.6	22 38.1	11 53.5	21 38.1	2 05.6	25 18.5	9 38.6	27 39.3	26 02.7	3 03.6
17 Su	13 43 33	24 00 48	16 43 56	22 39 42	5 53.9	24 19.9	11 32.8	22 20.4	2 23.0	25 12.4	9 45.8	27 37.2	26 02.0	3 04.6
18 M	13 47 29	25 00 21	28 34 51	4♓29 54	5 47.6	26 01.1	11 09.9	23 02.7	2 40.6	25 06.4	9 53.1	27 35.2	26 01.4	3 05.6
19 Tu	13 51 26	25 59 55	10♓25 21	16 21 37	5 38.7	27 41.5	10 44.9	23 45.1	2 58.3	25 00.6	10 00.3	27 33.1	26 00.7	3 06.7
20 W	13 55 22	26 59 31	22 19 03	28 17 58	5 27.6	29 21.4	10 17.9	24 27.5	3 16.1	24 54.9	10 07.5	27 31.1	26 00.1	3 07.8
21 Th	13 59 19	27 59 09	4♈18 39	10♈21 17	5 15.2	1♏00.6	9 49.1	25 10.0	3 34.1	24 49.4	10 14.7	27 29.1	25 59.6	3 08.9
22 F	14 03 15	28 58 48	16 26 03	22 33 04	5 02.5	2 39.1	9 18.5	25 52.5	3 52.2	24 44.1	10 21.8	27 27.2	25 59.0	3 10.1
23 Sa	14 07 12	29 58 30	28 42 26	4♉54 11	4 50.6	4 17.1	8 46.4	26 35.2	4 10.4	24 38.9	10 29.0	27 25.3	25 58.5	3 11.2
24 Su	14 11 09	0♏58 14	11♉08 24	17 25 05	4 40.6	5 54.5	8 13.0	27 17.9	4 28.8	24 33.9	10 36.1	27 23.4	25 58.0	3 12.5
25 M	14 15 05	1 58 00	23 44 19	0♊06 07	4 33.1	7 31.3	7 38.5	28 00.6	4 47.3	24 29.0	10 43.2	27 21.5	25 57.6	3 13.7
26 Tu	14 19 02	2 57 48	6♊30 33	12 57 44	4 28.3	9 07.6	7 03.1	28 43.4	5 05.9	24 24.4	10 50.2	27 19.7	25 57.2	3 14.9
27 W	14 22 58	3 57 38	19 27 46	26 00 48	4D 26.2	10 43.4	6 27.0	29 26.3	5 24.7	24 19.9	10 57.3	27 17.9	25 56.8	3 16.2
28 Th	14 26 55	4 57 30	2♋37 00	9♋16 33	4 25.9	12 18.6	5 50.6	0♐09.3	5 43.6	24 15.6	11 04.3	27 16.1	25 56.5	3 17.5
29 F	14 30 51	5 57 25	15 59 39	22 46 30	4 26.7	13 53.3	5 13.9	0 52.3	6 02.6	24 11.4	11 11.2	27 14.4	25 56.2	3 18.9
30 Sa	14 34 48	6 57 21	29 37 16	6♌32 06	4R 27.2	15 27.5	4 37.4	1 35.4	6 21.7	24 07.5	11 18.2	27 12.7	25 55.9	3 20.2
31 Su	14 38 44	7 57 20	13♌31 05	20 34 12	4 26.5	17 01.3	4 01.2	2 18.6	6 40.9	24 03.7	11 25.1	27 11.1	25 55.6	3 21.6

Astro Data

	Dy Hr Mn
♄0S	8 13:58
☽0S	8 15:45
☿D	12 23:12
♇D	14 4:37
♃☌♅	19 1:04
☽0N	22 10:45
⊙0S	23 3:11
☿0S	5 22:28
☽0S	6 2:17
♀R	8 7:06
♃⚺♆	8 22:15
☽0N	19 16:54
♄⚼♆	27 10:31

Planet Ingress

		Dy Hr Mn
♀	♏	8 15:46
♃	♓R	9 4:51
♂	♏	14 22:39
⊙	♎	23 3:10
☿	♎	3 15:05
⚳	♑	9 0:18
☿	♏	20 21:20
⊙	♏	23 12:36
♂	♐	28 6:49

Last Aspect / ☽ Ingress

Last Aspect Dy Hr Mn		☽ Ingress	Dy Hr Mn
31 23:14	♅ ⚹	♊	1 0:20
3 5:41	♅ □	♋	3 6:52
5 8:32	♅ △	♌	5 9:46
7 8:18	♀ ⚹	♍	7 9:54
9 9:00	♃ ☍	♎	9 9:02
11 5:17	♂ ☌	♏	11 9:22
13 11:54	♃ △	♐	13 12:53
15 18:53	♃ □	♑	15 20:31
18 5:14	♃ ⚹	♒	18 7:36
20 13:10	♆ ☌	♓	20 20:16
23 5:53	♅ ☌	♈	23 8:48
25 13:13	♆ ⚹	♉	25 20:18
28 3:04	♅ ⚹	♊	28 6:12
30 10:38	♅ □	♋	30 13:47

Last Aspect / ☽ Ingress

Last Aspect Dy Hr Mn		☽ Ingress	Dy Hr Mn
2 15:23	☿ ⚹	♌	2 18:22
4 13:53	♆ ☍	♍	4 20:01
6 16:44	♅ ☍	♎	6 19:53
8 13:39	♆ △	♏	8 19:53
10 18:28	♅ △	♐	10 22:10
13 0:09	♅ □	♑	13 4:18
15 9:50	♅ ⚹	♒	15 14:25
17 18:50	♆ ☌	♓	18 2:53
20 10:26	♅ ☌	♈	20 15:24
23 1:38	⊙ ☍	♉	23 2:31
25 7:50	♂ ☍	♊	25 11:49
27 14:20	♅ □	♋	27 19:15
29 19:49	♅ △	♌	30 0:40

☽ Phases & Eclipses

Dy Hr Mn		
1 17:23	☾	9♊10
8 10:31	●	15♍41
15 5:51	☽	22♐18
23 9:18	○	0♈15
1 3:53	☾	7♋52
7 18:46	●	14♎24
14 21:29	☽	21♑26
23 1:38	○	29♈33
30 12:47	☾	6♌59

Astro Data

1 September 2010
Julian Day # 40421
SVP 5♓06'21"
GC 26♐59.3 ⚴ 17♏13.7
Eris 22♈05.6R ⚵ 15♌08.0
⚷ 27♒57.3R ⚶ 11♎16.7
☽ Mean ☊ 8♑44.4

1 October 2010
Julian Day # 40451
SVP 5♓06'18"
GC 26♐59.4 ⚴ 27♏42.1
Eris 21♈50.2R ⚵ 29♌12.5
⚷ 26♒41.0R ⚶ 26♎33.8
☽ Mean ☊ 7♑09.1

November 2010 LONGITUDE

Day	Sid.Time	☉	0 hr ☽	Noon ☽	True ☊	☿	♀	♂	⚳	♃	♄	♅	♆	♇
1 M	14 42 41	8♏57 21	27♌41 22	4♍52 21	4♑23.7	18♏34.6	3♏25.5	3♐01.8	7♑00.2	24♓00.1	11♎32.0	27♓09.4	25♒55.4	3♑23.0
2 Tu	14 46 38	9 57 24	12♍06 49	19 24 16	4R 18.7	20 07.5	2R 50.7	3 45.0	7 19.7	23R 56.7	11 38.8	27R 07.8	25R 55.2	3 24.5
3 W	14 50 34	10 57 30	26 44 05	4♎05 30	4 11.7	21 39.9	2 17.0	4 28.4	7 39.3	23 53.5	11 45.6	27 06.3	25 55.1	3 25.9
4 Th	14 54 31	11 57 37	11♎27 39	18 49 34	4 03.4	23 11.9	1 44.5	5 11.8	7 58.9	23 50.5	11 52.4	27 04.8	25 55.0	3 27.4
5 F	14 58 27	12 57 46	26 10 17	3♏28 47	3 54.9	24 43.6	1 13.4	5 55.3	8 18.7	23 47.7	11 59.1	27 03.3	25 54.9	3 28.9
6 Sa	15 02 24	13 57 58	10♏44 07	17 55 26	3 47.2	26 14.8	0 44.0	6 38.8	8 38.6	23 45.1	12 05.8	27 01.9	25D 54.8	3 30.5
7 Su	15 06 20	14 58 11	25 01 57	2♐03 04	3 41.3	27 45.5	0 16.4	7 22.4	8 58.6	23 42.7	12 12.4	27 00.5	25 54.8	3 32.0
8 M	15 10 17	15 58 25	8♐58 19	15 47 25	3 37.6	29 15.9	29♎50.7	8 06.1	9 18.7	23 40.5	12 19.0	26 59.2	25 54.9	3 33.6
9 Tu	15 14 13	16 58 42	22 30 13	29 06 44	3D 36.0	0♐45.9	29 27.1	8 49.8	9 38.9	23 38.5	12 25.6	26 57.9	25 54.9	3 35.2
10 W	15 18 10	17 59 00	5♑37 08	12♑01 41	3 36.2	2 15.5	29 05.7	9 33.6	9 59.2	23 36.7	12 32.1	26 56.6	25 55.0	3 36.8
11 Th	15 22 07	18 59 19	18 20 47	24 34 53	3 37.5	3 44.6	28 46.5	10 17.5	10 19.6	23 35.1	12 38.6	26 55.4	25 55.2	3 38.5
12 F	15 26 03	19 59 40	0♒44 30	6♒50 15	3 38.9	5 13.4	28 29.6	11 01.4	10 40.1	23 33.7	12 45.0	26 54.2	25 55.3	3 40.2
13 Sa	15 30 00	21 00 02	12 52 43	18 52 34	3R 39.8	6 41.6	28 15.1	11 45.3	11 00.6	23 32.5	12 51.4	26 53.1	25 55.5	3 41.8
14 Su	15 33 56	22 00 26	24 50 24	0♓46 54	3 39.3	8 09.4	28 03.1	12 29.4	11 21.3	23 31.5	12 57.7	26 52.0	25 55.7	3 43.6
15 M	15 37 53	23 00 50	6♓42 40	12 38 19	3 37.1	9 36.6	27 53.5	13 13.4	11 42.1	23 30.7	13 04.0	26 51.0	25 56.0	3 45.3
16 Tu	15 41 49	24 01 17	18 34 25	24 31 31	3 33.1	11 03.3	27 46.4	13 57.6	12 02.9	23 30.2	13 10.2	26 50.0	25 56.3	3 47.0
17 W	15 45 46	25 01 44	0♈30 07	6♈30 39	3 27.6	12 29.4	27 41.8	14 41.8	12 23.8	23 29.8	13 16.3	26 49.1	25 56.6	3 48.8
18 Th	15 49 42	26 02 13	12 33 33	18 39 07	3 21.0	13 54.9	27D 39.6	15 26.0	12 44.8	23D 29.7	13 22.4	26 48.2	25 57.0	3 50.6
19 F	15 53 39	27 02 44	24 47 40	0♉59 24	3 14.1	15 19.6	27 39.9	16 10.3	13 05.9	23 29.7	13 28.5	26 47.3	25 57.4	3 52.4
20 Sa	15 57 36	28 03 15	7♉14 29	13 33 02	3 07.6	16 43.5	27 42.6	16 54.7	13 27.1	23 30.0	13 34.5	26 46.5	25 57.8	3 54.2
21 Su	16 01 32	29 03 49	19 55 04	26 20 36	3 02.3	18 06.5	27 47.6	17 39.1	13 48.3	23 30.5	13 40.4	26 45.7	25 58.3	3 56.0
22 M	16 05 29	0♐04 23	2♊49 35	9♊21 56	2 58.4	19 28.6	27 55.0	18 23.6	14 09.6	23 31.2	13 46.3	26 45.0	25 58.8	3 57.9
23 Tu	16 09 25	1 05 00	15 57 32	22 36 15	2D 56.4	20 49.4	28 04.7	19 08.2	14 31.0	23 32.1	13 52.1	26 44.4	25 59.3	3 59.8
24 W	16 13 22	2 05 38	29 17 56	6♋02 28	2 56.0	22 09.0	28 16.6	19 52.8	14 52.5	23 33.2	13 57.9	26 43.8	25 59.9	4 01.7
25 Th	16 17 18	3 06 17	12♋49 42	19 39 30	2 56.8	23 27.1	28 30.7	20 37.4	15 14.0	23 34.5	14 03.6	26 43.2	26 00.5	4 03.6
26 F	16 21 15	4 06 58	26 31 44	3♌26 17	2 58.4	24 43.6	28 46.9	21 22.1	15 35.7	23 36.0	14 09.3	26 42.7	26 01.2	4 05.5
27 Sa	16 25 11	5 07 40	10♌23 03	17 21 55	2 59.9	25 58.1	29 05.2	22 06.9	15 57.3	23 37.7	14 14.8	26 42.2	26 01.8	4 07.4
28 Su	16 29 08	6 08 24	24 22 44	1♍25 24	3R 00.8	27 10.4	29 25.5	22 51.7	16 19.1	23 39.6	14 20.3	26 41.8	26 02.5	4 09.4
29 M	16 33 05	7 09 10	8♍29 43	15 35 29	3 00.6	28 20.3	29 47.6	23 36.6	16 40.9	23 41.7	14 25.8	26 41.5	26 03.3	4 11.3
30 Tu	16 37 01	8 09 57	22 42 26	29 50 17	2 59.2	29 27.2	0♏11.7	24 21.5	17 02.8	23 44.0	14 31.2	26 41.1	26 04.1	4 13.3

December 2010 LONGITUDE

Day	Sid.Time	☉	0 hr ☽	Noon ☽	True ☊	☿	♀	♂	⚳	♃	♄	♅	♆	♇
1 W	16 40 58	9♐10 46	6♎58 39	14♎07 08	2♑56.8	0♑30.9	0♏37.5	25♐06.5	17♑24.8	23♓46.5	14♎36.5	26♓40.9	26♒04.9	4♑15.3
2 Th	16 44 54	10 11 36	21 15 15	28 22 29	2R 53.6	1 30.8	1 05.1	25 51.6	17 46.8	23 49.2	14 41.7	26R 40.7	26 05.7	4 17.3
3 F	16 48 51	11 12 28	5♏28 20	12♏32 13	2 50.3	2 26.4	1 34.3	26 36.7	18 08.9	23 52.2	14 46.9	26 40.5	26 06.6	4 19.3
4 Sa	16 52 47	12 13 21	19 33 37	26 31 58	2 47.3	3 17.1	2 05.1	27 21.8	18 31.0	23 55.3	14 52.0	26 40.4	26 07.5	4 21.4
5 Su	16 56 44	13 14 15	3♐26 49	10♐17 44	2 45.1	4 02.1	2 37.5	28 07.1	18 53.2	23 58.6	14 57.0	26D 40.3	26 08.4	4 23.4
6 M	17 00 40	14 15 10	17 04 21	23 46 24	2D 43.9	4 40.9	3 11.3	28 52.3	19 15.5	24 02.1	15 01.9	26 40.3	26 09.4	4 25.5
7 Tu	17 04 37	15 16 06	0♑23 42	6♑56 09	2 43.8	5 12.5	3 46.6	29 37.6	19 37.8	24 05.8	15 06.8	26 40.4	26 10.4	4 27.5
8 W	17 08 34	16 17 03	13 23 47	19 46 39	2 44.4	5 36.2	4 23.2	0♑23.0	20 00.2	24 09.7	15 11.6	26 40.5	26 11.4	4 29.6
9 Th	17 12 30	17 18 01	26 04 58	2♒18 59	2 45.7	5 51.0	5 01.1	1 08.4	20 22.6	24 13.8	15 16.3	26 40.6	26 12.5	4 31.7
10 F	17 16 27	18 19 00	8♒29 03	14 35 32	2 47.1	5R 56.2	5 40.3	1 53.9	20 45.1	24 18.1	15 20.9	26 40.8	26 13.6	4 33.8
11 Sa	17 20 23	19 19 59	20 38 55	26 39 41	2 48.4	5 50.9	6 20.8	2 39.4	21 07.7	24 22.6	15 25.5	26 41.1	26 14.7	4 35.9
12 Su	17 24 20	20 20 59	2♓38 23	8♓35 35	2 49.2	5 34.5	7 02.3	3 25.0	21 30.3	24 27.2	15 30.0	26 41.4	26 15.9	4 38.0
13 M	17 28 16	21 21 59	14 31 51	20 27 49	2R 49.6	5 06.6	7 45.0	4 10.6	21 52.9	24 32.1	15 34.3	26 41.7	26 17.0	4 40.1
14 Tu	17 32 13	22 23 00	26 24 04	2♈21 11	2 49.3	4 27.3	8 28.8	4 56.2	22 15.6	24 37.1	15 38.6	26 42.1	26 18.3	4 42.2
15 W	17 36 10	23 24 01	8♈19 47	14 20 26	2 48.6	3 36.8	9 13.7	5 41.9	22 38.3	24 42.3	15 42.9	26 42.6	26 19.5	4 44.3
16 Th	17 40 06	24 25 03	20 23 39	26 29 57	2 47.7	2 35.9	9 59.5	6 27.7	23 01.1	24 47.7	15 47.0	26 43.1	26 20.8	4 46.5
17 F	17 44 03	25 26 05	2♉39 47	8♉53 33	2 46.6	1 26.2	10 46.3	7 13.5	23 23.9	24 53.3	15 51.1	26 43.7	26 22.1	4 48.6
18 Sa	17 47 59	26 27 08	15 11 36	21 34 12	2 45.7	0 09.6	11 34.0	7 59.3	23 46.7	24 59.0	15 55.0	26 44.3	26 23.4	4 50.7
19 Su	17 51 56	27 28 12	28 01 32	4♊33 42	2 45.0	28♐48.5	12 22.7	8 45.2	24 09.6	25 05.0	15 58.9	26 45.0	26 24.8	4 52.9
20 M	17 55 52	28 29 15	11♊10 44	17 52 34	2 44.6	27 25.6	13 12.1	9 31.1	24 32.6	25 11.1	16 02.7	26 45.7	26 26.2	4 55.0
21 Tu	17 59 49	29 30 20	24 39 01	1♋29 51	2D 44.4	26 03.8	14 02.5	10 17.1	24 55.5	25 17.3	16 06.4	26 46.4	26 27.6	4 57.2
22 W	18 03 45	0♑31 25	8♋24 45	15 23 17	2 44.5	24 45.6	14 53.6	11 03.1	25 18.6	25 23.8	16 10.0	26 47.3	26 29.0	4 59.3
23 Th	18 07 42	1 32 30	22 25 02	29 29 28	2 44.6	23 33.5	15 45.5	11 49.1	25 41.6	25 30.4	16 13.5	26 48.1	26 30.5	5 01.5
24 F	18 11 39	2 33 36	6♌36 05	13♌44 19	2R 44.7	22 29.4	16 38.1	12 35.2	26 04.7	25 37.2	16 17.0	26 49.1	26 32.0	5 03.7
25 Sa	18 15 35	3 34 42	20 53 38	28 03 31	2 44.7	21 34.7	17 31.5	13 21.4	26 27.8	25 44.1	16 20.3	26 50.0	26 33.5	5 05.8
26 Su	18 19 32	4 35 49	5♍13 28	12♍23 01	2 44.5	20 50.2	18 25.5	14 07.5	26 51.0	25 51.2	16 23.5	26 51.0	26 35.1	5 08.0
27 M	18 23 28	5 36 57	19 31 45	26 39 19	2D 44.4	20 16.5	19 20.2	14 53.8	27 14.2	25 58.5	16 26.7	26 52.1	26 36.7	5 10.1
28 Tu	18 27 25	6 38 05	3♎45 22	10♎49 39	2 44.4	19 53.3	20 15.5	15 40.0	27 37.4	26 05.9	16 29.7	26 53.2	26 38.3	5 12.3
29 W	18 31 21	7 39 14	17 51 56	24 51 59	2 44.6	19D 40.6	21 11.5	16 26.3	28 00.6	26 13.5	16 32.7	26 54.4	26 39.9	5 14.5
30 Th	18 35 18	8 40 23	1♏49 40	8♏44 49	2 45.0	19 37.6	22 08.0	17 12.7	28 23.9	26 21.2	16 35.5	26 55.6	26 41.5	5 16.6
31 F	18 39 14	9 41 33	15 37 18	22 27 00	2 45.7	19 43.9	23 05.1	17 59.1	28 47.2	26 29.1	16 38.3	26 56.9	26 43.2	5 18.8

Astro Data	Dy Hr Mn
☽0S	2 10:38
♆D	7 6:05
☽0N	15 23:37
♃D	18 16:55
♀D	18 21:19
☽0S	29 16:25
♅D	6 1:51
☿R	10 12:06
☽0N	13 7:14
☽0S	26 21:34
☿D	30 7:21

Planet Ingress		Dy Hr Mn
♀	♎R	8 3:07
☿	♐	8 23:44
☉	♐	22 10:16
♀	♏	30 0:34
☿	♑	1 0:12
♂	♑	7 23:50
☿	♐R	18 14:54
☉	♑	21 23:40

Last Aspect Dy Hr Mn		☽ Ingress	Dy Hr Mn
31 21:02	♆ ☍	♍	1 3:52
3 0:37	♅ ☍	♎	3 5:20
4 23:35	♆ △	♏	5 6:17
7 3:45	☿ ☌	♐	7 8:29
9 12:36	♀ ⚹	♑	9 13:38
11 19:58	♀ □	♒	11 22:33
14 6:34	♀ △	♓	14 10:25
16 16:38	♅ ☌	♈	16 23:00
19 5:34	♀ ☍	♉	19 10:05
21 17:28	☉ ☍	♊	21 18:47
23 21:58	♀ △	♋	24 1:15
26 3:45	♀ □	♌	26 6:02
28 8:31	♀ ⚹	♍	28 9:35
30 11:18	☿ □	♎	30 12:16

Last Aspect Dy Hr Mn		☽ Ingress	Dy Hr Mn
2 8:09	♆ △	♏	2 14:45
4 12:15	♅ △	♐	4 18:00
6 21:47	♂ ☌	♑	6 23:17
9 1:08	♅ ⚹	♒	9 7:32
11 11:10	♅ ☌	♓	11 18:42
14 0:36	♅ ☌	♈	14 7:16
16 11:42	♆ ⚹	♉	16 18:50
18 21:38	♅ ⚹	♊	19 3:38
21 8:15	☉ ☍	♋	21 9:23
23 7:27	♅ △	♌	23 12:52
25 9:29	♆ ☍	♍	25 15:15
27 12:22	♅ ☍	♎	27 17:39
29 15:06	♆ △	♏	29 20:51

☽ Phases & Eclipses Dy Hr Mn		
6 4:53	●	13♏40
13 16:40	☽	21♒12
21 17:28	○	29♉18
28 20:38	☾	6♍30
5 17:37	●	13♐28
13 14:00	☽	21♓27
21 8:15	○	29♊21
21 8:18	•	T 1.256
28 4:20	☾	6♎19

Astro Data

1 November 2010
Julian Day # 40482
SVP 5♓06'15"
GC 26♐59.4 ⚴ 9♐46.7
Eris 21♈31.9R ⚵ 12♍03.8
⚷ 26♒04.7R ⚶ 12♏55.5
☽ Mean ☊ 5♑30.6

1 December 2010
Julian Day # 40512
SVP 5♓06'10"
GC 26♐59.5 ⚴ 22♐01.1
Eris 21♈17.0R ⚵ 22♍04.8
⚷ 26♒24.6 ⚶ 29♏01.5
☽ Mean ☊ 3♑55.3

LONGITUDE — January 2011

Day	Sid.Time	☉	0 hr ☽	Noon ☽	True ☊	☿	♀	♂	⚳	♃	♄	♅	♆	♇
1 Sa	18 43 11	10♑42 43	29♏13 48	5♐57 36	2♑46.4	19♐58.7	24♏02.7	18♑45.5	29♑10.6	26♓37.1	16♎40.9	26♓58.2	26♒44.9	5♑21.0
2 Su	18 47 08	11 43 54	12♐38 18	19 15 48	2 47.0	20 21.1	25 00.9	19 32.0	29 33.9	26 45.3	16 43.5	26 59.5	26 46.6	5 23.1
3 M	18 51 04	12 45 05	25 50 02	2♑20 55	2R47.3	20 50.6	25 59.5	20 18.5	29 57.3	26 53.7	16 46.0	27 01.0	26 48.4	5 25.3
4 Tu	18 55 01	13 46 15	8♑48 25	15 12 29	2 47.0	21 26.4	26 58.6	21 05.0	0♒20.8	27 02.2	16 48.3	27 02.4	26 50.2	5 27.4
5 W	18 58 57	14 47 26	21 33 09	27 50 27	2 46.1	22 07.8	27 58.2	21 51.6	0 44.2	27 10.8	16 50.6	27 03.9	26 52.0	5 29.6
6 Th	19 02 54	15 48 37	4♒04 28	10♒15 18	2 44.5	22 54.2	28 58.2	22 38.2	1 07.7	27 19.6	16 52.7	27 05.5	26 53.8	5 31.7
7 F	19 06 50	16 49 47	16 23 10	22 28 14	2 42.4	23 45.2	29 58.7	23 24.8	1 31.2	27 28.5	16 54.8	27 07.1	26 55.6	5 33.8
8 Sa	19 10 47	17 50 57	28 30 49	4♓31 12	2 40.0	24 40.2	0♐59.5	24 11.5	1 54.7	27 37.5	16 56.7	27 08.7	26 57.5	5 36.0
9 Su	19 14 43	18 52 07	10♓29 47	16 26 56	2 37.6	25 38.7	2 00.8	24 58.2	2 18.2	27 46.7	16 58.5	27 10.4	26 59.3	5 38.1
10 M	19 18 40	19 53 16	22 23 09	28 18 53	2 35.6	26 40.4	3 02.4	25 45.0	2 41.7	27 56.0	17 00.3	27 12.1	27 01.2	5 40.2
11 Tu	19 22 37	20 54 24	4♈14 41	10♈11 06	2D34.3	27 45.1	4 04.4	26 31.7	3 05.3	28 05.5	17 01.9	27 13.9	27 03.2	5 42.3
12 W	19 26 33	21 55 32	16 08 43	22 08 08	2 33.9	28 52.2	5 06.8	27 18.5	3 28.9	28 15.1	17 03.4	27 15.7	27 05.1	5 44.4
13 Th	19 30 30	22 56 40	28 09 55	4♉14 42	2 34.4	0♑01.7	6 09.5	28 05.3	3 52.4	28 24.8	17 04.8	27 17.6	27 07.0	5 46.5
14 F	19 34 26	23 57 47	10♉23 04	16 35 34	2 35.6	1 13.2	7 12.5	28 52.2	4 16.0	28 34.6	17 06.2	27 19.5	27 09.0	5 48.6
15 Sa	19 38 23	24 58 53	22 52 45	29 15 06	2 37.2	2 26.6	8 15.9	29 39.1	4 39.7	28 44.6	17 07.4	27 21.5	27 11.0	5 50.6
16 Su	19 42 19	25 59 59	5♊43 01	12♊16 50	2 38.8	3 41.7	9 19.5	0♒26.0	5 03.3	28 54.7	17 08.5	27 23.5	27 13.0	5 52.7
17 M	19 46 16	27 01 04	18 56 49	25 43 02	2R39.8	4 58.3	10 23.5	1 12.9	5 26.9	29 04.9	17 09.5	27 25.5	27 15.0	5 54.8
18 Tu	19 50 12	28 02 08	2♋35 31	9♋34 05	2 39.8	6 16.4	11 27.8	1 59.9	5 50.5	29 15.2	17 10.4	27 27.6	27 17.1	5 56.8
19 W	19 54 09	29 03 12	16 38 26	23 48 05	2 38.5	7 35.7	12 32.3	2 46.8	6 14.2	29 25.7	17 11.1	27 29.7	27 19.1	5 58.8
20 Th	19 58 06	0♒04 15	1♌02 25	8♌20 42	2 35.8	8 56.3	13 37.1	3 33.8	6 37.9	29 36.2	17 11.8	27 31.9	27 21.2	6 00.8
21 F	20 02 02	1 05 18	15 42 03	23 05 31	2 32.0	10 17.9	14 42.2	4 20.9	7 01.5	29 46.9	17 12.4	27 34.1	27 23.3	6 02.8
22 Sa	20 05 59	2 06 20	0♍30 06	7♍54 47	2 27.5	11 40.7	15 47.6	5 07.9	7 25.2	29 57.6	17 12.8	27 36.3	27 25.4	6 04.8
23 Su	20 09 55	3 07 21	15 18 36	22 40 38	2 23.2	13 04.4	16 53.2	5 55.0	7 48.9	0♈08.5	17 13.2	27 38.6	27 27.5	6 06.8
24 M	20 13 52	4 08 22	0♎00 04	7♎16 14	2 19.6	14 29.0	17 59.0	6 42.1	8 12.5	0 19.5	17 13.4	27 40.9	27 29.6	6 08.8
25 Tu	20 17 48	5 09 22	14 28 33	21 36 38	2 17.3	15 54.5	19 05.1	7 29.2	8 36.2	0 30.6	17R13.6	27 43.3	27 31.7	6 10.7
26 W	20 21 45	6 10 22	28 40 12	5♏39 06	2D16.5	17 20.9	20 11.4	8 16.3	8 59.9	0 41.8	17 13.6	27 45.7	27 33.9	6 12.7
27 Th	20 25 41	7 11 22	12♏33 19	19 22 54	2 17.1	18 48.1	21 17.9	9 03.5	9 23.6	0 53.1	17 13.5	27 48.1	27 36.0	6 14.6
28 F	20 29 38	8 12 20	26 07 58	2♐48 44	2 18.5	20 16.1	22 24.7	9 50.7	9 47.3	1 04.5	17 13.3	27 50.6	27 38.2	6 16.5
29 Sa	20 33 35	9 13 19	9♐25 24	15 58 14	2 20.1	21 44.9	23 31.6	10 37.9	10 11.0	1 16.0	17 13.0	27 53.1	27 40.4	6 18.4
30 Su	20 37 31	10 14 17	22 27 27	28 53 19	2R21.1	23 14.4	24 38.8	11 25.1	10 34.7	1 27.6	17 12.6	27 55.6	27 42.6	6 20.3
31 M	20 41 28	11 15 13	5♑16 02	11♑35 49	2 20.7	24 44.7	25 46.1	12 12.4	10 58.4	1 39.3	17 12.1	27 58.2	27 44.8	6 22.1

LONGITUDE — February 2011

Day	Sid.Time	☉	0 hr ☽	Noon ☽	True ☊	☿	♀	♂	⚳	♃	♄	♅	♆	♇
1 Tu	20 45 24	12♒16 09	17♑52 53	24♑07 21	2♑18.4	26♑15.7	26♐53.6	12♒59.6	11♒22.0	1♈51.1	17♎11.5	28♓00.8	27♒47.0	6♑24.0
2 W	20 49 21	13 17 04	0♒19 24	6♒29 09	2R14.0	27 47.5	28 01.2	13 46.9	11 45.7	2 03.0	17R10.8	28 03.4	27 49.2	6 25.8
3 Th	20 53 17	14 17 58	12 36 44	18 42 15	2 07.5	29 20.0	29 09.1	14 34.2	12 09.4	2 15.0	17 09.9	28 06.1	27 51.4	6 27.6
4 F	20 57 14	15 18 51	24 45 51	0♓47 39	1 59.5	0♒53.2	0♑17.0	15 21.5	12 33.1	2 27.0	17 09.0	28 08.8	27 53.7	6 29.4
5 Sa	21 01 11	16 19 43	6♓47 48	12 46 31	1 50.6	2 27.1	1 25.2	16 08.8	12 56.7	2 39.2	17 08.0	28 11.5	27 55.9	6 31.2
6 Su	21 05 07	17 20 33	18 43 59	24 40 28	1 41.6	4 01.9	2 33.5	16 56.1	13 20.4	2 51.4	17 06.8	28 14.3	27 58.2	6 32.9
7 M	21 09 04	18 21 22	0♈36 16	6♈31 42	1 33.4	5 37.3	3 41.9	17 43.5	13 44.0	3 03.7	17 05.6	28 17.1	28 00.4	6 34.6
8 Tu	21 13 00	19 22 09	12 27 09	18 23 04	1 26.9	7 13.6	4 50.5	18 30.8	14 07.6	3 16.1	17 04.2	28 19.9	28 02.7	6 36.3
9 W	21 16 57	20 22 55	24 19 55	0♉18 12	1 22.3	8 50.6	5 59.2	19 18.2	14 31.3	3 28.6	17 02.8	28 22.7	28 04.9	6 38.0
10 Th	21 20 53	21 23 40	6♉18 28	12 21 20	1D19.9	10 28.4	7 08.0	20 05.5	14 54.9	3 41.1	17 01.2	28 25.6	28 07.2	6 39.7
11 F	21 24 50	22 24 23	18 27 21	24 37 11	1 19.5	12 07.0	8 17.0	20 52.9	15 18.5	3 53.8	16 59.5	28 28.5	28 09.5	6 41.3
12 Sa	21 28 46	23 25 04	0♊51 27	7♊10 45	1 20.2	13 46.4	9 26.1	21 40.3	15 42.0	4 06.5	16 57.8	28 31.4	28 11.7	6 43.0
13 Su	21 32 43	24 25 44	13 35 39	20 06 43	1R21.3	15 26.6	10 35.3	22 27.6	16 05.6	4 19.2	16 55.9	28 34.4	28 14.0	6 44.6
14 M	21 36 40	25 26 22	26 44 24	3♋29 04	1 21.8	17 07.7	11 44.6	23 15.0	16 29.1	4 32.1	16 54.0	28 37.4	28 16.3	6 46.2
15 Tu	21 40 36	26 26 59	10♋20 56	17 20 06	1 20.6	18 49.6	12 54.1	24 02.4	16 52.7	4 45.0	16 51.9	28 40.4	28 18.6	6 47.7
16 W	21 44 33	27 27 34	24 26 29	1♌39 46	1 17.1	20 32.4	14 03.6	24 49.8	17 16.2	4 58.0	16 49.8	28 43.4	28 20.9	6 49.2
17 Th	21 48 29	28 28 07	8♌59 26	16 24 46	1 11.2	22 16.1	15 13.3	25 37.2	17 39.7	5 11.0	16 47.5	28 46.5	28 23.1	6 50.8
18 F	21 52 26	29 28 38	23 54 48	1♍28 26	1 03.2	24 00.7	16 23.0	26 24.5	18 03.1	5 24.1	16 45.2	28 49.6	28 25.4	6 52.2
19 Sa	21 56 22	0♓29 08	9♍04 22	16 41 15	0 54.0	25 46.2	17 32.9	27 11.9	18 26.6	5 37.3	16 42.8	28 52.7	28 27.7	6 53.7
20 Su	22 00 19	1 29 37	24 17 41	1♎52 21	0 44.6	27 32.6	18 42.9	27 59.3	18 50.0	5 50.5	16 40.3	28 55.8	28 30.0	6 55.1
21 M	22 04 15	2 30 04	9♎23 58	16 51 27	0 36.4	29 19.9	19 52.9	28 46.7	19 13.4	6 03.8	16 37.7	28 58.9	28 32.2	6 56.5
22 Tu	22 08 12	3 30 30	24 13 55	1♏30 38	0 30.1	1♓08.2	21 03.1	29 34.1	19 36.8	6 17.1	16 35.0	29 02.1	28 34.5	6 57.9
23 W	22 12 08	4 30 54	8♏41 08	15 45 09	0 26.3	2 57.4	22 13.4	0♓21.5	20 00.1	6 30.5	16 32.2	29 05.3	28 36.8	6 59.3
24 Th	22 16 05	5 31 17	22 42 36	29 33 34	0D24.7	4 47.5	23 23.7	1 08.9	20 23.5	6 44.0	16 29.3	29 08.5	28 39.1	7 00.6
25 F	22 20 02	6 31 39	6♐18 16	12♐57 02	0 24.7	6 38.4	24 34.2	1 56.3	20 46.8	6 57.5	16 26.4	29 11.7	28 41.3	7 01.9
26 Sa	22 23 58	7 32 00	19 30 15	25 58 22	0R25.2	8 30.3	25 44.7	2 43.7	21 10.1	7 11.1	16 23.3	29 14.9	28 43.6	7 03.2
27 Su	22 27 55	8 32 19	2♑21 51	8♑41 12	0 24.9	10 22.9	26 55.3	3 31.1	21 33.3	7 24.7	16 20.2	29 18.2	28 45.9	7 04.5
28 M	22 31 51	9 32 36	14 56 51	21 09 17	0 22.9	12 16.3	28 06.0	4 18.4	21 56.5	7 38.4	16 17.0	29 21.4	28 48.1	7 05.7

Astro Data

Aspect	Dy Hr Mn
♃⊻♆	2 16:52
♃☌♅	4 12:54
☽0N	9 15:25
☽0S	23 4:46
♄ R	26 6:11
♃0N	5 13:49
☽0N	5 23:19
☽0S	19 14:49
♃□♇	25 20:41

Planet Ingress

Planet	Sign	Dy Hr Mn
⚳	♒	3 14:43
♀	♐	7 12:32
☿	♑	13 11:26
♂	♒	15 22:42
☉	♒	20 10:20
♃	♈	22 17:12
☿	♒	3 22:20
♀	♑	4 5:59
☉	♓	19 0:26
☿	♓	21 20:54
♂	♓	23 1:07

Last Aspect / ☽ Ingress (January)

Last Aspect Dy Hr Mn			☽ Ingress	Dy Hr Mn
31 19:58	♅	△	♐	1 1:22
3 2:09	♅	□	♑	3 7:40
5 12:16	♀	⚹	♒	5 16:09
7 20:52	♆	☌	♓	8 2:58
10 11:13	♃	☌	♈	10 15:25
13 2:48	☿	△	♉	13 3:38
15 12:48	♂	△	♊	15 13:24
17 17:58	♃	□	♋	17 19:30
19 21:27	♃	△	♌	19 22:17
21 18:59	♆	☍	♍	21 23:11
23 20:09	♅	☍	♎	23 24:00
25 22:05	♆	△	♏	26 2:17
28 3:02	♅	△	♐	28 6:56
30 10:12	♅	□	♑	30 14:05

Last Aspect / ☽ Ingress (February)

Last Aspect Dy Hr Mn			☽ Ingress	Dy Hr Mn
1 19:33	♅	⚹	♒	1 23:22
4 6:12	♆	☌	♓	4 10:25
6 19:14	♅	☌	♈	6 22:47
9 7:32	♆	⚹	♉	9 11:24
11 19:28	♅	⚹	♊	11 22:22
14 3:20	♅	□	♋	14 5:50
16 7:07	♅	△	♌	16 9:15
18 8:37	☉	☍	♍	18 9:40
20 7:19	♅	☍	♎	20 9:02
22 8:36	♂	△	♏	22 9:30
24 11:16	♅	△	♐	24 12:47
26 18:10	♅	□	♑	26 19:33

☽ Phases & Eclipses

Dy Hr Mn	Phase	Position
4 9:04	●	13♑39
4 8:51:43	●	P 0.858
12 11:33	☽	21♈54
19 21:22	○	29♋27
26 12:58	☾	6♏13
3 2:32	●	13♒54
11 7:19	☽	22♉13
18 8:37	○	29♌20
24 23:27	☾	6♐00

Astro Data

1 January 2011
Julian Day # 40543
SVP 5♓06'04"
GC 26♐59.6 ⚴ 4♑42.3
Eris 21♈09.5R ⚵ 28♍32.0
⚷ 27♒38.7 ⚶ 15♐37.4
☽ Mean ☊ 2♑16.8

1 February 2011
Julian Day # 40574
SVP 5♓05'59"
GC 26♐59.6 ⚴ 16♑54.9
Eris 21♈12.2 ⚵ 29♍07.1R
⚷ 29♒30.5 ⚶ 1♑48.5
☽ Mean ☊ 0♑38.3

March 2011 LONGITUDE

Day	Sid.Time	☉	0 hr ☽	Noon ☽	True ☊	☿	♀	♂	⚳	♃	♄	♅	♆	♇
1 Tu	22 35 48	10♓32 52	27♑18 53	3♒26 02	0♑18.3	14♓10.4	29♑16.7	5♓05.8	22♒19.7	7♈52.1	16♎13.8	29♓24.7	28♒50.4	7♑06.9
2 W	22 39 44	11 33 06	9♒31 05	15 34 19	0R 10.8	16 05.1	0♒27.6	5 53.2	22 42.9	8 05.8	16R 10.4	29 28.0	28 52.6	7 08.1
3 Th	22 43 41	12 33 19	21 36 00	27 36 21	0 00.3	18 00.4	1 38.4	6 40.6	23 06.0	8 19.6	16 07.0	29 31.3	28 54.8	7 09.2
4 F	22 47 37	13 33 30	3♓35 34	9♓33 50	29♐47.6	19 55.9	2 49.4	7 27.9	23 29.1	8 33.5	16 03.5	29 34.6	28 57.1	7 10.4
5 Sa	22 51 34	14 33 39	15 31 16	21 28 04	29 33.5	21 51.7	4 00.4	8 15.3	23 52.2	8 47.4	15 59.9	29 38.0	28 59.3	7 11.4
6 Su	22 55 31	15 33 46	27 24 20	3♈20 17	29 19.2	23 47.5	5 11.5	9 02.6	24 15.2	9 01.3	15 56.3	29 41.3	29 01.5	7 12.5
7 M	22 59 27	16 33 51	9♈16 04	15 11 54	29 05.9	25 43.1	6 22.6	9 49.9	24 38.2	9 15.3	15 52.5	29 44.7	29 03.7	7 13.5
8 Tu	23 03 24	17 33 55	21 08 03	27 04 46	28 54.6	27 38.2	7 33.8	10 37.2	25 01.2	9 29.3	15 48.8	29 48.0	29 05.9	7 14.5
9 W	23 07 20	18 33 56	3♉02 24	9♉01 20	28 45.9	29 32.5	8 45.1	11 24.5	25 24.1	9 43.3	15 44.9	29 51.4	29 08.1	7 15.5
10 Th	23 11 17	19 33 55	15 01 59	21 04 48	28 40.3	1♈25.7	9 56.4	12 11.8	25 47.0	9 57.4	15 41.0	29 54.8	29 10.2	7 16.5
11 F	23 15 13	20 33 52	27 10 19	3♊19 04	28 37.3	3 17.5	11 07.7	12 59.1	26 09.8	10 11.5	15 37.1	29 58.2	29 12.4	7 17.4
12 Sa	23 19 10	21 33 47	9♊31 38	15 48 36	28 36.3	5 07.3	12 19.1	13 46.3	26 32.6	10 25.7	15 33.1	0♈01.6	29 14.6	7 18.3
13 Su	23 23 06	22 33 40	22 10 36	28 38 11	28 36.3	6 54.8	13 30.6	14 33.6	26 55.3	10 39.8	15 29.0	0 05.0	29 16.7	7 19.1
14 M	23 27 03	23 33 31	5♋11 56	11♋52 20	28 35.9	8 39.6	14 42.0	15 20.8	27 18.0	10 54.0	15 24.9	0 08.4	29 18.8	7 19.9
15 Tu	23 31 00	24 33 19	18 39 47	25 34 35	28 34.0	10 21.0	15 53.6	16 08.0	27 40.7	11 08.3	15 20.7	0 11.8	29 20.9	7 20.7
16 W	23 34 56	25 33 05	2♌36 53	9♌46 36	28 29.8	11 58.7	17 05.2	16 55.2	28 03.3	11 22.5	15 16.5	0 15.2	29 23.0	7 21.5
17 Th	23 38 53	26 32 49	17 03 30	24 27 04	28 22.8	13 32.1	18 16.8	17 42.3	28 25.9	11 36.8	15 12.2	0 18.7	29 25.1	7 22.2
18 F	23 42 49	27 32 30	1♍56 33	9♍30 59	28 13.3	15 00.7	19 28.4	18 29.5	28 48.4	11 51.1	15 07.9	0 22.1	29 27.2	7 22.9
19 Sa	23 46 46	28 32 09	17 09 09	24 49 41	28 02.2	16 24.1	20 40.2	19 16.6	29 10.8	12 05.4	15 03.6	0 25.5	29 29.3	7 23.6
20 Su	23 50 42	29 31 47	2♎31 06	10♎11 52	27 50.9	17 41.9	21 51.9	20 03.7	29 33.3	12 19.8	14 59.2	0 28.9	29 31.3	7 24.2
21 M	23 54 39	0♈31 22	17 50 29	25 25 35	27 40.6	18 53.6	23 03.7	20 50.7	29 55.6	12 34.1	14 54.8	0 32.4	29 33.3	7 24.8
22 Tu	23 58 35	1 30 56	2♏55 56	10♏20 32	27 32.4	19 58.9	24 15.5	21 37.8	0♓17.9	12 48.5	14 50.3	0 35.8	29 35.3	7 25.4
23 W	0 02 32	2 30 28	17 38 37	24 49 38	27 27.0	20 57.4	25 27.4	22 24.8	0 40.2	13 02.9	14 45.9	0 39.2	29 37.3	7 26.0
24 Th	0 06 29	3 29 58	1♐53 18	8♐49 33	27 24.2	21 48.8	26 39.3	23 11.8	1 02.4	13 17.3	14 41.3	0 42.6	29 39.3	7 26.5
25 F	0 10 25	4 29 26	15 38 30	22 20 24	27D 23.3	22 33.0	27 51.3	23 58.8	1 24.6	13 31.8	14 36.8	0 46.1	29 41.3	7 27.0
26 Sa	0 14 22	5 28 53	28 55 39	5♑24 42	27R 23.3	23 09.8	29 03.3	24 45.8	1 46.7	13 46.2	14 32.2	0 49.5	29 43.2	7 27.4
27 Su	0 18 18	6 28 18	11♑48 08	18 06 29	27 22.9	23 39.0	0♓15.3	25 32.8	2 08.7	14 00.7	14 27.7	0 52.9	29 45.2	7 27.9
28 M	0 22 15	7 27 41	24 20 21	0♒30 19	27 21.0	24 00.5	1 27.4	26 19.7	2 30.7	14 15.2	14 23.1	0 56.3	29 47.1	7 28.3
29 Tu	0 26 11	8 27 03	6♒36 56	12 40 45	27 16.7	24 14.5	2 39.5	27 06.6	2 52.7	14 29.6	14 18.4	0 59.7	29 49.0	7 28.6
30 W	0 30 08	9 26 22	18 42 16	24 41 57	27 09.5	24R 20.9	3 51.6	27 53.5	3 14.5	14 44.1	14 13.8	1 03.1	29 50.8	7 28.9
31 Th	0 34 04	10 25 40	0♓40 11	6♓37 22	26 59.5	24 19.9	5 03.8	28 40.3	3 36.3	14 58.6	14 09.1	1 06.5	29 52.7	7 29.2

April 2011 LONGITUDE

Day	Sid.Time	☉	0 hr ☽	Noon ☽	True ☊	☿	♀	♂	⚳	♃	♄	♅	♆	♇
1 F	0 38 01	11♈24 55	12♓33 48	18♓29 47	26♐47.3	24♈11.9	6♓15.9	29♓27.1	3♓58.1	15♈13.1	14♎04.5	1♈09.9	29♒54.5	7♑29.5
2 Sa	0 41 57	12 24 09	24 25 34	0♈21 20	26R 33.7	23R 57.0	7 28.2	0♈13.9	4 19.8	15 27.6	13R 59.8	1 13.3	29 56.3	7 29.7
3 Su	0 45 54	13 23 21	6♈17 19	12 13 39	26 19.8	23 35.8	8 40.4	1 00.7	4 41.4	15 42.2	13 55.1	1 16.7	29 58.1	7 29.9
4 M	0 49 51	14 22 30	18 10 31	24 08 05	26 06.8	23 08.8	9 52.6	1 47.4	5 02.9	15 56.7	13 50.5	1 20.1	29 59.9	7 30.1
5 Tu	0 53 47	15 21 38	0♉06 30	6♉05 59	25 55.8	22 36.6	11 04.9	2 34.1	5 24.4	16 11.2	13 45.8	1 23.4	0♓01.6	7 30.2
6 W	0 57 44	16 20 43	12 06 43	18 08 57	25 47.3	21 59.9	12 17.2	3 20.7	5 45.8	16 25.7	13 41.1	1 26.8	0 03.3	7 30.3
7 Th	1 01 40	17 19 47	24 12 58	0♊19 04	25 41.7	21 19.5	13 29.5	4 07.4	6 07.1	16 40.2	13 36.5	1 30.1	0 05.0	7 30.4
8 F	1 05 37	18 18 48	6♊27 37	12 39 00	25 38.8	20 36.3	14 41.9	4 54.0	6 28.4	16 54.7	13 31.8	1 33.4	0 06.7	7R 30.4
9 Sa	1 09 33	19 17 47	18 53 39	25 12 01	25D 38.1	19 51.1	15 54.2	5 40.5	6 49.6	17 09.3	13 27.2	1 36.7	0 08.4	7 30.5
10 Su	1 13 30	20 16 44	1♋34 35	8♋01 50	25 38.4	19 04.9	17 06.6	6 27.0	7 10.7	17 23.8	13 22.6	1 40.0	0 10.0	7 30.4
11 M	1 17 26	21 15 38	14 34 15	21 12 17	25R 38.8	18 18.5	18 19.0	7 13.5	7 31.7	17 38.3	13 18.0	1 43.3	0 11.6	7 30.4
12 Tu	1 21 23	22 14 30	27 56 20	4♌46 43	25 38.1	17 32.9	19 31.4	8 00.0	7 52.6	17 52.8	13 13.4	1 46.6	0 13.2	7 30.3
13 W	1 25 20	23 13 20	11♌43 40	18 47 15	25 35.5	16 48.7	20 43.8	8 46.4	8 13.5	18 07.2	13 08.8	1 49.9	0 14.7	7 30.2
14 Th	1 29 16	24 12 08	25 57 24	3♍13 51	25 30.6	16 06.9	21 56.3	9 32.7	8 34.3	18 21.7	13 04.3	1 53.1	0 16.3	7 30.0
15 F	1 33 13	25 10 53	10♍36 06	18 03 29	25 23.6	15 28.0	23 08.7	10 19.1	8 55.0	18 36.2	12 59.8	1 56.3	0 17.8	7 29.9
16 Sa	1 37 09	26 09 36	25 35 06	3♎09 49	25 15.1	14 52.7	24 21.2	11 05.4	9 15.6	18 50.6	12 55.3	1 59.5	0 19.3	7 29.7
17 Su	1 41 06	27 08 16	10♎46 27	18 23 37	25 06.2	14 21.3	25 33.7	11 51.6	9 36.2	19 05.0	12 50.8	2 02.7	0 20.7	7 29.4
18 M	1 45 02	28 06 55	25 59 57	3♏34 06	24 58.1	13 54.4	26 46.2	12 37.8	9 56.6	19 19.5	12 46.4	2 05.9	0 22.1	7 29.2
19 Tu	1 48 59	29 05 32	11♏04 48	18 30 54	24 51.6	13 32.2	27 58.7	13 24.0	10 17.0	19 33.9	12 42.0	2 09.0	0 23.6	7 28.9
20 W	1 52 55	0♉04 08	25 51 29	3♐05 47	24 47.4	13 14.9	29 11.3	14 10.2	10 37.3	19 48.2	12 37.6	2 12.2	0 24.9	7 28.5
21 Th	1 56 52	1 02 41	10♐13 18	17 13 42	24D 45.5	13 02.6	0♈23.8	14 56.3	10 57.5	20 02.6	12 33.3	2 15.3	0 26.3	7 28.2
22 F	2 00 49	2 01 13	24 06 54	0♑52 56	24 45.4	12D 55.3	1 36.4	15 42.3	11 17.6	20 17.0	12 29.1	2 18.4	0 27.6	7 27.8
23 Sa	2 04 45	2 59 43	7♑32 02	14 04 33	24 46.3	12 53.2	2 49.0	16 28.3	11 37.6	20 31.3	12 24.8	2 21.4	0 28.9	7 27.4
24 Su	2 08 42	3 58 12	20 30 55	26 51 38	24R 47.3	12 56.1	4 01.6	17 14.3	11 57.5	20 45.6	12 20.7	2 24.5	0 30.2	7 26.9
25 M	2 12 38	4 56 39	3♒07 16	9♒18 25	24 47.4	13 04.0	5 14.2	18 00.3	12 17.3	20 59.9	12 16.5	2 27.5	0 31.4	7 26.5
26 Tu	2 16 35	5 55 04	15 25 40	21 29 37	24 46.0	13 16.7	6 26.9	18 46.2	12 37.0	21 14.2	12 12.5	2 30.5	0 32.6	7 26.0
27 W	2 20 31	6 53 28	27 30 51	3♓29 56	24 42.6	13 34.1	7 39.5	19 32.0	12 56.7	21 28.4	12 08.4	2 33.5	0 33.8	7 25.4
28 Th	2 24 28	7 51 50	9♓27 25	15 23 45	24 37.2	13 56.1	8 52.2	20 17.8	13 16.2	21 42.6	12 04.4	2 36.5	0 35.0	7 24.9
29 F	2 28 24	8 50 10	21 19 27	27 14 53	24 30.1	14 22.5	10 04.9	21 03.6	13 35.6	21 56.8	12 00.5	2 39.4	0 36.1	7 24.3
30 Sa	2 32 21	9 48 29	3♈10 27	9♈06 29	24 21.9	14 53.1	11 17.6	21 49.3	13 54.9	22 11.0	11 56.7	2 42.3	0 37.2	7 23.6

Astro Data

	Dy Hr Mn
☽0N	5 6:09
☿0N	10 2:35
☽0S	19 2:09
☉0N	20 23:22
♄□♆	24 19:31
♃☍♄	28 21:56
☿ R	30 20:50
♃∠♆	31 0:42
☽0N	1 11:56
♂0N	4 21:49
♇ R	9 8:52
♅0N	9 19:31
☽0S	15 12:21
☿ D	23 10:05
♀0N	24 4:25

Planet Ingress

		Dy Hr Mn
♀	♒	2 2:40
☊	♐R	3 12:38
☿	♈	9 17:48
♅	♈	12 0:50
☉	♈	20 23:22
⚳	♓	21 16:42
♀	♓	27 6:54
♂	♈	2 4:52
♆	♓	4 13:52
☉	♉	20 10:19
♀	♈	21 4:07

☽0N28 17:33

Last Aspect / ☽ Ingress

Last Aspect Dy Hr Mn			☽ Ingress	Dy Hr Mn
1 4:04	♅	⚹	♒	1 5:15
3 14:38	♆	☌	♓	3 16:48
6 4:35	♅	☌	♈	6 5:15
8 16:05	♆	⚹	♉	8 17:53
11 5:27	♅	⚹	♊	11 5:32
13 13:11	♆	△	♋	13 14:31
15 10:06	☉	△	♌	15 19:34
17 19:59	♆	☍	♍	17 20:54
19 18:11	☉	☍	♎	19 20:04
21 18:36	♆	△	♏	21 19:18
23 20:09	♆	□	♐	23 20:46
26 1:26	♆	⚹	♑	26 1:58
28 3:18	♂	⚹	♒	28 11:01
30 22:22	♆	☌	♓	30 22:39

Last Aspect / ☽ Ingress

Last Aspect Dy Hr Mn			☽ Ingress	Dy Hr Mn
31 13:45	♇	⚹	♈	2 11:17
4 10:05	☿	☌	♉	4 23:47
5 23:03	♀	⚹	♊	7 11:23
9 2:25	☿	⚹	♋	9 21:03
11 12:06	☉	□	♌	12 3:38
13 19:59	☉	△	♍	14 6:41
15 20:50	♀	☍	♎	16 7:00
18 2:45	☉	☍	♏	18 6:20
20 4:54	♀	△	♐	20 6:51
21 16:58	♃	△	♑	22 10:25
24 0:14	♃	□	♒	24 18:00
26 11:29	♃	⚹	♓	27 4:59
27 19:54	♇	⚹	♈	29 17:34

☽ Phases & Eclipses

Dy Hr Mn		
4 20:47	●	13♓56
12 23:46	☽	22♊03
19 18:11	○	28♍48
26 12:08	☾	5♑29
3 14:33	●	13♈30
11 12:06	☽	21♋16
18 2:45	○	27♎44
25 2:48	☾	4♒34

Astro Data

1 March 2011
Julian Day # 40602
SVP 5♓05'55"
GC 26♐59.7 ⚴ 27♑03.3
Eris 21♈23.1 ⚵ 24♍10.6R
⚷ 1♓24.5 ⚶ 15♑40.3
☽ Mean ☊ 29♐09.3

1 April 2011
Julian Day # 40633
SVP 5♓05'53"
GC 26♐59.8 ⚴ 6♒36.7
Eris 21♈41.3 ⚵ 16♍56.2R
⚷ 3♓22.1 ⚶ 29♑35.0
☽ Mean ☊ 27♐30.8

LONGITUDE — May 2011

Day	Sid.Time	☉	0 hr ☽	Noon ☽	True ☊	☿	♀	♂	⚳	♃	♄	♅	♆	♇
1 Su	2 36 18	10♉46 46	15♈03 17	21♈01 07	24♐13.5	15♈27.8	12♈30.3	22♈35.0	14♓14.1	22♈25.1	11♎52.9	2♈45.2	0♓38.2	7♑23.0
2 M	2 40 14	11 45 02	27 00 11	3♉00 42	24R 05.6	16 06.4	13 43.0	23 20.7	14 33.2	22 39.2	11R 49.1	2 48.0	0 39.3	7R 22.3
3 Tu	2 44 11	12 43 16	9♉02 52	15 06 49	23 58.9	16 48.8	14 55.7	24 06.3	14 52.2	22 53.3	11 45.4	2 50.8	0 40.3	7 21.6
4 W	2 48 07	13 41 28	21 12 44	27 20 46	23 54.0	17 34.7	16 08.5	24 51.8	15 11.1	23 07.3	11 41.8	2 53.6	0 41.2	7 20.9
5 Th	2 52 04	14 39 38	3♊31 04	9♊43 50	23 51.1	18 24.1	17 21.2	25 37.3	15 29.8	23 21.3	11 38.3	2 56.4	0 42.2	7 20.2
6 F	2 56 00	15 37 47	15 59 13	22 17 27	23D 50.1	19 16.8	18 33.9	26 22.8	15 48.5	23 35.3	11 34.8	2 59.2	0 43.1	7 19.4
7 Sa	2 59 57	16 35 53	28 38 45	5♋03 22	23 50.6	20 12.8	19 46.7	27 08.2	16 07.0	23 49.2	11 31.4	3 01.9	0 44.0	7 18.6
8 Su	3 03 53	17 33 58	11♋31 33	18 03 35	23 52.0	21 11.7	20 59.5	27 53.5	16 25.4	24 03.1	11 28.1	3 04.5	0 44.8	7 17.7
9 M	3 07 50	18 32 01	24 39 43	1♌20 12	23 53.5	22 13.7	22 12.2	28 38.8	16 43.7	24 16.9	11 24.9	3 07.2	0 45.6	7 16.9
10 Tu	3 11 47	19 30 02	8♌05 17	14 55 09	23R 54.4	23 18.5	23 25.0	29 24.1	17 01.8	24 30.7	11 21.7	3 09.8	0 46.4	7 16.0
11 W	3 15 43	20 28 01	21 49 54	28 49 37	23 54.2	24 26.0	24 37.8	0♉09.3	17 19.8	24 44.5	11 18.6	3 12.4	0 47.2	7 15.1
12 Th	3 19 40	21 25 58	5♍54 12	13♍03 30	23 52.6	25 36.3	25 50.6	0 54.4	17 37.7	24 58.2	11 15.6	3 15.0	0 47.9	7 14.2
13 F	3 23 36	22 23 54	20 17 12	27 34 51	23 49.7	26 49.1	27 03.4	1 39.5	17 55.5	25 11.9	11 12.6	3 17.5	0 48.6	7 13.2
14 Sa	3 27 33	23 21 47	4♎55 51	12♎19 28	23 45.8	28 04.5	28 16.2	2 24.5	18 13.1	25 25.5	11 09.8	3 20.0	0 49.3	7 12.2
15 Su	3 31 29	24 19 39	19 44 51	27 11 03	23 41.7	29 22.4	29 29.0	3 09.5	18 30.6	25 39.1	11 07.0	3 22.4	0 49.9	7 11.2
16 M	3 35 26	25 17 29	4♏37 04	12♏01 52	23 37.8	0♉42.7	0♉41.8	3 54.5	18 48.0	25 52.6	11 04.3	3 24.8	0 50.5	7 10.2
17 Tu	3 39 22	26 15 18	19 24 26	26 43 49	23 34.8	2 05.5	1 54.6	4 39.4	19 05.2	26 06.1	11 01.7	3 27.2	0 51.0	7 09.2
18 W	3 43 19	27 13 05	3♐59 10	11♐09 43	23D 33.1	3 30.5	3 07.5	5 24.2	19 22.3	26 19.5	10 59.2	3 29.6	0 51.6	7 08.1
19 Th	3 47 16	28 10 51	18 14 54	25 14 14	23 32.6	4 58.0	4 20.3	6 09.0	19 39.2	26 32.9	10 56.8	3 31.9	0 52.1	7 07.0
20 F	3 51 12	29 08 36	2♑07 27	8♑54 24	23 33.3	6 27.7	5 33.2	6 53.7	19 56.0	26 46.2	10 54.4	3 34.2	0 52.5	7 05.9
21 Sa	3 55 09	0♊06 19	15 35 06	22 09 39	23 34.6	7 59.7	6 46.1	7 38.4	20 12.7	26 59.5	10 52.2	3 36.4	0 53.0	7 04.8
22 Su	3 59 05	1 04 02	28 38 20	5♒01 27	23 36.1	9 34.0	7 59.0	8 23.1	20 29.2	27 12.7	10 50.0	3 38.6	0 53.4	7 03.7
23 M	4 03 02	2 01 43	11♒19 26	17 32 45	23 37.4	11 10.6	9 11.8	9 07.7	20 45.6	27 25.9	10 47.9	3 40.8	0 53.8	7 02.5
24 Tu	4 06 58	2 59 23	23 41 55	29 47 30	23R 38.1	12 49.5	10 24.8	9 52.2	21 01.8	27 39.0	10 46.0	3 42.9	0 54.1	7 01.3
25 W	4 10 55	3 57 02	5♓50 03	11♓50 09	23 37.9	14 30.6	11 37.7	10 36.7	21 17.8	27 52.1	10 44.1	3 45.0	0 54.4	7 00.1
26 Th	4 14 51	4 54 40	17 48 23	23 45 19	23 36.9	16 13.9	12 50.6	11 21.1	21 33.7	28 05.0	10 42.3	3 47.1	0 54.7	6 58.9
27 F	4 18 48	5 52 18	29 41 30	5♈37 27	23 35.1	17 59.6	14 03.5	12 05.5	21 49.4	28 18.0	10 40.6	3 49.1	0 54.9	6 57.7
28 Sa	4 22 45	6 49 54	11♈33 40	17 30 38	23 32.8	19 47.4	15 16.5	12 49.8	22 05.0	28 30.8	10 39.0	3 51.0	0 55.1	6 56.4
29 Su	4 26 41	7 47 29	23 28 46	29 28 29	23 30.3	21 37.5	16 29.5	13 34.1	22 20.4	28 43.6	10 37.4	3 53.0	0 55.3	6 55.1
30 M	4 30 38	8 45 03	5♉30 06	11♉33 58	23 28.1	23 29.8	17 42.4	14 18.3	22 35.6	28 56.4	10 36.0	3 54.9	0 55.4	6 53.8
31 Tu	4 34 34	9 42 37	17 40 19	23 49 25	23 26.2	25 24.3	18 55.4	15 02.4	22 50.6	29 09.0	10 34.7	3 56.7	0 55.5	6 52.5

LONGITUDE — June 2011

Day	Sid.Time	☉	0 hr ☽	Noon ☽	True ☊	☿	♀	♂	⚳	♃	♄	♅	♆	♇
1 W	4 38 31	10♊40 09	0♊01 25	6♊16 31	23♐25.0	27♉20.9	20♉08.4	15♉46.5	23♓05.5	29♈21.6	10♎33.5	3♈58.5	0♓55.6	6♑51.2
2 Th	4 42 27	11 37 41	12 34 48	18 56 21	23D 24.5	29 19.7	21 21.4	16 30.6	23 20.2	29 34.2	10R 32.4	4 00.3	0R 55.6	6R 49.9
3 F	4 46 24	12 35 11	25 21 16	1♋49 33	23 24.6	1♊20.4	22 34.4	17 14.6	23 34.7	29 46.6	10 31.4	4 02.0	0 55.6	6 48.5
4 Sa	4 50 20	13 32 40	8♋21 14	14 56 19	23 25.1	3 23.1	23 47.5	17 58.5	23 49.0	29 59.0	10 30.4	4 03.7	0 55.6	6 47.2
5 Su	4 54 17	14 30 08	21 34 48	28 16 38	23 25.9	5 27.6	25 00.5	18 42.4	24 03.1	0♉11.3	10 29.6	4 05.4	0 55.6	6 45.8
6 M	4 58 14	15 27 35	5♌01 49	11♌50 16	23 26.7	7 33.8	26 13.5	19 26.2	24 17.1	0 23.5	10 28.9	4 07.0	0 55.5	6 44.4
7 Tu	5 02 10	16 25 01	18 41 56	25 36 44	23 27.3	9 41.5	27 26.6	20 10.0	24 30.8	0 35.7	10 28.3	4 08.5	0 55.4	6 43.0
8 W	5 06 07	17 22 25	2♍34 34	9♍35 16	23R 27.6	11 50.5	28 39.6	20 53.7	24 44.4	0 47.8	10 27.7	4 10.0	0 55.2	6 41.6
9 Th	5 10 03	18 19 49	16 38 40	23 44 32	23 27.6	14 00.7	29 52.7	21 37.3	24 57.7	0 59.7	10 27.3	4 11.5	0 55.0	6 40.2
10 F	5 14 00	19 17 11	0♎52 36	8♎02 32	23 27.4	16 11.7	1♊05.7	22 20.9	25 10.9	1 11.6	10 27.0	4 12.9	0 54.8	6 38.7
11 Sa	5 17 56	20 14 32	15 13 57	22 26 23	23 27.1	18 23.3	2 18.8	23 04.4	25 23.8	1 23.5	10 26.8	4 14.3	0 54.5	6 37.3
12 Su	5 21 53	21 11 52	29 39 21	6♏52 19	23 26.8	20 35.3	3 31.9	23 47.8	25 36.6	1 35.2	10D 26.7	4 15.6	0 54.3	6 35.8
13 M	5 25 49	22 09 11	14♏04 41	21 15 52	23 26.7	22 47.3	4 45.0	24 31.2	25 49.1	1 46.9	10 26.7	4 16.9	0 54.0	6 34.4
14 Tu	5 29 46	23 06 30	28 25 15	5♐32 14	23D 26.6	24 59.1	5 58.1	25 14.6	26 01.4	1 58.4	10 26.7	4 18.1	0 53.6	6 32.9
15 W	5 33 43	24 03 48	12♐36 16	19 36 48	23R 26.6	27 10.5	7 11.2	25 57.9	26 13.5	2 09.9	10 26.9	4 19.3	0 53.2	6 31.4
16 Th	5 37 39	25 01 05	26 33 23	3♑25 38	23 26.6	29 21.2	8 24.4	26 41.1	26 25.4	2 21.3	10 27.2	4 20.5	0 52.8	6 29.9
17 F	5 41 36	25 58 21	10♑13 13	16 55 56	23 26.5	1♋30.9	9 37.5	27 24.3	26 37.0	2 32.6	10 27.6	4 21.6	0 52.4	6 28.4
18 Sa	5 45 32	26 55 37	23 33 39	0♒06 20	23 26.2	3 39.4	10 50.7	28 07.4	26 48.5	2 43.8	10 28.1	4 22.7	0 51.9	6 27.0
19 Su	5 49 29	27 52 52	6♒34 02	12 56 54	23 25.7	5 46.5	12 03.9	28 50.4	26 59.7	2 54.9	10 28.7	4 23.7	0 51.4	6 25.4
20 M	5 53 25	28 50 08	19 15 11	25 29 10	23 25.1	7 52.1	13 17.1	29 33.4	27 10.6	3 06.0	10 29.3	4 24.6	0 50.9	6 23.9
21 Tu	5 57 22	29 47 22	1♓39 12	7♓45 44	23 24.5	9 56.0	14 30.3	0♊16.4	27 21.4	3 16.9	10 30.1	4 25.6	0 50.3	6 22.4
22 W	6 01 19	0♋44 37	13 49 14	19 50 12	23D 24.1	11 58.1	15 43.5	0 59.2	27 31.9	3 27.7	10 31.0	4 26.4	0 49.8	6 20.9
23 Th	6 05 15	1 41 52	25 49 10	1♈46 43	23 23.9	13 58.3	16 56.7	1 42.1	27 42.1	3 38.4	10 32.0	4 27.2	0 49.1	6 19.4
24 F	6 09 12	2 39 06	7♈43 23	13 39 47	23 24.1	15 56.5	18 10.0	2 24.8	27 52.1	3 49.1	10 33.1	4 28.0	0 48.5	6 17.9
25 Sa	6 13 08	3 36 20	19 36 29	25 34 03	23 24.7	17 52.7	19 23.3	3 07.5	28 01.8	3 59.6	10 34.3	4 28.7	0 47.8	6 16.3
26 Su	6 17 05	4 33 34	1♉33 01	7♉33 56	23 25.6	19 46.8	20 36.6	3 50.2	28 11.3	4 10.0	10 35.5	4 29.4	0 47.1	6 14.8
27 M	6 21 01	5 30 48	13 37 18	19 43 33	23 26.7	21 38.8	21 49.9	4 32.8	28 20.6	4 20.3	10 36.9	4 30.1	0 46.4	6 13.3
28 Tu	6 24 58	6 28 03	25 53 08	2♊06 23	23 27.8	23 28.7	23 03.2	5 15.3	28 29.5	4 30.5	10 38.4	4 30.6	0 45.6	6 11.7
29 W	6 28 54	7 25 17	8♊23 37	14 45 05	23R 28.5	25 16.4	24 16.6	5 57.8	28 38.2	4 40.6	10 40.0	4 31.2	0 44.8	6 10.2
30 Th	6 32 51	8 22 31	21 10 56	27 41 16	23 28.6	27 02.0	25 29.9	6 40.2	28 46.7	4 50.6	10 41.7	4 31.7	0 44.0	6 08.7

Astro Data Dy Hr Mn	Planet Ingress Dy Hr Mn	Last Aspect Dy Hr Mn	☽ Ingress Dy Hr Mn	Last Aspect Dy Hr Mn	☽ Ingress Dy Hr Mn	☽ Phases & Eclipses Dy Hr Mn	Astro Data
☽0S 12 20:07	♂ ♉ 11 7:05	1 15:21 ♂ ☌	♉ 2 5:59	3 8:09 ♃ ✶	♋ 3 8:37	3 6:52 ● 12♉31	1 May 2011
☽0N 26 0:02	♀ ♉ 15 22:13	3 6:52 ☉ ☌	♊ 4 17:10	5 5:34 ♀ ✶	♌ 5 15:04	10 20:34 ☽ 19♌51	Julian Day # 40663
	☿ ♉ 15 23:19	6 20:13 ♂ ✶	♋ 7 2:33	7 15:28 ♀ □	♍ 7 19:34	17 11:10 ○ 26♏13	SVP 5♓05'50"
♆R 3 7:29	☉ ♊ 21 9:22	9 6:54 ☉ □	♌ 9 9:36	9 8:14 ♂ △	♎ 9 22:32	24 18:53 ☾ 3♓16	GC 26♐59.9 ⚴ 13♒13.0
☽0S 9 1:53		11 4:53 ♃ △	♍ 11 14:00	11 8:05 ☉ △	♏ 12 0:34		Eris 22♈00.9 ⚵ 14♍00.1R
♃✶♆ 9 2:40	☿ ♊ 2 20:04	13 2:53 ☉ △	♎ 13 15:58	13 17:45 ♂ ☍	♐ 14 2:39	1 21:04 ● 11♊02	⚷ 4♓46.8 ⚶ 10♒41.2
♄D 13 3:52	♃ ♉ 4 13:57	15 16:02 ♀ ☍	♏ 15 16:33	16 3:32 ☿ ☍	♑ 16 6:00	1 21:17:14 • P 0.601	☽ Mean ☊ 25♐55.5
☽0N 22 7:51	♀ ♊ 9 14:24	17 11:10 ☉ ☍	♐ 17 17:24	18 8:08 ♂ △	♒ 18 11:48	9 2:12 ☽ 17♍56	
♃⚺♅ 28 12:21	☿ ♋ 16 19:10	19 14:19 ♃ △	♑ 19 20:17	20 20:24 ♂ △	♓ 20 20:46	15 20:15 ○ 24♐23	1 June 2011
	♂ ♊ 21 2:51	21 21:05 ♃ □	♒ 22 2:33	22 2:52 ♀ □	♈ 23 8:25	15 20:14 • T 1.700	Julian Day # 40694
	☉ ♋ 21 17:18	24 7:42 ♃ ✶	♓ 24 12:25	24 22:08 ♀ ✶	♉ 25 20:54	23 11:49 ☾ 1♈41	SVP 5♓05'45"
		25 18:16 ☿ ✶	♈ 27 0:37	27 16:25 ☿ ✶	♊ 28 7:57		GC 26♐59.9 ⚴ 15♒49.7R
		29 10:29 ♃ ☌	♉ 29 13:03	30 7:34 ♀ ☌	♋ 30 16:14		Eris 22♈18.0 ⚵ 16♍29.5
		31 15:38 ☿ ☌	♊ 31 23:57				⚷ 5♓27.5 ⚶ 18♒07.6
							☽ Mean ☊ 24♐17.0

July 2011 LONGITUDE

Day	Sid.Time	☉	0 hr ☽	Noon☽	True☊	☿	♀	♂	⚳	♃	♄	♅	♆	♇
1 F	6 36 48	9♋19 45	4♋16 06	10♋55 23	23♐28.0	28♋45.4	26♊43.3	7♊22.5	28♓54.8	5♉00.4	10♎43.4	4♈32.1	0♓43.2	6♑07.2
2 Sa	6 40 44	10 16 58	17 38 59	24 26 40	23R 26.5	0♌26.6	27 56.7	8 04.8	29 02.7	5 10.2	10 45.3	4 32.5	0R 42.3	6R 05.6
3 Su	6 44 41	11 14 12	1♌18 10	8♌13 10	23 24.5	2 05.6	29 10.1	8 47.0	29 10.3	5 19.8	10 47.3	4 32.8	0 41.4	6 04.1
4 M	6 48 37	12 11 25	15 11 15	22 12 02	23 22.1	3 42.5	0♋23.6	9 29.2	29 17.6	5 29.3	10 49.3	4 33.1	0 40.5	6 02.6
5 Tu	6 52 34	13 08 38	29 15 02	6♍19 51	23 19.6	5 17.2	1 37.0	10 11.3	29 24.6	5 38.7	10 51.5	4 33.4	0 39.5	6 01.1
6 W	6 56 30	14 05 51	13♍25 59	20 33 02	23 17.6	6 49.6	2 50.4	10 53.3	29 31.3	5 48.0	10 53.7	4 33.6	0 38.5	5 59.6
7 Th	7 00 27	15 03 03	27 40 34	4♎48 12	23D 16.4	8 19.9	4 03.9	11 35.2	29 37.7	5 57.1	10 56.1	4 33.7	0 37.5	5 58.1
8 F	7 04 23	16 00 15	11♎55 35	19 02 25	23 16.2	9 47.9	5 17.4	12 17.1	29 43.9	6 06.1	10 58.5	4 33.8	0 36.5	5 56.5
9 Sa	7 08 20	16 57 28	26 08 23	3♏13 13	23 16.8	11 13.6	6 30.9	12 59.0	29 49.7	6 15.0	11 01.1	4R 33.9	0 35.5	5 55.1
10 Su	7 12 17	17 54 39	10♏16 41	17 18 33	23 18.1	12 37.1	7 44.4	13 40.7	29 55.2	6 23.8	11 03.7	4 33.9	0 34.4	5 53.6
11 M	7 16 13	18 51 51	24 18 36	1♐16 37	23 19.5	13 58.2	8 57.9	14 22.4	0♈00.4	6 32.4	11 06.4	4 33.8	0 33.3	5 52.1
12 Tu	7 20 10	19 49 03	8♐12 23	15 05 42	23R 20.5	15 17.0	10 11.5	15 04.1	0 05.3	6 40.9	11 09.2	4 33.7	0 32.2	5 50.6
13 W	7 24 06	20 46 15	21 56 20	28 44 06	23 20.6	16 33.4	11 25.0	15 45.7	0 09.9	6 49.3	11 12.1	4 33.6	0 31.0	5 49.1
14 Th	7 28 03	21 43 27	5♑28 46	12♑10 08	23 19.4	17 47.3	12 38.6	16 27.2	0 14.2	6 57.5	11 15.1	4 33.4	0 29.8	5 47.7
15 F	7 31 59	22 40 39	18 48 04	25 22 23	23 16.8	18 58.6	13 52.2	17 08.7	0 18.1	7 05.6	11 18.2	4 33.2	0 28.7	5 46.2
16 Sa	7 35 56	23 37 52	1♒52 58	8♒19 46	23 12.9	20 07.4	15 05.8	17 50.0	0 21.8	7 13.6	11 21.3	4 32.9	0 27.4	5 44.8
17 Su	7 39 52	24 35 05	14 42 45	21 01 58	23 08.0	21 13.5	16 19.5	18 31.4	0 25.1	7 21.4	11 24.6	4 32.5	0 26.2	5 43.4
18 M	7 43 49	25 32 18	27 17 28	3♓29 27	23 02.7	22 16.9	17 33.1	19 12.6	0 28.1	7 29.1	11 27.9	4 32.2	0 25.0	5 41.9
19 Tu	7 47 46	26 29 32	9♓38 05	15 43 41	22 57.5	23 17.4	18 46.8	19 53.9	0 30.7	7 36.6	11 31.3	4 31.7	0 23.7	5 40.5
20 W	7 51 42	27 26 47	21 46 34	27 47 07	22 53.1	24 14.9	20 00.5	20 35.0	0 33.0	7 44.0	11 34.8	4 31.2	0 22.4	5 39.1
21 Th	7 55 39	28 24 02	3♈45 47	9♈43 02	22 49.8	25 09.4	21 14.2	21 16.1	0 35.0	7 51.2	11 38.4	4 30.7	0 21.1	5 37.8
22 F	7 59 35	29 21 18	15 39 25	21 35 28	22D 48.1	26 00.7	22 27.9	21 57.1	0 36.6	7 58.3	11 42.1	4 30.1	0 19.7	5 36.4
23 Sa	8 03 32	0♌18 35	27 31 47	3♉28 59	22 47.8	26 48.7	23 41.7	22 38.1	0 37.8	8 05.2	11 45.9	4 29.5	0 18.4	5 35.0
24 Su	8 07 28	1 15 53	9♉27 40	15 28 26	22 48.7	27 33.2	24 55.5	23 19.0	0 38.8	8 12.0	11 49.7	4 28.9	0 17.0	5 33.7
25 M	8 11 25	2 13 11	21 31 56	27 38 44	22 50.1	28 14.0	26 09.3	23 59.8	0 39.3	8 18.7	11 53.6	4 28.2	0 15.6	5 32.4
26 Tu	8 15 21	3 10 31	3♊49 24	10♊04 28	22 51.6	28 51.2	27 23.1	24 40.6	0R 39.6	8 25.2	11 57.6	4 27.4	0 14.2	5 31.0
27 W	8 19 18	4 07 51	16 24 24	22 49 34	22R 52.2	29 24.3	28 36.9	25 21.3	0 39.4	8 31.5	12 01.7	4 26.6	0 12.8	5 29.7
28 Th	8 23 15	5 05 13	29 20 19	5♋56 50	22 51.4	29 53.4	29 50.8	26 01.9	0 38.9	8 37.6	12 05.9	4 25.8	0 11.4	5 28.5
29 F	8 27 11	6 02 35	12♋39 12	19 27 24	22 48.8	0♍18.2	1♌04.7	26 42.5	0 38.1	8 43.6	12 10.1	4 24.9	0 09.9	5 27.2
30 Sa	8 31 08	6 59 58	26 21 14	3♌20 24	22 44.2	0 38.5	2 18.6	27 23.0	0 36.9	8 49.5	12 14.4	4 23.9	0 08.5	5 25.9
31 Su	8 35 04	7 57 22	10♌24 26	17 32 46	22 38.1	0 54.2	3 32.5	28 03.5	0 35.3	8 55.1	12 18.8	4 23.0	0 07.0	5 24.7

August 2011 LONGITUDE

Day	Sid.Time	☉	0 hr ☽	Noon☽	True☊	☿	♀	♂	⚳	♃	♄	♅	♆	♇
1 M	8 39 01	8♌54 46	24♌44 41	1♍59 26	22♐31.1	1♍05.0	4♌46.4	28♊43.8	0♈33.4	9♉00.6	12♎23.3	4♈21.9	0♓05.5	5♑23.5
2 Tu	8 42 57	9 52 11	9♍16 08	16 33 58	22R 24.0	1R 11.0	6 00.4	29 24.2	0R 31.0	9 06.0	12 27.8	4R 20.9	0R 04.0	5R 22.3
3 W	8 46 54	10 49 37	23 52 03	1♎09 36	22 17.8	1 11.8	7 14.3	0♋04.4	0 28.4	9 11.1	12 32.4	4 19.8	0 02.5	5 21.1
4 Th	8 50 50	11 47 04	8♎25 51	15 40 12	22 13.3	1 07.4	8 28.3	0 44.6	0 25.4	9 16.1	12 37.1	4 18.6	0 01.0	5 19.9
5 F	8 54 47	12 44 31	22 52 07	0♏01 09	22D 10.8	0 57.8	9 42.3	1 24.7	0 22.0	9 20.9	12 41.9	4 17.4	29♒59.4	5 18.8
6 Sa	8 58 44	13 41 59	7♏07 02	14 09 32	22 10.1	0 42.9	10 56.3	2 04.7	0 18.2	9 25.6	12 46.7	4 16.2	29 57.9	5 17.7
7 Su	9 02 40	14 39 28	21 08 35	28 04 07	22 10.6	0 22.7	12 10.4	2 44.7	0 14.1	9 30.0	12 51.6	4 14.9	29 56.3	5 16.6
8 M	9 06 37	15 36 57	4♐56 10	11♐44 49	22R 11.6	29♌57.5	13 24.4	3 24.6	0 09.7	9 34.3	12 56.6	4 13.6	29 54.7	5 15.5
9 Tu	9 10 33	16 34 27	18 30 09	25 12 16	22 11.9	29 27.3	14 38.5	4 04.4	0 04.9	9 38.4	13 01.6	4 12.2	29 53.2	5 14.5
10 W	9 14 30	17 31 58	1♑51 17	8♑27 15	22 10.6	28 52.5	15 52.5	4 44.1	29♓59.7	9 42.4	13 06.7	4 10.8	29 51.6	5 13.4
11 Th	9 18 26	18 29 30	15 00 17	21 30 24	22 07.2	28 13.4	17 06.6	5 23.8	29 54.2	9 46.1	13 11.9	4 09.4	29 50.0	5 12.4
12 F	9 22 23	19 27 03	27 57 40	4♒22 05	22 01.2	27 30.7	18 20.7	6 03.5	29 48.3	9 49.7	13 17.2	4 07.9	29 48.4	5 11.4
13 Sa	9 26 19	20 24 37	10♒43 40	17 02 26	21 52.9	26 44.8	19 34.9	6 43.0	29 42.1	9 53.1	13 22.5	4 06.4	29 46.8	5 10.5
14 Su	9 30 16	21 22 12	23 18 23	29 31 33	21 42.9	25 56.6	20 49.0	7 22.5	29 35.6	9 56.3	13 27.8	4 04.9	29 45.2	5 09.5
15 M	9 34 13	22 19 48	5♓42 00	11♓49 47	21 31.9	25 06.8	22 03.2	8 01.9	29 28.7	9 59.3	13 33.2	4 03.3	29 43.5	5 08.6
16 Tu	9 38 09	23 17 26	17 55 03	23 57 58	21 21.0	24 16.3	23 17.3	8 41.3	29 21.4	10 02.1	13 38.7	4 01.7	29 41.9	5 07.7
17 W	9 42 06	24 15 05	29 58 43	5♈57 36	21 11.1	23 26.1	24 31.5	9 20.6	29 13.9	10 04.8	13 44.3	4 00.0	29 40.3	5 06.8
18 Th	9 46 02	25 12 46	11♈54 56	17 51 04	21 03.1	22 37.3	25 45.7	9 59.8	29 06.0	10 07.2	13 49.9	3 58.3	29 38.6	5 06.0
19 F	9 49 59	26 10 28	23 46 28	29 41 34	20 57.4	21 50.7	26 59.9	10 38.9	28 57.8	10 09.5	13 55.5	3 56.6	29 37.0	5 05.1
20 Sa	9 53 55	27 08 11	5♉36 56	11♉33 06	20 54.0	21 07.4	28 14.2	11 18.0	28 49.2	10 11.5	14 01.3	3 54.8	29 35.4	5 04.3
21 Su	9 57 52	28 05 56	17 30 42	23 30 20	20D 52.7	20 28.3	29 28.4	11 57.0	28 40.4	10 13.4	14 07.0	3 53.0	29 33.7	5 03.6
22 M	10 01 48	29 03 43	29 32 40	5♊38 22	20 52.8	19 54.2	0♍42.7	12 36.0	28 31.2	10 15.1	14 12.9	3 51.2	29 32.1	5 02.8
23 Tu	10 05 45	0♍01 32	11♊48 04	18 02 26	20R 53.1	19 26.0	1 57.0	13 14.8	28 21.8	10 16.6	14 18.8	3 49.4	29 30.4	5 02.1
24 W	10 09 42	0 59 23	24 22 03	0♋47 29	20 52.8	19 04.3	3 11.3	13 53.6	28 12.0	10 17.8	14 24.7	3 47.5	29 28.8	5 01.4
25 Th	10 13 38	1 57 15	7♋19 12	13 57 35	20 50.8	18 49.7	4 25.7	14 32.4	28 02.0	10 18.9	14 30.7	3 45.6	29 27.2	5 00.7
26 F	10 17 35	2 55 09	20 42 54	27 35 13	20 46.4	18D 42.5	5 40.0	15 11.0	27 51.7	10 19.8	14 36.8	3 43.6	29 25.5	5 00.1
27 Sa	10 21 31	3 53 04	4♌34 30	11♌40 28	20 39.4	18 43.1	6 54.3	15 49.6	27 41.1	10 20.5	14 42.9	3 41.6	29 23.9	4 59.5
28 Su	10 25 28	4 51 01	18 52 41	26 10 28	20 30.2	18 51.8	8 08.7	16 28.1	27 30.3	10 21.0	14 49.0	3 39.6	29 22.3	4 58.9
29 M	10 29 24	5 49 00	3♍32 59	10♍59 14	20 19.6	19 08.7	9 23.1	17 06.6	27 19.2	10R 21.2	14 55.2	3 37.6	29 20.6	4 58.3
30 Tu	10 33 21	6 47 00	18 28 04	25 58 17	20 08.9	19 33.7	10 37.5	17 44.9	27 07.9	10 21.3	15 01.5	3 35.6	29 19.0	4 57.8
31 W	10 37 17	7 45 02	3♎28 40	10♎58 02	19 59.2	20 06.8	11 51.9	18 23.2	26 56.3	10 21.2	15 07.8	3 33.5	29 17.4	4 57.3

Astro Data

	Dy Hr Mn
☽0S	6 7:25
♃△♇	7 14:08
♅R	10 0:36
☽0N	19 16:25
⚳R	26 14:55
☽0S	2 14:31
☿R	3 3:50
☽0N	16 0:39
♄⚼♆	25 0:50
☿D	26 22:06
☽0S	29 23:46
♃R	30 9:18

Planet Ingress

	Dy Hr Mn
☿ ♌	2 5:39
♀ ♋	4 4:18
⚳ ♈	11 10:01
☉ ♌	23 4:13
♀ ♌	28 15:00
☿ ♍	28 18:00
♂ ♋	3 9:23
♆ ♒R	5 2:55
☿ ♌R	8 9:47
⚳ ♓R	10 10:39
♀ ♍	21 22:12
☉ ♍	23 11:22

Last Aspect / ☽ Ingress (July)

Last Aspect Dy Hr Mn		☽ Ingress Dy Hr Mn
1 11:38	♄ □	♌ 2 21:44
3 16:27	♄ ✶	♍ 5 1:16
6 0:20	☉ ✶	♎ 7 3:55
8 6:31	☉ □	♏ 9 6:32
10 13:06	☉ △	♐ 11 9:48
12 12:22	☿ △	♑ 13 14:15
15 6:41	☉ ☍	♒ 15 20:31
17 12:24	☿ ☍	♓ 18 5:14
20 11:16	☉ △	♈ 20 16:26
22 21:36	☿ △	♉ 23 4:59
25 13:13	☿ □	♊ 25 16:35
28 0:36	☿ ✶	♋ 28 1:13
28 23:04	♄ □	♌ 30 6:17

Last Aspect / ☽ Ingress (August)

Last Aspect Dy Hr Mn		☽ Ingress Dy Hr Mn
1 6:21	♂ ✶	♍ 1 8:43
1 23:39	♃ △	♎ 3 10:05
5 11:57	♆ △	♏ 5 11:58
7 15:15	♆ □	♐ 7 15:22
9 20:25	♆ ✶	♑ 9 20:39
10 20:35	♄ □	♒ 12 3:49
14 12:26	♆ ☌	♓ 14 12:55
15 8:22	♃ ✶	♈ 17 0:03
19 11:51	♆ ✶	♉ 19 12:37
22 0:00	♆ □	♊ 22 0:54
24 9:34	♆ △	♋ 24 10:32
25 13:05	♂ ☌	♌ 26 16:10
28 17:12	♆ ☍	♍ 28 18:14
29 22:16	♂ ✶	♎ 30 18:26

☽ Phases & Eclipses

Dy Hr Mn		
1 8:55	●	9♋12
1 8:39:31	◐	P 0.097
8 6:31	☽	15♎47
15 6:41	○	22♑28
23 5:03	☾	0♉02
30 18:41	●	7♌16
6 11:09	☽	13♏40
13 18:59	○	20♒41
21 21:56	☾	28♉30
29 3:05	●	5♍27

Astro Data

1 July 2011
Julian Day # 40724
SVP 5♓05'39"
GC 27♐00.0 ⚴ 12♒53.7R
Eris 22♈27.8 ⚵ 22♍40.3
⚷ 5♓14.4R ⚶ 19♒16.2R
☽ Mean ☊ 22♐41.7

1 August 2011
Julian Day # 40755
SVP 5♓05'34"
GC 27♐00.1 ⚴ 5♒20.3R
Eris 22♈28.6R ⚵ 1♎22.2
⚷ 4♓12.6R ⚶ 13♒39.1R
☽ Mean ☊ 21♐03.2

LONGITUDE — September 2011

Day	Sid.Time	☉	0 hr ☽	Noon ☽	True ☊	☿	♀	♂	?	♃	♄	♅	♆	♇
1 Th	10 41 14	8♍43 05	18♎25 16	25♎49 24	19♐51.7	20♌47.8	13♍06.3	19♋01.4	26♓44.5	10♉20.9	15♎14.1	3♈31.4	29♒15.8	4♑56.8
2 F	10 45 11	9 41 09	3♏09 39	10♏25 23	19R 46.8	21 36.6	14 20.7	19 39.5	26R 32.6	10R 20.4	15 20.5	3R 29.2	29R 14.1	4R 56.4
3 Sa	10 49 07	10 39 15	17 36 09	24 41 42	19 44.4	22 32.8	15 35.2	20 17.6	26 20.4	10 19.6	15 27.0	3 27.1	29 12.5	4 56.0
4 Su	10 53 04	11 37 23	1♐41 54	8♐36 47	19 43.7	23 36.1	16 49.6	20 55.5	26 08.1	10 18.7	15 33.4	3 24.9	29 10.9	4 55.6
5 M	10 57 00	12 35 32	15 26 29	22 11 13	19 43.7	24 46.1	18 04.1	21 33.4	25 55.6	10 17.6	15 39.9	3 22.7	29 09.4	4 55.2
6 Tu	11 00 57	13 33 42	28 51 16	5♑26 56	19 43.1	26 02.4	19 18.5	22 11.3	25 42.9	10 16.3	15 46.5	3 20.5	29 07.8	4 54.9
7 W	11 04 53	14 31 53	11♑58 33	18 26 25	19 40.8	27 24.3	20 33.0	22 49.0	25 30.1	10 14.7	15 53.1	3 18.3	29 06.2	4 54.6
8 Th	11 08 50	15 30 07	24 50 52	1♒12 11	19 35.8	28 51.5	21 47.4	23 26.6	25 17.2	10 13.0	15 59.7	3 16.0	29 04.6	4 54.3
9 F	11 12 46	16 28 21	7♒30 35	13 46 20	19 28.0	0♍23.4	23 01.9	24 04.2	25 04.1	10 11.1	16 06.4	3 13.8	29 03.1	4 54.1
10 Sa	11 16 43	17 26 38	19 59 36	26 10 33	19 17.3	1 59.4	24 16.4	24 41.7	24 51.0	10 09.0	16 13.1	3 11.5	29 01.6	4 53.9
11 Su	11 20 40	18 24 56	2♓19 19	8♓26 01	19 04.6	3 39.1	25 30.9	25 19.1	24 37.8	10 06.7	16 19.9	3 09.2	29 00.0	4 53.7
12 M	11 24 36	19 23 15	14 30 46	20 33 40	18 50.6	5 21.8	26 45.4	25 56.4	24 24.5	10 04.2	16 26.6	3 06.9	28 58.5	4 53.6
13 Tu	11 28 33	20 21 37	26 34 50	2♈34 25	18 36.7	7 07.1	27 59.9	26 33.7	24 11.1	10 01.4	16 33.4	3 04.5	28 57.0	4 53.5
14 W	11 32 29	21 20 00	8♈32 32	14 29 25	18 23.9	8 54.5	29 14.4	27 10.9	23 57.7	9 58.5	16 40.3	3 02.2	28 55.5	4 53.4
15 Th	11 36 26	22 18 26	20 25 16	26 20 21	18 13.2	10 43.6	0♎28.9	27 48.0	23 44.2	9 55.5	16 47.2	2 59.9	28 54.0	4 53.3
16 F	11 40 22	23 16 53	2♉15 01	8♉09 35	18 05.2	12 34.0	1 43.5	28 25.0	23 30.8	9 52.2	16 54.1	2 57.5	28 52.6	4D 53.3
17 Sa	11 44 19	24 15 23	14 04 31	20 00 15	18 00.1	14 25.2	2 58.0	29 01.9	23 17.3	9 48.7	17 01.0	2 55.1	28 51.1	4 53.3
18 Su	11 48 15	25 13 55	25 57 19	1♊56 15	17 57.4	16 17.1	4 12.5	29 38.7	23 03.9	9 45.0	17 08.0	2 52.7	28 49.7	4 53.3
19 M	11 52 12	26 12 28	7♊57 40	14 02 12	17D 56.6	18 09.2	5 27.1	0♌15.5	22 50.4	9 41.2	17 14.9	2 50.4	28 48.3	4 53.4
20 Tu	11 56 08	27 11 05	20 10 28	26 23 09	17R 56.7	20 01.5	6 41.6	0 52.2	22 37.0	9 37.2	17 22.0	2 48.0	28 46.9	4 53.5
21 W	12 00 05	28 09 43	2♋40 53	9♋04 18	17 56.3	21 53.6	7 56.2	1 28.8	22 23.7	9 33.0	17 29.0	2 45.6	28 45.5	4 53.6
22 Th	12 04 02	29 08 24	15 33 59	22 10 26	17 54.5	23 45.5	9 10.8	2 05.3	22 10.4	9 28.6	17 36.1	2 43.2	28 44.1	4 53.8
23 F	12 07 58	0♎07 06	28 54 03	5♌45 07	17 50.5	25 36.9	10 25.4	2 41.7	21 57.2	9 24.0	17 43.2	2 40.8	28 42.8	4 54.0
24 Sa	12 11 55	1 05 51	12♌43 46	19 49 55	17 44.0	27 27.8	11 40.0	3 18.0	21 44.1	9 19.3	17 50.3	2 38.3	28 41.4	4 54.2
25 Su	12 15 51	2 04 39	27 03 16	4♍23 19	17 35.1	29 18.1	12 54.6	3 54.3	21 31.1	9 14.3	17 57.4	2 35.9	28 40.1	4 54.5
26 M	12 19 48	3 03 28	11♍49 17	19 20 14	17 24.6	1♎07.6	14 09.2	4 30.4	21 18.3	9 09.2	18 04.6	2 33.5	28 38.8	4 54.8
27 Tu	12 23 44	4 02 19	26 54 59	4♎32 12	17 13.9	2 56.5	15 23.8	5 06.4	21 05.6	9 04.0	18 11.8	2 31.1	28 37.6	4 55.1
28 W	12 27 41	5 01 12	12♎10 31	19 48 28	17 04.2	4 44.5	16 38.4	5 42.4	20 53.0	8 58.6	18 18.9	2 28.7	28 36.3	4 55.4
29 Th	12 31 37	6 00 08	27 24 42	4♏57 57	16 56.5	6 31.6	17 53.0	6 18.2	20 40.6	8 53.0	18 26.2	2 26.3	28 35.1	4 55.8
30 F	12 35 34	6 59 05	12♏27 05	19 51 11	16 51.4	8 18.0	19 07.6	6 54.0	20 28.4	8 47.2	18 33.4	2 23.9	28 33.9	4 56.2

LONGITUDE — October 2011

Day	Sid.Time	☉	0 hr ☽	Noon ☽	True ☊	☿	♀	♂	?	♃	♄	♅	♆	♇
1 Sa	12 39 31	7♎58 04	27♏09 33	4♐21 43	16♐49.0	10♎03.4	20♎22.2	7♌29.6	20♓16.4	8♉41.3	18♎40.6	2♈21.5	28♒32.7	4♑56.7
2 Su	12 43 27	8 57 05	11♐27 24	18 26 29	16D 48.4	11 48.1	21 36.8	8 05.2	20R 04.5	8R 35.3	18 47.9	2R 19.1	28R 31.5	4 57.2
3 M	12 47 24	9 56 07	25 19 04	2♑05 21	16R 48.8	13 31.8	22 51.5	8 40.6	19 53.0	8 29.1	18 55.1	2 16.7	28 30.4	4 57.7
4 Tu	12 51 20	10 55 12	8♑45 37	15 20 16	16 48.9	15 14.7	24 06.1	9 16.0	19 41.6	8 22.8	19 02.4	2 14.3	28 29.3	4 58.2
5 W	12 55 17	11 54 18	21 49 43	28 14 25	16 47.6	16 56.8	25 20.7	9 51.2	19 30.5	8 16.4	19 09.7	2 11.9	28 28.2	4 58.8
6 Th	12 59 13	12 53 25	4♒34 49	10♒51 23	16 44.1	18 38.0	26 35.3	10 26.4	19 19.6	8 09.8	19 17.0	2 09.6	28 27.1	4 59.4
7 F	13 03 10	13 52 35	17 04 32	23 14 41	16 38.0	20 18.4	27 49.9	11 01.4	19 09.0	8 03.0	19 24.3	2 07.2	28 26.1	5 00.0
8 Sa	13 07 06	14 51 46	29 22 13	5♓27 27	16 29.5	21 58.0	29 04.5	11 36.3	18 58.6	7 56.2	19 31.6	2 04.9	28 25.1	5 00.7
9 Su	13 11 03	15 50 59	11♓30 42	17 32 13	16 19.0	23 36.8	0♏19.1	12 11.2	18 48.6	7 49.3	19 38.9	2 02.6	28 24.1	5 01.4
10 M	13 15 00	16 50 14	23 32 16	29 31 03	16 07.5	25 14.8	1 33.7	12 45.9	18 38.8	7 42.2	19 46.2	2 00.3	28 23.1	5 02.1
11 Tu	13 18 56	17 49 31	5♈28 46	11♈25 36	15 56.0	26 52.1	2 48.3	13 20.5	18 29.3	7 35.0	19 53.6	1 58.0	28 22.2	5 02.8
12 W	13 22 53	18 48 50	17 21 44	23 17 20	15 45.4	28 28.6	4 02.9	13 55.0	18 20.2	7 27.7	20 00.9	1 55.7	28 21.3	5 03.6
13 Th	13 26 49	19 48 12	29 12 36	5♉07 46	15 36.7	0♏04.5	5 17.6	14 29.4	18 11.3	7 20.4	20 08.2	1 53.4	28 20.4	5 04.4
14 F	13 30 46	20 47 35	11♉03 02	16 58 41	15 30.2	1 39.6	6 32.2	15 03.6	18 02.7	7 12.9	20 15.5	1 51.2	28 19.6	5 05.3
15 Sa	13 34 42	21 47 00	22 55 01	28 52 22	15 26.3	3 14.1	7 46.8	15 37.8	17 54.5	7 05.4	20 22.9	1 48.9	28 18.7	5 06.1
16 Su	13 38 39	22 46 28	4♊51 07	10♊51 40	15D 24.7	4 47.8	9 01.4	16 11.9	17 46.6	6 57.7	20 30.2	1 46.7	28 17.9	5 07.0
17 M	13 42 35	23 45 58	16 54 31	23 00 07	15 24.9	6 21.0	10 16.0	16 45.8	17 39.1	6 50.0	20 37.5	1 44.5	28 17.2	5 08.0
18 Tu	13 46 32	24 45 30	29 09 01	5♋21 46	15 25.9	7 53.5	11 30.6	17 19.6	17 31.8	6 42.2	20 44.8	1 42.4	28 16.4	5 08.9
19 W	13 50 29	25 45 05	11♋38 54	18 01 01	15R 27.0	9 25.3	12 45.2	17 53.3	17 25.0	6 34.4	20 52.2	1 40.2	28 15.7	5 09.9
20 Th	13 54 25	26 44 42	24 28 39	1♌02 18	15 27.2	10 56.5	13 59.8	18 26.9	17 18.4	6 26.5	20 59.5	1 38.1	28 15.1	5 10.9
21 F	13 58 22	27 44 21	7♌42 24	14 29 19	15 25.8	12 27.1	15 14.4	19 00.4	17 12.3	6 18.5	21 06.8	1 36.0	28 14.4	5 12.0
22 Sa	14 02 18	28 44 02	21 23 19	28 24 27	15 22.5	13 57.1	16 29.0	19 33.7	17 06.4	6 10.5	21 14.1	1 33.9	28 13.8	5 13.0
23 Su	14 06 15	29 43 46	5♍32 41	12♍47 44	15 17.3	15 26.5	17 43.6	20 06.9	17 01.0	6 02.5	21 21.4	1 31.9	28 13.2	5 14.1
24 M	14 10 11	0♏43 31	20 09 05	27 36 04	15 10.9	16 55.2	18 58.2	20 39.9	16 55.9	5 54.4	21 28.6	1 29.9	28 12.7	5 15.3
25 Tu	14 14 08	1 43 19	5♎07 45	12♎43 02	15 04.0	18 23.4	20 12.9	21 12.9	16 51.2	5 46.3	21 35.9	1 27.9	28 12.1	5 16.4
26 W	14 18 04	2 43 09	20 20 41	27 59 19	14 57.7	19 50.8	21 27.5	21 45.7	16 46.9	5 38.1	21 43.2	1 25.9	28 11.6	5 17.6
27 Th	14 22 01	3 43 01	5♏37 35	13♏14 06	14 52.8	21 17.7	22 42.1	22 18.3	16 42.9	5 30.0	21 50.4	1 24.0	28 11.2	5 18.8
28 F	14 25 57	4 42 55	20 47 36	28 16 58	14 49.8	22 43.8	23 56.7	22 50.8	16 39.3	5 21.8	21 57.6	1 22.1	28 10.8	5 20.1
29 Sa	14 29 54	5 42 51	5♐41 12	12♐59 33	14D 48.7	24 09.3	25 11.3	23 23.2	16 36.1	5 13.7	22 04.8	1 20.2	28 10.4	5 21.3
30 Su	14 33 51	6 42 49	20 11 28	27 16 36	14 49.2	25 34.0	26 25.9	23 55.4	16 33.3	5 05.5	22 12.0	1 18.4	28 10.0	5 22.6
31 M	14 37 47	7 42 48	4♑14 46	11♑06 00	14 50.6	26 57.9	27 40.5	24 27.5	16 30.8	4 57.4	22 19.2	1 16.5	28 09.7	5 23.9

Astro Data

	Dy Hr Mn
☽0N	12 7:40
♇ D	16 18:26
♀0S	17 11:17
☉0S	23 9:05
☽0S	26 10:21
☿0S	27 17:18
☽0N	9 13:22
♅0S	16 17:54
☽0S	23 20:33
♃△♇	28 16:30

Planet Ingress

		Dy Hr Mn
☿	♍	9 6:00
♀	♎	15 2:41
♂	♌	19 1:52
☉	♎	23 9:06
☿	♎	25 21:10
♀	♏	9 5:51
☿	♏	13 10:53
☉	♏	23 18:31

Last Aspect / ☽ Ingress (September)

Last Aspect Dy Hr Mn			☽ Ingress	Dy Hr Mn
1 17:36	♆	△	♏	1 18:49
3 19:42	♆	□	♐	3 21:05
6 0:31	♆	✶	♑	6 2:05
7 20:36	♂	☍	♒	8 9:43
10 17:33	♆	☌	♓	10 19:28
13 1:47	♀	☍	♈	13 6:50
15 17:11	♆	✶	♉	15 19:26
18 7:10	♂	✶	♊	18 8:07
20 16:35	♆	△	♋	20 18:55
23 1:23	☉	✶	♌	23 1:56
25 2:40	♆	☍	♍	25 4:50
25 19:48	♃	△	♎	27 4:52
29 1:52	♆	△	♏	29 4:06

Last Aspect / ☽ Ingress (October)

Last Aspect Dy Hr Mn			☽ Ingress	Dy Hr Mn
1 2:19	♆	□	♐	1 4:43
3 5:38	♆	✶	♑	3 8:17
5 5:59	♀	□	♒	5 15:19
7 22:09	♆	☌	♓	8 1:14
8 16:52	♃	✶	♈	10 12:58
13 0:09	☿	☍	♉	13 1:36
15 10:52	♆	□	♊	15 14:16
17 22:19	♆	△	♋	18 1:39
20 3:31	☉	□	♌	20 10:07
22 12:36	☉	✶	♍	22 14:42
23 20:48	♀	✶	♎	24 15:50
26 12:19	♆	△	♏	26 15:09
28 11:50	♆	□	♐	28 14:46
30 13:31	♆	✶	♑	30 16:40

☽ Phases & Eclipses

Dy Hr Mn		
4 17:40	☽	11♐51
12 9:28	○	19♓17
20 13:40	☾	27♊15
27 11:10	●	4♎00
4 3:16	☽	10♑34
12 2:07	○	18♈24
20 3:31	☾	26♋24
26 19:57	●	3♏03

Astro Data

1 September 2011
Julian Day # 40786
SVP 5♓05'31"
GC 27♐00.1 ⚳ 28♑43.6R
Eris 22♈19.8R ⚵ 11♎23.4
⚷ 2♓44.3R ⚶ 7♒11.0R
☽ Mean ☊ 19♐24.7

1 October 2011
Julian Day # 40816
SVP 5♓05'28"
GC 27♐00.2 ⚳ 27♑20.4
Eris 22♈04.4R ⚵ 21♎43.6
⚷ 1♓25.3R ⚶ 6♒49.8
☽ Mean ☊ 17♐49.4

November 2011 LONGITUDE

Day	Sid.Time	☉	0 hr ☽	Noon ☽	True ☊	☿	♀	♂	⚳	♃	♄	♅	♆	♇
1 Tu	14 41 44	8♏42 49	17♑50 26	24♑28 22	14♐52.1	28♏21.0	28♏55.1	24♌59.4	16♓28.8	4♉49.3	22♎26.3	1♈14.8	28♒09.4	5♑25.3
2 W	14 45 40	9 42 52	1♒00 08	7♒26 12	14R 52.9	29 43.3	0♐09.7	25 31.1	16R 27.1	4R 41.2	22 33.5	1R 13.0	28R 09.1	5 26.7
3 Th	14 49 37	10 42 55	13 47 02	20 03 10	14 52.4	1♐04.5	1 24.3	26 02.7	16 25.8	4 33.1	22 40.6	1 11.3	28 08.9	5 28.1
4 F	14 53 33	11 43 01	26 15 07	2♓23 24	14 50.4	2 24.8	2 38.9	26 34.2	16 24.8	4 25.1	22 47.6	1 09.7	28 08.7	5 29.5
5 Sa	14 57 30	12 43 08	8♓28 33	14 31 02	14 47.0	3 43.9	3 53.4	27 05.5	16D 24.3	4 17.1	22 54.7	1 08.0	28 08.5	5 30.9
6 Su	15 01 26	13 43 17	20 31 21	26 29 55	14 42.3	5 01.8	5 08.0	27 36.6	16 24.1	4 09.2	23 01.7	1 06.4	28 08.4	5 32.4
7 M	15 05 23	14 43 27	2♈27 09	8♈23 25	14 36.9	6 18.4	6 22.6	28 07.6	16 24.3	4 01.3	23 08.7	1 04.9	28 08.3	5 33.9
8 Tu	15 09 20	15 43 39	14 19 04	20 14 25	14 31.4	7 33.5	7 37.1	28 38.4	16 24.9	3 53.5	23 15.7	1 03.4	28 08.3	5 35.4
9 W	15 13 16	16 43 52	26 09 44	2♉05 17	14 26.4	8 46.9	8 51.7	29 09.0	16 25.8	3 45.7	23 22.7	1 01.9	28D 08.2	5 36.9
10 Th	15 17 13	17 44 08	8♉01 19	13 58 03	14 22.4	9 58.4	10 06.2	29 39.4	16 27.1	3 38.0	23 29.6	1 00.5	28 08.2	5 38.5
11 F	15 21 09	18 44 25	19 55 43	25 54 32	14 19.7	11 07.9	11 20.7	0♍09.7	16 28.7	3 30.4	23 36.5	0 59.1	28 08.3	5 40.0
12 Sa	15 25 06	19 44 43	1♊54 42	7♊56 29	14D 18.3	12 15.1	12 35.2	0 39.8	16 30.8	3 22.9	23 43.3	0 57.7	28 08.4	5 41.7
13 Su	15 29 02	20 45 04	14 00 05	20 05 47	14 18.3	13 19.7	13 49.8	1 09.8	16 33.2	3 15.5	23 50.1	0 56.4	28 08.5	5 43.3
14 M	15 32 59	21 45 26	26 13 52	2♋24 37	14 19.2	14 21.3	15 04.3	1 39.5	16 35.9	3 08.2	23 56.9	0 55.1	28 08.6	5 44.9
15 Tu	15 36 55	22 45 51	8♋38 22	14 55 26	14 20.8	15 19.6	16 18.8	2 09.1	16 39.0	3 00.9	24 03.7	0 53.9	28 08.8	5 46.6
16 W	15 40 52	23 46 17	21 16 12	27 41 00	14 22.4	16 14.2	17 33.3	2 38.5	16 42.4	2 53.8	24 10.4	0 52.7	28 09.0	5 48.3
17 Th	15 44 49	24 46 45	4♌10 12	10♌44 09	14 23.6	17 04.5	18 47.8	3 07.6	16 46.2	2 46.8	24 17.1	0 51.6	28 09.2	5 50.0
18 F	15 48 45	25 47 14	17 23 10	24 07 31	14R 24.2	17 50.2	20 02.3	3 36.6	16 50.4	2 39.9	24 23.7	0 50.5	28 09.5	5 51.7
19 Sa	15 52 42	26 47 46	0♍57 24	7♍52 58	14 23.8	18 30.4	21 16.8	4 05.4	16 54.9	2 33.1	24 30.3	0 49.4	28 09.8	5 53.5
20 Su	15 56 38	27 48 19	14 54 14	22 01 05	14 22.7	19 04.7	22 31.3	4 33.9	16 59.7	2 26.5	24 36.9	0 48.4	28 10.2	5 55.2
21 M	16 00 35	28 48 54	29 13 18	6♎30 29	14 21.0	19 32.2	23 45.7	5 02.3	17 04.9	2 19.9	24 43.4	0 47.5	28 10.6	5 57.0
22 Tu	16 04 31	29 49 31	13♎52 04	21 17 22	14 19.1	19 52.4	25 00.2	5 30.4	17 10.4	2 13.5	24 49.8	0 46.5	28 11.0	5 58.8
23 W	16 08 28	0♐50 10	28 45 32	6♏15 35	14 17.3	20R 04.2	26 14.7	5 58.3	17 16.2	2 07.3	24 56.3	0 45.7	28 11.4	6 00.6
24 Th	16 12 24	1 50 50	13♏46 29	21 17 07	14 16.0	20 07.1	27 29.2	6 26.0	17 22.3	2 01.2	25 02.6	0 44.9	28 11.9	6 02.5
25 F	16 16 21	2 51 32	28 46 21	6♐13 07	14D 15.4	20 00.2	28 43.6	6 53.4	17 28.8	1 55.3	25 09.0	0 44.1	28 12.5	6 04.3
26 Sa	16 20 18	3 52 15	13♐36 25	20 55 19	14 15.3	19 43.1	29 58.1	7 20.7	17 35.6	1 49.5	25 15.3	0 43.4	28 13.0	6 06.2
27 Su	16 24 14	4 52 59	28 09 06	5♑17 07	14 15.8	19 15.1	1♑12.5	7 47.6	17 42.8	1 43.8	25 21.5	0 42.7	28 13.6	6 08.1
28 M	16 28 11	5 53 45	12♑18 57	19 14 19	14 16.6	18 36.3	2 26.9	8 14.3	17 50.2	1 38.4	25 27.7	0 42.1	28 14.2	6 10.0
29 Tu	16 32 07	6 54 31	26 03 06	2♒45 19	14 17.4	17 46.7	3 41.4	8 40.8	17 58.0	1 33.1	25 33.8	0 41.5	28 14.9	6 11.9
30 W	16 36 04	7 55 19	9♒21 07	15 50 47	14 18.0	16 47.1	4 55.8	9 07.0	18 06.0	1 28.0	25 39.9	0 41.0	28 15.6	6 13.8

December 2011 LONGITUDE

Day	Sid.Time	☉	0 hr ☽	Noon ☽	True ☊	☿	♀	♂	⚳	♃	♄	♅	♆	♇
1 Th	16 40 00	8♐56 07	22♒14 40	28♒33 13	14♐18.4	15♐38.7	6♑10.2	9♍33.0	18♓14.4	1♉23.0	25♎45.9	0♈40.5	28♒16.3	6♑15.8
2 F	16 43 57	9 56 56	4♓46 54	10♓56 16	14R 18.5	14R 23.1	7 24.5	9 58.6	18 23.0	1R 18.2	25 51.8	0R 40.1	28 17.1	6 17.7
3 Sa	16 47 54	10 57 47	17 01 53	23 04 18	14 18.4	13 02.7	8 38.9	10 24.0	18 32.0	1 13.6	25 57.7	0 39.7	28 17.9	6 19.7
4 Su	16 51 50	11 58 38	29 04 06	5♈01 52	14 18.2	11 40.0	9 53.2	10 49.2	18 41.2	1 09.2	26 03.6	0 39.4	28 18.7	6 21.7
5 M	16 55 47	12 59 29	10♈58 09	16 53 28	14 18.0	10 17.8	11 07.6	11 14.0	18 50.7	1 05.0	26 09.4	0 39.1	28 19.5	6 23.7
6 Tu	16 59 43	14 00 22	22 48 20	28 43 15	14D 17.9	8 58.9	12 21.9	11 38.6	19 00.5	1 00.9	26 15.1	0 38.9	28 20.4	6 25.7
7 W	17 03 40	15 01 16	4♉38 39	10♉34 56	14 17.9	7 45.8	13 36.2	12 02.9	19 10.6	0 57.1	26 20.8	0 38.7	28 21.3	6 27.7
8 Th	17 07 36	16 02 10	16 32 29	22 31 39	14 18.0	6 40.6	14 50.4	12 26.9	19 20.9	0 53.4	26 26.4	0 38.6	28 22.3	6 29.7
9 F	17 11 33	17 03 06	28 32 43	4♊35 57	14R 18.2	5 45.1	16 04.7	12 50.5	19 31.6	0 49.9	26 31.9	0D 38.5	28 23.3	6 31.8
10 Sa	17 15 29	18 04 02	10♊41 34	16 49 48	14 18.2	5 00.3	17 18.9	13 13.9	19 42.5	0 46.7	26 37.4	0 38.5	28 24.3	6 33.8
11 Su	17 19 26	19 04 59	23 00 47	29 14 40	14 18.1	4 26.6	18 33.1	13 37.0	19 53.6	0 43.6	26 42.8	0 38.6	28 25.4	6 35.9
12 M	17 23 23	20 05 58	5♋31 34	11♋51 35	14 17.6	4 04.3	19 47.3	13 59.7	20 05.0	0 40.7	26 48.1	0 38.6	28 26.4	6 38.0
13 Tu	17 27 19	21 06 57	18 14 48	24 41 17	14 16.8	3D 53.0	21 01.5	14 22.1	20 16.6	0 38.0	26 53.4	0 38.8	28 27.5	6 40.1
14 W	17 31 16	22 07 57	1♌11 07	7♌44 21	14 15.8	3 52.3	22 15.6	14 44.2	20 28.5	0 35.5	26 58.6	0 39.0	28 28.7	6 42.1
15 Th	17 35 12	23 08 58	14 21 01	21 01 11	14 14.8	4 01.3	23 29.8	15 05.9	20 40.7	0 33.3	27 03.8	0 39.2	28 29.9	6 44.2
16 F	17 39 09	24 09 59	27 44 53	4♍32 08	14 13.9	4 19.4	24 43.9	15 27.3	20 53.1	0 31.2	27 08.8	0 39.5	28 31.1	6 46.3
17 Sa	17 43 05	25 11 02	11♍22 58	18 17 20	14D 13.3	4 45.7	25 58.0	15 48.3	21 05.7	0 29.3	27 13.8	0 39.8	28 32.3	6 48.4
18 Su	17 47 02	26 12 06	25 15 12	2♎16 29	14 13.3	5 19.4	27 12.0	16 09.0	21 18.6	0 27.7	27 18.7	0 40.2	28 33.6	6 50.5
19 M	17 50 58	27 13 11	9♎21 02	16 28 39	14 13.8	5 59.7	28 26.1	16 29.2	21 31.7	0 26.2	27 23.6	0 40.7	28 34.8	6 52.7
20 Tu	17 54 55	28 14 17	23 39 03	0♏51 53	14 14.8	6 45.8	29 40.1	16 49.1	21 45.0	0 25.0	27 28.3	0 41.2	28 36.2	6 54.8
21 W	17 58 52	29 15 23	8♏06 43	15 23 02	14 16.0	7 37.2	0♒54.1	17 08.6	21 58.5	0 23.9	27 33.0	0 41.7	28 37.5	6 56.9
22 Th	18 02 48	0♑16 30	22 40 16	29 57 44	14R 17.0	8 33.1	2 08.1	17 27.7	22 12.3	0 23.1	27 37.6	0 42.3	28 38.9	6 59.1
23 F	18 06 45	1 17 38	7♐14 45	14♐30 34	14 17.4	9 33.0	3 22.0	17 46.3	22 26.3	0 22.5	27 42.2	0 43.0	28 40.3	7 01.2
24 Sa	18 10 41	2 18 47	21 44 25	28 55 35	14 16.9	10 36.5	4 36.0	18 04.6	22 40.5	0 22.1	27 46.6	0 43.7	28 41.7	7 03.3
25 Su	18 14 38	3 19 56	6♑03 21	13♑07 05	14 15.4	11 43.1	5 49.8	18 22.3	22 55.0	0D 21.9	27 51.0	0 44.5	28 43.2	7 05.5
26 M	18 18 34	4 21 05	20 06 14	27 00 19	14 12.9	12 52.4	7 03.7	18 39.7	23 09.6	0 21.9	27 55.3	0 45.3	28 44.7	7 07.6
27 Tu	18 22 31	5 22 15	3♒49 01	10♒32 07	14 09.7	14 04.1	8 17.5	18 56.6	23 24.4	0 22.1	27 59.5	0 46.1	28 46.2	7 09.8
28 W	18 26 27	6 23 24	17 09 29	23 41 10	14 06.2	15 18.0	9 31.3	19 13.0	23 39.5	0 22.6	28 03.6	0 47.0	28 47.7	7 11.9
29 Th	18 30 24	7 24 34	0♓07 16	6♓28 04	14 03.0	16 33.7	10 45.1	19 29.0	23 54.7	0 23.2	28 07.7	0 48.0	28 49.3	7 14.1
30 F	18 34 21	8 25 43	12 43 52	18 55 05	14 00.5	17 51.1	11 58.8	19 44.5	24 10.1	0 24.1	28 11.6	0 49.0	28 50.9	7 16.2
31 Sa	18 38 17	9 26 52	25 02 11	1♈05 44	13D 59.0	19 10.0	13 12.5	19 59.5	24 25.8	0 25.1	28 15.5	0 50.1	28 52.5	7 18.3

Astro Data	Planet Ingress	Last Aspect	☽ Ingress	Last Aspect	☽ Ingress	☽ Phases & Eclipses
Dy Hr Mn	Dy Hr Mn	Dy Hr Mn	Dy Hr Mn	Dy Hr Mn	Dy Hr Mn	Dy Hr Mn
☽0N 5 18:44	♀ ♐ 2 8:52	1 21:01 ♀ ⚹	♒ 1 22:09	1 11:28 ♆ ☌	♓ 1 14:46	2 16:39 ☽ 9♒55
⚳ D 6 11:40	☿ ♐ 2 16:55	4 3:41 ♆ ☌	♓ 4 7:19	2 18:07 ♆ □	♈ 4 1:52	10 20:17 ○ 18♉05
♆ D 9 18:55	♂ ♍ 11 4:16	5 8:06 ☉ △	♈ 6 19:03	6 11:14 ♆ ⚹	♉ 6 14:36	18 15:10 ☾ 25♌55
☽0S 20 4:48	☉ ♐ 22 16:09	9 5:47 ♂ △	♉ 9 7:46	8 23:40 ♆ □	♊ 9 2:53	25 6:11 ● 2♐37
☿ R 24 7:20	♀ ♑ 26 12:37	11 16:28 ♆ □	♊ 11 20:11	11 10:25 ♆ △	♋ 11 13:27	25 6:21:21 ● P 0.905
		14 3:43 ♆ △	♋ 14 7:20	13 16:06 ♄ □	♌ 13 21:49	
☽0N 3 1:17	♀ ♒ 20 18:27	16 5:23 ♄ □	♌ 16 16:18	16 1:21 ♆ ☍	♍ 16 4:00	2 9:53 ☽ 9♓52
♅ D 10 7:05	☉ ♑ 22 5:31	18 19:06 ♆ ☍	♍ 18 22:20	18 2:30 ♀ △	♎ 18 8:07	10 14:37 ○ 18♊11
♃×♅ 13 5:24		20 22:23 ☉ ⚹	♎ 21 1:17	20 9:50 ♀ □	♏ 20 10:34	10 14:33 ● T 1.106
☿ D 14 1:43		22 23:05 ♆ △	♏ 23 1:59	22 9:50 ♀ □	♐ 22 12:04	18 0:49 ☾ 25♍44
☽0S 17 10:59		24 23:05 ♆ □	♐ 25 1:58	24 11:37 ♆ ⚹	♑ 24 13:48	24 18:08 ● 2♑34
♃ D 25 22:09		27 0:07 ♆ ⚹	♑ 27 3:06	26 13:37 ♄ □	♒ 26 17:15	
☽0N 30 9:50		28 23:02 ♄ □	♒ 29 7:03	28 21:32 ♆ ☌	♓ 28 23:46	
				30 13:39 ♂ ☍	♈ 31 9:49	

Astro Data

1 November 2011
Julian Day # 40847
SVP 5♓05'24"
GC 27♐00.3 ⚴ 0♒54.3
Eris 21♈46.1R ⚵ 2♏35.6
⚷ 0♓41.2R ⚶ 12♒50.4
☽ Mean ☊ 16♐10.9

1 December 2011
Julian Day # 40877
SVP 5♓05'20"
GC 27♐00.3 ⚴ 7♒36.3
Eris 21♈31.2R ⚵ 12♏50.4
⚷ 0♓51.3 ⚶ 22♒38.2
☽ Mean ☊ 14♐35.6

LONGITUDE — January 2012

Day	Sid.Time	☉	0 hr ☽	Noon☽	True☊	☿	♀	♂	⚳	♃	♄	♅	♆	♇
1 Su	18 42 14	10♑28 02	7♈06 16	13♈04 25	13♐58.7	20♐30.3	14♒26.1	20♍14.0	24♓41.6	0♉26.4	28♎19.2	0♈51.2	28♒54.2	7♑20.5
2 M	18 46 10	11 29 11	19 00 47	24 56 01	13 59.5	21 51.7	15 39.7	20 28.0	24 57.6	0 27.9	28 22.9	0 52.3	28 55.8	7 22.6
3 Tu	18 50 07	12 30 20	0♉50 43	6♉45 33	14 01.1	23 14.1	16 53.2	20 41.5	25 13.8	0 29.6	28 26.5	0 53.5	28 57.5	7 24.8
4 W	18 54 03	13 31 28	12 41 04	18 37 54	14 03.0	24 37.6	18 06.7	20 54.4	25 30.1	0 31.4	28 30.0	0 54.8	28 59.2	7 26.9
5 Th	18 58 00	14 32 37	24 36 33	0♊37 33	14 04.6	26 01.9	19 20.2	21 06.8	25 46.6	0 33.5	28 33.4	0 56.1	29 01.0	7 29.0
6 F	19 01 56	15 33 45	6♊41 21	12 48 22	14R 05.4	27 27.1	20 33.6	21 18.7	26 03.3	0 35.8	28 36.8	0 57.5	29 02.7	7 31.2
7 Sa	19 05 53	16 34 53	18 58 55	25 13 19	14 04.8	28 53.0	21 46.9	21 30.0	26 20.2	0 38.3	28 40.0	0 58.9	29 04.5	7 33.3
8 Su	19 09 50	17 36 01	1♋31 44	7♋54 20	14 02.5	0♑19.6	23 00.2	21 40.7	26 37.3	0 41.0	28 43.1	1 00.3	29 06.3	7 35.4
9 M	19 13 46	18 37 09	14 21 10	20 52 13	13 58.5	1 46.9	24 13.5	21 50.9	26 54.5	0 43.9	28 46.2	1 01.8	29 08.1	7 37.5
10 Tu	19 17 43	19 38 16	27 27 22	4♌06 29	13 53.1	3 14.8	25 26.7	22 00.5	27 11.8	0 47.0	28 49.1	1 03.4	29 10.0	7 39.7
11 W	19 21 39	20 39 23	10♌49 19	17 35 38	13 46.9	4 43.3	26 39.8	22 09.4	27 29.3	0 50.3	28 52.0	1 04.9	29 11.9	7 41.8
12 Th	19 25 36	21 40 30	24 25 05	1♍17 22	13 40.5	6 12.4	27 52.9	22 17.8	27 47.0	0 53.8	28 54.7	1 06.6	29 13.7	7 43.9
13 F	19 29 32	22 41 37	8♍12 07	15 08 59	13 34.8	7 42.0	29 05.9	22 25.5	28 04.8	0 57.5	28 57.4	1 08.3	29 15.6	7 45.9
14 Sa	19 33 29	23 42 44	22 07 40	29 07 50	13 30.6	9 12.2	0♓18.8	22 32.6	28 22.8	1 01.3	28 59.9	1 10.0	29 17.6	7 48.0
15 Su	19 37 25	24 43 50	6♎09 14	13♎11 35	13D 28.1	10 43.0	1 31.7	22 39.0	28 40.9	1 05.4	29 02.4	1 11.7	29 19.5	7 50.1
16 M	19 41 22	25 44 57	20 14 41	27 18 20	13 27.5	12 14.2	2 44.5	22 44.8	28 59.2	1 09.6	29 04.7	1 13.6	29 21.5	7 52.2
17 Tu	19 45 19	26 46 03	4♏22 23	11♏26 38	13 28.2	13 46.1	3 57.3	22 49.8	29 17.6	1 14.1	29 07.0	1 15.4	29 23.4	7 54.2
18 W	19 49 15	27 47 09	18 30 57	25 35 08	13 29.6	15 18.4	5 10.0	22 54.2	29 36.1	1 18.7	29 09.2	1 17.3	29 25.4	7 56.3
19 Th	19 53 12	28 48 15	2♐38 59	9♐42 16	13R 30.5	16 51.3	6 22.6	22 57.9	29 54.8	1 23.5	29 11.2	1 19.3	29 27.5	7 58.3
20 F	19 57 08	29 49 21	16 44 42	23 45 58	13 30.1	18 24.7	7 35.2	23 00.9	0♈13.6	1 28.5	29 13.2	1 21.3	29 29.5	8 00.4
21 Sa	20 01 05	0♒50 27	0♑45 43	7♑43 34	13 27.6	19 58.7	8 47.7	23 03.2	0 32.6	1 33.6	29 15.0	1 23.3	29 31.5	8 02.4
22 Su	20 05 01	1 51 31	14 39 05	21 31 52	13 22.7	21 33.2	10 00.2	23 04.7	0 51.7	1 39.0	29 16.8	1 25.4	29 33.6	8 04.4
23 M	20 08 58	2 52 35	28 21 30	5♒07 34	13 15.5	23 08.3	11 12.5	23R 05.5	1 10.9	1 44.5	29 18.4	1 27.5	29 35.7	8 06.4
24 Tu	20 12 55	3 53 39	11♒49 44	18 27 43	13 06.6	24 44.0	12 24.8	23 05.5	1 30.3	1 50.2	29 20.0	1 29.6	29 37.8	8 08.4
25 W	20 16 51	4 54 41	25 01 16	1♓30 16	12 56.8	26 20.3	13 37.0	23 04.8	1 49.7	1 56.1	29 21.4	1 31.8	29 39.9	8 10.3
26 Th	20 20 48	5 55 43	7♓54 40	14 14 29	12 47.2	27 57.2	14 49.1	23 03.3	2 09.3	2 02.2	29 22.7	1 34.1	29 42.0	8 12.3
27 F	20 24 44	6 56 43	20 29 53	26 41 06	12 38.8	29 34.7	16 01.1	23 01.0	2 29.0	2 08.4	29 24.0	1 36.3	29 44.1	8 14.2
28 Sa	20 28 41	7 57 42	2♈48 26	8♈52 16	12 32.2	1♒12.8	17 13.1	22 58.0	2 48.8	2 14.8	29 25.1	1 38.6	29 46.3	8 16.1
29 Su	20 32 37	8 58 41	14 53 05	20 51 24	12 27.9	2 51.6	18 24.9	22 54.1	3 08.8	2 21.3	29 26.1	1 41.0	29 48.4	8 18.0
30 M	20 36 34	9 59 38	26 47 48	2♉42 53	12D 25.9	4 31.0	19 36.6	22 49.5	3 28.8	2 28.1	29 27.0	1 43.4	29 50.6	8 19.9
31 Tu	20 40 30	11 00 34	8♉37 18	14 31 44	12 25.6	6 11.1	20 48.3	22 44.2	3 49.0	2 35.0	29 27.8	1 45.8	29 52.8	8 21.8

LONGITUDE — February 2012

Day	Sid.Time	☉	0 hr ☽	Noon☽	True☊	☿	♀	♂	⚳	♃	♄	♅	♆	♇
1 W	20 44 27	12♒01 28	20♉26 52	26♉23 22	12♐26.4	7♒52.0	21♓59.8	22♍38.0	4♈09.3	2♉42.0	29♎28.5	1♈48.3	29♒54.9	8♑23.7
2 Th	20 48 23	13 02 22	2♊21 56	8♊23 11	12R 27.1	9 33.5	23 11.3	22R 31.0	4 29.6	2 49.2	29 29.1	1 50.8	29 57.1	8 25.5
3 F	20 52 20	14 03 14	14 27 46	20 36 16	12 26.8	11 15.7	24 22.6	22 23.3	4 50.1	2 56.6	29 29.6	1 53.3	29 59.3	8 27.4
4 Sa	20 56 17	15 04 05	26 49 11	3♋06 59	12 24.6	12 58.7	25 33.8	22 14.8	5 10.7	3 04.1	29 30.0	1 55.8	0♓01.6	8 29.2
5 Su	21 00 13	16 04 54	9♋30 01	15 58 32	12 20.0	14 42.4	26 45.0	22 05.4	5 31.4	3 11.8	29 30.2	1 58.4	0 03.8	8 31.0
6 M	21 04 10	17 05 42	22 32 43	29 12 32	12 12.7	16 26.8	27 56.0	21 55.4	5 52.1	3 19.6	29 30.4	2 01.1	0 06.0	8 32.8
7 Tu	21 08 06	18 06 29	5♌57 55	12♌48 35	12 03.2	18 12.0	29 06.8	21 44.5	6 13.0	3 27.6	29R 30.5	2 03.7	0 08.3	8 34.5
8 W	21 12 03	19 07 15	19 44 09	26 44 09	11 52.1	19 57.9	0♈17.6	21 32.8	6 34.0	3 35.7	29 30.4	2 06.4	0 10.5	8 36.3
9 Th	21 15 59	20 07 59	3♍47 56	10♍54 51	11 40.8	21 44.5	1 28.2	21 20.4	6 55.0	3 43.9	29 30.3	2 09.2	0 12.7	8 38.0
10 F	21 19 56	21 08 42	18 04 08	25 15 03	11 30.5	23 31.8	2 38.7	21 07.2	7 16.2	3 52.3	29 30.0	2 11.9	0 15.0	8 39.7
11 Sa	21 23 52	22 09 24	2♎26 51	9♎38 49	11 22.1	25 19.8	3 49.1	20 53.3	7 37.4	4 00.9	29 29.7	2 14.7	0 17.3	8 41.3
12 Su	21 27 49	23 10 05	16 50 22	24 00 54	11 16.4	27 08.4	4 59.3	20 38.7	7 58.7	4 09.5	29 29.2	2 17.5	0 19.5	8 43.0
13 M	21 31 46	24 10 45	1♏10 01	8♏17 20	11 13.4	28 57.6	6 09.4	20 23.3	8 20.1	4 18.3	29 28.6	2 20.3	0 21.8	8 44.6
14 Tu	21 35 42	25 11 24	15 22 37	22 25 43	11D 12.5	0♓47.4	7 19.4	20 07.2	8 41.6	4 27.3	29 28.0	2 23.2	0 24.1	8 46.3
15 W	21 39 39	26 12 02	29 26 31	6♐25 01	11R 12.6	2 37.6	8 29.2	19 50.4	9 03.2	4 36.4	29 27.2	2 26.1	0 26.3	8 47.9
16 Th	21 43 35	27 12 38	13♐21 11	20 15 04	11 12.4	4 28.1	9 38.9	19 32.9	9 24.8	4 45.6	29 26.3	2 29.0	0 28.6	8 49.4
17 F	21 47 32	28 13 14	27 06 41	3♑56 02	11 10.6	6 18.9	10 48.5	19 14.8	9 46.5	4 54.9	29 25.3	2 32.0	0 30.9	8 51.0
18 Sa	21 51 28	29 13 48	10♑43 07	17 27 54	11 06.3	8 09.7	11 57.9	18 56.1	10 08.4	5 04.4	29 24.2	2 35.0	0 33.2	8 52.5
19 Su	21 55 25	0♓14 21	24 10 17	0♒50 10	10 58.9	10 00.4	13 07.1	18 36.8	10 30.2	5 14.0	29 23.0	2 38.0	0 35.5	8 54.0
20 M	21 59 21	1 14 52	7♒27 26	14 01 54	10 48.5	11 50.8	14 16.2	18 16.9	10 52.2	5 23.7	29 21.7	2 41.0	0 37.7	8 55.5
21 Tu	22 03 18	2 15 22	20 33 26	27 01 50	10 35.8	13 40.5	15 25.2	17 56.5	11 14.2	5 33.6	29 20.3	2 44.1	0 40.0	8 57.0
22 W	22 07 15	3 15 51	3♓26 59	9♓48 46	10 21.9	15 29.5	16 33.9	17 35.5	11 36.4	5 43.5	29 18.8	2 47.1	0 42.3	8 58.4
23 Th	22 11 11	4 16 17	16 07 06	22 21 58	10 08.0	17 17.2	17 42.5	17 14.2	11 58.5	5 53.6	29 17.2	2 50.2	0 44.6	8 59.8
24 F	22 15 08	5 16 42	28 33 25	4♈41 33	9 55.3	19 03.3	18 51.0	16 52.3	12 20.8	6 03.8	29 15.5	2 53.3	0 46.8	9 01.2
25 Sa	22 19 04	6 17 05	10♈46 32	16 48 38	9 44.9	20 47.4	19 59.2	16 30.1	12 43.1	6 14.1	29 13.8	2 56.5	0 49.1	9 02.5
26 Su	22 23 01	7 17 27	22 48 10	28 45 32	9 37.2	22 29.0	21 07.3	16 07.6	13 05.5	6 24.5	29 11.9	2 59.6	0 51.4	9 03.9
27 M	22 26 57	8 17 46	4♉41 10	10♉35 35	9 32.5	24 07.6	22 15.1	15 44.8	13 27.9	6 35.0	29 09.9	3 02.8	0 53.7	9 05.2
28 Tu	22 30 54	9 18 03	16 29 22	22 23 06	9 30.2	25 42.7	23 22.8	15 21.6	13 50.4	6 45.7	29 07.8	3 06.0	0 55.9	9 06.4
29 W	22 34 50	10 18 19	28 17 27	4♊13 05	9 29.5	27 13.7	24 30.3	14 58.3	14 13.0	6 56.4	29 05.6	3 09.2	0 58.2	9 07.7

Astro Data	Dy Hr Mn
☽ 0S	13 16:53
♃⚺♅	18 0:14
♂ R	24 0:55
☽ 0N	26 19:31
♅ 0N	28 3:37
♄ R	7 14:04
♀ 0N	9 3:28
☽ 0S	10 0:28
☽ 0N	23 4:31

Planet Ingress		Dy Hr Mn
☿	♑	8 6:35
♀	♓	14 5:48
⚳	♈	19 18:38
☉	♒	20 16:11
☿	♒	27 18:13
♆	♓	3 19:04
♀	♈	8 6:02
☿	♓	14 1:39
☉	♓	19 6:19

Last Aspect Dy Hr Mn			☽ Ingress	Dy Hr Mn
2 20:08	♆	⚹	♉	2 22:17
5 8:47	♆	□	♊	5 10:45
7 19:53	☿	☍	♋	7 21:06
10 2:26	♄	□	♌	10 4:36
12 8:24	♆	☍	♍	12 9:45
14 1:59	☉	△	♎	14 13:29
16 15:30	♆	△	♏	16 16:35
18 18:32	♆	□	♐	18 19:30
20 21:50	♆	⚹	♑	20 22:41
23 1:39	♄	□	♒	23 2:54
25 8:34	♆	☌	♓	25 9:12
27 4:54	♂	☍	♈	27 18:29
30 6:09	♆	⚹	♉	30 6:29

Last Aspect Dy Hr Mn			☽ Ingress	Dy Hr Mn
1 19:07	♆	□	♊	1 19:16
4 5:07	♄	△	♋	4 6:05
6 12:32	♄	□	♌	6 13:25
8 16:43	♄	⚹	♍	8 17:33
10 5:13	♂	☌	♎	10 19:55
12 21:10	♄	☌	♏	12 22:02
14 17:05	☉	□	♐	15 0:57
17 4:04	♄	⚹	♑	17 5:04
19 9:23	♄	□	♒	19 10:29
21 16:18	♄	△	♓	21 17:32
23 2:25	♂	☍	♈	24 2:49
26 12:53	♄	☍	♉	26 14:31
28 19:47	☿	⚹	♊	29 3:28

☽ Phases & Eclipses Dy Hr Mn		
1 6:16	☽	10♈13
9 7:31	○	18♋26
16 9:09	☾	25♎38
23 7:40	●	2♒42
31 4:11	☽	10♉41
7 21:55	○	18♌32
14 17:05	☾	25♏24
21 22:36	●	2♓42

Astro Data

1 January 2012
Julian Day # 40908
SVP 5♓05'15"
GC 27♐00.4 ⚴ 16♒30.2
Eris 21♈23.5R ⚵ 22♏34.8
⚷ 1♓55.5 ⚶ 5♓05.7
☽ Mean ☊ 12♐57.1

1 February 2012
Julian Day # 40939
SVP 5♓05'10"
GC 27♐00.5 ⚴ 26♒27.0
Eris 21♈26.1 ⚵ 0♐39.5
⚷ 3♓39.8 ⚶ 18♓49.1
☽ Mean ☊ 11♐18.6

March 2012 — LONGITUDE

Day	Sid.Time	☉	0 hr ☽	Noon ☽	True ☊	☿	♀	♂	⚳	♃	♄	♅	♆	♇
1 Th	22 38 47	11♓18 33	10♊10 42	16♊11 01	9♐29.5	28♓40.0	25♈37.5	14♍34.8	14♈35.6	7♉07.3	29♎03.4	3♈12.4	1♓00.4	9♑08.9
2 F	22 42 44	12 18 44	22 14 42	28 22 28	9R 28.8	0♈01.0	26 44.6	14R 11.2	14 58.3	7 18.2	29R 01.0	3 15.7	1 02.7	9 10.1
3 Sa	22 46 40	13 18 53	4♋34 58	10♋52 47	9 26.6	1 16.1	27 51.4	13 47.5	15 21.0	7 29.3	28 58.6	3 19.0	1 04.9	9 11.3
4 Su	22 50 37	14 19 01	17 16 27	23 46 24	9 21.9	2 24.8	28 58.0	13 23.8	15 43.8	7 40.4	28 56.0	3 22.2	1 07.2	9 12.4
5 M	22 54 33	15 19 06	0♌22 59	7♌06 22	9 14.5	3 26.4	0♉04.3	13 00.0	16 06.6	7 51.6	28 53.4	3 25.5	1 09.4	9 13.5
6 Tu	22 58 30	16 19 09	13 56 34	20 53 27	9 04.6	4 20.6	1 10.5	12 36.4	16 29.5	8 03.0	28 50.7	3 28.8	1 11.6	9 14.6
7 W	23 02 26	17 19 10	27 56 42	5♍05 47	8 53.1	5 06.8	2 16.3	12 12.8	16 52.5	8 14.4	28 47.9	3 32.1	1 13.8	9 15.7
8 Th	23 06 23	18 19 10	12♍20 01	19 38 34	8 41.2	5 44.8	3 21.9	11 49.3	17 15.5	8 25.9	28 45.0	3 35.5	1 16.0	9 16.7
9 F	23 10 19	19 19 07	27 00 26	4♎24 34	8 30.1	6 14.1	4 27.3	11 26.1	17 38.5	8 37.5	28 42.1	3 38.8	1 18.2	9 17.7
10 Sa	23 14 16	20 19 02	11♎49 54	19 15 20	8 21.1	6 34.7	5 32.4	11 03.0	18 01.6	8 49.2	28 39.0	3 42.2	1 20.4	9 18.7
11 Su	23 18 13	21 18 56	26 39 51	4♏02 33	8 14.8	6R 46.4	6 37.2	10 40.2	18 24.7	9 01.0	28 35.9	3 45.5	1 22.6	9 19.6
12 M	23 22 09	22 18 48	11♏22 37	18 39 26	8 11.3	6 49.2	7 41.7	10 17.7	18 47.9	9 12.8	28 32.7	3 48.9	1 24.8	9 20.6
13 Tu	23 26 06	23 18 39	25 52 30	3♐01 28	8D 10.1	6 43.4	8 46.0	9 55.6	19 11.1	9 24.8	28 29.4	3 52.3	1 26.9	9 21.4
14 W	23 30 02	24 18 28	10♐06 09	17 06 27	8R 10.1	6 29.3	9 49.9	9 33.8	19 34.4	9 36.8	28 26.1	3 55.7	1 29.1	9 22.3
15 Th	23 33 59	25 18 15	24 02 24	0♑54 06	8 10.1	6 07.2	10 53.6	9 12.5	19 57.7	9 48.9	28 22.7	3 59.1	1 31.2	9 23.1
16 F	23 37 55	26 18 00	7♑41 42	14 25 22	8 08.8	5 37.8	11 57.0	8 51.6	20 21.1	10 01.1	28 19.2	4 02.5	1 33.3	9 23.9
17 Sa	23 41 52	27 17 44	21 05 19	27 41 45	8 05.3	5 01.8	13 00.0	8 31.2	20 44.5	10 13.4	28 15.6	4 05.9	1 35.4	9 24.7
18 Su	23 45 48	28 17 26	4♒14 50	10♒44 45	7 58.9	4 20.1	14 02.7	8 11.3	21 07.9	10 25.7	28 12.0	4 09.3	1 37.5	9 25.4
19 M	23 49 45	29 17 07	17 11 37	23 35 34	7 49.9	3 33.7	15 05.1	7 51.9	21 31.4	10 38.1	28 08.3	4 12.7	1 39.6	9 26.1
20 Tu	23 53 42	0♈16 45	29 56 42	6♓15 04	7 38.8	2 43.6	16 07.1	7 33.2	21 54.9	10 50.6	28 04.6	4 16.1	1 41.7	9 26.8
21 W	23 57 38	1 16 21	12♓30 43	18 43 43	7 26.4	1 51.1	17 08.8	7 15.1	22 18.4	11 03.2	28 00.8	4 19.5	1 43.7	9 27.4
22 Th	0 01 35	2 15 56	24 54 07	1♈01 58	7 14.0	0 57.2	18 10.1	6 57.6	22 42.0	11 15.8	27 56.9	4 23.0	1 45.8	9 28.1
23 F	0 05 31	3 15 28	7♈07 22	13 10 24	7 02.7	0 03.1	19 11.1	6 40.7	23 05.6	11 28.5	27 52.9	4 26.4	1 47.8	9 28.6
24 Sa	0 09 28	4 14 59	19 11 14	25 10 03	6 53.3	29♓10.0	20 11.6	6 24.6	23 29.3	11 41.2	27 49.0	4 29.8	1 49.8	9 29.2
25 Su	0 13 24	5 14 27	1♉07 05	7♉02 37	6 46.4	28 18.7	21 11.7	6 09.1	23 53.0	11 54.0	27 44.9	4 33.2	1 51.8	9 29.7
26 M	0 17 21	6 13 53	12 56 59	18 50 34	6 42.2	27 30.4	22 11.5	5 54.4	24 16.7	12 06.9	27 40.8	4 36.7	1 53.7	9 30.2
27 Tu	0 21 17	7 13 17	24 43 48	0♊37 10	6D 40.4	26 45.7	23 10.8	5 40.4	24 40.4	12 19.8	27 36.7	4 40.1	1 55.7	9 30.7
28 W	0 25 14	8 12 39	6♊31 14	12 26 32	6 40.3	26 05.2	24 09.6	5 27.2	25 04.2	12 32.8	27 32.5	4 43.5	1 57.6	9 31.1
29 Th	0 29 10	9 11 58	18 23 42	24 23 21	6 41.2	25 29.6	25 08.0	5 14.7	25 28.0	12 45.9	27 28.3	4 47.0	1 59.5	9 31.5
30 F	0 33 07	10 11 16	0♋26 10	6♋32 48	6R 41.9	24 59.2	26 05.9	5 03.0	25 51.8	12 59.0	27 24.0	4 50.4	2 01.4	9 31.8
31 Sa	0 37 04	11 10 30	12 43 55	19 00 10	6 41.6	24 34.2	27 03.3	4 52.1	26 15.7	13 12.2	27 19.7	4 53.8	2 03.3	9 32.2

April 2012 — LONGITUDE

Day	Sid.Time	☉	0 hr ☽	Noon ☽	True ☊	☿	♀	♂	⚳	♃	♄	♅	♆	♇
1 Su	0 41 00	12♈09 43	25♋22 07	1♌50 21	6♐39.6	24♓14.9	28♉00.2	4♍41.9	26♈39.6	13♉25.4	27♎15.4	4♈57.2	2♓05.2	9♑32.5
2 M	0 44 57	13 08 53	8♌25 19	15 07 21	6R 35.5	24R 01.2	28 56.5	4R 32.6	27 03.5	13 38.6	27R 11.0	5 00.6	2 07.0	9 32.7
3 Tu	0 48 53	14 08 01	21 56 40	28 53 21	6 29.5	23D 53.3	29 52.3	4 24.0	27 27.4	13 51.9	27 06.6	5 04.0	2 08.8	9 33.0
4 W	0 52 50	15 07 07	5♍57 14	13♍08 01	6 22.0	23 50.9	0♊47.6	4 16.2	27 51.3	14 05.3	27 02.1	5 07.4	2 10.6	9 33.2
5 Th	0 56 46	16 06 10	20 25 09	27 47 54	6 14.0	23 54.0	1 42.2	4 09.2	28 15.3	14 18.7	26 57.7	5 10.8	2 12.4	9 33.4
6 F	1 00 43	17 05 11	5♎15 21	12♎46 25	6 06.5	24 02.5	2 36.2	4 03.0	28 39.3	14 32.2	26 53.2	5 14.2	2 14.2	9 33.5
7 Sa	1 04 39	18 04 10	20 19 54	27 54 34	6 00.4	24 16.1	3 29.6	3 57.6	29 03.3	14 45.6	26 48.7	5 17.5	2 15.9	9 33.6
8 Su	1 08 36	19 03 08	5♏29 07	13♏02 22	5 56.3	24 34.7	4 22.4	3 52.9	29 27.3	14 59.2	26 44.1	5 20.9	2 17.6	9 33.7
9 M	1 12 33	20 02 03	20 33 10	28 00 34	5D 54.4	24 58.0	5 14.4	3 49.0	29 51.3	15 12.8	26 39.6	5 24.2	2 19.3	9 33.7
10 Tu	1 16 29	21 00 57	5♐23 43	12♐41 58	5 54.3	25 25.8	6 05.8	3 45.9	0♉15.4	15 26.4	26 35.0	5 27.6	2 21.0	9R 33.8
11 W	1 20 26	21 59 49	19 54 52	27 02 06	5 55.3	25 57.9	6 56.4	3 43.6	0 39.4	15 40.0	26 30.4	5 30.9	2 22.6	9 33.8
12 Th	1 24 22	22 58 39	4♑03 31	10♑59 06	5R 56.6	26 34.2	7 46.3	3 42.0	1 03.5	15 53.7	26 25.8	5 34.2	2 24.2	9 33.7
13 F	1 28 19	23 57 27	17 48 58	24 33 18	5 57.1	27 14.3	8 35.5	3D 41.1	1 27.6	16 07.5	26 21.2	5 37.5	2 25.8	9 33.6
14 Sa	1 32 15	24 56 14	1♒12 20	7♒46 24	5 56.3	27 58.2	9 23.8	3 41.0	1 51.7	16 21.2	26 16.6	5 40.8	2 27.4	9 33.5
15 Su	1 36 12	25 54 59	14 15 47	20 40 51	5 53.7	28 45.6	10 11.3	3 41.6	2 15.9	16 35.0	26 12.0	5 44.1	2 28.9	9 33.4
16 M	1 40 08	26 53 42	27 01 56	3♓19 22	5 49.3	29 36.3	10 57.9	3 42.9	2 40.0	16 48.9	26 07.4	5 47.3	2 30.5	9 33.2
17 Tu	1 44 05	27 52 24	9♓33 28	15 44 31	5 43.6	0♈30.2	11 43.7	3 45.0	3 04.2	17 02.7	26 02.8	5 50.6	2 32.0	9 33.0
18 W	1 48 02	28 51 04	21 52 49	27 58 38	5 37.0	1 27.2	12 28.5	3 47.8	3 28.3	17 16.6	25 58.2	5 53.8	2 33.4	9 32.8
19 Th	1 51 58	29 49 42	4♈02 11	10♈03 42	5 30.3	2 27.1	13 12.4	3 51.2	3 52.5	17 30.5	25 53.6	5 57.0	2 34.9	9 32.5
20 F	1 55 55	0♉48 18	16 03 25	22 01 32	5 24.1	3 29.8	13 55.2	3 55.4	4 16.7	17 44.5	25 49.0	6 00.2	2 36.3	9 32.3
21 Sa	1 59 51	1 46 52	27 58 17	3♉53 52	5 19.2	4 35.1	14 37.1	4 00.3	4 40.9	17 58.5	25 44.4	6 03.4	2 37.7	9 31.9
22 Su	2 03 48	2 45 24	9♉48 31	15 42 31	5 15.8	5 43.0	15 17.8	4 05.8	5 05.1	18 12.5	25 39.8	6 06.5	2 39.0	9 31.6
23 M	2 07 44	3 43 55	21 36 06	27 29 35	5D 14.1	6 53.4	15 57.5	4 12.0	5 29.3	18 26.5	25 35.3	6 09.7	2 40.4	9 31.2
24 Tu	2 11 41	4 42 23	3♊23 18	9♊17 37	5 13.8	8 06.1	16 35.9	4 18.8	5 53.6	18 40.5	25 30.8	6 12.8	2 41.7	9 30.8
25 W	2 15 37	5 40 50	15 12 56	21 09 39	5 14.8	9 21.2	17 13.2	4 26.3	6 17.8	18 54.6	25 26.3	6 15.9	2 43.0	9 30.4
26 Th	2 19 34	6 39 15	27 08 16	3♋09 15	5 16.4	10 38.5	17 49.2	4 34.4	6 42.0	19 08.7	25 21.8	6 19.0	2 44.2	9 29.9
27 F	2 23 31	7 37 37	9♋13 08	15 20 26	5 18.1	11 58.0	18 23.9	4 43.2	7 06.2	19 22.8	25 17.3	6 22.0	2 45.4	9 29.4
28 Sa	2 27 27	8 35 57	21 31 44	27 47 33	5R 19.4	13 19.6	18 57.2	4 52.5	7 30.5	19 36.9	25 12.9	6 25.1	2 46.6	9 28.9
29 Su	2 31 24	9 34 16	4♌08 27	10♌34 55	5 19.8	14 43.3	19 29.1	5 02.5	7 54.7	19 51.1	25 08.5	6 28.1	2 47.8	9 28.3
30 M	2 35 20	10 32 32	17 07 27	23 46 25	5 19.2	16 09.0	19 59.5	5 13.0	8 18.9	20 05.2	25 04.1	6 31.1	2 48.9	9 27.8

Astro Data (Dy Hr Mn)	Planet Ingress (Dy Hr Mn)	Last Aspect (Dy Hr Mn)	☽ Ingress (Dy Hr Mn)	Last Aspect (Dy Hr Mn)	☽ Ingress (Dy Hr Mn)	☽ Phases & Eclipses (Dy Hr Mn)	Astro Data
☿0N 1 3:46	☿ ♈ 2 11:42	2 13:15 ♄ △	♋ 2 15:09	1 4:21 ♀ ⚹	♌ 1 8:37	1 1:23 ☽ 10♊52	1 March 2012
⚳0N 4 20:21	♀ ♉ 5 10:26	4 22:18 ♀ □	♌ 4 23:19	3 13:48 ♀ □	♍ 3 13:54	8 9:41 ○ 18♍13	Julian Day # 40968
☽0S 8 10:07	☉ ♈ 20 5:16	7 1:28 ♄ ⚹	♍ 7 3:28	5 5:38 ☿ ☍	♎ 5 15:33	15 1:26 ☾ 24♐52	SVP 5♓05'06"
☿ R 12 7:49	☿ ♓R 23 13:23	8 9:41 ☉ ☍	♎ 9 4:51	7 10:16 ♄ ☌	♏ 7 15:19	22 14:38 ● 2♈22	GC 27♐00.6 ⚴ 6♓05.5
♃△♇ 13 4:45		11 3:10 ♄ ☌	♏ 11 5:25	9 6:57 ☿ △	♐ 9 15:13	30 19:42 ☽ 10♋30	Eris 21♈37.3 ⚵ 5♐41.1
☉0N 20 5:15	♀ ♊ 3 15:19	12 18:31 ☉ △	♐ 13 6:55	11 11:07 ♄ ⚹	♑ 11 17:03		⚷ 5♓33.8 ⚶ 2♈11.1
☽0N 21 11:32	⚳ ♉ 9 20:41	15 7:35 ♄ ⚹	♑ 15 10:25	13 17:06 ☿ ⚹	♒ 13 21:49	6 19:20 ○ 17♎23	☽ Mean ☊ 9♐46.5
☿0S 28 21:19	☿ ♈ 16 22:43	17 13:02 ♄ □	♒ 17 16:13	15 22:43 ☉ ⚹	♓ 16 5:39	13 10:51 ☾ 23♑55	
	☉ ♉ 19 16:13	19 20:32 ♄ △	♓ 20 0:06	17 14:35 ♃ ⚹	♈ 18 16:00	21 7:20 ● 1♉35	1 April 2012
☿ D 4 10:12		21 8:40 ♀ ⚹	♈ 22 9:58	20 19:36 ♄ ☍	♉ 21 4:06	29 9:59 ☽ 9♌29	Julian Day # 40999
☽0S 4 20:35		24 17:18 ♄ ☍	♉ 24 21:44	22 17:11 ♃ ☌	♊ 23 17:06		SVP 5♓05'03"
♇ R 10 16:25		27 4:36 ☿ ⚹	♊ 27 10:44	25 20:32 ♄ △	♋ 26 5:43		GC 27♐00.6 ⚴ 16♓14.0
♂ D 14 3:54		29 18:06 ♄ △	♋ 29 23:08	28 7:07 ♄ □	♌ 28 16:12		Eris 21♈55.6 ⚵ 6♐57.2R
☽0N 17 16:52				30 14:18 ♄ ⚹	♍ 30 23:03		⚷ 7♓30.2 ⚶ 16♈35.9
☿0N 22 22:52							☽ Mean ☊ 8♐07.9

LONGITUDE — May 2012

Day	Sid.Time	☉	0 hr ☽	Noon ☽	True☊	☿	♀	♂	⚳	♃	♄	♅	♆	♇
1 Tu	2 39 17	11♉30 46	0♍32 08	7♍24 48	5♐17.5	17♈36.7	20♊28.4	5♍24.1	8♉43.2	20♉19.4	24♎59.8	6♈34.0	2♓50.0	9♑27.2
2 W	2 43 13	12 28 58	14 24 28	21 31 02	5R15.0	19 06.5	20 55.7	5 35.7	9 07.4	20 33.5	24R55.5	6 37.0	2 51.1	9R26.5
3 Th	2 47 10	13 27 08	28 44 14	6♎03 35	5 12.1	20 38.2	21 21.4	5 47.9	9 31.6	20 47.7	24 51.2	6 39.9	2 52.2	9 25.9
4 F	2 51 06	14 25 16	13♎28 26	20 57 57	5 09.3	22 11.8	21 45.3	6 00.6	9 55.8	21 01.9	24 47.0	6 42.8	2 53.2	9 25.2
5 Sa	2 55 03	15 23 22	28 31 07	6♏06 49	5 07.1	23 47.4	22 07.5	6 13.9	10 20.1	21 16.1	24 42.9	6 45.6	2 54.2	9 24.5
6 Su	2 59 00	16 21 27	13♏43 50	21 20 55	5D05.8	25 25.0	22 27.9	6 27.7	10 44.3	21 30.3	24 38.7	6 48.4	2 55.1	9 23.7
7 M	3 02 56	17 19 30	28 56 48	6♐30 19	5 05.4	27 04.4	22 46.3	6 41.9	11 08.5	21 44.5	24 34.7	6 51.3	2 56.1	9 23.0
8 Tu	3 06 53	18 17 31	14♐00 22	21 26 02	5 05.9	28 45.9	23 02.9	6 56.7	11 32.7	21 58.7	24 30.6	6 54.0	2 57.0	9 22.2
9 W	3 10 49	19 15 32	28 46 29	6♑01 09	5 06.9	0♉29.2	23 17.4	7 11.9	11 56.9	22 12.9	24 26.7	6 56.8	2 57.8	9 21.4
10 Th	3 14 46	20 13 30	13♑09 34	20 11 29	5 08.0	2 14.5	23 29.8	7 27.6	12 21.1	22 27.2	24 22.7	6 59.5	2 58.7	9 20.5
11 F	3 18 42	21 11 28	27 06 47	3♒55 31	5 09.0	4 01.8	23 40.2	7 43.8	12 45.3	22 41.4	24 18.9	7 02.2	2 59.5	9 19.7
12 Sa	3 22 39	22 09 24	10♒37 50	17 13 58	5R09.5	5 51.0	23 48.4	8 00.4	13 09.5	22 55.6	24 15.1	7 04.9	3 00.2	9 18.8
13 Su	3 26 35	23 07 18	23 44 16	0♓09 07	5 09.5	7 42.2	23 54.4	8 17.5	13 33.7	23 09.9	24 11.3	7 07.5	3 01.0	9 17.8
14 M	3 30 32	24 05 12	6♓28 56	12 44 12	5 08.9	9 35.3	23 58.1	8 35.0	13 57.9	23 24.1	24 07.6	7 10.1	3 01.7	9 16.9
15 Tu	3 34 29	25 03 04	18 55 23	25 02 55	5 07.9	11 30.3	23R59.5	8 53.0	14 22.1	23 38.3	24 04.0	7 12.6	3 02.4	9 15.9
16 W	3 38 25	26 00 55	1♈07 19	7♈08 59	5 06.7	13 27.2	23 58.6	9 11.3	14 46.2	23 52.5	24 00.4	7 15.2	3 03.0	9 15.0
17 Th	3 42 22	26 58 45	13 08 23	19 05 54	5 05.5	15 26.0	23 55.3	9 30.1	15 10.4	24 06.7	23 56.9	7 17.7	3 03.6	9 14.0
18 F	3 46 18	27 56 34	25 01 57	0♉56 53	5 04.4	17 26.7	23 49.6	9 49.3	15 34.5	24 20.9	23 53.5	7 20.1	3 04.2	9 12.9
19 Sa	3 50 15	28 54 21	6♉51 04	12 44 47	5 03.7	19 29.1	23 41.5	10 08.9	15 58.6	24 35.1	23 50.1	7 22.6	3 04.7	9 11.9
20 Su	3 54 11	29 52 07	18 38 23	24 32 09	5D03.3	21 33.2	23 31.0	10 28.9	16 22.8	24 49.3	23 46.9	7 25.0	3 05.3	9 10.8
21 M	3 58 08	0♊49 52	0♊26 21	6♊21 17	5 03.2	23 39.0	23 18.0	10 49.2	16 46.9	25 03.5	23 43.6	7 27.3	3 05.7	9 09.7
22 Tu	4 02 04	1 47 35	12 17 14	18 14 27	5 03.3	25 46.1	23 02.7	11 10.0	17 10.9	25 17.7	23 40.5	7 29.7	3 06.2	9 08.6
23 W	4 06 01	2 45 17	24 13 14	0♋13 53	5 03.5	27 54.6	22 45.0	11 31.1	17 35.0	25 31.8	23 37.4	7 32.0	3 06.6	9 07.5
24 Th	4 09 58	3 42 58	6♋16 43	12 22 01	5 03.7	0♊04.3	22 25.0	11 52.6	17 59.1	25 46.0	23 34.5	7 34.2	3 07.0	9 06.3
25 F	4 13 54	4 40 37	18 30 08	24 41 25	5R03.8	2 14.8	22 02.7	12 14.4	18 23.1	26 00.1	23 31.5	7 36.4	3 07.4	9 05.1
26 Sa	4 17 51	5 38 15	0♌56 13	7♌14 54	5 03.8	4 26.1	21 38.2	12 36.6	18 47.1	26 14.2	23 28.7	7 38.6	3 07.7	9 04.0
27 Su	4 21 47	6 35 51	13 37 49	20 05 21	5 03.7	6 37.9	21 11.7	12 59.1	19 11.1	26 28.3	23 26.0	7 40.8	3 08.0	9 02.7
28 M	4 25 44	7 33 26	26 37 48	3♍15 31	5D03.7	8 49.8	20 43.2	13 21.9	19 35.1	26 42.4	23 23.3	7 42.9	3 08.2	9 01.5
29 Tu	4 29 40	8 30 59	9♍58 43	16 47 38	5 03.7	11 01.7	20 13.0	13 45.1	19 59.1	26 56.5	23 20.7	7 44.9	3 08.4	9 00.3
30 W	4 33 37	9 28 31	23 42 23	0♎42 59	5 03.9	13 13.3	19 41.0	14 08.6	20 23.0	27 10.5	23 18.2	7 46.9	3 08.6	8 59.0
31 Th	4 37 33	10 26 01	7♎49 21	15 01 16	5 04.3	15 24.2	19 07.6	14 32.4	20 46.9	27 24.5	23 15.8	7 48.9	3 08.8	8 57.7

LONGITUDE — June 2012

Day	Sid.Time	☉	0 hr ☽	Noon ☽	True☊	☿	♀	♂	⚳	♃	♄	♅	♆	♇
1 F	4 41 30	11♊23 31	22♎18 22	29♎40 09	5♐04.8	17♊34.3	18♊32.9	14♍56.5	21♉10.8	27♉38.5	23♎13.5	7♈50.9	3♓08.9	8♑56.4
2 Sa	4 45 27	12 20 59	7♏05 58	14♏35 00	5 05.3	19 43.2	17R57.1	15 20.9	21 34.7	27 52.5	23R11.3	7 52.8	3 09.0	8R55.1
3 Su	4 49 23	13 18 26	22 06 19	29 38 56	5R05.6	21 50.8	17 20.4	15 45.5	21 58.5	28 06.4	23 09.1	7 54.6	3 09.1	8 53.8
4 M	4 53 20	14 15 52	7♐11 45	14♐43 38	5 05.6	23 56.7	16 43.1	16 10.5	22 22.4	28 20.3	23 07.1	7 56.5	3R09.1	8 52.5
5 Tu	4 57 16	15 13 17	22 13 29	29 40 15	5 05.0	26 01.0	16 05.5	16 35.8	22 46.2	28 34.2	23 05.1	7 58.3	3 09.1	8 51.1
6 W	5 01 13	16 10 41	7♑02 59	14♑20 49	5 04.0	28 03.3	15 27.7	17 01.3	23 09.9	28 48.1	23 03.3	8 00.0	3 09.0	8 49.8
7 Th	5 05 09	17 08 04	21 33 05	28 39 13	5 02.6	0♋03.6	14 50.1	17 27.1	23 33.7	29 01.9	23 01.5	8 01.7	3 09.0	8 48.4
8 F	5 09 06	18 05 27	5♒38 51	12♒31 48	5 01.1	2 01.7	14 12.8	17 53.1	23 57.4	29 15.7	22 59.8	8 03.4	3 08.9	8 47.0
9 Sa	5 13 02	19 02 49	19 17 59	25 57 31	4 59.8	3 57.6	13 36.2	18 19.4	24 21.1	29 29.5	22 58.2	8 05.0	3 08.7	8 45.6
10 Su	5 16 59	20 00 10	2♓30 35	8♓57 32	4D58.8	5 51.1	13 00.4	18 46.0	24 44.8	29 43.2	22 56.7	8 06.5	3 08.6	8 44.2
11 M	5 20 56	20 57 31	15 18 44	21 34 41	4 58.5	7 42.3	12 25.6	19 12.8	25 08.4	29 56.9	22 55.3	8 08.1	3 08.4	8 42.8
12 Tu	5 24 52	21 54 52	27 45 53	3♈52 54	4 58.9	9 31.1	11 52.1	19 39.9	25 32.0	0♊10.6	22 54.0	8 09.6	3 08.1	8 41.3
13 W	5 28 49	22 52 12	9♈56 17	15 56 37	4 59.9	11 17.5	11 20.1	20 07.2	25 55.6	0 24.2	22 52.8	8 11.0	3 07.9	8 39.9
14 Th	5 32 45	23 49 32	21 54 30	27 50 28	5 01.3	13 01.4	10 49.8	20 34.7	26 19.1	0 37.8	22 51.6	8 12.4	3 07.6	8 38.4
15 F	5 36 42	24 46 51	3♉45 04	9♉38 50	5 02.9	14 42.8	10 21.2	21 02.5	26 42.7	0 51.4	22 50.6	8 13.7	3 07.2	8 37.0
16 Sa	5 40 38	25 44 10	15 32 15	21 25 47	5 04.1	16 21.7	9 54.5	21 30.5	27 06.1	1 04.9	22 49.7	8 15.0	3 06.9	8 35.5
17 Su	5 44 35	26 41 28	27 19 51	3♊14 51	5R04.7	17 58.1	9 29.9	21 58.8	27 29.6	1 18.4	22 48.9	8 16.3	3 06.5	8 34.0
18 M	5 48 31	27 38 46	9♊11 09	15 09 04	5 04.3	19 31.9	9 07.4	22 27.3	27 53.0	1 31.8	22 48.1	8 17.5	3 06.1	8 32.6
19 Tu	5 52 28	28 36 04	21 08 53	27 10 52	5 02.8	21 03.2	8 47.1	22 56.0	28 16.4	1 45.2	22 47.5	8 18.7	3 05.6	8 31.1
20 W	5 56 25	29 33 21	3♋15 14	9♋22 11	5 00.2	22 32.0	8 29.1	23 24.9	28 39.7	1 58.6	22 47.0	8 19.8	3 05.1	8 29.6
21 Th	6 00 21	0♋30 38	15 31 54	21 44 32	4 56.6	23 58.1	8 13.5	23 54.1	29 03.0	2 11.9	22 46.5	8 20.9	3 04.6	8 28.1
22 F	6 04 18	1 27 54	28 00 14	4♌19 07	4 52.5	25 21.6	8 00.2	24 23.4	29 26.3	2 25.1	22 46.2	8 21.9	3 04.1	8 26.6
23 Sa	6 08 14	2 25 09	10♌41 20	17 06 58	4 48.3	26 42.5	7 49.3	24 53.0	29 49.5	2 38.3	22 46.0	8 22.9	3 03.5	8 25.1
24 Su	6 12 11	3 22 24	23 36 09	0♍09 00	4 44.6	28 00.6	7 40.7	25 22.8	0♊12.7	2 51.5	22D45.8	8 23.8	3 02.9	8 23.6
25 M	6 16 07	4 19 38	6♍45 38	13 26 09	4 41.8	29 16.0	7 34.5	25 52.7	0 35.8	3 04.6	22 45.8	8 24.7	3 02.3	8 22.0
26 Tu	6 20 04	5 16 52	20 10 39	26 59 12	4D40.3	0♌28.7	7 30.7	26 22.9	0 58.9	3 17.6	22 45.9	8 25.6	3 01.6	8 20.5
27 W	6 24 00	6 14 05	3♎51 53	10♎48 42	4 40.1	1 38.4	7D29.3	26 53.3	1 21.9	3 30.6	22 46.0	8 26.3	3 00.9	8 19.0
28 Th	6 27 57	7 11 18	17 49 38	24 54 35	4 41.0	2 45.2	7 30.1	27 23.8	1 44.9	3 43.6	22 46.3	8 27.1	3 00.2	8 17.5
29 F	6 31 54	8 08 30	2♏03 23	9♏15 49	4 42.4	3 49.0	7 33.3	27 54.5	2 07.9	3 56.5	22 46.7	8 27.8	2 59.5	8 16.0
30 Sa	6 35 50	9 05 42	16 31 30	23 49 59	4R43.6	4 49.7	7 38.6	28 25.5	2 30.8	4 09.3	22 47.1	8 28.4	2 58.7	8 14.4

Astro Data	Dy Hr Mn
☽ 0S	2 6:12
♃∠♅	8 2:10
☽ 0N	14 22:12
♀ R	15 14:34
♃⚻♄	16 22:43
♃⚼♇	17 23:23
☽ 0S	29 14:02
♆ R	4 21:05
☽ 0N	11 5:09
♅□♇	24 9:13
♃□♆	25 7:57
♄ D	25 8:01
☽ 0S	25 20:26
♀ D	27 15:08

Planet Ingress		Dy Hr Mn
☿	♉	9 5:16
☉	♊	20 15:17
☿	♊	24 11:13
☿	♋	7 11:17
♃	♊	11 17:23
☉	♋	20 23:10
⚳	♊	23 22:53
☿	♌	26 2:25

Last Aspect Dy Hr Mn			☽ Ingress	Dy Hr Mn
2 10:59	♀	□	♎	3 2:05
4 18:03	♄	☌	♏	5 2:21
6 12:15	♃	☍	♐	7 1:40
9 1:35	☿	△	♑	9 2:01
10 19:12	♄	□	♒	11 5:04
13 0:53	♄	△	♓	13 11:43
15 12:00	☉	⚹	♈	15 21:47
17 21:45	♄	☍	♉	18 10:04
20 12:36	♃	☌	♊	20 23:06
22 22:52	♄	△	♋	23 11:32
25 14:35	♃	⚹	♌	25 22:12
27 23:55	♃	□	♍	28 6:07
30 5:51	♃	△	♎	30 10:47

Last Aspect Dy Hr Mn			☽ Ingress	Dy Hr Mn
1 1:32	♄	☌	♏	1 12:32
3 9:31	♃	☍	♐	3 12:33
5 5:09	☿	☍	♑	5 12:32
7 12:39	♃	△	♒	7 14:18
9 18:34	♃	□	♓	9 19:23
11 10:42	☉	□	♈	12 4:22
14 3:10	☉	⚹	♉	14 16:23
16 12:10	♂	△	♊	17 5:25
19 15:03	☉	☌	♋	19 17:35
21 16:49	☿	☌	♌	22 3:48
23 22:27	♄	⚹	♍	24 11:44
26 10:54	♂	☌	♎	26 17:16
28 8:23	♄	☌	♏	28 20:33
30 19:47	♂	⚹	♐	30 22:05

☽ Phases & Eclipses Dy Hr Mn	
6 3:36	○ 16♏01
12 21:48	☾ 22♒33
20 23:48	● 0♊21
20 23:53:52	● A 05'36"
28 20:17	☽ 7♍53
4 11:13	○ 14♐14
4 11:04	● P 0.370
11 10:42	☾ 20♓54
19 15:03	● 28♊43
27 3:31	☽ 5♎54

Astro Data

1 May 2012
Julian Day # 41029
SVP 5♓05'00"
GC 27♐00.7 ⚴ 25♓23.7
Eris 22♈15.1 ⚵ 3♐19.6R
⚷ 8♓56.6 ⚶ 0♉21.7
☽ Mean ☊ 6♐32.6

1 June 2012
Julian Day # 41060
SVP 5♓04'56"
GC 27♐00.8 ⚴ 3♈33.1
Eris 22♈32.2 ⚵ 26♏37.5R
⚷ 9♓41.9 ⚶ 14♉06.9
☽ Mean ☊ 4♐54.1

July 2012 LONGITUDE

Day	Sid.Time	☉	0 hr ☽	Noon☽	True☊	☿	♀	♂	⚳	♃	♄	♅	♆	♇
1 Su	6 39 47	10♋02 53	1♐10 44	8♐33 04	4♐43.9	5♌47.2	7♊46.2	28♍56.6	2♊53.6	4♊22.1	22♎47.7	8♈29.0	2♓57.9	8♑12.9
2 M	6 43 43	11 00 05	15 56 14	23 19 24	4R42.7	6 41.4	7 55.8	29 27.8	3 16.4	4 34.8	22 48.4	8 29.6	2R57.0	8R11.4
3 Tu	6 47 40	11 57 16	0♑41 41	8♑02 10	4 39.8	7 32.3	8 07.6	29 59.3	3 39.2	4 47.4	22 49.1	8 30.1	2 56.2	8 09.9
4 W	6 51 36	12 54 27	15 19 57	22 34 11	4 35.3	8 19.6	8 21.4	0♎30.9	4 01.9	5 00.0	22 50.0	8 30.5	2 55.3	8 08.4
5 Th	6 55 33	13 51 37	29 44 05	6♒48 59	4 29.6	9 03.3	8 37.2	1 02.7	4 24.5	5 12.5	22 51.0	8 31.0	2 54.4	8 06.9
6 F	6 59 29	14 48 48	13♒48 19	20 41 42	4 23.4	9 43.2	8 54.9	1 34.6	4 47.1	5 25.0	22 52.0	8 31.3	2 53.5	8 05.4
7 Sa	7 03 26	15 46 00	27 28 52	4♓09 42	4 17.5	10 19.2	9 14.5	2 06.8	5 09.7	5 37.4	22 53.2	8 31.6	2 52.5	8 03.8
8 Su	7 07 23	16 43 11	10♓44 14	17 12 39	4 12.6	10 51.2	9 35.8	2 39.0	5 32.2	5 49.7	22 54.4	8 31.9	2 51.5	8 02.3
9 M	7 11 19	17 40 23	23 35 12	29 52 18	4 09.2	11 19.1	9 58.9	3 11.5	5 54.6	6 01.9	22 55.8	8 32.1	2 50.5	8 00.8
10 Tu	7 15 16	18 37 35	6♈04 24	12♈12 01	4D07.5	11 42.7	10 23.7	3 44.1	6 17.0	6 14.1	22 57.2	8 32.3	2 49.5	7 59.4
11 W	7 19 12	19 34 48	18 15 46	24 16 15	4 07.4	12 01.8	10 50.0	4 16.8	6 39.3	6 26.2	22 58.8	8 32.4	2 48.4	7 57.9
12 Th	7 23 09	20 32 01	0♉14 06	6♉09 58	4 08.3	12 16.5	11 18.0	4 49.8	7 01.6	6 38.3	23 00.4	8R32.4	2 47.3	7 56.4
13 F	7 27 05	21 29 15	12 04 30	17 58 21	4 09.7	12 26.5	11 47.4	5 22.9	7 23.8	6 50.2	23 02.1	8 32.5	2 46.2	7 54.9
14 Sa	7 31 02	22 26 29	23 52 07	29 46 25	4R10.7	12R31.7	12 18.3	5 56.1	7 45.9	7 02.1	23 04.0	8 32.4	2 45.1	7 53.5
15 Su	7 34 58	23 23 44	5♊41 47	11♊38 44	4 10.4	12 32.2	12 50.5	6 29.5	8 08.0	7 13.9	23 05.9	8 32.4	2 43.9	7 52.0
16 M	7 38 55	24 21 00	17 37 45	23 39 16	4 08.4	12 27.8	13 24.1	7 03.0	8 30.0	7 25.7	23 07.9	8 32.2	2 42.7	7 50.6
17 Tu	7 42 52	25 18 16	29 43 36	5♋51 06	4 04.3	12 18.6	13 59.0	7 36.7	8 52.0	7 37.3	23 10.0	8 32.1	2 41.5	7 49.1
18 W	7 46 48	26 15 32	12♋01 59	18 16 26	3 58.0	12 04.7	14 35.1	8 10.5	9 13.8	7 48.9	23 12.2	8 31.8	2 40.3	7 47.7
19 Th	7 50 45	27 12 49	24 34 32	0♌56 22	3 49.9	11 46.0	15 12.4	8 44.5	9 35.6	8 00.4	23 14.5	8 31.6	2 39.1	7 46.3
20 F	7 54 41	28 10 06	7♌21 55	13 51 07	3 40.6	11 22.9	15 50.8	9 18.7	9 57.4	8 11.8	23 16.9	8 31.3	2 37.8	7 44.9
21 Sa	7 58 38	29 07 24	20 23 52	27 00 02	3 31.3	10 55.6	16 30.3	9 52.9	10 19.0	8 23.1	23 19.4	8 30.9	2 36.5	7 43.5
22 Su	8 02 34	0♌04 42	3♍39 26	10♍21 56	3 22.7	10 24.4	17 10.9	10 27.4	10 40.6	8 34.3	23 22.0	8 30.5	2 35.2	7 42.1
23 M	8 06 31	1 02 00	17 07 19	23 55 26	3 15.8	9 49.6	17 52.5	11 01.9	11 02.1	8 45.4	23 24.7	8 30.0	2 33.9	7 40.7
24 Tu	8 10 27	1 59 19	0♎46 07	7♎39 15	3 11.1	9 11.7	18 35.1	11 36.6	11 23.5	8 56.5	23 27.5	8 29.5	2 32.5	7 39.4
25 W	8 14 24	2 56 38	14 34 42	21 32 21	3D08.7	8 31.4	19 18.5	12 11.4	11 44.9	9 07.4	23 30.3	8 28.9	2 31.2	7 38.0
26 Th	8 18 21	3 53 58	28 32 07	5♏33 54	3 08.2	7 49.3	20 02.9	12 46.4	12 06.2	9 18.3	23 33.2	8 28.3	2 29.8	7 36.7
27 F	8 22 17	4 51 18	12♏37 38	19 43 09	3R08.7	7 05.9	20 48.2	13 21.5	12 27.3	9 29.0	23 36.3	8 27.7	2 28.4	7 35.4
28 Sa	8 26 14	5 48 38	26 50 20	3♐58 56	3 09.0	6 22.2	21 34.3	13 56.7	12 48.4	9 39.7	23 39.4	8 27.0	2 27.0	7 34.1
29 Su	8 30 10	6 45 59	11♐08 43	18 19 19	3 08.2	5 38.8	22 21.3	14 32.1	13 09.5	9 50.2	23 42.6	8 26.3	2 25.6	7 32.8
30 M	8 34 07	7 43 20	25 30 20	2♑41 16	3 05.2	4 56.6	23 09.0	15 07.6	13 30.4	10 00.7	23 45.9	8 25.5	2 24.1	7 31.5
31 Tu	8 38 03	8 40 42	9♑51 33	17 00 36	2 59.6	4 16.3	23 57.5	15 43.2	13 51.3	10 11.0	23 49.3	8 24.6	2 22.7	7 30.3

August 2012 LONGITUDE

Day	Sid.Time	☉	0 hr ☽	Noon☽	True☊	☿	♀	♂	⚳	♃	♄	♅	♆	♇
1 W	8 42 00	9♌38 05	24♑07 44	1♒12 20	2♐51.6	3♌38.7	24♊46.7	16♎18.9	14♊12.0	10♊21.3	23♎52.7	8♈23.8	2♓21.2	7♑29.1
2 Th	8 45 57	10 35 29	8♒13 43	15 11 17	2R41.6	3R04.6	25 36.6	16 54.7	14 32.7	10 31.4	23 56.3	8R22.8	2R19.7	7R27.8
3 F	8 49 53	11 32 53	22 04 30	28 52 56	2 30.8	2 34.7	26 27.2	17 30.7	14 53.2	10 41.5	23 59.9	8 21.9	2 18.2	7 26.6
4 Sa	8 53 50	12 30 18	5♓36 12	12♓14 06	2 20.1	2 09.5	27 18.5	18 06.8	15 13.7	10 51.4	24 03.6	8 20.9	2 16.7	7 25.5
5 Su	8 57 46	13 27 45	18 46 32	25 13 29	2 10.7	1 49.6	28 10.4	18 43.0	15 34.1	11 01.2	24 07.4	8 19.8	2 15.2	7 24.3
6 M	9 01 43	14 25 13	1♈35 08	7♈51 42	2 03.4	1 35.4	29 03.0	19 19.3	15 54.4	11 10.9	24 11.3	8 18.7	2 13.6	7 23.2
7 Tu	9 05 39	15 22 41	14 03 32	20 11 04	1 58.4	1D27.4	29 56.1	19 55.7	16 14.6	11 20.5	24 15.2	8 17.6	2 12.1	7 22.0
8 W	9 09 36	16 20 12	26 14 49	2♉15 21	1 55.8	1 25.8	0♋49.9	20 32.3	16 34.7	11 30.0	24 19.2	8 16.4	2 10.5	7 20.9
9 Th	9 13 32	17 17 43	8♉13 17	14 09 15	1D54.9	1 31.0	1 44.2	21 09.0	16 54.7	11 39.4	24 23.3	8 15.2	2 09.0	7 19.8
10 F	9 17 29	18 15 16	20 03 56	25 58 02	1R55.0	1 43.0	2 39.0	21 45.8	17 14.6	11 48.6	24 27.5	8 13.9	2 07.4	7 18.8
11 Sa	9 21 25	19 12 50	1♊52 13	7♊47 10	1 54.9	2 01.9	3 34.3	22 22.7	17 34.3	11 57.8	24 31.8	8 12.6	2 05.8	7 17.7
12 Su	9 25 22	20 10 26	13 43 32	19 41 58	1 53.7	2 27.9	4 30.2	22 59.7	17 54.0	12 06.8	24 36.1	8 11.3	2 04.2	7 16.7
13 M	9 29 19	21 08 03	25 43 03	1♋47 18	1 50.5	3 00.9	5 26.5	23 36.9	18 13.5	12 15.6	24 40.5	8 09.9	2 02.6	7 15.7
14 Tu	9 33 15	22 05 42	7♋55 14	14 07 13	1 44.8	3 40.8	6 23.3	24 14.1	18 33.0	12 24.4	24 45.0	8 08.5	2 01.0	7 14.8
15 W	9 37 12	23 03 22	20 23 37	26 44 39	1 36.4	4 27.6	7 20.6	24 51.5	18 52.3	12 33.0	24 49.6	8 07.0	1 59.4	7 13.8
16 Th	9 41 08	24 01 03	3♌10 28	9♌41 05	1 25.8	5 21.1	8 18.3	25 29.0	19 11.5	12 41.5	24 54.2	8 05.5	1 57.8	7 12.9
17 F	9 45 05	24 58 46	16 16 27	22 56 25	1 13.7	6 21.2	9 16.5	26 06.6	19 30.6	12 49.9	24 58.9	8 04.0	1 56.2	7 12.0
18 Sa	9 49 01	25 56 30	29 40 41	6♍28 56	1 01.4	7 27.6	10 15.0	26 44.3	19 49.5	12 58.1	25 03.7	8 02.4	1 54.5	7 11.1
19 Su	9 52 58	26 54 15	13♍20 46	20 15 42	0 50.0	8 40.1	11 14.0	27 22.1	20 08.4	13 06.2	25 08.6	8 00.8	1 52.9	7 10.2
20 M	9 56 54	27 52 02	27 13 16	4♎12 59	0 40.6	9 58.4	12 13.3	28 00.1	20 27.1	13 14.1	25 13.5	7 59.1	1 51.2	7 09.4
21 Tu	10 00 51	28 49 49	11♎14 21	18 16 58	0 33.9	11 22.1	13 13.0	28 38.1	20 45.6	13 22.0	25 18.5	7 57.4	1 49.6	7 08.6
22 W	10 04 48	29 47 38	25 20 25	2♏24 23	0 30.0	12 51.0	14 13.1	29 16.3	21 04.0	13 29.6	25 23.5	7 55.7	1 48.0	7 07.8
23 Th	10 08 44	0♍45 28	9♏28 34	16 32 45	0D28.4	14 24.5	15 13.5	29 54.5	21 22.3	13 37.2	25 28.6	7 53.9	1 46.3	7 07.1
24 F	10 12 41	1 43 19	23 36 46	0♐40 29	0R28.2	16 02.4	16 14.3	0♏32.9	21 40.5	13 44.6	25 33.8	7 52.2	1 44.7	7 06.3
25 Sa	10 16 37	2 41 12	7♐43 47	14 46 34	0 28.0	17 44.0	17 15.4	1 11.4	21 58.5	13 51.8	25 39.1	7 50.3	1 43.0	7 05.6
26 Su	10 20 34	3 39 06	21 48 43	28 50 07	0 26.6	19 29.1	18 16.8	1 49.9	22 16.4	13 58.9	25 44.4	7 48.5	1 41.4	7 05.0
27 M	10 24 30	4 37 00	5♑50 36	12♑49 59	0 22.9	21 17.1	19 18.6	2 28.6	22 34.1	14 05.8	25 49.8	7 46.6	1 39.8	7 04.3
28 Tu	10 28 27	5 34 57	19 47 59	26 44 20	0 16.4	23 07.6	20 20.7	3 07.4	22 51.7	14 12.6	25 55.2	7 44.7	1 38.1	7 03.7
29 W	10 32 23	6 32 54	3♒38 43	10♒30 44	0 07.2	25 00.1	21 23.0	3 46.2	23 09.1	14 19.3	26 00.7	7 42.8	1 36.5	7 03.1
30 Th	10 36 20	7 30 53	17 20 03	24 06 15	29♏55.9	26 54.2	22 25.7	4 25.2	23 26.4	14 25.8	26 06.3	7 40.8	1 34.8	7 02.5
31 F	10 40 17	8 28 53	0♓49 01	7♓28 01	29 43.5	28 49.6	23 28.7	5 04.3	23 43.5	14 32.1	26 11.9	7 38.8	1 33.2	7 02.0

Astro Data	Dy Hr Mn
♂0S	5 0:43
☽0N	8 14:05
♅R	13 9:50
☿R	15 2:16
♃⊼♇	18 9:48
♃⚼♄	21 2:01
♃✱♅	22 4:05
☽0S	23 2:33
☽0N	4 23:55
☿D	8 5:40
☽0S	19 9:39

Planet Ingress	Dy Hr Mn
♂ ♎	3 12:33
☉ ♌	22 10:02
♀ ♋	7 13:44
☉ ♍	22 17:08
♂ ♏	23 15:25
☊ ♏R	30 3:41

Last Aspect Dy Hr Mn		☽ Ingress Dy Hr Mn
2 22:22	♂ □	♑ 2 22:52
4 12:26	♄ □	♒ 5 0:27
6 15:50	♄ △	♓ 7 4:30
8 11:01	☉ △	♈ 9 12:15
11 9:24	♄ ☍	♉ 11 23:32
13 19:47	☉ ✱	♊ 14 12:28
16 10:58	♄ △	♋ 17 0:32
19 4:25	☉ ☌	♌ 19 10:14
21 5:19	♄ ✱	♍ 21 17:25
23 0:45	♀ □	♎ 23 22:39
25 15:23	♄ ☌	♏ 26 2:30
26 15:39	☿ □	♐ 28 5:19
29 21:02	♄ ✱	♑ 30 7:30

Last Aspect Dy Hr Mn		☽ Ingress Dy Hr Mn
31 23:32	♄ □	♒ 1 9:57
3 7:25	♀ △	♓ 3 13:59
5 17:57	♀ □	♈ 5 21:00
7 20:05	♄ ☍	♉ 8 7:29
9 18:56	☉ □	♊ 10 20:12
12 21:51	♄ △	♋ 13 8:29
15 8:22	♄ □	♌ 15 18:06
17 17:56	♂ ✱	♍ 18 0:34
18 23:27	♃ □	♎ 20 4:46
22 7:14	☉ ✱	♏ 22 7:55
23 9:35	♀ △	♐ 24 10:51
26 6:40	♄ ✱	♑ 26 14:00
28 10:34	♄ □	♒ 28 17:40
30 17:49	☿ ☍	♓ 30 22:32

☽ Phases & Eclipses Dy Hr Mn	
3 18:53	○ 12♑14
11 1:49	☾ 19♈11
19 4:25	● 26♋55
26 8:57	☽ 3♏47
2 3:29	○ 10♒15
9 18:56	☾ 17♉34
17 15:55	● 25♌08
24 13:55	☽ 1♐48
31 13:59	○ 8♓34

Astro Data

1 July 2012
Julian Day # 41090
SVP 5♓04'51"
GC 27♐00.8 ⚴ 9♈16.2
Eris 22♈41.8 ⚵ 22♏01.3R
⚷ 9♓34.7R ⚶ 26♉40.3
☽ Mean ☊ 3♐18.8

1 August 2012
Julian Day # 41121
SVP 5♓04'46"
GC 27♐00.9 ⚴ 11♈28.8R
Eris 22♈42.5R ⚵ 22♏04.8
⚷ 8♓38.8R ⚶ 8♊25.1
☽ Mean ☊ 1♐40.3

LONGITUDE — September 2012

Day	Sid.Time	☉	0 hr ☽	Noon ☽	True ☊	☿	♀	♂	⚳	♃	♄	♅	♆	♇
1 Sa	10 44 13	9♍26 56	14♓02 57	20♓33 40	29♏31.3	0♍45.8	24♋32.0	5♏43.4	24♊00.4	14♊38.3	26♎17.5	7♈36.8	1♓31.6	7♑01.5
2 Su	10 48 10	10 24 59	27 00 00	3♈21 55	29R 20.3	2 42.6	25 35.5	6 22.7	24 17.2	14 44.3	26 23.3	7R 34.7	1R 30.0	7R 01.0
3 M	10 52 06	11 23 05	9♈39 29	15 52 49	29 11.4	4 39.6	26 39.3	7 02.0	24 33.8	14 50.1	26 29.0	7 32.7	1 28.3	7 00.5
4 Tu	10 56 03	12 21 12	22 02 10	28 07 50	29 05.2	6 36.7	27 43.4	7 41.5	24 50.3	14 55.8	26 34.9	7 30.6	1 26.7	7 00.1
5 W	10 59 59	13 19 21	4♉10 12	10♉09 45	29 01.6	8 33.5	28 47.8	8 21.0	25 06.6	15 01.4	26 40.8	7 28.4	1 25.1	6 59.7
6 Th	11 03 56	14 17 33	16 06 57	22 02 25	29D 00.1	10 29.9	29 52.4	9 00.7	25 22.7	15 06.7	26 46.7	7 26.3	1 23.5	6 59.3
7 F	11 07 52	15 15 46	27 56 45	3♊50 36	29 00.0	12 25.8	0♌57.3	9 40.4	25 38.6	15 11.9	26 52.7	7 24.1	1 22.0	6 59.0
8 Sa	11 11 49	16 14 01	9♊44 37	15 39 30	29R 00.2	14 21.0	2 02.4	10 20.3	25 54.4	15 17.0	26 58.7	7 21.9	1 20.4	6 58.7
9 Su	11 15 46	17 12 19	21 35 56	27 34 37	28 59.7	16 15.4	3 07.7	11 00.2	26 09.9	15 21.8	27 04.8	7 19.7	1 18.8	6 58.4
10 M	11 19 42	18 10 38	3♋36 12	9♋41 19	28 57.6	18 08.9	4 13.3	11 40.2	26 25.3	15 26.5	27 11.0	7 17.5	1 17.2	6 58.2
11 Tu	11 23 39	19 09 00	15 50 34	22 04 29	28 53.3	20 01.5	5 19.1	12 20.4	26 40.5	15 31.0	27 17.2	7 15.2	1 15.7	6 57.9
12 W	11 27 35	20 07 23	28 23 32	4♌48 04	28 46.5	21 53.2	6 25.1	13 00.6	26 55.5	15 35.3	27 23.4	7 13.0	1 14.2	6 57.8
13 Th	11 31 32	21 05 49	11♌18 22	17 54 33	28 37.5	23 43.8	7 31.4	13 40.9	27 10.3	15 39.5	27 29.7	7 10.7	1 12.6	6 57.6
14 F	11 35 28	22 04 16	24 36 39	1♍24 32	28 27.1	25 33.4	8 37.8	14 21.3	27 24.9	15 43.4	27 36.0	7 08.4	1 11.1	6 57.5
15 Sa	11 39 25	23 02 46	8♍17 56	15 16 26	28 16.3	27 21.9	9 44.5	15 01.8	27 39.2	15 47.2	27 42.4	7 06.1	1 09.6	6 57.4
16 Su	11 43 21	24 01 17	22 19 31	29 26 32	28 06.3	29 09.4	10 51.3	15 42.4	27 53.4	15 50.8	27 48.8	7 03.7	1 08.1	6 57.3
17 M	11 47 18	24 59 51	6♎36 46	13♎49 27	27 58.1	0♎55.8	11 58.4	16 23.1	28 07.3	15 54.2	27 55.3	7 01.4	1 06.6	6D 57.3
18 Tu	11 51 14	25 58 26	21 03 48	28 19 03	27 52.4	2 41.2	13 05.6	17 03.9	28 21.1	15 57.5	28 01.8	6 59.0	1 05.2	6 57.3
19 W	11 55 11	26 57 03	5♏34 27	12♏49 20	27 49.3	4 25.5	14 13.0	17 44.8	28 34.5	16 00.5	28 08.3	6 56.7	1 03.7	6 57.3
20 Th	11 59 08	27 55 41	20 03 08	27 15 22	27D 48.4	6 08.8	15 20.6	18 25.8	28 47.8	16 03.3	28 14.9	6 54.3	1 02.3	6 57.3
21 F	12 03 04	28 54 22	4♐25 37	11♐33 37	27 48.8	7 51.1	16 28.4	19 06.8	29 00.9	16 06.0	28 21.5	6 51.9	1 00.9	6 57.4
22 Sa	12 07 01	29 53 04	18 39 08	25 42 01	27R 49.5	9 32.4	17 36.3	19 48.0	29 13.7	16 08.5	28 28.2	6 49.5	0 59.5	6 57.5
23 Su	12 10 57	0♎51 48	2♑42 11	9♑39 35	27 49.2	11 12.7	18 44.5	20 29.2	29 26.2	16 10.8	28 34.9	6 47.1	0 58.1	6 57.7
24 M	12 14 54	1 50 33	16 34 12	23 25 59	27 47.1	12 52.0	19 52.8	21 10.5	29 38.5	16 12.8	28 41.6	6 44.7	0 56.8	6 57.9
25 Tu	12 18 50	2 49 20	0♒14 58	7♒01 05	27 42.7	14 30.4	21 01.2	21 51.9	29 50.6	16 14.7	28 48.3	6 42.3	0 55.4	6 58.1
26 W	12 22 47	3 48 09	13 44 19	20 24 37	27 36.2	16 07.8	22 09.8	22 33.4	0♋02.4	16 16.4	28 55.1	6 39.9	0 54.1	6 58.3
27 Th	12 26 43	4 46 59	27 01 54	3♓36 05	27 27.8	17 44.4	23 18.6	23 15.0	0 14.0	16 17.9	29 01.9	6 37.5	0 52.8	6 58.6
28 F	12 30 40	5 45 51	10♓07 07	16 34 54	27 18.6	19 20.0	24 27.5	23 56.7	0 25.3	16 19.2	29 08.8	6 35.1	0 51.5	6 58.9
29 Sa	12 34 37	6 44 46	22 59 22	29 20 28	27 09.4	20 54.7	25 36.6	24 38.4	0 36.4	16 20.3	29 15.7	6 32.7	0 50.3	6 59.2
30 Su	12 38 33	7 43 42	5♈38 13	11♈52 35	27 01.2	22 28.6	26 45.9	25 20.2	0 47.1	16 21.2	29 22.6	6 30.2	0 49.0	6 59.6

LONGITUDE — October 2012

Day	Sid.Time	☉	0 hr ☽	Noon ☽	True ☊	☿	♀	♂	⚳	♃	♄	♅	♆	♇
1 M	12 42 30	8♎42 40	18♈03 41	24♈11 37	26♏54.6	24♎01.6	27♌55.3	26♏02.1	0♋57.6	16♊22.0	29♎29.5	6♈27.8	0♓47.8	7♑00.0
2 Tu	12 46 26	9 41 40	0♉16 33	6♉18 42	26R 50.2	25 33.8	29 04.8	26 44.1	1 07.9	16 22.5	29 36.5	6R 25.4	0R 46.6	7 00.4
3 W	12 50 23	10 40 43	12 18 22	18 15 53	26D 47.9	27 05.1	0♍14.5	27 26.2	1 17.8	16 22.8	29 43.4	6 23.0	0 45.4	7 00.9
4 Th	12 54 19	11 39 48	24 11 38	0♊06 04	26 47.6	28 35.6	1 24.4	28 08.3	1 27.5	16R 22.9	29 50.4	6 20.6	0 44.3	7 01.4
5 F	12 58 16	12 38 55	5♊59 40	11 52 59	26 48.5	0♏05.2	2 34.4	28 50.5	1 36.9	16 22.8	29 57.5	6 18.2	0 43.2	7 01.9
6 Sa	13 02 12	13 38 04	17 46 34	23 41 02	26 50.1	1 34.0	3 44.5	29 32.9	1 46.0	16 22.5	0♏04.5	6 15.8	0 42.1	7 02.5
7 Su	13 06 09	14 37 16	29 37 00	5♋35 08	26R 51.4	3 01.9	4 54.8	0♐15.3	1 54.7	16 22.0	0 11.6	6 13.4	0 41.0	7 03.0
8 M	13 10 06	15 36 30	11♋36 03	17 40 26	26 51.8	4 29.0	6 05.2	0 57.7	2 03.2	16 21.3	0 18.7	6 11.0	0 39.9	7 03.7
9 Tu	13 14 02	16 35 46	23 48 54	0♌02 03	26 50.8	5 55.3	7 15.7	1 40.3	2 11.4	16 20.4	0 25.8	6 08.7	0 38.9	7 04.3
10 W	13 17 59	17 35 05	6♌20 27	12 44 36	26 48.1	7 20.6	8 26.3	2 23.0	2 19.2	16 19.3	0 32.9	6 06.3	0 37.9	7 05.0
11 Th	13 21 55	18 34 25	19 14 54	25 51 41	26 43.8	8 45.1	9 37.1	3 05.7	2 26.8	16 18.0	0 40.1	6 04.0	0 36.9	7 05.7
12 F	13 25 52	19 33 48	2♍35 08	9♍25 19	26 38.4	10 08.6	10 48.0	3 48.5	2 34.0	16 16.5	0 47.3	6 01.6	0 36.0	7 06.4
13 Sa	13 29 48	20 33 14	16 22 06	23 25 13	26 32.5	11 31.2	11 59.0	4 31.4	2 40.9	16 14.8	0 54.4	5 59.3	0 35.1	7 07.2
14 Su	13 33 45	21 32 41	0♎34 15	7♎48 36	26 27.0	12 52.7	13 10.2	5 14.3	2 47.4	16 12.9	1 01.6	5 57.0	0 34.2	7 08.0
15 M	13 37 41	22 32 11	15 07 30	22 30 05	26 22.6	14 13.2	14 21.4	5 57.4	2 53.6	16 10.8	1 08.8	5 54.7	0 33.3	7 08.8
16 Tu	13 41 38	23 31 42	29 55 24	7♏22 24	26 19.7	15 32.6	15 32.8	6 40.5	2 59.4	16 08.5	1 16.0	5 52.4	0 32.4	7 09.6
17 W	13 45 35	24 31 16	14♏50 04	22 17 22	26D 18.5	16 50.8	16 44.2	7 23.7	3 05.0	16 05.9	1 23.3	5 50.2	0 31.6	7 10.5
18 Th	13 49 31	25 30 52	29 43 23	7♐07 13	26 18.8	18 07.8	17 55.8	8 07.0	3 10.1	16 03.2	1 30.5	5 47.9	0 30.9	7 11.4
19 F	13 53 28	26 30 29	14♐28 09	21 45 32	26 20.0	19 23.4	19 07.5	8 50.4	3 14.9	16 00.3	1 37.7	5 45.7	0 30.1	7 12.4
20 Sa	13 57 24	27 30 08	28 58 54	6♑07 53	26 21.5	20 37.5	20 19.2	9 33.8	3 19.4	15 57.2	1 45.0	5 43.5	0 29.4	7 13.4
21 Su	14 01 21	28 29 49	13♑12 14	20 11 51	26R 22.6	21 50.1	21 31.1	10 17.3	3 23.4	15 54.0	1 52.2	5 41.3	0 28.7	7 14.4
22 M	14 05 17	29 29 32	27 06 39	3♒56 43	26 22.8	23 00.9	22 43.1	11 00.9	3 27.1	15 50.5	1 59.5	5 39.2	0 28.0	7 15.4
23 Tu	14 09 14	0♏29 16	10♒42 07	17 23 00	26 21.7	24 09.9	23 55.1	11 44.5	3 30.5	15 46.8	2 06.8	5 37.0	0 27.4	7 16.4
24 W	14 13 10	1 29 02	23 59 40	0♓31 59	26 19.5	25 16.8	25 07.3	12 28.2	3 33.4	15 42.9	2 14.0	5 34.9	0 26.8	7 17.5
25 Th	14 17 07	2 28 49	7♓00 27	13 25 12	26 16.3	26 21.5	26 19.5	13 12.0	3 36.0	15 38.9	2 21.3	5 32.8	0 26.2	7 18.6
26 F	14 21 04	3 28 38	19 46 26	26 04 20	26 12.6	27 23.6	27 31.8	13 55.9	3 38.2	15 34.7	2 28.5	5 30.8	0 25.7	7 19.8
27 Sa	14 25 00	4 28 29	2♈19 06	8♈30 55	26 09.0	28 23.0	28 44.2	14 39.8	3 40.1	15 30.3	2 35.8	5 28.7	0 25.2	7 20.9
28 Su	14 28 57	5 28 22	14 39 59	20 46 28	26 05.7	29 19.3	29 56.7	15 23.8	3 41.5	15 25.7	2 43.0	5 26.7	0 24.7	7 22.1
29 M	14 32 53	6 28 17	26 50 33	2♉52 26	26 03.3	0♐12.2	1♎09.3	16 07.9	3 42.6	15 20.9	2 50.3	5 24.8	0 24.3	7 23.3
30 Tu	14 36 50	7 28 13	8♉52 20	14 50 27	26D 01.9	1 01.3	2 22.0	16 52.0	3 43.2	15 16.0	2 57.5	5 22.8	0 23.9	7 24.6
31 W	14 40 46	8 28 12	20 47 03	26 42 22	26 01.5	1 46.2	3 34.7	17 36.2	3R 43.5	15 10.9	3 04.8	5 20.9	0 23.5	7 25.9

Astro Data Dy Hr Mn	Planet Ingress Dy Hr Mn	Last Aspect Dy Hr Mn	☽ Ingress Dy Hr Mn	Last Aspect Dy Hr Mn	☽ Ingress Dy Hr Mn	☽ Phases & Eclipses Dy Hr Mn	Astro Data
☽0N 1 9:06	☿ ♍ 1 2:33	1 20:03 ♀ △	♈ 2 5:38	1 22:33 ♄ ☍	♉ 1 23:27	8 13:16 ☾ 16♊17	1 September 2012
☽0S 15 18:20	♀ ♌ 6 14:49	4 11:07 ♀ □	♉ 4 15:42	4 7:45 ♂ ☍	♊ 4 11:48	16 2:12 ● 23♍37	Julian Day # 41152
♇D 18 5:08	☿ ♎ 16 23:23	5 18:56 ☉ △	♊ 7 4:11	5 21:09 ♃ ☌	♋ 7 0:46	22 19:42 ☽ 0♑12	SVP 5♓04'42"
☿0S 18 8:04	☉ ♎ 22 14:50	9 11:00 ♄ △	♋ 9 16:50	8 7:34 ☉ □	♌ 9 11:56	30 3:20 ○ 7♈22	GC 27♐01.0 ⚴ 8♈16.1R
♅□♇ 19 5:58	⚳ ♋ 26 7:01	11 22:00 ♄ □	♌ 12 3:02	10 21:41 ☉ ✶	♍ 11 19:25		Eris 22♈33.5R ⚵ 26♏35.0
☉0S 22 14:50		14 5:15 ♄ ✶	♍ 14 9:32	12 23:49 ♃ □	♎ 13 23:03	8 7:34 ☾ 15♋26	⚷ 7♓13.5R ⚶ 18♊07.4
☽0N 28 16:25	♀ ♍ 3 7:00	16 11:27 ☿ ☌	♎ 16 12:56	15 12:04 ☉ ☌	♏ 16 0:07	15 12:04 ● 22♎32	☽ Mean ☊ 0♐01.8
	☿ ♏ 5 10:36	18 11:31 ♄ ☌	♏ 18 14:47	17 2:24 ☿ ☌	♐ 18 0:27	22 3:33 ☽ 29♑09	
♃R 4 13:19	♄ ♏ 5 20:35	20 13:12 ☉ ✶	♐ 20 16:35	19 20:28 ☉ ✶	♑ 20 1:42	29 19:51 ○ 6♉48	1 October 2012
♄△♆ 11 2:40	♂ ♐ 7 3:22	22 16:46 ♄ ✶	♑ 22 19:22	22 3:33 ☉ □	♒ 22 5:03		Julian Day # 41182
☽0S 13 4:10	☉ ♏ 23 0:15	24 21:20 ♄ □	♒ 24 23:34	24 1:28 ☿ □	♓ 24 11:01		SVP 5♓04'40"
♃⚼♄ 15 16:57	♀ ♎ 28 13:05	27 3:34 ♄ △	♓ 27 5:25	26 15:05 ♀ ☍	♈ 26 19:32		GC 27♐01.0 ⚴ 0♈40.0R
☽0N 25 22:00	☿ ♐ 29 6:19	29 2:36 ♂ △	♈ 29 13:15	28 1:33 ♃ ✶	♉ 29 6:16		Eris 22♈18.1R ⚵ 3♐52.4
♀0S 31 13:37				29 21:03 ♇ △	♊ 31 18:41		⚷ 5♓53.3R ⚶ 24♊14.5
⚳R 31 15:47							☽ Mean ☊ 28♏26.5

November 2012 LONGITUDE

Day	Sid.Time	☉	0 hr ☽	Noon☽	True☊	☿	♀	♂	⚳	♃	♄	♅	♆	♇
1 Th	14 44 43	9♏28 13	2♊36 43	8♊30 24	26♏01.9	2♐26.4	4♎47.6	18♐20.5	3♋43.3	15♊05.6	3♏12.0	5♈19.0	0♓23.1	7♑27.2
2 F	14 48 39	10 28 15	14 23 48	20 17 17	26 03.0	3 01.4	6 00.5	19 04.8	3R42.8	15R00.2	3 19.2	5R17.2	0R22.8	7 28.5
3 Sa	14 52 36	11 28 20	26 11 16	2♋06 13	26 04.4	3 30.6	7 13.5	19 49.2	3 41.9	14 54.6	3 26.5	5 15.4	0 22.6	7 29.8
4 Su	14 56 32	12 28 26	8♋02 36	14 00 56	26 05.7	3 53.4	8 26.6	20 33.7	3 40.5	14 48.9	3 33.7	5 13.6	0 22.3	7 31.2
5 M	15 00 29	13 28 35	20 01 46	26 05 37	26 06.8	4 09.1	9 39.7	21 18.2	3 38.8	14 43.0	3 40.9	5 11.8	0 22.1	7 32.6
6 Tu	15 04 26	14 28 46	2♌13 05	8♌24 42	26R07.4	4R17.1	10 53.0	22 02.8	3 36.6	14 36.9	3 48.1	5 10.1	0 21.9	7 34.0
7 W	15 08 22	15 28 59	14 41 03	21 02 38	26 07.4	4 16.8	12 06.3	22 47.5	3 34.0	14 30.7	3 55.2	5 08.4	0 21.8	7 35.5
8 Th	15 12 19	16 29 14	27 29 57	4♍03 27	26 06.9	4 07.4	13 19.6	23 32.2	3 31.0	14 24.4	4 02.4	5 06.8	0 21.7	7 36.9
9 F	15 16 15	17 29 30	10♍43 28	17 30 16	26 06.1	3 48.5	14 33.1	24 17.0	3 27.6	14 17.9	4 09.5	5 05.2	0 21.6	7 38.4
10 Sa	15 20 12	18 29 49	24 23 59	1♎24 36	26 05.2	3 19.7	15 46.6	25 01.9	3 23.8	14 11.3	4 16.7	5 03.6	0D21.5	7 39.9
11 Su	15 24 08	19 30 10	8♎31 58	15 45 45	26 04.3	2 40.9	17 00.1	25 46.8	3 19.6	14 04.5	4 23.8	5 02.1	0 21.5	7 41.5
12 M	15 28 05	20 30 33	23 05 24	0♏30 15	26 03.7	1 52.2	18 13.8	26 31.8	3 14.9	13 57.6	4 30.9	5 00.6	0 21.5	7 43.0
13 Tu	15 32 01	21 30 57	7♏59 26	15 31 56	26D03.4	0 54.1	19 27.4	27 16.9	3 09.9	13 50.7	4 37.9	4 59.1	0 21.6	7 44.6
14 W	15 35 58	22 31 24	23 06 38	0♐42 22	26 03.3	29♏47.6	20 41.2	28 02.0	3 04.5	13 43.6	4 45.0	4 57.7	0 21.7	7 46.2
15 Th	15 39 55	23 31 51	8♐17 54	15 52 03	26 03.4	28 34.3	21 55.0	28 47.2	2 58.6	13 36.3	4 52.0	4 56.4	0 21.8	7 47.9
16 F	15 43 51	24 32 21	23 23 40	0♑51 45	26 03.6	27 16.1	23 08.8	29 32.4	2 52.4	13 29.0	4 59.0	4 55.0	0 22.0	7 49.5
17 Sa	15 47 48	25 32 52	8♑15 25	15 33 55	26R03.7	25 55.3	24 22.7	0♑17.7	2 45.7	13 21.6	5 06.0	4 53.7	0 22.2	7 51.2
18 Su	15 51 44	26 33 24	22 46 42	29 53 22	26 03.7	24 34.5	25 36.7	1 03.1	2 38.7	13 14.1	5 12.9	4 52.5	0 22.4	7 52.9
19 M	15 55 41	27 33 57	6♒53 43	13♒47 39	26 03.7	23 16.6	26 50.7	1 48.5	2 31.2	13 06.5	5 19.9	4 51.3	0 22.7	7 54.6
20 Tu	15 59 37	28 34 31	20 35 15	27 16 40	26D03.6	22 03.9	28 04.7	2 33.9	2 23.4	12 58.8	5 26.8	4 50.2	0 23.0	7 56.3
21 W	16 03 34	29 35 07	3♓52 10	10♓22 05	26 03.7	20 58.7	29 18.8	3 19.5	2 15.3	12 51.1	5 33.6	4 49.1	0 23.3	7 58.0
22 Th	16 07 30	0♐35 44	16 46 48	23 06 44	26 04.0	20 02.9	0♏32.9	4 05.0	2 06.7	12 43.3	5 40.4	4 48.0	0 23.7	7 59.8
23 F	16 11 27	1 36 22	29 22 19	5♈34 01	26 04.5	19 17.8	1 47.1	4 50.7	1 57.8	12 35.4	5 47.2	4 47.0	0 24.1	8 01.6
24 Sa	16 15 24	2 37 01	11♈42 14	17 47 26	26 05.2	18 44.0	3 01.3	5 36.3	1 48.6	12 27.4	5 54.0	4 46.0	0 24.5	8 03.4
25 Su	16 19 20	3 37 41	23 50 00	29 50 20	26 05.9	18 21.9	4 15.5	6 22.1	1 39.0	12 19.4	6 00.7	4 45.1	0 25.0	8 05.2
26 M	16 23 17	4 38 22	5♉48 49	11♉45 48	26 06.5	18D11.3	5 29.8	7 07.8	1 29.0	12 11.4	6 07.4	4 44.2	0 25.5	8 07.0
27 Tu	16 27 13	5 39 05	17 41 35	23 36 28	26R06.9	18 11.8	6 44.2	7 53.7	1 18.7	12 03.3	6 14.1	4 43.4	0 26.0	8 08.9
28 W	16 31 10	6 39 49	29 30 47	5♊24 45	26 06.7	18 22.8	7 58.5	8 39.6	1 08.2	11 55.2	6 20.7	4 42.6	0 26.6	8 10.8
29 Th	16 35 06	7 40 34	11♊18 41	17 12 48	26 05.9	18 43.3	9 12.9	9 25.5	0 57.3	11 47.1	6 27.3	4 41.9	0 27.2	8 12.6
30 F	16 39 03	8 41 21	23 07 23	29 02 42	26 04.5	19 12.6	10 27.4	10 11.5	0 46.1	11 38.9	6 33.8	4 41.2	0 27.9	8 14.5

December 2012 LONGITUDE

Day	Sid.Time	☉	0 hr ☽	Noon☽	True☊	☿	♀	♂	⚳	♃	♄	♅	♆	♇
1 Sa	16 43 00	9♐42 09	4♋59 00	10♋56 35	26♏02.6	19♏49.8	11♏41.9	10♑57.5	0♋34.6	11♊30.8	6♏40.3	4♈40.5	0♓28.6	8♑16.4
2 Su	16 46 56	10 42 58	16 55 46	22 56 50	26R00.3	20 33.9	12 56.4	11 43.6	0R22.8	11R22.6	6 46.8	4R40.0	0 29.3	8 18.4
3 M	16 50 53	11 43 49	29 00 10	5♌06 06	25 58.0	21 24.3	14 11.0	12 29.7	0 10.8	11 14.4	6 53.2	4 39.4	0 30.0	8 20.3
4 Tu	16 54 49	12 44 40	11♌15 03	17 27 24	25 55.9	22 20.1	15 25.6	13 15.8	29♊58.5	11 06.2	6 59.6	4 38.9	0 30.8	8 22.3
5 W	16 58 46	13 45 33	23 43 33	0♍03 58	25 54.5	23 20.6	16 40.2	14 02.1	29 46.0	10 58.0	7 05.9	4 38.5	0 31.6	8 24.2
6 Th	17 02 42	14 46 28	6♍29 04	12 59 14	25D53.9	24 25.3	17 54.9	14 48.3	29 33.2	10 49.9	7 12.2	4 38.1	0 32.4	8 26.2
7 F	17 06 39	15 47 23	19 34 53	26 16 21	25 54.2	25 33.6	19 09.5	15 34.6	29 20.3	10 41.7	7 18.4	4 37.8	0 33.3	8 28.2
8 Sa	17 10 35	16 48 20	3♎03 55	9♎57 47	25 55.3	26 45.0	20 24.3	16 21.0	29 07.1	10 33.6	7 24.6	4 37.5	0 34.2	8 30.2
9 Su	17 14 32	17 49 18	16 58 04	24 04 42	25 56.7	27 59.1	21 39.0	17 07.4	28 53.8	10 25.6	7 30.7	4 37.3	0 35.1	8 32.2
10 M	17 18 29	18 50 18	1♏17 32	8♏36 13	25 58.0	29 15.5	22 53.8	17 53.8	28 40.2	10 17.5	7 36.8	4 37.1	0 36.1	8 34.2
11 Tu	17 22 25	19 51 18	16 00 15	23 28 54	25R58.7	0♐34.0	24 08.6	18 40.3	28 26.6	10 09.6	7 42.8	4 36.9	0 37.1	8 36.3
12 W	17 26 22	20 52 20	1♐01 19	8♐36 27	25 58.3	1 54.2	25 23.4	19 26.8	28 12.8	10 01.6	7 48.8	4 36.9	0 38.1	8 38.3
13 Th	17 30 18	21 53 22	16 13 10	23 50 11	25 56.5	3 15.9	26 38.3	20 13.4	27 58.9	9 53.8	7 54.7	4D36.8	0 39.2	8 40.4
14 F	17 34 15	22 54 26	1♑26 15	9♑00 05	25 53.4	4 38.9	27 53.1	21 00.0	27 44.9	9 46.0	8 00.5	4 36.9	0 40.3	8 42.4
15 Sa	17 38 11	23 55 29	16 30 29	23 56 21	25 49.4	6 03.0	29 08.0	21 46.6	27 30.8	9 38.3	8 06.3	4 36.9	0 41.4	8 44.5
16 Su	17 42 08	24 56 34	1♒16 45	8♒30 58	25 45.1	7 28.2	0♐22.9	22 33.3	27 16.6	9 30.6	8 12.1	4 37.1	0 42.6	8 46.6
17 M	17 46 04	25 57 39	15 38 25	22 38 47	25 41.0	8 54.1	1 37.8	23 20.0	27 02.4	9 23.1	8 17.8	4 37.2	0 43.8	8 48.7
18 Tu	17 50 01	26 58 44	29 31 52	6♓17 44	25 37.9	10 20.9	2 52.8	24 06.8	26 48.2	9 15.6	8 23.4	4 37.5	0 45.0	8 50.7
19 W	17 53 58	27 59 49	12♓56 32	19 28 36	25D36.2	11 48.3	4 07.7	24 53.6	26 34.0	9 08.2	8 28.9	4 37.8	0 46.3	8 52.8
20 Th	17 57 54	29 00 55	25 54 19	2♈14 13	25 35.9	13 16.3	5 22.7	25 40.4	26 19.8	9 01.0	8 34.4	4 38.1	0 47.5	8 54.9
21 F	18 01 51	0♑02 00	8♈28 49	14 38 43	25 36.8	14 44.8	6 37.7	26 27.2	26 05.6	8 53.8	8 39.8	4 38.5	0 48.9	8 57.0
22 Sa	18 05 47	1 03 06	20 44 32	26 46 53	25 38.5	16 13.9	7 52.7	27 14.1	25 51.5	8 46.8	8 45.2	4 38.9	0 50.2	8 59.1
23 Su	18 09 44	2 04 13	2♉46 21	8♉43 32	25 40.3	17 43.3	9 07.7	28 01.0	25 37.4	8 39.8	8 50.5	4 39.4	0 51.6	9 01.3
24 M	18 13 40	3 05 19	14 39 00	20 33 15	25R41.4	19 13.2	10 22.7	28 47.9	25 23.4	8 33.0	8 55.7	4 39.9	0 52.9	9 03.4
25 Tu	18 17 37	4 06 26	26 26 48	2♊20 06	25 41.3	20 43.4	11 37.7	29 34.9	25 09.5	8 26.4	9 00.9	4 40.5	0 54.4	9 05.5
26 W	18 21 33	5 07 33	8♊13 32	14 07 30	25 39.4	22 14.0	12 52.7	0♒21.9	24 55.8	8 19.8	9 06.0	4 41.2	0 55.8	9 07.6
27 Th	18 25 30	6 08 40	20 02 18	25 58 14	25 35.5	23 45.0	14 07.8	1 08.9	24 42.1	8 13.4	9 11.0	4 41.9	0 57.3	9 09.7
28 F	18 29 27	7 09 48	1♋55 33	7♋54 27	25 29.5	25 16.3	15 22.8	1 55.9	24 28.7	8 07.2	9 15.9	4 42.6	0 58.8	9 11.9
29 Sa	18 33 23	8 10 55	13 55 08	19 57 47	25 22.0	26 47.9	16 37.9	2 43.0	24 15.3	8 01.0	9 20.8	4 43.4	1 00.3	9 14.0
30 Su	18 37 20	9 12 03	26 02 32	2♌09 32	25 13.4	28 19.8	17 53.0	3 30.1	24 02.2	7 55.1	9 25.6	4 44.3	1 01.9	9 16.1
31 M	18 41 16	10 13 11	8♌18 55	14 30 50	25 04.7	29 52.1	19 08.1	4 17.2	23 49.2	7 49.2	9 30.3	4 45.2	1 03.5	9 18.3

Astro Data Dy Hr Mn	Planet Ingress Dy Hr Mn	Last Aspect Dy Hr Mn	☽ Ingress Dy Hr Mn	Last Aspect Dy Hr Mn	☽ Ingress Dy Hr Mn	☽ Phases & Eclipses Dy Hr Mn
☿R 6 23:05	☿ ♏R 14 7:43	2 9:23 ♂ ☍	♋ 3 7:44	2 6:56 ☿ △	♌ 3 1:58	7 0:37 ☾ 15♌00
☽0S 9 13:56	♂ ♑ 17 2:37	4 8:38 ☉ △	♌ 5 19:40	4 22:09 ☿ □	♍ 5 11:53	13 22:09 ● 21♏57
♆D 11 7:53	☉ ♐ 21 21:51	7 15:28 ♂ △	♍ 8 4:36	7 10:37 ☿ ⚹	♎ 7 18:36	13 22:12:55 ● T 04'02"
♄⚻♅ 16 0:28	♀ ♏ 22 1:21	10 0:28 ♂ □	♎ 10 9:36	9 0:38 ☉ ⚹	♏ 9 21:52	20 14:33 ☽ 28♒41
☽0N 22 3:25		12 5:14 ♂ ⚹	♏ 12 11:11	11 13:09 ♀ ☌	♐ 11 22:23	28 14:47 ○ 6♊47
☿D 26 22:51	⚳ ♊R 4 9:07	14 10:40 ☿ ☌	♐ 14 10:53	13 8:43 ☉ ☌	♑ 13 21:44	28 14:34 • A 0.915
	☿ ♐ 11 1:41	16 9:45 ♂ ☌	♑ 16 10:37	15 21:16 ♀ ⚹	♒ 15 21:54	
☽0S 6 22:22	♀ ♐ 16 4:39	18 5:55 ☉ ⚹	♒ 18 12:11	17 18:13 ☉ ⚹	♓ 18 0:49	6 15:33 ☾ 14♍55
♅D 13 12:03	☉ ♑ 21 11:13	20 14:33 ☉ □	♓ 20 16:56	20 5:20 ☉ □	♈ 20 7:44	13 8:43 ● 21♐45
☽0N 19 10:47	♂ ♒ 26 0:50	22 6:33 ☿ △	♈ 23 1:13	22 12:58 ♂ □	♉ 22 18:26	20 5:20 ☽ 28♓44
♃⚻♇ 21 3:37	☿ ♑ 31 14:04	24 1:36 ♃ ⚹	♉ 25 12:19	25 5:59 ♂ △	♊ 25 7:14	28 10:22 ○ 7♋06
♃⚻♄ 22 15:04		27 0:58 ☿ ☍	♊ 28 0:59	27 6:51 ☿ ☍	♋ 27 20:08	
♄⚹♇ 27 1:42		29 1:05 ♃ ☌	♋ 30 13:56	28 14:44 ♄ △	♌ 30 7:46	

Astro Data

1 November 2012
Julian Day # 41213
SVP 5♓04'37"
GC 27♐01.1 ⚴ 23♓47.2R
Eris 21♈59.7R ⚵ 13♐20.5
⚷ 5♓04.1R ⚶ 25♊06.7R
☽ Mean ☊ 26♏48.0

1 December 2012
Julian Day # 41243
SVP 5♓04'32"
GC 27♐01.2 ⚴ 22♓48.2
Eris 21♈44.9R ⚵ 23♐38.6
⚷ 5♓07.0 ⚶ 19♊41.6R
☽ Mean ☊ 25♏12.7

LONGITUDE — January 2013

Day	Sid.Time	☉	0 hr ☽	Noon ☽	True ☊	☿	♀	♂	⚳	♃	♄	♅	♆	♇
1 Tu	18 45 13	11♑14 19	20♌45 26	27♌02 54	24♏56.8	1♑24.6	20♐23.2	5♒04.3	23♊36.5	7♊43.6	9♏35.0	4♈46.1	1♓05.1	9♑20.4
2 W	18 49 09	12 15 28	3♍23 24	9♍47 10	24R50.4	2 57.6	21 38.3	5 51.5	23R24.0	7R38.1	9 39.5	4 47.1	1 06.7	9 22.5
3 Th	18 53 06	13 16 36	16 14 26	22 45 25	24 46.0	4 30.8	22 53.5	6 38.7	23 11.7	7 32.7	9 44.0	4 48.2	1 08.3	9 24.6
4 F	18 57 02	14 17 45	29 20 25	5♎59 41	24D43.8	6 04.4	24 08.6	7 25.9	22 59.7	7 27.6	9 48.4	4 49.3	1 10.0	9 26.8
5 Sa	19 00 59	15 18 55	12♎43 28	19 32 01	24 43.5	7 38.4	25 23.8	8 13.1	22 47.9	7 22.6	9 52.8	4 50.4	1 11.7	9 28.9
6 Su	19 04 56	16 20 04	26 25 31	3♏24 07	24 44.4	9 12.7	26 38.9	9 00.3	22 36.5	7 17.7	9 57.0	4 51.6	1 13.5	9 31.0
7 M	19 08 52	17 21 14	10♏27 52	17 36 42	24R45.3	10 47.5	27 54.1	9 47.6	22 25.3	7 13.1	10 01.2	4 52.9	1 15.2	9 33.1
8 Tu	19 12 49	18 22 24	24 50 26	2♐08 45	24 45.3	12 22.6	29 09.3	10 34.9	22 14.4	7 08.6	10 05.3	4 54.2	1 17.0	9 35.2
9 W	19 16 45	19 23 34	9♐31 08	16 56 58	24 43.3	13 58.1	0♑24.4	11 22.2	22 03.8	7 04.3	10 09.3	4 55.5	1 18.8	9 37.3
10 Th	19 20 42	20 24 44	24 25 23	1♑55 27	24 38.7	15 34.1	1 39.6	12 09.5	21 53.6	7 00.2	10 13.2	4 56.9	1 20.6	9 39.4
11 F	19 24 38	21 25 53	9♑26 04	16 56 03	24 31.7	17 10.5	2 54.8	12 56.9	21 43.7	6 56.3	10 17.0	4 58.3	1 22.4	9 41.5
12 Sa	19 28 35	22 27 03	24 24 15	1♒49 28	24 22.7	18 47.3	4 10.0	13 44.2	21 34.2	6 52.6	10 20.8	4 59.8	1 24.3	9 43.6
13 Su	19 32 31	23 28 12	9♒10 36	16 26 43	24 12.8	20 24.7	5 25.2	14 31.6	21 25.0	6 49.0	10 24.4	5 01.4	1 26.2	9 45.7
14 M	19 36 28	24 29 20	23 36 57	0♓40 43	24 03.1	22 02.5	6 40.4	15 18.9	21 16.2	6 45.7	10 28.0	5 02.9	1 28.1	9 47.8
15 Tu	19 40 25	25 30 28	7♓37 35	14 27 17	23 54.8	23 40.8	7 55.6	16 06.3	21 07.7	6 42.5	10 31.5	5 04.6	1 30.0	9 49.9
16 W	19 44 21	26 31 35	21 09 49	27 45 18	23 48.6	25 19.6	9 10.8	16 53.7	20 59.7	6 39.6	10 34.9	5 06.2	1 31.9	9 51.9
17 Th	19 48 18	27 32 41	4♈14 01	10♈36 23	23 44.8	26 58.9	10 26.0	17 41.1	20 52.0	6 36.8	10 38.2	5 08.0	1 33.9	9 54.0
18 F	19 52 14	28 33 47	16 52 53	23 04 08	23D43.2	28 38.7	11 41.2	18 28.5	20 44.7	6 34.3	10 41.3	5 09.7	1 35.8	9 56.0
19 Sa	19 56 11	29 34 52	29 10 45	5♉13 25	23 43.2	0♒19.1	12 56.4	19 16.0	20 37.8	6 32.0	10 44.5	5 11.5	1 37.8	9 58.0
20 Su	20 00 07	0♒35 55	11♉12 49	17 09 41	23R43.8	2 00.0	14 11.6	20 03.4	20 31.4	6 29.8	10 47.5	5 13.4	1 39.8	10 00.1
21 M	20 04 04	1 36 58	23 04 39	28 58 25	23 43.8	3 41.5	15 26.7	20 50.8	20 25.3	6 27.9	10 50.4	5 15.3	1 41.9	10 02.1
22 Tu	20 08 00	2 38 00	4♊51 38	10♊44 52	23 42.2	5 23.5	16 41.9	21 38.2	20 19.7	6 26.1	10 53.2	5 17.2	1 43.9	10 04.1
23 W	20 11 57	3 39 01	16 38 41	22 33 36	23 38.3	7 06.1	17 57.1	22 25.7	20 14.5	6 24.6	10 55.9	5 19.2	1 46.0	10 06.1
24 Th	20 15 54	4 40 02	28 30 04	4♋28 28	23 31.6	8 49.1	19 12.3	23 13.1	20 09.7	6 23.3	10 58.6	5 21.2	1 48.0	10 08.1
25 F	20 19 50	5 41 01	10♋29 09	16 32 22	23 22.1	10 32.7	20 27.5	24 00.5	20 05.3	6 22.2	11 01.1	5 23.3	1 50.1	10 10.0
26 Sa	20 23 47	6 41 59	22 38 21	28 47 14	23 10.2	12 16.8	21 42.6	24 48.0	20 01.3	6 21.3	11 03.6	5 25.4	1 52.2	10 12.0
27 Su	20 27 43	7 42 57	4♌59 07	11♌14 03	22 56.9	14 01.2	22 57.8	25 35.4	19 57.8	6 20.5	11 05.9	5 27.5	1 54.3	10 13.9
28 M	20 31 40	8 43 53	17 32 01	23 53 01	22 43.3	15 46.1	24 13.0	26 22.8	19 54.7	6 20.0	11 08.1	5 29.7	1 56.4	10 15.9
29 Tu	20 35 36	9 44 49	0♍16 58	6♍43 48	22 30.6	17 31.3	25 28.2	27 10.2	19 52.0	6D19.7	11 10.3	5 32.0	1 58.6	10 17.8
30 W	20 39 33	10 45 44	13 13 28	19 45 55	22 19.9	19 16.7	26 43.3	27 57.7	19 49.7	6 19.6	11 12.3	5 34.2	2 00.7	10 19.7
31 Th	20 43 29	11 46 37	26 21 05	2♎58 59	22 12.0	21 02.3	27 58.5	28 45.1	19 47.9	6 19.7	11 14.3	5 36.5	2 02.9	10 21.5

LONGITUDE — February 2013

Day	Sid.Time	☉	0 hr ☽	Noon ☽	True ☊	☿	♀	♂	⚳	♃	♄	♅	♆	♇
1 F	20 47 26	12♒47 31	9♎39 36	16♎23 01	22♏07.1	22♒47.9	29♑13.7	29♒32.5	19♊46.4	6♊20.1	11♏16.1	5♈38.9	2♓05.0	10♑23.4
2 Sa	20 51 23	13 48 23	23 09 17	29 58 29	22R04.8	24 33.4	0♒28.8	0♓19.9	19R45.4	6 20.6	11 17.8	5 41.2	2 07.2	10 25.3
3 Su	20 55 19	14 49 15	6♏50 45	13♏46 09	22 04.3	26 18.7	1 44.0	1 07.3	19D44.9	6 21.3	11 19.5	5 43.6	2 09.4	10 27.1
4 M	20 59 16	15 50 06	20 44 47	27 46 40	22 04.3	28 03.4	2 59.2	1 54.8	19 44.7	6 22.2	11 21.0	5 46.1	2 11.6	10 28.9
5 Tu	21 03 12	16 50 56	4♐51 46	11♐59 59	22 03.3	29 47.3	4 14.3	2 42.2	19 45.0	6 23.3	11 22.4	5 48.6	2 13.8	10 30.7
6 W	21 07 09	17 51 45	19 11 05	26 24 46	22 00.3	1♓30.3	5 29.5	3 29.6	19 45.7	6 24.7	11 23.8	5 51.1	2 16.1	10 32.5
7 Th	21 11 05	18 52 33	3♑40 32	10♑57 50	21 54.3	3 11.8	6 44.6	4 17.0	19 46.8	6 26.2	11 25.0	5 53.7	2 18.3	10 34.3
8 F	21 15 02	19 53 20	18 15 57	25 34 04	21 45.5	4 51.6	7 59.8	5 04.3	19 48.3	6 27.9	11 26.1	5 56.3	2 20.5	10 36.0
9 Sa	21 18 59	20 54 06	2♒51 20	10♒06 48	21 34.2	6 29.3	9 14.9	5 51.7	19 50.2	6 29.8	11 27.2	5 58.9	2 22.8	10 37.8
10 Su	21 22 55	21 54 51	17 19 35	24 28 48	21 21.6	8 04.2	10 30.1	6 39.1	19 52.5	6 32.0	11 28.1	6 01.5	2 25.0	10 39.5
11 M	21 26 52	22 55 34	1♓33 38	8♓33 26	21 09.0	9 36.0	11 45.2	7 26.4	19 55.3	6 34.3	11 28.9	6 04.2	2 27.3	10 41.2
12 Tu	21 30 48	23 56 16	15 27 37	22 15 50	20 57.8	11 04.0	13 00.3	8 13.8	19 58.4	6 36.8	11 29.6	6 06.9	2 29.5	10 42.8
13 W	21 34 45	24 56 56	28 57 49	5♈33 32	20 49.0	12 27.5	14 15.5	9 01.1	20 02.0	6 39.5	11 30.2	6 09.7	2 31.8	10 44.5
14 Th	21 38 41	25 57 35	12♈03 03	18 26 35	20 42.9	13 45.9	15 30.6	9 48.4	20 05.9	6 42.4	11 30.7	6 12.5	2 34.0	10 46.1
15 F	21 42 38	26 58 12	24 44 29	0♉57 13	20 39.6	14 58.5	16 45.7	10 35.7	20 10.3	6 45.5	11 31.0	6 15.3	2 36.3	10 47.7
16 Sa	21 46 34	27 58 48	7♉05 17	13 09 18	20D38.3	16 04.6	18 00.8	11 23.0	20 15.0	6 48.8	11 31.3	6 18.1	2 38.6	10 49.3
17 Su	21 50 31	28 59 21	19 09 55	25 07 48	20R38.2	17 03.5	19 15.8	12 10.3	20 20.1	6 52.3	11 31.5	6 21.0	2 40.9	10 50.9
18 M	21 54 27	29 59 53	1♊03 39	6♊58 10	20 38.1	17 54.5	20 30.9	12 57.5	20 25.6	6 56.0	11R31.6	6 23.9	2 43.1	10 52.4
19 Tu	21 58 24	1♓00 23	12 52 04	18 46 02	20 36.8	18 37.0	21 46.0	13 44.7	20 31.5	6 59.9	11 31.5	6 26.8	2 45.4	10 53.9
20 W	22 02 21	2 00 52	24 40 42	0♋36 43	20 33.5	19 10.4	23 01.0	14 31.9	20 37.8	7 03.9	11 31.4	6 29.8	2 47.7	10 55.4
21 Th	22 06 17	3 01 18	6♋34 39	12 35 02	20 27.5	19 34.3	24 16.0	15 19.1	20 44.4	7 08.1	11 31.2	6 32.7	2 50.0	10 56.9
22 F	22 10 14	4 01 43	18 38 21	24 44 58	20 18.9	19R48.4	25 31.1	16 06.3	20 51.4	7 12.5	11 30.8	6 35.7	2 52.3	10 58.4
23 Sa	22 14 10	5 02 05	0♌55 13	7♌09 21	20 07.9	19 52.4	26 46.1	16 53.4	20 58.7	7 17.1	11 30.4	6 38.7	2 54.5	10 59.8
24 Su	22 18 07	6 02 26	13 27 32	19 49 49	19 55.4	19 46.5	28 01.1	17 40.5	21 06.4	7 21.9	11 29.8	6 41.8	2 56.8	11 01.2
25 M	22 22 03	7 02 46	26 16 13	2♍46 39	19 42.4	19 30.8	29 16.1	18 27.6	21 14.4	7 26.8	11 29.2	6 44.9	2 59.1	11 02.6
26 Tu	22 26 00	8 03 03	9♍20 56	15 58 52	19 30.3	19 05.7	0♓31.0	19 14.6	21 22.8	7 31.9	11 28.4	6 47.9	3 01.4	11 03.9
27 W	22 29 56	9 03 19	22 40 11	29 24 36	19 20.2	18 31.9	1 46.0	20 01.7	21 31.5	7 37.2	11 27.6	6 51.0	3 03.6	11 05.2
28 Th	22 33 53	10 03 33	6♎11 48	13♎01 28	19 12.6	17 50.2	3 01.0	20 48.7	21 40.5	7 42.7	11 26.6	6 54.2	3 05.9	11 06.5

Astro Data Dy Hr Mn	Planet Ingress Dy Hr Mn	Last Aspect Dy Hr Mn	☽ Ingress Dy Hr Mn	Last Aspect Dy Hr Mn	☽ Ingress Dy Hr Mn	☽ Phases & Eclipses Dy Hr Mn
☽0S 3 5:17	♀ ♑ 9 4:12	31 21:53 ♀ △	♍ 1 17:36	2 1:04 ☿ △	♏ 2 12:03	5 3:59 ☾ 14♎58
☽0N 15 20:41	☿ ♒ 19 7:26	3 12:16 ♀ □	♎ 4 1:12	4 12:32 ☿ □	♐ 4 15:46	11 19:45 ● 21♑46
♃ D 30 11:38	☉ ♒ 19 21:53	5 23:14 ♀ ⚹	♏ 6 6:10	5 20:43 ☉ ⚹	♑ 6 17:56	18 23:46 ☽ 29♈04
☽0S 30 11:44		7 11:32 ☉ ⚹	♐ 8 8:29	7 12:45 ♄ ⚹	♒ 8 19:18	27 4:39 ○ 7♌24
	♂ ♓ 2 1:55	9 2:29 ♂ ⚹	♑ 10 8:55	10 7:21 ☉ ☌	♓ 10 21:21	
⚳ D 4 8:50	♀ ♒ 2 2:48	11 19:45 ☉ ☌	♒ 12 9:02	11 17:04 ♄ △	♈ 13 1:52	3 13:57 ☾ 14♏54
☽0N 12 7:37	☿ ♓ 5 14:57	13 8:38 ♂ ☌	♓ 14 10:50	15 3:36 ☉ ⚹	♉ 15 10:09	10 7:21 ● 21♒43
♄ R 18 17:03	☉ ♓ 18 12:03	16 9:34 ☉ ⚹	♈ 16 16:08	17 20:32 ☉ □	♊ 17 21:51	17 20:32 ☽ 29♉21
☿ R 23 9:42	♀ ♓ 26 2:04	19 0:41 ☿ □	♉ 19 1:37	19 18:49 ♀ △	♋ 20 10:46	25 20:27 ○ 7♍24
☽0S 26 19:04		20 18:17 ♂ □	♊ 21 14:05	22 2:09 ☿ △	♌ 22 22:13	
		23 11:43 ♂ △	♋ 24 3:01	25 4:51 ♀ ☍	♍ 25 6:54	
		25 20:36 ♀ ☍	♌ 26 14:21	26 18:14 ♂ ☍	♎ 27 13:03	
		28 17:00 ♂ ☍	♍ 28 23:28			
		31 2:00 ♀ △	♎ 31 6:37			

Astro Data

1 January 2013
Julian Day # 41274
SVP 5♓04'27"
GC 27♐01.3 ⚴ 27♓40.1
Eris 21♈37.3R ⚵ 4♑52.9
⚷ 6♓03.7 ⚶ 12♊12.1R
☽ Mean ☊ 23♏34.2

1 February 2013
Julian Day # 41305
SVP 5♓04'22"
GC 27♐01.3 ⚴ 6♈43.8
Eris 21♈40.1 ⚵ 16♑12.5
⚷ 7♓41.8 ⚶ 9♊58.0
☽ Mean ☊ 21♏55.7

March 2013 LONGITUDE

Day	Sid.Time	☉	0 hr ☽	Noon ☽	True ☊	☿	♀	♂	⚳	♃	♄	♅	♆	♇
1 F	22 37 50	11♓03 45	19♎53 21	26♎47 09	19♏08.0	17♓01.8	4♓15.9	21♓35.7	21♊49.9	7♊48.3	11♏25.6	6♈57.3	3♓08.2	11♑07.8
2 Sa	22 41 46	12 03 56	3♏42 39	10♏39 40	19D 06.1	16R 07.9	5 30.8	22 22.6	21 59.5	7 54.1	11R 24.4	7 00.5	3 10.4	11 09.0
3 Su	22 45 43	13 04 06	17 38 03	24 37 41	19 05.9	15 09.9	6 45.8	23 09.6	22 09.5	8 00.0	11 23.2	7 03.7	3 12.7	11 10.3
4 M	22 49 39	14 04 14	1♐38 28	8♐40 18	19R 06.4	14 09.2	8 00.7	23 56.5	22 19.9	8 06.1	11 21.8	7 06.9	3 14.9	11 11.5
5 Tu	22 53 36	15 04 21	15 43 08	22 46 52	19 06.2	13 07.4	9 15.6	24 43.4	22 30.5	8 12.4	11 20.3	7 10.1	3 17.2	11 12.6
6 W	22 57 32	16 04 26	29 51 20	6♑56 23	19 04.4	12 05.8	10 30.5	25 30.2	22 41.4	8 18.8	11 18.8	7 13.4	3 19.4	11 13.8
7 Th	23 01 29	17 04 29	14♑01 46	21 07 11	19 00.2	11 05.9	11 45.4	26 17.1	22 52.7	8 25.4	11 17.1	7 16.6	3 21.7	11 14.9
8 F	23 05 25	18 04 31	28 12 17	5♒16 38	18 53.4	10 08.9	13 00.3	27 03.9	23 04.2	8 32.2	11 15.4	7 19.9	3 23.9	11 16.0
9 Sa	23 09 22	19 04 31	12♒19 44	19 21 05	18 44.6	9 15.8	14 15.2	27 50.7	23 16.0	8 39.1	11 13.6	7 23.2	3 26.1	11 17.0
10 Su	23 13 19	20 04 29	26 20 07	3♓16 19	18 34.6	8 27.4	15 30.0	28 37.4	23 28.1	8 46.1	11 11.6	7 26.5	3 28.3	11 18.1
11 M	23 17 15	21 04 26	10♓09 09	16 58 10	18 24.5	7 44.5	16 44.9	29 24.1	23 40.5	8 53.3	11 09.6	7 29.8	3 30.5	11 19.1
12 Tu	23 21 12	22 04 20	23 42 55	0♈23 07	18 15.4	7 07.6	17 59.7	0♈10.8	23 53.2	9 00.7	11 07.5	7 33.1	3 32.7	11 20.0
13 W	23 25 08	23 04 13	6♈58 31	13 29 00	18 08.3	6 36.9	19 14.5	0 57.4	24 06.2	9 08.2	11 05.2	7 36.5	3 34.9	11 21.0
14 Th	23 29 05	24 04 03	19 54 32	26 15 14	18 03.4	6 12.6	20 29.3	1 44.1	24 19.4	9 15.8	11 02.9	7 39.8	3 37.1	11 21.9
15 F	23 33 01	25 03 52	2♉31 15	8♉42 54	18D 01.0	5 54.8	21 44.1	2 30.6	24 32.9	9 23.6	11 00.5	7 43.2	3 39.2	11 22.8
16 Sa	23 36 58	26 03 38	14 50 31	20 54 33	18 00.6	5 43.4	22 58.9	3 17.2	24 46.7	9 31.6	10 58.0	7 46.5	3 41.4	11 23.6
17 Su	23 40 54	27 03 22	26 55 30	2♊53 56	18 01.4	5D 38.3	24 13.6	4 03.7	25 00.7	9 39.6	10 55.5	7 49.9	3 43.5	11 24.5
18 M	23 44 51	28 03 04	8♊50 26	14 45 38	18 02.7	5 39.3	25 28.4	4 50.2	25 15.0	9 47.8	10 52.8	7 53.3	3 45.6	11 25.3
19 Tu	23 48 47	29 02 44	20 40 11	26 34 45	18R 03.5	5 46.1	26 43.1	5 36.6	25 29.5	9 56.2	10 50.1	7 56.7	3 47.7	11 26.0
20 W	23 52 44	0♈02 22	2♋29 59	8♋26 34	18 03.1	5 58.5	27 57.8	6 23.0	25 44.3	10 04.7	10 47.3	8 00.1	3 49.8	11 26.8
21 Th	23 56 41	1 01 57	14 25 06	20 26 14	18 00.9	6 16.3	29 12.5	7 09.3	25 59.3	10 13.3	10 44.4	8 03.5	3 51.9	11 27.5
22 F	0 00 37	2 01 30	26 30 31	2♌38 30	17 56.8	6 39.0	0♈27.2	7 55.7	26 14.5	10 22.0	10 41.4	8 06.9	3 54.0	11 28.1
23 Sa	0 04 34	3 01 00	8♌50 37	15 07 16	17 50.9	7 06.6	1 41.8	8 41.9	26 30.0	10 30.8	10 38.3	8 10.3	3 56.1	11 28.8
24 Su	0 08 30	4 00 28	21 28 46	27 55 21	17 43.8	7 38.6	2 56.4	9 28.2	26 45.7	10 39.8	10 35.2	8 13.8	3 58.1	11 29.4
25 M	0 12 27	4 59 55	4♍27 06	11♍04 03	17 36.3	8 14.9	4 11.0	10 14.4	27 01.6	10 48.9	10 32.0	8 17.2	4 00.1	11 30.0
26 Tu	0 16 23	5 59 18	17 46 06	24 33 02	17 29.2	8 55.1	5 25.6	11 00.5	27 17.7	10 58.1	10 28.7	8 20.6	4 02.1	11 30.5
27 W	0 20 20	6 58 40	1♎24 33	8♎20 16	17 23.2	9 39.1	6 40.2	11 46.6	27 34.1	11 07.5	10 25.3	8 24.0	4 04.1	11 31.0
28 Th	0 24 16	7 58 00	15 19 43	22 22 21	17 19.0	10 26.7	7 54.8	12 32.7	27 50.7	11 16.9	10 21.9	8 27.5	4 06.1	11 31.5
29 F	0 28 13	8 57 18	29 27 39	6♏35 00	17D 16.8	11 17.6	9 09.3	13 18.7	28 07.4	11 26.5	10 18.4	8 30.9	4 08.1	11 32.0
30 Sa	0 32 10	9 56 34	13♏43 52	20 53 40	17 16.4	12 11.7	10 23.8	14 04.7	28 24.4	11 36.2	10 14.9	8 34.3	4 10.0	11 32.4
31 Su	0 36 06	10 55 48	28 03 54	5♐14 06	17 17.3	13 08.7	11 38.3	14 50.6	28 41.6	11 46.0	10 11.2	8 37.7	4 11.9	11 32.8

April 2013 LONGITUDE

Day	Sid.Time	☉	0 hr ☽	Noon ☽	True ☊	☿	♀	♂	⚳	♃	♄	♅	♆	♇
1 M	0 40 03	11♈55 01	12♐23 51	19♐32 47	17♏18.7	14♓08.6	12♈52.8	15♈36.5	28♊59.0	11♊55.9	10♏07.6	8♈41.2	4♓13.8	11♑33.2
2 Tu	0 43 59	12 54 12	26 40 35	3♑47 01	17R 19.9	15 11.1	14 07.3	16 22.4	29 16.5	12 05.9	10R 03.8	8 44.6	4 15.7	11 33.5
3 W	0 47 56	13 53 21	10♑51 49	17 54 49	17 20.2	16 16.3	15 21.8	17 08.2	29 34.3	12 16.0	10 00.0	8 48.0	4 17.6	11 33.8
4 Th	0 51 52	14 52 28	24 55 49	1♒54 40	17 19.0	17 23.8	16 36.3	17 54.0	29 52.2	12 26.2	9 56.2	8 51.4	4 19.4	11 34.1
5 F	0 55 49	15 51 33	8♒51 12	15 45 16	17 16.4	18 33.7	17 50.7	18 39.8	0♋10.4	12 36.6	9 52.2	8 54.8	4 21.3	11 34.4
6 Sa	0 59 45	16 50 37	22 36 43	29 25 22	17 12.6	19 45.8	19 05.1	19 25.5	0 28.7	12 47.0	9 48.3	8 58.2	4 23.1	11 34.6
7 Su	1 03 42	17 49 39	6♓11 04	12♓53 38	17 08.0	21 00.1	20 19.5	20 11.1	0 47.2	12 57.5	9 44.3	9 01.6	4 24.9	11 34.8
8 M	1 07 39	18 48 39	19 32 57	26 08 51	17 03.3	22 16.4	21 33.9	20 56.7	1 05.9	13 08.1	9 40.2	9 05.0	4 26.6	11 34.9
9 Tu	1 11 35	19 47 37	2♈41 13	9♈09 58	16 59.2	23 34.7	22 48.3	21 42.3	1 24.7	13 18.8	9 36.1	9 08.4	4 28.4	11 35.0
10 W	1 15 32	20 46 33	15 35 03	21 56 27	16 56.0	24 54.9	24 02.6	22 27.8	1 43.7	13 29.7	9 31.9	9 11.8	4 30.1	11 35.1
11 Th	1 19 28	21 45 27	28 14 11	4♉28 22	16 54.1	26 17.1	25 17.0	23 13.3	2 02.9	13 40.6	9 27.7	9 15.2	4 31.8	11 35.2
12 F	1 23 25	22 44 20	10♉39 08	16 46 39	16D 53.5	27 41.1	26 31.3	23 58.7	2 22.3	13 51.6	9 23.5	9 18.5	4 33.5	11R 35.2
13 Sa	1 27 21	23 43 10	22 51 12	28 53 04	16 54.0	29 06.8	27 45.6	24 44.1	2 41.8	14 02.7	9 19.2	9 21.9	4 35.1	11 35.2
14 Su	1 31 18	24 41 58	4♊52 36	10♊50 12	16 55.3	0♈34.4	28 59.9	25 29.4	3 01.5	14 13.8	9 14.9	9 25.2	4 36.8	11 35.1
15 M	1 35 14	25 40 43	16 46 19	22 41 26	16 56.9	2 03.6	0♉14.1	26 14.7	3 21.3	14 25.1	9 10.5	9 28.6	4 38.4	11 35.1
16 Tu	1 39 11	26 39 27	28 36 05	4♋30 47	16 58.5	3 34.6	1 28.4	26 59.9	3 41.3	14 36.4	9 06.1	9 31.9	4 40.0	11 35.0
17 W	1 43 08	27 38 08	10♋26 08	16 22 43	16 59.7	5 07.3	2 42.6	27 45.1	4 01.4	14 47.9	9 01.7	9 35.2	4 41.5	11 34.9
18 Th	1 47 04	28 36 48	22 21 08	28 22 00	17R 00.1	6 41.7	3 56.8	28 30.2	4 21.7	14 59.4	8 57.3	9 38.5	4 43.0	11 34.7
19 F	1 51 01	29 35 25	4♌25 53	10♌33 24	16 59.7	8 17.8	5 11.0	29 15.3	4 42.1	15 11.0	8 52.9	9 41.8	4 44.6	11 34.5
20 Sa	1 54 57	0♉33 59	16 45 04	23 01 24	16 58.5	9 55.5	6 25.1	0♉00.3	5 02.7	15 22.6	8 48.4	9 45.0	4 46.0	11 34.3
21 Su	1 58 54	1 32 32	29 22 52	5♍49 50	16 56.8	11 34.9	7 39.3	0 45.3	5 23.4	15 34.4	8 43.9	9 48.3	4 47.5	11 34.0
22 M	2 02 50	2 31 02	12♍22 37	19 01 24	16 54.9	13 16.0	8 53.4	1 30.2	5 44.3	15 46.2	8 39.4	9 51.5	4 48.9	11 33.8
23 Tu	2 06 47	3 29 30	25 46 18	2♎37 15	16 53.0	14 58.8	10 07.5	2 15.1	6 05.2	15 58.0	8 34.9	9 54.7	4 50.3	11 33.4
24 W	2 10 43	4 27 57	9♎34 07	16 36 34	16 51.5	16 43.2	11 21.5	2 59.9	6 26.3	16 10.0	8 30.3	9 57.9	4 51.7	11 33.1
25 Th	2 14 40	5 26 21	23 44 12	0♏56 26	16 50.6	18 29.4	12 35.6	3 44.7	6 47.6	16 22.0	8 25.8	10 01.1	4 53.0	11 32.7
26 F	2 18 36	6 24 44	8♏12 36	15 31 55	16D 50.3	20 17.2	13 49.6	4 29.4	7 08.9	16 34.1	8 21.2	10 04.2	4 54.4	11 32.3
27 Sa	2 22 33	7 23 04	22 53 35	0♐16 43	16 50.5	22 06.8	15 03.6	5 14.1	7 30.4	16 46.2	8 16.7	10 07.4	4 55.7	11 31.9
28 Su	2 26 30	8 21 23	7♐40 24	15 03 47	16 51.0	23 58.1	16 17.6	5 58.7	7 52.0	16 58.5	8 12.1	10 10.5	4 56.9	11 31.5
29 M	2 30 26	9 19 41	22 26 02	29 46 24	16 51.7	25 51.1	17 31.6	6 43.3	8 13.7	17 10.7	8 07.6	10 13.6	4 58.2	11 31.0
30 Tu	2 34 23	10 17 57	7♑04 12	14♑18 53	16 52.3	27 45.8	18 45.6	7 27.8	8 35.6	17 23.1	8 03.0	10 16.7	4 59.4	11 30.5

Astro Data	Dy Hr Mn
♄✱♇	8 7:07
☽0N	11 17:16
♂0N	14 10:50
☿D	17 20:05
☉0N	20 11:03
♃⚻♄	24 2:52
♀0N	24 16:51
☽0S	26 3:44
♃⚻♇	30 2:20
☽0N	8 0:27
♇R	12 19:35
♄⚻♅	13 3:30
☿0N	18 1:05
☽0S	22 13:11

Planet Ingress		Dy Hr Mn
♂	♈	12 6:27
☉	♈	20 11:03
♀	♈	22 3:16
⚳	♋	4 22:18
☿	♈	14 2:38
♀	♉	15 7:26
☉	♉	19 22:04
♂	♉	20 11:49

Last Aspect Dy Hr Mn		☽ Ingress	Dy Hr Mn
28 8:38	♇ □	♏	1 17:35
3 9:20	♂ △	♐	3 21:12
5 15:29	♂ □	♑	6 0:15
7 21:15	♂ ✱	♒	8 3:03
8 22:09	♄ □	♓	10 6:20
11 19:52	☉ ☌	♈	12 11:18
13 8:03	♇ □	♉	14 19:09
16 23:12	☉ ✱	♊	17 6:10
19 17:28	☉ □	♋	19 18:56
20 18:03	♇ ☍	♌	22 6:51
23 3:29	♄ □	♍	24 15:50
25 12:47	♇ △	♎	26 21:33
27 18:16	♂ ☍	♏	29 0:55
29 20:26	☿ △	♐	31 3:14

Last Aspect Dy Hr Mn		☽ Ingress	Dy Hr Mn
1 5:01	♂ △	♑	2 5:36
3 10:36	♂ □	♒	4 8:43
5 17:23	♂ ✱	♓	6 13:01
8 4:11	☿ ☌	♈	8 19:03
10 16:26	♀ ☌	♉	11 3:23
13 12:31	☿ ✱	♊	13 14:14
15 19:42	♂ ✱	♋	16 2:50
18 12:32	☉ □	♌	18 15:15
19 21:07	♃ ✱	♍	21 1:10
22 6:04	♃ □	♎	23 7:26
24 12:13	☿ ☍	♏	25 10:26
26 8:57	☿ ☍	♐	27 11:33
29 4:38	☿ △	♑	29 12:22

☽ Phases & Eclipses Dy Hr Mn	
4 21:54	☾ 14♐29
11 19:52	● 21♓24
19 17:28	☽ 29♊16
27 9:28	○ 6♎52
3 4:38	☾ 13♑35
10 9:36	● 20♈41
18 12:32	☽ 28♋38
25 19:58	○ 5♏46
25 20:09	• P 0.015

Astro Data

1 March 2013
Julian Day # 41333
SVP 5♓04'19"
GC 27♐01.4 ⚴ 17♈19.6
Eris 21♈50.9 ⚵ 26♑03.9
⚷ 9♓28.2 ⚶ 13♊34.7
☽ Mean ☊ 20♏26.7

1 April 2013
Julian Day # 41364
SVP 5♓04'16"
GC 27♐01.5 ⚴ 0♉56.0
Eris 22♈09.2 ⚵ 5♒58.0
⚷ 11♓23.8 ⚶ 21♊51.5
☽ Mean ☊ 18♏48.2

LONGITUDE — May 2013

Day	Sid.Time	☉	0 hr ☽	Noon ☽	True ☊	☿	♀	♂	⚳	♃	♄	♅	♆	♇
1 W	2 38 19	11♉16 11	21♑29 58	28♑37 04	16♏52.7	29♈42.2	19♉59.5	8♉12.3	8♋57.5	17♊35.5	7♏58.5	10♈19.8	5♓00.6	11♑29.9
2 Th	2 42 16	12 14 24	5♒39 58	12♒38 27	16R52.8	1♉40.3	21 13.5	8 56.8	9 19.6	17 47.9	7R53.9	10 22.8	5 01.7	11R29.4
3 F	2 46 12	13 12 36	19 32 29	26 22 01	16 52.7	3 40.1	22 27.4	9 41.1	9 41.8	18 00.5	7 49.4	10 25.8	5 02.8	11 28.8
4 Sa	2 50 09	14 10 46	3♓07 07	9♓47 52	16 52.5	5 41.5	23 41.3	10 25.5	10 04.1	18 13.0	7 44.9	10 28.8	5 03.9	11 28.2
5 Su	2 54 05	15 08 55	16 24 24	22 56 52	16 52.3	7 44.5	24 55.2	11 09.7	10 26.5	18 25.7	7 40.4	10 31.8	5 05.0	11 27.5
6 M	2 58 02	16 07 02	29 25 28	5♈50 20	16D52.1	9 49.0	26 09.0	11 54.0	10 49.0	18 38.4	7 35.9	10 34.7	5 06.0	11 26.8
7 Tu	3 01 59	17 05 07	12♈11 42	18 29 43	16 52.1	11 54.8	27 22.9	12 38.1	11 11.6	18 51.1	7 31.4	10 37.7	5 07.0	11 26.1
8 W	3 05 55	18 03 12	24 44 36	0♉56 32	16 52.1	14 02.0	28 36.7	13 22.3	11 34.4	19 03.9	7 26.9	10 40.6	5 08.0	11 25.4
9 Th	3 09 52	19 01 14	7♉05 42	13 12 19	16R52.2	16 10.2	29 50.6	14 06.3	11 57.2	19 16.7	7 22.5	10 43.4	5 08.9	11 24.6
10 F	3 13 48	19 59 15	19 16 34	25 18 39	16 52.2	18 19.5	1♊04.4	14 50.4	12 20.1	19 29.6	7 18.1	10 46.3	5 09.9	11 23.9
11 Sa	3 17 45	20 57 15	1♊18 50	7♊17 20	16 51.9	20 29.5	2 18.1	15 34.3	12 43.2	19 42.5	7 13.7	10 49.1	5 10.7	11 23.1
12 Su	3 21 41	21 55 13	13 14 25	19 10 23	16 51.5	22 40.1	3 31.9	16 18.3	13 06.3	19 55.5	7 09.4	10 51.9	5 11.6	11 22.2
13 M	3 25 38	22 53 09	25 05 31	1♋00 12	16 50.8	24 51.0	4 45.7	17 02.1	13 29.5	20 08.5	7 05.1	10 54.6	5 12.4	11 21.4
14 Tu	3 29 34	23 51 04	6♋54 47	12 49 40	16 49.9	27 02.0	5 59.4	17 45.9	13 52.9	20 21.6	7 00.8	10 57.4	5 13.2	11 20.5
15 W	3 33 31	24 48 57	18 45 17	24 42 06	16 48.9	29 12.7	7 13.1	18 29.7	14 16.3	20 34.7	6 56.6	11 00.1	5 14.0	11 19.6
16 Th	3 37 28	25 46 48	0♌40 35	6♌41 15	16 48.1	1♊22.9	8 26.8	19 13.4	14 39.8	20 47.9	6 52.4	11 02.7	5 14.7	11 18.7
17 F	3 41 24	26 44 38	12 44 38	18 51 16	16D47.6	3 32.4	9 40.5	19 57.0	15 03.4	21 01.0	6 48.2	11 05.4	5 15.4	11 17.7
18 Sa	3 45 21	27 42 25	25 01 40	1♍16 24	16 47.5	5 40.7	10 54.1	20 40.6	15 27.0	21 14.3	6 44.1	11 08.0	5 16.0	11 16.8
19 Su	3 49 17	28 40 11	7♍35 57	14 00 50	16 47.9	7 47.8	12 07.7	21 24.1	15 50.8	21 27.5	6 40.1	11 10.6	5 16.7	11 15.8
20 M	3 53 14	29 37 56	20 31 28	27 08 14	16 48.7	9 53.2	13 21.3	22 07.6	16 14.6	21 40.8	6 36.0	11 13.1	5 17.3	11 14.7
21 Tu	3 57 10	0♊35 39	3♎51 25	10♎41 13	16 49.8	11 56.8	14 34.9	22 51.1	16 38.5	21 54.1	6 32.1	11 15.6	5 17.8	11 13.7
22 W	4 01 07	1 33 20	17 37 41	24 40 46	16 50.8	13 58.4	15 48.5	23 34.4	17 02.5	22 07.5	6 28.1	11 18.1	5 18.4	11 12.6
23 Th	4 05 03	2 31 00	1♏50 13	9♏05 40	16R51.5	15 57.8	17 02.0	24 17.7	17 26.6	22 20.9	6 24.3	11 20.5	5 18.9	11 11.6
24 F	4 09 00	3 28 38	16 26 30	23 52 01	16 51.5	17 54.9	18 15.6	25 01.0	17 50.8	22 34.3	6 20.5	11 22.9	5 19.3	11 10.5
25 Sa	4 12 57	4 26 15	1♐21 19	8♐53 22	16 50.7	19 49.4	19 29.1	25 44.2	18 15.0	22 47.7	6 16.7	11 25.3	5 19.8	11 09.3
26 Su	4 16 53	5 23 51	16 27 04	24 01 13	16 49.0	21 41.4	20 42.6	26 27.4	18 39.3	23 01.2	6 13.0	11 27.7	5 20.2	11 08.2
27 M	4 20 50	6 21 26	1♑34 39	9♑06 13	16 46.8	23 30.6	21 56.0	27 10.5	19 03.7	23 14.7	6 09.4	11 30.0	5 20.5	11 07.0
28 Tu	4 24 46	7 19 00	16 34 49	23 59 32	16 44.2	25 17.2	23 09.5	27 53.5	19 28.1	23 28.2	6 05.9	11 32.2	5 20.9	11 05.9
29 W	4 28 43	8 16 33	1♒19 32	8♒34 10	16 41.9	27 00.9	24 22.9	28 36.5	19 52.7	23 41.7	6 02.3	11 34.5	5 21.2	11 04.7
30 Th	4 32 39	9 14 05	15 43 00	22 45 42	16 40.2	28 41.7	25 36.3	29 19.5	20 17.2	23 55.3	5 58.9	11 36.7	5 21.5	11 03.5
31 F	4 36 36	10 11 37	29 42 09	6♓32 20	16D39.4	0♋19.6	26 49.7	0♊02.4	20 41.9	24 08.9	5 55.5	11 38.8	5 21.7	11 02.2

LONGITUDE — June 2013

Day	Sid.Time	☉	0 hr ☽	Noon ☽	True ☊	☿	♀	♂	⚳	♃	♄	♅	♆	♇
1 Sa	4 40 32	11♊09 07	13♓16 24	19♓54 34	16♏39.6	1♋54.6	28♊03.1	0♊45.2	21♋06.6	24♊22.5	5♏52.2	11♈40.9	5♓21.9	11♑01.0
2 Su	4 44 29	12 06 37	26 27 08	2♈54 29	16 40.6	3 26.7	29 16.5	1 28.0	21 31.4	24 36.1	5R49.0	11 43.0	5 22.1	10R59.7
3 M	4 48 26	13 04 06	9♈17 01	15 35 09	16 42.2	4 55.7	0♋29.9	2 10.8	21 56.3	24 49.8	5 45.8	11 45.1	5 22.2	10 58.4
4 Tu	4 52 22	14 01 34	21 49 19	27 59 58	16 43.7	6 21.8	1 43.2	2 53.5	22 21.2	25 03.4	5 42.7	11 47.1	5 22.3	10 57.1
5 W	4 56 19	14 59 01	4♉07 29	10♉12 18	16R44.8	7 44.7	2 56.5	3 36.1	22 46.2	25 17.1	5 39.7	11 49.0	5 22.4	10 55.8
6 Th	5 00 15	15 56 28	16 14 47	22 15 16	16 44.8	9 04.6	4 09.8	4 18.7	23 11.3	25 30.8	5 36.8	11 50.9	5R22.4	10 54.5
7 F	5 04 12	16 53 54	28 14 07	4♊11 36	16 43.5	10 21.4	5 23.1	5 01.2	23 36.4	25 44.5	5 33.9	11 52.8	5 22.5	10 53.2
8 Sa	5 08 08	17 51 20	10♊08 01	16 03 38	16 40.6	11 34.9	6 36.4	5 43.7	24 01.6	25 58.3	5 31.1	11 54.7	5 22.4	10 51.8
9 Su	5 12 05	18 48 44	21 58 43	27 53 29	16 36.3	12 45.2	7 49.7	6 26.2	24 26.8	26 12.0	5 28.4	11 56.5	5 22.4	10 50.5
10 M	5 16 01	19 46 08	3♋48 11	9♋43 05	16 30.9	13 52.3	9 02.9	7 08.5	24 52.1	26 25.7	5 25.8	11 58.2	5 22.3	10 49.1
11 Tu	5 19 58	20 43 30	15 38 25	21 34 27	16 24.8	14 55.9	10 16.1	7 50.9	25 17.5	26 39.5	5 23.3	11 59.9	5 22.2	10 47.7
12 W	5 23 55	21 40 52	27 31 28	3♌29 47	16 18.8	15 56.2	11 29.3	8 33.1	25 42.9	26 53.2	5 20.8	12 01.6	5 22.0	10 46.3
13 Th	5 27 51	22 38 13	9♌29 45	15 31 41	16 13.3	16 52.9	12 42.5	9 15.3	26 08.3	27 07.0	5 18.5	12 03.2	5 21.8	10 44.9
14 F	5 31 48	23 35 33	21 36 01	27 43 09	16 09.0	17 46.0	13 55.7	9 57.5	26 33.9	27 20.8	5 16.2	12 04.8	5 21.6	10 43.5
15 Sa	5 35 44	24 32 52	3♍53 31	10♍07 35	16 06.3	18 35.4	15 08.8	10 39.6	26 59.4	27 34.5	5 14.0	12 06.4	5 21.4	10 42.0
16 Su	5 39 41	25 30 11	16 25 49	22 48 43	16D05.3	19 21.0	16 21.9	11 21.7	27 25.0	27 48.3	5 11.9	12 07.9	5 21.1	10 40.6
17 M	5 43 37	26 27 28	29 16 44	5♎50 19	16 05.6	20 02.7	17 35.0	12 03.7	27 50.7	28 02.1	5 09.9	12 09.3	5 20.8	10 39.1
18 Tu	5 47 34	27 24 44	12♎29 52	19 15 44	16 06.8	20 40.5	18 48.1	12 45.6	28 16.4	28 15.9	5 07.9	12 10.7	5 20.4	10 37.7
19 W	5 51 30	28 22 00	26 08 11	3♏07 21	16R08.0	21 14.1	20 01.1	13 27.5	28 42.2	28 29.6	5 06.1	12 12.1	5 20.1	10 36.2
20 Th	5 55 27	29 19 15	10♏13 15	17 25 45	16 08.5	21 43.5	21 14.1	14 09.3	29 08.0	28 43.4	5 04.4	12 13.4	5 19.7	10 34.7
21 F	5 59 24	0♋16 30	24 44 30	2♐08 59	16 07.6	22 08.6	22 27.1	14 51.1	29 33.9	28 57.1	5 02.7	12 14.7	5 19.2	10 33.3
22 Sa	6 03 20	1 13 43	9♐38 28	17 12 02	16 04.7	22 29.3	23 40.1	15 32.9	29 59.8	29 10.9	5 01.1	12 15.9	5 18.8	10 31.8
23 Su	6 07 17	2 10 57	24 48 34	2♑26 51	15 59.9	22 45.5	24 53.0	16 14.5	0♌25.7	29 24.7	4 59.7	12 17.1	5 18.3	10 30.3
24 M	6 11 13	3 08 10	10♑05 32	17 43 15	15 53.6	22 57.2	26 06.0	16 56.2	0 51.7	29 38.4	4 58.3	12 18.3	5 17.7	10 28.8
25 Tu	6 15 10	4 05 23	25 18 39	2♒50 28	15 46.6	23 04.3	27 18.9	17 37.8	1 17.7	29 52.2	4 57.0	12 19.3	5 17.2	10 27.3
26 W	6 19 06	5 02 35	10♒17 36	17 39 05	15 39.8	23R06.8	28 31.7	18 19.3	1 43.8	0♋05.9	4 55.8	12 20.4	5 16.6	10 25.8
27 Th	6 23 03	5 59 48	24 54 10	2♓02 22	15 34.1	23 04.8	29 44.6	19 00.8	2 09.9	0 19.6	4 54.7	12 21.4	5 16.0	10 24.3
28 F	6 27 00	6 57 00	9♓03 21	15 57 01	15 30.2	22 58.2	0♌57.4	19 42.2	2 36.1	0 33.3	4 53.7	12 22.3	5 15.3	10 22.8
29 Sa	6 30 56	7 54 12	22 43 26	29 22 51	15D28.2	22 47.1	2 10.2	20 23.6	3 02.3	0 47.0	4 52.8	12 23.2	5 14.7	10 21.3
30 Su	6 34 53	8 51 25	5♈55 36	12♈22 09	15 27.9	22 31.8	3 23.0	21 04.9	3 28.5	1 00.7	4 52.0	12 24.1	5 14.0	10 19.8

Astro Data

Dy Hr Mn

☽0N 5 5:56
☽0S 19 22:27
♃⚻♄ 20 5:22
♅□♇ 20 23:03

☽0N 1 11:45
♆R 7 8:26
♄△♆ 11 23:27
☽0S 16 6:43
☿R 26 13:09
☽0N 28 19:30

Planet Ingress

Dy Hr Mn

☿ ♉ 1 15:38
♀ ♊ 9 15:04
☿ ♊ 15 20:42
☉ ♊ 20 21:11
☿ ♋ 31 7:08
♂ ♊ 31 10:40

♀ ♋ 3 2:14
☉ ♋ 21 5:05
⚳ ♌ 22 12:14
♃ ♋ 26 1:41
♀ ♌ 27 17:04

Last Aspect / ☽ Ingress

Last Aspect Dy Hr Mn		☽ Ingress Dy Hr Mn
1 14:08	☿ □	♒ 1 14:21
3 4:26	♀ □	♓ 3 18:26
5 16:01	♀ ✶	♈ 6 1:04
7 12:42	♃ ✶	♉ 8 10:10
10 0:30	☉ ☌	♊ 10 21:22
12 13:33	♃ ☌	♋ 13 9:58
15 12:15	☉ ✶	♌ 15 22:39
18 4:36	☉ □	♍ 18 9:34
20 16:49	☉ △	♎ 20 17:08
22 7:36	♃ △	♏ 22 20:56
24 13:56	♃ ☍	♐ 24 21:50
26 10:23	♃ ☍	♑ 26 21:30
28 18:42	♂ △	♒ 28 21:49
30 23:58	♂ □	♓ 31 0:31

Last Aspect Dy Hr Mn		☽ Ingress Dy Hr Mn
2 4:31	♀ □	♈ 2 6:35
4 6:10	♃ ✶	♉ 4 15:55
5 13:26	♇ △	♊ 7 3:33
9 8:30	♃ ☌	♋ 9 16:17
10 21:16	☿ ☌	♌ 12 4:59
14 11:15	♃ ✶	♍ 14 16:27
16 21:27	♃ □	♎ 17 1:20
19 3:56	♃ △	♏ 19 6:40
20 19:17	☿ △	♐ 21 8:32
23 7:10	♃ ☍	♑ 23 8:09
25 2:25	♀ ☍	♒ 25 7:28
26 13:09	♂ △	♓ 27 8:33
29 0:17	☿ △	♈ 29 13:08

☽ Phases & Eclipses

Dy Hr Mn

2 11:15 ☾ 12♒13
10 0:30 ● 19♉31
10 0:26:21 • A 06'03"
18 4:36 ☽ 27♌25
25 4:26 ○ 4♐08
25 4:11 • A 0.015
31 18:59 ☾ 10♓28

8 15:57 ● 18♊01
16 17:25 ☽ 25♍43
23 11:33 ○ 2♑10
30 4:55 ☾ 8♈35

Astro Data

1 May 2013
Julian Day # 41394
SVP 5♓04'13"
GC 27♐01.5 ⚴ 15♉32.1
Eris 22♈28.7 ⚵ 13♒42.3
⚷ 12♓52.9 ⚶ 2♋25.7
☽ Mean ☊ 17♏12.9

1 June 2013
Julian Day # 41425
SVP 5♓04'09"
GC 27♐01.6 ⚴ 1♊49.2
Eris 22♈45.8 ⚵ 18♒26.5
⚷ 13♓43.8 ⚶ 14♋52.9
☽ Mean ☊ 15♏34.4

July 2013 LONGITUDE

Day	Sid.Time	☉	0 hr ☽	Noon ☽	True ☊	☿	♀	♂	⚳	♃	♄	♅	♆	♇
1 M	6 38 49	9♋48 38	18♈43 00	24♈58 43	15♏28.7	22♋12.4	4♌35.8	21♊46.2	3♌54.8	1♋14.4	4♏51.3	12♈24.9	5♓13.2	10♑18.3
2 Tu	6 42 46	10 45 51	1♉09 53	7♉17 07	15R 29.6	21R 49.1	5 48.6	22 27.4	4 21.1	1 28.1	4R 50.7	12 25.7	5R 12.5	10R 16.8
3 W	6 46 42	11 43 04	13 20 59	19 22 03	15 29.8	21 22.4	7 01.3	23 08.6	4 47.5	1 41.7	4 50.2	12 26.4	5 11.7	10 15.2
4 Th	6 50 39	12 40 17	25 20 51	1♊17 55	15 28.4	20 52.4	8 14.0	23 49.7	5 13.9	1 55.4	4 49.8	12 27.1	5 10.9	10 13.7
5 F	6 54 35	13 37 30	7♊13 41	13 08 37	15 24.8	20 19.8	9 26.7	24 30.8	5 40.3	2 09.0	4 49.5	12 27.7	5 10.0	10 12.2
6 Sa	6 58 32	14 34 44	19 03 03	24 57 23	15 18.7	19 45.0	10 39.3	25 11.8	6 06.8	2 22.6	4 49.2	12 28.3	5 09.1	10 10.7
7 Su	7 02 29	15 31 58	0♋51 52	6♋46 48	15 10.3	19 08.5	11 52.0	25 52.8	6 33.3	2 36.2	4D 49.1	12 28.8	5 08.2	10 09.2
8 M	7 06 25	16 29 12	12 42 25	18 38 55	14 59.9	18 31.0	13 04.6	26 33.8	6 59.8	2 49.7	4 49.1	12 29.3	5 07.3	10 07.7
9 Tu	7 10 22	17 26 26	24 36 30	0♌35 21	14 48.5	17 53.0	14 17.2	27 14.6	7 26.4	3 03.2	4 49.2	12 29.7	5 06.4	10 06.2
10 W	7 14 18	18 23 40	6♌35 38	12 37 32	14 36.9	17 15.3	15 29.7	27 55.5	7 53.0	3 16.8	4 49.3	12 30.1	5 05.4	10 04.7
11 Th	7 18 15	19 20 54	18 41 14	24 46 56	14 26.2	16 38.4	16 42.2	28 36.3	8 19.6	3 30.2	4 49.6	12 30.4	5 04.4	10 03.2
12 F	7 22 11	20 18 08	0♍54 53	7♍05 19	14 17.3	16 03.1	17 54.7	29 17.0	8 46.3	3 43.7	4 50.0	12 30.7	5 03.4	10 01.7
13 Sa	7 26 08	21 15 22	13 18 31	19 34 49	14 10.8	15 29.9	19 07.2	29 57.7	9 13.0	3 57.1	4 50.5	12 30.9	5 02.3	10 00.3
14 Su	7 30 04	22 12 36	25 54 33	2♎18 05	14 06.9	14 59.4	20 19.6	0♋38.3	9 39.7	4 10.5	4 51.0	12 31.1	5 01.2	9 58.8
15 M	7 34 01	23 09 50	8♎45 48	15 18 07	14D 05.2	14 32.3	21 32.0	1 18.8	10 06.5	4 23.9	4 51.7	12 31.2	5 00.1	9 57.3
16 Tu	7 37 58	24 07 05	21 55 25	28 38 03	14 05.0	14 09.0	22 44.4	1 59.4	10 33.3	4 37.2	4 52.5	12 31.3	4 59.0	9 55.9
17 W	7 41 54	25 04 19	5♏26 21	12♏20 35	14R 05.3	13 49.9	23 56.7	2 39.8	11 00.1	4 50.5	4 53.3	12R 31.3	4 57.9	9 54.4
18 Th	7 45 51	26 01 34	19 20 54	26 27 20	14 04.8	13 35.5	25 09.0	3 20.2	11 26.9	5 03.8	4 54.3	12 31.3	4 56.7	9 53.0
19 F	7 49 47	26 58 48	3♐39 48	10♐57 59	14 02.6	13 26.1	26 21.3	4 00.6	11 53.7	5 17.0	4 55.4	12 31.2	4 55.5	9 51.5
20 Sa	7 53 44	27 56 03	18 21 27	25 49 29	13 57.9	13D 21.9	27 33.5	4 40.9	12 20.6	5 30.2	4 56.5	12 31.1	4 54.3	9 50.1
21 Su	7 57 40	28 53 19	3♑21 13	10♑55 37	13 50.7	13 23.2	28 45.7	5 21.2	12 47.5	5 43.3	4 57.8	12 31.0	4 53.1	9 48.7
22 M	8 01 37	29 50 34	18 31 27	26 07 25	13 41.3	13 30.2	29 57.9	6 01.4	13 14.4	5 56.4	4 59.1	12 30.8	4 51.8	9 47.3
23 Tu	8 05 33	0♌47 50	3♒42 10	11♒14 22	13 30.9	13 42.9	1♍10.0	6 41.6	13 41.4	6 09.5	5 00.6	12 30.5	4 50.5	9 45.9
24 W	8 09 30	1 45 07	18 42 46	26 06 15	13 20.6	14 01.5	2 22.1	7 21.7	14 08.4	6 22.6	5 02.1	12 30.2	4 49.2	9 44.5
25 Th	8 13 27	2 42 25	3♓23 53	10♓34 55	13 11.5	14 26.0	3 34.1	8 01.8	14 35.4	6 35.6	5 03.8	12 29.9	4 47.9	9 43.2
26 F	8 17 23	3 39 43	17 38 53	24 35 28	13 04.7	14 56.4	4 46.1	8 41.8	15 02.4	6 48.5	5 05.5	12 29.5	4 46.6	9 41.8
27 Sa	8 21 20	4 37 02	1♈24 36	8♈06 23	13 00.3	15 32.7	5 58.1	9 21.8	15 29.4	7 01.4	5 07.3	12 29.0	4 45.2	9 40.5
28 Su	8 25 16	5 34 22	14 41 06	21 09 09	12 58.2	16 14.9	7 10.1	10 01.7	15 56.5	7 14.3	5 09.2	12 28.5	4 43.9	9 39.1
29 M	8 29 13	6 31 44	27 31 00	3♉47 15	12 57.6	17 03.0	8 22.0	10 41.6	16 23.5	7 27.1	5 11.2	12 28.0	4 42.5	9 37.8
30 Tu	8 33 09	7 29 06	9♉58 30	16 05 27	12 57.6	17 56.8	9 33.8	11 21.5	16 50.6	7 39.9	5 13.4	12 27.4	4 41.1	9 36.5
31 W	8 37 06	8 26 30	22 08 43	28 08 59	12 57.0	18 56.3	10 45.7	12 01.2	17 17.7	7 52.6	5 15.6	12 26.8	4 39.7	9 35.3

August 2013 LONGITUDE

Day	Sid.Time	☉	0 hr ☽	Noon ☽	True ☊	☿	♀	♂	⚳	♃	♄	♅	♆	♇
1 Th	8 41 02	9♌23 54	4♊06 54	10♊03 04	12♏54.8	20♋01.3	11♍57.4	12♋41.0	17♌44.9	8♋05.3	5♏17.9	12♈26.1	4♓38.2	9♑34.0
2 F	8 44 59	10 21 20	15 58 05	21 52 29	12R 50.2	21 11.8	13 09.2	13 20.7	18 12.0	8 17.9	5 20.2	12R 25.4	4R 36.8	9R 32.7
3 Sa	8 48 56	11 18 46	27 46 46	3♋41 24	12 42.9	22 27.6	14 20.9	14 00.4	18 39.2	8 30.4	5 22.7	12 24.6	4 35.3	9 31.5
4 Su	8 52 52	12 16 14	9♋36 45	15 33 10	12 32.9	23 48.5	15 32.6	14 40.0	19 06.4	8 42.9	5 25.3	12 23.8	4 33.8	9 30.3
5 M	8 56 49	13 13 43	21 30 57	27 30 21	12 20.7	25 14.3	16 44.2	15 19.5	19 33.6	8 55.4	5 27.9	12 22.9	4 32.3	9 29.1
6 Tu	9 00 45	14 11 13	3♌31 34	9♌34 45	12 07.2	26 44.9	17 55.8	15 59.0	20 00.8	9 07.8	5 30.7	12 22.0	4 30.8	9 27.9
7 W	9 04 42	15 08 44	15 40 02	21 47 31	11 53.5	28 19.9	19 07.4	16 38.5	20 28.1	9 20.1	5 33.5	12 21.1	4 29.3	9 26.7
8 Th	9 08 38	16 06 16	27 57 17	4♍09 24	11 40.7	29 59.0	20 18.9	17 17.9	20 55.3	9 32.4	5 36.5	12 20.1	4 27.8	9 25.6
9 F	9 12 35	17 03 48	10♍23 58	16 41 02	11 30.0	1♌42.0	21 30.4	17 57.3	21 22.6	9 44.6	5 39.5	12 19.0	4 26.2	9 24.5
10 Sa	9 16 31	18 01 22	23 00 44	29 23 11	11 22.0	3 28.6	22 41.8	18 36.6	21 49.8	9 56.8	5 42.6	12 17.9	4 24.7	9 23.4
11 Su	9 20 28	18 58 57	5♎48 32	12♎16 59	11 16.9	5 18.3	23 53.2	19 15.8	22 17.1	10 08.9	5 45.8	12 16.8	4 23.1	9 22.3
12 M	9 24 25	19 56 32	18 48 43	25 24 00	11 14.4	7 10.8	25 04.5	19 55.0	22 44.4	10 20.9	5 49.0	12 15.6	4 21.5	9 21.2
13 Tu	9 28 21	20 54 09	2♏03 04	8♏46 09	11 13.7	9 05.6	26 15.7	20 34.2	23 11.7	10 32.8	5 52.4	12 14.4	4 19.9	9 20.2
14 W	9 32 18	21 51 46	15 33 32	22 25 24	11 13.8	11 02.5	27 27.0	21 13.3	23 39.0	10 44.7	5 55.8	12 13.2	4 18.4	9 19.1
15 Th	9 36 14	22 49 25	29 21 55	6♐23 11	11 13.3	13 01.0	28 38.1	21 52.4	24 06.3	10 56.5	5 59.4	12 11.9	4 16.8	9 18.1
16 F	9 40 11	23 47 04	13♐29 10	20 39 45	11 11.1	15 00.7	29 49.3	22 31.4	24 33.6	11 08.2	6 03.0	12 10.5	4 15.2	9 17.2
17 Sa	9 44 07	24 44 45	27 54 39	5♑13 26	11 06.6	17 01.3	1♎00.3	23 10.4	25 01.0	11 19.9	6 06.7	12 09.2	4 13.5	9 16.2
18 Su	9 48 04	25 42 26	12♑35 30	20 00 06	10 59.5	19 02.5	2 11.3	23 49.3	25 28.3	11 31.5	6 10.5	12 07.7	4 11.9	9 15.3
19 M	9 52 00	26 40 09	27 26 20	4♒53 10	10 50.2	21 03.9	3 22.2	24 28.1	25 55.6	11 43.0	6 14.3	12 06.3	4 10.3	9 14.4
20 Tu	9 55 57	27 37 53	12♒19 32	19 44 18	10 39.8	23 05.3	4 33.1	25 07.0	26 23.0	11 54.4	6 18.2	12 04.8	4 08.7	9 13.5
21 W	9 59 54	28 35 38	27 06 22	4♓24 41	10 29.4	25 06.4	5 43.9	25 45.7	26 50.3	12 05.8	6 22.3	12 03.3	4 07.0	9 12.6
22 Th	10 03 50	29 33 24	11♓38 19	18 46 31	10 20.2	27 07.1	6 54.7	26 24.5	27 17.7	12 17.1	6 26.3	12 01.7	4 05.4	9 11.8
23 F	10 07 47	0♍31 12	25 48 40	2♈44 21	10 13.0	29 07.1	8 05.4	27 03.1	27 45.0	12 28.3	6 30.5	12 00.1	4 03.8	9 11.0
24 Sa	10 11 43	1 29 01	9♈33 20	16 15 33	10 08.4	1♍06.3	9 16.0	27 41.8	28 12.4	12 39.4	6 34.7	11 58.5	4 02.1	9 10.2
25 Su	10 15 40	2 26 53	22 51 07	29 20 15	10D 06.1	3 04.7	10 26.6	28 20.4	28 39.8	12 50.4	6 39.1	11 56.8	4 00.5	9 09.4
26 M	10 19 36	3 24 46	5♉43 22	12♉00 53	10 05.6	5 02.0	11 37.1	28 58.9	29 07.1	13 01.4	6 43.4	11 55.1	3 58.8	9 08.7
27 Tu	10 23 33	4 22 41	18 13 23	24 21 26	10R 06.1	6 58.3	12 47.6	29 37.4	29 34.5	13 12.2	6 47.9	11 53.3	3 57.2	9 08.0
28 W	10 27 29	5 20 37	0♊25 41	6♊26 48	10 06.4	8 53.4	13 58.0	0♌15.9	0♍01.9	13 23.0	6 52.5	11 51.6	3 55.5	9 07.3
29 Th	10 31 26	6 18 36	12 25 25	18 22 14	10 05.6	10 47.4	15 08.3	0 54.3	0 29.3	13 33.7	6 57.1	11 49.7	3 53.9	9 06.7
30 F	10 35 22	7 16 36	24 17 52	0♋12 56	10 02.9	12 40.2	16 18.6	1 32.6	0 56.6	13 44.2	7 01.7	11 47.9	3 52.3	9 06.0
31 Sa	10 39 19	8 14 38	6♋08 03	12 03 45	9 57.9	14 31.7	17 28.8	2 10.9	1 24.0	13 54.7	7 06.5	11 46.0	3 50.6	9 05.4

Astro Data (Dy Hr Mn)

♄ D 8 5:13
☽ 0S 13 13:49
♅ R 17 17:21
♃△♄ 17 17:33
♃△♆ 18 0:15
♄△♆ 19 13:21
☿ D 20 18:24
☽ 0N 26 5:20

♃☍♇ 7 23:47
☽ 0S 9 20:14
♀0S 17 22:52
♃□♅ 21 7:17
☽ 0N 22 16:01

Planet Ingress (Dy Hr Mn)

♂ ♋ 13 13:23
♀ ♍ 22 12:42
☉ ♌ 22 15:57

☿ ♌ 8 12:14
♀ ♎ 16 15:38
☉ ♍ 22 23:03
☿ ♍ 23 22:38
♂ ♌ 28 2:06
⚳ ♍ 28 10:21

Last Aspect Dy Hr Mn			☽ Ingress	Dy Hr Mn
1 6:49	☿	□	♉	1 21:44
3 15:52	☿	✶	♊	4 9:23
6 12:31	♂	☌	♋	6 22:15
8 11:45	☿	☌	♌	9 10:49
11 19:56	♂	✶	♍	11 22:13
13 15:27	☉	✶	♎	14 7:42
16 3:19	☉	□	♏	16 14:25
18 11:14	☉	△	♐	18 17:55
20 15:01	♀	△	♑	20 18:40
21 15:54	☿	☍	♒	22 18:08
23 14:02	♅	✶	♓	24 18:23
25 18:44	☿	△	♈	26 21:30
28 2:20	☿	□	♉	29 4:44
30 15:59	☿	✶	♊	31 15:43

Last Aspect Dy Hr Mn			☽ Ingress	Dy Hr Mn
1 16:50	♅	✶	♋	3 4:31
5 6:50	☿	☌	♌	5 16:59
6 21:52	☉	☌	♍	8 3:58
9 22:06	♀	☌	♎	10 13:09
12 1:30	♂	□	♏	12 20:19
14 21:31	♀	✶	♐	15 1:05
16 17:33	☉	△	♑	17 3:26
18 18:27	♂	☍	♒	19 4:08
21 1:46	☉	☍	♓	21 4:44
23 1:39	♂	△	♈	23 7:14
25 10:03	♂	□	♉	25 13:14
27 22:59	♂	✶	♊	27 23:09
29 4:46	♀	△	♋	30 11:34

☽ Phases & Eclipses (Dy Hr Mn)

8 7:15 ● 16♋18
16 3:19 ☽ 23♎46
22 18:17 ○ 0♒06
29 17:44 ☾ 6♉45

6 21:52 ● 14♌35
14 10:57 ☽ 21♏49
21 1:46 ○ 28♒11
28 9:36 ☾ 5♊15

Astro Data

1 July 2013
Julian Day # 41455
SVP 5♓04'04"
GC 27♐01.7 ⚴ 18♊30.1
Eris 22♈55.6 ⚵ 18♒10.8R
⚷ 13♓43.8R ⚶ 27♋49.3
☽ Mean ☊ 13♏59.1

1 August 2013
Julian Day # 41486
SVP 5♓03'59"
GC 27♐01.7 ⚴ 6♋21.1
Eris 22♈56.4R ⚵ 12♒27.6R
⚷ 12♓54.7R ⚶ 11♌44.7
☽ Mean ☊ 12♏20.6

LONGITUDE — September 2013

Day	Sid.Time	☉	0 hr ☽	Noon ☽	True ☊	☿	♀	♂	⚳	♃	♄	♅	♆	♇
1 Su	10 43 16	9♍12 42	18♋00 32	23♋58 51	9♏50.5	16♍22.0	18♎39.0	2♌49.2	1♍51.4	14♋05.1	7♏11.3	11♈44.1	3♓49.0	9♑04.8
2 M	10 47 12	10 10 48	29 59 06	6♌01 38	9R41.3	18 11.0	19 49.1	3 27.4	2 18.8	14 15.4	7 16.2	11R42.2	3R47.3	9R04.3
3 Tu	10 51 09	11 08 56	12♌06 44	18 14 37	9 30.8	19 58.8	20 59.1	4 05.6	2 46.1	14 25.6	7 21.2	11 40.2	3 45.7	9 03.8
4 W	10 55 05	12 07 05	24 25 26	0♍39 18	9 20.0	21 45.4	22 09.0	4 43.7	3 13.5	14 35.7	7 26.2	11 38.2	3 44.1	9 03.3
5 Th	10 59 02	13 05 16	6♍56 17	13 16 24	9 10.1	23 30.8	23 18.9	5 21.8	3 40.9	14 45.7	7 31.3	11 36.2	3 42.5	9 02.8
6 F	11 02 58	14 03 29	19 39 38	26 05 55	9 01.8	25 14.9	24 28.7	5 59.8	4 08.2	14 55.6	7 36.5	11 34.2	3 40.8	9 02.4
7 Sa	11 06 55	15 01 43	2♎35 13	9♎07 28	8 55.7	26 57.9	25 38.4	6 37.7	4 35.6	15 05.4	7 41.7	11 32.1	3 39.2	9 02.0
8 Su	11 10 51	16 00 00	15 42 35	22 20 32	8 52.2	28 39.7	26 48.1	7 15.6	5 02.9	15 15.0	7 47.0	11 30.0	3 37.6	9 01.6
9 M	11 14 48	16 58 17	29 01 15	5♏44 45	8D50.9	0♎20.3	27 57.6	7 53.5	5 30.2	15 24.6	7 52.3	11 27.9	3 36.0	9 01.2
10 Tu	11 18 45	17 56 37	12♏31 01	19 20 04	8 51.2	1 59.8	29 07.1	8 31.3	5 57.6	15 34.0	7 57.7	11 25.7	3 34.5	9 00.9
11 W	11 22 41	18 54 58	26 11 55	3♐06 35	8 52.2	3 38.1	0♏16.5	9 09.1	6 24.9	15 43.3	8 03.2	11 23.5	3 32.9	9 00.6
12 Th	11 26 38	19 53 20	10♐04 04	17 04 22	8R53.0	5 15.3	1 25.9	9 46.8	6 52.2	15 52.6	8 08.7	11 21.3	3 31.3	9 00.4
13 F	11 30 34	20 51 44	24 07 23	1♑13 00	8 52.5	6 51.5	2 35.1	10 24.4	7 19.5	16 01.7	8 14.3	11 19.1	3 29.8	9 00.2
14 Sa	11 34 31	21 50 10	8♑21 02	15 31 10	8 50.3	8 26.5	3 44.2	11 02.0	7 46.8	16 10.6	8 20.0	11 16.9	3 28.2	9 00.0
15 Su	11 38 27	22 48 37	22 43 01	29 56 09	8 46.1	10 00.4	4 53.3	11 39.6	8 14.0	16 19.5	8 25.7	11 14.7	3 26.7	8 59.8
16 M	11 42 24	23 47 06	7♒09 57	14♒23 48	8 40.3	11 33.3	6 02.2	12 17.1	8 41.3	16 28.2	8 31.4	11 12.4	3 25.2	8 59.7
17 Tu	11 46 20	24 45 36	21 37 00	28 48 47	8 33.5	13 05.1	7 11.0	12 54.5	9 08.5	16 36.9	8 37.2	11 10.1	3 23.6	8 59.5
18 W	11 50 17	25 44 08	5♓58 26	13♓05 13	8 26.7	14 35.8	8 19.8	13 31.9	9 35.7	16 45.3	8 43.1	11 07.8	3 22.2	8 59.5
19 Th	11 54 14	26 42 42	20 08 26	27 07 29	8 20.6	16 05.5	9 28.4	14 09.3	10 02.9	16 53.7	8 49.0	11 05.5	3 20.7	8 59.4
20 F	11 58 10	27 41 18	4♈01 52	10♈51 11	8 16.0	17 34.1	10 36.9	14 46.6	10 30.1	17 01.9	8 55.0	11 03.2	3 19.2	8D59.4
21 Sa	12 02 07	28 39 56	17 35 09	24 13 36	8 13.3	19 01.6	11 45.3	15 23.8	10 57.3	17 10.0	9 01.0	11 00.8	3 17.7	8 59.4
22 Su	12 06 03	29 38 36	0♉46 33	7♉14 03	8D12.3	20 28.1	12 53.7	16 01.0	11 24.5	17 18.0	9 07.0	10 58.5	3 16.3	8 59.4
23 M	12 10 00	0♎37 18	13 36 20	19 53 39	8 12.9	21 53.4	14 01.9	16 38.2	11 51.6	17 25.8	9 13.1	10 56.1	3 14.9	8 59.5
24 Tu	12 13 56	1 36 02	26 06 25	2♊15 04	8 14.3	23 17.7	15 09.9	17 15.3	12 18.7	17 33.5	9 19.3	10 53.7	3 13.5	8 59.6
25 W	12 17 53	2 34 49	8♊20 07	14 22 07	8 16.0	24 40.8	16 17.9	17 52.3	12 45.8	17 41.1	9 25.5	10 51.3	3 12.1	8 59.8
26 Th	12 21 49	3 33 37	20 21 39	26 19 19	8R17.2	26 02.7	17 25.8	18 29.3	13 12.9	17 48.5	9 31.8	10 49.0	3 10.7	8 59.9
27 F	12 25 46	4 32 28	2♋15 45	8♋11 35	8 17.4	27 23.5	18 33.5	19 06.2	13 40.0	17 55.8	9 38.1	10 46.6	3 09.4	9 00.1
28 Sa	12 29 43	5 31 22	14 07 25	20 03 52	8 16.3	28 42.9	19 41.1	19 43.1	14 07.1	18 02.9	9 44.4	10 44.1	3 08.0	9 00.4
29 Su	12 33 39	6 30 17	26 01 31	2♌00 55	8 13.7	0♏01.1	20 48.6	20 20.0	14 34.1	18 09.9	9 50.8	10 41.7	3 06.7	9 00.6
30 M	12 37 36	7 29 15	8♌02 34	14 06 58	8 09.9	1 17.9	21 56.0	20 56.7	15 01.1	18 16.8	9 57.2	10 39.3	3 05.4	9 00.9

LONGITUDE — October 2013

Day	Sid.Time	☉	0 hr ☽	Noon ☽	True ☊	☿	♀	♂	⚳	♃	♄	♅	♆	♇
1 Tu	12 41 32	8♎28 15	20♌14 31	26♌25 34	8♏05.2	2♏33.3	23♏03.2	21♌33.5	15♍28.1	18♋23.5	10♏03.7	10♈36.9	3♓04.2	9♑01.2
2 W	12 45 29	9 27 17	2♍40 25	8♍59 17	8R00.3	3 47.2	24 10.3	22 10.1	15 55.0	18 30.0	10 10.2	10R34.5	3R02.9	9 01.6
3 Th	12 49 25	10 26 22	15 22 19	21 49 37	7 55.7	4 59.5	25 17.3	22 46.7	16 21.9	18 36.4	10 16.7	10 32.0	3 01.7	9 02.0
4 F	12 53 22	11 25 28	28 21 09	4♎56 51	7 51.9	6 10.1	26 24.1	23 23.3	16 48.8	18 42.6	10 23.3	10 29.6	3 00.5	9 02.4
5 Sa	12 57 18	12 24 37	11♎36 36	18 20 12	7 49.4	7 18.9	27 30.8	23 59.8	17 15.7	18 48.7	10 29.9	10 27.2	2 59.3	9 02.8
6 Su	13 01 15	13 23 47	25 07 24	1♏57 56	7D48.2	8 25.6	28 37.3	24 36.2	17 42.5	18 54.6	10 36.6	10 24.8	2 58.1	9 03.3
7 M	13 05 11	14 23 00	8♏51 27	15 47 40	7 48.3	9 30.3	29 43.7	25 12.6	18 09.4	19 00.4	10 43.2	10 22.3	2 57.0	9 03.8
8 Tu	13 09 08	15 22 14	22 46 14	29 46 47	7 49.3	10 32.7	0♐49.9	25 48.9	18 36.1	19 06.0	10 50.0	10 19.9	2 55.8	9 04.3
9 W	13 13 05	16 21 30	6♐49 02	13♐52 39	7 50.7	11 32.6	1 55.9	26 25.2	19 02.9	19 11.4	10 56.7	10 17.5	2 54.8	9 04.9
10 Th	13 17 01	17 20 49	20 57 19	28 02 45	7 52.0	12 29.8	3 01.8	27 01.3	19 29.6	19 16.7	11 03.5	10 15.1	2 53.7	9 05.5
11 F	13 20 58	18 20 09	5♑08 41	12♑14 51	7R52.8	13 24.0	4 07.4	27 37.5	19 56.3	19 21.8	11 10.3	10 12.7	2 52.7	9 06.1
12 Sa	13 24 54	19 19 30	19 20 57	26 26 45	7 52.7	14 14.9	5 12.9	28 13.5	20 22.9	19 26.7	11 17.2	10 10.3	2 51.6	9 06.8
13 Su	13 28 51	20 18 53	3♒31 57	10♒36 16	7 51.8	15 02.3	6 18.2	28 49.5	20 49.5	19 31.4	11 24.0	10 08.0	2 50.6	9 07.5
14 M	13 32 47	21 18 18	17 39 24	24 41 03	7 50.2	15 45.8	7 23.3	29 25.5	21 16.0	19 36.0	11 30.9	10 05.6	2 49.7	9 08.2
15 Tu	13 36 44	22 17 45	1♓40 52	8♓38 33	7 48.2	16 25.0	8 28.1	0♍01.3	21 42.5	19 40.4	11 37.8	10 03.2	2 48.7	9 08.9
16 W	13 40 40	23 17 13	15 33 46	22 26 11	7 46.1	16 59.4	9 32.8	0 37.2	22 09.0	19 44.7	11 44.8	10 00.9	2 47.8	9 09.7
17 Th	13 44 37	24 16 44	29 15 30	6♈01 26	7 44.4	17 28.7	10 37.2	1 12.9	22 35.5	19 48.7	11 51.7	9 58.6	2 47.0	9 10.5
18 F	13 48 34	25 16 16	12♈43 45	19 22 14	7 43.2	17 52.3	11 41.4	1 48.6	23 01.8	19 52.6	11 58.7	9 56.2	2 46.1	9 11.4
19 Sa	13 52 30	26 15 50	25 56 44	2♉27 10	7D42.6	18 09.7	12 45.4	2 24.2	23 28.2	19 56.3	12 05.7	9 53.9	2 45.3	9 12.2
20 Su	13 56 27	27 15 27	8♉53 28	15 15 40	7 42.6	18R20.3	13 49.1	2 59.8	23 54.5	19 59.8	12 12.8	9 51.7	2 44.5	9 13.1
21 M	14 00 23	28 15 05	21 33 53	27 48 15	7 43.2	18 23.6	14 52.5	3 35.3	24 20.8	20 03.1	12 19.8	9 49.4	2 43.7	9 14.0
22 Tu	14 04 20	29 14 46	3♊58 59	10♊06 23	7 44.0	18 19.1	15 55.7	4 10.7	24 47.0	20 06.3	12 26.9	9 47.1	2 43.0	9 15.0
23 W	14 08 16	0♏14 29	16 10 46	22 12 31	7 44.8	18 06.3	16 58.7	4 46.0	25 13.2	20 09.3	12 34.0	9 44.9	2 42.3	9 16.0
24 Th	14 12 13	1 14 14	28 12 05	4♋09 56	7 45.6	17 44.8	18 01.3	5 21.3	25 39.3	20 12.0	12 41.0	9 42.7	2 41.6	9 17.0
25 F	14 16 09	2 14 01	10♋06 34	16 02 32	7 46.1	17 14.2	19 03.7	5 56.6	26 05.4	20 14.6	12 48.2	9 40.5	2 40.9	9 18.0
26 Sa	14 20 06	3 13 50	21 58 24	27 54 45	7R46.3	16 34.6	20 05.8	6 31.7	26 31.4	20 17.0	12 55.3	9 38.3	2 40.3	9 19.1
27 Su	14 24 03	4 13 42	3♌52 09	9♌51 12	7 46.4	15 46.0	21 07.6	7 06.8	26 57.4	20 19.3	13 02.4	9 36.2	2 39.7	9 20.2
28 M	14 27 59	5 13 36	15 52 30	21 56 36	7 46.2	14 49.1	22 09.0	7 41.8	27 23.3	20 21.3	13 09.6	9 34.1	2 39.2	9 21.3
29 Tu	14 31 56	6 13 32	28 04 03	4♍15 22	7 46.0	13 44.7	23 10.1	8 16.8	27 49.1	20 23.1	13 16.7	9 32.0	2 38.7	9 22.4
30 W	14 35 52	7 13 30	10♍31 00	16 51 22	7D45.9	12 34.1	24 10.9	8 51.6	28 14.9	20 24.7	13 23.9	9 29.9	2 38.2	9 23.6
31 Th	14 39 49	8 13 30	23 16 49	29 47 35	7 45.9	11 19.0	25 11.4	9 26.4	28 40.7	20 26.2	13 31.1	9 27.9	2 37.7	9 24.8

Astro Data	Planet Ingress	Last Aspect	☽ Ingress	Last Aspect	☽ Ingress	☽ Phases & Eclipses	Astro Data
Dy Hr Mn	Dy Hr Mn	Dy Hr Mn	Dy Hr Mn	Dy Hr Mn	Dy Hr Mn	Dy Hr Mn	
☽0S 6 2:57	☿ ♎ 9 7:08	1 0:08 ♀ □	♌ 2 0:02	1 4:49 ♀ □	♍ 1 18:53	5 11:37 ● 13♍04	1 September 2013
☿0S 10 1:26	♀ ♏ 11 6:17	3 17:53 ♀ ⚹	♍ 4 10:45	3 18:59 ♀ ⚹	♎ 4 3:01	12 17:09 ☽ 20♐06	Julian Day # 41517
☽0N 19 1:52	☉ ♎ 22 20:45	6 10:11 ☿ ☌	♎ 6 19:14	5 22:29 ♂ ⚹	♏ 6 8:34	19 11:14 ○ 26♓41	SVP 5♓03'56"
♇ D 20 15:30	☿ ♏ 29 11:39	8 20:47 ♀ ☌	♏ 9 1:45	8 4:55 ♂ □	♐ 8 12:23	27 3:57 ☾ 4♋13	GC 27♐01.8 ⚴ 24♋16.9
♄⚹♇ 21 5:46		10 9:22 ☉ ⚹	♐ 11 6:37	10 10:12 ♂ △	♑ 10 15:18		Eris 22♈47.5R ⚵ 5♒41.0R
☉0S 22 20:45	♀ ♐ 7 17:55	12 17:09 ☉ □	♑ 13 9:57	12 0:06 ♃ ☍	♒ 12 18:01	5 0:36 ● 11♎56	⚷ 11♓33.1R ⚶ 25♌58.6
♃□♆ 29 2:39	♂ ♍ 15 11:06	14 23:18 ☉ △	♒ 15 12:06	14 20:29 ♂ ☍	♓ 14 21:07	11 23:03 ☽ 18♑47	☽ Mean ☊ 10♏42.1
	☉ ♏ 23 6:11	16 8:20 ♂ ☍	♓ 17 13:59	16 7:16 ♃ △	♈ 17 1:19	18 23:39 ○ 25♈45	
☽0S 3 10:47		19 11:14 ☉ ☍	♈ 19 16:59	18 23:39 ☉ ☍	♉ 19 7:28	18 23:51 A 0.765	1 October 2013
♄⚻♅ 5 4:47		21 1:26 ☿ ☍	♉ 21 22:34	20 21:03 ♃ ⚹	♊ 21 16:15	26 23:42 ☾ 3♌43	Julian Day # 41547
☽0N 16 9:41		23 7:14 ♃ ⚹	♊ 24 7:35	23 0:36 ♀ ☍	♋ 24 3:37		SVP 5♓03'53"
☿R 21 10:30		26 11:22 ☿ △	♋ 26 19:26	25 20:32 ♃ ☌	♌ 26 16:13		GC 27♐01.9 ⚴ 10♌56.4
☽0S 30 19:52		29 7:31 ☿ □	♌ 29 7:58	28 12:27 ♀ △	♍ 29 3:46		Eris 22♈32.2R ⚵ 4♒01.7
				31 2:49 ♀ □	♎ 31 12:23		⚷ 10♓11.7R ⚶ 9♍48.4
							☽ Mean ☊ 9♏06.7

November 2013 LONGITUDE

Day	Sid.Time	☉	0 hr ☽	Noon ☽	True ☊	☿	♀	♂	⚳	♃	♄	♅	♆	♇
1 F	14 43 45	9♏13 32	6♎23 50	13♎05 39	7♏46.0	10♏01.5	26♐11.5	10♍01.1	29♍06.4	20♋27.4	13♏38.3	9♈25.8	2♓37.3	9♑26.0
2 Sa	14 47 42	10 13 36	19 52 58	26 45 37	7R46.1	8R43.9	27 11.2	10 35.8	29 32.0	20 28.4	13 45.5	9R23.8	2R36.9	9 27.3
3 Su	14 51 38	11 13 43	3♏43 20	10♏45 43	7 46.2	7 28.7	28 10.5	11 10.3	29 57.6	20 29.3	13 52.7	9 21.9	2 36.5	9 28.6
4 M	14 55 35	12 13 51	17 52 16	25 02 24	7 46.0	6 18.3	29 09.4	11 44.8	0♎23.1	20 29.9	13 59.9	9 20.0	2 36.2	9 29.9
5 Tu	14 59 32	13 14 01	2♐15 27	9♐30 41	7 45.6	5 14.8	0♑07.9	12 19.2	0 48.5	20 30.4	14 07.1	9 18.1	2 35.9	9 31.2
6 W	15 03 28	14 14 13	16 47 21	24 04 42	7 44.9	4 20.1	1 06.0	12 53.5	1 13.9	20R30.6	14 14.3	9 16.2	2 35.6	9 32.6
7 Th	15 07 25	15 14 26	1♑21 59	8♑38 30	7 44.1	3 35.6	2 03.6	13 27.7	1 39.2	20 30.6	14 21.5	9 14.4	2 35.4	9 33.9
8 F	15 11 21	16 14 41	15 53 37	23 06 45	7 43.3	3 02.2	3 00.8	14 01.9	2 04.4	20 30.5	14 28.7	9 12.6	2 35.2	9 35.4
9 Sa	15 15 18	17 14 57	0♒17 27	7♒25 18	7D42.8	2 40.4	3 57.4	14 35.9	2 29.6	20 30.1	14 35.9	9 10.8	2 35.1	9 36.8
10 Su	15 19 14	18 15 14	14 30 00	21 31 19	7 42.7	2D30.3	4 53.5	15 09.9	2 54.6	20 29.6	14 43.1	9 09.1	2 34.9	9 38.2
11 M	15 23 11	19 15 33	28 29 06	5♓23 17	7 43.1	2 31.6	5 49.1	15 43.7	3 19.7	20 28.8	14 50.3	9 07.4	2 34.8	9 39.7
12 Tu	15 27 07	20 15 53	12♓13 50	19 00 44	7 43.9	2 43.7	6 44.1	16 17.5	3 44.6	20 27.8	14 57.5	9 05.7	2 34.8	9 41.2
13 W	15 31 04	21 16 15	25 44 02	2♈23 48	7 45.1	3 05.9	7 38.5	16 51.2	4 09.4	20 26.7	15 04.6	9 04.1	2D34.7	9 42.7
14 Th	15 35 01	22 16 38	9♈00 07	15 33 03	7 46.2	3 37.4	8 32.3	17 24.8	4 34.2	20 25.3	15 11.8	9 02.5	2 34.8	9 44.3
15 F	15 38 57	23 17 03	22 02 41	28 29 06	7R47.1	4 17.2	9 25.4	17 58.3	4 58.9	20 23.8	15 19.0	9 01.0	2 34.8	9 45.8
16 Sa	15 42 54	24 17 29	4♉52 24	11♉12 38	7 47.3	5 04.6	10 18.0	18 31.7	5 23.5	20 22.0	15 26.1	8 59.5	2 34.9	9 47.4
17 Su	15 46 50	25 17 57	17 29 55	23 44 20	7 46.5	5 58.6	11 09.8	19 05.0	5 48.0	20 20.1	15 33.2	8 58.0	2 35.0	9 49.0
18 M	15 50 47	26 18 26	29 55 59	6♊05 00	7 44.8	6 58.3	12 00.9	19 38.3	6 12.4	20 17.9	15 40.4	8 56.6	2 35.1	9 50.6
19 Tu	15 54 43	27 18 57	12♊11 31	18 15 43	7 42.2	8 03.1	12 51.2	20 11.4	6 36.8	20 15.6	15 47.5	8 55.2	2 35.3	9 52.3
20 W	15 58 40	28 19 29	24 17 47	0♋17 57	7 38.9	9 12.3	13 40.8	20 44.4	7 01.1	20 13.0	15 54.6	8 53.9	2 35.5	9 54.0
21 Th	16 02 36	29 20 04	6♋16 29	12 13 43	7 35.2	10 25.3	14 29.6	21 17.3	7 25.2	20 10.3	16 01.7	8 52.6	2 35.8	9 55.7
22 F	16 06 33	0♐20 39	18 09 59	24 05 40	7 31.6	11 41.5	15 17.6	21 50.2	7 49.3	20 07.4	16 08.7	8 51.3	2 36.1	9 57.4
23 Sa	16 10 30	1 21 17	0♌01 12	5♌57 03	7 28.5	13 00.4	16 04.6	22 22.9	8 13.3	20 04.3	16 15.8	8 50.1	2 36.4	9 59.1
24 Su	16 14 26	2 21 56	11 53 43	17 51 44	7 26.4	14 21.6	16 50.8	22 55.5	8 37.2	20 00.9	16 22.8	8 49.0	2 36.7	10 00.8
25 M	16 18 23	3 22 36	23 51 40	29 54 05	7D25.4	15 44.8	17 36.1	23 28.0	9 01.0	19 57.4	16 29.8	8 47.8	2 37.1	10 02.6
26 Tu	16 22 19	4 23 18	5♍59 34	12♍08 44	7 25.6	17 09.7	18 20.3	24 00.4	9 24.7	19 53.8	16 36.8	8 46.8	2 37.5	10 04.4
27 W	16 26 16	5 24 02	18 22 09	24 40 23	7 26.8	18 36.0	19 03.6	24 32.7	9 48.2	19 49.9	16 43.8	8 45.7	2 38.0	10 06.2
28 Th	16 30 12	6 24 48	1♎03 58	7♎33 22	7 28.4	20 03.4	19 45.8	25 04.9	10 11.7	19 45.8	16 50.7	8 44.8	2 38.5	10 08.0
29 F	16 34 09	7 25 35	14 08 59	20 51 06	7 30.0	21 31.9	20 26.9	25 36.9	10 35.1	19 41.6	16 57.6	8 43.8	2 39.0	10 09.8
30 Sa	16 38 05	8 26 23	27 39 56	4♏35 32	7R30.9	23 01.1	21 06.8	26 08.9	10 58.4	19 37.2	17 04.5	8 42.9	2 39.6	10 11.7

December 2013 LONGITUDE

Day	Sid.Time	☉	0 hr ☽	Noon ☽	True ☊	☿	♀	♂	⚳	♃	♄	♅	♆	♇
1 Su	16 42 02	9♐27 13	11♏37 47	18♏46 23	7♏30.4	24♏31.0	21♑45.6	26♍40.7	11♎21.5	19♋32.6	17♏11.4	8♈42.1	2♓40.1	10♑13.5
2 M	16 45 59	10 28 04	26 00 55	3♐20 42	7R28.4	26 01.5	22 23.1	27 12.3	11 44.5	19R27.8	17 18.2	8R41.3	2 40.8	10 15.4
3 Tu	16 49 55	11 28 57	10♐44 56	18 12 39	7 24.6	27 32.5	22 59.3	27 43.9	12 07.5	19 22.8	17 25.0	8 40.5	2 41.4	10 17.3
4 W	16 53 52	12 29 50	25 42 46	3♑14 05	7 19.6	29 03.8	23 34.2	28 15.3	12 30.3	19 17.7	17 31.8	8 39.8	2 42.1	10 19.2
5 Th	16 57 48	13 30 45	10♑45 26	18 15 38	7 14.0	0♐35.5	24 07.6	28 46.6	12 52.9	19 12.5	17 38.6	8 39.2	2 42.9	10 21.1
6 F	17 01 45	14 31 40	25 43 34	3♒08 16	7 08.7	2 07.4	24 39.6	29 17.8	13 15.5	19 07.0	17 45.3	8 38.6	2 43.6	10 23.1
7 Sa	17 05 41	15 32 36	10♒28 51	17 44 41	7 04.4	3 39.5	25 10.0	29 48.8	13 37.9	19 01.4	17 51.9	8 38.1	2 44.4	10 25.0
8 Su	17 09 38	16 33 33	24 55 14	2♓00 13	7 01.6	5 11.8	25 38.9	0♎19.7	14 00.2	18 55.7	17 58.6	8 37.6	2 45.2	10 27.0
9 M	17 13 34	17 34 30	8♓59 26	15 52 53	7D00.6	6 44.3	26 06.1	0 50.4	14 22.3	18 49.8	18 05.2	8 37.1	2 46.1	10 28.9
10 Tu	17 17 31	18 35 28	22 40 41	29 23 03	7 01.1	8 17.0	26 31.5	1 21.0	14 44.4	18 43.7	18 11.7	8 36.7	2 47.0	10 30.9
11 W	17 21 28	19 36 26	6♈00 15	12♈32 38	7 02.4	9 49.7	26 55.2	1 51.4	15 06.3	18 37.5	18 18.3	8 36.4	2 47.9	10 32.9
12 Th	17 25 24	20 37 25	19 00 34	25 24 26	7R03.8	11 22.6	27 17.0	2 21.7	15 28.0	18 31.2	18 24.7	8 36.1	2 48.9	10 34.9
13 F	17 29 21	21 38 25	1♉44 35	8♉01 25	7 04.4	12 55.5	27 36.8	2 51.9	15 49.6	18 24.7	18 31.2	8 35.8	2 49.9	10 36.9
14 Sa	17 33 17	22 39 25	14 15 15	20 26 26	7 03.4	14 28.6	27 54.7	3 21.8	16 11.1	18 18.1	18 37.6	8 35.6	2 50.9	10 39.0
15 Su	17 37 14	23 40 26	26 35 13	2♊41 53	7 00.2	16 01.8	28 10.5	3 51.7	16 32.4	18 11.4	18 43.9	8 35.5	2 51.9	10 41.0
16 M	17 41 10	24 41 28	8♊46 39	14 49 42	6 54.5	17 35.1	28 24.2	4 21.4	16 53.6	18 04.6	18 50.2	8 35.4	2 53.0	10 43.0
17 Tu	17 45 07	25 42 30	20 51 15	26 51 27	6 46.7	19 08.6	28 35.7	4 50.9	17 14.6	17 57.7	18 56.5	8D35.4	2 54.1	10 45.1
18 W	17 49 03	26 43 33	2♋50 28	8♋48 27	6 37.2	20 42.1	28 45.0	5 20.2	17 35.4	17 50.6	19 02.7	8 35.4	2 55.3	10 47.1
19 Th	17 53 00	27 44 37	14 45 34	20 42 01	6 26.7	22 15.9	28 51.9	5 49.4	17 56.1	17 43.4	19 08.9	8 35.4	2 56.5	10 49.2
20 F	17 56 57	28 45 41	26 38 15	2♌33 46	6 16.2	23 49.7	28 56.5	6 18.4	18 16.7	17 36.2	19 15.0	8 35.6	2 57.7	10 51.3
21 Sa	18 00 53	29 46 46	8♌29 34	14 25 43	6 06.7	25 23.8	28R58.7	6 47.3	18 37.1	17 28.8	19 21.1	8 35.7	2 58.9	10 53.3
22 Su	18 04 50	0♑47 51	20 22 34	26 20 32	5 59.0	26 58.0	28 58.5	7 16.0	18 57.3	17 21.3	19 27.1	8 35.9	3 00.2	10 55.4
23 M	18 08 46	1 48 57	2♍20 01	8♍21 33	5 53.5	28 32.4	28 55.8	7 44.4	19 17.4	17 13.8	19 33.1	8 36.2	3 01.5	10 57.5
24 Tu	18 12 43	2 50 04	14 25 37	20 32 46	5 50.5	0♑07.0	28 50.7	8 12.7	19 37.2	17 06.2	19 39.0	8 36.5	3 02.8	10 59.6
25 W	18 16 39	3 51 11	26 43 36	2♎58 43	5D49.5	1 41.9	28 43.0	8 40.9	19 56.9	16 58.5	19 44.8	8 36.9	3 04.1	11 01.7
26 Th	18 20 36	4 52 19	9♎18 42	15 44 09	5 50.0	3 16.9	28 32.9	9 08.8	20 16.5	16 50.7	19 50.6	8 37.3	3 05.5	11 03.8
27 F	18 24 32	5 53 28	22 15 36	28 53 34	5R50.7	4 52.3	28 20.3	9 36.5	20 35.8	16 42.9	19 56.4	8 37.8	3 06.9	11 05.9
28 Sa	18 28 29	6 54 37	5♏38 28	12♏30 36	5 50.7	6 27.9	28 05.2	10 04.0	20 55.0	16 35.0	20 02.0	8 38.3	3 08.4	11 08.0
29 Su	18 32 26	7 55 47	19 30 07	26 37 03	5 48.9	8 03.8	27 47.7	10 31.3	21 13.9	16 27.1	20 07.7	8 38.9	3 09.8	11 10.1
30 M	18 36 22	8 56 57	3♐51 09	11♐11 59	5 44.5	9 40.0	27 27.9	10 58.4	21 32.7	16 19.1	20 13.2	8 39.6	3 11.3	11 12.2
31 Tu	18 40 19	9 58 08	18 38 54	26 10 59	5 37.5	11 16.5	27 05.8	11 25.3	21 51.3	16 11.1	20 18.7	8 40.2	3 12.8	11 14.3

Astro Data	Dy Hr Mn
♅□♇	1 10:31
♃ R	7 5:04
☿ D	10 21:15
☽ 0N	12 15:41
♆ D	13 18:43
☽ 0S	27 5:27
☽ 0N	9 21:45
♃△♄	13 0:02
♂0S	17 1:58
♅ D	17 17:40
♃⚻♆	17 22:20
♀ R	21 21:55
☽ 0S	24 14:22

Planet Ingress		Dy Hr Mn
⚳	♎	3 14:16
♀	♑	5 8:44
☉	♐	22 3:49
☿	♐	5 2:43
♂	♎	7 20:42
☉	♑	21 17:12
☿	♑	24 10:13

Last Aspect Dy Hr Mn			☽ Ingress	Dy Hr Mn
2 12:48	♀	⚹	♏	2 17:36
4 4:24	♃	△	♐	4 20:15
5 16:49	♂	□	♑	6 21:45
8 7:40	♃	☍	♒	8 23:31
10 5:58	☉	□	♓	11 2:37
12 14:35	♃	△	♈	13 7:40
14 20:58	♃	□	♉	15 14:50
17 15:17	☉	☍	♊	18 0:08
19 16:01	♂	□	♋	20 11:24
22 7:12	♂	⚹	♌	22 23:58
24 9:00	♄	□	♍	25 12:12
27 11:45	♂	☌	♎	27 22:01
29 11:15	♀	□	♏	30 4:04

Last Aspect Dy Hr Mn			☽ Ingress	Dy Hr Mn
2 1:35	♂	⚹	♐	2 6:32
4 3:46	♂	□	♑	4 6:50
6 5:33	♂	△	♒	6 6:54
7 12:12	♄	□	♓	8 8:35
10 6:42	♀	⚹	♈	10 13:07
12 15:38	♀	□	♉	12 20:41
15 2:55	♀	△	♊	15 6:42
17 9:29	☉	☍	♋	17 18:18
20 4:38	♀	☍	♌	20 6:49
22 13:27	☿	△	♍	22 19:20
25 3:56	♀	△	♎	25 6:18
27 11:01	♀	□	♏	27 13:59
29 13:55	♀	⚹	♐	29 17:38
30 11:37	♂	⚹	♑	31 18:02

☽ Phases & Eclipses Dy Hr Mn		
3 12:51	●	11♏16
3 12:47:36		AT01'40"
10 5:58	☽	18♒00
17 15:17	○	25♉26
25 19:29	☾	3♍42
3 0:23	●	10♐59
9 15:13	☽	17♓43
17 9:29	○	25♊36
25 13:49	☾	3♎56

Astro Data

1 November 2013
Julian Day # 41578
SVP 5♓03'50"
GC 27♐02.0 ⚴ 26♌18.6
Eris 22♈13.8R ⚵ 8♒38.1
⚷ 9♓16.6R ⚶ 23♍50.5
☽ Mean ☊ 7♏28.2

1 December 2013
Julian Day # 41608
SVP 5♓03'46"
GC 27♐02.0 ⚴ 7♍49.1
Eris 21♈58.9R ⚵ 17♒39.2
⚷ 9♓11.4 ⚶ 6♎41.8
☽ Mean ☊ 5♏52.9

LONGITUDE — January 2014

Day	Sid.Time	☉	0 hr ☽	Noon ☽	True☊	☿	♀	♂	⚳	♃	♄	♅	♆	♇
1 W	18 44 15	10♑59 19	3♑47 06	11♑25 58	5♏28.3	12♑53.4	26♑41.5	11♎51.9	22♎09.7	16♋03.0	20♏24.2	8♈41.0	3♓14.4	11♑16.5
2 Th	18 48 12	12 00 30	19 06 09	26 46 09	5R 17.9	14 30.5	26R 15.2	12 18.3	22 27.8	15R 54.9	20 29.5	8 41.8	3 15.9	11 18.6
3 F	18 52 08	13 01 41	4♒24 31	11♒59 50	5 07.6	16 08.0	25 46.9	12 44.5	22 45.8	15 46.8	20 34.9	8 42.6	3 17.5	11 20.7
4 Sa	18 56 05	14 02 51	19 30 52	26 56 33	4 58.6	17 45.9	25 16.8	13 10.5	23 03.5	15 38.7	20 40.1	8 43.5	3 19.2	11 22.8
5 Su	19 00 01	15 04 01	4♓16 03	11♓28 48	4 51.9	19 24.0	24 45.1	13 36.2	23 21.1	15 30.6	20 45.3	8 44.4	3 20.8	11 24.9
6 M	19 03 58	16 05 11	18 34 26	25 32 49	4 47.9	21 02.6	24 11.9	14 01.6	23 38.4	15 22.5	20 50.4	8 45.4	3 22.5	11 27.0
7 Tu	19 07 55	17 06 21	2♈24 00	9♈08 13	4D 46.1	22 41.4	23 37.6	14 26.8	23 55.4	15 14.4	20 55.4	8 46.5	3 24.2	11 29.1
8 W	19 11 51	18 07 30	15 45 50	22 17 15	4R 46.0	24 20.6	23 02.2	14 51.7	24 12.3	15 06.3	21 00.4	8 47.6	3 25.9	11 31.2
9 Th	19 15 48	19 08 38	28 43 01	5♉03 40	4 46.2	26 00.1	22 26.1	15 16.4	24 28.9	14 58.2	21 05.2	8 48.7	3 27.6	11 33.3
10 F	19 19 44	20 09 46	11♉19 46	17 31 54	4 45.5	27 39.9	21 49.5	15 40.8	24 45.3	14 50.1	21 10.1	8 49.9	3 29.4	11 35.4
11 Sa	19 23 41	21 10 54	23 40 35	29 46 23	4 42.9	29 19.9	21 12.6	16 05.0	25 01.5	14 42.1	21 14.8	8 51.1	3 31.2	11 37.5
12 Su	19 27 37	22 12 01	5♊49 45	11♊51 08	4 37.6	1♒00.2	20 35.8	16 28.9	25 17.4	14 34.1	21 19.5	8 52.4	3 33.0	11 39.6
13 M	19 31 34	23 13 08	17 50 56	23 49 30	4 29.2	2 40.6	19 59.2	16 52.5	25 33.1	14 26.2	21 24.1	8 53.8	3 34.8	11 41.7
14 Tu	19 35 30	24 14 14	29 47 08	5♋44 07	4 17.8	4 21.2	19 23.2	17 15.8	25 48.5	14 18.3	21 28.6	8 55.2	3 36.7	11 43.7
15 W	19 39 27	25 15 20	11♋40 39	17 36 57	4 04.2	6 01.7	18 47.9	17 38.8	26 03.7	14 10.4	21 33.0	8 56.6	3 38.5	11 45.8
16 Th	19 43 24	26 16 25	23 33 11	29 29 30	3 49.3	7 42.2	18 13.7	18 01.5	26 18.6	14 02.7	21 37.4	8 58.1	3 40.4	11 47.9
17 F	19 47 20	27 17 29	5♌26 03	11♌22 59	3 34.3	9 22.5	17 40.7	18 23.9	26 33.2	13 54.9	21 41.7	8 59.6	3 42.3	11 49.9
18 Sa	19 51 17	28 18 34	17 20 28	23 18 39	3 20.4	11 02.4	17 09.2	18 46.0	26 47.6	13 47.3	21 45.9	9 01.2	3 44.2	11 52.0
19 Su	19 55 13	29 19 37	29 17 47	5♍18 04	3 08.7	12 41.8	16 39.3	19 07.7	27 01.7	13 39.7	21 50.0	9 02.8	3 46.2	11 54.0
20 M	19 59 10	0♒20 40	11♍19 49	17 23 20	2 59.8	14 20.5	16 11.3	19 29.2	27 15.6	13 32.2	21 54.0	9 04.4	3 48.2	11 56.0
21 Tu	20 03 06	1 21 43	23 28 59	29 37 11	2 54.0	15 58.2	15 45.3	19 50.3	27 29.1	13 24.8	21 58.0	9 06.1	3 50.1	11 58.1
22 W	20 07 03	2 22 46	5♎48 24	12♎03 06	2 51.0	17 34.7	15 21.4	20 11.0	27 42.4	13 17.5	22 01.8	9 07.9	3 52.1	12 00.1
23 Th	20 10 59	3 23 47	18 21 49	24 45 05	2 50.1	19 09.6	14 59.7	20 31.4	27 55.4	13 10.3	22 05.6	9 09.7	3 54.1	12 02.1
24 F	20 14 56	4 24 49	1♏13 27	7♏47 25	2 50.0	20 42.6	14 40.4	20 51.5	28 08.1	13 03.2	22 09.3	9 11.5	3 56.2	12 04.0
25 Sa	20 18 53	5 25 50	14 27 30	21 14 06	2 49.5	22 13.1	14 23.4	21 11.1	28 20.5	12 56.2	22 12.9	9 13.4	3 58.2	12 06.0
26 Su	20 22 49	6 26 51	28 07 33	5♐08 02	2 47.3	23 40.8	14 08.9	21 30.4	28 32.6	12 49.3	22 16.5	9 15.4	4 00.3	12 08.0
27 M	20 26 46	7 27 51	12♐15 36	19 30 05	2 42.7	25 05.0	13 56.8	21 49.3	28 44.4	12 42.5	22 19.9	9 17.3	4 02.4	12 10.0
28 Tu	20 30 42	8 28 50	26 51 07	4♑18 04	2 35.1	26 25.1	13 47.3	22 07.8	28 55.9	12 35.9	22 23.2	9 19.3	4 04.5	12 11.9
29 W	20 34 39	9 29 49	11♑50 06	19 26 08	2 25.2	27 40.4	13 40.2	22 25.9	29 07.0	12 29.4	22 26.5	9 21.4	4 06.6	12 13.8
30 Th	20 38 35	10 30 47	27 04 54	4♒44 58	2 13.7	28 50.2	13 35.7	22 43.6	29 17.9	12 23.0	22 29.7	9 23.5	4 08.7	12 15.7
31 F	20 42 32	11 31 44	12♒24 53	20 03 06	2 02.1	29 53.8	13D 33.6	23 00.8	29 28.4	12 16.7	22 32.7	9 25.6	4 10.8	12 17.6

LONGITUDE — February 2014

Day	Sid.Time	☉	0 hr ☽	Noon ☽	True☊	☿	♀	♂	⚳	♃	♄	♅	♆	♇
1 Sa	20 46 29	12♒32 39	27♒38 13	5♓08 57	1♏51.8	0♓50.2	13♑33.9	23♎17.7	29♎38.6	12♋10.6	22♏35.7	9♈27.8	4♓13.0	12♑19.5
2 Su	20 50 25	13 33 34	12♓34 10	19 53 00	1R 43.7	1 38.8	13 36.6	23 34.0	29 48.4	12R 04.7	22 38.6	9 30.0	4 15.1	12 21.4
3 M	20 54 22	14 34 27	27 04 49	4♈09 12	1 38.5	2 18.7	13 41.6	23 49.9	29 57.9	11 58.8	22 41.4	9 32.3	4 17.3	12 23.3
4 Tu	20 58 18	15 35 19	11♈06 00	17 55 16	1 36.0	2 49.1	13 49.0	24 05.4	0♏07.0	11 53.2	22 44.1	9 34.6	4 19.5	12 25.1
5 W	21 02 15	16 36 09	24 37 11	1♉12 07	1D 35.3	3 09.5	13 58.6	24 20.4	0 15.8	11 47.7	22 46.6	9 36.9	4 21.6	12 26.9
6 Th	21 06 11	17 36 59	7♉40 32	14 02 59	1R 35.5	3R 19.4	14 10.4	24 34.9	0 24.3	11 42.3	22 49.1	9 39.3	4 23.8	12 28.7
7 F	21 10 08	18 37 46	20 20 04	26 32 25	1 35.3	3 18.3	14 24.3	24 48.9	0 32.3	11 37.2	22 51.5	9 41.7	4 26.0	12 30.5
8 Sa	21 14 04	19 38 32	2♊40 39	8♊45 25	1 33.5	3 06.3	14 40.3	25 02.4	0 40.1	11 32.1	22 53.9	9 44.2	4 28.3	12 32.3
9 Su	21 18 01	20 39 17	14 47 19	20 46 56	1 29.4	2 43.5	14 58.3	25 15.4	0 47.4	11 27.3	22 56.1	9 46.6	4 30.5	12 34.1
10 M	21 21 57	21 40 00	26 44 49	2♋41 28	1 22.5	2 10.4	15 18.2	25 27.9	0 54.4	11 22.6	22 58.2	9 49.2	4 32.7	12 35.8
11 Tu	21 25 54	22 40 42	8♋37 20	14 32 51	1 13.0	1 27.8	15 40.1	25 39.8	1 01.1	11 18.1	23 00.2	9 51.7	4 34.9	12 37.5
12 W	21 29 51	23 41 22	20 28 20	26 24 08	1 01.3	0 36.8	16 03.7	25 51.3	1 07.3	11 13.8	23 02.1	9 54.3	4 37.2	12 39.2
13 Th	21 33 47	24 42 00	2♌20 29	8♌17 38	0 48.4	29♒38.8	16 29.2	26 02.1	1 13.2	11 09.7	23 03.9	9 56.9	4 39.4	12 40.9
14 F	21 37 44	25 42 37	14 15 46	20 15 03	0 35.4	28 35.3	16 56.3	26 12.4	1 18.6	11 05.7	23 05.6	9 59.6	4 41.7	12 42.6
15 Sa	21 41 40	26 43 13	26 15 37	2♍17 36	0 23.3	27 28.3	17 25.0	26 22.2	1 23.7	11 01.9	23 07.2	10 02.2	4 44.0	12 44.2
16 Su	21 45 37	27 43 47	8♍21 09	14 26 22	0 13.0	26 19.5	17 55.4	26 31.3	1 28.4	10 58.3	23 08.7	10 04.9	4 46.2	12 45.8
17 M	21 49 33	28 44 20	20 33 26	26 42 29	0 05.4	25 10.7	18 27.2	26 39.9	1 32.7	10 54.9	23 10.2	10 07.7	4 48.5	12 47.4
18 Tu	21 53 30	29 44 51	2♎53 44	9♎07 23	0 00.6	24 03.7	19 00.6	26 47.9	1 36.6	10 51.7	23 11.5	10 10.5	4 50.7	12 49.0
19 W	21 57 26	0♓45 21	15 23 43	21 43 02	29♎58.3	23 00.0	19 35.3	26 55.2	1 40.1	10 48.7	23 12.7	10 13.3	4 53.0	12 50.5
20 Th	22 01 23	1 45 49	28 05 38	4♏31 53	29D 58.1	22 01.0	20 11.4	27 01.9	1 43.2	10 45.8	23 13.8	10 16.1	4 55.3	12 52.1
21 F	22 05 20	2 46 17	11♏02 08	17 36 46	29 58.9	21 07.6	20 48.8	27 08.0	1 45.9	10 43.2	23 14.8	10 19.0	4 57.6	12 53.6
22 Sa	22 09 16	3 46 43	24 16 08	1♐00 36	29R 59.5	20 20.6	21 27.4	27 13.4	1 48.1	10 40.7	23 15.7	10 21.8	4 59.9	12 55.1
23 Su	22 13 13	4 47 08	7♐50 24	14 45 46	29 59.1	19 40.6	22 07.2	27 18.1	1 50.0	10 38.4	23 16.5	10 24.8	5 02.1	12 56.5
24 M	22 17 09	5 47 31	21 46 47	28 53 27	29 56.8	19 07.9	22 48.2	27 22.2	1 51.4	10 36.4	23 17.2	10 27.7	5 04.4	12 58.0
25 Tu	22 21 06	6 47 53	6♑05 33	13♑22 46	29 52.2	18 42.5	23 30.3	27 25.6	1 52.4	10 34.5	23 17.8	10 30.7	5 06.7	12 59.4
26 W	22 25 02	7 48 14	20 44 33	28 10 12	29 45.7	18 24.5	24 13.4	27 28.3	1R 53.0	10 32.8	23 18.3	10 33.7	5 09.0	13 00.8
27 Th	22 28 59	8 48 33	5♒38 48	13♒09 20	29 37.9	18 13.6	24 57.5	27 30.2	1 53.1	10 31.3	23 18.6	10 36.7	5 11.3	13 02.2
28 F	22 32 55	9 48 50	20 40 37	28 11 29	29 29.8	18D 09.7	25 42.6	27 31.5	1 52.8	10 30.0	23 18.9	10 39.7	5 13.5	13 03.5

Astro Data

	Dy Hr Mn
☽0N	6 5:56
☽0S	20 21:57
⚳0S	26 6:43
♃☍♇	31 9:17
♀D	31 20:50
☽0N	2 16:36
☿R	6 21:47
⚳0N	12 10:38
☽0S	17 4:34
♃□♅	26 7:30
⚳R	27 8:09
☿D	28 14:01

Planet Ingress

	Dy Hr Mn
☿ ♒	11 21:36
☉ ♒	20 3:52
☿ ♓	31 14:30
⚳ ♏	3 17:30
☿ ♒R	13 3:31
☊ ♎R	18 16:20
☉ ♓	18 18:01

Last Aspect / ☽ Ingress (January)

Last Aspect Dy Hr Mn		☽ Ingress	Dy Hr Mn
2 11:13	♀ ☌	♒	2 17:04
4 1:48	♄ □	♓	4 16:59
6 9:45	♀ ⚹	♈	6 19:46
8 16:23	☿ □	♉	9 2:25
11 10:59	☿ △	♊	11 12:27
12 21:34	♂ △	♋	14 0:26
16 4:53	☉ ☍	♌	16 13:02
18 8:53	♄ □	♍	19 1:25
20 20:56	♄ ⚹	♎	21 12:44
23 3:52	♂ ☌	♏	23 21:45
25 13:56	☿ □	♐	26 3:14
27 22:03	☿ ⚹	♑	28 5:05
29 16:48	♂ □	♒	30 4:34

Last Aspect / ☽ Ingress (February)

Last Aspect Dy Hr Mn		☽ Ingress	Dy Hr Mn
31 16:46	♂ △	♓	1 3:46
2 16:36	♄ △	♈	3 4:56
4 23:15	♂ ☍	♉	5 9:48
7 4:51	♄ ☍	♊	7 18:45
9 21:10	♂ △	♋	10 6:34
12 10:52	♂ □	♌	12 19:16
15 3:14	☿ ☍	♍	15 7:27
17 5:06	♄ ⚹	♎	17 18:24
19 21:53	♂ ☌	♏	20 3:34
21 22:11	♄ ☌	♐	22 10:13
24 9:26	♂ ⚹	♑	24 13:51
26 10:52	♂ □	♒	26 14:57
28 10:56	♂ △	♓	28 14:54

☽ Phases & Eclipses

Dy Hr Mn	
1 11:15	● 10♑57
8 3:40	☽ 17♈46
16 4:53	○ 25♋58
24 5:20	☾ 4♏08
30 21:40	● 10♒55
6 19:23	☽ 17♉56
14 23:54	○ 26♌13
22 17:16	☾ 4♐00

Astro Data

1 January 2014
Julian Day # 41639
SVP 5♓03'41"
GC 27♐02.1 ⚴ 13♍37.6
Eris 21♈51.2R ⚵ 0♓05.2
⚷ 9♓59.5 ⚶ 18♎22.7
☽ Mean ☊ 4♏14.4

1 February 2014
Julian Day # 41670
SVP 5♓03'36"
GC 27♐02.2 ⚴ 10♍13.3R
Eris 21♈53.8 ⚵ 14♓37.2
⚷ 11♓30.8 ⚶ 26♎56.1
☽ Mean ☊ 2♏35.9

March 2014 LONGITUDE

Day	Sid.Time	☉	0 hr ☽	Noon☽	True☊	☿	♀	♂	⚳	♃	♄	♅	♆	♇
1 Sa	22 36 52	10♓49 06	5♓40 40	13♓07 00	29♎22.4	18♒12.4	26♑28.6	27♎32.0	1♏52.1	10♋29.0	23♏19.1	10♈42.8	5♓15.8	13♑04.8
2 Su	22 40 49	11 49 20	20 29 24	27 46 55	29R 16.8	18 21.4	27 15.5	27R 31.7	1R 51.0	10R 28.1	23R 19.2	10 45.9	5 18.1	13 06.1
3 M	22 44 45	12 49 32	4♈58 46	12♈04 22	29 13.3	18 36.3	28 03.2	27 30.7	1 49.4	10 27.4	23 19.1	10 49.0	5 20.3	13 07.4
4 Tu	22 48 42	13 49 42	19 03 18	25 55 24	29D 12.0	18 56.8	28 51.8	27 29.0	1 47.4	10 26.9	23 19.0	10 52.1	5 22.6	13 08.6
5 W	22 52 38	14 49 50	2♉40 36	9♉19 03	29 12.3	19 22.5	29 41.1	27 26.5	1 45.0	10D 26.6	23 18.8	10 55.3	5 24.9	13 09.9
6 Th	22 56 35	15 49 56	15 51 00	22 16 51	29 13.6	19 53.0	0♒31.2	27 23.3	1 42.1	10 26.5	23 18.4	10 58.4	5 27.1	13 11.1
7 F	23 00 31	16 50 00	28 37 02	4♊52 06	29 15.0	20 28.0	1 22.1	27 19.3	1 38.8	10 26.6	23 18.0	11 01.6	5 29.4	13 12.2
8 Sa	23 04 28	17 50 02	11♊02 37	17 09 12	29R 15.7	21 07.3	2 13.6	27 14.5	1 35.1	10 26.9	23 17.4	11 04.8	5 31.6	13 13.4
9 Su	23 08 24	18 50 02	23 12 28	29 13 02	29 15.0	21 50.6	3 05.8	27 09.0	1 31.0	10 27.4	23 16.8	11 08.0	5 33.8	13 14.5
10 M	23 12 21	19 50 00	5♋11 30	11♋08 29	29 12.6	22 37.4	3 58.6	27 02.7	1 26.5	10 28.1	23 16.0	11 11.3	5 36.1	13 15.5
11 Tu	23 16 18	20 49 55	17 04 31	23 00 09	29 08.5	23 27.8	4 52.0	26 55.6	1 21.5	10 29.0	23 15.2	11 14.5	5 38.3	13 16.6
12 W	23 20 14	21 49 48	28 55 53	4♌52 09	29 02.9	24 21.3	5 46.1	26 47.8	1 16.2	10 30.1	23 14.3	11 17.8	5 40.5	13 17.6
13 Th	23 24 11	22 49 39	10♌49 21	16 47 53	28 56.4	25 17.8	6 40.7	26 39.1	1 10.4	10 31.4	23 13.2	11 21.1	5 42.7	13 18.6
14 F	23 28 07	23 49 28	22 48 02	28 50 06	28 49.7	26 17.1	7 35.9	26 29.8	1 04.2	10 32.9	23 12.1	11 24.4	5 44.9	13 19.6
15 Sa	23 32 04	24 49 15	4♍54 16	11♍00 46	28 43.5	27 19.0	8 31.6	26 19.6	0 57.7	10 34.5	23 10.8	11 27.7	5 47.1	13 20.5
16 Su	23 36 00	25 49 00	17 09 45	23 21 18	28 38.3	28 23.5	9 27.9	26 08.7	0 50.7	10 36.4	23 09.5	11 31.0	5 49.3	13 21.4
17 M	23 39 57	26 48 42	29 35 34	5♎52 35	28 34.7	29 30.3	10 24.6	25 57.1	0 43.3	10 38.4	23 08.0	11 34.4	5 51.4	13 22.3
18 Tu	23 43 53	27 48 23	12♎12 27	18 35 13	28D 32.7	0♓39.4	11 21.8	25 44.7	0 35.6	10 40.7	23 06.5	11 37.7	5 53.6	13 23.2
19 W	23 47 50	28 48 02	25 00 56	1♏29 41	28 32.3	1 50.5	12 19.5	25 31.5	0 27.5	10 43.1	23 04.9	11 41.1	5 55.7	13 24.0
20 Th	23 51 46	29 47 39	8♏01 33	14 36 35	28 33.1	3 03.7	13 17.7	25 17.7	0 19.1	10 45.7	23 03.2	11 44.4	5 57.8	13 24.8
21 F	23 55 43	0♈47 15	21 14 54	27 56 34	28 34.6	4 18.8	14 16.3	25 03.1	0 10.2	10 48.5	23 01.4	11 47.8	6 00.0	13 25.6
22 Sa	23 59 40	1 46 49	4♐41 41	11♐30 20	28 36.2	5 35.8	15 15.3	24 47.8	0 01.1	10 51.5	22 59.4	11 51.2	6 02.1	13 26.3
23 Su	0 03 36	2 46 21	18 22 33	25 18 23	28R 37.2	6 54.6	16 14.7	24 31.9	29♎51.5	10 54.6	22 57.5	11 54.6	6 04.2	13 27.0
24 M	0 07 33	3 45 51	2♑17 47	9♑20 40	28 37.3	8 15.1	17 14.5	24 15.2	29 41.7	10 57.9	22 55.4	11 58.0	6 06.2	13 27.7
25 Tu	0 11 29	4 45 19	16 26 52	23 36 08	28 36.3	9 37.3	18 14.7	23 58.0	29 31.5	11 01.5	22 53.2	12 01.4	6 08.3	13 28.3
26 W	0 15 26	5 44 46	0♒48 07	8♒02 23	28 34.2	11 01.1	19 15.2	23 40.1	29 21.0	11 05.2	22 50.9	12 04.8	6 10.4	13 29.0
27 Th	0 19 22	6 44 11	15 18 24	22 35 30	28 31.5	12 26.5	20 16.1	23 21.6	29 10.2	11 09.0	22 48.6	12 08.2	6 12.4	13 29.5
28 F	0 23 19	7 43 34	29 53 01	7♓10 10	28 28.5	13 53.5	21 17.3	23 02.5	28 59.1	11 13.1	22 46.1	12 11.6	6 14.4	13 30.1
29 Sa	0 27 15	8 42 56	14♓26 10	21 40 14	28 25.8	15 22.0	22 18.8	22 42.9	28 47.8	11 17.3	22 43.6	12 15.0	6 16.4	13 30.6
30 Su	0 31 12	9 42 15	28 51 35	5♈59 31	28 23.9	16 52.0	23 20.6	22 22.8	28 36.2	11 21.7	22 41.0	12 18.5	6 18.4	13 31.1
31 M	0 35 09	10 41 32	13♈03 24	20 02 40	28D 22.9	18 23.4	24 22.7	22 02.2	28 24.3	11 26.2	22 38.3	12 21.9	6 20.4	13 31.6

April 2014 LONGITUDE

Day	Sid.Time	☉	0 hr ☽	Noon☽	True☊	☿	♀	♂	⚳	♃	♄	♅	♆	♇
1 Tu	0 39 05	11♈40 47	26♈56 53	3♉45 47	28♎22.8	19♓56.4	25♒25.1	21♎41.2	28♎12.2	11♋31.0	22♏35.5	12♈25.3	6♓22.3	13♑32.0
2 W	0 43 02	12 40 00	10♉29 08	17 06 53	28 23.4	21 30.8	26 27.8	21R 19.8	27R 59.9	11 35.9	22R 32.6	12 28.8	6 24.3	13 32.4
3 Th	0 46 58	13 39 11	23 39 05	0♊05 53	28 24.6	23 06.7	27 30.7	20 58.1	27 47.3	11 40.9	22 29.7	12 32.2	6 26.2	13 32.8
4 F	0 50 55	14 38 20	6♊27 33	12 44 23	28 25.8	24 44.0	28 33.9	20 36.0	27 34.6	11 46.2	22 26.7	12 35.6	6 28.1	13 33.1
5 Sa	0 54 51	15 37 26	18 56 49	25 05 19	28 26.9	26 22.7	29 37.4	20 13.7	27 21.8	11 51.6	22 23.6	12 39.0	6 30.0	13 33.4
6 Su	0 58 48	16 36 31	1♋10 22	7♋12 31	28R 27.6	28 03.0	0♓41.1	19 51.1	27 08.7	11 57.1	22 20.4	12 42.5	6 31.8	13 33.7
7 M	1 02 44	17 35 32	13 12 21	19 10 26	28 27.8	29 44.6	1 45.0	19 28.4	26 55.5	12 02.8	22 17.2	12 45.9	6 33.6	13 34.0
8 Tu	1 06 41	18 34 32	25 07 21	1♌03 42	28 27.5	1♈27.8	2 49.1	19 05.5	26 42.3	12 08.7	22 13.9	12 49.3	6 35.5	13 34.2
9 W	1 10 38	19 33 29	7♌00 02	12 56 55	28 26.8	3 12.4	3 53.5	18 42.5	26 28.9	12 14.7	22 10.5	12 52.7	6 37.3	13 34.4
10 Th	1 14 34	20 32 24	18 54 54	24 54 27	28 25.9	4 58.5	4 58.1	18 19.5	26 15.4	12 20.9	22 07.0	12 56.1	6 39.0	13 34.5
11 F	1 18 31	21 31 17	0♍56 04	7♍00 09	28 24.9	6 46.1	6 02.8	17 56.5	26 01.8	12 27.2	22 03.5	12 59.5	6 40.8	13 34.6
12 Sa	1 22 27	22 30 07	13 07 06	19 17 15	28 24.0	8 35.3	7 07.8	17 33.5	25 48.2	12 33.7	22 00.0	13 02.9	6 42.5	13 34.7
13 Su	1 26 24	23 28 56	25 30 51	1♎48 09	28 23.4	10 25.9	8 13.0	17 10.6	25 34.5	12 40.3	21 56.3	13 06.3	6 44.2	13 34.8
14 M	1 30 20	24 27 42	8♎09 17	14 34 22	28 23.0	12 18.1	9 18.4	16 47.8	25 20.9	12 47.1	21 52.6	13 09.7	6 45.9	13R 34.8
15 Tu	1 34 17	25 26 26	21 03 26	27 36 29	28D 22.9	14 11.7	10 23.9	16 25.2	25 07.2	12 54.0	21 48.9	13 13.1	6 47.6	13 34.8
16 W	1 38 13	26 25 08	4♏13 27	10♏54 12	28 23.0	16 07.0	11 29.7	16 02.8	24 53.5	13 01.0	21 45.1	13 16.4	6 49.2	13 34.8
17 Th	1 42 10	27 23 49	17 38 35	24 26 23	28 23.1	18 03.7	12 35.6	15 40.6	24 39.9	13 08.2	21 41.2	13 19.8	6 50.8	13 34.7
18 F	1 46 06	28 22 27	1♐17 23	8♐11 19	28R 23.1	20 01.9	13 41.7	15 18.7	24 26.3	13 15.6	21 37.3	13 23.1	6 52.4	13 34.6
19 Sa	1 50 03	29 21 04	15 07 54	22 06 51	28 23.1	22 01.6	14 47.9	14 57.2	24 12.8	13 23.0	21 33.3	13 26.5	6 54.0	13 34.5
20 Su	1 54 00	0♉19 40	29 07 51	6♑10 38	28 22.9	24 02.8	15 54.3	14 36.0	23 59.4	13 30.6	21 29.3	13 29.8	6 55.6	13 34.4
21 M	1 57 56	1 18 13	13♑14 52	20 20 15	28D 22.8	26 05.3	17 00.9	14 15.2	23 46.0	13 38.3	21 25.3	13 33.1	6 57.1	13 34.2
22 Tu	2 01 53	2 16 45	27 26 29	4♒33 16	28 22.8	28 09.1	18 07.6	13 54.9	23 32.8	13 46.2	21 21.2	13 36.4	6 58.6	13 34.0
23 W	2 05 49	3 15 16	11♒40 17	18 47 13	28 22.9	0♉14.2	19 14.5	13 35.1	23 19.7	13 54.2	21 17.0	13 39.7	7 00.0	13 33.7
24 Th	2 09 46	4 13 45	25 53 46	2♓59 34	28 23.3	2 20.4	20 21.5	13 15.7	23 06.7	14 02.3	21 12.8	13 43.0	7 01.5	13 33.5
25 F	2 13 42	5 12 12	10♓04 19	17 07 47	28 23.9	4 27.5	21 28.6	12 56.9	22 53.9	14 10.5	21 08.6	13 46.2	7 02.9	13 33.2
26 Sa	2 17 39	6 10 37	24 09 15	1♈08 43	28 24.5	6 35.4	22 35.9	12 38.7	22 41.3	14 18.9	21 04.4	13 49.5	7 04.3	13 32.8
27 Su	2 21 35	7 09 01	8♈05 43	14 59 55	28R 25.0	8 43.9	23 43.3	12 21.1	22 28.8	14 27.4	21 00.1	13 52.7	7 05.6	13 32.5
28 M	2 25 32	8 07 23	21 51 00	28 38 39	28 25.2	10 52.8	24 50.9	12 04.1	22 16.6	14 36.0	20 55.7	13 55.9	7 07.0	13 32.1
29 Tu	2 29 29	9 05 44	5♉22 38	12♉02 44	28 25.0	13 01.9	25 58.5	11 47.8	22 04.6	14 44.7	20 51.4	13 59.1	7 08.3	13 31.7
30 W	2 33 25	10 04 03	18 38 46	25 10 38	28 24.1	15 10.8	27 06.2	11 32.2	21 52.8	14 53.6	20 47.0	14 02.2	7 09.6	13 31.2

Astro Data	Dy Hr Mn
♂ R	1 16:25
☽ 0N	2 4:03
♄ R	2 16:20
♃ D	6 10:43
☽ 0S	16 11:17
☉ 0N	20 16:58
☽ 0N	29 14:06
☿ 0N	10 14:19
☽ 0S	12 18:57
♇ R	14 23:48
♃□♅	20 7:30
♃☍♇	20 23:27
♅□♇	21 19:22
☽ 0N	25 21:49

Planet Ingress		Dy Hr Mn
♀	♒	5 21:04
☿	♓	17 22:25
☉	♈	20 16:58
⚳	♎R	22 14:43
♀	♓	5 20:32
☿	♈	7 15:36
☉	♉	20 3:57
☿	♉	23 9:17

Last Aspect Dy Hr Mn			☽ Ingress	Dy Hr Mn
2 11:05	♀	⚹	♈	2 15:41
4 17:32	♀	□	♉	4 19:13
6 13:56	♄	☍	♊	7 2:38
9 7:54	♂	△	♋	9 13:34
11 19:52	♂	□	♌	12 2:10
14 7:25	♂	⚹	♍	14 14:19
16 17:09	☉	☍	♎	17 0:47
19 1:08	♂	☌	♏	19 9:14
21 3:13	♄	☌	♐	21 15:40
23 10:41	♂	⚹	♑	23 20:04
25 12:36	♂	□	♒	25 22:40
27 13:14	♂	△	♓	28 0:12
29 13:45	♄	△	♈	30 1:55

Last Aspect Dy Hr Mn			☽ Ingress	Dy Hr Mn
31 20:08	♀	⚹	♉	1 5:21
3 6:44	♀	□	♊	3 11:49
5 14:56	☿	□	♋	5 21:41
7 18:15	♄	△	♌	8 9:51
10 6:27	♄	□	♍	10 22:09
12 17:13	♄	⚹	♎	13 8:34
15 7:43	☉	☍	♏	15 16:21
17 7:10	♄	☌	♐	17 21:45
20 1:18	☉	△	♑	20 1:29
21 23:22	☿	□	♒	22 4:19
23 16:12	♄	□	♓	24 6:56
25 20:04	♀	☌	♈	26 10:02
27 11:03	♃	□	♉	28 14:24
30 15:54	♀	⚹	♊	30 20:57

☽ Phases & Eclipses Dy Hr Mn		
1 8:01	●	10♓39
8 13:28	☽	17♊54
16 17:09	○	26♍02
24 1:47	☾	3♑21
30 18:46	●	9♈59
7 8:32	☽	17♋27
15 7:43	○	25♎16
15 7:47	☍	T 1.290
22 7:53	☾	2♒07
29 6:15	●	8♉52
29 6:04:33	☌	A non-C

Astro Data

1 March 2014
Julian Day # 41698
SVP 5♓03'33"
GC 27♐02.2 ⚴ 1♍20.6R
Eris 22♈04.5 ⚵ 28♓59.0
⚷ 13♓13.5 ⚶ 29♎59.6
☽ Mean ☊ 1♏07.0

1 April 2014
Julian Day # 41729
SVP 5♓03'30"
GC 27♐02.3 ⚴ 25♌11.5R
Eris 22♈22.7 ⚵ 15♈50.5
⚷ 15♓08.1 ⚶ 26♎22.4R
☽ Mean ☊ 29♎28.4

LONGITUDE — May 2014

Day	Sid.Time	☉	0 hr ☽	Noon ☽	True ☊	☿	♀	♂	⚳	♃	♄	♅	♆	♇
1 Th	2 37 22	11♉02 20	1♊38 17	8♊01 46	28♎22.7	17♉19.4	28♓14.1	11♎17.3	21♎41.3	15♋02.5	20♏42.6	14♈05.4	7♓10.8	13♑30.8
2 F	2 41 18	12 00 35	14 21 08	20 36 34	28R 20.8	19 27.2	29 22.1	11R 03.1	21R 30.0	15 11.6	20R 38.2	14 08.5	7 12.1	13R 30.2
3 Sa	2 45 15	12 58 48	26 48 17	2♋56 33	28 18.7	21 34.0	0♈30.2	10 49.7	21 19.0	15 20.8	20 33.7	14 11.6	7 13.2	13 29.7
4 Su	2 49 11	13 56 59	9♋01 45	15 04 14	28 16.8	23 39.5	1 38.3	10 37.0	21 08.3	15 30.1	20 29.3	14 14.7	7 14.4	13 29.2
5 M	2 53 08	14 55 08	21 04 28	27 02 57	28 15.3	25 43.4	2 46.6	10 25.0	20 57.9	15 39.5	20 24.8	14 17.8	7 15.6	13 28.6
6 Tu	2 57 04	15 53 15	3♌00 11	8♌56 43	28D 14.4	27 45.5	3 55.0	10 13.9	20 47.8	15 49.0	20 20.3	14 20.9	7 16.7	13 28.0
7 W	3 01 01	16 51 21	14 53 08	20 50 00	28 14.3	29 45.4	5 03.4	10 03.6	20 38.0	15 58.6	20 15.8	14 23.9	7 17.7	13 27.3
8 Th	3 04 58	17 49 24	26 47 56	2♍47 29	28 14.9	1♊42.9	6 12.0	9 54.0	20 28.5	16 08.4	20 11.3	14 26.9	7 18.8	13 26.7
9 F	3 08 54	18 47 25	8♍49 16	14 53 50	28 16.2	3 37.8	7 20.6	9 45.3	20 19.4	16 18.2	20 06.8	14 29.9	7 19.8	13 26.0
10 Sa	3 12 51	19 45 25	21 01 43	27 13 24	28 17.8	5 29.9	8 29.3	9 37.3	20 10.6	16 28.1	20 02.3	14 32.8	7 20.8	13 25.3
11 Su	3 16 47	20 43 23	3♎29 21	9♎49 56	28 19.2	7 19.1	9 38.1	9 30.2	20 02.1	16 38.1	19 57.8	14 35.7	7 21.7	13 24.5
12 M	3 20 44	21 41 19	16 15 29	22 46 14	28R 20.0	9 05.2	10 47.0	9 23.8	19 54.0	16 48.2	19 53.3	14 38.6	7 22.7	13 23.7
13 Tu	3 24 40	22 39 13	29 22 18	6♏03 44	28 19.9	10 48.2	11 56.0	9 18.3	19 46.3	16 58.4	19 48.8	14 41.5	7 23.6	13 22.9
14 W	3 28 37	23 37 06	12♏50 28	19 42 19	28 18.7	12 27.8	13 05.1	9 13.5	19 38.9	17 08.7	19 44.3	14 44.4	7 24.4	13 22.1
15 Th	3 32 33	24 34 57	26 38 57	3♐39 59	28 16.2	14 04.0	14 14.2	9 09.6	19 31.9	17 19.1	19 39.8	14 47.2	7 25.3	13 21.3
16 F	3 36 30	25 32 47	10♐44 54	17 53 06	28 12.7	15 36.9	15 23.5	9 06.4	19 25.3	17 29.6	19 35.3	14 50.0	7 26.1	13 20.4
17 Sa	3 40 27	26 30 36	25 03 56	2♑16 41	28 08.8	17 06.2	16 32.8	9 04.1	19 19.1	17 40.1	19 30.8	14 52.8	7 26.9	13 19.5
18 Su	3 44 23	27 28 23	9♑30 38	16 45 05	28 04.9	18 31.9	17 42.1	9 02.5	19 13.2	17 50.8	19 26.4	14 55.5	7 27.6	13 18.6
19 M	3 48 20	28 26 09	23 59 20	1♒12 47	28 01.7	19 54.0	18 51.6	9D 01.6	19 07.7	18 01.5	19 22.0	14 58.2	7 28.3	13 17.7
20 Tu	3 52 16	29 23 55	8♒24 52	15 35 06	27 59.6	21 12.5	20 01.1	9 01.6	19 02.6	18 12.3	19 17.5	15 00.9	7 29.0	13 16.7
21 W	3 56 13	0♊21 38	22 43 06	29 48 33	27D 58.9	22 27.2	21 10.7	9 02.3	18 57.9	18 23.2	19 13.2	15 03.6	7 29.6	13 15.7
22 Th	4 00 09	1 19 21	6♓51 14	13♓51 00	27 59.4	23 38.2	22 20.4	9 03.8	18 53.6	18 34.2	19 08.8	15 06.2	7 30.3	13 14.7
23 F	4 04 06	2 17 03	20 47 45	27 41 24	28 00.7	24 45.4	23 30.1	9 06.0	18 49.7	18 45.3	19 04.4	15 08.8	7 30.8	13 13.7
24 Sa	4 08 02	3 14 44	4♈31 59	11♈19 27	28 02.1	25 48.7	24 39.9	9 09.0	18 46.1	18 56.4	19 00.1	15 11.3	7 31.4	13 12.7
25 Su	4 11 59	4 12 24	18 03 51	24 45 11	28R 03.0	26 48.1	25 49.8	9 12.7	18 43.0	19 07.6	18 55.8	15 13.8	7 31.9	13 11.6
26 M	4 15 56	5 10 03	1♉23 28	7♉58 43	28 02.6	27 43.4	26 59.7	9 17.1	18 40.3	19 18.9	18 51.6	15 16.3	7 32.4	13 10.5
27 Tu	4 19 52	6 07 41	14 30 54	21 00 03	28 00.5	28 34.7	28 09.7	9 22.2	18 37.9	19 30.2	18 47.4	15 18.8	7 32.8	13 09.4
28 W	4 23 49	7 05 17	27 26 08	3♊49 10	27 56.5	29 21.9	29 19.8	9 28.1	18 36.0	19 41.7	18 43.2	15 21.2	7 33.3	13 08.3
29 Th	4 27 45	8 02 53	10♊09 08	16 26 04	27 50.8	0♋04.8	0♉29.9	9 34.7	18 34.5	19 53.2	18 39.1	15 23.6	7 33.6	13 07.1
30 F	4 31 42	9 00 27	22 40 00	28 51 02	27 43.8	0 43.4	1 40.0	9 41.9	18 33.3	20 04.7	18 35.0	15 26.0	7 34.0	13 06.0
31 Sa	4 35 38	9 58 01	4♋59 16	11♋04 52	27 36.2	1 17.6	2 50.2	9 49.9	18 32.6	20 16.4	18 30.9	15 28.3	7 34.3	13 04.8

LONGITUDE — June 2014

Day	Sid.Time	☉	0 hr ☽	Noon ☽	True ☊	☿	♀	♂	⚳	♃	♄	♅	♆	♇
1 Su	4 39 35	10♊55 33	17♋08 03	23♋09 04	27♎28.7	1♋47.4	4♉00.5	9♎58.5	18♎32.3	20♋28.1	18♏26.9	15♈30.6	7♓34.6	13♑03.6
2 M	4 43 31	11 53 04	29 08 12	5♌05 51	27R 22.2	2 12.6	5 10.8	10 07.7	18D 32.3	20 39.9	18R 23.0	15 32.8	7 34.9	13R 02.4
3 Tu	4 47 28	12 50 33	11♌02 23	16 58 17	27 17.2	2 33.4	6 21.2	10 17.6	18 32.8	20 51.7	18 19.1	15 35.0	7 35.1	13 01.1
4 W	4 51 25	13 48 01	22 54 02	28 50 10	27 14.0	2 49.5	7 31.6	10 28.2	18 33.6	21 03.6	18 15.2	15 37.2	7 35.3	12 59.9
5 Th	4 55 21	14 45 28	4♍47 16	10♍45 55	27D 12.6	3 00.9	8 42.0	10 39.4	18 34.9	21 15.5	18 11.4	15 39.3	7 35.4	12 58.6
6 F	4 59 18	15 42 54	16 46 45	22 50 22	27 12.8	3R 07.8	9 52.5	10 51.1	18 36.5	21 27.5	18 07.7	15 41.4	7 35.6	12 57.3
7 Sa	5 03 14	16 40 19	28 57 25	5♎08 30	27 13.8	3 10.1	11 03.1	11 03.5	18 38.5	21 39.6	18 04.0	15 43.5	7 35.7	12 56.0
8 Su	5 07 11	17 37 43	11♎24 14	17 45 08	27R 14.9	3 07.8	12 13.7	11 16.5	18 40.9	21 51.7	18 00.3	15 45.5	7 35.7	12 54.7
9 M	5 11 07	18 35 05	24 11 43	0♏44 22	27 15.2	3 01.1	13 24.3	11 30.0	18 43.6	22 03.9	17 56.8	15 47.5	7R 35.7	12 53.4
10 Tu	5 15 04	19 32 27	7♏23 25	14 09 03	27 13.9	2 50.2	14 35.0	11 44.1	18 46.7	22 16.1	17 53.3	15 49.4	7 35.7	12 52.0
11 W	5 19 00	20 29 47	21 01 18	28 00 05	27 10.5	2 35.2	15 45.7	11 58.8	18 50.2	22 28.4	17 49.8	15 51.3	7 35.7	12 50.7
12 Th	5 22 57	21 27 07	5♐05 07	12♐15 54	27 05.0	2 16.3	16 56.5	12 14.0	18 54.1	22 40.7	17 46.4	15 53.2	7 35.6	12 49.3
13 F	5 26 54	22 24 26	19 31 49	26 52 04	26 57.6	1 54.0	18 07.4	12 29.7	18 58.3	22 53.1	17 43.1	15 55.0	7 35.5	12 47.9
14 Sa	5 30 50	23 21 45	4♑15 42	11♑41 41	26 49.3	1 28.5	19 18.2	12 46.0	19 02.9	23 05.5	17 39.9	15 56.8	7 35.4	12 46.6
15 Su	5 34 47	24 19 02	19 08 53	26 36 13	26 41.0	1 00.2	20 29.2	13 02.8	19 07.8	23 18.0	17 36.7	15 58.5	7 35.2	12 45.2
16 M	5 38 43	25 16 20	4♒02 34	11♒26 58	26 33.7	0 29.7	21 40.1	13 20.0	19 13.0	23 30.5	17 33.6	16 00.2	7 35.0	12 43.8
17 Tu	5 42 40	26 13 37	18 48 31	26 06 28	26 28.3	29♊57.4	22 51.2	13 37.8	19 18.6	23 43.0	17 30.6	16 01.8	7 34.8	12 42.3
18 W	5 46 36	27 10 53	3♓20 16	10♓29 29	26 25.1	29 23.8	24 02.2	13 56.0	19 24.6	23 55.6	17 27.7	16 03.4	7 34.5	12 40.9
19 Th	5 50 33	28 08 09	17 33 51	24 33 16	26D 23.9	28 49.6	25 13.4	14 14.7	19 30.9	24 08.3	17 24.8	16 05.0	7 34.2	12 39.5
20 F	5 54 29	29 05 25	1♈27 45	8♈17 22	26 24.1	28 15.3	26 24.5	14 33.9	19 37.5	24 20.9	17 22.0	16 06.5	7 33.9	12 38.0
21 Sa	5 58 26	0♋02 41	15 02 20	21 42 52	26R 24.6	27 41.5	27 35.7	14 53.5	19 44.4	24 33.7	17 19.3	16 08.0	7 33.6	12 36.6
22 Su	6 02 23	0 59 57	28 19 14	4♉51 42	26 24.4	27 08.8	28 47.0	15 13.6	19 51.7	24 46.4	17 16.6	16 09.4	7 33.2	12 35.1
23 M	6 06 19	1 57 13	11♉20 34	17 46 06	26 22.4	26 37.7	29 58.3	15 34.1	19 59.2	24 59.2	17 14.0	16 10.8	7 32.8	12 33.6
24 Tu	6 10 16	2 54 28	24 08 31	0♊28 03	26 18.0	26 08.8	1♊09.6	15 55.0	20 07.2	25 12.0	17 11.6	16 12.1	7 32.3	12 32.2
25 W	6 14 12	3 51 44	6♊44 54	12 59 14	26 10.9	25 42.5	2 21.0	16 16.4	20 15.4	25 24.9	17 09.2	16 13.4	7 31.8	12 30.7
26 Th	6 18 09	4 48 59	19 11 10	25 20 50	26 01.2	25 19.4	3 32.4	16 38.2	20 23.9	25 37.8	17 06.9	16 14.7	7 31.3	12 29.2
27 F	6 22 05	5 46 14	1♋28 21	7♋33 48	25 49.6	24 59.8	4 43.9	17 00.5	20 32.7	25 50.7	17 04.6	16 15.9	7 30.8	12 27.7
28 Sa	6 26 02	6 43 28	13 37 20	19 39 02	25 37.0	24 44.1	5 55.4	17 23.1	20 41.8	26 03.7	17 02.5	16 17.0	7 30.2	12 26.2
29 Su	6 29 59	7 40 43	25 39 04	1♌37 36	25 24.5	24 32.6	7 07.0	17 46.1	20 51.3	26 16.7	17 00.4	16 18.1	7 29.6	12 24.7
30 M	6 33 55	8 37 57	7♌34 51	13 31 03	25 13.1	24 25.4	8 18.5	18 09.5	21 01.0	26 29.7	16 58.5	16 19.2	7 29.0	12 23.2

Astro Data

Astro Data	Dy Hr Mn
♀0N	6 2:54
☽0S	10 3:44
♂D	20 1:32
☽0N	23 3:59
♃△♄	24 17:48
⚳D	1 20:16
☽0S	6 13:01
☿R	7 11:58
♆R	9 19:51
♃⚼♆	12 2:13
☽0N	19 10:22
⚳0S	22 8:56

Planet Ingress

Planet Ingress	Dy Hr Mn
♀ ♈	3 1:22
☿ ♊	7 14:58
☉ ♊	21 3:00
♀ ♉	29 1:47
☿ ♋	29 9:13
☿ ♊R	17 10:06
☉ ♋	21 10:52
♀ ♊	23 12:35

Last Aspect / ☽ Ingress (May)

Last Aspect Dy Hr Mn		☽ Ingress	Dy Hr Mn
1 23:33	♅ ⚹	♋	3 6:14
5 8:47	☿ ⚹	♌	5 17:57
7 10:52	♄ □	♍	8 6:25
9 22:09	♄ ⚹	♎	10 17:20
12 0:52	♃ □	♏	13 1:08
14 19:17	☉ ☍	♐	15 5:45
16 7:44	☿ ☍	♑	17 8:13
19 7:03	☉ △	♒	19 9:59
20 22:22	☿ △	♓	21 12:19
23 6:27	☿ □	♈	23 16:02
25 15:59	☿ ⚹	♉	25 21:29
27 9:11	♃ ⚹	♊	28 4:49
29 10:00	♅ ⚹	♋	30 14:14

Last Aspect / ☽ Ingress (June)

Last Aspect Dy Hr Mn		☽ Ingress	Dy Hr Mn
1 6:33	♃ ☌	♌	2 1:44
3 14:43	♄ □	♍	4 14:21
6 9:14	♃ ⚹	♎	7 2:02
8 19:48	♃ □	♏	9 10:39
11 2:22	♃ △	♐	11 15:24
13 4:13	☉ ☍	♑	13 17:06
15 6:36	♃ ☍	♒	15 17:28
17 18:08	☿ △	♓	17 18:27
19 19:07	☿ □	♈	19 21:27
21 22:25	☿ ⚹	♉	22 3:04
24 1:50	♃ ⚹	♊	24 11:07
26 11:57	☿ ☌	♋	26 21:07
29 1:04	♃ ☌	♌	29 8:44

☽ Phases & Eclipses

Dy Hr Mn		
7 3:16	☽	16♌30
14 19:17	○	23♏55
21 13:00	☾	0♓24
28 18:41	●	7♊21
5 20:40	☽	15♍06
13 4:13	○	22♐06
19 18:40	☾	28♓24
27 8:10	●	5♋37

Astro Data

1 May 2014
Julian Day # 41759
SVP 5♓03'28"
GC 27♐02.4 ⚴ 26♌55.0
Eris 22♈42.2 ⚵ 2♉48.5
⚷ 16♓39.5 ⚶ 19♎13.1R
☽ Mean ☊ 27♎53.1

1 June 2014
Julian Day # 41790
SVP 5♓03'23"
GC 27♐02.4 ⚴ 4♍10.2
Eris 22♈59.4 ⚵ 20♉43.5
⚷ 17♓35.6 ⚶ 16♎30.0
☽ Mean ☊ 26♎14.6

July 2014 — LONGITUDE

Day	Sid.Time	☉	0 hr ☽	Noon ☽	True ☊	☿	♀	♂	⚳	♃	♄	♅	♆	♇
1 Tu	6 37 52	9♋35 10	19♌26 31	25♌21 35	25♎03.7	24♊22.9	9♊30.2	18♎33.3	21♎11.0	26♋42.8	16♏56.6	16♈20.2	7♓28.3	12♑21.7
2 W	6 41 48	10 32 24	1♍16 38	7♍12 07	24R 56.9	24D 25.1	10 41.8	18 57.5	21 21.3	26 55.8	16R 54.8	16 21.2	7R 27.6	12R 20.2
3 Th	6 45 45	11 29 37	13 08 30	19 06 21	24 52.6	24 32.2	11 53.5	19 22.0	21 31.9	27 08.9	16 53.1	16 22.1	7 26.9	12 18.7
4 F	6 49 41	12 26 50	25 06 13	1♎08 42	24D 50.6	24 44.3	13 05.2	19 46.9	21 42.7	27 22.0	16 51.5	16 23.0	7 26.2	12 17.2
5 Sa	6 53 38	13 24 02	7♎14 26	13 24 04	24R 50.2	25 01.4	14 17.0	20 12.1	21 53.8	27 35.2	16 50.0	16 23.8	7 25.4	12 15.7
6 Su	6 57 34	14 21 14	19 38 14	25 57 34	24 50.3	25 23.5	15 28.8	20 37.7	22 05.2	27 48.3	16 48.6	16 24.6	7 24.6	12 14.2
7 M	7 01 31	15 18 26	2♏22 41	8♏54 07	24 49.7	25 50.6	16 40.6	21 03.6	22 16.8	28 01.5	16 47.2	16 25.3	7 23.7	12 12.7
8 Tu	7 05 27	16 15 38	15 32 20	22 17 42	24 47.5	26 22.8	17 52.5	21 29.9	22 28.7	28 14.7	16 46.0	16 26.0	7 22.9	12 11.2
9 W	7 09 24	17 12 50	29 10 26	6♐10 35	24 43.0	27 00.0	19 04.5	21 56.5	22 40.9	28 27.9	16 44.9	16 26.6	7 22.0	12 09.7
10 Th	7 13 21	18 10 01	13♐18 01	20 32 23	24 36.0	27 42.1	20 16.4	22 23.4	22 53.3	28 41.2	16 43.8	16 27.2	7 21.1	12 08.2
11 F	7 17 17	19 07 13	27 53 08	5♑19 26	24 26.7	28 29.1	21 28.4	22 50.6	23 05.9	28 54.4	16 42.9	16 27.8	7 20.2	12 06.7
12 Sa	7 21 14	20 04 25	12♑50 18	20 24 33	24 16.1	29 20.9	22 40.5	23 18.1	23 18.8	29 07.7	16 42.0	16 28.3	7 19.2	12 05.2
13 Su	7 25 10	21 01 37	28 00 52	5♒37 51	24 05.4	0♋17.6	23 52.5	23 45.9	23 31.9	29 20.9	16 41.3	16 28.7	7 18.2	12 03.8
14 M	7 29 07	21 58 49	13♒14 09	20 48 25	23 55.9	1 19.0	25 04.7	24 14.0	23 45.2	29 34.2	16 40.6	16 29.1	7 17.2	12 02.3
15 Tu	7 33 03	22 56 02	28 19 27	5♓46 13	23 48.5	2 25.1	26 16.8	24 42.4	23 58.8	29 47.5	16 40.0	16 29.4	7 16.2	12 00.8
16 W	7 37 00	23 53 15	13♓07 52	20 23 48	23 43.7	3 35.8	27 29.1	25 11.0	24 12.6	0♌00.8	16 39.6	16 29.7	7 15.1	11 59.3
17 Th	7 40 57	24 50 29	27 33 34	4♈36 59	23 41.4	4 51.0	28 41.3	25 40.0	24 26.6	0 14.1	16 39.2	16 30.0	7 14.0	11 57.9
18 F	7 44 53	25 47 43	11♈33 59	18 24 42	23 40.7	6 10.7	29 53.6	26 09.2	24 40.8	0 27.4	16 38.9	16 30.2	7 12.9	11 56.4
19 Sa	7 48 50	26 44 59	25 09 21	1♉48 16	23 40.7	7 34.8	1♋05.9	26 38.7	24 55.2	0 40.8	16 38.7	16 30.3	7 11.8	11 55.0
20 Su	7 52 46	27 42 15	8♉21 50	14 50 28	23 40.0	9 03.1	2 18.3	27 08.5	25 09.9	0 54.1	16D 38.6	16 30.4	7 10.6	11 53.6
21 M	7 56 43	28 39 32	21 14 37	27 34 44	23 37.6	10 35.6	3 30.8	27 38.5	25 24.7	1 07.4	16 38.7	16R 30.5	7 09.4	11 52.1
22 Tu	8 00 39	29 36 49	3♊51 14	10♊04 31	23 32.7	12 12.1	4 43.2	28 08.8	25 39.8	1 20.8	16 38.8	16 30.5	7 08.2	11 50.7
23 W	8 04 36	0♌34 08	16 14 58	22 22 55	23 25.0	13 52.4	5 55.7	28 39.3	25 55.1	1 34.1	16 39.0	16 30.5	7 07.0	11 49.3
24 Th	8 08 32	1 31 27	28 28 40	4♋32 30	23 14.6	15 36.4	7 08.3	29 10.1	26 10.5	1 47.5	16 39.3	16 30.4	7 05.7	11 47.9
25 F	8 12 29	2 28 47	10♋34 37	16 35 14	23 02.1	17 23.8	8 20.9	29 41.2	26 26.2	2 00.8	16 39.7	16 30.2	7 04.5	11 46.5
26 Sa	8 16 26	3 26 07	22 34 33	28 32 44	22 48.6	19 14.4	9 33.5	0♏12.5	26 42.1	2 14.2	16 40.2	16 30.0	7 03.2	11 45.1
27 Su	8 20 22	4 23 28	4♌29 56	10♌26 20	22 35.1	21 07.9	10 46.2	0 44.1	26 58.1	2 27.5	16 40.8	16 29.8	7 01.9	11 43.8
28 M	8 24 19	5 20 50	16 22 05	22 17 25	22 22.7	23 04.0	11 58.9	1 15.8	27 14.3	2 40.8	16 41.5	16 29.5	7 00.6	11 42.4
29 Tu	8 28 15	6 18 13	28 12 31	4♍07 39	22 12.4	25 02.4	13 11.6	1 47.9	27 30.7	2 54.2	16 42.3	16 29.2	6 59.2	11 41.1
30 W	8 32 12	7 15 36	10♍03 06	15 59 13	22 04.8	27 02.8	14 24.4	2 20.1	27 47.3	3 07.5	16 43.2	16 28.8	6 57.9	11 39.8
31 Th	8 36 08	8 13 00	21 56 21	27 54 55	21 59.9	29 04.8	15 37.2	2 52.6	28 04.1	3 20.8	16 44.2	16 28.4	6 56.5	11 38.5

August 2014 — LONGITUDE

Day	Sid.Time	☉	0 hr ☽	Noon ☽	True ☊	☿	♀	♂	⚳	♃	♄	♅	♆	♇
1 F	8 40 05	9♌10 24	3♎55 24	9♎58 18	21♎57.5	1♌08.0	16♋50.1	3♏25.3	28♎21.0	3♌34.1	16♏45.3	16♈27.9	6♓55.1	11♑37.2
2 Sa	8 44 01	10 07 49	16 04 09	22 13 31	21D 56.9	3 12.3	18 03.0	3 58.2	28 38.1	3 47.4	16 46.5	16R 27.4	6R 53.7	11R 35.9
3 Su	8 47 58	11 05 15	28 27 00	4♏45 12	21R 57.2	5 17.1	19 15.9	4 31.4	28 55.4	4 00.7	16 47.7	16 26.8	6 52.2	11 34.6
4 M	8 51 54	12 02 41	11♏08 43	17 38 06	21 57.2	7 22.2	20 28.9	5 04.7	29 12.9	4 14.0	16 49.1	16 26.2	6 50.8	11 33.4
5 Tu	8 55 51	13 00 08	24 13 52	0♐56 28	21 55.9	9 27.4	21 41.9	5 38.3	29 30.5	4 27.2	16 50.6	16 25.5	6 49.3	11 32.1
6 W	8 59 48	13 57 36	7♐46 15	14 43 23	21 52.5	11 32.3	22 54.9	6 12.1	29 48.2	4 40.5	16 52.2	16 24.8	6 47.9	11 30.9
7 Th	9 03 44	14 55 04	21 47 56	28 59 44	21 46.9	13 36.8	24 08.0	6 46.0	0♏06.1	4 53.7	16 53.8	16 24.0	6 46.4	11 29.7
8 F	9 07 41	15 52 33	6♑18 24	13♑43 18	21 39.1	15 40.6	25 21.1	7 20.2	0 24.2	5 06.9	16 55.6	16 23.2	6 44.9	11 28.5
9 Sa	9 11 37	16 50 03	21 13 38	28 48 19	21 30.1	17 43.5	26 34.3	7 54.6	0 42.4	5 20.1	16 57.4	16 22.4	6 43.4	11 27.4
10 Su	9 15 34	17 47 34	6♒26 07	14♒05 41	21 20.8	19 45.5	27 47.5	8 29.1	1 00.8	5 33.3	16 59.4	16 21.5	6 41.8	11 26.2
11 M	9 19 30	18 45 06	21 45 33	29 24 18	21 12.5	21 46.4	29 00.7	9 03.8	1 19.3	5 46.4	17 01.4	16 20.5	6 40.3	11 25.1
12 Tu	9 23 27	19 42 40	7♓00 33	14♓33 03	21 06.1	23 46.0	0♌14.0	9 38.8	1 37.9	5 59.5	17 03.6	16 19.6	6 38.8	11 24.0
13 W	9 27 24	20 40 14	22 00 44	29 22 43	21 02.0	25 44.4	1 27.3	10 13.9	1 56.7	6 12.6	17 05.8	16 18.5	6 37.2	11 22.9
14 Th	9 31 20	21 37 50	6♈38 21	13♈47 13	21D 00.2	27 41.5	2 40.7	10 49.1	2 15.6	6 25.7	17 08.1	16 17.5	6 35.6	11 21.9
15 F	9 35 17	22 35 27	20 49 05	27 43 56	21 00.1	29 37.3	3 54.1	11 24.6	2 34.6	6 38.8	17 10.5	16 16.3	6 34.0	11 20.8
16 Sa	9 39 13	23 33 06	4♉31 53	11♉13 12	21 00.9	1♍31.6	5 07.5	12 00.3	2 53.8	6 51.8	17 13.0	16 15.2	6 32.5	11 19.8
17 Su	9 43 10	24 30 47	17 48 14	24 17 25	21R 01.4	3 24.5	6 21.0	12 36.1	3 13.1	7 04.8	17 15.6	16 14.0	6 30.9	11 18.8
18 M	9 47 06	25 28 29	0♊41 15	7♊00 14	21 00.7	5 16.1	7 34.5	13 12.1	3 32.5	7 17.8	17 18.3	16 12.8	6 29.3	11 17.8
19 Tu	9 51 03	26 26 13	13 14 54	19 25 45	20 58.1	7 06.2	8 48.1	13 48.2	3 52.1	7 30.8	17 21.0	16 11.5	6 27.6	11 16.8
20 W	9 54 59	27 23 58	25 33 19	1♋38 03	20 53.2	8 54.8	10 01.7	14 24.6	4 11.8	7 43.7	17 23.9	16 10.1	6 26.0	11 15.9
21 Th	9 58 56	28 21 45	7♋40 25	13 40 49	20 46.3	10 42.1	11 15.3	15 01.1	4 31.6	7 56.6	17 26.8	16 08.8	6 24.4	11 15.0
22 F	10 02 52	29 19 33	19 39 39	25 37 14	20 37.6	12 28.0	12 29.0	15 37.8	4 51.6	8 09.4	17 29.9	16 07.4	6 22.8	11 14.1
23 Sa	10 06 49	0♍17 23	1♌33 54	7♌29 56	20 28.1	14 12.5	13 42.7	16 14.6	5 11.6	8 22.3	17 33.0	16 05.9	6 21.1	11 13.2
24 Su	10 10 46	1 15 15	13 25 33	19 21 01	20 18.6	15 55.6	14 56.5	16 51.7	5 31.8	8 35.1	17 36.2	16 04.5	6 19.5	11 12.4
25 M	10 14 42	2 13 08	25 16 32	1♍12 19	20 09.8	17 37.4	16 10.3	17 28.8	5 52.1	8 47.8	17 39.5	16 02.9	6 17.9	11 11.6
26 Tu	10 18 39	3 11 02	7♍08 33	13 05 27	20 02.7	19 17.8	17 24.1	18 06.2	6 12.5	9 00.5	17 42.8	16 01.4	6 16.2	11 10.8
27 W	10 22 35	4 08 58	19 03 16	25 02 12	19 57.6	20 56.9	18 38.0	18 43.7	6 33.0	9 13.2	17 46.3	15 59.8	6 14.6	11 10.0
28 Th	10 26 32	5 06 56	1♎02 33	7♎04 35	19 54.7	22 34.7	19 51.9	19 21.3	6 53.6	9 25.8	17 49.8	15 58.1	6 12.9	11 09.3
29 F	10 30 28	6 04 54	13 08 38	19 15 02	19D 53.7	24 11.1	21 05.8	19 59.2	7 14.3	9 38.4	17 53.5	15 56.5	6 11.3	11 08.6
30 Sa	10 34 25	7 02 55	25 24 12	1♏36 32	19 54.3	25 46.3	22 19.7	20 37.1	7 35.1	9 50.9	17 57.2	15 54.8	6 09.6	11 07.9
31 Su	10 38 21	8 00 56	7♏52 27	14 12 26	19 55.7	27 20.2	23 33.7	21 15.2	7 56.1	10 03.4	18 01.0	15 53.0	6 08.0	11 07.2

Astro Data

	Dy Hr Mn
☿ D	1 12:51
☽ 0S	3 21:48
☽ 0N	16 18:28
♄ D	20 20:37
♅ R	22 2:54
☽ 0S	31 5:24
☽ 0N	13 4:31
♃⊼♆	15 4:13
☽ 0S	27 11:52

Planet Ingress

		Dy Hr Mn
☿	♋	13 4:46
♃	♌	16 10:32
♀	♋	18 14:07
☉	♌	22 21:42
♂	♏	26 2:26
☿	♌	31 22:47
⚳	♏	7 3:49
♀	♌	12 7:25
☿	♍	15 16:45
☉	♍	23 4:47

Last Aspect / ☽ Ingress

Last Aspect Dy Hr Mn		☽ Ingress	Dy Hr Mn
1 10:01	☿ ⚹	♍	1 21:25
4 4:22	♃ ⚹	♎	4 9:44
6 15:32	♃ □	♏	6 19:35
8 22:34	♃ △	♐	9 1:26
11 0:20	☿ ☍	♑	11 3:26
13 1:57	♃ ☍	♒	13 3:08
14 19:24	♀ △	♓	15 2:41
17 0:58	♀ □	♈	17 4:08
19 2:19	♂ ☍	♉	19 8:44
21 14:14	☉ ⚹	♊	21 16:37
24 0:54	♂ △	♋	24 3:00
25 13:54	☿ ☌	♌	26 14:56
28 0:39	♄ □	♍	29 3:38
31 14:49	☿ ⚹	♎	31 16:10

Last Aspect / ☽ Ingress

Last Aspect Dy Hr Mn		☽ Ingress	Dy Hr Mn
2 2:59	♀ □	♏	3 2:58
4 17:44	♀ △	♐	5 10:20
6 14:53	♅ △	♑	7 13:40
9 8:10	♀ ☍	♒	9 13:53
10 22:13	☿ ☍	♓	11 12:56
12 16:02	♄ △	♈	13 13:01
15 15:51	☿ △	♉	15 15:59
17 12:27	☉ □	♊	17 22:42
20 2:55	☉ ⚹	♋	20 8:46
21 19:35	♄ △	♌	22 20:50
24 8:27	♄ □	♍	25 9:34
27 2:30	☿ ☌	♎	27 21:55
29 16:01	♀ ⚹	♏	30 8:54

☽ Phases & Eclipses

Dy Hr Mn	
5 12:00	☽ 13♎24
12 11:26	○ 20♑03
19 2:09	☾ 26♈21
26 22:43	● 3♌52
4 0:51	☽ 11♏36
10 18:10	○ 18♒02
17 12:27	☾ 24♉32
25 14:14	● 2♍19

Astro Data

1 July 2014
Julian Day # 41820
SVP 5♓03'18"
GC 27♐02.5 ⚴ 14♍06.9
Eris 23♈09.3 ⚵ 8♊08.1
⚷ 17♓42.2R ⚶ 20♎53.2
☽ Mean ☊ 24♎39.3

1 August 2014
Julian Day # 41851
SVP 5♓03'14"
GC 27♐02.6 ⚴ 26♍03.5
Eris 23♈10.2R ⚵ 25♊48.0
⚷ 16♓59.8R ⚶ 0♏33.5
☽ Mean ☊ 23♎00.8

LONGITUDE — September 2014

Day	Sid.Time	☉	0 hr ☽	Noon☽	True☊	☿	♀	♂	⚳	♃	♄	♅	♆	♇
1 M	10 42 18	8♍58 59	20♏36 56	27♏06 23	19♎57.0	28♍52.8	24♌47.7	21♏53.5	8♏17.1	10♌15.9	18♏04.8	15♈51.2	6♓06.3	11♑06.6
2 Tu	10 46 15	9 57 03	3♐41 14	10♐21 52	19R 57.5	0♎24.0	26 01.8	22 31.9	8 38.2	10 28.3	18 08.8	15R 49.4	6R 04.7	11R 06.0
3 W	10 50 11	10 55 09	17 08 35	24 01 37	19 56.7	1 54.0	27 15.9	23 10.5	8 59.5	10 40.6	18 12.8	15 47.6	6 03.1	11 05.4
4 Th	10 54 08	11 53 16	1♑01 05	8♑06 57	19 54.4	3 22.7	28 30.0	23 49.2	9 20.8	10 52.9	18 16.9	15 45.7	6 01.4	11 04.8
5 F	10 58 04	12 51 25	15 19 01	22 36 56	19 50.5	4 50.1	29 44.1	24 28.0	9 42.2	11 05.2	18 21.1	15 43.8	5 59.8	11 04.3
6 Sa	11 02 01	13 49 35	0♒00 05	7♒27 45	19 45.7	6 16.2	0♍58.3	25 07.0	10 03.7	11 17.4	18 25.3	15 41.9	5 58.2	11 03.8
7 Su	11 05 57	14 47 46	14 59 00	22 32 44	19 40.6	7 40.9	2 12.5	25 46.1	10 25.3	11 29.5	18 29.7	15 39.9	5 56.5	11 03.3
8 M	11 09 54	15 45 59	0♓07 46	7♓42 50	19 35.9	9 04.3	3 26.7	26 25.3	10 47.0	11 41.6	18 34.1	15 38.0	5 54.9	11 02.9
9 Tu	11 13 50	16 44 14	15 16 42	22 48 06	19 32.5	10 26.3	4 41.0	27 04.7	11 08.7	11 53.6	18 38.5	15 35.9	5 53.3	11 02.5
10 W	11 17 47	17 42 30	0♈15 57	7♈39 15	19D 30.5	11 46.8	5 55.3	27 44.2	11 30.6	12 05.6	18 43.1	15 33.9	5 51.7	11 02.1
11 Th	11 21 44	18 40 49	14 57 09	22 09 02	19 30.1	13 05.9	7 09.6	28 23.8	11 52.5	12 17.5	18 47.7	15 31.8	5 50.1	11 01.7
12 F	11 25 40	19 39 09	29 14 26	6♉13 06	19 30.8	14 23.5	8 24.0	29 03.5	12 14.5	12 29.3	18 52.4	15 29.7	5 48.5	11 01.4
13 Sa	11 29 37	20 37 32	13♉04 55	19 49 56	19 32.3	15 39.6	9 38.4	29 43.4	12 36.6	12 41.1	18 57.1	15 27.6	5 46.9	11 01.1
14 Su	11 33 33	21 35 57	26 28 22	3♊00 31	19 33.8	16 54.0	10 52.8	0♐23.4	12 58.8	12 52.8	19 02.0	15 25.5	5 45.3	11 00.8
15 M	11 37 30	22 34 23	9♊26 46	15 47 34	19R 34.8	18 06.7	12 07.2	1 03.5	13 21.0	13 04.5	19 06.9	15 23.3	5 43.8	11 00.6
16 Tu	11 41 26	23 32 52	22 03 26	28 14 53	19 34.9	19 17.7	13 21.7	1 43.8	13 43.4	13 16.1	19 11.8	15 21.1	5 42.2	11 00.4
17 W	11 45 23	24 31 24	4♋22 29	10♋26 48	19 33.9	20 26.8	14 36.2	2 24.2	14 05.8	13 27.6	19 16.8	15 18.9	5 40.7	11 00.2
18 Th	11 49 19	25 29 57	16 28 21	22 27 41	19 31.8	21 33.9	15 50.7	3 04.7	14 28.2	13 39.0	19 21.9	15 16.7	5 39.1	11 00.1
19 F	11 53 16	26 28 32	28 25 19	4♌21 44	19 28.7	22 38.8	17 05.3	3 45.3	14 50.8	13 50.4	19 27.1	15 14.4	5 37.6	10 59.9
20 Sa	11 57 13	27 27 10	10♌17 22	16 12 40	19 25.1	23 41.6	18 19.9	4 26.1	15 13.4	14 01.7	19 32.3	15 12.2	5 36.1	10 59.9
21 Su	12 01 09	28 25 49	22 08 00	28 03 44	19 21.5	24 42.0	19 34.5	5 06.9	15 36.1	14 13.0	19 37.6	15 09.9	5 34.6	10 59.8
22 M	12 05 06	29 24 31	4♍00 11	9♍57 39	19 18.2	25 39.8	20 49.2	5 47.9	15 58.9	14 24.1	19 43.0	15 07.6	5 33.2	10D 59.8
23 Tu	12 09 02	0♎23 15	15 56 24	21 56 40	19 15.7	26 34.8	22 03.8	6 29.0	16 21.7	14 35.2	19 48.4	15 05.3	5 31.7	10 59.8
24 W	12 12 59	1 22 00	27 58 40	4♎02 37	19 14.0	27 26.9	23 18.5	7 10.2	16 44.6	14 46.2	19 53.8	15 02.9	5 30.2	10 59.8
25 Th	12 16 55	2 20 48	10♎08 42	16 17 07	19D 13.4	28 15.8	24 33.2	7 51.6	17 07.6	14 57.1	19 59.4	15 00.6	5 28.8	10 59.9
26 F	12 20 52	3 19 37	22 28 03	28 41 41	19 13.6	29 01.2	25 48.0	8 33.0	17 30.6	15 07.9	20 05.0	14 58.2	5 27.4	10 59.9
27 Sa	12 24 48	4 18 29	4♏58 13	11♏17 50	19 14.4	29 42.8	27 02.7	9 14.6	17 53.7	15 18.7	20 10.6	14 55.8	5 26.0	11 00.1
28 Su	12 28 45	5 17 22	17 40 46	24 07 12	19 15.6	0♏20.3	28 17.5	9 56.3	18 16.9	15 29.3	20 16.3	14 53.5	5 24.6	11 00.2
29 M	12 32 41	6 16 17	0♐37 23	7♐11 30	19 16.8	0 53.4	29 32.3	10 38.1	18 40.1	15 39.9	20 22.0	14 51.1	5 23.2	11 00.4
30 Tu	12 36 38	7 15 14	13 49 46	20 32 21	19 17.6	1 21.7	0♎47.1	11 19.9	19 03.4	15 50.4	20 27.9	14 48.7	5 21.9	11 00.6

LONGITUDE — October 2014

Day	Sid.Time	☉	0 hr ☽	Noon☽	True☊	☿	♀	♂	⚳	♃	♄	♅	♆	♇
1 W	12 40 35	8♎14 13	27♐19 24	4♑11 03	19♎18.1	1♏44.9	2♎01.9	12♐01.9	19♏26.7	16♌00.7	20♏33.7	14♈46.3	5♓20.6	11♑00.9
2 Th	12 44 31	9 13 13	11♑07 18	18 08 09	19R 18.0	2 02.3	3 16.8	12 44.0	19 50.1	16 11.0	20 39.6	14R 43.9	5R 19.3	11 01.2
3 F	12 48 28	10 12 15	25 13 27	2♒23 00	19 17.5	2 13.7	4 31.6	13 26.2	20 13.5	16 21.2	20 45.6	14 41.4	5 18.0	11 01.5
4 Sa	12 52 24	11 11 19	9♒36 28	16 53 23	19 16.7	2R 18.6	5 46.5	14 08.5	20 37.0	16 31.3	20 51.6	14 39.0	5 16.7	11 01.8
5 Su	12 56 21	12 10 25	24 13 10	1♓35 11	19 15.8	2 16.5	7 01.4	14 50.9	21 00.6	16 41.3	20 57.7	14 36.6	5 15.5	11 02.2
6 M	13 00 17	13 09 32	8♓58 37	16 22 37	19 15.1	2 07.1	8 16.3	15 33.4	21 24.1	16 51.3	21 03.8	14 34.2	5 14.3	11 02.6
7 Tu	13 04 14	14 08 41	23 46 19	1♈08 46	19 14.6	1 50.0	9 31.2	16 16.0	21 47.8	17 01.1	21 09.9	14 31.7	5 13.1	11 03.0
8 W	13 08 10	15 07 52	8♈29 05	15 46 23	19D 14.4	1 24.9	10 46.2	16 58.7	22 11.5	17 10.8	21 16.1	14 29.3	5 11.9	11 03.5
9 Th	13 12 07	16 07 05	22 59 52	0♉08 52	19 14.5	0 51.7	12 01.1	17 41.5	22 35.2	17 20.4	21 22.4	14 26.9	5 10.7	11 04.0
10 F	13 16 04	17 06 21	7♉12 47	14 11 10	19 14.6	0 10.5	13 16.1	18 24.3	22 59.0	17 29.8	21 28.7	14 24.4	5 09.6	11 04.5
11 Sa	13 20 00	18 05 38	21 03 43	27 50 14	19 14.8	29♎21.5	14 31.1	19 07.3	23 22.8	17 39.2	21 35.0	14 22.0	5 08.5	11 05.0
12 Su	13 23 57	19 04 58	4♊30 42	11♊05 11	19R 14.9	28 25.3	15 46.1	19 50.4	23 46.7	17 48.5	21 41.4	14 19.6	5 07.4	11 05.6
13 M	13 27 53	20 04 20	17 33 51	23 57 01	19 14.8	27 22.8	17 01.1	20 33.5	24 10.6	17 57.7	21 47.8	14 17.2	5 06.4	11 06.2
14 Tu	13 31 50	21 03 44	0♋15 02	6♋28 20	19 14.7	26 15.1	18 16.2	21 16.7	24 34.6	18 06.7	21 54.2	14 14.8	5 05.3	11 06.9
15 W	13 35 46	22 03 11	12 37 24	18 42 48	19D 14.7	25 03.8	19 31.2	22 00.1	24 58.6	18 15.7	22 00.7	14 12.4	5 04.3	11 07.5
16 Th	13 39 43	23 02 40	24 45 03	0♌44 45	19 14.7	23 50.7	20 46.3	22 43.5	25 22.6	18 24.5	22 07.2	14 10.0	5 03.3	11 08.2
17 F	13 43 39	24 02 11	6♌42 29	12 38 50	19 15.0	22 37.8	22 01.4	23 27.0	25 46.7	18 33.2	22 13.8	14 07.6	5 02.4	11 09.0
18 Sa	13 47 36	25 01 45	18 34 22	24 29 39	19 15.4	21 27.1	23 16.5	24 10.6	26 10.9	18 41.8	22 20.4	14 05.2	5 01.5	11 09.7
19 Su	13 51 33	26 01 20	0♍25 13	6♍21 35	19 16.1	20 20.9	24 31.6	24 54.2	26 35.0	18 50.2	22 27.0	14 02.8	5 00.6	11 10.5
20 M	13 55 29	27 00 58	12 19 13	18 18 34	19 16.9	19 21.2	25 46.7	25 38.0	26 59.2	18 58.6	22 33.7	14 00.5	4 59.7	11 11.3
21 Tu	13 59 26	28 00 38	24 20 01	0♎23 57	19 17.7	18 29.5	27 01.9	26 21.9	27 23.5	19 06.8	22 40.4	13 58.1	4 58.9	11 12.2
22 W	14 03 22	29 00 20	6♎30 38	12 40 22	19R 18.1	17 47.3	28 17.0	27 05.8	27 47.8	19 14.8	22 47.1	13 55.8	4 58.0	11 13.1
23 Th	14 07 19	0♏00 05	18 53 20	25 09 43	19 18.1	17 15.7	29 32.2	27 49.8	28 12.1	19 22.8	22 53.9	13 53.5	4 57.3	11 14.0
24 F	14 11 15	0 59 51	1♏29 37	7♏53 07	19 17.6	16 55.2	0♏47.3	28 33.9	28 36.4	19 30.6	23 00.7	13 51.2	4 56.5	11 14.9
25 Sa	14 15 12	1 59 39	14 20 13	20 50 15	19 16.4	16D 46.1	2 02.5	29 18.1	29 00.8	19 38.3	23 07.5	13 48.9	4 55.8	11 15.9
26 Su	14 19 08	2 59 29	27 25 09	4♐02 52	19 14.6	16 48.3	3 17.7	0♑02.3	29 25.2	19 45.8	23 14.4	13 46.7	4 55.1	11 16.9
27 M	14 23 05	3 59 21	10♐43 56	17 28 15	19 12.6	17 01.4	4 32.9	0 46.7	29 49.7	19 53.2	23 21.2	13 44.4	4 54.4	11 17.9
28 Tu	14 27 01	4 59 15	24 15 40	1♑06 02	19 10.6	17 24.8	5 48.1	1 31.1	0♐14.2	20 00.5	23 28.1	13 42.2	4 53.8	11 18.9
29 W	14 30 58	5 59 10	7♑59 11	14 54 59	19 09.0	17 57.9	7 03.3	2 15.6	0 38.7	20 07.6	23 35.0	13 40.0	4 53.2	11 20.0
30 Th	14 34 55	6 59 07	21 53 14	28 53 47	19D 08.1	18 39.8	8 18.5	3 00.1	1 03.2	20 14.6	23 42.0	13 37.8	4 52.6	11 21.1
31 F	14 38 51	7 59 06	5♒56 25	13♒00 57	19 08.0	19 29.6	9 33.7	3 44.8	1 27.8	20 21.5	23 48.9	13 35.7	4 52.1	11 22.3

Astro Data (Dy Hr Mn)	Planet Ingress (Dy Hr Mn)	Last Aspect (Dy Hr Mn)	☽ Ingress (Dy Hr Mn)	Last Aspect (Dy Hr Mn)	☽ Ingress (Dy Hr Mn)
☿0S 2 2:54	☿ ♎ 2 5:39	1 15:41 ☿ ⚹	♐ 1 17:18	30 3:30 ♃ △	♑ 1 4:42
♃⚻♇ 5 10:24	♀ ♍ 5 17:08	3 18:07 ♀ △	♑ 3 22:16	2 16:19 ♄ ⚹	♒ 3 8:01
☽0N 9 15:31	♂ ♐ 13 21:58	5 15:09 ♂ ⚹	♒ 5 24:00	4 18:33 ♄ □	♓ 5 9:25
♇ D 23 0:37	☉ ♎ 23 2:30	7 17:20 ♂ □	♓ 7 23:48	6 19:39 ♄ △	♈ 7 10:08
☉0S 23 2:30	☿ ♏ 27 22:40	9 19:11 ♂ △	♈ 9 23:34	8 14:21 ♃ △	♉ 9 11:45
☽0S 23 18:05	♀ ♎ 29 20:53	11 0:59 ♅ ☌	♉ 12 1:18	11 0:50 ♄ ☍	♊ 11 15:52
♃△♅ 25 18:20		13 13:32 ☉ △	♊ 14 6:27	13 17:59 ☿ △	♋ 13 23:31
	☿ ♎R 10 17:28	16 2:06 ☉ □	♋ 16 15:25	15 23:28 ☿ □	♌ 16 10:30
♀0S 2 11:49	☉ ♏ 23 11:58	18 18:39 ☉ ⚹	♌ 19 3:11	18 13:11 ☉ ⚹	♍ 18 23:09
☿ R 4 17:04	♀ ♏ 23 20:53	21 4:34 ☿ ⚹	♍ 21 15:55	21 3:31 ♂ □	♎ 21 11:13
☽0N 7 1:56	♂ ♑ 26 10:44	23 12:16 ♀ ☌	♎ 24 4:00	23 17:23 ♂ ⚹	♏ 23 21:11
☽0S 21 1:14	⚳ ♐ 27 22:07	26 12:40 ☿ ☌	♏ 26 14:30	25 16:12 ♄ ☌	♐ 26 4:41
☿ D 25 19:20		28 20:32 ♀ ⚹	♐ 28 22:51	27 16:19 ♃ △	♑ 28 10:04
				30 3:02 ♄ ⚹	♒ 30 13:53

☽ Phases & Eclipses (Dy Hr Mn)		Astro Data
2 11:12	☽ 9♐55	1 September 2014
9 1:39	○ 16♓19	Julian Day # 41882
16 2:06	☾ 23♊09	SVP 5♓03'11"
24 6:15	● 1♎08	GC 27♐02.6 ⚴ 8♎59.1
		Eris 23♈01.5R ⚵ 12♋34.6
		⚷ 15♓42.1R ⚶ 13♏20.7
1 19:34	☽ 8♑33	☽ Mean ☊ 21♎22.3
8 10:52	○ 15♈05	
8 10:56	◐ T 1.166	1 October 2014
15 19:13	☾ 22♋21	Julian Day # 41912
23 21:58	● 0♏25	SVP 5♓03'08"
23 21:45:39	◐ P 0.811	GC 27♐02.7 ⚴ 22♎01.6
31 2:49	☽ 7♒36	Eris 22♈46.2R ⚵ 27♋11.9
		⚷ 14♓20.2R ⚶ 27♏28.6
		☽ Mean ☊ 19♎47.0

November 2014 — LONGITUDE

Day	Sid.Time	☉	0 hr ☽	Noon ☽	True ☊	☿	♀	♂	⚳	♃	♄	♅	♆	♇
1 Sa	14 42 48	8♏59 06	20♒07 09	27♒14 45	19♎08.7	20♎26.5	10♏49.0	4♑29.5	1♐52.3	20♌28.2	23♏55.9	13♈33.5	4♓51.6	11♑23.4
2 Su	14 46 44	9 59 08	4♓23 27	11♓32 57	19 09.9	21 29.6	12 04.2	5 14.2	2 16.9	20 34.7	24 02.9	13R 31.4	4R 51.1	11 24.6
3 M	14 50 41	10 59 11	18 42 52	25 52 46	19 11.3	22 38.2	13 19.4	5 59.1	2 41.6	20 41.1	24 09.9	13 29.3	4 50.7	11 25.8
4 Tu	14 54 37	11 59 16	3♈02 14	10♈10 44	19R 12.4	23 51.4	14 34.6	6 44.0	3 06.2	20 47.3	24 17.0	13 27.3	4 50.3	11 27.0
5 W	14 58 34	12 59 22	17 17 47	24 22 51	19 12.5	25 08.8	15 49.9	7 28.9	3 30.9	20 53.4	24 24.0	13 25.2	4 49.9	11 28.3
6 Th	15 02 30	13 59 30	1♉25 23	8♉24 53	19 11.4	26 29.5	17 05.1	8 13.9	3 55.6	20 59.3	24 31.1	13 23.3	4 49.5	11 29.6
7 F	15 06 27	14 59 40	15 20 51	22 12 51	19 09.0	27 53.2	18 20.3	8 59.0	4 20.3	21 05.1	24 38.2	13 21.3	4 49.2	11 30.9
8 Sa	15 10 24	15 59 52	29 00 31	5♊43 32	19 05.3	29 19.2	19 35.6	9 44.2	4 45.0	21 10.7	24 45.3	13 19.3	4 48.9	11 32.2
9 Su	15 14 20	17 00 06	12♊21 43	18 54 56	19 00.8	0♏47.3	20 50.9	10 29.4	5 09.8	21 16.2	24 52.4	13 17.4	4 48.7	11 33.6
10 M	15 18 17	18 00 22	25 23 10	1♋46 29	18 56.0	2 17.1	22 06.1	11 14.6	5 34.5	21 21.5	24 59.5	13 15.6	4 48.5	11 35.0
11 Tu	15 22 13	19 00 40	8♋05 04	14 19 10	18 51.6	3 48.2	23 21.4	12 00.0	5 59.3	21 26.6	25 06.6	13 13.7	4 48.3	11 36.4
12 W	15 26 10	20 00 59	20 29 06	26 35 19	18 47.9	5 20.4	24 36.7	12 45.4	6 24.1	21 31.6	25 13.7	13 11.9	4 48.2	11 37.8
13 Th	15 30 06	21 01 20	2♌38 15	8♌38 26	18 45.6	6 53.5	25 51.9	13 30.8	6 48.9	21 36.4	25 20.9	13 10.1	4 48.1	11 39.3
14 F	15 34 03	22 01 44	14 36 25	20 32 50	18D 44.7	8 27.2	27 07.2	14 16.3	7 13.8	21 41.0	25 28.0	13 08.4	4 48.0	11 40.8
15 Sa	15 37 59	23 02 09	26 28 17	2♍23 23	18 45.1	10 01.5	28 22.5	15 01.9	7 38.6	21 45.5	25 35.1	13 06.7	4D 47.9	11 42.3
16 Su	15 41 56	24 02 36	8♍18 47	14 15 08	18 46.5	11 36.1	29 37.8	15 47.5	8 03.5	21 49.8	25 42.3	13 05.0	4 47.9	11 43.8
17 M	15 45 53	25 03 05	20 13 03	26 13 06	18 48.3	13 11.1	0♐53.1	16 33.1	8 28.4	21 53.9	25 49.4	13 03.4	4 47.9	11 45.3
18 Tu	15 49 49	26 03 36	2♎15 54	8♎21 56	18R 49.8	14 46.2	2 08.4	17 18.9	8 53.3	21 57.8	25 56.6	13 01.8	4 48.0	11 46.9
19 W	15 53 46	27 04 08	14 31 42	20 45 35	18 50.3	16 21.5	3 23.7	18 04.6	9 18.2	22 01.6	26 03.8	13 00.2	4 48.1	11 48.5
20 Th	15 57 42	28 04 42	27 03 58	3♏27 04	18 49.2	17 56.8	4 39.0	18 50.5	9 43.1	22 05.2	26 10.9	12 58.7	4 48.2	11 50.1
21 F	16 01 39	29 05 18	9♏55 03	16 28 01	18 46.1	19 32.2	5 54.3	19 36.3	10 08.0	22 08.6	26 18.1	12 57.2	4 48.4	11 51.7
22 Sa	16 05 35	0♐05 55	23 05 53	29 48 33	18 41.1	21 07.5	7 09.7	20 22.3	10 32.9	22 11.8	26 25.2	12 55.8	4 48.6	11 53.4
23 Su	16 09 32	1 06 34	6♐35 45	13♐27 10	18 34.6	22 42.8	8 25.0	21 08.3	10 57.8	22 14.8	26 32.4	12 54.4	4 48.8	11 55.1
24 M	16 13 28	2 07 15	20 22 21	27 20 51	18 27.1	24 17.9	9 40.3	21 54.3	11 22.8	22 17.7	26 39.5	12 53.0	4 49.1	11 56.7
25 Tu	16 17 25	3 07 56	4♑22 06	11♑25 34	18 19.7	25 53.0	10 55.6	22 40.4	11 47.7	22 20.3	26 46.6	12 51.7	4 49.4	11 58.5
26 W	16 21 22	4 08 39	18 30 41	25 36 53	18 13.3	27 28.0	12 10.9	23 26.5	12 12.7	22 22.8	26 53.8	12 50.5	4 49.7	12 00.2
27 Th	16 25 18	5 09 23	2♒43 40	9♒50 34	18 08.6	29 02.9	13 26.3	24 12.7	12 37.6	22 25.1	27 00.9	12 49.3	4 50.1	12 01.9
28 F	16 29 15	6 10 08	16 57 12	24 03 12	18D 05.9	0♐37.7	14 41.6	24 58.9	13 02.6	22 27.2	27 08.0	12 48.1	4 50.5	12 03.7
29 Sa	16 33 11	7 10 53	1♓08 20	8♓12 21	18 05.2	2 12.4	15 56.9	25 45.1	13 27.5	22 29.1	27 15.1	12 46.9	4 51.0	12 05.5
30 Su	16 37 08	8 11 40	15 15 07	22 16 29	18 05.9	3 47.0	17 12.2	26 31.4	13 52.5	22 30.8	27 22.1	12 45.9	4 51.4	12 07.3

December 2014 — LONGITUDE

Day	Sid.Time	☉	0 hr ☽	Noon ☽	True ☊	☿	♀	♂	⚳	♃	♄	♅	♆	♇
1 M	16 41 04	9♐12 27	29♓16 23	6♈14 43	18♎07.0	5♐21.5	18♐27.5	27♑17.7	14♐17.4	22♌32.3	27♏29.2	12♈44.8	4♓51.9	12♑09.1
2 Tu	16 45 01	10 13 16	13♈11 24	20 06 19	18R 07.4	6 55.9	19 42.8	28 04.1	14 42.4	22 33.7	27 36.2	12R 43.8	4 52.5	12 10.9
3 W	16 48 57	11 14 05	26 59 22	3♉50 23	18 06.2	8 30.2	20 58.1	28 50.4	15 07.3	22 34.8	27 43.3	12 42.9	4 53.1	12 12.8
4 Th	16 52 54	12 14 55	10♉39 12	17 25 37	18 02.7	10 04.5	22 13.4	29 36.9	15 32.3	22 35.8	27 50.3	12 42.0	4 53.7	12 14.6
5 F	16 56 51	13 15 47	24 09 24	0♊50 19	17 56.5	11 38.8	23 28.7	0♒23.3	15 57.2	22 36.5	27 57.3	12 41.1	4 54.3	12 16.5
6 Sa	17 00 47	14 16 39	7♊28 08	14 02 38	17 47.9	13 13.0	24 44.0	1 09.8	16 22.1	22 37.1	28 04.3	12 40.3	4 55.0	12 18.4
7 Su	17 04 44	15 17 32	20 33 36	27 00 54	17 37.5	14 47.2	25 59.3	1 56.3	16 47.0	22 37.4	28 11.2	12 39.6	4 55.7	12 20.3
8 M	17 08 40	16 18 27	3♋24 24	9♋44 04	17 26.3	16 21.4	27 14.6	2 42.8	17 12.0	22R 37.6	28 18.1	12 38.9	4 56.5	12 22.2
9 Tu	17 12 37	17 19 22	15 59 56	22 12 04	17 15.4	17 55.6	28 29.9	3 29.4	17 36.9	22 37.6	28 25.1	12 38.2	4 57.2	12 24.1
10 W	17 16 33	18 20 19	28 20 39	4♌25 56	17 05.7	19 29.9	29 45.2	4 16.0	18 01.8	22 37.4	28 31.9	12 37.6	4 58.0	12 26.1
11 Th	17 20 30	19 21 17	10♌28 14	16 27 56	16 58.1	21 04.2	1♑00.5	5 02.6	18 26.7	22 36.9	28 38.8	12 37.0	4 58.9	12 28.0
12 F	17 24 26	20 22 15	22 25 30	28 21 26	16 53.0	22 38.6	2 15.8	5 49.3	18 51.6	22 36.3	28 45.6	12 36.5	4 59.8	12 30.0
13 Sa	17 28 23	21 23 15	4♍16 18	10♍10 42	16 50.3	24 13.1	3 31.1	6 35.9	19 16.4	22 35.5	28 52.5	12 36.0	5 00.7	12 32.0
14 Su	17 32 20	22 24 16	16 05 17	22 00 43	16D 49.5	25 47.7	4 46.4	7 22.6	19 41.3	22 34.5	28 59.2	12 35.6	5 01.6	12 33.9
15 M	17 36 16	23 25 18	27 57 41	3♎56 53	16 49.8	27 22.3	6 01.6	8 09.4	20 06.2	22 33.3	29 06.0	12 35.3	5 02.6	12 35.9
16 Tu	17 40 13	24 26 21	9♎58 59	16 04 40	16R 50.2	28 57.1	7 16.9	8 56.1	20 31.0	22 31.9	29 12.7	12 35.0	5 03.6	12 37.9
17 W	17 44 09	25 27 25	22 14 35	28 29 17	16 49.6	0♑32.0	8 32.2	9 42.9	20 55.8	22 30.3	29 19.4	12 34.7	5 04.6	12 40.0
18 Th	17 48 06	26 28 29	4♏49 20	11♏15 10	16 47.0	2 07.1	9 47.5	10 29.7	21 20.7	22 28.5	29 26.0	12 34.5	5 05.7	12 42.0
19 F	17 52 02	27 29 35	17 47 06	24 25 22	16 41.7	3 42.3	11 02.8	11 16.5	21 45.5	22 26.5	29 32.7	12 34.3	5 06.8	12 44.0
20 Sa	17 55 59	28 30 41	1♐10 02	8♐01 01	16 33.7	5 17.6	12 18.0	12 03.3	22 10.2	22 24.3	29 39.2	12 34.2	5 07.9	12 46.0
21 Su	17 59 55	29 31 49	14 58 04	22 00 46	16 23.3	6 53.1	13 33.3	12 50.2	22 35.0	22 21.9	29 45.8	12D 34.2	5 09.1	12 48.1
22 M	18 03 52	0♑32 56	29 08 31	6♑20 38	16 11.6	8 28.7	14 48.6	13 37.1	22 59.8	22 19.3	29 52.3	12 34.2	5 10.3	12 50.2
23 Tu	18 07 49	1 34 04	13♑36 13	20 54 23	15 59.7	10 04.5	16 03.9	14 24.0	23 24.5	22 16.6	29 58.8	12 34.2	5 11.5	12 52.2
24 W	18 11 45	2 35 13	28 14 07	5♒34 27	15 49.1	11 40.3	17 19.1	15 10.9	23 49.2	22 13.6	0♐05.2	12 34.4	5 12.8	12 54.3
25 Th	18 15 42	3 36 21	12♒54 28	20 13 16	15 40.7	13 16.3	18 34.4	15 57.8	24 13.9	22 10.4	0 11.6	12 34.5	5 14.0	12 56.4
26 F	18 19 38	4 37 30	27 30 09	4♓44 29	15 35.2	14 52.3	19 49.6	16 44.7	24 38.5	22 07.1	0 17.9	12 34.7	5 15.4	12 58.4
27 Sa	18 23 35	5 38 39	11♓55 46	19 03 41	15 32.4	16 28.3	21 04.8	17 31.7	25 03.2	22 03.6	0 24.2	12 35.0	5 16.7	13 00.5
28 Su	18 27 31	6 39 47	26 08 01	3♈08 41	15 31.6	18 04.3	22 20.1	18 18.6	25 27.8	21 59.9	0 30.5	12 35.3	5 18.1	13 02.6
29 M	18 31 28	7 40 56	10♈05 39	16 59 00	15 31.6	19 40.3	23 35.3	19 05.6	25 52.4	21 56.0	0 36.7	12 35.7	5 19.5	13 04.7
30 Tu	18 35 25	8 42 04	23 48 52	0♉35 23	15 31.1	21 16.1	24 50.5	19 52.6	26 16.9	21 51.9	0 42.8	12 36.1	5 20.9	13 06.8
31 W	18 39 21	9 43 13	7♉18 43	13 59 01	15 28.6	22 51.6	26 05.7	20 39.5	26 41.4	21 47.7	0 48.9	12 36.5	5 22.3	13 08.9

Astro Data

	Dy Hr Mn
☽0N	3 10:33
♆D	16 7:07
☽0S	17 9:54
♄∠♇	27 16:48
☽0N	30 17:22
♄⚼♅	3 10:47
♃R	8 20:42
☽0S	14 19:35
♅□♇	15 5:15
♅D	21 22:46
☽0N	27 23:59

Planet Ingress

	Dy Hr Mn
☿ ♏	8 23:10
♀ ♐	16 19:05
☉ ♐	22 9:39
☿ ♐	28 2:27
♂ ♒	4 23:58
♀ ♑	10 16:43
☿ ♑	17 3:54
☉ ♑	21 23:04
♄ ♐	23 16:35

Last Aspect / ☽ Ingress

Last Aspect Dy Hr Mn		☽ Ingress Dy Hr Mn
1 6:23	♄ □	♓ 1 16:38
3 9:06	♄ △	♈ 3 18:54
5 13:26	☿ ☍	♉ 5 21:34
7 16:18	♄ ☍	♊ 8 1:46
9 16:23	♃ ⚹	♋ 10 8:39
12 9:17	♄ △	♌ 12 18:45
15 2:54	♀ □	♍ 15 7:09
17 11:12	♄ ⚹	♎ 17 19:31
19 14:26	♃ ⚹	♏ 20 5:32
22 5:54	♄ ☌	♐ 22 12:20
24 3:17	♃ △	♑ 24 16:33
26 15:31	☿ ⚹	♒ 26 19:24
28 17:15	♄ □	♓ 28 22:04

Last Aspect / ☽ Ingress

Last Aspect Dy Hr Mn		☽ Ingress Dy Hr Mn
30 20:48	♄ △	♈ 1 1:15
3 2:43	♂ □	♉ 3 5:16
5 6:46	♄ ☍	♊ 5 10:29
7 9:53	♀ ☍	♋ 7 17:35
10 0:16	♄ △	♌ 10 3:15
12 12:50	♄ □	♍ 12 15:20
15 2:12	♄ ⚹	♎ 15 4:06
17 5:41	☉ ⚹	♏ 17 14:53
19 21:12	♄ ☌	♐ 19 21:56
21 12:36	♃ △	♑ 22 1:26
23 3:18	♀ ☌	♒ 24 2:53
25 15:12	♃ ☍	♓ 26 4:08
27 15:45	♀ ⚹	♈ 28 6:36
30 0:47	♀ □	♉ 30 10:57

☽ Phases & Eclipses

Dy Hr Mn	
6 22:24	○ 14♉26
14 15:17	☾ 22♌10
22 12:33	● 0♐07
29 10:07	☽ 7♓06
6 12:28	○ 14♊18
14 12:52	☾ 22♍26
22 1:37	● 0♑06
28 18:33	☽ 6♈56

Astro Data

1 November 2014
Julian Day # 41943
SVP 5♓03'05"
GC 27♐02.8 ⚴ 5♏44.2
Eris 22♈27.9R ⚵ 9♌22.5
⚷ 13♓20.1R ⚶ 13♐09.9
☽ Mean ☊ 18♎08.4

1 December 2014
Julian Day # 41973
SVP 5♓03'01"
GC 27♐02.9 ⚴ 18♏54.6
Eris 22♈12.9R ⚵ 16♌21.5
⚷ 13♓07.4 ⚶ 28♐56.4
☽ Mean ☊ 16♎33.1

LONGITUDE — January 2015

Day	Sid.Time	☉	0 hr ☽	Noon ☽	True ☊	☿	♀	♂	⚳	♃	♄	♅	♆	♇
1 Th	18 43 18	10♑44 21	20♉36 24	27♉11 01	15♎23.5	24♑26.9	27♑20.8	21♒26.5	27♐05.9	21♌43.3	0♐55.0	12♈37.1	5♓23.8	13♑10.9
2 F	18 47 14	11 45 29	3♊42 54	10♊12 08	15R 15.1	26 01.6	28 36.0	22 13.5	27 30.4	21R 38.7	1 01.0	12 37.6	5 25.3	13 13.0
3 Sa	18 51 11	12 46 37	16 38 41	23 02 35	15 03.9	27 35.8	29 51.2	23 00.5	27 54.8	21 34.0	1 07.0	12 38.3	5 26.9	13 15.1
4 Su	18 55 07	13 47 45	29 23 48	5♋42 17	14 50.4	29 09.2	1♒06.3	23 47.4	28 19.2	21 29.1	1 12.9	12 38.9	5 28.4	13 17.2
5 M	18 59 04	14 48 53	11♋58 00	18 10 57	14 35.9	0♒41.7	2 21.4	24 34.4	28 43.6	21 24.0	1 18.7	12 39.7	5 30.0	13 19.3
6 Tu	19 03 00	15 50 01	24 21 08	0♌28 36	14 21.5	2 12.8	3 36.6	25 21.4	29 08.0	21 18.8	1 24.5	12 40.5	5 31.6	13 21.4
7 W	19 06 57	16 51 09	6♌33 26	12 35 47	14 08.4	3 42.5	4 51.7	26 08.4	29 32.3	21 13.4	1 30.2	12 41.3	5 33.2	13 23.5
8 Th	19 10 54	17 52 17	18 35 51	24 33 52	13 57.7	5 10.4	6 06.7	26 55.3	29 56.5	21 07.9	1 35.9	12 42.2	5 34.9	13 25.6
9 F	19 14 50	18 53 25	0♍30 11	6♍25 09	13 49.8	6 35.9	7 21.8	27 42.3	0♑20.8	21 02.2	1 41.5	12 43.1	5 36.6	13 27.7
10 Sa	19 18 47	19 54 33	12 19 12	18 12 51	13 44.9	7 58.9	8 36.9	28 29.3	0 45.0	20 56.3	1 47.1	12 44.1	5 38.3	13 29.8
11 Su	19 22 43	20 55 41	24 06 38	0♎01 09	13 42.6	9 18.6	9 51.9	29 16.3	1 09.1	20 50.4	1 52.6	12 45.1	5 40.0	13 31.9
12 M	19 26 40	21 56 48	5♎57 01	11 54 55	13 42.0	10 34.6	11 07.0	0♓03.2	1 33.3	20 44.2	1 58.0	12 46.2	5 41.8	13 33.9
13 Tu	19 30 36	22 57 56	17 55 32	23 59 33	13 42.0	11 46.1	12 22.0	0 50.2	1 57.3	20 38.0	2 03.4	12 47.3	5 43.5	13 36.0
14 W	19 34 33	23 59 04	0♏07 41	6♏20 37	13 41.5	12 52.6	13 37.0	1 37.1	2 21.4	20 31.6	2 08.7	12 48.5	5 45.3	13 38.1
15 Th	19 38 29	25 00 11	12 39 00	19 03 25	13 39.3	13 53.1	14 52.0	2 24.1	2 45.4	20 25.1	2 14.0	12 49.7	5 47.1	13 40.1
16 F	19 42 26	26 01 19	25 34 24	2♐12 22	13 34.7	14 47.0	16 07.0	3 11.0	3 09.4	20 18.5	2 19.2	12 51.0	5 49.0	13 42.2
17 Sa	19 46 23	27 02 26	8♐57 34	15 50 08	13 27.5	15 33.2	17 22.0	3 58.0	3 33.3	20 11.7	2 24.3	12 52.3	5 50.8	13 44.3
18 Su	19 50 19	28 03 33	22 50 00	29 56 54	13 17.8	16 11.0	18 36.9	4 44.9	3 57.1	20 04.8	2 29.3	12 53.7	5 52.7	13 46.3
19 M	19 54 16	29 04 39	7♑10 22	14♑29 41	13 06.5	16 39.4	19 51.9	5 31.8	4 21.0	19 57.9	2 34.3	12 55.1	5 54.6	13 48.3
20 Tu	19 58 12	0♒05 45	21 53 59	29 22 10	12 55.0	16 57.7	21 06.8	6 18.7	4 44.8	19 50.8	2 39.2	12 56.6	5 56.5	13 50.4
21 W	20 02 09	1 06 51	6♒53 05	14♒25 27	12 44.4	17R 05.1	22 21.7	7 05.6	5 08.5	19 43.6	2 44.0	12 58.1	5 58.5	13 52.4
22 Th	20 06 05	2 07 55	21 57 59	29 29 27	12 36.1	17 01.2	23 36.6	7 52.5	5 32.2	19 36.4	2 48.8	12 59.7	6 00.4	13 54.4
23 F	20 10 02	3 08 59	6♓58 43	14♓24 48	12 30.5	16 45.8	24 51.4	8 39.4	5 55.8	19 29.0	2 53.5	13 01.3	6 02.4	13 56.4
24 Sa	20 13 58	4 10 02	21 46 51	29 04 14	12D 27.7	16 18.8	26 06.3	9 26.3	6 19.3	19 21.6	2 58.1	13 02.9	6 04.4	13 58.4
25 Su	20 17 55	5 11 03	6♈16 31	13♈23 24	12 27.1	15 40.7	27 21.1	10 13.1	6 42.9	19 14.1	3 02.6	13 04.6	6 06.4	14 00.4
26 M	20 21 52	6 12 04	20 24 47	27 20 40	12R 27.5	14 52.4	28 35.9	10 59.9	7 06.3	19 06.5	3 07.1	13 06.4	6 08.4	14 02.4
27 Tu	20 25 48	7 13 03	4♉11 13	10♉56 37	12 27.6	13 54.9	29 50.6	11 46.7	7 29.7	18 58.8	3 11.5	13 08.2	6 10.5	14 04.3
28 W	20 29 45	8 14 02	17 37 09	24 13 07	12 26.3	12 50.1	1♓05.3	12 33.5	7 53.1	18 51.1	3 15.8	13 10.0	6 12.5	14 06.3
29 Th	20 33 41	9 14 59	0♊44 52	7♊12 42	12 22.8	11 39.7	2 20.0	13 20.3	8 16.3	18 43.4	3 20.0	13 11.9	6 14.6	14 08.2
30 F	20 37 38	10 15 55	13 36 57	19 57 54	12 16.6	10 25.9	3 34.7	14 07.0	8 39.6	18 35.6	3 24.1	13 13.8	6 16.7	14 10.2
31 Sa	20 41 34	11 16 50	26 15 48	2♋30 54	12 07.9	9 11.0	4 49.4	14 53.8	9 02.7	18 27.7	3 28.2	13 15.8	6 18.8	14 12.1

LONGITUDE — February 2015

Day	Sid.Time	☉	0 hr ☽	Noon ☽	True ☊	☿	♀	♂	⚳	♃	♄	♅	♆	♇
1 Su	20 45 31	12♒17 44	8♋43 24	14♋53 30	11♎57.2	7♒57.1	6♓04.0	15♓40.4	9♑25.8	18♌19.8	3♐32.2	13♈17.8	6♓20.9	14♑14.0
2 M	20 49 27	13 18 36	21 01 19	27 07 01	11R 45.6	6R 46.1	7 18.5	16 27.1	9 48.9	18R 11.9	3 36.1	13 19.9	6 23.0	14 15.9
3 Tu	20 53 24	14 19 27	3♌10 44	9♌12 35	11 34.0	5 39.8	8 33.1	17 13.8	10 11.8	18 04.0	3 39.9	13 21.9	6 25.2	14 17.7
4 W	20 57 21	15 20 18	15 12 42	21 11 14	11 23.5	4 39.6	9 47.6	18 00.4	10 34.7	17 56.1	3 43.6	13 24.1	6 27.3	14 19.6
5 Th	21 01 17	16 21 07	27 08 21	3♍04 15	11 14.9	3 46.5	11 02.1	18 47.0	10 57.6	17 48.1	3 47.3	13 26.2	6 29.5	14 21.4
6 F	21 05 14	17 21 55	8♍59 11	14 53 23	11 08.8	3 01.3	12 16.5	19 33.6	11 20.4	17 40.1	3 50.8	13 28.5	6 31.6	14 23.3
7 Sa	21 09 10	18 22 42	20 47 12	26 40 59	11 05.1	2 24.2	13 30.9	20 20.1	11 43.1	17 32.1	3 54.3	13 30.7	6 33.8	14 25.1
8 Su	21 13 07	19 23 27	2♎35 08	8♎30 06	11D 03.8	1 55.5	14 45.3	21 06.6	12 05.7	17 24.2	3 57.7	13 33.0	6 36.0	14 26.9
9 M	21 17 03	20 24 12	14 26 23	20 24 31	11 04.2	1 35.1	15 59.6	21 53.1	12 28.3	17 16.2	4 01.0	13 35.3	6 38.2	14 28.7
10 Tu	21 21 00	21 24 56	26 25 05	2♏28 40	11 05.4	1 22.7	17 14.0	22 39.6	12 50.8	17 08.3	4 04.2	13 37.7	6 40.4	14 30.4
11 W	21 24 56	22 25 38	8♏35 54	14 47 25	11R 06.6	1D 18.1	18 28.2	23 26.0	13 13.2	17 00.3	4 07.3	13 40.1	6 42.6	14 32.2
12 Th	21 28 53	23 26 20	21 03 50	27 25 46	11 06.8	1 20.8	19 42.5	24 12.4	13 35.5	16 52.4	4 10.3	13 42.5	6 44.9	14 33.9
13 F	21 32 50	24 27 01	3♐53 47	10♐28 23	11 05.4	1 30.3	20 56.7	24 58.8	13 57.8	16 44.6	4 13.2	13 45.0	6 47.1	14 35.6
14 Sa	21 36 46	25 27 40	17 09 58	23 58 50	11 02.1	1 46.3	22 10.8	25 45.2	14 20.0	16 36.7	4 16.1	13 47.5	6 49.3	14 37.3
15 Su	21 40 43	26 28 19	0♑55 09	7♑58 51	10 56.9	2 08.2	23 25.0	26 31.5	14 42.1	16 29.0	4 18.8	13 50.1	6 51.6	14 39.0
16 M	21 44 39	27 28 56	15 09 46	22 27 25	10 50.5	2 35.7	24 39.1	27 17.8	15 04.1	16 21.2	4 21.5	13 52.6	6 53.8	14 40.6
17 Tu	21 48 36	28 29 32	29 51 10	7♒20 09	10 43.6	3 08.2	25 53.1	28 04.1	15 26.1	16 13.6	4 24.0	13 55.2	6 56.1	14 42.3
18 W	21 52 32	29 30 06	14♒53 19	22 29 28	10 37.2	3 45.4	27 07.1	28 50.3	15 47.9	16 06.0	4 26.5	13 57.9	6 58.4	14 43.9
19 Th	21 56 29	0♓30 39	0♓07 17	7♓45 25	10 32.2	4 26.9	28 21.1	29 36.5	16 09.7	15 58.4	4 28.8	14 00.6	7 00.6	14 45.5
20 F	22 00 25	1 31 10	15 22 30	22 57 18	10 29.1	5 12.4	29 35.0	0♈22.7	16 31.4	15 50.9	4 31.1	14 03.3	7 02.9	14 47.0
21 Sa	22 04 22	2 31 40	0♈28 39	7♈55 34	10D 27.9	6 01.6	0♈48.9	1 08.8	16 53.0	15 43.5	4 33.3	14 06.0	7 05.2	14 48.6
22 Su	22 08 18	3 32 08	15 17 15	22 33 05	10 28.4	6 54.1	2 02.7	1 54.9	17 14.5	15 36.2	4 35.3	14 08.8	7 07.5	14 50.1
23 M	22 12 15	4 32 34	29 42 41	6♉45 48	10 29.7	7 49.7	3 16.5	2 41.0	17 35.9	15 29.0	4 37.3	14 11.6	7 09.7	14 51.6
24 Tu	22 16 12	5 32 58	13♉42 22	20 32 29	10 31.2	8 48.2	4 30.3	3 27.0	17 57.2	15 21.9	4 39.2	14 14.4	7 12.0	14 53.1
25 W	22 20 08	6 33 20	27 16 20	3♊54 12	10R 32.0	9 49.5	5 44.0	4 13.0	18 18.4	15 14.9	4 41.0	14 17.3	7 14.3	14 54.5
26 Th	22 24 05	7 33 40	10♊26 26	16 53 27	10 31.6	10 53.2	6 57.6	4 59.0	18 39.5	15 08.0	4 42.6	14 20.2	7 16.6	14 56.0
27 F	22 28 01	8 33 58	23 15 40	29 33 32	10 29.7	11 59.2	8 11.2	5 44.9	19 00.5	15 01.2	4 44.2	14 23.1	7 18.8	14 57.4
28 Sa	22 31 58	9 34 15	5♋47 29	11♋57 56	10 26.4	13 07.4	9 24.7	6 30.8	19 21.5	14 54.5	4 45.7	14 26.0	7 21.1	14 58.8

Astro Data

	Dy Hr Mn
☽0S	11 4:58
☿R	21 15:56
☽0N	24 8:19
☽0S	7 12:56
☿D	11 14:58
☽0N	20 18:51
♂0N	21 17:30
♀0N	22 15:29
♃⚻♇	27 23:12

Planet Ingress

	Dy Hr Mn
♀ ♒	3 14:49
☿ ♒	5 1:09
⚳ ♑	8 15:25
♂ ♓	12 10:21
☉ ♒	20 9:44
♀ ♓	27 15:01
☉ ♓	18 23:51
♂ ♈	20 0:12
♀ ♈	20 20:07

Last Aspect / ☽ Ingress

Last Aspect Dy Hr Mn		☽ Ingress Dy Hr Mn
1 12:20 ♀ △	♊	1 17:10
3 11:56 ♂ △	♋	4 1:09
5 4:54 ☉ ☍	♌	6 11:04
8 17:06 ♂ ☍	♍	8 22:59
10 15:47 ☉ △	♎	11 11:58
13 9:48 ☉ □	♏	13 23:45
15 23:53 ☉ ⚹	♐	16 8:02
17 19:26 ♃ △	♑	18 12:05
19 10:52 ♇ ☌	♒	20 13:01
22 1:46 ♀ ☌	♓	22 12:49
23 11:14 ♇ ⚹	♈	24 13:32
26 14:24 ♀ ⚹	♉	26 16:38
28 2:20 ♃ □	♊	28 22:37
30 9:25 ♃ ⚹	♋	31 7:10

Last Aspect Dy Hr Mn		☽ Ingress Dy Hr Mn
1 13:38 ♂ △	♌	2 17:42
4 5:32 ♃ ☌	♍	5 5:47
6 22:10 ♂ ☍	♎	7 18:45
9 11:59 ☉ △	♏	10 7:06
12 5:33 ♂ △	♐	12 16:48
14 15:16 ♂ □	♑	14 22:25
16 20:18 ♂ ⚹	♒	17 0:14
18 23:48 ☉ ☌	♓	18 23:49
19 23:03 ♇ ⚹	♈	20 23:14
22 0:37 ♃ △	♉	23 0:29
24 2:58 ♃ □	♊	25 4:55
26 8:45 ♃ ⚹	♋	27 12:51

☽ Phases & Eclipses

Dy Hr Mn	
5 4:54	○ 14♋31
13 9:48	☾ 22♎52
20 13:15	● 0♒09
27 4:50	☽ 6♉55
3 23:10	○ 14♌48
12 3:51	☾ 23♏06
18 23:48	● 0♓00
25 17:15	☽ 6♊47

Astro Data

1 January 2015
Julian Day # 42004
SVP 5♓02'56"
GC 27♐02.9 ⚴ 1♐59.5
Eris 22♈05.0R ⚵ 16♌04.2R
⚷ 13♓47.5 ⚶ 15♑29.0
☽ Mean ☊ 14♎54.7

1 February 2015
Julian Day # 42035
SVP 5♓02'51"
GC 27♐03.0 ⚴ 13♐53.6
Eris 22♈07.5 ⚵ 9♌03.0R
⚷ 15♓12.2 ⚶ 1♒56.2
☽ Mean ☊ 13♎16.2

March 2015 LONGITUDE

Day	Sid.Time	☉	0 hr ☽	Noon ☽	True ☊	☿	♀	♂	⚳	♃	♄	♅	♆	♇
1 Su	22 35 54	10♓34 29	18♋05 19	24♋10 01	10♎21.9	14♒17.7	10♈38.1	7♈16.6	19♑42.3	14♌47.9	4♐47.1	14♈29.0	7♓23.4	15♑00.1
2 M	22 39 51	11 34 41	0♌12 24	6♌12 49	10R 16.7	15 30.0	11 51.5	8 02.4	20 03.0	14R 41.5	4 48.4	14 32.0	7 25.7	15 01.5
3 Tu	22 43 47	12 34 51	12 11 34	18 08 56	10 11.6	16 44.0	13 04.9	8 48.1	20 23.6	14 35.1	4 49.5	14 35.0	7 28.0	15 02.8
4 W	22 47 44	13 35 00	24 05 13	0♍00 39	10 06.9	17 59.8	14 18.2	9 33.8	20 44.1	14 28.9	4 50.6	14 38.0	7 30.2	15 04.1
5 Th	22 51 41	14 35 06	5♍55 30	11 50 00	10 03.2	19 17.3	15 31.4	10 19.5	21 04.5	14 22.9	4 51.6	14 41.1	7 32.5	15 05.3
6 F	22 55 37	15 35 10	17 44 22	23 38 53	10 00.8	20 36.4	16 44.6	11 05.1	21 24.8	14 17.0	4 52.5	14 44.1	7 34.8	15 06.6
7 Sa	22 59 34	16 35 13	29 33 47	5♎29 20	9D 59.7	21 57.0	17 57.7	11 50.7	21 44.9	14 11.2	4 53.2	14 47.2	7 37.0	15 07.8
8 Su	23 03 30	17 35 14	11♎25 50	17 23 36	9 59.9	23 19.0	19 10.7	12 36.2	22 05.0	14 05.5	4 53.9	14 50.4	7 39.3	15 09.0
9 M	23 07 27	18 35 13	23 22 58	29 24 18	10 00.9	24 42.5	20 23.7	13 21.7	22 24.9	14 00.0	4 54.5	14 53.5	7 41.5	15 10.1
10 Tu	23 11 23	19 35 11	5♏28 00	11♏34 28	10 02.4	26 07.4	21 36.6	14 07.2	22 44.7	13 54.7	4 54.9	14 56.7	7 43.8	15 11.3
11 W	23 15 20	20 35 07	17 44 09	23 57 31	10 04.0	27 33.7	22 49.5	14 52.6	23 04.4	13 49.5	4 55.3	14 59.9	7 46.0	15 12.4
12 Th	23 19 16	21 35 01	0♐15 02	6♐37 08	10 05.3	29 01.3	24 02.3	15 38.0	23 24.0	13 44.5	4 55.6	15 03.1	7 48.2	15 13.4
13 F	23 23 13	22 34 54	13 04 19	19 36 58	10R 05.9	0♓30.2	25 15.0	16 23.3	23 43.5	13 39.6	4 55.7	15 06.3	7 50.5	15 14.5
14 Sa	23 27 10	23 34 45	26 15 29	3♑00 09	10 05.7	2 00.4	26 27.7	17 08.6	24 02.8	13 34.9	4R 55.8	15 09.5	7 52.7	15 15.5
15 Su	23 31 06	24 34 34	9♑51 14	16 48 48	10 04.7	3 31.9	27 40.2	17 53.9	24 22.0	13 30.4	4 55.8	15 12.8	7 54.9	15 16.5
16 M	23 35 03	25 34 22	23 52 52	1♒03 15	10 03.2	5 04.6	28 52.8	18 39.1	24 41.1	13 26.0	4 55.6	15 16.0	7 57.1	15 17.5
17 Tu	23 38 59	26 34 07	8♒19 35	15 41 22	10 01.5	6 38.6	0♉05.2	19 24.2	25 00.1	13 21.8	4 55.4	15 19.3	7 59.3	15 18.4
18 W	23 42 56	27 33 51	23 07 55	0♓38 21	9 59.9	8 13.8	1 17.6	20 09.4	25 18.9	13 17.7	4 55.0	15 22.6	8 01.5	15 19.3
19 Th	23 46 52	28 33 36	8♓11 40	15 46 45	9 58.7	9 50.3	2 30.0	20 54.4	25 37.6	13 13.9	4 54.6	15 25.9	8 03.6	15 20.2
20 F	23 50 49	29 33 14	23 22 23	0♈57 23	9D 58.1	11 28.0	3 42.2	21 39.5	25 56.1	13 10.2	4 54.0	15 29.2	8 05.8	15 21.1
21 Sa	23 54 45	0♈32 52	8♈30 31	16 00 40	9 58.0	13 07.0	4 54.4	22 24.5	26 14.5	13 06.7	4 53.4	15 32.6	8 07.9	15 21.9
22 Su	23 58 42	1 32 28	23 26 48	0♉48 02	9 58.4	14 47.3	6 06.5	23 09.4	26 32.8	13 03.4	4 52.6	15 35.9	8 10.1	15 22.7
23 M	0 02 38	2 32 02	8♉03 39	15 13 05	9 59.0	16 28.8	7 18.5	23 54.3	26 50.9	13 00.2	4 51.8	15 39.3	8 12.2	15 23.5
24 Tu	0 06 35	3 31 34	22 15 59	29 12 09	9 59.7	18 11.6	8 30.5	24 39.2	27 08.8	12 57.3	4 50.9	15 42.7	8 14.3	15 24.2
25 W	0 10 32	4 31 04	6♊01 31	12♊44 11	10 00.2	19 55.7	9 42.3	25 24.0	27 26.6	12 54.5	4 49.8	15 46.0	8 16.4	15 24.9
26 Th	0 14 28	5 30 31	19 20 23	25 50 26	10R 00.5	21 41.1	10 54.1	26 08.7	27 44.3	12 51.9	4 48.7	15 49.4	8 18.5	15 25.6
27 F	0 18 25	6 29 56	2♋14 42	8♋33 40	10 00.6	23 27.8	12 05.8	26 53.4	28 01.8	12 49.5	4 47.4	15 52.8	8 20.6	15 26.2
28 Sa	0 22 21	7 29 18	14 47 49	20 57 40	10 00.5	25 15.9	13 17.4	27 38.1	28 19.1	12 47.3	4 46.1	15 56.2	8 22.6	15 26.8
29 Su	0 26 18	8 28 39	27 03 45	3♌06 38	10 00.4	27 05.3	14 28.9	28 22.7	28 36.3	12 45.3	4 44.7	15 59.6	8 24.7	15 27.4
30 M	0 30 14	9 27 57	9♌06 48	15 04 48	10D 00.3	28 56.0	15 40.4	29 07.2	28 53.3	12 43.4	4 43.1	16 03.0	8 26.7	15 28.0
31 Tu	0 34 11	10 27 12	21 01 07	26 56 14	10 00.2	0♈48.1	16 51.7	29 51.7	29 10.2	12 41.8	4 41.5	16 06.4	8 28.7	15 28.5

April 2015 LONGITUDE

Day	Sid.Time	☉	0 hr ☽	Noon ☽	True ☊	☿	♀	♂	⚳	♃	♄	♅	♆	♇
1 W	0 38 07	11♈26 26	2♍50 34	8♍44 34	10♎00.4	2♈41.5	18♉02.9	0♉36.2	29♑26.9	12♌40.3	4♐39.8	16♈09.9	8♓30.7	15♑29.0
2 Th	0 42 04	12 25 37	14 38 35	20 33 00	10 00.5	4 36.3	19 14.1	1 20.6	29 43.4	12R 39.1	4R 38.0	16 13.3	8 32.7	15 29.5
3 F	0 46 01	13 24 46	26 28 08	2♎24 18	10R 00.7	6 32.4	20 25.1	2 04.9	29 59.8	12 38.0	4 36.1	16 16.7	8 34.6	15 29.9
4 Sa	0 49 57	14 23 53	8♎21 46	14 20 49	10 00.7	8 29.8	21 36.0	2 49.3	0♒15.9	12 37.1	4 34.1	16 20.1	8 36.6	15 30.3
5 Su	0 53 54	15 22 58	20 21 40	26 24 33	10 00.5	10 28.6	22 46.9	3 33.5	0 31.9	12 36.4	4 32.1	16 23.6	8 38.5	15 30.7
6 M	0 57 50	16 22 01	2♏29 43	8♏37 21	10 00.0	12 28.6	23 57.6	4 17.7	0 47.8	12 35.9	4 29.9	16 27.0	8 40.4	15 31.0
7 Tu	1 01 47	17 21 02	14 47 41	21 00 56	9 59.1	14 29.8	25 08.3	5 01.9	1 03.4	12 35.6	4 27.7	16 30.4	8 42.3	15 31.3
8 W	1 05 43	18 20 01	27 17 18	3♐37 00	9 58.1	16 32.1	26 18.8	5 46.0	1 18.9	12D 35.4	4 25.3	16 33.8	8 44.1	15 31.6
9 Th	1 09 40	19 18 59	10♐00 15	16 27 18	9 56.9	18 35.4	27 29.2	6 30.0	1 34.2	12 35.5	4 22.9	16 37.3	8 46.0	15 31.9
10 F	1 13 36	20 17 54	22 58 20	29 33 35	9 56.0	20 39.7	28 39.6	7 14.1	1 49.3	12 35.7	4 20.4	16 40.7	8 47.8	15 32.1
11 Sa	1 17 33	21 16 48	6♑13 14	12♑57 27	9D 55.4	22 44.8	29 49.8	7 58.0	2 04.2	12 36.2	4 17.8	16 44.1	8 49.6	15 32.3
12 Su	1 21 30	22 15 40	19 46 22	26 40 04	9 55.3	24 50.4	0♊59.9	8 41.9	2 18.9	12 36.8	4 15.1	16 47.6	8 51.4	15 32.4
13 M	1 25 26	23 14 31	3♒38 34	10♒41 49	9 55.8	26 56.5	2 09.9	9 25.8	2 33.4	12 37.6	4 12.4	16 51.0	8 53.2	15 32.6
14 Tu	1 29 23	24 13 20	17 49 39	25 01 51	9 56.7	29 02.8	3 19.8	10 09.6	2 47.7	12 38.6	4 09.6	16 54.4	8 54.9	15 32.7
15 W	1 33 19	25 12 07	2♓18 01	9♓37 40	9 57.8	1♉09.0	4 29.6	10 53.4	3 01.8	12 39.8	4 06.7	16 57.8	8 56.6	15 32.7
16 Th	1 37 16	26 10 52	17 00 14	24 24 57	9 58.7	3 14.9	5 39.2	11 37.1	3 15.6	12 41.1	4 03.7	17 01.2	8 58.3	15R 32.8
17 F	1 41 12	27 09 35	1♈51 02	9♈17 35	9R 59.2	5 20.1	6 48.8	12 20.8	3 29.3	12 42.7	4 00.6	17 04.6	9 00.0	15 32.8
18 Sa	1 45 09	28 08 17	16 43 39	24 08 16	9 58.7	7 24.4	7 58.2	13 04.5	3 42.8	12 44.4	3 57.5	17 08.0	9 01.7	15 32.7
19 Su	1 49 05	29 06 57	1♉30 27	8♉49 19	9 57.4	9 27.3	9 07.5	13 48.0	3 56.0	12 46.3	3 54.3	17 11.4	9 03.3	15 32.7
20 M	1 53 02	0♉05 35	16 04 01	23 13 50	9 55.1	11 28.7	10 16.7	14 31.6	4 09.0	12 48.4	3 51.0	17 14.7	9 04.9	15 32.6
21 Tu	1 56 59	1 04 10	0♊18 10	7♊16 34	9 52.2	13 28.1	11 25.7	15 15.1	4 21.8	12 50.7	3 47.7	17 18.1	9 06.5	15 32.5
22 W	2 00 55	2 02 44	14 08 42	20 54 26	9 49.1	15 25.3	12 34.7	15 58.5	4 34.4	12 53.2	3 44.3	17 21.4	9 08.0	15 32.3
23 Th	2 04 52	3 01 16	27 33 46	4♋06 48	9 46.3	17 19.9	13 43.4	16 41.9	4 46.7	12 55.8	3 40.8	17 24.8	9 09.6	15 32.2
24 F	2 08 48	3 59 45	10♋33 47	16 55 03	9 44.2	19 11.6	14 52.1	17 25.2	4 58.8	12 58.6	3 37.3	17 28.1	9 11.1	15 32.0
25 Sa	2 12 45	4 58 13	23 11 02	29 22 13	9D 43.1	21 00.2	16 00.6	18 08.5	5 10.7	13 01.6	3 33.7	17 31.4	9 12.6	15 31.7
26 Su	2 16 41	5 56 38	5♌29 09	11♌32 25	9 43.1	22 45.5	17 08.9	18 51.7	5 22.3	13 04.8	3 30.0	17 34.7	9 14.0	15 31.5
27 M	2 20 38	6 55 01	17 32 37	23 30 22	9 44.1	24 27.2	18 17.1	19 34.9	5 33.7	13 08.1	3 26.3	17 38.0	9 15.5	15 31.2
28 Tu	2 24 34	7 53 21	29 26 16	5♍20 56	9 45.7	26 05.2	19 25.2	20 18.0	5 44.8	13 11.6	3 22.5	17 41.3	9 16.9	15 30.8
29 W	2 28 31	8 51 40	11♍14 58	17 08 54	9 47.5	27 39.3	20 33.0	21 01.1	5 55.7	13 15.3	3 18.7	17 44.6	9 18.2	15 30.5
30 Th	2 32 27	9 49 57	23 03 19	28 58 40	9R 48.9	29 09.3	21 40.7	21 44.1	6 06.3	13 19.1	3 14.8	17 47.8	9 19.6	15 30.1

Astro Data	Dy Hr Mn
♃△♅	3 12:26
☽0S	6 19:29
♄ R	14 15:03
♅□♇	17 2:55
☽0N	20 6:15
☉0N	20 22:46
☿0N	2 6:38
☽0S	3 1:41
♃ D	8 16:58
☽0N	16 16:42
♇ R	17 3:56
☽0S	30 8:48

Planet Ingress		Dy Hr Mn
☿	♓	13 3:53
♀	♉	17 10:16
☉	♈	20 22:46
☿	♈	31 1:45
♂	♉	31 16:28
⚳	♒	3 12:22
♀	♊	11 15:30
☿	♉	14 22:53
☉	♉	20 9:43

Last Aspect Dy Hr Mn			☽ Ingress	Dy Hr Mn
28 17:54	♇	☍	♌	1 23:35
3 8:49	☿	☍	♍	4 11:59
5 18:38	♇	△	♎	7 0:53
9 1:25	☿	△	♏	9 13:11
11 19:47	☿	□	♐	11 23:32
13 23:12	♀	△	♑	14 6:41
16 8:03	♀	□	♒	16 10:15
17 18:19	♂	⚹	♓	18 10:59
20 9:37	☉	☌	♈	20 10:29
21 22:52	♂	☌	♉	22 10:41
23 14:26	☿	⚹	♊	24 13:24
26 12:36	♂	⚹	♋	26 19:46
29 1:59	♂	□	♌	29 5:49
30 13:58	♅	△	♍	31 18:13

Last Aspect Dy Hr Mn			☽ Ingress	Dy Hr Mn
2 9:02	♀	△	♎	3 7:09
4 16:00	♅	☍	♏	5 19:05
7 20:43	♀	☍	♐	8 5:09
9 17:43	☉	△	♑	10 12:48
12 8:16	☿	□	♒	12 17:45
14 19:46	☿	⚹	♓	14 20:13
15 21:38	♇	⚹	♈	16 21:01
18 18:58	☉	☌	♉	18 21:32
19 23:08	♇	△	♊	20 23:29
22 5:39	♅	⚹	♋	23 4:27
24 17:05	☿	⚹	♌	25 13:14
27 14:13	☿	□	♍	28 1:08
30 12:25	☿	△	♎	30 14:04

☽ Phases & Eclipses Dy Hr Mn		
5 18:07	○	14♍50
13 17:49	☾	22♐49
20 9:37	●	29♓27
20 9:46:46	●	T 02'47"
27 7:44	☽	6♋19
4 12:07	○	14♎24
4 12:01	○	T 1.001
12 3:46	☾	21♑55
18 18:58	●	28♈25
25 23:56	☽	5♌27

Astro Data

1 March 2015
Julian Day # 42063
SVP 5♓02'48"
GC 27♐03.1 ⚴ 22♐48.7
Eris 22♈18.1 ⚵ 3♌47.9R
⚷ 16♓51.3 ⚶ 16♒26.9
☽ Mean ☊ 11♎47.2

1 April 2015
Julian Day # 42094
SVP 5♓02'46"
GC 27♐03.1 ⚴ 29♐13.2
Eris 22♈36.2 ⚵ 4♌26.4
⚷ 18♓44.8 ⚶ 1♓48.4
☽ Mean ☊ 10♎08.7

LONGITUDE — May 2015

Day	Sid.Time	☉	0 hr ☽	Noon ☽	True ☊	☿	♀	♂	⚳	♃	♄	♅	♆	♇
1 F	2 36 24	10♉48 12	4♎55 28	10♎54 07	9♎49.4	0♊35.2	22♊48.3	22♉27.1	6♒16.7	13♌23.2	3♐10.9	17♈51.0	9♓20.9	15♑29.7
2 Sa	2 40 21	11 46 25	16 54 59	22 58 24	9R 48.5	1 56.9	23 55.7	23 10.0	6 26.8	13 27.3	3R 06.9	17 54.2	9 22.2	15R 29.3
3 Su	2 44 17	12 44 36	29 04 39	5♏13 58	9 46.1	3 14.2	25 02.9	23 52.8	6 36.6	13 31.7	3 02.9	17 57.4	9 23.5	15 28.8
4 M	2 48 14	13 42 45	11♏26 31	17 42 27	9 42.2	4 27.0	26 09.9	24 35.7	6 46.2	13 36.2	2 58.9	18 00.6	9 24.7	15 28.3
5 Tu	2 52 10	14 40 53	24 01 49	0♐24 41	9 37.0	5 35.4	27 16.8	25 18.4	6 55.5	13 40.8	2 54.8	18 03.8	9 25.9	15 27.8
6 W	2 56 07	15 38 59	6♐51 04	13 20 54	9 31.1	6 39.2	28 23.4	26 01.1	7 04.6	13 45.7	2 50.6	18 06.9	9 27.1	15 27.2
7 Th	3 00 03	16 37 04	19 54 10	26 30 46	9 25.1	7 38.4	29 29.9	26 43.8	7 13.4	13 50.6	2 46.4	18 10.0	9 28.2	15 26.7
8 F	3 04 00	17 35 07	3♑10 40	9♑53 44	9 19.8	8 32.8	0♋36.2	27 26.4	7 21.8	13 55.8	2 42.2	18 13.1	9 29.4	15 26.1
9 Sa	3 07 56	18 33 09	16 39 54	23 29 04	9 15.8	9 22.5	1 42.3	28 09.0	7 30.1	14 01.1	2 38.0	18 16.2	9 30.5	15 25.4
10 Su	3 11 53	19 31 09	0♒21 11	7♒16 08	9D 13.4	10 07.4	2 48.2	28 51.5	7 38.0	14 06.5	2 33.7	18 19.3	9 31.5	15 24.8
11 M	3 15 50	20 29 08	14 13 51	21 14 15	9 12.7	10 47.4	3 53.9	29 34.0	7 45.6	14 12.1	2 29.4	18 22.3	9 32.6	15 24.1
12 Tu	3 19 46	21 27 06	28 17 12	5♓22 33	9 13.4	11 22.4	4 59.4	0♊16.5	7 52.9	14 17.9	2 25.1	18 25.3	9 33.6	15 23.4
13 W	3 23 43	22 25 02	12♓30 10	19 39 46	9 14.6	11 52.5	6 04.7	0 58.8	8 00.0	14 23.7	2 20.7	18 28.3	9 34.5	15 22.7
14 Th	3 27 39	23 22 58	26 51 06	4♈03 47	9R 15.5	12 17.6	7 09.7	1 41.2	8 06.7	14 29.8	2 16.3	18 31.3	9 35.5	15 21.9
15 F	3 31 36	24 20 52	11♈17 23	18 31 24	9 15.3	12 37.7	8 14.6	2 23.5	8 13.1	14 36.0	2 11.9	18 34.2	9 36.4	15 21.1
16 Sa	3 35 32	25 18 44	25 45 15	2♉58 18	9 13.2	12 52.8	9 19.2	3 05.7	8 19.2	14 42.3	2 07.5	18 37.1	9 37.3	15 20.3
17 Su	3 39 29	26 16 36	10♉09 53	17 19 18	9 08.9	13 02.9	10 23.6	3 47.9	8 25.0	14 48.8	2 03.1	18 40.0	9 38.1	15 19.5
18 M	3 43 25	27 14 26	24 25 51	1♊28 52	9 02.6	13R 08.1	11 27.7	4 30.1	8 30.5	14 55.4	1 58.6	18 42.9	9 39.0	15 18.6
19 Tu	3 47 22	28 12 14	8♊27 47	15 22 02	8 54.9	13 08.5	12 31.6	5 12.2	8 35.7	15 02.1	1 54.2	18 45.7	9 39.7	15 17.8
20 W	3 51 19	29 10 01	22 11 14	28 55 02	8 46.6	13 04.1	13 35.3	5 54.2	8 40.5	15 09.0	1 49.7	18 48.5	9 40.5	15 16.9
21 Th	3 55 15	0♊07 47	5♋33 17	12♋05 53	8 38.5	12 55.3	14 38.6	6 36.3	8 45.0	15 16.0	1 45.2	18 51.3	9 41.2	15 15.9
22 F	3 59 12	1 05 31	18 32 56	24 54 35	8 31.7	12 42.1	15 41.7	7 18.2	8 49.2	15 23.2	1 40.8	18 54.1	9 41.9	15 15.0
23 Sa	4 03 08	2 03 14	1♌11 08	7♌22 57	8 26.7	12 25.0	16 44.6	8 00.1	8 53.0	15 30.5	1 36.3	18 56.8	9 42.6	15 14.0
24 Su	4 07 05	3 00 55	13 30 29	19 34 16	8 23.7	12 04.1	17 47.1	8 42.0	8 56.5	15 37.9	1 31.8	18 59.5	9 43.2	15 13.0
25 M	4 11 01	3 58 34	25 34 52	1♍32 54	8D 22.6	11 39.8	18 49.3	9 23.8	8 59.7	15 45.4	1 27.3	19 02.2	9 43.8	15 12.0
26 Tu	4 14 58	4 56 12	7♍29 02	13 23 54	8 22.9	11 12.7	19 51.3	10 05.6	9 02.6	15 53.1	1 22.9	19 04.8	9 44.4	15 11.0
27 W	4 18 54	5 53 48	19 18 10	25 12 30	8 23.8	10 43.2	20 52.9	10 47.3	9 05.1	16 00.9	1 18.4	19 07.4	9 44.9	15 09.9
28 Th	4 22 51	6 51 23	1♎07 34	7♎03 59	8R 24.4	10 11.7	21 54.2	11 29.0	9 07.2	16 08.8	1 14.0	19 10.0	9 45.4	15 08.8
29 F	4 26 48	7 48 57	13 02 20	19 03 11	8 23.8	9 38.9	22 55.1	12 10.6	9 09.0	16 16.9	1 09.5	19 12.5	9 45.9	15 07.7
30 Sa	4 30 44	8 46 29	25 07 02	1♏14 20	8 21.3	9 05.3	23 55.7	12 52.2	9 10.5	16 25.0	1 05.1	19 15.0	9 46.3	15 06.6
31 Su	4 34 41	9 44 00	7♏25 28	13 40 43	8 16.4	8 31.5	24 56.0	13 33.7	9 11.6	16 33.3	1 00.7	19 17.5	9 46.7	15 05.5

LONGITUDE — June 2015

Day	Sid.Time	☉	0 hr ☽	Noon ☽	True ☊	☿	♀	♂	⚳	♃	♄	♅	♆	♇
1 M	4 38 37	10♊41 30	20♏00 20	26♏24 27	8♎09.2	7♊58.1	25♋55.8	14♊15.2	9♒12.4	16♌41.7	0♐56.3	19♈19.9	9♓47.1	15♑04.3
2 Tu	4 42 34	11 38 59	2♐53 06	9♐26 14	8R 00.0	7R 25.7	26 55.3	14 56.6	9R 12.8	16 50.2	0R 52.0	19 22.3	9 47.4	15R 03.2
3 W	4 46 30	12 36 26	16 03 43	22 45 21	7 49.6	6 54.7	27 54.4	15 38.0	9 12.9	16 58.8	0 47.6	19 24.7	9 47.7	15 02.0
4 Th	4 50 27	13 33 53	29 30 50	6♑19 49	7 39.1	6 25.8	28 53.1	16 19.3	9 12.6	17 07.5	0 43.3	19 27.0	9 48.0	15 00.8
5 F	4 54 23	14 31 19	13♑11 56	20 06 45	7 29.5	5 59.4	29 51.4	17 00.7	9 11.9	17 16.4	0 39.0	19 29.3	9 48.3	14 59.5
6 Sa	4 58 20	15 28 44	27 03 53	4♒02 54	7 21.8	5 36.0	0♌49.2	17 41.9	9 10.9	17 25.3	0 34.8	19 31.6	9 48.5	14 58.3
7 Su	5 02 17	16 26 09	11♒03 27	18 05 10	7 16.5	5 15.9	1 46.6	18 23.1	9 09.6	17 34.4	0 30.6	19 33.8	9 48.7	14 57.1
8 M	5 06 13	17 23 32	25 07 46	2♓10 59	7 13.7	4 59.4	2 43.6	19 04.3	9 07.8	17 43.5	0 26.4	19 36.0	9 48.8	14 55.8
9 Tu	5 10 10	18 20 56	9♓14 39	16 18 33	7D 12.9	4 46.8	3 40.1	19 45.4	9 05.7	17 52.8	0 22.2	19 38.1	9 48.9	14 54.5
10 W	5 14 06	19 18 18	23 22 34	0♈26 35	7R 13.0	4 38.4	4 36.1	20 26.5	9 03.3	18 02.1	0 18.1	19 40.2	9 49.0	14 53.2
11 Th	5 18 03	20 15 41	7♈30 26	14 34 01	7 13.0	4D 34.2	5 31.6	21 07.6	9 00.5	18 11.6	0 14.0	19 42.3	9R 49.0	14 51.9
12 F	5 21 59	21 13 02	21 37 08	28 39 35	7 11.5	4 34.5	6 26.6	21 48.6	8 57.3	18 21.1	0 10.0	19 44.4	9 49.0	14 50.5
13 Sa	5 25 56	22 10 24	5♉41 08	12♉41 28	7 07.7	4 39.2	7 21.1	22 29.5	8 53.7	18 30.8	0 06.0	19 46.4	9 49.0	14 49.2
14 Su	5 29 52	23 07 45	19 40 14	26 37 05	7 01.0	4 48.6	8 15.0	23 10.5	8 49.8	18 40.5	0 02.1	19 48.3	9 49.0	14 47.9
15 M	5 33 49	24 05 05	3♊31 34	10♊23 16	6 51.8	5 02.5	9 08.4	23 51.3	8 45.6	18 50.4	29♏58.2	19 50.2	9 48.9	14 46.5
16 Tu	5 37 46	25 02 25	17 11 47	23 56 43	6 40.6	5 20.9	10 01.1	24 32.2	8 40.9	19 00.3	29 54.3	19 52.1	9 48.8	14 45.1
17 W	5 41 42	25 59 44	0♋37 43	7♋14 29	6 28.4	5 43.9	10 53.3	25 13.0	8 36.0	19 10.3	29 50.5	19 53.9	9 48.6	14 43.7
18 Th	5 45 39	26 57 03	13 46 48	20 14 33	6 16.4	6 11.3	11 44.8	25 53.7	8 30.6	19 20.5	29 46.8	19 55.7	9 48.4	14 42.3
19 F	5 49 35	27 54 21	26 37 46	2♌56 19	6 05.8	6 43.2	12 35.7	26 34.4	8 25.0	19 30.7	29 43.1	19 57.5	9 48.2	14 40.9
20 Sa	5 53 32	28 51 38	9♌10 32	15 20 36	5 57.4	7 19.4	13 25.9	27 15.1	8 18.9	19 41.0	29 39.5	19 59.2	9 48.0	14 39.5
21 Su	5 57 28	29 48 54	21 26 52	27 29 44	5 51.5	8 00.0	14 15.4	27 55.7	8 12.6	19 51.3	29 35.9	20 00.9	9 47.7	14 38.1
22 M	6 01 25	0♋46 10	3♍29 41	9♍27 16	5 48.1	8 44.8	15 04.1	28 36.3	8 05.9	20 01.8	29 32.4	20 02.5	9 47.4	14 36.6
23 Tu	6 05 22	1 43 25	15 23 04	21 17 42	5D 46.7	9 33.7	15 52.1	29 16.9	7 58.8	20 12.3	29 29.0	20 04.0	9 47.1	14 35.2
24 W	6 09 18	2 40 40	27 11 50	3♎06 10	5R 46.5	10 26.8	16 39.2	29 57.4	7 51.4	20 23.0	29 25.6	20 05.6	9 46.7	14 33.7
25 Th	6 13 15	3 37 53	9♎01 21	14 58 05	5 46.4	11 23.9	17 25.6	0♋37.8	7 43.8	20 33.7	29 22.3	20 07.1	9 46.3	14 32.3
26 F	6 17 11	4 35 07	20 57 03	26 58 55	5 45.3	12 24.9	18 11.1	1 18.2	7 35.7	20 44.4	29 19.0	20 08.5	9 45.8	14 30.8
27 Sa	6 21 08	5 32 19	3♏04 16	9♏13 41	5 42.3	13 29.9	18 55.7	1 58.6	7 27.4	20 55.3	29 15.9	20 09.9	9 45.4	14 29.4
28 Su	6 25 04	6 29 32	15 27 41	21 46 41	5 37.0	14 38.8	19 39.4	2 38.9	7 18.8	21 06.2	29 12.8	20 11.3	9 44.9	14 27.9
29 M	6 29 01	7 26 44	28 11 02	4♐40 56	5 29.0	15 51.5	20 22.1	3 19.2	7 09.9	21 17.2	29 09.7	20 12.6	9 44.4	14 26.4
30 Tu	6 32 57	8 23 55	11♐16 31	17 57 46	5 18.9	17 07.9	21 03.8	3 59.5	7 00.7	21 28.3	29 06.8	20 13.8	9 43.8	14 24.9

Astro Data Dy Hr Mn	Planet Ingress Dy Hr Mn	Last Aspect Dy Hr Mn	☽ Ingress Dy Hr Mn	Last Aspect Dy Hr Mn	☽ Ingress Dy Hr Mn	☽ Phases & Eclipses Dy Hr Mn
♄□♅ 4 6:13	☿ ♊ 1 2:01	2 14:04 ♀ △	♏ 3 1:48	1 11:02 ♀ △	♐ 1 18:40	4 3:43 ○ 13♏23
☽0N 14 1:12	♀ ♋ 7 22:53	5 1:50 ♂ ☍	♐ 5 11:14	3 6:00 ♅ △	♑ 4 0:52	11 10:37 ☾ 20♒26
☿R 19 1:49	♂ ♊ 12 2:41	7 17:53 ♀ ☍	♑ 7 18:17	5 10:55 ♅ □	♒ 6 5:03	18 4:14 ● 26♉56
♃⚻♇ 21 11:40	☉ ♊ 21 8:46	9 20:36 ♂ △	♒ 9 23:23	7 14:32 ♅ ⚹	♓ 8 8:17	25 17:20 ☽ 4♍11
☽0S 27 17:18		11 10:37 ☉ □	♓ 12 2:54	9 18:09 ♂ □	♈ 10 11:15	
	♀ ♌ 5 15:34	13 16:56 ☉ ⚹	♈ 14 5:15	11 23:44 ♂ ⚹	♉ 12 14:17	2 16:20 ○ 11♐49
⚳R 3 4:21	♄ ♏R 15 0:37	15 12:05 ♅ ☌	♉ 16 7:03	13 22:07 ♃ □	♊ 14 17:52	9 15:43 ☾ 18♓30
☽0N 10 8:07	☉ ♋ 21 16:39	18 4:14 ☉ ☌	♊ 18 9:28	16 14:07 ☉ ☌	♋ 16 22:52	16 14:07 ● 25♊07
☿D 11 22:35	♂ ♋ 24 13:34	19 17:59 ♅ ⚹	♋ 20 13:57	19 5:53 ♄ △	♌ 19 6:24	24 11:04 ☽ 2♎38
♆R 12 9:09		22 0:37 ♅ □	♌ 22 21:43	21 16:11 ♄ □	♍ 21 17:00	
♄∠♇ 20 11:46		24 10:51 ♅ △	♍ 25 8:53	24 5:13 ♂ □	♎ 24 5:42	
♃△♅ 22 13:48		27 2:22 ♀ ⚹	♎ 27 21:43	25 23:23 ♃ ⚹	♏ 26 17:58	
☽0S 24 2:42		29 20:21 ♀ □	♏ 30 9:35	29 1:51 ♄ ☌	♐ 29 3:22	

Astro Data

1 May 2015
Julian Day # 42124
SVP 5♓02'43"
GC 27♐03.2 ⚴ 29♐56.2R
Eris 22♈55.7 ⚵ 10♌23.2
⚷ 20♓18.1 ⚶ 15♓34.5
☽ Mean ☊ 8♎33.3

1 June 2015
Julian Day # 42155
SVP 5♓02'39"
GC 27♐03.3 ⚴ 23♐51.0R
Eris 23♈12.9 ⚵ 19♌39.4
⚷ 21♓19.0 ⚶ 28♓04.5
☽ Mean ☊ 6♎54.8

July 2015 LONGITUDE

Day	Sid.Time	☉	0 hr ☽	Noon ☽	True ☊	☿	♀	♂	⚳	♃	♄	♅	♆	♇
1 W	6 36 54	9♋21 07	24♐44 31	1♑36 30	5♎07.4	18♊28.1	21♌44.4	4♋39.7	6♒51.2	21♌39.4	29♏03.9	20♈15.1	9♓43.2	14♑23.4
2 Th	6 40 51	10 18 18	8♑33 19	15 34 24	4R 55.7	19 52.0	22 24.0	5 19.9	6R 41.4	21 50.6	29R 01.1	20 16.2	9R 42.6	14R 22.0
3 F	6 44 47	11 15 29	22 39 11	29 46 57	4 44.9	21 19.5	23 02.5	6 00.0	6 31.3	22 01.9	28 58.4	20 17.4	9 42.0	14 20.5
4 Sa	6 48 44	12 12 40	6♒56 58	14♒08 32	4 36.2	22 50.5	23 39.8	6 40.1	6 21.0	22 13.2	28 55.7	20 18.5	9 41.3	14 19.0
5 Su	6 52 40	13 09 51	21 20 56	28 33 29	4 30.1	24 25.1	24 15.9	7 20.1	6 10.5	22 24.6	28 53.1	20 19.5	9 40.6	14 17.5
6 M	6 56 37	14 07 02	5♓45 37	12♓56 49	4 26.7	26 03.2	24 50.7	8 00.2	5 59.7	22 36.1	28 50.6	20 20.5	9 39.9	14 16.0
7 Tu	7 00 33	15 04 14	20 06 40	27 14 50	4D 25.5	27 44.7	25 24.3	8 40.2	5 48.6	22 47.6	28 48.2	20 21.4	9 39.1	14 14.5
8 W	7 04 30	16 01 26	4♈21 05	11♈25 15	4R 25.5	29 29.4	25 56.5	9 20.1	5 37.4	22 59.2	28 45.9	20 22.3	9 38.3	14 13.0
9 Th	7 08 26	16 58 39	18 27 13	25 26 56	4 25.3	1♋17.3	26 27.4	10 00.0	5 25.9	23 10.9	28 43.7	20 23.2	9 37.5	14 11.5
10 F	7 12 23	17 55 51	2♉24 20	9♉19 25	4 23.9	3 08.2	26 56.8	10 39.9	5 14.2	23 22.6	28 41.5	20 24.0	9 36.6	14 10.0
11 Sa	7 16 20	18 53 05	16 12 07	23 02 25	4 20.2	5 02.0	27 24.7	11 19.7	5 02.3	23 34.3	28 39.4	20 24.7	9 35.8	14 08.5
12 Su	7 20 16	19 50 19	29 50 14	6♊35 29	4 13.8	6 58.4	27 51.1	11 59.6	4 50.2	23 46.2	28 37.4	20 25.4	9 34.9	14 07.0
13 M	7 24 13	20 47 33	13♊18 02	19 57 46	4 04.9	8 57.3	28 15.8	12 39.3	4 38.0	23 58.1	28 35.5	20 26.1	9 34.0	14 05.6
14 Tu	7 28 09	21 44 48	26 34 30	3♋08 07	3 54.1	10 58.4	28 38.9	13 19.1	4 25.6	24 10.0	28 33.7	20 26.7	9 33.0	14 04.1
15 W	7 32 06	22 42 03	9♋38 27	16 05 23	3 42.2	13 01.4	29 00.3	13 58.8	4 13.1	24 22.0	28 32.0	20 27.3	9 32.0	14 02.6
16 Th	7 36 02	23 39 18	22 28 47	28 48 38	3 30.6	15 06.0	29 19.9	14 38.5	4 00.4	24 34.0	28 30.4	20 27.8	9 31.0	14 01.1
17 F	7 39 59	24 36 34	5♌04 53	11♌17 36	3 20.1	17 12.0	29 37.7	15 18.1	3 47.6	24 46.1	28 28.8	20 28.2	9 30.0	13 59.7
18 Sa	7 43 55	25 33 50	17 26 53	23 32 56	3 11.7	19 19.0	29 53.6	15 57.7	3 34.7	24 58.2	28 27.4	20 28.6	9 28.9	13 58.2
19 Su	7 47 52	26 31 06	29 35 58	5♍36 17	3 05.9	21 26.7	0♍07.5	16 37.2	3 21.7	25 10.4	28 26.0	20 29.0	9 27.9	13 56.7
20 M	7 51 49	27 28 23	11♍34 17	17 30 22	3 02.5	23 34.8	0 19.4	17 16.8	3 08.7	25 22.6	28 24.7	20 29.3	9 26.8	13 55.3
21 Tu	7 55 45	28 25 39	23 25 02	29 18 50	3D 01.2	25 43.0	0 29.1	17 56.3	2 55.5	25 34.9	28 23.6	20 29.6	9 25.6	13 53.9
22 W	7 59 42	29 22 56	5♎12 19	11♎06 07	3 01.4	27 51.0	0 36.8	18 35.7	2 42.4	25 47.2	28 22.5	20 29.8	9 24.5	13 52.4
23 Th	8 03 38	0♌20 14	17 00 52	22 57 14	3R 02.0	29 58.6	0 42.3	19 15.1	2 29.2	25 59.5	28 21.5	20 30.0	9 23.3	13 51.0
24 F	8 07 35	1 17 31	28 55 53	4♏57 30	3 02.2	2♌05.6	0R 45.5	19 54.5	2 16.0	26 11.9	28 20.6	20 30.1	9 22.1	13 49.6
25 Sa	8 11 31	2 14 49	11♏02 45	17 12 16	3 00.9	4 11.7	0 46.4	20 33.9	2 02.7	26 24.4	28 19.8	20R 30.1	9 20.9	13 48.2
26 Su	8 15 28	3 12 08	23 26 39	29 46 26	2 57.8	6 16.9	0 45.0	21 13.2	1 49.5	26 36.8	28 19.1	20 30.2	9 19.7	13 46.8
27 M	8 19 24	4 09 27	6♐12 05	12♐43 57	2 52.5	8 20.8	0 41.2	21 52.4	1 36.4	26 49.3	28 18.5	20 30.1	9 18.4	13 45.4
28 Tu	8 23 21	5 06 46	19 22 19	26 07 16	2 45.3	10 23.5	0 35.0	22 31.7	1 23.2	27 01.9	28 18.0	20 30.1	9 17.2	13 44.0
29 W	8 27 18	6 04 06	2♑58 47	9♑56 40	2 36.8	12 24.9	0 26.5	23 10.9	1 10.1	27 14.4	28 17.6	20 29.9	9 15.9	13 42.7
30 Th	8 31 14	7 01 27	17 00 32	24 09 53	2 28.0	14 24.8	0 15.5	23 50.1	0 57.1	27 27.0	28 17.3	20 29.8	9 14.6	13 41.3
31 F	8 35 11	7 58 48	1♒24 02	8♒42 09	2 19.9	16 23.2	0 02.1	24 29.2	0 44.1	27 39.7	28 17.1	20 29.5	9 13.2	13 40.0

August 2015 LONGITUDE

Day	Sid.Time	☉	0 hr ☽	Noon ☽	True ☊	☿	♀	♂	⚳	♃	♄	♅	♆	♇
1 Sa	8 39 07	8♌56 10	16♒03 21	23♒26 39	2♎13.5	18♌20.0	29♌46.4	25♋08.3	0♒31.3	27♌52.3	28♏17.0	20♈29.3	9♓11.9	13♑38.7
2 Su	8 43 04	9 53 33	0♓51 03	8♓15 36	2R 09.1	20 15.3	29R 28.4	25 47.4	0R 18.5	28 05.0	28D 17.0	20R 29.0	9R 10.5	13R 37.4
3 M	8 47 00	10 50 57	15 39 21	23 01 29	2D 07.1	22 09.0	29 08.0	26 26.5	0 05.8	28 17.7	28 17.0	20 28.6	9 09.1	13 36.1
4 Tu	8 50 57	11 48 22	0♈21 16	7♈38 07	2 06.8	24 01.1	28 45.5	27 05.5	29♑53.3	28 30.5	28 17.2	20 28.2	9 07.7	13 34.8
5 W	8 54 53	12 45 48	14 51 32	22 01 10	2 07.7	25 51.6	28 20.9	27 44.5	29 40.9	28 43.3	28 17.5	20 27.7	9 06.3	13 33.6
6 Th	8 58 50	13 43 15	29 06 48	6♉08 18	2R 08.7	27 40.5	27 54.3	28 23.4	29 28.7	28 56.1	28 17.8	20 27.2	9 04.8	13 32.3
7 F	9 02 47	14 40 44	13♉05 35	19 58 42	2 08.7	29 27.8	27 25.8	29 02.4	29 16.6	29 08.9	28 18.3	20 26.7	9 03.4	13 31.1
8 Sa	9 06 43	15 38 14	26 47 42	3♊32 40	2 07.3	1♍13.6	26 55.6	29 41.3	29 04.7	29 21.7	28 18.8	20 26.1	9 01.9	13 29.9
9 Su	9 10 40	16 35 46	10♊13 45	16 51 04	2 03.8	2 57.7	26 23.8	0♌20.2	28 53.0	29 34.6	28 19.5	20 25.4	9 00.4	13 28.7
10 M	9 14 36	17 33 19	23 24 44	29 54 53	1 58.5	4 40.4	25 50.6	0 59.0	28 41.5	29 47.5	28 20.3	20 24.7	8 59.0	13 27.5
11 Tu	9 18 33	18 30 53	6♋21 39	12♋45 07	1 51.8	6 21.4	25 16.1	1 37.8	28 30.2	0♍00.4	28 21.1	20 24.0	8 57.4	13 26.3
12 W	9 22 29	19 28 28	19 05 24	25 22 34	1 44.3	8 01.0	24 40.7	2 16.6	28 19.2	0 13.4	28 22.1	20 23.2	8 55.9	13 25.2
13 Th	9 26 26	20 26 05	1♌36 45	7♌48 03	1 36.9	9 39.0	24 04.5	2 55.4	28 08.3	0 26.3	28 23.1	20 22.3	8 54.4	13 24.1
14 F	9 30 22	21 23 43	13 56 33	20 02 24	1 30.4	11 15.5	23 27.7	3 34.1	27 57.7	0 39.3	28 24.2	20 21.5	8 52.8	13 22.9
15 Sa	9 34 19	22 21 22	26 05 45	2♍06 48	1 25.2	12 50.4	22 50.6	4 12.8	27 47.4	0 52.2	28 25.5	20 20.5	8 51.3	13 21.9
16 Su	9 38 16	23 19 02	8♍05 44	14 02 50	1 21.9	14 23.9	22 13.3	4 51.5	27 37.3	1 05.2	28 26.8	20 19.6	8 49.7	13 20.8
17 M	9 42 12	24 16 44	19 58 22	25 52 42	1D 20.3	15 55.8	21 36.2	5 30.1	27 27.5	1 18.2	28 28.2	20 18.6	8 48.1	13 19.7
18 Tu	9 46 09	25 14 26	1♎46 10	7♎39 12	1 20.3	17 26.2	20 59.4	6 08.7	27 18.0	1 31.3	28 29.8	20 17.5	8 46.6	13 18.7
19 W	9 50 05	26 12 10	13 32 16	19 25 51	1 21.5	18 55.0	20 23.2	6 47.3	27 08.8	1 44.3	28 31.4	20 16.4	8 45.0	13 17.7
20 Th	9 54 02	27 09 55	25 20 29	1♏16 44	1 23.2	20 22.4	19 47.9	7 25.8	26 59.9	1 57.3	28 33.1	20 15.2	8 43.4	13 16.7
21 F	9 57 58	28 07 41	7♏15 10	13 16 35	1 24.8	21 48.1	19 13.5	8 04.3	26 51.2	2 10.3	28 34.9	20 14.0	8 41.7	13 15.8
22 Sa	10 01 55	29 05 28	19 21 04	25 29 46	1R 25.6	23 12.3	18 40.5	8 42.8	26 42.9	2 23.4	28 36.8	20 12.8	8 40.1	13 14.8
23 Su	10 05 51	0♍03 17	1♐43 05	8♐01 36	1 25.4	24 34.9	18 08.8	9 21.3	26 34.9	2 36.4	28 38.8	20 11.5	8 38.5	13 13.9
24 M	10 09 48	1 01 06	14 25 51	20 56 17	1 23.8	25 55.8	17 38.8	9 59.7	26 27.3	2 49.5	28 40.9	20 10.2	8 36.9	13 13.0
25 Tu	10 13 44	1 58 57	27 33 18	4♑17 10	1 21.1	27 15.0	17 10.5	10 38.1	26 19.9	3 02.5	28 43.1	20 08.9	8 35.3	13 12.2
26 W	10 17 41	2 56 49	11♑08 01	18 05 52	1 17.5	28 32.6	16 44.1	11 16.5	26 12.9	3 15.6	28 45.4	20 07.5	8 33.6	13 11.3
27 Th	10 21 38	3 54 42	25 10 31	2♒21 38	1 13.6	29 48.3	16 19.7	11 54.8	26 06.2	3 28.6	28 47.7	20 06.1	8 32.0	13 10.5
28 F	10 25 34	4 52 37	9♒38 42	17 01 00	1 09.9	1♎02.2	15 57.5	12 33.1	25 59.9	3 41.7	28 50.2	20 04.6	8 30.3	13 09.7
29 Sa	10 29 31	5 50 33	24 27 40	1♓57 43	1 07.0	2 14.2	15 37.5	13 11.4	25 53.9	3 54.7	28 52.7	20 03.1	8 28.7	13 09.0
30 Su	10 33 27	6 48 30	9♓30 03	17 03 30	1D 05.3	3 24.2	15 19.8	13 49.7	25 48.2	4 07.8	28 55.4	20 01.5	8 27.0	13 08.2
31 M	10 37 24	7 46 29	24 36 56	2♈09 12	1 04.8	4 32.1	15 04.5	14 27.9	25 42.9	4 20.8	28 58.1	19 59.9	8 25.4	13 07.5

Astro Data

	Dy Hr Mn
☽ 0N	7 14:44
☽ 0S	21 11:48
♀ R	25 9:30
♅ R	26 10:39
♄ D	2 5:54
♃□♄	3 10:37
☽ 0N	3 22:31
♃⚻♇	4 19:23
♄∠♇	13 22:18
☽ 0S	17 19:40
☿0S	25 22:04
☽ 0N	31 8:06

Planet Ingress

		Dy Hr Mn
☿	♋	8 18:53
♀	♍	18 22:39
☉	♌	23 3:32
☿	♌	23 12:15
♀	♌R	31 15:28
⚳	♑R	3 23:09
☿	♍	7 19:16
♂	♌	8 23:33
♃	♍	11 11:12
☉	♍	23 10:38
☿	♎	27 15:46

Last Aspect / ☽ Ingress

Dy Hr Mn				Dy Hr Mn
30 18:19	♃	△	♑	1 9:12
3 10:39	♄	✶	♒	3 12:22
5 12:33	♄	□	♓	5 14:24
7 14:37	♄	△	♈	7 16:39
9 13:48	♀	△	♉	9 19:51
11 21:53	♄	☍	♊	12 0:17
14 3:32	♀	✶	♋	14 6:15
16 11:25	♄	△	♌	16 14:16
18 21:42	♄	□	♍	19 0:48
21 10:08	♄	✶	♎	21 13:24
23 18:13	♃	✶	♏	24 2:08
26 9:16	♄	☌	♐	26 12:26
28 13:38	♃	△	♑	28 18:49
30 18:51	♄	✶	♒	30 21:41

Last Aspect / ☽ Ingress

Dy Hr Mn				Dy Hr Mn
1 22:04	♀	☍	♓	1 22:37
3 20:36	♄	△	♈	3 23:25
5 23:30	♃	△	♉	6 1:30
8 4:47	♂	✶	♊	8 5:41
10 11:46	♃	✶	♋	10 12:09
12 17:45	♄	△	♌	12 20:53
15 4:37	♄	□	♍	15 7:47
17 17:17	♄	✶	♎	17 20:24
20 2:58	☉	✶	♏	20 9:25
22 19:32	☉	□	♐	22 20:42
24 22:05	☿	□	♑	25 4:23
27 7:21	☿	△	♒	27 8:05
29 7:04	♄	□	♓	29 8:52
31 6:55	♄	△	♈	31 8:34

☽ Phases & Eclipses

Dy Hr Mn		
2 2:21	○	9♑55
8 20:25	☾	16♈22
16 1:25	●	23♋14
24 4:05	☽	0♏59
31 10:44	○	7♒56
7 2:04	☾	14♉17
14 14:55	●	21♌31
22 19:32	☽	29♏24
29 18:36	○	6♓06

Astro Data

1 July 2015
Julian Day # 42185
SVP 5♓02'34"
GC 27♐03.3 ⚴ 15♐31.2R
Eris 23♈23.0 ⚵ 0♍11.9
⚷ 21♓32.0R ⚶ 7♈33.2
☽ Mean ☊ 5♎19.5

1 August 2015
Julian Day # 42216
SVP 5♓02'29"
GC 27♐03.4 ⚴ 11♐39.8R
Eris 23♈24.0R ⚵ 11♍52.5
⚷ 20♓56.1R ⚶ 12♈58.5
☽ Mean ☊ 3♎41.0

LONGITUDE — September 2015

Day	Sid.Time	☉	0 hr ☽	Noon ☽	True ☊	☿	♀	♂	⚳	♃	♄	♅	♆	♇
1 Tu	10 41 20	8♍44 30	9♈39 15	17♈06 10	1♎05.3	5♎37.9	14♌51.6	15♌06.1	25♑37.9	4♍33.9	29♏00.9	19♈58.3	8♓23.7	13♑06.8
2 W	10 45 17	9 42 33	24 29 06	1♉47 24	1 06.5	6 41.3	14R41.1	15 44.3	25R33.3	4 46.9	29 03.8	19R56.6	8R22.1	13R06.1
3 Th	10 49 13	10 40 38	9♉00 35	16 08 15	1 07.9	7 42.4	14 33.0	16 22.4	25 29.1	4 59.9	29 06.8	19 54.9	8 20.5	13 05.5
4 F	10 53 10	11 38 45	23 10 14	0♊06 25	1R08.9	8 40.9	14 27.4	17 00.5	25 25.2	5 12.9	29 09.9	19 53.2	8 18.8	13 04.9
5 Sa	10 57 07	12 36 53	6♊56 50	13 41 38	1 09.2	9 36.7	14D24.2	17 38.7	25 21.6	5 26.0	29 13.0	19 51.5	8 17.2	13 04.3
6 Su	11 01 03	13 35 04	20 20 58	26 55 08	1 08.7	10 29.7	14 23.3	18 16.7	25 18.5	5 39.0	29 16.3	19 49.7	8 15.5	13 03.7
7 M	11 05 00	14 33 17	3♋24 24	9♋49 06	1 07.5	11 19.6	14 24.8	18 54.8	25 15.6	5 51.9	29 19.6	19 47.8	8 13.9	13 03.2
8 Tu	11 08 56	15 31 32	16 09 33	22 26 07	1 05.6	12 06.2	14 28.7	19 32.8	25 13.2	6 04.9	29 23.0	19 46.0	8 12.2	13 02.7
9 W	11 12 53	16 29 48	28 39 07	4♌48 53	1 03.5	12 49.4	14 34.8	20 10.8	25 11.1	6 17.9	29 26.5	19 44.1	8 10.6	13 02.2
10 Th	11 16 49	17 28 07	10♌55 45	17 00 00	1 01.3	13 28.8	14 43.1	20 48.8	25 09.4	6 30.8	29 30.1	19 42.1	8 09.0	13 01.8
11 F	11 20 46	18 26 28	23 01 57	29 01 52	0 59.6	14 04.2	14 53.5	21 26.7	25 08.0	6 43.7	29 33.7	19 40.2	8 07.4	13 01.3
12 Sa	11 24 42	19 24 50	5♍00 02	10♍56 42	0 58.3	14 35.3	15 06.1	22 04.7	25 07.0	6 56.6	29 37.5	19 38.2	8 05.8	13 00.9
13 Su	11 28 39	20 23 14	16 52 08	22 46 37	0D57.6	15 01.8	15 20.7	22 42.6	25 06.3	7 09.5	29 41.3	19 36.2	8 04.2	13 00.6
14 M	11 32 36	21 21 40	28 40 24	4♎33 47	0 57.5	15 23.3	15 37.3	23 20.4	25D06.0	7 22.4	29 45.2	19 34.1	8 02.6	13 00.2
15 Tu	11 36 32	22 20 08	10♎27 04	16 20 32	0 57.8	15 39.6	15 55.8	23 58.3	25 06.1	7 35.2	29 49.2	19 32.1	8 01.0	12 59.9
16 W	11 40 29	23 18 38	22 14 32	28 09 25	0 58.5	15 50.3	16 16.2	24 36.1	25 06.5	7 48.1	29 53.3	19 30.0	7 59.4	12 59.6
17 Th	11 44 25	24 17 09	4♏05 35	10♏03 25	0 59.2	15R55.1	16 38.4	25 13.9	25 07.3	8 00.8	29 57.4	19 27.9	7 57.8	12 59.4
18 F	11 48 22	25 15 43	16 03 21	22 05 51	0 59.9	15 53.5	17 02.3	25 51.6	25 08.5	8 13.6	0♐01.6	19 25.7	7 56.2	12 59.2
19 Sa	11 52 18	26 14 18	28 11 23	4♐20 26	1 00.4	15 45.3	17 27.9	26 29.4	25 10.0	8 26.3	0 05.9	19 23.5	7 54.7	12 59.0
20 Su	11 56 15	27 12 54	10♐33 30	16 51 04	1R00.7	15 30.3	17 55.2	27 07.1	25 11.8	8 39.1	0 10.3	19 21.4	7 53.2	12 58.8
21 M	12 00 11	28 11 32	23 13 38	29 41 38	1 00.7	15 08.2	18 24.0	27 44.7	25 14.0	8 51.7	0 14.7	19 19.1	7 51.6	12 58.7
22 Tu	12 04 08	29 10 12	6♑15 31	12♑55 36	1 00.7	14 39.0	18 54.3	28 22.4	25 16.5	9 04.4	0 19.2	19 16.9	7 50.1	12 58.6
23 W	12 08 05	0♎08 54	19 42 10	26 35 24	1D00.6	14 02.6	19 26.2	29 00.0	25 19.4	9 17.0	0 23.8	19 14.7	7 48.6	12 58.5
24 Th	12 12 01	1 07 37	3♒35 22	10♒41 57	1 00.6	13 19.4	19 59.4	29 37.6	25 22.7	9 29.6	0 28.5	19 12.4	7 47.1	12D58.5
25 F	12 15 58	2 06 22	17 54 55	25 13 50	1 00.6	12 29.7	20 34.0	0♍15.2	25 26.2	9 42.1	0 33.2	19 10.1	7 45.7	12 58.5
26 Sa	12 19 54	3 05 09	2♓38 08	10♓07 01	1 00.8	11 34.1	21 09.9	0 52.7	25 30.1	9 54.6	0 38.0	19 07.8	7 44.2	12 58.5
27 Su	12 23 51	4 03 58	17 39 36	25 14 47	1R00.9	10 33.5	21 47.1	1 30.2	25 34.3	10 07.1	0 42.8	19 05.5	7 42.8	12 58.6
28 M	12 27 47	5 02 48	2♈51 27	10♈28 21	1 00.8	9 29.1	22 25.5	2 07.7	25 38.9	10 19.5	0 47.8	19 03.2	7 41.3	12 58.6
29 Tu	12 31 44	6 01 41	18 04 16	25 38 00	1 00.6	8 22.3	23 05.2	2 45.1	25 43.7	10 31.9	0 52.8	19 00.8	7 39.9	12 58.8
30 W	12 35 40	7 00 35	3♉08 26	10♉34 34	1 00.0	7 14.6	23 45.9	3 22.6	25 48.9	10 44.2	0 57.8	18 58.5	7 38.5	12 58.9

LONGITUDE — October 2015

Day	Sid.Time	☉	0 hr ☽	Noon ☽	True ☊	☿	♀	♂	⚳	♃	♄	♅	♆	♇
1 Th	12 39 37	7♎59 32	17♉55 33	25♉10 42	0♎59.3	6♎07.7	24♌27.8	4♍00.0	25♑54.4	10♍56.5	1♐03.0	18♈56.1	7♓37.2	12♑59.1
2 F	12 43 33	8 58 31	2♊19 30	9♊21 39	0R58.5	5R03.4	25 10.8	4 37.4	26 00.2	11 08.8	1 08.1	18R53.7	7R35.8	12 59.3
3 Sa	12 47 30	9 57 33	16 16 59	23 05 29	0 57.8	4 03.6	25 54.7	5 14.7	26 06.4	11 21.0	1 13.4	18 51.3	7 34.5	12 59.5
4 Su	12 51 27	10 56 37	29 47 18	6♋22 41	0D57.4	3 09.8	26 39.7	5 52.1	26 12.8	11 33.2	1 18.7	18 48.9	7 33.2	12 59.8
5 M	12 55 23	11 55 43	12♋51 58	19 15 34	0 57.5	2 23.5	27 25.6	6 29.4	26 19.5	11 45.3	1 24.1	18 46.5	7 31.9	13 00.1
6 Tu	12 59 20	12 54 52	25 33 57	1♌47 36	0 58.0	1 46.0	28 12.5	7 06.7	26 26.6	11 57.4	1 29.5	18 44.1	7 30.6	13 00.4
7 W	13 03 16	13 54 02	7♌57 04	14 02 51	0 59.0	1 18.2	29 00.2	7 43.9	26 33.9	12 09.4	1 35.0	18 41.7	7 29.3	13 00.8
8 Th	13 07 13	14 53 15	20 05 29	26 05 27	1 00.3	1 00.8	29 48.7	8 21.2	26 41.5	12 21.4	1 40.6	18 39.2	7 28.1	13 01.1
9 F	13 11 09	15 52 31	2♍03 15	7♍59 21	1 01.6	0D54.1	0♍38.1	8 58.4	26 49.5	12 33.3	1 46.2	18 36.8	7 26.9	13 01.6
10 Sa	13 15 06	16 51 48	13 54 10	19 48 07	1R02.6	0 58.1	1 28.3	9 35.6	26 57.7	12 45.1	1 51.8	18 34.4	7 25.7	13 02.0
11 Su	13 19 02	17 51 08	25 41 35	1♎34 54	1 02.9	1 12.7	2 19.2	10 12.7	27 06.2	12 56.9	1 57.6	18 31.9	7 24.5	13 02.5
12 M	13 22 59	18 50 29	7♎28 24	13 22 22	1 02.4	1 37.5	3 10.9	10 49.8	27 14.9	13 08.7	2 03.3	18 29.5	7 23.4	13 03.0
13 Tu	13 26 56	19 49 53	19 17 05	25 12 49	1 01.0	2 12.0	4 03.3	11 26.9	27 24.0	13 20.3	2 09.2	18 27.0	7 22.3	13 03.5
14 W	13 30 52	20 49 19	1♏09 49	7♏08 19	0 58.5	2 55.4	4 56.3	12 04.0	27 33.3	13 31.9	2 15.0	18 24.6	7 21.2	13 04.1
15 Th	13 34 49	21 48 47	13 08 34	19 10 47	0 55.4	3 47.1	5 50.0	12 41.0	27 42.9	13 43.5	2 21.0	18 22.2	7 20.1	13 04.7
16 F	13 38 45	22 48 16	25 15 14	1♐22 10	0 51.8	4 46.3	6 44.4	13 18.0	27 52.8	13 55.0	2 27.0	18 19.7	7 19.1	13 05.3
17 Sa	13 42 42	23 47 48	7♐31 51	13 44 34	0 48.2	5 52.1	7 39.3	13 55.0	28 02.9	14 06.4	2 33.0	18 17.3	7 18.0	13 06.0
18 Su	13 46 38	24 47 21	20 00 37	26 20 18	0 45.1	7 03.8	8 34.9	14 31.9	28 13.3	14 17.7	2 39.1	18 14.9	7 17.0	13 06.7
19 M	13 50 35	25 46 57	2♑43 56	9♑11 51	0 42.9	8 20.6	9 31.0	15 08.9	28 24.0	14 29.0	2 45.2	18 12.5	7 16.1	13 07.4
20 Tu	13 54 31	26 46 34	15 44 22	22 21 47	0D41.9	9 41.8	10 27.6	15 45.7	28 34.9	14 40.2	2 51.4	18 10.1	7 15.1	13 08.1
21 W	13 58 28	27 46 12	29 04 22	5♒52 21	0 42.1	11 06.7	11 24.9	16 22.6	28 46.0	14 51.4	2 57.6	18 07.7	7 14.2	13 08.9
22 Th	14 02 25	28 45 53	12♒45 56	19 45 12	0 43.2	12 34.9	12 22.6	16 59.4	28 57.4	15 02.4	3 03.8	18 05.3	7 13.3	13 09.7
23 F	14 06 21	29 45 34	26 50 07	4♓00 36	0 44.7	14 05.6	13 20.8	17 36.2	29 09.1	15 13.4	3 10.1	18 02.9	7 12.5	13 10.6
24 Sa	14 10 18	0♏45 18	11♓16 22	18 37 01	0R46.0	15 38.5	14 19.5	18 13.0	29 20.9	15 24.3	3 16.5	18 00.5	7 11.7	13 11.4
25 Su	14 14 14	1 45 04	26 01 58	3♈30 30	0 46.3	17 13.2	15 18.7	18 49.7	29 33.0	15 35.1	3 22.9	17 58.2	7 10.9	13 12.3
26 M	14 18 11	2 44 51	11♈01 43	18 34 38	0 45.3	18 49.3	16 18.4	19 26.4	29 45.4	15 45.8	3 29.3	17 55.9	7 10.1	13 13.2
27 Tu	14 22 07	3 44 40	26 08 07	3♉41 00	0 42.6	20 26.4	17 18.5	20 03.0	29 57.9	15 56.5	3 35.7	17 53.5	7 09.4	13 14.2
28 W	14 26 04	4 44 31	11♉12 05	18 40 13	0 38.4	22 04.4	18 19.0	20 39.7	0♒10.7	16 07.1	3 42.2	17 51.2	7 08.7	13 15.2
29 Th	14 30 00	5 44 24	26 04 19	3♊23 25	0 33.2	23 43.0	19 20.0	21 16.3	0 23.7	16 17.6	3 48.8	17 48.9	7 08.0	13 16.2
30 F	14 33 57	6 44 19	10♊36 45	17 43 39	0 27.6	25 22.1	20 21.4	21 52.9	0 36.9	16 28.0	3 55.3	17 46.7	7 07.3	13 17.2
31 Sa	14 37 53	7 44 17	24 43 44	1♋36 42	0 22.5	27 01.3	21 23.2	22 29.4	0 50.3	16 38.3	4 02.0	17 44.4	7 06.7	13 18.3

Astro Data	Dy Hr Mn
♃⚻♅	3 3:53
♀ D	6 8:30
☽ 0S	14 2:10
⚳ D	14 19:15
♃☍♆	17 6:55
☿ R	17 18:11
☉ 0S	23 8:22
♇ D	25 6:59
☽ 0N	27 19:04
☿ 0N	9 10:24
☿ D	9 14:59
☽ 0S	11 8:12
♃△♇	11 23:52
☿ 0S	15 12:32
♄⚻♅	22 16:00

Planet Ingress	Dy Hr Mn
♄ ♐	18 2:50
☉ ♎	23 8:22
♂ ♍	25 2:19
♀ ♍	8 17:30
☉ ♏	23 17:48
⚳ ♒	27 15:57
☽ 0N	25 6:03

Last Aspect Dy Hr Mn		☽ Ingress	Dy Hr Mn
1 16:39	♅ ☌	♉	2 9:03
4 10:21	♄ ☍	♊	4 11:49
5 23:05	♅ ⚹	♋	6 17:41
9 1:29	♄ △	♌	9 2:37
11 13:04	♄ □	♍	11 13:57
14 2:09	♄ ⚹	♎	14 2:42
16 4:23	♂ ⚹	♏	16 15:44
18 19:50	♂ □	♐	19 3:33
21 9:00	☉ □	♑	21 12:34
22 23:14	♅ □	♒	23 17:52
25 4:03	♀ ☍	♓	25 19:45
26 16:33	♇ ⚹	♈	27 19:30
29 7:46	♀ △	♉	29 18:58

Last Aspect Dy Hr Mn		☽ Ingress	Dy Hr Mn
1 10:45	♀ □	♊	1 20:05
3 17:20	♀ ⚹	♋	4 0:23
5 11:05	♅ □	♌	6 8:32
7 21:11	♅ △	♍	8 19:52
9 22:13	♇ △	♎	11 8:47
13 0:07	☉ ☌	♏	13 21:39
15 0:59	♃ ⚹	♐	16 9:19
18 8:50	☉ ⚹	♑	18 18:53
20 20:32	☉ □	♒	21 1:39
23 4:23	☉ △	♓	23 5:19
24 11:19	♂ ☍	♈	25 6:23
26 12:26	☿ ☍	♉	27 6:08
28 15:21	♂ △	♊	29 6:25
31 2:53	☿ △	♋	31 9:10

☽ Phases & Eclipses Dy Hr Mn	
5 9:55	☾ 12♊32
13 6:42	● 20♍10
13 6:55:19	● P 0.788
21 9:00	☽ 28♐04
28 2:52	○ 4♈40
28 2:48	● T 1.276
4 21:07	☾ 11♋19
13 0:07	● 19♎20
20 20:32	☽ 27♑08
27 12:06	○ 3♉45

Astro Data

1 September 2015
Julian Day # 42247
SVP 5♓02'26"
GC 27♐03.5 ⚴ 14♐13.2
Eris 23♈15.4R ⚵ 23♍51.1
⚷ 19♓42.5R ⚶ 11♈50.0R
☽ Mean ☊ 2♎02.5

1 October 2015
Julian Day # 42277
SVP 5♓02'24"
GC 27♐03.6 ⚴ 20♐54.6
Eris 23♈00.2R ⚵ 5♎23.3
⚷ 18♓20.6R ⚶ 5♈04.5R
☽ Mean ☊ 0♎27.2

November 2015 LONGITUDE

Day	Sid.Time	☉	0 hr ☽	Noon ☽	True☊	☿	♀	♂	⚳	♃	♄	♅	♆	♇
1 Su	14 41 50	8♏44 16	8♋22 32	15♋01 19	0♎18.5	28♎40.8	22♍25.4	23♍05.9	1♒04.0	16♍48.5	4♐08.6	17♈42.2	7♓06.1	13♑19.4
2 M	14 45 47	9 44 18	21 33 17	27 58 49	0R16.0	0♏20.2	23 27.9	23 42.4	1 17.8	16 58.7	4 15.3	17R40.0	7R05.6	13 20.5
3 Tu	14 49 43	10 44 22	4♌18 23	10♌32 30	0D15.2	1 59.6	24 30.8	24 18.9	1 31.9	17 08.7	4 22.0	17 37.8	7 05.1	13 21.6
4 W	14 53 40	11 44 27	16 41 47	22 46 50	0 15.8	3 38.9	25 34.1	24 55.3	1 46.1	17 18.6	4 28.7	17 35.6	7 04.6	13 22.8
5 Th	14 57 36	12 44 35	28 48 19	4♍46 52	0 17.3	5 17.9	26 37.7	25 31.7	2 00.5	17 28.5	4 35.5	17 33.5	7 04.1	13 24.0
6 F	15 01 33	13 44 45	10♍43 08	16 37 44	0 18.8	6 56.8	27 41.6	26 08.0	2 15.2	17 38.2	4 42.2	17 31.3	7 03.7	13 25.2
7 Sa	15 05 29	14 44 57	22 31 16	28 24 17	0R19.7	8 35.4	28 45.9	26 44.4	2 30.0	17 47.9	4 49.1	17 29.3	7 03.3	13 26.4
8 Su	15 09 26	15 45 11	4♎17 20	10♎10 52	0 19.1	10 13.7	29 50.5	27 20.6	2 45.1	17 57.4	4 55.9	17 27.2	7 02.9	13 27.7
9 M	15 13 22	16 45 27	16 05 21	22 01 10	0 16.5	11 51.7	0♎55.3	27 56.9	3 00.3	18 06.9	5 02.8	17 25.1	7 02.6	13 29.0
10 Tu	15 17 19	17 45 45	27 58 38	3♏58 03	0 11.6	13 29.3	2 00.5	28 33.1	3 15.7	18 16.2	5 09.6	17 23.1	7 02.3	13 30.3
11 W	15 21 16	18 46 04	9♏59 40	16 03 41	0 04.6	15 06.7	3 05.9	29 09.3	3 31.3	18 25.4	5 16.6	17 21.1	7 02.0	13 31.7
12 Th	15 25 12	19 46 26	22 10 15	28 19 29	29♍55.8	16 43.7	4 11.6	29 45.4	3 47.0	18 34.5	5 23.5	17 19.2	7 01.8	13 33.0
13 F	15 29 09	20 46 49	4♐31 28	10♐46 17	29 46.0	18 20.5	5 17.6	0♎21.5	4 02.9	18 43.5	5 30.4	17 17.3	7 01.6	13 34.4
14 Sa	15 33 05	21 47 13	17 03 58	23 24 34	29 36.2	19 56.9	6 23.8	0 57.6	4 19.1	18 52.4	5 37.4	17 15.4	7 01.4	13 35.8
15 Su	15 37 02	22 47 40	29 48 08	6♑14 43	29 27.3	21 33.0	7 30.3	1 33.6	4 35.3	19 01.2	5 44.4	17 13.5	7 01.3	13 37.3
16 M	15 40 58	23 48 07	12♑44 22	19 17 11	29 20.2	23 08.8	8 37.0	2 09.6	4 51.8	19 09.8	5 51.4	17 11.7	7 01.2	13 38.8
17 Tu	15 44 55	24 48 36	25 53 15	2♒32 42	29 15.5	24 44.4	9 43.9	2 45.5	5 08.4	19 18.3	5 58.4	17 09.9	7 01.2	13 40.2
18 W	15 48 51	25 49 06	9♒15 40	16 02 16	29D13.1	26 19.7	10 51.1	3 21.4	5 25.2	19 26.8	6 05.5	17 08.2	7D01.1	13 41.7
19 Th	15 52 48	26 49 38	22 52 39	29 46 56	29 12.7	27 54.7	11 58.5	3 57.2	5 42.1	19 35.0	6 12.5	17 06.4	7 01.2	13 43.3
20 F	15 56 45	27 50 10	6♓45 11	13♓47 28	29 13.3	29 29.5	13 06.1	4 33.0	5 59.2	19 43.2	6 19.6	17 04.8	7 01.2	13 44.8
21 Sa	16 00 41	28 50 44	20 53 43	28 03 48	29R13.9	1♐04.0	14 13.9	5 08.8	6 16.4	19 51.2	6 26.6	17 03.1	7 01.3	13 46.4
22 Su	16 04 38	29 51 19	5♈17 30	12♈34 24	29 13.2	2 38.4	15 21.9	5 44.5	6 33.8	19 59.1	6 33.7	17 01.5	7 01.4	13 48.0
23 M	16 08 34	0♐51 55	19 54 03	27 15 47	29 10.3	4 12.6	16 30.1	6 20.2	6 51.3	20 06.9	6 40.8	16 59.9	7 01.5	13 49.6
24 Tu	16 12 31	1 52 32	4♉38 50	12♉02 20	29 04.6	5 46.6	17 38.5	6 55.8	7 09.0	20 14.5	6 47.9	16 58.4	7 01.7	13 51.2
25 W	16 16 27	2 53 11	19 25 19	26 46 47	28 56.4	7 20.4	18 47.1	7 31.4	7 26.8	20 22.0	6 55.0	16 56.9	7 01.9	13 52.9
26 Th	16 20 24	3 53 51	4♊05 43	11♊21 09	28 46.3	8 54.1	19 55.9	8 07.0	7 44.8	20 29.4	7 02.1	16 55.5	7 02.2	13 54.6
27 F	16 24 20	4 54 33	18 32 12	25 38 04	28 35.3	10 27.7	21 04.9	8 42.5	8 02.9	20 36.7	7 09.2	16 54.1	7 02.5	13 56.3
28 Sa	16 28 17	5 55 16	2♋38 09	9♋31 58	28 24.8	12 01.1	22 14.0	9 17.9	8 21.1	20 43.8	7 16.3	16 52.7	7 02.8	13 58.0
29 Su	16 32 14	6 56 00	16 19 15	22 59 51	28 15.7	13 34.5	23 23.4	9 53.4	8 39.5	20 50.7	7 23.5	16 51.4	7 03.2	13 59.7
30 M	16 36 10	7 56 46	29 33 51	6♌01 25	28 08.9	15 07.8	24 32.8	10 28.7	8 58.0	20 57.5	7 30.6	16 50.1	7 03.5	14 01.4

December 2015 LONGITUDE

Day	Sid.Time	☉	0 hr ☽	Noon ☽	True☊	☿	♀	♂	⚳	♃	♄	♅	♆	♇
1 Tu	16 40 07	8♐57 33	12♌22 53	18♌38 42	28♍04.6	16♐41.0	25♎42.5	11♎04.1	9♒16.6	21♍04.2	7♐37.7	16♈48.9	7♓04.0	14♑03.2
2 W	16 44 03	9 58 22	24 49 23	0♍55 33	28D02.6	18 14.1	26 52.3	11 39.3	9 35.3	21 10.7	7 44.8	16R47.7	7 04.4	14 05.0
3 Th	16 48 00	10 59 12	6♍57 49	12 56 53	28 02.2	19 47.1	28 02.3	12 14.6	9 54.2	21 17.1	7 51.9	16 46.5	7 04.9	14 06.8
4 F	16 51 56	12 00 04	18 53 27	24 48 13	28R02.5	21 20.1	29 12.4	12 49.8	10 13.2	21 23.3	7 59.0	16 45.4	7 05.4	14 08.6
5 Sa	16 55 53	13 00 57	0♎43 51	6♎35 08	28 02.2	22 53.0	0♏22.6	13 24.9	10 32.3	21 29.4	8 06.1	16 44.4	7 06.0	14 10.4
6 Su	16 59 49	14 01 51	12 28 38	18 23 00	28 00.3	24 25.8	1 33.0	14 00.0	10 51.6	21 35.3	8 13.2	16 43.4	7 06.6	14 12.2
7 M	17 03 46	15 02 46	24 18 48	0♏16 34	27 56.1	25 58.6	2 43.6	14 35.0	11 10.9	21 41.1	8 20.3	16 42.4	7 07.2	14 14.1
8 Tu	17 07 43	16 03 43	6♏16 46	12 19 48	27 48.9	27 31.3	3 54.2	15 10.0	11 30.4	21 46.7	8 27.4	16 41.5	7 07.9	14 16.0
9 W	17 11 39	17 04 41	18 26 00	24 35 37	27 38.9	29 03.8	5 05.0	15 44.9	11 50.0	21 52.1	8 34.5	16 40.6	7 08.6	14 17.9
10 Th	17 15 36	18 05 40	0♐48 51	7♐05 47	27 26.6	0♑36.2	6 15.9	16 19.7	12 09.7	21 57.4	8 41.5	16 39.8	7 09.3	14 19.8
11 F	17 19 32	19 06 40	13 26 27	19 50 50	27 12.8	2 08.5	7 26.9	16 54.5	12 29.5	22 02.6	8 48.6	16 39.0	7 10.1	14 21.7
12 Sa	17 23 29	20 07 41	26 18 49	2♑50 14	26 59.0	3 40.5	8 38.1	17 29.3	12 49.4	22 07.5	8 55.6	16 38.3	7 10.9	14 23.6
13 Su	17 27 25	21 08 42	9♑24 56	16 02 40	26 46.2	5 12.2	9 49.3	18 03.9	13 09.4	22 12.3	9 02.7	16 37.6	7 11.7	14 25.5
14 M	17 31 22	22 09 44	22 43 13	29 26 23	26 35.7	6 43.7	11 00.7	18 38.6	13 29.5	22 16.9	9 09.7	16 37.0	7 12.6	14 27.5
15 Tu	17 35 19	23 10 47	6♒11 58	12♒59 45	26 28.2	8 14.7	12 12.1	19 13.1	13 49.8	22 21.4	9 16.7	16 36.4	7 13.5	14 29.4
16 W	17 39 15	24 11 50	19 49 39	26 41 32	26 23.7	9 45.2	13 23.7	19 47.6	14 10.1	22 25.7	9 23.6	16 35.9	7 14.4	14 31.4
17 Th	17 43 12	25 12 54	3♓35 20	10♓31 02	26 21.8	11 15.1	14 35.3	20 22.0	14 30.5	22 29.8	9 30.6	16 35.4	7 15.4	14 33.4
18 F	17 47 08	26 13 58	17 28 37	24 28 04	26 21.5	12 44.3	15 47.0	20 56.4	14 51.0	22 33.7	9 37.5	16 35.0	7 16.4	14 35.4
19 Sa	17 51 05	27 15 02	1♈29 23	8♈32 32	26 21.3	14 12.6	16 58.8	21 30.7	15 11.6	22 37.5	9 44.4	16 34.7	7 17.4	14 37.4
20 Su	17 55 01	28 16 07	15 37 25	22 43 54	26 20.0	15 39.8	18 10.8	22 04.9	15 32.3	22 41.1	9 51.3	16 34.3	7 18.4	14 39.4
21 M	17 58 58	29 17 12	29 51 46	7♉00 42	26 16.3	17 05.7	19 22.7	22 39.0	15 53.1	22 44.5	9 58.2	16 34.1	7 19.5	14 41.4
22 Tu	18 02 54	0♑18 17	14♉10 18	21 20 05	26 09.6	18 30.1	20 34.8	23 13.1	16 13.9	22 47.7	10 05.0	16 33.8	7 20.6	14 43.4
23 W	18 06 51	1 19 22	28 29 28	5♊37 48	26 00.1	19 52.6	21 47.0	23 47.1	16 34.9	22 50.7	10 11.8	16 33.7	7 21.8	14 45.4
24 Th	18 10 48	2 20 28	12♊44 25	19 48 35	25 48.4	21 13.0	22 59.2	24 21.1	16 55.9	22 53.6	10 18.6	16 33.6	7 23.0	14 47.5
25 F	18 14 44	3 21 34	26 49 38	3♋46 54	25 35.5	22 30.9	24 11.5	24 55.0	17 17.0	22 56.3	10 25.4	16D33.5	7 24.2	14 49.5
26 Sa	18 18 41	4 22 41	10♋39 49	17 27 54	25 22.9	23 45.7	25 23.9	25 28.8	17 38.2	22 58.8	10 32.1	16 33.5	7 25.4	14 51.6
27 Su	18 22 37	5 23 48	24 10 47	0♌48 13	25 11.8	24 57.0	26 36.4	26 02.5	17 59.5	23 01.1	10 38.8	16 33.5	7 26.7	14 53.6
28 M	18 26 34	6 24 55	7♌20 06	13 46 28	25 03.1	26 04.2	27 49.0	26 36.2	18 20.9	23 03.3	10 45.5	16 33.6	7 28.0	14 55.7
29 Tu	18 30 30	7 26 03	20 07 27	26 23 19	24 57.1	27 06.6	29 01.6	27 09.7	18 42.3	23 05.2	10 52.1	16 33.8	7 29.3	14 57.7
30 W	18 34 27	8 27 11	2♍34 26	8♍41 15	24 53.9	28 03.6	0♐14.3	27 43.2	19 03.8	23 07.0	10 58.7	16 34.0	7 30.7	14 59.8
31 Th	18 38 23	9 28 19	14 44 18	20 44 10	24D52.8	28 54.2	1 27.0	28 16.7	19 25.4	23 08.6	11 05.3	16 34.2	7 32.0	15 01.9

Astro Data	Dy Hr Mn
♃⊼♅	5 22:03
☽0S	7 15:05
♀0S	11 10:40
♂0S	18 9:59
♆D	18 16:32
☽0N	21 15:33
♄□♆	26 12:16
☽0S	4 23:36
☽0N	18 23:03
♅D	26 3:54

Planet Ingress		Dy Hr Mn
☿	♏	2 7:07
♀	♎	8 15:32
☊	♍R	12 0:58
♂	♎	12 21:42
☿	♐	20 19:44
☉	♐	22 15:26
♀	♏	5 4:16
☿	♑	10 2:35
☉	♑	22 4:49
♀	♐	30 7:18

Last Aspect Dy Hr Mn		☽ Ingress Dy Hr Mn
2 3:36	♂ ⚹	♌ 2 15:49
4 1:47	♅ △	♍ 5 2:24
7 12:48	♀ ☌	♎ 7 15:15
9 2:43	♅ ☍	♏ 10 4:04
12 14:55	♂ ⚹	♐ 12 15:15
14 3:20	♃ □	♑ 15 0:22
16 20:54	☉ ⚹	♒ 17 7:25
19 8:20	☿ □	♓ 19 12:23
21 13:24	☉ △	♈ 21 15:13
22 19:17	♅ ☌	♉ 23 16:27
25 1:27	♃ △	♊ 25 17:16
27 3:36	♀ △	♋ 27 19:28
29 12:47	♀ □	♌ 30 0:48

Last Aspect Dy Hr Mn		☽ Ingress Dy Hr Mn
2 3:10	♀ ⚹	♍ 2 10:10
4 5:00	♃ ☌	♎ 4 22:35
7 2:04	☿ ⚹	♏ 7 11:27
9 6:40	♃ ⚹	♐ 9 22:26
11 16:07	♃ □	♑ 12 6:48
13 23:08	♃ △	♒ 14 13:00
16 7:18	☉ ⚹	♓ 16 17:46
18 15:15	☉ □	♈ 18 21:27
20 22:02	☉ △	♉ 21 0:14
22 14:27	♃ △	♊ 23 2:32
24 20:05	♂ △	♋ 25 5:28
27 3:37	♀ △	♌ 27 10:32
29 17:39	♀ □	♍ 29 18:59

☽ Phases & Eclipses Dy Hr Mn	
3 12:25	☾ 10♌45
11 17:48	● 19♏01
19 6:28	☽ 26♒36
25 22:45	○ 3♊20
3 7:41	☾ 10♍48
11 10:30	● 19♐03
18 15:15	☽ 26♓22
25 11:13	○ 3♋20

Astro Data

1 November 2015
Julian Day # 42308
SVP 5♓02'21"
GC 27♐03.6 ⚴ 0♑20.6
Eris 22♈41.9R ⚵ 16♎54.1
⚷ 17♓16.2R ⚶ 29♓09.1R
☽ Mean ☊ 28♍48.7

1 December 2015
Julian Day # 42338
SVP 5♓02'16"
GC 27♐03.7 ⚴ 10♑47.0
Eris 22♈26.8R ⚵ 27♎12.5
⚷ 16♓56.6 ⚶ 29♓42.5
☽ Mean ☊ 27♍13.3

LONGITUDE — January 2016

Day	Sid.Time	☉	0 hr ☽	Noon ☽	True☊	☿	♀	♂	⚳	♃	♄	♅	♆	♇
1 F	18 42 20	10♑29 28	26♍41 29	2♎36 55	24♍52.9	29♑37.8	2♐39.8	28♎50.0	19♒47.0	23♍09.9	11♐11.8	16♈34.5	7♓33.5	15♑03.9
2 Sa	18 46 17	11 30 37	8♎31 11	14 24 58	24R 53.0	0♒13.3	3 52.7	29 23.3	20 08.7	23 11.1	11 18.3	16 34.9	7 34.9	15 06.0
3 Su	18 50 13	12 31 47	20 18 58	26 13 54	24 52.0	0 39.8	5 05.7	29 56.5	20 30.5	23 12.1	11 24.8	16 35.3	7 36.4	15 08.1
4 M	18 54 10	13 32 56	2♏10 24	8♏09 08	24 49.1	0 56.5	6 18.7	0♏29.6	20 52.4	23 13.0	11 31.2	16 35.7	7 37.9	15 10.2
5 Tu	18 58 06	14 34 07	14 10 42	20 15 38	24 43.6	1R 02.6	7 31.7	1 02.6	21 14.3	23 13.6	11 37.6	16 36.3	7 39.4	15 12.2
6 W	19 02 03	15 35 17	26 24 24	2♐37 25	24 35.5	0 57.4	8 44.8	1 35.5	21 36.3	23 14.0	11 43.9	16 36.8	7 40.9	15 14.3
7 Th	19 05 59	16 36 27	8♐55 00	15 17 22	24 25.2	0 40.4	9 58.0	2 08.3	21 58.3	23R 14.2	11 50.2	16 37.4	7 42.5	15 16.4
8 F	19 09 56	17 37 38	21 44 38	28 16 48	24 13.4	0 11.6	11 11.2	2 41.0	22 20.5	23 14.3	11 56.4	16 38.1	7 44.1	15 18.5
9 Sa	19 13 52	18 38 48	4♑53 48	11♑35 23	24 01.3	29♑31.2	12 24.4	3 13.7	22 42.6	23 14.1	12 02.6	16 38.8	7 45.7	15 20.6
10 Su	19 17 49	19 39 58	18 21 19	25 11 10	23 50.2	28 39.9	13 37.7	3 46.2	23 04.9	23 13.8	12 08.8	16 39.6	7 47.4	15 22.6
11 M	19 21 46	20 41 08	2♒04 33	9♒00 56	23 41.0	27 38.9	14 51.1	4 18.6	23 27.2	23 13.2	12 14.9	16 40.4	7 49.0	15 24.7
12 Tu	19 25 42	21 42 18	15 59 50	23 00 46	23 34.6	26 30.0	16 04.4	4 50.9	23 49.5	23 12.5	12 20.9	16 41.3	7 50.7	15 26.8
13 W	19 29 39	22 43 27	0♓03 12	7♓06 44	23 30.9	25 15.2	17 17.9	5 23.2	24 11.9	23 11.5	12 26.9	16 42.2	7 52.5	15 28.8
14 Th	19 33 35	23 44 35	14 10 56	21 15 29	23D 29.8	23 56.9	18 31.3	5 55.3	24 34.4	23 10.4	12 32.9	16 43.2	7 54.2	15 30.9
15 F	19 37 32	24 45 43	28 20 05	5♈24 30	23 30.1	22 37.5	19 44.8	6 27.3	24 56.9	23 09.1	12 38.8	16 44.2	7 56.0	15 33.0
16 Sa	19 41 28	25 46 50	12♈28 34	19 32 08	23R 30.9	21 19.7	20 58.3	6 59.1	25 19.4	23 07.6	12 44.6	16 45.3	7 57.7	15 35.0
17 Su	19 45 25	26 47 56	26 35 06	3♉37 19	23 30.8	20 05.6	22 11.8	7 30.9	25 42.0	23 05.9	12 50.4	16 46.4	7 59.6	15 37.1
18 M	19 49 21	27 49 02	10♉38 41	17 39 05	23 28.9	18 57.2	23 25.4	8 02.6	26 04.7	23 04.0	12 56.2	16 47.6	8 01.4	15 39.1
19 Tu	19 53 18	28 50 06	24 38 21	1♊36 16	23 24.7	17 56.0	24 39.0	8 34.1	26 27.4	23 01.9	13 01.9	16 48.8	8 03.2	15 41.2
20 W	19 57 15	29 51 10	8♊32 38	15 27 09	23 18.2	17 03.1	25 52.7	9 05.5	26 50.1	22 59.6	13 07.5	16 50.1	8 05.1	15 43.2
21 Th	20 01 11	0♒52 13	22 19 32	29 09 29	23 09.9	16 19.2	27 06.3	9 36.9	27 12.9	22 57.2	13 13.0	16 51.4	8 07.0	15 45.2
22 F	20 05 08	1 53 16	5♋56 38	12♋40 41	23 00.6	15 44.5	28 20.0	10 08.0	27 35.8	22 54.5	13 18.5	16 52.7	8 08.9	15 47.2
23 Sa	20 09 04	2 54 17	19 21 20	25 58 17	22 51.4	15 19.2	29 33.7	10 39.1	27 58.6	22 51.7	13 24.0	16 54.2	8 10.8	15 49.2
24 Su	20 13 01	3 55 18	2♌31 19	9♌00 17	22 43.3	15 02.9	0♑47.5	11 10.0	28 21.5	22 48.7	13 29.4	16 55.6	8 12.8	15 51.2
25 M	20 16 57	4 56 18	15 25 05	21 45 42	22 37.0	14D 55.4	2 01.3	11 40.9	28 44.5	22 45.5	13 34.7	16 57.1	8 14.8	15 53.2
26 Tu	20 20 54	5 57 17	28 02 12	4♍14 42	22 32.9	14 56.1	3 15.1	12 11.5	29 07.5	22 42.1	13 39.9	16 58.7	8 16.7	15 55.2
27 W	20 24 50	6 58 15	10♍23 26	16 28 42	22D 31.0	15 04.5	4 28.9	12 42.1	29 30.5	22 38.6	13 45.1	17 00.3	8 18.7	15 57.2
28 Th	20 28 47	7 59 13	22 30 51	28 30 20	22 30.9	15 20.0	5 42.8	13 12.5	29 53.5	22 34.8	13 50.2	17 01.9	8 20.7	15 59.1
29 F	20 32 44	9 00 10	4♎27 37	10♎23 14	22 32.1	15 42.0	6 56.7	13 42.8	0♓16.6	22 30.9	13 55.3	17 03.6	8 22.8	16 01.1
30 Sa	20 36 40	10 01 06	16 17 45	22 11 48	22 33.8	16 10.1	8 10.6	14 12.9	0 39.8	22 26.9	14 00.3	17 05.4	8 24.8	16 03.0
31 Su	20 40 37	11 02 02	28 06 01	4♏01 01	22R 35.1	16 43.6	9 24.5	14 42.9	1 02.9	22 22.6	14 05.2	17 07.1	8 26.9	16 05.0

LONGITUDE — February 2016

Day	Sid.Time	☉	0 hr ☽	Noon ☽	True☊	☿	♀	♂	⚳	♃	♄	♅	♆	♇
1 M	20 44 33	12♒02 57	9♏57 30	15♏56 06	22♍35.3	17♑22.2	10♑38.5	15♏12.7	1♓26.1	22♍18.2	14♐10.0	17♈09.0	8♓29.0	16♑06.9
2 Tu	20 48 30	13 03 51	21 57 29	28 02 14	22R 33.9	18 05.3	11 52.5	15 42.4	1 49.3	22R 13.6	14 14.8	17 10.8	8 31.1	16 08.8
3 W	20 52 26	14 04 44	4♐10 59	10♐24 15	22 30.8	18 52.5	13 06.5	16 11.9	2 12.6	22 08.9	14 19.5	17 12.8	8 33.2	16 10.7
4 Th	20 56 23	15 05 37	16 42 29	23 06 07	22 26.2	19 43.5	14 20.5	16 41.3	2 35.9	22 04.0	14 24.2	17 14.7	8 35.3	16 12.5
5 F	21 00 19	16 06 29	29 35 27	6♑10 38	22 20.4	20 37.9	15 34.5	17 10.5	2 59.2	21 58.9	14 28.7	17 16.7	8 37.4	16 14.4
6 Sa	21 04 16	17 07 19	12♑51 47	19 38 50	22 14.3	21 35.4	16 48.6	17 39.5	3 22.5	21 53.7	14 33.2	17 18.8	8 39.6	16 16.3
7 Su	21 08 13	18 08 09	26 31 35	3♒29 42	22 08.6	22 35.8	18 02.6	18 08.4	3 45.9	21 48.3	14 37.6	17 20.9	8 41.7	16 18.1
8 M	21 12 09	19 08 58	10♒32 46	17 40 11	22 03.9	23 38.8	19 16.7	18 37.0	4 09.3	21 42.8	14 41.9	17 23.0	8 43.9	16 19.9
9 Tu	21 16 06	20 09 45	24 51 17	2♓05 22	22 00.8	24 44.3	20 30.8	19 05.5	4 32.7	21 37.1	14 46.2	17 25.1	8 46.1	16 21.7
10 W	21 20 02	21 10 31	9♓21 37	16 39 15	21D 59.5	25 51.9	21 44.9	19 33.8	4 56.1	21 31.3	14 50.3	17 27.3	8 48.3	16 23.5
11 Th	21 23 59	22 11 15	23 57 30	1♈15 36	21 59.6	27 01.6	22 59.0	20 01.9	5 19.6	21 25.4	14 54.4	17 29.6	8 50.5	16 25.3
12 F	21 27 55	23 11 58	8♈32 52	15 48 41	22 00.8	28 13.2	24 13.1	20 29.8	5 43.1	21 19.3	14 58.4	17 31.9	8 52.7	16 27.0
13 Sa	21 31 52	24 12 39	23 02 32	0♉13 59	22 02.3	29 26.6	25 27.2	20 57.6	6 06.6	21 13.1	15 02.4	17 34.2	8 54.9	16 28.7
14 Su	21 35 48	25 13 19	7♉22 40	14 28 20	22R 03.6	0♒41.7	26 41.4	21 25.1	6 30.1	21 06.7	15 06.2	17 36.6	8 57.1	16 30.5
15 M	21 39 45	26 13 57	21 30 46	28 29 50	22 03.9	1 58.4	27 55.5	21 52.4	6 53.6	21 00.3	15 09.9	17 39.0	8 59.3	16 32.2
16 Tu	21 43 42	27 14 33	5♊25 28	12♊17 37	22 03.1	3 16.5	29 09.6	22 19.5	7 17.1	20 53.7	15 13.6	17 41.4	9 01.6	16 33.8
17 W	21 47 38	28 15 07	19 06 16	25 51 26	22 01.1	4 36.0	0♒23.8	22 46.4	7 40.7	20 47.1	15 17.2	17 43.9	9 03.8	16 35.5
18 Th	21 51 35	29 15 40	2♋33 07	9♋11 22	21 58.2	5 56.9	1 37.9	23 13.1	8 04.2	20 40.3	15 20.7	17 46.4	9 06.1	16 37.1
19 F	21 55 31	0♓16 11	15 46 12	22 17 38	21 54.8	7 19.0	2 52.1	23 39.5	8 27.8	20 33.4	15 24.1	17 48.9	9 08.3	16 38.8
20 Sa	21 59 28	1 16 40	28 45 44	5♌10 32	21 51.4	8 42.5	4 06.3	24 05.8	8 51.4	20 26.4	15 27.5	17 51.5	9 10.6	16 40.4
21 Su	22 03 24	2 17 08	11♌32 04	17 50 24	21 48.5	10 07.0	5 20.4	24 31.8	9 15.0	20 19.4	15 30.7	17 54.1	9 12.8	16 41.9
22 M	22 07 21	3 17 33	24 05 36	0♍17 47	21 46.3	11 32.8	6 34.6	24 57.6	9 38.6	20 12.2	15 33.8	17 56.7	9 15.1	16 43.5
23 Tu	22 11 17	4 17 57	6♍27 03	12 33 34	21D 45.1	12 59.7	7 48.8	25 23.1	10 02.2	20 05.0	15 36.9	17 59.4	9 17.4	16 45.0
24 W	22 15 14	5 18 20	18 37 30	24 39 05	21 44.9	14 27.7	9 03.0	25 48.4	10 25.8	19 57.7	15 39.9	18 02.1	9 19.6	16 46.5
25 Th	22 19 11	6 18 41	0♎38 33	6♎36 13	21 45.5	15 56.8	10 17.2	26 13.5	10 49.5	19 50.3	15 42.7	18 04.8	9 21.9	16 48.0
26 F	22 23 07	7 19 00	12 32 25	18 27 31	21 46.6	17 27.0	11 31.4	26 38.2	11 13.1	19 42.8	15 45.5	18 07.6	9 24.2	16 49.5
27 Sa	22 27 04	8 19 18	24 21 56	0♏16 07	21 47.9	18 58.2	12 45.6	27 02.8	11 36.7	19 35.3	15 48.2	18 10.4	9 26.5	16 51.0
28 Su	22 31 00	9 19 34	6♏10 33	12 05 45	21 49.2	20 30.5	13 59.8	27 27.0	12 00.4	19 27.8	15 50.8	18 13.2	9 28.8	16 52.4
29 M	22 34 57	10 19 49	18 02 16	24 00 39	21 50.2	22 03.9	15 14.0	27 51.0	12 24.0	19 20.1	15 53.3	18 16.1	9 31.0	16 53.8

Astro Data (Dy Hr Mn)	Planet Ingress (Dy Hr Mn)	Last Aspect (Dy Hr Mn)	☽ Ingress (Dy Hr Mn)	Last Aspect (Dy Hr Mn)	☽ Ingress (Dy Hr Mn)	☽ Phases & Eclipses (Dy Hr Mn)
☽0S 1 9:22	☿ ♒ 2 2:21	1 5:35 ☿ △	♎ 1 6:42	2 0:36 ♃ ✱	♐ 2 15:51	2 5:32 ☾ 11♎14
☿R 5 13:07	♂ ♏ 3 14:34	2 16:25 ♅ ☍	♏ 3 19:37	4 10:05 ♃ □	♑ 5 0:45	10 1:32 ● 19♑13
♃R 8 4:41	☿ ♑R 8 19:37	5 17:49 ♃ ✱	♐ 6 6:57	6 15:55 ♃ △	♒ 7 6:00	16 23:27 ☽ 26♈16
☽0N 15 5:41	☉ ♒ 20 15:28	8 2:45 ♃ □	♑ 8 15:08	8 14:40 ☉ ☌	♓ 9 8:32	24 1:47 ○ 3♌29
☿D 25 21:52	♀ ♑ 23 20:33	10 17:41 ☿ ☌	♒ 10 20:24	11 4:26 ☿ ✱	♈ 11 9:56	
☽0S 28 18:58	⚳ ♓ 28 18:43	12 1:10 ♅ ✱	♓ 12 23:55	13 10:33 ☿ □	♉ 13 11:37	1 3:29 ☾ 11♏41
		14 16:32 ☉ ✱	♈ 15 2:49	15 10:55 ♀ △	♊ 15 14:36	8 14:40 ● 19♒16
☽0N 11 13:26	☿ ♒ 13 22:44	16 23:27 ☉ □	♉ 17 5:49	17 16:38 ☉ △	♋ 17 19:25	15 7:48 ☽ 26♉03
☽0S 25 3:10	♀ ♒ 17 4:18	19 6:51 ☉ △	♊ 19 9:14	19 14:37 ♂ △	♌ 20 2:18	22 18:21 ○ 3♍34
	☉ ♓ 19 5:35	21 8:02 ♀ ☍	♋ 21 13:29	22 1:18 ♂ □	♍ 22 11:25	
		23 6:22 ♃ ✱	♌ 23 19:22	24 14:24 ♂ ✱	♎ 24 22:43	
		25 2:52 ♅ △	♍ 26 3:47	26 11:19 ♅ ☍	♏ 27 11:27	
		28 0:12 ♃ ☌	♎ 28 15:00	29 19:56 ♂ ☌	♐ 29 23:57	
		30 1:35 ♅ ☍	♏ 31 3:51			

Astro Data

1 January 2016
Julian Day # 42369
SVP 5♓02'11"
GC 27♐03.8 ⚴ 22♑09.3
Eris 22♈18.8R ⚵ 6♏18.9
⚷ 17♓29.0 ⚶ 6♈06.0
☽ Mean ☊ 25♍34.9

1 February 2016
Julian Day # 42400
SVP 5♓02'07"
GC 27♐03.8 ⚴ 3♒31.6
Eris 22♈21.0 ⚵ 12♏47.8
⚷ 18♓47.4 ⚶ 16♈07.5
☽ Mean ☊ 23♍56.4

March 2016 LONGITUDE

Day	Sid.Time	☉	0 hr ☽	Noon ☽	True ☊	☿	♀	♂	⚳	♃	♄	♅	♆	♇
1 Tu	22 38 53	11♓20 02	0♐01 29	6♐05 21	21♍50.7	23♒38.3	16♒28.3	28♏14.7	12♓47.7	19♍12.5	15♐55.8	18♈18.9	9♓33.3	16♑55.2
2 W	22 42 50	12 20 14	12 12 51	18 24 32	21R 50.7	25 13.8	17 42.5	28 38.1	13 11.4	19R 04.8	15 58.1	18 21.8	9 35.6	16 56.5
3 Th	22 46 46	13 20 25	24 40 58	1♑02 39	21 50.2	26 50.3	18 56.7	29 01.3	13 35.0	18 57.0	16 00.3	18 24.8	9 37.9	16 57.9
4 F	22 50 43	14 20 33	7♑30 03	14 03 31	21 49.5	28 27.9	20 11.0	29 24.1	13 58.7	18 49.2	16 02.4	18 27.7	9 40.1	16 59.2
5 Sa	22 54 39	15 20 41	20 43 23	27 29 47	21 48.7	0♓06.6	21 25.2	29 46.6	14 22.3	18 41.4	16 04.5	18 30.7	9 42.4	17 00.5
6 Su	22 58 36	16 20 46	4♒22 49	11♒22 21	21 47.9	1 46.3	22 39.5	0♐08.7	14 46.0	18 33.6	16 06.4	18 33.7	9 44.7	17 01.7
7 M	23 02 33	17 20 50	18 28 11	25 39 53	21 47.4	3 27.2	23 53.7	0 30.6	15 09.6	18 25.8	16 08.3	18 36.8	9 47.0	17 02.9
8 Tu	23 06 29	18 20 52	2♓56 54	10♓18 31	21D 47.2	5 09.1	25 08.0	0 52.1	15 33.3	18 18.0	16 10.0	18 39.8	9 49.2	17 04.2
9 W	23 10 26	19 20 52	17 43 53	25 12 03	21 47.1	6 52.2	26 22.2	1 13.3	15 56.9	18 10.1	16 11.6	18 42.9	9 51.5	17 05.3
10 Th	23 14 22	20 20 51	2♈41 58	10♈12 34	21 47.2	8 36.4	27 36.4	1 34.1	16 20.6	18 02.3	16 13.2	18 46.0	9 53.7	17 06.5
11 F	23 18 19	21 20 47	17 42 46	25 11 32	21R 47.2	10 21.7	28 50.7	1 54.5	16 44.2	17 54.5	16 14.6	18 49.1	9 56.0	17 07.6
12 Sa	23 22 15	22 20 41	2♉37 54	10♉01 01	21 47.2	12 08.2	0♓04.9	2 14.6	17 07.8	17 46.7	16 16.0	18 52.3	9 58.2	17 08.7
13 Su	23 26 12	23 20 33	17 20 08	24 34 40	21 47.1	13 55.8	1 19.1	2 34.3	17 31.5	17 38.9	16 17.2	18 55.4	10 00.4	17 09.8
14 M	23 30 08	24 20 23	1♊44 09	8♊48 19	21 47.0	15 44.7	2 33.3	2 53.6	17 55.1	17 31.1	16 18.3	18 58.6	10 02.7	17 10.8
15 Tu	23 34 05	25 20 10	15 46 57	22 40 01	21D 46.9	17 34.7	3 47.6	3 12.6	18 18.6	17 23.4	16 19.4	19 01.8	10 04.9	17 11.8
16 W	23 38 02	26 19 56	29 27 35	6♋09 46	21 47.0	19 25.9	5 01.8	3 31.1	18 42.2	17 15.8	16 20.3	19 05.0	10 07.1	17 12.8
17 Th	23 41 58	27 19 39	12♋46 48	19 18 55	21 47.3	21 18.3	6 16.0	3 49.2	19 05.8	17 08.1	16 21.2	19 08.3	10 09.3	17 13.8
18 F	23 45 55	28 19 19	25 46 26	2♌09 40	21 47.8	23 11.8	7 30.2	4 06.9	19 29.4	17 00.5	16 21.9	19 11.5	10 11.5	17 14.7
19 Sa	23 49 51	29 18 58	8♌28 57	14 44 37	21 48.6	25 06.6	8 44.4	4 24.2	19 52.9	16 53.0	16 22.6	19 14.8	10 13.7	17 15.6
20 Su	23 53 48	0♈18 34	20 56 58	27 06 21	21 49.4	27 02.4	9 58.6	4 41.1	20 16.4	16 45.6	16 23.1	19 18.1	10 15.9	17 16.5
21 M	23 57 44	1 18 08	3♍13 04	9♍17 24	21 50.0	28 59.4	11 12.7	4 57.5	20 39.9	16 38.2	16 23.5	19 21.4	10 18.0	17 17.4
22 Tu	0 01 41	2 17 40	15 19 37	21 20 00	21R 50.3	0♈57.5	12 26.9	5 13.5	21 03.4	16 30.8	16 23.9	19 24.7	10 20.2	17 18.2
23 W	0 05 37	3 17 10	27 18 48	3♎16 16	21 50.0	2 56.6	13 41.1	5 29.0	21 26.9	16 23.6	16 24.1	19 28.0	10 22.3	17 19.0
24 Th	0 09 34	4 16 38	9♎12 38	15 08 11	21 49.1	4 56.6	14 55.3	5 44.1	21 50.3	16 16.4	16R 24.3	19 31.3	10 24.4	17 19.7
25 F	0 13 30	5 16 03	21 03 08	26 57 47	21 47.5	6 57.4	16 09.4	5 58.6	22 13.8	16 09.3	16 24.3	19 34.7	10 26.6	17 20.5
26 Sa	0 17 27	6 15 27	2♏52 23	8♏47 16	21 45.4	8 59.0	17 23.6	6 12.7	22 37.2	16 02.4	16 24.3	19 38.0	10 28.7	17 21.2
27 Su	0 21 24	7 14 49	14 42 45	20 39 11	21 43.0	11 01.1	18 37.7	6 26.3	23 00.6	15 55.5	16 24.1	19 41.4	10 30.8	17 21.9
28 M	0 25 20	8 14 09	26 36 55	2♐36 24	21 40.6	13 03.6	19 51.9	6 39.4	23 24.0	15 48.7	16 23.8	19 44.7	10 32.8	17 22.5
29 Tu	0 29 17	9 13 28	8♐38 01	14 42 15	21 38.6	15 06.3	21 06.0	6 51.9	23 47.3	15 42.0	16 23.5	19 48.1	10 34.9	17 23.1
30 W	0 33 13	10 12 44	20 49 34	27 00 27	21 37.1	17 08.9	22 20.2	7 03.9	24 10.6	15 35.4	16 23.0	19 51.5	10 36.9	17 23.7
31 Th	0 37 10	11 11 59	3♑15 23	9♑34 54	21D 36.6	19 11.2	23 34.3	7 15.3	24 33.9	15 28.9	16 22.5	19 54.9	10 39.0	17 24.3

April 2016 LONGITUDE

Day	Sid.Time	☉	0 hr ☽	Noon ☽	True ☊	☿	♀	♂	⚳	♃	♄	♅	♆	♇
1 F	0 41 06	12♈11 12	15♑59 28	22♑29 32	21♍36.9	21♈13.0	24♓48.5	7♐26.2	24♓57.2	15♍22.5	16♐21.8	19♈58.3	10♓41.0	17♑24.8
2 Sa	0 45 03	13 10 23	29 05 31	5♒47 47	21 37.9	23 13.7	26 02.6	7 36.5	25 20.5	15R 16.3	16R 21.1	20 01.7	10 43.0	17 25.3
3 Su	0 48 59	14 09 33	12♒36 35	19 32 05	21 39.3	25 13.2	27 16.7	7 46.2	25 43.7	15 10.2	16 20.2	20 05.2	10 45.0	17 25.8
4 M	0 52 56	15 08 41	26 34 20	3♓43 12	21 40.7	27 11.1	28 30.9	7 55.3	26 06.9	15 04.2	16 19.3	20 08.6	10 47.0	17 26.2
5 Tu	0 56 53	16 07 46	10♓58 24	18 19 28	21R 41.4	29 06.9	29 45.0	8 03.8	26 30.1	14 58.3	16 18.2	20 12.0	10 48.9	17 26.6
6 W	1 00 49	17 06 50	25 45 46	3♈16 26	21 41.1	1♉00.3	0♈59.1	8 11.6	26 53.3	14 52.6	16 17.1	20 15.4	10 50.8	17 27.0
7 Th	1 04 46	18 05 52	10♈50 29	18 26 46	21 39.4	2 50.9	2 13.2	8 18.8	27 16.4	14 47.0	16 15.8	20 18.9	10 52.7	17 27.3
8 F	1 08 42	19 04 52	26 04 03	3♉41 02	21 36.5	4 38.4	3 27.3	8 25.4	27 39.5	14 41.5	16 14.5	20 22.3	10 54.6	17 27.6
9 Sa	1 12 39	20 03 50	11♉16 26	18 49 01	21 32.7	6 22.5	4 41.4	8 31.3	28 02.5	14 36.3	16 13.1	20 25.7	10 56.5	17 27.9
10 Su	1 16 35	21 02 46	26 17 39	3♊41 23	21 28.6	8 02.7	5 55.5	8 36.6	28 25.5	14 31.1	16 11.6	20 29.2	10 58.4	17 28.2
11 M	1 20 32	22 01 39	10♊59 24	18 11 07	21 24.7	9 38.8	7 09.5	8 41.2	28 48.5	14 26.1	16 09.9	20 32.6	11 00.2	17 28.4
12 Tu	1 24 28	23 00 31	25 16 06	2♋14 09	21 21.9	11 10.5	8 23.6	8 45.1	29 11.5	14 21.3	16 08.2	20 36.0	11 02.0	17 28.6
13 W	1 28 25	23 59 20	9♋05 15	15 49 30	21D 20.3	12 37.6	9 37.7	8 48.3	29 34.4	14 16.6	16 06.4	20 39.5	11 03.8	17 28.7
14 Th	1 32 22	24 58 06	22 27 09	28 58 33	21 20.0	13 59.9	10 51.7	8 50.8	29 57.3	14 12.1	16 04.6	20 42.9	11 05.6	17 28.9
15 F	1 36 18	25 56 51	5♌24 08	11♌44 23	21 21.0	15 17.2	12 05.7	8 52.6	0♈20.1	14 07.7	16 02.6	20 46.3	11 07.4	17 29.0
16 Sa	1 40 15	26 55 33	17 59 49	24 10 59	21 22.6	16 29.3	13 19.7	8 53.7	0 42.9	14 03.5	16 00.5	20 49.7	11 09.1	17 29.1
17 Su	1 44 11	27 54 13	0♍18 25	6♍22 39	21 24.2	17 36.1	14 33.7	8R 54.0	1 05.6	13 59.5	15 58.4	20 53.2	11 10.8	17R 29.1
18 M	1 48 08	28 52 51	12 24 11	18 23 31	21R 25.1	18 37.4	15 47.7	8 53.7	1 28.3	13 55.6	15 56.1	20 56.6	11 12.5	17 29.1
19 Tu	1 52 04	29 51 26	24 21 05	0♎17 20	21 24.7	19 33.1	17 01.7	8 52.6	1 51.0	13 51.9	15 53.8	21 00.0	11 14.2	17 29.1
20 W	1 56 01	0♉50 00	6♎12 37	12 07 18	21 22.5	20 23.2	18 15.7	8 50.8	2 13.6	13 48.4	15 51.4	21 03.4	11 15.8	17 29.0
21 Th	1 59 57	1 48 31	18 01 43	23 56 08	21 18.5	21 07.6	19 29.7	8 48.2	2 36.2	13 45.0	15 48.9	21 06.8	11 17.4	17 29.0
22 F	2 03 54	2 47 01	29 50 50	5♏46 02	21 12.6	21 46.2	20 43.6	8 44.9	2 58.7	13 41.9	15 46.3	21 10.1	11 19.0	17 28.8
23 Sa	2 07 51	3 45 29	11♏41 59	17 38 52	21 05.2	22 19.0	21 57.6	8 40.8	3 21.2	13 38.9	15 43.7	21 13.5	11 20.6	17 28.7
24 Su	2 11 47	4 43 55	23 36 55	29 36 20	20 57.0	22 46.0	23 11.5	8 35.9	3 43.7	13 36.0	15 40.9	21 16.9	11 22.1	17 28.5
25 M	2 15 44	5 42 19	5♐37 21	11♐40 11	20 48.8	23 07.1	24 25.5	8 30.3	4 06.1	13 33.4	15 38.1	21 20.2	11 23.6	17 28.3
26 Tu	2 19 40	6 40 41	17 45 06	23 52 23	20 41.4	23 22.4	25 39.4	8 23.9	4 28.4	13 30.9	15 35.3	21 23.6	11 25.1	17 28.1
27 W	2 23 37	7 39 02	0♑02 19	6♑15 14	20 35.5	23 32.0	26 53.3	8 16.8	4 50.7	13 28.6	15 32.3	21 26.9	11 26.6	17 27.9
28 Th	2 27 33	8 37 22	12 31 29	18 51 28	20 31.4	23R 36.0	28 07.2	8 08.9	5 13.0	13 26.5	15 29.3	21 30.2	11 28.0	17 27.6
29 F	2 31 30	9 35 39	25 15 33	1♒44 08	20D 29.5	23 34.5	29 21.2	8 00.2	5 35.2	13 24.6	15 26.2	21 33.6	11 29.5	17 27.3
30 Sa	2 35 26	10 33 56	8♒17 37	14 56 23	20 29.2	23 27.7	0♉35.1	7 50.8	5 57.3	13 22.8	15 23.0	21 36.8	11 30.9	17 26.9

Astro Data

	Dy Hr Mn
♃⚻♅	6 11:46
☽0N	9 23:14
♃△♇	16 20:07
☉0N	20 4:32
☽0S	23 9:50
♃□♄	23 10:17
☿0N	23 13:25
♄ R	25 10:02
☽0N	6 10:19
♀0N	8 12:09
♂ R	17 12:15
♇ R	18 7:27
☽0S	19 16:00
☿ R	28 17:21

Planet Ingress

	Dy Hr Mn
☿ ♓	5 10:25
♂ ♐	6 2:30
♀ ♓	12 10:25
☉ ♈	20 4:31
☿ ♈	22 0:20
♀ ♈	5 16:52
☿ ♉	5 23:10
⚳ ♈	14 14:53
☉ ♉	19 15:31
♀ ♉	30 0:37

Last Aspect / ☽ Ingress (March)

Last Aspect Dy Hr Mn		☽ Ingress	Dy Hr Mn
3 2:56	☿ ⚹	♑	3 10:03
5 16:06	♂ ⚹	♒	5 16:23
7 8:47	♀ ☌	♓	7 19:10
9 1:56	☉ ☌	♈	9 19:41
11 18:25	♀ ⚹	♉	11 19:45
13 9:48	☉ ⚹	♊	13 21:05
15 17:04	☉ □	♋	16 0:58
18 4:10	☉ △	♌	18 7:56
19 20:44	♅ △	♍	20 17:40
22 3:56	♇ △	♎	23 5:24
24 20:56	♅ ☍	♏	25 18:10
27 7:27	♀ △	♐	28 6:47
30 1:56	♀ □	♑	30 17:46

Last Aspect / ☽ Ingress (April)

Last Aspect Dy Hr Mn		☽ Ingress	Dy Hr Mn
1 16:40	♀ ⚹	♒	2 1:38
3 23:17	☿ ⚹	♓	4 5:47
5 10:34	♇ ⚹	♈	6 6:47
7 14:57	♅ ☌	♉	8 6:12
9 9:51	♇ △	♊	10 6:00
11 18:58	☉ ⚹	♋	12 8:08
14 4:00	☉ □	♌	14 13:54
16 17:50	☉ △	♍	16 23:24
18 12:30	☿ △	♎	19 11:25
21 6:14	♅ ☍	♏	22 0:19
23 21:47	☿ ☍	♐	24 12:47
26 15:52	♀ △	♑	26 23:56
29 7:08	♀ □	♒	29 8:48

☽ Phases & Eclipses

Dy Hr Mn	
1 23:12	☾ 11♐48
9 1:56	● 18♓56
9 1:58:20	● T 04'10"
15 17:04	☽ 25♊33
23 12:02	○ 3♎17
23 11:48	● A 0.775
31 15:18	☾ 11♑20
7 11:25	● 18♈04
14 4:00	☽ 24♋39
22 5:25	○ 2♏31
30 3:30	☾ 10♒13

Astro Data

1 March 2016
Julian Day # 42429
SVP 5♓02'04"
GC 27♐03.9 ⚴ 13♒40.7
Eris 22♈32.0 ⚵ 15♏10.3
⚷ 20♓26.6 ⚶ 27♈19.5
☽ Mean ☊ 22♍24.2

1 April 2016
Julian Day # 42460
SVP 5♓02'01"
GC 27♐04.0 ⚴ 23♒27.5
Eris 22♈50.2 ⚵ 12♏35.7R
⚷ 22♓18.8 ⚶ 10♉18.6
☽ Mean ☊ 20♍45.7

LONGITUDE   May 2016

Day	Sid.Time	☉	0 hr ☽	Noon ☽	True ☊	☿	♀	♂	⚳	♃	♄	♅	♆	♇
1 Su	2 39 23	11♉32 11	21♒40 47	28♒31 06	20♍30.0	23♉15.9	1♉49.0	7♐40.6	6♈19.4	13♍21.3	15♐19.7	21♈40.1	11♓32.2	17♑26.5
2 M	2 43 20	12 30 24	5♓27 32	12♓30 11	20R 31.0	22R 59.5	3 02.9	7R 29.7	6 41.5	13R 19.9	15R 16.4	21 43.4	11 33.6	17R 26.1
3 Tu	2 47 16	13 28 36	19 39 02	26 53 53	20 31.0	22 38.6	4 16.8	7 18.0	7 03.4	13 18.7	15 13.0	21 46.7	11 34.9	17 25.7
4 W	2 51 13	14 26 46	4♈14 22	11♈39 57	20 29.3	22 13.9	5 30.7	7 05.7	7 25.4	13 17.6	15 09.6	21 49.9	11 36.1	17 25.3
5 Th	2 55 09	15 24 55	19 09 53	26 43 12	20 25.3	21 45.7	6 44.5	6 52.6	7 47.2	13 16.8	15 06.1	21 53.1	11 37.4	17 24.8
6 F	2 59 06	16 23 02	4♉18 48	11♉55 27	20 19.0	21 14.6	7 58.4	6 38.8	8 09.0	13 16.2	15 02.5	21 56.3	11 38.6	17 24.3
7 Sa	3 03 02	17 21 08	19 31 50	27 06 37	20 11.0	20 41.2	9 12.3	6 24.3	8 30.8	13 15.7	14 58.9	21 59.5	11 39.8	17 23.7
8 Su	3 06 59	18 19 12	4♊38 29	12♊06 13	20 02.2	20 06.1	10 26.2	6 09.2	8 52.5	13 15.4	14 55.2	22 02.7	11 41.0	17 23.2
9 M	3 10 55	19 17 14	19 28 46	26 45 16	19 53.7	19 29.9	11 40.0	5 53.5	9 14.1	13D 15.3	14 51.5	22 05.8	11 42.1	17 22.6
10 Tu	3 14 52	20 15 14	3♋55 03	10♋57 40	19 46.5	18 53.3	12 53.9	5 37.2	9 35.7	13 15.4	14 47.7	22 09.0	11 43.2	17 22.0
11 W	3 18 49	21 13 13	17 52 52	24 40 40	19 41.3	18 16.9	14 07.7	5 20.3	9 57.1	13 15.7	14 43.8	22 12.1	11 44.3	17 21.3
12 Th	3 22 45	22 11 10	1♌21 10	7♌54 41	19 38.4	17 41.4	15 21.5	5 02.9	10 18.6	13 16.1	14 39.9	22 15.2	11 45.4	17 20.6
13 F	3 26 42	23 09 05	14 21 38	20 42 31	19D 37.4	17 07.3	16 35.4	4 44.9	10 39.9	13 16.8	14 36.0	22 18.2	11 46.4	17 19.9
14 Sa	3 30 38	24 06 58	26 57 55	3♍08 28	19 37.6	16 35.3	17 49.2	4 26.5	11 01.2	13 17.6	14 32.0	22 21.3	11 47.4	17 19.2
15 Su	3 34 35	25 04 49	9♍14 47	15 17 32	19R 38.1	16 05.7	19 03.0	4 07.7	11 22.4	13 18.6	14 28.0	22 24.3	11 48.3	17 18.5
16 M	3 38 31	26 02 39	21 17 22	27 14 54	19 37.9	15 39.2	20 16.8	3 48.5	11 43.5	13 19.8	14 23.9	22 27.3	11 49.3	17 17.7
17 Tu	3 42 28	27 00 27	3♎10 44	9♎05 25	19 36.1	15 16.0	21 30.5	3 28.9	12 04.6	13 21.1	14 19.8	22 30.3	11 50.2	17 16.9
18 W	3 46 24	27 58 13	14 59 29	20 53 24	19 31.9	14 56.5	22 44.3	3 08.9	12 25.6	13 22.7	14 15.6	22 33.2	11 51.0	17 16.1
19 Th	3 50 21	28 55 58	26 47 35	2♏42 26	19 25.0	14 41.0	23 58.1	2 48.7	12 46.5	13 24.4	14 11.5	22 36.2	11 51.9	17 15.2
20 F	3 54 17	29 53 41	8♏38 17	14 35 23	19 15.6	14 29.7	25 11.9	2 28.3	13 07.3	13 26.3	14 07.3	22 39.1	11 52.7	17 14.4
21 Sa	3 58 14	0♊51 23	20 34 00	26 34 20	19 04.2	14 22.8	26 25.6	2 07.6	13 28.1	13 28.3	14 03.0	22 41.9	11 53.5	17 13.5
22 Su	4 02 11	1 49 04	2♐36 32	8♐40 45	18 51.6	14D 20.3	27 39.4	1 46.8	13 48.7	13 30.6	13 58.7	22 44.8	11 54.2	17 12.5
23 M	4 06 07	2 46 43	14 47 06	20 55 42	18 38.9	14 22.3	28 53.1	1 25.8	14 09.3	13 33.0	13 54.4	22 47.6	11 54.9	17 11.6
24 Tu	4 10 04	3 44 21	27 06 37	3♑20 00	18 27.1	14 28.8	0♊06.9	1 04.8	14 29.8	13 35.6	13 50.1	22 50.4	11 55.6	17 10.7
25 W	4 14 00	4 41 58	9♑35 56	15 54 34	18 17.3	14 39.9	1 20.6	0 43.7	14 50.3	13 38.3	13 45.8	22 53.2	11 56.2	17 09.7
26 Th	4 17 57	5 39 34	22 16 04	28 40 37	18 10.1	14 55.4	2 34.4	0 22.6	15 10.6	13 41.3	13 41.4	22 55.9	11 56.9	17 08.7
27 F	4 21 53	6 37 09	5♒08 25	11♒39 44	18 05.7	15 15.4	3 48.1	0 01.6	15 30.9	13 44.4	13 37.0	22 58.6	11 57.4	17 07.6
28 Sa	4 25 50	7 34 43	18 14 49	24 53 55	18 03.6	15 39.7	5 01.9	29♏40.7	15 51.1	13 47.6	13 32.6	23 01.3	11 58.0	17 06.6
29 Su	4 29 47	8 32 16	1♓37 20	8♓25 19	18 03.2	16 08.2	6 15.6	29 20.0	16 11.1	13 51.0	13 28.2	23 03.9	11 58.5	17 05.5
30 M	4 33 43	9 29 49	15 18 04	22 15 46	18 03.2	16 41.0	7 29.3	28 59.4	16 31.1	13 54.6	13 23.8	23 06.6	11 59.0	17 04.5
31 Tu	4 37 40	10 27 20	29 18 29	6♈26 10	18 02.4	17 17.7	8 43.1	28 39.0	16 51.0	13 58.4	13 19.3	23 09.1	11 59.5	17 03.3

LONGITUDE   June 2016

Day	Sid.Time	☉	0 hr ☽	Noon ☽	True ☊	☿	♀	♂	⚳	♃	♄	♅	♆	♇
1 W	4 41 36	11♊24 51	13♈38 42	20♈55 45	17♍59.7	17♉58.5	9♊56.8	28♏18.9	17♈10.8	14♍02.3	13♐14.9	23♈11.7	11♓59.9	17♑02.2
2 Th	4 45 33	12 22 21	28 16 49	5♉41 18	17R 54.4	18 43.1	11 10.6	27R 59.2	17 30.5	14 06.4	13R 10.5	23 14.2	12 00.3	17R 01.1
3 F	4 49 29	13 19 50	13♉08 21	20 37 01	17 46.4	19 31.4	12 24.3	27 39.8	17 50.1	14 10.6	13 06.0	23 16.7	12 00.6	16 59.9
4 Sa	4 53 26	14 17 19	28 06 13	5♊34 47	17 36.3	20 23.4	13 38.1	27 20.8	18 09.7	14 15.0	13 01.6	23 19.2	12 00.9	16 58.7
5 Su	4 57 22	15 14 47	13♊01 32	20 25 20	17 25.1	21 19.0	14 51.8	27 02.3	18 29.1	14 19.6	12 57.1	23 21.6	12 01.2	16 57.5
6 M	5 01 19	16 12 13	27 45 05	4♋59 51	17 14.1	22 18.0	16 05.5	26 44.3	18 48.4	14 24.3	12 52.7	23 24.0	12 01.5	16 56.3
7 Tu	5 05 16	17 09 39	12♋08 51	19 11 28	17 04.4	23 20.5	17 19.3	26 26.8	19 07.6	14 29.2	12 48.2	23 26.3	12 01.7	16 55.1
8 W	5 09 12	18 07 04	26 07 19	2♌56 11	16 57.0	24 26.3	18 33.0	26 09.9	19 26.6	14 34.2	12 43.8	23 28.6	12 01.9	16 53.9
9 Th	5 13 09	19 04 27	9♌38 04	16 13 05	16 52.2	25 35.3	19 46.7	25 53.6	19 45.6	14 39.4	12 39.4	23 30.9	12 02.1	16 52.6
10 F	5 17 05	20 01 50	22 41 33	29 03 51	16 49.8	26 47.6	21 00.5	25 37.9	20 04.5	14 44.7	12 35.0	23 33.2	12 02.2	16 51.3
11 Sa	5 21 02	20 59 11	5♍20 31	11♍32 06	16 49.1	28 03.1	22 14.2	25 22.9	20 23.2	14 50.2	12 30.6	23 35.4	12 02.3	16 50.0
12 Su	5 24 58	21 56 32	17 39 16	23 42 39	16 49.0	29 21.6	23 27.9	25 08.5	20 41.8	14 55.9	12 26.3	23 37.5	12 02.4	16 48.7
13 M	5 28 55	22 53 51	29 42 55	5♎40 47	16 48.6	0♊43.3	24 41.6	24 54.9	21 00.4	15 01.6	12 21.9	23 39.7	12R 02.4	16 47.4
14 Tu	5 32 51	23 51 10	11♎36 53	17 31 53	16 46.7	2 08.0	25 55.3	24 42.0	21 18.8	15 07.5	12 17.6	23 41.7	12 02.4	16 46.1
15 W	5 36 48	24 48 27	23 26 33	29 20 57	16 42.6	3 35.7	27 09.0	24 29.8	21 37.0	15 13.6	12 13.3	23 43.8	12 02.4	16 44.7
16 Th	5 40 45	25 45 44	5♏16 09	11♏12 27	16 35.9	5 06.5	28 22.8	24 18.4	21 55.2	15 19.8	12 09.1	23 45.8	12 02.3	16 43.4
17 F	5 44 41	26 43 00	17 10 17	23 10 01	16 26.7	6 40.2	29 36.5	24 07.8	22 13.2	15 26.1	12 04.8	23 47.8	12 02.2	16 42.0
18 Sa	5 48 38	27 40 16	29 11 59	5♐16 25	16 15.4	8 16.9	0♋50.2	23 58.0	22 31.1	15 32.6	12 00.6	23 49.7	12 02.1	16 40.6
19 Su	5 52 34	28 37 31	11♐23 32	17 33 28	16 02.8	9 56.5	2 03.9	23 48.9	22 48.9	15 39.2	11 56.5	23 51.6	12 01.9	16 39.3
20 M	5 56 31	29 34 45	23 46 19	0♑02 07	15 50.1	11 39.0	3 17.6	23 40.7	23 06.5	15 46.0	11 52.3	23 53.5	12 01.7	16 37.9
21 Tu	6 00 27	0♋31 59	6♑20 54	12 42 39	15 38.4	13 24.4	4 31.3	23 33.3	23 24.0	15 52.8	11 48.2	23 55.3	12 01.5	16 36.5
22 W	6 04 24	1 29 12	19 07 19	25 34 52	15 28.6	15 12.6	5 45.0	23 26.7	23 41.4	15 59.8	11 44.2	23 57.0	12 01.2	16 35.1
23 Th	6 08 20	2 26 26	2♒05 16	8♒38 29	15 21.4	17 03.5	6 58.7	23 20.9	23 58.6	16 07.0	11 40.2	23 58.8	12 00.9	16 33.6
24 F	6 12 17	3 23 39	15 14 31	21 53 22	15 16.9	18 57.1	8 12.4	23 15.9	24 15.7	16 14.2	11 36.2	24 00.4	12 00.6	16 32.2
25 Sa	6 16 14	4 20 51	28 35 05	5♓19 44	15D 15.0	20 53.2	9 26.1	23 11.8	24 32.7	16 21.6	11 32.2	24 02.1	12 00.2	16 30.8
26 Su	6 20 10	5 18 04	12♓07 22	18 58 05	15 14.7	22 51.7	10 39.9	23 08.5	24 49.5	16 29.1	11 28.4	24 03.7	11 59.9	16 29.3
27 M	6 24 07	6 15 17	25 51 57	2♈49 03	15R 15.0	24 52.5	11 53.6	23 06.0	25 06.2	16 36.7	11 24.5	24 05.2	11 59.4	16 27.9
28 Tu	6 28 03	7 12 30	9♈49 24	16 52 57	15 14.7	26 55.3	13 07.3	23 04.4	25 22.7	16 44.5	11 20.7	24 06.8	11 59.0	16 26.4
29 W	6 32 00	8 09 43	23 59 37	1♉09 12	15 12.8	29 00.1	14 21.0	23D 03.6	25 39.1	16 52.4	11 17.0	24 08.2	11 58.5	16 24.9
30 Th	6 35 56	9 06 56	8♉21 22	15 35 45	15 08.6	1♋06.4	15 34.8	23 03.6	25 55.3	17 00.4	11 13.3	24 09.6	11 58.0	16 23.5

Astro Data	Dy Hr Mn
☽ 0N	3 21:05
♃ D	9 12:15
☽ 0S	16 22:56
☿ D	22 13:21
♃□♄	26 12:29
☽ 0N	31 6:15
☽ 0S	13 7:15
♆ R	13 20:43
♄□♆	18 3:30
⚳0N	18 12:28
♃△♇	26 12:31
☽ 0N	27 13:33
♂ D	29 23:40

Planet Ingress		Dy Hr Mn
☉	♊	20 14:38
♀	♊	24 9:46
♂	♏R	27 13:52
☿	♊	12 23:24
♀	♋	17 19:40
☉	♋	20 22:35
☿	♋	29 23:25

Last Aspect Dy Hr Mn			☽ Ingress	Dy Hr Mn
1 2:57	☿	□	♓	1 14:35
3 5:09	☿	⚹	♈	3 17:05
5 4:18	♅	☌	♉	5 17:11
7 2:12	☿	☌	♊	7 16:36
9 4:16	♅	⚹	♋	9 17:25
11 7:35	♅	□	♌	11 21:33
13 17:03	☉	□	♍	14 5:53
16 9:21	☉	△	♎	16 17:34
18 15:24	♅	☍	♏	19 6:31
21 11:41	♀	☍	♐	21 18:49
23 15:39	♅	△	♑	24 5:35
26 1:13	♅	□	♒	26 14:28
28 20:20	♂	□	♓	28 21:07
30 23:11	♂	△	♈	31 1:10

Last Aspect Dy Hr Mn			☽ Ingress	Dy Hr Mn
1 15:43	♅	☌	♉	2 2:48
3 23:04	♂	☍	♊	4 3:02
5 16:49	♅	⚹	♋	6 3:42
8 0:19	♂	△	♌	8 6:48
10 7:15	☿	□	♍	10 13:47
12 14:48	♂	⚹	♎	13 0:34
15 7:01	♀	△	♏	15 13:19
17 13:54	♂	☌	♐	18 1:35
20 11:03	☉	☍	♑	20 11:56
22 8:58	♅	□	♒	22 20:10
24 15:49	♅	⚹	♓	25 2:32
26 19:56	☿	□	♈	27 7:09
29 7:47	☿	⚹	♉	29 10:04

☽ Phases & Eclipses Dy Hr Mn		
6 19:31	●	16♉41
13 17:03	☽	23♌21
21 21:16	○	1♐14
29 12:13	☾	8♓33
5 3:01	●	14♊53
12 8:11	☽	21♍47
20 11:03	○	29♐33
27 18:20	☾	6♈30

Astro Data

1 May 2016
Julian Day # 42490
SVP 5♓01'58"
GC 27♐04.0 ⚴ 1♓10.1
Eris 23♈09.7 ⚵ 6♏16.6R
⚷ 23♓53.1 ⚶ 23♉19.3
☽ Mean ☊ 19♍10.4

1 June 2016
Julian Day # 42521
SVP 5♓01'54"
GC 27♐04.1 ⚴ 6♓15.8
Eris 23♈26.9 ⚵ 0♏38.1R
⚷ 24♓57.2 ⚶ 6♊51.8
☽ Mean ☊ 17♍31.9

July 2016 — LONGITUDE

Day	Sid.Time	☉	0 hr ☽	Noon ☽	True ☊	☿	♀	♂	⚳	♃	♄	♅	♆	♇
1 F	6 39 53	10♋04 09	22♉51 47	0♊08 49	15♍02.0	3♋14.1	16♋48.5	23♏04.4	26♈11.3	17♍08.5	11♐09.7	24♈11.0	11♓57.5	16♑22.0
2 Sa	6 43 49	11 01 23	7♊26 08	14 42 55	14R 53.5	5 23.0	18 02.2	23 06.1	26 27.2	17 16.7	11R 06.2	24 12.4	11R 56.9	16R 20.5
3 Su	6 47 46	11 58 36	21 58 18	29 11 26	14 43.9	7 32.6	19 16.0	23 08.6	26 42.9	17 25.1	11 02.7	24 13.6	11 56.3	16 19.0
4 M	6 51 43	12 55 50	6♋21 28	13♋27 37	14 34.4	9 42.8	20 29.7	23 11.9	26 58.5	17 33.5	10 59.2	24 14.9	11 55.7	16 17.6
5 Tu	6 55 39	13 53 04	20 29 13	27 25 43	14 26.0	11 53.1	21 43.5	23 16.0	27 13.9	17 42.1	10 55.9	24 16.1	11 55.0	16 16.1
6 W	6 59 36	14 50 17	4♌16 40	11♌01 48	14 19.6	14 03.5	22 57.2	23 20.9	27 29.1	17 50.8	10 52.5	24 17.2	11 54.3	16 14.6
7 Th	7 03 32	15 47 30	17 41 00	24 14 14	14 15.5	16 13.5	24 11.0	23 26.5	27 44.2	17 59.6	10 49.3	24 18.3	11 53.6	16 13.1
8 F	7 07 29	16 44 44	0♍41 41	7♍03 35	14D 13.6	18 22.9	25 24.7	23 33.0	27 59.0	18 08.5	10 46.1	24 19.4	11 52.9	16 11.6
9 Sa	7 11 25	17 41 57	13 20 18	19 32 17	14 13.5	20 31.6	26 38.5	23 40.3	28 13.7	18 17.5	10 43.0	24 20.4	11 52.1	16 10.1
10 Su	7 15 22	18 39 10	25 40 03	1♎44 11	14 14.3	22 39.2	27 52.2	23 48.3	28 28.2	18 26.6	10 40.0	24 21.4	11 51.3	16 08.7
11 M	7 19 18	19 36 23	7♎45 16	13 43 57	14R 15.2	24 45.7	29 06.0	23 57.0	28 42.5	18 35.8	10 37.0	24 22.3	11 50.5	16 07.2
12 Tu	7 23 15	20 33 36	19 40 53	25 36 44	14 15.2	26 50.9	0♌19.7	24 06.5	28 56.6	18 45.1	10 34.1	24 23.1	11 49.6	16 05.7
13 W	7 27 12	21 30 49	1♏32 06	7♏27 39	14 13.6	28 54.6	1 33.4	24 16.7	29 10.5	18 54.5	10 31.3	24 23.9	11 48.7	16 04.2
14 Th	7 31 08	22 28 02	13 23 59	19 21 38	14 10.2	0♌56.8	2 47.2	24 27.7	29 24.3	19 04.0	10 28.6	24 24.7	11 47.8	16 02.7
15 F	7 35 05	23 25 15	25 21 11	1♐23 04	14 04.7	2 57.4	4 00.9	24 39.3	29 37.8	19 13.5	10 25.9	24 25.4	11 46.9	16 01.3
16 Sa	7 39 01	24 22 28	7♐27 44	13 35 33	13 57.6	4 56.3	5 14.7	24 51.6	29 51.1	19 23.2	10 23.4	24 26.1	11 45.9	15 59.8
17 Su	7 42 58	25 19 42	19 46 48	26 01 43	13 49.4	6 53.5	6 28.4	25 04.6	0♉04.2	19 33.0	10 20.9	24 26.7	11 44.9	15 58.3
18 M	7 46 54	26 16 55	2♑20 29	8♑43 09	13 41.0	8 49.0	7 42.1	25 18.2	0 17.2	19 42.9	10 18.4	24 27.3	11 43.9	15 56.9
19 Tu	7 50 51	27 14 09	15 09 46	21 40 16	13 33.3	10 42.6	8 55.9	25 32.5	0 29.9	19 52.8	10 16.1	24 27.9	11 42.9	15 55.4
20 W	7 54 47	28 11 24	28 14 33	4♒52 29	13 26.9	12 34.5	10 09.6	25 47.5	0 42.4	20 02.9	10 13.9	24 28.3	11 41.8	15 54.0
21 Th	7 58 44	29 08 39	11♒33 51	18 18 26	13 22.5	14 24.6	11 23.3	26 03.0	0 54.7	20 13.0	10 11.7	24 28.8	11 40.7	15 52.5
22 F	8 02 41	0♌05 55	25 06 00	1♓56 18	13D 20.1	16 12.9	12 37.1	26 19.2	1 06.7	20 23.2	10 09.6	24 29.1	11 39.6	15 51.1
23 Sa	8 06 37	1 03 11	8♓49 06	15 44 10	13 19.5	17 59.4	13 50.8	26 36.0	1 18.5	20 33.5	10 07.6	24 29.5	11 38.5	15 49.7
24 Su	8 10 34	2 00 28	22 41 16	29 40 14	13 20.3	19 44.1	15 04.5	26 53.3	1 30.2	20 43.9	10 05.7	24 29.8	11 37.3	15 48.3
25 M	8 14 30	2 57 46	6♈40 51	13♈42 58	13 21.6	21 27.1	16 18.3	27 11.3	1 41.5	20 54.4	10 03.9	24 30.0	11 36.1	15 46.9
26 Tu	8 18 27	3 55 05	20 46 23	27 50 56	13R 22.6	23 08.3	17 32.0	27 29.8	1 52.7	21 04.9	10 02.1	24 30.2	11 34.9	15 45.5
27 W	8 22 23	4 52 25	4♉56 24	12♉02 36	13 22.5	24 47.7	18 45.7	27 48.8	2 03.6	21 15.5	10 00.5	24 30.3	11 33.7	15 44.1
28 Th	8 26 20	5 49 46	19 09 15	26 16 05	13 21.0	26 25.4	19 59.5	28 08.4	2 14.2	21 26.2	9 58.9	24 30.4	11 32.5	15 42.7
29 F	8 30 16	6 47 09	3♊22 45	10♊28 51	13 17.8	28 01.3	21 13.2	28 28.6	2 24.6	21 37.0	9 57.5	24R 30.5	11 31.2	15 41.3
30 Sa	8 34 13	7 44 32	17 34 00	24 37 44	13 13.4	29 35.5	22 26.9	28 49.3	2 34.8	21 47.8	9 56.1	24 30.5	11 29.9	15 40.0
31 Su	8 38 10	8 41 56	1♋39 35	8♋39 03	13 08.2	1♍07.9	23 40.7	29 10.5	2 44.7	21 58.8	9 54.8	24 30.4	11 28.6	15 38.6

August 2016 — LONGITUDE

Day	Sid.Time	☉	0 hr ☽	Noon ☽	True ☊	☿	♀	♂	⚳	♃	♄	♅	♆	♇
1 M	8 42 06	9♌39 22	15♋35 41	22♋29 02	13♍03.0	2♍38.5	24♌54.4	29♏32.3	2♉54.3	22♍09.8	9♐53.6	24♈30.3	11♓27.3	15♑37.3
2 Tu	8 46 03	10 36 48	29 18 42	6♌04 20	12R 58.5	4 07.4	26 08.2	29 54.5	3 03.7	22 20.8	9R 52.5	24R 30.1	11R 26.0	15R 36.0
3 W	8 49 59	11 34 15	12♌45 38	19 22 26	12 55.1	5 34.5	27 21.9	0♐17.3	3 12.8	22 32.0	9 51.5	24 29.9	11 24.6	15 34.7
4 Th	8 53 56	12 31 43	25 54 36	2♍22 07	12D 53.2	6 59.7	28 35.6	0 40.5	3 21.6	22 43.2	9 50.6	24 29.7	11 23.2	15 33.4
5 F	8 57 52	13 29 12	8♍45 01	15 03 29	12 52.8	8 23.1	29 49.4	1 04.2	3 30.2	22 54.2	9 49.8	24 29.4	11 21.8	15 32.1
6 Sa	9 01 49	14 26 41	21 17 42	27 28 00	12 53.5	9 44.6	1♍03.1	1 28.4	3 38.4	23 05.8	9 49.1	24 29.0	11 20.4	15 30.9
7 Su	9 05 45	15 24 12	3♎34 44	9♎38 19	12 55.0	11 04.2	2 16.8	1 53.0	3 46.4	23 17.2	9 48.4	24 28.6	11 19.0	15 29.6
8 M	9 09 42	16 21 43	15 39 15	21 38 01	12 56.7	12 21.9	3 30.5	2 18.1	3 54.1	23 28.6	9 47.9	24 28.2	11 17.5	15 28.4
9 Tu	9 13 39	17 19 15	27 35 12	3♏31 21	12 58.2	13 37.5	4 44.2	2 43.7	4 01.5	23 40.1	9 47.5	24 27.7	11 16.1	15 27.2
10 W	9 17 35	18 16 48	9♏27 05	15 22 59	12R 58.9	14 51.1	5 57.9	3 09.6	4 08.7	23 51.7	9 47.2	24 27.2	11 14.6	15 26.0
11 Th	9 21 32	19 14 22	21 19 40	27 17 43	12 58.6	16 02.6	7 11.6	3 36.0	4 15.5	24 03.3	9 46.9	24 26.6	11 13.1	15 24.8
12 F	9 25 28	20 11 57	3♐17 45	9♐20 18	12 57.4	17 11.8	8 25.3	4 02.8	4 22.0	24 15.0	9D 46.8	24 25.9	11 11.6	15 23.6
13 Sa	9 29 25	21 09 33	15 25 54	21 35 02	12 55.2	18 18.7	9 39.0	4 30.0	4 28.2	24 26.8	9 46.7	24 25.3	11 10.1	15 22.5
14 Su	9 33 21	22 07 10	27 48 08	4♑05 35	12 52.5	19 23.2	10 52.6	4 57.6	4 34.1	24 38.6	9 46.8	24 24.5	11 08.5	15 21.4
15 M	9 37 18	23 04 47	10♑27 41	16 54 39	12 49.5	20 25.3	12 06.3	5 25.6	4 39.7	24 50.4	9 47.0	24 23.8	11 07.0	15 20.3
16 Tu	9 41 14	24 02 26	23 26 38	0♒03 40	12 46.8	21 24.7	13 20.0	5 53.9	4 45.0	25 02.3	9 47.2	24 22.9	11 05.5	15 19.2
17 W	9 45 11	25 00 06	6♒45 43	13 32 37	12 44.6	22 21.3	14 33.6	6 22.7	4 49.9	25 14.3	9 47.6	24 22.1	11 03.9	15 18.1
18 Th	9 49 08	25 57 48	20 24 09	27 19 59	12 43.2	23 15.1	15 47.2	6 51.7	4 54.6	25 26.3	9 48.0	24 21.2	11 02.3	15 17.1
19 F	9 53 04	26 55 30	4♓19 44	11♓22 55	12D 42.7	24 05.8	17 00.9	7 21.2	4 58.9	25 38.3	9 48.5	24 20.2	11 00.7	15 16.1
20 Sa	9 57 01	27 53 14	18 29 02	25 37 30	12 43.0	24 53.4	18 14.5	7 50.9	5 02.9	25 50.4	9 49.2	24 19.2	10 59.2	15 15.1
21 Su	10 00 57	28 51 00	2♈47 47	9♈59 18	12 43.8	25 37.5	19 28.1	8 21.1	5 06.5	26 02.6	9 49.9	24 18.2	10 57.6	15 14.1
22 M	10 04 54	29 48 47	17 11 29	24 23 48	12 44.8	26 18.0	20 41.7	8 51.5	5 09.8	26 14.8	9 50.7	24 17.1	10 55.9	15 13.1
23 Tu	10 08 50	0♍46 35	1♉35 45	8♉46 52	12 45.7	26 54.7	21 55.3	9 22.3	5 12.8	26 27.0	9 51.7	24 15.9	10 54.3	15 12.2
24 W	10 12 47	1 44 26	15 56 44	23 04 59	12R 46.3	27 27.4	23 08.9	9 53.4	5 15.4	26 39.3	9 52.7	24 14.8	10 52.7	15 11.3
25 Th	10 16 43	2 42 19	0♊11 18	7♊15 24	12 46.4	27 55.8	24 22.4	10 24.8	5 17.7	26 51.6	9 53.8	24 13.5	10 51.1	15 10.4
26 F	10 20 40	3 40 13	14 17 03	21 16 03	12 46.0	28 19.7	25 36.0	10 56.5	5 19.6	27 03.9	9 55.0	24 12.3	10 49.5	15 09.5
27 Sa	10 24 37	4 38 09	28 12 13	5♋05 24	12 45.3	28 38.8	26 49.6	11 28.5	5 21.2	27 16.3	9 56.3	24 11.0	10 47.8	15 08.7
28 Su	10 28 33	5 36 07	11♋55 29	18 42 20	12 44.5	28 52.8	28 03.1	12 00.9	5 22.4	27 28.8	9 57.7	24 09.6	10 46.2	15 07.8
29 M	10 32 30	6 34 07	25 25 53	2♌06 02	12 43.7	29 01.5	29 16.7	12 33.5	5 23.2	27 41.2	9 59.2	24 08.3	10 44.5	15 07.0
30 Tu	10 36 26	7 32 08	8♌42 43	15 15 54	12 43.0	29R 04.6	0♎30.3	13 06.4	5R 23.7	27 53.7	10 00.8	24 06.8	10 42.9	15 06.3
31 W	10 40 23	8 30 11	21 45 33	28 11 40	12 42.7	29 02.0	1 43.8	13 39.6	5 23.8	28 06.3	10 02.5	24 05.4	10 41.2	15 05.5

Astro Data	Dy Hr Mn
☽0S	10 16:32
☽0N	24 19:54
♅ R	29 21:07
☽0S	7 1:44
♃⚻♅	13 9:03
♄ D	13 9:51
☿0S	19 19:19
☽0N	21 2:55
☿ R	30 13:05
⚳ R	31 7:10

Planet Ingress		Dy Hr Mn
♀	♌	12 5:35
☿	♌	14 0:48
⚳	♉	17 4:11
☉	♌	22 9:31
☿	♍	30 18:19
♂	♐	2 17:50
♀	♍	5 15:28
☉	♍	22 16:40
♀	♎	30 2:08

Last Aspect Dy Hr Mn			☽ Ingress	Dy Hr Mn
1 0:20	♂	☍	♊	1 11:45
3 3:44	♅	⚹	♋	3 13:21
5 6:31	♅	□	♌	5 16:29
7 12:08	♅	△	♍	7 22:42
10 3:29	♀	⚹	♎	10 8:33
12 15:02	☿	□	♏	12 20:53
14 22:23	♂	☌	♐	15 9:15
17 8:58	♅	△	♑	17 19:34
19 22:58	☉	☍	♒	20 3:11
22 1:57	♂	□	♓	22 8:36
24 7:07	♂	△	♈	24 12:34
26 6:20	♅	☌	♉	26 15:39
28 15:14	♂	☍	♊	28 18:18
30 11:48	♅	⚹	♋	30 21:10

Last Aspect Dy Hr Mn			☽ Ingress	Dy Hr Mn
2 0:45	♂	△	♌	2 1:13
4 4:14	♀	☌	♍	4 7:35
6 3:21	♃	☌	♎	6 16:58
8 17:42	♅	☍	♏	9 4:53
11 5:23	♃	⚹	♐	11 17:25
13 17:38	♃	□	♑	14 4:13
16 2:46	♃	△	♒	16 11:53
18 9:28	☉	☍	♓	18 16:35
20 12:22	♃	☍	♈	20 19:20
22 11:49	♅	☌	♉	22 21:20
24 19:39	☿	△	♊	24 23:41
27 0:31	☿	□	♋	27 3:07
29 6:24	☿	⚹	♌	29 8:13
31 4:21	♅	△	♍	31 15:23

☽ Phases & Eclipses Dy Hr Mn	
4 11:02	● 12♋54
12 0:53	☽ 20♎07
19 22:58	○ 27♑40
26 23:01	☾ 4♉21
2 20:46	● 10♌58
10 18:22	☽ 18♏32
18 9:28	○ 25♒52
25 3:42	☾ 2♊22

Astro Data

1 July 2016
Julian Day # 42551
SVP 5♓01'49"
GC 27♐04.2 ⚴ 7♓02.3R
Eris 23♈36.8 ⚵ 29♎35.8
⚷ 25♓14.6R ⚶ 19♊47.6
☽ Mean ☊ 15♍56.6

1 August 2016
Julian Day # 42582
SVP 5♓01'45"
GC 27♐04.3 ⚴ 2♓34.0R
Eris 23♈37.7R ⚵ 3♏05.9
⚷ 24♓43.5R ⚶ 2♋41.7
☽ Mean ☊ 14♍18.1

LONGITUDE — September 2016

Day	Sid.Time	☉	0 hr ☽	Noon ☽	True ☊	☿	♀	♂	⚳	♃	♄	♅	♆	♇
1 Th	10 44 19	9♍28 16	4♍34 16	10♍53 25	12♍42.5	28♍53.3	2♎57.3	14♐13.1	5♉23.5	28♍18.8	10♐04.3	24♈03.9	10♓39.6	15♑04.8
2 F	10 48 16	10 26 22	17 09 11	23 21 42	12D42.6	28R38.4	4 10.8	14 46.9	5R22.9	28 31.4	10 06.2	24R02.3	10R37.9	15R04.1
3 Sa	10 52 12	11 24 30	29 31 08	5♎37 40	12 42.7	28 17.2	5 24.3	15 20.9	5 21.9	28 44.1	10 08.2	24 00.7	10 36.3	15 03.4
4 Su	10 56 09	12 22 40	11♎41 33	17 43 05	12R42.8	27 49.7	6 37.8	15 55.2	5 20.5	28 56.7	10 10.2	23 59.1	10 34.6	15 02.8
5 M	11 00 05	13 20 51	23 42 35	29 40 25	12 42.7	27 16.1	7 51.3	16 29.8	5 18.8	29 09.4	10 12.4	23 57.5	10 33.0	15 02.1
6 Tu	11 04 02	14 19 04	5♏36 58	11♏32 43	12 42.6	26 36.5	9 04.8	17 04.6	5 16.7	29 22.1	10 14.7	23 55.8	10 31.3	15 01.6
7 W	11 07 59	15 17 18	17 28 08	23 23 42	12 42.4	25 51.3	10 18.2	17 39.7	5 14.2	29 34.8	10 17.0	23 54.1	10 29.7	15 01.0
8 Th	11 11 55	16 15 34	29 19 57	5♐17 28	12D42.2	25 01.1	11 31.7	18 15.0	5 11.3	29 47.6	10 19.4	23 52.3	10 28.1	15 00.5
9 F	11 15 52	17 13 51	11♐16 47	17 18 29	12 42.1	24 06.5	12 45.1	18 50.6	5 08.1	0♎00.4	10 22.0	23 50.5	10 26.4	14 59.9
10 Sa	11 19 48	18 12 10	23 23 09	29 31 20	12 42.2	23 08.6	13 58.5	19 26.4	5 04.4	0 13.2	10 24.6	23 48.7	10 24.8	14 59.5
11 Su	11 23 45	19 10 31	5♑43 34	12♑00 23	12 42.6	22 08.4	15 11.9	20 02.4	5 00.5	0 26.0	10 27.3	23 46.8	10 23.2	14 59.0
12 M	11 27 41	20 08 53	18 22 14	24 49 31	12 43.3	21 07.1	16 25.3	20 38.7	4 56.1	0 38.8	10 30.1	23 44.9	10 21.5	14 58.6
13 Tu	11 31 38	21 07 17	1♒22 35	8♒01 40	12 44.0	20 06.2	17 38.6	21 15.1	4 51.4	0 51.7	10 33.0	23 43.0	10 19.9	14 58.2
14 W	11 35 34	22 05 42	14 46 54	21 38 19	12 44.7	19 07.0	18 52.0	21 51.8	4 46.3	1 04.5	10 36.0	23 41.1	10 18.3	14 57.8
15 Th	11 39 31	23 04 09	28 35 47	5♓39 03	12R45.2	18 11.0	20 05.3	22 28.7	4 40.8	1 17.4	10 39.0	23 39.1	10 16.7	14 57.5
16 F	11 43 28	24 02 37	12♓47 44	20 01 16	12 45.2	17 19.6	21 18.6	23 05.8	4 35.0	1 30.3	10 42.2	23 37.1	10 15.1	14 57.2
17 Sa	11 47 24	25 01 08	27 19 00	4♈40 08	12 44.6	16 34.1	22 31.9	23 43.1	4 28.8	1 43.2	10 45.4	23 35.0	10 13.5	14 56.9
18 Su	11 51 21	25 59 40	12♈03 47	19 29 00	12 43.4	15 55.8	23 45.2	24 20.6	4 22.2	1 56.1	10 48.7	23 33.0	10 11.9	14 56.6
19 M	11 55 17	26 58 15	26 54 49	4♉20 16	12 41.7	15 25.5	24 58.4	24 58.3	4 15.3	2 09.1	10 52.1	23 30.9	10 10.4	14 56.4
20 Tu	11 59 14	27 56 52	11♉44 24	19 06 22	12 39.9	15 04.0	26 11.6	25 36.1	4 08.1	2 22.0	10 55.6	23 28.8	10 08.8	14 56.2
21 W	12 03 10	28 55 31	26 25 25	3♊40 54	12 38.3	14D52.0	27 24.9	26 14.2	4 00.5	2 35.0	10 59.1	23 26.6	10 07.3	14 56.0
22 Th	12 07 07	29 54 12	10♊52 17	17 59 13	12D37.2	14 49.7	28 38.1	26 52.4	3 52.5	2 47.9	11 02.8	23 24.5	10 05.7	14 55.9
23 F	12 11 03	0♎52 56	25 01 25	1♋58 45	12 36.9	14 57.3	29 51.3	27 30.8	3 44.2	3 00.9	11 06.5	23 22.3	10 04.2	14 55.8
24 Sa	12 15 00	1 51 41	8♋51 11	15 38 46	12 37.3	15 14.8	1♏04.5	28 09.4	3 35.6	3 13.9	11 10.3	23 20.1	10 02.7	14 55.7
25 Su	12 18 57	2 50 30	22 21 37	28 59 56	12 38.5	15 41.9	2 17.6	28 48.2	3 26.6	3 26.8	11 14.2	23 17.8	10 01.2	14 55.7
26 M	12 22 53	3 49 20	5♌33 55	12♌03 48	12 40.0	16 18.3	3 30.8	29 27.2	3 17.3	3 39.8	11 18.2	23 15.6	9 59.7	14D55.6
27 Tu	12 26 50	4 48 12	18 29 50	24 52 18	12 41.4	17 03.5	4 43.9	0♑06.3	3 07.7	3 52.8	11 22.2	23 13.3	9 58.3	14 55.6
28 W	12 30 46	5 47 07	1♍11 25	7♍27 27	12R42.2	17 56.8	5 57.0	0 45.6	2 57.8	4 05.8	11 26.3	23 11.0	9 56.8	14 55.7
29 Th	12 34 43	6 46 04	13 40 37	19 51 07	12 42.1	18 57.8	7 10.1	1 25.1	2 47.6	4 18.7	11 30.5	23 08.7	9 55.4	14 55.8
30 F	12 38 39	7 45 03	25 59 11	2♎05 00	12 40.8	20 05.7	8 23.2	2 04.7	2 37.1	4 31.7	11 34.8	23 06.4	9 54.0	14 55.9

LONGITUDE — October 2016

Day	Sid.Time	☉	0 hr ☽	Noon ☽	True ☊	☿	♀	♂	⚳	♃	♄	♅	♆	♇
1 Sa	12 42 36	8♎44 04	8♎08 45	14♎10 38	12♍38.1	21♍19.7	9♏36.3	2♑44.5	2♉26.4	4♎44.7	11♐39.2	23♈04.1	9♓52.6	14♑56.0
2 Su	12 46 32	9 43 07	20 10 51	26 09 35	12R34.2	22 39.3	10 49.3	3 24.5	2R15.3	4 57.6	11 43.6	23R01.7	9R51.2	14 56.2
3 M	12 50 29	10 42 12	2♏07 04	8♏03 32	12 29.4	24 03.6	12 02.4	4 04.6	2 04.0	5 10.6	11 48.1	22 59.3	9 49.8	14 56.3
4 Tu	12 54 25	11 41 18	13 59 16	19 54 32	12 24.1	25 32.1	13 15.4	4 44.8	1 52.4	5 23.5	11 52.7	22 57.0	9 48.5	14 56.6
5 W	12 58 22	12 40 27	25 49 41	1♐45 04	12 19.0	27 04.2	14 28.4	5 25.2	1 40.6	5 36.5	11 57.3	22 54.6	9 47.1	14 56.8
6 Th	13 02 19	13 39 38	7♐41 06	13 38 11	12 14.7	28 39.2	15 41.4	6 05.8	1 28.6	5 49.4	12 02.0	22 52.2	9 45.8	14 57.1
7 F	13 06 15	14 38 50	19 36 49	25 37 28	12 11.5	0♎16.6	16 54.3	6 46.5	1 16.4	6 02.3	12 06.8	22 49.8	9 44.5	14 57.4
8 Sa	13 10 12	15 38 05	1♑40 42	7♑47 01	12D09.8	1 56.0	18 07.2	7 27.3	1 04.0	6 15.2	12 11.7	22 47.4	9 43.3	14 57.8
9 Su	13 14 08	16 37 21	13 57 02	20 11 16	12 09.6	3 37.0	19 20.1	8 08.3	0 51.4	6 28.1	12 16.6	22 44.9	9 42.0	14 58.2
10 M	13 18 05	17 36 38	26 30 19	2♒54 42	12 10.5	5 19.2	20 33.0	8 49.4	0 38.6	6 41.0	12 21.6	22 42.5	9 40.8	14 58.6
11 Tu	13 22 01	18 35 58	9♒24 56	16 01 26	12 12.0	7 02.2	21 45.9	9 30.6	0 25.6	6 53.8	12 26.6	22 40.1	9 39.6	14 59.0
12 W	13 25 58	19 35 19	22 44 36	29 34 40	12R13.4	8 45.9	22 58.7	10 12.0	0 12.5	7 06.6	12 31.7	22 37.6	9 38.4	14 59.5
13 Th	13 29 54	20 34 42	6♓31 46	13♓35 52	12 13.9	10 29.9	24 11.5	10 53.4	29♈59.3	7 19.5	12 36.9	22 35.2	9 37.3	15 00.0
14 F	13 33 51	21 34 07	20 46 46	28 04 05	12 12.9	12 14.1	25 24.3	11 35.0	29 45.9	7 32.2	12 42.2	22 32.8	9 36.1	15 00.5
15 Sa	13 37 48	22 33 34	5♈27 13	12♈55 21	12 10.1	13 58.4	26 37.0	12 16.7	29 32.5	7 45.0	12 47.5	22 30.3	9 35.0	15 01.0
16 Su	13 41 44	23 33 03	20 27 30	28 02 31	12 05.4	15 42.6	27 49.7	12 58.5	29 18.9	7 57.8	12 52.8	22 27.9	9 33.9	15 01.6
17 M	13 45 41	24 32 33	5♉39 08	13♉16 02	11 59.3	17 26.5	29 02.4	13 40.4	29 05.3	8 10.5	12 58.3	22 25.4	9 32.9	15 02.2
18 Tu	13 49 37	25 32 07	20 51 53	28 25 23	11 52.7	19 10.2	0♐15.0	14 22.5	28 51.6	8 23.2	13 03.7	22 23.0	9 31.9	15 02.9
19 W	13 53 34	26 31 42	5♊55 21	13♊20 48	11 46.4	20 53.5	1 27.7	15 04.6	28 37.9	8 35.8	13 09.3	22 20.5	9 30.9	15 03.6
20 Th	13 57 30	27 31 19	20 40 52	27 54 56	11 41.4	22 36.4	2 40.3	15 46.9	28 24.1	8 48.5	13 14.9	22 18.1	9 29.9	15 04.3
21 F	14 01 27	28 30 59	5♋02 34	12♋03 33	11 38.2	24 18.9	3 52.9	16 29.2	28 10.4	9 01.1	13 20.5	22 15.7	9 28.9	15 05.0
22 Sa	14 05 23	29 30 41	18 57 51	25 45 33	11D36.8	26 00.8	5 05.4	17 11.7	27 56.6	9 13.7	13 26.2	22 13.3	9 28.0	15 05.8
23 Su	14 09 20	0♏30 26	2♌26 54	9♌02 15	11 37.1	27 42.3	6 17.9	17 54.2	27 42.8	9 26.2	13 32.0	22 10.9	9 27.1	15 06.6
24 M	14 13 17	1 30 12	15 32 01	21 56 38	11 38.2	29 23.2	7 30.4	18 36.8	27 29.1	9 38.7	13 37.8	22 08.4	9 26.2	15 07.4
25 Tu	14 17 13	2 30 01	28 16 37	4♍32 27	11R39.3	1♏03.6	8 42.9	19 19.6	27 15.4	9 51.2	13 43.7	22 06.0	9 25.4	15 08.2
26 W	14 21 10	3 29 52	10♍44 36	16 53 35	11 39.3	2 43.4	9 55.3	20 02.4	27 01.8	10 03.7	13 49.6	22 03.7	9 24.6	15 09.1
27 Th	14 25 06	4 29 45	22 59 47	29 03 40	11 37.6	4 22.8	11 07.7	20 45.4	26 48.2	10 16.1	13 55.6	22 01.3	9 23.8	15 10.0
28 F	14 29 03	5 29 40	5♎05 34	11♎05 50	11 33.4	6 01.6	12 20.1	21 28.4	26 34.8	10 28.4	14 01.6	21 58.9	9 23.0	15 11.0
29 Sa	14 32 59	6 29 37	17 04 45	23 02 36	11 26.7	7 39.9	13 32.5	22 11.5	26 21.4	10 40.8	14 07.7	21 56.6	9 22.3	15 11.9
30 Su	14 36 56	7 29 37	28 59 36	4♏55 58	11 17.6	9 17.6	14 44.8	22 54.7	26 08.2	10 53.0	14 13.8	21 54.2	9 21.6	15 12.9
31 M	14 40 52	8 29 38	10♏51 54	16 47 34	11 06.7	10 54.9	15 57.1	23 38.0	25 55.1	11 05.3	14 20.0	21 51.9	9 20.9	15 13.9

Astro Data (Dy Hr Mn)	Planet Ingress (Dy Hr Mn)	Last Aspect (Dy Hr Mn)	☽ Ingress (Dy Hr Mn)	Last Aspect (Dy Hr Mn)	☽ Ingress (Dy Hr Mn)	☽ Phases & Eclipses (Dy Hr Mn)
♀0S 1 1:32	♃ ♎ 9 11:19	2 22:14 ♃ ☌	♎ 3 0:57	2 5:44 ♅ ☍	♏ 2 19:44	1 9:04 ● 9♍21
☽0S 3 9:53	☉ ♎ 22 14:22	5 0:31 ♅ ☍	♏ 5 12:40	5 1:05 ☿ ⚹	♐ 5 8:27	1 9:08:02 ● A 03'05"
♄□♆ 10 13:05	♀ ♏ 23 14:52	8 0:44 ♄ ⚹	♐ 8 1:21	7 6:27 ♅ △	♑ 7 20:41	9 11:50 ☽ 17♐13
☿0N 12 0:25	♂ ♑ 27 8:08	10 0:52 ♅ △	♑ 10 12:56	9 16:52 ♅ □	♒ 10 6:34	16 19:06 ○ 24♓20
☽0N 17 11:47		12 10:01 ♅ □	♒ 12 21:30	11 23:50 ♅ ⚹	♓ 12 12:44	16 18:55 • A 0.908
♃0S 21 5:01	☿ ♎ 7 7:57	14 15:32 ♅ ⚹	♓ 15 2:24	14 7:14 ♀ △	♈ 14 15:09	23 9:57 ☾ 0♋48
☿ D 22 5:30	⚳ ♈R 13 10:42	16 19:06 ☉ ☍	♈ 17 4:23	16 4:24 ☉ ☍	♉ 16 15:05	
☉0S 22 14:22	♀ ♐ 18 7:02	18 20:12 ♂ △	♉ 19 4:59	17 14:48 ♇ △	♊ 18 14:31	1 0:13 ● 8♎15
♇ D 26 15:03	☉ ♏ 22 23:47	21 3:33 ☉ △	♊ 21 5:54	20 11:18 ☉ △	♋ 20 15:29	9 4:34 ☽ 16♑19
☽0S 30 16:47	☿ ♏ 24 20:47	23 7:58 ♀ △	♋ 23 8:34	22 19:15 ☉ □	♌ 22 19:35	16 4:24 ○ 23♈14
⚳0S 1 18:17		25 1:43 ♅ □	♌ 25 13:49	24 12:22 ♅ △	♍ 25 3:17	22 19:15 ☾ 29♋49
☿0S 9 23:52		27 8:54 ♅ △	♍ 27 21:44	26 18:34 ♂ △	♎ 27 13:52	30 17:39 ● 7♏44
☽0N 14 22:33		29 10:06 ☿ ☌	♎ 30 7:53	29 10:10 ♂ □	♏ 30 2:02	
♃⚻♆ 23 13:34						
☽0S 27 23:04						

Astro Data

1 September 2016
Julian Day # 42613
SVP 5♓01'41"
GC 27♐04.3 ⚵ 24♒53.7R
Eris 23♈28.9R ⚶ 9♏51.6
⚷ 23♓33.3R ⚴ 14♋43.6
☽ Mean ☊ 12♍39.6

1 October 2016
Julian Day # 42643
SVP 5♓01'39"
GC 27♐04.4 ⚵ 19♒37.9R
Eris 23♈13.6R ⚶ 18♏21.7
⚷ 22♓11.8R ⚴ 24♋53.9
☽ Mean ☊ 11♍04.2

November 2016 LONGITUDE

Day	Sid.Time	☉	0 hr ☽	Noon ☽	True ☊	☿	♀	♂	⚳	♃	♄	♅	♆	♇
1 Tu	14 44 49	9♏29 41	22♏43 09	28♏38 51	10♍54.9	12♏31.8	17♐09.3	24♑21.4	25♈42.2	11♎17.5	14♐26.2	21♈49.6	9♓20.3	15♑15.0
2 W	14 48 45	10 29 46	4♐34 51	10♐31 22	10R 43.2	14 08.1	18 21.5	25 04.9	25R 29.4	11 29.6	14 32.4	21R 47.3	9R 19.7	15 16.0
3 Th	14 52 42	11 29 52	16 28 39	22 26 59	10 32.6	15 44.0	19 33.7	25 48.4	25 16.9	11 41.7	14 38.7	21 45.1	9 19.1	15 17.1
4 F	14 56 39	12 30 00	28 26 41	4♑28 05	10 24.1	17 19.5	20 45.8	26 32.0	25 04.5	11 53.8	14 45.1	21 42.8	9 18.6	15 18.3
5 Sa	15 00 35	13 30 10	10♑31 37	16 37 41	10 18.0	18 54.6	21 57.9	27 15.7	24 52.3	12 05.7	14 51.4	21 40.6	9 18.1	15 19.4
6 Su	15 04 32	14 30 22	22 46 47	28 59 26	10 14.5	20 29.2	23 09.9	27 59.5	24 40.4	12 17.7	14 57.9	21 38.4	9 17.6	15 20.6
7 M	15 08 28	15 30 35	5♒16 08	11♒37 27	10D 13.2	22 03.5	24 21.9	28 43.3	24 28.7	12 29.6	15 04.3	21 36.2	9 17.2	15 21.8
8 Tu	15 12 25	16 30 49	18 03 56	24 36 07	10 13.3	23 37.4	25 33.9	29 27.3	24 17.2	12 41.4	15 10.8	21 34.1	9 16.8	15 23.0
9 W	15 16 21	17 31 05	1♓14 28	7♓59 27	10R 13.8	25 11.0	26 45.8	0♒11.2	24 06.1	12 53.2	15 17.3	21 31.9	9 16.4	15 24.3
10 Th	15 20 18	18 31 22	14 51 23	21 50 28	10 13.3	26 44.2	27 57.6	0 55.3	23 55.1	13 04.9	15 23.9	21 29.8	9 16.1	15 25.6
11 F	15 24 14	19 31 41	28 56 48	6♈10 14	10 10.8	28 17.1	29 09.4	1 39.3	23 44.5	13 16.5	15 30.5	21 27.7	9 15.7	15 26.9
12 Sa	15 28 11	20 32 01	13♈30 26	20 56 50	10 05.8	29 49.7	0♑21.1	2 23.5	23 34.2	13 28.1	15 37.1	21 25.7	9 15.5	15 28.2
13 Su	15 32 08	21 32 22	28 28 37	6♉04 45	9 58.1	1♐22.0	1 32.8	3 07.7	23 24.1	13 39.6	15 43.8	21 23.7	9 15.2	15 29.6
14 M	15 36 04	22 32 46	13♉44 00	21 24 59	9 48.2	2 54.0	2 44.4	3 52.0	23 14.4	13 51.1	15 50.5	21 21.7	9 15.0	15 30.9
15 Tu	15 40 01	23 33 11	29 06 11	6♊46 06	9 37.3	4 25.7	3 56.0	4 36.3	23 04.9	14 02.5	15 57.2	21 19.7	9 14.8	15 32.3
16 W	15 43 57	24 33 37	14♊23 16	21 56 20	9 26.7	5 57.1	5 07.5	5 20.6	22 55.8	14 13.8	16 03.9	21 17.8	9 14.7	15 33.8
17 Th	15 47 54	25 34 06	29 24 08	6♋45 43	9 17.6	7 28.2	6 18.9	6 05.0	22 47.1	14 25.1	16 10.7	21 15.9	9 14.6	15 35.2
18 F	15 51 50	26 34 36	14♋00 23	21 07 40	9 10.9	8 59.1	7 30.3	6 49.5	22 38.6	14 36.3	16 17.5	21 14.0	9 14.5	15 36.7
19 Sa	15 55 47	27 35 08	28 07 20	4♌59 23	9 06.8	10 29.6	8 41.6	7 34.0	22 30.6	14 47.4	16 24.3	21 12.2	9D 14.5	15 38.2
20 Su	15 59 44	28 35 42	11♌43 59	18 21 27	9D 05.0	11 59.9	9 52.8	8 18.5	22 22.8	14 58.4	16 31.2	21 10.4	9 14.5	15 39.7
21 M	16 03 40	29 36 17	24 52 15	1♍16 54	9R 04.7	13 29.9	11 04.0	9 03.1	22 15.4	15 09.4	16 38.1	21 08.6	9 14.5	15 41.2
22 Tu	16 07 37	0♐36 54	7♍36 00	13 50 09	9 04.7	14 59.5	12 15.1	9 47.8	22 08.4	15 20.3	16 44.9	21 06.9	9 14.6	15 42.8
23 W	16 11 33	1 37 33	19 59 59	26 06 09	9 03.8	16 28.8	13 26.1	10 32.5	22 01.8	15 31.1	16 51.9	21 05.2	9 14.6	15 44.3
24 Th	16 15 30	2 38 13	2♎09 13	8♎09 48	9 00.8	17 57.7	14 37.1	11 17.2	21 55.5	15 41.8	16 58.8	21 03.5	9 14.8	15 45.9
25 F	16 19 26	3 38 55	14 08 25	20 05 34	8 55.1	19 26.2	15 48.0	12 02.0	21 49.6	15 52.4	17 05.8	21 01.9	9 14.9	15 47.6
26 Sa	16 23 23	4 39 39	26 01 41	1♏57 11	8 46.2	20 54.1	16 58.8	12 46.8	21 44.1	16 03.0	17 12.7	21 00.3	9 15.1	15 49.2
27 Su	16 27 19	5 40 24	7♏52 23	13 47 36	8 34.5	22 21.6	18 09.5	13 31.6	21 38.9	16 13.5	17 19.7	20 58.7	9 15.4	15 50.8
28 M	16 31 16	6 41 11	19 43 06	25 39 04	8 20.5	23 48.5	19 20.2	14 16.5	21 34.2	16 23.8	17 26.7	20 57.2	9 15.6	15 52.5
29 Tu	16 35 12	7 41 58	1♐35 42	7♐33 10	8 05.4	25 14.6	20 30.7	15 01.5	21 29.8	16 34.1	17 33.7	20 55.8	9 16.0	15 54.2
30 W	16 39 09	8 42 47	13 31 35	19 31 07	7 50.3	26 40.0	21 41.2	15 46.4	21 25.9	16 44.3	17 40.8	20 54.4	9 16.3	15 55.9

December 2016 LONGITUDE

Day	Sid.Time	☉	0 hr ☽	Noon ☽	True ☊	☿	♀	♂	⚳	♃	♄	♅	♆	♇
1 Th	16 43 06	9♐43 38	25♐31 52	1♑33 59	7♍36.4	28♐04.5	22♑51.6	16♒31.4	21♈22.3	16♎54.4	17♐47.8	20♈53.0	9♓16.7	15♑57.7
2 F	16 47 02	10 44 29	7♑37 39	13 43 03	7R 24.9	29 27.9	24 01.9	17 16.4	21R 19.1	17 04.5	17 54.9	20R 51.7	9 17.1	15 59.4
3 Sa	16 50 59	11 45 21	19 50 24	25 59 58	7 16.3	0♑50.1	25 12.1	18 01.5	21 16.3	17 14.4	18 01.9	20 50.4	9 17.5	16 01.2
4 Su	16 54 55	12 46 15	2♒12 03	8♒27 00	7 10.9	2 11.0	26 22.1	18 46.6	21 14.0	17 24.2	18 09.0	20 49.1	9 18.0	16 03.0
5 M	16 58 52	13 47 09	14 45 11	21 07 03	7 08.2	3 30.1	27 32.1	19 31.7	21 12.0	17 33.9	18 16.1	20 47.9	9 18.5	16 04.7
6 Tu	17 02 48	14 48 04	27 33 00	4♓03 31	7 07.5	4 47.4	28 41.9	20 16.8	21 10.4	17 43.5	18 23.2	20 46.8	9 19.1	16 06.6
7 W	17 06 45	15 48 59	10♓39 02	17 20 00	7 07.5	6 02.6	29 51.7	21 02.0	21 09.2	17 53.0	18 30.3	20 45.6	9 19.6	16 08.4
8 Th	17 10 42	16 49 55	24 06 46	0♈59 39	7 07.0	7 15.1	1♒01.3	21 47.2	21 08.4	18 02.4	18 37.4	20 44.6	9 20.3	16 10.2
9 F	17 14 38	17 50 52	7♈58 52	15 04 29	7 04.6	8 24.8	2 10.7	22 32.4	21D 08.0	18 11.7	18 44.4	20 43.5	9 20.9	16 12.1
10 Sa	17 18 35	18 51 49	22 16 23	29 34 19	6 59.7	9 31.1	3 20.1	23 17.6	21 08.0	18 20.9	18 51.5	20 42.6	9 21.6	16 13.9
11 Su	17 22 31	19 52 47	6♉57 46	14♉26 02	6 52.1	10 33.4	4 29.3	24 02.8	21 08.4	18 30.0	18 58.6	20 41.6	9 22.3	16 15.8
12 M	17 26 28	20 53 46	21 58 11	29 33 06	6 42.1	11 31.3	5 38.3	24 48.0	21 09.2	18 38.9	19 05.7	20 40.8	9 23.0	16 17.7
13 Tu	17 30 24	21 54 46	7♊09 31	14♊46 04	6 31.0	12 24.0	6 47.3	25 33.3	21 10.3	18 47.8	19 12.8	20 39.9	9 23.8	16 19.6
14 W	17 34 21	22 55 46	22 21 20	29 53 57	6 19.9	13 10.9	7 56.0	26 18.5	21 11.9	18 56.5	19 19.9	20 39.2	9 24.6	16 21.5
15 Th	17 38 17	23 56 47	7♋22 39	14♋46 18	6 10.2	13 51.1	9 04.6	27 03.8	21 13.8	19 05.1	19 27.0	20 38.4	9 25.5	16 23.5
16 F	17 42 14	24 57 49	22 03 58	29 14 58	6 02.9	14 23.7	10 13.1	27 49.0	21 16.1	19 13.6	19 34.1	20 37.7	9 26.4	16 25.4
17 Sa	17 46 11	25 58 52	6♌18 47	13♌15 12	5 58.2	14 48.0	11 21.3	28 34.3	21 18.7	19 22.0	19 41.1	20 37.1	9 27.3	16 27.4
18 Su	17 50 07	26 59 55	20 04 08	26 45 44	5D 56.1	15R 03.0	12 29.4	29 19.6	21 21.8	19 30.3	19 48.2	20 36.5	9 28.2	16 29.3
19 M	17 54 04	28 00 59	3♍20 17	9♍48 13	5 55.9	15 07.8	13 37.4	0♓04.9	21 25.2	19 38.4	19 55.3	20 36.0	9 29.2	16 31.3
20 Tu	17 58 00	29 02 04	16 10 02	22 26 20	5R 56.3	15 01.8	14 45.1	0 50.2	21 28.9	19 46.4	20 02.3	20 35.5	9 30.2	16 33.3
21 W	18 01 57	0♑03 10	28 37 43	4♎44 52	5 56.4	14 44.3	15 52.7	1 35.5	21 33.0	19 54.3	20 09.3	20 35.1	9 31.3	16 35.3
22 Th	18 05 53	1 04 17	10♎48 25	16 49 04	5 54.9	14 15.1	17 00.1	2 20.8	21 37.5	20 02.0	20 16.3	20 34.7	9 32.3	16 37.3
23 F	18 09 50	2 05 24	22 47 25	28 44 07	5 51.3	13 34.2	18 07.2	3 06.1	21 42.4	20 09.6	20 23.4	20 34.3	9 33.4	16 39.3
24 Sa	18 13 46	3 06 32	4♏39 42	10♏34 43	5 45.0	12 42.2	19 14.2	3 51.5	21 47.6	20 17.1	20 30.3	20 34.1	9 34.6	16 41.3
25 Su	18 17 43	4 07 41	16 29 40	22 24 57	5 36.2	11 40.1	20 21.0	4 36.8	21 53.1	20 24.5	20 37.3	20 33.8	9 35.7	16 43.3
26 M	18 21 40	5 08 50	28 20 59	4♐18 06	5 25.4	10 29.6	21 27.6	5 22.1	21 59.0	20 31.7	20 44.3	20 33.7	9 36.9	16 45.3
27 Tu	18 25 36	6 10 00	10♐16 33	16 16 35	5 13.4	9 12.6	22 33.9	6 07.4	22 05.2	20 38.7	20 51.2	20 33.5	9 38.2	16 47.3
28 W	18 29 33	7 11 10	22 18 24	28 22 08	5 01.4	7 51.8	23 40.0	6 52.8	22 11.8	20 45.6	20 58.1	20D 33.5	9 39.4	16 49.4
29 Th	18 33 29	8 12 20	4♑27 54	10♑35 48	4 50.4	6 29.7	24 45.9	7 38.1	22 18.7	20 52.4	21 05.1	20 33.4	9 40.7	16 51.4
30 F	18 37 26	9 13 30	16 45 55	22 58 19	4 41.4	5 09.2	25 51.5	8 23.4	22 26.0	20 59.1	21 11.9	20 33.5	9 42.0	16 53.5
31 Sa	18 41 22	10 14 41	29 13 04	5♒30 16	4 34.8	3 52.7	26 56.8	9 08.8	22 33.5	21 05.5	21 18.8	20 33.6	9 43.4	16 55.5

Astro Data	Planet Ingress	Last Aspect	☽ Ingress	Last Aspect	☽ Ingress	☽ Phases & Eclipses	Astro Data
Dy Hr Mn	Dy Hr Mn	Dy Hr Mn	Dy Hr Mn	Dy Hr Mn	Dy Hr Mn	Dy Hr Mn	1 November 2016
♄⚺♇ 10 19:40	♂ ♒ 9 5:53	1 2:45 ♂ ⚹	♐ 1 14:44	1 4:09 ☿ ☌	♑ 1 8:53	7 19:52 ☽ 15♒50	Julian Day # 42674
☽0N 11 9:53	♀ ♑ 12 4:55	3 10:36 ♅ △	♑ 4 3:06	3 10:17 ♀ ☌	♒ 3 19:45	14 13:53 ○ 22♉38	SVP 5♓01'36"
♆D 20 4:40	☿ ♐ 12 14:41	6 9:58 ♂ ☌	♒ 6 13:56	5 11:24 ♅ ⚹	♓ 6 4:32	21 8:34 ☾ 29♌28	GC 27♐04.5 ⚴ 19♒26.6
☽0S 24 5:55	☉ ♐ 21 21:24	8 13:56 ♀ ⚹	♓ 8 21:46	7 14:06 ♄ □	♈ 8 10:17	29 12:19 ● 7♐43	Eris 22♈55.3R ⚵ 28♏21.0
♃□♇ 24 23:02		10 23:17 ♀ □	♈ 11 1:46	10 1:07 ♂ ⚹	♉ 10 12:42		⚷ 21♓04.6R ⚶ 2♌41.4
	☿ ♑ 2 21:19	12 12:46 ♅ ☌	♉ 13 2:25	12 4:06 ♂ □	♊ 12 12:42	7 9:04 ☽ 15♓42	☽ Mean ☊ 9♍25.7
☽0N 8 19:52	♀ ♒ 7 14:52	14 13:53 ☉ ☍	♊ 15 1:24	14 5:59 ♂ △	♋ 14 12:10	14 0:07 ○ 22♊26	
⚳D 10 0:27	♂ ♓ 19 9:24	16 10:59 ♅ ⚹	♋ 17 0:58	15 21:38 ♅ □	♌ 16 13:16	21 1:57 ☾ 29♍38	1 December 2016
⚳0N 14 21:24	☉ ♑ 21 10:45	18 22:04 ☉ △	♌ 19 3:16	18 16:56 ♂ ☍	♍ 18 17:53	29 6:54 ● 7♑59	Julian Day # 42704
☿R 19 10:56		21 8:34 ☉ □	♍ 21 9:35	21 1:57 ☉ □	♎ 21 2:41		SVP 5♓01'32"
☽0S 21 14:13		22 17:43 ♄ □	♎ 23 19:43	22 19:33 ♅ ☍	♏ 23 14:34		GC 27♐04.5 ⚴ 23♒43.7
♄△♅ 25 0:22		25 13:53 ♅ ☍	♏ 26 8:03	25 7:23 ♀ □	♐ 26 3:20		Eris 22♈40.3R ⚵ 8♐36.1
♃☍♅ 26 18:36		27 21:49 ♀ ⚹	♐ 28 20:47	28 1:46 ♀ ⚹	♑ 28 15:13		⚷ 20♓40.2 ⚶ 5♌42.5
♅D 29 9:30				30 8:08 ♃ □	♒ 31 1:30		☽ Mean ☊ 7♍50.4

LONGITUDE — January 2017

Day	Sid.Time	☉	0 hr ☽	Noon ☽	True ☊	☿	♀	♂	⚳	♃	♄	♅	♆	♇
1 Su	18 45 19	11♑15 51	11♒50 00	18♒12 25	4♍30.9	2♑42.4	28♒01.9	9♓54.1	22♈41.4	21♎11.9	21♐25.6	20♈33.7	9♓44.7	16♑57.6
2 M	18 49 15	12 17 02	24 37 39	1♓05 53	4D 29.4	1R 40.1	29 06.8	10 39.4	22 49.6	21 18.1	21 32.4	20 33.9	9 46.1	16 59.6
3 Tu	18 53 12	13 18 12	7♓37 19	14 12 12	4 29.7	0 46.9	0♓11.3	11 24.7	22 58.2	21 24.1	21 39.2	20 34.1	9 47.6	17 01.7
4 W	18 57 09	14 19 22	20 50 46	27 33 14	4 30.9	0 03.6	1 15.5	12 10.0	23 07.0	21 30.0	21 46.0	20 34.4	9 49.0	17 03.7
5 Th	19 01 05	15 20 31	4♈19 51	11♈10 48	4R 31.7	29♐30.6	2 19.4	12 55.3	23 16.1	21 35.7	21 52.7	20 34.8	9 50.5	17 05.8
6 F	19 05 02	16 21 40	18 06 14	25 06 13	4 31.4	29 07.7	3 23.0	13 40.5	23 25.6	21 41.3	21 59.4	20 35.1	9 52.0	17 07.9
7 Sa	19 08 58	17 22 49	2♉10 43	9♉19 36	4 29.3	28D 54.6	4 26.3	14 25.8	23 35.3	21 46.7	22 06.0	20 35.6	9 53.5	17 09.9
8 Su	19 12 55	18 23 57	16 32 35	23 49 15	4 25.1	28 51.0	5 29.2	15 11.0	23 45.3	21 51.9	22 12.6	20 36.1	9 55.1	17 12.0
9 M	19 16 51	19 25 05	1♊09 02	8♊31 12	4 19.2	28 56.1	6 31.7	15 56.3	23 55.7	21 57.0	22 19.2	20 36.7	9 56.7	17 14.0
10 Tu	19 20 48	20 26 12	15 54 56	23 19 17	4 12.2	29 09.3	7 33.9	16 41.5	24 06.3	22 01.9	22 25.8	20 37.3	9 58.3	17 16.1
11 W	19 24 44	21 27 19	0♋43 14	8♋05 45	4 05.2	29 29.9	8 35.7	17 26.7	24 17.1	22 06.7	22 32.3	20 37.9	9 59.9	17 18.2
12 Th	19 28 41	22 28 26	15 25 47	22 42 24	3 59.0	29 57.3	9 37.1	18 11.8	24 28.3	22 11.3	22 38.8	20 38.6	10 01.6	17 20.2
13 F	19 32 38	23 29 32	29 54 44	7♌02 02	3 54.3	0♑30.9	10 38.0	18 57.0	24 39.7	22 15.7	22 45.3	20 39.4	10 03.3	17 22.3
14 Sa	19 36 34	24 30 38	14♌03 42	20 59 21	3D 51.6	1 09.9	11 38.6	19 42.1	24 51.4	22 20.0	22 51.7	20 40.2	10 05.0	17 24.3
15 Su	19 40 31	25 31 44	27 48 41	4♍31 38	3 50.9	1 53.9	12 38.7	20 27.2	25 03.3	22 24.1	22 58.0	20 41.1	10 06.7	17 26.4
16 M	19 44 27	26 32 49	11♍08 15	17 38 42	3 51.6	2 42.3	13 38.3	21 12.3	25 15.5	22 28.0	23 04.4	20 42.0	10 08.5	17 28.4
17 Tu	19 48 24	27 33 54	24 03 18	0♎22 26	3 53.2	3 34.8	14 37.5	21 57.4	25 28.0	22 31.7	23 10.7	20 42.9	10 10.3	17 30.5
18 W	19 52 20	28 34 59	6♎36 35	12 46 18	3 54.9	4 30.9	15 36.2	22 42.5	25 40.7	22 35.3	23 16.9	20 43.9	10 12.1	17 32.5
19 Th	19 56 17	29 36 03	18 52 09	24 54 44	3R 56.0	5 30.2	16 34.3	23 27.5	25 53.6	22 38.7	23 23.1	20 45.0	10 13.9	17 34.5
20 F	20 00 13	0♒37 07	0♏54 41	6♏52 37	3 55.9	6 32.4	17 32.0	24 12.5	26 06.8	22 41.9	23 29.2	20 46.1	10 15.7	17 36.5
21 Sa	20 04 10	1 38 11	12 49 11	18 44 58	3 54.3	7 37.3	18 29.1	24 57.5	26 20.3	22 45.0	23 35.3	20 47.3	10 17.6	17 38.6
22 Su	20 08 07	2 39 14	24 40 34	0♐36 31	3 51.2	8 44.6	19 25.7	25 42.5	26 33.9	22 47.8	23 41.4	20 48.5	10 19.5	17 40.6
23 M	20 12 03	3 40 17	6♐33 22	12 31 34	3 46.9	9 54.1	20 21.7	26 27.4	26 47.8	22 50.5	23 47.4	20 49.7	10 21.4	17 42.6
24 Tu	20 16 00	4 41 19	18 31 14	24 33 44	3 41.9	11 05.5	21 17.1	27 12.3	27 02.0	22 53.0	23 53.4	20 51.0	10 23.3	17 44.6
25 W	20 19 56	5 42 21	0♑38 25	6♑45 53	3 36.6	12 18.8	22 11.8	27 57.3	27 16.3	22 55.3	23 59.3	20 52.4	10 25.2	17 46.6
26 Th	20 23 53	6 43 22	12 56 21	19 09 59	3 31.8	13 33.7	23 06.0	28 42.1	27 30.9	22 57.4	24 05.1	20 53.8	10 27.2	17 48.5
27 F	20 27 49	7 44 22	25 26 55	1♒47 11	3 28.0	14 50.1	23 59.4	29 27.0	27 45.7	22 59.4	24 10.9	20 55.3	10 29.2	17 50.5
28 Sa	20 31 46	8 45 22	8♒10 50	14 37 51	3 25.4	16 08.0	24 52.2	0♈11.8	28 00.7	23 01.1	24 16.7	20 56.8	10 31.2	17 52.5
29 Su	20 35 42	9 46 20	21 08 11	27 41 46	3D 24.2	17 27.2	25 44.2	0 56.6	28 15.9	23 02.7	24 22.4	20 58.3	10 33.2	17 54.4
30 M	20 39 39	10 47 17	4♓18 31	10♓58 21	3 24.2	18 47.6	26 35.5	1 41.4	28 31.4	23 04.1	24 28.0	20 59.9	10 35.2	17 56.3
31 Tu	20 43 36	11 48 14	17 41 09	24 26 50	3 25.2	20 09.2	27 26.0	2 26.2	28 47.0	23 05.3	24 33.6	21 01.6	10 37.2	17 58.3

LONGITUDE — February 2017

Day	Sid.Time	☉	0 hr ☽	Noon ☽	True ☊	☿	♀	♂	⚳	♃	♄	♅	♆	♇
1 W	20 47 32	12♒49 08	1♈15 19	8♈06 28	3♍26.7	21♑31.9	28♓15.6	3♈10.9	29♈02.8	23♎06.3	24♐39.1	21♈03.2	10♓39.3	18♑00.2
2 Th	20 51 29	13 50 02	15 00 14	21 56 30	3 28.1	22 55.7	29 04.4	3 55.6	29 18.9	23 07.1	24 44.5	21 05.0	10 41.4	18 02.1
3 F	20 55 25	14 50 54	28 55 09	5♉56 04	3R 29.0	24 20.4	29 52.4	4 40.2	29 35.1	23 07.7	24 49.9	21 06.7	10 43.4	18 04.0
4 Sa	20 59 22	15 51 45	12♉59 04	20 04 00	3 29.2	25 46.1	0♈39.4	5 24.9	29 51.5	23 08.1	24 55.3	21 08.6	10 45.5	18 05.8
5 Su	21 03 18	16 52 35	27 10 36	4♊18 35	3 28.5	27 12.8	1 25.4	6 09.5	0♉08.1	23R 08.4	25 00.5	21 10.4	10 47.7	18 07.7
6 M	21 07 15	17 53 23	11♊27 36	18 37 17	3 27.1	28 40.4	2 10.4	6 54.0	0 24.9	23 08.4	25 05.7	21 12.3	10 49.8	18 09.6
7 Tu	21 11 11	18 54 09	25 47 08	2♋56 41	3 25.2	0♒08.9	2 54.4	7 38.5	0 41.9	23 08.3	25 10.9	21 14.3	10 51.9	18 11.4
8 W	21 15 08	19 54 54	10♋05 23	17 12 41	3 23.4	1 38.2	3 37.3	8 23.0	0 59.0	23 08.0	25 15.9	21 16.3	10 54.1	18 13.2
9 Th	21 19 05	20 55 38	24 17 59	1♌20 45	3 21.7	3 08.4	4 19.1	9 07.5	1 16.3	23 07.4	25 20.9	21 18.3	10 56.2	18 15.0
10 F	21 23 01	21 56 20	8♌20 27	15 16 35	3 20.6	4 39.5	4 59.7	9 51.9	1 33.8	23 06.7	25 25.9	21 20.4	10 58.4	18 16.8
11 Sa	21 26 58	22 57 01	22 08 44	28 56 32	3D 20.2	6 11.4	5 39.0	10 36.3	1 51.4	23 05.8	25 30.7	21 22.5	11 00.6	18 18.6
12 Su	21 30 54	23 57 40	5♍39 43	12♍18 07	3 20.2	7 44.2	6 17.2	11 20.6	2 09.2	23 04.8	25 35.5	21 24.7	11 02.8	18 20.3
13 M	21 34 51	24 58 18	18 51 37	25 20 15	3 20.7	9 17.8	6 53.9	12 04.9	2 27.2	23 03.5	25 40.2	21 26.9	11 05.0	18 22.1
14 Tu	21 38 47	25 58 55	1♎44 06	8♎03 20	3 21.5	10 52.3	7 29.4	12 49.2	2 45.3	23 02.0	25 44.9	21 29.1	11 07.2	18 23.8
15 W	21 42 44	26 59 30	14 18 14	20 29 07	3 22.2	12 27.7	8 03.4	13 33.4	3 03.6	23 00.4	25 49.5	21 31.4	11 09.4	18 25.5
16 Th	21 46 40	28 00 05	26 36 23	2♏40 28	3 22.9	14 03.9	8 35.9	14 17.6	3 22.0	22 58.6	25 54.0	21 33.7	11 11.6	18 27.2
17 F	21 50 37	29 00 38	8♏41 53	14 41 09	3 23.3	15 41.0	9 07.0	15 01.8	3 40.6	22 56.5	25 58.4	21 36.1	11 13.9	18 28.9
18 Sa	21 54 34	0♓01 09	20 38 49	26 35 29	3R 23.4	17 19.0	9 36.4	15 45.9	3 59.3	22 54.3	26 02.7	21 38.4	11 16.1	18 30.5
19 Su	21 58 30	1 01 40	2♐31 43	8♐28 07	3 23.4	18 57.9	10 04.2	16 30.0	4 18.2	22 51.9	26 07.0	21 40.9	11 18.4	18 32.1
20 M	22 02 27	2 02 09	14 25 17	20 23 47	3 23.3	20 37.8	10 30.3	17 14.1	4 37.2	22 49.4	26 11.2	21 43.3	11 20.6	18 33.7
21 Tu	22 06 23	3 02 37	26 24 11	2♑27 01	3D 23.2	22 18.5	10 54.7	17 58.1	4 56.4	22 46.6	26 15.3	21 45.8	11 22.9	18 35.3
22 W	22 10 20	4 03 04	8♑32 46	14 41 54	3 23.3	24 00.2	11 17.2	18 42.1	5 15.7	22 43.7	26 19.4	21 48.4	11 25.1	18 36.9
23 Th	22 14 16	5 03 29	20 54 49	27 11 51	3 23.4	25 42.9	11 37.9	19 26.1	5 35.1	22 40.6	26 23.3	21 50.9	11 27.4	18 38.5
24 F	22 18 13	6 03 53	3♒33 17	9♒59 18	3 23.6	27 26.5	11 56.6	20 10.0	5 54.7	22 37.3	26 27.2	21 53.5	11 29.7	18 40.0
25 Sa	22 22 09	7 04 15	16 30 03	23 05 33	3R 23.8	29 11.1	12 13.3	20 53.8	6 14.4	22 33.8	26 31.0	21 56.2	11 31.9	18 41.5
26 Su	22 26 06	8 04 35	29 45 44	6♓30 30	3 23.9	0♓56.7	12 28.0	21 37.7	6 34.2	22 30.1	26 34.7	21 58.8	11 34.2	18 43.0
27 M	22 30 03	9 04 54	13♓19 36	20 12 45	3 23.7	2 43.3	12 40.5	22 21.5	6 54.2	22 26.3	26 38.3	22 01.5	11 36.5	18 44.4
28 Tu	22 33 59	10 05 11	27 09 34	4♈09 38	3 23.1	4 30.9	12 50.8	23 05.3	7 14.2	22 22.3	26 41.9	22 04.3	11 38.8	18 45.9

Astro Data

	Dy Hr Mn
☽0N	5 3:24
☿ D	8 9:44
☽0S	17 23:47
♂0N	29 12:09
♀0N	30 8:04
☽0N	1 9:31
♃ R	6 6:54
☽0S	14 9:30
☽0N	28 16:23

Planet Ingress

		Dy Hr Mn
♀	♓	3 7:48
☿	♐R	4 14:18
☿	♑	12 14:04
☉	♒	19 21:25
♂	♈	28 5:40
♀	♈	3 15:52
⚳	♉	5 0:18
☿	♒	7 9:36
☉	♓	18 11:32
☿	♓	25 23:08

Last Aspect / ☽ Ingress (January)

Last Aspect Dy Hr Mn			☽ Ingress	Dy Hr Mn
2 8:00	♀	☌	♓	2 9:58
4 16:15	☿	□	♈	4 16:21
6 18:43	☿	△	♉	6 20:19
8 2:24	☉	△	♊	8 22:07
10 21:40	☿	☍	♋	10 22:50
12 11:35	☉	☍	♌	13 0:09
14 15:18	♄	△	♍	15 3:53
17 6:11	☉	△	♎	17 11:17
19 8:56	♄	⚹	♏	19 22:10
22 1:25	♂	△	♐	22 10:46
24 17:34	♂	□	♑	24 22:44
27 7:19	♂	⚹	♒	27 8:38
29 5:53	♄	⚹	♓	29 16:11
31 17:37	♀	☌	♈	31 21:48

Last Aspect / ☽ Ingress (February)

Last Aspect Dy Hr Mn			☽ Ingress	Dy Hr Mn
2 16:51	♄	△	♉	3 1:51
4 22:43	☿	△	♊	5 4:45
6 22:55	♄	☍	♋	7 7:04
8 22:01	♃	□	♌	9 9:42
11 5:53	♄	△	♍	11 13:53
13 12:38	♄	□	♎	13 20:44
16 1:55	☉	△	♏	16 6:42
17 19:39	♇	⚹	♐	18 18:53
20 23:38	♄	☌	♑	21 7:09
23 3:25	♃	□	♒	23 17:18
25 18:12	♄	⚹	♓	26 0:26
27 23:09	♄	□	♈	28 4:53

☽ Phases & Eclipses

Dy Hr Mn		
5 19:48	☽	15♈40
12 11:35	○	22♋27
19 22:15	☾	0♏02
28 0:08	●	8♒15
4 4:20	☽	15♉32
11 0:34	○	22♌28
11 0:45	•	A 0.988
18 19:34	☾	0♐20
26 14:59	●	8♓12
26 14:54:32	•	A 00'44"

Astro Data

1 January 2017
Julian Day # 42735
SVP 5♓01'27"
GC 27♐04.6 ⚴ 1♓13.5
Eris 22♈32.4R ⚵ 19♐16.2
⚷ 21♓07.0 ⚶ 2♌12.2R
☽ Mean ☊ 6♍11.9

1 February 2017
Julian Day # 42766
SVP 5♓01'22"
GC 27♐04.7 ⚴ 10♓36.0
Eris 22♈34.9 ⚵ 29♐26.6
⚷ 22♓20.7 ⚶ 24♋23.7R
☽ Mean ☊ 4♍33.4

March 2017 — LONGITUDE

Day	Sid.Time	☉	0 hr ☽	Noon ☽	True ☊	☿	♀	♂	⚳	♃	♄	♅	♆	♇
1 W	22 37 56	11♓05 26	11♈12 28	18♈17 34	3♍22.3	6♓19.6	12♈58.8	23♈49.0	7♉34.4	22♎18.2	26♐45.3	22♈07.0	11♓41.1	18♑47.3
2 Th	22 41 52	12 05 39	25 24 26	2♉32 31	3R 21.3	8 09.3	13 04.5	24 32.7	7 54.8	22R 13.8	26 48.7	22 09.8	11 43.3	18 48.7
3 F	22 45 49	13 05 50	9♉41 19	16 50 22	3 20.3	9 59.9	13R 07.9	25 16.3	8 15.2	22 09.3	26 52.0	22 12.6	11 45.6	18 50.1
4 Sa	22 49 45	14 05 59	23 59 12	1♊07 26	3D 19.5	11 51.6	13 08.8	25 59.9	8 35.8	22 04.7	26 55.2	22 15.5	11 47.9	18 51.4
5 Su	22 53 42	15 06 06	8♊14 41	15 20 39	3 19.3	13 44.3	13 07.3	26 43.5	8 56.4	21 59.9	26 58.3	22 18.4	11 50.2	18 52.7
6 M	22 57 38	16 06 11	22 25 02	29 27 37	3 19.6	15 37.9	13 03.3	27 27.0	9 17.2	21 54.9	27 01.3	22 21.3	11 52.4	18 54.0
7 Tu	23 01 35	17 06 13	6♋28 12	13♋26 35	3 20.4	17 32.5	12 56.7	28 10.5	9 38.1	21 49.8	27 04.2	22 24.2	11 54.7	18 55.3
8 W	23 05 32	18 06 14	20 22 37	27 16 09	3 21.6	19 27.9	12 47.7	28 53.9	9 59.1	21 44.6	27 07.1	22 27.2	11 57.0	18 56.6
9 Th	23 09 28	19 06 12	4♌07 03	10♌55 11	3 22.8	21 24.1	12 36.1	29 37.3	10 20.1	21 39.2	27 09.8	22 30.1	11 59.3	18 57.8
10 F	23 13 25	20 06 08	17 40 25	24 22 38	3R 23.6	23 21.0	12 22.0	0♉20.6	10 41.3	21 33.7	27 12.4	22 33.1	12 01.5	18 59.0
11 Sa	23 17 21	21 06 02	1♍01 43	7♍37 34	3 23.8	25 18.6	12 05.4	1 03.9	11 02.6	21 28.0	27 15.0	22 36.2	12 03.8	19 00.2
12 Su	23 21 18	22 05 54	14 10 04	20 39 10	3 23.0	27 16.6	11 46.4	1 47.2	11 24.0	21 22.2	27 17.5	22 39.2	12 06.0	19 01.3
13 M	23 25 14	23 05 44	27 04 48	3♎26 59	3 21.1	29 14.9	11 25.0	2 30.4	11 45.5	21 16.2	27 19.8	22 42.3	12 08.3	19 02.4
14 Tu	23 29 11	24 05 33	9♎45 43	16 01 05	3 18.4	1♈13.4	11 01.3	3 13.5	12 07.1	21 10.2	27 22.1	22 45.4	12 10.5	19 03.5
15 W	23 33 07	25 05 19	22 13 12	28 22 13	3 14.9	3 11.7	10 35.5	3 56.7	12 28.7	21 04.0	27 24.3	22 48.5	12 12.8	19 04.6
16 Th	23 37 04	26 05 03	4♏28 21	10♏31 53	3 11.1	5 09.7	10 07.7	4 39.7	12 50.5	20 57.7	27 26.4	22 51.6	12 15.0	19 05.6
17 F	23 41 00	27 04 46	16 33 08	22 32 27	3 07.5	7 07.1	9 37.9	5 22.8	13 12.3	20 51.3	27 28.4	22 54.8	12 17.2	19 06.6
18 Sa	23 44 57	28 04 27	28 30 17	4♐27 04	3 04.6	9 03.5	9 06.4	6 05.8	13 34.3	20 44.7	27 30.3	22 58.0	12 19.4	19 07.6
19 Su	23 48 54	29 04 07	10♐23 19	16 19 34	3 02.6	10 58.6	8 33.4	6 48.7	13 56.3	20 38.1	27 32.1	23 01.2	12 21.6	19 08.6
20 M	23 52 50	0♈03 44	22 16 21	28 14 18	3D 01.8	12 52.0	7 59.0	7 31.7	14 18.4	20 31.4	27 33.8	23 04.4	12 23.8	19 09.5
21 Tu	23 56 47	1 03 20	4♑13 58	10♑16 00	3 02.1	14 43.3	7 23.4	8 14.5	14 40.6	20 24.5	27 35.4	23 07.6	12 26.0	19 10.4
22 W	0 00 43	2 02 54	16 20 58	22 29 28	3 03.4	16 32.0	6 47.0	8 57.4	15 02.9	20 17.6	27 36.9	23 10.9	12 28.2	19 11.3
23 Th	0 04 40	3 02 26	28 42 05	4♒59 19	3 05.1	18 17.7	6 09.8	9 40.2	15 25.2	20 10.6	27 38.3	23 14.1	12 30.4	19 12.2
24 F	0 08 36	4 01 57	11♒21 39	17 49 29	3 06.7	20 00.0	5 32.3	10 22.9	15 47.6	20 03.5	27 39.6	23 17.4	12 32.5	19 13.0
25 Sa	0 12 33	5 01 26	24 23 09	1♓02 51	3R 07.4	21 38.5	4 54.6	11 05.6	16 10.2	19 56.3	27 40.9	23 20.7	12 34.7	19 13.8
26 Su	0 16 29	6 00 52	7♓48 41	14 40 37	3 06.9	23 12.6	4 16.9	11 48.3	16 32.7	19 49.1	27 42.0	23 24.0	12 36.8	19 14.5
27 M	0 20 26	7 00 17	21 38 28	28 41 55	3 04.8	24 42.0	3 39.6	12 30.9	16 55.4	19 41.8	27 43.0	23 27.3	12 38.9	19 15.3
28 Tu	0 24 23	7 59 40	5♈50 27	13♈03 29	3 01.0	26 06.3	3 02.8	13 13.5	17 18.1	19 34.4	27 43.9	23 30.7	12 41.0	19 16.0
29 W	0 28 19	8 59 01	20 20 13	27 39 49	2 56.0	27 25.2	2 26.8	13 56.0	17 40.9	19 26.9	27 44.7	23 34.0	12 43.1	19 16.6
30 Th	0 32 16	9 58 19	5♉01 20	12♉23 50	2 50.3	28 38.3	1 51.9	14 38.5	18 03.8	19 19.4	27 45.4	23 37.4	12 45.2	19 17.3
31 F	0 36 12	10 57 36	19 46 19	27 07 52	2 44.9	29 45.4	1 18.1	15 21.0	18 26.8	19 11.9	27 46.1	23 40.7	12 47.3	19 17.9

April 2017 — LONGITUDE

Day	Sid.Time	☉	0 hr ☽	Noon ☽	True ☊	☿	♀	♂	⚳	♃	♄	♅	♆	♇
1 Sa	0 40 09	11♈56 50	4♊27 40	11♊44 56	2♍40.4	0♉46.3	0♈45.9	16♉03.4	18♉49.8	19♎04.3	27♐46.6	23♈44.1	12♓49.3	19♑18.5
2 Su	0 44 05	12 56 02	18 59 05	26 09 37	2R 37.4	1 40.6	0R 15.2	16 45.8	19 12.9	18R 56.7	27 47.0	23 47.5	12 51.4	19 19.0
3 M	0 48 02	13 55 12	3♋16 10	10♋18 32	2D 36.2	2 28.3	29♓46.3	17 28.1	19 36.0	18 49.1	27 47.3	23 50.9	12 53.4	19 19.6
4 Tu	0 51 58	14 54 19	17 16 35	24 10 18	2 36.5	3 09.2	29 19.4	18 10.4	19 59.2	18 41.4	27 47.5	23 54.3	12 55.4	19 20.1
5 W	0 55 55	15 53 24	0♌59 46	7♌45 06	2 37.7	3 43.2	28 54.5	18 52.6	20 22.5	18 33.7	27R 47.7	23 57.7	12 57.4	19 20.5
6 Th	0 59 52	16 52 26	14 26 29	21 04 05	2R 39.0	4 10.3	28 31.8	19 34.8	20 45.8	18 26.0	27 47.7	24 01.1	12 59.4	19 21.0
7 F	1 03 48	17 51 27	27 38 08	4♍08 48	2 39.5	4 30.4	28 11.3	20 17.0	21 09.2	18 18.3	27 47.6	24 04.5	13 01.4	19 21.4
8 Sa	1 07 45	18 50 25	10♍36 19	17 00 49	2 38.4	4 43.7	27 53.2	20 59.1	21 32.6	18 10.6	27 47.4	24 08.0	13 03.3	19 21.7
9 Su	1 11 41	19 49 21	23 22 29	29 41 27	2 35.2	4R 50.1	27 37.5	21 41.1	21 56.1	18 02.9	27 47.2	24 11.4	13 05.2	19 22.1
10 M	1 15 38	20 48 14	5♎57 48	12♎11 41	2 29.8	4 49.9	27 24.2	22 23.1	22 19.7	17 55.2	27 46.8	24 14.8	13 07.1	19 22.4
11 Tu	1 19 34	21 47 06	18 23 09	24 32 20	2 22.2	4 43.3	27 13.3	23 05.1	22 43.3	17 47.5	27 46.3	24 18.3	13 09.0	19 22.7
12 W	1 23 31	22 45 56	0♏39 17	6♏44 09	2 13.1	4 30.6	27 05.0	23 47.0	23 06.9	17 39.8	27 45.7	24 21.7	13 10.9	19 22.9
13 Th	1 27 27	23 44 43	12 47 04	18 48 09	2 03.2	4 12.2	26 59.1	24 28.9	23 30.6	17 32.2	27 45.1	24 25.1	13 12.7	19 23.2
14 F	1 31 24	24 43 29	24 47 39	0♐45 45	1 53.5	3 48.5	26D 55.6	25 10.8	23 54.4	17 24.6	27 44.3	24 28.6	13 14.5	19 23.4
15 Sa	1 35 20	25 42 13	6♐42 45	12 38 59	1 44.9	3 20.0	26 54.6	25 52.6	24 18.2	17 17.0	27 43.5	24 32.0	13 16.3	19 23.5
16 Su	1 39 17	26 40 56	18 34 48	24 30 38	1 38.0	2 47.5	26 55.9	26 34.3	24 42.0	17 09.5	27 42.5	24 35.4	13 18.1	19 23.7
17 M	1 43 14	27 39 36	0♑26 55	6♑24 12	1 33.2	2 11.4	26 59.6	27 16.0	25 05.9	17 02.0	27 41.5	24 38.9	13 19.9	19 23.8
18 Tu	1 47 10	28 38 15	12 22 59	18 23 52	1D 30.8	1 32.6	27 05.6	27 57.7	25 29.9	16 54.5	27 40.3	24 42.3	13 21.6	19 23.9
19 W	1 51 07	29 36 53	24 27 28	0♒34 24	1 30.1	0 51.9	27 13.9	28 39.4	25 53.9	16 47.1	27 39.1	24 45.7	13 23.4	19 23.9
20 Th	1 55 03	0♉35 28	6♒45 17	13 00 46	1 30.7	0 09.9	27 24.3	29 21.0	26 17.9	16 39.8	27 37.7	24 49.2	13 25.1	19R 23.9
21 F	1 59 00	1 34 02	19 21 25	25 47 50	1R 31.4	29♈27.6	27 36.8	0♊02.5	26 42.0	16 32.5	27 36.3	24 52.6	13 26.7	19 23.9
22 Sa	2 02 56	2 32 35	2♓20 31	8♓59 51	1 31.3	28 45.7	27 51.4	0 44.0	27 06.1	16 25.3	27 34.8	24 56.0	13 28.4	19 23.9
23 Su	2 06 53	3 31 05	15 46 10	22 39 37	1 29.4	28 04.8	28 08.0	1 25.5	27 30.3	16 18.2	27 33.2	24 59.4	13 30.0	19 23.8
24 M	2 10 49	4 29 34	29 40 12	6♈47 44	1 25.1	27 25.8	28 26.6	2 06.9	27 54.5	16 11.1	27 31.5	25 02.8	13 31.6	19 23.7
25 Tu	2 14 46	5 28 01	14♈01 49	21 21 51	1 18.5	26 49.3	28 47.0	2 48.3	28 18.8	16 04.2	27 29.7	25 06.2	13 33.2	19 23.5
26 W	2 18 43	6 26 27	28 47 01	6♉16 19	1 09.7	26 15.8	29 09.1	3 29.7	28 43.1	15 57.3	27 27.8	25 09.6	13 34.8	19 23.4
27 Th	2 22 39	7 24 50	13♉48 35	21 22 32	0 59.9	25 45.7	29 33.1	4 11.0	29 07.4	15 50.5	27 25.8	25 13.0	13 36.3	19 23.2
28 F	2 26 36	8 23 12	28 56 53	6♊30 17	0 50.2	25 19.6	29 58.6	4 52.3	29 31.8	15 43.8	27 23.7	25 16.4	13 37.8	19 23.0
29 Sa	2 30 32	9 21 32	14♊01 32	21 29 29	0 41.8	24 57.6	0♈25.8	5 33.6	29 56.2	15 37.2	27 21.6	25 19.7	13 39.3	19 22.7
30 Su	2 34 29	10 19 50	28 53 11	6♋11 54	0 35.5	24 40.2	0 54.5	6 14.8	0♊20.7	15 30.8	27 19.4	25 23.1	13 40.8	19 22.4

Astro Data	Dy Hr Mn
♃☍♅	3 1:17
♀R	4 9:10
☽0S	13 18:08
☿0N	14 17:45
☉0N	20 10:30
☽0N	28 1:22
♃□♇	30 18:20
♄R	6 5:07
☿R	9 23:17
☽0S	10 1:21
♀D	15 10:19
♇R	20 12:50
☽0N	24 12:00

Planet Ingress	Dy Hr Mn
♂ ♉	10 0:35
☿ ♈	13 21:08
☉ ♈	20 10:30
☿ ♉	31 17:32
♀ ♓R	3 0:26
☉ ♉	19 21:28
☿ ♈R	20 17:38
♂ ♊	21 10:33
♀ ♈	28 13:14
⚳ ♊	29 15:43

Last Aspect Dy Hr Mn		☽ Ingress Dy Hr Mn
2 2:20	♄ △	♉ 2 7:44
3 15:21	♇ △	♊ 4 10:07
6 8:23	♂ ✶	♋ 6 12:55
8 15:00	♂ □	♌ 8 16:47
10 17:07	♄ △	♍ 10 22:08
13 2:37	☿ ☍	♎ 13 5:29
15 10:06	♄ ✶	♏ 15 15:12
17 21:58	☉ △	♐ 18 3:01
20 10:39	♄ ☌	♑ 20 15:32
22 13:21	♅ □	♒ 23 2:29
25 5:57	♄ ✶	♓ 25 10:08
27 10:20	♄ □	♈ 27 14:12
29 12:08	♄ △	♉ 29 15:49
30 23:13	♇ △	♊ 31 16:41

Last Aspect Dy Hr Mn		☽ Ingress Dy Hr Mn
2 14:44	♄ ☍	♋ 2 18:28
4 20:46	♀ △	♌ 4 22:14
7 0:17	♄ △	♍ 7 4:21
9 8:22	♄ □	♎ 9 12:35
11 18:20	♄ ✶	♏ 11 22:43
14 4:19	♀ △	♐ 14 10:28
16 18:27	♄ ☌	♑ 16 23:06
19 9:58	☉ □	♒ 19 10:53
21 18:24	☿ ✶	♓ 21 19:44
23 21:35	♀ ☌	♈ 24 0:34
25 21:54	♄ △	♉ 26 1:57
28 1:20	♀ ✶	♊ 28 1:40
29 21:29	♄ ☍	♋ 30 1:49

☽ Phases & Eclipses Dy Hr Mn		
5 11:34	☽	15♊05
12 14:55	○	22♍13
20 15:59	☾	0♑14
28 2:58	●	7♈37
3 18:41	☽	14♋12
11 6:09	○	21♎33
19 9:58	☾	29♑32
26 12:17	●	6♉27

Astro Data

1 March 2017
Julian Day # 42794
SVP 5♓01'19"
GC 27♐04.7 ⚴ 19♓58.3
Eris 22♈45.5 ⚵ 7♑37.0
⚷ 23♓53.2 ⚶ 20♋15.2R
☽ Mean ☊ 3♍04.4

1 April 2017
Julian Day # 42825
SVP 5♓01'17"
GC 27♐04.8 ⚴ 0♈48.7
Eris 23♈03.6 ⚵ 14♑38.3
⚷ 25♓44.4 ⚶ 22♋19.5
☽ Mean ☊ 1♍25.9

LONGITUDE — May 2017

Day	Sid.Time	☉	0 hr ☽	Noon☽	True☊	☿	♀	♂	⚳	♃	♄	♅	♆	♇
1 M	2 38 25	11♉18 06	13♋25 04	20♋32 18	0♍31.8	24♈27.3	1♈24.7	6♊55.9	0♊45.1	15♎24.4	27♐17.0	25♈26.4	13♓42.2	19♑22.1
2 Tu	2 42 22	12 16 20	27 33 27	4♌28 30	0D 30.2	24R 19.2	1 56.4	7 37.0	1 09.7	15R 18.2	27R 14.6	25 29.8	13 43.6	19R 21.8
3 W	2 46 18	13 14 31	11♌17 36	18 00 58	0R 30.0	24D 15.9	2 29.4	8 18.1	1 34.2	15 12.1	27 12.2	25 33.1	13 45.0	19 21.4
4 Th	2 50 15	14 12 41	24 38 56	1♍11 52	0 30.2	24 17.4	3 03.7	8 59.2	1 58.8	15 06.0	27 09.6	25 36.4	13 46.3	19 21.0
5 F	2 54 12	15 10 49	7♍40 12	14 04 20	0 29.6	24 23.6	3 39.3	9 40.2	2 23.4	15 00.2	27 07.0	25 39.7	13 47.6	19 20.6
6 Sa	2 58 08	16 08 54	20 24 41	26 41 39	0 27.0	24 34.6	4 16.2	10 21.1	2 48.0	14 54.4	27 04.2	25 42.9	13 48.9	19 20.2
7 Su	3 02 05	17 06 58	2♎55 36	9♎06 53	0 21.8	24 50.2	4 54.2	11 02.0	3 12.7	14 48.8	27 01.4	25 46.2	13 50.2	19 19.7
8 M	3 06 01	18 05 00	15 15 49	21 22 38	0 13.8	25 10.2	5 33.3	11 42.9	3 37.3	14 43.3	26 58.6	25 49.5	13 51.4	19 19.2
9 Tu	3 09 58	19 03 00	27 27 35	3♏30 52	0 03.1	25 34.7	6 13.6	12 23.7	4 02.1	14 38.0	26 55.6	25 52.7	13 52.7	19 18.7
10 W	3 13 54	20 00 59	9♏32 40	15 33 09	29♌50.4	26 03.4	6 54.9	13 04.5	4 26.8	14 32.8	26 52.6	25 55.9	13 53.8	19 18.1
11 Th	3 17 51	20 58 56	21 32 26	27 30 42	29 36.6	26 36.2	7 37.2	13 45.3	4 51.6	14 27.7	26 49.5	25 59.1	13 55.0	19 17.5
12 F	3 21 47	21 56 51	3♐28 05	9♐24 46	29 23.0	27 13.0	8 20.5	14 26.0	5 16.4	14 22.8	26 46.3	26 02.3	13 56.1	19 16.9
13 Sa	3 25 44	22 54 45	15 20 55	21 16 47	29 10.5	27 53.6	9 04.7	15 06.7	5 41.2	14 18.1	26 43.1	26 05.4	13 57.2	19 16.3
14 Su	3 29 41	23 52 38	27 12 37	3♑08 42	29 00.2	28 37.9	9 49.9	15 47.3	6 06.0	14 13.5	26 39.8	26 08.6	13 58.3	19 15.6
15 M	3 33 37	24 50 29	9♑05 23	15 03 04	28 52.5	29 25.9	10 35.9	16 27.9	6 30.9	14 09.0	26 36.5	26 11.7	13 59.3	19 14.9
16 Tu	3 37 34	25 48 20	21 02 10	27 03 11	28 47.7	0♉17.2	11 22.7	17 08.5	6 55.8	14 04.7	26 33.0	26 14.8	14 00.3	19 14.2
17 W	3 41 30	26 46 08	3♒06 38	9♒13 03	28 45.3	1 11.9	12 10.3	17 49.0	7 20.7	14 00.6	26 29.5	26 17.9	14 01.3	19 13.5
18 Th	3 45 27	27 43 56	15 23 03	21 37 13	28 44.6	2 09.8	12 58.8	18 29.5	7 45.6	13 56.6	26 26.0	26 20.9	14 02.2	19 12.7
19 F	3 49 23	28 41 43	27 56 11	4♓20 33	28 44.5	3 10.8	13 47.9	19 10.0	8 10.6	13 52.8	26 22.4	26 24.0	14 03.2	19 11.9
20 Sa	3 53 20	29 39 28	10♓50 52	17 27 39	28 43.9	4 14.9	14 37.8	19 50.4	8 35.5	13 49.2	26 18.7	26 27.0	14 04.0	19 11.1
21 Su	3 57 16	0♊37 12	24 11 21	1♈02 17	28 41.7	5 21.9	15 28.3	20 30.8	9 00.5	13 45.7	26 15.0	26 30.0	14 04.9	19 10.3
22 M	4 01 13	1 34 56	8♈00 38	15 06 23	28 37.2	6 31.7	16 19.5	21 11.2	9 25.6	13 42.4	26 11.2	26 32.9	14 05.7	19 09.4
23 Tu	4 05 10	2 32 38	22 19 22	29 39 08	28 30.0	7 44.4	17 11.3	21 51.5	9 50.6	13 39.2	26 07.4	26 35.9	14 06.5	19 08.5
24 W	4 09 06	3 30 19	7♉05 03	14♉36 11	28 20.6	8 59.8	18 03.8	22 31.8	10 15.6	13 36.3	26 03.5	26 38.8	14 07.3	19 07.6
25 Th	4 13 03	4 27 59	22 11 26	29 49 32	28 09.9	10 17.8	18 56.8	23 12.1	10 40.7	13 33.5	25 59.6	26 41.7	14 08.0	19 06.7
26 F	4 16 59	5 25 38	7♊29 03	15♊08 33	27 59.2	11 38.5	19 50.3	23 52.3	11 05.8	13 30.8	25 55.6	26 44.6	14 08.7	19 05.7
27 Sa	4 20 56	6 23 15	22 46 32	0♋21 41	27 49.7	13 01.8	20 44.5	24 32.5	11 30.9	13 28.4	25 51.6	26 47.4	14 09.4	19 04.8
28 Su	4 24 52	7 20 52	7♋52 44	15 18 40	27 42.4	14 27.7	21 39.1	25 12.7	11 56.0	13 26.1	25 47.6	26 50.2	14 10.0	19 03.8
29 M	4 28 49	8 18 27	22 38 40	29 52 09	27 37.8	15 56.1	22 34.2	25 52.8	12 21.1	13 24.1	25 43.5	26 53.0	14 10.6	19 02.8
30 Tu	4 32 45	9 16 00	6♌58 46	13♌58 21	27D 35.6	17 27.0	23 29.8	26 32.9	12 46.3	13 22.1	25 39.4	26 55.8	14 11.2	19 01.7
31 W	4 36 42	10 13 32	20 50 58	27 36 46	27 35.1	19 00.4	24 25.8	27 13.0	13 11.4	13 20.4	25 35.2	26 58.5	14 11.7	19 00.7

LONGITUDE — June 2017

Day	Sid.Time	☉	0 hr ☽	Noon☽	True☊	☿	♀	♂	⚳	♃	♄	♅	♆	♇
1 Th	4 40 39	11♊11 03	4♍16 05	10♍49 20	27♌35.2	20♉36.3	25♈22.4	27♊53.0	13♊36.6	13♎18.9	25♐31.0	27♈01.2	14♓12.2	18♑59.6
2 F	4 44 35	12 08 33	17 16 59	23 39 32	27R 34.7	22 14.7	26 19.3	28 33.0	14 01.8	13R 17.5	25R 26.8	27 03.8	14 12.7	18R 58.5
3 Sa	4 48 32	13 06 01	29 57 30	6♎11 27	27 32.6	23 55.6	27 16.6	29 13.0	14 26.9	13 16.3	25 22.5	27 06.5	14 13.1	18 57.4
4 Su	4 52 28	14 03 28	12♎21 51	18 29 14	27 28.2	25 38.9	28 14.4	29 52.9	14 52.1	13 15.3	25 18.2	27 09.1	14 13.5	18 56.3
5 M	4 56 25	15 00 53	24 34 01	0♏36 40	27 21.1	27 24.7	29 12.6	0♋32.8	15 17.3	13 14.5	25 13.9	27 11.6	14 13.9	18 55.1
6 Tu	5 00 21	15 58 18	6♏37 31	12 36 57	27 11.5	29 13.0	0♉11.1	1 12.6	15 42.5	13 13.8	25 09.6	27 14.2	14 14.2	18 53.9
7 W	5 04 18	16 55 42	18 35 15	24 32 41	27 00.0	1♊03.6	1 10.0	1 52.4	16 07.7	13 13.4	25 05.3	27 16.7	14 14.6	18 52.8
8 Th	5 08 14	17 53 04	0♐29 30	6♐25 56	26 47.5	2 56.6	2 09.3	2 32.2	16 33.0	13 13.1	25 00.9	27 19.1	14 14.8	18 51.6
9 F	5 12 11	18 50 26	12 22 06	18 18 16	26 35.1	4 51.9	3 08.9	3 12.0	16 58.2	13D 13.0	24 56.5	27 21.6	14 15.1	18 50.3
10 Sa	5 16 08	19 47 47	24 14 34	0♑11 13	26 23.8	6 49.5	4 08.9	3 51.7	17 23.4	13 13.0	24 52.1	27 24.0	14 15.3	18 49.1
11 Su	5 20 04	20 45 07	6♑08 23	12 06 19	26 14.4	8 49.3	5 09.1	4 31.4	17 48.7	13 13.3	24 47.7	27 26.3	14 15.5	18 47.9
12 M	5 24 01	21 42 27	18 05 14	24 05 25	26 07.5	10 51.1	6 09.8	5 11.1	18 13.9	13 13.7	24 43.3	27 28.7	14 15.6	18 46.6
13 Tu	5 27 57	22 39 46	0♒07 11	6♒10 52	26 03.2	12 54.9	7 10.7	5 50.7	18 39.1	13 14.3	24 38.9	27 31.0	14 15.7	18 45.3
14 W	5 31 54	23 37 05	12 16 52	18 25 37	26D 01.3	15 00.4	8 11.9	6 30.4	19 04.4	13 15.1	24 34.5	27 33.2	14 15.8	18 44.0
15 Th	5 35 50	24 34 23	24 37 33	0♓53 09	26 01.1	17 07.6	9 13.4	7 09.9	19 29.6	13 16.1	24 30.1	27 35.5	14R 15.9	18 42.7
16 F	5 39 47	25 31 41	7♓12 56	13 37 25	26R 01.8	19 16.1	10 15.2	7 49.5	19 54.9	13 17.2	24 25.6	27 37.6	14 15.9	18 41.4
17 Sa	5 43 43	26 28 58	20 07 04	26 42 23	26 02.2	21 25.9	11 17.2	8 29.0	20 20.2	13 18.6	24 21.2	27 39.8	14 15.9	18 40.1
18 Su	5 47 40	27 26 15	3♈23 47	10♈11 36	26 01.5	23 36.5	12 19.6	9 08.5	20 45.4	13 20.0	24 16.8	27 41.9	14 15.8	18 38.7
19 M	5 51 37	28 23 32	17 06 06	24 07 22	25 58.9	25 47.7	13 22.1	9 48.0	21 10.7	13 21.7	24 12.4	27 44.0	14 15.7	18 37.4
20 Tu	5 55 33	29 20 49	1♉15 23	8♉29 53	25 54.1	27 59.4	14 25.0	10 27.5	21 36.0	13 23.6	24 08.0	27 46.0	14 15.6	18 36.0
21 W	5 59 30	0♋18 05	15 50 26	23 16 23	25 47.5	0♋11.1	15 28.0	11 06.9	22 01.2	13 25.6	24 03.6	27 48.0	14 15.5	18 34.6
22 Th	6 03 26	1 15 22	0♊46 53	8♊20 51	25 39.8	2 22.6	16 31.3	11 46.3	22 26.5	13 27.8	23 59.2	27 50.0	14 15.3	18 33.2
23 F	6 07 23	2 12 38	15 57 07	23 34 19	25 31.8	4 33.7	17 34.8	12 25.7	22 51.8	13 30.2	23 54.8	27 51.9	14 15.1	18 31.9
24 Sa	6 11 19	3 09 53	1♋11 08	8♋46 11	25 24.8	6 44.1	18 38.6	13 05.0	23 17.0	13 32.7	23 50.5	27 53.7	14 14.8	18 30.5
25 Su	6 15 16	4 07 09	16 18 13	23 46 05	25 19.4	8 53.5	19 42.5	13 44.3	23 42.3	13 35.4	23 46.1	27 55.6	14 14.6	18 29.0
26 M	6 19 12	5 04 24	1♌08 48	8♌25 35	25 16.2	11 01.8	20 46.7	14 23.6	24 07.5	13 38.3	23 41.8	27 57.4	14 14.3	18 27.6
27 Tu	6 23 09	6 01 38	15 35 52	22 39 18	25D 15.0	13 08.8	21 51.0	15 02.9	24 32.8	13 41.4	23 37.5	27 59.1	14 13.9	18 26.2
28 W	6 27 06	6 58 52	29 35 43	6♍25 08	25 15.4	15 14.2	22 55.6	15 42.1	24 58.0	13 44.6	23 33.3	28 00.8	14 13.6	18 24.8
29 Th	6 31 02	7 56 06	13♍07 42	19 43 43	25 16.5	17 18.1	24 00.3	16 21.4	25 23.3	13 48.0	23 29.1	28 02.5	14 13.2	18 23.3
30 F	6 34 59	8 53 19	26 13 34	2♎37 43	25R 17.5	19 20.3	25 05.2	17 00.6	25 48.5	13 51.5	23 24.9	28 04.1	14 12.7	18 21.9

Astro Data

	Dy Hr Mn
☿ D	3 16:34
☽ 0S	7 7:47
♃⚻♆	17 8:38
♄△♅	19 6:16
☽ 0N	21 22:45
☽ 0S	3 14:34
♃ D	9 14:04
♆ R	16 11:11
☽ 0N	18 7:58
☽ 0S	30 22:27

Planet Ingress

		Dy Hr Mn
☊	♌R	9 18:08
☿	♉	16 4:08
☉	♊	20 20:32
♂	♋	4 16:17
♀	♉	6 7:28
☿	♊	6 22:16
☉	♋	21 4:25
☿	♋	21 9:59

Last Aspect / ☽ Ingress

Last Aspect Dy Hr Mn			☽ Ingress	Dy Hr Mn
1 20:24	♅	□	♌	2 4:13
4 4:36	♄	△	♍	4 9:48
6 12:43	♄	□	♎	6 18:21
8 23:00	♄	⚹	♏	9 5:02
10 21:44	☉	☍	♐	11 17:01
14 2:15	☿	△	♑	14 5:39
16 10:23	♅	□	♒	16 17:51
19 0:34	☉	□	♓	19 3:53
21 3:40	♄	□	♈	21 10:12
23 7:00	♅	☌	♉	23 12:34
24 19:09	♇	△	♊	25 12:16
27 6:19	♅	⚹	♋	27 11:26
29 7:00	♅	□	♌	29 12:13
31 11:15	♂	⚹	♍	31 16:17

Last Aspect / ☽ Ingress

Last Aspect Dy Hr Mn			☽ Ingress	Dy Hr Mn
2 21:50	♂	□	♎	3 0:05
5 8:58	♀	☍	♏	5 10:47
7 0:36	♇	⚹	♐	7 23:00
10 6:21	♅	△	♑	10 11:37
12 18:46	♅	□	♒	12 23:46
15 5:41	♅	⚹	♓	15 10:19
17 11:34	☉	□	♈	17 17:56
19 19:43	☉	⚹	♉	19 21:54
21 4:27	♇	△	♊	21 22:45
23 18:47	♅	⚹	♋	23 22:08
25 18:46	♅	□	♌	25 22:08
27 21:13	♅	△	♍	28 0:42
29 20:36	♀	△	♎	30 7:03

☽ Phases & Eclipses

Dy Hr Mn		
3 2:48	☽	12♌52
10 21:44	○	20♏24
19 0:34	☾	28♒14
25 19:46	●	4♊47
1 12:43	☽	11♍13
9 13:11	○	18♐53
17 11:34	☾	26♓28
24 2:32	●	2♋47

Astro Data

1 May 2017
Julian Day # 42855
SVP 5♓01'13"
GC 27♐04.9 ⚴ 11♈21.6
Eris 23♈23.1 ⚵ 18♑08.7
⚷ 27♓20.4 ⚶ 29♋32.6
☽ Mean ☊ 29♌50.6

1 June 2017
Julian Day # 42886
SVP 5♓01'09"
GC 27♐05.0 ⚴ 21♈54.8
Eris 23♈40.4 ⚵ 16♑52.9R
⚷ 28♓28.7 ⚶ 10♌18.4
☽ Mean ☊ 28♌12.1

July 2017 — LONGITUDE

Day	Sid.Time	☉	0 hr ☽	Noon ☽	True ☊	☿	♀	♂	⚳	♃	♄	♅	♆	♇
1 Sa	6 38 55	9♋50 31	8♎56 41	15♎11 00	25♌17.5	21♋20.6	26♉10.3	17♋39.7	26♊13.7	13♎55.2	23♐20.7	28♈05.7	14♓12.3	18♑20.4
2 Su	6 42 52	10 47 44	21 21 15	27 27 58	25R16.0	23 19.1	27 15.5	18 18.9	26 38.9	13 59.1	23R16.6	28 07.2	14R11.8	18R18.9
3 M	6 46 48	11 44 55	3♏31 42	9♏33 00	25 12.6	25 15.6	28 21.0	18 58.0	27 04.1	14 03.1	23 12.5	28 08.7	14 11.2	18 17.5
4 Tu	6 50 45	12 42 07	15 32 21	21 30 13	25 07.5	27 10.2	29 26.6	19 37.1	27 29.3	14 07.3	23 08.4	28 10.1	14 10.7	18 16.0
5 W	6 54 41	13 39 18	27 27 03	3♐23 15	25 01.0	29 02.8	0♊32.3	20 16.1	27 54.5	14 11.7	23 04.4	28 11.5	14 10.1	18 14.6
6 Th	6 58 38	14 36 30	9♐19 10	15 15 08	24 53.8	0♌53.5	1 38.3	20 55.2	28 19.6	14 16.2	23 00.5	28 12.9	14 09.5	18 13.1
7 F	7 02 35	15 33 41	21 11 26	27 08 21	24 46.5	2 42.1	2 44.4	21 34.2	28 44.8	14 20.9	22 56.6	28 14.2	14 08.8	18 11.6
8 Sa	7 06 31	16 30 52	3♑06 07	9♑04 58	24 40.0	4 28.7	3 50.6	22 13.2	29 10.0	14 25.7	22 52.7	28 15.4	14 08.2	18 10.1
9 Su	7 10 28	17 28 04	15 05 04	21 06 39	24 34.6	6 13.2	4 57.0	22 52.1	29 35.1	14 30.7	22 48.9	28 16.7	14 07.5	18 08.7
10 M	7 14 24	18 25 15	27 09 54	3♒15 00	24 31.0	7 55.8	6 03.6	23 31.1	0♋00.2	14 35.8	22 45.1	28 17.8	14 06.7	18 07.2
11 Tu	7 18 21	19 22 27	9♒22 11	15 31 38	24D29.0	9 36.3	7 10.3	24 10.0	0 25.3	14 41.1	22 41.4	28 19.0	14 06.0	18 05.7
12 W	7 22 17	20 19 39	21 43 36	27 58 21	24 28.7	11 14.9	8 17.1	24 48.9	0 50.4	14 46.5	22 37.7	28 20.0	14 05.2	18 04.2
13 Th	7 26 14	21 16 51	4♓16 08	10♓37 16	24 29.6	12 51.4	9 24.1	25 27.8	1 15.5	14 52.1	22 34.1	28 21.1	14 04.4	18 02.8
14 F	7 30 10	22 14 04	17 02 01	23 30 44	24 31.1	14 25.8	10 31.3	26 06.6	1 40.6	14 57.8	22 30.5	28 22.0	14 03.5	18 01.3
15 Sa	7 34 07	23 11 17	0♈03 41	6♈41 12	24 32.5	15 58.3	11 38.5	26 45.5	2 05.6	15 03.6	22 27.0	28 23.0	14 02.7	17 59.8
16 Su	7 38 04	24 08 31	13 23 31	20 10 53	24R33.4	17 28.7	12 46.0	27 24.3	2 30.6	15 09.6	22 23.6	28 23.9	14 01.8	17 58.3
17 M	7 42 00	25 05 46	27 03 27	4♉01 18	24 33.1	18 57.1	13 53.5	28 03.1	2 55.7	15 15.8	22 20.2	28 24.7	14 00.9	17 56.9
18 Tu	7 45 57	26 03 01	11♉04 23	18 12 35	24 31.7	20 23.4	15 01.2	28 41.9	3 20.7	15 22.1	22 16.9	28 25.5	13 59.9	17 55.4
19 W	7 49 53	27 00 18	25 25 35	2♊42 59	24 29.1	21 47.6	16 09.0	29 20.7	3 45.7	15 28.5	22 13.7	28 26.2	13 58.9	17 54.0
20 Th	7 53 50	27 57 35	10♊04 11	17 28 29	24 25.8	23 09.6	17 16.9	29 59.4	4 10.6	15 35.0	22 10.5	28 26.9	13 57.9	17 52.5
21 F	7 57 46	28 54 52	24 55 00	2♋22 47	24 22.3	24 29.5	18 25.0	0♌38.2	4 35.6	15 41.7	22 07.4	28 27.6	13 56.9	17 51.1
22 Sa	8 01 43	29 52 11	9♋50 49	17 18 01	24 19.2	25 47.2	19 33.2	1 16.9	5 00.5	15 48.6	22 04.4	28 28.2	13 55.9	17 49.6
23 Su	8 05 40	0♌49 30	24 43 22	2♌05 50	24 17.0	27 02.6	20 41.4	1 55.6	5 25.4	15 55.5	22 01.4	28 28.7	13 54.8	17 48.2
24 M	8 09 36	1 46 49	9♌24 30	16 38 36	24D15.8	28 15.7	21 49.8	2 34.3	5 50.3	16 02.6	21 58.5	28 29.2	13 53.7	17 46.8
25 Tu	8 13 33	2 44 09	23 47 26	0♍50 31	24 15.8	29 26.4	22 58.3	3 13.0	6 15.1	16 09.9	21 55.7	28 29.7	13 52.6	17 45.4
26 W	8 17 29	3 41 30	7♍47 30	14 38 11	24 16.6	0♍34.6	24 07.0	3 51.6	6 40.0	16 17.2	21 52.9	28 30.1	13 51.4	17 43.9
27 Th	8 21 26	4 38 51	21 22 32	28 00 38	24 17.9	1 40.3	25 15.7	4 30.2	7 04.8	16 24.7	21 50.3	28 30.5	13 50.3	17 42.5
28 F	8 25 22	5 36 12	4♎32 41	10♎59 00	24 19.3	2 43.4	26 24.5	5 08.8	7 29.5	16 32.3	21 47.7	28 30.8	13 49.1	17 41.2
29 Sa	8 29 19	6 33 34	17 19 57	23 36 00	24 20.3	3 43.7	27 33.4	5 47.4	7 54.3	16 40.0	21 45.2	28 31.0	13 47.9	17 39.8
30 Su	8 33 15	7 30 57	29 47 38	5♏55 24	24R20.8	4 41.1	28 42.5	6 26.0	8 19.0	16 47.9	21 42.8	28 31.2	13 46.6	17 38.4
31 M	8 37 12	8 28 20	11♏59 50	18 01 30	24 20.5	5 35.6	29 51.6	7 04.6	8 43.7	16 55.9	21 40.4	28 31.4	13 45.4	17 37.0

August 2017 — LONGITUDE

Day	Sid.Time	☉	0 hr ☽	Noon ☽	True ☊	☿	♀	♂	⚳	♃	♄	♅	♆	♇
1 Tu	8 41 08	9♌25 43	24♏00 59	29♏58 48	24♌19.6	6♍26.9	1♋00.8	7♌43.1	9♋08.3	17♎04.0	21♐38.2	28♈31.5	13♓44.1	17♑35.7
2 W	8 45 05	10 23 07	5♐55 31	11♐51 39	24R18.1	7 15.0	2 10.2	8 21.6	9 32.9	17 12.2	21R36.0	28R31.5	13R42.8	17R34.4
3 Th	8 49 02	11 20 32	17 47 41	23 44 05	24 16.3	7 59.6	3 19.6	9 00.1	9 57.5	17 20.5	21 33.9	28 31.6	13 41.5	17 33.0
4 F	8 52 58	12 17 58	29 41 16	5♑39 37	24 14.5	8 40.7	4 29.1	9 38.6	10 22.1	17 28.9	21 31.9	28 31.5	13 40.1	17 31.7
5 Sa	8 56 55	13 15 24	11♑39 32	17 41 18	24 12.9	9 18.0	5 38.8	10 17.1	10 46.6	17 37.5	21 30.0	28 31.4	13 38.8	17 30.4
6 Su	9 00 51	14 12 52	23 45 12	29 51 30	24 11.7	9 51.4	6 48.5	10 55.5	11 11.1	17 46.1	21 28.2	28 31.3	13 37.4	17 29.1
7 M	9 04 48	15 10 20	6♒00 25	12♒12 06	24D11.1	10 20.6	7 58.3	11 34.0	11 35.6	17 54.9	21 26.4	28 31.1	13 36.0	17 27.9
8 Tu	9 08 44	16 07 49	18 26 44	24 44 26	24 10.8	10 45.5	9 08.2	12 12.4	12 00.0	18 03.8	21 24.8	28 30.9	13 34.6	17 26.6
9 W	9 12 41	17 05 19	1♓05 19	7♓29 27	24 11.0	11 05.8	10 18.3	12 50.8	12 24.4	18 12.8	21 23.2	28 30.6	13 33.2	17 25.4
10 Th	9 16 37	18 02 51	13 56 54	20 27 44	24 11.5	11 21.4	11 28.4	13 29.2	12 48.7	18 21.8	21 21.8	28 30.3	13 31.8	17 24.1
11 F	9 20 34	19 00 24	27 02 00	3♈39 43	24 12.0	11 32.1	12 38.6	14 07.6	13 13.0	18 31.0	21 20.4	28 29.9	13 30.3	17 22.9
12 Sa	9 24 31	19 57 58	10♈20 55	17 05 37	24 12.5	11R37.6	13 48.9	14 46.0	13 37.3	18 40.3	21 19.1	28 29.5	13 28.8	17 21.7
13 Su	9 28 27	20 55 33	23 53 47	0♉45 25	24 12.8	11 37.8	14 59.3	15 24.4	14 01.5	18 49.7	21 17.9	28 29.0	13 27.4	17 20.6
14 M	9 32 24	21 53 10	7♉40 26	14 38 45	24R12.9	11 32.6	16 09.8	16 02.7	14 25.7	18 59.2	21 16.8	28 28.5	13 25.9	17 19.4
15 Tu	9 36 20	22 50 49	21 40 15	28 44 44	24 12.9	11 21.9	17 20.3	16 41.1	14 49.8	19 08.8	21 15.8	28 27.9	13 24.4	17 18.3
16 W	9 40 17	23 48 29	5♊51 57	13♊01 37	24D12.9	11 05.5	18 31.0	17 19.4	15 14.0	19 18.5	21 14.9	28 27.3	13 22.8	17 17.1
17 Th	9 44 13	24 46 11	20 13 22	27 26 45	24 12.9	10 43.6	19 41.8	17 57.7	15 38.0	19 28.3	21 14.0	28 26.6	13 21.3	17 16.0
18 F	9 48 10	25 43 54	4♋41 16	11♋56 22	24 13.0	10 16.3	20 52.6	18 36.0	16 02.0	19 38.1	21 13.3	28 25.9	13 19.8	17 15.0
19 Sa	9 52 06	26 41 39	19 11 26	26 25 50	24 13.2	9 43.6	22 03.6	19 14.3	16 26.0	19 48.1	21 12.7	28 25.1	13 18.2	17 13.9
20 Su	9 56 03	27 39 26	3♌38 53	10♌49 56	24R13.4	9 05.9	23 14.6	19 52.6	16 49.9	19 58.2	21 12.2	28 24.3	13 16.6	17 12.9
21 M	10 00 00	28 37 13	17 58 19	25 03 27	24 13.5	8 23.7	24 25.7	20 30.9	17 13.8	20 08.3	21 11.7	28 23.5	13 15.1	17 11.8
22 Tu	10 03 56	29 35 03	2♍04 45	9♍01 46	24 13.4	7 37.4	25 36.8	21 09.2	17 37.6	20 18.6	21 11.4	28 22.6	13 13.5	17 10.8
23 W	10 07 53	0♍32 53	15 54 06	22 41 26	24 12.9	6 47.7	26 48.1	21 47.4	18 01.4	20 28.9	21 11.1	28 21.7	13 11.9	17 09.8
24 Th	10 11 49	1 30 45	29 23 36	6♎00 29	24 12.1	5 55.5	27 59.4	22 25.7	18 25.1	20 39.3	21 11.0	28 20.7	13 10.3	17 08.9
25 F	10 15 46	2 28 38	12♎32 06	18 58 35	24 11.1	5 01.7	29 10.8	23 03.9	18 48.7	20 49.8	21D10.9	28 19.6	13 08.7	17 07.9
26 Sa	10 19 42	3 26 33	25 20 06	1♏36 56	24 10.0	4 07.3	0♌22.3	23 42.1	19 12.3	21 00.4	21 11.0	28 18.6	13 07.0	17 07.0
27 Su	10 23 39	4 24 29	7♏49 27	13 58 04	24 09.1	3 13.4	1 33.9	24 20.4	19 35.8	21 11.0	21 11.1	28 17.4	13 05.4	17 06.1
28 M	10 27 35	5 22 26	20 03 15	26 05 31	24D08.4	2 21.1	2 45.5	24 58.6	19 59.3	21 21.7	21 11.4	28 16.3	13 03.8	17 05.3
29 Tu	10 31 32	6 20 24	2♐05 24	8♐03 29	24 08.2	1 31.6	3 57.2	25 36.8	20 22.7	21 32.6	21 11.7	28 15.1	13 02.1	17 04.4
30 W	10 35 29	7 18 24	14 00 19	19 56 31	24 08.6	0 46.1	5 09.0	26 14.9	20 46.1	21 43.5	21 12.2	28 13.8	13 00.5	17 03.6
31 Th	10 39 25	8 16 25	25 52 39	1♑49 18	24 09.5	0 05.4	6 20.8	26 53.1	21 09.4	21 54.4	21 12.7	28 12.5	12 58.9	17 02.8

Astro Data
Dy Hr Mn
♃⚹♆ 5 4:20
☽0N 15 15:05
☽0S 28 7:23

♅R 3 5:32
♃□♇ 4 18:49
☽0N 11 20:50
♅⚹♆ 11 21:50
☿R 13 1:01
☽0S 24 16:42
♄D 25 12:09
♃⚹♄ 27 12:16

Planet Ingress
Dy Hr Mn
♀ ♊ 5 0:13
☿ ♌ 6 0:21
⚳ ♋ 10 11:48
♂ ♌ 20 12:21
☉ ♌ 22 15:16
☿ ♍ 25 23:42
♀ ♋ 31 14:55

☉ ♍ 22 22:21
♀ ♌ 26 4:31
☿ ♌R 31 15:29

Last Aspect / ☽ Ingress
Dy Hr Mn — Dy Hr Mn
2 13:18 ♅☍ ♏ 2 17:00
5 1:35 ☿△ ♐ 5 5:09
7 14:13 ♅△ ♑ 7 17:46
10 2:13 ♅□ ♒ 10 5:36
12 12:42 ♅⚹ ♓ 12 15:53
14 17:02 ♂△ ♈ 14 23:53
17 2:20 ♅☌ ♉ 17 5:05
19 6:12 ♂⚹ ♊ 19 7:32
21 5:42 ♅⚹ ♋ 21 8:11
23 6:06 ♅□ ♌ 23 8:35
25 9:23 ♅☍ ♍ 25 10:33
27 6:32 ♀□ ♎ 27 15:38
29 21:31 ♅☍ ♏ 30 0:24

Last Aspect / ☽ Ingress
Dy Hr Mn — Dy Hr Mn
31 11:11 ♇⚹ ♐ 1 12:02
3 21:40 ♅△ ♑ 4 0:38
6 9:23 ♅□ ♒ 6 12:17
8 19:09 ♅⚹ ♓ 8 21:57
10 13:39 ♄□ ♈ 11 5:23
13 8:02 ♅☌ ♉ 13 10:41
15 1:16 ☉□ ♊ 15 14:07
17 13:39 ♅⚹ ♋ 17 16:14
19 15:18 ♅□ ♌ 19 17:56
21 18:31 ☉☌ ♍ 21 20:26
23 20:03 ♀⚹ ♎ 24 1:06
26 5:40 ♅☍ ♏ 26 8:54
28 9:39 ♂□ ♐ 28 19:49
31 4:43 ♅△ ♑ 31 8:20

☽ Phases & Eclipses
Dy Hr Mn
1 0:52 ☽ 9♎24
9 4:08 ○ 17♑09
16 19:27 ☾ 24♈26
23 9:47 ● 0♌44
30 15:24 ☽ 7♏39

7 18:12 ○ 15♒25
7 18:22 • P 0.246
15 1:16 ☾ 22♉25
21 18:31 ● 28♌53
21 18:26:40 • T 02'40"
29 8:14 ☽ 6♐11

Astro Data
1 July 2017
Julian Day # 42916
SVP 5♓01'04"
GC 27♐05.0 ⚴ 1♉17.8
Eris 23♈50.4 ⚵ 11♑05.4R
⚷ 28♓51.9R ⚶ 22♌40.0
☽ Mean ☊ 26♌36.8

1 August 2017
Julian Day # 42947
SVP 5♓01'00"
GC 27♐05.1 ⚴ 9♉16.7
Eris 23♈51.4R ⚵ 4♑39.6R
⚷ 28♓27.0R ⚶ 6♍43.0
☽ Mean ☊ 24♌58.3

LONGITUDE September 2017

Day	Sid.Time	☉	0 hr ☽	Noon ☽	True ☊	☿	♀	♂	⚳	♃	♄	♅	♆	♇
1 F	10 43 22	9♍14 28	7♑47 02	13♑46 22	24♌10.8	29♌30.7	7♌32.8	27♌31.3	21♋32.6	22♎05.5	21♐13.3	28♈11.2	12♓57.2	17♑02.0
2 Sa	10 47 18	10 12 32	19 47 49	25 51 51	24 12.1	29R 02.7	8 44.8	28 09.4	21 55.8	22 16.6	21 14.1	28R 09.8	12R 55.6	17R 01.3
3 Su	10 51 15	11 10 37	1♒58 53	8♒09 18	24 13.3	28 42.2	9 56.8	28 47.6	22 18.9	22 27.7	21 14.9	28 08.4	12 53.9	17 00.5
4 M	10 55 11	12 08 44	14 23 25	20 41 29	24R 13.9	28D 29.6	11 09.0	29 25.7	22 41.9	22 39.0	21 15.8	28 07.0	12 52.3	16 59.8
5 Tu	10 59 08	13 06 53	27 03 42	3♓30 11	24 13.7	28 25.5	12 21.2	0♍03.8	23 04.8	22 50.3	21 16.8	28 05.5	12 50.6	16 59.2
6 W	11 03 04	14 05 03	10♓00 58	16 36 03	24 12.5	28 30.0	13 33.5	0 41.9	23 27.7	23 01.7	21 18.0	28 03.9	12 49.0	16 58.5
7 Th	11 07 01	15 03 15	23 15 19	29 58 37	24 10.4	28 43.4	14 45.8	1 20.0	23 50.5	23 13.1	21 19.2	28 02.4	12 47.3	16 57.9
8 F	11 10 58	16 01 28	6♈45 42	13♈36 19	24 07.5	29 05.6	15 58.2	1 58.1	24 13.2	23 24.6	21 20.5	28 00.8	12 45.7	16 57.3
9 Sa	11 14 54	16 59 44	20 30 08	27 26 46	24 04.3	29 36.5	17 10.7	2 36.2	24 35.9	23 36.2	21 21.9	27 59.1	12 44.0	16 56.7
10 Su	11 18 51	17 58 02	4♉25 53	11♉27 04	24 01.2	0♍16.0	18 23.3	3 14.3	24 58.5	23 47.8	21 23.4	27 57.4	12 42.4	16 56.2
11 M	11 22 47	18 56 21	18 29 56	25 34 06	23 58.7	1 03.6	19 36.0	3 52.4	25 21.0	23 59.5	21 25.0	27 55.7	12 40.7	16 55.7
12 Tu	11 26 44	19 54 43	2♊39 14	9♊44 59	23D 57.2	1 59.0	20 48.7	4 30.5	25 43.4	24 11.3	21 26.7	27 54.0	12 39.1	16 55.2
13 W	11 30 40	20 53 07	16 51 03	23 57 08	23 56.9	3 01.8	22 01.4	5 08.6	26 05.8	24 23.1	21 28.5	27 52.2	12 37.5	16 54.7
14 Th	11 34 37	21 51 34	1♋02 58	8♋08 19	23 57.6	4 11.5	23 14.3	5 46.6	26 28.0	24 35.0	21 30.3	27 50.4	12 35.8	16 54.3
15 F	11 38 33	22 50 02	15 12 56	22 16 36	23 59.0	5 27.4	24 27.2	6 24.7	26 50.2	24 46.9	21 32.3	27 48.5	12 34.2	16 53.9
16 Sa	11 42 30	23 48 33	29 19 02	6♌20 02	24 00.5	6 49.0	25 40.2	7 02.8	27 12.3	24 58.9	21 34.4	27 46.6	12 32.6	16 53.5
17 Su	11 46 27	24 47 05	13♌19 18	20 16 35	24R 01.3	8 15.7	26 53.2	7 40.8	27 34.3	25 10.9	21 36.5	27 44.7	12 31.0	16 53.2
18 M	11 50 23	25 45 40	27 11 35	4♍04 01	24 01.0	9 46.9	28 06.3	8 18.9	27 56.2	25 23.0	21 38.8	27 42.8	12 29.4	16 52.8
19 Tu	11 54 20	26 44 17	10♍53 36	17 40 01	23 59.1	11 22.1	29 19.5	8 56.9	28 18.0	25 35.2	21 41.1	27 40.8	12 27.8	16 52.6
20 W	11 58 16	27 42 55	24 23 01	1♎02 21	23 55.5	13 00.6	0♍32.7	9 35.0	28 39.7	25 47.3	21 43.6	27 38.8	12 26.2	16 52.3
21 Th	12 02 13	28 41 36	7♎37 50	14 09 18	23 50.4	14 41.8	1 46.0	10 13.0	29 01.3	25 59.6	21 46.1	27 36.7	12 24.6	16 52.1
22 F	12 06 09	29 40 18	20 36 40	26 59 53	23 44.3	16 25.4	2 59.3	10 51.0	29 22.8	26 11.8	21 48.7	27 34.7	12 23.1	16 51.8
23 Sa	12 10 06	0♎39 03	3♏19 01	9♏34 11	23 37.9	18 10.9	4 12.7	11 29.1	29 44.2	26 24.2	21 51.4	27 32.6	12 21.5	16 51.7
24 Su	12 14 02	1 37 49	15 45 34	21 53 25	23 31.9	19 57.7	5 26.2	12 07.1	0♌05.5	26 36.5	21 54.2	27 30.5	12 20.0	16 51.5
25 M	12 17 59	2 36 37	27 58 05	3♐59 56	23 26.9	21 45.6	6 39.7	12 45.1	0 26.7	26 49.0	21 57.1	27 28.3	12 18.5	16 51.4
26 Tu	12 21 55	3 35 26	9♐59 27	15 57 06	23 23.4	23 34.3	7 53.2	13 23.1	0 47.8	27 01.4	22 00.1	27 26.2	12 16.9	16 51.3
27 W	12 25 52	4 34 18	21 53 27	27 49 05	23D 21.7	25 23.4	9 06.8	14 01.1	1 08.7	27 13.9	22 03.2	27 24.0	12 15.4	16 51.3
28 Th	12 29 49	5 33 11	3♑44 35	9♑40 35	23 21.5	27 12.7	10 20.5	14 39.1	1 29.6	27 26.4	22 06.3	27 21.8	12 13.9	16D 51.2
29 F	12 33 45	6 32 06	15 37 45	21 36 41	23 22.5	29 02.1	11 34.2	15 17.1	1 50.3	27 39.0	22 09.6	27 19.6	12 12.5	16 51.3
30 Sa	12 37 42	7 31 03	27 38 02	3♒42 25	23 24.0	0♎51.3	12 48.0	15 55.0	2 10.9	27 51.6	22 12.9	27 17.3	12 11.0	16 51.3

LONGITUDE October 2017

Day	Sid.Time	☉	0 hr ☽	Noon ☽	True ☊	☿	♀	♂	⚳	♃	♄	♅	♆	♇
1 Su	12 41 38	8♎30 01	9♒50 24	16♒02 33	23♌25.2	2♎40.2	14♍01.8	16♍33.0	2♌31.4	28♎04.2	22♐16.3	27♈15.0	12♓09.6	16♑51.4
2 M	12 45 35	9 29 01	22 19 20	28 41 11	23R 25.3	4 28.7	15 15.6	17 11.0	2 51.8	28 16.9	22 19.8	27R 12.7	12R 08.1	16 51.4
3 Tu	12 49 31	10 28 03	5♓08 25	11♓41 15	23 23.6	6 16.7	16 29.5	17 48.9	3 12.0	28 29.6	22 23.4	27 10.4	12 06.7	16 51.6
4 W	12 53 28	11 27 07	18 19 49	25 04 07	23 19.9	8 04.1	17 43.5	18 26.9	3 32.2	28 42.3	22 27.0	27 08.1	12 05.3	16 51.7
5 Th	12 57 24	12 26 13	1♈53 59	8♈49 09	23 14.1	9 50.8	18 57.5	19 04.8	3 52.1	28 55.1	22 30.7	27 05.8	12 04.0	16 51.9
6 F	13 01 21	13 25 21	15 49 13	22 53 38	23 06.6	11 36.9	20 11.5	19 42.8	4 12.0	29 07.9	22 34.6	27 03.4	12 02.6	16 52.1
7 Sa	13 05 18	14 24 31	0♉01 46	7♉12 53	22 58.3	13 22.3	21 25.6	20 20.7	4 31.7	29 20.7	22 38.5	27 01.1	12 01.3	16 52.4
8 Su	13 09 14	15 23 43	14 26 11	21 40 53	22 50.2	15 07.0	22 39.7	20 58.7	4 51.3	29 33.5	22 42.4	26 58.7	11 59.9	16 52.6
9 M	13 13 11	16 22 57	28 56 10	6♊11 17	22 43.2	16 51.0	23 53.9	21 36.6	5 10.7	29 46.4	22 46.5	26 56.3	11 58.6	16 52.9
10 Tu	13 17 07	17 22 14	13♊25 33	20 38 20	22 38.1	18 34.2	25 08.2	22 14.6	5 30.0	29 59.3	22 50.6	26 53.9	11 57.4	16 53.3
11 W	13 21 04	18 21 33	27 49 10	4♋57 38	22 35.3	20 16.6	26 22.5	22 52.5	5 49.2	0♏12.2	22 54.8	26 51.5	11 56.1	16 53.6
12 Th	13 25 00	19 20 55	12♋03 28	19 06 27	22D 34.5	21 58.4	27 36.8	23 30.5	6 08.2	0 25.1	22 59.1	26 49.1	11 54.9	16 54.0
13 F	13 28 57	20 20 19	26 06 30	3♌03 33	22 35.0	23 39.4	28 51.2	24 08.4	6 27.0	0 38.1	23 03.5	26 46.6	11 53.7	16 54.5
14 Sa	13 32 53	21 19 45	9♌57 37	16 48 45	22R 35.7	25 19.7	0♎05.6	24 46.3	6 45.7	0 51.0	23 07.9	26 44.2	11 52.5	16 54.9
15 Su	13 36 50	22 19 13	23 37 01	0♍22 28	22 35.5	26 59.2	1 20.0	25 24.3	7 04.2	1 04.0	23 12.4	26 41.8	11 51.3	16 55.4
16 M	13 40 47	23 18 44	7♍05 09	13 45 06	22 33.5	28 38.1	2 34.5	26 02.2	7 22.6	1 17.0	23 17.0	26 39.3	11 50.2	16 55.9
17 Tu	13 44 43	24 18 16	20 22 20	26 56 49	22 28.9	0♏16.3	3 49.0	26 40.1	7 40.8	1 30.1	23 21.6	26 36.9	11 49.0	16 56.5
18 W	13 48 40	25 17 51	3♎28 32	9♎57 25	22 21.5	1 53.9	5 03.6	27 18.1	7 58.8	1 43.1	23 26.4	26 34.4	11 47.9	16 57.0
19 Th	13 52 36	26 17 28	16 23 24	22 46 25	22 11.6	3 30.8	6 18.2	27 56.0	8 16.7	1 56.2	23 31.2	26 32.0	11 46.9	16 57.6
20 F	13 56 33	27 17 08	29 06 25	5♏23 22	21 59.9	5 07.1	7 32.8	28 33.9	8 34.3	2 09.2	23 36.0	26 29.5	11 45.8	16 58.3
21 Sa	14 00 29	28 16 49	11♏37 15	17 48 06	21 47.5	6 42.8	8 47.5	29 11.8	8 51.8	2 22.3	23 40.9	26 27.1	11 44.8	16 58.9
22 Su	14 04 26	29 16 32	23 56 01	0♐01 06	21 35.4	8 17.9	10 02.2	29 49.7	9 09.1	2 35.4	23 45.9	26 24.6	11 43.8	16 59.6
23 M	14 08 22	0♏16 17	6♐03 36	12 03 43	21 24.7	9 52.4	11 17.0	0♎27.6	9 26.2	2 48.4	23 51.0	26 22.2	11 42.8	17 00.4
24 Tu	14 12 19	1 16 03	18 01 49	23 58 15	21 16.2	11 26.4	12 31.7	1 05.5	9 43.2	3 01.5	23 56.1	26 19.7	11 41.9	17 01.1
25 W	14 16 15	2 15 52	29 53 28	5♑47 57	21 10.4	12 59.8	13 46.5	1 43.4	9 59.9	3 14.6	24 01.3	26 17.3	11 41.0	17 01.9
26 Th	14 20 12	3 15 42	11♑42 16	17 36 59	21 07.1	14 32.6	15 01.3	2 21.3	10 16.4	3 27.7	24 06.6	26 14.9	11 40.1	17 02.7
27 F	14 24 09	4 15 34	23 32 45	29 30 12	21D 05.9	16 05.0	16 16.2	2 59.2	10 32.7	3 40.8	24 11.9	26 12.4	11 39.3	17 03.5
28 Sa	14 28 05	5 15 27	5♒30 00	11♒32 53	21R 05.9	17 36.8	17 31.0	3 37.1	10 48.8	3 53.9	24 17.3	26 10.0	11 38.4	17 04.4
29 Su	14 32 02	6 15 23	17 39 30	23 50 32	21 06.0	19 08.2	18 45.9	4 15.0	11 04.7	4 07.0	24 22.7	26 07.6	11 37.6	17 05.3
30 M	14 35 58	7 15 19	0♓06 36	6♓28 19	21 05.1	20 39.0	20 00.9	4 52.9	11 20.4	4 20.1	24 28.2	26 05.2	11 36.9	17 06.2
31 Tu	14 39 55	8 15 18	12 56 11	19 30 37	21 02.2	22 09.3	21 15.8	5 30.7	11 35.9	4 33.2	24 33.8	26 02.8	11 36.1	17 07.2

Astro Data	Planet Ingress	Last Aspect	☽ Ingress	Last Aspect	☽ Ingress	☽ Phases & Eclipses	Astro Data
Dy Hr Mn	Dy Hr Mn	Dy Hr Mn	Dy Hr Mn	Dy Hr Mn	Dy Hr Mn	Dy Hr Mn	1 September 2017
☿D 5 11:30	♂ ♍ 5 9:36	2 16:31 ♅ □	♒ 2 20:07	2 11:14 ♃ △	♓ 2 14:27	6 7:04 ○ 13♓53	Julian Day # 42978
☽0N 8 3:04	☿ ♍ 10 2:53	5 5:17 ♂ ☍	♓ 5 5:29	4 7:20 ♄ □	♈ 4 20:41	13 6:26 ☾ 20♊40	SVP 5♓00'56"
☽0S 21 1:30	♀ ♍ 20 1:16	6 20:30 ♄ □	♈ 7 12:02	6 22:39 ♃ ☍	♉ 6 23:57	20 5:31 ● 27♍27	GC 27♐05.2 ⚴ 13♉54.7
⊙0S 22 20:04	⊙ ♎ 22 20:03	9 15:53 ☿ △	♉ 9 16:24	8 13:46 ♀ △	♊ 9 1:46	28 2:55 ☽ 5♑11	Eris 23♈42.8R ⚵ 2♑49.2
♃□♆ 27 14:38	⚳ ♌ 24 5:46	11 0:55 ♀ □	♊ 11 19:30	10 22:26 ♅ ⚹	♋ 11 3:39		⚷ 27♓21.2R ⚶ 21♍38.4
♃☍♅ 28 4:26	☿ ♎ 30 0:43	13 18:37 ♅ ⚹	♋ 13 22:13	13 4:01 ♀ ⚹	♌ 13 6:42	5 18:41 ○ 12♈43	☽ Mean ☊ 23♌19.8
♇D 28 19:37		15 21:24 ♅ □	♌ 16 1:10	15 5:29 ♅ △	♍ 15 11:20	12 12:27 ☾ 19♋22	
	♃ ♏ 10 13:21	18 0:56 ♅ △	♍ 18 4:53	17 11:28 ♂ ☌	♎ 17 17:36	19 19:13 ● 26♎35	1 October 2017
☿0S 2 3:13	☿ ♎ 14 10:12	20 5:31 ⊙ ☌	♎ 20 10:07	19 19:13 ⊙ ☌	♏ 20 1:42	27 22:23 ☽ 4♒41	Julian Day # 43008
☽0N 5 11:19	♀ ♏ 17 8:00	22 13:06 ♅ ☍	♏ 22 17:41	22 11:36 ♂ ⚹	♐ 22 11:58		SVP 5♓00'54"
♅∠♆ 7 7:15	♂ ♎ 22 18:30	24 7:34 ☿ ⚹	♐ 25 4:02	24 16:46 ♅ △	♑ 25 0:13		GC 27♐05.2 ⚴ 12♉44.7R
♀0S 17 6:21	⊙ ♏ 23 5:28	27 11:09 ♅ △	♑ 27 16:25	27 5:24 ♅ □	♒ 27 13:00		Eris 23♈27.6R ⚵ 6♑18.6
☽0S 18 9:13		30 0:15 ♃ □	♒ 30 4:41	29 16:23 ♅ ⚹	♓ 29 23:47		⚷ 26♓00.4R ⚶ 6♎38.4
♂0S 26 23:01							☽ Mean ☊ 21♌44.4

November 2017 — LONGITUDE

Day	Sid.Time	☉	0 hr ☽	Noon ☽	True ☊	☿	♀	♂	⚳	♃	♄	♅	♆	♇
1 W	14 43 51	9♏15 18	26♓11 54	3♈00 13	20♌56.7	23♏39.1	22♎30.8	6♎08.6	11♌51.1	4♏46.3	24♐39.4	26♈00.5	11♓35.4	17♑08.2
2 Th	14 47 48	10 15 19	9♈55 32	16 57 39	20R 48.5	25 08.4	23 45.8	6 46.4	12 06.1	4 59.4	24 45.1	25R 58.1	11R 34.7	17 09.2
3 F	14 51 44	11 15 23	24 06 10	1♉20 29	20 38.1	26 37.2	25 00.8	7 24.3	12 20.9	5 12.4	24 50.8	25 55.8	11 34.1	17 10.2
4 Sa	14 55 41	12 15 28	8♉39 49	16 03 14	20 26.5	28 05.5	26 15.8	8 02.2	12 35.5	5 25.5	24 56.6	25 53.4	11 33.5	17 11.3
5 Su	14 59 38	13 15 35	23 29 38	0♊57 51	20 14.9	29 33.3	27 30.9	8 40.0	12 49.8	5 38.6	25 02.4	25 51.1	11 32.9	17 12.3
6 M	15 03 34	14 15 45	8♊26 42	15 55 00	20 04.7	1♐00.5	28 46.0	9 17.9	13 03.9	5 51.6	25 08.3	25 48.8	11 32.3	17 13.4
7 Tu	15 07 31	15 15 56	23 21 41	0♋45 45	19 56.9	2 27.1	0♏01.1	9 55.7	13 17.7	6 04.6	25 14.2	25 46.6	11 31.8	17 14.6
8 W	15 11 27	16 16 09	8♋06 23	15 22 58	19 51.9	3 53.2	1 16.2	10 33.6	13 31.3	6 17.7	25 20.2	25 44.3	11 31.3	17 15.8
9 Th	15 15 24	17 16 24	22 34 59	29 42 10	19 49.5	5 18.6	2 31.4	11 11.4	13 44.6	6 30.7	25 26.2	25 42.1	11 30.9	17 16.9
10 F	15 19 20	18 16 41	6♌44 21	13♌41 32	19 48.9	6 43.2	3 46.5	11 49.3	13 57.7	6 43.7	25 32.3	25 39.8	11 30.4	17 18.2
11 Sa	15 23 17	19 17 00	20 33 48	27 21 21	19 48.9	8 07.2	5 01.7	12 27.1	14 10.5	6 56.6	25 38.4	25 37.7	11 30.1	17 19.4
12 Su	15 27 13	20 17 22	4♍04 25	10♍43 17	19 48.0	9 30.3	6 16.9	13 05.0	14 23.0	7 09.6	25 44.6	25 35.5	11 29.7	17 20.7
13 M	15 31 10	21 17 45	17 18 13	23 49 31	19 45.1	10 52.5	7 32.2	13 42.8	14 35.3	7 22.5	25 50.8	25 33.3	11 29.4	17 22.0
14 Tu	15 35 07	22 18 10	0♎17 27	6♎42 16	19 39.4	12 13.7	8 47.4	14 20.6	14 47.2	7 35.4	25 57.1	25 31.2	11 29.1	17 23.3
15 W	15 39 03	23 18 36	13 04 11	19 23 23	19 30.6	13 33.8	10 02.7	14 58.5	14 58.9	7 48.3	26 03.4	25 29.1	11 28.8	17 24.6
16 Th	15 43 00	24 19 05	25 39 59	1♏54 09	19 19.0	14 52.7	11 18.0	15 36.3	15 10.3	8 01.2	26 09.7	25 27.1	11 28.6	17 26.0
17 F	15 46 56	25 19 35	8♏05 56	14 15 26	19 05.3	16 10.2	12 33.3	16 14.1	15 21.3	8 14.0	26 16.1	25 25.0	11 28.4	17 27.4
18 Sa	15 50 53	26 20 07	20 22 44	26 27 52	18 50.6	17 26.1	13 48.6	16 52.0	15 32.1	8 26.8	26 22.5	25 23.0	11 28.2	17 28.8
19 Su	15 54 49	27 20 41	2♐30 58	8♐32 05	18 36.2	18 40.3	15 03.9	17 29.8	15 42.6	8 39.6	26 29.0	25 21.0	11 28.1	17 30.2
20 M	15 58 46	28 21 16	14 31 24	20 29 04	18 23.3	19 52.5	16 19.3	18 07.6	15 52.7	8 52.4	26 35.5	25 19.1	11 28.0	17 31.6
21 Tu	16 02 42	29 21 52	26 25 17	2♑20 20	18 12.8	21 02.4	17 34.6	18 45.4	16 02.6	9 05.1	26 42.0	25 17.2	11 28.0	17 33.1
22 W	16 06 39	0♐22 30	8♑14 32	14 08 14	18 05.2	22 09.7	18 50.0	19 23.2	16 12.1	9 17.8	26 48.6	25 15.3	11D 27.9	17 34.6
23 Th	16 10 36	1 23 09	20 01 52	25 55 54	18 00.6	23 14.1	20 05.4	20 01.0	16 21.3	9 30.4	26 55.2	25 13.4	11 27.9	17 36.1
24 F	16 14 32	2 23 49	1♒50 52	7♒47 20	17D 58.5	24 15.1	21 20.8	20 38.8	16 30.1	9 43.1	27 01.9	25 11.6	11 28.0	17 37.7
25 Sa	16 18 29	3 24 30	13 45 54	19 47 14	17 58.1	25 12.3	22 36.2	21 16.5	16 38.7	9 55.6	27 08.5	25 09.8	11 28.1	17 39.2
26 Su	16 22 25	4 25 12	25 52 00	2♓00 51	17R 58.3	26 05.2	23 51.6	21 54.3	16 46.8	10 08.2	27 15.2	25 08.1	11 28.2	17 40.8
27 M	16 26 22	5 25 56	8♓14 30	14 33 35	17 58.0	26 53.2	25 07.0	22 32.1	16 54.7	10 20.7	27 22.0	25 06.4	11 28.3	17 42.4
28 Tu	16 30 18	6 26 40	20 58 44	27 30 30	17 56.0	27 35.7	26 22.4	23 09.8	17 02.1	10 33.1	27 28.7	25 04.7	11 28.5	17 44.0
29 W	16 34 15	7 27 25	4♈09 23	10♈55 41	17 51.8	28 11.8	27 37.8	23 47.6	17 09.3	10 45.5	27 35.5	25 03.1	11 28.7	17 45.7
30 Th	16 38 11	8 28 11	17 49 38	24 51 15	17 45.0	28 41.0	28 53.2	24 25.3	17 16.0	10 57.9	27 42.3	25 01.5	11 29.0	17 47.3

December 2017 — LONGITUDE

Day	Sid.Time	☉	0 hr ☽	Noon ☽	True ☊	☿	♀	♂	⚳	♃	♄	♅	♆	♇
1 F	16 42 08	9♐28 59	2♉00 19	9♉16 27	17♌36.0	29♐02.2	0♐08.6	25♎03.0	17♌22.4	11♏10.2	27♐49.1	24♈59.9	11♓29.3	17♑49.0
2 Sa	16 46 05	10 29 47	16 39 00	24 07 05	17R 25.7	29R 14.9	1 24.1	25 40.7	17 28.5	11 22.5	27 56.0	24R 58.4	11 29.6	17 50.7
3 Su	16 50 01	11 30 37	1♊39 38	9♊15 23	17 15.3	29 18.0	2 39.5	26 18.5	17 34.1	11 34.7	28 02.9	24 56.9	11 30.0	17 52.4
4 M	16 53 58	12 31 27	16 53 00	24 31 04	17 06.0	29 10.9	3 55.0	26 56.2	17 39.4	11 46.9	28 09.8	24 55.5	11 30.4	17 54.2
5 Tu	16 57 54	13 32 19	2♋08 10	9♋43 01	16 58.8	28 53.0	5 10.4	27 33.9	17 44.3	11 59.0	28 16.7	24 54.1	11 30.8	17 55.9
6 W	17 01 51	14 33 12	17 14 26	24 41 24	16 54.3	28 23.8	6 25.9	28 11.6	17 48.8	12 11.1	28 23.6	24 52.8	11 31.3	17 57.7
7 Th	17 05 47	15 34 06	2♌03 08	9♌19 02	16D 52.4	27 43.4	7 41.4	28 49.3	17 53.0	12 23.1	28 30.6	24 51.5	11 31.8	17 59.4
8 F	17 09 44	16 35 01	16 28 44	23 32 02	16 52.3	26 52.0	8 56.8	29 27.0	17 56.7	12 35.1	28 37.5	24 50.2	11 32.3	18 01.2
9 Sa	17 13 40	17 35 58	0♍28 56	7♍19 32	16R 53.0	25 50.5	10 12.3	0♏04.7	18 00.0	12 47.0	28 44.5	24 49.0	11 32.9	18 03.0
10 Su	17 17 37	18 36 56	14 04 06	20 42 56	16 53.4	24 40.3	11 27.8	0 42.4	18 02.9	12 58.9	28 51.5	24 47.8	11 33.5	18 04.9
11 M	17 21 34	19 37 55	27 16 24	3♎44 57	16 52.3	23 23.3	12 43.3	1 20.1	18 05.4	13 10.6	28 58.5	24 46.7	11 34.1	18 06.7
12 Tu	17 25 30	20 38 55	10♎08 59	16 28 57	16 49.0	22 01.9	13 58.8	1 57.7	18 07.5	13 22.4	29 05.6	24 45.6	11 34.7	18 08.6
13 W	17 29 27	21 39 56	22 45 14	28 58 15	16 43.2	20 38.9	15 14.3	2 35.4	18 09.2	13 34.0	29 12.6	24 44.6	11 35.4	18 10.4
14 Th	17 33 23	22 40 58	5♏08 22	11♏15 53	16 35.1	19 16.9	16 29.8	3 13.0	18 10.5	13 45.6	29 19.7	24 43.6	11 36.2	18 12.3
15 F	17 37 20	23 42 01	17 21 08	23 24 22	16 25.3	17 58.9	17 45.3	3 50.7	18 11.3	13 57.1	29 26.7	24 42.6	11 36.9	18 14.2
16 Sa	17 41 16	24 43 05	29 25 50	5♐25 43	16 14.6	16 47.1	19 00.9	4 28.3	18R 11.7	14 08.6	29 33.8	24 41.7	11 37.7	18 16.1
17 Su	17 45 13	25 44 10	11♐24 14	17 21 34	16 04.1	15 43.6	20 16.4	5 05.9	18 11.7	14 20.0	29 40.9	24 40.9	11 38.6	18 18.0
18 M	17 49 09	26 45 15	23 17 54	29 13 23	15 54.7	14 49.7	21 31.9	5 43.6	18 11.2	14 31.3	29 47.9	24 40.1	11 39.4	18 19.9
19 Tu	17 53 06	27 46 21	5♑08 14	11♑02 40	15 47.2	14 06.4	22 47.5	6 21.2	18 10.3	14 42.6	29 55.0	24 39.4	11 40.3	18 21.9
20 W	17 57 03	28 47 28	16 56 53	22 51 10	15 41.9	13 34.1	24 03.0	6 58.8	18 09.0	14 53.7	0♑02.1	24 38.7	11 41.3	18 23.8
21 Th	18 00 59	29 48 35	28 45 49	4♒41 10	15D 39.1	13 12.6	25 18.5	7 36.3	18 07.2	15 04.8	0 09.2	24 38.0	11 42.2	18 25.8
22 F	18 04 56	0♑49 42	10♒37 35	16 35 30	15 38.3	13D 01.8	26 34.0	8 13.9	18 05.0	15 15.8	0 16.3	24 37.4	11 43.2	18 27.7
23 Sa	18 08 52	1 50 50	22 35 21	28 37 39	15 39.1	13 01.0	27 49.6	8 51.4	18 02.4	15 26.7	0 23.4	24 36.9	11 44.3	18 29.7
24 Su	18 12 49	2 51 57	4♓42 56	10♓51 44	15 40.6	13 09.6	29 05.1	9 29.0	17 59.3	15 37.6	0 30.5	24 36.4	11 45.3	18 31.7
25 M	18 16 45	3 53 05	17 04 38	23 22 13	15R 42.0	13 26.8	0♑20.6	10 06.5	17 55.8	15 48.3	0 37.5	24 35.9	11 46.4	18 33.7
26 Tu	18 20 42	4 54 13	29 45 03	6♈13 41	15 42.5	13 51.8	1 36.1	10 44.0	17 51.9	15 59.0	0 44.6	24 35.5	11 47.5	18 35.7
27 W	18 24 39	5 55 21	12♈48 36	19 30 14	15 41.5	14 23.8	2 51.6	11 21.5	17 47.6	16 09.6	0 51.7	24 35.2	11 48.7	18 37.7
28 Th	18 28 35	6 56 28	26 18 55	3♉14 49	15 38.8	15 02.2	4 07.1	11 58.9	17 42.8	16 20.1	0 58.8	24 34.9	11 49.9	18 39.7
29 F	18 32 32	7 57 36	10♉17 59	17 28 18	15 34.6	15 46.3	5 22.6	12 36.4	17 37.6	16 30.5	1 05.8	24 34.7	11 51.1	18 41.7
30 Sa	18 36 28	8 58 44	24 45 23	2♊08 42	15 29.2	16 35.3	6 38.1	13 13.9	17 31.9	16 40.8	1 12.9	24 34.5	11 52.3	18 43.7
31 Su	18 40 25	9 59 52	9♊37 28	17 10 42	15 23.6	17 28.9	7 53.6	13 51.3	17 25.9	16 51.0	1 19.9	24 34.3	11 53.6	18 45.7

Astro Data	Planet Ingress	Last Aspect	☽ Ingress	Last Aspect	☽ Ingress	☽ Phases & Eclipses
Dy Hr Mn	Dy Hr Mn	Dy Hr Mn	Dy Hr Mn	Dy Hr Mn	Dy Hr Mn	Dy Hr Mn
☽0N 1 21:46	☿ ♐ 5 19:20	31 21:09 ♄ □	♈ 1 6:44	2 1:55 ♇ △	♊ 2 21:22	4 5:24 ○ 11♉59
♄△♅ 11 9:46	♀ ♏ 7 11:40	3 3:04 ♅ ☌	♉ 3 9:47	4 19:14 ☿ ☍	♋ 4 20:38	10 20:38 ☾ 18♌38
☽0S 14 15:58	☉ ♐ 22 3:06	5 9:30 ☿ ☍	♊ 5 10:27	6 17:57 ♂ ☌	♌ 6 20:38	18 11:43 ● 26♏19
♆D 22 14:22		7 10:41 ♀ △	♋ 7 10:46	8 22:42 ♂ ⚹	♍ 8 23:10	26 17:04 ☽ 4♓38
☽0N 29 8:54	♀ ♐ 1 9:15	9 5:15 ♅ □	♌ 9 12:30	11 3:04 ♄ □	♎ 11 5:02	
	♂ ♏ 9 9:00	11 8:57 ♅ △	♍ 11 16:42	13 12:28 ♄ ⚹	♏ 13 14:00	3 15:48 ○ 11♊40
♃△♆ 3 2:21	♄ ♑ 20 4:50	13 15:46 ♄ □	♎ 13 23:27	15 1:43 ♇ ⚹	♐ 16 1:08	10 7:53 ☾ 18♍26
☿R 3 7:35	☉ ♑ 21 16:29	16 0:51 ♄ ⚹	♏ 16 8:20	18 13:11 ♄ ☌	♑ 18 13:35	18 6:32 ● 26♐31
☽0S 11 22:37	♀ ♑ 25 5:27	18 11:43 ☉ ☌	♐ 18 19:00	20 15:38 ♅ □	♒ 21 2:30	26 9:21 ☽ 4♈47
⚳R 16 22:30		21 0:28 ♄ ☌	♑ 21 7:15	23 10:14 ♀ ⚹	♓ 23 14:43	
♃∠♄ 22 14:56		23 10:34 ♅ □	♒ 23 20:15	25 2:49 ♇ ⚹	♈ 26 0:28	
☿D 23 1:51		26 2:38 ♄ ⚹	♓ 26 8:05	27 20:58 ♅ ☌	♉ 28 6:24	
☽0N 26 18:28		28 12:10 ♅ ☌	♈ 28 16:31	29 14:02 ♇ △	♊ 30 8:32	
		30 18:38 ☿ △	♉ 30 20:39			

Astro Data

1 November 2017
Julian Day # 43039
SVP 5♓00'51"
GC 27♐05.3 ⚴ 4♉35.8R
Eris 23♈09.2R ⚵ 14♑01.1
⚷ 24♓49.9R ⚶ 22♎28.1
☽ Mean ☊ 20♌05.9

1 December 2017
Julian Day # 43069
SVP 5♓00'47"
GC 27♐05.4 ⚴ 26♈27.3R
Eris 22♈54.2R ⚵ 24♑08.1
⚷ 24♓19.4R ⚶ 7♏50.0
☽ Mean ☊ 18♌30.6

LONGITUDE January 2018

Day	Sid.Time	☉	0 hr ☽	Noon ☽	True ☊	☿	♀	♂	⚳	♃	♄	♅	♆	♇
1 M	18 44 21	11♑01 00	24♊47 15	2♋25 50	15♌18.6	18♐26.4	9♑09.1	14♏28.7	17♌19.4	17♏01.2	1♑26.9	24♈34.3	11♓54.9	18♑47.8
2 Tu	18 48 18	12 02 08	10♋05 07	17 43 42	15R 14.8	19 27.3	10 24.6	15 06.1	17R 12.6	17 11.2	1 33.9	24D 34.2	11 56.2	18 49.8
3 W	18 52 14	13 03 15	25 20 16	2♌53 34	15D 12.6	20 31.5	11 40.1	15 43.5	17 05.3	17 21.1	1 40.9	24 34.2	11 57.6	18 51.8
4 Th	18 56 11	14 04 23	10♌22 31	17 46 13	15 12.1	21 38.3	12 55.6	16 20.9	16 57.6	17 30.9	1 47.9	24 34.3	11 59.0	18 53.9
5 F	19 00 08	15 05 31	25 03 55	2♍15 08	15 12.9	22 47.7	14 11.1	16 58.3	16 49.6	17 40.7	1 54.9	24 34.4	12 00.4	18 55.9
6 Sa	19 04 04	16 06 40	9♍19 32	16 16 59	15 14.4	23 59.2	15 26.6	17 35.6	16 41.1	17 50.3	2 01.9	24 34.6	12 01.8	18 58.0
7 Su	19 08 01	17 07 48	23 07 31	29 51 18	15 16.0	25 12.7	16 42.1	18 13.0	16 32.3	17 59.8	2 08.8	24 34.8	12 03.3	19 00.0
8 M	19 11 57	18 08 56	6♎28 37	12♎59 49	15R 17.0	26 28.0	17 57.6	18 50.3	16 23.1	18 09.2	2 15.7	24 35.1	12 04.8	19 02.0
9 Tu	19 15 54	19 10 05	19 25 21	25 45 42	15 16.9	27 44.9	19 13.0	19 27.6	16 13.5	18 18.5	2 22.6	24 35.4	12 06.3	19 04.1
10 W	19 19 50	20 11 14	2♏01 20	8♏12 49	15 15.6	29 03.2	20 28.5	20 04.9	16 03.5	18 27.7	2 29.5	24 35.8	12 07.9	19 06.1
11 Th	19 23 47	21 12 22	14 20 37	20 25 15	15 13.1	0♑22.8	21 44.0	20 42.2	15 53.2	18 36.8	2 36.3	24 36.3	12 09.5	19 08.2
12 F	19 27 43	22 13 31	26 27 13	2♐26 57	15 09.7	1 43.6	22 59.5	21 19.4	15 42.6	18 45.8	2 43.2	24 36.8	12 11.1	19 10.2
13 Sa	19 31 40	23 14 39	8♐24 54	14 21 27	15 05.9	3 05.5	24 14.9	21 56.7	15 31.7	18 54.6	2 50.0	24 37.3	12 12.7	19 12.3
14 Su	19 35 37	24 15 48	20 16 59	26 11 50	15 02.0	4 28.4	25 30.4	22 33.9	15 20.4	19 03.4	2 56.8	24 37.9	12 14.3	19 14.3
15 M	19 39 33	25 16 56	2♑06 19	8♑00 43	14 58.7	5 52.2	26 45.9	23 11.1	15 08.9	19 12.0	3 03.5	24 38.5	12 16.0	19 16.3
16 Tu	19 43 30	26 18 04	13 55 18	19 50 19	14 56.1	7 17.0	28 01.3	23 48.2	14 57.0	19 20.5	3 10.2	24 39.2	12 17.7	19 18.4
17 W	19 47 26	27 19 11	25 46 02	1♒42 39	14 54.5	8 42.5	29 16.8	24 25.4	14 44.9	19 28.8	3 16.9	24 40.0	12 19.4	19 20.4
18 Th	19 51 23	28 20 17	7♒40 25	13 39 34	14D 53.9	10 08.8	0♒32.2	25 02.5	14 32.5	19 37.1	3 23.6	24 40.8	12 21.2	19 22.4
19 F	19 55 19	29 21 23	19 40 21	25 43 02	14 54.3	11 35.9	1 47.7	25 39.6	14 19.9	19 45.2	3 30.2	24 41.6	12 22.9	19 24.5
20 Sa	19 59 16	0♒22 29	1♓47 54	7♓55 14	14 55.2	13 03.7	3 03.1	26 16.7	14 07.1	19 53.1	3 36.8	24 42.5	12 24.7	19 26.5
21 Su	20 03 12	1 23 33	14 05 21	20 18 36	14 56.5	14 32.2	4 18.5	26 53.7	13 54.0	20 01.0	3 43.4	24 43.5	12 26.5	19 28.5
22 M	20 07 09	2 24 36	26 35 19	2♈55 53	14 57.7	16 01.4	5 33.9	27 30.7	13 40.8	20 08.7	3 49.9	24 44.5	12 28.4	19 30.5
23 Tu	20 11 06	3 25 39	9♈20 40	15 50 00	14 58.7	17 31.2	6 49.3	28 07.7	13 27.4	20 16.3	3 56.4	24 45.5	12 30.2	19 32.5
24 W	20 15 02	4 26 40	22 24 16	29 03 45	14R 59.2	19 01.7	8 04.7	28 44.7	13 13.8	20 23.7	4 02.9	24 46.6	12 32.1	19 34.5
25 Th	20 18 59	5 27 41	5♉48 44	12♉39 24	14 59.1	20 32.8	9 20.1	29 21.6	13 00.1	20 31.0	4 09.3	24 47.8	12 34.0	19 36.5
26 F	20 22 55	6 28 40	19 35 53	26 38 10	14 58.7	22 04.6	10 35.4	29 58.5	12 46.3	20 38.2	4 15.7	24 49.0	12 35.9	19 38.5
27 Sa	20 26 52	7 29 39	3♊46 08	10♊59 32	14 57.9	23 37.1	11 50.8	0♐35.4	12 32.3	20 45.2	4 22.0	24 50.3	12 37.8	19 40.4
28 Su	20 30 48	8 30 36	18 17 56	25 40 47	14 57.1	25 10.1	13 06.1	1 12.3	12 18.3	20 52.1	4 28.3	24 51.6	12 39.8	19 42.4
29 M	20 34 45	9 31 32	3♋07 21	10♋36 46	14 56.5	26 43.9	14 21.5	1 49.1	12 04.2	20 58.9	4 34.6	24 52.9	12 41.8	19 44.4
30 Tu	20 38 41	10 32 27	18 08 03	25 40 08	14 56.0	28 18.3	15 36.8	2 25.9	11 50.1	21 05.5	4 40.8	24 54.3	12 43.8	19 46.3
31 W	20 42 38	11 33 21	3♌11 55	10♌42 15	14D 55.9	29 53.4	16 52.1	3 02.7	11 36.0	21 11.9	4 46.9	24 55.8	12 45.8	19 48.2

LONGITUDE February 2018

Day	Sid.Time	☉	0 hr ☽	Noon ☽	True ☊	☿	♀	♂	⚳	♃	♄	♅	♆	♇
1 Th	20 46 35	12♒34 14	18♌10 03	25♌34 18	14♌55.9	1♒29.1	18♒07.4	3♐39.4	11♌21.8	21♏18.2	4♑53.0	24♈57.3	12♓47.8	19♑50.2
2 F	20 50 31	13 35 05	2♍54 05	10♍08 38	14 56.0	3 05.6	19 22.6	4 16.1	11R 07.6	21 24.3	4 59.1	24 58.8	12 49.8	19 52.1
3 Sa	20 54 28	14 35 56	17 17 21	24 19 46	14R 56.1	4 42.7	20 37.9	4 52.8	10 53.5	21 30.3	5 05.1	25 00.4	12 51.9	19 54.0
4 Su	20 58 24	15 36 46	1♎15 36	8♎04 44	14 56.1	6 20.6	21 53.2	5 29.5	10 39.4	21 36.2	5 11.1	25 02.0	12 53.9	19 55.8
5 M	21 02 21	16 37 35	14 47 11	21 23 06	14 56.0	7 59.2	23 08.4	6 06.1	10 25.3	21 41.9	5 17.0	25 03.7	12 56.0	19 57.7
6 Tu	21 06 17	17 38 23	27 52 45	4♏16 31	14 55.8	9 38.6	24 23.6	6 42.7	10 11.4	21 47.4	5 22.9	25 05.4	12 58.1	19 59.6
7 W	21 10 14	18 39 10	10♏34 50	16 48 11	14D 55.7	11 18.8	25 38.9	7 19.3	9 57.5	21 52.8	5 28.7	25 07.2	13 00.2	20 01.4
8 Th	21 14 10	19 39 56	22 57 07	29 02 12	14 55.8	12 59.7	26 54.1	7 55.8	9 43.8	21 58.0	5 34.4	25 09.0	13 02.3	20 03.3
9 F	21 18 07	20 40 42	5♐04 01	11♐03 08	14 56.1	14 41.4	28 09.3	8 32.3	9 30.2	22 03.0	5 40.2	25 10.8	13 04.4	20 05.1
10 Sa	21 22 04	21 41 26	17 00 10	22 55 38	14 56.7	16 24.0	29 24.5	9 08.8	9 16.7	22 07.9	5 45.8	25 12.7	13 06.6	20 06.9
11 Su	21 26 00	22 42 09	28 50 06	4♑44 06	14 57.6	18 07.3	0♓39.6	9 45.2	9 03.5	22 12.7	5 51.4	25 14.7	13 08.8	20 08.7
12 M	21 29 57	23 42 51	10♑38 05	16 32 31	14 58.5	19 51.5	1 54.8	10 21.6	8 50.4	22 17.2	5 56.9	25 16.7	13 10.9	20 10.5
13 Tu	21 33 53	24 43 32	22 27 49	28 24 23	14 59.3	21 36.5	3 09.9	10 57.9	8 37.5	22 21.6	6 02.4	25 18.7	13 13.1	20 12.2
14 W	21 37 50	25 44 12	4♒22 32	10♒22 35	14R 59.7	23 22.4	4 25.1	11 34.2	8 24.8	22 25.8	6 07.8	25 20.8	13 15.3	20 14.0
15 Th	21 41 46	26 44 50	16 24 48	22 29 25	14 59.7	25 09.1	5 40.2	12 10.5	8 12.4	22 29.8	6 13.2	25 22.9	13 17.5	20 15.7
16 F	21 45 43	27 45 26	28 36 38	4♓46 38	14 58.9	26 56.7	6 55.3	12 46.7	8 00.2	22 33.7	6 18.5	25 25.0	13 19.7	20 17.4
17 Sa	21 49 39	28 46 01	10♓59 33	17 15 30	14 57.5	28 45.1	8 10.4	13 22.8	7 48.3	22 37.4	6 23.7	25 27.2	13 21.9	20 19.1
18 Su	21 53 36	29 46 35	23 34 36	29 56 57	14 55.5	0♓34.3	9 25.4	13 58.9	7 36.7	22 40.9	6 28.9	25 29.5	13 24.1	20 20.8
19 M	21 57 33	0♓47 07	6♈22 36	12♈51 39	14 53.1	2 24.3	10 40.5	14 35.0	7 25.3	22 44.3	6 34.0	25 31.7	13 26.4	20 22.4
20 Tu	22 01 29	1 47 37	19 24 10	26 00 12	14 50.8	4 15.0	11 55.5	15 11.0	7 14.3	22 47.4	6 39.0	25 34.0	13 28.6	20 24.1
21 W	22 05 26	2 48 05	2♉39 50	9♉23 05	14 48.8	6 06.5	13 10.5	15 47.0	7 03.6	22 50.4	6 43.9	25 36.4	13 30.8	20 25.7
22 Th	22 09 22	3 48 32	16 10 02	23 00 41	14D 47.6	7 58.6	14 25.5	16 22.9	6 53.3	22 53.2	6 48.8	25 38.8	13 33.1	20 27.3
23 F	22 13 19	4 48 56	29 55 02	6♊53 03	14 47.3	9 51.2	15 40.4	16 58.8	6 43.3	22 55.9	6 53.6	25 41.2	13 35.3	20 28.9
24 Sa	22 17 15	5 49 19	13♊54 41	20 59 47	14 47.9	11 44.3	16 55.4	17 34.6	6 33.6	22 58.3	6 58.4	25 43.6	13 37.6	20 30.4
25 Su	22 21 12	6 49 39	28 08 09	5♋19 31	14 49.1	13 37.8	18 10.3	18 10.3	6 24.3	23 00.6	7 03.1	25 46.1	13 39.9	20 32.0
26 M	22 25 08	7 49 58	12♋33 32	19 49 46	14 50.6	15 31.5	19 25.2	18 46.1	6 15.4	23 02.7	7 07.7	25 48.7	13 42.1	20 33.5
27 Tu	22 29 05	8 50 15	27 07 40	4♌26 37	14R 51.7	17 25.2	20 40.0	19 21.7	6 06.9	23 04.6	7 12.2	25 51.2	13 44.4	20 35.0
28 W	22 33 02	9 50 30	11♌45 57	19 04 54	14 51.9	19 18.7	21 54.9	19 57.3	5 58.7	23 06.3	7 16.7	25 53.8	13 46.7	20 36.5

Astro Data	Planet Ingress	Last Aspect	☽ Ingress	Last Aspect	☽ Ingress	☽ Phases & Eclipses	Astro Data
Dy Hr Mn	Dy Hr Mn	Dy Hr Mn	Dy Hr Mn	Dy Hr Mn	Dy Hr Mn	Dy Hr Mn	1 January 2018
♅ D 2 14:12	☿ ♑ 11 5:10	31 23:40 ♅ ⚹	♋ 1 8:11	1 11:00 ♅ △	♍ 1 19:14	2 2:25 ○ 11♋38	Julian Day # 43100
☽ 0S 8 6:21	♀ ♒ 18 1:45	2 22:47 ♅ □	♌ 3 7:24	3 7:08 ♃ ⚹	♎ 3 21:48	8 22:26 ☾ 18♎36	SVP 5♓00'41"
♃⚹♇ 16 4:15	☉ ♒ 20 3:10	4 23:11 ♅ △	♍ 5 8:13	5 18:47 ♅ ☍	♏ 6 3:58	17 2:18 ● 26♑54	GC 27♐05.4 ⚴ 26♈06.1
☽ 0N 23 1:24	♂ ♐ 26 12:57	7 2:52 ☿ □	♎ 7 12:16	8 7:17 ♀ □	♐ 8 13:55	24 22:22 ☽ 4♉53	Eris 22♈46.2R ⚵ 6♒23.2
	☿ ♒ 31 13:40	9 16:14 ☿ ⚹	♏ 9 20:07	10 16:39 ♅ △	♑ 11 2:22	31 13:28 ○ 11♌37	⚷ 24♓39.2 ⚶ 23♏22.5
☽ 0S 4 15:38		11 14:54 ♀ ⚹	♐ 12 7:05	13 5:44 ♅ □	♒ 13 15:13	31 13:31 ☍ T 1.316	☽ Mean ☊ 16♌52.1
☽ 0N 19 6:49	♀ ♓ 10 23:21	14 8:49 ♅ △	♑ 14 19:43	15 21:06 ☉ ☌	♓ 16 2:43		
	☿ ♓ 18 4:29	17 6:31 ♀ ☌	♒ 17 8:33	17 22:15 ♃ △	♈ 18 12:06	7 15:55 ☾ 18♏49	1 February 2018
	☉ ♓ 18 17:19	19 11:53 ♂ □	♓ 19 20:28	20 11:12 ♅ ☌	♉ 20 19:13	15 21:06 ● 27♒08	Julian Day # 43131
		22 1:14 ♂ △	♈ 22 6:28	22 11:47 ♃ ☍	♊ 23 0:09	15 20:52:32 ☌ P 0.599	SVP 5♓00'36"
		24 4:17 ♅ ☌	♉ 24 13:41	24 19:59 ♅ ⚹	♋ 25 3:07	23 8:10 ☽ 4♊39	GC 27♐05.5 ⚴ 3♉54.2
		26 3:18 ☿ △	♊ 26 17:41	26 21:52 ♅ □	♌ 27 4:43		Eris 22♈48.5 ⚵ 19♒49.7
		28 10:40 ♅ ⚹	♋ 28 18:59				⚷ 25♓47.0 ⚶ 8♐01.1
		30 16:41 ☿ ☍	♌ 30 18:54				☽ Mean ☊ 15♌13.7

March 2018 — LONGITUDE

Day	Sid.Time	☉	0 hr ☽	Noon ☽	True ☊	☿	♀	♂	⚳	♃	♄	♅	♆	♇
1 Th	22 36 58	10♓50 42	26♌22 41	3♍38 30	14♌50.9	21♓11.7	23♓09.7	20♐32.9	5♌51.0	23♏07.8	7♑21.1	25♈56.5	13♓49.0	20♑37.9
2 F	22 40 55	11 50 53	10♍51 33	18 01 07	14R48.4	23 04.1	24 24.5	21 08.4	5R43.6	23 09.2	7 25.4	25 59.1	13 51.2	20 39.4
3 Sa	22 44 51	12 51 03	25 06 29	2♎07 05	14 44.7	24 55.4	25 39.2	21 43.8	5 36.7	23 10.3	7 29.6	26 01.8	13 53.5	20 40.8
4 Su	22 48 48	13 51 10	9♎02 25	15 52 08	14 40.2	26 45.3	26 54.0	22 19.2	5 30.1	23 11.3	7 33.8	26 04.5	13 55.8	20 42.1
5 M	22 52 44	14 51 16	22 36 00	29 13 56	14 35.4	28 33.4	28 08.7	22 54.5	5 24.0	23 12.1	7 37.8	26 07.3	13 58.1	20 43.5
6 Tu	22 56 41	15 51 20	5♏45 57	12♏12 12	14 31.0	0♈19.3	29 23.4	23 29.8	5 18.3	23 12.7	7 41.8	26 10.1	14 00.3	20 44.8
7 W	23 00 37	16 51 23	18 32 57	24 48 34	14 27.5	2 02.4	0♈38.0	24 05.0	5 13.0	23 13.1	7 45.8	26 12.9	14 02.6	20 46.2
8 Th	23 04 34	17 51 24	0♐59 28	7♐06 10	14D25.4	3 42.3	1 52.7	24 40.2	5 08.2	23R13.3	7 49.6	26 15.7	14 04.9	20 47.5
9 F	23 08 30	18 51 24	13 09 13	19 09 14	14 24.7	5 18.5	3 07.3	25 15.3	5 03.7	23 13.4	7 53.3	26 18.6	14 07.2	20 48.7
10 Sa	23 12 27	19 51 22	25 06 48	1♑02 35	14 25.3	6 50.4	4 21.9	25 50.3	4 59.7	23 13.2	7 57.0	26 21.5	14 09.4	20 50.0
11 Su	23 16 24	20 51 18	6♑57 14	12 51 22	14 26.9	8 17.5	5 36.5	26 25.2	4 56.2	23 12.9	8 00.6	26 24.4	14 11.7	20 51.2
12 M	23 20 20	21 51 12	18 45 38	24 40 37	14 28.6	9 39.3	6 51.0	27 00.1	4 53.0	23 12.3	8 04.1	26 27.4	14 14.0	20 52.4
13 Tu	23 24 17	22 51 05	0♒36 54	6♒35 02	14R30.0	10 55.2	8 05.5	27 34.9	4 50.3	23 11.6	8 07.5	26 30.4	14 16.2	20 53.6
14 W	23 28 13	23 50 56	12 35 31	18 38 46	14 30.2	12 04.8	9 20.0	28 09.6	4 48.1	23 10.7	8 10.9	26 33.4	14 18.5	20 54.7
15 Th	23 32 10	24 50 46	24 45 13	0♓55 10	14 28.7	13 07.7	10 34.5	28 44.2	4 46.2	23 09.6	8 14.1	26 36.4	14 20.8	20 55.8
16 F	23 36 06	25 50 33	7♓08 52	13 26 32	14 25.3	14 03.4	11 49.0	29 18.8	4 44.9	23 08.3	8 17.3	26 39.4	14 23.0	20 56.9
17 Sa	23 40 03	26 50 18	19 48 17	26 14 07	14 19.9	14 51.6	13 03.4	29 53.3	4 43.9	23 06.8	8 20.3	26 42.5	14 25.2	20 58.0
18 Su	23 43 59	27 50 02	2♈44 03	9♈17 58	14 13.0	15 32.1	14 17.8	0♑27.7	4D43.4	23 05.2	8 23.3	26 45.6	14 27.5	20 59.0
19 M	23 47 56	28 49 43	15 55 41	22 37 02	14 05.2	16 04.6	15 32.1	1 02.0	4 43.3	23 03.3	8 26.2	26 48.7	14 29.7	21 00.0
20 Tu	23 51 53	29 49 22	29 21 44	6♉09 32	13 57.5	16 29.1	16 46.5	1 36.2	4 43.7	23 01.3	8 29.0	26 51.9	14 31.9	21 01.0
21 W	23 55 49	0♈49 00	13♉00 06	19 53 10	13 50.6	16 45.3	18 00.8	2 10.3	4 44.5	22 59.1	8 31.7	26 55.0	14 34.1	21 01.9
22 Th	23 59 46	1 48 35	26 48 27	3♊45 40	13 45.4	16R53.4	19 15.0	2 44.3	4 45.7	22 56.7	8 34.3	26 58.2	14 36.3	21 02.9
23 F	0 03 42	2 48 07	10♊44 34	17 44 56	13 42.3	16 53.5	20 29.2	3 18.2	4 47.3	22 54.1	8 36.9	27 01.4	14 38.5	21 03.8
24 Sa	0 07 39	3 47 38	24 46 35	1♋49 21	13D41.3	16 45.9	21 43.4	3 52.1	4 49.4	22 51.4	8 39.3	27 04.6	14 40.7	21 04.6
25 Su	0 11 35	4 47 06	8♋53 04	15 57 35	13 41.7	16 30.8	22 57.6	4 25.8	4 51.9	22 48.4	8 41.6	27 07.8	14 42.9	21 05.5
26 M	0 15 32	5 46 32	23 02 45	0♌08 23	13R42.7	16 08.7	24 11.7	4 59.5	4 54.8	22 45.3	8 43.9	27 11.1	14 45.0	21 06.3
27 Tu	0 19 28	6 45 55	7♌14 17	14 20 11	13 43.2	15 40.3	25 25.8	5 33.0	4 58.1	22 42.1	8 46.0	27 14.4	14 47.2	21 07.1
28 W	0 23 25	7 45 16	21 25 49	28 30 49	13 42.3	15 06.1	26 39.9	6 06.4	5 01.8	22 38.6	8 48.1	27 17.6	14 49.3	21 07.8
29 Th	0 27 22	8 44 35	5♍34 47	12♍37 18	13 39.1	14 26.9	27 53.9	6 39.8	5 06.0	22 35.0	8 50.1	27 20.9	14 51.5	21 08.6
30 F	0 31 18	9 43 51	19 37 52	26 36 01	13 33.4	13 43.7	29 07.9	7 13.0	5 10.5	22 31.2	8 51.9	27 24.2	14 53.6	21 09.3
31 Sa	0 35 15	10 43 06	3♎31 13	10♎23 02	13 25.3	12 57.4	0♉21.8	7 46.1	5 15.4	22 27.2	8 53.7	27 27.6	14 55.7	21 09.9

April 2018 — LONGITUDE

Day	Sid.Time	☉	0 hr ☽	Noon ☽	True ☊	☿	♀	♂	⚳	♃	♄	♅	♆	♇
1 Su	0 39 11	11♈42 18	17♎10 59	23♎54 44	13♌15.6	12♈09.0	1♉35.7	8♑19.1	5♌20.7	22♏23.1	8♑55.4	27♈30.9	14♓57.8	21♑10.6
2 M	0 43 08	12 41 29	0♏33 56	7♏08 24	13R05.2	11R19.4	2 49.6	8 52.0	5 26.3	22R18.8	8 56.9	27 34.2	14 59.8	21 11.2
3 Tu	0 47 04	13 40 37	13 37 59	20 02 41	12 55.1	10 29.8	4 03.5	9 24.8	5 32.4	22 14.4	8 58.4	27 37.6	15 01.9	21 11.8
4 W	0 51 01	14 39 44	26 22 35	2♐37 51	12 46.4	9 41.0	5 17.3	9 57.5	5 38.8	22 09.8	8 59.8	27 40.9	15 04.0	21 12.3
5 Th	0 54 57	15 38 49	8♐48 47	14 55 45	12 39.7	8 54.0	6 31.0	10 30.1	5 45.6	22 05.0	9 01.1	27 44.3	15 06.0	21 12.9
6 F	0 58 54	16 37 52	20 59 10	26 59 34	12 35.4	8 09.5	7 44.8	11 02.5	5 52.8	22 00.1	9 02.3	27 47.7	15 08.0	21 13.4
7 Sa	1 02 50	17 36 53	2♑57 30	8♑53 35	12D33.3	7 28.3	8 58.5	11 34.8	6 00.3	21 55.1	9 03.4	27 51.1	15 10.0	21 13.8
8 Su	1 06 47	18 35 53	14 48 27	20 42 47	12 32.9	6 51.0	10 12.1	12 06.9	6 08.2	21 49.9	9 04.4	27 54.5	15 12.0	21 14.3
9 M	1 10 44	19 34 51	26 37 14	2♒32 30	12R33.4	6 18.1	11 25.8	12 39.0	6 16.5	21 44.5	9 05.3	27 57.9	15 14.0	21 14.7
10 Tu	1 14 40	20 33 47	8♒29 17	14 28 12	12 33.6	5 49.9	12 39.4	13 10.8	6 25.1	21 39.0	9 06.1	28 01.3	15 15.9	21 15.1
11 W	1 18 37	21 32 41	20 29 55	26 35 01	12 32.7	5 26.7	13 52.9	13 42.6	6 34.0	21 33.4	9 06.8	28 04.8	15 17.8	21 15.4
12 Th	1 22 33	22 31 34	2♓44 01	8♓57 26	12 29.7	5 08.7	15 06.5	14 14.2	6 43.3	21 27.6	9 07.4	28 08.2	15 19.8	21 15.7
13 F	1 26 30	23 30 24	15 15 37	21 38 54	12 24.1	4 56.1	16 20.0	14 45.6	6 52.9	21 21.7	9 07.9	28 11.6	15 21.7	21 16.0
14 Sa	1 30 26	24 29 13	28 07 28	4♈41 25	12 16.0	4D48.7	17 33.4	15 16.9	7 02.8	21 15.7	9 08.3	28 15.1	15 23.5	21 16.3
15 Su	1 34 23	25 28 00	11♈20 42	18 05 09	12 05.7	4 46.7	18 46.8	15 48.0	7 13.0	21 09.6	9 08.6	28 18.5	15 25.4	21 16.5
16 M	1 38 19	26 26 45	24 54 31	1♉48 23	11 54.1	4 49.8	20 00.2	16 18.9	7 23.6	21 03.3	9 08.8	28 21.9	15 27.2	21 16.7
17 Tu	1 42 16	27 25 28	8♉46 16	15 47 35	11 42.4	4 58.1	21 13.5	16 49.7	7 34.5	20 57.0	9R08.9	28 25.4	15 29.0	21 16.8
18 W	1 46 13	28 24 09	22 51 43	29 58 01	11 31.9	5 11.3	22 26.8	17 20.2	7 45.7	20 50.5	9 08.9	28 28.8	15 30.8	21 17.0
19 Th	1 50 09	29 22 48	7♊05 49	14♊14 29	11 23.5	5 29.3	23 40.1	17 50.7	7 57.3	20 43.9	9 08.8	28 32.2	15 32.6	21 17.1
20 F	1 54 06	0♉21 25	21 23 27	28 32 13	11 17.9	5 51.9	24 53.3	18 20.9	8 09.1	20 37.2	9 08.6	28 35.7	15 34.4	21 17.2
21 Sa	1 58 02	1 20 00	5♋40 19	12♋47 26	11 14.9	6 19.0	26 06.5	18 50.9	8 21.2	20 30.5	9 08.4	28 39.1	15 36.1	21 17.2
22 Su	2 01 59	2 18 32	19 53 18	26 57 42	11D14.0	6 50.3	27 19.6	19 20.8	8 33.6	20 23.6	9 08.0	28 42.6	15 37.8	21R17.2
23 M	2 05 55	3 17 03	4♌00 31	11♌01 40	11R14.0	7 25.7	28 32.7	19 50.4	8 46.3	20 16.6	9 07.5	28 46.0	15 39.5	21 17.2
24 Tu	2 09 52	4 15 31	18 01 06	24 58 45	11 13.5	8 05.0	29 45.8	20 19.9	8 59.3	20 09.6	9 06.9	28 49.4	15 41.2	21 17.2
25 W	2 13 48	5 13 57	1♍54 36	8♍48 35	11 11.5	8 48.0	0♊58.7	20 49.1	9 12.5	20 02.5	9 06.2	28 52.9	15 42.8	21 17.1
26 Th	2 17 45	6 12 20	15 40 37	22 30 34	11 07.0	9 34.5	2 11.7	21 18.2	9 26.0	19 55.3	9 05.5	28 56.3	15 44.4	21 17.0
27 F	2 21 42	7 10 42	29 18 19	6♎03 40	10 59.5	10 24.5	3 24.6	21 47.0	9 39.8	19 48.1	9 04.6	28 59.7	15 46.0	21 16.9
28 Sa	2 25 38	8 09 01	12♎46 24	19 26 19	10 49.4	11 17.7	4 37.4	22 15.7	9 53.8	19 40.8	9 03.6	29 03.1	15 47.6	21 16.7
29 Su	2 29 35	9 07 19	26 03 10	2♏36 45	10 37.2	12 14.0	5 50.2	22 44.1	10 08.1	19 33.4	9 02.6	29 06.5	15 49.1	21 16.5
30 M	2 33 31	10 05 35	9♏06 52	15 33 21	10 24.1	13 13.4	7 03.0	23 12.3	10 22.7	19 26.0	9 01.4	29 09.9	15 50.7	21 16.3

Astro Data

	Dy Hr Mn
☽0S	4 1:39
☿0N	6 4:59
♃ R	9 4:47
♀0N	9 5:56
♃∠♄	14 11:04
☽0N	18 13:03
⚳ D	19 4:13
☉0N	20 16:17
☿ R	23 0:18
☽0S	31 11:04
♃⚹♇	14 9:59
☽0N	14 21:23
☿ D	15 9:22
♄ R	18 1:48
♇ R	22 15:27

Planet Ingress

		Dy Hr Mn
☿	♈	6 7:35
♀	♈	6 23:47
♂	♑	17 16:41
☉	♈	20 16:17
♀	♉	31 4:55
☉	♉	20 3:14
♀	♊	24 16:41

☽0S27 19:02

Last Aspect / ☽ Ingress

Last Aspect Dy Hr Mn			☽ Ingress	Dy Hr Mn
28 23:14	♅	△	♍	1 5:59
2 23:51	♀	☍	♎	3 8:22
5 6:20	♅	☍	♏	5 13:24
7 8:56	♃	☌	♐	7 22:04
10 2:29	♅	△	♑	10 9:53
12 15:37	♅	□	♒	12 22:46
15 7:34	♂	⚹	♓	15 10:13
17 13:13	☉	☌	♈	17 18:58
19 19:30	♅	☌	♉	20 1:08
21 17:22	♃	☍	♊	22 5:31
24 3:53	♅	⚹	♋	24 8:54
26 6:59	♅	□	♌	26 11:46
28 9:55	♅	△	♍	28 14:31
30 5:00	♃	⚹	♎	30 17:53

Last Aspect / ☽ Ingress

Last Aspect Dy Hr Mn			☽ Ingress	Dy Hr Mn
1 18:30	♅	☍	♏	1 22:58
3 16:07	♃	☌	♐	4 6:56
6 13:37	♅	△	♑	6 18:02
9 2:41	♅	□	♒	9 6:51
11 14:57	♅	⚹	♓	11 18:41
13 11:28	♃	△	♈	14 3:27
16 6:00	♅	☌	♉	16 8:52
17 22:06	♀	☌	♊	18 12:03
20 12:06	♅	⚹	♋	20 14:28
22 14:59	♅	□	♌	22 17:10
24 18:41	♅	△	♍	24 20:41
26 9:51	♇	△	♎	27 1:14
29 5:33	♅	☍	♏	29 7:13

☽ Phases & Eclipses

Dy Hr Mn		
2 0:52	○	11♍23
9 11:21	☾	18♐50
17 13:13	●	26♓53
24 15:36	☽	3♋57
31 12:38	○	10♎45
8 7:19	☾	18♑24
16 1:58	●	26♈02
22 21:47	☽	2♌42
30 0:59	○	9♏39

Astro Data

1 March 2018
Julian Day # 43159
SVP 5♓00'33"
GC 27♐05.6 ⚴ 15♉30.0
Eris 22♈59.0 ⚵ 2♓37.3
⚷ 27♓16.2 ⚶ 19♐45.8
☽ Mean ☊ 13♌44.7

1 April 2018
Julian Day # 43190
SVP 5♓00'31"
GC 27♐05.6 ⚴ 1♊19.2
Eris 23♈17.0 ⚵ 17♓12.7
⚷ 29♓06.2 ⚶ 29♐51.1
☽ Mean ☊ 12♌06.2

LONGITUDE — May 2018

Day	Sid.Time	☉	0 hr ☽	Noon ☽	True ☊	☿	♀	♂	⚳	♃	♄	♅	♆	♇
1 Tu	2 37 28	11♉03 49	21♏56 06	28♏15 04	10♌11.3	14♈15.6	8♊15.7	23♑40.2	10♌37.5	19♏18.5	9♑00.2	29♈13.3	15♓52.2	21♑16.1
2 W	2 41 24	12 02 02	4♐30 16	10♐41 48	9R 59.9	15 20.6	9 28.4	24 08.0	10 52.5	19R 11.0	8R 58.8	29 16.7	15 53.6	21R 15.8
3 Th	2 45 21	13 00 13	16 49 49	22 54 34	9 50.7	16 28.3	10 41.0	24 35.4	11 07.8	19 03.5	8 57.4	29 20.1	15 55.1	21 15.5
4 F	2 49 17	13 58 23	28 56 21	4♑55 35	9 44.2	17 38.6	11 53.6	25 02.7	11 23.3	18 55.9	8 55.9	29 23.4	15 56.5	21 15.2
5 Sa	2 53 14	14 56 31	10♑52 42	16 48 12	9 40.4	18 51.4	13 06.1	25 29.6	11 39.1	18 48.3	8 54.3	29 26.8	15 57.9	21 14.8
6 Su	2 57 11	15 54 37	22 42 39	28 36 39	9D 38.7	20 06.7	14 18.6	25 56.3	11 55.0	18 40.7	8 52.6	29 30.1	15 59.3	21 14.4
7 M	3 01 07	16 52 42	4♒30 50	10♒25 53	9R 38.4	21 24.3	15 31.0	26 22.8	12 11.2	18 33.1	8 50.8	29 33.4	16 00.6	21 14.0
8 Tu	3 05 04	17 50 46	16 22 29	22 21 18	9 38.4	22 44.2	16 43.4	26 48.9	12 27.6	18 25.4	8 48.9	29 36.8	16 01.9	21 13.6
9 W	3 09 00	18 48 48	28 23 03	4♓28 23	9 37.6	24 06.4	17 55.7	27 14.8	12 44.3	18 17.8	8 46.9	29 40.1	16 03.2	21 13.1
10 Th	3 12 57	19 46 49	10♓37 58	16 52 21	9 35.0	25 30.9	19 08.0	27 40.3	13 01.1	18 10.1	8 44.9	29 43.3	16 04.4	21 12.6
11 F	3 16 53	20 44 48	23 12 06	29 37 39	9 30.1	26 57.5	20 20.3	28 05.6	13 18.2	18 02.5	8 42.7	29 46.6	16 05.7	21 12.1
12 Sa	3 20 50	21 42 47	6♈09 20	12♈47 24	9 22.7	28 26.4	21 32.5	28 30.5	13 35.4	17 54.9	8 40.5	29 49.9	16 06.9	21 11.5
13 Su	3 24 46	22 40 43	19 31 54	26 22 46	9 13.0	29 57.4	22 44.6	28 55.1	13 52.9	17 47.2	8 38.2	29 53.1	16 08.0	21 11.0
14 M	3 28 43	23 38 39	3♉19 46	10♉22 31	9 02.1	1♉30.5	23 56.7	29 19.4	14 10.6	17 39.6	8 35.8	29 56.4	16 09.2	21 10.4
15 Tu	3 32 40	24 36 33	17 30 25	24 42 47	8 50.9	3 05.7	25 08.8	29 43.3	14 28.4	17 32.1	8 33.3	29 59.6	16 10.3	21 09.7
16 W	3 36 36	25 34 26	1♊58 47	9♊17 32	8 40.7	4 43.1	26 20.8	0♒06.9	14 46.5	17 24.5	8 30.7	0♉02.8	16 11.4	21 09.1
17 Th	3 40 33	26 32 17	16 38 02	23 59 21	8 32.6	6 22.6	27 32.7	0 30.1	15 04.7	17 17.0	8 28.1	0 05.9	16 12.4	21 08.4
18 F	3 44 29	27 30 07	1♋20 35	8♋40 50	8 27.2	8 04.1	28 44.6	0 53.0	15 23.2	17 09.6	8 25.4	0 09.1	16 13.4	21 07.7
19 Sa	3 48 26	28 27 55	15 59 24	23 15 37	8 24.4	9 47.8	29 56.4	1 15.5	15 41.8	17 02.2	8 22.6	0 12.2	16 14.4	21 07.0
20 Su	3 52 22	29 25 41	0♌28 59	7♌39 08	8D 23.6	11 33.6	1♋08.2	1 37.6	16 00.6	16 54.8	8 19.7	0 15.3	16 15.4	21 06.2
21 M	3 56 19	0♊23 25	14 45 48	21 48 50	8R 23.9	13 21.5	2 19.9	1 59.3	16 19.5	16 47.5	8 16.8	0 18.4	16 16.3	21 05.4
22 Tu	4 00 15	1 21 08	28 48 10	5♍43 48	8 24.0	15 11.5	3 31.6	2 20.6	16 38.7	16 40.3	8 13.8	0 21.5	16 17.2	21 04.6
23 W	4 04 12	2 18 50	12♍35 48	19 24 16	8 22.7	17 03.6	4 43.2	2 41.5	16 58.0	16 33.2	8 10.7	0 24.6	16 18.1	21 03.8
24 Th	4 08 09	3 16 29	26 09 16	2♎50 56	8 19.4	18 57.7	5 54.7	3 02.0	17 17.5	16 26.1	8 07.5	0 27.6	16 18.9	21 02.9
25 F	4 12 05	4 14 07	9♎29 21	16 04 36	8 13.5	20 53.9	7 06.2	3 22.1	17 37.1	16 19.1	8 04.3	0 30.6	16 19.8	21 02.1
26 Sa	4 16 02	5 11 44	22 36 46	29 05 53	8 05.3	22 52.2	8 17.6	3 41.7	17 56.9	16 12.1	8 01.0	0 33.6	16 20.5	21 01.2
27 Su	4 19 58	6 09 19	5♏31 58	11♏55 04	7 55.3	24 52.3	9 28.9	4 00.9	18 16.8	16 05.3	7 57.7	0 36.5	16 21.3	21 00.3
28 M	4 23 55	7 06 54	18 15 11	24 32 19	7 44.5	26 54.4	10 40.2	4 19.7	18 36.9	15 58.6	7 54.2	0 39.4	16 22.0	20 59.3
29 Tu	4 27 51	8 04 27	0♐46 31	6♐57 50	7 33.9	28 58.3	11 51.4	4 38.0	18 57.2	15 51.9	7 50.8	0 42.4	16 22.7	20 58.4
30 W	4 31 48	9 01 58	13 06 19	19 12 06	7 24.5	1♊03.8	13 02.5	4 55.8	19 17.6	15 45.4	7 47.2	0 45.2	16 23.3	20 57.4
31 Th	4 35 44	9 59 29	25 15 20	1♑16 11	7 17.0	3 11.0	14 13.6	5 13.1	19 38.1	15 38.9	7 43.6	0 48.1	16 23.9	20 56.4

LONGITUDE — June 2018

Day	Sid.Time	☉	0 hr ☽	Noon ☽	True ☊	☿	♀	♂	⚳	♃	♄	♅	♆	♇
1 F	4 39 41	10♊56 59	7♑14 55	13♑11 50	7♌11.8	5♊19.4	15♋24.6	5♒30.0	19♌58.8	15♏32.6	7♑40.0	0♉50.9	16♓24.5	20♑55.3
2 Sa	4 43 38	11 54 28	19 07 15	25 01 36	7R 08.9	7 29.1	16 35.5	5 46.3	20 19.6	15R 26.4	7R 36.3	0 53.7	16 25.1	20R 54.3
3 Su	4 47 34	12 51 56	0♒55 17	6♒48 50	7D 08.0	9 39.8	17 46.4	6 02.1	20 40.5	15 20.3	7 32.5	0 56.5	16 25.6	20 53.2
4 M	4 51 31	13 49 23	12 42 45	18 37 38	7 08.6	11 51.2	18 57.2	6 17.3	21 01.6	15 14.3	7 28.7	0 59.2	16 26.1	20 52.2
5 Tu	4 55 27	14 46 50	24 34 04	0♓32 42	7 09.7	14 03.1	20 07.9	6 32.0	21 22.9	15 08.4	7 24.9	1 01.9	16 26.6	20 51.1
6 W	4 59 24	15 44 15	6♓34 10	12 39 06	7R 10.4	16 15.2	21 18.5	6 46.2	21 44.2	15 02.7	7 21.0	1 04.6	16 27.0	20 49.9
7 Th	5 03 20	16 41 41	18 48 10	25 02 00	7 10.1	18 27.3	22 29.1	6 59.8	22 05.7	14 57.0	7 17.0	1 07.3	16 27.4	20 48.8
8 F	5 07 17	17 39 05	1♈21 10	7♈46 13	7 08.1	20 39.1	23 39.6	7 12.7	22 27.3	14 51.5	7 13.0	1 09.9	16 27.7	20 47.6
9 Sa	5 11 13	18 36 29	14 17 36	20 55 40	7 04.2	22 50.2	24 50.0	7 25.1	22 49.0	14 46.2	7 09.0	1 12.5	16 28.1	20 46.5
10 Su	5 15 10	19 33 52	27 40 40	4♉32 40	6 58.6	25 00.5	26 00.4	7 36.9	23 10.9	14 41.0	7 04.9	1 15.0	16 28.4	20 45.3
11 M	5 19 07	20 31 15	11♉31 37	18 37 15	6 51.9	27 09.7	27 10.7	7 48.0	23 32.9	14 35.9	7 00.8	1 17.5	16 28.6	20 44.1
12 Tu	5 23 03	21 28 38	25 49 08	3♊06 37	6 44.8	29 17.6	28 20.9	7 58.5	23 55.0	14 31.0	6 56.6	1 20.0	16 28.8	20 42.8
13 W	5 27 00	22 25 59	10♊28 56	17 55 08	6 38.4	1♋24.0	29 31.0	8 08.3	24 17.2	14 26.2	6 52.4	1 22.5	16 29.0	20 41.6
14 Th	5 30 56	23 23 21	25 24 09	2♋54 51	6 33.4	3 28.8	0♌41.1	8 17.5	24 39.5	14 21.6	6 48.2	1 24.9	16 29.2	20 40.4
15 F	5 34 53	24 20 41	10♋26 06	17 56 45	6 30.2	5 31.7	1 51.1	8 26.0	25 01.9	14 17.2	6 44.0	1 27.3	16 29.3	20 39.1
16 Sa	5 38 49	25 18 01	25 25 46	2♌52 12	6D 28.9	7 32.7	3 00.9	8 33.8	25 24.5	14 12.9	6 39.7	1 29.7	16 29.4	20 37.8
17 Su	5 42 46	26 15 20	10♌15 12	17 34 08	6 29.3	9 31.7	4 10.7	8 40.9	25 47.2	14 08.7	6 35.4	1 32.0	16 29.5	20 36.5
18 M	5 46 42	27 12 37	24 48 27	1♍57 48	6 30.4	11 28.5	5 20.4	8 47.3	26 09.9	14 04.7	6 31.1	1 34.3	16R 29.5	20 35.2
19 Tu	5 50 39	28 09 55	9♍01 58	16 00 50	6R 31.7	13 23.3	6 30.0	8 53.1	26 32.8	14 00.9	6 26.7	1 36.5	16 29.5	20 33.9
20 W	5 54 36	29 07 11	22 54 26	29 42 49	6 32.2	15 15.7	7 39.6	8 58.1	26 55.8	13 57.3	6 22.4	1 38.7	16 29.5	20 32.5
21 Th	5 58 32	0♋04 26	6♎26 11	13♎04 43	6 31.4	17 06.0	8 49.0	9 02.4	27 18.8	13 53.8	6 18.0	1 40.9	16 29.4	20 31.2
22 F	6 02 29	1 01 41	19 38 41	26 08 20	6 29.1	18 54.0	9 58.3	9 06.0	27 42.0	13 50.5	6 13.6	1 43.0	16 29.3	20 29.8
23 Sa	6 06 25	1 58 55	2♏33 55	8♏55 44	6 25.3	20 39.7	11 07.5	9 08.8	28 05.2	13 47.3	6 09.2	1 45.1	16 29.2	20 28.5
24 Su	6 10 22	2 56 08	15 14 02	21 29 05	6 20.3	22 23.1	12 16.6	9 11.0	28 28.6	13 44.3	6 04.8	1 47.1	16 29.1	20 27.1
25 M	6 14 18	3 53 21	27 41 05	3♐50 19	6 14.8	24 04.2	13 25.6	9 12.4	28 52.0	13 41.5	6 00.4	1 49.1	16 28.9	20 25.7
26 Tu	6 18 15	4 50 34	9♐56 58	16 01 15	6 09.4	25 43.0	14 34.5	9R 13.0	29 15.6	13 38.9	5 56.0	1 51.1	16 28.6	20 24.3
27 W	6 22 11	5 47 46	22 03 23	28 03 35	6 04.7	27 19.5	15 43.3	9 12.9	29 39.2	13 36.4	5 51.6	1 53.1	16 28.4	20 22.9
28 Th	6 26 08	6 44 58	4♑02 04	9♑59 02	6 01.1	28 53.6	16 51.9	9 12.1	0♍02.9	13 34.1	5 47.2	1 54.9	16 28.1	20 21.5
29 F	6 30 05	7 42 10	15 54 46	21 49 30	5 58.8	0♌25.4	18 00.5	9 10.5	0 26.7	13 32.0	5 42.8	1 56.8	16 27.8	20 20.1
30 Sa	6 34 01	8 39 22	27 43 33	3♒37 12	5D 57.9	1 54.9	19 08.9	9 08.2	0 50.5	13 30.1	5 38.3	1 58.6	16 27.4	20 18.7

Astro Data

	Dy Hr Mn
☽0N	12 7:22
☽0S	25 1:42
♃△♆	25 9:53
☽0N	8 17:27
♅∠♆	16 9:42
♆R	18 23:28
☽0S	21 8:04
♂R	26 21:06

Planet Ingress

		Dy Hr Mn
☿	♉	13 12:41
♅	♉	15 15:18
♂	♒	16 4:56
♀	♋	19 13:12
☉	♊	21 2:16
☿	♊	29 23:50
☿	♋	12 20:01
♀	♌	13 21:55
☉	♋	21 10:08
⚳	♍	28 9:05
☿	♌	29 5:17

Last Aspect / ☽ Ingress (May)

Last Aspect Dy Hr Mn			☽ Ingress	Dy Hr Mn
1 2:57	♂	⚹	♐	1 15:21
4 0:51	♅	△	♑	4 2:07
6 13:49	♅	□	♒	6 14:50
9 2:30	♅	⚹	♓	9 3:12
11 9:03	♂	⚹	♈	11 12:41
13 18:06	♅	☌	♉	13 18:16
15 20:31	♂	△	♊	15 20:44
17 18:19	♀	☌	♋	17 21:48
19 21:15	☉	⚹	♌	19 23:12
21 3:31	♃	□	♍	22 2:04
23 14:56	♇	△	♎	24 6:53
25 21:05	♇	□	♏	26 13:41
28 17:26	☿	☍	♐	28 22:30
30 6:27	♆	□	♑	31 9:28

Last Aspect / ☽ Ingress (June)

Last Aspect Dy Hr Mn			☽ Ingress	Dy Hr Mn
2 3:38	♇	☌	♒	2 22:07
4 5:11	♃	□	♓	5 10:55
7 6:36	♀	△	♈	7 21:27
9 19:38	♀	□	♉	10 4:05
12 3:30	♀	⚹	♊	12 6:54
13 19:44	☉	☌	♋	14 7:21
15 16:20	♇	☍	♌	16 7:22
18 3:27	☉	⚹	♍	18 8:42
20 10:52	☉	□	♎	20 12:30
22 1:35	♇	□	♏	22 19:12
24 14:01	☿	△	♐	25 4:30
26 12:54	♆	□	♑	27 15:53
29 8:59	♇	☌	♒	30 4:38

☽ Phases & Eclipses

Dy Hr Mn		
8 2:10	☾	17♒27
15 11:49	●	24♉36
22 3:50	☽	1♍02
29 14:21	○	8♐10
6 18:33	☾	16♓00
13 19:44	●	22♊44
20 10:52	☽	29♍04
28 4:54	○	6♑28

Astro Data

1 May 2018
Julian Day # 43220
SVP 5♓00'28"
GC 27♐05.7 ⚵ 18♊15.9
Eris 23♈36.5 ⚴ 1♈31.0
⚷ 0♈43.7 ⚶ 4♑43.4
☽ Mean ☊ 10♌30.8

1 June 2018
Julian Day # 43251
SVP 5♓00'23"
GC 27♐05.8 ⚵ 6♋27.0
Eris 23♈53.8 ⚴ 16♈13.9
⚷ 1♈56.1 ⚶ 2♑34.3R
☽ Mean ☊ 8♌52.3

July 2018

LONGITUDE

Day	Sid.Time	☉	0 hr ☽	Noon ☽	True ☊	☿	♀	♂	⚳	♃	♄	♅	♆	♇
1 Su	6 37 58	9♋36 33	9♒30 48	15♒24 45	5♌58.2	3♌21.9	20♌17.2	9♒05.1	1♍14.5	13♏28.4	5♑33.9	2♉00.4	16♓27.0	20♑17.2
2 M	6 41 54	10 33 45	21 19 26	27 15 18	5 59.4	4 46.6	21 25.4	9R 01.2	1 38.5	13R 26.8	5R 29.5	2 02.1	16R 26.6	20R 15.8
3 Tu	6 45 51	11 30 56	3♓12 49	9♓12 29	6 01.0	6 08.8	22 33.5	8 56.6	2 02.6	13 25.4	5 25.2	2 03.8	16 26.2	20 14.4
4 W	6 49 47	12 28 08	15 14 49	21 20 22	6 02.6	7 28.5	23 41.4	8 51.2	2 26.8	13 24.2	5 20.8	2 05.4	16 25.7	20 12.9
5 Th	6 53 44	13 25 20	27 29 41	3♈43 18	6R 03.7	8 45.7	24 49.3	8 45.1	2 51.1	13 23.1	5 16.4	2 07.0	16 25.2	20 11.5
6 F	6 57 40	14 22 32	10♈01 46	16 25 36	6 04.0	10 00.4	25 57.0	8 38.3	3 15.4	13 22.3	5 12.1	2 08.6	16 24.7	20 10.0
7 Sa	7 01 37	15 19 45	22 55 16	29 31 11	6 03.4	11 12.4	27 04.5	8 30.7	3 39.9	13 21.6	5 07.7	2 10.1	16 24.1	20 08.5
8 Su	7 05 34	16 16 58	6♉13 39	13♉02 56	6 01.9	12 21.7	28 12.0	8 22.4	4 04.4	13 21.1	5 03.4	2 11.6	16 23.5	20 07.1
9 M	7 09 30	17 14 11	19 59 05	27 02 05	5 59.9	13 28.3	29 19.3	8 13.5	4 28.9	13 20.8	4 59.2	2 13.0	16 22.9	20 05.6
10 Tu	7 13 27	18 11 25	4♊11 42	11♊27 33	5 57.6	14 32.1	0♍26.4	8 03.8	4 53.6	13D 20.7	4 54.9	2 14.4	16 22.2	20 04.1
11 W	7 17 23	19 08 39	18 49 02	26 15 26	5 55.5	15 32.9	1 33.5	7 53.5	5 18.3	13 20.7	4 50.7	2 15.7	16 21.5	20 02.7
12 Th	7 21 20	20 05 54	3♋45 49	11♋19 08	5 53.9	16 30.6	2 40.3	7 42.5	5 43.1	13 21.0	4 46.5	2 17.0	16 20.8	20 01.2
13 F	7 25 16	21 03 08	18 54 16	26 29 59	5D 53.0	17 25.3	3 47.1	7 30.9	6 07.9	13 21.4	4 42.3	2 18.2	16 20.1	19 59.8
14 Sa	7 29 13	22 00 23	4♌05 07	11♌38 29	5 53.0	18 16.6	4 53.6	7 18.8	6 32.8	13 22.0	4 38.2	2 19.4	16 19.3	19 58.3
15 Su	7 33 10	22 57 39	19 08 59	26 35 40	5 53.5	19 04.6	6 00.1	7 06.1	6 57.8	13 22.7	4 34.1	2 20.6	16 18.5	19 56.8
16 M	7 37 06	23 54 54	3♍57 42	11♍14 25	5 54.3	19 49.1	7 06.3	6 52.9	7 22.9	13 23.7	4 30.1	2 21.7	16 17.7	19 55.4
17 Tu	7 41 03	24 52 09	18 25 18	25 30 03	5 55.3	20 29.9	8 12.4	6 39.2	7 48.0	13 24.8	4 26.1	2 22.7	16 16.8	19 53.9
18 W	7 44 59	25 49 24	2♎28 28	9♎20 30	5 56.0	21 06.9	9 18.3	6 25.0	8 13.1	13 26.2	4 22.1	2 23.7	16 16.0	19 52.4
19 Th	7 48 56	26 46 40	16 06 15	22 45 55	5R 56.3	21 39.9	10 24.1	6 10.5	8 38.3	13 27.7	4 18.2	2 24.7	16 15.0	19 51.0
20 F	7 52 52	27 43 56	29 19 45	5♏48 06	5 56.2	22 08.8	11 29.6	5 55.5	9 03.6	13 29.3	4 14.3	2 25.6	16 14.1	19 49.5
21 Sa	7 56 49	28 41 12	12♏11 21	18 29 54	5 55.8	22 33.4	12 35.0	5 40.3	9 29.0	13 31.2	4 10.5	2 26.4	16 13.1	19 48.1
22 Su	8 00 45	29 38 28	24 44 11	0♐54 40	5 55.2	22 53.6	13 40.1	5 24.8	9 54.3	13 33.2	4 06.7	2 27.2	16 12.2	19 46.6
23 M	8 04 42	0♌35 44	7♐01 45	13 05 54	5 54.5	23 09.2	14 45.1	5 09.0	10 19.8	13 35.4	4 03.0	2 28.0	16 11.1	19 45.2
24 Tu	8 08 39	1 33 01	19 07 29	25 06 56	5 53.9	23 20.1	15 49.9	4 53.0	10 45.3	13 37.8	3 59.3	2 28.7	16 10.1	19 43.8
25 W	8 12 35	2 30 19	1♑04 37	7♑00 52	5 53.4	23R 26.1	16 54.4	4 36.8	11 10.8	13 40.4	3 55.7	2 29.4	16 09.1	19 42.3
26 Th	8 16 32	3 27 37	12 56 04	18 50 30	5 53.2	23 27.2	17 58.8	4 20.5	11 36.4	13 43.1	3 52.2	2 30.0	16 08.0	19 40.9
27 F	8 20 28	4 24 55	24 44 30	0♒38 21	5D 53.1	23 23.2	19 02.9	4 04.2	12 02.1	13 46.0	3 48.7	2 30.6	16 06.9	19 39.5
28 Sa	8 24 25	5 22 15	6♒32 20	12 26 46	5R 53.1	23 14.1	20 06.8	3 47.8	12 27.8	13 49.1	3 45.2	2 31.1	16 05.7	19 38.1
29 Su	8 28 21	6 19 35	18 21 53	24 18 01	5 53.1	23 00.0	21 10.4	3 31.4	12 53.5	13 52.3	3 41.9	2 31.6	16 04.6	19 36.7
30 M	8 32 18	7 16 55	0♓15 27	6♓14 28	5 53.0	22 40.9	22 13.9	3 15.0	13 19.3	13 55.7	3 38.5	2 32.0	16 03.4	19 35.3
31 Tu	8 36 14	8 14 17	12 15 25	18 18 37	5 52.8	22 17.0	23 17.0	2 58.8	13 45.1	13 59.3	3 35.3	2 32.4	16 02.2	19 34.0

August 2018

LONGITUDE

Day	Sid.Time	☉	0 hr ☽	Noon ☽	True ☊	☿	♀	♂	⚳	♃	♄	♅	♆	♇
1 W	8 40 11	9♌11 40	24♓24 24	0♈33 09	5♌52.4	21♌48.4	24♍20.0	2♒42.7	14♍11.0	14♏03.0	3♑32.1	2♉32.7	16♓01.0	19♑32.6
2 Th	8 44 07	10 09 03	6♈45 15	13 01 03	5R 52.0	21R 15.5	25 22.6	2R 26.7	14 36.9	14 06.9	3R 29.0	2 33.0	15R 59.7	19R 31.2
3 F	8 48 04	11 06 28	19 20 58	25 45 22	5 51.6	20 38.7	26 25.0	2 11.0	15 02.9	14 10.9	3 26.0	2 33.2	15 58.5	19 29.9
4 Sa	8 52 01	12 03 54	2♉14 38	8♉49 06	5D 51.4	19 58.4	27 27.2	1 55.6	15 28.9	14 15.2	3 23.0	2 33.4	15 57.2	19 28.6
5 Su	8 55 57	13 01 21	15 29 05	22 14 50	5 51.5	19 15.2	28 29.1	1 40.4	15 55.0	14 19.5	3 20.1	2 33.5	15 55.9	19 27.2
6 M	8 59 54	13 58 50	29 06 31	6♊04 13	5 51.9	18 29.9	29 30.7	1 25.7	16 21.1	14 24.1	3 17.3	2 33.6	15 54.5	19 25.9
7 Tu	9 03 50	14 56 20	13♊07 55	20 17 29	5 52.6	17 43.0	0♎32.0	1 11.3	16 47.2	14 28.8	3 14.6	2R 33.7	15 53.2	19 24.6
8 W	9 07 47	15 53 51	27 32 35	4♋52 48	5 53.4	16 55.6	1 33.0	0 57.3	17 13.4	14 33.7	3 11.9	2 33.6	15 51.8	19 23.3
9 Th	9 11 43	16 51 24	12♋17 31	19 45 59	5 54.0	16 08.3	2 33.7	0 43.9	17 39.6	14 38.7	3 09.3	2 33.6	15 50.5	19 22.1
10 F	9 15 40	17 48 58	27 17 18	4♌50 28	5R 54.3	15 22.2	3 34.0	0 30.9	18 05.9	14 43.9	3 06.8	2 33.5	15 49.1	19 20.8
11 Sa	9 19 37	18 46 33	12♌24 23	19 57 54	5 54.1	14 38.2	4 34.1	0 18.5	18 32.2	14 49.2	3 04.4	2 33.3	15 47.7	19 19.6
12 Su	9 23 33	19 44 08	27 29 52	4♍59 10	5 53.1	13 57.0	5 33.8	0 06.7	18 58.6	14 54.7	3 02.0	2 33.1	15 46.2	19 18.4
13 M	9 27 30	20 41 45	12♍24 46	19 45 45	5 51.6	13 19.6	6 33.2	29♑55.5	19 24.9	15 00.3	2 59.8	2 32.8	15 44.8	19 17.2
14 Tu	9 31 26	21 39 23	27 01 20	4♎10 53	5 49.6	12 46.8	7 32.2	29 45.0	19 51.3	15 06.1	2 57.6	2 32.5	15 43.3	19 16.0
15 W	9 35 23	22 37 02	11♎14 00	18 10 23	5 47.6	12 19.1	8 30.8	29 35.2	20 17.8	15 12.0	2 55.5	2 32.1	15 41.8	19 14.8
16 Th	9 39 19	23 34 42	24 59 55	1♏42 41	5 45.9	11 57.4	9 29.0	29 26.0	20 44.3	15 18.1	2 53.5	2 31.7	15 40.3	19 13.6
17 F	9 43 16	24 32 23	8♏18 51	14 48 41	5D 44.8	11 42.0	10 26.9	29 17.6	21 10.8	15 24.3	2 51.6	2 31.3	15 38.8	19 12.5
18 Sa	9 47 12	25 30 06	21 12 36	27 31 03	5 44.6	11D 33.5	11 24.3	29 10.0	21 37.3	15 30.7	2 49.7	2 30.8	15 37.3	19 11.4
19 Su	9 51 09	26 27 49	3♐44 32	9♐53 35	5 45.1	11 32.2	12 21.3	29 03.1	22 03.9	15 37.2	2 48.0	2 30.2	15 35.8	19 10.3
20 M	9 55 05	27 25 33	15 58 48	22 00 44	5 46.4	11 38.2	13 17.8	28 57.0	22 30.4	15 43.9	2 46.3	2 29.6	15 34.3	19 09.2
21 Tu	9 59 02	28 23 18	27 59 58	3♑57 03	5 48.0	11 51.9	14 13.8	28 51.7	22 57.1	15 50.7	2 44.8	2 29.0	15 32.7	19 08.1
22 W	10 02 59	29 21 05	9♑52 31	15 46 53	5 49.6	12 13.2	15 09.4	28 47.1	23 23.7	15 57.6	2 43.3	2 28.3	15 31.1	19 07.1
23 Th	10 06 55	0♍18 53	21 40 39	27 34 15	5R 50.7	12 42.2	16 04.5	28 43.4	23 50.4	16 04.7	2 41.9	2 27.5	15 29.6	19 06.1
24 F	10 10 52	1 16 42	3♒28 07	9♒22 37	5 50.9	13 18.9	16 59.1	28 40.5	24 17.1	16 11.9	2 40.7	2 26.7	15 28.0	19 05.1
25 Sa	10 14 48	2 14 32	15 18 08	21 14 57	5 49.9	14 03.0	17 53.1	28 38.4	24 43.8	16 19.2	2 39.5	2 25.9	15 26.4	19 04.1
26 Su	10 18 45	3 12 24	27 13 22	3♓13 38	5 47.6	14 54.4	18 46.6	28 37.1	25 10.6	16 26.7	2 38.4	2 25.0	15 24.8	19 03.1
27 M	10 22 41	4 10 17	9♓15 58	15 20 36	5 44.0	15 52.8	19 39.4	28D 36.6	25 37.3	16 34.2	2 37.4	2 24.1	15 23.2	19 02.2
28 Tu	10 26 38	5 08 12	21 27 40	27 37 23	5 39.5	16 58.1	20 31.7	28 36.9	26 04.1	16 42.0	2 36.4	2 23.1	15 21.6	19 01.3
29 W	10 30 34	6 06 09	3♈49 53	10♈05 19	5 34.4	18 09.7	21 23.4	28 38.1	26 30.9	16 49.8	2 35.6	2 22.1	15 20.0	19 00.4
30 Th	10 34 31	7 04 07	16 23 52	22 45 40	5 29.5	19 27.4	22 14.5	28 40.0	26 57.8	16 57.8	2 34.9	2 21.1	15 18.3	18 59.5
31 F	10 38 28	8 02 07	29 10 52	5♉39 39	5 25.2	20 50.7	23 04.9	28 42.8	27 24.6	17 05.9	2 34.3	2 19.9	15 16.7	18 58.7

Astro Data

	Dy Hr Mn
☽0N	6 2:03
♃D	10 17:04
☽0S	18 15:16
☿R	26 5:03
☽0N	2 8:32
♀0S	6 2:33
♅R	7 16:50
☽0S	14 23:52
☿D	19 4:25
♃△♆	19 7:45
♂D	27 14:06
☽0N	29 13:48

Planet Ingress

	Dy Hr Mn
♀ ♍	10 2:33
☉ ♌	22 21:01
♀ ♎	6 23:29
♂ ♑R	13 2:15
☉ ♍	23 4:10

Last Aspect Dy Hr Mn		☽ Ingress Dy Hr Mn
1 22:57	♀ ☍	♓ 2 17:32
4 9:48	♇ ⚹	♈ 5 4:51
7 7:10	♀ △	♉ 7 12:52
9 16:11	♀ □	♊ 9 16:59
10 20:01	♆ □	♋ 11 18:00
13 2:49	☉ ☌	♌ 13 17:32
14 23:13	☿ ☌	♍ 15 17:32
17 10:51	☉ ⚹	♎ 17 19:43
19 19:53	☉ □	♏ 20 1:14
22 9:19	☉ △	♐ 22 10:13
24 8:23	☿ △	♑ 24 21:50
26 13:42	♇ ☌	♒ 27 10:42
29 9:26	☿ ☍	♓ 29 23:29

Last Aspect Dy Hr Mn		☽ Ingress Dy Hr Mn
31 22:43	♀ ☍	♈ 1 10:56
3 2:53	☿ △	♉ 3 19:52
5 23:48	♀ △	♊ 6 1:33
7 7:56	☿ ⚹	♋ 8 4:02
9 11:22	♇ ☍	♌ 10 4:19
11 9:59	☉ ☌	♍ 12 4:00
14 4:38	♂ △	♎ 14 4:58
16 7:57	♂ □	♏ 16 8:55
18 15:08	♂ ⚹	♐ 18 16:46
20 23:48	☉ △	♑ 21 4:02
23 14:20	♂ ☌	♒ 23 16:57
25 4:40	♀ ☍	♓ 26 5:34
28 13:56	♂ ⚹	♈ 28 16:36
30 23:05	♂ □	♉ 31 1:31

☽ Phases & Eclipses

Dy Hr Mn	
6 7:52	☾ 14♈13
13 2:49	● 20♋41
13 3:02:18	● P 0.337
19 19:53	☽ 27♎05
27 20:22	○ 4♒45
27 20:23	● T 1.609
4 18:19	☾ 12♉19
11 9:59	● 18♌42
11 9:47:27	● P 0.737
18 7:50	☽ 25♏20
26 11:57	○ 3♓12

Astro Data

1 July 2018
Julian Day # 43281
SVP 5♓00'18"
GC 27♐05.9 ⚴ 24♋00.4
Eris 24♈04.0 ⚵ 0♉03.6
⚷ 2♈25.0 ⚶ 25♐46.8R
☽ Mean ☊ 7♌17.0

1 August 2018
Julian Day # 43312
SVP 5♓00'14"
GC 27♐05.9 ⚴ 11♌37.9
Eris 24♈05.2R ⚵ 13♉16.8
⚷ 2♈06.2R ⚶ 22♐08.2
☽ Mean ☊ 5♌38.5

LONGITUDE — September 2018

Day	Sid.Time	☉	0 hr ☽	Noon☽	True☊	☿	♀	♂	⚳	♃	♄	♅	♆	♇
1 Sa	10 42 24	9♍00 09	12♉12 10	18♉48 36	5♌22.1	22♌19.2	23♎54.6	28♑46.4	27♍51.5	17♏14.1	2♑33.7	2♉18.8	15♓15.1	18♑57.8
2 Su	10 46 21	9 58 13	25 29 07	2♊13 51	5D 20.5	23 52.4	24 43.6	28 50.8	28 18.4	17 22.4	2R 33.3	2R 17.6	15R 13.4	18R 57.0
3 M	10 50 17	10 56 19	9♊02 58	15 56 33	5 20.3	25 29.7	25 31.9	28 55.9	28 45.3	17 30.9	2 33.0	2 16.4	15 11.8	18 56.3
4 Tu	10 54 14	11 54 27	22 54 39	29 57 15	5 21.2	27 10.8	26 19.4	29 01.9	29 12.3	17 39.4	2 32.7	2 15.1	15 10.1	18 55.5
5 W	10 58 10	12 52 37	7♋04 17	14♋15 33	5 22.6	28 55.0	27 06.1	29 08.6	29 39.3	17 48.1	2D 32.6	2 13.8	15 08.5	18 54.8
6 Th	11 02 07	13 50 49	21 30 45	28 49 29	5R 23.7	0♍41.9	27 52.0	29 16.2	0♎06.2	17 56.9	2 32.5	2 12.4	15 06.8	18 54.1
7 F	11 06 03	14 49 03	6♌11 11	13♌35 12	5 23.6	2 31.0	28 37.1	29 24.5	0 33.2	18 05.9	2 32.6	2 11.0	15 05.2	18 53.4
8 Sa	11 10 00	15 47 18	21 00 44	28 26 55	5 21.7	4 21.9	29 21.3	29 33.5	1 00.3	18 14.9	2 32.7	2 09.6	15 03.5	18 52.8
9 Su	11 13 57	16 45 36	5♍52 45	13♍17 15	5 17.9	6 14.1	0♏04.6	29 43.4	1 27.3	18 24.0	2 33.0	2 08.1	15 01.9	18 52.1
10 M	11 17 53	17 43 55	20 39 24	27 58 14	5 12.4	8 07.3	0 46.9	29 54.0	1 54.3	18 33.3	2 33.3	2 06.6	15 00.2	18 51.5
11 Tu	11 21 50	18 42 16	5♎12 51	12♎22 28	5 05.7	10 01.2	1 28.2	0♒05.3	2 21.4	18 42.6	2 33.8	2 05.0	14 58.6	18 51.0
12 W	11 25 46	19 40 39	19 26 26	26 24 15	4 58.6	11 55.5	2 08.5	0 17.4	2 48.5	18 52.1	2 34.3	2 03.4	14 56.9	18 50.4
13 Th	11 29 43	20 39 04	3♏15 36	10♏00 20	4 52.1	13 49.8	2 47.7	0 30.2	3 15.6	19 01.7	2 35.0	2 01.8	14 55.3	18 49.9
14 F	11 33 39	21 37 30	16 38 27	23 10 04	4 46.9	15 44.1	3 25.8	0 43.7	3 42.7	19 11.4	2 35.7	2 00.1	14 53.6	18 49.4
15 Sa	11 37 36	22 35 57	29 35 30	5♐55 06	4 43.4	17 38.1	4 02.7	0 57.9	4 09.8	19 21.1	2 36.5	1 58.4	14 52.0	18 48.9
16 Su	11 41 32	23 34 27	12♐09 21	18 18 49	4D 41.9	19 31.6	4 38.4	1 12.8	4 36.9	19 31.0	2 37.5	1 56.7	14 50.4	18 48.5
17 M	11 45 29	24 32 58	24 24 04	0♑25 45	4 41.9	21 24.5	5 12.8	1 28.3	5 04.0	19 41.0	2 38.5	1 54.9	14 48.7	18 48.1
18 Tu	11 49 26	25 31 30	6♑24 32	12 21 03	4 42.9	23 16.8	5 45.9	1 44.5	5 31.1	19 51.1	2 39.6	1 53.1	14 47.1	18 47.7
19 W	11 53 22	26 30 05	18 15 58	24 09 56	4R 44.1	25 08.3	6 17.6	2 01.4	5 58.3	20 01.2	2 40.9	1 51.2	14 45.5	18 47.4
20 Th	11 57 19	27 28 41	0♒03 34	5♒57 27	4 44.6	26 59.0	6 47.8	2 18.9	6 25.4	20 11.5	2 42.2	1 49.3	14 43.9	18 47.0
21 F	12 01 15	28 27 18	11 52 09	17 48 10	4 43.5	28 48.8	7 16.6	2 37.0	6 52.6	20 21.8	2 43.6	1 47.4	14 42.3	18 46.7
22 Sa	12 05 12	29 25 58	23 45 57	29 45 57	4 40.4	0♎37.7	7 43.8	2 55.7	7 19.7	20 32.3	2 45.1	1 45.5	14 40.7	18 46.5
23 Su	12 09 08	0♎24 39	5♓48 28	11♓53 50	4 34.9	2 25.7	8 09.5	3 14.9	7 46.9	20 42.8	2 46.7	1 43.5	14 39.1	18 46.2
24 M	12 13 05	1 23 22	18 02 15	24 13 55	4 27.1	4 12.7	8 33.4	3 34.8	8 14.0	20 53.4	2 48.4	1 41.5	14 37.6	18 46.0
25 Tu	12 17 01	2 22 07	0♈28 55	6♈47 19	4 17.5	5 58.8	8 55.6	3 55.2	8 41.2	21 04.1	2 50.2	1 39.5	14 36.0	18 45.8
26 W	12 20 58	3 20 54	13 09 08	19 34 19	4 07.0	7 44.0	9 16.1	4 16.1	9 08.4	21 14.9	2 52.1	1 37.4	14 34.5	18 45.7
27 Th	12 24 54	4 19 43	26 02 48	2♉34 30	3 56.5	9 28.2	9 34.7	4 37.6	9 35.6	21 25.8	2 54.1	1 35.3	14 32.9	18 45.6
28 F	12 28 51	5 18 35	9♉09 16	15 47 02	3 47.1	11 11.5	9 51.4	4 59.6	10 02.7	21 36.7	2 56.2	1 33.2	14 31.4	18 45.5
29 Sa	12 32 48	6 17 28	22 27 39	29 11 04	3 39.7	12 53.8	10 06.1	5 22.1	10 29.9	21 47.7	2 58.4	1 31.1	14 29.9	18 45.4
30 Su	12 36 44	7 16 24	5♊57 09	12♊45 54	3 34.8	14 35.3	10 18.8	5 45.1	10 57.1	21 58.9	3 00.7	1 28.9	14 28.4	18D 45.4

LONGITUDE — October 2018

Day	Sid.Time	☉	0 hr ☽	Noon☽	True☊	☿	♀	♂	⚳	♃	♄	♅	♆	♇
1 M	12 40 41	8♎15 22	19♊37 14	26♊31 10	3♌32.3	16♎15.9	10♏29.5	6♒08.6	11♎24.3	22♏10.1	3♑03.0	1♉26.8	14♓26.9	18♑45.4
2 Tu	12 44 37	9 14 22	3♋27 41	10♋26 46	3D 31.7	17 55.6	10 38.0	6 32.5	11 51.5	22 21.3	3 05.5	1R 24.6	14R 25.4	18 45.4
3 W	12 48 34	10 13 25	17 28 23	24 32 29	3R 32.1	19 34.4	10 44.3	6 56.9	12 18.6	22 32.7	3 08.0	1 22.3	14 24.0	18 45.5
4 Th	12 52 30	11 12 30	1♌38 57	8♌47 38	3 32.1	21 12.5	10 48.4	7 21.8	12 45.8	22 44.1	3 10.7	1 20.1	14 22.6	18 45.5
5 F	12 56 27	12 11 38	15 58 16	23 10 31	3 30.7	22 49.6	10R 50.3	7 47.1	13 13.0	22 55.6	3 13.4	1 17.8	14 21.1	18 45.7
6 Sa	13 00 23	13 10 48	0♍23 56	7♍38 00	3 26.9	24 26.0	10 49.8	8 12.9	13 40.2	23 07.1	3 16.2	1 15.5	14 19.7	18 45.8
7 Su	13 04 20	14 09 59	14 52 04	22 05 27	3 20.3	26 01.7	10 47.0	8 39.1	14 07.3	23 18.8	3 19.1	1 13.2	14 18.3	18 46.0
8 M	13 08 17	15 09 13	29 17 23	6♎27 07	3 11.0	27 36.5	10 41.8	9 05.7	14 34.5	23 30.5	3 22.1	1 10.9	14 17.0	18 46.2
9 Tu	13 12 13	16 08 29	13♎33 51	20 36 52	2 59.9	29 10.6	10 34.2	9 32.8	15 01.7	23 42.2	3 25.2	1 08.5	14 15.6	18 46.4
10 W	13 16 10	17 07 48	27 35 31	4♏29 13	2 48.0	0♏43.9	10 24.2	10 00.2	15 28.8	23 54.1	3 28.4	1 06.2	14 14.3	18 46.7
11 Th	13 20 06	18 07 08	11♏17 34	18 00 13	2 36.7	2 16.5	10 11.8	10 28.1	15 56.0	24 06.0	3 31.6	1 03.8	14 13.0	18 47.0
12 F	13 24 03	19 06 30	24 37 02	1♐07 59	2 26.9	3 48.4	9 57.0	10 56.3	16 23.1	24 17.9	3 35.0	1 01.4	14 11.7	18 47.3
13 Sa	13 27 59	20 05 54	7♐33 11	13 52 52	2 19.5	5 19.5	9 39.9	11 24.9	16 50.2	24 30.0	3 38.4	0 59.0	14 10.4	18 47.7
14 Su	13 31 56	21 05 19	20 07 22	26 17 09	2 14.8	6 49.9	9 20.5	11 53.9	17 17.3	24 42.1	3 41.9	0 56.6	14 09.2	18 48.1
15 M	13 35 52	22 04 47	2♑22 42	8♑24 39	2 12.4	8 19.7	8 58.8	12 23.2	17 44.5	24 54.2	3 45.5	0 54.2	14 07.9	18 48.5
16 Tu	13 39 49	23 04 16	14 23 36	20 20 13	2D 11.8	9 48.7	8 35.0	12 52.8	18 11.5	25 06.4	3 49.2	0 51.8	14 06.7	18 48.9
17 W	13 43 46	24 03 47	26 15 13	2♒09 16	2R 11.8	11 16.9	8 09.1	13 22.8	18 38.6	25 18.7	3 53.0	0 49.4	14 05.6	18 49.4
18 Th	13 47 42	25 03 20	8♒03 06	13 57 22	2 11.4	12 44.5	7 41.3	13 53.2	19 05.7	25 31.0	3 56.8	0 46.9	14 04.4	18 49.9
19 F	13 51 39	26 02 55	19 52 45	25 49 54	2 09.5	14 11.3	7 11.7	14 23.8	19 32.7	25 43.3	4 00.7	0 44.5	14 03.3	18 50.4
20 Sa	13 55 35	27 02 31	1♓49 22	7♓51 43	2 05.3	15 37.3	6 40.4	14 54.7	19 59.8	25 55.7	4 04.7	0 42.0	14 02.2	18 51.0
21 Su	13 59 32	28 02 09	13 57 25	20 06 53	1 58.3	17 02.6	6 07.7	15 26.0	20 26.8	26 08.2	4 08.8	0 39.6	14 01.1	18 51.6
22 M	14 03 28	29 01 49	26 20 26	2♈38 19	1 48.7	18 27.1	5 33.8	15 57.5	20 53.8	26 20.7	4 13.0	0 37.1	14 00.0	18 52.2
23 Tu	14 07 25	0♏01 31	9♈00 40	15 27 32	1 36.8	19 50.7	4 58.8	16 29.3	21 20.8	26 33.3	4 17.2	0 34.7	13 59.0	18 52.9
24 W	14 11 21	1 01 14	21 58 54	28 34 36	1 23.7	21 13.4	4 23.0	17 01.4	21 47.7	26 45.9	4 21.5	0 32.2	13 58.0	18 53.6
25 Th	14 15 18	2 01 00	5♉14 25	11♉58 04	1 10.6	22 35.3	3 46.7	17 33.8	22 14.7	26 58.5	4 25.9	0 29.8	13 57.0	18 54.3
26 F	14 19 14	3 00 48	18 45 12	25 35 24	0 58.8	23 56.1	3 10.0	18 06.4	22 41.6	27 11.2	4 30.4	0 27.3	13 56.1	18 55.0
27 Sa	14 23 11	4 00 38	2♊28 17	9♊23 25	0 49.2	25 15.9	2 33.3	18 39.2	23 08.5	27 23.9	4 34.9	0 24.9	13 55.1	18 55.8
28 Su	14 27 08	5 00 30	16 20 24	23 18 54	0 42.6	26 34.5	1 56.8	19 12.3	23 35.4	27 36.7	4 39.5	0 22.4	13 54.2	18 56.6
29 M	14 31 04	6 00 24	0♋18 33	7♋19 07	0 38.9	27 51.9	1 20.7	19 45.6	24 02.3	27 49.5	4 44.2	0 20.0	13 53.4	18 57.4
30 Tu	14 35 01	7 00 20	14 20 23	21 22 10	0D 37.5	29 08.0	0 45.3	20 19.2	24 29.2	28 02.4	4 48.9	0 17.5	13 52.5	18 58.3
31 W	14 38 57	8 00 19	28 24 21	5♌26 49	0R 37.4	0♐22.7	0 10.8	20 53.0	24 56.0	28 15.3	4 53.8	0 15.1	13 51.7	18 59.1

Astro Data	Dy Hr Mn
♃∠♄	3 17:43
♄ D	6 11:10
☽0S	11 9:36
♃⚹♇	12 7:56
☉0S	23 1:55
☿0S	23 19:14
☽0N	25 19:39
♇ D	1 2:04
♀ R	5 19:06
☽0S	8 19:23
⚳0S	12 12:17
☽0N	23 3:31

Planet Ingress		Dy Hr Mn
☿	♍	6 2:40
⚳	♎	6 6:27
♀	♏	9 9:26
♂	♒	11 0:57
☿	♎	22 3:41
☉	♎	23 1:55
☿	♏	10 0:41
☉	♏	23 11:24
☿	♐	31 4:39
♀	♎R	31 19:43

Last Aspect Dy Hr Mn		☽ Ingress	Dy Hr Mn
2 5:58	♂ △	♊	2 8:03
4 6:38	☿ ⚹	♋	4 12:05
6 12:44	♂ ☍	♌	6 13:55
8 13:32	♀ ⚹	♍	8 14:30
10 15:14	♂ △	♎	10 15:21
11 22:59	♇ □	♏	12 18:16
14 8:55	☉ ⚹	♐	15 0:46
16 23:16	☉ □	♑	17 11:09
19 17:11	☉ △	♒	19 23:53
21 17:14	♃ □	♓	22 12:28
24 5:27	♃ △	♈	24 23:05
26 10:29	♇ □	♉	27 7:17
28 22:37	♃ ☍	♊	29 13:27

Last Aspect Dy Hr Mn		☽ Ingress	Dy Hr Mn
30 15:39	☿ △	♋	1 18:02
3 8:34	♃ △	♌	3 21:13
5 11:35	♃ □	♍	5 23:20
7 14:04	♃ ⚹	♎	8 1:11
9 8:51	♇ □	♏	10 4:10
11 23:13	♃ ☌	♐	12 9:54
14 0:59	☉ ⚹	♑	14 19:18
16 21:50	♃ ⚹	♒	17 7:37
19 12:28	☉ △	♓	19 20:22
21 23:48	♃ △	♈	22 6:59
23 18:19	♇ □	♉	24 14:34
26 14:50	♃ ☍	♊	26 19:42
28 4:39	♂ △	♋	28 23:28
31 2:32	☿ △	♌	31 2:43

☽ Phases & Eclipses Dy Hr Mn	
3 2:39	☾ 10♊34
9 18:03	● 17♍00
16 23:16	☽ 24♐02
25 2:54	○ 2♈00
2 9:47	☾ 9♋09
9 3:48	● 15♎48
16 18:03	☽ 23♑19
24 16:46	○ 1♉13
31 16:41	☾ 8♌12

Astro Data

1 September 2018
Julian Day # 43343
SVP 5♓00'10"
GC 27♐06.0 ⚳ 28♌26.8
Eris 23♈56.7R ⚵ 24♉08.4
⚷ 1♈04.9R ⚶ 25♐41.6
☽ Mean ☊ 4♌00.0

1 October 2018
Julian Day # 43373
SVP 5♓00'08"
GC 27♐06.1 ⚳ 13♍46.3
Eris 23♈41.6R ⚵ 0♊09.0
⚷ 29♓45.1R ⚶ 4♑18.4
☽ Mean ☊ 2♌24.7

November 2018 LONGITUDE

Day	Sid.Time	☉	0 hr ☽	Noon ☽	True ☊	☿	♀	♂	⚳	♃	♄	♅	♆	♇
1 Th	14 42 54	9♏00 20	12♌29 31	19♌32 21	0♌37.1	1♐35.7	29♎37.5	21♒27.0	25♎22.8	28♏28.2	4♑58.7	0♉12.7	13♓50.9	19♑00.0
2 F	14 46 50	10 00 23	26 35 13	3♍37 58	0R35.5	2 47.0	29R05.6	22 01.2	25 49.6	28 41.2	5 03.6	0R10.3	13R50.2	19 01.0
3 Sa	14 50 47	11 00 28	10♍40 28	17 42 27	0 31.4	3 56.3	28 35.2	22 35.7	26 16.3	28 54.2	5 08.6	0 07.8	13 49.5	19 01.9
4 Su	14 54 43	12 00 35	24 43 38	1♎43 40	0 24.4	5 03.5	28 06.5	23 10.4	26 43.1	29 07.2	5 13.7	0 05.4	13 48.8	19 02.9
5 M	14 58 40	13 00 44	8♎42 10	15 38 41	0 14.7	6 08.3	27 39.7	23 45.2	27 09.8	29 20.3	5 18.9	0 03.1	13 48.1	19 04.0
6 Tu	15 02 37	14 00 55	22 32 46	29 23 55	0 02.9	7 10.3	27 14.9	24 20.3	27 36.4	29 33.4	5 24.1	0 00.7	13 47.5	19 05.0
7 W	15 06 33	15 01 08	6♏11 44	12♏55 45	29♋50.3	8 09.4	26 52.3	24 55.5	28 03.1	29 46.5	5 29.4	29♈58.3	13 46.9	19 06.1
8 Th	15 10 30	16 01 23	19 35 39	26 11 08	29 38.0	9 05.0	26 31.8	25 31.0	28 29.7	29 59.6	5 34.7	29 56.0	13 46.3	19 07.2
9 F	15 14 26	17 01 40	2♐42 01	9♐08 11	29 27.4	9 56.9	26 13.7	26 06.6	28 56.3	0♐12.8	5 40.2	29 53.7	13 45.7	19 08.3
10 Sa	15 18 23	18 01 58	15 29 39	21 46 31	29 19.1	10 44.5	25 57.9	26 42.5	29 22.9	0 26.0	5 45.6	29 51.4	13 45.2	19 09.4
11 Su	15 22 19	19 02 18	27 58 59	4♑07 21	29 13.5	11 27.3	25 44.6	27 18.5	29 49.4	0 39.2	5 51.2	29 49.1	13 44.8	19 10.6
12 M	15 26 16	20 02 39	10♑11 58	16 13 19	29 10.6	12 04.8	25 33.6	27 54.6	0♏15.9	0 52.5	5 56.8	29 46.8	13 44.3	19 11.8
13 Tu	15 30 12	21 03 02	22 11 54	28 08 18	29D09.8	12 36.3	25 25.2	28 31.0	0 42.3	1 05.7	6 02.4	29 44.6	13 43.9	19 13.1
14 W	15 34 09	22 03 26	4♒03 08	9♒57 03	29 10.1	13 01.2	25 19.2	29 07.5	1 08.7	1 19.0	6 08.1	29 42.3	13 43.5	19 14.3
15 Th	15 38 06	23 03 52	15 50 43	21 44 50	29R10.5	13 18.7	25D15.6	29 44.1	1 35.1	1 32.3	6 13.9	29 40.1	13 43.2	19 15.6
16 F	15 42 02	24 04 19	27 40 07	3♓37 13	29 10.0	13R28.0	25 14.5	0♓20.9	2 01.4	1 45.6	6 19.7	29 38.0	13 42.9	19 16.9
17 Sa	15 45 59	25 04 47	9♓36 50	15 39 36	29 07.7	13 28.6	25 15.9	0 57.9	2 27.7	1 59.0	6 25.5	29 35.8	13 42.6	19 18.2
18 Su	15 49 55	26 05 16	21 46 07	27 56 57	29 03.0	13 19.7	25 19.6	1 34.9	2 53.9	2 12.3	6 31.4	29 33.7	13 42.4	19 19.6
19 M	15 53 52	27 05 47	4♈12 33	10♈33 18	28 56.0	13 00.7	25 25.6	2 12.2	3 20.2	2 25.7	6 37.4	29 31.6	13 42.2	19 20.9
20 Tu	15 57 48	28 06 19	16 59 32	23 31 23	28 47.0	12 31.3	25 33.9	2 49.5	3 46.3	2 39.0	6 43.4	29 29.5	13 42.0	19 22.3
21 W	16 01 45	29 06 53	0♉08 57	6♉52 09	28 36.7	11 51.3	25 44.5	3 27.0	4 12.4	2 52.4	6 49.5	29 27.4	13 41.9	19 23.7
22 Th	16 05 41	0♐07 28	13 40 46	20 34 29	28 26.3	11 00.9	25 57.3	4 04.5	4 38.5	3 05.8	6 55.6	29 25.4	13 41.7	19 25.2
23 F	16 09 38	1 08 04	27 32 51	4♊35 20	28 16.8	10 00.8	26 12.3	4 42.2	5 04.5	3 19.2	7 01.7	29 23.4	13 41.7	19 26.6
24 Sa	16 13 35	2 08 42	11♊41 16	18 49 58	28 09.3	8 52.2	26 29.3	5 20.1	5 30.5	3 32.5	7 07.9	29 21.5	13D41.6	19 28.1
25 Su	16 17 31	3 09 21	26 00 44	3♋12 51	28 04.3	7 36.8	26 48.4	5 58.0	5 56.5	3 45.9	7 14.2	29 19.5	13 41.6	19 29.6
26 M	16 21 28	4 10 02	10♋25 37	17 38 26	28D01.8	6 16.7	27 09.4	6 36.0	6 22.4	3 59.3	7 20.5	29 17.6	13 41.7	19 31.2
27 Tu	16 25 24	5 10 45	24 50 42	2♌01 58	28 01.4	4 54.4	27 32.3	7 14.2	6 48.2	4 12.7	7 26.8	29 15.8	13 41.7	19 32.7
28 W	16 29 21	6 11 29	9♌11 49	16 19 55	28 02.2	3 32.8	27 57.1	7 52.4	7 14.0	4 26.1	7 33.2	29 13.9	13 41.8	19 34.3
29 Th	16 33 17	7 12 14	23 26 04	0♍30 04	28R03.1	2 14.6	28 23.6	8 30.7	7 39.7	4 39.6	7 39.6	29 12.2	13 42.0	19 35.9
30 F	16 37 14	8 13 01	7♍31 48	14 31 11	28 03.1	1 02.3	28 51.8	9 09.1	8 05.4	4 53.0	7 46.0	29 10.4	13 42.1	19 37.5

December 2018 LONGITUDE

Day	Sid.Time	☉	0 hr ☽	Noon ☽	True ☊	☿	♀	♂	⚳	♃	♄	♅	♆	♇
1 Sa	16 41 11	9♐13 50	21♍28 08	28♍22 37	28♋01.4	29♏58.1	29♎21.7	9♓47.7	8♏31.1	5♐06.4	7♑52.5	29♈08.7	13♓42.3	19♑39.1
2 Su	16 45 07	10 14 40	5♎14 34	12♎03 56	27R57.4	29R03.5	29 53.2	10 26.3	8 56.7	5 19.7	7 59.0	29R07.0	13 42.6	19 40.7
3 M	16 49 04	11 15 31	18 50 38	25 34 34	27 51.4	28 19.8	0♏26.2	11 05.0	9 22.2	5 33.1	8 05.6	29 05.3	13 42.8	19 42.4
4 Tu	16 53 00	12 16 24	2♏15 39	8♏53 43	27 43.8	27 47.5	1 00.6	11 43.8	9 47.6	5 46.5	8 12.2	29 03.7	13 43.2	19 44.1
5 W	16 56 57	13 17 18	15 28 42	22 00 25	27 35.5	27 26.6	1 36.5	12 22.7	10 13.1	5 59.9	8 18.8	29 02.1	13 43.5	19 45.8
6 Th	17 00 53	14 18 14	28 28 48	4♐53 45	27 27.4	27D17.0	2 13.7	13 01.7	10 38.4	6 13.3	8 25.5	29 00.6	13 43.9	19 47.5
7 F	17 04 50	15 19 10	11♐15 13	17 33 09	27 20.4	27 18.1	2 52.2	13 40.7	11 03.7	6 26.6	8 32.2	28 59.1	13 44.3	19 49.2
8 Sa	17 08 46	16 20 08	23 47 37	29 58 40	27 15.0	27 29.2	3 32.0	14 19.9	11 28.9	6 40.0	8 38.9	28 57.7	13 44.7	19 50.9
9 Su	17 12 43	17 21 06	6♑06 27	12♑11 09	27 11.7	27 49.5	4 12.9	14 59.1	11 54.1	6 53.3	8 45.7	28 56.3	13 45.2	19 52.7
10 M	17 16 40	18 22 05	18 13 01	24 12 23	27D10.4	28 18.1	4 55.0	15 38.4	12 19.2	7 06.6	8 52.4	28 54.9	13 45.7	19 54.5
11 Tu	17 20 36	19 23 05	0♒09 37	6♒05 06	27 10.8	28 54.2	5 38.2	16 17.8	12 44.2	7 19.9	8 59.2	28 53.6	13 46.3	19 56.3
12 W	17 24 33	20 24 06	11 59 21	17 52 52	27 12.2	29 36.9	6 22.5	16 57.2	13 09.1	7 33.1	9 06.1	28 52.3	13 46.9	19 58.1
13 Th	17 28 29	21 25 07	23 46 12	29 39 57	27 14.1	0♐25.6	7 07.8	17 36.7	13 34.0	7 46.4	9 12.9	28 51.1	13 47.5	19 59.9
14 F	17 32 26	22 26 09	5♓34 43	11♓31 09	27R15.6	1 19.4	7 54.0	18 16.2	13 58.8	7 59.6	9 19.8	28 49.9	13 48.1	20 01.8
15 Sa	17 36 22	23 27 11	17 29 54	23 31 37	27 16.2	2 17.8	8 41.2	18 55.9	14 23.6	8 12.8	9 26.7	28 48.8	13 48.8	20 03.6
16 Su	17 40 19	24 28 13	29 36 56	5♈46 28	27 15.5	3 20.1	9 29.3	19 35.5	14 48.2	8 26.0	9 33.6	28 47.7	13 49.5	20 05.5
17 M	17 44 15	25 29 16	12♈00 48	18 20 28	27 13.3	4 26.0	10 18.3	20 15.3	15 12.8	8 39.2	9 40.5	28 46.6	13 50.3	20 07.3
18 Tu	17 48 12	26 30 20	24 45 55	1♉17 32	27 09.8	5 34.9	11 08.2	20 55.0	15 37.3	8 52.3	9 47.5	28 45.6	13 51.1	20 09.2
19 W	17 52 09	27 31 23	7♉55 34	14 40 11	27 05.4	6 46.5	11 58.8	21 34.9	16 01.7	9 05.4	9 54.5	28 44.7	13 51.9	20 11.1
20 Th	17 56 05	28 32 28	21 31 22	28 28 58	27 00.7	8 00.5	12 50.2	22 14.8	16 26.1	9 18.4	10 01.5	28 43.8	13 52.8	20 13.0
21 F	18 00 02	29 33 32	5♊32 41	12♊42 02	26 56.4	9 16.4	13 42.4	22 54.7	16 50.3	9 31.5	10 08.5	28 42.9	13 53.6	20 14.9
22 Sa	18 03 58	0♑34 37	19 56 26	27 15 05	26 53.1	10 34.2	14 35.3	23 34.6	17 14.5	9 44.5	10 15.5	28 42.1	13 54.6	20 16.9
23 Su	18 07 55	1 35 43	4♋37 10	12♋01 43	26D51.1	11 53.6	15 28.9	24 14.6	17 38.6	9 57.5	10 22.5	28 41.3	13 55.5	20 18.8
24 M	18 11 51	2 36 49	19 27 45	26 54 16	26 50.4	13 14.3	16 23.2	24 54.7	18 02.6	10 10.4	10 29.5	28 40.6	13 56.5	20 20.8
25 Tu	18 15 48	3 37 55	4♌20 19	11♌44 59	26 51.0	14 36.3	17 18.2	25 34.7	18 26.6	10 23.3	10 36.6	28 40.0	13 57.5	20 22.7
26 W	18 19 44	4 39 03	19 07 27	26 27 02	26 52.2	15 59.3	18 13.8	26 14.9	18 50.4	10 36.2	10 43.7	28 39.4	13 58.6	20 24.7
27 Th	18 23 41	5 40 10	3♍43 07	10♍55 15	26 53.7	17 23.3	19 09.9	26 55.0	19 14.1	10 49.0	10 50.7	28 38.8	13 59.6	20 26.6
28 F	18 27 38	6 41 18	18 03 05	25 06 24	26R54.8	18 48.3	20 06.7	27 35.2	19 37.8	11 01.8	10 57.8	28 38.3	14 00.7	20 28.6
29 Sa	18 31 34	7 42 27	2♎05 04	8♎59 03	26 55.1	20 13.9	21 04.0	28 15.4	20 01.4	11 14.5	11 04.9	28 37.8	14 01.9	20 30.6
30 Su	18 35 31	8 43 36	15 48 22	22 33 08	26 54.6	21 40.4	22 01.9	28 55.6	20 24.8	11 27.2	11 12.0	28 37.4	14 03.0	20 32.6
31 M	18 39 27	9 44 46	29 13 29	5♏49 34	26 53.2	23 07.4	23 00.3	29 35.9	20 48.2	11 39.8	11 19.1	28 37.1	14 04.2	20 34.6

Astro Data	Planet Ingress
Dy Hr Mn	Dy Hr Mn
☽0S 5 4:01	☊ ♋R 6 17:38
♃⚻♅ 8 6:21	♅ ♈R 6 19:01
♀D 16 10:52	♃ ♐ 8 12:40
☿R 17 1:33	⚳ ♏ 11 21:38
☽0N 19 13:20	♂ ♓ 15 22:22
♆D 25 1:09	☉ ♐ 22 9:03
♃∠♇ 29 4:29	
	☿ ♏R 1 11:13
☽0S 2 10:57	♀ ♏ 2 17:03
☿D 6 21:25	☿ ♐ 12 23:44
♅∠♆ 15 11:13	☉ ♑ 21 22:24
☽0N 16 23:27	
♃⚺♄ 27 19:19	
☽0S 29 17:02	

Last Aspect Dy Hr Mn	☽ Ingress Dy Hr Mn	Last Aspect Dy Hr Mn	☽ Ingress Dy Hr Mn
2 4:33 ♀ ⚹	♍ 2 5:49	1 14:35 ♅ ⚹	♎ 1 14:50
4 7:27 ♃ ⚹	♎ 4 9:02	3 18:17 ♅ ☍	♏ 3 19:56
6 8:20 ♀ ☌	♏ 6 13:03	5 21:54 ☿ ☌	♐ 6 2:50
8 10:43 ♂ □	♐ 8 19:01	8 10:01 ♅ △	♑ 8 12:03
11 3:36 ♅ △	♑ 11 3:56	10 21:28 ♅ □	♒ 10 23:41
13 15:14 ♅ □	♒ 13 15:46	13 10:21 ♅ ⚹	♓ 13 12:41
16 4:00 ♅ ⚹	♓ 16 4:43	15 11:50 ☉ □	♈ 16 0:45
18 8:05 ☉ △	♈ 18 15:57	18 7:22 ♅ ☌	♉ 18 9:38
20 22:47 ♅ ☌	♉ 20 23:44	20 0:43 ♂ ⚹	♊ 20 14:36
22 10:00 ♇ △	♊ 23 4:12	22 14:22 ♅ ⚹	♋ 22 16:29
25 5:32 ♅ ⚹	♋ 25 6:39	24 14:51 ♅ □	♌ 24 17:00
27 7:23 ♅ □	♌ 27 8:36	26 15:38 ♅ △	♍ 26 17:51
29 9:48 ♅ △	♍ 29 11:09	28 16:28 ♂ ☍	♎ 28 20:24
		30 22:55 ♅ ☍	♏ 31 1:24

☽ Phases & Eclipses Dy Hr Mn	
7 16:03	● 15♏11
15 14:55	☽ 23♒11
23 5:40	○ 0♊52
30 0:20	☾ 7♍43
7 7:22	● 15♐07
15 11:50	☽ 23♓27
22 17:50	○ 0♋49
29 9:35	☾ 7♎36

Astro Data

1 November 2018
Julian Day # 43404
SVP 5♓00'04"
GC 27♐06.1 ⚴ 28♍24.6
Eris 23♈23.2R ⚵ 28♉52.3R
⚷ 28♓31.7R ⚶ 16♑23.1
☽ Mean ☊ 0♌46.2

1 December 2018
Julian Day # 43434
SVP 5♓00'00"
GC 27♐06.2 ⚴ 11♎01.8
Eris 23♈08.1R ⚵ 22♉35.6R
⚷ 27♓55.6R ⚶ 29♑49.8
☽ Mean ☊ 29♋10.9

LONGITUDE January 2019

Day	Sid.Time	☉	0 hr ☽	Noon ☽	True☊	☿	♀	♂	⚳	♃	♄	♅	♆	♇
1 Tu	18 43 24	10♑45 56	12♏21 35	18♏49 44	26♋51.1	24♐35.1	23♏59.1	0♈16.2	21♏11.5	11♐52.4	11♑26.1	28♈36.8	14♓05.5	20♑36.6
2 W	18 47 20	11 47 06	25 14 11	1♐35 10	26R48.8	26 03.3	24 58.5	0 56.5	21 34.6	12 05.0	11 33.2	28R36.5	14 06.7	20 38.6
3 Th	18 51 17	12 48 17	7♐52 52	14 07 28	26 46.5	27 32.1	25 58.3	1 36.9	21 57.7	12 17.5	11 40.3	28 36.3	14 08.0	20 40.6
4 F	18 55 13	13 49 28	20 19 08	26 28 04	26 44.6	29 01.4	26 58.5	2 17.3	22 20.7	12 30.0	11 47.4	28 36.1	14 09.3	20 42.6
5 Sa	18 59 10	14 50 39	2♑34 27	8♑38 27	26 43.3	0♑31.2	27 59.2	2 57.7	22 43.5	12 42.4	11 54.5	28 36.1	14 10.7	20 44.7
6 Su	19 03 07	15 51 50	14 40 17	20 40 08	26D42.7	2 01.4	29 00.3	3 38.2	23 06.3	12 54.7	12 01.6	28D36.0	14 12.1	20 46.7
7 M	19 07 03	16 53 01	26 38 13	2♒34 48	26 42.7	3 32.1	0♐01.8	4 18.7	23 28.9	13 07.0	12 08.7	28 36.0	14 13.5	20 48.7
8 Tu	19 11 00	17 54 11	8♒30 08	14 24 32	26 43.2	5 03.2	1 03.6	4 59.2	23 51.4	13 19.2	12 15.8	28 36.1	14 14.9	20 50.7
9 W	19 14 56	18 55 21	20 18 17	26 11 47	26 43.9	6 34.8	2 05.8	5 39.7	24 13.8	13 31.4	12 22.8	28 36.2	14 16.4	20 52.8
10 Th	19 18 53	19 56 31	2♓05 23	7♓59 33	26 44.8	8 06.8	3 08.4	6 20.2	24 36.1	13 43.5	12 29.9	28 36.4	14 17.8	20 54.8
11 F	19 22 49	20 57 41	13 54 43	19 51 21	26 45.5	9 39.2	4 11.2	7 00.8	24 58.3	13 55.6	12 36.9	28 36.6	14 19.4	20 56.8
12 Sa	19 26 46	21 58 49	25 50 00	1♈51 11	26 46.0	11 12.1	5 14.5	7 41.3	25 20.3	14 07.5	12 44.0	28 36.8	14 20.9	20 58.9
13 Su	19 30 42	22 59 58	7♈55 28	14 03 23	26R46.3	12 45.5	6 18.0	8 21.9	25 42.2	14 19.5	12 51.0	28 37.2	14 22.5	21 00.9
14 M	19 34 39	24 01 05	20 15 31	26 32 25	26 46.3	14 19.3	7 21.8	9 02.5	26 04.0	14 31.3	12 58.0	28 37.5	14 24.0	21 02.9
15 Tu	19 38 36	25 02 12	2♉54 37	9♉22 34	26 46.3	15 53.5	8 26.0	9 43.1	26 25.7	14 43.1	13 05.0	28 38.0	14 25.7	21 04.9
16 W	19 42 32	26 03 18	15 56 44	22 37 25	26D46.2	17 28.3	9 30.4	10 23.7	26 47.2	14 54.8	13 12.0	28 38.4	14 27.3	21 07.0
17 Th	19 46 29	27 04 24	29 24 55	6♊19 19	26 46.2	19 03.6	10 35.1	11 04.4	27 08.6	15 06.4	13 19.0	28 39.0	14 29.0	21 09.0
18 F	19 50 25	28 05 29	13♊20 37	20 28 38	26 46.3	20 39.3	11 40.1	11 45.0	27 29.9	15 18.0	13 25.9	28 39.6	14 30.7	21 11.0
19 Sa	19 54 22	29 06 33	27 43 02	5♋03 17	26 46.4	22 15.6	12 45.3	12 25.6	27 51.0	15 29.5	13 32.8	28 40.2	14 32.4	21 13.0
20 Su	19 58 18	0♒07 36	12♋28 41	19 58 21	26R46.6	23 52.5	13 50.8	13 06.3	28 12.0	15 40.9	13 39.8	28 40.9	14 34.1	21 15.0
21 M	20 02 15	1 08 39	27 31 16	5♌06 20	26 46.6	25 29.9	14 56.5	13 46.9	28 32.9	15 52.2	13 46.6	28 41.6	14 35.9	21 17.1
22 Tu	20 06 12	2 09 41	12♌42 19	20 18 02	26 46.3	27 07.8	16 02.5	14 27.5	28 53.6	16 03.5	13 53.5	28 42.4	14 37.6	21 19.1
23 W	20 10 08	3 10 42	27 52 14	5♍23 48	26 45.7	28 46.4	17 08.7	15 08.2	29 14.1	16 14.7	14 00.4	28 43.3	14 39.4	21 21.1
24 Th	20 14 05	4 11 43	12♍51 42	20 15 03	26 44.9	0♒25.5	18 15.1	15 48.8	29 34.6	16 25.8	14 07.2	28 44.1	14 41.3	21 23.0
25 F	20 18 01	5 12 43	27 33 07	4♎45 21	26 44.0	2 05.3	19 21.7	16 29.5	29 54.8	16 36.8	14 14.0	28 45.1	14 43.1	21 25.0
26 Sa	20 21 58	6 13 43	11♎51 22	18 50 57	26 43.2	3 45.6	20 28.6	17 10.1	0♐14.9	16 47.7	14 20.7	28 46.1	14 45.0	21 27.0
27 Su	20 25 54	7 14 42	25 44 03	2♏30 45	26D42.7	5 26.7	21 35.6	17 50.7	0 34.9	16 58.5	14 27.5	28 47.1	14 46.9	21 29.0
28 M	20 29 51	8 15 41	9♏11 14	15 45 48	26 42.8	7 08.3	22 42.9	18 31.4	0 54.7	17 09.3	14 34.2	28 48.2	14 48.8	21 30.9
29 Tu	20 33 47	9 16 39	22 14 47	28 38 36	26 43.4	8 50.7	23 50.3	19 12.0	1 14.4	17 19.9	14 40.9	28 49.3	14 50.7	21 32.9
30 W	20 37 44	10 17 36	4♐57 41	11♐12 28	26 44.5	10 33.6	24 57.9	19 52.7	1 33.9	17 30.5	14 47.5	28 50.5	14 52.6	21 34.8
31 Th	20 41 41	11 18 33	17 23 26	23 31 01	26 45.9	12 17.3	26 05.7	20 33.3	1 53.2	17 41.0	14 54.1	28 51.8	14 54.6	21 36.8

LONGITUDE February 2019

Day	Sid.Time	☉	0 hr ☽	Noon ☽	True☊	☿	♀	♂	⚳	♃	♄	♅	♆	♇
1 F	20 45 37	12♒19 29	29♐35 40	5♑37 46	26♋47.2	14♒01.6	27♐13.7	21♈13.9	2♐12.3	17♐51.3	15♑00.7	28♈53.1	14♓56.6	21♑38.7
2 Sa	20 49 34	13 20 24	11♑37 44	17 35 55	26R48.2	15 46.6	28 21.8	21 54.6	2 31.3	18 01.6	15 07.3	28 54.4	14 58.6	21 40.6
3 Su	20 53 30	14 21 18	23 32 41	29 28 19	26 48.4	17 32.1	29 30.1	22 35.2	2 50.1	18 11.8	15 13.8	28 55.8	15 00.6	21 42.5
4 M	20 57 27	15 22 11	5♒23 07	11♒17 23	26 47.7	19 18.3	0♑38.5	23 15.9	3 08.7	18 21.9	15 20.3	28 57.2	15 02.6	21 44.4
5 Tu	21 01 23	16 23 02	17 11 21	23 05 17	26 45.9	21 05.0	1 47.1	23 56.5	3 27.2	18 31.8	15 26.7	28 58.7	15 04.6	21 46.3
6 W	21 05 20	17 23 53	28 59 26	4♓54 03	26 43.1	22 52.3	2 55.8	24 37.1	3 45.4	18 41.7	15 33.1	29 00.3	15 06.7	21 48.2
7 Th	21 09 16	18 24 42	10♓49 22	16 45 40	26 39.6	24 40.0	4 04.6	25 17.8	4 03.5	18 51.5	15 39.5	29 01.8	15 08.8	21 50.1
8 F	21 13 13	19 25 30	22 43 13	28 42 20	26 35.6	26 28.2	5 13.6	25 58.4	4 21.4	19 01.1	15 45.8	29 03.5	15 10.9	21 51.9
9 Sa	21 17 09	20 26 17	4♈43 20	10♈46 33	26 31.6	28 16.6	6 22.6	26 39.0	4 39.1	19 10.6	15 52.1	29 05.1	15 13.0	21 53.8
10 Su	21 21 06	21 27 02	16 52 23	23 01 13	26 28.2	0♓05.2	7 31.8	27 19.6	4 56.6	19 20.1	15 58.3	29 06.8	15 15.1	21 55.6
11 M	21 25 03	22 27 45	29 13 28	5♉29 33	26 25.8	1 53.8	8 41.2	28 00.2	5 13.8	19 29.4	16 04.5	29 08.6	15 17.2	21 57.4
12 Tu	21 28 59	23 28 27	11♉49 57	18 15 05	26D24.7	3 42.3	9 50.6	28 40.8	5 30.9	19 38.6	16 10.6	29 10.4	15 19.3	21 59.2
13 W	21 32 56	24 29 07	24 45 24	1♊21 17	26 24.7	5 30.4	11 00.1	29 21.3	5 47.8	19 47.7	16 16.7	29 12.3	15 21.5	22 01.0
14 Th	21 36 52	25 29 46	8♊03 08	14 51 13	26 25.8	7 18.0	12 09.8	0♉01.9	6 04.5	19 56.6	16 22.8	29 14.1	15 23.7	22 02.7
15 F	21 40 49	26 30 23	21 45 47	28 46 54	26 27.4	9 04.8	13 19.6	0 42.5	6 20.9	20 05.5	16 28.8	29 16.1	15 25.8	22 04.5
16 Sa	21 44 45	27 30 58	5♋54 34	13♋08 35	26R28.8	10 50.3	14 29.4	1 23.0	6 37.2	20 14.2	16 34.7	29 18.1	15 28.0	22 06.2
17 Su	21 48 42	28 31 31	20 28 36	27 54 04	26 29.3	12 34.4	15 39.4	2 03.5	6 53.2	20 22.8	16 40.6	29 20.1	15 30.2	22 07.9
18 M	21 52 38	29 32 03	5♌24 14	12♌58 12	26 28.3	14 16.5	16 49.4	2 44.0	7 09.0	20 31.3	16 46.4	29 22.2	15 32.4	22 09.6
19 Tu	21 56 35	0♓32 33	20 34 51	28 12 58	26 25.7	15 56.2	17 59.6	3 24.5	7 24.6	20 39.6	16 52.2	29 24.3	15 34.6	22 11.3
20 W	22 00 32	1 33 02	5♍51 15	13♍28 21	26 21.5	17 33.0	19 09.8	4 05.0	7 40.0	20 47.8	16 58.0	29 26.4	15 36.8	22 13.0
21 Th	22 04 28	2 33 29	21 02 58	28 33 52	26 16.1	19 06.3	20 20.2	4 45.4	7 55.1	20 55.9	17 03.7	29 28.6	15 39.1	22 14.6
22 F	22 08 25	3 33 54	5♎59 57	13♎20 16	26 10.4	20 35.6	21 30.6	5 25.8	8 10.0	21 03.9	17 09.3	29 30.8	15 41.3	22 16.2
23 Sa	22 12 21	4 34 18	20 34 06	27 40 57	26 05.2	22 00.2	22 41.1	6 06.3	8 24.7	21 11.7	17 14.8	29 33.1	15 43.5	22 17.8
24 Su	22 16 18	5 34 41	4♏40 29	11♏32 37	26 01.1	23 19.4	23 51.7	6 46.7	8 39.1	21 19.4	17 20.3	29 35.4	15 45.8	22 19.4
25 M	22 20 14	6 35 02	18 17 24	24 55 04	25D58.6	24 32.8	25 02.4	7 27.0	8 53.3	21 27.0	17 25.8	29 37.7	15 48.0	22 21.0
26 Tu	22 24 11	7 35 22	1♐25 58	7♐50 34	25 57.9	25 39.5	26 13.1	8 07.4	9 07.2	21 34.4	17 31.2	29 40.1	15 50.3	22 22.5
27 W	22 28 07	8 35 41	14 09 24	20 23 01	25 58.5	26 39.1	27 24.0	8 47.8	9 20.9	21 41.7	17 36.5	29 42.5	15 52.6	22 24.1
28 Th	22 32 04	9 35 58	26 32 03	2♑37 07	26 00.0	27 30.9	28 34.9	9 28.1	9 34.3	21 48.8	17 41.8	29 45.0	15 54.8	22 25.6

Astro Data Dy Hr Mn	Planet Ingress Dy Hr Mn	Last Aspect Dy Hr Mn	☽ Ingress Dy Hr Mn	Last Aspect Dy Hr Mn	☽ Ingress Dy Hr Mn	☽ Phases & Eclipses Dy Hr Mn	Astro Data
♂0N 2 0:58	♂ ♈ 1 2:21	1 22:27 ♀ ☌	♐ 2 9:00	31 22:34 ♅ △	♑ 1 0:48	6 1:29 ● 15♑25	1 January 2019
♅ D 6 20:28	☿ ♑ 5 3:41	4 17:43 ☿ ☌	♑ 4 18:56	3 10:54 ♅ □	♒ 3 13:04	6 1:42:40 ◐ P 0.715	Julian Day # 43465
♃⚼♅ 9 21:34	♀ ♐ 7 11:19	7 6:21 ♀ ⚹	♒ 7 6:47	6 0:00 ♅ ⚹	♓ 6 2:03	14 6:47 ☽ 23♈48	SVP 4♓59'55"
☽0N 13 7:53	☉ ♒ 20 9:01	9 16:54 ♅ ⚹	♓ 9 19:45	7 22:15 ♇ ⚹	♈ 8 14:35	21 5:17 ○ 0♌52	GC 27♐06.3 ⚴ 21♎40.4
♃□♆ 13 18:59	☿ ♒ 24 5:50	11 14:26 ☉ ⚹	♈ 12 8:19	10 23:49 ♅ ☌	♉ 11 1:30	21 5:13 ◑ T 1.195	Eris 22♈59.9R ⚵ 20♉38.9
☽0S 26 0:07	⚳ ♐ 25 18:09	14 15:57 ♅ ☌	♉ 14 18:32	12 22:27 ☉ □	♊ 13 9:33	27 21:12 ☾ 7♏38	⚷ 28♓08.7 ⚶ 14♒42.3
♄⚹♆ 31 14:16		16 18:35 ☉ △	♊ 17 1:01	15 12:50 ♅ ⚹	♋ 15 14:04		☽ Mean ☊ 27♋32.4
	♀ ♑ 3 22:30	19 1:34 ♅ ⚹	♋ 19 3:45	17 14:18 ♅ □	♌ 17 15:22	4 21:05 ● 15♒45	1 February 2019
☽0N 9 14:02	☿ ♓ 10 10:52	21 1:51 ♅ □	♌ 21 3:56	19 13:52 ♅ △	♍ 19 14:48	12 22:27 ☽ 23♉55	Julian Day # 43496
☽0S 22 9:19	♂ ♉ 14 10:52	23 1:21 ♅ △	♍ 23 3:23	21 1:53 ♇ △	♎ 21 14:18	19 15:55 ○ 0♍42	SVP 4♓59'50"
☿0N 27 6:28	☉ ♓ 18 23:05	24 13:52 ♇ △	♎ 25 4:04	23 15:12 ♅ ☍	♏ 23 15:57	26 11:29 ☾ 7♐34	GC 27♐06.4 ⚴ 28♎21.5
		27 5:22 ♅ ☍	♏ 27 7:32	25 12:15 ♀ ⚹	♐ 25 21:21		Eris 23♈02.1 ⚵ 26♉50.2
		28 22:40 ♇ ⚹	♐ 29 14:34	28 6:18 ♅ △	♑ 28 6:49		⚷ 29♓10.6 ⚶ 0♓01.1
							☽ Mean ☊ 25♋53.9

March 2019 LONGITUDE

Day	Sid.Time	☉	0 hr ☽	Noon ☽	True ☊	☿	♀	♂	⚳	♃	♄	♅	♆	♇
1 F	22 36 01	10♓36 14	8♑38 49	14♑37 47	26♋01.4	28♓14.4	29♑45.9	10♉08.5	9♐47.5	21♐55.8	17♑47.0	29♈47.4	15♓57.1	22♑27.1
2 Sa	22 39 57	11 36 28	20 34 34	26 29 45	26R02.0	28 49.2	0♒56.9	10 48.8	10 00.4	22 02.7	17 52.1	29 50.0	15 59.4	22 28.5
3 Su	22 43 54	12 36 40	2♒23 48	8♒17 14	26 01.1	29 15.0	2 08.0	11 29.1	10 13.0	22 09.4	17 57.2	29 52.5	16 01.6	22 30.0
4 M	22 47 50	13 36 51	14 10 27	20 03 51	25 58.0	29 31.5	3 19.2	12 09.4	10 25.4	22 15.9	18 02.2	29 55.1	16 03.9	22 31.4
5 Tu	22 51 47	14 37 00	25 57 46	1♓52 30	25 52.6	29R38.6	4 30.4	12 49.6	10 37.4	22 22.3	18 07.1	29 57.7	16 06.2	22 32.8
6 W	22 55 43	15 37 07	7♓48 18	13 45 26	25 45.0	29 36.5	5 41.7	13 29.9	10 49.2	22 28.6	18 12.0	0♉00.4	16 08.5	22 34.2
7 Th	22 59 40	16 37 12	19 44 04	25 44 23	25 35.7	29 25.2	6 53.0	14 10.1	11 00.7	22 34.7	18 16.8	0 03.1	16 10.8	22 35.5
8 F	23 03 36	17 37 16	1♈46 33	7♈50 42	25 25.4	29 05.1	8 04.4	14 50.3	11 11.9	22 40.6	18 21.5	0 05.8	16 13.0	22 36.9
9 Sa	23 07 33	18 37 17	13 57 00	20 05 36	25 15.1	28 36.9	9 15.9	15 30.5	11 22.8	22 46.4	18 26.2	0 08.6	16 15.3	22 38.2
10 Su	23 11 30	19 37 17	26 16 39	2♉30 22	25 05.9	28 01.2	10 27.4	16 10.7	11 33.5	22 52.0	18 30.8	0 11.3	16 17.6	22 39.5
11 M	23 15 26	20 37 14	8♉46 55	15 06 34	24 58.4	27 19.0	11 38.9	16 50.9	11 43.8	22 57.5	18 35.3	0 14.1	16 19.9	22 40.7
12 Tu	23 19 23	21 37 09	21 29 33	27 56 09	24 53.3	26 31.3	12 50.5	17 31.0	11 53.8	23 02.8	18 39.7	0 17.0	16 22.1	22 42.0
13 W	23 23 19	22 37 02	4♊26 40	11♊01 26	24D50.6	25 39.2	14 02.1	18 11.1	12 03.5	23 07.9	18 44.1	0 19.9	16 24.4	22 43.2
14 Th	23 27 16	23 36 53	17 40 43	24 24 52	24 49.9	24 44.0	15 13.7	18 51.3	12 12.9	23 12.9	18 48.4	0 22.8	16 26.7	22 44.3
15 F	23 31 12	24 36 42	1♋14 06	8♋08 40	24 50.5	23 47.0	16 25.5	19 31.3	12 22.0	23 17.7	18 52.6	0 25.7	16 28.9	22 45.5
16 Sa	23 35 09	25 36 28	15 08 42	22 14 14	24R51.0	22 49.5	17 37.2	20 11.4	12 30.8	23 22.3	18 56.7	0 28.6	16 31.2	22 46.6
17 Su	23 39 05	26 36 12	29 25 11	6♌41 19	24 50.5	21 52.7	18 49.0	20 51.4	12 39.2	23 26.8	19 00.7	0 31.6	16 33.5	22 47.8
18 M	23 43 02	27 35 54	14♌02 14	21 27 22	24 48.0	20 57.7	20 00.8	21 31.4	12 47.3	23 31.1	19 04.7	0 34.6	16 35.7	22 48.8
19 Tu	23 46 59	28 35 34	28 55 56	6♍27 02	24 42.8	20 05.7	21 12.7	22 11.4	12 55.1	23 35.3	19 08.6	0 37.6	16 37.9	22 49.9
20 W	23 50 55	29 35 11	13♍59 35	21 32 22	24 35.1	19 17.5	22 24.6	22 51.4	13 02.6	23 39.2	19 12.4	0 40.7	16 40.2	22 50.9
21 Th	23 54 52	0♈34 46	29 04 11	6♎33 44	24 25.5	18 33.8	23 36.5	23 31.3	13 09.7	23 43.0	19 16.1	0 43.7	16 42.4	22 51.9
22 F	23 58 48	1 34 20	13♎59 51	21 21 24	24 15.1	17 55.2	24 48.5	24 11.3	13 16.5	23 46.6	19 19.8	0 46.8	16 44.6	22 52.9
23 Sa	0 02 45	2 33 51	28 37 28	5♏47 15	24 05.1	17 22.2	26 00.5	24 51.2	13 22.9	23 50.1	19 23.3	0 49.9	16 46.8	22 53.8
24 Su	0 06 41	3 33 21	12♏50 14	19 46 01	23 56.5	16 54.9	27 12.5	25 31.0	13 29.0	23 53.4	19 26.8	0 53.1	16 49.0	22 54.8
25 M	0 10 38	4 32 49	26 34 28	3♐15 39	23 50.3	16 33.7	28 24.6	26 10.9	13 34.7	23 56.4	19 30.2	0 56.2	16 51.2	22 55.7
26 Tu	0 14 34	5 32 15	9♐49 44	16 17 05	23 46.5	16 18.4	29 36.7	26 50.7	13 40.1	23 59.4	19 33.5	0 59.4	16 53.4	22 56.5
27 W	0 18 31	6 31 39	22 38 10	28 53 31	23D44.8	16 09.1	0♓48.9	27 30.5	13 45.2	24 02.1	19 36.8	1 02.6	16 55.6	22 57.4
28 Th	0 22 27	7 31 02	5♑03 46	11♑09 35	23 44.6	16D05.8	2 01.1	28 10.3	13 49.8	24 04.7	19 39.9	1 05.8	16 57.8	22 58.2
29 F	0 26 24	8 30 23	17 11 38	23 10 37	23R44.8	16 08.1	3 13.3	28 50.1	13 54.1	24 07.0	19 42.9	1 09.1	16 59.9	22 59.0
30 Sa	0 30 21	9 29 42	29 07 12	5♒02 05	23 44.3	16 16.0	4 25.5	29 29.8	13 58.0	24 09.2	19 45.9	1 12.3	17 02.1	22 59.7
31 Su	0 34 17	10 28 59	10♒55 53	16 49 12	23 42.1	16 29.3	5 37.8	0♊09.6	14 01.6	24 11.2	19 48.8	1 15.6	17 04.2	23 00.5

April 2019 LONGITUDE

Day	Sid.Time	☉	0 hr ☽	Noon ☽	True ☊	☿	♀	♂	⚳	♃	♄	♅	♆	♇
1 M	0 38 14	11♈28 14	22♒42 37	28♒36 39	23♋37.4	16♓47.6	6♓50.1	0♊49.3	14♐04.8	24♐13.1	19♑51.6	1♉18.8	17♓06.3	23♑01.2
2 Tu	0 42 10	12 27 28	4♓31 45	10♓28 19	23R29.8	17 10.8	8 02.4	1 29.0	14 07.5	24 14.7	19 54.3	1 22.1	17 08.5	23 01.8
3 W	0 46 07	13 26 39	16 26 44	22 27 15	23 19.5	17 38.5	9 14.8	2 08.6	14 10.0	24 16.1	19 56.9	1 25.4	17 10.6	23 02.5
4 Th	0 50 03	14 25 49	28 30 08	4♈35 34	23 07.1	18 10.7	10 27.1	2 48.3	14 12.0	24 17.4	19 59.4	1 28.8	17 12.6	23 03.1
5 F	0 54 00	15 24 56	10♈43 39	16 54 30	22 53.4	18 47.0	11 39.5	3 27.9	14 13.6	24 18.5	20 01.8	1 32.1	17 14.7	23 03.7
6 Sa	0 57 56	16 24 02	23 08 08	29 24 36	22 39.6	19 27.2	12 51.9	4 07.5	14 14.9	24 19.4	20 04.1	1 35.5	17 16.8	23 04.2
7 Su	1 01 53	17 23 05	5♉43 53	12♉05 58	22 27.0	20 11.2	14 04.4	4 47.1	14 15.7	24 20.0	20 06.3	1 38.8	17 18.8	23 04.7
8 M	1 05 50	18 22 07	18 30 52	24 58 33	22 16.5	20 58.7	15 16.8	5 26.7	14R16.2	24 20.6	20 08.5	1 42.2	17 20.8	23 05.2
9 Tu	1 09 46	19 21 06	1♊29 04	8♊02 27	22 08.9	21 49.5	16 29.3	6 06.2	14 16.3	24 20.9	20 10.5	1 45.6	17 22.8	23 05.7
10 W	1 13 43	20 20 03	14 38 46	21 18 07	22 04.3	22 43.4	17 41.8	6 45.8	14 15.9	24R21.0	20 12.5	1 49.0	17 24.8	23 06.1
11 Th	1 17 39	21 18 57	28 00 39	4♋46 29	22 02.2	23 40.4	18 54.3	7 25.3	14 15.2	24 21.0	20 14.3	1 52.4	17 26.8	23 06.5
12 F	1 21 36	22 17 50	11♋35 46	18 28 39	22 01.8	24 40.3	20 06.8	8 04.7	14 14.1	24 20.7	20 16.1	1 55.8	17 28.8	23 06.9
13 Sa	1 25 32	23 16 40	25 25 15	2♌25 37	22 01.7	25 42.8	21 19.3	8 44.2	14 12.6	24 20.3	20 17.7	1 59.2	17 30.7	23 07.3
14 Su	1 29 29	24 15 28	9♌29 47	16 37 39	22 00.7	26 48.0	22 31.8	9 23.6	14 10.7	24 19.7	20 19.3	2 02.6	17 32.6	23 07.6
15 M	1 33 25	25 14 13	23 49 00	1♍03 34	21 57.6	27 55.7	23 44.4	10 03.0	14 08.5	24 18.9	20 20.8	2 06.0	17 34.5	23 07.9
16 Tu	1 37 22	26 12 56	8♍20 51	15 40 16	21 51.8	29 05.8	24 56.9	10 42.4	14 05.8	24 17.9	20 22.1	2 09.4	17 36.4	23 08.1
17 W	1 41 19	27 11 37	23 01 07	0♎22 33	21 43.3	0♈18.2	26 09.5	11 21.8	14 02.7	24 16.7	20 23.4	2 12.9	17 38.3	23 08.3
18 Th	1 45 15	28 10 16	7♎43 38	15 03 23	21 32.7	1 32.9	27 22.1	12 01.1	13 59.3	24 15.3	20 24.6	2 16.3	17 40.1	23 08.5
19 F	1 49 12	29 08 53	22 20 50	29 35 01	21 21.1	2 49.7	28 34.7	12 40.4	13 55.4	24 13.8	20 25.7	2 19.8	17 42.0	23 08.7
20 Sa	1 53 08	0♉07 28	6♏45 03	13♏50 11	21 09.7	4 08.6	29 47.3	13 19.7	13 51.2	24 12.0	20 26.6	2 23.2	17 43.8	23 08.8
21 Su	1 57 05	1 06 01	20 49 46	27 43 20	20 59.9	5 29.5	0♈59.9	13 59.0	13 46.6	24 10.1	20 27.5	2 26.6	17 45.6	23 09.0
22 M	2 01 01	2 04 33	4♐30 36	11♐11 26	20 52.3	6 52.5	2 12.6	14 38.2	13 41.6	24 08.0	20 28.3	2 30.1	17 47.3	23 09.0
23 Tu	2 04 58	3 03 02	17 45 51	24 14 01	20 47.3	8 17.4	3 25.3	15 17.4	13 36.2	24 05.8	20 29.0	2 33.5	17 49.1	23 09.1
24 W	2 08 54	4 01 30	0♑36 16	6♑52 59	20 44.8	9 44.3	4 38.0	15 56.7	13 30.5	24 03.3	20 29.6	2 37.0	17 50.8	23R09.1
25 Th	2 12 51	4 59 57	13 04 40	19 11 55	20D44.1	11 13.0	5 50.6	16 35.8	13 24.4	24 00.7	20 30.1	2 40.4	17 52.5	23 09.1
26 F	2 16 48	5 58 22	25 15 20	1♒15 34	20R44.2	12 43.6	7 03.4	17 15.0	13 17.9	23 57.8	20 30.5	2 43.9	17 54.2	23 09.1
27 Sa	2 20 44	6 56 45	7♒13 19	13 09 15	20 44.2	14 16.1	8 16.1	17 54.1	13 11.0	23 54.8	20 30.8	2 47.3	17 55.8	23 09.0
28 Su	2 24 41	7 55 07	19 04 04	24 58 25	20 42.8	15 50.4	9 28.8	18 33.3	13 03.8	23 51.7	20 31.0	2 50.7	17 57.5	23 08.9
29 M	2 28 37	8 53 27	0♓52 57	6♓48 17	20 39.4	17 26.5	10 41.6	19 12.4	12 56.2	23 48.3	20R31.1	2 54.2	17 59.1	23 08.8
30 Tu	2 32 34	9 51 45	12 44 59	18 43 33	20 33.5	19 04.5	11 54.3	19 51.5	12 48.3	23 44.8	20 31.1	2 57.6	18 00.6	23 08.6

Astro Data

	Dy Hr Mn
☿R	5 18:21
♃⊻♇	7 16:34
☽0N	8 19:14
☿0S	16 21:56
☉0N	20 21:59
☽0S	21 19:54
☿D	28 14:00
☽0N	5 1:20
⚳R	9 4:36
♃R	10 17:02
☽0S	18 6:09
☿0N	22 1:52
♀0N	23 16:20
♇R	24 18:49
♄R	30 0:55

Planet Ingress

		Dy Hr Mn
♀	♒	1 16:46
♅	♉	6 8:28
☉	♈	20 22:00
♀	♓	26 19:44
♂	♊	31 6:13
☿	♈	17 6:02
☉	♉	20 8:56
♀	♈	20 16:12

Last Aspect / ☽ Ingress (March)

Last Aspect Dy Hr Mn		☽ Ingress	Dy Hr Mn
2 18:48	♅ □	♒	2 19:07
5 8:06	♅ ⚹	♓	5 8:12
7 19:09	☿ ☌	♈	7 20:29
9 17:15	♃ △	♉	10 7:11
12 9:32	☿ ⚹	♊	12 15:49
14 12:32	☿ □	♋	14 21:50
16 18:04	☉ △	♌	17 0:58
18 15:20	♃ △	♍	19 1:42
20 15:23	♃ □	♎	21 1:29
22 18:11	♀ △	♏	23 2:17
25 2:25	♀ □	♐	25 6:07
27 2:38	♃ ☌	♑	27 14:09
30 0:06	♂ △	♒	30 1:47

Last Aspect / ☽ Ingress (April)

Last Aspect Dy Hr Mn		☽ Ingress	Dy Hr Mn
1 3:03	♃ ⚹	♓	1 14:49
3 15:37	♃ □	♈	4 2:58
6 2:16	♃ △	♉	6 13:07
8 8:30	♇ △	♊	8 21:16
10 17:28	♃ ☍	♋	11 3:32
12 23:34	☿ △	♌	13 7:51
15 1:40	☉ △	♍	15 10:15
17 4:30	♀ ☍	♎	17 11:23
19 11:13	☉ ☍	♏	19 12:42
21 4:01	♇ ⚹	♐	21 16:00
23 11:45	♃ ☌	♑	23 22:51
25 19:49	♇ ☌	♒	26 9:28
28 9:45	♃ ⚹	♓	28 22:13

☽ Phases & Eclipses

Dy Hr Mn	
6 16:05	● 15♓47
14 10:28	☽ 23♊33
21 1:44	○ 0♎09
28 4:11	☾ 7♑12
5 8:52	● 15♈17
12 19:07	☽ 22♋35
19 11:13	○ 29♎07
26 22:19	☾ 6♒23

Astro Data

1 March 2019
Julian Day # 43524
SVP 4♓59'46"
GC 27♐06.4 ⚴ 29♎00.3R
Eris 23♈12.5 ⚵ 7♊01.5
⚷ 0♈36.4 ⚶ 13♓53.1
☽ Mean ☊ 24♋24.9

1 April 2019
Julian Day # 43555
SVP 4♓59'43"
GC 27♐06.5 ⚴ 22♎31.7R
Eris 23♈30.4 ⚵ 20♊49.7
⚷ 2♈25.2 ⚶ 28♓58.4
☽ Mean ☊ 22♋46.4

LONGITUDE — May 2019

Day	Sid.Time	☉	0 hr ☽	Noon☽	True☊	☿	♀	♂	⚳	♃	♄	♅	♆	♇
1 W	2 36 30	10♉50 02	24♓44 29	0♈48 10	20♋25.1	20♈44.2	13♈07.1	20♊30.5	12♐40.0	23♐41.1	20♑31.0	3♉01.0	18♓02.2	23♑08.4
2 Th	2 40 27	11 48 17	6♈54 57	13 05 06	20R 14.6	22 25.8	14 19.9	21 09.6	12R 31.4	23R 37.2	20R 30.8	3 04.5	18 03.7	23R 08.2
3 F	2 44 23	12 46 31	19 18 47	25 36 10	20 03.0	24 09.2	15 32.7	21 48.6	12 22.5	23 33.2	20 30.5	3 07.9	18 05.2	23 08.0
4 Sa	2 48 20	13 44 43	1♉57 17	8♉22 06	19 51.2	25 54.5	16 45.5	22 27.6	12 13.2	23 29.0	20 30.2	3 11.3	18 06.7	23 07.7
5 Su	2 52 16	14 42 53	14 50 34	21 22 34	19 40.4	27 41.6	17 58.3	23 06.6	12 03.7	23 24.7	20 29.7	3 14.7	18 08.2	23 07.4
6 M	2 56 13	15 41 02	27 57 55	4♊36 26	19 31.5	29 30.5	19 11.1	23 45.6	11 53.8	23 20.1	20 29.1	3 18.1	18 09.6	23 07.1
7 Tu	3 00 10	16 39 08	11♊17 55	18 02 10	19 25.2	1♉21.2	20 23.9	24 24.5	11 43.7	23 15.5	20 28.4	3 21.5	18 11.0	23 06.7
8 W	3 04 06	17 37 14	24 48 59	1♋38 12	19 21.5	3 13.8	21 36.8	25 03.5	11 33.2	23 10.6	20 27.6	3 24.8	18 12.4	23 06.4
9 Th	3 08 03	18 35 17	8♋29 40	15 23 15	19D 20.2	5 08.2	22 49.6	25 42.4	11 22.5	23 05.7	20 26.8	3 28.2	18 13.8	23 06.0
10 F	3 11 59	19 33 18	22 18 52	29 16 26	19 20.4	7 04.5	24 02.5	26 21.3	11 11.6	23 00.5	20 25.8	3 31.5	18 15.1	23 05.5
11 Sa	3 15 56	20 31 18	6♌15 51	13♌17 05	19R 21.0	9 02.5	25 15.3	27 00.2	11 00.4	22 55.3	20 24.7	3 34.9	18 16.4	23 05.1
12 Su	3 19 52	21 29 15	20 20 02	27 24 35	19 21.0	11 02.4	26 28.2	27 39.0	10 48.9	22 49.9	20 23.6	3 38.2	18 17.7	23 04.6
13 M	3 23 49	22 27 11	4♍30 34	11♍37 46	19 19.5	13 03.9	27 41.0	28 17.9	10 37.2	22 44.3	20 22.3	3 41.5	18 18.9	23 04.0
14 Tu	3 27 46	23 25 05	18 45 55	25 54 39	19 15.8	15 07.1	28 53.9	28 56.7	10 25.4	22 38.6	20 21.0	3 44.8	18 20.1	23 03.5
15 W	3 31 42	24 22 57	3♎03 33	10♎12 06	19 09.9	17 11.8	0♉06.7	29 35.5	10 13.3	22 32.8	20 19.6	3 48.1	18 21.3	23 02.9
16 Th	3 35 39	25 20 47	17 19 45	24 25 56	19 02.3	19 18.1	1 19.6	0♋14.3	10 01.0	22 26.9	20 18.0	3 51.4	18 22.4	23 02.3
17 F	3 39 35	26 18 36	1♏30 00	8♏31 20	18 53.8	21 25.7	2 32.5	0 53.0	9 48.6	22 20.8	20 16.4	3 54.6	18 23.6	23 01.7
18 Sa	3 43 32	27 16 23	15 29 23	22 23 36	18 45.5	23 34.5	3 45.4	1 31.7	9 36.0	22 14.7	20 14.7	3 57.9	18 24.7	23 01.1
19 Su	3 47 28	28 14 09	29 13 30	5♐58 44	18 38.2	25 44.3	4 58.3	2 10.5	9 23.3	22 08.4	20 12.9	4 01.1	18 25.7	23 00.4
20 M	3 51 25	29 11 53	12♐39 02	19 14 13	18 32.7	27 54.9	6 11.2	2 49.2	9 10.4	22 02.0	20 11.1	4 04.3	18 26.8	22 59.7
21 Tu	3 55 21	0♊09 37	25 44 15	2♑09 11	18 29.3	0♊06.1	7 24.1	3 27.8	8 57.4	21 55.5	20 09.1	4 07.5	18 27.8	22 59.0
22 W	3 59 18	1 07 19	8♑29 12	14 44 32	18D 28.0	2 17.7	8 37.0	4 06.5	8 44.4	21 48.9	20 07.0	4 10.6	18 28.8	22 58.2
23 Th	4 03 15	2 04 59	20 55 32	27 02 38	18 28.2	4 29.3	9 50.0	4 45.2	8 31.2	21 42.2	20 04.9	4 13.8	18 29.7	22 57.5
24 F	4 07 11	3 02 39	3♒06 19	9♒07 07	18 29.4	6 40.7	11 02.9	5 23.8	8 17.9	21 35.4	20 02.7	4 16.9	18 30.6	22 56.7
25 Sa	4 11 08	4 00 18	15 05 36	21 02 23	18 30.8	8 51.7	12 15.9	6 02.4	8 04.6	21 28.5	20 00.4	4 20.0	18 31.5	22 55.8
26 Su	4 15 04	4 57 56	26 58 05	2♓53 21	18R 31.6	11 01.9	13 28.9	6 41.0	7 51.3	21 21.5	19 58.0	4 23.1	18 32.4	22 55.0
27 M	4 19 01	5 55 32	8♓48 48	14 45 06	18 31.2	13 11.1	14 41.9	7 19.6	7 37.9	21 14.4	19 55.5	4 26.2	18 33.2	22 54.1
28 Tu	4 22 57	6 53 08	20 42 51	26 42 39	18 29.1	15 19.0	15 54.9	7 58.2	7 24.5	21 07.3	19 53.0	4 29.2	18 34.0	22 53.3
29 W	4 26 54	7 50 43	2♈45 02	8♈50 31	18 25.4	17 25.4	17 07.9	8 36.7	7 11.1	21 00.1	19 50.3	4 32.2	18 34.8	22 52.3
30 Th	4 30 50	8 48 17	14 59 35	21 12 36	18 20.2	19 30.1	18 20.9	9 15.3	6 57.7	20 52.8	19 47.6	4 35.2	18 35.5	22 51.4
31 F	4 34 47	9 45 50	27 29 54	3♉51 43	18 14.0	21 32.9	19 33.9	9 53.8	6 44.3	20 45.5	19 44.8	4 38.2	18 36.2	22 50.5

LONGITUDE — June 2019

Day	Sid.Time	☉	0 hr ☽	Noon☽	True☊	☿	♀	♂	⚳	♃	♄	♅	♆	♇
1 Sa	4 38 44	10♊43 22	10♉18 14	16♉49 31	18♋07.7	23♊33.6	20♉46.9	10♋32.3	6♐31.0	20♐38.1	19♑42.0	4♉41.2	18♓36.9	22♑49.5
2 Su	4 42 40	11 40 54	23 25 31	0♊06 10	18R 01.8	25 32.1	22 00.0	11 10.8	6R 17.8	20R 30.6	19R 39.0	4 44.1	18 37.5	22R 48.5
3 M	4 46 37	12 38 24	6♊51 13	13 40 27	17 57.1	27 28.3	23 13.1	11 49.3	6 04.7	20 23.1	19 36.0	4 47.0	18 38.1	22 47.5
4 Tu	4 50 33	13 35 53	20 33 29	27 29 56	17 53.9	29 22.2	24 26.1	12 27.8	5 51.6	20 15.6	19 32.9	4 49.8	18 38.7	22 46.4
5 W	4 54 30	14 33 22	4♋29 23	11♋31 22	17D 52.4	1♋13.5	25 39.2	13 06.3	5 38.6	20 08.0	19 29.8	4 52.7	18 39.2	22 45.4
6 Th	4 58 26	15 30 49	18 35 26	25 41 07	17 52.5	3 02.3	26 52.3	13 44.7	5 25.8	20 00.4	19 26.6	4 55.5	18 39.7	22 44.3
7 F	5 02 23	16 28 15	2♌47 59	9♌55 37	17 53.6	4 48.6	28 05.4	14 23.2	5 13.1	19 52.8	19 23.3	4 58.3	18 40.2	22 43.2
8 Sa	5 06 19	17 25 40	17 03 38	24 11 42	17 55.0	6 32.2	29 18.5	15 01.6	5 00.6	19 45.2	19 19.9	5 01.1	18 40.7	22 42.1
9 Su	5 10 16	18 23 04	1♍19 29	8♍26 42	17R 56.1	8 13.1	0♊31.6	15 40.0	4 48.2	19 37.5	19 16.5	5 03.8	18 41.1	22 41.0
10 M	5 14 13	19 20 27	15 33 04	22 38 20	17 56.4	9 51.4	1 44.7	16 18.4	4 36.0	19 29.9	19 13.1	5 06.5	18 41.4	22 39.8
11 Tu	5 18 09	20 17 48	29 42 16	6♎44 37	17 55.5	11 27.0	2 57.8	16 56.8	4 24.0	19 22.2	19 09.5	5 09.2	18 41.8	22 38.7
12 W	5 22 06	21 15 09	13♎45 08	20 43 36	17 53.4	12 59.9	4 10.9	17 35.1	4 12.3	19 14.6	19 05.9	5 11.8	18 42.1	22 37.5
13 Th	5 26 02	22 12 28	27 39 46	4♏33 22	17 50.3	14 30.1	5 24.1	18 13.5	4 00.7	19 06.9	19 02.3	5 14.4	18 42.4	22 36.3
14 F	5 29 59	23 09 47	11♏24 11	18 11 58	17 46.8	15 57.5	6 37.2	18 51.8	3 49.3	18 59.3	18 58.6	5 17.0	18 42.6	22 35.1
15 Sa	5 33 55	24 07 04	24 56 30	1♐37 35	17 43.3	17 22.1	7 50.4	19 30.1	3 38.2	18 51.7	18 54.8	5 19.5	18 42.8	22 33.8
16 Su	5 37 52	25 04 21	8♐15 03	14 48 45	17 40.3	18 43.9	9 03.6	20 08.5	3 27.4	18 44.1	18 51.0	5 22.0	18 43.0	22 32.6
17 M	5 41 48	26 01 38	21 18 36	27 44 33	17 38.2	20 02.9	10 16.7	20 46.8	3 16.8	18 36.6	18 47.2	5 24.5	18 43.2	22 31.3
18 Tu	5 45 45	26 58 54	4♑06 37	10♑24 51	17D 37.1	21 18.9	11 29.9	21 25.0	3 06.5	18 29.0	18 43.3	5 26.9	18 43.3	22 30.1
19 W	5 49 42	27 56 09	16 39 24	22 50 25	17 37.0	22 32.0	12 43.2	22 03.3	2 56.4	18 21.6	18 39.3	5 29.3	18 43.4	22 28.8
20 Th	5 53 38	28 53 24	28 58 09	5♒02 53	17 37.7	23 42.1	13 56.4	22 41.6	2 46.6	18 14.1	18 35.3	5 31.7	18 43.4	22 27.5
21 F	5 57 35	29 50 39	11♒04 59	17 04 48	17 39.0	24 49.1	15 09.6	23 19.8	2 37.1	18 06.8	18 31.3	5 34.1	18R 43.5	22 26.2
22 Sa	6 01 31	0♋47 53	23 02 47	28 59 25	17 40.5	25 53.0	16 22.9	23 58.1	2 28.0	17 59.4	18 27.2	5 36.4	18 43.4	22 24.9
23 Su	6 05 28	1 45 07	4♓55 12	10♓50 39	17 41.7	26 53.6	17 36.2	24 36.3	2 19.1	17 52.2	18 23.1	5 38.6	18 43.4	22 23.5
24 M	6 09 24	2 42 21	16 46 21	22 42 52	17R 42.6	27 51.0	18 49.5	25 14.5	2 10.5	17 44.9	18 19.0	5 40.8	18 43.3	22 22.2
25 Tu	6 13 21	3 39 35	28 40 48	4♈40 42	17 42.9	28 45.0	20 02.8	25 52.8	2 02.3	17 37.8	18 14.8	5 43.0	18 43.2	22 20.8
26 W	6 17 17	4 36 48	10♈43 10	16 48 46	17 42.5	29 35.4	21 16.1	26 31.0	1 54.4	17 30.7	18 10.6	5 45.2	18 43.1	22 19.5
27 Th	6 21 14	5 34 02	22 58 02	29 11 29	17 41.6	0♌22.3	22 29.4	27 09.2	1 46.8	17 23.8	18 06.3	5 47.3	18 42.9	22 18.1
28 F	6 25 11	6 31 16	5♉29 33	11♉52 39	17 40.4	1 05.5	23 42.8	27 47.4	1 39.5	17 16.9	18 02.0	5 49.4	18 42.7	22 16.7
29 Sa	6 29 07	7 28 29	18 21 06	24 55 08	17 39.1	1 44.8	24 56.2	28 25.6	1 32.6	17 10.1	17 57.8	5 51.4	18 42.4	22 15.3
30 Su	6 33 04	8 25 43	1♊34 54	8♊20 24	17 37.9	2 20.2	26 09.6	29 03.8	1 26.1	17 03.3	17 53.4	5 53.4	18 42.2	22 13.9

Astro Data

Aspect	Dy Hr Mn
♅∠♆	2 2:51
☽0N	2 9:07
♃⊻♇	9 10:31
☽0S	15 14:38
☽0N	29 18:06
♃⚼♅	6 23:20
☽0S	11 21:11
♃⊻♄	14 16:29
♃□♆	16 15:23
♄✶♆	18 11:48
♆ R	21 14:37
☽0N	26 3:00

Planet Ingress

Planet	Sign	Dy Hr Mn
☿	♉	6 18:26
♀	♉	15 9:47
♂	♋	16 3:10
☉	♊	21 8:00
☿	♊	21 10:53
☿	♋	4 20:06
♀	♊	9 1:38
☉	♋	21 15:55
☿	♌	27 0:21

Last Aspect / ☽ Ingress (May)

Last Aspect Dy Hr Mn		☽ Ingress	Dy Hr Mn
30 21:58	♃ □	♈	1 10:25
3 8:48	☿ ☌	♉	3 20:19
5 15:11	♇ △	♊	6 3:41
7 23:51	♂ ☌	♋	8 9:08
10 2:07	♀ □	♌	10 13:15
12 12:26	♂ ✶	♍	12 16:23
14 17:20	♂ □	♎	14 18:52
16 9:39	♇ □	♏	16 21:27
18 21:13	☉ ☍	♐	19 1:22
20 17:06	♃ ☌	♑	21 7:57
23 3:59	♇ ☌	♒	23 17:50
25 12:52	♃ ✶	♓	26 6:09
28 4:22	♇ ✶	♈	28 18:33
30 15:09	♇ □	♉	31 4:44

Last Aspect / ☽ Ingress (June)

Last Aspect Dy Hr Mn		☽ Ingress	Dy Hr Mn
1 22:54	♇ △	♊	2 11:49
4 15:43	☿ ☌	♋	4 16:18
6 14:11	♀ ✶	♌	6 19:17
8 21:24	♀ □	♍	8 21:46
10 12:03	♇ △	♎	11 0:30
12 15:16	♇ □	♏	13 4:04
14 19:47	♇ ✶	♐	15 9:04
17 8:32	☉ ☍	♑	17 16:14
19 11:20	☿ ☍	♒	20 2:02
21 14:03	♃ ✶	♓	22 14:03
24 23:11	☿ △	♈	25 2:39
27 7:52	♂ □	♉	27 13:33
29 18:39	♂ ✶	♊	29 21:10

☽ Phases & Eclipses

Dy Hr Mn	Phase	Position
4 22:47	●	14♉11
12 1:13	☽	21♌03
18 21:13	○	27♏39
26 16:35	☾	5♓09
3 10:03	●	12♊34
10 6:00	☽	19♍06
17 8:32	○	25♐53
25 9:48	☾	3♈34

Astro Data

1 May 2019
Julian Day # 43585
SVP 4♓59'40"
GC 27♐06.6 ⚵ 13♋49.9R
Eris 23♈49.9 ⚶ 5♋15.4
⚷ 4♈04.2 ⚴ 13♈02.3
☽ Mean ☊ 21♋11.1

1 June 2019
Julian Day # 43616
SVP 4♓59'36"
GC 27♐06.6 ⚵ 10♋23.0
Eris 24♈07.4 ⚶ 20♋26.8
⚷ 5♈20.6 ⚴ 26♈42.1
☽ Mean ☊ 19♋32.6

July 2019 LONGITUDE

Day	Sid.Time	☉	0 hr ☽	Noon ☽	True ☊	☿	♀	♂	⚳	♃	♄	♅	♆	♇
1 M	6 37 00	9♋22 57	15♊11 35	22♊08 13	17♋37.0	2♌51.5	27♊23.0	29♋42.0	1♐19.9	16♐56.7	17♑49.1	5♉55.4	18♓41.9	22♑12.5
2 Tu	6 40 57	10 20 11	29 09 59	6♋16 27	17D 36.5	3 18.6	28 36.4	0♌20.1	1R 14.1	16R 50.2	17R 44.7	5 57.3	18R 41.5	22R 11.1
3 W	6 44 53	11 17 25	13♋27 03	20 41 08	17 36.4	3 41.4	29 49.8	0 58.3	1 08.6	16 43.8	17 40.4	5 59.2	18 41.2	22 09.7
4 Th	6 48 50	12 14 38	27 58 00	5♌16 51	17 36.6	3 59.7	1♋03.3	1 36.5	1 03.5	16 37.5	17 36.0	6 01.0	18 40.8	22 08.2
5 F	6 52 46	13 11 52	12♌36 55	19 57 22	17 36.9	4 13.6	2 16.8	2 14.6	0 58.8	16 31.3	17 31.6	6 02.8	18 40.3	22 06.8
6 Sa	6 56 43	14 09 05	27 17 27	4♍36 26	17 37.3	4 22.8	3 30.3	2 52.8	0 54.4	16 25.3	17 27.2	6 04.5	18 39.9	22 05.4
7 Su	7 00 40	15 06 17	11♍53 38	19 08 28	17 37.6	4R 27.4	4 43.8	3 30.9	0 50.4	16 19.3	17 22.8	6 06.2	18 39.4	22 03.9
8 M	7 04 36	16 03 30	26 20 26	3♎29 07	17 37.7	4 27.2	5 57.3	4 09.1	0 46.8	16 13.5	17 18.3	6 07.9	18 38.9	22 02.5
9 Tu	7 08 33	17 00 42	10♎34 12	17 35 27	17 37.7	4 22.4	7 10.8	4 47.2	0 43.5	16 07.9	17 13.9	6 09.5	18 38.3	22 01.0
10 W	7 12 29	17 57 55	24 32 42	1♏25 53	17 37.7	4 12.8	8 24.3	5 25.3	0 40.6	16 02.3	17 09.5	6 11.1	18 37.7	21 59.6
11 Th	7 16 26	18 55 07	8♏14 58	14 59 57	17 37.8	3 58.7	9 37.9	6 03.4	0 38.1	15 56.9	17 05.1	6 12.6	18 37.1	21 58.1
12 F	7 20 22	19 52 19	21 40 56	28 17 58	17 38.0	3 40.2	10 51.5	6 41.5	0 36.0	15 51.6	17 00.6	6 14.1	18 36.5	21 56.7
13 Sa	7 24 19	20 49 31	4♐51 11	11♐20 42	17 38.2	3 17.4	12 05.0	7 19.6	0 34.2	15 46.5	16 56.2	6 15.6	18 35.8	21 55.2
14 Su	7 28 15	21 46 43	17 46 38	24 09 10	17 38.6	2 50.6	13 18.6	7 57.7	0 32.8	15 41.6	16 51.8	6 17.0	18 35.1	21 53.7
15 M	7 32 12	22 43 55	0♑28 25	6♑44 32	17R 38.9	2 20.2	14 32.3	8 35.8	0 31.8	15 36.7	16 47.4	6 18.3	18 34.4	21 52.3
16 Tu	7 36 09	23 41 08	12 57 41	19 08 03	17 39.0	1 46.6	15 45.9	9 13.9	0 31.2	15 32.1	16 43.1	6 19.6	18 33.6	21 50.8
17 W	7 40 05	24 38 21	25 15 47	1♒21 05	17 38.8	1 10.3	16 59.6	9 52.0	0D 30.9	15 27.5	16 38.7	6 20.9	18 32.9	21 49.4
18 Th	7 44 02	25 35 34	7♒24 09	13 25 14	17 38.2	0 31.8	18 13.2	10 30.1	0 30.9	15 23.2	16 34.4	6 22.1	18 32.1	21 47.9
19 F	7 47 58	26 32 48	19 24 33	25 22 25	17 37.2	29♋51.8	19 26.9	11 08.1	0 31.4	15 19.0	16 30.0	6 23.3	18 31.2	21 46.5
20 Sa	7 51 55	27 30 02	1♓19 06	7♓14 58	17 35.9	29 10.8	20 40.6	11 46.2	0 32.2	15 14.9	16 25.7	6 24.4	18 30.4	21 45.0
21 Su	7 55 51	28 27 17	13 10 21	19 05 40	17 34.4	28 29.7	21 54.4	12 24.3	0 33.3	15 11.1	16 21.4	6 25.5	18 29.5	21 43.6
22 M	7 59 48	29 24 33	25 01 21	0♈57 50	17 33.0	27 49.1	23 08.1	13 02.3	0 34.8	15 07.4	16 17.2	6 26.5	18 28.5	21 42.1
23 Tu	8 03 44	0♌21 49	6♈55 38	12 55 14	17 31.9	27 09.7	24 21.9	13 40.4	0 36.7	15 03.8	16 13.0	6 27.5	18 27.6	21 40.7
24 W	8 07 41	1 19 06	18 57 09	25 01 57	17D 31.2	26 32.4	25 35.7	14 18.5	0 38.9	15 00.4	16 08.8	6 28.4	18 26.6	21 39.2
25 Th	8 11 38	2 16 24	1♉10 11	7♉22 21	17 31.2	25 57.7	26 49.5	14 56.6	0 41.5	14 57.2	16 04.6	6 29.3	18 25.6	21 37.8
26 F	8 15 34	3 13 43	13 39 02	20 00 42	17 31.8	25 26.3	28 03.3	15 34.6	0 44.4	14 54.2	16 00.5	6 30.1	18 24.6	21 36.4
27 Sa	8 19 31	4 11 03	26 27 49	3♊00 48	17 32.9	24 58.8	29 17.2	16 12.7	0 47.6	14 51.3	15 56.4	6 30.9	18 23.5	21 35.0
28 Su	8 23 27	5 08 24	9♊39 59	16 25 35	17 34.1	24 35.9	0♌31.0	16 50.8	0 51.2	14 48.7	15 52.3	6 31.7	18 22.5	21 33.6
29 M	8 27 24	6 05 46	23 17 45	0♋16 27	17 35.3	24 17.8	1 44.9	17 28.8	0 55.2	14 46.2	15 48.3	6 32.4	18 21.4	21 32.1
30 Tu	8 31 20	7 03 09	7♋21 32	14 32 41	17R 35.9	24 05.2	2 58.9	18 06.9	0 59.4	14 43.8	15 44.3	6 33.0	18 20.3	21 30.8
31 W	8 35 17	8 00 33	21 49 25	29 11 04	17 35.6	23D 58.2	4 12.8	18 45.0	1 04.0	14 41.7	15 40.4	6 33.6	18 19.1	21 29.4

August 2019 LONGITUDE

Day	Sid.Time	☉	0 hr ☽	Noon ☽	True ☊	☿	♀	♂	⚳	♃	♄	♅	♆	♇
1 Th	8 39 14	8♌57 57	6♌36 50	14♌05 46	17♋34.3	23♋57.2	5♌26.7	19♌23.1	1♐09.0	14♐39.7	15♑36.5	6♉34.2	18♓18.0	21♑28.0
2 F	8 43 10	9 55 23	21 36 48	29 08 48	17R 32.0	24 02.4	6 40.7	20 01.2	1 14.2	14R 38.0	15R 32.6	6 34.7	18R 16.8	21R 26.6
3 Sa	8 47 07	10 52 49	6♍40 39	14♍11 11	17 29.1	24 13.9	7 54.7	20 39.2	1 19.8	14 36.4	15 28.9	6 35.1	18 15.6	21 25.3
4 Su	8 51 03	11 50 16	21 39 20	29 04 09	17 26.0	24 31.9	9 08.7	21 17.3	1 25.7	14 35.0	15 25.1	6 35.5	18 14.3	21 23.9
5 M	8 55 00	12 47 43	6♎24 48	13♎40 35	17 23.2	24 56.3	10 22.7	21 55.4	1 32.0	14 33.7	15 21.4	6 35.8	18 13.1	21 22.6
6 Tu	8 58 56	13 45 11	20 51 01	27 55 44	17 21.3	25 27.3	11 36.7	22 33.5	1 38.5	14 32.7	15 17.8	6 36.1	18 11.8	21 21.2
7 W	9 02 53	14 42 40	4♏54 34	11♏47 27	17D 20.4	26 04.8	12 50.8	23 11.6	1 45.3	14 31.8	15 14.3	6 36.4	18 10.5	21 19.9
8 Th	9 06 49	15 40 10	18 34 29	25 15 50	17 20.7	26 48.8	14 04.8	23 49.7	1 52.5	14 31.2	15 10.8	6 36.6	18 09.2	21 18.6
9 F	9 10 46	16 37 40	1♐51 46	8♐22 36	17 21.9	27 39.1	15 18.9	24 27.7	1 59.9	14 30.7	15 07.3	6 36.7	18 07.8	21 17.3
10 Sa	9 14 42	17 35 11	14 48 42	21 10 27	17 23.5	28 35.7	16 33.0	25 05.8	2 07.7	14 30.4	15 03.9	6 36.9	18 06.5	21 16.1
11 Su	9 18 39	18 32 43	27 28 15	3♑42 28	17 25.0	29 38.4	17 47.1	25 43.9	2 15.7	14D 30.3	15 00.6	6R 36.9	18 05.1	21 14.8
12 M	9 22 36	19 30 16	9♑53 30	16 01 43	17R 25.7	0♌47.0	19 01.2	26 22.0	2 24.0	14 30.4	14 57.4	6 36.9	18 03.7	21 13.5
13 Tu	9 26 32	20 27 51	22 07 27	28 11 00	17 25.1	2 01.4	20 15.3	27 00.1	2 32.6	14 30.6	14 54.2	6 36.9	18 02.3	21 12.3
14 W	9 30 29	21 25 26	4♒12 42	10♒12 47	17 23.0	3 21.3	21 29.5	27 38.2	2 41.5	14 31.1	14 51.1	6 36.8	18 00.9	21 11.1
15 Th	9 34 25	22 23 02	16 11 32	22 09 10	17 19.2	4 46.4	22 43.6	28 16.3	2 50.7	14 31.7	14 48.0	6 36.6	17 59.5	21 09.9
16 F	9 38 22	23 20 39	28 05 55	4♓02 01	17 13.9	6 16.5	23 57.8	28 54.4	3 00.1	14 32.5	14 45.1	6 36.4	17 58.0	21 08.7
17 Sa	9 42 18	24 18 18	9♓57 42	15 53 10	17 07.4	7 51.1	25 12.0	29 32.5	3 09.8	14 33.5	14 42.2	6 36.2	17 56.6	21 07.5
18 Su	9 46 15	25 15 58	21 48 42	27 44 32	17 00.5	9 30.0	26 26.2	0♍10.6	3 19.8	14 34.7	14 39.3	6 35.9	17 55.1	21 06.4
19 M	9 50 11	26 13 40	3♈40 58	9♈38 18	16 53.7	11 12.7	27 40.4	0 48.7	3 30.0	14 36.1	14 36.6	6 35.6	17 53.6	21 05.3
20 Tu	9 54 08	27 11 23	15 36 54	21 37 08	16 47.8	12 58.8	28 54.6	1 26.8	3 40.5	14 37.6	14 33.9	6 35.2	17 52.1	21 04.1
21 W	9 58 05	28 09 07	27 39 25	3♉44 10	16 43.3	14 48.0	0♍08.9	2 05.0	3 51.2	14 39.4	14 31.3	6 34.7	17 50.5	21 03.0
22 Th	10 02 01	29 06 54	9♉51 52	16 03 00	16 40.6	16 39.7	1 23.2	2 43.1	4 02.2	14 41.3	14 28.8	6 34.3	17 49.0	21 02.0
23 F	10 05 58	0♍04 42	22 18 05	28 37 38	16D 39.7	18 33.6	2 37.4	3 21.3	4 13.4	14 43.4	14 26.4	6 33.7	17 47.5	21 00.9
24 Sa	10 09 54	1 02 31	5♊02 09	11♊32 09	16 40.1	20 29.2	3 51.7	3 59.4	4 24.9	14 45.7	14 24.0	6 33.1	17 45.9	20 59.9
25 Su	10 13 51	2 00 23	18 08 04	24 50 19	16 41.3	22 26.2	5 06.1	4 37.6	4 36.6	14 48.1	14 21.8	6 32.5	17 44.3	20 58.8
26 M	10 17 47	2 58 16	1♋39 13	8♋34 58	16R 42.4	24 24.2	6 20.4	5 15.8	4 48.5	14 50.8	14 19.6	6 31.8	17 42.8	20 57.8
27 Tu	10 21 44	3 56 11	15 37 39	22 47 12	16 42.5	26 22.8	7 34.7	5 53.9	5 00.7	14 53.6	14 17.5	6 31.1	17 41.2	20 56.9
28 W	10 25 40	4 54 08	0♌03 19	7♌25 32	16 40.8	28 21.7	8 49.1	6 32.1	5 13.1	14 56.6	14 15.5	6 30.3	17 39.6	20 55.9
29 Th	10 29 37	5 52 07	14 53 11	22 25 22	16 37.0	0♍20.7	10 03.5	7 10.3	5 25.8	14 59.7	14 13.5	6 29.5	17 38.0	20 55.0
30 F	10 33 34	6 50 07	0♍01 00	7♍38 51	16 31.2	2 19.6	11 17.9	7 48.5	5 38.7	15 03.1	14 11.7	6 28.7	17 36.4	20 54.0
31 Sa	10 37 30	7 48 08	15 17 34	22 55 46	16 23.9	4 18.0	12 32.3	8 26.8	5 51.7	15 06.6	14 10.0	6 27.8	17 34.7	20 53.1

Astro Data Dy Hr Mn	Planet Ingress Dy Hr Mn	Last Aspect Dy Hr Mn	☽ Ingress Dy Hr Mn	Last Aspect Dy Hr Mn	☽ Ingress Dy Hr Mn	☽ Phases & Eclipses Dy Hr Mn
☿R 7 23:16	♂ ♌ 1 23:20	1 21:49 ♀ ☌	♋ 2 1:25	1 20:49 ♂ ☌	♍ 2 13:22	2 19:17 ● 10♋38
☽0S 9 2:54	♀ ♋ 3 15:19	3 14:26 ♇ ☍	♌ 4 3:20	4 4:28 ☿ ✶	♎ 4 13:31	2 19:24:09 ● T 04'33"
⚳D 17 19:07	☿ ♋R 19 7:07	5 6:26 ♃ △	♍ 6 4:26	6 7:37 ☿ □	♏ 6 15:33	9 10:56 ☽ 16♎58
☽0N 23 10:38	☉ ♌ 23 2:52	7 16:51 ♇ △	♎ 8 6:08	8 14:59 ☿ △	♐ 8 20:36	16 21:39 ○ 24♑04
	♀ ♌ 28 1:55	9 19:37 ♇ □	♏ 10 9:30	10 19:52 ♂ △	♑ 11 4:51	16 21:32 ● P 0.653
☿D 1 3:58		12 0:30 ♇ ✶	♐ 12 15:06	12 22:13 ♇ ☌	♒ 13 15:37	25 1:19 ☾ 1♉51
☽0S 5 9:28	☿ ♌ 11 19:47	14 1:31 ♆ □	♑ 14 23:06	16 1:03 ♂ ☍	♓ 16 3:51	
♃D 11 13:38	♂ ♍ 18 5:19	16 21:39 ☉ ☍	♒ 17 9:20	17 22:36 ♇ ✶	♈ 18 16:34	1 3:13 ● 8♌37
♅R 12 2:28	♀ ♍ 21 9:08	18 15:55 ♃ ✶	♓ 19 21:20	21 4:08 ♀ △	♉ 21 4:38	7 17:32 ☽ 14♏56
♃✶♄ 19 14:48	☉ ♍ 23 10:03	22 8:35 ☉ △	♈ 22 10:03	22 21:34 ♇ △	♊ 23 14:35	15 12:30 ○ 22♒24
☽0N 19 16:42	☿ ♍ 29 7:49	24 14:49 ♀ □	♉ 24 21:43	25 7:00 ☿ ✶	♋ 25 21:06	23 14:57 ☾ 0♊12
		27 4:29 ♀ ✶	♊ 27 6:30	27 8:56 ♇ ☍	♌ 27 23:55	30 10:38 ● 6♍47
		28 15:25 ♆ □	♋ 29 11:32	29 0:08 ♃ △	♍ 29 23:58	
		31 3:34 ☿ ☌	♌ 31 13:19	31 8:47 ♇ △	♎ 31 23:09	

Astro Data

1 July 2019
Julian Day # 43646
SVP 4♓59'31"
GC 27♐06.7 ⚵ 13♎39.6
Eris 24♈17.7 ⚴ 5♌00.8
⚷ 5♈54.9 ⚶ 8♉39.6
☽ Mean ☊ 17♋57.3

1 August 2019
Julian Day # 43677
SVP 4♓59'26"
GC 27♐06.8 ⚵ 21♎36.4
Eris 24♈19.0R ⚴ 19♌41.3
⚷ 5♈42.3R ⚶ 18♉58.6
☽ Mean ☊ 16♋18.8

LONGITUDE September 2019

Day	Sid.Time	☉	0 hr ☽	Noon ☽	True ☊	☿	♀	♂	⚳	♃	♄	♅	♆	♇
1 Su	10 41 27	8♍46 11	0♎32 05	8♎05 10	16♋16.1	6♍15.9	13♍46.7	9♍05.0	6♐05.0	15♐10.3	14♑08.3	6♉26.8	17♓33.1	20♑52.3
2 M	10 45 23	9 44 16	15 33 54	22 57 15	16R 08.7	8 13.1	15 01.1	9 43.2	6 18.6	15 14.2	14R 06.7	6R 25.8	17R 31.5	20R 51.4
3 Tu	10 49 20	10 42 22	0♏14 27	7♏24 57	16 02.8	10 09.5	16 15.5	10 21.5	6 32.3	15 18.2	14 05.3	6 24.7	17 29.8	20 50.6
4 W	10 53 16	11 40 30	14 28 22	21 24 36	15 58.8	12 05.0	17 29.9	10 59.7	6 46.2	15 22.4	14 03.9	6 23.7	17 28.2	20 49.8
5 Th	10 57 13	12 38 39	28 13 40	4♐55 47	15D 57.0	13 59.5	18 44.4	11 38.0	7 00.4	15 26.8	14 02.6	6 22.5	17 26.6	20 49.0
6 F	11 01 09	13 36 49	11♐31 18	18 00 36	15 56.8	15 53.0	19 58.8	12 16.2	7 14.7	15 31.3	14 01.4	6 21.3	17 24.9	20 48.3
7 Sa	11 05 06	14 35 01	24 24 14	0♑42 42	15 57.5	17 45.4	21 13.3	12 54.5	7 29.3	15 36.0	14 00.3	6 20.1	17 23.3	20 47.5
8 Su	11 09 03	15 33 14	6♑56 36	13 06 30	15R 58.1	19 36.7	22 27.7	13 32.8	7 44.0	15 40.9	13 59.3	6 18.9	17 21.6	20 46.8
9 M	11 12 59	16 31 29	19 12 56	25 16 29	15 57.7	21 26.8	23 42.2	14 11.1	7 58.9	15 46.0	13 58.4	6 17.6	17 20.0	20 46.2
10 Tu	11 16 56	17 29 46	1♒17 38	7♒16 52	15 55.4	23 15.8	24 56.7	14 49.3	8 14.0	15 51.2	13 57.6	6 16.2	17 18.3	20 45.5
11 W	11 20 52	18 28 04	13 14 38	19 11 19	15 50.6	25 03.7	26 11.1	15 27.7	8 29.3	15 56.5	13 56.9	6 14.8	17 16.7	20 44.9
12 Th	11 24 49	19 26 23	25 07 17	1♓02 49	15 43.2	26 50.4	27 25.6	16 06.0	8 44.8	16 02.0	13 56.3	6 13.4	17 15.0	20 44.3
13 F	11 28 45	20 24 45	6♓58 13	12 53 44	15 33.3	28 36.1	28 40.1	16 44.3	9 00.4	16 07.7	13 55.7	6 11.9	17 13.4	20 43.7
14 Sa	11 32 42	21 23 08	18 49 33	24 45 53	15 21.7	0♎20.6	29 54.6	17 22.6	9 16.2	16 13.5	13 55.3	6 10.4	17 11.7	20 43.2
15 Su	11 36 38	22 21 33	0♈42 53	6♈40 46	15 09.1	2 03.9	1♎09.1	18 01.0	9 32.2	16 19.5	13 55.0	6 08.9	17 10.1	20 42.6
16 M	11 40 35	23 20 00	12 39 40	18 39 47	14 56.7	3 46.3	2 23.6	18 39.3	9 48.4	16 25.7	13 54.8	6 07.3	17 08.4	20 42.1
17 Tu	11 44 32	24 18 29	24 41 19	0♉44 29	14 45.5	5 27.5	3 38.1	19 17.7	10 04.7	16 31.9	13D 54.6	6 05.6	17 06.8	20 41.7
18 W	11 48 28	25 17 00	6♉49 32	12 56 46	14 36.5	7 07.7	4 52.6	19 56.1	10 21.2	16 38.4	13 54.6	6 04.0	17 05.1	20 41.2
19 Th	11 52 25	26 15 33	19 06 30	25 19 05	14 30.0	8 46.8	6 07.2	20 34.5	10 37.8	16 45.0	13 54.6	6 02.3	17 03.5	20 40.8
20 F	11 56 21	27 14 09	1♊34 54	7♊54 25	14 26.2	10 25.0	7 21.7	21 12.9	10 54.6	16 51.7	13 54.8	6 00.6	17 01.9	20 40.4
21 Sa	12 00 18	28 12 46	14 18 02	20 46 14	14D 24.7	12 02.1	8 36.2	21 51.3	11 11.6	16 58.6	13 55.1	5 58.8	17 00.3	20 40.1
22 Su	12 04 14	29 11 26	27 19 27	3♋58 09	14R 24.5	13 38.3	9 50.8	22 29.8	11 28.7	17 05.6	13 55.4	5 57.0	16 58.7	20 39.7
23 M	12 08 11	0♎10 08	10♋42 43	17 33 29	14 24.6	15 13.4	11 05.3	23 08.2	11 46.0	17 12.8	13 55.9	5 55.2	16 57.1	20 39.4
24 Tu	12 12 07	1 08 53	24 30 41	1♌34 26	14 23.7	16 47.7	12 19.9	23 46.7	12 03.4	17 20.1	13 56.4	5 53.3	16 55.5	20 39.2
25 W	12 16 04	2 07 40	8♌44 42	16 01 14	14 20.8	18 20.9	13 34.5	24 25.2	12 21.0	17 27.5	13 57.1	5 51.4	16 53.9	20 38.9
26 Th	12 20 01	3 06 29	23 23 38	0♍51 15	14 15.2	19 53.3	14 49.1	25 03.7	12 38.7	17 35.1	13 57.8	5 49.4	16 52.3	20 38.7
27 F	12 23 57	4 05 19	8♍23 14	15 58 29	14 06.9	21 24.6	16 03.6	25 42.2	12 56.6	17 42.8	13 58.7	5 47.5	16 50.7	20 38.5
28 Sa	12 27 54	5 04 13	23 35 47	1♎13 47	13 56.6	22 55.1	17 18.2	26 20.8	13 14.6	17 50.7	13 59.6	5 45.5	16 49.2	20 38.4
29 Su	12 31 50	6 03 08	8♎51 02	16 26 09	13 45.3	24 24.6	18 32.8	26 59.3	13 32.7	17 58.7	14 00.7	5 43.5	16 47.6	20 38.2
30 M	12 35 47	7 02 05	23 57 46	1♏24 42	13 34.5	25 53.2	19 47.4	27 37.9	13 51.0	18 06.8	14 01.8	5 41.4	16 46.1	20 38.1

LONGITUDE October 2019

Day	Sid.Time	☉	0 hr ☽	Noon ☽	True ☊	☿	♀	♂	⚳	♃	♄	♅	♆	♇
1 Tu	12 39 43	8♎01 04	8♏45 55	16♏00 37	13♋25.4	27♎20.9	21♎02.0	28♍16.4	14♐09.4	18♐15.1	14♑03.1	5♉39.3	16♓44.6	20♑38.1
2 W	12 43 40	9 00 05	23 08 13	0♐08 24	13R 18.6	28 47.6	22 16.6	28 55.0	14 27.9	18 23.4	14 04.4	5R 37.2	16R 43.1	20D 38.0
3 Th	12 47 36	9 59 07	7♐01 02	13 46 11	13 14.6	0♏13.3	23 31.2	29 33.6	14 46.6	18 32.0	14 05.9	5 35.1	16 41.6	20 38.0
4 F	12 51 33	10 58 12	20 24 07	26 55 13	13 12.8	1 38.1	24 45.7	0♎12.3	15 05.4	18 40.6	14 07.4	5 32.9	16 40.1	20 38.0
5 Sa	12 55 29	11 57 18	3♑19 57	9♑38 54	13 12.4	3 01.8	26 00.3	0 50.9	15 24.3	18 49.4	14 09.1	5 30.7	16 38.6	20 38.1
6 Su	12 59 26	12 56 26	15 52 41	22 01 58	13 12.3	4 24.5	27 14.9	1 29.5	15 43.4	18 58.2	14 10.8	5 28.5	16 37.2	20 38.2
7 M	13 03 23	13 55 36	28 07 22	4♒09 34	13 11.3	5 46.1	28 29.5	2 08.2	16 02.5	19 07.3	14 12.6	5 26.3	16 35.8	20 38.3
8 Tu	13 07 19	14 54 47	10♒09 12	16 06 52	13 08.4	7 06.6	29 44.1	2 46.9	16 21.8	19 16.4	14 14.6	5 24.1	16 34.4	20 38.4
9 W	13 11 16	15 54 01	22 03 08	27 58 31	13 02.8	8 26.0	0♏58.7	3 25.5	16 41.2	19 25.6	14 16.6	5 21.8	16 33.0	20 38.6
10 Th	13 15 12	16 53 16	3♓53 31	9♓48 33	12 54.4	9 44.1	2 13.3	4 04.2	17 00.7	19 35.0	14 18.7	5 19.5	16 31.6	20 38.8
11 F	13 19 09	17 52 33	15 44 00	21 40 10	12 43.3	11 00.9	3 27.8	4 42.9	17 20.4	19 44.4	14 20.9	5 17.2	16 30.2	20 39.0
12 Sa	13 23 05	18 51 52	27 37 21	3♈35 47	12 30.1	12 16.3	4 42.4	5 21.7	17 40.1	19 54.0	14 23.2	5 14.9	16 28.9	20 39.3
13 Su	13 27 02	19 51 12	9♈35 39	15 37 05	12 16.0	13 30.2	5 57.0	6 00.4	17 59.9	20 03.7	14 25.6	5 12.5	16 27.6	20 39.6
14 M	13 30 58	20 50 35	21 40 15	27 45 13	12 01.9	14 42.6	7 11.5	6 39.2	18 19.8	20 13.5	14 28.1	5 10.2	16 26.3	20 39.9
15 Tu	13 34 55	21 50 00	3♉52 06	10♉00 59	11 49.2	15 53.3	8 26.1	7 18.0	18 39.9	20 23.4	14 30.6	5 07.8	16 25.0	20 40.2
16 W	13 38 52	22 49 28	16 11 59	22 25 13	11 38.7	17 02.2	9 40.7	7 56.8	19 00.0	20 33.4	14 33.3	5 05.4	16 23.7	20 40.6
17 Th	13 42 48	23 48 57	28 40 49	4♊58 58	11 31.1	18 09.0	10 55.3	8 35.6	19 20.3	20 43.5	14 36.1	5 03.0	16 22.5	20 41.0
18 F	13 46 45	24 48 29	11♊19 51	17 43 42	11 26.5	19 13.7	12 09.8	9 14.4	19 40.6	20 53.8	14 38.9	5 00.6	16 21.3	20 41.5
19 Sa	13 50 41	25 48 03	24 10 49	0♋41 29	11D 24.4	20 16.0	13 24.4	9 53.3	20 01.1	21 04.1	14 41.9	4 58.2	16 20.1	20 41.9
20 Su	13 54 38	26 47 39	7♋16 00	13 54 42	11 24.1	21 15.7	14 39.0	10 32.1	20 21.6	21 14.5	14 44.9	4 55.8	16 18.9	20 42.4
21 M	13 58 34	27 47 17	20 37 55	27 25 54	11R 24.3	22 12.5	15 53.5	11 11.0	20 42.3	21 25.0	14 48.0	4 53.3	16 17.8	20 42.9
22 Tu	14 02 31	28 46 58	4♌18 54	11♌17 06	11 23.7	23 06.2	17 08.1	11 50.0	21 03.0	21 35.7	14 51.2	4 50.9	16 16.7	20 43.5
23 W	14 06 27	29 46 41	18 20 32	25 29 09	11 21.4	23 56.3	18 22.7	12 28.9	21 23.8	21 46.4	14 54.5	4 48.5	16 15.6	20 44.1
24 Th	14 10 24	0♏46 27	2♍42 44	10♍00 55	11 16.5	24 42.6	19 37.3	13 07.8	21 44.7	21 57.2	14 57.9	4 46.0	16 14.5	20 44.7
25 F	14 14 21	1 46 14	17 23 07	24 48 35	11 09.1	25 24.6	20 51.8	13 46.8	22 05.7	22 08.1	15 01.4	4 43.5	16 13.4	20 45.3
26 Sa	14 18 17	2 46 04	2♎16 27	9♎45 39	10 59.6	26 01.9	22 06.4	14 25.8	22 26.8	22 19.1	15 04.9	4 41.1	16 12.4	20 46.0
27 Su	14 22 14	3 45 56	17 15 01	24 43 23	10 49.1	26 33.9	23 21.0	15 04.8	22 48.0	22 30.2	15 08.5	4 38.6	16 11.4	20 46.7
28 M	14 26 10	4 45 49	2♏09 32	9♏32 20	10 38.9	27 00.1	24 35.5	15 43.8	23 09.2	22 41.4	15 12.3	4 36.1	16 10.4	20 47.4
29 Tu	14 30 07	5 45 45	16 50 44	24 03 52	10 30.0	27 20.0	25 50.1	16 22.9	23 30.6	22 52.6	15 16.1	4 33.7	16 09.5	20 48.2
30 W	14 34 03	6 45 43	1♐11 01	8♐11 40	10 23.5	27 32.9	27 04.7	17 02.0	23 52.0	23 04.0	15 20.0	4 31.2	16 08.6	20 49.0
31 Th	14 38 00	7 45 42	15 05 30	21 52 23	10 19.6	27R 38.2	28 19.3	17 41.0	24 13.5	23 15.4	15 23.9	4 28.7	16 07.7	20 49.8

Astro Data

	Dy Hr Mn
☽0S	1 18:02
☿0S	15 10:28
☽0N	15 22:03
♀0S	16 22:08
♄ D	18 8:48
♃□♆	21 16:45
☉0S	23 7:51
☽0S	29 4:26
♇ D	3 6:40
♂0S	7 14:19
☽0N	13 4:03
♃⚼♅	14 5:27
♃⚺♇	17 5:46
☽0S	26 15:09
☿ R	31 15:43

Planet Ingress

		Dy Hr Mn
☿	♎	14 7:16
♀	♎	14 13:44
☉	♎	23 7:51
☿	♏	3 8:15
♂	♎	4 4:23
♀	♏	8 17:07
☉	♏	23 17:21

Last Aspect / ☽ Ingress (September)

Last Aspect Dy Hr Mn			☽ Ingress	Dy Hr Mn
2 8:35	♇	□	♏	2 23:36
4 10:59	♇	⚹	♐	5 3:09
6 16:04	♀	□	♑	7 10:38
9 8:31	♀	△	♒	9 21:25
11 5:24	♃	⚹	♓	12 9:53
14 4:34	☉	☍	♈	14 22:34
16 16:04	♇	□	♉	17 10:32
19 13:58	☉	△	♊	19 20:59
22 2:42	☉	□	♋	22 4:51
23 22:06	♂	⚹	♌	24 9:21
25 16:15	☿	⚹	♍	26 10:38
28 3:59	♂	☌	♎	28 10:04
30 2:07	☿	☌	♏	30 9:43

Last Aspect / ☽ Ingress (October)

Last Aspect Dy Hr Mn			☽ Ingress	Dy Hr Mn
2 9:47	♂	⚹	♐	2 11:45
4 7:35	♀	⚹	♑	4 17:44
6 23:27	♀	□	♒	7 3:43
8 18:28	♃	⚹	♓	9 16:06
11 9:56	♇	⚹	♈	12 4:47
13 22:00	♇	□	♉	14 16:25
16 8:39	♇	△	♊	17 2:31
19 2:15	☉	△	♋	19 10:44
21 12:40	☉	□	♌	21 16:30
23 9:15	☿	□	♍	23 19:31
25 13:01	☿	⚹	♎	25 20:21
27 8:23	♃	⚹	♏	27 20:30
29 17:36	☿	☌	♐	29 22:00

☽ Phases & Eclipses

Dy Hr Mn		
6 3:12	☽	13♐15
14 4:34	○	21♓05
22 2:42	☾	28♊49
28 18:28	●	5♎20
5 16:48	☽	12♑09
13 21:09	○	20♈14
21 12:40	☾	27♋49
28 3:40	●	4♏25

Astro Data

1 September 2019
Julian Day # 43708
SVP 4♓59'22"
GC 27♐06.8 ⚴ 2♏15.3
Eris 24♈10.7R ⚵ 3♍48.3
⚷ 4♈45.6R ⚶ 25♉54.3
☽ Mean ☊ 14♋40.3

1 October 2019
Julian Day # 43738
SVP 4♓59'20"
GC 27♐06.9 ⚴ 14♏02.2
Eris 23♈55.7R ⚵ 16♍44.4
⚷ 3♈27.2R ⚶ 27♉27.2R
☽ Mean ☊ 13♋05.0

November 2019 LONGITUDE

Day	Sid.Time	☉	0 hr ☽	Noon ☽	True ☊	☿	♀	♂	⚳	♃	♄	♅	♆	♇
1 F	14 41 56	8♏45 43	28♐32 23	5♑05 41	10♋18.0	27♏35.2	29♏33.8	18♎20.1	24♐35.1	23♐26.9	15♑28.0	4♉26.3	16♓06.9	20♑50.6
2 Sa	14 45 53	9 45 46	11♑32 38	17 53 41	10D 18.1	27R 23.5	0♐48.4	18 59.3	24 56.7	23 38.5	15 32.1	4R 23.8	16R 06.0	20 51.5
3 Su	14 49 50	10 45 51	24 09 20	0♒20 12	10R 18.8	27 02.6	2 02.9	19 38.4	25 18.5	23 50.2	15 36.3	4 21.4	16 05.2	20 52.4
4 M	14 53 46	11 45 57	6♒26 54	12 30 05	10 19.3	26 32.1	3 17.5	20 17.5	25 40.3	24 01.9	15 40.6	4 18.9	16 04.5	20 53.3
5 Tu	14 57 43	12 46 04	18 30 24	24 28 32	10 18.4	25 51.9	4 32.0	20 56.7	26 02.1	24 13.8	15 44.9	4 16.5	16 03.7	20 54.3
6 W	15 01 39	13 46 13	0♓25 07	6♓20 46	10 15.5	25 02.3	5 46.5	21 35.9	26 24.1	24 25.7	15 49.4	4 14.1	16 03.0	20 55.3
7 Th	15 05 36	14 46 24	12 16 04	18 11 33	10 10.3	24 03.7	7 01.0	22 15.1	26 46.1	24 37.6	15 53.9	4 11.7	16 02.3	20 56.3
8 F	15 09 32	15 46 36	24 07 44	0♈05 05	10 02.9	22 57.3	8 15.6	22 54.3	27 08.2	24 49.7	15 58.5	4 09.3	16 01.7	20 57.3
9 Sa	15 13 29	16 46 49	6♈03 58	12 04 44	9 53.7	21 44.3	9 30.1	23 33.5	27 30.3	25 01.8	16 03.1	4 06.9	16 01.1	20 58.4
10 Su	15 17 25	17 47 05	18 07 42	24 13 04	9 43.6	20 26.9	10 44.6	24 12.8	27 52.5	25 14.0	16 07.8	4 04.5	16 00.5	20 59.5
11 M	15 21 22	18 47 22	0♉21 01	6♉31 42	9 33.6	19 07.1	11 59.0	24 52.1	28 14.7	25 26.2	16 12.6	4 02.1	15 59.9	21 00.6
12 Tu	15 25 19	19 47 40	12 45 11	19 01 31	9 24.4	17 47.6	13 13.5	25 31.4	28 37.1	25 38.5	16 17.5	3 59.8	15 59.4	21 01.7
13 W	15 29 15	20 48 01	25 20 43	1♊42 47	9 17.1	16 31.0	14 28.0	26 10.7	28 59.4	25 50.9	16 22.4	3 57.4	15 58.9	21 02.9
14 Th	15 33 12	21 48 23	8♊07 42	14 35 26	9 12.0	15 19.7	15 42.5	26 50.0	29 21.9	26 03.3	16 27.4	3 55.1	15 58.5	21 04.1
15 F	15 37 08	22 48 47	21 05 59	27 39 20	9D 09.2	14 15.9	16 56.9	27 29.4	29 44.4	26 15.8	16 32.5	3 52.8	15 58.1	21 05.3
16 Sa	15 41 05	23 49 13	4♋15 31	10♋54 32	9 08.6	13 21.5	18 11.4	28 08.8	0♑06.9	26 28.4	16 37.6	3 50.6	15 57.7	21 06.5
17 Su	15 45 01	24 49 40	17 36 27	24 21 19	9 09.4	12 37.7	19 25.9	28 48.2	0 29.6	26 41.0	16 42.8	3 48.3	15 57.3	21 07.8
18 M	15 48 58	25 50 10	1♌09 13	8♌00 14	9 10.7	12 05.4	20 40.3	29 27.6	0 52.2	26 53.7	16 48.1	3 46.1	15 57.0	21 09.1
19 Tu	15 52 54	26 50 41	14 54 23	21 51 44	9R 11.7	11 44.7	21 54.7	0♏07.1	1 14.9	27 06.4	16 53.4	3 43.8	15 56.7	21 10.4
20 W	15 56 51	27 51 14	28 52 14	5♍55 50	9 11.6	11D 35.7	23 09.2	0 46.6	1 37.7	27 19.2	16 58.8	3 41.7	15 56.4	21 11.7
21 Th	16 00 48	28 51 49	13♍02 23	20 11 37	9 09.7	11 37.9	24 23.6	1 26.1	2 00.5	27 32.1	17 04.3	3 39.5	15 56.2	21 13.1
22 F	16 04 44	29 52 25	27 23 13	4♎36 43	9 06.0	11 50.6	25 38.0	2 05.6	2 23.4	27 45.0	17 09.8	3 37.3	15 56.0	21 14.4
23 Sa	16 08 41	0♐53 03	11♎51 35	19 07 11	9 00.8	12 13.0	26 52.5	2 45.1	2 46.3	27 57.9	17 15.4	3 35.2	15 55.9	21 15.8
24 Su	16 12 37	1 53 43	26 22 48	3♏37 39	8 54.9	12 44.4	28 06.9	3 24.7	3 09.3	28 10.9	17 21.0	3 33.1	15 55.7	21 17.3
25 M	16 16 34	2 54 25	10♏50 57	18 01 54	8 49.0	13 23.7	29 21.3	4 04.3	3 32.3	28 23.9	17 26.7	3 31.1	15 55.6	21 18.7
26 Tu	16 20 30	3 55 08	25 09 43	2♐13 44	8 43.9	14 10.1	0♑35.7	4 43.9	3 55.4	28 37.0	17 32.4	3 29.0	15 55.6	21 20.2
27 W	16 24 27	4 55 53	9♐13 20	16 08 01	8 40.3	15 02.8	1 50.1	5 23.5	4 18.5	28 50.2	17 38.2	3 27.0	15D 55.6	21 21.7
28 Th	16 28 23	5 56 38	22 57 24	29 41 14	8D 38.4	16 00.9	3 04.4	6 03.1	4 41.7	29 03.3	17 44.1	3 25.0	15 55.6	21 23.2
29 F	16 32 20	6 57 25	6♑19 25	12♑51 58	8 38.1	17 03.9	4 18.8	6 42.8	5 04.8	29 16.6	17 50.0	3 23.1	15 55.6	21 24.7
30 Sa	16 36 17	7 58 13	19 18 59	25 40 44	8 39.1	18 11.0	5 33.2	7 22.5	5 28.1	29 29.8	17 56.0	3 21.2	15 55.7	21 26.3

December 2019 LONGITUDE

Day	Sid.Time	☉	0 hr ☽	Noon ☽	True ☊	☿	♀	♂	⚳	♃	♄	♅	♆	♇
1 Su	16 40 13	8♐59 02	1♒57 32	8♒09 47	8♋40.9	19♏21.7	6♑47.5	8♏02.2	5♑51.4	29♐43.1	18♑02.0	3♉19.3	15♓55.8	21♑27.9
2 M	16 44 10	9 59 52	14 17 59	20 22 38	8 42.6	20 35.5	8 01.8	8 41.9	6 14.7	29 56.5	18 08.0	3R 17.5	15 56.0	21 29.4
3 Tu	16 48 06	11 00 43	26 24 19	2♓23 38	8R 43.9	21 51.9	9 16.1	9 21.6	6 38.0	0♑09.8	18 14.1	3 15.7	15 56.2	21 31.1
4 W	16 52 03	12 01 35	8♓21 11	14 17 35	8 44.2	23 10.6	10 30.4	10 01.4	7 01.4	0 23.2	18 20.3	3 13.9	15 56.4	21 32.7
5 Th	16 55 59	13 02 27	20 13 29	26 09 28	8 43.4	24 31.2	11 44.7	10 41.2	7 24.8	0 36.7	18 26.5	3 12.2	15 56.7	21 34.3
6 F	16 59 56	14 03 21	2♈06 08	8♈04 03	8 41.3	25 53.5	12 59.0	11 20.9	7 48.3	0 50.1	18 32.7	3 10.5	15 57.0	21 36.0
7 Sa	17 03 52	15 04 15	14 03 43	20 05 40	8 38.3	27 17.3	14 13.2	12 00.8	8 11.7	1 03.6	18 39.0	3 08.8	15 57.3	21 37.7
8 Su	17 07 49	16 05 10	26 10 19	2♉18 04	8 34.7	28 42.2	15 27.4	12 40.6	8 35.2	1 17.2	18 45.3	3 07.2	15 57.6	21 39.4
9 M	17 11 46	17 06 05	8♉29 15	14 44 08	8 31.0	0♐08.2	16 41.6	13 20.4	8 58.8	1 30.7	18 51.7	3 05.6	15 58.0	21 41.1
10 Tu	17 15 42	18 07 02	21 02 54	27 25 44	8 27.6	1 35.1	17 55.8	14 00.3	9 22.3	1 44.3	18 58.1	3 04.0	15 58.5	21 42.8
11 W	17 19 39	19 07 59	3♊52 36	10♊23 34	8 25.0	3 02.8	19 09.9	14 40.2	9 45.9	1 57.9	19 04.6	3 02.5	15 58.9	21 44.6
12 Th	17 23 35	20 08 58	16 58 34	23 37 28	8 23.4	4 31.1	20 24.1	15 20.1	10 09.6	2 11.5	19 11.1	3 01.1	15 59.4	21 46.3
13 F	17 27 32	21 09 57	0♋20 05	7♋06 11	8D 22.8	6 00.0	21 38.2	16 00.1	10 33.2	2 25.2	19 17.6	2 59.7	16 00.0	21 48.1
14 Sa	17 31 28	22 10 57	13 55 31	20 47 48	8 23.2	7 29.5	22 52.3	16 40.1	10 56.9	2 38.9	19 24.2	2 58.3	16 00.5	21 49.9
15 Su	17 35 25	23 11 58	27 42 44	4♌40 01	8 24.1	8 59.3	24 06.3	17 20.0	11 20.6	2 52.6	19 30.8	2 57.0	16 01.1	21 51.7
16 M	17 39 21	24 13 00	11♌39 21	18 40 25	8 25.3	10 29.5	25 20.4	18 00.1	11 44.3	3 06.3	19 37.4	2 55.7	16 01.8	21 53.5
17 Tu	17 43 18	25 14 03	25 42 57	2♍46 38	8 26.4	12 00.1	26 34.4	18 40.1	12 08.0	3 20.0	19 44.1	2 54.4	16 02.5	21 55.4
18 W	17 47 15	26 15 06	9♍51 12	16 56 24	8R 27.1	13 31.0	27 48.4	19 20.2	12 31.8	3 33.7	19 50.8	2 53.2	16 03.2	21 57.2
19 Th	17 51 11	27 16 11	24 01 58	1♎07 38	8 27.2	15 02.2	29 02.4	20 00.2	12 55.6	3 47.5	19 57.5	2 52.1	16 03.9	21 59.1
20 F	17 55 08	28 17 17	8♎13 08	15 18 10	8 26.8	16 33.6	0♒16.3	20 40.3	13 19.4	4 01.3	20 04.2	2 50.9	16 04.7	22 00.9
21 Sa	17 59 04	29 18 23	22 22 28	29 25 43	8 26.0	18 05.3	1 30.2	21 20.5	13 43.2	4 15.1	20 11.0	2 49.9	16 05.5	22 02.8
22 Su	18 03 01	0♑19 30	6♏27 36	13♏27 47	8 24.9	19 37.3	2 44.1	22 00.6	14 07.1	4 28.9	20 17.8	2 48.9	16 06.3	22 04.7
23 M	18 06 57	1 20 38	20 25 56	27 21 42	8 24.0	21 09.5	3 58.0	22 40.8	14 30.9	4 42.7	20 24.7	2 47.9	16 07.2	22 06.6
24 Tu	18 10 54	2 21 47	4♐14 45	11♐04 46	8 23.2	22 41.9	5 11.8	23 21.0	14 54.8	4 56.5	20 31.5	2 47.0	16 08.1	22 08.5
25 W	18 14 50	3 22 56	17 51 27	24 34 33	8 22.8	24 14.5	6 25.6	24 01.2	15 18.7	5 10.3	20 38.4	2 46.1	16 09.0	22 10.4
26 Th	18 18 47	4 24 06	1♑13 49	7♑49 06	8D 22.6	25 47.4	7 39.4	24 41.4	15 42.6	5 24.1	20 45.3	2 45.3	16 10.0	22 12.4
27 F	18 22 44	5 25 16	14 20 18	20 47 20	8 22.7	27 20.6	8 53.1	25 21.7	16 06.5	5 38.0	20 52.3	2 44.5	16 11.0	22 14.3
28 Sa	18 26 40	6 26 26	27 10 14	3♒29 04	8 22.9	28 54.0	10 06.8	26 02.0	16 30.5	5 51.8	20 59.2	2 43.8	16 12.0	22 16.3
29 Su	18 30 37	7 27 36	9♒44 01	15 55 15	8R 23.1	0♑27.6	11 20.5	26 42.2	16 54.4	6 05.6	21 06.2	2 43.1	16 13.1	22 18.2
30 M	18 34 33	8 28 46	22 03 05	28 07 50	8 23.1	2 01.5	12 34.1	27 22.5	17 18.4	6 19.5	21 13.2	2 42.5	16 14.2	22 20.2
31 Tu	18 38 30	9 29 56	4♓09 53	10♓09 42	8 23.1	3 35.7	13 47.7	28 02.9	17 42.3	6 33.3	21 20.2	2 41.9	16 15.3	22 22.2

Astro Data	Planet Ingress
Dy Hr Mn	Dy Hr Mn
♄⚹♆ 9 2:47	♀ ♐ 1 20:26
☽0N 9 11:33	⚳ ♑ 16 4:37
☿ D 20 19:15	♂ ♏ 19 7:41
☽0S 23 0:16	☉ ♐ 22 15:00
♆ D 27 12:33	♀ ♑ 26 0:30
☽0N 6 20:14	♃ ♑ 2 18:21
♃△♅ 15 19:02	☿ ♐ 9 9:43
☽0S 20 6:52	♀ ♒ 20 6:43
	☉ ♑ 22 4:21
	☿ ♑ 29 4:56

Last Aspect	☽ Ingress	Last Aspect	☽ Ingress
Dy Hr Mn	Dy Hr Mn	Dy Hr Mn	Dy Hr Mn
31 14:31 ♃ ☌	♑ 1 2:39	2 12:28 ☿ □	♓ 3 7:12
3 5:48 ☿ ⚹	♒ 3 11:21	5 8:16 ☿ △	♈ 5 19:46
5 14:38 ☿ □	♓ 5 23:09	7 15:03 ♇ □	♉ 8 7:30
8 1:14 ♃ □	♈ 8 11:50	10 1:14 ♇ △	♊ 10 16:48
10 14:02 ♃ △	♉ 10 23:19	12 5:13 ☉ ☍	♋ 12 23:24
12 15:49 ♇ △	♊ 13 8:47	14 15:58 ♀ ☍	♌ 15 3:57
15 11:41 ♂ △	♋ 15 16:16	16 22:11 ☉ △	♍ 17 7:17
17 20:16 ♂ □	♌ 17 21:58	19 8:08 ♀ △	♎ 19 10:06
19 21:12 ☉ □	♍ 20 1:56	21 11:47 ☉ ⚹	♏ 21 12:58
22 3:33 ☉ ⚹	♎ 22 4:21	23 3:28 ♂ ☌	♐ 23 16:35
24 2:51 ♃ ⚹	♏ 24 5:59	25 11:19 ☿ ☌	♑ 25 21:46
25 17:31 ♇ ⚹	♐ 26 8:12	27 21:04 ♂ ⚹	♒ 28 5:22
28 10:51 ♃ ☌	♑ 28 12:34	30 10:25 ♂ □	♓ 30 15:43
30 3:58 ♇ ☌	♒ 30 20:14		

☽ Phases & Eclipses	
Dy Hr Mn	
4 10:24	☽ 11♒42
12 13:36	○ 19♉52
19 21:12	☾ 27♌14
26 15:07	● 4♐03
4 6:59	☽ 11♓49
12 5:13	○ 19♊52
19 4:58	☾ 26♍58
26 5:14	● 4♑07
26 5:18:54	● A 03'39"

Astro Data

1 November 2019
Julian Day # 43769
SVP 4♓59'16"
GC 27♐07.0 ⚴ 27♏02.1
Eris 23♈37.3R ⚵ 29♍02.0
⚷ 2♈11.2R ⚶ 22♉27.5R
☽ Mean ☊ 11♋26.5

1 December 2019
Julian Day # 43799
SVP 4♓59'11"
GC 27♐07.0 ⚴ 9♐55.0
Eris 23♈22.1R ⚵ 9♎21.5
⚷ 1♈29.8R ⚶ 15♉03.8R
☽ Mean ☊ 9♋51.2

LONGITUDE — January 2020

Day	Sid.Time	☉	0 hr ☽	Noon ☽	True ☊	☿	♀	♂	⚳	♃	♄	♅	♆	♇
1 W	18 42 26	10♑31 06	16♓07 44	22♓04 31	8♋22.9	5♑10.2	15♒01.3	28♏43.2	18♑06.3	6♑47.1	21♑27.2	2♉41.4	16♓16.5	22♑24.1
2 Th	18 46 23	11 32 16	28 00 35	3♈56 32	8D 22.8	6 45.0	16 14.8	29 23.6	18 30.3	7 00.9	21 34.2	2R 40.9	16 17.6	22 26.1
3 F	18 50 20	12 33 26	9♈52 55	15 50 21	8 22.7	8 20.1	17 28.2	0♐04.0	18 54.2	7 14.8	21 41.3	2 40.5	16 18.9	22 28.1
4 Sa	18 54 16	13 34 35	21 49 26	27 50 45	8 22.9	9 55.6	18 41.6	0 44.4	19 18.2	7 28.6	21 48.3	2 40.1	16 20.1	22 30.1
5 Su	18 58 13	14 35 45	3♉54 51	10♉02 19	8 23.4	11 31.4	19 55.0	1 24.8	19 42.2	7 42.4	21 55.4	2 39.8	16 21.4	22 32.1
6 M	19 02 09	15 36 53	16 13 39	22 29 18	8 24.1	13 07.6	21 08.3	2 05.2	20 06.2	7 56.1	22 02.5	2 39.5	16 22.7	22 34.1
7 Tu	19 06 06	16 38 02	28 49 41	5♊15 08	8 24.9	14 44.2	22 21.5	2 45.7	20 30.2	8 09.9	22 09.6	2 39.3	16 24.0	22 36.1
8 W	19 10 02	17 39 11	11♊45 54	18 22 09	8 25.7	16 21.1	23 34.7	3 26.2	20 54.1	8 23.7	22 16.7	2 39.2	16 25.4	22 38.1
9 Th	19 13 59	18 40 19	25 03 56	1♋51 11	8R 26.2	17 58.5	24 47.8	4 06.7	21 18.1	8 37.4	22 23.8	2 39.1	16 26.8	22 40.1
10 F	19 17 55	19 41 26	8♋43 44	15 41 18	8 26.2	19 36.3	26 00.9	4 47.2	21 42.1	8 51.2	22 30.9	2D 39.0	16 28.2	22 42.1
11 Sa	19 21 52	20 42 34	22 43 29	29 49 45	8 25.5	21 14.5	27 13.9	5 27.8	22 06.1	9 04.9	22 38.0	2 39.0	16 29.6	22 44.1
12 Su	19 25 49	21 43 41	6♌59 30	14♌12 04	8 24.2	22 53.2	28 26.9	6 08.3	22 30.1	9 18.6	22 45.1	2 39.0	16 31.1	22 46.2
13 M	19 29 45	22 44 48	21 26 44	28 42 42	8 22.4	24 32.4	29 39.8	6 48.9	22 54.0	9 32.3	22 52.2	2 39.1	16 32.6	22 48.2
14 Tu	19 33 42	23 45 55	5♍59 14	13♍15 36	8 20.4	26 12.0	0♓52.6	7 29.5	23 18.0	9 45.9	22 59.3	2 39.3	16 34.1	22 50.2
15 W	19 37 38	24 47 02	20 31 06	27 45 07	8 18.6	27 52.0	2 05.3	8 10.2	23 42.0	9 59.6	23 06.4	2 39.5	16 35.7	22 52.2
16 Th	19 41 35	25 48 08	4♎57 06	12♎06 37	8 17.3	29 32.6	3 18.0	8 50.8	24 05.9	10 13.2	23 13.5	2 39.8	16 37.3	22 54.2
17 F	19 45 31	26 49 15	19 13 18	26 16 52	8D 16.8	1♒13.5	4 30.6	9 31.5	24 29.9	10 26.8	23 20.6	2 40.1	16 38.9	22 56.2
18 Sa	19 49 28	27 50 21	3♏17 09	10♏14 01	8 17.2	2 55.0	5 43.2	10 12.2	24 53.8	10 40.3	23 27.7	2 40.4	16 40.5	22 58.2
19 Su	19 53 24	28 51 27	17 07 25	23 57 20	8 18.4	4 36.8	6 55.7	10 53.0	25 17.8	10 53.9	23 34.8	2 40.8	16 42.1	23 00.2
20 M	19 57 21	29 52 32	0♐43 49	7♐26 54	8 19.9	6 19.1	8 08.1	11 33.7	25 41.7	11 07.4	23 41.9	2 41.3	16 43.8	23 02.2
21 Tu	20 01 18	0♒53 38	14 06 39	20 43 09	8 21.4	8 01.7	9 20.5	12 14.5	26 05.6	11 20.8	23 49.0	2 41.8	16 45.5	23 04.2
22 W	20 05 14	1 54 43	27 16 28	3♑46 39	8R 22.2	9 44.6	10 32.7	12 55.3	26 29.5	11 34.3	23 56.1	2 42.4	16 47.3	23 06.2
23 Th	20 09 11	2 55 47	10♑13 46	16 37 53	8 22.1	11 27.8	11 44.9	13 36.1	26 53.4	11 47.7	24 03.1	2 43.0	16 49.0	23 08.2
24 F	20 13 07	3 56 51	22 59 03	29 17 18	8 20.5	13 11.2	12 57.0	14 16.9	27 17.3	12 01.1	24 10.2	2 43.7	16 50.8	23 10.2
25 Sa	20 17 04	4 57 54	5♒32 43	11♒45 21	8 17.5	14 54.7	14 09.0	14 57.7	27 41.1	12 14.4	24 17.2	2 44.4	16 52.6	23 12.2
26 Su	20 21 00	5 58 56	17 55 19	24 02 42	8 13.3	16 38.1	15 21.0	15 38.6	28 05.0	12 27.7	24 24.3	2 45.2	16 54.4	23 14.2
27 M	20 24 57	6 59 57	0♓07 41	6♓10 25	8 08.1	18 21.4	16 32.8	16 19.5	28 28.8	12 41.0	24 31.3	2 46.0	16 56.2	23 16.1
28 Tu	20 28 53	8 00 57	12 11 08	18 10 07	8 02.6	20 04.3	17 44.6	17 00.4	28 52.6	12 54.2	24 38.3	2 46.9	16 58.1	23 18.1
29 W	20 32 50	9 01 56	24 07 39	0♈04 06	7 57.3	21 46.8	18 56.2	17 41.3	29 16.4	13 07.4	24 45.3	2 47.8	16 59.9	23 20.1
30 Th	20 36 47	10 02 54	5♈59 52	11 55 24	7 52.8	23 28.4	20 07.8	18 22.2	29 40.2	13 20.5	24 52.2	2 48.8	17 01.8	23 22.0
31 F	20 40 43	11 03 51	17 51 10	23 47 42	7 49.7	25 09.1	21 19.3	19 03.1	0♒03.9	13 33.6	24 59.1	2 49.8	17 03.8	23 24.0

LONGITUDE — February 2020

Day	Sid.Time	☉	0 hr ☽	Noon ☽	True ☊	☿	♀	♂	⚳	♃	♄	♅	♆	♇
1 Sa	20 44 40	12♒04 46	29♈45 34	5♉45 20	7♋48.1	26♒48.4	22♓30.6	19♐44.1	0♒27.6	13♑46.7	25♑06.1	2♉50.9	17♓05.7	23♑25.9
2 Su	20 48 36	13 05 41	11♉47 36	17 52 59	7D 48.0	28 26.0	23 41.9	20 25.1	0 51.3	13 59.7	25 13.0	2 52.1	17 07.6	23 27.8
3 M	20 52 33	14 06 33	24 02 07	0♊15 34	7 49.0	0♓01.4	24 53.0	21 06.1	1 15.0	14 12.6	25 19.8	2 53.2	17 09.6	23 29.7
4 Tu	20 56 29	15 07 25	6♊33 57	12 57 46	7 50.7	1 34.2	26 04.0	21 47.1	1 38.7	14 25.5	25 26.7	2 54.5	17 11.6	23 31.6
5 W	21 00 26	16 08 15	19 27 31	26 03 36	7R 52.1	3 04.0	27 14.9	22 28.1	2 02.3	14 38.3	25 33.5	2 55.8	17 13.6	23 33.5
6 Th	21 04 22	17 09 04	2♋46 19	9♋35 48	7 52.7	4 29.9	28 25.7	23 09.2	2 25.9	14 51.1	25 40.3	2 57.1	17 15.6	23 35.4
7 F	21 08 19	18 09 52	16 32 07	23 35 07	7 51.6	5 51.5	29 36.3	23 50.2	2 49.4	15 03.9	25 47.1	2 58.5	17 17.7	23 37.3
8 Sa	21 12 16	19 10 38	0♌44 27	7♌59 39	7 48.5	7 08.1	0♈46.8	24 31.3	3 13.0	15 16.5	25 53.8	2 59.9	17 19.7	23 39.1
9 Su	21 16 12	20 11 22	15 19 59	22 44 36	7 43.6	8 18.8	1 57.2	25 12.4	3 36.5	15 29.2	26 00.5	3 01.4	17 21.8	23 41.0
10 M	21 20 09	21 12 06	0♍12 29	7♍42 30	7 37.1	9 23.1	3 07.5	25 53.6	4 00.0	15 41.7	26 07.2	3 02.9	17 23.9	23 42.8
11 Tu	21 24 05	22 12 48	15 13 28	22 44 11	7 30.1	10 20.0	4 17.6	26 34.7	4 23.4	15 54.2	26 13.9	3 04.5	17 26.0	23 44.6
12 W	21 28 02	23 13 29	0♎13 28	7♎40 14	7 23.3	11 08.9	5 27.5	27 15.9	4 46.8	16 06.6	26 20.5	3 06.1	17 28.1	23 46.5
13 Th	21 31 58	24 14 09	15 03 34	22 22 40	7 17.8	11 49.1	6 37.4	27 57.1	5 10.2	16 19.0	26 27.1	3 07.7	17 30.2	23 48.2
14 F	21 35 55	25 14 47	29 36 55	6♏45 53	7 14.2	12 20.0	7 47.0	28 38.3	5 33.5	16 31.3	26 33.6	3 09.4	17 32.3	23 50.0
15 Sa	21 39 51	26 15 25	13♏49 19	20 47 07	7D 12.5	12 41.1	8 56.6	29 19.5	5 56.8	16 43.6	26 40.1	3 11.2	17 34.5	23 51.8
16 Su	21 43 48	27 16 02	27 39 18	4♐26 02	7 12.6	12R 51.9	10 06.0	0♑00.7	6 20.1	16 55.8	26 46.6	3 13.0	17 36.6	23 53.5
17 M	21 47 45	28 16 37	11♐07 34	17 44 11	7 13.6	12 52.3	11 15.2	0 42.0	6 43.3	17 07.9	26 53.1	3 14.8	17 38.8	23 55.3
18 Tu	21 51 41	29 17 11	24 16 14	0♑44 05	7R 14.6	12 42.3	12 24.3	1 23.3	7 06.6	17 19.9	26 59.5	3 16.7	17 41.0	23 57.0
19 W	21 55 38	0♓17 44	7♑08 05	13 28 37	7 14.6	12 22.1	13 33.2	2 04.6	7 29.7	17 31.9	27 05.8	3 18.6	17 43.2	23 58.7
20 Th	21 59 34	1 18 16	19 46 00	26 00 32	7 12.7	11 52.2	14 42.0	2 45.9	7 52.8	17 43.8	27 12.2	3 20.6	17 45.4	24 00.4
21 F	22 03 31	2 18 46	2♒12 31	8♒22 12	7 08.3	11 13.4	15 50.6	3 27.2	8 15.9	17 55.6	27 18.4	3 22.6	17 47.6	24 02.1
22 Sa	22 07 27	3 19 15	14 29 46	20 35 26	7 01.2	10 26.6	16 59.0	4 08.6	8 39.0	18 07.3	27 24.7	3 24.7	17 49.8	24 03.7
23 Su	22 11 24	4 19 42	26 39 21	2♓41 39	6 51.7	9 33.1	18 07.2	4 49.9	9 01.9	18 19.0	27 30.8	3 26.8	17 52.0	24 05.4
24 M	22 15 20	5 20 07	8♓42 30	14 42 02	6 40.4	8 34.4	19 15.2	5 31.3	9 24.9	18 30.6	27 37.0	3 28.9	17 54.2	24 07.0
25 Tu	22 19 17	6 20 30	20 40 23	26 37 43	6 28.3	7 32.0	20 23.1	6 12.7	9 47.8	18 42.0	27 43.1	3 31.1	17 56.5	24 08.6
26 W	22 23 14	7 20 52	2♈34 14	8♈30 08	6 16.5	6 27.5	21 30.8	6 54.1	10 10.6	18 53.5	27 49.1	3 33.3	17 58.7	24 10.1
27 Th	22 27 10	8 21 12	14 25 41	20 21 10	6 05.8	5 22.5	22 38.2	7 35.5	10 33.4	19 04.8	27 55.1	3 35.6	18 01.0	24 11.7
28 F	22 31 07	9 21 30	26 16 56	2♉13 21	5 57.2	4 18.6	23 45.5	8 16.9	10 56.2	19 16.0	28 01.1	3 37.9	18 03.2	24 13.2
29 Sa	22 35 03	10 21 46	8♉10 53	14 10 00	5 51.2	3 17.3	24 52.5	8 58.3	11 18.9	19 27.2	28 06.9	3 40.2	18 05.5	24 14.8

Astro Data	Planet Ingress	Last Aspect	☽ Ingress	Last Aspect	☽ Ingress	☽ Phases & Eclipses	Astro Data
Dy Hr Mn	Dy Hr Mn	Dy Hr Mn	Dy Hr Mn	Dy Hr Mn	Dy Hr Mn	Dy Hr Mn	
☽0N 3 4:52	♂ ♐ 3 9:39	2 2:15 ♂ △	♈ 2 4:02	31 15:11 ☿ ✱	♉ 1 0:29	3 4:47 ☽ 12♈15	1 January 2020
♅D 11 1:50	♀ ♓ 13 18:40	4 1:19 ♇ □	♉ 4 16:16	3 11:29 ☿ □	♊ 3 11:30	10 19:22 ○ 20♋00	Julian Day # 43830
♄☌♇ 12 17:00	☿ ♒ 16 18:32	6 12:09 ♇ △	♊ 7 2:12	5 14:21 ♀ □	♋ 5 19:04	10 19:11 • A 0.895	SVP 4♓59'06"
☽0S 16 12:13	☉ ♒ 20 14:56	8 22:17 ♀ △	♋ 9 8:44	7 15:44 ♄ ☍	♌ 7 22:46	17 13:00 ☾ 26♎52	GC 27♐07.1 ⚴ 23♐04.0
☽0N 30 12:19	⚳ ♒ 31 8:02	10 23:59 ♇ ☍	♌ 11 12:17	9 16:10 ♂ △	♍ 9 23:40	24 21:43 ● 4♒22	Eris 23♈13.8R ⚵ 17♎27.9
		13 13:43 ♀ ☍	♍ 13 14:08	11 18:27 ♂ □	♎ 11 23:38		⚷ 1♈36.3 ⚶ 12♉06.9
♀0N 8 16:26	☿ ♓ 3 11:39	15 12:13 ♀ △	♎ 15 15:44	13 21:41 ♂ ✱	♏ 14 0:39	2 1:43 ☽ 12♉40	☽ Mean ☊ 8♋12.7
☽0S 12 18:54	♀ ♈ 7 20:04	17 13:00 ☉ □	♏ 17 18:22	15 22:21 ♄ ✱	♐ 16 4:08	9 7:34 ○ 20♌00	
☿R 17 0:53	♂ ♑ 16 11:34	19 21:23 ☉ ✱	♐ 19 22:42	18 9:04 ☉ ✱	♑ 18 10:38	15 22:18 ☾ 26♏41	1 February 2020
♃✱♆ 20 15:57	☉ ♓ 19 4:58	21 4:47 ♆ □	♑ 22 5:01	20 14:19 ♄ ☌	♒ 20 19:43	23 15:33 ● 4♓29	Julian Day # 43861
☽0N 26 18:30		24 2:10 ♄ ☌	♒ 24 13:22	22 4:09 ♀ ✱	♓ 23 6:38		SVP 4♓59'01"
		25 19:08 ☿ ☌	♓ 26 23:45	25 14:13 ♄ ✱	♈ 25 18:48		GC 27♐07.2 ⚴ 5♑31.7
		29 1:10 ♄ ✱	♈ 29 11:52	28 3:26 ♄ □	♉ 28 7:31		Eris 23♈15.8 ⚵ 21♎29.5
							⚷ 2♈32.6 ⚶ 15♉46.7
							☽ Mean ☊ 6♋34.2

March 2020 LONGITUDE

Day	Sid.Time	☉	0 hr ☽	Noon ☽	True ☊	☿	♀	♂	⚳	♃	♄	♅	♆	♇
1 Su	22 39 00	11♓22 01	20♉11 12	26♉15 05	5♋47.8	2♓19.7	25♈59.3	9♑39.8	11♒41.5	19♑38.2	28♑12.8	3♉42.6	18♓07.7	24♑16.3
2 M	22 42 56	12 22 13	2♊22 12	8♊33 12	5D46.6	1R26.9	27 05.9	10 21.2	12 04.1	19 49.2	28 18.6	3 45.0	18 10.0	24 17.7
3 Tu	22 46 53	13 22 23	14 48 40	21 09 16	5 46.7	0 39.7	28 12.3	11 02.7	12 26.6	20 00.0	28 24.3	3 47.4	18 12.3	24 19.2
4 W	22 50 49	14 22 31	27 35 34	4♋08 07	5R47.1	29♒58.7	29 18.4	11 44.2	12 49.1	20 10.8	28 30.0	3 49.9	18 14.6	24 20.6
5 Th	22 54 46	15 22 37	10♋47 26	17 33 53	5 46.6	29 24.2	0♉24.3	12 25.7	13 11.5	20 21.5	28 35.6	3 52.4	18 16.8	24 22.0
6 F	22 58 43	16 22 41	24 27 45	1♌29 08	5 44.1	28 56.5	1 29.9	13 07.2	13 33.9	20 32.1	28 41.2	3 55.0	18 19.1	24 23.4
7 Sa	23 02 39	17 22 42	8♌37 56	15 53 52	5 39.1	28 35.6	2 35.3	13 48.7	13 56.2	20 42.6	28 46.7	3 57.6	18 21.4	24 24.8
8 Su	23 06 36	18 22 42	23 16 25	0♍44 48	5 31.5	28 21.5	3 40.3	14 30.2	14 18.5	20 52.9	28 52.1	4 00.2	18 23.7	24 26.1
9 M	23 10 32	19 22 40	8♍18 01	15 54 53	5 21.7	28D14.1	4 45.1	15 11.8	14 40.6	21 03.2	28 57.5	4 02.8	18 25.9	24 27.5
10 Tu	23 14 29	20 22 35	23 34 02	1♎14 00	5 10.8	28 13.1	5 49.6	15 53.3	15 02.8	21 13.4	29 02.8	4 05.5	18 28.2	24 28.8
11 W	23 18 25	21 22 29	8♎53 19	16 30 33	5 00.2	28 18.2	6 53.9	16 34.9	15 24.8	21 23.5	29 08.1	4 08.2	18 30.5	24 30.0
12 Th	23 22 22	22 22 21	24 04 21	1♏33 33	4 51.0	28 29.2	7 57.8	17 16.5	15 46.8	21 33.4	29 13.2	4 11.0	18 32.8	24 31.3
13 F	23 26 18	23 22 11	8♏57 14	16 14 38	4 44.3	28 45.8	9 01.4	17 58.1	16 08.7	21 43.3	29 18.4	4 13.7	18 35.0	24 32.5
14 Sa	23 30 15	24 21 59	23 25 18	0♐28 57	4 40.1	29 07.7	10 04.7	18 39.7	16 30.6	21 53.0	29 23.4	4 16.6	18 37.3	24 33.7
15 Su	23 34 11	25 21 46	7♐25 32	14 15 09	4D38.4	29 34.5	11 07.7	19 21.3	16 52.4	22 02.6	29 28.4	4 19.4	18 39.6	24 34.9
16 M	23 38 08	26 21 32	20 58 06	27 34 44	4R38.0	0♓05.9	12 10.3	20 03.0	17 14.1	22 12.2	29 33.4	4 22.3	18 41.9	24 36.0
17 Tu	23 42 05	27 21 15	4♑05 29	10♑30 53	4 38.0	0 41.7	13 12.7	20 44.6	17 35.8	22 21.6	29 38.2	4 25.1	18 44.1	24 37.2
18 W	23 46 01	28 20 57	16 51 28	23 07 44	4 37.0	1 21.6	14 14.6	21 26.3	17 57.4	22 30.9	29 43.0	4 28.1	18 46.4	24 38.3
19 Th	23 49 58	29 20 37	29 20 15	5♒29 30	4 33.9	2 05.3	15 16.2	22 07.9	18 18.9	22 40.0	29 47.8	4 31.0	18 48.6	24 39.4
20 F	23 53 54	0♈20 16	11♒35 58	17 40 05	4 28.1	2 52.6	16 17.5	22 49.6	18 40.3	22 49.1	29 52.4	4 34.0	18 50.9	24 40.4
21 Sa	23 57 51	1 19 52	23 42 14	29 42 47	4 19.2	3 43.3	17 18.3	23 31.3	19 01.7	22 58.0	29 57.0	4 37.0	18 53.1	24 41.4
22 Su	0 01 47	2 19 26	5♓42 01	11♓40 12	4 07.5	4 37.1	18 18.8	24 13.0	19 23.0	23 06.8	0♒01.5	4 40.0	18 55.3	24 42.4
23 M	0 05 44	3 18 59	17 37 35	23 34 21	3 53.8	5 33.9	19 18.8	24 54.7	19 44.2	23 15.5	0 05.9	4 43.0	18 57.6	24 43.4
24 Tu	0 09 40	4 18 29	29 30 41	5♈26 45	3 39.0	6 33.5	20 18.5	25 36.4	20 05.3	23 24.0	0 10.3	4 46.1	18 59.8	24 44.3
25 W	0 13 37	5 17 58	11♈22 41	17 18 41	3 24.3	7 35.8	21 17.7	26 18.1	20 26.4	23 32.4	0 14.6	4 49.2	19 02.0	24 45.3
26 Th	0 17 34	6 17 24	23 14 54	29 11 31	3 11.0	8 40.6	22 16.4	26 59.7	20 47.3	23 40.7	0 18.8	4 52.3	19 04.2	24 46.1
27 F	0 21 30	7 16 48	5♉08 46	11♉06 55	3 00.0	9 47.8	23 14.7	27 41.4	21 08.2	23 48.8	0 22.9	4 55.5	19 06.4	24 47.0
28 Sa	0 25 27	8 16 11	17 06 14	23 07 05	2 51.9	10 57.3	24 12.5	28 23.1	21 29.0	23 56.8	0 26.9	4 58.6	19 08.6	24 47.8
29 Su	0 29 23	9 15 31	29 09 49	5♊14 53	2 46.8	12 08.9	25 09.8	29 04.8	21 49.7	24 04.7	0 30.9	5 01.8	19 10.7	24 48.6
30 M	0 33 20	10 14 48	11♊22 44	17 33 54	2 44.3	13 22.6	26 06.6	29 46.6	22 10.3	24 12.5	0 34.8	5 05.0	19 12.9	24 49.4
31 Tu	0 37 16	11 14 04	23 48 53	0♋08 16	2 43.6	14 38.4	27 02.9	0♒28.3	22 30.8	24 20.1	0 38.6	5 08.2	19 15.1	24 50.2

April 2020 LONGITUDE

Day	Sid.Time	☉	0 hr ☽	Noon ☽	True ☊	☿	♀	♂	⚳	♃	♄	♅	♆	♇
1 W	0 41 13	12♈13 17	6♋32 36	13♋02 27	2♋43.6	15♓56.0	27♉58.6	1♒10.0	22♒51.2	24♑27.5	0♒42.3	5♉11.4	19♓17.2	24♑50.9
2 Th	0 45 09	13 12 27	19 38 19	26 20 40	2R43.1	17 15.6	28 53.7	1 51.7	23 11.5	24 34.8	0 46.0	5 14.7	19 19.3	24 51.6
3 F	0 49 06	14 11 36	3♌09 53	10♌06 13	2 41.0	18 36.9	29 48.3	2 33.4	23 31.8	24 42.0	0 49.5	5 17.9	19 21.5	24 52.3
4 Sa	0 53 03	15 10 42	17 09 47	24 20 31	2 36.5	20 00.0	0♊42.2	3 15.1	23 51.9	24 49.0	0 53.0	5 21.2	19 23.6	24 52.9
5 Su	0 56 59	16 09 45	1♍38 07	9♍02 05	2 29.4	21 24.8	1 35.5	3 56.8	24 11.9	24 55.9	0 56.4	5 24.5	19 25.6	24 53.5
6 M	1 00 56	17 08 47	16 31 40	24 05 54	2 20.1	22 51.4	2 28.1	4 38.5	24 31.8	25 02.6	0 59.7	5 27.8	19 27.7	24 54.1
7 Tu	1 04 52	18 07 46	1♎43 35	9♎23 21	2 09.6	24 19.5	3 20.0	5 20.2	24 51.7	25 09.2	1 02.9	5 31.1	19 29.8	24 54.6
8 W	1 08 49	19 06 43	17 03 47	24 43 23	1 59.2	25 49.4	4 11.2	6 01.9	25 11.4	25 15.6	1 06.0	5 34.5	19 31.8	24 55.1
9 Th	1 12 45	20 05 38	2♏20 41	9♏54 21	1 50.1	27 20.8	5 01.7	6 43.6	25 31.0	25 21.9	1 09.1	5 37.8	19 33.9	24 55.6
10 F	1 16 42	21 04 32	17 23 12	24 46 15	1 43.3	28 53.8	5 51.4	7 25.3	25 50.5	25 28.0	1 12.0	5 41.2	19 35.9	24 56.1
11 Sa	1 20 38	22 03 23	2♐02 46	9♐12 12	1 39.0	0♈28.5	6 40.3	8 07.0	26 09.9	25 34.0	1 14.9	5 44.6	19 37.9	24 56.5
12 Su	1 24 35	23 02 13	16 14 18	23 08 59	1D37.2	2 04.7	7 28.4	8 48.7	26 29.3	25 39.8	1 17.7	5 47.9	19 39.9	24 56.9
13 M	1 28 32	24 01 01	29 56 22	6♑36 41	1 37.0	3 42.5	8 15.7	9 30.4	26 48.4	25 45.5	1 20.4	5 51.3	19 41.8	24 57.3
14 Tu	1 32 28	24 59 47	13♑10 21	19 37 50	1R37.4	5 21.9	9 02.1	10 12.1	27 07.5	25 51.0	1 23.0	5 54.7	19 43.8	24 57.7
15 W	1 36 25	25 58 32	25 59 39	2♒16 24	1 37.3	7 02.9	9 47.6	10 53.8	27 26.5	25 56.3	1 25.5	5 58.1	19 45.7	24 58.0
16 Th	1 40 21	26 57 15	8♒28 39	14 37 01	1 35.7	8 45.4	10 32.1	11 35.5	27 45.3	26 01.5	1 27.9	6 01.6	19 47.6	24 58.3
17 F	1 44 18	27 55 56	20 42 05	26 44 24	1 31.9	10 29.6	11 15.7	12 17.1	28 04.1	26 06.5	1 30.3	6 05.0	19 49.5	24 58.5
18 Sa	1 48 14	28 54 35	2♓44 30	8♓42 52	1 25.5	12 15.3	11 58.3	12 58.8	28 22.7	26 11.3	1 32.5	6 08.4	19 51.4	24 58.8
19 Su	1 52 11	29 53 13	14 39 58	20 36 11	1 16.8	14 02.7	12 39.8	13 40.4	28 41.1	26 16.0	1 34.6	6 11.8	19 53.3	24 59.0
20 M	1 56 07	0♉51 49	26 31 53	2♈27 24	1 06.3	15 51.7	13 20.2	14 22.1	28 59.5	26 20.4	1 36.7	6 15.3	19 55.1	24 59.1
21 Tu	2 00 04	1 50 23	8♈23 00	14 18 57	0 54.8	17 42.3	13 59.5	15 03.7	29 17.7	26 24.8	1 38.6	6 18.7	19 56.9	24 59.3
22 W	2 04 00	2 48 55	20 15 27	26 12 42	0 43.4	19 34.5	14 37.6	15 45.3	29 35.8	26 28.9	1 40.5	6 22.2	19 58.7	24 59.4
23 Th	2 07 57	3 47 26	2♉10 53	8♉10 10	0 33.1	21 28.4	15 14.5	16 26.9	29 53.8	26 32.9	1 42.2	6 25.6	20 00.5	24 59.5
24 F	2 11 54	4 45 54	14 10 43	20 12 42	0 24.6	23 23.9	15 50.2	17 08.4	0♓11.6	26 36.7	1 43.9	6 29.1	20 02.2	24 59.5
25 Sa	2 15 50	5 44 21	26 16 20	2♊21 48	0 18.5	25 21.0	16 24.5	17 49.9	0 29.3	26 40.3	1 45.5	6 32.5	20 04.0	24R59.5
26 Su	2 19 47	6 42 46	8♊29 21	14 39 15	0 15.0	27 19.8	16 57.4	18 31.5	0 46.9	26 43.7	1 47.0	6 36.0	20 05.7	24 59.5
27 M	2 23 43	7 41 08	20 51 48	27 07 20	0D13.6	29 20.1	17 28.9	19 13.0	1 04.3	26 47.0	1 48.3	6 39.4	20 07.4	24 59.5
28 Tu	2 27 40	8 39 29	3♋26 11	9♋48 45	0 14.0	1♉21.9	17 58.9	19 54.4	1 21.5	26 50.1	1 49.6	6 42.9	20 09.1	24 59.4
29 W	2 31 36	9 37 48	16 15 26	22 46 37	0 15.0	3 25.1	18 27.4	20 35.9	1 38.6	26 53.0	1 50.8	6 46.3	20 10.7	24 59.3
30 Th	2 35 33	10 36 04	29 22 43	6♌04 03	0R15.9	5 29.8	18 54.3	21 17.3	1 55.6	26 55.7	1 51.9	6 49.8	20 12.3	24 59.2

Astro Data

	Dy Hr Mn
☿ D	10 3:49
☽ 0S	11 4:16
☉ 0N	20 3:51
☽ 0N	25 0:14
♃☌♇	5 2:46
☽ 0S	7 15:21
☿ 0N	14 16:08
☽ 0N	21 6:27
♇ R	25 18:55

Planet Ingress

	Dy Hr Mn
☿ ♒R	4 11:09
♀ ♉	5 3:08
☿ ♓	16 7:44
☉ ♈	20 3:51
♄ ♒	22 3:59
♂ ♒	30 19:44
♀ ♊	3 17:12
☿ ♈	11 4:49
☉ ♉	19 14:47
⚳ ♓	23 20:21
☿ ♉	27 19:54

Last Aspect / ☽ Ingress (March)

Last Aspect Dy Hr Mn		☽ Ingress Dy Hr Mn
1 15:53	♄ △	♊ 1 19:22
4 2:21	♀ ⚹	♋ 4 4:26
6 7:13	♄ ☍	♌ 6 9:29
8 8:14	☿ ☍	♍ 8 10:48
10 8:33	♄ △	♎ 10 10:04
12 8:13	♄ □	♏ 12 9:29
14 10:07	♄ ⚹	♐ 14 11:10
16 9:35	☉ □	♑ 16 16:26
19 0:49	♄ ☌	♒ 19 1:17
20 9:01	♀ □	♓ 21 12:34
23 14:52	♂ ⚹	♈ 24 0:59
26 7:18	♂ □	♉ 26 13:38
28 23:06	♂ △	♊ 29 1:39
30 15:11	♆ □	♋ 31 11:44

Last Aspect / ☽ Ingress (April)

Last Aspect Dy Hr Mn		☽ Ingress Dy Hr Mn
2 16:50	♀ ⚹	♌ 2 18:27
3 19:30	☉ △	♍ 4 21:20
6 13:30	♃ △	♎ 6 21:17
8 12:51	♃ □	♏ 8 20:18
10 19:36	☿ △	♐ 10 20:36
12 11:47	☉ △	♑ 13 0:06
14 23:49	♃ ☌	♒ 15 7:38
17 14:35	☉ ⚹	♓ 17 18:31
19 23:32	♃ ⚹	♈ 20 7:01
22 12:33	♃ □	♉ 22 19:37
25 0:44	♃ △	♊ 25 7:21
27 17:01	☿ ⚹	♋ 27 17:29
29 19:31	♃ ☍	♌ 30 1:07

☽ Phases & Eclipses

Dy Hr Mn	
2 19:59	☽ 12♊42
9 17:49	○ 19♍37
16 9:35	☾ 26♐16
24 9:29	● 4♈12
1 10:22	☽ 12♋09
8 2:36	○ 18♎44
14 22:57	☾ 25♑27
23 2:27	● 3♉24
30 20:39	☽ 10♌57

Astro Data

1 March 2020
Julian Day # 43890
SVP 4♓58'58"
GC 27♐07.3 ⚴ 15♑58.1
Eris 23♈26.5 ⚵ 20♎09.0R
⚷ 3♈58.3 ⚶ 23♉23.5
☽ Mean ☊ 5♋02.0

1 April 2020
Julian Day # 43921
SVP 4♓58'54"
GC 27♐07.3 ⚴ 24♑56.0
Eris 23♈44.6 ⚵ 13♎51.4R
⚷ 5♈46.1 ⚶ 4♊08.1
☽ Mean ☊ 3♋23.5

LONGITUDE May 2020

Day	Sid.Time	☉	0 hr ☽	Noon ☽	True ☊	☿	♀	♂	⚳	♃	♄	♅	♆	♇
1 F	2 39 30	11♉34 19	12♌50 58	19♌43 41	0♋15.6	7♉35.7	19♊19.5	21♒58.7	2♓12.4	26♑58.3	1♒52.9	6♉53.2	20♓13.9	24♑59.1
2 Sa	2 43 26	12 32 31	26 42 20	3♍46 56	0R13.7	9 42.9	19 43.0	22 40.0	2 29.1	27 00.6	1 53.8	6 56.7	20 15.5	24R58.9
3 Su	2 47 23	13 30 41	10♍57 21	18 13 16	0 09.9	11 51.0	20 04.7	23 21.4	2 45.6	27 02.8	1 54.6	7 00.1	20 17.0	24 58.7
4 M	2 51 19	14 28 49	25 34 12	2♎59 29	0 04.4	14 00.0	20 24.5	24 02.7	3 02.0	27 04.8	1 55.3	7 03.5	20 18.6	24 58.4
5 Tu	2 55 16	15 26 56	10♎28 15	17 59 31	29♊58.0	16 09.6	20 42.5	24 44.0	3 18.2	27 06.6	1 55.9	7 07.0	20 20.0	24 58.2
6 W	2 59 12	16 25 00	25 32 07	3♏04 52	29 51.4	18 19.6	20 58.4	25 25.2	3 34.2	27 08.2	1 56.4	7 10.4	20 21.5	24 57.9
7 Th	3 03 09	17 23 03	10♏36 32	18 05 54	29 45.7	20 29.9	21 12.4	26 06.5	3 50.1	27 09.6	1 56.8	7 13.8	20 23.0	24 57.6
8 F	3 07 05	18 21 04	25 31 50	2♐53 20	29 41.5	22 40.0	21 24.2	26 47.7	4 05.8	27 10.9	1 57.1	7 17.2	20 24.4	24 57.2
9 Sa	3 11 02	19 19 04	10♐09 33	17 19 49	29D39.1	24 49.8	21 33.9	27 28.8	4 21.4	27 11.9	1 57.3	7 20.6	20 25.8	24 56.8
10 Su	3 14 58	20 17 02	24 23 39	1♑20 45	29 38.5	26 58.9	21 41.4	28 10.0	4 36.7	27 12.8	1R57.4	7 24.0	20 27.2	24 56.4
11 M	3 18 55	21 14 59	8♑11 02	14 54 31	29 39.2	29 07.0	21 46.7	28 51.1	4 51.9	27 13.5	1 57.4	7 27.4	20 28.5	24 56.0
12 Tu	3 22 52	22 12 55	21 31 24	28 02 00	29 40.7	1♊14.0	21R49.7	29 32.1	5 07.0	27 14.0	1 57.3	7 30.8	20 29.8	24 55.5
13 W	3 26 48	23 10 49	4♒26 42	10♒45 59	29 42.1	3 19.4	21 50.4	0♓13.1	5 21.8	27 14.3	1 57.2	7 34.1	20 31.1	24 55.1
14 Th	3 30 45	24 08 42	17 00 22	23 10 25	29R42.8	5 23.1	21 48.7	0 54.1	5 36.5	27R14.4	1 56.9	7 37.5	20 32.4	24 54.6
15 F	3 34 41	25 06 34	29 16 43	5♓19 51	29 42.2	7 24.7	21 44.6	1 35.1	5 51.0	27 14.3	1 56.5	7 40.8	20 33.6	24 54.0
16 Sa	3 38 38	26 04 24	11♓20 25	17 18 57	29 40.2	9 24.2	21 38.1	2 16.0	6 05.3	27 14.1	1 56.0	7 44.1	20 34.8	24 53.4
17 Su	3 42 34	27 02 14	23 16 02	29 12 10	29 36.7	11 21.2	21 29.2	2 56.8	6 19.4	27 13.6	1 55.5	7 47.4	20 36.0	24 52.9
18 M	3 46 31	28 00 02	5♈07 50	11♈03 30	29 32.1	13 15.7	21 17.8	3 37.6	6 33.3	27 13.0	1 54.8	7 50.7	20 37.1	24 52.2
19 Tu	3 50 27	28 57 49	16 59 35	22 56 26	29 26.9	15 07.5	21 04.1	4 18.3	6 47.0	27 12.1	1 54.0	7 54.0	20 38.2	24 51.6
20 W	3 54 24	29 55 34	28 54 25	4♉53 48	29 21.6	16 56.5	20 48.0	4 59.0	7 00.5	27 11.1	1 53.2	7 57.3	20 39.3	24 50.9
21 Th	3 58 21	0♊53 19	10♉54 53	16 57 52	29 16.9	18 42.6	20 29.5	5 39.6	7 13.8	27 09.9	1 52.2	8 00.5	20 40.3	24 50.2
22 F	4 02 17	1 51 02	23 02 57	29 10 20	29 13.1	20 25.8	20 08.8	6 20.1	7 26.9	27 08.5	1 51.2	8 03.8	20 41.4	24 49.5
23 Sa	4 06 14	2 48 44	5♊20 09	11♊32 33	29 10.6	22 05.8	19 45.9	7 00.6	7 39.8	27 06.9	1 50.0	8 07.0	20 42.4	24 48.8
24 Su	4 10 10	3 46 25	17 47 40	24 05 37	29D09.5	23 42.8	19 20.8	7 41.1	7 52.5	27 05.1	1 48.8	8 10.2	20 43.3	24 48.0
25 M	4 14 07	4 44 04	0♋26 32	6♋50 34	29 09.6	25 16.7	18 53.7	8 21.4	8 04.9	27 03.1	1 47.5	8 13.4	20 44.3	24 47.2
26 Tu	4 18 03	5 41 42	13 17 50	19 48 28	29 10.6	26 47.3	18 24.6	9 01.7	8 17.2	27 01.0	1 46.0	8 16.6	20 45.2	24 46.4
27 W	4 22 00	6 39 19	26 22 38	3♌00 27	29 12.0	28 14.7	17 53.9	9 41.9	8 29.2	26 58.7	1 44.5	8 19.7	20 46.1	24 45.6
28 Th	4 25 57	7 36 54	9♌42 04	16 27 37	29 13.4	29 38.9	17 21.5	10 22.0	8 41.0	26 56.1	1 42.9	8 22.8	20 46.9	24 44.7
29 F	4 29 53	8 34 28	23 17 10	0♍10 47	29R14.3	0♋59.7	16 47.7	11 02.1	8 52.5	26 53.4	1 41.2	8 25.9	20 47.7	24 43.9
30 Sa	4 33 50	9 32 00	7♍08 28	14 10 08	29 14.4	2 17.2	16 12.7	11 42.1	9 03.9	26 50.6	1 39.4	8 29.0	20 48.5	24 43.0
31 Su	4 37 46	10 29 31	21 15 40	28 24 49	29 13.7	3 31.3	15 36.6	12 21.9	9 14.9	26 47.5	1 37.6	8 32.1	20 49.2	24 42.0

LONGITUDE June 2020

Day	Sid.Time	☉	0 hr ☽	Noon ☽	True ☊	☿	♀	♂	⚳	♃	♄	♅	♆	♇
1 M	4 41 43	11♊27 00	5♎37 14	12♎52 30	29♊12.2	4♋42.0	14♊59.8	13♓01.8	9♓25.8	26♑44.3	1♒35.6	8♉35.1	20♓50.0	24♑41.1
2 Tu	4 45 39	12 24 28	20 10 03	27 29 14	29R10.3	5 49.1	14R22.4	13 41.5	9 36.4	26R40.8	1R33.6	8 38.1	20 50.6	24R40.1
3 W	4 49 36	13 21 55	4♏49 22	12♏09 37	29 08.2	6 52.7	13 44.7	14 21.1	9 46.8	26 37.3	1 31.4	8 41.1	20 51.3	24 39.1
4 Th	4 53 32	14 19 21	19 29 10	26 47 12	29 06.5	7 52.7	13 06.9	15 00.7	9 56.9	26 33.5	1 29.2	8 44.1	20 51.9	24 38.1
5 F	4 57 29	15 16 46	4♐02 52	11♐15 24	29 05.3	8 48.9	12 29.4	15 40.2	10 06.8	26 29.6	1 26.9	8 47.0	20 52.5	24 37.1
6 Sa	5 01 26	16 14 10	18 24 06	25 28 22	29D04.8	9 41.4	11 52.2	16 19.6	10 16.4	26 25.5	1 24.5	8 49.9	20 53.1	24 36.1
7 Su	5 05 22	17 11 33	2♑27 41	9♑21 41	29 05.0	10 30.0	11 15.8	16 58.9	10 25.8	26 21.2	1 22.1	8 52.8	20 53.6	24 35.0
8 M	5 09 19	18 08 55	16 10 06	22 52 48	29 05.6	11 14.6	10 40.2	17 38.1	10 34.9	26 16.8	1 19.5	8 55.7	20 54.1	24 33.9
9 Tu	5 13 15	19 06 17	29 29 47	6♒01 10	29 06.5	11 55.3	10 05.8	18 17.2	10 43.7	26 12.3	1 16.9	8 58.5	20 54.6	24 32.8
10 W	5 17 12	20 03 38	12♒27 07	18 47 56	29 07.4	12 31.7	9 32.7	18 56.2	10 52.3	26 07.5	1 14.2	9 01.3	20 55.0	24 31.7
11 Th	5 21 08	21 00 59	25 04 00	1♓15 44	29 08.1	13 04.0	9 01.1	19 35.1	11 00.6	26 02.6	1 11.4	9 04.1	20 55.4	24 30.6
12 F	5 25 05	21 58 19	7♓23 36	13 28 08	29R08.5	13 31.9	8 31.2	20 13.8	11 08.6	25 57.6	1 08.6	9 06.8	20 55.7	24 29.4
13 Sa	5 29 01	22 55 38	19 29 53	25 29 25	29 08.6	13 55.5	8 03.1	20 52.5	11 16.4	25 52.4	1 05.7	9 09.6	20 56.1	24 28.2
14 Su	5 32 58	23 52 57	1♈27 16	7♈24 03	29 08.4	14 14.6	7 37.1	21 31.0	11 23.8	25 47.1	1 02.7	9 12.2	20 56.4	24 27.0
15 M	5 36 55	24 50 16	13 20 19	19 16 36	29 08.0	14 29.2	7 13.1	22 09.5	11 31.0	25 41.6	0 59.6	9 14.9	20 56.6	24 25.8
16 Tu	5 40 51	25 47 34	25 13 27	1♉11 21	29 07.6	14 39.2	6 51.3	22 47.8	11 37.9	25 35.9	0 56.4	9 17.5	20 56.9	24 24.6
17 W	5 44 48	26 44 52	7♉10 48	13 12 14	29 07.3	14R44.7	6 31.7	23 25.9	11 44.5	25 30.2	0 53.2	9 20.1	20 57.1	24 23.4
18 Th	5 48 44	27 42 10	19 16 02	25 22 34	29 07.0	14 45.6	6 14.5	24 03.9	11 50.7	25 24.3	0 49.9	9 22.7	20 57.2	24 22.1
19 F	5 52 41	28 39 27	1♊32 07	7♊44 59	29D07.0	14 42.1	5 59.6	24 41.8	11 56.7	25 18.3	0 46.6	9 25.2	20 57.4	24 20.9
20 Sa	5 56 37	29 36 44	14 01 20	20 21 21	29R07.0	14 34.1	5 47.1	25 19.5	12 02.4	25 12.1	0 43.2	9 27.7	20 57.5	24 19.6
21 Su	6 00 34	0♋34 01	26 45 08	3♋12 43	29 07.0	14 21.9	5 37.0	25 57.1	12 07.8	25 05.9	0 39.7	9 30.2	20 57.6	24 18.3
22 M	6 04 30	1 31 17	9♋44 07	16 19 19	29 06.9	14 05.5	5 29.2	26 34.5	12 12.8	24 59.5	0 36.2	9 32.6	20R57.6	24 17.0
23 Tu	6 08 27	2 28 33	22 58 11	29 40 39	29 06.7	13 45.3	5 23.9	27 11.8	12 17.6	24 53.0	0 32.6	9 35.0	20 57.6	24 15.7
24 W	6 12 24	3 25 48	6♌26 32	13♌15 39	29 06.2	13 21.5	5D20.9	27 48.8	12 22.0	24 46.4	0 28.9	9 37.4	20 57.6	24 14.4
25 Th	6 16 20	4 23 03	20 07 50	27 02 49	29 05.7	12 54.5	5 20.2	28 25.8	12 26.1	24 39.6	0 25.2	9 39.7	20 57.5	24 13.0
26 F	6 20 17	5 20 17	4♍00 25	11♍00 21	29 05.2	12 24.7	5 21.9	29 02.5	12 29.9	24 32.8	0 21.5	9 42.0	20 57.4	24 11.7
27 Sa	6 24 13	6 17 30	18 02 22	25 06 12	29D04.7	11 52.5	5 25.8	29 39.1	12 33.3	24 25.9	0 17.7	9 44.2	20 57.3	24 10.3
28 Su	6 28 10	7 14 43	2♎11 34	9♎18 12	29 04.6	11 18.4	5 31.9	0♈15.5	12 36.4	24 18.9	0 13.8	9 46.4	20 57.1	24 09.0
29 M	6 32 06	8 11 55	16 25 45	23 33 56	29 04.9	10 43.1	5 40.1	0 51.7	12 39.2	24 11.9	0 09.9	9 48.6	20 56.9	24 07.6
30 Tu	6 36 03	9 09 07	0♏42 24	7♏50 46	29 05.5	10 07.1	5 50.5	1 27.7	12 41.7	24 04.7	0 05.9	9 50.8	20 56.7	24 06.2

Astro Data

	Dy Hr Mn
☽0S	5 1:59
♄ R	11 4:10
♀ R	13 6:46
♃ R	14 14:33
☽0N	18 13:32
☽0S	1 10:27
☽0N	14 21:17
☿ R	18 4:59
♆ R	23 4:32
♀ D	25 6:49
☽0S	28 16:31
♃☌♇	30 5:48

Planet Ingress

	Dy Hr Mn
☊ ♊R	5 4:41
☿ ♊	11 21:59
♂ ♓	13 4:18
☉ ♊	20 13:50
☿ ♋	28 18:10
☉ ♋	20 21:45
♂ ♈	28 1:46

Last Aspect / ☽ Ingress (May)

Last Aspect Dy Hr Mn		☽ Ingress Dy Hr Mn
1 16:05	♂ ☍	♍ 2 5:36
4 2:26	♃ △	♎ 4 7:11
6 2:32	♃ □	♏ 6 7:06
8 2:40	♃ ⚹	♐ 8 7:16
10 6:12	♂ ⚹	♑ 10 9:40
12 10:31	♃ ☌	♒ 12 15:40
14 14:04	☉ □	♓ 15 1:26
17 8:00	♃ ⚹	♈ 17 13:37
19 20:34	♃ □	♉ 20 2:12
22 8:02	♃ △	♊ 22 13:37
24 11:11	☿ ☌	♋ 24 23:10
27 1:07	♃ ☍	♌ 27 6:34
28 13:31	♀ ⚹	♍ 29 11:41
31 9:18	♃ △	♎ 31 14:39

Last Aspect / ☽ Ingress (June)

Last Aspect Dy Hr Mn		☽ Ingress Dy Hr Mn
2 10:41	♃ □	♏ 2 16:07
4 11:38	♃ ⚹	♐ 4 17:18
6 4:12	♆ □	♑ 6 19:45
8 18:07	♃ ☌	♒ 9 0:55
10 14:36	☉ △	♓ 11 9:33
13 12:46	♃ ⚹	♈ 13 21:04
16 0:51	♃ □	♉ 16 9:37
18 12:03	♃ △	♊ 18 21:01
20 21:49	♂ □	♋ 21 6:03
23 7:21	♂ △	♌ 23 12:34
24 5:35	♅ □	♍ 25 17:06
27 20:03	♂ ☍	♎ 27 20:18
29 13:03	♃ □	♏ 29 22:49

☽ Phases & Eclipses

Dy Hr Mn		
7 10:46	○	17♏20
14 14:04	☾	24♒14
22 17:40	●	2♊05
30 3:31	☽	9♍12
5 19:14	○	15♐34
5 19:26	•	A 0.568
13 6:25	☾	22♓42
21 6:43	●	0♋21
21 6:41:15	•	A 00'38"
28 8:17	☽	7♎06

Astro Data

1 May 2020
Julian Day # 43951
SVP 4♓58'51"
GC 27♐07.4 ⚳ 0♒09.1
Eris 24♈04.1 ⚵ 7♎41.1R
⚷ 7♈26.0 ⚶ 15♊58.4
☽ Mean ☊ 1♋48.2

1 June 2020
Julian Day # 43982
SVP 4♓58'46"
GC 27♐07.5 ⚳ 0♒10.1R
Eris 24♈21.5 ⚵ 5♎53.1
⚷ 8♈45.1 ⚶ 29♊01.0
☽ Mean ☊ 0♋09.7

July 2020 LONGITUDE

Day	Sid.Time	☉	0 hr ☽	Noon ☽	True ☊	☿	♀	♂	⚳	♃	♄	♅	♆	♇
1 W	6 39 59	10♋06 19	14♏58 41	22♏05 45	29♊06.4	9♋30.9	6♊02.9	2♈03.6	12♓43.8	23♑57.5	0♒02.0	9♉52.8	20♓56.5	24♑04.8
2 Th	6 43 56	11 03 30	29 11 32	6♐15 38	29 07.2	8R 55.4	6 17.4	2 39.2	12 45.6	23R 50.2	29♑57.9	9 54.9	20R 56.2	24R 03.4
3 F	6 47 53	12 00 41	13♐17 38	20 17 05	29R 07.8	8 20.9	6 33.8	3 14.7	12 47.0	23 42.8	29R 53.8	9 56.9	20 55.9	24 02.0
4 Sa	6 51 49	12 57 52	27 13 37	4♑06 51	29 07.9	7 48.2	6 52.0	3 49.9	12 48.1	23 35.4	29 49.7	9 58.9	20 55.5	24 00.6
5 Su	6 55 46	13 55 03	10♑56 26	17 42 04	29 07.3	7 17.9	7 12.1	4 25.0	12 48.9	23 27.9	29 45.6	10 00.8	20 55.1	23 59.2
6 M	6 59 42	14 52 14	24 23 33	1♒00 40	29 05.9	6 50.4	7 34.0	4 59.8	12R 49.3	23 20.4	29 41.4	10 02.7	20 54.7	23 57.8
7 Tu	7 03 39	15 49 25	7♒33 21	14 01 32	29 03.9	6 26.3	7 57.6	5 34.4	12 49.4	23 12.8	29 37.2	10 04.6	20 54.3	23 56.3
8 W	7 07 35	16 46 36	20 25 18	26 44 44	29 01.4	6 06.0	8 22.9	6 08.8	12 49.1	23 05.2	29 32.9	10 06.4	20 53.8	23 54.9
9 Th	7 11 32	17 43 48	3♓00 03	9♓11 31	28 58.8	5 49.9	8 49.7	6 43.0	12 48.4	22 57.6	29 28.7	10 08.2	20 53.3	23 53.5
10 F	7 15 29	18 40 59	15 19 26	21 24 13	28 56.4	5 38.2	9 18.1	7 16.9	12 47.4	22 49.9	29 24.4	10 09.9	20 52.8	23 52.0
11 Sa	7 19 25	19 38 12	27 26 17	3♈26 07	28 54.7	5D 31.4	9 48.0	7 50.5	12 46.1	22 42.2	29 20.0	10 11.6	20 52.2	23 50.6
12 Su	7 23 22	20 35 24	9♈24 15	15 21 13	28D 53.8	5 29.6	10 19.3	8 24.0	12 44.3	22 34.5	29 15.7	10 13.3	20 51.6	23 49.1
13 M	7 27 18	21 32 37	21 17 36	27 13 59	28 53.8	5 33.0	10 52.0	8 57.1	12 42.3	22 26.7	29 11.3	10 14.9	20 51.0	23 47.7
14 Tu	7 31 15	22 29 51	3♉10 57	9♉09 07	28 54.6	5 41.7	11 26.0	9 30.0	12 39.8	22 19.0	29 06.9	10 16.4	20 50.4	23 46.2
15 W	7 35 11	23 27 05	15 09 03	21 11 20	28 56.1	5 55.8	12 01.2	10 02.6	12 37.0	22 11.3	29 02.5	10 17.9	20 49.7	23 44.8
16 Th	7 39 08	24 24 20	27 16 30	3♊25 03	28 57.7	6 15.4	12 37.7	10 34.9	12 33.9	22 03.5	28 58.1	10 19.4	20 49.0	23 43.3
17 F	7 43 04	25 21 36	9♊37 28	15 54 07	28 59.1	6 40.5	13 15.4	11 06.9	12 30.4	21 55.8	28 53.7	10 20.8	20 48.2	23 41.9
18 Sa	7 47 01	26 18 52	22 15 23	28 41 29	28R 59.6	7 11.1	13 54.2	11 38.6	12 26.5	21 48.1	28 49.3	10 22.2	20 47.5	23 40.4
19 Su	7 50 58	27 16 09	5♋12 38	11♋48 53	28 59.0	7 47.2	14 34.1	12 10.0	12 22.3	21 40.4	28 44.8	10 23.5	20 46.7	23 39.0
20 M	7 54 54	28 13 26	18 30 14	25 16 33	28 57.1	8 28.7	15 15.0	12 41.1	12 17.7	21 32.8	28 40.4	10 24.8	20 45.8	23 37.5
21 Tu	7 58 51	29 10 44	2♌07 37	9♌03 04	28 53.8	9 15.7	15 57.0	13 11.8	12 12.7	21 25.1	28 36.0	10 26.1	20 45.0	23 36.1
22 W	8 02 47	0♌08 02	16 02 31	23 05 26	28 49.5	10 08.0	16 39.9	13 42.2	12 07.4	21 17.6	28 31.5	10 27.3	20 44.1	23 34.6
23 Th	8 06 44	1 05 21	0♍11 15	7♍19 23	28 44.8	11 05.6	17 23.7	14 12.3	12 01.8	21 10.0	28 27.1	10 28.4	20 43.2	23 33.2
24 F	8 10 40	2 02 40	14 29 10	21 40 00	28 40.4	12 08.5	18 08.4	14 42.0	11 55.8	21 02.5	28 22.7	10 29.5	20 42.3	23 31.8
25 Sa	8 14 37	2 59 59	28 51 15	6♎02 21	28 36.8	13 16.5	18 53.9	15 11.4	11 49.5	20 55.1	28 18.2	10 30.6	20 41.3	23 30.3
26 Su	8 18 33	3 57 19	13♎12 48	20 22 09	28 34.6	14 29.5	19 40.3	15 40.4	11 42.8	20 47.7	28 13.8	10 31.6	20 40.3	23 28.9
27 M	8 22 30	4 54 39	27 30 01	4♏36 06	28D 33.8	15 47.4	20 27.5	16 09.0	11 35.8	20 40.4	28 09.4	10 32.5	20 39.3	23 27.5
28 Tu	8 26 27	5 52 00	11♏40 08	18 41 58	28 34.4	17 10.1	21 15.5	16 37.2	11 28.5	20 33.2	28 05.0	10 33.4	20 38.3	23 26.1
29 W	8 30 23	6 49 21	25 41 26	2♐38 26	28 35.7	18 37.4	22 04.2	17 05.0	11 20.8	20 26.0	28 00.7	10 34.3	20 37.2	23 24.7
30 Th	8 34 20	7 46 43	9♐32 53	16 24 45	28R 37.0	20 09.2	22 53.6	17 32.5	11 12.8	20 18.9	27 56.3	10 35.1	20 36.1	23 23.3
31 F	8 38 16	8 44 05	23 13 55	0♑00 22	28 37.5	21 45.2	23 43.7	17 59.5	11 04.5	20 11.9	27 52.0	10 35.9	20 35.0	23 21.9

August 2020 LONGITUDE

Day	Sid.Time	☉	0 hr ☽	Noon ☽	True ☊	☿	♀	♂	⚳	♃	♄	♅	♆	♇
1 Sa	8 42 13	9♌41 28	6♑44 01	13♑24 46	28♊36.5	23♋25.3	24♊34.5	18♈26.1	10♓55.9	20♑05.0	27♑47.7	10♉36.6	20♓33.9	23♑20.5
2 Su	8 46 09	10 38 51	20 02 33	26 37 16	28R 33.6	25 09.1	25 26.0	18 52.3	10R 47.0	19R 58.2	27R 43.4	10 37.3	20R 32.8	23R 19.1
3 M	8 50 06	11 36 16	3♒08 50	9♒37 10	28 28.7	26 56.4	26 18.1	19 18.1	10 37.8	19 51.5	27 39.2	10 37.9	20 31.6	23 17.8
4 Tu	8 54 02	12 33 41	16 02 12	22 23 54	28 22.1	28 46.9	27 10.8	19 43.4	10 28.4	19 44.9	27 35.0	10 38.5	20 30.4	23 16.4
5 W	8 57 59	13 31 07	28 42 15	4♓57 18	28 14.4	0♌40.2	28 04.0	20 08.3	10 18.6	19 38.4	27 30.8	10 39.0	20 29.2	23 15.1
6 Th	9 01 56	14 28 35	11♓09 09	17 17 53	28 06.1	2 35.9	28 57.9	20 32.7	10 08.5	19 32.0	27 26.6	10 39.5	20 27.9	23 13.8
7 F	9 05 52	15 26 03	23 23 45	29 26 58	27 58.3	4 33.8	29 52.3	20 56.6	9 58.2	19 25.8	27 22.5	10 39.9	20 26.7	23 12.4
8 Sa	9 09 49	16 23 33	5♈27 50	11♈26 44	27 51.7	6 33.4	0♋47.3	21 20.0	9 47.7	19 19.6	27 18.4	10 40.3	20 25.4	23 11.1
9 Su	9 13 45	17 21 04	17 24 04	23 20 19	27 46.8	8 34.4	1 42.7	21 42.9	9 36.8	19 13.6	27 14.4	10 40.6	20 24.1	23 09.8
10 M	9 17 42	18 18 36	29 15 59	5♉11 38	27 43.8	10 36.4	2 38.7	22 05.2	9 25.8	19 07.7	27 10.4	10 40.9	20 22.7	23 08.5
11 Tu	9 21 38	19 16 10	11♉07 50	17 05 12	27D 42.7	12 39.1	3 35.1	22 27.1	9 14.5	19 01.9	27 06.5	10 41.1	20 21.4	23 07.3
12 W	9 25 35	20 13 45	23 04 23	29 06 00	27 43.0	14 42.1	4 32.1	22 48.3	9 03.0	18 56.3	27 02.5	10 41.3	20 20.0	23 06.0
13 Th	9 29 31	21 11 21	5♊10 43	11♊19 09	27 44.0	16 45.2	5 29.4	23 09.1	8 51.3	18 50.8	26 58.7	10 41.4	20 18.7	23 04.8
14 F	9 33 28	22 09 00	17 31 54	23 49 31	27R 44.8	18 48.2	6 27.3	23 29.2	8 39.3	18 45.4	26 54.9	10 41.5	20 17.3	23 03.5
15 Sa	9 37 25	23 06 39	0♋12 33	6♋41 23	27 44.5	20 50.7	7 25.5	23 48.7	8 27.2	18 40.2	26 51.1	10R 41.5	20 15.9	23 02.3
16 Su	9 41 21	24 04 20	13 16 21	19 57 42	27 42.4	22 52.6	8 24.2	24 07.7	8 14.9	18 35.2	26 47.4	10 41.5	20 14.4	23 01.1
17 M	9 45 18	25 02 03	26 45 29	3♌39 37	27 37.9	24 53.8	9 23.2	24 26.0	8 02.5	18 30.3	26 43.8	10 41.4	20 13.0	22 59.9
18 Tu	9 49 14	25 59 47	10♌39 54	17 45 54	27 31.2	26 54.1	10 22.6	24 43.7	7 49.9	18 25.6	26 40.2	10 41.3	20 11.5	22 58.8
19 W	9 53 11	26 57 32	24 57 03	2♍12 37	27 22.8	28 53.3	11 22.5	25 00.7	7 37.1	18 21.0	26 36.7	10 41.1	20 10.0	22 57.6
20 Th	9 57 07	27 55 19	9♍31 44	16 53 27	27 13.5	0♍51.5	12 22.6	25 17.1	7 24.3	18 16.6	26 33.2	10 40.9	20 08.6	22 56.5
21 F	10 01 04	28 53 06	24 16 44	1♎40 33	27 04.5	2 48.4	13 23.1	25 32.7	7 11.3	18 12.3	26 29.8	10 40.6	20 07.0	22 55.4
22 Sa	10 05 00	29 50 55	9♎03 53	16 25 49	26 56.9	4 44.2	14 24.0	25 47.8	6 58.2	18 08.2	26 26.5	10 40.3	20 05.5	22 54.3
23 Su	10 08 57	0♍48 46	23 45 31	1♏02 16	26 51.4	6 38.6	15 25.2	26 02.1	6 45.1	18 04.3	26 23.2	10 39.9	20 04.0	22 53.2
24 M	10 12 53	1 46 37	8♏15 31	15 24 51	26 48.3	8 31.8	16 26.7	26 15.7	6 31.9	18 00.6	26 20.0	10 39.5	20 02.5	22 52.1
25 Tu	10 16 50	2 44 30	22 30 00	29 30 50	26D 47.2	10 23.6	17 28.5	26 28.6	6 18.6	17 57.0	26 16.9	10 39.1	20 00.9	22 51.1
26 W	10 20 47	3 42 23	6♐27 19	13♐19 32	26R 47.4	12 14.2	18 30.6	26 40.7	6 05.3	17 53.6	26 13.8	10 38.6	19 59.3	22 50.1
27 Th	10 24 43	4 40 19	20 07 35	26 51 40	26 47.7	14 03.4	19 33.1	26 52.2	5 52.0	17 50.4	26 10.8	10 38.0	19 57.8	22 49.1
28 F	10 28 40	5 38 15	3♑31 58	10♑08 42	26 47.0	15 51.3	20 35.8	27 02.8	5 38.6	17 47.4	26 07.9	10 37.4	19 56.2	22 48.1
29 Sa	10 32 36	6 36 13	16 42 05	23 12 19	26 44.3	17 37.9	21 38.8	27 12.8	5 25.3	17 44.6	26 05.1	10 36.7	19 54.6	22 47.2
30 Su	10 36 33	7 34 12	29 39 32	6♒03 55	26 38.9	19 23.2	22 42.1	27 21.9	5 12.0	17 41.9	26 02.3	10 36.0	19 53.0	22 46.2
31 M	10 40 29	8 32 12	12♒25 33	18 44 33	26 30.8	21 07.2	23 45.7	27 30.3	4 58.7	17 39.4	25 59.6	10 35.3	19 51.4	22 45.3

Astro Data (Dy Hr Mn)

Event	Dy Hr Mn
⚳R	7 4:02
♂0N	11 12:19
☽0N	12 5:03
☿D	12 8:27
☽0S	25 21:35
♃⚹♆	27 16:08
☽0N	8 12:17
♅R	15 14:28
☽0S	22 3:50

Planet Ingress (Dy Hr Mn)

Planet	Sign	Dy Hr Mn
♄	♑R	1 23:39
☉	♌	22 8:38
☿	♌	5 3:33
♀	♋	7 15:22
☿	♍	20 1:31
☉	♍	22 15:46

Last Aspect / ☽ Ingress (July)

Last Aspect Dy Hr Mn	Aspect	☽ Ingress	Dy Hr Mn
2 1:22	♄⚹	♐	2 1:22
3 13:07	♆□	♑	4 4:49
6 9:36	♄☌	♒	6 10:09
7 4:39	♅□	♓	8 18:14
11 3:50	♄⚹	♈	11 5:07
13 15:55	♄□	♉	13 17:35
16 3:22	♄△	♊	16 5:20
17 21:16	♆□	♋	18 14:25
20 17:56	♄☍	♌	20 20:17
22 0:28	♀⚹	♍	22 23:41
24 23:09	♄△	♎	25 1:55
27 1:10	♄□	♏	27 4:13
29 4:02	♄⚹	♐	29 7:26
31 0:09	♀☍	♑	31 11:59

Last Aspect / ☽ Ingress (August)

Last Aspect Dy Hr Mn	Aspect	☽ Ingress	Dy Hr Mn
2 14:01	♄☌	♒	2 18:12
4 21:47	♀△	♓	5 2:29
7 12:55	♀□	♈	7 13:06
9 19:51	♄□	♉	10 1:29
12 7:56	♄△	♊	12 13:47
14 11:20	♂⚹	♋	14 23:37
17 0:00	♄☍	♌	17 5:40
19 5:39	☿☌	♍	19 8:21
21 3:38	♄△	♎	21 9:17
23 4:21	♄□	♏	23 10:17
25 6:28	♄⚹	♐	25 12:50
27 12:01	♂△	♑	27 17:38
29 19:32	♂□	♒	30 0:38

☽ Phases & Eclipses (Dy Hr Mn)

Dy Hr Mn	Phase
5 4:46	○ 13♑38
5 4:31	• A 0.354
12 23:30	☾ 21♈03
20 17:34	● 28♋27
27 12:34	☽ 4♏56
3 16:00	○ 11♒46
11 16:46	☾ 19♉28
19 2:43	● 26♌35
25 17:59	☽ 2♐59

Astro Data

1 July 2020
Julian Day # 44012
SVP 4♓58'41"
GC 27♐07.5 ⚴ 24♑19.4R
Eris 24♈31.6 ✻ 8♎53.8
⚷ 9♈23.4 ⚶ 12♋02.4
☽ Mean ☊ 28♊34.4

1 August 2020
Julian Day # 44043
SVP 4♓58'36"
GC 27♐07.6 ⚴ 16♑12.2R
Eris 24♈32.8R ✻ 15♎25.1
⚷ 9♈15.3R ⚶ 25♋38.3
☽ Mean ☊ 26♊55.9

LONGITUDE — September 2020

Day	Sid.Time	☉	0 hr ☽	Noon☽	True☊	☿	♀	♂	⚳	♃	♄	♅	♆	♇
1 Tu	10 44 26	9♍30 14	25♒00 58	1♓14 52	26♊20.1	22♍49.9	24♋49.5	27♈37.8	4♓45.4	17♑37.2	25♑57.0	10♉34.5	19♓49.8	22♑44.4
2 W	10 48 22	10 28 18	7♓26 20	13 35 23	26R 07.7	24 31.4	25 53.6	27 44.6	4R 32.2	17R 35.1	25R 54.5	10R 33.6	19R 48.1	22R 43.5
3 Th	10 52 19	11 26 23	19 42 06	25 46 35	25 54.5	26 11.6	26 58.0	27 50.5	4 19.1	17 33.1	25 52.0	10 32.7	19 46.5	22 42.7
4 F	10 56 16	12 24 30	1♈48 58	7♈49 23	25 41.8	27 50.7	28 02.6	27 55.6	4 06.1	17 31.4	25 49.7	10 31.8	19 44.9	22 41.9
5 Sa	11 00 12	13 22 39	13 48 03	19 45 13	25 30.5	29 28.5	29 07.4	27 59.9	3 53.2	17 29.9	25 47.4	10 30.8	19 43.2	22 41.1
6 Su	11 04 09	14 20 50	25 41 12	1♉36 19	25 21.4	1♎05.1	0♌12.6	28 03.3	3 40.4	17 28.5	25 45.2	10 29.8	19 41.6	22 40.3
7 M	11 08 05	15 19 02	7♉31 01	13 25 45	25 15.1	2 40.6	1 17.9	28 05.9	3 27.7	17 27.3	25 43.1	10 28.7	19 40.0	22 39.5
8 Tu	11 12 02	16 17 17	19 21 01	25 17 22	25 11.3	4 14.9	2 23.5	28 07.6	3 15.1	17 26.4	25 41.1	10 27.6	19 38.3	22 38.8
9 W	11 15 58	17 15 34	1♊15 25	7♊15 46	25D 09.8	5 48.0	3 29.3	28R 08.4	3 02.7	17 25.6	25 39.2	10 26.4	19 36.7	22 38.1
10 Th	11 19 55	18 13 52	13 19 05	19 26 03	25R 09.5	7 20.0	4 35.3	28 08.4	2 50.5	17 25.0	25 37.3	10 25.2	19 35.0	22 37.4
11 F	11 23 51	19 12 13	25 37 18	1♋53 31	25 09.4	8 50.8	5 41.5	28 07.4	2 38.4	17 24.6	25 35.6	10 24.0	19 33.3	22 36.8
12 Sa	11 27 48	20 10 36	8♋15 19	14 43 17	25 08.4	10 20.5	6 48.0	28 05.6	2 26.6	17D 24.4	25 33.9	10 22.7	19 31.7	22 36.1
13 Su	11 31 45	21 09 01	21 17 52	27 59 30	25 05.5	11 49.0	7 54.6	28 02.9	2 14.9	17 24.4	25 32.3	10 21.4	19 30.0	22 35.5
14 M	11 35 41	22 07 29	4♌48 25	11♌44 43	25 00.0	13 16.3	9 01.5	27 59.2	2 03.4	17 24.6	25 30.9	10 20.0	19 28.4	22 35.0
15 Tu	11 39 38	23 05 58	18 48 19	25 58 53	24 51.9	14 42.4	10 08.5	27 54.7	1 52.2	17 25.0	25 29.5	10 18.6	19 26.7	22 34.4
16 W	11 43 34	24 04 29	3♍15 56	10♍38 43	24 41.7	16 07.4	11 15.8	27 49.4	1 41.2	17 25.6	25 28.2	10 17.1	19 25.1	22 33.9
17 Th	11 47 31	25 03 02	18 06 17	25 37 30	24 30.4	17 31.1	12 23.2	27 43.1	1 30.4	17 26.3	25 27.0	10 15.6	19 23.4	22 33.4
18 F	11 51 27	26 01 37	3♎11 08	10♎45 51	24 19.2	18 53.6	13 30.8	27 36.0	1 19.9	17 27.3	25 25.9	10 14.1	19 21.8	22 32.9
19 Sa	11 55 24	27 00 14	18 20 19	25 53 14	24 09.6	20 14.9	14 38.6	27 28.0	1 09.7	17 28.4	25 24.9	10 12.5	19 20.2	22 32.5
20 Su	11 59 20	27 58 53	3♏23 25	10♏49 51	24 02.3	21 34.8	15 46.5	27 19.2	0 59.7	17 29.8	25 24.0	10 10.9	19 18.5	22 32.0
21 M	12 03 17	28 57 33	18 11 42	25 28 19	23 57.9	22 53.3	16 54.7	27 09.7	0 50.0	17 31.3	25 23.2	10 09.2	19 16.9	22 31.7
22 Tu	12 07 14	29 56 15	2♐39 17	9♐44 19	23 55.9	24 10.4	18 02.9	26 59.3	0 40.7	17 33.1	25 22.4	10 07.5	19 15.3	22 31.3
23 W	12 11 10	0♎54 59	16 43 23	23 36 32	23 55.4	25 26.1	19 11.4	26 48.1	0 31.6	17 35.0	25 21.8	10 05.8	19 13.7	22 31.0
24 Th	12 15 07	1 53 45	0♑23 58	7♑05 57	23 55.4	26 40.2	20 20.0	26 36.2	0 22.8	17 37.1	25 21.3	10 04.1	19 12.0	22 30.7
25 F	12 19 03	2 52 32	13 42 49	20 14 57	23 54.5	27 52.6	21 28.8	26 23.6	0 14.4	17 39.4	25 20.9	10 02.3	19 10.5	22 30.4
26 Sa	12 23 00	3 51 21	26 42 45	3♒06 35	23 51.6	29 03.3	22 37.7	26 10.3	0 06.3	17 41.9	25 20.6	10 00.4	19 08.9	22 30.1
27 Su	12 26 56	4 50 12	9♒26 51	15 43 54	23 46.1	0♏12.2	23 46.7	25 56.4	29♒58.4	17 44.6	25 20.4	9 58.6	19 07.3	22 29.9
28 M	12 30 53	5 49 04	21 58 02	28 09 33	23 37.6	1 19.1	24 56.0	25 41.8	29 51.0	17 47.5	25D 20.3	9 56.7	19 05.7	22 29.7
29 Tu	12 34 49	6 47 58	4♓18 43	10♓25 44	23 26.6	2 23.9	26 05.3	25 26.6	29 43.8	17 50.5	25 20.2	9 54.7	19 04.1	22 29.6
30 W	12 38 46	7 46 54	16 30 47	22 34 04	23 13.8	3 26.5	27 14.9	25 10.9	29 37.0	17 53.7	25 20.3	9 52.8	19 02.6	22 29.4

LONGITUDE — October 2020

Day	Sid.Time	☉	0 hr ☽	Noon☽	True☊	☿	♀	♂	⚳	♃	♄	♅	♆	♇
1 Th	12 42 43	8♎45 52	28♓35 42	4♈35 51	23♊00.2	4♏26.6	28♌24.5	24♈54.6	29♒30.6	17♑57.2	25♑20.5	9♉50.8	19♓01.1	22♑29.3
2 F	12 46 39	9 44 52	10♈34 38	16 32 14	22R 47.0	5 24.1	29 34.3	24R 37.9	29R 24.5	18 00.8	25 20.8	9R 48.8	18R 59.5	22R 29.3
3 Sa	12 50 36	10 43 54	22 28 47	28 24 29	22 35.2	6 18.8	0♍44.3	24 20.7	29 18.7	18 04.5	25 21.1	9 46.7	18 58.0	22 29.2
4 Su	12 54 32	11 42 59	4♉19 34	10♉14 16	22 25.6	7 10.3	1 54.3	24 03.1	29 13.3	18 08.5	25 21.6	9 44.7	18 56.5	22D 29.2
5 M	12 58 29	12 42 05	16 08 54	22 03 49	22 18.9	7 58.5	3 04.6	23 45.1	29 08.3	18 12.6	25 22.2	9 42.5	18 55.0	22 29.2
6 Tu	13 02 25	13 41 14	27 59 23	3♊56 03	22 14.8	8 43.0	4 14.9	23 26.8	29 03.6	18 16.9	25 22.9	9 40.4	18 53.6	22 29.3
7 W	13 06 22	14 40 25	9♊54 17	15 54 38	22D 13.2	9 23.5	5 25.4	23 08.3	28 59.3	18 21.4	25 23.6	9 38.3	18 52.1	22 29.3
8 Th	13 10 18	15 39 38	21 57 39	28 03 56	22 13.1	9 59.6	6 36.0	22 49.5	28 55.3	18 26.1	25 24.5	9 36.1	18 50.7	22 29.4
9 F	13 14 15	16 38 54	4♋14 06	10♋28 47	22R 13.6	10 30.9	7 46.8	22 30.5	28 51.8	18 30.9	25 25.5	9 33.9	18 49.2	22 29.6
10 Sa	13 18 11	17 38 11	16 48 35	23 14 08	22 13.6	10 57.0	8 57.6	22 11.4	28 48.5	18 35.9	25 26.6	9 31.7	18 47.8	22 29.7
11 Su	13 22 08	18 37 32	29 45 58	6♌24 35	22 12.1	11 17.4	10 08.6	21 52.2	28 45.7	18 41.1	25 27.7	9 29.4	18 46.5	22 29.9
12 M	13 26 05	19 36 54	13♌10 22	20 03 34	22 08.5	11 31.6	11 19.7	21 33.0	28 43.2	18 46.5	25 29.0	9 27.2	18 45.1	22 30.1
13 Tu	13 30 01	20 36 19	27 04 19	4♍12 29	22 02.5	11R 39.1	12 30.9	21 13.8	28 41.1	18 52.0	25 30.4	9 24.9	18 43.7	22 30.4
14 W	13 33 58	21 35 46	11♍27 47	18 49 42	21 54.5	11 39.4	13 42.3	20 54.7	28 39.3	18 57.7	25 31.8	9 22.6	18 42.4	22 30.7
15 Th	13 37 54	22 35 15	26 17 26	3♎50 02	21 45.4	11 32.0	14 53.7	20 35.7	28 38.0	19 03.5	25 33.4	9 20.2	18 41.1	22 31.0
16 F	13 41 51	23 34 46	11♎26 17	19 04 53	21 36.3	11 16.6	16 05.3	20 16.9	28 37.0	19 09.5	25 35.1	9 17.9	18 39.8	22 31.3
17 Sa	13 45 47	24 34 20	26 44 24	4♏23 25	21 28.4	10 52.7	17 16.9	19 58.3	28 36.3	19 15.7	25 36.8	9 15.5	18 38.5	22 31.7
18 Su	13 49 44	25 33 55	12♏00 32	19 34 28	21 22.5	10 20.2	18 28.7	19 40.0	28D 36.1	19 22.0	25 38.7	9 13.2	18 37.3	22 32.1
19 M	13 53 40	26 33 33	27 04 05	4♐28 27	21 19.1	9 39.1	19 40.5	19 22.1	28 36.2	19 28.5	25 40.6	9 10.8	18 36.0	22 32.5
20 Tu	13 57 37	27 33 12	11♐46 51	18 58 48	21D 17.9	8 49.6	20 52.4	19 04.5	28 36.6	19 35.2	25 42.7	9 08.4	18 34.8	22 33.0
21 W	14 01 34	28 32 53	26 03 59	3♑02 20	21 18.3	7 52.2	22 04.5	18 47.4	28 37.5	19 42.0	25 44.8	9 06.0	18 33.7	22 33.5
22 Th	14 05 30	29 32 36	9♑53 53	16 38 50	21 19.3	6 47.9	23 16.6	18 30.7	28 38.7	19 49.0	25 47.1	9 03.5	18 32.5	22 34.0
23 F	14 09 27	0♏32 20	23 17 31	29 50 19	21R 19.9	5 38.0	24 28.8	18 14.6	28 40.3	19 56.1	25 49.4	9 01.1	18 31.4	22 34.5
24 Sa	14 13 23	1 32 06	6♒17 40	12♒40 03	21 19.2	4 24.1	25 41.1	17 58.9	28 42.2	20 03.4	25 51.9	8 58.7	18 30.3	22 35.1
25 Su	14 17 20	2 31 54	18 57 57	25 11 53	21 16.5	3 08.2	26 53.5	17 43.9	28 44.5	20 10.8	25 54.4	8 56.2	18 29.2	22 35.7
26 M	14 21 16	3 31 43	1♓22 18	7♓29 40	21 11.7	1 52.5	28 06.0	17 29.4	28 47.1	20 18.4	25 57.0	8 53.8	18 28.1	22 36.3
27 Tu	14 25 13	4 31 34	13 34 25	19 36 56	21 05.0	0 39.4	29 18.5	17 15.6	28 50.1	20 26.1	25 59.7	8 51.3	18 27.1	22 37.0
28 W	14 29 09	5 31 27	25 37 36	1♈36 44	20 56.8	29♎31.1	0♎31.2	17 02.5	28 53.4	20 33.9	26 02.5	8 48.8	18 26.1	22 37.7
29 Th	14 33 06	6 31 21	7♈34 38	13 31 34	20 48.0	28 29.7	1 43.9	16 50.0	28 57.1	20 41.9	26 05.4	8 46.4	18 25.1	22 38.4
30 F	14 37 03	7 31 18	19 27 47	25 23 30	20 39.3	27 37.0	2 56.7	16 38.3	29 01.1	20 50.1	26 08.4	8 43.9	18 24.1	22 39.2
31 Sa	14 40 59	8 31 16	1♉18 56	7♉14 18	20 31.7	26 54.4	4 09.6	16 27.2	29 05.4	20 58.3	26 11.5	8 41.4	18 23.2	22 39.9

Astro Data

	Dy Hr Mn
☽ 0N	4 18:51
☿0S	6 6:27
♂ R	9 22:24
♃ D	13 0:42
☽ 0S	18 12:37
☉0S	22 13:32
♄ D	29 5:13
☽ 0N	2 1:01
♇ D	4 13:34
♃⚹♆	12 7:07
☿ R	14 1:05
☽ 0S	15 23:32
⚳ D	18 17:01
☽ 0N	29 7:18
♀0S	31 2:05

Planet Ingress

		Dy Hr Mn
☿	♎	5 19:47
♀	♌	6 7:23
☉	♎	22 13:32
⚳	♒R	27 7:09
☿	♏	27 7:42
♀	♍	2 20:49
☉	♏	22 23:01
☿	♎R	28 1:35
♀	♎	28 1:42

Last Aspect / ☽ Ingress (September)

Last Aspect Dy Hr Mn		☽ Ingress Dy Hr Mn
1 4:57	♂ ⚹	♓ 1 9:35
3 14:35	♀ △	♈ 3 20:23
6 4:46	♂ ☌	♉ 6 8:45
8 12:48	♄ △	♊ 8 21:29
11 4:49	♂ ⚹	♋ 11 8:24
13 12:06	♂ □	♌ 13 15:34
15 15:11	♂ △	♍ 15 18:38
17 11:43	♄ △	♎ 17 18:57
19 14:30	♂ ☍	♏ 19 18:34
21 18:14	☉ ⚹	♐ 21 19:33
23 17:33	♂ △	♑ 23 23:17
26 3:37	☿ □	♒ 26 6:09
28 7:19	♂ ⚹	♓ 28 15:35

Last Aspect / ☽ Ingress (October)

Last Aspect Dy Hr Mn		☽ Ingress Dy Hr Mn
30 17:31	♄ ⚹	♈ 1 2:48
3 5:48	♄ □	♉ 3 15:14
5 18:42	♄ △	♊ 6 4:04
8 1:58	♂ ⚹	♋ 8 15:47
10 16:05	♄ ☍	♌ 11 0:26
12 14:31	♂ △	♍ 13 4:57
14 22:48	♄ △	♎ 15 5:55
16 22:13	♄ □	♏ 17 5:07
18 21:44	♄ ⚹	♐ 19 4:44
21 3:39	☉ ⚹	♑ 21 6:45
23 4:36	♄ ☌	♒ 23 12:18
24 21:55	♂ ⚹	♓ 25 21:19
28 0:47	♄ ⚹	♈ 28 8:46
30 16:14	☿ ☍	♉ 30 21:20

☽ Phases & Eclipses

Dy Hr Mn		
2 5:23	○	10♓12
10 9:27	☾	18♊08
17 11:01	●	25♍01
24 1:56	☽	1♑29
1 21:06	○	9♈08
10 0:41	☾	17♋10
16 19:32	●	23♎53
23 13:24	☽	0♒36
31 14:50	○	8♉38

Astro Data

1 September 2020
Julian Day # 44074
SVP 4♓58'32"
GC 27♐07.7 ⚴ 12♑16.2R
Eris 24♈24.3R ⚵ 24♎03.8
⚷ 8♈22.2R ⚶ 9♌07.3
☽ Mean ☊ 25♊17.4

1 October 2020
Julian Day # 44104
SVP 4♓58'29"
GC 27♐07.7 ⚴ 14♑00.5
Eris 24♈09.2R ⚵ 3♏36.0
⚷ 7♈05.0R ⚶ 21♌44.5
☽ Mean ☊ 23♊42.1

November 2020 LONGITUDE

Day	Sid.Time	☉	0 hr ☽	Noon☽	True☊	☿	♀	♂	⚳	♃	♄	♅	♆	♇
1 Su	14 44 56	9♏31 16	13♉09 47	19♉05 37	20♊25.7	26♎22.8	5♎22.5	16♈16.9	29♒10.1	21♑06.8	26♑14.6	8♉39.0	18♓22.3	22♑40.7
2 M	14 48 52	10 31 18	25 02 00	0♊59 13	20R 21.7	26R 02.7	6 35.6	16R 07.4	29 15.1	21 15.3	26 17.9	8R 36.5	18R 21.5	22 41.6
3 Tu	14 52 49	11 31 22	6♊57 31	12 57 12	20D 19.8	25D 54.2	7 48.7	15 58.6	29 20.4	21 24.0	26 21.2	8 34.0	18 20.6	22 42.4
4 W	14 56 45	12 31 29	18 58 36	25 02 05	20 19.6	25 57.0	9 01.9	15 50.5	29 26.1	21 32.8	26 24.7	8 31.6	18 19.8	22 43.3
5 Th	15 00 42	13 31 37	1♋08 02	7♋16 54	20 20.6	26 10.7	10 15.1	15 43.3	29 32.1	21 41.7	26 28.2	8 29.1	18 19.0	22 44.2
6 F	15 04 38	14 31 47	13 29 07	19 45 10	20 22.3	26 34.6	11 28.5	15 36.8	29 38.4	21 50.8	26 31.8	8 26.6	18 18.3	22 45.2
7 Sa	15 08 35	15 31 59	26 05 31	2♌30 40	20 23.8	27 07.9	12 41.9	15 31.2	29 45.0	22 00.0	26 35.5	8 24.2	18 17.5	22 46.2
8 Su	15 12 32	16 32 13	9♌01 05	15 37 12	20R 24.5	27 49.6	13 55.4	15 26.3	29 51.9	22 09.3	26 39.2	8 21.8	18 16.9	22 47.1
9 M	15 16 28	17 32 30	22 19 22	29 07 54	20 24.0	28 38.9	15 08.9	15 22.3	29 59.1	22 18.8	26 43.1	8 19.3	18 16.2	22 48.2
10 Tu	15 20 25	18 32 48	6♍03 00	13♍04 42	20 21.9	29 35.0	16 22.5	15 19.0	0♓06.7	22 28.4	26 47.0	8 16.9	18 15.6	22 49.2
11 W	15 24 21	19 33 08	20 12 56	27 27 26	20 18.5	0♏37.0	17 36.2	15 16.6	0 14.5	22 38.0	26 51.0	8 14.5	18 15.0	22 50.3
12 Th	15 28 18	20 33 30	4♎47 43	12♎13 08	20 14.4	1 44.0	18 49.9	15 14.9	0 22.6	22 47.9	26 55.1	8 12.1	18 14.4	22 51.4
13 F	15 32 14	21 33 54	19 42 52	27 15 53	20 10.1	2 55.5	20 03.7	15D 14.1	0 31.0	22 57.8	26 59.3	8 09.7	18 13.8	22 52.5
14 Sa	15 36 11	22 34 20	4♏51 02	12♏27 06	20 06.3	4 10.8	21 17.5	15 14.1	0 39.8	23 07.8	27 03.5	8 07.3	18 13.3	22 53.7
15 Su	15 40 07	23 34 48	20 02 48	27 36 50	20 03.6	5 29.4	22 31.4	15 14.9	0 48.8	23 18.0	27 07.9	8 04.9	18 12.9	22 54.8
16 M	15 44 04	24 35 17	5♐08 02	12♐35 17	20D 02.2	6 50.6	23 45.3	15 16.5	0 58.1	23 28.3	27 12.3	8 02.6	18 12.4	22 56.0
17 Tu	15 48 01	25 35 48	19 57 39	27 14 21	20 02.2	8 14.2	24 59.3	15 18.8	1 07.6	23 38.7	27 16.8	8 00.3	18 12.0	22 57.3
18 W	15 51 57	26 36 20	4♑24 50	11♑28 41	20 03.2	9 39.7	26 13.4	15 22.0	1 17.5	23 49.2	27 21.3	7 58.0	18 11.7	22 58.5
19 Th	15 55 54	27 36 54	18 25 42	25 15 50	20 04.7	11 06.8	27 27.4	15 26.0	1 27.6	23 59.8	27 26.0	7 55.7	18 11.3	22 59.8
20 F	15 59 50	28 37 29	1♒59 12	8♒36 01	20 06.2	12 35.3	28 41.6	15 30.7	1 38.0	24 10.5	27 30.7	7 53.4	18 11.0	23 01.1
21 Sa	16 03 47	29 38 05	15 06 38	21 31 27	20R 07.2	14 04.8	29 55.7	15 36.1	1 48.6	24 21.3	27 35.5	7 51.1	18 10.7	23 02.4
22 Su	16 07 43	0♐38 42	27 50 57	4♓05 39	20 07.3	15 35.3	1♏09.9	15 42.3	1 59.5	24 32.2	27 40.3	7 48.9	18 10.5	23 03.8
23 M	16 11 40	1 39 20	10♓16 05	16 22 47	20 06.6	17 06.4	2 24.2	15 49.3	2 10.7	24 43.2	27 45.3	7 46.7	18 10.3	23 05.1
24 Tu	16 15 36	2 39 59	22 26 19	28 27 13	20 05.0	18 38.2	3 38.5	15 56.9	2 22.1	24 54.3	27 50.2	7 44.5	18 10.1	23 06.5
25 W	16 19 33	3 40 39	4♈26 00	10♈23 09	20 02.8	20 10.4	4 52.8	16 05.3	2 33.8	25 05.5	27 55.3	7 42.4	18 10.0	23 07.9
26 Th	16 23 30	4 41 21	16 19 10	22 14 27	20 00.3	21 43.0	6 07.2	16 14.3	2 45.7	25 16.8	28 00.4	7 40.2	18 09.9	23 09.4
27 F	16 27 26	5 42 04	28 09 26	4♉04 29	19 57.8	23 15.9	7 21.6	16 24.0	2 57.8	25 28.2	28 05.6	7 38.1	18 09.8	23 10.8
28 Sa	16 31 23	6 42 48	9♉59 55	15 56 04	19 55.8	24 49.1	8 36.0	16 34.4	3 10.2	25 39.7	28 10.9	7 36.1	18D 09.8	23 12.3
29 Su	16 35 19	7 43 33	21 53 13	27 51 37	19 54.3	26 22.4	9 50.5	16 45.5	3 22.8	25 51.3	28 16.2	7 34.0	18 09.8	23 13.8
30 M	16 39 16	8 44 19	3♊51 30	9♊53 05	19D 53.4	27 55.8	11 05.0	16 57.1	3 35.7	26 02.9	28 21.6	7 32.0	18 09.8	23 15.3

December 2020 LONGITUDE

Day	Sid.Time	☉	0 hr ☽	Noon☽	True☊	☿	♀	♂	⚳	♃	♄	♅	♆	♇
1 Tu	16 43 12	9♐45 07	15♊56 35	22♊02 11	19♊53.2	29♏29.3	12♏19.5	17♈09.4	3♓48.7	26♑14.7	28♑27.0	7♉30.0	18♓09.9	23♑16.9
2 W	16 47 09	10 45 56	28 10 06	4♋20 30	19 53.6	1♐02.9	13 34.1	17 22.3	4 02.0	26 26.5	28 32.5	7R 28.0	18 10.0	23 18.4
3 Th	16 51 05	11 46 46	10♋33 37	16 49 38	19 54.2	2 36.5	14 48.7	17 35.8	4 15.5	26 38.4	28 38.1	7 26.1	18 10.1	23 20.0
4 F	16 55 02	12 47 37	23 08 47	29 31 16	19 55.0	4 10.2	16 03.4	17 49.8	4 29.2	26 50.4	28 43.7	7 24.2	18 10.3	23 21.6
5 Sa	16 58 59	13 48 30	5♌57 19	12♌27 10	19 55.7	5 43.9	17 18.0	18 04.5	4 43.2	27 02.5	28 49.4	7 22.4	18 10.5	23 23.2
6 Su	17 02 55	14 49 24	19 01 02	25 39 09	19 56.2	7 17.7	18 32.8	18 19.7	4 57.3	27 14.7	28 55.2	7 20.6	18 10.7	23 24.8
7 M	17 06 52	15 50 19	2♍21 41	9♍08 49	19R 56.5	8 51.4	19 47.5	18 35.4	5 11.7	27 26.9	29 01.0	7 18.8	18 11.0	23 26.5
8 Tu	17 10 48	16 51 16	16 00 39	22 57 14	19 56.5	10 25.2	21 02.3	18 51.6	5 26.2	27 39.2	29 06.8	7 17.0	18 11.3	23 28.1
9 W	17 14 45	17 52 13	29 58 32	7♎04 26	19 56.4	11 59.0	22 17.1	19 08.4	5 41.0	27 51.6	29 12.7	7 15.3	18 11.7	23 29.8
10 Th	17 18 41	18 53 12	14♎14 43	21 29 01	19D 56.2	13 32.8	23 31.9	19 25.7	5 55.9	28 04.1	29 18.7	7 13.6	18 12.0	23 31.5
11 F	17 22 38	19 54 12	28 46 54	6♏07 46	19 56.2	15 06.7	24 46.7	19 43.5	6 11.1	28 16.6	29 24.7	7 12.0	18 12.4	23 33.2
12 Sa	17 26 35	20 55 13	13♏30 55	20 55 34	19 56.2	16 40.7	26 01.6	20 01.8	6 26.4	28 29.3	29 30.8	7 10.4	18 12.9	23 35.0
13 Su	17 30 31	21 56 16	28 20 50	5♐45 47	19R 56.3	18 14.7	27 16.5	20 20.6	6 42.0	28 41.9	29 36.9	7 08.8	18 13.4	23 36.7
14 M	17 34 28	22 57 19	13♐09 28	20 30 56	19 56.4	19 48.8	28 31.4	20 39.8	6 57.7	28 54.7	29 43.0	7 07.3	18 13.9	23 38.5
15 Tu	17 38 24	23 58 23	27 49 17	5♑03 42	19 56.3	21 23.0	29 46.3	20 59.5	7 13.6	29 07.5	29 49.3	7 05.8	18 14.5	23 40.3
16 W	17 42 21	24 59 28	12♑13 27	19 17 58	19 55.9	22 57.3	1♐01.3	21 19.6	7 29.7	29 20.4	29 55.5	7 04.4	18 15.0	23 42.1
17 Th	17 46 17	26 00 33	26 16 45	3♒09 30	19 55.3	24 31.7	2 16.3	21 40.2	7 45.9	29 33.3	0♒01.8	7 03.0	18 15.7	23 43.9
18 F	17 50 14	27 01 38	9♒56 01	16 36 18	19 54.4	26 06.3	3 31.2	22 01.3	8 02.3	29 46.3	0 08.2	7 01.7	18 16.3	23 45.7
19 Sa	17 54 10	28 02 44	23 10 26	29 38 36	19 53.5	27 41.0	4 46.2	22 22.7	8 18.9	29 59.4	0 14.6	7 00.3	18 17.0	23 47.5
20 Su	17 58 07	29 03 50	6♓01 07	12♓18 24	19 52.7	29 15.9	6 01.2	22 44.5	8 35.7	0♒12.5	0 21.0	6 59.1	18 17.7	23 49.4
21 M	18 02 04	0♑04 57	18 30 54	24 39 07	19D 52.2	0♑51.0	7 16.3	23 06.8	8 52.6	0 25.7	0 27.4	6 57.9	18 18.5	23 51.2
22 Tu	18 06 00	1 06 03	0♈43 38	6♈45 01	19 52.2	2 26.2	8 31.3	23 29.4	9 09.7	0 38.9	0 34.0	6 56.7	18 19.3	23 53.1
23 W	18 09 57	2 07 10	12 43 52	18 40 48	19 52.8	4 01.7	9 46.3	23 52.4	9 27.0	0 52.2	0 40.5	6 55.6	18 20.1	23 55.0
24 Th	18 13 53	3 08 17	24 36 23	0♉31 14	19 53.8	5 37.4	11 01.4	24 15.7	9 44.4	1 05.5	0 47.1	6 54.5	18 21.0	23 56.8
25 F	18 17 50	4 09 24	6♉25 54	12 20 56	19 55.2	7 13.3	12 16.4	24 39.4	10 01.9	1 18.9	0 53.7	6 53.5	18 21.8	23 58.7
26 Sa	18 21 46	5 10 31	18 16 50	24 14 05	19 56.6	8 49.4	13 31.5	25 03.5	10 19.6	1 32.3	1 00.3	6 52.5	18 22.8	24 00.6
27 Su	18 25 43	6 11 39	0♊13 07	6♊14 20	19 57.7	10 25.8	14 46.6	25 27.9	10 37.5	1 45.8	1 07.0	6 51.6	18 23.7	24 02.6
28 M	18 29 39	7 12 46	12 18 04	18 24 36	19R 58.2	12 02.5	16 01.7	25 52.6	10 55.5	1 59.3	1 13.7	6 50.7	18 24.7	24 04.5
29 Tu	18 33 36	8 13 54	24 34 12	0♋47 03	19 57.9	13 39.4	17 16.8	26 17.6	11 13.6	2 12.9	1 20.5	6 49.8	18 25.7	24 06.4
30 W	18 37 33	9 15 02	7♋03 18	13 23 02	19 56.5	15 16.6	18 31.9	26 42.9	11 31.9	2 26.5	1 27.3	6 49.0	18 26.8	24 08.4
31 Th	18 41 29	10 16 10	19 46 19	26 13 08	19 54.2	16 54.0	19 47.0	27 08.5	11 50.3	2 40.1	1 34.1	6 48.3	18 27.9	24 10.3

Astro Data Dy Hr Mn	Planet Ingress Dy Hr Mn	Last Aspect Dy Hr Mn	☽ Ingress Dy Hr Mn	Last Aspect Dy Hr Mn	☽ Ingress Dy Hr Mn	☽ Phases & Eclipses Dy Hr Mn	Astro Data
☿ D 3 17:53	⚳ ♓ 9 14:49	2 2:31 ♄ △	♊ 2 10:01	1 4:23 ♆ □	♋ 2 3:34	8 13:47 ☾ 16♌37	1 November 2020
☽ 0S 12 10:34	☿ ♏ 10 21:57	4 13:50 ☿ △	♋ 4 21:47	4 10:30 ♄ ☍	♌ 4 12:54	15 5:08 ● 23♏18	Julian Day # 44135
♃☌♇ 12 21:40	♀ ♏ 21 13:23	7 1:28 ☿ □	♌ 7 7:19	5 22:29 ♂ △	♍ 6 19:47	22 4:46 ☽ 0♓20	SVP 4♓58'26"
♂ D 14 0:37	☉ ♐ 21 20:41	9 11:06 ☿ ⚹	♍ 9 13:31	8 22:36 ♄ △	♎ 9 0:02	30 9:31 ○ 8♊38	GC 27♐07.8 ⚴ 19♑58.1
☽ 0N 25 14:04		11 11:00 ♄ △	♎ 11 16:11	11 0:57 ♄ □	♏ 11 2:00	30 9:44 ☍ A 0.828	Eris 23♈50.9R ⚵ 14♏03.5
♆ D 29 0:37	☿ ♐ 1 19:52	13 11:34 ♄ □	♏ 13 16:20	13 1:59 ♄ ⚹	♐ 13 2:40		⚷ 5♈47.4R ⚶ 3♍48.2
	♀ ♐ 15 16:22	15 11:14 ♄ ⚹	♐ 15 15:48	14 16:18 ☉ ☌	♑ 15 3:36	8 0:38 ☾ 16♍22	☽ Mean ☊ 22♊03.6
☽ 0S 9 19:22	♄ ♒ 17 5:05	17 7:56 ♀ ⚹	♑ 17 16:36	17 5:36 ♃ ☌	♒ 17 6:28	14 16:18 ● 23♐08	
♃☌♄ 21 18:22	♃ ♒ 19 13:08	19 16:31 ☉ ⚹	♒ 19 20:26	19 8:46 ☉ ⚹	♓ 19 12:40	14 16:14:39 ● T 02'10"	1 December 2020
☽ 0N 22 21:25	☿ ♑ 20 23:08	21 0:50 ♂ ⚹	♓ 22 4:07	21 10:26 ♇ ⚹	♈ 21 22:33	21 23:42 ☽ 0♈35	Julian Day # 44165
	☉ ♑ 21 10:03	24 10:46 ♄ ⚹	♈ 24 15:06	23 22:52 ♂ ☌	♉ 24 10:57	30 3:29 ○ 8♋53	SVP 4♓58'21"
		26 23:47 ♄ □	♉ 27 3:44	26 11:33 ♇ △	♊ 26 23:34		GC 27♐07.9 ⚴ 28♑10.3
		29 12:50 ♄ △	♊ 29 16:17	29 3:02 ♂ ⚹	♋ 29 10:29		Eris 23♈35.7R ⚵ 24♏16.7
				31 13:46 ♂ □	♌ 31 18:59		⚷ 5♈02.2R ⚶ 13♍37.5
							☽ Mean ☊ 20♊28.3

LONGITUDE — January 2021

Day	Sid.Time	☉	0 hr ☽	Noon ☽	True ☊	☿	♀	♂	⚳	♃	♄	♅	♆	♇
1 F	18 45 26	11♑17 18	2♌43 29	9♌17 16	19♊51.0	18♑31.7	21♐02.2	27♈34.4	12♓08.8	2♒53.8	1♒40.9	6♉47.6	18♓29.0	24♑12.3
2 Sa	18 49 22	12 18 27	15 54 26	22 34 51	19R47.5	20 09.6	22 17.3	28 00.6	12 27.5	3 07.5	1 47.8	6R47.0	18 30.1	24 14.2
3 Su	18 53 19	13 19 36	29 18 24	6♍04 58	19 44.1	21 47.7	23 32.5	28 27.1	12 46.3	3 21.3	1 54.6	6 46.4	18 31.3	24 16.2
4 M	18 57 15	14 20 44	12♍54 25	19 46 36	19 41.3	23 26.0	24 47.7	28 53.8	13 05.3	3 35.1	2 01.5	6 45.9	18 32.5	24 18.2
5 Tu	19 01 12	15 21 53	26 41 25	3♎38 42	19D39.6	25 04.4	26 02.8	29 20.8	13 24.3	3 48.9	2 08.5	6 45.4	18 33.7	24 20.1
6 W	19 05 08	16 23 03	10♎38 20	17 40 10	19 39.1	26 42.9	27 18.0	29 48.0	13 43.5	4 02.8	2 15.4	6 44.9	18 35.0	24 22.1
7 Th	19 09 05	17 24 12	24 44 03	1♏49 46	19 39.7	28 21.5	28 33.2	0♉15.5	14 02.8	4 16.7	2 22.4	6 44.5	18 36.3	24 24.1
8 F	19 13 02	18 25 22	8♏57 08	16 05 52	19 41.1	29 59.9	29 48.4	0 43.3	14 22.2	4 30.7	2 29.4	6 44.2	18 37.6	24 26.1
9 Sa	19 16 58	19 26 32	23 15 39	0♐26 09	19 42.7	1♒38.3	1♑03.6	1 11.3	14 41.8	4 44.6	2 36.4	6 43.9	18 38.9	24 28.1
10 Su	19 20 55	20 27 41	7♐36 55	14 47 30	19R43.7	3 16.4	2 18.8	1 39.5	15 01.4	4 58.6	2 43.4	6 43.7	18 40.3	24 30.1
11 M	19 24 51	21 28 51	21 57 22	29 05 57	19 43.4	4 54.1	3 34.0	2 07.9	15 21.2	5 12.6	2 50.5	6 43.5	18 41.7	24 32.1
12 Tu	19 28 48	22 30 01	6♑12 41	13♑16 56	19 41.5	6 31.2	4 49.3	2 36.6	15 41.1	5 26.7	2 57.6	6 43.4	18 43.2	24 34.1
13 W	19 32 44	23 31 10	20 18 09	27 15 46	19 37.8	8 07.6	6 04.5	3 05.5	16 01.1	5 40.8	3 04.6	6D43.3	18 44.6	24 36.1
14 Th	19 36 41	24 32 19	4♒09 17	10♒58 18	19 32.6	9 43.0	7 19.7	3 34.6	16 21.2	5 54.9	3 11.7	6 43.3	18 46.1	24 38.1
15 F	19 40 38	25 33 28	17 42 27	24 21 30	19 26.3	11 17.1	8 34.9	4 03.9	16 41.4	6 09.0	3 18.8	6 43.3	18 47.6	24 40.1
16 Sa	19 44 34	26 34 35	0♓55 21	7♓23 57	19 19.8	12 49.7	9 50.2	4 33.5	17 01.7	6 23.1	3 25.9	6 43.4	18 49.2	24 42.1
17 Su	19 48 31	27 35 42	13 47 23	20 05 52	19 13.8	14 20.3	11 05.4	5 03.2	17 22.1	6 37.2	3 33.1	6 43.6	18 50.7	24 44.1
18 M	19 52 27	28 36 49	26 19 39	2♈29 08	19 08.9	15 48.5	12 20.6	5 33.1	17 42.6	6 51.4	3 40.2	6 43.8	18 52.3	24 46.1
19 Tu	19 56 24	29 37 54	8♈34 45	14 37 01	19 05.7	17 13.9	13 35.8	6 03.2	18 03.2	7 05.6	3 47.3	6 44.0	18 53.9	24 48.1
20 W	20 00 20	0♒38 59	20 36 29	26 33 45	19D04.3	18 35.8	14 51.0	6 33.5	18 23.9	7 19.8	3 54.4	6 44.3	18 55.6	24 50.0
21 Th	20 04 17	1 40 02	2♉29 26	8♉24 13	19 04.4	19 53.8	16 06.2	7 03.9	18 44.7	7 34.0	4 01.6	6 44.6	18 57.3	24 52.0
22 F	20 08 13	2 41 05	14 18 44	20 13 40	19 05.7	21 07.0	17 21.4	7 34.5	19 05.6	7 48.2	4 08.7	6 45.0	18 58.9	24 54.0
23 Sa	20 12 10	3 42 07	26 09 37	2♊07 16	19 07.3	22 14.8	18 36.7	8 05.3	19 26.6	8 02.4	4 15.9	6 45.5	19 00.7	24 56.0
24 Su	20 16 07	4 43 08	8♊07 12	14 09 57	19R08.4	23 16.4	19 51.9	8 36.2	19 47.7	8 16.7	4 23.0	6 46.0	19 02.4	24 58.0
25 M	20 20 03	5 44 08	20 16 05	26 26 01	19 08.2	24 11.0	21 07.1	9 07.3	20 08.8	8 30.9	4 30.2	6 46.6	19 04.2	25 00.0
26 Tu	20 24 00	6 45 07	2♋40 10	8♋58 49	19 06.1	24 57.6	22 22.3	9 38.6	20 30.0	8 45.1	4 37.3	6 47.2	19 05.9	25 01.9
27 W	20 27 56	7 46 05	15 22 12	21 50 27	19 01.8	25 35.5	23 37.5	10 10.0	20 51.3	8 59.4	4 44.5	6 47.8	19 07.7	25 03.9
28 Th	20 31 53	8 47 02	28 23 34	5♌01 31	18 55.3	26 03.8	24 52.6	10 41.5	21 12.7	9 13.6	4 51.6	6 48.6	19 09.6	25 05.8
29 F	20 35 49	9 47 58	11♌44 05	18 31 01	18 47.0	26 22.0	26 07.8	11 13.2	21 34.2	9 27.9	4 58.7	6 49.3	19 11.4	25 07.8
30 Sa	20 39 46	10 48 53	25 21 56	2♍16 25	18 37.9	26R29.3	27 23.0	11 45.0	21 55.7	9 42.1	5 05.9	6 50.1	19 13.3	25 09.7
31 Su	20 43 42	11 49 47	9♍13 58	16 14 04	18 28.9	26 25.5	28 38.2	12 16.9	22 17.3	9 56.4	5 13.0	6 51.0	19 15.2	25 11.7

LONGITUDE — February 2021

Day	Sid.Time	☉	0 hr ☽	Noon ☽	True ☊	☿	♀	♂	⚳	♃	♄	♅	♆	♇
1 M	20 47 39	12♒50 40	23♍16 11	0♎19 47	18♊21.0	26♒10.4	29♑53.4	12♉49.0	22♓39.0	10♒10.6	5♒20.1	6♉51.9	19♓17.1	25♑13.6
2 Tu	20 51 36	13 51 32	7♎24 23	14 29 32	18R15.2	25R44.2	1♒08.6	13 21.1	23 00.8	10 24.9	5 27.2	6 52.9	19 19.0	25 15.5
3 W	20 55 32	14 52 24	21 34 50	28 39 57	18 11.7	25 07.5	2 23.8	13 53.4	23 22.6	10 39.1	5 34.3	6 53.9	19 20.9	25 17.4
4 Th	20 59 29	15 53 15	5♏44 36	12♏48 37	18D10.5	24 21.0	3 38.9	14 25.9	23 44.5	10 53.4	5 41.4	6 55.0	19 22.9	25 19.3
5 F	21 03 25	16 54 05	19 51 48	26 54 03	18 10.7	23 26.0	4 54.1	14 58.4	24 06.5	11 07.6	5 48.4	6 56.1	19 24.9	25 21.2
6 Sa	21 07 22	17 54 54	3♐55 16	10♐55 22	18R11.5	22 24.0	6 09.3	15 31.1	24 28.5	11 21.8	5 55.5	6 57.3	19 26.9	25 23.1
7 Su	21 11 18	18 55 42	17 54 16	24 51 50	18 11.4	21 16.9	7 24.5	16 03.8	24 50.7	11 36.0	6 02.5	6 58.5	19 28.9	25 25.0
8 M	21 15 15	19 56 30	1♑47 58	8♑42 27	18 09.6	20 06.5	8 39.6	16 36.7	25 12.8	11 50.2	6 09.6	6 59.8	19 30.9	25 26.8
9 Tu	21 19 11	20 57 16	15 35 08	22 25 43	18 05.1	18 54.9	9 54.8	17 09.7	25 35.1	12 04.4	6 16.6	7 01.1	19 33.0	25 28.7
10 W	21 23 08	21 58 01	29 13 58	5♒59 33	17 57.8	17 44.0	11 10.0	17 42.8	25 57.4	12 18.6	6 23.6	7 02.5	19 35.0	25 30.5
11 Th	21 27 05	22 58 45	12♒42 12	19 21 37	17 47.9	16 35.6	12 25.1	18 16.0	26 19.7	12 32.8	6 30.5	7 03.9	19 37.1	25 32.3
12 F	21 31 01	23 59 27	25 57 30	2♓29 39	17 36.1	15 31.4	13 40.3	18 49.3	26 42.1	12 46.9	6 37.5	7 05.3	19 39.2	25 34.1
13 Sa	21 34 58	25 00 08	8♓57 51	15 22 00	17 23.7	14 32.5	14 55.4	19 22.7	27 04.6	13 01.0	6 44.4	7 06.8	19 41.3	25 35.9
14 Su	21 38 54	26 00 48	21 42 03	27 58 02	17 11.7	13 40.0	16 10.5	19 56.2	27 27.2	13 15.1	6 51.3	7 08.4	19 43.4	25 37.7
15 M	21 42 51	27 01 26	4♈10 06	10♈18 25	17 01.3	12 54.6	17 25.6	20 29.8	27 49.7	13 29.2	6 58.2	7 10.0	19 45.5	25 39.5
16 Tu	21 46 47	28 02 02	16 23 17	22 25 05	16 53.2	12 16.8	18 40.7	21 03.4	28 12.4	13 43.3	7 05.0	7 11.7	19 47.7	25 41.2
17 W	21 50 44	29 02 36	28 24 13	4♉21 12	16 47.8	11 46.7	19 55.8	21 37.2	28 35.1	13 57.3	7 11.8	7 13.4	19 49.8	25 43.0
18 Th	21 54 40	0♓03 09	10♉16 35	16 10 59	16 44.9	11 24.4	21 10.9	22 11.0	28 57.8	14 11.3	7 18.6	7 15.1	19 52.0	25 44.7
19 F	21 58 37	1 03 40	22 05 02	27 59 23	16D43.9	11 09.7	22 26.0	22 45.0	29 20.6	14 25.3	7 25.4	7 16.9	19 54.2	25 46.4
20 Sa	22 02 33	2 04 09	3♊54 45	9♊51 48	16R44.0	11D02.4	23 41.1	23 19.0	29 43.4	14 39.3	7 32.1	7 18.7	19 56.3	25 48.1
21 Su	22 06 30	3 04 36	15 51 16	21 53 49	16 44.0	11 02.1	24 56.1	23 53.1	0♈06.3	14 53.2	7 38.8	7 20.6	19 58.5	25 49.8
22 M	22 10 27	4 05 02	28 00 06	4♋10 45	16 42.8	11 08.5	26 11.2	24 27.2	0 29.2	15 07.1	7 45.5	7 22.5	20 00.7	25 51.4
23 Tu	22 14 23	5 05 26	10♋26 18	16 47 16	16 39.5	11 21.2	27 26.2	25 01.4	0 52.2	15 21.0	7 52.2	7 24.5	20 03.0	25 53.1
24 W	22 18 20	6 05 47	23 14 01	29 46 51	16 33.5	11 39.8	28 41.2	25 35.7	1 15.2	15 34.8	7 58.8	7 26.5	20 05.2	25 54.7
25 Th	22 22 16	7 06 07	6♌25 54	13♌11 11	16 24.8	12 03.9	29 56.2	26 10.1	1 38.2	15 48.6	8 05.3	7 28.5	20 07.4	25 56.3
26 F	22 26 13	8 06 25	20 02 33	26 59 41	16 13.9	12 33.2	1♓11.2	26 44.5	2 01.3	16 02.4	8 11.9	7 30.6	20 09.6	25 57.9
27 Sa	22 30 09	9 06 41	4♍02 08	11♍09 18	16 01.7	13 07.1	2 26.2	27 19.0	2 24.4	16 16.1	8 18.4	7 32.8	20 11.9	25 59.4
28 Su	22 34 06	10 06 56	18 20 25	25 34 39	15 49.6	13 45.5	3 41.2	27 53.6	2 47.6	16 29.8	8 24.8	7 34.9	20 14.1	26 01.0

Astro Data

	Dy Hr Mn
♃∠♆	4 6:59
☽0S	6 1:11
♅D	14 8:38
♃□♅	17 22:51
☽0N	19 5:08
♄∠♆	20 16:59
☿R	30 15:54
☽0S	2 6:00
☽0N	15 12:51
♄□♅	17 19:10
☿D	21 0:53

Planet Ingress

	Dy Hr Mn
♂ ♉	6 22:28
☿ ♒	8 12:01
♀ ♑	8 15:42
☉ ♒	19 20:41
♀ ♒	1 14:07
☉ ♓	18 10:45
⚳ ♈	21 5:24
♀ ♓	25 13:13

Last Aspect / ☽ Ingress

Last Aspect Dy Hr Mn		☽ Ingress Dy Hr Mn
2 22:01 ♂ △	♍	3 1:14
4 21:35 ♀ □	♎	5 5:43
7 5:56 ♀ ⚹	♏	7 8:55
9 2:00 ♇ ⚹	♐	9 11:16
10 18:30 ♆ □	♑	11 13:31
13 7:23 ♇ ☌	♒	13 16:45
14 9:29 ☿ ☌	♓	15 22:18
18 3:46 ☉ ⚹	♈	18 7:08
20 8:30 ♇ □	♉	20 18:57
22 21:29 ♇ △	♊	23 7:44
25 7:18 ☿ △	♋	25 18:53
27 17:56 ♇ ☍	♌	28 2:55
30 1:54 ☿ ☍	♍	30 8:04

Last Aspect Dy Hr Mn		☽ Ingress Dy Hr Mn
1 11:11 ♀ △	♎	1 11:26
3 6:16 ☿ △	♏	3 14:16
5 9:21 ♇ ⚹	♐	5 17:18
7 6:17 ☿ ⚹	♑	7 20:53
9 17:23 ♇ ☌	♒	10 1:21
11 19:07 ☉ ☌	♓	12 7:24
14 7:30 ♇ ⚹	♈	14 15:55
17 0:18 ☉ ⚹	♉	17 3:13
19 7:29 ♇ △	♊	19 16:05
21 18:40 ♀ △	♋	22 3:54
24 4:55 ♇ ☍	♌	24 12:24
26 11:33 ♂ □	♍	26 17:08
28 15:59 ♂ △	♎	28 19:18

☽ Phases & Eclipses

Dy Hr Mn		
6 9:38	☾	16♎17
13 5:01	●	23♑13
20 21:03	☽	1♉02
28 19:17	○	9♌06
4 17:38	☾	16♏08
11 19:07	●	23♒17
19 18:48	☽	1♊21
27 8:18	○	8♍57

Astro Data

1 January 2021
Julian Day # 44196
SVP 4♓58'15"
GC 27♐08.0 ⚴ 8♒01.0
Eris 23♈27.6R ⚵ 4♐24.3
⚷ 5♈04.0 ⚶ 20♍12.4
☽ Mean ☊ 18♊49.8

1 February 2021
Julian Day # 44227
SVP 4♓58'10"
GC 27♐08.0 ⚴ 18♒27.6
Eris 23♈29.8 ⚵ 13♐24.7
⚷ 5♈56.1 ⚶ 20♍42.9R
☽ Mean ☊ 17♊11.3

March 2021 LONGITUDE

Day	Sid.Time	☉	0 hr ☽	Noon ☽	True ☊	☿	♀	♂	⚳	♃	♄	♅	♆	♇
1 M	22 38 02	11♓07 08	2♎51 08	10♎08 55	15♊38.8	14♒28.0	4♓56.1	28♉28.2	3♈10.8	16♒43.4	8♒31.2	7♉37.1	20♓16.4	26♑02.5
2 Tu	22 41 59	12 07 20	17 27 07	24 44 54	15R 30.4	15 14.2	6 11.1	29 02.8	3 34.0	16 57.0	8 37.6	7 39.4	20 18.6	26 04.0
3 W	22 45 56	13 07 29	2♏01 29	9♏16 15	15 24.9	16 04.0	7 26.0	29 37.5	3 57.3	17 10.6	8 43.9	7 41.7	20 20.9	26 05.5
4 Th	22 49 52	14 07 37	16 28 39	23 38 18	15 22.1	16 57.0	8 40.9	0♊12.3	4 20.6	17 24.1	8 50.2	7 44.0	20 23.2	26 07.0
5 F	22 53 49	15 07 44	0♐44 55	7♐48 21	15 21.3	17 53.1	9 55.9	0 47.1	4 43.9	17 37.6	8 56.5	7 46.3	20 25.4	26 08.4
6 Sa	22 57 45	16 07 49	14 48 30	21 45 24	15 21.2	18 52.0	11 10.8	1 22.0	5 07.3	17 51.1	9 02.7	7 48.7	20 27.7	26 09.8
7 Su	23 01 42	17 07 52	28 39 04	5♑29 38	15 20.5	19 53.6	12 25.7	1 57.0	5 30.7	18 04.5	9 08.9	7 51.2	20 30.0	26 11.2
8 M	23 05 38	18 07 54	12♑17 11	19 01 48	15 18.0	20 57.7	13 40.6	2 32.0	5 54.1	18 17.8	9 15.0	7 53.7	20 32.3	26 12.6
9 Tu	23 09 35	19 07 55	25 43 36	2♒22 38	15 12.8	22 04.2	14 55.5	3 07.0	6 17.6	18 31.1	9 21.0	7 56.2	20 34.5	26 14.0
10 W	23 13 31	20 07 53	8♒58 57	15 32 31	15 04.5	23 12.8	16 10.3	3 42.1	6 41.1	18 44.3	9 27.0	7 58.7	20 36.8	26 15.3
11 Th	23 17 28	21 07 50	22 03 22	28 31 24	14 53.4	24 23.5	17 25.2	4 17.3	7 04.6	18 57.5	9 33.0	8 01.3	20 39.1	26 16.6
12 F	23 21 25	22 07 45	4♓56 36	11♓18 52	14 40.3	25 36.3	18 40.0	4 52.5	7 28.2	19 10.6	9 38.9	8 03.9	20 41.4	26 17.9
13 Sa	23 25 21	23 07 38	17 38 10	23 54 27	14 26.4	26 50.9	19 54.8	5 27.7	7 51.7	19 23.7	9 44.8	8 06.6	20 43.6	26 19.2
14 Su	23 29 18	24 07 29	0♈07 42	6♈17 57	14 12.8	28 07.3	21 09.7	6 03.0	8 15.3	19 36.7	9 50.6	8 09.2	20 45.9	26 20.4
15 M	23 33 14	25 07 18	12 25 15	18 29 46	14 00.8	29 25.4	22 24.4	6 38.3	8 38.9	19 49.7	9 56.3	8 11.9	20 48.2	26 21.6
16 Tu	23 37 11	26 07 05	24 31 38	0♉31 08	13 51.1	0♓45.2	23 39.2	7 13.7	9 02.6	20 02.6	10 02.0	8 14.7	20 50.5	26 22.8
17 W	23 41 07	27 06 50	6♉28 34	12 24 17	13 44.3	2 06.6	24 54.0	7 49.1	9 26.2	20 15.4	10 07.7	8 17.5	20 52.7	26 24.0
18 Th	23 45 04	28 06 32	18 18 44	24 12 23	13 40.3	3 29.6	26 08.7	8 24.6	9 49.9	20 28.2	10 13.2	8 20.3	20 55.0	26 25.1
19 F	23 49 00	29 06 13	0♊05 46	5♊59 30	13D 38.7	4 54.1	27 23.5	9 00.1	10 13.6	20 40.9	10 18.8	8 23.1	20 57.3	26 26.3
20 Sa	23 52 57	0♈05 51	11 54 10	17 50 27	13 38.5	6 20.1	28 38.2	9 35.6	10 37.3	20 53.6	10 24.2	8 26.0	20 59.5	26 27.4
21 Su	23 56 54	1 05 27	23 49 00	29 50 32	13R 38.7	7 47.5	29 52.9	10 11.2	11 01.0	21 06.1	10 29.6	8 28.8	21 01.8	26 28.4
22 M	0 00 50	2 05 01	5♋55 44	12♋05 17	13 38.3	9 16.3	1♈07.6	10 46.8	11 24.8	21 18.6	10 35.0	8 31.8	21 04.0	26 29.5
23 Tu	0 04 47	3 04 33	18 19 49	24 39 58	13 36.2	10 46.6	2 22.2	11 22.5	11 48.5	21 31.1	10 40.2	8 34.7	21 06.3	26 30.5
24 W	0 08 43	4 04 02	1♌06 16	7♌39 09	13 31.8	12 18.2	3 36.8	11 58.1	12 12.3	21 43.4	10 45.4	8 37.7	21 08.5	26 31.5
25 Th	0 12 40	5 03 28	14 18 57	21 05 51	13 25.0	13 51.2	4 51.5	12 33.9	12 36.1	21 55.7	10 50.6	8 40.7	21 10.7	26 32.4
26 F	0 16 36	6 02 53	27 59 53	5♍00 53	13 16.1	15 25.6	6 06.1	13 09.6	12 59.9	22 07.9	10 55.7	8 43.7	21 13.0	26 33.4
27 Sa	0 20 33	7 02 15	12♍08 32	19 22 14	13 06.0	17 01.4	7 20.6	13 45.3	13 23.7	22 20.1	11 00.7	8 46.7	21 15.2	26 34.3
28 Su	0 24 29	8 01 35	26 41 17	4♎04 45	12 55.7	18 38.5	8 35.2	14 21.1	13 47.5	22 32.1	11 05.6	8 49.8	21 17.4	26 35.2
29 M	0 28 26	9 00 53	11♎31 36	19 00 41	12 46.5	20 17.0	9 49.7	14 57.0	14 11.3	22 44.1	11 10.5	8 52.9	21 19.6	26 36.0
30 Tu	0 32 23	10 00 09	26 30 51	4♏00 53	12 39.3	21 56.9	11 04.3	15 32.8	14 35.1	22 56.0	11 15.3	8 56.0	21 21.8	26 36.9
31 W	0 36 19	10 59 24	11♏29 42	18 56 17	12 34.8	23 38.1	12 18.8	16 08.7	14 59.0	23 07.8	11 20.1	8 59.1	21 23.9	26 37.7

April 2021 LONGITUDE

Day	Sid.Time	☉	0 hr ☽	Noon ☽	True ☊	☿	♀	♂	⚳	♃	♄	♅	♆	♇
1 Th	0 40 16	11♈58 36	26♏19 46	3♐39 26	12♊32.7	25♓20.7	13♈33.3	16♊44.6	15♈22.8	23♒19.6	11♒24.7	9♉02.3	21♓26.1	26♑38.4
2 F	0 44 12	12 57 47	10♐54 44	18 05 18	12D 32.5	27 04.8	14 47.8	17 20.5	15 46.7	23 31.2	11 29.3	9 05.4	21 28.3	26 39.2
3 Sa	0 48 09	13 56 56	25 10 52	2♑11 22	12R 33.2	28 50.2	16 02.2	17 56.4	16 10.5	23 42.8	11 33.9	9 08.6	21 30.4	26 39.9
4 Su	0 52 05	14 56 03	9♑06 49	15 57 18	12 33.6	0♈37.1	17 16.7	18 32.4	16 34.4	23 54.3	11 38.3	9 11.9	21 32.5	26 40.6
5 M	0 56 02	15 55 08	22 43 01	29 24 10	12 32.7	2 25.4	18 31.1	19 08.4	16 58.3	24 05.7	11 42.7	9 15.1	21 34.7	26 41.3
6 Tu	0 59 58	16 54 12	6♒01 00	12♒33 47	12 29.7	4 15.1	19 45.5	19 44.4	17 22.2	24 17.0	11 47.0	9 18.3	21 36.8	26 41.9
7 W	1 03 55	17 53 14	19 02 46	25 28 12	12 24.4	6 06.3	20 59.9	20 20.5	17 46.0	24 28.2	11 51.2	9 21.6	21 38.9	26 42.5
8 Th	1 07 52	18 52 14	1♓50 18	8♓09 18	12 16.8	7 59.0	22 14.3	20 56.5	18 09.9	24 39.3	11 55.4	9 24.9	21 41.0	26 43.1
9 F	1 11 48	19 51 12	14 25 21	20 38 39	12 07.7	9 53.1	23 28.7	21 32.6	18 33.8	24 50.4	11 59.4	9 28.2	21 43.0	26 43.6
10 Sa	1 15 45	20 50 08	26 49 19	2♈57 31	11 57.9	11 48.6	24 43.0	22 08.8	18 57.7	25 01.3	12 03.4	9 31.5	21 45.1	26 44.1
11 Su	1 19 41	21 49 03	9♈03 23	15 07 02	11 48.3	13 45.6	25 57.4	22 44.9	19 21.6	25 12.1	12 07.3	9 34.8	21 47.1	26 44.6
12 M	1 23 38	22 47 55	21 08 37	27 08 18	11 39.8	15 44.0	27 11.7	23 21.1	19 45.4	25 22.8	12 11.2	9 38.1	21 49.1	26 45.1
13 Tu	1 27 34	23 46 45	3♉06 15	9♉02 43	11 33.1	17 43.8	28 26.0	23 57.3	20 09.3	25 33.5	12 14.9	9 41.5	21 51.2	26 45.5
14 W	1 31 31	24 45 34	14 57 54	20 52 06	11 28.6	19 44.9	29 40.2	24 33.5	20 33.2	25 44.0	12 18.6	9 44.9	21 53.2	26 45.9
15 Th	1 35 27	25 44 20	26 45 39	2♊38 54	11D 26.3	21 47.3	0♉54.5	25 09.7	20 57.1	25 54.4	12 22.2	9 48.2	21 55.1	26 46.3
16 F	1 39 24	26 43 04	8♊32 17	14 26 13	11 25.9	23 50.9	2 08.7	25 46.0	21 20.9	26 04.7	12 25.7	9 51.6	21 57.1	26 46.6
17 Sa	1 43 20	27 41 46	20 21 13	26 17 49	11 26.8	25 55.6	3 23.0	26 22.3	21 44.8	26 14.9	12 29.1	9 55.0	21 59.0	26 46.9
18 Su	1 47 17	28 40 26	2♋16 34	8♋18 04	11 28.3	28 01.3	4 37.2	26 58.6	22 08.7	26 25.0	12 32.4	9 58.4	22 01.0	26 47.2
19 M	1 51 14	29 39 04	14 22 56	20 31 46	11R 29.6	0♉07.9	5 51.3	27 34.9	22 32.5	26 35.0	12 35.6	10 01.8	22 02.9	26 47.5
20 Tu	1 55 10	0♉37 39	26 45 12	3♌03 50	11 29.9	2 15.1	7 05.5	28 11.2	22 56.3	26 44.9	12 38.8	10 05.3	22 04.8	26 47.7
21 W	1 59 07	1 36 12	9♌28 14	15 58 54	11 28.8	4 22.8	8 19.6	28 47.5	23 20.2	26 54.6	12 41.9	10 08.7	22 06.6	26 47.9
22 Th	2 03 03	2 34 43	22 36 15	29 20 39	11 26.1	6 30.7	9 33.7	29 23.9	23 44.0	27 04.2	12 44.8	10 12.1	22 08.5	26 48.1
23 F	2 07 00	3 33 12	6♍12 16	13♍11 10	11 22.0	8 38.6	10 47.8	0♋00.3	24 07.8	27 13.8	12 47.7	10 15.6	22 10.3	26 48.2
24 Sa	2 10 56	4 31 39	20 17 11	27 30 02	11 16.8	10 46.3	12 01.9	0 36.6	24 31.5	27 23.2	12 50.5	10 19.0	22 12.1	26 48.3
25 Su	2 14 53	5 30 03	4♎49 09	12♎13 51	11 11.4	12 53.3	13 15.9	1 13.0	24 55.3	27 32.4	12 53.3	10 22.4	22 13.9	26 48.4
26 M	2 18 49	6 28 26	19 43 11	27 16 07	11 06.5	14 59.5	14 29.9	1 49.4	25 19.1	27 41.6	12 55.9	10 25.9	22 15.7	26 48.5
27 Tu	2 22 46	7 26 46	4♏51 26	12♏27 54	11 02.8	17 04.4	15 43.9	2 25.8	25 42.8	27 50.6	12 58.4	10 29.3	22 17.4	26R 48.5
28 W	2 26 43	8 25 05	20 04 15	27 39 13	11D 00.7	19 07.9	16 57.9	3 02.3	26 06.6	27 59.5	13 00.9	10 32.8	22 19.1	26 48.5
29 Th	2 30 39	9 23 23	5♐11 40	12♐40 33	11 00.1	21 09.5	18 11.9	3 38.7	26 30.3	28 08.3	13 03.2	10 36.3	22 20.8	26 48.4
30 F	2 34 36	10 21 39	20 05 02	27 24 22	11 00.8	23 09.1	19 25.8	4 15.2	26 54.0	28 17.0	13 05.5	10 39.7	22 22.5	26 48.4

Astro Data

	Dy Hr Mn
☽ 0S	1 12:41
☽ 0N	14 20:07
☉ 0N	20 9:38
♃⚺♆	21 1:52
♀ 0N	24 3:40
☽ 0S	28 22:14
⚳ 0N	4 15:01
☿ 0N	6 18:32
☽ 0N	11 2:43
♃⚺♇	20 19:10
☽ 0S	25 9:15
♇ R	27 20:03

Planet Ingress

	Dy Hr Mn
♂ ♊	4 3:31
☿ ♓	15 22:28
☉ ♈	20 9:39
♀ ♈	21 14:17
☿ ♈	4 3:42
♀ ♉	14 18:23
☿ ♉	19 10:30
☉ ♉	19 20:35
♂ ♋	23 11:50

Last Aspect / ☽ Ingress (March)

Last Aspect Dy Hr Mn		☽ Ingress	Dy Hr Mn
2 14:11	♇ □	♏	2 20:39
4 16:11	♇ ⚹	♐	4 22:44
6 9:45	♆ □	♑	7 2:21
9 0:54	♇ ☌	♒	9 7:42
11 3:33	☿ ☌	♓	11 14:45
13 16:39	♇ ⚹	♈	13 23:45
16 3:41	♇ □	♉	16 10:57
18 20:41	☉ ⚹	♊	18 23:48
21 12:05	♀ □	♋	21 12:19
23 15:27	♇ ☍	♌	23 21:57
25 13:29	♃ ☍	♍	26 3:27
27 23:49	♇ △	♎	28 5:23
30 0:09	♇ □	♏	30 5:34

Last Aspect / ☽ Ingress (April)

Last Aspect Dy Hr Mn		☽ Ingress	Dy Hr Mn
1 0:30	♇ ⚹	♐	1 6:00
3 5:25	☿ □	♑	3 8:14
5 7:06	♇ ☌	♒	5 13:05
7 10:06	♃ ☌	♓	7 20:32
9 23:49	♇ ⚹	♈	10 6:12
12 12:08	♀ ☌	♉	12 17:45
15 0:01	♇ △	♊	15 6:36
17 15:04	☉ ⚹	♋	17 19:26
20 0:05	♇ ☍	♌	20 6:12
22 12:06	♂ ⚹	♍	22 13:09
24 10:51	♇ △	♎	24 16:07
26 12:41	♃ △	♏	26 16:19
28 12:33	♃ □	♐	28 15:44
30 13:28	♃ ⚹	♑	30 16:17

☽ Phases & Eclipses

Dy Hr Mn		
6 1:31	☾	15♐42
13 10:22	●	23♓04
21 14:42	☽	1♋12
28 18:49	○	8♎18
4 10:04	☾	14♑51
12 2:32	●	22♈25
20 7:00	☽	0♌25
27 3:33	○	7♏06

Astro Data

1 March 2021
Julian Day # 44255
SVP 4♓58'07"
GC 27♐08.1 ⚵ 27♒53.6
Eris 23♈40.2 ⚴ 19♐47.7
⚷ 7♈16.0 ⚶ 15♍13.8R
☽ Mean ☊ 15♊42.4

1 April 2021
Julian Day # 44286
SVP 4♓58'04"
GC 27♐08.2 ⚵ 7♓50.2
Eris 23♈58.2 ⚴ 23♐43.0
⚷ 9♈02.5 ⚶ 8♍07.9R
☽ Mean ☊ 14♊03.9

LONGITUDE — May 2021

Day	Sid.Time	☉	0 hr ☽	Noon ☽	True ☊	☿	♀	♂	⚳	♃	♄	♅	♆	♇
1 Sa	2 38 32	11♉19 53	4♑38 03	11♑45 44	11♊02.2	25♉06.2	20♉39.8	4♋51.7	27♈17.7	28♒25.5	13♒07.6	10♉43.2	22♓24.2	26♑48.3
2 Su	2 42 29	12 18 06	18 47 13	25 42 27	11 03.6	27 00.8	21 53.7	5 28.1	27 41.4	28 33.9	13 09.7	10 46.6	22 25.8	26R48.2
3 M	2 46 25	13 16 17	2♒31 31	9♒14 37	11R04.5	28 52.5	23 07.6	6 04.6	28 05.0	28 42.2	13 11.7	10 50.1	22 27.4	26 48.0
4 Tu	2 50 22	14 14 27	15 51 58	22 23 55	11 04.3	0♊41.1	24 21.5	6 41.2	28 28.7	28 50.3	13 13.6	10 53.6	22 29.0	26 47.9
5 W	2 54 19	15 12 35	28 50 49	5♓13 04	11 02.9	2 26.5	25 35.3	7 17.7	28 52.3	28 58.3	13 15.4	10 57.0	22 30.6	26 47.7
6 Th	2 58 15	16 10 42	11♓31 02	17 45 08	11 00.3	4 08.6	26 49.2	7 54.2	29 15.9	29 06.1	13 17.1	11 00.5	22 32.1	26 47.4
7 F	3 02 12	17 08 47	23 55 45	0♈03 15	10 57.0	5 47.2	28 03.0	8 30.8	29 39.5	29 13.8	13 18.7	11 03.9	22 33.6	26 47.2
8 Sa	3 06 08	18 06 51	6♈08 01	12 10 23	10 53.2	7 22.1	29 16.8	9 07.4	0♉03.0	29 21.4	13 20.2	11 07.3	22 35.1	26 46.9
9 Su	3 10 05	19 04 54	18 10 39	24 09 09	10 49.5	8 53.4	0♊30.6	9 43.9	0 26.6	29 28.8	13 21.6	11 10.8	22 36.5	26 46.5
10 M	3 14 01	20 02 55	0♉06 10	6♉01 58	10 46.4	10 20.9	1 44.4	10 20.5	0 50.1	29 36.1	13 22.9	11 14.2	22 38.0	26 46.2
11 Tu	3 17 58	21 00 54	11 56 49	17 50 59	10 44.0	11 44.6	2 58.2	10 57.2	1 13.6	29 43.2	13 24.1	11 17.6	22 39.4	26 45.8
12 W	3 21 54	21 58 52	23 44 45	29 38 21	10D42.6	13 04.3	4 11.9	11 33.8	1 37.0	29 50.2	13 25.2	11 21.1	22 40.8	26 45.4
13 Th	3 25 51	22 56 48	5♊32 05	11♊26 14	10 42.2	14 20.1	5 25.6	12 10.4	2 00.5	29 57.0	13 26.2	11 24.5	22 42.1	26 45.0
14 F	3 29 47	23 54 43	17 21 07	23 17 04	10 42.6	15 31.9	6 39.4	12 47.1	2 23.9	0♓03.7	13 27.2	11 27.9	22 43.5	26 44.5
15 Sa	3 33 44	24 52 37	29 14 27	5♋13 37	10 43.7	16 39.5	7 53.0	13 23.7	2 47.3	0 10.2	13 28.0	11 31.3	22 44.8	26 44.1
16 Su	3 37 41	25 50 28	11♋14 59	17 18 59	10 45.0	17 43.0	9 06.7	14 00.4	3 10.6	0 16.6	13 28.7	11 34.7	22 46.0	26 43.6
17 M	3 41 37	26 48 18	23 26 04	29 36 40	10 46.2	18 42.3	10 20.4	14 37.1	3 33.9	0 22.8	13 29.3	11 38.0	22 47.3	26 43.0
18 Tu	3 45 34	27 46 06	5♌51 18	12♌10 24	10 47.2	19 37.3	11 34.0	15 13.8	3 57.2	0 28.9	13 29.9	11 41.4	22 48.5	26 42.5
19 W	3 49 30	28 43 53	18 34 28	25 03 53	10R47.6	20 28.0	12 47.6	15 50.5	4 20.5	0 34.7	13 30.3	11 44.8	22 49.7	26 41.9
20 Th	3 53 27	29 41 38	1♍39 06	8♍20 25	10 47.5	21 14.2	14 01.2	16 27.2	4 43.7	0 40.5	13 30.6	11 48.1	22 50.8	26 41.3
21 F	3 57 23	0♊39 21	15 08 06	22 02 19	10 46.9	21 56.0	15 14.7	17 04.0	5 06.9	0 46.0	13 30.9	11 51.4	22 52.0	26 40.6
22 Sa	4 01 20	1 37 02	29 03 05	6♎10 19	10 46.1	22 33.2	16 28.3	17 40.7	5 30.0	0 51.4	13R31.0	11 54.7	22 53.1	26 40.0
23 Su	4 05 16	2 34 42	13♎23 43	20 42 53	10 45.1	23 05.8	17 41.8	18 17.4	5 53.2	0 56.7	13 31.0	11 58.0	22 54.1	26 39.3
24 M	4 09 13	3 32 21	28 07 12	5♏35 54	10 44.3	23 33.7	18 55.3	18 54.2	6 16.2	1 01.8	13 31.0	12 01.3	22 55.2	26 38.6
25 Tu	4 13 10	4 29 58	13♏08 02	20 42 34	10 43.7	23 56.9	20 08.8	19 31.0	6 39.3	1 06.7	13 30.8	12 04.6	22 56.2	26 37.8
26 W	4 17 06	5 27 34	28 18 22	5♐54 13	10D43.5	24 15.4	21 22.2	20 07.7	7 02.3	1 11.4	13 30.6	12 07.8	22 57.2	26 37.1
27 Th	4 21 03	6 25 09	13♐28 55	21 01 19	10 43.5	24 29.2	22 35.7	20 44.5	7 25.3	1 16.0	13 30.2	12 11.1	22 58.1	26 36.3
28 F	4 24 59	7 22 42	28 30 21	5♑55 02	10 43.7	24 38.2	23 49.1	21 21.3	7 48.2	1 20.4	13 29.8	12 14.3	22 59.1	26 35.5
29 Sa	4 28 56	8 20 15	13♑14 34	20 28 18	10 44.0	24R42.6	25 02.5	21 58.1	8 11.1	1 24.6	13 29.2	12 17.5	22 59.9	26 34.7
30 Su	4 32 52	9 17 47	27 35 45	4♒36 37	10 44.2	24 42.3	26 15.9	22 34.9	8 34.0	1 28.6	13 28.6	12 20.7	23 00.8	26 33.8
31 M	4 36 49	10 15 17	11♒30 45	18 18 09	10R44.3	24 37.5	27 29.3	23 11.7	8 56.8	1 32.5	13 27.9	12 23.8	23 01.6	26 33.0

LONGITUDE — June 2021

Day	Sid.Time	☉	0 hr ☽	Noon ☽	True ☊	☿	♀	♂	⚳	♃	♄	♅	♆	♇
1 Tu	4 40 46	11♊12 47	24♒58 56	1♓33 23	10♊44.3	24♊28.4	28♊42.6	23♋48.6	9♉19.6	1♓36.2	13♒27.0	12♉27.0	23♓02.4	26♑32.1
2 W	4 44 42	12 10 17	8♓01 48	14 24 36	10D44.3	24R15.2	29 55.9	24 25.4	9 42.3	1 39.7	13R26.1	12 30.1	23 03.2	26R31.2
3 Th	4 48 39	13 07 45	20 42 15	26 55 13	10 44.3	23 58.0	1♋09.3	25 02.3	10 05.0	1 43.0	13 25.1	12 33.2	23 03.9	26 30.2
4 F	4 52 35	14 05 13	3♈04 02	9♈09 13	10 44.5	23 37.2	2 22.6	25 39.1	10 27.6	1 46.2	13 24.0	12 36.2	23 04.6	26 29.3
5 Sa	4 56 32	15 02 40	15 11 18	21 10 47	10 44.9	23 13.2	3 35.8	26 16.0	10 50.2	1 49.2	13 22.8	12 39.3	23 05.3	26 28.3
6 Su	5 00 28	16 00 06	27 08 09	3♉03 54	10 45.5	22 46.3	4 49.1	26 52.9	11 12.8	1 51.9	13 21.5	12 42.3	23 06.0	26 27.3
7 M	5 04 25	16 57 32	8♉58 28	14 52 17	10 46.1	22 17.0	6 02.3	27 29.8	11 35.3	1 54.5	13 20.1	12 45.3	23 06.6	26 26.3
8 Tu	5 08 21	17 54 57	20 45 45	26 39 14	10 46.6	21 45.9	7 15.6	28 06.7	11 57.7	1 57.0	13 18.6	12 48.3	23 07.1	26 25.2
9 W	5 12 18	18 52 21	2♊33 06	8♊27 38	10R46.8	21 13.3	8 28.8	28 43.7	12 20.1	1 59.2	13 17.0	12 51.3	23 07.7	26 24.2
10 Th	5 16 15	19 49 44	14 23 10	20 19 58	10 46.7	20 39.9	9 42.0	29 20.6	12 42.5	2 01.2	13 15.3	12 54.2	23 08.2	26 23.1
11 F	5 20 11	20 47 07	26 18 19	2♋18 27	10 46.1	20 06.3	10 55.2	29 57.6	13 04.8	2 03.1	13 13.6	12 57.1	23 08.7	26 22.0
12 Sa	5 24 08	21 44 29	8♋20 37	14 25 04	10 45.0	19 33.0	12 08.3	0♌34.5	13 27.0	2 04.7	13 11.7	13 00.0	23 09.1	26 20.9
13 Su	5 28 04	22 41 50	20 32 03	26 41 48	10 43.4	19 00.6	13 21.5	1 11.5	13 49.2	2 06.2	13 09.8	13 02.9	23 09.6	26 19.8
14 M	5 32 01	23 39 11	2♌54 34	9♌10 35	10 41.7	18 29.6	14 34.6	1 48.5	14 11.3	2 07.5	13 07.8	13 05.7	23 09.9	26 18.6
15 Tu	5 35 57	24 36 30	15 30 07	21 53 27	10 40.0	18 00.6	15 47.7	2 25.5	14 33.4	2 08.5	13 05.6	13 08.5	23 10.3	26 17.4
16 W	5 39 54	25 33 49	28 20 48	4♍52 26	10 38.6	17 34.1	17 00.7	3 02.5	14 55.4	2 09.4	13 03.4	13 11.3	23 10.6	26 16.3
17 Th	5 43 50	26 31 06	11♍28 35	18 09 29	10D37.8	17 10.5	18 13.8	3 39.6	15 17.3	2 10.1	13 01.2	13 14.0	23 10.9	26 15.1
18 F	5 47 47	27 28 23	24 55 19	1♎46 12	10 37.6	16 50.1	19 26.8	4 16.6	15 39.2	2 10.6	12 58.8	13 16.7	23 11.1	26 13.9
19 Sa	5 51 44	28 25 39	8♎42 13	15 43 21	10 38.2	16 33.5	20 39.8	4 53.6	16 01.0	2 10.9	12 56.3	13 19.4	23 11.3	26 12.6
20 Su	5 55 40	29 22 54	22 49 33	0♏00 34	10 39.3	16 20.7	21 52.8	5 30.7	16 22.8	2R11.1	12 53.8	13 22.0	23 11.5	26 11.4
21 M	5 59 37	0♋20 08	7♏16 07	14 35 45	10 40.5	16 12.2	23 05.7	6 07.8	16 44.5	2 11.0	12 51.2	13 24.7	23 11.7	26 10.1
22 Tu	6 03 33	1 17 22	21 58 53	29 24 50	10R41.5	16D08.0	24 18.6	6 44.8	17 06.1	2 10.7	12 48.5	13 27.2	23 11.8	26 08.9
23 W	6 07 30	2 14 36	6♐52 46	14♐21 46	10 41.7	16 08.4	25 31.5	7 21.9	17 27.7	2 10.3	12 45.7	13 29.8	23 11.9	26 07.6
24 Th	6 11 26	3 11 49	21 50 52	29 19 01	10 40.9	16 13.4	26 44.4	7 59.0	17 49.2	2 09.6	12 42.9	13 32.3	23 12.0	26 06.3
25 F	6 15 23	4 09 01	6♑45 12	14♑08 25	10 39.0	16 23.2	27 57.2	8 36.1	18 10.6	2 08.8	12 40.0	13 34.8	23R12.0	26 05.0
26 Sa	6 19 19	5 06 13	21 27 44	28 42 20	10 36.2	16 37.7	29 10.1	9 13.3	18 32.0	2 07.8	12 37.0	13 37.3	23 12.0	26 03.7
27 Su	6 23 16	6 03 25	5♒51 31	12♒54 44	10 32.7	16 57.1	0♌22.8	9 50.4	18 53.2	2 06.6	12 33.9	13 39.7	23 11.9	26 02.4
28 M	6 27 13	7 00 37	19 51 36	26 41 54	10 29.1	17 21.2	1 35.6	10 27.5	19 14.5	2 05.1	12 30.8	13 42.1	23 11.9	26 01.0
29 Tu	6 31 09	7 57 49	3♓25 34	10♓02 38	10 26.0	17 50.0	2 48.4	11 04.7	19 35.6	2 03.5	12 27.6	13 44.4	23 11.8	25 59.7
30 W	6 35 06	8 55 01	16 33 21	22 58 00	10 23.7	18 23.6	4 01.1	11 41.9	19 56.7	2 01.7	12 24.3	13 46.7	23 11.6	25 58.3

Astro Data

	Dy Hr Mn
☽0N	8 8:51
☽0S	22 19:29
♄R	23 9:20
☿R	29 22:36
☽0N	4 15:02
♄□♅	14 22:02
☽0S	19 3:18
♃R	20 15:06
☿D	22 22:02
♆R	25 19:23

Planet Ingress

	Dy Hr Mn
☿ ♊	4 2:50
⚳ ♉	8 8:55
♀ ♊	9 2:02
♃ ♓	13 22:37
☉ ♊	20 19:38
♀ ♋	2 13:20
♂ ♌	11 13:35
☉ ♋	21 3:33
♀ ♌	27 4:28

Last Aspect / ☽ Ingress (May)

Last Aspect Dy Hr Mn		☽ Ingress	Dy Hr Mn
2 14:39	☿ △	♒	2 19:32
5 0:07	♃ ☌	♓	5 2:10
7 7:37	♀ ⚹	♈	7 11:54
9 22:51	♃ ⚹	♉	9 23:48
12 12:24	♃ □	♊	12 12:44
14 10:52	♆ □	♋	15 1:32
17 6:24	♇ ☍	♌	17 12:45
19 19:14	☉ □	♍	19 21:00
21 19:57	♇ △	♎	22 1:37
23 21:38	♇ □	♏	24 3:02
25 21:21	♇ ⚹	♐	26 2:40
27 17:37	♀ ☍	♑	28 2:25
29 22:16	♇ ☌	♒	30 4:05

Last Aspect / ☽ Ingress (June)

Last Aspect Dy Hr Mn		☽ Ingress	Dy Hr Mn
1 6:15	♀ △	♓	1 9:09
3 11:12	♇ ⚹	♈	3 18:00
5 22:48	♂ □	♉	6 5:47
8 15:08	♂ ⚹	♊	8 18:49
10 17:39	♆ □	♋	11 7:24
13 11:17	♇ ☍	♌	13 18:24
15 17:28	☉ ⚹	♍	16 3:03
18 3:55	☉ □	♎	18 8:55
20 10:53	☉ △	♏	20 11:59
22 6:44	♇ ⚹	♐	22 12:57
24 2:10	♆ □	♑	24 13:06
26 12:51	♀ ☍	♒	26 14:10
27 19:09	☿ △	♓	28 17:52

☽ Phases & Eclipses

Dy Hr Mn	
3 19:51	☾ 13♒35
11 19:01	● 21♉18
19 19:14	☽ 29♌01
26 11:15	○ 5♐26
26 11:20	• T 1.009
2 7:26	☾ 11♓59
10 10:54	● 19♊47
10 10:43:05	• A 03'51"
18 3:55	☽ 27♍09
24 18:41	○ 3♑28

Astro Data

1 May 2021
Julian Day # 44316
SVP 4♓58'00"
GC 27♐08.2 ⚴ 16♓24.6
Eris 24♈17.7 * 23♐01.8R
⚷ 10♈43.9 ⚵ 7♍11.1
☽ Mean ☊ 12♊28.5

1 June 2021
Julian Day # 44347
SVP 4♓57'55"
GC 27♐08.3 ⚴ 23♓24.9
Eris 24♈35.2 * 17♐37.0R
⚷ 12♈06.8 ⚵ 12♍56.9
☽ Mean ☊ 10♊50.1

July 2021 — LONGITUDE

Day	Sid.Time	☉	0 hr ☽	Noon ☽	True ☊	☿	♀	♂	⚳	♃	♄	♅	♆	♇
1 Th	6 39 02	9♋52 13	29♓16 59	5♈30 49	10♊22.7	19♊01.9	5♌13.8	12♌19.0	20♉17.6	1♓59.8	12♒21.0	13♉49.0	23♓11.4	25♑57.0
2 F	6 42 59	10 49 26	11♈40 00	17 45 08	10D 22.8	19 44.7	6 26.5	12 56.2	20 38.5	1R 57.6	12R 17.6	13 51.2	23R 11.2	25R 55.6
3 Sa	6 46 55	11 46 38	23 46 49	29 45 39	10 23.9	20 32.2	7 39.1	13 33.5	20 59.4	1 55.2	12 14.1	13 53.4	23 11.0	25 54.2
4 Su	6 50 52	12 43 51	5♉42 16	11♉37 16	10 25.5	21 24.2	8 51.7	14 10.7	21 20.1	1 52.7	12 10.6	13 55.6	23 10.7	25 52.8
5 M	6 54 48	13 41 04	17 31 13	23 24 44	10 27.2	22 20.6	10 04.3	14 47.9	21 40.8	1 49.9	12 07.0	13 57.7	23 10.4	25 51.4
6 Tu	6 58 45	14 38 17	29 18 19	5♊12 29	10R 28.3	23 21.5	11 16.9	15 25.2	22 01.4	1 47.0	12 03.4	13 59.8	23 10.1	25 50.0
7 W	7 02 42	15 35 30	11♊07 42	17 04 24	10 28.2	24 26.6	12 29.5	16 02.5	22 21.9	1 43.9	11 59.7	14 01.9	23 09.8	25 48.6
8 Th	7 06 38	16 32 44	23 02 56	29 03 40	10 26.5	25 36.1	13 42.0	16 39.8	22 42.3	1 40.6	11 55.9	14 03.9	23 09.4	25 47.2
9 F	7 10 35	17 29 58	5♋06 53	11♋12 48	10 23.2	26 49.8	14 54.5	17 17.1	23 02.6	1 37.1	11 52.1	14 05.8	23 08.9	25 45.8
10 Sa	7 14 31	18 27 12	17 21 39	23 33 33	10 18.2	28 07.7	16 07.0	17 54.4	23 22.8	1 33.5	11 48.2	14 07.8	23 08.5	25 44.3
11 Su	7 18 28	19 24 26	29 48 39	6♌07 00	10 12.0	29 29.6	17 19.4	18 31.8	23 42.9	1 29.7	11 44.3	14 09.6	23 08.0	25 42.9
12 M	7 22 24	20 21 40	12♌28 39	18 53 39	10 05.2	0♋55.6	18 31.8	19 09.1	24 02.9	1 25.6	11 40.3	14 11.5	23 07.5	25 41.5
13 Tu	7 26 21	21 18 54	25 22 00	1♍53 41	9 58.6	2 25.6	19 44.2	19 46.5	24 22.9	1 21.5	11 36.3	14 13.3	23 06.9	25 40.0
14 W	7 30 18	22 16 09	8♍28 42	15 07 03	9 52.8	3 59.4	20 56.6	20 23.9	24 42.7	1 17.1	11 32.3	14 15.0	23 06.4	25 38.6
15 Th	7 34 14	23 13 23	21 48 43	28 33 41	9 48.6	5 36.9	22 08.9	21 01.3	25 02.4	1 12.6	11 28.2	14 16.8	23 05.8	25 37.1
16 F	7 38 11	24 10 38	5♎21 58	12♎13 33	9D 46.2	7 18.1	23 21.2	21 38.7	25 22.0	1 07.9	11 24.1	14 18.4	23 05.1	25 35.7
17 Sa	7 42 07	25 07 52	19 08 27	26 06 36	9 45.6	9 02.8	24 33.4	22 16.2	25 41.6	1 03.1	11 19.9	14 20.1	23 04.4	25 34.3
18 Su	7 46 04	26 05 07	3♏07 59	10♏12 30	9 46.2	10 50.8	25 45.7	22 53.6	26 01.0	0 58.1	11 15.7	14 21.6	23 03.8	25 32.8
19 M	7 50 00	27 02 22	17 20 00	24 30 17	9 47.3	12 41.9	26 57.8	23 31.1	26 20.3	0 53.0	11 11.5	14 23.2	23 03.0	25 31.4
20 Tu	7 53 57	27 59 37	1♐43 03	8♐57 57	9R 47.9	14 35.8	28 10.0	24 08.5	26 39.5	0 47.7	11 07.2	14 24.7	23 02.3	25 29.9
21 W	7 57 53	28 56 52	16 14 30	23 32 08	9 47.2	16 32.4	29 22.1	24 46.0	26 58.5	0 42.2	11 02.9	14 26.1	23 01.5	25 28.5
22 Th	8 01 50	29 54 08	0♑50 13	8♑08 01	9 44.5	18 31.4	0♍34.1	25 23.6	27 17.5	0 36.6	10 58.6	14 27.5	23 00.7	25 27.1
23 F	8 05 47	0♌51 24	15 24 46	22 39 39	9 39.5	20 32.4	1 46.2	26 01.1	27 36.4	0 30.9	10 54.3	14 28.9	22 59.9	25 25.6
24 Sa	8 09 43	1 48 41	29 51 53	7♒00 39	9 32.6	22 35.1	2 58.1	26 38.6	27 55.1	0 25.0	10 49.9	14 30.2	22 59.0	25 24.2
25 Su	8 13 40	2 45 58	14♒05 16	21 05 06	9 24.3	24 39.3	4 10.1	27 16.2	28 13.7	0 19.0	10 45.5	14 31.5	22 58.1	25 22.8
26 M	8 17 36	3 43 16	27 59 38	4♓48 30	9 15.6	26 44.5	5 22.0	27 53.7	28 32.2	0 12.9	10 41.1	14 32.7	22 57.2	25 21.3
27 Tu	8 21 33	4 40 35	11♓31 27	18 08 23	9 07.5	28 50.4	6 33.8	28 31.3	28 50.6	0 06.6	10 36.7	14 33.9	22 56.2	25 19.9
28 W	8 25 29	5 37 54	24 39 20	1♈04 27	9 00.9	0♌56.9	7 45.7	29 08.9	29 08.8	0 00.2	10 32.3	14 35.0	22 55.3	25 18.5
29 Th	8 29 26	6 35 15	7♈24 02	13 38 27	8 56.1	3 03.4	8 57.5	29 46.6	29 27.0	29♒53.7	10 27.8	14 36.1	22 54.3	25 17.1
30 F	8 33 22	7 32 37	19 48 10	25 53 43	8 53.5	5 09.8	10 09.2	0♍24.2	29 44.9	29 47.1	10 23.4	14 37.1	22 53.3	25 15.7
31 Sa	8 37 19	8 29 59	1♉55 42	7♉54 44	8D 52.7	7 15.9	11 20.9	1 01.9	0♊02.8	29 40.3	10 18.9	14 38.1	22 52.2	25 14.3

August 2021 — LONGITUDE

Day	Sid.Time	☉	0 hr ☽	Noon ☽	True ☊	☿	♀	♂	⚳	♃	♄	♅	♆	♇
1 Su	8 41 16	9♌27 23	13♉51 29	19♉46 36	8♊53.1	9♌21.3	12♍32.6	1♍39.6	0♊20.5	29♒33.5	10♒14.5	14♉39.1	22♓51.1	25♑12.9
2 M	8 45 12	10 24 48	25 40 47	1♊34 40	8R 53.9	11 26.0	13 44.2	2 17.3	0 38.1	29R 26.5	10R 10.0	14 39.9	22R 50.0	25R 11.5
3 Tu	8 49 09	11 22 14	7♊28 55	13 24 10	8 54.0	13 29.7	14 55.8	2 55.0	0 55.5	29 19.5	10 05.5	14 40.8	22 48.9	25 10.1
4 W	8 53 05	12 19 42	19 20 59	25 19 56	8 52.5	15 32.4	16 07.3	3 32.8	1 12.8	29 12.3	10 01.1	14 41.6	22 47.8	25 08.8
5 Th	8 57 02	13 17 10	1♋21 30	7♋26 07	8 49.0	17 33.8	17 18.8	4 10.6	1 30.0	29 05.1	9 56.6	14 42.3	22 46.6	25 07.4
6 F	9 00 58	14 14 40	13 34 11	19 45 59	8 42.9	19 34.0	18 30.3	4 48.4	1 47.0	28 57.8	9 52.2	14 43.0	22 45.4	25 06.1
7 Sa	9 04 55	15 12 11	26 01 44	2♌21 35	8 34.4	21 32.8	19 41.7	5 26.2	2 03.8	28 50.4	9 47.7	14 43.7	22 44.2	25 04.7
8 Su	9 08 51	16 09 43	8♌45 37	15 13 47	8 24.0	23 30.1	20 53.1	6 04.0	2 20.5	28 42.9	9 43.3	14 44.3	22 43.0	25 03.4
9 M	9 12 48	17 07 15	21 46 02	28 22 10	8 12.7	25 26.1	22 04.4	6 41.9	2 37.0	28 35.4	9 38.9	14 44.8	22 41.7	25 02.1
10 Tu	9 16 45	18 04 49	5♍01 59	11♍45 13	8 01.5	27 20.6	23 15.7	7 19.8	2 53.4	28 27.8	9 34.5	14 45.3	22 40.5	25 00.8
11 W	9 20 41	19 02 24	18 31 34	25 20 44	7 51.6	29 13.5	24 26.9	7 57.7	3 09.6	28 20.2	9 30.1	14 45.8	22 39.2	24 59.5
12 Th	9 24 38	20 00 00	2♎12 24	9♎06 16	7 43.8	1♍05.0	25 38.1	8 35.6	3 25.6	28 12.5	9 25.7	14 46.2	22 37.9	24 58.2
13 F	9 28 34	20 57 36	16 02 05	22 59 35	7 38.6	2 55.0	26 49.2	9 13.5	3 41.5	28 04.7	9 21.4	14 46.5	22 36.5	24 56.9
14 Sa	9 32 31	21 55 14	29 58 34	6♏58 53	7 36.0	4 43.5	28 00.3	9 51.5	3 57.2	27 57.0	9 17.1	14 46.8	22 35.2	24 55.7
15 Su	9 36 27	22 52 53	14♏00 22	21 02 55	7D 35.3	6 30.5	29 11.3	10 29.5	4 12.7	27 49.2	9 12.8	14 47.1	22 33.8	24 54.4
16 M	9 40 24	23 50 32	28 06 26	5♐10 48	7R 35.4	8 16.0	0♎22.3	11 07.5	4 28.0	27 41.3	9 08.6	14 47.3	22 32.4	24 53.2
17 Tu	9 44 20	24 48 13	12♐15 53	19 21 31	7 35.1	10 00.1	1 33.2	11 45.5	4 43.2	27 33.5	9 04.3	14 47.4	22 31.0	24 52.0
18 W	9 48 17	25 45 55	26 27 31	3♑33 36	7 33.1	11 42.7	2 44.0	12 23.6	4 58.1	27 25.6	9 00.2	14 47.5	22 29.6	24 50.8
19 Th	9 52 14	26 43 38	10♑39 26	17 44 39	7 28.7	13 23.9	3 54.8	13 01.6	5 12.9	27 17.8	8 56.0	14R 47.6	22 28.2	24 49.6
20 F	9 56 10	27 41 21	24 48 48	1♒51 22	7 21.4	15 03.6	5 05.5	13 39.7	5 27.5	27 09.9	8 51.9	14 47.6	22 26.7	24 48.5
21 Sa	10 00 07	28 39 06	8♒51 50	15 49 39	7 11.6	16 41.9	6 16.2	14 17.8	5 41.9	27 02.0	8 47.8	14 47.5	22 25.2	24 47.3
22 Su	10 04 03	29 36 53	22 44 17	29 35 14	7 00.0	18 18.9	7 26.8	14 56.0	5 56.1	26 54.2	8 43.8	14 47.4	22 23.8	24 46.2
23 M	10 08 00	0♍34 41	6♓22 03	13♓04 21	6 47.7	19 54.4	8 37.3	15 34.1	6 10.1	26 46.3	8 39.8	14 47.3	22 22.3	24 45.1
24 Tu	10 11 56	1 32 30	19 41 52	26 14 25	6 36.0	21 28.5	9 47.7	16 12.3	6 23.9	26 38.5	8 35.9	14 47.1	22 20.8	24 44.0
25 W	10 15 53	2 30 21	2♈41 55	9♈04 25	6 25.9	23 01.3	10 58.1	16 50.5	6 37.5	26 30.7	8 32.0	14 46.8	22 19.2	24 42.9
26 Th	10 19 49	3 28 13	15 22 03	21 35 05	6 18.2	24 32.7	12 08.5	17 28.7	6 50.9	26 22.9	8 28.2	14 46.5	22 17.7	24 41.9
27 F	10 23 46	4 26 07	27 43 51	3♉48 46	6 13.1	26 02.7	13 18.7	18 07.0	7 04.1	26 15.2	8 24.4	14 46.2	22 16.1	24 40.8
28 Sa	10 27 43	5 24 03	9♉50 20	15 49 07	6 10.4	27 31.2	14 28.9	18 45.3	7 17.0	26 07.5	8 20.7	14 45.8	22 14.6	24 39.8
29 Su	10 31 39	6 22 01	21 45 42	27 40 46	6 09.5	28 58.4	15 39.1	19 23.6	7 29.7	25 59.9	8 17.0	14 45.4	22 13.0	24 38.8
30 M	10 35 36	7 20 01	3♊34 57	9♊28 58	6 09.4	0♎24.2	16 49.1	20 01.9	7 42.2	25 52.3	8 13.4	14 44.9	22 11.4	24 37.8
31 Tu	10 39 32	8 18 02	15 23 29	21 19 12	6 09.1	1 48.5	17 59.1	20 40.3	7 54.5	25 44.7	8 09.8	14 44.3	22 09.8	24 36.9

Astro Data Dy Hr Mn	Planet Ingress Dy Hr Mn	Last Aspect Dy Hr Mn	☽ Ingress Dy Hr Mn	Last Aspect Dy Hr Mn	☽ Ingress Dy Hr Mn	☽ Phases & Eclipses Dy Hr Mn
☽0N 1 21:46	☿ ♋ 11 20:36	30 17:41 ♇ ⚹	♈ 1 1:22	2 7:42 ♃ □	♊ 2 8:47	1 21:12 ☾ 10♈14
☽0S 16 8:42	♀ ♍ 22 0:38	3 4:16 ♇ □	♉ 3 12:29	4 19:39 ♃ △	♋ 4 21:18	10 1:18 ● 18♋02
☽0N 29 5:17	☉ ♌ 22 14:28	5 16:58 ♇ △	♊ 6 1:25	6 22:13 ♇ ☍	♌ 7 7:33	17 10:12 ☽ 25♎04
	☿ ♌ 28 1:13	8 4:21 ☿ ☌	♋ 8 13:52	9 12:24 ♃ ☍	♍ 9 14:57	24 2:38 ○ 1♒26
☽0S 12 13:25	♃ ♒R 28 12:44	10 16:11 ♇ ☍	♌ 11 0:22	11 11:23 ♇ △	♎ 11 20:09	31 13:17 ☾ 8♉33
♀0S 17 11:00	♂ ♍ 29 20:34	12 12:30 ♂ ☌	♍ 13 8:32	13 20:40 ♃ △	♏ 14 0:02	
♅R 20 1:41	⚳ ♊ 31 8:14	15 6:47 ♇ △	♎ 15 14:33	16 3:06 ♀ ⚹	♐ 16 3:13	8 13:51 ● 16♌14
☽0N 25 13:17		17 11:05 ♇ □	♏ 17 18:39	18 1:44 ♃ ⚹	♑ 18 5:59	15 15:21 ☽ 23♏01
☿0S 29 13:41	☿ ♍ 11 21:58	19 16:31 ☉ △	♐ 19 21:09	20 0:00 ♇ ☌	♒ 20 8:50	22 12:03 ○ 29♒37
	♀ ♎ 16 4:28	21 22:27 ♀ ☍	♑ 21 22:37	22 12:03 ☉ ☍	♓ 22 12:44	30 7:14 ☾ 7♊09
	☉ ♍ 22 21:36	23 16:35 ♇ ☌	♒ 24 0:14	24 9:14 ♇ ⚹	♈ 24 18:58	
	☿ ♎ 30 5:11	25 23:15 ♂ ☍	♓ 26 3:31	26 21:16 ♃ ⚹	♉ 27 4:28	
		28 1:14 ♇ ⚹	♈ 28 9:59	29 15:00 ☿ △	♊ 29 16:43	
		30 19:39 ♃ ⚹	♉ 30 20:09			

Astro Data

1 July 2021
Julian Day # 44377
SVP 4♓57'50"
GC 27♐08.4 ⚴ 27♓17.7
Eris 24♈45.4 ⚵ 11♐15.1R
⚷ 12♈50.5 ⚶ 22♍50.9
☽ Mean ☊ 9♊14.8

1 August 2021
Julian Day # 44408
SVP 4♓57'45"
GC 27♐08.4 ⚴ 26♓47.6R
Eris 24♈46.8R ⚵ 8♐20.8R
⚷ 12♈48.6R ⚶ 5♎46.0
☽ Mean ☊ 7♊36.3

LONGITUDE — September 2021

Day	Sid.Time	☉	0 hr ☽	Noon ☽	True ☊	☿	♀	♂	⚳	♃	♄	♅	♆	♇
1 W	10 43 29	9♍16 06	27♊16 48	3♋16 55	6♊07.4	3♎11.4	19♎09.0	21♍18.7	8♊06.5	25♒37.3	8♒06.3	14♉43.8	22♓08.3	24♑35.9
2 Th	10 47 25	10 14 11	9♋20 11	15 27 07	6R 03.6	4 32.8	20 18.9	21 57.1	8 18.3	25R 29.9	8R 02.9	14R 43.1	22R 06.6	24R 35.0
3 F	10 51 22	11 12 19	21 38 16	27 54 01	5 57.2	5 52.7	21 28.7	22 35.5	8 29.9	25 22.6	7 59.5	14 42.4	22 05.0	24 34.1
4 Sa	10 55 18	12 10 28	4♌14 43	10♌40 35	5 48.2	7 11.0	22 38.4	23 14.0	8 41.2	25 15.3	7 56.2	14 41.7	22 03.4	24 33.3
5 Su	10 59 15	13 08 39	17 11 45	23 48 13	5 37.2	8 27.6	23 48.0	23 52.5	8 52.2	25 08.2	7 53.0	14 40.9	22 01.8	24 32.4
6 M	11 03 12	14 06 51	0♍29 53	7♍16 30	5 25.0	9 42.6	24 57.6	24 31.0	9 03.0	25 01.1	7 49.8	14 40.1	22 00.2	24 31.6
7 Tu	11 07 08	15 05 06	14 07 43	21 03 05	5 12.9	10 55.8	26 07.1	25 09.6	9 13.5	24 54.1	7 46.7	14 39.2	21 58.5	24 30.8
8 W	11 11 05	16 03 22	28 02 06	5♎04 10	5 02.1	12 07.3	27 16.5	25 48.2	9 23.8	24 47.3	7 43.7	14 38.3	21 56.9	24 30.0
9 Th	11 15 01	17 01 40	12♎08 39	19 14 58	4 53.6	13 16.8	28 25.8	26 26.8	9 33.8	24 40.5	7 40.7	14 37.3	21 55.2	24 29.3
10 F	11 18 58	17 59 59	26 22 29	3♏30 39	4 47.9	14 24.3	29 35.0	27 05.4	9 43.5	24 33.9	7 37.9	14 36.3	21 53.6	24 28.5
11 Sa	11 22 54	18 58 20	10♏38 59	17 47 02	4 45.0	15 29.6	0♏44.2	27 44.1	9 52.9	24 27.4	7 35.1	14 35.3	21 51.9	24 27.8
12 Su	11 26 51	19 56 43	24 54 28	2♐00 59	4D 44.1	16 32.8	1 53.2	28 22.8	10 02.1	24 21.0	7 32.4	14 34.2	21 50.3	24 27.1
13 M	11 30 47	20 55 07	9♐06 23	16 10 29	4R 44.2	17 33.5	3 02.2	29 01.5	10 11.0	24 14.7	7 29.7	14 33.0	21 48.6	24 26.5
14 Tu	11 34 44	21 53 33	23 13 13	0♑14 26	4 44.0	18 31.7	4 11.0	29 40.2	10 19.6	24 08.6	7 27.2	14 31.8	21 47.0	24 25.9
15 W	11 38 40	22 52 00	7♑14 06	14 12 08	4 42.4	19 27.2	5 19.8	0♎19.0	10 27.8	24 02.6	7 24.7	14 30.6	21 45.3	24 25.3
16 Th	11 42 37	23 50 29	21 08 25	28 02 49	4 38.4	20 19.7	6 28.4	0 57.8	10 35.8	23 56.7	7 22.4	14 29.3	21 43.7	24 24.7
17 F	11 46 34	24 49 00	4♒55 13	11♒45 25	4 31.7	21 09.2	7 37.0	1 36.6	10 43.5	23 51.0	7 20.1	14 28.0	21 42.0	24 24.1
18 Sa	11 50 30	25 47 32	18 33 13	25 18 22	4 22.6	21 55.2	8 45.4	2 15.5	10 50.9	23 45.4	7 17.9	14 26.6	21 40.4	24 23.6
19 Su	11 54 27	26 46 06	2♓00 37	8♓39 44	4 11.8	22 37.7	9 53.7	2 54.3	10 58.0	23 40.0	7 15.7	14 25.2	21 38.7	24 23.1
20 M	11 58 23	27 44 42	15 15 29	21 47 39	4 00.3	23 16.2	11 01.9	3 33.2	11 04.8	23 34.7	7 13.7	14 23.8	21 37.1	24 22.6
21 Tu	12 02 20	28 43 19	28 16 03	4♈40 36	3 49.3	23 50.6	12 10.0	4 12.2	11 11.2	23 29.6	7 11.7	14 22.3	21 35.4	24 22.2
22 W	12 06 16	29 41 59	11♈01 13	17 17 56	3 39.7	24 20.4	13 18.0	4 51.1	11 17.4	23 24.6	7 09.9	14 20.8	21 33.8	24 21.8
23 Th	12 10 13	0♎40 40	23 30 48	29 40 01	3 32.4	24 45.3	14 25.9	5 30.1	11 23.2	23 19.9	7 08.1	14 19.2	21 32.1	24 21.4
24 F	12 14 09	1 39 24	5♉45 46	11♉48 24	3 27.6	25 04.9	15 33.6	6 09.1	11 28.6	23 15.2	7 06.5	14 17.6	21 30.5	24 21.0
25 Sa	12 18 06	2 38 10	17 48 15	23 45 47	3D 25.2	25 18.8	16 41.2	6 48.2	11 33.8	23 10.8	7 04.9	14 16.0	21 28.9	24 20.7
26 Su	12 22 03	3 36 58	29 41 29	5♊35 53	3 24.7	25R 26.7	17 48.7	7 27.3	11 38.6	23 06.5	7 03.4	14 14.3	21 27.3	24 20.4
27 M	12 25 59	4 35 49	11♊29 34	17 23 11	3 25.3	25 28.2	18 56.0	8 06.4	11 43.0	23 02.4	7 02.0	14 12.6	21 25.7	24 20.1
28 Tu	12 29 56	5 34 41	23 17 21	29 12 44	3R 26.1	25 22.7	20 03.3	8 45.6	11 47.1	22 58.4	7 00.7	14 10.8	21 24.1	24 19.8
29 W	12 33 52	6 33 36	5♋10 03	11♋09 56	3 26.2	25 10.2	21 10.4	9 24.8	11 50.9	22 54.7	6 59.5	14 09.1	21 22.5	24 19.6
30 Th	12 37 49	7 32 34	17 13 04	23 20 05	3 24.8	24 50.2	22 17.3	10 04.0	11 54.3	22 51.1	6 58.4	14 07.2	21 20.9	24 19.4

LONGITUDE — October 2021

Day	Sid.Time	☉	0 hr ☽	Noon ☽	True ☊	☿	♀	♂	⚳	♃	♄	♅	♆	♇
1 F	12 41 45	8♎31 33	29♋31 36	5♌48 08	3♊21.3	24♎22.5	23♏24.1	10♎43.2	11♊57.3	22♒47.7	6♒57.4	14♉05.4	21♓19.4	24♑19.3
2 Sa	12 45 42	9 30 35	12♌10 10	18 38 05	3R 15.6	23R 47.2	24 30.8	11 22.5	12 00.0	22R 44.5	6R 56.5	14R 03.5	21R 17.8	24R 19.1
3 Su	12 49 38	10 29 39	25 12 10	1♍52 32	3 08.2	23 04.4	25 37.3	12 01.9	12 02.3	22 41.5	6 55.7	14 01.6	21 16.2	24 19.0
4 M	12 53 35	11 28 45	8♍39 13	15 32 05	2 59.8	22 14.4	26 43.6	12 41.2	12 04.2	22 38.6	6 54.9	13 59.6	21 14.7	24 18.9
5 Tu	12 57 32	12 27 53	22 30 49	29 34 59	2 51.2	21 17.8	27 49.8	13 20.6	12 05.8	22 36.0	6 54.3	13 57.6	21 13.2	24 18.9
6 W	13 01 28	13 27 03	6♎44 00	13♎57 08	2 43.5	20 15.6	28 55.9	14 00.0	12 07.0	22 33.6	6 53.8	13 55.6	21 11.7	24D 18.9
7 Th	13 05 25	14 26 16	21 13 36	28 32 30	2 37.6	19 08.9	0♐01.7	14 39.5	12 07.8	22 31.3	6 53.4	13 53.6	21 10.2	24 18.9
8 F	13 09 21	15 25 30	5♏52 57	13♏14 03	2 33.9	17 59.2	1 07.4	15 18.9	12R 08.2	22 29.3	6 53.1	13 51.5	21 08.7	24 18.9
9 Sa	13 13 18	16 24 47	20 34 57	27 54 51	2D 32.4	16 48.2	2 12.9	15 58.5	12 08.2	22 27.4	6 52.9	13 49.4	21 07.2	24 19.0
10 Su	13 17 14	17 24 05	5♐13 04	12♐29 00	2 32.6	15 37.9	3 18.3	16 38.0	12 07.8	22 25.8	6D 52.7	13 47.3	21 05.8	24 19.1
11 M	13 21 11	18 23 25	19 42 12	26 52 16	2 33.8	14 30.2	4 23.4	17 17.6	12 07.1	22 24.3	6 52.7	13 45.1	21 04.4	24 19.2
12 Tu	13 25 07	19 22 47	3♑58 56	11♑02 02	2R 34.9	13 27.0	5 28.3	17 57.2	12 06.0	22 23.1	6 52.8	13 43.0	21 02.9	24 19.4
13 W	13 29 04	20 22 10	18 01 29	24 57 13	2 35.0	12 30.3	6 33.0	18 36.9	12 04.4	22 22.0	6 53.0	13 40.8	21 01.5	24 19.5
14 Th	13 33 01	21 21 35	1♒49 16	8♒37 39	2 33.6	11 41.6	7 37.5	19 16.5	12 02.5	22 21.2	6 53.3	13 38.5	21 00.2	24 19.8
15 F	13 36 57	22 21 02	15 22 26	22 03 41	2 30.4	11 02.2	8 41.8	19 56.2	12 00.2	22 20.5	6 53.7	13 36.3	20 58.8	24 20.0
16 Sa	13 40 54	23 20 31	28 41 29	5♓15 53	2 25.4	10 33.0	9 45.8	20 36.0	11 57.5	22 20.1	6 54.2	13 34.0	20 57.5	24 20.3
17 Su	13 44 50	24 20 01	11♓46 57	18 14 43	2 19.2	10 14.8	10 49.6	21 15.8	11 54.4	22D 19.8	6 54.8	13 31.7	20 56.1	24 20.6
18 M	13 48 47	25 19 34	24 39 16	1♈00 37	2 12.6	10D 07.7	11 53.1	21 55.6	11 50.9	22 19.8	6 55.5	13 29.4	20 54.8	24 20.9
19 Tu	13 52 43	26 19 08	7♈18 49	13 33 57	2 06.2	10 11.7	12 56.4	22 35.4	11 47.0	22 19.9	6 56.3	13 27.1	20 53.6	24 21.3
20 W	13 56 40	27 18 44	19 46 05	25 55 19	2 00.7	10 26.5	13 59.4	23 15.3	11 42.7	22 20.3	6 57.2	13 24.8	20 52.3	24 21.7
21 Th	14 00 36	28 18 22	2♉01 47	8♉05 37	1 56.6	10 51.5	15 02.1	23 55.2	11 38.0	22 20.8	6 58.2	13 22.4	20 51.1	24 22.1
22 F	14 04 33	29 18 02	14 07 01	20 06 14	1D 54.3	11 26.2	16 04.6	24 35.1	11 33.0	22 21.6	6 59.3	13 20.0	20 49.8	24 22.5
23 Sa	14 08 29	0♏17 44	26 03 32	1♊59 14	1 53.5	12 09.7	17 06.7	25 15.1	11 27.5	22 22.6	7 00.5	13 17.7	20 48.7	24 23.0
24 Su	14 12 26	1 17 29	7♊53 42	13 47 21	1 54.2	13 01.2	18 08.6	25 55.1	11 21.7	22 23.7	7 01.8	13 15.3	20 47.5	24 23.5
25 M	14 16 23	2 17 15	19 40 36	25 33 58	1 55.7	13 59.9	19 10.1	26 35.2	11 15.5	22 25.1	7 03.2	13 12.8	20 46.3	24 24.1
26 Tu	14 20 19	3 17 04	1♋27 57	7♋23 07	1 57.5	15 04.9	20 11.3	27 15.3	11 08.9	22 26.6	7 04.7	13 10.4	20 45.2	24 24.6
27 W	14 24 16	4 16 55	13 20 04	19 19 22	1 59.2	16 15.5	21 12.2	27 55.4	11 01.9	22 28.4	7 06.2	13 08.0	20 44.1	24 25.2
28 Th	14 28 12	5 16 48	25 21 40	1♌27 33	2R 00.0	17 30.9	22 12.7	28 35.6	10 54.5	22 30.4	7 07.9	13 05.6	20 43.0	24 25.8
29 F	14 32 09	6 16 43	7♌37 39	13 52 32	1 59.9	18 50.4	23 12.9	29 15.8	10 46.8	22 32.5	7 09.7	13 03.1	20 42.0	24 26.5
30 Sa	14 36 05	7 16 41	20 12 47	26 38 52	1 58.5	20 13.4	24 12.7	29 56.0	10 38.7	22 34.9	7 11.6	13 00.6	20 41.0	24 27.2
31 Su	14 40 02	8 16 41	3♍11 13	9♍50 10	1 56.2	21 39.4	25 12.1	0♏36.3	10 30.3	22 37.4	7 13.6	12 58.2	20 40.0	24 27.9

Astro Data	Planet Ingress	Last Aspect	☽ Ingress	Last Aspect	☽ Ingress	☽ Phases & Eclipses	Astro Data
Dy Hr Mn	Dy Hr Mn	Dy Hr Mn	Dy Hr Mn	Dy Hr Mn	Dy Hr Mn	Dy Hr Mn	1 September 2021
☽0S 8 19:42	♀ ♏ 10 20:40	31 20:50 ♃ △	♋ 1 5:27	30 14:50 ☿ □	♌ 1 0:55	7 0:53 ● 14♍38	Julian Day # 44439
♃×♇ 11 10:07	♂ ♎ 15 0:15	3 5:39 ♇ ☍	♌ 3 15:59	2 23:44 ♀ □	♍ 3 8:39	13 20:41 ☽ 21♐16	SVP 4♓57'40"
♂0S 17 20:33	☉ ♎ 22 19:22	5 14:23 ♃ ☍	♍ 5 23:07	5 8:47 ♀ ⚹	♎ 5 12:42	20 23:56 ○ 28♓14	GC 27♐08.5 ⚴ 21♓01.9R
☽0N 21 21:10		7 19:25 ♂ ☌	♎ 8 3:22	7 5:04 ♇ □	♏ 7 14:23	29 1:58 ☾ 6♋09	Eris 24♈38.5R ⚵ 10♐35.6
☉0S 22 19:22	♀ ♐ 7 11:22	10 4:49 ♀ ☌	♏ 10 6:06	9 6:06 ♇ ⚹	♐ 9 15:25		⚷ 12♈00.4R ⚶ 20♎22.6
☿R 27 5:11	☉ ♏ 23 4:52	12 5:34 ♂ ⚹	♐ 12 8:36	11 4:32 ♃ ⚹	♑ 11 17:16	6 11:07 ● 13♎25	☽ Mean ☊ 5♊57.8
	♂ ♏ 30 14:22	14 10:59 ♂ □	♑ 14 11:35	13 10:54 ♇ ☌	♒ 13 20:48	13 3:26 ☽ 20♑01	
☽0S 6 4:40		16 5:41 ♇ ☌	♒ 16 15:24	15 12:34 ☉ △	♓ 16 2:23	20 14:58 ○ 27♈26	1 October 2021
♇D 6 18:30		18 9:16 ♃ ☌	♓ 18 20:24	17 23:25 ♇ ⚹	♈ 18 10:05	28 20:06 ☾ 5♌37	Julian Day # 44469
⚳R 9 1:32		20 23:56 ☉ ☍	♈ 21 3:14	20 14:58 ☉ ☍	♉ 20 20:00		SVP 4♓57'37"
♄D 11 2:18		23 2:06 ☿ ☍	♉ 23 12:39	22 20:36 ♇ △	♊ 23 7:58		GC 27♐08.6 ⚴ 13♓27.7R
♃D 18 5:31		25 13:10 ♇ △	♊ 26 0:38	25 14:12 ☉ △	♋ 25 21:01		Eris 24♈23.4R ⚵ 16♐38.5
☿D 18 15:19		28 4:19 ☿ △	♋ 28 13:35	28 6:03 ♂ □	♌ 28 9:08		⚷ 10♈45.0R ⚶ 5♏32.9
☽0N 19 4:18				30 7:06 ♀ △	♍ 30 18:11		☽ Mean ☊ 4♊22.4

November 2021 LONGITUDE

Day	Sid.Time	☉	0 hr ☽	Noon ☽	True ☊	☿	♀	♂	⚳	♃	♄	♅	♆	♇
1 M	14 43 59	9♏16 42	16♍35 56	23♍28 36	1♊53.1	23♎07.8	26♐11.1	1♏16.6	10♊21.4	22♒40.1	7♒15.7	12♉55.7	20♓39.0	24♑28.6
2 Tu	14 47 55	10 16 46	0♎28 05	7♎34 09	1R 49.9	24 38.2	27 09.7	1 57.0	10R 12.3	22 43.1	7 17.9	12R 53.2	20R 38.1	24 29.4
3 W	14 51 52	11 16 52	14 46 23	22 04 12	1 47.0	26 10.2	28 07.9	2 37.4	10 02.8	22 46.2	7 20.2	12 50.7	20 37.2	24 30.2
4 Th	14 55 48	12 17 00	29 26 51	6♏53 26	1 44.8	27 43.6	29 05.7	3 17.8	9 52.9	22 49.5	7 22.5	12 48.3	20 36.3	24 31.0
5 F	14 59 45	13 17 09	14♏22 57	21 54 18	1D 43.7	29 18.0	0♑03.0	3 58.3	9 42.8	22 53.0	7 25.0	12 45.8	20 35.4	24 31.9
6 Sa	15 03 41	14 17 21	29 26 23	6♐58 03	1 43.5	0♏53.3	0 59.8	4 38.8	9 32.3	22 56.8	7 27.6	12 43.3	20 34.6	24 32.7
7 Su	15 07 38	15 17 34	14♐28 14	21 55 58	1 44.2	2 29.1	1 56.1	5 19.3	9 21.5	23 00.7	7 30.2	12 40.8	20 33.8	24 33.6
8 M	15 11 34	16 17 49	29 20 22	6♑40 42	1 45.3	4 05.4	2 51.9	5 59.9	9 10.5	23 04.7	7 33.0	12 38.4	20 33.0	24 34.6
9 Tu	15 15 31	17 18 06	13♑56 22	21 06 56	1 46.4	5 42.1	3 47.1	6 40.5	8 59.1	23 09.0	7 35.8	12 35.9	20 32.3	24 35.5
10 W	15 19 28	18 18 23	28 12 05	5♒11 41	1 47.3	7 18.9	4 41.8	7 21.1	8 47.5	23 13.5	7 38.8	12 33.4	20 31.6	24 36.5
11 Th	15 23 24	19 18 43	12♒05 40	18 54 06	1R 47.6	8 55.8	5 35.9	8 01.8	8 35.6	23 18.1	7 41.8	12 31.0	20 30.9	24 37.5
12 F	15 27 21	20 19 03	25 37 08	2♓14 57	1 47.3	10 32.8	6 29.3	8 42.5	8 23.5	23 23.0	7 44.9	12 28.5	20 30.3	24 38.6
13 Sa	15 31 17	21 19 25	8♓47 50	15 16 04	1 46.5	12 09.7	7 22.2	9 23.3	8 11.1	23 28.0	7 48.2	12 26.1	20 29.6	24 39.6
14 Su	15 35 14	22 19 48	21 39 58	27 59 50	1 45.4	13 46.5	8 14.3	10 04.1	7 58.6	23 33.1	7 51.5	12 23.6	20 29.1	24 40.7
15 M	15 39 10	23 20 13	4♈16 00	10♈28 48	1 44.2	15 23.2	9 05.7	10 44.9	7 45.8	23 38.5	7 54.9	12 21.2	20 28.5	24 41.8
16 Tu	15 43 07	24 20 39	16 38 31	22 45 28	1 43.0	16 59.8	9 56.5	11 25.7	7 32.8	23 44.0	7 58.3	12 18.8	20 28.0	24 43.0
17 W	15 47 03	25 21 06	28 49 56	4♉52 10	1 42.2	18 36.2	10 46.4	12 06.6	7 19.6	23 49.8	8 01.9	12 16.4	20 27.5	24 44.2
18 Th	15 51 00	26 21 35	10♉52 26	16 51 01	1 41.7	20 12.4	11 35.6	12 47.6	7 06.3	23 55.6	8 05.5	12 14.0	20 27.0	24 45.3
19 F	15 54 57	27 22 06	22 48 08	28 44 02	1D 41.5	21 48.4	12 23.9	13 28.5	6 52.9	24 01.7	8 09.3	12 11.6	20 26.6	24 46.6
20 Sa	15 58 53	28 22 38	4♊38 59	10♊33 15	1 41.5	23 24.2	13 11.4	14 09.6	6 39.3	24 07.9	8 13.1	12 09.3	20 26.2	24 47.8
21 Su	16 02 50	29 23 12	16 27 05	22 20 48	1 41.7	24 59.9	13 58.0	14 50.6	6 25.5	24 14.3	8 17.0	12 06.9	20 25.9	24 49.1
22 M	16 06 46	0♐23 47	28 14 42	4♋09 07	1 41.9	26 35.3	14 43.7	15 31.7	6 11.7	24 20.9	8 21.0	12 04.6	20 25.5	24 50.3
23 Tu	16 10 43	1 24 24	10♋04 24	16 00 57	1R 42.0	28 10.6	15 28.4	16 12.8	5 57.8	24 27.6	8 25.1	12 02.3	20 25.3	24 51.7
24 W	16 14 39	2 25 02	21 59 11	27 59 31	1 41.9	29 45.7	16 12.1	16 54.0	5 43.8	24 34.4	8 29.2	12 00.0	20 25.0	24 53.0
25 Th	16 18 36	3 25 42	4♌02 26	10♌08 24	1 41.8	1♐20.6	16 54.8	17 35.2	5 29.8	24 41.5	8 33.5	11 57.8	20 24.8	24 54.3
26 F	16 22 32	4 26 24	16 17 55	22 31 31	1 41.7	2 55.3	17 36.4	18 16.5	5 15.7	24 48.7	8 37.8	11 55.5	20 24.6	24 55.7
27 Sa	16 26 29	5 27 07	28 49 40	5♍12 53	1D 41.6	4 30.0	18 16.8	18 57.7	5 01.6	24 56.0	8 42.1	11 53.3	20 24.4	24 57.1
28 Su	16 30 26	6 27 52	11♍41 36	18 16 17	1 41.7	6 04.5	18 56.1	19 39.1	4 47.5	25 03.5	8 46.6	11 51.1	20 24.3	24 58.5
29 M	16 34 22	7 28 38	24 57 15	1♎44 48	1 42.0	7 38.9	19 34.2	20 20.4	4 33.4	25 11.2	8 51.2	11 48.9	20 24.2	25 00.0
30 Tu	16 38 19	8 29 26	8♎39 05	15 40 09	1 42.6	9 13.2	20 11.0	21 01.8	4 19.3	25 19.0	8 55.8	11 46.8	20 24.2	25 01.4

December 2021 LONGITUDE

Day	Sid.Time	☉	0 hr ☽	Noon ☽	True ☊	☿	♀	♂	⚳	♃	♄	♅	♆	♇
1 W	16 42 15	9♐30 15	22♎47 55	0♏02 05	1♊43.3	10♐47.4	20♑46.5	21♏43.3	4♊05.3	25♒27.0	9♒00.5	11♉44.7	20♓24.1	25♑02.9
2 Th	16 46 12	10 31 06	7♏22 13	14 47 42	1 43.9	12 21.6	21 20.6	22 24.8	3R 51.3	25 35.1	9 05.2	11R 42.6	20D 24.2	25 04.4
3 F	16 50 08	11 31 58	22 17 42	29 51 16	1R 44.2	13 55.7	21 53.3	23 06.3	3 37.4	25 43.4	9 10.1	11 40.5	20 24.2	25 06.0
4 Sa	16 54 05	12 32 51	7♐27 18	15♐04 34	1 44.0	15 29.8	22 24.5	23 47.9	3 23.6	25 51.8	9 15.0	11 38.5	20 24.3	25 07.5
5 Su	16 58 01	13 33 46	22 41 50	0♑17 50	1 43.2	17 03.8	22 54.2	24 29.5	3 10.0	26 00.4	9 20.0	11 36.5	20 24.4	25 09.1
6 M	17 01 58	14 34 41	7♑51 20	15 21 13	1 41.8	18 37.9	23 22.2	25 11.1	2 56.4	26 09.1	9 25.0	11 34.5	20 24.6	25 10.7
7 Tu	17 05 55	15 35 38	22 46 29	0♒06 18	1 40.0	20 11.9	23 48.6	25 52.8	2 43.1	26 17.9	9 30.2	11 32.6	20 24.8	25 12.3
8 W	17 09 51	16 36 34	7♒20 01	14 27 10	1 38.2	21 46.0	24 13.2	26 34.5	2 29.8	26 26.9	9 35.4	11 30.7	20 25.0	25 13.9
9 Th	17 13 48	17 37 32	21 27 30	28 20 54	1 36.8	23 20.1	24 36.0	27 16.3	2 16.8	26 36.0	9 40.6	11 28.8	20 25.3	25 15.5
10 F	17 17 44	18 38 30	5♓07 25	11♓47 15	1D 35.9	24 54.2	24 56.9	27 58.1	2 04.0	26 45.2	9 45.9	11 26.9	20 25.6	25 17.2
11 Sa	17 21 41	19 39 29	18 20 42	24 48 09	1 35.8	26 28.4	25 15.8	28 39.9	1 51.3	26 54.6	9 51.3	11 25.1	20 25.9	25 18.8
12 Su	17 25 37	20 40 28	1♈10 04	7♈26 55	1 36.6	28 02.6	25 32.7	29 21.8	1 38.9	27 04.1	9 56.8	11 23.4	20 26.3	25 20.5
13 M	17 29 34	21 41 28	13 39 15	19 47 35	1 38.0	29 36.9	25 47.6	0♐03.7	1 26.8	27 13.7	10 02.3	11 21.6	20 26.7	25 22.2
14 Tu	17 33 30	22 42 29	25 52 27	1♉54 23	1 39.7	1♑11.2	26 00.3	0 45.6	1 14.8	27 23.5	10 07.9	11 20.0	20 27.1	25 23.9
15 W	17 37 27	23 43 30	7♉53 52	13 51 24	1 41.3	2 45.5	26 10.8	1 27.6	1 03.2	27 33.4	10 13.5	11 18.3	20 27.6	25 25.7
16 Th	17 41 24	24 44 31	19 47 26	25 42 17	1R 42.3	4 19.9	26 19.0	2 09.6	0 51.8	27 43.4	10 19.2	11 16.7	20 28.1	25 27.4
17 F	17 45 20	25 45 33	1♊36 27	7♊30 15	1 42.3	5 54.3	26 24.8	2 51.6	0 40.7	27 53.5	10 24.9	11 15.1	20 28.6	25 29.2
18 Sa	17 49 17	26 46 36	13 23 59	19 17 58	1 41.0	7 28.7	26R 28.3	3 33.7	0 29.9	28 03.8	10 30.8	11 13.6	20 29.2	25 31.0
19 Su	17 53 13	27 47 40	25 12 27	1♋07 42	1 38.3	9 03.1	26 29.4	4 15.9	0 19.5	28 14.1	10 36.6	11 12.1	20 29.8	25 32.7
20 M	17 57 10	28 48 44	7♋03 56	13 01 22	1 34.4	10 37.5	26 28.0	4 58.0	0 09.3	28 24.6	10 42.5	11 10.6	20 30.4	25 34.5
21 Tu	18 01 06	29 49 48	19 00 15	25 00 46	1 29.5	12 11.7	26 24.2	5 40.3	29♉59.5	28 35.2	10 48.5	11 09.2	20 31.1	25 36.4
22 W	18 05 03	0♑50 53	1♌03 11	7♌07 42	1 24.1	13 45.7	26 17.8	6 22.5	29 50.0	28 45.9	10 54.5	11 07.9	20 31.8	25 38.2
23 Th	18 09 00	1 51 59	13 14 35	19 24 07	1 18.9	15 19.6	26 09.0	7 04.8	29 40.8	28 56.7	11 00.6	11 06.6	20 32.5	25 40.0
24 F	18 12 56	2 53 05	25 36 35	1♍52 17	1 14.4	16 53.1	25 57.6	7 47.1	29 32.0	29 07.6	11 06.7	11 05.3	20 33.3	25 41.9
25 Sa	18 16 53	3 54 12	8♍11 35	14 34 47	1 11.1	18 26.2	25 43.8	8 29.5	29 23.5	29 18.6	11 12.9	11 04.0	20 34.1	25 43.7
26 Su	18 20 49	4 55 20	21 02 17	27 34 24	1D 09.4	19 58.8	25 27.5	9 11.9	29 15.5	29 29.7	11 19.1	11 02.9	20 34.9	25 45.6
27 M	18 24 46	5 56 28	4♎11 30	10♎53 53	1 09.3	21 30.7	25 08.8	9 54.4	29 07.8	29 41.0	11 25.4	11 01.7	20 35.8	25 47.5
28 Tu	18 28 42	6 57 37	17 41 51	24 35 36	1 10.3	23 01.8	24 47.9	10 36.9	29 00.4	29 52.3	11 31.7	11 00.6	20 36.7	25 49.4
29 W	18 32 39	7 58 46	1♏35 15	8♏40 50	1 11.8	24 31.9	24 24.7	11 19.4	28 53.5	0♓03.7	11 38.1	10 59.6	20 37.7	25 51.3
30 Th	18 36 35	8 59 56	15 52 13	23 09 10	1R 13.0	26 00.7	23 59.4	12 02.0	28 46.9	0 15.3	11 44.5	10 58.6	20 38.6	25 53.2
31 F	18 40 32	10 01 06	0♐31 13	7♐57 47	1 13.0	27 27.9	23 32.1	12 44.6	28 40.8	0 26.9	11 50.9	10 57.6	20 39.6	25 55.1

Astro Data

Dy Hr Mn
☽0S 2 15:28
☽0N 15 10:28
♃⚺♇ 27 16:17
☽0S 30 1:49
♆D 1 13:23
☽0N 12 16:16
♀R 19 10:37
♄□♅ 24 7:18
☽0S 27 9:30

Planet Ingress

Dy Hr Mn
♀ ♑ 5 10:45
☿ ♏ 5 22:36
☉ ♐ 22 2:35
☿ ♐ 24 15:38
♂ ♐ 13 9:54
☿ ♑ 13 17:53
⚳ ♉R 21 10:40
☉ ♑ 21 16:00
♃ ♓ 29 4:11

Last Aspect / ☽ Ingress

Dy Hr Mn		☽ Ingress Dy Hr Mn
1 17:01 ♀ □	♎	1 23:12
3 22:33 ♀ ⚹	♏	4 0:54
5 16:11 ♇ ⚹	♐	6 0:54
7 13:45 ♃ ⚹	♑	8 1:05
9 17:53 ♇ ☌	♒	10 3:04
11 19:53 ♃ ☌	♓	12 7:55
14 5:41 ♇ ⚹	♈	14 15:49
16 15:52 ♇ □	♉	17 2:19
19 8:59 ☉ ☍	♊	19 14:34
21 15:53 ♃ △	♋	22 3:34
24 5:47 ♇ ☍	♌	24 16:00
26 16:25 ♃ ☍	♍	27 2:13
29 0:04 ♇ △	♎	29 8:56

Last Aspect / ☽ Ingress

Dy Hr Mn		☽ Ingress Dy Hr Mn
1 4:21 ♃ △	♏	1 11:57
3 5:23 ♃ □	♐	3 12:14
5 5:09 ♃ ⚹	♑	5 11:32
7 4:43 ♂ ⚹	♒	7 11:50
9 10:01 ♂ □	♓	9 14:54
11 19:41 ♂ △	♈	11 21:47
14 2:53 ♃ ⚹	♉	14 8:12
16 16:10 ♃ □	♊	16 20:44
19 6:03 ♃ △	♋	19 9:43
21 14:45 ♀ ☍	♌	21 21:55
24 6:41 ♃ ☍	♍	24 8:25
26 8:41 ♇ △	♎	26 16:25
28 21:12 ♃ △	♏	28 21:17
30 17:11 ☿ ⚹	♐	30 23:09

☽ Phases & Eclipses

Dy Hr Mn	
4 21:16	● 12♏40
11 12:47	☽ 19♒21
19 8:59	○ 27♉14
19 9:04	P 0.974
27 12:29	☾ 5♍28
4 7:44	● 12♐22
4 7:34:36	T 01'55"
11 1:37	☽ 19♓13
19 4:37	○ 27♊29
27 2:25	☾ 5♎32

Astro Data

1 November 2021
Julian Day # 44500
SVP 4♓57'34"
GC 27♐08.7 ⚴ 9♓12.3R
Eris 24♈05.1R ⚵ 25♐34.2
⚷ 9♈25.4R ⚶ 21♏53.7
☽ Mean ☊ 2♊43.9

1 December 2021
Julian Day # 44530
SVP 4♓57'29"
GC 27♐08.7 ⚴ 10♓35.2
Eris 23♈49.9R ⚵ 5♑52.8
⚷ 8♈35.2R ⚶ 8♐03.3
☽ Mean ☊ 1♊08.6

LONGITUDE — January 2022

Day	Sid.Time	☉	0 hr ☽	Noon ☽	True ☊	☿	♀	♂	⚳	♃	♄	♅	♆	♇
1 Sa	18 44 29	11♑02 17	15♐28 04	23♐01 07	1♊11.3	28♑53.3	23♑02.9	13♐27.2	28♉35.0	0♓38.6	11♒57.4	10♉56.7	20♓40.7	25♑57.0
2 Su	18 48 25	12 03 28	0♑35 49	8♑11 00	1R 07.5	0♒16.5	22R 32.1	14 09.9	28R 29.7	0 50.4	12 03.9	10R 55.9	20 41.7	25 59.0
3 M	18 52 22	13 04 39	15 45 21	23 17 39	1 01.9	1 37.0	21 59.7	14 52.7	28 24.8	1 02.4	12 10.5	10 55.1	20 42.8	26 00.9
4 Tu	18 56 18	14 05 49	0♒46 38	8♒11 13	0 55.0	2 54.3	21 26.1	15 35.4	28 20.2	1 14.4	12 17.1	10 54.3	20 44.0	26 02.9
5 W	19 00 15	15 07 00	15 30 24	22 43 24	0 47.7	4 08.0	20 51.3	16 18.2	28 16.1	1 26.4	12 23.8	10 53.6	20 45.1	26 04.8
6 Th	19 04 11	16 08 10	29 49 37	6♓48 40	0 41.2	5 17.3	20 15.7	17 01.1	28 12.4	1 38.6	12 30.5	10 53.0	20 46.3	26 06.8
7 F	19 08 08	17 09 20	13♓40 22	20 24 43	0 36.0	6 21.5	19 39.4	17 43.9	28 09.1	1 50.9	12 37.2	10 52.3	20 47.5	26 08.7
8 Sa	19 12 04	18 10 30	27 01 54	3♈32 13	0 32.8	7 19.9	19 02.8	18 26.9	28 06.3	2 03.2	12 43.9	10 51.8	20 48.8	26 10.7
9 Su	19 16 01	19 11 39	9♈56 06	16 14 04	0D 31.5	8 11.7	18 26.0	19 09.8	28 03.8	2 15.6	12 50.7	10 51.3	20 50.1	26 12.7
10 M	19 19 58	20 12 47	22 26 44	28 34 41	0 31.8	8 56.0	17 49.4	19 52.8	28 01.8	2 28.1	12 57.5	10 50.8	20 51.4	26 14.6
11 Tu	19 23 54	21 13 55	4♉38 36	10♉39 09	0 33.0	9 31.8	17 13.1	20 35.8	28 00.2	2 40.7	13 04.3	10 50.4	20 52.7	26 16.6
12 W	19 27 51	22 15 03	16 36 59	22 32 44	0R 34.2	9 58.4	16 37.5	21 18.8	27 59.0	2 53.3	13 11.2	10 50.1	20 54.1	26 18.6
13 Th	19 31 47	23 16 10	28 27 02	4♊20 27	0 34.4	10R 14.7	16 02.7	22 01.9	27 58.2	3 06.0	13 18.1	10 49.8	20 55.5	26 20.6
14 F	19 35 44	24 17 17	10♊13 33	16 06 48	0 32.9	10 20.2	15 29.1	22 45.1	27D 57.9	3 18.8	13 25.0	10 49.6	20 56.9	26 22.6
15 Sa	19 39 40	25 18 22	22 00 41	27 55 34	0 29.0	10 14.3	14 56.9	23 28.2	27 57.9	3 31.7	13 31.9	10 49.4	20 58.3	26 24.5
16 Su	19 43 37	26 19 28	3♋51 50	9♋49 47	0 22.6	9 56.7	14 26.1	24 11.4	27 58.4	3 44.6	13 38.9	10 49.2	20 59.8	26 26.5
17 M	19 47 33	27 20 33	15 49 39	21 51 38	0 13.7	9 27.3	13 57.1	24 54.7	27 59.2	3 57.6	13 45.9	10 49.1	21 01.3	26 28.5
18 Tu	19 51 30	28 21 37	27 55 55	4♌02 37	0 03.0	8 46.6	13 30.0	25 37.9	28 00.5	4 10.7	13 52.9	10D 49.1	21 02.8	26 30.5
19 W	19 55 27	29 22 41	10♌11 50	16 23 37	29♉51.4	7 55.5	13 05.0	26 21.2	28 02.1	4 23.8	13 59.9	10 49.1	21 04.4	26 32.5
20 Th	19 59 23	0♒23 44	22 38 02	28 55 09	29 39.9	6 55.2	12 42.1	27 04.6	28 04.2	4 37.0	14 07.0	10 49.2	21 06.0	26 34.4
21 F	20 03 20	1 24 47	5♍15 00	11♍37 40	29 29.5	5 47.5	12 21.5	27 48.0	28 06.7	4 50.2	14 14.1	10 49.3	21 07.6	26 36.4
22 Sa	20 07 16	2 25 49	18 03 14	24 31 47	29 21.3	4 34.4	12 03.2	28 31.4	28 09.5	5 03.5	14 21.1	10 49.5	21 09.2	26 38.4
23 Su	20 11 13	3 26 50	1♎03 28	7♎38 25	29 15.7	3 18.1	11 47.4	29 14.9	28 12.7	5 16.9	14 28.2	10 49.7	21 10.9	26 40.4
24 M	20 15 09	4 27 51	14 16 50	20 58 54	29 12.7	2 01.2	11 34.0	29 58.4	28 16.3	5 30.3	14 35.3	10 50.0	21 12.5	26 42.3
25 Tu	20 19 06	5 28 52	27 44 48	4♏34 44	29D 11.8	0 45.7	11 23.1	0♑41.9	28 20.3	5 43.8	14 42.5	10 50.3	21 14.2	26 44.3
26 W	20 23 02	6 29 53	11♏28 53	18 27 20	29R 12.1	29♑33.9	11 14.8	1 25.5	28 24.7	5 57.3	14 49.6	10 50.7	21 16.0	26 46.3
27 Th	20 26 59	7 30 52	25 30 10	2♐37 20	29 12.3	28 27.4	11 08.9	2 09.1	28 29.5	6 10.9	14 56.8	10 51.2	21 17.7	26 48.2
28 F	20 30 56	8 31 52	9♐48 41	17 03 58	29 11.1	27 27.7	11D 05.5	2 52.8	28 34.6	6 24.6	15 03.9	10 51.6	21 19.5	26 50.2
29 Sa	20 34 52	9 32 50	24 22 45	1♑44 27	29 07.6	26 35.7	11 04.6	3 36.5	28 40.1	6 38.3	15 11.1	10 52.2	21 21.3	26 52.1
30 Su	20 38 49	10 33 49	9♑08 22	16 33 36	29 01.1	25 52.1	11 06.2	4 20.2	28 46.0	6 52.0	15 18.3	10 52.8	21 23.1	26 54.1
31 M	20 42 45	11 34 46	23 59 12	1♒24 06	28 51.9	25 17.2	11 10.1	5 03.9	28 52.2	7 05.8	15 25.5	10 53.4	21 25.0	26 56.0

LONGITUDE — February 2022

Day	Sid.Time	☉	0 hr ☽	Noon ☽	True ☊	☿	♀	♂	⚳	♃	♄	♅	♆	♇
1 Tu	20 46 42	12♒35 42	8♒47 13	16♒07 28	28♉40.8	24♑51.1	11♑16.3	5♑47.7	28♉58.8	7♓19.6	15♒32.7	10♉54.1	21♓26.8	26♑57.9
2 W	20 50 38	13 36 37	23 23 49	0♓35 22	28R 28.8	24R 33.6	11 24.9	6 31.6	29 05.7	7 33.5	15 39.9	10 54.9	21 28.7	26 59.9
3 Th	20 54 35	14 37 31	7♓41 21	14 41 10	28 17.5	24D 24.3	11 35.6	7 15.4	29 13.0	7 47.4	15 47.1	10 55.7	21 30.6	27 01.8
4 F	20 58 31	15 38 23	21 34 24	28 20 49	28 07.9	24 23.0	11 48.5	7 59.3	29 20.6	8 01.4	15 54.3	10 56.6	21 32.5	27 03.7
5 Sa	21 02 28	16 39 14	5♈00 22	11♈33 10	28 00.7	24 29.0	12 03.5	8 43.2	29 28.6	8 15.3	16 01.4	10 57.5	21 34.4	27 05.6
6 Su	21 06 25	17 40 04	17 59 30	24 19 44	27 56.3	24 42.0	12 20.6	9 27.2	29 36.9	8 29.4	16 08.6	10 58.4	21 36.4	27 07.4
7 M	21 10 21	18 40 52	0♉34 23	6♉44 00	27 54.3	25 01.3	12 39.6	10 11.2	29 45.6	8 43.4	16 15.8	10 59.4	21 38.4	27 09.3
8 Tu	21 14 18	19 41 39	12 49 14	18 50 46	27 53.8	25 26.6	13 00.5	10 55.2	29 54.5	8 57.5	16 23.0	11 00.5	21 40.3	27 11.2
9 W	21 18 14	20 42 25	24 49 17	0♊45 29	27 53.8	25 57.3	13 23.3	11 39.2	0♊03.8	9 11.7	16 30.2	11 01.6	21 42.3	27 13.0
10 Th	21 22 11	21 43 09	6♊40 06	12 33 48	27 53.2	26 32.9	13 47.9	12 23.3	0 13.4	9 25.8	16 37.4	11 02.8	21 44.4	27 14.9
11 F	21 26 07	22 43 51	18 27 15	24 21 05	27 50.7	27 13.2	14 14.2	13 07.4	0 23.3	9 40.0	16 44.6	11 04.0	21 46.4	27 16.7
12 Sa	21 30 04	23 44 32	0♋15 53	6♋12 12	27 45.8	27 57.6	14 42.1	13 51.5	0 33.6	9 54.2	16 51.8	11 05.2	21 48.5	27 18.5
13 Su	21 34 00	24 45 11	12 10 31	18 11 15	27 38.0	28 45.9	15 11.7	14 35.7	0 44.1	10 08.5	16 58.9	11 06.5	21 50.5	27 20.3
14 M	21 37 57	25 45 49	24 14 44	0♌21 17	27 27.4	29 37.7	15 42.8	15 19.9	0 54.9	10 22.8	17 06.1	11 07.9	21 52.6	27 22.1
15 Tu	21 41 54	26 46 25	6♌31 07	12 44 21	27 14.6	0♒32.7	16 15.4	16 04.2	1 06.0	10 37.1	17 13.2	11 09.3	21 54.7	27 23.9
16 W	21 45 50	27 46 59	19 01 04	25 21 18	27 00.6	1 30.7	16 49.4	16 48.4	1 17.4	10 51.4	17 20.3	11 10.8	21 56.8	27 25.7
17 Th	21 49 47	28 47 32	1♍44 58	8♍11 59	26 46.7	2 31.4	17 24.8	17 32.7	1 29.1	11 05.7	17 27.4	11 12.3	21 58.9	27 27.4
18 F	21 53 43	29 48 04	14 42 13	21 15 31	26 34.1	3 34.8	18 01.5	18 17.0	1 41.1	11 20.1	17 34.5	11 13.8	22 01.1	27 29.2
19 Sa	21 57 40	0♓48 34	27 51 42	4♎30 36	26 23.8	4 40.4	18 39.5	19 01.4	1 53.3	11 34.5	17 41.6	11 15.4	22 03.2	27 30.9
20 Su	22 01 36	1 49 02	11♎12 05	17 56 00	26 16.6	5 48.3	19 18.7	19 45.8	2 05.8	11 48.9	17 48.7	11 17.0	22 05.4	27 32.6
21 M	22 05 33	2 49 30	24 42 16	1♏30 49	26 12.3	6 58.2	19 59.1	20 30.2	2 18.6	12 03.3	17 55.7	11 18.7	22 07.5	27 34.3
22 Tu	22 09 29	3 49 56	8♏21 37	15 14 39	26D 10.6	8 10.1	20 40.7	21 14.7	2 31.6	12 17.7	18 02.7	11 20.4	22 09.7	27 36.0
23 W	22 13 26	4 50 20	22 09 58	29 07 33	26R 10.3	9 23.8	21 23.3	21 59.2	2 44.9	12 32.1	18 09.8	11 22.2	22 11.9	27 37.6
24 Th	22 17 23	5 50 44	6♐07 25	13♐09 35	26 10.3	10 39.2	22 06.9	22 43.7	2 58.4	12 46.6	18 16.8	11 24.0	22 14.1	27 39.3
25 F	22 21 19	6 51 06	20 13 58	27 20 27	26 09.0	11 56.2	22 51.6	23 28.3	3 12.2	13 01.1	18 23.7	11 25.9	22 16.3	27 40.9
26 Sa	22 25 16	7 51 27	4♑28 49	11♑38 48	26 05.5	13 14.8	23 37.2	24 12.8	3 26.3	13 15.6	18 30.7	11 27.8	22 18.5	27 42.5
27 Su	22 29 12	8 51 46	18 50 00	26 01 54	25 59.2	14 34.9	24 23.7	24 57.5	3 40.6	13 30.1	18 37.6	11 29.8	22 20.8	27 44.1
28 M	22 33 09	9 52 04	3♒13 56	10♒25 26	25 50.1	15 56.3	25 11.1	25 42.1	3 55.1	13 44.6	18 44.5	11 31.8	22 23.0	27 45.7

Astro Data

	Dy Hr Mn
☽ 0N	8 22:52
☿ R	14 11:43
⚳ D	14 21:21
♅ D	18 15:27
☽ 0S	23 14:33
♀ D	29 8:47
☿ D	4 4:14
☽ 0N	5 7:02
♃✶♅	18 0:14
☽ 0S	19 19:22
♃∠♇	23 22:18

Planet Ingress

	Dy Hr Mn
☿ ♒	2 7:11
☊ ♉R	18 18:22
☉ ♒	20 2:40
♂ ♑	24 12:54
☿ ♑R	26 3:06
⚳ ♊	9 2:14
☿ ♒	14 21:55
☉ ♓	18 16:44

Last Aspect / ☽ Ingress (January)

Last Aspect Dy Hr Mn		☽ Ingress Dy Hr Mn
1 8:17 ♆ □	♑	1 23:03
3 16:22 ♇ ☌	♒	3 22:45
5 0:46 ♂ ✶	♓	6 0:18
7 22:24 ♇ ✶	♈	8 5:27
10 7:24 ♇ □	♉	10 14:48
12 19:40 ♇ △	♊	13 3:09
15 2:23 ♂ ☍	♋	15 16:12
17 23:50 ☉ ☍	♌	18 4:04
20 8:17 ♂ △	♍	20 14:03
22 19:47 ♂ □	♎	22 22:04
24 22:11 ♇ □	♏	25 3:58
27 5:29 ☿ ✶	♐	27 7:36
28 19:01 ♆ □	♑	29 9:10
31 4:45 ♇ ☌	♒	31 9:44

Last Aspect / ☽ Ingress (February)

Last Aspect Dy Hr Mn		☽ Ingress Dy Hr Mn
1 11:02 ♄ ☌	♓	2 11:01
4 9:42 ♇ ✶	♈	4 14:58
6 17:22 ♇ □	♉	6 22:54
9 4:49 ♇ △	♊	9 10:28
11 8:24 ☉ △	♋	11 23:28
14 10:28 ☿ ☍	♌	14 11:18
16 16:58 ☉ ☍	♍	16 20:44
18 23:21 ♇ △	♎	19 3:52
21 5:03 ♇ □	♏	21 9:20
23 9:25 ♇ ✶	♐	23 13:30
25 3:26 ♆ □	♑	25 16:29
27 14:51 ♇ ☌	♒	27 18:37

☽ Phases & Eclipses

Dy Hr Mn	
2 18:35	● 12♑20
9 18:12	☽ 19♈27
17 23:50	○ 27♋51
25 13:42	☾ 5♏33
1 5:47	● 12♒20
8 13:51	☽ 19♉46
16 16:58	○ 28♌00
23 22:34	☾ 5♐17

Astro Data

1 January 2022
Julian Day # 44561
SVP 4♓57'23"
GC 27♐08.8 ⚴ 16♓35.0
Eris 23♈41.6R ⚵ 17♑34.6
⚷ 8♈30.7 ⚶ 24♐47.7
☽ Mean ☊ 29♉30.2

1 February 2022
Julian Day # 44592
SVP 4♓57'17"
GC 27♐08.9 ⚴ 25♓39.3
Eris 23♈43.7 ⚵ 29♑48.9
⚷ 9♈17.2 ⚶ 11♑13.8
☽ Mean ☊ 27♉51.7

March 2022 — LONGITUDE

Day	Sid.Time	☉	0 hr ☽	Noon ☽	True ☊	☿	♀	♂	⚳	♃	♄	♅	♆	♇
1 Tu	22 37 05	10♓52 20	17♒35 39	24♒43 50	25♉39.0	17♒19.2	25♑59.4	26♑26.8	4♊09.8	13♓59.1	18♒51.4	11♉33.8	22♓25.2	27♑47.3
2 W	22 41 02	11 52 35	1♓49 15	8♓51 09	25R 27.0	18 43.3	26 48.4	27 11.5	4 24.8	14 13.6	18 58.2	11 35.9	22 27.5	27 48.8
3 Th	22 44 58	12 52 47	15 48 55	22 41 57	25 15.4	20 08.8	27 38.2	27 56.2	4 40.1	14 28.1	19 05.0	11 38.0	22 29.7	27 50.3
4 F	22 48 55	13 52 58	29 29 50	6♈12 15	25 05.4	21 35.5	28 28.7	28 40.9	4 55.5	14 42.6	19 11.8	11 40.2	22 32.0	27 51.8
5 Sa	22 52 52	14 53 07	12♈49 00	19 20 04	24 57.7	23 03.4	29 20.0	29 25.7	5 11.2	14 57.2	19 18.5	11 42.4	22 34.2	27 53.3
6 Su	22 56 48	15 53 14	25 45 31	2♉05 34	24 52.8	24 32.6	0♒11.9	0♒10.5	5 27.1	15 11.7	19 25.3	11 44.6	22 36.5	27 54.7
7 M	23 00 45	16 53 19	8♉20 33	14 30 51	24D 50.4	26 02.9	1 04.5	0 55.3	5 43.2	15 26.2	19 31.9	11 46.9	22 38.8	27 56.2
8 Tu	23 04 41	17 53 21	20 37 01	26 39 33	24 50.0	27 34.4	1 57.7	1 40.1	5 59.5	15 40.7	19 38.6	11 49.2	22 41.0	27 57.6
9 W	23 08 38	18 53 22	2♊39 07	8♊36 20	24R 50.4	29 07.1	2 51.6	2 24.9	6 16.0	15 55.2	19 45.2	11 51.6	22 43.3	27 59.0
10 Th	23 12 34	19 53 20	14 31 52	20 26 25	24 50.8	0♓41.0	3 46.0	3 09.8	6 32.7	16 09.7	19 51.8	11 54.0	22 45.6	28 00.3
11 F	23 16 31	20 53 17	26 20 41	2♋15 19	24 50.0	2 16.0	4 40.9	3 54.7	6 49.6	16 24.2	19 58.3	11 56.4	22 47.9	28 01.7
12 Sa	23 20 27	21 53 11	8♋11 00	14 08 22	24 47.3	3 52.2	5 36.5	4 39.6	7 06.7	16 38.7	20 04.8	11 58.9	22 50.1	28 03.0
13 Su	23 24 24	22 53 03	20 07 59	26 10 25	24 42.3	5 29.5	6 32.5	5 24.6	7 24.0	16 53.2	20 11.3	12 01.4	22 52.4	28 04.3
14 M	23 28 21	23 52 53	2♌16 10	8♌25 37	24 34.9	7 08.0	7 29.0	6 09.5	7 41.5	17 07.7	20 17.7	12 03.9	22 54.7	28 05.6
15 Tu	23 32 17	24 52 40	14 39 10	20 57 02	24 25.6	8 47.7	8 26.1	6 54.5	7 59.2	17 22.1	20 24.1	12 06.5	22 57.0	28 06.8
16 W	23 36 14	25 52 26	27 19 25	3♍46 23	24 15.3	10 28.6	9 23.6	7 39.5	8 17.0	17 36.6	20 30.4	12 09.1	22 59.2	28 08.1
17 Th	23 40 10	26 52 09	10♍17 56	16 53 58	24 04.8	12 10.7	10 21.5	8 24.5	8 35.1	17 51.0	20 36.7	12 11.7	23 01.5	28 09.3
18 F	23 44 07	27 51 51	23 34 16	0♎18 35	23 55.3	13 54.0	11 19.9	9 09.6	8 53.3	18 05.4	20 42.9	12 14.4	23 03.8	28 10.5
19 Sa	23 48 03	28 51 30	7♎06 36	13 57 56	23 47.6	15 38.5	12 18.8	9 54.6	9 11.6	18 19.8	20 49.1	12 17.1	23 06.1	28 11.6
20 Su	23 52 00	29 51 07	20 52 11	27 48 55	23 42.4	17 24.3	13 18.0	10 39.7	9 30.2	18 34.2	20 55.3	12 19.8	23 08.3	28 12.8
21 M	23 55 56	0♈50 43	4♏47 44	11♏48 15	23D 39.7	19 11.3	14 17.6	11 24.8	9 48.9	18 48.5	21 01.4	12 22.6	23 10.6	28 13.9
22 Tu	23 59 53	1 50 17	18 50 05	25 52 56	23 39.1	20 59.6	15 17.6	12 10.0	10 07.7	19 02.9	21 07.4	12 25.4	23 12.9	28 15.0
23 W	0 03 50	2 49 49	2♐56 30	10♐00 33	23 39.8	22 49.2	16 18.0	12 55.1	10 26.7	19 17.2	21 13.4	12 28.2	23 15.1	28 16.0
24 Th	0 07 46	3 49 19	17 04 53	24 09 18	23R 40.8	24 40.1	17 18.8	13 40.3	10 45.9	19 31.5	21 19.4	12 31.1	23 17.4	28 17.1
25 F	0 11 43	4 48 48	1♑13 39	8♑17 46	23 41.1	26 32.2	18 19.9	14 25.5	11 05.2	19 45.8	21 25.3	12 34.0	23 19.6	28 18.1
26 Sa	0 15 39	5 48 15	15 21 29	22 24 36	23 39.9	28 25.6	19 21.3	15 10.7	11 24.7	20 00.0	21 31.2	12 36.9	23 21.9	28 19.1
27 Su	0 19 36	6 47 40	29 26 56	6♒28 13	23 36.6	0♈20.4	20 23.0	15 55.9	11 44.4	20 14.3	21 37.0	12 39.8	23 24.1	28 20.0
28 M	0 23 32	7 47 04	13♒28 11	20 26 31	23 31.3	2 16.3	21 25.1	16 41.1	12 04.2	20 28.5	21 42.7	12 42.8	23 26.3	28 20.9
29 Tu	0 27 29	8 46 25	27 22 52	4♓16 53	23 24.5	4 13.6	22 27.4	17 26.4	12 24.1	20 42.6	21 48.4	12 45.8	23 28.5	28 21.8
30 W	0 31 25	9 45 45	11♓08 12	17 56 26	23 17.0	6 12.0	23 30.0	18 11.6	12 44.2	20 56.8	21 54.0	12 48.8	23 30.7	28 22.7
31 Th	0 35 22	10 45 02	24 41 16	1♈22 24	23 09.7	8 11.6	24 32.9	18 56.9	13 04.4	21 10.9	21 59.6	12 51.8	23 32.9	28 23.6

April 2022 — LONGITUDE

Day	Sid.Time	☉	0 hr ☽	Noon ☽	True ☊	☿	♀	♂	⚳	♃	♄	♅	♆	♇
1 F	0 39 19	11♈44 18	7♈59 33	14♈32 33	23♉03.4	10♈12.3	25♒36.1	19♒42.2	13♊24.7	21♓24.9	22♒05.1	12♉54.9	23♓35.1	28♑24.4
2 Sa	0 43 15	12 43 32	21 01 16	27 25 40	22R 58.7	12 14.0	26 39.5	20 27.5	13 45.2	21 39.0	22 10.5	12 58.0	23 37.3	28 25.2
3 Su	0 47 12	13 42 43	3♉45 45	10♉01 40	22 56.0	14 16.7	27 43.1	21 12.8	14 05.8	21 53.0	22 15.9	13 01.1	23 39.5	28 26.0
4 M	0 51 08	14 41 53	16 13 36	22 21 48	22D 55.1	16 20.1	28 47.0	21 58.1	14 26.6	22 07.0	22 21.2	13 04.2	23 41.7	28 26.7
5 Tu	0 55 05	15 41 00	28 26 37	4♊28 28	22 55.7	18 24.2	29 51.1	22 43.4	14 47.5	22 20.9	22 26.5	13 07.4	23 43.8	28 27.4
6 W	0 59 01	16 40 05	10♊27 47	16 25 05	22 57.2	20 28.8	0♓55.5	23 28.7	15 08.5	22 34.8	22 31.7	13 10.5	23 45.9	28 28.1
7 Th	1 02 58	17 39 08	22 20 55	28 15 52	22 58.9	22 33.6	2 00.0	24 14.0	15 29.6	22 48.6	22 36.8	13 13.7	23 48.1	28 28.7
8 F	1 06 54	18 38 08	4♋10 33	10♋05 34	23R 00.2	24 38.4	3 04.8	24 59.4	15 50.8	23 02.4	22 41.9	13 17.0	23 50.2	28 29.4
9 Sa	1 10 51	19 37 06	16 01 34	21 59 11	23 00.6	26 43.0	4 09.7	25 44.7	16 12.2	23 16.2	22 46.9	13 20.2	23 52.3	28 30.0
10 Su	1 14 47	20 36 02	27 59 02	4♌01 43	22 59.6	28 47.1	5 14.9	26 30.0	16 33.7	23 29.9	22 51.8	13 23.4	23 54.4	28 30.5
11 M	1 18 44	21 34 56	10♌07 50	16 17 53	22 57.2	0♉50.3	6 20.2	27 15.4	16 55.3	23 43.6	22 56.6	13 26.7	23 56.5	28 31.1
12 Tu	1 22 41	22 33 47	22 32 23	28 51 44	22 53.6	2 52.4	7 25.7	28 00.7	17 17.0	23 57.2	23 01.4	13 30.0	23 58.5	28 31.6
13 W	1 26 37	23 32 36	5♍16 15	11♍46 12	22 49.3	4 52.9	8 31.4	28 46.1	17 38.8	24 10.8	23 06.1	13 33.3	24 00.6	28 32.1
14 Th	1 30 34	24 31 23	18 21 44	25 02 53	22 44.7	6 51.5	9 37.3	29 31.4	18 00.7	24 24.3	23 10.8	13 36.6	24 02.6	28 32.5
15 F	1 34 30	25 30 08	1♎49 33	8♎41 33	22 40.6	8 47.9	10 43.3	0♓16.8	18 22.8	24 37.8	23 15.3	13 39.9	24 04.6	28 33.0
16 Sa	1 38 27	26 28 50	15 38 35	22 40 11	22 37.3	10 41.8	11 49.5	1 02.2	18 44.9	24 51.2	23 19.8	13 43.2	24 06.6	28 33.4
17 Su	1 42 23	27 27 31	29 45 53	6♏55 02	22 35.3	12 32.8	12 55.9	1 47.5	19 07.1	25 04.6	23 24.3	13 46.6	24 08.6	28 33.7
18 M	1 46 20	28 26 10	14♏07 01	21 21 08	22D 34.6	14 20.6	14 02.4	2 32.9	19 29.4	25 17.9	23 28.6	13 50.0	24 10.6	28 34.1
19 Tu	1 50 16	29 24 47	28 36 40	5♐52 55	22 35.0	16 05.0	15 09.1	3 18.3	19 51.9	25 31.2	23 32.9	13 53.3	24 12.5	28 34.4
20 W	1 54 13	0♉23 23	13♐09 13	20 24 56	22 36.1	17 45.6	16 15.9	4 03.6	20 14.4	25 44.4	23 37.1	13 56.7	24 14.5	28 34.7
21 Th	1 58 10	1 21 56	27 39 31	4♑52 28	22 37.5	19 22.4	17 22.9	4 49.0	20 37.0	25 57.5	23 41.2	14 00.1	24 16.4	28 34.9
22 F	2 02 06	2 20 28	12♑03 21	19 11 48	22 38.6	20 55.0	18 30.0	5 34.4	20 59.7	26 10.6	23 45.2	14 03.5	24 18.3	28 35.2
23 Sa	2 06 03	3 18 59	26 17 33	3♒20 20	22R 39.0	22 23.3	19 37.3	6 19.8	21 22.6	26 23.6	23 49.2	14 06.9	24 20.2	28 35.4
24 Su	2 09 59	4 17 28	10♒20 00	17 16 25	22 38.6	23 47.1	20 44.7	7 05.1	21 45.5	26 36.6	23 53.1	14 10.4	24 22.0	28 35.5
25 M	2 13 56	5 15 55	24 09 28	0♓59 07	22 37.3	25 06.4	21 52.2	7 50.5	22 08.4	26 49.5	23 56.9	14 13.8	24 23.9	28 35.7
26 Tu	2 17 52	6 14 21	7♓45 18	14 27 59	22 35.4	26 21.0	22 59.9	8 35.8	22 31.5	27 02.4	24 00.6	14 17.2	24 25.7	28 35.8
27 W	2 21 49	7 12 45	21 07 11	27 42 52	22 33.3	27 30.8	24 07.6	9 21.2	22 54.7	27 15.1	24 04.2	14 20.7	24 27.5	28 35.9
28 Th	2 25 45	8 11 07	4♈15 04	10♈43 47	22 31.2	28 35.7	25 15.5	10 06.5	23 17.9	27 27.8	24 07.8	14 24.1	24 29.3	28 35.9
29 F	2 29 42	9 09 27	17 09 04	23 30 57	22 29.4	29 35.6	26 23.5	10 51.9	23 41.3	27 40.5	24 11.3	14 27.6	24 31.0	28R 35.9
30 Sa	2 33 39	10 07 46	29 49 31	6♉04 50	22 28.3	0♊30.5	27 31.6	11 37.2	24 04.7	27 53.0	24 14.6	14 31.0	24 32.7	28 35.9

Astro Data	Dy Hr Mn
☽0N	4 16:08
☽0S	19 2:18
☉0N	20 15:35
☿0N	29 5:57
☽0N	1 0:46
♃⚺♄	6 3:25
♃☌♆	12 14:44
☽0S	15 11:35
☽0N	28 7:51
♇R	29 18:38

Planet Ingress		Dy Hr Mn
♂	♒	6 6:24
♀	♒	6 6:31
☿	♓	10 1:33
☉	♈	20 15:35
☿	♈	27 7:46
♀	♓	5 15:19
☿	♉	11 2:11
♂	♓	15 3:07
☉	♉	20 2:25
☿	♊	29 22:24

Last Aspect Dy Hr Mn		☽ Ingress	Dy Hr Mn
1 2:02	♄ ☌	♓	1 20:55
3 21:46	♂ ⚹	♈	4 0:54
6 4:03	♇ □	♉	6 8:01
8 14:36	♇ △	♊	8 18:41
10 16:44	♆ □	♋	11 7:25
13 15:45	♇ ☍	♌	13 19:33
15 10:57	♄ ☍	♍	16 5:00
18 8:12	♇ △	♎	18 11:27
20 12:41	♇ □	♏	20 15:46
22 16:02	♇ ⚹	♐	22 19:00
24 13:00	☿ □	♑	24 21:55
26 23:52	☿ ⚹	♒	27 0:56
28 14:12	♄ ☌	♓	29 4:33
31 6:38	♇ ⚹	♈	31 9:32

Last Aspect Dy Hr Mn		☽ Ingress	Dy Hr Mn
2 13:52	♇ □	♉	2 16:51
5 1:54	♀ □	♊	5 3:05
7 3:16	♂ △	♋	7 15:31
10 1:02	♇ ☍	♌	10 4:01
12 10:18	♂ ☍	♍	12 14:09
14 18:13	♇ △	♎	14 20:47
16 21:58	♇ □	♏	17 0:24
18 23:56	♇ ⚹	♐	19 2:18
20 20:57	♃ □	♑	21 3:53
23 3:54	♇ ☌	♒	23 6:18
25 0:35	☿ □	♓	25 10:16
27 13:37	♇ ⚹	♈	27 16:11
29 21:40	♇ □	♉	30 0:20

☽ Phases & Eclipses Dy Hr Mn	
2 17:36	● 12♓07
10 10:47	☽ 19♊50
18 7:19	○ 27♍40
25 5:38	☾ 4♑33
1 6:26	● 11♈31
9 6:49	☽ 19♋24
16 18:56	○ 26♎46
23 11:58	☾ 3♒19
30 20:29	● 10♉28
30 20:42:37	P 0.640

Astro Data

1 March 2022
Julian Day # 44620
SVP 4♓57'14"
GC 27♐08.9 ⚴ 5♈33.2
Eris 23♈54.0 ⚵ 10♒57.3
⚷ 10♈33.7 ⚶ 25♑28.5
☽ Mean ☊ 26♉22.7

1 April 2022
Julian Day # 44651
SVP 4♓57'11"
GC 27♐09.0 ⚴ 17♈46.3
Eris 24♈11.9 ⚵ 22♒58.1
⚷ 12♈19.0 ⚶ 10♒06.4
☽ Mean ☊ 24♉44.2

LONGITUDE May 2022

Day	Sid.Time	☉	0 hr ☽	Noon ☽	True ☊	☿	♀	♂	⚳	♃	♄	♅	♆	♇
1 Su	2 37 35	11♉06 04	12♉17 01	18♉26 13	22♉27.8	1♊20.2	28♓39.8	12♓22.5	24♊28.2	28♓05.5	24♒17.9	14♉34.5	24♓34.5	28♑35.9
2 M	2 41 32	12 04 19	24 32 38	0♊36 26	22D27.9	2 04.8	29 48.1	13 07.8	24 51.8	28 17.9	24 21.2	14 38.0	24 36.1	28R35.8
3 Tu	2 45 28	13 02 33	6♊37 54	12 37 17	22 28.4	2 44.1	0♈56.4	13 53.0	25 15.5	28 30.3	24 24.3	14 41.4	24 37.8	28 35.7
4 W	2 49 25	14 00 44	18 34 56	24 31 13	22 29.2	3 18.2	2 04.9	14 38.3	25 39.2	28 42.5	24 27.3	14 44.9	24 39.5	28 35.6
5 Th	2 53 21	14 58 54	0♋26 30	6♋21 15	22 30.1	3 47.0	3 13.5	15 23.5	26 03.0	28 54.7	24 30.3	14 48.4	24 41.1	28 35.5
6 F	2 57 18	15 57 02	12 15 55	18 11 00	22 30.8	4 10.4	4 22.2	16 08.8	26 26.9	29 06.8	24 33.1	14 51.8	24 42.7	28 35.3
7 Sa	3 01 14	16 55 08	24 07 02	0♌04 32	22 31.3	4 28.6	5 30.9	16 54.0	26 50.9	29 18.9	24 35.9	14 55.3	24 44.3	28 35.1
8 Su	3 05 11	17 53 13	6♌04 06	12 06 16	22R31.6	4 41.4	6 39.7	17 39.2	27 14.9	29 30.8	24 38.6	14 58.8	24 45.8	28 34.9
9 M	3 09 08	18 51 15	18 11 38	24 20 45	22 31.6	4R49.0	7 48.6	18 24.3	27 39.0	29 42.7	24 41.2	15 02.2	24 47.3	28 34.6
10 Tu	3 13 04	19 49 15	0♍34 10	6♍52 23	22 31.4	4 51.5	8 57.6	19 09.5	28 03.1	29 54.4	24 43.6	15 05.7	24 48.8	28 34.3
11 W	3 17 01	20 47 14	13 15 53	19 45 04	22 31.2	4 49.0	10 06.7	19 54.6	28 27.4	0♈06.1	24 46.1	15 09.2	24 50.3	28 34.0
12 Th	3 20 57	21 45 10	26 20 16	3♎01 43	22D31.1	4 41.7	11 15.9	20 39.7	28 51.7	0 17.7	24 48.4	15 12.6	24 51.8	28 33.7
13 F	3 24 54	22 43 05	9♎49 32	16 43 45	22 31.1	4 29.7	12 25.1	21 24.7	29 16.0	0 29.2	24 50.6	15 16.1	24 53.2	28 33.3
14 Sa	3 28 50	23 40 58	23 44 13	0♏50 39	22 31.1	4 13.5	13 34.4	22 09.8	29 40.4	0 40.7	24 52.7	15 19.5	24 54.6	28 32.9
15 Su	3 32 47	24 38 49	8♏02 37	15 19 32	22R31.2	3 53.3	14 43.7	22 54.8	0♋04.9	0 52.0	24 54.7	15 22.9	24 55.9	28 32.5
16 M	3 36 43	25 36 39	22 40 42	0♐05 16	22 31.2	3 29.5	15 53.2	23 39.8	0 29.4	1 03.2	24 56.7	15 26.4	24 57.3	28 32.0
17 Tu	3 40 40	26 34 28	7♐32 18	15 00 48	22 31.0	3 02.5	17 02.7	24 24.8	0 54.0	1 14.4	24 58.5	15 29.8	24 58.6	28 31.5
18 W	3 44 37	27 32 16	22 29 44	29 58 06	22 30.6	2 32.9	18 12.3	25 09.8	1 18.7	1 25.4	25 00.3	15 33.2	24 59.9	28 31.0
19 Th	3 48 33	28 30 02	7♑24 53	14♑49 13	22 30.0	2 01.2	19 22.0	25 54.7	1 43.4	1 36.4	25 01.9	15 36.6	25 01.1	28 30.5
20 F	3 52 30	29 27 47	22 10 17	29 27 24	22 29.4	1 27.9	20 31.7	26 39.6	2 08.2	1 47.2	25 03.5	15 40.0	25 02.4	28 30.0
21 Sa	3 56 26	0♊25 30	6♒40 01	13♒47 44	22 28.8	0 53.6	21 41.5	27 24.5	2 33.0	1 58.0	25 05.0	15 43.4	25 03.6	28 29.4
22 Su	4 00 23	1 23 13	20 50 17	27 47 31	22D28.5	0 19.1	22 51.4	28 09.3	2 57.9	2 08.6	25 06.3	15 46.8	25 04.8	28 28.8
23 M	4 04 19	2 20 55	4♓39 22	11♓25 56	22 28.6	29♉44.7	24 01.3	28 54.1	3 22.8	2 19.1	25 07.6	15 50.1	25 05.9	28 28.1
24 Tu	4 08 16	3 18 35	18 07 20	24 43 46	22 29.1	29 11.2	25 11.3	29 38.9	3 47.8	2 29.6	25 08.8	15 53.5	25 07.0	28 27.5
25 W	4 12 12	4 16 15	1♈15 30	7♈42 48	22 30.1	28 39.1	26 21.3	0♈23.7	4 12.9	2 39.9	25 09.8	15 56.8	25 08.1	28 26.8
26 Th	4 16 09	5 13 53	14 05 58	20 25 18	22 31.2	28 09.0	27 31.5	1 08.4	4 38.0	2 50.1	25 10.8	16 00.2	25 09.2	28 26.1
27 F	4 20 06	6 11 31	26 41 07	2♉53 43	22 32.2	27 41.3	28 41.6	1 53.0	5 03.1	3 00.2	25 11.7	16 03.5	25 10.2	28 25.4
28 Sa	4 24 02	7 09 08	9♉03 23	15 10 25	22R32.9	27 16.4	29 51.8	2 37.6	5 28.3	3 10.2	25 12.5	16 06.8	25 11.2	28 24.6
29 Su	4 27 59	8 06 43	21 15 05	27 17 38	22 32.9	26 54.8	1♉02.1	3 22.2	5 53.6	3 20.1	25 13.2	16 10.1	25 12.2	28 23.8
30 M	4 31 55	9 04 18	3♊18 18	9♊17 22	22 32.2	26 36.8	2 12.4	4 06.8	6 18.9	3 29.9	25 13.7	16 13.3	25 13.1	28 23.0
31 Tu	4 35 52	10 01 51	15 15 03	21 11 36	22 30.6	26 22.7	3 22.8	4 51.3	6 44.2	3 39.5	25 14.2	16 16.6	25 14.0	28 22.2

LONGITUDE June 2022

Day	Sid.Time	☉	0 hr ☽	Noon ☽	True ☊	☿	♀	♂	⚳	♃	♄	♅	♆	♇
1 W	4 39 48	10♊59 23	27♊07 17	3♋02 21	22♉28.2	26♉12.6	4♉33.3	5♈35.7	7♋09.6	3♈49.0	25♒14.6	16♉19.8	25♓14.9	28♑21.4
2 Th	4 43 45	11 56 55	8♋57 05	14 51 48	22R25.3	26D06.8	5 43.7	6 20.1	7 35.0	3 58.5	25 14.9	16 23.0	25 15.7	28R20.5
3 F	4 47 42	12 54 25	20 46 48	26 42 27	22 22.0	26 05.3	6 54.3	7 04.4	8 00.5	4 07.7	25 15.1	16 26.2	25 16.6	28 19.6
4 Sa	4 51 38	13 51 53	2♌39 07	8♌37 13	22 19.0	26 08.3	8 04.8	7 48.7	8 26.1	4 16.9	25R15.2	16 29.4	25 17.4	28 18.7
5 Su	4 55 35	14 49 21	14 37 10	20 39 27	22 16.4	26 15.7	9 15.4	8 33.0	8 51.6	4 25.9	25 15.2	16 32.6	25 18.1	28 17.8
6 M	4 59 31	15 46 47	26 44 31	2♍52 53	22 14.7	26 27.6	10 26.1	9 17.2	9 17.2	4 34.8	25 15.1	16 35.7	25 18.8	28 16.8
7 Tu	5 03 28	16 44 13	9♍05 04	15 21 34	22D14.1	26 44.1	11 36.8	10 01.3	9 42.9	4 43.6	25 14.8	16 38.8	25 19.5	28 15.9
8 W	5 07 24	17 41 37	21 42 54	28 09 32	22 14.4	27 04.9	12 47.5	10 45.4	10 08.5	4 52.2	25 14.5	16 41.9	25 20.2	28 14.9
9 Th	5 11 21	18 38 59	4♎41 55	11♎20 28	22 15.6	27 30.1	13 58.3	11 29.4	10 34.3	5 00.8	25 14.1	16 45.0	25 20.8	28 13.9
10 F	5 15 17	19 36 21	18 05 28	24 57 10	22 17.1	27 59.7	15 09.1	12 13.4	11 00.0	5 09.1	25 13.6	16 48.0	25 21.4	28 12.8
11 Sa	5 19 14	20 33 42	1♏55 39	9♏00 53	22R18.3	28 33.5	16 20.0	12 57.3	11 25.8	5 17.4	25 13.0	16 51.1	25 21.9	28 11.8
12 Su	5 23 11	21 31 02	16 12 40	23 30 36	22 18.8	29 11.5	17 30.9	13 41.1	11 51.6	5 25.5	25 12.4	16 54.1	25 22.5	28 10.7
13 M	5 27 07	22 28 21	0♐54 08	8♐22 30	22 18.0	29 53.6	18 41.9	14 24.9	12 17.5	5 33.5	25 11.6	16 57.0	25 23.0	28 09.6
14 Tu	5 31 04	23 25 39	15 54 46	23 29 51	22 15.8	0♊39.7	19 52.9	15 08.6	12 43.4	5 41.3	25 10.7	17 00.0	25 23.4	28 08.5
15 W	5 35 00	24 22 57	1♑06 33	8♑43 36	22 12.3	1 29.7	21 03.9	15 52.3	13 09.3	5 49.0	25 09.7	17 02.9	25 23.9	28 07.4
16 Th	5 38 57	25 20 14	16 19 41	23 53 03	22 07.8	2 23.6	22 15.0	16 35.9	13 35.3	5 56.5	25 08.7	17 05.8	25 24.3	28 06.3
17 F	5 42 53	26 17 31	1♒24 02	8♒50 06	22 03.2	3 21.3	23 26.2	17 19.5	14 01.3	6 03.9	25 07.5	17 08.7	25 24.7	28 05.1
18 Sa	5 46 50	27 14 47	16 10 52	23 25 39	21 59.0	4 22.7	24 37.4	18 03.0	14 27.3	6 11.2	25 06.2	17 11.6	25 25.0	28 03.9
19 Su	5 50 46	28 12 03	0♓34 00	7♓35 35	21 55.9	5 27.8	25 48.6	18 46.4	14 53.4	6 18.3	25 04.9	17 14.4	25 25.3	28 02.7
20 M	5 54 43	29 09 18	14 30 20	21 18 17	21D54.3	6 36.4	26 59.9	19 29.7	15 19.5	6 25.3	25 03.4	17 17.2	25 25.6	28 01.5
21 Tu	5 58 40	0♋06 34	27 59 38	4♈34 41	21 54.1	7 48.7	28 11.2	20 13.0	15 45.6	6 32.1	25 01.9	17 19.9	25 25.8	28 00.3
22 W	6 02 36	1 03 49	11♈03 49	17 27 31	21 55.0	9 04.4	29 22.5	20 56.2	16 11.8	6 38.7	25 00.3	17 22.7	25 26.0	27 59.1
23 Th	6 06 33	2 01 04	23 46 14	0♉00 31	21 56.5	10 23.6	0♊33.9	21 39.4	16 37.9	6 45.2	24 58.5	17 25.4	25 26.2	27 57.8
24 F	6 10 29	2 58 19	6♉10 51	12 17 46	21R57.8	11 46.2	1 45.4	22 22.4	17 04.2	6 51.5	24 56.7	17 28.1	25 26.3	27 56.6
25 Sa	6 14 26	3 55 34	18 21 45	24 23 15	21 58.2	13 12.2	2 56.9	23 05.4	17 30.4	6 57.7	24 54.8	17 30.7	25 26.4	27 55.3
26 Su	6 18 22	4 52 49	0♊22 44	6♊20 36	21 57.0	14 41.5	4 08.4	23 48.3	17 56.7	7 03.8	24 52.8	17 33.3	25 26.5	27 54.0
27 M	6 22 19	5 50 03	12 17 12	18 12 53	21 53.9	16 14.2	5 20.0	24 31.1	18 23.0	7 09.6	24 50.7	17 35.9	25R26.5	27 52.7
28 Tu	6 26 15	6 47 18	24 07 57	0♋02 42	21 48.7	17 50.1	6 31.6	25 13.8	18 49.3	7 15.3	24 48.6	17 38.4	25 26.6	27 51.4
29 W	6 30 12	7 44 32	5♋57 22	11 52 11	21 41.7	19 29.2	7 43.2	25 56.5	19 15.7	7 20.8	24 46.3	17 41.0	25 26.5	27 50.1
30 Th	6 34 09	8 41 46	17 47 23	23 43 11	21 33.4	21 11.5	8 54.9	26 39.0	19 42.1	7 26.2	24 44.0	17 43.4	25 26.5	27 48.8

Astro Data	Dy Hr Mn
♃⚹♇	3 22:35
♀0N	5 17:44
☿ R	10 11:49
♃∠♅	11 20:53
☽0S	12 21:43
♄⚺♆	17 15:40
♃0N	25 8:20
☽0N	25 13:30
♂0N	30 9:20
♄⚺♆	31 22:04
☿ D	3 8:01
♄ R	4 21:48
☽0S	9 6:45
☽0N	21 18:54
♆ R	28 7:56

Planet Ingress		Dy Hr Mn
♀	♈	2 16:12
♃	♈	10 23:23
⚳	♋	15 7:12
☉	♊	21 1:24
☿	♉R	23 1:16
♂	♈	24 23:19
♀	♉	28 14:47
☿	♊	13 15:28
☉	♋	21 9:15
♀	♊	23 0:36

Last Aspect Dy Hr Mn		☽ Ingress	Dy Hr Mn
2 10:14	♀ ⚹	♊	2 10:48
4 20:38	♃ □	♋	4 23:06
7 10:27	♃ △	♌	7 11:51
9 12:40	♄ ☍	♍	9 22:54
12 4:01	♇ △	♎	12 6:36
14 8:08	♇ □	♏	14 10:35
16 9:29	♇ ⚹	♐	16 11:52
18 4:01	♄ ⚹	♑	18 12:03
20 12:01	☉ △	♒	20 12:54
22 7:20	♄ ☌	♓	22 15:51
24 21:35	♂ ☌	♈	24 21:41
27 3:21	♇ □	♉	27 6:24
29 14:12	♇ △	♊	29 17:24

Last Aspect Dy Hr Mn		☽ Ingress	Dy Hr Mn
31 20:11	♄ △	♋	1 5:50
3 15:16	♇ ☍	♌	3 18:39
5 23:13	☿ □	♍	6 6:23
8 12:10	♇ △	♎	8 15:24
10 17:38	♇ □	♏	10 20:42
12 21:41	☿ ☍	♐	12 22:33
14 14:59	♆ □	♑	14 22:15
16 18:43	♇ ☌	♒	16 21:45
18 18:51	☉ △	♓	18 23:02
21 3:12	☉ □	♈	21 3:38
23 8:04	♇ □	♉	23 11:59
25 19:04	♇ △	♊	25 23:14
28 2:39	♆ □	♋	28 11:55

☽ Phases & Eclipses Dy Hr Mn	
9 0:23	☽ 18♌23
16 4:15	○ 25♏18
16 4:13	☍ T 1.413
22 18:44	☾ 1♓39
30 11:31	● 9♊03
7 14:50	☽ 16♍51
14 11:53	○ 23♐25
21 3:12	☾ 29♓46
29 2:53	● 7♋23

Astro Data

1 May 2022
Julian Day # 44681
SVP 4♓57'07"
GC 27♐09.1 ⚴ 0♉29.6
Eris 24♈31.4 ⚵ 3♓46.3
⚷ 14♈01.7 ⚶ 22♒26.7
☽ Mean ☊ 23♉08.9

1 June 2022
Julian Day # 44712
SVP 4♓57'02"
GC 27♐09.1 ⚴ 14♉20.5
Eris 24♈48.9 ⚵ 13♓18.2
⚷ 15♈28.4 ⚶ 2♓08.3
☽ Mean ☊ 21♉30.4

July 2022 LONGITUDE

Day	Sid.Time	☉	0 hr ☽	Noon ☽	True ☊	☿	♀	♂	⚳	♃	♄	♅	♆	♇
1 F	6 38 05	9♋39 00	29♋39 48	5♌37 27	21♉24.4	22♊56.9	10♊06.6	27♈21.5	20♋08.5	7♈31.4	24♒41.6	17♉45.9	25♓26.4	27♑47.4
2 Sa	6 42 02	10 36 13	11♌36 23	17 36 51	21R 15.6	24 45.3	11 18.4	28 03.8	20 34.9	7 36.4	24R 39.1	17 48.3	25R 26.3	27R 46.1
3 Su	6 45 58	11 33 27	23 39 08	29 43 31	21 07.9	26 36.6	12 30.2	28 46.1	21 01.3	7 41.2	24 36.5	17 50.7	25 26.1	27 44.7
4 M	6 49 55	12 30 40	5♍50 22	12♍00 02	21 01.9	28 30.6	13 42.0	29 28.3	21 27.8	7 45.9	24 33.8	17 53.0	25 25.9	27 43.4
5 Tu	6 53 51	13 27 52	18 12 54	24 29 25	20 58.0	0♋27.3	14 53.9	0♉10.4	21 54.3	7 50.4	24 31.1	17 55.3	25 25.7	27 42.0
6 W	6 57 48	14 25 05	0♎50 00	7♎15 06	20D 56.1	2 26.3	16 05.8	0 52.3	22 20.8	7 54.7	24 28.2	17 57.6	25 25.5	27 40.6
7 Th	7 01 44	15 22 17	13 45 09	20 20 37	20 56.0	4 27.6	17 17.7	1 34.2	22 47.3	7 58.9	24 25.3	17 59.8	25 25.2	27 39.2
8 F	7 05 41	16 19 29	27 01 53	3♏49 17	20 56.7	6 30.9	18 29.7	2 16.0	23 13.8	8 02.9	24 22.4	18 02.0	25 24.9	27 37.8
9 Sa	7 09 38	17 16 40	10♏43 05	17 43 27	20R 57.4	8 35.8	19 41.7	2 57.6	23 40.4	8 06.6	24 19.3	18 04.1	25 24.5	27 36.4
10 Su	7 13 34	18 13 52	24 50 24	2♐03 48	20 57.0	10 42.2	20 53.7	3 39.2	24 07.0	8 10.2	24 16.2	18 06.2	25 24.1	27 35.0
11 M	7 17 31	19 11 04	9♐23 19	16 48 26	20 54.6	12 49.8	22 05.8	4 20.7	24 33.6	8 13.7	24 13.0	18 08.3	25 23.7	27 33.6
12 Tu	7 21 27	20 08 16	24 18 25	1♑52 19	20 50.0	14 58.2	23 17.9	5 02.0	25 00.2	8 16.9	24 09.7	18 10.3	25 23.3	27 32.2
13 W	7 25 24	21 05 28	9♑29 02	17 07 18	20 43.1	17 07.1	24 30.1	5 43.3	25 26.8	8 20.0	24 06.4	18 12.3	25 22.8	27 30.8
14 Th	7 29 20	22 02 40	24 45 46	2♒23 00	20 34.6	19 16.3	25 42.3	6 24.4	25 53.5	8 22.9	24 03.0	18 14.3	25 22.3	27 29.3
15 F	7 33 17	22 59 52	9♒57 40	17 28 29	20 25.6	21 25.5	26 54.5	7 05.4	26 20.1	8 25.6	23 59.6	18 16.2	25 21.8	27 27.9
16 Sa	7 37 14	23 57 05	24 54 19	2♓14 14	20 17.1	23 34.4	28 06.8	7 46.4	26 46.8	8 28.1	23 56.0	18 18.1	25 21.3	27 26.5
17 Su	7 41 10	24 54 18	9♓27 29	16 33 36	20 10.1	25 42.7	29 19.1	8 27.2	27 13.5	8 30.4	23 52.5	18 19.9	25 20.7	27 25.1
18 M	7 45 07	25 51 32	23 32 17	0♈23 28	20 05.3	27 50.2	0♋31.5	9 07.9	27 40.2	8 32.5	23 48.8	18 21.7	25 20.0	27 23.6
19 Tu	7 49 03	26 48 47	7♈07 17	13 43 59	20 02.7	29 56.8	1 43.9	9 48.4	28 06.9	8 34.4	23 45.1	18 23.4	25 19.4	27 22.2
20 W	7 53 00	27 46 02	20 13 59	26 37 45	20D 02.0	2♌02.3	2 56.4	10 28.9	28 33.6	8 36.2	23 41.4	18 25.1	25 18.7	27 20.7
21 Th	7 56 56	28 43 18	2♉55 52	9♉08 56	20R 02.2	4 06.6	4 08.8	11 09.2	29 00.3	8 37.7	23 37.6	18 26.8	25 18.0	27 19.3
22 F	8 00 53	29 40 35	15 17 35	21 22 27	20 02.5	6 09.5	5 21.4	11 49.4	29 27.1	8 39.1	23 33.7	18 28.4	25 17.3	27 17.9
23 Sa	8 04 49	0♌37 53	27 24 09	3♊23 19	20 01.7	8 10.9	6 34.0	12 29.4	29 53.9	8 40.2	23 29.8	18 30.0	25 16.5	27 16.4
24 Su	8 08 46	1 35 11	9♊20 30	15 16 15	19 58.9	10 10.8	7 46.6	13 09.3	0♌20.6	8 41.2	23 25.8	18 31.5	25 15.7	27 15.0
25 M	8 12 43	2 32 31	21 11 04	27 05 24	19 53.6	12 09.1	8 59.2	13 49.1	0 47.4	8 41.9	23 21.8	18 33.0	25 14.9	27 13.6
26 Tu	8 16 39	3 29 51	2♋59 40	8♋54 13	19 45.6	14 05.8	10 11.9	14 28.8	1 14.2	8 42.5	23 17.7	18 34.4	25 14.1	27 12.2
27 W	8 20 36	4 27 12	14 49 21	20 45 22	19 35.1	16 00.9	11 24.7	15 08.3	1 41.0	8 42.9	23 13.6	18 35.8	25 13.2	27 10.7
28 Th	8 24 32	5 24 33	26 42 29	2♌40 54	19 22.7	17 54.3	12 37.4	15 47.6	2 07.8	8R 43.0	23 09.5	18 37.1	25 12.3	27 09.3
29 F	8 28 29	6 21 56	8♌40 47	14 42 17	19 09.4	19 46.0	13 50.2	16 26.8	2 34.7	8 43.0	23 05.3	18 38.4	25 11.3	27 07.9
30 Sa	8 32 25	7 19 19	20 45 33	26 50 41	18 56.3	21 36.0	15 03.1	17 05.8	3 01.5	8 42.8	23 01.1	18 39.7	25 10.4	27 06.5
31 Su	8 36 22	8 16 43	2♍57 52	9♍07 13	18 44.6	23 24.3	16 16.0	17 44.7	3 28.3	8 42.4	22 56.8	18 40.9	25 09.4	27 05.1

August 2022 LONGITUDE

Day	Sid.Time	☉	0 hr ☽	Noon ☽	True ☊	☿	♀	♂	⚳	♃	♄	♅	♆	♇
1 M	8 40 18	9♌14 07	15♍18 55	21♍33 09	18♉35.1	25♌11.0	17♋28.9	18♉23.5	3♌55.2	8♈41.7	22♒52.6	18♉42.1	25♓08.4	27♑03.7
2 Tu	8 44 15	10 11 32	27 50 10	4♎10 11	18R 28.3	26 56.0	18 41.8	19 02.0	4 22.0	8R 40.9	22R 48.2	18 43.2	25R 07.4	27R 02.3
3 W	8 48 12	11 08 58	10♎33 32	17 00 29	18 24.3	28 39.4	19 54.8	19 40.4	4 48.8	8 39.9	22 43.9	18 44.2	25 06.3	27 00.9
4 Th	8 52 08	12 06 24	23 31 24	0♏06 38	18D 22.6	0♍21.1	21 07.9	20 18.7	5 15.7	8 38.7	22 39.5	18 45.2	25 05.2	26 59.5
5 F	8 56 05	13 03 51	6♏46 30	13 31 20	18R 22.3	2 01.2	22 20.9	20 56.7	5 42.5	8 37.3	22 35.1	18 46.2	25 04.1	26 58.2
6 Sa	9 00 01	14 01 19	20 21 26	27 17 01	18 22.2	3 39.7	23 34.0	21 34.6	6 09.4	8 35.7	22 30.7	18 47.1	25 03.0	26 56.8
7 Su	9 03 58	14 58 47	4♐18 13	11♐25 02	18 21.0	5 16.5	24 47.2	22 12.3	6 36.2	8 33.9	22 26.3	18 48.0	25 01.8	26 55.4
8 M	9 07 54	15 56 17	18 37 22	25 54 53	18 17.8	6 51.7	26 00.3	22 49.9	7 03.1	8 31.9	22 21.9	18 48.8	25 00.7	26 54.1
9 Tu	9 11 51	16 53 47	3♑17 08	10♑43 27	18 12.0	8 25.3	27 13.5	23 27.3	7 29.9	8 29.7	22 17.4	18 49.6	24 59.5	26 52.8
10 W	9 15 47	17 51 18	18 12 59	25 44 41	18 03.6	9 57.2	28 26.8	24 04.5	7 56.8	8 27.3	22 12.9	18 50.3	24 58.2	26 51.5
11 Th	9 19 44	18 48 50	3♒17 25	10♒49 56	17 53.3	11 27.5	29 40.1	24 41.5	8 23.6	8 24.7	22 08.5	18 51.0	24 57.0	26 50.2
12 F	9 23 41	19 46 23	18 20 58	25 49 14	17 42.2	12 56.2	0♌53.4	25 18.3	8 50.4	8 22.0	22 04.0	18 51.6	24 55.7	26 48.9
13 Sa	9 27 37	20 43 57	3♓13 34	10♓32 57	17 31.6	14 23.2	2 06.8	25 55.0	9 17.3	8 19.0	21 59.5	18 52.2	24 54.5	26 47.6
14 Su	9 31 34	21 41 32	17 46 31	24 53 35	17 22.7	15 48.6	3 20.2	26 31.4	9 44.1	8 15.9	21 55.0	18 52.7	24 53.2	26 46.3
15 M	9 35 30	22 39 09	1♈53 43	8♈46 40	17 16.1	17 12.3	4 33.6	27 07.7	10 10.9	8 12.6	21 50.5	18 53.2	24 51.8	26 45.0
16 Tu	9 39 27	23 36 47	15 32 23	22 10 59	17 12.1	18 34.2	5 47.1	27 43.8	10 37.8	8 09.0	21 46.0	18 53.6	24 50.5	26 43.8
17 W	9 43 23	24 34 27	28 42 45	5♉08 06	17D 10.3	19 54.4	7 00.6	28 19.6	11 04.6	8 05.3	21 41.5	18 54.0	24 49.1	26 42.5
18 Th	9 47 20	25 32 08	11♉27 32	17 41 37	17R 09.9	21 12.8	8 14.2	28 55.3	11 31.4	8 01.5	21 37.0	18 54.3	24 47.7	26 41.3
19 F	9 51 16	26 29 51	23 50 59	29 56 18	17 09.9	22 29.3	9 27.8	29 30.7	11 58.3	7 57.4	21 32.5	18 54.6	24 46.4	26 40.1
20 Sa	9 55 13	27 27 36	5♊58 13	11♊57 25	17 09.2	23 44.0	10 41.4	0♊05.9	12 25.1	7 53.2	21 28.1	18 54.8	24 44.9	26 38.9
21 Su	9 59 10	28 25 22	17 54 33	23 50 15	17 06.7	24 56.7	11 55.1	0 40.9	12 51.9	7 48.8	21 23.6	18 55.0	24 43.5	26 37.7
22 M	10 03 06	29 23 10	29 45 07	5♋39 43	17 01.9	26 07.3	13 08.8	1 15.7	13 18.7	7 44.2	21 19.2	18 55.1	24 42.1	26 36.6
23 Tu	10 07 03	0♍21 00	11♋34 33	17 30 06	16 54.3	27 15.8	14 22.6	1 50.2	13 45.5	7 39.4	21 14.7	18 55.2	24 40.6	26 35.4
24 W	10 10 59	1 18 51	23 26 46	29 24 55	16 44.3	28 22.2	15 36.3	2 24.5	14 12.3	7 34.5	21 10.3	18R 55.3	24 39.1	26 34.3
25 Th	10 14 56	2 16 43	5♌24 52	11♌26 50	16 32.3	29 26.2	16 50.2	2 58.6	14 39.0	7 29.4	21 06.0	18 55.2	24 37.6	26 33.2
26 F	10 18 52	3 14 38	17 31 02	23 37 38	16 19.4	0♎27.7	18 04.0	3 32.4	15 05.8	7 24.2	21 01.6	18 55.2	24 36.1	26 32.1
27 Sa	10 22 49	4 12 33	29 46 42	5♍58 21	16 06.7	1 26.8	19 17.9	4 05.9	15 32.5	7 18.8	20 57.3	18 55.0	24 34.6	26 31.1
28 Su	10 26 45	5 10 31	12♍12 37	18 29 32	15 55.3	2 23.1	20 31.9	4 39.2	15 59.3	7 13.2	20 53.0	18 54.9	24 33.1	26 30.0
29 M	10 30 42	6 08 29	24 49 06	1♎11 22	15 46.0	3 16.5	21 45.8	5 12.2	16 26.0	7 07.5	20 48.7	18 54.6	24 31.5	26 29.0
30 Tu	10 34 39	7 06 30	7♎36 22	14 04 08	15 39.5	4 07.0	22 59.8	5 45.0	16 52.7	7 01.6	20 44.5	18 54.4	24 30.0	26 27.9
31 W	10 38 35	8 04 31	20 34 45	27 08 20	15 35.7	4 54.2	24 13.8	6 17.4	17 19.4	6 55.6	20 40.3	18 54.0	24 28.4	26 26.9

Astro Data

	Dy Hr Mn
☽0S	6 13:32
☽0N	19 1:24
♃∠♄	21 11:18
♃ R	28 20:39
☽0S	2 18:30
☽0N	15 9:42
☿0S	22 22:28
♅ R	24 13:55
☽0S	29 23:22

Planet Ingress

		Dy Hr Mn
♂	♉	5 6:05
☿	♋	5 6:26
♀	♋	18 1:33
☿	♌	19 12:36
☉	♌	22 20:08
⚳	♌	23 17:30
☿	♍	4 6:59
♀	♌	11 18:31
♂	♊	20 7:57
☉	♍	23 3:17
☿	♎	26 1:04

Last Aspect / ☽ Ingress (July)

Last Aspect Dy Hr Mn		☽ Ingress	Dy Hr Mn
30 20:15	♇ ☍	♌	1 0:41
3 10:00	♂ △	♍	3 12:32
5 18:05	♇ △	♎	5 22:26
8 1:05	♇ □	♏	8 5:16
10 4:35	♇ ⚹	♐	10 8:35
12 1:44	♆ □	♑	12 9:02
14 4:18	♇ ☌	♒	14 8:14
16 4:38	♀ △	♓	16 8:19
18 6:44	♇ ⚹	♈	18 11:19
20 14:20	☉ □	♉	20 18:24
22 23:46	♇ △	♊	23 5:12
25 8:16	♆ □	♋	25 17:55
28 0:55	♇ ☍	♌	28 6:37
30 4:30	♄ ☍	♍	30 18:12

Last Aspect / ☽ Ingress (August)

Last Aspect Dy Hr Mn		☽ Ingress	Dy Hr Mn
1 22:30	♇ △	♎	2 4:07
4 6:21	♇ □	♏	4 11:48
6 11:25	♇ ⚹	♐	6 16:40
8 10:31	♆ □	♑	8 18:40
10 16:41	♀ ☍	♒	10 18:46
12 11:08	♂ □	♓	12 18:45
14 15:12	♇ ⚹	♈	14 20:44
16 20:19	♇ □	♉	17 2:23
19 11:07	♂ ☌	♊	19 12:07
21 22:08	☉ ⚹	♋	22 0:30
24 9:41	☿ ⚹	♌	24 13:10
26 6:56	♄ ☍	♍	27 0:26
29 3:09	♇ △	♎	29 9:46
31 10:45	♇ □	♏	31 17:12

☽ Phases & Eclipses

Dy Hr Mn		
7 2:15	☽	14♎59
13 18:39	○	21♑21
20 14:20	☾	27♈52
28 17:56	●	5♌39
5 11:08	☽	13♏02
12 1:37	○	19♒21
19 4:37	☾	26♉12
27 8:18	●	4♍04

Astro Data

1 July 2022
Julian Day # 44742
SVP 4♓56'56"
GC 27♐09.2 ⚴ 28♉16.9
Eris 24♈59.4 ✱ 19♓41.6
⚷ 16♈17.5 ⚶ 6♓44.2
☽ Mean ☊ 19♉55.1

1 August 2022
Julian Day # 44773
SVP 4♓56'51"
GC 27♐09.3 ⚴ 13♊03.2
Eris 25♈00.9R ✱ 21♓20.3R
⚷ 16♈21.7R ⚶ 4♓32.4R
☽ Mean ☊ 18♉16.6

LONGITUDE — September 2022

Day	Sid.Time	☉	0 hr ☽	Noon ☽	True ☊	☿	♀	♂	⚳	♃	♄	♅	♆	♇
1 Th	10 42 32	9♍02 34	3♏44 59	10♏24 52	15♉34.3	5♎38.0	25♌27.9	6♊49.6	17♌46.1	6♈49.4	20♒36.1	18♉53.7	24♓26.8	26♑26.0
2 F	10 46 28	10 00 39	17 08 08	23 54 56	15D34.4	6 18.1	26 42.0	7 21.5	18 12.7	6R43.2	20R32.0	18R53.2	24R25.3	26R25.0
3 Sa	10 50 25	10 58 45	0♐45 28	7♐39 49	15R34.8	6 54.3	27 56.1	7 53.2	18 39.4	6 36.7	20 27.9	18 52.8	24 23.7	26 24.1
4 Su	10 54 21	11 56 52	14 38 06	21 40 19	15 34.5	7 26.4	29 10.2	8 24.5	19 06.0	6 30.2	20 23.9	18 52.3	24 22.1	26 23.2
5 M	10 58 18	12 55 01	28 46 24	5♑56 12	15 32.4	7 54.0	0♍24.4	8 55.5	19 32.6	6 23.5	20 19.9	18 51.7	24 20.4	26 22.3
6 Tu	11 02 14	13 53 11	13♑09 24	20 25 34	15 28.1	8 16.9	1 38.6	9 26.3	19 59.2	6 16.8	20 16.0	18 51.1	24 18.8	26 21.4
7 W	11 06 11	14 51 22	27 44 09	5♒04 27	15 21.4	8 34.8	2 52.8	9 56.7	20 25.7	6 09.9	20 12.1	18 50.4	24 17.2	26 20.6
8 Th	11 10 08	15 49 35	12♒25 40	19 46 53	15 13.1	8 47.3	4 07.1	10 26.8	20 52.3	6 02.9	20 08.3	18 49.7	24 15.6	26 19.8
9 F	11 14 04	16 47 50	27 07 10	4♓25 32	15 03.9	8R54.2	5 21.4	10 56.6	21 18.8	5 55.8	20 04.5	18 49.0	24 13.9	26 19.0
10 Sa	11 18 01	17 46 06	11♓41 02	18 52 48	14 55.1	8 55.1	6 35.7	11 26.1	21 45.3	5 48.6	20 00.8	18 48.1	24 12.3	26 18.2
11 Su	11 21 57	18 44 24	26 00 02	3♈02 05	14 47.6	8 49.8	7 50.0	11 55.2	22 11.8	5 41.3	19 57.1	18 47.3	24 10.7	26 17.4
12 M	11 25 54	19 42 44	9♈58 27	16 48 47	14 42.2	8 38.0	9 04.4	12 24.0	22 38.2	5 33.9	19 53.5	18 46.4	24 09.0	26 16.7
13 Tu	11 29 50	20 41 06	23 32 54	0♉10 46	14 39.1	8 19.6	10 18.8	12 52.5	23 04.6	5 26.4	19 49.9	18 45.4	24 07.4	26 16.0
14 W	11 33 47	21 39 30	6♉42 29	13 08 17	14D38.0	7 54.4	11 33.3	13 20.6	23 31.0	5 18.9	19 46.5	18 44.5	24 05.7	26 15.3
15 Th	11 37 43	22 37 56	19 28 32	25 43 40	14 38.5	7 22.5	12 47.7	13 48.3	23 57.4	5 11.2	19 43.1	18 43.4	24 04.0	26 14.7
16 F	11 41 40	23 36 25	1♊54 11	8♊00 39	14 39.6	6 44.0	14 02.2	14 15.7	24 23.7	5 03.5	19 39.7	18 42.3	24 02.4	26 14.0
17 Sa	11 45 36	24 34 55	14 03 41	20 03 55	14R40.5	5 59.2	15 16.7	14 42.7	24 50.1	4 55.8	19 36.4	18 41.2	24 00.7	26 13.4
18 Su	11 49 33	25 33 28	26 01 59	1♋58 33	14 40.4	5 08.5	16 31.3	15 09.3	25 16.3	4 48.0	19 33.2	18 40.0	23 59.1	26 12.8
19 M	11 53 30	26 32 03	7♋54 14	13 49 40	14 38.6	4 12.8	17 45.9	15 35.5	25 42.6	4 40.1	19 30.1	18 38.8	23 57.4	26 12.3
20 Tu	11 57 26	27 30 40	19 45 27	25 42 08	14 34.8	3 12.8	19 00.5	16 01.3	26 08.8	4 32.2	19 27.0	18 37.6	23 55.8	26 11.8
21 W	12 01 23	28 29 19	1♌40 15	7♌40 16	14 29.2	2 09.9	20 15.1	16 26.6	26 35.0	4 24.3	19 24.0	18 36.3	23 54.1	26 11.3
22 Th	12 05 19	29 28 00	13 42 36	19 47 39	14 22.0	1 05.2	21 29.8	16 51.6	27 01.2	4 16.3	19 21.1	18 34.9	23 52.5	26 10.8
23 F	12 09 16	0♎26 43	25 55 41	2♍06 57	14 14.1	0 00.3	22 44.4	17 16.1	27 27.3	4 08.3	19 18.3	18 33.5	23 50.8	26 10.3
24 Sa	12 13 12	1 25 29	8♍21 38	14 39 51	14 06.1	28♍56.7	23 59.1	17 40.1	27 53.4	4 00.3	19 15.6	18 32.1	23 49.2	26 09.9
25 Su	12 17 09	2 24 16	21 01 40	27 27 03	13 59.0	27 56.2	25 13.9	18 03.7	28 19.4	3 52.2	19 12.9	18 30.6	23 47.5	26 09.5
26 M	12 21 05	3 23 05	3♎55 59	10♎28 21	13 53.3	27 00.4	26 28.6	18 26.8	28 45.5	3 44.2	19 10.3	18 29.1	23 45.9	26 09.2
27 Tu	12 25 02	4 21 57	17 04 02	23 42 54	13 49.6	26 10.6	27 43.4	18 49.5	29 11.4	3 36.1	19 07.8	18 27.6	23 44.3	26 08.8
28 W	12 28 59	5 20 50	0♏24 48	7♏09 32	13D47.9	25 28.3	28 58.2	19 11.6	29 37.4	3 28.1	19 05.4	18 26.0	23 42.7	26 08.5
29 Th	12 32 55	6 19 45	13 56 59	20 46 59	13 47.9	24 54.6	0♎13.0	19 33.3	0♍03.2	3 20.1	19 03.0	18 24.3	23 41.1	26 08.2
30 F	12 36 52	7 18 42	27 39 25	4♐34 07	13 49.0	24 30.3	1 27.8	19 54.4	0 29.1	3 12.1	19 00.8	18 22.7	23 39.5	26 08.0

LONGITUDE — October 2022

Day	Sid.Time	☉	0 hr ☽	Noon ☽	True ☊	☿	♀	♂	⚳	♃	♄	♅	♆	♇
1 Sa	12 40 48	8♎17 41	11♐31 00	18♐29 57	13♉50.5	24♍16.0	2♎42.6	20♊15.1	0♍54.9	3♈04.1	18♒58.6	18♉21.0	23♓37.9	26♑07.7
2 Su	12 44 45	9 16 42	25 30 50	2♑33 32	13R51.6	24D12.0	3 57.5	20 35.2	1 20.6	2R56.1	18R56.6	18R19.2	23R36.3	26R07.6
3 M	12 48 41	10 15 44	9♑37 52	16 43 39	13 51.5	24 18.5	5 12.4	20 54.8	1 46.3	2 48.2	18 54.6	18 17.5	23 34.7	26 07.4
4 Tu	12 52 38	11 14 48	23 50 38	0♒58 32	13 50.1	24 35.2	6 27.3	21 13.8	2 12.0	2 40.4	18 52.7	18 15.7	23 33.1	26 07.2
5 W	12 56 34	12 13 54	8♒07 01	15 15 38	13 47.3	25 01.9	7 42.2	21 32.3	2 37.6	2 32.5	18 50.9	18 13.8	23 31.6	26 07.1
6 Th	13 00 31	13 13 02	22 23 57	29 31 28	13 43.3	25 38.0	8 57.1	21 50.2	3 03.1	2 24.8	18 49.2	18 11.9	23 30.0	26 07.1
7 F	13 04 28	14 12 11	6♓37 37	13♓41 52	13 38.8	26 23.1	10 12.0	22 07.5	3 28.6	2 17.1	18 47.6	18 10.0	23 28.5	26 07.0
8 Sa	13 08 24	15 11 22	20 43 39	27 42 26	13 34.5	27 16.3	11 27.0	22 24.2	3 54.1	2 09.4	18 46.1	18 08.1	23 27.0	26D07.0
9 Su	13 12 21	16 10 35	4♈37 44	11♈29 06	13 30.8	28 17.0	12 41.9	22 40.4	4 19.5	2 01.8	18 44.7	18 06.1	23 25.5	26 07.0
10 M	13 16 17	17 09 50	18 16 10	24 58 38	13 28.3	29 24.4	13 56.9	22 55.9	4 44.8	1 54.3	18 43.4	18 04.1	23 24.0	26 07.0
11 Tu	13 20 14	18 09 07	1♉36 20	8♉09 10	13D27.2	0♎37.8	15 11.9	23 10.8	5 10.1	1 46.9	18 42.2	18 02.1	23 22.5	26 07.1
12 W	13 24 10	19 08 26	14 37 08	21 00 18	13 27.3	1 56.4	16 26.9	23 25.1	5 35.3	1 39.6	18 41.1	18 00.0	23 21.1	26 07.2
13 Th	13 28 07	20 07 48	27 18 52	3♊33 06	13 28.3	3 19.5	17 41.9	23 38.7	6 00.5	1 32.4	18 40.0	17 57.9	23 19.6	26 07.3
14 F	13 32 03	21 07 12	9♊43 20	15 49 57	13 29.9	4 46.4	18 56.9	23 51.6	6 25.6	1 25.3	18 39.1	17 55.8	23 18.2	26 07.4
15 Sa	13 36 00	22 06 38	21 53 26	27 54 15	13 31.6	6 16.6	20 12.0	24 03.9	6 50.7	1 18.2	18 38.3	17 53.6	23 16.8	26 07.6
16 Su	13 39 57	23 06 06	3♋52 59	9♋50 10	13 32.9	7 49.5	21 27.1	24 15.5	7 15.6	1 11.3	18 37.6	17 51.5	23 15.4	26 07.8
17 M	13 43 53	24 05 37	15 46 25	21 42 18	13R33.5	9 24.7	22 42.1	24 26.3	7 40.6	1 04.5	18 36.9	17 49.3	23 14.0	26 08.1
18 Tu	13 47 50	25 05 09	27 38 28	3♌35 29	13 33.3	11 01.6	23 57.2	24 36.5	8 05.4	0 57.8	18 36.4	17 47.1	23 12.7	26 08.3
19 W	13 51 46	26 04 45	9♌33 57	15 34 26	13 32.2	12 39.9	25 12.3	24 45.9	8 30.2	0 51.3	18 36.0	17 44.8	23 11.4	26 08.6
20 Th	13 55 43	27 04 22	21 37 28	27 43 35	13 30.4	14 19.4	26 27.5	24 54.5	8 54.9	0 44.8	18 35.7	17 42.5	23 10.0	26 09.0
21 F	13 59 39	28 04 01	3♍53 12	10♍06 45	13 28.2	15 59.6	27 42.6	25 02.4	9 19.6	0 38.5	18 35.5	17 40.3	23 08.8	26 09.3
22 Sa	14 03 36	29 03 43	16 24 33	22 46 26	13 26.0	17 40.4	28 57.7	25 09.5	9 44.1	0 32.4	18D35.3	17 38.0	23 07.5	26 09.7
23 Su	14 07 32	0♏03 27	29 13 54	5♎45 45	13 24.0	19 21.6	0♏12.9	25 15.8	10 08.6	0 26.3	18 35.3	17 35.6	23 06.2	26 10.1
24 M	14 11 29	1 03 13	12♎22 25	19 03 51	13 22.6	21 03.0	1 28.1	25 21.3	10 33.0	0 20.5	18 35.4	17 33.3	23 05.0	26 10.5
25 Tu	14 15 26	2 03 01	25 49 53	2♏40 16	13D21.8	22 44.5	2 43.2	25 25.9	10 57.4	0 14.7	18 35.6	17 30.9	23 03.8	26 11.0
26 W	14 19 22	3 02 51	9♏34 40	16 32 44	13 21.6	24 25.9	3 58.4	25 29.8	11 21.6	0 09.2	18 35.9	17 28.5	23 02.6	26 11.5
27 Th	14 23 19	4 02 43	23 33 59	0♐37 57	13 22.0	26 07.2	5 13.6	25 32.8	11 45.8	0 03.8	18 36.3	17 26.2	23 01.4	26 12.1
28 F	14 27 15	5 02 37	7♐44 07	14 51 59	13 22.6	27 48.2	6 28.8	25 35.0	12 09.9	29♓58.5	18 36.8	17 23.8	23 00.3	26 12.6
29 Sa	14 31 12	6 02 33	22 01 01	29 10 44	13 23.3	29 29.0	7 44.0	25 36.4	12 33.9	29 53.5	18 37.4	17 21.3	22 59.2	26 13.2
30 Su	14 35 08	7 02 30	6♑20 37	13♑30 16	13 23.9	1♏09.5	8 59.2	25R36.8	12 57.8	29 48.6	18 38.1	17 18.9	22 58.1	26 13.8
31 M	14 39 05	8 02 29	20 39 14	27 47 12	13R24.3	2 49.6	10 14.4	25 36.5	13 21.6	29 43.8	18 38.9	17 16.5	22 57.1	26 14.5

Astro Data

	Dy Hr Mn
☿ R	10 3:39
☽ 0N	11 19:11
♃∠♄	21 13:09
☉0S	23 1:06
☽ 0S	26 5:55
♃0S	26 10:58
☿0N	27 7:37
♃∠♅	28 19:59
♀0S	1 22:34
☿ D	2 9:08
♇ D	8 21:58
☽ 0N	9 4:26
☿0S	14 8:13
♄ D	23 4:09
☽ 0S	23 14:38

Planet Ingress

		Dy Hr Mn
♀	♍	5 4:06
☉	♎	23 1:05
☿	♍R	23 12:06
♀	♎	29 7:50
⚳	♍	29 9:00
☿	♎	10 23:52
♀	♏	23 7:53
☉	♏	23 10:37
♃	♓R	28 5:11
☿	♏	29 19:23
♂	R30	13:27

Last Aspect / ☽ Ingress (September)

Last Aspect Dy Hr Mn			☽ Ingress	Dy Hr Mn
2 17:23	♀	□	♐	2 22:41
5 1:52	♀	△	♑	5 2:04
6 21:44	♇	☌	♒	7 3:42
8 12:35	♄	☌	♓	9 4:43
11 0:30	♇	⚹	♈	11 6:48
13 4:54	♇	□	♉	13 11:40
15 13:00	♇	△	♊	15 20:17
17 21:53	☉	□	♋	18 8:00
20 15:58	☉	⚹	♌	20 20:39
22 11:08	♄	☍	♍	23 7:55
25 12:50	☿	☌	♎	25 16:44
27 16:22	♇	□	♏	27 23:16
29 21:21	♇	⚹	♐	30 4:05

Last Aspect / ☽ Ingress (October)

Last Aspect Dy Hr Mn			☽ Ingress	Dy Hr Mn
1 21:47	☿	□	♑	2 7:39
4 3:50	♇	☌	♒	4 10:22
5 22:47	♂	△	♓	6 12:48
8 11:12	☿	☍	♈	8 15:58
10 14:03	♇	□	♉	10 21:05
12 21:43	♇	△	♊	13 5:09
15 4:12	♂	☌	♋	15 16:12
17 20:58	♇	☍	♌	18 4:46
20 10:36	☉	⚹	♍	20 16:27
22 18:19	♇	△	♎	23 1:25
25 0:37	♇	□	♏	25 7:20
27 4:29	♇	⚹	♐	27 10:56
29 13:11	♃	□	♑	29 13:23
31 15:16	♃	⚹	♒	31 15:44

☽ Phases & Eclipses

Dy Hr Mn		
3 18:09	☽	11♐14
10 10:00	○	17♓41
17 21:53	☾	24♊59
25 21:56	●	2♎49
3 0:15	☽	9♑47
9 20:56	○	16♈33
17 17:16	☾	24♋19
25 10:50	●	2♏00
25 11:01:21	●	P 0.862

Astro Data

1 September 2022
Julian Day # 44804
SVP 4♓56'47"
GC 27♐09.4 ⚵ 27♊48.4
Eris 24♈52.7R ⚶ 16♓33.2R
⚷ 15♈38.6R ⚴ 27♒18.0R
☽ Mean ☊ 16♉38.1

1 October 2022
Julian Day # 44834
SVP 4♓56'44"
GC 27♐09.4 ⚵ 11♋12.8
Eris 24♈37.7R ⚶ 9♓41.2R
⚷ 14♈25.4R ⚴ 23♒02.4R
☽ Mean ☊ 15♉02.8

November 2022 LONGITUDE

Day	Sid.Time	☉	0 hr ☽	Noon ☽	True ☊	☿	♀	♂	⚳	♃	♄	♅	♆	♇
1 Tu	14 43 01	9♏02 29	4♒53 48	11♒58 45	13♉24.4	4♏29.3	11♏29.6	25♊35.2	13♍45.4	29♓39.3	18♒39.8	17♉14.0	22♓56.0	26♑15.1
2 W	14 46 58	10 02 31	19 01 49	26 02 46	13R 24.2	6 08.7	12 44.9	25R 33.1	14 09.0	29R 34.9	18 40.8	17R 11.6	22R 55.0	26 15.8
3 Th	14 50 55	11 02 35	3♓01 23	9♓57 30	13 24.0	7 47.6	14 00.1	25 30.1	14 32.5	29 30.7	18 41.9	17 09.1	22 54.0	26 16.6
4 F	14 54 51	12 02 39	16 50 57	23 41 35	13 23.8	9 26.1	15 15.3	25 26.2	14 56.0	29 26.7	18 43.2	17 06.6	22 53.1	26 17.3
5 Sa	14 58 48	13 02 46	0♈29 16	7♈13 51	13D 23.7	11 04.2	16 30.5	25 21.5	15 19.3	29 22.9	18 44.5	17 04.2	22 52.2	26 18.1
6 Su	15 02 44	14 02 54	13 55 14	20 33 18	13 23.7	12 41.9	17 45.8	25 15.9	15 42.5	29 19.3	18 45.9	17 01.7	22 51.3	26 18.9
7 M	15 06 41	15 03 04	27 07 58	3♉39 10	13R 23.8	14 19.2	19 01.0	25 09.4	16 05.7	29 15.8	18 47.4	16 59.2	22 50.4	26 19.8
8 Tu	15 10 37	16 03 16	10♉06 51	16 31 01	13 23.8	15 56.1	20 16.2	25 02.0	16 28.7	29 12.6	18 49.0	16 56.7	22 49.5	26 20.6
9 W	15 14 34	17 03 29	22 51 40	29 08 52	13 23.7	17 32.6	21 31.5	24 53.8	16 51.6	29 09.5	18 50.8	16 54.2	22 48.7	26 21.5
10 Th	15 18 30	18 03 44	5♊22 44	11♊33 23	13 23.3	19 08.7	22 46.7	24 44.6	17 14.4	29 06.7	18 52.6	16 51.7	22 47.9	26 22.5
11 F	15 22 27	19 04 02	17 41 02	23 45 54	13 22.6	20 44.5	24 02.0	24 34.6	17 37.1	29 04.0	18 54.5	16 49.3	22 47.2	26 23.4
12 Sa	15 26 24	20 04 21	29 48 16	5♋48 29	13 21.8	22 20.0	25 17.2	24 23.8	17 59.7	29 01.6	18 56.5	16 46.8	22 46.5	26 24.4
13 Su	15 30 20	21 04 42	11♋46 55	17 43 58	13 20.8	23 55.2	26 32.5	24 12.1	18 22.2	28 59.3	18 58.6	16 44.3	22 45.8	26 25.4
14 M	15 34 17	22 05 04	23 40 07	29 35 51	13 19.8	25 30.0	27 47.8	23 59.6	18 44.5	28 57.2	19 00.9	16 41.8	22 45.1	26 26.4
15 Tu	15 38 13	23 05 29	5♌31 42	11♌28 11	13 19.1	27 04.5	29 03.0	23 46.2	19 06.8	28 55.4	19 03.2	16 39.4	22 44.5	26 27.5
16 W	15 42 10	24 05 55	17 25 54	23 25 25	13D 18.8	28 38.8	0♐18.3	23 32.0	19 28.9	28 53.7	19 05.6	16 36.9	22 43.9	26 28.6
17 Th	15 46 06	25 06 24	29 27 21	5♍32 15	13 19.1	0♐12.9	1 33.6	23 17.1	19 50.8	28 52.3	19 08.1	16 34.4	22 43.3	26 29.7
18 F	15 50 03	26 06 54	11♍40 42	17 53 16	13 19.8	1 46.6	2 48.9	23 01.3	20 12.7	28 51.0	19 10.7	16 32.0	22 42.8	26 30.8
19 Sa	15 53 59	27 07 26	24 10 27	0♎32 44	13 20.9	3 20.2	4 04.2	22 44.8	20 34.4	28 50.0	19 13.4	16 29.6	22 42.3	26 31.9
20 Su	15 57 56	28 07 59	7♎00 30	13 34 04	13 22.2	4 53.5	5 19.5	22 27.6	20 56.0	28 49.2	19 16.2	16 27.1	22 41.8	26 33.1
21 M	16 01 53	29 08 35	20 13 40	26 59 25	13 23.3	6 26.7	6 34.8	22 09.7	21 17.4	28 48.5	19 19.1	16 24.7	22 41.4	26 34.3
22 Tu	16 05 49	0♐09 12	3♏51 17	10♏49 08	13R 23.8	7 59.7	7 50.1	21 51.2	21 38.7	28 48.1	19 22.0	16 22.3	22 40.9	26 35.5
23 W	16 09 46	1 09 50	17 52 40	25 01 25	13 23.5	9 32.4	9 05.4	21 32.0	21 59.9	28D 47.9	19 25.1	16 19.9	22 40.6	26 36.8
24 Th	16 13 42	2 10 31	2♐14 50	9♐32 10	13 22.3	11 05.1	10 20.7	21 12.2	22 20.9	28 47.9	19 28.3	16 17.6	22 40.2	26 38.1
25 F	16 17 39	3 11 12	16 52 36	24 15 15	13 20.1	12 37.5	11 36.0	20 51.9	22 41.7	28 48.2	19 31.5	16 15.2	22 39.9	26 39.4
26 Sa	16 21 35	4 11 55	1♑39 07	9♑03 15	13 17.3	14 09.8	12 51.3	20 31.1	23 02.4	28 48.6	19 34.9	16 12.9	22 39.7	26 40.7
27 Su	16 25 32	5 12 39	16 26 42	23 48 35	13 14.3	15 41.9	14 06.6	20 09.9	23 22.9	28 49.2	19 38.3	16 10.6	22 39.4	26 42.0
28 M	16 29 28	6 13 24	1♒08 06	8♒24 32	13 11.7	17 13.9	15 21.9	19 48.2	23 43.3	28 50.1	19 41.9	16 08.3	22 39.2	26 43.4
29 Tu	16 33 25	7 14 10	15 37 21	22 46 05	13 09.9	18 45.7	16 37.2	19 26.2	24 03.5	28 51.1	19 45.5	16 06.0	22 39.0	26 44.8
30 W	16 37 22	8 14 57	29 50 27	6♓50 16	13D 09.2	20 17.3	17 52.5	19 03.8	24 23.6	28 52.4	19 49.2	16 03.7	22 38.9	26 46.2

December 2022 LONGITUDE

Day	Sid.Time	☉	0 hr ☽	Noon ☽	True ☊	☿	♀	♂	⚳	♃	♄	♅	♆	♇
1 Th	16 41 18	9♐15 45	13♓45 27	20♓36 02	13♉09.6	21♐48.7	19♐07.8	18♊41.2	24♍43.4	28♓53.8	19♒53.0	16♉01.5	22♓38.8	26♑47.6
2 F	16 45 15	10 16 33	27 22 06	4♈03 48	13 10.9	23 20.0	20 23.1	18R 18.4	25 03.1	28 55.5	19 56.9	15R 59.3	22R 38.7	26 49.1
3 Sa	16 49 11	11 17 23	10♈41 21	17 14 56	13 12.6	24 50.9	21 38.4	17 55.4	25 22.6	28 57.4	20 00.8	15 57.1	22D 38.7	26 50.6
4 Su	16 53 08	12 18 13	23 44 48	0♉11 11	13 14.1	26 21.6	22 53.7	17 32.3	25 42.0	28 59.5	20 04.9	15 54.9	22 38.7	26 52.0
5 M	16 57 04	13 19 04	6♉34 18	12 54 21	13R 14.7	27 52.0	24 09.0	17 09.1	26 01.1	29 01.7	20 09.0	15 52.8	22 38.7	26 53.6
6 Tu	17 01 01	14 19 57	19 11 33	25 26 04	13 14.0	29 22.0	25 24.2	16 46.0	26 20.1	29 04.2	20 13.2	15 50.7	22 38.8	26 55.1
7 W	17 04 57	15 20 50	1♊38 04	7♊47 41	13 11.6	0♑51.6	26 39.5	16 22.8	26 38.9	29 06.9	20 17.5	15 48.6	22 38.9	26 56.6
8 Th	17 08 54	16 21 44	13 55 05	20 00 25	13 07.5	2 20.7	27 54.8	15 59.7	26 57.5	29 09.8	20 21.8	15 46.6	22 39.0	26 58.2
9 F	17 12 51	17 22 39	26 03 48	2♋05 24	13 01.9	3 49.2	29 10.1	15 36.8	27 15.9	29 12.9	20 26.3	15 44.6	22 39.2	26 59.8
10 Sa	17 16 47	18 23 36	8♋05 24	14 03 59	12 55.2	5 17.1	0♑25.3	15 14.1	27 34.1	29 16.2	20 30.8	15 42.6	22 39.4	27 01.4
11 Su	17 20 44	19 24 33	20 01 23	25 57 51	12 48.2	6 44.1	1 40.6	14 51.5	27 52.1	29 19.6	20 35.4	15 40.6	22 39.7	27 03.0
12 M	17 24 40	20 25 31	1♌53 42	7♌49 14	12 41.4	8 10.1	2 55.9	14 29.3	28 09.9	29 23.3	20 40.1	15 38.7	22 40.0	27 04.7
13 Tu	17 28 37	21 26 30	13 44 51	19 40 57	12 35.7	9 35.0	4 11.1	14 07.4	28 27.5	29 27.2	20 44.9	15 36.8	22 40.3	27 06.3
14 W	17 32 33	22 27 31	25 38 00	1♍36 31	12 31.5	10 58.5	5 26.4	13 45.8	28 44.9	29 31.2	20 49.7	15 35.0	22 40.6	27 08.0
15 Th	17 36 30	23 28 32	7♍37 00	13 40 02	12D 29.1	12 20.4	6 41.7	13 24.6	29 02.0	29 35.4	20 54.6	15 33.1	22 41.0	27 09.7
16 F	17 40 27	24 29 34	19 46 12	25 56 06	12 28.5	13 40.5	7 56.9	13 03.9	29 19.0	29 39.9	20 59.6	15 31.3	22 41.4	27 11.4
17 Sa	17 44 23	25 30 37	2♎10 19	8♎29 28	12 29.2	14 58.4	9 12.2	12 43.6	29 35.7	29 44.5	21 04.6	15 29.6	22 41.9	27 13.1
18 Su	17 48 20	26 31 41	14 54 07	21 24 47	12 30.7	16 13.7	10 27.4	12 23.9	29 52.1	29 49.3	21 09.7	15 27.9	22 42.3	27 14.8
19 M	17 52 16	27 32 46	28 01 54	4♏45 52	12R 31.9	17 25.9	11 42.7	12 04.8	0♎08.4	29 54.3	21 14.9	15 26.2	22 42.9	27 16.6
20 Tu	17 56 13	28 33 52	11♏36 55	18 35 08	12 31.9	18 34.7	12 57.9	11 46.2	0 24.4	29 59.4	21 20.1	15 24.6	22 43.4	27 18.3
21 W	18 00 09	29 34 59	25 40 27	2♐52 38	12 30.1	19 39.5	14 13.2	11 28.3	0 40.1	0♈04.8	21 25.5	15 23.0	22 44.0	27 20.1
22 Th	18 04 06	0♑36 07	10♐11 11	17 35 25	12 26.1	20 39.5	15 28.4	11 11.0	0 55.6	0 10.3	21 30.9	15 21.4	22 44.6	27 21.9
23 F	18 08 02	1 37 15	25 04 27	2♑37 13	12 19.9	21 34.1	16 43.7	10 54.4	1 10.8	0 16.0	21 36.3	15 19.9	22 45.3	27 23.7
24 Sa	18 11 59	2 38 23	10♑12 28	17 48 54	12 12.2	22 22.5	17 58.9	10 38.5	1 25.8	0 21.9	21 41.8	15 18.5	22 46.0	27 25.5
25 Su	18 15 56	3 39 32	25 25 08	2♒59 49	12 03.9	23 03.9	19 14.1	10 23.3	1 40.5	0 28.0	21 47.4	15 17.0	22 46.7	27 27.4
26 M	18 19 52	4 40 41	10♒31 44	17 59 43	11 56.1	23 37.4	20 29.4	10 09.0	1 54.9	0 34.3	21 53.1	15 15.7	22 47.5	27 29.2
27 Tu	18 23 49	5 41 50	25 22 51	2♓40 23	11 49.9	24 02.0	21 44.6	9 55.3	2 09.1	0 40.7	21 58.8	15 14.3	22 48.3	27 31.0
28 W	18 27 45	6 42 59	9♓51 47	16 56 45	11 45.8	24R 17.0	22 59.8	9 42.5	2 23.0	0 47.2	22 04.5	15 13.0	22 49.1	27 32.9
29 Th	18 31 42	7 44 08	23 55 09	0♈47 01	11D 43.9	24 21.3	24 15.0	9 30.5	2 36.6	0 54.0	22 10.3	15 11.8	22 49.9	27 34.8
30 F	18 35 38	8 45 16	7♈32 32	14 12 01	11 43.8	24 14.5	25 30.2	9 19.3	2 49.9	1 00.9	22 16.2	15 10.6	22 50.8	27 36.6
31 Sa	18 39 35	9 46 25	20 45 50	27 14 26	11 44.6	23 55.9	26 45.3	9 08.8	3 02.9	1 08.0	22 22.1	15 09.4	22 51.8	27 38.5

Astro Data (Dy Hr Mn)

	Dy Hr Mn
☽0N	5 12:00
☽0S	20 0:23
♃D	23 23:04
☽0N	2 17:34
♆D	4 0:15
☽0S	17 9:06
♃∠♅	24 0:44
☿R	29 9:32
☽0N	29 22:39

Planet Ingress (Dy Hr Mn)

		Dy Hr Mn
♀	♐	16 6:10
☿	♐	17 8:43
☉	♐	22 8:22
☿	♑	6 22:09
♀	♑	10 3:55
⚳	♎	18 23:35
♃	♈	20 14:33
☉	♑	21 21:49

Last Aspect / ☽ Ingress

Last Aspect Dy Hr Mn		☽ Ingress	Dy Hr Mn
2 11:09	♂ △	♓	2 18:48
4 22:06	♃ ☌	♈	4 23:08
6 22:31	♇ □	♉	7 5:16
9 12:01	♃ ⚹	♊	9 13:38
11 22:30	♃ □	♋	12 0:23
14 10:42	♃ △	♌	14 12:49
16 23:57	☿ □	♍	17 1:05
19 8:48	♃ ☍	♎	19 10:59
21 11:16	♇ □	♏	21 17:17
23 18:17	♃ △	♐	23 20:17
25 19:23	♃ □	♑	25 21:19
27 20:12	♃ ⚹	♒	27 22:08
29 6:55	♄ ☌	♓	30 0:16

Last Aspect Dy Hr Mn		☽ Ingress	Dy Hr Mn
2 2:46	♃ ☌	♈	2 4:42
4 5:47	♇ □	♉	4 11:39
6 19:03	♃ ⚹	♊	6 20:50
9 6:15	♃ □	♋	9 7:50
11 18:50	♃ △	♌	11 20:10
13 15:53	☉ △	♍	14 8:47
16 19:14	♃ ☍	♎	16 19:50
18 22:37	♇ □	♏	19 3:32
21 2:46	♇ ⚹	♐	21 7:14
22 20:17	♆ □	♑	23 7:51
25 3:12	♇ ☌	♒	25 7:15
26 18:21	♄ ☌	♓	27 7:35
29 6:22	♇ ⚹	♈	29 10:37
31 12:45	♇ □	♉	31 17:10

☽ Phases & Eclipses (Dy Hr Mn)

Dy Hr Mn		
1 6:38	☽	8♒49
8 11:03	○	16♉01
8 11:00	•	T 1.359
16 13:28	☾	24♌10
23 22:58	●	1♐38
30 14:38	☽	8♓22
8 4:09	○	16♊02
16 8:57	☾	24♍22
23 10:18	●	1♑33
30 1:22	☽	8♈18

Astro Data

1 November 2022
Julian Day # 44865
SVP 4♓56'40"
GC 27♐09.5 ⚴ 22♋14.0
Eris 24♈19.4R ⚵ 8♓01.9
⚷ 13♈04.1R ⚶ 25♒31.1
☽ Mean ☊ 13♉24.3

1 December 2022
Julian Day # 44895
SVP 4♓56'35"
GC 27♐09.6 ⚴ 26♋32.5R
Eris 24♈04.1R ⚵ 13♓37.2
⚷ 12♈09.2R ⚶ 3♓08.2
☽ Mean ☊ 11♉49.0

LONGITUDE — January 2023

Day	Sid.Time	☉	0 hr ☽	Noon ☽	True ☊	☿	♀	♂	⚳	♃	♄	♅	♆	♇
1 Su	18 43 31	10♑47 33	3♉38 16	9♉57 50	11♉45.2	23♑25.4	28♑00.5	8♊59.3	3♎15.6	1♈15.2	22♒28.1	15♉08.3	22♓52.7	27♑40.4
2 M	18 47 28	11 48 42	16 13 36	22 26 01	11R44.6	22R43.3	29 15.6	8R50.5	3 28.1	1 22.6	22 34.2	15R07.2	22 53.7	27 42.3
3 Tu	18 51 25	12 49 50	28 35 33	4♊42 33	11 41.9	21 50.3	0♒30.7	8 42.6	3 40.2	1 30.2	22 40.3	15 06.2	22 54.7	27 44.2
4 W	18 55 21	13 50 58	10♊47 26	16 50 28	11 36.4	20 47.5	1 45.9	8 35.5	3 52.0	1 37.9	22 46.4	15 05.3	22 55.8	27 46.2
5 Th	18 59 18	14 52 06	22 51 58	28 52 09	11 28.1	19 36.7	3 01.0	8 29.2	4 03.5	1 45.7	22 52.6	15 04.4	22 56.9	27 48.1
6 F	19 03 14	15 53 14	4♋51 15	10♋49 27	11 17.3	18 20.1	4 16.1	8 23.7	4 14.7	1 53.7	22 58.8	15 03.5	22 58.0	27 50.0
7 Sa	19 07 11	16 54 22	16 46 55	22 43 47	11 04.6	17 00.1	5 31.1	8 19.1	4 25.6	2 01.9	23 05.1	15 02.7	22 59.1	27 51.9
8 Su	19 11 07	17 55 30	28 40 15	4♌36 26	10 51.2	15 39.4	6 46.2	8 15.2	4 36.1	2 10.2	23 11.5	15 01.9	23 00.3	27 53.9
9 M	19 15 04	18 56 37	10♌32 33	16 28 45	10 38.0	14 20.5	8 01.2	8 12.2	4 46.3	2 18.7	23 17.9	15 01.2	23 01.5	27 55.8
10 Tu	19 19 01	19 57 45	22 25 18	28 22 27	10 26.2	13 05.9	9 16.3	8 09.9	4 56.1	2 27.3	23 24.3	15 00.5	23 02.7	27 57.8
11 W	19 22 57	20 58 52	4♍20 30	10♍19 48	10 16.8	11 57.4	10 31.3	8 08.5	5 05.7	2 36.0	23 30.7	14 59.9	23 04.0	27 59.7
12 Th	19 26 54	21 59 59	16 20 44	22 23 46	10 10.1	10 56.7	11 46.3	8D 07.8	5 14.8	2 44.9	23 37.3	14 59.3	23 05.3	28 01.7
13 F	19 30 50	23 01 06	28 29 21	4♎38 01	10 06.2	10 04.7	13 01.3	8 07.9	5 23.6	2 53.9	23 43.8	14 58.8	23 06.6	28 03.6
14 Sa	19 34 47	24 02 13	10♎50 19	17 06 51	10D 04.6	9 22.3	14 16.3	8 08.8	5 32.1	3 03.0	23 50.4	14 58.3	23 08.0	28 05.6
15 Su	19 38 43	25 03 20	23 28 10	29 54 52	10R 04.5	8 49.6	15 31.2	8 10.4	5 40.2	3 12.3	23 57.0	14 57.9	23 09.3	28 07.6
16 M	19 42 40	26 04 27	6♏27 31	13♏06 37	10 04.6	8 26.5	16 46.2	8 12.7	5 47.9	3 21.7	24 03.7	14 57.5	23 10.7	28 09.5
17 Tu	19 46 36	27 05 34	19 52 35	26 45 46	10 03.7	8 12.9	18 01.1	8 15.8	5 55.2	3 31.3	24 10.4	14 57.2	23 12.2	28 11.5
18 W	19 50 33	28 06 41	3♐46 20	10♐54 18	10 00.6	8D 08.2	19 16.0	8 19.7	6 02.2	3 41.0	24 17.2	14 56.9	23 13.6	28 13.5
19 Th	19 54 30	29 07 47	18 09 29	25 31 27	9 54.8	8 11.8	20 30.9	8 24.2	6 08.7	3 50.8	24 23.9	14 56.7	23 15.1	28 15.4
20 F	19 58 26	0♒08 53	2♑59 32	10♑32 49	9 46.2	8 23.3	21 45.8	8 29.5	6 14.9	4 00.7	24 30.8	14 56.6	23 16.7	28 17.4
21 Sa	20 02 23	1 09 58	18 10 10	25 50 15	9 35.5	8 41.9	23 00.7	8 35.4	6 20.7	4 10.8	24 37.6	14 56.5	23 18.2	28 19.4
22 Su	20 06 19	2 11 03	3♒31 36	11♒12 42	9 23.7	9 07.1	24 15.5	8 42.0	6 26.1	4 20.9	24 44.5	14D 56.4	23 19.8	28 21.4
23 M	20 10 16	3 12 07	18 52 00	26 28 05	9 12.4	9 38.2	25 30.3	8 49.3	6 31.1	4 31.2	24 51.4	14 56.4	23 21.4	28 23.3
24 Tu	20 14 12	4 13 10	3♓59 39	11♓25 37	9 02.9	10 14.8	26 45.1	8 57.3	6 35.6	4 41.6	24 58.3	14 56.5	23 23.0	28 25.3
25 W	20 18 09	5 14 12	18 45 09	25 57 36	8 55.9	10 56.2	27 59.9	9 05.9	6 39.8	4 52.2	25 05.3	14 56.6	23 24.6	28 27.2
26 Th	20 22 05	6 15 13	3♈02 39	10♈00 10	8 51.8	11 42.1	29 14.7	9 15.1	6 43.5	5 02.8	25 12.3	14 56.8	23 26.3	28 29.2
27 F	20 26 02	7 16 13	16 50 12	23 33 01	8 50.0	12 32.1	0♓29.4	9 25.0	6 46.9	5 13.6	25 19.3	14 57.0	23 28.0	28 31.1
28 Sa	20 29 59	8 17 12	0♉08 58	6♉38 33	8 49.7	13 25.6	1 44.1	9 35.5	6 49.8	5 24.4	25 26.3	14 57.2	23 29.7	28 33.1
29 Su	20 33 55	9 18 09	13 02 17	19 20 47	8 49.5	14 22.5	2 58.7	9 46.5	6 52.3	5 35.4	25 33.4	14 57.6	23 31.4	28 35.0
30 M	20 37 52	10 19 06	25 34 38	1♊44 28	8 48.3	15 22.3	4 13.3	9 58.2	6 54.3	5 46.5	25 40.4	14 57.9	23 33.2	28 37.0
31 Tu	20 41 48	11 20 01	7♊50 53	13 54 25	8 45.0	16 24.9	5 27.9	10 10.4	6 56.0	5 57.6	25 47.5	14 58.4	23 35.0	28 38.9

LONGITUDE — February 2023

Day	Sid.Time	☉	0 hr ☽	Noon ☽	True ☊	☿	♀	♂	⚳	♃	♄	♅	♆	♇
1 W	20 45 45	12♒20 55	19♊55 38	25♊55 00	8♉38.8	17♑30.0	6♓42.5	10♊23.1	6♎57.2	6♈08.9	25♒54.6	14♉58.8	23♓36.8	28♑40.8
2 Th	20 49 41	13 21 48	1♋52 59	7♋49 58	8R29.6	18 37.4	7 57.0	10 36.4	6 58.0	6 20.3	26 01.8	14 59.4	23 38.6	28 42.7
3 F	20 53 38	14 22 40	13 46 17	19 42 16	8 17.6	19 46.8	9 11.5	10 50.2	6R58.3	6 31.8	26 08.9	14 59.9	23 40.5	28 44.7
4 Sa	20 57 34	15 23 30	25 38 10	1♌34 12	8 03.7	20 58.2	10 26.0	11 04.6	6 58.2	6 43.3	26 16.1	15 00.6	23 42.3	28 46.6
5 Su	21 01 31	16 24 19	7♌30 33	13 27 23	7 48.8	22 11.4	11 40.4	11 19.4	6 57.7	6 55.0	26 23.3	15 01.3	23 44.2	28 48.5
6 M	21 05 28	17 25 07	19 24 51	25 23 06	7 34.1	23 26.2	12 54.8	11 34.7	6 56.8	7 06.8	26 30.5	15 02.0	23 46.1	28 50.3
7 Tu	21 09 24	18 25 54	1♍22 15	7♍22 30	7 20.9	24 42.7	14 09.2	11 50.5	6 55.4	7 18.6	26 37.7	15 02.8	23 48.1	28 52.2
8 W	21 13 21	19 26 40	13 23 59	19 26 55	7 10.1	26 00.5	15 23.5	12 06.7	6 53.5	7 30.5	26 44.9	15 03.6	23 50.0	28 54.1
9 Th	21 17 17	20 27 24	25 31 32	1♎38 06	7 02.3	27 19.8	16 37.8	12 23.4	6 51.2	7 42.6	26 52.1	15 04.5	23 52.0	28 55.9
10 F	21 21 14	21 28 08	7♎46 56	13 58 23	6 57.5	28 40.3	17 52.1	12 40.6	6 48.5	7 54.7	26 59.3	15 05.5	23 53.9	28 57.8
11 Sa	21 25 10	22 28 50	20 12 50	26 30 43	6D 55.4	0♒02.1	19 06.3	12 58.2	6 45.4	8 06.8	27 06.6	15 06.5	23 55.9	28 59.6
12 Su	21 29 07	23 29 31	2♏52 30	9♏18 40	6 55.0	1 25.1	20 20.4	13 16.2	6 41.8	8 19.1	27 13.8	15 07.5	23 57.9	29 01.5
13 M	21 33 03	24 30 12	15 49 40	22 25 58	6R 55.2	2 49.2	21 34.6	13 34.6	6 37.7	8 31.5	27 21.1	15 08.6	24 00.0	29 03.3
14 Tu	21 37 00	25 30 51	29 08 01	5♐56 11	6 54.8	4 14.4	22 48.7	13 53.4	6 33.3	8 43.9	27 28.3	15 09.7	24 02.0	29 05.1
15 W	21 40 57	26 31 29	12♐50 43	19 51 48	6 52.7	5 40.7	24 02.8	14 12.6	6 28.4	8 56.4	27 35.6	15 10.9	24 04.1	29 06.9
16 Th	21 44 53	27 32 06	26 59 26	4♑13 27	6 48.2	7 08.0	25 16.8	14 32.2	6 23.0	9 09.0	27 42.8	15 12.2	24 06.2	29 08.7
17 F	21 48 50	28 32 42	11♑33 27	18 58 51	6 41.1	8 36.3	26 30.8	14 52.2	6 17.3	9 21.7	27 50.1	15 13.5	24 08.2	29 10.4
18 Sa	21 52 46	29 33 17	26 28 50	4♒02 24	6 31.8	10 05.7	27 44.7	15 12.5	6 11.1	9 34.4	27 57.4	15 14.8	24 10.4	29 12.2
19 Su	21 56 43	0♓33 50	11♒38 20	19 15 19	6 21.6	11 36.0	28 58.6	15 33.2	6 04.5	9 47.2	28 04.6	15 16.2	24 12.5	29 13.9
20 M	22 00 39	1 34 21	26 51 58	4♓26 52	6 11.5	13 07.3	0♈12.5	15 54.3	5 57.5	10 00.1	28 11.9	15 17.7	24 14.6	29 15.7
21 Tu	22 04 36	2 34 51	11♓58 42	19 26 14	6 02.8	14 39.6	1 26.3	16 15.7	5 50.1	10 13.1	28 19.1	15 19.1	24 16.7	29 17.4
22 W	22 08 32	3 35 19	26 48 26	4♈04 29	5 56.4	16 12.8	2 40.0	16 37.5	5 42.3	10 26.1	28 26.4	15 20.7	24 18.9	29 19.1
23 Th	22 12 29	4 35 46	11♈13 44	18 15 49	5 52.7	17 47.0	3 53.8	16 59.6	5 34.1	10 39.1	28 33.6	15 22.3	24 21.1	29 20.7
24 F	22 16 26	5 36 11	25 10 33	1♉57 58	5D 51.3	19 22.1	5 07.4	17 22.0	5 25.5	10 52.3	28 40.8	15 23.9	24 23.2	29 22.4
25 Sa	22 20 22	6 36 33	8♉38 14	15 11 42	5 51.5	20 58.3	6 21.0	17 44.7	5 16.5	11 05.5	28 48.1	15 25.6	24 25.4	29 24.1
26 Su	22 24 19	7 36 54	21 38 47	28 00 00	5R 52.3	22 35.4	7 34.6	18 07.7	5 07.2	11 18.7	28 55.3	15 27.3	24 27.6	29 25.7
27 M	22 28 15	8 37 13	4♊15 57	10♊27 15	5 52.7	24 13.5	8 48.1	18 31.0	4 57.6	11 32.1	29 02.5	15 29.0	24 29.8	29 27.3
28 Tu	22 32 12	9 37 30	16 34 30	22 38 21	5 51.6	25 52.6	10 01.5	18 54.7	4 47.6	11 45.4	29 09.7	15 30.9	24 32.0	29 28.9

Astro Data

	Dy Hr Mn
♄⚺♆	6 7:57
♂ D	12 20:58
♃0N	13 5:57
☽0S	13 15:34
☿ D	18 13:13
♅ D	22 22:59
☽0N	26 5:33
⚳ R	3 19:14
☽0S	9 20:32
♀0N	22 2:56
☽0N	22 15:01

Planet Ingress

		Dy Hr Mn
♀	♒	3 2:11
☉	♒	20 8:31
♀	♓	27 2:34
☿	♒	11 11:23
☉	♓	18 22:35
♀	♈	20 7:57

Last Aspect / ☽ Ingress

Last Aspect Dy Hr Mn			☽ Ingress	Dy Hr Mn
2 22:18	♇	△	♊	3 2:45
5 0:09	♆	□	♋	5 14:16
7 22:24	♇	☍	♌	8 2:41
10 1:54	♄	☍	♍	10 15:16
12 23:08	♇	△	♎	13 2:58
15 8:41	♇	□	♏	15 12:09
17 14:28	♇	⚹	♐	17 17:34
19 10:10	♄	⚹	♑	19 19:13
21 15:53	♇	☌	♒	21 18:30
23 10:20	♀	☌	♓	23 17:37
25 16:13	♇	⚹	♈	25 18:49
27 21:02	♇	□	♉	27 23:44
30 5:53	♇	△	♊	30 8:36

Last Aspect / ☽ Ingress

Last Aspect Dy Hr Mn			☽ Ingress	Dy Hr Mn
1 11:59	♄	△	♋	1 20:13
4 6:20	♇	☍	♌	4 8:50
6 14:17	♄	☍	♍	6 21:15
9 6:41	♇	△	♎	9 8:48
11 16:42	♇	□	♏	11 18:36
13 23:53	♇	⚹	♐	14 1:32
16 1:07	♄	⚹	♑	16 5:01
18 4:19	♇	☌	♒	18 5:36
20 2:01	♄	☌	♓	20 4:57
22 4:07	♇	⚹	♈	22 5:15
24 7:23	♇	□	♉	24 8:30
26 14:44	♇	△	♊	26 15:49

☽ Phases & Eclipses

Dy Hr Mn		
6 23:09	○	16♋22
15 2:11	☾	24♎38
21 20:54	●	1♒33
28 15:20	☽	8♉26
5 18:30	○	16♌41
13 16:02	☾	24♏40
20 7:07	●	1♓22
27 8:07	☽	8♊27

Astro Data

1 January 2023
Julian Day # 44926
SVP 4♓56'29"
GC 27♐09.6 ⚴ 20♋39.7R
Eris 23♈55.7R ⚵ 24♓46.8
⚷ 11♈58.4 ⚶ 14♓12.9
☽ Mean ☊ 10♉10.5

1 February 2023
Julian Day # 44957
SVP 4♓56'23"
GC 27♐09.7 ⚴ 11♋42.0R
Eris 23♈57.6 ⚵ 9♈21.2
⚷ 12♈39.2 ⚶ 27♓04.8
☽ Mean ☊ 8♉32.1

March 2023

LONGITUDE

Day	Sid.Time	☉	0 hr ☽	Noon☽	True☊	☿	♀	♂	⚳	♃	♄	♅	♆	♇
1 W	22 36 08	10♓37 45	28♊39 25	4♋38 19	5♉48.4	27♒32.7	11♈14.9	19♊18.5	4♎37.3	11♈58.9	29♒16.8	15♉32.7	24♓34.2	29♑30.5
2 Th	22 40 05	11 37 58	10♋35 35	16 31 46	5R43.0	29 13.8	12 28.2	19 42.7	4R26.6	12 12.3	29 24.0	15 34.6	24 36.5	29 32.0
3 F	22 44 01	12 38 09	22 27 21	28 22 47	5 35.3	0♓56.0	13 41.5	20 07.1	4 15.7	12 25.9	29 31.1	15 36.6	24 38.7	29 33.6
4 Sa	22 47 58	13 38 18	4♌18 27	10♌14 44	5 26.1	2 39.2	14 54.7	20 31.8	4 04.4	12 39.5	29 38.3	15 38.5	24 40.9	29 35.1
5 Su	22 51 55	14 38 25	16 11 54	22 10 14	5 16.0	4 23.4	16 07.9	20 56.8	3 52.9	12 53.1	29 45.4	15 40.6	24 43.2	29 36.6
6 M	22 55 51	15 38 30	28 09 57	4♍11 15	5 06.0	6 08.8	17 20.9	21 21.9	3 41.1	13 06.8	29 52.5	15 42.6	24 45.4	29 38.1
7 Tu	22 59 48	16 38 33	10♍14 16	16 19 10	4 57.0	7 55.3	18 33.9	21 47.4	3 29.1	13 20.5	29 59.5	15 44.7	24 47.7	29 39.5
8 W	23 03 44	17 38 34	22 26 04	28 35 05	4 49.8	9 42.8	19 46.9	22 13.0	3 16.8	13 34.2	0♓06.6	15 46.9	24 50.0	29 41.0
9 Th	23 07 41	18 38 33	4♎46 19	10♎59 55	4 44.8	11 31.5	20 59.8	22 38.9	3 04.3	13 48.0	0 13.6	15 49.1	24 52.2	29 42.4
10 F	23 11 37	19 38 30	17 16 01	23 34 46	4D42.1	13 21.2	22 12.6	23 05.0	2 51.6	14 01.9	0 20.6	15 51.3	24 54.5	29 43.8
11 Sa	23 15 34	20 38 26	29 56 21	6♏20 59	4 41.5	15 12.1	23 25.3	23 31.3	2 38.7	14 15.8	0 27.6	15 53.6	24 56.8	29 45.2
12 Su	23 19 30	21 38 20	12♏48 53	19 20 18	4 42.3	17 04.2	24 38.0	23 57.8	2 25.6	14 29.7	0 34.5	15 55.9	24 59.0	29 46.5
13 M	23 23 27	22 38 13	25 55 29	2♐34 41	4 43.7	18 57.3	25 50.6	24 24.6	2 12.4	14 43.7	0 41.5	15 58.2	25 01.3	29 47.9
14 Tu	23 27 23	23 38 04	9♐18 09	16 06 06	4R44.9	20 51.5	27 03.2	24 51.5	1 59.0	14 57.7	0 48.4	16 00.6	25 03.6	29 49.2
15 W	23 31 20	24 37 53	22 58 41	29 56 01	4 45.0	22 46.8	28 15.7	25 18.7	1 45.5	15 11.7	0 55.2	16 03.1	25 05.9	29 50.5
16 Th	23 35 17	25 37 41	6♑58 06	14♑04 50	4 43.5	24 43.1	29 28.1	25 46.0	1 31.9	15 25.8	1 02.1	16 05.5	25 08.1	29 51.8
17 F	23 39 13	26 37 27	21 15 59	28 31 13	4 40.4	26 40.4	0♉40.4	26 13.5	1 18.2	15 39.9	1 08.9	16 08.0	25 10.4	29 53.0
18 Sa	23 43 10	27 37 11	5♒50 01	13♒11 42	4 35.8	28 38.6	1 52.7	26 41.3	1 04.5	15 54.0	1 15.7	16 10.5	25 12.7	29 54.2
19 Su	23 47 06	28 36 54	20 35 31	28 00 33	4 30.4	0♈37.7	3 04.9	27 09.2	0 50.6	16 08.2	1 22.4	16 13.1	25 15.0	29 55.4
20 M	23 51 03	29 36 34	5♓25 48	12♓50 16	4 25.0	2 37.4	4 17.0	27 37.2	0 36.8	16 22.4	1 29.2	16 15.7	25 17.2	29 56.6
21 Tu	23 54 59	0♈36 13	20 12 54	27 32 43	4 20.3	4 37.7	5 29.1	28 05.5	0 22.9	16 36.6	1 35.8	16 18.3	25 19.5	29 57.8
22 W	23 58 56	1 35 49	4♈48 47	12♈00 19	4 17.0	6 38.5	6 41.0	28 34.0	0 09.0	16 50.9	1 42.5	16 21.0	25 21.8	29 58.9
23 Th	0 02 52	2 35 24	19 06 37	26 07 12	4D15.4	8 39.4	7 52.9	29 02.6	29♍55.2	17 05.2	1 49.1	16 23.7	25 24.0	29 60.0
24 F	0 06 49	3 34 56	3♉01 41	9♉49 54	4 15.2	10 40.4	9 04.7	29 31.3	29 41.4	17 19.4	1 55.6	16 26.4	25 26.3	0♒01.1
25 Sa	0 10 46	4 34 27	16 31 47	23 07 26	4 16.2	12 41.2	10 16.4	0♋00.3	29 27.7	17 33.8	2 02.2	16 29.2	25 28.6	0 02.1
26 Su	0 14 42	5 33 55	29 37 05	6♊01 02	4 17.9	14 41.4	11 28.1	0 29.4	29 14.0	17 48.1	2 08.7	16 32.0	25 30.8	0 03.1
27 M	0 18 39	6 33 21	12♊19 42	18 33 34	4 19.5	16 40.8	12 39.6	0 58.6	29 00.4	18 02.5	2 15.1	16 34.8	25 33.1	0 04.1
28 Tu	0 22 35	7 32 44	24 43 09	0♋49 01	4R20.6	18 38.9	13 51.1	1 28.0	28 47.0	18 16.8	2 21.5	16 37.7	25 35.3	0 05.1
29 W	0 26 32	8 32 05	6♋51 45	12 51 57	4 20.7	20 35.6	15 02.5	1 57.6	28 33.7	18 31.2	2 27.9	16 40.5	25 37.6	0 06.1
30 Th	0 30 28	9 31 24	18 50 14	24 47 10	4 19.6	22 30.3	16 13.7	2 27.2	28 20.6	18 45.6	2 34.2	16 43.5	25 39.8	0 07.0
31 F	0 34 25	10 30 41	0♌43 20	6♌39 17	4 17.5	24 22.6	17 24.9	2 57.1	28 07.6	19 00.0	2 40.4	16 46.4	25 42.0	0 07.9

April 2023

LONGITUDE

Day	Sid.Time	☉	0 hr ☽	Noon☽	True☊	☿	♀	♂	⚳	♃	♄	♅	♆	♇
1 Sa	0 38 21	11♈29 55	12♌35 33	18♌32 36	4♉14.5	26♈12.2	18♉36.0	3♋27.0	27♍54.8	19♈14.5	2♓46.6	16♉49.4	25♓44.2	0♒08.8
2 Su	0 42 18	12 29 07	24 30 53	0♍30 49	4R11.0	27 58.7	19 47.0	3 57.1	27R42.2	19 28.9	2 52.8	16 52.3	25 46.4	0 09.6
3 M	0 46 15	13 28 17	6♍32 47	12 37 04	4 07.5	29 41.6	20 57.8	4 27.3	27 29.8	19 43.3	2 58.9	16 55.3	25 48.6	0 10.4
4 Tu	0 50 11	14 27 24	18 43 57	24 53 39	4 04.4	1♉20.6	22 08.6	4 57.6	27 17.7	19 57.8	3 05.0	16 58.4	25 50.8	0 11.2
5 W	0 54 08	15 26 30	1♎06 22	7♎22 13	4 01.9	2 55.4	23 19.3	5 28.1	27 05.8	20 12.3	3 11.0	17 01.4	25 53.0	0 12.0
6 Th	0 58 04	16 25 33	13 41 19	20 03 42	4 00.5	4 25.5	24 29.8	5 58.7	26 54.1	20 26.7	3 17.0	17 04.5	25 55.1	0 12.7
7 F	1 02 01	17 24 34	26 29 26	2♏58 30	4D00.0	5 50.8	25 40.3	6 29.4	26 42.7	20 41.2	3 22.9	17 07.6	25 57.3	0 13.4
8 Sa	1 05 57	18 23 34	9♏30 53	16 06 34	4 00.3	7 11.0	26 50.6	7 00.2	26 31.6	20 55.7	3 28.8	17 10.8	25 59.4	0 14.1
9 Su	1 09 54	19 22 31	22 45 30	29 27 37	4 01.2	8 25.8	28 00.8	7 31.1	26 20.8	21 10.1	3 34.6	17 13.9	26 01.6	0 14.7
10 M	1 13 50	20 21 27	6♐12 52	13♐01 12	4 02.3	9 35.1	29 11.0	8 02.1	26 10.3	21 24.6	3 40.3	17 17.1	26 03.7	0 15.3
11 Tu	1 17 47	21 20 21	19 52 31	26 46 44	4 03.4	10 38.6	0♊21.0	8 33.2	26 00.2	21 39.1	3 46.0	17 20.3	26 05.8	0 15.9
12 W	1 21 44	22 19 14	3♑43 45	10♑43 27	4R04.1	11 36.2	1 30.9	9 04.5	25 50.3	21 53.6	3 51.7	17 23.5	26 07.9	0 16.5
13 Th	1 25 40	23 18 05	17 45 39	24 50 09	4 04.3	12 27.8	2 40.6	9 35.8	25 40.8	22 08.1	3 57.2	17 26.7	26 10.0	0 17.1
14 F	1 29 37	24 16 54	1♒56 44	9♒05 07	4 04.0	13 13.2	3 50.3	10 07.3	25 31.6	22 22.6	4 02.8	17 30.0	26 12.1	0 17.6
15 Sa	1 33 33	25 15 41	16 14 55	23 25 46	4 03.3	13 52.5	4 59.9	10 38.8	25 22.7	22 37.0	4 08.2	17 33.2	26 14.1	0 18.1
16 Su	1 37 30	26 14 26	0♓37 12	7♓48 43	4 02.4	14 25.5	6 09.3	11 10.5	25 14.3	22 51.5	4 13.6	17 36.5	26 16.2	0 18.5
17 M	1 41 26	27 13 10	14 59 47	22 09 48	4 01.5	14 52.2	7 18.6	11 42.3	25 06.2	23 06.0	4 18.9	17 39.8	26 18.2	0 18.9
18 Tu	1 45 23	28 11 52	29 18 13	6♈24 26	4 00.9	15 12.7	8 27.7	12 14.1	24 58.4	23 20.4	4 24.2	17 43.1	26 20.2	0 19.3
19 W	1 49 19	29 10 32	13♈27 53	20 28 03	4D00.5	15 27.0	9 36.8	12 46.1	24 51.1	23 34.9	4 29.4	17 46.4	26 22.2	0 19.7
20 Th	1 53 16	0♉09 10	27 24 27	4♉16 40	4 00.4	15R35.1	10 45.7	13 18.1	24 44.1	23 49.3	4 34.6	17 49.8	26 24.2	0 20.0
21 F	1 57 13	1 07 47	11♉04 24	17 47 23	4 00.5	15 37.2	11 54.5	13 50.2	24 37.6	24 03.7	4 39.6	17 53.1	26 26.1	0 20.3
22 Sa	2 01 09	2 06 21	24 25 28	0♊58 36	4 00.6	15 33.5	13 03.1	14 22.5	24 31.4	24 18.1	4 44.6	17 56.5	26 28.1	0 20.6
23 Su	2 05 06	3 04 53	7♊26 49	13 50 15	4R00.8	15 24.2	14 11.6	14 54.8	24 25.7	24 32.5	4 49.6	17 59.9	26 30.0	0 20.9
24 M	2 09 02	4 03 24	20 09 04	26 23 35	4 00.8	15 09.7	15 20.0	15 27.2	24 20.4	24 46.9	4 54.4	18 03.3	26 31.9	0 21.1
25 Tu	2 12 59	5 01 52	2♋34 09	8♋41 09	4 00.8	14 50.2	16 28.2	15 59.7	24 15.5	25 01.3	4 59.2	18 06.7	26 33.8	0 21.3
26 W	2 16 55	6 00 18	14 45 03	20 46 22	4 00.7	14 26.2	17 36.2	16 32.3	24 11.0	25 15.6	5 03.9	18 10.1	26 35.7	0 21.5
27 Th	2 20 52	6 58 42	26 45 37	2♌43 21	4D00.6	13 58.2	18 44.1	17 04.9	24 06.9	25 29.9	5 08.6	18 13.5	26 37.5	0 21.6
28 F	2 24 48	7 57 04	8♌40 09	14 36 35	4 00.6	13 26.8	19 51.8	17 37.7	24 03.2	25 44.2	5 13.2	18 17.0	26 39.4	0 21.7
29 Sa	2 28 45	8 55 24	20 33 15	26 30 43	4 00.8	12 52.6	20 59.4	18 10.5	24 00.0	25 58.5	5 17.7	18 20.4	26 41.2	0 21.8
30 Su	2 32 42	9 53 41	2♍29 33	8♍30 16	4 01.3	12 16.2	22 06.8	18 43.3	23 57.1	26 12.8	5 22.1	18 23.8	26 42.9	0 21.8

Astro Data	Dy Hr Mn
♄⚺♇	3 22:27
☽0S	9 1:55
♃⚺♅	19 22:07
☿0N	20 10:54
☉0N	20 21:26
♃∠♄	21 9:27
☽0N	22 1:33
☽0S	5 8:55
☽0N	18 10:57
☿R	21 8:36

Planet Ingress	Dy Hr Mn
☿ ♓	2 22:53
♄ ♓	7 13:36
♀ ♉	16 22:35
☿ ♈	19 4:25
☉ ♈	20 21:26
⚳ ♍R	23 3:39
♇ ♒	23 12:14
♂ ♋	25 11:46
☿ ♉	3 16:23
♀ ♊	11 4:48
☉ ♉	20 8:15

Last Aspect Dy Hr Mn		☽ Ingress Dy Hr Mn
1 1:08	♄ △	♋ 1 2:41
3 14:24	♇ ☍	♌ 3 15:17
6 3:20	♄ ☍	♍ 6 3:40
8 14:08	♇ △	♎ 8 14:45
10 23:38	♇ □	♏ 11 0:07
13 7:00	♇ ⚹	♐ 13 7:22
15 8:51	♀ △	♑ 15 12:07
17 14:15	♇ ☌	♒ 17 14:26
19 10:34	♂ △	♓ 19 15:13
21 15:59	♇ ⚹	♈ 21 16:02
23 17:14	♂ ⚹	♉ 23 18:43
25 16:20	♆ ⚹	♊ 26 0:43
28 1:40	♆ □	♋ 28 10:23
30 13:47	♆ △	♌ 30 22:32

Last Aspect Dy Hr Mn		☽ Ingress Dy Hr Mn
2 6:04	☿ △	♍ 2 10:58
4 13:51	♆ ☍	♎ 4 21:52
6 12:44	♃ ☍	♏ 7 6:30
9 9:10	♀ ☍	♐ 9 12:58
11 10:49	♆ □	♑ 11 17:34
13 14:15	♆ ⚹	♒ 13 20:43
15 15:17	☉ ⚹	♓ 15 22:58
17 18:58	♆ ☌	♈ 18 1:10
20 4:14	☉ ☌	♉ 20 4:31
22 3:42	♆ ⚹	♊ 22 10:12
24 12:16	♆ □	♋ 24 19:00
26 23:42	♆ △	♌ 27 6:31
29 10:54	♃ △	♍ 29 19:00

☽ Phases & Eclipses Dy Hr Mn	
7 12:42	○ 16♍40
15 2:09	☾ 24♐13
21 17:24	● 0♈50
29 2:34	☽ 8♋09
6 4:36	○ 16♎07
13 9:13	☾ 23♑11
20 4:14	● 29♈50
20 4:17:56	● AT01'16"
27 21:21	☽ 7♌21

Astro Data

1 March 2023
Julian Day # 44985
SVP 4♓56'20"
GC 27♐09.8 ⚴ 11♋16.6
Eris 24♈07.8 ⚵ 24♈17.8
⚷ 13♈52.3 ⚶ 9♈28.7
☽ Mean ☊ 7♉03.1

1 April 2023
Julian Day # 45016
SVP 4♓56'16"
GC 27♐09.8 ⚴ 18♋32.8
Eris 24♈25.6 ⚵ 11♉57.9
⚷ 15♈36.3 ⚶ 23♈32.5
☽ Mean ☊ 5♉24.6

LONGITUDE — May 2023

Day	Sid.Time	☉	0 hr ☽	Noon ☽	True ☊	☿	♀	♂	⚳	♃	♄	♅	♆	♇
1 M	2 36 38	10♉51 57	14♍33 23	20♍39 24	4♉01.9	11♉38.3	23♊14.0	19♋16.3	23♍54.7	26♈27.0	5♓26.4	18♉27.3	26♓44.7	0♒21.9
2 Tu	2 40 35	11 50 10	26 48 44	3♎01 45	4 02.7	10R 59.6	24 21.0	19 49.3	23R 52.7	26 41.2	5 30.7	18 30.7	26 46.5	0R 21.8
3 W	2 44 31	12 48 22	9♎18 47	15 40 05	4 03.4	10 20.8	25 27.9	20 22.4	23 51.1	26 55.4	5 34.9	18 34.2	26 48.2	0 21.8
4 Th	2 48 28	13 46 32	22 05 52	28 36 12	4R 03.8	9 42.6	26 34.5	20 55.6	23 50.0	27 09.6	5 39.0	18 37.7	26 49.9	0 21.7
5 F	2 52 24	14 44 40	5♏11 10	11♏50 40	4 03.7	9 05.7	27 41.0	21 28.8	23 49.2	27 23.7	5 43.1	18 41.1	26 51.6	0 21.7
6 Sa	2 56 21	15 42 47	18 34 37	25 22 48	4 03.1	8 30.6	28 47.2	22 02.1	23D 48.9	27 37.8	5 47.0	18 44.6	26 53.2	0 21.5
7 Su	3 00 17	16 40 51	2♐14 55	9♐10 39	4 01.9	7 58.1	29 53.3	22 35.5	23 49.0	27 51.9	5 50.9	18 48.1	26 54.9	0 21.4
8 M	3 04 14	17 38 55	16 09 35	23 11 18	4 00.3	7 28.4	0♋59.2	23 08.9	23 49.5	28 05.9	5 54.7	18 51.5	26 56.5	0 21.2
9 Tu	3 08 11	18 36 57	0♑15 18	7♑21 08	3 58.5	7 02.1	2 04.9	23 42.4	23 50.4	28 19.9	5 58.4	18 55.0	26 58.1	0 21.0
10 W	3 12 07	19 34 57	14 28 17	21 36 18	3 56.9	6 39.6	3 10.3	24 15.9	23 51.7	28 33.9	6 02.1	18 58.5	26 59.6	0 20.8
11 Th	3 16 04	20 32 56	28 44 43	5♒53 07	3 55.7	6 21.1	4 15.5	24 49.6	23 53.4	28 47.8	6 05.6	19 02.0	27 01.2	0 20.5
12 F	3 20 00	21 30 54	13♒01 07	20 08 22	3D 55.2	6 06.9	5 20.6	25 23.3	23 55.4	29 01.7	6 09.1	19 05.4	27 02.7	0 20.2
13 Sa	3 23 57	22 28 51	27 14 32	4♓19 22	3 55.5	5 57.2	6 25.3	25 57.0	23 57.9	29 15.6	6 12.5	19 08.9	27 04.2	0 19.9
14 Su	3 27 53	23 26 46	11♓22 36	18 24 02	3 56.5	5D 51.9	7 29.9	26 30.8	24 00.8	29 29.4	6 15.8	19 12.4	27 05.6	0 19.6
15 M	3 31 50	24 24 40	25 23 27	2♈20 39	3 57.8	5 51.3	8 34.2	27 04.7	24 04.1	29 43.2	6 19.0	19 15.9	27 07.1	0 19.2
16 Tu	3 35 46	25 22 33	9♈15 28	16 07 43	3 59.1	5 55.3	9 38.3	27 38.6	24 07.7	29 56.9	6 22.1	19 19.3	27 08.5	0 18.8
17 W	3 39 43	26 20 24	22 57 14	29 43 51	3R 59.8	6 03.9	10 42.1	28 12.6	24 11.8	0♉10.6	6 25.1	19 22.8	27 09.9	0 18.4
18 Th	3 43 40	27 18 14	6♉27 23	13♉07 42	3 59.6	6 17.0	11 45.7	28 46.7	24 16.2	0 24.3	6 28.1	19 26.2	27 11.2	0 18.0
19 F	3 47 36	28 16 03	19 44 39	26 18 07	3 58.2	6 34.6	12 49.0	29 20.8	24 21.0	0 37.9	6 30.9	19 29.7	27 12.5	0 17.5
20 Sa	3 51 33	29 13 51	2♊48 01	9♊14 17	3 55.6	6 56.6	13 52.1	29 55.0	24 26.1	0 51.5	6 33.7	19 33.1	27 13.8	0 17.0
21 Su	3 55 29	0♊11 37	15 36 53	21 55 53	3 51.9	7 22.9	14 54.8	0♌29.2	24 31.7	1 05.0	6 36.4	19 36.6	27 15.1	0 16.5
22 M	3 59 26	1 09 22	28 11 20	4♋23 22	3 47.5	7 53.3	15 57.3	1 03.5	24 37.6	1 18.5	6 39.0	19 40.0	27 16.4	0 15.9
23 Tu	4 03 22	2 07 05	10♋32 12	16 38 03	3 42.9	8 27.8	16 59.5	1 37.8	24 43.8	1 31.9	6 41.5	19 43.4	27 17.6	0 15.3
24 W	4 07 19	3 04 47	22 41 15	28 42 09	3 38.6	9 06.3	18 01.4	2 12.2	24 50.5	1 45.3	6 43.9	19 46.8	27 18.8	0 14.7
25 Th	4 11 15	4 02 27	4♌41 08	10♌38 40	3 35.3	9 48.6	19 02.9	2 46.7	24 57.4	1 58.6	6 46.2	19 50.2	27 19.9	0 14.1
26 F	4 15 12	5 00 06	16 35 16	22 31 26	3 33.1	10 34.5	20 04.1	3 21.2	25 04.7	2 11.9	6 48.4	19 53.6	27 21.1	0 13.4
27 Sa	4 19 09	5 57 43	28 27 44	4♍24 46	3D 32.3	11 24.1	21 05.0	3 55.7	25 12.4	2 25.1	6 50.5	19 57.0	27 22.2	0 12.8
28 Su	4 23 05	6 55 19	10♍23 07	16 23 23	3 32.7	12 17.2	22 05.5	4 30.3	25 20.4	2 38.2	6 52.5	20 00.4	27 23.3	0 12.1
29 M	4 27 02	7 52 53	22 26 12	28 32 09	3 34.0	13 13.7	23 05.7	5 05.0	25 28.7	2 51.3	6 54.4	20 03.7	27 24.3	0 11.3
30 Tu	4 30 58	8 50 26	4♎41 48	10♎55 42	3 35.6	14 13.5	24 05.5	5 39.7	25 37.3	3 04.3	6 56.3	20 07.1	27 25.3	0 10.6
31 W	4 34 55	9 47 57	17 14 21	23 38 10	3R 36.9	15 16.5	25 04.9	6 14.4	25 46.3	3 17.3	6 58.0	20 10.4	27 26.3	0 09.8

LONGITUDE — June 2023

Day	Sid.Time	☉	0 hr ☽	Noon ☽	True ☊	☿	♀	♂	⚳	♃	♄	♅	♆	♇
1 Th	4 38 51	10♊45 28	0♏07 30	6♏42 38	3♉37.2	16♉22.7	26♋03.9	6♌49.2	25♍55.6	3♉30.2	6♓59.6	20♉13.7	27♓27.3	0♒09.0
2 F	4 42 48	11 42 57	13 23 42	20 10 44	3R 36.1	17 31.9	27 02.5	7 24.0	26 05.2	3 43.0	7 01.2	20 17.0	27 28.2	0R 08.2
3 Sa	4 46 44	12 40 25	27 03 38	4♐02 09	3 33.2	18 44.2	28 00.7	7 58.9	26 15.1	3 55.8	7 02.6	20 20.3	27 29.1	0 07.4
4 Su	4 50 41	13 37 52	11♐05 53	18 14 18	3 28.7	19 59.4	28 58.4	8 33.8	26 25.3	4 08.5	7 04.0	20 23.6	27 29.9	0 06.5
5 M	4 54 38	14 35 18	25 26 45	2♑42 28	3 22.9	21 17.6	29 55.7	9 08.8	26 35.7	4 21.2	7 05.2	20 26.8	27 30.8	0 05.6
6 Tu	4 58 34	15 32 43	10♑00 35	17 20 14	3 16.6	22 38.6	0♌52.6	9 43.8	26 46.5	4 33.8	7 06.4	20 30.0	27 31.6	0 04.7
7 W	5 02 31	16 30 07	24 40 30	2♒00 29	3 10.7	24 02.5	1 48.9	10 18.9	26 57.6	4 46.3	7 07.5	20 33.3	27 32.4	0 03.8
8 Th	5 06 27	17 27 31	9♒19 22	16 36 26	3 05.9	25 29.3	2 44.8	10 54.0	27 08.9	4 58.7	7 08.4	20 36.5	27 33.1	0 02.9
9 F	5 10 24	18 24 54	23 51 01	1♓02 37	3 02.8	26 58.8	3 40.1	11 29.2	27 20.6	5 11.1	7 09.3	20 39.6	27 33.8	0 01.9
10 Sa	5 14 20	19 22 17	8♓10 50	15 15 24	3D 01.5	28 31.1	4 34.9	12 04.4	27 32.5	5 23.4	7 10.1	20 42.8	27 34.5	0 00.9
11 Su	5 18 17	20 19 39	22 16 09	29 13 01	3 01.7	0♊06.2	5 29.2	12 39.6	27 44.6	5 35.6	7 10.7	20 45.9	27 35.1	29♑59.9
12 M	5 22 14	21 17 00	6♈05 59	12♈55 09	3 02.7	1 44.0	6 23.0	13 14.9	27 57.1	5 47.8	7 11.3	20 49.1	27 35.7	29 58.9
13 Tu	5 26 10	22 14 21	19 40 35	26 22 28	3R 03.7	3 24.5	7 16.1	13 50.3	28 09.7	5 59.9	7 11.8	20 52.1	27 36.3	29 57.8
14 W	5 30 07	23 11 42	3♉00 54	9♉36 03	3 03.7	5 07.8	8 08.7	14 25.6	28 22.7	6 11.8	7 12.1	20 55.2	27 36.9	29 56.8
15 Th	5 34 03	24 09 02	16 08 02	22 37 00	3 01.9	6 53.7	9 00.6	15 01.1	28 35.9	6 23.8	7 12.4	20 58.3	27 37.4	29 55.7
16 F	5 38 00	25 06 22	29 03 01	5♊26 11	2 57.8	8 42.3	9 51.9	15 36.6	28 49.4	6 35.6	7 12.6	21 01.3	27 37.9	29 54.6
17 Sa	5 41 56	26 03 41	11♊46 34	18 04 13	2 51.4	10 33.5	10 42.6	16 12.1	29 03.1	6 47.3	7R 12.6	21 04.3	27 38.3	29 53.5
18 Su	5 45 53	27 01 00	24 19 11	0♋31 33	2 43.0	12 27.1	11 32.5	16 47.7	29 17.0	6 59.0	7 12.6	21 07.3	27 38.7	29 52.3
19 M	5 49 49	27 58 18	6♋41 21	12 48 43	2 33.1	14 23.3	12 21.8	17 23.3	29 31.2	7 10.6	7 12.5	21 10.2	27 39.1	29 51.2
20 Tu	5 53 46	28 55 36	18 53 43	24 56 32	2 22.7	16 21.7	13 10.3	17 58.9	29 45.6	7 22.1	7 12.3	21 13.2	27 39.5	29 50.0
21 W	5 57 43	29 52 53	0♌57 21	6♌56 24	2 12.8	18 22.4	13 58.0	18 34.6	0♎00.3	7 33.5	7 11.9	21 16.1	27 39.8	29 48.9
22 Th	6 01 39	0♋50 09	12 53 58	18 50 23	2 04.2	20 25.2	14 44.9	19 10.4	0 15.2	7 44.8	7 11.5	21 18.9	27 40.1	29 47.7
23 F	6 05 36	1 47 25	24 46 02	0♍41 21	1 57.5	22 29.8	15 31.0	19 46.1	0 30.3	7 56.0	7 11.0	21 21.8	27 40.4	29 46.4
24 Sa	6 09 32	2 44 40	6♍36 48	12 32 56	1 53.2	24 36.1	16 16.2	20 22.0	0 45.6	8 07.1	7 10.4	21 24.6	27 40.6	29 45.2
25 Su	6 13 29	3 41 54	18 30 17	24 29 28	1D 51.0	26 43.9	17 00.6	20 57.8	1 01.1	8 18.1	7 09.6	21 27.4	27 40.8	29 44.0
26 M	6 17 25	4 39 08	0♎31 06	6♎35 49	1 50.6	28 52.9	17 44.0	21 33.7	1 16.9	8 29.0	7 08.8	21 30.1	27 40.9	29 42.7
27 Tu	6 21 22	5 36 21	12 44 15	18 57 03	1 51.1	1♋02.8	18 26.4	22 09.7	1 32.8	8 39.9	7 07.9	21 32.9	27 41.0	29 41.5
28 W	6 25 18	6 33 34	25 14 50	1♏38 11	1R 51.5	3 13.4	19 07.8	22 45.7	1 49.0	8 50.6	7 06.9	21 35.6	27 41.1	29 40.2
29 Th	6 29 15	7 30 46	8♏07 36	14 43 32	1 50.8	5 24.3	19 48.1	23 21.7	2 05.3	9 01.2	7 05.8	21 38.2	27 41.2	29 38.9
30 F	6 33 12	8 27 58	21 26 18	28 16 05	1 48.2	7 35.4	20 27.4	23 57.7	2 21.9	9 11.7	7 04.6	21 40.9	27R 41.2	29 37.6

Astro Data

	Dy Hr Mn
♇ R	1 17:10
☽ 0S	2 17:17
♃⚺♆	2 22:05
⚳ D	6 19:26
☿ D	15 3:17
☽ 0N	15 17:55
♃□♇	18 1:12
☽ 0S	30 1:50
☽ 0N	11 22:58
♄ R	17 17:29
♃⚹♄	19 15:54
☽ 0S	26 9:23
♆ R	30 21:08

Planet Ingress

		Dy Hr Mn
♀	♋	7 14:26
♃	♉	16 17:21
♂	♌	20 15:33
☉	♊	21 7:10
♀	♌	5 13:48
♇	♑R	11 9:48
☿	♊	11 10:28
⚳	♎	21 11:31
☉	♋	21 14:59
☿	♋	27 0:25

Last Aspect / ☽ Ingress (May)

Last Aspect Dy Hr Mn			☽ Ingress	Dy Hr Mn
1 23:54	♆	☍	♎	2 6:10
4 9:18	♃	☍	♏	4 14:33
6 14:39	♆	△	♐	6 20:05
8 20:29	♃	△	♑	8 23:34
10 23:53	♃	□	♒	11 2:07
13 3:16	♃	⚹	♓	13 4:40
15 2:58	♆	☌	♈	15 7:57
17 9:11	♂	□	♉	17 12:29
19 17:52	♂	⚹	♊	19 18:49
21 22:13	♆	□	♋	22 3:30
24 9:13	♆	△	♌	24 14:36
26 6:39	♅	□	♍	27 3:06
29 9:47	♆	☍	♎	29 14:52
31 14:55	♀	□	♏	31 23:46

Last Aspect / ☽ Ingress (June)

Last Aspect Dy Hr Mn			☽ Ingress	Dy Hr Mn
3 0:52	♀	△	♐	3 5:05
5 3:25	♆	□	♑	5 7:32
7 4:41	♆	⚹	♒	7 8:43
9 4:25	☿	□	♓	9 10:15
11 13:21	♇	⚹	♈	11 13:22
13 18:28	♇	□	♉	13 18:32
16 1:38	♇	△	♊	16 1:47
18 6:25	♆	□	♋	18 10:59
20 21:44	♇	☍	♌	20 22:05
22 17:02	♅	□	♍	23 10:36
25 22:25	♇	△	♎	25 22:58
28 8:20	♇	□	♏	28 8:57
30 14:21	♇	⚹	♐	30 15:01

☽ Phases & Eclipses

Dy Hr Mn		
5 17:35	○	14♏58
5 17:24	☍	A 0.963
12 14:29	☾	21♒37
19 15:54	●	28♉25
27 15:23	☽	6♍06
4 3:43	○	13♐18
10 19:33	☾	19♓40
18 4:38	●	26♊43
26 7:51	☽	4♎29

Astro Data

1 May 2023
Julian Day # 45046
SVP 4♓56'12"
GC 27♐09.9 ⚵ 29♋30.8
Eris 24♈45.2 ✱ 29♉35.1
⚷ 17♈20.2 ⚶ 7♉08.2
☽ Mean ☊ 3♉49.3

1 June 2023
Julian Day # 45077
SVP 4♓56'08"
GC 27♐10.0 ⚵ 12♌36.6
Eris 25♈02.8 ✱ 17♊49.9
⚷ 18♈50.6 ⚶ 20♉52.8
☽ Mean ☊ 2♉10.8

July 2023 — LONGITUDE

Day	Sid.Time	☉	0 hr ☽	Noon ☽	True☊	☿	♀	♂	⚳	♃	♄	♅	♆	♇
1 Sa	6 37 08	9♋25 09	5♐12 57	12♐16 44	1♉43.2	9♋46.3	21♌05.5	24♌33.8	2♎38.6	9♉22.1	7♓03.3	21♉43.5	27♓41.2	29♑36.3
2 Su	6 41 05	10 22 21	19 27 06	26 43 30	1R 35.9	11 56.7	21 42.4	25 10.0	2 55.5	9 32.4	7R 01.9	21 46.0	27R 41.2	29R 35.0
3 M	6 45 01	11 19 32	4♑05 12	11♑31 16	1 26.7	14 06.4	22 18.1	25 46.2	3 12.6	9 42.7	7 00.4	21 48.6	27 41.1	29 33.6
4 Tu	6 48 58	12 16 43	19 00 36	26 32 02	1 16.7	16 15.2	22 52.6	26 22.4	3 29.9	9 52.7	6 58.9	21 51.1	27 41.0	29 32.3
5 W	6 52 54	13 13 54	4♒04 18	11♒36 08	1 07.0	18 22.9	23 25.7	26 58.6	3 47.3	10 02.7	6 57.2	21 53.6	27 40.9	29 31.0
6 Th	6 56 51	14 11 05	19 06 20	26 33 50	0 58.9	20 29.4	23 57.4	27 34.9	4 05.0	10 12.6	6 55.5	21 56.0	27 40.7	29 29.6
7 F	7 00 47	15 08 16	3♓57 41	11♓17 05	0 52.9	22 34.4	24 27.8	28 11.2	4 22.8	10 22.4	6 53.6	21 58.4	27 40.5	29 28.2
8 Sa	7 04 44	16 05 28	18 31 29	25 40 29	0 49.5	24 37.9	24 56.6	28 47.6	4 40.7	10 32.0	6 51.7	22 00.8	27 40.3	29 26.9
9 Su	7 08 41	17 02 39	2♈43 51	9♈41 33	0D 48.2	26 39.7	25 24.0	29 24.0	4 58.9	10 41.5	6 49.6	22 03.1	27 40.0	29 25.5
10 M	7 12 37	17 59 52	16 33 39	23 20 20	0R 48.1	28 39.9	25 49.8	0♍00.5	5 17.2	10 50.9	6 47.5	22 05.4	27 39.7	29 24.1
11 Tu	7 16 34	18 57 05	0♉01 52	6♉38 33	0 48.0	0♌38.3	26 13.9	0 37.0	5 35.6	11 00.2	6 45.3	22 07.6	27 39.4	29 22.7
12 W	7 20 30	19 54 18	13 10 45	19 38 49	0 46.9	2 34.8	26 36.4	1 13.5	5 54.2	11 09.4	6 43.0	22 09.9	27 39.0	29 21.3
13 Th	7 24 27	20 51 32	26 03 07	2♊23 59	0 43.7	4 29.6	26 57.2	1 50.1	6 13.0	11 18.4	6 40.7	22 12.0	27 38.6	29 19.9
14 F	7 28 23	21 48 46	8♊41 44	14 56 40	0 37.7	6 22.5	27 16.1	2 26.7	6 32.0	11 27.3	6 38.2	22 14.2	27 38.2	29 18.5
15 Sa	7 32 20	22 46 01	21 09 02	27 19 03	0 28.9	8 13.5	27 33.2	3 03.4	6 51.0	11 36.1	6 35.7	22 16.3	27 37.8	29 17.1
16 Su	7 36 17	23 43 16	3♋26 54	9♋32 46	0 17.6	10 02.6	27 48.4	3 40.1	7 10.3	11 44.8	6 33.0	22 18.3	27 37.3	29 15.6
17 M	7 40 13	24 40 32	15 36 46	21 39 05	0 04.5	11 49.9	28 01.6	4 16.8	7 29.6	11 53.3	6 30.3	22 20.4	27 36.8	29 14.2
18 Tu	7 44 10	25 37 48	27 39 48	3♌39 06	29♈50.6	13 35.3	28 12.7	4 53.6	7 49.2	12 01.7	6 27.5	22 22.4	27 36.2	29 12.8
19 W	7 48 06	26 35 04	9♌37 06	15 33 59	29 37.3	15 18.8	28 21.8	5 30.4	8 08.8	12 09.9	6 24.7	22 24.3	27 35.7	29 11.4
20 Th	7 52 03	27 32 21	21 29 58	27 25 17	29 25.4	17 00.4	28 28.7	6 07.3	8 28.6	12 18.0	6 21.7	22 26.2	27 35.1	29 09.9
21 F	7 55 59	28 29 38	3♍20 12	9♍15 03	29 15.8	18 40.2	28 33.4	6 44.2	8 48.5	12 26.0	6 18.7	22 28.0	27 34.4	29 08.5
22 Sa	7 59 56	29 26 55	15 10 13	21 06 06	29 09.0	20 18.1	28R 35.8	7 21.1	9 08.6	12 33.8	6 15.6	22 29.9	27 33.8	29 07.1
23 Su	8 03 52	0♌24 12	27 03 10	3♎01 57	29 05.0	21 54.2	28 36.0	7 58.1	9 28.8	12 41.5	6 12.4	22 31.6	27 33.1	29 05.7
24 M	8 07 49	1 21 30	9♎03 00	15 06 53	29 03.2	23 28.3	28 33.8	8 35.2	9 49.1	12 49.1	6 09.2	22 33.4	27 32.4	29 04.2
25 Tu	8 11 45	2 18 49	21 14 15	27 25 42	29 02.8	25 00.6	28 29.2	9 12.2	10 09.6	12 56.5	6 05.9	22 35.0	27 31.6	29 02.8
26 W	8 15 42	3 16 07	3♏41 53	10♏03 26	29 02.7	26 31.0	28 22.3	9 49.3	10 30.1	13 03.7	6 02.5	22 36.7	27 30.8	29 01.4
27 Th	8 19 39	4 13 26	16 30 56	23 04 56	29 01.9	27 59.5	28 13.0	10 26.5	10 50.8	13 10.8	5 59.0	22 38.3	27 30.0	29 00.0
28 F	8 23 35	5 10 46	29 45 53	6♐34 07	28 59.2	29 26.1	28 01.2	11 03.6	11 11.6	13 17.8	5 55.5	22 39.8	27 29.2	28 58.5
29 Sa	8 27 32	6 08 06	13♐29 52	20 33 08	28 54.1	0♍50.8	27 47.1	11 40.8	11 32.5	13 24.6	5 52.0	22 41.3	27 28.3	28 57.1
30 Su	8 31 28	7 05 26	27 43 46	5♑01 23	28 46.5	2 13.4	27 30.6	12 18.1	11 53.6	13 31.2	5 48.3	22 42.8	27 27.4	28 55.7
31 M	8 35 25	8 02 48	12♑25 20	19 54 46	28 36.9	3 34.1	27 11.7	12 55.4	12 14.7	13 37.7	5 44.6	22 44.2	27 26.5	28 54.3

August 2023 — LONGITUDE

Day	Sid.Time	☉	0 hr ☽	Noon ☽	True☊	☿	♀	♂	⚳	♃	♄	♅	♆	♇
1 Tu	8 39 21	9♌00 09	27♑28 37	5♒05 37	28♈26.4	4♍52.7	26♌50.7	13♍32.7	12♎36.0	13♉44.1	5♓40.9	22♉45.6	27♓25.6	28♑52.9
2 W	8 43 18	9 57 32	12♒44 25	20 23 34	28R 16.2	6 09.3	26R 27.4	14 10.1	12 57.3	13 50.3	5R 37.1	22 46.9	27R 24.6	28R 51.5
3 Th	8 47 15	10 54 55	28 01 38	5♓37 15	28 07.3	7 23.6	26 02.0	14 47.5	13 18.8	13 56.3	5 33.2	22 48.2	27 23.6	28 50.1
4 F	8 51 11	11 52 20	13♓09 11	20 36 25	28 00.9	8 35.8	25 34.7	15 24.9	13 40.3	14 02.2	5 29.3	22 49.5	27 22.6	28 48.7
5 Sa	8 55 08	12 49 45	27 58 06	5♈13 37	27 57.0	9 45.7	25 05.5	16 02.4	14 02.0	14 07.8	5 25.3	22 50.6	27 21.6	28 47.4
6 Su	8 59 04	13 47 12	12♈22 34	19 24 47	27D 55.4	10 53.2	24 34.6	16 40.0	14 23.8	14 13.4	5 21.3	22 51.8	27 20.5	28 46.0
7 M	9 03 01	14 44 40	26 20 13	3♉09 03	27R 55.2	11 58.3	24 02.2	17 17.5	14 45.6	14 18.7	5 17.3	22 52.9	27 19.4	28 44.6
8 Tu	9 06 57	15 42 10	9♉51 32	16 28 01	27 55.4	13 00.8	23 28.5	17 55.1	15 07.6	14 23.9	5 13.2	22 53.9	27 18.3	28 43.3
9 W	9 10 54	16 39 40	22 58 57	29 24 46	27 54.7	14 00.7	22 53.6	18 32.8	15 29.6	14 29.0	5 09.0	22 54.9	27 17.1	28 41.9
10 Th	9 14 50	17 37 13	5♊45 58	12♊03 23	27 52.3	14 57.9	22 17.9	19 10.5	15 51.8	14 33.8	5 04.8	22 55.9	27 16.0	28 40.6
11 F	9 18 47	18 34 46	18 16 25	24 26 36	27 47.3	15 52.1	21 41.3	19 48.2	16 14.0	14 38.5	5 00.6	22 56.8	27 14.8	28 39.3
12 Sa	9 22 44	19 32 21	0♋33 58	6♋38 56	27 39.8	16 43.2	21 04.4	20 26.0	16 36.4	14 43.0	4 56.3	22 57.6	27 13.6	28 37.9
13 Su	9 26 40	20 29 57	12 41 50	18 42 59	27 29.9	17 31.2	20 27.1	21 03.8	16 58.8	14 47.3	4 52.0	22 58.4	27 12.4	28 36.6
14 M	9 30 37	21 27 35	24 42 39	0♌41 05	27 18.3	18 15.8	19 49.9	21 41.7	17 21.3	14 51.5	4 47.7	22 59.2	27 11.1	28 35.3
15 Tu	9 34 33	22 25 14	6♌38 31	12 35 08	27 06.1	18 56.8	19 12.8	22 19.6	17 43.9	14 55.4	4 43.3	22 59.9	27 09.8	28 34.1
16 W	9 38 30	23 22 54	18 31 08	24 26 42	26 54.2	19 34.0	18 36.2	22 57.6	18 06.6	14 59.2	4 38.9	23 00.6	27 08.5	28 32.8
17 Th	9 42 26	24 20 35	0♍22 02	6♍17 19	26 43.7	20 07.3	18 00.3	23 35.6	18 29.4	15 02.8	4 34.5	23 01.2	27 07.2	28 31.5
18 F	9 46 23	25 18 18	12 12 46	18 08 38	26 35.3	20 36.4	17 25.3	24 13.6	18 52.2	15 06.2	4 30.1	23 01.7	27 05.9	28 30.3
19 Sa	9 50 19	26 16 01	24 05 11	0♎02 44	26 29.5	21 01.1	16 51.5	24 51.7	19 15.1	15 09.5	4 25.6	23 02.2	27 04.5	28 29.1
20 Su	9 54 16	27 13 46	6♎01 37	12 02 13	26 26.1	21 21.1	16 18.9	25 29.8	19 38.1	15 12.5	4 21.1	23 02.7	27 03.2	28 27.8
21 M	9 58 13	28 11 32	18 04 59	24 10 21	26D 25.0	21 36.2	15 47.8	26 08.0	20 01.2	15 15.3	4 16.6	23 03.1	27 01.8	28 26.6
22 Tu	10 02 09	29 09 19	0♏18 50	6♏30 58	26 25.3	21 46.2	15 18.4	26 46.2	20 24.4	15 18.0	4 12.1	23 03.4	27 00.4	28 25.4
23 W	10 06 06	0♍07 08	12 47 16	19 08 18	26R 26.2	21R 50.8	14 50.8	27 24.4	20 47.6	15 20.5	4 07.6	23 03.7	26 58.9	28 24.3
24 Th	10 10 02	1 04 57	25 34 37	2♐06 43	26 26.6	21 49.9	14 25.1	28 02.7	21 10.9	15 22.7	4 03.0	23 04.0	26 57.5	28 23.1
25 F	10 13 59	2 02 48	8♐45 04	15 30 04	26 25.7	21 43.2	14 01.5	28 41.1	21 34.3	15 24.8	3 58.5	23 04.2	26 56.0	28 22.0
26 Sa	10 17 55	3 00 40	22 21 59	29 21 00	26 22.9	21 30.6	13 40.0	29 19.4	21 57.7	15 26.7	3 54.0	23 04.3	26 54.6	28 20.9
27 Su	10 21 52	3 58 34	6♑27 05	13♑40 03	26 18.1	21 12.0	13 20.8	29 57.8	22 21.2	15 28.4	3 49.4	23 04.5	26 53.1	28 19.8
28 M	10 25 48	4 56 28	20 59 30	28 24 48	26 11.7	20 47.4	13 03.9	0♎36.3	22 44.8	15 29.9	3 44.9	23R 04.5	26 51.6	28 18.7
29 Tu	10 29 45	5 54 24	5♒55 08	13♒29 26	26 04.3	20 17.0	12 49.3	1 14.8	23 08.5	15 31.2	3 40.3	23 04.5	26 50.1	28 17.6
30 W	10 33 42	6 52 21	21 06 31	28 45 03	25 56.9	19 40.8	12 37.1	1 53.3	23 32.2	15 32.3	3 35.8	23 04.5	26 48.6	28 16.6
31 Th	10 37 38	7 50 20	6♓23 40	14♓00 58	25 50.7	18 59.3	12 27.4	2 31.9	23 55.9	15 33.3	3 31.3	23 04.4	26 47.0	28 15.5

Astro Data Dy Hr Mn	Planet Ingress Dy Hr Mn	Last Aspect Dy Hr Mn	☽ Ingress Dy Hr Mn	Last Aspect Dy Hr Mn	☽ Ingress Dy Hr Mn	☽ Phases & Eclipses Dy Hr Mn
☽0N 9 4:01	♂ ♍ 10 11:41	2 13:34 ♆ □	♑ 2 17:21	1 2:14 ♇ ☌	♒ 1 3:59	3 11:40 ○ 11♑19
♃∠♆ 22 11:48	☿ ♌ 11 4:12	4 16:47 ♇ ☌	♒ 4 17:31	2 21:17 ♀ ☍	♓ 3 3:07	10 1:49 ☾ 17♈36
♀ R 23 1:34	☊ ♈R 17 19:47	6 13:43 ♂ ☍	♓ 6 17:34	5 1:22 ♇ ⚹	♈ 5 3:20	17 18:33 ● 24♋56
☽0S 23 15:31	☉ ♌ 23 1:52	8 18:23 ♇ ⚹	♈ 8 19:20	7 4:14 ♇ □	♉ 7 6:26	25 22:08 ☽ 2♏43
	☿ ♍ 28 21:32	10 23:12 ☿ □	♉ 10 23:57	9 10:40 ♇ △	♊ 9 13:06	
☽0N 5 11:00		13 6:12 ♇ △	♊ 13 7:27	11 17:28 ♆ □	♋ 11 22:53	1 18:33 ○ 9♒16
⚳0S 9 20:31	☉ ♍ 23 9:02	15 12:37 ♆ □	♋ 15 17:15	14 7:48 ♇ ☍	♌ 14 10:37	8 10:30 ☾ 15♉39
☽0S 19 20:47	♂ ♎ 27 13:21	18 3:07 ♇ ☍	♌ 18 4:41	16 9:39 ☉ ☌	♍ 16 23:15	16 9:39 ● 23♌17
☿0S 21 3:28		20 14:10 ♀ ☌	♍ 20 17:14	19 8:52 ♇ △	♎ 19 11:55	24 9:58 ☽ 1♐00
☿ R 23 20:01		23 4:07 ♇ △	♎ 23 5:55	21 20:32 ☉ ⚹	♏ 21 23:23	31 1:37 ○ 7♓25
♅ R 29 2:39		25 15:06 ♇ □	♏ 25 16:56	24 5:11 ♇ ⚹	♐ 24 8:09	
♂0S 29 22:10		27 22:37 ♇ ⚹	♐ 28 0:25	26 11:57 ♂ □	♑ 26 13:06	
☿0N 30 18:51		29 23:52 ♀ △	♑ 30 3:45	28 11:50 ♇ ☌	♒ 28 14:33	
				30 3:05 ♅ □	♓ 30 13:58	

Astro Data

1 July 2023
Julian Day # 45107
SVP 4♓56'02"
GC 27♐10.0 ⚴ 26♌00.5
Eris 25♈13.3 ⚵ 5♋08.9
⚷ 19♈45.2 ⚶ 3♊36.9
☽ Mean ☊ 0♉35.5

1 August 2023
Julian Day # 45138
SVP 4♓55'56"
GC 27♐10.1 ⚴ 10♍09.4
Eris 25♈15.0R ⚵ 22♋21.9
⚷ 19♈55.7R ⚶ 15♊49.1
☽ Mean ☊ 28♈57.0

LONGITUDE — September 2023

Day	Sid.Time	☉	0 hr ☽	Noon☽	True☊	☿	♀	♂	⚳	♃	♄	♅	♆	♇
1 F	10 41 35	8♍48 21	21♓35 37	29♓06 27	25♈46.1	18♍12.9	12♌20.0	3♎10.5	24♎19.7	15♉34.0	3♓26.8	23♉04.2	26♓45.5	28♑14.5
2 Sa	10 45 31	9 46 23	6♈32 25	13♈52 41	25D43.7	17R22.2	12R15.1	3 49.2	24 43.6	15 34.5	3R22.3	23R04.0	26R43.9	28R13.5
3 Su	10 49 28	10 44 27	21 06 36	28 13 46	25 43.2	16 28.0	12D12.6	4 27.9	25 07.5	15 34.8	3 17.8	23 03.8	26 42.3	28 12.5
4 M	10 53 24	11 42 33	5♉13 57	12♉07 06	25 44.0	15 31.3	12 12.5	5 06.6	25 31.5	15R34.9	3 13.3	23 03.5	26 40.8	28 11.6
5 Tu	10 57 21	12 40 40	18 53 20	25 32 55	25 45.3	14 33.2	12 14.7	5 45.4	25 55.6	15 34.8	3 08.8	23 03.1	26 39.2	28 10.7
6 W	11 01 17	13 38 50	2♊06 11	8♊33 34	25R46.3	13 34.8	12 19.2	6 24.3	26 19.7	15 34.6	3 04.4	23 02.8	26 37.6	28 09.8
7 Th	11 05 14	14 37 02	14 55 33	21 12 39	25 46.2	12 37.5	12 26.0	7 03.2	26 43.9	15 34.1	3 00.0	23 02.3	26 36.0	28 08.9
8 F	11 09 11	15 35 17	27 25 23	3♋34 19	25 44.5	11 42.5	12 34.9	7 42.1	27 08.1	15 33.4	2 55.6	23 01.8	26 34.4	28 08.0
9 Sa	11 13 07	16 33 33	9♋39 59	15 42 52	25 41.0	10 51.2	12 46.1	8 21.1	27 32.4	15 32.5	2 51.2	23 01.3	26 32.7	28 07.2
10 Su	11 17 04	17 31 51	21 43 28	27 42 14	25 36.0	10 04.8	12 59.3	9 00.1	27 56.7	15 31.4	2 46.9	23 00.7	26 31.1	28 06.3
11 M	11 21 00	18 30 11	3♌39 37	9♌35 58	25 29.8	9 24.4	13 14.5	9 39.2	28 21.1	15 30.1	2 42.6	23 00.1	26 29.5	28 05.5
12 Tu	11 24 57	19 28 33	15 31 41	21 27 04	25 23.1	8 51.0	13 31.8	10 18.3	28 45.5	15 28.6	2 38.4	22 59.4	26 27.8	28 04.8
13 W	11 28 53	20 26 56	27 22 24	3♍17 58	25 16.5	8 25.6	13 50.9	10 57.5	29 10.0	15 26.9	2 34.1	22 58.6	26 26.2	28 04.0
14 Th	11 32 50	21 25 22	9♍14 01	15 10 46	25 10.8	8 08.7	14 11.9	11 36.7	29 34.5	15 25.0	2 29.9	22 57.8	26 24.5	28 03.3
15 F	11 36 46	22 23 50	21 08 27	27 07 16	25 06.3	8D00.8	14 34.6	12 15.9	29 59.1	15 22.9	2 25.8	22 57.0	26 22.9	28 02.6
16 Sa	11 40 43	23 22 19	3♎07 26	9♎09 11	25 03.5	8 02.2	14 59.1	12 55.2	0♏23.7	15 20.6	2 21.7	22 56.1	26 21.2	28 01.9
17 Su	11 44 39	24 20 51	15 12 44	21 18 20	25D02.3	8 13.1	15 25.3	13 34.6	0 48.4	15 18.1	2 17.6	22 55.2	26 19.6	28 01.2
18 M	11 48 36	25 19 24	27 26 16	3♏36 49	25 02.6	8 33.4	15 53.0	14 14.0	1 13.1	15 15.5	2 13.6	22 54.2	26 17.9	28 00.6
19 Tu	11 52 33	26 17 59	9♏50 18	16 07 02	25 03.8	9 02.9	16 22.3	14 53.4	1 37.9	15 12.6	2 09.7	22 53.2	26 16.2	28 00.0
20 W	11 56 29	27 16 35	22 27 23	28 51 42	25 05.4	9 41.4	16 53.1	15 32.9	2 02.7	15 09.5	2 05.8	22 52.1	26 14.6	27 59.4
21 Th	12 00 26	28 15 14	5♐20 21	11♐53 40	25 06.9	10 28.4	17 25.4	16 12.5	2 27.5	15 06.2	2 02.0	22 51.0	26 12.9	27 58.9
22 F	12 04 22	29 13 54	18 32 00	25 15 37	25R07.7	11 23.4	17 59.1	16 52.0	2 52.4	15 02.8	1 58.2	22 49.9	26 11.3	27 58.3
23 Sa	12 08 19	0♎12 36	2♑04 46	8♑59 33	25 07.5	12 25.8	18 34.0	17 31.7	3 17.3	14 59.1	1 54.4	22 48.7	26 09.6	27 57.8
24 Su	12 12 15	1 11 19	16 00 03	23 06 11	25 06.2	13 35.2	19 10.3	18 11.3	3 42.3	14 55.3	1 50.8	22 47.4	26 08.0	27 57.4
25 M	12 16 12	2 10 04	0♒17 42	7♒34 15	25 03.9	14 50.7	19 47.9	18 51.0	4 07.2	14 51.3	1 47.2	22 46.2	26 06.3	27 56.9
26 Tu	12 20 08	3 08 51	14 55 18	22 20 09	25 01.1	16 11.7	20 26.6	19 30.8	4 32.3	14 47.1	1 43.6	22 44.8	26 04.7	27 56.5
27 W	12 24 05	4 07 39	29 47 59	7♓17 48	24 58.3	17 37.6	21 06.5	20 10.6	4 57.3	14 42.7	1 40.2	22 43.4	26 03.0	27 56.1
28 Th	12 28 02	5 06 30	14♓48 35	22 19 12	24 55.9	19 07.8	21 47.6	20 50.4	5 22.4	14 38.2	1 36.8	22 42.0	26 01.4	27 55.7
29 F	12 31 58	6 05 22	29 48 32	7♈15 30	24 54.2	20 41.6	22 29.7	21 30.3	5 47.5	14 33.5	1 33.4	22 40.6	25 59.8	27 55.4
30 Sa	12 35 55	7 04 16	14♈39 04	21 58 21	24D53.6	22 18.5	23 12.9	22 10.3	6 12.7	14 28.6	1 30.2	22 39.1	25 58.1	27 55.1

LONGITUDE — October 2023

Day	Sid.Time	☉	0 hr ☽	Noon☽	True☊	☿	♀	♂	⚳	♃	♄	♅	♆	♇
1 Su	12 39 51	8♎03 12	29♈12 33	6♉21 05	24♈53.8	23♍57.9	23♌57.1	22♎50.3	6♏37.8	14♉23.5	1♓27.0	22♉37.5	25♓56.5	27♑54.8
2 M	12 43 48	9 02 11	13♉23 30	20 19 29	24 54.7	25 39.3	24 42.3	23 30.3	7 03.0	14R18.3	1R23.8	22R36.0	25R54.9	27R54.6
3 Tu	12 47 44	10 01 12	27 08 56	3♊51 51	24 55.9	27 22.4	25 28.4	24 10.4	7 28.3	14 12.9	1 20.8	22 34.4	25 53.3	27 54.3
4 W	12 51 41	11 00 15	10♊28 23	16 58 48	24 57.1	29 06.8	26 15.4	24 50.5	7 53.5	14 07.3	1 17.8	22 32.7	25 51.7	27 54.1
5 Th	12 55 37	11 59 20	23 23 27	29 42 46	24 57.9	0♎52.0	27 03.3	25 30.7	8 18.8	14 01.6	1 14.9	22 31.0	25 50.2	27 54.0
6 F	12 59 34	12 58 28	5♋57 13	12♋07 19	24R58.3	2 37.9	27 52.1	26 10.9	8 44.2	13 55.7	1 12.1	22 29.3	25 48.6	27 53.8
7 Sa	13 03 31	13 57 38	18 13 38	24 16 44	24 58.1	4 24.1	28 41.6	26 51.2	9 09.5	13 49.7	1 09.4	22 27.5	25 47.0	27 53.7
8 Su	13 07 27	14 56 51	0♌17 10	6♌15 31	24 57.3	6 10.6	29 32.0	27 31.5	9 34.9	13 43.6	1 06.8	22 25.7	25 45.5	27 53.6
9 M	13 11 24	15 56 05	12 12 19	18 08 05	24 56.3	7 57.0	0♍23.1	28 11.9	10 00.3	13 37.3	1 04.2	22 23.9	25 43.9	27 53.6
10 Tu	13 15 20	16 55 22	24 03 21	29 58 34	24 55.1	9 43.3	1 14.9	28 52.4	10 25.7	13 30.8	1 01.7	22 22.0	25 42.4	27D53.5
11 W	13 19 17	17 54 41	5♍54 11	11♍50 37	24 54.0	11 29.3	2 07.5	29 32.8	10 51.2	13 24.2	0 59.4	22 20.1	25 40.9	27 53.5
12 Th	13 23 13	18 54 02	17 48 13	23 47 21	24 53.2	13 14.9	3 00.7	0♏13.4	11 16.7	13 17.5	0 57.1	22 18.2	25 39.4	27 53.5
13 F	13 27 10	19 53 26	29 48 18	5♎51 19	24 52.6	15 00.2	3 54.5	0 54.0	11 42.2	13 10.7	0 54.8	22 16.2	25 37.9	27 53.6
14 Sa	13 31 06	20 52 51	11♎56 40	18 04 32	24D52.4	16 44.9	4 49.0	1 34.6	12 07.7	13 03.7	0 52.7	22 14.2	25 36.4	27 53.7
15 Su	13 35 03	21 52 19	24 15 06	0♏28 30	24 52.3	18 29.1	5 44.1	2 15.3	12 33.2	12 56.7	0 50.7	22 12.2	25 35.0	27 53.8
16 M	13 39 00	22 51 49	6♏44 53	13 04 22	24 52.5	20 12.7	6 39.8	2 56.0	12 58.8	12 49.5	0 48.8	22 10.1	25 33.6	27 54.0
17 Tu	13 42 56	23 51 20	19 27 02	25 52 59	24 52.6	21 55.7	7 36.0	3 36.8	13 24.4	12 42.2	0 46.9	22 08.0	25 32.1	27 54.1
18 W	13 46 53	24 50 54	2♐22 18	8♐55 05	24R52.6	23 38.1	8 32.8	4 17.6	13 50.0	12 34.8	0 45.2	22 05.9	25 30.7	27 54.3
19 Th	13 50 49	25 50 29	15 31 22	22 11 14	24 52.6	25 19.9	9 30.2	4 58.5	14 15.6	12 27.4	0 43.6	22 03.8	25 29.4	27 54.6
20 F	13 54 46	26 50 06	28 54 43	5♑41 53	24 52.5	27 01.0	10 28.0	5 39.4	14 41.2	12 19.8	0 42.0	22 01.6	25 28.0	27 54.8
21 Sa	13 58 42	27 49 45	12♑32 44	19 27 14	24D52.3	28 41.6	11 26.3	6 20.4	15 06.8	12 12.2	0 40.6	21 59.4	25 26.6	27 55.1
22 Su	14 02 39	28 49 26	26 25 21	3♒26 58	24 52.3	0♏21.5	12 25.1	7 01.4	15 32.5	12 04.4	0 39.2	21 57.2	25 25.3	27 55.5
23 M	14 06 35	29 49 08	10♒31 55	17 40 00	24 52.5	2 00.8	13 24.4	7 42.5	15 58.2	11 56.7	0 38.0	21 55.0	25 24.0	27 55.8
24 Tu	14 10 32	0♏48 52	24 50 52	2♓04 10	24 52.9	3 39.5	14 24.1	8 23.6	16 23.8	11 48.8	0 36.8	21 52.7	25 22.7	27 56.2
25 W	14 14 29	1 48 37	9♓19 26	16 36 08	24 53.5	5 17.6	15 24.3	9 04.7	16 49.5	11 40.9	0 35.8	21 50.4	25 21.5	27 56.6
26 Th	14 18 25	2 48 25	23 53 38	1♈11 16	24 54.1	6 55.1	16 24.9	9 46.0	17 15.2	11 33.0	0 34.8	21 48.1	25 20.2	27 57.0
27 F	14 22 22	3 48 14	8♈28 20	15 44 06	24R54.6	8 32.1	17 25.9	10 27.2	17 40.9	11 24.9	0 33.9	21 45.8	25 19.0	27 57.5
28 Sa	14 26 18	4 48 04	22 57 48	0♉08 44	24 54.6	10 08.5	18 27.3	11 08.5	18 06.6	11 16.9	0 33.2	21 43.4	25 17.8	27 58.0
29 Su	14 30 15	5 47 57	7♉16 13	14 19 38	24 54.2	11 44.5	19 29.2	11 49.9	18 32.3	11 08.8	0 32.5	21 41.1	25 16.6	27 58.5
30 M	14 34 11	6 47 52	21 18 29	28 12 19	24 53.1	13 19.9	20 31.4	12 31.3	18 58.1	11 00.7	0 32.0	21 38.7	25 15.5	27 59.1
31 Tu	14 38 08	7 47 49	5♊00 49	11♊43 47	24 51.5	14 54.9	21 33.9	13 12.7	19 23.8	10 52.6	0 31.6	21 36.3	25 14.4	27 59.6

Astro Data

	Dy Hr Mn
☽ 0N	1 20:26
♀ D	4 1:21
♃ R	4 14:12
☿ D	15 20:24
☽ 0S	16 2:18
☉ 0S	23 6:51
☽ 0N	29 7:12
☿ 0S	7 9:37
♇ D	11 1:12
☽ 0S	13 8:55
☽ 0N	26 17:08

Planet Ingress

	Dy Hr Mn
⚳ ♏	15 12:51
☉ ♎	23 6:51
☿ ♎	5 0:10
♀ ♍	9 1:12
♂ ♏	12 4:05
☿ ♏	22 6:50
☉ ♏	23 16:22

Last Aspect / ☽ Ingress (September)

Last Aspect Dy Hr Mn		☽ Ingress Dy Hr Mn
1 10:37	♇ ⚹	♈ 1 13:26
3 11:58	♇ □	♉ 3 15:01
5 16:47	♇ △	♊ 5 20:08
7 22:23	♆ □	♋ 8 5:01
10 12:48	♇ ☍	♌ 10 16:37
12 15:07	♅ □	♍ 13 5:19
15 13:51	♇ △	♎ 15 17:46
18 1:07	♇ □	♏ 18 4:59
20 10:23	♇ ⚹	♐ 20 14:07
22 19:33	☉ □	♑ 22 20:21
24 20:07	♇ ☌	♒ 24 23:31
26 12:40	♅ □	♓ 27 0:19
28 20:59	♇ ⚹	♈ 29 0:18

Last Aspect / ☽ Ingress (October)

Last Aspect Dy Hr Mn		☽ Ingress Dy Hr Mn
30 21:51	♇ □	♉ 1 1:19
3 1:21	♇ △	♊ 3 5:04
5 6:36	♀ ⚹	♋ 5 12:33
7 19:13	♇ ☍	♌ 7 23:26
10 9:38	♂ ⚹	♍ 10 12:03
12 20:12	♇ △	♎ 13 0:23
15 7:02	♇ □	♏ 15 11:05
17 15:45	♇ ⚹	♐ 17 19:38
19 19:03	☉ ⚹	♑ 20 1:56
22 6:02	☿ □	♒ 22 6:07
23 19:05	♅ □	♓ 24 8:34
26 6:40	♇ ⚹	♈ 26 10:03
28 8:21	♇ □	♉ 28 11:45
30 11:37	♇ △	♊ 30 15:09

☽ Phases & Eclipses

Dy Hr Mn		
6 22:22	☾	14♊04
15 1:41	●	21♍59
22 19:33	☽	29♐32
29 9:59	○	6♈00
6 13:49	☾	13♋03
14 17:56	●	21♎08
14 18:00:41	●	A 05'17"
22 3:31	☽	28♑28
28 20:25	○	5♉09
28 20:15	●	P 0.122

Astro Data

1 September 2023
Julian Day # 45169
SVP 4♓55'52"
GC 27♐10.2 ⚴ 24♍24.1
Eris 25♈07.0R ⚵ 8♌35.3
⚷ 19♈18.0R ⚶ 26♊25.0
☽ Mean ☊ 27♈18.5

1 October 2023
Julian Day # 45199
SVP 4♓55'49"
GC 27♐10.3 ⚴ 8♎08.6
Eris 24♈52.1R ⚵ 22♌59.3
⚷ 18♈07.2R ⚶ 4♋05.1
☽ Mean ☊ 25♈43.2

November 2023 LONGITUDE

Day	Sid.Time	☉	0 hr ☽	Noon ☽	True ☊	☿	♀	♂	⚳	♃	♄	♅	♆	♇
1 W	14 42 04	8♏47 48	18♊21 09	24♊52 56	24♈49.5	16♏29.4	22♍36.9	13♏54.3	19♏49.5	10♉44.5	0♓31.2	21♉33.9	25♓13.3	28♑00.3
2 Th	14 46 01	9 47 49	1♋19 16	7♋40 23	24R 47.6	18 03.4	23 40.2	14 35.8	20 15.3	10R 36.3	0R 31.0	21R 31.5	25R 12.2	28 00.9
3 F	14 49 58	10 47 52	13 56 36	20 08 19	24 45.9	19 37.0	24 43.8	15 17.4	20 41.0	10 28.1	0D 30.9	21 29.1	25 11.2	28 01.6
4 Sa	14 53 54	11 47 58	26 16 00	2♌20 09	24D 44.9	21 10.2	25 47.8	15 59.1	21 06.8	10 20.0	0 30.8	21 26.6	25 10.1	28 02.3
5 Su	14 57 51	12 48 05	8♌21 20	14 20 07	24 44.6	22 43.0	26 52.1	16 40.8	21 32.6	10 11.8	0 30.9	21 24.2	25 09.1	28 03.0
6 M	15 01 47	13 48 14	20 17 06	26 12 55	24 45.1	24 15.3	27 56.7	17 22.6	21 58.3	10 03.7	0 31.1	21 21.7	25 08.2	28 03.7
7 Tu	15 05 44	14 48 26	2♍08 08	8♍03 24	24 46.3	25 47.3	29 01.5	18 04.4	22 24.1	9 55.6	0 31.4	21 19.2	25 07.2	28 04.5
8 W	15 09 40	15 48 39	13 59 16	19 56 19	24 47.9	27 18.9	0♎06.7	18 46.3	22 49.9	9 47.5	0 31.7	21 16.8	25 06.3	28 05.3
9 Th	15 13 37	16 48 55	25 55 05	1♎56 04	24 49.6	28 50.2	1 12.2	19 28.2	23 15.6	9 39.5	0 32.2	21 14.3	25 05.4	28 06.1
10 F	15 17 33	17 49 12	7♎59 43	14 06 26	24R 50.9	0♐21.0	2 17.9	20 10.2	23 41.4	9 31.5	0 32.8	21 11.8	25 04.6	28 07.0
11 Sa	15 21 30	18 49 31	20 16 35	26 30 26	24 51.3	1 51.5	3 23.9	20 52.2	24 07.2	9 23.5	0 33.5	21 09.3	25 03.7	28 07.9
12 Su	15 25 27	19 49 52	2♏48 13	9♏10 05	24 50.5	3 21.7	4 30.2	21 34.3	24 32.9	9 15.6	0 34.3	21 06.8	25 02.9	28 08.8
13 M	15 29 23	20 50 15	15 36 07	22 06 19	24 48.3	4 51.4	5 36.7	22 16.4	24 58.7	9 07.7	0 35.2	21 04.3	25 02.2	28 09.7
14 Tu	15 33 20	21 50 40	28 40 38	5♐18 56	24 44.9	6 20.7	6 43.5	22 58.6	25 24.4	9 00.0	0 36.2	21 01.8	25 01.4	28 10.7
15 W	15 37 16	22 51 06	12♐01 02	18 46 42	24 40.6	7 49.7	7 50.4	23 40.8	25 50.2	8 52.3	0 37.4	20 59.3	25 00.7	28 11.7
16 Th	15 41 13	23 51 34	25 35 39	2♑27 33	24 36.0	9 18.2	8 57.6	24 23.1	26 15.9	8 44.6	0 38.6	20 56.8	25 00.0	28 12.7
17 F	15 45 09	24 52 03	9♑22 07	16 18 59	24 31.6	10 46.3	10 05.1	25 05.5	26 41.7	8 37.1	0 39.9	20 54.3	24 59.4	28 13.8
18 Sa	15 49 06	25 52 34	23 17 49	0♒18 20	24 28.1	12 13.9	11 12.7	25 47.8	27 07.4	8 29.6	0 41.3	20 51.9	24 58.8	28 14.8
19 Su	15 53 02	26 53 05	7♒20 12	14 23 11	24D 25.9	13 40.9	12 20.5	26 30.2	27 33.1	8 22.3	0 42.9	20 49.4	24 58.2	28 15.9
20 M	15 56 59	27 53 38	21 26 59	28 31 24	24 25.3	15 07.4	13 28.6	27 12.7	27 58.9	8 15.0	0 44.5	20 46.9	24 57.6	28 17.1
21 Tu	16 00 56	28 54 12	5♓36 13	12♓41 13	24 25.9	16 33.2	14 36.8	27 55.2	28 24.6	8 07.9	0 46.2	20 44.4	24 57.1	28 18.2
22 W	16 04 52	29 54 47	19 46 13	26 50 58	24 27.4	17 58.3	15 45.3	28 37.8	28 50.2	8 00.8	0 48.1	20 42.0	24 56.6	28 19.4
23 Th	16 08 49	0♐55 24	3♈55 16	10♈58 52	24R 28.8	19 22.7	16 53.9	29 20.4	29 15.9	7 53.9	0 50.0	20 39.5	24 56.2	28 20.6
24 F	16 12 45	1 56 01	18 01 27	25 02 43	24 29.4	20 46.1	18 02.7	0♐03.1	29 41.6	7 47.1	0 52.1	20 37.1	24 55.7	28 21.8
25 Sa	16 16 42	2 56 40	2♉02 21	8♉59 56	24 28.5	22 08.5	19 11.6	0 45.8	0♐07.2	7 40.5	0 54.2	20 34.7	24 55.4	28 23.0
26 Su	16 20 38	3 57 20	15 55 08	22 47 31	24 25.6	23 29.8	20 20.8	1 28.6	0 32.8	7 33.9	0 56.4	20 32.3	24 55.0	28 24.3
27 M	16 24 35	4 58 01	29 36 45	6♊22 26	24 20.7	24 49.8	21 30.1	2 11.4	0 58.5	7 27.5	0 58.8	20 29.9	24 54.7	28 25.6
28 Tu	16 28 31	5 58 44	13♊04 16	19 41 59	24 14.0	26 08.3	22 39.6	2 54.2	1 24.1	7 21.3	1 01.2	20 27.5	24 54.4	28 26.9
29 W	16 32 28	6 59 28	26 15 23	2♋44 20	24 06.3	27 25.0	23 49.3	3 37.2	1 49.6	7 15.2	1 03.7	20 25.1	24 54.1	28 28.2
30 Th	16 36 25	8 00 14	9♋08 49	15 28 50	23 58.3	28 39.9	24 59.1	4 20.1	2 15.2	7 09.2	1 06.4	20 22.8	24 53.9	28 29.6

December 2023 LONGITUDE

Day	Sid.Time	☉	0 hr ☽	Noon ☽	True ☊	☿	♀	♂	⚳	♃	♄	♅	♆	♇
1 F	16 40 21	9♐01 01	21♋44 33	27♋56 10	23♈50.8	29♐52.5	26♎09.0	5♐03.1	2♐40.8	7♉03.4	1♓09.1	20♉20.4	24♓53.7	28♑31.0
2 Sa	16 44 18	10 01 49	4♌03 59	10♌08 22	23R 44.8	1♑02.4	27 19.2	5 46.2	3 06.3	6R 57.8	1 11.9	20R 18.1	24R 53.6	28 32.3
3 Su	16 48 14	11 02 39	16 09 45	22 08 39	23 40.5	2 09.5	28 29.4	6 29.3	3 31.8	6 52.3	1 14.8	20 15.8	24 53.5	28 33.8
4 M	16 52 11	12 03 30	28 05 36	4♍01 13	23D 38.3	3 13.1	29 39.8	7 12.5	3 57.3	6 46.9	1 17.9	20 13.6	24 53.4	28 35.2
5 Tu	16 56 07	13 04 22	9♍56 05	15 50 54	23 37.9	4 12.8	0♏50.4	7 55.7	4 22.8	6 41.8	1 21.0	20 11.3	24 53.3	28 36.7
6 W	17 00 04	14 05 16	21 46 17	27 42 56	23 38.8	5 08.1	2 01.1	8 39.0	4 48.2	6 36.8	1 24.2	20 09.1	24D 53.3	28 38.1
7 Th	17 04 00	15 06 10	3♎41 30	9♎42 37	23 40.0	5 58.3	3 11.9	9 22.3	5 13.6	6 32.0	1 27.4	20 06.9	24 53.3	28 39.6
8 F	17 07 57	16 07 07	15 46 56	21 55 01	23R 40.8	6 42.6	4 22.8	10 05.7	5 39.0	6 27.3	1 30.8	20 04.7	24 53.4	28 41.2
9 Sa	17 11 54	17 08 04	28 07 24	4♏24 32	23 40.2	7 20.4	5 33.8	10 49.1	6 04.4	6 22.9	1 34.3	20 02.6	24 53.4	28 42.7
10 Su	17 15 50	18 09 03	10♏46 49	17 14 30	23 37.4	7 50.8	6 45.0	11 32.6	6 29.8	6 18.6	1 37.9	20 00.4	24 53.6	28 44.2
11 M	17 19 47	19 10 02	23 47 47	0♐26 43	23 32.2	8 13.0	7 56.3	12 16.1	6 55.1	6 14.5	1 41.5	19 58.3	24 53.7	28 45.8
12 Tu	17 23 43	20 11 03	7♐11 13	14 01 05	23 24.7	8R 26.0	9 07.6	12 59.7	7 20.4	6 10.6	1 45.3	19 56.3	24 53.9	28 47.4
13 W	17 27 40	21 12 05	20 55 58	27 55 23	23 15.3	8 29.1	10 19.1	13 43.3	7 45.7	6 06.9	1 49.1	19 54.2	24 54.1	28 49.0
14 Th	17 31 36	22 13 07	4♑58 46	12♑05 27	23 05.1	8 21.5	11 30.7	14 26.9	8 10.9	6 03.4	1 53.0	19 52.2	24 54.4	28 50.7
15 F	17 35 33	23 14 10	19 14 43	26 25 47	22 55.3	8 02.7	12 42.4	15 10.7	8 36.1	6 00.1	1 57.0	19 50.3	24 54.7	28 52.3
16 Sa	17 39 30	24 15 14	3♒37 54	10♒50 20	22 46.9	7 32.2	13 54.2	15 54.4	9 01.3	5 57.0	2 01.1	19 48.3	24 55.0	28 54.0
17 Su	17 43 26	25 16 18	18 02 27	25 13 38	22 40.8	6 50.2	15 06.0	16 38.2	9 26.4	5 54.1	2 05.3	19 46.4	24 55.4	28 55.6
18 M	17 47 23	26 17 22	2♓23 25	9♓31 24	22 37.3	5 57.2	16 18.0	17 22.1	9 51.5	5 51.4	2 09.5	19 44.5	24 55.8	28 57.3
19 Tu	17 51 19	27 18 27	16 37 17	23 40 54	22D 36.1	4 54.1	17 30.0	18 06.0	10 16.6	5 48.9	2 13.9	19 42.7	24 56.2	28 59.0
20 W	17 55 16	28 19 32	0♈42 06	7♈40 52	22 36.3	3 42.7	18 42.1	18 49.9	10 41.6	5 46.6	2 18.3	19 40.9	24 56.7	29 00.8
21 Th	17 59 12	29 20 37	14 37 10	21 31 01	22R 36.7	2 24.8	19 54.3	19 33.9	11 06.6	5 44.5	2 22.8	19 39.1	24 57.2	29 02.5
22 F	18 03 09	0♑21 42	28 22 29	5♉11 35	22 36.0	1 03.2	21 06.5	20 17.9	11 31.6	5 42.6	2 27.4	19 37.4	24 57.8	29 04.2
23 Sa	18 07 05	1 22 48	11♉58 19	18 42 40	22 33.2	29♐40.4	22 18.9	21 02.0	11 56.5	5 40.9	2 32.0	19 35.7	24 58.3	29 06.0
24 Su	18 11 02	2 23 54	25 24 37	2♊04 04	22 27.6	28 19.4	23 31.3	21 46.1	12 21.3	5 39.4	2 36.8	19 34.1	24 58.9	29 07.8
25 M	18 14 59	3 25 00	8♊40 56	15 15 05	22 19.0	27 02.6	24 43.8	22 30.3	12 46.2	5 38.1	2 41.6	19 32.5	24 59.6	29 09.6
26 Tu	18 18 55	4 26 06	21 46 22	28 14 39	22 07.8	25 52.4	25 56.4	23 14.5	13 11.0	5 37.1	2 46.5	19 30.9	25 00.3	29 11.4
27 W	18 22 52	5 27 13	4♋39 49	11♋01 44	21 54.8	24 50.5	27 09.0	23 58.7	13 35.7	5 36.2	2 51.4	19 29.4	25 01.0	29 13.2
28 Th	18 26 48	6 28 20	17 20 20	23 35 36	21 41.2	23 58.1	28 21.7	24 43.0	14 00.4	5 35.6	2 56.5	19 27.9	25 01.7	29 15.0
29 F	18 30 45	7 29 28	29 47 32	5♌56 14	21 28.2	23 16.1	29 34.5	25 27.4	14 25.1	5 35.1	3 01.6	19 26.5	25 02.5	29 16.8
30 Sa	18 34 41	8 30 35	12♌01 51	18 04 36	21 16.8	22 44.6	0♐47.3	26 11.8	14 49.7	5D 34.9	3 06.7	19 25.1	25 03.3	29 18.7
31 Su	18 38 38	9 31 43	24 04 48	0♍02 46	21 07.9	22 23.6	2 00.2	26 56.2	15 14.2	5 34.9	3 12.0	19 23.7	25 04.1	29 20.5

Astro Data	Dy Hr Mn
♄ D	4 7:04
♃∠♆	5 21:05
☽ 0S	9 16:38
♀0S	11 5:22
☽ 0N	23 0:26
♆ D	6 13:23
☽ 0S	7 0:37
☿ R	13 7:09
☽ 0N	20 5:18
♃ D	31 2:42

Planet Ingress	Dy Hr Mn
♀ ♎	8 9:32
☿ ♐	10 6:26
☉ ♐	22 14:04
♂ ♐	24 10:16
⚳ ♐	25 5:15
☿ ♑	1 14:33
♀ ♏	4 18:52
☉ ♑	22 3:28
☿ ♐R	23 6:19
♀ ♐	29 20:25

Last Aspect Dy Hr Mn		☽ Ingress	Dy Hr Mn
1 12:38	♆ □	♋	1 21:31
4 3:29	♇ ☍	♌	4 7:22
6 7:26	☿ □	♍	6 19:40
9 4:56	☿ ⚹	♎	9 8:09
11 15:07	♇ □	♏	11 18:40
13 23:05	♇ ⚹	♐	14 2:24
15 22:58	♆ □	♑	16 7:43
18 8:29	♇ ☌	♒	18 11:29
20 10:51	☉ □	♓	20 14:30
22 15:11	♂ △	♈	22 17:21
24 17:42	♇ □	♉	24 20:30
26 21:53	♇ △	♊	27 0:41
29 1:04	☿ ☍	♋	29 6:55

Last Aspect Dy Hr Mn		☽ Ingress	Dy Hr Mn
1 13:08	♇ ☍	♌	1 16:02
4 2:12	♀ ⚹	♍	4 3:51
6 13:51	♇ △	♎	6 16:36
9 1:06	♇ □	♏	9 3:36
11 8:58	♇ ⚹	♐	11 11:12
13 6:50	♆ □	♑	13 15:33
15 16:05	♇ ☌	♒	15 17:57
17 12:05	☉ ⚹	♓	17 19:59
19 21:05	♇ ⚹	♈	19 22:48
22 2:48	☉ △	♉	22 2:51
24 6:41	♇ △	♊	24 8:16
26 7:57	☿ ☍	♋	26 15:16
28 22:58	♇ ☍	♌	29 0:24
31 5:19	♂ △	♍	31 11:54

☽ Phases & Eclipses Dy Hr Mn	
5 8:38	☾ 12♌40
13 9:29	● 20♏44
20 10:51	☽ 27♒51
27 9:17	○ 4♊51
5 5:50	☾ 12♍49
12 23:33	● 20♐40
19 18:40	☽ 27♓35
27 0:34	○ 4♋58

Astro Data

1 November 2023
Julian Day # 45230
SVP 4♓55'45"
GC 27♐10.3 ⚴ 22♎07.9
Eris 24♈33.8R ⚵ 5♍57.5
⚷ 16♈44.6R ⚶ 7♋29.6
☽ Mean ☊ 24♈04.7

1 December 2023
Julian Day # 45260
SVP 4♓55'40"
GC 27♐10.4 ⚴ 5♏12.1
Eris 24♈18.4R ⚵ 15♍44.2
⚷ 15♈45.0R ⚶ 4♋33.3R
☽ Mean ☊ 22♈29.4

LONGITUDE — January 2024

Day	Sid.Time	☉	0 hr ☽	Noon ☽	True ☊	☿	♀	♂	⚳	♃	♄	♅	♆	♇
1 M	18 42 34	10♑32 52	5♍58 58	11♍53 51	21♈01.9	22♐12.7	3♐13.2	27♐40.7	15♐38.8	5♉35.1	3♓17.3	19♉22.4	25♓05.0	29♑22.4
2 Tu	18 46 31	11 34 00	17 47 59	23 41 57	20R58.5	22D11.5	4 26.2	28 25.2	16 03.2	5 35.5	3 22.6	19R21.1	25 05.9	29 24.3
3 W	18 50 28	12 35 09	29 36 22	5♎31 54	20D57.3	22 19.2	5 39.3	29 09.8	16 27.6	5 36.1	3 28.1	19 19.9	25 06.9	29 26.1
4 Th	18 54 24	13 36 19	11♎29 15	17 29 06	20R57.2	22 35.1	6 52.4	29 54.4	16 52.0	5 36.9	3 33.6	19 18.7	25 07.8	29 28.0
5 F	18 58 21	14 37 28	23 32 11	29 39 10	20 57.0	22 58.6	8 05.6	0♑39.1	17 16.3	5 37.9	3 39.2	19 17.6	25 08.8	29 29.9
6 Sa	19 02 17	15 38 38	5♏50 44	12♏07 30	20 55.6	23 28.8	9 18.8	1 23.8	17 40.6	5 39.1	3 44.8	19 16.5	25 09.9	29 31.8
7 Su	19 06 14	16 39 48	18 30 02	24 58 48	20 52.1	24 05.2	10 32.1	2 08.6	18 04.8	5 40.5	3 50.5	19 15.5	25 10.9	29 33.7
8 M	19 10 10	17 40 58	1♐34 11	8♐16 25	20 45.7	24 47.1	11 45.4	2 53.4	18 28.9	5 42.2	3 56.3	19 14.5	25 12.0	29 35.7
9 Tu	19 14 07	18 42 08	15 05 34	22 01 33	20 36.6	25 33.8	12 58.8	3 38.2	18 53.0	5 44.0	4 02.1	19 13.5	25 13.2	29 37.6
10 W	19 18 04	19 43 19	29 04 05	6♑12 41	20 25.3	26 25.0	14 12.2	4 23.1	19 17.1	5 46.0	4 08.0	19 12.7	25 14.3	29 39.5
11 Th	19 22 00	20 44 29	13♑26 42	20 45 18	20 12.9	27 20.1	15 25.7	5 08.1	19 41.1	5 48.3	4 13.9	19 11.8	25 15.5	29 41.4
12 F	19 25 57	21 45 38	28 07 29	5♒32 12	20 00.7	28 18.7	16 39.2	5 53.0	20 05.0	5 50.8	4 19.9	19 11.0	25 16.7	29 43.4
13 Sa	19 29 53	22 46 48	12♒58 19	20 24 41	19 50.0	29 20.4	17 52.7	6 38.0	20 28.8	5 53.4	4 26.0	19 10.3	25 18.0	29 45.3
14 Su	19 33 50	23 47 56	27 50 14	5♓13 59	19 42.0	0♑24.9	19 06.3	7 23.1	20 52.6	5 56.3	4 32.1	19 09.6	25 19.3	29 47.3
15 M	19 37 46	24 49 04	12♓35 04	19 52 48	19 37.0	1 32.0	20 19.9	8 08.2	21 16.3	5 59.3	4 38.2	19 09.0	25 20.6	29 49.2
16 Tu	19 41 43	25 50 12	27 06 38	4♈16 11	19 34.6	2 41.3	21 33.5	8 53.3	21 40.0	6 02.6	4 44.4	19 08.4	25 21.9	29 51.2
17 W	19 45 39	26 51 18	11♈21 16	18 21 45	19 34.1	3 52.7	22 47.2	9 38.4	22 03.5	6 06.0	4 50.7	19 07.8	25 23.3	29 53.1
18 Th	19 49 36	27 52 24	25 17 41	2♉09 12	19 34.1	5 05.9	24 00.8	10 23.6	22 27.1	6 09.6	4 57.0	19 07.3	25 24.7	29 55.1
19 F	19 53 33	28 53 29	8♉56 26	15 39 38	19 33.2	6 20.8	25 14.6	11 08.9	22 50.5	6 13.5	5 03.4	19 06.9	25 26.1	29 57.0
20 Sa	19 57 29	29 54 33	22 19 02	28 54 51	19 30.3	7 37.3	26 28.3	11 54.2	23 13.9	6 17.5	5 09.8	19 06.5	25 27.6	29 59.0
21 Su	20 01 26	0♒55 36	5♊27 20	11♊56 41	19 24.6	8 55.2	27 42.1	12 39.5	23 37.2	6 21.7	5 16.2	19 06.2	25 29.0	0♒00.9
22 M	20 05 22	1 56 39	18 23 04	24 46 39	19 15.9	10 14.4	28 55.9	13 24.8	24 00.4	6 26.1	5 22.7	19 05.9	25 30.5	0 02.9
23 Tu	20 09 19	2 57 41	1♋07 32	7♋25 48	19 04.5	11 34.8	0♑09.7	14 10.2	24 23.5	6 30.7	5 29.3	19 05.7	25 32.1	0 04.8
24 W	20 13 15	3 58 41	13 41 31	19 54 45	18 51.3	12 56.4	1 23.5	14 55.6	24 46.6	6 35.4	5 35.8	19 05.5	25 33.6	0 06.8
25 Th	20 17 12	4 59 41	26 05 31	2♌13 54	18 37.4	14 19.0	2 37.4	15 41.1	25 09.6	6 40.4	5 42.5	19 05.4	25 35.2	0 08.7
26 F	20 21 08	6 00 40	8♌19 55	14 23 41	18 24.0	15 42.6	3 51.3	16 26.6	25 32.5	6 45.5	5 49.1	19D05.3	25 36.8	0 10.7
27 Sa	20 25 05	7 01 39	20 25 17	26 24 54	18 12.2	17 07.1	5 05.2	17 12.1	25 55.3	6 50.8	5 55.8	19 05.3	25 38.4	0 12.6
28 Su	20 29 02	8 02 36	2♍22 43	8♍18 59	18 02.8	18 32.6	6 19.1	17 57.7	26 18.1	6 56.3	6 02.6	19 05.3	25 40.1	0 14.5
29 M	20 32 58	9 03 33	14 13 59	20 08 05	17 56.3	19 59.0	7 33.1	18 43.3	26 40.7	7 02.0	6 09.3	19 05.4	25 41.8	0 16.5
30 Tu	20 36 55	10 04 29	26 01 41	1♎55 15	17 52.5	21 26.2	8 47.1	19 28.9	27 03.3	7 07.8	6 16.1	19 05.6	25 43.5	0 18.4
31 W	20 40 51	11 05 24	7♎49 17	13 44 21	17D51.2	22 54.2	10 01.1	20 14.6	27 25.8	7 13.8	6 23.0	19 05.8	25 45.2	0 20.3

LONGITUDE — February 2024

Day	Sid.Time	☉	0 hr ☽	Noon ☽	True ☊	☿	♀	♂	⚳	♃	♄	♅	♆	♇
1 Th	20 44 48	12♒06 18	19♎41 02	25♎39 59	17♈51.3	24♑23.0	11♑15.1	21♑00.3	27♐48.2	7♉19.9	6♓29.8	19♉06.0	25♓47.0	0♒22.2
2 F	20 48 44	13 07 12	1♏41 51	7♏47 18	17R51.9	25 52.7	12 29.2	21 46.0	28 10.5	7 26.3	6 36.8	19 06.3	25 48.7	0 24.2
3 Sa	20 52 41	14 08 05	13 57 01	20 11 42	17 51.8	27 23.1	13 43.2	22 31.8	28 32.7	7 32.8	6 43.7	19 06.7	25 50.5	0 26.1
4 Su	20 56 37	15 08 57	26 31 57	2♐58 22	17 50.1	28 54.2	14 57.3	23 17.6	28 54.9	7 39.4	6 50.7	19 07.1	25 52.3	0 28.0
5 M	21 00 34	16 09 48	9♐31 28	16 11 40	17 46.3	0♒26.2	16 11.4	24 03.5	29 16.9	7 46.3	6 57.7	19 07.5	25 54.2	0 29.9
6 Tu	21 04 31	17 10 39	22 59 14	29 54 19	17 40.0	1 58.9	17 25.5	24 49.3	29 38.9	7 53.3	7 04.7	19 08.0	25 56.0	0 31.8
7 W	21 08 27	18 11 29	6♑56 51	14♑06 34	17 31.8	3 32.4	18 39.7	25 35.2	0♑00.7	8 00.4	7 11.7	19 08.6	25 57.9	0 33.7
8 Th	21 12 24	19 12 17	21 22 59	28 45 24	17 22.4	5 06.6	19 53.8	26 21.2	0 22.5	8 07.7	7 18.8	19 09.2	25 59.8	0 35.5
9 F	21 16 20	20 13 04	6♒12 54	13♒44 24	17 12.9	6 41.7	21 08.0	27 07.2	0 44.1	8 15.2	7 25.9	19 09.9	26 01.7	0 37.4
10 Sa	21 20 17	21 13 51	21 18 40	28 54 23	17 04.7	8 17.5	22 22.2	27 53.2	1 05.7	8 22.8	7 33.1	19 10.6	26 03.7	0 39.3
11 Su	21 24 13	22 14 35	6♓30 15	14♓04 55	16 58.5	9 54.1	23 36.3	28 39.2	1 27.1	8 30.6	7 40.2	19 11.4	26 05.6	0 41.1
12 M	21 28 10	23 15 18	21 37 13	29 06 04	16 54.8	11 31.5	24 50.5	29 25.2	1 48.4	8 38.5	7 47.4	19 12.2	26 07.6	0 42.9
13 Tu	21 32 06	24 16 00	6♈30 34	13♈50 01	16D53.4	13 09.8	26 04.7	0♒11.3	2 09.6	8 46.5	7 54.6	19 13.1	26 09.6	0 44.8
14 W	21 36 03	25 16 40	21 03 55	28 11 56	16 53.8	14 48.8	27 18.9	0 57.4	2 30.7	8 54.7	8 01.8	19 14.0	26 11.6	0 46.6
15 Th	21 40 00	26 17 18	5♉13 54	12♉09 51	16 54.8	16 28.7	28 33.1	1 43.6	2 51.7	9 03.1	8 09.0	19 15.0	26 13.6	0 48.4
16 F	21 43 56	27 17 55	18 59 52	25 44 11	16R55.5	18 09.5	29 47.3	2 29.7	3 12.6	9 11.6	8 16.2	19 16.0	26 15.6	0 50.2
17 Sa	21 47 53	28 18 30	2♊23 06	8♊56 56	16 54.9	19 51.2	1♒01.5	3 15.9	3 33.3	9 20.2	8 23.5	19 17.1	26 17.7	0 51.9
18 Su	21 51 49	29 19 03	15 26 04	21 50 52	16 52.3	21 33.7	2 15.7	4 02.1	3 54.0	9 29.0	8 30.7	19 18.3	26 19.8	0 53.7
19 M	21 55 46	0♓19 34	28 11 43	4♋28 58	16 47.6	23 17.1	3 30.0	4 48.3	4 14.5	9 37.9	8 38.0	19 19.4	26 21.8	0 55.5
20 Tu	21 59 42	1 20 04	10♋42 58	16 54 02	16 41.0	25 01.5	4 44.2	5 34.6	4 34.9	9 46.9	8 45.3	19 20.7	26 23.9	0 57.2
21 W	22 03 39	2 20 32	23 02 28	29 08 32	16 33.0	26 46.8	5 58.4	6 20.8	4 55.2	9 56.1	8 52.6	19 22.0	26 26.1	0 58.9
22 Th	22 07 35	3 20 58	5♌12 27	11♌14 29	16 24.4	28 33.0	7 12.6	7 07.1	5 15.3	10 05.3	8 59.9	19 23.3	26 28.2	1 00.6
23 F	22 11 32	4 21 22	17 14 48	23 13 36	16 16.1	0♓20.2	8 26.9	7 53.4	5 35.4	10 14.8	9 07.2	19 24.7	26 30.3	1 02.3
24 Sa	22 15 29	5 21 44	29 11 05	5♍07 27	16 08.9	2 08.3	9 41.1	8 39.8	5 55.3	10 24.3	9 14.5	19 26.1	26 32.5	1 04.0
25 Su	22 19 25	6 22 05	11♍02 54	16 57 38	16 03.3	3 57.3	10 55.4	9 26.1	6 15.0	10 33.9	9 21.8	19 27.6	26 34.6	1 05.7
26 M	22 23 22	7 22 25	22 51 54	28 45 59	15 59.7	5 47.3	12 09.6	10 12.5	6 34.7	10 43.7	9 29.1	19 29.1	26 36.8	1 07.3
27 Tu	22 27 18	8 22 42	4♎40 09	10♎34 45	15D58.0	7 38.2	13 23.9	10 58.9	6 54.2	10 53.6	9 36.5	19 30.6	26 38.9	1 09.0
28 W	22 31 15	9 22 58	16 30 09	22 26 45	15 58.1	9 30.0	14 38.1	11 45.3	7 13.5	11 03.6	9 43.8	19 32.2	26 41.1	1 10.6
29 Th	22 35 11	10 23 13	28 24 59	4♏25 21	15 59.3	11 22.7	15 52.4	12 31.8	7 32.7	11 13.7	9 51.1	19 33.9	26 43.3	1 12.2

Astro Data	Dy Hr Mn	Planet Ingress	Dy Hr Mn
☿ D	2 3:08	♂ ♑	4 14:59
☽ 0S	3 7:54	☿ ♑	14 2:51
☽ 0N	16 10:19	☉ ♒	20 14:08
♅ D	27 7:37	♇ ♒	21 0:51
☽ 0S	30 14:13	♀ ♑	23 8:51
☽ 0N	12 18:06	☿ ♒	5 5:11
☽ 0S	26 20:06	⚳ ♑	7 11:13
		♂ ♒	13 6:06
		♀ ♒	16 16:06
		☉ ♓	19 4:14
		☿ ♓	23 7:30

Last Aspect Dy Hr Mn		☽ Ingress	Dy Hr Mn	Last Aspect Dy Hr Mn		☽ Ingress	Dy Hr Mn
2 23:37	♇ △	♎	3 0:48	1 9:04	☿ □	♏	1 20:38
5 11:42	♇ □	♏	5 12:41	4 3:25	☿ ⚹	♐	4 6:29
7 20:23	♇ ⚹	♐	7 21:10	6 5:07	♆ □	♑	6 12:10
9 18:26	☿ ☌	♑	10 1:34	8 7:53	♂ ☌	♒	8 14:01
12 2:34	♇ ☌	♒	12 3:02	9 23:00	☉ ☌	♓	10 13:44
13 10:00	♅ □	♓	14 3:30	12 12:33	♂ ⚹	♈	12 13:27
16 4:34	♇ ⚹	♈	16 4:50	14 10:22	♀ □	♉	14 15:03
18 8:04	♇ □	♉	18 8:13	16 15:02	☉ □	♊	16 19:41
20 13:58	☉ △	♊	20 13:59	19 3:22	☉ △	♋	19 3:26
22 20:41	♀ ☍	♋	22 21:52	21 6:39	♆ △	♌	21 13:42
24 22:59	♆ △	♌	25 7:38	23 4:19	♅ □	♍	24 1:39
26 21:20	♅ □	♍	27 19:12	26 7:36	♆ ☍	♎	26 14:31
29 23:21	♆ ☍	♎	30 8:05	27 18:23	♀ △	♏	29 3:10

☽ Phases & Eclipses Dy Hr Mn		
4 3:32	☾	13♎15
11 11:58	●	20♑44
18 3:54	☽	27♈32
25 17:55	○	5♌15
2 23:19	☾	13♏36
9 23:00	●	20♒41
16 15:02	☽	27♉26
24 12:32	○	5♍23

Astro Data

1 January 2024
Julian Day # 45291
SVP 4♓55'34"
GC 27♐10.5 ⚴ 17♏45.6
Eris 24♈09.9R ⚵ 21♍21.7
⚷ 15♈27.9 ⚶ 26♊52.3R
☽ Mean ☊ 20♈50.9

1 February 2024
Julian Day # 45322
SVP 4♓55'28"
GC 27♐10.5 ⚴ 28♏33.1
Eris 24♈11.6 ⚵ 20♍28.4R
⚷ 16♈02.9 ⚶ 21♊55.4R
☽ Mean ☊ 19♈12.5

March 2024 LONGITUDE

Day	Sid.Time	☉	0 hr ☽	Noon ☽	True ☊	☿	♀	♂	⚳	♃	♄	♅	♆	♇
1 F	22 39 08	11♓23 26	10♏28 21	16♏34 31	16♈01.1	13♓16.2	17♒06.7	13♒18.2	7♑51.8	11♉24.0	9♓58.4	19♉35.6	26♓45.5	1♒13.8
2 Sa	22 43 04	12 23 37	22 44 24	28 58 35	16 02.6	15 10.5	18 20.9	14 04.7	8 10.8	11 34.3	10 05.8	19 37.4	26 47.7	1 15.3
3 Su	22 47 01	13 23 47	5♐17 36	11♐42 01	16R 03.4	17 05.5	19 35.2	14 51.2	8 29.6	11 44.8	10 13.1	19 39.2	26 50.0	1 16.9
4 M	22 50 58	14 23 56	18 12 20	24 49 00	16 02.9	19 01.0	20 49.5	15 37.7	8 48.2	11 55.4	10 20.4	19 41.0	26 52.2	1 18.4
5 Tu	22 54 54	15 24 03	1♑32 23	8♑22 44	16 01.0	20 57.0	22 03.8	16 24.3	9 06.7	12 06.0	10 27.8	19 42.9	26 54.4	1 19.9
6 W	22 58 51	16 24 08	15 20 11	22 24 43	15 57.9	22 53.4	23 18.1	17 10.8	9 25.1	12 16.8	10 35.1	19 44.8	26 56.7	1 21.4
7 Th	23 02 47	17 24 12	29 36 07	6♒53 59	15 54.0	24 49.9	24 32.4	17 57.4	9 43.2	12 27.7	10 42.4	19 46.8	26 58.9	1 22.9
8 F	23 06 44	18 24 14	14♒17 41	21 46 26	15 49.9	26 46.4	25 46.6	18 44.0	10 01.3	12 38.7	10 49.7	19 48.8	27 01.2	1 24.3
9 Sa	23 10 40	19 24 15	29 19 15	6♓54 59	15 46.2	28 42.5	27 00.9	19 30.6	10 19.1	12 49.7	10 57.0	19 50.9	27 03.5	1 25.8
10 Su	23 14 37	20 24 13	14♓32 24	22 10 12	15 43.6	0♈38.1	28 15.2	20 17.2	10 36.8	13 00.9	11 04.2	19 53.0	27 05.7	1 27.2
11 M	23 18 33	21 24 10	29 47 04	7♈21 46	15D 42.3	2 32.8	29 29.5	21 03.8	10 54.4	13 12.2	11 11.5	19 55.1	27 08.0	1 28.6
12 Tu	23 22 30	22 24 04	14♈53 09	22 20 12	15 42.2	4 26.3	0♓43.8	21 50.4	11 11.7	13 23.6	11 18.7	19 57.3	27 10.2	1 29.9
13 W	23 26 27	23 23 57	29 42 04	6♉58 06	15 43.1	6 18.2	1 58.0	22 37.1	11 28.9	13 35.0	11 26.0	19 59.5	27 12.5	1 31.3
14 Th	23 30 23	24 23 47	14♉07 49	21 10 57	15 44.5	8 08.0	3 12.3	23 23.7	11 45.9	13 46.6	11 33.2	20 01.8	27 14.8	1 32.6
15 F	23 34 20	25 23 35	28 07 22	4♊57 05	15 45.8	9 55.4	4 26.5	24 10.3	12 02.8	13 58.2	11 40.4	20 04.1	27 17.1	1 33.9
16 Sa	23 38 16	26 23 21	11♊40 17	18 17 13	15R 46.8	11 39.8	5 40.8	24 57.0	12 19.4	14 09.9	11 47.6	20 06.4	27 19.4	1 35.2
17 Su	23 42 13	27 23 05	24 48 13	1♋13 42	15 46.9	13 20.7	6 55.0	25 43.7	12 35.9	14 21.7	11 54.8	20 08.8	27 21.6	1 36.4
18 M	23 46 09	28 22 46	7♋34 06	13 49 54	15 46.2	14 57.8	8 09.3	26 30.3	12 52.2	14 33.6	12 01.9	20 11.2	27 23.9	1 37.7
19 Tu	23 50 06	29 22 25	20 01 35	26 09 38	15 44.7	16 30.5	9 23.5	27 17.0	13 08.3	14 45.6	12 09.0	20 13.7	27 26.2	1 38.9
20 W	23 54 02	0♈22 02	2♌14 32	8♌16 43	15 42.7	17 58.4	10 37.7	28 03.7	13 24.2	14 57.6	12 16.2	20 16.2	27 28.5	1 40.1
21 Th	23 57 59	1 21 37	14 16 38	20 14 43	15 40.4	19 21.0	11 52.0	28 50.4	13 39.9	15 09.7	12 23.2	20 18.7	27 30.7	1 41.3
22 F	0 01 56	2 21 09	26 11 20	2♍06 51	15 38.2	20 37.8	13 06.2	29 37.0	13 55.4	15 21.9	12 30.3	20 21.2	27 33.0	1 42.4
23 Sa	0 05 52	3 20 39	8♍01 38	13 55 58	15 36.4	21 48.7	14 20.4	0♓23.7	14 10.7	15 34.2	12 37.3	20 23.8	27 35.3	1 43.5
24 Su	0 09 49	4 20 08	19 50 10	25 44 31	15 35.1	22 53.1	15 34.6	1 10.4	14 25.9	15 46.5	12 44.3	20 26.4	27 37.5	1 44.6
25 M	0 13 45	5 19 33	1♎39 16	7♎34 42	15D 34.5	23 50.8	16 48.8	1 57.1	14 40.8	15 58.9	12 51.3	20 29.1	27 39.8	1 45.7
26 Tu	0 17 42	6 18 57	13 31 05	19 28 39	15 34.4	24 41.5	18 03.0	2 43.8	14 55.5	16 11.4	12 58.3	20 31.8	27 42.1	1 46.7
27 W	0 21 38	7 18 19	25 27 40	1♏28 26	15 34.7	25 25.1	19 17.1	3 30.5	15 10.0	16 23.9	13 05.2	20 34.5	27 44.3	1 47.7
28 Th	0 25 35	8 17 40	7♏31 13	13 36 19	15 35.3	26 01.4	20 31.3	4 17.2	15 24.3	16 36.5	13 12.1	20 37.3	27 46.6	1 48.7
29 F	0 29 31	9 16 58	19 44 03	25 54 45	15 36.0	26 30.3	21 45.5	5 03.9	15 38.4	16 49.2	13 18.9	20 40.0	27 48.8	1 49.7
30 Sa	0 33 28	10 16 14	2♐08 46	8♐26 27	15 36.7	26 51.8	22 59.7	5 50.6	15 52.2	17 02.0	13 25.8	20 42.9	27 51.0	1 50.6
31 Su	0 37 24	11 15 29	14 48 10	21 14 16	15 37.1	27 05.8	24 13.9	6 37.3	16 05.9	17 14.8	13 32.6	20 45.7	27 53.3	1 51.5

April 2024 LONGITUDE

Day	Sid.Time	☉	0 hr ☽	Noon ☽	True ☊	☿	♀	♂	⚳	♃	♄	♅	♆	♇
1 M	0 41 21	12♈14 42	27♐45 06	4♑21 00	15♈37.3	27♈12.5	25♓28.0	7♓24.0	16♑19.3	17♉27.6	13♓39.3	20♉48.6	27♓55.5	1♒52.4
2 Tu	0 45 18	13 13 53	11♑02 14	17 49 02	15R 37.3	27R 12.0	26 42.2	8 10.7	16 32.4	17 40.5	13 46.0	20 51.5	27 57.7	1 53.3
3 W	0 49 14	14 13 03	24 41 34	1♒39 54	15 37.3	27 04.5	27 56.3	8 57.3	16 45.4	17 53.5	13 52.7	20 54.4	27 59.9	1 54.1
4 Th	0 53 11	15 12 11	8♒43 59	15 53 39	15D 37.2	26 50.5	29 10.5	9 44.0	16 58.1	18 06.6	13 59.4	20 57.4	28 02.1	1 54.9
5 F	0 57 07	16 11 16	23 08 35	0♓28 21	15 37.2	26 30.2	0♈24.6	10 30.7	17 10.6	18 19.6	14 06.0	21 00.4	28 04.3	1 55.7
6 Sa	1 01 04	17 10 20	7♓52 20	15 19 46	15 37.3	26 04.3	1 38.8	11 17.4	17 22.8	18 32.8	14 12.6	21 03.4	28 06.5	1 56.5
7 Su	1 05 00	18 09 23	22 49 47	0♈21 24	15 37.5	25 33.3	2 52.9	12 04.1	17 34.8	18 46.0	14 19.1	21 06.4	28 08.7	1 57.2
8 M	1 08 57	19 08 23	7♈53 32	15 25 04	15R 37.5	24 57.9	4 07.0	12 50.7	17 46.5	18 59.2	14 25.6	21 09.5	28 10.8	1 57.9
9 Tu	1 12 53	20 07 21	22 54 55	0♉22 00	15 37.4	24 18.8	5 21.2	13 37.4	17 57.9	19 12.5	14 32.0	21 12.5	28 13.0	1 58.6
10 W	1 16 50	21 06 17	7♉45 21	15 04 05	15 37.0	23 36.9	6 35.3	14 24.0	18 09.2	19 25.9	14 38.5	21 15.6	28 15.1	1 59.2
11 Th	1 20 47	22 05 12	22 17 27	29 24 54	15 36.4	22 53.0	7 49.4	15 10.6	18 20.1	19 39.2	14 44.8	21 18.8	28 17.3	1 59.8
12 F	1 24 43	23 04 04	6♊26 00	13♊20 31	15 35.5	22 08.0	9 03.5	15 57.2	18 30.8	19 52.7	14 51.1	21 21.9	28 19.4	2 00.4
13 Sa	1 28 40	24 02 53	20 08 20	26 49 30	15 34.7	21 22.7	10 17.5	16 43.8	18 41.2	20 06.2	14 57.4	21 25.1	28 21.5	2 01.0
14 Su	1 32 36	25 01 41	3♋24 13	9♋52 46	15 34.0	20 38.0	11 31.6	17 30.4	18 51.3	20 19.7	15 03.6	21 28.3	28 23.6	2 01.5
15 M	1 36 33	26 00 26	16 15 30	22 32 54	15D 33.6	19 54.7	12 45.7	18 17.0	19 01.2	20 33.2	15 09.8	21 31.5	28 25.6	2 02.0
16 Tu	1 40 29	26 59 09	28 45 27	4♌53 42	15 33.7	19 13.5	13 59.7	19 03.5	19 10.8	20 46.8	15 15.9	21 34.7	28 27.7	2 02.5
17 W	1 44 26	27 57 50	10♌58 12	16 59 32	15 34.3	18 35.1	15 13.7	19 50.0	19 20.1	21 00.4	15 21.9	21 38.0	28 29.8	2 02.9
18 Th	1 48 22	28 56 29	22 58 16	28 55 00	15 35.4	18 00.1	16 27.8	20 36.5	19 29.1	21 14.1	15 28.0	21 41.2	28 31.8	2 03.4
19 F	1 52 19	29 55 05	4♍50 14	10♍44 32	15 36.7	17 28.9	17 41.8	21 23.0	19 37.8	21 27.8	15 33.9	21 44.5	28 33.8	2 03.7
20 Sa	1 56 16	0♉53 39	16 38 24	22 32 17	15 38.0	17 02.0	18 55.8	22 09.5	19 46.2	21 41.5	15 39.8	21 47.8	28 35.8	2 04.1
21 Su	2 00 12	1 52 11	28 26 38	4♎21 53	15R 38.9	16 39.6	20 09.8	22 55.9	19 54.4	21 55.3	15 45.6	21 51.1	28 37.8	2 04.4
22 M	2 04 09	2 50 41	10♎18 22	16 16 26	15 39.3	16 22.0	21 23.7	23 42.4	20 02.2	22 09.1	15 51.4	21 54.5	28 39.8	2 04.7
23 Tu	2 08 05	3 49 09	22 16 24	28 18 30	15 38.8	16 09.3	22 37.7	24 28.8	20 09.8	22 22.9	15 57.2	21 57.8	28 41.7	2 05.0
24 W	2 12 02	4 47 36	4♏22 59	10♏30 04	15 37.3	16 01.6	23 51.7	25 15.2	20 17.0	22 36.7	16 02.8	22 01.2	28 43.6	2 05.3
25 Th	2 15 58	5 46 00	16 39 55	22 52 41	15 35.0	15D 58.9	25 05.6	26 01.6	20 23.9	22 50.6	16 08.5	22 04.5	28 45.6	2 05.5
26 F	2 19 55	6 44 23	29 08 31	5♐27 32	15 32.0	16 01.2	26 19.6	26 47.9	20 30.6	23 04.5	16 14.0	22 07.9	28 47.4	2 05.7
27 Sa	2 23 51	7 42 44	11♐49 49	18 15 30	15 28.6	16 08.4	27 33.5	27 34.3	20 36.9	23 18.4	16 19.5	22 11.3	28 49.3	2 05.8
28 Su	2 27 48	8 41 03	24 44 40	1♑17 24	15 25.4	16 20.4	28 47.5	28 20.6	20 42.9	23 32.4	16 24.9	22 14.7	28 51.2	2 06.0
29 M	2 31 45	9 39 21	7♑53 47	14 33 54	15 22.7	16 37.1	0♉01.4	29 06.9	20 48.5	23 46.3	16 30.3	22 18.1	28 53.0	2 06.1
30 Tu	2 35 41	10 37 38	21 17 50	28 05 37	15D 21.0	16 58.4	1 15.3	29 53.1	20 53.9	24 00.3	16 35.6	22 21.5	28 54.9	2 06.2

Astro Data Dy Hr Mn	Planet Ingress Dy Hr Mn	Last Aspect Dy Hr Mn	☽ Ingress Dy Hr Mn	Last Aspect Dy Hr Mn	☽ Ingress Dy Hr Mn	☽ Phases & Eclipses Dy Hr Mn	Astro Data
♃∠♆ 4 2:58	☿ ♈ 10 4:04	2 7:49 ♆ △	♐ 2 13:57	1 0:17 ♆ □	♑ 1 4:06	3 15:25 ☾ 13♐32	1 March 2024
☿0N 10 16:34	♀ ♓ 11 21:52	4 15:42 ♆ □	♑ 4 21:16	3 5:42 ♆ ✱	♒ 3 9:09	10 9:02 ● 20♓17	Julian Day # 45351
☽0N 11 4:39	☉ ♈ 20 3:08	6 19:36 ♆ ✱	♒ 7 0:40	5 5:41 ♆ ✱	♓ 5 11:14	17 4:12 ☽ 27♊04	SVP 4♓55'25"
⊙0N 20 3:07	♂ ♓ 22 23:48	8 18:57 ♀ ☌	♓ 9 1:05	7 8:28 ♆ ☌	♈ 7 11:26	25 7:01 ○ 5♎07	GC 27♐10.6 ⚵ 5♐50.3
☽0S 25 2:10		10 19:47 ♆ ☌	♈ 11 0:20	9 2:40 ♆ ☌	♉ 9 11:24	25 7:14 • A 0.956	Eris 24♈22.1 ⚴ 14♍13.2R
	♀ ♈ 5 4:01	12 11:09 ♂ ✱	♉ 13 0:29	11 10:05 ♆ ✱	♊ 11 13:00		⚷ 17♈15.5 ⚶ 23♊25.8
☿R 1 22:17	☉ ♉ 19 14:01	14 22:30 ♆ ✱	♊ 15 3:17	13 14:47 ♆ □	♋ 13 17:46	2 3:16 ☾ 12♑52	☽ Mean ☊ 17♈40.3
☽0N 7 15:47	♀ ♉ 29 11:32	17 4:44 ♆ □	♋ 17 9:42	15 23:23 ♆ △	♌ 16 2:25	8 18:22 ● 19♈24	
♀0N 7 23:08	♂ ♈ 30 15:34	19 18:53 ⊙ △	♌ 19 19:34	18 12:03 ⊙ △	♍ 18 14:12	8 18:18:29 • T 04'28"	1 April 2024
♃☌♅ 21 2:28		22 6:35 ♂ ☍	♍ 22 7:43	21 0:21 ♆ ☍	♎ 21 3:09	15 19:14 ☽ 26♋18	Julian Day # 45382
☽0S 21 8:41		24 15:50 ♆ ☍	♎ 24 20:39	22 23:25 ♀ ☍	♏ 23 15:21	23 23:50 ○ 4♏18	SVP 4♓55'21"
☿D 25 12:55		26 23:10 ☿ ☍	♏ 27 9:04	25 23:18 ♆ △	♐ 26 1:38		GC 27♐10.7 ⚵ 8♐33.7R
		29 15:41 ♆ △	♐ 29 19:53	28 7:32 ♆ □	♑ 28 9:39		Eris 24♈40.0 ⚴ 7♍40.9R
				30 15:20 ♂ ✱	♒ 30 15:21		⚷ 18♈58.6 ⚶ 0♋17.6
							☽ Mean ☊ 16♈01.8

LONGITUDE — May 2024

Day	Sid.Time	☉	0 hr ☽	Noon☽	True☊	☿	♀	♂	⚳	♃	♄	♅	♆	♇
1 W	2 39 38	11♉35 53	4♒57 19	11♒52 54	15♈20.5	17♈24.1	2♉29.3	0♈39.4	20♑58.9	24♉14.3	16♓40.9	22♉25.0	28♓56.7	2♒06.2
2 Th	2 43 34	12 34 06	18 52 22	25 55 38	15 21.0	17 54.0	3 43.2	1 25.6	21 03.5	24 28.4	16 46.0	22 28.4	28 58.4	2R 06.2
3 F	2 47 31	13 32 18	3♓02 32	10♓12 51	15 22.2	18 28.1	4 57.1	2 11.8	21 07.9	24 42.4	16 51.2	22 31.9	29 00.2	2 06.2
4 Sa	2 51 27	14 30 28	17 26 18	24 42 27	15 23.7	19 06.0	6 11.0	2 57.9	21 11.9	24 56.5	16 56.2	22 35.3	29 01.9	2 06.2
5 Su	2 55 24	15 28 37	2♈00 50	9♈20 51	15R 24.6	19 47.8	7 24.9	3 44.1	21 15.5	25 10.6	17 01.2	22 38.8	29 03.6	2 06.1
6 M	2 59 20	16 26 45	16 41 49	24 02 59	15 24.5	20 33.1	8 38.8	4 30.2	21 18.8	25 24.7	17 06.1	22 42.2	29 05.3	2 06.0
7 Tu	3 03 17	17 24 51	1♉23 32	8♉42 37	15 22.8	21 22.0	9 52.7	5 16.2	21 21.8	25 38.8	17 10.9	22 45.7	29 07.0	2 05.9
8 W	3 07 14	18 22 55	15 59 24	23 13 03	15 19.6	22 14.2	11 06.6	6 02.3	21 24.4	25 52.9	17 15.7	22 49.2	29 08.7	2 05.8
9 Th	3 11 10	19 20 58	0♊22 48	7♊27 58	15 15.1	23 09.7	12 20.4	6 48.3	21 26.6	26 07.0	17 20.4	22 52.7	29 10.3	2 05.6
10 F	3 15 07	20 18 59	14 27 58	21 22 23	15 09.6	24 08.3	13 34.3	7 34.3	21 28.5	26 21.2	17 25.0	22 56.2	29 11.9	2 05.4
11 Sa	3 19 03	21 16 59	28 10 52	4♋53 17	15 04.1	25 09.8	14 48.2	8 20.2	21 30.0	26 35.3	17 29.5	22 59.6	29 13.5	2 05.2
12 Su	3 23 00	22 14 56	11♋29 34	17 59 50	14 59.1	26 14.3	16 02.0	9 06.1	21 31.2	26 49.5	17 34.0	23 03.1	29 15.0	2 04.9
13 M	3 26 56	23 12 52	24 24 18	0♌43 17	14 55.3	27 21.6	17 15.9	9 51.9	21 32.0	27 03.6	17 38.4	23 06.6	29 16.5	2 04.6
14 Tu	3 30 53	24 10 46	6♌57 11	13 06 31	14D 53.0	28 31.6	18 29.7	10 37.8	21R 32.5	27 17.8	17 42.7	23 10.1	29 18.0	2 04.3
15 W	3 34 49	25 08 39	19 11 48	25 13 38	14 52.3	29 44.2	19 43.5	11 23.5	21 32.6	27 31.9	17 46.9	23 13.6	29 19.5	2 04.0
16 Th	3 38 46	26 06 29	1♍12 38	7♍09 26	14 52.9	0♉59.5	20 57.3	12 09.3	21 32.3	27 46.1	17 51.1	23 17.1	29 21.0	2 03.6
17 F	3 42 43	27 04 18	13 04 41	18 59 01	14 54.3	2 17.2	22 11.1	12 55.0	21 31.6	28 00.2	17 55.1	23 20.6	29 22.4	2 03.2
18 Sa	3 46 39	28 02 05	24 53 03	0♎47 25	14 55.8	3 37.5	23 24.9	13 40.6	21 30.6	28 14.4	17 59.1	23 24.0	29 23.8	2 02.8
19 Su	3 50 36	28 59 50	6♎42 41	12 39 23	14R 56.7	5 00.2	24 38.7	14 26.2	21 29.3	28 28.5	18 03.0	23 27.5	29 25.1	2 02.3
20 M	3 54 32	29 57 34	18 38 02	24 39 06	14 56.2	6 25.3	25 52.5	15 11.8	21 27.5	28 42.7	18 06.9	23 31.0	29 26.5	2 01.9
21 Tu	3 58 29	0♊55 17	0♏42 58	6♏49 59	14 53.8	7 52.8	27 06.3	15 57.3	21 25.4	28 56.8	18 10.6	23 34.4	29 27.8	2 01.4
22 W	4 02 25	1 52 58	13 00 26	19 14 32	14 49.4	9 22.7	28 20.0	16 42.8	21 22.9	29 11.0	18 14.3	23 37.9	29 29.1	2 00.8
23 Th	4 06 22	2 50 37	25 32 26	1♐54 14	14 43.1	10 54.9	29 33.8	17 28.3	21 20.1	29 25.1	18 17.9	23 41.4	29 30.4	2 00.3
24 F	4 10 18	3 48 16	8♐19 56	14 49 29	14 35.3	12 29.5	0♊47.6	18 13.7	21 16.9	29 39.3	18 21.4	23 44.8	29 31.6	1 59.7
25 Sa	4 14 15	4 45 53	21 22 47	27 59 42	14 26.9	14 06.4	2 01.3	18 59.0	21 13.3	29 53.4	18 24.8	23 48.2	29 32.8	1 59.1
26 Su	4 18 12	5 43 29	4♑40 03	11♑23 37	14 18.6	15 45.6	3 15.1	19 44.3	21 09.4	0♊07.5	18 28.1	23 51.7	29 34.0	1 58.5
27 M	4 22 08	6 41 05	18 10 10	24 59 29	14 11.4	17 27.1	4 28.8	20 29.6	21 05.1	0 21.6	18 31.3	23 55.1	29 35.1	1 57.9
28 Tu	4 26 05	7 38 39	1♒51 20	8♒45 31	14 06.1	19 10.9	5 42.6	21 14.9	21 00.5	0 35.7	18 34.5	23 58.5	29 36.3	1 57.2
29 W	4 30 01	8 36 12	15 41 50	22 40 07	14 02.9	20 57.0	6 56.3	22 00.0	20 55.4	0 49.8	18 37.6	24 01.9	29 37.4	1 56.5
30 Th	4 33 58	9 33 44	29 40 12	6♓41 58	14D 01.7	22 45.4	8 10.1	22 45.2	20 50.1	1 03.8	18 40.5	24 05.3	29 38.4	1 55.8
31 F	4 37 54	10 31 16	13♓45 15	20 49 57	14 02.0	24 36.1	9 23.8	23 30.3	20 44.3	1 17.9	18 43.4	24 08.7	29 39.4	1 55.0

LONGITUDE — June 2024

Day	Sid.Time	☉	0 hr ☽	Noon☽	True☊	☿	♀	♂	⚳	♃	♄	♅	♆	♇
1 Sa	4 41 51	11♊28 47	27♓55 53	5♈02 54	14♈02.7	26♉29.0	10♊37.6	24♈15.3	20♑38.3	1♊31.9	18♓46.2	24♉12.1	29♓40.4	1♒54.3
2 Su	4 45 48	12 26 17	12♈10 45	19 19 10	14R 02.9	28 24.2	11 51.3	25 00.3	20R 31.8	1 45.9	18 48.9	24 15.4	29 41.4	1R 53.5
3 M	4 49 44	13 23 46	26 27 49	3♉36 18	14 01.3	0♊21.5	13 05.1	25 45.2	20 25.0	1 59.9	18 51.5	24 18.8	29 42.4	1 52.7
4 Tu	4 53 41	14 21 15	10♉44 10	17 50 55	13 57.5	2 21.0	14 18.8	26 30.1	20 17.9	2 13.9	18 54.0	24 22.1	29 43.3	1 51.8
5 W	4 57 37	15 18 43	24 55 58	1♊58 47	13 51.1	4 22.4	15 32.6	27 15.0	20 10.5	2 27.9	18 56.5	24 25.4	29 44.2	1 51.0
6 Th	5 01 34	16 16 10	8♊58 45	15 55 19	13 42.4	6 25.8	16 46.3	27 59.8	20 02.7	2 41.8	18 58.8	24 28.7	29 45.0	1 50.1
7 F	5 05 30	17 13 36	22 47 59	29 36 17	13 32.3	8 31.0	18 00.1	28 44.5	19 54.6	2 55.7	19 01.0	24 32.0	29 45.8	1 49.2
8 Sa	5 09 27	18 11 01	6♋19 51	12♋58 25	13 21.7	10 37.7	19 13.8	29 29.1	19 46.1	3 09.6	19 03.2	24 35.3	29 46.6	1 48.3
9 Su	5 13 23	19 08 26	19 31 49	26 00 01	13 11.8	12 46.0	20 27.5	0♉13.8	19 37.4	3 23.5	19 05.2	24 38.6	29 47.4	1 47.3
10 M	5 17 20	20 05 49	2♌23 05	8♌41 10	13 03.4	14 55.5	21 41.3	0 58.3	19 28.4	3 37.3	19 07.2	24 41.8	29 48.1	1 46.4
11 Tu	5 21 17	21 03 11	14 54 34	21 03 39	12 57.2	17 06.0	22 55.0	1 42.8	19 19.0	3 51.1	19 09.0	24 45.0	29 48.8	1 45.4
12 W	5 25 13	22 00 33	27 08 50	3♍10 40	12 53.4	19 17.2	24 08.7	2 27.2	19 09.4	4 04.9	19 10.8	24 48.2	29 49.5	1 44.4
13 Th	5 29 10	22 57 53	9♍09 42	15 06 33	12D 51.7	21 29.0	25 22.5	3 11.6	18 59.5	4 18.6	19 12.5	24 51.4	29 50.1	1 43.4
14 F	5 33 06	23 55 12	21 01 52	26 56 19	12 51.5	23 41.0	26 36.2	3 55.9	18 49.3	4 32.3	19 14.0	24 54.5	29 50.7	1 42.3
15 Sa	5 37 03	24 52 31	2♎50 34	8♎45 19	12R 51.8	25 53.0	27 49.9	4 40.1	18 38.9	4 46.0	19 15.5	24 57.7	29 51.2	1 41.3
16 Su	5 40 59	25 49 48	14 41 14	20 38 58	12 51.6	28 04.6	29 03.6	5 24.3	18 28.2	4 59.7	19 16.9	25 00.8	29 51.8	1 40.2
17 M	5 44 56	26 47 05	26 39 08	2♏42 19	12 50.0	0♋15.6	0♋17.3	6 08.4	18 17.3	5 13.3	19 18.1	25 03.9	29 52.3	1 39.1
18 Tu	5 48 52	27 44 21	8♏49 03	14 59 47	12 46.2	2 25.8	1 31.0	6 52.5	18 06.2	5 26.8	19 19.3	25 07.0	29 52.7	1 38.0
19 W	5 52 49	28 41 36	21 14 56	27 34 47	12 39.8	4 34.9	2 44.8	7 36.4	17 54.8	5 40.4	19 20.4	25 10.0	29 53.2	1 36.9
20 Th	5 56 46	29 38 51	3♐59 34	10♐29 22	12 31.0	6 42.8	3 58.5	8 20.4	17 43.2	5 53.9	19 21.4	25 13.0	29 53.6	1 35.7
21 F	6 00 42	0♋36 05	17 04 13	23 43 58	12 20.3	8 49.3	5 12.2	9 04.2	17 31.4	6 07.3	19 22.2	25 16.0	29 54.0	1 34.6
22 Sa	6 04 39	1 33 19	0♑28 26	7♑17 16	12 08.6	10 54.1	6 25.9	9 48.0	17 19.5	6 20.7	19 23.0	25 19.0	29 54.3	1 33.4
23 Su	6 08 35	2 30 32	14 10 05	21 06 25	11 57.1	12 57.2	7 39.6	10 31.8	17 07.4	6 34.1	19 23.7	25 22.0	29 54.6	1 32.2
24 M	6 12 32	3 27 45	28 05 43	5♒07 27	11 47.0	14 58.5	8 53.3	11 15.4	16 55.1	6 47.5	19 24.3	25 24.9	29 54.9	1 31.0
25 Tu	6 16 28	4 24 58	12♒11 03	19 15 59	11 39.1	16 57.9	10 07.0	11 59.0	16 42.6	7 00.7	19 24.8	25 27.8	29 55.1	1 29.8
26 W	6 20 25	5 22 11	26 21 46	3♓27 58	11 34.0	18 55.3	11 20.7	12 42.6	16 30.0	7 14.0	19 25.1	25 30.7	29 55.3	1 28.6
27 Th	6 24 21	6 19 24	10♓34 11	17 40 07	11 31.4	20 50.7	12 34.4	13 26.1	16 17.3	7 27.2	19 25.4	25 33.5	29 55.5	1 27.3
28 F	6 28 18	7 16 36	24 45 31	1♈50 11	11 30.6	22 44.0	13 48.1	14 09.5	16 04.5	7 40.3	19 25.6	25 36.3	29 55.7	1 26.1
29 Sa	6 32 15	8 13 49	8♈54 00	15 56 49	11 30.6	24 35.3	15 01.9	14 52.8	15 51.5	7 53.4	19R 25.7	25 39.1	29 55.8	1 24.8
30 Su	6 36 11	9 11 02	22 58 35	29 59 10	11 30.0	26 24.4	16 15.6	15 36.1	15 38.5	8 06.5	19 25.7	25 41.8	29 55.9	1 23.5

Astro Data	Dy Hr Mn
♇ R	2 17:48
♂0N	4 10:19
☽0N	5 1:04
♄∠♇	6 11:51
⚳ R	15 5:35
☽0S	18 15:36
♃⚹♆	23 21:45
☽0N	1 7:31
♃△♇	3 0:14
☽0S	14 22:39
☽0N	28 12:11
♄ R	29 19:07

Planet Ingress		Dy Hr Mn
☿	♉	15 17:06
☉	♊	20 13:01
♀	♊	23 20:31
♃	♊	25 23:16
☿	♊	3 7:38
♂	♉	9 4:36
♀	♋	17 6:21
☿	♋	17 9:08
☉	♋	20 20:52

Last Aspect Dy Hr Mn		☽ Ingress	Dy Hr Mn
2 9:30	♃ □	♓	2 18:53
4 19:07	♆ ☌	♈	4 20:42
6 5:58	☿ ☌	♉	6 21:43
8 21:56	♆ ⚹	♊	8 23:22
11 1:50	♆ □	♋	11 3:14
13 9:14	♆ △	♌	13 10:37
15 16:42	♃ □	♍	15 21:34
18 9:10	♆ ☍	♎	18 10:24
19 15:49	♂ ☍	♏	20 22:35
23 7:29	♆ △	♐	23 8:25
25 14:48	♆ □	♑	25 15:37
27 20:03	♆ ⚹	♒	27 20:46
29 14:21	♅ □	♓	30 0:34

Last Aspect Dy Hr Mn		☽ Ingress	Dy Hr Mn
1 2:56	♆ ☌	♈	1 3:29
2 22:05	♂ ☌	♉	3 5:56
5 8:10	♆ ⚹	♊	5 8:37
7 12:17	♆ □	♋	7 12:42
9 19:07	♆ △	♌	9 19:30
11 19:18	♅ □	♍	12 5:40
14 17:55	♆ ☍	♎	14 18:13
17 6:06	☿ △	♏	17 6:39
19 16:20	♆ △	♐	19 16:33
21 22:59	♆ □	♑	21 23:10
24 3:07	♆ ⚹	♒	24 3:15
25 22:31	♅ □	♓	26 6:09
28 8:46	♆ ☌	♈	28 8:53
30 4:58	☿ □	♉	30 12:01

☽ Phases & Eclipses Dy Hr Mn	
1 11:28	☾ 11♒35
8 3:23	● 18♉02
15 11:49	☽ 25♌08
23 13:54	○ 2♐55
30 17:14	☾ 9♓46
6 12:39	● 16♊18
14 5:20	☽ 23♍39
22 1:09	○ 1♑07
28 21:55	☾ 7♈40

Astro Data

1 May 2024
Julian Day # 45412
SVP 4♓55'17"
GC 27♐10.7 ⚴ 4♐18.0R
Eris 24♈59.6 ⚵ 6♍33.9
⚷ 20♈43.6 ⚶ 10♋07.6
☽ Mean ☊ 14♈26.5

1 June 2024
Julian Day # 45443
SVP 4♓55'12"
GC 27♐10.8 ⚴ 25♏21.5R
Eris 25♈17.1 ⚵ 10♍40.3
⚷ 22♈17.0 ⚶ 22♋13.0
☽ Mean ☊ 12♈48.0

July 2024 LONGITUDE

Day	Sid.Time	☉	0 hr ☽	Noon ☽	True ☊	☿	♀	♂	⚳	♃	♄	♅	♆	♇
1 M	6 40 08	10♋08 15	6♉58 28	13♉56 23	11♈27.6	28♋11.4	17♋29.3	16♉19.3	15♑25.4	8♊19.5	19♓25.5	25♉44.6	29♓55.9	1♒22.2
2 Tu	6 44 04	11 05 29	20 52 43	27 47 17	11R 22.6	29 56.3	18 43.0	17 02.4	15R 12.2	8 32.4	19R 25.3	25 47.3	29R 55.9	1R 20.9
3 W	6 48 01	12 02 42	4♊39 50	11♊30 06	11 14.8	1♌39.1	19 56.8	17 45.4	14 59.0	8 45.3	19 25.0	25 49.9	29 55.9	1 19.6
4 Th	6 51 57	12 59 56	18 17 48	25 02 37	11 04.5	3 19.7	21 10.5	18 28.4	14 45.8	8 58.2	19 24.6	25 52.6	29 55.8	1 18.3
5 F	6 55 54	13 57 10	1♋44 15	8♋22 25	10 52.5	4 58.3	22 24.3	19 11.3	14 32.6	9 11.0	19 24.1	25 55.2	29 55.8	1 16.9
6 Sa	6 59 51	14 54 23	14 56 50	21 27 20	10 39.8	6 34.6	23 38.0	19 54.1	14 19.3	9 23.7	19 23.5	25 57.7	29 55.6	1 15.6
7 Su	7 03 47	15 51 37	27 53 46	4♌16 02	10 27.7	8 08.9	24 51.7	20 36.9	14 06.1	9 36.3	19 22.7	26 00.3	29 55.5	1 14.2
8 M	7 07 44	16 48 51	10♌34 10	16 48 14	10 17.3	9 40.9	26 05.5	21 19.5	13 52.9	9 48.9	19 21.9	26 02.8	29 55.3	1 12.9
9 Tu	7 11 40	17 46 04	22 58 25	29 04 59	10 09.3	11 10.8	27 19.2	22 02.1	13 39.7	10 01.5	19 21.0	26 05.2	29 55.1	1 11.5
10 W	7 15 37	18 43 18	5♍08 15	11♍08 36	10 03.9	12 38.5	28 33.0	22 44.6	13 26.6	10 14.0	19 20.0	26 07.7	29 54.9	1 10.1
11 Th	7 19 33	19 40 31	17 06 32	23 02 34	10 01.0	14 04.0	29 46.7	23 27.0	13 13.6	10 26.4	19 18.9	26 10.1	29 54.6	1 08.8
12 F	7 23 30	20 37 45	28 57 16	4♎51 15	10D 00.0	15 27.3	1♌00.4	24 09.3	13 00.6	10 38.7	19 17.7	26 12.4	29 54.3	1 07.4
13 Sa	7 27 26	21 34 58	10♎45 10	16 39 41	10R 00.0	16 48.2	2 14.2	24 51.5	12 47.8	10 51.0	19 16.4	26 14.7	29 53.9	1 06.0
14 Su	7 31 23	22 32 12	22 35 29	28 33 16	9 59.9	18 06.9	3 27.9	25 33.7	12 35.0	11 03.2	19 15.0	26 17.0	29 53.5	1 04.6
15 M	7 35 20	23 29 25	4♏33 42	10♏37 28	9 58.8	19 23.2	4 41.6	26 15.8	12 22.4	11 15.3	19 13.5	26 19.3	29 53.1	1 03.2
16 Tu	7 39 16	24 26 39	16 45 09	22 57 22	9 55.7	20 37.0	5 55.3	26 57.8	12 10.0	11 27.4	19 11.9	26 21.5	29 52.7	1 01.8
17 W	7 43 13	25 23 53	29 14 37	5♐37 20	9 50.3	21 48.4	7 09.1	27 39.7	11 57.7	11 39.3	19 10.2	26 23.6	29 52.2	1 00.4
18 Th	7 47 09	26 21 07	12♐05 52	18 40 25	9 42.5	22 57.2	8 22.8	28 21.5	11 45.5	11 51.2	19 08.4	26 25.8	29 51.7	0 58.9
19 F	7 51 06	27 18 22	25 21 05	2♑07 50	9 32.8	24 03.4	9 36.5	29 03.2	11 33.6	12 03.1	19 06.6	26 27.9	29 51.2	0 57.5
20 Sa	7 55 02	28 15 36	9♑00 28	15 58 37	9 22.1	25 06.8	10 50.2	29 44.9	11 21.8	12 14.8	19 04.6	26 29.9	29 50.7	0 56.1
21 Su	7 58 59	29 12 51	23 01 50	0♒09 27	9 11.5	26 07.5	12 03.9	0♊26.4	11 10.2	12 26.5	19 02.6	26 31.9	29 50.1	0 54.7
22 M	8 02 55	0♌10 07	7♒20 47	14 35 02	9 02.1	27 05.2	13 17.6	1 07.9	10 58.8	12 38.1	19 00.4	26 33.9	29 49.5	0 53.3
23 Tu	8 06 52	1 07 23	21 51 20	29 08 51	8 54.9	27 59.9	14 31.3	1 49.3	10 47.7	12 49.6	18 58.2	26 35.8	29 48.8	0 51.9
24 W	8 10 49	2 04 40	6♓26 45	13♓44 17	8 50.3	28 51.4	15 45.0	2 30.6	10 36.7	13 01.1	18 55.9	26 37.7	29 48.1	0 50.4
25 Th	8 14 45	3 01 58	21 00 45	28 15 33	8D 48.1	29 39.6	16 58.7	3 11.8	10 26.0	13 12.4	18 53.5	26 39.6	29 47.4	0 49.0
26 F	8 18 42	3 59 16	5♈28 14	12♈38 24	8 47.8	0♍24.3	18 12.4	3 52.9	10 15.6	13 23.7	18 51.0	26 41.4	29 46.7	0 47.6
27 Sa	8 22 38	4 56 36	19 45 47	26 50 12	8R 48.2	1 05.5	19 26.1	4 33.9	10 05.4	13 34.9	18 48.4	26 43.1	29 45.9	0 46.2
28 Su	8 26 35	5 53 57	3♉51 32	10♉49 45	8 48.3	1 42.9	20 39.8	5 14.8	9 55.5	13 45.9	18 45.8	26 44.8	29 45.1	0 44.8
29 M	8 30 31	6 51 18	17 44 49	24 36 45	8 47.0	2 16.4	21 53.6	5 55.7	9 45.8	13 56.9	18 43.1	26 46.5	29 44.3	0 43.3
30 Tu	8 34 28	7 48 41	1♊25 35	8♊11 20	8 43.5	2 45.8	23 07.3	6 36.4	9 36.4	14 07.8	18 40.2	26 48.2	29 43.5	0 41.9
31 W	8 38 24	8 46 05	14 54 02	21 33 41	8 37.5	3 11.0	24 21.0	7 17.1	9 27.4	14 18.7	18 37.3	26 49.7	29 42.6	0 40.5

August 2024 LONGITUDE

Day	Sid.Time	☉	0 hr ☽	Noon ☽	True ☊	☿	♀	♂	⚳	♃	♄	♅	♆	♇
1 Th	8 42 21	9♌43 30	28♊10 15	4♋43 44	8♈29.4	3♍31.6	25♌34.7	7♊57.6	9♑18.6	14♊29.4	18♓34.4	26♉51.3	29♓41.7	0♒39.1
2 F	8 46 18	10 40 56	11♋14 06	17 41 16	8R 19.9	3 47.6	26 48.4	8 38.1	9R 10.1	14 40.0	18R 31.3	26 52.8	29R 40.8	0R 37.7
3 Sa	8 50 14	11 38 23	24 05 15	0♌25 59	8 09.7	3 58.8	28 02.1	9 18.4	9 02.0	14 50.5	18 28.2	26 54.2	29 39.8	0 36.4
4 Su	8 54 11	12 35 51	6♌43 28	12 57 44	8 00.0	4R 05.0	29 15.8	9 58.6	8 54.1	15 00.9	18 25.0	26 55.6	29 38.8	0 35.0
5 M	8 58 07	13 33 20	19 08 50	25 16 52	7 51.7	4 06.1	0♍29.5	10 38.8	8 46.6	15 11.3	18 21.7	26 57.0	29 37.8	0 33.6
6 Tu	9 02 04	14 30 50	1♍21 58	7♍24 21	7 45.4	4 01.9	1 43.2	11 18.8	8 39.4	15 21.5	18 18.4	26 58.3	29 36.8	0 32.2
7 W	9 06 00	15 28 20	13 24 16	19 22 01	7 41.3	3 52.4	2 56.8	11 58.7	8 32.5	15 31.6	18 14.9	26 59.6	29 35.7	0 30.8
8 Th	9 09 57	16 25 52	25 17 58	1♎12 31	7D 39.4	3 37.5	4 10.5	12 38.5	8 26.0	15 41.6	18 11.4	27 00.8	29 34.7	0 29.5
9 F	9 13 53	17 23 24	7♎06 09	12 59 21	7 39.3	3 17.4	5 24.2	13 18.2	8 19.9	15 51.4	18 07.9	27 02.0	29 33.6	0 28.1
10 Sa	9 17 50	18 20 58	18 52 41	24 46 43	7 40.3	2 52.0	6 37.9	13 57.8	8 14.0	16 01.2	18 04.3	27 03.1	29 32.4	0 26.8
11 Su	9 21 47	19 18 32	0♏42 05	6♏39 25	7 41.6	2 21.5	7 51.5	14 37.3	8 08.6	16 10.9	18 00.6	27 04.2	29 31.3	0 25.5
12 M	9 25 43	20 16 07	12 39 22	18 42 35	7R 42.3	1 46.4	9 05.2	15 16.6	8 03.4	16 20.4	17 56.9	27 05.2	29 30.1	0 24.1
13 Tu	9 29 40	21 13 43	24 49 42	1♐01 22	7 41.7	1 06.9	10 18.8	15 55.9	7 58.7	16 29.9	17 53.1	27 06.2	29 28.9	0 22.8
14 W	9 33 36	22 11 20	7♐18 10	13 40 37	7 39.5	0 23.5	11 32.4	16 35.0	7 54.3	16 39.2	17 49.2	27 07.1	29 27.7	0 21.5
15 Th	9 37 33	23 08 58	20 09 11	26 44 14	7 35.5	29♌36.9	12 46.1	17 14.0	7 50.2	16 48.4	17 45.3	27 08.0	29 26.4	0 20.2
16 F	9 41 29	24 06 37	3♑26 01	10♑14 38	7 30.0	28 47.8	13 59.7	17 52.9	7 46.5	16 57.5	17 41.3	27 08.8	29 25.2	0 19.0
17 Sa	9 45 26	25 04 17	17 10 04	24 12 04	7 23.7	27 57.0	15 13.3	18 31.7	7 43.2	17 06.4	17 37.3	27 09.6	29 23.9	0 17.7
18 Su	9 49 22	26 01 58	1♒20 17	8♒34 09	7 17.2	27 05.5	16 26.9	19 10.3	7 40.2	17 15.2	17 33.3	27 10.3	29 22.6	0 16.5
19 M	9 53 19	26 59 41	15 52 57	23 15 49	7 11.5	26 14.3	17 40.4	19 48.9	7 37.6	17 23.9	17 29.1	27 11.0	29 21.3	0 15.2
20 Tu	9 57 16	27 57 24	0♓41 47	8♓09 48	7 07.3	25 24.4	18 54.0	20 27.3	7 35.4	17 32.5	17 25.0	27 11.7	29 19.9	0 14.0
21 W	10 01 12	28 55 09	15 38 48	23 07 43	7D 04.8	24 36.8	20 07.6	21 05.6	7 33.5	17 41.0	17 20.8	27 12.3	29 18.6	0 12.8
22 Th	10 05 09	29 52 56	0♈35 32	8♈01 20	7 04.1	23 52.5	21 21.1	21 43.8	7 31.9	17 49.3	17 16.5	27 12.8	29 17.2	0 11.6
23 F	10 09 05	0♍50 44	15 24 18	22 43 44	7 04.8	23 12.5	22 34.6	22 21.9	7 30.7	17 57.5	17 12.3	27 13.3	29 15.8	0 10.4
24 Sa	10 13 02	1 48 34	29 59 07	7♉10 02	7 06.2	22 37.8	23 48.2	22 59.8	7 29.9	18 05.5	17 07.9	27 13.7	29 14.4	0 09.2
25 Su	10 16 58	2 46 26	14♉16 12	21 17 29	7R 07.4	22 09.1	25 01.7	23 37.6	7D 29.4	18 13.4	17 03.6	27 14.1	29 12.9	0 08.1
26 M	10 20 55	3 44 19	28 13 47	5♊05 10	7 07.9	21 47.0	26 15.2	24 15.3	7 29.3	18 21.2	16 59.2	27 14.4	29 11.5	0 07.0
27 Tu	10 24 51	4 42 15	11♊51 44	18 33 37	7 07.1	21 32.2	27 28.7	24 52.8	7 29.6	18 28.9	16 54.8	27 14.7	29 10.0	0 05.8
28 W	10 28 48	5 40 12	25 10 59	1♋44 05	7 04.8	21D 25.1	28 42.2	25 30.3	7 30.2	18 36.4	16 50.3	27 15.0	29 08.6	0 04.7
29 Th	10 32 45	6 38 11	8♋13 06	14 38 16	7 01.2	21 26.1	29 55.7	26 07.5	7 31.1	18 43.7	16 45.9	27 15.2	29 07.1	0 03.7
30 F	10 36 41	7 36 12	20 59 49	27 17 57	6 56.7	21 35.3	1♎09.2	26 44.7	7 32.4	18 50.9	16 41.4	27 15.3	29 05.6	0 02.6
31 Sa	10 40 38	8 34 15	3♌32 52	9♌44 47	6 51.9	21 52.8	2 22.7	27 21.7	7 34.1	18 58.0	16 36.9	27 15.4	29 04.0	0 01.5

Astro Data

	Dy Hr Mn
♆ R	2 10:43
☽ 0S	12 5:34
☽ 0N	25 17:23
☿ R	5 4:57
♃□♇	7 10:29
☽ 0S	8 12:13
♃□♄	19 21:47
☽ 0N	22 1:01
⚳ D	26 7:38
☿ D	28 21:17
♀0S	31 12:30

Planet Ingress

	Dy Hr Mn
☿ ♌	2 12:51
♀ ♌	11 16:20
♂ ♊	20 20:44
☉ ♌	22 7:46
☿ ♍	25 22:43
♀ ♍	5 2:24
☿ ♌R	15 0:17
☉ ♍	22 14:56
♀ ♎	29 13:24

Last Aspect / ☽ Ingress (July)

Last Aspect Dy Hr Mn		☽ Ingress Dy Hr Mn
2 15:44	♆ ⚹	♊ 2 15:51
4 20:45	♆ □	♋ 4 20:53
7 3:49	♆ △	♌ 7 3:57
9 6:05	♅ □	♍ 9 13:49
12 1:56	♆ ☍	♎ 12 2:08
13 22:50	☉ □	♏ 14 14:54
17 1:12	♆ △	♐ 17 1:26
19 7:59	♆ □	♑ 19 8:15
21 11:27	♆ ⚹	♒ 21 11:44
23 9:59	☿ ☍	♓ 23 13:24
25 14:33	♆ ☌	♈ 25 14:53
26 22:16	♀ △	♉ 27 17:24
29 21:01	♆ ⚹	♊ 29 21:29

Last Aspect / ☽ Ingress (August)

Last Aspect Dy Hr Mn		☽ Ingress Dy Hr Mn
1 2:47	♆ □	♋ 1 3:20
3 10:33	♆ △	♌ 3 11:11
5 15:17	♅ □	♍ 5 21:18
8 8:41	♆ ☍	♎ 8 9:33
9 21:46	☉ ⚹	♏ 10 22:35
13 9:02	♆ △	♐ 13 10:02
15 16:53	☿ △	♑ 15 17:52
17 20:44	♆ ⚹	♒ 17 21:46
19 18:27	☉ ☍	♓ 19 22:53
21 21:55	♆ ☌	♈ 21 23:03
23 12:46	☿ △	♉ 24 0:01
26 1:42	♆ ⚹	♊ 26 3:05
28 7:15	♆ □	♋ 28 8:49
30 15:26	♆ △	♌ 30 17:10

☽ Phases & Eclipses

Dy Hr Mn	
5 22:59	● 14♋23
13 22:50	☽ 22♎01
21 10:18	○ 29♑09
28 2:53	☾ 5♉32
4 11:14	● 12♌34
12 15:20	☽ 20♏24
19 18:27	○ 27♒15
26 9:27	☾ 3♊38

Astro Data

1 July 2024
Julian Day # 45473
SVP 4♓55'06"
GC 27♐10.9 ⚴ 20♏03.1R
Eris 25♈27.5 ⚵ 17♍54.6
⚷ 23♈15.7 ⚶ 5♌03.2
☽ Mean ☊ 11♈12.7

1 August 2024
Julian Day # 45504
SVP 4♓55'00"
GC 27♐11.0 ⚴ 21♏27.1
Eris 25♈29.0R ⚵ 27♍18.6
⚷ 23♈31.2R ⚶ 19♌03.7
☽ Mean ☊ 9♈34.2

LONGITUDE — September 2024

Day	Sid.Time	☉	0 hr ☽	Noon ☽	True ☊	☿	♀	♂	⚳	♃	♄	♅	♆	♇
1 Su	10 44 34	9♍32 19	15♌53 53	22♌00 22	6♈47.3	22♌18.6	3♎36.1	27♊58.5	7♑36.1	19♊04.9	16♓32.3	27♉15.4	29♓02.5	0♒00.5
2 M	10 48 31	10 30 25	28 04 25	4♍06 14	6R43.4	22 52.7	4 49.6	28 35.2	7 38.4	19 11.6	16R27.8	27R15.4	29R01.0	29♑59.5
3 Tu	10 52 27	11 28 33	10♍06 02	16 04 01	6 40.6	23 34.9	6 03.0	29 11.8	7 41.1	19 18.3	16 23.2	27 15.3	28 59.4	29R58.5
4 W	10 56 24	12 26 42	22 00 27	27 55 34	6D39.1	24 24.8	7 16.5	29 48.2	7 44.1	19 24.7	16 18.6	27 15.2	28 57.8	29 57.5
5 Th	11 00 20	13 24 53	3♎49 40	9♎43 05	6 38.9	25 22.3	8 29.9	0♋24.5	7 47.4	19 31.0	16 14.0	27 15.0	28 56.3	29 56.6
6 F	11 04 17	14 23 06	15 36 08	21 29 14	6 39.6	26 26.8	9 43.3	1 00.6	7 51.1	19 37.1	16 09.4	27 14.8	28 54.7	29 55.7
7 Sa	11 08 14	15 21 20	27 22 47	3♏17 14	6 41.0	27 37.9	10 56.7	1 36.5	7 55.2	19 43.1	16 04.8	27 14.5	28 53.1	29 54.8
8 Su	11 12 10	16 19 36	9♏13 05	15 10 48	6 42.6	28 55.3	12 10.1	2 12.3	7 59.5	19 48.9	16 00.2	27 14.2	28 51.5	29 53.9
9 M	11 16 07	17 17 54	21 10 57	27 14 05	6 44.0	0♍18.2	13 23.4	2 47.9	8 04.2	19 54.5	15 55.6	27 13.8	28 49.8	29 53.0
10 Tu	11 20 03	18 16 13	3♐20 45	9♐31 32	6R45.0	1 46.3	14 36.8	3 23.4	8 09.2	20 00.0	15 51.0	27 13.4	28 48.2	29 52.2
11 W	11 24 00	19 14 33	15 46 59	22 07 39	6 45.2	3 18.9	15 50.1	3 58.7	8 14.5	20 05.3	15 46.5	27 13.0	28 46.6	29 51.3
12 Th	11 27 56	20 12 55	28 34 01	5♑06 32	6 44.6	4 55.5	17 03.4	4 33.8	8 20.2	20 10.5	15 41.9	27 12.4	28 45.0	29 50.6
13 F	11 31 53	21 11 19	11♑45 34	18 31 24	6 43.3	6 35.5	18 16.7	5 08.8	8 26.1	20 15.5	15 37.3	27 11.9	28 43.3	29 49.8
14 Sa	11 35 49	22 09 44	25 24 10	2♒23 53	6 41.7	8 18.4	19 30.0	5 43.6	8 32.4	20 20.3	15 32.7	27 11.3	28 41.7	29 49.0
15 Su	11 39 46	23 08 11	9♒30 24	16 43 25	6 39.9	10 03.7	20 43.2	6 18.2	8 38.9	20 24.9	15 28.2	27 10.6	28 40.0	29 48.3
16 M	11 43 43	24 06 40	24 02 24	1♓26 42	6 38.4	11 51.0	21 56.5	6 52.7	8 45.8	20 29.3	15 23.7	27 09.9	28 38.4	29 47.6
17 Tu	11 47 39	25 05 10	8♓55 28	16 27 42	6 37.3	13 39.8	23 09.7	7 26.9	8 52.9	20 33.6	15 19.2	27 09.1	28 36.7	29 46.9
18 W	11 51 36	26 03 42	24 02 18	1♈38 05	6D36.8	15 29.7	24 22.9	8 01.0	9 00.4	20 37.7	15 14.7	27 08.3	28 35.1	29 46.3
19 Th	11 55 32	27 02 16	9♈13 52	16 48 26	6 36.9	17 20.4	25 36.0	8 35.0	9 08.1	20 41.6	15 10.2	27 07.4	28 33.4	29 45.6
20 F	11 59 29	28 00 52	24 20 41	1♉49 33	6 37.4	19 11.7	26 49.2	9 08.7	9 16.1	20 45.4	15 05.8	27 06.5	28 31.8	29 45.0
21 Sa	12 03 25	28 59 30	9♉14 10	16 33 47	6 38.0	21 03.1	28 02.3	9 42.3	9 24.4	20 48.9	15 01.4	27 05.6	28 30.1	29 44.5
22 Su	12 07 22	29 58 10	23 47 49	0♊55 51	6 38.7	22 54.6	29 15.5	10 15.6	9 33.0	20 52.3	14 57.0	27 04.6	28 28.4	29 43.9
23 M	12 11 18	0♎56 53	7♊57 38	14 53 04	6 39.1	24 45.9	0♏28.6	10 48.8	9 41.8	20 55.5	14 52.7	27 03.6	28 26.8	29 43.4
24 Tu	12 15 15	1 55 38	21 42 10	28 25 05	6R39.3	26 37.0	1 41.7	11 21.8	9 51.0	20 58.5	14 48.4	27 02.5	28 25.1	29 42.9
25 W	12 19 12	2 54 26	5♋02 03	11♋33 23	6 39.3	28 27.5	2 54.7	11 54.5	10 00.4	21 01.3	14 44.2	27 01.3	28 23.5	29 42.4
26 Th	12 23 08	3 53 15	17 59 25	24 20 34	6 39.1	0♎17.5	4 07.8	12 27.1	10 10.0	21 04.0	14 39.9	27 00.2	28 21.8	29 42.0
27 F	12 27 05	4 52 07	0♌37 15	6♌49 54	6 38.9	2 06.9	5 20.8	12 59.5	10 19.9	21 06.4	14 35.8	26 58.9	28 20.2	29 41.5
28 Sa	12 31 01	5 51 01	12 58 57	19 04 49	6D38.7	3 55.6	6 33.9	13 31.6	10 30.1	21 08.6	14 31.6	26 57.7	28 18.5	29 41.1
29 Su	12 34 58	6 49 57	25 07 54	1♍08 36	6 38.7	5 43.6	7 46.9	14 03.5	10 40.5	21 10.7	14 27.5	26 56.4	28 16.9	29 40.8
30 M	12 38 54	7 48 55	7♍07 18	13 04 20	6 38.8	7 30.7	8 59.9	14 35.2	10 51.2	21 12.5	14 23.5	26 55.0	28 15.2	29 40.4

LONGITUDE — October 2024

Day	Sid.Time	☉	0 hr ☽	Noon ☽	True ☊	☿	♀	♂	⚳	♃	♄	♅	♆	♇
1 Tu	12 42 51	8♎47 56	19♍00 03	24♍54 45	6♈38.9	9♎17.1	10♏12.9	15♋06.7	11♑02.1	21♊14.2	14♓19.5	26♉53.6	28♓13.6	29♑40.1
2 W	12 46 47	9 46 58	0♎48 45	6♎42 20	6R38.9	11 02.6	11 25.8	15 37.9	11 13.3	21 15.6	14R15.6	26R52.2	28R12.0	29R39.8
3 Th	12 50 44	10 46 03	12 35 46	18 29 20	6 38.8	12 47.3	12 38.8	16 08.9	11 24.7	21 16.9	14 11.7	26 50.7	28 10.4	29 39.6
4 F	12 54 40	11 45 09	24 23 20	0♏18 00	6 38.5	14 31.2	13 51.7	16 39.7	11 36.4	21 18.0	14 07.9	26 49.1	28 08.8	29 39.3
5 Sa	12 58 37	12 44 18	6♏13 40	12 10 37	6 37.8	16 14.3	15 04.6	17 10.2	11 48.3	21 18.8	14 04.2	26 47.6	28 07.2	29 39.1
6 Su	13 02 34	13 43 28	18 09 10	24 09 40	6 36.9	17 56.5	16 17.4	17 40.4	12 00.4	21 19.5	14 00.5	26 46.0	28 05.6	29 39.0
7 M	13 06 30	14 42 41	0♐12 28	6♐17 56	6 35.8	19 37.9	17 30.3	18 10.5	12 12.8	21 19.9	13 56.8	26 44.3	28 04.0	29 38.8
8 Tu	13 10 27	15 41 55	12 26 28	18 38 28	6 34.8	21 18.5	18 43.1	18 40.2	12 25.3	21R20.2	13 53.3	26 42.7	28 02.4	29 38.7
9 W	13 14 23	16 41 11	24 54 22	1♑14 35	6 34.0	22 58.4	19 55.9	19 09.7	12 38.1	21 20.3	13 49.8	26 40.9	28 00.9	29 38.6
10 Th	13 18 20	17 40 29	7♑39 31	14 09 36	6D33.6	24 37.5	21 08.7	19 38.9	12 51.2	21 20.1	13 46.4	26 39.2	27 59.3	29 38.6
11 F	13 22 16	18 39 49	20 45 11	27 26 37	6 33.7	26 15.8	22 21.5	20 07.9	13 04.4	21 19.8	13 43.0	26 37.4	27 57.8	29D38.5
12 Sa	13 26 13	19 39 10	4♒14 08	11♒07 56	6 34.4	27 53.4	23 34.2	20 36.6	13 17.8	21 19.2	13 39.8	26 35.6	27 56.3	29 38.5
13 Su	13 30 09	20 38 33	18 08 04	25 14 31	6 35.4	29 30.2	24 46.9	21 05.0	13 31.5	21 18.5	13 36.6	26 33.7	27 54.8	29 38.6
14 M	13 34 06	21 37 58	2♓27 04	9♓45 22	6 36.5	1♏06.4	25 59.5	21 33.1	13 45.3	21 17.5	13 33.5	26 31.8	27 53.3	29 38.6
15 Tu	13 38 03	22 37 25	17 08 54	24 36 59	6R37.3	2 41.9	27 12.2	22 00.9	13 59.4	21 16.4	13 30.4	26 29.9	27 51.8	29 38.7
16 W	13 41 59	23 36 53	2♈08 45	9♈43 12	6 37.5	4 16.7	28 24.8	22 28.5	14 13.6	21 15.0	13 27.4	26 27.9	27 50.3	29 38.8
17 Th	13 45 56	24 36 23	17 19 13	24 55 36	6 36.9	5 50.9	29 37.4	22 55.7	14 28.1	21 13.5	13 24.6	26 25.9	27 48.9	29 38.9
18 F	13 49 52	25 35 56	2♉31 07	10♉04 32	6 35.3	7 24.4	0♐49.9	23 22.6	14 42.7	21 11.7	13 21.8	26 23.9	27 47.5	29 39.1
19 Sa	13 53 49	26 35 30	17 34 43	25 00 34	6 32.9	8 57.3	2 02.4	23 49.3	14 57.5	21 09.8	13 19.0	26 21.9	27 46.1	29 39.3
20 Su	13 57 45	27 35 07	2♊21 13	9♊35 54	6 30.1	10 29.6	3 14.9	24 15.6	15 12.5	21 07.7	13 16.4	26 19.8	27 44.7	29 39.5
21 M	14 01 42	28 34 46	16 44 03	23 45 18	6 27.2	12 01.3	4 27.3	24 41.5	15 27.7	21 05.3	13 13.9	26 17.7	27 43.3	29 39.8
22 Tu	14 05 38	29 34 28	0♋39 28	7♋26 33	6 24.9	13 32.4	5 39.8	25 07.2	15 43.1	21 02.8	13 11.4	26 15.5	27 41.9	29 40.1
23 W	14 09 35	0♏34 11	14 06 39	20 40 04	6D23.4	15 02.9	6 52.2	25 32.5	15 58.6	21 00.0	13 09.1	26 13.4	27 40.6	29 40.4
24 Th	14 13 32	1 33 57	27 07 09	3♌28 22	6 23.1	16 32.9	8 04.5	25 57.5	16 14.3	20 57.1	13 06.8	26 11.2	27 39.3	29 40.8
25 F	14 17 28	2 33 45	9♌44 14	15 55 18	6 23.7	18 02.2	9 16.9	26 22.1	16 30.2	20 54.0	13 04.6	26 09.0	27 38.0	29 41.1
26 Sa	14 21 25	3 33 35	22 02 09	28 05 23	6 25.2	19 31.0	10 29.2	26 46.3	16 46.3	20 50.7	13 02.5	26 06.7	27 36.7	29 41.5
27 Su	14 25 21	4 33 28	4♍05 34	10♍03 18	6 27.0	20 59.1	11 41.4	27 10.2	17 02.5	20 47.1	13 00.5	26 04.5	27 35.4	29 42.0
28 M	14 29 18	5 33 22	15 59 08	21 53 35	6 28.6	22 26.7	12 53.7	27 33.7	17 18.9	20 43.4	12 58.6	26 02.2	27 34.2	29 42.4
29 Tu	14 33 14	6 33 19	27 47 09	3♎40 17	6R29.5	23 53.6	14 05.9	27 56.8	17 35.5	20 39.5	12 56.8	25 59.9	27 33.0	29 42.9
30 W	14 37 11	7 33 17	9♎33 26	15 26 57	6 29.1	25 19.9	15 18.0	28 19.5	17 52.2	20 35.5	12 55.1	25 57.6	27 31.8	29 43.4
31 Th	14 41 07	8 33 18	21 21 13	27 16 30	6 27.2	26 45.5	16 30.2	28 41.8	18 09.1	20 31.2	12 53.5	25 55.2	27 30.6	29 44.0

Astro Data	Planet Ingress	Last Aspect	☽ Ingress	Last Aspect	☽ Ingress	☽ Phases & Eclipses	Astro Data
Dy Hr Mn	Dy Hr Mn	Dy Hr Mn	Dy Hr Mn	Dy Hr Mn	Dy Hr Mn	Dy Hr Mn	1 September 2024
♅R 1 15:19	♇ ♑R 2 0:11	2 0:26 ♂ ⚹	♍ 2 3:50	1 21:40 ♇ △	♎ 1 22:21	3 1:57 ● 11♍04	Julian Day # 45535
☽0S 4 18:35	♂ ♋ 4 19:47	4 16:08 ♇ △	♎ 4 16:13	4 10:42 ♇ □	♏ 4 11:23	11 6:07 ☽ 19♐00	SVP 4♓54'56"
☽0N 18 11:15	☿ ♍ 9 6:51	7 5:10 ♇ □	♏ 7 5:20	6 22:54 ♇ ⚹	♐ 6 23:35	18 2:36 ○ 25♓41	GC 27♐11.0 ⚴ 28♏02.9
☉0S 22 12:45	☉ ♎ 22 12:45	9 17:13 ♇ ⚹	♐ 9 17:27	9 5:55 ♆ □	♑ 9 9:39	18 2:45 • P 0.085	Eris 25♈20.9R ⚵ 7♎46.4
♄∠♇ 25 23:10	♀ ♏ 23 2:37	12 0:22 ♆ □	♑ 12 2:39	11 15:54 ♇ ☌	♒ 11 16:32	24 18:51 ☾ 2♋12	⚷ 22♈57.6R ⚶ 3♍32.5
☿0S 28 6:05	☿ ♎ 26 8:10	14 7:36 ♇ ☌	♒ 14 7:55	13 14:12 ♅ □	♓ 13 19:56		☽ Mean ☊ 7♈55.8
		16 5:05 ♅ □	♓ 16 9:40	15 20:01 ♇ ⚹	♈ 15 20:35	2 18:50 ● 10♎04	
☽0S 2 0:44	☿ ♏ 13 19:25	18 9:04 ♇ ⚹	♈ 18 9:25	17 19:28 ♇ □	♉ 17 20:01	2 18:46:13 • A 07'25"	1 October 2024
♃R 9 7:06	♀ ♐ 17 19:29	20 8:40 ♇ □	♉ 20 9:04	19 19:35 ♇ △	♊ 19 20:08	10 18:56 ☽ 17♑58	Julian Day # 45565
♇D 12 0:36	☉ ♏ 22 22:16	22 10:15 ☉ △	♊ 22 10:25	21 21:01 ☉ △	♋ 21 22:51	17 11:28 ○ 24♈35	SVP 4♓54'53"
☽0N 15 22:26		24 12:00 ♆ □	♋ 24 14:51	24 4:49 ♇ ☍	♌ 24 5:25	24 8:04 ☾ 1♌24	GC 27♐11.1 ⚴ 7♐19.9
☽0S 29 6:49		26 22:13 ♇ ☍	♌ 26 22:48	26 8:05 ♅ □	♍ 26 15:49		Eris 25♈05.9R ⚵ 18♎21.9
		29 3:37 ♅ □	♍ 29 9:43	29 3:56 ♇ △	♎ 29 4:31		⚷ 21♈48.7R ⚶ 17♍46.8
				31 16:58 ♇ □	♏ 31 17:30		☽ Mean ☊ 6♈20.4

November 2024 LONGITUDE

Day	Sid.Time	☉	0 hr ☽	Noon ☽	True ☊	☿	♀	♂	⚳	♃	♄	♅	♆	♇
1 F	14 45 04	9♏33 21	3♏13 07	9♏11 16	6♈23.5	28♏10.4	17♐42.3	29♋03.6	18♑26.1	20♊26.8	12♓52.0	25♉52.9	27♓29.5	29♑44.5
2 Sa	14 49 01	10 33 25	15 11 13	21 13 07	6R18.4	29 34.5	18 54.3	29 25.1	18 43.3	20R22.1	12R50.5	25R50.5	27R28.4	29 45.1
3 Su	14 52 57	11 33 32	27 17 11	3♐23 33	6 12.1	0♐57.9	20 06.3	29 46.1	19 00.6	20 17.3	12 49.2	25 48.1	27 27.3	29 45.8
4 M	14 56 54	12 33 40	9♐32 24	15 43 53	6 05.3	2 20.4	21 18.3	0♌06.7	19 18.1	20 12.4	12 48.0	25 45.7	27 26.2	29 46.4
5 Tu	15 00 50	13 33 50	21 58 11	28 15 28	5 58.8	3 41.9	22 30.2	0 26.8	19 35.7	20 07.2	12 46.9	25 43.3	27 25.2	29 47.1
6 W	15 04 47	14 34 02	4♑35 55	10♑59 45	5 53.3	5 02.5	23 42.1	0 46.4	19 53.5	20 01.9	12 45.9	25 40.8	27 24.2	29 47.9
7 Th	15 08 43	15 34 15	17 27 11	23 58 27	5 49.4	6 21.9	24 54.0	1 05.6	20 11.4	19 56.5	12 45.0	25 38.4	27 23.2	29 48.6
8 F	15 12 40	16 34 29	0♒33 47	7♒13 26	5D47.2	7 40.2	26 05.7	1 24.3	20 29.4	19 50.8	12 44.2	25 35.9	27 22.3	29 49.4
9 Sa	15 16 36	17 34 45	13 57 36	20 46 31	5 46.8	8 57.0	27 17.5	1 42.6	20 47.6	19 45.0	12 43.5	25 33.5	27 21.3	29 50.2
10 Su	15 20 33	18 35 03	27 40 20	4♓39 09	5 47.7	10 12.4	28 29.2	2 00.3	21 05.9	19 39.1	12 42.9	25 31.0	27 20.4	29 51.0
11 M	15 24 30	19 35 21	11♓42 58	18 51 45	5 49.0	11 26.1	29 40.8	2 17.5	21 24.3	19 33.0	12 42.4	25 28.5	27 19.6	29 51.8
12 Tu	15 28 26	20 35 41	26 05 16	3♈23 13	5R49.9	12 38.0	0♑52.3	2 34.2	21 42.9	19 26.8	12 42.1	25 26.0	27 18.7	29 52.7
13 W	15 32 23	21 36 03	10♈45 05	18 10 16	5 49.3	13 47.7	2 03.8	2 50.4	22 01.6	19 20.4	12 41.8	25 23.5	27 17.9	29 53.6
14 Th	15 36 19	22 36 26	25 37 57	3♉07 14	5 46.6	14 55.1	3 15.2	3 06.0	22 20.4	19 13.9	12 41.6	25 21.0	27 17.1	29 54.6
15 F	15 40 16	23 36 51	10♉37 05	18 06 23	5 41.7	15 59.8	4 26.6	3 21.1	22 39.3	19 07.3	12D41.6	25 18.5	27 16.4	29 55.5
16 Sa	15 44 12	24 37 17	25 34 01	2♊58 50	5 34.8	17 01.5	5 37.9	3 35.7	22 58.3	19 00.5	12 41.6	25 16.0	27 15.6	29 56.5
17 Su	15 48 09	25 37 45	10♊19 48	17 35 57	5 26.7	17 59.8	6 49.1	3 49.7	23 17.5	18 53.7	12 41.8	25 13.5	27 14.9	29 57.5
18 M	15 52 05	26 38 15	24 46 28	1♋50 44	5 18.3	18 54.3	8 00.3	4 03.1	23 36.8	18 46.7	12 42.0	25 11.0	27 14.3	29 58.6
19 Tu	15 56 02	27 38 46	8♋48 17	15 38 51	5 10.6	19 44.4	9 11.4	4 15.9	23 56.1	18 39.6	12 42.4	25 08.5	27 13.7	29 59.6
20 W	15 59 59	28 39 19	22 22 22	28 58 54	5 04.6	20 29.6	10 22.4	4 28.1	24 15.6	18 32.3	12 42.8	25 06.0	27 13.1	0♒00.7
21 Th	16 03 55	29 39 54	5♌28 43	11♌52 10	5 00.6	21 09.3	11 33.4	4 39.6	24 35.2	18 25.0	12 43.4	25 03.5	27 12.5	0 01.8
22 F	16 07 52	0♐40 31	18 09 43	24 21 56	4D58.8	21 42.8	12 44.3	4 50.6	24 55.0	18 17.6	12 44.1	25 01.0	27 11.9	0 03.0
23 Sa	16 11 48	1 41 09	0♍29 24	6♍32 48	4 58.7	22 09.3	13 55.1	5 00.9	25 14.8	18 10.1	12 44.9	24 58.6	27 11.4	0 04.1
24 Su	16 15 45	2 41 48	12 32 48	18 30 05	4 59.5	22 28.2	15 05.8	5 10.5	25 34.7	18 02.5	12 45.7	24 56.1	27 11.0	0 05.3
25 M	16 19 41	3 42 30	24 25 19	0♎19 12	5R00.3	22R38.5	16 16.4	5 19.5	25 54.7	17 54.8	12 46.7	24 53.6	27 10.5	0 06.5
26 Tu	16 23 38	4 43 13	6♎12 21	12 05 22	5 00.1	22 39.6	17 27.0	5 27.7	26 14.8	17 47.0	12 47.8	24 51.1	27 10.1	0 07.7
27 W	16 27 35	5 43 57	17 58 51	23 53 19	4 58.1	22 30.7	18 37.4	5 35.3	26 35.1	17 39.2	12 49.0	24 48.7	27 09.7	0 09.0
28 Th	16 31 31	6 44 44	29 49 14	5♏47 00	4 53.5	22 11.2	19 47.8	5 42.2	26 55.4	17 31.3	12 50.3	24 46.3	27 09.4	0 10.3
29 F	16 35 28	7 45 31	11♏47 00	17 49 32	4 46.2	21 40.8	20 58.1	5 48.3	27 15.8	17 23.3	12 51.8	24 43.8	27 09.1	0 11.6
30 Sa	16 39 24	8 46 20	23 54 50	0♐03 04	4 36.4	20 59.4	22 08.3	5 53.7	27 36.3	17 15.3	12 53.3	24 41.4	27 08.8	0 12.9

December 2024 LONGITUDE

Day	Sid.Time	☉	0 hr ☽	Noon ☽	True ☊	☿	♀	♂	⚳	♃	♄	♅	♆	♇
1 Su	16 43 21	9♐47 10	6♐14 21	12♐28 46	4♈24.7	20♐07.3	23♑18.4	5♌58.4	27♑56.9	17♊07.3	12♓54.9	24♉39.0	27♓08.6	0♒14.2
2 M	16 47 17	10 48 02	18 46 20	25 07 02	4R12.1	19R05.4	24 28.4	6 02.3	28 17.6	16R59.2	12 56.6	24R36.6	27R08.4	0 15.6
3 Tu	16 51 14	11 48 54	1♑30 48	7♑57 35	3 59.8	17 54.9	25 38.3	6 05.4	28 38.4	16 51.1	12 58.5	24 34.3	27 08.2	0 17.0
4 W	16 55 10	12 49 47	14 27 19	20 59 54	3 49.0	16 37.8	26 48.0	6 07.8	28 59.3	16 42.9	13 00.4	24 31.9	27 08.1	0 18.4
5 Th	16 59 07	13 50 42	27 35 19	4♒13 29	3 40.5	15 16.5	27 57.7	6 09.4	29 20.2	16 34.8	13 02.4	24 29.6	27 08.0	0 19.8
6 F	17 03 04	14 51 37	10♒54 26	17 38 09	3 34.9	13 53.6	29 07.2	6R10.2	29 41.3	16 26.6	13 04.6	24 27.3	27 07.9	0 21.3
7 Sa	17 07 00	15 52 33	24 24 41	1♓14 05	3 31.9	12 31.8	0♒16.6	6 10.2	0♒02.4	16 18.4	13 06.8	24 25.0	27D07.9	0 22.7
8 Su	17 10 57	16 53 29	8♓06 27	15 01 50	3D31.1	11 14.1	1 25.9	6 09.3	0 23.6	16 10.2	13 09.2	24 22.7	27 07.9	0 24.2
9 M	17 14 53	17 54 26	22 00 19	29 01 53	3R31.3	10 02.8	2 35.1	6 07.7	0 44.9	16 02.1	13 11.6	24 20.5	27 07.9	0 25.7
10 Tu	17 18 50	18 55 24	6♈06 33	13♈14 12	3 31.0	8 59.8	3 44.0	6 05.3	1 06.2	15 53.9	13 14.2	24 18.3	27 08.0	0 27.3
11 W	17 22 46	19 56 22	20 24 37	27 37 32	3 29.1	8 06.8	4 52.9	6 02.0	1 27.6	15 45.8	13 16.8	24 16.1	27 08.1	0 28.8
12 Th	17 26 43	20 57 21	4♉52 31	12♉09 02	3 24.7	7 24.5	6 01.6	5 57.9	1 49.1	15 37.6	13 19.5	24 13.9	27 08.2	0 30.4
13 F	17 30 39	21 58 21	19 26 26	26 43 58	3 17.2	6 53.4	7 10.1	5 53.0	2 10.7	15 29.6	13 22.4	24 11.8	27 08.4	0 31.9
14 Sa	17 34 36	22 59 21	4♊00 47	11♊16 01	3 07.0	6 33.5	8 18.5	5 47.2	2 32.3	15 21.5	13 25.3	24 09.7	27 08.6	0 33.5
15 Su	17 38 33	24 00 22	18 28 45	25 38 09	2 55.0	6D24.5	9 26.7	5 40.6	2 54.0	15 13.5	13 28.3	24 07.6	27 08.8	0 35.2
16 M	17 42 29	25 01 24	2♋43 25	9♋43 49	2 42.4	6 25.7	10 34.7	5 33.2	3 15.8	15 05.6	13 31.5	24 05.5	27 09.1	0 36.8
17 Tu	17 46 26	26 02 26	16 38 48	23 27 56	2 30.5	6 36.5	11 42.6	5 24.9	3 37.6	14 57.7	13 34.7	24 03.5	27 09.4	0 38.4
18 W	17 50 22	27 03 29	0♌10 57	6♌47 44	2 20.5	6 56.0	12 50.2	5 15.8	3 59.5	14 49.8	13 38.0	24 01.5	27 09.8	0 40.1
19 Th	17 54 19	28 04 33	13 18 19	19 42 53	2 13.1	7 23.5	13 57.7	5 05.9	4 21.4	14 42.1	13 41.4	23 59.6	27 10.2	0 41.8
20 F	17 58 15	29 05 38	26 01 45	2♍15 20	2 08.4	7 58.2	15 05.0	4 55.1	4 43.5	14 34.4	13 44.9	23 57.6	27 10.6	0 43.5
21 Sa	18 02 12	0♑06 43	8♍24 08	14 28 43	2 06.2	8 39.2	16 12.1	4 43.5	5 05.5	14 26.8	13 48.5	23 55.8	27 11.0	0 45.2
22 Su	18 06 08	1 07 49	20 29 43	26 27 50	2 05.6	9 25.9	17 18.9	4 31.1	5 27.7	14 19.2	13 52.2	23 53.9	27 11.5	0 46.9
23 M	18 10 05	2 08 56	2♎23 45	8♎18 11	2 05.5	10 17.6	18 25.6	4 17.8	5 49.9	14 11.8	13 55.9	23 52.1	27 12.1	0 48.6
24 Tu	18 14 02	3 10 03	14 11 49	20 05 23	2 04.8	11 13.7	19 32.0	4 03.8	6 12.1	14 04.4	13 59.8	23 50.3	27 12.6	0 50.4
25 W	18 17 58	4 11 11	25 59 33	1♏54 58	2 02.4	12 13.8	20 38.3	3 49.0	6 34.4	13 57.2	14 03.7	23 48.5	27 13.2	0 52.2
26 Th	18 21 55	5 12 20	7♏52 14	13 51 54	1 57.5	13 17.2	21 44.2	3 33.4	6 56.8	13 50.1	14 07.7	23 46.8	27 13.8	0 53.9
27 F	18 25 51	6 13 30	19 54 29	26 00 25	1 49.6	14 23.8	22 50.0	3 17.1	7 19.2	13 43.0	14 11.9	23 45.2	27 14.5	0 55.7
28 Sa	18 29 48	7 14 39	2♐10 01	8♐23 36	1 39.0	15 33.0	23 55.5	3 00.1	7 41.7	13 36.1	14 16.1	23 43.5	27 15.2	0 57.5
29 Su	18 33 44	8 15 50	14 41 20	21 03 18	1 26.3	16 44.6	25 00.7	2 42.3	8 04.2	13 29.3	14 20.4	23 41.9	27 15.9	0 59.3
30 M	18 37 41	9 17 00	27 29 32	3♑59 55	1 12.5	17 58.2	26 05.7	2 23.9	8 26.8	13 22.7	14 24.7	23 40.4	27 16.7	1 01.1
31 Tu	18 41 38	10 18 11	10♑34 19	17 12 30	0 59.0	19 13.7	27 10.4	2 04.9	8 49.4	13 16.1	14 29.2	23 38.9	27 17.5	1 03.0

Astro Data

	Dy Hr Mn
☽ 0N	12 8:06
♄ D	15 14:21
☽ 0S	25 13:06
☿ R	26 2:42
♂ R	6 23:34
♆ D	7 23:44
☽ 0N	9 14:39
♃⚼♇	13 6:05
☿ D	15 20:59
☽ 0S	22 19:52
♃□♄	24 22:01

Planet Ingress

		Dy Hr Mn
☿	♐	2 19:19
♂	♌	4 4:11
♀	♑	11 18:27
♇	♒	19 20:30
☉	♐	21 19:58
♀	♒	7 6:14
⚳	♒	7 9:17
☉	♑	21 9:22

Last Aspect / ☽ Ingress

Last Aspect Dy Hr Mn		☽ Ingress	Dy Hr Mn
3 4:52	♇ ⚹	♐	3 5:21
5 10:25	♆ □	♑	5 15:18
7 22:39	♇ ☌	♒	7 22:59
10 0:25	♀ ⚹	♓	10 4:01
12 6:14	♇ ⚹	♈	12 6:27
14 6:51	♇ □	♉	14 7:00
16 7:04	♇ △	♊	16 7:10
18 4:10	♆ □	♋	18 8:51
20 11:21	☉ △	♌	20 13:52
22 13:16	♅ □	♍	22 23:02
25 5:36	♆ ☍	♎	25 11:21
27 9:15	☿ ⚹	♏	28 0:22
30 6:20	♆ △	♐	30 11:54

Last Aspect / ☽ Ingress

Last Aspect Dy Hr Mn		☽ Ingress	Dy Hr Mn
2 15:48	♆ □	♑	2 21:10
4 23:35	♀ ☌	♒	5 4:22
7 0:03	♅ □	♓	7 9:50
9 8:46	♆ ☌	♈	9 13:39
10 22:15	☉ △	♉	11 15:56
13 12:40	♆ ⚹	♊	13 17:23
15 14:33	♆ □	♋	15 19:22
17 18:35	♆ △	♌	17 23:40
20 5:21	☉ △	♍	20 7:38
22 13:28	♆ ☍	♎	22 19:09
24 10:45	♀ △	♏	25 8:07
27 14:25	♆ △	♐	27 19:48
29 23:35	♆ □	♑	30 4:38

☽ Phases & Eclipses

Dy Hr Mn		
1 12:48	●	9♏35
9 5:57	☽	17♒20
15 21:30	○	24♉01
23 1:29	☾	1♍15
1 6:23	●	9♐33
8 15:28	☽	17♓02
15 9:03	○	23♊53
22 22:19	☾	1♎34
30 22:28	●	9♑44

Astro Data

1 November 2024
Julian Day # 45596
SVP 4♓54'49"
GC 27♐11.2 ⚴ 18♐34.0
Eris 24♈47.5R ⚵ 29♎21.0
⚷ 20♈25.0R ⚶ 2♎27.4
☽ Mean ☊ 4♈41.9

1 December 2024
Julian Day # 45626
SVP 4♓54'44"
GC 27♐11.2 ⚴ 0♑13.2
Eris 24♈32.3R ⚵ 9♏34.6
⚷ 19♈22.1R ⚶ 16♎14.6
☽ Mean ☊ 3♈06.6

LONGITUDE — January 2025

Day	Sid.Time	☉	0 hr ☽	Noon☽	True☊	☿	♀	♂	⚳	♃	♄	♅	♆	♇
1 W	18 45 34	11♑19 21	23♑54 10	0♒39 01	0♈46.9	20♐30.9	28♒14.8	1♌45.2	9♒12.1	13♊09.8	14♓33.7	23♉37.4	27♓18.3	1♒04.8
2 Th	18 49 31	12 20 32	7♒26 42	14 16 51	0R37.3	21 49.6	29 19.0	1R24.9	9 34.8	13R03.5	14 38.3	23R36.0	27 19.1	1 06.7
3 F	18 53 27	13 21 43	21 09 10	28 03 19	0 30.8	23 09.5	0♓22.8	1 04.1	9 57.5	12 57.4	14 43.0	23 34.6	27 20.0	1 08.5
4 Sa	18 57 24	14 22 53	4♓59 03	11♓56 09	0 27.2	24 30.7	1 26.3	0 42.8	10 20.3	12 51.5	14 47.8	23 33.3	27 21.0	1 10.4
5 Su	19 01 20	15 24 03	18 54 25	25 53 44	0D26.1	25 53.0	2 29.4	0 21.0	10 43.2	12 45.7	14 52.7	23 32.0	27 21.9	1 12.3
6 M	19 05 17	16 25 12	2♈54 01	9♈55 11	0R26.1	27 16.2	3 32.2	29♋58.8	11 06.0	12 40.0	14 57.6	23 30.8	27 22.9	1 14.1
7 Tu	19 09 13	17 26 21	16 57 10	23 59 54	0 26.1	28 40.3	4 34.7	29 36.3	11 29.0	12 34.6	15 02.6	23 29.6	27 23.9	1 16.0
8 W	19 13 10	18 27 30	1♉03 18	8♉07 14	0 24.6	0♑05.3	5 36.7	29 13.3	11 51.9	12 29.2	15 07.7	23 28.4	27 25.0	1 17.9
9 Th	19 17 07	19 28 38	15 11 31	22 15 54	0 20.7	1 31.0	6 38.4	28 50.1	12 14.9	12 24.1	15 12.8	23 27.3	27 26.1	1 19.8
10 F	19 21 03	20 29 46	29 20 05	6♊23 41	0 14.1	2 57.5	7 39.7	28 26.7	12 37.9	12 19.1	15 18.0	23 26.3	27 27.2	1 21.7
11 Sa	19 25 00	21 30 53	13♊26 15	20 27 18	0 04.9	4 24.6	8 40.5	28 03.0	13 00.9	12 14.3	15 23.3	23 25.3	27 28.3	1 23.6
12 Su	19 28 56	22 32 00	27 26 17	4♋22 42	29♓53.9	5 52.4	9 40.9	27 39.2	13 24.0	12 09.7	15 28.7	23 24.3	27 29.5	1 25.6
13 M	19 32 53	23 33 06	11♋16 00	18 05 41	29 42.2	7 20.8	10 40.9	27 15.3	13 47.1	12 05.3	15 34.1	23 23.4	27 30.7	1 27.5
14 Tu	19 36 49	24 34 12	24 51 19	1♌32 31	29 31.1	8 49.9	11 40.4	26 51.3	14 10.3	12 01.0	15 39.6	23 22.5	27 32.0	1 29.4
15 W	19 40 46	25 35 18	8♌09 02	14 40 40	29 21.6	10 19.5	12 39.4	26 27.3	14 33.5	11 57.0	15 45.1	23 21.7	27 33.2	1 31.3
16 Th	19 44 42	26 36 23	21 07 23	27 29 11	29 14.4	11 49.7	13 38.0	26 03.3	14 56.7	11 53.1	15 50.8	23 21.0	27 34.5	1 33.3
17 F	19 48 39	27 37 27	3♍46 14	9♍58 47	29 10.0	13 20.4	14 36.0	25 39.4	15 19.9	11 49.4	15 56.5	23 20.3	27 35.8	1 35.2
18 Sa	19 52 36	28 38 32	16 07 09	22 11 45	29D08.0	14 51.7	15 33.5	25 15.6	15 43.1	11 45.9	16 02.2	23 19.6	27 37.2	1 37.1
19 Su	19 56 32	29 39 36	28 13 06	4♎11 43	29 07.8	16 23.6	16 30.4	24 51.9	16 06.4	11 42.6	16 08.0	23 19.0	27 38.6	1 39.1
20 M	20 00 29	0♒40 39	10♎08 13	16 03 13	29 08.6	17 56.1	17 26.8	24 28.5	16 29.7	11 39.4	16 13.9	23 18.4	27 40.0	1 41.0
21 Tu	20 04 25	1 41 42	21 57 24	27 51 25	29R09.4	19 29.1	18 22.5	24 05.3	16 53.0	11 36.5	16 19.8	23 17.9	27 41.4	1 42.9
22 W	20 08 22	2 42 45	3♏45 57	9♏41 43	29 09.2	21 02.7	19 17.7	23 42.5	17 16.4	11 33.8	16 25.8	23 17.5	27 42.9	1 44.9
23 Th	20 12 18	3 43 48	15 39 22	21 39 33	29 07.2	22 36.9	20 12.2	23 19.9	17 39.8	11 31.2	16 31.8	23 17.0	27 44.4	1 46.8
24 F	20 16 15	4 44 50	27 42 52	3♐49 54	29 03.0	24 11.7	21 06.1	22 57.8	18 03.2	11 28.9	16 37.9	23 16.7	27 45.9	1 48.7
25 Sa	20 20 11	5 45 51	10♐01 07	16 16 59	28 56.6	25 47.1	21 59.3	22 36.1	18 26.6	11 26.8	16 44.1	23 16.4	27 47.4	1 50.7
26 Su	20 24 08	6 46 52	22 37 50	29 03 55	28 48.5	27 23.1	22 51.8	22 14.8	18 50.0	11 24.9	16 50.3	23 16.2	27 49.0	1 52.6
27 M	20 28 05	7 47 52	5♑35 21	12♑12 11	28 39.3	28 59.7	23 43.6	21 54.1	19 13.5	11 23.1	16 56.6	23 16.0	27 50.6	1 54.6
28 Tu	20 32 01	8 48 52	18 54 19	25 41 32	28 30.1	0♒37.0	24 34.6	21 33.8	19 36.9	11 21.6	17 02.9	23 15.8	27 52.2	1 56.5
29 W	20 35 58	9 49 50	2♒33 31	9♒29 50	28 21.8	2 14.9	25 24.8	21 14.2	20 00.4	11 20.3	17 09.3	23 15.7	27 53.9	1 58.4
30 Th	20 39 54	10 50 48	16 29 58	23 33 22	28 15.4	3 53.5	26 14.1	20 55.2	20 23.9	11 19.2	17 15.7	23D15.7	27 55.5	2 00.3
31 F	20 43 51	11 51 44	0♓39 24	7♓47 26	28 11.3	5 32.7	27 02.7	20 36.8	20 47.4	11 18.3	17 22.2	23 15.7	27 57.2	2 02.2

LONGITUDE — February 2025

Day	Sid.Time	☉	0 hr ☽	Noon☽	True☊	☿	♀	♂	⚳	♃	♄	♅	♆	♇
1 Sa	20 47 47	12♒52 40	14♓56 51	22♓07 04	28♓09.5	7♒12.7	27♓50.3	20♋19.0	21♒10.9	11♊17.6	17♓28.7	23♉15.8	27♓58.9	2♒04.2
2 Su	20 51 44	13 53 34	29 17 31	6♈27 44	28D09.6	8 53.4	28 37.0	20R01.9	21 34.5	11R17.1	17 35.2	23 15.9	28 00.7	2 06.1
3 M	20 55 40	14 54 26	13♈37 16	20 45 47	28 10.8	10 34.8	29 22.7	19 45.6	21 58.0	11D16.8	17 41.8	23 16.1	28 02.4	2 08.0
4 Tu	20 59 37	15 55 18	27 53 00	4♉58 40	28R12.0	12 16.9	0♈07.4	19 30.0	22 21.6	11 16.7	17 48.5	23 16.3	28 04.2	2 09.9
5 W	21 03 34	16 56 07	12♉02 36	19 04 39	28 12.4	13 59.8	0 51.1	19 15.1	22 45.1	11 16.8	17 55.1	23 16.6	28 06.0	2 11.7
6 Th	21 07 30	17 56 56	26 04 43	3♊02 39	28 11.3	15 43.4	1 33.7	19 01.0	23 08.7	11 17.2	18 01.9	23 16.9	28 07.9	2 13.6
7 F	21 11 27	18 57 43	9♊58 21	16 51 42	28 08.4	17 27.8	2 15.1	18 47.6	23 32.2	11 17.7	18 08.6	23 17.3	28 09.7	2 15.5
8 Sa	21 15 23	19 58 28	23 42 36	0♋30 53	28 03.8	19 13.0	2 55.3	18 35.0	23 55.8	11 18.4	18 15.4	23 17.8	28 11.6	2 17.4
9 Su	21 19 20	20 59 12	7♋16 25	13 59 02	27 57.9	20 58.9	3 34.3	18 23.2	24 19.4	11 19.4	18 22.3	23 18.3	28 13.5	2 19.2
10 M	21 23 16	21 59 55	20 38 35	27 14 55	27 51.5	22 45.6	4 12.0	18 12.2	24 43.0	11 20.5	18 29.1	23 18.8	28 15.4	2 21.1
11 Tu	21 27 13	23 00 36	3♌47 53	10♌17 22	27 45.4	24 33.0	4 48.4	18 02.0	25 06.5	11 21.8	18 36.1	23 19.4	28 17.3	2 22.9
12 W	21 31 10	24 01 15	16 43 17	23 05 35	27 40.2	26 21.1	5 23.3	17 52.6	25 30.1	11 23.4	18 43.0	23 20.1	28 19.2	2 24.8
13 Th	21 35 06	25 01 53	29 24 16	5♍39 22	27 36.5	28 10.0	5 56.9	17 44.0	25 53.7	11 25.1	18 50.0	23 20.8	28 21.2	2 26.6
14 F	21 39 03	26 02 30	11♍51 00	17 59 19	27D34.5	29 59.4	6 28.9	17 36.1	26 17.3	11 27.0	18 57.0	23 21.5	28 23.2	2 28.4
15 Sa	21 42 59	27 03 05	24 04 33	0♎06 58	27 34.1	1♓49.5	6 59.4	17 29.1	26 40.8	11 29.2	19 04.0	23 22.3	28 25.2	2 30.2
16 Su	21 46 56	28 03 39	6♎06 54	12 04 44	27 34.9	3 40.1	7 28.3	17 22.9	27 04.4	11 31.5	19 11.1	23 23.2	28 27.2	2 32.0
17 M	21 50 52	29 04 12	18 00 53	23 55 52	27 36.6	5 31.1	7 55.5	17 17.4	27 28.0	11 34.0	19 18.1	23 24.1	28 29.2	2 33.7
18 Tu	21 54 49	0♓04 43	29 50 11	5♏44 23	27 38.5	7 22.4	8 20.9	17 12.7	27 51.5	11 36.7	19 25.3	23 25.0	28 31.3	2 35.5
19 W	21 58 45	1 05 13	11♏39 03	17 34 48	27 40.0	9 13.9	8 44.6	17 08.9	28 15.1	11 39.6	19 32.4	23 26.1	28 33.3	2 37.3
20 Th	22 02 42	2 05 42	23 32 15	29 32 01	27R40.8	11 05.5	9 06.5	17 05.8	28 38.6	11 42.7	19 39.6	23 27.1	28 35.4	2 39.0
21 F	22 06 38	3 06 10	5♐34 44	11♐40 59	27 40.5	12 56.9	9 26.4	17 03.4	29 02.2	11 46.0	19 46.8	23 28.2	28 37.5	2 40.7
22 Sa	22 10 35	4 06 36	17 51 23	24 06 28	27 39.1	14 47.8	9 44.4	17 01.9	29 25.7	11 49.4	19 54.0	23 29.4	28 39.6	2 42.4
23 Su	22 14 32	5 07 01	0♑26 43	6♑52 33	27 36.7	16 38.2	10 00.3	17D01.0	29 49.3	11 53.1	20 01.2	23 30.6	28 41.7	2 44.1
24 M	22 18 28	6 07 25	13 24 19	20 02 14	27 33.7	18 27.5	10 14.1	17 01.0	0♓12.8	11 56.9	20 08.5	23 31.9	28 43.8	2 45.8
25 Tu	22 22 25	7 07 47	26 46 25	3♒36 52	27 30.5	20 15.5	10 25.8	17 01.7	0 36.3	12 00.9	20 15.7	23 33.2	28 46.0	2 47.5
26 W	22 26 21	8 08 07	10♒33 25	17 35 45	27 27.7	22 01.8	10 35.3	17 03.1	0 59.8	12 05.1	20 23.0	23 34.6	28 48.1	2 49.1
27 Th	22 30 18	9 08 26	24 43 28	1♓55 57	27 25.6	23 45.9	10 42.5	17 05.2	1 23.3	12 09.5	20 30.3	23 36.0	28 50.3	2 50.8
28 F	22 34 14	10 08 43	9♓12 30	16 32 21	27D24.4	25 27.4	10 47.3	17 08.1	1 46.8	12 14.1	20 37.7	23 37.4	28 52.4	2 52.4

Astro Data
Dy Hr Mn
☽0N 5 19:10
☽0S 19 3:16
♄∠♇ 27 0:47
♀0N 30 7:32
♅ D 30 16:23

☽0N 2 0:39
♃ D 4 9:41
☽0S 15 10:56
♂ D 24 2:01

Planet Ingress
Dy Hr Mn
♀ ♓ 3 3:25
♂ ♋R 6 10:45
☿ ♑ 8 10:31
☊ ♓R 11 23:04
☉ ♒ 19 20:01
☿ ♒ 28 2:54

♀ ♈ 4 7:58
☿ ♓ 14 12:08
☉ ♓ 18 10:08
⚳ ♓ 23 22:56

Last Aspect / ☽ Ingress

Last Aspect Dy Hr Mn		☽ Ingress Dy Hr Mn
1 6:03	♆ ⚹	♒ 1 10:51
3 4:14	♅ □	♓ 3 15:22
5 14:31	♆ ☌	♈ 5 19:02
7 21:17	♂ □	♉ 7 22:12
9 22:51	♂ ⚹	♊ 10 1:08
12 0:05	♆ □	♋ 12 4:25
14 4:47	♆ △	♌ 14 9:13
16 4:11	♅ □	♍ 16 16:47
19 2:02	☉ △	♎ 19 3:34
21 4:35	♂ △	♏ 21 16:21
24 0:04	♆ △	♐ 24 4:30
26 9:41	♆ □	♑ 26 13:44
28 15:50	♆ ⚹	♒ 28 19:33
30 11:30	♅ □	♓ 30 22:54

Last Aspect Dy Hr Mn		☽ Ingress Dy Hr Mn
1 22:07	♀ ☌	♈ 2 1:11
3 10:21	♂ □	♉ 4 3:35
6 3:31	♆ ⚹	♊ 6 6:45
8 7:53	♆ □	♋ 8 11:05
10 13:51	♆ △	♌ 10 17:02
12 19:13	♆ ☍	♍ 13 1:08
15 8:37	♆ ☍	♎ 15 11:46
17 23:25	☉ △	♏ 18 0:20
20 10:07	♆ △	♐ 20 12:56
22 20:40	♆ □	♑ 22 23:10
25 3:29	♆ ⚹	♒ 25 5:41
26 22:06	♅ □	♓ 27 8:48

☽ Phases & Eclipses
Dy Hr Mn
6 23:57 ☽ 16♈56
13 22:28 ○ 24♋00
21 20:32 ☾ 2♏03
29 12:37 ● 9♒51

5 8:03 ☽ 16♉46
12 13:55 ○ 24♌06
20 17:34 ☾ 2♐20
28 0:46 ● 9♓41

Astro Data
1 January 2025
Julian Day # 45657
SVP 4♓54'38"
GC 27♐11.3 ⚳ 12♑28.0
Eris 24♈23.9R ⚴ 19♏08.0
⚷ 19♈00.2 ⚶ 29♎25.1
☽ Mean ☊ 1♈28.2

1 February 2025
Julian Day # 45688
SVP 4♓54'32"
GC 27♐11.4 ⚳ 24♑23.6
Eris 24♈25.8 ⚴ 26♏48.1
⚷ 19♈31.0 ⚶ 10♏24.5
☽ Mean ☊ 29♓49.7

March 2025 — LONGITUDE

Day	Sid.Time	☉	0 hr ☽	Noon ☽	True☊	☿	♀	♂	⚳	♃	♄	♅	♆	♇
1 Sa	22 38 11	11♓08 58	23♓54 35	1♈18 19	27♓24.2	27♓05.7	10♈49.8	17♋11.6	2♓10.3	12♊18.8	20♓45.0	23♉38.9	28♓54.6	2♒54.0
2 Su	22 42 07	12 09 12	8♈42 36	16 06 34	27 24.7	28 40.4	10R 49.9	17 15.9	2 33.7	12 23.7	20 52.3	23 40.5	28 56.8	2 55.6
3 M	22 46 04	13 09 23	23 29 21	0♉50 11	27 25.7	0♈10.7	10 47.5	17 20.8	2 57.1	12 28.8	20 59.7	23 42.1	28 59.0	2 57.2
4 Tu	22 50 01	14 09 33	8♉08 23	15 23 22	27 26.8	1 36.3	10 42.6	17 26.4	3 20.5	12 34.1	21 07.1	23 43.7	29 01.2	2 58.7
5 W	22 53 57	15 09 40	22 34 42	29 42 01	27 27.7	2 56.4	10 35.2	17 32.7	3 43.9	12 39.5	21 14.5	23 45.4	29 03.5	3 00.2
6 Th	22 57 54	16 09 45	6♊45 04	13♊43 42	27R 28.1	4 10.5	10 25.2	17 39.6	4 07.3	12 45.1	21 21.8	23 47.2	29 05.7	3 01.8
7 F	23 01 50	17 09 49	20 37 51	27 27 32	27 27.9	5 18.0	10 12.8	17 47.1	4 30.7	12 50.9	21 29.2	23 49.0	29 07.9	3 03.3
8 Sa	23 05 47	18 09 49	4♋12 48	10♋53 45	27 27.3	6 18.5	9 57.8	17 55.3	4 54.0	12 56.8	21 36.6	23 50.8	29 10.2	3 04.7
9 Su	23 09 43	19 09 48	17 30 32	24 03 17	27 26.3	7 11.5	9 40.4	18 04.0	5 17.3	13 02.9	21 44.0	23 52.7	29 12.4	3 06.2
10 M	23 13 40	20 09 45	0♌32 12	6♌57 27	27 25.3	7 56.6	9 20.6	18 13.4	5 40.6	13 09.2	21 51.4	23 54.6	29 14.7	3 07.6
11 Tu	23 17 36	21 09 39	13 19 14	19 37 42	27 24.4	8 33.5	8 58.4	18 23.3	6 03.8	13 15.6	21 58.8	23 56.5	29 16.9	3 09.1
12 W	23 21 33	22 09 32	25 53 03	2♍05 28	27 23.8	9 01.9	8 33.9	18 33.8	6 27.0	13 22.2	22 06.3	23 58.5	29 19.2	3 10.5
13 Th	23 25 30	23 09 22	8♍15 08	14 22 13	27 23.4	9 21.7	8 07.3	18 44.9	6 50.2	13 28.9	22 13.7	24 00.6	29 21.4	3 11.8
14 F	23 29 26	24 09 10	20 26 55	26 29 27	27D 23.2	9R 32.7	7 38.8	18 56.5	7 13.4	13 35.8	22 21.1	24 02.7	29 23.7	3 13.2
15 Sa	23 33 23	25 08 57	2♎30 01	8♎28 50	27 23.3	9 35.1	7 08.3	19 08.6	7 36.6	13 42.8	22 28.5	24 04.8	29 26.0	3 14.5
16 Su	23 37 19	26 08 41	14 26 10	20 22 18	27 23.4	9 29.1	6 36.2	19 21.3	7 59.7	13 49.9	22 35.9	24 07.0	29 28.2	3 15.8
17 M	23 41 16	27 08 24	26 17 31	2♏12 10	27R 23.5	9 14.9	6 02.6	19 34.4	8 22.8	13 57.3	22 43.3	24 09.2	29 30.5	3 17.1
18 Tu	23 45 12	28 08 04	8♏06 35	14 01 12	27 23.5	8 53.1	5 27.7	19 48.1	8 45.8	14 04.7	22 50.7	24 11.4	29 32.8	3 18.4
19 W	23 49 09	29 07 43	19 56 24	25 52 39	27 23.3	8 24.1	4 51.7	20 02.2	9 08.9	14 12.3	22 58.0	24 13.7	29 35.1	3 19.6
20 Th	23 53 05	0♈07 21	1♐50 27	7♐50 16	27 23.1	7 48.8	4 14.9	20 16.8	9 31.9	14 20.1	23 05.4	24 16.0	29 37.3	3 20.9
21 F	23 57 02	1 06 56	13 52 40	19 58 09	27D 22.8	7 07.9	3 37.5	20 31.9	9 54.8	14 28.0	23 12.8	24 18.4	29 39.6	3 22.1
22 Sa	0 00 59	2 06 30	26 07 17	2♑20 37	27 22.7	6 22.4	2 59.8	20 47.4	10 17.8	14 36.0	23 20.1	24 20.8	29 41.9	3 23.2
23 Su	0 04 55	3 06 02	8♑38 40	15 01 56	27 22.9	5 33.4	2 22.0	21 03.4	10 40.7	14 44.1	23 27.5	24 23.2	29 44.2	3 24.4
24 M	0 08 52	4 05 32	21 30 53	28 05 55	27 23.3	4 42.0	1 44.4	21 19.8	11 03.5	14 52.4	23 34.8	24 25.7	29 46.4	3 25.5
25 Tu	0 12 48	5 05 01	4♒47 21	11♒35 24	27 23.9	3 49.3	1 07.3	21 36.7	11 26.4	15 00.8	23 42.2	24 28.2	29 48.7	3 26.6
26 W	0 16 45	6 04 28	18 30 11	25 31 39	27 24.7	2 56.4	0 30.8	21 53.9	11 49.2	15 09.4	23 49.5	24 30.8	29 51.0	3 27.7
27 Th	0 20 41	7 03 53	2♓39 37	9♓53 43	27 25.4	2 04.3	29♓55.2	22 11.6	12 11.9	15 18.1	23 56.8	24 33.4	29 53.2	3 28.8
28 F	0 24 38	8 03 15	17 13 26	24 38 04	27R 25.7	1 14.1	29 20.7	22 29.7	12 34.6	15 26.9	24 04.0	24 36.0	29 55.5	3 29.8
29 Sa	0 28 34	9 02 36	2♈06 45	9♈38 28	27 25.5	0 26.7	28 47.6	22 48.2	12 57.3	15 35.8	24 11.3	24 38.6	29 57.7	3 30.8
30 Su	0 32 31	10 01 55	17 12 08	24 46 34	27 24.7	29♓42.7	28 16.0	23 07.0	13 19.9	15 44.9	24 18.5	24 41.3	29 60.0	3 31.8
31 M	0 36 28	11 01 12	2♉20 34	9♉52 59	27 23.3	29 03.0	27 46.1	23 26.3	13 42.5	15 54.0	24 25.8	24 44.0	0♈02.2	3 32.8

April 2025 — LONGITUDE

Day	Sid.Time	☉	0 hr ☽	Noon ☽	True☊	☿	♀	♂	⚳	♃	♄	♅	♆	♇
1 Tu	0 40 24	12♈00 27	17♉22 43	24♉48 45	27♓21.5	28♓27.8	27♓18.0	23♋45.9	14♓05.1	16♊03.3	24♓33.0	24♉46.8	0♈04.5	3♒33.7
2 W	0 44 21	12 59 39	2♊10 15	9♊26 32	27R 19.7	27R 57.8	26R 51.9	24 05.9	14 27.6	16 12.7	24 40.1	24 49.6	0 06.7	3 34.6
3 Th	0 48 17	13 58 50	16 37 05	23 41 32	27 18.2	27 33.1	26 28.0	24 26.2	14 50.0	16 22.3	24 47.3	24 52.4	0 09.0	3 35.5
4 F	0 52 14	14 57 58	0♋39 42	7♋31 35	27D 17.3	27 13.8	26 06.2	24 46.9	15 12.4	16 31.9	24 54.4	24 55.2	0 11.2	3 36.3
5 Sa	0 56 10	15 57 03	14 17 14	20 56 53	27 17.3	27 00.2	25 46.7	25 07.9	15 34.7	16 41.7	25 01.5	24 58.1	0 13.4	3 37.2
6 Su	1 00 07	16 56 06	27 30 48	3♌59 22	27 18.0	26D 52.1	25 29.6	25 29.2	15 57.0	16 51.5	25 08.6	25 01.0	0 15.6	3 38.0
7 M	1 04 03	17 55 07	10♌22 57	16 41 58	27 19.3	26 49.6	25 14.8	25 50.8	16 19.3	17 01.5	25 15.7	25 03.9	0 17.8	3 38.7
8 Tu	1 08 00	18 54 06	22 56 54	29 08 09	27 20.9	26 52.5	25 02.5	26 12.8	16 41.5	17 11.6	25 22.7	25 06.9	0 20.0	3 39.5
9 W	1 11 57	19 53 02	5♍16 09	11♍21 19	27 22.3	27 00.6	24 52.7	26 35.1	17 03.6	17 21.7	25 29.7	25 09.8	0 22.2	3 40.2
10 Th	1 15 53	20 51 56	17 24 04	23 24 44	27R 23.1	27 13.9	24 45.3	26 57.6	17 25.7	17 32.0	25 36.6	25 12.8	0 24.3	3 40.9
11 F	1 19 50	21 50 48	29 23 42	5♎21 15	27 22.9	27 32.0	24 40.4	27 20.5	17 47.7	17 42.4	25 43.6	25 15.9	0 26.5	3 41.5
12 Sa	1 23 46	22 49 38	11♎17 43	17 13 22	27 21.5	27 54.9	24D 37.8	27 43.6	18 09.7	17 52.8	25 50.5	25 18.9	0 28.6	3 42.2
13 Su	1 27 43	23 48 26	23 08 27	29 03 14	27 18.7	28 22.3	24 37.7	28 07.0	18 31.6	18 03.4	25 57.3	25 22.0	0 30.7	3 42.8
14 M	1 31 39	24 47 12	4♏57 58	10♏52 53	27 14.7	28 54.0	24 40.0	28 30.6	18 53.5	18 14.0	26 04.1	25 25.1	0 32.9	3 43.4
15 Tu	1 35 36	25 45 56	16 48 14	22 44 17	27 09.9	29 29.8	24 44.6	28 54.6	19 15.3	18 24.8	26 10.9	25 28.2	0 35.0	3 43.9
16 W	1 39 32	26 44 38	28 41 18	4♐39 34	27 04.7	0♈09.5	24 51.5	29 18.8	19 37.0	18 35.6	26 17.7	25 31.4	0 37.1	3 44.5
17 Th	1 43 29	27 43 19	10♐39 24	16 41 09	26 59.7	0 53.0	25 00.6	29 43.2	19 58.7	18 46.6	26 24.4	25 34.5	0 39.2	3 45.0
18 F	1 47 26	28 41 58	22 45 10	28 51 50	26 55.4	1 40.0	25 11.8	0♌07.9	20 20.3	18 57.6	26 31.1	25 37.7	0 41.2	3 45.4
19 Sa	1 51 22	29 40 35	5♑01 34	11♑14 49	26 52.4	2 30.4	25 25.2	0 32.8	20 41.9	19 08.7	26 37.7	25 40.9	0 43.3	3 45.9
20 Su	1 55 19	0♉39 10	17 32 00	23 53 37	26D 50.9	3 23.9	25 40.6	0 58.0	21 03.4	19 19.9	26 44.3	25 44.1	0 45.3	3 46.3
21 M	1 59 15	1 37 44	0♒20 05	6♒51 51	26 50.8	4 20.6	25 58.0	1 23.4	21 24.8	19 31.2	26 50.9	25 47.4	0 47.3	3 46.7
22 Tu	2 03 12	2 36 16	13 29 20	20 12 52	26 51.8	5 20.2	26 17.3	1 49.0	21 46.2	19 42.5	26 57.4	25 50.7	0 49.4	3 47.0
23 W	2 07 08	3 34 47	27 02 46	3♓59 11	26 53.2	6 22.7	26 38.4	2 14.9	22 07.5	19 54.0	27 03.9	25 53.9	0 51.3	3 47.4
24 Th	2 11 05	4 33 16	11♓02 13	18 11 46	26R 54.4	7 27.8	27 01.4	2 40.9	22 28.7	20 05.5	27 10.3	25 57.2	0 53.3	3 47.7
25 F	2 15 01	5 31 43	25 27 36	2♈49 17	26 54.5	8 35.5	27 26.0	3 07.2	22 49.8	20 17.1	27 16.7	26 00.6	0 55.3	3 47.9
26 Sa	2 18 58	6 30 09	10♈16 11	17 47 31	26 53.0	9 45.8	27 52.3	3 33.7	23 10.9	20 28.7	27 23.0	26 03.9	0 57.2	3 48.2
27 Su	2 22 54	7 28 32	25 22 14	2♉59 13	26 49.6	10 58.4	28 20.2	4 00.5	23 31.9	20 40.5	27 29.3	26 07.2	0 59.2	3 48.4
28 M	2 26 51	8 26 55	10♉37 11	18 14 47	26 44.5	12 13.4	28 49.6	4 27.4	23 52.8	20 52.3	27 35.5	26 10.6	1 01.1	3 48.6
29 Tu	2 30 48	9 25 15	25 50 42	3♊23 39	26 38.2	13 30.7	29 20.4	4 54.5	24 13.7	21 04.2	27 41.7	26 14.0	1 02.9	3 48.7
30 W	2 34 44	10 23 34	10♊52 25	18 16 01	26 31.7	14 50.2	29 52.7	5 21.8	24 34.5	21 16.2	27 47.9	26 17.3	1 04.8	3 48.9

Astro Data	Dy Hr Mn
☽0N	1 9:09
♀R	2 0:37
☿0N	2 12:32
☽0S	14 18:05
☿R	15 6:46
☉0N	20 9:03
☽0N	28 19:54
☿0S	3 5:49
♄✶♅	4 16:22
☿D	7 11:09
☽0S	11 0:18
♀D	13 1:03
♃□♇	17 8:17
☿0N	23 4:16
☽0N	25 6:33

Planet Ingress	Dy Hr Mn
☿ ♈	3 9:05
☉ ♈	20 9:03
♀ ♓R	27 8:42
☿ ♓R	30 2:19
♆ ♈	30 12:01
☿ ♈	16 6:26
♂ ♌	18 4:22
☉ ♉	19 19:57
♀ ♈	30 17:17

Last Aspect Dy Hr Mn		☽ Ingress Dy Hr Mn
1 8:06	♆ ☌	♈ 1 9:53
2 13:53	♂ □	♉ 3 10:38
5 10:55	♆ ✶	♊ 5 12:30
7 14:58	♆ □	♋ 7 16:30
9 21:33	♆ △	♌ 9 23:00
11 20:17	♅ □	♍ 12 7:57
14 17:49	♆ ☍	♎ 14 19:00
16 9:54	♂ □	♏ 17 7:32
19 19:29	♆ △	♐ 19 20:18
22 6:54	♆ □	♑ 22 7:30
24 15:02	♆ ✶	♒ 24 15:26
26 10:16	♅ □	♓ 26 19:33
28 20:31	♆ ☌	♈ 28 20:37
30 9:19	♂ □	♉ 30 20:17

Last Aspect Dy Hr Mn		☽ Ingress Dy Hr Mn
1 17:44	☿ ✶	♊ 1 20:27
3 18:28	♅ □	♋ 3 22:51
5 22:56	☿ △	♌ 6 4:35
8 4:09	♅ □	♍ 8 13:41
10 19:50	☿ ☍	♎ 11 1:13
13 10:02	♂ □	♏ 13 13:55
16 2:25	☿ △	♐ 16 2:38
18 11:39	☉ △	♑ 18 14:13
20 17:22	♄ ✶	♒ 20 23:23
22 21:57	♅ □	♓ 23 5:08
25 2:58	♀ ☌	♈ 25 7:25
26 16:19	♃ ✶	♉ 27 7:18
29 5:19	♀ ✶	♊ 29 6:36

☽ Phases & Eclipses Dy Hr Mn	
6 16:33	☽ 16♊21
14 6:56	○ 23♍57
14 7:00	• T 1.179
22 11:31	☾ 2♑05
29 10:59	● 9♈00
29 10:48:35	• P 0.938
5 2:16	☽ 15♋33
13 0:23	○ 23♎20
21 1:37	☾ 1♒12
27 19:32	● 7♉47

Astro Data

1 March 2025
Julian Day # 45716
SVP 4♓54'28"
GC 27♐11.4 ⚴ 4♒26.2
Eris 24♈35.9 ⚵ 1♐04.5
⚷ 20♈38.1 ⚶ 16♏54.8
☽ Mean ☊ 28♓20.7

1 April 2025
Julian Day # 45747
SVP 4♓54'25"
GC 27♐11.5 ⚴ 14♒08.4
Eris 24♈53.8 ⚵ 1♐29.8R
⚷ 22♈19.7 ⚶ 17♏57.2R
☽ Mean ☊ 26♓42.2

LONGITUDE — May 2025

Day	Sid.Time	☉	0 hr ☽	Noon ☽	True ☊	☿	♀	♂	⚳	♃	♄	♅	♆	♇
1 Th	2 38 41	11♉21 50	25♊33 35	2♋44 30	26♓25.9	16♈11.8	0♈26.3	5♌49.4	24♓55.2	21♊28.2	27♓53.9	26♉20.7	1♈06.7	3♒49.0
2 F	2 42 37	12 20 05	9♋48 22	16 44 57	26R 21.4	17 35.6	1 01.3	6 17.1	25 15.8	21 40.3	28 00.0	26 24.2	1 08.5	3 49.1
3 Sa	2 46 34	13 18 17	23 34 15	0♌16 25	26 18.7	19 01.5	1 37.4	6 45.0	25 36.3	21 52.4	28 05.9	26 27.6	1 10.3	3 49.1
4 Su	2 50 30	14 16 28	6♌51 44	13 20 35	26D 17.8	20 29.4	2 14.8	7 13.0	25 56.7	22 04.7	28 11.9	26 31.0	1 12.1	3R 49.1
5 M	2 54 27	15 14 36	19 43 29	26 00 58	26 18.3	21 59.3	2 53.3	7 41.3	26 17.1	22 16.9	28 17.7	26 34.4	1 13.9	3 49.1
6 Tu	2 58 24	16 12 42	2♍13 37	8♍22 00	26 19.5	23 31.2	3 33.0	8 09.7	26 37.3	22 29.3	28 23.5	26 37.9	1 15.6	3 49.1
7 W	3 02 20	17 10 47	14 26 46	20 28 28	26R 20.5	25 05.2	4 13.7	8 38.3	26 57.5	22 41.7	28 29.2	26 41.3	1 17.3	3 49.0
8 Th	3 06 17	18 08 49	26 27 41	2♎24 58	26 20.5	26 41.1	4 55.5	9 07.0	27 17.6	22 54.1	28 34.9	26 44.8	1 19.0	3 48.9
9 F	3 10 13	19 06 50	8♎20 48	14 15 39	26 18.7	28 19.0	5 38.2	9 35.9	27 37.6	23 06.6	28 40.6	26 48.3	1 20.7	3 48.8
10 Sa	3 14 10	20 04 49	20 09 58	26 04 06	26 14.6	29 58.9	6 21.9	10 05.0	27 57.5	23 19.2	28 46.1	26 51.7	1 22.4	3 48.6
11 Su	3 18 06	21 02 47	1♏58 25	7♏53 12	26 08.2	1♉40.7	7 06.5	10 34.2	28 17.3	23 31.8	28 51.6	26 55.2	1 24.0	3 48.5
12 M	3 22 03	22 00 42	13 48 43	19 45 13	25 59.6	3 24.6	7 52.0	11 03.6	28 37.0	23 44.5	28 57.0	26 58.7	1 25.6	3 48.3
13 Tu	3 25 59	22 58 37	25 42 54	1♐41 57	25 49.5	5 10.4	8 38.4	11 33.1	28 56.6	23 57.2	29 02.4	27 02.2	1 27.2	3 48.0
14 W	3 29 56	23 56 30	7♐42 32	13 44 50	25 38.6	6 58.2	9 25.5	12 02.7	29 16.1	24 10.0	29 07.7	27 05.7	1 28.8	3 47.8
15 Th	3 33 53	24 54 21	19 49 00	25 55 14	25 28.0	8 48.0	10 13.5	12 32.5	29 35.5	24 22.8	29 13.0	27 09.2	1 30.3	3 47.5
16 F	3 37 49	25 52 11	2♑03 41	8♑14 36	25 18.6	10 39.8	11 02.2	13 02.5	29 54.9	24 35.6	29 18.1	27 12.7	1 31.8	3 47.2
17 Sa	3 41 46	26 50 00	14 28 12	20 44 44	25 11.2	12 33.6	11 51.7	13 32.6	0♈14.1	24 48.5	29 23.3	27 16.2	1 33.3	3 46.8
18 Su	3 45 42	27 47 48	27 04 30	3♒27 49	25 06.1	14 29.3	12 41.8	14 02.8	0 33.2	25 01.5	29 28.3	27 19.6	1 34.8	3 46.5
19 M	3 49 39	28 45 34	9♒55 01	16 26 26	25 03.5	16 27.0	13 32.7	14 33.2	0 52.2	25 14.5	29 33.3	27 23.1	1 36.2	3 46.1
20 Tu	3 53 35	29 43 20	23 02 26	29 43 22	25D 02.8	18 26.5	14 24.2	15 03.7	1 11.1	25 27.5	29 38.2	27 26.6	1 37.6	3 45.7
21 W	3 57 32	0♊41 04	6♓29 32	13♓21 12	25R 03.2	20 27.9	15 16.3	15 34.3	1 29.9	25 40.6	29 43.0	27 30.1	1 39.0	3 45.2
22 Th	4 01 28	1 38 47	20 18 34	27 21 43	25 03.4	22 31.1	16 09.0	16 05.0	1 48.5	25 53.7	29 47.8	27 33.6	1 40.4	3 44.8
23 F	4 05 25	2 36 29	4♈30 37	11♈45 06	25 02.4	24 35.9	17 02.3	16 35.9	2 07.1	26 06.8	29 52.4	27 37.1	1 41.7	3 44.3
24 Sa	4 09 22	3 34 10	19 04 49	26 29 13	24 59.3	26 42.3	17 56.1	17 06.9	2 25.5	26 20.0	29 57.0	27 40.6	1 43.0	3 43.7
25 Su	4 13 18	4 31 51	3♉57 36	11♉29 01	24 53.5	28 50.2	18 50.5	17 38.1	2 43.8	26 33.2	0♈01.6	27 44.1	1 44.3	3 43.2
26 M	4 17 15	5 29 30	19 02 25	26 36 35	24 45.4	0♊59.3	19 45.4	18 09.3	3 02.0	26 46.5	0 06.0	27 47.5	1 45.6	3 42.6
27 Tu	4 21 11	6 27 08	4♊10 16	11♊42 09	24 35.5	3 09.4	20 40.8	18 40.7	3 20.1	26 59.8	0 10.4	27 51.0	1 46.8	3 42.0
28 W	4 25 08	7 24 45	19 10 59	26 35 35	24 25.1	5 20.4	21 36.6	19 12.3	3 38.0	27 13.1	0 14.7	27 54.5	1 48.0	3 41.4
29 Th	4 29 04	8 22 21	3♋54 57	11♋08 14	24 15.3	7 32.0	22 32.9	19 43.9	3 55.8	27 26.5	0 18.9	27 57.9	1 49.1	3 40.8
30 F	4 33 01	9 19 55	18 14 50	25 14 18	24 07.2	9 44.0	23 29.7	20 15.6	4 13.5	27 39.8	0 23.1	28 01.4	1 50.3	3 40.1
31 Sa	4 36 57	10 17 28	2♌06 28	8♌51 17	24 01.4	11 56.1	24 26.9	20 47.5	4 31.1	27 53.2	0 27.2	28 04.8	1 51.4	3 39.4

LONGITUDE — June 2025

Day	Sid.Time	☉	0 hr ☽	Noon ☽	True ☊	☿	♀	♂	⚳	♃	♄	♅	♆	♇
1 Su	4 40 54	11♊15 00	15♌28 57	21♌59 47	23♓58.1	14♊07.9	25♈24.4	21♌19.5	4♈48.5	28♊06.7	0♈31.1	28♉08.3	1♈52.5	3♒38.7
2 M	4 44 51	12 12 30	28 24 11	4♍42 42	23D 56.8	16 19.3	26 22.4	21 51.6	5 05.8	28 20.1	0 35.0	28 11.7	1 53.5	3R 37.9
3 Tu	4 48 47	13 09 59	10♍55 56	17 04 30	23R 56.7	18 30.0	27 20.8	22 23.7	5 22.9	28 33.6	0 38.8	28 15.1	1 54.5	3 37.2
4 W	4 52 44	14 07 26	23 09 05	29 10 20	23 56.6	20 39.7	28 19.5	22 56.0	5 39.9	28 47.1	0 42.6	28 18.5	1 55.5	3 36.4
5 Th	4 56 40	15 04 53	5♎08 56	11♎05 31	23 55.6	22 48.1	29 18.6	23 28.4	5 56.8	29 00.6	0 46.2	28 21.9	1 56.5	3 35.6
6 F	5 00 37	16 02 18	17 00 43	22 55 07	23 52.8	24 55.1	0♉18.0	24 00.9	6 13.5	29 14.2	0 49.8	28 25.3	1 57.4	3 34.7
7 Sa	5 04 33	16 59 42	28 49 14	4♏43 36	23 47.3	27 00.5	1 17.8	24 33.5	6 30.0	29 27.7	0 53.2	28 28.6	1 58.3	3 33.9
8 Su	5 08 30	17 57 06	10♏38 38	16 34 46	23 39.2	29 04.1	2 17.9	25 06.2	6 46.4	29 41.3	0 56.6	28 32.0	1 59.2	3 33.0
9 M	5 12 26	18 54 28	22 32 18	28 31 32	23 28.5	1♋05.7	3 18.4	25 39.0	7 02.7	29 54.9	0 59.9	28 35.3	2 00.0	3 32.1
10 Tu	5 16 23	19 51 49	4♐32 43	10♐36 02	23 16.0	3 05.2	4 19.1	26 11.9	7 18.8	0♋08.5	1 03.2	28 38.6	2 00.8	3 31.2
11 W	5 20 20	20 49 10	16 41 38	22 49 38	23 02.6	5 02.6	5 20.2	26 44.9	7 34.8	0 22.1	1 06.3	28 41.9	2 01.6	3 30.3
12 Th	5 24 16	21 46 30	29 00 05	5♑13 05	22 49.4	6 57.8	6 21.5	27 18.0	7 50.5	0 35.7	1 09.3	28 45.2	2 02.3	3 29.3
13 F	5 28 13	22 43 49	11♑28 40	17 46 52	22 37.6	8 50.6	7 23.1	27 51.1	8 06.2	0 49.4	1 12.3	28 48.5	2 03.0	3 28.3
14 Sa	5 32 09	23 41 08	24 07 45	0♒31 22	22 28.1	10 41.1	8 25.0	28 24.4	8 21.7	1 03.0	1 15.1	28 51.8	2 03.7	3 27.3
15 Su	5 36 06	24 38 26	6♒57 50	13 27 14	22 21.4	12 29.2	9 27.2	28 57.8	8 37.0	1 16.7	1 17.9	28 55.0	2 04.4	3 26.3
16 M	5 40 02	25 35 44	19 59 43	26 35 27	22 17.5	14 15.0	10 29.7	29 31.2	8 52.1	1 30.4	1 20.6	28 58.2	2 05.0	3 25.3
17 Tu	5 43 59	26 33 01	3♓14 37	9♓57 24	22D 15.9	15 58.3	11 32.4	0♍04.7	9 07.0	1 44.0	1 23.1	29 01.4	2 05.6	3 24.2
18 W	5 47 56	27 30 18	16 44 02	23 34 40	22R 15.6	17 39.1	12 35.3	0 38.4	9 21.8	1 57.7	1 25.6	29 04.6	2 06.1	3 23.2
19 Th	5 51 52	28 27 35	0♈29 29	7♈28 35	22 15.5	19 17.5	13 38.5	1 12.1	9 36.4	2 11.4	1 28.0	29 07.8	2 06.6	3 22.1
20 F	5 55 49	29 24 52	14 31 59	21 39 38	22 14.2	20 53.5	14 41.9	1 45.9	9 50.9	2 25.1	1 30.3	29 10.9	2 07.1	3 21.0
21 Sa	5 59 45	0♋22 08	28 51 20	6♉06 46	22 10.9	22 26.9	15 45.5	2 19.8	10 05.1	2 38.8	1 32.5	29 14.0	2 07.6	3 19.9
22 Su	6 03 42	1 19 25	13♉25 28	20 46 48	22 05.0	23 57.9	16 49.4	2 53.8	10 19.2	2 52.5	1 34.6	29 17.1	2 08.0	3 18.7
23 M	6 07 38	2 16 41	28 10 01	5♊34 14	21 56.5	25 26.4	17 53.4	3 27.8	10 33.0	3 06.2	1 36.6	29 20.2	2 08.4	3 17.6
24 Tu	6 11 35	3 13 57	12♊58 26	20 21 36	21 46.3	26 52.3	18 57.7	4 02.0	10 46.7	3 20.0	1 38.6	29 23.2	2 08.8	3 16.4
25 W	6 15 31	4 11 13	27 42 40	5♋00 36	21 35.3	28 15.6	20 02.2	4 36.2	11 00.2	3 33.7	1 40.4	29 26.3	2 09.1	3 15.2
26 Th	6 19 28	5 08 29	12♋14 28	19 23 26	21 24.9	29 36.4	21 06.8	5 10.6	11 13.4	3 47.4	1 42.1	29 29.3	2 09.4	3 14.0
27 F	6 23 25	6 05 44	26 26 49	3♌24 07	21 16.0	0♌54.5	22 11.6	5 45.0	11 26.5	4 01.1	1 43.7	29 32.2	2 09.6	3 12.8
28 Sa	6 27 21	7 02 58	10♌14 59	16 59 16	21 09.6	2 09.9	23 16.7	6 19.5	11 39.3	4 14.8	1 45.2	29 35.2	2 09.9	3 11.6
29 Su	6 31 18	8 00 13	23 36 58	0♍08 16	21 05.7	3 22.6	24 21.8	6 54.1	11 52.0	4 28.4	1 46.7	29 38.1	2 10.1	3 10.4
30 M	6 35 14	8 57 26	6♍33 26	12 52 53	21D 04.0	4 32.4	25 27.2	7 28.7	12 04.4	4 42.1	1 48.0	29 41.0	2 10.2	3 09.1

Astro Data Dy Hr Mn	Planet Ingress Dy Hr Mn	Last Aspect Dy Hr Mn	☽ Ingress Dy Hr Mn	Last Aspect Dy Hr Mn	☽ Ingress Dy Hr Mn	☽ Phases & Eclipses Dy Hr Mn
♇ R 4 15:28	☿ ♉ 10 12:16	1 3:50 ♄ □	♋ 1 7:24	1 23:39 ♃ ⚹	♍ 2 3:01	4 13:53 ☽ 14♌21
☽ 0S 8 5:52	⚳ ♈ 16 18:24	3 8:03 ♄ △	♌ 3 11:30	4 11:13 ♃ □	♎ 4 13:39	12 16:57 ○ 22♏13
☽ 0N 22 15:02	☉ ♊ 20 18:56	5 13:05 ♅ □	♍ 5 19:41	7 1:06 ♃ △	♏ 7 2:24	20 12:00 ☾ 29♒43
	♄ ♈ 25 3:37	8 4:12 ♄ ☍	♎ 8 7:07	9 12:08 ♅ ☍	♐ 9 14:57	27 3:04 ● 6♊06
♃⚺♅ 1 15:49	☿ ♊ 26 1:00	10 6:19 ♃ △	♏ 10 19:59	11 19:59 ♂ △	♑ 12 1:56	
☽ 0S 4 11:36		13 6:38 ♄ △	♐ 13 8:36	14 8:53 ♅ △	♒ 14 11:01	3 3:42 ☽ 12♍50
♃□♄ 15 14:37	♀ ♉ 6 4:44	15 18:30 ♄ □	♑ 15 19:59	16 17:32 ♂ ☍	♓ 16 18:10	11 7:45 ○ 20♐39
☽ 0N 18 20:53	☿ ♋ 8 22:59	18 4:28 ♄ ⚹	♒ 18 5:31	18 21:35 ♅ ⚹	♈ 18 23:09	18 19:20 ☾ 27♓48
♃□♆ 19 3:17	♃ ♋ 9 21:03	20 12:00 ☉ □	♓ 20 12:30	21 1:50 ☉ ⚹	♉ 21 1:54	25 10:33 ● 4♋08
♃⚻♇ 24 6:17	♂ ♍ 17 8:37	22 16:08 ♄ ☌	♈ 22 16:27	23 1:52 ♅ ☌	♊ 23 2:58	
	☉ ♋ 21 2:43	24 11:45 ♃ ⚹	♉ 24 17:39	23 8:27 ♂ ☌	♋ 25 3:45	
	☿ ♌ 26 19:10	26 13:53 ♅ ☌	♊ 26 17:23	27 5:17 ♅ ⚹	♌ 27 6:06	
		28 13:02 ♃ ☌	♋ 28 17:34	29 11:04 ♅ □	♍ 29 11:45	
		30 16:52 ♅ ⚹	♌ 30 20:18			

Astro Data

1 May 2025
Julian Day # 45777
SVP 4♓54'21"
GC 27♐11.6 ⚴ 21♒16.9
Eris 25♈13.4 ⚵ 27♏05.9R
⚷ 24♈06.0 ⚶ 12♏17.9R
☽ Mean ☊ 25♓06.9

1 June 2025
Julian Day # 45808
SVP 4♓54'16"
GC 27♐11.7 ⚴ 25♒03.1
Eris 25♈31.0 ⚵ 20♏21.9R
⚷ 25♈43.3 ⚶ 6♏04.7R
☽ Mean ☊ 23♓28.4

July 2025 LONGITUDE

Day	Sid.Time	☉	0 hr ☽	Noon ☽	True ☊	☿	♀	♂	⚳	♃	♄	♅	♆	♇
1 Tu	6 39 11	9♋54 40	19♍07 06	25♍16 39	21♓03.8	5♌39.4	26♉32.7	8♍03.5	12♈16.6	4♋55.8	1♈49.2	29♉43.9	2♈10.3	3♒07.8
2 W	6 43 07	10 51 53	1♎22 10	7♎24 16	21R 04.1	6 43.4	27 38.4	8 38.3	12 28.6	5 09.5	1 50.3	29 46.7	2 10.4	3R 06.6
3 Th	6 47 04	11 49 05	13 23 37	19 20 55	21 03.9	7 44.3	28 44.3	9 13.2	12 40.4	5 23.1	1 51.3	29 49.5	2 10.5	3 05.3
4 F	6 51 00	12 46 18	25 16 48	1♏11 55	21 02.2	8 42.2	29 50.3	9 48.1	12 51.9	5 36.7	1 52.3	29 52.3	2R 10.5	3 04.0
5 Sa	6 54 57	13 43 30	7♏06 53	13 02 19	20 58.4	9 36.7	0♊56.4	10 23.2	13 03.2	5 50.4	1 53.1	29 55.1	2 10.5	3 02.7
6 Su	6 58 54	14 40 41	18 58 43	24 56 37	20 52.2	10 28.0	2 02.7	10 58.3	13 14.3	6 04.0	1 53.8	29 57.8	2 10.5	3 01.4
7 M	7 02 50	15 37 53	0♐56 27	6♐58 35	20 43.7	11 15.7	3 09.2	11 33.5	13 25.2	6 17.6	1 54.4	0♊00.5	2 10.4	3 00.0
8 Tu	7 06 47	16 35 05	13 03 23	19 11 05	20 33.6	11 59.9	4 15.8	12 08.8	13 35.8	6 31.1	1 55.0	0 03.1	2 10.3	2 58.7
9 W	7 10 43	17 32 17	25 21 54	1♑35 57	20 22.6	12 40.3	5 22.6	12 44.1	13 46.1	6 44.7	1 55.4	0 05.8	2 10.2	2 57.3
10 Th	7 14 40	18 29 29	7♑53 21	14 14 05	20 11.8	13 16.9	6 29.5	13 19.5	13 56.3	6 58.2	1 55.7	0 08.4	2 10.0	2 56.0
11 F	7 18 36	19 26 41	20 38 10	27 05 31	20 02.1	13 49.5	7 36.5	13 55.0	14 06.1	7 11.8	1 55.9	0 10.9	2 09.8	2 54.6
12 Sa	7 22 33	20 23 53	3♒36 03	10♒09 40	19 54.4	14 17.9	8 43.7	14 30.5	14 15.7	7 25.3	1R 56.0	0 13.4	2 09.6	2 53.3
13 Su	7 26 29	21 21 05	16 46 15	23 25 40	19 49.1	14 42.1	9 51.0	15 06.1	14 25.1	7 38.7	1 56.1	0 15.9	2 09.3	2 51.9
14 M	7 30 26	22 18 18	0♓07 51	6♓52 42	19D 46.4	15 01.8	10 58.5	15 41.8	14 34.2	7 52.2	1 56.0	0 18.4	2 09.1	2 50.5
15 Tu	7 34 23	23 15 31	13 40 09	20 30 08	19 45.6	15 17.0	12 06.0	16 17.6	14 43.0	8 05.6	1 55.8	0 20.8	2 08.7	2 49.1
16 W	7 38 19	24 12 45	27 22 39	4♈17 40	19 46.2	15 27.5	13 13.7	16 53.4	14 51.6	8 19.0	1 55.5	0 23.2	2 08.4	2 47.7
17 Th	7 42 16	25 09 59	11♈15 08	18 15 03	19R 47.0	15R 33.3	14 21.6	17 29.3	14 59.9	8 32.4	1 55.1	0 25.6	2 08.0	2 46.3
18 F	7 46 12	26 07 15	25 17 20	2♉21 52	19 47.0	15 34.3	15 29.5	18 05.3	15 07.9	8 45.8	1 54.6	0 27.9	2 07.6	2 44.9
19 Sa	7 50 09	27 04 31	9♉28 30	16 36 59	19 45.4	15 30.4	16 37.6	18 41.4	15 15.7	8 59.1	1 54.0	0 30.2	2 07.1	2 43.5
20 Su	7 54 05	28 01 48	23 47 01	0♊58 12	19 41.7	15 21.6	17 45.8	19 17.5	15 23.1	9 12.4	1 53.4	0 32.4	2 06.6	2 42.1
21 M	7 58 02	28 59 05	8♊10 03	15 22 00	19 36.1	15 08.0	18 54.2	19 53.7	15 30.3	9 25.7	1 52.6	0 34.6	2 06.1	2 40.7
22 Tu	8 01 58	29 56 24	22 33 26	29 43 40	19 29.0	14 49.6	20 02.6	20 30.0	15 37.2	9 38.9	1 51.7	0 36.8	2 05.6	2 39.3
23 W	8 05 55	0♌53 43	6♋52 01	13♋57 46	19 21.3	14 26.7	21 11.1	21 06.3	15 43.7	9 52.1	1 50.7	0 38.9	2 05.0	2 37.9
24 Th	8 09 52	1 51 03	21 00 16	27 58 56	19 13.9	13 59.4	22 19.8	21 42.7	15 50.0	10 05.3	1 49.6	0 41.0	2 04.4	2 36.5
25 F	8 13 48	2 48 23	4♌53 13	11♌42 41	19 07.8	13 28.0	23 28.6	22 19.2	15 56.0	10 18.4	1 48.4	0 43.0	2 03.8	2 35.1
26 Sa	8 17 45	3 45 44	18 27 03	25 06 06	19 03.3	12 53.0	24 37.4	22 55.8	16 01.6	10 31.5	1 47.1	0 45.0	2 03.1	2 33.7
27 Su	8 21 41	4 43 05	1♍39 45	8♍08 04	19D 00.9	12 14.8	25 46.4	23 32.4	16 07.0	10 44.5	1 45.8	0 47.0	2 02.4	2 32.3
28 M	8 25 38	5 40 27	14 31 10	20 49 43	19 00.4	11 34.0	26 55.4	24 09.1	16 12.0	10 57.5	1 44.3	0 48.9	2 01.7	2 30.8
29 Tu	8 29 34	6 37 50	27 02 55	3♎12 18	19 01.1	10 51.1	28 04.6	24 45.8	16 16.7	11 10.5	1 42.7	0 50.8	2 01.0	2 29.4
30 W	8 33 31	7 35 13	9♎17 59	15 20 30	19 02.6	10 07.0	29 13.9	25 22.7	16 21.1	11 23.4	1 41.0	0 52.6	2 00.2	2 28.0
31 Th	8 37 27	8 32 36	21 20 25	27 18 21	19 04.0	9 22.3	0♋23.2	25 59.5	16 25.2	11 36.3	1 39.3	0 54.4	1 59.4	2 26.6

August 2025 LONGITUDE

Day	Sid.Time	☉	0 hr ☽	Noon ☽	True ☊	☿	♀	♂	⚳	♃	♄	♅	♆	♇
1 F	8 41 24	9♌30 00	3♏14 54	9♏10 43	19♓04.6	8♌37.9	1♋32.7	26♍36.5	16♈28.9	11♋49.2	1♈37.4	0♊56.2	1♈58.6	2♒25.2
2 Sa	8 45 21	10 27 25	15 06 25	21 02 37	19R 03.9	7R 54.6	2 42.2	27 13.5	16 32.3	12 02.0	1R 35.4	0 57.9	1R 57.7	2R 23.8
3 Su	8 49 17	11 24 50	26 59 55	2♐58 54	19 01.7	7 13.2	3 51.8	27 50.6	16 35.4	12 14.7	1 33.4	0 59.5	1 56.8	2 22.4
4 M	8 53 14	12 22 17	9♐00 06	15 04 01	18 57.9	6 34.5	5 01.6	28 27.8	16 38.1	12 27.4	1 31.3	1 01.1	1 55.9	2 21.0
5 Tu	8 57 10	13 19 44	21 11 05	27 21 42	18 53.0	5 59.2	6 11.4	29 05.0	16 40.6	12 40.0	1 29.0	1 02.7	1 54.9	2 19.6
6 W	9 01 07	14 17 11	3♑36 11	9♑54 46	18 47.4	5 28.1	7 21.3	29 42.3	16 42.6	12 52.6	1 26.7	1 04.3	1 54.0	2 18.3
7 Th	9 05 03	15 14 40	16 17 40	22 44 57	18 41.8	5 01.8	8 31.3	0♎19.6	16 44.3	13 05.2	1 24.3	1 05.7	1 53.0	2 16.9
8 F	9 09 00	16 12 09	29 16 39	5♒52 41	18 36.8	4 40.9	9 41.4	0 57.0	16 45.7	13 17.7	1 21.8	1 07.2	1 52.0	2 15.5
9 Sa	9 12 57	17 09 39	12♒32 57	19 17 14	18 32.9	4 25.9	10 51.6	1 34.5	16 46.7	13 30.1	1 19.3	1 08.6	1 50.9	2 14.2
10 Su	9 16 53	18 07 11	26 05 17	2♓56 47	18 30.6	4D 17.2	12 01.9	2 12.0	16 47.4	13 42.5	1 16.6	1 09.9	1 49.9	2 12.8
11 M	9 20 50	19 04 43	9♓51 25	16 48 49	18D 29.7	4 15.1	13 12.3	2 49.6	16R 47.7	13 54.8	1 13.8	1 11.2	1 48.8	2 11.5
12 Tu	9 24 46	20 02 17	23 48 36	0♈50 24	18 30.1	4 19.8	14 22.8	3 27.3	16 47.7	14 07.0	1 11.0	1 12.5	1 47.6	2 10.1
13 W	9 28 43	20 59 52	7♈53 52	14 58 38	18 31.3	4 31.6	15 33.3	4 05.0	16 47.3	14 19.2	1 08.1	1 13.7	1 46.5	2 08.8
14 Th	9 32 39	21 57 29	22 04 22	29 10 45	18 32.8	4 50.5	16 44.0	4 42.8	16 46.6	14 31.4	1 05.1	1 14.8	1 45.3	2 07.5
15 F	9 36 36	22 55 07	6♉17 30	13♉24 19	18R 33.8	5 16.7	17 54.7	5 20.6	16 45.4	14 43.5	1 02.1	1 15.9	1 44.2	2 06.2
16 Sa	9 40 32	23 52 47	20 30 56	27 37 05	18 34.0	5 49.9	19 05.5	5 58.6	16 44.0	14 55.5	0 58.9	1 17.0	1 42.9	2 04.9
17 Su	9 44 29	24 50 28	4♊42 28	11♊46 50	18 33.2	6 30.4	20 16.5	6 36.5	16 42.1	15 07.4	0 55.7	1 18.0	1 41.7	2 03.6
18 M	9 48 26	25 48 11	18 49 54	25 51 21	18 31.3	7 17.8	21 27.5	7 14.6	16 39.9	15 19.3	0 52.4	1 19.0	1 40.5	2 02.4
19 Tu	9 52 22	26 45 56	2♋50 54	9♋48 13	18 28.7	8 12.1	22 38.5	7 52.7	16 37.3	15 31.1	0 49.0	1 19.9	1 39.2	2 01.1
20 W	9 56 19	27 43 42	16 43 02	23 35 00	18 25.8	9 13.0	23 49.7	8 30.9	16 34.4	15 42.9	0 45.6	1 20.8	1 37.9	1 59.9
21 Th	10 00 15	28 41 30	0♌23 51	7♌09 20	18 23.0	10 20.3	25 00.9	9 09.2	16 31.1	15 54.5	0 42.1	1 21.6	1 36.6	1 58.6
22 F	10 04 12	29 39 19	13 51 11	20 29 14	18 20.7	11 33.8	26 12.3	9 47.5	16 27.4	16 06.1	0 38.5	1 22.4	1 35.3	1 57.4
23 Sa	10 08 08	0♍37 10	27 03 18	3♍33 20	18 19.2	12 53.0	27 23.7	10 25.9	16 23.3	16 17.7	0 34.8	1 23.1	1 33.9	1 56.2
24 Su	10 12 05	1 35 01	9♍59 17	16 21 10	18D 18.7	14 17.7	28 35.1	11 04.3	16 18.9	16 29.1	0 31.1	1 23.7	1 32.5	1 55.0
25 M	10 16 01	2 32 55	22 39 05	28 53 11	18 18.9	15 47.4	29 46.7	11 42.9	16 14.1	16 40.5	0 27.3	1 24.4	1 31.1	1 53.8
26 Tu	10 19 58	3 30 49	5♎03 41	11♎10 52	18 19.8	17 21.8	0♌58.3	12 21.4	16 08.9	16 51.8	0 23.5	1 24.9	1 29.7	1 52.7
27 W	10 23 54	4 28 45	17 15 03	23 16 37	18 21.0	19 00.3	2 10.0	13 00.1	16 03.4	17 03.0	0 19.6	1 25.4	1 28.3	1 51.5
28 Th	10 27 51	5 26 43	29 16 01	5♏13 41	18 22.2	20 42.5	3 21.7	13 38.8	15 57.6	17 14.1	0 15.7	1 25.9	1 26.9	1 50.4
29 F	10 31 48	6 24 42	11♏10 10	17 05 58	18 23.3	22 28.0	4 33.6	14 17.6	15 51.4	17 25.1	0 11.7	1 26.3	1 25.4	1 49.3
30 Sa	10 35 44	7 22 42	23 01 39	28 57 47	18R 23.9	24 16.3	5 45.5	14 56.4	15 44.8	17 36.1	0 07.6	1 26.7	1 23.9	1 48.2
31 Su	10 39 41	8 20 43	4♐54 58	10♐53 47	18 24.0	26 06.9	6 57.4	15 35.3	15 37.9	17 46.9	0 03.5	1 27.0	1 22.4	1 47.1

Astro Data Dy Hr Mn	Planet Ingress Dy Hr Mn
☽0S 1 18:18	♀ ♊ 4 15:32
♆R 4 21:34	♅ ♊ 7 7:46
♄R 13 4:08	☉ ♌ 22 13:31
☽0N 16 1:31	♀ ♋ 31 3:58
☿R 18 4:46	
☽0S 29 2:04	♂ ♎ 6 23:24
	☉ ♍ 22 20:35
♂0S 8 21:33	♀ ♌ 25 16:28
☿D 11 7:30	
⚳R 11 21:37	
♄⚹♅ 12 3:33	
☽0N 12 7:10	
♃∠♅ 24 0:02	
☽0S 25 10:13	
♅⚹♆ 29 0:10	

Last Aspect Dy Hr Mn	☽ Ingress Dy Hr Mn	Last Aspect Dy Hr Mn	☽ Ingress Dy Hr Mn
1 20:48 ♅ △	♎ 1 21:18	3 1:08 ♂ ⚹	♐ 3 6:02
2 19:31 ☉ □	♏ 4 9:34	5 15:30 ♂ □	♑ 5 17:05
6 22:05 ♅ ☍	♐ 6 22:07	6 17:41 ♃ ☍	♒ 8 1:19
7 21:31 ♂ □	♑ 9 8:56	9 7:56 ☉ ☍	♓ 10 6:51
10 20:38 ☉ ☍	♒ 11 17:22	11 6:56 ♃ △	♈ 12 10:34
12 19:46 ☿ ☍	♓ 13 23:46	13 22:55 ☉ △	♉ 14 13:23
15 17:11 ☉ △	♈ 16 4:33	16 5:13 ☉ □	♊ 16 16:02
18 0:39 ☉ □	♉ 18 8:00	18 11:54 ☉ ⚹	♋ 18 19:06
20 6:45 ☉ ⚹	♊ 20 10:23	20 12:28 ♀ ☌	♌ 20 23:18
21 19:53 ♂ □	♋ 22 12:27	21 18:15 ☿ ☌	♍ 23 5:25
24 0:43 ♂ ⚹	♌ 24 15:30	25 13:55 ♀ ⚹	♎ 25 14:09
26 11:03 ♀ ⚹	♍ 26 20:57	27 2:08 ☿ ⚹	♏ 28 1:28
29 0:58 ♀ □	♎ 29 5:44	30 0:48 ☿ □	♐ 30 14:06
30 4:00 ♃ □	♏ 31 17:26		

☽ Phases & Eclipses Dy Hr Mn	
2 19:31	☽ 11♎10
10 20:38	○ 18♑50
18 0:39	☾ 25♈40
24 19:12	● 2♌08
1 12:42	☽ 9♏32
9 7:56	○ 17♒00
16 5:13	☾ 23♉36
23 6:08	● 0♍23
31 6:26	☽ 8♐07

Astro Data

1 July 2025
Julian Day # 45838
SVP 4♓54'10"
GC 27♐11.7 ⚴ 23♒45.2R
Eris 25♈41.5 ⚵ 16♏29.5R
⚷ 26♈47.6 ⚶ 6♏28.1
☽ Mean ☊ 21♓53.1

1 August 2025
Julian Day # 45869
SVP 4♓54'05"
GC 27♐11.8 ⚴ 17♒16.7R
Eris 25♈43.2R ⚵ 17♏23.0
⚷ 27♈09.7R ⚶ 13♏26.6
☽ Mean ☊ 20♓14.6

LONGITUDE — September 2025

Day	Sid.Time	☉	0 hr ☽	Noon ☽	True ☊	☿	♀	♂	⚳	♃	♄	♅	♆	♇
1 M	10 43 37	9♍18 46	16♐54 49	22♐58 38	18♓23.7	27♌59.4	8♌09.5	16♎14.2	15♈30.6	17♋57.7	29♓59.3	1♊27.3	1♈20.9	1♒46.0
2 Tu	10 47 34	10 16 50	29 05 46	5♑16 44	18R 23.0	29 53.3	9 21.6	16 53.3	15R 23.0	18 08.4	29R 55.1	1 27.5	1R 19.4	1R 45.0
3 W	10 51 30	11 14 56	11♑32 00	17 52 00	18 22.2	1♍48.3	10 33.8	17 32.4	15 15.1	18 19.0	29 50.9	1 27.6	1 17.9	1 44.0
4 Th	10 55 27	12 13 03	24 17 02	0♒47 24	18 21.4	3 44.1	11 46.0	18 11.5	15 06.9	18 29.5	29 46.6	1 27.8	1 16.4	1 43.0
5 F	10 59 24	13 11 12	7♒23 16	14 04 42	18 20.7	5 40.3	12 58.4	18 50.7	14 58.3	18 39.9	29 42.3	1R 27.8	1 14.8	1 42.0
6 Sa	11 03 20	14 09 22	20 51 40	27 44 02	18 20.3	7 36.7	14 10.8	19 30.0	14 49.4	18 50.2	29 37.9	1 27.8	1 13.2	1 41.0
7 Su	11 07 17	15 07 33	4♓41 32	11♓43 47	18D 20.1	9 33.0	15 23.2	20 09.3	14 40.2	19 00.4	29 33.5	1 27.8	1 11.7	1 40.1
8 M	11 11 13	16 05 47	18 50 20	26 00 36	18 20.1	11 29.0	16 35.7	20 48.7	14 30.7	19 10.5	29 29.0	1 27.7	1 10.1	1 39.1
9 Tu	11 15 10	17 04 02	3♈13 55	10♈29 36	18 20.2	13 24.6	17 48.3	21 28.1	14 20.9	19 20.5	29 24.6	1 27.5	1 08.5	1 38.2
10 W	11 19 06	18 02 19	17 46 54	25 05 03	18R 20.2	15 19.5	19 01.0	22 07.6	14 10.8	19 30.4	29 20.1	1 27.4	1 06.9	1 37.4
11 Th	11 23 03	19 00 38	2♉23 19	9♉40 59	18 20.2	17 13.8	20 13.7	22 47.2	14 00.4	19 40.2	29 15.6	1 27.1	1 05.3	1 36.5
12 F	11 26 59	19 58 59	16 57 23	24 11 57	18 20.1	19 07.3	21 26.5	23 26.9	13 49.8	19 49.9	29 11.0	1 26.8	1 03.7	1 35.7
13 Sa	11 30 56	20 57 23	1♊24 08	8♊33 31	18D 20.0	20 59.9	22 39.4	24 06.6	13 38.9	19 59.5	29 06.4	1 26.5	1 02.0	1 34.8
14 Su	11 34 52	21 55 48	15 39 45	22 42 35	18 19.9	22 51.6	23 52.3	24 46.3	13 27.8	20 09.0	29 01.8	1 26.1	1 00.4	1 34.0
15 M	11 38 49	22 54 16	29 41 48	6♋37 17	18 20.0	24 42.3	25 05.3	25 26.2	13 16.4	20 18.3	28 57.2	1 25.7	0 58.8	1 33.3
16 Tu	11 42 46	23 52 46	13♋28 59	20 16 53	18 20.4	26 32.0	26 18.4	26 06.1	13 04.7	20 27.6	28 52.6	1 25.2	0 57.1	1 32.5
17 W	11 46 42	24 51 18	27 01 00	3♌41 22	18 20.9	28 20.7	27 31.5	26 46.0	12 52.9	20 36.7	28 48.0	1 24.6	0 55.5	1 31.8
18 Th	11 50 39	25 49 52	10♌18 04	16 51 11	18 21.6	0♎08.4	28 44.7	27 26.1	12 40.8	20 45.7	28 43.3	1 24.0	0 53.8	1 31.1
19 F	11 54 35	26 48 29	23 20 48	29 47 02	18 22.3	1 55.1	29 57.9	28 06.2	12 28.5	20 54.6	28 38.7	1 23.4	0 52.2	1 30.4
20 Sa	11 58 32	27 47 07	6♍09 57	12♍29 41	18R 22.7	3 40.7	1♍11.3	28 46.3	12 16.1	21 03.4	28 34.0	1 22.7	0 50.5	1 29.8
21 Su	12 02 28	28 45 47	18 46 20	25 00 02	18 22.6	5 25.3	2 24.6	29 26.6	12 03.4	21 12.1	28 29.4	1 22.0	0 48.8	1 29.1
22 M	12 06 25	29 44 29	1♎10 54	7♎19 06	18 22.0	7 08.9	3 38.0	0♏06.8	11 50.6	21 20.6	28 24.7	1 21.2	0 47.2	1 28.5
23 Tu	12 10 21	0♎43 13	13 24 48	19 28 12	18 20.8	8 51.6	4 51.5	0 47.2	11 37.7	21 29.0	28 20.0	1 20.3	0 45.5	1 28.0
24 W	12 14 18	1 41 59	25 29 30	1♏28 58	18 19.1	10 33.2	6 05.0	1 27.6	11 24.6	21 37.3	28 15.4	1 19.5	0 43.8	1 27.4
25 Th	12 18 15	2 40 47	7♏26 53	13 23 34	18 16.9	12 13.9	7 18.6	2 08.1	11 11.4	21 45.4	28 10.8	1 18.5	0 42.2	1 26.9
26 F	12 22 11	3 39 37	19 19 23	25 14 42	18 14.6	13 53.6	8 32.2	2 48.6	10 58.1	21 53.4	28 06.1	1 17.5	0 40.5	1 26.4
27 Sa	12 26 08	4 38 28	1♐09 58	7♐05 38	18 12.5	15 32.4	9 45.9	3 29.2	10 44.7	22 01.3	28 01.5	1 16.5	0 38.9	1 25.9
28 Su	12 30 04	5 37 21	13 02 12	19 00 11	18 11.0	17 10.3	10 59.6	4 09.9	10 31.3	22 09.0	27 56.9	1 15.4	0 37.2	1 25.5
29 M	12 34 01	6 36 16	25 00 07	1♑02 34	18D 10.1	18 47.3	12 13.4	4 50.6	10 17.8	22 16.6	27 52.3	1 14.3	0 35.6	1 25.0
30 Tu	12 37 57	7 35 13	7♑08 06	13 17 17	18 10.1	20 23.4	13 27.2	5 31.4	10 04.2	22 24.1	27 47.8	1 13.2	0 33.9	1 24.7

LONGITUDE — October 2025

Day	Sid.Time	☉	0 hr ☽	Noon ☽	True ☊	☿	♀	♂	⚳	♃	♄	♅	♆	♇
1 W	12 41 54	8♎34 12	19♑30 42	25♑48 52	18♓10.9	21♎58.6	14♍41.1	6♏12.3	9♈50.6	22♋31.4	27♓43.2	1♊12.0	0♈32.3	1♒24.3
2 Th	12 45 50	9 33 12	2♒12 18	8♒41 27	18 12.3	23 33.0	15 55.0	6 53.2	9R 37.0	22 38.6	27R 38.7	1R 10.7	0R 30.6	1R 23.9
3 F	12 49 47	10 32 14	15 16 42	21 58 22	18 13.8	25 06.6	17 09.0	7 34.2	9 23.4	22 45.6	27 34.2	1 09.4	0 29.0	1 23.6
4 Sa	12 53 44	11 31 18	28 46 36	5♓41 29	18R 15.0	26 39.3	18 23.0	8 15.2	9 09.8	22 52.5	27 29.8	1 08.1	0 27.4	1 23.3
5 Su	12 57 40	12 30 23	12♓42 56	19 50 42	18 15.4	28 11.2	19 37.0	8 56.3	8 56.2	22 59.3	27 25.4	1 06.7	0 25.7	1 23.1
6 M	13 01 37	13 29 31	27 04 20	4♈23 17	18 14.6	29 42.3	20 51.1	9 37.4	8 42.7	23 05.9	27 21.0	1 05.3	0 24.1	1 22.9
7 Tu	13 05 33	14 28 40	11♈46 46	19 13 53	18 12.6	1♏12.5	22 05.3	10 18.7	8 29.3	23 12.3	27 16.6	1 03.8	0 22.5	1 22.7
8 W	13 09 30	15 27 52	26 43 35	4♉14 47	18 09.4	2 42.0	23 19.4	10 59.9	8 15.9	23 18.6	27 12.3	1 02.3	0 20.9	1 22.5
9 Th	13 13 26	16 27 05	11♉46 17	19 16 58	18 05.5	4 10.7	24 33.7	11 41.3	8 02.6	23 24.7	27 08.0	1 00.8	0 19.3	1 22.3
10 F	13 17 23	17 26 21	26 45 42	4♊11 30	18 01.5	5 38.5	25 48.0	12 22.7	7 49.4	23 30.7	27 03.8	0 59.2	0 17.8	1 22.2
11 Sa	13 21 19	18 25 40	11♊33 28	18 50 54	17 58.0	7 05.5	27 02.3	13 04.1	7 36.3	23 36.5	26 59.6	0 57.5	0 16.2	1 22.1
12 Su	13 25 16	19 25 00	26 03 13	3♋10 02	17 55.6	8 31.7	28 16.6	13 45.7	7 23.3	23 42.2	26 55.5	0 55.9	0 14.7	1 22.1
13 M	13 29 13	20 24 23	10♋11 09	17 06 27	17D 54.5	9 57.1	29 31.1	14 27.3	7 10.5	23 47.7	26 51.4	0 54.2	0 13.1	1D 22.0
14 Tu	13 33 09	21 23 49	23 56 00	0♌39 59	17 54.8	11 21.5	0♎45.5	15 08.9	6 57.9	23 53.0	26 47.4	0 52.4	0 11.6	1 22.0
15 W	13 37 06	22 23 16	7♌18 36	13 52 11	17 56.1	12 45.1	2 00.0	15 50.6	6 45.4	23 58.2	26 43.5	0 50.7	0 10.1	1 22.1
16 Th	13 41 02	23 22 46	20 21 05	26 45 38	17 57.7	14 07.7	3 14.5	16 32.4	6 33.1	24 03.2	26 39.5	0 48.8	0 08.6	1 22.1
17 F	13 44 59	24 22 18	3♍06 15	9♍23 17	17R 59.0	15 29.4	4 29.1	17 14.3	6 21.0	24 08.0	26 35.7	0 47.0	0 07.1	1 22.2
18 Sa	13 48 55	25 21 52	15 37 06	21 48 01	17 59.3	16 50.0	5 43.7	17 56.2	6 09.0	24 12.7	26 31.9	0 45.1	0 05.6	1 22.3
19 Su	13 52 52	26 21 29	27 56 23	4♎02 27	17 57.9	18 09.5	6 58.3	18 38.2	5 57.4	24 17.1	26 28.2	0 43.2	0 04.1	1 22.4
20 M	13 56 48	27 21 07	10♎06 30	16 08 45	17 54.5	19 27.9	8 13.0	19 20.2	5 45.9	24 21.4	26 24.5	0 41.2	0 02.7	1 22.6
21 Tu	14 00 45	28 20 48	22 09 27	28 08 46	17 49.2	20 45.0	9 27.7	20 02.3	5 34.7	24 25.6	26 20.9	0 39.2	0 01.3	1 22.8
22 W	14 04 42	29 20 30	4♏06 55	10♏04 05	17 42.1	22 00.8	10 42.4	20 44.5	5 23.8	24 29.5	26 17.4	0 37.2	29♓59.9	1 23.0
23 Th	14 08 38	0♏20 15	16 00 28	21 56 15	17 33.9	23 15.1	11 57.2	21 26.7	5 13.1	24 33.3	26 13.9	0 35.2	29 58.5	1 23.3
24 F	14 12 35	1 20 01	27 51 41	3♐47 00	17 25.3	24 27.9	13 12.0	22 09.0	5 02.7	24 36.9	26 10.6	0 33.1	29 57.1	1 23.6
25 Sa	14 16 31	2 19 50	9♐42 29	15 38 26	17 17.1	25 39.0	14 26.8	22 51.4	4 52.6	24 40.3	26 07.3	0 31.0	29 55.8	1 23.9
26 Su	14 20 28	3 19 40	21 35 13	27 33 12	17 10.1	26 48.1	15 41.7	23 33.8	4 42.8	24 43.5	26 04.0	0 28.9	29 54.4	1 24.2
27 M	14 24 24	4 19 32	3♑32 48	9♑34 30	17 04.9	27 55.3	16 56.6	24 16.2	4 33.3	24 46.5	26 00.9	0 26.7	29 53.1	1 24.6
28 Tu	14 28 21	5 19 25	15 38 47	21 46 11	17 01.7	29 00.1	18 11.5	24 58.8	4 24.1	24 49.4	25 57.8	0 24.5	29 51.8	1 25.0
29 W	14 32 17	6 19 21	27 57 14	4♒12 32	17D 00.6	0♐02.4	19 26.4	25 41.4	4 15.2	24 52.1	25 54.9	0 22.3	29 50.6	1 25.4
30 Th	14 36 14	7 19 17	10♒32 38	16 58 05	17 01.0	1 01.9	20 41.3	26 24.0	4 06.7	24 54.5	25 52.0	0 20.1	29 49.3	1 25.9
31 F	14 40 11	8 19 16	23 29 26	0♓07 08	17 02.1	1 58.3	21 56.3	27 06.7	3 58.5	24 56.8	25 49.2	0 17.8	29 48.1	1 26.4

Astro Data

	Dy Hr Mn
♅ R	6 4:52
☽ 0N	8 15:14
☿ 0S	19 20:51
☽ 0S	21 17:45
☉ 0S	22 18:20
☽ 0N	6 1:28
♇ D	14 2:55
♀ 0S	16 17:17
☽ 0S	18 23:59

Planet Ingress

	Dy Hr Mn
♄ ♓R	1 8:08
☿ ♍	2 13:24
☿ ♎	18 10:07
♀ ♍	19 12:40
♂ ♏	22 7:56
☉ ♎	22 18:20
☿ ♏	6 16:42
♀ ♎	13 21:20
♆ ♓R	22 9:49
☉ ♏	23 3:52
☿ ♐	29 11:03

Last Aspect / ☽ Ingress (September)

Last Aspect Dy Hr Mn		☽ Ingress	Dy Hr Mn
2 1:40	♄ □	♑	2 1:46
4 10:09	♄ ⚹	♒	4 10:33
5 20:53	♂ △	♓	6 15:55
8 17:45	♄ ☌	♈	8 18:38
10 6:55	♂ ☍	♉	10 20:05
12 20:15	♄ ⚹	♊	12 21:39
14 22:48	♄ □	♋	15 0:31
17 3:15	♄ △	♌	17 5:21
19 12:23	♀ ☌	♍	19 12:24
21 19:55	☉ ☌	♎	21 21:42
23 16:03	♃ □	♏	24 9:01
26 17:45	♄ △	♐	26 21:38
29 5:45	♄ □	♑	29 9:56

Last Aspect / ☽ Ingress (October)

Last Aspect Dy Hr Mn		☽ Ingress	Dy Hr Mn
1 15:35	♄ ⚹	♒	1 19:53
3 18:16	☿ △	♓	4 2:08
6 0:31	♄ ☌	♈	6 4:49
7 18:25	♃ □	♉	8 5:14
10 0:32	♄ ⚹	♊	10 5:13
12 2:57	♀ □	♋	12 6:38
14 5:06	♄ △	♌	14 10:48
16 5:07	☉ ⚹	♍	16 18:07
18 21:12	♄ ☍	♎	19 4:03
21 12:26	☉ ☌	♏	21 15:43
24 4:15	♆ △	♐	24 4:20
26 16:43	♆ □	♑	26 16:54
29 3:39	♆ ⚹	♒	29 3:56
31 6:16	♂ □	♓	31 11:47

☽ Phases & Eclipses

Dy Hr Mn	
7 18:10	○ 15♓23
7 18:13	• T 1.362
14 10:34	☾ 21♊52
21 19:55	● 29♍05
21 19:43:04	• P 0.855
29 23:55	☽ 7♑06
7 3:49	○ 14♈08
13 18:14	☾ 20♋40
21 12:26	● 28♎22
29 16:22	☽ 6♒30

Astro Data

1 September 2025
Julian Day # 45900
SVP 4♓54'00"
GC 27♐11.9 ⚴ 9♒49.3R
Eris 25♈35.1R ⚵ 22♏27.3
⚷ 26♈41.9R ⚶ 24♏39.3
☽ Mean ☊ 18♓36.2

1 October 2025
Julian Day # 45930
SVP 4♓53'57"
GC 27♐11.9 ⚴ 6♒41.0R
Eris 25♈20.2R ⚵ 0♐02.9
⚷ 25♈36.2R ⚶ 7♐51.7
☽ Mean ☊ 17♓00.8

November 2025 LONGITUDE

Day	Sid.Time	☉	0 hr ☽	Noon ☽	True ☊	☿	♀	♂	⚳	♃	♄	♅	♆	♇
1 Sa	14 44 07	9♏19 16	6♓51 37	13♓43 11	17♓02.9	2♐51.2	23♎11.3	27♏49.5	3♈50.6	24♋58.9	25♓46.4	0♊15.5	29♓46.9	1♒26.9
2 Su	14 48 04	10 19 17	20 41 59	27 48 02	17R 02.4	3 40.2	24 26.3	28 32.3	3R 43.1	25 00.8	25R 43.8	0R 13.2	29R 45.7	1 27.4
3 M	14 52 00	11 19 20	5♈01 10	12♈20 59	16 59.9	4 24.9	25 41.3	29 15.2	3 35.9	25 02.5	25 41.2	0 10.9	29 44.6	1 28.0
4 Tu	14 55 57	12 19 25	19 46 52	27 17 59	16 55.0	5 04.8	26 56.4	29 58.1	3 29.1	25 04.0	25 38.8	0 08.6	29 43.5	1 28.6
5 W	14 59 53	13 19 32	4♉53 18	12♉31 33	16 47.9	5 39.3	28 11.5	0♐41.1	3 22.7	25 05.3	25 36.4	0 06.2	29 42.4	1 29.2
6 Th	15 03 50	14 19 40	20 11 24	27 51 22	16 39.3	6 07.9	29 26.6	1 24.2	3 16.6	25 06.5	25 34.1	0 03.8	29 41.3	1 29.9
7 F	15 07 46	15 19 51	5♊30 01	13♊05 58	16 30.2	6 29.9	0♏41.7	2 07.3	3 10.9	25 07.4	25 32.0	0 01.4	29 40.2	1 30.6
8 Sa	15 11 43	16 20 03	20 37 55	28 04 47	16 21.8	6 44.6	1 56.9	2 50.5	3 05.5	25 08.1	25 29.9	29♉59.0	29 39.2	1 31.3
9 Su	15 15 40	17 20 18	5♋25 42	12♋39 59	16 15.1	6R 51.3	3 12.0	3 33.7	3 00.6	25 08.7	25 27.9	29 56.6	29 38.2	1 32.0
10 M	15 19 36	18 20 34	19 47 13	26 47 13	16 10.8	6 49.5	4 27.2	4 17.1	2 56.0	25 09.0	25 26.0	29 54.2	29 37.2	1 32.8
11 Tu	15 23 33	19 20 52	3♌39 58	10♌25 39	16D 08.6	6 38.4	5 42.4	5 00.4	2 51.8	25R 09.2	25 24.2	29 51.7	29 36.3	1 33.6
12 W	15 27 29	20 21 13	17 04 33	23 37 05	16 08.3	6 17.5	6 57.6	5 43.8	2 47.9	25 09.1	25 22.5	29 49.3	29 35.4	1 34.4
13 Th	15 31 26	21 21 35	0♍03 45	6♍25 05	16R 08.8	5 46.6	8 12.9	6 27.3	2 44.4	25 08.8	25 20.9	29 46.8	29 34.5	1 35.2
14 F	15 35 22	22 21 59	12 41 39	18 54 02	16 09.1	5 05.5	9 28.2	7 10.9	2 41.4	25 08.4	25 19.4	29 44.3	29 33.6	1 36.1
15 Sa	15 39 19	23 22 25	25 02 46	1♎08 25	16 07.9	4 14.4	10 43.4	7 54.5	2 38.7	25 07.7	25 18.0	29 41.8	29 32.8	1 37.0
16 Su	15 43 15	24 22 53	7♎11 29	13 12 26	16 04.4	3 14.0	11 58.7	8 38.1	2 36.4	25 06.8	25 16.7	29 39.3	29 32.0	1 37.9
17 M	15 47 12	25 23 22	19 11 41	25 09 38	15 58.1	2 05.5	13 14.0	9 21.8	2 34.4	25 05.8	25 15.5	29 36.8	29 31.2	1 38.9
18 Tu	15 51 09	26 23 53	1♏06 37	7♏02 55	15 48.9	0 50.5	14 29.4	10 05.6	2 32.9	25 04.5	25 14.5	29 34.3	29 30.5	1 39.8
19 W	15 55 05	27 24 26	12 58 47	18 54 27	15 37.1	29♏31.0	15 44.7	10 49.5	2 31.7	25 03.0	25 13.5	29 31.8	29 29.8	1 40.8
20 Th	15 59 02	28 25 01	24 50 06	0♐45 55	15 23.4	28 09.7	17 00.1	11 33.4	2 31.0	25 01.4	25 12.6	29 29.3	29 29.1	1 41.9
21 F	16 02 58	29 25 37	6♐42 03	12 38 40	15 09.1	26 49.0	18 15.4	12 17.3	2D 30.6	24 59.5	25 11.8	29 26.8	29 28.4	1 42.9
22 Sa	16 06 55	0♐26 15	18 35 55	24 33 59	14 55.1	25 31.8	19 30.8	13 01.3	2 30.6	24 57.4	25 11.2	29 24.3	29 27.8	1 44.0
23 Su	16 10 51	1 26 54	0♑33 04	6♑33 24	14 42.8	24 20.6	20 46.2	13 45.4	2 31.0	24 55.2	25 10.6	29 21.8	29 27.2	1 45.1
24 M	16 14 48	2 27 34	12 35 14	18 38 52	14 33.0	23 17.4	22 01.6	14 29.5	2 31.7	24 52.7	25 10.2	29 19.3	29 26.7	1 46.2
25 Tu	16 18 44	3 28 15	24 44 40	0♒53 00	14 26.1	22 23.9	23 17.0	15 13.7	2 32.9	24 50.1	25 09.8	29 16.8	29 26.2	1 47.4
26 W	16 22 41	4 28 57	7♒04 18	13 19 02	14 22.1	21 41.4	24 32.4	15 57.9	2 34.4	24 47.2	25 09.6	29 14.2	29 25.7	1 48.6
27 Th	16 26 38	5 29 41	19 37 42	26 00 49	14D 20.5	21 10.3	25 47.8	16 42.2	2 36.3	24 44.2	25D 09.5	29 11.8	29 25.2	1 49.8
28 F	16 30 34	6 30 25	2♓28 54	9♓02 28	14R 20.3	20 50.8	27 03.2	17 26.6	2 38.5	24 41.0	25 09.5	29 09.3	29 24.8	1 51.0
29 Sa	16 34 31	7 31 10	15 42 00	22 27 56	14 20.2	20D 42.7	28 18.7	18 11.0	2 41.2	24 37.5	25 09.6	29 06.8	29 24.4	1 52.2
30 Su	16 38 27	8 31 57	29 20 35	6♈20 10	14 18.9	20 45.5	29 34.1	18 55.4	2 44.1	24 33.9	25 09.7	29 04.3	29 24.1	1 53.5

December 2025 LONGITUDE

Day	Sid.Time	☉	0 hr ☽	Noon ☽	True ☊	☿	♀	♂	⚳	♃	♄	♅	♆	♇
1 M	16 42 24	9♐32 44	13♈26 47	20♈40 17	14♓15.4	20♏58.4	0♐49.5	19♐39.9	2♈47.5	24♋30.2	25♓10.1	29♉01.8	29♓23.7	1♒54.8
2 Tu	16 46 20	10 33 32	28 00 22	5♉26 29	14R 09.1	21 20.7	2 05.0	20 24.4	2 51.2	24R 26.2	25 10.5	28R 59.4	29R 23.4	1 56.1
3 W	16 50 17	11 34 21	12♉57 49	20 33 22	14 00.1	21 51.4	3 20.4	21 09.0	2 55.3	24 22.0	25 11.0	28 57.0	29 23.2	1 57.4
4 Th	16 54 13	12 35 12	28 11 55	5♊52 03	13 49.1	22 29.7	4 35.9	21 53.7	2 59.7	24 17.7	25 11.6	28 54.5	29 23.0	1 58.8
5 F	16 58 10	13 36 03	13♊32 19	21 11 13	13 37.3	23 14.8	5 51.3	22 38.4	3 04.4	24 13.2	25 12.4	28 52.1	29 22.8	2 00.2
6 Sa	17 02 07	14 36 56	28 47 16	6♋19 09	13 26.1	24 05.8	7 06.8	23 23.2	3 09.5	24 08.5	25 13.2	28 49.7	29 22.6	2 01.6
7 Su	17 06 03	15 37 49	13♋45 41	21 05 57	13 16.8	25 02.1	8 22.3	24 08.0	3 15.0	24 03.7	25 14.2	28 47.4	29 22.5	2 03.0
8 M	17 10 00	16 38 44	28 19 13	5♌25 01	13 10.2	26 02.9	9 37.7	24 52.8	3 20.8	23 58.7	25 15.2	28 45.0	29 22.4	2 04.4
9 Tu	17 13 56	17 39 40	12♌23 10	19 13 38	13 06.3	27 07.8	10 53.2	25 37.8	3 26.9	23 53.5	25 16.4	28 42.7	29 22.4	2 05.9
10 W	17 17 53	18 40 37	25 56 36	2♍32 24	13D 04.8	28 16.1	12 08.7	26 22.7	3 33.3	23 48.2	25 17.7	28 40.3	29D 22.4	2 07.4
11 Th	17 21 49	19 41 35	9♍01 29	15 24 24	13R 04.5	29 27.4	13 24.2	27 07.7	3 40.0	23 42.6	25 19.0	28 38.0	29 22.4	2 08.9
12 F	17 25 46	20 42 34	21 41 44	27 54 09	13 04.4	0♐41.3	14 39.7	27 52.8	3 47.1	23 37.0	25 20.5	28 35.7	29 22.4	2 10.4
13 Sa	17 29 43	21 43 35	4♎02 18	10♎06 50	13 03.2	1 57.5	15 55.2	28 37.9	3 54.5	23 31.2	25 22.1	28 33.5	29 22.5	2 11.9
14 Su	17 33 39	22 44 36	16 08 23	22 07 34	12 59.8	3 15.7	17 10.7	29 23.1	4 02.2	23 25.2	25 23.8	28 31.2	29 22.6	2 13.5
15 M	17 37 36	23 45 39	28 04 57	4♏01 04	12 53.7	4 35.6	18 26.2	0♑08.3	4 10.3	23 19.1	25 25.6	28 29.0	29 22.8	2 15.0
16 Tu	17 41 32	24 46 42	9♏56 24	15 51 24	12 44.6	5 56.9	19 41.8	0 53.6	4 18.6	23 12.8	25 27.5	28 26.8	29 23.0	2 16.6
17 W	17 45 29	25 47 46	21 46 25	27 41 47	12 32.8	7 19.6	20 57.3	1 38.9	4 27.2	23 06.5	25 29.5	28 24.7	29 23.2	2 18.2
18 Th	17 49 25	26 48 52	3♐37 49	9♐34 43	12 19.1	8 43.4	22 12.8	2 24.3	4 36.2	22 59.9	25 31.6	28 22.6	29 23.5	2 19.8
19 F	17 53 22	27 49 57	15 32 41	21 31 54	12 04.6	10 08.1	23 28.3	3 09.7	4 45.4	22 53.3	25 33.9	28 20.5	29 23.8	2 21.5
20 Sa	17 57 18	28 51 04	27 32 29	3♑34 34	11 50.5	11 33.8	24 43.9	3 55.2	4 54.9	22 46.5	25 36.2	28 18.4	29 24.1	2 23.1
21 Su	18 01 15	29 52 11	9♑38 15	15 43 38	11 37.9	13 00.2	25 59.4	4 40.7	5 04.7	22 39.6	25 38.6	28 16.3	29 24.5	2 24.8
22 M	18 05 12	0♑53 18	21 50 52	28 00 04	11 27.9	14 27.3	27 14.9	5 26.3	5 14.8	22 32.6	25 41.1	28 14.3	29 24.9	2 26.5
23 Tu	18 09 08	1 54 26	4♒11 25	10♒25 06	11 20.8	15 55.0	28 30.5	6 11.9	5 25.2	22 25.5	25 43.8	28 12.4	29 25.3	2 28.2
24 W	18 13 05	2 55 34	16 41 21	23 00 26	11 16.7	17 23.2	29 46.0	6 57.5	5 35.9	22 18.3	25 46.5	28 10.4	29 25.8	2 29.9
25 Th	18 17 01	3 56 42	29 22 40	5♓48 23	11D 15.1	18 52.0	1♑01.5	7 43.2	5 46.8	22 11.0	25 49.3	28 08.5	29 26.3	2 31.6
26 F	18 20 58	4 57 50	12♓17 56	18 51 43	11 15.1	20 21.2	2 17.0	8 29.0	5 58.0	22 03.6	25 52.2	28 06.6	29 26.8	2 33.4
27 Sa	18 24 54	5 58 58	25 30 04	2♈13 21	11R 15.6	21 50.9	3 32.6	9 14.7	6 09.5	21 56.1	25 55.2	28 04.8	29 27.4	2 35.1
28 Su	18 28 51	7 00 06	9♈01 53	15 55 55	11 15.3	23 20.9	4 48.1	10 00.6	6 21.2	21 48.5	25 58.4	28 03.0	29 28.0	2 36.9
29 M	18 32 47	8 01 14	22 55 35	0♉00 55	11 13.2	24 51.3	6 03.6	10 46.4	6 33.2	21 40.9	26 01.6	28 01.2	29 28.7	2 38.6
30 Tu	18 36 44	9 02 22	7♉11 47	14 27 56	11 08.7	26 22.1	7 19.1	11 32.3	6 45.4	21 33.2	26 04.9	27 59.5	29 29.3	2 40.4
31 W	18 40 41	10 03 30	21 48 51	29 13 54	11 01.8	27 53.3	8 34.6	12 18.3	6 57.8	21 25.4	26 08.3	27 57.8	29 30.0	2 42.2

Astro Data

	Dy Hr Mn
☽ 0N	2 11:59
☿ R	9 19:03
♃ R	11 16:43
☽ 0S	15 5:08
♅⚹♆	20 14:40
⚳ D	21 23:58
♄ D	28 3:53
☿ D	29 17:41
☽ 0N	29 20:35
♆ D	10 12:25
☽ 0S	12 10:34
☽ 0N	27 2:25

Planet Ingress

	Dy Hr Mn
♂ ♐	4 13:02
♀ ♏	6 22:41
♅ ♉R	8 2:23
☿ ♏R	19 3:21
☉ ♐	22 1:37
♀ ♐	30 20:15
☿ ♐	11 22:41
♂ ♑	15 7:35
☉ ♑	21 15:04
♀ ♑	24 16:27

Last Aspect / ☽ Ingress (November)

Last Aspect Dy Hr Mn		☽ Ingress Dy Hr Mn
2 15:16 ♆ ☌	♈	2 15:41
4 11:22 ♀ ☍	♉	4 16:17
6 14:52 ♆ ⚹	♊	6 15:22
8 14:33 ♆ □	♋	8 15:07
10 17:24 ♅ ⚹	♌	10 17:35
12 23:31 ♅ □	♍	12 23:53
15 9:10 ♅ △	♎	15 9:45
17 11:52 ♃ □	♏	17 21:46
20 9:26 ♅ ☍	♐	20 10:27
22 21:49 ♅ □	♑	22 22:54
25 9:11 ♆ ⚹	♒	25 10:17
27 17:54 ♅ □	♓	27 19:25
30 0:06 ♆ ☌	♈	30 1:08

Last Aspect / ☽ Ingress (December)

Last Aspect Dy Hr Mn		☽ Ingress Dy Hr Mn
1 18:16 ♃ □	♉	2 3:14
4 1:51 ♆ ⚹	♊	4 2:49
6 0:56 ♆ □	♋	6 1:55
8 1:46 ♆ △	♌	8 2:49
10 4:58 ♅ □	♍	10 7:21
12 14:52 ♆ ☍	♎	12 16:05
15 3:37 ♂ ⚹	♏	15 3:52
17 15:25 ♅ △	♐	17 16:40
20 3:42 ♆ □	♑	20 4:54
22 14:45 ♆ ⚹	♒	22 15:53
24 21:43 ♅ □	♓	25 1:10
27 7:05 ♆ ☌	♈	27 8:03
29 2:14 ♀ △	♉	29 11:58
31 12:26 ♆ ⚹	♊	31 13:14

☽ Phases & Eclipses

Dy Hr Mn		
5 13:20	○	13♉23
12 5:29	☾	20♌05
20 6:48	●	28♏12
28 7:00	☽	6♓18
4 23:15	○	13♊04
11 20:53	☾	20♍04
20 1:44	●	28♐25
27 19:11	☽	6♈17

Astro Data

1 November 2025
Julian Day # 45961
SVP 4♓53'53"
GC 27♐12.0 ♀ 8♒42.9
Eris 25♈01.9R ✱ 9♐38.7
⚷ 24♈11.6R ⚵ 22♐55.9
☽ Mean ☊ 15♓22.3

1 December 2025
Julian Day # 45991
SVP 4♓53'48"
GC 27♐12.1 ♀ 14♒26.1
Eris 24♈46.5R ✱ 19♐56.2
⚷ 23♈04.2R ⚵ 8♑17.9
☽ Mean ☊ 13♓47.0

LONGITUDE — January 2026

Day	Sid.Time	☉	0 hr ☽	Noon ☽	True ☊	☿	♀	♂	⚳	♃	♄	♅	♆	♇
1 Th	18 44 37	11♑04 38	6♊42 13	14♊12 48	10♓53.1	29♐24.8	9♑50.1	13♑04.2	7♈10.6	21♋17.5	26♓11.8	27♉56.1	29♓30.8	2♒44.0
2 F	18 48 34	12 05 46	21 44 29	29 16 03	10R43.5	0♑56.7	11 05.6	13 50.3	7 23.5	21R09.7	26 15.4	27R54.5	29 31.6	2 45.8
3 Sa	18 52 30	13 06 54	6♋46 15	14♋13 49	10 34.3	2 28.9	12 21.1	14 36.3	7 36.7	21 01.7	26 19.1	27 53.0	29 32.4	2 47.7
4 Su	18 56 27	14 08 02	21 37 38	28 56 41	10 26.5	4 01.5	13 36.6	15 22.4	7 50.1	20 53.8	26 22.8	27 51.4	29 33.2	2 49.5
5 M	19 00 23	15 09 09	6♌10 05	13♌17 13	10 21.0	5 34.5	14 52.0	16 08.6	8 03.8	20 45.7	26 26.7	27 50.0	29 34.1	2 51.4
6 Tu	19 04 20	16 10 17	20 17 37	27 11 01	10D18.0	7 07.8	16 07.5	16 54.7	8 17.6	20 37.7	26 30.7	27 48.5	29 35.0	2 53.2
7 W	19 08 17	17 11 25	3♍57 22	10♍36 46	10 17.1	8 41.5	17 23.0	17 41.0	8 31.7	20 29.6	26 34.7	27 47.1	29 35.9	2 55.1
8 Th	19 12 13	18 12 33	17 09 28	23 35 50	10 17.8	10 15.6	18 38.5	18 27.2	8 46.0	20 21.6	26 38.8	27 45.8	29 36.9	2 56.9
9 F	19 16 10	19 13 41	29 56 22	6♎11 35	10 19.0	11 50.1	19 54.0	19 13.5	9 00.5	20 13.5	26 43.0	27 44.5	29 37.9	2 58.8
10 Sa	19 20 06	20 14 49	12♎22 05	18 28 30	10R19.7	13 25.1	21 09.4	19 59.8	9 15.2	20 05.4	26 47.3	27 43.2	29 39.0	3 00.7
11 Su	19 24 03	21 15 57	24 31 29	0♏31 41	10 19.2	15 00.4	22 24.9	20 46.2	9 30.2	19 57.3	26 51.7	27 42.0	29 40.0	3 02.6
12 M	19 27 59	22 17 06	6♏29 44	12 26 15	10 16.8	16 36.2	23 40.4	21 32.6	9 45.3	19 49.2	26 56.2	27 40.8	29 41.1	3 04.5
13 Tu	19 31 56	23 18 14	18 21 49	24 17 02	10 12.2	18 12.5	24 55.8	22 19.0	10 00.6	19 41.1	27 00.7	27 39.7	29 42.3	3 06.4
14 W	19 35 52	24 19 22	0♐12 22	6♐08 19	10 05.6	19 49.2	26 11.3	23 05.5	10 16.2	19 33.0	27 05.3	27 38.6	29 43.4	3 08.3
15 Th	19 39 49	25 20 30	12 05 18	18 03 41	9 57.6	21 26.4	27 26.8	23 52.0	10 31.9	19 25.0	27 10.1	27 37.6	29 44.6	3 10.2
16 F	19 43 46	26 21 37	24 03 48	0♑05 54	9 48.9	23 04.2	28 42.2	24 38.6	10 47.8	19 17.0	27 14.8	27 36.6	29 45.8	3 12.1
17 Sa	19 47 42	27 22 44	6♑10 14	12 16 58	9 40.3	24 42.4	29 57.7	25 25.2	11 03.9	19 09.1	27 19.7	27 35.7	29 47.1	3 14.0
18 Su	19 51 39	28 23 51	18 26 13	24 38 06	9 32.7	26 21.2	1♒13.1	26 11.8	11 20.2	19 01.1	27 24.7	27 34.8	29 48.4	3 15.9
19 M	19 55 35	29 24 57	0♒52 40	7♒09 58	9 26.8	28 00.5	2 28.5	26 58.4	11 36.7	18 53.3	27 29.7	27 33.9	29 49.7	3 17.8
20 Tu	19 59 32	0♒26 03	13 30 03	19 52 56	9 22.8	29 40.4	3 44.0	27 45.1	11 53.4	18 45.5	27 34.8	27 33.2	29 51.0	3 19.8
21 W	20 03 28	1 27 07	26 18 39	2♓47 13	9D21.0	1♒20.8	4 59.4	28 31.8	12 10.2	18 37.7	27 40.0	27 32.4	29 52.4	3 21.7
22 Th	20 07 25	2 28 11	9♓18 43	15 53 12	9 21.0	3 01.8	6 14.8	29 18.5	12 27.2	18 30.0	27 45.2	27 31.7	29 53.8	3 23.6
23 F	20 11 21	3 29 14	22 30 45	29 11 27	9 22.2	4 43.3	7 30.2	0♒05.3	12 44.4	18 22.4	27 50.5	27 31.1	29 55.2	3 25.5
24 Sa	20 15 18	4 30 16	5♈55 25	12♈42 44	9 23.8	6 25.5	8 45.6	0 52.0	13 01.7	18 14.9	27 55.9	27 30.5	29 56.7	3 27.4
25 Su	20 19 15	5 31 17	19 33 30	26 27 47	9R25.0	8 08.2	10 01.0	1 38.8	13 19.2	18 07.5	28 01.4	27 30.0	29 58.1	3 29.4
26 M	20 23 11	6 32 17	3♉25 35	10♉26 53	9 25.3	9 51.5	11 16.3	2 25.7	13 36.9	18 00.1	28 06.9	27 29.5	29 59.6	3 31.3
27 Tu	20 27 08	7 33 16	17 31 35	24 39 28	9 24.1	11 35.3	12 31.7	3 12.5	13 54.7	17 52.9	28 12.5	27 29.1	0♈01.2	3 33.2
28 W	20 31 04	8 34 13	1♊50 15	9♊03 33	9 21.5	13 19.6	13 47.0	3 59.4	14 12.7	17 45.8	28 18.1	27 28.7	0 02.7	3 35.1
29 Th	20 35 01	9 35 10	16 18 52	23 35 34	9 17.7	15 04.4	15 02.3	4 46.3	14 30.9	17 38.7	28 23.9	27 28.4	0 04.3	3 37.0
30 F	20 38 57	10 36 05	0♋52 59	8♋10 21	9 13.4	16 49.7	16 17.7	5 33.2	14 49.1	17 31.8	28 29.6	27 28.1	0 05.9	3 39.0
31 Sa	20 42 54	11 36 59	15 26 50	22 41 39	9 09.1	18 35.4	17 32.9	6 20.2	15 07.6	17 25.0	28 35.5	27 27.9	0 07.6	3 40.9

LONGITUDE — February 2026

Day	Sid.Time	☉	0 hr ☽	Noon ☽	True ☊	☿	♀	♂	⚳	♃	♄	♅	♆	♇
1 Su	20 46 50	12♒37 52	29♋53 58	7♌03 01	9♓05.6	20♒21.4	18♒48.2	7♒07.1	15♈26.1	17♋18.3	28♓41.4	27♉27.8	0♈09.2	3♒42.8
2 M	20 50 47	13 38 44	14♌08 06	21 08 39	9R03.2	22 07.6	20 03.5	7 54.1	15 44.8	17R11.7	28 47.4	27R27.7	0 10.9	3 44.7
3 Tu	20 54 44	14 39 35	28 04 10	4♍54 17	9D02.2	23 54.0	21 18.8	8 41.1	16 03.7	17 05.3	28 53.4	27D27.6	0 12.6	3 46.6
4 W	20 58 40	15 40 25	11♍38 48	18 17 37	9 02.4	25 40.3	22 34.0	9 28.1	16 22.6	16 59.0	28 59.5	27 27.6	0 14.3	3 48.5
5 Th	21 02 37	16 41 13	24 50 44	1♎18 19	9 03.5	27 26.6	23 49.2	10 15.2	16 41.7	16 52.8	29 05.6	27 27.6	0 16.1	3 50.4
6 F	21 06 33	17 42 01	7♎40 37	13 57 56	9 05.1	29 12.4	25 04.5	11 02.2	17 01.0	16 46.8	29 11.8	27 27.7	0 17.9	3 52.2
7 Sa	21 10 30	18 42 48	20 10 42	26 19 24	9 06.7	0♓57.8	26 19.7	11 49.3	17 20.3	16 40.9	29 18.1	27 27.9	0 19.6	3 54.1
8 Su	21 14 26	19 43 34	2♏24 31	8♏26 38	9 07.9	2 42.2	27 34.9	12 36.4	17 39.8	16 35.2	29 24.4	27 28.1	0 21.5	3 56.0
9 M	21 18 23	20 44 19	14 26 21	20 24 14	9R08.4	4 25.6	28 50.1	13 23.5	17 59.4	16 29.6	29 30.7	27 28.4	0 23.3	3 57.8
10 Tu	21 22 19	21 45 03	26 20 54	2♐16 57	9 08.0	6 07.5	0♓05.2	14 10.7	18 19.2	16 24.2	29 37.1	27 28.7	0 25.1	3 59.7
11 W	21 26 16	22 45 46	8♐12 59	14 09 35	9 06.8	7 47.5	1 20.4	14 57.8	18 39.1	16 18.9	29 43.6	27 29.0	0 27.0	4 01.5
12 Th	21 30 13	23 46 28	20 07 16	26 06 35	9 04.9	9 25.2	2 35.5	15 45.0	18 59.0	16 13.8	29 50.1	27 29.5	0 28.9	4 03.4
13 F	21 34 09	24 47 08	2♑07 59	8♑11 55	9 02.8	11 00.1	3 50.7	16 32.2	19 19.1	16 08.9	29 56.6	27 29.9	0 30.8	4 05.2
14 Sa	21 38 06	25 47 48	14 18 46	20 28 52	9 00.6	12 31.5	5 05.8	17 19.4	19 39.4	16 04.1	0♈03.2	27 30.5	0 32.8	4 07.0
15 Su	21 42 02	26 48 26	26 42 29	2♒59 49	8 58.8	13 59.0	6 20.9	18 06.6	19 59.7	15 59.5	0 09.9	27 31.0	0 34.7	4 08.8
16 M	21 45 59	27 49 03	9♒21 02	15 46 12	8 57.4	15 21.9	7 36.0	18 53.8	20 20.1	15 55.1	0 16.6	27 31.7	0 36.7	4 10.6
17 Tu	21 49 55	28 49 38	22 15 22	28 48 28	8D56.7	16 39.4	8 51.1	19 41.0	20 40.7	15 50.8	0 23.3	27 32.4	0 38.7	4 12.4
18 W	21 53 52	29 50 12	5♓25 26	12♓06 07	8 56.5	17 51.0	10 06.1	20 28.3	21 01.3	15 46.8	0 30.1	27 33.1	0 40.7	4 14.2
19 Th	21 57 48	0♓50 44	18 50 20	25 37 53	8 56.9	18 55.9	11 21.1	21 15.5	21 22.1	15 42.9	0 36.9	27 33.9	0 42.7	4 15.9
20 F	22 01 45	1 51 15	2♈28 30	9♈21 55	8 57.4	19 53.4	12 36.1	22 02.8	21 42.9	15 39.2	0 43.8	27 34.7	0 44.8	4 17.7
21 Sa	22 05 42	2 51 43	16 17 54	23 16 07	8 58.1	20 43.0	13 51.1	22 50.0	22 03.9	15 35.6	0 50.7	27 35.6	0 46.8	4 19.4
22 Su	22 09 38	3 52 10	0♉16 19	7♉18 13	8 58.6	21 23.9	15 06.1	23 37.3	22 24.9	15 32.3	0 57.6	27 36.6	0 48.9	4 21.1
23 M	22 13 35	4 52 36	14 21 32	21 25 58	8 58.9	21 55.8	16 21.0	24 24.6	22 46.1	15 29.2	1 04.5	27 37.6	0 50.9	4 22.9
24 Tu	22 17 31	5 52 59	28 31 16	5♊37 10	8R59.0	22 18.2	17 36.0	25 11.8	23 07.3	15 26.2	1 11.6	27 38.6	0 53.0	4 24.6
25 W	22 21 28	6 53 20	12♊43 21	19 49 33	8 59.0	22R30.9	18 50.9	25 59.1	23 28.7	15 23.5	1 18.6	27 39.7	0 55.2	4 26.2
26 Th	22 25 24	7 53 39	26 55 28	4♋00 46	8 58.9	22 33.7	20 05.7	26 46.4	23 50.1	15 20.9	1 25.6	27 40.9	0 57.3	4 27.9
27 F	22 29 21	8 53 57	11♋05 08	18 08 14	8D58.8	22 26.7	21 20.6	27 33.7	24 11.6	15 18.5	1 32.7	27 42.1	0 59.4	4 29.6
28 Sa	22 33 17	9 54 12	25 09 43	2♌09 12	8 58.9	22 10.1	22 35.4	28 21.0	24 33.2	15 16.4	1 39.9	27 43.3	1 01.6	4 31.2

Astro Data

	Dy Hr Mn
☽0S	8 17:46
♄✶♅	20 5:21
☽0N	23 7:07
⚳0N	4 1:58
♅D	4 2:34
☽0S	5 2:51
☽0N	19 13:15
♄☌♆	20 16:54
☿R	26 6:48

Planet Ingress

	Dy Hr Mn
☿ ♑	1 21:12
♀ ♒	17 12:45
☉ ♒	20 1:46
☿ ♒	20 16:42
♂ ♒	23 9:18
♆ ♈	26 17:38
☿ ♓	6 22:49
♀ ♓	10 10:20
♄ ♈	14 0:13
☉ ♓	18 15:53

Last Aspect / ☽ Ingress

Last Aspect Dy Hr Mn		☽ Ingress Dy Hr Mn
2 12:25 ♆ □	♋	2 13:10
4 13:01 ♆ △	♌	4 13:45
6 13:06 ♅ □	♍	6 16:58
8 23:24 ♆ ☍	♎	9 0:07
10 17:55 ♀ □	♏	11 10:56
13 23:00 ♆ △	♐	13 23:35
16 11:20 ♆ □	♑	16 11:48
18 21:58 ♆ ✶	♒	18 22:19
21 2:18 ♅ □	♓	21 6:51
23 13:18 ♆ ☌	♈	23 13:27
24 21:37 ♃ □	♉	25 18:06
27 17:59 ♄ ✶	♊	27 20:56
29 19:58 ♄ □	♋	29 22:33

Last Aspect / ☽ Ingress

Last Aspect Dy Hr Mn		☽ Ingress Dy Hr Mn
31 21:53 ♄ △	♌	1 0:10
2 22:56 ♅ □	♍	3 3:22
5 7:50 ♄ ☍	♎	5 9:34
7 12:01 ♀ △	♏	7 19:14
10 7:02 ♀ □	♐	10 7:23
12 19:30 ♄ □	♑	12 19:46
15 1:33 ♅ △	♒	15 6:18
17 12:02 ☉ ☌	♓	17 14:10
19 15:24 ♅ ✶	♈	19 19:40
21 11:13 ♂ ✶	♉	21 23:32
23 22:30 ♅ ☌	♊	24 2:30
25 23:01 ♂ △	♋	26 5:12
28 4:22 ♅ ✶	♌	28 8:18

☽ Phases & Eclipses

Dy Hr Mn		
3 10:04	○	13♋02
10 15:50	☾	20♎25
18 19:53	●	28♑44
26 4:49	☽	6♉14
1 22:10	○	13♌04
9 12:44	☾	20♏46
17 12:02	●	28♒50
17 12:13:04	●	A 02'20"
24 12:29	☽	5♊54

Astro Data

1 January 2026
Julian Day # 46022
SVP 4♓53'42"
GC 27♐12.1 ⚴ 22♒44.2
Eris 24♈38.0R ⚵ 1♑02.5
⚷ 22♈36.0R ⚶ 24♑32.9
☽ Mean ☊ 12♓08.6

1 February 2026
Julian Day # 46053
SVP 4♓53'36"
GC 27♐12.2 ⚴ 2♓23.8
Eris 24♈39.7 ⚵ 12♑06.3
⚷ 23♈00.7 ⚶ 10♒49.0
☽ Mean ☊ 10♓30.1

March 2026 — LONGITUDE

Day	Sid.Time	☉	0 hr ☽	Noon ☽	True ☊	☿	♀	♂	⚳	♃	♄	♅	♆	♇
1 Su	22 37 14	10♓54 25	9♌06 21	16♌00 49	8♓59.0	21♓44.5	23♓50.2	29♒08.2	24♈54.9	15♋14.4	1♈47.0	27♉44.6	1♈03.7	4♒32.8
2 M	22 41 11	11 54 36	22 52 15	29 40 21	8R 59.1	21R 10.4	25 05.0	29 55.5	25 16.6	15R 12.6	1 54.2	27 45.9	1 05.9	4 34.4
3 Tu	22 45 07	12 54 46	6♍24 50	13♍05 30	8 59.2	20 28.8	26 19.7	0♓42.8	25 38.5	15 11.0	2 01.4	27 47.3	1 08.1	4 36.0
4 W	22 49 04	13 54 53	19 42 08	26 14 38	8 59.0	19 40.7	27 34.4	1 30.1	26 00.4	15 09.6	2 08.6	27 48.8	1 10.2	4 37.6
5 Th	22 53 00	14 54 59	2♎42 56	9♎07 03	8 58.5	18 47.3	28 49.1	2 17.3	26 22.4	15 08.4	2 15.9	27 50.3	1 12.4	4 39.1
6 F	22 56 57	15 55 03	15 27 03	21 43 05	8 57.7	17 50.1	0♈03.8	3 04.6	26 44.5	15 07.4	2 23.1	27 51.8	1 14.6	4 40.7
7 Sa	23 00 53	16 55 06	27 55 22	4♏04 09	8 56.6	16 50.3	1 18.4	3 51.9	27 06.6	15 06.5	2 30.4	27 53.4	1 16.8	4 42.2
8 Su	23 04 50	17 55 07	10♏09 47	16 12 38	8 55.4	15 49.5	2 33.1	4 39.1	27 28.8	15 05.9	2 37.8	27 55.0	1 19.1	4 43.7
9 M	23 08 46	18 55 06	22 13 10	28 11 51	8 54.4	14 49.1	3 47.6	5 26.4	27 51.1	15 05.5	2 45.1	27 56.7	1 21.3	4 45.2
10 Tu	23 12 43	19 55 04	4♐09 11	10♐05 44	8D 53.7	13 50.4	5 02.2	6 13.7	28 13.5	15D 05.3	2 52.5	27 58.4	1 23.5	4 46.7
11 W	23 16 40	20 55 00	16 02 03	21 58 44	8 53.5	12 54.5	6 16.8	7 00.9	28 35.9	15 05.3	2 59.8	28 00.2	1 25.8	4 48.1
12 Th	23 20 36	21 54 54	27 56 21	3♑55 31	8 53.8	12 02.4	7 31.3	7 48.2	28 58.4	15 05.4	3 07.2	28 02.0	1 28.0	4 49.5
13 F	23 24 33	22 54 47	9♑56 49	16 00 48	8 54.7	11 15.1	8 45.8	8 35.4	29 21.0	15 05.8	3 14.6	28 03.8	1 30.3	4 50.9
14 Sa	23 28 29	23 54 38	22 08 02	28 19 00	8 56.0	10 33.1	10 00.2	9 22.7	29 43.7	15 06.3	3 22.0	28 05.7	1 32.5	4 52.3
15 Su	23 32 26	24 54 27	4♒34 11	10♒53 58	8 57.3	9 56.9	11 14.7	10 09.9	0♉06.4	15 07.1	3 29.5	28 07.7	1 34.8	4 53.7
16 M	23 36 22	25 54 14	17 18 41	23 48 36	8 58.4	9 26.9	12 29.1	10 57.1	0 29.1	15 08.0	3 36.9	28 09.7	1 37.1	4 55.0
17 Tu	23 40 19	26 54 00	0♓23 52	7♓04 32	8R 59.0	9 03.1	13 43.5	11 44.3	0 52.0	15 09.2	3 44.4	28 11.7	1 39.3	4 56.4
18 W	23 44 15	27 53 43	13 50 34	20 41 46	8 58.6	8 45.7	14 57.8	12 31.5	1 14.8	15 10.5	3 51.8	28 13.8	1 41.6	4 57.7
19 Th	23 48 12	28 53 25	27 37 52	4♈38 29	8 57.3	8 34.7	16 12.2	13 18.7	1 37.8	15 12.0	3 59.3	28 15.9	1 43.9	4 58.9
20 F	23 52 08	29 53 05	11♈43 06	18 51 09	8 55.0	8D 29.7	17 26.5	14 05.9	2 00.8	15 13.7	4 06.8	28 18.1	1 46.1	5 00.2
21 Sa	23 56 05	0♈52 42	26 01 58	3♉14 51	8 52.0	8 30.8	18 40.7	14 53.0	2 23.9	15 15.6	4 14.3	28 20.3	1 48.4	5 01.4
22 Su	0 00 02	1 52 18	10♉29 04	17 43 53	8 48.8	8 37.7	19 55.0	15 40.2	2 47.0	15 17.7	4 21.7	28 22.5	1 50.7	5 02.6
23 M	0 03 58	2 51 51	24 58 37	2♊12 36	8 45.9	8 50.1	21 09.2	16 27.3	3 10.2	15 20.0	4 29.2	28 24.8	1 53.0	5 03.8
24 Tu	0 07 55	3 51 22	9♊25 16	16 36 07	8 43.9	9 07.7	22 23.3	17 14.4	3 33.4	15 22.5	4 36.7	28 27.1	1 55.2	5 05.0
25 W	0 11 51	4 50 51	23 44 41	0♋50 41	8D 42.9	9 30.4	23 37.5	18 01.5	3 56.7	15 25.2	4 44.2	28 29.4	1 57.5	5 06.1
26 Th	0 15 48	5 50 17	7♋53 51	14 53 59	8 43.2	9 57.7	24 51.6	18 48.6	4 20.0	15 28.0	4 51.7	28 31.8	1 59.8	5 07.3
27 F	0 19 44	6 49 41	21 51 01	28 44 51	8 44.3	10 29.6	26 05.6	19 35.6	4 43.4	15 31.0	4 59.2	28 34.3	2 02.1	5 08.4
28 Sa	0 23 41	7 49 03	5♌35 29	12♌22 56	8 45.9	11 05.7	27 19.6	20 22.6	5 06.8	15 34.2	5 06.7	28 36.7	2 04.3	5 09.4
29 Su	0 27 37	8 48 22	19 07 13	25 48 22	8R 47.3	11 45.7	28 33.6	21 09.6	5 30.2	15 37.6	5 14.2	28 39.2	2 06.6	5 10.5
30 M	0 31 34	9 47 39	2♍26 26	9♍01 26	8 47.8	12 29.5	29 47.6	21 56.6	5 53.7	15 41.2	5 21.7	28 41.8	2 08.9	5 11.5
31 Tu	0 35 31	10 46 54	15 33 24	22 02 21	8 47.1	13 16.9	1♉01.5	22 43.6	6 17.3	15 44.9	5 29.1	28 44.4	2 11.1	5 12.5

April 2026 — LONGITUDE

Day	Sid.Time	☉	0 hr ☽	Noon ☽	True ☊	☿	♀	♂	⚳	♃	♄	♅	♆	♇
1 W	0 39 27	11♈46 07	28♍28 18	4♎51 15	8♓44.6	14♓07.6	2♉15.4	23♓30.5	6♉40.9	15♋48.8	5♈36.6	28♉47.0	2♈13.4	5♒13.5
2 Th	0 43 24	12 45 17	11♎11 14	17 28 18	8R 40.6	15 01.4	3 29.2	24 17.4	7 04.5	15 52.9	5 44.0	28 49.6	2 15.6	5 14.4
3 F	0 47 20	13 44 26	23 42 28	29 53 50	8 35.0	15 58.3	4 43.0	25 04.3	7 28.2	15 57.2	5 51.5	28 52.3	2 17.9	5 15.3
4 Sa	0 51 17	14 43 32	6♏02 29	12♏08 35	8 28.6	16 58.0	5 56.7	25 51.2	7 51.9	16 01.6	5 58.9	28 55.0	2 20.1	5 16.2
5 Su	0 55 13	15 42 37	18 12 19	24 13 54	8 21.8	18 00.4	7 10.5	26 38.0	8 15.6	16 06.2	6 06.4	28 57.7	2 22.3	5 17.1
6 M	0 59 10	16 41 40	0♐13 37	6♐11 48	8 15.5	19 05.4	8 24.2	27 24.8	8 39.4	16 10.9	6 13.8	29 00.5	2 24.5	5 17.9
7 Tu	1 03 06	17 40 41	12 08 48	18 05 05	8 10.2	20 12.9	9 37.8	28 11.6	9 03.2	16 15.8	6 21.2	29 03.3	2 26.8	5 18.8
8 W	1 07 03	18 39 41	24 01 04	29 57 17	8 06.5	21 22.7	10 51.4	28 58.4	9 27.1	16 20.9	6 28.6	29 06.1	2 29.0	5 19.6
9 Th	1 11 00	19 38 38	5♑54 17	11♑52 37	8D 04.5	22 34.8	12 05.0	29 45.2	9 51.0	16 26.2	6 36.0	29 09.0	2 31.2	5 20.3
10 F	1 14 56	20 37 34	17 52 53	23 55 43	8 04.2	23 49.0	13 18.5	0♈31.9	10 15.0	16 31.6	6 43.3	29 11.9	2 33.4	5 21.1
11 Sa	1 18 53	21 36 28	0♒01 43	6♒11 30	8 05.1	25 05.3	14 32.1	1 18.6	10 38.9	16 37.1	6 50.7	29 14.8	2 35.5	5 21.8
12 Su	1 22 49	22 35 21	12 25 42	18 44 50	8 06.5	26 23.7	15 45.5	2 05.2	11 02.9	16 42.9	6 58.0	29 17.7	2 37.7	5 22.5
13 M	1 26 46	23 34 11	25 09 27	1♓40 00	8R 07.6	27 44.1	16 59.0	2 51.9	11 27.0	16 48.7	7 05.3	29 20.7	2 39.9	5 23.1
14 Tu	1 30 42	24 33 00	8♓16 51	15 00 14	8 07.6	29 06.3	18 12.3	3 38.5	11 51.0	16 54.8	7 12.6	29 23.7	2 42.0	5 23.8
15 W	1 34 39	25 31 47	21 50 17	28 46 57	8 05.7	0♈30.4	19 25.7	4 25.1	12 15.1	17 01.0	7 19.8	29 26.7	2 44.2	5 24.4
16 Th	1 38 35	26 30 32	5♈50 04	12♈59 14	8 01.7	1 56.4	20 39.0	5 11.6	12 39.2	17 07.3	7 27.1	29 29.8	2 46.3	5 24.9
17 F	1 42 32	27 29 15	20 13 53	27 33 17	7 55.8	3 24.2	21 52.3	5 58.1	13 03.4	17 13.8	7 34.3	29 32.8	2 48.4	5 25.5
18 Sa	1 46 29	28 27 57	4♉56 33	12♉22 39	7 48.3	4 53.7	23 05.5	6 44.6	13 27.6	17 20.4	7 41.5	29 35.9	2 50.5	5 26.0
19 Su	1 50 25	29 26 36	19 50 29	27 18 54	7 40.3	6 25.0	24 18.7	7 31.0	13 51.8	17 27.2	7 48.6	29 39.1	2 52.6	5 26.5
20 M	1 54 22	0♉25 14	4♊46 47	12♊13 01	7 32.8	7 58.0	25 31.9	8 17.4	14 16.0	17 34.1	7 55.8	29 42.2	2 54.7	5 27.0
21 Tu	1 58 18	1 23 49	19 36 41	26 56 54	7 26.8	9 32.7	26 45.0	9 03.8	14 40.3	17 41.2	8 02.9	29 45.4	2 56.7	5 27.4
22 W	2 02 15	2 22 22	4♋13 01	11♋24 30	7 22.8	11 09.2	27 58.1	9 50.2	15 04.6	17 48.4	8 10.0	29 48.6	2 58.8	5 27.8
23 Th	2 06 11	3 20 53	18 31 02	25 32 26	7D 20.9	12 47.3	29 11.1	10 36.4	15 28.9	17 55.7	8 17.0	29 51.8	3 00.8	5 28.2
24 F	2 10 08	4 19 22	2♌28 37	9♌19 41	7 20.7	14 27.2	0♊24.1	11 22.7	15 53.2	18 03.2	8 24.0	29 55.0	3 02.8	5 28.5
25 Sa	2 14 04	5 17 48	16 05 47	22 47 09	7 21.4	16 08.8	1 37.0	12 08.9	16 17.6	18 10.8	8 31.0	29 58.3	3 04.8	5 28.9
26 Su	2 18 01	6 16 12	29 24 03	5♍56 49	7R 22.0	17 52.1	2 49.9	12 55.1	16 41.9	18 18.5	8 38.0	0♊01.5	3 06.8	5 29.2
27 M	2 21 58	7 14 35	12♍25 44	18 51 08	7 21.4	19 37.1	4 02.7	13 41.2	17 06.3	18 26.4	8 44.9	0 04.8	3 08.8	5 29.4
28 Tu	2 25 54	8 12 55	25 13 18	1♎32 29	7 18.7	21 23.8	5 15.5	14 27.3	17 30.7	18 34.3	8 51.7	0 08.1	3 10.7	5 29.7
29 W	2 29 51	9 11 13	7♎48 56	14 02 53	7 13.5	23 12.3	6 28.2	15 13.4	17 55.1	18 42.5	8 58.6	0 11.4	3 12.7	5 29.9
30 Th	2 33 47	10 09 29	20 14 29	26 23 55	7 05.6	25 02.5	7 40.9	15 59.4	18 19.5	18 50.7	9 05.4	0 14.7	3 14.6	5 30.1

Astro Data	Dy Hr Mn
☽ 0S	4 12:12
♀0N	8 16:43
♃ D	11 3:31
☽ 0N	18 21:49
☉0N	20 14:47
☿ D	20 19:35
♄0N	26 21:27
♄⚹♇	28 22:14
☽ 0S	31 20:04
♂0N	12 18:24
☽ 0N	15 7:43
☿0N	19 6:44
♆0N	24 4:41
☽ 0S	28 1:51

Planet Ingress	Dy Hr Mn
♂ ♓	2 14:17
♀ ♈	6 10:47
⚳ ♉	15 5:17
☉ ♈	20 14:47
♀ ♉	30 16:02
♂ ♈	9 19:37
☿ ♈	15 3:23
☉ ♉	20 1:40
♀ ♊	24 4:05
♅ ♊	26 0:51

Last Aspect Dy Hr Mn		☽ Ingress	Dy Hr Mn
2 12:29	♂ ☍	♍	2 12:35
4 14:54	♅ △	♎	4 18:57
5 23:23	♃ □	♏	7 4:03
9 11:29	♅ ☍	♐	9 15:38
11 9:40	☉ □	♑	12 4:08
14 11:34	♅ △	♒	14 15:15
16 19:58	♅ □	♓	16 23:17
19 1:25	☉ ☌	♈	19 4:04
20 9:24	♀ ☌	♉	21 6:36
23 5:41	♅ ☌	♊	23 8:20
24 22:38	♀ ⚹	♋	25 10:34
27 11:41	♅ ⚹	♌	27 14:11
29 17:29	♀ △	♍	29 19:34

Last Aspect Dy Hr Mn		☽ Ingress	Dy Hr Mn
1 0:33	♅ △	♎	1 2:52
2 8:56	♃ □	♏	3 12:12
5 21:30	♅ ☍	♐	5 23:33
8 9:53	♂ □	♑	8 12:05
10 22:25	♅ △	♒	10 23:57
13 7:43	♅ □	♓	13 8:57
15 13:08	♅ ⚹	♈	15 14:05
17 11:53	☉ ☌	♉	17 15:59
19 15:46	♅ ☌	♊	19 16:19
20 5:19	♂ ⚹	♋	21 17:01
23 19:29	♅ ⚹	♌	23 19:42
24 22:22	☿ △	♍	26 1:06
27 11:13	♃ ⚹	♎	28 9:04
30 8:53	☿ ☍	♏	30 19:03

☽ Phases & Eclipses Dy Hr Mn	
3 11:39	○ 12♍54
3 11:35	☊ T 1.151
11 9:40	☾ 20♐49
19 1:25	● 28♓27
25 19:19	☽ 5♋09
2 2:13	○ 12♎21
10 4:53	☾ 20♑20
17 11:53	● 27♈29
24 2:33	☽ 3♌56

Astro Data

1 March 2026
Julian Day # 46081
SVP 4♓53'32"
GC 27♐12.3 ⚳ 11♓39.9
Eris 24♈49.8 ✱ 21♑35.2
⚷ 24♈04.1 ⚶ 25♒15.3
☽ Mean ☊ 9♓01.1

1 April 2026
Julian Day # 46112
SVP 4♓53'29"
GC 27♐12.4 ⚳ 22♓00.6
Eris 25♈07.5 ✱ 0♒51.1
⚷ 25♈44.1 ⚶ 10♓39.6
☽ Mean ☊ 7♓22.6

LONGITUDE May 2026

Day	Sid.Time	☉	0 hr ☽	Noon ☽	True ☊	☿	♀	♂	⚳	♃	♄	♅	♆	♇
1 F	2 37 44	11♉07 43	2♏31 19	8♏36 48	6♓55.5	26♈54.5	8♊53.6	16♈45.3	18♉44.0	18♋59.1	9♈12.2	0♊18.1	3♈16.5	5♒30.2
2 Sa	2 41 40	12 05 56	14 40 29	20 42 31	6R43.7	28 48.2	10 06.2	17 31.3	19 08.4	19 07.5	9 18.9	0 21.4	3 18.4	5 30.3
3 Su	2 45 37	13 04 07	26 43 01	2♐42 08	6 31.4	0♉43.7	11 18.7	18 17.2	19 32.9	19 16.1	9 25.6	0 24.8	3 20.2	5 30.4
4 M	2 49 33	14 02 17	8♐40 03	14 36 59	6 19.6	2 40.8	12 31.2	19 03.0	19 57.4	19 24.9	9 32.2	0 28.2	3 22.1	5 30.5
5 Tu	2 53 30	15 00 25	20 33 11	26 28 57	6 09.2	4 39.7	13 43.6	19 48.8	20 21.9	19 33.7	9 38.8	0 31.6	3 23.9	5 30.6
6 W	2 57 27	15 58 31	2♑24 37	8♑20 35	6 01.0	6 40.3	14 56.0	20 34.6	20 46.4	19 42.6	9 45.4	0 35.0	3 25.7	5R30.6
7 Th	3 01 23	16 56 36	14 17 16	20 15 11	5 55.4	8 42.5	16 08.4	21 20.3	21 11.0	19 51.7	9 51.9	0 38.4	3 27.5	5 30.6
8 F	3 05 20	17 54 39	26 14 49	2♒16 45	5 52.3	10 46.3	17 20.7	22 06.0	21 35.5	20 00.9	9 58.4	0 41.9	3 29.2	5 30.5
9 Sa	3 09 16	18 52 41	8♒21 36	14 29 56	5D51.1	12 51.5	18 32.9	22 51.6	22 00.1	20 10.1	10 04.8	0 45.3	3 31.0	5 30.5
10 Su	3 13 13	19 50 42	20 42 26	26 59 42	5R51.2	14 58.1	19 45.1	23 37.2	22 24.6	20 19.5	10 11.2	0 48.8	3 32.7	5 30.4
11 M	3 17 09	20 48 41	3♓22 21	9♓50 58	5 51.2	17 05.9	20 57.2	24 22.8	22 49.2	20 29.0	10 17.5	0 52.2	3 34.4	5 30.2
12 Tu	3 21 06	21 46 40	16 26 03	23 08 02	5 50.2	19 14.8	22 09.3	25 08.3	23 13.8	20 38.6	10 23.7	0 55.7	3 36.0	5 30.1
13 W	3 25 02	22 44 36	29 57 14	6♈53 48	5 47.2	21 24.7	23 21.4	25 53.8	23 38.4	20 48.3	10 30.0	0 59.2	3 37.7	5 29.9
14 Th	3 28 59	23 42 32	13♈57 44	21 08 49	5 41.6	23 35.2	24 33.4	26 39.2	24 03.0	20 58.1	10 36.1	1 02.6	3 39.3	5 29.7
15 F	3 32 56	24 40 26	28 26 37	5♉50 28	5 33.5	25 46.1	25 45.3	27 24.5	24 27.6	21 08.0	10 42.3	1 06.1	3 40.9	5 29.5
16 Sa	3 36 52	25 38 19	13♉19 29	20 52 35	5 23.5	27 57.3	26 57.2	28 09.9	24 52.2	21 18.0	10 48.3	1 09.6	3 42.5	5 29.2
17 Su	3 40 49	26 36 10	28 28 30	6♊05 53	5 12.6	0♊08.4	28 09.0	28 55.1	25 16.9	21 28.1	10 54.3	1 13.1	3 44.0	5 28.9
18 M	3 44 45	27 34 00	13♊43 18	21 19 22	5 02.2	2 19.2	29 20.8	29 40.3	25 41.5	21 38.2	11 00.3	1 16.6	3 45.6	5 28.6
19 Tu	3 48 42	28 31 49	28 52 47	6♋22 22	4 53.5	4 29.3	0♋32.5	0♉25.5	26 06.1	21 48.5	11 06.2	1 20.1	3 47.1	5 28.3
20 W	3 52 38	29 29 36	13♋47 08	21 06 20	4 47.2	6 38.6	1 44.2	1 10.6	26 30.8	21 58.9	11 12.0	1 23.6	3 48.6	5 27.9
21 Th	3 56 35	0♊27 21	28 19 23	5♌25 59	4 43.5	8 46.6	2 55.8	1 55.7	26 55.4	22 09.3	11 17.8	1 27.1	3 50.0	5 27.5
22 F	4 00 31	1 25 05	12♌25 58	19 19 23	4D42.0	10 53.2	4 07.4	2 40.7	27 20.0	22 19.9	11 23.5	1 30.7	3 51.4	5 27.1
23 Sa	4 04 28	2 22 47	26 06 25	2♍47 21	4R41.8	12 58.2	5 18.8	3 25.6	27 44.7	22 30.5	11 29.2	1 34.1	3 52.8	5 26.7
24 Su	4 08 25	3 20 27	9♍22 34	15 52 30	4 41.6	15 01.3	6 30.2	4 10.5	28 09.3	22 41.2	11 34.8	1 37.6	3 54.2	5 26.2
25 M	4 12 21	4 18 06	22 17 37	28 38 24	4 40.3	17 02.2	7 41.6	4 55.4	28 33.9	22 52.0	11 40.3	1 41.1	3 55.6	5 25.7
26 Tu	4 16 18	5 15 43	4♎55 18	11♎08 47	4 36.9	19 01.0	8 52.9	5 40.2	28 58.6	23 02.9	11 45.8	1 44.6	3 56.9	5 25.2
27 W	4 20 14	6 13 19	17 19 16	23 27 10	4 30.7	20 57.4	10 04.1	6 24.9	29 23.2	23 13.8	11 51.2	1 48.1	3 58.2	5 24.6
28 Th	4 24 11	7 10 54	29 32 49	5♏36 32	4 21.8	22 51.2	11 15.2	7 09.6	29 47.8	23 24.9	11 56.5	1 51.6	3 59.4	5 24.1
29 F	4 28 07	8 08 27	11♏38 36	17 39 15	4 10.3	24 42.5	12 26.3	7 54.2	0♊12.4	23 36.0	12 01.8	1 55.1	4 00.7	5 23.5
30 Sa	4 32 04	9 05 59	23 38 42	29 37 09	3 57.1	26 31.2	13 37.3	8 38.8	0 37.0	23 47.1	12 07.0	1 58.6	4 01.9	5 22.8
31 Su	4 36 00	10 03 30	5♐34 46	11♐31 43	3 43.3	28 17.1	14 48.2	9 23.3	1 01.7	23 58.4	12 12.1	2 02.1	4 03.1	5 22.2

LONGITUDE June 2026

Day	Sid.Time	☉	0 hr ☽	Noon ☽	True ☊	☿	♀	♂	⚳	♃	♄	♅	♆	♇
1 M	4 39 57	11♊01 00	17♐28 09	23♐24 16	3♓29.9	0♋00.2	15♋59.1	10♉07.8	1♊26.3	24♋09.7	12♈17.2	2♊05.6	4♈04.2	5♒21.5
2 Tu	4 43 54	11 58 29	29 20 14	5♑16 17	3R18.0	1 40.5	17 09.9	10 52.2	1 50.9	24 21.1	12 22.2	2 09.0	4 05.3	5R20.8
3 W	4 47 50	12 55 57	11♑12 39	17 09 36	3 08.4	3 18.0	18 20.6	11 36.6	2 15.5	24 32.6	12 27.1	2 12.5	4 06.4	5 20.1
4 Th	4 51 47	13 53 24	23 07 28	29 06 37	3 01.6	4 52.6	19 31.2	12 20.9	2 40.1	24 44.1	12 32.0	2 16.0	4 07.5	5 19.4
5 F	4 55 43	14 50 51	5♒07 27	11♒10 25	2 57.6	6 24.3	20 41.8	13 05.1	3 04.6	24 55.7	12 36.8	2 19.4	4 08.5	5 18.6
6 Sa	4 59 40	15 48 16	17 15 59	23 24 43	2D55.9	7 53.1	21 52.3	13 49.3	3 29.2	25 07.4	12 41.5	2 22.9	4 09.5	5 17.9
7 Su	5 03 36	16 45 41	29 37 09	5♓53 51	2R55.6	9 18.9	23 02.7	14 33.4	3 53.8	25 19.1	12 46.1	2 26.3	4 10.5	5 17.0
8 M	5 07 33	17 43 06	12♓15 24	18 42 22	2 55.7	10 41.8	24 13.0	15 17.5	4 18.3	25 30.9	12 50.6	2 29.7	4 11.4	5 16.2
9 Tu	5 11 30	18 40 30	25 15 17	1♈54 39	2 55.1	12 01.6	25 23.3	16 01.6	4 42.9	25 42.7	12 55.1	2 33.1	4 12.4	5 15.4
10 W	5 15 26	19 37 53	8♈40 50	15 34 07	2 52.8	13 18.3	26 33.4	16 45.5	5 07.4	25 54.6	12 59.5	2 36.5	4 13.2	5 14.5
11 Th	5 19 23	20 35 16	22 34 40	29 42 27	2 48.2	14 32.0	27 43.5	17 29.4	5 32.0	26 06.6	13 03.8	2 39.9	4 14.1	5 13.6
12 F	5 23 19	21 32 38	6♉57 12	14♉18 29	2 41.2	15 42.4	28 53.6	18 13.3	5 56.5	26 18.6	13 08.1	2 43.2	4 14.9	5 12.7
13 Sa	5 27 16	22 30 00	21 45 35	29 17 36	2 32.3	16 49.7	0♌03.5	18 57.1	6 21.0	26 30.7	13 12.3	2 46.6	4 15.7	5 11.8
14 Su	5 31 12	23 27 21	6♊53 25	14♊31 44	2 22.5	17 53.6	1 13.4	19 40.8	6 45.5	26 42.8	13 16.3	2 50.0	4 16.5	5 10.8
15 M	5 35 09	24 24 42	22 11 09	29 50 13	2 13.0	18 54.2	2 23.1	20 24.5	7 10.0	26 55.0	13 20.3	2 53.3	4 17.2	5 09.8
16 Tu	5 39 05	25 22 03	7♋27 30	15♋01 41	2 04.9	19 51.4	3 32.8	21 08.1	7 34.4	27 07.3	13 24.3	2 56.6	4 17.9	5 08.9
17 W	5 43 02	26 19 22	22 31 34	29 56 10	1 59.1	20 45.0	4 42.4	21 51.7	7 58.9	27 19.6	13 28.1	2 59.9	4 18.6	5 07.8
18 Th	5 46 59	27 16 41	7♌14 40	14♌26 33	1 55.8	21 34.9	5 51.9	22 35.2	8 23.3	27 31.9	13 31.8	3 03.2	4 19.2	5 06.8
19 F	5 50 55	28 13 58	21 31 27	28 29 14	1D54.6	22 21.2	7 01.3	23 18.6	8 47.7	27 44.3	13 35.5	3 06.4	4 19.8	5 05.8
20 Sa	5 54 52	29 11 15	5♍19 58	12♍03 51	1 54.8	23 03.6	8 10.6	24 02.0	9 12.1	27 56.7	13 39.1	3 09.7	4 20.4	5 04.7
21 Su	5 58 48	0♋08 31	18 41 11	25 12 24	1R55.4	23 42.0	9 19.8	24 45.3	9 36.5	28 09.2	13 42.6	3 12.9	4 20.9	5 03.6
22 M	6 02 45	1 05 47	1♎37 58	7♎58 25	1 55.2	24 16.4	10 28.9	25 28.5	10 00.8	28 21.7	13 45.9	3 16.1	4 21.4	5 02.5
23 Tu	6 06 41	2 03 02	14 14 17	20 26 07	1 53.5	24 46.6	11 37.8	26 11.7	10 25.2	28 34.3	13 49.3	3 19.3	4 21.9	5 01.4
24 W	6 10 38	3 00 16	26 34 26	2♏39 47	1 49.6	25 12.6	12 46.7	26 54.8	10 49.5	28 46.9	13 52.5	3 22.4	4 22.3	5 00.3
25 Th	6 14 34	3 57 29	8♏42 38	14 43 26	1 43.4	25 34.2	13 55.5	27 37.8	11 13.8	28 59.5	13 55.6	3 25.6	4 22.7	4 59.1
26 F	6 18 31	4 54 43	20 42 37	26 40 33	1 35.1	25 51.3	15 04.1	28 20.8	11 38.0	29 12.2	13 58.6	3 28.7	4 23.1	4 58.0
27 Sa	6 22 28	5 51 55	2♐37 34	8♐34 00	1 25.4	26 03.9	16 12.6	29 03.8	12 02.2	29 24.9	14 01.6	3 31.8	4 23.4	4 56.8
28 Su	6 26 24	6 49 08	14 30 07	20 26 09	1 15.1	26 11.9	17 21.1	29 46.6	12 26.5	29 37.7	14 04.5	3 34.9	4 23.8	4 55.6
29 M	6 30 21	7 46 20	26 22 19	2♑18 51	1 05.2	26R15.3	18 29.3	0♊29.4	12 50.7	29 50.4	14 07.2	3 37.9	4 24.0	4 54.4
30 Tu	6 34 17	8 43 32	8♑15 55	14 13 44	0 56.4	26 14.1	19 37.5	1 12.1	13 14.8	0♌03.3	14 09.9	3 40.9	4 24.3	4 53.2

Astro Data

	Dy Hr Mn
♇ R	6 15:36
☽ 0N	12 17:02
☽ 0S	25 6:37
☽ 0N	9 0:28
☽ 0S	21 12:13
☿ R	29 17:38

Planet Ingress

		Dy Hr Mn
☿	♉	3 2:58
☿	♊	17 10:28
♂	♉	18 22:27
♀	♋	19 1:06
☉	♊	21 0:38
⚳	♊	28 23:53
☿	♋	1 11:57
♀	♌	13 10:48
☉	♋	21 8:26
♂	♊	28 19:30
♃	♌	30 5:53

Last Aspect / ☽ Ingress

Dy Hr Mn			☽ Ingress	Dy Hr Mn
2 8:49	♃	△	♐	3 6:35
4 21:35	♂	△	♑	5 19:07
7 14:20	♂	□	♒	8 7:29
10 5:10	♂	⚹	♓	10 17:41
12 10:05	♀	□	♈	13 0:05
14 21:34	♂	☌	♉	15 2:32
17 1:03	☿	☌	♊	17 2:24
17 19:37	♄	⚹	♋	19 1:47
20 13:28	♃	☌	♌	21 2:49
21 22:07	♄	△	♍	23 6:58
25 0:55	♃	⚹	♎	25 14:35
27 11:33	♃	□	♏	28 0:54
30 0:06	♃	△	♐	30 12:46

Last Aspect / ☽ Ingress

Dy Hr Mn			☽ Ingress	Dy Hr Mn
31 13:22	♄	△	♑	2 1:20
4 3:05	♃	☍	♒	4 13:47
5 19:52	☉	△	♓	7 0:44
9 0:40	♃	△	♈	9 8:35
11 8:23	♀	□	♉	11 12:29
13 7:31	♃	⚹	♊	13 13:07
15 2:55	☉	☌	♋	15 12:15
17 7:42	♃	☌	♌	17 12:06
19 11:32	☉	⚹	♍	19 14:38
21 17:34	♃	⚹	♎	21 20:56
24 4:12	♃	□	♏	24 6:44
26 17:11	♃	△	♐	26 18:42
28 5:06	♀	△	♑	29 7:20

☽ Phases & Eclipses

Dy Hr Mn		
1 17:24	○	11♏21
9 21:12	☾	19♒15
16 20:02	●	25♉58
23 11:12	☽	2♍21
31 8:46	○	9♐56
8 10:02	☾	17♓38
15 2:55	●	24♊03
21 21:57	☽	0♎32
29 23:58	○	8♑15

Astro Data

1 May 2026
Julian Day # 46142
SVP 4♓53'26"
GC 27♐12.4 ⚴ 1♈39.0
Eris 25♈27.1 ⚵ 7♒38.8
⚷ 27♈31.7 ⚶ 24♓39.8
☽ Mean ☊ 5♓47.3

1 June 2026
Julian Day # 46173
SVP 4♓53'20"
GC 27♐12.5 ⚴ 10♈41.2
Eris 25♈44.8 ⚵ 10♒56.6
⚷ 29♈12.8 ⚶ 7♈43.6
☽ Mean ☊ 4♓08.8

July 2026 LONGITUDE

Day	Sid.Time	☉	0 hr ☽	Noon ☽	True☊	☿	♀	♂	⚳	♃	♄	♅	♆	♇
1 W	6 38 14	9♋40 43	20♑12 29	26♑12 22	0♓49.5	26♋08.3	20♌45.5	1♊54.8	13♊39.0	0♌16.1	14♈12.5	3♊44.0	4♈24.5	4♒52.0
2 Th	6 42 10	10 37 55	2♒13 39	8♒16 33	0R 44.8	25R 58.0	21 53.4	2 37.4	14 03.1	0 29.0	14 15.0	3 46.9	4 24.7	4R 50.7
3 F	6 46 07	11 35 07	14 21 21	20 28 22	0D 42.3	25 43.3	23 01.2	3 20.0	14 27.2	0 41.9	14 17.4	3 49.9	4 24.8	4 49.5
4 Sa	6 50 03	12 32 18	26 37 56	2♓50 24	0 41.8	25 24.4	24 08.9	4 02.4	14 51.2	0 54.9	14 19.7	3 52.8	4 24.9	4 48.2
5 Su	6 54 00	13 29 30	9♓06 12	15 25 43	0 42.5	25 01.5	25 16.4	4 44.8	15 15.2	1 07.8	14 21.9	3 55.7	4 25.0	4 46.9
6 M	6 57 57	14 26 42	21 49 25	28 17 41	0 43.8	24 35.0	26 23.7	5 27.2	15 39.2	1 20.8	14 24.0	3 58.6	4R 25.1	4 45.6
7 Tu	7 01 53	15 23 55	4♈50 58	11♈29 39	0R 44.6	24 05.1	27 31.0	6 09.5	16 03.2	1 33.8	14 26.0	4 01.4	4 25.1	4 44.3
8 W	7 05 50	16 21 08	18 14 04	25 04 29	0 44.4	23 32.5	28 38.0	6 51.7	16 27.2	1 46.9	14 27.9	4 04.2	4 25.1	4 43.0
9 Th	7 09 46	17 18 21	2♉01 03	9♉03 50	0 42.5	22 57.4	29 45.0	7 33.9	16 51.1	2 00.0	14 29.7	4 07.0	4 25.0	4 41.7
10 F	7 13 43	18 15 35	16 12 42	23 27 24	0 38.9	22 20.6	0♍51.8	8 16.0	17 14.9	2 13.0	14 31.4	4 09.7	4 24.9	4 40.3
11 Sa	7 17 39	19 12 49	0♊47 26	8♊12 11	0 33.8	21 42.5	1 58.4	8 58.0	17 38.8	2 26.2	14 33.0	4 12.5	4 24.8	4 39.0
12 Su	7 21 36	20 10 03	15 40 49	23 12 19	0 28.1	21 03.8	3 04.9	9 40.0	18 02.6	2 39.3	14 34.5	4 15.2	4 24.7	4 37.7
13 M	7 25 33	21 07 19	0♋45 35	8♋19 24	0 22.4	20 25.2	4 11.3	10 21.9	18 26.4	2 52.5	14 35.9	4 17.8	4 24.5	4 36.3
14 Tu	7 29 29	22 04 34	15 52 32	23 23 44	0 17.6	19 47.4	5 17.5	11 03.7	18 50.1	3 05.6	14 37.2	4 20.4	4 24.3	4 35.0
15 W	7 33 26	23 01 50	0♌51 51	8♌15 52	0 14.2	19 10.9	6 23.5	11 45.4	19 13.8	3 18.8	14 38.5	4 23.0	4 24.1	4 33.6
16 Th	7 37 22	23 59 05	15 34 51	22 48 07	0D 12.6	18 36.5	7 29.3	12 27.1	19 37.4	3 32.0	14 39.6	4 25.6	4 23.8	4 32.2
17 F	7 41 19	24 56 21	29 55 08	6♍55 32	0 12.6	18 04.8	8 35.0	13 08.7	20 01.1	3 45.3	14 40.6	4 28.1	4 23.5	4 30.8
18 Sa	7 45 15	25 53 37	13♍49 12	20 36 05	0 13.6	17 36.3	9 40.5	13 50.3	20 24.6	3 58.5	14 41.5	4 30.6	4 23.1	4 29.4
19 Su	7 49 12	26 50 54	27 16 22	3♎50 18	0 15.2	17 11.7	10 45.8	14 31.7	20 48.1	4 11.7	14 42.3	4 33.1	4 22.8	4 28.1
20 M	7 53 08	27 48 10	10♎18 14	16 40 38	0R 16.5	16 51.3	11 50.9	15 13.1	21 11.6	4 25.0	14 43.0	4 35.5	4 22.3	4 26.7
21 Tu	7 57 05	28 45 27	22 57 57	29 10 45	0 17.0	16 35.6	12 55.7	15 54.5	21 35.1	4 38.2	14 43.5	4 37.9	4 21.9	4 25.3
22 W	8 01 02	29 42 44	5♏19 34	11♏24 58	0 16.3	16 24.9	14 00.4	16 35.7	21 58.4	4 51.5	14 44.0	4 40.2	4 21.5	4 23.9
23 Th	8 04 58	0♌40 01	17 27 31	23 27 44	0 14.3	16D 19.6	15 04.9	17 16.9	22 21.8	5 04.8	14 44.4	4 42.5	4 21.0	4 22.5
24 F	8 08 55	1 37 18	29 26 09	5♐23 17	0 11.1	16 19.8	16 09.2	17 58.0	22 45.1	5 18.0	14 44.7	4 44.8	4 20.4	4 21.1
25 Sa	8 12 51	2 34 37	11♐19 36	17 15 31	0 07.0	16 25.8	17 13.2	18 39.1	23 08.3	5 31.3	14 44.9	4 47.0	4 19.9	4 19.7
26 Su	8 16 48	3 31 55	23 11 27	29 07 46	0 02.5	16 37.8	18 17.0	19 20.0	23 31.5	5 44.6	14R 45.0	4 49.2	4 19.3	4 18.3
27 M	8 20 44	4 29 14	5♑04 49	11♑02 53	29♒58.2	16 55.7	19 20.6	20 00.9	23 54.7	5 57.9	14 45.0	4 51.4	4 18.7	4 16.9
28 Tu	8 24 41	5 26 34	17 02 14	23 03 08	29 54.4	17 19.6	20 23.9	20 41.8	24 17.8	6 11.2	14 44.9	4 53.5	4 18.0	4 15.4
29 W	8 28 37	6 23 54	29 05 48	5♒10 25	29 51.6	17 49.6	21 27.0	21 22.5	24 40.8	6 24.5	14 44.6	4 55.6	4 17.4	4 14.0
30 Th	8 32 34	7 21 15	11♒17 12	17 26 17	29D 49.9	18 25.7	22 29.8	22 03.2	25 03.8	6 37.8	14 44.3	4 57.6	4 16.7	4 12.6
31 F	8 36 31	8 18 37	23 37 54	29 52 10	29 49.4	19 07.9	23 32.3	22 43.8	25 26.7	6 51.0	14 43.9	4 59.6	4 15.9	4 11.2

August 2026 LONGITUDE

Day	Sid.Time	☉	0 hr ☽	Noon ☽	True☊	☿	♀	♂	⚳	♃	♄	♅	♆	♇
1 Sa	8 40 27	9♌15 59	6♓09 17	12♓29 26	29♒49.8	19♋56.0	24♍34.6	23♊24.3	25♊49.6	7♌04.3	14♈43.4	5♊01.6	4♈15.2	4♒09.8
2 Su	8 44 24	10 13 23	18 52 48	25 19 33	29 50.9	20 50.0	25 36.6	24 04.8	26 12.4	7 17.6	14R 42.7	5 03.5	4R 14.4	4R 08.4
3 M	8 48 20	11 10 48	1♈49 55	8♈24 04	29 52.3	21 49.8	26 38.3	24 45.2	26 35.2	7 30.9	14 42.0	5 05.3	4 13.5	4 07.0
4 Tu	8 52 17	12 08 13	15 02 12	21 44 27	29 53.6	22 55.3	27 39.8	25 25.5	26 57.9	7 44.1	14 41.2	5 07.2	4 12.7	4 05.6
5 W	8 56 13	13 05 40	28 31 00	5♉21 56	29R 54.3	24 06.4	28 40.9	26 05.8	27 20.5	7 57.4	14 40.2	5 08.9	4 11.8	4 04.3
6 Th	9 00 10	14 03 09	12♉17 17	19 17 03	29 54.4	25 22.8	29 41.7	26 46.0	27 43.1	8 10.7	14 39.2	5 10.7	4 10.9	4 02.9
7 F	9 04 06	15 00 39	26 21 07	3♊29 16	29 53.8	26 44.5	0♎42.2	27 26.1	28 05.6	8 23.9	14 38.0	5 12.4	4 10.0	4 01.5
8 Sa	9 08 03	15 58 10	10♊41 13	17 56 32	29 52.6	28 11.1	1 42.4	28 06.1	28 28.1	8 37.1	14 36.8	5 14.0	4 09.1	4 00.1
9 Su	9 12 00	16 55 42	25 14 42	2♋35 03	29 51.1	29 42.4	2 42.3	28 46.1	28 50.5	8 50.4	14 35.5	5 15.7	4 08.1	3 58.8
10 M	9 15 56	17 53 16	9♋56 53	17 19 22	29 49.6	1♌18.2	3 41.8	29 26.0	29 12.8	9 03.6	14 34.0	5 17.2	4 07.1	3 57.4
11 Tu	9 19 53	18 50 51	24 41 38	2♌02 48	29 48.4	2 58.1	4 41.0	0♋05.8	29 35.1	9 16.8	14 32.5	5 18.7	4 06.0	3 56.1
12 W	9 23 49	19 48 27	9♌22 00	16 38 23	29D 47.7	4 41.8	5 39.8	0 45.5	29 57.2	9 30.0	14 30.9	5 20.2	4 05.0	3 54.7
13 Th	9 27 46	20 46 05	23 51 09	0♍59 39	29 47.5	6 28.9	6 38.2	1 25.1	0♋19.3	9 43.1	14 29.2	5 21.6	4 03.9	3 53.4
14 F	9 31 42	21 43 43	8♍03 16	15 01 35	29 47.7	8 19.1	7 36.2	2 04.7	0 41.4	9 56.3	14 27.3	5 23.0	4 02.8	3 52.0
15 Sa	9 35 39	22 41 23	21 54 15	28 41 05	29 48.3	10 11.9	8 33.9	2 44.2	1 03.3	10 09.4	14 25.4	5 24.4	4 01.7	3 50.7
16 Su	9 39 35	23 39 03	5♎22 02	11♎57 08	29 48.9	12 07.0	9 31.1	3 23.6	1 25.2	10 22.5	14 23.4	5 25.6	4 00.5	3 49.4
17 M	9 43 32	24 36 45	18 26 34	24 50 35	29 49.4	14 03.9	10 27.8	4 02.9	1 47.0	10 35.6	14 21.3	5 26.9	3 59.3	3 48.1
18 Tu	9 47 29	25 34 27	1♏09 32	7♏23 50	29 49.8	16 02.3	11 24.1	4 42.1	2 08.7	10 48.6	14 19.1	5 28.1	3 58.1	3 46.8
19 W	9 51 25	26 32 11	13 33 56	19 40 22	29R 50.0	18 01.8	12 20.0	5 21.3	2 30.3	11 01.7	14 16.8	5 29.2	3 56.9	3 45.6
20 Th	9 55 22	27 29 56	25 43 39	1♐44 21	29 50.0	20 02.1	13 15.3	6 00.3	2 51.9	11 14.7	14 14.4	5 30.3	3 55.7	3 44.3
21 F	9 59 18	28 27 42	7♐43 03	13 40 19	29 50.0	22 02.8	14 10.2	6 39.3	3 13.3	11 27.6	14 11.9	5 31.3	3 54.4	3 43.0
22 Sa	10 03 15	29 25 29	19 36 41	25 32 44	29D 49.9	24 03.6	15 04.5	7 18.2	3 34.7	11 40.6	14 09.4	5 32.3	3 53.1	3 41.8
23 Su	10 07 11	0♍23 17	1♑29 00	7♑25 47	29 49.9	26 04.3	15 58.2	7 57.0	3 56.0	11 53.5	14 06.7	5 33.3	3 51.8	3 40.6
24 M	10 11 08	1 21 07	13 24 06	19 23 52	29 50.1	28 04.7	16 51.5	8 35.8	4 17.2	12 06.4	14 04.0	5 34.2	3 50.5	3 39.4
25 Tu	10 15 04	2 18 58	25 25 40	1♒29 51	29 50.3	0♍04.5	17 44.1	9 14.4	4 38.2	12 19.3	14 01.2	5 35.0	3 49.1	3 38.2
26 W	10 19 01	3 16 50	7♒36 45	13 46 38	29 50.5	2 03.7	18 36.1	9 53.0	4 59.2	12 32.1	13 58.2	5 35.8	3 47.8	3 37.0
27 Th	10 22 58	4 14 43	19 59 43	26 16 11	29R 50.7	4 02.0	19 27.5	10 31.5	5 20.1	12 44.9	13 55.3	5 36.6	3 46.4	3 35.8
28 F	10 26 54	5 12 38	2♓36 11	8♓59 47	29 50.6	5 59.4	20 18.2	11 09.9	5 41.0	12 57.6	13 52.2	5 37.3	3 45.0	3 34.6
29 Sa	10 30 51	6 10 35	15 27 02	21 57 56	29 50.2	7 55.8	21 08.3	11 48.2	6 01.7	13 10.3	13 49.0	5 37.9	3 43.6	3 33.5
30 Su	10 34 47	7 08 33	28 32 27	5♈10 30	29 49.6	9 51.2	21 57.6	12 26.4	6 22.3	13 23.0	13 45.8	5 38.5	3 42.1	3 32.4
31 M	10 38 44	8 06 32	11♈52 01	18 36 52	29 48.6	11 45.3	22 46.2	13 04.5	6 42.8	13 35.7	13 42.5	5 39.1	3 40.7	3 31.3

Astro Data Dy Hr Mn	Planet Ingress Dy Hr Mn	Last Aspect Dy Hr Mn	☽ Ingress Dy Hr Mn	Last Aspect Dy Hr Mn	☽ Ingress Dy Hr Mn	☽ Phases & Eclipses Dy Hr Mn	Astro Data
☽0N 6 6:03	♀ ♍ 9 17:23	1 11:52 ☿ ☍	♒ 1 19:34	2 12:34 ♀ ☍	♈ 2 20:38	7 19:30 ☾ 15♈42	1 July 2026
♆R 7 10:56	☉ ♌ 22 19:14	3 17:29 ♀ ☍	♓ 4 6:31	4 18:53 ♂ ⚹	♉ 5 2:37	14 9:45 ● 21♋59	Julian Day # 46203
♅⚹♆ 15 20:33	☊ ♒R 27 1:43	6 5:22 ☿ △	♈ 6 15:08	6 23:26 ☿ ⚹	♊ 7 6:09	21 11:07 ☽ 28♎43	SVP 4♓53'14"
♅△♇ 18 4:47		8 18:43 ♀ △	♉ 8 20:32	9 5:28 ♂ ☌	♋ 9 7:47	29 14:37 ○ 6♒30	GC 27♐12.6 ⚴ 17♈47.4
☽0S 18 19:49	♀ ♎ 6 19:14	10 10:14 ☿ ⚹	♊ 10 22:43	10 7:31 ♄ □	♌ 11 8:39		Eris 25♈55.5 ✱ 8♒59.4R
♃△♆ 20 7:24	☿ ♌ 9 16:29	11 22:13 ♄ ⚹	♋ 12 22:48	12 17:38 ☉ ☌	♍ 13 10:19	6 2:23 ☾ 13♉40	⚷ 0♉22.8 ⚵ 18♈17.1
♃☍♇ 20 14:47	♂ ♋ 11 8:32	14 9:45 ☉ ☌	♌ 14 22:36	13 19:25 ♅ □	♎ 15 14:21	12 17:38 ● 20♌02	☽ Mean ☊ 2♓33.5
♃⚹♅ 21 11:12	⚳ ♋ 12 14:59	15 22:28 ♄ △	♍ 17 0:08	17 11:32 ☉ ⚹	♏ 17 21:47	12 17:47:04 ● T 02'18"	
☿D 23 23:00	☉ ♍ 23 2:20	18 22:14 ☉ ⚹	♎ 19 4:58	20 2:47 ☉ □	♐ 20 8:31	20 2:47 ☽ 27♏08	1 August 2026
♆⚹♇ 25 5:50	☿ ♍ 25 11:05	21 11:07 ☉ □	♏ 21 13:36	22 20:32 ☉ △	♑ 22 21:00	28 4:20 ○ 4♓54	Julian Day # 46234
♄R 26 19:57		22 21:50 ☿ △	♐ 24 1:08	24 6:31 ♀ □	♒ 25 9:03	28 4:14 ● P 0.930	SVP 4♓53'09"
☽0N 2 11:07		25 14:59 ♂ ☍	♑ 26 13:45	26 22:01 ♀ △	♓ 27 19:05		GC 27♐12.6 ⚴ 22♈09.7
♀0S 5 18:47		28 6:12 ♀ △	♒ 29 1:47	28 16:15 ♂ △	♈ 30 2:39		Eris 25♈57.3R ✱ 2♒20.1R
☽0S 15 5:09		30 21:28 ♂ △	♓ 31 12:15				⚷ 0♉51.9 ⚵ 25♈44.4
☽0N 29 17:15	♃△△31 22:18						☽ Mean ☊ 0♓55.1

LONGITUDE September 2026

Day	Sid.Time	☉	0 hr ☽	Noon ☽	True ☊	☿	♀	♂	⚳	♃	♄	♅	♆	♇
1 Tu	10 42 40	9♍04 34	25♈24 53	2♉15 57	29♒47.5	13♍38.4	23♎34.1	13♋42.6	7♋03.2	13♌48.3	13♈39.1	5♊39.6	3♈39.2	3♒30.2
2 W	10 46 37	10 02 38	9♉09 51	16 06 26	29R46.6	15 30.2	24 21.2	14 20.6	7 23.5	14 00.8	13R35.7	5 40.0	3R37.7	3R29.1
3 Th	10 50 33	11 00 43	23 05 28	0♊06 47	29D45.9	17 20.8	25 07.5	14 58.5	7 43.6	14 13.4	13 32.2	5 40.4	3 36.3	3 28.1
4 F	10 54 30	11 58 51	7♊10 07	14 15 15	29 45.7	19 10.2	25 53.0	15 36.3	8 03.7	14 25.8	13 28.6	5 40.8	3 34.7	3 27.0
5 Sa	10 58 27	12 57 01	21 21 54	28 29 47	29 46.1	20 58.4	26 37.6	16 14.0	8 23.7	14 38.3	13 24.9	5 41.1	3 33.2	3 26.0
6 Su	11 02 23	13 55 12	5♋38 35	12♋47 58	29 47.0	22 45.4	27 21.3	16 51.6	8 43.5	14 50.7	13 21.2	5 41.3	3 31.7	3 25.0
7 M	11 06 20	14 53 26	19 57 32	27 06 52	29 48.1	24 31.2	28 04.0	17 29.1	9 03.2	15 03.0	13 17.4	5 41.5	3 30.1	3 24.0
8 Tu	11 10 16	15 51 41	4♌15 32	11♌23 04	29 49.1	26 15.8	28 45.8	18 06.5	9 22.8	15 15.3	13 13.6	5 41.7	3 28.6	3 23.1
9 W	11 14 13	16 49 59	18 28 59	25 32 47	29R49.7	27 59.2	29 26.6	18 43.9	9 42.3	15 27.5	13 09.6	5 41.8	3 27.0	3 22.1
10 Th	11 18 09	17 48 18	2♍33 59	9♍32 07	29 49.5	29 41.5	0♏06.3	19 21.1	10 01.6	15 39.7	13 05.7	5R41.8	3 25.4	3 21.2
11 F	11 22 06	18 46 39	16 26 45	23 17 29	29 48.4	1♎22.7	0 45.0	19 58.2	10 20.8	15 51.8	13 01.6	5 41.8	3 23.8	3 20.3
12 Sa	11 26 02	19 45 02	0♎04 01	6♎46 04	29 46.3	3 02.7	1 22.5	20 35.3	10 39.9	16 03.9	12 57.5	5 41.7	3 22.2	3 19.4
13 Su	11 29 59	20 43 27	13 23 26	19 56 04	29 43.4	4 41.6	1 58.8	21 12.2	10 58.8	16 15.9	12 53.4	5 41.6	3 20.6	3 18.6
14 M	11 33 55	21 41 53	26 23 54	2♏47 03	29 40.0	6 19.4	2 33.8	21 49.0	11 17.6	16 27.9	12 49.2	5 41.5	3 19.0	3 17.7
15 Tu	11 37 52	22 40 21	9♏05 40	15 19 59	29 36.7	7 56.1	3 07.6	22 25.8	11 36.3	16 39.8	12 44.9	5 41.3	3 17.4	3 16.9
16 W	11 41 49	23 38 51	21 30 19	27 37 03	29 33.8	9 31.8	3 40.1	23 02.4	11 54.8	16 51.6	12 40.7	5 41.0	3 15.7	3 16.1
17 Th	11 45 45	24 37 22	3♐40 37	9♐41 32	29 31.7	11 06.4	4 11.1	23 38.9	12 13.2	17 03.4	12 36.3	5 40.7	3 14.1	3 15.3
18 F	11 49 42	25 35 55	15 40 18	21 37 30	29D30.7	12 39.9	4 40.7	24 15.3	12 31.4	17 15.1	12 31.9	5 40.3	3 12.5	3 14.6
19 Sa	11 53 38	26 34 30	27 33 43	3♑29 33	29 30.9	14 12.5	5 08.8	24 51.6	12 49.4	17 26.8	12 27.5	5 39.9	3 10.8	3 13.9
20 Su	11 57 35	27 33 06	9♑25 37	15 22 32	29 32.0	15 44.0	5 35.3	25 27.8	13 07.3	17 38.3	12 23.1	5 39.4	3 09.2	3 13.2
21 M	12 01 31	28 31 44	21 20 54	27 21 17	29 33.7	17 14.4	6 00.1	26 03.9	13 25.1	17 49.8	12 18.6	5 38.9	3 07.5	3 12.5
22 Tu	12 05 28	29 30 24	3♒24 15	9♒30 20	29 35.4	18 43.8	6 23.3	26 39.9	13 42.7	18 01.3	12 14.1	5 38.3	3 05.9	3 11.9
23 W	12 09 25	0♎29 05	15 39 59	21 53 39	29R36.6	20 12.2	6 44.7	27 15.8	14 00.1	18 12.6	12 09.5	5 37.7	3 04.2	3 11.2
24 Th	12 13 21	1 27 49	28 11 39	4♓34 18	29 36.7	21 39.6	7 04.3	27 51.5	14 17.4	18 23.9	12 05.0	5 37.1	3 02.5	3 10.6
25 F	12 17 18	2 26 33	11♓01 47	17 34 11	29 35.4	23 05.8	7 22.1	28 27.2	14 34.4	18 35.2	12 00.4	5 36.3	3 00.9	3 10.1
26 Sa	12 21 14	3 25 20	24 11 33	0♈53 45	29 32.4	24 31.1	7 37.9	29 02.7	14 51.4	18 46.3	11 55.7	5 35.6	2 59.2	3 09.5
27 Su	12 25 11	4 24 09	7♈40 37	14 31 50	29 28.0	25 55.2	7 51.7	29 38.2	15 08.1	18 57.4	11 51.1	5 34.8	2 57.5	3 09.0
28 M	12 29 07	5 23 00	21 27 04	28 25 49	29 22.6	27 18.2	8 03.4	0♌13.5	15 24.6	19 08.4	11 46.4	5 33.9	2 55.9	3 08.5
29 Tu	12 33 04	6 21 53	5♉27 36	12♉31 51	29 16.8	28 40.1	8 13.0	0 48.7	15 41.0	19 19.3	11 41.8	5 33.0	2 54.2	3 08.0
30 W	12 37 00	7 20 48	19 38 00	26 45 28	29 11.5	0♏00.8	8 20.5	1 23.8	15 57.2	19 30.1	11 37.1	5 32.1	2 52.5	3 07.6

LONGITUDE October 2026

Day	Sid.Time	☉	0 hr ☽	Noon ☽	True ☊	☿	♀	♂	⚳	♃	♄	♅	♆	♇
1 Th	12 40 57	8♎19 46	3♊53 43	11♊02 13	29♒07.3	1♏20.3	8♏25.7	1♌58.7	16♋13.2	19♌40.8	11♈32.4	5♊31.1	2♈50.9	3♒07.1
2 F	12 44 53	9 18 46	18 10 31	25 18 12	29R04.7	2 38.5	8R28.7	2 33.6	16 29.0	19 51.5	11R27.7	5R30.0	2R49.2	3R06.8
3 Sa	12 48 50	10 17 48	2♋24 57	9♋30 29	29D03.8	3 55.4	8 29.4	3 08.3	16 44.7	20 02.1	11 22.9	5 28.9	2 47.6	3 06.4
4 Su	12 52 47	11 16 53	16 34 33	23 37 00	29 04.3	5 10.8	8 27.8	3 42.9	17 00.1	20 12.6	11 18.2	5 27.8	2 46.0	3 06.1
5 M	12 56 43	12 16 00	0♌37 42	7♌36 31	29 05.6	6 24.8	8 23.8	4 17.4	17 15.3	20 23.0	11 13.5	5 26.6	2 44.3	3 05.7
6 Tu	13 00 40	13 15 09	14 33 22	21 28 09	29R06.7	7 37.2	8 17.5	4 51.8	17 30.3	20 33.3	11 08.8	5 25.4	2 42.7	3 05.5
7 W	13 04 36	14 14 20	28 20 46	5♍11 04	29 06.7	8 47.9	8 08.7	5 26.0	17 45.0	20 43.5	11 04.1	5 24.1	2 41.1	3 05.2
8 Th	13 08 33	15 13 34	11♍58 57	18 44 14	29 05.0	9 56.7	7 57.6	6 00.1	17 59.6	20 53.6	10 59.4	5 22.8	2 39.4	3 05.0
9 F	13 12 29	16 12 49	25 26 47	2♎06 23	29 01.0	11 03.7	7 44.0	6 34.0	18 13.9	21 03.6	10 54.7	5 21.4	2 37.8	3 04.8
10 Sa	13 16 26	17 12 07	8♎42 52	15 16 05	28 54.7	12 08.5	7 28.2	7 07.8	18 28.0	21 13.5	10 50.0	5 20.0	2 36.2	3 04.6
11 Su	13 20 22	18 11 27	21 45 51	28 12 05	28 46.6	13 11.0	7 10.0	7 41.5	18 41.9	21 23.3	10 45.3	5 18.5	2 34.6	3 04.4
12 M	13 24 19	19 10 49	4♏34 41	10♏53 37	28 37.2	14 11.0	6 49.5	8 15.0	18 55.6	21 33.0	10 40.7	5 17.0	2 33.0	3 04.3
13 Tu	13 28 16	20 10 13	17 08 56	23 20 44	28 27.7	15 08.3	6 26.9	8 48.4	19 09.0	21 42.6	10 36.0	5 15.5	2 31.5	3 04.2
14 W	13 32 12	21 09 38	29 29 10	5♐34 28	28 18.8	16 02.6	6 02.2	9 21.6	19 22.1	21 52.1	10 31.4	5 13.9	2 29.9	3 04.2
15 Th	13 36 09	22 09 06	11♐36 56	17 36 55	28 11.4	16 53.5	5 35.4	9 54.7	19 35.0	22 01.5	10 26.8	5 12.3	2 28.3	3D04.1
16 F	13 40 05	23 08 36	23 34 52	29 31 15	28 06.2	17 40.9	5 06.8	10 27.7	19 47.7	22 10.8	10 22.3	5 10.7	2 26.8	3 04.1
17 Sa	13 44 02	24 08 07	5♑26 37	11♑21 31	28 03.1	18 24.3	4 36.5	11 00.4	20 00.1	22 20.0	10 17.8	5 09.0	2 25.3	3 04.2
18 Su	13 47 58	25 07 40	17 16 34	23 12 24	28D02.1	19 03.4	4 04.7	11 33.1	20 12.2	22 29.1	10 13.3	5 07.3	2 23.8	3 04.2
19 M	13 51 55	26 07 15	29 09 41	5♒09 06	28 02.4	19 37.6	3 31.4	12 05.5	20 24.1	22 38.0	10 08.8	5 05.5	2 22.3	3 04.3
20 Tu	13 55 51	27 06 51	11♒11 18	17 16 56	28R03.3	20 06.5	2 57.1	12 37.8	20 35.7	22 46.8	10 04.4	5 03.7	2 20.8	3 04.4
21 W	13 59 48	28 06 29	23 26 38	29 41 00	28 03.7	20 29.6	2 21.7	13 10.0	20 47.0	22 55.5	10 00.1	5 01.8	2 19.3	3 04.5
22 Th	14 03 45	29 06 09	6♓00 33	12♓25 45	28 02.6	20 46.4	1 45.7	13 42.0	20 58.0	23 04.1	9 55.7	5 00.0	2 17.9	3 04.7
23 F	14 07 41	0♏05 51	18 56 58	25 34 27	27 59.4	20R56.2	1 09.2	14 13.8	21 08.8	23 12.6	9 51.4	4 58.1	2 16.5	3 04.9
24 Sa	14 11 38	1 05 34	2♈18 18	9♈08 31	27 53.6	20 58.6	0 32.4	14 45.4	21 19.3	23 20.9	9 47.2	4 56.1	2 15.0	3 05.1
25 Su	14 15 34	2 05 19	16 04 52	23 07 00	27 45.5	20 52.9	29♎55.7	15 16.9	21 29.5	23 29.1	9 43.0	4 54.1	2 13.6	3 05.4
26 M	14 19 31	3 05 07	0♉14 25	7♉26 25	27 35.6	20 38.7	29 19.3	15 48.2	21 39.4	23 37.2	9 38.9	4 52.1	2 12.3	3 05.7
27 Tu	14 23 27	4 04 56	14 42 12	22 00 50	27 25.0	20 15.5	28 43.4	16 19.4	21 49.0	23 45.2	9 34.8	4 50.1	2 10.9	3 06.0
28 W	14 27 24	5 04 47	29 21 22	6♊42 48	27 15.0	19 43.1	28 08.3	16 50.3	21 58.3	23 53.0	9 30.8	4 48.0	2 09.6	3 06.3
29 Th	14 31 20	6 04 41	14♊04 09	21 24 30	27 06.6	19 01.5	27 34.2	17 21.1	22 07.2	24 00.7	9 26.8	4 45.9	2 08.2	3 06.7
30 F	14 35 17	7 04 36	28 43 03	5♋59 07	27 00.6	18 11.0	27 01.4	17 51.7	22 15.9	24 08.3	9 22.9	4 43.8	2 06.9	3 07.1
31 Sa	14 39 14	8 04 34	13♋12 09	20 21 43	26 57.3	17 12.1	26 29.9	18 22.1	22 24.2	24 15.7	9 19.1	4 41.7	2 05.7	3 07.5

Astro Data	Dy Hr Mn
♅R	10 18:29
☿0S	11 13:24
☽0S	11 14:46
♆✶♇	16 1:48
♆0S	16 2:36
♃□♆	22 20:25
☉0S	23 0:06
☽0N	26 1:12
♀R	3 7:17
☽0S	8 22:54
♇D	16 2:42
☽0N	23 10:27
☿R	24 7:13
♃□♄	31 19:15

Planet Ingress	Dy Hr Mn
♀ ♏	10 8:08
☿ ♎	10 16:22
☉ ♎	23 0:06
♂ ♌	28 2:50
☿ ♏	30 11:46
☉ ♏	23 9:39
♀ ♎R	25 9:11

Last Aspect Dy Hr Mn	☽ Ingress Dy Hr Mn
31 19:48 ♀ ☍	♉ 1 8:02
2 10:48 ☿ △	♊ 3 11:48
5 8:41 ☿ △	♋ 5 14:32
7 13:41 ♀ □	♌ 7 16:51
9 18:59 ♀ ✶	♍ 9 19:36
11 5:53 ♂ ✶	♎ 11 23:53
13 14:28 ♂ □	♏ 14 6:45
16 3:31 ☉ ✶	♐ 16 16:42
18 20:45 ☉ □	♑ 19 4:56
21 14:33 ☉ △	♒ 21 17:16
23 8:19 ☿ △	♓ 24 3:25
26 8:33 ♂ △	♈ 26 10:24
28 9:52 ☿ ☍	♉ 28 14:41
29 23:37 ♃ □	♊ 30 17:27

Last Aspect Dy Hr Mn	☽ Ingress Dy Hr Mn
2 2:43 ♃ ✶	♋ 2 19:55
3 15:10 ♄ □	♌ 4 22:55
6 10:23 ♃ ☌	♍ 7 2:54
7 18:58 ☿ ✶	♎ 9 8:12
10 23:08 ♃ ✶	♏ 11 15:22
13 8:47 ♃ □	♐ 14 1:01
15 21:57 ☉ ✶	♑ 16 12:58
18 16:14 ☉ □	♒ 19 1:41
21 8:43 ☉ △	♓ 21 12:36
23 3:32 ☿ △	♈ 23 19:55
25 23:01 ♀ ☍	♉ 25 23:36
27 14:52 ♃ □	♊ 28 1:03
29 21:45 ♀ △	♋ 30 2:07

☽ Phases & Eclipses Dy Hr Mn	
4 7:52	☾ 11♊49
11 3:28	● 18♍26
18 20:45	☽ 25♐57
26 16:50	○ 3♈37
3 13:26	☾ 10♋21
10 15:51	● 17♎22
18 16:14	☽ 25♑18
26 4:13	○ 2♉46

Astro Data

1 September 2026
Julian Day # 46265
SVP 4♓53'05"
GC 27♐12.7 ⚴ 21♈35.7R
Eris 25♈49.3R ⚵ 26♑30.3R
⚷ 0♉30.4R ⚶ 27♈38.0R
☽ Mean ☊ 29♒16.6

1 October 2026
Julian Day # 46295
SVP 4♓53'02"
GC 27♐12.8 ⚴ 15♈16.5R
Eris 25♈34.5R ⚵ 26♑22.1
⚷ 29♈28.1R ⚶ 22♈55.7R
☽ Mean ☊ 27♒41.2

November 2026 LONGITUDE

Day	Sid.Time	☉	0 hr ☽	Noon☽	True☊	☿	♀	♂	⚳	♃	♄	♅	♆	♇
1 Su	14 43 10	9♏04 34	27♋27 34	4♌29 31	26♒56.1	16♏05.7	26♎00.2	18♌52.4	22♋32.3	24♌23.0	9♈15.3	4♊39.5	2♈04.4	3♒08.0
2 M	14 47 07	10 04 36	11♌27 34	18 21 44	26R 56.1	14R 53.5	25R 32.2	19 22.4	22 39.9	24 30.2	9R 11.6	4R 37.3	2R 03.2	3 08.4
3 Tu	14 51 03	11 04 41	25 12 08	1♍58 54	26 56.2	13 37.1	25 06.2	19 52.2	22 47.3	24 37.2	9 08.0	4 35.0	2 02.0	3 08.9
4 W	14 55 00	12 04 47	8♍42 13	15 22 15	26 54.9	12 18.8	24 42.2	20 21.8	22 54.3	24 44.0	9 04.4	4 32.8	2 00.8	3 09.5
5 Th	14 58 56	13 04 55	21 59 11	28 33 09	26 51.3	11 01.0	24 20.5	20 51.2	23 00.9	24 50.8	9 00.9	4 30.5	1 59.6	3 10.0
6 F	15 02 53	14 05 06	5♎04 15	11♎32 36	26 44.8	9 46.1	24 01.0	21 20.4	23 07.2	24 57.3	8 57.5	4 28.2	1 58.5	3 10.6
7 Sa	15 06 49	15 05 18	17 58 15	24 21 14	26 35.2	8 36.6	23 43.8	21 49.4	23 13.2	25 03.8	8 54.1	4 25.9	1 57.3	3 11.3
8 Su	15 10 46	16 05 32	0♏41 33	6♏59 12	26 23.0	7 34.6	23 29.1	22 18.1	23 18.7	25 10.0	8 50.8	4 23.5	1 56.2	3 11.9
9 M	15 14 43	17 05 49	13 14 11	19 26 31	26 09.2	6 41.9	23 16.8	22 46.7	23 24.0	25 16.1	8 47.7	4 21.2	1 55.2	3 12.6
10 Tu	15 18 39	18 06 07	25 36 12	1♐43 17	25 54.8	5 59.7	23 06.9	23 15.0	23 28.8	25 22.1	8 44.5	4 18.8	1 54.1	3 13.3
11 W	15 22 36	19 06 26	7♐47 53	13 50 06	25 41.2	5 28.9	22 59.5	23 43.0	23 33.3	25 27.9	8 41.5	4 16.4	1 53.1	3 14.0
12 Th	15 26 32	20 06 47	19 50 07	25 48 11	25 29.4	5 09.7	22 54.6	24 10.8	23 37.3	25 33.5	8 38.6	4 14.0	1 52.1	3 14.8
13 F	15 30 29	21 07 10	1♑44 36	7♑39 43	25 20.1	5D 02.2	22D 52.1	24 38.4	23 41.0	25 39.0	8 35.7	4 11.5	1 51.2	3 15.6
14 Sa	15 34 25	22 07 34	13 33 56	19 27 44	25 13.9	5 05.9	22 52.1	25 05.7	23 44.4	25 44.4	8 33.0	4 09.1	1 50.3	3 16.4
15 Su	15 38 22	23 08 00	25 21 39	1♒16 14	25 10.4	5 20.2	22 54.4	25 32.8	23 47.3	25 49.5	8 30.3	4 06.6	1 49.4	3 17.2
16 M	15 42 18	24 08 27	7♒12 06	13 09 54	25 09.0	5 44.4	22 59.1	25 59.6	23 49.8	25 54.5	8 27.7	4 04.2	1 48.5	3 18.1
17 Tu	15 46 15	25 08 55	19 10 20	25 14 03	25 08.8	6 17.6	23 06.2	26 26.1	23 51.9	25 59.3	8 25.3	4 01.7	1 47.6	3 19.0
18 W	15 50 12	26 09 25	1♓21 47	7♓34 13	25 08.6	6 58.8	23 15.5	26 52.4	23 53.7	26 04.0	8 22.9	3 59.2	1 46.8	3 19.9
19 Th	15 54 08	27 09 56	13 51 59	20 15 43	25 07.2	7 47.3	23 27.0	27 18.4	23 55.0	26 08.4	8 20.6	3 56.7	1 46.0	3 20.9
20 F	15 58 05	28 10 28	26 45 57	3♈23 07	25 03.6	8 42.1	23 40.6	27 44.1	23 55.9	26 12.8	8 18.4	3 54.2	1 45.3	3 21.8
21 Sa	16 02 01	29 11 01	10♈07 33	16 59 24	24 57.4	9 42.5	23 56.4	28 09.5	23R 56.4	26 16.9	8 16.3	3 51.7	1 44.6	3 22.8
22 Su	16 05 58	0♐11 36	23 58 39	1♉05 06	24 48.5	10 47.8	24 14.2	28 34.7	23 56.5	26 20.9	8 14.3	3 49.2	1 43.9	3 23.8
23 M	16 09 54	1 12 11	8♉18 17	15 37 34	24 37.6	11 57.2	24 34.0	28 59.5	23 56.2	26 24.6	8 12.4	3 46.7	1 43.2	3 24.9
24 Tu	16 13 51	2 12 49	23 02 05	0♊30 47	24 25.8	13 10.2	24 55.7	29 24.1	23 55.5	26 28.3	8 10.6	3 44.2	1 42.6	3 26.0
25 W	16 17 47	3 13 28	8♊02 29	15 35 52	24 14.4	14 26.3	25 19.4	29 48.3	23 54.3	26 31.7	8 08.8	3 41.7	1 42.0	3 27.1
26 Th	16 21 44	4 14 08	23 09 39	0♋42 31	24 04.7	15 45.1	25 44.8	0♍12.3	23 52.8	26 35.0	8 07.2	3 39.1	1 41.4	3 28.2
27 F	16 25 41	5 14 50	8♋13 17	15 40 52	23 57.6	17 06.0	26 11.9	0 35.9	23 50.8	26 38.0	8 05.8	3 36.6	1 40.9	3 29.3
28 Sa	16 29 37	6 15 33	23 04 24	0♌23 10	23 53.4	18 28.9	26 40.8	0 59.2	23 48.4	26 40.9	8 04.4	3 34.1	1 40.4	3 30.5
29 Su	16 33 34	7 16 18	7♌36 39	14 44 34	23D 51.7	19 53.4	27 11.3	1 22.2	23 45.6	26 43.6	8 03.1	3 31.6	1 39.9	3 31.7
30 M	16 37 30	8 17 04	21 46 45	28 43 14	23R 51.5	21 19.3	27 43.3	1 44.8	23 42.3	26 46.1	8 01.9	3 29.1	1 39.4	3 32.9

December 2026 LONGITUDE

Day	Sid.Time	☉	0 hr ☽	Noon☽	True☊	☿	♀	♂	⚳	♃	♄	♅	♆	♇
1 Tu	16 41 27	9♐17 52	5♍34 07	12♍19 40	23♒51.6	22♏46.3	28♎16.9	2♍07.1	23♋38.7	26♌48.5	8♈00.8	3♊26.6	1♈39.0	3♒34.1
2 W	16 45 23	10 18 41	19 00 08	25 35 53	23R 50.6	24 14.2	28 51.9	2 29.0	23R 34.6	26 50.6	7R 59.8	3R 24.1	1R 38.7	3 35.4
3 Th	16 49 20	11 19 31	2♎07 16	8♎34 38	23 47.6	25 43.0	29 28.3	2 50.6	23 30.1	26 52.6	7 58.9	3 21.6	1 38.3	3 36.7
4 F	16 53 16	12 20 23	14 58 20	21 18 42	23 41.8	27 12.4	0♏06.0	3 11.8	23 25.1	26 54.3	7 58.2	3 19.1	1 38.0	3 38.0
5 Sa	16 57 13	13 21 17	27 36 01	3♏50 33	23 33.1	28 42.4	0 45.0	3 32.6	23 19.7	26 55.9	7 57.5	3 16.6	1 37.7	3 39.3
6 Su	17 01 10	14 22 11	10♏02 33	16 12 11	23 21.9	0♐12.9	1 25.3	3 53.0	23 14.0	26 57.3	7 57.0	3 14.1	1 37.5	3 40.6
7 M	17 05 06	15 23 07	22 19 38	28 25 03	23 09.0	1 43.8	2 06.7	4 13.0	23 07.8	26 58.5	7 56.5	3 11.7	1 37.3	3 42.0
8 Tu	17 09 03	16 24 04	4♐28 34	10♐30 17	22 55.6	3 15.1	2 49.3	4 32.6	23 01.2	26 59.4	7 56.2	3 09.2	1 37.1	3 43.4
9 W	17 12 59	17 25 02	16 30 21	22 28 53	22 42.8	4 46.6	3 32.9	4 51.7	22 54.2	27 00.2	7 56.0	3 06.8	1 37.0	3 44.8
10 Th	17 16 56	18 26 01	28 26 03	4♑22 01	22 31.7	6 18.4	4 17.6	5 10.5	22 46.8	27 00.8	7D 55.9	3 04.4	1 36.9	3 46.2
11 F	17 20 52	19 27 01	10♑17 00	16 11 14	22 23.0	7 50.3	5 03.3	5 28.8	22 39.0	27 01.2	7 55.9	3 02.0	1 36.8	3 47.7
12 Sa	17 24 49	20 28 01	22 05 02	27 58 44	22 17.1	9 22.5	5 50.0	5 46.6	22 30.8	27R 01.4	7 56.0	2 59.6	1D 36.8	3 49.2
13 Su	17 28 46	21 29 02	3♒52 43	9♒47 25	22 13.9	10 54.9	6 37.6	6 04.1	22 22.2	27 01.5	7 56.2	2 57.3	1 36.8	3 50.7
14 M	17 32 42	22 30 04	15 43 19	21 40 57	22D 13.0	12 27.3	7 26.1	6 21.0	22 13.3	27 01.3	7 56.5	2 54.9	1 36.8	3 52.2
15 Tu	17 36 39	23 31 06	27 40 53	3♓43 44	22 13.5	14 00.0	8 15.4	6 37.5	22 04.0	27 00.9	7 57.0	2 52.6	1 36.9	3 53.7
16 W	17 40 35	24 32 09	9♓50 08	16 00 42	22R 14.4	15 32.8	9 05.6	6 53.5	21 54.3	27 00.3	7 57.5	2 50.3	1 37.0	3 55.2
17 Th	17 44 32	25 33 12	22 16 06	28 36 58	22 14.6	17 05.7	9 56.6	7 09.0	21 44.3	26 59.5	7 58.2	2 48.0	1 37.1	3 56.8
18 F	17 48 28	26 34 15	5♈03 53	11♈37 24	22 13.3	18 38.7	10 48.3	7 24.0	21 33.9	26 58.5	7 59.0	2 45.8	1 37.3	3 58.4
19 Sa	17 52 25	27 35 19	18 17 59	25 05 57	22 10.0	20 12.0	11 40.8	7 38.4	21 23.3	26 57.4	7 59.8	2 43.5	1 37.5	3 59.9
20 Su	17 56 21	28 36 23	2♉01 30	9♉04 40	22 04.4	21 45.3	12 34.0	7 52.4	21 12.3	26 56.0	8 00.8	2 41.3	1 37.8	4 01.6
21 M	18 00 18	29 37 28	16 15 16	23 32 53	21 57.1	23 18.9	13 27.8	8 05.9	21 01.0	26 54.4	8 01.9	2 39.2	1 38.0	4 03.2
22 Tu	18 04 15	0♑38 33	0♊56 54	8♊26 28	21 48.9	24 52.6	14 22.4	8 18.8	20 49.4	26 52.7	8 03.1	2 37.0	1 38.4	4 04.8
23 W	18 08 11	1 39 38	16 00 30	23 37 46	21 40.7	26 26.4	15 17.5	8 31.1	20 37.6	26 50.7	8 04.5	2 34.9	1 38.7	4 06.5
24 Th	18 12 08	2 40 44	1♋16 54	8♋56 31	21 33.8	28 00.5	16 13.3	8 42.9	20 25.5	26 48.6	8 05.9	2 32.8	1 39.1	4 08.2
25 F	18 16 04	3 41 50	16 35 10	24 11 33	21 28.8	29 34.8	17 09.7	8 54.1	20 13.1	26 46.3	8 07.4	2 30.7	1 39.5	4 09.8
26 Sa	18 20 01	4 42 56	1♌44 25	9♌12 44	21D 26.1	1♑09.4	18 06.7	9 04.8	20 00.5	26 43.8	8 09.0	2 28.7	1 40.0	4 11.5
27 Su	18 23 57	5 44 03	16 35 39	23 52 32	21 25.5	2 44.1	19 04.2	9 14.8	19 47.6	26 41.1	8 10.8	2 26.7	1 40.5	4 13.3
28 M	18 27 54	6 45 11	1♍02 57	8♍06 40	21 26.4	4 19.2	20 02.3	9 24.2	19 34.6	26 38.2	8 12.6	2 24.8	1 41.0	4 15.0
29 Tu	18 31 50	7 46 18	15 03 39	21 53 58	21 27.8	5 54.5	21 00.8	9 33.0	19 21.3	26 35.1	8 14.6	2 22.8	1 41.5	4 16.7
30 W	18 35 47	8 47 27	28 37 51	5♎15 36	21R 28.7	7 30.1	21 59.9	9 41.2	19 07.9	26 31.8	8 16.6	2 20.9	1 42.1	4 18.5
31 Th	18 39 44	9 48 36	11♎47 38	18 14 21	21 28.4	9 06.0	22 59.4	9 48.7	18 54.3	26 28.3	8 18.8	2 19.1	1 42.8	4 20.2

Astro Data Dy Hr Mn	Planet Ingress Dy Hr Mn
☽0S 5 4:44	☉ ♐ 22 7:24
☿D 13 15:56	♂ ♍ 25 23:38
♀D 14 0:28	
☽0N 19 19:30	♀ ♏ 4 8:14
⚳R 22 5:59	☿ ♐ 6 8:34
♅△♇ 29 11:22	☉ ♑ 21 20:51
	☿ ♑ 25 18:24
☽0S 2 9:16	
♄D 10 23:32	
♆D 12 22:19	
♃R 13 0:58	
☽0N 17 2:54	
☽0S 29 15:04	

Last Aspect Dy Hr Mn	☽ Ingress Dy Hr Mn
31 22:01 ♀ □	♌ 1 4:19
3 0:12 ♀ ✶	♍ 3 8:29
4 6:59 ☿ ✶	♎ 5 14:39
7 13:21 ♃ ✶	♏ 7 22:41
9 23:26 ♃ □	♐ 10 8:37
12 11:30 ♃ △	♑ 12 20:28
14 18:57 ♀ □	♒ 15 9:25
17 14:27 ♂ ☍	♓ 17 21:21
20 1:47 ☉ △	♈ 20 5:53
22 7:40 ♂ △	♉ 22 10:11
24 10:10 ♂ □	♊ 24 11:11
26 5:25 ♃ ✶	♋ 26 10:52
28 5:41 ♀ □	♌ 28 11:22
30 10:12 ♀ ✶	♍ 30 14:14

Last Aspect Dy Hr Mn	☽ Ingress Dy Hr Mn
2 9:12 ☿ ✶	♎ 2 20:05
4 22:42 ♃ ✶	♏ 5 4:36
7 9:09 ♃ □	♐ 7 15:08
9 21:07 ♃ △	♑ 10 3:10
10 19:14 ♄ □	♒ 12 16:07
14 22:41 ♃ ☍	♓ 15 4:37
17 5:44 ☉ □	♈ 17 14:36
19 16:41 ☉ △	♉ 19 20:31
21 17:27 ♃ □	♊ 21 22:28
23 17:02 ♃ ✶	♋ 23 22:00
25 0:11 ♀ △	♌ 25 21:13
27 16:40 ♃ ☌	♍ 27 22:14
29 10:19 ♀ ✶	♎ 30 2:28

☽ Phases & Eclipses Dy Hr Mn	
1 20:30	☾ 9♌26
9 7:03	● 16♏53
17 11:49	☽ 25♒08
24 14:55	○ 2♊20
1 6:10	☾ 9♍03
9 0:53	● 16♐57
17 5:44	☽ 25♓17
24 1:29	○ 2♋14
30 19:01	☾ 9♎05

Astro Data

1 November 2026
Julian Day # 46326
SVP 4♓52'57"
GC 27♐12.8 ⚴ 6♈42.9R
Eris 25♈16.2R ⚵ 2♒00.7
⚷ 28♈03.1R ⚶ 15♈24.2R
☽ Mean ☊ 26♒02.7

1 December 2026
Julian Day # 46356
SVP 4♓52'53"
GC 27♐12.9 ⚴ 3♈17.6
Eris 25♈00.7R ⚵ 11♒27.5
⚷ 26♈51.4R ⚶ 12♈42.6
☽ Mean ☊ 24♒27.4

LONGITUDE — January 2027

Day	Sid.Time	☉	0 hr ☽	Noon ☽	True ☊	☿	♀	♂	⚳	♃	♄	♅	♆	♇
1 F	18 43 40	10♑49 45	24♎36 14	0♏53 44	21♒26.3	10♑42.2	23♏59.4	9♍55.6	18♋40.5	26♌24.7	8♈21.1	2♊17.2	1♈43.4	4♒22.0
2 Sa	18 47 37	11 50 55	7♏07 20	13 17 28	21R 22.2	12 18.7	24 59.9	10 01.8	18R 26.6	26R 20.9	8 23.4	2R 15.4	1 44.1	4 23.8
3 Su	18 51 33	12 52 05	19 24 35	25 29 04	21 16.6	13 55.6	26 00.7	10 07.3	18 12.6	26 16.9	8 25.9	2 13.7	1 44.8	4 25.6
4 M	18 55 30	13 53 15	1♐31 19	7♐31 39	21 09.7	15 32.9	27 02.0	10 12.1	17 58.5	26 12.7	8 28.5	2 12.0	1 45.6	4 27.4
5 Tu	18 59 26	14 54 26	13 30 23	19 27 49	21 02.4	17 10.5	28 03.6	10 16.2	17 44.4	26 08.3	8 31.2	2 10.3	1 46.4	4 29.2
6 W	19 03 23	15 55 36	25 24 12	1♑19 46	20 55.4	18 48.5	29 05.7	10 19.6	17 30.2	26 03.8	8 34.0	2 08.7	1 47.2	4 31.0
7 Th	19 07 20	16 56 47	7♑14 45	13 09 22	20 49.4	20 26.9	0♐08.1	10 22.2	17 15.9	25 59.1	8 36.8	2 07.1	1 48.1	4 32.8
8 F	19 11 16	17 57 57	19 03 50	24 58 23	20 44.9	22 05.6	1 10.8	10 24.2	17 01.6	25 54.2	8 39.8	2 05.5	1 49.0	4 34.7
9 Sa	19 15 13	18 59 08	0♒53 15	6♒48 39	20 42.2	23 44.7	2 13.9	10 25.3	16 47.4	25 49.2	8 42.9	2 04.0	1 49.9	4 36.5
10 Su	19 19 09	20 00 18	12 44 53	18 42 15	20D 41.1	25 24.2	3 17.3	10R 25.7	16 33.1	25 44.0	8 46.1	2 02.6	1 50.9	4 38.4
11 M	19 23 06	21 01 27	24 41 04	0♓41 42	20 41.6	27 04.0	4 21.0	10 25.4	16 18.9	25 38.7	8 49.4	2 01.1	1 51.9	4 40.3
12 Tu	19 27 02	22 02 36	6♓44 32	12 49 59	20 43.0	28 44.2	5 25.0	10 24.3	16 04.7	25 33.2	8 52.7	1 59.8	1 52.9	4 42.1
13 W	19 30 59	23 03 44	18 58 31	25 10 36	20 44.8	0♒24.7	6 29.3	10 22.4	15 50.6	25 27.5	8 56.2	1 58.4	1 53.9	4 44.0
14 Th	19 34 55	24 04 52	1♈26 43	7♈47 22	20 46.4	2 05.4	7 33.8	10 19.7	15 36.6	25 21.7	8 59.8	1 57.1	1 55.0	4 45.9
15 F	19 38 52	25 05 59	14 13 01	20 44 09	20R 47.3	3 46.4	8 38.7	10 16.2	15 22.8	25 15.8	9 03.4	1 55.9	1 56.1	4 47.8
16 Sa	19 42 49	26 07 06	27 21 10	4♉04 27	20 47.1	5 27.6	9 43.8	10 12.0	15 09.0	25 09.7	9 07.2	1 54.7	1 57.3	4 49.6
17 Su	19 46 45	27 08 12	10♉54 14	17 50 43	20 45.8	7 08.9	10 49.2	10 06.9	14 55.4	25 03.5	9 11.0	1 53.6	1 58.5	4 51.5
18 M	19 50 42	28 09 17	24 53 54	2♊03 38	20 43.5	8 50.1	11 54.8	10 01.1	14 42.0	24 57.2	9 14.9	1 52.5	1 59.7	4 53.4
19 Tu	19 54 38	29 10 21	9♊19 38	16 41 23	20 40.6	10 31.4	13 00.6	9 54.5	14 28.8	24 50.7	9 18.9	1 51.4	2 00.9	4 55.3
20 W	19 58 35	0♒11 24	24 08 11	1♋39 09	20 37.7	12 12.4	14 06.7	9 47.0	14 15.8	24 44.1	9 23.1	1 50.4	2 02.2	4 57.2
21 Th	20 02 31	1 12 27	9♋13 16	16 49 23	20 35.2	13 53.0	15 13.0	9 38.8	14 02.9	24 37.4	9 27.3	1 49.5	2 03.5	4 59.1
22 F	20 06 28	2 13 29	24 26 14	2♌02 32	20 33.5	15 33.0	16 19.5	9 29.8	13 50.3	24 30.6	9 31.5	1 48.6	2 04.8	5 01.1
23 Sa	20 10 24	3 14 30	9♌37 04	17 08 36	20D 32.8	17 12.3	17 26.3	9 19.9	13 38.0	24 23.7	9 35.9	1 47.7	2 06.2	5 03.0
24 Su	20 14 21	4 15 31	24 36 06	1♍58 37	20 33.0	18 50.6	18 33.2	9 09.3	13 25.9	24 16.7	9 40.4	1 46.9	2 07.5	5 04.9
25 M	20 18 18	5 16 30	9♍15 25	16 25 56	20 33.9	20 27.5	19 40.4	8 57.9	13 14.1	24 09.6	9 44.9	1 46.1	2 09.0	5 06.8
26 Tu	20 22 14	6 17 30	23 29 46	0♎26 44	20 35.1	22 02.7	20 47.7	8 45.7	13 02.5	24 02.4	9 49.5	1 45.4	2 10.4	5 08.7
27 W	20 26 11	7 18 28	7♎16 47	14 00 02	20 36.3	23 35.9	21 55.3	8 32.8	12 51.3	23 55.0	9 54.2	1 44.8	2 11.9	5 10.6
28 Th	20 30 07	8 19 26	20 36 42	27 07 07	20R 37.1	25 06.5	23 03.0	8 19.1	12 40.3	23 47.7	9 59.0	1 44.2	2 13.3	5 12.5
29 F	20 34 04	9 20 24	3♏31 41	9♏50 53	20 37.3	26 34.0	24 10.9	8 04.6	12 29.7	23 40.2	10 03.8	1 43.6	2 14.9	5 14.4
30 Sa	20 38 00	10 21 21	16 05 14	22 15 15	20 37.0	27 57.9	25 18.9	7 49.3	12 19.4	23 32.7	10 08.8	1 43.1	2 16.4	5 16.3
31 Su	20 41 57	11 22 17	28 21 29	4♐24 28	20 36.3	29 17.5	26 27.2	7 33.4	12 09.5	23 25.1	10 13.8	1 42.7	2 18.0	5 18.2

LONGITUDE — February 2027

Day	Sid.Time	☉	0 hr ☽	Noon ☽	True ☊	☿	♀	♂	⚳	♃	♄	♅	♆	♇
1 M	20 45 53	12♒23 12	10♐24 46	16♐22 53	20♒35.3	0♓32.2	27♐35.5	7♍16.7	11♋59.9	23♌17.4	10♈18.9	1♊42.3	2♈19.6	5♒20.1
2 Tu	20 49 50	13 24 07	22 19 19	28 14 31	20R 34.2	1 41.0	28 44.1	6R 59.4	11R 50.7	23R 09.7	10 24.1	1R 41.9	2 21.2	5 22.0
3 W	20 53 47	14 25 01	4♑08 58	10♑03 02	20 33.2	2 43.4	29 52.8	6 41.4	11 41.8	23 01.9	10 29.3	1 41.6	2 22.8	5 23.9
4 Th	20 57 43	15 25 54	15 57 08	21 51 35	20 32.4	3 38.5	1♑01.6	6 22.8	11 33.3	22 54.1	10 34.6	1 41.4	2 24.5	5 25.8
5 F	21 01 40	16 26 46	27 46 43	3♒42 49	20 32.0	4 25.5	2 10.5	6 03.5	11 25.2	22 46.2	10 40.0	1 41.2	2 26.2	5 27.7
6 Sa	21 05 36	17 27 36	9♒40 10	15 39 00	20D 31.8	5 03.6	3 19.6	5 43.7	11 17.6	22 38.3	10 45.5	1 41.1	2 27.9	5 29.5
7 Su	21 09 33	18 28 26	21 39 34	27 42 04	20 31.8	5 32.2	4 28.8	5 23.3	11 10.3	22 30.4	10 51.0	1 41.0	2 29.7	5 31.4
8 M	21 13 29	19 29 14	3♓46 43	9♓53 44	20 31.9	5 50.7	5 38.1	5 02.4	11 03.4	22 22.5	10 56.6	1D 41.0	2 31.4	5 33.3
9 Tu	21 17 26	20 30 01	16 03 18	22 15 40	20R 31.9	5R 58.6	6 47.6	4 41.0	10 56.9	22 14.5	11 02.3	1 41.0	2 33.2	5 35.1
10 W	21 21 22	21 30 46	28 31 02	4♈49 37	20 31.9	5 55.7	7 57.1	4 19.2	10 50.9	22 06.5	11 08.0	1 41.1	2 35.0	5 37.0
11 Th	21 25 19	22 31 30	11♈11 40	17 37 24	20 31.7	5 42.0	9 06.8	3 57.0	10 45.3	21 58.6	11 13.8	1 41.2	2 36.8	5 38.8
12 F	21 29 16	23 32 12	24 07 03	0♉40 52	20 31.4	5 17.7	10 16.5	3 34.4	10 40.1	21 50.6	11 19.7	1 41.4	2 38.7	5 40.7
13 Sa	21 33 12	24 32 53	7♉19 03	14 01 48	20D 31.2	4 43.5	11 26.4	3 11.5	10 35.3	21 42.7	11 25.6	1 41.6	2 40.5	5 42.5
14 Su	21 37 09	25 33 32	20 49 17	27 41 36	20 31.1	4 00.0	12 36.4	2 48.3	10 31.0	21 34.7	11 31.6	1 41.9	2 42.4	5 44.3
15 M	21 41 05	26 34 09	4♊38 47	11♊40 50	20 31.3	3 08.5	13 46.4	2 24.9	10 27.1	21 26.8	11 37.6	1 42.3	2 44.3	5 46.1
16 Tu	21 45 02	27 34 45	18 47 36	25 58 51	20 31.8	2 10.4	14 56.6	2 01.4	10 23.7	21 19.0	11 43.7	1 42.7	2 46.3	5 47.9
17 W	21 48 58	28 35 19	3♋14 15	10♋33 19	20 32.5	1 07.2	16 06.8	1 37.6	10 20.7	21 11.1	11 49.9	1 43.1	2 48.2	5 49.7
18 Th	21 52 55	29 35 51	17 55 27	25 19 58	20 33.2	0 00.8	17 17.1	1 13.8	10 18.1	21 03.3	11 56.1	1 43.6	2 50.2	5 51.5
19 F	21 56 51	0♓36 22	2♌46 02	10♌12 44	20R 33.7	28♒52.9	18 27.6	0 50.0	10 15.9	20 55.5	12 02.4	1 44.2	2 52.2	5 53.3
20 Sa	22 00 48	1 36 50	17 39 09	25 04 17	20 33.8	27 45.2	19 38.1	0 26.1	10 14.2	20 47.8	12 08.7	1 44.8	2 54.2	5 55.0
21 Su	22 04 45	2 37 17	2♍27 10	9♍46 53	20 33.3	26 39.5	20 48.7	0 02.2	10 13.0	20 40.2	12 15.1	1 45.5	2 56.2	5 56.8
22 M	22 08 41	3 37 43	17 02 34	24 13 29	20 32.2	25 37.1	21 59.3	29♌38.5	10 12.1	20 32.6	12 21.5	1 46.2	2 58.2	5 58.5
23 Tu	22 12 38	4 38 06	1♎19 00	8♎18 39	20 30.4	24 39.4	23 10.1	29 14.8	10D 11.7	20 25.0	12 28.0	1 47.0	3 00.2	6 00.2
24 W	22 16 34	5 38 29	15 12 07	21 59 11	20 28.4	23 47.3	24 20.9	28 51.3	10 11.7	20 17.6	12 34.5	1 47.8	3 02.3	6 02.0
25 Th	22 20 31	6 38 50	28 39 50	5♏14 10	20 26.3	23 01.6	25 31.8	28 28.0	10 12.1	20 10.2	12 41.1	1 48.6	3 04.4	6 03.6
26 F	22 24 27	7 39 10	11♏42 24	18 04 51	20 24.6	22 22.7	26 42.8	28 05.0	10 13.0	20 02.9	12 47.7	1 49.6	3 06.4	6 05.3
27 Sa	22 28 24	8 39 28	24 21 55	0♐34 05	20D 23.5	21 51.0	27 53.8	27 42.3	10 14.3	19 55.6	12 54.4	1 50.5	3 08.5	6 07.0
28 Su	22 32 20	9 39 45	6♐41 53	12 45 53	20 23.4	21 26.4	29 05.0	27 19.9	10 16.0	19 48.5	13 01.1	1 51.6	3 10.7	6 08.7

Astro Data

	Dy Hr Mn
♂ R	10 13:00
☽ 0N	13 8:38
♅⚹♆	15 9:32
♃⚼♄	22 10:03
☽ 0S	25 23:47
♅ D	8 12:31
☽ 0N	9 14:05
☿ R	9 17:39
☽ 0S	22 10:34
⚳ D	23 23:25
♆ 0N	26 17:35

Planet Ingress

	Dy Hr Mn
♀ ♐	7 8:55
☿ ♒	13 6:07
☉ ♒	20 7:31
☿ ♓	1 1:27
♀ ♑	3 14:32
☿ ♒R	18 12:17
☉ ♓	18 21:35
♂ ♌R	21 14:15

Last Aspect / ☽ Ingress (January)

Last Aspect Dy Hr Mn		☽ Ingress Dy Hr Mn
1 3:29 ♃ ⚹	♏	1 10:17
3 13:34 ♃ □	♐	3 20:58
6 1:24 ♃ △	♑	6 9:18
8 5:12 ☿ ☌	♒	8 22:12
11 2:00 ♃ ☍	♓	11 10:37
13 7:33 ☉ ⚹	♈	13 21:15
15 20:36 ☉ □	♉	16 4:45
18 4:59 ☉ △	♊	18 8:34
20 1:02 ♃ ⚹	♋	20 9:22
21 0:47 ♂ ⚹	♌	22 8:46
23 23:35 ♃ ☌	♍	24 8:46
25 17:57 ♀ □	♎	26 11:13
28 7:47 ☿ △	♏	28 17:22
31 0:37 ☿ □	♐	31 3:15

Last Aspect / ☽ Ingress (February)

Last Aspect Dy Hr Mn		☽ Ingress Dy Hr Mn
2 13:06 ♀ ☌	♑	2 15:34
3 12:54 ♄ □	♒	5 4:30
7 1:48 ♃ ☍	♓	7 16:33
8 3:54 ☿ ☌	♈	10 2:50
11 21:50 ☉ ⚹	♉	12 10:46
14 8:00 ☉ □	♊	14 16:00
16 14:51 ☉ △	♋	16 18:40
17 21:50 ♀ ☍	♌	18 19:32
20 16:03 ☿ ☍	♍	20 20:00
22 7:55 ♀ △	♎	22 21:46
24 24:00 ♂ ⚹	♏	25 2:25
27 6:36 ♂ □	♐	27 10:54

☽ Phases & Eclipses

Dy Hr Mn	
7 20:26	● 17♑18
15 20:36	☽ 25♈28
22 12:19	○ 2♌14
29 10:57	☾ 9♏18
6 15:57	● 17♒38
6 16:00:47	• A 07'51"
14 8:00	☽ 25♉23
20 23:25	○ 2♍06
20 23:14	• A 0.927
28 5:18	☾ 9♐23

Astro Data

1 January 2027
Julian Day # 46387
SVP 4♓52'47"
GC 27♐13.0 ⚴ 6♈46.8
Eris 24♈52.0R ⚵ 23♒56.6
⚷ 26♈16.6R ⚶ 16♈30.7
☽ Mean ☊ 22♒49.0

1 February 2027
Julian Day # 46418
SVP 4♓52'41"
GC 27♐13.1 ⚴ 15♈37.8
Eris 24♈53.6 ⚵ 8♓16.6
⚷ 26♈35.1 ⚶ 24♈56.5
☽ Mean ☊ 21♒10.5

March 2027 — LONGITUDE

Day	Sid.Time	☉	0 hr ☽	Noon ☽	True ☊	☿	♀	♂	⚳	♃	♄	♅	♆	♇
1 M	22 36 17	10♓40 00	18♐46 41	24♐44 54	20♒24.0	21♒09.1	0♒16.2	26♌57.8	10♋18.1	19♌41.5	13♈07.9	1♊52.6	3♈12.8	6♒10.3
2 Tu	22 40 14	11 40 14	0♑41 09	6♑36 02	20 25.4	20R 58.9	1 27.4	26R 36.2	10 20.7	19R 34.5	13 14.7	1 53.8	3 14.9	6 11.9
3 W	22 44 10	12 40 26	12 30 08	18 24 03	20 27.1	20D 55.4	2 38.7	26 15.0	10 23.6	19 27.7	13 21.5	1 54.9	3 17.1	6 13.5
4 Th	22 48 07	13 40 37	24 18 18	0♒13 25	20 28.8	20 58.4	3 50.1	25 54.3	10 27.0	19 21.0	13 28.4	1 56.2	3 19.2	6 15.1
5 F	22 52 03	14 40 46	6♒09 52	12 08 06	20R 29.9	21 07.7	5 01.5	25 34.2	10 30.8	19 14.4	13 35.4	1 57.4	3 21.4	6 16.7
6 Sa	22 56 00	15 40 53	18 08 29	24 11 22	20 30.2	21 22.8	6 13.0	25 14.5	10 34.9	19 07.9	13 42.3	1 58.8	3 23.6	6 18.3
7 Su	22 59 56	16 40 59	0♓17 02	6♓25 44	20 29.1	21 43.4	7 24.5	24 55.5	10 39.5	19 01.6	13 49.3	2 00.1	3 25.8	6 19.8
8 M	23 03 53	17 41 02	12 37 40	18 52 57	20 26.7	22 09.1	8 36.1	24 37.1	10 44.5	18 55.3	13 56.4	2 01.6	3 28.0	6 21.3
9 Tu	23 07 49	18 41 04	25 11 41	1♈33 55	20 22.9	22 39.7	9 47.7	24 19.3	10 49.8	18 49.2	14 03.4	2 03.0	3 30.2	6 22.8
10 W	23 11 46	19 41 04	7♈59 41	14 28 55	20 18.3	23 14.7	10 59.4	24 02.2	10 55.6	18 43.3	14 10.6	2 04.6	3 32.4	6 24.3
11 Th	23 15 43	20 41 02	21 01 36	27 37 38	20 13.2	23 53.9	12 11.1	23 45.7	11 01.7	18 37.4	14 17.7	2 06.1	3 34.6	6 25.8
12 F	23 19 39	21 40 57	4♉16 57	10♉59 27	20 08.4	24 37.1	13 22.8	23 30.0	11 08.2	18 31.7	14 24.9	2 07.7	3 36.9	6 27.3
13 Sa	23 23 36	22 40 51	17 45 02	24 33 35	20 04.5	25 23.9	14 34.6	23 15.0	11 15.1	18 26.2	14 32.1	2 09.4	3 39.1	6 28.7
14 Su	23 27 32	23 40 42	1♊25 02	8♊19 17	20 01.9	26 14.1	15 46.5	23 00.7	11 22.4	18 20.8	14 39.3	2 11.1	3 41.4	6 30.1
15 M	23 31 29	24 40 32	15 16 13	22 15 45	20D 00.9	27 07.6	16 58.3	22 47.1	11 30.0	18 15.6	14 46.6	2 12.9	3 43.6	6 31.5
16 Tu	23 35 25	25 40 19	29 17 46	6♋22 06	20 01.3	28 04.0	18 10.2	22 34.4	11 38.0	18 10.5	14 53.8	2 14.7	3 45.9	6 32.9
17 W	23 39 22	26 40 04	13♋28 37	20 37 04	20 02.6	29 03.2	19 22.2	22 22.4	11 46.3	18 05.6	15 01.1	2 16.5	3 48.1	6 34.2
18 Th	23 43 18	27 39 46	27 47 12	4♌58 41	20 04.0	0♓05.1	20 34.2	22 11.2	11 55.0	18 00.9	15 08.5	2 18.4	3 50.4	6 35.6
19 F	23 47 15	28 39 26	12♌11 07	19 24 02	20R 04.7	1 09.5	21 46.2	22 00.7	12 04.0	17 56.3	15 15.8	2 20.3	3 52.6	6 36.9
20 Sa	23 51 12	29 39 04	26 36 55	3♍49 11	20 03.9	2 16.3	22 58.2	21 51.1	12 13.4	17 51.9	15 23.2	2 22.3	3 54.9	6 38.2
21 Su	23 55 08	0♈38 39	11♍00 11	18 09 16	20 01.2	3 25.3	24 10.3	21 42.2	12 23.1	17 47.6	15 30.6	2 24.3	3 57.2	6 39.4
22 M	23 59 05	1 38 13	25 15 46	2♎19 04	19 56.5	4 36.4	25 22.4	21 34.1	12 33.1	17 43.6	15 38.0	2 26.4	3 59.5	6 40.7
23 Tu	0 03 01	2 37 44	9♎18 32	16 13 39	19 50.2	5 49.6	26 34.5	21 26.8	12 43.4	17 39.7	15 45.4	2 28.5	4 01.7	6 41.9
24 W	0 06 58	3 37 14	23 03 58	29 49 08	19 42.7	7 04.8	27 46.7	21 20.2	12 54.1	17 35.9	15 52.9	2 30.6	4 04.0	6 43.1
25 Th	0 10 54	4 36 42	6♏28 56	13♏03 14	19 35.1	8 21.8	28 58.9	21 14.5	13 05.0	17 32.4	16 00.4	2 32.8	4 06.3	6 44.3
26 F	0 14 51	5 36 08	19 32 02	25 55 28	19 28.2	9 40.7	0♓11.2	21 09.5	13 16.3	17 29.0	16 07.8	2 35.0	4 08.5	6 45.4
27 Sa	0 18 47	6 35 32	2♐13 46	8♐27 14	19 22.7	11 01.3	1 23.4	21 05.3	13 27.9	17 25.8	16 15.3	2 37.3	4 10.8	6 46.6
28 Su	0 22 44	7 34 54	14 36 18	20 41 26	19 19.0	12 23.6	2 35.7	21 01.8	13 39.8	17 22.8	16 22.8	2 39.6	4 13.1	6 47.7
29 M	0 26 40	8 34 15	26 43 11	2♑42 09	19D 17.2	13 47.6	3 48.1	20 59.1	13 51.9	17 19.9	16 30.4	2 41.9	4 15.4	6 48.8
30 Tu	0 30 37	9 33 34	8♑38 57	14 34 13	19 17.1	15 13.2	5 00.4	20 57.2	14 04.4	17 17.3	16 37.9	2 44.3	4 17.6	6 49.8
31 W	0 34 34	10 32 51	20 28 38	26 22 52	19 18.1	16 40.4	6 12.8	20 56.0	14 17.2	17 14.8	16 45.4	2 46.7	4 19.9	6 50.9

April 2027 — LONGITUDE

Day	Sid.Time	☉	0 hr ☽	Noon ☽	True ☊	☿	♀	♂	⚳	♃	♄	♅	♆	♇
1 Th	0 38 30	11♈32 06	2♒17 34	8♒13 24	19♒19.3	18♓09.1	7♓25.2	20♌55.6	14♋30.2	17♌12.5	16♈53.0	2♊49.2	4♈22.2	6♒51.9
2 F	0 42 27	12 31 19	14 10 57	20 10 49	19R 19.8	19 39.4	8 37.7	20D 55.9	14 43.5	17R 10.4	17 00.5	2 51.7	4 24.4	6 52.9
3 Sa	0 46 23	13 30 31	26 13 32	2♓19 37	19 18.8	21 11.2	9 50.1	20 56.9	14 57.1	17 08.5	17 08.1	2 54.2	4 26.7	6 53.8
4 Su	0 50 20	14 29 40	8♓29 27	14 43 25	19 15.7	22 44.5	11 02.6	20 58.7	15 10.9	17 06.8	17 15.7	2 56.8	4 28.9	6 54.8
5 M	0 54 16	15 28 48	21 01 46	27 24 42	19 10.2	24 19.3	12 15.1	21 01.1	15 25.0	17 05.2	17 23.2	2 59.4	4 31.2	6 55.7
6 Tu	0 58 13	16 27 53	3♈52 18	10♈24 33	19 02.5	25 55.5	13 27.6	21 04.3	15 39.4	17 03.9	17 30.8	3 02.0	4 33.4	6 56.5
7 W	1 02 09	17 26 57	17 01 22	23 42 33	18 53.0	27 33.3	14 40.2	21 08.2	15 54.0	17 02.7	17 38.4	3 04.6	4 35.6	6 57.4
8 Th	1 06 06	18 25 59	0♉27 49	7♉16 51	18 42.8	29 12.5	15 52.7	21 12.7	16 08.9	17 01.7	17 45.9	3 07.3	4 37.9	6 58.2
9 F	1 10 03	19 24 58	14 09 12	21 04 29	18 32.9	0♈53.3	17 05.3	21 17.9	16 24.1	17 01.0	17 53.5	3 10.1	4 40.1	6 59.1
10 Sa	1 13 59	20 23 56	28 02 11	5♊01 54	18 24.4	2 35.5	18 17.9	21 23.8	16 39.4	17 00.4	18 01.1	3 12.8	4 42.3	6 59.8
11 Su	1 17 56	21 22 51	12♊03 09	19 05 34	18 18.1	4 19.2	19 30.4	21 30.3	16 55.0	17 00.0	18 08.7	3 15.6	4 44.5	7 00.6
12 M	1 21 52	22 21 44	26 08 46	3♋12 26	18 14.3	6 04.5	20 43.1	21 37.5	17 10.9	16D 59.8	18 16.2	3 18.5	4 46.7	7 01.3
13 Tu	1 25 49	23 20 35	10♋16 21	17 20 16	18D 12.8	7 51.2	21 55.7	21 45.3	17 27.0	16 59.7	18 23.8	3 21.3	4 48.9	7 02.0
14 W	1 29 45	24 19 24	24 24 03	1♌27 33	18 12.8	9 39.5	23 08.3	21 53.7	17 43.3	16 59.9	18 31.3	3 24.2	4 51.1	7 02.7
15 Th	1 33 42	25 18 10	8♌30 39	15 33 14	18R 13.2	11 29.3	24 20.9	22 02.7	17 59.8	17 00.3	18 38.9	3 27.1	4 53.2	7 03.4
16 F	1 37 38	26 16 53	22 35 11	29 36 20	18 12.8	13 20.7	25 33.6	22 12.3	18 16.6	17 00.8	18 46.4	3 30.1	4 55.4	7 04.0
17 Sa	1 41 35	27 15 35	6♍36 30	13♍35 28	18 10.4	15 13.6	26 46.3	22 22.5	18 33.5	17 01.5	18 53.9	3 33.0	4 57.5	7 04.6
18 Su	1 45 32	28 14 14	20 32 58	27 28 40	18 05.5	17 08.1	27 58.9	22 33.2	18 50.7	17 02.5	19 01.5	3 36.0	4 59.7	7 05.1
19 M	1 49 28	29 12 51	4♎22 15	11♎13 20	17 57.7	19 04.1	29 11.6	22 44.5	19 08.0	17 03.6	19 09.0	3 39.0	5 01.8	7 05.7
20 Tu	1 53 25	0♉11 26	18 01 33	24 46 31	17 47.5	21 01.6	0♈24.3	22 56.3	19 25.6	17 04.8	19 16.4	3 42.1	5 03.9	7 06.2
21 W	1 57 21	1 10 00	1♏27 54	8♏05 23	17 35.7	23 00.7	1 37.0	23 08.7	19 43.4	17 06.3	19 23.9	3 45.1	5 06.0	7 06.7
22 Th	2 01 18	2 08 31	14 38 44	21 07 47	17 23.5	25 01.2	2 49.8	23 21.6	20 01.3	17 08.0	19 31.4	3 48.2	5 08.1	7 07.1
23 F	2 05 14	3 07 01	27 32 27	3♐52 42	17 11.9	27 03.2	4 02.5	23 35.0	20 19.5	17 09.8	19 38.8	3 51.4	5 10.1	7 07.6
24 Sa	2 09 11	4 05 29	10♐08 39	16 20 28	17 02.1	29 06.6	5 15.3	23 48.8	20 37.8	17 11.8	19 46.3	3 54.5	5 12.2	7 08.0
25 Su	2 13 07	5 03 55	22 28 26	28 32 52	16 54.6	1♉11.2	6 28.0	24 03.2	20 56.4	17 14.0	19 53.7	3 57.7	5 14.2	7 08.3
26 M	2 17 04	6 02 19	4♑34 13	10♑32 58	16 49.7	3 17.0	7 40.8	24 18.1	21 15.1	17 16.4	20 01.1	4 00.8	5 16.2	7 08.7
27 Tu	2 21 01	7 00 42	16 29 39	22 24 53	16 47.2	5 23.9	8 53.6	24 33.4	21 34.0	17 18.9	20 08.4	4 04.0	5 18.3	7 09.0
28 W	2 24 57	7 59 04	28 19 16	4♒13 30	16D 46.4	7 31.7	10 06.4	24 49.2	21 53.0	17 21.6	20 15.8	4 07.3	5 20.2	7 09.3
29 Th	2 28 54	8 57 23	10♒08 15	16 04 12	16R 46.4	9 40.2	11 19.2	25 05.4	22 12.2	17 24.5	20 23.1	4 10.5	5 22.2	7 09.6
30 F	2 32 50	9 55 42	22 02 03	28 02 28	16 46.1	11 49.3	12 32.1	25 22.1	22 31.7	17 27.6	20 30.4	4 13.8	5 24.2	7 09.8

Astro Data

	Dy Hr Mn
☿ D	3 12:33
☽ 0N	8 20:37
♃⊼♆	11 20:25
☉0N	20 20:26
☽ 0S	21 20:52
♂ D	1 14:09
♃△♄	3 13:00
☽ 0N	5 4:24
☿0N	12 1:22
♄∠♅	12 23:24
♃ D	13 2:13
☽ 0S	18 4:41
♀0N	23 3:56

Planet Ingress

	Dy Hr Mn
♀ ♒	1 6:33
☿ ♓	18 10:03
☉ ♈	20 20:26
♀ ♓	26 8:18
☿ ♈	8 23:21
♀ ♈	20 3:58
☉ ♉	20 7:19
☿ ♉	24 22:19

Last Aspect / ☽ Ingress (March)

Last Aspect Dy Hr Mn		☽ Ingress Dy Hr Mn
1 16:20 ♂ △	♑	1 22:37
3 1:39 ♄ □	♒	4 11:33
6 14:02 ♂ ☍	♓	6 23:27
8 9:31 ☉ ☌	♈	9 9:04
11 5:08 ♂ △	♉	11 16:17
13 13:34 ☿ □	♊	13 21:32
15 20:53 ☿ △	♋	16 1:12
17 22:53 ☉ △	♌	18 3:42
19 16:18 ♀ ☍	♍	20 5:38
20 9:35 ♅ □	♎	22 8:03
24 8:00 ♀ △	♏	24 12:19
26 3:05 ♂ □	♐	26 19:44
28 12:40 ♂ △	♑	29 6:34
30 16:14 ♄ □	♒	31 19:21

Last Aspect / ☽ Ingress (April)

Last Aspect Dy Hr Mn		☽ Ingress Dy Hr Mn
2 13:30 ♂ ☍	♓	3 7:26
5 5:23 ☿ ☌	♈	5 16:50
7 7:22 ♂ △	♉	7 23:11
9 12:23 ♂ □	♊	10 3:22
11 16:11 ☉ ⚹	♋	12 6:33
13 22:58 ☉ □	♌	14 9:31
16 5:53 ☉ △	♍	16 12:41
18 12:58 ♀ ☍	♎	18 16:23
20 8:41 ♂ ⚹	♏	20 21:22
22 16:14 ♂ □	♐	23 4:38
25 2:56 ♂ △	♑	25 14:53
27 7:20 ♄ □	♒	28 3:25
30 6:33 ♂ ☍	♓	30 15:53

☽ Phases & Eclipses

Dy Hr Mn	
8 9:31	● 17♓35
15 16:26	☽ 24♊52
22 10:45	○ 1♎35
30 0:55	☾ 9♑06
6 23:52	● 16♈57
13 22:58	☽ 23♋47
20 22:28	○ 0♏37
28 20:19	☾ 8♒19

Astro Data

1 March 2027
Julian Day # 46446
SVP 4♓52'37"
GC 27♐13.1 ⚴ 26♈42.1
Eris 25♈03.5 ⚵ 22♓19.5
⚷ 27♈34.4 ⚶ 4♉51.6
☽ Mean ☊ 19♒41.5

1 April 2027
Julian Day # 46477
SVP 4♓52'34"
GC 27♐13.2 ⚴ 11♉17.9
Eris 25♈21.2 ⚵ 8♈44.3
⚷ 29♈12.8 ⚶ 17♉13.7
☽ Mean ☊ 18♒03.0

LONGITUDE — May 2027

Day	Sid.Time	☉	0 hr ☽	Noon ☽	True ☊	☿	♀	♂	⚳	♃	♄	♅	♆	♇
1 Sa	2 36 47	10♉53 58	4♓06 07	10♓13 37	16♒44.4	13♉58.6	13♈44.9	25♌39.2	22♋51.2	17♌30.8	20♈37.7	4♊17.1	5♈26.1	7♒10.0
2 Su	2 40 43	11 52 13	16 25 30	22 42 17	16R 40.5	16 08.0	14 57.8	25 56.7	23 11.0	17 34.2	20 45.0	4 20.4	5 28.1	7 10.2
3 M	2 44 40	12 50 27	29 04 23	5♈32 06	16 34.0	18 17.1	16 10.6	26 14.6	23 30.9	17 37.8	20 52.2	4 23.7	5 30.0	7 10.4
4 Tu	2 48 36	13 48 39	12♈05 37	18 45 02	16 24.9	20 25.7	17 23.5	26 33.0	23 50.9	17 41.6	20 59.4	4 27.0	5 31.8	7 10.5
5 W	2 52 33	14 46 49	25 30 14	2♉21 03	16 13.8	22 33.5	18 36.4	26 51.7	24 11.1	17 45.5	21 06.6	4 30.3	5 33.7	7 10.6
6 Th	2 56 30	15 44 58	9♉17 06	16 17 54	16 01.7	24 40.1	19 49.3	27 10.9	24 31.5	17 49.6	21 13.7	4 33.7	5 35.6	7 10.6
7 F	3 00 26	16 43 05	23 22 50	0♊31 13	15 49.9	26 45.4	21 02.1	27 30.4	24 52.0	17 53.8	21 20.8	4 37.1	5 37.4	7 10.7
8 Sa	3 04 23	17 41 11	7♊42 16	14 55 13	15 39.7	28 48.9	22 15.0	27 50.4	25 12.7	17 58.2	21 27.9	4 40.5	5 39.2	7R 10.7
9 Su	3 08 19	18 39 15	22 09 15	29 23 36	15 31.9	0♊50.5	23 27.9	28 10.7	25 33.5	18 02.8	21 35.0	4 43.9	5 41.0	7 10.7
10 M	3 12 16	19 37 17	6♋37 37	13♋50 39	15 26.9	2 49.9	24 40.9	28 31.3	25 54.5	18 07.6	21 42.0	4 47.3	5 42.8	7 10.6
11 Tu	3 16 12	20 35 17	21 02 13	28 11 54	15 24.5	4 46.8	25 53.8	28 52.3	26 15.6	18 12.5	21 49.0	4 50.7	5 44.5	7 10.6
12 W	3 20 09	21 33 15	5♌19 24	12♌24 31	15 23.8	6 41.1	27 06.7	29 13.7	26 36.9	18 17.5	21 55.9	4 54.2	5 46.3	7 10.5
13 Th	3 24 05	22 31 11	19 27 06	26 27 06	15 23.8	8 32.6	28 19.6	29 35.4	26 58.2	18 22.7	22 02.8	4 57.6	5 48.0	7 10.3
14 F	3 28 02	23 29 05	3♍24 29	10♍19 16	15 23.1	10 21.2	29 32.5	29 57.4	27 19.7	18 28.1	22 09.7	5 01.1	5 49.6	7 10.2
15 Sa	3 31 59	24 26 58	17 11 27	24 01 04	15 20.5	12 06.7	0♉45.4	0♍19.7	27 41.4	18 33.6	22 16.5	5 04.5	5 51.3	7 10.0
16 Su	3 35 55	25 24 49	0♎48 07	7♎32 34	15 15.4	13 49.1	1 58.4	0 42.4	28 03.1	18 39.3	22 23.3	5 08.0	5 52.9	7 09.8
17 M	3 39 52	26 22 38	14 14 22	20 53 28	15 07.4	15 28.2	3 11.3	1 05.4	28 25.0	18 45.1	22 30.1	5 11.5	5 54.5	7 09.6
18 Tu	3 43 48	27 20 25	27 29 44	4♏03 05	14 57.1	17 04.0	4 24.3	1 28.6	28 47.0	18 51.0	22 36.8	5 15.0	5 56.1	7 09.3
19 W	3 47 45	28 18 11	10♏33 24	17 00 33	14 45.1	18 36.4	5 37.2	1 52.2	29 09.1	18 57.1	22 43.4	5 18.5	5 57.7	7 09.0
20 Th	3 51 41	29 15 56	23 24 27	29 45 01	14 32.5	20 05.3	6 50.2	2 16.1	29 31.4	19 03.4	22 50.0	5 22.0	5 59.2	7 08.7
21 F	3 55 38	0♊13 39	6♐02 14	12♐16 05	14 20.6	21 30.8	8 03.1	2 40.2	29 53.7	19 09.8	22 56.6	5 25.5	6 00.7	7 08.4
22 Sa	3 59 34	1 11 21	18 26 39	24 34 02	14 10.4	22 52.8	9 16.1	3 04.6	0♌16.2	19 16.3	23 03.2	5 29.0	6 02.2	7 08.0
23 Su	4 03 31	2 09 02	0♑38 26	6♑40 06	14 02.4	24 11.2	10 29.1	3 29.3	0 38.8	19 22.9	23 09.6	5 32.5	6 03.7	7 07.6
24 M	4 07 28	3 06 42	12 39 21	18 36 32	13 57.1	25 26.0	11 42.1	3 54.2	1 01.5	19 29.7	23 16.1	5 36.0	6 05.1	7 07.2
25 Tu	4 11 24	4 04 20	24 32 06	0♒26 32	13 54.3	26 37.1	12 55.1	4 19.4	1 24.3	19 36.7	23 22.5	5 39.5	6 06.6	7 06.8
26 W	4 15 21	5 01 58	6♒20 22	12 14 11	13D 53.4	27 44.4	14 08.1	4 44.9	1 47.2	19 43.7	23 28.8	5 43.0	6 07.9	7 06.3
27 Th	4 19 17	5 59 34	18 08 37	24 04 17	13 53.7	28 48.0	15 21.2	5 10.6	2 10.2	19 50.9	23 35.1	5 46.5	6 09.3	7 05.8
28 F	4 23 14	6 57 09	0♓01 52	6♓02 03	13R 54.0	29 47.7	16 34.2	5 36.6	2 33.3	19 58.2	23 41.3	5 50.0	6 10.6	7 05.3
29 Sa	4 27 10	7 54 44	12 05 30	18 12 52	13 53.5	0♋43.6	17 47.2	6 02.8	2 56.5	20 05.7	23 47.5	5 53.6	6 12.0	7 04.7
30 Su	4 31 07	8 52 18	24 24 49	0♈41 55	13 51.3	1 35.4	19 00.3	6 29.3	3 19.9	20 13.3	23 53.6	5 57.1	6 13.2	7 04.2
31 M	4 35 03	9 49 51	7♈04 42	13 33 37	13 46.9	2 23.2	20 13.4	6 56.0	3 43.3	20 21.0	23 59.7	6 00.6	6 14.5	7 03.6

LONGITUDE — June 2027

Day	Sid.Time	☉	0 hr ☽	Noon ☽	True ☊	☿	♀	♂	⚳	♃	♄	♅	♆	♇
1 Tu	4 39 00	10♊47 23	20♈09 00	26♈51 04	13♒40.3	3♋06.8	21♉26.5	7♍22.9	4♌06.8	20♌28.8	24♈05.7	6♊04.1	6♈15.7	7♒02.9
2 W	4 42 57	11 44 54	3♉39 53	10♉35 22	13R 31.9	3 46.2	22 39.5	7 50.0	4 30.4	20 36.8	24 11.6	6 07.6	6 16.9	7R 02.3
3 Th	4 46 53	12 42 24	17 37 13	24 45 01	13 22.5	4 21.3	23 52.6	8 17.4	4 54.1	20 44.8	24 17.5	6 11.1	6 18.1	7 01.6
4 F	4 50 50	13 39 54	1♊58 08	9♊15 48	13 13.2	4 52.0	25 05.8	8 45.0	5 17.9	20 53.0	24 23.4	6 14.6	6 19.2	7 00.9
5 Sa	4 54 46	14 37 23	16 37 07	24 01 05	13 05.1	5 18.3	26 18.9	9 12.9	5 41.8	21 01.3	24 29.2	6 18.1	6 20.3	7 00.2
6 Su	4 58 43	15 34 50	1♋26 40	8♋52 48	12 59.0	5 40.1	27 32.0	9 40.9	6 05.8	21 09.8	24 34.9	6 21.6	6 21.4	6 59.5
7 M	5 02 39	16 32 17	16 18 29	23 42 47	12 55.4	5 57.4	28 45.1	10 09.2	6 29.9	21 18.3	24 40.5	6 25.1	6 22.5	6 58.7
8 Tu	5 06 36	17 29 42	1♌04 51	8♌24 01	12D 53.9	6 10.0	29 58.3	10 37.6	6 54.0	21 27.0	24 46.1	6 28.5	6 23.5	6 58.0
9 W	5 10 33	18 27 07	15 39 41	22 51 27	12 54.1	6 18.1	1♊11.4	11 06.3	7 18.3	21 35.7	24 51.6	6 32.0	6 24.5	6 57.2
10 Th	5 14 29	19 24 30	29 59 01	7♍02 13	12R 55.0	6R 21.5	2 24.6	11 35.2	7 42.6	21 44.6	24 57.1	6 35.5	6 25.4	6 56.3
11 F	5 18 26	20 21 52	14♍00 58	20 55 17	12 55.5	6 20.4	3 37.8	12 04.2	8 07.0	21 53.6	25 02.5	6 38.9	6 26.4	6 55.5
12 Sa	5 22 22	21 19 13	27 45 15	4♎31 00	12 54.6	6 14.9	4 50.9	12 33.5	8 31.4	22 02.7	25 07.8	6 42.3	6 27.3	6 54.6
13 Su	5 26 19	22 16 33	11♎12 40	17 50 25	12 51.8	6 05.1	6 04.1	13 02.9	8 56.0	22 11.9	25 13.1	6 45.8	6 28.1	6 53.7
14 M	5 30 15	23 13 52	24 24 26	0♏54 53	12 47.0	5 51.1	7 17.3	13 32.5	9 20.6	22 21.1	25 18.3	6 49.2	6 29.0	6 52.8
15 Tu	5 34 12	24 11 10	7♏21 55	13 45 40	12 40.3	5 33.2	8 30.5	14 02.3	9 45.3	22 30.5	25 23.4	6 52.6	6 29.8	6 51.9
16 W	5 38 08	25 08 27	20 06 17	26 23 52	12 32.4	5 11.7	9 43.7	14 32.3	10 10.1	22 40.0	25 28.4	6 56.0	6 30.5	6 50.9
17 Th	5 42 05	26 05 44	2♐38 33	8♐50 27	12 24.0	4 46.8	10 56.9	15 02.5	10 34.9	22 49.6	25 33.4	6 59.3	6 31.3	6 50.0
18 F	5 46 02	27 03 00	14 59 39	21 06 17	12 16.0	4 19.1	12 10.2	15 32.8	10 59.8	22 59.3	25 38.3	7 02.7	6 32.0	6 49.0
19 Sa	5 49 58	28 00 16	27 10 30	3♑12 28	12 09.3	3 48.9	13 23.4	16 03.3	11 24.8	23 09.0	25 43.1	7 06.1	6 32.7	6 48.0
20 Su	5 53 55	28 57 31	9♑12 21	15 10 23	12 04.2	3 16.8	14 36.7	16 33.9	11 49.9	23 18.9	25 47.9	7 09.4	6 33.3	6 47.0
21 M	5 57 51	29 54 45	21 06 50	27 02 00	12 01.0	2 43.2	15 49.9	17 04.8	12 15.0	23 28.9	25 52.6	7 12.7	6 34.0	6 45.9
22 Tu	6 01 48	0♋51 59	2♒56 12	8♒49 49	11D 59.8	2 08.7	17 03.2	17 35.7	12 40.1	23 38.9	25 57.2	7 16.0	6 34.6	6 44.9
23 W	6 05 44	1 49 13	14 43 16	20 37 02	12 00.1	1 33.9	18 16.5	18 06.9	13 05.4	23 49.0	26 01.7	7 19.3	6 35.1	6 43.8
24 Th	6 09 41	2 46 27	26 31 36	2♓27 30	12 01.3	0 59.5	19 29.9	18 38.2	13 30.7	23 59.3	26 06.1	7 22.5	6 35.6	6 42.7
25 F	6 13 37	3 43 41	8♓25 18	14 25 35	12 02.9	0 26.0	20 43.2	19 09.6	13 56.1	24 09.6	26 10.5	7 25.8	6 36.1	6 41.6
26 Sa	6 17 34	4 40 54	20 28 57	26 36 02	12R 04.2	29♊53.9	21 56.5	19 41.2	14 21.5	24 19.9	26 14.8	7 29.0	6 36.6	6 40.5
27 Su	6 21 31	5 38 07	2♈47 26	9♈03 44	12 04.4	29 23.9	23 09.9	20 13.0	14 47.0	24 30.4	26 19.0	7 32.2	6 37.0	6 39.3
28 M	6 25 27	6 35 21	15 25 29	21 53 13	12 03.3	28 56.4	24 23.3	20 44.9	15 12.5	24 41.0	26 23.1	7 35.4	6 37.4	6 38.2
29 Tu	6 29 24	7 32 34	28 27 20	5♉08 11	12 00.8	28 32.0	25 36.7	21 17.0	15 38.1	24 51.6	26 27.2	7 38.6	6 37.8	6 37.0
30 W	6 33 20	8 29 48	11♉56 00	18 50 50	11 57.0	28 11.0	26 50.1	21 49.2	16 03.8	25 02.3	26 31.1	7 41.7	6 38.1	6 35.8

Astro Data

	Dy Hr Mn
☽0N	2 12:42
♇R	8 12:58
☽0S	15 10:00
☽0N	29 20:32
♅⚹♆	6 10:09
♃⚻♆	8 1:03
☿R	10 18:17
☽0S	11 14:39
♅△♇	15 8:14
☽0N	26 3:24
♆⚹♇	29 0:10

Planet Ingress

		Dy Hr Mn
☿	♊	9 1:59
♂	♍	14 14:48
♀	♉	14 21:03
☉	♊	21 6:19
⚳	♌	21 18:42
☿	♋	28 17:08
♀	♊	8 12:34
☉	♋	21 14:12
☿	♊R	26 7:20

Last Aspect / ☽ Ingress (May)

Last Aspect Dy Hr Mn		☽ Ingress	Dy Hr Mn
1 20:48	☿ ⚹	♈	3 1:44
5 2:10	♂ △	♉	5 7:54
7 6:50	♂ □	♊	7 11:08
9 9:56	♂ ⚹	♋	9 13:00
11 7:47	♀ □	♌	11 15:02
13 17:33	♂ ☌	♍	13 18:07
15 12:49	☉ △	♎	15 22:35
17 14:57	♄ ☍	♏	18 4:34
20 11:00	☉ ☍	♐	20 12:28
22 9:00	♄ △	♑	22 22:44
24 21:31	♄ □	♒	25 11:06
27 22:25	☿ △	♓	27 23:56
29 11:05	♀ ⚹	♈	30 10:40

Last Aspect / ☽ Ingress (June)

Last Aspect Dy Hr Mn		☽ Ingress	Dy Hr Mn
1 7:03	♄ ☌	♉	1 17:34
3 10:24	♀ ☌	♊	3 20:44
5 12:46	♄ ⚹	♋	5 21:40
7 20:56	♀ ⚹	♌	7 22:14
9 15:23	♄ △	♍	10 0:02
11 10:57	☉ □	♎	12 3:58
14 1:35	♄ ☍	♏	14 10:18
16 4:47	♃ □	♐	16 18:55
19 0:46	☉ ☍	♑	19 5:37
21 9:38	♄ □	♒	21 18:02
23 23:04	♄ ⚹	♓	24 7:02
26 18:09	☿ □	♈	26 18:37
29 0:29	☿ ⚹	♉	29 2:48

☽ Phases & Eclipses

Dy Hr Mn	
6 11:00	● 15♉43
13 4:45	☽ 22♌14
20 11:00	○ 29♏14
28 13:59	☾ 7♓02
4 19:41	● 13♊58
11 10:57	☽ 20♍19
19 0:46	○ 27♐33
27 4:55	☾ 5♈21

Astro Data

1 May 2027
Julian Day # 46507
SVP 4♓52'30"
GC 27♐13.3 ⚴ 27♉06.9
Eris 25♈40.8 ⚵ 25♈13.7
⚷ 1♉01.6 ⚶ 29♉54.6
☽ Mean ☊ 16♒27.7

1 June 2027
Julian Day # 46538
SVP 4♓52'26"
GC 27♐13.3 ⚴ 14♊41.4
Eris 25♈58.5 ⚵ 12♉39.3
⚷ 2♉46.6 ⚶ 13♊18.6
☽ Mean ☊ 14♒49.2

July 2027 LONGITUDE

Day	Sid.Time	☉	0 hr ☽	Noon☽	True☊	☿	♀	♂	⚳	♃	♄	♅	♆	♇
1 Th	6 37 17	9♋27 02	25♉52 37	3♊01 06	11♒52.5	27♊53.9	28♊03.6	22♍21.5	16♌29.5	25♌13.1	26♈35.0	7♊44.8	6♈38.4	6♒34.6
2 F	6 41 13	10 24 16	10♊15 49	17 36 09	11R47.9	27R40.9	29 17.0	22 54.0	16 55.3	25 24.0	26 38.8	7 48.0	6 38.6	6R33.4
3 Sa	6 45 10	11 21 29	25 01 18	2♋30 19	11 43.9	27 32.3	0♋30.5	23 26.7	17 21.2	25 34.9	26 42.5	7 51.0	6 38.9	6 32.2
4 Su	6 49 06	12 18 43	10♋02 06	17 35 31	11 41.1	27D28.4	1 44.0	23 59.5	17 47.1	25 45.9	26 46.1	7 54.1	6 39.1	6 30.9
5 M	6 53 03	13 15 57	25 09 24	2♌42 33	11D39.6	27 29.3	2 57.5	24 32.4	18 13.0	25 57.0	26 49.7	7 57.1	6 39.2	6 29.7
6 Tu	6 57 00	14 13 11	10♌13 52	17 42 21	11 39.4	27 35.1	4 11.0	25 05.5	18 39.0	26 08.2	26 53.1	8 00.1	6 39.4	6 28.4
7 W	7 00 56	15 10 24	25 07 06	2♍27 25	11 40.3	27 46.0	5 24.5	25 38.7	19 05.1	26 19.4	26 56.5	8 03.1	6 39.5	6 27.2
8 Th	7 04 53	16 07 37	9♍42 42	16 52 33	11 41.7	28 01.9	6 38.1	26 12.0	19 31.2	26 30.7	26 59.7	8 06.1	6 39.5	6 25.9
9 F	7 08 49	17 04 50	23 56 42	0♎55 01	11 43.0	28 23.0	7 51.6	26 45.5	19 57.3	26 42.0	27 02.9	8 09.0	6R39.6	6 24.6
10 Sa	7 12 46	18 02 03	7♎47 31	14 34 17	11R43.7	28 49.2	9 05.2	27 19.1	20 23.5	26 53.4	27 06.0	8 11.9	6 39.6	6 23.3
11 Su	7 16 42	18 59 16	21 15 30	27 51 25	11 43.4	29 20.6	10 18.8	27 52.8	20 49.7	27 04.9	27 09.0	8 14.7	6 39.5	6 22.0
12 M	7 20 39	19 56 28	4♏22 19	10♏48 32	11 42.2	29 57.0	11 32.4	28 26.7	21 16.0	27 16.4	27 11.8	8 17.6	6 39.5	6 20.6
13 Tu	7 24 35	20 53 41	17 10 23	23 28 14	11 40.1	0♋38.6	12 46.0	29 00.7	21 42.3	27 28.0	27 14.6	8 20.4	6 39.4	6 19.3
14 W	7 28 32	21 50 54	29 42 25	5♐53 17	11 37.4	1 25.1	13 59.6	29 34.8	22 08.7	27 39.7	27 17.3	8 23.2	6 39.2	6 18.0
15 Th	7 32 29	22 48 07	12♐01 09	18 06 20	11 34.5	2 16.7	15 13.2	0♎09.0	22 35.1	27 51.4	27 20.0	8 25.9	6 39.1	6 16.6
16 F	7 36 25	23 45 20	24 09 09	0♑09 53	11 31.7	3 13.2	16 26.9	0 43.3	23 01.6	28 03.2	27 22.5	8 28.6	6 38.9	6 15.3
17 Sa	7 40 22	24 42 33	6♑08 48	12 06 12	11 29.4	4 14.6	17 40.6	1 17.8	23 28.0	28 15.0	27 24.9	8 31.3	6 38.7	6 13.9
18 Su	7 44 18	25 39 46	18 02 18	23 57 25	11 27.9	5 20.7	18 54.3	1 52.4	23 54.6	28 26.9	27 27.2	8 34.0	6 38.4	6 12.5
19 M	7 48 15	26 37 00	29 51 48	5♒45 42	11D27.2	6 31.6	20 08.0	2 27.1	24 21.1	28 38.8	27 29.4	8 36.6	6 38.1	6 11.2
20 Tu	7 52 11	27 34 15	11♒39 27	17 33 20	11 27.2	7 47.1	21 21.7	3 01.9	24 47.7	28 50.8	27 31.6	8 39.2	6 37.8	6 09.8
21 W	7 56 08	28 31 30	23 27 40	29 22 47	11 27.8	9 07.2	22 35.5	3 36.8	25 14.4	29 02.8	27 33.6	8 41.7	6 37.4	6 08.4
22 Th	8 00 05	29 28 45	5♓19 05	11♓16 56	11 28.7	10 31.8	23 49.2	4 11.8	25 41.0	29 14.9	27 35.5	8 44.3	6 37.1	6 07.0
23 F	8 04 01	0♌26 01	17 16 45	23 18 58	11 29.8	12 00.7	25 03.0	4 47.0	26 07.8	29 27.0	27 37.4	8 46.8	6 36.6	6 05.6
24 Sa	8 07 58	1 23 18	29 24 04	5♈32 29	11 30.8	13 33.8	26 16.8	5 22.2	26 34.5	29 39.2	27 39.1	8 49.2	6 36.2	6 04.2
25 Su	8 11 54	2 20 36	11♈44 43	18 01 16	11 31.5	15 10.9	27 30.6	5 57.6	27 01.3	29 51.4	27 40.7	8 51.6	6 35.7	6 02.8
26 M	8 15 51	3 17 55	24 22 35	0♉49 08	11R31.7	16 51.9	28 44.5	6 33.1	27 28.1	0♍03.7	27 42.2	8 54.0	6 35.2	6 01.5
27 Tu	8 19 47	4 15 14	7♉21 19	13 59 32	11 31.6	18 36.5	29 58.4	7 08.7	27 55.0	0 16.0	27 43.7	8 56.3	6 34.7	6 00.1
28 W	8 23 44	5 12 35	20 44 03	27 35 03	11 31.3	20 24.6	1♌12.2	7 44.4	28 21.8	0 28.3	27 45.0	8 58.6	6 34.1	5 58.7
29 Th	8 27 40	6 09 57	4♊32 39	11♊36 48	11 30.7	22 15.7	2 26.1	8 20.2	28 48.8	0 40.7	27 46.2	9 00.9	6 33.5	5 57.3
30 F	8 31 37	7 07 20	18 47 16	26 03 43	11 30.2	24 09.8	3 40.1	8 56.1	29 15.7	0 53.1	27 47.3	9 03.1	6 32.9	5 55.9
31 Sa	8 35 34	8 04 44	3♋25 36	10♋52 13	11 29.8	26 06.3	4 54.0	9 32.1	29 42.7	1 05.6	27 48.4	9 05.3	6 32.2	5 54.5

August 2027 LONGITUDE

Day	Sid.Time	☉	0 hr ☽	Noon☽	True☊	☿	♀	♂	⚳	♃	♄	♅	♆	♇
1 Su	8 39 30	9♌02 09	18♋22 42	25♋56 04	11♒29.6	28♋05.0	6♌08.0	10♎08.3	0♍09.7	1♍18.1	27♈49.3	9♊07.5	6♈31.5	5♒53.1
2 M	8 43 27	9 59 34	3♌31 13	11♌06 57	11D29.6	0♌05.6	7 22.0	10 44.5	0 36.8	1 30.6	27 50.1	9 09.6	6R30.8	5R51.7
3 Tu	8 47 23	10 57 01	18 42 05	26 15 27	11R29.6	2 07.7	8 36.0	11 20.9	1 03.9	1 43.2	27 50.8	9 11.7	6 30.1	5 50.3
4 W	8 51 20	11 54 28	3♍45 55	11♍12 31	11 29.6	4 10.9	9 50.0	11 57.3	1 31.0	1 55.8	27 51.4	9 13.7	6 29.3	5 48.9
5 Th	8 55 16	12 51 56	18 34 20	25 50 41	11 29.5	6 14.9	11 04.0	12 33.9	1 58.1	2 08.4	27 51.9	9 15.7	6 28.5	5 47.5
6 F	8 59 13	13 49 25	3♎01 00	10♎04 54	11 29.3	8 19.4	12 18.0	13 10.6	2 25.2	2 21.1	27 52.3	9 17.6	6 27.6	5 46.1
7 Sa	9 03 09	14 46 54	17 02 12	23 52 50	11 29.1	10 24.0	13 32.1	13 47.3	2 52.4	2 33.8	27 52.6	9 19.5	6 26.8	5 44.7
8 Su	9 07 06	15 44 25	0♏36 52	7♏14 30	11D28.9	12 28.6	14 46.2	14 24.2	3 19.6	2 46.5	27 52.7	9 21.4	6 25.9	5 43.4
9 M	9 11 03	16 41 56	13 46 03	20 11 51	11 28.8	14 32.9	16 00.3	15 01.2	3 46.8	2 59.3	27R52.8	9 23.2	6 25.0	5 42.0
10 Tu	9 14 59	17 39 28	26 32 22	2♐48 03	11 29.0	16 36.6	17 14.4	15 38.2	4 14.1	3 12.0	27 52.8	9 25.0	6 24.0	5 40.6
11 W	9 18 56	18 37 00	8♐59 23	15 06 53	11 29.5	18 39.6	18 28.5	16 15.4	4 41.3	3 24.8	27 52.7	9 26.7	6 23.1	5 39.3
12 Th	9 22 52	19 34 34	21 11 04	27 12 25	11 30.3	20 41.6	19 42.6	16 52.7	5 08.6	3 37.7	27 52.4	9 28.4	6 22.1	5 37.9
13 F	9 26 49	20 32 09	3♑11 25	9♑08 32	11 31.2	22 42.7	20 56.7	17 30.0	5 35.9	3 50.5	27 52.1	9 30.1	6 21.1	5 36.6
14 Sa	9 30 45	21 29 44	15 04 13	20 58 52	11 32.0	24 42.7	22 10.9	18 07.5	6 03.2	4 03.4	27 51.7	9 31.7	6 20.0	5 35.2
15 Su	9 34 42	22 27 21	26 52 54	2♒46 39	11R32.6	26 41.4	23 25.1	18 45.0	6 30.6	4 16.2	27 51.1	9 33.2	6 19.0	5 33.9
16 M	9 38 38	23 24 59	8♒40 29	14 34 42	11 32.7	28 38.8	24 39.2	19 22.6	6 57.9	4 29.1	27 50.5	9 34.7	6 17.9	5 32.6
17 Tu	9 42 35	24 22 38	20 29 36	26 25 28	11 32.2	0♍35.0	25 53.4	20 00.4	7 25.3	4 42.0	27 49.7	9 36.2	6 16.7	5 31.3
18 W	9 46 32	25 20 18	2♓22 35	8♓21 11	11 31.1	2 29.8	27 07.6	20 38.2	7 52.7	4 55.0	27 48.9	9 37.6	6 15.6	5 30.0
19 Th	9 50 28	26 17 59	14 21 32	20 23 52	11 29.3	4 23.2	28 21.9	21 16.1	8 20.1	5 07.9	27 47.9	9 39.0	6 14.4	5 28.7
20 F	9 54 25	27 15 42	26 28 28	2♈35 34	11 27.1	6 15.2	29 36.1	21 54.1	8 47.6	5 20.9	27 46.8	9 40.3	6 13.2	5 27.4
21 Sa	9 58 21	28 13 27	8♈45 26	14 58 21	11 24.7	8 05.8	0♍50.3	22 32.2	9 15.0	5 33.8	27 45.7	9 41.6	6 12.0	5 26.1
22 Su	10 02 18	29 11 13	21 14 36	27 34 27	11 22.4	9 55.1	2 04.6	23 10.4	9 42.5	5 46.8	27 44.4	9 42.8	6 10.8	5 24.9
23 M	10 06 14	0♍09 01	3♉58 13	10♉26 12	11 20.7	11 42.9	3 18.9	23 48.6	10 09.9	5 59.8	27 43.1	9 44.0	6 09.5	5 23.6
24 Tu	10 10 11	1 06 50	16 58 40	23 35 53	11D19.7	13 29.4	4 33.2	24 27.0	10 37.4	6 12.8	27 41.6	9 45.1	6 08.3	5 22.4
25 W	10 14 07	2 04 42	0♊18 07	7♊05 34	11 19.6	15 14.5	5 47.5	25 05.5	11 04.9	6 25.8	27 40.0	9 46.2	6 07.0	5 21.2
26 Th	10 18 04	3 02 35	13 58 22	20 56 36	11 20.3	16 58.3	7 01.8	25 44.0	11 32.4	6 38.9	27 38.4	9 47.2	6 05.7	5 20.0
27 F	10 22 01	4 00 30	28 00 14	5♋09 10	11 21.6	18 40.7	8 16.2	26 22.7	12 00.0	6 51.9	27 36.6	9 48.2	6 04.3	5 18.8
28 Sa	10 25 57	4 58 27	12♋23 09	19 41 47	11 22.9	20 21.8	9 30.5	27 01.4	12 27.5	7 04.9	27 34.8	9 49.2	6 03.0	5 17.6
29 Su	10 29 54	5 56 25	27 04 32	4♌30 45	11R23.8	22 01.6	10 44.9	27 40.3	12 55.1	7 18.0	27 32.8	9 50.0	6 01.6	5 16.4
30 M	10 33 50	6 54 26	11♌59 36	19 30 11	11 23.7	23 40.1	11 59.3	28 19.2	13 22.7	7 31.0	27 30.7	9 50.9	6 00.2	5 15.3
31 Tu	10 37 47	7 52 28	27 01 28	4♍32 20	11 22.4	25 17.3	13 13.6	28 58.2	13 50.2	7 44.0	27 28.6	9 51.7	5 58.8	5 14.1

Astro Data	Dy Hr Mn
☿ D	4 19:41
☽ 0S	8 20:52
♆ R	9 22:42
♃△♄	11 23:17
♂0S	16 18:50
☽ 0N	23 9:26
☽ 0S	5 5:40
♄ R	9 18:07
☽ 0N	19 15:16
♃⚻♇	20 23:01
♃⚻♆	24 4:22

Planet Ingress	Dy Hr Mn
♀ ♋	3 2:03
☿ ♋	12 13:49
♂ ♎	15 5:42
☉ ♌	23 1:06
♃ ♍	26 4:50
♀ ♌	27 12:32
⚳ ♍	1 3:21
☿ ♌	2 10:54
☿ ♍	17 4:44
♀ ♍	20 19:44
☉ ♍	23 8:15

Last Aspect Dy Hr Mn		☽ Ingress	Dy Hr Mn
30 22:43	♃ □	♊	1 6:57
3 4:06	☿ ☌	♋	3 8:00
5 2:37	♄ □	♌	5 7:41
7 4:12	☿ ⚹	♍	7 7:58
9 7:30	☿ □	♎	9 10:25
11 14:51	☿ △	♏	11 15:56
13 23:10	♂ ⚹	♐	14 0:34
16 7:42	♃ △	♑	16 11:40
18 19:07	♄ □	♒	19 0:17
21 11:19	♃ ☍	♓	21 13:15
23 15:49	♀ △	♈	24 1:11
26 7:45	♀ □	♉	26 10:29
27 21:29	☿ ⚹	♊	28 16:11
30 14:50	♄ ⚹	♋	30 18:26

Last Aspect Dy Hr Mn		☽ Ingress	Dy Hr Mn
1 15:55	☿ ☌	♌	1 18:26
3 14:32	♄ △	♍	3 17:58
4 8:47	♅ □	♎	5 18:56
7 19:06	♄ ☍	♏	7 22:54
9 4:55	☉ □	♐	10 6:37
12 13:20	♄ △	♑	12 17:36
15 1:59	♄ □	♒	15 6:21
17 14:50	♄ ⚹	♓	17 19:13
18 14:33	♅ □	♈	20 6:56
22 15:17	☉ △	♉	22 16:34
23 14:44	☿ △	♊	24 23:28
26 23:22	♄ ⚹	♋	27 3:22
29 0:47	♄ □	♌	29 4:44
31 2:42	♂ ⚹	♍	31 4:45

☽ Phases & Eclipses Dy Hr Mn	
4 3:03	● 11♋57
10 18:40	☽ 18♎18
18 15:46	○ 25♑49
18 16:04	• A 0.001
26 16:56	☾ 3♉30
2 10:06	● 9♌55
2 10:07:50	• T 06'23"
9 4:55	☽ 16♏25
17 7:30	○ 24♒12
17 7:15	• A 0.545
25 2:28	☾ 1♊42
31 17:42	● 8♍06

Astro Data

1 July 2027
Julian Day # 46568
SVP 4♓52'20"
GC 27♐13.4 ⚴ 2♋25.0
Eris 26♈09.3 ⚵ 29♉37.9
⚷ 4♉02.6 ⚶ 26♊16.7
☽ Mean ☊ 13♒13.9

1 August 2027
Julian Day # 46599
SVP 4♓52'14"
GC 27♐13.5 ⚴ 20♋55.4
Eris 26♈11.3R ⚵ 16♊54.0
⚷ 4♉38.9 ⚶ 9♋24.8
☽ Mean ☊ 11♒35.4

LONGITUDE — September 2027

Day	Sid.Time	☉	0 hr ☽	Noon ☽	True ☊	☿	♀	♂	⚳	♃	♄	♅	♆	♇
1 W	10 41 43	8♍50 31	12♍01 43	19♍28 30	11♒19.8	26♍53.3	14♍28.0	29♎37.3	14♍17.8	7♍57.1	27♈26.3	9♊52.4	5♈57.4	5♒13.0
2 Th	10 45 40	9 48 36	26 51 39	4♎10 16	11R16.1	28 28.0	15 42.5	0♏16.5	14 45.4	8 10.1	27R24.0	9 53.1	5R55.9	5R11.9
3 F	10 49 36	10 46 43	11♎23 31	18 30 49	11 11.8	0♎01.4	16 56.9	0 55.8	15 13.0	8 23.2	27 21.6	9 53.7	5 54.5	5 10.8
4 Sa	10 53 33	11 44 51	25 31 40	2♏25 46	11 07.6	1 33.6	18 11.3	1 35.2	15 40.6	8 36.2	27 19.0	9 54.3	5 53.0	5 09.8
5 Su	10 57 29	12 43 00	9♏13 02	15 53 28	11 04.0	3 04.5	19 25.7	2 14.6	16 08.2	8 49.2	27 16.4	9 54.8	5 51.5	5 08.7
6 M	11 01 26	13 41 11	22 27 17	28 54 45	11 01.6	4 34.2	20 40.2	2 54.2	16 35.8	9 02.2	27 13.7	9 55.3	5 50.0	5 07.7
7 Tu	11 05 23	14 39 24	5♐16 17	11♐32 22	11D00.6	6 02.6	21 54.6	3 33.8	17 03.5	9 15.3	27 10.9	9 55.7	5 48.5	5 06.7
8 W	11 09 19	15 37 38	17 43 32	23 50 23	11 00.9	7 29.7	23 09.1	4 13.5	17 31.1	9 28.3	27 08.1	9 56.1	5 47.0	5 05.7
9 Th	11 13 16	16 35 53	29 53 31	5♑53 33	11 02.1	8 55.5	24 23.5	4 53.4	17 58.7	9 41.3	27 05.1	9 56.5	5 45.4	5 04.7
10 F	11 17 12	17 34 10	11♑51 06	17 46 48	11 03.8	10 20.1	25 38.0	5 33.2	18 26.3	9 54.2	27 02.1	9 56.7	5 43.9	5 03.7
11 Sa	11 21 09	18 32 29	23 41 13	29 34 56	11R05.3	11 43.3	26 52.5	6 13.2	18 54.0	10 07.2	26 58.9	9 57.0	5 42.3	5 02.8
12 Su	11 25 05	19 30 49	5♒28 28	11♒22 20	11 05.9	13 05.1	28 06.9	6 53.2	19 21.6	10 20.2	26 55.7	9 57.1	5 40.7	5 01.9
13 M	11 29 02	20 29 11	17 16 58	23 12 48	11 05.1	14 25.6	29 21.4	7 33.4	19 49.2	10 33.1	26 52.5	9 57.3	5 39.1	5 01.0
14 Tu	11 32 58	21 27 34	29 10 12	5♓09 29	11 02.4	15 44.6	0♎35.9	8 13.6	20 16.8	10 46.0	26 49.1	9R57.3	5 37.5	5 00.1
15 W	11 36 55	22 26 00	11♓10 56	17 14 47	10 57.9	17 02.1	1 50.4	8 53.9	20 44.4	10 58.9	26 45.6	9 57.3	5 35.9	4 59.3
16 Th	11 40 52	23 24 27	23 21 13	29 30 24	10 51.6	18 18.1	3 04.9	9 34.2	21 12.1	11 11.8	26 42.1	9 57.3	5 34.3	4 58.4
17 F	11 44 48	24 22 56	5♈42 27	11♈57 28	10 44.1	19 32.5	4 19.4	10 14.7	21 39.7	11 24.7	26 38.5	9 57.2	5 32.7	4 57.6
18 Sa	11 48 45	25 21 26	18 15 29	24 36 36	10 36.1	20 45.3	5 33.9	10 55.2	22 07.3	11 37.5	26 34.9	9 57.1	5 31.0	4 56.8
19 Su	11 52 41	26 20 00	1♉00 49	7♉28 11	10 28.5	21 56.2	6 48.4	11 35.8	22 34.9	11 50.4	26 31.2	9 56.9	5 29.4	4 56.1
20 M	11 56 38	27 18 35	13 58 45	20 32 34	10 22.0	23 05.3	8 02.9	12 16.5	23 02.5	12 03.2	26 27.4	9 56.7	5 27.8	4 55.3
21 Tu	12 00 34	28 17 12	27 09 41	3♊50 11	10 17.4	24 12.5	9 17.4	12 57.3	23 30.1	12 15.9	26 23.5	9 56.4	5 26.1	4 54.6
22 W	12 04 31	29 15 52	10♊34 08	17 21 36	10D14.8	25 17.6	10 31.9	13 38.2	23 57.7	12 28.7	26 19.6	9 56.1	5 24.5	4 53.9
23 Th	12 08 27	0♎14 34	24 12 41	1♋07 26	10 14.1	26 20.4	11 46.5	14 19.1	24 25.3	12 41.4	26 15.6	9 55.7	5 22.8	4 53.3
24 F	12 12 24	1 13 18	8♋05 54	15 08 03	10 14.7	27 20.8	13 01.0	15 00.2	24 52.9	12 54.1	26 11.6	9 55.2	5 21.2	4 52.6
25 Sa	12 16 21	2 12 04	22 13 50	29 23 06	10R15.7	28 18.7	14 15.5	15 41.3	25 20.5	13 06.8	26 07.5	9 54.8	5 19.5	4 52.0
26 Su	12 20 17	3 10 53	6♌35 37	13♌51 02	10 16.0	29 13.8	15 30.1	16 22.5	25 48.1	13 19.5	26 03.3	9 54.2	5 17.8	4 51.4
27 M	12 24 14	4 09 44	21 08 54	28 28 38	10 14.6	0♏06.0	16 44.6	17 03.7	26 15.7	13 32.1	25 59.1	9 53.6	5 16.2	4 50.8
28 Tu	12 28 10	5 08 37	5♍49 34	13♍10 53	10 11.0	0 54.9	17 59.2	17 45.1	26 43.2	13 44.7	25 54.8	9 53.0	5 14.5	4 50.3
29 W	12 32 07	6 07 32	20 31 45	27 51 13	10 04.8	1 40.3	19 13.8	18 26.5	27 10.8	13 57.2	25 50.5	9 52.3	5 12.8	4 49.7
30 Th	12 36 03	7 06 29	5♎08 22	12♎22 19	9 56.6	2 21.9	20 28.3	19 08.1	27 38.3	14 09.7	25 46.1	9 51.6	5 11.2	4 49.2

LONGITUDE — October 2027

Day	Sid.Time	☉	0 hr ☽	Noon ☽	True ☊	☿	♀	♂	⚳	♃	♄	♅	♆	♇
1 F	12 40 00	8♎05 28	19♎32 12	26♎37 17	9♒47.1	2♏59.4	21♎42.9	19♏49.7	28♍05.8	14♍22.2	25♈41.7	9♊50.8	5♈09.5	4♒48.8
2 Sa	12 43 56	9 04 30	3♏36 57	10♏30 43	9R37.5	3 32.4	22 57.5	20 31.3	28 33.4	14 34.6	25R37.3	9R49.9	5R07.8	4R48.3
3 Su	12 47 53	10 03 33	17 18 16	23 59 26	9 28.7	4 00.5	24 12.0	21 13.1	29 00.9	14 47.0	25 32.8	9 49.1	5 06.2	4 47.9
4 M	12 51 50	11 02 38	0♐34 14	7♐02 48	9 21.7	4 23.4	25 26.6	21 54.9	29 28.3	14 59.4	25 28.3	9 48.1	5 04.5	4 47.5
5 Tu	12 55 46	12 01 44	13 25 24	19 42 26	9 16.9	4 40.5	26 41.2	22 36.8	29 55.8	15 11.7	25 23.7	9 47.1	5 02.9	4 47.2
6 W	12 59 43	13 00 53	25 54 21	2♑01 44	9D14.4	4 51.4	27 55.7	23 18.8	0♎23.3	15 23.9	25 19.1	9 46.1	5 01.2	4 46.8
7 Th	13 03 39	14 00 03	8♑05 09	14 05 17	9 13.8	4R55.6	29 10.3	24 00.9	0 50.7	15 36.1	25 14.5	9 45.0	4 59.6	4 46.5
8 F	13 07 36	14 59 15	20 02 47	25 58 21	9 14.2	4 52.8	0♏24.8	24 43.0	1 18.1	15 48.3	25 09.9	9 43.9	4 57.9	4 46.2
9 Sa	13 11 32	15 58 29	1♒52 40	7♒46 25	9R14.6	4 42.4	1 39.4	25 25.2	1 45.5	16 00.4	25 05.2	9 42.8	4 56.3	4 46.0
10 Su	13 15 29	16 57 44	13 40 14	19 34 46	9 14.1	4 24.2	2 54.0	26 07.5	2 12.9	16 12.5	25 00.5	9 41.6	4 54.7	4 45.7
11 M	13 19 25	17 57 02	25 30 35	1♓28 15	9 11.7	3 57.9	4 08.5	26 49.9	2 40.2	16 24.5	24 55.8	9 40.3	4 53.1	4 45.5
12 Tu	13 23 22	18 56 21	7♓28 14	13 30 59	9 06.8	3 23.3	5 23.0	27 32.3	3 07.5	16 36.4	24 51.0	9 39.0	4 51.4	4 45.4
13 W	13 27 19	19 55 42	19 36 52	25 46 10	8 59.2	2 40.5	6 37.6	28 14.8	3 34.8	16 48.4	24 46.3	9 37.6	4 49.8	4 45.2
14 Th	13 31 15	20 55 05	1♈59 07	8♈15 51	8 49.2	1 49.9	7 52.1	28 57.3	4 02.1	17 00.2	24 41.5	9 36.3	4 48.3	4 45.1
15 F	13 35 12	21 54 30	14 36 26	21 00 53	8 37.3	0 52.0	9 06.7	29 40.0	4 29.4	17 12.0	24 36.8	9 34.8	4 46.7	4 45.0
16 Sa	13 39 08	22 53 57	27 29 06	4♉00 58	8 24.7	29♎47.9	10 21.2	0♐22.7	4 56.6	17 23.7	24 32.0	9 33.3	4 45.1	4 44.9
17 Su	13 43 05	23 53 26	10♉36 18	17 14 53	8 12.5	28 38.7	11 35.7	1 05.5	5 23.8	17 35.4	24 27.2	9 31.8	4 43.5	4D44.9
18 M	13 47 01	24 52 57	23 56 28	0♊40 50	8 01.9	27 26.2	12 50.3	1 48.3	5 51.0	17 47.0	24 22.4	9 30.3	4 42.0	4 44.9
19 Tu	13 50 58	25 52 31	7♊27 42	14 16 53	7 53.7	26 12.2	14 04.8	2 31.3	6 18.2	17 58.6	24 17.7	9 28.7	4 40.5	4 44.9
20 W	13 54 54	26 52 06	21 08 11	28 01 26	7 48.4	24 58.7	15 19.3	3 14.3	6 45.3	18 10.1	24 12.9	9 27.0	4 39.0	4 45.0
21 Th	13 58 51	27 51 44	4♋56 30	11♋53 18	7 45.8	23 48.1	16 33.9	3 57.4	7 12.4	18 21.5	24 08.1	9 25.4	4 37.4	4 45.1
22 F	14 02 48	28 51 25	18 51 46	25 51 51	7 45.1	22 42.4	17 48.4	4 40.5	7 39.5	18 32.8	24 03.4	9 23.7	4 36.0	4 45.2
23 Sa	14 06 44	29 51 07	2♌53 31	9♌56 42	7 45.1	21 43.6	19 02.9	5 23.7	8 06.5	18 44.1	23 58.6	9 21.9	4 34.5	4 45.3
24 Su	14 10 41	0♏50 52	17 01 19	24 07 14	7 44.4	20 53.5	20 17.5	6 07.0	8 33.5	18 55.3	23 53.9	9 20.1	4 33.0	4 45.5
25 M	14 14 37	1 50 39	1♍14 14	8♍22 05	7 41.9	20 13.2	21 32.0	6 50.4	9 00.5	19 06.5	23 49.2	9 18.3	4 31.6	4 45.7
26 Tu	14 18 34	2 50 29	15 30 25	22 38 48	7 36.7	19 43.7	22 46.5	7 33.9	9 27.5	19 17.5	23 44.5	9 16.4	4 30.2	4 45.9
27 W	14 22 30	3 50 20	29 46 43	6♎53 35	7 28.5	19 25.5	24 01.0	8 17.4	9 54.4	19 28.5	23 39.8	9 14.5	4 28.7	4 46.1
28 Th	14 26 27	4 50 13	13♎58 48	21 01 43	7 17.6	19D18.8	25 15.6	9 00.9	10 21.3	19 39.5	23 35.1	9 12.6	4 27.3	4 46.4
29 F	14 30 23	5 50 09	28 01 39	4♏58 01	7 05.1	19 23.3	26 30.1	9 44.6	10 48.1	19 50.3	23 30.5	9 10.6	4 26.0	4 46.7
30 Sa	14 34 20	6 50 07	11♏50 14	18 37 51	6 52.2	19 38.7	27 44.6	10 28.3	11 14.9	20 01.0	23 25.9	9 08.6	4 24.6	4 47.1
31 Su	14 38 17	7 50 06	25 20 28	1♐57 51	6 40.1	20 04.2	28 59.2	11 12.1	11 41.7	20 11.7	23 21.3	9 06.6	4 23.3	4 47.4

Astro Data

	Dy Hr Mn
☽0S	1 16:13
☿0S	3 13:08
♃□♅	10 16:42
♅ R	15 9:10
☽0N	15 21:35
♀0S	16 8:38
♃⚻♄	18 8:10
☉0S	23 6:03
☽0S	29 2:33
☿ R	7 14:38
☽0N	13 4:42
♄∠♅	16 2:06
♆⚹♇	16 14:29
♇ D	18 3:51
☽0S	26 10:41

Planet Ingress

	Dy Hr Mn
♂ ♏	2 1:53
☿ ♎	3 11:38
♀ ♎	14 0:26
☉ ♎	23 6:03
☿ ♏	27 9:11
⚳ ♎	5 15:40
♀ ♏	8 4:00
♂ ♐	15 23:15
☿ ♎R	16 7:37
☉ ♏	23 15:34
☿ D	28 14:12
♃⚻⚻	29 3:51

Last Aspect / ☽ Ingress

Last Aspect Dy Hr Mn		☽ Ingress	Dy Hr Mn
2 1:30	☿ ☌	♎	2 5:08
4 3:07	♄ ☍	♏	4 7:45
5 19:07	♀ ⚹	♐	6 14:02
8 18:30	♄ △	♑	9 0:13
11 6:44	♄ □	♒	11 12:51
13 19:21	♄ ⚹	♓	14 1:40
15 23:05	☉ ☍	♈	16 12:57
18 15:41	♄ ☌	♉	18 22:06
21 1:14	☉ △	♊	21 5:07
23 3:36	♄ ⚹	♋	23 10:03
25 10:05	☿ □	♌	25 13:02
27 7:57	♄ △	♍	27 14:29
28 19:50	♂ ⚹	♎	29 15:32

Last Aspect / ☽ Ingress

Last Aspect Dy Hr Mn		☽ Ingress	Dy Hr Mn
1 10:26	♄ ☍	♏	1 17:47
3 6:44	♂ ☌	♐	3 22:57
6 3:03	♀ ⚹	♑	6 8:01
8 10:22	♄ □	♒	8 20:11
11 2:05	♂ □	♓	11 9:03
13 17:05	♂ △	♈	13 20:11
15 18:39	♄ ☌	♉	16 4:38
17 12:37	♃ △	♊	18 10:48
20 9:50	☉ △	♋	20 15:26
22 17:30	☉ □	♌	22 19:04
24 11:38	♄ △	♍	24 21:55
26 12:14	♀ ⚹	♎	27 0:22
28 16:21	♄ ☍	♏	29 3:24
31 6:01	♀ ☌	♐	31 8:25

☽ Phases & Eclipses

Dy Hr Mn	
7 18:32	☽ 14♐55
15 23:05	○ 22♓53
23 10:22	☾ 0♋11
30 2:37	● 6♎43
7 11:49	☽ 14♑00
15 13:48	○ 21♈59
22 17:30	☾ 29♋05
29 13:38	● 5♏54

Astro Data

1 September 2027
Julian Day # 46630
SVP 4♓52'10"
GC 27♐13.5 ⚴ 9♌00.8
Eris 26♈03.5R ⚵ 3♋16.6
⚷ 4♉24.1R ⚶ 21♋56.6
☽ Mean ☊ 9♒56.9

1 October 2027
Julian Day # 46660
SVP 4♓52'07"
GC 27♐13.6 ⚴ 25♌31.6
Eris 25♈48.8R ⚵ 17♋20.1
⚷ 3♉25.9R ⚶ 2♌59.1
☽ Mean ☊ 8♒21.6

November 2027 LONGITUDE

Day	Sid.Time	☉	0 hr ☽	Noon ☽	True ☊	☿	♀	♂	⚳	♃	♄	♅	♆	♇
1 M	14 42 13	8♏50 07	8♐29 51	14♐56 27	6♒30.0	20♎39.1	0♐13.7	11♐56.0	12♎08.4	20♍22.3	23♈16.8	9♊04.5	4♈22.0	4♒47.8
2 Tu	14 46 10	9 50 10	21 17 46	27 34 02	6R 22.5	21 22.6	1 28.2	12 39.9	12 35.1	20 32.8	23R 12.3	9R 02.4	4R 20.7	4 48.2
3 W	14 50 06	10 50 15	3♑45 35	9♑52 50	6 17.8	22 13.8	2 42.7	13 23.9	13 01.8	20 43.2	23 07.9	9 00.3	4 19.4	4 48.7
4 Th	14 54 03	11 50 21	15 56 17	21 56 31	6 15.6	23 11.8	3 57.2	14 08.0	13 28.4	20 53.5	23 03.5	8 58.2	4 18.2	4 49.2
5 F	14 57 59	12 50 29	27 54 08	3♒49 47	6 15.0	24 15.8	5 11.7	14 52.1	13 54.9	21 03.8	22 59.1	8 56.0	4 17.0	4 49.7
6 Sa	15 01 56	13 50 38	9♒44 11	15 38 00	6 15.0	25 25.0	6 26.2	15 36.3	14 21.4	21 13.9	22 54.8	8 53.8	4 15.7	4 50.2
7 Su	15 05 52	14 50 49	21 31 57	27 26 44	6 14.5	26 38.6	7 40.7	16 20.5	14 47.9	21 24.0	22 50.6	8 51.6	4 14.6	4 50.8
8 M	15 09 49	15 51 01	3♓23 02	9♓21 30	6 12.3	27 56.2	8 55.1	17 04.8	15 14.3	21 33.9	22 46.4	8 49.3	4 13.4	4 51.4
9 Tu	15 13 46	16 51 15	15 22 45	21 27 21	6 07.8	29 17.0	10 09.6	17 49.2	15 40.6	21 43.7	22 42.2	8 47.0	4 12.3	4 52.0
10 W	15 17 42	17 51 30	27 35 47	3♈48 31	6 00.6	0♏40.5	11 24.1	18 33.7	16 06.9	21 53.5	22 38.1	8 44.7	4 11.2	4 52.6
11 Th	15 21 39	18 51 47	10♈05 52	16 28 06	5 50.9	2 06.3	12 38.5	19 18.1	16 33.2	22 03.1	22 34.1	8 42.4	4 10.1	4 53.3
12 F	15 25 35	19 52 06	22 55 20	29 27 38	5 39.2	3 34.1	13 52.9	20 02.7	16 59.4	22 12.7	22 30.1	8 40.1	4 09.0	4 54.0
13 Sa	15 29 32	20 52 26	6♉04 55	12♉47 00	5 26.6	5 03.4	15 07.4	20 47.3	17 25.6	22 22.1	22 26.2	8 37.7	4 08.0	4 54.7
14 Su	15 33 28	21 52 47	19 33 34	26 24 16	5 14.4	6 34.1	16 21.8	21 32.0	17 51.7	22 31.5	22 22.4	8 35.3	4 07.0	4 55.5
15 M	15 37 25	22 53 11	3♊18 37	10♊16 07	5 03.8	8 05.7	17 36.2	22 16.7	18 17.7	22 40.7	22 18.6	8 32.9	4 06.0	4 56.3
16 Tu	15 41 21	23 53 36	17 16 14	24 18 24	4 55.6	9 38.3	18 50.6	23 01.5	18 43.7	22 49.8	22 14.9	8 30.5	4 05.1	4 57.1
17 W	15 45 18	24 54 03	1♋22 06	8♋26 50	4 50.3	11 11.4	20 05.0	23 46.4	19 09.6	22 58.8	22 11.2	8 28.1	4 04.2	4 57.9
18 Th	15 49 15	25 54 32	15 32 08	22 37 38	4D 47.7	12 45.1	21 19.4	24 31.3	19 35.5	23 07.7	22 07.7	8 25.6	4 03.3	4 58.8
19 F	15 53 11	26 55 02	29 43 00	6♌48 00	4 47.2	14 19.2	22 33.8	25 16.3	20 01.3	23 16.5	22 04.2	8 23.2	4 02.4	4 59.7
20 Sa	15 57 08	27 55 35	13♌52 25	20 56 07	4R 47.6	15 53.6	23 48.2	26 01.3	20 27.1	23 25.2	22 00.8	8 20.7	4 01.6	5 00.6
21 Su	16 01 04	28 56 09	27 58 59	5♍00 54	4 47.6	17 28.2	25 02.6	26 46.4	20 52.8	23 33.7	21 57.5	8 18.2	4 00.8	5 01.5
22 M	16 05 01	29 56 45	12♍01 49	19 01 36	4 46.0	19 02.9	26 16.9	27 31.6	21 18.4	23 42.2	21 54.2	8 15.7	4 00.0	5 02.5
23 Tu	16 08 57	0♐57 22	26 00 08	2♎57 17	4 42.0	20 37.7	27 31.3	28 16.8	21 43.9	23 50.5	21 51.0	8 13.2	3 59.3	5 03.5
24 W	16 12 54	1 58 02	9♎52 51	16 46 36	4 35.4	22 12.5	28 45.6	29 02.1	22 09.4	23 58.6	21 48.0	8 10.7	3 58.6	5 04.5
25 Th	16 16 50	2 58 42	23 38 15	0♏27 33	4 26.5	23 47.3	29 60.0	29 47.4	22 34.9	24 06.7	21 45.0	8 08.2	3 57.9	5 05.5
26 F	16 20 47	3 59 25	7♏14 10	13 57 46	4 15.9	25 22.2	1♑14.3	0♑32.8	23 00.2	24 14.6	21 42.1	8 05.7	3 57.2	5 06.6
27 Sa	16 24 44	5 00 09	20 38 05	27 14 49	4 04.9	26 56.9	2 28.6	1 18.3	23 25.5	24 22.4	21 39.2	8 03.2	3 56.6	5 07.7
28 Su	16 28 40	6 00 54	3♐47 44	10♐16 39	3 54.6	28 31.6	3 43.0	2 03.8	23 50.7	24 30.1	21 36.5	8 00.6	3 56.0	5 08.8
29 M	16 32 37	7 01 41	16 41 27	23 02 07	3 45.9	0♐06.3	4 57.3	2 49.3	24 15.8	24 37.6	21 33.9	7 58.1	3 55.5	5 09.9
30 Tu	16 36 33	8 02 29	29 18 39	5♑31 11	3 39.5	1 40.8	6 11.6	3 34.9	24 40.9	24 45.0	21 31.4	7 55.6	3 55.0	5 11.1

December 2027 LONGITUDE

Day	Sid.Time	☉	0 hr ☽	Noon ☽	True ☊	☿	♀	♂	⚳	♃	♄	♅	♆	♇
1 W	16 40 30	9♐03 18	11♑39 55	17♑45 08	3♒35.7	3♐15.3	7♑25.8	4♑20.6	25♎05.9	24♍52.2	21♈28.9	7♊53.1	3♈54.5	5♒12.3
2 Th	16 44 26	10 04 08	23 47 10	29 46 28	3D 34.2	4 49.7	8 40.1	5 06.3	25 30.8	24 59.3	21R 26.6	7R 50.5	3R 54.0	5 13.5
3 F	16 48 23	11 04 59	5♒43 28	11♒38 45	3 34.4	6 24.1	9 54.4	5 52.1	25 55.6	25 06.3	21 24.3	7 48.0	3 53.6	5 14.7
4 Sa	16 52 19	12 05 51	17 32 51	23 26 25	3 35.6	7 58.4	11 08.6	6 37.9	26 20.3	25 13.1	21 22.2	7 45.5	3 53.2	5 16.0
5 Su	16 56 16	13 06 43	29 20 05	5♓14 31	3R 36.7	9 32.7	12 22.8	7 23.7	26 44.9	25 19.8	21 20.1	7 42.9	3 52.8	5 17.3
6 M	17 00 13	14 07 36	11♓10 23	17 08 23	3 37.0	11 06.9	13 37.0	8 09.7	27 09.5	25 26.4	21 18.2	7 40.4	3 52.5	5 18.6
7 Tu	17 04 09	15 08 31	23 09 09	29 13 22	3 35.7	12 41.1	14 51.2	8 55.6	27 33.9	25 32.7	21 16.3	7 37.9	3 52.2	5 19.9
8 W	17 08 06	16 09 25	5♈21 37	11♈34 29	3 32.4	14 15.3	16 05.3	9 41.6	27 58.3	25 39.0	21 14.6	7 35.4	3 52.0	5 21.2
9 Th	17 12 02	17 10 21	17 52 27	24 15 56	3 27.2	15 49.5	17 19.4	10 27.6	28 22.6	25 45.1	21 12.9	7 32.9	3 51.8	5 22.6
10 F	17 15 59	18 11 17	0♉45 17	7♉20 41	3 20.4	17 23.7	18 33.6	11 13.7	28 46.7	25 51.0	21 11.4	7 30.5	3 51.6	5 24.0
11 Sa	17 19 55	19 12 15	14 02 13	20 49 50	3 12.8	18 57.9	19 47.6	11 59.9	29 10.8	25 56.8	21 10.0	7 28.0	3 51.4	5 25.4
12 Su	17 23 52	20 13 12	27 43 20	4♊42 23	3 05.2	20 32.3	21 01.7	12 46.0	29 34.8	26 02.4	21 08.7	7 25.5	3 51.3	5 26.8
13 M	17 27 48	21 14 11	11♊46 30	18 55 04	2 58.6	22 06.6	22 15.7	13 32.3	29 58.7	26 07.9	21 07.5	7 23.1	3 51.2	5 28.2
14 Tu	17 31 45	22 15 11	26 07 24	3♋22 43	2 53.7	23 41.1	23 29.7	14 18.5	0♏22.5	26 13.2	21 06.3	7 20.7	3D 51.2	5 29.7
15 W	17 35 42	23 16 11	10♋40 10	17 58 55	2 50.8	25 15.6	24 43.7	15 04.8	0 46.2	26 18.3	21 05.3	7 18.3	3 51.2	5 31.2
16 Th	17 39 38	24 17 12	25 18 09	2♌37 04	2D 49.9	26 50.3	25 57.7	15 51.2	1 09.8	26 23.3	21 04.5	7 15.9	3 51.2	5 32.7
17 F	17 43 35	25 18 14	9♌54 59	17 11 15	2 50.5	28 25.1	27 11.6	16 37.6	1 33.3	26 28.1	21 03.7	7 13.5	3 51.2	5 34.2
18 Sa	17 47 31	26 19 17	24 25 22	1♍36 53	2 51.9	0♑00.1	28 25.5	17 24.0	1 56.6	26 32.8	21 03.0	7 11.1	3 51.3	5 35.7
19 Su	17 51 28	27 20 21	8♍45 29	15 50 54	2R 53.3	1 35.1	29 39.4	18 10.5	2 19.9	26 37.2	21 02.4	7 08.8	3 51.4	5 37.2
20 M	17 55 24	28 21 26	22 52 59	29 51 39	2 53.8	3 10.4	0♒53.3	18 57.0	2 43.1	26 41.6	21 02.0	7 06.5	3 51.6	5 38.8
21 Tu	17 59 21	29 22 31	6♎46 49	13♎38 29	2 52.9	4 45.8	2 07.1	19 43.5	3 06.1	26 45.7	21 01.6	7 04.2	3 51.8	5 40.4
22 W	18 03 17	0♑23 38	20 26 41	27 11 26	2 50.3	6 21.4	3 20.9	20 30.1	3 29.0	26 49.7	21 01.4	7 01.9	3 52.0	5 42.0
23 Th	18 07 14	1 24 45	3♏52 46	10♏30 43	2 46.4	7 57.2	4 34.7	21 16.8	3 51.8	26 53.4	21D 01.3	6 59.6	3 52.3	5 43.6
24 F	18 11 11	2 25 53	17 05 21	23 36 39	2 41.5	9 33.1	5 48.4	22 03.4	4 14.5	26 57.1	21 01.2	6 57.4	3 52.6	5 45.2
25 Sa	18 15 07	3 27 01	0♐04 41	6♐29 28	2 36.2	11 09.2	7 02.1	22 50.2	4 37.1	27 00.5	21 01.3	6 55.2	3 52.9	5 46.9
26 Su	18 19 04	4 28 10	12 51 02	19 09 25	2 31.3	12 45.5	8 15.8	23 36.9	4 59.5	27 03.8	21 01.6	6 53.1	3 53.3	5 48.5
27 M	18 23 00	5 29 20	25 24 41	1♑36 53	2 27.2	14 21.8	9 29.4	24 23.7	5 21.8	27 06.8	21 01.9	6 50.9	3 53.7	5 50.2
28 Tu	18 26 57	6 30 29	7♑46 09	13 52 36	2 24.5	15 58.4	10 43.0	25 10.5	5 44.0	27 09.7	21 02.3	6 48.8	3 54.1	5 51.9
29 W	18 30 53	7 31 39	19 56 23	25 57 44	2D 23.1	17 35.0	11 56.6	25 57.4	6 06.1	27 12.5	21 02.9	6 46.7	3 54.6	5 53.6
30 Th	18 34 50	8 32 49	1♒56 53	7♒54 08	2 23.0	19 11.6	13 10.1	26 44.3	6 28.0	27 15.0	21 03.5	6 44.7	3 55.1	5 55.3
31 F	18 38 47	9 34 00	13 49 48	19 44 16	2 24.0	20 48.3	14 23.6	27 31.2	6 49.7	27 17.3	21 04.3	6 42.6	3 55.6	5 57.0

Astro Data

	Dy Hr Mn
☽ 0N	9 12:23
♃⚻♄	13 19:22
⚳ 0S	16 13:43
☽ 0S	22 16:08
☽ 0N	6 20:03
♆ D	15 9:09
☽ 0S	19 20:46
♄ D	24 2:47

Planet Ingress

		Dy Hr Mn
♀	♐	1 7:36
☿	♏	10 0:27
☉	♐	22 13:17
♀	♑	25 12:01
♂	♑	25 18:39
☿	♐	29 10:25
⚳	♏	13 13:18
☿	♑	18 11:59
♀	♒	19 18:41
☉	♑	22 2:43

Last Aspect / ☽ Ingress

Last Aspect Dy Hr Mn			☽ Ingress	Dy Hr Mn
2 3:41	♄	△	♑	2 16:42
4 14:45	☿	□	♒	5 4:14
7 10:11	☿	△	♓	7 17:10
9 12:33	♃	☍	♈	10 4:40
11 23:17	♄	☌	♉	12 12:59
14 5:08	♃	△	♊	14 18:16
16 9:42	♂	☍	♋	16 21:41
18 17:59	☉	△	♌	19 0:29
21 0:49	☉	□	♍	21 3:26
23 3:28	♂	□	♎	23 6:54
25 11:06	♀	⚹	♏	25 11:11
27 11:23	☿	☌	♐	27 17:02
29 15:04	♃	□	♑	30 1:20

Last Aspect / ☽ Ingress

Last Aspect Dy Hr Mn			☽ Ingress	Dy Hr Mn
2 2:19	♃	△	♒	2 12:27
4 7:48	♄	⚹	♓	5 1:21
7 4:41	♃	☍	♈	7 13:32
9 6:18	♄	☌	♉	9 22:37
11 20:59	♃	△	♊	12 3:56
14 0:05	♃	□	♋	14 6:25
16 1:43	♃	⚹	♌	16 7:42
18 8:58	☿	△	♍	18 9:18
20 9:12	☉	□	♎	20 12:14
22 1:02	♄	☍	♏	22 17:02
24 18:13	♃	⚹	♐	24 23:51
27 3:15	♃	□	♑	27 8:52
29 14:30	♃	△	♒	29 20:05

☽ Phases & Eclipses

Dy Hr Mn		
6 8:01	☽	13♒41
14 3:27	○	21♉31
21 0:49	☾	28♌28
28 3:26	●	5♐39
6 5:23	☽	13♓51
13 16:10	○	21♊25
20 9:12	☾	28♍14
27 20:13	●	5♑50

Astro Data

1 November 2027
Julian Day # 46691
SVP 4♓52'03"
GC 27♐13.7 ⚴ 10♍53.8
Eris 25♈30.4R ⚵ 28♋22.8
⚷ 2♉00.7R ⚶ 12♌20.1
☽ Mean ☊ 6♒43.1

1 December 2027
Julian Day # 46721
SVP 4♓51'58"
GC 27♐13.8 ⚴ 23♍15.9
Eris 25♈14.9R ⚵ 3♌13.2
⚷ 0♉44.9R ⚶ 17♌49.2
☽ Mean ☊ 5♒07.8

LONGITUDE — January 2028

Day	Sid.Time	☉	0 hr ☽	Noon ☽	True☊	☿	♀	♂	⚳	♃	♄	♅	♆	♇
1 Sa	18 42 43	10♑35 10	25♒37 57	1♓31 19	2♒25.6	22♑24.9	15♒37.0	28♑18.1	7♏11.3	27♍19.5	21♈05.2	6♊40.7	3♈56.2	5♒58.8
2 Su	18 46 40	11 36 19	7♓24 52	13 19 08	2 27.4	24 01.3	16 50.4	29 05.1	7 32.8	27 21.4	21 06.2	6R 38.7	3 56.8	6 00.5
3 M	18 50 36	12 37 29	19 14 40	25 12 04	2 28.9	25 37.6	18 03.8	29 52.1	7 54.1	27 23.2	21 07.3	6 36.8	3 57.5	6 02.3
4 Tu	18 54 33	13 38 39	1♈11 55	7♈14 51	2R 29.8	27 13.5	19 17.1	0♒39.1	8 15.3	27 24.8	21 08.5	6 34.9	3 58.2	6 04.1
5 W	18 58 29	14 39 48	13 21 28	19 32 21	2 29.9	28 48.9	20 30.3	1 26.1	8 36.4	27 26.2	21 09.8	6 33.1	3 58.9	6 05.8
6 Th	19 02 26	15 40 57	25 48 06	2♉09 14	2 29.1	0♒23.7	21 43.5	2 13.2	8 57.2	27 27.4	21 11.2	6 31.2	3 59.6	6 07.6
7 F	19 06 22	16 42 05	8♉36 13	15 09 29	2 27.6	1 57.7	22 56.6	3 00.3	9 18.0	27 28.5	21 12.8	6 29.5	4 00.4	6 09.4
8 Sa	19 10 19	17 43 14	21 49 17	28 35 51	2 25.7	3 30.7	24 09.7	3 47.4	9 38.5	27 29.3	21 14.4	6 27.7	4 01.2	6 11.2
9 Su	19 14 16	18 44 21	5♊29 13	12♊29 18	2 23.7	5 02.4	25 22.7	4 34.6	9 58.9	27 29.9	21 16.2	6 26.0	4 02.0	6 13.1
10 M	19 18 12	19 45 29	19 35 49	26 48 21	2 22.0	6 32.4	26 35.6	5 21.8	10 19.2	27 30.4	21 18.0	6 24.4	4 02.9	6 14.9
11 Tu	19 22 09	20 46 36	4♋06 19	11♋28 58	2 20.9	8 00.6	27 48.5	6 08.9	10 39.2	27R 30.7	21 20.0	6 22.8	4 03.8	6 16.7
12 W	19 26 05	21 47 43	18 55 24	26 24 38	2D 20.3	9 26.4	29 01.3	6 56.1	10 59.1	27 30.7	21 22.1	6 21.2	4 04.8	6 18.6
13 Th	19 30 02	22 48 50	3♌55 35	11♌27 09	2 20.4	10 49.3	0♓14.1	7 43.4	11 18.9	27 30.6	21 24.3	6 19.7	4 05.8	6 20.4
14 F	19 33 58	23 49 56	18 58 15	26 27 48	2 20.9	12 08.9	1 26.8	8 30.6	11 38.4	27 30.3	21 26.5	6 18.2	4 06.8	6 22.3
15 Sa	19 37 55	24 51 02	3♍54 51	11♍18 33	2 21.5	13 24.6	2 39.4	9 17.9	11 57.8	27 29.8	21 28.9	6 16.7	4 07.8	6 24.1
16 Su	19 41 51	25 52 08	18 38 09	25 53 05	2 22.2	14 35.6	3 51.9	10 05.2	12 17.0	27 29.1	21 31.4	6 15.3	4 08.9	6 26.0
17 M	19 45 48	26 53 13	3♎02 54	10♎07 19	2 22.7	15 41.3	5 04.4	10 52.5	12 36.1	27 28.2	21 34.0	6 14.0	4 10.0	6 27.9
18 Tu	19 49 45	27 54 18	17 06 11	23 59 26	2R 22.9	16 40.9	6 16.8	11 39.8	12 54.9	27 27.1	21 36.7	6 12.7	4 11.1	6 29.7
19 W	19 53 41	28 55 24	0♏47 09	7♏29 28	2 22.8	17 33.5	7 29.1	12 27.1	13 13.5	27 25.8	21 39.5	6 11.4	4 12.3	6 31.6
20 Th	19 57 38	29 56 29	14 06 37	20 38 51	2 22.7	18 18.2	8 41.3	13 14.5	13 32.0	27 24.4	21 42.4	6 10.2	4 13.5	6 33.5
21 F	20 01 34	0♒57 33	27 06 28	3♐29 47	2 22.5	18 54.2	9 53.5	14 01.9	13 50.2	27 22.7	21 45.4	6 09.0	4 14.7	6 35.4
22 Sa	20 05 31	1 58 38	9♐49 08	16 04 50	2D 22.4	19 20.6	11 05.6	14 49.3	14 08.3	27 20.8	21 48.5	6 07.9	4 15.9	6 37.3
23 Su	20 09 27	2 59 41	22 17 12	28 26 34	2 22.4	19R 36.7	12 17.6	15 36.7	14 26.2	27 18.8	21 51.7	6 06.8	4 17.2	6 39.2
24 M	20 13 24	4 00 45	4♑33 13	10♑37 25	2 22.5	19 41.9	13 29.5	16 24.1	14 43.8	27 16.6	21 55.0	6 05.8	4 18.5	6 41.1
25 Tu	20 17 21	5 01 47	16 39 28	22 39 37	2R 22.7	19 35.7	14 41.3	17 11.5	15 01.2	27 14.1	21 58.4	6 04.8	4 19.9	6 43.0
26 W	20 21 17	6 02 49	28 38 06	4♒35 11	2 22.7	19 18.0	15 53.1	17 58.9	15 18.4	27 11.5	22 01.9	6 03.9	4 21.2	6 44.9
27 Th	20 25 14	7 03 50	10♒31 06	16 26 06	2 22.5	18 49.0	17 04.7	18 46.4	15 35.4	27 08.7	22 05.5	6 03.0	4 22.6	6 46.8
28 F	20 29 10	8 04 50	22 20 26	28 14 22	2 22.1	18 09.0	18 16.3	19 33.8	15 52.2	27 05.8	22 09.2	6 02.2	4 24.1	6 48.7
29 Sa	20 33 07	9 05 49	4♓08 12	10♓02 14	2 21.3	17 19.2	19 27.7	20 21.3	16 08.7	27 02.6	22 13.0	6 01.4	4 25.5	6 50.5
30 Su	20 37 03	10 06 47	15 56 48	21 52 15	2 20.2	16 20.8	20 39.1	21 08.8	16 25.0	26 59.2	22 16.9	6 00.6	4 27.0	6 52.4
31 M	20 41 00	11 07 44	27 48 59	3♈47 24	2 19.0	15 15.4	21 50.3	21 56.2	16 41.1	26 55.7	22 20.8	6 00.0	4 28.5	6 54.3

LONGITUDE — February 2028

Day	Sid.Time	☉	0 hr ☽	Noon ☽	True☊	☿	♀	♂	⚳	♃	♄	♅	♆	♇
1 Tu	20 44 56	12♒08 39	9♈47 56	15♈51 04	2♒17.8	14♒04.9	23♓01.5	22♒43.7	16♏56.9	26♍52.0	22♈24.9	5♊59.3	4♈30.0	6♒56.2
2 W	20 48 53	13 09 34	21 57 16	28 07 03	2R 16.8	12R 51.6	24 12.5	23 31.2	17 12.5	26R 48.1	22 29.0	5R 58.7	4 31.6	6 58.1
3 Th	20 52 49	14 10 27	4♉20 55	10♉39 23	2D 16.4	11 37.5	25 23.4	24 18.7	17 27.9	26 44.1	22 33.2	5 58.2	4 33.2	7 00.0
4 F	20 56 46	15 11 19	17 02 56	23 32 04	2 16.5	10 24.8	26 34.2	25 06.2	17 43.0	26 39.9	22 37.6	5 57.8	4 34.8	7 01.9
5 Sa	21 00 43	16 12 09	0♊07 10	6♊48 38	2 17.2	9 15.3	27 44.8	25 53.6	17 57.8	26 35.5	22 42.0	5 57.3	4 36.4	7 03.7
6 Su	21 04 39	17 12 58	13 36 44	20 31 37	2 18.3	8 10.6	28 55.4	26 41.1	18 12.4	26 30.9	22 46.5	5 57.0	4 38.1	7 05.6
7 M	21 08 36	18 13 46	27 33 22	4♋41 51	2 19.6	7 12.0	0♈05.8	27 28.6	18 26.8	26 26.2	22 51.0	5 56.7	4 39.8	7 07.5
8 Tu	21 12 32	19 14 32	11♋56 48	19 17 46	2R 20.5	6 20.5	1 16.0	28 16.1	18 40.8	26 21.4	22 55.7	5 56.4	4 41.5	7 09.4
9 W	21 16 29	20 15 16	26 44 06	4♌14 58	2 20.8	5 36.8	2 26.1	29 03.5	18 54.7	26 16.4	23 00.5	5 56.2	4 43.2	7 11.2
10 Th	21 20 25	21 16 00	11♌49 23	19 26 13	2 20.2	5 01.2	3 36.1	29 51.0	19 08.2	26 11.2	23 05.3	5 56.0	4 45.0	7 13.1
11 F	21 24 22	22 16 42	27 04 13	4♍42 06	2 18.6	4 33.7	4 45.9	0♓38.5	19 21.5	26 05.8	23 10.2	5 55.9	4 46.7	7 14.9
12 Sa	21 28 19	23 17 22	12♍18 34	19 52 22	2 16.1	4 14.4	5 55.6	1 25.9	19 34.4	26 00.4	23 15.1	5D 55.9	4 48.5	7 16.7
13 Su	21 32 15	24 18 01	27 22 22	4♎47 33	2 13.0	4 03.0	7 05.1	2 13.4	19 47.1	25 54.8	23 20.2	5 55.9	4 50.3	7 18.6
14 M	21 36 12	25 18 40	12♎07 06	19 20 22	2 10.0	3D 59.1	8 14.5	3 00.8	19 59.6	25 49.0	23 25.3	5 55.9	4 52.2	7 20.4
15 Tu	21 40 08	26 19 17	26 26 55	3♏26 29	2 07.5	4 02.5	9 23.7	3 48.3	20 11.7	25 43.1	23 30.5	5 56.0	4 54.0	7 22.2
16 W	21 44 05	27 19 53	10♏19 01	17 04 36	2D 05.9	4 12.5	10 32.8	4 35.7	20 23.5	25 37.1	23 35.8	5 56.2	4 55.9	7 24.0
17 Th	21 48 01	28 20 27	23 43 27	0♐15 54	2 05.5	4 28.9	11 41.7	5 23.1	20 35.1	25 30.9	23 41.2	5 56.4	4 57.8	7 25.8
18 F	21 51 58	29 21 01	6♐42 22	13 03 21	2 06.2	4 51.1	12 50.4	6 10.5	20 46.3	25 24.6	23 46.6	5 56.7	4 59.7	7 27.6
19 Sa	21 55 54	0♓21 34	19 19 20	25 30 52	2 07.8	5 18.8	13 59.0	6 58.0	20 57.2	25 18.2	23 52.1	5 57.0	5 01.6	7 29.4
20 Su	21 59 51	1 22 05	1♑38 30	7♑42 46	2 09.6	5 51.4	15 07.4	7 45.4	21 07.8	25 11.7	23 57.7	5 57.4	5 03.6	7 31.2
21 M	22 03 48	2 22 34	13 44 12	19 43 18	2 11.1	6 28.7	16 15.6	8 32.8	21 18.1	25 05.1	24 03.3	5 57.8	5 05.6	7 32.9
22 Tu	22 07 44	3 23 03	25 40 30	1♒36 17	2R 11.8	7 10.3	17 23.6	9 20.2	21 28.0	24 58.3	24 09.0	5 58.3	5 07.6	7 34.7
23 W	22 11 41	4 23 30	7♒31 02	13 25 07	2 11.1	7 55.8	18 31.5	10 07.5	21 37.7	24 51.5	24 14.8	5 58.8	5 09.6	7 36.4
24 Th	22 15 37	5 23 55	19 18 52	25 12 35	2 08.8	8 44.9	19 39.1	10 54.9	21 46.9	24 44.5	24 20.7	5 59.4	5 11.6	7 38.1
25 F	22 19 34	6 24 18	1♓06 33	7♓01 01	2 04.7	9 37.4	20 46.5	11 42.2	21 55.9	24 37.5	24 26.6	6 00.1	5 13.6	7 39.8
26 Sa	22 23 30	7 24 40	12 56 12	18 52 21	1 59.0	10 33.0	21 53.8	12 29.6	22 04.5	24 30.3	24 32.5	6 00.8	5 15.7	7 41.5
27 Su	22 27 27	8 25 00	24 49 39	0♈48 20	1 52.2	11 31.4	23 00.8	13 16.9	22 12.8	24 23.1	24 38.6	6 01.5	5 17.7	7 43.2
28 M	22 31 23	9 25 19	6♈48 37	12 50 43	1 45.0	12 32.6	24 07.6	14 04.2	22 20.7	24 15.8	24 44.7	6 02.3	5 19.8	7 44.9
29 Tu	22 35 20	10 25 35	18 54 53	25 01 23	1 38.0	13 36.3	25 14.2	14 51.4	22 28.2	24 08.5	24 50.8	6 03.1	5 21.9	7 46.5

Astro Data	Planet Ingress
Dy Hr Mn	Dy Hr Mn
☽0N 3 3:13	♂ ♒ 3 16:03
♄∠♅ 12 6:19	☿ ♒ 6 5:59
♃R 12 8:54	♀ ♓ 13 7:21
♅△♇ 13 6:40	☉ ♒ 20 13:23
☽0S 16 3:34	
☿R 24 11:03	♀ ♈ 7 10:02
☽0N 30 9:50	♂ ♓ 10 16:33
	☉ ♓ 19 3:27
♀0N 8 5:20	
☽0S 12 13:33	
♅D 12 23:51	
☿D 14 12:39	
♃⊼♄ 26 8:01	
☽0N 26 16:08	

Last Aspect	☽ Ingress	Last Aspect	☽ Ingress
Dy Hr Mn	Dy Hr Mn	Dy Hr Mn	Dy Hr Mn
31 14:43 ♄ ⚹	♓ 1 8:54	2 2:27 ♂ ⚹	♉ 2 15:38
3 16:24 ♃ ☍	♈ 3 21:37	4 18:06 ♀ ⚹	♊ 4 23:47
5 15:08 ♄ ☌	♉ 6 7:57	7 3:36 ♀ □	♋ 7 4:08
8 10:03 ♃ △	♊ 8 14:28	8 23:20 ♃ ⚹	♌ 9 5:14
10 13:09 ♃ □	♋ 10 17:16	10 17:46 ♄ △	♍ 11 4:36
12 13:46 ♃ ⚹	♌ 12 17:44	12 21:45 ♃ ☌	♎ 13 4:14
14 3:56 ♄ △	♍ 14 17:41	14 22:51 ☉ △	♏ 15 6:04
16 14:40 ♃ ☌	♎ 16 18:53	17 8:09 ☉ □	♐ 17 11:31
18 19:27 ☉ □	♏ 18 22:36	19 11:36 ♃ □	♑ 19 20:46
21 0:32 ♃ ⚹	♐ 21 5:25	21 22:42 ♃ △	♒ 22 8:45
23 9:48 ♃ □	♑ 23 15:03	24 10:13 ♄ ⚹	♓ 24 21:45
25 21:09 ♃ △	♒ 26 2:45	26 23:14 ♃ ☍	♈ 27 10:23
27 23:33 ♄ ⚹	♓ 28 15:35	29 12:28 ♀ ☌	♉ 29 21:43
30 22:17 ♃ ☍	♈ 31 4:24		

☽ Phases & Eclipses	Astro Data
Dy Hr Mn	1 January 2028
5 1:42 ☽ 14♈14	Julian Day # 46752
12 4:04 ○ 21♋28	SVP 4♓51'52"
12 4:14 ☍ P 0.066	GC 27♐13.8 ⚴ 1♎57.8
18 19:27 ☾ 28♎13	Eris 25♈06.0R ⚵ 29♋57.9R
26 15:14 ● 6♒11	⚷ 0♉03.4R ⚶ 17♌30.7R
26 15:08:59 ✱ A 10'27"	☽ Mean ☊ 3♒29.3
3 19:12 ☽ 14♉29	1 February 2028
10 15:05 ○ 21♌24	Julian Day # 46783
17 8:09 ☾ 28♏11	SVP 4♓51'47"
25 10:39 ● 6♓21	GC 27♐13.9 ⚴ 4♎02.5R
	Eris 25♈07.4 ⚵ 22♋35.0R
	⚷ 0♉15.3 ⚶ 10♌49.4R
	☽ Mean ☊ 1♒50.9

March 2028 LONGITUDE

Day	Sid.Time	☉	0 hr ☽	Noon ☽	True ☊	☿	♀	♂	⚳	♃	♄	♅	♆	♇
1 W	22 39 16	11♓25 50	1♉10 31	7♉22 35	1♒32.2	14♒42.3	26♈20.5	15♓38.7	22♏35.4	24♍01.0	24♈57.0	6♊04.0	5♈24.0	7♒48.2
2 Th	22 43 13	12 26 02	13 37 56	19 56 55	1R 27.9	15 50.5	27 26.6	16 25.9	22 42.3	23R 53.5	25 03.3	6 05.0	5 26.1	7 49.8
3 F	22 47 10	13 26 13	26 19 54	2♊47 18	1D 25.5	17 00.8	28 32.5	17 13.1	22 48.8	23 46.0	25 09.6	6 06.0	5 28.3	7 51.4
4 Sa	22 51 06	14 26 21	9♊19 30	15 56 51	1 24.9	18 13.0	29 38.1	18 00.3	22 54.9	23 38.4	25 16.0	6 07.1	5 30.4	7 53.0
5 Su	22 55 03	15 26 28	22 39 44	29 28 25	1 25.6	19 27.1	0♉43.4	18 47.5	23 00.6	23 30.8	25 22.4	6 08.2	5 32.6	7 54.6
6 M	22 58 59	16 26 32	6♋23 07	13♋24 00	1 26.9	20 42.9	1 48.5	19 34.7	23 06.0	23 23.1	25 28.9	6 09.3	5 34.7	7 56.1
7 Tu	23 02 56	17 26 34	20 31 04	27 44 10	1R 27.8	22 00.4	2 53.3	20 21.8	23 11.0	23 15.4	25 35.5	6 10.5	5 36.9	7 57.7
8 W	23 06 52	18 26 34	5♌03 01	12♌27 07	1 27.4	23 19.6	3 57.8	21 08.9	23 15.6	23 07.6	25 42.0	6 11.8	5 39.1	7 59.2
9 Th	23 10 49	19 26 32	19 55 48	27 28 11	1 24.9	24 40.3	5 02.0	21 55.9	23 19.8	22 59.9	25 48.7	6 13.1	5 41.3	8 00.7
10 F	23 14 45	20 26 27	5♍03 15	12♍39 49	1 20.3	26 02.4	6 05.9	22 43.0	23 23.7	22 52.1	25 55.3	6 14.5	5 43.5	8 02.2
11 Sa	23 18 42	21 26 21	20 16 35	27 52 14	1 13.6	27 26.1	7 09.5	23 30.0	23 27.1	22 44.3	26 02.1	6 15.9	5 45.7	8 03.7
12 Su	23 22 39	22 26 13	5♎25 26	12♎54 57	1 05.6	28 51.2	8 12.8	24 17.0	23 30.2	22 36.5	26 08.8	6 17.3	5 47.9	8 05.1
13 M	23 26 35	23 26 03	20 19 39	27 38 35	0 57.4	0♓17.6	9 15.7	25 03.9	23 32.9	22 28.6	26 15.7	6 18.8	5 50.1	8 06.6
14 Tu	23 30 32	24 25 51	4♏51 00	11♏56 21	0 49.9	1 45.4	10 18.3	25 50.9	23 35.1	22 20.8	26 22.5	6 20.4	5 52.4	8 08.0
15 W	23 34 28	25 25 38	18 54 19	25 44 47	0 44.1	3 14.6	11 20.5	26 37.8	23 37.0	22 13.0	26 29.4	6 21.9	5 54.6	8 09.4
16 Th	23 38 25	26 25 23	2♐27 49	9♐03 39	0 40.4	4 45.0	12 22.4	27 24.7	23 38.5	22 05.3	26 36.4	6 23.6	5 56.9	8 10.8
17 F	23 42 21	27 25 06	15 32 39	21 55 18	0D 38.8	6 16.8	13 24.0	28 11.5	23 39.5	21 57.5	26 43.3	6 25.3	5 59.1	8 12.2
18 Sa	23 46 18	28 24 47	28 12 10	4♑23 50	0 38.8	7 49.9	14 25.1	28 58.4	23 40.2	21 49.8	26 50.4	6 27.0	6 01.4	8 13.5
19 Su	23 50 14	29 24 27	10♑30 58	16 34 13	0 39.6	9 24.2	15 25.9	29 45.2	23R 40.4	21 42.1	26 57.4	6 28.8	6 03.6	8 14.8
20 M	23 54 11	0♈24 05	22 34 15	28 31 44	0R 40.3	10 59.8	16 26.3	0♈31.9	23 40.2	21 34.4	27 04.5	6 30.6	6 05.9	8 16.1
21 Tu	23 58 08	1 23 41	4♒27 16	10♒21 28	0 39.7	12 36.8	17 26.2	1 18.7	23 39.7	21 26.8	27 11.7	6 32.5	6 08.2	8 17.4
22 W	0 02 04	2 23 16	16 14 53	22 08 01	0 37.2	14 15.0	18 25.8	2 05.4	23 38.6	21 19.2	27 18.8	6 34.4	6 10.4	8 18.7
23 Th	0 06 01	3 22 48	28 01 22	3♓55 18	0 32.2	15 54.4	19 24.9	2 52.0	23 37.2	21 11.7	27 26.0	6 36.4	6 12.7	8 19.9
24 F	0 09 57	4 22 19	9♓50 14	15 46 28	0 24.5	17 35.2	20 23.5	3 38.7	23 35.4	21 04.2	27 33.2	6 38.4	6 15.0	8 21.1
25 Sa	0 13 54	5 21 47	21 44 15	27 43 50	0 14.3	19 17.3	21 21.7	4 25.3	23 33.1	20 56.8	27 40.5	6 40.4	6 17.2	8 22.3
26 Su	0 17 50	6 21 14	3♈45 23	9♈49 04	0 02.4	21 00.7	22 19.4	5 11.9	23 30.5	20 49.5	27 47.8	6 42.5	6 19.5	8 23.5
27 M	0 21 47	7 20 38	15 54 59	22 03 14	29♑49.7	22 45.4	23 16.6	5 58.4	23 27.4	20 42.2	27 55.1	6 44.6	6 21.8	8 24.6
28 Tu	0 25 43	8 20 01	28 13 55	4♉27 06	29 37.3	24 31.5	24 13.3	6 44.9	23 23.9	20 35.0	28 02.4	6 46.8	6 24.1	8 25.7
29 W	0 29 40	9 19 21	10♉42 53	17 01 22	29 26.4	26 18.9	25 09.4	7 31.4	23 20.0	20 27.9	28 09.8	6 49.0	6 26.3	8 26.8
30 Th	0 33 37	10 18 39	23 22 39	29 46 54	29 17.8	28 07.7	26 05.0	8 17.8	23 15.7	20 20.9	28 17.2	6 51.2	6 28.6	8 27.9
31 F	0 37 33	11 17 55	6♊14 17	12♊44 59	29 12.0	29 57.8	27 00.0	9 04.2	23 11.0	20 14.0	28 24.6	6 53.5	6 30.9	8 28.9

April 2028 LONGITUDE

Day	Sid.Time	☉	0 hr ☽	Noon ☽	True ☊	☿	♀	♂	⚳	♃	♄	♅	♆	♇
1 Sa	0 41 30	12♈17 09	19♊19 14	25♊57 16	29♑08.9	1♈49.3	27♉54.4	9♈50.5	23♏05.9	20♍07.2	28♈32.1	6♊55.9	6♈33.1	8♒30.0
2 Su	0 45 26	13 16 20	2♋39 20	9♋25 40	29D 07.9	3 42.2	28 48.2	10 36.8	23R 00.4	20R 00.5	28 39.5	6 58.2	6 35.4	8 31.0
3 M	0 49 23	14 15 29	16 16 31	23 12 02	29R 08.0	5 36.4	29 41.4	11 23.1	22 54.5	19 53.9	28 47.0	7 00.6	6 37.7	8 31.9
4 Tu	0 53 19	15 14 36	0♌12 20	7♌17 28	29 07.8	7 32.1	0♊33.9	12 09.3	22 48.2	19 47.4	28 54.5	7 03.1	6 39.9	8 32.9
5 W	0 57 16	16 13 40	14 27 19	21 41 42	29 06.3	9 29.0	1 25.6	12 55.5	22 41.5	19 41.0	29 02.0	7 05.6	6 42.2	8 33.8
6 Th	1 01 12	17 12 42	29 00 14	6♍22 23	29 02.4	11 27.3	2 16.7	13 41.6	22 34.5	19 34.8	29 09.6	7 08.1	6 44.4	8 34.7
7 F	1 05 09	18 11 42	13♍47 27	21 14 34	28 55.7	13 27.0	3 07.0	14 27.7	22 27.1	19 28.7	29 17.1	7 10.6	6 46.7	8 35.6
8 Sa	1 09 06	19 10 39	28 42 46	6♎10 56	28 46.5	15 27.8	3 56.6	15 13.8	22 19.3	19 22.7	29 24.7	7 13.2	6 48.9	8 36.5
9 Su	1 13 02	20 09 34	13♎37 55	21 02 35	28 35.5	17 29.9	4 45.3	15 59.8	22 11.2	19 16.8	29 32.2	7 15.8	6 51.1	8 37.3
10 M	1 16 59	21 08 28	28 23 48	5♏40 34	28 23.9	19 33.0	5 33.2	16 45.7	22 02.7	19 11.0	29 39.8	7 18.5	6 53.3	8 38.1
11 Tu	1 20 55	22 07 19	12♏52 01	19 57 25	28 13.1	21 37.2	6 20.3	17 31.7	21 53.9	19 05.4	29 47.4	7 21.2	6 55.6	8 38.8
12 W	1 24 52	23 06 09	26 56 16	3♐48 14	28 04.1	23 42.2	7 06.4	18 17.5	21 44.7	19 00.0	29 55.0	7 23.9	6 57.8	8 39.6
13 Th	1 28 48	24 04 57	10♐33 12	17 11 12	27 57.7	25 48.0	7 51.6	19 03.4	21 35.3	18 54.7	0♉02.6	7 26.6	7 00.0	8 40.3
14 F	1 32 45	25 03 43	23 42 27	0♑07 17	27 53.8	27 54.3	8 35.9	19 49.2	21 25.5	18 49.5	0 10.3	7 29.4	7 02.2	8 41.0
15 Sa	1 36 41	26 02 27	6♑26 08	12 39 35	27 52.1	0♉00.9	9 19.2	20 34.9	21 15.4	18 44.5	0 17.9	7 32.2	7 04.3	8 41.7
16 Su	1 40 38	27 01 10	18 48 13	24 52 42	27 51.7	2 07.7	10 01.5	21 20.7	21 05.0	18 39.6	0 25.5	7 35.1	7 06.5	8 42.3
17 M	1 44 35	27 59 51	0♒53 42	6♒51 54	27 51.7	4 14.2	10 42.7	22 06.3	20 54.3	18 34.9	0 33.2	7 38.0	7 08.7	8 42.9
18 Tu	1 48 31	28 58 30	12 48 02	18 42 44	27 50.7	6 20.3	11 22.8	22 51.9	20 43.3	18 30.3	0 40.8	7 40.9	7 10.8	8 43.5
19 W	1 52 28	29 57 08	24 36 41	0♓30 30	27 47.9	8 25.7	12 01.7	23 37.5	20 32.0	18 25.9	0 48.5	7 43.8	7 13.0	8 44.1
20 Th	1 56 24	0♉55 43	6♓24 45	12 20 00	27 42.5	10 29.9	12 39.4	24 23.1	20 20.5	18 21.7	0 56.1	7 46.8	7 15.1	8 44.6
21 F	2 00 21	1 54 17	18 16 43	24 15 20	27 34.3	12 32.8	13 16.0	25 08.5	20 08.8	18 17.6	1 03.8	7 49.7	7 17.2	8 45.1
22 Sa	2 04 17	2 52 50	0♈16 12	6♈19 39	27 23.6	14 33.9	13 51.2	25 54.0	19 56.8	18 13.7	1 11.4	7 52.7	7 19.3	8 45.6
23 Su	2 08 14	3 51 20	12 25 54	18 35 08	27 11.0	16 32.9	14 25.1	26 39.4	19 44.6	18 09.9	1 19.1	7 55.8	7 21.4	8 46.1
24 M	2 12 10	4 49 49	24 47 29	1♉02 59	26 57.5	18 29.6	14 57.6	27 24.7	19 32.3	18 06.4	1 26.7	7 58.9	7 23.5	8 46.5
25 Tu	2 16 07	5 48 16	7♉21 40	13 43 29	26 44.3	20 23.7	15 28.6	28 10.0	19 19.7	18 03.0	1 34.4	8 01.9	7 25.5	8 46.9
26 W	2 20 03	6 46 41	20 08 24	26 36 19	26 32.6	22 14.9	15 58.2	28 55.3	19 07.0	17 59.7	1 42.0	8 05.1	7 27.6	8 47.3
27 Th	2 24 00	7 45 04	3♊07 10	9♊40 51	26 23.3	24 02.9	16 26.2	29 40.5	18 54.1	17 56.7	1 49.6	8 08.2	7 29.6	8 47.6
28 F	2 27 57	8 43 25	16 17 18	22 56 28	26 16.9	25 47.5	16 52.6	0♉25.6	18 41.1	17 53.8	1 57.2	8 11.4	7 31.6	8 47.9
29 Sa	2 31 53	9 41 45	29 38 20	6♋22 54	26 13.3	27 28.6	17 17.4	1 10.7	18 27.9	17 51.1	2 04.9	8 14.5	7 33.6	8 48.2
30 Su	2 35 50	10 40 02	13♋10 10	20 00 13	26D 12.0	29 06.0	17 40.3	1 55.8	18 14.7	17 48.6	2 12.5	8 17.7	7 35.6	8 48.5

Astro Data	Dy Hr Mn	Planet Ingress	Dy Hr Mn	Last Aspect Dy Hr Mn		☽ Ingress Dy Hr Mn	Last Aspect Dy Hr Mn		☽ Ingress Dy Hr Mn	☽ Phases & Eclipses Dy Hr Mn	
♃□♇	9 9:44	♀ ♉	4 20:02	2 19:21	♃ △	♊ 3 6:50	1 16:41	♄ ⚹	♋ 1 19:16	4 9:04	☽ 14♊19
☽0S	11 1:02	☿ ♓	13 7:09	5 4:44	♄ ⚹	♋ 5 12:55	3 21:40	♄ □	♌ 3 23:39	11 1:07	○ 20♍59
⚳R	19 13:48	♂ ♈	19 19:37	7 8:25	♄ □	♌ 7 15:44	6 0:09	♄ △	♍ 6 1:38	17 23:24	☾ 27♐53
☉0N	20 2:18	☉ ♈	20 2:18	9 9:21	♄ △	♍ 9 16:01	7 9:11	♃ ☌	♎ 8 2:04	26 4:32	● 6♈03
♂0N	22 4:40	☊ ♑R	26 16:32	11 4:43	♂ ☍	♎ 11 15:23	10 2:00	♄ ☍	♏ 10 2:38		
☽0N	24 22:23	☿ ♈	31 12:29	13 9:42	♄ ☍	♏ 13 15:54	11 10:32	♃ ⚹	♐ 12 5:20	2 19:17	☽ 13♋34
				15 13:40	♂ △	♐ 15 19:34	14 7:01	☿ △	♑ 14 11:46	9 10:28	○ 20♎06
☿0N	2 20:07	♀ ♊	3 20:29	18 0:47	♂ □	♑ 18 3:28	16 16:38	☉ □	♒ 16 22:13	16 16:38	☾ 27♑13
☽0S	7 11:19	♄ ♉	13 3:41	20 9:02	♄ □	♒ 20 14:58	19 10:46	☉ ⚹	♓ 19 10:58	24 19:48	● 5♉09
☽0N	21 4:50	☿ ♉	15 11:49	22 22:40	♄ ⚹	♓ 23 4:02	21 0:06	♃ ☍	♈ 21 23:28		
		☉ ♉	19 13:11	24 22:33	♃ ☍	♈ 25 16:32	24 4:35	♂ ☌	♉ 24 10:00		
		♂ ♉	27 22:22	27 23:30	♄ ☌	♉ 28 3:25	26 2:35	☿ ☌	♊ 26 18:16		
				30 8:24	☿ ⚹	♊ 30 12:24	28 2:56	♃ □	♋ 29 0:39		

Astro Data

1 March 2028
Julian Day # 46812
SVP 4♓51'44"
GC 27♐14.0 ⚴ 28♍21.1R
Eris 25♈17.7 ⚵ 20♋11.2
⚷ 1♉13.1 ⚶ 4♌24.3R
☽ Mean ☊ 0♒18.7

1 April 2028
Julian Day # 46843
SVP 4♓51'40"
GC 27♐14.0 ⚴ 18♍53.9R
Eris 25♈35.5 ⚵ 24♋21.6
⚷ 2♉50.5 ⚶ 3♌45.3
☽ Mean ☊ 28♑40.2

LONGITUDE May 2028

Day	Sid.Time	☉	0 hr ☽	Noon☽	True☊	☿	♀	♂	⚳	♃	♄	♅	♆	♇
1 M	2 39 46	11♉38 17	26♋53 06	3♌48 52	26♑12.0	0♊39.6	18♊01.5	2♉40.8	18♏01.3	17♍46.3	2♉20.1	8♊21.0	7♈37.6	8♒48.7
2 Tu	2 43 43	12 36 30	10♌47 32	17 49 09	26R 12.0	2 09.2	18 20.9	3 25.7	17R 47.9	17R 44.1	2 27.6	8 24.2	7 39.5	8 48.9
3 W	2 47 39	13 34 41	24 53 37	2♍00 51	26 10.9	3 34.7	18 38.3	4 10.6	17 34.4	17 42.1	2 35.2	8 27.5	7 41.5	8 49.1
4 Th	2 51 36	14 32 49	9♍10 36	16 22 34	26 07.6	4 56.0	18 53.7	4 55.4	17 20.9	17 40.4	2 42.7	8 30.8	7 43.4	8 49.2
5 F	2 55 32	15 30 56	23 36 20	0♎51 22	26 01.7	6 13.1	19 07.0	5 40.2	17 07.4	17 38.7	2 50.3	8 34.0	7 45.3	8 49.3
6 Sa	2 59 29	16 29 01	8♎07 00	15 22 32	25 53.5	7 25.9	19 18.2	6 25.0	16 53.9	17 37.3	2 57.8	8 37.4	7 47.1	8 49.4
7 Su	3 03 26	17 27 04	22 37 10	29 50 03	25 43.6	8 34.3	19 27.3	7 09.6	16 40.3	17 36.1	3 05.3	8 40.7	7 49.0	8 49.5
8 M	3 07 22	18 25 06	7♏00 24	14♏07 24	25 33.1	9 38.2	19 34.1	7 54.3	16 26.8	17 35.0	3 12.8	8 44.0	7 50.8	8R 49.5
9 Tu	3 11 19	19 23 05	21 10 19	28 08 33	25 23.2	10 37.7	19 38.7	8 38.8	16 13.4	17 34.1	3 20.2	8 47.4	7 52.7	8 49.5
10 W	3 15 15	20 21 04	5♐01 34	11♐49 00	25 14.9	11 32.5	19R 41.0	9 23.4	15 59.9	17 33.4	3 27.7	8 50.8	7 54.5	8 49.5
11 Th	3 19 12	21 19 01	18 30 39	25 06 24	25 08.8	12 22.6	19 40.9	10 07.9	15 46.6	17 32.9	3 35.1	8 54.2	7 56.3	8 49.5
12 F	3 23 08	22 16 56	1♑36 19	8♑00 34	25 05.2	13 08.1	19 38.4	10 52.3	15 33.3	17 32.6	3 42.5	8 57.6	7 58.0	8 49.4
13 Sa	3 27 05	23 14 50	14 19 28	20 33 23	25D 03.8	13 48.8	19 33.5	11 36.7	15 20.2	17D 32.4	3 49.9	9 01.0	7 59.8	8 49.3
14 Su	3 31 02	24 12 43	26 42 48	2♒48 16	25 03.9	14 24.7	19 26.2	12 21.0	15 07.1	17 32.5	3 57.3	9 04.4	8 01.5	8 49.2
15 M	3 34 58	25 10 34	8♒50 21	14 49 41	25R 04.7	14 55.7	19 16.5	13 05.2	14 54.2	17 32.7	4 04.6	9 07.9	8 03.2	8 49.0
16 Tu	3 38 55	26 08 25	20 46 56	26 42 45	25 05.1	15 21.8	19 04.3	13 49.5	14 41.4	17 33.1	4 11.9	9 11.3	8 04.8	8 48.8
17 W	3 42 51	27 06 14	2♓37 48	8♓32 44	25 04.3	15 43.0	18 49.8	14 33.6	14 28.8	17 33.6	4 19.2	9 14.8	8 06.5	8 48.6
18 Th	3 46 48	28 04 02	14 28 12	20 24 48	25 01.7	15 59.2	18 32.8	15 17.7	14 16.4	17 34.4	4 26.4	9 18.2	8 08.1	8 48.4
19 F	3 50 44	29 01 48	26 23 07	2♈23 41	24 56.9	16 10.6	18 13.6	16 01.8	14 04.1	17 35.3	4 33.6	9 21.7	8 09.7	8 48.1
20 Sa	3 54 41	29 59 34	8♈26 59	14 33 25	24 50.0	16R 17.1	17 52.1	16 45.8	13 52.1	17 36.4	4 40.8	9 25.2	8 11.3	8 47.8
21 Su	3 58 37	0♊57 18	20 43 21	26 57 04	24 41.5	16 18.8	17 28.4	17 29.8	13 40.2	17 37.7	4 48.0	9 28.7	8 12.8	8 47.5
22 M	4 02 34	1 55 01	3♉14 47	9♉36 37	24 32.3	16 15.9	17 02.6	18 13.7	13 28.6	17 39.2	4 55.1	9 32.2	8 14.4	8 47.2
23 Tu	4 06 30	2 52 43	16 02 36	22 32 43	24 23.1	16 08.4	16 34.8	18 57.5	13 17.2	17 40.9	5 02.2	9 35.7	8 15.9	8 46.8
24 W	4 10 27	3 50 24	29 06 53	5♊44 55	24 15.0	15 56.6	16 05.2	19 41.3	13 06.1	17 42.7	5 09.3	9 39.2	8 17.4	8 46.4
25 Th	4 14 24	4 48 04	12♊26 36	19 13 48	24 08.7	15 40.8	15 33.9	20 25.1	12 55.2	17 44.7	5 16.3	9 42.7	8 18.8	8 46.0
26 F	4 18 20	5 45 42	25 59 53	2♋50 54	24 04.6	15 21.1	15 01.1	21 08.8	12 44.7	17 46.9	5 23.3	9 46.3	8 20.2	8 45.6
27 Sa	4 22 17	6 43 20	9♋44 27	16 40 12	24D 02.7	14 58.1	14 26.9	21 52.4	12 34.4	17 49.2	5 30.2	9 49.8	8 21.6	8 45.1
28 Su	4 26 13	7 40 55	23 37 55	0♌37 20	24 02.6	14 32.0	13 51.6	22 36.0	12 24.4	17 51.8	5 37.1	9 53.3	8 23.0	8 44.6
29 M	4 30 10	8 38 30	7♌38 14	14 40 24	24 03.6	14 03.4	13 15.4	23 19.5	12 14.7	17 54.5	5 44.0	9 56.8	8 24.4	8 44.1
30 Tu	4 34 06	9 36 02	21 43 39	28 47 48	24R 04.7	13 32.7	12 38.4	24 03.0	12 05.3	17 57.4	5 50.8	10 00.4	8 25.7	8 43.5
31 W	4 38 03	10 33 34	5♍52 40	12♍58 04	24 05.1	13 00.4	12 00.9	24 46.4	11 56.2	18 00.4	5 57.6	10 03.9	8 27.0	8 43.0

LONGITUDE June 2028

Day	Sid.Time	☉	0 hr ☽	Noon☽	True☊	☿	♀	♂	⚳	♃	♄	♅	♆	♇
1 Th	4 42 00	11♊31 04	20♍03 48	27♍09 36	24♑04.0	12♊27.2	11♊23.2	25♉29.7	11♏47.5	18♍03.6	6♉04.3	10♊07.4	8♈28.2	8♒42.4
2 F	4 45 56	12 28 32	4♎15 12	11♎20 18	24R 01.2	11R 53.6	10R 45.5	26 13.0	11R 39.1	18 07.0	6 11.0	10 10.9	8 29.5	8R 41.8
3 Sa	4 49 53	13 26 00	18 24 31	25 27 28	23 56.7	11 20.1	10 08.1	26 56.2	11 31.0	18 10.5	6 17.7	10 14.5	8 30.7	8 41.1
4 Su	4 53 49	14 23 26	2♏28 44	9♏27 51	23 51.1	10 47.4	9 31.1	27 39.4	11 23.3	18 14.2	6 24.3	10 18.0	8 31.9	8 40.5
5 M	4 57 46	15 20 51	16 24 24	23 17 57	23 45.0	10 16.0	8 54.9	28 22.5	11 16.0	18 18.1	6 30.8	10 21.5	8 33.0	8 39.8
6 Tu	5 01 42	16 18 15	0♐08 04	6♐54 24	23 39.2	9 46.5	8 19.7	29 05.6	11 09.0	18 22.1	6 37.3	10 25.0	8 34.2	8 39.1
7 W	5 05 39	17 15 38	13 36 39	20 14 36	23 34.4	9 19.2	7 45.6	29 48.6	11 02.3	18 26.3	6 43.8	10 28.5	8 35.3	8 38.3
8 Th	5 09 35	18 13 01	26 48 03	3♑16 57	23 31.1	8 54.8	7 13.0	0♊31.6	10 56.1	18 30.7	6 50.2	10 32.0	8 36.3	8 37.6
9 F	5 13 32	19 10 22	9♑41 18	16 01 13	23D 29.5	8 33.6	6 41.8	1 14.5	10 50.2	18 35.2	6 56.6	10 35.5	8 37.4	8 36.8
10 Sa	5 17 29	20 07 43	22 16 51	28 28 28	23 29.3	8 15.9	6 12.5	1 57.3	10 44.6	18 39.9	7 02.9	10 39.0	8 38.4	8 36.0
11 Su	5 21 25	21 05 04	4♒36 23	10♒41 01	23 30.3	8 02.0	5 45.0	2 40.1	10 39.4	18 44.7	7 09.1	10 42.5	8 39.3	8 35.2
12 M	5 25 22	22 02 23	16 42 47	22 42 10	23 32.0	7 52.2	5 19.5	3 22.9	10 34.6	18 49.6	7 15.3	10 46.0	8 40.3	8 34.3
13 Tu	5 29 18	22 59 43	28 39 44	4♓36 02	23 33.6	7D 46.7	4 56.2	4 05.6	10 30.2	18 54.8	7 21.5	10 49.5	8 41.2	8 33.5
14 W	5 33 15	23 57 01	10♓31 39	16 27 12	23R 34.8	7 45.5	4 35.1	4 48.2	10 26.2	19 00.0	7 27.6	10 52.9	8 42.1	8 32.6
15 Th	5 37 11	24 54 20	22 23 17	28 20 30	23 35.0	7 48.9	4 16.2	5 30.8	10 22.5	19 05.4	7 33.6	10 56.4	8 43.0	8 31.7
16 F	5 41 08	25 51 38	4♈19 29	10♈20 48	23 34.0	7 56.9	3 59.7	6 13.3	10 19.2	19 11.0	7 39.6	10 59.8	8 43.8	8 30.8
17 Sa	5 45 04	26 48 55	16 25 00	22 32 38	23 31.9	8 09.4	3 45.6	6 55.8	10 16.3	19 16.7	7 45.5	11 03.3	8 44.6	8 29.8
18 Su	5 49 01	27 46 13	28 44 08	4♉59 57	23 28.9	8 26.6	3 33.9	7 38.2	10 13.8	19 22.6	7 51.3	11 06.7	8 45.3	8 28.9
19 M	5 52 58	28 43 30	11♉20 25	17 45 47	23 25.3	8 48.3	3 24.6	8 20.5	10 11.7	19 28.6	7 57.1	11 10.1	8 46.1	8 27.9
20 Tu	5 56 54	29 40 47	24 16 16	0♊51 57	23 21.6	9 14.6	3 17.7	9 02.9	10 09.9	19 34.7	8 02.8	11 13.5	8 46.8	8 26.9
21 W	6 00 51	0♋38 04	7♊32 48	14 18 43	23 18.4	9 45.4	3 13.2	9 45.1	10 08.6	19 41.0	8 08.5	11 16.9	8 47.4	8 25.9
22 Th	6 04 47	1 35 20	21 09 30	28 04 49	23 16.0	10 20.7	3D 11.0	10 27.3	10 07.6	19 47.4	8 14.1	11 20.3	8 48.1	8 24.8
23 F	6 08 44	2 32 36	5♋04 17	12♋07 26	23D 14.7	11 00.4	3 11.2	11 09.5	10 07.0	19 54.0	8 19.7	11 23.6	8 48.7	8 23.8
24 Sa	6 12 40	3 29 52	19 13 45	26 22 38	23 14.4	11 44.4	3 13.6	11 51.5	10D 06.8	20 00.7	8 25.1	11 27.0	8 49.3	8 22.7
25 Su	6 16 37	4 27 07	3♌33 30	10♌45 45	23 15.0	12 32.7	3 18.3	12 33.6	10 07.0	20 07.5	8 30.5	11 30.3	8 49.8	8 21.6
26 M	6 20 33	5 24 21	17 58 47	25 12 02	23 16.1	13 25.2	3 25.2	13 15.5	10 07.5	20 14.5	8 35.9	11 33.6	8 50.3	8 20.5
27 Tu	6 24 30	6 21 35	2♍24 58	9♍37 06	23 17.3	14 21.8	3 34.2	13 57.5	10 08.4	20 21.6	8 41.1	11 36.9	8 50.8	8 19.4
28 W	6 28 27	7 18 48	16 47 59	23 57 14	23 18.1	15 22.5	3 45.3	14 39.3	10 09.7	20 28.8	8 46.3	11 40.1	8 51.2	8 18.2
29 Th	6 32 23	8 16 01	1♎04 31	8♎09 33	23R 18.5	16 27.2	3 58.5	15 21.1	10 11.4	20 36.1	8 51.4	11 43.4	8 51.6	8 17.1
30 F	6 36 20	9 13 14	15 12 05	22 11 54	23 18.1	17 35.9	4 13.6	16 02.9	10 13.4	20 43.6	8 56.5	11 46.6	8 52.0	8 15.9

Astro Data	Dy Hr Mn
♃⚼♄	4 5:49
☽0S	4 18:48
♇ R	9 9:34
♅△♇	10 3:08
♀ R	10 23:04
♃ D	13 20:01
☽0N	18 11:41
☿ R	21 8:44
☽0S	31 23:59
♆⚹♇	9 4:38
☿ D	14 6:07
☽0N	14 18:57
♀ D	22 22:14
♄□♇	24 3:03
⚳ D	24 13:31

Planet Ingress	Dy Hr Mn
☿ ♊	1 1:43
☉ ♊	20 12:11
♂ ♊	7 18:21
☉ ♋	20 20:03
☽0S	28 5:00
♄ ⊻⊻	29 12:59

Last Aspect Dy Hr Mn		☽ Ingress	Dy Hr Mn
30 8:10	♃ ⚹	♌	1 5:24
2 12:55	♀ ⚹	♍	3 8:37
4 16:15	♀ □	♎	5 10:35
6 18:35	♀ △	♏	7 12:17
8 19:50	☉ ☍	♐	9 15:13
11 2:08	♀ ☍	♑	11 21:01
13 17:40	☉ △	♒	14 6:28
16 10:44	☉ □	♓	16 18:40
19 4:42	☉ ⚹	♈	19 7:14
20 18:16	♀ ⚹	♉	21 17:50
23 5:00	♂ ☌	♊	24 1:36
25 9:25	♃ □	♋	26 7:01
27 21:28	♂ ⚹	♌	28 10:56
30 3:31	♂ □	♍	30 14:02

Last Aspect Dy Hr Mn		☽ Ingress	Dy Hr Mn
1 9:02	♂ △	♎	1 16:48
2 14:04	☉ △	♏	3 19:45
5 21:24	♂ ☍	♐	5 23:46
7 8:42	♃ □	♑	8 5:54
9 16:56	♃ △	♒	10 14:58
12 10:33	☉ △	♓	13 2:42
15 4:29	☉ □	♈	15 15:20
17 20:59	☉ ⚹	♉	18 2:26
19 15:12	♃ △	♊	20 10:26
21 21:30	♃ □	♋	22 15:18
24 1:14	♃ ⚹	♌	24 18:04
25 15:09	☿ ⚹	♍	26 19:59
28 6:07	♃ ☌	♎	28 22:11

☽ Phases & Eclipses Dy Hr Mn	
2 2:27	☽ 12♌13
8 19:50	○ 18♏44
16 10:44	☾ 26♒05
24 8:17	● 3♊41
31 7:38	☽ 10♍23
7 6:10	○ 17♐02
15 4:29	☾ 24♓36
22 18:29	● 1♋51
29 12:12	☽ 8♎16

Astro Data

1 May 2028
Julian Day # 46873
SVP 4♓51'36"
GC 27♐14.1 ⚴ 15♍02.4R
Eris 25♈55.1 ⚵ 2♌38.3
⚷ 4♉40.6 ⚶ 9♌16.8
☽ Mean ☊ 27♑04.9

1 June 2028
Julian Day # 46904
SVP 4♓51'32"
GC 27♐14.2 ⚴ 18♍13.1
Eris 26♈12.7 ⚵ 13♌27.3
⚷ 6♉29.2 ⚶ 19♌07.8
☽ Mean ☊ 25♑26.4

July 2028 LONGITUDE

Day	Sid.Time	☉	0 hr ☽	Noon ☽	True ☊	☿	♀	♂	⚳	♃	♄	♅	♆	♇
1 Sa	6 40 16	10♋10 26	29♎08 49	6♏02 43	23♑17.2	18♊48.5	4♊30.6	16♊44.5	10♏15.8	20♍51.2	9♉01.5	11♊49.8	8♈52.4	8♒14.7
2 Su	6 44 13	11 07 37	12♏53 28	19 40 56	23R 15.9	20 05.0	4 49.5	17 26.2	10 18.5	20 58.9	9 06.4	11 53.0	8 52.7	8R 13.5
3 M	6 48 09	12 04 49	26 25 04	3♐05 47	23 14.4	21 25.3	5 10.2	18 07.7	10 21.7	21 06.8	9 11.2	11 56.2	8 52.9	8 12.3
4 Tu	6 52 06	13 02 00	9♐43 00	16 16 43	23 13.1	22 49.4	5 32.7	18 49.3	10 25.1	21 14.7	9 15.9	11 59.3	8 53.2	8 11.1
5 W	6 56 02	13 59 11	22 46 53	29 13 31	23 12.1	24 17.2	5 56.8	19 30.7	10 28.9	21 22.8	9 20.6	12 02.5	8 53.4	8 09.9
6 Th	6 59 59	14 56 22	5♑36 39	11♑56 19	23D 11.5	25 48.7	6 22.6	20 12.1	10 33.1	21 31.0	9 25.2	12 05.6	8 53.6	8 08.6
7 F	7 03 56	15 53 33	18 12 37	24 25 40	23 11.4	27 23.8	6 49.9	20 53.5	10 37.6	21 39.3	9 29.7	12 08.7	8 53.7	8 07.4
8 Sa	7 07 52	16 50 44	0♒35 38	6♒42 41	23 11.6	29 02.4	7 18.8	21 34.8	10 42.4	21 47.7	9 34.2	12 11.7	8 53.9	8 06.1
9 Su	7 11 49	17 47 56	12 47 05	18 49 04	23 12.0	0♋44.4	7 49.1	22 16.0	10 47.6	21 56.2	9 38.5	12 14.7	8 53.9	8 04.9
10 M	7 15 45	18 45 07	24 48 59	0♓47 10	23 12.5	2 29.8	8 20.8	22 57.2	10 53.1	22 04.8	9 42.8	12 17.7	8 54.0	8 03.6
11 Tu	7 19 42	19 42 19	6♓44 01	12 39 57	23 12.9	4 18.3	8 53.9	23 38.3	10 58.9	22 13.6	9 47.0	12 20.7	8R 54.0	8 02.3
12 W	7 23 38	20 39 32	18 35 26	24 30 57	23 13.2	6 09.9	9 28.3	24 19.4	11 05.1	22 22.4	9 51.1	12 23.7	8 54.0	8 01.0
13 Th	7 27 35	21 36 44	0♈27 00	6♈24 10	23 13.4	8 04.2	10 04.0	25 00.4	11 11.5	22 31.4	9 55.1	12 26.6	8 54.0	7 59.6
14 F	7 31 31	22 33 58	12 22 57	18 23 57	23 13.5	10 01.2	10 40.9	25 41.4	11 18.3	22 40.4	9 59.1	12 29.5	8 53.9	7 58.3
15 Sa	7 35 28	23 31 12	24 27 42	0♉34 48	23 13.5	12 00.6	11 18.9	26 22.3	11 25.4	22 49.6	10 03.0	12 32.4	8 53.8	7 57.0
16 Su	7 39 25	24 28 26	6♉45 46	13 01 06	23 13.5	14 02.1	11 58.1	27 03.2	11 32.8	22 58.9	10 06.7	12 35.2	8 53.6	7 55.6
17 M	7 43 21	25 25 42	19 21 19	25 46 49	23 13.7	16 05.4	12 38.3	27 44.0	11 40.5	23 08.2	10 10.4	12 38.0	8 53.4	7 54.3
18 Tu	7 47 18	26 22 58	2♊17 58	8♊55 02	23 13.9	18 10.3	13 19.6	28 24.8	11 48.5	23 17.7	10 14.0	12 40.8	8 53.2	7 52.9
19 W	7 51 14	27 20 14	15 38 11	22 27 30	23 14.3	20 16.3	14 01.9	29 05.5	11 56.8	23 27.2	10 17.5	12 43.6	8 53.0	7 51.6
20 Th	7 55 11	28 17 32	29 22 54	6♋24 11	23 14.6	22 23.2	14 45.1	29 46.1	12 05.4	23 36.9	10 20.9	12 46.3	8 52.7	7 50.2
21 F	7 59 07	29 14 50	13♋31 02	20 42 56	23R 14.8	24 30.8	15 29.3	0♋26.7	12 14.3	23 46.6	10 24.3	12 49.0	8 52.4	7 48.9
22 Sa	8 03 04	0♌12 08	27 59 18	5♌19 23	23 14.7	26 38.5	16 14.3	1 07.3	12 23.5	23 56.5	10 27.5	12 51.6	8 52.1	7 47.5
23 Su	8 07 01	1 09 27	12♌42 20	20 07 15	23 14.2	28 46.3	17 00.2	1 47.8	12 33.0	24 06.4	10 30.6	12 54.3	8 51.7	7 46.1
24 M	8 10 57	2 06 46	27 33 10	4♍59 08	23 13.4	0♌53.8	17 46.9	2 28.2	12 42.7	24 16.4	10 33.7	12 56.9	8 51.3	7 44.7
25 Tu	8 14 54	3 04 06	12♍24 11	19 47 27	23 12.3	3 00.8	18 34.3	3 08.6	12 52.7	24 26.5	10 36.6	12 59.4	8 50.9	7 43.3
26 W	8 18 50	4 01 27	27 08 08	4♎25 31	23 11.3	5 07.1	19 22.6	3 48.9	13 03.0	24 36.7	10 39.5	13 01.9	8 50.4	7 41.9
27 Th	8 22 47	4 58 47	11♎39 02	18 48 14	23 10.4	7 12.4	20 11.5	4 29.1	13 13.5	24 47.0	10 42.3	13 04.4	8 49.9	7 40.5
28 F	8 26 43	5 56 08	25 52 48	2♏52 30	23D 10.0	9 16.7	21 01.2	5 09.3	13 24.4	24 57.4	10 44.9	13 06.9	8 49.4	7 39.2
29 Sa	8 30 40	6 53 30	9♏47 16	16 37 04	23 10.2	11 19.8	21 51.5	5 49.5	13 35.4	25 07.8	10 47.5	13 09.3	8 48.9	7 37.8
30 Su	8 34 36	7 50 52	23 22 01	0♐02 14	23 10.9	13 21.6	22 42.5	6 29.6	13 46.8	25 18.3	10 50.0	13 11.6	8 48.3	7 36.4
31 M	8 38 33	8 48 15	6♐37 55	13 09 17	23 12.0	15 22.0	23 34.2	7 09.6	13 58.3	25 28.9	10 52.3	13 14.0	8 47.7	7 35.0

August 2028 LONGITUDE

Day	Sid.Time	☉	0 hr ☽	Noon ☽	True ☊	☿	♀	♂	⚳	♃	♄	♅	♆	♇
1 Tu	8 42 30	9♌45 38	19♐36 36	26♐00 06	23♑13.3	17♌21.0	24♊26.4	7♋49.6	14♏10.2	25♍39.6	10♉54.6	13♊16.3	8♈47.0	7♒33.6
2 W	8 46 26	10 43 02	2♑20 03	8♑36 43	23 14.4	19 18.4	25 19.3	8 29.5	14 22.2	25 50.4	10 56.8	13 18.6	8R 46.3	7R 32.2
3 Th	8 50 23	11 40 27	14 50 21	21 01 11	23R 14.9	21 14.4	26 12.7	9 09.4	14 34.5	26 01.2	10 58.9	13 20.8	8 45.6	7 30.8
4 F	8 54 19	12 37 52	27 09 27	3♒15 23	23 14.6	23 08.7	27 06.8	9 49.2	14 47.0	26 12.1	11 00.9	13 23.0	8 44.9	7 29.4
5 Sa	8 58 16	13 35 19	9♒19 12	15 21 06	23 13.3	25 01.6	28 01.3	10 28.9	14 59.8	26 23.1	11 02.7	13 25.1	8 44.1	7 28.1
6 Su	9 02 12	14 32 46	21 21 20	27 20 05	23 11.0	26 52.8	28 56.4	11 08.6	15 12.8	26 34.1	11 04.5	13 27.2	8 43.4	7 26.7
7 M	9 06 09	15 30 15	3♓17 38	9♓14 11	23 07.8	28 42.5	29 52.0	11 48.3	15 26.0	26 45.2	11 06.2	13 29.3	8 42.5	7 25.3
8 Tu	9 10 05	16 27 44	15 10 03	21 05 30	23 04.1	0♍30.6	0♋48.0	12 27.9	15 39.4	26 56.4	11 07.7	13 31.3	8 41.7	7 23.9
9 W	9 14 02	17 25 15	27 00 51	2♈56 27	23 00.1	2 17.1	1 44.6	13 07.4	15 53.1	27 07.6	11 09.2	13 33.3	8 40.8	7 22.6
10 Th	9 17 59	18 22 47	8♈52 42	14 49 59	22 56.5	4 02.1	2 41.6	13 46.9	16 06.9	27 18.9	11 10.6	13 35.2	8 39.9	7 21.2
11 F	9 21 55	19 20 20	20 48 45	26 49 28	22 53.7	5 45.5	3 39.1	14 26.3	16 21.0	27 30.3	11 11.8	13 37.1	8 39.0	7 19.8
12 Sa	9 25 52	20 17 55	2♉52 38	8♉58 46	22D 51.9	7 27.5	4 37.0	15 05.7	16 35.2	27 41.7	11 13.0	13 39.0	8 38.0	7 18.5
13 Su	9 29 48	21 15 31	15 08 23	21 22 02	22 51.3	9 07.9	5 35.3	15 45.0	16 49.7	27 53.2	11 14.1	13 40.8	8 37.1	7 17.1
14 M	9 33 45	22 13 09	27 40 15	4♊03 32	22 51.8	10 46.8	6 34.1	16 24.3	17 04.4	28 04.8	11 15.0	13 42.6	8 36.1	7 15.8
15 Tu	9 37 41	23 10 49	10♊32 23	17 07 14	22 53.1	12 24.2	7 33.2	17 03.5	17 19.2	28 16.4	11 15.9	13 44.3	8 35.0	7 14.5
16 W	9 41 38	24 08 31	23 48 26	0♋36 16	22 54.6	14 00.2	8 32.8	17 42.7	17 34.3	28 28.1	11 16.6	13 46.0	8 34.0	7 13.1
17 Th	9 45 34	25 06 12	7♋30 55	14 32 22	22R 55.8	15 34.6	9 32.7	18 21.8	17 49.5	28 39.8	11 17.2	13 47.6	8 32.9	7 11.8
18 F	9 49 31	26 03 56	21 40 30	28 55 00	22 55.9	17 07.6	10 32.9	19 00.9	18 05.0	28 51.6	11 17.8	13 49.2	8 31.8	7 10.5
19 Sa	9 53 28	27 01 42	6♌15 22	13♌40 53	22 54.5	18 39.1	11 33.6	19 39.9	18 20.6	29 03.5	11 18.2	13 50.8	8 30.7	7 09.2
20 Su	9 57 24	27 59 28	21 10 42	28 43 46	22 51.5	20 09.1	12 34.5	20 18.8	18 36.4	29 15.4	11 18.5	13 52.3	8 29.5	7 08.0
21 M	10 01 21	28 57 17	6♍18 54	13♍54 51	22 47.1	21 37.7	13 35.8	20 57.7	18 52.4	29 27.3	11 18.7	13 53.7	8 28.3	7 06.7
22 Tu	10 05 17	29 55 06	21 30 20	29 04 04	22 41.8	23 04.7	14 37.4	21 36.5	19 08.6	29 39.3	11R 18.8	13 55.1	8 27.1	7 05.4
23 W	10 09 14	0♍52 57	6♎34 53	14♎01 42	22 36.4	24 30.1	15 39.3	22 15.3	19 24.9	29 51.4	11 18.8	13 56.5	8 25.9	7 04.2
24 Th	10 13 10	1 50 49	21 23 37	28 39 55	22 31.8	25 54.1	16 41.5	22 54.0	19 41.4	0♎03.5	11 18.7	13 57.8	8 24.7	7 02.9
25 F	10 17 07	2 48 42	5♏50 05	12♏53 48	22 28.5	27 16.4	17 44.0	23 32.6	19 58.1	0 15.6	11 18.5	13 59.1	8 23.4	7 01.7
26 Sa	10 21 03	3 46 36	19 50 53	26 41 24	22D 26.9	28 37.2	18 46.8	24 11.2	20 15.0	0 27.8	11 18.1	14 00.3	8 22.1	7 00.5
27 Su	10 25 00	4 44 32	3♐25 29	10♐03 25	22 26.8	29 56.3	19 49.8	24 49.7	20 32.0	0 40.0	11 17.7	14 01.4	8 20.8	6 59.3
28 M	10 28 57	5 42 29	16 35 32	23 02 18	22 27.8	1♎13.6	20 53.2	25 28.2	20 49.1	0 52.3	11 17.2	14 02.6	8 19.5	6 58.1
29 Tu	10 32 53	6 40 27	29 24 08	5♑41 32	22 29.2	2 29.3	21 56.8	26 06.6	21 06.4	1 04.6	11 16.5	14 03.6	8 18.1	6 56.9
30 W	10 36 50	7 38 27	11♑55 00	18 04 59	22R 30.1	3 43.1	23 00.7	26 45.0	21 23.9	1 16.9	11 15.8	14 04.6	8 16.8	6 55.8
31 Th	10 40 46	8 36 28	24 11 58	0♒16 22	22 29.9	4 55.1	24 04.8	27 23.3	21 41.5	1 29.3	11 14.9	14 05.6	8 15.4	6 54.6

Astro Data

	Dy Hr Mn
♆ R	11 13:05
☽ 0N	12 2:20
♃♇♇	16 4:44
☽ 0S	25 11:57
♃♇♄	3 5:41
☽ 0N	8 9:27
☽ 0S	21 21:26
♄ R	22 22:18
☿0S	26 4:21

Planet Ingress

		Dy Hr Mn
☿	♋	9 1:39
♂	♋	20 20:11
☉	♌	22 6:55
☿	♌	24 1:52
♀	♋	7 15:27
☿	♍	8 5:11
☉	♍	22 14:02
♃	♎	24 5:09
☿	♎	27 13:09

Last Aspect / ☽ Ingress (July)

Last Aspect Dy Hr Mn			☽ Ingress	Dy Hr Mn
30 3:23	☿	△	♏	1 1:29
2 14:20	♃	⚹	♐	3 6:25
5 1:36	☿	☍	♑	5 13:27
7 6:34	♃	△	♒	7 22:50
9 19:19	♂	△	♓	10 10:25
12 11:35	♂	□	♈	12 23:05
15 3:16	♂	⚹	♉	15 10:52
17 11:18	☉	⚹	♊	17 19:47
20 0:05	♂	☌	♋	20 1:04
22 3:03	☉	☌	♌	22 3:18
23 6:41	♀	⚹	♍	24 3:57
25 19:41	♃	☌	♎	26 4:42
27 14:29	♀	△	♏	28 7:03
30 3:22	♃	⚹	♐	30 11:56

Last Aspect / ☽ Ingress (August)

Last Aspect Dy Hr Mn			☽ Ingress	Dy Hr Mn
1 11:21	♃	□	♑	1 19:34
3 21:55	♃	△	♒	4 5:35
6 15:30	♀	△	♓	6 17:22
9 0:02	♃	☍	♈	9 6:03
10 19:45	☉	△	♉	11 18:18
14 0:36	♃	△	♊	14 4:24
16 8:12	♃	□	♋	16 10:56
18 11:54	♃	⚹	♌	18 13:47
20 10:45	☉	☌	♍	20 14:01
22 12:57	♃	☌	♎	22 13:29
24 2:02	♂	□	♏	24 14:13
26 15:48	☿	⚹	♐	26 17:52
27 19:16	♅	☍	♑	29 1:08
31 5:58	♂	☍	♒	31 11:28

☽ Phases & Eclipses

Dy Hr Mn		
6 18:12	○	15♑11
6 18:21	•	P 0.389
14 20:58	☾	22♈55
22 3:03	●	29♋51
22 2:56:40	•	T 05'10"
28 17:41	☽	6♏10
5 8:11	○	13♒26
13 11:46	☾	21♉15
20 10:45	●	27♌56
27 1:37	☽	4♐19

Astro Data

1 July 2028
Julian Day # 46934
SVP 4♓51'26"
GC 27♐14.2 ⚵ 25♍51.4
Eris 26♈23.4 ⚶ 24♌58.7
⚷ 7♉50.2 ⚴ 1♍05.7
☽ Mean ☊ 23♑51.1

1 August 2028
Julian Day # 46965
SVP 4♓51'21"
GC 27♐14.3 ⚵ 6♎27.3
Eris 26♈25.2R ⚶ 7♍20.6
⚷ 8♉32.5 ⚴ 15♍01.9
☽ Mean ☊ 22♑12.6

LONGITUDE — September 2028

Day	Sid.Time	☉	0 hr ☽	Noon ☽	True ☊	☿	♀	♂	⚳	♃	♄	♅	♆	♇
1 F	10 44 43	9♍34 30	6♒18 36	12♒19 02	22♑27.8	6♎05.1	25♋09.2	28♋01.5	21♏59.3	1♎41.8	11♉14.0	14♊06.5	8♈14.0	6♒53.5
2 Sa	10 48 39	10 32 34	18 17 59	24 15 47	22R 23.6	7 13.0	26 13.8	28 39.7	22 17.2	1 54.2	11R 12.9	14 07.4	8R 12.6	6R 52.4
3 Su	10 52 36	11 30 40	0♓12 42	6♓08 58	22 17.1	8 18.8	27 18.7	29 17.8	22 35.3	2 06.7	11 11.8	14 08.2	8 11.1	6 51.3
4 M	10 56 32	12 28 47	12 04 49	18 00 28	22 08.8	9 22.3	28 23.8	29 55.8	22 53.5	2 19.2	11 10.5	14 09.0	8 09.7	6 50.2
5 Tu	11 00 29	13 26 56	23 56 08	29 51 59	21 59.2	10 23.4	29 29.1	0♌33.8	23 11.8	2 31.8	11 09.1	14 09.7	8 08.2	6 49.1
6 W	11 04 25	14 25 07	5♈48 15	11♈45 09	21 49.2	11 22.0	0♌34.7	1 11.8	23 30.2	2 44.4	11 07.7	14 10.4	8 06.7	6 48.1
7 Th	11 08 22	15 23 19	17 42 54	23 41 48	21 39.7	12 17.9	1 40.5	1 49.7	23 48.8	2 57.0	11 06.1	14 11.0	8 05.2	6 47.1
8 F	11 12 19	16 21 34	29 42 08	5♉44 13	21 31.5	13 10.9	2 46.5	2 27.5	24 07.6	3 09.6	11 04.4	14 11.6	8 03.7	6 46.1
9 Sa	11 16 15	17 19 50	11♉48 24	17 55 07	21 25.3	14 00.9	3 52.7	3 05.3	24 26.4	3 22.3	11 02.7	14 12.1	8 02.2	6 45.1
10 Su	11 20 12	18 18 09	24 04 45	0♊17 48	21 21.4	14 47.6	4 59.2	3 43.0	24 45.4	3 35.0	11 00.8	14 12.6	8 00.6	6 44.1
11 M	11 24 08	19 16 29	6♊34 43	12 56 02	21D 19.6	15 30.8	6 05.8	4 20.7	25 04.5	3 47.8	10 58.8	14 13.0	7 59.1	6 43.1
12 Tu	11 28 05	20 14 52	19 22 13	25 53 48	21 19.6	16 10.2	7 12.7	4 58.3	25 23.7	4 00.5	10 56.7	14 13.4	7 57.5	6 42.2
13 W	11 32 01	21 13 17	2♋31 13	9♋14 53	21R 20.2	16 45.6	8 19.7	5 35.8	25 43.1	4 13.3	10 54.6	14 13.7	7 56.0	6 41.3
14 Th	11 35 58	22 11 44	16 05 08	23 02 13	21 20.6	17 16.7	9 27.0	6 13.3	26 02.6	4 26.1	10 52.3	14 13.9	7 54.4	6 40.4
15 F	11 39 54	23 10 13	0♌06 12	7♌17 01	21 19.6	17 43.2	10 34.4	6 50.7	26 22.2	4 38.9	10 50.0	14 14.1	7 52.8	6 39.5
16 Sa	11 43 51	24 08 45	14 34 25	21 57 55	21 16.4	18 04.6	11 42.0	7 28.1	26 41.9	4 51.8	10 47.5	14 14.3	7 51.2	6 38.7
17 Su	11 47 48	25 07 18	29 26 49	7♍00 13	21 10.6	18 20.7	12 49.8	8 05.3	27 01.7	5 04.6	10 45.0	14 14.4	7 49.6	6 37.9
18 M	11 51 44	26 05 53	14♍36 59	22 15 52	21 02.6	18 31.2	13 57.7	8 42.6	27 21.6	5 17.5	10 42.3	14R 14.5	7 47.9	6 37.1
19 Tu	11 55 41	27 04 30	29 55 26	7♎34 15	20 53.0	18R 35.5	15 05.9	9 19.7	27 41.7	5 30.4	10 39.6	14 14.5	7 46.3	6 36.3
20 W	11 59 37	28 03 10	15♎10 54	22 44 01	20 43.1	18 33.5	16 14.1	9 56.8	28 01.8	5 43.3	10 36.8	14 14.4	7 44.7	6 35.5
21 Th	12 03 34	29 01 50	0♏12 24	7♏35 04	20 34.1	18 24.8	17 22.6	10 33.8	28 22.1	5 56.3	10 33.8	14 14.3	7 43.0	6 34.8
22 F	12 07 30	0♎00 33	14 51 12	22 00 16	20 26.9	18 09.0	18 31.2	11 10.8	28 42.5	6 09.2	10 30.8	14 14.1	7 41.4	6 34.1
23 Sa	12 11 27	0 59 18	29 01 56	5♐56 07	20 22.2	17 46.1	19 40.0	11 47.7	29 02.9	6 22.1	10 27.8	14 13.9	7 39.7	6 33.4
24 Su	12 15 23	1 58 04	12♐42 53	19 22 30	20 19.7	17 15.9	20 48.9	12 24.5	29 23.5	6 35.1	10 24.6	14 13.7	7 38.1	6 32.7
25 M	12 19 20	2 56 52	25 55 20	2♑21 52	20D 19.1	16 38.5	21 57.9	13 01.3	29 44.2	6 48.1	10 21.4	14 13.4	7 36.4	6 32.1
26 Tu	12 23 17	3 55 42	8♑42 40	14 58 20	20R 19.3	15 54.0	23 07.2	13 38.0	0♐05.0	7 01.0	10 18.0	14 13.0	7 34.8	6 31.5
27 W	12 27 13	4 54 33	21 09 27	27 16 41	20 19.2	15 03.0	24 16.5	14 14.6	0 25.8	7 14.0	10 14.6	14 12.6	7 33.1	6 30.9
28 Th	12 31 10	5 53 26	3♒20 37	9♒21 51	20 17.7	14 06.1	25 26.0	14 51.1	0 46.8	7 27.0	10 11.1	14 12.2	7 31.4	6 30.3
29 F	12 35 06	6 52 21	15 20 56	21 18 24	20 13.9	13 04.2	26 35.6	15 27.6	1 07.8	7 40.0	10 07.6	14 11.6	7 29.8	6 29.8
30 Sa	12 39 03	7 51 17	27 14 42	3♓10 18	20 07.3	11 58.6	27 45.4	16 04.0	1 28.9	7 53.0	10 03.9	14 11.1	7 28.1	6 29.2

LONGITUDE — October 2028

Day	Sid.Time	☉	0 hr ☽	Noon ☽	True ☊	☿	♀	♂	⚳	♃	♄	♅	♆	♇
1 Su	12 42 59	8♎50 16	9♓05 32	15♓00 46	19♑57.9	10♎50.7	28♌55.3	16♌40.4	1♐50.1	8♎05.9	10♉00.2	14♊10.5	7♈26.4	6♒28.7
2 M	12 46 56	9 49 16	20 56 16	26 52 18	19R 46.0	9R 42.1	0♍05.4	17 16.6	2 11.4	8 18.9	9R 56.4	14R 09.8	7R 24.8	6R 28.3
3 Tu	12 50 52	10 48 18	2♈49 04	8♈46 44	19 32.4	8 34.6	1 15.6	17 52.8	2 32.8	8 31.9	9 52.6	14 09.1	7 23.1	6 27.8
4 W	12 54 49	11 47 22	14 45 29	20 45 27	19 18.1	7 30.1	2 25.9	18 29.0	2 54.3	8 44.9	9 48.7	14 08.3	7 21.4	6 27.4
5 Th	12 58 46	12 46 29	26 46 47	2♉49 36	19 04.4	6 30.3	3 36.3	19 05.0	3 15.8	8 57.8	9 44.7	14 07.5	7 19.8	6 27.0
6 F	13 02 42	13 45 37	8♉54 04	15 00 21	18 52.4	5 37.0	4 46.9	19 41.0	3 37.5	9 10.8	9 40.7	14 06.7	7 18.1	6 26.7
7 Sa	13 06 39	14 44 48	21 08 38	27 19 11	18 42.9	4 51.7	5 57.6	20 16.9	3 59.2	9 23.8	9 36.6	14 05.8	7 16.5	6 26.3
8 Su	13 10 35	15 44 01	3♊32 13	9♊48 05	18 36.3	4 15.5	7 08.4	20 52.8	4 20.9	9 36.7	9 32.4	14 04.8	7 14.8	6 26.0
9 M	13 14 32	16 43 17	16 07 05	22 29 36	18 32.5	3 49.2	8 19.4	21 28.6	4 42.8	9 49.7	9 28.2	14 03.8	7 13.2	6 25.7
10 Tu	13 18 28	17 42 34	28 56 02	5♋26 48	18D 31.1	3D 33.6	9 30.5	22 04.3	5 04.7	10 02.6	9 23.9	14 02.8	7 11.5	6 25.5
11 W	13 22 25	18 41 54	12♋02 18	18 42 56	18R 30.9	3 28.9	10 41.6	22 39.9	5 26.8	10 15.6	9 19.6	14 01.7	7 09.9	6 25.3
12 Th	13 26 21	19 41 17	25 29 04	2♌21 01	18 30.6	3 34.9	11 52.9	23 15.4	5 48.8	10 28.5	9 15.2	14 00.5	7 08.3	6 25.1
13 F	13 30 18	20 40 41	9♌18 59	16 23 03	18 29.1	3 51.6	13 04.4	23 50.9	6 11.0	10 41.4	9 10.8	13 59.3	7 06.7	6 24.9
14 Sa	13 34 15	21 40 08	23 33 11	0♍49 09	18 25.4	4 18.4	14 15.9	24 26.3	6 33.2	10 54.3	9 06.4	13 58.1	7 05.1	6 24.7
15 Su	13 38 11	22 39 37	8♍10 32	15 36 41	18 18.8	4 54.8	15 27.5	25 01.6	6 55.5	11 07.2	9 01.8	13 56.8	7 03.5	6 24.6
16 M	13 42 08	23 39 09	23 06 47	0♎39 48	18 09.7	5 40.0	16 39.2	25 36.8	7 17.9	11 20.0	8 57.3	13 55.5	7 01.9	6 24.5
17 Tu	13 46 04	24 38 42	8♎14 31	15 49 41	17 58.7	6 33.2	17 51.1	26 12.0	7 40.3	11 32.8	8 52.7	13 54.1	7 00.3	6 24.5
18 W	13 50 01	25 38 18	23 23 53	0♏55 49	17 47.1	7 33.6	19 03.0	26 47.0	8 02.8	11 45.7	8 48.1	13 52.7	6 58.7	6D 24.4
19 Th	13 53 57	26 37 55	8♏24 10	15 47 50	17 36.4	8 40.4	20 15.0	27 22.0	8 25.4	11 58.5	8 43.4	13 51.3	6 57.2	6 24.4
20 F	13 57 54	27 37 35	23 05 49	0♐17 21	17 27.6	9 52.9	21 27.1	27 56.9	8 48.0	12 11.2	8 38.7	13 49.8	6 55.6	6 24.4
21 Sa	14 01 50	28 37 16	7♐21 56	14 19 13	17 21.4	11 10.3	22 39.3	28 31.7	9 10.7	12 24.0	8 34.0	13 48.2	6 54.1	6 24.5
22 Su	14 05 47	29 37 00	21 09 07	27 51 42	17 17.9	12 31.9	23 51.6	29 06.4	9 33.4	12 36.7	8 29.3	13 46.6	6 52.6	6 24.6
23 M	14 09 44	0♏36 45	4♑27 14	10♑56 05	17D 16.6	13 57.0	25 04.0	29 41.0	9 56.2	12 49.4	8 24.5	13 45.0	6 51.1	6 24.7
24 Tu	14 13 40	1 36 31	17 18 45	23 35 48	17R 16.5	15 25.1	26 16.4	0♍15.5	10 19.1	13 02.1	8 19.8	13 43.4	6 49.6	6 24.8
25 W	14 17 37	2 36 20	29 47 50	5♒55 32	17 16.6	16 55.8	27 29.0	0 50.0	10 42.0	13 14.7	8 15.0	13 41.7	6 48.1	6 25.0
26 Th	14 21 33	3 36 10	11♒59 34	18 00 34	17 15.6	18 28.4	28 41.6	1 24.3	11 05.0	13 27.3	8 10.2	13 39.9	6 46.7	6 25.2
27 F	14 25 30	4 36 01	23 59 13	29 56 07	17 12.7	20 02.7	29 54.3	1 58.5	11 28.0	13 39.9	8 05.3	13 38.1	6 45.2	6 25.4
28 Sa	14 29 26	5 35 54	5♓51 53	11♓47 03	17 07.2	21 38.3	1♎07.1	2 32.7	11 51.0	13 52.4	8 00.5	13 36.3	6 43.8	6 25.7
29 Su	14 33 23	6 35 49	17 42 07	23 37 34	16 59.0	23 14.9	2 19.9	3 06.7	12 14.1	14 04.9	7 55.7	13 34.5	6 42.4	6 25.9
30 M	14 37 19	7 35 46	29 33 47	5♈31 07	16 48.4	24 52.4	3 32.9	3 40.7	12 37.3	14 17.3	7 50.8	13 32.6	6 41.0	6 26.3
31 Tu	14 41 16	8 35 44	11♈29 52	17 30 17	16 36.1	26 30.3	4 45.9	4 14.5	13 00.5	14 29.8	7 46.0	13 30.7	6 39.7	6 26.6

Astro Data

	Dy Hr Mn
☽0N	4 15:57
♃0S	5 14:47
☽0S	18 8:22
♅R	19 0:03
☿R	19 16:35
☉0S	22 11:46
♃△♇	24 7:48
♃☍♆	28 19:17
☽0N	1 21:56
♃⚻♄	8 5:56
☿D	11 10:28
☽0S	15 18:39
♇D	19 3:43
♃△♅	27 9:07
☽0N	29 3:52

Planet Ingress

		Dy Hr Mn
♂	♌	4 14:37
♀	♌	5 23:19
☉	♎	22 11:46
⚳	♐	26 6:17
♀	♍	2 10:09
☉	♏	22 21:14
♂	♍	24 1:12
♀	♎	27 13:53

♀0S30 14:06

Last Aspect / ☽ Ingress (September)

Dy Hr Mn		☽ Ingress	Dy Hr Mn
1 15:36	♅ △	♓	2 23:34
5 11:09	♀ △	♈	5 12:16
6 16:53	♅ ⚹	♉	8 0:36
9 10:45	☉ △	♊	10 11:26
12 0:47	☉ □	♋	12 19:27
14 10:27	☉ ⚹	♌	14 23:50
16 5:34	☿ ⚹	♍	17 0:53
18 18:25	☉ ☌	♎	19 0:07
20 5:23	☿ ☌	♏	20 23:40
22 5:37	♀ □	♐	23 1:40
24 14:52	♀ △	♑	25 7:34
26 13:41	☿ □	♒	27 17:22
29 23:51	♀ ☍	♓	30 5:35

Last Aspect / ☽ Ingress (October)

Dy Hr Mn		☽ Ingress	Dy Hr Mn
1 10:18	♅ □	♈	2 18:19
4 7:13	♂ △	♉	5 6:24
6 21:37	♂ □	♊	7 17:11
9 10:00	♂ ⚹	♋	10 1:58
11 11:58	☉ □	♌	12 7:55
14 1:01	♂ ☌	♍	14 10:39
15 11:44	♀ ☌	♎	16 10:57
18 5:07	♂ ⚹	♏	18 10:31
20 7:55	♂ □	♐	20 11:31
22 15:26	☉ ⚹	♑	22 15:52
24 17:43	♀ △	♒	25 0:24
26 13:04	☿ △	♓	27 12:08
28 15:41	♅ □	♈	30 0:53

☽ Phases & Eclipses

Dy Hr Mn		
3 23:49	○	11♓59
12 0:47	☾	19♊48
18 18:25	●	26♍22
25 13:11	☽	3♑00
3 16:26	○	10♈59
11 11:58	☾	18♋42
18 2:58	●	25♎16
25 4:54	☽	2♒19

Astro Data

1 September 2028
Julian Day # 46996
SVP 4♓51'17"
GC 27♐14.4 ⚵ 18♎39.0
Eris 26♈17.2R ⚴ 19♍47.0
⚷ 8♉23.4R ⚶ 0♎01.8
☽ Mean ☊ 20♑34.1

1 October 2028
Julian Day # 47026
SVP 4♓51'14"
GC 27♐14.5 ⚵ 1♏20.3
Eris 26♈02.4R ⚴ 1♎36.2
⚷ 7♉28.4R ⚶ 15♎13.8
☽ Mean ☊ 18♑58.8

November 2028 LONGITUDE

Day	Sid.Time	☉	0 hr ☽	Noon ☽	True ☊	☿	♀	♂	⚳	♃	♄	♅	♆	♇
1 W	14 45 12	9♏35 45	23♈32 34	29♈36 51	16♑23.2	28♎08.7	5♎59.0	4♍48.3	13♐23.8	14♎42.1	7♉41.2	13♊28.7	6♈38.3	6♒26.9
2 Th	14 49 09	10 35 47	5♉43 17	11♉51 55	16R 10.7	29 47.3	7 12.1	5 22.0	13 47.1	14 54.5	7R 36.3	13R 26.7	6R 37.0	6 27.3
3 F	14 53 06	11 35 51	18 02 51	24 16 08	15 59.8	1♏26.0	8 25.3	5 55.5	14 10.4	15 06.8	7 31.5	13 24.7	6 35.7	6 27.8
4 Sa	14 57 02	12 35 57	0♊31 48	6♊49 56	15 51.2	3 04.8	9 38.6	6 29.0	14 33.8	15 19.0	7 26.7	13 22.6	6 34.4	6 28.2
5 Su	15 00 59	13 36 05	13 10 36	19 33 53	15 45.4	4 43.5	10 52.0	7 02.3	14 57.3	15 31.2	7 21.9	13 20.6	6 33.2	6 28.7
6 M	15 04 55	14 36 15	25 59 54	2♋28 50	15 42.3	6 22.1	12 05.5	7 35.6	15 20.7	15 43.4	7 17.1	13 18.4	6 31.9	6 29.2
7 Tu	15 08 52	15 36 26	9♋00 50	15 36 06	15D 41.5	8 00.5	13 19.0	8 08.7	15 44.3	15 55.5	7 12.3	13 16.3	6 30.7	6 29.7
8 W	15 12 48	16 36 40	22 14 52	28 57 21	15 42.0	9 38.8	14 32.5	8 41.7	16 07.8	16 07.6	7 07.6	13 14.1	6 29.5	6 30.3
9 Th	15 16 45	17 36 56	5♌43 46	12♌34 20	15R 42.7	11 16.8	15 46.2	9 14.7	16 31.4	16 19.6	7 02.9	13 11.9	6 28.4	6 30.9
10 F	15 20 42	18 37 14	19 29 11	26 28 24	15 42.5	12 54.5	16 59.9	9 47.5	16 55.0	16 31.6	6 58.2	13 09.7	6 27.2	6 31.5
11 Sa	15 24 38	19 37 34	3♍32 00	10♍39 52	15 40.6	14 31.9	18 13.6	10 20.2	17 18.7	16 43.5	6 53.5	13 07.5	6 26.1	6 32.1
12 Su	15 28 35	20 37 56	17 51 47	25 07 21	15 36.3	16 09.1	19 27.4	10 52.7	17 42.4	16 55.4	6 48.9	13 05.2	6 25.0	6 32.8
13 M	15 32 31	21 38 20	2♎26 04	9♎47 15	15 29.9	17 46.0	20 41.3	11 25.2	18 06.2	17 07.2	6 44.3	13 02.9	6 23.9	6 33.5
14 Tu	15 36 28	22 38 45	17 10 05	24 33 41	15 21.9	19 22.6	21 55.2	11 57.5	18 30.0	17 18.9	6 39.7	13 00.6	6 22.9	6 34.2
15 W	15 40 24	23 39 13	1♏57 01	9♏19 05	15 13.3	20 59.0	23 09.2	12 29.7	18 53.8	17 30.6	6 35.2	12 58.2	6 21.9	6 35.0
16 Th	15 44 21	24 39 42	16 38 49	23 55 16	15 05.2	22 35.0	24 23.3	13 01.8	19 17.6	17 42.2	6 30.7	12 55.9	6 20.9	6 35.8
17 F	15 48 17	25 40 13	1♐07 32	8♐14 51	14 58.5	24 10.8	25 37.3	13 33.7	19 41.5	17 53.7	6 26.3	12 53.5	6 19.9	6 36.6
18 Sa	15 52 14	26 40 45	15 16 36	22 12 20	14 53.9	25 46.3	26 51.5	14 05.5	20 05.4	18 05.2	6 21.9	12 51.1	6 19.0	6 37.4
19 Su	15 56 11	27 41 19	29 01 46	5♑44 48	14D 51.6	27 21.6	28 05.6	14 37.2	20 29.4	18 16.7	6 17.5	12 48.7	6 18.1	6 38.3
20 M	16 00 07	28 41 54	12♑21 27	18 51 53	14 51.3	28 56.7	29 19.8	15 08.7	20 53.3	18 28.0	6 13.2	12 46.2	6 17.2	6 39.1
21 Tu	16 04 04	29 42 31	25 16 26	1♒35 28	14 52.3	0♐31.5	0♏34.1	15 40.1	21 17.3	18 39.3	6 09.0	12 43.8	6 16.4	6 40.1
22 W	16 08 00	0♐43 08	7♒49 30	13 59 03	14 53.8	2 06.2	1 48.4	16 11.4	21 41.4	18 50.5	6 04.8	12 41.3	6 15.6	6 41.0
23 Th	16 11 57	1 43 47	20 04 43	26 07 07	14R 54.9	3 40.6	3 02.7	16 42.5	22 05.4	19 01.7	6 00.7	12 38.9	6 14.8	6 41.9
24 F	16 15 53	2 44 26	2♓06 54	8♓04 42	14 54.9	5 14.9	4 17.1	17 13.4	22 29.5	19 12.7	5 56.7	12 36.4	6 14.0	6 42.9
25 Sa	16 19 50	3 45 07	14 01 09	19 56 54	14 53.2	6 49.0	5 31.5	17 44.2	22 53.6	19 23.7	5 52.7	12 33.9	6 13.3	6 43.9
26 Su	16 23 46	4 45 49	25 52 31	1♈48 35	14 49.8	8 23.0	6 45.9	18 14.9	23 17.7	19 34.6	5 48.7	12 31.4	6 12.6	6 45.0
27 M	16 27 43	5 46 32	7♈45 37	13 44 07	14 44.6	9 56.9	8 00.4	18 45.4	23 41.8	19 45.4	5 44.9	12 28.9	6 11.9	6 46.0
28 Tu	16 31 40	6 47 16	19 44 31	25 47 11	14 38.2	11 30.6	9 14.9	19 15.8	24 05.9	19 56.2	5 41.1	12 26.3	6 11.3	6 47.1
29 W	16 35 36	7 48 01	1♉52 27	8♉00 36	14 31.3	13 04.3	10 29.4	19 45.9	24 30.1	20 06.8	5 37.4	12 23.8	6 10.7	6 48.2
30 Th	16 39 33	8 48 47	14 11 50	20 26 18	14 24.5	14 37.8	11 44.0	20 16.0	24 54.3	20 17.4	5 33.7	12 21.3	6 10.1	6 49.4

December 2028 LONGITUDE

Day	Sid.Time	☉	0 hr ☽	Noon ☽	True ☊	☿	♀	♂	⚳	♃	♄	♅	♆	♇
1 F	16 43 29	9♐49 35	26♉44 06	3♊05 17	14♑18.6	16♐11.3	12♏58.6	20♍45.9	25♐18.5	20♎27.9	5♉30.2	12♊18.7	6♈09.6	6♒50.5
2 Sa	16 47 26	10 50 24	9♊29 50	15 57 44	14R 14.1	17 44.8	14 13.2	21 15.6	25 42.7	20 38.3	5R 26.7	12R 16.2	6R 09.1	6 51.7
3 Su	16 51 22	11 51 13	22 28 54	29 03 13	14 11.4	19 18.2	15 27.9	21 45.1	26 06.9	20 48.6	5 23.3	12 13.7	6 08.6	6 52.9
4 M	16 55 19	12 52 04	5♋40 38	12♋20 59	14D 10.4	20 51.5	16 42.6	22 14.5	26 31.2	20 58.9	5 20.0	12 11.1	6 08.2	6 54.1
5 Tu	16 59 15	13 52 57	19 04 10	25 50 06	14 10.8	22 24.9	17 57.3	22 43.7	26 55.4	21 09.0	5 16.7	12 08.6	6 07.8	6 55.4
6 W	17 03 12	14 53 50	2♌38 40	9♌29 46	14 12.2	23 58.1	19 12.1	23 12.7	27 19.7	21 19.0	5 13.6	12 06.1	6 07.4	6 56.6
7 Th	17 07 09	15 54 45	16 23 20	23 19 16	14 13.8	25 31.4	20 26.8	23 41.5	27 44.0	21 29.0	5 10.5	12 03.5	6 07.0	6 57.9
8 F	17 11 05	16 55 41	0♍17 29	7♍17 53	14R 15.0	27 04.6	21 41.6	24 10.2	28 08.3	21 38.8	5 07.5	12 01.0	6 06.7	6 59.2
9 Sa	17 15 02	17 56 38	14 20 20	21 24 40	14 15.3	28 37.7	22 56.5	24 38.6	28 32.6	21 48.6	5 04.6	11 58.5	6 06.5	7 00.6
10 Su	17 18 58	18 57 36	28 30 41	5♎38 07	14 14.4	0♑10.8	24 11.4	25 06.9	28 56.9	21 58.2	5 01.8	11 55.9	6 06.2	7 01.9
11 M	17 22 55	19 58 35	12♎46 38	19 55 53	14 12.3	1 43.8	25 26.2	25 34.9	29 21.2	22 07.8	4 59.1	11 53.4	6 06.0	7 03.3
12 Tu	17 26 51	20 59 36	27 05 23	4♏14 40	14 09.3	3 16.7	26 41.2	26 02.8	29 45.5	22 17.2	4 56.5	11 50.9	6 05.8	7 04.7
13 W	17 30 48	22 00 38	11♏23 11	18 30 22	14 06.0	4 49.4	27 56.1	26 30.4	0♑09.9	22 26.5	4 54.0	11 48.4	6 05.7	7 06.1
14 Th	17 34 44	23 01 41	25 35 36	2♐38 20	14 02.8	6 21.9	29 11.1	26 57.9	0 34.2	22 35.8	4 51.6	11 45.9	6 05.6	7 07.5
15 F	17 38 41	24 02 44	9♐38 00	16 34 06	14 00.3	7 54.2	0♐26.0	27 25.1	0 58.6	22 44.9	4 49.2	11 43.5	6 05.5	7 09.0
16 Sa	17 42 38	25 03 49	23 26 10	0♑13 51	13 58.7	9 26.2	1 41.0	27 52.0	1 22.9	22 53.9	4 47.0	11 41.0	6D 05.5	7 10.4
17 Su	17 46 34	26 04 54	6♑56 50	13 34 58	13D 58.2	10 57.8	2 56.0	28 18.8	1 47.3	23 02.8	4 44.9	11 38.6	6 05.5	7 11.9
18 M	17 50 31	27 05 59	20 08 09	26 36 22	13 58.6	12 28.9	4 11.1	28 45.3	2 11.7	23 11.5	4 42.9	11 36.1	6 05.6	7 13.4
19 Tu	17 54 27	28 07 05	2♒59 45	9♒18 28	13 59.7	13 59.3	5 26.1	29 11.6	2 36.0	23 20.2	4 41.0	11 33.7	6 05.6	7 15.0
20 W	17 58 24	29 08 12	15 32 49	21 43 07	14 01.1	15 29.1	6 41.1	29 37.6	3 00.4	23 28.7	4 39.2	11 31.3	6 05.7	7 16.5
21 Th	18 02 20	0♑09 18	27 49 49	3♓53 21	14 02.4	16 57.9	7 56.2	0♎03.4	3 24.7	23 37.1	4 37.5	11 28.9	6 05.9	7 18.1
22 F	18 06 17	1 10 25	9♓54 14	15 53 01	14 03.5	18 25.6	9 11.3	0 29.0	3 49.1	23 45.4	4 35.9	11 26.6	6 06.1	7 19.6
23 Sa	18 10 13	2 11 32	21 50 17	27 46 37	14R 04.0	19 52.0	10 26.3	0 54.3	4 13.4	23 53.5	4 34.4	11 24.3	6 06.3	7 21.2
24 Su	18 14 10	3 12 39	3♈42 36	9♈38 52	14 03.9	21 16.8	11 41.4	1 19.3	4 37.8	24 01.6	4 33.0	11 21.9	6 06.5	7 22.8
25 M	18 18 07	4 13 46	15 36 00	21 34 35	14 03.4	22 39.7	12 56.5	1 44.0	5 02.1	24 09.5	4 31.7	11 19.6	6 06.8	7 24.4
26 Tu	18 22 03	5 14 53	27 35 10	3♉38 18	14 02.5	24 00.3	14 11.6	2 08.5	5 26.4	24 17.2	4 30.6	11 17.4	6 07.1	7 26.1
27 W	18 26 00	6 16 01	9♉44 28	15 54 07	14 01.4	25 18.3	15 26.8	2 32.7	5 50.7	24 24.9	4 29.5	11 15.1	6 07.5	7 27.7
28 Th	18 29 56	7 17 08	22 07 38	28 25 20	14 00.4	26 33.1	16 41.9	2 56.6	6 15.1	24 32.4	4 28.6	11 12.9	6 07.9	7 29.4
29 F	18 33 53	8 18 16	4♊47 30	11♊14 18	13 59.6	27 44.3	17 57.0	3 20.3	6 39.4	24 39.7	4 27.7	11 10.7	6 08.3	7 31.1
30 Sa	18 37 49	9 19 24	17 45 49	24 22 05	13 59.0	28 51.2	19 12.2	3 43.6	7 03.7	24 47.0	4 27.0	11 08.6	6 08.7	7 32.8
31 Su	18 41 46	10 20 31	1♋03 01	7♋48 28	13D 58.8	29 53.0	20 27.3	4 06.7	7 27.9	24 54.1	4 26.4	11 06.4	6 09.2	7 34.5

Astro Data	Dy Hr Mn
♆⚹♇	8 1:35
☽0S	12 2:29
♄□♇	15 12:56
♄⚺♆	19 8:01
☽0N	25 10:25
☽0S	9 7:53
♆D	16 20:45
☽0N	22 18:03

Planet Ingress	Dy Hr Mn
☿ ♏	2 15:05
♀ ♏	21 0:59
☿ ♐	21 4:01
☉ ♐	21 18:56
☿ ♑	10 9:13
⚳ ♑	13 2:16
♀ ♐	15 3:40
☉ ♑	21 8:21
♂ ♎	21 8:47
♇ ♒	31 14:50

Last Aspect Dy Hr Mn		☽ Ingress Dy Hr Mn
1 8:39	☿ ☍	♉ 1 12:46
2 9:19	☉ ☍	♊ 3 22:59
5 4:17	♃ △	♋ 6 7:25
7 12:36	♃ □	♌ 8 13:51
9 21:27	☉ □	♍ 10 18:01
12 4:02	☉ ⚹	♎ 12 20:01
14 7:19	♀ ☌	♏ 14 20:50
16 13:19	☉ ☌	♐ 16 22:07
18 20:59	♀ ⚹	♑ 19 1:43
21 8:06	☉ ⚹	♒ 21 8:58
22 21:42	♃ △	♓ 23 19:46
25 7:19	♂ ☍	♈ 26 8:21
28 0:13	♃ ☍	♉ 28 20:19

Last Aspect Dy Hr Mn		☽ Ingress Dy Hr Mn
30 11:39	♂ △	♊ 1 6:11
2 22:08	♂ □	♋ 3 13:43
5 6:18	♂ ⚹	♌ 5 19:21
7 16:16	☿ △	♍ 7 23:30
10 1:41	☿ □	♎ 10 2:31
11 15:44	♃ ☌	♏ 12 4:53
14 5:32	♀ ☌	♐ 14 7:30
16 7:40	♂ □	♑ 16 11:35
18 16:10	♂ △	♒ 18 18:21
21 3:55	☉ ⚹	♓ 21 4:17
22 17:50	☿ ⚹	♈ 23 16:30
25 17:13	♃ ☍	♉ 26 4:48
28 8:04	☿ △	♊ 28 14:59
30 12:45	♃ △	♋ 30 22:07

☽ Phases & Eclipses Dy Hr Mn	
2 9:19	○ 10♉29
9 21:27	☾ 18♌01
16 13:19	● 24♏43
24 0:16	☽ 2♓15
2 1:41	○ 10♊24
9 5:40	☾ 17♍41
16 2:08	● 24♐39
23 21:46	☽ 2♈36
31 16:50	○ 10♋33
31 16:53	☊ T 1.246

Astro Data

1 November 2028
Julian Day # 47057
SVP 4♓51'11"
GC 27♐14.5 ⚴ 14♏55.4
Eris 25♈44.0R ⚵ 13♎15.2
⚷ 6♉03.3R ⚶ 1♏22.5
☽ Mean ☊ 17♑20.3

1 December 2028
Julian Day # 47087
SVP 4♓51'06"
GC 27♐14.6 ⚴ 28♏08.9
Eris 25♈28.5R ⚵ 23♎31.7
⚷ 4♉44.0R ⚶ 17♏09.5
☽ Mean ☊ 15♑45.0

LONGITUDE — January 2029

Day	Sid.Time	☉	0 hr ☽	Noon ☽	True ☊	☿	♀	♂	⚳	♃	♄	♅	♆	♇
1 M	18 45 43	11♑21 39	14♋38 12	21♋31 53	13♑58.8	0♒49.2	21♐42.5	4♎29.4	7♑52.2	25♎01.0	4♉25.9	11♊04.3	6♈09.8	7♒36.2
2 Tu	18 49 39	12 22 47	28 29 09	5♌29 34	13 58.9	1 38.8	22 57.6	4 51.9	8 16.5	25 07.8	4R 25.5	11R 02.3	6 10.3	7 37.9
3 W	18 53 36	13 23 55	12♌32 39	19 37 56	13R 59.0	2 21.0	24 12.8	5 14.0	8 40.7	25 14.5	4 25.2	11 00.2	6 10.9	7 39.6
4 Th	18 57 32	14 25 03	26 44 52	3♍52 58	13 59.1	2 54.9	25 28.0	5 35.8	9 04.9	25 21.0	4 25.1	10 58.2	6 11.5	7 41.4
5 F	19 01 29	15 26 12	11♍01 44	18 10 42	13 59.0	3 19.6	26 43.2	5 57.2	9 29.2	25 27.4	4D 25.0	10 56.2	6 12.2	7 43.2
6 Sa	19 05 25	16 27 20	25 19 26	2♎27 32	13 58.8	3R 34.2	27 58.4	6 18.3	9 53.4	25 33.6	4 25.0	10 54.3	6 12.9	7 44.9
7 Su	19 09 22	17 28 29	9♎34 41	16 40 31	13D 58.7	3 37.9	29 13.6	6 39.1	10 17.5	25 39.7	4 25.2	10 52.4	6 13.6	7 46.7
8 M	19 13 18	18 29 38	23 44 49	0♏47 18	13 58.8	3 30.1	0♑28.8	6 59.5	10 41.7	25 45.6	4 25.5	10 50.5	6 14.4	7 48.5
9 Tu	19 17 15	19 30 47	7♏47 47	14 46 04	13 59.2	3 10.6	1 44.0	7 19.5	11 05.9	25 51.4	4 25.9	10 48.7	6 15.2	7 50.3
10 W	19 21 12	20 31 56	21 41 59	28 35 23	13 59.8	2 39.3	2 59.3	7 39.2	11 30.0	25 57.0	4 26.4	10 46.9	6 16.0	7 52.1
11 Th	19 25 08	21 33 05	5♐26 07	12♐14 03	14 00.5	1 56.5	4 14.5	7 58.4	11 54.1	26 02.4	4 27.0	10 45.1	6 16.9	7 53.9
12 F	19 29 05	22 34 14	18 59 02	25 40 58	14 01.2	1 03.2	5 29.8	8 17.3	12 18.2	26 07.7	4 27.7	10 43.4	6 17.8	7 55.7
13 Sa	19 33 01	23 35 23	2♑19 41	8♑55 07	14R 01.6	0 00.7	6 45.0	8 35.8	12 42.3	26 12.9	4 28.6	10 41.7	6 18.7	7 57.6
14 Su	19 36 58	24 36 32	15 27 09	21 55 44	14 01.5	28♑50.7	8 00.2	8 53.8	13 06.3	26 17.8	4 29.5	10 40.1	6 19.7	7 59.4
15 M	19 40 54	25 37 40	28 20 49	4♒42 25	14 00.8	27 35.4	9 15.5	9 11.4	13 30.4	26 22.6	4 30.6	10 38.5	6 20.6	8 01.2
16 Tu	19 44 51	26 38 47	11♒00 32	17 15 16	13 59.5	26 17.2	10 30.7	9 28.6	13 54.4	26 27.3	4 31.8	10 36.9	6 21.7	8 03.1
17 W	19 48 47	27 39 54	23 26 44	29 35 06	13 57.5	24 58.6	11 46.0	9 45.4	14 18.3	26 31.7	4 33.1	10 35.4	6 22.7	8 05.0
18 Th	19 52 44	28 41 01	5♓40 37	11♓43 33	13 55.2	23 41.9	13 01.2	10 01.7	14 42.3	26 36.0	4 34.5	10 33.9	6 23.8	8 06.8
19 F	19 56 41	29 42 06	17 44 13	23 43 00	13 52.8	22 29.4	14 16.4	10 17.5	15 06.2	26 40.1	4 36.0	10 32.5	6 24.9	8 08.7
20 Sa	20 00 37	0♒43 11	29 40 19	5♈36 39	13 50.7	21 22.8	15 31.7	10 32.9	15 30.0	26 44.1	4 37.6	10 31.1	6 26.1	8 10.5
21 Su	20 04 34	1 44 14	11♈32 29	17 28 22	13 49.2	20 23.5	16 46.9	10 47.8	15 53.9	26 47.9	4 39.3	10 29.8	6 27.3	8 12.4
22 M	20 08 30	2 45 17	23 24 51	29 22 31	13D 48.4	19 32.6	18 02.1	11 02.2	16 17.7	26 51.5	4 41.2	10 28.5	6 28.5	8 14.3
23 Tu	20 12 27	3 46 19	5♉21 58	11♉23 48	13 48.6	18 50.6	19 17.4	11 16.1	16 41.5	26 54.9	4 43.1	10 27.3	6 29.7	8 16.1
24 W	20 16 23	4 47 20	17 28 38	23 37 02	13 49.6	18 17.7	20 32.6	11 29.5	17 05.2	26 58.1	4 45.2	10 26.1	6 31.0	8 18.0
25 Th	20 20 20	5 48 20	29 49 33	6♊06 45	13 51.1	17 54.0	21 47.8	11 42.4	17 28.9	27 01.2	4 47.3	10 24.9	6 32.3	8 19.9
26 F	20 24 16	6 49 19	12♊29 04	18 56 54	13 52.8	17 39.1	23 03.0	11 54.8	17 52.6	27 04.1	4 49.6	10 23.8	6 33.6	8 21.8
27 Sa	20 28 13	7 50 17	25 30 36	2♋10 21	13R 54.1	17D 32.8	24 18.2	12 06.6	18 16.3	27 06.8	4 52.0	10 22.8	6 35.0	8 23.7
28 Su	20 32 10	8 51 13	8♋56 17	15 48 21	13 54.5	17 34.5	25 33.4	12 17.9	18 39.9	27 09.4	4 54.5	10 21.8	6 36.3	8 25.6
29 M	20 36 06	9 52 09	22 46 24	29 50 06	13 53.6	17 43.7	26 48.6	12 28.7	19 03.4	27 11.7	4 57.1	10 20.8	6 37.8	8 27.4
30 Tu	20 40 03	10 53 04	6♌58 58	14♌12 24	13 51.4	17 59.9	28 03.8	12 38.9	19 26.9	27 13.9	4 59.7	10 19.9	6 39.2	8 29.3
31 W	20 43 59	11 53 57	21 29 39	28 49 53	13 48.0	18 22.5	29 19.0	12 48.4	19 50.4	27 15.9	5 02.5	10 19.0	6 40.7	8 31.2

LONGITUDE — February 2029

Day	Sid.Time	☉	0 hr ☽	Noon ☽	True ☊	☿	♀	♂	⚳	♃	♄	♅	♆	♇
1 Th	20 47 56	12♒54 50	6♍12 08	13♍35 28	13♑43.7	18♑50.9	0♒34.2	12♎57.5	20♑13.8	27♎17.7	5♉05.4	10♊18.2	6♈42.2	8♒33.1
2 F	20 51 52	13 55 42	20 58 53	28 21 26	13R 39.3	19 24.7	1 49.4	13 05.9	20 37.2	27 19.3	5 08.4	10R 17.5	6 43.7	8 34.9
3 Sa	20 55 49	14 56 32	5♎42 57	13♎00 37	13 35.4	20 03.5	3 04.6	13 13.6	21 00.6	27 20.7	5 11.5	10 16.8	6 45.2	8 36.8
4 Su	20 59 45	15 57 22	20 15 48	27 27 19	13 32.6	20 46.7	4 19.8	13 20.8	21 23.9	27 22.0	5 14.7	10 16.1	6 46.8	8 38.7
5 M	21 03 42	16 58 12	4♏34 46	11♏37 53	13D 31.2	21 33.9	5 35.0	13 27.3	21 47.2	27 23.0	5 18.0	10 15.5	6 48.4	8 40.5
6 Tu	21 07 39	17 59 00	18 36 33	25 30 44	13 31.3	22 24.9	6 50.2	13 33.2	22 10.4	27 23.9	5 21.4	10 15.0	6 50.0	8 42.4
7 W	21 11 35	18 59 48	2♐20 28	9♐05 53	13 32.5	23 19.3	8 05.3	13 38.4	22 33.6	27 24.5	5 24.8	10 14.5	6 51.6	8 44.3
8 Th	21 15 32	20 00 34	15 47 10	22 24 30	13 34.1	24 16.8	9 20.5	13 43.0	22 56.7	27 25.0	5 28.4	10 14.0	6 53.3	8 46.1
9 F	21 19 28	21 01 20	28 58 06	5♑28 12	13R 35.4	25 17.1	10 35.7	13 46.8	23 19.8	27 25.3	5 32.1	10 13.6	6 55.0	8 48.0
10 Sa	21 23 25	22 02 05	11♑55 01	18 18 45	13 35.6	26 20.0	11 50.9	13 49.9	23 42.8	27R 25.4	5 35.9	10 13.3	6 56.7	8 49.8
11 Su	21 27 21	23 02 48	24 39 34	0♒57 38	13 34.0	27 25.4	13 06.0	13 52.4	24 05.8	27 25.3	5 39.7	10 13.0	6 58.5	8 51.7
12 M	21 31 18	24 03 30	7♒13 05	13 26 05	13 30.4	28 33.0	14 21.2	13 54.1	24 28.7	27 25.1	5 43.7	10 12.7	7 00.2	8 53.5
13 Tu	21 35 14	25 04 11	19 36 42	25 45 03	13 24.7	29 42.6	15 36.3	13R 55.1	24 51.5	27 24.6	5 47.7	10 12.6	7 02.0	8 55.3
14 W	21 39 11	26 04 50	1♓51 16	7♓55 28	13 17.2	0♒54.2	16 51.5	13 55.3	25 14.3	27 23.9	5 51.9	10 12.4	7 03.8	8 57.1
15 Th	21 43 08	27 05 28	13 57 45	19 58 19	13 08.6	2 07.5	18 06.6	13 54.9	25 37.1	27 23.1	5 56.1	10D 12.4	7 05.6	8 58.9
16 F	21 47 04	28 06 04	25 57 20	1♈55 01	12 59.6	3 22.6	19 21.7	13 53.6	25 59.7	27 22.0	6 00.4	10 12.3	7 07.5	9 00.7
17 Sa	21 51 01	29 06 38	7♈51 39	13 47 32	12 51.2	4 39.2	20 36.8	13 51.6	26 22.4	27 20.8	6 04.8	10 12.4	7 09.4	9 02.5
18 Su	21 54 57	0♓07 11	19 43 00	25 38 28	12 44.1	5 57.3	21 51.9	13 48.9	26 44.9	27 19.4	6 09.3	10 12.4	7 11.2	9 04.3
19 M	21 58 54	1 07 42	1♉34 23	7♉31 13	12 38.9	7 16.9	23 07.0	13 45.4	27 07.4	27 17.8	6 13.9	10 12.6	7 13.2	9 06.1
20 Tu	22 02 50	2 08 12	13 29 31	19 29 49	12 35.9	8 37.8	24 22.1	13 41.1	27 29.9	27 16.0	6 18.6	10 12.8	7 15.1	9 07.9
21 W	22 06 47	3 08 39	25 32 45	1♊38 53	12D 34.8	10 00.0	25 37.1	13 36.0	27 52.2	27 14.0	6 23.3	10 13.0	7 17.0	9 09.6
22 Th	22 10 43	4 09 05	7♊48 53	14 03 21	12 35.3	11 23.5	26 52.2	13 30.2	28 14.5	27 11.8	6 28.1	10 13.3	7 19.0	9 11.3
23 F	22 14 40	5 09 29	20 22 54	26 48 07	12 36.4	12 48.3	28 07.2	13 23.6	28 36.8	27 09.5	6 33.1	10 13.7	7 21.0	9 13.1
24 Sa	22 18 37	6 09 51	3♋19 31	9♋57 32	12R 37.2	14 14.2	29 22.3	13 16.2	28 58.9	27 07.0	6 38.0	10 14.1	7 23.0	9 14.8
25 Su	22 22 33	7 10 11	16 42 32	23 34 44	12 36.6	15 41.2	0♓37.3	13 08.0	29 21.0	27 04.3	6 43.1	10 14.5	7 25.0	9 16.5
26 M	22 26 30	8 10 29	0♌34 10	7♌40 43	12 34.0	17 09.4	1 52.3	12 59.1	29 43.0	27 01.4	6 48.3	10 15.1	7 27.0	9 18.2
27 Tu	22 30 26	9 10 45	14 54 04	22 13 40	12 29.0	18 38.7	3 07.3	12 49.4	0♒05.0	26 58.3	6 53.5	10 15.6	7 29.0	9 19.9
28 W	22 34 23	10 10 59	29 38 46	7♍08 24	12 21.8	20 09.1	4 22.2	12 39.0	0 26.8	26 55.0	6 58.8	10 16.2	7 31.1	9 21.6

Astro Data

	Dy Hr Mn
♂0S	5 6:10
♄ D	5 12:40
☽0S	5 13:09
☿ R	7 7:57
♃□♅	9 3:24
☽0N	19 2:20
☿ D	27 18:42
☽0S	1 20:46
♃ R	10 13:08
♂ R	14 8:17
☽0N	15 10:15
♅ D	16 10:53

Planet Ingress

	Dy Hr Mn
♀ ♑	8 2:48
☿ ♑R	13 12:15
☉ ♒	19 19:02
♀ ♒	1 1:04
☿ ♒	13 17:53
☉ ♓	18 9:09
♀ ♓	25 0:05
⚳ ♒	27 6:34

Last Aspect / ☽ Ingress (January)

Last Aspect Dy Hr Mn		☽ Ingress Dy Hr Mn
1 18:05	♃ □	♌ 2 2:36
3 21:32	♃ ⚹	♍ 4 5:28
6 3:44	♀ □	♎ 6 7:52
8 3:22	♃ ☌	♏ 8 10:39
9 20:52	☉ ⚹	♐ 10 14:28
12 12:49	♃ ⚹	♑ 12 19:47
14 23:48	☿ ☌	♒ 15 3:06
17 5:59	♃ △	♓ 17 12:49
19 9:45	☿ ⚹	♈ 20 0:40
22 6:55	♃ ☍	♉ 22 13:15
24 5:20	♀ △	♊ 25 0:20
27 2:52	♃ △	♋ 27 8:06
29 7:31	♃ □	♌ 29 12:17
31 9:26	♃ ⚹	♍ 31 13:54

Last Aspect / ☽ Ingress (February)

Last Aspect Dy Hr Mn		☽ Ingress Dy Hr Mn
1 20:51	☿ △	♎ 2 14:41
4 11:51	♃ ☌	♏ 4 16:16
6 6:14	☿ ⚹	♐ 6 19:52
8 21:09	♃ ⚹	♑ 9 1:54
11 5:15	♃ □	♒ 11 10:10
13 15:15	♃ △	♓ 13 20:21
14 16:32	♅ □	♈ 16 8:08
18 15:24	♃ ☍	♉ 18 20:49
20 22:47	♀ □	♊ 21 8:46
23 14:42	♀ △	♋ 23 17:54
25 18:00	♃ □	♌ 25 23:02
27 19:40	♃ ⚹	♍ 28 0:34

☽ Phases & Eclipses

Dy Hr Mn	
7 13:28	☾ 17♎32
14 17:26	● 24♑50
14 17:13:48	● P 0.871
22 19:24	☽ 3♉04
30 6:05	○ 10♌38
5 21:53	☾ 17♏23
13 10:33	● 25♒01
21 15:11	☽ 3♊17
28 17:11	○ 10♍24

Astro Data

1 January 2029
Julian Day # 47118
SVP 4♓50'59"
GC 27♐14.7 ⚴ 11♐27.2
Eris 25♈19.9R ⚵ 2♏22.5
⚷ 3♉57.2R ⚶ 3♐17.5
☽ Mean ☊ 14♑06.5

1 February 2029
Julian Day # 47149
SVP 4♓50'54"
GC 27♐14.7 ⚴ 23♐48.9
Eris 25♈21.4 ⚵ 8♏16.6
⚷ 4♉04.0 ⚶ 18♐47.4
☽ Mean ☊ 12♑28.0

March 2029 LONGITUDE

Day	Sid.Time	☉	0 hr ☽	Noon ☽	True ☊	☿	♀	♂	⚳	♃	♄	♅	♆	♇
1 Th	22 38 19	11♓11 11	14♍41 26	22♍16 37	12♑12.9	21♒40.6	5♓37.2	12♎27.7	0♒48.6	26♎51.6	7♉04.1	10♊16.9	7♈33.2	9♒23.2
2 F	22 42 16	12 11 22	29 52 35	7♎27 59	12R 03.6	23 13.2	6 52.1	12R 15.7	1 10.4	26R 48.0	7 09.6	10 17.6	7 35.3	9 24.8
3 Sa	22 46 12	13 11 31	15♎01 31	22 31 57	11 54.9	24 46.9	8 07.1	12 03.0	1 32.0	26 44.3	7 15.1	10 18.4	7 37.4	9 26.5
4 Su	22 50 09	14 11 38	29 58 15	7♏19 33	11 47.9	26 21.7	9 22.0	11 49.5	1 53.6	26 40.3	7 20.7	10 19.2	7 39.5	9 28.1
5 M	22 54 06	15 11 44	14♏35 13	21 44 46	11 43.2	27 57.5	10 36.9	11 35.3	2 15.1	26 36.2	7 26.3	10 20.1	7 41.6	9 29.7
6 Tu	22 58 02	16 11 49	28 47 59	5♐44 48	11D 40.9	29 34.5	11 51.9	11 20.4	2 36.5	26 32.0	7 32.0	10 21.0	7 43.7	9 31.3
7 W	23 01 59	17 11 52	12♐35 19	19 19 45	11 40.5	1♓12.5	13 06.8	11 04.8	2 57.8	26 27.5	7 37.8	10 22.0	7 45.9	9 32.8
8 Th	23 05 55	18 11 53	25 58 26	2♑31 44	11R 40.9	2 51.7	14 21.6	10 48.4	3 19.0	26 22.9	7 43.7	10 23.0	7 48.0	9 34.4
9 F	23 09 52	19 11 53	9♑00 05	15 23 58	11 41.0	4 31.9	15 36.5	10 31.5	3 40.2	26 18.2	7 49.6	10 24.1	7 50.2	9 35.9
10 Sa	23 13 48	20 11 51	21 43 48	28 00 04	11 39.8	6 13.3	16 51.4	10 13.8	4 01.3	26 13.3	7 55.6	10 25.3	7 52.4	9 37.4
11 Su	23 17 45	21 11 47	4♒13 09	10♒23 28	11 36.2	7 55.8	18 06.3	9 55.6	4 22.2	26 08.2	8 01.6	10 26.4	7 54.6	9 38.9
12 M	23 21 41	22 11 42	16 31 21	22 37 07	11 29.8	9 39.5	19 21.1	9 36.7	4 43.1	26 03.0	8 07.7	10 27.7	7 56.8	9 40.4
13 Tu	23 25 38	23 11 35	28 41 03	4♓43 22	11 20.4	11 24.3	20 35.9	9 17.3	5 03.9	25 57.7	8 13.9	10 29.0	7 59.0	9 41.9
14 W	23 29 35	24 11 26	10♓44 18	16 44 01	11 08.5	13 10.3	21 50.7	8 57.3	5 24.6	25 52.2	8 20.1	10 30.3	8 01.2	9 43.3
15 Th	23 33 31	25 11 15	22 42 40	28 40 25	10 54.9	14 57.5	23 05.5	8 36.9	5 45.2	25 46.5	8 26.4	10 31.7	8 03.4	9 44.7
16 F	23 37 28	26 11 01	4♈37 24	10♈33 47	10 40.7	16 45.9	24 20.3	8 15.9	6 05.7	25 40.8	8 32.7	10 33.1	8 05.7	9 46.1
17 Sa	23 41 24	27 10 46	16 29 44	22 25 27	10 27.1	18 35.5	25 35.1	7 54.6	6 26.1	25 34.9	8 39.1	10 34.6	8 07.9	9 47.5
18 Su	23 45 21	28 10 29	28 21 09	4♉17 06	10 15.1	20 26.3	26 49.8	7 32.8	6 46.4	25 28.8	8 45.6	10 36.1	8 10.1	9 48.9
19 M	23 49 17	29 10 10	10♉13 36	16 11 00	10 05.7	22 18.3	28 04.6	7 10.7	7 06.6	25 22.7	8 52.1	10 37.7	8 12.4	9 50.3
20 Tu	23 53 14	0♈09 49	22 09 43	28 10 10	9 59.1	24 11.6	29 19.3	6 48.3	7 26.7	25 16.4	8 58.7	10 39.3	8 14.6	9 51.6
21 W	23 57 10	1 09 25	4♊12 51	10♊18 17	9 55.3	26 06.0	0♈34.0	6 25.6	7 46.7	25 10.0	9 05.3	10 41.0	8 16.9	9 52.9
22 Th	0 01 07	2 08 59	16 27 03	22 39 44	9D 53.8	28 01.6	1 48.7	6 02.7	8 06.6	25 03.5	9 11.9	10 42.7	8 19.1	9 54.2
23 F	0 05 03	3 08 31	28 56 56	5♋19 16	9R 53.6	29 58.4	3 03.3	5 39.6	8 26.4	24 56.9	9 18.6	10 44.5	8 21.4	9 55.4
24 Sa	0 09 00	4 08 01	11♋47 19	18 21 38	9 53.5	1♈56.3	4 18.0	5 16.4	8 46.0	24 50.2	9 25.4	10 46.3	8 23.7	9 56.7
25 Su	0 12 57	5 07 28	25 02 43	1♌50 56	9 52.2	3 55.2	5 32.6	4 53.1	9 05.6	24 43.4	9 32.2	10 48.1	8 26.0	9 57.9
26 M	0 16 53	6 06 53	8♌46 34	15 49 43	9 48.9	5 55.2	6 47.2	4 29.7	9 25.0	24 36.5	9 39.0	10 50.0	8 28.2	9 59.1
27 Tu	0 20 50	7 06 15	23 00 17	0♍18 00	9 42.9	7 56.1	8 01.8	4 06.4	9 44.3	24 29.5	9 45.9	10 52.0	8 30.5	10 00.3
28 W	0 24 46	8 05 35	7♍42 16	15 12 21	9 34.3	9 57.7	9 16.3	3 43.0	10 03.5	24 22.5	9 52.9	10 53.9	8 32.8	10 01.4
29 Th	0 28 43	9 04 53	22 47 11	0♎25 34	9 23.8	12 00.1	10 30.9	3 19.8	10 22.6	24 15.3	9 59.8	10 56.0	8 35.0	10 02.6
30 F	0 32 39	10 04 09	8♎06 05	15 47 15	9 12.4	14 02.9	11 45.4	2 56.7	10 41.5	24 08.1	10 06.8	10 58.0	8 37.3	10 03.7
31 Sa	0 36 36	11 03 23	23 27 34	1♏05 33	9 01.7	16 06.1	12 59.9	2 33.7	11 00.3	24 00.8	10 13.9	11 00.1	8 39.6	10 04.8

April 2029 LONGITUDE

Day	Sid.Time	☉	0 hr ☽	Noon ☽	True ☊	☿	♀	♂	⚳	♃	♄	♅	♆	♇
1 Su	0 40 32	12♈02 35	8♏39 50	16♏09 17	8♑52.8	18♈09.3	14♈14.4	2♎10.9	11♒19.0	23♎53.5	10♉21.0	11♊02.3	8♈41.8	10♒05.8
2 M	0 44 29	13 01 46	23 32 53	0♐49 57	8R 46.5	20 12.5	15 28.9	1R 48.4	11 37.6	23R 46.1	10 28.1	11 04.5	8 44.1	10 06.9
3 Tu	0 48 26	14 00 54	7♐59 59	15 02 44	8 42.8	22 15.2	16 43.3	1 26.2	11 56.1	23 38.6	10 35.3	11 06.7	8 46.4	10 07.9
4 W	0 52 22	15 00 01	21 58 10	28 46 25	8D 41.4	24 17.1	17 57.8	1 04.3	12 14.4	23 31.1	10 42.5	11 09.0	8 48.6	10 08.9
5 Th	0 56 19	15 59 06	5♑27 45	12♑02 34	8R 41.2	26 18.0	19 12.2	0 42.8	12 32.6	23 23.6	10 49.7	11 11.3	8 50.9	10 09.8
6 F	1 00 15	16 58 10	18 31 21	24 54 38	8 41.1	28 17.5	20 26.6	0 21.7	12 50.7	23 16.0	10 56.9	11 13.7	8 53.2	10 10.8
7 Sa	1 04 12	17 57 11	1♒12 59	7♒26 58	8 39.8	0♉15.2	21 41.0	0 01.0	13 08.6	23 08.4	11 04.2	11 16.0	8 55.4	10 11.7
8 Su	1 08 08	18 56 11	13 37 08	19 44 03	8 36.3	2 10.8	22 55.4	29♍40.8	13 26.3	23 00.7	11 11.6	11 18.5	8 57.7	10 12.6
9 M	1 12 05	19 55 09	25 48 13	1♓50 07	8 30.2	4 03.8	24 09.7	29 21.1	13 44.0	22 53.0	11 18.9	11 20.9	8 59.9	10 13.5
10 Tu	1 16 01	20 54 05	7♓50 11	13 48 48	8 21.2	5 53.9	25 24.1	29 02.0	14 01.5	22 45.4	11 26.3	11 23.4	9 02.2	10 14.3
11 W	1 19 58	21 52 59	19 46 19	25 43 02	8 09.7	7 40.9	26 38.4	28 43.4	14 18.8	22 37.7	11 33.7	11 26.0	9 04.4	10 15.1
12 Th	1 23 55	22 51 51	1♈39 15	7♈35 09	7 56.5	9 24.3	27 52.7	28 25.4	14 36.0	22 29.9	11 41.1	11 28.5	9 06.6	10 15.9
13 F	1 27 51	23 50 42	13 30 58	19 26 53	7 42.6	11 03.8	29 07.0	28 08.1	14 53.0	22 22.2	11 48.6	11 31.2	9 08.8	10 16.7
14 Sa	1 31 48	24 49 30	25 23 04	1♉19 40	7 29.3	12 39.2	0♉21.3	27 51.4	15 09.9	22 14.5	11 56.1	11 33.8	9 11.0	10 17.4
15 Su	1 35 44	25 48 17	7♉16 53	13 14 53	7 17.5	14 10.3	1 35.5	27 35.4	15 26.6	22 06.9	12 03.6	11 36.5	9 13.2	10 18.1
16 M	1 39 41	26 47 01	19 13 52	25 14 04	7 08.2	15 36.8	2 49.8	27 20.2	15 43.2	21 59.2	12 11.1	11 39.2	9 15.4	10 18.8
17 Tu	1 43 37	27 45 44	1♊15 45	7♊19 13	7 01.7	16 58.6	4 04.0	27 05.6	15 59.6	21 51.5	12 18.7	11 41.9	9 17.6	10 19.5
18 W	1 47 34	28 44 24	13 24 48	19 32 53	6 57.9	18 15.4	5 18.2	26 51.8	16 15.8	21 43.9	12 26.2	11 44.7	9 19.8	10 20.1
19 Th	1 51 30	29 43 02	25 43 52	1♋58 14	6D 56.5	19 27.1	6 32.3	26 38.7	16 31.9	21 36.3	12 33.8	11 47.5	9 22.0	10 20.7
20 F	1 55 27	0♉41 38	8♋16 27	14 39 01	6 56.6	20 33.6	7 46.5	26 26.4	16 47.8	21 28.8	12 41.4	11 50.4	9 24.1	10 21.3
21 Sa	1 59 24	1 40 12	21 06 25	27 39 09	6R 57.0	21 34.8	9 00.6	26 14.8	17 03.5	21 21.3	12 49.0	11 53.2	9 26.3	10 21.9
22 Su	2 03 20	2 38 43	4♌17 41	11♌02 25	6 56.8	22 30.5	10 14.7	26 04.1	17 19.0	21 13.8	12 56.7	11 56.1	9 28.4	10 22.4
23 M	2 07 17	3 37 13	17 53 39	24 51 35	6 54.9	23 20.8	11 28.8	25 54.1	17 34.4	21 06.4	13 04.3	11 59.0	9 30.5	10 22.9
24 Tu	2 11 13	4 35 40	1♍56 18	9♍07 39	6 50.8	24 05.5	12 42.8	25 44.9	17 49.6	20 59.1	13 12.0	12 02.0	9 32.6	10 23.3
25 W	2 15 10	5 34 05	16 25 22	23 48 53	6 44.5	24 44.5	13 56.9	25 36.5	18 04.6	20 51.8	13 19.6	12 05.0	9 34.7	10 23.8
26 Th	2 19 06	6 32 28	1♎17 28	8♎50 11	6 36.4	25 17.9	15 10.9	25 28.9	18 19.4	20 44.6	13 27.3	12 08.0	9 36.8	10 24.2
27 F	2 23 03	7 30 48	16 25 54	24 03 18	6 27.5	25 45.6	16 24.9	25 22.1	18 34.1	20 37.5	13 35.0	12 11.0	9 38.9	10 24.6
28 Sa	2 26 59	8 29 08	1♏41 03	9♏17 44	6 19.0	26 07.6	17 38.9	25 16.1	18 48.5	20 30.4	13 42.7	12 14.1	9 40.9	10 25.0
29 Su	2 30 56	9 27 25	16 52 01	24 22 38	6 11.9	26 23.9	18 52.8	25 10.9	19 02.8	20 23.5	13 50.4	12 17.1	9 42.9	10 25.3
30 M	2 34 53	10 25 41	1♐48 28	9♐08 37	6 06.9	26 34.6	20 06.7	25 06.4	19 16.8	20 16.6	13 58.1	12 20.3	9 45.0	10 25.6

Astro Data	Dy Hr Mn	Planet Ingress	Dy Hr Mn	Last Aspect Dy Hr Mn		☽ Ingress	Dy Hr Mn	Last Aspect Dy Hr Mn		☽ Ingress	Dy Hr Mn	☽ Phases & Eclipses Dy Hr Mn	
☽0S	1 7:03	☿ ♓	6 18:16	28 17:11	☉ ☍	♎	2 0:12	1 2:37	♄ ☍	♐	2 10:37	7 7:53	☾ 17♐02
♄⊻♆	9 15:59	☉ ♈	20 8:03	3 18:44	♃ ☌	♏	4 0:03	4 2:48	♃ ⚹	♑	4 14:11	15 4:20	● 24♓52
☽0N	14 16:55	♀ ♈	21 1:05	5 23:56	☿ □	♐	6 2:04	6 19:36	☿ □	♒	6 21:40	23 7:34	☽ 2♋58
♂0N	17 7:13	☿ ♈	23 12:20	8 0:49	♃ ⚹	♑	8 7:21	8 19:01	♀ ⚹	♓	9 8:20	30 2:28	○ 9♎41
♃♇♅	17 12:52			10 8:36	♃ □	♒	10 15:51	11 17:55	♂ ☍	♈	11 20:39		
☉0N	20 8:03	☿ ♉	7 8:53	12 18:44	♃ △	♓	13 2:37	13 21:41	☉ ☌	♉	14 9:19	5 19:53	☾ 16♑18
♀0N	23 14:17	♂ ♍R	7 13:11	15 4:20	☉ ☌	♈	15 14:40	16 16:06	♂ △	♊	16 21:29	13 21:41	● 24♈14
☿0N	25 4:02	♀ ♉	14 5:07	17 18:20	♃ ☍	♉	18 3:20	19 7:19	☉ ⚹	♋	19 8:13	21 19:51	☽ 1♌59
☽0S	28 18:10	☉ ♉	19 18:57	20 14:33	♀ ⚹	♊	20 15:39	21 9:28	♂ ⚹	♌	21 16:16	28 10:38	○ 8♏26
♄□♇	29 23:13			23 0:07	☿ □	♋	23 1:59	23 9:15	☿ □	♍	23 20:44		
				24 23:32	♃ □	♌	25 8:46	25 14:52	♂ ☌	♎	25 21:56		
♄⊻♅	9 21:55			27 2:32	♃ ⚹	♍	27 11:31	27 6:39	♃ ☌	♏	27 21:21		
☽0N	10 22:26			28 5:07	♅ □	♎	29 11:20	29 15:18	☿ ☍	♐	29 21:04		
☽0S	25 3:50			31 0:57	♃ ☌	♏	31 10:17						

Astro Data

1 March 2029
Julian Day # 47177
SVP 4♓50'51"
GC 27♐14.8 ⚳ 3♑29.2
Eris 25♈31.4 ⚵ 9♏47.0R
⚷ 4♉56.0 ⚶ 1♑42.4
☽ Mean ☊ 10♑59.1

1 April 2029
Julian Day # 47208
SVP 4♓50'48"
GC 27♐14.9 ⚳ 11♑23.1
Eris 25♈49.1 ⚵ 6♏17.5R
⚷ 6♉31.4 ⚶ 13♑53.9
☽ Mean ☊ 9♑20.6

LONGITUDE May 2029

Day	Sid.Time	☉	0 hr ☽	Noon ☽	True ☊	☿	♀	♂	⚳	♃	♄	♅	♆	♇
1 Tu	2 38 49	11♉23 55	16♐22 23	23♐29 16	6♑04.2	26♉39.8	21♉20.7	25♍02.7	19♒30.7	20♎09.8	14♉05.8	12♊23.4	9♈47.0	10♒25.9
2 W	2 42 46	12 22 07	0♑29 01	7♑21 33	6D 03.5	26R 39.6	22 34.6	24R 59.9	19 44.4	20R 03.1	14 13.5	12 26.5	9 49.0	10 26.1
3 Th	2 46 42	13 20 18	14 06 56	20 45 27	6 04.2	26 34.2	23 48.4	24 57.7	19 57.8	19 56.5	14 21.2	12 29.7	9 51.0	10 26.4
4 F	2 50 39	14 18 28	27 17 27	3♒43 23	6R 05.2	26 23.8	25 02.3	24 56.4	20 11.1	19 50.0	14 28.9	12 32.9	9 52.9	10 26.6
5 Sa	2 54 35	15 16 36	10♒03 45	16 19 08	6 05.7	26 08.8	26 16.1	24D 55.8	20 24.1	19 43.6	14 36.6	12 36.1	9 54.9	10 26.7
6 Su	2 58 32	16 14 42	22 30 06	28 37 16	6 04.8	25 49.4	27 30.0	24 55.9	20 37.0	19 37.4	14 44.3	12 39.4	9 56.8	10 26.9
7 M	3 02 28	17 12 47	4♓41 11	10♓42 28	6 02.0	25 26.0	28 43.8	24 56.8	20 49.6	19 31.2	14 52.0	12 42.6	9 58.7	10 27.0
8 Tu	3 06 25	18 10 51	16 41 37	22 39 11	5 57.1	24 59.2	29 57.6	24 58.5	21 02.0	19 25.2	14 59.8	12 45.9	10 00.6	10 27.1
9 W	3 10 22	19 08 53	28 35 37	4♈31 23	5 50.4	24 29.4	1♊11.4	25 00.9	21 14.1	19 19.3	15 07.5	12 49.2	10 02.4	10 27.1
10 Th	3 14 18	20 06 54	10♈26 52	16 22 25	5 42.4	23 57.1	2 25.1	25 04.0	21 26.1	19 13.5	15 15.2	12 52.5	10 04.3	10R 27.2
11 F	3 18 15	21 04 54	22 18 22	28 15 00	5 33.9	23 23.0	3 38.8	25 07.8	21 37.8	19 07.8	15 22.9	12 55.9	10 06.1	10 27.2
12 Sa	3 22 11	22 02 52	4♉12 34	10♉11 17	5 25.7	22 47.7	4 52.6	25 12.3	21 49.2	19 02.3	15 30.5	12 59.2	10 07.9	10 27.2
13 Su	3 26 08	23 00 49	16 11 21	22 12 57	5 18.4	22 11.8	6 06.3	25 17.5	22 00.5	18 56.9	15 38.2	13 02.6	10 09.7	10 27.1
14 M	3 30 04	23 58 44	28 16 15	4♊21 26	5 12.9	21 35.9	7 20.0	25 23.5	22 11.4	18 51.7	15 45.9	13 05.9	10 11.5	10 27.0
15 Tu	3 34 01	24 56 37	10♊28 39	16 38 06	5 09.2	21 00.7	8 33.6	25 30.1	22 22.2	18 46.6	15 53.6	13 09.3	10 13.3	10 26.9
16 W	3 37 57	25 54 29	22 49 59	29 04 30	5D 07.6	20 26.8	9 47.3	25 37.3	22 32.7	18 41.6	16 01.2	13 12.8	10 15.0	10 26.8
17 Th	3 41 54	26 52 20	5♋21 53	11♋42 23	5 07.6	19 54.7	11 00.9	25 45.3	22 42.9	18 36.8	16 08.9	13 16.2	10 16.7	10 26.6
18 F	3 45 51	27 50 09	18 06 18	24 33 53	5 08.7	19 24.9	12 14.5	25 53.8	22 52.9	18 32.2	16 16.5	13 19.6	10 18.4	10 26.5
19 Sa	3 49 47	28 47 56	1♌05 27	7♌41 18	5 10.2	18 57.9	13 28.1	26 03.0	23 02.6	18 27.7	16 24.1	13 23.1	10 20.0	10 26.3
20 Su	3 53 44	29 45 41	14 21 41	21 06 52	5R 11.4	18 34.2	14 41.7	26 12.9	23 12.1	18 23.4	16 31.7	13 26.5	10 21.7	10 26.0
21 M	3 57 40	0♊43 25	27 57 03	4♍52 20	5 11.6	18 14.0	15 55.2	26 23.3	23 21.3	18 19.2	16 39.3	13 30.0	10 23.3	10 25.7
22 Tu	4 01 37	1 41 07	11♍52 46	18 58 18	5 10.4	17 57.7	17 08.7	26 34.4	23 30.2	18 15.2	16 46.8	13 33.5	10 24.9	10 25.5
23 W	4 05 33	2 38 47	26 08 42	3♎23 39	5 07.9	17 45.4	18 22.2	26 46.0	23 38.9	18 11.3	16 54.4	13 36.9	10 26.4	10 25.1
24 Th	4 09 30	3 36 26	10♎42 39	18 05 04	5 04.3	17 37.5	19 35.7	26 58.2	23 47.3	18 07.6	17 01.9	13 40.4	10 28.0	10 24.8
25 F	4 13 26	4 34 04	25 30 08	2♏56 55	5 00.0	17D 33.9	20 49.1	27 11.0	23 55.4	18 04.1	17 09.4	13 43.9	10 29.5	10 24.4
26 Sa	4 17 23	5 31 40	10♏24 27	17 51 41	4 55.9	17 34.7	22 02.6	27 24.3	24 03.2	18 00.8	17 16.8	13 47.4	10 31.0	10 24.0
27 Su	4 21 20	6 29 15	25 17 33	2♐41 01	4 52.5	17 40.1	23 16.0	27 38.2	24 10.8	17 57.6	17 24.3	13 50.9	10 32.5	10 23.6
28 M	4 25 16	7 26 48	10♐01 07	17 16 59	4 50.3	17 50.0	24 29.4	27 52.5	24 18.0	17 54.6	17 31.7	13 54.5	10 33.9	10 23.2
29 Tu	4 29 13	8 24 21	24 27 53	1♑33 14	4D 49.4	18 04.4	25 42.7	28 07.5	24 25.0	17 51.8	17 39.1	13 58.0	10 35.3	10 22.7
30 W	4 33 09	9 21 53	8♑32 37	15 25 44	4 49.7	18 23.2	26 56.1	28 22.9	24 31.7	17 49.1	17 46.5	14 01.5	10 36.7	10 22.2
31 Th	4 37 06	10 19 23	22 12 30	28 52 57	4 50.8	18 46.3	28 09.4	28 38.8	24 38.1	17 46.6	17 53.9	14 05.1	10 38.1	10 21.7

LONGITUDE June 2029

Day	Sid.Time	☉	0 hr ☽	Noon ☽	True ☊	☿	♀	♂	⚳	♃	♄	♅	♆	♇
1 F	4 41 02	11♊16 53	5♒27 12	11♒55 33	4♑52.3	19♉13.8	29♊22.7	28♍55.2	24♒44.2	17♎44.3	18♉01.2	14♊08.6	10♈39.4	10♒21.2
2 Sa	4 44 59	12 14 22	18 18 21	24 36 01	4 53.7	19 45.5	0♋36.0	29 12.1	24 50.0	17R 42.2	18 08.5	14 12.1	10 40.7	10R 20.6
3 Su	4 48 55	13 11 50	0♓49 03	6♓57 59	4R 54.6	20 21.3	1 49.3	29 29.4	24 55.4	17 40.2	18 15.7	14 15.7	10 42.0	10 20.0
4 M	4 52 52	14 09 18	13 03 21	19 05 43	4 54.7	21 01.1	3 02.6	29 47.2	25 00.6	17 38.4	18 23.0	14 19.2	10 43.3	10 19.4
5 Tu	4 56 49	15 06 44	25 05 42	1♈03 50	4 53.8	21 44.8	4 15.8	0♎05.5	25 05.4	17 36.8	18 30.2	14 22.7	10 44.5	10 18.7
6 W	5 00 45	16 04 10	7♈00 41	12 56 48	4 52.1	22 32.4	5 29.0	0 24.2	25 09.9	17 35.4	18 37.3	14 26.3	10 45.7	10 18.1
7 Th	5 04 42	17 01 36	18 52 41	24 48 49	4 49.8	23 23.7	6 42.2	0 43.4	25 14.1	17 34.1	18 44.5	14 29.8	10 46.8	10 17.4
8 F	5 08 38	17 59 00	0♉45 41	6♉43 40	4 47.3	24 18.6	7 55.4	1 03.0	25 18.0	17 33.0	18 51.6	14 33.3	10 48.0	10 16.7
9 Sa	5 12 35	18 56 25	12 43 09	18 44 29	4 44.8	25 17.1	9 08.6	1 23.0	25 21.6	17 32.2	18 58.6	14 36.9	10 49.1	10 15.9
10 Su	5 16 31	19 53 48	24 47 58	0♊53 51	4 42.7	26 19.0	10 21.7	1 43.4	25 24.8	17 31.5	19 05.7	14 40.4	10 50.2	10 15.2
11 M	5 20 28	20 51 11	7♊02 22	13 13 41	4 41.2	27 24.4	11 34.8	2 04.3	25 27.6	17 30.9	19 12.7	14 43.9	10 51.2	10 14.4
12 Tu	5 24 24	21 48 33	19 27 59	25 45 23	4D 40.4	28 33.2	12 48.0	2 25.5	25 30.2	17 30.6	19 19.6	14 47.5	10 52.3	10 13.6
13 W	5 28 21	22 45 55	2♋05 58	8♋29 49	4 40.2	29 45.2	14 01.0	2 47.2	25 32.4	17D 30.4	19 26.5	14 51.0	10 53.3	10 12.8
14 Th	5 32 18	23 43 15	14 57 00	21 27 32	4 40.7	1♊00.5	15 14.1	3 09.2	25 34.2	17 30.5	19 33.4	14 54.5	10 54.2	10 12.0
15 F	5 36 14	24 40 35	28 01 29	4♌38 50	4 41.4	2 19.0	16 27.2	3 31.6	25 35.8	17 30.7	19 40.2	14 58.0	10 55.2	10 11.1
16 Sa	5 40 11	25 37 54	11♌19 37	18 03 49	4 42.3	3 40.7	17 40.2	3 54.4	25 36.9	17 31.0	19 47.0	15 01.5	10 56.1	10 10.2
17 Su	5 44 07	26 35 12	24 51 25	1♍42 24	4 43.0	5 05.5	18 53.2	4 17.5	25 37.7	17 31.6	19 53.7	15 05.0	10 56.9	10 09.3
18 M	5 48 04	27 32 30	8♍36 41	15 34 12	4R 43.4	6 33.4	20 06.1	4 41.0	25R 38.2	17 32.3	20 00.4	15 08.5	10 57.8	10 08.4
19 Tu	5 52 00	28 29 46	22 34 49	29 38 22	4 43.6	8 04.4	21 19.1	5 04.9	25 38.3	17 33.3	20 07.0	15 12.0	10 58.6	10 07.5
20 W	5 55 57	29 27 01	6♎44 37	13♎53 18	4 43.4	9 38.5	22 32.0	5 29.0	25 38.1	17 34.4	20 13.6	15 15.4	10 59.4	10 06.5
21 Th	5 59 53	0♋24 16	21 04 03	28 16 29	4 43.1	11 15.6	23 44.9	5 53.6	25 37.5	17 35.6	20 20.2	15 18.9	11 00.1	10 05.5
22 F	6 03 50	1 21 31	5♏30 07	12♏44 24	4 42.7	12 55.7	24 57.8	6 18.4	25 36.6	17 37.1	20 26.7	15 22.3	11 00.8	10 04.5
23 Sa	6 07 47	2 18 44	19 58 46	27 12 36	4 42.4	14 38.7	26 10.6	6 43.6	25 35.3	17 38.7	20 33.1	15 25.7	11 01.5	10 03.5
24 Su	6 11 43	3 15 57	4♐25 15	11♐36 04	4 42.3	16 24.6	27 23.4	7 09.1	25 33.6	17 40.5	20 39.5	15 29.2	11 02.2	10 02.5
25 M	6 15 40	4 13 10	18 44 25	25 49 43	4 42.2	18 13.4	28 36.2	7 34.8	25 31.6	17 42.5	20 45.8	15 32.6	11 02.8	10 01.4
26 Tu	6 19 36	5 10 22	2♑51 23	9♑48 58	4 42.2	20 05.0	29 49.0	8 00.9	25 29.3	17 44.7	20 52.1	15 36.0	11 03.4	10 00.4
27 W	6 23 33	6 07 34	16 42 04	23 30 20	4 42.2	21 59.2	1♌01.7	8 27.3	25 26.6	17 47.0	20 58.3	15 39.3	11 03.9	9 59.3
28 Th	6 27 29	7 04 46	0♒13 35	6♒51 41	4 42.0	23 55.9	2 14.4	8 54.0	25 23.5	17 49.5	21 04.5	15 42.7	11 04.5	9 58.2
29 F	6 31 26	8 01 58	13 24 37	19 52 28	4 41.7	25 55.1	3 27.1	9 20.9	25 20.1	17 52.1	21 10.6	15 46.0	11 05.0	9 57.1
30 Sa	6 35 23	8 59 10	26 15 24	2♓33 38	4 41.2	27 56.4	4 39.7	9 48.2	25 16.3	17 55.0	21 16.7	15 49.4	11 05.4	9 55.9

Astro Data

	Dy Hr Mn
☿R	1 23:08
♂D	5 19:01
☽0N	8 3:52
♇R	11 4:19
☽0S	22 11:02
♆✶♇	22 19:28
☿D	25 19:23
♃⚻♄	30 18:16
☽0N	4 10:23
♂0S	8 18:39
♃D	13 21:08
☽0S	18 16:31
⚳R	19 8:03

Planet Ingress

	Dy Hr Mn
♀ ♊	8 12:47
☉ ♊	20 17:57
♀ ♋	2 0:12
♂ ♎	5 4:50
☿ ♊	13 16:48
☉ ♋	21 1:49
♀ ♌	26 15:39

Last Aspect / ☽ Ingress (May)

Last Aspect Dy Hr Mn		☽ Ingress Dy Hr Mn
1 14:39	♂□	♑ 1 23:10
3 22:33	☿△	♒ 4 5:02
6 9:33	♀□	♓ 6 14:43
8 16:42	♂☍	♈ 9 2:51
10 17:43	♃☍	♉ 11 15:32
13 18:09	♂△	♊ 14 3:25
16 5:18	♂□	♋ 16 13:46
18 18:31	☉✶	♌ 18 22:00
20 7:37	☿□	♍ 21 3:34
23 0:53	♂☌	♎ 23 6:24
24 14:40	♀△	♏ 25 7:15
27 3:40	♂✶	♐ 27 7:38
29 6:04	♂□	♑ 29 9:21
31 11:34	♂△	♒ 31 14:02

Last Aspect / ☽ Ingress (June)

Last Aspect Dy Hr Mn		☽ Ingress Dy Hr Mn
2 2:20	☿□	♓ 2 22:25
4 16:05	☿✶	♈ 5 9:51
6 21:23	♃☍	♉ 7 22:28
10 2:09	☿☌	♊ 10 10:14
12 3:52	☉☌	♋ 12 20:02
14 8:28	♄✶	♌ 15 3:35
17 2:22	☉✶	♍ 17 9:01
19 9:55	☉□	♎ 19 12:37
21 3:46	♀□	♏ 21 14:52
23 10:08	♀△	♐ 23 16:38
24 22:14	♃✶	♑ 25 19:07
27 7:29	♄△	♒ 27 23:36
30 1:30	☿△	♓ 30 7:07

☽ Phases & Eclipses

Dy Hr Mn	
5 9:49	☾ 15♒11
13 13:43	● 23♉05
21 4:17	☽ 0♍25
27 18:39	○ 6♐45
4 1:20	☾ 13♓44
12 3:52	● 21♊29
12 4:06:08	● P 0.458
19 9:55	☽ 28♍25
26 3:24	○ 4♑50
26 3:23	● T 1.844

Astro Data

1 May 2029
Julian Day # 47238
SVP 4♓50'44"
GC 27♐14.9 ⚴ 14♑30.6
Eris 26♈08.6 ⚵ 29♎41.3R
⚷ 8♉22.6 ⚶ 22♑08.3
☽ Mean ☊ 7♑45.2

1 June 2029
Julian Day # 47269
SVP 4♓50'39"
GC 27♐15.0 ⚴ 11♑13.1R
Eris 26♈26.4 ⚵ 24♎43.1R
⚷ 10♉15.5 ⚶ 24♑41.9R
☽ Mean ☊ 6♑06.7

July 2029 — LONGITUDE

Day	Sid.Time	☉	0 hr ☽	Noon ☽	True ☊	☿	♀	♂	⚳	♃	♄	♅	♆	♇
1 Su	6 39 19	9♋56 21	8♓47 31	14♓57 26	4♑40.7	29♊59.8	5♌52.4	10♎15.7	25♒12.2	17♎58.0	21♉22.7	15♊52.7	11♈05.9	9♒54.8
2 M	6 43 16	10 53 33	21 03 49	27 07 10	4R 40.3	2♋04.9	7 05.0	10 43.4	25R 07.7	18 01.1	21 28.6	15 56.0	11 06.3	9R 53.6
3 Tu	6 47 12	11 50 45	3♈07 58	9♈06 48	4D 40.1	4 11.6	8 17.5	11 11.5	25 02.9	18 04.5	21 34.5	15 59.2	11 06.6	9 52.4
4 W	6 51 09	12 47 57	15 04 13	21 00 48	4 40.2	6 19.6	9 30.1	11 39.8	24 57.7	18 08.0	21 40.3	16 02.5	11 06.9	9 51.3
5 Th	6 55 05	13 45 10	26 57 08	2♉53 46	4 40.6	8 28.5	10 42.6	12 08.4	24 52.2	18 11.6	21 46.1	16 05.7	11 07.2	9 50.1
6 F	6 59 02	14 42 23	8♉51 16	14 50 12	4 41.4	10 38.1	11 55.1	12 37.2	24 46.3	18 15.5	21 51.8	16 09.0	11 07.5	9 48.8
7 Sa	7 02 58	15 39 36	20 51 03	26 54 20	4 42.4	12 48.2	13 07.6	13 06.3	24 40.0	18 19.5	21 57.4	16 12.2	11 07.7	9 47.6
8 Su	7 06 55	16 36 49	3♊00 28	9♊09 52	4 43.5	14 58.3	14 20.0	13 35.6	24 33.5	18 23.6	22 03.0	16 15.3	11 08.0	9 46.4
9 M	7 10 52	17 34 03	15 22 52	21 39 46	4 44.3	17 08.2	15 32.4	14 05.2	24 26.6	18 27.9	22 08.5	16 18.5	11 08.1	9 45.1
10 Tu	7 14 48	18 31 17	28 00 47	4♋26 04	4R 44.6	19 17.8	16 44.8	14 35.0	24 19.3	18 32.4	22 13.9	16 21.6	11 08.3	9 43.9
11 W	7 18 45	19 28 31	10♋55 43	17 29 44	4 44.2	21 26.6	17 57.2	15 05.1	24 11.8	18 37.0	22 19.2	16 24.7	11 08.4	9 42.6
12 Th	7 22 41	20 25 46	24 08 05	0♌50 36	4 43.2	23 34.6	19 09.5	15 35.4	24 03.9	18 41.8	22 24.5	16 27.8	11 08.4	9 41.3
13 F	7 26 38	21 23 00	7♌37 06	14 27 20	4 41.4	25 41.5	20 21.8	16 05.9	23 55.7	18 46.7	22 29.7	16 30.9	11R 08.5	9 40.0
14 Sa	7 30 34	22 20 15	21 20 59	28 17 42	4 39.1	27 47.2	21 34.1	16 36.6	23 47.2	18 51.8	22 34.9	16 33.9	11 08.5	9 38.7
15 Su	7 34 31	23 17 30	5♍17 06	12♍18 46	4 36.8	29 51.6	22 46.3	17 07.6	23 38.3	18 57.1	22 39.9	16 36.9	11 08.4	9 37.4
16 M	7 38 27	24 14 44	19 22 19	26 27 19	4 34.7	1♌54.5	23 58.5	17 38.8	23 29.2	19 02.5	22 44.9	16 39.9	11 08.4	9 36.1
17 Tu	7 42 24	25 11 59	3♎33 24	10♎40 09	4 33.2	3 55.8	25 10.7	18 10.2	23 19.8	19 08.0	22 49.8	16 42.9	11 08.3	9 34.8
18 W	7 46 21	26 09 14	17 47 13	24 54 17	4D 32.7	5 55.5	26 22.8	18 41.9	23 10.1	19 13.7	22 54.7	16 45.8	11 08.2	9 33.4
19 Th	7 50 17	27 06 30	2♏01 02	9♏07 11	4 33.0	7 53.5	27 34.9	19 13.7	23 00.2	19 19.5	22 59.4	16 48.7	11 08.0	9 32.1
20 F	7 54 14	28 03 45	16 12 27	23 16 34	4 34.1	9 49.8	28 46.9	19 45.7	22 50.0	19 25.5	23 04.1	16 51.6	11 07.8	9 30.7
21 Sa	7 58 10	29 01 01	0♐19 19	7♐20 25	4 35.5	11 44.4	29 58.9	20 18.0	22 39.5	19 31.6	23 08.7	16 54.4	11 07.6	9 29.4
22 Su	8 02 07	29 58 17	14 19 39	21 16 45	4R 36.7	13 37.2	1♍10.9	20 50.4	22 28.8	19 37.9	23 13.3	16 57.2	11 07.3	9 28.0
23 M	8 06 03	0♌55 33	28 11 27	5♑03 31	4 37.2	15 28.2	2 22.8	21 23.0	22 17.8	19 44.3	23 17.7	17 00.0	11 07.0	9 26.7
24 Tu	8 10 00	1 52 50	11♑52 42	18 38 44	4 36.6	17 17.5	3 34.7	21 55.8	22 06.7	19 50.8	23 22.1	17 02.8	11 06.7	9 25.3
25 W	8 13 56	2 50 07	25 21 25	2♒00 32	4 34.5	19 05.1	4 46.5	22 28.8	21 55.3	19 57.5	23 26.4	17 05.5	11 06.4	9 23.9
26 Th	8 17 53	3 47 25	8♒35 55	15 07 27	4 31.1	20 50.8	5 58.3	23 02.0	21 43.7	20 04.3	23 30.6	17 08.2	11 06.0	9 22.6
27 F	8 21 50	4 44 44	21 35 03	27 58 40	4 26.7	22 34.9	7 10.1	23 35.4	21 31.9	20 11.2	23 34.7	17 10.8	11 05.6	9 21.2
28 Sa	8 25 46	5 42 03	4♓18 23	10♓34 16	4 21.6	24 17.2	8 21.8	24 09.0	21 19.9	20 18.3	23 38.7	17 13.5	11 05.1	9 19.8
29 Su	8 29 43	6 39 24	16 46 29	22 55 17	4 16.5	25 57.7	9 33.4	24 42.7	21 07.7	20 25.5	23 42.6	17 16.1	11 04.7	9 18.4
30 M	8 33 39	7 36 45	29 00 56	5♈03 49	4 11.9	27 36.6	10 45.0	25 16.6	20 55.4	20 32.8	23 46.5	17 18.6	11 04.2	9 17.0
31 Tu	8 37 36	8 34 07	11♈04 19	17 02 55	4 08.4	29 13.7	11 56.6	25 50.7	20 42.9	20 40.2	23 50.3	17 21.1	11 03.6	9 15.7

August 2029 — LONGITUDE

Day	Sid.Time	☉	0 hr ☽	Noon ☽	True ☊	☿	♀	♂	⚳	♃	♄	♅	♆	♇
1 W	8 41 32	9♌31 30	23♈00 06	28♈56 24	4♑06.3	0♍49.1	13♍08.2	26♎24.9	20♒30.3	20♎47.8	23♉53.9	17♊23.6	11♈03.0	9♒14.3
2 Th	8 45 29	10 28 55	4♉52 24	10♉48 42	4D 05.6	2 22.7	14 19.7	26 59.3	20R 17.6	20 55.5	23 57.5	17 26.1	11R 02.4	9R 12.9
3 F	8 49 25	11 26 21	16 45 54	22 44 38	4 06.2	3 54.7	15 31.1	27 33.9	20 04.7	21 03.3	24 01.0	17 28.5	11 01.8	9 11.5
4 Sa	8 53 22	12 23 48	28 45 30	4♊49 06	4 07.6	5 24.9	16 42.5	28 08.7	19 51.8	21 11.3	24 04.5	17 30.9	11 01.2	9 10.1
5 Su	8 57 19	13 21 16	10♊56 03	17 06 53	4 09.2	6 53.4	17 53.9	28 43.6	19 38.7	21 19.4	24 07.8	17 33.2	11 00.5	9 08.7
6 M	9 01 15	14 18 45	23 22 05	29 42 09	4R 10.2	8 20.1	19 05.2	29 18.7	19 25.6	21 27.5	24 11.0	17 35.5	10 59.8	9 07.4
7 Tu	9 05 12	15 16 16	6♋07 24	12♋38 09	4 09.9	9 45.0	20 16.5	29 54.0	19 12.4	21 35.8	24 14.1	17 37.8	10 59.0	9 06.0
8 W	9 09 08	16 13 47	19 14 35	25 56 44	4 08.0	11 08.2	21 27.7	0♏29.4	18 59.2	21 44.3	24 17.2	17 40.0	10 58.2	9 04.6
9 Th	9 13 05	17 11 20	2♌44 35	9♌37 54	4 04.1	12 29.4	22 38.9	1 05.0	18 45.9	21 52.8	24 20.1	17 42.2	10 57.4	9 03.2
10 F	9 17 01	18 08 54	16 36 22	23 39 32	3 58.5	13 48.9	23 50.0	1 40.8	18 32.7	22 01.4	24 22.9	17 44.3	10 56.6	9 01.9
11 Sa	9 20 58	19 06 29	0♍46 48	7♍57 30	3 51.7	15 06.3	25 01.1	2 16.7	18 19.4	22 10.2	24 25.7	17 46.4	10 55.8	9 00.5
12 Su	9 24 54	20 04 05	15 10 52	22 26 06	3 44.7	16 21.9	26 12.1	2 52.8	18 06.1	22 19.1	24 28.3	17 48.5	10 54.9	8 59.2
13 M	9 28 51	21 01 42	29 42 23	6♎58 55	3 38.1	17 35.3	27 23.1	3 29.0	17 52.9	22 28.0	24 30.9	17 50.5	10 54.0	8 57.8
14 Tu	9 32 48	21 59 20	14♎14 55	21 29 44	3 33.0	18 46.7	28 34.0	4 05.3	17 39.7	22 37.1	24 33.3	17 52.5	10 53.0	8 56.5
15 W	9 36 44	22 56 59	28 42 46	5♏53 32	3 29.8	19 55.9	29 44.9	4 41.9	17 26.6	22 46.3	24 35.7	17 54.4	10 52.0	8 55.1
16 Th	9 40 41	23 54 39	13♏01 38	20 06 49	3D 28.6	21 02.8	0♎55.7	5 18.5	17 13.5	22 55.6	24 37.9	17 56.3	10 51.0	8 53.8
17 F	9 44 37	24 52 20	27 08 52	4♐07 43	3 28.8	22 07.4	2 06.4	5 55.3	17 00.5	23 05.0	24 40.1	17 58.2	10 50.0	8 52.5
18 Sa	9 48 34	25 50 02	11♐03 19	17 55 41	3 29.8	23 09.5	3 17.1	6 32.3	16 47.7	23 14.5	24 42.1	18 00.0	10 49.0	8 51.2
19 Su	9 52 30	26 47 46	24 44 53	1♑30 57	3R 30.4	24 08.9	4 27.7	7 09.4	16 34.9	23 24.1	24 44.1	18 01.7	10 47.9	8 49.9
20 M	9 56 27	27 45 30	8♑13 59	14 54 01	3 29.8	25 05.7	5 38.3	7 46.6	16 22.3	23 33.7	24 45.9	18 03.5	10 46.8	8 48.6
21 Tu	10 00 23	28 43 15	21 31 09	28 05 22	3 27.2	25 59.6	6 48.7	8 24.0	16 09.7	23 43.5	24 47.6	18 05.1	10 45.7	8 47.3
22 W	10 04 20	29 41 02	4♒36 44	11♒05 12	3 22.2	26 50.4	7 59.1	9 01.4	15 57.4	23 53.4	24 49.3	18 06.8	10 44.6	8 46.0
23 Th	10 08 17	0♍38 50	17 30 47	23 53 28	3 14.7	27 38.1	9 09.5	9 39.1	15 45.2	24 03.4	24 50.8	18 08.4	10 43.4	8 44.7
24 F	10 12 13	1 36 39	0♓13 14	6♓30 04	3 05.3	28 22.4	10 19.8	10 16.8	15 33.2	24 13.4	24 52.2	18 09.9	10 42.2	8 43.5
25 Sa	10 16 10	2 34 29	12 43 59	18 55 03	2 54.6	29 03.0	11 30.0	10 54.7	15 21.3	24 23.5	24 53.6	18 11.4	10 41.0	8 42.2
26 Su	10 20 06	3 32 22	25 03 20	1♈08 58	2 43.6	29 39.9	12 40.1	11 32.7	15 09.7	24 33.8	24 54.8	18 12.8	10 39.8	8 41.0
27 M	10 24 03	4 30 16	7♈12 07	13 13 02	2 33.4	0♎12.7	13 50.1	12 10.9	14 58.2	24 44.1	24 55.9	18 14.2	10 38.5	8 39.8
28 Tu	10 27 59	5 28 11	19 11 58	25 09 18	2 24.8	0 41.2	15 00.1	12 49.1	14 47.0	24 54.5	24 56.9	18 15.6	10 37.2	8 38.6
29 W	10 31 56	6 26 09	1♉05 23	7♉00 42	2 18.4	1 05.1	16 10.1	13 27.5	14 36.0	25 05.0	24 57.8	18 16.9	10 35.9	8 37.4
30 Th	10 35 52	7 24 08	12 55 45	18 51 03	2 14.4	1 24.2	17 19.9	14 06.1	14 25.2	25 15.5	24 58.6	18 18.1	10 34.6	8 36.2
31 F	10 39 49	8 22 09	24 47 12	0♊44 48	2D 12.6	1 38.2	18 29.7	14 44.7	14 14.7	25 26.2	24 59.3	18 19.3	10 33.3	8 35.0

Astro Data

	Dy Hr Mn
☽0N	1 18:22
♆R	14 2:10
☽0S	15 22:08
☽0N	29 3:06
☽0S	12 5:28
♀0S	16 22:58
☿0S	20 11:57
☽0N	25 11:21
♃⊼♄	28 18:03

Planet Ingress

		Dy Hr Mn
☿	♋	1 12:03
☿	♌	15 13:38
♀	♍	21 12:22
☉	♌	22 12:43
☿	♍	31 23:36
♂	♏	7 16:04
♀	♎	15 17:08
☉	♍	22 19:53
☿	♎	27 2:22

Last Aspect / ☽ Ingress (July)

Last Aspect Dy Hr Mn			☽ Ingress	Dy Hr Mn
2 0:43	♄	⚹	♈	2 17:44
4 6:09	♃	☍	♉	5 6:09
7 2:07	♄	☌	♊	7 18:06
9 5:52	♃	△	♋	10 3:44
11 20:48	♄	⚹	♌	12 10:30
14 2:04	♄	□	♍	14 14:56
16 7:59	☉	⚹	♎	16 18:00
18 14:43	♀	⚹	♏	18 20:36
20 22:15	♀	□	♐	20 23:27
22 11:13	♂	⚹	♑	23 3:09
24 20:29	♄	△	♒	25 8:22
27 3:41	♄	□	♓	27 15:49
29 13:33	♄	⚹	♈	30 1:57

Last Aspect / ☽ Ingress (August)

Last Aspect Dy Hr Mn			☽ Ingress	Dy Hr Mn
1 6:38	♂	☍	♉	1 14:09
3 14:34	♄	☌	♊	4 2:28
6 11:14	♂	△	♋	6 12:34
8 9:02	♄	⚹	♌	8 19:11
10 13:14	♄	□	♍	10 22:41
12 18:46	♀	☌	♎	13 0:29
14 13:53	♃	☌	♏	15 2:09
16 19:43	♄	☍	♐	17 4:54
19 2:59	☉	△	♑	19 9:18
21 7:53	☿	△	♒	21 15:30
23 13:49	♄	□	♓	23 23:35
26 8:55	☿	☍	♈	26 9:44
28 11:30	♃	☍	♉	28 21:48
31 0:24	♄	☌	♊	31 10:30

☽ Phases & Eclipses

Dy Hr Mn		
3 17:59	☾	12♈05
11 15:52	●	19♋38
11 15:37:20	●	P 0.230
18 14:16	☽	26♎15
25 13:37	○	2♒54
2 11:17	☾	10♉27
10 1:57	●	17♌45
16 18:57	☽	24♏11
24 1:52	○	1♓12

Astro Data

1 July 2029
Julian Day # 47299
SVP 4♓50'34"
GC 27♐15.1 ⚴ 3♑09.4R
Eris 26♈37.2 ⚵ 24♎35.6
⚷ 11♉42.9 ⚶ 20♑14.4R
☽ Mean ☊ 4♑31.4

1 August 2029
Julian Day # 47330
SVP 4♓50'29"
GC 27♐15.2 ⚴ 26♐37.5R
Eris 26♈39.1R ⚵ 28♎49.0
⚷ 12♉33.4 ⚶ 13♑26.0R
☽ Mean ☊ 2♑53.0

LONGITUDE — September 2029

Day	Sid.Time	☉	0 hr ☽	Noon ☽	True ☊	☿	♀	♂	⚳	♃	♄	♅	♆	♇
1 Sa	10 43 46	9♍20 12	6♊44 32	12♊47 01	2♑12.3	1♎46.9	19♎39.4	15♏23.5	14♒04.5	25♎36.9	24♉59.9	18♊20.5	10♈31.9	8♒33.9
2 Su	10 47 42	10 18 17	18 52 56	25 02 56	2R12.7	1R49.9	20 49.0	16 02.4	13R54.5	25 47.8	25 00.3	18 21.6	10R30.6	8R32.7
3 M	10 51 39	11 16 24	1♋17 39	7♋37 41	2 12.8	1 46.9	21 58.5	16 41.5	13 44.7	25 58.6	25 00.7	18 22.7	10 29.2	8 31.6
4 Tu	10 55 35	12 14 33	14 03 35	20 35 47	2 11.4	1 37.9	23 08.0	17 20.6	13 35.3	26 09.6	25 01.0	18 23.7	10 27.8	8 30.5
5 W	10 59 32	13 12 44	27 14 38	4♌00 23	2 07.8	1 22.6	24 17.4	17 59.9	13 26.1	26 20.7	25R01.1	18 24.6	10 26.3	8 29.4
6 Th	11 03 28	14 10 56	10♌53 04	17 52 36	2 01.6	1 00.9	25 26.7	18 39.3	13 17.3	26 31.8	25 01.1	18 25.6	10 24.9	8 28.3
7 F	11 07 25	15 09 11	24 58 40	2♍10 48	1 53.0	0 32.9	26 35.9	19 18.8	13 08.7	26 43.0	25 01.1	18 26.4	10 23.4	8 27.3
8 Sa	11 11 21	16 07 27	9♍28 19	16 50 20	1 42.7	29♍58.5	27 45.1	19 58.4	13 00.5	26 54.2	25 00.9	18 27.2	10 22.0	8 26.2
9 Su	11 15 18	17 05 45	24 15 50	1♎43 43	1 31.8	29 18.0	28 54.1	20 38.2	12 52.6	27 05.5	25 00.6	18 28.0	10 20.5	8 25.2
10 M	11 19 14	18 04 05	9♎12 47	16 41 51	1 21.6	28 31.8	0♏03.1	21 18.1	12 45.0	27 16.9	25 00.2	18 28.7	10 18.9	8 24.2
11 Tu	11 23 11	19 02 26	24 09 47	1♏35 30	1 13.2	27 40.6	1 12.0	21 58.1	12 37.7	27 28.4	24 59.7	18 29.3	10 17.4	8 23.2
12 W	11 27 08	20 00 50	8♏58 08	16 16 55	1 07.3	26 45.0	2 20.7	22 38.2	12 30.8	27 39.9	24 59.1	18 29.9	10 15.9	8 22.3
13 Th	11 31 04	20 59 14	23 31 17	0♐40 49	1 04.1	25 45.9	3 29.4	23 18.4	12 24.2	27 51.5	24 58.4	18 30.5	10 14.4	8 21.3
14 F	11 35 01	21 57 41	7♐45 18	14 44 39	1D02.9	24 44.6	4 38.0	23 58.7	12 18.0	28 03.2	24 57.6	18 31.0	10 12.8	8 20.4
15 Sa	11 38 57	22 56 09	21 38 54	28 28 11	1R02.8	23 42.4	5 46.4	24 39.2	12 12.1	28 14.9	24 56.6	18 31.5	10 11.2	8 19.5
16 Su	11 42 54	23 54 38	5♑12 45	11♑52 50	1 02.6	22 40.6	6 54.8	25 19.7	12 06.6	28 26.7	24 55.6	18 31.9	10 09.6	8 18.6
17 M	11 46 50	24 53 09	18 28 44	25 00 45	1 01.0	21 40.7	8 03.0	26 00.4	12 01.4	28 38.5	24 54.4	18 32.2	10 08.1	8 17.8
18 Tu	11 50 47	25 51 42	1♒29 11	7♒54 20	0 57.0	20 44.3	9 11.1	26 41.1	11 56.6	28 50.4	24 53.2	18 32.5	10 06.5	8 16.9
19 W	11 54 43	26 50 16	14 16 24	20 35 39	0 50.1	19 52.7	10 19.2	27 22.0	11 52.1	29 02.3	24 51.8	18 32.7	10 04.8	8 16.1
20 Th	11 58 40	27 48 52	26 52 16	3♓06 24	0 40.3	19 07.4	11 27.0	28 03.0	11 48.0	29 14.3	24 50.4	18 32.9	10 03.2	8 15.3
21 F	12 02 37	28 47 30	9♓18 10	15 27 42	0 28.1	18 29.4	12 34.8	28 44.0	11 44.3	29 26.4	24 48.8	18 33.1	10 01.6	8 14.5
22 Sa	12 06 33	29 46 10	21 35 06	27 40 27	0 14.3	17 59.8	13 42.4	29 25.2	11 40.9	29 38.5	24 47.2	18 33.2	10 00.0	8 13.8
23 Su	12 10 30	0♎44 51	3♈43 50	9♈45 24	0 00.2	17 39.4	14 49.9	0♐06.4	11 37.9	29 50.6	24 45.4	18R33.2	9 58.3	8 13.0
24 M	12 14 26	1 43 35	15 45 14	21 43 32	29♐46.8	17D28.6	15 57.3	0 47.8	11 35.2	0♏02.8	24 43.5	18 33.2	9 56.7	8 12.3
25 Tu	12 18 23	2 42 21	27 40 28	3♉36 18	29 35.3	17 27.7	17 04.5	1 29.3	11 32.9	0 15.1	24 41.6	18 33.1	9 55.0	8 11.6
26 W	12 22 19	3 41 09	9♉31 17	15 25 48	29 26.3	17 36.9	18 11.6	2 10.8	11 31.0	0 27.4	24 39.5	18 33.0	9 53.4	8 11.0
27 Th	12 26 16	4 39 59	21 20 11	27 14 55	29 20.2	17 56.0	19 18.6	2 52.5	11 29.4	0 39.7	24 37.3	18 32.8	9 51.7	8 10.3
28 F	12 30 12	5 38 51	3♊10 28	9♊07 22	29 16.7	18 24.8	20 25.4	3 34.3	11 28.2	0 52.1	24 35.1	18 32.6	9 50.1	8 09.7
29 Sa	12 34 09	6 37 46	15 06 12	21 07 35	29D15.4	19 02.9	21 32.0	4 16.1	11 27.3	1 04.5	24 32.7	18 32.3	9 48.4	8 09.1
30 Su	12 38 06	7 36 43	27 12 08	3♋20 33	29R15.3	19 49.6	22 38.5	4 58.1	11D26.8	1 17.0	24 30.3	18 32.0	9 46.7	8 08.6

LONGITUDE — October 2029

Day	Sid.Time	☉	0 hr ☽	Noon ☽	True ☊	☿	♀	♂	⚳	♃	♄	♅	♆	♇
1 M	12 42 02	8♎35 42	9♋33 28	15♋51 33	29♐15.2	20♍44.5	23♏44.9	5♐40.1	11♒26.7	1♏29.5	24♉27.7	18♊31.6	9♈45.1	8♒08.0
2 Tu	12 45 59	9 34 44	22 15 25	28 45 38	29R14.0	21 46.8	24 51.1	6 22.3	11 26.9	1 42.1	24R25.1	18R31.2	9R43.4	8R07.5
3 W	12 49 55	10 33 47	5♌22 43	12♌07 03	29 10.7	22 55.9	25 57.1	7 04.5	11 27.5	1 54.7	24 22.3	18 30.7	9 41.7	8 07.0
4 Th	12 53 52	11 32 53	18 58 52	25 58 16	29 04.9	24 10.9	27 03.0	7 46.9	11 28.5	2 07.3	24 19.5	18 30.2	9 40.0	8 06.5
5 F	12 57 48	12 32 02	3♍05 08	10♍19 08	28 56.6	25 31.3	28 08.7	8 29.3	11 29.8	2 20.0	24 16.6	18 29.6	9 38.4	8 06.1
6 Sa	13 01 45	13 31 12	17 39 43	25 06 05	28 46.5	26 56.2	29 14.2	9 11.9	11 31.4	2 32.7	24 13.6	18 29.0	9 36.7	8 05.7
7 Su	13 05 41	14 30 25	2♎37 14	10♎11 58	28 35.5	28 25.1	0♐19.6	9 54.5	11 33.4	2 45.4	24 10.5	18 28.3	9 35.0	8 05.3
8 M	13 09 38	15 29 39	17 48 57	25 26 48	28 25.2	29 57.3	1 24.7	10 37.2	11 35.8	2 58.2	24 07.3	18 27.6	9 33.4	8 04.9
9 Tu	13 13 35	16 28 56	3♏04 06	10♏39 29	28 16.5	1♎32.3	2 29.7	11 20.0	11 38.5	3 11.0	24 04.0	18 26.8	9 31.7	8 04.6
10 W	13 17 31	17 28 15	18 11 45	25 39 48	28 10.4	3 09.6	3 34.4	12 02.9	11 41.5	3 23.8	24 00.6	18 26.0	9 30.1	8 04.3
11 Th	13 21 28	18 27 36	3♐02 46	10♐20 01	28 07.0	4 48.7	4 39.0	12 45.9	11 44.9	3 36.6	23 57.2	18 25.1	9 28.4	8 04.0
12 F	13 25 24	19 26 58	17 31 06	24 35 46	28D05.9	6 29.3	5 43.3	13 29.0	11 48.7	3 49.5	23 53.7	18 24.1	9 26.8	8 03.8
13 Sa	13 29 21	20 26 22	1♑33 58	8♑25 48	28R06.1	8 10.9	6 47.4	14 12.1	11 52.7	4 02.4	23 50.1	18 23.2	9 25.1	8 03.6
14 Su	13 33 17	21 25 48	15 11 28	21 51 18	28 06.4	9 53.4	7 51.3	14 55.4	11 57.1	4 15.3	23 46.4	18 22.1	9 23.5	8 03.4
15 M	13 37 14	22 25 16	28 25 39	4♒54 58	28 05.6	11 36.4	8 54.9	15 38.7	12 01.9	4 28.3	23 42.7	18 21.1	9 21.9	8 03.2
16 Tu	13 41 10	23 24 45	11♒19 40	17 40 12	28 02.9	13 19.8	9 58.2	16 22.1	12 06.9	4 41.3	23 38.9	18 20.0	9 20.3	8 03.1
17 W	13 45 07	24 24 16	23 57 00	0♓10 29	27 57.6	15 03.3	11 01.3	17 05.6	12 12.3	4 54.2	23 35.0	18 18.8	9 18.7	8 02.9
18 Th	13 49 04	25 23 49	6♓21 01	12 28 58	27 49.8	16 46.8	12 04.2	17 49.2	12 18.0	5 07.2	23 31.1	18 17.6	9 17.1	8 02.8
19 F	13 53 00	26 23 23	18 34 38	24 38 19	27 39.8	18 30.2	13 06.7	18 32.8	12 24.0	5 20.3	23 27.0	18 16.3	9 15.5	8 02.8
20 Sa	13 56 57	27 23 00	0♈40 15	6♈40 39	27 28.4	20 13.4	14 09.0	19 16.6	12 30.3	5 33.3	23 23.0	18 15.0	9 13.9	8D02.8
21 Su	14 00 53	28 22 38	12 39 44	18 37 40	27 16.6	21 56.3	15 10.9	20 00.4	12 37.0	5 46.4	23 18.8	18 13.7	9 12.4	8 02.8
22 M	14 04 50	29 22 18	24 34 38	0♉30 48	27 05.4	23 38.9	16 12.5	20 44.2	12 43.9	5 59.4	23 14.6	18 12.3	9 10.8	8 02.8
23 Tu	14 08 46	0♏22 01	6♉26 22	12 21 30	26 55.9	25 21.1	17 13.9	21 28.2	12 51.1	6 12.5	23 10.4	18 10.8	9 09.3	8 02.8
24 W	14 12 43	1 21 45	18 16 27	24 11 26	26 48.5	27 02.8	18 14.8	22 12.2	12 58.7	6 25.6	23 06.1	18 09.3	9 07.8	8 02.9
25 Th	14 16 39	2 21 32	0♊06 44	6♊02 41	26 43.7	28 44.0	19 15.5	22 56.3	13 06.5	6 38.7	23 01.7	18 07.8	9 06.3	8 03.0
26 F	14 20 36	3 21 20	11 59 37	17 57 57	26D41.3	0♏24.8	20 15.8	23 40.5	13 14.6	6 51.8	22 57.3	18 06.3	9 04.8	8 03.2
27 Sa	14 24 32	4 21 11	23 58 07	0♋00 35	26 40.9	2 05.1	21 15.7	24 24.8	13 23.0	7 04.9	22 52.8	18 04.7	9 03.3	8 03.3
28 Su	14 28 29	5 21 04	6♋05 52	12 14 32	26 41.8	3 44.9	22 15.2	25 09.1	13 31.7	7 18.0	22 48.3	18 03.0	9 01.8	8 03.5
29 M	14 32 26	6 20 59	18 27 07	24 44 13	26R43.0	5 24.1	23 14.4	25 53.5	13 40.7	7 31.2	22 43.8	18 01.3	9 00.4	8 03.7
30 Tu	14 36 22	7 20 57	1♌06 25	7♌34 15	26 43.5	7 02.9	24 13.1	26 38.0	13 49.9	7 44.3	22 39.2	17 59.6	8 59.0	8 04.0
31 W	14 40 19	8 20 56	14 08 13	20 48 47	26 42.7	8 41.2	25 11.4	27 22.5	13 59.4	7 57.4	22 34.5	17 57.9	8 57.5	8 04.3

Astro Data	Dy Hr Mn
☿ R	2 12:19
♄ R	6 8:35
☽ 0S	8 14:53
☿ 0N	16 9:43
☽ 0N	21 18:11
☉ 0S	22 17:40
♅ R	23 16:23
☿ D	25 2:01
⚳ D	1 8:43
☽ 0S	6 1:21
♃□♅	10 15:49
☿ 0S	11 7:45
☽ 0N	18 23:36
♇ D	21 3:55

Planet Ingress		Dy Hr Mn
☿	♍R	8 11:01
♀	♏	10 10:56
☉	♎	22 17:40
♂	♐	23 8:15
☊	♐R	23 12:19
♃	♏	24 6:25
♀	♐	7 4:49
☿	♎	8 12:42
☉	♏	23 3:09
☿	♏	26 6:05

Last Aspect Dy Hr Mn		☽ Ingress Dy Hr Mn
2 13:28	♃ △	♋ 2 21:32
4 22:12	♃ □	♌ 5 4:55
7 2:47	♃ ⚹	♍ 7 8:23
9 8:17	☿ ☌	♎ 9 9:14
11 5:15	♃ ☌	♏ 11 9:25
13 4:17	☿ ⚹	♐ 13 10:51
15 11:36	♃ ⚹	♑ 15 14:43
17 18:49	♃ □	♒ 17 21:14
20 4:26	♃ △	♓ 20 6:01
22 16:30	☉ ☍	♈ 22 16:36
24 5:37	♅ ⚹	♉ 25 4:42
27 6:41	♄ ☌	♊ 27 17:35
29 7:37	☿ □	♋ 30 5:29

Last Aspect Dy Hr Mn		☽ Ingress Dy Hr Mn
2 4:09	♀ △	♌ 2 14:16
4 13:59	♀ □	♍ 4 18:49
6 19:08	♀ ⚹	♎ 6 19:50
8 1:01	♅ △	♏ 8 19:10
10 9:21	♄ ☍	♐ 10 19:02
12 2:36	☉ ⚹	♑ 12 21:17
14 15:28	♄ △	♒ 15 2:54
16 23:55	☉ △	♓ 17 11:40
19 9:39	♄ ⚹	♈ 19 22:40
22 9:29	☉ ☍	♉ 22 10:58
24 9:48	♄ ☌	♊ 24 23:46
27 0:10	♂ ☍	♋ 27 11:59
29 8:12	♄ ⚹	♌ 29 21:56

☽ Phases & Eclipses Dy Hr Mn		
1 4:34	☾	9♊02
8 10:45	●	16♍04
15 1:30	☽	22♐31
22 16:30	○	29♓57
30 20:58	☾	7♋59
7 19:16	●	14♎48
14 11:10	☽	21♑24
22 9:29	○	29♈16
30 11:33	☾	7♌20

Astro Data

1 September 2029
Julian Day # 47361
SVP 4♓50'26"
GC 27♐15.2 ⚴ 26♐17.5
Eris 26♈31.3R ⚵ 6♏01.6
⚷ 12♉32.1R ⚶ 12♑14.2
☽ Mean ☊ 1♑14.5

1 October 2029
Julian Day # 47391
SVP 4♓50'22"
GC 27♐15.3 ⚴ 0♑59.3
Eris 26♈16.5R ⚵ 14♏45.8
⚷ 11♉42.4R ⚶ 17♑34.8
☽ Mean ☊ 29♐39.1

November 2029 LONGITUDE

Day	Sid.Time	☉	0 hr ☽	Noon ☽	True ☊	☿	♀	♂	⚳	♃	♄	♅	♆	♇
1 Th	14 44 15	9♏20 58	27♌36 18	4♍30 59	26♐40.0	10♏19.0	26♐09.3	28♐07.1	14♒09.2	8♏10.6	22♉29.9	17♊56.1	8♈56.1	8♒04.6
2 F	14 48 12	10 21 01	11♍32 55	18 42 00	26R35.3	11 56.4	27 06.7	28 51.8	14 19.2	8 23.7	22R25.2	17R54.2	8R54.8	8 04.9
3 Sa	14 52 08	11 21 07	25 57 56	3♎20 11	26 29.2	13 33.3	28 03.7	29 36.6	14 29.6	8 36.9	22 20.4	17 52.3	8 53.4	8 05.3
4 Su	14 56 05	12 21 15	10♎48 00	18 20 27	26 22.2	15 09.7	29 00.2	0♑21.4	14 40.1	8 50.0	22 15.6	17 50.4	8 52.1	8 05.7
5 M	15 00 01	13 21 25	25 56 24	3♏34 33	26 15.5	16 45.8	29 56.1	1 06.3	14 51.0	9 03.1	22 10.9	17 48.5	8 50.8	8 06.1
6 Tu	15 03 58	14 21 37	11♏13 33	18 52 00	26 09.9	18 21.4	0♑51.6	1 51.3	15 02.0	9 16.3	22 06.0	17 46.5	8 49.5	8 06.5
7 W	15 07 55	15 21 50	26 28 32	4♐01 54	26 06.1	19 56.6	1 46.5	2 36.3	15 13.4	9 29.4	22 01.2	17 44.5	8 48.2	8 07.0
8 Th	15 11 51	16 22 06	11♐30 59	18 54 50	26D04.4	21 31.5	2 40.8	3 21.4	15 25.0	9 42.5	21 56.4	17 42.4	8 46.9	8 07.5
9 F	15 15 48	17 22 23	26 12 43	3♑24 06	26 04.4	23 06.0	3 34.5	4 06.6	15 36.8	9 55.6	21 51.5	17 40.4	8 45.7	8 08.0
10 Sa	15 19 44	18 22 41	10♑28 41	17 26 18	26 05.5	24 40.1	4 27.7	4 51.8	15 48.8	10 08.7	21 46.6	17 38.3	8 44.5	8 08.6
11 Su	15 23 41	19 23 01	24 17 01	1♒00 59	26 07.1	26 13.9	5 20.1	5 37.1	16 01.1	10 21.8	21 41.8	17 36.1	8 43.3	8 09.2
12 M	15 27 37	20 23 22	7♒38 29	14 09 54	26R08.2	27 47.4	6 11.9	6 22.4	16 13.7	10 34.8	21 36.9	17 34.0	8 42.2	8 09.8
13 Tu	15 31 34	21 23 45	20 35 42	26 56 20	26 08.2	29 20.6	7 03.0	7 07.8	16 26.4	10 47.9	21 32.0	17 31.8	8 41.1	8 10.4
14 W	15 35 30	22 24 09	3♓12 20	9♓24 13	26 06.7	0♐53.5	7 53.3	7 53.3	16 39.4	11 00.9	21 27.1	17 29.6	8 39.9	8 11.1
15 Th	15 39 27	23 24 34	15 32 29	21 37 40	26 03.7	2 26.1	8 42.8	8 38.8	16 52.6	11 13.9	21 22.2	17 27.3	8 38.9	8 11.8
16 F	15 43 24	24 25 01	27 40 13	3♈40 36	25 59.3	3 58.4	9 31.6	9 24.4	17 06.0	11 26.9	21 17.3	17 25.0	8 37.8	8 12.5
17 Sa	15 47 20	25 25 29	9♈39 15	15 36 33	25 54.0	5 30.5	10 19.5	10 10.0	17 19.6	11 39.9	21 12.4	17 22.7	8 36.8	8 13.3
18 Su	15 51 17	26 25 58	21 32 52	27 28 30	25 48.4	7 02.3	11 06.5	10 55.7	17 33.5	11 52.9	21 07.6	17 20.4	8 35.8	8 14.0
19 M	15 55 13	27 26 29	3♉23 48	9♉19 00	25 43.1	8 33.9	11 52.7	11 41.4	17 47.5	12 05.8	21 02.7	17 18.1	8 34.8	8 14.9
20 Tu	15 59 10	28 27 01	15 14 22	21 10 08	25 38.6	10 05.2	12 37.9	12 27.2	18 01.8	12 18.7	20 57.9	17 15.7	8 33.9	8 15.7
21 W	16 03 06	29 27 35	27 06 32	3♊03 47	25 35.4	11 36.3	13 22.1	13 13.0	18 16.2	12 31.6	20 53.1	17 13.4	8 32.9	8 16.5
22 Th	16 07 03	0♐28 10	9♊02 07	15 01 45	25D33.5	13 07.1	14 05.3	13 58.9	18 30.8	12 44.4	20 48.3	17 11.0	8 32.1	8 17.4
23 F	16 10 59	1 28 47	21 02 55	27 05 52	25 33.1	14 37.6	14 47.4	14 44.8	18 45.7	12 57.2	20 43.5	17 08.5	8 31.2	8 18.3
24 Sa	16 14 56	2 29 26	3♋10 54	9♋18 17	25 33.7	16 07.9	15 28.4	15 30.8	19 00.7	13 10.0	20 38.8	17 06.1	8 30.4	8 19.3
25 Su	16 18 53	3 30 05	15 28 21	21 41 27	25 35.1	17 37.9	16 08.3	16 16.8	19 15.9	13 22.8	20 34.1	17 03.7	8 29.6	8 20.2
26 M	16 22 49	4 30 47	27 57 55	4♌18 08	25 36.8	19 07.5	16 46.9	17 02.9	19 31.3	13 35.5	20 29.4	17 01.2	8 28.8	8 21.2
27 Tu	16 26 46	5 31 30	10♌40 29	17 11 20	25 38.2	20 36.7	17 24.3	17 49.0	19 46.9	13 48.2	20 24.8	16 58.7	8 28.0	8 22.2
28 W	16 30 42	6 32 14	23 45 04	0♍23 59	25R39.0	22 05.6	18 00.4	18 35.2	20 02.6	14 00.9	20 20.2	16 56.2	8 27.3	8 23.2
29 Th	16 34 39	7 33 00	7♍08 23	13 58 29	25 39.0	23 34.0	18 35.2	19 21.4	20 18.5	14 13.5	20 15.6	16 53.7	8 26.6	8 24.3
30 F	16 38 35	8 33 48	20 54 25	27 56 12	25 38.2	25 01.9	19 08.6	20 07.7	20 34.6	14 26.1	20 11.1	16 51.2	8 26.0	8 25.4

December 2029 LONGITUDE

Day	Sid.Time	☉	0 hr ☽	Noon ☽	True ☊	☿	♀	♂	⚳	♃	♄	♅	♆	♇
1 Sa	16 42 32	9♐34 37	5♎03 43	12♎16 43	25♐36.6	26♐29.2	19♑40.5	20♑54.0	20♒50.9	14♏38.7	20♉06.6	16♊48.7	8♈25.4	8♒26.5
2 Su	16 46 28	10 35 28	19 34 47	26 57 21	25R34.7	27 55.8	20 10.9	21 40.3	21 07.4	14 51.2	20R02.2	16R46.2	8R24.8	8 27.6
3 M	16 50 25	11 36 20	4♏23 41	11♏52 54	25 32.8	29 21.6	20 39.7	22 26.7	21 24.0	15 03.7	19 57.8	16 43.7	8 24.2	8 28.7
4 Tu	16 54 22	12 37 13	19 23 59	26 55 53	25 31.3	0♑46.6	21 06.9	23 13.2	21 40.8	15 16.1	19 53.5	16 41.1	8 23.7	8 29.9
5 W	16 58 18	13 38 08	4♐27 25	11♐57 29	25D30.4	2 10.5	21 32.4	23 59.6	21 57.7	15 28.5	19 49.2	16 38.6	8 23.2	8 31.1
6 Th	17 02 15	14 39 03	19 24 57	26 48 50	25 30.1	3 33.1	21 56.1	24 46.2	22 14.8	15 40.8	19 45.0	16 36.0	8 22.8	8 32.3
7 F	17 06 11	15 40 00	4♑08 12	11♑22 18	25 30.4	4 54.3	22 18.0	25 32.7	22 32.1	15 53.1	19 40.9	16 33.5	8 22.4	8 33.6
8 Sa	17 10 08	16 40 57	18 30 33	25 32 29	25 31.1	6 13.9	22 38.0	26 19.3	22 49.5	16 05.3	19 36.8	16 30.9	8 22.0	8 34.8
9 Su	17 14 04	17 41 56	2♒27 53	9♒16 36	25 31.9	7 31.5	22 56.0	27 06.0	23 07.0	16 17.5	19 32.8	16 28.4	8 21.6	8 36.1
10 M	17 18 01	18 42 54	15 58 42	22 34 22	25 32.7	8 46.9	23 12.0	27 52.6	23 24.7	16 29.6	19 28.8	16 25.8	8 21.3	8 37.4
11 Tu	17 21 58	19 43 54	29 03 52	5♓27 34	25 33.2	9 59.7	23 25.8	28 39.3	23 42.6	16 41.7	19 24.9	16 23.3	8 21.0	8 38.7
12 W	17 25 54	20 44 54	11♓45 55	17 59 26	25R33.4	11 09.4	23 37.5	29 26.0	24 00.6	16 53.7	19 21.1	16 20.7	8 20.7	8 40.1
13 Th	17 29 51	21 45 54	24 08 38	0♈14 05	25 33.3	12 15.6	23 47.0	0♒12.8	24 18.7	17 05.7	19 17.4	16 18.2	8 20.5	8 41.4
14 F	17 33 47	22 46 55	6♈16 22	12 16 03	25 33.1	13 17.8	23 54.2	0 59.6	24 36.9	17 17.6	19 13.7	16 15.7	8 20.3	8 42.8
15 Sa	17 37 44	23 47 56	18 13 41	24 09 51	25 32.9	14 15.2	23 59.0	1 46.4	24 55.3	17 29.4	19 10.2	16 13.1	8 20.2	8 44.2
16 Su	17 41 40	24 48 58	0♉05 02	5♉59 46	25D32.7	15 07.4	24R01.4	2 33.2	25 13.9	17 41.2	19 06.7	16 10.6	8 20.1	8 45.7
17 M	17 45 37	25 50 01	11 54 31	17 49 42	25 32.7	15 53.4	24 01.4	3 20.1	25 32.5	17 52.9	19 03.2	16 08.1	8 20.0	8 47.1
18 Tu	17 49 33	26 51 04	23 45 44	29 42 59	25 32.8	16 32.5	23 58.9	4 07.0	25 51.3	18 04.5	18 59.9	16 05.6	8D19.9	8 48.6
19 W	17 53 30	27 52 07	5♊41 46	11♊42 24	25 32.9	17 03.8	23 53.9	4 53.9	26 10.2	18 16.1	18 56.7	16 03.1	8 19.9	8 50.0
20 Th	17 57 27	28 53 11	17 45 07	23 50 09	25R33.0	17 26.4	23 46.4	5 40.8	26 29.2	18 27.6	18 53.5	16 00.7	8 19.9	8 51.5
21 F	18 01 23	29 54 16	29 57 42	6♋07 56	25 33.0	17R39.5	23 36.4	6 27.8	26 48.4	18 39.0	18 50.4	15 58.2	8 20.0	8 53.1
22 Sa	18 05 20	0♑55 21	12♋20 59	18 37 01	25 32.6	17 42.1	23 23.9	7 14.8	27 07.7	18 50.4	18 47.4	15 55.8	8 20.1	8 54.6
23 Su	18 09 16	1 56 26	24 56 06	1♌18 21	25 31.9	17 33.6	23 08.9	8 01.8	27 27.0	19 01.7	18 44.6	15 53.3	8 20.2	8 56.1
24 M	18 13 13	2 57 33	7♌43 52	14 12 43	25 31.0	17 13.5	22 51.4	8 48.8	27 46.5	19 12.9	18 41.8	15 50.9	8 20.4	8 57.7
25 Tu	18 17 09	3 58 39	20 45 00	27 20 47	25 30.0	16 41.6	22 31.7	9 35.8	28 06.1	19 24.0	18 39.1	15 48.5	8 20.6	8 59.3
26 W	18 21 06	4 59 46	4♍00 08	10♍43 07	25 29.0	15 58.1	22 09.6	10 22.9	28 25.9	19 35.1	18 36.4	15 46.1	8 20.8	9 00.9
27 Th	18 25 02	6 00 54	17 29 48	24 20 11	25D28.2	15 03.7	21 45.3	11 10.0	28 45.7	19 46.1	18 33.9	15 43.8	8 21.1	9 02.5
28 F	18 28 59	7 02 02	1♎14 17	8♎12 05	25 28.0	13 59.5	21 19.0	11 57.1	29 05.6	19 57.0	18 31.5	15 41.5	8 21.4	9 04.1
29 Sa	18 32 56	8 03 11	15 13 28	22 18 20	25 28.3	12 47.4	20 50.8	12 44.2	29 25.7	20 07.8	18 29.2	15 39.1	8 21.7	9 05.7
30 Su	18 36 52	9 04 21	29 26 27	6♏37 33	25 29.2	11 29.5	20 20.8	13 31.3	29 45.8	20 18.5	18 27.0	15 36.9	8 22.1	9 07.4
31 M	18 40 49	10 05 30	13♏51 15	21 07 07	25 30.4	10 08.4	19 49.2	14 18.5	0♓06.0	20 29.2	18 24.9	15 34.6	8 22.5	9 09.1

Astro Data

	Dy Hr Mn
♃□♇	1 0:45
☽0S	2 11:04
♃⚻♆	4 15:27
☽0N	15 4:50
☽0S	29 18:41
♆⚹♇	30 20:58
♃⚻♅	10 5:46
☽0N	12 11:35
♀R	16 23:49
♆D	19 8:25
☿R	22 5:50
♃☍♄	22 7:04
☽0S	27 0:31

Planet Ingress

	Dy Hr Mn
♂ ♑	4 0:33
♀ ♑	5 13:40
☿ ♐	13 22:11
☉ ♐	22 0:51
☿ ♑	3 22:48
♂ ♒	13 5:26
☉ ♑	21 14:15
⚳ ♓	31 4:51

Last Aspect / ☽ Ingress

Last Aspect Dy Hr Mn		☽ Ingress Dy Hr Mn
1 0:16 ♂ △	♍	1 4:11
3 5:38 ♂ □	♎	3 6:35
5 5:55 ♀ ⚹	♏	5 6:23
6 17:04 ♄ ☍	♐	7 5:35
8 10:02 ♅ ☍	♑	9 6:18
11 2:20 ☿ ⚹	♒	11 10:11
13 17:14 ☿ □	♓	13 17:51
15 15:51 ☉ △	♈	16 4:39
17 15:34 ♅ ⚹	♉	18 17:07
21 4:04 ☉ ☍	♊	21 5:50
22 16:17 ♅ ☌	♋	23 17:44
25 9:51 ♄ ⚹	♌	26 3:52
27 19:05 ☿ △	♍	28 11:17
30 6:29 ☿ □	♎	30 15:29

Last Aspect / ☽ Ingress

Last Aspect Dy Hr Mn		☽ Ingress Dy Hr Mn
2 13:45 ☿ ⚹	♏	2 16:55
4 5:46 ♂ ⚹	♐	4 16:53
5 19:30 ♅ ☍	♑	6 17:12
8 13:25 ♂ ☌	♒	8 19:42
10 6:23 ♄ □	♓	11 1:45
12 23:08 ♀ ⚹	♈	13 11:32
15 11:38 ♀ □	♉	15 23:50
18 0:30 ♀ △	♊	18 12:34
20 22:48 ☉ ☍	♋	21 0:04
22 20:55 ♀ ☍	♌	23 9:33
24 21:19 ♃ □	♍	25 16:48
27 7:37 ♀ △	♎	27 21:51
29 9:37 ♀ □	♏	30 0:56

☽ Phases & Eclipses

Dy Hr Mn	
6 4:25	● 14♏03
13 0:36	☽ 20♒55
21 4:04	○ 29♉08
28 23:49	☾ 7♍02
5 14:53	● 13♐45
5 15:03:54	● P 0.891
12 17:51	☽ 21♓00
20 22:48	○ 29♊21
20 22:43	● T 1.117
28 9:50	☾ 6♎57

Astro Data

1 November 2029
Julian Day # 47422
SVP 4♓50'19"
GC 27♐15.4 ⚵ 9♑02.9
Eris 25♈58.2R ⚶ 24♏50.8
⚷ 10♉18.1R ⚴ 27♑34.3
☽ Mean ☊ 28♐00.6

1 December 2029
Julian Day # 47452
SVP 4♓50'15"
GC 27♐15.4 ⚵ 18♑35.5
Eris 25♈42.6R ⚶ 5♐04.3
⚷ 8♉55.0R ⚴ 9♒45.2
☽ Mean ☊ 26♐25.3

LONGITUDE — January 2030

Day	Sid.Time	☉	0 hr ☽	Noon ☽	True ☊	☿	♀	♂	⚳	♃	♄	♅	♆	♇
1 Tu	18 44 45	11♑06 41	28♏24 36	5♐43 04	25♐31.4	8♑46.8	19♑16.2	15♒05.6	0♓26.4	20♏39.7	18♉22.9	15♊32.3	8♈22.9	9♒10.7
2 W	18 48 42	12 07 51	13♐01 51	20 20 12	25R 32.1	7R 27.2	18R 42.0	15 52.8	0 46.8	20 50.2	18R 21.0	15R 30.1	8 23.4	9 12.4
3 Th	18 52 38	13 09 02	27 37 21	4♑52 29	25 32.0	6 12.3	18 06.9	16 40.0	1 07.4	21 00.6	18 19.2	15 28.0	8 23.9	9 14.1
4 F	18 56 35	14 10 13	12♑04 51	19 13 43	25 30.8	5 03.9	17 31.0	17 27.2	1 28.0	21 10.9	18 17.5	15 25.8	8 24.4	9 15.9
5 Sa	19 00 32	15 11 24	26 18 26	3♒18 25	25 28.7	4 03.8	16 54.6	18 14.4	1 48.7	21 21.1	18 15.9	15 23.7	8 25.0	9 17.6
6 Su	19 04 28	16 12 34	10♒13 13	17 02 29	25 25.7	3 12.8	16 17.9	19 01.7	2 09.6	21 31.1	18 14.5	15 21.6	8 25.6	9 19.3
7 M	19 08 25	17 13 45	23 46 00	0♓23 41	25 22.3	2 31.8	15 41.3	19 48.9	2 30.5	21 41.1	18 13.1	15 19.5	8 26.3	9 21.1
8 Tu	19 12 21	18 14 54	6♓55 34	13 21 47	25 19.0	2 00.9	15 04.9	20 36.1	2 51.5	21 51.0	18 11.8	15 17.5	8 27.0	9 22.8
9 W	19 16 18	19 16 04	19 42 36	25 58 22	25 16.2	1 39.9	14 29.0	21 23.4	3 12.5	22 00.8	18 10.7	15 15.5	8 27.7	9 24.6
10 Th	19 20 14	20 17 13	2♈09 31	8♈16 31	25 14.4	1D 28.7	13 53.9	22 10.6	3 33.7	22 10.5	18 09.7	15 13.5	8 28.4	9 26.4
11 F	19 24 11	21 18 21	14 19 56	20 20 20	25D 13.7	1 26.5	13 19.8	22 57.9	3 54.9	22 20.1	18 08.7	15 11.6	8 29.2	9 28.2
12 Sa	19 28 07	22 19 29	26 18 20	2♉14 34	25 14.1	1 32.9	12 46.9	23 45.1	4 16.2	22 29.5	18 07.9	15 09.7	8 30.0	9 30.0
13 Su	19 32 04	23 20 36	8♉09 39	14 04 14	25 15.5	1 47.2	12 15.4	24 32.3	4 37.6	22 38.9	18 07.2	15 07.8	8 30.9	9 31.8
14 M	19 36 00	24 21 43	19 58 54	25 54 17	25 17.4	2 08.7	11 45.5	25 19.6	4 59.1	22 48.1	18 06.7	15 06.0	8 31.7	9 33.6
15 Tu	19 39 57	25 22 49	1♊50 56	7♊49 23	25 19.2	2 36.8	11 17.4	26 06.8	5 20.6	22 57.3	18 06.2	15 04.2	8 32.7	9 35.4
16 W	19 43 54	26 23 55	13 50 08	19 53 39	25R 20.3	3 10.8	10 51.3	26 54.1	5 42.2	23 06.3	18 05.8	15 02.5	8 33.6	9 37.2
17 Th	19 47 50	27 24 59	26 00 17	2♋10 25	25 20.2	3 50.2	10 27.2	27 41.3	6 03.9	23 15.2	18 05.6	15 00.8	8 34.6	9 39.1
18 F	19 51 47	28 26 04	8♋24 17	14 42 05	25 18.5	4 34.5	10 05.4	28 28.5	6 25.7	23 24.0	18D 05.5	14 59.1	8 35.6	9 40.9
19 Sa	19 55 43	29 27 07	21 03 57	27 29 57	25 15.1	5 23.1	9 45.9	29 15.8	6 47.5	23 32.6	18 05.4	14 57.5	8 36.6	9 42.7
20 Su	19 59 40	0♒28 10	4♌00 02	10♌34 09	25 10.2	6 15.6	9 28.7	0♓03.0	7 09.4	23 41.2	18 05.5	14 55.9	8 37.7	9 44.6
21 M	20 03 36	1 29 12	17 12 07	23 53 45	25 04.1	7 11.7	9 14.0	0 50.2	7 31.3	23 49.6	18 05.7	14 54.4	8 38.8	9 46.4
22 Tu	20 07 33	2 30 14	0♍38 48	7♍26 58	24 57.7	8 11.0	9 01.8	1 37.4	7 53.3	23 57.9	18 06.0	14 52.9	8 39.9	9 48.3
23 W	20 11 30	3 31 15	14 17 57	21 11 28	24 51.7	9 13.1	8 52.0	2 24.6	8 15.4	24 06.1	18 06.5	14 51.4	8 41.1	9 50.1
24 Th	20 15 26	4 32 16	28 07 10	5♎04 47	24 46.8	10 17.9	8 44.8	3 11.8	8 37.5	24 14.1	18 07.0	14 50.0	8 42.3	9 52.0
25 F	20 19 23	5 33 16	12♎04 03	19 04 42	24 43.6	11 25.0	8 40.1	3 59.0	8 59.7	24 22.1	18 07.7	14 48.6	8 43.5	9 53.9
26 Sa	20 23 19	6 34 16	26 06 30	3♏09 17	24D 42.4	12 34.4	8D 37.9	4 46.2	9 22.0	24 29.8	18 08.4	14 47.3	8 44.8	9 55.7
27 Su	20 27 16	7 35 15	10♏12 52	17 17 05	24 42.7	13 45.7	8 38.1	5 33.3	9 44.3	24 37.5	18 09.3	14 46.1	8 46.1	9 57.6
28 M	20 31 12	8 36 14	24 21 45	1♐26 42	24 43.9	14 58.8	8 40.8	6 20.5	10 06.7	24 45.0	18 10.3	14 44.8	8 47.4	9 59.5
29 Tu	20 35 09	9 37 12	8♐31 45	15 36 39	24R 45.1	16 13.5	8 45.9	7 07.7	10 29.1	24 52.4	18 11.4	14 43.7	8 48.7	10 01.3
30 W	20 39 05	10 38 09	22 41 09	29 44 56	24 45.3	17 29.9	8 53.2	7 54.8	10 51.6	24 59.6	18 12.7	14 42.5	8 50.1	10 03.2
31 Th	20 43 02	11 39 06	6♑47 39	13♑48 54	24 43.6	18 47.6	9 02.9	8 41.9	11 14.1	25 06.7	18 14.0	14 41.4	8 51.5	10 05.1

LONGITUDE — February 2030

Day	Sid.Time	☉	0 hr ☽	Noon ☽	True ☊	☿	♀	♂	⚳	♃	♄	♅	♆	♇
1 F	20 46 59	12♒40 02	20♑48 14	27♑45 14	24♐39.6	20♑06.8	9♑14.7	9♓29.0	11♓36.7	25♏13.7	18♉15.4	14♊40.4	8♈52.9	10♒06.9
2 Sa	20 50 55	13 40 57	4♒39 26	11♒30 22	24R 33.3	21 27.1	9 28.7	10 16.2	11 59.3	25 20.5	18 17.0	14R 39.4	8 54.4	10 08.8
3 Su	20 54 52	14 41 50	18 17 37	25 00 51	24 25.0	22 48.7	9 44.8	11 03.2	12 22.0	25 27.2	18 18.7	14 38.5	8 55.8	10 10.7
4 M	20 58 48	15 42 43	1♓39 43	8♓14 02	24 15.5	24 11.4	10 02.8	11 50.3	12 44.7	25 33.7	18 20.4	14 37.6	8 57.4	10 12.5
5 Tu	21 02 45	16 43 34	14 43 38	21 08 29	24 05.9	25 35.1	10 22.9	12 37.4	13 07.5	25 40.1	18 22.3	14 36.8	8 58.9	10 14.4
6 W	21 06 41	17 44 24	27 28 39	3♈44 17	23 57.0	26 59.9	10 44.8	13 24.4	13 30.3	25 46.3	18 24.3	14 36.0	9 00.4	10 16.2
7 Th	21 10 38	18 45 12	9♈55 38	16 03 02	23 49.9	28 25.7	11 08.5	14 11.4	13 53.2	25 52.3	18 26.4	14 35.2	9 02.0	10 18.1
8 F	21 14 34	19 45 59	22 06 53	28 07 40	23 44.9	29 52.4	11 33.9	14 58.4	14 16.1	25 58.3	18 28.6	14 34.6	9 03.6	10 19.9
9 Sa	21 18 31	20 46 45	4♉05 57	10♉02 17	23D 42.2	1♒20.1	12 01.1	15 45.4	14 39.0	26 04.0	18 30.9	14 33.9	9 05.3	10 21.8
10 Su	21 22 28	21 47 29	15 57 19	21 51 42	23 41.4	2 48.7	12 29.9	16 32.3	15 02.0	26 09.6	18 33.4	14 33.4	9 06.9	10 23.6
11 M	21 26 24	22 48 11	27 46 07	3♊41 14	23 41.9	4 18.3	13 00.2	17 19.2	15 25.0	26 15.0	18 35.9	14 32.8	9 08.6	10 25.5
12 Tu	21 30 21	23 48 52	9♊37 45	15 36 19	23R 42.8	5 48.7	13 32.1	18 06.1	15 48.1	26 20.3	18 38.5	14 32.4	9 10.3	10 27.3
13 W	21 34 17	24 49 32	21 37 35	27 42 10	23 43.0	7 20.0	14 05.4	18 53.0	16 11.2	26 25.4	18 41.3	14 31.9	9 12.0	10 29.1
14 Th	21 38 14	25 50 09	3♋50 37	10♋03 28	23 41.5	8 52.1	14 40.1	19 39.8	16 34.3	26 30.4	18 44.1	14 31.6	9 13.8	10 30.9
15 F	21 42 10	26 50 45	16 21 07	22 43 55	23 37.8	10 25.2	15 16.1	20 26.6	16 57.4	26 35.2	18 47.0	14 31.3	9 15.6	10 32.7
16 Sa	21 46 07	27 51 20	29 12 06	5♌45 48	23 31.4	11 59.1	15 53.5	21 13.4	17 20.6	26 39.8	18 50.1	14 31.0	9 17.4	10 34.5
17 Su	21 50 03	28 51 52	12♌25 01	19 09 38	23 22.6	13 33.9	16 32.1	22 00.2	17 43.8	26 44.3	18 53.2	14 30.8	9 19.2	10 36.3
18 M	21 54 00	29 52 24	25 59 23	2♍53 53	23 12.0	15 09.6	17 11.9	22 46.9	18 07.1	26 48.6	18 56.5	14 30.6	9 21.0	10 38.1
19 Tu	21 57 57	0♓52 53	9♍52 39	16 55 05	23 00.6	16 46.3	17 52.8	23 33.6	18 30.3	26 52.7	18 59.8	14 30.5	9 22.9	10 39.9
20 W	22 01 53	1 53 21	24 00 33	1♎08 19	22 49.8	18 23.8	18 34.9	24 20.3	18 53.6	26 56.6	19 03.2	14D 30.5	9 24.7	10 41.7
21 Th	22 05 50	2 53 48	8♎17 42	15 27 59	22 40.7	20 02.2	19 18.0	25 06.9	19 16.9	27 00.4	19 06.8	14 30.5	9 26.6	10 43.4
22 F	22 09 46	3 54 13	22 38 31	29 48 44	22 34.0	21 41.6	20 02.1	25 53.5	19 40.3	27 04.0	19 10.4	14 30.5	9 28.6	10 45.2
23 Sa	22 13 43	4 54 37	6♏58 07	14♏06 16	22 30.0	23 21.9	20 47.3	26 40.1	20 03.7	27 07.4	19 14.1	14 30.6	9 30.5	10 46.9
24 Su	22 17 39	5 55 00	21 12 51	28 17 40	22D 28.4	25 03.2	21 33.3	27 26.7	20 27.1	27 10.7	19 17.9	14 30.8	9 32.4	10 48.6
25 M	22 21 36	6 55 22	5♐20 32	12♐21 24	22R 28.3	26 45.5	22 20.3	28 13.2	20 50.5	27 13.8	19 21.8	14 31.0	9 34.4	10 50.4
26 Tu	22 25 32	7 55 42	19 20 11	26 16 55	22 28.4	28 28.8	23 08.2	28 59.7	21 14.0	27 16.7	19 25.8	14 31.3	9 36.4	10 52.1
27 W	22 29 29	8 56 00	3♑11 35	10♑04 10	22 27.3	0♓13.0	23 56.8	29 46.2	21 37.4	27 19.4	19 29.9	14 31.6	9 38.4	10 53.8
28 Th	22 33 26	9 56 18	16 54 39	23 43 00	22 24.1	1 58.3	24 46.3	0♈32.6	22 00.9	27 21.9	19 34.1	14 32.0	9 40.4	10 55.4

Astro Data

	Dy Hr Mn
☽ 0N	8 20:31
☿ D	11 5:46
♄ D	19 3:55
♃□♆	20 0:45
☽ 0S	23 6:31
♀ D	26 21:35
☽ 0N	5 6:26
☽ 0S	19 14:21
♅ D	20 23:24

Planet Ingress

		Dy Hr Mn
☉	♒	20 0:56
♂	♓	20 10:29
☿	♒	8 14:05
☉	♓	18 15:01
☿	♓	27 9:01
♂	♈	27 19:08

Last Aspect / ☽ Ingress

Last Aspect Dy Hr Mn			☽ Ingress	Dy Hr Mn
31 10:57	♃	☌	♐	1 2:37
2 4:16	♂	⚹	♑	3 3:56
4 15:20	♃	⚹	♒	5 6:19
6 20:04	♃	□	♓	7 11:17
9 4:18	♃	△	♈	9 19:48
11 17:39	♂	⚹	♉	12 7:28
14 10:45	♂	□	♊	14 20:16
17 2:41	♂	△	♋	17 7:47
19 15:55	☉	☍	♌	19 16:38
21 11:53	♃	□	♍	21 22:51
23 17:06	♃	⚹	♎	24 3:15
25 4:43	♅	△	♏	26 6:38
28 0:33	♃	☌	♐	28 9:33
29 10:30	♅	☍	♑	30 12:26

Last Aspect / ☽ Ingress

Last Aspect Dy Hr Mn			☽ Ingress	Dy Hr Mn
1 7:36	♃	⚹	♒	1 15:54
3 12:48	♃	□	♓	3 20:59
5 21:27	☿	⚹	♈	6 4:49
7 17:49	☉	⚹	♉	8 15:45
10 20:48	♃	☍	♊	11 4:32
13 5:49	☉	△	♋	13 16:30
15 19:13	♃	△	♌	16 1:28
18 6:21	☉	☍	♍	18 6:59
20 4:55	♃	⚹	♎	20 10:05
21 20:38	☿	△	♏	22 12:19
24 10:28	♂	△	♐	24 14:54
26 16:59	♂	□	♑	26 18:27
28 18:29	♃	⚹	♒	28 23:08

☽ Phases & Eclipses

Dy Hr Mn		
4 2:51	●	13♑47
11 14:07	☽	21♈24
19 15:55	○	29♋37
26 18:16	☾	6♏50
2 16:09	●	13♒51
10 11:51	☽	21♉47
18 6:21	○	29♌38
25 1:59	☾	6♐30

Astro Data

1 January 2030
Julian Day # 47483
SVP 4♓50'09"
GC 27♐15.5 ⚵ 29♑20.1
Eris 25♈33.8R ⚶ 15♐35.6
⚷ 8♉01.0R ⚴ 23♒46.2
☽ Mean ☊ 24♐46.8

1 February 2030
Julian Day # 47514
SVP 4♓50'03"
GC 27♐15.6 ⚵ 10♒18.5
Eris 25♈35.2 ⚶ 25♐28.6
⚷ 8♉00.5 ⚴ 8♓30.4
☽ Mean ☊ 23♐08.4

March 2030 — LONGITUDE

Day	Sid.Time	☉	0 hr ☽	Noon ☽	True ☊	☿	♀	♂	⚳	♃	♄	♅	♆	♇
1 F	22 37 22	10♓56 33	0♒29 08	7♒12 55	22♐17.9	3♓44.6	25♑36.5	1♈19.0	22♓24.4	27♏24.3	19♉38.4	14♊32.4	9♈42.5	10♒57.1
2 Sa	22 41 19	11 56 47	13 54 13	20 32 51	22R 08.6	5 32.0	26 27.5	2 05.4	22 48.0	27 26.5	19 42.8	14 32.9	9 44.5	10 58.8
3 Su	22 45 15	12 56 59	27 08 39	3♓41 23	21 56.8	7 20.4	27 19.2	2 51.7	23 11.5	27 28.4	19 47.2	14 33.4	9 46.6	11 00.4
4 M	22 49 12	13 57 10	10♓10 55	16 37 03	21 43.4	9 09.8	28 11.5	3 38.0	23 35.1	27 30.2	19 51.8	14 34.0	9 48.7	11 02.0
5 Tu	22 53 08	14 57 19	22 59 40	29 18 42	21 29.5	11 00.3	29 04.5	4 24.3	23 58.7	27 31.8	19 56.4	14 34.7	9 50.7	11 03.6
6 W	22 57 05	15 57 25	5♈34 08	11♈46 01	21 16.5	12 51.8	29 58.0	5 10.5	24 22.3	27 33.3	20 01.1	14 35.4	9 52.8	11 05.2
7 Th	23 01 01	16 57 30	17 54 28	23 59 41	21 05.4	14 44.4	0♒52.2	5 56.7	24 45.9	27 34.5	20 05.9	14 36.1	9 55.0	11 06.8
8 F	23 04 58	17 57 33	0♉01 56	6♉01 33	20 56.9	16 37.9	1 47.0	6 42.8	25 09.5	27 35.6	20 10.8	14 36.9	9 57.1	11 08.4
9 Sa	23 08 54	18 57 34	11 58 57	17 54 37	20 51.2	18 32.4	2 42.3	7 29.0	25 33.1	27 36.4	20 15.7	14 37.8	9 59.2	11 09.9
10 Su	23 12 51	19 57 32	23 49 04	29 42 53	20 48.2	20 27.9	3 38.1	8 15.0	25 56.7	27 37.1	20 20.7	14 38.7	10 01.4	11 11.5
11 M	23 16 48	20 57 29	5♊36 41	11♊31 07	20 47.2	22 24.2	4 34.5	9 01.1	26 20.4	27 37.6	20 25.9	14 39.6	10 03.6	11 13.0
12 Tu	23 20 44	21 57 23	17 26 54	23 24 42	20 47.1	24 21.3	5 31.3	9 47.0	26 44.0	27 37.9	20 31.0	14 40.7	10 05.7	11 14.5
13 W	23 24 41	22 57 15	29 25 14	5♋29 11	20 46.7	26 19.1	6 28.6	10 33.0	27 07.7	27R 38.0	20 36.3	14 41.7	10 07.9	11 16.0
14 Th	23 28 37	23 57 05	11♋37 15	17 50 03	20 45.1	28 17.5	7 26.4	11 18.9	27 31.4	27 37.9	20 41.7	14 42.8	10 10.1	11 17.5
15 F	23 32 34	24 56 53	24 08 10	0♌32 06	20 41.3	0♈16.3	8 24.6	12 04.8	27 55.0	27 37.7	20 47.1	14 44.0	10 12.3	11 18.9
16 Sa	23 36 30	25 56 39	7♌02 17	13 39 00	20 34.8	2 15.4	9 23.3	12 50.6	28 18.7	27 37.2	20 52.6	14 45.2	10 14.5	11 20.3
17 Su	23 40 27	26 56 22	20 22 24	27 12 30	20 25.8	4 14.5	10 22.3	13 36.4	28 42.4	27 36.6	20 58.1	14 46.5	10 16.8	11 21.7
18 M	23 44 23	27 56 03	4♍09 06	11♍11 53	20 14.8	6 13.4	11 21.8	14 22.1	29 06.1	27 35.8	21 03.7	14 47.8	10 19.0	11 23.1
19 Tu	23 48 20	28 55 42	18 20 18	25 33 39	20 02.8	8 11.9	12 21.7	15 07.8	29 29.7	27 34.7	21 09.4	14 49.1	10 21.2	11 24.5
20 W	23 52 17	29 55 19	2♎51 07	10♎11 44	19 51.3	10 09.7	13 21.9	15 53.4	29 53.4	27 33.5	21 15.2	14 50.5	10 23.4	11 25.9
21 Th	23 56 13	0♈54 54	17 34 28	24 58 17	19 41.5	12 06.3	14 22.5	16 39.0	0♈17.1	27 32.2	21 21.0	14 52.0	10 25.7	11 27.2
22 F	0 00 10	1 54 27	2♏22 10	9♏45 07	19 34.1	14 01.5	15 23.4	17 24.6	0 40.8	27 30.6	21 26.9	14 53.5	10 27.9	11 28.5
23 Sa	0 04 06	2 53 59	17 06 18	24 24 58	19 29.7	15 54.9	16 24.7	18 10.1	1 04.5	27 28.8	21 32.9	14 55.1	10 30.2	11 29.8
24 Su	0 08 03	3 53 28	1♐40 31	8♐52 30	19D 27.7	17 46.0	17 26.3	18 55.5	1 28.1	27 26.9	21 38.9	14 56.7	10 32.4	11 31.1
25 M	0 11 59	4 52 56	16 00 37	23 04 40	19R 27.5	19 34.4	18 28.2	19 41.0	1 51.8	27 24.8	21 45.0	14 58.3	10 34.7	11 32.3
26 Tu	0 15 56	5 52 23	0♑04 36	7♑00 26	19 27.6	21 19.7	19 30.5	20 26.3	2 15.5	27 22.5	21 51.1	15 00.0	10 37.0	11 33.6
27 W	0 19 52	6 51 47	13 52 14	20 40 10	19 26.9	23 01.4	20 33.0	21 11.7	2 39.2	27 20.0	21 57.3	15 01.7	10 39.2	11 34.8
28 Th	0 23 49	7 51 10	27 24 22	4♒05 02	19 24.3	24 39.2	21 35.8	21 57.0	3 02.9	27 17.3	22 03.6	15 03.5	10 41.5	11 36.0
29 F	0 27 46	8 50 31	10♒42 18	17 16 20	19 19.0	26 12.6	22 38.9	22 42.2	3 26.5	27 14.5	22 09.9	15 05.4	10 43.8	11 37.1
30 Sa	0 31 42	9 49 50	23 47 17	0♓15 13	19 11.0	27 41.2	23 42.2	23 27.4	3 50.2	27 11.5	22 16.3	15 07.2	10 46.1	11 38.3
31 Su	0 35 39	10 49 08	6♓40 15	13 02 25	19 00.5	29 04.7	24 45.8	24 12.6	4 13.8	27 08.3	22 22.8	15 09.1	10 48.3	11 39.4

April 2030 — LONGITUDE

Day	Sid.Time	☉	0 hr ☽	Noon ☽	True ☊	☿	♀	♂	⚳	♃	♄	♅	♆	♇
1 M	0 39 35	11♈48 23	19♓21 46	25♓38 21	18♐48.6	0♉22.8	25♒49.6	24♈57.7	4♈37.5	27♏04.9	22♉29.3	15♊11.1	10♈50.6	11♒40.5
2 Tu	0 43 32	12 47 36	1♈52 11	8♈03 18	18R 36.2	1 35.2	26 53.7	25 42.8	5 01.1	27R 01.3	22 35.8	15 13.1	10 52.9	11 41.6
3 W	0 47 28	13 46 48	14 11 46	20 17 39	18 24.5	2 41.7	27 58.0	26 27.8	5 24.7	26 57.6	22 42.4	15 15.2	10 55.1	11 42.6
4 Th	0 51 25	14 45 57	26 21 05	2♉22 12	18 14.4	3 41.9	29 02.5	27 12.8	5 48.3	26 53.7	22 49.0	15 17.3	10 57.4	11 43.7
5 F	0 55 21	15 45 04	8♉21 13	14 18 22	18 06.7	4 35.8	0♓07.2	27 57.7	6 11.9	26 49.7	22 55.7	15 19.4	10 59.7	11 44.7
6 Sa	0 59 18	16 44 09	20 13 58	26 08 21	18 01.7	5 23.2	1 12.1	28 42.6	6 35.5	26 45.5	23 02.5	15 21.6	11 01.9	11 45.6
7 Su	1 03 14	17 43 12	2♊01 56	7♊55 10	17D 59.1	6 04.0	2 17.2	29 27.4	6 59.1	26 41.1	23 09.3	15 23.8	11 04.2	11 46.6
8 M	1 07 11	18 42 13	13 48 34	19 42 40	17 58.6	6 38.0	3 22.5	0♉12.2	7 22.6	26 36.5	23 16.1	15 26.1	11 06.5	11 47.5
9 Tu	1 11 08	19 41 12	25 38 05	1♋35 24	17 59.2	7 05.3	4 28.0	0 56.9	7 46.2	26 31.9	23 23.0	15 28.4	11 08.7	11 48.4
10 W	1 15 04	20 40 08	7♋35 17	13 38 24	18R 00.1	7 25.8	5 33.7	1 41.6	8 09.7	26 27.0	23 30.0	15 30.7	11 11.0	11 49.3
11 Th	1 19 01	21 39 02	19 45 25	25 57 00	18 00.2	7 39.6	6 39.6	2 26.2	8 33.2	26 22.0	23 36.9	15 33.1	11 13.2	11 50.2
12 F	1 22 57	22 37 53	2♌13 45	8♌36 17	17 58.8	7R 46.8	7 45.6	3 10.8	8 56.7	26 16.9	23 43.9	15 35.5	11 15.5	11 51.0
13 Sa	1 26 54	23 36 43	15 05 08	21 40 42	17 55.3	7 47.5	8 51.7	3 55.3	9 20.1	26 11.6	23 51.0	15 37.9	11 17.7	11 51.8
14 Su	1 30 50	24 35 30	28 23 21	5♍13 14	17 49.9	7 41.9	9 58.1	4 39.8	9 43.6	26 06.2	23 58.1	15 40.4	11 19.9	11 52.6
15 M	1 34 47	25 34 15	12♍10 22	19 14 37	17 42.8	7 30.3	11 04.6	5 24.2	10 07.0	26 00.6	24 05.2	15 42.9	11 22.1	11 53.3
16 Tu	1 38 43	26 32 57	26 25 36	3♎42 46	17 34.8	7 13.2	12 11.2	6 08.6	10 30.4	25 54.9	24 12.4	15 45.5	11 24.3	11 54.1
17 W	1 42 40	27 31 38	11♎05 20	18 32 23	17 26.9	6 50.8	13 18.0	6 52.9	10 53.7	25 49.1	24 19.6	15 48.1	11 26.5	11 54.8
18 Th	1 46 37	28 30 16	26 02 50	3♏35 30	17 20.2	6 23.7	14 24.9	7 37.2	11 17.1	25 43.1	24 26.8	15 50.7	11 28.7	11 55.5
19 F	1 50 33	29 28 53	11♏09 09	18 42 33	17 15.3	5 52.5	15 32.0	8 21.4	11 40.4	25 37.1	24 34.1	15 53.4	11 30.9	11 56.1
20 Sa	1 54 30	0♉27 28	26 14 33	3♐44 03	17D 12.6	5 17.8	16 39.2	9 05.5	12 03.7	25 30.9	24 41.4	15 56.1	11 33.1	11 56.7
21 Su	1 58 26	1 26 01	11♐10 08	18 32 01	17 11.9	4 40.3	17 46.6	9 49.7	12 27.0	25 24.6	24 48.7	15 58.8	11 35.3	11 57.3
22 M	2 02 23	2 24 33	25 49 06	3♑00 56	17 12.7	4 00.8	18 54.1	10 33.7	12 50.3	25 18.2	24 56.1	16 01.6	11 37.4	11 57.9
23 Tu	2 06 19	3 23 03	10♑07 16	17 07 57	17 13.9	3 20.0	20 01.7	11 17.7	13 13.5	25 11.7	25 03.5	16 04.4	11 39.6	11 58.5
24 W	2 10 16	4 21 32	24 03 00	0♒52 30	17R 14.8	2 38.6	21 09.4	12 01.7	13 36.7	25 05.0	25 10.9	16 07.2	11 41.7	11 59.0
25 Th	2 14 12	5 19 58	7♒36 39	14 15 41	17 14.4	1 57.5	22 17.3	12 45.6	13 59.9	24 58.3	25 18.4	16 10.1	11 43.9	11 59.5
26 F	2 18 09	6 18 23	20 49 54	27 19 34	17 12.4	1 17.3	23 25.3	13 29.5	14 23.0	24 51.5	25 25.9	16 12.9	11 46.0	11 59.9
27 Sa	2 22 06	7 16 47	3♓45 03	10♓06 37	17 08.6	0 38.8	24 33.3	14 13.3	14 46.1	24 44.6	25 33.4	16 15.9	11 48.1	12 00.4
28 Su	2 26 02	8 15 09	16 24 36	22 39 17	17 03.2	0 02.6	25 41.5	14 57.1	15 09.2	24 37.6	25 40.9	16 18.8	11 50.2	12 00.8
29 M	2 29 59	9 13 29	28 50 57	4♈59 51	16 56.8	29♈29.2	26 49.8	15 40.8	15 32.3	24 30.5	25 48.4	16 21.8	11 52.2	12 01.2
30 Tu	2 33 55	10 11 48	11♈06 14	17 10 18	16 50.0	28 59.1	27 58.2	16 24.5	15 55.3	24 23.4	25 56.0	16 24.8	11 54.3	12 01.5

Astro Data

	Dy Hr Mn
♂0N	1 16:47
☽0N	4 15:17
♃ R	13 14:35
☿0N	16 8:20
☽0S	18 23:59
☉0N	20 13:54
☽0N	31 21:55
♃∥♆	12 16:34
☿ R	13 2:33
☽0S	15 10:02
♃☍♄	24 1:58
☽0N	28 2:57

Planet Ingress

		Dy Hr Mn
♀	♒	6 12:52
☿	♈	15 8:43
☉	♈	20 13:53
⚳	♈	20 18:40
☿	♉	1 4:48
♀	♓	5 9:20
♂	♉	8 5:28
☉	♉	20 0:45
☿	♈R	28 13:46

Last Aspect / ☽ Ingress

Last Aspect Dy Hr Mn			☽ Ingress	Dy Hr Mn
3 0:34	♃	□	♓	3 5:13
5 11:31	♀	⚹	♈	5 13:19
6 17:31	♅	⚹	♉	7 23:56
10 7:44	♃	☍	♊	10 12:35
12 14:16	☿	□	♋	13 1:09
15 6:34	♃	△	♌	15 11:00
17 12:42	♃	□	♍	17 16:51
19 17:58	☉	☍	♎	19 19:19
20 21:46	♂	☍	♏	21 20:09
23 17:03	♃	☌	♐	23 21:13
25 5:54	♂	△	♑	25 23:52
27 23:50	♃	⚹	♒	28 4:39
30 6:37	☿	⚹	♓	30 11:32

Last Aspect / ☽ Ingress

Last Aspect Dy Hr Mn			☽ Ingress	Dy Hr Mn
1 14:45	♃	△	♈	1 20:23
4 4:42	♀	⚹	♉	4 7:16
6 13:15	♃	☍	♊	6 19:52
8 9:46	☉	⚹	♋	9 8:48
11 12:48	♃	△	♌	11 19:46
13 20:03	♃	□	♍	14 2:51
15 23:14	♃	⚹	♎	16 5:54
18 3:21	☉	☍	♏	18 6:18
19 22:56	♃	☌	♐	20 6:01
21 10:40	♀	□	♑	22 6:57
24 1:53	♃	⚹	♒	24 10:27
26 8:27	♄	□	♓	26 16:59
28 18:28	♀	☌	♈	29 2:14

☽ Phases & Eclipses

Dy Hr Mn		
4 6:36	●	13♓44
12 8:49	☽	21♊49
19 17:58	○	29♍11
26 9:53	☾	5♑47
2 22:04	●	13♈12
11 2:58	☽	21♋17
18 3:21	○	28♎09
24 18:40	☾	4♒38

Astro Data

1 March 2030
Julian Day # 47542
SVP 4♓50'00"
GC 27♐15.6 ⚴ 19♒56.9
Eris 25♈45.0 ⚵ 3♑13.2
⚷ 8♉47.6 ⚶ 22♓01.2
☽ Mean ☊ 21♐39.4

1 April 2030
Julian Day # 47573
SVP 4♓49'57"
GC 27♐15.7 ⚴ 29♒48.4
Eris 26♈02.6 ⚵ 9♑30.3
⚷ 10♉20.7 ⚶ 6♈51.8
☽ Mean ☊ 20♐00.9

LONGITUDE — May 2030

Day	Sid.Time	☉	0 hr ☽	Noon☽	True☊	☿	♀	♂	⚳	♃	♄	♅	♆	♇
1 W	2 37 52	11♉10 05	23♈12 17	29♈12 23	16♐43.5	28♈32.8	29♓06.7	17♉08.1	16♈18.3	24♏16.1	26♉03.6	16♊27.8	11♈56.3	12♒01.8
2 Th	2 41 48	12 08 20	5♉10 48	11♉07 46	16R38.1	28R10.5	0♈15.3	17 51.7	16 41.2	24R08.9	26 11.2	16 30.8	11 58.4	12 02.1
3 F	2 45 45	13 06 34	17 03 30	22 58 13	16 34.1	27 52.6	1 24.0	18 35.2	17 04.1	24 01.5	26 18.8	16 33.9	12 00.4	12 02.4
4 Sa	2 49 41	14 04 46	28 52 13	4♊45 44	16D31.8	27 39.2	2 32.8	19 18.7	17 27.0	23 54.1	26 26.5	16 37.0	12 02.4	12 02.7
5 Su	2 53 38	15 02 56	10♊39 07	16 32 42	16 31.1	27 30.5	3 41.6	20 02.1	17 49.8	23 46.7	26 34.1	16 40.2	12 04.4	12 02.9
6 M	2 57 35	16 01 04	22 26 52	28 22 02	16 31.7	27D26.5	4 50.5	20 45.5	18 12.6	23 39.2	26 41.8	16 43.3	12 06.4	12 03.1
7 Tu	3 01 31	16 59 11	4♋18 39	10♋17 11	16 33.2	27 27.2	5 59.6	21 28.8	18 35.4	23 31.7	26 49.5	16 46.5	12 08.3	12 03.2
8 W	3 05 28	17 57 15	16 18 09	22 22 05	16 34.9	27 32.7	7 08.6	22 12.0	18 58.1	23 24.1	26 57.2	16 49.7	12 10.2	12 03.4
9 Th	3 09 24	18 55 18	28 29 32	4♌41 03	16 36.4	27 42.8	8 17.8	22 55.3	19 20.8	23 16.5	27 04.9	16 52.9	12 12.2	12 03.5
10 F	3 13 21	19 53 19	10♌57 13	17 18 34	16R37.1	27 57.5	9 27.0	23 38.4	19 43.4	23 08.9	27 12.6	16 56.1	12 14.1	12 03.6
11 Sa	3 17 17	20 51 17	23 45 36	0♍18 46	16 36.8	28 16.8	10 36.3	24 21.5	20 06.0	23 01.3	27 20.4	16 59.4	12 15.9	12 03.6
12 Su	3 21 14	21 49 14	6♍58 28	13 45 00	16 35.3	28 40.4	11 45.7	25 04.6	20 28.5	22 53.6	27 28.1	17 02.7	12 17.8	12R03.7
13 M	3 25 10	22 47 10	20 38 31	27 39 04	16 33.0	29 08.2	12 55.2	25 47.6	20 51.0	22 46.0	27 35.9	17 06.0	12 19.6	12 03.7
14 Tu	3 29 07	23 45 03	4♎46 30	12♎00 31	16 30.1	29 40.2	14 04.7	26 30.5	21 13.4	22 38.3	27 43.6	17 09.3	12 21.4	12 03.6
15 W	3 33 04	24 42 54	19 20 35	26 46 03	16 27.1	0♉16.2	15 14.3	27 13.4	21 35.8	22 30.7	27 51.4	17 12.6	12 23.2	12 03.6
16 Th	3 37 00	25 40 45	4♏16 00	11♏49 27	16 24.6	0 56.1	16 23.9	27 56.2	21 58.1	22 23.1	27 59.1	17 16.0	12 25.0	12 03.5
17 F	3 40 57	26 38 33	19 25 15	27 02 09	16 22.9	1 39.7	17 33.6	28 39.0	22 20.4	22 15.5	28 06.9	17 19.3	12 26.8	12 03.4
18 Sa	3 44 53	27 36 20	4♐38 56	12♐14 20	16D22.2	2 26.9	18 43.4	29 21.8	22 42.7	22 07.9	28 14.7	17 22.7	12 28.5	12 03.3
19 Su	3 48 50	28 34 06	19 47 13	27 16 32	16 22.3	3 17.6	19 53.3	0♊04.5	23 04.9	22 00.3	28 22.4	17 26.1	12 30.2	12 03.1
20 M	3 52 46	29 31 51	4♑41 21	12♑00 55	16 23.2	4 11.7	21 03.2	0 47.1	23 27.0	21 52.8	28 30.2	17 29.5	12 31.9	12 02.9
21 Tu	3 56 43	0♊29 34	19 14 40	26 22 13	16 24.4	5 09.0	22 13.2	1 29.7	23 49.1	21 45.3	28 38.0	17 32.9	12 33.6	12 02.7
22 W	4 00 39	1 27 17	3♒23 18	10♒17 51	16 25.4	6 09.5	23 23.3	2 12.2	24 11.1	21 37.8	28 45.7	17 36.4	12 35.3	12 02.5
23 Th	4 04 36	2 24 58	17 05 55	23 47 40	16R26.1	7 13.2	24 33.4	2 54.7	24 33.1	21 30.4	28 53.5	17 39.8	12 36.9	12 02.2
24 F	4 08 33	3 22 38	0♓23 21	6♓53 18	16 26.3	8 19.8	25 43.5	3 37.2	24 55.0	21 23.0	29 01.2	17 43.3	12 38.5	12 01.9
25 Sa	4 12 29	4 20 17	13 17 55	19 37 37	16 25.8	9 29.3	26 53.7	4 19.6	25 16.9	21 15.7	29 09.0	17 46.7	12 40.1	12 01.6
26 Su	4 16 26	5 17 56	25 52 51	2♈04 04	16 24.9	10 41.7	28 04.0	5 01.9	25 38.7	21 08.4	29 16.7	17 50.2	12 41.6	12 01.2
27 M	4 20 22	6 15 33	8♈11 43	14 16 15	16 23.6	11 56.9	29 14.4	5 44.2	26 00.5	21 01.2	29 24.5	17 53.7	12 43.2	12 00.9
28 Tu	4 24 19	7 13 09	20 18 06	26 17 41	16 22.3	13 14.8	0♉24.8	6 26.5	26 22.2	20 54.1	29 32.2	17 57.2	12 44.7	12 00.5
29 W	4 28 15	8 10 45	2♉15 24	8♉11 36	16 21.1	14 35.4	1 35.2	7 08.7	26 43.8	20 47.1	29 39.9	18 00.7	12 46.2	12 00.1
30 Th	4 32 12	9 08 19	14 06 40	20 00 55	16 20.2	15 58.7	2 45.7	7 50.8	27 05.3	20 40.1	29 47.6	18 04.2	12 47.6	11 59.6
31 F	4 36 08	10 05 52	25 54 41	1♊48 15	16 19.6	17 24.6	3 56.2	8 32.9	27 26.8	20 33.2	29 55.3	18 07.7	12 49.0	11 59.1

LONGITUDE — June 2030

Day	Sid.Time	☉	0 hr ☽	Noon☽	True☊	☿	♀	♂	⚳	♃	♄	♅	♆	♇
1 Sa	4 40 05	11♊03 25	7♊41 54	13♊35 57	16♐19.4	18♉53.1	5♉06.8	9♊15.0	27♈48.3	20♏26.4	0♊03.0	18♊11.3	12♈50.4	11♒58.6
2 Su	4 44 02	12 00 56	19 30 39	25 26 18	16D19.4	20 24.2	6 17.4	9 57.0	28 09.6	20R19.7	0 10.7	18 14.8	12 51.8	11R58.1
3 M	4 47 58	12 58 26	1♋23 11	7♋21 35	16 19.7	21 57.9	7 28.1	10 38.9	28 30.9	20 13.1	0 18.3	18 18.4	12 53.2	11 57.6
4 Tu	4 51 55	13 55 55	13 21 50	19 24 14	16 19.9	23 34.2	8 38.8	11 20.9	28 52.1	20 06.6	0 26.0	18 21.9	12 54.5	11 57.0
5 W	4 55 51	14 53 24	25 29 08	1♌36 52	16 20.2	25 12.9	9 49.6	12 02.7	29 13.3	20 00.2	0 33.6	18 25.4	12 55.8	11 56.4
6 Th	4 59 48	15 50 50	7♌47 50	14 02 22	16R20.3	26 54.2	11 00.4	12 44.5	29 34.3	19 54.0	0 41.2	18 29.0	12 57.1	11 55.8
7 F	5 03 44	16 48 16	20 20 53	26 43 43	16 20.3	28 38.1	12 11.2	13 26.3	29 55.3	19 47.8	0 48.8	18 32.5	12 58.3	11 55.2
8 Sa	5 07 41	17 45 40	3♍11 19	9♍43 58	16D20.2	0♊24.4	13 22.1	14 08.0	0♉16.2	19 41.8	0 56.4	18 36.1	12 59.5	11 54.5
9 Su	5 11 37	18 43 04	16 22 00	23 05 41	16 20.2	2 13.2	14 33.0	14 49.7	0 37.1	19 35.8	1 03.9	18 39.6	13 00.7	11 53.8
10 M	5 15 34	19 40 26	29 55 14	6♎50 45	16 20.4	4 04.5	15 44.0	15 31.3	0 57.8	19 30.0	1 11.4	18 43.2	13 01.9	11 53.1
11 Tu	5 19 31	20 37 47	13♎52 16	20 59 38	16 20.6	5 58.1	16 55.0	16 12.8	1 18.5	19 24.4	1 18.9	18 46.7	13 03.0	11 52.4
12 W	5 23 27	21 35 07	28 12 39	5♏30 54	16 21.1	7 54.1	18 06.0	16 54.3	1 39.1	19 18.8	1 26.4	18 50.3	13 04.1	11 51.6
13 Th	5 27 24	22 32 27	12♏53 51	20 20 48	16 21.5	9 52.4	19 17.1	17 35.8	1 59.6	19 13.4	1 33.8	18 53.8	13 05.2	11 50.8
14 F	5 31 20	23 29 45	27 50 54	5♐23 12	16R21.9	11 52.8	20 28.2	18 17.2	2 20.0	19 08.2	1 41.3	18 57.4	13 06.2	11 50.1
15 Sa	5 35 17	24 27 03	12♐56 40	20 30 09	16 22.0	13 55.3	21 39.4	18 58.6	2 40.3	19 03.1	1 48.7	19 00.9	13 07.2	11 49.2
16 Su	5 39 13	25 24 20	28 02 32	5♑32 41	16 21.7	15 59.7	22 50.6	19 39.9	3 00.6	18 58.1	1 56.0	19 04.5	13 08.2	11 48.4
17 M	5 43 10	26 21 36	12♑59 35	20 22 14	16 20.9	18 05.8	24 01.9	20 21.2	3 20.8	18 53.3	2 03.4	19 08.0	13 09.1	11 47.6
18 Tu	5 47 07	27 18 52	27 39 51	4♒51 43	16 19.7	20 13.4	25 13.2	21 02.4	3 40.8	18 48.6	2 10.7	19 11.5	13 10.1	11 46.7
19 W	5 51 03	28 16 08	11♒57 22	18 56 26	16 18.3	22 22.4	26 24.5	21 43.6	4 00.8	18 44.1	2 17.9	19 15.1	13 11.0	11 45.8
20 Th	5 55 00	29 13 23	25 48 46	2♓34 18	16 17.0	24 32.4	27 35.9	22 24.7	4 20.7	18 39.7	2 25.2	19 18.6	13 11.8	11 44.9
21 F	5 58 56	0♋10 38	9♓13 11	15 45 38	16 16.0	26 43.1	28 47.3	23 05.8	4 40.5	18 35.5	2 32.4	19 22.1	13 12.6	11 43.9
22 Sa	6 02 53	1 07 53	22 12 00	28 32 41	16D15.5	28 54.5	29 58.8	23 46.9	5 00.2	18 31.4	2 39.6	19 25.6	13 13.4	11 43.0
23 Su	6 06 49	2 05 08	4♈48 11	10♈59 00	16 15.7	1♋06.0	1♊10.3	24 27.9	5 19.8	18 27.5	2 46.7	19 29.1	13 14.2	11 42.0
24 M	6 10 46	3 02 22	17 05 42	23 08 51	16 16.5	3 17.5	2 21.8	25 08.8	5 39.3	18 23.8	2 53.8	19 32.6	13 14.9	11 41.0
25 Tu	6 14 42	3 59 37	29 09 01	5♉06 46	16 17.8	5 28.7	3 33.4	25 49.7	5 58.7	18 20.2	3 00.9	19 36.0	13 15.6	11 40.0
26 W	6 18 39	4 56 51	11♉02 39	16 57 12	16 19.3	7 39.4	4 45.0	26 30.6	6 18.0	18 16.8	3 07.9	19 39.5	13 16.3	11 38.9
27 Th	6 22 36	5 54 06	22 50 55	28 44 18	16 20.7	9 49.2	5 56.7	27 11.4	6 37.2	18 13.6	3 14.9	19 42.9	13 17.0	11 37.9
28 F	6 26 32	6 51 20	4♊37 45	10♊31 44	16R21.5	11 58.0	7 08.4	27 52.2	6 56.3	18 10.6	3 21.8	19 46.4	13 17.6	11 36.8
29 Sa	6 30 29	7 48 34	16 26 36	22 22 42	16 21.5	14 05.6	8 20.2	28 33.0	7 15.3	18 07.7	3 28.7	19 49.8	13 18.2	11 35.8
30 Su	6 34 25	8 45 48	28 20 20	4♋19 48	16 20.4	16 11.8	9 31.9	29 13.7	7 34.1	18 05.0	3 35.6	19 53.2	13 18.7	11 34.7

Astro Data Dy Hr Mn	Planet Ingress Dy Hr Mn	Last Aspect Dy Hr Mn	☽ Ingress Dy Hr Mn	Last Aspect Dy Hr Mn	☽ Ingress Dy Hr Mn	☽ Phases & Eclipses Dy Hr Mn
♆⚹♇ 4 15:42	♀ ♈ 2 6:39	1 10:43 ☿ ☌	♉ 1 13:35	1 21:22 ♅ ☌	♋ 2 21:12	2 14:13 ● 12♉14
♀0N 5 8:13	☿ ♉ 15 1:31	3 18:52 ♄ ☌	♊ 4 2:18	4 21:30 ☿ ⚹	♌ 5 8:51	10 17:13 ☽ 20♌06
☿ D 6 20:17	♂ ♊ 19 9:30	6 10:08 ☿ ⚹	♋ 6 15:18	7 16:07 ☿ □	♍ 7 18:06	17 11:20 ○ 26♏37
⚳0N 7 1:56	☉ ♊ 20 23:42	8 22:16 ☿ □	♌ 9 2:56	9 5:50 ♃ ⚹	♎ 10 0:08	24 4:59 ☾ 3♓06
♄∠♆ 10 17:48	♀ ♉ 28 3:34	11 8:12 ☿ △	♍ 11 11:26	11 11:21 ☉ △	♏ 12 2:57	
☽0S 12 19:01		13 11:54 ♄ △	♎ 13 15:59	13 10:12 ♃ ☌	♐ 14 3:26	1 6:23 ● 10♊50
♇ R 12 23:15	♄ ♊ 1 2:35	14 20:28 ♅ △	♏ 15 17:11	15 18:42 ☉ ☍	♑ 16 3:07	1 6:29:11 ● A 05'21"
☽0N 25 8:19	⚳ ♉ 7 17:23	17 14:40 ♂ ☍	♐ 17 16:40	17 18:32 ☿ △	♒ 18 3:53	9 3:37 ☽ 18♍23
	☿ ♊ 8 6:32	18 23:10 ♀ △	♑ 19 16:24	20 5:35 ☉ △	♓ 20 7:25	15 18:42 ○ 24♐43
☽0S 9 2:18	☉ ♋ 21 7:32	21 15:53 ♄ △	♒ 21 18:11	22 12:50 ☿ □	♈ 22 14:47	15 18:35 P 0.502
♃⊼♅ 15 18:00	♀ ♊ 22 12:25	23 21:21 ♄ □	♓ 23 23:17	24 16:14 ♂ ⚹	♉ 25 1:42	22 17:21 ☾ 1♈21
☽0N 21 15:35	☿ ♋ 22 23:58	26 6:31 ♄ ⚹	♈ 26 7:59	26 14:41 ♃ ☍	♊ 27 14:34	30 21:36 ● 9♋09
		27 19:14 ♅ ⚹	♉ 28 19:27	30 1:10 ♂ ☌	♋ 30 3:20	
		31 8:08 ♄ ☌	♊ 31 8:20			

Astro Data

1 May 2030
Julian Day # 47603
SVP 4♓49'54"
GC 27♐15.8 ⚴ 7♓55.0
Eris 26♈22.2 ⚵ 11♉58.4
⚷ 12♉13.0 ⚶ 20♈50.4
☽ Mean ☊ 18♐25.5

1 June 2030
Julian Day # 47634
SVP 4♓49'50"
GC 27♐15.8 ⚴ 13♓53.9
Eris 26♈40.0 ⚵ 9♉29.1R
⚷ 14♉10.1 ⚶ 4♉35.3
☽ Mean ☊ 16♐47.0

July 2030 — LONGITUDE

Day	Sid.Time	☉	0 hr ☽	Noon ☽	True ☊	☿	♀	♂	⚳	♃	♄	♅	♆	♇
1 M	6 38 22	9♋43 02	10♋21 21	16♋25 12	16♐18.2	18♋16.5	10♊43.8	29♊54.3	7♉52.9	18♏02.4	3♊42.4	19♊56.6	13♈19.2	11♒33.6
2 Tu	6 42 18	10 40 16	22 31 33	28 40 36	16R 15.0	20 19.6	11 55.6	0♋34.9	8 11.5	18R 00.1	3 49.2	20 00.0	13 19.7	11R 32.4
3 W	6 46 15	11 37 30	4♌52 30	11♌07 25	16 11.2	22 20.9	13 07.5	1 15.5	8 30.0	17 57.9	3 55.9	20 03.4	13 20.1	11 31.3
4 Th	6 50 11	12 34 43	17 25 30	23 46 54	16 07.1	24 20.4	14 19.4	1 56.0	8 48.4	17 55.9	4 02.6	20 06.7	13 20.6	11 30.1
5 F	6 54 08	13 31 56	0♍11 45	6♍40 12	16 03.3	26 18.0	15 31.4	2 36.5	9 06.7	17 54.0	4 09.2	20 10.1	13 20.9	11 29.0
6 Sa	6 58 05	14 29 09	13 12 24	19 48 28	16 00.2	28 13.8	16 43.4	3 16.9	9 24.8	17 52.4	4 15.8	20 13.4	13 21.3	11 27.8
7 Su	7 02 01	15 26 21	26 28 34	3♎12 49	15D 58.4	0♌07.5	17 55.4	3 57.3	9 42.8	17 50.9	4 22.3	20 16.7	13 21.6	11 26.6
8 M	7 05 58	16 23 34	10♎01 18	16 54 07	15 57.8	1 59.4	19 07.4	4 37.7	10 00.7	17 49.7	4 28.8	20 20.0	13 21.9	11 25.4
9 Tu	7 09 54	17 20 46	23 51 16	0♏52 45	15 58.4	3 49.2	20 19.5	5 18.0	10 18.4	17 48.5	4 35.2	20 23.3	13 22.1	11 24.1
10 W	7 13 51	18 17 58	7♏58 29	15 08 16	15 59.7	5 37.1	21 31.7	5 58.2	10 36.0	17 47.6	4 41.6	20 26.5	13 22.3	11 22.9
11 Th	7 17 47	19 15 10	22 21 51	29 38 50	16 01.0	7 23.0	22 43.8	6 38.4	10 53.5	17 46.9	4 47.9	20 29.7	13 22.5	11 21.7
12 F	7 21 44	20 12 22	6♐58 46	14♐21 00	16R 01.7	9 06.9	23 56.0	7 18.6	11 10.9	17 46.3	4 54.2	20 32.9	13 22.7	11 20.4
13 Sa	7 25 40	21 09 34	21 44 51	29 09 31	16 01.1	10 48.9	25 08.3	7 58.7	11 28.1	17 46.0	5 00.4	20 36.1	13 22.8	11 19.1
14 Su	7 29 37	22 06 46	6♑34 05	13♑57 40	15 58.9	12 28.8	26 20.6	8 38.8	11 45.1	17D 45.8	5 06.5	20 39.3	13 22.9	11 17.9
15 M	7 33 34	23 03 58	21 19 17	28 38 01	15 55.1	14 06.8	27 32.9	9 18.8	12 02.0	17 45.8	5 12.6	20 42.4	13 23.0	11 16.6
16 Tu	7 37 30	24 01 11	5♒52 59	13♒03 25	15 49.8	15 42.8	28 45.2	9 58.8	12 18.8	17 45.9	5 18.6	20 45.5	13R 23.0	11 15.3
17 W	7 41 27	24 58 24	20 08 38	27 08 06	15 43.9	17 16.8	29 57.6	10 38.8	12 35.4	17 46.3	5 24.6	20 48.6	13 23.0	11 14.0
18 Th	7 45 23	25 55 38	4♓01 26	10♓48 23	15 38.0	18 48.8	1♋10.1	11 18.7	12 51.9	17 46.8	5 30.5	20 51.7	13 22.9	11 12.7
19 F	7 49 20	26 52 52	17 28 54	24 03 01	15 32.8	20 18.9	2 22.5	11 58.6	13 08.2	17 47.5	5 36.4	20 54.7	13 22.8	11 11.4
20 Sa	7 53 16	27 50 07	0♈30 58	6♈53 02	15 29.1	21 46.9	3 35.0	12 38.4	13 24.4	17 48.4	5 42.1	20 57.7	13 22.7	11 10.0
21 Su	7 57 13	28 47 22	13 09 37	19 21 14	15D 27.0	23 12.8	4 47.6	13 18.2	13 40.4	17 49.5	5 47.9	21 00.7	13 22.6	11 08.7
22 M	8 01 09	29 44 39	25 28 25	1♉31 46	15 26.5	24 36.7	6 00.2	13 58.0	13 56.2	17 50.7	5 53.5	21 03.7	13 22.4	11 07.4
23 Tu	8 05 06	0♌41 56	7♉31 54	13 29 28	15 27.2	25 58.5	7 12.8	14 37.7	14 11.9	17 52.1	5 59.1	21 06.6	13 22.2	11 06.0
24 W	8 09 03	1 39 14	19 25 07	25 19 29	15 28.5	27 18.2	8 25.5	15 17.4	14 27.4	17 53.7	6 04.6	21 09.5	13 22.0	11 04.7
25 Th	8 12 59	2 36 33	1♊13 13	7♊06 54	15R 29.7	28 35.7	9 38.2	15 57.0	14 42.7	17 55.5	6 10.1	21 12.4	13 21.7	11 03.3
26 F	8 16 56	3 33 53	13 01 07	18 56 25	15 30.0	29 51.0	10 51.0	16 36.7	14 57.9	17 57.5	6 15.5	21 15.3	13 21.4	11 01.9
27 Sa	8 20 52	4 31 14	24 53 18	0♋52 13	15 28.7	1♍04.0	12 03.8	17 16.2	15 12.8	17 59.6	6 20.8	21 18.1	13 21.1	11 00.6
28 Su	8 24 49	5 28 35	6♋53 33	12 57 40	15 25.3	2 14.6	13 16.6	17 55.8	15 27.6	18 01.9	6 26.0	21 20.9	13 20.7	10 59.2
29 M	8 28 45	6 25 57	19 04 50	25 15 17	15 19.7	3 22.9	14 29.5	18 35.3	15 42.2	18 04.4	6 31.2	21 23.6	13 20.3	10 57.8
30 Tu	8 32 42	7 23 21	1♌29 11	7♌46 37	15 12.1	4 28.6	15 42.4	19 14.7	15 56.7	18 07.1	6 36.3	21 26.4	13 19.9	10 56.5
31 W	8 36 38	8 20 44	14 07 39	20 32 16	15 03.3	5 31.7	16 55.4	19 54.1	16 10.9	18 09.9	6 41.3	21 29.1	13 19.4	10 55.1

August 2030 — LONGITUDE

Day	Sid.Time	☉	0 hr ☽	Noon ☽	True ☊	☿	♀	♂	⚳	♃	♄	♅	♆	♇
1 Th	8 40 35	9♌18 09	27♌00 26	3♍32 02	14♐53.9	6♍32.0	18♋08.3	20♋33.5	16♉24.9	18♏12.9	6♊46.2	21♊31.7	13♈18.9	10♒53.7
2 F	8 44 32	10 15 34	10♍06 59	16 45 08	14R 45.0	7 29.6	19 21.4	21 12.8	16 38.7	18 16.1	6 51.1	21 34.3	13R 18.4	10R 52.3
3 Sa	8 48 28	11 13 00	23 26 21	0♎10 30	14 37.5	8 24.2	20 34.4	21 52.1	16 52.3	18 19.5	6 55.8	21 36.9	13 17.9	10 51.0
4 Su	8 52 25	12 10 27	6♎57 27	13 47 04	14 32.0	9 15.7	21 47.5	22 31.4	17 05.8	18 23.0	7 00.5	21 39.5	13 17.3	10 49.6
5 M	8 56 21	13 07 54	20 39 17	27 34 00	14 28.9	10 04.0	23 00.6	23 10.6	17 19.0	18 26.7	7 05.2	21 42.0	13 16.7	10 48.2
6 Tu	9 00 18	14 05 23	4♏31 09	11♏30 40	14D 27.8	10 48.9	24 13.8	23 49.8	17 32.0	18 30.5	7 09.7	21 44.5	13 16.0	10 46.8
7 W	9 04 14	15 02 51	18 32 28	25 36 28	14 28.1	11 30.2	25 27.0	24 28.9	17 44.8	18 34.6	7 14.2	21 46.9	13 15.4	10 45.5
8 Th	9 08 11	16 00 21	2♐42 34	9♐50 33	14R 28.7	12 07.8	26 40.2	25 08.0	17 57.3	18 38.7	7 18.5	21 49.4	13 14.7	10 44.1
9 F	9 12 07	16 57 51	17 00 14	24 11 17	14 28.4	12 41.4	27 53.5	25 47.1	18 09.7	18 43.1	7 22.8	21 51.7	13 13.9	10 42.7
10 Sa	9 16 04	17 55 23	1♑23 21	8♑35 56	14 26.3	13 10.9	29 06.8	26 26.1	18 21.8	18 47.6	7 27.0	21 54.1	13 13.2	10 41.4
11 Su	9 20 01	18 52 55	15 48 31	23 00 30	14 21.7	13 36.0	0♌20.1	27 05.1	18 33.7	18 52.3	7 31.2	21 56.4	13 12.4	10 40.0
12 M	9 23 57	19 50 28	0♒11 11	7♒19 53	14 14.5	13 56.6	1 33.5	27 44.0	18 45.4	18 57.1	7 35.2	21 58.6	13 11.6	10 38.6
13 Tu	9 27 54	20 48 02	14 25 55	21 28 34	14 05.2	14 12.4	2 46.9	28 23.0	18 56.8	19 02.1	7 39.1	22 00.9	13 10.7	10 37.3
14 W	9 31 50	21 45 37	28 27 14	5♓21 20	13 54.7	14 23.2	4 00.3	29 01.8	19 08.0	19 07.2	7 43.0	22 03.0	13 09.9	10 35.9
15 Th	9 35 47	22 43 13	12♓10 26	18 54 12	13 43.9	14R 28.9	5 13.8	29 40.7	19 18.9	19 12.5	7 46.8	22 05.2	13 09.0	10 34.6
16 F	9 39 43	23 40 51	25 32 23	2♈04 57	13 34.1	14 29.2	6 27.3	0♌19.5	19 29.6	19 17.9	7 50.5	22 07.3	13 08.0	10 33.3
17 Sa	9 43 40	24 38 31	8♈31 54	14 53 25	13 26.1	14 24.0	7 40.9	0 58.2	19 40.1	19 23.5	7 54.0	22 09.3	13 07.1	10 31.9
18 Su	9 47 36	25 36 11	21 09 47	27 21 21	13 20.4	14 13.2	8 54.5	1 37.0	19 50.3	19 29.3	7 57.5	22 11.4	13 06.1	10 30.6
19 M	9 51 33	26 33 54	3♉28 37	9♉32 05	13 17.2	13 56.7	10 08.1	2 15.7	20 00.2	19 35.2	8 01.0	22 13.3	13 05.1	10 29.3
20 Tu	9 55 30	27 31 38	15 32 20	21 30 02	13D 15.9	13 34.5	11 21.8	2 54.3	20 09.9	19 41.2	8 04.3	22 15.3	13 04.1	10 28.0
21 W	9 59 26	28 29 23	27 25 48	3♊20 21	13R 15.8	13 06.7	12 35.5	3 33.0	20 19.3	19 47.4	8 07.5	22 17.2	13 03.0	10 26.7
22 Th	10 03 23	29 27 11	9♊14 22	15 08 30	13 15.9	12 33.5	13 49.3	4 11.6	20 28.4	19 53.7	8 10.6	22 19.0	13 01.9	10 25.4
23 F	10 07 19	0♍25 00	21 03 28	26 59 53	13 15.2	11 55.3	15 03.1	4 50.1	20 37.3	20 00.2	8 13.6	22 20.8	13 00.8	10 24.1
24 Sa	10 11 16	1 22 51	2♋58 23	8♋59 32	13 12.7	11 12.3	16 16.9	5 28.7	20 45.8	20 06.8	8 16.6	22 22.6	12 59.7	10 22.8
25 Su	10 15 12	2 20 43	15 03 51	21 11 48	13 07.7	10 25.2	17 30.8	6 07.2	20 54.1	20 13.6	8 19.4	22 24.3	12 58.5	10 21.6
26 M	10 19 09	3 18 37	27 23 45	3♌40 01	13 00.1	9 34.6	18 44.7	6 45.6	21 02.1	20 20.5	8 22.2	22 26.0	12 57.4	10 20.3
27 Tu	10 23 05	4 16 33	10♌00 48	16 26 14	12 50.0	8 41.4	19 58.6	7 24.0	21 09.8	20 27.5	8 24.8	22 27.6	12 56.2	10 19.1
28 W	10 27 02	5 14 30	22 56 20	29 31 00	12 38.2	7 46.6	21 12.6	8 02.4	21 17.2	20 34.7	8 27.3	22 29.2	12 54.9	10 17.9
29 Th	10 30 59	6 12 29	6♍10 05	12♍53 18	12 25.7	6 51.1	22 26.5	8 40.8	21 24.3	20 42.0	8 29.8	22 30.7	12 53.7	10 16.6
30 F	10 34 55	7 10 29	19 40 20	26 30 48	12 13.7	5 56.2	23 40.6	9 19.1	21 31.1	20 49.4	8 32.1	22 32.2	12 52.4	10 15.4
31 Sa	10 38 52	8 08 31	3♎24 15	10♎20 16	12 03.4	5 03.1	24 54.6	9 57.4	21 37.6	20 57.0	8 34.3	22 33.6	12 51.1	10 14.3

Astro Data	Dy Hr Mn
☽ 0S	6 8:24
♃ D	15 1:28
♆ R	16 16:30
☽ 0N	19 0:51
☽ 0S	2 14:31
☽ 0N	15 10:53
☿ R	16 1:21
☽ 0S	29 21:45

Planet Ingress	Dy Hr Mn
♂ ♋	1 15:21
☿ ♌	7 10:24
♀ ♋	17 12:47
☉ ♌	22 18:26
☿ ♍	26 14:55
♀ ♌	11 5:25
♂ ♌	15 23:57
☉ ♍	23 1:38

Last Aspect Dy Hr Mn		☽ Ingress	Dy Hr Mn
1 16:24	☿ ☌	♌	2 14:34
4 5:03	♅ ⚹	♍	4 23:38
7 5:37	☿ ⚹	♎	7 6:18
8 17:58	♅ △	♏	9 10:30
10 17:38	☉ △	♐	11 12:35
13 4:55	♀ ☍	♑	13 13:22
15 2:13	☉ ☍	♒	15 14:15
17 1:06	♅ △	♓	17 16:58
19 17:39	☉ △	♈	19 23:02
22 8:09	☉ □	♉	22 8:58
24 16:32	☿ □	♊	24 21:31
26 16:42	♅ ☌	♋	27 10:16
28 22:18	♂ ☌	♌	29 21:09

Last Aspect Dy Hr Mn		☽ Ingress	Dy Hr Mn
31 13:46	♅ ⚹	♍	1 5:31
2 20:41	♅ □	♎	3 11:41
5 4:01	♂ □	♏	5 16:12
7 11:42	♀ △	♐	7 19:26
9 8:06	♅ ☍	♑	9 21:41
11 19:08	♂ ☍	♒	11 23:41
13 12:55	♅ △	♓	14 2:41
15 17:45	♅ □	♈	16 8:10
18 8:18	☉ △	♉	18 17:10
21 1:17	☉ □	♊	21 5:13
23 2:35	♅ ☌	♋	23 18:02
25 10:05	♃ △	♌	26 5:00
27 23:09	♅ ⚹	♍	28 12:53
30 5:01	♅ □	♎	30 18:05

☽ Phases & Eclipses Dy Hr Mn	
8 11:03	☽ 16♎21
15 2:13	○ 22♑41
22 8:09	☾ 29♈35
30 11:12	● 7♌21
6 16:44	☽ 14♏17
13 10:46	○ 20♒45
21 1:17	☾ 28♉04
28 23:09	● 5♍41

Astro Data

1 July 2030
Julian Day # 47664
SVP 4♓49'44"
GC 27♐15.9 ⚴ 16♓06.3R
Eris 26♈51.0 ⚵ 3♑09.3R
⚷ 15♉44.4 ⚶ 16♉52.3
☽ Mean ☊ 15♐11.8

1 August 2030
Julian Day # 47695
SVP 4♓49'39"
GC 27♐16.0 ⚴ 13♓20.1R
Eris 26♈53.0R ⚵ 27♐25.8R
⚷ 16♉43.5 ⚶ 27♉55.2
☽ Mean ☊ 13♐33.3

LONGITUDE — September 2030

Day	Sid.Time	☉	0 hr ☽	Noon ☽	True ☊	☿	♀	♂	⚳	♃	♄	♅	♆	♇
1 Su	10 42 48	9♍06 34	17♎18 23	24♎18 11	11♐55.6	4♍12.8	26♌08.7	10♌35.6	21♉43.8	21♏04.7	8♊36.4	22♊35.0	12♈49.8	10♒13.1
2 M	10 46 45	10 04 39	1♏19 16	8♏21 19	11R 50.8	3R 26.6	27 22.8	11 13.8	21 49.7	21 12.5	8 38.5	22 36.3	12R 48.5	10R 11.9
3 Tu	10 50 41	11 02 45	15 24 01	22 27 09	11 48.4	2 45.5	28 37.0	11 52.0	21 55.2	21 20.5	8 40.4	22 37.6	12 47.2	10 10.8
4 W	10 54 38	12 00 52	29 30 31	6♐34 00	11 47.9	2 10.5	29 51.2	12 30.1	22 00.4	21 28.6	8 42.2	22 38.9	12 45.8	10 09.6
5 Th	10 58 34	12 59 01	13♐37 26	20 40 46	11 47.8	1 42.5	1♍05.4	13 08.2	22 05.3	21 36.8	8 43.9	22 40.1	12 44.4	10 08.5
6 F	11 02 31	13 57 12	27 43 51	4♑46 36	11 46.9	1 22.1	2 19.6	13 46.3	22 09.8	21 45.1	8 45.5	22 41.2	12 43.0	10 07.4
7 Sa	11 06 28	14 55 24	11♑48 50	18 50 23	11 44.1	1D 10.0	3 33.9	14 24.3	22 14.0	21 53.6	8 47.0	22 42.3	12 41.6	10 06.4
8 Su	11 10 24	15 53 37	25 51 00	2♒50 23	11 38.6	1 06.5	4 48.1	15 02.3	22 17.9	22 02.1	8 48.4	22 43.4	12 40.2	10 05.3
9 M	11 14 21	16 51 52	9♒48 13	16 44 06	11 30.3	1 11.9	6 02.5	15 40.2	22 21.4	22 10.8	8 49.7	22 44.4	12 38.7	10 04.2
10 Tu	11 18 17	17 50 08	23 37 39	0♓28 25	11 19.6	1 26.3	7 16.8	16 18.1	22 24.6	22 19.6	8 50.9	22 45.3	12 37.2	10 03.2
11 W	11 22 14	18 48 26	7♓16 01	14 00 02	11 07.4	1 49.7	8 31.2	16 56.0	22 27.5	22 28.5	8 52.0	22 46.2	12 35.8	10 02.2
12 Th	11 26 10	19 46 46	20 40 08	27 16 03	10 54.9	2 21.9	9 45.5	17 33.9	22 30.0	22 37.6	8 52.9	22 47.1	12 34.3	10 01.2
13 F	11 30 07	20 45 08	3♈47 33	10♈14 31	10 43.3	3 02.7	11 00.0	18 11.7	22 32.1	22 46.7	8 53.8	22 47.9	12 32.7	10 00.2
14 Sa	11 34 03	21 43 31	16 36 55	22 54 49	10 33.6	3 51.6	12 14.4	18 49.4	22 33.9	22 55.9	8 54.5	22 48.6	12 31.2	9 59.3
15 Su	11 38 00	22 41 57	29 08 22	5♉17 50	10 26.5	4 48.4	13 28.9	19 27.2	22 35.3	23 05.3	8 55.2	22 49.3	12 29.7	9 58.3
16 M	11 41 56	23 40 25	11♉23 32	17 25 53	10 22.0	5 52.5	14 43.4	20 04.9	22 36.3	23 14.7	8 55.7	22 50.0	12 28.1	9 57.4
17 Tu	11 45 53	24 38 55	23 25 22	29 22 31	10D 19.9	7 03.3	15 57.9	20 42.6	22 37.0	23 24.3	8 56.1	22 50.6	12 26.6	9 56.5
18 W	11 49 50	25 37 27	5♊17 55	11♊12 12	10 19.5	8 20.3	17 12.5	21 20.2	22R 37.3	23 34.0	8 56.5	22 51.1	12 25.0	9 55.6
19 Th	11 53 46	26 36 01	17 06 02	23 00 06	10R 19.7	9 42.8	18 27.1	21 57.8	22 37.2	23 43.8	8 56.7	22 51.6	12 23.4	9 54.8
20 F	11 57 43	27 34 38	28 55 04	4♋51 38	10 19.5	11 10.3	19 41.7	22 35.4	22 36.8	23 53.6	8R 56.8	22 52.0	12 21.8	9 53.9
21 Sa	12 01 39	28 33 16	10♋50 29	16 52 17	10 17.9	12 42.1	20 56.3	23 13.0	22 36.0	24 03.6	8 56.8	22 52.4	12 20.2	9 53.1
22 Su	12 05 36	29 31 57	22 57 39	29 07 09	10 14.3	14 17.6	22 11.0	23 50.5	22 34.8	24 13.7	8 56.6	22 52.8	12 18.6	9 52.3
23 M	12 09 32	0♎30 40	5♌21 19	11♌40 34	10 08.1	15 56.3	23 25.7	24 27.9	22 33.2	24 23.8	8 56.4	22 53.0	12 17.0	9 51.6
24 Tu	12 13 29	1 29 25	18 05 15	24 35 36	9 59.6	17 37.6	24 40.4	25 05.4	22 31.2	24 34.1	8 56.1	22 53.3	12 15.3	9 50.8
25 W	12 17 25	2 28 12	1♍11 44	7♍53 38	9 49.4	19 21.1	25 55.2	25 42.8	22 28.8	24 44.5	8 55.6	22 53.4	12 13.7	9 50.1
26 Th	12 21 22	3 27 02	14 41 09	21 34 00	9 38.3	21 06.2	27 09.9	26 20.1	22 26.1	24 54.9	8 55.0	22 53.6	12 12.0	9 49.4
27 F	12 25 19	4 25 53	28 31 45	5♎33 53	9 27.7	22 52.7	28 24.7	26 57.5	22 23.0	25 05.5	8 54.4	22R 53.6	12 10.4	9 48.7
28 Sa	12 29 15	5 24 47	12♎39 46	19 48 42	9 18.6	24 40.1	29 39.5	27 34.7	22 19.4	25 16.1	8 53.6	22 53.7	12 08.7	9 48.0
29 Su	12 33 12	6 23 42	26 59 57	4♏12 46	9 11.8	26 28.2	0♎54.3	28 12.0	22 15.5	25 26.8	8 52.7	22 53.6	12 07.1	9 47.4
30 M	12 37 08	7 22 39	11♏26 24	18 40 12	9 07.7	28 16.6	2 09.1	28 49.2	22 11.3	25 37.6	8 51.7	22 53.5	12 05.4	9 46.8

LONGITUDE — October 2030

Day	Sid.Time	☉	0 hr ☽	Noon ☽	True ☊	☿	♀	♂	⚳	♃	♄	♅	♆	♇
1 Tu	12 41 05	8♎21 39	25♏53 33	3♐05 53	9♐06.1	0♎05.2	3♎24.0	29♌26.4	22♉06.6	25♏48.5	8♊50.6	22♊53.4	12♈03.7	9♒46.2
2 W	12 45 01	9 20 40	10♐16 48	17 25 55	9D 06.1	1 53.8	4 38.9	0♍03.5	22R 01.5	25 59.5	8R 49.4	22R 53.2	12R 02.1	9R 45.6
3 Th	12 48 58	10 19 42	24 32 59	1♑37 49	9R 06.8	3 42.2	5 53.7	0 40.6	21 56.1	26 10.5	8 48.1	22 53.0	12 00.4	9 45.1
4 F	12 52 54	11 18 47	8♑40 15	15 40 14	9 07.0	5 30.2	7 08.6	1 17.7	21 50.3	26 21.7	8 46.6	22 52.7	11 58.7	9 44.6
5 Sa	12 56 51	12 17 53	22 37 42	29 32 35	9 05.6	7 17.9	8 23.6	1 54.7	21 44.1	26 32.9	8 45.1	22 52.3	11 57.1	9 44.1
6 Su	13 00 48	13 17 01	6♒24 54	13♒14 33	9 02.0	9 05.1	9 38.5	2 31.7	21 37.6	26 44.2	8 43.5	22 51.9	11 55.4	9 43.7
7 M	13 04 44	14 16 10	20 01 32	26 45 44	8 56.1	10 51.6	10 53.4	3 08.6	21 30.7	26 55.6	8 41.7	22 51.5	11 53.7	9 43.2
8 Tu	13 08 41	15 15 22	3♓27 06	10♓05 29	8 48.2	12 37.6	12 08.4	3 45.5	21 23.4	27 07.0	8 39.9	22 51.0	11 52.1	9 42.8
9 W	13 12 37	16 14 35	16 40 49	23 12 58	8 39.0	14 22.9	13 23.3	4 22.4	21 15.8	27 18.5	8 37.9	22 50.4	11 50.4	9 42.4
10 Th	13 16 34	17 13 50	29 41 49	6♈07 17	8 29.5	16 07.5	14 38.3	4 59.2	21 07.8	27 30.1	8 35.9	22 49.8	11 48.7	9 42.1
11 F	13 20 30	18 13 07	12♈29 18	18 47 51	8 20.8	17 51.4	15 53.3	5 36.0	20 59.5	27 41.7	8 33.7	22 49.2	11 47.1	9 41.7
12 Sa	13 24 27	19 12 26	25 02 56	1♉14 37	8 13.5	19 34.6	17 08.3	6 12.7	20 50.9	27 53.5	8 31.5	22 48.5	11 45.4	9 41.4
13 Su	13 28 23	20 11 48	7♉23 01	13 28 20	8 08.3	21 17.1	18 23.3	6 49.4	20 41.9	28 05.3	8 29.1	22 47.7	11 43.8	9 41.2
14 M	13 32 20	21 11 11	19 30 46	25 30 38	8 05.3	22 58.9	19 38.3	7 26.1	20 32.5	28 17.1	8 26.7	22 46.9	11 42.1	9 40.9
15 Tu	13 36 16	22 10 37	1♊28 17	7♊24 08	8D 04.3	24 40.0	20 53.4	8 02.7	20 22.9	28 29.0	8 24.2	22 46.1	11 40.5	9 40.7
16 W	13 40 13	23 10 05	13 18 38	19 12 16	8 04.9	26 20.4	22 08.4	8 39.3	20 12.9	28 41.0	8 21.5	22 45.2	11 38.8	9 40.5
17 Th	13 44 10	24 09 35	25 05 37	0♋59 16	8 06.4	28 00.1	23 23.5	9 15.9	20 02.7	28 53.1	8 18.8	22 44.2	11 37.2	9 40.3
18 F	13 48 06	25 09 08	6♋53 48	12 49 53	8 07.8	29 39.1	24 38.6	9 52.4	19 52.1	29 05.2	8 16.0	22 43.2	11 35.6	9 40.2
19 Sa	13 52 03	26 08 42	18 48 09	24 49 17	8R 08.6	1♏17.5	25 53.7	10 28.9	19 41.2	29 17.3	8 13.1	22 42.2	11 34.0	9 40.1
20 Su	13 55 59	27 08 19	0♌53 54	7♌02 38	8 08.0	2 55.3	27 08.8	11 05.3	19 30.1	29 29.6	8 10.1	22 41.1	11 32.4	9 40.0
21 M	13 59 56	28 07 59	13 16 06	19 34 51	8 05.8	4 32.4	28 23.9	11 41.7	19 18.7	29 41.9	8 07.0	22 40.0	11 30.8	9 39.9
22 Tu	14 03 52	29 07 40	25 59 21	2♍30 00	8 01.9	6 08.9	29 39.1	12 18.0	19 07.0	29 54.2	8 03.8	22 38.8	11 29.2	9D 39.9
23 W	14 07 49	0♏07 24	9♍07 05	15 50 47	7 56.7	7 44.9	0♏54.2	12 54.4	18 55.1	0♐06.6	8 00.5	22 37.5	11 27.6	9 39.9
24 Th	14 11 45	1 07 10	22 41 08	29 37 58	7 50.7	9 20.2	2 09.4	13 30.6	18 43.0	0 19.0	7 57.1	22 36.3	11 26.1	9 39.9
25 F	14 15 42	2 06 58	6♎41 01	13♎49 50	7 44.9	10 55.0	3 24.6	14 06.8	18 30.6	0 31.5	7 53.7	22 34.9	11 24.5	9 40.0
26 Sa	14 19 39	3 06 48	21 03 47	28 22 07	7 39.9	12 29.3	4 39.7	14 43.0	18 18.0	0 44.1	7 50.2	22 33.6	11 23.0	9 40.1
27 Su	14 23 35	4 06 40	5♏43 58	13♏08 23	7 36.3	14 03.1	5 54.9	15 19.1	18 05.2	0 56.7	7 46.6	22 32.1	11 21.5	9 40.2
28 M	14 27 32	5 06 34	20 34 21	28 00 52	7D 34.5	15 36.3	7 10.1	15 55.2	17 52.3	1 09.3	7 42.9	22 30.7	11 20.0	9 40.3
29 Tu	14 31 28	6 06 30	5♐26 58	12♐51 43	7 34.2	17 09.0	8 25.3	16 31.3	17 39.1	1 22.0	7 39.1	22 29.2	11 18.5	9 40.5
30 W	14 35 25	7 06 28	20 14 19	27 34 03	7 35.2	18 41.3	9 40.5	17 07.2	17 25.9	1 34.8	7 35.3	22 27.6	11 17.0	9 40.7
31 Th	14 39 21	8 06 28	4♑50 20	12♑02 42	7 36.7	20 13.1	10 55.7	17 43.2	17 12.5	1 47.6	7 31.4	22 26.1	11 15.6	9 40.9

Astro Data

	Dy Hr Mn
☿ D	8 9:28
☽ 0N	11 19:57
♃⚻♅	13 15:22
⚳ R	18 19:43
♄ R	20 21:31
☉0S	22 23:27
☽ 0S	26 6:26
♅ R	28 8:28
♀0S	1 9:09
☿0S	3 15:10
♃⚼♆	7 8:39
☽ 0N	9 2:56
♇ D	23 3:08
☽ 0S	23 15:58

Planet Ingress

	Dy Hr Mn
♀ ♍	4 14:52
☉ ♎	22 23:28
♀ ♎	28 18:35
☿ ♎	1 10:51
♂ ♍	2 9:43
☿ ♏	18 17:04
♀ ♏	22 18:41
♃ ♐	22 23:15
☉ ♏	23 9:02

Last Aspect / ☽ Ingress (September)

Last Aspect Dy Hr Mn		☽ Ingress Dy Hr Mn
1 15:27	♀ ⚹	♏ 1 21:45
3 23:29	♀ □	♐ 4 0:50
5 15:23	♅ ☍	♑ 6 3:52
7 17:17	♃ ⚹	♒ 8 7:07
9 22:28	♅ △	♓ 10 11:10
12 3:50	♅ □	♈ 12 17:01
14 11:48	♅ ⚹	♉ 15 1:40
17 1:37	☉ △	♊ 17 13:16
19 19:58	☉ □	♋ 20 2:11
22 12:52	☉ ⚹	♌ 22 13:42
24 12:57	♂ ☌	♍ 24 21:50
26 22:36	♀ ☌	♎ 27 2:31
29 1:33	♂ ⚹	♏ 29 5:00

Last Aspect / ☽ Ingress (October)

Last Aspect Dy Hr Mn		☽ Ingress Dy Hr Mn
1 6:16	☿ ⚹	♐ 1 6:50
2 21:11	♅ ☍	♑ 3 9:14
5 6:43	♃ ⚹	♒ 5 12:48
7 12:18	♃ □	♓ 7 17:48
9 19:41	♃ △	♈ 10 0:34
11 19:42	♅ ⚹	♉ 12 9:35
14 17:40	♃ ☍	♊ 14 21:02
17 4:56	☿ △	♋ 17 9:59
19 20:59	♃ △	♌ 19 22:14
22 7:10	♃ □	♍ 22 7:25
23 23:53	♅ □	♎ 24 12:38
26 2:29	♅ △	♏ 26 14:40
27 15:40	♂ ⚹	♐ 28 15:12
30 3:39	♅ ☍	♑ 30 16:00

☽ Phases & Eclipses

Dy Hr Mn	
4 21:57	☽ 12♐25
11 21:19	○ 19♓11
19 19:58	☾ 26♊55
27 9:56	● 4♎21
4 3:57	☽ 10♑59
11 10:48	○ 18♈10
19 14:52	☾ 26♋16
26 20:18	● 3♏28

Astro Data

1 September 2030
Julian Day # 47726
SVP 4♓49'36"
GC 27♐16.1 ⚴ 6♓10.1R
Eris 26♈45.4R ⚵ 26♐42.7
⚷ 16♉50.9R ⚶ 6♊14.8
☽ Mean ☊ 11♐54.8

1 October 2030
Julian Day # 47756
SVP 4♓49'33"
GC 27♐16.1 ⚴ 29♒37.0R
Eris 26♈30.7R ⚵ 0♑57.1
⚷ 16♉07.2R ⚶ 10♊01.8
☽ Mean ☊ 10♐19.4

November 2030 LONGITUDE

Day	Sid.Time	☉	0 hr ☽	Noon ☽	True ☊	☿	♀	♂	⚷	♃	♄	♅	♆	♇
1 F	14 43 18	9♏06 29	19♑10 50	26♑14 29	7♐38.0	21♏44.4	12♏10.9	18♍19.1	16♉58.9	2♐00.4	7♊27.4	22♊24.4	11♈14.1	9♒41.2
2 Sa	14 47 14	10 06 31	3♒13 34	10♒08 01	7R38.6	23 15.2	13 26.2	18 54.9	16R45.3	2 13.2	7R23.4	22R22.8	11R12.7	9 41.4
3 Su	14 51 11	11 06 35	16 57 54	23 43 18	7 38.0	24 45.5	14 41.4	19 30.7	16 31.6	2 26.1	7 19.3	22 21.1	11 11.3	9 41.7
4 M	14 55 08	12 06 41	0♓24 20	7♓01 11	7 36.1	26 15.4	15 56.6	20 06.4	16 17.8	2 39.1	7 15.1	22 19.3	11 09.9	9 42.1
5 Tu	14 59 04	13 06 48	13 34 00	20 02 59	7 33.1	27 44.8	17 11.8	20 42.1	16 03.9	2 52.1	7 10.9	22 17.5	11 08.6	9 42.4
6 W	15 03 01	14 06 56	26 28 19	2♈50 11	7 29.5	29 13.8	18 27.0	21 17.7	15 50.0	3 05.1	7 06.6	22 15.7	11 07.2	9 42.8
7 Th	15 06 57	15 07 07	9♈08 46	15 24 12	7 25.7	0♐42.2	19 42.3	21 53.3	15 36.1	3 18.1	7 02.3	22 13.8	11 05.9	9 43.2
8 F	15 10 54	16 07 19	21 36 42	27 46 24	7 22.2	2 10.2	20 57.5	22 28.8	15 22.1	3 31.2	6 57.9	22 11.9	11 04.6	9 43.7
9 Sa	15 14 50	17 07 32	3♉53 29	9♉58 07	7 19.4	3 37.6	22 12.7	23 04.3	15 08.2	3 44.3	6 53.4	22 10.0	11 03.3	9 44.2
10 Su	15 18 47	18 07 48	16 00 29	22 00 47	7 17.6	5 04.4	23 28.0	23 39.7	14 54.3	3 57.4	6 48.9	22 08.0	11 02.1	9 44.7
11 M	15 22 43	19 08 05	27 59 15	3♊56 06	7D16.8	6 30.7	24 43.2	24 15.1	14 40.4	4 10.6	6 44.4	22 06.1	11 00.8	9 45.2
12 Tu	15 26 40	20 08 24	9♊51 37	15 46 06	7 17.0	7 56.4	25 58.5	24 50.5	14 26.6	4 23.8	6 39.8	22 04.0	10 59.6	9 45.8
13 W	15 30 37	21 08 45	21 39 52	27 33 17	7 17.9	9 21.4	27 13.7	25 25.7	14 12.8	4 37.0	6 35.2	22 02.0	10 58.4	9 46.3
14 Th	15 34 33	22 09 07	3♋26 45	9♋20 43	7 19.3	10 45.6	28 29.0	26 00.9	13 59.2	4 50.2	6 30.5	21 59.9	10 57.2	9 47.0
15 F	15 38 30	23 09 32	15 15 37	21 11 57	7 20.7	12 09.1	29 44.2	26 36.1	13 45.6	5 03.5	6 25.8	21 57.7	10 56.1	9 47.6
16 Sa	15 42 26	24 09 58	27 10 16	3♌11 05	7 21.9	13 31.6	0♐59.5	27 11.2	13 32.1	5 16.8	6 21.1	21 55.6	10 55.0	9 48.3
17 Su	15 46 23	25 10 26	9♌14 58	15 22 30	7R22.7	14 53.2	2 14.7	27 46.3	13 18.8	5 30.1	6 16.3	21 53.4	10 53.9	9 49.0
18 M	15 50 19	26 10 56	21 34 15	27 50 45	7 22.9	16 13.6	3 30.0	28 21.3	13 05.6	5 43.4	6 11.5	21 51.2	10 52.8	9 49.7
19 Tu	15 54 16	27 11 28	4♍12 34	10♍40 10	7 22.6	17 32.9	4 45.3	28 56.2	12 52.6	5 56.8	6 06.7	21 49.0	10 51.8	9 50.4
20 W	15 58 12	28 12 02	17 13 59	23 54 22	7 21.8	18 50.7	6 00.6	29 31.1	12 39.7	6 10.1	6 01.9	21 46.7	10 50.8	9 51.2
21 Th	16 02 09	29 12 37	0♎41 33	7♎35 40	7 20.9	20 06.9	7 15.9	0♎05.9	12 27.1	6 23.5	5 57.0	21 44.4	10 49.8	9 52.0
22 F	16 06 06	0♐13 14	14 36 40	21 44 23	7 19.9	21 21.4	8 31.1	0 40.7	12 14.6	6 36.9	5 52.1	21 42.1	10 48.8	9 52.8
23 Sa	16 10 02	1 13 53	28 58 28	6♏18 21	7 19.2	22 33.8	9 46.4	1 15.3	12 02.4	6 50.3	5 47.2	21 39.8	10 47.9	9 53.7
24 Su	16 13 59	2 14 33	13♏43 20	21 12 32	7 18.7	23 43.9	11 01.7	1 50.0	11 50.4	7 03.7	5 42.3	21 37.4	10 47.0	9 54.5
25 M	16 17 55	3 15 15	28 44 56	6♐19 25	7D18.6	24 51.4	12 17.0	2 24.5	11 38.6	7 17.2	5 37.4	21 35.0	10 46.1	9 55.4
26 Tu	16 21 52	4 15 58	13♐54 48	21 29 52	7 18.7	25 55.8	13 32.3	2 59.0	11 27.1	7 30.6	5 32.4	21 32.6	10 45.2	9 56.4
27 W	16 25 48	5 16 43	29 03 27	6♑34 26	7 18.9	26 56.8	14 47.6	3 33.4	11 15.9	7 44.1	5 27.5	21 30.2	10 44.4	9 57.3
28 Th	16 29 45	6 17 29	14♑01 49	21 24 44	7 19.0	27 53.9	16 02.9	4 07.8	11 04.9	7 57.5	5 22.6	21 27.8	10 43.6	9 58.3
29 F	16 33 41	7 18 15	28 42 29	5♒54 33	7R19.1	28 46.5	17 18.2	4 42.0	10 54.3	8 11.0	5 17.6	21 25.3	10 42.9	9 59.3
30 Sa	16 37 38	8 19 03	13♒00 33	20 00 17	7 19.0	29 34.1	18 33.5	5 16.2	10 43.9	8 24.4	5 12.7	21 22.9	10 42.2	10 00.3

December 2030 LONGITUDE

Day	Sid.Time	☉	0 hr ☽	Noon ☽	True ☊	☿	♀	♂	⚷	♃	♄	♅	♆	♇
1 Su	16 41 35	9♐19 51	26♒53 42	3♓40 51	7♐19.0	0♑15.9	19♐48.8	5♎50.4	10♉33.9	8♐37.9	5♊07.8	21♊20.4	10♈41.5	10♒01.4
2 M	16 45 31	10 20 41	10♓21 56	16 57 11	7D19.0	0 51.1	21 04.1	6 24.4	10R24.2	8 51.4	5R02.9	21R17.9	10R40.8	10 02.5
3 Tu	16 49 28	11 21 31	23 26 58	29 51 39	7 19.2	1 19.1	22 19.4	6 58.4	10 14.8	9 04.8	4 58.0	21 15.4	10 40.2	10 03.6
4 W	16 53 24	12 22 22	6♈11 38	12♈27 21	7 19.6	1 39.0	23 34.6	7 32.3	10 05.8	9 18.3	4 53.1	21 12.9	10 39.6	10 04.7
5 Th	16 57 21	13 23 14	18 39 15	24 47 43	7 20.2	1R50.0	24 49.9	8 06.1	9 57.1	9 31.7	4 48.3	21 10.4	10 39.0	10 05.8
6 F	17 01 17	14 24 07	0♉53 12	6♉56 05	7 21.0	1 51.1	26 05.2	8 39.9	9 48.7	9 45.2	4 43.5	21 07.8	10 38.5	10 07.0
7 Sa	17 05 14	15 25 00	12 56 45	18 55 32	7 21.7	1 41.8	27 20.4	9 13.5	9 40.8	9 58.6	4 38.7	21 05.3	10 38.0	10 08.2
8 Su	17 09 10	16 25 55	24 52 48	0♊48 51	7R22.1	1 21.4	28 35.7	9 47.1	9 33.2	10 12.1	4 33.9	21 02.7	10 37.5	10 09.4
9 M	17 13 07	17 26 51	6♊43 58	12 38 26	7 22.1	0 49.7	29 51.0	10 20.6	9 25.9	10 25.5	4 29.1	21 00.2	10 37.0	10 10.6
10 Tu	17 17 04	18 27 47	18 32 32	24 26 30	7 21.6	0 06.6	1♑06.2	10 54.0	9 19.0	10 38.9	4 24.4	20 57.6	10 36.6	10 11.9
11 W	17 21 00	19 28 45	0♋20 36	6♋15 06	7 20.4	29♐12.6	2 21.5	11 27.4	9 12.6	10 52.3	4 19.7	20 55.1	10 36.3	10 13.2
12 Th	17 24 57	20 29 43	12 10 16	18 06 23	7 18.6	28 08.8	3 36.7	12 00.7	9 06.5	11 05.7	4 15.1	20 52.5	10 35.9	10 14.5
13 F	17 28 53	21 30 42	24 03 43	0♌02 37	7 16.4	26 56.7	4 52.0	12 33.8	9 00.7	11 19.1	4 10.5	20 50.0	10 35.6	10 15.8
14 Sa	17 32 50	22 31 42	6♌03 23	12 06 24	7 14.1	25 38.4	6 07.2	13 06.9	8 55.4	11 32.5	4 06.0	20 47.4	10 35.4	10 17.1
15 Su	17 36 46	23 32 44	18 12 01	24 20 40	7 11.9	24 16.3	7 22.5	13 39.9	8 50.5	11 45.8	4 01.5	20 44.9	10 35.1	10 18.5
16 M	17 40 43	24 33 46	0♍32 44	6♍48 41	7 10.2	22 53.3	8 37.7	14 12.8	8 45.9	11 59.1	3 57.0	20 42.3	10 34.9	10 19.8
17 Tu	17 44 40	25 34 49	13 08 57	19 33 58	7D09.3	21 32.1	9 52.9	14 45.6	8 41.8	12 12.5	3 52.6	20 39.7	10 34.7	10 21.2
18 W	17 48 36	26 35 53	26 04 09	2♎39 54	7 09.3	20 15.4	11 08.2	15 18.4	8 38.1	12 25.7	3 48.2	20 37.2	10 34.6	10 22.7
19 Th	17 52 33	27 36 58	9♎21 35	16 09 28	7 10.1	19 05.5	12 23.4	15 51.0	8 34.7	12 39.0	3 43.9	20 34.7	10 34.5	10 24.1
20 F	17 56 29	28 38 03	23 03 46	0♏04 33	7 11.5	18 04.2	13 38.6	16 23.5	8 31.8	12 52.3	3 39.7	20 32.1	10 34.4	10 25.5
21 Sa	18 00 26	29 39 10	7♏11 47	14 25 17	7 12.9	17 12.8	14 53.9	16 55.9	8 29.3	13 05.5	3 35.5	20 29.6	10D34.4	10 27.0
22 Su	18 04 22	0♑40 18	21 44 41	29 09 26	7R13.9	16 32.0	16 09.1	17 28.3	8 27.1	13 18.7	3 31.4	20 27.1	10 34.4	10 28.5
23 M	18 08 19	1 41 26	6♐38 49	14♐11 54	7 14.0	16 02.1	17 24.3	18 00.5	8 25.4	13 31.9	3 27.4	20 24.6	10 34.4	10 30.0
24 Tu	18 12 15	2 42 35	21 47 39	29 24 53	7 12.7	15 42.9	18 39.5	18 32.6	8 24.1	13 45.0	3 23.4	20 22.1	10 34.5	10 31.5
25 W	18 16 12	3 43 44	7♑02 18	14♑38 38	7 10.1	15D34.2	19 54.7	19 04.6	8 23.2	13 58.1	3 19.5	20 19.6	10 34.6	10 33.1
26 Th	18 20 09	4 44 53	22 12 35	29 42 58	7 06.4	15 35.2	21 09.9	19 36.4	8D22.7	14 11.2	3 15.6	20 17.2	10 34.8	10 34.6
27 F	18 24 05	5 46 03	7♒08 42	14♒28 52	7 02.1	15 45.4	22 25.1	20 08.2	8 22.6	14 24.2	3 11.9	20 14.7	10 35.0	10 36.2
28 Sa	18 28 02	6 47 13	21 42 44	28 49 47	6 57.8	16 03.9	23 40.3	20 39.8	8 22.9	14 37.2	3 08.2	20 12.3	10 35.2	10 37.8
29 Su	18 31 58	7 48 22	5♓49 42	12♓42 20	6 54.4	16 30.0	24 55.5	21 11.4	8 23.6	14 50.2	3 04.6	20 09.9	10 35.4	10 39.4
30 M	18 35 55	8 49 32	19 27 44	26 06 06	6 52.1	17 02.9	26 10.7	21 42.8	8 24.7	15 03.1	3 01.1	20 07.5	10 35.7	10 41.0
31 Tu	18 39 51	9 50 41	2♈37 47	9♈03 10	6D51.3	17 42.0	27 25.8	22 14.0	8 26.2	15 16.0	2 57.6	20 05.1	10 36.0	10 42.6

Astro Data Dy Hr Mn	Planet Ingress Dy Hr Mn	Last Aspect Dy Hr Mn	☽ Ingress Dy Hr Mn	Last Aspect Dy Hr Mn	☽ Ingress Dy Hr Mn	☽ Phases & Eclipses Dy Hr Mn
☽0N 5 8:10	☿ ♐ 7 0:32	1 3:25 ☿ ⚹	♒ 1 18:26	30 14:23 ♅ △	♓ 1 5:28	2 11:57 ☽ 10♒06
♃☍♄ 20 1:07	♀ ♐ 15 17:02	3 14:05 ☿ □	♓ 3 23:16	2 20:24 ♀ □	♈ 3 12:16	10 3:31 ○ 17♉47
☽0S 20 1:09	♂ ♎ 21 7:56	6 4:17 ☿ △	♈ 6 6:38	5 12:05 ♀ △	♉ 5 22:15	18 8:33 ☾ 26♌02
♂0S 27 17:18	☉ ♐ 22 6:46	8 1:10 ♅ ⚹	♉ 8 16:21	6 18:21 ♇ □	♊ 8 10:21	25 6:48 ● 3♐02
		10 15:29 ♂ △	♊ 11 4:03	10 22:45 ☿ ☍	♋ 10 23:18	25 6:51:36 ● T 03'44"
☽0N 2 13:39	☿ ♑ 1 2:28	13 7:26 ♂ □	♋ 13 16:59	11 23:04 ♂ □	♌ 13 11:55	
☿R 6 2:47	♀ ♑ 9 14:53	15 23:25 ♂ ⚹	♌ 16 5:39	15 11:52 ☿ △	♍ 15 22:57	1 22:58 ☽ 9♓48
♃⚹♇ 8 6:45	☿ ♐R 10 15:12	18 8:33 ☉ □	♍ 18 16:05	18 0:02 ☉ □	♎ 18 7:10	9 22:42 ○ 17♊54
♃△♆ 10 8:03	☉ ♑ 21 20:11	20 22:23 ♂ ☌	♎ 20 22:47	20 9:21 ☉ ⚹	♏ 20 11:52	9 22:29 ☍ A 0.941
☽0S 17 8:57		22 11:56 ♅ △	♏ 23 1:41	21 12:51 ♀ ⚹	♐ 22 13:21	18 0:02 ☾ 26♍05
♆D 21 20:42		23 17:50 ♇ □	♐ 25 1:59	23 21:47 ♅ ☍	♑ 24 12:55	24 17:33 ● 2♑57
☿D 25 21:17		26 19:33 ☿ ☌	♑ 27 1:30	25 21:06 ♀ ☌	♒ 26 12:27	31 13:37 ☽ 9♈55
♆⚹♇ 26 14:22		27 18:41 ♆ □	♒ 29 2:08	27 21:44 ♂ △	♓ 28 14:00	
⚷D 27 5:38				30 12:09 ♀ ⚹	♈ 30 19:09	
☽0N 29 21:29						

Astro Data

1 November 2030
Julian Day # 47787
SVP 4♓49'30"
GC 27♐16.2 ⚵ 27♒39.1
Eris 26♈12.3R ⚴ 9♑01.0
⚷ 14♉44.5R ⚶ 7♊33.3R
☽ Mean ☊ 8♐40.9

1 December 2030
Julian Day # 47817
SVP 4♓49'25"
GC 27♐16.3 ⚵ 0♓43.3
Eris 25♈56.6R ⚴ 19♑11.2
⚷ 13♉17.8R ⚶ 0♊16.3R
☽ Mean ☊ 7♐05.6

LONGITUDE January 2031

Day	Sid.Time	☉	0 hr ☽	Noon ☽	True ☊	☿	♀	♂	⚳	♃	♄	♅	♆	♇
1 W	18 43 48	10♑51 50	15♈22 47	21♈37 11	6♐51.9	18♐26.5	28♑40.9	22♎45.2	8♉28.1	15♐28.9	2♊54.3	20♊02.8	10♈36.4	10♒44.3
2 Th	18 47 44	11 52 59	27 46 57	3♉52 41	6 53.4	19 15.9	29 56.1	23 16.2	8 30.4	15 41.7	2R 51.0	20R 00.4	10 36.8	10 45.9
3 F	18 51 41	12 54 08	9♉55 00	15 54 30	6 55.2	20 09.6	1♒11.2	23 47.1	8 33.1	15 54.5	2 47.8	19 58.1	10 37.2	10 47.6
4 Sa	18 55 38	13 55 17	21 51 45	27 47 17	6R 56.7	21 07.2	2 26.3	24 17.9	8 36.1	16 07.2	2 44.7	19 55.8	10 37.7	10 49.3
5 Su	18 59 34	14 56 25	3♊41 38	9♊35 17	6 57.0	22 08.2	3 41.3	24 48.5	8 39.6	16 19.8	2 41.7	19 53.6	10 38.1	10 51.0
6 M	19 03 31	15 57 34	15 28 38	21 22 07	6 55.8	23 12.3	4 56.4	25 19.0	8 43.4	16 32.5	2 38.8	19 51.3	10 38.7	10 52.7
7 Tu	19 07 27	16 58 42	27 16 04	3♋10 48	6 52.5	24 19.1	6 11.5	25 49.3	8 47.5	16 45.0	2 36.0	19 49.1	10 39.2	10 54.4
8 W	19 11 24	17 59 50	9♋06 36	15 03 42	6 47.3	25 28.3	7 26.5	26 19.6	8 52.1	16 57.6	2 33.3	19 47.0	10 39.8	10 56.2
9 Th	19 15 20	19 00 58	21 02 19	27 02 38	6 40.2	26 39.6	8 41.5	26 49.6	8 57.0	17 10.0	2 30.7	19 44.8	10 40.5	10 57.9
10 F	19 19 17	20 02 05	3♌04 49	9♌09 02	6 31.9	27 53.0	9 56.5	27 19.6	9 02.2	17 22.4	2 28.2	19 42.7	10 41.1	10 59.6
11 Sa	19 23 13	21 03 12	15 15 26	21 24 09	6 23.1	29 08.0	11 11.5	27 49.3	9 07.9	17 34.8	2 25.8	19 40.6	10 41.8	11 01.4
12 Su	19 27 10	22 04 20	27 35 22	3♍49 15	6 14.8	0♑24.7	12 26.5	28 19.0	9 13.8	17 47.1	2 23.4	19 38.6	10 42.6	11 03.2
13 M	19 31 07	23 05 27	10♍06 00	16 25 48	6 07.7	1 42.7	13 41.5	28 48.4	9 20.1	17 59.3	2 21.2	19 36.5	10 43.3	11 04.9
14 Tu	19 35 03	24 06 33	22 48 55	29 15 36	6 02.6	3 02.1	14 56.4	29 17.8	9 26.8	18 11.5	2 19.1	19 34.5	10 44.1	11 06.7
15 W	19 39 00	25 07 40	5♎46 06	12♎20 44	5 59.6	4 22.7	16 11.3	29 46.9	9 33.8	18 23.7	2 17.1	19 32.6	10 44.9	11 08.5
16 Th	19 42 56	26 08 47	18 59 47	25 43 30	5D 58.7	5 44.5	17 26.2	0♏15.9	9 41.1	18 35.7	2 15.2	19 30.7	10 45.8	11 10.3
17 F	19 46 53	27 09 53	2♏32 10	9♏25 57	5 59.2	7 07.2	18 41.0	0 44.7	9 48.8	18 47.7	2 13.4	19 28.8	10 46.7	11 12.1
18 Sa	19 50 49	28 10 59	16 25 02	23 29 25	6R 00.3	8 30.9	19 56.0	1 13.4	9 56.8	18 59.6	2 11.7	19 26.9	10 47.6	11 13.9
19 Su	19 54 46	29 12 06	0♐39 05	7♐53 47	6 00.7	9 55.5	21 10.9	1 41.8	10 05.1	19 11.5	2 10.1	19 25.1	10 48.6	11 15.7
20 M	19 58 42	0♒13 11	15 13 11	22 36 46	5 59.5	11 21.0	22 25.7	2 10.1	10 13.8	19 23.3	2 08.6	19 23.4	10 49.6	11 17.6
21 Tu	20 02 39	1 14 17	0♑03 48	7♑33 28	5 56.0	12 47.2	23 40.5	2 38.2	10 22.7	19 35.0	2 07.3	19 21.6	10 50.6	11 19.4
22 W	20 06 36	2 15 22	15 04 42	22 36 25	5 49.9	14 14.3	24 55.3	3 06.1	10 32.0	19 46.7	2 06.0	19 19.9	10 51.7	11 21.2
23 Th	20 10 32	3 16 26	0♒07 24	7♒36 26	5 41.6	15 42.1	26 10.1	3 33.8	10 41.6	19 58.3	2 04.9	19 18.3	10 52.8	11 23.1
24 F	20 14 29	4 17 29	15 02 19	22 23 58	5 31.9	17 10.6	27 24.9	4 01.3	10 51.5	20 09.8	2 03.8	19 16.7	10 53.9	11 24.9
25 Sa	20 18 25	5 18 32	29 40 23	6♓50 47	5 22.1	18 39.8	28 39.6	4 28.6	11 01.6	20 21.2	2 02.9	19 15.1	10 55.0	11 26.8
26 Su	20 22 22	6 19 33	13♓54 33	20 51 18	5 13.2	20 09.7	29 54.3	4 55.7	11 12.1	20 32.5	2 02.1	19 13.6	10 56.2	11 28.6
27 M	20 26 18	7 20 34	27 40 49	4♈23 05	5 06.3	21 40.3	1♓09.0	5 22.5	11 22.9	20 43.8	2 01.4	19 12.1	10 57.4	11 30.5
28 Tu	20 30 15	8 21 33	10♈58 15	17 26 39	5 01.7	23 11.6	2 23.6	5 49.2	11 34.0	20 55.0	2 00.8	19 10.7	10 58.7	11 32.3
29 W	20 34 11	9 22 31	23 48 42	0♉04 55	4D 59.5	24 43.6	3 38.2	6 15.6	11 45.3	21 06.1	2 00.4	19 09.3	10 59.9	11 34.2
30 Th	20 38 08	10 23 28	6♉15 54	12 22 18	4 59.0	26 16.2	4 52.8	6 41.8	11 56.9	21 17.1	2 00.0	19 07.9	11 01.2	11 36.0
31 F	20 42 05	11 24 24	18 24 48	24 24 06	4R 59.5	27 49.5	6 07.4	7 07.8	12 08.8	21 28.0	1 59.8	19 06.6	11 02.6	11 37.9

LONGITUDE February 2031

Day	Sid.Time	☉	0 hr ☽	Noon ☽	True ☊	☿	♀	♂	⚳	♃	♄	♅	♆	♇
1 Sa	20 46 01	12♒25 19	0♊20 53	6♊15 50	4♐59.8	29♑23.5	7♓21.9	7♏33.5	12♉21.0	21♐38.8	1♊59.6	19♊05.4	11♈03.9	11♒39.7
2 Su	20 49 58	13 26 12	12 09 35	18 02 48	4R 58.9	0♒58.2	8 36.4	7 59.0	12 33.4	21 49.5	1D 59.6	19R 04.2	11 05.3	11 41.6
3 M	20 53 54	14 27 04	23 56 03	29 49 52	4 55.9	2 33.6	9 50.9	8 24.3	12 46.1	22 00.2	1 59.7	19 03.0	11 06.7	11 43.4
4 Tu	20 57 51	15 27 55	5♋44 44	11♋41 07	4 50.1	4 09.7	11 05.3	8 49.3	12 59.0	22 10.7	1 59.9	19 01.9	11 08.2	11 45.3
5 W	21 01 47	16 28 44	17 39 22	23 39 48	4 41.6	5 46.6	12 19.7	9 14.0	13 12.2	22 21.2	2 00.3	19 00.8	11 09.6	11 47.1
6 Th	21 05 44	17 29 32	29 42 42	5♌48 14	4 30.4	7 24.1	13 34.0	9 38.5	13 25.7	22 31.6	2 00.7	18 59.8	11 11.1	11 49.0
7 F	21 09 40	18 30 19	11♌56 34	18 07 47	4 17.5	9 02.5	14 48.3	10 02.8	13 39.3	22 41.8	2 01.3	18 58.9	11 12.6	11 50.8
8 Sa	21 13 37	19 31 04	24 21 56	0♍39 01	4 03.9	10 41.5	16 02.6	10 26.7	13 53.3	22 52.0	2 01.9	18 58.0	11 14.2	11 52.7
9 Su	21 17 34	20 31 49	6♍59 01	13 21 53	3 50.7	12 21.4	17 16.8	10 50.4	14 07.4	23 02.1	2 02.7	18 57.1	11 15.8	11 54.5
10 M	21 21 30	21 32 32	19 47 37	26 16 08	3 39.2	14 02.1	18 31.0	11 13.8	14 21.8	23 12.0	2 03.6	18 56.3	11 17.4	11 56.3
11 Tu	21 25 27	22 33 14	2♎47 26	9♎21 29	3 30.2	15 43.6	19 45.1	11 36.9	14 36.4	23 21.9	2 04.6	18 55.5	11 19.0	11 58.2
12 W	21 29 23	23 33 55	15 58 21	22 38 03	3 24.2	17 25.9	20 59.2	11 59.8	14 51.2	23 31.6	2 05.7	18 54.8	11 20.6	12 00.0
13 Th	21 33 20	24 34 35	29 20 40	6♏06 19	3 21.1	19 09.1	22 13.3	12 22.3	15 06.3	23 41.2	2 06.9	18 54.1	11 22.3	12 01.8
14 F	21 37 16	25 35 14	12♏55 06	19 47 10	3 20.1	20 53.1	23 27.3	12 44.5	15 21.5	23 50.8	2 08.3	18 53.5	11 24.0	12 03.6
15 Sa	21 41 13	26 35 51	26 42 36	3♐41 31	3 20.0	22 37.9	24 41.3	13 06.4	15 37.0	24 00.2	2 09.7	18 53.0	11 25.7	12 05.4
16 Su	21 45 09	27 36 28	10♐43 55	17 49 47	3 19.6	24 23.7	25 55.3	13 27.9	15 52.7	24 09.5	2 11.3	18 52.5	11 27.4	12 07.3
17 M	21 49 06	28 37 03	24 58 59	2♑11 16	3 17.4	26 10.3	27 09.2	13 49.1	16 08.6	24 18.7	2 13.0	18 52.0	11 29.2	12 09.1
18 Tu	21 53 03	29 37 38	9♑26 16	16 43 29	3 12.7	27 57.8	28 23.1	14 10.0	16 24.7	24 27.8	2 14.8	18 51.6	11 31.0	12 10.8
19 W	21 56 59	0♓38 10	24 02 18	1♒21 56	3 04.9	29 46.2	29 36.9	14 30.5	16 41.0	24 36.7	2 16.7	18 51.3	11 32.8	12 12.6
20 Th	22 00 56	1 38 42	8♒41 34	16 00 15	2 54.5	1♓35.4	0♈50.7	14 50.7	16 57.5	24 45.6	2 18.7	18 51.0	11 34.6	12 14.4
21 F	22 04 52	2 39 12	23 17 02	0♓30 58	2 42.4	3 25.4	2 04.4	15 10.5	17 14.2	24 54.3	2 20.8	18 50.7	11 36.5	12 16.2
22 Sa	22 08 49	3 39 40	7♓41 10	14 46 48	2 29.8	5 16.3	3 18.1	15 29.9	17 31.1	25 02.8	2 23.0	18 50.6	11 38.3	12 17.9
23 Su	22 12 45	4 40 07	21 47 13	28 41 51	2 18.1	7 07.9	4 31.7	15 48.9	17 48.2	25 11.3	2 25.3	18 50.4	11 40.2	12 19.7
24 M	22 16 42	5 40 31	5♈30 21	12♈12 30	2 08.5	9 00.2	5 45.3	16 07.5	18 05.4	25 19.6	2 27.7	18D 50.3	11 42.1	12 21.4
25 Tu	22 20 38	6 40 54	18 48 15	25 17 44	2 01.6	10 53.2	6 58.8	16 25.7	18 22.9	25 27.8	2 30.3	18 50.3	11 44.1	12 23.1
26 W	22 24 35	7 41 16	1♉41 10	7♉58 57	1 57.4	12 46.7	8 12.3	16 43.5	18 40.5	25 35.9	2 32.9	18 50.3	11 46.0	12 24.8
27 Th	22 28 32	8 41 35	14 11 31	20 19 27	1D 55.6	14 40.7	9 25.7	17 00.9	18 58.3	25 43.8	2 35.7	18 50.4	11 48.0	12 26.5
28 F	22 32 28	9 41 52	26 23 21	2♊23 52	1R 55.2	16 35.0	10 39.1	17 17.9	19 16.2	25 51.6	2 38.5	18 50.6	11 49.9	12 28.2

Astro Data	Dy Hr Mn
☽ 0S	13 15:32
♃☍♅	20 12:05
☽ 0N	26 7:53
♄ D	2 2:26
☽ 0S	9 22:00
♀0N	21 14:08
☽ 0N	22 18:54
♅ D	25 11:25

Planet Ingress	Dy Hr Mn
♀ ♒	2 13:16
☿ ♑	12 4:20
♂ ♏	15 22:49
☉ ♒	20 6:49
♀ ♓	26 13:50
☿ ♒	1 21:16
☉ ♓	18 20:52
☿ ♓	19 15:03
♀ ♈	19 19:31

Last Aspect Dy Hr Mn		☽ Ingress Dy Hr Mn
2 3:20	♀ □	♉ 2 4:21
3 5:24	☉ △	♊ 4 16:29
6 20:24	♂ △	♋ 7 5:33
9 11:33	♂ □	♌ 9 17:53
12 0:58	♂ ✶	♍ 12 4:39
14 1:36	☉ △	♎ 14 13:22
16 12:48	☉ □	♏ 16 19:33
18 20:29	☉ ✶	♐ 18 22:55
20 11:40	♀ ✶	♑ 20 23:54
21 21:14	☿ ☌	♒ 22 23:48
24 21:02	♀ ☌	♓ 25 0:33
26 11:27	♃ □	♈ 27 4:08
29 0:19	☿ □	♉ 29 11:51
31 19:57	☿ △	♊ 31 23:18

Last Aspect Dy Hr Mn		☽ Ingress Dy Hr Mn
2 19:49	♃ ☍	♋ 3 12:21
4 10:53	♆ □	♌ 6 0:34
7 20:55	♃ △	♍ 8 10:46
10 6:15	♃ □	♎ 10 18:53
12 13:48	☉ △	♏ 13 1:10
14 22:51	☉ □	♐ 15 5:40
17 5:37	☉ ✶	♑ 17 8:22
19 8:52	♀ ✶	♒ 19 9:46
21 2:35	♃ ✶	♓ 21 11:08
23 5:49	♃ □	♈ 23 14:17
25 12:19	♃ △	♉ 25 20:49
27 5:21	♂ ☍	♊ 28 7:12

☽ Phases & Eclipses Dy Hr Mn	
8 18:27	○ 18♋16
16 12:48	☾ 26♎11
23 4:32	● 2♒57
30 7:44	☽ 10♉13
7 12:47	○ 18♌32
14 22:51	☾ 26♏03
21 15:50	● 2♓49

Astro Data

1 January 2031
Julian Day # 47848
SVP 4♓49'20"
GC 27♐16.3 ⚴ 7♓33.4
Eris 25♈47.7R ⚵ 1♒16.8
⚷ 12♉16.5R ⚶ 24♉47.7R
☽ Mean ☊ 5♐27.1

1 February 2031
Julian Day # 47879
SVP 4♓49'15"
GC 27♐16.4 ⚴ 16♓44.1
Eris 25♈48.9 ⚵ 14♒23.5
⚷ 12♉08.0 ⚶ 25♉57.5
☽ Mean ☊ 3♐48.6

March 2031 — LONGITUDE

Day	Sid.Time	☉	0 hr ☽	Noon ☽	True ☊	☿	♀	♂	⚳	♃	♄	♅	♆	♇
1 Sa	22 36 25	10♓42 07	8♊21 42	14♊17 32	1♐55.2	18♓29.4	11♈52.4	17♏34.4	19♉34.4	25♐59.3	2♊41.5	18♊50.8	11♈51.9	12♒29.9
2 Su	22 40 21	11 42 21	20 12 04	26 06 00	1R 54.4	20 23.8	13 05.6	17 50.5	19 52.7	26 06.8	2 44.5	18 51.0	11 53.9	12 31.6
3 M	22 44 18	12 42 32	2♋00 01	7♋54 45	1 51.8	22 18.0	14 18.8	18 06.1	20 11.1	26 14.2	2 47.7	18 51.3	11 56.0	12 33.2
4 Tu	22 48 14	13 42 41	13 50 50	19 48 48	1 46.8	24 11.6	15 31.9	18 21.3	20 29.7	26 21.4	2 50.9	18 51.7	11 58.0	12 34.9
5 W	22 52 11	14 42 48	25 49 10	1♌52 23	1 39.0	26 04.4	16 44.9	18 36.0	20 48.5	26 28.6	2 54.3	18 52.1	12 00.1	12 36.5
6 Th	22 56 07	15 42 53	7♌58 49	14 08 48	1 28.7	27 56.1	17 57.9	18 50.2	21 07.4	26 35.5	2 57.7	18 52.5	12 02.1	12 38.1
7 F	23 00 04	16 42 56	20 22 32	26 40 11	1 16.6	29 46.2	19 10.8	19 03.9	21 26.5	26 42.3	3 01.3	18 53.0	12 04.2	12 39.7
8 Sa	23 04 01	17 42 57	3♍01 47	9♍27 21	1 03.7	1♈34.3	20 23.7	19 17.2	21 45.7	26 49.0	3 04.9	18 53.6	12 06.3	12 41.3
9 Su	23 07 57	18 42 56	15 56 46	22 29 56	0 51.2	3 20.1	21 36.4	19 29.9	22 05.0	26 55.5	3 08.6	18 54.2	12 08.4	12 42.9
10 M	23 11 54	19 42 53	29 06 36	5♎46 33	0 40.2	5 03.0	22 49.1	19 42.0	22 24.5	27 01.9	3 12.5	18 54.9	12 10.6	12 44.4
11 Tu	23 15 50	20 42 49	12♎29 32	19 15 16	0 31.7	6 42.5	24 01.8	19 53.7	22 44.2	27 08.1	3 16.4	18 55.6	12 12.7	12 45.9
12 W	23 19 47	21 42 42	26 03 28	2♏53 56	0 26.0	8 18.1	25 14.3	20 04.8	23 03.9	27 14.2	3 20.4	18 56.4	12 14.8	12 47.5
13 Th	23 23 43	22 42 34	9♏46 24	16 40 42	0D 23.2	9 49.3	26 26.8	20 15.3	23 23.9	27 20.1	3 24.5	18 57.2	12 17.0	12 49.0
14 F	23 27 40	23 42 25	23 36 41	0♐34 15	0 22.4	11 15.6	27 39.2	20 25.3	23 43.9	27 25.8	3 28.7	18 58.1	12 19.2	12 50.5
15 Sa	23 31 36	24 42 13	7♐33 17	14 33 43	0R 22.8	12 36.4	28 51.6	20 34.7	24 04.1	27 31.4	3 33.0	18 59.0	12 21.3	12 51.9
16 Su	23 35 33	25 42 00	21 35 30	28 38 32	0 23.0	13 51.4	0♉03.9	20 43.5	24 24.4	27 36.9	3 37.3	19 00.0	12 23.5	12 53.4
17 M	23 39 29	26 41 46	5♑42 43	12♑47 55	0 21.9	15 00.0	1 16.1	20 51.7	24 44.8	27 42.1	3 41.8	19 01.0	12 25.7	12 54.8
18 Tu	23 43 26	27 41 29	19 53 55	27 00 26	0 18.6	16 01.8	2 28.2	20 59.2	25 05.3	27 47.2	3 46.4	19 02.1	12 27.9	12 56.3
19 W	23 47 23	28 41 11	4♒07 10	11♒13 41	0 12.8	16 56.6	3 40.3	21 06.1	25 26.0	27 52.2	3 51.0	19 03.2	12 30.2	12 57.7
20 Th	23 51 19	29 40 52	18 19 32	25 24 09	0 04.8	17 43.9	4 52.2	21 12.4	25 46.8	27 57.0	3 55.7	19 04.4	12 32.4	12 59.0
21 F	23 55 16	0♈40 30	2♓27 00	9♓27 29	29♏55.1	18 23.6	6 04.1	21 18.0	26 07.7	28 01.6	4 00.5	19 05.7	12 34.6	13 00.4
22 Sa	23 59 12	1 40 06	16 25 02	23 19 05	29 45.0	18 55.5	7 15.9	21 23.0	26 28.8	28 06.0	4 05.4	19 06.9	12 36.8	13 01.7
23 Su	0 03 09	2 39 40	0♈09 11	6♈54 52	29 35.6	19 19.5	8 27.7	21 27.2	26 49.9	28 10.3	4 10.3	19 08.3	12 39.1	13 03.1
24 M	0 07 05	3 39 13	13 35 51	20 11 53	29 27.8	19 35.4	9 39.3	21 30.8	27 11.2	28 14.4	4 15.4	19 09.7	12 41.3	13 04.4
25 Tu	0 11 02	4 38 43	26 42 51	3♉08 46	29 22.2	19R 43.5	10 50.9	21 33.7	27 32.5	28 18.3	4 20.5	19 11.1	12 43.6	13 05.6
26 W	0 14 58	5 38 11	9♉29 43	15 45 56	29 19.0	19 43.7	12 02.4	21 35.9	27 54.0	28 22.1	4 25.7	19 12.6	12 45.8	13 06.9
27 Th	0 18 55	6 37 37	21 57 41	28 05 23	29D 17.9	19 36.4	13 13.8	21 37.3	28 15.6	28 25.6	4 31.0	19 14.1	12 48.1	13 08.1
28 F	0 22 52	7 37 01	4♊09 28	10♊10 29	29 18.4	19 21.9	14 25.1	21R 38.1	28 37.3	28 29.0	4 36.3	19 15.7	12 50.4	13 09.4
29 Sa	0 26 48	8 36 22	16 08 58	22 05 32	29 19.6	19 00.5	15 36.3	21 38.1	28 59.0	28 32.3	4 41.7	19 17.3	12 52.6	13 10.6
30 Su	0 30 45	9 35 41	28 00 50	3♋55 31	29R 20.6	18 33.0	16 47.4	21 37.4	29 20.9	28 35.3	4 47.2	19 19.0	12 54.9	13 11.7
31 M	0 34 41	10 34 58	9♋50 14	15 45 38	29 20.6	17 59.8	17 58.4	21 35.9	29 42.9	28 38.2	4 52.8	19 20.7	12 57.2	13 12.9

April 2031 — LONGITUDE

Day	Sid.Time	☉	0 hr ☽	Noon ☽	True ☊	☿	♀	♂	⚳	♃	♄	♅	♆	♇
1 Tu	0 38 38	11♈34 13	21♋42 24	27♋41 09	29♏19.0	17♈21.9	19♉09.3	21♏33.7	0♊05.0	28♐40.9	4♊58.4	19♊22.5	12♈59.4	13♒14.0
2 W	0 42 34	12 33 25	3♌42 28	9♌46 55	29R 15.5	16R 39.9	20 20.1	21R 30.8	0 27.1	28 43.4	5 04.1	19 24.3	13 01.7	13 15.1
3 Th	0 46 31	13 32 35	15 55 01	22 07 11	29 10.1	15 54.8	21 30.7	21 27.1	0 49.4	28 45.7	5 09.9	19 26.1	13 04.0	13 16.2
4 F	0 50 27	14 31 42	28 23 49	4♍45 11	29 03.3	15 07.7	22 41.3	21 22.6	1 11.7	28 47.8	5 15.7	19 28.0	13 06.2	13 17.3
5 Sa	0 54 24	15 30 47	11♍11 29	17 42 49	28 55.8	14 19.3	23 51.8	21 17.4	1 34.2	28 49.8	5 21.6	19 30.0	13 08.5	13 18.3
6 Su	0 58 21	16 29 51	24 19 11	1♎00 28	28 48.3	13 30.8	25 02.2	21 11.4	1 56.7	28 51.6	5 27.6	19 32.0	13 10.8	13 19.3
7 M	1 02 17	17 28 52	7♎46 29	14 36 54	28 41.8	12 43.0	26 12.4	21 04.7	2 19.3	28 53.1	5 33.6	19 34.0	13 13.0	13 20.3
8 Tu	1 06 14	18 27 51	21 31 22	28 29 26	28 36.9	11 56.8	27 22.5	20 57.2	2 42.0	28 54.5	5 39.7	19 36.1	13 15.3	13 21.3
9 W	1 10 10	19 26 48	5♏30 36	12♏34 21	28 34.0	11 13.1	28 32.5	20 48.9	3 04.7	28 55.8	5 45.9	19 38.2	13 17.6	13 22.2
10 Th	1 14 07	20 25 43	19 40 09	26 47 28	28D 33.0	10 32.5	29 42.4	20 39.8	3 27.6	28 56.8	5 52.1	19 40.3	13 19.8	13 23.2
11 F	1 18 03	21 24 37	3♐55 48	11♐04 41	28 33.4	9 55.6	0♊52.2	20 30.1	3 50.5	28 57.6	5 58.4	19 42.5	13 22.1	13 24.1
12 Sa	1 22 00	22 23 28	18 13 41	25 22 26	28 34.8	9 22.9	2 01.9	20 19.5	4 13.5	28 58.3	6 04.7	19 44.8	13 24.3	13 24.9
13 Su	1 25 56	23 22 18	2♑30 35	9♑37 51	28 36.1	8 54.8	3 11.4	20 08.2	4 36.6	28 58.8	6 11.1	19 47.1	13 26.6	13 25.8
14 M	1 29 53	24 21 07	16 43 59	23 48 45	28R 36.8	8 31.6	4 20.8	19 56.2	4 59.8	28 59.1	6 17.5	19 49.4	13 28.8	13 26.6
15 Tu	1 33 50	25 19 53	0♒51 57	7♒53 24	28 36.1	8 13.5	5 30.1	19 43.4	5 23.0	28R 59.2	6 24.0	19 51.7	13 31.1	13 27.4
16 W	1 37 46	26 18 38	14 52 54	21 50 17	28 34.0	8 00.6	6 39.2	19 29.9	5 46.3	28 59.1	6 30.6	19 54.1	13 33.3	13 28.2
17 Th	1 41 43	27 17 21	28 45 20	5♓37 53	28 30.5	7D 52.9	7 48.3	19 15.7	6 09.7	28 58.8	6 37.2	19 56.6	13 35.5	13 28.9
18 F	1 45 39	28 16 03	12♓27 44	19 14 39	28 26.1	7 50.5	8 57.2	19 00.8	6 33.1	28 58.3	6 43.9	19 59.0	13 37.7	13 29.6
19 Sa	1 49 36	29 14 42	25 58 29	2♈39 00	28 21.4	7 53.2	10 05.9	18 45.2	6 56.7	28 57.6	6 50.6	20 01.5	13 40.0	13 30.3
20 Su	1 53 32	0♉13 20	9♈16 05	15 49 33	28 17.0	8 01.0	11 14.5	18 29.0	7 20.3	28 56.8	6 57.3	20 04.1	13 42.2	13 31.0
21 M	1 57 29	1 11 56	22 19 18	28 45 17	28 13.4	8 13.7	12 23.0	18 12.1	7 43.9	28 55.8	7 04.1	20 06.7	13 44.3	13 31.6
22 Tu	2 01 25	2 10 30	5♉07 29	11♉25 55	28 11.0	8 31.1	13 31.3	17 54.7	8 07.6	28 54.5	7 11.0	20 09.3	13 46.5	13 32.3
23 W	2 05 22	3 09 03	17 40 41	23 51 56	28D 09.9	8 53.2	14 39.5	17 36.7	8 31.4	28 53.1	7 17.9	20 11.9	13 48.7	13 32.8
24 Th	2 09 18	4 07 33	29 59 51	6♊04 43	28 10.1	9 19.7	15 47.6	17 18.1	8 55.3	28 51.5	7 24.8	20 14.6	13 50.9	13 33.4
25 F	2 13 15	5 06 01	12♊06 50	18 06 35	28 11.2	9 50.5	16 55.4	16 59.1	9 19.2	28 49.7	7 31.8	20 17.3	13 53.0	13 33.9
26 Sa	2 17 12	6 04 28	24 04 22	0♋00 39	28 12.8	10 25.4	18 03.2	16 39.6	9 43.2	28 47.8	7 38.8	20 20.1	13 55.2	13 34.5
27 Su	2 21 08	7 02 52	5♋55 56	11 50 44	28 14.4	11 04.1	19 10.7	16 19.6	10 07.2	28 45.6	7 45.9	20 22.9	13 57.3	13 34.9
28 M	2 25 05	8 01 14	17 45 38	23 41 12	28 15.7	11 46.6	20 18.1	15 59.2	10 31.3	28 43.3	7 53.0	20 25.7	13 59.4	13 35.4
29 Tu	2 29 01	8 59 34	29 38 01	5♌36 43	28R 16.4	12 32.7	21 25.3	15 38.5	10 55.4	28 40.8	8 00.2	20 28.5	14 01.5	13 35.8
30 W	2 32 58	9 57 52	11♌37 52	17 42 05	28 16.2	13 22.2	22 32.3	15 17.5	11 19.6	28 38.1	8 07.3	20 31.4	14 03.6	13 36.2

Astro Data	Planet Ingress	Last Aspect	☽ Ingress	Last Aspect	☽ Ingress	☽ Phases & Eclipses	Astro Data
Dy Hr Mn	Dy Hr Mn	Dy Hr Mn	Dy Hr Mn	Dy Hr Mn	Dy Hr Mn	Dy Hr Mn	1 March 2031
☿0N 7 17:29	☿ ♈ 7 15:03	2 12:02 ♃ ☍	♋ 2 19:56	31 23:45 ♂ △	♌ 1 16:37	1 4:03 ☽ 10♊22	Julian Day # 47907
☽0S 9 5:23	♀ ♉ 16 10:43	4 22:23 ☿ △	♌ 5 8:18	4 0:44 ♃ △	♍ 4 3:02	9 4:31 ○ 18♍24	SVP 4♓49'12"
☉0N 20 19:41	☉ ♈ 20 19:42	7 12:04 ♃ △	♍ 7 18:18	6 8:09 ♃ □	♎ 6 10:12	16 6:37 ☾ 25♐29	GC 27♐16.5 ⚵ 26♓14.5
♃∠♇ 21 3:05	☊ ♏R 21 0:12	9 20:07 ♃ □	♎ 10 1:36	8 12:43 ♃ ✱	♏ 8 14:35	23 3:50 ● 2♈19	Eris 25♈58.6 ⚶ 26♒44.8
☽0N 22 4:12		12 2:00 ♃ ✱	♏ 12 6:55	10 17:20 ♀ ☍	♐ 10 17:24	31 0:33 ☽ 10♋07	⚷ 12♉49.8 ⚴ 1♊47.8
☿R 26 0:43	⚳ ♊ 1 6:36	13 23:15 ☉ △	♐ 14 11:01	12 18:03 ♃ ☌	♑ 12 19:47		☽ Mean ☊ 2♐19.7
♂R 29 0:36	♀ ♊ 10 18:02	16 10:14 ♃ ☌	♑ 16 14:18	14 12:59 ☉ □	♒ 14 22:31	7 17:22 ○ 17♎42	
	☉ ♉ 20 6:32	18 13:14 ☉ ✱	♒ 18 17:03	17 0:24 ♃ ✱	♓ 17 2:10	14 12:59 ☾ 24♑24	1 April 2031
☽0S 5 13:51		20 16:21 ♃ ✱	♓ 20 19:49	19 5:22 ♃ □	♈ 19 7:13	21 16:58 ● 1♉24	Julian Day # 47938
♆✱♇ 12 22:07		22 20:26 ♃ □	♈ 22 23:44	21 12:20 ♃ △	♉ 21 14:20	29 19:21 ☽ 9♌17	SVP 4♓49'09"
♃R 15 12:05		25 2:55 ♃ △	♉ 25 6:07	23 0:10 ♂ ☍	♊ 24 0:00		GC 27♐16.5 ⚵ 7♈33.0
☽0N 18 10:53		26 23:19 ♂ ☍	♊ 27 15:46	26 9:33 ♃ ☍	♋ 26 11:59		Eris 26♈16.2 ⚶ 10♓40.8
☿D 18 11:17		30 1:07 ♃ ☍	♋ 30 4:02	27 20:50 ♂ △	♌ 29 0:44		⚷ 14♉20.1 ⚴ 11♊31.6
							☽ Mean ☊ 0♐41.2

LONGITUDE May 2031

Day	Sid.Time	☉	0 hr ☽	Noon☽	True☊	☿	♀	♂	⚳	♃	♄	♅	♆	♇
1 Th	2 36 54	10♉56 08	23♌49 56	0♍01 56	28♏15.3	14♈15.0	23♊39.2	14♏56.2	11♊43.9	28♐35.2	8♊14.5	20♊34.3	14♈05.7	13♒36.6
2 F	2 40 51	11 54 21	6♍18 35	12 40 21	28R13.6	15 11.0	24 45.8	14R34.6	12 08.2	28R32.1	8 21.8	20 37.3	14 07.8	13 36.9
3 Sa	2 44 47	12 52 33	19 07 33	25 40 30	28 11.7	16 10.0	25 52.3	14 12.9	12 32.5	28 28.9	8 29.1	20 40.2	14 09.8	13 37.3
4 Su	2 48 44	13 50 43	2♎19 21	9♎04 11	28 09.6	17 11.9	26 58.5	13 51.0	12 56.9	28 25.5	8 36.4	20 43.2	14 11.9	13 37.6
5 M	2 52 41	14 48 51	15 54 57	22 51 27	28 07.9	18 16.6	28 04.6	13 29.0	13 21.4	28 21.9	8 43.7	20 46.2	14 13.9	13 37.8
6 Tu	2 56 37	15 46 57	29 53 23	7♏00 19	28 06.7	19 24.0	29 10.4	13 06.9	13 45.9	28 18.2	8 51.1	20 49.3	14 15.9	13 38.1
7 W	3 00 34	16 45 02	14♏11 41	21 26 49	28D06.1	20 34.1	0♋16.0	12 44.8	14 10.4	28 14.3	8 58.5	20 52.3	14 17.9	13 38.3
8 Th	3 04 30	17 43 05	28 44 59	6♐05 22	28 06.1	21 46.7	1 21.5	12 22.8	14 35.0	28 10.2	9 06.0	20 55.4	14 19.9	13 38.5
9 F	3 08 27	18 41 06	13♐27 07	20 49 24	28 06.6	23 01.8	2 26.6	12 00.8	14 59.7	28 06.0	9 13.4	20 58.6	14 21.8	13 38.6
10 Sa	3 12 23	19 39 06	28 11 23	5♑32 17	28 07.3	24 19.3	3 31.6	11 38.9	15 24.3	28 01.6	9 20.9	21 01.7	14 23.8	13 38.8
11 Su	3 16 20	20 37 05	12♑51 23	20 08 03	28 08.0	25 39.2	4 36.3	11 17.1	15 49.1	27 57.1	9 28.5	21 04.9	14 25.7	13 38.9
12 M	3 20 16	21 35 02	27 21 44	4♒31 59	28 08.5	27 01.4	5 40.8	10 55.6	16 13.8	27 52.4	9 36.0	21 08.1	14 27.6	13 39.0
13 Tu	3 24 13	22 32 58	11♒38 29	18 40 57	28R08.7	28 25.9	6 45.1	10 34.2	16 38.7	27 47.5	9 43.6	21 11.3	14 29.5	13 39.0
14 W	3 28 10	23 30 53	25 39 14	2♓33 15	28 08.7	29 52.6	7 49.1	10 13.2	17 03.5	27 42.5	9 51.2	21 14.5	14 31.4	13R39.0
15 Th	3 32 06	24 28 46	9♓22 58	16 08 24	28 08.5	1♉21.6	8 52.9	9 52.5	17 28.4	27 37.4	9 58.8	21 17.8	14 33.2	13 39.0
16 F	3 36 03	25 26 38	22 49 40	29 26 49	28 08.2	2 52.7	9 56.4	9 32.1	17 53.4	27 32.1	10 06.4	21 21.0	14 35.0	13 39.0
17 Sa	3 39 59	26 24 29	6♈00 02	12♈29 25	28 07.9	4 26.1	10 59.6	9 12.2	18 18.4	27 26.6	10 14.0	21 24.3	14 36.9	13 38.9
18 Su	3 43 56	27 22 19	18 55 09	25 17 23	28D07.8	6 01.6	12 02.6	8 52.7	18 43.4	27 21.0	10 21.7	21 27.6	14 38.6	13 38.8
19 M	3 47 52	28 20 08	1♉36 17	7♉52 01	28 07.7	7 39.3	13 05.2	8 33.7	19 08.5	27 15.3	10 29.4	21 31.0	14 40.4	13 38.7
20 Tu	3 51 49	29 17 55	14 04 45	20 14 40	28R07.8	9 19.2	14 07.6	8 15.2	19 33.6	27 09.5	10 37.1	21 34.3	14 42.2	13 38.6
21 W	3 55 45	0♊15 41	26 21 58	2♊26 49	28 07.8	11 01.2	15 09.7	7 57.2	19 58.7	27 03.5	10 44.8	21 37.7	14 43.9	13 38.4
22 Th	3 59 42	1 13 26	8♊29 26	14 30 04	28 07.7	12 45.3	16 11.5	7 39.9	20 23.9	26 57.4	10 52.5	21 41.1	14 45.6	13 38.2
23 F	4 03 39	2 11 09	20 28 56	26 26 19	28 07.4	14 31.7	17 13.0	7 23.2	20 49.1	26 51.2	11 00.3	21 44.5	14 47.3	13 38.0
24 Sa	4 07 35	3 08 51	2♋22 30	8♋17 50	28 06.8	16 20.1	18 14.1	7 07.1	21 14.3	26 44.8	11 08.0	21 47.9	14 49.0	13 37.8
25 Su	4 11 32	4 06 31	14 12 39	20 07 21	28 06.1	18 10.8	19 14.9	6 51.7	21 39.6	26 38.4	11 15.8	21 51.3	14 50.6	13 37.5
26 M	4 15 28	5 04 10	26 02 20	1♌58 03	28 05.2	20 03.5	20 15.4	6 37.0	22 04.9	26 31.8	11 23.6	21 54.7	14 52.2	13 37.2
27 Tu	4 19 25	6 01 48	7♌54 59	13 53 36	28 04.4	21 58.4	21 15.4	6 23.1	22 30.3	26 25.2	11 31.3	21 58.2	14 53.8	13 36.9
28 W	4 23 21	6 59 24	19 54 28	25 58 04	28D03.9	23 55.3	22 15.2	6 09.8	22 55.6	26 18.4	11 39.1	22 01.7	14 55.4	13 36.6
29 Th	4 27 18	7 56 58	2♍04 58	8♍15 43	28 03.7	25 54.2	23 14.5	5 57.3	23 21.0	26 11.6	11 46.9	22 05.1	14 56.9	13 36.2
30 F	4 31 14	8 54 31	14 30 50	20 50 50	28 03.9	27 55.1	24 13.4	5 45.6	23 46.4	26 04.7	11 54.7	22 08.6	14 58.4	13 35.8
31 Sa	4 35 11	9 52 03	27 16 13	3♎47 22	28 04.6	29 57.9	25 11.9	5 34.7	24 11.9	25 57.7	12 02.5	22 12.1	14 59.9	13 35.4

LONGITUDE June 2031

Day	Sid.Time	☉	0 hr ☽	Noon☽	True☊	☿	♀	♂	⚳	♃	♄	♅	♆	♇
1 Su	4 39 08	10♊49 34	10♎24 41	17♎08 25	28♏05.6	2♊02.5	26♋10.0	5♏24.6	24♊37.4	25♐50.6	12♊10.3	22♊15.6	15♈01.4	13♒34.9
2 M	4 43 04	11 47 03	23 58 44	0♏55 40	28 06.6	4 08.7	27 07.6	5R15.3	25 02.9	25R43.4	12 18.1	22 19.1	15 02.8	13R34.4
3 Tu	4 47 01	12 44 31	7♏59 09	15 08 53	28R07.4	6 16.4	28 04.8	5 06.8	25 28.4	25 36.2	12 25.9	22 22.6	15 04.3	13 33.9
4 W	4 50 57	13 41 58	22 24 28	29 45 18	28 07.7	8 25.4	29 01.5	4 59.0	25 53.9	25 28.9	12 33.7	22 26.2	15 05.7	13 33.4
5 Th	4 54 54	14 39 24	7♐10 38	14♐39 34	28 07.2	10 35.6	29 57.7	4 52.2	26 19.5	25 21.5	12 41.5	22 29.7	15 07.0	13 32.9
6 F	4 58 50	15 36 48	22 11 04	29 44 01	28 05.9	12 46.6	0♌53.5	4 46.1	26 45.1	25 14.1	12 49.3	22 33.3	15 08.4	13 32.3
7 Sa	5 02 47	16 34 13	7♑17 16	14♑49 40	28 03.9	14 58.2	1 48.6	4 40.8	27 10.8	25 06.7	12 57.1	22 36.8	15 09.7	13 31.7
8 Su	5 06 44	17 31 36	22 20 04	29 47 29	28 01.6	17 10.3	2 43.3	4 36.4	27 36.4	24 59.2	13 04.9	22 40.4	15 11.0	13 31.1
9 M	5 10 40	18 28 59	7♒10 57	14♒29 45	27 59.2	19 22.4	3 37.4	4 32.7	28 02.1	24 51.7	13 12.7	22 43.9	15 12.2	13 30.5
10 Tu	5 14 37	19 26 21	21 43 15	28 51 02	27 57.3	21 34.3	4 31.0	4 29.9	28 27.8	24 44.1	13 20.4	22 47.5	15 13.5	13 29.8
11 W	5 18 33	20 23 42	5♓52 49	12♓48 29	27D56.3	23 45.8	5 23.9	4 27.9	28 53.5	24 36.5	13 28.2	22 51.0	15 14.7	13 29.1
12 Th	5 22 30	21 21 03	19 38 04	26 21 41	27 56.2	25 56.6	6 16.2	4D26.7	29 19.2	24 28.8	13 36.0	22 54.6	15 15.8	13 28.4
13 F	5 26 26	22 18 24	2♈59 34	9♈32 01	27 57.0	28 06.5	7 08.0	4 26.3	29 45.0	24 21.2	13 43.7	22 58.2	15 17.0	13 27.7
14 Sa	5 30 23	23 15 44	15 59 24	22 22 06	27 58.4	0♋15.1	7 59.0	4 26.7	0♋10.8	24 13.5	13 51.5	23 01.7	15 18.1	13 26.9
15 Su	5 34 19	24 13 04	28 40 31	4♉55 05	28 00.0	2 22.4	8 49.4	4 27.9	0 36.6	24 05.9	13 59.2	23 05.3	15 19.2	13 26.2
16 M	5 38 16	25 10 23	11♉06 11	17 14 13	28R01.2	4 28.1	9 39.1	4 29.9	1 02.4	23 58.2	14 06.9	23 08.8	15 20.2	13 25.4
17 Tu	5 42 13	26 07 42	23 19 34	29 22 36	28 01.7	6 32.1	10 28.1	4 32.7	1 28.2	23 50.6	14 14.6	23 12.4	15 21.3	13 24.6
18 W	5 46 09	27 05 01	5♊23 38	11♊22 59	28 00.9	8 34.2	11 16.3	4 36.2	1 54.1	23 42.9	14 22.3	23 16.0	15 22.3	13 23.7
19 Th	5 50 06	28 02 19	17 20 56	23 17 45	27 58.6	10 34.5	12 03.8	4 40.6	2 20.0	23 35.3	14 30.0	23 19.5	15 23.2	13 22.9
20 F	5 54 02	28 59 36	29 13 42	5♋09 02	27 54.9	12 32.6	12 50.5	4 45.7	2 45.8	23 27.6	14 37.6	23 23.1	15 24.2	13 22.0
21 Sa	5 57 59	29 56 53	11♋03 59	16 58 47	27 49.9	14 28.7	13 36.3	4 51.5	3 11.7	23 20.1	14 45.3	23 26.6	15 25.1	13 21.1
22 Su	6 01 55	0♋54 10	22 53 42	28 48 59	27 44.2	16 22.7	14 21.2	4 58.1	3 37.7	23 12.5	14 52.9	23 30.2	15 26.0	13 20.2
23 M	6 05 52	1 51 26	4♌44 56	10♌41 49	27 38.2	18 14.4	15 05.2	5 05.5	4 03.6	23 05.0	15 00.5	23 33.7	15 26.8	13 19.2
24 Tu	6 09 48	2 48 41	16 39 59	22 39 46	27 32.6	20 04.0	15 48.3	5 13.5	4 29.5	22 57.5	15 08.1	23 37.3	15 27.6	13 18.3
25 W	6 13 45	3 45 56	28 41 34	4♍45 46	27 28.1	21 51.3	16 30.4	5 22.3	4 55.5	22 50.1	15 15.6	23 40.8	15 28.4	13 17.3
26 Th	6 17 42	4 43 10	10♍52 50	17 03 12	27 25.0	23 36.4	17 11.5	5 31.8	5 21.5	22 42.7	15 23.2	23 44.3	15 29.1	13 16.3
27 F	6 21 38	5 40 23	23 17 21	29 35 47	27D23.5	25 19.2	17 51.5	5 42.0	5 47.4	22 35.4	15 30.7	23 47.8	15 29.9	13 15.3
28 Sa	6 25 35	6 37 36	5♎58 59	12♎27 25	27 23.4	26 59.8	18 30.4	5 52.8	6 13.4	22 28.1	15 38.1	23 51.3	15 30.6	13 14.3
29 Su	6 29 31	7 34 49	19 01 33	25 41 46	27 24.4	28 38.1	19 08.2	6 04.3	6 39.4	22 20.9	15 45.6	23 54.8	15 31.2	13 13.2
30 M	6 33 28	8 32 01	2♏28 25	9♏21 44	27 25.8	0♌14.1	19 44.7	6 16.5	7 05.4	22 13.8	15 53.0	23 58.3	15 31.8	13 12.2

Astro Data	Dy Hr Mn
♃∠♇	1 1:39
☽0S	2 22:50
♇ R	14 20:29
☽0N	15 16:07
☽0S	30 7:30
♄△♇	11 14:39
☽0N	11 22:04
♂ D	13 11:58
♃☍♅	20 21:48
☽0S	26 15:17
♄⚹♆	27 9:12

Planet Ingress	Dy Hr Mn
♀ ♋	7 6:08
☿ ♉	14 14:01
☉ ♊	21 5:29
☿ ♊	31 12:24
♀ ♌	5 12:58
⚳ ♋	14 1:59
☿ ♋	14 9:10
☉ ♋	21 13:18
☿ ♌	30 8:26

Last Aspect Dy Hr Mn		☽ Ingress Dy Hr Mn
1 9:13	♃ △	♍ 1 11:56
3 17:04	♃ □	♎ 3 19:50
5 21:40	♀ △	♏ 6 0:11
7 3:41	☉ ☍	♐ 8 2:03
9 23:48	♃ ☌	♑ 10 2:57
11 22:06	☿ □	♒ 12 4:24
14 6:47	☿ ⚹	♓ 14 7:33
16 8:33	♃ □	♈ 16 13:00
18 15:53	♃ △	♉ 18 20:56
19 23:09	♇ □	♊ 21 7:10
23 12:50	♃ ☍	♋ 23 19:12
25 10:04	♀ ☌	♌ 26 8:01
28 12:40	♃ △	♍ 28 19:56
31 3:40	☿ △	♎ 31 5:03

Last Aspect Dy Hr Mn		☽ Ingress Dy Hr Mn
2 4:58	♀ □	♏ 2 10:25
4 10:44	♀ △	♐ 4 12:24
6 4:55	♃ ☌	♑ 6 12:25
7 12:32	♆ □	♒ 8 12:20
10 5:07	♃ ⚹	♓ 10 13:57
12 11:06	☿ □	♈ 12 18:34
14 15:29	♃ △	♉ 15 2:32
16 4:32	♇ □	♊ 17 13:14
19 22:26	☉ ☌	♋ 20 1:34
21 8:50	♆ □	♌ 22 14:24
24 13:55	♅ ⚹	♍ 25 2:36
27 2:37	☿ ⚹	♎ 27 12:46
29 17:56	☿ □	♏ 29 19:39

☽ Phases & Eclipses Dy Hr Mn	
7 3:41	○ 16♏25
7 3:52	• A 0.881
13 19:08	☾ 22♒50
21 7:18	● 0♊04
21 7:16:05	• A 05'25"
29 11:21	☽ 7♍55
5 12:00	○ 14♐39
5 11:45	• A 0.129
12 2:22	☾ 20♓58
19 22:26	● 28♊27
28 0:20	☽ 6♎10

Astro Data

1 May 2031
Julian Day # 47968
SVP 4♓49'06"
GC 27♐16.6 ⚴ 18♈53.7
Eris 26♈35.8 ⚵ 24♓08.5
⚷ 16♉13.4 ⚶ 22♊50.0
☽ Mean ☊ 29♏05.8

1 June 2031
Julian Day # 47999
SVP 4♓49'02"
GC 27♐16.7 ⚴ 0♉43.3
Eris 26♈53.7 ⚵ 7♈41.0
⚷ 18♉14.9 ⚶ 5♋37.4
☽ Mean ☊ 27♏27.3

July 2031 — LONGITUDE

Day	Sid.Time	☉	0 hr ☽	Noon ☽	True ☊	☿	♀	♂	⚳	♃	♄	♅	♆	♇
1 Tu	6 37 24	9♋29 13	16♏21 50	23♏28 44	27♏26.7	1♌47.8	20♌20.0	6♏29.3	7♋31.4	22♐06.8	16♊00.4	24♊01.8	15♈32.4	13♒11.1
2 W	6 41 21	10 26 24	0♐42 13	8♐01 55	27R 26.3	3 19.3	20 54.1	6 42.8	7 57.4	21R 59.8	16 07.8	24 05.2	15 33.0	13R 10.0
3 Th	6 45 17	11 23 35	15 27 17	22 57 31	27 24.2	4 48.4	21 26.7	6 56.8	8 23.4	21 52.9	16 15.1	24 08.7	15 33.5	13 08.9
4 F	6 49 14	12 20 46	0♑31 40	8♑08 36	27 20.1	6 15.2	21 58.0	7 11.5	8 49.5	21 46.2	16 22.4	24 12.1	15 34.0	13 07.8
5 Sa	6 53 11	13 17 57	15 47 03	23 25 39	27 14.4	7 39.6	22 27.9	7 26.8	9 15.5	21 39.5	16 29.7	24 15.6	15 34.5	13 06.7
6 Su	6 57 07	14 15 08	1♒03 04	8♒37 56	27 07.6	9 01.6	22 56.3	7 42.6	9 41.6	21 32.9	16 36.9	24 19.0	15 34.9	13 05.5
7 M	7 01 04	15 12 19	16 09 01	23 35 16	27 00.8	10 21.2	23 23.1	7 59.0	10 07.6	21 26.4	16 44.1	24 22.4	15 35.3	13 04.3
8 Tu	7 05 00	16 09 30	0♓55 44	8♓09 46	26 54.8	11 38.3	23 48.3	8 16.0	10 33.7	21 20.0	16 51.3	24 25.7	15 35.7	13 03.2
9 W	7 08 57	17 06 41	15 16 51	22 16 46	26 50.4	12 52.9	24 11.8	8 33.5	10 59.7	21 13.8	16 58.4	24 29.1	15 36.0	13 02.0
10 Th	7 12 53	18 03 53	29 09 25	5♈54 55	26D 47.9	14 04.9	24 33.7	8 51.5	11 25.8	21 07.6	17 05.5	24 32.4	15 36.3	13 00.8
11 F	7 16 50	19 01 05	12♈33 31	19 05 35	26 47.1	15 14.3	24 53.7	9 10.1	11 51.8	21 01.6	17 12.6	24 35.8	15 36.6	12 59.5
12 Sa	7 20 46	19 58 18	25 31 36	1♉52 03	26 47.6	16 20.9	25 12.0	9 29.2	12 17.9	20 55.7	17 19.6	24 39.1	15 36.8	12 58.3
13 Su	7 24 43	20 55 32	8♉07 30	14 18 32	26 48.6	17 24.7	25 28.4	9 48.8	12 44.0	20 49.9	17 26.6	24 42.4	15 37.0	12 57.1
14 M	7 28 40	21 52 45	20 25 45	26 29 42	26R 49.2	18 25.7	25 42.8	10 08.9	13 10.1	20 44.3	17 33.5	24 45.7	15 37.2	12 55.8
15 Tu	7 32 36	22 50 00	2♊30 55	8♊29 57	26 48.4	19 23.6	25 55.3	10 29.5	13 36.1	20 38.8	17 40.4	24 48.9	15 37.4	12 54.6
16 W	7 36 33	23 47 15	14 27 17	20 23 20	26 45.7	20 18.5	26 05.6	10 50.6	14 02.2	20 33.4	17 47.3	24 52.1	15 37.5	12 53.3
17 Th	7 40 29	24 44 30	26 18 31	2♋13 13	26 40.5	21 10.1	26 13.9	11 12.2	14 28.3	20 28.2	17 54.1	24 55.4	15 37.5	12 52.0
18 F	7 44 26	25 41 46	8♋07 44	14 02 21	26 32.8	21 58.4	26 20.0	11 34.3	14 54.4	20 23.1	18 00.8	24 58.6	15R 37.6	12 50.7
19 Sa	7 48 22	26 39 02	19 57 21	25 52 55	26 23.1	22 43.2	26 23.9	11 56.8	15 20.5	20 18.1	18 07.5	25 01.7	15 37.6	12 49.4
20 Su	7 52 19	27 36 19	1♌49 18	7♌46 40	26 12.0	23 24.4	26R 25.6	12 19.8	15 46.5	20 13.4	18 14.2	25 04.9	15 37.6	12 48.1
21 M	7 56 15	28 33 36	13 45 12	19 45 05	26 00.4	24 01.7	26 24.9	12 43.2	16 12.6	20 08.7	18 20.8	25 08.0	15 37.5	12 46.8
22 Tu	8 00 12	29 30 53	25 46 30	1♍49 41	25 49.4	24 35.2	26 21.9	13 07.1	16 38.7	20 04.2	18 27.4	25 11.1	15 37.4	12 45.5
23 W	8 04 09	0♌28 11	7♍54 49	14 02 11	25 39.9	25 04.5	26 16.5	13 31.3	17 04.7	19 59.9	18 33.9	25 14.2	15 37.3	12 44.2
24 Th	8 08 05	1 25 29	20 12 03	26 24 43	25 32.7	25 29.6	26 08.8	13 56.1	17 30.8	19 55.8	18 40.3	25 17.2	15 37.1	12 42.8
25 F	8 12 02	2 22 48	2♎40 34	8♎59 56	25 27.9	25 50.2	25 58.6	14 21.2	17 56.9	19 51.8	18 46.7	25 20.2	15 36.9	12 41.5
26 Sa	8 15 58	3 20 07	15 23 13	21 50 51	25D 25.6	26 06.3	25 46.1	14 46.7	18 22.9	19 48.0	18 53.1	25 23.2	15 36.7	12 40.1
27 Su	8 19 55	4 17 26	28 23 14	5♏00 47	25 25.1	26 17.6	25 31.2	15 12.6	18 48.9	19 44.3	18 59.3	25 26.2	15 36.5	12 38.8
28 M	8 23 51	5 14 46	11♏43 52	18 32 49	25R 25.3	26R 24.0	25 13.9	15 38.9	19 15.0	19 40.8	19 05.6	25 29.1	15 36.2	12 37.4
29 Tu	8 27 48	6 12 06	25 27 54	2♐29 14	25 25.3	26 25.5	24 54.4	16 05.6	19 41.0	19 37.5	19 11.8	25 32.0	15 35.9	12 36.1
30 W	8 31 44	7 09 27	9♐36 52	16 50 38	25 23.8	26 21.8	24 32.5	16 32.7	20 07.0	19 34.4	19 17.9	25 34.9	15 35.5	12 34.7
31 Th	8 35 41	8 06 49	24 10 14	1♑35 07	25 20.0	26 13.0	24 08.5	17 00.1	20 33.0	19 31.4	19 23.9	25 37.8	15 35.1	12 33.3

August 2031 — LONGITUDE

Day	Sid.Time	☉	0 hr ☽	Noon ☽	True ☊	☿	♀	♂	⚳	♃	♄	♅	♆	♇
1 F	8 39 38	9♌04 10	9♑04 34	16♑37 39	25♏13.7	25♌59.1	23♌42.5	17♏27.8	20♋59.0	19♐28.6	19♊29.9	25♊40.6	15♈34.7	12♒32.0
2 Sa	8 43 34	10 01 33	24 13 14	1♒50 05	25R 05.0	25R 40.1	23R 14.5	17 55.9	21 24.9	19R 26.0	19 35.8	25 43.4	15R 34.3	12R 30.6
3 Su	8 47 31	10 58 56	9♒26 51	17 02 08	24 54.8	25 16.1	22 44.7	18 24.4	21 50.9	19 23.6	19 41.7	25 46.2	15 33.8	12 29.3
4 M	8 51 27	11 56 21	24 34 38	2♓03 03	24 44.4	24 47.4	22 13.2	18 53.2	22 16.9	19 21.3	19 47.5	25 48.9	15 33.3	12 27.9
5 Tu	8 55 24	12 53 46	9♓26 19	16 43 32	24 34.9	24 14.2	21 40.3	19 22.3	22 42.8	19 19.3	19 53.3	25 51.6	15 32.8	12 26.5
6 W	8 59 20	13 51 12	23 54 00	0♈57 15	24 27.2	23 37.0	21 06.0	19 51.7	23 08.7	19 17.4	19 58.9	25 54.2	15 32.2	12 25.1
7 Th	9 03 17	14 48 40	7♈53 03	14 41 22	24 22.1	22 56.1	20 30.7	20 21.4	23 34.6	19 15.7	20 04.5	25 56.9	15 31.6	12 23.8
8 F	9 07 13	15 46 09	21 22 21	27 56 17	24 19.3	22 12.2	19 54.6	20 51.5	24 00.5	19 14.1	20 10.1	25 59.5	15 31.0	12 22.4
9 Sa	9 11 10	16 43 39	4♉23 36	10♉44 49	24D 18.3	21 26.0	19 17.8	21 21.8	24 26.4	19 12.8	20 15.5	26 02.0	15 30.3	12 21.0
10 Su	9 15 07	17 41 10	17 00 32	23 11 22	24R 18.3	20 38.3	18 40.6	21 52.5	24 52.3	19 11.6	20 20.9	26 04.6	15 29.7	12 19.7
11 M	9 19 03	18 38 43	29 17 58	5♊21 00	24 18.0	19 49.8	18 03.3	22 23.4	25 18.1	19 10.7	20 26.3	26 07.0	15 29.0	12 18.3
12 Tu	9 23 00	19 36 18	11♊21 08	17 18 59	24 16.4	19 01.5	17 26.0	22 54.7	25 44.0	19 09.9	20 31.5	26 09.5	15 28.2	12 17.0
13 W	9 26 56	20 33 54	23 15 10	29 10 14	24 12.6	18 14.3	16 49.0	23 26.2	26 09.8	19 09.3	20 36.7	26 11.9	15 27.4	12 15.6
14 Th	9 30 53	21 31 31	5♋04 42	10♋59 05	24 06.2	17 29.1	16 12.6	23 58.0	26 35.6	19 08.9	20 41.8	26 14.3	15 26.6	12 14.2
15 F	9 34 49	22 29 09	16 53 45	22 49 08	23 56.9	16 46.9	15 37.0	24 30.1	27 01.4	19D 08.7	20 46.8	26 16.6	15 25.8	12 12.9
16 Sa	9 38 46	23 26 49	28 45 31	4♌43 11	23 45.2	16 08.5	15 02.4	25 02.5	27 27.2	19 08.6	20 51.8	26 18.9	15 25.0	12 11.6
17 Su	9 42 42	24 24 30	10♌42 23	16 43 16	23 31.9	15 34.7	14 28.9	25 35.1	27 52.9	19 08.8	20 56.7	26 21.2	15 24.1	12 10.2
18 M	9 46 39	25 22 13	22 46 01	28 50 45	23 18.0	15 06.3	13 56.9	26 08.1	28 18.6	19 09.1	21 01.5	26 23.4	15 23.2	12 08.9
19 Tu	9 50 36	26 19 57	4♍57 34	11♍06 33	23 04.7	14 44.0	13 26.4	26 41.2	28 44.3	19 09.6	21 06.2	26 25.6	15 22.2	12 07.6
20 W	9 54 32	27 17 42	17 17 48	23 31 25	22 53.1	14 28.2	12 57.6	27 14.7	29 10.0	19 10.3	21 10.8	26 27.8	15 21.3	12 06.3
21 Th	9 58 29	28 15 28	29 47 30	6♎06 11	22 44.0	14D 19.4	12 30.7	27 48.4	29 35.6	19 11.2	21 15.4	26 29.9	15 20.3	12 04.9
22 F	10 02 25	29 13 15	12♎27 37	18 52 01	22 37.8	14 18.0	12 05.8	28 22.3	0♌01.2	19 12.3	21 19.8	26 31.9	15 19.2	12 03.6
23 Sa	10 06 22	0♍11 04	25 19 34	1♏50 32	22 34.5	14 24.2	11 42.9	28 56.5	0 26.8	19 13.6	21 24.2	26 33.9	15 18.2	12 02.3
24 Su	10 10 18	1 08 54	8♏25 11	15 03 47	22D 33.2	14 38.2	11 22.3	29 30.9	0 52.4	19 15.0	21 28.5	26 35.9	15 17.1	12 01.1
25 M	10 14 15	2 06 45	21 46 38	28 34 00	22R 33.2	15 00.1	11 03.9	0♐05.6	1 17.9	19 16.7	21 32.7	26 37.8	15 16.0	11 59.8
26 Tu	10 18 11	3 04 37	5♐26 06	12♐23 05	22 33.0	15 29.7	10 47.8	0 40.5	1 43.4	19 18.5	21 36.9	26 39.7	15 14.9	11 58.5
27 W	10 22 08	4 02 31	19 25 04	26 32 01	22 31.5	16 07.1	10 34.0	1 15.6	2 08.9	19 20.5	21 40.9	26 41.6	15 13.8	11 57.3
28 Th	10 26 05	5 00 26	3♑43 46	11♑00 01	22 27.8	16 52.2	10 22.7	1 50.9	2 34.3	19 22.7	21 44.9	26 43.4	15 12.6	11 56.0
29 F	10 30 01	5 58 22	18 20 17	25 43 56	22 21.5	17 44.6	10 13.7	2 26.4	2 59.7	19 25.1	21 48.7	26 45.1	15 11.4	11 54.8
30 Sa	10 33 58	6 56 19	3♒10 08	10♒37 57	22 12.9	18 44.1	10 07.2	3 02.2	3 25.0	19 27.6	21 52.5	26 46.8	15 10.2	11 53.6
31 Su	10 37 54	7 54 18	18 06 17	25 34 01	22 02.6	19 50.4	10 03.0	3 38.2	3 50.4	19 30.4	21 56.2	26 48.5	15 09.0	11 52.4

Astro Data (Dy Hr Mn)

Astro Data	Dy Hr Mn
☽0N	9 6:14
♆R	19 6:12
♀R	20 17:09
☽0S	23 22:06
☿R	29 6:48
♃☍♄	1 8:28
☽0N	5 16:26
♃D	16 5:00
☽0S	20 4:27
☿D	22 4:28

Planet Ingress (Dy Hr Mn)

Planet Ingress	Dy Hr Mn
☉ ♌	23 0:12
⚳ ♌	22 10:51
☉ ♍	23 7:24
♂ ♐	25 8:10

Last Aspect Dy Hr Mn		☽ Ingress Dy Hr Mn	Last Aspect Dy Hr Mn		☽ Ingress Dy Hr Mn
1 6:30	♀ □	♐ 1 22:50	1 13:22	♂ ⚹	♒ 2 9:07
3 13:54	♅ ☍	♑ 3 23:10	4 1:57	♅ △	♓ 4 8:42
4 23:40	♆ □	♒ 5 22:21	6 3:22	♅ □	♈ 6 10:22
7 13:17	♅ △	♓ 7 22:28	8 8:25	♅ ⚹	♉ 8 15:49
9 15:51	♅ □	♈ 10 1:29	10 9:19	♂ ☍	♊ 11 1:23
11 23:05	♀ △	♉ 12 8:27	13 5:57	♅ ☌	♋ 13 13:41
14 10:25	♀ □	♊ 14 18:59	15 15:34	♂ △	♌ 16 2:30
16 23:43	♀ ⚹	♋ 17 7:30	18 7:09	♅ ⚹	♍ 18 14:16
19 13:41	☉ ☌	♌ 19 20:19	20 19:28	♂ ⚹	♎ 21 0:24
22 1:14	♀ ☌	♍ 22 8:23	23 2:16	♀ ⚹	♏ 23 8:37
24 9:49	♅ □	♎ 24 18:53	24 11:13	☿ □	♐ 25 14:31
26 19:58	☿ ⚹	♏ 27 2:56	27 12:16	♅ ☍	♑ 27 17:48
29 1:39	☿ □	♐ 29 7:46	28 18:53	♆ □	♒ 29 18:54
31 3:26	☿ △	♑ 31 9:27	31 14:00	♅ △	♓ 31 19:09

☽ Phases & Eclipses (Dy Hr Mn)

Dy Hr Mn	
4 19:03	○ 12♑38
11 11:51	☾ 19♈01
19 13:41	● 26♋43
27 10:36	☽ 4♏14
3 1:47	○ 10♒35
10 0:25	☾ 17♉13
18 4:33	● 25♌04
25 18:41	☽ 2♐23

Astro Data

1 July 2031
Julian Day # 48029
SVP 4♓48'57"
GC 27♐16.8 ⚴ 11♉57.4
Eris 27♈04.7 ⚵ 19♈56.2
⚷ 19♉56.2 ⚶ 18♋36.4
☽ Mean ☊ 25♏52.0

1 August 2031
Julian Day # 48060
SVP 4♓48'52"
GC 27♐16.8 ⚴ 22♉50.8
Eris 27♈07.0R ⚵ 0♉46.2
⚷ 21♉04.6 ⚶ 2♌20.5
☽ Mean ☊ 24♏13.5

LONGITUDE — September 2031

Day	Sid.Time	☉	0 hr ☽	Noon ☽	True ☊	☿	♀	♂	⚸	♃	♄	♅	♆	♇
1 M	10 41 51	8♍52 18	2♓59 59	10♓23 02	21♏52.0	21♌03.1	10♌01.3	4♐14.3	4♌15.7	19♐33.3	21♊59.8	26♊50.1	15♈07.7	11♒51.2
2 Tu	10 45 47	9 50 20	17 42 07	24 56 18	21R42.2	22 21.9	10D01.8	4 50.7	4 40.9	19 36.3	22 03.3	26 51.7	15R06.5	11R50.0
3 W	10 49 44	10 48 23	2♈04 50	9♈07 07	21 34.2	23 46.1	10 04.8	5 27.3	5 06.2	19 39.6	22 06.7	26 53.2	15 05.2	11 48.8
4 Th	10 53 40	11 46 29	16 02 46	22 51 34	21 28.7	25 15.5	10 10.0	6 04.0	5 31.3	19 43.0	22 10.0	26 54.7	15 03.8	11 47.7
5 F	10 57 37	12 44 36	29 33 30	6♉08 42	21 25.6	26 49.4	10 17.4	6 41.0	5 56.5	19 46.6	22 13.2	26 56.1	15 02.5	11 46.6
6 Sa	11 01 33	13 42 46	12♉37 27	19 00 08	21D24.6	28 27.3	10 27.0	7 18.1	6 21.6	19 50.4	22 16.3	26 57.5	15 01.1	11 45.4
7 Su	11 05 30	14 40 57	25 17 16	1♊29 23	21 24.8	0♍08.7	10 38.8	7 55.4	6 46.7	19 54.4	22 19.3	26 58.9	14 59.8	11 44.3
8 M	11 09 27	15 39 10	7♊37 06	13 41 05	21R25.3	1 53.2	10 52.7	8 32.9	7 11.7	19 58.5	22 22.3	27 00.1	14 58.4	11 43.2
9 Tu	11 13 23	16 37 26	19 41 58	25 40 26	21 24.9	3 40.2	11 08.5	9 10.6	7 36.7	20 02.8	22 25.1	27 01.4	14 57.0	11 42.2
10 W	11 17 20	17 35 43	1♋37 08	7♋32 42	21 22.8	5 29.2	11 26.4	9 48.5	8 01.6	20 07.3	22 27.8	27 02.6	14 55.5	11 41.1
11 Th	11 21 16	18 34 03	13 27 46	19 22 52	21 18.4	7 19.9	11 46.1	10 26.6	8 26.5	20 11.9	22 30.4	27 03.7	14 54.1	11 40.1
12 F	11 25 13	19 32 24	25 18 34	1♌15 19	21 11.6	9 11.8	12 07.6	11 04.8	8 51.4	20 16.7	22 33.0	27 04.8	14 52.6	11 39.0
13 Sa	11 29 09	20 30 48	7♌13 36	13 13 45	21 02.7	11 04.5	12 31.0	11 43.2	9 16.2	20 21.7	22 35.4	27 05.9	14 51.2	11 38.0
14 Su	11 33 06	21 29 13	19 16 06	25 20 56	20 52.3	12 57.8	12 56.0	12 21.8	9 40.9	20 26.8	22 37.7	27 06.9	14 49.7	11 37.0
15 M	11 37 02	22 27 41	1♍28 25	7♍38 44	20 41.2	14 51.4	13 22.7	13 00.6	10 05.6	20 32.1	22 39.9	27 07.8	14 48.2	11 36.1
16 Tu	11 40 59	23 26 10	13 51 59	20 08 12	20 30.7	16 45.1	13 51.0	13 39.5	10 30.3	20 37.5	22 42.0	27 08.7	14 46.6	11 35.1
17 W	11 44 56	24 24 41	26 27 25	2♎49 37	20 21.5	18 38.5	14 20.8	14 18.6	10 54.8	20 43.1	22 44.0	27 09.5	14 45.1	11 34.2
18 Th	11 48 52	25 23 15	9♎14 46	15 42 50	20 14.5	20 31.7	14 52.1	14 57.8	11 19.4	20 48.9	22 45.9	27 10.3	14 43.6	11 33.3
19 F	11 52 49	26 21 50	22 13 47	28 47 34	20 10.0	22 24.3	15 24.8	15 37.2	11 43.9	20 54.8	22 47.7	27 11.0	14 42.0	11 32.4
20 Sa	11 56 45	27 20 26	5♏24 11	12♏03 37	20D07.9	24 16.4	15 58.9	16 16.8	12 08.3	21 00.9	22 49.4	27 11.7	14 40.4	11 31.5
21 Su	12 00 42	28 19 05	18 45 54	25 31 03	20 07.7	26 07.7	16 34.3	16 56.5	12 32.6	21 07.1	22 51.0	27 12.4	14 38.8	11 30.6
22 M	12 04 38	29 17 45	2♐19 09	9♐10 13	20 08.6	27 58.4	17 11.0	17 36.4	12 56.9	21 13.5	22 52.5	27 12.9	14 37.2	11 29.8
23 Tu	12 08 35	0♎16 27	16 04 19	23 01 28	20R09.5	29 48.2	17 48.9	18 16.4	13 21.2	21 20.1	22 53.8	27 13.5	14 35.6	11 29.0
24 W	12 12 31	1 15 11	0♑01 41	7♑04 53	20 09.6	1♎37.1	18 28.0	18 56.6	13 45.3	21 26.8	22 55.1	27 14.0	14 34.0	11 28.2
25 Th	12 16 28	2 13 56	14 10 56	21 19 39	20 08.0	3 25.2	19 08.2	19 36.9	14 09.4	21 33.6	22 56.2	27 14.4	14 32.4	11 27.4
26 F	12 20 25	3 12 43	28 30 42	5♒43 40	20 04.4	5 12.3	19 49.6	20 17.3	14 33.5	21 40.6	22 57.3	27 14.7	14 30.8	11 26.7
27 Sa	12 24 21	4 11 32	12♒58 04	20 13 16	19 59.0	6 58.5	20 32.0	20 57.9	14 57.4	21 47.7	22 58.2	27 15.1	14 29.2	11 26.0
28 Su	12 28 18	5 10 22	27 28 36	4♓43 18	19 52.4	8 43.9	21 15.4	21 38.6	15 21.3	21 55.0	22 59.0	27 15.3	14 27.5	11 25.3
29 M	12 32 14	6 09 14	11♓56 35	19 07 40	19 45.3	10 28.3	21 59.9	22 19.5	15 45.1	22 02.4	22 59.7	27 15.5	14 25.9	11 24.6
30 Tu	12 36 11	7 08 09	26 15 47	3♈20 13	19 38.8	12 11.8	22 45.3	23 00.4	16 08.9	22 09.9	23 00.3	27 15.7	14 24.2	11 24.0

LONGITUDE — October 2031

Day	Sid.Time	☉	0 hr ☽	Noon ☽	True ☊	☿	♀	♂	⚸	♃	♄	♅	♆	♇
1 W	12 40 07	8♎07 05	10♈20 20	17♈15 38	19♏33.5	13♎54.4	23♌31.6	23♐41.5	16♌32.6	22♐17.6	23♊00.8	27♊15.8	14♈22.6	11♒23.3
2 Th	12 44 04	9 06 03	24 05 42	0♉50 16	19R30.1	15 36.1	24 18.8	24 22.7	16 56.2	22 25.4	23 01.2	27R15.9	14R20.9	11R22.7
3 F	12 48 00	10 05 03	7♉29 12	14 02 28	19D28.5	17 16.9	25 06.9	25 04.1	17 19.7	22 33.4	23 01.5	27 15.9	14 19.2	11 22.1
4 Sa	12 51 57	11 04 06	20 30 11	26 52 34	19 28.6	18 56.9	25 55.8	25 45.6	17 43.1	22 41.5	23R01.6	27 15.8	14 17.6	11 21.6
5 Su	12 55 54	12 03 11	3♊09 57	9♊22 43	19 29.8	20 36.1	26 45.6	26 27.1	18 06.5	22 49.7	23 01.7	27 15.7	14 15.9	11 21.1
6 M	12 59 50	13 02 18	15 31 19	21 36 19	19 31.5	22 14.4	27 36.1	27 08.8	18 29.8	22 58.1	23 01.6	27 15.6	14 14.2	11 20.6
7 Tu	13 03 47	14 01 27	27 38 15	3♋37 43	19R33.0	23 51.9	28 27.3	27 50.7	18 53.0	23 06.5	23 01.4	27 15.4	14 12.6	11 20.1
8 W	13 07 43	15 00 39	9♋35 21	15 31 45	19 33.5	25 28.7	29 19.3	28 32.6	19 16.1	23 15.1	23 01.1	27 15.1	14 10.9	11 19.6
9 Th	13 11 40	15 59 53	21 27 34	27 23 24	19 32.8	27 04.7	0♍12.0	29 14.7	19 39.1	23 23.9	23 00.8	27 14.8	14 09.2	11 19.2
10 F	13 15 36	16 59 10	3♌19 52	9♌17 31	19 30.5	28 39.9	1 05.3	29 56.8	20 02.1	23 32.7	23 00.2	27 14.5	14 07.5	11 18.8
11 Sa	13 19 33	17 58 28	15 16 55	21 18 33	19 27.0	0♏14.4	1 59.4	0♑39.1	20 24.9	23 41.7	22 59.6	27 14.1	14 05.9	11 18.4
12 Su	13 23 29	18 57 49	27 22 54	3♍30 19	19 22.4	1 48.2	2 54.0	1 21.5	20 47.7	23 50.8	22 58.9	27 13.6	14 04.2	11 18.1
13 M	13 27 26	19 57 12	9♍41 11	15 55 45	19 17.3	3 21.2	3 49.2	2 04.0	21 10.3	24 00.0	22 58.1	27 13.1	14 02.5	11 17.7
14 Tu	13 31 22	20 56 38	22 14 15	28 36 47	19 12.4	4 53.6	4 45.0	2 46.6	21 32.9	24 09.3	22 57.1	27 12.5	14 00.9	11 17.4
15 W	13 35 19	21 56 05	5♎03 27	11♎34 13	19 08.1	6 25.3	5 41.4	3 29.3	21 55.3	24 18.8	22 56.1	27 11.9	13 59.2	11 17.2
16 Th	13 39 16	22 55 35	18 09 01	24 47 44	19 05.0	7 56.3	6 38.3	4 12.1	22 17.7	24 28.4	22 54.9	27 11.2	13 57.6	11 16.9
17 F	13 43 12	23 55 06	1♏30 11	8♏16 07	19D03.3	9 26.6	7 35.8	4 55.1	22 39.9	24 38.1	22 53.6	27 10.5	13 55.9	11 16.7
18 Sa	13 47 09	24 54 40	15 05 18	21 57 25	19 03.0	10 56.2	8 33.7	5 38.1	23 02.1	24 47.8	22 52.2	27 09.7	13 54.3	11 16.5
19 Su	13 51 05	25 54 15	28 52 12	5♐49 21	19 03.7	12 25.2	9 32.2	6 21.2	23 24.1	24 57.8	22 50.7	27 08.9	13 52.6	11 16.3
20 M	13 55 02	26 53 53	12♐48 32	19 49 30	19 05.0	13 53.4	10 31.1	7 04.4	23 46.0	25 07.8	22 49.1	27 08.0	13 51.0	11 16.2
21 Tu	13 58 58	27 53 32	26 51 57	3♑55 37	19 06.5	15 21.0	11 30.5	7 47.8	24 07.8	25 17.9	22 47.4	27 07.1	13 49.4	11 16.1
22 W	14 02 55	28 53 13	11♑00 14	18 05 33	19R07.5	16 47.8	12 30.3	8 31.2	24 29.5	25 28.1	22 45.6	27 06.1	13 47.8	11 16.0
23 Th	14 06 51	29 52 56	25 11 19	2♒17 16	19 07.8	18 14.0	13 30.5	9 14.7	24 51.0	25 38.4	22 43.7	27 05.1	13 46.2	11 16.0
24 F	14 10 48	0♏52 40	9♒23 08	16 28 39	19 07.2	19 39.3	14 31.2	9 58.2	25 12.4	25 48.9	22 41.7	27 04.1	13 44.6	11D15.9
25 Sa	14 14 45	1 52 26	23 33 30	0♓37 22	19 05.7	21 03.9	15 32.3	10 41.9	25 33.7	25 59.4	22 39.6	27 02.9	13 43.0	11 15.9
26 Su	14 18 41	2 52 13	7♓39 54	14 40 47	19 03.8	22 27.7	16 33.8	11 25.6	25 54.9	26 10.0	22 37.3	27 01.8	13 41.5	11 16.0
27 M	14 22 38	3 52 02	21 39 38	28 36 05	19 01.6	23 50.6	17 35.6	12 09.5	26 15.9	26 20.7	22 35.0	27 00.6	13 39.9	11 16.0
28 Tu	14 26 34	4 51 53	5♈29 46	12♈20 23	18 59.7	25 12.6	18 37.9	12 53.4	26 36.8	26 31.5	22 32.6	26 59.3	13 38.4	11 16.1
29 W	14 30 31	5 51 46	19 07 36	25 51 08	18 58.2	26 33.7	19 40.5	13 37.4	26 57.6	26 42.5	22 30.1	26 58.0	13 36.9	11 16.2
30 Th	14 34 27	6 51 41	2♉30 46	9♉06 20	18D57.4	27 53.7	20 43.4	14 21.4	27 18.3	26 53.5	22 27.5	26 56.7	13 35.4	11 16.3
31 F	14 38 24	7 51 37	15 37 43	22 04 52	18 57.2	29 12.6	21 46.7	15 05.5	27 38.8	27 04.5	22 24.7	26 55.3	13 33.9	11 16.5

Astro Data

	Dy Hr Mn
♀ D	1 17:58
♅□♇	1 21:17
☽ 0N	2 3:14
☽ 0S	16 11:09
☉0S	23 5:17
☿0S	25 8:01
☽ 0N	29 12:51
♅ R	3 2:44
♄ R	5 10:51
♃☍♄	6 21:55
☽ 0S	13 18:52
♇ D	24 23:14
☽ 0N	26 20:11
♃∠♇	27 1:23
♃☍♅	30 18:12

Planet Ingress

		Dy Hr Mn
☿	♍	7 9:58
☉	♎	23 5:16
☿	♎	23 14:36
♀	♍	9 6:34
♂	♑	10 13:48
☿	♏	11 8:20
☉	♏	23 14:51

Last Aspect / ☽ Ingress

Last Aspect Dy Hr Mn			☽ Ingress	Dy Hr Mn
2 15:13	♅	□	♈	2 20:29
4 19:15	♅	⚹	♉	5 0:48
7 8:58	☿	□	♊	7 9:06
9 14:43	♅	☌	♋	9 20:44
11 10:12	☉	⚹	♌	12 9:28
14 15:28	♅	⚹	♍	14 21:07
17 1:19	♅	□	♎	17 6:41
19 9:04	♅	△	♏	19 14:12
21 17:20	☉	⚹	♐	21 19:55
23 19:13	♅	☍	♑	23 23:57
25 0:37	♆	□	♒	26 2:29
27 23:38	♅	△	♓	28 4:11
30 1:41	♅	□	♈	30 6:20

Last Aspect / ☽ Ingress

Last Aspect Dy Hr Mn			☽ Ingress	Dy Hr Mn
2 5:37	♅	⚹	♉	2 10:30
4 10:05	♀	□	♊	4 17:56
7 0:50	♀	⚹	♋	7 4:43
9 11:16	☿	□	♌	9 17:17
11 23:42	♅	⚹	♍	12 5:09
14 9:22	♅	□	♎	14 14:36
16 16:17	♅	△	♏	16 21:19
17 17:18	♇	□	♐	19 1:57
21 0:58	☉	⚹	♑	21 5:20
23 7:38	☉	□	♒	23 8:08
25 5:56	♅	△	♓	25 10:56
27 9:15	♅	□	♈	27 14:26
29 14:00	♅	⚹	♉	29 19:28

☽ Phases & Eclipses

Dy Hr Mn		
1 9:22	○	8♓46
8 16:16	☾	15♊50
16 18:48	●	23♍43
24 1:21	☽	0♑49
30 18:59	○	7♈25
8 10:51	☾	14♋58
16 8:22	●	22♎47
23 7:38	☽	29♑42
30 7:34	○	6♉41
30 7:47	☍	A 0.716

Astro Data

1 September 2031
Julian Day # 48091
SVP 4♓48'48"
GC 27♐16.9 ⚳ 2♊01.4
Eris 26♈59.4R ⚴ 7♉55.9
⚷ 21♉21.6R ⚶ 16♌09.4
☽ Mean ☊ 22♏35.0

1 October 2031
Julian Day # 48121
SVP 4♓48'46"
GC 27♐17.0 ⚳ 7♊20.6
Eris 26♈44.8R ⚴ 8♉43.9R
⚷ 20♉45.0R ⚶ 29♌20.1
☽ Mean ☊ 20♏59.7

November 2031 LONGITUDE

Day	Sid.Time	☉	0 hr ☽	Noon ☽	True ☊	☿	♀	♂	⚳	♃	♄	♅	♆	♇
1 Sa	14 42 20	8♏51 36	28♉27 49	4♊46 39	18♏57.6	0♐30.3	22♍50.4	15♑49.7	27♌59.1	27♐15.7	22♊21.9	26♊53.8	13♈32.4	11♒16.7
2 Su	14 46 17	9 51 37	11♊01 32	17 12 42	18 58.3	1 46.6	23 54.4	16 34.0	28 19.3	27 27.0	22R 19.0	26R 52.4	13R 30.9	11 16.9
3 M	14 50 14	10 51 40	23 20 26	29 25 05	18 59.2	3 01.5	24 58.7	17 18.3	28 39.4	27 38.3	22 16.1	26 50.8	13 29.5	11 17.2
4 Tu	14 54 10	11 51 45	5♋27 02	11♋26 45	19 00.1	4 14.8	26 03.3	18 02.8	28 59.3	27 49.8	22 13.0	26 49.3	13 28.0	11 17.5
5 W	14 58 07	12 51 51	17 24 42	23 21 25	19 00.7	5 26.3	27 08.2	18 47.2	29 19.1	28 01.3	22 09.8	26 47.7	13 26.6	11 17.8
6 Th	15 02 03	13 52 00	29 17 27	5♌13 22	19R 01.1	6 35.9	28 13.4	19 31.8	29 38.7	28 12.9	22 06.5	26 46.0	13 25.2	11 18.1
7 F	15 06 00	14 52 11	11♌09 45	17 07 11	19 01.1	7 43.2	29 18.9	20 16.4	29 58.1	28 24.6	22 03.2	26 44.3	13 23.9	11 18.5
8 Sa	15 09 56	15 52 24	23 06 17	29 07 37	19 01.0	8 48.2	0♎24.7	21 01.1	0♍17.4	28 36.3	21 59.8	26 42.6	13 22.5	11 18.9
9 Su	15 13 53	16 52 40	5♍11 45	11♍19 14	19 00.8	9 50.3	1 30.7	21 45.8	0 36.5	28 48.2	21 56.2	26 40.9	13 21.2	11 19.3
10 M	15 17 49	17 52 57	17 30 33	23 46 09	19 00.6	10 49.4	2 37.0	22 30.6	0 55.4	29 00.1	21 52.6	26 39.0	13 19.9	11 19.7
11 Tu	15 21 46	18 53 16	0♎06 27	6♎31 45	19D 00.6	11 45.0	3 43.5	23 15.5	1 14.2	29 12.1	21 49.0	26 37.2	13 18.6	11 20.2
12 W	15 25 43	19 53 37	13 02 19	19 38 17	19 00.6	12 36.8	4 50.3	24 00.4	1 32.8	29 24.1	21 45.2	26 35.3	13 17.3	11 20.7
13 Th	15 29 39	20 53 59	26 19 41	3♏06 29	19 00.7	13 24.1	5 57.3	24 45.4	1 51.1	29 36.3	21 41.4	26 33.4	13 16.0	11 21.2
14 F	15 33 36	21 54 24	9♏58 30	16 55 28	19R 00.8	14 06.6	7 04.6	25 30.5	2 09.3	29 48.5	21 37.5	26 31.4	13 14.8	11 21.8
15 Sa	15 37 32	22 54 50	23 56 57	1♐02 30	19 00.7	14 43.5	8 12.0	26 15.6	2 27.3	0♑00.8	21 33.5	26 29.5	13 13.6	11 22.4
16 Su	15 41 29	23 55 18	8♐11 30	15 23 20	19 00.4	15 14.3	9 19.7	27 00.8	2 45.2	0 13.1	21 29.5	26 27.4	13 12.4	11 23.0
17 M	15 45 25	24 55 48	22 37 18	29 52 39	18 59.8	15 38.2	10 27.6	27 46.0	3 02.8	0 25.5	21 25.4	26 25.4	13 11.3	11 23.6
18 Tu	15 49 22	25 56 19	7♑08 41	14♑24 42	18 59.1	15 54.5	11 35.7	28 31.3	3 20.2	0 38.0	21 21.2	26 23.3	13 10.1	11 24.3
19 W	15 53 18	26 56 51	21 40 00	28 54 01	18 58.3	16R 02.5	12 43.9	29 16.6	3 37.4	0 50.5	21 17.0	26 21.2	13 09.0	11 25.0
20 Th	15 57 15	27 57 25	6♒06 11	13♒16 04	18 57.6	16 01.4	13 52.4	0♒01.9	3 54.4	1 03.1	21 12.7	26 19.0	13 07.9	11 25.7
21 F	16 01 12	28 57 59	20 23 17	27 27 33	18D 57.4	15 50.6	15 01.0	0 47.4	4 11.2	1 15.8	21 08.3	26 16.9	13 06.9	11 26.5
22 Sa	16 05 08	29 58 35	4♓28 38	11♓26 25	18 57.6	15 29.5	16 09.9	1 32.8	4 27.7	1 28.5	21 03.9	26 14.7	13 05.9	11 27.2
23 Su	16 09 05	0♐59 12	18 20 46	25 11 40	18 58.3	14 57.7	17 18.9	2 18.3	4 44.0	1 41.3	20 59.4	26 12.4	13 04.9	11 28.0
24 M	16 13 01	1 59 50	1♈59 06	8♈43 05	18 59.3	14 15.2	18 28.0	3 03.8	5 00.1	1 54.1	20 54.9	26 10.2	13 03.9	11 28.8
25 Tu	16 16 58	3 00 29	15 23 40	22 00 54	19 00.5	13 22.4	19 37.4	3 49.4	5 16.0	2 06.9	20 50.4	26 07.9	13 02.9	11 29.7
26 W	16 20 54	4 01 09	28 34 49	5♉05 30	19 01.5	12 20.1	20 46.9	4 35.0	5 31.7	2 19.9	20 45.8	26 05.6	13 02.0	11 30.6
27 Th	16 24 51	5 01 51	11♉32 58	17 57 19	19R 01.9	11 09.4	21 56.5	5 20.7	5 47.1	2 32.8	20 41.1	26 03.3	13 01.1	11 31.5
28 F	16 28 47	6 02 34	24 18 36	0♊36 51	19 01.6	9 52.4	23 06.3	6 06.3	6 02.3	2 45.9	20 36.4	26 00.9	13 00.3	11 32.4
29 Sa	16 32 44	7 03 18	6♊52 11	13 04 41	19 00.2	8 31.3	24 16.3	6 52.0	6 17.2	2 58.9	20 31.7	25 58.5	12 59.4	11 33.3
30 Su	16 36 41	8 04 04	19 14 27	25 21 38	18 57.9	7 08.7	25 26.4	7 37.8	6 31.9	3 12.1	20 27.0	25 56.2	12 58.6	11 34.3

December 2031 LONGITUDE

Day	Sid.Time	☉	0 hr ☽	Noon ☽	True ☊	☿	♀	♂	⚳	♃	♄	♅	♆	♇
1 M	16 40 37	9♐04 50	1♋26 23	7♋28 54	18♏54.8	5♐47.5	26♎36.7	8♒23.6	6♍46.3	3♑25.2	20♊22.2	25♊53.7	12♈57.9	11♒35.3
2 Tu	16 44 34	10 05 39	13 29 27	19 28 16	18R 51.2	4R 30.3	27 47.1	9 09.4	7 00.4	3 38.4	20R 17.4	25R 51.3	12R 57.1	11 36.3
3 W	16 48 30	11 06 28	25 25 43	1♌22 07	18 47.5	3 19.6	28 57.7	9 55.2	7 14.3	3 51.7	20 12.5	25 48.9	12 56.4	11 37.4
4 Th	16 52 27	12 07 19	7♌17 53	13 13 28	18 44.3	2 17.5	0♏08.3	10 41.0	7 27.9	4 05.0	20 07.6	25 46.4	12 55.7	11 38.5
5 F	16 56 23	13 08 11	19 09 20	25 06 00	18 41.8	1 25.4	1 19.2	11 26.9	7 41.3	4 18.3	20 02.8	25 43.9	12 55.1	11 39.5
6 Sa	17 00 20	14 09 04	1♍04 01	7♍03 57	18D 40.4	0 44.3	2 30.1	12 12.8	7 54.4	4 31.7	19 57.8	25 41.4	12 54.5	11 40.7
7 Su	17 04 16	15 09 59	13 06 23	19 11 54	18 40.2	0 14.6	3 41.2	12 58.8	8 07.1	4 45.1	19 52.9	25 38.9	12 53.9	11 41.8
8 M	17 08 13	16 10 55	25 21 08	1♎34 37	18 41.1	29♏56.2	4 52.3	13 44.7	8 19.6	4 58.5	19 48.0	25 36.4	12 53.3	11 43.0
9 Tu	17 12 10	17 11 52	7♎52 58	14 16 39	18 42.7	29D 49.0	6 03.6	14 30.7	8 31.8	5 12.0	19 43.0	25 33.9	12 52.8	11 44.1
10 W	17 16 06	18 12 51	20 46 11	27 21 54	18 44.4	29 52.2	7 15.0	15 16.7	8 43.7	5 25.5	19 38.1	25 31.3	12 52.3	11 45.3
11 Th	17 20 03	19 13 50	4♏04 08	10♏53 02	18R 45.6	0♐05.1	8 26.5	16 02.8	8 55.3	5 39.1	19 33.1	25 28.8	12 51.9	11 46.6
12 F	17 23 59	20 14 51	17 48 38	24 50 48	18 45.7	0 27.0	9 38.1	16 48.8	9 06.6	5 52.7	19 28.2	25 26.3	12 51.4	11 47.8
13 Sa	17 27 56	21 15 53	1♐59 15	9♐13 30	18 44.2	0 56.9	10 49.9	17 34.9	9 17.5	6 06.3	19 23.2	25 23.7	12 51.0	11 49.1
14 Su	17 31 52	22 16 56	16 32 52	23 56 34	18 41.0	1 34.0	12 01.7	18 21.0	9 28.1	6 19.9	19 18.3	25 21.1	12 50.7	11 50.4
15 M	17 35 49	23 17 59	1♑23 35	8♑52 53	18 36.4	2 17.5	13 13.6	19 07.1	9 38.5	6 33.6	19 13.3	25 18.6	12 50.4	11 51.7
16 Tu	17 39 45	24 19 04	16 23 16	23 53 35	18 30.9	3 06.8	14 25.6	19 53.3	9 48.4	6 47.2	19 08.4	25 16.0	12 50.1	11 53.0
17 W	17 43 42	25 20 08	1♒22 41	8♒49 30	18 25.4	4 01.0	15 37.6	20 39.4	9 58.0	7 01.0	19 03.5	25 13.4	12 49.8	11 54.4
18 Th	17 47 39	26 21 13	16 13 05	23 32 37	18 20.6	4 59.7	16 49.8	21 25.6	10 07.3	7 14.7	18 58.6	25 10.9	12 49.6	11 55.8
19 F	17 51 35	27 22 19	0♓47 27	7♓57 08	18 17.2	6 02.2	18 02.0	22 11.7	10 16.3	7 28.4	18 53.7	25 08.3	12 49.4	11 57.2
20 Sa	17 55 32	28 23 24	15 01 22	22 00 00	18D 15.5	7 08.1	19 14.3	22 57.9	10 24.9	7 42.2	18 48.8	25 05.7	12 49.3	11 58.6
21 Su	17 59 28	29 24 30	28 53 03	5♈40 37	18 15.5	8 16.9	20 26.7	23 44.1	10 33.1	7 56.0	18 44.0	25 03.2	12 49.2	12 00.0
22 M	18 03 25	0♑25 36	12♈22 55	19 00 14	18 16.7	9 28.4	21 39.1	24 30.3	10 41.0	8 09.8	18 39.2	25 00.6	12 49.1	12 01.4
23 Tu	18 07 21	1 26 42	25 32 52	2♉01 12	18 18.2	10 42.1	22 51.6	25 16.5	10 48.5	8 23.6	18 34.4	24 58.1	12D 49.0	12 02.9
24 W	18 11 18	2 27 49	8♉25 35	14 46 21	18R 19.1	11 57.9	24 04.2	26 02.7	10 55.6	8 37.4	18 29.7	24 55.5	12 49.0	12 04.4
25 Th	18 15 14	3 28 56	21 03 53	27 18 29	18 18.7	13 15.4	25 16.9	26 48.9	11 02.4	8 51.3	18 24.9	24 53.0	12 49.0	12 05.9
26 F	18 19 11	4 30 03	3♊30 26	9♊40 01	18 16.3	14 34.5	26 29.6	27 35.1	11 08.7	9 05.1	18 20.3	24 50.5	12 49.1	12 07.4
27 Sa	18 23 08	5 31 10	15 47 27	21 52 58	18 11.6	15 54.9	27 42.4	28 21.3	11 14.7	9 19.0	18 15.7	24 48.0	12 49.2	12 08.9
28 Su	18 27 04	6 32 17	27 56 42	3♋58 52	18 04.5	17 16.6	28 55.3	29 07.5	11 20.4	9 32.8	18 11.1	24 45.5	12 49.3	12 10.5
29 M	18 31 01	7 33 25	9♋59 36	15 59 03	17 55.5	18 39.3	0♐08.2	29 53.7	11 25.6	9 46.7	18 06.5	24 43.0	12 49.5	12 12.1
30 Tu	18 34 57	8 34 33	21 57 23	27 54 46	17 45.2	20 03.0	1 21.2	0♓39.9	11 30.4	10 00.6	18 02.1	24 40.5	12 49.7	12 13.6
31 W	18 38 54	9 35 41	3♌51 23	9♌47 27	17 34.6	21 27.7	2 34.2	1 26.1	11 34.8	10 14.5	17 57.6	24 38.0	12 49.9	12 15.2

Astro Data	Planet Ingress	Last Aspect	☽ Ingress	Last Aspect	☽ Ingress	☽ Phases & Eclipses	Astro Data
Dy Hr Mn	Dy Hr Mn	Dy Hr Mn	Dy Hr Mn	Dy Hr Mn	Dy Hr Mn	Dy Hr Mn	1 November 2031
☽0S 10 3:36	☿ ♐ 1 2:36	31 11:23 ♀ △	♊ 1 2:55	3 6:36 ♀ □	♌ 3 9:14	7 7:03 ☾ 14♌40	Julian Day # 48152
♀0S 10 23:27	⚳ ♍ 7 14:20	3 8:25 ♃ ☍	♋ 3 13:09	5 13:16 ♅ ⚹	♍ 5 21:51	14 21:11 ● 22♏18	SVP 4♓48'43"
♅□♇ 18 3:27	♀ ♎ 8 3:00	5 20:25 ♀ ⚹	♌ 6 1:26	8 8:54 ☿ ⚹	♎ 8 8:58	14 21:07:31 ● AT01'08"	GC 27♐17.0 ⚴ 5♊45.0R
☿ R 19 21:17	♃ ♑ 15 10:30	8 10:57 ♃ △	♍ 8 13:44	10 8:41 ♅ △	♏ 10 16:44	21 14:46 ☽ 29♒05	Eris 26♈26.4R ⚵ 2♉54.2R
☽0N 23 1:51	♂ ♒ 20 10:58	10 22:04 ♃ □	♎ 10 23:48	11 21:29 ♂ □	♐ 12 20:41	28 23:20 ○ 6♊31	⚷ 19♉24.8R ⚶ 12♍20.1
	☉ ♐ 22 12:34	13 5:43 ♃ ⚹	♏ 13 6:31	14 14:16 ♅ ☍	♑ 14 21:46		☽ Mean ☊ 19♏21.2
☽0S 7 12:41		15 3:28 ♂ ⚹	♐ 15 10:15	15 19:33 ♀ ⚹	♒ 16 21:47	7 3:21 ☾ 14♍48	
☿ D 9 16:25	♀ ♏ 4 9:10	17 6:18 ♅ ☍	♑ 17 12:12	18 16:59 ☉ ⚹	♓ 18 22:41	14 9:07 ● 22♐10	1 December 2031
☽0N 20 8:04	☿ ♏R 8 5:38	19 12:40 ♂ ☌	♒ 19 13:50	21 0:02 ☉ □	♈ 21 1:58	21 0:02 ☽ 28♓54	Julian Day # 48182
♆ D 24 7:41	☿ ♐ 11 4:23	21 14:46 ☉ □	♓ 21 16:20	22 22:58 ♅ ⚹	♉ 23 8:14	28 17:34 ○ 6♋46	SVP 4♓48'38"
	☉ ♑ 22 1:57	23 13:47 ♅ □	♈ 23 20:29	25 10:59 ♂ □	♊ 25 17:12		GC 27♐17.1 ⚴ 26♉43.6R
	♀ ♐ 29 9:18	25 19:29 ♅ ⚹	♉ 26 2:36	28 1:41 ♂ △	♋ 28 4:05		Eris 26♈10.7R ⚵ 28♈25.5R
	♂ ♓ 29 15:17	26 23:56 ♇ □	♊ 28 10:50	29 5:40 ♆ □	♌ 30 16:13		⚷ 17♉54.8R ⚶ 23♍38.6
		30 13:08 ♅ ☌	♋ 30 21:09				☽ Mean ☊ 17♏45.9

LONGITUDE — January 2032

Day	Sid.Time	☉	0 hr ☽	Noon ☽	True ☊	☿	♀	♂	⚳	♃	♄	♅	♆	♇
1 Th	18 42 50	10♑36 50	15♌43 12	21♌38 56	17♏24.7	22♐53.1	3♐47.3	2♓12.3	11♍38.8	10♑28.3	17♊53.3	24♊35.6	12♈50.2	12♒16.8
2 F	18 46 47	11 37 58	27 34 58	3♍31 41	17R16.3	24 19.2	5 00.5	2 58.4	11 42.4	10 42.2	17R48.9	24R33.1	12 50.5	12 18.4
3 Sa	18 50 44	12 39 07	9♍29 28	15 28 48	17 10.0	25 46.1	6 13.7	3 44.6	11 45.6	10 56.1	17 44.7	24 30.7	12 50.8	12 20.1
4 Su	18 54 40	13 40 16	21 30 10	27 34 07	17 06.2	27 13.5	7 26.9	4 30.8	11 48.4	11 10.0	17 40.5	24 28.3	12 51.2	12 21.7
5 M	18 58 37	14 41 26	3♎41 12	9♎52 01	17D04.5	28 41.6	8 40.3	5 17.0	11 50.7	11 23.9	17 36.3	24 26.0	12 51.6	12 23.4
6 Tu	19 02 33	15 42 36	16 07 11	22 27 18	17 04.6	0♑10.2	9 53.6	6 03.1	11 52.6	11 37.8	17 32.2	24 23.6	12 52.0	12 25.1
7 W	19 06 30	16 43 45	28 52 57	5♏24 41	17R05.4	1 39.3	11 07.0	6 49.3	11 54.1	11 51.7	17 28.2	24 21.3	12 52.5	12 26.7
8 Th	19 10 26	17 44 56	12♏03 00	18 48 19	17 05.8	3 09.0	12 20.5	7 35.4	11 55.2	12 05.5	17 24.3	24 19.0	12 53.0	12 28.4
9 F	19 14 23	18 46 06	25 40 55	2♐40 56	17 04.7	4 39.2	13 34.0	8 21.6	11R55.8	12 19.4	17 20.4	24 16.7	12 53.6	12 30.1
10 Sa	19 18 19	19 47 16	9♐48 21	17 02 54	17 01.3	6 09.8	14 47.5	9 07.7	11 56.0	12 33.3	17 16.7	24 14.4	12 54.2	12 31.9
11 Su	19 22 16	20 48 27	24 24 07	1♑51 19	16 55.2	7 40.9	16 01.1	9 53.8	11 55.7	12 47.1	17 12.9	24 12.2	12 54.8	12 33.6
12 M	19 26 13	21 49 37	9♑23 34	16 59 42	16 46.7	9 12.5	17 14.7	10 39.9	11 55.0	13 00.9	17 09.3	24 10.0	12 55.4	12 35.3
13 Tu	19 30 09	22 50 47	24 38 25	2♒18 16	16 36.6	10 44.6	18 28.4	11 26.0	11 53.9	13 14.8	17 05.8	24 07.9	12 56.1	12 37.1
14 W	19 34 06	23 51 56	9♒57 47	17 35 31	16 26.1	12 17.1	19 42.0	12 12.1	11 52.3	13 28.6	17 02.3	24 05.7	12 56.8	12 38.8
15 Th	19 38 02	24 53 05	25 10 04	2♓40 15	16 16.5	13 50.2	20 55.7	12 58.2	11 50.2	13 42.4	16 58.9	24 03.6	12 57.6	12 40.6
16 F	19 41 59	25 54 13	10♓05 03	17 23 40	16 09.0	15 23.7	22 09.5	13 44.3	11 47.7	13 56.1	16 55.6	24 01.5	12 58.4	12 42.4
17 Sa	19 45 55	26 55 20	24 35 33	1♈40 23	16 03.9	16 57.7	23 23.2	14 30.3	11 44.8	14 09.9	16 52.4	23 59.5	12 59.2	12 44.2
18 Su	19 49 52	27 56 27	8♈38 04	15 28 40	16 01.5	18 32.2	24 37.0	15 16.3	11 41.5	14 23.6	16 49.3	23 57.5	13 00.0	12 46.0
19 M	19 53 48	28 57 33	22 12 26	28 49 43	16D00.8	20 07.2	25 50.8	16 02.3	11 37.6	14 37.3	16 46.3	23 55.5	13 00.9	12 47.7
20 Tu	19 57 45	29 58 38	5♉20 58	11♉46 41	16R01.0	21 42.7	27 04.7	16 48.3	11 33.4	14 51.0	16 43.4	23 53.5	13 01.8	12 49.5
21 W	20 01 42	0♒59 42	18 07 26	24 23 44	16 00.8	23 18.8	28 18.5	17 34.3	11 28.7	15 04.7	16 40.5	23 51.6	13 02.8	12 51.4
22 Th	20 05 38	2 00 45	0♊36 09	6♊45 14	15 59.0	24 55.5	29 32.4	18 20.2	11 23.6	15 18.3	16 37.8	23 49.7	13 03.7	12 53.2
23 F	20 09 35	3 01 47	12 51 27	18 55 17	15 54.7	26 32.7	0♑46.3	19 06.1	11 18.1	15 31.9	16 35.2	23 47.9	13 04.8	12 55.0
24 Sa	20 13 31	4 02 48	24 57 10	0♋57 27	15 47.4	28 10.5	2 00.3	19 52.0	11 12.2	15 45.5	16 32.6	23 46.1	13 05.8	12 56.8
25 Su	20 17 28	5 03 49	6♋56 29	12 54 32	15 37.1	29 48.9	3 14.2	20 37.9	11 05.8	15 59.0	16 30.2	23 44.4	13 06.9	12 58.6
26 M	20 21 24	6 04 49	18 51 52	24 48 41	15 24.2	1♒27.9	4 28.2	21 23.7	10 59.0	16 12.6	16 27.8	23 42.7	13 08.0	13 00.5
27 Tu	20 25 21	7 05 47	0♌45 10	6♌41 30	15 09.7	3 07.6	5 42.2	22 09.5	10 51.8	16 26.0	16 25.6	23 41.0	13 09.1	13 02.3
28 W	20 29 17	8 06 45	12 37 49	18 34 16	14 54.6	4 47.8	6 56.2	22 55.3	10 44.2	16 39.5	16 23.5	23 39.3	13 10.3	13 04.1
29 Th	20 33 14	9 07 42	24 31 01	0♍28 13	14 40.2	6 28.8	8 10.3	23 41.0	10 36.2	16 52.9	16 21.4	23 37.7	13 11.5	13 06.0
30 F	20 37 11	10 08 38	6♍26 04	12 24 47	14 27.7	8 10.4	9 24.3	24 26.8	10 27.8	17 06.3	16 19.5	23 36.2	13 12.7	13 07.8
31 Sa	20 41 07	11 09 33	18 24 39	24 25 56	14 17.8	9 52.7	10 38.4	25 12.5	10 19.1	17 19.6	16 17.7	23 34.7	13 14.0	13 09.6

LONGITUDE — February 2032

Day	Sid.Time	☉	0 hr ☽	Noon ☽	True ☊	☿	♀	♂	⚳	♃	♄	♅	♆	♇
1 Su	20 45 04	12♒10 28	0♎29 00	6♎34 14	14♏10.9	11♒35.7	11♑52.5	25♓58.1	10♍09.9	17♑32.9	16♊16.0	23♊33.2	13♈15.2	13♒11.5
2 M	20 49 00	13 11 21	12 42 03	18 52 57	14R07.0	13 19.3	13 06.6	26 43.8	10R00.4	17 46.2	16R14.4	23R31.8	13 16.5	13 13.3
3 Tu	20 52 57	14 12 14	25 07 27	1♏26 03	14D05.5	15 03.7	14 20.8	27 29.4	9 50.5	17 59.4	16 12.9	23 30.4	13 17.9	13 15.2
4 W	20 56 53	15 13 06	7♏49 20	14 17 50	14R05.2	16 48.7	15 34.9	28 15.0	9 40.3	18 12.6	16 11.5	23 29.1	13 19.3	13 17.0
5 Th	21 00 50	16 13 57	20 52 06	27 32 36	14 05.0	18 34.4	16 49.1	29 00.5	9 29.8	18 25.7	16 10.2	23 27.8	13 20.7	13 18.8
6 F	21 04 46	17 14 48	4♐19 46	11♐13 53	14 03.6	20 20.8	18 03.3	29 46.1	9 18.9	18 38.8	16 09.1	23 26.6	13 22.1	13 20.7
7 Sa	21 08 43	18 15 37	18 15 10	25 23 36	13 59.9	22 07.8	19 17.5	0♈31.6	9 07.7	18 51.8	16 08.0	23 25.4	13 23.5	13 22.5
8 Su	21 12 40	19 16 26	2♑39 00	10♑00 58	13 53.4	23 55.3	20 31.7	1 17.1	8 56.2	19 04.8	16 07.1	23 24.2	13 25.0	13 24.4
9 M	21 16 36	20 17 13	17 28 49	25 01 40	13 44.3	25 43.4	21 45.9	2 02.5	8 44.4	19 17.7	16 06.2	23 23.2	13 26.5	13 26.2
10 Tu	21 20 33	21 18 00	2♒38 25	10♒17 44	13 33.3	27 32.0	23 00.2	2 47.9	8 32.4	19 30.6	16 05.5	23 22.1	13 28.1	13 28.0
11 W	21 24 29	22 18 45	17 58 11	25 38 17	13 21.6	29 20.9	24 14.4	3 33.3	8 20.1	19 43.5	16 04.9	23 21.1	13 29.6	13 29.9
12 Th	21 28 26	23 19 29	3♓16 31	10♓51 29	13 10.8	1♓10.2	25 28.6	4 18.6	8 07.5	19 56.2	16 04.4	23 20.2	13 31.2	13 31.7
13 F	21 32 22	24 20 11	18 21 53	25 46 40	13 01.9	2 59.5	26 42.9	5 03.9	7 54.8	20 08.9	16 04.0	23 19.3	13 32.8	13 33.5
14 Sa	21 36 19	25 20 51	3♈04 58	10♈16 11	12 55.7	4 48.9	27 57.2	5 49.2	7 41.8	20 21.6	16 03.8	23 18.4	13 34.5	13 35.3
15 Su	21 40 15	26 21 30	17 19 59	24 16 12	12 52.2	6 38.1	29 11.4	6 34.5	7 28.6	20 34.2	16D03.6	23 17.6	13 36.1	13 37.1
16 M	21 44 12	27 22 08	1♉04 55	7♉46 22	12D51.0	8 27.0	0♒25.7	7 19.7	7 15.3	20 46.7	16 03.6	23 16.9	13 37.8	13 38.9
17 Tu	21 48 09	28 22 43	14 20 55	20 49 03	12R51.1	10 15.1	1 40.0	8 04.8	7 01.8	20 59.2	16 03.7	23 16.2	13 39.5	13 40.7
18 W	21 52 05	29 23 17	27 11 18	3♊28 16	12 51.1	12 02.4	2 54.2	8 50.0	6 48.2	21 11.6	16 03.9	23 15.6	13 41.2	13 42.5
19 Th	21 56 02	0♓23 49	9♊40 35	15 48 53	12 50.0	13 48.3	4 08.5	9 35.1	6 34.5	21 23.9	16 04.2	23 15.0	13 43.0	13 44.3
20 F	21 59 58	1 24 19	21 53 46	27 55 51	12 46.8	15 32.6	5 22.8	10 20.1	6 20.7	21 36.2	16 04.6	23 14.5	13 44.8	13 46.1
21 Sa	22 03 55	2 24 48	3♋55 40	9♋53 47	12 40.9	17 14.8	6 37.1	11 05.1	6 06.8	21 48.4	16 05.1	23 14.0	13 46.6	13 47.8
22 Su	22 07 51	3 25 14	15 50 39	21 46 44	12 32.2	18 54.5	7 51.4	11 50.1	5 52.8	22 00.6	16 05.8	23 13.6	13 48.4	13 49.6
23 M	22 11 48	4 25 39	27 42 23	3♌37 59	12 21.3	20 31.1	9 05.7	12 35.0	5 38.8	22 12.6	16 06.6	23 13.2	13 50.2	13 51.3
24 Tu	22 15 44	5 26 02	9♌33 48	15 30 06	12 08.7	22 04.0	10 20.0	13 19.9	5 24.8	22 24.6	16 07.4	23 12.9	13 52.1	13 53.1
25 W	22 19 41	6 26 23	21 27 05	27 24 57	11 55.6	23 32.7	11 34.3	14 04.8	5 10.8	22 36.5	16 08.4	23 12.6	13 53.9	13 54.8
26 Th	22 23 37	7 26 43	3♍23 52	9♍23 59	11 43.1	24 56.5	12 48.6	14 49.6	4 56.8	22 48.3	16 09.5	23 12.4	13 55.8	13 56.5
27 F	22 27 34	8 27 00	15 25 25	21 28 19	11 32.1	26 14.9	14 02.9	15 34.3	4 42.8	23 00.1	16 10.7	23 12.2	13 57.7	13 58.2
28 Sa	22 31 31	9 27 16	27 32 50	3♎39 07	11 23.6	27 27.1	15 17.2	16 19.0	4 28.9	23 11.8	16 12.0	23 12.1	13 59.7	13 59.9
29 Su	22 35 27	10 27 31	9♎47 23	15 57 50	11 17.8	28 32.7	16 31.5	17 03.7	4 15.0	23 23.4	16 13.5	23D12.0	14 01.6	14 01.6

Astro Data

	Dy Hr Mn
☽0S	3 21:07
♃⚺♇	10 9:15
⚳R	10 9:45
♃□♆	12 1:56
☽0N	16 16:49
♃⚻♄	27 11:21
☽0S	31 4:25
♂0N	8 6:11
♆✶♇	10 15:03
☽0N	13 3:54
♄D	16 7:01
☽0S	27 10:56
☿0N	28 7:03
♃⚻♅	28 12:38
♆✶♇	29 11:17

Planet Ingress

		Dy Hr Mn
☿	♑	6 9:15
☉	♒	20 12:32
♀	♑	22 20:57
☿	♒	25 14:42
♂	♈	6 19:21
☿	♓	11 20:35
♀	♒	16 3:42
☉	♓	19 2:33

Last Aspect / ☽ Ingress (January)

Last Aspect Dy Hr Mn		☽ Ingress	Dy Hr Mn
1 17:56	♅ ✶	♍	2 4:53
4 11:14	☿ □	♎	4 16:47
6 15:38	♅ △	♏	7 2:04
8 9:59	☉ ✶	♐	9 7:26
10 23:43	♅ ☍	♑	11 9:02
12 20:08	☉ ☌	♒	13 8:24
14 22:16	♅ △	♓	15 7:43
17 3:18	☉ ✶	♈	17 9:09
19 12:16	☉ □	♉	19 14:09
21 9:37	☿ △	♊	21 22:50
23 21:40	♅ ☌	♋	24 10:05
26 4:38	♂ △	♌	26 22:29
28 22:14	♅ ✶	♍	29 11:03
31 13:39	♂ ☍	♎	31 23:03

Last Aspect / ☽ Ingress (February)

Last Aspect Dy Hr Mn		☽ Ingress	Dy Hr Mn
2 20:56	♅ △	♏	3 9:17
5 14:46	♂ △	♐	5 16:22
7 8:43	♅ ☍	♑	7 19:38
9 6:22	♀ ☌	♒	9 19:51
11 18:37	☿ ☌	♓	11 18:51
13 13:40	♀ ✶	♈	13 18:55
15 21:31	♀ □	♉	15 22:05
18 3:30	☉ □	♊	18 5:21
20 2:40	♅ ☌	♋	20 16:08
22 12:28	♃ ☍	♌	23 4:39
25 3:33	♅ ✶	♍	25 17:11
27 22:30	☿ ☍	♎	28 4:50

☽ Phases & Eclipses

Dy Hr Mn		
5 22:05	☾	15♎07
12 20:08	●	22♑10
19 12:16	☽	28♈58
27 12:54	○	7♌08
4 13:50	☾	15♏18
11 6:25	●	22♒05
18 3:30	☽	29♉02
26 7:44	○	7♍16

Astro Data

1 January 2032
Julian Day # 48213
SVP 4♓48'33"
GC 27♐17.2 ⚳ 20♉09.5R
Eris 26♈01.6R ⚵ 1♉53.0
⚷ 16♉46.0R ⚶ 2♎45.8
☽ Mean ☊ 16♏07.4

1 February 2032
Julian Day # 48244
SVP 4♓48'28"
GC 27♐17.2 ⚳ 24♉01.9
Eris 26♈02.7 ⚵ 12♉11.7
⚷ 16♉29.0 ⚶ 7♎09.0
☽ Mean ☊ 14♏28.9

March 2032 LONGITUDE

Day	Sid.Time	☉	0 hr ☽	Noon ☽	True ☊	☿	♀	♂	⚳	♃	♄	♅	♆	♇
1 M	22 39 24	11♓27 44	22♎10 43	28♎26 20	11♏14.7	29♓31.0	17♒45.8	17♈48.4	4♍01.2	23♑34.9	16♊15.0	23♊12.0	14♈03.6	14♒03.3
2 Tu	22 43 20	12 27 55	4♏44 59	11♏07 03	11D13.8	0♈21.4	19 00.1	18 32.9	3R47.6	23 46.3	16 16.7	23 12.1	14 05.6	14 05.0
3 W	22 47 17	13 28 05	17 32 52	24 02 50	11 14.3	1 03.6	20 14.4	19 17.5	3 34.0	23 57.7	16 18.4	23 12.2	14 07.6	14 06.6
4 Th	22 51 13	14 28 13	0♐37 22	7♐16 48	11R15.2	1 37.1	21 28.7	20 02.0	3 20.6	24 08.9	16 20.3	23 12.3	14 09.6	14 08.3
5 F	22 55 10	15 28 20	14 01 31	20 51 46	11 15.2	2 01.7	22 43.1	20 46.5	3 07.4	24 20.1	16 22.3	23 12.6	14 11.6	14 09.9
6 Sa	22 59 06	16 28 25	27 47 46	4♑49 36	11 13.7	2 17.1	23 57.4	21 30.9	2 54.3	24 31.2	16 24.4	23 12.8	14 13.7	14 11.5
7 Su	23 03 03	17 28 29	11♑57 13	19 10 25	11 09.9	2R23.4	25 11.7	22 15.3	2 41.5	24 42.2	16 26.5	23 13.1	14 15.8	14 13.1
8 M	23 07 00	18 28 31	26 28 49	3♒51 50	11 04.1	2 20.5	26 26.0	22 59.7	2 28.8	24 53.1	16 28.8	23 13.5	14 17.8	14 14.7
9 Tu	23 10 56	19 28 31	11♒18 43	18 48 31	10 56.7	2 08.8	27 40.4	23 44.0	2 16.4	25 03.9	16 31.3	23 13.9	14 19.9	14 16.3
10 W	23 14 53	20 28 29	26 20 10	3♓52 29	10 48.6	1 48.5	28 54.7	24 28.3	2 04.2	25 14.6	16 33.8	23 14.4	14 22.0	14 17.8
11 Th	23 18 49	21 28 26	11♓24 12	18 54 05	10 40.9	1 20.4	0♓09.0	25 12.5	1 52.2	25 25.2	16 36.4	23 15.0	14 24.1	14 19.4
12 F	23 22 46	22 28 21	26 20 57	3♈43 42	10 34.6	0 45.0	1 23.3	25 56.7	1 40.6	25 35.7	16 39.1	23 15.5	14 26.3	14 20.9
13 Sa	23 26 42	23 28 14	11♈01 25	18 13 19	10 30.3	0 03.4	2 37.6	26 40.8	1 29.2	25 46.1	16 41.9	23 16.2	14 28.4	14 22.4
14 Su	23 30 39	24 28 04	25 18 51	2♉17 38	10D28.3	29♓16.4	3 51.9	27 24.9	1 18.1	25 56.4	16 44.8	23 16.9	14 30.6	14 23.9
15 M	23 34 35	25 27 53	9♉09 30	15 54 27	10 28.1	28 25.2	5 06.2	28 09.0	1 07.3	26 06.6	16 47.9	23 17.6	14 32.7	14 25.3
16 Tu	23 38 32	26 27 39	22 32 38	29 04 20	10 29.1	27 31.1	6 20.5	28 53.0	0 56.9	26 16.7	16 51.0	23 18.4	14 34.9	14 26.8
17 W	23 42 29	27 27 23	5♊29 56	11♊49 55	10 30.6	26 35.2	7 34.8	29 36.9	0 46.8	26 26.7	16 54.2	23 19.3	14 37.1	14 28.2
18 Th	23 46 25	28 27 05	18 04 50	24 15 15	10R31.6	25 38.9	8 49.1	0♉20.8	0 37.1	26 36.6	16 57.6	23 20.2	14 39.3	14 29.7
19 F	23 50 22	29 26 45	0♋21 46	6♋25 00	10 31.4	24 43.3	10 03.4	1 04.7	0 27.7	26 46.3	17 01.0	23 21.1	14 41.5	14 31.1
20 Sa	23 54 18	0♈26 22	12 25 35	18 24 06	10 29.5	23 49.5	11 17.6	1 48.5	0 18.6	26 56.0	17 04.5	23 22.1	14 43.7	14 32.5
21 Su	23 58 15	1 25 57	24 21 07	0♌17 12	10 25.9	22 58.5	12 31.9	2 32.3	0 10.0	27 05.5	17 08.1	23 23.2	14 45.9	14 33.8
22 M	0 02 11	2 25 30	6♌12 53	12 08 36	10 20.7	22 11.3	13 46.1	3 16.0	0 01.7	27 14.9	17 11.8	23 24.3	14 48.1	14 35.2
23 Tu	0 06 08	3 25 00	18 04 49	24 01 55	10 14.4	21 28.4	15 00.4	3 59.7	29♌53.8	27 24.2	17 15.6	23 25.5	14 50.4	14 36.5
24 W	0 10 04	4 24 29	0♍00 15	6♍00 08	10 07.7	20 50.4	16 14.6	4 43.3	29 46.4	27 33.4	17 19.5	23 26.7	14 52.6	14 37.8
25 Th	0 14 01	5 23 55	12 01 48	18 05 30	10 01.2	20 17.9	17 28.8	5 26.9	29 39.3	27 42.5	17 23.5	23 27.9	14 54.8	14 39.1
26 F	0 17 57	6 23 19	24 11 24	0♎19 40	9 55.6	19 51.0	18 43.0	6 10.4	29 32.6	27 51.4	17 27.6	23 29.3	14 57.1	14 40.4
27 Sa	0 21 54	7 22 41	6♎30 25	12 43 46	9 51.3	19 30.0	19 57.3	6 53.9	29 26.3	28 00.2	17 31.8	23 30.6	14 59.3	14 41.6
28 Su	0 25 51	8 22 01	18 59 48	25 18 37	9 48.8	19 14.8	21 11.5	7 37.3	29 20.5	28 08.9	17 36.0	23 32.0	15 01.6	14 42.8
29 M	0 29 47	9 21 18	1♏40 18	8♏04 56	9D47.8	19 05.6	22 25.7	8 20.7	29 15.0	28 17.5	17 40.4	23 33.5	15 03.9	14 44.0
30 Tu	0 33 44	10 20 35	14 32 37	21 03 26	9 48.3	19D02.1	23 39.9	9 04.1	29 10.0	28 25.9	17 44.8	23 35.0	15 06.1	14 45.2
31 W	0 37 40	11 19 49	27 37 31	4♐14 59	9 49.6	19 04.4	24 54.1	9 47.4	29 05.4	28 34.2	17 49.3	23 36.5	15 08.4	14 46.4

April 2032 LONGITUDE

Day	Sid.Time	☉	0 hr ☽	Noon ☽	True ☊	☿	♀	♂	⚳	♃	♄	♅	♆	♇
1 Th	0 41 37	12♈19 01	10♐55 57	17♐40 31	9♏51.2	19♓12.0	26♓08.2	10♉30.6	29♌01.2	28♑42.4	17♊53.9	23♊38.1	15♈10.7	14♒47.5
2 F	0 45 33	13 18 12	24 28 48	1♑20 52	9R52.5	19 25.0	27 22.4	11 13.8	28R57.5	28 50.4	17 58.6	23 39.8	15 12.9	14 48.7
3 Sa	0 49 30	14 17 21	8♑16 45	15 16 25	9 52.9	19 43.1	28 36.6	11 57.0	28 54.2	28 58.3	18 03.4	23 41.5	15 15.2	14 49.8
4 Su	0 53 26	15 16 28	22 19 48	29 26 42	9 52.3	20 05.9	29 50.8	12 40.1	28 51.3	29 06.1	18 08.2	23 43.2	15 17.5	14 50.8
5 M	0 57 23	16 15 34	6♒36 52	13♒49 55	9 50.5	20 33.4	1♈04.9	13 23.2	28 48.8	29 13.7	18 13.1	23 45.0	15 19.7	14 51.9
6 Tu	1 01 20	17 14 37	21 05 23	28 22 41	9 48.0	21 05.3	2 19.1	14 06.2	28 46.8	29 21.2	18 18.1	23 46.8	15 22.0	14 52.9
7 W	1 05 16	18 13 39	5♓41 09	13♓00 02	9 45.0	21 41.3	3 33.3	14 49.2	28 45.2	29 28.5	18 23.2	23 48.7	15 24.3	14 53.9
8 Th	1 09 13	19 12 39	20 18 33	27 35 52	9 42.1	22 21.2	4 47.4	15 32.2	28 44.1	29 35.7	18 28.4	23 50.6	15 26.5	14 54.9
9 F	1 13 09	20 11 37	4♈51 09	12♈03 36	9 39.9	23 04.8	6 01.5	16 15.0	28 43.3	29 42.8	18 33.6	23 52.6	15 28.8	14 55.9
10 Sa	1 17 06	21 10 33	19 12 30	26 17 12	9D38.5	23 52.0	7 15.7	16 57.9	28D43.0	29 49.7	18 39.0	23 54.6	15 31.1	14 56.8
11 Su	1 21 02	22 09 28	3♉17 09	10♉11 55	9 38.1	24 42.6	8 29.8	17 40.7	28 43.2	29 56.4	18 44.3	23 56.7	15 33.3	14 57.7
12 M	1 24 59	23 08 20	17 01 13	23 44 52	9 38.5	25 36.3	9 43.9	18 23.5	28 43.7	0♒03.0	18 49.8	23 58.7	15 35.6	14 58.6
13 Tu	1 28 55	24 07 10	0♊22 48	6♊55 06	9 39.5	26 33.0	10 58.0	19 06.2	28 44.7	0 09.5	18 55.4	24 00.9	15 37.8	14 59.5
14 W	1 32 52	25 05 57	13 21 57	19 43 36	9 40.8	27 32.7	12 12.1	19 48.8	28 46.1	0 15.7	19 01.0	24 03.1	15 40.1	15 00.3
15 Th	1 36 49	26 04 43	26 00 24	2♋12 47	9 42.0	28 35.1	13 26.2	20 31.5	28 48.0	0 21.9	19 06.6	24 05.3	15 42.3	15 01.1
16 F	1 40 45	27 03 26	8♋21 12	14 26 12	9 42.8	29 40.1	14 40.3	21 14.0	28 50.2	0 27.9	19 12.4	24 07.6	15 44.6	15 01.9
17 Sa	1 44 42	28 02 07	20 28 19	26 28 07	9R43.2	0♈47.7	15 54.3	21 56.6	28 52.9	0 33.7	19 18.2	24 09.9	15 46.8	15 02.7
18 Su	1 48 38	29 00 46	2♌26 11	8♌23 05	9 43.0	1 57.7	17 08.4	22 39.0	28 55.9	0 39.3	19 24.1	24 12.2	15 49.0	15 03.4
19 M	1 52 35	29 59 23	14 19 26	20 15 46	9 42.4	3 10.1	18 22.4	23 21.5	28 59.4	0 44.8	19 30.0	24 14.6	15 51.3	15 04.1
20 Tu	1 56 31	0♉57 57	26 12 38	2♍10 34	9 41.4	4 24.7	19 36.4	24 03.8	29 03.3	0 50.2	19 36.0	24 17.0	15 53.5	15 04.8
21 W	2 00 28	1 56 29	8♍10 03	14 11 32	9 40.3	5 41.5	20 50.4	24 46.2	29 07.5	0 55.4	19 42.1	24 19.4	15 55.7	15 05.4
22 Th	2 04 24	2 54 59	20 15 25	26 22 05	9 39.3	7 00.4	22 04.4	25 28.5	29 12.2	1 00.4	19 48.2	24 21.9	15 57.9	15 06.1
23 F	2 08 21	3 53 28	2♎31 51	8♎44 59	9 38.6	8 21.4	23 18.4	26 10.7	29 17.2	1 05.2	19 54.4	24 24.5	16 00.1	15 06.7
24 Sa	2 12 18	4 51 54	15 01 41	21 22 07	9 38.1	9 44.4	24 32.4	26 52.9	29 22.6	1 09.9	20 00.7	24 27.0	16 02.2	15 07.3
25 Su	2 16 14	5 50 18	27 46 22	4♏14 30	9D37.9	11 09.4	25 46.4	27 35.0	29 28.4	1 14.4	20 07.0	24 29.6	16 04.4	15 07.8
26 M	2 20 11	6 48 40	10♏46 30	17 22 19	9 37.9	12 36.4	27 00.3	28 17.1	29 34.6	1 18.7	20 13.3	24 32.3	16 06.6	15 08.3
27 Tu	2 24 07	7 47 01	24 01 51	0♐44 57	9 38.0	14 05.3	28 14.3	28 59.2	29 41.2	1 22.9	20 19.8	24 34.9	16 08.7	15 08.8
28 W	2 28 04	8 45 20	7♐31 27	14 21 09	9R38.1	15 36.2	29 28.2	29 41.2	29 48.1	1 26.9	20 26.2	24 37.6	16 10.8	15 09.3
29 Th	2 32 00	9 43 37	21 13 50	28 09 15	9 38.2	17 08.9	0♉42.2	0♊23.1	29 55.3	1 30.7	20 32.8	24 40.4	16 13.0	15 09.8
30 F	2 35 57	10 41 53	5♑07 08	12♑07 14	9 38.1	18 43.5	1 56.1	1 05.1	0♍02.9	1 34.3	20 39.3	24 43.1	16 15.1	15 10.2

Astro Data Dy Hr Mn	Planet Ingress Dy Hr Mn	Last Aspect Dy Hr Mn	☽ Ingress Dy Hr Mn	Last Aspect Dy Hr Mn	☽ Ingress Dy Hr Mn	☽ Phases & Eclipses Dy Hr Mn
♅ D 1 1:36	☿ ♈ 2 1:20	1 2:33 ♃ □	♏ 1 14:59	2 4:23 ♀ □	♑ 2 9:39	5 1:48 ☾ 15♐03
☿ R 7 16:24	♀ ♓ 11 9:05	3 11:50 ♃ ⚹	♐ 3 22:52	4 12:44 ♀ ⚹	♒ 4 12:56	11 16:26 ● 21♓40
☽0N 11 15:16	☿ ♓R 13 13:48	5 16:05 ♅ ☍	♑ 6 3:47	6 4:25 ♅ △	♓ 6 14:40	18 20:58 ☽ 28♊49
☉0N 20 1:24	♂ ♉ 18 0:37	7 21:12 ♃ ☌	♒ 8 5:44	8 15:19 ♃ ⚹	♈ 8 15:58	27 0:47 ○ 6♎55
☿0S 20 21:03	☉ ♈ 20 1:23	10 3:24 ♀ ☌	♓ 10 5:50	10 18:06 ♃ □	♉ 10 18:21	
☽0S 25 17:33	⚳ ♌R 22 17:10	11 22:37 ♃ ⚹	♈ 12 5:55	12 15:36 ☿ ⚹	♊ 12 23:18	3 10:11 ☾ 14♑13
☿ D 30 14:30		14 3:08 ♂ ☌	♉ 14 8:02	15 4:19 ☿ □	♋ 15 7:42	10 2:41 ● 20♈48
	♀ ♈ 4 14:59	16 9:19 ☿ ⚹	♊ 16 13:43	17 15:26 ☉ □	♌ 17 19:06	17 15:26 ☽ 28♋10
♀0N 7 9:56	♃ ♒ 12 1:00	18 20:58 ☉ □	♋ 18 23:17	19 20:04 ♅ ⚹	♍ 20 7:38	25 15:11 ○ 5♏58
☽0N 8 0:51	☿ ♈ 16 19:09	21 5:27 ♃ ☍	♌ 21 11:25	22 10:09 ♂ △	♎ 22 19:05	25 15:15 • T 1.191
⚳ D 10 16:39	☉ ♉ 19 12:15	23 10:46 ♅ ⚹	♍ 23 23:59	24 18:35 ♀ ☍	♏ 25 4:09	
☿0N 21 23:21	♀ ♉ 28 22:19	26 7:07 ♃ △	♎ 26 11:22	27 8:41 ♂ ☍	♐ 27 10:40	
☽0S 22 1:00	♂ ♊ 28 22:46	28 17:26 ♃ □	♏ 28 20:51	29 5:57 ♅ ☍	♑ 29 15:11	
	⚳ ♍ 30 2:52	31 1:37 ♃ ⚹	♐ 31 4:19			

Astro Data

1 March 2032
Julian Day # 48273
SVP 4♓48'25"
GC 27♐17.3 ⚴ 4♊33.9
Eris 26♈12.7 ⚵ 25♉17.4
⚷ 17♉06.9 ⚶ 4♎52.0R
☽ Mean ☊ 12♏56.7

1 April 2032
Julian Day # 48304
SVP 4♓48'22"
GC 27♐17.4 ⚴ 19♊34.0
Eris 26♈30.4 ⚵ 11♊00.6
⚷ 18♉35.3 ⚶ 27♍24.0R
☽ Mean ☊ 11♏18.2

LONGITUDE — May 2032

Day	Sid.Time	☉	0 hr ☽	Noon ☽	True ☊	☿	♀	♂	⚳	♃	♄	♅	♆	♇
1 Sa	2 39 53	11♉40 07	19♑09 16	26♑12 58	9♏38.0	20♈19.9	3♉10.0	1♊46.9	0♍10.9	1♒37.8	20♊46.0	24♊45.9	16♈17.2	15♒10.6
2 Su	2 43 50	12 38 20	3♒18 01	10♒24 10	9D38.0	21 58.3	4 24.0	2 28.8	0 19.2	1 41.1	20 52.7	24 48.8	16 19.3	15 11.0
3 M	2 47 47	13 36 31	17 31 06	24 38 30	9 38.0	23 38.4	5 37.9	3 10.6	0 27.9	1 44.2	20 59.4	24 51.6	16 21.4	15 11.3
4 Tu	2 51 43	14 34 41	1♓46 02	8♓53 23	9 38.3	25 20.5	6 51.8	3 52.3	0 36.8	1 47.1	21 06.2	24 54.5	16 23.4	15 11.6
5 W	2 55 40	15 32 49	16 00 12	23 06 06	9 38.7	27 04.4	8 05.7	4 34.0	0 46.1	1 49.9	21 13.0	24 57.5	16 25.5	15 11.9
6 Th	2 59 36	16 30 56	0♈10 42	7♈13 37	9 39.3	28 50.2	9 19.6	5 15.7	0 55.8	1 52.4	21 19.9	25 00.4	16 27.5	15 12.2
7 F	3 03 33	17 29 02	14 14 29	21 12 53	9 39.9	0♉37.8	10 33.5	5 57.3	1 05.7	1 54.8	21 26.8	25 03.4	16 29.5	15 12.4
8 Sa	3 07 29	18 27 06	28 08 27	5♉00 50	9R40.2	2 27.4	11 47.4	6 38.9	1 16.0	1 57.0	21 33.7	25 06.4	16 31.5	15 12.6
9 Su	3 11 26	19 25 08	11♉49 43	18 34 49	9 40.1	4 18.8	13 01.3	7 20.4	1 26.6	1 59.0	21 40.8	25 09.4	16 33.5	15 12.8
10 M	3 15 22	20 23 09	25 15 54	1♊52 48	9 39.5	6 12.1	14 15.2	8 01.9	1 37.5	2 00.8	21 47.8	25 12.5	16 35.5	15 12.9
11 Tu	3 19 19	21 21 09	8♊25 24	14 53 40	9 38.4	8 07.2	15 29.0	8 43.4	1 48.7	2 02.5	21 54.9	25 15.6	16 37.4	15 13.1
12 W	3 23 16	22 19 06	21 17 37	27 37 22	9 36.7	10 04.2	16 42.9	9 24.8	2 00.3	2 03.9	22 02.0	25 18.7	16 39.4	15 13.2
13 Th	3 27 12	23 17 02	3♋53 04	10♋04 58	9 34.8	12 03.0	17 56.7	10 06.2	2 12.1	2 05.2	22 09.2	25 21.8	16 41.3	15 13.2
14 F	3 31 09	24 14 56	16 13 21	22 18 37	9 33.0	14 03.6	19 10.6	10 47.5	2 24.2	2 06.2	22 16.4	25 25.0	16 43.2	15 13.3
15 Sa	3 35 05	25 12 49	28 21 08	4♌21 23	9 31.4	16 05.9	20 24.4	11 28.8	2 36.5	2 07.1	22 23.6	25 28.2	16 45.1	15R13.3
16 Su	3 39 02	26 10 40	10♌19 52	16 17 06	9D30.3	18 09.9	21 38.2	12 10.0	2 49.2	2 07.8	22 30.9	25 31.4	16 46.9	15 13.3
17 M	3 42 58	27 08 29	22 13 39	28 10 06	9 30.0	20 15.4	22 52.1	12 51.2	3 02.1	2 08.3	22 38.2	25 34.6	16 48.8	15 13.2
18 Tu	3 46 55	28 06 16	4♍07 01	10♍05 00	9 30.5	22 22.4	24 05.9	13 32.4	3 15.3	2 08.6	22 45.5	25 37.9	16 50.6	15 13.2
19 W	3 50 51	29 04 02	16 04 39	22 06 30	9 31.6	24 30.6	25 19.7	14 13.5	3 28.8	2R08.7	22 52.9	25 41.2	16 52.4	15 13.1
20 Th	3 54 48	0♊01 46	28 11 09	4♎19 05	9 33.1	26 40.0	26 33.5	14 54.5	3 42.5	2 08.6	23 00.3	25 44.4	16 54.2	15 13.0
21 F	3 58 44	0 59 28	10♎30 47	16 46 42	9 34.6	28 50.3	27 47.2	15 35.5	3 56.5	2 08.4	23 07.7	25 47.7	16 55.9	15 12.8
22 Sa	4 02 41	1 57 09	23 07 11	29 32 33	9R35.6	1♊01.4	29 01.0	16 16.5	4 10.7	2 07.9	23 15.2	25 51.1	16 57.7	15 12.7
23 Su	4 06 38	2 54 48	6♏03 00	12♏38 39	9 35.9	3 12.9	0♊14.8	16 57.5	4 25.2	2 07.3	23 22.7	25 54.4	16 59.4	15 12.5
24 M	4 10 34	3 52 27	19 19 32	26 05 33	9 35.1	5 24.6	1 28.5	17 38.4	4 39.9	2 06.5	23 30.2	25 57.8	17 01.1	15 12.2
25 Tu	4 14 31	4 50 03	2♐56 32	9♐52 10	9 33.1	7 36.3	2 42.3	18 19.2	4 54.9	2 05.4	23 37.7	26 01.2	17 02.8	15 12.0
26 W	4 18 27	5 47 39	16 52 03	23 55 41	9 30.0	9 47.7	3 56.1	19 00.0	5 10.1	2 04.2	23 45.3	26 04.6	17 04.4	15 11.7
27 Th	4 22 24	6 45 14	1♑02 31	8♑11 54	9 26.3	11 58.5	5 09.8	19 40.8	5 25.5	2 02.9	23 52.9	26 08.0	17 06.0	15 11.4
28 F	4 26 20	7 42 48	15 23 10	22 35 40	9 22.4	14 08.4	6 23.6	20 21.6	5 41.1	2 01.3	24 00.5	26 11.4	17 07.6	15 11.1
29 Sa	4 30 17	8 40 20	29 48 43	7♒01 40	9 19.0	16 17.2	7 37.3	21 02.3	5 57.0	1 59.5	24 08.1	26 14.8	17 09.2	15 10.8
30 Su	4 34 14	9 37 52	14♒13 58	21 25 05	9 16.6	18 24.6	8 51.1	21 42.9	6 13.1	1 57.6	24 15.7	26 18.3	17 10.8	15 10.4
31 M	4 38 10	10 35 23	28 34 33	5♓42 01	9D15.4	20 30.4	10 04.8	22 23.5	6 29.4	1 55.4	24 23.4	26 21.8	17 12.3	15 10.0

LONGITUDE — June 2032

Day	Sid.Time	☉	0 hr ☽	Noon ☽	True ☊	☿	♀	♂	⚳	♃	♄	♅	♆	♇
1 Tu	4 42 07	11♊32 53	12♓47 12	19♓49 52	9♏15.6	22♊34.5	11♊18.6	23♊04.1	6♍45.9	1♒53.1	24♊31.1	26♊25.2	17♈13.8	15♒09.6
2 W	4 46 03	12 30 23	26 49 50	3♈47 02	9 16.7	24 36.6	12 32.3	23 44.7	7 02.6	1R50.6	24 38.8	26 28.7	17 15.3	15R09.1
3 Th	4 50 00	13 27 51	10♈41 21	17 32 47	9 18.1	26 36.6	13 46.1	24 25.2	7 19.5	1 47.9	24 46.5	26 32.2	17 16.8	15 08.7
4 F	4 53 56	14 25 19	24 21 16	1♉06 48	9R19.3	28 34.4	14 59.8	25 05.7	7 36.6	1 45.0	24 54.2	26 35.7	17 18.2	15 08.2
5 Sa	4 57 53	15 22 47	7♉49 21	14 28 54	9 19.4	0♋29.9	16 13.5	25 46.1	7 53.9	1 42.0	25 01.9	26 39.3	17 19.6	15 07.6
6 Su	5 01 49	16 20 13	21 05 26	27 38 54	9 18.0	2 23.0	17 27.3	26 26.6	8 11.4	1 38.7	25 09.7	26 42.8	17 21.0	15 07.1
7 M	5 05 46	17 17 39	4♊09 16	10♊36 29	9 14.8	4 13.6	18 41.0	27 06.9	8 29.1	1 35.3	25 17.5	26 46.3	17 22.4	15 06.5
8 Tu	5 09 43	18 15 04	17 00 33	23 21 27	9 09.7	6 01.8	19 54.8	27 47.3	8 47.0	1 31.8	25 25.2	26 49.9	17 23.7	15 05.9
9 W	5 13 39	19 12 28	29 39 11	5♋53 48	9 03.3	7 47.4	21 08.5	28 27.6	9 05.1	1 28.0	25 33.0	26 53.4	17 25.0	15 05.3
10 Th	5 17 36	20 09 52	12♋05 23	18 14 04	8 56.0	9 30.4	22 22.3	29 07.8	9 23.3	1 24.1	25 40.8	26 57.0	17 26.3	15 04.7
11 F	5 21 32	21 07 14	24 19 59	0♌23 24	8 48.7	11 10.9	23 36.0	29 48.1	9 41.8	1 20.0	25 48.6	27 00.5	17 27.5	15 04.0
12 Sa	5 25 29	22 04 35	6♌24 33	12 23 47	8 42.0	12 48.7	24 49.7	0♋28.3	10 00.4	1 15.7	25 56.4	27 04.1	17 28.7	15 03.3
13 Su	5 29 25	23 01 56	18 21 28	24 18 01	8 36.6	14 23.9	26 03.4	1 08.4	10 19.1	1 11.3	26 04.2	27 07.7	17 29.9	15 02.6
14 M	5 33 22	23 59 15	0♍13 56	6♍09 42	8 33.0	15 56.5	27 17.2	1 48.5	10 38.1	1 06.7	26 12.0	27 11.2	17 31.1	15 01.9
15 Tu	5 37 18	24 56 34	12 05 54	18 03 05	8D31.2	17 26.4	28 30.9	2 28.6	10 57.2	1 02.0	26 19.9	27 14.8	17 32.2	15 01.1
16 W	5 41 15	25 53 52	24 01 52	0♎02 53	8 31.0	18 53.5	29 44.6	3 08.7	11 16.4	0 57.0	26 27.7	27 18.4	17 33.3	15 00.4
17 Th	5 45 12	26 51 09	6♎06 44	12 14 05	8 31.9	20 18.0	0♋58.3	3 48.7	11 35.9	0 52.0	26 35.5	27 22.0	17 34.4	14 59.6
18 F	5 49 08	27 48 25	18 25 30	24 41 36	8 33.1	21 39.7	2 12.0	4 28.7	11 55.4	0 46.8	26 43.3	27 25.5	17 35.4	14 58.7
19 Sa	5 53 05	28 45 40	1♏02 53	7♏29 50	8R33.7	22 58.6	3 25.7	5 08.6	12 15.2	0 41.5	26 51.1	27 29.1	17 36.4	14 57.9
20 Su	5 57 01	29 42 55	14 02 51	20 42 11	8 33.1	24 14.6	4 39.4	5 48.5	12 35.0	0 36.0	26 58.9	27 32.7	17 37.4	14 57.1
21 M	6 00 58	0♋40 09	27 28 02	4♐20 23	8 30.4	25 27.8	5 53.1	6 28.4	12 55.1	0 30.3	27 06.7	27 36.3	17 38.4	14 56.2
22 Tu	6 04 54	1 37 22	11♐19 06	18 23 53	8 25.7	26 38.0	7 06.8	7 08.2	13 15.2	0 24.6	27 14.5	27 39.9	17 39.3	14 55.3
23 W	6 08 51	2 34 35	25 34 14	2♑49 31	8 19.0	27 45.2	8 20.5	7 48.0	13 35.5	0 18.7	27 22.3	27 43.4	17 40.2	14 54.4
24 Th	6 12 47	3 31 48	10♑08 54	17 31 27	8 11.0	28 49.3	9 34.2	8 27.8	13 56.0	0 12.7	27 30.1	27 47.0	17 41.1	14 53.4
25 F	6 16 44	4 29 01	24 56 11	2♒21 58	8 02.6	29 50.2	10 47.9	9 07.5	14 16.6	0 06.5	27 37.9	27 50.6	17 41.9	14 52.5
26 Sa	6 20 41	5 26 13	9♒47 47	17 12 34	7 55.0	0♌47.9	12 01.6	9 47.3	14 37.3	0 00.3	27 45.7	27 54.1	17 42.7	14 51.5
27 Su	6 24 37	6 23 25	24 35 22	1♓55 23	7 48.9	1 42.3	13 15.3	10 26.9	14 58.1	29♑53.9	27 53.4	27 57.7	17 43.5	14 50.5
28 M	6 28 34	7 20 37	9♓11 55	16 24 26	7 45.0	2 33.1	14 29.1	11 06.6	15 19.1	29 47.4	28 01.2	28 01.2	17 44.2	14 49.5
29 Tu	6 32 30	8 17 49	23 32 34	0♈36 04	7D43.2	3 20.5	15 42.8	11 46.2	15 40.1	29 40.8	28 08.9	28 04.8	17 44.9	14 48.5
30 W	6 36 27	9 15 02	7♈34 52	14 28 57	7 43.1	4 04.1	16 56.5	12 25.8	16 01.4	29 34.0	28 16.7	28 08.3	17 45.6	14 47.5

Astro Data (Dy Hr Mn)

Astro Data	Dy Hr Mn
☽0N	5 8:01
♇R	15 15:55
☽0S	19 9:26
♃R	19 14:49
☽0N	1 13:56
☽0S	15 18:21
♄☌♅	28 12:05
☽0N	28 20:29

Planet Ingress (Dy Hr Mn)

Planet Ingress	Dy Hr Mn
☿ ♉	7 3:37
☉ ♊	20 11:16
☿ ♊	22 0:46
♀ ♊	23 7:11
☿ ♋	5 5:45
♂ ♋	11 19:07
♀ ♋	16 17:01
☉ ♋	20 19:10
☿ ♌	25 15:58
♃ ♑R	26 12:58

Last Aspect / ☽ Ingress (May)

Last Aspect Dy Hr Mn		☽ Ingress Dy Hr Mn
1 0:43	♅ □	♒ 1 18:25
3 12:22	♅ △	♓ 3 21:01
5 15:09	♅ □	♈ 5 23:42
7 18:40	♅ ⚹	♉ 8 3:14
9 13:37	☉ ☌	♊ 10 8:35
12 7:35	♅ ☌	♋ 12 16:32
14 16:11	☉ ⚹	♌ 15 3:17
17 9:45	☉ □	♍ 17 15:42
20 2:54	☉ △	♎ 20 3:34
22 5:06	♅ △	♏ 22 12:51
23 16:37	♇ □	♐ 24 18:52
26 15:39	♅ ☍	♑ 26 22:15
28 2:53	♆ □	♒ 29 0:19
30 20:13	♅ △	♓ 31 2:24

Last Aspect / ☽ Ingress (June)

Last Aspect Dy Hr Mn		☽ Ingress Dy Hr Mn
1 23:21	♅ □	♈ 2 5:28
4 6:43	☿ ⚹	♉ 4 10:01
5 13:10	♇ □	♊ 6 16:20
8 20:55	♂ ☌	♋ 9 0:40
10 10:26	♆ □	♌ 11 11:14
13 17:45	♅ ⚹	♍ 13 23:32
16 11:20	♀ □	♎ 16 11:54
18 18:23	☉ △	♏ 18 22:02
20 18:56	☿ △	♐ 21 4:27
23 3:32	♅ ☍	♑ 23 7:20
25 7:37	☿ ☍	♒ 25 8:11
27 5:29	♅ △	♓ 27 8:51
29 10:26	♃ ⚹	♈ 29 10:58

☽ Phases & Eclipses (Dy Hr Mn)

Dy Hr Mn	Phase
2 16:03	☾ 12♒48
9 13:37	● 19♉29
9 13:26:43	A 00'22"
17 9:45	☽ 27♌03
25 2:38	○ 4♐28
31 20:52	☾ 10♓57
8 1:33	● 17♊50
16 3:01	☽ 25♍32
23 11:34	○ 2♑34
30 2:13	☾ 8♈52

Astro Data

1 May 2032
Julian Day # 48334
SVP 4♓48'19"
GC 27♐17.5 ⚴ 5♋37.2
Eris 26♈50.0 ⚵ 26♊49.6
⚷ 20♉29.8 ⚶ 23♍01.9R
☽ Mean ☊ 9♏42.9

1 June 2032
Julian Day # 48365
SVP 4♓48'15"
GC 27♐17.5 ⚴ 22♋34.4
Eris 27♈07.8 ⚵ 13♋09.5
⚷ 22♉35.8 ⚶ 25♍48.1
☽ Mean ☊ 8♏04.4

July 2032 LONGITUDE

Day	Sid.Time	☉	0 hr ☽	Noon ☽	True☊	☿	♀	♂	⚳	♃	♄	♅	♆	♇
1 Th	6 40 23	10♋12 14	21♈18 26	28♈03 29	7♏43.7	4♌44.0	18♋10.2	13♋05.4	16♍22.7	29♑27.2	28♊24.4	28♊11.8	17♈46.2	14♒46.4
2 F	6 44 20	11 09 27	4♉44 19	11♉21 11	7R 43.9	5 19.9	19 23.9	13 44.9	16 44.2	29R 20.3	28 32.1	28 15.3	17 46.8	14R 45.3
3 Sa	6 48 16	12 06 40	17 54 19	24 23 59	7 42.6	5 51.9	20 37.6	14 24.4	17 05.7	29 13.3	28 39.8	28 18.8	17 47.4	14 44.2
4 Su	6 52 13	13 03 53	0♊50 25	7♊13 49	7 39.1	6 19.6	21 51.3	15 03.9	17 27.4	29 06.2	28 47.5	28 22.3	17 48.0	14 43.1
5 M	6 56 10	14 01 06	13 34 21	19 52 12	7 33.0	6 43.1	23 05.1	15 43.3	17 49.2	28 59.1	28 55.1	28 25.8	17 48.5	14 42.0
6 Tu	7 00 06	14 58 20	26 07 30	2♋20 21	7 24.2	7 02.1	24 18.8	16 22.8	18 11.2	28 51.8	29 02.7	28 29.3	17 49.0	14 40.9
7 W	7 04 03	15 55 33	8♋30 51	14 39 07	7 13.3	7 16.7	25 32.5	17 02.2	18 33.2	28 44.5	29 10.4	28 32.8	17 49.4	14 39.7
8 Th	7 07 59	16 52 47	20 45 12	26 49 14	7 01.1	7 26.6	26 46.2	17 41.5	18 55.4	28 37.1	29 18.0	28 36.2	17 49.9	14 38.6
9 F	7 11 56	17 50 01	2♌51 21	8♌51 40	6 48.6	7R 31.8	28 00.0	18 20.9	19 17.6	28 29.7	29 25.5	28 39.6	17 50.2	14 37.4
10 Sa	7 15 52	18 47 14	14 50 23	20 47 43	6 36.8	7 32.3	29 13.7	19 00.2	19 40.0	28 22.1	29 33.1	28 43.1	17 50.6	14 36.2
11 Su	7 19 49	19 44 28	26 43 57	2♍39 23	6 26.8	7 28.1	0♌27.4	19 39.4	20 02.4	28 14.6	29 40.6	28 46.5	17 50.9	14 35.0
12 M	7 23 45	20 41 42	8♍34 22	14 29 20	6 19.2	7 19.1	1 41.1	20 18.7	20 25.0	28 07.0	29 48.1	28 49.9	17 51.2	14 33.8
13 Tu	7 27 42	21 38 55	20 24 44	26 21 05	6 14.2	7 05.5	2 54.8	20 57.9	20 47.6	27 59.4	29 55.6	28 53.2	17 51.5	14 32.6
14 W	7 31 39	22 36 09	2♎18 56	8♎18 52	6 11.7	6 47.4	4 08.5	21 37.1	21 10.4	27 51.7	0♋03.0	28 56.6	17 51.7	14 31.3
15 Th	7 35 35	23 33 23	14 21 30	20 27 29	6D 10.9	6 24.9	5 22.3	22 16.3	21 33.2	27 44.0	0 10.4	28 59.9	17 51.9	14 30.1
16 F	7 39 32	24 30 37	26 37 38	2♏52 05	6R 10.9	5 58.3	6 36.0	22 55.4	21 56.2	27 36.3	0 17.8	29 03.2	17 52.0	14 28.8
17 Sa	7 43 28	25 27 51	9♏11 58	15 37 44	6 10.7	5 27.9	7 49.7	23 34.5	22 19.2	27 28.6	0 25.2	29 06.5	17 52.1	14 27.6
18 Su	7 47 25	26 25 05	22 09 53	28 48 53	6 09.2	4 54.2	9 03.4	24 13.6	22 42.3	27 20.8	0 32.5	29 09.8	17 52.2	14 26.3
19 M	7 51 21	27 22 20	5♐35 02	12♐28 33	6 05.5	4 17.6	10 17.1	24 52.7	23 05.5	27 13.1	0 39.8	29 13.1	17 52.3	14 25.0
20 Tu	7 55 18	28 19 34	19 29 27	26 37 32	5 59.2	3 38.7	11 30.8	25 31.7	23 28.8	27 05.3	0 47.0	29 16.3	17R 52.3	14 23.7
21 W	7 59 14	29 16 49	3♑52 25	11♑13 29	5 50.6	2 58.0	12 44.4	26 10.7	23 52.2	26 57.6	0 54.2	29 19.6	17 52.3	14 22.4
22 Th	8 03 11	0♌14 05	18 39 54	26 10 37	5 40.3	2 16.3	13 58.1	26 49.7	24 15.6	26 49.9	1 01.4	29 22.8	17 52.3	14 21.1
23 F	8 07 08	1 11 21	3♒44 28	11♒20 07	5 29.5	1 34.2	15 11.8	27 28.6	24 39.2	26 42.2	1 08.6	29 25.9	17 52.2	14 19.8
24 Sa	8 11 04	2 08 37	18 56 12	26 31 22	5 19.4	0 52.6	16 25.5	28 07.5	25 02.8	26 34.5	1 15.7	29 29.1	17 52.1	14 18.5
25 Su	8 15 01	3 05 55	4♓04 21	11♓33 59	5 11.2	0 12.1	17 39.2	28 46.5	25 26.4	26 26.8	1 22.8	29 32.2	17 52.0	14 17.2
26 M	8 18 57	4 03 13	18 59 17	26 19 29	5 05.5	29♋33.5	18 52.8	29 25.3	25 50.2	26 19.2	1 29.8	29 35.3	17 51.8	14 15.8
27 Tu	8 22 54	5 00 32	3♈34 01	10♈42 29	5 02.3	28 57.5	20 06.5	0♌04.2	26 14.0	26 11.6	1 36.8	29 38.4	17 51.6	14 14.5
28 W	8 26 50	5 57 52	17 44 44	24 40 46	5 01.2	28 24.8	21 20.2	0 43.0	26 37.9	26 04.0	1 43.7	29 41.5	17 51.4	14 13.1
29 Th	8 30 47	6 55 13	1♉30 41	8♉14 45	5 01.1	27 56.1	22 33.9	1 21.9	27 01.9	25 56.5	1 50.6	29 44.5	17 51.1	14 11.8
30 F	8 34 43	7 52 35	14 53 17	21 26 39	5 00.8	27 31.9	23 47.5	2 00.7	27 26.0	25 49.1	1 57.5	29 47.5	17 50.8	14 10.4
31 Sa	8 38 40	8 49 59	27 55 18	4♊19 37	4 59.0	27 12.8	25 01.2	2 39.4	27 50.1	25 41.7	2 04.3	29 50.5	17 50.5	14 09.1

August 2032 LONGITUDE

Day	Sid.Time	☉	0 hr ☽	Noon ☽	True☊	☿	♀	♂	⚳	♃	♄	♅	♆	♇
1 Su	8 42 37	9♌47 23	10♊40 02	16♊56 57	4♏55.0	26♋59.1	26♌14.9	3♌18.2	28♍14.3	25♑34.3	2♋11.1	29♊53.4	17♈50.1	14♒07.7
2 M	8 46 33	10 44 49	23 10 46	29 21 47	4R 48.2	26D 51.2	27 28.5	3 56.9	28 38.6	25R 27.1	2 17.8	29 56.3	17R 49.7	14R 06.4
3 Tu	8 50 30	11 42 15	5♋30 21	11♋36 42	4 38.6	26 49.4	28 42.2	4 35.6	29 02.9	25 19.9	2 24.5	29 59.2	17 49.3	14 05.0
4 W	8 54 26	12 39 43	17 41 07	23 43 47	4 26.6	26 53.9	29 55.9	5 14.3	29 27.3	25 12.8	2 31.1	0♋02.1	17 48.8	14 03.6
5 Th	8 58 23	13 37 12	29 44 53	5♌44 35	4 13.2	27 05.0	1♍09.5	5 53.0	29 51.8	25 05.8	2 37.7	0 04.9	17 48.4	14 02.3
6 F	9 02 19	14 34 41	11♌43 04	17 40 28	3 59.5	27 22.6	2 23.2	6 31.7	0♎16.3	24 58.9	2 44.2	0 07.7	17 47.8	14 00.9
7 Sa	9 06 16	15 32 12	23 36 58	29 32 43	3 46.6	27 47.0	3 36.8	7 10.3	0 40.9	24 52.0	2 50.7	0 10.5	17 47.3	13 59.6
8 Su	9 10 12	16 29 43	5♍27 57	11♍22 53	3 35.5	28 18.0	4 50.5	7 48.9	1 05.6	24 45.3	2 57.1	0 13.2	17 46.7	13 58.2
9 M	9 14 09	17 27 16	17 17 47	23 12 58	3 26.9	28 55.7	6 04.1	8 27.5	1 30.3	24 38.7	3 03.5	0 15.9	17 46.1	13 56.8
10 Tu	9 18 06	18 24 49	29 08 46	5♎05 36	3 21.1	29 40.0	7 17.7	9 06.1	1 55.0	24 32.2	3 09.8	0 18.6	17 45.5	13 55.5
11 W	9 22 02	19 22 24	11♎03 53	17 04 08	3 17.9	0♌30.9	8 31.3	9 44.6	2 19.9	24 25.8	3 16.0	0 21.2	17 44.8	13 54.1
12 Th	9 25 59	20 19 59	23 06 52	29 12 38	3D 16.8	1 28.1	9 44.9	10 23.1	2 44.8	24 19.5	3 22.2	0 23.8	17 44.1	13 52.7
13 F	9 29 55	21 17 35	5♏22 02	11♏35 40	3R 16.9	2 31.5	10 58.5	11 01.6	3 09.7	24 13.3	3 28.3	0 26.4	17 43.4	13 51.4
14 Sa	9 33 52	22 15 13	17 54 09	24 18 06	3 17.0	3 40.9	12 12.1	11 40.1	3 34.7	24 07.3	3 34.4	0 28.9	17 42.6	13 50.0
15 Su	9 37 48	23 12 51	0♐48 04	7♐24 33	3 16.2	4 56.2	13 25.7	12 18.6	3 59.7	24 01.4	3 40.4	0 31.4	17 41.8	13 48.7
16 M	9 41 45	24 10 30	14 08 01	20 58 45	3 13.5	6 17.0	14 39.3	12 57.0	4 24.8	23 55.6	3 46.3	0 33.9	17 41.0	13 47.4
17 Tu	9 45 41	25 08 10	27 56 56	5♑02 35	3 08.6	7 43.0	15 52.8	13 35.4	4 49.9	23 50.0	3 52.2	0 36.3	17 40.2	13 46.0
18 W	9 49 38	26 05 52	12♑15 28	19 35 11	3 01.3	9 13.9	17 06.4	14 13.8	5 15.1	23 44.5	3 58.0	0 38.7	17 39.3	13 44.7
19 Th	9 53 35	27 03 34	27 01 04	4♒32 12	2 52.5	10 49.3	18 19.9	14 52.2	5 40.3	23 39.2	4 03.8	0 41.0	17 38.4	13 43.4
20 F	9 57 31	28 01 18	12♒07 31	19 45 45	2 43.0	12 28.9	19 33.4	15 30.6	6 05.6	23 34.0	4 09.4	0 43.3	17 37.5	13 42.1
21 Sa	10 01 28	28 59 02	27 25 28	5♓05 16	2 34.1	14 12.2	20 46.9	16 08.9	6 30.9	23 29.0	4 15.1	0 45.6	17 36.5	13 40.8
22 Su	10 05 24	29 56 49	12♓43 41	20 19 24	2 26.8	15 58.8	22 00.4	16 47.3	6 56.3	23 24.1	4 20.6	0 47.8	17 35.6	13 39.5
23 M	10 09 21	0♍54 36	27 51 10	5♈17 57	2 21.8	17 48.3	23 13.9	17 25.6	7 21.7	23 19.4	4 26.1	0 50.0	17 34.5	13 38.2
24 Tu	10 13 17	1 52 26	12♈38 57	19 53 34	2D 19.3	19 40.2	24 27.4	18 03.9	7 47.2	23 14.8	4 31.5	0 52.1	17 33.5	13 36.9
25 W	10 17 14	2 50 17	27 01 23	4♉02 15	2 18.7	21 34.1	25 40.9	18 42.1	8 12.6	23 10.4	4 36.8	0 54.2	17 32.5	13 35.6
26 Th	10 21 10	3 48 10	10♉56 10	17 43 17	2 19.2	23 29.6	26 54.3	19 20.4	8 38.2	23 06.1	4 42.1	0 56.3	17 31.4	13 34.3
27 F	10 25 07	4 46 05	24 23 52	0♊58 18	2R 19.9	25 26.4	28 07.8	19 58.7	9 03.8	23 02.1	4 47.3	0 58.3	17 30.3	13 33.1
28 Sa	10 29 04	5 44 02	7♊27 02	13 50 32	2 19.6	27 23.9	29 21.2	20 36.9	9 29.4	22 58.2	4 52.4	1 00.3	17 29.2	13 31.8
29 Su	10 33 00	6 42 00	20 09 18	26 23 53	2 17.6	29 22.0	0♎34.6	21 15.1	9 55.0	22 54.4	4 57.4	1 02.2	17 28.0	13 30.6
30 M	10 36 57	7 40 01	2♋34 44	8♋42 23	2 13.4	1♍20.4	1 48.1	21 53.3	10 20.7	22 50.9	5 02.4	1 04.1	17 26.8	13 29.4
31 Tu	10 40 53	8 38 03	14 47 16	20 49 50	2 07.0	3 18.7	3 01.5	22 31.5	10 46.5	22 47.5	5 07.2	1 06.0	17 25.6	13 28.2

Astro Data	Dy Hr Mn
♃⊼♄	5 18:22
♃⊼♅	8 13:59
☿ R	10 2:34
♄⚼♇	10 20:38
☽ 0S	13 2:49
♆ R	20 20:44
♅⚼♇	22 3:14
☽ 0N	26 4:58
☿ D	3 6:53
☽ 0S	9 10:11
☽ 0N	22 15:22
♀ 0S	30 23:29

Planet Ingress		Dy Hr Mn
♀	♌	11 3:05
♄	♋	14 2:17
☉	♌	22 6:06
☿	♋R	25 19:21
♂	♌	27 9:25
♅	♋	3 18:21
♀	♍	4 13:21
⚳	♎	5 20:02
☿	♌	10 21:48
☉	♍	22 13:19
♀	♎	29 0:41
☿	♍	29 19:42

Last Aspect Dy Hr Mn		☽ Ingress	Dy Hr Mn
1 14:29	♃ □	♉	1 15:29
3 20:54	♃ △	♊	3 22:26
6 5:34	♄ ☌	♋	6 7:28
8 15:32	♃ ☍	♌	8 18:19
11 5:54	♄ ⚹	♍	11 6:37
13 19:17	♄ □	♎	13 19:21
16 4:39	♅ △	♏	16 6:30
18 9:24	♃ ⚹	♐	18 14:07
20 16:25	♅ ☍	♑	20 17:37
22 13:05	♂ ☍	♒	22 18:04
24 16:43	♅ △	♓	24 17:31
26 17:25	♅ □	♈	26 18:04
28 20:49	♅ ⚹	♉	28 21:20
30 22:59	☿ ⚹	♊	31 3:53

Last Aspect Dy Hr Mn		☽ Ingress	Dy Hr Mn
2 13:08	♅ ☌	♋	2 13:14
4 18:23	☿ ☌	♌	5 0:30
6 12:15	♆ △	♍	7 12:55
10 0:18	☿ ⚹	♎	10 1:44
12 2:28	♃ □	♏	12 13:33
14 11:40	♃ ⚹	♐	14 22:32
16 17:56	☉ △	♑	17 3:29
18 18:41	♃ ☌	♒	19 4:46
21 1:48	☉ ☍	♓	21 4:02
22 16:52	♃ ⚹	♈	23 3:27
24 17:36	♃ □	♉	25 5:04
27 6:15	♀ △	♊	27 10:13
29 18:51	☿ ⚹	♋	29 18:59

☽ Phases & Eclipses Dy Hr Mn		
7 14:43	●	16♋02
15 18:33	☽	23♎49
22 18:53	○	0♒30
29 9:27	☾	6♉49
6 5:13	●	14♌18
14 7:52	☽	22♏05
21 1:48	○	28♒34
27 19:35	☾	5♊04

Astro Data

1 July 2032
Julian Day # 48395
SVP 4♓48'10"
GC 27♐17.6 ⚴ 8♌45.2
Eris 27♈18.7 ⚵ 28♋37.0
⚷ 24♉23.8 ⚶ 4♎00.9
☽ Mean ☊ 6♏29.1

1 August 2032
Julian Day # 48426
SVP 4♓48'05"
GC 27♐17.7 ⚴ 24♌59.3
Eris 27♈20.8R ⚵ 14♌01.8
⚷ 25♉40.8 ⚶ 15♎59.8
☽ Mean ☊ 4♏50.6

LONGITUDE September 2032

Day	Sid.Time	☉	0 hr ☽	Noon ☽	True ☊	☿	♀	♂	⚳	♃	♄	♅	♆	♇
1 W	10 44 50	9♍36 07	26♋50 27	2♌49 29	1♏58.6	5♍16.7	4♎14.9	23♌09.7	11♎12.2	22♑44.3	5♋12.0	1♋07.8	17♈24.4	13♒27.0
2 Th	10 48 46	10 34 12	8♌47 17	14 44 06	1R49.1	7 14.4	5 28.3	23 47.9	11 38.0	22R41.3	5 16.8	1 09.5	17R23.2	13R25.8
3 F	10 52 43	11 32 20	20 40 13	26 35 52	1 39.2	9 11.4	6 41.6	24 26.0	12 03.9	22 38.4	5 21.4	1 11.2	17 21.9	13 24.6
4 Sa	10 56 39	12 30 29	2♍31 17	8♍26 40	1 30.0	11 07.7	7 55.0	25 04.1	12 29.8	22 35.8	5 25.9	1 12.9	17 20.6	13 23.5
5 Su	11 00 36	13 28 40	14 22 13	20 18 08	1 22.1	13 03.2	9 08.3	25 42.3	12 55.7	22 33.3	5 30.4	1 14.5	17 19.3	13 22.3
6 M	11 04 32	14 26 53	26 14 39	2♎11 59	1 16.1	14 57.7	10 21.7	26 20.4	13 21.6	22 31.0	5 34.8	1 16.1	17 18.0	13 21.2
7 Tu	11 08 29	15 25 07	8♎10 24	14 10 10	1 12.4	16 51.3	11 35.0	26 58.4	13 47.6	22 28.9	5 39.1	1 17.6	17 16.6	13 20.1
8 W	11 12 26	16 23 23	20 11 37	26 15 04	1D10.8	18 43.8	12 48.3	27 36.5	14 13.6	22 27.0	5 43.3	1 19.1	17 15.3	13 19.0
9 Th	11 16 22	17 21 41	2♏20 54	8♏29 32	1 10.9	20 35.3	14 01.6	28 14.6	14 39.6	22 25.3	5 47.4	1 20.5	17 13.9	13 17.9
10 F	11 20 19	18 20 00	14 41 23	20 56 57	1 12.1	22 25.7	15 14.9	28 52.6	15 05.7	22 23.8	5 51.5	1 21.9	17 12.5	13 16.8
11 Sa	11 24 15	19 18 21	27 16 40	3♐41 02	1 13.5	24 15.0	16 28.1	29 30.6	15 31.7	22 22.5	5 55.4	1 23.2	17 11.1	13 15.7
12 Su	11 28 12	20 16 43	10♐10 31	16 45 33	1R14.4	26 03.2	17 41.4	0♍08.6	15 57.8	22 21.4	5 59.3	1 24.5	17 09.6	13 14.7
13 M	11 32 08	21 15 07	23 26 32	0♑13 47	1 14.0	27 50.3	18 54.6	0 46.6	16 24.0	22 20.4	6 03.0	1 25.7	17 08.2	13 13.7
14 Tu	11 36 05	22 13 32	7♑07 32	14 07 51	1 12.1	29 36.2	20 07.8	1 24.6	16 50.1	22 19.7	6 06.7	1 26.9	17 06.7	13 12.7
15 W	11 40 01	23 11 59	21 14 43	28 27 54	1 08.7	1♎21.1	21 21.0	2 02.5	17 16.3	22 19.1	6 10.3	1 28.1	17 05.2	13 11.7
16 Th	11 43 58	24 10 28	5♒46 58	13♒11 21	1 04.0	3 04.9	22 34.2	2 40.5	17 42.5	22 18.8	6 13.7	1 29.1	17 03.7	13 10.8
17 F	11 47 55	25 08 58	20 40 13	28 12 37	0 58.7	4 47.6	23 47.3	3 18.4	18 08.8	22D18.6	6 17.1	1 30.2	17 02.2	13 09.8
18 Sa	11 51 51	26 07 30	5♓47 24	13♓23 21	0 53.7	6 29.2	25 00.4	3 56.3	18 35.0	22 18.7	6 20.4	1 31.2	17 00.7	13 08.9
19 Su	11 55 48	27 06 04	20 59 11	28 33 36	0 49.7	8 09.9	26 13.5	4 34.2	19 01.3	22 18.9	6 23.6	1 32.1	16 59.1	13 08.0
20 M	11 59 44	28 04 40	6♈05 24	13♈33 27	0 47.1	9 49.5	27 26.6	5 12.1	19 27.5	22 19.3	6 26.7	1 33.0	16 57.6	13 07.1
21 Tu	12 03 41	29 03 17	20 56 45	28 14 32	0D46.1	11 28.1	28 39.6	5 50.0	19 53.8	22 19.9	6 29.7	1 33.8	16 56.0	13 06.2
22 W	12 07 37	0♎01 57	5♉26 08	12♉31 10	0 46.5	13 05.7	29 52.7	6 27.9	20 20.2	22 20.7	6 32.6	1 34.6	16 54.4	13 05.4
23 Th	12 11 34	1 00 40	19 29 23	26 20 42	0 47.8	14 42.3	1♏05.7	7 05.7	20 46.5	22 21.7	6 35.4	1 35.3	16 52.8	13 04.5
24 F	12 15 30	1 59 24	3♊05 14	9♊43 10	0 49.4	16 18.0	2 18.7	7 43.6	21 12.9	22 22.9	6 38.1	1 36.0	16 51.3	13 03.7
25 Sa	12 19 27	2 58 11	16 14 49	22 40 37	0R50.6	17 52.8	3 31.7	8 21.4	21 39.2	22 24.3	6 40.7	1 36.6	16 49.6	13 03.0
26 Su	12 23 24	3 57 00	29 01 02	5♋16 33	0 51.0	19 26.6	4 44.7	8 59.2	22 05.6	22 25.9	6 43.2	1 37.2	16 48.0	13 02.2
27 M	12 27 20	4 55 51	11♋27 44	17 35 07	0 50.3	20 59.6	5 57.6	9 37.0	22 32.1	22 27.6	6 45.6	1 37.7	16 46.4	13 01.5
28 Tu	12 31 17	5 54 44	23 39 15	29 40 40	0 48.4	22 31.6	7 10.5	10 14.8	22 58.5	22 29.6	6 47.9	1 38.2	16 44.8	13 00.8
29 W	12 35 13	6 53 40	5♌39 54	11♌37 28	0 45.5	24 02.7	8 23.5	10 52.6	23 24.9	22 31.8	6 50.1	1 38.6	16 43.1	13 00.1
30 Th	12 39 10	7 52 38	17 33 48	23 29 22	0 41.9	25 32.9	9 36.4	11 30.4	23 51.4	22 34.1	6 52.2	1 39.0	16 41.5	12 59.4

LONGITUDE October 2032

Day	Sid.Time	☉	0 hr ☽	Noon ☽	True ☊	☿	♀	♂	⚳	♃	♄	♅	♆	♇
1 F	12 43 06	8♎51 38	29♌24 34	5♍19 47	0♏38.1	27♎02.2	10♏49.2	12♍08.2	24♎17.9	22♑36.6	6♋54.2	1♋39.3	16♈39.8	12♒58.7
2 Sa	12 47 03	9 50 40	11♍15 21	17 11 34	0R34.6	28 30.6	12 02.1	12 45.9	24 44.3	22 39.3	6 56.0	1 39.5	16R38.2	12R58.1
3 Su	12 50 59	10 49 44	23 08 44	29 07 06	0 31.6	29 58.2	13 14.9	13 23.6	25 10.8	22 42.3	6 57.8	1 39.7	16 36.5	12 57.5
4 M	12 54 56	11 48 51	5♎06 54	11♎08 22	0 29.6	1♏24.7	14 27.7	14 01.4	25 37.3	22 45.3	6 59.4	1 39.9	16 34.8	12 56.9
5 Tu	12 58 52	12 47 59	17 11 41	23 17 04	0D28.5	2 50.4	15 40.5	14 39.1	26 03.8	22 48.6	7 01.0	1 40.0	16 33.2	12 56.4
6 W	13 02 49	13 47 09	29 24 42	5♏34 48	0 28.5	4 15.1	16 53.3	15 16.8	26 30.4	22 52.1	7 02.4	1R40.0	16 31.5	12 55.9
7 Th	13 06 46	14 46 22	11♏47 34	18 03 12	0 29.1	5 38.8	18 06.1	15 54.5	26 56.9	22 55.7	7 03.7	1 40.0	16 29.8	12 55.4
8 F	13 10 42	15 45 36	24 21 56	0♐43 59	0 30.3	7 01.6	19 18.8	16 32.1	27 23.4	22 59.6	7 04.9	1 39.9	16 28.2	12 54.9
9 Sa	13 14 39	16 44 53	7♐09 36	13 39 01	0 31.5	8 23.2	20 31.5	17 09.8	27 50.0	23 03.6	7 06.0	1 39.8	16 26.5	12 54.4
10 Su	13 18 35	17 44 11	20 12 29	26 50 13	0 32.6	9 43.8	21 44.2	17 47.5	28 16.5	23 07.8	7 07.0	1 39.7	16 24.8	12 54.0
11 M	13 22 32	18 43 31	3♑32 24	10♑19 14	0R33.2	11 03.2	22 56.8	18 25.1	28 43.1	23 12.2	7 07.9	1 39.4	16 23.1	12 53.6
12 Tu	13 26 28	19 42 52	17 10 50	24 07 14	0 33.3	12 21.5	24 09.4	19 02.7	29 09.6	23 16.7	7 08.7	1 39.2	16 21.5	12 53.2
13 W	13 30 25	20 42 15	1♒08 25	8♒14 16	0 32.9	13 38.4	25 22.0	19 40.3	29 36.2	23 21.4	7 09.4	1 38.9	16 19.8	12 52.9
14 Th	13 34 21	21 41 40	15 24 33	22 38 54	0 32.1	14 54.0	26 34.6	20 17.9	0♏02.7	23 26.3	7 09.9	1 38.5	16 18.1	12 52.6
15 F	13 38 18	22 41 07	29 56 52	7♓17 50	0 31.2	16 08.1	27 47.1	20 55.5	0 29.3	23 31.4	7 10.3	1 38.0	16 16.5	12 52.3
16 Sa	13 42 15	23 40 36	14♓41 05	22 05 50	0 30.3	17 20.7	28 59.6	21 33.0	0 55.9	23 36.7	7 10.7	1 37.6	16 14.8	12 52.0
17 Su	13 46 11	24 40 06	29 31 10	6♈56 09	0 29.7	18 31.5	0♐12.0	22 10.6	1 22.4	23 42.1	7 10.9	1 37.0	16 13.2	12 51.8
18 M	13 50 08	25 39 38	14♈19 50	21 41 17	0D29.4	19 40.6	1 24.5	22 48.1	1 49.0	23 47.6	7R11.0	1 36.4	16 11.5	12 51.6
19 Tu	13 54 04	26 39 12	28 59 35	6♉13 57	0 29.4	20 47.6	2 36.9	23 25.6	2 15.5	23 53.4	7 11.0	1 35.8	16 09.9	12 51.4
20 W	13 58 01	27 38 49	13♉23 40	20 28 10	0 29.5	21 52.5	3 49.2	24 03.1	2 42.1	23 59.3	7 10.9	1 35.1	16 08.2	12 51.2
21 Th	14 01 57	28 38 27	27 26 58	4♊19 48	0 29.7	22 54.9	5 01.5	24 40.6	3 08.6	24 05.4	7 10.6	1 34.4	16 06.6	12 51.1
22 F	14 05 54	29 38 08	11♊06 29	17 47 00	0R29.9	23 54.7	6 13.8	25 18.1	3 35.2	24 11.6	7 10.3	1 33.6	16 05.0	12 51.0
23 Sa	14 09 50	0♏37 51	24 21 26	0♋50 00	0 29.9	24 51.6	7 26.1	25 55.6	4 01.7	24 18.0	7 09.8	1 32.8	16 03.4	12 50.9
24 Su	14 13 47	1 37 36	7♋12 59	13 30 48	0 29.9	25 45.3	8 38.3	26 33.1	4 28.3	24 24.6	7 09.3	1 31.9	16 01.8	12 50.8
25 M	14 17 44	2 37 24	19 43 52	25 52 42	0D29.8	26 35.4	9 50.5	27 10.6	4 54.8	24 31.3	7 08.6	1 30.9	16 00.2	12D50.8
26 Tu	14 21 40	3 37 13	1♌57 51	7♌59 53	0 29.8	27 21.6	11 02.7	27 48.0	5 21.3	24 38.2	7 07.8	1 30.0	15 58.6	12 50.8
27 W	14 25 37	4 37 05	13 59 22	19 56 53	0 30.0	28 03.4	12 14.8	28 25.4	5 47.9	24 45.2	7 06.9	1 28.9	15 57.0	12 50.8
28 Th	14 29 33	5 36 59	25 53 03	1♍48 24	0 30.4	28 40.3	13 26.9	29 02.9	6 14.4	24 52.4	7 05.9	1 27.8	15 55.5	12 50.9
29 F	14 33 30	6 36 55	7♍43 30	13 38 54	0 31.0	29 11.9	14 38.9	29 40.3	6 40.9	24 59.7	7 04.8	1 26.7	15 53.9	12 51.0
30 Sa	14 37 26	7 36 54	19 35 03	25 32 28	0 31.7	29 37.5	15 50.9	0♎17.7	7 07.4	25 07.2	7 03.6	1 25.5	15 52.4	12 51.1
31 Su	14 41 23	8 36 54	1♎31 33	7♎32 42	0 32.5	29 56.6	17 02.9	0 55.1	7 33.9	25 14.8	7 02.2	1 24.3	15 50.9	12 51.2

Astro Data	Dy Hr Mn
☽0S	5 16:32
⚳0S	11 5:34
☿0S	15 22:56
♃ D	17 19:53
☽0N	19 2:26
☉0S	22 11:12
☽0S	2 22:41
♅ R	6 19:54
☽0N	16 12:33
♄ R	18 22:27
♇ D	25 21:11
☽0S	30 5:44

Planet Ingress		Dy Hr Mn
♂	♍	12 6:33
☿	♎	14 17:25
☉	♎	22 11:12
♀	♏	22 14:24
☿	♏	3 12:31
⚳	♏	14 9:31
♀	♐	17 8:01
☉	♏	22 20:47
♂	♎	30 0:40
☿	♐	31 17:34

Last Aspect Dy Hr Mn			☽ Ingress	Dy Hr Mn
31 15:53	♃	☍	♌	1 6:20
3 7:22	♂	☌	♍	3 18:53
5 16:32	♃	△	♎	6 7:34
8 14:50	♂	⚹	♏	8 19:23
11 3:48	♂	□	♐	11 5:07
13 7:10	☿	□	♑	13 11:36
15 2:38	☉	△	♒	15 14:32
17 4:21	♀	△	♓	17 14:50
19 9:32	☉	☍	♈	19 14:17
21 12:46	♀	☍	♉	21 14:55
23 5:00	♃	△	♊	23 18:29
25 1:47	☿	△	♋	26 1:52
27 21:39	♃	☍	♌	28 12:39

Last Aspect Dy Hr Mn			☽ Ingress	Dy Hr Mn
30 16:47	☿	⚹	♍	1 1:12
2 23:03	♃	△	♎	3 13:46
5 11:04	♃	□	♏	6 1:09
7 21:19	♃	⚹	♐	8 10:37
9 18:46	♂	□	♑	10 17:41
12 12:04	♀	⚹	♒	12 22:04
14 19:03	♀	□	♓	15 0:05
17 0:08	♀	△	♈	17 0:47
18 18:59	☉	☍	♉	19 1:40
20 18:26	♂	△	♊	21 4:26
23 2:26	♂	□	♋	23 10:27
25 14:41	♂	⚹	♌	25 20:07
28 5:19	☿	□	♍	28 8:20
30 20:27	☿	⚹	♎	30 20:57

☽ Phases & Eclipses Dy Hr Mn		
4 20:58	●	12♍52
12 18:50	☽	20♐33
19 9:32	○	27♓00
26 9:14	☾	3♋50
4 13:28	●	11♎52
12 3:49	☽	19♑23
18 18:59	○	25♈57
18 19:04	☍	T 1.103
26 2:30	☾	3♌14

Astro Data

1 September 2032
Julian Day # 48457
SVP 4♓48'02"
GC 27♐17.7 ⚴ 10♍38.6
Eris 27♈13.1R ⚵ 28♌42.7
⚷ 26♉06.6R ⚶ 0♏06.8
☽ Mean ☊ 3♏12.1

1 October 2032
Julian Day # 48487
SVP 4♓47'59"
GC 27♐17.8 ⚴ 25♍11.1
Eris 26♈58.4R ⚵ 12♍01.5
⚷ 25♉36.5R ⚶ 15♏02.0
☽ Mean ☊ 1♏36.8

November 2032 — LONGITUDE

Day	Sid.Time	☉	0 hr ☽	Noon ☽	True ☊	☿	♀	♂	⚳	♃	♄	♅	♆	♇
1 M	14 45 19	9♏36 56	13♎36 14	19♎42 29	0♏33.1	0♐08.5	18♐14.8	1♎32.4	8♏00.4	25♑22.6	7♋00.8	1♋23.0	15♈49.4	12♒51.4
2 Tu	14 49 16	10 37 01	25 51 41	2♏04 02	0R33.2	0R12.6	19 26.7	2 09.8	8 26.9	25 30.5	6R59.2	1R21.7	15R47.9	12 51.6
3 W	14 53 13	11 37 07	8♏19 42	14 38 47	0 32.9	0 08.3	20 38.6	2 47.1	8 53.3	25 38.5	6 57.5	1 20.3	15 46.4	12 51.8
4 Th	14 57 09	12 37 15	21 01 22	27 27 29	0 31.9	29♏54.9	21 50.4	3 24.5	9 19.8	25 46.7	6 55.8	1 18.9	15 44.9	12 52.1
5 F	15 01 06	13 37 25	3♐57 06	10♐30 13	0 30.4	29 32.2	23 02.2	4 01.8	9 46.2	25 55.1	6 53.9	1 17.5	15 43.5	12 52.4
6 Sa	15 05 02	14 37 37	17 06 46	23 46 39	0 28.4	28 59.7	24 13.9	4 39.1	10 12.6	26 03.6	6 51.9	1 16.0	15 42.1	12 52.7
7 Su	15 08 59	15 37 50	0♑29 47	7♑16 04	0 26.4	28 17.4	25 25.5	5 16.3	10 39.1	26 12.2	6 49.8	1 14.4	15 40.7	12 53.0
8 M	15 12 55	16 38 05	14 05 22	20 57 34	0 24.6	27 25.6	26 37.2	5 53.6	11 05.4	26 21.0	6 47.6	1 12.9	15 39.3	12 53.4
9 Tu	15 16 52	17 38 21	27 52 33	4♒50 09	0D23.4	26 24.9	27 48.7	6 30.9	11 31.8	26 29.9	6 45.3	1 11.2	15 37.9	12 53.8
10 W	15 20 48	18 38 39	11♒50 13	18 52 36	0 23.0	25 16.5	29 00.2	7 08.1	11 58.2	26 38.9	6 43.0	1 09.6	15 36.6	12 54.2
11 Th	15 24 45	19 38 58	25 57 06	3♓03 29	0 23.4	24 02.0	0♑11.7	7 45.3	12 24.5	26 48.0	6 40.5	1 07.9	15 35.3	12 54.6
12 F	15 28 42	20 39 18	10♓11 31	17 20 53	0 24.5	22 43.4	1 23.0	8 22.5	12 50.8	26 57.3	6 37.9	1 06.1	15 34.0	12 55.1
13 Sa	15 32 38	21 39 40	24 31 14	1♈42 12	0 26.0	21 23.0	2 34.3	8 59.7	13 17.1	27 06.7	6 35.2	1 04.3	15 32.7	12 55.6
14 Su	15 36 35	22 40 03	8♈53 19	16 04 06	0 27.2	20 03.5	3 45.6	9 36.8	13 43.3	27 16.2	6 32.4	1 02.5	15 31.4	12 56.2
15 M	15 40 31	23 40 28	23 14 02	0♉22 33	0R27.7	18 47.5	4 56.7	10 14.0	14 09.6	27 25.9	6 29.5	1 00.6	15 30.2	12 56.7
16 Tu	15 44 28	24 40 54	7♉29 04	14 33 03	0 27.1	17 37.5	6 07.8	10 51.1	14 35.8	27 35.6	6 26.5	0 58.7	15 28.9	12 57.3
17 W	15 48 24	25 41 22	21 33 55	28 31 09	0 25.1	16 35.6	7 18.9	11 28.2	15 02.0	27 45.5	6 23.5	0 56.8	15 27.8	12 57.9
18 Th	15 52 21	26 41 51	5♊24 18	12♊12 59	0 21.9	15 43.4	8 29.8	12 05.3	15 28.2	27 55.5	6 20.3	0 54.8	15 26.6	12 58.5
19 F	15 56 17	27 42 22	18 56 52	25 35 46	0 17.7	15 02.1	9 40.7	12 42.4	15 54.3	28 05.6	6 17.1	0 52.8	15 25.4	12 59.2
20 Sa	16 00 14	28 42 55	2♋09 32	8♋38 11	0 13.0	14 32.3	10 51.5	13 19.5	16 20.4	28 15.8	6 13.8	0 50.8	15 24.3	12 59.9
21 Su	16 04 11	29 43 30	15 01 48	21 20 33	0 08.4	14 14.3	12 02.2	13 56.5	16 46.5	28 26.2	6 10.4	0 48.7	15 23.2	13 00.6
22 M	16 08 07	0♐44 06	27 34 43	3♌44 40	0 04.4	14D07.8	13 12.8	14 33.6	17 12.6	28 36.6	6 06.9	0 46.6	15 22.2	13 01.4
23 Tu	16 12 04	1 44 43	9♌50 49	15 53 39	0 01.7	14 12.2	14 23.4	15 10.6	17 38.6	28 47.2	6 03.3	0 44.5	15 21.1	13 02.1
24 W	16 16 00	2 45 23	21 53 42	27 51 33	0D00.3	14 27.0	15 33.8	15 47.6	18 04.6	28 57.8	5 59.6	0 42.3	15 20.1	13 02.9
25 Th	16 19 57	3 46 04	3♍47 49	9♍43 06	0 00.3	14 51.3	16 44.2	16 24.6	18 30.6	29 08.6	5 55.9	0 40.1	15 19.1	13 03.7
26 F	16 23 53	4 46 46	15 38 04	21 33 20	0 01.5	15 24.1	17 54.5	17 01.5	18 56.5	29 19.5	5 52.1	0 37.9	15 18.2	13 04.6
27 Sa	16 27 50	5 47 30	27 29 33	3♎27 20	0 03.3	16 04.7	19 04.7	17 38.5	19 22.5	29 30.5	5 48.2	0 35.7	15 17.2	13 05.5
28 Su	16 31 46	6 48 16	9♎27 16	15 29 55	0 05.0	16 52.0	20 14.8	18 15.4	19 48.3	29 41.5	5 44.2	0 33.4	15 16.3	13 06.4
29 M	16 35 43	7 49 03	21 35 47	27 45 20	0R05.9	17 45.5	21 24.8	18 52.3	20 14.2	29 52.7	5 40.2	0 31.1	15 15.4	13 07.3
30 Tu	16 39 40	8 49 52	3♏58 58	10♏17 00	0 05.3	18 44.2	22 34.7	19 29.2	20 40.0	0♒04.0	5 36.1	0 28.8	15 14.6	13 08.2

December 2032 — LONGITUDE

Day	Sid.Time	☉	0 hr ☽	Noon ☽	True ☊	☿	♀	♂	⚳	♃	♄	♅	♆	♇
1 W	16 43 36	9♐50 42	16♏39 41	23♏07 09	0♏03.0	19♏47.5	23♑44.5	20♎06.1	21♏05.8	0♒15.4	5♋31.9	0♋26.4	15♈13.8	13♒09.2
2 Th	16 47 33	10 51 33	29 39 27	6♐16 34	29♎58.6	20 54.8	24 54.2	20 43.0	21 31.5	0 26.8	5R27.7	0R24.1	15R13.0	13 10.2
3 F	16 51 29	11 52 26	12♐58 19	19 44 30	29R52.5	22 05.5	26 03.7	21 19.8	21 57.2	0 38.4	5 23.4	0 21.7	15 12.2	13 11.2
4 Sa	16 55 26	12 53 19	26 34 45	3♑28 41	29 45.2	23 19.2	27 13.2	21 56.6	22 22.9	0 50.0	5 19.0	0 19.3	15 11.5	13 12.3
5 Su	16 59 22	13 54 14	10♑25 50	17 25 42	29 37.6	24 35.5	28 22.5	22 33.4	22 48.5	1 01.8	5 14.6	0 16.8	15 10.8	13 13.3
6 M	17 03 19	14 55 09	24 27 45	1♒31 27	29 30.6	25 53.9	29 31.7	23 10.1	23 14.1	1 13.6	5 10.2	0 14.4	15 10.1	13 14.4
7 Tu	17 07 15	15 56 06	8♒36 18	15 41 50	29 25.2	27 14.3	0♒40.8	23 46.9	23 39.6	1 25.5	5 05.7	0 11.9	15 09.5	13 15.5
8 W	17 11 12	16 57 03	22 47 37	29 53 18	29 21.7	28 36.3	1 49.7	24 23.6	24 05.1	1 37.5	5 01.1	0 09.5	15 08.9	13 16.7
9 Th	17 15 09	17 58 00	6♓58 34	14♓03 10	29D20.3	29 59.7	2 58.5	25 00.2	24 30.5	1 49.6	4 56.5	0 07.0	15 08.3	13 17.8
10 F	17 19 05	18 58 58	21 06 56	28 09 40	29 20.6	1♐24.2	4 07.1	25 36.9	24 55.9	2 01.7	4 51.8	0 04.5	15 07.8	13 19.0
11 Sa	17 23 02	19 59 57	5♈11 17	12♈11 40	29 21.6	2 49.8	5 15.6	26 13.5	25 21.2	2 14.0	4 47.2	0 01.9	15 07.3	13 20.2
12 Su	17 26 58	21 00 56	19 10 43	26 08 19	29R22.5	4 16.3	6 23.9	26 50.1	25 46.5	2 26.3	4 42.4	29♊59.4	15 06.8	13 21.4
13 M	17 30 55	22 01 56	3♉04 20	9♉58 37	29 22.0	5 43.6	7 32.0	27 26.7	26 11.8	2 38.7	4 37.7	29 56.9	15 06.4	13 22.7
14 Tu	17 34 51	23 02 57	16 50 59	23 41 13	29 19.4	7 11.5	8 40.0	28 03.2	26 37.0	2 51.1	4 32.9	29 54.3	15 06.0	13 23.9
15 W	17 38 48	24 03 58	0♊29 05	7♊14 18	29 14.1	8 40.0	9 47.7	28 39.7	27 02.1	3 03.6	4 28.0	29 51.8	15 05.6	13 25.2
16 Th	17 42 44	25 04 59	13 56 36	20 35 44	29 06.4	10 09.1	10 55.3	29 16.2	27 27.2	3 16.2	4 23.2	29 49.2	15 05.3	13 26.5
17 F	17 46 41	26 06 02	27 11 26	3♋43 30	28 56.6	11 38.6	12 02.7	29 52.7	27 52.2	3 28.9	4 18.3	29 46.7	15 05.0	13 27.9
18 Sa	17 50 38	27 07 05	10♋11 45	16 36 04	28 45.6	13 08.5	13 09.9	0♏29.2	28 17.2	3 41.7	4 13.4	29 44.1	15 04.7	13 29.2
19 Su	17 54 34	28 08 09	22 56 24	29 12 47	28 34.5	14 38.7	14 16.9	1 05.6	28 42.1	3 54.5	4 08.5	29 41.5	15 04.5	13 30.6
20 M	17 58 31	29 09 13	5♌25 19	11♌34 11	28 24.3	16 09.3	15 23.7	1 42.0	29 07.0	4 07.3	4 03.6	29 38.9	15 04.3	13 32.0
21 Tu	18 02 27	0♑10 18	17 39 39	23 42 03	28 16.0	17 40.3	16 30.3	2 18.3	29 31.8	4 20.3	3 58.7	29 36.4	15 04.1	13 33.4
22 W	18 06 24	1 11 24	29 41 48	5♍39 21	28 10.0	19 11.5	17 36.6	2 54.7	29 56.6	4 33.3	3 53.7	29 33.8	15 04.0	13 34.8
23 Th	18 10 20	2 12 31	11♍35 15	17 30 04	28 06.5	20 43.0	18 42.7	3 31.0	0♐21.2	4 46.3	3 48.7	29 31.2	15 03.9	13 36.2
24 F	18 14 17	3 13 38	23 24 25	29 18 58	28D05.2	22 14.8	19 48.6	4 07.3	0 45.9	4 59.4	3 43.8	29 28.6	15 03.8	13 37.7
25 Sa	18 18 13	4 14 46	5♎14 22	11♎11 21	28 05.3	23 46.8	20 54.2	4 43.5	1 10.4	5 12.6	3 38.8	29 26.1	15D03.8	13 39.1
26 Su	18 22 10	5 15 54	17 10 34	23 12 43	28R05.8	25 19.1	21 59.6	5 19.7	1 34.9	5 25.8	3 33.8	29 23.5	15 03.8	13 40.6
27 M	18 26 07	6 17 03	29 18 28	5♏28 26	28 05.6	26 51.7	23 04.7	5 55.9	1 59.4	5 39.1	3 28.9	29 21.0	15 03.8	13 42.1
28 Tu	18 30 03	7 18 13	11♏43 12	18 03 17	28 03.7	28 24.6	24 09.6	6 32.1	2 23.8	5 52.4	3 23.9	29 18.4	15 03.9	13 43.7
29 W	18 34 00	8 19 23	24 29 06	1♐00 57	27 59.4	29 57.7	25 14.2	7 08.2	2 48.1	6 05.8	3 19.0	29 15.9	15 04.0	13 45.2
30 Th	18 37 56	9 20 33	7♐39 02	14 23 24	27 52.3	1♑31.1	26 18.5	7 44.3	3 12.3	6 19.3	3 14.0	29 13.3	15 04.2	13 46.8
31 F	18 41 53	10 21 44	21 13 58	28 10 25	27 42.6	3 04.8	27 22.4	8 20.3	3 36.5	6 32.8	3 09.1	29 10.8	15 04.3	13 48.3

Astro Data	Dy Hr Mn
☿ R	2 11:58
♂ 0S	3 15:01
☽ 0N	12 20:37
☿ D	22 14:02
☽ 0S	26 14:14
♃⚻♅	2 7:14
☽ 0N	10 3:04
♃⚻♄	20 6:58
☽ 0S	23 23:43
♆ D	25 21:03

Planet Ingress	Dy Hr Mn
☿ ♏R	4 4:39
♀ ♑	11 8:05
☉ ♐	21 18:32
♃ ♒	30 3:33
☊ ♎R	2 5:15
♀ ♒	6 21:49
☿ ♐	9 12:06
♅ ♊R	12 6:23
♂ ♏	17 16:48
☉ ♑	21 7:57
⚳ ♐	22 15:21
☿ ♑	29 12:36

Last Aspect Dy Hr Mn		☽ Ingress Dy Hr Mn
1 23:11	♃ □	♏ 2 8:01
4 16:27	☿ ☌	♐ 4 16:43
6 12:54	♀ ☌	♑ 6 23:07
8 22:29	☿ ⚹	♒ 9 3:40
11 6:44	♀ ⚹	♓ 11 6:51
13 4:15	♃ ⚹	♈ 13 9:09
15 6:59	♃ □	♉ 15 11:22
17 10:40	♃ △	♊ 17 14:34
18 17:44	♆ ⚹	♋ 19 20:02
22 1:51	♃ ☍	♌ 22 4:42
23 10:55	♆ △	♍ 24 16:19
27 3:56	♃ △	♎ 27 5:03
29 16:10	♃ □	♏ 29 16:20

Last Aspect Dy Hr Mn		☽ Ingress Dy Hr Mn
1 13:16	♀ ⚹	♐ 2 0:37
3 14:56	♂ ⚹	♑ 4 5:58
6 8:19	♀ ☌	♒ 6 9:25
8 9:36	☿ □	♓ 8 12:11
9 19:10	☉ □	♈ 10 15:08
12 18:38	♅ ⚹	♉ 12 18:41
13 17:56	♇ □	♊ 14 23:09
17 4:46	♅ ☌	♋ 17 5:09
18 9:08	♆ □	♌ 19 13:31
21 23:47	♅ ⚹	♍ 22 0:37
24 12:20	♅ □	♎ 24 13:23
27 0:07	♅ △	♏ 27 1:21
29 0:26	♀ □	♐ 29 10:09
31 13:43	♅ ☍	♑ 31 15:08

☽ Phases & Eclipses Dy Hr Mn	
3 5:46	● 11♏22
3 5:34:13	● P 0.856
10 11:34	☽ 18♒38
17 6:43	○ 25♉28
24 22:49	☾ 3♍13
2 20:54	● 11♐14
9 19:10	☽ 18♓16
16 20:50	○ 25♊27
24 20:40	☾ 3♎36

Astro Data

1 November 2032
Julian Day # 48518
SVP 4♓47'57"
GC 27♐17.9 ⚴ 9♎27.7
Eris 26♈40.0R ⚵ 24♍30.5
⚷ 24♉18.8R ⚶ 1♐15.3
☽ Mean ☊ 29♎58.2

1 December 2032
Julian Day # 48548
SVP 4♓47'53"
GC 27♐17.9 ⚴ 22♎16.0
Eris 26♈24.4R ⚵ 4♎46.0
⚷ 22♉46.2R ⚶ 17♐22.6
☽ Mean ☊ 28♎22.9

LONGITUDE — January 2033

Day	Sid.Time	☉	0 hr ☽	Noon ☽	True ☊	☿	♀	♂	⚳	♃	♄	♅	♆	♇
1 Sa	18 45 49	11♑22 55	5♑12 22	12♑19 13	27♎31.2	4♑38.9	28♒26.1	8♏56.3	4♐00.6	6♒46.3	3♋04.2	29♊08.3	15♈04.6	13♒49.9
2 Su	18 49 46	12 24 06	19 30 14	26 44 36	27R19.1	6 13.2	29 29.5	9 32.3	4 24.6	6 59.9	2R59.3	29R05.8	15 04.8	13 51.5
3 M	18 53 42	13 25 17	4♒01 24	11♒19 42	27 07.8	7 47.9	0♓32.5	10 08.2	4 48.5	7 13.5	2 54.5	29 03.3	15 05.1	13 53.1
4 Tu	18 57 39	14 26 28	18 38 33	25 57 05	26 58.5	9 22.9	1 35.2	10 44.1	5 12.4	7 27.2	2 49.7	29 00.9	15 05.4	13 54.8
5 W	19 01 36	15 27 39	3♓14 27	10♓30 00	26 51.8	10 58.2	2 37.6	11 20.0	5 36.2	7 40.9	2 44.9	28 58.4	15 05.8	13 56.4
6 Th	19 05 32	16 28 49	17 43 07	24 53 23	26 48.1	12 34.0	3 39.5	11 55.8	5 59.9	7 54.7	2 40.1	28 56.0	15 06.2	13 58.1
7 F	19 09 29	17 29 59	2♈00 29	9♈04 14	26D46.6	14 10.1	4 41.1	12 31.5	6 23.5	8 08.5	2 35.4	28 53.6	15 06.6	13 59.7
8 Sa	19 13 25	18 31 08	16 04 33	23 01 25	26R46.5	15 46.6	5 42.2	13 07.2	6 47.0	8 22.3	2 30.7	28 51.2	15 07.0	14 01.4
9 Su	19 17 22	19 32 17	29 54 54	6♉45 08	26 46.3	17 23.5	6 43.0	13 42.9	7 10.5	8 36.1	2 26.1	28 48.8	15 07.5	14 03.1
10 M	19 21 18	20 33 25	13♉32 13	20 16 18	26 44.7	19 00.9	7 43.3	14 18.5	7 33.8	8 50.0	2 21.5	28 46.5	15 08.1	14 04.8
11 Tu	19 25 15	21 34 33	26 57 31	3♊35 57	26 40.6	20 38.7	8 43.1	14 54.1	7 57.1	9 04.0	2 16.9	28 44.2	15 08.6	14 06.5
12 W	19 29 11	22 35 40	10♊11 40	16 44 45	26 33.5	22 17.0	9 42.5	15 29.6	8 20.3	9 17.9	2 12.4	28 41.9	15 09.2	14 08.2
13 Th	19 33 08	23 36 47	23 15 10	29 42 55	26 23.3	23 55.7	10 41.4	16 05.1	8 43.4	9 31.9	2 08.0	28 39.6	15 09.9	14 09.9
14 F	19 37 05	24 37 53	6♋07 58	12♋30 15	26 10.6	25 34.9	11 39.8	16 40.6	9 06.4	9 45.9	2 03.6	28 37.3	15 10.5	14 11.7
15 Sa	19 41 01	25 38 59	18 49 43	25 06 19	25 56.4	27 14.6	12 37.6	17 16.0	9 29.3	9 59.9	1 59.2	28 35.1	15 11.2	14 13.4
16 Su	19 44 58	26 40 05	1♌20 02	7♌30 51	25 41.8	28 54.8	13 35.0	17 51.4	9 52.1	10 14.0	1 54.9	28 32.9	15 12.0	14 15.2
17 M	19 48 54	27 41 09	13 38 51	19 44 06	25 28.3	0♒35.5	14 31.7	18 26.7	10 14.8	10 28.1	1 50.7	28 30.8	15 12.7	14 16.9
18 Tu	19 52 51	28 42 14	25 46 45	1♍47 01	25 16.7	2 16.6	15 27.9	19 01.9	10 37.4	10 42.2	1 46.6	28 28.6	15 13.5	14 18.7
19 W	19 56 47	29 43 18	7♍45 10	13 41 32	25 07.9	3 58.3	16 23.5	19 37.2	11 00.0	10 56.3	1 42.5	28 26.5	15 14.4	14 20.5
20 Th	20 00 44	0♒44 21	19 36 32	25 30 35	25 02.0	5 40.4	17 18.4	20 12.3	11 22.4	11 10.5	1 38.5	28 24.5	15 15.2	14 22.3
21 F	20 04 41	1 45 24	1♎24 13	7♎18 00	24 58.9	7 23.0	18 12.7	20 47.4	11 44.7	11 24.7	1 34.5	28 22.4	15 16.1	14 24.1
22 Sa	20 08 37	2 46 27	13 12 32	19 08 27	24D57.9	9 05.9	19 06.4	21 22.5	12 06.9	11 38.9	1 30.6	28 20.4	15 17.1	14 25.9
23 Su	20 12 34	3 47 29	25 06 26	1♏07 11	24R57.8	10 49.3	19 59.3	21 57.5	12 29.0	11 53.1	1 26.8	28 18.4	15 18.0	14 27.6
24 M	20 16 30	4 48 31	7♏11 23	13 19 45	24 57.6	12 33.0	20 51.6	22 32.5	12 51.0	12 07.3	1 23.1	28 16.5	15 19.0	14 29.5
25 Tu	20 20 27	5 49 33	19 32 58	25 51 40	24 56.1	14 16.9	21 43.1	23 07.4	13 12.9	12 21.5	1 19.4	28 14.6	15 20.0	14 31.3
26 W	20 24 23	6 50 34	2♐16 25	8♐47 43	24 52.4	16 01.1	22 33.8	23 42.2	13 34.7	12 35.8	1 15.9	28 12.7	15 21.1	14 33.1
27 Th	20 28 20	7 51 34	15 25 58	22 11 25	24 46.0	17 45.3	23 23.7	24 17.0	13 56.4	12 50.1	1 12.4	28 10.9	15 22.2	14 34.9
28 F	20 32 16	8 52 34	29 04 09	6♑04 05	24 37.1	19 29.5	24 12.8	24 51.7	14 17.9	13 04.3	1 09.0	28 09.1	15 23.3	14 36.7
29 Sa	20 36 13	9 53 32	13♑10 54	20 24 07	24 26.3	21 13.5	25 01.0	25 26.4	14 39.4	13 18.6	1 05.6	28 07.4	15 24.5	14 38.5
30 Su	20 40 10	10 54 31	27 43 01	5♒06 41	24 14.7	22 57.1	25 48.3	26 01.0	15 00.7	13 32.9	1 02.4	28 05.7	15 25.7	14 40.4
31 M	20 44 06	11 55 28	12♒34 04	20 04 00	24 03.6	24 40.2	26 34.7	26 35.5	15 21.9	13 47.2	0 59.3	28 04.0	15 26.9	14 42.2

LONGITUDE — February 2033

Day	Sid.Time	☉	0 hr ☽	Noon ☽	True ☊	☿	♀	♂	⚳	♃	♄	♅	♆	♇
1 Tu	20 48 03	12♒56 24	27♒35 15	5♓06 33	23♎54.3	26♒22.4	27♓20.1	27♏09.9	15♐42.9	14♒01.5	0♋56.2	28♊02.4	15♈28.1	14♒44.0
2 W	20 51 59	13 57 18	12♓36 43	20 04 41	23R47.7	28 03.5	28 04.5	27 44.3	16 03.9	14 15.8	0R53.3	28R00.8	15 29.4	14 45.9
3 Th	20 55 56	14 58 12	27 29 28	4♈50 19	23 43.9	29 43.2	28 47.8	28 18.6	16 24.7	14 30.1	0 50.4	27 59.3	15 30.7	14 47.7
4 F	20 59 52	15 59 04	12♈06 37	19 17 57	23D42.6	1♓21.0	29 30.0	28 52.9	16 45.3	14 44.4	0 47.6	27 57.8	15 32.0	14 49.5
5 Sa	21 03 49	16 59 54	26 24 04	3♉24 52	23 42.7	2 56.6	0♈11.1	29 27.0	17 05.9	14 58.7	0 45.0	27 56.3	15 33.4	14 51.3
6 Su	21 07 45	18 00 44	10♉20 23	17 10 46	23R43.1	4 29.4	0 50.9	0♐01.1	17 26.3	15 13.0	0 42.4	27 54.9	15 34.7	14 53.2
7 M	21 11 42	19 01 31	23 56 11	0♊36 55	23 42.5	5 58.9	1 29.5	0 35.1	17 46.5	15 27.3	0 40.0	27 53.6	15 36.2	14 55.0
8 Tu	21 15 38	20 02 18	7♊13 16	13 45 31	23 39.8	7 24.5	2 06.8	1 09.0	18 06.6	15 41.6	0 37.6	27 52.3	15 37.6	14 56.8
9 W	21 19 35	21 03 02	20 13 59	26 38 56	23 34.6	8 45.5	2 42.8	1 42.9	18 26.6	15 55.8	0 35.3	27 51.0	15 39.1	14 58.6
10 Th	21 23 32	22 03 45	3♋00 39	9♋19 22	23 26.8	10 01.2	3 17.3	2 16.7	18 46.5	16 10.1	0 33.2	27 49.8	15 40.6	15 00.5
11 F	21 27 28	23 04 27	15 35 17	21 48 35	23 16.8	11 11.0	3 50.4	2 50.4	19 06.1	16 24.4	0 31.1	27 48.6	15 42.1	15 02.3
12 Sa	21 31 25	24 05 07	27 59 25	4♌07 56	23 05.5	12 14.0	4 21.9	3 24.0	19 25.7	16 38.6	0 29.2	27 47.5	15 43.6	15 04.1
13 Su	21 35 21	25 05 46	10♌14 16	16 18 31	22 53.8	13 09.5	4 51.9	3 57.5	19 45.1	16 52.9	0 27.3	27 46.4	15 45.2	15 05.9
14 M	21 39 18	26 06 23	22 20 48	28 21 16	22 42.9	13 56.9	5 20.2	4 31.0	20 04.3	17 07.1	0 25.6	27 45.4	15 46.8	15 07.7
15 Tu	21 43 14	27 06 58	4♍20 03	10♍17 20	22 33.7	14 35.5	5 46.8	5 04.4	20 23.4	17 21.3	0 23.9	27 44.4	15 48.4	15 09.5
16 W	21 47 11	28 07 33	16 13 20	22 08 16	22 26.7	15 04.6	6 11.7	5 37.6	20 42.3	17 35.5	0 22.4	27 43.5	15 50.1	15 11.3
17 Th	21 51 07	29 08 06	28 02 26	3♎56 10	22 22.2	15 24.0	6 34.7	6 10.8	21 01.1	17 49.7	0 21.0	27 42.6	15 51.7	15 13.1
18 F	21 55 04	0♓08 37	9♎49 51	15 43 53	22D20.2	15R33.1	6 55.9	6 43.9	21 19.7	18 03.8	0 19.7	27 41.8	15 53.4	15 14.9
19 Sa	21 59 01	1 09 07	21 38 46	27 34 59	22 20.1	15 32.0	7 15.1	7 17.0	21 38.1	18 18.0	0 18.5	27 41.0	15 55.1	15 16.6
20 Su	22 02 57	2 09 36	3♏33 05	9♏33 40	22 21.1	15 20.6	7 32.3	7 49.9	21 56.4	18 32.1	0 17.4	27 40.3	15 56.9	15 18.4
21 M	22 06 54	3 10 04	15 37 21	21 44 45	22 22.4	14 59.3	7 47.5	8 22.7	22 14.5	18 46.2	0 16.4	27 39.6	15 58.6	15 20.2
22 Tu	22 10 50	4 10 30	27 56 31	4♐13 16	22R23.0	14 28.6	8 00.5	8 55.4	22 32.5	19 00.2	0 15.6	27 39.0	16 00.4	15 21.9
23 W	22 14 47	5 10 55	10♐35 37	17 04 06	22 22.2	13 49.3	8 11.4	9 28.0	22 50.2	19 14.3	0 14.8	27 38.4	16 02.2	15 23.7
24 Th	22 18 43	6 11 18	23 39 13	0♑21 23	22 19.5	13 02.3	8 20.0	10 00.6	23 07.8	19 28.3	0 14.2	27 37.9	16 04.1	15 25.4
25 F	22 22 40	7 11 41	7♑10 51	14 07 44	22 15.0	12 09.0	8 26.3	10 33.0	23 25.2	19 42.3	0 13.6	27 37.5	16 05.9	15 27.1
26 Sa	22 26 36	8 12 01	21 11 59	28 23 21	22 08.9	11 10.7	8 30.3	11 05.3	23 42.4	19 56.3	0 13.2	27 37.0	16 07.8	15 28.9
27 Su	22 30 33	9 12 20	5♒41 22	13♒05 21	22 02.1	10 09.0	8R31.8	11 37.4	23 59.4	20 10.2	0 12.9	27 36.7	16 09.7	15 30.6
28 M	22 34 30	10 12 38	20 34 24	28 07 29	21 55.4	9 05.5	8 31.0	12 09.5	24 16.2	20 24.1	0 12.7	27 36.4	16 11.6	15 32.3

Astro Data

Aspect	Dy Hr Mn
♅□♇	5 23:53
☽0N	6 9:51
☽0S	20 8:53
♃□♅	28 19:10
♀0N	30 8:02
☽0N	2 18:42
♃☌♇	4 21:51
♃✶♆	8 4:35
♃□♄	8 6:15
☽0S	16 16:41
☿R	18 21:23
♄□♇	20 3:29
♀R	27 15:42

Planet Ingress

Planet	Dy Hr Mn
♀ ♓	2 23:36
☿ ♒	17 3:33
☉ ♒	19 18:34
☿ ♓	3 16:05
♀ ♈	5 5:28
♂ ♐	6 11:13
☉ ♓	18 8:35

Last Aspect / ☽ Ingress (January)

Last Aspect Dy Hr Mn		☽ Ingress Dy Hr Mn
1 16:37	♆ □	♒ 2 17:22
4 17:01	♅ △	♓ 4 18:40
6 18:47	♅ □	♈ 6 20:36
8 22:07	♅ ✶	♉ 9 0:09
10 12:33	☉ △	♊ 11 5:29
13 10:02	♅ ☌	♋ 13 12:32
15 16:45	☿ ☍	♌ 15 21:25
18 5:24	♅ ✶	♍ 18 8:26
20 17:53	♅ □	♎ 20 21:09
23 6:25	♅ △	♏ 23 9:46
25 6:34	♂ ☌	♐ 25 19:46
27 22:26	♅ ☍	♑ 28 1:36
29 20:37	♂ ✶	♒ 30 3:43

Last Aspect / ☽ Ingress (February)

Last Aspect Dy Hr Mn		☽ Ingress Dy Hr Mn
1 0:44	♅ △	♓ 1 3:51
3 1:37	♀ ☌	♈ 3 4:05
5 2:38	♅ ✶	♉ 5 6:08
6 13:35	☉ □	♊ 7 10:53
9 14:15	♅ ☌	♋ 9 18:19
11 0:12	♆ □	♌ 12 3:55
14 10:48	♅ ✶	♍ 14 15:18
16 23:21	♅ □	♎ 17 3:59
19 12:12	♅ △	♏ 19 16:52
21 6:04	♃ □	♐ 22 3:57
24 7:09	♅ ☍	♑ 24 11:22
25 15:22	♆ □	♒ 26 14:40
28 11:11	♅ △	♓ 28 14:58

☽ Phases & Eclipses

Dy Hr Mn		
1 10:18	●	11♑19
8 3:36	☽	18♈10
15 13:08	○	25♋42
23 17:47	☾	4♏02
30 22:01	●	11♒20
6 13:35	☽	18♉05
14 7:05	○	25♌54
22 11:54	☾	4♐10

Astro Data

1 January 2033
Julian Day # 48579
SVP 4♓47'47"
GC 27♐18.0 ⚴ 3♏51.9
Eris 26♈15.4R ⚵ 12♎25.7
⚷ 21♉30.8R ⚶ 4♑09.1
☽ Mean ☊ 26♎44.4

1 February 2033
Julian Day # 48610
SVP 4♓47'42"
GC 27♐18.1 ⚴ 12♏40.3
Eris 26♈16.7 ⚵ 15♎28.8
⚷ 21♉06.4 ⚶ 20♑42.8
☽ Mean ☊ 25♎06.0

March 2033 LONGITUDE

Day	Sid.Time	☉	0 hr ☽	Noon ☽	True ☊	☿	♀	♂	⚳	♃	♄	♅	♆	♇
1 Tu	22 38 26	11♓12 54	5♓43 21	13♓20 43	21♎49.8	8♓01.6	8♈27.7	12♐41.4	24♐32.9	20♒38.0	0♋12.7	27♊36.1	16♈13.5	15♒33.9
2 W	22 42 23	12 13 08	20 58 15	28 34 37	21R46.0	6R59.0	8R21.9	13 13.2	24 49.3	20 51.9	0D12.7	27R35.9	16 15.4	15 35.6
3 Th	22 46 19	13 13 20	6♈08 35	13♈39 03	21D44.1	5 58.9	8 13.6	13 44.9	25 05.5	21 05.7	0 12.9	27 35.8	16 17.4	15 37.3
4 F	22 50 16	14 13 30	21 05 03	28 25 51	21 44.0	5 02.6	8 02.8	14 16.5	25 21.6	21 19.4	0 13.1	27 35.7	16 19.4	15 38.9
5 Sa	22 54 12	15 13 38	5♉40 50	12♉49 40	21 45.1	4 11.0	7 49.5	14 47.9	25 37.4	21 33.2	0 13.5	27D35.7	16 21.4	15 40.6
6 Su	22 58 09	16 13 44	19 52 07	26 48 09	21 46.6	3 24.9	7 33.6	15 19.2	25 53.0	21 46.8	0 14.0	27 35.7	16 23.4	15 42.2
7 M	23 02 05	17 13 48	3♊37 51	10♊21 25	21R47.8	2 44.8	7 15.4	15 50.3	26 08.4	22 00.5	0 14.6	27 35.8	16 25.4	15 43.8
8 Tu	23 06 02	18 13 50	16 59 08	23 31 20	21 47.8	2 11.2	6 54.8	16 21.4	26 23.6	22 14.1	0 15.3	27 35.9	16 27.5	15 45.4
9 W	23 09 59	19 13 49	29 58 26	6♋20 50	21 46.4	1 44.2	6 31.8	16 52.2	26 38.5	22 27.7	0 16.2	27 36.1	16 29.5	15 47.0
10 Th	23 13 55	20 13 47	12♋38 57	18 53 13	21 43.6	1 24.0	6 06.6	17 23.0	26 53.3	22 41.2	0 17.1	27 36.3	16 31.6	15 48.6
11 F	23 17 52	21 13 42	25 04 02	1♌11 48	21 39.4	1 10.3	5 39.3	17 53.6	27 07.8	22 54.6	0 18.2	27 36.6	16 33.7	15 50.1
12 Sa	23 21 48	22 13 35	7♌16 54	13 19 40	21 34.4	1D03.2	5 10.1	18 24.0	27 22.1	23 08.1	0 19.3	27 37.0	16 35.8	15 51.7
13 Su	23 25 45	23 13 26	19 20 25	25 19 28	21 29.2	1 02.5	4 39.0	18 54.3	27 36.1	23 21.4	0 20.6	27 37.4	16 37.9	15 53.2
14 M	23 29 41	24 13 15	1♍17 06	7♍13 34	21 24.3	1 07.8	4 06.4	19 24.4	27 49.9	23 34.7	0 22.0	27 37.8	16 40.0	15 54.7
15 Tu	23 33 38	25 13 01	13 09 07	19 04 01	21 20.2	1 18.8	3 32.2	19 54.4	28 03.5	23 48.0	0 23.5	27 38.3	16 42.1	15 56.2
16 W	23 37 34	26 12 46	24 58 28	0♎52 44	21 17.4	1 35.4	2 56.9	20 24.2	28 16.9	24 01.2	0 25.1	27 38.9	16 44.3	15 57.7
17 Th	23 41 31	27 12 29	6♎47 05	12 41 45	21D15.8	1 57.2	2 20.6	20 53.9	28 30.0	24 14.4	0 26.8	27 39.5	16 46.4	15 59.1
18 F	23 45 27	28 12 10	18 37 01	24 33 13	21 15.6	2 23.9	1 43.5	21 23.4	28 42.8	24 27.5	0 28.6	27 40.1	16 48.6	16 00.6
19 Sa	23 49 24	29 11 49	0♏30 39	6♏29 42	21 16.3	2 55.2	1 05.9	21 52.7	28 55.4	24 40.5	0 30.5	27 40.8	16 50.8	16 02.0
20 Su	23 53 21	0♈11 26	12 30 43	18 34 08	21 17.7	3 30.8	0 28.1	22 21.9	29 07.8	24 53.5	0 32.6	27 41.6	16 53.0	16 03.4
21 M	23 57 17	1 11 01	24 40 23	0♐49 55	21 19.3	4 10.5	29♓50.3	22 50.8	29 19.9	25 06.4	0 34.7	27 42.4	16 55.2	16 04.8
22 Tu	0 01 14	2 10 35	7♐03 12	13 20 43	21 20.7	4 54.1	29 12.8	23 19.6	29 31.7	25 19.3	0 37.0	27 43.3	16 57.4	16 06.2
23 W	0 05 10	3 10 07	19 42 57	26 10 21	21R21.6	5 41.2	28 35.8	23 48.2	29 43.3	25 32.1	0 39.3	27 44.2	16 59.6	16 07.5
24 Th	0 09 07	4 09 37	2♑43 21	9♑22 20	21 21.7	6 31.7	27 59.6	24 16.6	29 54.6	25 44.9	0 41.8	27 45.2	17 01.8	16 08.9
25 F	0 13 03	5 09 06	16 07 35	22 59 20	21 20.9	7 25.4	27 24.3	24 44.8	0♑05.6	25 57.6	0 44.4	27 46.2	17 04.0	16 10.2
26 Sa	0 17 00	6 08 32	29 57 39	7♒02 32	21 19.6	8 22.1	26 50.3	25 12.8	0 16.3	26 10.2	0 47.0	27 47.3	17 06.3	16 11.5
27 Su	0 20 56	7 07 57	14♒13 45	21 30 57	21 17.9	9 21.6	26 17.8	25 40.6	0 26.8	26 22.7	0 49.8	27 48.4	17 08.5	16 12.8
28 M	0 24 53	8 07 20	28 53 34	6♓20 53	21 16.2	10 23.8	25 46.8	26 08.2	0 37.0	26 35.2	0 52.7	27 49.6	17 10.7	16 14.0
29 Tu	0 28 50	9 06 41	13♓52 00	21 25 53	21 14.8	11 28.5	25 17.7	26 35.5	0 46.8	26 47.6	0 55.6	27 50.8	17 13.0	16 15.2
30 W	0 32 46	10 06 00	29 01 24	6♈37 20	21D13.9	12 35.6	24 50.4	27 02.6	0 56.4	26 59.9	0 58.7	27 52.1	17 15.2	16 16.5
31 Th	0 36 43	11 05 18	14♈12 28	21 45 35	21 13.6	13 45.1	24 25.2	27 29.4	1 05.7	27 12.2	1 01.9	27 53.5	17 17.5	16 17.7

April 2033 LONGITUDE

Day	Sid.Time	☉	0 hr ☽	Noon ☽	True ☊	☿	♀	♂	⚳	♃	♄	♅	♆	♇
1 F	0 40 39	12♈04 33	29♈15 35	6♉41 26	21♎13.9	14♓56.7	24♓02.2	27♐56.1	1♑14.7	27♒24.4	1♋05.1	27♊54.8	17♈19.8	16♒18.8
2 Sa	0 44 36	13 03 46	14♉02 18	21 17 29	21 14.5	16 10.5	23R41.4	28 22.4	1 23.3	27 36.5	1 08.5	27 56.3	17 22.0	16 20.0
3 Su	0 48 32	14 02 57	28 26 26	5♊28 49	21 15.2	17 26.2	23 22.9	28 48.6	1 31.7	27 48.5	1 12.0	27 57.7	17 24.3	16 21.1
4 M	0 52 29	15 02 05	12♊24 28	19 13 21	21 15.8	18 44.0	23 06.8	29 14.4	1 39.8	28 00.4	1 15.5	27 59.3	17 26.6	16 22.2
5 Tu	0 56 25	16 01 11	25 55 35	2♋31 24	21 16.2	20 03.6	22 53.1	29 40.1	1 47.5	28 12.3	1 19.2	28 00.9	17 28.8	16 23.3
6 W	1 00 22	17 00 15	9♋01 06	15 25 07	21R16.3	21 25.1	22 41.8	0♑05.4	1 54.9	28 24.1	1 22.9	28 02.5	17 31.1	16 24.4
7 Th	1 04 19	17 59 17	21 43 53	27 57 54	21 16.3	22 48.4	22 33.0	0 30.5	2 02.0	28 35.7	1 26.8	28 04.1	17 33.4	16 25.4
8 F	1 08 15	18 58 16	4♌07 41	10♌13 45	21 16.1	24 13.4	22 26.6	0 55.3	2 08.8	28 47.4	1 30.7	28 05.9	17 35.6	16 26.4
9 Sa	1 12 12	19 57 13	16 16 38	22 16 51	21 15.9	25 40.1	22 22.6	1 19.8	2 15.3	28 58.9	1 34.7	28 07.6	17 37.9	16 27.4
10 Su	1 16 08	20 56 07	28 14 55	4♍11 17	21D15.8	27 08.5	22D21.1	1 44.0	2 21.4	29 10.3	1 38.8	28 09.4	17 40.2	16 28.4
11 M	1 20 05	21 55 00	10♍06 27	16 00 49	21 15.8	28 38.6	22 21.9	2 07.9	2 27.1	29 21.6	1 43.0	28 11.3	17 42.4	16 29.3
12 Tu	1 24 01	22 53 50	21 54 47	27 48 45	21 16.0	0♈10.3	22 25.1	2 31.6	2 32.6	29 32.9	1 47.3	28 13.2	17 44.7	16 30.2
13 W	1 27 58	23 52 38	3♎43 02	9♎37 59	21R16.1	1 43.7	22 30.6	2 54.9	2 37.7	29 44.0	1 51.7	28 15.1	17 47.0	16 31.1
14 Th	1 31 54	24 51 24	15 33 54	21 31 02	21 16.2	3 18.7	22 38.3	3 17.9	2 42.5	29 55.1	1 56.2	28 17.1	17 49.2	16 32.0
15 F	1 35 51	25 50 08	27 29 40	3♏30 04	21 16.1	4 55.3	22 48.3	3 40.6	2 46.9	0♓06.0	2 00.7	28 19.1	17 51.5	16 32.9
16 Sa	1 39 47	26 48 50	9♏32 25	15 37 00	21 15.7	6 33.5	23 00.3	4 02.9	2 50.9	0 16.9	2 05.3	28 21.2	17 53.7	16 33.7
17 Su	1 43 44	27 47 31	21 44 02	27 53 43	21 15.0	8 13.3	23 14.5	4 24.9	2 54.6	0 27.7	2 10.0	28 23.3	17 56.0	16 34.5
18 M	1 47 41	28 46 09	4♐06 19	10♐22 03	21 14.1	9 54.8	23 30.7	4 46.6	2 58.0	0 38.3	2 14.8	28 25.5	17 58.2	16 35.3
19 Tu	1 51 37	29 44 46	16 41 10	23 03 53	21 13.0	11 37.9	23 48.8	5 07.9	3 01.0	0 48.9	2 19.7	28 27.7	18 00.5	16 36.0
20 W	1 55 34	0♉43 21	29 30 29	6♑01 10	21 12.0	13 22.6	24 08.9	5 28.8	3 03.6	0 59.3	2 24.6	28 29.9	18 02.7	16 36.7
21 Th	1 59 30	1 41 55	12♑36 12	19 15 46	21D11.3	15 08.9	24 30.7	5 49.4	3 05.9	1 09.7	2 29.7	28 32.2	18 04.9	16 37.4
22 F	2 03 27	2 40 27	26 00 04	2♒49 13	21 11.1	16 56.9	24 54.3	6 09.6	3 07.8	1 20.0	2 34.8	28 34.5	18 07.1	16 38.1
23 Sa	2 07 23	3 38 57	9♒43 20	16 42 26	21 11.4	18 46.6	25 19.7	6 29.3	3 09.3	1 30.1	2 40.0	28 36.9	18 09.3	16 38.8
24 Su	2 11 20	4 37 26	23 46 26	0♓55 10	21 12.1	20 37.9	25 46.6	6 48.7	3 10.5	1 40.1	2 45.2	28 39.3	18 11.5	16 39.4
25 M	2 15 16	5 35 53	8♓08 24	15 25 42	21 13.2	22 30.8	26 15.2	7 07.6	3 11.3	1 50.0	2 50.6	28 41.7	18 13.7	16 40.0
26 Tu	2 19 13	6 34 18	22 46 34	0♈10 21	21 14.2	24 25.5	26 45.2	7 26.2	3R11.7	1 59.8	2 56.0	28 44.2	18 15.9	16 40.6
27 W	2 23 10	7 32 42	7♈36 19	15 03 36	21R14.8	26 21.7	27 16.7	7 44.2	3 11.7	2 09.5	3 01.4	28 46.7	18 18.1	16 41.1
28 Th	2 27 06	8 31 04	22 31 16	29 58 20	21 14.7	28 19.7	27 49.6	8 01.8	3 11.3	2 19.1	3 07.0	28 49.2	18 20.2	16 41.6
29 F	2 31 03	9 29 24	7♉23 48	14♉46 42	21 13.8	0♉19.2	28 23.8	8 19.0	3 10.6	2 28.5	3 12.6	28 51.8	18 22.4	16 42.1
30 Sa	2 34 59	10 27 43	22 06 05	29 21 09	21 11.9	2 20.3	28 59.3	8 35.6	3 09.5	2 37.9	3 18.3	28 54.4	18 24.5	16 42.6

Astro Data (Dy Hr Mn)

	Dy Hr Mn
♄ D	1 16:04
☽ 0N	2 5:34
♅ D	5 14:43
☿ D	13 2:58
☽ 0S	15 23:06
☉0N	20 7:24
☽ 0N	29 16:50
♃△♅	4 9:21
♄□♇	7 0:22
♀ D	10 15:29
☽ 0S	12 5:11
☿0N	16 0:41
☽ 0N	26 2:47
⚳ R	27 1:30

Planet Ingress (Dy Hr Mn)

	Dy Hr Mn
☉ ♈	20 7:24
♀ ♓R	21 5:50
⚳ ♑	24 23:45
♂ ♑	6 6:52
☿ ♈	12 9:19
♃ ♓	14 22:46
☉ ♉	19 18:14
☿ ♉	29 8:10

Last Aspect / ☽ Ingress

Last Aspect Dy Hr Mn		☽ Ingress Dy Hr Mn
2 10:27	♅ □	♈ 2 14:15
4 10:38	♅ ✶	♉ 4 14:35
6 3:09	♃ □	♊ 6 17:36
8 19:34	♅ ☌	♋ 9 0:03
10 14:50	☉ △	♌ 11 9:39
13 16:37	♅ ✶	♍ 13 21:25
16 5:26	♅ □	♎ 16 10:13
18 18:17	♅ △	♏ 18 22:58
21 10:10	♀ △	♐ 21 10:23
23 16:16	♀ □	♑ 23 19:02
25 19:19	♀ ✶	♒ 26 0:04
27 22:15	♅ △	♓ 28 1:47
29 22:09	♅ □	♈ 30 1:33

Last Aspect Dy Hr Mn		☽ Ingress Dy Hr Mn
31 21:49	♅ ✶	♉ 1 1:11
2 22:45	♃ □	♊ 3 2:39
5 6:37	♂ ☍	♋ 5 7:23
7 1:41	♀ △	♌ 7 15:57
10 1:42	♃ ☍	♍ 10 3:32
12 12:50	♅ □	♎ 12 16:27
15 1:37	♅ △	♏ 15 5:01
17 2:46	♀ △	♐ 17 16:05
19 22:05	♅ ☍	♑ 20 0:55
21 21:38	♀ ✶	♒ 22 7:03
24 8:12	♀ □	♓ 24 10:28
26 9:40	♅ □	♈ 26 11:43
28 10:08	♅ ✶	♉ 28 12:03
30 11:22	♀ ✶	♊ 30 13:05

☽ Phases & Eclipses

Dy Hr Mn	
1 8:25	● 11♓04
8 1:28	☽ 17♊47
16 1:39	○ 25♍47
24 1:51	☾ 3♑44
30 17:53	● 10♈21
30 18:02:35	✔ T 02'37"
6 15:15	☽ 17♋08
14 19:19	○ 25♎09
14 19:14	• T 1.094
22 11:43	☾ 2♒40
29 2:47	● 9♉07

Astro Data

1 March 2033
Julian Day # 48638
SVP 4♓47'39"
GC 27♐18.2 ⚴ 16♏36.3
Eris 26♈26.4 ⚵ 13♎03.3R
⚷ 21♉37.1 ⚶ 5♒11.4
☽ Mean ☊ 23♎37.0

1 April 2033
Julian Day # 48669
SVP 4♓47'37"
GC 27♐18.2 ⚴ 14♏16.2R
Eris 26♈44.0 ⚵ 6♎08.7R
⚷ 23♉01.8 ⚶ 20♒17.5
☽ Mean ☊ 21♎58.5

LONGITUDE — May 2033

Day	Sid.Time	☉	0 hr ☽	Noon ☽	True ☊	☿	♀	♂	⚳	♃	♄	♅	♆	♇
1 Su	2 38 56	11♉25 59	6♊31 09	13♊35 32	21♎09.3	4♉23.0	29♓36.1	8♑51.8	3♑08.0	2♓47.1	3♋24.1	28♊57.1	18♈26.7	16♒43.0
2 M	2 42 52	12 24 14	20 33 49	27 25 45	21R 06.3	6 27.0	0♈14.0	9 07.5	3R 06.1	2 56.1	3 29.9	28 59.8	18 28.8	16 43.4
3 Tu	2 46 49	13 22 27	4♋11 12	10♋50 11	21 03.5	8 32.5	0 53.0	9 22.7	3 03.9	3 05.1	3 35.8	29 02.5	18 30.9	16 43.8
4 W	2 50 45	14 20 38	17 22 50	23 49 25	21 01.3	10 39.2	1 33.2	9 37.4	3 01.2	3 13.9	3 41.7	29 05.3	18 33.0	16 44.2
5 Th	2 54 42	15 18 47	0♌10 18	6♌25 55	20D 59.9	12 47.0	2 14.4	9 51.6	2 58.2	3 22.6	3 47.7	29 08.1	18 35.1	16 44.5
6 F	2 58 39	16 16 53	12 36 46	18 43 25	20 59.6	14 55.8	2 56.6	10 05.2	2 54.8	3 31.2	3 53.8	29 10.9	18 37.2	16 44.8
7 Sa	3 02 35	17 14 58	24 46 26	0♍46 26	21 00.4	17 05.4	3 39.8	10 18.3	2 51.0	3 39.6	3 59.9	29 13.7	18 39.2	16 45.1
8 Su	3 06 32	18 13 01	6♍44 02	12 39 49	21 01.8	19 15.5	4 23.9	10 30.9	2 46.9	3 47.9	4 06.1	29 16.6	18 41.2	16 45.4
9 M	3 10 28	19 11 02	18 34 24	24 28 21	21 03.6	21 25.9	5 08.9	10 42.9	2 42.4	3 56.1	4 12.4	29 19.5	18 43.3	16 45.6
10 Tu	3 14 25	20 09 02	0♎22 14	6♎16 33	21 05.1	23 36.4	5 54.7	10 54.3	2 37.5	4 04.1	4 18.7	29 22.5	18 45.3	16 45.8
11 W	3 18 21	21 06 59	12 11 49	18 08 28	21R 06.0	25 46.7	6 41.5	11 05.1	2 32.3	4 12.0	4 25.1	29 25.4	18 47.3	16 46.0
12 Th	3 22 18	22 04 55	24 06 55	0♏07 31	21 05.6	27 56.5	7 29.0	11 15.4	2 26.7	4 19.7	4 31.5	29 28.4	18 49.2	16 46.1
13 F	3 26 14	23 02 49	6♏10 35	12 16 24	21 03.8	0♊05.5	8 17.2	11 25.0	2 20.7	4 27.3	4 38.0	29 31.5	18 51.2	16 46.2
14 Sa	3 30 11	24 00 42	18 25 11	24 37 06	21 00.4	2 13.4	9 06.3	11 34.1	2 14.4	4 34.8	4 44.5	29 34.5	18 53.1	16 46.3
15 Su	3 34 08	24 58 33	0♐52 17	7♐10 49	20 55.7	4 20.0	9 56.0	11 42.5	2 07.7	4 42.1	4 51.1	29 37.6	18 55.1	16 46.4
16 M	3 38 04	25 56 23	13 32 46	19 58 09	20 50.1	6 25.0	10 46.5	11 50.3	2 00.7	4 49.3	4 57.7	29 40.7	18 57.0	16 46.4
17 Tu	3 42 01	26 54 11	26 26 57	2♑59 09	20 44.2	8 28.2	11 37.6	11 57.4	1 53.3	4 56.3	5 04.4	29 43.8	18 58.9	16R 46.4
18 W	3 45 57	27 51 58	9♑34 42	16 13 34	20 38.7	10 29.3	12 29.3	12 03.8	1 45.6	5 03.2	5 11.1	29 47.0	19 00.8	16 46.4
19 Th	3 49 54	28 49 44	22 55 42	29 41 01	20 34.3	12 28.1	13 21.7	12 09.6	1 37.6	5 10.0	5 17.9	29 50.2	19 02.6	16 46.4
20 F	3 53 50	29 47 29	6♒29 30	13♒21 05	20 31.4	14 24.5	14 14.7	12 14.7	1 29.2	5 16.5	5 24.7	29 53.4	19 04.4	16 46.3
21 Sa	3 57 47	0♊45 13	20 15 43	27 13 20	20D 30.2	16 18.3	15 08.2	12 19.1	1 20.6	5 23.0	5 31.6	29 56.6	19 06.3	16 46.2
22 Su	4 01 43	1 42 56	4♓13 51	11♓17 10	20 30.5	18 09.5	16 02.3	12 22.8	1 11.6	5 29.2	5 38.5	29 59.8	19 08.0	16 46.1
23 M	4 05 40	2 40 37	18 23 09	25 31 36	20 31.6	19 57.8	16 56.9	12 25.7	1 02.3	5 35.3	5 45.5	0♋03.1	19 09.8	16 46.0
24 Tu	4 09 37	3 38 18	2♈42 16	9♈54 50	20R 32.8	21 43.3	17 52.0	12 28.0	0 52.7	5 41.3	5 52.5	0 06.4	19 11.6	16 45.8
25 W	4 13 33	4 35 58	17 08 55	24 24 01	20 33.1	23 25.9	18 47.6	12 29.5	0 42.8	5 47.1	5 59.5	0 09.7	19 13.3	16 45.6
26 Th	4 17 30	5 33 36	1♉39 36	8♉55 02	20 31.8	25 05.4	19 43.7	12R 30.2	0 32.6	5 52.7	6 06.6	0 13.0	19 15.0	16 45.4
27 F	4 21 26	6 31 14	16 09 37	23 22 39	20 28.4	26 42.0	20 40.3	12 30.2	0 22.1	5 58.2	6 13.7	0 16.4	19 16.7	16 45.1
28 Sa	4 25 23	7 28 51	0♊33 24	7♊41 08	20 22.9	28 15.4	21 37.3	12 29.4	0 11.4	6 03.5	6 20.9	0 19.7	19 18.4	16 44.8
29 Su	4 29 19	8 26 26	14 45 10	21 44 52	20 15.8	29 45.8	22 34.7	12 27.9	0 00.5	6 08.6	6 28.1	0 23.1	19 20.0	16 44.5
30 M	4 33 16	9 24 00	28 39 45	5♋29 21	20 07.8	1♋13.0	23 32.5	12 25.6	29♐49.3	6 13.6	6 35.3	0 26.5	19 21.6	16 44.2
31 Tu	4 37 12	10 21 33	12♋13 24	18 51 44	19 59.7	2 37.0	24 30.6	12 22.6	29 37.9	6 18.4	6 42.6	0 29.9	19 23.2	16 43.9

LONGITUDE — June 2033

Day	Sid.Time	☉	0 hr ☽	Noon ☽	True ☊	☿	♀	♂	⚳	♃	♄	♅	♆	♇
1 W	4 41 09	11♊19 05	25♋24 18	1♌51 12	19♎52.7	3♋57.7	25♈29.2	12♑18.8	29♐26.2	6♓23.0	6♋49.9	0♋33.3	19♈24.8	16♒43.5
2 Th	4 45 06	12 16 36	8♌12 38	14 28 54	19R 47.2	5 15.3	26 28.1	12R 14.3	29R 14.4	6 27.4	6 57.2	0 36.8	19 26.3	16R 43.1
3 F	4 49 02	13 14 05	20 40 25	26 47 40	19 43.7	6 29.5	27 27.4	12 09.0	29 02.3	6 31.7	7 04.6	0 40.2	19 27.9	16 42.6
4 Sa	4 52 59	14 11 33	2♍51 10	8♍51 31	19D 42.1	7 40.3	28 27.0	12 03.0	28 50.1	6 35.8	7 12.0	0 43.7	19 29.4	16 42.2
5 Su	4 56 55	15 09 00	14 49 21	20 45 18	19 42.1	8 47.7	29 27.0	11 56.2	28 37.7	6 39.7	7 19.4	0 47.2	19 30.8	16 41.7
6 M	5 00 52	16 06 25	26 40 03	2♎34 16	19 43.0	9 51.6	0♉27.3	11 48.7	28 25.2	6 43.4	7 26.8	0 50.7	19 32.3	16 41.2
7 Tu	5 04 48	17 03 49	8♎28 35	14 23 39	19R 43.8	10 52.0	1 27.8	11 40.5	28 12.5	6 47.0	7 34.3	0 54.2	19 33.7	16 40.7
8 W	5 08 45	18 01 13	20 20 05	26 18 28	19 43.7	11 48.7	2 28.7	11 31.6	27 59.7	6 50.4	7 41.8	0 57.7	19 35.1	16 40.1
9 Th	5 12 41	18 58 35	2♏19 19	8♏23 09	19 41.9	12 41.7	3 29.9	11 21.9	27 46.8	6 53.6	7 49.3	1 01.2	19 36.5	16 39.6
10 F	5 16 38	19 55 56	14 30 21	20 41 19	19 37.9	13 30.9	4 31.4	11 11.6	27 33.8	6 56.6	7 56.9	1 04.8	19 37.8	16 39.0
11 Sa	5 20 35	20 53 17	26 56 19	3♐15 32	19 31.4	14 16.3	5 33.1	11 00.6	27 20.8	6 59.4	8 04.5	1 08.3	19 39.1	16 38.4
12 Su	5 24 31	21 50 36	9♐39 07	16 07 05	19 22.9	14 57.6	6 35.1	10 49.0	27 07.6	7 02.1	8 12.0	1 11.9	19 40.4	16 37.7
13 M	5 28 28	22 47 55	22 39 22	29 15 52	19 12.9	15 34.9	7 37.4	10 36.7	26 54.4	7 04.5	8 19.7	1 15.4	19 41.7	16 37.1
14 Tu	5 32 24	23 45 13	5♑56 21	12♑40 34	19 02.3	16 08.0	8 40.0	10 23.8	26 41.2	7 06.8	8 27.3	1 19.0	19 42.9	16 36.4
15 W	5 36 21	24 42 31	19 28 10	26 18 50	18 52.4	16 36.8	9 42.8	10 10.4	26 27.9	7 08.9	8 35.0	1 22.6	19 44.1	16 35.7
16 Th	5 40 17	25 39 48	3♒12 11	10♒07 51	18 44.0	17 01.3	10 45.8	9 56.3	26 14.6	7 10.8	8 42.6	1 26.1	19 45.3	16 34.9
17 F	5 44 14	26 37 05	17 05 27	24 04 42	18 37.9	17 21.4	11 49.1	9 41.7	26 01.3	7 12.5	8 50.3	1 29.7	19 46.4	16 34.2
18 Sa	5 48 10	27 34 21	1♓05 16	8♓06 55	18 34.3	17 36.9	12 52.6	9 26.5	25 48.0	7 14.1	8 58.0	1 33.3	19 47.6	16 33.4
19 Su	5 52 07	28 31 38	15 09 25	22 12 37	18D 32.9	17 48.0	13 56.3	9 10.9	25 34.8	7 15.4	9 05.7	1 36.9	19 48.7	16 32.6
20 M	5 56 04	29 28 54	29 16 20	6♈20 28	18R 32.9	17R 54.4	15 00.2	8 54.8	25 21.6	7 16.5	9 13.5	1 40.5	19 49.7	16 31.8
21 Tu	6 00 00	0♋26 09	13♈24 51	20 29 23	18 33.1	17 56.3	16 04.4	8 38.3	25 08.4	7 17.5	9 21.2	1 44.1	19 50.7	16 31.0
22 W	6 03 57	1 23 25	27 33 53	4♉38 09	18 32.2	17 53.7	17 08.7	8 21.3	24 55.3	7 18.2	9 29.0	1 47.7	19 51.7	16 30.1
23 Th	6 07 53	2 20 41	11♉41 56	18 44 57	18 29.4	17 46.7	18 13.3	8 04.0	24 42.3	7 18.8	9 36.7	1 51.2	19 52.7	16 29.2
24 F	6 11 50	3 17 56	25 46 51	2♊47 14	18 23.8	17 35.3	19 18.0	7 46.5	24 29.4	7 19.2	9 44.5	1 54.8	19 53.7	16 28.4
25 Sa	6 15 46	4 15 11	9♊45 40	16 41 42	18 15.5	17 19.7	20 23.0	7 28.6	24 16.6	7R 19.4	9 52.3	1 58.4	19 54.6	16 27.4
26 Su	6 19 43	5 12 27	23 34 51	0♋24 40	18 05.0	17 00.1	21 28.1	7 10.5	24 04.0	7 19.3	10 00.1	2 02.0	19 55.5	16 26.5
27 M	6 23 40	6 09 41	7♋10 45	13 52 43	17 53.2	16 36.9	22 33.4	6 52.3	23 51.5	7 19.1	10 07.9	2 05.6	19 56.3	16 25.6
28 Tu	6 27 36	7 06 56	20 30 17	27 03 14	17 41.1	16 10.2	23 38.8	6 33.9	23 39.1	7 18.7	10 15.7	2 09.2	19 57.1	16 24.6
29 W	6 31 33	8 04 10	3♌31 26	9♌54 52	17 30.1	15 40.7	24 44.4	6 15.4	23 27.0	7 18.1	10 23.5	2 12.8	19 57.9	16 23.6
30 Th	6 35 29	9 01 24	16 13 38	22 27 53	17 21.0	15 08.6	25 50.2	5 56.9	23 15.0	7 17.3	10 31.3	2 16.4	19 58.7	16 22.6

Astro Data

	Dy Hr Mn
♃∠♆	7 10:28
☽0S	9 12:13
♇ R	17 13:01
☽0N	23 10:45
♂ R	26 23:49
☽0S	5 20:41
♅⚼♇	18 12:43
☽0N	19 17:23
☿ R	21 10:06
♃ R	25 21:53

Planet Ingress

		Dy Hr Mn
♀	♈	2 3:14
☿	♊	13 10:59
☉	♊	20 17:12
♅	♋	22 13:16
⚳	♐R	29 13:01
☿	♋	29 15:51
♀	♉	6 1:10
☉	♋	21 1:02

Last Aspect / ☽ Ingress (May)

Last Aspect Dy Hr Mn		☽ Ingress Dy Hr Mn
2 14:47 ♅ ☌	♋	2 16:33
4 2:08 ♆ □	♌	4 23:40
7 8:53 ♅ ⚹	♍	7 10:27
9 21:55 ♅ □	♎	9 23:15
12 10:42 ♅ △	♏	12 11:45
14 10:44 ☉ ☍	♐	14 22:20
17 6:01 ♅ ☍	♑	17 6:32
19 10:22 ☉ △	♒	19 12:34
21 16:41 ♅ △	♓	21 16:46
23 1:19 ♅ □	♈	23 19:29
25 10:11 ☿ ⚹	♉	25 21:15
27 0:59 ♇ □	♊	27 23:04
29 13:32 ♀ ⚹	♋	30 2:20

Last Aspect / ☽ Ingress (June)

Last Aspect Dy Hr Mn		☽ Ingress Dy Hr Mn
31 23:11 ♀ □	♌	1 8:32
3 13:25 ♀ △	♍	3 18:20
4 23:40 ☉ □	♎	6 6:46
7 22:28 ♆ ☍	♏	8 19:23
10 4:11 ♇ □	♐	11 5:50
12 23:20 ☉ ☍	♑	13 13:20
15 0:27 ♆ □	♒	15 18:26
17 16:40 ☉ △	♓	17 22:08
19 23:31 ☉ □	♈	20 1:14
21 10:54 ♆ ☌	♉	22 4:08
23 11:02 ♀ ☌	♊	24 7:13
25 17:36 ♆ ⚹	♋	26 11:16
28 5:10 ♀ ⚹	♌	28 17:27

☽ Phases & Eclipses

Dy Hr Mn	
6 6:46	☽ 16♌04
14 10:44	○ 23♏58
21 18:30	☾ 1♓01
28 11:38	● 7♊28
4 23:40	☽ 14♍39
12 23:20	○ 22♐18
19 23:31	☾ 28♓59
26 21:08	● 5♋34

Astro Data

1 May 2033
Julian Day # 48699
SVP 4♓47'34"
GC 27♐18.3 ⚴ 5♍59.8R
Eris 27♈03.6 ⚵ 0♋38.0R
⚷ 24♉56.8 ⚶ 3♓27.8
☽ Mean ☊ 20♎23.1

1 June 2033
Julian Day # 48730
SVP 4♓47'30"
GC 27♐18.4 ⚴ 28♌46.9R
Eris 27♈21.5 ⚵ 0♋03.2
⚷ 27♉07.5 ⚶ 14♓43.2
☽ Mean ☊ 18♎44.6

July 2033 — LONGITUDE

Day	Sid.Time	☉	0 hr ☽	Noon ☽	True ☊	☿	♀	♂	⚳	♃	♄	♅	♆	♇
1 F	6 39 26	9♋58 37	28♌37 56	4♍44 06	17♎14.4	14♋34.4	26♉56.2	5♑38.5	23♐03.2	7♓16.3	10♋39.1	2♋19.9	19♈59.4	16♒21.6
2 Sa	6 43 22	10 55 51	10♍46 51	16 46 41	17R 10.4	13R 58.8	28 02.2	5R 20.1	22R 51.6	7R 15.1	10 46.9	2 23.5	20 00.1	16R 20.5
3 Su	6 47 19	11 53 03	22 44 08	28 39 50	17 08.5	13 22.4	29 08.5	5 01.8	22 40.2	7 13.8	10 54.7	2 27.0	20 00.8	16 19.5
4 M	6 51 15	12 50 16	4♎34 26	10♎28 34	17 08.0	12 45.6	0♊14.8	4 43.7	22 29.0	7 12.2	11 02.5	2 30.6	20 01.4	16 18.4
5 Tu	6 55 12	13 47 28	16 22 57	22 18 15	17 08.0	12 09.3	1 21.4	4 25.8	22 18.1	7 10.4	11 10.3	2 34.1	20 02.0	16 17.3
6 W	6 59 08	14 44 40	28 15 10	4♏14 21	17 07.3	11 33.9	2 28.0	4 08.1	22 07.5	7 08.5	11 18.1	2 37.7	20 02.6	16 16.2
7 Th	7 03 05	15 41 52	10♏16 27	16 22 05	17 05.0	11 00.1	3 34.8	3 50.8	21 57.1	7 06.3	11 25.9	2 41.2	20 03.1	16 15.1
8 F	7 07 02	16 39 03	22 31 45	28 45 59	17 00.4	10 28.5	4 41.8	3 33.8	21 46.9	7 04.0	11 33.7	2 44.7	20 03.6	16 14.0
9 Sa	7 10 58	17 36 15	5♐05 09	11♐29 34	16 53.2	9 59.8	5 48.9	3 17.2	21 37.1	7 01.5	11 41.5	2 48.2	20 04.1	16 12.8
10 Su	7 14 55	18 33 27	17 59 26	24 34 50	16 43.6	9 34.3	6 56.1	3 01.0	21 27.5	6 58.8	11 49.3	2 51.7	20 04.5	16 11.7
11 M	7 18 51	19 30 38	1♑15 43	8♑01 55	16 32.4	9 12.5	8 03.4	2 45.2	21 18.2	6 55.9	11 57.1	2 55.2	20 04.9	16 10.5
12 Tu	7 22 48	20 27 50	14 53 09	21 48 59	16 20.5	8 55.0	9 10.9	2 29.9	21 09.3	6 52.9	12 04.8	2 58.7	20 05.3	16 09.3
13 W	7 26 44	21 25 02	28 48 55	5♒52 20	16 09.2	8 41.9	10 18.5	2 15.2	21 00.6	6 49.6	12 12.6	3 02.1	20 05.6	16 08.1
14 Th	7 30 41	22 22 14	12♒58 36	20 07 00	15 59.6	8 33.7	11 26.2	2 01.0	20 52.2	6 46.2	12 20.3	3 05.6	20 05.9	16 06.9
15 F	7 34 38	23 19 27	27 16 53	4♓27 35	15 52.5	8D 30.6	12 34.1	1 47.4	20 44.2	6 42.6	12 28.0	3 09.0	20 06.2	16 05.7
16 Sa	7 38 34	24 16 40	11♓38 29	18 49 03	15 48.2	8 32.8	13 42.1	1 34.4	20 36.4	6 38.8	12 35.7	3 12.4	20 06.4	16 04.5
17 Su	7 42 31	25 13 54	25 58 50	3♈07 27	15D 46.3	8 40.3	14 50.2	1 22.0	20 29.0	6 34.8	12 43.4	3 15.8	20 06.7	16 03.2
18 M	7 46 27	26 11 08	10♈14 39	17 20 10	15R 45.9	8 53.4	15 58.4	1 10.3	20 21.9	6 30.7	12 51.1	3 19.2	20 06.8	16 02.0
19 Tu	7 50 24	27 08 24	24 23 53	1♉25 42	15 45.9	9 12.1	17 06.7	0 59.3	20 15.2	6 26.4	12 58.8	3 22.6	20 07.0	16 00.7
20 W	7 54 20	28 05 40	8♉25 31	15 23 19	15 45.0	9 36.5	18 15.2	0 49.0	20 08.8	6 21.9	13 06.4	3 25.9	20 07.1	15 59.4
21 Th	7 58 17	29 02 57	22 19 01	29 12 35	15 42.2	10 06.4	19 23.7	0 39.5	20 02.7	6 17.3	13 14.1	3 29.3	20 07.2	15 58.2
22 F	8 02 13	0♌00 14	6♊03 54	12♊52 53	15 36.8	10 42.1	20 32.4	0 30.7	19 57.0	6 12.5	13 21.7	3 32.6	20R 07.2	15 56.9
23 Sa	8 06 10	0 57 33	19 39 23	26 23 15	15 28.6	11 23.3	21 41.2	0 22.6	19 51.7	6 07.5	13 29.3	3 35.9	20 07.2	15 55.6
24 Su	8 10 07	1 54 52	3♋04 18	9♋42 21	15 18.3	12 10.1	22 50.1	0 15.4	19 46.7	6 02.4	13 36.8	3 39.2	20 07.2	15 54.3
25 M	8 14 03	2 52 12	16 17 11	22 48 39	15 06.6	13 02.4	23 59.1	0 09.0	19 42.1	5 57.1	13 44.4	3 42.4	20 07.2	15 53.0
26 Tu	8 18 00	3 49 33	29 16 36	5♌40 54	14 54.7	14 00.2	25 08.2	0 03.4	19 37.8	5 51.7	13 51.9	3 45.7	20 07.1	15 51.7
27 W	8 21 56	4 46 54	12♌01 29	18 18 21	14 43.7	15 03.3	26 17.4	29♐58.6	19 33.9	5 46.1	13 59.4	3 48.9	20 06.9	15 50.3
28 Th	8 25 53	5 44 16	24 31 33	0♍41 11	14 34.6	16 11.6	27 26.6	29 54.7	19 30.3	5 40.4	14 06.9	3 52.1	20 06.8	15 49.0
29 F	8 29 49	6 41 38	6♍47 28	12 50 39	14 27.8	17 25.1	28 36.0	29 51.6	19 27.1	5 34.5	14 14.3	3 55.2	20 06.6	15 47.7
30 Sa	8 33 46	7 39 02	18 51 04	24 49 06	14 23.6	18 43.6	29 45.5	29 49.4	19 24.3	5 28.5	14 21.7	3 58.4	20 06.4	15 46.3
31 Su	8 37 42	8 36 25	0♎45 12	6♎39 53	14D 21.8	20 06.9	0♋55.0	29 48.0	19 21.9	5 22.3	14 29.1	4 01.5	20 06.1	15 45.0

August 2033 — LONGITUDE

Day	Sid.Time	☉	0 hr ☽	Noon ☽	True ☊	☿	♀	♂	⚳	♃	♄	♅	♆	♇
1 M	8 41 39	9♌33 49	12♎33 41	18♎27 13	14♎21.6	21♋35.0	2♋04.7	29♐47.5	19♐19.8	5♓16.1	14♋36.4	4♋04.6	20♈05.9	15♒43.6
2 Tu	8 45 36	10 31 14	24 21 06	0♏16 00	14R 22.1	23 07.5	3 14.4	29D 47.9	19R 18.1	5R 09.7	14 43.8	4 07.6	20R 05.5	15R 42.3
3 W	8 49 32	11 28 40	6♏12 35	12 11 31	14 22.4	24 44.3	4 24.3	29 49.0	19 16.7	5 03.2	14 51.0	4 10.7	20 05.2	15 40.9
4 Th	8 53 29	12 26 06	18 13 29	24 19 08	14 21.7	26 25.1	5 34.2	29 51.1	19 15.7	4 56.5	14 58.3	4 13.7	20 04.8	15 39.6
5 F	8 57 25	13 23 33	0♐29 06	6♐43 58	14 19.1	28 09.6	6 44.2	29 54.0	19 15.1	4 49.8	15 05.5	4 16.7	20 04.4	15 38.2
6 Sa	9 01 22	14 21 01	13 04 15	19 30 23	14 14.3	29 57.5	7 54.3	29 57.7	19D 14.8	4 43.0	15 12.7	4 19.6	20 04.0	15 36.9
7 Su	9 05 18	15 18 29	26 02 42	2♑41 26	14 07.5	1♌48.5	9 04.5	0♑02.2	19 14.9	4 36.0	15 19.8	4 22.5	20 03.5	15 35.5
8 M	9 09 15	16 15 58	9♑26 40	16 18 18	13 59.2	3 42.2	10 14.8	0 07.6	19 15.4	4 29.0	15 26.9	4 25.4	20 03.0	15 34.2
9 Tu	9 13 11	17 13 29	23 16 09	0♒19 47	13 50.2	5 38.3	11 25.1	0 13.7	19 16.2	4 21.9	15 34.0	4 28.3	20 02.5	15 32.8
10 W	9 17 08	18 11 00	7♒28 41	14 42 08	13 41.5	7 36.3	12 35.6	0 20.7	19 17.3	4 14.6	15 41.0	4 31.1	20 01.9	15 31.4
11 Th	9 21 05	19 08 32	21 59 22	29 19 27	13 34.3	9 35.9	13 46.1	0 28.4	19 18.8	4 07.3	15 48.0	4 34.0	20 01.3	15 30.1
12 F	9 25 01	20 06 05	6♓41 27	14♓04 26	13 29.0	11 36.7	14 56.7	0 37.0	19 20.7	3 59.9	15 55.0	4 36.7	20 00.7	15 28.7
13 Sa	9 28 58	21 03 40	21 27 26	28 49 37	13D 26.1	13 38.5	16 07.4	0 46.2	19 22.9	3 52.5	16 01.8	4 39.5	20 00.1	15 27.4
14 Su	9 32 54	22 01 16	6♈10 11	13♈28 27	13 25.3	15 40.7	17 18.2	0 56.3	19 25.4	3 45.0	16 08.7	4 42.2	19 59.4	15 26.0
15 M	9 36 51	22 58 53	20 43 53	27 56 03	13 25.8	17 43.3	18 29.1	1 07.0	19 28.3	3 37.4	16 15.5	4 44.8	19 58.7	15 24.7
16 Tu	9 40 47	23 56 32	5♉04 38	12♉09 24	13R 26.8	19 45.8	19 40.1	1 18.5	19 31.5	3 29.7	16 22.3	4 47.5	19 57.9	15 23.4
17 W	9 44 44	24 54 13	19 10 15	26 07 09	13 27.3	21 48.0	20 51.1	1 30.7	19 35.1	3 22.0	16 29.0	4 50.1	19 57.2	15 22.0
18 Th	9 48 40	25 51 55	3♊00 04	9♊49 06	13 26.4	23 49.7	22 02.3	1 43.7	19 38.9	3 14.3	16 35.7	4 52.7	19 56.4	15 20.7
19 F	9 52 37	26 49 39	16 34 19	23 15 49	13 23.5	25 50.8	23 13.5	1 57.3	19 43.1	3 06.5	16 42.3	4 55.2	19 55.5	15 19.4
20 Sa	9 56 33	27 47 25	29 53 42	6♋28 03	13 18.7	27 51.1	24 24.8	2 11.7	19 47.7	2 58.7	16 48.9	4 57.7	19 54.7	15 18.0
21 Su	10 00 30	28 45 12	12♋59 00	19 26 35	13 12.3	29 50.4	25 36.1	2 26.7	19 52.5	2 50.9	16 55.4	5 00.2	19 53.8	15 16.7
22 M	10 04 27	29 43 01	25 50 55	2♌12 04	13 04.8	1♍48.8	26 47.6	2 42.4	19 57.7	2 43.0	17 01.8	5 02.6	19 52.9	15 15.4
23 Tu	10 08 23	0♍40 51	8♌30 05	14 45 03	12 57.1	3 45.9	27 59.1	2 58.7	20 03.2	2 35.1	17 08.2	5 05.0	19 52.0	15 14.1
24 W	10 12 20	1 38 43	20 57 03	27 06 12	12 50.1	5 42.0	29 10.7	3 15.7	20 09.0	2 27.2	17 14.6	5 07.3	19 51.0	15 12.8
25 Th	10 16 16	2 36 36	3♍12 36	9♍16 25	12 44.3	7 36.7	0♌22.4	3 33.4	20 15.2	2 19.3	17 20.9	5 09.6	19 50.0	15 11.5
26 F	10 20 13	3 34 30	15 17 49	21 17 02	12 40.2	9 30.3	1 34.1	3 51.7	20 21.6	2 11.4	17 27.1	5 11.9	19 49.0	15 10.2
27 Sa	10 24 09	4 32 27	27 14 19	3♎09 59	12D 38.0	11 22.5	2 46.0	4 10.6	20 28.3	2 03.5	17 33.3	5 14.1	19 47.9	15 09.0
28 Su	10 28 06	5 30 24	9♎04 23	14 57 53	12 37.6	13 13.5	3 57.8	4 30.1	20 35.4	1 55.6	17 39.4	5 16.3	19 46.9	15 07.7
29 M	10 32 02	6 28 23	20 50 56	26 44 00	12 38.4	15 03.2	5 09.8	4 50.2	20 42.7	1 47.7	17 45.5	5 18.5	19 45.8	15 06.5
30 Tu	10 35 59	7 26 23	2♏37 35	8♏32 16	12 40.0	16 51.5	6 21.8	5 10.9	20 50.3	1 39.9	17 51.5	5 20.6	19 44.7	15 05.2
31 W	10 39 56	8 24 25	14 28 35	20 27 09	12 41.7	18 38.6	7 33.9	5 32.1	20 58.2	1 32.1	17 57.4	5 22.6	19 43.5	15 04.0

Astro Data Dy Hr Mn	Planet Ingress Dy Hr Mn	Last Aspect Dy Hr Mn	☽ Ingress Dy Hr Mn	Last Aspect Dy Hr Mn	☽ Ingress Dy Hr Mn	☽ Phases & Eclipses Dy Hr Mn	Astro Data
☽0S 3 6:03	♀ ♊ 4 6:38	30 19:11 ♀ □	♍ 1 2:41	2 11:03 ♂ ⚹	♏ 2 11:28	4 17:13 ☽ 13♎03	1 July 2033
☿ D 15 14:21	☉ ♌ 22 11:54	3 13:04 ♀ △	♎ 3 14:43	4 16:46 ☿ △	♐ 4 23:04	12 9:30 ○ 20♑22	Julian Day # 48760
☽0N 17 0:08	♂ ♐R 27 4:36	5 7:24 ♆ ☍	♏ 6 3:31	6 13:02 ♆ △	♑ 7 7:10	19 4:08 ☾ 26♈50	SVP 4♓47'25"
♆ R 23 10:27	♀ ♋ 30 17:01	7 11:46 ♇ □	♐ 8 14:21	8 18:28 ♆ □	♒ 9 11:27	26 8:14 ● 3♌41	GC 27♐18.4 ⚴ 28♎27.9
☽0S 30 15:07		10 3:49 ♆ △	♑ 10 21:45	10 20:47 ♆ ⚹	♓ 11 13:06		Eris 27♈32.6 ⚵ 4♎02.2
	☿ ♌ 6 12:33	12 9:30 ☉ ☍	♒ 13 2:01	12 15:01 ♄ △	♈ 13 13:55	3 10:27 ☽ 11♏25	⚷ 29♉03.6 ⚶ 21♓56.9
♂ D 1 14:26	♂ ♑ 7 0:49	14 11:58 ♆ ⚹	♓ 15 4:33	15 3:09 ☉ △	♉ 15 15:28	10 18:09 ○ 18♒26	☽ Mean ☊ 17♎09.3
♃∠♆ 3 4:08	☿ ♍ 21 13:56	16 21:48 ☉ △	♈ 17 6:45	17 9:44 ☉ □	♊ 17 18:45	17 9:44 ☾ 24♉49	
⚳ D 6 17:39	☉ ♍ 22 19:03	19 4:08 ☉ □	♉ 19 9:33	19 18:56 ☉ ⚹	♋ 20 0:11	24 21:41 ● 2♍02	1 August 2033
♃△♅ 8 20:31	♀ ♌ 25 4:30	21 11:42 ☉ ⚹	♊ 21 13:23	22 0:43 ♀ ☌	♌ 22 7:50		Julian Day # 48791
♄⊼♇ 9 8:35		23 2:50 ♀ ☌	♋ 23 18:28	23 21:53 ♆ △	♍ 24 17:41		SVP 4♓47'21"
☽0N 13 8:18		25 7:02 ♆ □	♌ 26 1:21	26 4:15 ♄ ⚹	♎ 27 5:35		GC 27♐18.5 ⚴ 4♏03.7
♃⚼♄ 25 9:17		28 10:30 ♂ △	♍ 28 10:39	28 21:48 ♆ ☍	♏ 29 18:39		Eris 27♈34.8R ⚵ 11♎14.0
☽0S 26 22:54		30 22:06 ♂ □	♎ 30 22:28				⚷ 0♊31.5 ⚶ 23♓29.7R
							☽ Mean ☊ 15♎30.8

LONGITUDE — September 2033

Day	Sid.Time	☉	0 hr ☽	Noon☽	True☊	☿	♀	♂	⚳	♃	♄	♅	♆	♇
1 Th	10 43 52	9♍22 28	26♏28 36	2♐33 31	12♎42.8	20♍24.5	8♌46.1	5♑53.9	21♐06.5	1♓24.3	18♋03.3	5♋24.6	19♈42.4	15♒02.8
2 F	10 47 49	10 20 32	8♐42 32	14 56 16	12R42.9	22 09.0	9 58.3	6 16.3	21 14.9	1R16.6	18 09.1	5 26.6	19R41.2	15R01.6
3 Sa	10 51 45	11 18 38	21 15 16	27 40 04	12 41.7	23 52.3	11 10.6	6 39.2	21 23.7	1 09.0	18 14.8	5 28.6	19 40.0	15 00.4
4 Su	10 55 42	12 16 45	4♑11 06	10♑48 44	12 39.2	25 34.4	12 22.9	7 02.6	21 32.8	1 01.3	18 20.5	5 30.4	19 38.7	14 59.2
5 M	10 59 38	13 14 54	17 33 13	24 24 41	12 35.7	27 15.3	13 35.4	7 26.5	21 42.1	0 53.8	18 26.1	5 32.3	19 37.5	14 58.1
6 Tu	11 03 35	14 13 04	1♒23 04	8♒28 12	12 31.7	28 54.9	14 47.9	7 50.9	21 51.6	0 46.3	18 31.6	5 34.1	19 36.2	14 56.9
7 W	11 07 31	15 11 15	15 39 40	22 56 56	12 27.7	0♎33.4	16 00.4	8 15.7	22 01.5	0 38.9	18 37.1	5 35.8	19 34.9	14 55.8
8 Th	11 11 28	16 09 29	0♓19 17	7♓45 48	12 24.4	2 10.7	17 13.0	8 41.1	22 11.6	0 31.5	18 42.4	5 37.6	19 33.6	14 54.6
9 F	11 15 25	17 07 44	15 15 31	22 47 18	12 22.1	3 46.8	18 25.7	9 06.9	22 21.9	0 24.3	18 47.8	5 39.2	19 32.3	14 53.5
10 Sa	11 19 21	18 06 00	0♈20 03	7♈52 37	12D21.2	5 21.8	19 38.5	9 33.1	22 32.5	0 17.1	18 53.0	5 40.8	19 30.9	14 52.4
11 Su	11 23 18	19 04 19	15 23 53	22 52 52	12 21.4	6 55.6	20 51.3	9 59.8	22 43.4	0 10.0	18 58.2	5 42.4	19 29.5	14 51.4
12 M	11 27 14	20 02 39	0♉18 37	7♉40 25	12 22.4	8 28.4	22 04.2	10 26.9	22 54.4	0 03.0	19 03.3	5 43.9	19 28.1	14 50.3
13 Tu	11 31 11	21 01 02	14 57 35	22 09 42	12 23.7	10 00.0	23 17.1	10 54.4	23 05.8	29♒56.1	19 08.3	5 45.4	19 26.7	14 49.2
14 W	11 35 07	21 59 27	29 16 24	6♊17 31	12 24.9	11 30.4	24 30.1	11 22.3	23 17.3	29 49.4	19 13.2	5 46.8	19 25.3	14 48.2
15 Th	11 39 04	22 57 54	13♊12 59	20 02 49	12R25.5	12 59.8	25 43.2	11 50.7	23 29.1	29 42.7	19 18.1	5 48.2	19 23.8	14 47.2
16 F	11 43 00	23 56 24	26 47 11	3♋26 15	12 25.3	14 28.0	26 56.4	12 19.4	23 41.2	29 36.1	19 22.8	5 49.5	19 22.4	14 46.2
17 Sa	11 46 57	24 54 55	10♋00 16	16 29 32	12 24.2	15 55.1	28 09.6	12 48.5	23 53.4	29 29.7	19 27.5	5 50.8	19 20.9	14 45.2
18 Su	11 50 54	25 53 29	22 54 20	29 15 00	12 22.5	17 21.1	29 22.8	13 18.0	24 05.9	29 23.4	19 32.1	5 52.0	19 19.4	14 44.3
19 M	11 54 50	26 52 04	5♌31 52	11♌45 13	12 20.3	18 45.8	0♍36.1	13 47.8	24 18.6	29 17.2	19 36.7	5 53.2	19 17.9	14 43.3
20 Tu	11 58 47	27 50 42	17 55 23	24 02 40	12 18.0	20 09.4	1 49.5	14 18.0	24 31.5	29 11.2	19 41.1	5 54.4	19 16.4	14 42.4
21 W	12 02 43	28 49 22	0♍07 21	6♍09 42	12 16.0	21 31.8	3 03.0	14 48.6	24 44.7	29 05.3	19 45.5	5 55.4	19 14.9	14 41.5
22 Th	12 06 40	29 48 04	12 10 00	18 08 30	12 14.4	22 53.0	4 16.4	15 19.5	24 58.0	28 59.5	19 49.8	5 56.5	19 13.3	14 40.6
23 F	12 10 36	0♎46 48	24 05 27	0♎01 08	12 13.5	24 12.8	5 30.0	15 50.8	25 11.6	28 53.9	19 53.9	5 57.4	19 11.7	14 39.8
24 Sa	12 14 33	1 45 33	5♎55 46	11 49 39	12D13.2	25 31.3	6 43.6	16 22.4	25 25.4	28 48.4	19 58.0	5 58.4	19 10.2	14 38.9
25 Su	12 18 29	2 44 21	17 43 04	23 36 19	12 13.4	26 48.4	7 57.2	16 54.3	25 39.4	28 43.1	20 02.0	5 59.3	19 08.6	14 38.1
26 M	12 22 26	3 43 11	29 29 42	5♏23 34	12 14.0	28 04.1	9 10.9	17 26.6	25 53.5	28 37.9	20 05.9	6 00.1	19 07.0	14 37.3
27 Tu	12 26 22	4 42 02	11♏18 18	17 14 17	12 14.8	29 18.2	10 24.7	17 59.1	26 07.9	28 32.9	20 09.8	6 00.8	19 05.4	14 36.5
28 W	12 30 19	5 40 56	23 11 56	29 11 41	12 15.6	0♏30.8	11 38.5	18 32.0	26 22.5	28 28.1	20 13.5	6 01.6	19 03.8	14 35.8
29 Th	12 34 16	6 39 51	5♐14 02	11♐19 27	12 16.2	1 41.6	12 52.3	19 05.2	26 37.2	28 23.5	20 17.1	6 02.2	19 02.1	14 35.1
30 F	12 38 12	7 38 48	17 28 27	23 41 32	12 16.6	2 50.6	14 06.2	19 38.6	26 52.2	28 19.0	20 20.7	6 02.9	19 00.5	14 34.3

LONGITUDE — October 2033

Day	Sid.Time	☉	0 hr ☽	Noon☽	True☊	☿	♀	♂	⚳	♃	♄	♅	♆	♇
1 Sa	12 42 09	8♎37 47	29♐59 12	6♑21 56	12♎16.7	3♏57.6	15♍20.1	20♑12.4	27♐07.3	28♒14.7	20♋24.1	6♋03.4	18♈58.9	14♒33.7
2 Su	12 46 05	9 36 47	12♑50 13	19 24 28	12R16.7	5 02.5	16 34.1	20 46.4	27 22.6	28R10.5	20 27.5	6 03.9	18R57.2	14R33.0
3 M	12 50 02	10 35 49	26 05 01	2♒52 09	12 16.6	6 05.2	17 48.1	21 20.6	27 38.1	28 06.6	20 30.7	6 04.4	18 55.6	14 32.4
4 Tu	12 53 58	11 34 53	9♒46 01	16 46 41	12D16.5	7 05.5	19 02.2	21 55.2	27 53.8	28 02.8	20 33.9	6 04.8	18 53.9	14 31.7
5 W	12 57 55	12 33 59	23 54 00	1♓07 43	12 16.4	8 03.1	20 16.3	22 30.0	28 09.6	27 59.2	20 36.9	6 05.1	18 52.3	14 31.2
6 Th	13 01 51	13 33 06	8♓27 23	15 52 22	12 16.5	8 57.8	21 30.4	23 05.0	28 25.6	27 55.8	20 39.9	6 05.4	18 50.6	14 30.6
7 F	13 05 48	14 32 15	23 21 53	0♈54 59	12R16.6	9 49.5	22 44.6	23 40.2	28 41.8	27 52.6	20 42.7	6 05.7	18 48.9	14 30.0
8 Sa	13 09 45	15 31 27	8♈30 34	16 07 28	12 16.6	10 37.7	23 58.9	24 15.7	28 58.1	27 49.5	20 45.5	6 05.9	18 47.3	14 29.5
9 Su	13 13 41	16 30 40	23 44 28	1♉20 18	12 16.5	11 22.1	25 13.2	24 51.4	29 14.6	27 46.7	20 48.2	6 06.0	18 45.6	14 29.0
10 M	13 17 38	17 29 55	8♉53 48	16 23 52	12 16.1	12 02.5	26 27.5	25 27.4	29 31.3	27 44.0	20 50.7	6 06.1	18 43.9	14 28.5
11 Tu	13 21 34	18 29 13	23 49 30	1♊09 53	12 15.5	12 38.5	27 41.8	26 03.5	29 48.1	27 41.6	20 53.2	6R06.1	18 42.3	14 28.1
12 W	13 25 31	19 28 33	8♊24 22	15 32 28	12 14.7	13 09.5	28 56.2	26 39.8	0♑05.0	27 39.3	20 55.5	6 06.1	18 40.6	14 27.7
13 Th	13 29 27	20 27 56	22 33 54	29 28 31	12 14.0	13 35.3	0♎10.7	27 16.4	0 22.1	27 37.2	20 57.7	6 06.0	18 38.9	14 27.3
14 F	13 33 24	21 27 20	6♋16 21	12♋57 33	12D13.5	13 55.2	1 25.2	27 53.1	0 39.4	27 35.4	20 59.9	6 05.9	18 37.2	14 26.9
15 Sa	13 37 20	22 26 47	19 32 23	26 01 12	12 13.4	14 08.8	2 39.7	28 30.1	0 56.8	27 33.7	21 01.9	6 05.7	18 35.6	14 26.6
16 Su	13 41 17	23 26 16	2♌24 26	8♌42 32	12 13.8	14R15.5	3 54.3	29 07.2	1 14.4	27 32.2	21 03.8	6 05.5	18 33.9	14 26.3
17 M	13 45 14	24 25 48	14 56 00	21 05 20	12 14.7	14 14.9	5 08.9	29 44.6	1 32.0	27 30.9	21 05.7	6 05.2	18 32.2	14 26.0
18 Tu	13 49 10	25 25 21	27 11 05	3♍13 43	12 15.9	14 06.4	6 23.5	0♒22.1	1 49.9	27 29.9	21 07.4	6 04.9	18 30.6	14 25.7
19 W	13 53 07	26 24 57	9♍13 45	15 11 39	12 17.2	13 49.6	7 38.2	0 59.8	2 07.9	27 29.0	21 09.0	6 04.5	18 28.9	14 25.5
20 Th	13 57 03	27 24 35	21 07 52	27 02 48	12 18.3	13 24.2	8 52.9	1 37.7	2 26.0	27 28.3	21 10.4	6 04.1	18 27.3	14 25.3
21 F	14 01 00	28 24 16	2♎56 52	8♎50 24	12R18.8	12 50.1	10 07.6	2 15.7	2 44.2	27 27.9	21 11.8	6 03.6	18 25.6	14 25.1
22 Sa	14 04 56	29 23 58	14 43 46	20 37 15	12 18.7	12 07.1	11 22.4	2 54.0	3 02.6	27D27.6	21 13.1	6 03.0	18 24.0	14 24.9
23 Su	14 08 53	0♏23 42	26 31 09	2♏25 45	12 17.5	11 15.8	12 37.2	3 32.3	3 21.1	27 27.5	21 14.2	6 02.4	18 22.3	14 24.8
24 M	14 12 49	1 23 29	8♏21 17	14 18 00	12 15.4	10 16.5	13 52.0	4 10.9	3 39.7	27 27.7	21 15.3	6 01.8	18 20.7	14 24.7
25 Tu	14 16 46	2 23 17	20 16 10	26 16 00	12 12.5	9 10.5	15 06.9	4 49.6	3 58.5	27 28.0	21 16.2	6 01.1	18 19.1	14 24.6
26 W	14 20 42	3 23 07	2♐17 45	8♐21 42	12 09.0	7 59.1	16 21.8	5 28.5	4 17.4	27 28.6	21 17.0	6 00.3	18 17.5	14 24.6
27 Th	14 24 39	4 22 59	14 28 06	20 37 13	12 05.4	6 44.0	17 36.7	6 07.5	4 36.4	27 29.3	21 17.8	5 59.5	18 15.9	14D24.5
28 F	14 28 36	5 22 53	26 49 23	3♑04 55	12 02.2	5 27.3	18 51.6	6 46.7	4 55.5	27 30.3	21 18.4	5 58.6	18 14.3	14 24.5
29 Sa	14 32 32	6 22 48	9♑24 07	15 47 21	11 59.6	4 11.4	20 06.6	7 26.0	5 14.7	27 31.4	21 18.8	5 57.7	18 12.7	14 24.6
30 Su	14 36 29	7 22 45	22 14 57	28 47 15	11D58.2	2 58.6	21 21.6	8 05.4	5 34.1	27 32.8	21 19.2	5 56.8	18 11.1	14 24.6
31 M	14 40 25	8 22 44	5♒24 34	12♒07 13	11 58.0	1 51.1	22 36.6	8 45.0	5 53.6	27 34.4	21 19.5	5 55.8	18 09.6	14 24.7

Astro Data	Planet Ingress	Last Aspect	☽ Ingress	Last Aspect	☽ Ingress	☽ Phases & Eclipses	Astro Data
Dy Hr Mn	Dy Hr Mn	Dy Hr Mn	Dy Hr Mn	Dy Hr Mn	Dy Hr Mn	Dy Hr Mn	1 September 2033
☿0S 7 17:45	☿ ♎ 7 3:50	31 7:45 ☿ ⚹	♐ 1 6:58	30 20:47 ♃ ⚹	♑ 1 0:02	2 2:25 ☽ 9♐57	Julian Day # 48822
☽0N 9 18:16	♃ ♒R 12 22:30	3 3:49 ☿ □	♑ 3 16:19	2 14:35 ♂ ☌	♒ 3 6:57	9 2:22 ○ 16♓44	SVP 4♓47'17"
♄□♆ 16 10:15	♀ ♍ 19 0:10	5 17:35 ☿ △	♒ 5 21:38	5 6:49 ♃ ☌	♓ 5 10:08	15 17:35 ☾ 23♊11	GC 27♐18.6 ⚵ 13♏19.9
☉0S 22 16:53	☉ ♎ 22 16:53	7 6:29 ♆ ⚹	♓ 7 23:29	7 0:01 ♂ ⚹	♈ 7 10:33	23 13:41 ● 0♎51	Eris 27♈27.3R ⚵ 20♎17.7
☽0S 23 5:20	☿ ♏ 28 1:45	9 5:36 ♄ △	♈ 9 23:28	9 6:23 ♃ ⚹	♉ 9 9:53	23 13:54:30 ● P 0.689	⚷ 1♊09.0 ⚶ 18♓06.8R
		11 8:27 ♀ △	♉ 11 23:30	11 6:19 ♃ □	♊ 11 10:05		☽ Mean ☊ 13♎52.3
☽0N 7 5:19	⚳ ♑ 12 4:55	14 1:01 ♃ □	♊ 14 1:14	13 8:46 ♃ △	♋ 13 12:55	1 16:34 ☽ 8♑49	
♅R 11 16:05	♀ ♎ 13 8:33	16 5:07 ♃ △	♋ 16 5:47	15 16:53 ♂ ☍	♌ 15 19:27	8 10:59 ○ 15♈29	1 October 2033
♀0S 16 4:21	♂ ♒ 17 21:53	18 5:06 ☉ ⚹	♌ 18 13:26	18 0:38 ♃ ☍	♍ 18 5:35	8 10:56 ● T 1.350	Julian Day # 48852
☿R 16 22:05	☉ ♏ 23 2:29	20 22:04 ♃ ☍	♍ 20 23:45	20 0:04 ♄ ⚹	♎ 20 18:00	15 4:49 ☾ 22♋09	SVP 4♓47'15"
☽0S 20 11:19		22 15:25 ♄ ⚹	♎ 23 11:58	23 1:55 ♃ △	♏ 23 7:04	23 7:30 ● 0♏12	GC 27♐18.6 ⚵ 24♏17.0
♃D 23 7:20		25 22:21 ♃ △	♏ 26 1:02	25 14:24 ♃ □	♐ 25 19:26	31 4:48 ☽ 8♒05	Eris 27♈12.6R ⚵ 0♏04.0
♇D 27 16:42		28 10:34 ♃ □	♐ 28 13:36	28 1:18 ♃ ⚹	♑ 28 6:06		⚷ 0♊48.6R ⚶ 11♓15.8R
				29 22:17 ♄ ☍	♒ 30 14:13		☽ Mean ☊ 12♎17.0

November 2033 LONGITUDE

Day	Sid.Time	☉	0 hr ☽	Noon ☽	True ☊	☿	♀	♂	⚳	♃	♄	♅	♆	♇
1 Tu	14 44 22	9♏22 44	18♒55 25	25♒49 22	11♎58.8	0♏51.1	23♎51.6	9♒24.7	6♑13.1	27♒36.1	21♋19.6	5♋54.7	18♈08.1	14♒24.9
2 W	14 48 18	10 22 46	2♓49 09	9♓54 46	12 00.2	0R 00.3	25 06.6	10 04.5	6 32.8	27 38.1	21R 19.6	5R 53.6	18R 06.5	14 25.0
3 Th	14 52 15	11 22 49	17 06 05	24 22 48	12 01.7	29♎19.8	26 21.7	10 44.5	6 52.6	27 40.3	21 19.6	5 52.5	18 05.0	14 25.2
4 F	14 56 11	12 22 54	1♈44 30	9♈10 33	12R 02.5	28 50.6	27 36.8	11 24.5	7 12.5	27 42.6	21 19.4	5 51.3	18 03.5	14 25.4
5 Sa	15 00 08	13 23 00	16 40 13	24 12 34	12 02.0	28 33.0	28 51.9	12 04.7	7 32.5	27 45.2	21 19.1	5 50.0	18 02.0	14 25.6
6 Su	15 04 05	14 23 09	1♉46 33	9♉21 00	12 00.0	28D 26.9	0♏07.0	12 45.0	7 52.6	27 47.9	21 18.7	5 48.7	18 00.6	14 25.9
7 M	15 08 01	15 23 19	16 54 42	24 26 28	11 56.3	28 32.2	1 22.1	13 25.4	8 12.8	27 50.9	21 18.1	5 47.4	17 59.1	14 26.1
8 Tu	15 11 58	16 23 31	1♊55 07	9♊19 32	11 51.4	28 48.1	2 37.3	14 05.8	8 33.0	27 54.0	21 17.5	5 46.0	17 57.7	14 26.4
9 W	15 15 54	17 23 44	16 38 48	23 52 06	11 45.9	29 14.0	3 52.5	14 46.4	8 53.4	27 57.3	21 16.8	5 44.6	17 56.3	14 26.8
10 Th	15 19 51	18 24 00	0♋58 52	7♋58 39	11 40.5	29 48.9	5 07.7	15 27.1	9 13.9	28 00.9	21 15.9	5 43.1	17 54.9	14 27.2
11 F	15 23 47	19 24 18	14 51 16	21 36 39	11 36.1	0♏32.1	6 22.9	16 07.8	9 34.5	28 04.6	21 14.9	5 41.6	17 53.5	14 27.6
12 Sa	15 27 44	20 24 38	28 14 58	4♌46 28	11 33.1	1 22.6	7 38.1	16 48.7	9 55.1	28 08.5	21 13.8	5 40.1	17 52.2	14 28.0
13 Su	15 31 40	21 24 59	11♌11 32	17 30 39	11D 31.8	2 19.6	8 53.4	17 29.6	10 15.9	28 12.6	21 12.7	5 38.5	17 50.8	14 28.4
14 M	15 35 37	22 25 23	23 44 22	29 53 18	11 32.0	3 22.2	10 08.7	18 10.7	10 36.7	28 16.8	21 11.3	5 36.8	17 49.5	14 28.9
15 Tu	15 39 34	23 25 48	5♍58 04	11♍59 19	11 33.2	4 29.8	11 23.9	18 51.8	10 57.6	28 21.3	21 09.9	5 35.1	17 48.2	14 29.4
16 W	15 43 30	24 26 15	17 57 42	23 53 50	11 34.9	5 41.5	12 39.3	19 33.0	11 18.6	28 26.0	21 08.4	5 33.4	17 46.9	14 29.9
17 Th	15 47 27	25 26 44	29 48 21	5♎41 49	11R 36.1	6 56.9	13 54.6	20 14.3	11 39.7	28 30.8	21 06.8	5 31.7	17 45.7	14 30.5
18 F	15 51 23	26 27 15	11♎34 48	17 27 48	11 36.0	8 15.4	15 09.9	20 55.6	12 00.9	28 35.8	21 05.0	5 29.8	17 44.4	14 31.1
19 Sa	15 55 20	27 27 48	23 21 18	29 15 42	11 34.1	9 36.5	16 25.3	21 37.1	12 22.1	28 41.0	21 03.2	5 28.0	17 43.2	14 31.7
20 Su	15 59 16	28 28 22	5♏11 22	11♏08 39	11 30.0	10 59.8	17 40.6	22 18.6	12 43.5	28 46.3	21 01.2	5 26.1	17 42.1	14 32.3
21 M	16 03 13	29 28 58	17 07 49	23 09 05	11 23.7	12 25.0	18 56.0	23 00.2	13 04.9	28 51.9	20 59.2	5 24.2	17 40.9	14 33.0
22 Tu	16 07 09	0♐29 35	29 12 39	5♐18 41	11 15.3	13 51.7	20 11.4	23 41.9	13 26.4	28 57.6	20 57.0	5 22.3	17 39.8	14 33.7
23 W	16 11 06	1 30 14	11♐27 16	17 38 31	11 05.7	15 19.7	21 26.8	24 23.6	13 47.9	29 03.5	20 54.8	5 20.3	17 38.7	14 34.4
24 Th	16 15 03	2 30 54	23 52 31	0♑09 18	10 55.7	16 48.8	22 42.2	25 05.4	14 09.5	29 09.6	20 52.4	5 18.2	17 37.6	14 35.1
25 F	16 18 59	3 31 36	6♑28 57	12 51 31	10 46.3	18 18.7	23 57.6	25 47.3	14 31.2	29 15.8	20 49.9	5 16.2	17 36.5	14 35.9
26 Sa	16 22 56	4 32 18	19 17 06	25 45 46	10 38.5	19 49.4	25 13.0	26 29.2	14 53.0	29 22.2	20 47.4	5 14.1	17 35.5	14 36.7
27 Su	16 26 52	5 33 02	2♒17 39	8♒52 52	10 32.8	21 20.7	26 28.4	27 11.2	15 14.9	29 28.8	20 44.7	5 12.0	17 34.5	14 37.5
28 M	16 30 49	6 33 47	15 31 34	22 13 55	10 29.6	22 52.4	27 43.9	27 53.2	15 36.8	29 35.6	20 41.9	5 09.8	17 33.5	14 38.4
29 Tu	16 34 45	7 34 32	29 00 06	5♓50 14	10D 28.5	24 24.5	28 59.3	28 35.3	15 58.7	29 42.5	20 39.1	5 07.7	17 32.6	14 39.2
30 W	16 38 42	8 35 19	12♓44 30	19 42 57	10 28.9	25 56.9	0♐14.7	29 17.5	16 20.8	29 49.5	20 36.1	5 05.4	17 31.7	14 40.1

December 2033 LONGITUDE

Day	Sid.Time	☉	0 hr ☽	Noon ☽	True ☊	☿	♀	♂	⚳	♃	♄	♅	♆	♇
1 Th	16 42 38	9♐36 06	26♓45 40	3♈52 34	10♎29.7	27♏29.6	1♐30.2	29♒59.7	16♑42.9	29♒56.8	20♋33.1	5♋03.2	17♈30.8	14♒41.0
2 F	16 46 35	10 36 55	11♈03 32	18 18 17	10R 29.6	29 02.4	2 45.6	0♓41.9	17 05.0	0♓04.1	20R 30.0	5R 00.9	17R 29.9	14 42.0
3 Sa	16 50 32	11 37 44	25 36 26	2♉57 26	10 27.5	0♐35.4	4 01.1	1 24.2	17 27.2	0 11.7	20 26.7	4 58.7	17 29.1	14 43.0
4 Su	16 54 28	12 38 34	10♉20 36	17 45 08	10 23.0	2 08.5	5 16.5	2 06.5	17 49.5	0 19.4	20 23.4	4 56.3	17 28.3	14 43.9
5 M	16 58 25	13 39 25	25 10 07	2♊34 30	10 15.7	3 41.7	6 32.0	2 48.9	18 11.8	0 27.2	20 20.0	4 54.0	17 27.5	14 45.0
6 Tu	17 02 21	14 40 18	9♊57 16	17 17 22	10 06.1	5 15.0	7 47.5	3 31.3	18 34.2	0 35.2	20 16.6	4 51.7	17 26.8	14 46.0
7 W	17 06 18	15 41 11	24 33 48	1♋45 39	9 55.4	6 48.3	9 02.9	4 13.7	18 56.6	0 43.4	20 13.0	4 49.3	17 26.1	14 47.1
8 Th	17 10 14	16 42 05	8♋52 09	15 52 40	9 44.5	8 21.7	10 18.4	4 56.2	19 19.1	0 51.6	20 09.4	4 46.9	17 25.4	14 48.2
9 F	17 14 11	17 43 01	22 46 45	29 34 09	9 34.8	9 55.2	11 33.9	5 38.7	19 41.6	1 00.1	20 05.7	4 44.5	17 24.7	14 49.3
10 Sa	17 18 07	18 43 58	6♌14 45	12♌48 37	9 27.2	11 28.7	12 49.4	6 21.2	20 04.2	1 08.6	20 01.9	4 42.0	17 24.1	14 50.4
11 Su	17 22 04	19 44 55	19 16 01	25 37 15	9 22.0	13 02.3	14 04.9	7 03.7	20 26.8	1 17.4	19 58.0	4 39.6	17 23.5	14 51.6
12 M	17 26 01	20 45 54	1♍52 49	8♍03 15	9 19.3	14 35.9	15 20.4	7 46.3	20 49.5	1 26.2	19 54.1	4 37.1	17 23.0	14 52.7
13 Tu	17 29 57	21 46 54	14 09 09	20 11 12	9D 18.5	16 09.6	16 35.9	8 28.9	21 12.2	1 35.2	19 50.0	4 34.6	17 22.5	14 53.9
14 W	17 33 54	22 47 55	26 10 05	2♎06 29	9R 18.7	17 43.4	17 51.4	9 11.6	21 35.0	1 44.3	19 46.0	4 32.1	17 22.0	14 55.1
15 Th	17 37 50	23 48 57	8♎01 08	13 54 43	9 18.7	19 17.3	19 06.9	9 54.2	21 57.8	1 53.6	19 41.8	4 29.6	17 21.5	14 56.4
16 F	17 41 47	24 50 00	19 47 55	25 41 31	9 17.5	20 51.3	20 22.4	10 36.9	22 20.7	2 03.0	19 37.6	4 27.0	17 21.1	14 57.6
17 Sa	17 45 43	25 51 04	1♏35 41	7♏31 25	9 14.1	22 25.4	21 37.9	11 19.6	22 43.6	2 12.5	19 33.3	4 24.5	17 20.7	14 58.9
18 Su	17 49 40	26 52 08	13 29 06	19 29 10	9 07.9	23 59.6	22 53.5	12 02.4	23 06.6	2 22.1	19 29.0	4 22.0	17 20.3	15 00.2
19 M	17 53 36	27 53 14	25 31 59	1♐37 54	8 58.8	25 34.0	24 09.0	12 45.1	23 29.6	2 31.9	19 24.6	4 19.4	17 20.0	15 01.5
20 Tu	17 57 33	28 54 20	7♐47 08	13 59 51	8 47.1	27 08.5	25 24.5	13 27.9	23 52.6	2 41.8	19 20.1	4 16.8	17 19.7	15 02.9
21 W	18 01 30	29 55 27	20 16 09	26 36 04	8 33.6	28 43.2	26 40.1	14 10.7	24 15.7	2 51.9	19 15.6	4 14.3	17 19.5	15 04.2
22 Th	18 05 26	0♑56 35	2♑59 33	9♑26 30	8 19.5	0♑18.1	27 55.6	14 53.5	24 38.8	3 02.0	19 11.1	4 11.7	17 19.3	15 05.6
23 F	18 09 23	1 57 43	15 56 47	22 30 14	8 06.1	1 53.2	29 11.1	15 36.4	25 01.9	3 12.3	19 06.5	4 09.1	17 19.1	15 07.0
24 Sa	18 13 19	2 58 51	29 06 39	5♒45 51	7 54.6	3 28.5	0♑26.7	16 19.2	25 25.1	3 22.7	19 01.9	4 06.5	17 18.9	15 08.4
25 Su	18 17 16	3 59 59	12♒27 38	19 11 51	7 45.8	5 04.1	1 42.2	17 02.1	25 48.3	3 33.2	18 57.2	4 04.0	17 18.8	15 09.9
26 M	18 21 12	5 01 08	25 58 23	2♓47 06	7 40.2	6 39.8	2 57.7	17 45.0	26 11.6	3 43.8	18 52.5	4 01.4	17 18.7	15 11.3
27 Tu	18 25 09	6 02 16	9♓37 57	16 30 55	7 37.4	8 15.9	4 13.2	18 27.9	26 34.8	3 54.5	18 47.7	3 58.8	17D 18.7	15 12.8
28 W	18 29 06	7 03 25	23 25 59	0♈23 09	7 36.7	9 52.2	5 28.7	19 10.8	26 58.1	4 05.4	18 42.9	3 56.2	17 18.7	15 14.3
29 Th	18 33 02	8 04 33	7♈22 28	14 23 53	7 36.6	11 28.8	6 44.3	19 53.7	27 21.5	4 16.3	18 38.1	3 53.6	17 18.7	15 15.8
30 F	18 36 59	9 05 42	21 27 25	28 32 56	7 35.8	13 05.6	7 59.8	20 36.6	27 44.8	4 27.4	18 33.3	3 51.1	17 18.8	15 17.3
31 Sa	18 40 55	10 06 50	5♉40 17	12♉49 14	7 33.1	14 42.7	9 15.3	21 19.5	28 08.2	4 38.5	18 28.4	3 48.5	17 18.9	15 18.8

Astro Data

	Dy Hr Mn
♄R	2 7:05
☽0N	3 15:59
☿D	6 12:41
☽0S	16 18:14
☽0N	1 0:55
☽0S	14 2:56
♃∠♆	18 7:41
♃⚼♄	27 1:29
♃△♅	27 19:39
♆D	28 7:36
☽0N	28 8:00

Planet Ingress

	Dy Hr Mn
☿ ♎R	2 12:09
♀ ♏	6 9:46
☿ ♏	10 18:35
☉ ♐	22 0:17
♀ ♐	30 7:19
♂ ♓	1 12:11
♃ ♓	1 22:35
☿ ♐	3 2:52
☉ ♑	21 13:47
☿ ♑	22 7:25
♀ ♑	24 3:32

Last Aspect / ☽ Ingress (November)

Last Aspect Dy Hr Mn		☽ Ingress Dy Hr Mn
1 15:04 ♃ ☌	♓	1 19:11
3 6:59 ♄ △	♈	3 21:10
5 20:03 ♀ ☍	♉	5 21:11
7 17:28 ♃ □	♊	7 20:55
9 21:23 ☿ △	♋	9 22:20
11 11:21 ♄ ☌	♌	12 3:12
14 8:50 ♃ ☍	♍	14 12:13
16 13:12 ☉ ✶	♎	17 0:24
19 10:49 ♃ △	♏	19 13:30
21 23:24 ♃ □	♐	22 1:33
24 10:05 ♃ ✶	♑	24 11:42
26 10:53 ♀ ✶	♒	26 19:48
29 1:09 ♃ ☌	♓	29 1:46

Last Aspect / ☽ Ingress (December)

Last Aspect Dy Hr Mn		☽ Ingress Dy Hr Mn
30 23:55 ☿ △	♈	1 5:29
2 15:36 ♄ □	♉	3 7:11
4 16:15 ♄ ✶	♊	5 7:49
6 12:15 ♆ ✶	♋	7 9:03
8 19:23 ♄ ☌	♌	9 12:46
10 23:57 ☉ △	♍	11 20:23
13 15:29 ☉ □	♎	14 7:44
16 10:06 ☉ ✶	♏	16 20:46
18 12:00 ♄ △	♐	19 8:48
21 16:33 ☿ ☌	♑	21 18:24
23 5:50 ♄ ☍	♒	24 1:37
25 8:39 ♆ ✶	♓	26 7:06
27 15:56 ♄ △	♈	28 11:20
29 19:10 ♄ □	♉	30 14:27

☽ Phases & Eclipses

Dy Hr Mn		
6 20:33	○	14♉45
13 20:10	☾	21♌46
22 1:40	●	0♐03
29 15:16	☽	7♓43
6 7:23	○	14♊29
13 15:29	☾	21♍56
21 18:48	●	0♑13
29 0:21	☽	7♈35

Astro Data

1 November 2033
Julian Day # 48883
SVP 4♓47'12"
GC 27♐18.7 ⚴ 6♐42.3
Eris 26♈54.2R ⚵ 10♏37.9
⚷ 29♉35.8R ⚶ 9♓45.2
☽ Mean ☊ 10♎38.5

1 December 2033
Julian Day # 48913
SVP 4♓47'08"
GC 27♐18.8 ⚴ 19♐11.5
Eris 26♈38.5R ⚵ 20♏50.4
⚷ 28♉01.1R ⚶ 14♓35.1
☽ Mean ☊ 9♎03.1

LONGITUDE — January 2034

Day	Sid.Time	☉	0 hr ☽	Noon ☽	True ☊	☿	♀	♂	⚳	♃	♄	♅	♆	♇
1 Su	18 44 52	11♑07 58	19♉59 26	27♉10 26	7♎27.7	16♑20.2	10♑30.8	22♓02.4	28♑31.6	4♓49.8	18♋23.5	3♋45.9	17♈19.0	15♒20.4
2 M	18 48 48	12 09 06	4♊21 43	11♊32 39	7R 19.2	17 57.9	11 46.3	22 45.3	28 55.0	5 01.1	18R 18.6	3R 43.4	17 19.2	15 21.9
3 Tu	18 52 45	13 10 14	18 42 32	25 50 39	7 08.2	19 35.9	13 01.7	23 28.2	29 18.5	5 12.6	18 13.7	3 40.8	17 19.4	15 23.5
4 W	18 56 41	14 11 22	2♋56 15	9♋58 37	6 55.7	21 14.1	14 17.2	24 11.1	29 41.9	5 24.1	18 08.8	3 38.3	17 19.6	15 25.1
5 Th	19 00 38	15 12 30	16 57 03	23 50 58	6 42.9	22 52.6	15 32.7	24 54.0	0♒05.4	5 35.8	18 03.8	3 35.8	17 19.9	15 26.7
6 F	19 04 35	16 13 38	0♌39 53	7♌23 27	6 31.2	24 31.4	16 48.2	25 36.9	0 28.9	5 47.5	17 58.9	3 33.3	17 20.2	15 28.3
7 Sa	19 08 31	17 14 45	14 01 25	20 33 41	6 21.6	26 10.3	18 03.7	26 19.8	0 52.5	5 59.4	17 53.9	3 30.8	17 20.5	15 30.0
8 Su	19 12 28	18 15 53	27 00 19	3♍21 28	6 14.7	27 49.4	19 19.1	27 02.7	1 16.0	6 11.3	17 48.9	3 28.3	17 20.9	15 31.6
9 M	19 16 24	19 17 01	9♍37 26	15 48 35	6 10.6	29 28.6	20 34.6	27 45.6	1 39.6	6 23.3	17 44.0	3 25.9	17 21.3	15 33.3
10 Tu	19 20 21	20 18 09	21 55 23	27 58 25	6D 08.9	1♒07.8	21 50.1	28 28.4	2 03.2	6 35.4	17 39.0	3 23.4	17 21.7	15 34.9
11 W	19 24 17	21 19 16	3♎58 15	9♎55 33	6 08.7	2 47.0	23 05.5	29 11.3	2 26.8	6 47.6	17 34.1	3 21.0	17 22.2	15 36.6
12 Th	19 28 14	22 20 24	15 50 59	21 45 16	6R 08.9	4 26.0	24 21.0	29 54.2	2 50.4	6 59.8	17 29.1	3 18.6	17 22.7	15 38.3
13 F	19 32 10	23 21 32	27 39 05	3♏33 08	6 08.4	6 04.7	25 36.5	0♈37.0	3 14.0	7 12.2	17 24.2	3 16.2	17 23.3	15 40.0
14 Sa	19 36 07	24 22 40	9♏28 08	15 24 42	6 06.2	7 43.1	26 51.9	1 19.9	3 37.6	7 24.6	17 19.3	3 13.8	17 23.8	15 41.7
15 Su	19 40 04	25 23 47	21 23 30	27 25 05	6 01.6	9 20.8	28 07.4	2 02.7	4 01.3	7 37.1	17 14.4	3 11.5	17 24.5	15 43.4
16 M	19 44 00	26 24 54	3♐30 00	9♐38 42	5 54.3	10 57.8	29 22.8	2 45.5	4 25.0	7 49.7	17 09.5	3 09.1	17 25.1	15 45.1
17 Tu	19 47 57	27 26 02	15 51 33	22 08 52	5 44.6	12 33.7	0♒38.3	3 28.4	4 48.6	8 02.4	17 04.7	3 06.8	17 25.8	15 46.9
18 W	19 51 53	28 27 08	28 30 50	4♑57 34	5 33.2	14 08.2	1 53.7	4 11.2	5 12.3	8 15.1	16 59.9	3 04.6	17 26.5	15 48.6
19 Th	19 55 50	29 28 15	11♑29 04	18 05 12	5 21.0	15 41.1	3 09.1	4 54.0	5 36.0	8 27.9	16 55.1	3 02.3	17 27.3	15 50.4
20 F	19 59 46	0♒29 20	24 45 48	1♒30 34	5 09.4	17 12.0	4 24.6	5 36.8	5 59.7	8 40.8	16 50.3	3 00.1	17 28.0	15 52.1
21 Sa	20 03 43	1 30 26	8♒19 08	15 11 05	4 59.4	18 40.3	5 40.0	6 19.6	6 23.4	8 53.8	16 45.6	2 57.9	17 28.9	15 53.9
22 Su	20 07 39	2 31 30	22 05 59	29 03 21	4 51.8	20 05.6	6 55.4	7 02.4	6 47.1	9 06.8	16 40.9	2 55.8	17 29.7	15 55.7
23 M	20 11 36	3 32 34	6♓02 43	13♓03 39	4 47.1	21 27.4	8 10.8	7 45.1	7 10.8	9 19.9	16 36.2	2 53.6	17 30.6	15 57.5
24 Tu	20 15 33	4 33 36	20 05 45	27 08 38	4D 45.1	22 44.9	9 26.2	8 27.9	7 34.5	9 33.0	16 31.6	2 51.5	17 31.5	15 59.2
25 W	20 19 29	5 34 38	4♈12 02	11♈15 42	4 45.0	23 57.5	10 41.5	9 10.6	7 58.3	9 46.2	16 27.1	2 49.5	17 32.5	16 01.0
26 Th	20 23 26	6 35 38	18 19 24	25 22 59	4R 45.7	25 04.5	11 56.9	9 53.3	8 22.0	9 59.5	16 22.6	2 47.4	17 33.4	16 02.8
27 F	20 27 22	7 36 37	2♉26 21	9♉29 20	4 46.1	26 04.9	13 12.2	10 36.0	8 45.7	10 12.8	16 18.1	2 45.4	17 34.5	16 04.6
28 Sa	20 31 19	8 37 36	16 31 52	23 33 47	4 45.0	26 58.1	14 27.6	11 18.7	9 09.4	10 26.2	16 13.7	2 43.5	17 35.5	16 06.4
29 Su	20 35 15	9 38 33	0♊34 56	7♊35 09	4 41.7	27 43.2	15 42.9	12 01.3	9 33.1	10 39.7	16 09.4	2 41.6	17 36.6	16 08.2
30 M	20 39 12	10 39 29	14 34 11	21 31 47	4 36.1	28 19.3	16 58.2	12 44.0	9 56.8	10 53.2	16 05.1	2 39.7	17 37.7	16 10.0
31 Tu	20 43 08	11 40 23	28 27 37	5♋21 23	4 28.4	28 45.7	18 13.5	13 26.6	10 20.5	11 06.7	16 00.9	2 37.8	17 38.8	16 11.9

LONGITUDE — February 2034

Day	Sid.Time	☉	0 hr ☽	Noon ☽	True ☊	☿	♀	♂	⚳	♃	♄	♅	♆	♇
1 W	20 47 05	12♒41 17	12♋12 42	19♋01 12	4♎19.4	29♒01.8	19♒28.8	14♈09.2	10♒44.2	11♓20.3	15♋56.7	2♋36.0	17♈40.0	16♒13.7
2 Th	20 51 02	13 42 09	25 46 32	2♌28 22	4R 10.2	29R 07.0	20 44.1	14 51.7	11 07.8	11 34.0	15R 52.6	2R 34.2	17 41.2	16 15.5
3 F	20 54 58	14 43 00	9♌06 25	15 40 26	4 01.6	29 01.1	21 59.3	15 34.3	11 31.5	11 47.7	15 48.6	2 32.5	17 42.4	16 17.3
4 Sa	20 58 55	15 43 50	22 10 16	28 35 48	3 54.6	28 44.1	23 14.5	16 16.8	11 55.2	12 01.4	15 44.6	2 30.8	17 43.7	16 19.1
5 Su	21 02 51	16 44 39	4♍57 02	11♍14 01	3 49.8	28 16.2	24 29.8	16 59.3	12 18.8	12 15.2	15 40.7	2 29.2	17 45.0	16 20.9
6 M	21 06 48	17 45 27	17 26 56	23 36 00	3D 47.2	27 37.9	25 45.0	17 41.8	12 42.5	12 29.0	15 36.9	2 27.6	17 46.3	16 22.7
7 Tu	21 10 44	18 46 14	29 41 32	5♎43 54	3 46.6	26 50.3	27 00.2	18 24.2	13 06.1	12 42.9	15 33.2	2 26.0	17 47.6	16 24.6
8 W	21 14 41	19 47 00	11♎43 33	17 40 58	3 47.4	25 54.6	28 15.4	19 06.6	13 29.7	12 56.8	15 29.5	2 24.5	17 49.0	16 26.4
9 Th	21 18 37	20 47 44	23 36 44	29 31 24	3 49.0	24 52.4	29 30.5	19 49.0	13 53.3	13 10.8	15 25.9	2 23.0	17 50.4	16 28.2
10 F	21 22 34	21 48 28	5♏25 36	11♏19 58	3R 50.5	23 45.4	0♓45.7	20 31.4	14 16.9	13 24.8	15 22.4	2 21.6	17 51.8	16 30.0
11 Sa	21 26 31	22 49 11	17 15 09	23 11 49	3 51.1	22 35.5	2 00.8	21 13.7	14 40.5	13 38.8	15 19.0	2 20.2	17 53.3	16 31.8
12 Su	21 30 27	23 49 53	29 10 38	5♐12 12	3 50.3	21 24.8	3 16.0	21 56.1	15 04.1	13 52.9	15 15.7	2 18.8	17 54.7	16 33.6
13 M	21 34 24	24 50 33	11♐17 10	17 26 05	3 47.7	20 15.0	4 31.1	22 38.4	15 27.7	14 07.0	15 12.4	2 17.5	17 56.2	16 35.4
14 Tu	21 38 20	25 51 13	23 39 29	29 57 49	3 43.6	19 08.0	5 46.2	23 20.6	15 51.2	14 21.1	15 09.3	2 16.3	17 57.8	16 37.2
15 W	21 42 17	26 51 51	6♑21 27	12♑50 41	3 38.1	18 05.1	7 01.3	24 02.9	16 14.7	14 35.3	15 06.2	2 15.1	17 59.3	16 39.0
16 Th	21 46 13	27 52 28	19 25 40	26 06 28	3 32.0	17 07.8	8 16.4	24 45.1	16 38.2	14 49.5	15 03.2	2 13.9	18 00.9	16 40.8
17 F	21 50 10	28 53 04	2♒53 01	9♒45 06	3 26.0	16 16.7	9 31.4	25 27.3	17 01.7	15 03.8	15 00.3	2 12.8	18 02.5	16 42.6
18 Sa	21 54 06	29 53 38	16 42 24	23 44 28	3 20.9	15 32.7	10 46.5	26 09.5	17 25.2	15 18.0	14 57.6	2 11.7	18 04.2	16 44.4
19 Su	21 58 03	0♓54 11	0♓50 45	8♓00 35	3 17.1	14 56.2	12 01.5	26 51.7	17 48.6	15 32.3	14 54.9	2 10.7	18 05.8	16 46.1
20 M	22 02 00	1 54 42	15 13 17	22 28 06	3D 15.1	14 27.2	13 16.5	27 33.8	18 12.0	15 46.6	14 52.3	2 09.8	18 07.5	16 47.9
21 Tu	22 05 56	2 55 12	29 44 17	7♈01 05	3 14.8	14 05.9	14 31.5	28 15.9	18 35.4	16 01.0	14 49.8	2 08.9	18 09.2	16 49.7
22 W	22 09 53	3 55 39	14♈17 47	21 33 46	3 15.6	13 52.0	15 46.4	28 58.0	18 58.8	16 15.3	14 47.4	2 08.0	18 10.9	16 51.4
23 Th	22 13 49	4 56 05	28 48 27	6♉01 19	3 17.1	13D 45.4	17 01.4	29 40.0	19 22.1	16 29.7	14 45.1	2 07.2	18 12.7	16 53.2
24 F	22 17 46	5 56 29	13♉11 59	20 20 06	3 18.5	13 45.7	18 16.3	0♉22.0	19 45.4	16 44.1	14 42.9	2 06.4	18 14.5	16 54.9
25 Sa	22 21 42	6 56 51	27 25 24	4♊27 42	3R 19.3	13 52.5	19 31.2	1 04.0	20 08.7	16 58.5	14 40.8	2 05.7	18 16.3	16 56.6
26 Su	22 25 39	7 57 11	11♊26 52	18 22 47	3 18.9	14 05.6	20 46.0	1 46.0	20 32.0	17 12.9	14 38.8	2 05.1	18 18.1	16 58.4
27 M	22 29 35	8 57 29	25 15 25	2♋04 42	3 17.3	14 24.4	22 00.8	2 27.9	20 55.2	17 27.4	14 37.0	2 04.5	18 19.9	17 00.1
28 Tu	22 33 32	9 57 45	8♋50 38	15 33 12	3 14.7	14 48.7	23 15.7	3 09.8	21 18.4	17 41.8	14 35.2	2 03.9	18 21.8	17 01.8

Astro Data	Planet Ingress	Last Aspect	☽ Ingress	Last Aspect	☽ Ingress	☽ Phases & Eclipses	Astro Data
Dy Hr Mn	Dy Hr Mn	Dy Hr Mn	Dy Hr Mn	Dy Hr Mn	Dy Hr Mn	Dy Hr Mn	
☽0S 10 12:54	⚳ ♒ 5 6:28	1 2:59 ♂ ✶	♊ 1 16:43	1 9:36 ♆ □	♌ 2 7:33	4 19:48 ○ 14♋31	1 January 2034
♂0N 13 15:56	☿ ♒ 9 19:36	3 7:47 ♂ □	♋ 3 19:01	4 12:15 ☿ ☍	♍ 4 14:38	12 13:18 ☾ 22♎24	Julian Day # 48944
♄□♆ 13 16:08	♂ ♈ 12 15:17	5 13:57 ♂ △	♌ 5 22:49	5 20:32 ♄ ✶	♎ 7 0:37	20 10:03 ● 0♒24	SVP 4♓47'03"
☽0N 24 14:46	♀ ♒ 16 23:50	7 6:04 ♆ △	♍ 8 5:38	9 11:58 ♀ △	♏ 9 12:58	27 8:33 ☽ 7♉28	GC 27♐18.9 ⚴ 2♑03.9
♄⊼♇ 29 16:27	☉ ♒ 20 0:28	10 13:04 ♂ ☍	♎ 10 16:03	11 11:10 ☉ □	♐ 12 1:39		Eris 26♈29.4R ⚵ 0♐49.6
		12 17:55 ♀ □	♏ 13 4:47	14 3:31 ☉ ✶	♑ 14 12:04	3 10:06 ○ 14♌38	⚷ 26♉37.5R ⚶ 23♓52.8
☿R 2 11:23	♀ ♓ 9 21:24	15 13:33 ♀ ✶	♐ 15 17:07	16 9:27 ♂ □	♒ 16 18:55	11 11:10 ☾ 22♏47	☽ Mean ☊ 7♎24.7
☽0S 6 22:39	☉ ♓ 18 14:31	17 3:00 ♆ △	♑ 18 2:47	18 16:18 ♂ ✶	♓ 18 22:35	18 23:11 ● 0♓22	
♃△♄ 17 7:12	♂ ♉ 23 23:25	19 10:51 ♆ □	♒ 20 9:20	20 0:44 ♃ ☌	♈ 21 0:26	25 16:35 ☽ 7♊08	1 February 2034
☽0N 20 23:00		21 18:46 ☿ ☌	♓ 22 13:37	23 0:53 ♂ ☌	♉ 23 1:59		Julian Day # 48975
☿D 23 22:56		23 18:01 ♄ △	♈ 24 16:51	24 8:11 ♀ ✶	♊ 25 4:23		SVP 4♓46'58"
♃⊼♇ 25 8:30		26 11:26 ♆ ✶	♉ 26 19:51	26 16:34 ♀ □	♋ 27 8:20		GC 27♐18.9 ⚴ 14♑23.8
		28 18:10 ☿ □	♊ 28 23:00				Eris 26♈30.5 ⚵ 9♐31.6
		31 0:11 ☿ △	♋ 31 2:40				⚷ 26♉03.0R ⚶ 5♈38.8
							☽ Mean ☊ 5♎46.2

March 2034 — LONGITUDE

Day	Sid.Time	☉	0 hr ☽	Noon ☽	True ☊	☿	♀	♂	⚳	♃	♄	♅	♆	♇
1 W	22 37 28	10♓57 59	22♋12 25	28♋48 15	3♎11.4	15♒18.0	24♓30.4	3♉51.7	21♒41.5	17♓56.3	14♋33.5	2♋03.5	18♈23.7	17♒03.5
2 Th	22 41 25	11 58 11	5♌20 44	11♌49 52	3R 08.0	15 52.0	25 45.2	4 33.5	22 04.6	18 10.8	14R 32.0	2R 03.0	18 25.5	17 05.2
3 F	22 45 22	12 58 22	18 15 40	24 38 09	3 04.8	16 30.3	26 59.9	5 15.3	22 27.7	18 25.3	14 30.5	2 02.6	18 27.5	17 06.8
4 Sa	22 49 18	13 58 30	0♍57 23	7♍13 25	3 02.4	17 12.7	28 14.6	5 57.0	22 50.8	18 39.8	14 29.2	2 02.3	18 29.4	17 08.5
5 Su	22 53 15	14 58 36	13 26 20	19 36 16	3 00.8	17 58.9	29 29.3	6 38.8	23 13.8	18 54.3	14 28.0	2 02.0	18 31.3	17 10.1
6 M	22 57 11	15 58 41	25 43 21	1♎47 46	3D 00.3	18 48.6	0♈44.0	7 20.4	23 36.7	19 08.8	14 26.8	2 01.8	18 33.3	17 11.8
7 Tu	23 01 08	16 58 43	7♎49 45	13 49 34	3 00.6	19 41.6	1 58.6	8 02.1	23 59.7	19 23.3	14 25.8	2 01.6	18 35.3	17 13.4
8 W	23 05 04	17 58 44	19 47 32	25 43 58	3 01.6	20 37.6	3 13.2	8 43.7	24 22.6	19 37.8	14 24.9	2 01.5	18 37.3	17 15.0
9 Th	23 09 01	18 58 44	1♏39 15	7♏33 51	3 02.9	21 36.4	4 27.7	9 25.3	24 45.4	19 52.3	14 24.1	2D 01.4	18 39.3	17 16.6
10 F	23 12 57	19 58 41	13 28 12	19 22 47	3 04.2	22 37.9	5 42.3	10 06.9	25 08.3	20 06.8	14 23.4	2 01.4	18 41.3	17 18.2
11 Sa	23 16 54	20 58 37	25 18 09	1♐14 51	3 05.3	23 41.9	6 56.8	10 48.4	25 31.0	20 21.4	14 22.9	2 01.4	18 43.4	17 19.8
12 Su	23 20 51	21 58 32	7♐13 26	13 14 29	3R 06.0	24 48.3	8 11.3	11 29.9	25 53.8	20 35.9	14 22.4	2 01.5	18 45.4	17 21.3
13 M	23 24 47	22 58 24	19 18 37	25 26 24	3 06.1	25 56.9	9 25.8	12 11.4	26 16.5	20 50.4	14 22.1	2 01.7	18 47.5	17 22.9
14 Tu	23 28 44	23 58 15	1♑38 23	7♑55 08	3 05.8	27 07.7	10 40.2	12 52.9	26 39.1	21 04.9	14 21.8	2 01.9	18 49.6	17 24.4
15 W	23 32 40	24 58 05	14 17 08	20 44 50	3 05.1	28 20.4	11 54.6	13 34.3	27 01.7	21 19.4	14D 21.7	2 02.1	18 51.7	17 25.9
16 Th	23 36 37	25 57 52	27 18 34	3♒58 39	3 04.3	29 35.0	13 09.0	14 15.7	27 24.3	21 34.0	14 21.7	2 02.4	18 53.8	17 27.4
17 F	23 40 33	26 57 38	10♒45 13	17 38 18	3 03.5	0♓51.5	14 23.4	14 57.0	27 46.8	21 48.5	14 21.8	2 02.8	18 56.0	17 28.9
18 Sa	23 44 30	27 57 22	24 37 48	1♓43 27	3 02.8	2 09.7	15 37.7	15 38.3	28 09.3	22 02.9	14 22.0	2 03.2	18 58.1	17 30.4
19 Su	23 48 26	28 57 04	8♓54 50	16 11 23	3 02.5	3 29.7	16 52.0	16 19.6	28 31.7	22 17.4	14 22.3	2 03.7	19 00.3	17 31.8
20 M	23 52 23	29 56 45	23 32 23	0♈56 59	3D 02.3	4 51.2	18 06.2	17 00.9	28 54.0	22 31.9	14 22.8	2 04.2	19 02.4	17 33.2
21 Tu	23 56 20	0♈56 23	8♈24 15	15 53 09	3 02.4	6 14.4	19 20.5	17 42.1	29 16.3	22 46.4	14 23.3	2 04.8	19 04.6	17 34.6
22 W	0 00 16	1 55 59	23 22 39	0♉51 43	3 02.5	7 39.1	20 34.7	18 23.3	29 38.6	23 00.8	14 24.0	2 05.4	19 06.8	17 36.0
23 Th	0 04 13	2 55 33	8♉19 19	15 44 33	3R 02.5	9 05.3	21 48.9	19 04.5	0♓00.8	23 15.2	14 24.7	2 06.1	19 09.0	17 37.4
24 F	0 08 09	3 55 05	23 06 34	0♊24 41	3 02.5	10 32.9	23 03.0	19 45.6	0 22.9	23 29.6	14 25.6	2 06.8	19 11.2	17 38.8
25 Sa	0 12 06	4 54 34	7♊38 20	14 47 05	3 02.4	12 02.1	24 17.1	20 26.7	0 45.0	23 44.0	14 26.6	2 07.6	19 13.4	17 40.1
26 Su	0 16 02	5 54 02	21 50 39	28 48 52	3D 02.3	13 32.6	25 31.2	21 07.8	1 07.0	23 58.4	14 27.7	2 08.5	19 15.6	17 41.4
27 M	0 19 59	6 53 26	5♋41 40	12♋29 08	3 02.3	15 04.6	26 45.2	21 48.8	1 29.0	24 12.7	14 28.9	2 09.4	19 17.8	17 42.7
28 Tu	0 23 55	7 52 49	19 11 23	25 48 37	3 02.5	16 38.0	27 59.2	22 29.8	1 50.9	24 27.1	14 30.3	2 10.3	19 20.0	17 44.0
29 W	0 27 52	8 52 09	2♌21 04	8♌49 02	3 02.9	18 12.7	29 13.1	23 10.8	2 12.7	24 41.4	14 31.7	2 11.3	19 22.3	17 45.3
30 Th	0 31 48	9 51 27	15 12 48	21 32 41	3 03.6	19 48.9	0♉27.0	23 51.7	2 34.5	24 55.7	14 33.3	2 12.4	19 24.5	17 46.5
31 F	0 35 45	10 50 43	27 48 59	4♍02 01	3 04.3	21 26.5	1 40.9	24 32.6	2 56.2	25 09.9	14 34.9	2 13.5	19 26.8	17 47.8

April 2034 — LONGITUDE

Day	Sid.Time	☉	0 hr ☽	Noon ☽	True ☊	☿	♀	♂	⚳	♃	♄	♅	♆	♇
1 Sa	0 39 42	11♈49 56	10♍12 05	16♍19 27	3♎05.0	23♓05.4	2♉54.7	25♉13.5	3♓17.8	25♓24.1	14♋36.7	2♋14.6	19♈29.0	17♒49.0
2 Su	0 43 38	12 49 07	22 24 26	28 27 15	3R 05.4	24 45.8	4 08.5	25 54.3	3 39.4	25 38.3	14 38.5	2 15.8	19 31.3	17 50.1
3 M	0 47 35	13 48 16	4♎28 10	10♎27 27	3 05.3	26 27.6	5 22.3	26 35.1	4 00.9	25 52.5	14 40.5	2 17.1	19 33.5	17 51.3
4 Tu	0 51 31	14 47 23	16 25 20	22 22 03	3 04.7	28 10.8	6 36.0	27 15.9	4 22.3	26 06.6	14 42.6	2 18.4	19 35.8	17 52.4
5 W	0 55 28	15 46 28	28 17 51	4♏13 01	3 03.4	29 55.4	7 49.7	27 56.6	4 43.6	26 20.8	14 44.8	2 19.7	19 38.1	17 53.5
6 Th	0 59 24	16 45 31	10♏07 48	16 02 29	3 01.5	1♈41.5	9 03.3	28 37.3	5 04.9	26 34.8	14 47.0	2 21.1	19 40.3	17 54.6
7 F	1 03 21	17 44 33	21 57 25	27 52 54	2 59.3	3 29.0	10 16.9	29 18.0	5 26.2	26 48.9	14 49.4	2 22.5	19 42.6	17 55.7
8 Sa	1 07 17	18 43 32	3♐49 19	9♐47 03	2 57.0	5 18.0	11 30.5	29 58.6	5 47.3	27 02.9	14 51.9	2 24.0	19 44.9	17 56.8
9 Su	1 11 14	19 42 30	15 46 30	21 48 09	2 54.8	7 08.4	12 44.0	0♊39.2	6 08.4	27 16.9	14 54.5	2 25.6	19 47.1	17 57.8
10 M	1 15 11	20 41 25	27 52 25	3♑59 50	2 53.2	9 00.4	13 57.5	1 19.7	6 29.4	27 30.8	14 57.2	2 27.2	19 49.4	17 58.8
11 Tu	1 19 07	21 40 20	10♑10 52	16 26 02	2D 52.4	10 53.8	15 11.0	2 00.3	6 50.3	27 44.7	15 00.0	2 28.8	19 51.7	17 59.8
12 W	1 23 04	22 39 12	22 45 50	29 10 46	2 52.5	12 48.7	16 24.4	2 40.8	7 11.1	27 58.6	15 02.9	2 30.5	19 53.9	18 00.7
13 Th	1 27 00	23 38 03	5♒41 15	12♒17 44	2 53.3	14 45.0	17 37.8	3 21.3	7 31.9	28 12.4	15 05.9	2 32.2	19 56.2	18 01.7
14 F	1 30 57	24 36 51	19 00 33	25 49 56	2 54.6	16 42.9	18 51.1	4 01.7	7 52.6	28 26.2	15 09.0	2 34.0	19 58.5	18 02.6
15 Sa	1 34 53	25 35 38	2♓46 03	9♓48 53	2 56.0	18 42.1	20 04.4	4 42.1	8 13.1	28 39.9	15 12.2	2 35.9	20 00.7	18 03.5
16 Su	1 38 50	26 34 24	16 58 19	24 14 02	2R 57.0	20 42.8	21 17.6	5 22.5	8 33.6	28 53.6	15 15.5	2 37.7	20 03.0	18 04.3
17 M	1 42 46	27 33 07	1♈35 32	9♈02 07	2 57.1	22 44.7	22 30.9	6 02.9	8 54.1	29 07.2	15 18.9	2 39.6	20 05.2	18 05.2
18 Tu	1 46 43	28 31 49	16 32 57	24 06 59	2 56.0	24 48.0	23 44.0	6 43.2	9 14.4	29 20.8	15 22.3	2 41.6	20 07.5	18 06.0
19 W	1 50 40	29 30 29	1♉43 06	9♉20 01	2 53.6	26 52.5	24 57.2	7 23.5	9 34.6	29 34.4	15 25.9	2 43.6	20 09.7	18 06.8
20 Th	1 54 36	0♉29 07	16 56 29	24 31 12	2 50.1	28 58.0	26 10.3	8 03.7	9 54.8	29 47.9	15 29.6	2 45.7	20 12.0	18 07.5
21 F	1 58 33	1 27 43	2♊02 59	9♊30 45	2 46.2	1♉04.4	27 23.3	8 44.0	10 14.8	0♈01.3	15 33.4	2 47.7	20 14.2	18 08.3
22 Sa	2 02 29	2 26 17	16 53 32	24 10 36	2 42.3	3 11.7	28 36.3	9 24.2	10 34.8	0 14.7	15 37.2	2 49.9	20 16.5	18 09.0
23 Su	2 06 26	3 24 48	1♋21 22	8♋25 28	2 39.1	5 19.5	29 49.3	10 04.4	10 54.6	0 28.0	15 41.2	2 52.1	20 18.7	18 09.7
24 M	2 10 22	4 23 18	15 22 43	22 13 07	2D 37.1	7 27.8	1♊02.2	10 44.5	11 14.4	0 41.3	15 45.2	2 54.3	20 20.9	18 10.3
25 Tu	2 14 19	5 21 45	28 56 47	5♌33 58	2 36.5	9 36.1	2 15.1	11 24.6	11 34.0	0 54.5	15 49.3	2 56.5	20 23.1	18 11.0
26 W	2 18 15	6 20 10	12♌05 03	18 30 27	2 37.1	11 44.4	3 27.9	12 04.7	11 53.6	1 07.7	15 53.5	2 58.8	20 25.3	18 11.6
27 Th	2 22 12	7 18 33	24 50 39	1♍06 08	2 38.5	13 52.2	4 40.6	12 44.8	12 13.0	1 20.8	15 57.8	3 01.2	20 27.5	18 12.2
28 F	2 26 09	8 16 54	7♍17 28	13 25 08	2 40.2	15 59.4	5 53.4	13 24.8	12 32.3	1 33.8	16 02.2	3 03.6	20 29.7	18 12.7
29 Sa	2 30 05	9 15 12	19 29 40	25 31 33	2R 41.4	18 05.5	7 06.0	14 04.8	12 51.6	1 46.8	16 06.7	3 06.0	20 31.9	18 13.3
30 Su	2 34 02	10 13 29	1♎31 16	7♎29 13	2 41.5	20 10.3	8 18.6	14 44.7	13 10.7	1 59.7	16 11.2	3 08.4	20 34.1	18 13.8

Astro Data

	Dy Hr Mn
♅□♇	1 11:43
♃⚺♆	3 16:11
☽0S	6 6:50
♀0N	8 3:35
♅ D	10 6:50
♄ D	16 2:31
☽0N	20 9:08
☉0N	20 13:19
☽0S	2 13:25
☿0N	8 6:55
☽0N	16 20:07
☽0S	29 19:31

Planet Ingress

	Dy Hr Mn
♀ ♈	5 21:52
☿ ♓	16 19:54
☉ ♈	20 13:19
⚳ ♓	23 11:09
♀ ♉	30 3:13
☿ ♈	5 13:03
♂ ♊	8 12:50
☉ ♉	20 0:05
☿ ♉	20 23:47
♃ ♈	21 9:41
♀ ♊	23 15:31

Last Aspect / ☽ Ingress (March)

Last Aspect Dy Hr Mn		☽ Ingress Dy Hr Mn
1 3:21 ♀ △	♌	1 14:11
3 0:20 ♆ △	♍	3 22:11
5 10:36 ♃ ☍	♎	6 8:27
8 0:47 ☿ △	♏	8 20:39
10 19:14 ☿ □	♐	11 9:29
13 13:06 ☿ ⚹	♑	13 20:50
15 20:22 ☉ ⚹	♒	16 4:52
17 14:14 ♆ ⚹	♓	18 9:06
20 10:16 ☉ ☌	♈	20 10:28
21 18:02 ♀ ☌	♉	22 10:37
24 0:26 ♃ ⚹	♊	24 11:19
26 5:45 ♀ ⚹	♋	26 14:03
28 16:23 ♀ □	♌	28 19:40
30 16:41 ♂ □	♍	31 4:12

Last Aspect / ☽ Ingress (April)

Last Aspect Dy Hr Mn		☽ Ingress Dy Hr Mn
2 6:38 ♂ △	♎	2 15:05
4 6:23 ♆ ☍	♏	5 3:27
7 15:02 ♂ ☍	♐	7 16:17
9 23:03 ♃ □	♑	10 4:11
12 9:43 ♃ ⚹	♒	12 13:31
14 9:42 ☉ ⚹	♓	14 19:14
16 19:44 ♃ ☌	♈	16 21:25
18 19:27 ☉ ☌	♉	18 21:17
20 20:32 ♃ ⚹	♊	20 20:43
22 5:32 ♆ ⚹	♋	22 21:43
24 8:42 ♆ □	♌	25 1:54
26 15:37 ♆ △	♍	27 9:53
28 18:08 ☿ △	♎	29 20:57

☽ Phases & Eclipses

Dy Hr Mn	
5 2:11	○ 14♍34
13 6:46	☾ 22♐45
20 10:16	● 29♓52
20 10:18:45	● T 04'09"
27 1:20	☽ 6♋27
3 19:20	○ 14♎06
3 19:07	○ A 0.855
11 22:46	☾ 22♑07
18 19:27	● 28♈50
25 11:36	☽ 5♌21

Astro Data

1 March 2034
Julian Day # 49003
SVP 4♓46'55"
GC 27♐19.0 ⚴ 24♑34.3
Eris 26♈40.1 ⚵ 15♐26.4
⚷ 26♉26.0 ⚶ 17♈24.4
☽ Mean ☊ 4♎17.2

1 April 2034
Julian Day # 49034
SVP 4♓46'52"
GC 27♐19.1 ⚴ 4♒02.7
Eris 26♈57.6 ⚵ 18♐34.0
⚷ 27♉46.1 ⚶ 1♉01.0
☽ Mean ☊ 2♎38.7

LONGITUDE — May 2034

Day	Sid.Time	☉	0 hr ☽	Noon ☽	True ☊	☿	♀	♂	⚳	♃	♄	♅	♆	♇
1 M	2 37 58	11♉11 44	13♎25 50	19♎21 28	2♎40.0	22♉13.5	9♊31.2	15♊24.6	13♓29.7	2♈12.6	16♋15.8	3♋10.9	20♈36.2	18♒14.3
2 Tu	2 41 55	12 09 57	25 16 27	1♏11 07	2R36.7	24 14.7	10 43.7	16 04.5	13 48.6	2 25.3	16 20.6	3 13.4	20 38.4	18 14.7
3 W	2 45 51	13 08 08	7♏05 42	13 00 30	2 31.5	26 13.8	11 56.1	16 44.4	14 07.4	2 38.1	16 25.3	3 16.0	20 40.5	18 15.2
4 Th	2 49 48	14 06 18	18 55 43	24 51 35	2 24.7	28 10.4	13 08.6	17 24.2	14 26.1	2 50.7	16 30.2	3 18.6	20 42.6	18 15.6
5 F	2 53 44	15 04 26	0♐48 20	6♐46 09	2 16.9	0♊04.4	14 20.9	18 04.0	14 44.6	3 03.3	16 35.2	3 21.2	20 44.7	18 15.9
6 Sa	2 57 41	16 02 32	12 45 18	18 45 59	2 08.8	1 55.5	15 33.2	18 43.8	15 03.1	3 15.8	16 40.2	3 23.9	20 46.8	18 16.3
7 Su	3 01 37	17 00 37	24 48 27	0♑53 00	2 01.2	3 43.5	16 45.5	19 23.5	15 21.4	3 28.2	16 45.3	3 26.6	20 48.9	18 16.6
8 M	3 05 34	17 58 40	6♑59 54	13 09 30	1 54.8	5 28.3	17 57.7	20 03.3	15 39.6	3 40.6	16 50.5	3 29.4	20 51.0	18 16.9
9 Tu	3 09 31	18 56 42	19 22 08	25 38 11	1 50.3	7 09.8	19 09.8	20 43.0	15 57.7	3 52.9	16 55.7	3 32.1	20 53.1	18 17.2
10 W	3 13 27	19 54 43	1♒58 03	8♒22 08	1D47.7	8 47.8	20 21.9	21 22.6	16 15.6	4 05.1	17 01.0	3 34.9	20 55.1	18 17.4
11 Th	3 17 24	20 52 42	14 50 51	21 24 37	1 47.0	10 22.3	21 33.9	22 02.3	16 33.4	4 17.2	17 06.4	3 37.8	20 57.1	18 17.7
12 F	3 21 20	21 50 40	28 03 49	4♓48 48	1 47.6	11 53.1	22 45.9	22 41.9	16 51.1	4 29.3	17 11.9	3 40.6	20 59.2	18 17.8
13 Sa	3 25 17	22 48 36	11♓39 51	18 37 09	1R48.6	13 20.3	23 57.9	23 21.5	17 08.7	4 41.2	17 17.4	3 43.5	21 01.2	18 18.0
14 Su	3 29 13	23 46 31	25 40 48	2♈50 43	1 49.1	14 43.7	25 09.7	24 01.0	17 26.1	4 53.1	17 23.0	3 46.5	21 03.2	18 18.1
15 M	3 33 10	24 44 26	10♈06 43	17 28 22	1 48.1	16 03.3	26 21.6	24 40.5	17 43.4	5 04.9	17 28.7	3 49.4	21 05.1	18 18.3
16 Tu	3 37 06	25 42 18	24 55 05	2♉26 03	1 45.0	17 19.0	27 33.3	25 20.1	18 00.5	5 16.7	17 34.5	3 52.4	21 07.1	18 18.3
17 W	3 41 03	26 40 10	10♉00 17	17 36 38	1 39.6	18 30.8	28 45.1	25 59.6	18 17.5	5 28.3	17 40.3	3 55.4	21 09.0	18 18.4
18 Th	3 45 00	27 38 00	25 13 51	2♊50 34	1 32.3	19 38.7	29 56.7	26 39.0	18 34.3	5 39.8	17 46.1	3 58.5	21 10.9	18R18.4
19 F	3 48 56	28 35 49	10♊25 27	17 57 11	1 23.8	20 42.4	1♋08.3	27 18.5	18 51.0	5 51.3	17 52.1	4 01.5	21 12.8	18 18.4
20 Sa	3 52 53	29 33 36	25 24 35	2♋46 38	1 15.2	21 42.1	2 19.9	27 57.9	19 07.6	6 02.6	17 58.1	4 04.6	21 14.7	18 18.4
21 Su	3 56 49	0♊31 22	10♋02 28	17 11 29	1 07.6	22 37.6	3 31.4	28 37.3	19 24.0	6 13.9	18 04.1	4 07.8	21 16.6	18 18.4
22 M	4 00 46	1 29 06	24 13 17	1♌07 39	1 01.9	23 28.8	4 42.8	29 16.6	19 40.2	6 25.1	18 10.3	4 10.9	21 18.4	18 18.3
23 Tu	4 04 42	2 26 48	7♌54 37	14 34 21	0 58.3	24 15.8	5 54.1	29 56.0	19 56.3	6 36.2	18 16.4	4 14.1	21 20.3	18 18.2
24 W	4 08 39	3 24 29	21 07 11	27 33 32	0D56.8	24 58.3	7 05.4	0♋35.3	20 12.2	6 47.1	18 22.7	4 17.3	21 22.1	18 18.1
25 Th	4 12 35	4 22 09	3♍53 55	10♍08 56	0 56.8	25 36.4	8 16.6	1 14.6	20 28.0	6 58.0	18 29.0	4 20.5	21 23.8	18 17.9
26 F	4 16 32	5 19 46	16 19 13	22 25 22	0R57.4	26 10.0	9 27.8	1 53.8	20 43.6	7 08.8	18 35.3	4 23.7	21 25.6	18 17.8
27 Sa	4 20 29	6 17 23	28 28 03	4♎27 54	0 57.5	26 38.9	10 38.8	2 33.1	20 59.0	7 19.4	18 41.7	4 27.0	21 27.4	18 17.5
28 Su	4 24 25	7 14 58	10♎25 31	16 21 29	0 56.3	27 03.3	11 49.8	3 12.3	21 14.2	7 30.0	18 48.2	4 30.3	21 29.1	18 17.3
29 M	4 28 22	8 12 31	22 16 20	28 10 34	0 53.0	27 23.0	13 00.8	3 51.5	21 29.3	7 40.5	18 54.7	4 33.6	21 30.8	18 17.1
30 Tu	4 32 18	9 10 03	4♏04 38	9♏58 57	0 47.0	27 38.0	14 11.6	4 30.6	21 44.2	7 50.8	19 01.2	4 36.9	21 32.4	18 16.8
31 W	4 36 15	10 07 34	15 53 52	21 49 43	0 38.5	27 48.3	15 22.4	5 09.7	21 59.0	8 01.1	19 07.9	4 40.2	21 34.1	18 16.5

LONGITUDE — June 2034

Day	Sid.Time	☉	0 hr ☽	Noon ☽	True ☊	☿	♀	♂	⚳	♃	♄	♅	♆	♇
1 Th	4 40 11	11♊05 04	27♏46 44	3♐45 11	0♎27.8	27♊53.9	16♋33.1	5♋48.9	22♓13.5	8♈11.2	19♋14.5	4♋43.6	21♈35.7	18♒16.1
2 F	4 44 08	12 02 33	9♐45 13	15 47 02	0R15.5	27R55.0	17 43.7	6 27.9	22 27.9	8 21.2	19 21.2	4 47.0	21 37.3	18R15.8
3 Sa	4 48 04	13 00 01	21 50 45	27 56 30	0 02.8	27 51.5	18 54.3	7 07.0	22 42.1	8 31.1	19 28.0	4 50.4	21 38.9	18 15.4
4 Su	4 52 01	13 57 28	4♑04 24	10♑14 35	29♍50.7	27 43.6	20 04.8	7 46.0	22 56.1	8 40.9	19 34.8	4 53.8	21 40.5	18 15.0
5 M	4 55 58	14 54 54	16 27 09	22 42 15	29 40.3	27 31.5	21 15.1	8 25.1	23 09.9	8 50.6	19 41.6	4 57.2	21 42.0	18 14.6
6 Tu	4 59 54	15 52 20	29 00 04	5♒20 46	29 32.2	27 15.5	22 25.5	9 04.1	23 23.5	9 00.2	19 48.5	5 00.7	21 43.5	18 14.1
7 W	5 03 51	16 49 44	11♒44 36	18 11 48	29 26.9	26 55.7	23 35.7	9 43.0	23 36.9	9 09.6	19 55.4	5 04.1	21 45.0	18 13.6
8 Th	5 07 47	17 47 08	24 42 38	1♓17 23	29 24.1	26 32.6	24 45.8	10 22.0	23 50.1	9 19.0	20 02.4	5 07.6	21 46.5	18 13.1
9 F	5 11 44	18 44 31	7♓56 22	14 39 52	29D23.3	26 06.4	25 55.9	11 00.9	24 03.1	9 28.2	20 09.4	5 11.1	21 47.9	18 12.6
10 Sa	5 15 40	19 41 54	21 28 08	28 21 26	29R23.3	25 37.7	27 05.9	11 39.9	24 15.9	9 37.2	20 16.5	5 14.6	21 49.3	18 12.1
11 Su	5 19 37	20 39 16	5♈19 53	12♈23 34	29 22.9	25 07.0	28 15.8	12 18.8	24 28.5	9 46.2	20 23.6	5 18.1	21 50.7	18 11.5
12 M	5 23 33	21 36 38	19 32 27	26 46 19	29 21.0	24 34.7	29 25.6	12 57.7	24 40.9	9 55.0	20 30.7	5 21.6	21 52.1	18 10.9
13 Tu	5 27 30	22 34 00	4♉04 49	11♉27 27	29 16.7	24 01.3	0♌35.3	13 36.5	24 53.1	10 03.7	20 37.9	5 25.1	21 53.4	18 10.3
14 W	5 31 27	23 31 21	18 53 29	26 22 03	29 09.7	23 27.5	1 45.0	14 15.4	25 05.0	10 12.3	20 45.1	5 28.7	21 54.7	18 09.6
15 Th	5 35 23	24 28 41	3♊52 09	11♊22 38	29 00.3	22 53.9	2 54.5	14 54.2	25 16.7	10 20.7	20 52.3	5 32.2	21 56.0	18 09.0
16 F	5 39 20	25 26 01	18 52 17	26 19 55	28 49.4	22 21.0	4 04.0	15 33.0	25 28.2	10 29.0	20 59.6	5 35.8	21 57.2	18 08.3
17 Sa	5 43 16	26 23 21	3♋44 20	11♋04 28	28 38.3	21 49.3	5 13.3	15 11.8	25 39.5	10 37.1	21 06.9	5 39.3	21 58.5	18 07.6
18 Su	5 47 13	27 20 39	18 19 22	25 28 18	28 28.1	21 19.5	6 22.6	16 50.6	25 50.5	10 45.2	21 14.2	5 42.9	21 59.7	18 06.9
19 M	5 51 09	28 17 57	2♌30 41	9♌26 09	28 20.0	20 51.9	7 31.8	17 29.4	26 01.3	10 53.0	21 21.6	5 46.5	22 00.8	18 06.1
20 Tu	5 55 06	29 15 14	16 14 32	22 55 51	28 14.4	20 27.1	8 40.8	18 08.1	26 11.8	11 00.8	21 29.0	5 50.1	22 02.0	18 05.3
21 W	5 59 03	0♋12 31	29 30 18	5♍58 11	28 11.3	20 05.6	9 49.8	18 46.8	26 22.1	11 08.4	21 36.4	5 53.7	22 03.1	18 04.5
22 Th	6 02 59	1 09 47	12♍19 57	18 36 07	28D10.1	19 47.6	10 58.6	19 25.5	26 32.1	11 15.8	21 43.9	5 57.3	22 04.1	18 03.7
23 F	6 06 56	2 07 02	24 47 17	0♎54 06	28R10.0	19 33.5	12 07.3	20 04.2	26 41.9	11 23.1	21 51.3	6 00.9	22 05.2	18 02.9
24 Sa	6 10 52	3 04 16	6♎57 13	12 57 19	28 09.8	19 23.5	13 15.9	20 42.9	26 51.4	11 30.2	21 58.8	6 04.5	22 06.2	18 02.0
25 Su	6 14 49	4 01 30	18 55 04	24 51 08	28 08.4	19D17.9	14 24.4	21 21.6	27 00.7	11 37.2	22 06.3	6 08.1	22 07.2	18 01.1
26 M	6 18 45	4 58 43	0♏46 09	6♏40 42	28 05.1	19 16.9	15 32.8	22 00.2	27 09.7	11 44.1	22 13.9	6 11.7	22 08.2	18 00.2
27 Tu	6 22 42	5 55 56	12 35 21	18 30 36	27 59.2	19 20.5	16 41.1	22 38.8	27 18.5	11 50.8	22 21.5	6 15.3	22 09.1	17 59.3
28 W	6 26 38	6 53 08	24 26 57	0♐24 46	27 50.6	19 28.9	17 49.2	23 17.4	27 27.0	11 57.3	22 29.0	6 18.9	22 10.0	17 58.4
29 Th	6 30 35	7 50 20	6♐24 26	12 26 14	27 39.8	19 42.1	18 57.2	23 56.0	27 35.2	12 03.7	22 36.6	6 22.5	22 10.9	17 57.5
30 F	6 34 32	8 47 32	18 30 24	24 37 07	27 27.4	20 00.2	20 05.0	24 34.6	27 43.1	12 09.9	22 44.3	6 26.1	22 11.7	17 56.5

Astro Data

	Dy Hr Mn
♃0N	2 23:20
♅⊡♇	3 2:25
♃∠♇	6 12:59
♃□♅	7 8:02
☽0N	14 6:27
♇ R	19 7:02
♄⊼♇	23 18:42
☽0S	27 2:34
☿ R	2 5:24
☽0N	10 15:06
☽0S	23 11:09
♄□♆	25 15:06
☿ D	26 5:24

Planet Ingress

		Dy Hr Mn
☿	♊	5 11:04
♀	♋	18 13:06
☉	♊	20 22:58
♂	♋	23 14:27
☊	♍R	3 17:25
♀	♌	12 23:50
☉	♋	21 6:45

Last Aspect / ☽ Ingress

Last Aspect Dy Hr Mn			☽ Ingress	Dy Hr Mn
1 14:32	♆	☍	♏	2 9:36
4 19:59	☿	☍	♐	4 22:23
6 16:01	♆	△	♑	7 10:16
9 2:53	♆	□	♒	9 20:17
11 13:12	♂	△	♓	12 3:28
13 21:56	♀	□	♈	14 7:15
16 3:33	♀	⚹	♉	16 8:07
18 3:14	☉	☌	♊	18 7:31
20 3:47	♂	☌	♋	20 7:27
21 18:58	♆	□	♌	22 10:02
24 6:53	☿	⚹	♍	24 16:36
26 19:45	☿	□	♎	27 3:03
29 10:21	☿	△	♏	29 15:43

Last Aspect / ☽ Ingress

Last Aspect Dy Hr Mn			☽ Ingress	Dy Hr Mn
31 6:30	♄	△	♐	1 4:28
3 11:50	☿	☍	♑	3 16:02
5 10:05	♆	□	♒	6 1:54
8 3:37	☿	△	♓	8 9:39
10 9:37	♀	△	♈	10 14:50
12 16:45	♀	□	♉	12 17:19
14 2:55	♄	⚹	♊	14 17:49
16 10:27	☉	☌	♋	16 17:56
18 6:08	♆	□	♌	18 19:42
21 0:27	☉	⚹	♍	21 0:55
22 18:07	♄	⚹	♎	23 10:13
25 6:28	♆	☍	♏	25 22:26
27 20:50	♂	△	♐	28 11:10
30 7:15	♆	△	♑	30 22:30

☽ Phases & Eclipses

Dy Hr Mn		
3 12:17	○	13♏09
11 10:57	☾	20♒50
18 3:14	●	27♉17
24 23:59	☽	3♍53
2 3:55	○	11♐43
9 19:45	☾	19♓03
16 10:27	●	25♊22
23 14:36	☽	2♎13

Astro Data

1 May 2034
Julian Day # 49064
SVP 4♓46'50"
GC 27♐19.1 ⚵ 10♒23.0
Eris 27♈17.2 ⚶ 16♐55.9R
⚷ 29♉41.2 ⚴ 14♉21.7
☽ Mean ☊ 1♎03.3

1 June 2034
Julian Day # 49095
SVP 4♓46'46"
GC 27♐19.2 ⚵ 12♒26.0R
Eris 27♈35.3 ⚶ 10♐56.0R
⚷ 1♊56.6 ⚴ 28♉01.0
☽ Mean ☊ 29♍24.8

July 2034 LONGITUDE

Day	Sid.Time	☉	0 hr ☽	Noon ☽	True ☊	☿	♀	♂	⚳	♃	♄	♅	♆	♇
1 Sa	6 38 28	9♋44 43	0♑46 32	6♑58 44	27♍14.6	20♊23.2	21♌12.8	25♋13.1	27♓50.8	12♈16.0	22♋51.9	6♋29.7	22♈12.5	17♒55.5
2 Su	6 42 25	10 41 54	13 13 44	19 31 36	27R 02.3	20 51.0	22 20.4	25 51.6	27 58.2	12 21.9	22 59.6	6 33.3	22 13.3	17R 54.5
3 M	6 46 21	11 39 06	25 52 18	2♒15 50	26 51.7	21 23.6	23 27.8	26 30.2	28 05.3	12 27.6	23 07.2	6 36.9	22 14.0	17 53.5
4 Tu	6 50 18	12 36 17	8♒42 11	15 11 21	26 43.4	22 01.0	24 35.1	27 08.7	28 12.1	12 33.2	23 14.9	6 40.5	22 14.7	17 52.5
5 W	6 54 14	13 33 28	21 43 19	28 18 09	26 38.0	22 43.2	25 42.3	27 47.2	28 18.6	12 38.6	23 22.6	6 44.1	22 15.4	17 51.4
6 Th	6 58 11	14 30 39	4♓55 52	11♓36 34	26 35.2	23 30.0	26 49.3	28 25.7	28 24.8	12 43.9	23 30.3	6 47.7	22 16.1	17 50.3
7 F	7 02 07	15 27 51	18 20 21	25 07 19	26D 34.4	24 21.5	27 56.2	29 04.1	28 30.7	12 49.0	23 38.1	6 51.2	22 16.7	17 49.2
8 Sa	7 06 04	16 25 03	1♈57 35	8♈51 16	26R 34.6	25 17.6	29 02.9	29 42.6	28 36.3	12 53.9	23 45.8	6 54.8	22 17.3	17 48.1
9 Su	7 10 01	17 22 16	15 48 25	22 49 06	26 34.6	26 18.2	0♍09.5	0♌21.0	28 41.6	12 58.6	23 53.5	6 58.4	22 17.8	17 47.0
10 M	7 13 57	18 19 29	29 53 15	7♉00 46	26 33.4	27 23.2	1 15.9	0 59.5	28 46.6	13 03.2	24 01.3	7 01.9	22 18.3	17 45.9
11 Tu	7 17 54	19 16 42	14♉11 26	21 24 54	26 30.0	28 32.7	2 22.1	1 37.9	28 51.3	13 07.6	24 09.1	7 05.5	22 18.8	17 44.8
12 W	7 21 50	20 13 56	28 40 43	5♊58 19	26 24.1	29 46.5	3 28.2	2 16.3	28 55.7	13 11.8	24 16.8	7 09.0	22 19.3	17 43.6
13 Th	7 25 47	21 11 11	13♊16 59	20 35 55	26 16.1	1♋04.6	4 34.1	2 54.7	28 59.7	13 15.8	24 24.6	7 12.6	22 19.7	17 42.4
14 F	7 29 43	22 08 25	27 54 16	5♋11 08	26 06.7	2 26.9	5 39.8	3 33.2	29 03.4	13 19.6	24 32.4	7 16.1	22 20.1	17 41.3
15 Sa	7 33 40	23 05 41	12♋25 35	19 36 46	25 57.0	3 53.3	6 45.4	4 11.5	29 06.8	13 23.3	24 40.2	7 19.6	22 20.5	17 40.1
16 Su	7 37 36	24 02 56	26 43 54	3♌46 16	25 48.1	5 23.8	7 50.8	4 49.9	29 09.8	13 26.8	24 48.0	7 23.1	22 20.8	17 38.9
17 M	7 41 33	25 00 12	10♌43 20	17 34 40	25 40.9	6 58.2	8 56.0	5 28.3	29 12.5	13 30.1	24 55.7	7 26.6	22 21.1	17 37.6
18 Tu	7 45 30	25 57 28	24 20 00	0♍59 16	25 36.0	8 36.4	10 01.0	6 06.7	29 14.9	13 33.2	25 03.5	7 30.1	22 21.3	17 36.4
19 W	7 49 26	26 54 44	7♍32 27	13 59 46	25D 33.4	10 18.2	11 05.8	6 45.0	29 16.9	13 36.1	25 11.3	7 33.5	22 21.6	17 35.2
20 Th	7 53 23	27 52 01	20 21 29	26 37 59	25 32.8	12 03.5	12 10.4	7 23.4	29 18.6	13 38.9	25 19.1	7 37.0	22 21.8	17 33.9
21 F	7 57 19	28 49 18	2♎49 44	8♎57 17	25 33.3	13 52.2	13 14.8	8 01.7	29 19.9	13 41.4	25 26.9	7 40.4	22 21.9	17 32.7
22 Sa	8 01 16	29 46 34	15 01 14	21 02 10	25R 34.2	15 43.9	14 18.9	8 40.0	29 20.9	13 43.8	25 34.6	7 43.8	22 22.1	17 31.4
23 Su	8 05 12	0♌43 52	27 00 45	2♏57 37	25 34.5	17 38.4	15 22.9	9 18.3	29 21.5	13 45.9	25 42.4	7 47.2	22 22.1	17 30.1
24 M	8 09 09	1 41 09	8♏53 27	14 48 52	25 33.5	19 35.5	16 26.6	9 56.6	29R 21.8	13 47.9	25 50.1	7 50.6	22 22.2	17 28.8
25 Tu	8 13 05	2 38 27	20 44 28	26 40 53	25 30.5	21 34.9	17 30.0	10 34.9	29 21.8	13 49.7	25 57.9	7 53.9	22R 22.2	17 27.6
26 W	8 17 02	3 35 46	2♐38 38	8♐38 15	25 25.5	23 36.2	18 33.3	11 13.2	29 21.4	13 51.3	26 05.6	7 57.3	22 22.2	17 26.3
27 Th	8 20 59	4 33 05	14 40 11	20 44 50	25 18.7	25 39.1	19 36.2	11 51.5	29 20.6	13 52.7	26 13.4	8 00.6	22 22.2	17 25.0
28 F	8 24 55	5 30 24	26 52 33	3♑03 37	25 10.6	27 43.2	20 38.9	12 29.7	29 19.5	13 53.9	26 21.1	8 03.9	22 22.1	17 23.6
29 Sa	8 28 52	6 27 44	9♑18 14	15 36 33	25 01.9	29 48.3	21 41.4	13 08.0	29 18.0	13 54.9	26 28.8	8 07.2	22 22.0	17 22.3
30 Su	8 32 48	7 25 05	21 58 38	28 24 30	24 53.6	1♌54.0	22 43.5	13 46.2	29 16.2	13 55.7	26 36.5	8 10.5	22 21.9	17 21.0
31 M	8 36 45	8 22 26	4♒54 06	11♒27 21	24 46.6	4 00.1	23 45.4	14 24.5	29 14.0	13 56.4	26 44.2	8 13.7	22 21.7	17 19.7

August 2034 LONGITUDE

Day	Sid.Time	☉	0 hr ☽	Noon ☽	True ☊	☿	♀	♂	⚳	♃	♄	♅	♆	♇
1 Tu	8 40 41	9♌19 48	18♒04 05	24♒44 08	24♍41.3	6♌06.1	24♍47.0	15♌02.7	29♓11.4	13♈56.8	26♋51.9	8♋16.9	22♈21.5	17♒18.3
2 W	8 44 38	10 17 11	1♓27 19	8♓13 25	24R 38.1	8 12.0	25 48.3	15 41.0	29R 08.5	13R 57.0	26 59.5	8 20.1	22R 21.3	17R 17.0
3 Th	8 48 34	11 14 35	15 02 14	21 53 34	24D 36.9	10 17.3	26 49.2	16 19.2	29 05.2	13 57.0	27 07.1	8 23.3	22 21.1	17 15.7
4 F	8 52 31	12 12 00	28 47 14	5♈43 03	24 37.3	12 22.0	27 49.9	16 57.4	29 01.6	13 56.9	27 14.8	8 26.5	22 20.8	17 14.3
5 Sa	8 56 28	13 09 27	12♈40 51	19 40 30	24 38.5	14 25.8	28 50.2	17 35.6	28 57.6	13 56.5	27 22.4	8 29.6	22 20.4	17 13.0
6 Su	9 00 24	14 06 54	26 41 51	3♉44 45	24R 39.7	16 28.7	29 50.2	18 13.8	28 53.2	13 55.9	27 29.9	8 32.7	22 20.1	17 11.6
7 M	9 04 21	15 04 24	10♉49 02	17 54 31	24 40.0	18 30.4	0♎49.9	18 52.0	28 48.5	13 55.2	27 37.5	8 35.8	22 19.7	17 10.3
8 Tu	9 08 17	16 01 53	25 00 58	2♊08 09	24 38.9	20 30.9	1 49.2	19 30.3	28 43.5	13 54.2	27 45.0	8 38.8	22 19.3	17 08.9
9 W	9 12 14	16 59 25	9♊15 44	16 23 21	24 36.3	22 30.1	2 48.1	20 08.5	28 38.1	13 53.1	27 52.6	8 41.8	22 18.8	17 07.6
10 Th	9 16 10	17 56 58	23 30 36	0♋37 01	24 32.1	24 27.9	3 46.7	20 46.7	28 32.3	13 51.7	28 00.1	8 44.8	22 18.3	17 06.2
11 F	9 20 07	18 54 32	7♋42 07	14 45 22	24 27.0	26 24.3	4 44.9	21 24.9	28 26.2	13 50.2	28 07.5	8 47.8	22 17.8	17 04.9
12 Sa	9 24 03	19 52 08	21 46 16	28 44 17	24 21.6	28 19.3	5 42.7	22 03.1	28 19.7	13 48.4	28 15.0	8 50.7	22 17.3	17 03.5
13 Su	9 28 00	20 49 45	5♌38 57	12♌29 50	24 16.6	0♍12.9	6 40.1	22 41.3	28 12.9	13 46.5	28 22.4	8 53.6	22 16.7	17 02.2
14 M	9 31 57	21 47 23	19 16 34	25 58 51	24 12.7	2 05.0	7 37.0	23 19.5	28 05.7	13 44.3	28 29.8	8 56.5	22 16.1	17 00.8
15 Tu	9 35 53	22 45 02	2♍36 28	9♍09 20	24 10.3	3 55.6	8 33.6	23 57.7	27 58.2	13 42.0	28 37.1	8 59.4	22 15.5	16 59.5
16 W	9 39 50	23 42 43	15 37 24	22 00 45	24D 09.3	5 44.7	9 29.6	24 35.9	27 50.4	13 39.4	28 44.4	9 02.2	22 14.8	16 58.1
17 Th	9 43 46	24 40 24	28 19 32	4♎34 00	24 09.7	7 32.4	10 25.2	25 14.1	27 42.2	13 36.7	28 51.7	9 05.0	22 14.1	16 56.8
18 F	9 47 43	25 38 07	10♎44 27	16 51 18	24 11.0	9 18.6	11 20.3	25 52.3	27 33.8	13 33.8	28 59.0	9 07.7	22 13.4	16 55.5
19 Sa	9 51 39	26 35 50	22 54 57	28 55 56	24 12.7	11 03.4	12 14.9	26 30.5	27 25.0	13 30.7	29 06.2	9 10.4	22 12.6	16 54.1
20 Su	9 55 36	27 33 35	4♏54 44	10♏51 58	24 14.3	12 46.8	13 08.9	27 08.6	27 15.9	13 27.4	29 13.4	9 13.1	22 11.8	16 52.8
21 M	9 59 32	28 31 21	16 48 11	22 43 59	24R 15.3	14 28.7	14 02.4	27 46.8	27 06.5	13 23.9	29 20.6	9 15.8	22 11.0	16 51.5
22 Tu	10 03 29	29 29 08	28 39 59	4♐36 47	24 15.3	16 09.3	14 55.4	28 25.0	26 56.8	13 20.2	29 27.7	9 18.4	22 10.2	16 50.2
23 W	10 07 25	0♍26 57	10♐35 00	16 35 11	24 14.2	17 48.4	15 47.7	29 03.2	26 46.9	13 16.4	29 34.7	9 20.9	22 09.3	16 48.9
24 Th	10 11 22	1 24 46	22 37 53	28 43 39	24 12.2	19 26.2	16 39.4	29 41.4	26 36.7	13 12.4	29 41.8	9 23.5	22 08.4	16 47.6
25 F	10 15 19	2 22 37	4♑52 54	11♑06 06	24 09.5	21 02.6	17 30.5	0♍19.5	26 26.2	13 08.1	29 48.8	9 26.0	22 07.5	16 46.3
26 Sa	10 19 15	3 20 29	17 23 34	23 45 37	24 06.4	22 37.6	18 20.9	0 57.7	26 15.4	13 03.8	29 55.7	9 28.5	22 06.5	16 45.0
27 Su	10 23 12	4 18 22	0♒12 25	6♒44 07	24 03.4	24 11.3	19 10.6	1 35.9	26 04.4	12 59.2	0♌02.6	9 30.9	22 05.6	16 43.7
28 M	10 27 08	5 16 17	13 20 44	20 02 13	24 00.8	25 43.7	19 59.6	2 14.0	25 53.2	12 54.5	0 09.5	9 33.3	22 04.6	16 42.4
29 Tu	10 31 05	6 14 13	26 48 23	3♓39 02	23 59.1	27 14.6	20 47.9	2 52.2	25 41.8	12 49.6	0 16.3	9 35.6	22 03.5	16 41.2
30 W	10 35 01	7 12 11	10♓33 50	17 32 24	23D 58.3	28 44.3	21 35.4	3 30.4	25 30.1	12 44.6	0 23.1	9 37.9	22 02.5	16 39.9
31 Th	10 38 58	8 10 10	24 34 17	1♈39 00	23 58.3	0♎12.5	22 22.1	4 08.6	25 18.2	12 39.3	0 29.8	9 40.2	22 01.4	16 38.7

Astro Data	Dy Hr Mn
☽ 0N	7 22:07
☽ 0S	20 20:45
⚳ R	24 19:54
♆ R	25 22:32
♃ R	3 3:43
☽ 0N	4 4:34
♀ 0S	5 11:32
☽ 0S	17 6:12
☿ 0S	30 22:35
☽ 0N	31 11:57

Planet Ingress	Dy Hr Mn
♂ ♌	8 22:52
♀ ♍	9 8:35
☿ ♋	12 16:14
☉ ♌	22 17:37
☿ ♌	29 14:14
♀ ♎	6 15:56
☿ ♍	13 9:16
☉ ♍	23 0:49
♂ ♍	24 23:43
♄ ♌	27 2:48
☿ ♎	31 8:35

Last Aspect Dy Hr Mn		☽ Ingress	Dy Hr Mn
3 0:37	♂ ☍	♒	3 7:46
5 6:50	♀ ☍	♓	5 15:05
7 19:17	♂ △	♈	7 20:34
9 18:24	☿ ✶	♉	10 0:11
11 16:34	♄ ✶	♊	12 2:11
13 14:50	♆ ✶	♋	14 3:27
15 20:35	♄ ☌	♌	16 5:33
17 20:28	♆ △	♍	18 10:12
20 14:35	☉ ✶	♎	20 18:30
22 21:13	♄ □	♏	23 6:01
25 10:32	♄ △	♐	25 18:41
27 15:11	♆ △	♑	28 6:05
30 8:37	♄ ☍	♒	30 14:57

Last Aspect Dy Hr Mn		☽ Ingress	Dy Hr Mn
1 7:44	♆ ✶	♓	1 21:25
3 21:16	♀ ☍	♈	4 2:06
6 1:16	♄ □	♉	6 5:38
8 4:33	♄ ✶	♊	8 8:24
9 23:57	☿ ✶	♋	10 10:57
12 11:09	♄ ☌	♌	12 14:11
14 7:00	♂ ☌	♍	14 19:16
17 0:55	♄ ✶	♎	17 3:12
19 12:21	♄ □	♏	19 14:08
22 1:30	♄ △	♐	22 2:42
24 13:59	♂ △	♑	24 14:29
26 23:35	♄ ☍	♒	26 23:37
28 15:37	♆ ✶	♓	29 5:37
29 22:21	♅ △	♈	31 9:13

☽ Phases & Eclipses Dy Hr Mn		
1 17:46	○	9♑58
9 2:00	☾	16♈58
15 18:17	●	23♋21
23 7:06	☽	0♏32
31 5:56	○	8♒08
7 6:51	☾	14♉52
14 3:54	●	21♌28
22 0:45	☽	29♏02
29 16:50	○	6♓26

Astro Data

1 July 2034
Julian Day # 49125
SVP 4♓46'41"
GC 27♐19.3 ⚴ 8♒46.1R
Eris 27♈46.4 ⚵ 4♐57.6R
⚷ 4♊01.1 ⚶ 10♊50.4
☽ Mean ☊ 27♍49.5

1 August 2034
Julian Day # 49156
SVP 4♓46'36"
GC 27♐19.3 ⚴ 0♒52.6R
Eris 27♈48.8R ⚵ 2♐57.9
⚷ 5♊40.9 ⚶ 23♊21.7
☽ Mean ☊ 26♍11.0

LONGITUDE — September 2034

Day	Sid.Time	☉	0 hr ☽	Noon ☽	True ☊	☿	♀	♂	⚳	♃	♄	♅	♆	♇
1 F	10 42 54	9♍08 11	8♈46 02	15♈54 50	23♍59.0	1♎39.4	23♎08.0	4♍46.7	25♓06.1	12♈34.0	0♌36.5	9♋42.4	22♈00.3	16♒37.5
2 Sa	10 46 51	10 06 14	23 04 53	0♉15 39	24 00.0	3 04.9	23 53.0	5 24.9	24R53.9	12R28.4	0 43.2	9 44.6	21R59.2	16R36.2
3 Su	10 50 48	11 04 18	7♉26 39	14 37 25	24 01.0	4 29.0	24 37.1	6 03.1	24 41.4	12 22.7	0 49.7	9 46.8	21 58.0	16 35.0
4 M	10 54 44	12 02 25	21 47 31	28 56 34	24 01.7	5 51.6	25 20.3	6 41.3	24 28.9	12 16.9	0 56.3	9 48.9	21 56.9	16 33.8
5 Tu	10 58 41	13 00 34	6♊04 13	13♊10 09	24R02.0	7 12.8	26 02.5	7 19.5	24 16.1	12 10.9	1 02.8	9 51.0	21 55.7	16 32.6
6 W	11 02 37	13 58 45	20 14 06	27 15 51	24 01.7	8 32.5	26 43.8	7 57.7	24 03.2	12 04.8	1 09.2	9 53.0	21 54.4	16 31.5
7 Th	11 06 34	14 56 58	4♋15 08	11♋11 49	24 01.1	9 50.7	27 24.0	8 35.9	23 50.2	11 58.6	1 15.6	9 55.0	21 53.2	16 30.3
8 F	11 10 30	15 55 13	18 05 41	24 56 36	24 00.2	11 07.3	28 03.1	9 14.1	23 37.1	11 52.2	1 21.9	9 56.9	21 51.9	16 29.2
9 Sa	11 14 27	16 53 30	1♌44 24	8♌29 00	23 59.3	12 22.2	28 41.2	9 52.3	23 23.9	11 45.6	1 28.1	9 58.8	21 50.6	16 28.0
10 Su	11 18 23	17 51 48	15 10 15	21 48 04	23 58.5	13 35.4	29 18.0	10 30.6	23 10.6	11 39.0	1 34.3	10 00.6	21 49.3	16 26.9
11 M	11 22 20	18 50 09	28 22 23	4♍53 08	23 58.0	14 46.8	29 53.7	11 08.8	22 57.3	11 32.2	1 40.5	10 02.4	21 48.0	16 25.8
12 Tu	11 26 17	19 48 32	11♍20 18	17 43 52	23D57.7	15 56.3	0♏28.1	11 47.0	22 43.9	11 25.3	1 46.6	10 04.2	21 46.7	16 24.7
13 W	11 30 13	20 46 56	24 03 54	0♎20 28	23 57.7	17 03.8	1 01.2	12 25.2	22 30.4	11 18.3	1 52.6	10 05.9	21 45.3	16 23.7
14 Th	11 34 10	21 45 22	6♎33 41	12 43 43	23 57.8	18 09.2	1 33.0	13 03.5	22 17.0	11 11.2	1 58.5	10 07.6	21 43.9	16 22.6
15 F	11 38 06	22 43 50	18 50 45	24 55 03	23 58.0	19 12.4	2 03.3	13 41.7	22 03.5	11 04.0	2 04.4	10 09.2	21 42.5	16 21.6
16 Sa	11 42 03	23 42 20	0♏56 55	6♏56 40	23R58.1	20 13.2	2 32.2	14 20.0	21 50.1	10 56.7	2 10.3	10 10.8	21 41.1	16 20.5
17 Su	11 45 59	24 40 51	12 54 41	18 51 24	23 58.0	21 11.5	2 59.5	14 58.2	21 36.6	10 49.3	2 16.0	10 12.3	21 39.6	16 19.5
18 M	11 49 56	25 39 24	24 47 16	0♐42 47	23 57.9	22 07.1	3 25.3	15 36.5	21 23.3	10 41.8	2 21.7	10 13.8	21 38.2	16 18.5
19 Tu	11 53 52	26 37 59	6♐38 26	12 34 48	23 57.7	22 59.7	3 49.4	16 14.7	21 09.9	10 34.2	2 27.3	10 15.2	21 36.7	16 17.6
20 W	11 57 49	27 36 35	18 32 25	24 31 52	23D57.6	23 49.3	4 11.7	16 53.0	20 56.7	10 26.6	2 32.9	10 16.6	21 35.2	16 16.6
21 Th	12 01 45	28 35 14	0♑33 43	6♑38 33	23 57.7	24 35.4	4 32.3	17 31.2	20 43.5	10 18.9	2 38.4	10 17.9	21 33.7	16 15.7
22 F	12 05 42	29 33 53	12 46 55	18 59 23	23 58.0	25 17.9	4 51.1	18 09.5	20 30.4	10 11.2	2 43.8	10 19.2	21 32.2	16 14.8
23 Sa	12 09 39	0♎32 35	25 16 25	1♒38 30	23 58.5	25 56.5	5 08.0	18 47.8	20 17.4	10 03.3	2 49.1	10 20.4	21 30.7	16 13.9
24 Su	12 13 35	1 31 18	8♒06 00	14 39 14	23 59.2	26 30.8	5 22.8	19 26.1	20 04.6	9 55.5	2 54.4	10 21.6	21 29.1	16 13.0
25 M	12 17 32	2 30 03	21 18 27	28 03 45	23 59.9	27 00.5	5 35.7	20 04.3	19 51.9	9 47.6	2 59.6	10 22.7	21 27.6	16 12.2
26 Tu	12 21 28	3 28 50	4♓55 07	11♓52 26	24R00.5	27 25.3	5 46.5	20 42.6	19 39.3	9 39.6	3 04.7	10 23.8	21 26.0	16 11.3
27 W	12 25 25	4 27 38	18 55 26	26 03 41	24 00.7	27 44.6	5 55.1	21 20.9	19 26.9	9 31.6	3 09.8	10 24.8	21 24.4	16 10.5
28 Th	12 29 21	5 26 29	3♈16 38	10♈33 38	24 00.3	27 58.2	6 01.5	21 59.2	19 14.7	9 23.6	3 14.7	10 25.8	21 22.9	16 09.7
29 F	12 33 18	6 25 21	17 53 52	25 16 29	23 59.3	28R05.7	6 05.7	22 37.5	19 02.7	9 15.6	3 19.6	10 26.7	21 21.3	16 09.0
30 Sa	12 37 14	7 24 16	2♉40 33	10♉05 08	23 57.9	28 06.5	6R07.6	23 15.9	18 50.9	9 07.6	3 24.4	10 27.6	21 19.6	16 08.2

LONGITUDE — October 2034

Day	Sid.Time	☉	0 hr ☽	Noon ☽	True ☊	☿	♀	♂	⚳	♃	♄	♅	♆	♇
1 Su	12 41 11	8♎23 13	17♉29 16	24♉52 05	23♍56.1	28♎00.4	6♏07.2	23♍54.2	18♓39.2	8♈59.5	3♌29.1	10♋28.4	21♈18.0	16♒07.5
2 M	12 45 08	9 22 12	2♊12 45	9♊30 34	23R54.4	27R46.9	6R04.4	24 32.5	18R27.8	8R51.5	3 33.8	10 29.2	21R16.4	16R06.8
3 Tu	12 49 04	10 21 14	16 44 54	23 55 17	23 53.2	27 25.9	5 59.3	25 10.9	18 16.7	8 43.4	3 38.3	10 29.9	21 14.8	16 06.1
4 W	12 53 01	11 20 18	1♋01 22	8♋02 53	23D52.6	26 57.0	5 51.7	25 49.2	18 05.8	8 35.4	3 42.8	10 30.5	21 13.1	16 05.4
5 Th	12 56 57	12 19 24	14 59 44	21 51 52	23 52.8	26 20.4	5 41.8	26 27.6	17 55.1	8 27.3	3 47.2	10 31.1	21 11.5	16 04.8
6 F	13 00 54	13 18 32	28 39 21	5♌22 18	23 53.7	25 36.1	5 29.5	27 06.0	17 44.7	8 19.3	3 51.5	10 31.7	21 09.8	16 04.2
7 Sa	13 04 50	14 17 43	12♌00 52	18 35 16	23 55.1	24 44.6	5 14.8	27 44.4	17 34.5	8 11.3	3 55.7	10 32.2	21 08.2	16 03.6
8 Su	13 08 47	15 16 56	25 05 42	1♍32 25	23 56.6	23 46.5	4 57.8	28 22.8	17 24.7	8 03.4	3 59.8	10 32.7	21 06.5	16 03.0
9 M	13 12 43	16 16 11	7♍55 37	14 15 33	23R57.7	22 42.8	4 38.5	29 01.2	17 15.1	7 55.5	4 03.9	10 33.1	21 04.8	16 02.5
10 Tu	13 16 40	17 15 29	20 32 26	26 46 27	23 58.0	21 34.7	4 17.0	29 39.6	17 05.9	7 47.6	4 07.8	10 33.4	21 03.2	16 02.0
11 W	13 20 37	18 14 48	2♎57 48	9♎06 40	23 57.1	20 23.9	3 53.4	0♎18.0	16 56.9	7 39.8	4 11.7	10 33.7	21 01.5	16 01.5
12 Th	13 24 33	19 14 10	15 13 14	21 17 41	23 54.9	19 12.0	3 27.7	0 56.4	16 48.3	7 32.1	4 15.4	10 33.9	20 59.8	16 01.0
13 F	13 28 30	20 13 34	27 20 10	3♏20 53	23 51.4	18 01.2	3 00.1	1 34.9	16 40.0	7 24.4	4 19.1	10 34.1	20 58.1	16 00.6
14 Sa	13 32 26	21 12 59	9♏20 03	15 17 52	23 46.9	16 53.5	2 30.7	2 13.3	16 32.0	7 16.8	4 22.7	10 34.2	20 56.5	16 00.2
15 Su	13 36 23	22 12 27	21 14 35	27 10 28	23 41.8	15 50.8	1 59.7	2 51.8	16 24.4	7 09.2	4 26.1	10R34.3	20 54.8	15 59.8
16 M	13 40 19	23 11 57	3♐05 51	9♐01 02	23 36.6	14 54.9	1 27.3	3 30.2	16 17.1	7 01.8	4 29.5	10 34.3	20 53.1	15 59.4
17 Tu	13 44 16	24 11 28	14 56 24	20 52 23	23 32.0	14 07.5	0 53.5	4 08.7	16 10.1	6 54.4	4 32.8	10 34.3	20 51.4	15 59.1
18 W	13 48 12	25 11 01	26 49 25	2♑47 59	23 28.4	13 29.8	0 18.7	4 47.2	16 03.5	6 47.1	4 36.0	10 34.2	20 49.8	15 58.8
19 Th	13 52 09	26 10 36	8♑48 36	14 51 48	23D26.3	13 02.6	29♎43.1	5 25.7	15 57.3	6 40.0	4 39.1	10 34.1	20 48.1	15 58.5
20 F	13 56 06	27 10 13	20 58 09	27 08 14	23 25.6	12D46.6	29 06.9	6 04.2	15 51.4	6 32.9	4 42.1	10 33.9	20 46.4	15 58.2
21 Sa	14 00 02	28 09 51	3♒22 37	9♒41 52	23 26.2	12 41.7	28 30.3	6 42.7	15 45.9	6 26.0	4 44.9	10 33.7	20 44.8	15 58.0
22 Su	14 03 59	29 09 32	16 06 31	22 37 04	23 27.6	12 48.0	27 53.6	7 21.2	15 40.8	6 19.1	4 47.7	10 33.4	20 43.1	15 57.8
23 M	14 07 55	0♏09 13	29 13 58	5♓57 33	23 29.1	13 04.9	27 17.0	7 59.7	15 36.0	6 12.4	4 50.4	10 33.0	20 41.5	15 57.6
24 Tu	14 11 52	1 08 57	12♓48 04	19 45 38	23R30.1	13 32.0	26 40.7	8 38.3	15 31.6	6 05.8	4 53.0	10 32.6	20 39.8	15 57.5
25 W	14 15 48	2 08 42	26 50 10	4♈01 27	23 29.7	14 08.5	26 05.1	9 16.8	15 27.6	5 59.3	4 55.5	10 32.1	20 38.2	15 57.3
26 Th	14 19 45	3 08 29	11♈19 04	18 42 23	23 27.5	14 53.7	25 30.4	9 55.4	15 23.9	5 53.0	4 57.8	10 31.6	20 36.6	15 57.2
27 F	14 23 41	4 08 18	26 10 33	3♉42 35	23 23.4	15 46.5	24 56.8	10 33.9	15 20.6	5 46.8	5 00.1	10 31.1	20 34.9	15 57.2
28 Sa	14 27 38	5 08 09	11♉17 19	18 53 28	23 17.8	16 46.4	24 24.4	11 12.5	15 17.7	5 40.8	5 02.3	10 30.5	20 33.3	15 57.1
29 Su	14 31 34	6 08 02	26 29 43	4♊04 45	23 11.2	17 52.3	23 53.6	11 51.1	15 15.2	5 34.9	5 04.3	10 29.8	20 31.7	15D57.1
30 M	14 35 31	7 07 57	11♊37 19	19 06 16	23 04.7	19 03.5	23 24.5	12 29.7	15 13.0	5 29.1	5 06.3	10 29.1	20 30.1	15 57.1
31 Tu	14 39 28	8 07 55	26 30 38	3♋49 36	22 59.2	20 19.3	22 57.3	13 08.3	15 11.2	5 23.5	5 08.1	10 28.3	20 28.5	15 57.2

Astro Data

Astro Data	Dy Hr Mn
☽0S	13 14:29
♃□♅	21 14:44
☉0S	22 22:41
☽0N	27 21:15
☿R	30 3:01
♀R	30 19:38
☽0S	10 21:23
♂0S	14 17:07
♅R	16 10:17
☿D	21 10:23
☽0N	25 8:09
♇D	29 13:44

Planet Ingress

Planet Ingress	Dy Hr Mn
♀ ♏	11 16:19
☉ ♎	22 22:41
♂ ♎	11 0:45
♀ ♎R	19 0:41
☉ ♏	23 8:18

Last Aspect / ☽ Ingress (September)

Last Aspect Dy Hr Mn		☽ Ingress	Dy Hr Mn
2 0:45	♀ ☍	♉	2 11:34
3 15:16	♇ □	♊	4 13:47
6 11:02	♀ △	♋	6 16:41
8 17:45	♀ □	♌	8 20:55
11 2:22	♀ ✶	♍	11 2:59
12 16:15	☉ ☌	♎	13 11:21
15 5:40	♆ ☍	♏	15 22:06
18 0:50	☉ ✶	♐	18 10:33
20 18:41	☉ □	♑	20 22:53
23 0:43	♅ □	♒	23 8:55
25 10:04	♅ △	♓	25 15:25
27 3:43	♂ ☍	♈	27 18:34
29 16:36	☿ ☍	♉	29 19:40

Last Aspect / ☽ Ingress (October)

Last Aspect Dy Hr Mn		☽ Ingress	Dy Hr Mn
1 10:21	♂ △	♊	1 20:23
3 17:44	☿ △	♋	3 22:16
5 20:30	♂ ✶	♌	6 2:23
7 22:35	☿ ✶	♍	8 9:07
10 17:53	♂ ☌	♎	10 18:15
12 11:25	♆ ☍	♏	13 5:19
14 13:25	♇ □	♐	15 17:43
17 19:18	☉ ✶	♑	18 6:23
20 15:38	♀ □	♒	20 17:31
23 0:49	☉ △	♓	23 1:23
23 20:04	♅ △	♈	25 5:18
26 22:32	♀ ☍	♉	27 6:06
28 7:22	♇ □	♊	29 5:32
30 18:45	♀ △	♋	31 5:42

☽ Phases & Eclipses

Dy Hr Mn	
5 11:43	☾ 13♊00
12 16:15	● 19♍59
12 16:19:28	● A 02'58"
20 18:41	☽ 27♐53
28 2:58	○ 5♈04
28 2:48	• P 0.014
4 18:06	☾ 11♋35
12 7:34	● 19♎03
20 12:04	☽ 27♑10
27 12:44	○ 4♉10

Astro Data

1 September 2034
Julian Day # 49187
SVP 4♓46'33"
GC 27♐19.4 ⚴ 24♑47.0R
Eris 27♈41.4R ⚵ 5♐56.5
⚷ 6♊31.7 ⚶ 4♋38.0
☽ Mean ☊ 24♍32.5

1 October 2034
Julian Day # 49217
SVP 4♓46'31"
GC 27♐19.5 ⚴ 24♑09.9
Eris 27♈26.9R ⚵ 12♐22.8
⚷ 6♊22.8R ⚶ 13♋29.7
☽ Mean ☊ 22♍57.2

November 2034 LONGITUDE

Day	Sid.Time	☉	0 hr ☽	Noon ☽	True ☊	☿	♀	♂	⚳	♃	♄	♅	♆	♇
1 W	14 43 24	9♏07 54	11♋02 37	18♋09 15	22♍55.3	21♎39.0	22♎32.0	13♎46.9	15♓09.8	5♈18.1	5♌09.8	10♋27.5	20♈27.0	15♒57.2
2 Th	14 47 21	10 07 56	25 09 21	2♌02 52	22D53.3	23 02.1	22R08.9	14 25.6	15R08.8	5R12.8	5 11.5	10R26.6	20R25.4	15 57.3
3 F	14 51 17	11 07 59	8♌49 56	15 30 49	22 53.1	24 27.9	21 48.1	15 04.2	15 08.1	5 07.7	5 13.0	10 25.7	20 23.9	15 57.4
4 Sa	14 55 14	12 08 05	22 05 51	28 35 27	22 54.0	25 56.1	21 29.5	15 42.9	15D07.8	5 02.8	5 14.4	10 24.8	20 22.3	15 57.6
5 Su	14 59 10	13 08 13	5♍00 04	11♍20 10	22R55.2	27 26.1	21 13.3	16 21.6	15 07.9	4 58.0	5 15.7	10 23.7	20 20.8	15 57.8
6 M	15 03 07	14 08 23	17 36 15	23 48 46	22 55.7	28 57.8	20 59.6	17 00.3	15 08.3	4 53.4	5 16.9	10 22.7	20 19.3	15 58.0
7 Tu	15 07 03	15 08 35	29 58 10	6♎04 54	22 54.7	0♏30.7	20 48.3	17 39.0	15 09.1	4 49.0	5 17.9	10 21.6	20 17.8	15 58.2
8 W	15 11 00	16 08 49	12♎09 18	18 11 46	22 51.4	2 04.5	20 39.5	18 17.7	15 10.3	4 44.7	5 18.9	10 20.4	20 16.3	15 58.4
9 Th	15 14 57	17 09 05	24 12 34	0♏12 01	22 45.6	3 39.2	20 33.2	18 56.4	15 11.9	4 40.7	5 19.7	10 19.2	20 14.9	15 58.7
10 F	15 18 53	18 09 22	6♏10 20	12 07 45	22 37.2	5 14.5	20 29.3	19 35.1	15 13.8	4 36.8	5 20.5	10 17.9	20 13.4	15 59.0
11 Sa	15 22 50	19 09 42	18 04 27	24 00 38	22 26.8	6 50.2	20D27.9	20 13.9	15 16.1	4 33.1	5 21.1	10 16.6	20 12.0	15 59.4
12 Su	15 26 46	20 10 03	29 56 27	5♐52 06	22 15.2	8 26.2	20 28.9	20 52.6	15 18.7	4 29.6	5 21.6	10 15.3	20 10.6	15 59.8
13 M	15 30 43	21 10 26	11♐47 45	17 43 38	22 03.3	10 02.4	20 32.3	21 31.4	15 21.7	4 26.4	5 22.0	10 13.9	20 09.2	16 00.2
14 Tu	15 34 39	22 10 50	23 39 57	29 36 58	21 52.1	11 38.7	20 38.0	22 10.2	15 25.1	4 23.3	5 22.3	10 12.4	20 07.8	16 00.6
15 W	15 38 36	23 11 16	5♑34 59	11♑34 19	21 42.8	13 15.1	20 46.0	22 49.0	15 28.8	4 20.4	5 22.5	10 10.9	20 06.5	16 01.0
16 Th	15 42 32	24 11 43	17 35 22	23 38 33	21 35.8	14 51.4	20 56.2	23 27.8	15 32.9	4 17.7	5R22.5	10 09.4	20 05.2	16 01.5
17 F	15 46 29	25 12 12	29 44 18	5♒53 08	21 31.4	16 27.7	21 08.7	24 06.6	15 37.3	4 15.2	5 22.5	10 07.8	20 03.9	16 02.0
18 Sa	15 50 26	26 12 42	12♒05 34	18 22 10	21D29.4	18 03.9	21 23.3	24 45.4	15 42.0	4 12.9	5 22.3	10 06.2	20 02.6	16 02.5
19 Su	15 54 22	27 13 13	24 43 28	1♓10 04	21 29.2	19 39.9	21 39.9	25 24.2	15 47.1	4 10.8	5 22.0	10 04.5	20 01.3	16 03.1
20 M	15 58 19	28 13 45	7♓42 28	14 21 11	21R29.6	21 15.9	21 58.5	26 03.1	15 52.5	4 08.9	5 21.6	10 02.8	20 00.1	16 03.7
21 Tu	16 02 15	29 14 19	21 06 39	27 59 11	21 29.6	22 51.6	22 19.1	26 41.9	15 58.3	4 07.2	5 21.1	10 01.1	19 58.9	16 04.3
22 W	16 06 12	0♐14 53	4♈58 59	12♈06 06	21 28.0	24 27.2	22 41.6	27 20.8	16 04.3	4 05.8	5 20.5	9 59.3	19 57.7	16 04.9
23 Th	16 10 08	1 15 29	19 20 22	26 41 25	21 23.9	26 02.7	23 05.9	27 59.6	16 10.7	4 04.5	5 19.7	9 57.5	19 56.5	16 05.6
24 F	16 14 05	2 16 07	4♉08 38	11♉41 10	21 17.1	27 37.9	23 32.0	28 38.5	16 17.5	4 03.4	5 18.9	9 55.6	19 55.3	16 06.3
25 Sa	16 18 01	3 16 45	19 17 56	26 57 41	21 07.9	29 13.0	23 59.8	29 17.4	16 24.5	4 02.6	5 17.9	9 53.7	19 54.2	16 07.0
26 Su	16 21 58	4 17 25	4♊38 58	12♊20 18	20 57.1	0♐48.0	24 29.3	29 56.3	16 31.8	4 02.0	5 16.9	9 51.8	19 53.1	16 07.7
27 M	16 25 55	5 18 07	20 00 09	27 37 03	20 46.2	2 22.8	25 00.4	0♏35.2	16 39.5	4 01.5	5 15.7	9 49.9	19 52.1	16 08.5
28 Tu	16 29 51	6 18 49	5♋09 42	12♋36 56	20 36.4	3 57.5	25 33.0	1 14.2	16 47.4	4D01.3	5 14.4	9 47.9	19 51.0	16 09.3
29 W	16 33 48	7 19 34	19 57 51	27 11 47	20 28.8	5 32.1	26 07.1	1 53.1	16 55.7	4 01.3	5 13.0	9 45.8	19 50.0	16 10.1
30 Th	16 37 44	8 20 19	4♌18 19	11♌17 14	20 23.8	7 06.6	26 42.6	2 32.1	17 04.2	4 01.5	5 11.5	9 43.8	19 49.0	16 11.0

December 2034 LONGITUDE

Day	Sid.Time	☉	0 hr ☽	Noon ☽	True ☊	☿	♀	♂	⚳	♃	♄	♅	♆	♇
1 F	16 41 41	9♐21 07	18♌08 35	24♌52 33	20♍21.2	8♐41.0	27♎19.5	3♏11.0	17♓13.1	4♈01.8	5♌09.9	9♋41.7	19♈48.1	16♒11.8
2 Sa	16 45 37	10 21 55	1♍29 30	7♍59 51	20R20.5	10 15.3	27 57.7	3 50.0	17 22.2	4 02.4	5R08.2	9R39.5	19R47.1	16 12.7
3 Su	16 49 34	11 22 45	14 24 11	20 43 03	20 20.6	11 49.5	28 37.2	4 29.0	17 31.6	4 03.3	5 06.4	9 37.4	19 46.2	16 13.7
4 M	16 53 30	12 23 37	26 57 05	3♎06 55	20 20.1	13 23.7	29 18.0	5 08.0	17 41.3	4 04.3	5 04.5	9 35.2	19 45.3	16 14.6
5 Tu	16 57 27	13 24 30	9♎13 09	15 16 23	20 17.9	14 57.9	29 59.8	5 47.1	17 51.3	4 05.5	5 02.4	9 32.9	19 44.5	16 15.6
6 W	17 01 24	14 25 24	21 17 11	27 16 02	20 13.2	16 32.0	0♏42.9	6 26.1	18 01.5	4 06.9	5 00.3	9 30.7	19 43.7	16 16.5
7 Th	17 05 20	15 26 19	3♏13 27	9♏09 50	20 05.3	18 06.2	1 26.9	7 05.1	18 12.1	4 08.5	4 58.0	9 28.4	19 42.9	16 17.6
8 F	17 09 17	16 27 16	15 05 34	21 00 59	19 54.5	19 40.4	2 12.1	7 44.2	18 22.9	4 10.4	4 55.7	9 26.1	19 42.1	16 18.6
9 Sa	17 13 13	17 28 14	26 56 20	2♐51 54	19 41.1	21 14.6	2 58.2	8 23.3	18 33.9	4 12.4	4 53.3	9 23.8	19 41.4	16 19.7
10 Su	17 17 10	18 29 12	8♐47 51	14 44 23	19 26.1	22 48.8	3 45.3	9 02.4	18 45.2	4 14.7	4 50.7	9 21.4	19 40.7	16 20.7
11 M	17 21 06	19 30 12	20 41 37	26 39 44	19 10.8	24 23.1	4 33.3	9 41.4	18 56.8	4 17.1	4 48.1	9 19.0	19 40.0	16 21.9
12 Tu	17 25 03	20 31 13	2♑38 51	8♑39 05	18 56.3	25 57.5	5 22.1	10 20.6	19 08.6	4 19.8	4 45.3	9 16.7	19 39.4	16 23.0
13 W	17 28 59	21 32 14	14 40 38	20 43 39	18 43.8	27 31.9	6 11.8	10 59.7	19 20.7	4 22.6	4 42.5	9 14.2	19 38.8	16 24.1
14 Th	17 32 56	22 33 16	26 48 21	2♒55 00	18 34.0	29 06.4	7 02.4	11 38.8	19 33.0	4 25.7	4 39.6	9 11.8	19 38.2	16 25.3
15 F	17 36 53	23 34 18	9♒03 51	15 15 15	18 27.5	0♑41.0	7 53.7	12 17.9	19 45.6	4 29.0	4 36.5	9 09.4	19 37.7	16 26.5
16 Sa	17 40 49	24 35 21	21 29 34	27 47 12	18 23.9	2 15.6	8 45.7	12 57.1	19 58.4	4 32.4	4 33.4	9 06.9	19 37.2	16 27.7
17 Su	17 44 46	25 36 25	4♓08 36	10♓34 14	18D22.6	3 50.4	9 38.5	13 36.2	20 11.4	4 36.1	4 30.2	9 04.4	19 36.7	16 29.0
18 M	17 48 42	26 37 29	17 04 33	23 40 03	18R22.5	5 25.2	10 32.0	14 15.4	20 24.7	4 39.9	4 26.9	9 01.9	19 36.3	16 30.2
19 Tu	17 52 39	27 38 33	0♈21 09	7♈08 15	18 22.3	7 00.0	11 26.1	14 54.5	20 38.2	4 43.9	4 23.5	8 59.4	19 35.9	16 31.5
20 W	17 56 35	28 39 37	14 01 38	21 01 32	18 20.7	8 35.0	12 20.9	15 33.7	20 51.9	4 48.2	4 20.1	8 56.9	19 35.5	16 32.8
21 Th	18 00 32	29 40 42	28 07 58	5♉20 51	18 16.8	10 09.9	13 16.3	16 12.9	21 05.8	4 52.6	4 16.5	8 54.3	19 35.2	16 34.1
22 F	18 04 28	0♑41 47	12♉39 51	20 04 26	18 10.1	11 44.8	14 12.4	16 52.1	21 19.9	4 57.2	4 12.9	8 51.8	19 34.9	16 35.4
23 Sa	18 08 25	1 42 52	27 33 52	5♊07 08	18 00.9	13 19.7	15 09.0	17 31.3	21 34.3	5 02.0	4 09.2	8 49.2	19 34.6	16 36.8
24 Su	18 12 22	2 43 58	12♊43 07	20 20 29	17 50.1	14 54.5	16 06.1	18 10.5	21 48.8	5 06.9	4 05.4	8 46.6	19 34.4	16 38.2
25 M	18 16 18	3 45 03	27 57 50	5♋33 44	17 38.8	16 29.2	17 03.9	18 49.7	22 03.6	5 12.1	4 01.6	8 44.1	19 34.2	16 39.6
26 Tu	18 20 15	4 46 10	13♋06 49	20 35 48	17 28.5	18 03.6	18 02.1	19 29.0	22 18.6	5 17.4	3 57.7	8 41.5	19 34.0	16 41.0
27 W	18 24 11	5 47 17	27 59 34	5♌17 13	17 20.2	19 37.8	19 00.9	20 08.2	22 33.7	5 22.9	3 53.7	8 38.9	19 33.9	16 42.4
28 Th	18 28 08	6 48 24	12♌28 04	19 31 39	17 14.6	21 11.5	20 00.1	20 47.5	22 49.1	5 28.6	3 49.6	8 36.3	19 33.8	16 43.8
29 F	18 32 04	7 49 31	26 27 45	3♍16 21	17 11.7	22 44.7	20 59.8	21 26.8	23 04.6	5 34.5	3 45.5	8 33.8	19 33.7	16 45.3
30 Sa	18 36 01	8 50 39	9♍57 36	16 31 50	17D10.8	24 17.2	22 00.0	22 06.0	23 20.3	5 40.5	3 41.3	8 31.2	19D33.7	16 46.8
31 Su	18 39 58	9 51 48	22 59 28	29 21 02	17R11.2	25 48.9	23 00.6	22 45.3	23 36.2	5 46.8	3 37.1	8 28.6	19 33.7	16 48.3

Astro Data

	Dy Hr Mn
♃△♄	2 16:50
⚳ D	4 19:08
☽0S	7 3:40
♀ D	11 14:03
♄ R	16 12:02
☽0N	21 19:12
♃ D	29 2:26
☽0S	4 10:42
♃△♄	16 15:36
☽0N	19 4:35
♆ D	30 20:10
☽0S	31 19:27

Planet Ingress

	Dy Hr Mn
☿ ♏	7 4:07
☉ ♐	22 6:06
☿ ♐	25 23:52
♂ ♏	26 14:17
♀ ♏	5 12:05
☿ ♑	15 1:36
☉ ♑	21 19:35

Last Aspect / ☽ Ingress

Last Aspect Dy Hr Mn		☽ Ingress Dy Hr Mn
1 19:17	♀ □	♌ 2 8:25
4 6:26	☿ ⚹	♍ 4 14:38
5 15:44	☉ ⚹	♎ 7 0:04
8 16:51	♀ ☌	♏ 9 11:36
11 1:17	☉ ☌	♐ 12 0:07
13 20:07	♂ ⚹	♑ 14 12:46
16 13:11	☉ ⚹	♒ 17 0:31
19 4:03	☉ □	♓ 19 9:50
21 14:20	☉ △	♈ 21 15:28
23 14:12	♂ ☍	♉ 23 17:21
25 15:56	☿ ☍	♊ 25 16:45
27 7:44	♀ △	♋ 27 15:47
29 10:07	♀ □	♌ 29 16:42

Last Aspect / ☽ Ingress

Last Aspect Dy Hr Mn		☽ Ingress Dy Hr Mn
1 16:38	♀ ⚹	♍ 1 21:17
2 16:48	☿ □	♎ 4 5:55
5 20:54	♆ ☍	♏ 6 17:30
8 2:27	♇ □	♐ 9 6:12
11 6:44	☿ ☌	♑ 11 18:42
13 9:52	♆ □	♒ 14 6:17
16 5:23	☉ ⚹	♓ 16 16:12
18 17:46	☉ □	♈ 18 23:22
21 1:52	☉ △	♉ 21 3:07
22 6:35	♂ ☍	♊ 23 3:53
24 10:47	♆ ⚹	♋ 25 3:13
26 10:21	♆ □	♌ 27 3:17
28 14:17	♂ □	♍ 29 6:12
31 4:24	☿ △	♎ 31 13:14

☽ Phases & Eclipses

Dy Hr Mn	
3 3:29	☾ 10♌47
11 1:17	● 18♏43
19 4:03	☽ 26♒53
25 22:33	○ 3♊43
2 16:48	☾ 10♍34
10 20:16	● 18♐50
18 17:46	☽ 26♓52
25 8:56	○ 3♋37

Astro Data

1 November 2034
Julian Day # 49248
SVP 4♓46'27"
GC 27♐19.6 ⚵ 28♑21.2
Eris 27♈08.5R ⚴ 21♐27.5
⚷ 5♊16.7R ⚶ 18♋58.7
☽ Mean ☊ 21♍18.7

1 December 2034
Julian Day # 49278
SVP 4♓46'23"
GC 27♐19.6 ⚵ 5♒26.8
Eris 26♈52.7R ⚴ 1♑44.0
⚷ 3♊40.9R ⚶ 18♋38.8R
☽ Mean ☊ 19♍43.4

LONGITUDE — January 2035

Day	Sid.Time	☉	0 hr ☽	Noon ☽	True ☊	☿	♀	♂	⚳	♃	♄	♅	♆	♇
1 M	18 43 54	10♑52 56	5♎37 08	11♎48 22	17♍11.5	27♑19.4	24♏01.6	23♏24.6	23♓52.3	5♈53.1	3♌32.7	8♋26.0	19♈33.8	16♒49.8
2 Tu	18 47 51	11 54 06	17 55 26	23 58 58	17R10.7	28 48.7	25 03.1	24 04.0	24 08.6	5 59.7	3R28.4	8R23.4	19 33.8	16 51.3
3 W	18 51 47	12 55 15	29 59 37	5♏58 01	17 07.8	0♒16.3	26 04.9	24 43.3	24 25.0	6 06.4	3 24.0	8 20.8	19 33.9	16 52.8
4 Th	18 55 44	13 56 25	11♏54 46	17 50 26	17 02.4	1 42.0	27 07.1	25 22.6	24 41.7	6 13.3	3 19.5	8 18.2	19 34.1	16 54.4
5 F	18 59 40	14 57 35	23 45 31	29 40 29	16 54.4	3 05.4	28 09.7	26 02.0	24 58.5	6 20.3	3 15.0	8 15.7	19 34.3	16 56.0
6 Sa	19 03 37	15 58 45	5♐35 46	11♐31 44	16 44.1	4 25.9	29 12.6	26 41.4	25 15.4	6 27.5	3 10.4	8 13.1	19 34.5	16 57.6
7 Su	19 07 33	16 59 56	17 28 42	23 26 56	16 32.4	5 43.2	0♐15.8	27 20.7	25 32.6	6 34.9	3 05.8	8 10.5	19 34.7	16 59.2
8 M	19 11 30	18 01 06	29 26 38	5♑28 01	16 20.3	6 56.5	1 19.4	28 00.1	25 49.9	6 42.4	3 01.1	8 08.0	19 35.0	17 00.8
9 Tu	19 15 27	19 02 16	11♑31 12	17 36 19	16 08.8	8 05.4	2 23.3	28 39.5	26 07.3	6 50.1	2 56.4	8 05.5	19 35.4	17 02.4
10 W	19 19 23	20 03 26	23 43 28	29 52 44	15 58.9	9 08.9	3 27.4	29 18.9	26 24.9	6 58.0	2 51.7	8 02.9	19 35.7	17 04.0
11 Th	19 23 20	21 04 36	6♒04 12	12♒17 58	15 51.4	10 06.4	4 31.9	29 58.3	26 42.7	7 06.0	2 46.9	8 00.4	19 36.1	17 05.7
12 F	19 27 16	22 05 45	18 34 08	24 52 50	15 46.5	10 57.0	5 36.6	0♐37.7	27 00.6	7 14.1	2 42.1	7 57.9	19 36.5	17 07.3
13 Sa	19 31 13	23 06 54	1♓14 13	7♓38 27	15D44.2	11 39.8	6 41.6	1 17.1	27 18.7	7 22.4	2 37.3	7 55.5	19 37.0	17 09.0
14 Su	19 35 09	24 08 02	14 05 46	20 36 23	15 44.0	12 14.0	7 46.9	1 56.5	27 36.9	7 30.8	2 32.5	7 53.0	19 37.5	17 10.7
15 M	19 39 06	25 09 10	27 10 35	3♈48 35	15 44.9	12 38.5	8 52.4	2 35.9	27 55.3	7 39.4	2 27.6	7 50.5	19 38.0	17 12.4
16 Tu	19 43 02	26 10 17	10♈30 42	17 17 08	15R46.0	12R52.8	9 58.2	3 15.4	28 13.8	7 48.1	2 22.7	7 48.1	19 38.6	17 14.1
17 W	19 46 59	27 11 23	24 08 06	1♉03 46	15 46.3	12 56.0	11 04.2	3 54.8	28 32.4	7 57.0	2 17.8	7 45.7	19 39.2	17 15.8
18 Th	19 50 56	28 12 28	8♉04 12	15 09 21	15 44.9	12 47.6	12 10.4	4 34.2	28 51.2	8 06.0	2 12.9	7 43.3	19 39.8	17 17.5
19 F	19 54 52	29 13 33	22 19 04	29 33 03	15 41.4	12 27.6	13 16.8	5 13.7	29 10.1	8 15.1	2 08.0	7 41.0	19 40.5	17 19.2
20 Sa	19 58 49	0♒14 37	6♊50 51	14♊11 51	15 36.1	11 56.0	14 23.4	5 53.1	29 29.1	8 24.4	2 03.0	7 38.6	19 41.2	17 21.0
21 Su	20 02 45	1 15 40	21 35 19	29 00 22	15 29.5	11 13.3	15 30.3	6 32.6	29 48.3	8 33.8	1 58.1	7 36.3	19 41.9	17 22.7
22 M	20 06 42	2 16 42	6♋26 01	13♋51 11	15 22.3	10 20.5	16 37.4	7 12.1	0♈07.6	8 43.3	1 53.2	7 34.0	19 42.7	17 24.5
23 Tu	20 10 38	3 17 43	21 14 50	28 35 54	15 15.8	9 19.0	17 44.6	7 51.6	0 27.0	8 53.0	1 48.2	7 31.8	19 43.5	17 26.2
24 W	20 14 35	4 18 44	5♌53 24	13♌06 28	15 10.5	8 10.5	18 52.1	8 31.0	0 46.5	9 02.8	1 43.3	7 29.5	19 44.3	17 28.0
25 Th	20 18 31	5 19 43	20 14 22	27 16 31	15 07.1	6 57.2	19 59.7	9 10.5	1 06.1	9 12.7	1 38.4	7 27.3	19 45.2	17 29.7
26 F	20 22 28	6 20 42	4♍12 30	11♍02 05	15D05.7	5 41.3	21 07.5	9 50.0	1 25.9	9 22.7	1 33.4	7 25.1	19 46.1	17 31.5
27 Sa	20 26 25	7 21 41	17 45 11	24 21 52	15 06.0	4 25.2	22 15.5	10 29.5	1 45.8	9 32.8	1 28.5	7 23.0	19 47.0	17 33.3
28 Su	20 30 21	8 22 38	0♎52 21	7♎16 56	15 07.4	3 10.9	23 23.6	11 09.1	2 05.7	9 43.1	1 23.6	7 20.9	19 48.0	17 35.1
29 M	20 34 18	9 23 35	13 36 03	19 50 11	15 09.1	2 00.5	24 32.0	11 48.6	2 25.8	9 53.5	1 18.8	7 18.8	19 49.0	17 36.9
30 Tu	20 38 14	10 24 32	25 59 52	2♏05 42	15R10.4	0 55.7	25 40.4	12 28.1	2 46.0	10 04.0	1 13.9	7 16.7	19 50.0	17 38.6
31 W	20 42 11	11 25 28	8♏08 16	14 08 14	15 10.7	29♑57.7	26 49.1	13 07.7	3 06.3	10 14.6	1 09.1	7 14.7	19 51.1	17 40.4

LONGITUDE — February 2035

Day	Sid.Time	☉	0 hr ☽	Noon ☽	True ☊	☿	♀	♂	⚳	♃	♄	♅	♆	♇
1 Th	20 46 07	12♒26 23	20♏06 11	26♏02 45	15♍09.7	29♑07.5	27♐57.9	13♐47.2	3♈26.8	10♈25.3	1♌04.3	7♋12.7	19♈52.2	17♒42.2
2 F	20 50 04	13 27 17	1♐58 33	7♐54 08	15R07.1	28R25.5	29 06.8	14 26.8	3 47.3	10 36.1	0R59.5	7R10.7	19 53.3	17 44.0
3 Sa	20 54 00	14 28 11	13 50 03	19 46 49	15 03.1	27 52.2	0♑15.8	15 06.3	4 07.9	10 47.1	0 54.8	7 08.8	19 54.4	17 45.8
4 Su	20 57 57	15 29 03	25 44 53	1♑44 41	14 58.3	27 27.5	1 25.0	15 45.9	4 28.6	10 58.1	0 50.1	7 06.9	19 55.6	17 47.6
5 M	21 01 54	16 29 55	7♑46 34	13 50 53	14 53.0	27 11.2	2 34.3	16 25.5	4 49.4	11 09.3	0 45.4	7 05.1	19 56.8	17 49.4
6 Tu	21 05 50	17 30 46	19 57 52	26 07 45	14 48.0	27D03.0	3 43.8	17 05.0	5 10.4	11 20.5	0 40.8	7 03.3	19 58.1	17 51.2
7 W	21 09 47	18 31 35	2♒20 41	8♒36 47	14 43.7	27 02.5	4 53.3	17 44.6	5 31.4	11 31.9	0 36.2	7 01.5	19 59.3	17 53.1
8 Th	21 13 43	19 32 24	14 56 07	21 18 44	14 40.6	27 09.3	6 03.0	18 24.2	5 52.5	11 43.3	0 31.6	6 59.8	20 00.6	17 54.9
9 F	21 17 40	20 33 11	27 44 38	4♓13 46	14D38.9	27 22.9	7 12.8	19 03.7	6 13.7	11 54.9	0 27.1	6 58.1	20 02.0	17 56.7
10 Sa	21 21 36	21 33 57	10♓46 06	17 21 35	14 38.5	27 42.7	8 22.6	19 43.3	6 34.9	12 06.5	0 22.7	6 56.5	20 03.3	17 58.5
11 Su	21 25 33	22 34 41	24 00 08	0♈41 43	14 39.2	28 08.3	9 32.6	20 22.9	6 56.3	12 18.2	0 18.3	6 54.9	20 04.7	18 00.3
12 M	21 29 29	23 35 24	7♈26 14	14 13 39	14 40.6	28 39.3	10 42.7	21 02.5	7 17.7	12 30.1	0 14.0	6 53.3	20 06.1	18 02.1
13 Tu	21 33 26	24 36 05	21 03 53	27 56 52	14 42.1	29 15.1	11 52.8	21 42.0	7 39.3	12 42.0	0 09.7	6 51.8	20 07.6	18 03.9
14 W	21 37 23	25 36 45	4♉52 32	11♉50 48	14 43.2	29 55.5	13 03.1	22 21.6	8 00.9	12 54.0	0 05.5	6 50.3	20 09.0	18 05.7
15 Th	21 41 19	26 37 23	18 51 32	25 54 36	14R43.7	0♒40.0	14 13.4	23 01.2	8 22.6	13 06.1	0 01.3	6 48.9	20 10.5	18 07.4
16 F	21 45 16	27 37 59	2♊59 48	10♊06 54	14 43.3	1 28.2	15 23.9	23 40.7	8 44.3	13 18.2	29♋57.2	6 47.5	20 12.1	18 09.2
17 Sa	21 49 12	28 38 33	17 15 34	24 25 29	14 42.1	2 20.0	16 34.4	24 20.3	9 06.2	13 30.5	29 53.2	6 46.2	20 13.6	18 11.0
18 Su	21 53 09	29 39 06	1♋36 12	8♋47 14	14 40.4	3 15.0	17 45.0	24 59.9	9 28.1	13 42.8	29 49.2	6 44.9	20 15.2	18 12.8
19 M	21 57 05	0♓39 37	15 58 03	23 08 06	14 38.5	4 12.9	18 55.6	25 39.5	9 50.1	13 55.2	29 45.4	6 43.7	20 16.8	18 14.6
20 Tu	22 01 02	1 40 06	0♌16 45	7♌23 24	14 36.8	5 13.6	20 06.4	26 19.0	10 12.1	14 07.7	29 41.6	6 42.5	20 18.4	18 16.3
21 W	22 04 58	2 40 33	14 27 29	21 28 26	14 35.5	6 16.9	21 17.2	26 58.6	10 34.3	14 20.3	29 37.8	6 41.4	20 20.0	18 18.1
22 Th	22 08 55	3 40 59	28 25 43	5♍18 55	14D34.7	7 22.5	22 28.1	27 38.2	10 56.4	14 32.9	29 34.2	6 40.3	20 21.7	18 19.8
23 F	22 12 52	4 41 23	12♍07 40	18 51 40	14 34.6	8 30.3	23 39.1	28 17.8	11 18.7	14 45.6	29 30.6	6 39.2	20 23.4	18 21.6
24 Sa	22 16 48	5 41 46	25 30 46	2♎04 52	14 35.0	9 40.1	24 50.1	28 57.3	11 41.0	14 58.4	29 27.1	6 38.3	20 25.1	18 23.3
25 Su	22 20 45	6 42 06	8♎33 59	14 58 13	14 35.7	10 52.0	26 01.3	29 36.9	12 03.4	15 11.2	29 23.7	6 37.3	20 26.9	18 25.1
26 M	22 24 41	7 42 26	21 17 46	27 32 54	14 36.5	12 05.6	27 12.4	0♑16.5	12 25.8	15 24.1	29 20.3	6 36.4	20 28.6	18 26.8
27 Tu	22 28 38	8 42 44	3♏43 58	9♏51 22	14 37.2	13 21.0	28 23.7	0 56.1	12 48.3	15 37.1	29 17.1	6 35.6	20 30.4	18 28.5
28 W	22 32 34	9 43 01	15 55 34	21 57 03	14 37.7	14 38.0	29 35.0	1 35.7	13 10.9	15 50.1	29 13.9	6 34.8	20 32.2	18 30.2

Astro Data (Dy Hr Mn)

	Dy Hr Mn
☽0N	15 11:43
♃□♅	16 11:58
☿R	17 6:44
☽0S	28 5:35
☿D	7 1:25
☽0N	11 17:57
☽0S	24 15:41

Planet Ingress (Dy Hr Mn)

		Dy Hr Mn
☿	♒	3 7:30
♀	♐	7 6:01
♂	♐	11 13:02
☉	♒	20 6:15
⚳	♈	22 2:37
☿	♑R	31 11:00
♀	♑	3 6:30
☿	♒	14 14:33
♄	♋R	15 19:36
☉	♓	18 20:17
♂	♑	26 1:59
♀	♒	28 20:24

Last Aspect / ☽ Ingress (January)

Last Aspect Dy Hr Mn		☽ Ingress Dy Hr Mn
2 22:59	☿ □	♏ 3 0:01
5 8:38	♀ ☌	♐ 5 12:40
7 4:13	♆ △	♑ 8 1:07
10 10:50	♂ ⚹	♒ 10 12:14
12 1:59	♆ ⚹	♓ 12 21:40
14 19:00	☉ ⚹	♈ 15 5:07
17 4:47	☉ □	♉ 17 10:10
19 11:25	☉ △	♊ 19 12:45
20 20:55	♆ ⚹	♋ 21 13:36
22 21:31	♆ □	♌ 23 14:18
24 23:10	♆ △	♍ 25 16:42
27 7:48	♀ □	♎ 27 22:23
29 22:04	♀ ⚹	♏ 30 7:52

Last Aspect / ☽ Ingress (February)

Last Aspect Dy Hr Mn		☽ Ingress Dy Hr Mn
1 17:51	☿ ⚹	♐ 1 20:00
3 12:15	♆ △	♑ 4 8:31
6 13:46	☿ ☌	♒ 6 19:29
8 9:33	♆ ⚹	♓ 9 4:11
11 7:16	☿ ⚹	♈ 11 10:45
13 14:22	☿ □	♉ 13 15:34
15 13:18	☉ □	♊ 15 18:56
17 19:35	☉ △	♋ 17 21:19
19 23:04	♄ ☌	♌ 19 23:32
21 21:58	♂ △	♍ 22 2:44
24 7:12	♄ ⚹	♎ 24 8:11
26 15:27	♄ □	♏ 26 16:45

☽ Phases & Eclipses (Dy Hr Mn)

Dy Hr Mn	
1 10:02	☾ 10♎48
9 15:04	● 19♑10
17 4:47	☽ 26♈53
23 20:18	○ 3♌39
31 6:04	☾ 11♏10
8 8:23	● 19♒23
15 13:18	☽ 26♉41
22 8:55	○ 3♍33
22 9:06	• A 0.965

Astro Data

1 January 2035
Julian Day # 49309
SVP 4♓46'18"
GC 27♐19.7 ⚴ 14♒35.3
Eris 26♈43.4R ⚵ 13♑14.8
⚷ 2♊09.2R ⚶ 12♋06.7R
☽ Mean ☊ 18♍04.9

1 February 2035
Julian Day # 49340
SVP 4♓46'14"
GC 27♐19.8 ⚴ 24♒39.5
Eris 26♈44.4 ⚵ 25♑09.3
⚷ 1♊23.4R ⚶ 5♋12.5R
☽ Mean ☊ 16♍26.4

March 2035 LONGITUDE

Day	Sid.Time	☉	0 hr ☽	Noon ☽	True ☊	☿	♀	♂	⚳	♃	♄	♅	♆	♇
1 Th	22 36 31	10♓43 16	27♏56 23	3♐54 06	14♍37.9	15♒56.6	0♒46.4	2♑15.3	13♈33.5	16♈03.2	29♋10.8	6♋34.0	20♈34.0	18♒31.9
2 F	22 40 27	11 43 29	9♐50 48	15 47 05	14R 37.9	17 16.8	1 57.9	2 54.8	13 56.2	16 16.4	29R 07.9	6R 33.4	20 35.9	18 33.6
3 Sa	22 44 24	12 43 41	21 43 30	27 40 40	14 37.8	18 38.3	3 09.4	3 34.4	14 19.0	16 29.6	29 05.0	6 32.7	20 37.7	18 35.3
4 Su	22 48 20	13 43 52	3♑39 10	9♑39 31	14D 37.7	20 01.3	4 20.9	4 14.0	14 41.8	16 42.9	29 02.2	6 32.1	20 39.6	18 36.9
5 M	22 52 17	14 44 01	15 42 15	21 47 52	14 37.7	21 25.6	5 32.5	4 53.6	15 04.6	16 56.2	28 59.5	6 31.6	20 41.5	18 38.6
6 Tu	22 56 14	15 44 08	27 56 48	4♒09 26	14 37.8	22 51.2	6 44.2	5 33.1	15 27.5	17 09.6	28 56.9	6 31.1	20 43.4	18 40.3
7 W	23 00 10	16 44 14	10♒26 05	16 47 02	14 38.0	24 18.1	7 55.9	6 12.7	15 50.5	17 23.1	28 54.3	6 30.7	20 45.4	18 41.9
8 Th	23 04 07	17 44 18	23 12 29	29 42 30	14 38.2	25 46.3	9 07.6	6 52.2	16 13.5	17 36.6	28 51.9	6 30.3	20 47.3	18 43.5
9 F	23 08 03	18 44 20	6♓17 10	12♓56 24	14R 38.3	27 15.7	10 19.4	7 31.8	16 36.5	17 50.1	28 49.6	6 30.0	20 49.3	18 45.1
10 Sa	23 12 00	19 44 20	19 40 05	26 28 01	14 38.2	28 46.3	11 31.3	8 11.3	16 59.6	18 03.7	28 47.4	6 29.7	20 51.3	18 46.7
11 Su	23 15 56	20 44 19	3♈19 53	10♈15 22	14 37.8	0♓18.1	12 43.2	8 50.8	17 22.8	18 17.4	28 45.3	6 29.5	20 53.3	18 48.3
12 M	23 19 53	21 44 15	17 14 04	24 15 31	14 37.1	1 51.2	13 55.1	9 30.3	17 46.0	18 31.1	28 43.3	6 29.4	20 55.3	18 49.9
13 Tu	23 23 49	22 44 09	1♉19 17	8♉24 51	14 36.1	3 25.4	15 07.0	10 09.8	18 09.2	18 44.8	28 41.4	6 29.3	20 57.4	18 51.4
14 W	23 27 46	23 44 01	15 31 45	22 39 30	14 35.1	5 00.8	16 19.0	10 49.3	18 32.5	18 58.6	28 39.6	6D 29.2	20 59.4	18 53.0
15 Th	23 31 43	24 43 51	29 47 40	6♊55 50	14 34.3	6 37.4	17 31.0	11 28.8	18 55.8	19 12.4	28 37.9	6 29.2	21 01.5	18 54.5
16 F	23 35 39	25 43 39	14♊03 35	21 10 35	14D 33.9	8 15.2	18 43.1	12 08.2	19 19.1	19 26.3	28 36.3	6 29.3	21 03.6	18 56.0
17 Sa	23 39 36	26 43 25	28 16 31	5♋21 07	14 34.0	9 54.2	19 55.2	12 47.7	19 42.5	19 40.2	28 34.8	6 29.4	21 05.7	18 57.5
18 Su	23 43 32	27 43 08	12♋24 09	19 25 22	14 34.6	11 34.4	21 07.3	13 27.1	20 06.0	19 54.1	28 33.5	6 29.6	21 07.8	18 59.0
19 M	23 47 29	28 42 49	26 24 34	3♌21 35	14 35.7	13 15.9	22 19.5	14 06.5	20 29.4	20 08.1	28 32.2	6 29.8	21 09.9	19 00.5
20 Tu	23 51 25	29 42 27	10♌16 14	17 08 21	14 36.8	14 58.5	23 31.6	14 46.0	20 52.9	20 22.1	28 31.0	6 30.1	21 12.1	19 01.9
21 W	23 55 22	0♈42 03	23 57 46	0♍44 19	14 37.8	16 42.5	24 43.9	15 25.4	21 16.5	20 36.1	28 30.0	6 30.4	21 14.2	19 03.3
22 Th	23 59 18	1 41 38	7♍27 51	14 08 13	14R 38.2	18 27.6	25 56.1	16 04.7	21 40.0	20 50.2	28 29.1	6 30.8	21 16.4	19 04.8
23 F	0 03 15	2 41 09	20 45 18	27 18 58	14 37.8	20 14.1	27 08.4	16 44.1	22 03.6	21 04.3	28 28.2	6 31.2	21 18.5	19 06.2
24 Sa	0 07 12	3 40 39	3♎49 08	10♎15 44	14 36.4	22 01.8	28 20.7	17 23.5	22 27.3	21 18.4	28 27.5	6 31.7	21 20.7	19 07.5
25 Su	0 11 08	4 40 07	16 38 46	22 58 15	14 34.0	23 50.8	29 33.0	18 02.8	22 50.9	21 32.6	28 26.9	6 32.2	21 22.9	19 08.9
26 M	0 15 05	5 39 33	29 14 14	5♏26 52	14 30.8	25 41.1	0♓45.4	18 42.2	23 14.6	21 46.8	28 26.4	6 32.8	21 25.1	19 10.2
27 Tu	0 19 01	6 38 58	11♏36 18	17 42 46	14 27.2	27 32.7	1 57.7	19 21.5	23 38.3	22 01.0	28 26.0	6 33.5	21 27.3	19 11.6
28 W	0 22 58	7 38 20	23 46 32	29 47 58	14 23.6	29 25.7	3 10.2	20 00.8	24 02.1	22 15.2	28 25.7	6 34.2	21 29.5	19 12.9
29 Th	0 26 54	8 37 40	5♐47 26	11♐45 22	14 20.5	1♈19.9	4 22.6	20 40.1	24 25.8	22 29.5	28 25.5	6 34.9	21 31.7	19 14.2
30 F	0 30 51	9 36 59	17 42 14	23 38 33	14 18.3	3 15.5	5 35.1	21 19.4	24 49.6	22 43.7	28D 25.5	6 35.7	21 33.9	19 15.4
31 Sa	0 34 47	10 36 16	29 34 51	5♑31 43	14D 17.1	5 12.3	6 47.6	21 58.6	25 13.5	22 58.0	28 25.5	6 36.6	21 36.2	19 16.7

April 2035 LONGITUDE

Day	Sid.Time	☉	0 hr ☽	Noon ☽	True ☊	☿	♀	♂	⚳	♃	♄	♅	♆	♇
1 Su	0 38 44	11♈35 31	11♑29 45	17♑29 31	14♍17.2	7♈10.4	8♓00.1	22♑37.9	25♈37.3	23♈12.3	28♋25.7	6♋37.5	21♈38.4	19♒17.9
2 M	0 42 40	12 34 45	23 31 39	29 36 44	14 18.2	9 09.7	9 12.6	23 17.1	26 01.2	23 26.7	28 26.0	6 38.5	21 40.6	19 19.1
3 Tu	0 46 37	13 33 56	5♒45 21	11♒58 04	14 19.8	11 10.2	10 25.2	23 56.3	26 25.1	23 41.0	28 26.3	6 39.5	21 42.9	19 20.3
4 W	0 50 34	14 33 06	18 15 23	24 37 46	14 21.5	13 11.8	11 37.8	24 35.4	26 49.0	23 55.4	28 26.8	6 40.5	21 45.1	19 21.5
5 Th	0 54 30	15 32 14	1♓05 35	7♓39 10	14R 22.6	15 14.3	12 50.4	25 14.6	27 12.9	24 09.8	28 27.4	6 41.7	21 47.4	19 22.6
6 F	0 58 27	16 31 20	14 18 41	21 04 13	14 22.6	17 17.8	14 03.0	25 53.7	27 36.9	24 24.2	28 28.1	6 42.8	21 49.7	19 23.8
7 Sa	1 02 23	17 30 24	27 55 43	4♈53 00	14 21.0	19 22.0	15 15.6	26 32.8	28 00.9	24 38.6	28 29.0	6 44.0	21 51.9	19 24.9
8 Su	1 06 20	18 29 26	11♈55 42	19 03 21	14 17.9	21 26.8	16 28.3	27 11.8	28 24.9	24 53.0	28 29.9	6 45.3	21 54.2	19 25.9
9 M	1 10 16	19 28 26	26 15 19	3♉30 52	14 13.3	23 32.0	17 41.0	27 50.8	28 48.9	25 07.4	28 30.9	6 46.6	21 56.5	19 27.0
10 Tu	1 14 13	20 27 25	10♉49 10	18 09 18	14 07.9	25 37.4	18 53.6	28 29.8	29 12.9	25 21.9	28 32.1	6 48.0	21 58.7	19 28.0
11 W	1 18 09	21 26 21	25 30 21	2♊51 24	14 02.4	27 42.7	20 06.3	29 08.8	29 37.0	25 36.3	28 33.3	6 49.4	22 01.0	19 29.1
12 Th	1 22 06	22 25 14	10♊11 34	17 30 03	13 57.6	29 47.6	21 19.0	29 47.7	0♉01.0	25 50.7	28 34.7	6 50.9	22 03.3	19 30.0
13 F	1 26 03	23 24 06	24 46 09	1♋59 17	13 54.1	1♉51.9	22 31.7	0♒26.5	0 25.1	26 05.2	28 36.2	6 52.4	22 05.5	19 31.0
14 Sa	1 29 59	24 22 55	9♋09 00	16 14 57	13D 52.3	3 55.3	23 44.5	1 05.4	0 49.2	26 19.6	28 37.8	6 54.0	22 07.8	19 32.0
15 Su	1 33 56	25 21 42	23 16 57	0♌14 51	13 52.2	5 57.3	24 57.2	1 44.2	1 13.3	26 34.1	28 39.5	6 55.6	22 10.1	19 32.9
16 M	1 37 52	26 20 27	7♌08 40	13 58 27	13 53.1	7 57.7	26 09.9	2 22.9	1 37.4	26 48.5	28 41.3	6 57.3	22 12.3	19 33.8
17 Tu	1 41 49	27 19 09	20 44 17	27 26 21	13 54.5	9 56.1	27 22.7	3 01.7	2 01.5	27 03.0	28 43.2	6 59.0	22 14.6	19 34.7
18 W	1 45 45	28 17 49	4♍04 48	10♍39 48	13R 55.4	11 52.1	28 35.5	3 40.3	2 25.6	27 17.4	28 45.2	7 00.7	22 16.9	19 35.5
19 Th	1 49 42	29 16 27	17 11 32	23 40 09	13 54.9	13 45.5	29 48.2	4 19.0	2 49.8	27 31.9	28 47.3	7 02.5	22 19.1	19 36.3
20 F	1 53 38	0♉15 03	0♎05 48	6♎28 36	13 52.6	15 36.0	1♈01.0	4 57.6	3 13.9	27 46.3	28 49.5	7 04.4	22 21.4	19 37.1
21 Sa	1 57 35	1 13 37	12 48 39	19 06 04	13 48.0	17 23.2	2 13.8	5 36.1	3 38.0	28 00.7	28 51.8	7 06.2	22 23.6	19 37.9
22 Su	2 01 32	2 12 08	25 20 54	1♏33 15	13 41.3	19 06.9	3 26.6	6 14.7	4 02.2	28 15.2	28 54.2	7 08.2	22 25.9	19 38.7
23 M	2 05 28	3 10 38	7♏43 11	13 50 48	13 32.8	20 46.9	4 39.4	6 53.1	4 26.3	28 29.6	28 56.7	7 10.1	22 28.1	19 39.4
24 Tu	2 09 25	4 09 06	19 56 13	25 59 32	13 23.3	22 23.1	5 52.2	7 31.6	4 50.5	28 44.0	28 59.3	7 12.2	22 30.3	19 40.1
25 W	2 13 21	5 07 33	2♐00 58	8♐00 41	13 13.7	23 55.1	7 05.1	8 10.0	5 14.7	28 58.4	29 02.1	7 14.2	22 32.6	19 40.8
26 Th	2 17 18	6 05 57	13 58 56	19 56 02	13 04.8	25 22.9	8 17.9	8 48.3	5 38.8	29 12.8	29 04.9	7 16.3	22 34.8	19 41.4
27 F	2 21 14	7 04 20	25 52 18	1♑48 08	12 57.4	26 46.3	9 30.8	9 26.6	6 03.0	29 27.1	29 07.8	7 18.5	22 37.0	19 42.1
28 Sa	2 25 11	8 02 42	7♑43 57	13 40 15	12 52.1	28 05.2	10 43.7	10 04.8	6 27.2	29 41.5	29 10.8	7 20.7	22 39.2	19 42.7
29 Su	2 29 07	9 01 02	19 37 34	25 36 25	12 49.0	29 19.5	11 56.6	10 43.0	6 51.4	29 55.8	29 13.9	7 22.9	22 41.4	19 43.2
30 M	2 33 04	9 59 20	1♒37 26	7♒41 13	12D 47.9	0♊29.1	13 09.5	11 21.1	7 15.5	0♉10.2	29 17.1	7 25.2	22 43.6	19 43.8

Astro Data	Planet Ingress	Last Aspect	☽ Ingress	Last Aspect	☽ Ingress	☽ Phases & Eclipses	Astro Data
Dy Hr Mn	Dy Hr Mn	Dy Hr Mn	Dy Hr Mn	Dy Hr Mn	Dy Hr Mn	Dy Hr Mn	1 March 2035
⚳0N 7 14:00	☿ ♓ 11 7:17	1 2:32 ♄ △	♐ 1 4:09	2 9:41 ♄ ☍	♒ 2 12:46	2 3:02 ☾ 11♐21	Julian Day # 49368
☽0N 11 1:17	☉ ♈ 20 19:04	2 21:45 ♆ △	♑ 3 16:40	4 10:39 ♃ ⚹	♓ 4 21:59	9 23:11 ● 19♓12	SVP 4♓46'11"
♃⚹♇ 14 0:58	♀ ♓ 25 20:58	6 1:59 ♄ ☍	♒ 6 3:59	7 0:57 ♄ △	♈ 7 3:35	9 23:05:53 ● A 00'46"	GC 27♐19.8 ⚴ 3♓59.5
♅D 14 21:32	☿ ♈ 28 19:14	8 3:49 ☿ ☌	♓ 8 12:32	9 3:44 ♄ □	♉ 9 6:12	16 20:16 ☽ 26♊04	Eris 26♈53.9 ⚵ 5♒51.1
☉0N 20 19:04		10 16:04 ♄ △	♈ 10 18:11	11 5:40 ♂ △	♊ 11 7:20	23 22:43 ○ 3♎08	⚷ 1♊37.6 ⚶ 4♋13.3
☽0S 24 0:25	⚳ ♉ 12 10:58	12 19:34 ♄ □	♉ 12 21:46	13 2:01 ♃ ⚹	♋ 13 8:41	31 23:08 ☾ 11♑04	☽ Mean ☊ 14♍57.4
♃☌♆ 24 16:33	☿ ♉ 12 14:23	14 22:04 ♄ ⚹	♊ 15 0:21	15 9:15 ♄ ☌	♌ 15 11:34		
♄D 30 13:14	♂ ♒ 12 19:37	16 20:16 ☉ □	♋ 17 2:55	17 11:46 ☉ △	♍ 17 16:37	8 10:59 ● 18♈27	1 April 2035
☿0N 30 20:06	♀ ♈ 19 15:53	19 3:41 ♄ ☌	♌ 19 6:11	19 21:35 ♄ ⚹	♎ 19 23:49	15 2:56 ☽ 25♋00	Julian Day # 49399
	☉ ♉ 20 5:50	21 0:19 ♀ ☍	♍ 21 10:41	22 6:51 ♄ □	♏ 22 8:59	22 13:22 ○ 2♏15	SVP 4♓46'08"
☽0N 7 10:35	♃ ♉ 29 18:58	23 14:07 ♄ ⚹	♎ 23 16:56	24 17:59 ♄ △	♐ 24 19:59	30 16:55 ☾ 10♒11	GC 27♐19.9 ⚴ 14♓05.1
☽0S 20 7:33	☿ ♊ 30 1:46	25 22:29 ♄ □	♏ 26 1:28	27 7:09 ♃ △	♑ 27 8:21		Eris 27♈11.3 ⚵ 17♒09.7
♀0N 22 15:41		28 11:07 ☿ △	♐ 28 12:24	29 20:14 ☿ △	♒ 29 20:46		⚷ 2♊51.8 ⚶ 9♋11.0
♃□♄ 25 19:36		30 10:07 ♃ △	♑ 31 0:51				☽ Mean ☊ 13♍18.9

LONGITUDE May 2035

Day	Sid.Time	☉	0 hr ☽	Noon ☽	True ☊	☿	♀	♂	⚳	♃	♄	♅	♆	♇
1 Tu	2 37 01	10♉57 36	13♒48 23	19♒59 35	12♍48.2	1♊34.0	14♈22.4	11♒59.2	7♉39.7	0♉24.5	29♋20.4	7♋27.5	22♈45.8	19♒44.3
2 W	2 40 57	11 55 52	26 15 26	2♓36 31	12R 49.0	2 34.0	15 35.3	12 37.2	8 03.9	0 38.8	29 23.8	7 29.9	22 48.0	19 44.8
3 Th	2 44 54	12 54 05	9♓03 24	15 36 34	12 49.3	3 29.1	16 48.2	13 15.1	8 28.1	0 53.1	29 27.3	7 32.3	22 50.1	19 45.3
4 F	2 48 50	13 52 17	22 16 24	29 03 10	12 48.1	4 19.2	18 01.1	13 53.0	8 52.2	1 07.3	29 30.9	7 34.7	22 52.3	19 45.7
5 Sa	2 52 47	14 50 28	5♈57 02	12♈57 55	12 44.8	5 04.2	19 14.1	14 30.8	9 16.4	1 21.5	29 34.5	7 37.2	22 54.4	19 46.2
6 Su	2 56 43	15 48 37	20 05 38	27 19 44	12 39.0	5 44.2	20 27.0	15 08.5	9 40.6	1 35.8	29 38.3	7 39.7	22 56.5	19 46.5
7 M	3 00 40	16 46 45	4♉39 36	12♉04 23	12 31.0	6 19.0	21 40.0	15 46.1	10 04.8	1 49.9	29 42.1	7 42.2	22 58.7	19 46.9
8 Tu	3 04 36	17 44 51	19 33 04	27 04 30	12 21.6	6 48.7	22 52.9	16 23.7	10 28.9	2 04.1	29 46.1	7 44.8	23 00.8	19 47.3
9 W	3 08 33	18 42 55	4♊37 26	12♊10 35	12 11.8	7 13.2	24 05.9	17 01.1	10 53.1	2 18.2	29 50.1	7 47.4	23 02.9	19 47.6
10 Th	3 12 29	19 40 57	19 42 40	27 12 29	12 02.9	7 32.4	25 18.9	17 38.5	11 17.2	2 32.3	29 54.2	7 50.1	23 05.0	19 47.9
11 F	3 16 26	20 38 58	4♋39 00	12♋01 18	11 55.9	7 46.5	26 31.9	18 15.8	11 41.4	2 46.4	29 58.4	7 52.8	23 07.0	19 48.1
12 Sa	3 20 23	21 36 57	19 18 41	26 30 38	11 51.4	7 55.4	27 44.8	18 53.0	12 05.5	3 00.5	0♌02.7	7 55.5	23 09.1	19 48.4
13 Su	3 24 19	22 34 54	3♌36 49	10♌37 06	11D 49.1	7R 59.3	28 57.8	19 30.2	12 29.6	3 14.5	0 07.1	7 58.2	23 11.1	19 48.6
14 M	3 28 16	23 32 49	17 31 31	24 20 10	11 48.6	7 58.2	0♉10.8	20 07.2	12 53.7	3 28.5	0 11.6	8 01.0	23 13.2	19 48.8
15 Tu	3 32 12	24 30 43	1♍03 18	7♍41 15	11R 48.8	7 52.4	1 23.8	20 44.1	13 17.8	3 42.4	0 16.1	8 03.9	23 15.2	19 48.9
16 W	3 36 09	25 28 34	14 14 22	20 43 03	11 48.6	7 41.9	2 36.8	21 20.9	13 41.9	3 56.3	0 20.7	8 06.7	23 17.2	19 49.0
17 Th	3 40 05	26 26 24	27 07 41	3♎28 39	11 46.8	7 27.1	3 49.8	21 57.7	14 06.0	4 10.2	0 25.4	8 09.6	23 19.1	19 49.1
18 F	3 44 02	27 24 12	9♎46 20	16 01 04	11 42.7	7 08.3	5 02.8	22 34.3	14 30.0	4 24.0	0 30.2	8 12.5	23 21.1	19 49.2
19 Sa	3 47 58	28 21 59	22 13 10	28 22 54	11 35.7	6 45.8	6 15.8	23 10.9	14 54.0	4 37.8	0 35.1	8 15.4	23 23.0	19 49.3
20 Su	3 51 55	29 19 44	4♏30 30	10♏36 11	11 25.9	6 20.1	7 28.8	23 47.3	15 18.1	4 51.6	0 40.0	8 18.4	23 25.0	19R 49.3
21 M	3 55 52	0♊17 27	16 40 09	22 42 32	11 14.0	5 51.6	8 41.8	24 23.6	15 42.1	5 05.3	0 45.0	8 21.4	23 26.9	19 49.3
22 Tu	3 59 48	1 15 09	28 43 30	4♐43 10	11 00.6	5 20.8	9 54.8	24 59.8	16 06.1	5 19.0	0 50.1	8 24.4	23 28.8	19 49.3
23 W	4 03 45	2 12 50	10♐41 42	16 39 15	10 46.9	4 48.3	11 07.9	25 35.9	16 30.1	5 32.6	0 55.2	8 27.5	23 30.6	19 49.2
24 Th	4 07 41	3 10 30	22 36 00	28 32 08	10 34.1	4 14.7	12 20.9	26 11.9	16 54.0	5 46.2	1 00.5	8 30.6	23 32.5	19 49.1
25 F	4 11 38	4 08 08	4♑27 54	10♑23 35	10 23.2	3 40.5	13 34.0	26 47.8	17 18.0	5 59.7	1 05.8	8 33.7	23 34.3	19 49.0
26 Sa	4 15 34	5 05 46	16 19 29	22 15 59	10 14.7	3 06.3	14 47.0	27 23.5	17 41.9	6 13.2	1 11.2	8 36.8	23 36.1	19 48.9
27 Su	4 19 31	6 03 22	28 13 28	4♒12 25	10 09.0	2 32.8	16 00.1	27 59.2	18 05.8	6 26.7	1 16.6	8 40.0	23 37.9	19 48.8
28 M	4 23 28	7 00 58	10♒13 20	16 16 45	10 05.9	2 00.5	17 13.2	28 34.6	18 29.7	6 40.1	1 22.1	8 43.2	23 39.7	19 48.6
29 Tu	4 27 24	7 58 32	22 23 14	28 33 24	10 04.8	1 29.9	18 26.3	29 10.0	18 53.6	6 53.4	1 27.7	8 46.4	23 41.5	19 48.4
30 W	4 31 21	8 56 06	4♓47 52	11♓07 15	10 04.6	1 01.6	19 39.4	29 45.2	19 17.4	7 06.7	1 33.3	8 49.6	23 43.2	19 48.1
31 Th	4 35 17	9 53 38	17 32 09	24 03 08	10 04.3	0 36.0	20 52.5	0♓20.2	19 41.2	7 19.9	1 39.0	8 52.9	23 44.9	19 47.9

LONGITUDE June 2035

Day	Sid.Time	☉	0 hr ☽	Noon ☽	True ☊	☿	♀	♂	⚳	♃	♄	♅	♆	♇
1 F	4 39 14	10♊51 10	0♈40 42	7♈25 16	10♍02.8	0♊13.5	22♉05.6	0♓55.1	20♉05.1	7♉33.1	1♌44.8	8♋56.1	23♈46.6	19♒47.6
2 Sa	4 43 10	11 48 41	14 17 08	21 16 26	9R 59.0	29♉54.5	23 18.7	1 29.8	20 28.8	7 46.3	1 50.7	8 59.4	23 48.3	19R 47.3
3 Su	4 47 07	12 46 12	28 23 09	5♉37 01	9 52.7	29R 39.3	24 31.9	2 04.4	20 52.6	7 59.3	1 56.6	9 02.8	23 49.9	19 46.9
4 M	4 51 03	13 43 41	12♉57 35	20 24 07	9 44.0	29 28.0	25 45.0	2 38.8	21 16.3	8 12.4	2 02.5	9 06.1	23 51.5	19 46.6
5 Tu	4 55 00	14 41 10	27 55 42	5♊31 10	9 33.7	29 21.0	26 58.2	3 13.0	21 40.0	8 25.3	2 08.6	9 09.5	23 53.1	19 46.2
6 W	4 58 57	15 38 38	13♊09 14	20 48 27	9 22.8	29D 18.2	28 11.4	3 47.0	22 03.7	8 38.2	2 14.6	9 12.8	23 54.7	19 45.8
7 Th	5 02 53	16 36 05	28 27 24	6♋04 37	9 12.8	29 19.9	29 24.5	4 20.9	22 27.4	8 51.1	2 20.8	9 16.2	23 56.3	19 45.4
8 F	5 06 50	17 33 31	13♋38 48	21 08 45	9 04.7	29 26.1	0♊37.7	4 54.5	22 51.0	9 03.8	2 27.0	9 19.6	23 57.8	19 44.9
9 Sa	5 10 46	18 30 56	28 33 30	5♌52 17	8 59.2	29 36.7	1 50.9	5 28.0	23 14.6	9 16.5	2 33.3	9 23.1	23 59.3	19 44.4
10 Su	5 14 43	19 28 19	13♌04 34	20 10 02	8 56.2	29 51.9	3 04.1	6 01.2	23 38.2	9 29.2	2 39.6	9 26.5	24 00.8	19 43.9
11 M	5 18 39	20 25 42	27 08 36	4♍00 17	8D 55.2	0♊11.6	4 17.3	6 34.3	24 01.7	9 41.7	2 45.9	9 30.0	24 02.2	19 43.4
12 Tu	5 22 36	21 23 04	10♍45 21	17 24 05	8R 55.2	0 35.6	5 30.5	7 07.1	24 25.2	9 54.2	2 52.4	9 33.4	24 03.7	19 42.8
13 W	5 26 32	22 20 24	23 56 55	0♎24 18	8 55.1	1 04.1	6 43.8	7 39.7	24 48.6	10 06.7	2 58.8	9 36.9	24 05.1	19 42.2
14 Th	5 30 29	23 17 44	6♎46 46	13 04 47	8 53.6	1 36.8	7 57.0	8 12.1	25 12.1	10 19.0	3 05.4	9 40.4	24 06.4	19 41.6
15 F	5 34 26	24 15 02	19 18 53	25 29 34	8 49.9	2 13.9	9 10.2	8 44.3	25 35.5	10 31.3	3 11.9	9 43.9	24 07.8	19 41.0
16 Sa	5 38 22	25 12 20	1♏37 17	7♏42 28	8 43.7	2 55.0	10 23.5	9 16.2	25 58.8	10 43.5	3 18.6	9 47.5	24 09.1	19 40.4
17 Su	5 42 19	26 09 37	13 45 32	19 46 49	8 34.8	3 40.3	11 36.7	9 48.0	26 22.1	10 55.6	3 25.2	9 51.0	24 10.4	19 39.7
18 M	5 46 15	27 06 53	25 46 38	1♐45 17	8 23.8	4 29.6	12 50.0	10 19.4	26 45.4	11 07.7	3 31.9	9 54.5	24 11.6	19 39.0
19 Tu	5 50 12	28 04 09	7♐43 01	13 40 03	8 11.5	5 22.8	14 03.3	10 50.7	27 08.6	11 19.7	3 38.7	9 58.1	24 12.9	19 38.3
20 W	5 54 08	29 01 24	19 36 34	25 32 47	7 58.9	6 20.0	15 16.6	11 21.7	27 31.8	11 31.6	3 45.5	10 01.7	24 14.1	19 37.6
21 Th	5 58 05	29 58 38	1♑28 52	7♑25 00	7 47.0	7 20.9	16 29.9	11 52.4	27 55.0	11 43.4	3 52.4	10 05.2	24 15.3	19 36.8
22 F	6 02 01	0♋55 52	13 21 22	19 18 12	7 36.9	8 25.6	17 43.2	12 22.8	28 18.1	11 55.1	3 59.2	10 08.8	24 16.4	19 36.1
23 Sa	6 05 58	1 53 06	25 15 43	1♒14 10	7 29.1	9 33.9	18 56.5	12 53.0	28 41.2	12 06.8	4 06.2	10 12.4	24 17.5	19 35.3
24 Su	6 09 55	2 50 20	7♒13 52	13 15 09	7 23.9	10 46.0	20 09.9	13 22.9	29 04.3	12 18.3	4 13.1	10 16.0	24 18.6	19 34.4
25 M	6 13 51	3 47 33	19 18 22	25 23 57	7D 21.3	12 01.6	21 23.2	13 52.5	29 27.3	12 29.8	4 20.2	10 19.6	24 19.7	19 33.6
26 Tu	6 17 48	4 44 46	1♓32 20	7♓44 01	7 20.6	13 20.8	22 36.6	14 21.8	29 50.2	12 41.2	4 27.2	10 23.2	24 20.7	19 32.8
27 W	6 21 44	5 41 59	13 59 30	20 19 17	7 21.0	14 43.5	23 50.0	14 50.8	0♊13.1	12 52.5	4 34.3	10 26.8	24 21.8	19 31.9
28 Th	6 25 41	6 39 12	26 43 56	3♈13 55	7R 21.6	16 09.6	25 03.4	15 19.4	0 36.0	13 03.7	4 41.4	10 30.4	24 22.7	19 31.0
29 F	6 29 37	7 36 25	9♈49 44	16 31 49	7 21.3	17 39.2	26 16.8	15 47.8	0 58.8	13 14.8	4 48.6	10 34.0	24 23.7	19 30.1
30 Sa	6 33 34	8 33 38	23 20 29	0♉15 58	7 19.3	19 12.3	27 30.3	16 15.8	1 21.6	13 25.8	4 55.8	10 37.6	24 24.6	19 29.1

Astro Data Dy Hr Mn	Planet Ingress Dy Hr Mn	Last Aspect Dy Hr Mn	☽ Ingress Dy Hr Mn	Last Aspect Dy Hr Mn	☽ Ingress Dy Hr Mn	☽ Phases & Eclipses Dy Hr Mn	Astro Data
☽0N 4 21:11	♄ ♌ 11 20:46	1 17:20 ♆ ✶	♓ 2 7:06	2 16:18 ♆ ☌	♉ 3 2:42	7 20:05 ● 17♉06	1 May 2035
☿R 13 18:42	♀ ♉ 14 8:27	4 12:49 ♄ △	♈ 4 13:40	5 2:19 ☿ ☌	♊ 5 3:17	14 10:30 ☽ 23♌29	Julian Day # 49429
☽0S 17 13:58	☉ ♊ 21 4:45	6 15:49 ♄ □	♉ 6 16:23	6 16:53 ♆ ✶	♋ 7 2:26	22 4:27 ○ 0♐57	SVP 4♓46'05"
♇R 20 23:01	♂ ♓ 30 22:09	8 16:18 ♄ ✶	♊ 8 16:39	9 1:35 ☿ ✶	♌ 9 2:21	30 7:32 ☾ 8♓45	GC 27♐20.0 ⚴ 23♓06.6
		10 8:42 ♀ ✶	♋ 10 16:29	10 18:36 ♆ △	♍ 11 4:58		Eris 27♈30.9 ⚵ 26♒58.3
☽0N 1 7:32	☿ ♉R 2 4:34	12 14:16 ♀ □	♌ 12 17:52	12 19:51 ☉ □	♎ 13 11:15	6 3:22 ● 15♊18	⚷ 4♊46.4 ⚶ 18♋00.5
☿D 6 14:54	♀ ♊ 7 23:38	14 10:30 ☉ □	♍ 14 22:06	15 9:23 ☉ △	♏ 15 20:49	12 19:51 ☽ 21♍42	☽ Mean ☊ 11♍43.6
♃✶♅ 10 5:03	☿ ♊ 10 22:33	16 21:37 ☉ △	♎ 17 5:25	17 11:46 ♇ □	♐ 18 8:28	20 19:39 ○ 29♐20	
☽0S 13 20:58	☉ ♋ 21 12:34	19 2:14 ♆ ☍	♏ 19 15:10	20 19:39 ☉ ☍	♑ 20 21:00	28 18:44 ☾ 6♈55	1 June 2035
☽0N 28 16:18	⚳ ♊ 26 22:15	21 15:32 ♂ □	♐ 22 2:33	22 22:02 ♆ □	♒ 23 9:31		Julian Day # 49460
		24 7:01 ♂ ✶	♑ 24 14:58	25 9:54 ♆ ✶	♓ 25 21:00		SVP 4♓46'01"
		26 14:42 ♆ □	♒ 27 3:34	27 19:17 ♀ □	♈ 28 6:03		GC 27♐20.0 ⚴ 1♈00.4
		29 13:14 ♂ ☌	♓ 29 14:47	30 6:47 ♀ ✶	♉ 30 11:33		Eris 27♈49.0 ⚵ 4♓57.7
		31 5:34 ♀ ✶	♈ 31 22:47				⚷ 7♊06.4 ⚶ 29♋35.7
							☽ Mean ☊ 10♍05.1

July 2035 — LONGITUDE

Day	Sid.Time	☉	0 hr ☽	Noon ☽	True ☊	☿	♀	♂	⚳	♃	♄	♅	♆	♇
1 Su	6 37 30	9♋30 51	7♉18 22	14♉27 35	7♍15.2	20♊48.6	28♊43.7	16♓43.4	1♊44.3	13♉36.8	5♌03.0	10♋41.3	24♈25.5	19♒28.2
2 M	6 41 27	10 28 05	21 43 20	29 05 09	7R09.1	22 28.3	29 57.2	17 10.7	2 07.0	13 47.6	5 10.3	10 44.9	24 26.3	19R27.2
3 Tu	6 45 24	11 25 18	6♊32 19	14♊03 55	7 01.5	24 11.1	1♋10.7	17 37.6	2 29.6	13 58.3	5 17.5	10 48.5	24 27.2	19 26.2
4 W	6 49 20	12 22 32	21 38 51	29 15 53	6 53.4	25 57.1	2 24.2	18 04.1	2 52.2	14 08.9	5 24.9	10 52.1	24 28.0	19 25.2
5 Th	6 53 17	13 19 46	6♋53 38	14♋30 46	6 45.8	27 46.2	3 37.7	18 30.2	3 14.7	14 19.5	5 32.2	10 55.7	24 28.7	19 24.2
6 F	6 57 13	14 16 59	22 05 54	29 37 48	6 39.7	29 38.1	4 51.3	18 55.9	3 37.1	14 29.9	5 39.6	10 59.4	24 29.4	19 23.2
7 Sa	7 01 10	15 14 13	7♌05 19	14♌27 30	6 35.7	1♋32.8	6 04.8	19 21.2	3 59.5	14 40.2	5 47.0	11 03.0	24 30.1	19 22.1
8 Su	7 05 06	16 11 26	21 43 39	28 53 12	6D33.8	3 30.0	7 18.4	19 46.1	4 21.9	14 50.4	5 54.4	11 06.6	24 30.8	19 21.1
9 M	7 09 03	17 08 40	5♍55 52	12♍51 30	6 33.7	5 29.7	8 32.0	20 10.5	4 44.1	15 00.5	6 01.9	11 10.2	24 31.4	19 20.0
10 Tu	7 12 59	18 05 53	19 40 09	26 22 00	6 34.7	7 31.4	9 45.6	20 34.5	5 06.4	15 10.5	6 09.4	11 13.8	24 32.1	19 18.9
11 W	7 16 56	19 03 06	2♎57 23	9♎26 42	6R35.8	9 35.1	10 59.2	20 58.1	5 28.5	15 20.3	6 16.9	11 17.4	24 32.6	19 17.8
12 Th	7 20 53	20 00 18	15 50 24	22 09 01	6 36.1	11 40.4	12 12.8	21 21.2	5 50.6	15 30.1	6 24.4	11 21.0	24 33.2	19 16.7
13 F	7 24 49	20 57 31	28 23 06	4♏33 11	6 35.1	13 47.0	13 26.5	21 43.8	6 12.6	15 39.7	6 31.9	11 24.6	24 33.7	19 15.5
14 Sa	7 28 46	21 54 44	10♏39 50	16 43 34	6 32.2	15 54.6	14 40.1	22 06.0	6 34.6	15 49.2	6 39.5	11 28.2	24 34.1	19 14.4
15 Su	7 32 42	22 51 57	22 44 54	28 44 19	6 27.5	18 02.9	15 53.8	22 27.6	6 56.5	15 58.6	6 47.1	11 31.7	24 34.6	19 13.2
16 M	7 36 39	23 49 10	4♐42 17	10♐39 12	6 21.2	20 11.7	17 07.4	22 48.8	7 18.3	16 07.9	6 54.7	11 35.3	24 35.0	19 12.0
17 Tu	7 40 35	24 46 23	16 35 27	22 31 23	6 14.0	22 20.6	18 21.1	23 09.4	7 40.1	16 17.1	7 02.3	11 38.9	24 35.4	19 10.8
18 W	7 44 32	25 43 37	28 27 19	4♑23 31	6 06.5	24 29.3	19 34.9	23 29.5	8 01.7	16 26.1	7 09.9	11 42.4	24 35.7	19 09.6
19 Th	7 48 28	26 40 50	10♑20 14	16 17 43	5 59.4	26 37.6	20 48.6	23 49.1	8 23.4	16 35.0	7 17.6	11 45.9	24 36.0	19 08.4
20 F	7 52 25	27 38 05	22 16 11	28 15 49	5 53.5	28 45.3	22 02.3	24 08.2	8 44.9	16 43.8	7 25.2	11 49.5	24 36.3	19 07.2
21 Sa	7 56 22	28 35 19	4♒16 50	10♒19 26	5 49.1	0♌52.1	23 16.1	24 26.6	9 06.4	16 52.4	7 32.9	11 53.0	24 36.6	19 06.0
22 Su	8 00 18	29 32 34	16 23 49	22 30 14	5 46.5	2 57.9	24 29.9	24 44.5	9 27.8	17 01.0	7 40.6	11 56.5	24 36.8	19 04.7
23 M	8 04 15	0♌29 50	28 38 53	4♓50 03	5D45.6	5 02.5	25 43.7	25 01.8	9 49.1	17 09.4	7 48.2	12 00.0	24 36.9	19 03.5
24 Tu	8 08 11	1 27 06	11♓03 59	17 21 01	5 46.1	7 05.9	26 57.5	25 18.5	10 10.3	17 17.6	7 55.9	12 03.4	24 37.1	19 02.2
25 W	8 12 08	2 24 24	23 41 28	0♈05 38	5 47.5	9 07.9	28 11.3	25 34.6	10 31.5	17 25.7	8 03.6	12 06.9	24 37.2	19 00.9
26 Th	8 16 04	3 21 42	6♈33 52	13 06 30	5 49.0	11 08.4	29 25.2	25 50.1	10 52.6	17 33.7	8 11.4	12 10.3	24 37.3	18 59.6
27 F	8 20 01	4 19 01	19 43 51	26 26 13	5R50.2	13 07.3	0♌39.0	26 04.8	11 13.6	17 41.6	8 19.1	12 13.7	24 37.3	18 58.4
28 Sa	8 23 57	5 16 20	3♉13 48	10♉06 48	5 50.3	15 04.7	1 52.9	26 19.0	11 34.5	17 49.3	8 26.8	12 17.2	24R37.4	18 57.1
29 Su	8 27 54	6 13 42	17 05 17	24 09 11	5 49.2	17 00.5	3 06.8	26 32.4	11 55.3	17 56.8	8 34.5	12 20.6	24 37.3	18 55.8
30 M	8 31 51	7 11 04	1♊18 23	8♊32 32	5 46.9	18 54.6	4 20.8	26 45.2	12 16.0	18 04.2	8 42.3	12 23.9	24 37.3	18 54.5
31 Tu	8 35 47	8 08 27	15 51 12	23 13 45	5 43.6	20 47.1	5 34.7	26 57.2	12 36.7	18 11.5	8 50.0	12 27.3	24 37.2	18 53.1

August 2035 — LONGITUDE

Day	Sid.Time	☉	0 hr ☽	Noon ☽	True ☊	☿	♀	♂	⚳	♃	♄	♅	♆	♇
1 W	8 39 44	9♌05 51	0♋39 24	8♋07 16	5♍40.0	22♌38.0	6♌48.7	27♓08.5	12♊57.2	18♉18.6	8♌57.7	12♋30.6	24♈37.1	18♒51.8
2 Th	8 43 40	10 03 17	15 36 21	23 05 35	5R36.6	24 27.2	8 02.7	27 19.1	13 17.7	18 25.6	9 05.5	12 34.0	24R37.0	18R50.5
3 F	8 47 37	11 00 43	0♌33 51	8♌00 06	5 33.9	26 14.8	9 16.7	27 29.0	13 38.1	18 32.4	9 13.2	12 37.3	24 36.8	18 49.2
4 Sa	8 51 33	11 58 10	15 23 17	22 42 30	5D32.3	28 00.7	10 30.7	27 38.1	13 58.3	18 39.1	9 20.9	12 40.5	24 36.6	18 47.8
5 Su	8 55 30	12 55 38	29 56 57	7♍05 59	5 31.9	29 45.0	11 44.7	27 46.4	14 18.5	18 45.6	9 28.7	12 43.8	24 36.3	18 46.5
6 M	8 59 26	13 53 06	14♍09 06	21 05 59	5 32.5	1♍27.7	12 58.8	27 53.9	14 38.6	18 51.9	9 36.4	12 47.0	24 36.0	18 45.2
7 Tu	9 03 23	14 50 36	27 56 29	4♎40 33	5 33.7	3 08.7	14 12.8	28 00.7	14 58.5	18 58.1	9 44.1	12 50.2	24 35.7	18 43.8
8 W	9 07 20	15 48 06	11♎18 19	17 50 01	5 35.1	4 48.2	15 26.9	28 06.6	15 18.4	19 04.2	9 51.8	12 53.4	24 35.4	18 42.5
9 Th	9 11 16	16 45 37	24 15 58	0♏36 33	5 36.3	6 26.1	16 41.0	28 11.8	15 38.1	19 10.0	9 59.5	12 56.6	24 35.0	18 41.1
10 F	9 15 13	17 43 09	6♏52 16	13 03 36	5R37.0	8 02.4	17 55.1	28 16.2	15 57.8	19 15.7	10 07.2	12 59.7	24 34.6	18 39.8
11 Sa	9 19 09	18 40 42	19 11 06	25 15 19	5 36.9	9 37.1	19 09.2	28 19.8	16 17.3	19 21.3	10 14.9	13 02.8	24 34.2	18 38.4
12 Su	9 23 06	19 38 15	1♐16 48	7♐16 08	5 36.1	11 10.2	20 23.3	28 22.6	16 36.7	19 26.6	10 22.6	13 05.9	24 33.7	18 37.1
13 M	9 27 02	20 35 50	13 13 50	19 10 27	5 34.6	12 41.7	21 37.5	28 24.5	16 56.0	19 31.8	10 30.3	13 09.0	24 33.2	18 35.8
14 Tu	9 30 59	21 33 25	25 06 29	1♑02 25	5 32.8	14 11.7	22 51.6	28R25.7	17 15.1	19 36.8	10 37.9	13 12.0	24 32.7	18 34.4
15 W	9 34 55	22 31 02	6♑58 41	12 55 43	5 30.8	15 40.0	24 05.8	28 26.0	17 34.2	19 41.7	10 45.5	13 15.0	24 32.1	18 33.1
16 Th	9 38 52	23 28 40	18 53 53	24 53 31	5 29.0	17 06.7	25 20.0	28 25.6	17 53.1	19 46.4	10 53.2	13 18.0	24 31.5	18 31.7
17 F	9 42 49	24 26 18	0♒54 56	6♒58 25	5 27.6	18 31.7	26 34.2	28 24.3	18 11.9	19 50.9	11 00.8	13 20.9	24 30.9	18 30.4
18 Sa	9 46 45	25 23 58	13 04 12	19 12 29	5 26.6	19 55.1	27 48.4	28 22.2	18 30.6	19 55.2	11 08.3	13 23.8	24 30.3	18 29.1
19 Su	9 50 42	26 21 39	25 23 27	1♓37 16	5D26.2	21 16.8	29 02.6	28 19.2	18 49.2	19 59.4	11 15.9	13 26.7	24 29.6	18 27.7
20 M	9 54 38	27 19 22	7♓54 04	14 13 58	5 26.3	22 36.8	0♍16.8	28 15.5	19 07.6	20 03.4	11 23.5	13 29.6	24 28.9	18 26.4
21 Tu	9 58 35	28 17 06	20 37 03	27 03 25	5 26.7	23 55.0	1 31.1	28 11.0	19 25.9	20 07.1	11 31.0	13 32.4	24 28.1	18 25.1
22 W	10 02 31	29 14 51	3♈33 09	10♈06 18	5 27.3	25 11.4	2 45.3	28 05.6	19 44.1	20 10.8	11 38.5	13 35.2	24 27.4	18 23.8
23 Th	10 06 28	0♍12 38	16 42 58	23 23 11	5 27.9	26 25.9	3 59.6	27 59.5	20 02.1	20 14.2	11 46.0	13 38.0	24 26.6	18 22.4
24 F	10 10 24	1 10 27	0♉06 59	6♉54 23	5 28.3	27 38.5	5 13.9	27 52.6	20 20.0	20 17.4	11 53.4	13 40.7	24 25.8	18 21.1
25 Sa	10 14 21	2 08 17	13 45 24	20 40 00	5R28.5	28 49.1	6 28.2	27 44.9	20 37.7	20 20.5	12 00.9	13 43.4	24 24.9	18 19.8
26 Su	10 18 17	3 06 09	27 38 06	4♊39 35	5 28.6	29 57.6	7 42.5	27 36.4	20 55.3	20 23.4	12 08.3	13 46.0	24 24.0	18 18.5
27 M	10 22 14	4 04 03	11♊44 17	18 51 57	5 28.5	1♎03.9	8 56.8	27 27.2	21 12.7	20 26.0	12 15.7	13 48.6	24 23.1	18 17.3
28 Tu	10 26 11	5 01 59	26 02 18	3♋14 55	5D28.5	2 07.9	10 11.1	27 17.3	21 30.0	20 28.5	12 23.1	13 51.2	24 22.2	18 16.0
29 W	10 30 07	5 59 57	10♋29 21	17 45 05	5 28.5	3 09.5	11 25.5	27 06.6	21 47.1	20 30.8	12 30.4	13 53.8	24 21.2	18 14.7
30 Th	10 34 04	6 57 57	25 01 31	2♌18 00	5 28.6	4 08.5	12 39.8	26 55.3	22 04.1	20 32.9	12 37.7	13 56.3	24 20.2	18 13.4
31 F	10 38 00	7 55 58	9♌33 50	16 48 20	5 28.8	5 04.9	13 54.2	26 43.4	22 20.9	20 34.8	12 45.0	13 58.8	24 19.2	18 12.1

Astro Data

	Dy Hr Mn
☽0S	11 5:17
☽0N	25 23:09
♆ R	28 12:29
♃□♇	5 14:49
☽0S	7 14:46
♂ R	15 10:02
☽0N	22 5:00
☿0S	24 1:29

Planet Ingress

	Dy Hr Mn
♀ ♋	2 12:55
☿ ♋	6 16:38
☿ ♌	21 2:07
☉ ♌	22 23:30
♀ ♌	26 23:19
☿ ♍	5 15:29
♀ ♍	20 6:34
☉ ♍	23 6:45
☿ ♎	26 12:52

Last Aspect / ☽ Ingress (July)

Last Aspect Dy Hr Mn		☽ Ingress Dy Hr Mn
1 20:17	♇ □	♊ 2 13:29
4 6:06	☿ ☌	♋ 4 13:09
6 3:48	♆ □	♌ 6 12:36
8 4:39	♆ △	♍ 8 13:53
10 1:18	♂ ☍	♎ 10 18:36
12 16:37	♆ ☍	♏ 13 3:08
14 23:13	☉ △	♐ 15 14:32
17 16:11	♆ △	♑ 18 3:07
20 13:11	☿ ☍	♒ 20 15:28
22 16:08	♆ ⚹	♓ 23 2:38
25 8:04	♀ △	♈ 25 11:50
27 8:46	♆ ☌	♉ 27 18:19
29 16:05	♂ ⚹	♊ 29 21:49
31 18:06	♂ □	♋ 31 22:57

Last Aspect / ☽ Ingress (August)

Last Aspect Dy Hr Mn		☽ Ingress Dy Hr Mn
2 18:52	♂ △	♌ 2 23:06
4 21:59	☿ ☌	♍ 5 0:05
7 0:02	♂ ☍	♎ 7 3:39
9 0:36	♆ ☍	♏ 9 10:50
11 18:08	♂ △	♐ 11 21:27
14 6:43	♂ □	♑ 14 9:54
16 19:02	♂ ⚹	♒ 16 22:11
19 6:30	♀ ☍	♓ 19 8:53
21 14:04	♂ ☌	♈ 21 17:27
23 13:53	♆ ☌	♉ 23 23:48
26 3:17	☿ △	♊ 26 4:03
28 2:12	♂ □	♋ 28 6:36
30 3:15	♂ △	♌ 30 8:12

☽ Phases & Eclipses

Dy Hr Mn	
5 10:01	● 13♋15
12 7:34	☽ 19♎50
20 10:38	○ 27♑35
28 2:57	☾ 4♉55
3 17:13	● 11♌13
10 21:54	☽ 18♏07
19 1:01	○ 25♒55
19 1:12	P 0.104
26 9:09	☾ 2♊59

Astro Data

1 July 2035
Julian Day # 49490
SVP 4♓45'56"
GC 27♐20.1 ⚴ 6♈19.0
Eris 28♈00.3 ⚵ 9♓06.4
⚷ 9♊19.8 ⚶ 12♌15.9
☽ Mean ☊ 8♍29.7

1 August 2035
Julian Day # 49521
SVP 4♓45'52"
GC 27♐20.2 ⚴ 7♈54.7R
Eris 28♈02.9R ⚵ 7♓43.1R
⚷ 11♊12.4 ⚶ 26♌19.4
☽ Mean ☊ 6♍51.3

LONGITUDE — September 2035

Day	Sid.Time	☉	0 hr ☽	Noon ☽	True ☊	☿	♀	♂	⚳	♃	♄	♅	♆	♇
1 Sa	10 41 57	8♍54 01	24♌00 46	1♍10 28	5♍28.9	5♎58.4	15♍08.6	26♓30.8	22♊37.6	20♉36.6	12♌52.2	14♋01.2	24♈18.2	18♒10.9
2 Su	10 45 53	9 52 06	8♍16 48	15 19 11	5R28.8	6 49.0	16 23.0	26R17.7	22 54.1	20 38.1	12 59.4	14 03.6	24R17.1	18R09.7
3 M	10 49 50	10 50 12	22 17 08	29 10 13	5 28.5	7 36.3	17 37.4	26 04.0	23 10.4	20 39.4	13 06.6	14 06.0	24 16.0	18 08.5
4 Tu	10 53 46	11 48 20	5♎58 11	12♎40 48	5 27.9	8 20.1	18 51.8	25 49.8	23 26.5	20 40.5	13 13.7	14 08.3	24 14.9	18 07.3
5 W	10 57 43	12 46 29	19 18 01	25 49 50	5 27.1	9 00.3	20 06.2	25 35.2	23 42.4	20 41.4	13 20.8	14 10.6	24 13.8	18 06.1
6 Th	11 01 40	13 44 40	2♏16 23	8♏37 54	5 26.1	9 36.6	21 20.7	25 20.1	23 58.2	20 42.1	13 27.9	14 12.8	24 12.6	18 04.9
7 F	11 05 36	14 42 52	14 54 40	21 07 04	5 25.1	10 08.8	22 35.1	25 04.7	24 13.8	20 42.7	13 34.9	14 15.0	24 11.4	18 03.7
8 Sa	11 09 33	15 41 06	27 15 31	3♐20 32	5 24.4	10 36.4	23 49.5	24 48.9	24 29.2	20 43.0	13 41.9	14 17.2	24 10.2	18 02.5
9 Su	11 13 29	16 39 22	9♐22 36	15 22 19	5D24.1	10 59.3	25 04.0	24 32.9	24 44.4	20R43.1	13 48.8	14 19.3	24 09.0	18 01.4
10 M	11 17 26	17 37 39	21 20 13	27 16 55	5 24.3	11 17.1	26 18.4	24 16.7	24 59.4	20 43.0	13 55.7	14 21.3	24 07.7	18 00.2
11 Tu	11 21 22	18 35 57	3♑12 59	9♑09 00	5 25.1	11 29.5	27 32.9	24 00.2	25 14.2	20 42.7	14 02.6	14 23.4	24 06.4	17 59.1
12 W	11 25 19	19 34 17	15 05 32	21 03 10	5 26.2	11R36.2	28 47.3	23 43.6	25 28.8	20 42.2	14 09.4	14 25.4	24 05.1	17 58.0
13 Th	11 29 15	20 32 39	27 02 23	3♒03 42	5 27.5	11 36.8	0♎01.8	23 26.9	25 43.2	20 41.6	14 16.1	14 27.3	24 03.8	17 56.9
14 F	11 33 12	21 31 02	9♒07 34	15 14 23	5 28.8	11 31.1	1 16.3	23 10.2	25 57.4	20 40.7	14 22.9	14 29.2	24 02.5	17 55.8
15 Sa	11 37 09	22 29 27	21 24 32	27 38 17	5R29.6	11 18.8	2 30.7	22 53.5	26 11.4	20 39.6	14 29.5	14 31.0	24 01.1	17 54.8
16 Su	11 41 05	23 27 54	3♓55 54	10♓17 34	5 29.7	10 59.8	3 45.2	22 36.8	26 25.2	20 38.3	14 36.2	14 32.8	23 59.8	17 53.7
17 M	11 45 02	24 26 23	16 43 22	23 13 21	5 28.9	10 33.8	4 59.7	22 20.2	26 38.7	20 36.8	14 42.7	14 34.6	23 58.4	17 52.7
18 Tu	11 48 58	25 24 53	29 47 31	6♈25 44	5 27.1	10 01.0	6 14.1	22 03.7	26 52.1	20 35.1	14 49.2	14 36.3	23 57.0	17 51.7
19 W	11 52 55	26 23 25	13♈07 53	19 53 44	5 24.5	9 21.4	7 28.6	21 47.5	27 05.2	20 33.3	14 55.7	14 38.0	23 55.5	17 50.7
20 Th	11 56 51	27 22 00	26 43 01	3♉35 28	5 21.4	8 35.5	8 43.1	21 31.4	27 18.1	20 31.2	15 02.1	14 39.6	23 54.1	17 49.7
21 F	12 00 48	28 20 36	10♉30 44	17 28 29	5 18.2	7 43.6	9 57.6	21 15.6	27 30.7	20 28.9	15 08.5	14 41.2	23 52.6	17 48.7
22 Sa	12 04 44	29 19 15	24 28 22	1♊30 03	5 15.5	6 46.6	11 12.1	21 00.1	27 43.1	20 26.4	15 14.8	14 42.7	23 51.1	17 47.8
23 Su	12 08 41	0♎17 56	8♊33 10	15 37 25	5 13.7	5 45.4	12 26.6	20 45.0	27 55.3	20 23.8	15 21.0	14 44.2	23 49.6	17 46.9
24 M	12 12 38	1 16 39	22 42 30	29 48 06	5D13.0	4 41.2	13 41.1	20 30.3	28 07.2	20 20.9	15 27.2	14 45.6	23 48.1	17 46.0
25 Tu	12 16 34	2 15 25	6♋53 59	13♋59 53	5 13.4	3 35.4	14 55.6	20 16.0	28 18.9	20 17.8	15 33.4	14 47.0	23 46.6	17 45.1
26 W	12 20 31	3 14 13	21 05 33	28 10 43	5 14.6	2 29.6	16 10.1	20 02.1	28 30.3	20 14.6	15 39.4	14 48.3	23 45.1	17 44.2
27 Th	12 24 27	4 13 03	5♌15 09	12♌18 35	5 16.1	1 25.5	17 24.6	19 48.8	28 41.4	20 11.2	15 45.5	14 49.6	23 43.5	17 43.4
28 F	12 28 24	5 11 55	19 20 45	26 21 19	5R17.3	0 24.7	18 39.2	19 36.0	28 52.3	20 07.5	15 51.4	14 50.8	23 42.0	17 42.5
29 Sa	12 32 20	6 10 50	3♍20 01	10♍16 29	5 17.4	29♍28.9	19 53.7	19 23.7	29 02.9	20 03.7	15 57.3	14 52.0	23 40.4	17 41.7
30 Su	12 36 17	7 09 47	17 10 23	24 01 25	5 16.1	28 39.6	21 08.2	19 12.1	29 13.3	19 59.7	16 03.1	14 53.1	23 38.8	17 40.9

LONGITUDE — October 2035

Day	Sid.Time	☉	0 hr ☽	Noon ☽	True ☊	☿	♀	♂	⚳	♃	♄	♅	♆	♇
1 M	12 40 13	8♎08 45	0♎49 14	7♎33 33	5♍13.2	27♍58.1	22♎22.8	19♓01.1	29♊23.3	19♉55.5	16♌08.9	14♋54.2	23♈37.2	17♒40.2
2 Tu	12 44 10	9 07 46	14 14 04	20 50 36	5R08.6	27R25.4	23 37.3	18R50.8	29 33.1	19R51.1	16 14.6	14 55.2	23R35.6	17R39.4
3 W	12 48 06	10 06 49	27 22 59	3♏51 06	5 02.9	27 02.5	24 51.8	18 41.2	29 42.6	19 46.5	16 20.2	14 56.2	23 34.0	17 38.7
4 Th	12 52 03	11 05 54	10♏14 56	16 34 32	4 56.6	26D49.9	26 06.4	18 32.3	29 51.7	19 41.8	16 25.7	14 57.1	23 32.4	17 38.0
5 F	12 56 00	12 05 00	22 50 02	29 01 37	4 50.5	26 47.7	27 20.9	18 24.1	0♋00.6	19 36.9	16 31.2	14 58.0	23 30.7	17 37.3
6 Sa	12 59 56	13 04 09	5♐09 36	11♐14 18	4 45.1	26 56.1	28 35.4	18 16.7	0 09.2	19 31.8	16 36.6	14 58.8	23 29.1	17 36.7
7 Su	13 03 53	14 03 19	17 16 08	23 15 35	4 41.2	27 14.7	29 50.0	18 10.1	0 17.5	19 26.6	16 42.0	14 59.6	23 27.4	17 36.1
8 M	13 07 49	15 02 31	29 13 09	5♑09 25	4D39.0	27 43.3	1♏04.5	18 04.2	0 25.5	19 21.2	16 47.2	15 00.3	23 25.8	17 35.5
9 Tu	13 11 46	16 01 45	11♑04 57	17 00 22	4 38.4	28 21.3	2 19.0	17 59.1	0 33.1	19 15.6	16 52.4	15 00.9	23 24.1	17 34.9
10 W	13 15 42	17 01 01	22 56 19	28 53 27	4 39.1	29 08.1	3 33.5	17 54.9	0 40.4	19 09.9	16 57.5	15 01.5	23 22.5	17 34.3
11 Th	13 19 39	18 00 18	4♒52 23	10♒53 45	4 40.5	0♎02.8	4 48.1	17 51.4	0 47.5	19 04.0	17 02.6	15 02.1	23 20.8	17 33.8
12 F	13 23 35	18 59 37	16 58 10	23 06 12	4R41.9	1 04.8	6 02.6	17 48.7	0 54.1	18 58.0	17 07.5	15 02.6	23 19.1	17 33.3
13 Sa	13 27 32	19 58 58	29 18 22	5♓35 10	4 42.5	2 13.4	7 17.1	17 46.8	1 00.5	18 51.9	17 12.4	15 03.0	23 17.5	17 32.8
14 Su	13 31 29	20 58 21	11♓56 58	18 24 05	4 41.5	3 27.6	8 31.6	17D45.7	1 06.5	18 45.5	17 17.2	15 03.4	23 15.8	17 32.3
15 M	13 35 25	21 57 46	24 56 44	1♈34 59	4 38.5	4 46.8	9 46.1	17 45.4	1 12.2	18 39.1	17 21.9	15 03.7	23 14.1	17 31.9
16 Tu	13 39 22	22 57 12	8♈18 50	15 08 07	4 33.3	6 10.3	11 00.6	17 45.9	1 17.5	18 32.5	17 26.5	15 04.0	23 12.4	17 31.5
17 W	13 43 18	23 56 41	22 02 33	29 01 41	4 26.3	7 37.5	12 15.1	17 47.2	1 22.5	18 25.8	17 31.1	15 04.3	23 10.8	17 31.1
18 Th	13 47 15	24 56 12	6♉05 02	13♉11 55	4 18.2	9 07.7	13 29.6	17 49.3	1 27.1	18 19.0	17 35.5	15 04.4	23 09.1	17 30.8
19 F	13 51 11	25 55 44	20 21 40	27 33 30	4 09.8	10 40.5	14 44.1	17 52.2	1 31.4	18 12.1	17 39.9	15 04.6	23 07.4	17 30.4
20 Sa	13 55 08	26 55 19	4♊46 41	12♊00 25	4 02.3	12 15.4	15 58.6	17 55.8	1 35.3	18 05.0	17 44.2	15R04.6	23 05.7	17 30.1
21 Su	13 59 04	27 54 57	19 14 01	26 26 50	3 56.4	13 51.9	17 13.1	18 00.2	1 38.9	17 57.8	17 48.4	15 04.6	23 04.1	17 29.8
22 M	14 03 01	28 54 36	3♋38 19	10♋48 00	3 52.8	15 29.8	18 27.6	18 05.4	1 42.1	17 50.6	17 52.5	15 04.6	23 02.4	17 29.6
23 Tu	14 06 58	29 54 18	17 55 32	25 00 39	3D51.3	17 08.7	19 42.0	18 11.2	1 44.9	17 43.2	17 56.6	15 04.5	23 00.7	17 29.4
24 W	14 10 54	0♏54 03	2♌03 10	9♌03 00	3 51.4	18 48.3	20 56.5	18 17.9	1 47.3	17 35.7	18 00.5	15 04.4	22 59.1	17 29.2
25 Th	14 14 51	1 53 49	16 00 06	22 54 28	3R52.2	20 28.5	22 11.0	18 25.2	1 49.4	17 28.1	18 04.4	15 04.2	22 57.4	17 29.0
26 F	14 18 47	2 53 38	29 46 08	6♍35 09	3 52.5	22 09.0	23 25.5	18 33.3	1 51.0	17 20.5	18 08.1	15 03.9	22 55.8	17 28.8
27 Sa	14 22 44	3 53 29	13♍21 31	20 05 17	3 51.3	23 49.7	24 40.0	18 42.1	1 52.3	17 12.8	18 11.8	15 03.6	22 54.1	17 28.7
28 Su	14 26 40	4 53 22	26 46 26	3♎24 55	3 47.6	25 30.4	25 54.5	18 51.6	1 53.1	17 05.0	18 15.4	15 03.3	22 52.5	17 28.6
29 M	14 30 37	5 53 17	10♎00 43	16 33 44	3 41.2	27 11.1	27 09.0	19 01.9	1R53.6	16 57.1	18 18.8	15 02.8	22 50.8	17 28.6
30 Tu	14 34 33	6 53 14	23 03 53	29 31 05	3 32.2	28 51.7	28 23.4	19 12.8	1 53.7	16 49.2	18 22.2	15 02.4	22 49.2	17D28.5
31 W	14 38 30	7 53 13	5♏55 13	12♏16 13	3 21.0	0♏32.1	29 37.9	19 24.3	1 53.4	16 41.2	18 25.5	15 01.9	22 47.6	17 28.5

Astro Data

	Dy Hr Mn
☽0S	4 0:32
♃R	9 14:16
☿R	13 2:29
♀0S	15 19:26
♄⊻♅	15 19:30
☽0N	18 11:37
☉0S	23 4:39
☽0S	1 9:34
☿0N	1 16:00
☿D	5 4:53
☿0S	15 5:48
♂D	15 8:33
☽0N	15 20:18
♄☍♇	17 12:13
♅R	21 8:03

Planet Ingress

		Dy Hr Mn
♀	♎	13 11:25
☉	♎	23 4:40
☿	♍R	28 22:19
⚳	♋	5 10:17
♀	♏	7 15:14
☿	♎	11 10:50
☉	♏	23 14:17
☿	♏	31 4:19
♀	♐	31 19:07

Last Aspect / ☽ Ingress (September)

Last Aspect Dy Hr Mn			☽ Ingress	Dy Hr Mn
1 0:30	♆	△	♍	1 10:02
3 6:40	♂	☍	♎	3 13:27
5 9:03	♆	☍	♏	5 19:45
7 19:34	♂	△	♐	8 5:24
10 9:48	♀	□	♑	10 17:30
13 5:16	♀	△	♒	13 5:55
15 5:03	♆	⚹	♓	15 16:31
17 14:25	☉	☍	♈	18 0:23
19 19:05	♆	☌	♉	20 5:45
22 8:00	☉	△	♊	22 9:26
24 1:52	♆	⚹	♋	24 12:20
26 4:31	♆	□	♌	26 15:05
28 7:27	♆	△	♍	28 18:16
30 19:45	☿	☌	♎	30 22:33

Last Aspect / ☽ Ingress (October)

Last Aspect Dy Hr Mn			☽ Ingress	Dy Hr Mn
2 17:37	♀	☌	♏	3 4:50
5 7:39	☿	⚹	♐	5 13:54
7 20:19	☿	□	♑	8 1:35
10 12:32	☿	△	♒	10 14:14
12 12:25	♆	⚹	♓	13 1:20
14 12:39	♃	⚹	♈	15 9:09
17 2:37	☉	☍	♉	17 13:40
18 20:31	♃	☌	♊	19 16:04
21 14:38	☉	△	♋	21 17:55
23 8:37	♆	□	♌	23 20:30
25 12:05	♆	△	♍	26 0:24
27 21:03	♀	⚹	♎	28 5:49
30 10:36	☿	☌	♏	30 12:54

☽ Phases & Eclipses

Dy Hr Mn		
2 2:01	●	9♍28
2 1:56:46	●	T 02'54"
9 14:48	☽	16♐46
17 14:25	○	24♓32
24 14:41	☾	1♋23
1 13:08	●	8♎12
9 9:51	☽	15♑56
17 2:37	○	23♈33
23 20:58	☾	0♌17
31 3:00	●	7♏31

Astro Data

1 September 2035
Julian Day # 49552
SVP 4♓45'48"
GC 27♐20.2 ⚴ 4♈03.5R
Eris 27♈55.6R ⚵ 0♓57.9R
⚷ 12♊18.2 ⚶ 11♍02.1
☽ Mean ☊ 5♍12.8

1 October 2035
Julian Day # 49582
SVP 4♓45'46"
GC 27♐20.3 ⚴ 26♓20.6R
Eris 27♈41.2R ⚵ 25♒24.2R
⚷ 12♊22.9R ⚶ 25♍39.5
☽ Mean ☊ 3♍37.4

November 2035 LONGITUDE

Day	Sid.Time	☉	0 hr ☽	Noon ☽	True ☊	☿	♀	♂	⚳	♃	♄	♅	♆	♇
1 Th	14 42 27	8♏53 14	18♏34 03	24♏48 40	3♍08.7	2♏12.2	0♐52.4	19♓36.6	1♋52.6	16♉33.2	18♌28.7	15♋01.3	22♈46.0	17♒28.5
2 F	14 46 23	9 53 17	1♐00 08	7♐08 31	2R 56.3	3 52.0	2 06.9	19 49.5	1R 51.5	16R 25.1	18 31.7	15R 00.7	22R 44.4	17 28.6
3 Sa	14 50 20	10 53 21	13 13 58	19 16 41	2 45.1	5 31.5	3 21.3	20 03.1	1 50.0	16 17.0	18 34.7	15 00.0	22 42.8	17 28.6
4 Su	14 54 16	11 53 28	25 16 58	1♑15 07	2 35.8	7 10.6	4 35.8	20 17.2	1 48.0	16 08.9	18 37.6	14 59.3	22 41.3	17 28.7
5 M	14 58 13	12 53 36	7♑11 34	13 06 45	2 29.1	8 49.4	5 50.3	20 32.0	1 45.7	16 00.8	18 40.4	14 58.5	22 39.7	17 28.8
6 Tu	15 02 09	13 53 45	19 01 11	24 55 26	2 25.0	10 27.8	7 04.7	20 47.5	1 42.9	15 52.6	18 43.1	14 57.6	22 38.2	17 29.0
7 W	15 06 06	14 53 56	0♒50 07	6♒45 51	2D 23.2	12 05.8	8 19.1	21 03.4	1 39.7	15 44.5	18 45.6	14 56.8	22 36.7	17 29.2
8 Th	15 10 02	15 54 09	12 43 19	18 43 12	2 22.9	13 43.4	9 33.6	21 20.0	1 36.2	15 36.3	18 48.1	14 55.8	22 35.1	17 29.4
9 F	15 13 59	16 54 23	24 46 11	0♓52 58	2R 23.1	15 20.6	10 48.0	21 37.2	1 32.2	15 28.1	18 50.4	14 54.8	22 33.6	17 29.6
10 Sa	15 17 56	17 54 39	7♓04 12	13 20 31	2 22.7	16 57.5	12 02.4	21 54.8	1 27.8	15 20.0	18 52.7	14 53.8	22 32.2	17 29.9
11 Su	15 21 52	18 54 56	19 42 30	26 10 38	2 20.6	18 34.0	13 16.8	22 13.1	1 23.0	15 11.8	18 54.9	14 52.7	22 30.7	17 30.2
12 M	15 25 49	19 55 14	2♈45 19	9♈26 50	2 16.0	20 10.2	14 31.2	22 31.8	1 17.8	15 03.7	18 56.9	14 51.6	22 29.2	17 30.5
13 Tu	15 29 45	20 55 34	16 15 17	23 10 37	2 08.6	21 46.0	15 45.6	22 51.1	1 12.2	14 55.6	18 58.8	14 50.4	22 27.8	17 30.8
14 W	15 33 42	21 55 56	0♉12 38	7♉20 54	1 58.8	23 21.5	17 00.0	23 10.8	1 06.3	14 47.6	19 00.7	14 49.2	22 26.4	17 31.2
15 Th	15 37 38	22 56 19	14 34 47	21 53 29	1 47.3	24 56.8	18 14.3	23 31.0	0 59.9	14 39.6	19 02.4	14 47.9	22 25.0	17 31.6
16 F	15 41 35	23 56 43	29 16 04	6♊41 27	1 35.4	26 31.7	19 28.7	23 51.7	0 53.1	14 31.6	19 04.0	14 46.6	22 23.6	17 32.0
17 Sa	15 45 31	24 57 10	14♊08 30	21 36 02	1 24.5	28 06.3	20 43.0	24 12.9	0 46.0	14 23.7	19 05.5	14 45.2	22 22.2	17 32.5
18 Su	15 49 28	25 57 38	29 02 57	6♋28 11	1 15.6	29 40.7	21 57.4	24 34.5	0 38.5	14 15.9	19 06.9	14 43.8	22 20.9	17 33.0
19 M	15 53 25	26 58 08	13♋50 49	21 10 05	1 09.5	1♐14.9	23 11.7	24 56.5	0 30.6	14 08.1	19 08.2	14 42.4	22 19.6	17 33.5
20 Tu	15 57 21	27 58 40	28 25 23	5♌36 17	1 06.2	2 48.9	24 26.0	25 19.0	0 22.3	14 00.4	19 09.4	14 40.9	22 18.3	17 34.0
21 W	16 01 18	28 59 14	12♌42 31	19 43 58	1 05.1	4 22.6	25 40.4	25 41.8	0 13.6	13 52.7	19 10.4	14 39.3	22 17.0	17 34.6
22 Th	16 05 14	29 59 49	26 40 37	3♍32 35	1 05.0	5 56.1	26 54.7	26 05.1	0 04.6	13 45.2	19 11.4	14 37.7	22 15.8	17 35.1
23 F	16 09 11	1♐00 26	10♍20 03	17 03 15	1 04.6	7 29.5	28 09.0	26 28.8	29♊55.3	13 37.7	19 12.2	14 36.1	22 14.5	17 35.7
24 Sa	16 13 07	2 01 05	23 42 26	0♎17 52	1 02.5	9 02.7	29 23.2	26 52.8	29 45.5	13 30.4	19 13.0	14 34.4	22 13.3	17 36.4
25 Su	16 17 04	3 01 45	6♎49 49	13 18 31	0 57.9	10 35.8	0♑37.5	27 17.3	29 35.5	13 23.1	19 13.6	14 32.7	22 12.1	17 37.0
26 M	16 21 00	4 02 27	19 44 12	26 07 02	0 50.2	12 08.7	1 51.8	27 42.1	29 25.1	13 15.9	19 14.1	14 31.0	22 11.0	17 37.7
27 Tu	16 24 57	5 03 11	2♏27 11	8♏44 44	0 39.4	13 41.5	3 06.1	28 07.3	29 14.4	13 08.9	19 14.5	14 29.2	22 09.8	17 38.4
28 W	16 28 53	6 03 56	14 59 49	21 12 28	0 26.3	15 14.1	4 20.3	28 32.8	29 03.4	13 01.9	19 14.8	14 27.3	22 08.7	17 39.2
29 Th	16 32 50	7 04 42	27 22 46	3♐30 46	0 11.8	16 46.6	5 34.6	28 58.7	28 52.1	12 55.1	19R 14.9	14 25.5	22 07.7	17 40.0
30 F	16 36 47	8 05 30	9♐36 31	15 40 05	29♌57.1	18 19.0	6 48.8	29 24.9	28 40.5	12 48.4	19 15.0	14 23.5	22 06.6	17 40.8

December 2035 LONGITUDE

Day	Sid.Time	☉	0 hr ☽	Noon ☽	True ☊	☿	♀	♂	⚳	♃	♄	♅	♆	♇
1 Sa	16 40 43	9♐06 19	21♐41 36	27♐41 11	29♌43.6	19♐51.3	8♑03.0	29♓51.5	28♊28.6	12♉41.9	19♌14.9	14♋21.6	22♈05.6	17♒41.6
2 Su	16 44 40	10 07 09	3♑39 01	9♑35 20	29R 32.1	21 23.4	9 17.2	0♈18.4	28R 16.5	12R 35.5	19R 14.7	14R 19.6	22R 04.6	17 42.4
3 M	16 48 36	11 08 00	15 30 24	21 24 32	29 23.5	22 55.4	10 31.4	0 45.5	28 04.2	12 29.2	19 14.5	14 17.6	22 03.6	17 43.3
4 Tu	16 52 33	12 08 53	27 18 09	3♒11 40	29 17.8	24 27.2	11 45.6	1 13.0	27 51.5	12 23.1	19 14.1	14 15.6	22 02.6	17 44.2
5 W	16 56 29	13 09 45	9♒05 35	15 00 26	29 14.9	25 58.8	12 59.7	1 40.8	27 38.7	12 17.1	19 13.5	14 13.5	22 01.7	17 45.1
6 Th	17 00 26	14 10 39	20 56 49	26 55 22	29D 14.1	27 30.2	14 13.9	2 08.9	27 25.7	12 11.3	19 12.9	14 11.3	22 00.8	17 46.0
7 F	17 04 23	15 11 34	2♓56 42	9♓01 33	29R 14.2	29 01.4	15 28.0	2 37.3	27 12.5	12 05.6	19 12.2	14 09.2	22 00.0	17 47.0
8 Sa	17 08 19	16 12 29	15 10 34	21 24 26	29 14.2	0♑32.3	16 42.1	3 05.9	26 59.1	12 00.1	19 11.3	14 07.0	21 59.1	17 48.0
9 Su	17 12 16	17 13 25	27 43 49	4♈09 21	29 12.9	2 02.8	17 56.1	3 34.8	26 45.6	11 54.8	19 10.4	14 04.8	21 58.3	17 49.0
10 M	17 16 12	18 14 22	10♈41 33	17 20 53	29 09.5	3 32.9	19 10.2	4 04.0	26 31.9	11 49.6	19 09.3	14 02.6	21 57.6	17 50.0
11 Tu	17 20 09	19 15 19	24 07 41	1♉02 07	29 03.5	5 02.5	20 24.2	4 33.4	26 18.1	11 44.6	19 08.1	14 00.3	21 56.8	17 51.1
12 W	17 24 05	20 16 17	8♉04 09	15 13 36	28 55.2	6 31.6	21 38.2	5 03.1	26 04.2	11 39.8	19 06.8	13 58.0	21 56.1	17 52.2
13 Th	17 28 02	21 17 15	22 29 59	29 52 40	28 45.1	7 59.9	22 52.1	5 32.9	25 50.2	11 35.2	19 05.4	13 55.7	21 55.4	17 53.3
14 F	17 31 58	22 18 15	7♊20 43	14♊53 03	28 34.5	9 27.4	24 06.1	6 03.0	25 36.1	11 30.7	19 03.9	13 53.4	21 54.8	17 54.4
15 Sa	17 35 55	23 19 15	22 28 25	0♋05 27	28 24.6	10 54.0	25 20.0	6 33.4	25 22.0	11 26.4	19 02.3	13 51.0	21 54.2	17 55.6
16 Su	17 39 52	24 20 16	7♋42 46	15 19 01	28 16.5	12 19.3	26 33.9	7 03.9	25 07.8	11 22.3	19 00.6	13 48.6	21 53.6	17 56.7
17 M	17 43 48	25 21 18	22 52 54	0♌23 17	28 11.0	13 43.3	27 47.7	7 34.6	24 53.6	11 18.4	18 58.8	13 46.2	21 53.0	17 57.9
18 Tu	17 47 45	26 22 20	7♌49 12	15 09 55	28D 08.1	15 05.6	29 01.5	8 05.6	24 39.4	11 14.7	18 56.9	13 43.8	21 52.5	17 59.1
19 W	17 51 41	27 23 24	22 24 51	29 33 42	28 07.4	16 26.0	0♒15.3	8 36.7	24 25.3	11 11.2	18 54.8	13 41.4	21 52.0	18 00.4
20 Th	17 55 38	28 24 28	6♍36 16	13♍32 34	28 08.0	17 44.1	1 29.1	9 08.1	24 11.1	11 07.9	18 52.7	13 38.9	21 51.6	18 01.6
21 F	17 59 34	29 25 33	20 22 44	27 07 00	28R 08.6	18 59.5	2 42.8	9 39.6	23 57.0	11 04.8	18 50.5	13 36.4	21 51.2	18 02.9
22 Sa	18 03 31	0♑26 39	3♎45 41	10♎19 11	28 08.1	20 11.8	3 56.5	10 11.3	23 42.9	11 01.8	18 48.1	13 33.9	21 50.8	18 04.2
23 Su	18 07 27	1 27 45	16 47 52	23 12 09	28 05.7	21 20.4	5 10.2	10 43.2	23 29.0	10 59.1	18 45.7	13 31.4	21 50.4	18 05.5
24 M	18 11 24	2 28 53	29 32 28	5♏49 11	28 00.7	22 24.8	6 23.8	11 15.2	23 15.1	10 56.6	18 43.2	13 28.9	21 50.1	18 06.8
25 Tu	18 15 21	3 30 01	12♏02 42	18 13 19	27 53.4	23 24.3	7 37.4	11 47.5	23 01.3	10 54.2	18 40.5	13 26.3	21 49.8	18 08.2
26 W	18 19 17	4 31 10	24 21 23	0♐27 09	27 44.1	24 18.2	8 51.0	12 19.9	22 47.7	10 52.1	18 37.8	13 23.8	21 49.6	18 09.5
27 Th	18 23 14	5 32 19	6♐30 52	12 32 46	27 33.6	25 05.6	10 04.5	12 52.4	22 34.2	10 50.2	18 35.0	13 21.2	21 49.3	18 10.9
28 F	18 27 10	6 33 28	18 33 03	24 31 53	27 22.9	25 45.7	11 18.0	13 25.2	22 20.9	10 48.5	18 32.0	13 18.7	21 49.2	18 12.3
29 Sa	18 31 07	7 34 38	0♑29 26	6♑25 55	27 13.1	26 17.7	12 31.5	13 58.1	22 07.8	10 47.0	18 29.0	13 16.1	21 49.0	18 13.8
30 Su	18 35 03	8 35 48	12 21 28	18 16 17	27 04.8	26 40.5	13 44.9	14 31.1	21 54.9	10 45.7	18 25.9	13 13.5	21 48.9	18 15.2
31 M	18 39 00	9 36 59	24 10 37	0♒04 40	26 58.7	26R 53.3	14 58.3	15 04.3	21 42.2	10 44.6	18 22.7	13 10.9	21 48.8	18 16.7

Astro Data

	Dy Hr Mn
☽0N	12 6:52
♃✶♅	14 6:17
☽0S	24 23:58
♄ R	30 11:08
♂0N	4 10:31
☽0N	9 17:40
☽0S	22 6:51

Planet Ingress

	Dy Hr Mn
☿ ♐	18 16:54
☉ ♐	22 12:04
⚳ ♊R	22 23:58
♀ ♑	24 23:52
☊ ♌R	30 7:13
♂ ♈	1 19:39
☿ ♑	8 3:28
♀ ♒	19 7:01
☉ ♑	22 1:32

Last Aspect / ☽ Ingress

Last Aspect Dy Hr Mn		☽ Ingress Dy Hr Mn
1 1:50 ♂ △	♐	1 22:03
3 18:51 ♆ △	♑	4 9:29
6 7:22 ♆ □	♒	6 22:18
8 19:40 ♆ ✶	♓	9 10:17
11 4:30 ♂ ☌	♈	11 19:00
13 10:46 ♆ ☌	♉	13 23:39
15 17:35 ☿ ☍	♊	16 1:11
17 16:19 ♂ □	♋	18 1:32
19 22:18 ☉ △	♌	20 2:37
22 5:18 ☉ □	♍	22 5:47
24 10:10 ♀ □	♎	24 11:27
26 4:36 ♆ ☍	♏	26 19:21
29 2:48 ♂ △	♐	29 5:07

Last Aspect / ☽ Ingress

Last Aspect Dy Hr Mn		☽ Ingress Dy Hr Mn
1 16:32 ♂ □	♑	1 16:39
3 13:19 ♆ □	♒	4 5:30
6 13:20 ☿ ✶	♓	6 18:09
8 1:57 ♀ ✶	♈	9 4:16
10 20:11 ♆ ☌	♉	11 10:13
12 23:33 ♀ △	♊	13 12:12
15 0:34 ☉ ☍	♋	15 11:51
17 7:28 ♀ ☍	♌	17 11:23
19 8:03 ☉ △	♍	19 12:45
21 16:30 ☉ □	♎	21 17:11
23 9:26 ♆ ☍	♏	24 0:52
25 22:58 ♆ ✶	♐	26 11:06
28 6:33 ♆ △	♑	28 23:01
31 5:26 ☿ ☌	♒	31 11:51

☽ Phases & Eclipses

Dy Hr Mn	
8 5:52	☽ 15♒39
15 13:50	○ 23♉01
22 5:18	☾ 29♌43
29 19:39	● 7♐24
8 1:06	☽ 15♓45
15 0:34	○ 22♊50
21 16:30	☾ 29♍37
29 14:32	● 7♑41

Astro Data

1 November 2035
Julian Day # 49613
SVP 4♓45'43"
GC 27♐20.4 ⚴ 20♓01.1R
Eris 27♈22.8R ⚵ 26♒21.9
⚷ 11♊25.9R ⚶ 10♎55.5
☽ Mean ☊ 1♍58.9

1 December 2035
Julian Day # 49643
SVP 4♓45'39"
GC 27♐20.5 ⚴ 19♓34.6
Eris 27♈06.9R ⚵ 3♓36.2
⚷ 9♊50.6R ⚶ 25♎32.3
☽ Mean ☊ 0♍23.6

LONGITUDE — January 2036

Day	Sid.Time	☉	0 hr ☽	Noon ☽	True ☊	☿	♀	♂	⚳	♃	♄	♅	♆	♇
1 Tu	18 42 56	10♑38 09	5♒58 44	11♒53 07	26♌55.1	26♑55.3	16♒11.6	15♈37.7	21♊29.7	10♉43.8	18♌19.4	13♋08.3	21♈48.8	18♒18.1
2 W	18 46 53	11 39 19	17 48 10	23 44 18	26D53.6	26R46.0	17 24.9	16 11.1	21R17.5	10R43.1	18R16.1	13R05.7	21D48.8	18 19.6
3 Th	18 50 50	12 40 29	29 41 55	5♓41 30	26 53.9	26 24.8	18 38.1	16 44.8	21 05.5	10 42.6	18 12.6	13 03.1	21 48.8	18 21.1
4 F	18 54 46	13 41 39	11♓43 34	17 48 41	26 55.3	25 51.7	19 51.3	17 18.5	20 53.8	10D42.4	18 09.1	13 00.5	21 48.8	18 22.6
5 Sa	18 58 43	14 42 49	23 57 23	0♈10 16	26 56.9	25 07.2	21 04.4	17 52.4	20 42.4	10 42.4	18 05.5	12 58.0	21 48.9	18 24.2
6 Su	19 02 39	15 43 58	6♈27 55	12 50 56	26R57.8	24 12.0	22 17.5	18 26.4	20 31.3	10 42.5	18 01.8	12 55.4	21 49.1	18 25.7
7 M	19 06 36	16 45 07	19 19 50	25 55 07	26 57.3	23 07.5	23 30.5	19 00.5	20 20.5	10 42.9	17 58.0	12 52.8	21 49.2	18 27.3
8 Tu	19 10 32	17 46 16	2♉37 13	9♉26 26	26 55.2	21 55.5	24 43.4	19 34.7	20 10.0	10 43.5	17 54.2	12 50.2	21 49.4	18 28.9
9 W	19 14 29	18 47 24	16 22 56	23 26 46	26 51.5	20 38.3	25 56.3	20 09.1	19 59.9	10 44.3	17 50.3	12 47.6	21 49.7	18 30.5
10 Th	19 18 25	19 48 32	0♊37 44	7♊55 28	26 46.4	19 18.4	27 09.1	20 43.5	19 50.1	10 45.3	17 46.3	12 45.0	21 49.9	18 32.1
11 F	19 22 22	20 49 39	15 19 23	22 48 40	26 40.8	17 58.3	28 21.9	21 18.1	19 40.6	10 46.5	17 42.3	12 42.5	21 50.3	18 33.7
12 Sa	19 26 19	21 50 46	0♋22 20	7♋59 12	26 35.5	16 40.6	29 34.5	21 52.8	19 31.5	10 48.0	17 38.2	12 39.9	21 50.6	18 35.3
13 Su	19 30 15	22 51 52	15 37 58	23 17 17	26 31.1	15 27.6	0♓47.2	22 27.5	19 22.8	10 49.6	17 34.0	12 37.4	21 51.0	18 36.9
14 M	19 34 12	23 52 59	0♌55 47	8♌32 07	26 28.3	14 21.0	1 59.7	23 02.4	19 14.4	10 51.4	17 29.8	12 34.8	21 51.4	18 38.6
15 Tu	19 38 08	24 54 04	16 05 06	23 33 38	26D27.2	13 22.2	3 12.1	23 37.3	19 06.4	10 53.4	17 25.5	12 32.3	21 51.8	18 40.3
16 W	19 42 05	25 55 10	0♍56 51	8♍14 04	26 27.6	12 32.4	4 24.5	24 12.3	18 58.8	10 55.7	17 21.2	12 29.8	21 52.3	18 41.9
17 Th	19 46 01	26 56 15	15 24 46	22 28 41	26 29.0	11 52.0	5 36.8	24 47.4	18 51.6	10 58.1	17 16.8	12 27.3	21 52.8	18 43.6
18 F	19 49 58	27 57 20	29 25 42	6♎15 51	26 30.6	11 21.1	6 49.0	25 22.6	18 44.8	11 00.7	17 12.3	12 24.8	21 53.4	18 45.3
19 Sa	19 53 54	28 58 25	12♎59 18	19 36 22	26R31.8	10 59.8	8 01.2	25 57.9	18 38.4	11 03.5	17 07.8	12 22.4	21 53.9	18 47.0
20 Su	19 57 51	29 59 29	26 07 24	2♏32 50	26 32.1	10D47.7	9 13.3	26 33.3	18 32.4	11 06.5	17 03.3	12 19.9	21 54.6	18 48.7
21 M	20 01 48	1♒00 33	8♏53 08	15 08 49	26 31.3	10 44.3	10 25.2	27 08.7	18 26.8	11 09.8	16 58.7	12 17.5	21 55.2	18 50.4
22 Tu	20 05 44	2 01 37	21 20 22	27 28 18	26 29.2	10 49.0	11 37.1	27 44.2	18 21.6	11 13.2	16 54.1	12 15.1	21 55.9	18 52.1
23 W	20 09 41	3 02 40	3♐33 05	9♐35 12	26 26.0	11 01.4	12 49.0	28 19.8	18 16.8	11 16.8	16 49.4	12 12.7	21 56.6	18 53.9
24 Th	20 13 37	4 03 43	15 35 06	21 33 12	26 22.3	11 20.8	14 00.7	28 55.5	18 12.5	11 20.6	16 44.7	12 10.3	21 57.4	18 55.6
25 F	20 17 34	5 04 46	27 29 52	3♑25 29	26 18.4	11 46.5	15 12.3	29 31.2	18 08.5	11 24.6	16 40.0	12 08.0	21 58.1	18 57.4
26 Sa	20 21 30	6 05 47	9♑20 21	15 14 48	26 14.8	12 18.1	16 23.9	0♉07.1	18 05.0	11 28.7	16 35.2	12 05.7	21 59.0	18 59.1
27 Su	20 25 27	7 06 48	21 09 07	27 03 32	26 11.9	12 55.0	17 35.3	0 43.0	18 01.9	11 33.1	16 30.4	12 03.4	21 59.8	19 00.9
28 M	20 29 23	8 07 49	2♒58 19	8♒53 42	26 10.0	13 36.7	18 46.6	1 18.9	17 59.3	11 37.7	16 25.6	12 01.1	22 00.7	19 02.6
29 Tu	20 33 20	9 08 48	14 49 57	20 47 17	26D09.1	14 22.8	19 57.9	1 54.9	17 57.1	11 42.4	16 20.8	11 58.9	22 01.6	19 04.4
30 W	20 37 17	10 09 46	26 45 56	2♓46 12	26 09.1	15 12.8	21 09.0	2 31.0	17 55.3	11 47.3	16 15.9	11 56.7	22 02.6	19 06.2
31 Th	20 41 13	11 10 43	8♓48 20	14 52 37	26 09.9	16 06.4	22 20.0	3 07.2	17 53.9	11 52.4	16 11.0	11 54.5	22 03.5	19 07.9

LONGITUDE — February 2036

Day	Sid.Time	☉	0 hr ☽	Noon ☽	True ☊	☿	♀	♂	⚳	♃	♄	♅	♆	♇
1 F	20 45 10	12♒11 39	20♓59 24	27♓08 59	26♌11.1	17♑03.2	23♓30.9	3♉43.4	17♊52.9	11♉57.7	16♌06.2	11♋52.4	22♈04.6	19♒09.7
2 Sa	20 49 06	13 12 34	3♈21 44	9♈38 02	26 12.4	18 03.1	24 41.7	4 19.7	17D52.4	12 03.1	16R01.3	11R50.2	22 05.6	19 11.5
3 Su	20 53 03	14 13 27	15 58 14	22 22 45	26 13.5	19 05.6	25 52.4	4 56.0	17 52.3	12 08.8	15 56.4	11 48.2	22 06.7	19 13.3
4 M	20 56 59	15 14 20	28 51 57	5♉26 10	26R14.1	20 10.6	27 02.9	5 32.4	17 52.6	12 14.6	15 51.4	11 46.1	22 07.8	19 15.1
5 Tu	21 00 56	16 15 10	12♉05 46	18 50 59	26 14.3	21 17.9	28 13.3	6 08.8	17 53.4	12 20.5	15 46.5	11 44.1	22 08.9	19 16.9
6 W	21 04 52	17 16 00	25 42 01	2♊39 00	26 14.0	22 27.2	29 23.6	6 45.3	17 54.5	12 26.7	15 41.6	11 42.1	22 10.1	19 18.7
7 Th	21 08 49	18 16 48	9♊41 54	16 50 37	26 13.3	23 38.5	0♈33.7	7 21.8	17 56.1	12 33.0	15 36.7	11 40.2	22 11.3	19 20.5
8 F	21 12 46	19 17 34	24 04 50	1♋24 08	26 12.5	24 51.6	1 43.7	7 58.4	17 58.1	12 39.5	15 31.9	11 38.3	22 12.5	19 22.2
9 Sa	21 16 42	20 18 19	8♋47 55	16 15 26	26 11.8	26 06.4	2 53.6	8 35.0	18 00.5	12 46.1	15 27.0	11 36.4	22 13.8	19 24.0
10 Su	21 20 39	21 19 03	23 45 46	1♌17 56	26 11.2	27 22.8	4 03.2	9 11.6	18 03.2	12 52.9	15 22.1	11 34.6	22 15.1	19 25.8
11 M	21 24 35	22 19 45	8♌50 50	16 23 19	26D11.0	28 40.6	5 12.8	9 48.3	18 06.4	12 59.9	15 17.3	11 32.8	22 16.4	19 27.6
12 Tu	21 28 32	23 20 25	23 54 16	1♍22 32	26 10.9	29 59.8	6 22.2	10 25.0	18 10.0	13 07.0	15 12.4	11 31.0	22 17.7	19 29.4
13 W	21 32 28	24 21 04	8♍47 09	16 07 10	26 11.0	1♒20.3	7 31.4	11 01.8	18 14.0	13 14.3	15 07.6	11 29.3	22 19.1	19 31.2
14 Th	21 36 25	25 21 42	23 21 51	0♎30 36	26R11.1	2 42.1	8 40.4	11 38.5	18 18.3	13 21.7	15 02.8	11 27.6	22 20.5	19 33.0
15 F	21 40 21	26 22 19	7♎32 58	14 28 41	26 11.2	4 05.1	9 49.3	12 15.4	18 23.1	13 29.2	14 58.1	11 26.0	22 21.9	19 34.8
16 Sa	21 44 18	27 22 55	21 17 38	27 59 53	26 11.1	5 29.3	10 58.0	12 52.2	18 28.2	13 37.0	14 53.3	11 24.4	22 23.4	19 36.5
17 Su	21 48 15	28 23 29	4♏35 35	11♏05 02	26 10.9	6 54.6	12 06.6	13 29.1	18 33.7	13 44.8	14 48.6	11 22.9	22 24.8	19 38.3
18 M	21 52 11	29 24 02	17 28 36	23 46 43	26D10.8	8 20.9	13 14.9	14 06.0	18 39.5	13 52.8	14 43.9	11 21.4	22 26.3	19 40.1
19 Tu	21 56 08	0♓24 34	29 59 54	6♐08 42	26 10.8	9 48.4	14 23.1	14 43.0	18 45.8	14 01.0	14 39.3	11 19.9	22 27.9	19 41.9
20 W	22 00 04	1 25 05	12♐13 41	18 15 24	26 11.1	11 16.9	15 31.1	15 20.0	18 52.4	14 09.3	14 34.7	11 18.5	22 29.4	19 43.6
21 Th	22 04 01	2 25 35	24 14 27	0♑11 24	26 11.6	12 46.4	16 38.9	15 57.0	18 59.3	14 17.7	14 30.2	11 17.1	22 31.0	19 45.4
22 F	22 07 57	3 26 03	6♑06 49	12 01 12	26 12.3	14 17.0	17 46.5	16 34.0	19 06.6	14 26.3	14 25.6	11 15.8	22 32.6	19 47.1
23 Sa	22 11 54	4 26 29	17 55 06	23 48 57	26 13.2	15 48.5	18 54.0	17 11.1	19 14.3	14 35.0	14 21.2	11 14.5	22 34.3	19 48.9
24 Su	22 15 50	5 26 55	29 43 14	5♒38 19	26 14.1	17 21.1	20 01.2	17 48.2	19 22.3	14 43.9	14 16.8	11 13.3	22 35.9	19 50.6
25 M	22 19 47	6 27 18	11♒34 36	17 32 24	26R14.6	18 54.6	21 08.2	18 25.3	19 30.7	14 52.9	14 12.4	11 12.1	22 37.6	19 52.4
26 Tu	22 23 44	7 27 40	23 32 01	29 33 44	26 14.8	20 29.2	22 14.9	19 02.5	19 39.4	15 02.0	14 08.1	11 11.0	22 39.3	19 54.1
27 W	22 27 40	8 28 01	5♓37 47	11♓44 20	26 14.3	22 04.7	23 21.5	19 39.7	19 48.4	15 11.2	14 03.8	11 09.9	22 41.0	19 55.8
28 Th	22 31 37	9 28 19	17 53 36	24 05 43	26 13.1	23 41.2	24 27.8	20 16.9	19 57.8	15 20.6	13 59.6	11 08.9	22 42.8	19 57.5
29 F	22 35 33	10 28 36	0♈20 50	6♈39 03	26 11.3	25 18.8	25 33.9	20 54.1	20 07.4	15 30.1	13 55.5	11 07.9	22 44.6	19 59.2

Astro Data

	Dy Hr Mn
☿R	1 4:24
♄☍♇	1 18:32
♆D	2 6:34
♃D	5 4:00
☽0N	6 2:42
☽0S	18 15:12
☿D	21 9:43
♃⚹♅	31 18:50
☽0N	2 9:18
⚳D	3 5:45
♀0N	7 18:36
☽0S	15 1:12
♃□♄	22 10:45
☽0N	29 14:55

Planet Ingress

	Dy Hr Mn
♀ ♓	12 20:25
☉ ♒	20 12:12
♂ ♉	26 7:16
♀ ♈	7 0:27
☿ ♒	12 12:04
☉ ♓	19 2:15

Last Aspect / ☽ Ingress (January)

Last Aspect Dy Hr Mn		☽ Ingress Dy Hr Mn
2 8:07 ♆ ⚹	♓	3 0:36
5 2:51 ☿ ⚹	♈	5 11:40
7 7:20 ☿ □	♉	7 19:20
9 16:34 ♀ □	♊	9 22:57
11 21:35 ♀ △	♋	11 23:25
13 11:17 ☉ ☍	♌	13 22:32
15 12:06 ♂ △	♍	15 22:27
17 20:17 ☉ △	♎	18 1:00
20 6:48 ☉ □	♏	20 7:13
21 19:10 ♇ □	♐	22 16:59
25 3:40 ♂ △	♑	25 5:04
27 1:42 ♆ □	♒	27 17:58
29 14:30 ♆ ⚹	♓	30 6:28

Last Aspect / ☽ Ingress (February)

Last Aspect Dy Hr Mn		☽ Ingress Dy Hr Mn
1 4:11 ♀ ☌	♈	1 17:31
3 11:30 ♆ ☌	♉	4 2:05
6 5:53 ♀ ⚹	♊	6 7:27
7 20:53 ♆ ⚹	♋	8 9:43
10 5:11 ☿ ☍	♌	10 9:56
11 22:10 ☉ ☍	♍	12 9:47
13 7:14 ♃ △	♎	14 11:08
16 10:48 ☉ △	♏	16 15:37
18 23:48 ☉ □	♐	19 0:00
20 20:30 ♆ △	♑	21 11:37
23 9:28 ♆ □	♒	24 0:34
25 22:13 ♆ ⚹	♓	26 12:52
28 4:15 ♂ ⚹	♈	28 23:20

☽ Phases & Eclipses

Dy Hr Mn	
6 17:49	☽ 15♈59
13 11:17	○ 22♋50
20 6:48	☾ 29♎46
28 10:18	● 8♒04
5 7:02	☽ 16♉03
11 22:10	○ 22♌45
11 22:13	• T 1.300
18 23:48	☾ 29♏54
27 5:00	● 8♓10
27 4:46:48	• P 0.629

Astro Data

1 January 2036
Julian Day # 49674
SVP 4♓45'33"
GC 27♐20.5 ⚴ 24♓39.9
Eris 26♈57.5R ⚵ 15♓31.5
⚷ 8♊11.0R ⚶ 9♏59.2
☽ Mean ☊ 28♌45.1

1 February 2036
Julian Day # 49705
SVP 4♓45'29"
GC 27♐20.6 ⚴ 3♈39.4
Eris 26♈58.3 ⚵ 0♈19.9
⚷ 7♊12.8R ⚶ 22♏59.3
☽ Mean ☊ 27♌06.6

March 2036 LONGITUDE

Day	Sid.Time	☉	0 hr ☽	Noon ☽	True ☊	☿	♀	♂	⚳	♃	♄	♅	♆	♇
1 Sa	22 39 30	11♓28 51	13♈00 30	19♈25 15	26♌09.1	26♒57.4	26♈39.7	21♉31.4	20♊17.4	15♉39.7	13♌51.4	11♋07.0	22♈46.3	20♒00.9
2 Su	22 43 26	12 29 04	25 53 26	2♉25 08	26R 06.7	28 37.0	27 45.3	22 08.7	20 27.8	15 49.4	13R 47.4	11R 06.1	22 48.2	20 02.6
3 M	22 47 23	13 29 15	9♉00 26	15 39 25	26 04.6	0♓17.6	28 50.7	22 45.9	20 38.4	15 59.3	13 43.5	11 05.3	22 50.0	20 04.3
4 Tu	22 51 19	14 29 24	22 22 10	29 08 45	26 03.1	1 59.3	29 55.7	23 23.3	20 49.3	16 09.3	13 39.7	11 04.5	22 51.8	20 05.9
5 W	22 55 16	15 29 31	5♊59 12	12♊53 33	26D 02.5	3 42.1	1♉00.5	24 00.6	21 00.6	16 19.3	13 35.9	11 03.8	22 53.7	20 07.6
6 Th	22 59 13	16 29 36	19 51 45	26 53 46	26 02.8	5 25.9	2 05.0	24 38.0	21 12.1	16 29.5	13 32.1	11 03.1	22 55.6	20 09.2
7 F	23 03 09	17 29 38	3♋59 26	11♋08 35	26 03.8	7 10.9	3 09.2	25 15.3	21 23.9	16 39.8	13 28.5	11 02.5	22 57.5	20 10.9
8 Sa	23 07 06	18 29 39	18 20 53	25 36 00	26 05.2	8 56.9	4 13.1	25 52.7	21 36.1	16 50.3	13 25.0	11 01.9	22 59.5	20 12.5
9 Su	23 11 02	19 29 37	2♌53 26	10♌12 37	26 06.5	10 44.1	5 16.6	26 30.1	21 48.4	17 00.8	13 21.5	11 01.4	23 01.4	20 14.1
10 M	23 14 59	20 29 33	17 32 56	24 53 37	26R 07.1	12 32.4	6 19.9	27 07.5	22 01.1	17 11.4	13 18.1	11 00.9	23 03.4	20 15.7
11 Tu	23 18 55	21 29 27	2♍13 54	9♍32 58	26 06.6	14 21.8	7 22.8	27 44.9	22 14.0	17 22.1	13 14.8	11 00.5	23 05.4	20 17.3
12 W	23 22 52	22 29 19	16 49 57	24 04 04	26 04.7	16 12.4	8 25.3	28 22.3	22 27.3	17 33.0	13 11.5	11 00.2	23 07.4	20 18.9
13 Th	23 26 48	23 29 09	1♎14 32	8♎20 40	26 01.5	18 04.1	9 27.5	28 59.7	22 40.7	17 43.9	13 08.4	10 59.9	23 09.4	20 20.4
14 F	23 30 45	24 28 57	15 21 52	22 17 39	25 57.3	19 56.9	10 29.4	29 37.2	22 54.4	17 54.9	13 05.3	10 59.6	23 11.4	20 21.9
15 Sa	23 34 41	25 28 44	29 07 40	5♏51 42	25 52.6	21 50.9	11 30.9	0♊14.6	23 08.4	18 06.0	13 02.3	10 59.4	23 13.4	20 23.5
16 Su	23 38 38	26 28 28	12♏29 41	19 01 40	25 48.1	23 46.0	12 31.9	0 52.1	23 22.6	18 17.2	12 59.4	10 59.3	23 15.5	20 25.0
17 M	23 42 35	27 28 11	25 27 49	1♐48 25	25 44.4	25 42.2	13 32.6	1 29.5	23 37.1	18 28.5	12 56.6	10 59.2	23 17.6	20 26.5
18 Tu	23 46 31	28 27 52	8♐03 51	14 14 33	25 41.9	27 39.4	14 32.9	2 07.0	23 51.8	18 39.9	12 53.9	10D 59.2	23 19.7	20 28.0
19 W	23 50 28	29 27 32	20 21 03	26 23 55	25D 40.8	29 37.5	15 32.8	2 44.5	24 06.8	18 51.4	12 51.3	10 59.2	23 21.8	20 29.4
20 Th	23 54 24	0♈27 10	2♑23 44	8♑21 10	25 41.0	1♈36.6	16 32.2	3 22.0	24 22.0	19 03.0	12 48.8	10 59.3	23 23.9	20 30.9
21 F	23 58 21	1 26 46	14 16 49	20 11 20	25 42.3	3 36.5	17 31.2	3 59.5	24 37.4	19 14.6	12 46.4	10 59.4	23 26.0	20 32.3
22 Sa	0 02 17	2 26 20	26 05 22	1♒59 32	25 44.1	5 37.0	18 29.8	4 37.0	24 53.0	19 26.4	12 44.1	10 59.6	23 28.2	20 33.8
23 Su	0 06 14	3 25 53	7♒54 25	13 50 35	25R 45.6	7 38.1	19 27.8	5 14.5	25 08.9	19 38.2	12 41.9	10 59.8	23 30.3	20 35.2
24 M	0 10 10	4 25 23	19 48 34	25 48 51	25 46.3	9 39.5	20 25.4	5 52.0	25 25.0	19 50.1	12 39.8	11 00.1	23 32.5	20 36.5
25 Tu	0 14 07	5 24 52	1♓51 51	7♓57 57	25 45.5	11 41.2	21 22.5	6 29.6	25 41.3	20 02.1	12 37.7	11 00.4	23 34.6	20 37.9
26 W	0 18 04	6 24 19	14 07 29	20 20 40	25 42.8	13 42.7	22 19.1	7 07.1	25 57.8	20 14.2	12 35.8	11 00.8	23 36.8	20 39.3
27 Th	0 22 00	7 23 43	26 37 41	2♈58 40	25 38.1	15 43.9	23 15.1	7 44.7	26 14.6	20 26.3	12 34.0	11 01.3	23 39.0	20 40.6
28 F	0 25 57	8 23 06	9♈23 38	15 52 34	25 31.7	17 44.5	24 10.5	8 22.2	26 31.5	20 38.5	12 32.3	11 01.8	23 41.2	20 41.9
29 Sa	0 29 53	9 22 27	22 25 23	29 01 56	25 24.2	19 44.1	25 05.4	8 59.8	26 48.7	20 50.8	12 30.7	11 02.3	23 43.4	20 43.2
30 Su	0 33 50	10 21 46	5♉42 02	12♉25 27	25 16.5	21 42.3	25 59.7	9 37.4	27 06.0	21 03.1	12 29.2	11 02.9	23 45.6	20 44.5
31 M	0 37 46	11 21 02	19 11 58	26 01 17	25 09.3	23 38.9	26 53.4	10 14.9	27 23.5	21 15.6	12 27.8	11 03.6	23 47.8	20 45.7

April 2036 LONGITUDE

Day	Sid.Time	☉	0 hr ☽	Noon ☽	True ☊	☿	♀	♂	⚳	♃	♄	♅	♆	♇
1 Tu	0 41 43	12♈20 16	2♊53 10	9♊47 22	25♌03.5	25♈33.5	27♉46.4	10♊52.5	27♊41.3	21♉28.1	12♌26.5	11♋04.3	23♈50.1	20♒47.0
2 W	0 45 39	13 19 28	16 43 39	23 41 48	24R 59.7	27 25.5	28 38.7	11 30.1	27 59.2	21 40.6	12R 25.3	11 05.1	23 52.3	20 48.2
3 Th	0 49 36	14 18 38	0♋41 38	7♋42 59	24D 58.0	29 14.7	29 30.4	12 07.7	28 17.3	21 53.3	12 24.3	11 05.9	23 54.5	20 49.4
4 F	0 53 33	15 17 45	14 45 42	21 49 37	24 58.0	1♉00.6	0♊21.3	12 45.3	28 35.6	22 05.9	12 23.3	11 06.8	23 56.8	20 50.5
5 Sa	0 57 29	16 16 50	28 54 36	6♌00 29	24 58.9	2 43.0	1 11.5	13 22.9	28 54.1	22 18.7	12 22.4	11 07.7	23 59.0	20 51.7
6 Su	1 01 26	17 15 53	13♌07 04	20 14 06	24R 59.7	4 21.3	2 00.9	14 00.4	29 12.7	22 31.5	12 21.7	11 08.7	24 01.3	20 52.8
7 M	1 05 22	18 14 53	27 21 20	4♍28 26	24 59.4	5 55.4	2 49.4	14 38.0	29 31.5	22 44.4	12 21.0	11 09.7	24 03.5	20 53.9
8 Tu	1 09 19	19 13 51	11♍34 58	18 40 33	24 57.2	7 24.8	3 37.2	15 15.6	29 50.5	22 57.3	12 20.5	11 10.8	24 05.8	20 55.0
9 W	1 13 15	20 12 47	25 44 39	2♎46 46	24 52.4	8 49.4	4 24.0	15 53.2	0♋09.6	23 10.2	12 20.1	11 12.0	24 08.1	20 56.1
10 Th	1 17 12	21 11 41	9♎46 22	16 42 55	24 45.3	10 09.0	5 10.0	16 30.8	0 28.9	23 23.3	12 19.8	11 13.1	24 10.3	20 57.1
11 F	1 21 08	22 10 32	23 35 55	0♏24 54	24 36.3	11 23.2	5 55.0	17 08.3	0 48.4	23 36.3	12 19.5	11 14.4	24 12.6	20 58.2
12 Sa	1 25 05	23 09 22	7♏09 29	13 49 22	24 26.2	12 31.9	6 39.0	17 45.9	1 08.0	23 49.5	12D 19.4	11 15.7	24 14.9	20 59.2
13 Su	1 29 01	24 08 10	20 24 20	26 54 16	24 16.2	13 35.1	7 22.0	18 23.5	1 27.7	24 02.6	12 19.4	11 17.0	24 17.1	21 00.1
14 M	1 32 58	25 06 56	3♐19 11	9♐39 11	24 07.1	14 32.4	8 04.0	19 01.1	1 47.7	24 15.9	12 19.6	11 18.4	24 19.4	21 01.1
15 Tu	1 36 55	26 05 40	15 54 28	22 05 21	23 59.9	15 23.9	8 44.9	19 38.6	2 07.7	24 29.1	12 19.8	11 19.8	24 21.7	21 02.0
16 W	1 40 51	27 04 23	28 12 12	4♑15 30	23 54.9	16 09.3	9 24.6	20 16.2	2 27.9	24 42.5	12 20.1	11 21.3	24 23.9	21 03.0
17 Th	1 44 48	28 03 04	10♑15 46	16 13 34	23 52.3	16 48.8	10 03.2	20 53.8	2 48.3	24 55.8	12 20.6	11 22.8	24 26.2	21 03.8
18 F	1 48 44	29 01 43	22 09 33	28 04 21	23D 51.5	17 22.1	10 40.6	21 31.4	3 08.8	25 09.2	12 21.1	11 24.4	24 28.5	21 04.7
19 Sa	1 52 41	0♉00 20	3♒58 38	9♒53 06	23 51.8	17 49.4	11 16.8	22 08.9	3 29.4	25 22.7	12 21.8	11 26.0	24 30.7	21 05.5
20 Su	1 56 37	0 58 56	15 48 25	21 45 15	23R 52.2	18 10.5	11 51.6	22 46.5	3 50.2	25 36.2	12 22.5	11 27.7	24 33.0	21 06.4
21 M	2 00 34	1 57 30	27 44 15	3♓46 03	23 51.8	18 25.6	12 25.1	23 24.1	4 11.1	25 49.7	12 23.4	11 29.4	24 35.2	21 07.1
22 Tu	2 04 30	2 56 03	9♓51 12	16 00 14	23 49.6	18 34.6	12 57.1	24 01.7	4 32.2	26 03.3	12 24.4	11 31.2	24 37.5	21 07.9
23 W	2 08 27	3 54 33	22 13 36	28 31 41	23 44.9	18R 37.8	13 27.7	24 39.2	4 53.3	26 16.9	12 25.5	11 33.0	24 39.7	21 08.7
24 Th	2 12 24	4 53 02	4♈54 44	11♈22 57	23 37.7	18 35.3	13 56.8	25 16.8	5 14.6	26 30.5	12 26.6	11 34.8	24 42.0	21 09.4
25 F	2 16 20	5 51 30	17 56 23	24 34 59	23 28.1	18 27.3	14 24.4	25 54.4	5 36.1	26 44.2	12 27.9	11 36.8	24 44.2	21 10.1
26 Sa	2 20 17	6 49 55	1♉18 36	8♉06 56	23 16.8	18 14.1	14 50.3	26 32.0	5 57.6	26 57.9	12 29.4	11 38.7	24 46.4	21 10.7
27 Su	2 24 13	7 48 19	14 59 37	21 56 09	23 05.1	17 56.1	15 14.5	27 09.6	6 19.3	27 11.6	12 30.9	11 40.7	24 48.7	21 11.4
28 M	2 28 10	8 46 41	28 56 00	5♊58 35	22 54.2	17 33.6	15 37.0	27 47.1	6 41.1	27 25.4	12 32.5	11 42.7	24 50.9	21 12.0
29 Tu	2 32 06	9 45 00	13♊03 17	20 09 29	22 45.0	17 07.0	15 57.6	28 24.7	7 03.0	27 39.2	12 34.2	11 44.8	24 53.1	21 12.6
30 W	2 36 03	10 43 18	27 16 37	4♋24 09	22 38.4	16 37.1	16 16.4	29 02.3	7 25.1	27 53.0	12 36.0	11 46.9	24 55.3	21 13.1

Astro Data	Planet Ingress	Last Aspect	☽ Ingress	Last Aspect	☽ Ingress	☽ Phases & Eclipses	Astro Data
Dy Hr Mn	Dy Hr Mn	Dy Hr Mn	Dy Hr Mn	Dy Hr Mn	Dy Hr Mn	Dy Hr Mn	
☽0S 13 11:40	☿ ♓ 3 7:49	2 4:00 ☿ ⚹	♉ 2 7:34	2 19:22 ☿ ⚹	♋ 2 22:49	5 16:50 ☽ 15♊42	1 March 2036
♅D 18 15:31	♀ ♉ 4 13:35	4 1:19 ♂ ☌	♊ 4 13:30	4 15:36 ♆ □	♌ 5 1:51	12 9:11 ○ 22♍22	Julian Day # 49734
☉0N 20 1:03	♂ ♊ 15 2:38	6 5:14 ♆ ⚹	♋ 6 17:16	6 18:24 ♆ △	♍ 7 4:27	19 18:40 ☾ 29♐44	SVP 4♓45'26"
☿0N 21 1:44	☿ ♈ 19 16:33	8 12:29 ♂ ⚹	♌ 8 19:15	8 19:22 ♃ △	♎ 9 7:15	27 20:58 ● 7♈46	GC 27♐20.7 ⚴ 14♈24.6
☽0N 27 21:34	☉ ♈ 20 1:04	10 15:48 ♂ □	♍ 10 20:21	11 1:02 ♆ ☍	♏ 11 11:16		Eris 27♈08.1 ⚵ 15♈51.4
♃□♇ 28 19:26		12 19:31 ♂ △	♎ 12 21:55	13 6:37 ♃ ☍	♐ 13 17:46	4 0:05 ☽ 14♋48	⚷ 7♊17.7 ⚶ 2♐40.8
	☿ ♉ 3 22:10	14 13:34 ♆ ☍	♏ 15 1:33	15 20:32 ☉ △	♑ 16 3:33	10 20:24 ○ 21♎32	☽ Mean ☊ 25♌34.5
☽0S 9 21:09	♀ ♊ 4 1:55	17 3:05 ☉ △	♐ 17 8:34	18 14:07 ☉ □	♒ 18 15:55	18 14:07 ☾ 29♑07	
♄D 12 22:38	⚳ ♋ 8 23:58	19 18:40 ☉ □	♑ 19 19:12	20 19:53 ♃ □	♓ 21 4:31	26 9:34 ● 6♉44	1 April 2036
♃⚺♆ 14 19:42	☉ ♉ 19 11:52	21 18:37 ♆ □	♒ 22 7:57	23 7:40 ♃ ⚹	♈ 23 14:47		Julian Day # 49765
☿R 23 13:19		24 7:27 ♆ ⚹	♓ 24 20:19	25 14:29 ♂ ⚹	♉ 25 21:40		SVP 4♓45'23"
☽0N 24 6:09		26 16:05 ♀ ⚹	♈ 27 6:23	27 21:10 ♃ ☌	♊ 28 1:49		GC 27♐20.7 ⚴ 27♈38.8
♃∠♅ 24 20:53		29 2:21 ♆ ☌	♉ 29 13:45	30 2:33 ♂ ☌	♋ 30 4:35		Eris 27♈25.7 ⚵ 3♉34.1
		31 13:38 ♀ ☌	♊ 31 18:58				⚷ 8♊26.6 ⚶ 8♐23.1
							☽ Mean ☊ 23♌55.9

LONGITUDE — May 2036

Day	Sid.Time	☉	0 hr ☽	Noon ☽	True ☊	☿	♀	♂	⚳	♃	♄	♅	♆	♇
1 Th	2 39 59	11♉41 34	11♋31 38	18♋38 40	22♌34.6	16♉04.2	16♊33.3	29♊39.9	7♋47.2	28♉06.8	12♌38.0	11♋49.1	24♈57.5	21♒13.7
2 F	2 43 56	12 39 48	25 44 56	2♌50 13	22D33.0	15R29.0	16 48.1	0♋17.4	8 09.5	28 20.7	12 40.0	11 51.3	24 59.7	21 14.2
3 Sa	2 47 53	13 38 00	9♌54 19	16 57 07	22R32.9	14 52.2	17 00.9	0 55.0	8 31.8	28 34.6	12 42.2	11 53.6	25 01.9	21 14.7
4 Su	2 51 49	14 36 10	23 58 32	0♍58 30	22 32.7	14 14.5	17 11.5	1 32.6	8 54.3	28 48.5	12 44.4	11 55.9	25 04.0	21 15.2
5 M	2 55 46	15 34 17	7♍56 57	14 53 49	22 31.4	13 36.5	17 20.0	2 10.1	9 16.8	29 02.4	12 46.7	11 58.2	25 06.2	21 15.6
6 Tu	2 59 42	16 32 23	21 49 00	28 42 22	22 27.9	12 58.9	17 26.2	2 47.7	9 39.5	29 16.4	12 49.2	12 00.6	25 08.3	21 16.0
7 W	3 03 39	17 30 27	5♎33 46	12♎23 00	22 21.6	12 22.3	17 30.1	3 25.2	10 02.3	29 30.3	12 51.7	12 03.0	25 10.5	21 16.4
8 Th	3 07 35	18 28 28	19 09 50	25 54 03	22 12.4	11 47.5	17R31.7	4 02.8	10 25.1	29 44.3	12 54.3	12 05.4	25 12.6	21 16.7
9 F	3 11 32	19 26 29	2♏35 21	9♏13 30	22 01.0	11 14.9	17 30.9	4 40.3	10 48.1	29 58.3	12 57.1	12 07.9	25 14.7	21 17.1
10 Sa	3 15 28	20 24 27	15 48 14	22 19 22	21 48.3	10 45.1	17 27.7	5 17.9	11 11.2	0♊12.3	12 59.9	12 10.4	25 16.8	21 17.4
11 Su	3 19 25	21 22 24	28 46 42	5♐10 09	21 35.4	10 18.5	17 22.0	5 55.4	11 34.3	0 26.4	13 02.8	12 13.0	25 18.9	21 17.7
12 M	3 23 22	22 20 20	11♐29 40	17 45 16	21 23.6	9 55.4	17 14.0	6 32.9	11 57.6	0 40.4	13 05.9	12 15.6	25 21.0	21 17.9
13 Tu	3 27 18	23 18 14	23 57 04	0♑05 15	21 13.8	9 36.3	17 03.5	7 10.5	12 20.9	0 54.4	13 09.0	12 18.2	25 23.0	21 18.1
14 W	3 31 15	24 16 07	6♑10 05	12 11 54	21 06.5	9 21.3	16 50.5	7 48.0	12 44.3	1 08.5	13 12.2	12 20.9	25 25.1	21 18.3
15 Th	3 35 11	25 13 59	18 11 07	24 08 12	21 01.9	9 10.7	16 35.2	8 25.5	13 07.8	1 22.6	13 15.5	12 23.6	25 27.1	21 18.5
16 F	3 39 08	26 11 49	0♒03 40	5♒58 07	20 59.7	9D04.5	16 17.5	9 03.1	13 31.4	1 36.7	13 18.9	12 26.3	25 29.1	21 18.7
17 Sa	3 43 04	27 09 38	11 52 09	17 46 25	20 59.0	9 02.9	15 57.4	9 40.6	13 55.1	1 50.7	13 22.4	12 29.1	25 31.1	21 18.8
18 Su	3 47 01	28 07 26	23 41 36	29 38 24	20 59.0	9 05.9	15 35.2	10 18.1	14 18.9	2 04.8	13 26.0	12 31.9	25 33.1	21 18.9
19 M	3 50 57	29 05 13	5♓37 28	11♓39 31	20 58.6	9 13.4	15 10.7	10 55.6	14 42.7	2 18.9	13 29.6	12 34.7	25 35.1	21 19.0
20 Tu	3 54 54	0♊02 58	17 45 12	23 55 08	20 56.6	9 25.5	14 44.3	11 33.2	15 06.7	2 33.0	13 33.4	12 37.6	25 37.1	21 19.0
21 W	3 58 51	1 00 42	0♈09 54	6♈30 00	20 52.5	9 42.1	14 15.8	12 10.7	15 30.7	2 47.1	13 37.2	12 40.5	25 39.0	21R19.0
22 Th	4 02 47	1 58 26	12 55 52	19 27 48	20 45.8	10 03.0	13 45.6	12 48.2	15 54.8	3 01.2	13 41.2	12 43.4	25 40.9	21 19.0
23 F	4 06 44	2 56 08	26 05 58	2♉50 28	20 36.8	10 28.3	13 13.8	13 25.7	16 18.9	3 15.3	13 45.2	12 46.4	25 42.8	21 19.0
24 Sa	4 10 40	3 53 49	9♉41 09	16 37 46	20 26.1	10 57.8	12 40.5	14 03.3	16 43.2	3 29.4	13 49.3	12 49.4	25 44.7	21 18.9
25 Su	4 14 37	4 51 29	23 39 55	0♊47 00	20 14.8	11 31.4	12 05.9	14 40.8	17 07.5	3 43.5	13 53.5	12 52.4	25 46.6	21 18.8
26 M	4 18 33	5 49 08	7♊58 20	15 13 05	20 04.1	12 09.0	11 30.3	15 18.3	17 31.9	3 57.6	13 57.8	12 55.4	25 48.4	21 18.7
27 Tu	4 22 30	6 46 46	22 30 24	29 49 22	19 55.1	12 50.4	10 53.8	15 55.9	17 56.4	4 11.7	14 02.1	12 58.5	25 50.2	21 18.6
28 W	4 26 26	7 44 22	7♋09 03	14♋28 36	19 48.7	13 35.7	10 16.7	16 33.4	18 20.9	4 25.8	14 06.6	13 01.6	25 52.1	21 18.4
29 Th	4 30 23	8 41 57	21 47 13	29 04 13	19 45.0	14 24.5	9 39.2	17 10.9	18 45.5	4 39.9	14 11.1	13 04.7	25 53.8	21 18.2
30 F	4 34 20	9 39 31	6♌19 00	13♌31 08	19D43.5	15 17.0	9 01.6	17 48.5	19 10.2	4 54.0	14 15.7	13 07.9	25 55.6	21 18.0
31 Sa	4 38 16	10 37 03	20 40 15	27 46 08	19R43.6	16 12.9	8 24.0	18 26.0	19 34.9	5 08.0	14 20.4	13 11.0	25 57.4	21 17.8

LONGITUDE — June 2036

Day	Sid.Time	☉	0 hr ☽	Noon ☽	True ☊	☿	♀	♂	⚳	♃	♄	♅	♆	♇
1 Su	4 42 13	11♊34 34	4♍48 38	11♍47 43	19♌43.8	17♉12.1	7♊46.8	19♋03.5	19♋59.7	5♊22.1	14♌25.2	13♋14.2	25♈59.1	21♒17.5
2 M	4 46 09	12 32 03	18 43 21	25 35 35	19R43.1	18 14.6	7R10.1	19 41.0	20 24.6	5 36.1	14 30.0	13 17.5	26 00.8	21R17.2
3 Tu	4 50 06	13 29 31	2♎24 31	9♎10 11	19 40.6	19 20.4	6 34.2	20 18.5	20 49.5	5 50.1	14 34.9	13 20.7	26 02.5	21 16.9
4 W	4 54 02	14 26 58	15 52 40	22 32 03	19 35.5	20 29.3	5 59.3	20 56.1	21 14.5	6 04.1	14 39.9	13 24.0	26 04.1	21 16.6
5 Th	4 57 59	15 24 24	29 08 22	5♏41 38	19 28.1	21 41.3	5 25.7	21 33.6	21 39.5	6 18.1	14 45.0	13 27.3	26 05.7	21 16.2
6 F	5 01 55	16 21 49	12♏11 52	18 39 04	19 18.6	22 56.3	4 53.5	22 11.1	22 04.6	6 32.1	14 50.1	13 30.6	26 07.4	21 15.8
7 Sa	5 05 52	17 19 12	25 03 13	1♐24 18	19 08.0	24 14.4	4 22.9	22 48.6	22 29.8	6 46.0	14 55.3	13 33.9	26 08.9	21 15.4
8 Su	5 09 49	18 16 35	7♐42 20	13 57 19	18 57.2	25 35.4	3 54.1	23 26.1	22 55.0	7 00.0	15 00.6	13 37.3	26 10.5	21 15.0
9 M	5 13 45	19 13 57	20 09 18	26 18 20	18 47.2	26 59.3	3 27.2	24 03.6	23 20.3	7 13.9	15 05.9	13 40.6	26 12.0	21 14.5
10 Tu	5 17 42	20 11 18	2♑24 33	8♑28 05	18 39.0	28 26.1	3 02.4	24 41.1	23 45.6	7 27.8	15 11.3	13 44.0	26 13.6	21 14.0
11 W	5 21 38	21 08 39	14 29 10	20 28 03	18 33.0	29 55.8	2 39.7	25 18.6	24 11.0	7 41.7	15 16.8	13 47.4	26 15.1	21 13.5
12 Th	5 25 35	22 05 58	26 25 02	2♒20 29	18 29.4	1♊28.3	2 19.3	25 56.2	24 36.5	7 55.5	15 22.4	13 50.9	26 16.5	21 13.0
13 F	5 29 31	23 03 18	8♒14 49	14 08 31	18D27.9	3 03.7	2 01.1	26 33.7	25 01.9	8 09.3	15 28.0	13 54.3	26 18.0	21 12.4
14 Sa	5 33 28	24 00 36	20 02 04	25 56 02	18 28.0	4 41.9	1 45.3	27 11.2	25 27.5	8 23.2	15 33.7	13 57.8	26 19.4	21 11.8
15 Su	5 37 24	24 57 55	1♓51 01	7♓47 36	18 29.0	6 22.8	1 31.9	27 48.7	25 53.1	8 36.9	15 39.4	14 01.2	26 20.8	21 11.2
16 M	5 41 21	25 55 13	13 46 27	19 48 13	18R29.9	8 06.6	1 21.0	28 26.2	26 18.7	8 50.7	15 45.2	14 04.7	26 22.1	21 10.6
17 Tu	5 45 18	26 52 30	25 53 32	2♈03 04	18 30.0	9 53.1	1 12.4	29 03.8	26 44.4	9 04.4	15 51.1	14 08.2	26 23.5	21 10.0
18 W	5 49 14	27 49 47	8♈17 25	14 37 11	18 28.5	11 42.2	1 06.3	29 41.3	27 10.1	9 18.1	15 57.0	14 11.7	26 24.8	21 09.3
19 Th	5 53 11	28 47 04	21 02 51	27 34 53	18 25.1	13 34.0	1 02.5	0♌18.8	27 35.9	9 31.8	16 03.0	14 15.2	26 26.0	21 08.6
20 F	5 57 07	29 44 21	4♉13 35	10♉59 11	18 19.9	15 28.3	1D01.1	0 56.3	28 01.8	9 45.4	16 09.0	14 18.8	26 27.3	21 07.9
21 Sa	6 01 04	0♋41 38	17 51 42	24 51 03	18 13.3	17 25.1	1 02.1	1 33.9	28 27.7	9 59.0	16 15.2	14 22.3	26 28.5	21 07.2
22 Su	6 05 00	1 38 54	1♊56 56	9♊08 53	18 06.1	19 24.2	1 05.3	2 11.4	28 53.6	10 12.6	16 21.3	14 25.9	26 29.7	21 06.4
23 M	6 08 57	2 36 10	16 26 15	23 48 12	17 59.2	21 25.5	1 10.8	2 49.0	29 19.6	10 26.1	16 27.5	14 29.5	26 30.9	21 05.6
24 Tu	6 12 53	3 33 26	1♋13 49	8♋42 01	17 53.5	23 28.9	1 18.4	3 26.6	29 45.6	10 39.6	16 33.8	14 33.0	26 32.0	21 04.8
25 W	6 16 50	4 30 42	16 11 43	23 41 47	17 49.5	25 34.1	1 28.2	4 04.1	0♌11.7	10 53.0	16 40.1	14 36.6	26 33.1	21 04.0
26 Th	6 20 47	5 27 57	1♌11 09	8♌38 47	17D47.6	27 40.8	1 40.1	4 41.7	0 37.8	11 06.4	16 46.5	14 40.2	26 34.2	21 03.2
27 F	6 24 43	6 25 12	16 03 48	23 25 26	17 47.8	29 49.0	1 53.9	5 19.3	1 03.9	11 19.8	16 53.0	14 43.8	26 35.3	21 02.3
28 Sa	6 28 40	7 22 26	0♍43 02	7♍56 10	17 48.3	1♋58.2	2 09.7	5 56.8	1 30.1	11 33.1	16 59.4	14 47.4	26 36.3	21 01.5
29 Su	6 32 36	8 19 39	15 04 27	22 07 44	17 49.6	4 08.2	2 27.4	6 34.4	1 56.3	11 46.4	17 06.0	14 51.1	26 37.3	21 00.6
30 M	6 36 33	9 16 52	29 05 54	5♎58 59	17R50.4	6 18.8	2 47.0	7 12.0	2 22.6	11 59.7	17 12.5	14 54.7	26 38.3	20 59.6

Astro Data	Dy Hr Mn
☽0S	7 4:58
♀R	8 15:59
☿D	17 8:30
♇R	21 15:39
☽0N	21 16:04
☽0S	3 11:34
☽0N	18 1:51
♀D	20 14:13
♃∠♆	28 18:09
☽0S	30 18:08

Planet Ingress	Dy Hr Mn
♂ ♋	2 0:51
♃ ♊	9 14:53
☉ ♊	20 10:46
☿ ♊	11 13:07
♂ ♌	18 23:58
☉ ♋	20 18:33
⚳ ♌	25 1:16
☿ ♋	27 14:03

Last Aspect Dy Hr Mn	☽ Ingress Dy Hr Mn
2 4:16 ♃ ✱	♌ 2 7:12
4 8:13 ♃ □	♍ 4 10:20
6 13:00 ♃ △	♎ 6 14:16
8 10:46 ♆ ☍	♏ 8 19:21
10 10:05 ♇ □	♐ 11 2:17
13 2:46 ♆ △	♑ 13 11:50
15 14:40 ♆ □	♒ 15 23:53
18 8:41 ☉ □	♓ 18 12:43
19 18:43 ♀ □	♈ 20 23:41
22 23:17 ♆ ☌	♉ 23 6:58
24 20:00 ♇ □	♊ 25 10:41
27 5:27 ♆ ✱	♋ 27 12:17
29 6:45 ♆ □	♌ 29 13:32
31 8:55 ♆ △	♍ 31 15:47

Last Aspect Dy Hr Mn	☽ Ingress Dy Hr Mn
2 1:11 ♂ ✱	♎ 2 19:45
4 18:25 ♆ ☍	♏ 5 1:34
6 20:55 ♆ ☍	♐ 7 9:20
9 11:48 ♆ △	♑ 9 19:15
11 23:41 ♆ □	♒ 12 7:15
14 12:48 ♆ ✱	♓ 14 20:15
17 5:53 ♂ △	♈ 17 8:01
19 14:21 ☉ ✱	♉ 19 16:23
21 5:37 ♇ □	♊ 21 20:43
23 16:24 ♆ ✱	♋ 23 22:01
25 16:35 ♆ □	♌ 25 22:06
27 17:12 ♆ △	♍ 27 22:49
28 23:34 ♅ ✱	♎ 30 1:34

☽ Phases & Eclipses Dy Hr Mn	
3 5:56	☽ 13♌23
10 8:11	○ 20♏15
18 8:41	☾ 27♒59
25 19:18	● 5♊09
1 11:36	☽ 11♍34
8 21:03	○ 18♐38
17 1:04	☾ 26♓26
24 3:11	● 3♋12
30 18:14	☽ 9♎32

Astro Data

1 May 2036
Julian Day # 49795
SVP 4♓45'20"
GC 27♐20.8 ⚴ 11♉45.7
Eris 27♈45.3 ⚵ 21♉18.6
⚷ 10♊21.0 ⚶ 7♐05.6R
☽ Mean ☊ 22♌20.6

1 June 2036
Julian Day # 49826
SVP 4♓45'16"
GC 27♐20.9 ⚴ 27♉27.1
Eris 28♈03.3 ⚵ 9♊49.1
⚷ 12♊45.7 ⚶ 0♐13.5R
☽ Mean ☊ 20♌42.1

July 2036 — LONGITUDE

Day	Sid.Time	☉	0 hr ☽	Noon ☽	True ☊	☿	♀	♂	⚳	♃	♄	♅	♆	♇
1 Tu	6 40 29	10♋14 05	12♎47 04	19♎30 19	17♌50.1	8♋29.7	3♊08.3	7♌49.6	2♌48.9	12♊12.9	17♌19.2	14♋58.3	26♈39.2	20♒58.7
2 W	6 44 26	11 11 17	26 08 55	2♏43 05	17R48.2	10 40.4	3 31.3	8 27.1	3 15.2	12 26.0	17 25.8	15 01.9	26 40.1	20R57.8
3 Th	6 48 22	12 08 29	9♏13 04	15 39 07	17 44.8	12 50.9	3 56.0	9 04.7	3 41.5	12 39.1	17 32.6	15 05.5	26 41.0	20 56.8
4 F	6 52 19	13 05 40	22 01 28	28 20 22	17 40.0	15 00.9	4 22.3	9 42.3	4 07.9	12 52.2	17 39.3	15 09.2	26 41.8	20 55.8
5 Sa	6 56 16	14 02 52	4♐36 02	10♐48 41	17 34.5	17 10.0	4 50.1	10 19.9	4 34.4	13 05.1	17 46.1	15 12.8	26 42.6	20 54.8
6 Su	7 00 12	15 00 03	16 58 31	23 05 44	17 28.9	19 18.2	5 19.4	10 57.5	5 00.8	13 18.1	17 53.0	15 16.5	26 43.4	20 53.8
7 M	7 04 09	15 57 14	29 10 33	5♑13 09	17 23.7	21 25.1	5 50.2	11 35.1	5 27.3	13 31.0	17 59.8	15 20.1	26 44.1	20 52.8
8 Tu	7 08 05	16 54 26	11♑13 43	17 12 30	17 19.6	23 30.8	6 22.4	12 12.7	5 53.8	13 43.8	18 06.8	15 23.7	26 44.9	20 51.7
9 W	7 12 02	17 51 37	23 09 41	29 05 33	17 16.8	25 35.0	6 55.9	12 50.3	6 20.4	13 56.6	18 13.7	15 27.3	26 45.5	20 50.6
10 Th	7 15 58	18 48 49	5♒00 22	10♒54 24	17D15.4	27 37.6	7 30.7	13 28.0	6 47.0	14 09.3	18 20.7	15 31.0	26 46.2	20 49.6
11 F	7 19 55	19 46 01	16 48 00	22 41 31	17 15.3	29 38.6	8 06.7	14 05.6	7 13.6	14 22.0	18 27.8	15 34.6	26 46.8	20 48.5
12 Sa	7 23 52	20 43 13	28 35 22	4♓29 56	17 16.3	1♌37.8	8 43.9	14 43.2	7 40.2	14 34.6	18 34.8	15 38.2	26 47.4	20 47.4
13 Su	7 27 48	21 40 25	10♓25 42	16 23 09	17 17.9	3 35.3	9 22.3	15 20.9	8 06.9	14 47.2	18 41.9	15 41.9	26 48.0	20 46.2
14 M	7 31 45	22 37 38	22 22 47	28 25 10	17 19.5	5 31.0	10 01.8	15 58.5	8 33.6	14 59.7	18 49.1	15 45.5	26 48.5	20 45.1
15 Tu	7 35 41	23 34 52	4♈30 50	10♈40 20	17 20.8	7 24.9	10 42.4	16 36.2	9 00.4	15 12.1	18 56.3	15 49.1	26 49.0	20 43.9
16 W	7 39 38	24 32 06	16 54 15	23 13 07	17R21.4	9 17.0	11 24.0	17 13.8	9 27.1	15 24.4	19 03.5	15 52.7	26 49.4	20 42.8
17 Th	7 43 34	25 29 21	29 37 27	6♉07 42	17 21.0	11 07.2	12 06.6	17 51.5	9 53.9	15 36.7	19 10.7	15 56.3	26 49.9	20 41.6
18 F	7 47 31	26 26 36	12♉44 18	19 27 32	17 19.7	12 55.5	12 50.1	18 29.2	10 20.7	15 49.0	19 18.0	15 59.9	26 50.3	20 40.4
19 Sa	7 51 27	27 23 53	26 17 36	3♊14 36	17 17.7	14 42.1	13 34.5	19 06.9	10 47.6	16 01.1	19 25.3	16 03.5	26 50.6	20 39.2
20 Su	7 55 24	28 21 10	10♊18 25	17 28 49	17 15.3	16 26.7	14 19.9	19 44.6	11 14.4	16 13.2	19 32.6	16 07.1	26 51.0	20 38.0
21 M	7 59 21	29 18 28	24 45 22	2♋07 27	17 13.0	18 09.6	15 06.0	20 22.3	11 41.3	16 25.2	19 39.9	16 10.6	26 51.3	20 36.8
22 Tu	8 03 17	0♌15 46	9♋34 18	17 04 58	17 11.1	19 50.6	15 53.0	21 00.1	12 08.2	16 37.2	19 47.3	16 14.2	26 51.5	20 35.6
23 W	8 07 14	1 13 05	24 38 23	2♌13 25	17D09.9	21 29.8	16 40.8	21 37.8	12 35.2	16 49.1	19 54.7	16 17.7	26 51.8	20 34.3
24 Th	8 11 10	2 10 25	9♌48 51	17 23 31	17 09.5	23 07.2	17 29.3	22 15.6	13 02.1	17 00.9	20 02.1	16 21.3	26 52.0	20 33.1
25 F	8 15 07	3 07 45	24 56 14	2♍25 58	17 09.8	24 42.7	18 18.5	22 53.3	13 29.1	17 12.6	20 09.6	16 24.8	26 52.1	20 31.8
26 Sa	8 19 03	4 05 06	9♍51 46	17 12 51	17 10.6	26 16.4	19 08.4	23 31.1	13 56.1	17 24.2	20 17.1	16 28.3	26 52.3	20 30.5
27 Su	8 23 00	5 02 27	24 28 36	1♎38 32	17 11.6	27 48.3	19 59.0	24 08.9	14 23.1	17 35.8	20 24.5	16 31.8	26 52.4	20 29.3
28 M	8 26 56	5 59 48	8♎42 22	15 39 55	17 12.5	29 18.3	20 50.2	24 46.7	14 50.2	17 47.2	20 32.0	16 35.3	26 52.4	20 28.0
29 Tu	8 30 53	6 57 10	22 31 12	29 16 18	17R13.0	0♍46.5	21 42.0	25 24.5	15 17.2	17 58.6	20 39.6	16 38.8	26R52.5	20 26.7
30 W	8 34 50	7 54 32	5♏55 25	12♏28 50	17 13.0	2 12.7	22 34.5	26 02.3	15 44.3	18 09.9	20 47.1	16 42.2	26 52.5	20 25.4
31 Th	8 38 46	8 51 55	18 56 52	25 19 55	17 12.7	3 37.1	23 27.5	26 40.1	16 11.4	18 21.1	20 54.7	16 45.7	26 52.4	20 24.1

August 2036 — LONGITUDE

Day	Sid.Time	☉	0 hr ☽	Noon ☽	True ☊	☿	♀	♂	⚳	♃	♄	♅	♆	♇
1 F	8 42 43	9♌49 19	1♐38 23	7♐52 41	17♌12.0	4♍59.5	24♊21.1	27♌17.9	16♌38.5	18♊32.3	21♌02.2	16♋49.1	26♈52.4	20♒22.8
2 Sa	8 46 39	10 46 43	14 03 15	20 10 29	17R11.2	6 20.0	25 15.3	27 55.8	17 05.6	18 43.3	21 09.8	16 52.5	26R52.3	20R21.5
3 Su	8 50 36	11 44 08	26 14 48	2♑16 36	17 10.4	7 38.4	26 10.0	28 33.6	17 32.7	18 54.3	21 17.4	16 55.9	26 52.1	20 20.1
4 M	8 54 32	12 41 33	8♑16 14	14 14 09	17 09.8	8 54.8	27 05.2	29 11.5	17 59.8	19 05.1	21 25.0	16 59.3	26 52.0	20 18.8
5 Tu	8 58 29	13 39 00	20 10 36	26 05 57	17 09.4	10 09.1	28 00.9	29 49.4	18 27.0	19 15.9	21 32.7	17 02.6	26 51.8	20 17.5
6 W	9 02 25	14 36 27	2♒00 29	7♒54 32	17D09.2	11 21.2	28 57.1	0♍27.3	18 54.2	19 26.5	21 40.3	17 05.9	26 51.6	20 16.2
7 Th	9 06 22	15 33 55	13 48 22	19 42 16	17 09.2	12 31.0	29 53.7	1 05.2	19 21.3	19 37.1	21 47.9	17 09.3	26 51.3	20 14.8
8 F	9 10 19	16 31 25	25 36 33	1♓31 27	17R09.2	13 38.6	0♋50.9	1 43.1	19 48.5	19 47.6	21 55.6	17 12.5	26 51.0	20 13.5
9 Sa	9 14 15	17 28 55	7♓27 19	13 24 25	17 09.2	14 43.6	1 48.4	2 21.0	20 15.7	19 57.9	22 03.2	17 15.8	26 50.7	20 12.2
10 Su	9 18 12	18 26 27	19 23 05	25 23 39	17 09.1	15 46.2	2 46.4	2 58.9	20 43.0	20 08.2	22 10.9	17 19.1	26 50.3	20 10.8
11 M	9 22 08	19 24 00	1♈26 27	7♈31 52	17 08.9	16 46.2	3 44.8	3 36.9	21 10.2	20 18.4	22 18.5	17 22.3	26 49.9	20 09.5
12 Tu	9 26 05	20 21 34	13 40 17	19 52 04	17 08.6	17 43.3	4 43.7	4 14.8	21 37.4	20 28.4	22 26.2	17 25.5	26 49.5	20 08.1
13 W	9 30 01	21 19 09	26 07 39	2♉27 26	17 08.3	18 37.6	5 42.9	4 52.8	22 04.7	20 38.4	22 33.9	17 28.6	26 49.1	20 06.8
14 Th	9 33 58	22 16 46	8♉51 48	15 21 09	17D08.0	19 28.9	6 42.5	5 30.8	22 31.9	20 48.2	22 41.5	17 31.8	26 48.6	20 05.5
15 F	9 37 54	23 14 25	21 55 50	28 36 10	17 08.0	20 17.0	7 42.5	6 08.8	22 59.2	20 58.0	22 49.2	17 34.9	26 48.1	20 04.1
16 Sa	9 41 51	24 12 05	5♊22 24	12♊14 43	17 08.3	21 01.7	8 42.8	6 46.9	23 26.5	21 07.6	22 56.9	17 38.0	26 47.5	20 02.8
17 Su	9 45 47	25 09 47	19 13 11	26 17 47	17 08.9	21 42.9	9 43.5	7 24.9	23 53.8	21 17.1	23 04.6	17 41.1	26 47.0	20 01.5
18 M	9 49 44	26 07 31	3♋28 19	10♋44 28	17 09.6	22 20.3	10 44.5	8 03.0	24 21.0	21 26.5	23 12.2	17 44.1	26 46.4	20 00.1
19 Tu	9 53 41	27 05 16	18 05 46	25 31 33	17 10.3	22 53.7	11 45.9	8 41.1	24 48.3	21 35.8	23 19.9	17 47.2	26 45.7	19 58.8
20 W	9 57 37	28 03 02	3♌01 04	10♌33 21	17R10.7	23 23.0	12 47.5	9 19.2	25 15.7	21 45.0	23 27.6	17 50.2	26 45.1	19 57.5
21 Th	10 01 34	29 00 50	18 07 21	25 41 58	17 10.7	23 47.8	13 49.5	9 57.3	25 43.0	21 54.0	23 35.2	17 53.1	26 44.4	19 56.2
22 F	10 05 30	29 58 39	3♍16 01	10♍48 19	17 10.0	24 07.9	14 51.8	10 35.5	26 10.3	22 02.9	23 42.9	17 56.0	26 43.7	19 54.8
23 Sa	10 09 27	0♍56 30	18 17 46	25 43 20	17 08.8	24 23.2	15 54.4	11 13.6	26 37.6	22 11.7	23 50.5	17 58.9	26 42.9	19 53.5
24 Su	10 13 23	1 54 22	3♎04 06	10♎19 19	17 07.0	24 33.2	16 57.2	11 51.8	27 04.9	22 20.3	23 58.1	18 01.8	26 42.1	19 52.2
25 M	10 17 20	2 52 15	17 28 24	24 30 56	17 05.1	24R37.8	18 00.3	12 30.0	27 32.2	22 28.9	24 05.8	18 04.6	26 41.3	19 50.9
26 Tu	10 21 16	3 50 09	1♏26 41	8♏15 34	17 03.3	24 36.8	19 03.7	13 08.2	27 59.5	22 37.3	24 13.4	18 07.4	26 40.5	19 49.6
27 W	10 25 13	4 48 05	14 57 39	21 33 10	17 02.1	24 30.0	20 07.4	13 46.4	28 26.8	22 45.6	24 21.0	18 10.2	26 39.6	19 48.3
28 Th	10 29 10	5 46 02	28 02 24	4♐25 46	17D01.6	24 17.2	21 11.3	14 24.6	28 54.2	22 53.7	24 28.6	18 12.9	26 38.7	19 47.0
29 F	10 33 06	6 44 00	10♐43 44	16 56 49	17 01.9	23 58.3	22 15.4	15 02.9	29 21.5	23 01.7	24 36.1	18 15.6	26 37.8	19 45.8
30 Sa	10 37 03	7 42 00	23 05 33	29 10 31	17 03.0	23 33.3	23 19.8	15 41.2	29 48.8	23 09.6	24 43.7	18 18.3	26 36.8	19 44.5
31 Su	10 40 59	8 40 01	5♑12 16	11♑11 22	17 04.5	23 02.3	24 24.5	16 19.4	0♍16.1	23 17.3	24 51.2	18 20.9	26 35.9	19 43.3

Astro Data

	Dy Hr Mn
☽ 0N	15 10:05
♃⚺♅	19 18:35
♄☍♇	28 0:54
☽ 0S	28 1:49
♆ R	30 0:20
♃△♇	10 17:27
☽ 0N	11 16:25
☿ 0S	19 9:51
☽ 0S	24 11:03
☿ R	25 19:49

Planet Ingress

	Dy Hr Mn
☿ ♌	11 16:17
☉ ♌	22 5:24
☿ ♍	28 23:17
♂ ♍	5 18:44
♀ ♋	7 14:38
☉ ♍	22 12:34
⚳ ♍	30 21:52

Last Aspect / ☽ Ingress

Last Aspect Dy Hr Mn		☽ Ingress	Dy Hr Mn
2 0:56	♆ ☍	♏	2 7:01
3 21:57	♇ □	♐	4 15:10
6 19:09	♆ △	♑	7 1:38
9 7:16	♆ □	♒	9 13:50
11 20:20	♆ ⚹	♓	12 2:52
13 23:30	☉ △	♈	14 15:07
16 18:47	♆ ☌	♉	17 0:42
19 1:10	☉ ⚹	♊	19 6:25
21 3:26	♆ ⚹	♋	21 8:33
23 3:31	♆ □	♌	23 8:29
25 3:05	♆ △	♍	25 8:06
26 15:22	♀ □	♎	27 9:14
29 7:43	♆ ☍	♏	29 13:18
31 14:40	♂ □	♐	31 20:52

Last Aspect / ☽ Ingress

Last Aspect Dy Hr Mn		☽ Ingress	Dy Hr Mn
3 4:11	♂ △	♑	3 7:28
5 13:33	♆ □	♒	5 19:55
8 2:31	♆ ⚹	♓	8 8:55
10 1:21	♃ □	♈	10 21:09
13 1:19	♆ ☌	♉	13 7:21
15 1:37	☉ □	♊	15 14:29
17 12:49	♆ ⚹	♋	17 18:13
19 13:59	♆ □	♌	19 19:11
21 17:37	☉ ☌	♍	21 18:49
23 9:48	☿ ☌	♎	23 18:58
25 15:44	♆ ☍	♏	25 21:29
27 17:21	☿ ⚹	♐	28 3:40
30 6:56	♆ △	♑	30 13:38

☽ Phases & Eclipses

Dy Hr Mn	
8 11:21	○ 16♑53
16 14:41	☾ 24♈38
23 10:18	● 1♌09
23 10:32:08	P 0.199
30 2:58	☽ 7♏33
7 2:50	○ 15♒12
7 2:53	T 1.454
15 1:37	☾ 22♉49
21 17:37	● 29♌14
21 17:25:44	P 0.862
28 14:45	☽ 5♐53

Astro Data

1 July 2036
Julian Day # 49856
SVP 4♓45'11"
GC 27♐20.9 ⚵ 13♊31.6
Eris 28♈14.5 ⚶ 27♊30.9
⚷ 15♊08.1 ⚴ 26♏02.3R
☽ Mean ☊ 19♌06.8

1 August 2036
Julian Day # 49887
SVP 4♓45'06"
GC 27♐21.0 ⚵ 0♋48.0
Eris 28♈16.9R ⚶ 15♋12.0
⚷ 17♊13.7 ⚴ 28♏54.8
☽ Mean ☊ 17♌28.3

LONGITUDE — September 2036

Day	Sid.Time	☉	0 hr ☽	Noon☽	True☊	☿	♀	♂	⚳	♃	♄	♅	♆	♇
1 M	10 44 56	9♍38 04	17♑08 22	23♑03 48	17♌06.2	22♍25.5	25♋29.4	16♍57.7	0♍43.4	23♊24.9	24♌58.7	18♋23.5	26♈34.9	19♒42.0
2 Tu	10 48 52	10 36 07	28 58 09	4♒51 53	17 07.5	21R43.2	26 34.5	17 36.1	1 10.7	23 32.3	25 06.2	18 26.1	26R33.8	19R40.8
3 W	10 52 49	11 34 13	10♒45 28	16 39 17	17R08.0	20 55.9	27 39.8	18 14.4	1 38.0	23 39.6	25 13.7	18 28.6	26 32.8	19 39.5
4 Th	10 56 45	12 32 20	22 33 42	28 29 04	17 07.4	20 04.2	28 45.4	18 52.8	2 05.2	23 46.8	25 21.2	18 31.1	26 31.7	19 38.3
5 F	11 00 42	13 30 28	4♓25 40	10♓23 48	17 05.6	19 09.0	29 51.2	19 31.2	2 32.5	23 53.8	25 28.6	18 33.5	26 30.6	19 37.1
6 Sa	11 04 39	14 28 38	16 23 42	22 25 35	17 02.5	18 11.2	0♌57.2	20 09.5	2 59.8	24 00.6	25 36.0	18 35.9	26 29.5	19 35.9
7 Su	11 08 35	15 26 50	28 29 39	4♈36 07	16 58.3	17 12.0	2 03.4	20 48.0	3 27.1	24 07.3	25 43.4	18 38.3	26 28.3	19 34.7
8 M	11 12 32	16 25 04	10♈45 08	16 56 53	16 53.4	16 12.6	3 09.8	21 26.4	3 54.3	24 13.9	25 50.8	18 40.6	26 27.2	19 33.6
9 Tu	11 16 28	17 23 20	23 11 32	29 29 16	16 48.4	15 14.4	4 16.4	22 04.9	4 21.6	24 20.3	25 58.1	18 42.9	26 26.0	19 32.4
10 W	11 20 25	18 21 37	5♉50 15	12♉14 40	16 43.9	14 18.6	5 23.3	22 43.3	4 48.8	24 26.5	26 05.4	18 45.2	26 24.7	19 31.3
11 Th	11 24 21	19 19 57	18 42 43	25 14 36	16 40.4	13 26.8	6 30.3	23 21.9	5 16.0	24 32.6	26 12.7	18 47.4	26 23.5	19 30.1
12 F	11 28 18	20 18 19	1♊50 31	8♊30 38	16D38.3	12 40.0	7 37.5	24 00.4	5 43.3	24 38.6	26 20.0	18 49.5	26 22.2	19 29.0
13 Sa	11 32 14	21 16 43	15 15 10	22 04 15	16 37.7	11 59.6	8 44.9	24 38.9	6 10.5	24 44.3	26 27.2	18 51.6	26 20.9	19 27.9
14 Su	11 36 11	22 15 09	28 58 00	5♋56 29	16 38.3	11 26.5	9 52.5	25 17.5	6 37.7	24 49.9	26 34.4	18 53.7	26 19.6	19 26.8
15 M	11 40 08	23 13 38	12♋59 41	20 07 31	16 39.6	11 01.5	11 00.3	25 56.1	7 04.9	24 55.4	26 41.5	18 55.8	26 18.3	19 25.8
16 Tu	11 44 04	24 12 08	27 19 47	4♌36 09	16R40.9	10 45.4	12 08.2	26 34.7	7 32.0	25 00.6	26 48.7	18 57.8	26 17.0	19 24.7
17 W	11 48 01	25 10 41	11♌56 11	19 19 17	16 41.3	10D38.5	13 16.3	27 13.4	7 59.2	25 05.8	26 55.8	18 59.7	26 15.6	19 23.7
18 Th	11 51 57	26 09 16	26 44 46	4♍11 46	16 40.2	10 41.2	14 24.6	27 52.1	8 26.4	25 10.7	27 02.8	19 01.6	26 14.2	19 22.6
19 F	11 55 54	27 07 52	11♍39 20	19 06 30	16 37.2	10 53.4	15 33.1	28 30.8	8 53.5	25 15.4	27 09.8	19 03.5	26 12.8	19 21.6
20 Sa	11 59 50	28 06 31	26 32 10	3♎55 20	16 32.2	11 15.2	16 41.7	29 09.5	9 20.6	25 20.0	27 16.8	19 05.3	26 11.4	19 20.6
21 Su	12 03 47	29 05 11	11♎14 59	18 30 12	16 25.9	11 46.4	17 50.4	29 48.2	9 47.7	25 24.4	27 23.8	19 07.0	26 09.9	19 19.7
22 M	12 07 43	0♎03 54	25 40 13	2♏44 23	16 18.9	12 26.4	18 59.3	0♎27.0	10 14.8	25 28.6	27 30.7	19 08.7	26 08.5	19 18.7
23 Tu	12 11 40	1 02 38	9♏42 14	16 33 28	16 12.2	13 15.0	20 08.4	1 05.8	10 41.8	25 32.7	27 37.5	19 10.4	26 07.0	19 17.8
24 W	12 15 36	2 01 24	23 17 56	29 55 41	16 06.6	14 11.5	21 17.6	1 44.6	11 08.9	25 36.6	27 44.3	19 12.0	26 05.5	19 16.8
25 Th	12 19 33	3 00 12	6♐26 54	12♐51 52	16 02.6	15 15.3	22 26.9	2 23.4	11 35.9	25 40.2	27 51.1	19 13.6	26 04.0	19 15.9
26 F	12 23 30	3 59 01	19 11 00	25 24 48	16D00.5	16 25.8	23 36.4	3 02.3	12 02.9	25 43.7	27 57.8	19 15.1	26 02.5	19 15.1
27 Sa	12 27 26	4 57 53	1♑33 50	7♑38 43	16 00.1	17 42.4	24 46.0	3 41.1	12 29.9	25 47.1	28 04.5	19 16.6	26 01.0	19 14.2
28 Su	12 31 23	5 56 46	13 40 04	19 38 34	16 00.9	19 04.3	25 55.8	4 20.1	12 56.8	25 50.2	28 11.1	19 18.0	25 59.4	19 13.4
29 M	12 35 19	6 55 40	25 34 51	1♒29 36	16 02.2	20 30.8	27 05.7	4 59.0	13 23.7	25 53.1	28 17.7	19 19.4	25 57.9	19 12.6
30 Tu	12 39 16	7 54 37	7♒23 26	13 16 58	16R03.0	22 01.4	28 15.7	5 37.9	13 50.6	25 55.9	28 24.2	19 20.7	25 56.3	19 11.8

LONGITUDE — October 2036

Day	Sid.Time	☉	0 hr ☽	Noon☽	True☊	☿	♀	♂	⚳	♃	♄	♅	♆	♇
1 W	12 43 12	8♎53 35	19♒10 47	25♒05 24	16♌02.6	23♍35.5	29♌25.8	6♎16.9	14♍17.5	25♊58.5	28♌30.7	19♋22.0	25♈54.7	19♒11.0
2 Th	12 47 09	9 52 35	1♓01 20	6♓59 00	16R00.2	25 12.4	0♍36.1	6 55.9	14 44.3	26 00.8	28 37.1	19 23.2	25R53.1	19R10.2
3 F	12 51 05	10 51 37	12 58 49	19 01 07	15 55.4	26 51.7	1 46.5	7 34.9	15 11.1	26 03.0	28 43.5	19 24.4	25 51.5	19 09.5
4 Sa	12 55 02	11 50 41	25 06 09	1♈14 09	15 48.3	28 32.9	2 57.0	8 14.0	15 37.9	26 05.0	28 49.8	19 25.5	25 49.9	19 08.8
5 Su	12 58 59	12 49 47	7♈25 16	13 39 37	15 39.2	0♎15.6	4 07.7	8 53.0	16 04.6	26 06.8	28 56.1	19 26.6	25 48.3	19 08.1
6 M	13 02 55	13 48 55	19 57 14	26 18 09	15 28.8	1 59.5	5 18.5	9 32.1	16 31.3	26 08.4	29 02.3	19 27.6	25 46.7	19 07.4
7 Tu	13 06 52	14 48 05	2♉42 19	9♉09 41	15 18.1	3 44.1	6 29.4	10 11.2	16 58.0	26 09.8	29 08.4	19 28.6	25 45.0	19 06.8
8 W	13 10 48	15 47 17	15 40 10	22 13 42	15 08.2	5 29.3	7 40.4	10 50.4	17 24.7	26 11.0	29 14.5	19 29.5	25 43.4	19 06.2
9 Th	13 14 45	16 46 31	28 50 11	5♊29 33	14 59.9	7 14.9	8 51.5	11 29.6	17 51.3	26 12.0	29 20.6	19 30.4	25 41.7	19 05.6
10 F	13 18 41	17 45 48	12♊11 45	18 56 44	14 54.0	9 00.6	10 02.8	12 08.8	18 17.9	26 12.9	29 26.5	19 31.2	25 40.1	19 05.0
11 Sa	13 22 38	18 45 07	25 44 30	2♋35 01	14 50.7	10 46.2	11 14.1	12 48.0	18 44.4	26 13.5	29 32.4	19 32.0	25 38.4	19 04.4
12 Su	13 26 34	19 44 28	9♋28 20	16 24 28	14D49.5	12 31.7	12 25.6	13 27.3	19 10.9	26 13.9	29 38.3	19 32.7	25 36.8	19 03.9
13 M	13 30 31	20 43 52	23 23 25	0♌25 10	14 49.7	14 16.9	13 37.2	14 06.6	19 37.4	26R14.1	29 44.1	19 33.3	25 35.1	19 03.4
14 Tu	13 34 28	21 43 18	7♌29 40	14 36 48	14R50.1	16 01.8	14 48.9	14 45.9	20 03.8	26 14.1	29 49.8	19 33.9	25 33.4	19 02.9
15 W	13 38 24	22 42 47	21 46 24	28 58 11	14 49.3	17 46.2	16 00.7	15 25.3	20 30.2	26 13.9	29 55.4	19 34.5	25 31.7	19 02.5
16 Th	13 42 21	23 42 17	6♍11 46	13♍26 40	14 46.5	19 30.1	17 12.6	16 04.7	20 56.6	26 13.5	0♍01.0	19 35.0	25 30.1	19 02.1
17 F	13 46 17	24 41 50	20 42 19	27 58 02	14 40.9	21 13.6	18 24.5	16 44.1	21 22.9	26 12.9	0 06.5	19 35.4	25 28.4	19 01.6
18 Sa	13 50 14	25 41 25	5♎13 03	12♎26 35	14 32.5	22 56.4	19 36.6	17 23.5	21 49.2	26 12.1	0 12.0	19 35.8	25 26.7	19 01.3
19 Su	13 54 10	26 41 02	19 37 47	26 45 52	14 21.9	24 38.7	20 48.8	18 03.0	22 15.4	26 11.1	0 17.3	19 36.1	25 25.0	19 00.9
20 M	13 58 07	27 40 41	3♏50 04	10♏49 42	14 10.2	26 20.5	22 01.1	18 42.5	22 41.6	26 09.9	0 22.6	19 36.4	25 23.3	19 00.6
21 Tu	14 02 03	28 40 22	17 44 12	24 33 09	13 58.5	28 01.6	23 13.4	19 22.0	23 07.7	26 08.5	0 27.9	19 36.6	25 21.7	19 00.3
22 W	14 06 00	29 40 05	1♐16 13	7♐53 17	13 48.1	29 42.1	24 25.8	20 01.6	23 33.8	26 06.9	0 33.0	19 36.8	25 20.0	19 00.0
23 Th	14 09 57	0♏39 50	14 24 20	20 49 32	13 39.9	1♏22.1	25 38.4	20 41.1	23 59.8	26 05.1	0 38.1	19 36.9	25 18.3	18 59.8
24 F	14 13 53	1 39 37	27 09 06	3♑23 27	13 34.3	3 01.4	26 51.0	21 20.7	24 25.8	26 03.1	0 43.1	19R37.0	25 16.6	18 59.5
25 Sa	14 17 50	2 39 25	9♑33 01	15 38 22	13 31.2	4 40.2	28 03.6	22 00.4	24 51.7	26 00.9	0 48.0	19 37.0	25 15.0	18 59.4
26 Su	14 21 46	3 39 15	21 40 05	27 38 50	13D30.1	6 18.4	29 16.4	22 40.0	25 17.6	25 58.5	0 52.8	19 37.0	25 13.3	18 59.2
27 M	14 25 43	4 39 07	3♒35 17	9♒30 09	13R30.0	7 56.1	0♎29.2	23 19.7	25 43.4	25 55.9	0 57.6	19 36.9	25 11.7	18 59.0
28 Tu	14 29 39	5 39 00	15 24 06	21 17 52	13 29.9	9 33.3	1 42.1	23 59.5	26 09.1	25 53.1	1 02.2	19 36.7	25 10.0	18 58.9
29 W	14 33 36	6 38 55	27 12 06	3♓07 29	13 28.6	11 09.9	2 55.1	24 39.2	26 34.8	25 50.1	1 06.8	19 36.5	25 08.4	18 58.8
30 Th	14 37 32	7 38 52	9♓04 37	15 04 05	13 25.2	12 46.0	4 08.2	25 19.0	27 00.5	25 46.9	1 11.3	19 36.2	25 06.7	18 58.8
31 F	14 41 29	8 38 50	21 06 25	27 12 02	13 19.0	14 21.6	5 21.3	25 58.8	27 26.0	25 43.5	1 15.7	19 35.9	25 05.1	18D58.7

Astro Data

	Dy Hr Mn
☿0N	4 12:46
☽0N	7 21:51
♄△♆	12 18:23
☿ D	17 17:23
☽0S	20 21:17
☉0S	22 10:25
♂0S	24 20:40
♅⊼♇	26 11:25
♃⚹♆	30 14:18
☽0N	5 4:05
☿0S	7 20:04
♃ R	14 1:39
☽0S	18 7:16
♅ R	25 3:24
♀0S	30 2:26

Planet Ingress

	Dy Hr Mn
♀ ♌	5 15:13
♂ ♎	21 19:18
☉ ♎	22 10:24
♀ ♍	1 23:41
☿ ♎	5 8:22
♄ ♍	16 7:36
☿ ♏	22 16:17
☉ ♏	22 20:00
♀ ♎	27 2:22

Last Aspect / ☽ Ingress (September)

Last Aspect Dy Hr Mn		☽ Ingress Dy Hr Mn
1 19:08	♆ □	♒ 2 2:06
4 8:03	♆ ⚹	♓ 4 15:04
6 15:10	♃ □	♈ 7 2:58
9 6:12	♆ ☌	♉ 9 12:58
11 13:47	♄ □	♊ 11 20:40
13 19:43	♄ ⚹	♋ 14 1:47
15 22:17	♆ □	♌ 16 4:25
18 0:24	♄ ☌	♍ 18 5:15
20 3:54	♂ ☌	♎ 20 5:37
22 3:02	♄ ⚹	♏ 22 7:20
24 7:59	♄ □	♐ 24 12:08
26 17:00	♄ △	♑ 26 20:56
29 0:48	♆ □	♒ 29 8:58

Last Aspect / ☽ Ingress (October)

Last Aspect Dy Hr Mn		☽ Ingress Dy Hr Mn
1 21:45	♀ ☍	♓ 1 21:56
4 5:55	☿ ☍	♈ 4 9:35
6 17:11	♄ △	♉ 6 18:57
9 0:50	♄ □	♊ 9 2:06
11 6:38	♄ ⚹	♋ 11 7:29
13 3:46	♆ □	♌ 13 11:17
15 13:36	♄ ☌	♍ 15 13:43
17 9:06	♃ □	♎ 17 15:22
19 11:51	☉ ☌	♏ 19 17:29
21 9:25	♀ ⚹	♐ 21 21:43
23 22:05	♀ □	♑ 24 5:28
26 15:39	♀ △	♒ 26 16:45
28 21:17	♃ △	♓ 29 5:41
31 9:07	♃ □	♈ 31 17:28

☽ Phases & Eclipses

Dy Hr Mn	
5 18:47	○ 13♓47
13 10:30	☾ 21♊13
20 1:53	● 27♍42
27 6:14	☽ 4♑44
5 10:16	○ 12♈46
12 18:11	☾ 20♋00
19 11:51	● 26♎41
27 1:15	☽ 4♒12

Astro Data

1 September 2036
Julian Day # 49918
SVP 4♓45'03"
GC 27♐21.1 ⚵ 18♋16.6
Eris 28♈09.5R ⚶ 1♌52.6
⚷ 18♊34.5 ⚴ 7♐34.7
☽ Mean ☊ 15♌49.8

1 October 2036
Julian Day # 49948
SVP 4♓45'00"
GC 27♐21.2 ⚵ 4♌36.4
Eris 27♈54.9R ⚶ 16♌35.6
⚷ 18♊53.3R ⚴ 19♐16.9
☽ Mean ☊ 14♌14.5

November 2036 LONGITUDE

Day	Sid.Time	☉	0 hr ☽	Noon ☽	True ☊	☿	♀	♂	⚳	♃	♄	♅	♆	♇
1 Sa	14 45 25	9♏38 50	3♈21 22	9♈34 42	13♌10.1	15♏56.8	6♎34.5	26♎38.6	27♍51.5	25♊40.0	1♍20.1	19♋35.5	25♈03.5	18♒58.7
2 Su	14 49 22	10 38 52	15 52 14	22 14 08	12R 58.8	17 31.5	7 47.7	27 18.5	28 17.0	25R 36.2	1 24.3	19R 35.1	25R 01.9	18 58.8
3 M	14 53 19	11 38 55	28 40 24	5♉11 00	12 45.8	19 05.8	9 01.1	27 58.4	28 42.4	25 32.3	1 28.5	19 34.6	25 00.3	18 58.8
4 Tu	14 57 15	12 39 00	11♉45 47	18 24 32	12 32.4	20 39.7	10 14.5	28 38.3	29 07.7	25 28.2	1 32.6	19 34.1	24 58.7	18 58.9
5 W	15 01 12	13 39 08	25 06 58	1♊52 44	12 19.8	22 13.1	11 27.9	29 18.2	29 32.9	25 23.9	1 36.5	19 33.5	24 57.1	18 59.0
6 Th	15 05 08	14 39 17	8♊41 29	15 32 50	12 09.2	23 46.2	12 41.5	29 58.2	29 58.1	25 19.4	1 40.4	19 32.9	24 55.6	18 59.1
7 F	15 09 05	15 39 28	22 26 25	29 21 52	12 01.4	25 18.9	13 55.1	0♏38.2	0♎23.2	25 14.7	1 44.2	19 32.2	24 54.0	18 59.3
8 Sa	15 13 01	16 39 41	6♋18 53	13♋17 10	11 56.5	26 51.2	15 08.7	1 18.3	0 48.2	25 09.9	1 48.0	19 31.5	24 52.5	18 59.4
9 Su	15 16 58	17 39 56	20 16 30	27 16 43	11 54.4	28 23.2	16 22.5	1 58.4	1 13.2	25 04.9	1 51.6	19 30.7	24 51.0	18 59.7
10 M	15 20 55	18 40 14	4♌17 40	11♌19 16	11 53.9	29 54.8	17 36.3	2 38.5	1 38.1	24 59.7	1 55.1	19 29.8	24 49.4	18 59.9
11 Tu	15 24 51	19 40 33	18 21 26	25 24 06	11 53.9	1♐26.1	18 50.1	3 18.6	2 02.9	24 54.4	1 58.5	19 29.0	24 48.0	19 00.2
12 W	15 28 48	20 40 54	2♍27 10	9♍30 32	11 52.9	2 57.1	20 04.0	3 58.8	2 27.7	24 48.9	2 01.9	19 28.0	24 46.5	19 00.4
13 Th	15 32 44	21 41 17	16 34 04	23 37 33	11 49.8	4 27.7	21 18.0	4 39.0	2 52.3	24 43.2	2 05.1	19 27.0	24 45.0	19 00.8
14 F	15 36 41	22 41 42	0♎40 43	7♎43 14	11 43.9	5 58.0	22 32.0	5 19.3	3 16.9	24 37.4	2 08.2	19 26.0	24 43.6	19 01.1
15 Sa	15 40 37	23 42 09	14 44 43	21 44 43	11 35.0	7 27.9	23 46.0	5 59.6	3 41.4	24 31.4	2 11.3	19 24.9	24 42.1	19 01.5
16 Su	15 44 34	24 42 38	28 42 45	5♏38 19	11 23.9	8 57.5	25 00.1	6 39.9	4 05.8	24 25.3	2 14.2	19 23.7	24 40.7	19 01.9
17 M	15 48 30	25 43 08	12♏30 54	19 20 02	11 11.4	10 26.7	26 14.3	7 20.2	4 30.1	24 19.1	2 17.0	19 22.5	24 39.3	19 02.3
18 Tu	15 52 27	26 43 40	26 05 16	2♐46 14	10 58.8	11 55.5	27 28.5	8 00.6	4 54.3	24 12.6	2 19.8	19 21.3	24 38.0	19 02.8
19 W	15 56 23	27 44 14	9♐22 37	15 54 15	10 47.4	13 23.8	28 42.7	8 41.0	5 18.4	24 06.1	2 22.4	19 20.0	24 36.6	19 03.2
20 Th	16 00 20	28 44 49	22 21 02	28 42 58	10 38.2	14 51.8	29 57.0	9 21.5	5 42.5	23 59.4	2 24.9	19 18.7	24 35.3	19 03.8
21 F	16 04 17	29 45 25	5♑00 11	11♑12 54	10 31.7	16 19.2	1♏11.3	10 01.9	6 06.4	23 52.6	2 27.3	19 17.3	24 34.0	19 04.3
22 Sa	16 08 13	0♐46 03	17 21 24	23 26 08	10 27.9	17 46.0	2 25.7	10 42.4	6 30.3	23 45.7	2 29.7	19 15.9	24 32.7	19 04.9
23 Su	16 12 10	1 46 41	29 27 31	5♒26 08	10D 26.5	19 12.2	3 40.1	11 23.0	6 54.0	23 38.7	2 31.9	19 14.4	24 31.4	19 05.4
24 M	16 16 06	2 47 21	11♒22 32	17 17 23	10 26.5	20 37.8	4 54.5	12 03.5	7 17.6	23 31.5	2 34.0	19 12.9	24 30.2	19 06.1
25 Tu	16 20 03	3 48 03	23 11 19	29 05 01	10R 27.0	22 02.5	6 09.0	12 44.1	7 41.1	23 24.3	2 36.0	19 11.3	24 29.0	19 06.7
26 W	16 23 59	4 48 45	4♓59 13	10♓54 34	10 26.9	23 26.4	7 23.5	13 24.7	8 04.6	23 16.9	2 37.9	19 09.7	24 27.8	19 07.4
27 Th	16 27 56	5 49 28	16 51 47	22 51 32	10 25.2	24 49.3	8 38.0	14 05.4	8 27.9	23 09.5	2 39.6	19 08.1	24 26.6	19 08.1
28 F	16 31 52	6 50 12	28 54 25	5♈01 03	10 21.3	26 11.0	9 52.6	14 46.1	8 51.1	23 01.9	2 41.3	19 06.4	24 25.4	19 08.8
29 Sa	16 35 49	7 50 57	11♈11 58	17 27 35	10 15.0	27 31.3	11 07.2	15 26.8	9 14.2	22 54.3	2 42.9	19 04.7	24 24.3	19 09.5
30 Su	16 39 46	8 51 43	23 48 19	0♉14 25	10 06.5	28 50.2	12 21.8	16 07.5	9 37.1	22 46.6	2 44.3	19 02.9	24 23.2	19 10.3

December 2036 LONGITUDE

Day	Sid.Time	☉	0 hr ☽	Noon ☽	True ☊	☿	♀	♂	⚳	♃	♄	♅	♆	♇
1 M	16 43 42	9♐52 31	6♉46 02	13♉23 13	9♌56.4	0♑07.3	13♏36.4	16♏48.3	10♎00.0	22♊38.9	2♍45.7	19♋01.1	24♈22.2	19♒11.1
2 Tu	16 47 39	10 53 19	20 05 53	26 53 48	9R 45.8	1 22.4	14 51.1	17 29.1	10 22.7	22R 31.0	2 46.9	18R 59.2	24R 21.1	19 11.9
3 W	16 51 35	11 54 09	3♊46 40	10♊44 00	9 35.7	2 35.3	16 05.8	18 10.0	10 45.3	22 23.1	2 48.1	18 57.4	24 20.1	19 12.7
4 Th	16 55 32	12 54 59	17 45 17	24 49 53	9 27.3	3 45.4	17 20.6	18 50.8	11 07.8	22 15.2	2 49.1	18 55.4	24 19.1	19 13.6
5 F	16 59 28	13 55 51	1♋57 09	9♋06 25	9 21.2	4 52.5	18 35.4	19 31.8	11 30.2	22 07.2	2 50.0	18 53.5	24 18.1	19 14.5
6 Sa	17 03 25	14 56 44	16 17 00	23 28 15	9 17.8	5 56.0	19 50.2	20 12.7	11 52.5	21 59.2	2 50.8	18 51.5	24 17.2	19 15.4
7 Su	17 07 22	15 57 38	0♌39 35	7♌50 30	9D 16.7	6 55.5	21 05.0	20 53.7	12 14.6	21 51.1	2 51.5	18 49.5	24 16.3	19 16.4
8 M	17 11 18	16 58 34	15 00 32	22 09 20	9 17.1	7 50.4	22 19.9	21 34.7	12 36.6	21 43.0	2 52.1	18 47.4	24 15.4	19 17.3
9 Tu	17 15 15	17 59 30	29 16 37	6♍22 08	9R 18.2	8 40.0	23 34.7	22 15.8	12 58.4	21 34.8	2 52.5	18 45.3	24 14.6	19 18.3
10 W	17 19 11	19 00 28	13♍25 46	20 27 22	9 18.6	9 23.5	24 49.6	22 56.8	13 20.1	21 26.7	2 52.9	18 43.2	24 13.8	19 19.3
11 Th	17 23 08	20 01 27	27 26 51	4♎24 08	9 17.6	10 00.3	26 04.6	23 38.0	13 41.7	21 18.5	2 53.1	18 41.0	24 13.0	19 20.4
12 F	17 27 04	21 02 27	11♎19 09	18 11 50	9 14.5	10 29.3	27 19.5	24 19.1	14 03.1	21 10.3	2R 53.2	18 38.8	24 12.2	19 21.4
13 Sa	17 31 01	22 03 29	25 02 04	1♏49 46	9 09.2	10 49.9	28 34.5	25 00.3	14 24.4	21 02.1	2 53.3	18 36.6	24 11.5	19 22.5
14 Su	17 34 57	23 04 31	8♏34 48	15 17 01	9 02.1	11R 01.0	29 49.5	25 41.5	14 45.5	20 54.0	2 53.2	18 34.3	24 10.8	19 23.6
15 M	17 38 54	24 05 34	21 56 17	28 32 25	8 53.9	11 01.9	1♐04.5	26 22.8	15 06.5	20 45.8	2 53.0	18 32.1	24 10.1	19 24.7
16 Tu	17 42 51	25 06 38	5♐05 17	11♐34 44	8 45.6	10 51.9	2 19.5	27 04.1	15 27.3	20 37.7	2 52.6	18 29.8	24 09.5	19 25.9
17 W	17 46 47	26 07 43	18 00 41	24 23 03	8 38.1	10 30.5	3 34.6	27 45.4	15 47.9	20 29.6	2 52.2	18 27.4	24 08.9	19 27.0
18 Th	17 50 44	27 08 49	0♑41 48	6♑56 57	8 32.2	9 57.3	4 49.6	28 26.8	16 08.4	20 21.5	2 51.7	18 25.1	24 08.3	19 28.2
19 F	17 54 40	28 09 55	13 08 36	19 16 53	8 28.1	9 12.7	6 04.7	29 08.2	16 28.8	20 13.4	2 51.0	18 22.7	24 07.8	19 29.4
20 Sa	17 58 37	29 11 01	25 22 00	1♒24 12	8D 26.2	8 17.2	7 19.8	29 49.6	16 48.9	20 05.4	2 50.2	18 20.3	24 07.3	19 30.7
21 Su	18 02 33	0♑12 08	7♒23 50	13 21 16	8 26.0	7 12.0	8 34.9	0♐31.0	17 08.9	19 57.5	2 49.3	18 17.9	24 06.8	19 31.9
22 M	18 06 30	1 13 15	19 16 55	25 11 18	8 27.2	5 58.9	9 50.0	1 12.5	17 28.7	19 49.6	2 48.4	18 15.5	24 06.4	19 33.2
23 Tu	18 10 26	2 14 23	1♓04 56	6♓58 23	8 29.0	4 40.1	11 05.1	1 54.0	17 48.3	19 41.8	2 47.3	18 13.0	24 06.0	19 34.5
24 W	18 14 23	3 15 30	12 52 15	18 47 10	8 30.7	3 18.1	12 20.3	2 35.6	18 07.8	19 34.0	2 46.0	18 10.5	24 05.6	19 35.8
25 Th	18 18 20	4 16 38	24 43 45	0♈42 40	8R 31.6	1 55.8	13 35.4	3 17.2	18 27.0	19 26.4	2 44.7	18 08.0	24 05.3	19 37.1
26 F	18 22 16	5 17 46	6♈44 34	12 50 05	8 31.4	0 35.7	14 50.5	3 58.8	18 46.1	19 18.8	2 43.3	18 05.5	24 05.0	19 38.4
27 Sa	18 26 13	6 18 53	18 59 50	25 14 22	8 29.6	29♐20.5	16 05.7	4 40.4	19 05.0	19 11.3	2 41.8	18 03.0	24 04.7	19 39.8
28 Su	18 30 09	7 20 01	1♉34 14	7♉59 50	8 26.5	28 12.3	17 20.8	5 22.1	19 23.7	19 03.9	2 40.1	18 00.5	24 04.5	19 41.2
29 M	18 34 06	8 21 09	14 31 34	21 09 39	8 22.3	27 12.6	18 36.0	6 03.8	19 42.2	18 56.5	2 38.4	17 57.9	24 04.3	19 42.6
30 Tu	18 38 02	9 22 17	27 54 13	4♊45 14	8 17.7	26 22.6	19 51.2	6 45.5	20 00.4	18 49.3	2 36.5	17 55.4	24 04.1	19 44.0
31 W	18 41 59	10 23 25	11♊42 34	18 45 51	8 13.1	25 42.9	21 06.4	7 27.3	20 18.5	18 42.2	2 34.6	17 52.8	24 04.0	19 45.4

Astro Data

	Dy Hr Mn
♇ D	1 7:55
☽ 0N	1 12:17
♃⚹♆	13 1:58
☽ 0S	14 15:47
♅⚻♇	27 12:17
☽ 0N	28 22:07
☽ 0S	11 22:32
♄ R	13 3:00
☿ R	15 2:05
♃△♇	24 7:24
☽ 0N	26 7:55

Planet Ingress

	Dy Hr Mn
♂ ♏	6 13:04
⚳ ♎	6 13:49
☿ ♐	10 13:21
♀ ♏	20 12:58
☉ ♐	21 17:46
☿ ♑	1 9:42
♀ ♐	14 15:22
♂ ♐	20 18:02
☉ ♑	21 7:14
☿ ♐R	26 23:10

Last Aspect / ☽ Ingress (November)

Last Aspect Dy Hr Mn		☽ Ingress Dy Hr Mn
2 21:59	♂ ☍	♉ 3 2:27
4 16:34	☿ ☍	♊ 5 8:41
7 4:55	♃ ☌	♋ 7 13:06
9 14:08	☿ △	♌ 9 16:39
11 11:10	♃ ⚹	♍ 11 19:50
13 13:51	♃ □	♎ 13 22:51
15 17:05	♆ ☍	♏ 16 2:13
18 0:16	☉ ☌	♐ 18 7:01
20 4:13	♆ △	♑ 20 14:26
22 14:12	♆ □	♒ 23 1:05
25 2:39	♆ ⚹	♓ 25 13:52
27 16:24	☿ □	♈ 28 2:09
30 9:06	☿ △	♉ 30 11:33

Last Aspect / ☽ Ingress (December)

Last Aspect Dy Hr Mn		☽ Ingress Dy Hr Mn
1 22:23	♇ □	♊ 2 17:26
4 11:08	♆ ⚹	♋ 4 20:43
6 13:22	♆ □	♌ 6 22:54
8 15:32	♆ △	♍ 9 1:13
10 20:14	♀ ⚹	♎ 11 4:24
12 22:32	♆ ☍	♏ 13 8:46
15 7:51	♂ ☌	♐ 15 14:40
17 15:36	☉ ☌	♑ 17 22:40
20 8:40	♂ ⚹	♒ 20 9:12
22 9:48	♆ ⚹	♓ 22 21:48
24 13:34	♃ □	♈ 25 10:35
27 19:08	☿ △	♉ 27 21:02
29 9:23	♇ □	♊ 30 3:42

☽ Phases & Eclipses

Dy Hr Mn	
4 0:45	○ 12♉11
11 1:30	☾ 19♌14
18 0:16	● 26♏14
25 22:29	☽ 4♓15
3 14:10	○ 12♊00
10 9:20	☾ 18♍54
17 15:36	● 26♐17
25 19:46	☽ 4♈36

Astro Data

1 November 2036
Julian Day # 49979
SVP 4♓44'57"
GC 27♐21.2 ⚴ 19♌34.9
Eris 27♈36.5R ⚵ 29♌37.2
⚷ 18♊06.3R ⚶ 3♑21.1
☽ Mean ☊ 12♌35.9

1 December 2036
Julian Day # 50009
SVP 4♓44'53"
GC 27♐21.3 ⚴ 0♍14.8
Eris 27♈20.6R ⚵ 8♍58.2
⚷ 16♊32.8R ⚶ 18♑03.3
☽ Mean ☊ 11♌00.6

LONGITUDE — January 2037

Day	Sid.Time	☉	0 hr ☽	Noon☽	True☊	☿	♀	♂	⚳	♃	♄	♅	♆	♇
1 Th	18 45 55	11♑24 33	25♊54 39	3♋08 19	8♌09.4	25♐13.7	22♐21.5	8♐09.1	20♎36.4	18♊35.3	2♍32.5	17♋50.2	24♈03.9	19♒46.9
2 F	18 49 52	12 25 40	10♋26 08	17 47 13	8R06.8	24R54.7	23 36.7	8 50.9	20 54.1	18R28.4	2R30.4	17R47.7	24R03.8	19 48.4
3 Sa	18 53 49	13 26 48	25 10 41	2♌35 33	8D05.7	24D45.7	24 51.9	9 32.8	21 11.5	18 21.7	2 28.1	17 45.1	24D03.8	19 49.9
4 Su	18 57 45	14 27 56	10♌00 51	17 25 40	8 05.8	24 46.1	26 07.1	10 14.7	21 28.8	18 15.0	2 25.8	17 42.5	24 03.8	19 51.3
5 M	19 01 42	15 29 04	24 49 09	2♍10 29	8 06.9	24 55.1	27 22.4	10 56.7	21 45.8	18 08.6	2 23.3	17 39.9	24 03.8	19 52.9
6 Tu	19 05 38	16 30 13	9♍29 01	16 44 12	8 08.3	25 12.2	28 37.6	11 38.6	22 02.6	18 02.2	2 20.8	17 37.3	24 03.9	19 54.4
7 W	19 09 35	17 31 21	23 55 34	1♎02 48	8 09.6	25 36.6	29 52.8	12 20.7	22 19.1	17 56.0	2 18.1	17 34.7	24 04.0	19 55.9
8 Th	19 13 31	18 32 29	8♎05 42	15 04 07	8R10.3	26 07.5	1♑08.1	13 02.7	22 35.5	17 49.9	2 15.4	17 32.1	24 04.2	19 57.5
9 F	19 17 28	19 33 38	21 58 01	28 47 26	8 10.0	26 44.4	2 23.3	13 44.8	22 51.5	17 44.0	2 12.5	17 29.5	24 04.4	19 59.0
10 Sa	19 21 24	20 34 47	5♏32 27	12♏13 11	8 08.9	27 26.7	3 38.5	14 26.9	23 07.4	17 38.3	2 09.6	17 26.9	24 04.6	20 00.6
11 Su	19 25 21	21 35 56	18 49 46	25 22 24	8 07.1	28 13.7	4 53.8	15 09.1	23 23.0	17 32.6	2 06.6	17 24.3	24 04.8	20 02.2
12 M	19 29 18	22 37 04	1♐51 13	8♐16 24	8 04.8	29 05.1	6 09.1	15 51.2	23 38.3	17 27.2	2 03.5	17 21.7	24 05.1	20 03.8
13 Tu	19 33 14	23 38 13	14 38 09	20 56 37	8 02.5	0♑00.3	7 24.3	16 33.5	23 53.4	17 21.9	2 00.3	17 19.1	24 05.4	20 05.5
14 W	19 37 11	24 39 21	27 11 59	3♑24 24	8 00.4	0 58.9	8 39.6	17 15.7	24 08.2	17 16.8	1 57.0	17 16.5	24 05.8	20 07.1
15 Th	19 41 07	25 40 30	9♑34 02	15 41 03	7 58.9	2 00.5	9 54.9	17 58.0	24 22.8	17 11.9	1 53.7	17 14.0	24 06.2	20 08.7
16 F	19 45 04	26 41 37	21 45 39	27 47 59	7D58.0	3 05.0	11 10.1	18 40.3	24 37.0	17 07.1	1 50.2	17 11.4	24 06.6	20 10.4
17 Sa	19 49 00	27 42 44	3♒48 17	9♒46 45	7 57.8	4 12.0	12 25.4	19 22.7	24 51.1	17 02.5	1 46.7	17 08.8	24 07.1	20 12.0
18 Su	19 52 57	28 43 51	15 43 39	21 39 13	7 58.1	5 21.2	13 40.7	20 05.0	25 04.8	16 58.1	1 43.1	17 06.3	24 07.6	20 13.7
19 M	19 56 53	29 44 57	27 33 48	3♓27 42	7 58.8	6 32.4	14 55.9	20 47.5	25 18.2	16 53.9	1 39.4	17 03.8	24 08.1	20 15.4
20 Tu	20 00 50	0♒46 02	9♓21 17	15 14 58	7 59.7	7 45.5	16 11.2	21 29.9	25 31.4	16 49.8	1 35.6	17 01.3	24 08.7	20 17.1
21 W	20 04 47	1 47 06	21 09 11	27 04 23	8 00.5	9 00.3	17 26.4	22 12.4	25 44.2	16 46.0	1 31.8	16 58.8	24 09.3	20 18.8
22 Th	20 08 43	2 48 09	3♈01 05	8♈59 47	8 01.1	10 16.6	18 41.7	22 54.9	25 56.8	16 42.3	1 27.9	16 56.3	24 09.9	20 20.5
23 F	20 12 40	3 49 12	15 01 03	21 05 26	8 01.4	11 34.3	19 56.9	23 37.4	26 09.0	16 38.9	1 24.0	16 53.8	24 10.6	20 22.2
24 Sa	20 16 36	4 50 13	27 13 30	3♉25 48	8R01.6	12 53.4	21 12.2	24 19.9	26 21.0	16 35.6	1 19.9	16 51.4	24 11.3	20 23.9
25 Su	20 20 33	5 51 13	9♉42 55	16 05 21	8 01.5	14 13.7	22 27.4	25 02.5	26 32.6	16 32.5	1 15.8	16 49.0	24 12.0	20 25.7
26 M	20 24 29	6 52 13	22 33 34	29 08 01	8 01.4	15 35.1	23 42.7	25 45.1	26 44.0	16 29.6	1 11.7	16 46.5	24 12.8	20 27.4
27 Tu	20 28 26	7 53 11	5♊49 00	12♊36 47	8D01.4	16 57.7	24 57.9	26 27.8	26 55.0	16 26.9	1 07.5	16 44.2	24 13.6	20 29.1
28 W	20 32 22	8 54 08	19 31 27	26 32 58	8 01.4	18 21.2	26 13.1	27 10.5	27 05.7	16 24.5	1 03.2	16 41.8	24 14.4	20 30.9
29 Th	20 36 19	9 55 04	3♋41 09	10♋55 38	8 01.6	19 45.8	27 28.3	27 53.2	27 16.0	16 22.2	0 58.9	16 39.5	24 15.3	20 32.6
30 F	20 40 16	10 55 59	18 15 52	25 41 08	8R01.7	21 11.2	28 43.6	28 35.9	27 26.0	16 20.1	0 54.5	16 37.2	24 16.2	20 34.4
31 Sa	20 44 12	11 56 53	3♌10 34	10♌43 09	8 01.8	22 37.6	29 58.8	29 18.7	27 35.7	16 18.2	0 50.1	16 34.9	24 17.1	20 36.2

LONGITUDE — February 2037

Day	Sid.Time	☉	0 hr ☽	Noon☽	True☊	☿	♀	♂	⚳	♃	♄	♅	♆	♇
1 Su	20 48 09	12♒57 45	18♌17 44	25♌53 09	8♌01.6	24♑04.8	1♒14.0	0♑01.5	27♎45.1	16♊16.5	0♍45.6	16♋32.6	24♈18.1	20♒37.9
2 M	20 52 05	13 58 37	3♍28 11	11♍01 39	8R01.2	25 32.9	2 29.2	0 44.4	27 54.1	16R15.0	0R41.1	16R30.4	24 19.1	20 39.7
3 Tu	20 56 02	14 59 28	18 32 26	25 59 32	8 00.4	27 01.8	3 44.4	1 27.2	28 02.8	16 13.7	0 36.6	16 28.2	24 20.1	20 41.5
4 W	20 59 58	16 00 17	3♎22 05	10♎39 23	7 59.5	28 31.6	4 59.6	2 10.1	28 11.1	16 12.7	0 32.0	16 26.0	24 21.2	20 43.2
5 Th	21 03 55	17 01 06	17 50 55	24 56 19	7 58.7	0♒02.1	6 14.8	2 53.1	28 19.0	16 11.8	0 27.4	16 23.9	24 22.3	20 45.0
6 F	21 07 51	18 01 54	1♏55 23	8♏48 04	7D58.1	1 33.4	7 30.0	3 36.0	28 26.6	16 11.1	0 22.7	16 21.8	24 23.4	20 46.8
7 Sa	21 11 48	19 02 42	15 34 28	22 14 46	7 58.0	3 05.6	8 45.1	4 19.0	28 33.8	16 10.6	0 18.0	16 19.7	24 24.5	20 48.6
8 Su	21 15 45	20 03 28	28 49 16	5♐18 17	7 58.4	4 38.5	10 00.3	5 02.1	28 40.6	16D10.4	0 13.3	16 17.6	24 25.7	20 50.4
9 M	21 19 41	21 04 13	11♐42 14	18 01 33	7 59.4	6 12.3	11 15.5	5 45.2	28 47.1	16 10.3	0 08.5	16 15.6	24 26.9	20 52.1
10 Tu	21 23 38	22 04 58	24 16 38	0♑27 58	8 00.6	7 46.8	12 30.7	6 28.3	28 53.2	16 10.4	0 03.8	16 13.6	24 28.2	20 53.9
11 W	21 27 34	23 05 41	6♑35 57	12 41 00	8 02.0	9 22.2	13 45.9	7 11.4	28 58.9	16 10.8	29♌59.0	16 11.7	24 29.4	20 55.7
12 Th	21 31 31	24 06 23	18 43 33	24 43 57	8 03.1	10 58.4	15 01.0	7 54.5	29 04.1	16 11.3	29 54.1	16 09.8	24 30.7	20 57.5
13 F	21 35 27	25 07 03	0♒42 33	6♒39 40	8R03.6	12 35.4	16 16.2	8 37.7	29 09.0	16 12.1	29 49.3	16 07.9	24 32.1	20 59.3
14 Sa	21 39 24	26 07 43	12 35 39	18 30 44	8 03.2	14 13.2	17 31.3	9 20.9	29 13.5	16 13.0	29 44.5	16 06.1	24 33.4	21 01.0
15 Su	21 43 20	27 08 21	24 25 12	0♓19 20	8 01.8	15 51.9	18 46.5	10 04.2	29 17.6	16 14.2	29 39.6	16 04.3	24 34.8	21 02.8
16 M	21 47 17	28 08 57	6♓13 21	12 07 31	7 59.4	17 31.5	20 01.6	10 47.5	29 21.3	16 15.5	29 34.8	16 02.6	24 36.2	21 04.6
17 Tu	21 51 14	29 09 32	18 02 05	23 57 18	7 56.1	19 12.0	21 16.7	11 30.7	29 24.6	16 17.1	29 29.9	16 00.9	24 37.7	21 06.3
18 W	21 55 10	0♓10 05	29 53 26	5♈50 49	7 52.3	20 53.3	22 31.8	12 14.1	29 27.4	16 18.8	29 25.1	15 59.2	24 39.1	21 08.1
19 Th	21 59 07	1 10 37	11♈49 43	17 50 29	7 48.3	22 35.5	23 47.0	12 57.4	29 29.9	16 20.8	29 20.2	15 57.6	24 40.6	21 09.9
20 F	22 03 03	2 11 07	23 53 30	29 59 08	7 44.7	24 18.7	25 02.0	13 40.8	29 31.9	16 22.9	29 15.3	15 56.0	24 42.1	21 11.6
21 Sa	22 07 00	3 11 35	6♉07 47	12♉19 55	7 42.0	26 02.8	26 17.1	14 24.2	29 33.5	16 25.2	29 10.5	15 54.5	24 43.7	21 13.4
22 Su	22 10 56	4 12 01	18 35 58	24 56 23	7D40.4	27 47.8	27 32.2	15 07.6	29 34.7	16 27.8	29 05.7	15 53.0	24 45.2	21 15.1
23 M	22 14 53	5 12 25	1♊21 37	7♊52 08	7 40.0	29 33.8	28 47.2	15 51.1	29 35.4	16 30.5	29 00.8	15 51.5	24 46.8	21 16.9
24 Tu	22 18 49	6 12 48	14 28 20	21 10 34	7 40.8	1♓20.8	0♓02.3	16 34.5	29R35.8	16 33.4	28 56.0	15 50.1	24 48.5	21 18.6
25 W	22 22 46	7 13 08	27 59 09	4♋54 17	7 42.3	3 08.7	1 17.3	17 18.0	29 35.7	16 36.5	28 51.3	15 48.8	24 50.1	21 20.3
26 Th	22 26 43	8 13 27	11♋56 03	19 04 24	7 43.8	4 57.6	2 32.3	18 01.6	29 35.2	16 39.8	28 46.5	15 47.5	24 51.8	21 22.0
27 F	22 30 39	9 13 43	26 19 09	3♌39 53	7R44.7	6 47.5	3 47.3	18 45.1	29 34.3	16 43.3	28 41.8	15 46.2	24 53.5	21 23.8
28 Sa	22 34 36	10 13 58	11♌06 03	18 36 51	7 44.4	8 38.3	5 02.3	19 28.7	29 32.9	16 47.0	28 37.0	15 45.0	24 55.2	21 25.5

Astro Data

	Dy Hr Mn
♆ D	3 17:46
☿ D	3 23:00
☽ 0S	8 4:49
♃⚺♅	14 14:45
☽ 0N	22 15:59
☽ 0S	4 12:33
♃ D	9 7:43
♃⚺♅	11 21:19
☽ 0N	18 22:06
⚳ R	24 19:12

Planet Ingress

		Dy Hr Mn
♀	♑	7 14:17
☿	♑	13 11:54
☉	♒	19 17:55
♀	♒	31 12:24
♂	♑	1 11:09
☿	♒	5 11:27
♄	♌R	11 6:47
☉	♓	18 8:00
☿	♓	23 17:53
♀	♓	24 11:16

Last Aspect / ☽ Ingress (January)

Last Aspect Dy Hr Mn		☽ Ingress	Dy Hr Mn
31 23:15	☿ ☍	♋	1 6:48
2 22:12	♆ □	♌	3 7:48
5 3:26	♀ △	♍	5 8:27
7 9:50	♀ □	♎	7 10:14
9 8:12	☿ ⚹	♏	9 14:08
11 4:29	☉ ⚹	♐	11 20:33
13 18:02	♆ △	♑	14 5:24
16 9:36	☉ ☌	♒	16 16:23
18 17:01	♆ ⚹	♓	19 4:57
21 1:31	♂ □	♈	21 17:55
23 18:03	♆ ☌	♉	24 5:23
26 1:04	♀ △	♊	26 13:34
28 13:07	♂ ☍	♋	28 17:49
30 17:20	♀ ☍	♌	30 18:55

Last Aspect / ☽ Ingress (February)

Last Aspect Dy Hr Mn		☽ Ingress	Dy Hr Mn
1 9:30	♆ △	♍	1 18:30
3 13:52	☿ △	♎	3 18:30
5 11:02	♆ ☍	♏	5 20:41
7 9:24	♇ □	♐	8 2:10
10 0:21	♆ △	♑	10 11:06
12 11:33	♆ □	♒	12 22:34
15 10:40	♄ ☍	♓	15 11:21
16 20:25	♃ □	♈	18 0:13
20 10:35	♄ △	♉	20 12:02
22 19:44	♄ □	♊	22 21:28
25 1:35	♄ ⚹	♋	25 3:31
26 21:37	♆ □	♌	27 6:02

☽ Phases & Eclipses

Dy Hr Mn		
2 2:36	○	12♋02
8 18:30	☾	18♎49
16 9:36	●	26♑35
16 9:48:57	●	P 0.705
24 14:56	☽	4♉58
31 14:05	○	12♌02
31 14:02	○	T 1.207
7 5:45	☾	18♏47
15 4:55	●	26♒50
23 6:42	☽	4♊59

Astro Data

1 January 2037
Julian Day # 50040
SVP 4♓44'47"
GC 27♐21.4 ⚴ 4♍03.5R
Eris 27♈11.4R ⚵ 13♍21.6
⚷ 14♊46.3R ⚶ 3♒49.0
☽ Mean ☊ 9♌22.2

1 February 2037
Julian Day # 50071
SVP 4♓44'42"
GC 27♐21.4 ⚴ 27♌55.7R
Eris 27♈12.4 ⚵ 10♍33.8R
⚷ 13♊36.4R ⚶ 19♒44.4
☽ Mean ☊ 7♌43.7

March 2037 LONGITUDE

Day	Sid.Time	☉	0 hr ☽	Noon ☽	True ☊	☿	♀	♂	⚳	♃	♄	♅	♆	♇
1 Su	22 38 32	11♓14 10	26♌11 20	3♍48 24	7♌42.4	10♓30.1	6♓17.3	20♑12.3	29♎31.1	16♊50.8	28♌32.4	15♋43.8	24♈56.9	21♒27.2
2 M	22 42 29	12 14 21	11♍26 47	19 05 11	7R38.8	12 22.8	7 32.2	20 55.9	29R 28.9	16 54.8	28R 27.7	15R 42.7	24 58.7	21 28.8
3 Tu	22 46 25	13 14 30	26 42 16	4♎16 41	7 33.8	14 16.3	8 47.2	21 39.6	29 26.2	16 59.0	28 23.1	15 41.7	25 00.5	21 30.5
4 W	22 50 22	14 14 37	11♎47 15	19 12 53	7 28.2	16 10.7	10 02.1	22 23.3	29 23.2	17 03.4	28 18.5	15 40.6	25 02.3	21 32.2
5 Th	22 54 18	15 14 43	26 32 40	3♏45 54	7 22.8	18 05.9	11 17.0	23 07.0	29 19.7	17 08.0	28 14.0	15 39.7	25 04.1	21 33.9
6 F	22 58 15	16 14 47	10♏52 07	17 51 02	7 18.3	20 01.7	12 31.9	23 50.7	29 15.8	17 12.7	28 09.5	15 38.7	25 05.9	21 35.5
7 Sa	23 02 12	17 14 50	24 42 33	1♐26 47	7 15.4	21 58.0	13 46.8	24 34.5	29 11.4	17 17.6	28 05.0	15 37.9	25 07.8	21 37.1
8 Su	23 06 08	18 14 51	8♐03 58	14 34 28	7D14.1	23 54.9	15 01.7	25 18.3	29 06.7	17 22.7	28 00.6	15 37.1	25 09.7	21 38.8
9 M	23 10 05	19 14 50	20 58 46	27 17 22	7 14.3	25 52.0	16 16.6	26 02.1	29 01.5	17 27.9	27 56.2	15 36.3	25 11.6	21 40.4
10 Tu	23 14 01	20 14 48	3♑30 51	9♑39 50	7 15.6	27 49.2	17 31.5	26 46.0	28 55.9	17 33.3	27 51.9	15 35.6	25 13.5	21 42.0
11 W	23 17 58	21 14 44	15 44 55	21 46 43	7 17.1	29 46.2	18 46.3	27 29.8	28 49.9	17 38.9	27 47.7	15 34.9	25 15.4	21 43.6
12 Th	23 21 54	22 14 39	27 45 49	3♒42 47	7R18.1	1♈42.9	20 01.2	28 13.7	28 43.5	17 44.7	27 43.4	15 34.3	25 17.4	21 45.2
13 F	23 25 51	23 14 31	9♒38 09	15 32 24	7 17.7	3 39.0	21 16.0	28 57.6	28 36.7	17 50.6	27 39.3	15 33.8	25 19.4	21 46.7
14 Sa	23 29 47	24 14 22	21 26 00	27 19 22	7 15.5	5 34.0	22 30.8	29 41.6	28 29.5	17 56.7	27 35.2	15 33.3	25 21.4	21 48.3
15 Su	23 33 44	25 14 11	3♓12 52	9♓06 49	7 10.9	7 27.6	23 45.6	0♒25.5	28 21.9	18 02.9	27 31.2	15 32.8	25 23.4	21 49.8
16 M	23 37 41	26 13 58	15 01 30	20 57 12	7 04.1	9 19.5	25 00.4	1 09.5	28 13.9	18 09.3	27 27.2	15 32.4	25 25.4	21 51.4
17 Tu	23 41 37	27 13 44	26 54 08	2♈52 28	6 55.4	11 09.3	26 15.2	1 53.5	28 05.5	18 15.8	27 23.3	15 32.1	25 27.4	21 52.9
18 W	23 45 34	28 13 27	8♈52 25	14 54 07	6 45.4	12 56.4	27 29.9	2 37.5	27 56.8	18 22.5	27 19.5	15 31.8	25 29.5	21 54.4
19 Th	23 49 30	29 13 08	20 57 45	27 03 28	6 35.2	14 40.4	28 44.7	3 21.5	27 47.7	18 29.4	27 15.8	15 31.5	25 31.5	21 55.9
20 F	23 53 27	0♈12 47	3♉11 27	9♉21 52	6 25.6	16 20.8	29 59.4	4 05.6	27 38.3	18 36.4	27 12.1	15 31.3	25 33.6	21 57.3
21 Sa	23 57 23	1 12 24	15 34 57	21 50 54	6 17.5	17 57.3	1♈14.1	4 49.6	27 28.6	18 43.6	27 08.5	15 31.2	25 35.7	21 58.8
22 Su	0 01 20	2 11 58	28 09 59	4♊32 30	6 11.6	19 29.2	2 28.8	5 33.7	27 18.5	18 50.9	27 04.9	15D31.1	25 37.8	22 00.2
23 M	0 05 16	3 11 31	10♊58 45	17 29 02	6 08.2	20 56.3	3 43.5	6 17.8	27 08.1	18 58.3	27 01.5	15 31.1	25 39.9	22 01.7
24 Tu	0 09 13	4 11 01	24 03 42	0♋43 05	6D06.9	22 18.0	4 58.1	7 01.9	26 57.4	19 05.9	26 58.1	15 31.2	25 42.1	22 03.1
25 W	0 13 09	5 10 29	7♋27 29	14 17 40	6 07.1	23 34.1	6 12.7	7 46.0	26 46.4	19 13.6	26 54.8	15 31.2	25 44.2	22 04.4
26 Th	0 17 06	6 09 54	21 12 23	28 13 13	6R07.8	24 44.0	7 27.3	8 30.1	26 35.1	19 21.5	26 51.6	15 31.4	25 46.4	22 05.8
27 F	0 21 03	7 09 17	5♌19 44	12♌31 48	6 07.9	25 47.6	8 41.9	9 14.3	26 23.6	19 29.5	26 48.5	15 31.6	25 48.5	22 07.2
28 Sa	0 24 59	8 08 38	19 49 09	27 11 22	6 06.2	26 44.6	9 56.5	9 58.5	26 11.9	19 37.6	26 45.5	15 31.8	25 50.7	22 08.5
29 Su	0 28 56	9 07 57	4♍37 48	12♍07 40	6 02.0	27 34.8	11 11.0	10 42.6	25 59.8	19 45.9	26 42.5	15 32.1	25 52.9	22 09.8
30 M	0 32 52	10 07 13	19 39 59	27 13 37	5 55.3	28 17.9	12 25.5	11 26.8	25 47.6	19 54.3	26 39.7	15 32.5	25 55.1	22 11.1
31 Tu	0 36 49	11 06 27	4♎47 20	12♎19 53	5 46.5	28 53.8	13 40.0	12 11.0	25 35.2	20 02.8	26 36.9	15 32.9	25 57.3	22 12.4

April 2037 LONGITUDE

Day	Sid.Time	☉	0 hr ☽	Noon ☽	True ☊	☿	♀	♂	⚳	♃	♄	♅	♆	♇
1 W	0 40 45	12♈05 39	19♎49 59	27♎16 25	5♌36.4	29♈22.5	14♈54.5	12♒55.3	25♎22.5	20♊11.4	26♌34.2	15♋33.4	25♈59.5	22♒13.7
2 Th	0 44 42	13 04 49	4♏38 05	11♏54 04	5R26.2	29 44.0	16 09.0	13 39.5	25R09.7	20 20.2	26R31.6	15 33.9	26 01.7	22 14.9
3 F	0 48 38	14 03 58	19 03 38	26 06 14	5 17.3	29 58.2	17 23.4	14 23.8	24 56.8	20 29.1	26 29.2	15 34.5	26 03.9	22 16.1
4 Sa	0 52 35	15 03 04	3♐01 34	9♐49 31	5 10.3	0♉05.2	18 37.9	15 08.0	24 43.6	20 38.1	26 26.8	15 35.1	26 06.2	22 17.3
5 Su	0 56 32	16 02 09	16 30 09	23 03 42	5 05.8	0R05.3	19 52.3	15 52.3	24 30.4	20 47.3	26 24.5	15 35.8	26 08.4	22 18.5
6 M	1 00 28	17 01 12	29 30 33	5♑51 10	5D03.5	29♈58.5	21 06.7	16 36.6	24 17.0	20 56.5	26 22.3	15 36.5	26 10.6	22 19.7
7 Tu	1 04 25	18 00 14	12♑06 09	18 16 05	5 03.0	29 45.4	22 21.1	17 20.9	24 03.5	21 05.9	26 20.1	15 37.3	26 12.9	22 20.8
8 W	1 08 21	18 59 13	24 21 39	0♒23 32	5R03.2	29 26.1	23 35.5	18 05.3	23 50.0	21 15.4	26 18.1	15 38.1	26 15.1	22 21.9
9 Th	1 12 18	19 58 11	6♒22 25	12 18 59	5 03.1	29 01.4	24 49.8	18 49.6	23 36.4	21 24.9	26 16.2	15 39.0	26 17.4	22 23.0
10 F	1 16 14	20 57 07	18 13 52	24 07 43	5 01.5	28 31.6	26 04.1	19 33.9	23 22.7	21 34.6	26 14.4	15 39.9	26 19.6	22 24.1
11 Sa	1 20 11	21 56 01	0♓01 06	5♓54 35	4 57.7	27 57.4	27 18.4	20 18.3	23 09.0	21 44.5	26 12.7	15 40.9	26 21.9	22 25.2
12 Su	1 24 07	22 54 53	11 48 39	17 43 45	4 51.1	27 19.7	28 32.7	21 02.6	22 55.3	21 54.4	26 11.1	15 42.0	26 24.2	22 26.2
13 M	1 28 04	23 53 44	23 40 15	29 38 31	4 41.8	26 39.1	29 47.0	21 47.0	22 41.6	22 04.4	26 09.6	15 43.1	26 26.4	22 27.2
14 Tu	1 32 01	24 52 32	5♈38 49	11♈41 21	4 30.0	25 56.4	1♉01.3	22 31.3	22 27.9	22 14.5	26 08.2	15 44.2	26 28.7	22 28.2
15 W	1 35 57	25 51 19	17 46 18	23 53 49	4 16.7	25 12.5	2 15.5	23 15.7	22 14.2	22 24.8	26 06.9	15 45.4	26 31.0	22 29.2
16 Th	1 39 54	26 50 04	0♉03 57	6♉16 47	4 02.9	24 28.3	3 29.7	24 00.1	22 00.7	22 35.1	26 05.7	15 46.6	26 33.2	22 30.1
17 F	1 43 50	27 48 46	12 32 20	18 50 37	3 49.8	23 44.5	4 44.0	24 44.4	21 47.2	22 45.5	26 04.6	15 47.9	26 35.5	22 31.0
18 Sa	1 47 47	28 47 27	25 11 38	1♊35 26	3 38.6	23 02.0	5 58.1	25 28.8	21 33.7	22 56.0	26 03.6	15 49.3	26 37.8	22 31.9
19 Su	1 51 43	29 46 06	8♊02 03	14 31 30	3 30.1	22 21.5	7 12.3	26 13.2	21 20.5	23 06.7	26 02.8	15 50.7	26 40.0	22 32.8
20 M	1 55 40	0♉44 43	21 03 55	27 39 22	3 24.5	21 43.5	8 26.4	26 57.5	21 07.3	23 17.4	26 02.0	15 52.1	26 42.3	22 33.6
21 Tu	1 59 36	1 43 17	4♋18 00	10♋59 59	3 21.6	21 08.8	9 40.6	27 41.9	20 54.3	23 28.2	26 01.3	15 53.6	26 44.6	22 34.5
22 W	2 03 33	2 41 49	17 45 29	24 34 39	3 20.7	20 37.8	10 54.7	28 26.2	20 41.4	23 39.1	26 00.8	15 55.2	26 46.8	22 35.3
23 Th	2 07 30	3 40 19	1♌27 41	8♌24 40	3 20.6	20 10.8	12 08.7	29 10.6	20 28.7	23 50.1	26 00.3	15 56.8	26 49.1	22 36.1
24 F	2 11 26	4 38 47	15 25 41	22 30 45	3 20.1	19 48.3	13 22.8	29 54.9	20 16.3	24 01.1	26 00.0	15 58.4	26 51.3	22 36.8
25 Sa	2 15 23	5 37 13	29 39 43	6♍52 24	3 17.8	19 30.4	14 36.8	0♓39.2	20 04.0	24 12.3	25 59.8	16 00.1	26 53.6	22 37.5
26 Su	2 19 19	6 35 36	14♍08 25	21 27 17	3 13.1	19 17.3	15 50.8	1 23.6	19 51.9	24 23.5	25D59.6	16 01.8	26 55.8	22 38.2
27 M	2 23 16	7 33 58	28 48 20	6♎10 49	3 05.6	19 09.1	17 04.8	2 07.9	19 40.1	24 34.8	25 59.6	16 03.6	26 58.1	22 38.9
28 Tu	2 27 12	8 32 17	13♎33 49	20 56 23	2 55.8	19D05.8	18 18.8	2 52.2	19 28.5	24 46.2	25 59.7	16 05.5	27 00.3	22 39.6
29 W	2 31 09	9 30 35	28 17 28	5♏36 03	2 44.5	19 07.4	19 32.7	3 36.5	19 17.2	24 57.7	25 59.9	16 07.3	27 02.5	22 40.2
30 Th	2 35 05	10 28 50	12♏51 09	20 01 54	2 33.0	19 13.9	20 46.6	4 20.8	19 06.1	25 09.2	26 00.2	16 09.2	27 04.7	22 40.8

Astro Data	Planet Ingress	Last Aspect	☽ Ingress	Last Aspect	☽ Ingress	☽ Phases & Eclipses
Dy Hr Mn	Dy Hr Mn	Dy Hr Mn	Dy Hr Mn	Dy Hr Mn	Dy Hr Mn	Dy Hr Mn
☽0S 3 22:24	☿ ♈ 11 14:49	1 3:45 ♄ ☌	♍ 1 6:01	1 15:31 ☿ ☍	♏ 1 16:26	2 0:29 ○ 11♍45
☿0N 12 6:45	♂ ♒ 14 22:04	2 15:03 ♂ △	♎ 3 5:13	3 12:39 ♄ □	♐ 3 18:44	8 19:26 ☾ 18♐33
☽0N 18 3:34	☉ ♈ 20 6:51	5 2:50 ♄ ⚹	♏ 5 5:43	5 18:11 ♄ △	♑ 6 0:55	16 23:37 ● 26♓43
☉0N 20 6:52	♀ ♈ 20 12:12	7 6:01 ♄ □	♐ 7 9:24	8 10:09 ☿ □	♒ 8 11:13	24 18:41 ☽ 4♋28
♀0N 23 1:13		9 13:14 ♄ △	♑ 9 17:12	10 20:34 ☿ ⚹	♓ 10 23:58	31 9:55 ○ 11♎01
♅D 23 8:27	☿ ♉ 3 16:25	12 0:13 ♂ ☌	♒ 12 4:30	12 20:34 ♃ □	♈ 13 12:43	
☽0S 31 9:19	☿ ♈R 6 8:18	14 12:32 ♄ ☍	♓ 14 17:27	15 17:07 ♆ ☌	♉ 15 23:52	7 11:26 ☾ 17♑59
	♀ ♉ 13 16:12	16 23:37 ☉ ☌	♈ 17 6:14	18 1:39 ♄ □	♊ 18 9:01	15 16:09 ● 26♈01
☿R 5 0:05	☉ ♉ 19 17:41	19 12:24 ♄ △	♉ 19 17:46	20 10:40 ♂ △	♋ 20 16:15	23 3:13 ☽ 3♌19
♄△♆ 9 5:16	♂ ♓ 24 14:46	21 22:01 ♄ □	♊ 22 3:28	22 15:52 ♆ □	♌ 22 21:28	29 18:55 ○ 9♏47
☽0N 14 9:57		24 5:17 ♄ ⚹	♋ 24 10:43	24 19:19 ♆ △	♍ 25 0:34	
♃△♇ 15 23:18		26 7:49 ♆ □	♌ 26 15:01	26 16:52 ♃ □	♎ 27 1:57	
♄D 27 4:58		28 11:18 ♄ ☌	♍ 28 16:33	28 21:55 ♆ ☍	♏ 29 2:48	
☽0S 27 19:30		30 0:16 ♃ □	♎ 30 16:24			
☿D 28 15:57						

Astro Data

1 March 2037
Julian Day # 50099
SVP 4♓44'39"
GC 27♐21.5 ⚴ 19♌04.7R
Eris 27♈21.9 ⚵ 3♍44.4R
⚷ 13♊29.9 ⚶ 3♓58.4
☽ Mean ☊ 6♌14.7

1 April 2037
Julian Day # 50130
SVP 4♓44'37"
GC 27♐21.6 ⚴ 15♌50.8
Eris 27♈39.4 ⚵ 28♌27.6R
⚷ 14♊29.7 ⚶ 19♓16.8
☽ Mean ☊ 4♌36.2

LONGITUDE — May 2037

Day	Sid.Time	☉	0 hr ☽	Noon ☽	True ☊	☿	♀	♂	⚳	♃	♄	♅	♆	♇
1 F	2 39 02	11♉27 04	27♏07 32	4♐07 24	2♌22.7	19♈25.2	22♉00.5	5♓05.1	18♎55.4	25♊20.8	26♌00.6	16♋11.2	27♈06.9	22♒41.4
2 Sa	2 42 58	12 25 17	11♐01 06	17 48 20	2R 14.3	19 41.2	23 14.4	5 49.4	18R 44.9	25 32.5	26 01.1	16 13.2	27 09.2	22 41.9
3 Su	2 46 55	13 23 28	24 29 00	1♑03 10	2 08.6	20 01.8	24 28.3	6 33.7	18 34.7	25 44.3	26 01.7	16 15.3	27 11.4	22 42.5
4 M	2 50 52	14 21 37	7♑31 03	13 52 58	2 05.3	20 26.7	25 42.1	7 18.0	18 24.8	25 56.1	26 02.4	16 17.4	27 13.5	22 43.0
5 Tu	2 54 48	15 19 45	20 09 21	26 20 44	2D 04.1	20 55.9	26 55.9	8 02.3	18 15.2	26 08.0	26 03.3	16 19.5	27 15.7	22 43.5
6 W	2 58 45	16 17 52	2♒27 43	8♒30 54	2R 04.1	21 29.2	28 09.7	8 46.5	18 06.0	26 20.0	26 04.2	16 21.7	27 17.9	22 43.9
7 Th	3 02 41	17 15 57	14 30 58	20 28 37	2 04.2	22 06.5	29 23.5	9 30.8	17 57.1	26 32.0	26 05.2	16 23.9	27 20.1	22 44.3
8 F	3 06 38	18 14 01	26 24 30	2♓19 18	2 03.3	22 47.6	0♊37.3	10 15.0	17 48.6	26 44.1	26 06.4	16 26.1	27 22.2	22 44.7
9 Sa	3 10 34	19 12 03	8♓13 41	14 08 16	2 00.6	23 32.3	1 51.0	10 59.2	17 40.4	26 56.2	26 07.6	16 28.4	27 24.4	22 45.1
10 Su	3 14 31	20 10 04	20 03 40	26 00 25	1 55.4	24 20.6	3 04.8	11 43.4	17 32.5	27 08.5	26 09.0	16 30.8	27 26.5	22 45.5
11 M	3 18 27	21 08 03	1♈59 01	7♈59 56	1 47.8	25 12.3	4 18.5	12 27.6	17 25.0	27 20.7	26 10.4	16 33.2	27 28.6	22 45.8
12 Tu	3 22 24	22 06 01	14 03 31	20 10 05	1 37.8	26 07.3	5 32.2	13 11.7	17 17.9	27 33.1	26 12.0	16 35.6	27 30.7	22 46.1
13 W	3 26 21	23 03 58	26 19 55	2♉33 10	1 26.4	27 05.4	6 45.9	13 55.9	17 11.2	27 45.5	26 13.7	16 38.0	27 32.8	22 46.4
14 Th	3 30 17	24 01 53	8♉49 57	15 10 19	1 14.5	28 06.5	7 59.5	14 40.0	17 04.9	27 57.9	26 15.4	16 40.5	27 34.9	22 46.6
15 F	3 34 14	24 59 47	21 34 15	28 01 40	1 03.2	29 10.6	9 13.2	15 24.0	16 58.9	28 10.5	26 17.3	16 43.1	27 37.0	22 46.8
16 Sa	3 38 10	25 57 40	4♊32 29	11♊06 33	0 53.5	0♉17.6	10 26.8	16 08.1	16 53.3	28 23.0	26 19.3	16 45.7	27 39.0	22 47.0
17 Su	3 42 07	26 55 31	17 43 42	24 23 45	0 46.2	1 27.4	11 40.4	16 52.1	16 48.1	28 35.6	26 21.3	16 48.3	27 41.1	22 47.2
18 M	3 46 03	27 53 20	1♋06 34	7♋52 00	0 41.5	2 39.8	12 54.0	17 36.1	16 43.4	28 48.3	26 23.5	16 50.9	27 43.1	22 47.3
19 Tu	3 50 00	28 51 08	14 39 54	21 30 09	0D 39.4	3 54.9	14 07.6	18 20.0	16 39.0	29 01.0	26 25.8	16 53.6	27 45.1	22 47.4
20 W	3 53 56	29 48 54	28 22 42	5♌17 28	0 39.2	5 12.6	15 21.1	19 03.9	16 35.0	29 13.8	26 28.2	16 56.3	27 47.1	22 47.5
21 Th	3 57 53	0♊46 39	12♌14 25	19 13 29	0R 39.8	6 32.8	16 34.6	19 47.8	16 31.5	29 26.6	26 30.6	16 59.1	27 49.1	22 47.6
22 F	4 01 50	1 44 22	26 14 38	3♍17 46	0 40.1	7 55.5	17 48.1	20 31.7	16 28.3	29 39.4	26 33.2	17 01.9	27 51.0	22R 47.6
23 Sa	4 05 46	2 42 03	10♍22 47	17 29 30	0 39.2	9 20.7	19 01.6	21 15.5	16 25.5	29 52.3	26 35.9	17 04.7	27 53.0	22 47.6
24 Su	4 09 43	3 39 43	24 37 41	1♎47 02	0 36.2	10 48.3	20 15.0	21 59.2	16 23.2	0♋05.3	26 38.6	17 07.5	27 54.9	22 47.6
25 M	4 13 39	4 37 21	8♎57 07	16 07 30	0 31.0	12 18.3	21 28.5	22 43.0	16 21.2	0 18.2	26 41.5	17 10.4	27 56.8	22 47.6
26 Tu	4 17 36	5 34 57	23 17 37	0♏26 52	0 23.9	13 50.7	22 41.9	23 26.7	16 19.6	0 31.3	26 44.4	17 13.3	27 58.7	22 47.5
27 W	4 21 32	6 32 33	7♏34 37	14 40 11	0 15.7	15 25.5	23 55.3	24 10.3	16 18.5	0 44.3	26 47.5	17 16.2	28 00.6	22 47.4
28 Th	4 25 29	7 30 07	21 42 56	28 42 14	0 07.1	17 02.7	25 08.6	24 53.9	16 17.7	0 57.4	26 50.6	17 19.2	28 02.4	22 47.3
29 F	4 29 25	8 27 39	5♐37 32	12♐28 23	29♋59.4	18 42.3	26 22.0	25 37.5	16D 17.3	1 10.5	26 53.9	17 22.2	28 04.3	22 47.1
30 Sa	4 33 22	9 25 11	19 14 22	25 55 15	29 53.2	20 24.2	27 35.3	26 21.1	16 17.4	1 23.7	26 57.2	17 25.2	28 06.1	22 47.0
31 Su	4 37 19	10 22 42	2♑30 52	9♑01 12	29 49.1	22 08.5	28 48.6	27 04.6	16 17.8	1 36.9	27 00.6	17 28.3	28 07.9	22 46.8

LONGITUDE — June 2037

Day	Sid.Time	☉	0 hr ☽	Noon ☽	True ☊	☿	♀	♂	⚳	♃	♄	♅	♆	♇
1 M	4 41 15	11♊20 12	15♑26 19	21♑46 24	29♋47.1	23♉55.1	0♋01.8	27♓48.0	16♎18.6	1♋50.1	27♌04.1	17♋31.4	28♈09.7	22♒46.6
2 Tu	4 45 12	12 17 41	28 01 45	4♒12 43	29D 46.8	25 44.1	1 15.1	28 31.4	16 19.8	2 03.3	27 07.7	17 34.5	28 11.4	22R 46.3
3 W	4 49 08	13 15 09	10♒19 46	16 23 22	29 47.8	27 35.4	2 28.3	29 14.8	16 21.3	2 16.6	27 11.4	17 37.6	28 13.2	22 46.1
4 Th	4 53 05	14 12 37	22 24 06	28 22 33	29 49.2	29 29.0	3 41.6	29 58.1	16 23.3	2 29.9	27 15.1	17 40.8	28 14.9	22 45.8
5 F	4 57 01	15 10 03	4♓19 20	10♓15 04	29R 50.2	1♊24.8	4 54.7	0♈41.3	16 25.6	2 43.3	27 19.0	17 44.0	28 16.6	22 45.4
6 Sa	5 00 58	16 07 29	16 10 24	22 05 58	29 50.1	3 22.8	6 07.9	1 24.5	16 28.3	2 56.6	27 22.9	17 47.2	28 18.2	22 45.1
7 Su	5 04 54	17 04 54	28 02 24	4♈00 19	29 48.5	5 22.9	7 21.1	2 07.7	16 31.4	3 10.0	27 26.9	17 50.4	28 19.9	22 44.7
8 M	5 08 51	18 02 19	10♈00 16	16 02 48	29 45.1	7 25.1	8 34.2	2 50.7	16 34.8	3 23.5	27 31.0	17 53.7	28 21.5	22 44.3
9 Tu	5 12 48	18 59 43	22 08 25	28 17 34	29 40.2	9 29.1	9 47.3	3 33.8	16 38.7	3 36.9	27 35.2	17 57.0	28 23.1	22 43.9
10 W	5 16 44	19 57 07	4♉30 35	10♉47 48	29 34.2	11 34.9	11 00.4	4 16.7	16 42.8	3 50.4	27 39.5	18 00.3	28 24.7	22 43.5
11 Th	5 20 41	20 54 30	17 09 25	23 35 35	29 27.6	13 42.2	12 13.5	4 59.6	16 47.4	4 03.8	27 43.8	18 03.6	28 26.2	22 43.0
12 F	5 24 37	21 51 52	0♊06 22	6♊41 43	29 21.3	15 51.0	13 26.6	5 42.4	16 52.3	4 17.3	27 48.3	18 06.9	28 27.8	22 42.5
13 Sa	5 28 34	22 49 14	13 21 31	20 05 35	29 16.0	18 00.8	14 39.6	6 25.2	16 57.5	4 30.9	27 52.8	18 10.3	28 29.3	22 42.0
14 Su	5 32 30	23 46 35	26 53 39	3♋45 23	29 12.2	20 11.7	15 52.6	7 07.8	17 03.1	4 44.4	27 57.4	18 13.7	28 30.8	22 41.5
15 M	5 36 27	24 43 56	10♋40 26	17 38 23	29D 10.1	22 23.1	17 05.6	7 50.4	17 09.1	4 58.0	28 02.1	18 17.1	28 32.2	22 40.9
16 Tu	5 40 24	25 41 15	24 38 50	1♌41 22	29 09.6	24 34.9	18 18.6	8 33.0	17 15.4	5 11.5	28 06.8	18 20.5	28 33.6	22 40.3
17 W	5 44 20	26 38 34	8♌45 33	15 51 01	29 10.4	26 46.9	19 31.6	9 15.4	17 22.0	5 25.1	28 11.6	18 24.0	28 35.0	22 39.7
18 Th	5 48 17	27 35 52	22 57 24	0♍04 20	29 11.8	28 58.7	20 44.5	9 57.8	17 29.0	5 38.7	28 16.5	18 27.4	28 36.4	22 39.1
19 F	5 52 13	28 33 10	7♍11 31	14 18 38	29 13.1	1♋10.0	21 57.4	10 40.0	17 36.3	5 52.3	28 21.5	18 30.9	28 37.8	22 38.4
20 Sa	5 56 10	29 30 26	21 25 27	28 31 40	29R 13.7	3 20.6	23 10.3	11 22.2	17 43.9	6 05.9	28 26.6	18 34.4	28 39.1	22 37.8
21 Su	6 00 06	0♋27 41	5♎37 03	12♎41 20	29 13.1	5 30.3	24 23.1	12 04.3	17 51.8	6 19.5	28 31.7	18 37.9	28 40.4	22 37.1
22 M	6 04 03	1 24 56	19 44 16	26 45 35	29 11.4	7 38.8	25 35.9	12 46.4	18 00.1	6 33.1	28 36.9	18 41.4	28 41.7	22 36.3
23 Tu	6 07 59	2 22 10	3♏45 01	10♏42 17	29 08.5	9 46.0	26 48.7	13 28.3	18 08.6	6 46.8	28 42.1	18 44.9	28 42.9	22 35.6
24 W	6 11 56	3 19 24	17 37 05	24 29 10	29 05.0	11 51.7	28 01.5	14 10.1	18 17.5	7 00.4	28 47.4	18 48.4	28 44.1	22 34.9
25 Th	6 15 53	4 16 37	1♐18 15	8♐04 03	29 01.3	13 55.8	29 14.2	14 51.9	18 26.6	7 14.0	28 52.8	18 52.0	28 45.3	22 34.1
26 F	6 19 49	5 13 50	14 46 22	21 24 59	28 58.0	15 58.1	0♌26.9	15 33.5	18 36.1	7 27.7	28 58.3	18 55.6	28 46.4	22 33.3
27 Sa	6 23 46	6 11 02	27 59 45	4♑30 34	28 55.4	17 58.6	1 39.6	16 15.1	18 45.8	7 41.3	29 03.8	18 59.1	28 47.6	22 32.5
28 Su	6 27 42	7 08 14	10♑57 22	17 20 10	28D 53.9	19 57.2	2 52.2	16 56.6	18 55.9	7 55.0	29 09.4	19 02.7	28 48.7	22 31.6
29 M	6 31 39	8 05 26	23 39 01	29 54 03	28 53.5	21 53.7	4 04.8	17 38.0	19 06.2	8 08.7	29 15.1	19 06.3	28 49.7	22 30.8
30 Tu	6 35 35	9 02 38	6♒05 29	12♒13 31	28 54.0	23 48.3	5 17.4	18 19.2	19 16.8	8 22.2	29 20.8	19 09.9	28 50.8	22 29.9

Astro Data Dy Hr Mn	Planet Ingress Dy Hr Mn	Last Aspect Dy Hr Mn	☽ Ingress Dy Hr Mn	Last Aspect Dy Hr Mn	☽ Ingress Dy Hr Mn	☽ Phases & Eclipses Dy Hr Mn	Astro Data
♃✶♆ 5 1:45	♀ ♊ 7 23:52	30 22:06 ♄ □	♐ 1 4:55	2 0:17 ♆ □	♒ 2 3:49	7 4:57 ☾ 16♒59	1 May 2037
☽0N 11 17:53	☿ ♉ 16 5:47	3 4:54 ♆ △	♑ 3 10:04	4 14:40 ♆ □	♓ 4 15:16	15 5:56 ● 24♉45	Julian Day # 50160
♃✶♆ 12 6:26	☉ ♊ 20 16:37	5 13:48 ♆ □	♒ 5 19:09	6 3:14 ♅ △	♈ 7 3:57	22 9:10 ☽ 1♍38	SVP 4♓44'34"
♇ R 23 7:50	♃ ♋ 24 2:14	8 1:55 ♆ ✶	♓ 8 7:17	9 12:11 ♆ ☌	♉ 9 15:19	29 4:25 ○ 8♐09	GC 27♐21.6 ⚴ 20♌05.6
☽0S 25 3:45	☊ ♋R 29 10:03	10 14:19 ♃ □	♈ 10 20:01	11 19:41 ♄ □	♊ 11 23:48		Eris 27♈59.0 ⚵ 29♌13.2
⚳ D 29 22:34		13 2:36 ♃ ✶	♉ 13 7:05	14 2:49 ♆ ✶	♋ 14 5:27	5 22:50 ☾ 15♓36	⚷ 16♊21.5 ⚶ 3♈21.2
	♀ ♋ 1 11:24	15 8:46 ♄ □	♊ 15 15:39	16 6:40 ♆ □	♌ 16 9:08	13 17:11 ● 23♊02	☽ Mean ☊ 3♌00.8
☽0N 8 2:48	♂ ♈ 4 13:04	17 19:38 ♃ ☌	♋ 17 22:01	18 9:49 ☿ ✶	♍ 18 11:53	20 13:47 ☽ 29♍35	
♂0N 11 6:55	☿ ♊ 4 18:28	20 1:47 ☉ ✶	♌ 20 2:49	20 13:47 ☉ □	♎ 20 14:29	27 15:21 ○ 6♑19	1 June 2037
☽0S 21 10:08	☿ ♋ 18 23:12	22 5:43 ♃ ✶	♍ 22 6:24	22 15:19 ♆ ☍	♏ 22 17:33		Julian Day # 50191
♄△♆ 23 16:34	☉ ♋ 21 0:24	23 18:41 ♂ ☍	♎ 24 9:01	24 19:37 ♄ □	♐ 24 21:42		SVP 4♓44'29"
♃⚼♇ 26 21:19	♀ ♌ 26 3:07	26 7:51 ♆ ☍	♏ 26 11:15	27 1:53 ♄ △	♑ 27 3:41		GC 27♐21.7 ⚴ 28♌57.2
⚳0S 28 7:28		28 8:47 ♄ □	♐ 28 14:14	29 9:56 ♆ □	♒ 29 12:11		Eris 28♈17.1 ⚵ 4♍50.1
		30 15:58 ♆ △	♑ 30 19:24				⚷ 18♊50.1 ⚶ 16♈44.8
							☽ Mean ☊ 1♌22.4

July 2037 — LONGITUDE

Day	Sid.Time	☉	0 hr ☽	Noon ☽	True ☊	☿	♀	♂	⚳	♃	♄	♅	♆	♇
1 W	6 39 32	9♋59 50	18♒18 29	24♒20 45	28♋55.2	25♋40.9	6♌30.0	19♈00.4	19♎27.7	8♋35.9	29♌26.5	19♋13.5	28♈51.8	22♒29.0
2 Th	6 43 28	10 57 02	0♓20 42	6♓18 48	28 56.6	27 31.3	7 42.5	19 41.5	19 38.8	8 49.5	29 32.4	19 17.1	28 52.8	22R 28.1
3 F	6 47 25	11 54 14	12 15 31	18 11 24	28 58.0	29 19.7	8 55.0	20 22.4	19 50.2	9 03.1	29 38.3	19 20.7	28 53.7	22 27.2
4 Sa	6 51 22	12 51 26	24 06 58	0♈02 48	28 59.1	1♌06.1	10 07.5	21 03.3	20 01.8	9 16.8	29 44.2	19 24.4	28 54.6	22 26.2
5 Su	6 55 18	13 48 38	5♈59 29	11 57 35	28R 59.5	2 50.3	11 19.9	21 44.0	20 13.8	9 30.4	29 50.2	19 28.0	28 55.5	22 25.2
6 M	6 59 15	14 45 51	17 57 43	24 00 26	28 59.3	4 32.5	12 32.3	22 24.6	20 25.9	9 44.0	29 56.3	19 31.6	28 56.4	22 24.3
7 Tu	7 03 11	15 43 04	0♉06 19	6♉15 52	28 58.5	6 12.5	13 44.7	23 05.1	20 38.3	9 57.6	0♍02.4	19 35.3	28 57.2	22 23.3
8 W	7 07 08	16 40 17	12 29 35	18 47 56	28 57.2	7 50.5	14 57.1	23 45.5	20 51.0	10 11.2	0 08.6	19 38.9	28 58.0	22 22.2
9 Th	7 11 04	17 37 31	25 11 15	1♊39 52	28 55.8	9 26.4	16 09.4	24 25.7	21 03.9	10 24.8	0 14.8	19 42.6	28 58.8	22 21.2
10 F	7 15 01	18 34 45	8♊13 59	14 53 43	28 54.4	11 00.2	17 21.7	25 05.8	21 17.1	10 38.3	0 21.1	19 46.2	28 59.5	22 20.2
11 Sa	7 18 57	19 31 59	21 39 05	28 29 57	28 53.3	12 31.8	18 34.0	25 45.8	21 30.5	10 51.9	0 27.5	19 49.9	29 00.2	22 19.1
12 Su	7 22 54	20 29 14	5♋26 08	12♋27 17	28 52.6	14 01.4	19 46.2	26 25.7	21 44.1	11 05.4	0 33.9	19 53.5	29 00.9	22 18.0
13 M	7 26 51	21 26 29	19 32 57	26 42 35	28D 52.3	15 28.8	20 58.4	27 05.3	21 57.9	11 19.0	0 40.3	19 57.2	29 01.5	22 16.9
14 Tu	7 30 47	22 23 44	3♌55 33	11♌11 10	28 52.4	16 54.0	22 10.6	27 44.9	22 12.0	11 32.5	0 46.8	20 00.8	29 02.1	22 15.8
15 W	7 34 44	23 20 59	18 28 41	25 47 20	28 52.8	18 17.0	23 22.7	28 24.3	22 26.3	11 46.0	0 53.3	20 04.5	29 02.7	22 14.7
16 Th	7 38 40	24 18 15	3♍06 22	10♍25 02	28 53.2	19 37.8	24 34.8	29 03.5	22 40.8	11 59.4	0 59.9	20 08.1	29 03.3	22 13.6
17 F	7 42 37	25 15 30	17 42 40	24 58 37	28 53.6	20 56.3	25 46.9	29 42.6	22 55.6	12 12.9	1 06.5	20 11.8	29 03.8	22 12.4
18 Sa	7 46 33	26 12 46	2♎12 21	9♎23 22	28 53.8	22 12.5	26 58.9	0♉21.5	23 10.5	12 26.3	1 13.2	20 15.4	29 04.3	22 11.2
19 Su	7 50 30	27 10 02	16 31 18	23 35 51	28R 53.9	23 26.3	28 10.9	1 00.3	23 25.6	12 39.7	1 19.9	20 19.0	29 04.7	22 10.1
20 M	7 54 26	28 07 18	0♏36 46	7♏33 54	28D 53.9	24 37.7	29 22.9	1 38.9	23 41.0	12 53.1	1 26.7	20 22.7	29 05.1	22 08.9
21 Tu	7 58 23	29 04 34	14 27 11	21 16 32	28 53.9	25 46.5	0♍34.8	2 17.3	23 56.5	13 06.4	1 33.5	20 26.3	29 05.5	22 07.7
22 W	8 02 20	0♌01 50	28 01 59	4♐43 34	28 54.0	26 52.7	1 46.6	2 55.6	24 12.3	13 19.7	1 40.3	20 29.9	29 05.8	22 06.5
23 Th	8 06 16	0 59 07	11♐21 19	17 55 22	28 54.1	27 56.3	2 58.4	3 33.7	24 28.2	13 33.0	1 47.2	20 33.5	29 06.2	22 05.3
24 F	8 10 13	1 56 24	24 25 46	0♑52 38	28 54.4	28 57.1	4 10.2	4 11.6	24 44.3	13 46.3	1 54.1	20 37.1	29 06.4	22 04.0
25 Sa	8 14 09	2 53 42	7♑16 06	13 36 16	28 54.7	29 54.9	5 21.9	4 49.3	25 00.6	13 59.5	2 01.0	20 40.7	29 06.7	22 02.8
26 Su	8 18 06	3 51 00	19 53 17	26 07 16	28R 54.8	0♍49.8	6 33.6	5 26.9	25 17.1	14 12.7	2 08.0	20 44.3	29 06.9	22 01.5
27 M	8 22 02	4 48 19	2♒18 23	8♒26 49	28 54.7	1 41.5	7 45.3	6 04.3	25 33.7	14 25.9	2 15.0	20 47.8	29 07.1	22 00.3
28 Tu	8 25 59	5 45 39	14 32 42	20 36 17	28 54.3	2 30.0	8 56.8	6 41.5	25 50.6	14 39.0	2 22.1	20 51.4	29 07.2	21 59.0
29 W	8 29 55	6 42 59	26 37 47	2♓37 27	28 53.6	3 15.0	10 08.4	7 18.5	26 07.6	14 52.1	2 29.2	20 55.0	29 07.4	21 57.8
30 Th	8 33 52	7 40 20	8♓35 34	14 32 27	28 52.5	3 56.4	11 19.9	7 55.3	26 24.7	15 05.2	2 36.3	20 58.5	29 07.4	21 56.5
31 F	8 37 49	8 37 42	20 28 26	26 23 55	28 51.2	4 34.2	12 31.3	8 32.0	26 42.1	15 18.2	2 43.5	21 02.0	29 07.5	21 55.2

August 2037 — LONGITUDE

Day	Sid.Time	☉	0 hr ☽	Noon ☽	True ☊	☿	♀	♂	⚳	♃	♄	♅	♆	♇
1 Sa	8 41 45	9♌35 05	2♈19 19	8♈15 02	28♋49.8	5♍07.9	13♍42.7	9♉08.4	26♎59.6	15♋31.2	2♍50.6	21♋05.5	29♈07.5	21♒53.9
2 Su	8 45 42	10 32 29	14 11 35	20 09 27	28R 48.7	5 37.6	14 54.1	9 44.6	27 17.2	15 44.2	2 57.8	21 09.0	29R 07.5	21R 52.6
3 M	8 49 38	11 29 55	26 09 08	2♉11 12	28D 47.9	6 03.1	16 05.4	10 20.6	27 35.0	15 57.1	3 05.1	21 12.5	29 07.5	21 51.3
4 Tu	8 53 35	12 27 21	8♉16 11	14 24 39	28 47.7	6 24.0	17 16.7	10 56.3	27 53.0	16 09.9	3 12.3	21 16.0	29 07.4	21 50.0
5 W	8 57 31	13 24 49	20 37 07	26 54 08	28 48.1	6 40.3	18 27.9	11 31.9	28 11.1	16 22.8	3 19.6	21 19.4	29 07.3	21 48.7
6 Th	9 01 28	14 22 18	3♊16 12	9♊43 45	28 49.1	6 51.7	19 39.1	12 07.2	28 29.4	16 35.5	3 26.9	21 22.9	29 07.1	21 47.4
7 F	9 05 24	15 19 48	16 17 12	22 56 51	28 50.3	6R 58.1	20 50.2	12 42.3	28 47.8	16 48.3	3 34.3	21 26.3	29 07.0	21 46.0
8 Sa	9 09 21	16 17 20	29 42 56	6♋35 31	28 51.5	6 59.4	22 01.3	13 17.1	29 06.4	17 01.0	3 41.7	21 29.7	29 06.7	21 44.7
9 Su	9 13 18	17 14 53	13♋34 35	20 39 56	28R 52.3	6 55.4	23 12.3	13 51.7	29 25.1	17 13.6	3 49.0	21 33.1	29 06.5	21 43.4
10 M	9 17 14	18 12 27	27 51 14	5♌07 58	28 52.3	6 46.0	24 23.3	14 26.0	29 44.0	17 26.2	3 56.5	21 36.5	29 06.2	21 42.1
11 Tu	9 21 11	19 10 02	12♌29 27	19 54 52	28 51.4	6 31.1	25 34.2	15 00.1	0♏03.0	17 38.8	4 03.9	21 39.8	29 05.9	21 40.7
12 W	9 25 07	20 07 38	27 23 16	4♍53 34	28 49.6	6 10.9	26 45.0	15 33.9	0 22.1	17 51.2	4 11.3	21 43.1	29 05.6	21 39.4
13 Th	9 29 04	21 05 15	12♍24 42	19 55 30	28 46.9	5 45.3	27 55.9	16 07.4	0 41.4	18 03.7	4 18.8	21 46.4	29 05.2	21 38.0
14 F	9 33 00	22 02 54	27 24 52	4♎51 48	28 43.9	5 14.6	29 06.6	16 40.6	1 00.8	18 16.0	4 26.3	21 49.7	29 04.8	21 36.7
15 Sa	9 36 57	23 00 33	12♎15 21	19 34 45	28 41.0	4 39.0	0♎17.3	17 13.6	1 20.4	18 28.4	4 33.8	21 53.0	29 04.4	21 35.4
16 Su	9 40 53	23 58 13	26 49 20	3♏58 39	28 38.9	3 58.9	1 27.9	17 46.2	1 40.0	18 40.6	4 41.3	21 56.2	29 03.9	21 34.0
17 M	9 44 50	24 55 55	11♏02 24	18 00 23	28D 37.7	3 14.9	2 38.5	18 18.6	1 59.8	18 52.8	4 48.8	21 59.4	29 03.4	21 32.7
18 Tu	9 48 47	25 53 37	24 52 36	1♐39 08	28 37.6	2 27.5	3 49.0	18 50.7	2 19.7	19 05.0	4 56.3	22 02.6	29 02.9	21 31.4
19 W	9 52 43	26 51 20	8♐20 10	14 55 57	28 38.6	1 37.5	4 59.4	19 22.4	2 39.7	19 17.0	5 03.9	22 05.8	29 02.3	21 30.1
20 Th	9 56 40	27 49 05	21 26 48	27 53 04	28 40.1	0 45.8	6 09.8	19 53.9	2 59.9	19 29.0	5 11.4	22 08.9	29 01.8	21 28.7
21 F	10 00 36	28 46 51	4♑15 07	10♑33 20	28 41.7	29♌53.3	7 20.1	20 25.0	3 20.2	19 41.0	5 19.0	22 12.0	29 01.1	21 27.4
22 Sa	10 04 33	29 44 37	16 48 03	22 59 40	28R 42.7	29 01.1	8 30.3	20 55.8	3 40.5	19 52.9	5 26.6	22 15.1	29 00.5	21 26.1
23 Su	10 08 29	0♍42 25	29 08 29	5♒14 50	28 42.6	28 10.1	9 40.5	21 26.3	4 01.0	20 04.7	5 34.1	22 18.2	28 59.8	21 24.8
24 M	10 12 26	1 40 15	11♒19 01	17 21 18	28 41.1	27 21.5	10 50.5	21 56.5	4 21.6	20 16.4	5 41.7	22 21.2	28 59.1	21 23.5
25 Tu	10 16 22	2 38 05	23 21 56	29 21 10	28 37.9	26 36.4	12 00.5	22 26.3	4 42.3	20 28.1	5 49.3	22 24.2	28 58.4	21 22.2
26 W	10 20 19	3 35 58	5♓19 12	11♓16 17	28 33.1	25 55.7	13 10.4	22 55.8	5 03.1	20 39.7	5 56.9	22 27.2	28 57.6	21 20.9
27 Th	10 24 16	4 33 51	17 12 38	23 08 28	28 27.1	25 20.3	14 20.3	23 24.9	5 24.0	20 51.2	6 04.5	22 30.1	28 56.8	21 19.6
28 F	10 28 12	5 31 46	29 04 00	4♈59 31	28 20.4	24 51.1	15 30.1	23 53.6	5 45.0	21 02.7	6 12.1	22 33.0	28 56.0	21 18.3
29 Sa	10 32 09	6 29 43	10♈55 16	16 51 34	28 13.6	24 28.8	16 39.8	24 22.0	6 06.1	21 14.0	6 19.7	22 35.9	28 55.1	21 17.0
30 Su	10 36 05	7 27 42	22 48 45	28 47 09	28 07.4	24 14.0	17 49.4	24 50.0	6 27.3	21 25.3	6 27.3	22 38.7	28 54.2	21 15.7
31 M	10 40 02	8 25 42	4♉47 11	10♉49 16	28 02.5	24D 07.1	18 58.9	25 17.6	6 48.6	21 36.6	6 34.9	22 41.5	28 53.3	21 14.4

Astro Data

	Dy Hr Mn
☽0N	5 11:32
☽0S	18 16:00
♆R	1 13:58
☽0N	1 19:03
☿R	8 5:46
♅⚻♇	11 16:39
☽0S	14 23:02
♀0S	16 11:15
☽0N	29 1:12
♃⚻♇	29 17:37
♃∠♄	31 0:49
☿D	31 20:10

Planet Ingress

		Dy Hr Mn
☿	♌	3 21:02
♄	♍	7 2:32
♂	♉	17 22:44
♀	♍	21 0:24
☉	♌	22 11:14
☿	♍	25 14:10
⚳	♏	11 8:13
♀	♎	15 6:08
☿	♌R	21 8:57
☉	♍	22 18:23

Last Aspect / ☽ Ingress (July)

Last Aspect Dy Hr Mn		☽ Ingress	Dy Hr Mn
1 22:16	♄ ☍	♓	1 23:18
3 14:21	♅ △	♈	4 11:54
6 23:46	♄ △	♉	6 23:48
8 18:43	♇ □	♊	9 8:56
11 12:53	♆ ⚹	♋	11 14:37
13 15:52	♆ □	♌	13 17:29
15 17:21	♆ △	♍	15 18:54
17 12:30	☉ ⚹	♎	17 20:20
19 21:22	♆ ☍	♏	19 22:57
22 2:55	☉ △	♐	22 3:31
24 8:42	♆ △	♑	24 10:22
26 17:48	♆ □	♒	26 19:31
29 4:59	♆ ⚹	♓	29 6:44
31 1:05	♅ △	♈	31 19:18

Last Aspect / ☽ Ingress (August)

Last Aspect Dy Hr Mn		☽ Ingress	Dy Hr Mn
3 5:55	♆ ☌	♉	3 7:40
5 2:18	♇ □	♊	5 17:52
7 22:57	♆ ⚹	♋	8 0:30
10 2:04	♆ □	♌	10 3:33
12 2:44	♆ △	♍	12 4:11
14 1:56	♀ ☌	♎	14 4:09
16 3:45	♆ ☍	♏	16 5:19
18 1:01	☉ □	♐	18 9:04
20 14:09	♆ △	♑	20 15:58
22 23:44	♆ □	♒	23 1:41
25 11:14	♆ ⚹	♓	25 13:18
27 12:35	♂ ⚹	♈	28 1:53
30 12:14	♆ ☌	♉	30 14:26

☽ Phases & Eclipses

Dy Hr Mn		
5 16:02	☾	13♈58
13 2:33	●	21♋04
13 2:40:37	●	T 03'58"
19 18:32	☽	27♎26
27 4:16	○	4♒30
27 4:10	●	P 0.810
4 7:52	☾	12♉17
11 10:43	●	19♌07
18 1:01	☽	25♏27
25 19:11	○	2♓55

Astro Data

1 July 2037
Julian Day # 50221
SVP 4♓44'24"
GC 27♐21.8 ⚴ 9♍48.8
Eris 28♈28.4 ⚵ 13♍03.1
⚷ 21♊22.2 ⚶ 28♈01.8
☽ Mean ☊ 29♋47.1

1 August 2037
Julian Day # 50252
SVP 4♓44'19"
GC 27♐21.9 ⚴ 22♍19.2
Eris 28♈31.0R ⚵ 23♍07.1
⚷ 23♊43.0 ⚶ 6♉56.9
☽ Mean ☊ 28♋08.6

LONGITUDE — September 2037

Day	Sid.Time	☉	0 hr ☽	Noon ☽	True ☊	☿	♀	♂	⚳	♃	♄	♅	♆	♇
1 Tu	10 43 58	9♍23 45	16♉53 52	23♉01 28	27♋59.3	24♌08.5	20♎08.4	25♉44.8	7♏10.0	21♋47.7	6♍42.5	22♋44.3	28♈52.4	21♒13.2
2 W	10 47 55	10 21 49	29 12 35	5♊27 44	27D57.8	24 18.3	21 17.7	26 11.5	7 31.5	21 58.8	6 50.1	22 47.1	28R51.4	21R11.9
3 Th	10 51 51	11 19 55	11♊47 27	18 12 15	27 57.9	24 36.6	22 27.0	26 37.9	7 53.1	22 09.7	6 57.7	22 49.8	28 50.5	21 10.7
4 F	10 55 48	12 18 04	24 42 38	1♋19 04	27 59.0	25 03.4	23 36.2	27 03.8	8 14.8	22 20.6	7 05.2	22 52.5	28 49.4	21 09.5
5 Sa	10 59 45	13 16 14	8♋01 57	14 51 33	28R00.2	25 38.6	24 45.3	27 29.3	8 36.5	22 31.4	7 12.8	22 55.1	28 48.4	21 08.3
6 Su	11 03 41	14 14 26	21 48 06	28 51 39	28 00.8	26 22.0	25 54.4	27 54.3	8 58.4	22 42.1	7 20.4	22 57.7	28 47.3	21 07.0
7 M	11 07 38	15 12 40	6♌02 03	13♌19 01	27 59.8	27 13.2	27 03.3	28 18.9	9 20.3	22 52.8	7 28.0	23 00.3	28 46.3	21 05.8
8 Tu	11 11 34	16 10 56	20 42 02	28 10 22	27 56.8	28 11.9	28 12.2	28 42.9	9 42.4	23 03.3	7 35.5	23 02.8	28 45.1	21 04.7
9 W	11 15 31	17 09 14	5♍43 05	13♍19 05	27 51.7	29 17.6	29 20.9	29 06.5	10 04.5	23 13.7	7 43.1	23 05.3	28 44.0	21 03.5
10 Th	11 19 27	18 07 34	20 57 05	28 35 45	27 44.9	0♍30.0	0♏29.6	29 29.6	10 26.7	23 24.1	7 50.6	23 07.8	28 42.8	21 02.3
11 F	11 23 24	19 05 55	6♎13 40	13♎49 28	27 37.1	1 48.4	1 38.2	29 52.1	10 49.0	23 34.3	7 58.1	23 10.2	28 41.6	21 01.2
12 Sa	11 27 20	20 04 18	21 21 52	28 49 44	27 29.5	3 12.3	2 46.6	0♊14.2	11 11.3	23 44.4	8 05.6	23 12.5	28 40.4	21 00.0
13 Su	11 31 17	21 02 43	6♏12 08	13♏28 18	27 23.1	4 41.2	3 55.0	0 35.7	11 33.8	23 54.5	8 13.1	23 14.9	28 39.2	20 58.9
14 M	11 35 13	22 01 09	20 37 44	27 40 08	27 18.4	6 14.4	5 03.3	0 56.7	11 56.3	24 04.4	8 20.6	23 17.2	28 37.9	20 57.8
15 Tu	11 39 10	22 59 37	4♐35 22	11♐23 34	27D15.9	7 51.5	6 11.4	1 17.1	12 18.8	24 14.2	8 28.0	23 19.4	28 36.7	20 56.7
16 W	11 43 07	23 58 07	18 04 54	24 39 46	27 15.3	9 31.8	7 19.4	1 36.9	12 41.5	24 23.9	8 35.4	23 21.6	28 35.4	20 55.6
17 Th	11 47 03	24 56 38	1♑08 35	7♑31 50	27 15.8	11 14.8	8 27.3	1 56.2	13 04.2	24 33.6	8 42.9	23 23.8	28 34.0	20 54.6
18 F	11 51 00	25 55 11	13 50 05	20 03 54	27R16.6	13 00.1	9 35.1	2 14.9	13 27.0	24 43.1	8 50.2	23 25.9	28 32.7	20 53.5
19 Sa	11 54 56	26 53 45	26 13 48	2♒20 23	27 16.7	14 47.2	10 42.8	2 33.0	13 49.9	24 52.5	8 57.6	23 28.0	28 31.4	20 52.5
20 Su	11 58 53	27 52 21	8♒24 08	14 25 33	27 15.1	16 35.6	11 50.3	2 50.5	14 12.8	25 01.7	9 05.0	23 30.1	28 30.0	20 51.5
21 M	12 02 49	28 50 59	20 25 07	26 23 13	27 11.2	18 25.1	12 57.7	3 07.4	14 35.8	25 10.9	9 12.3	23 32.1	28 28.6	20 50.5
22 Tu	12 06 46	29 49 38	2♓20 13	8♓16 29	27 04.6	20 15.3	14 04.9	3 23.7	14 58.9	25 20.0	9 19.6	23 34.0	28 27.2	20 49.5
23 W	12 10 42	0♎48 20	14 12 17	20 07 52	26 55.5	22 05.8	15 12.0	3 39.3	15 22.0	25 28.9	9 26.8	23 35.9	28 25.7	20 48.5
24 Th	12 14 39	1 47 03	26 03 30	1♈59 21	26 44.3	23 56.6	16 19.0	3 54.3	15 45.2	25 37.7	9 34.1	23 37.8	28 24.3	20 47.6
25 F	12 18 36	2 45 48	7♈55 36	13 52 27	26 31.9	25 47.3	17 25.8	4 08.6	16 08.4	25 46.4	9 41.3	23 39.6	28 22.8	20 46.6
26 Sa	12 22 32	3 44 36	19 50 03	25 48 36	26 19.3	27 37.8	18 32.5	4 22.2	16 31.7	25 55.0	9 48.5	23 41.3	28 21.3	20 45.7
27 Su	12 26 29	4 43 25	1♉48 16	7♉49 18	26 07.5	29 27.9	19 39.0	4 35.1	16 55.0	26 03.4	9 55.6	23 43.1	28 19.8	20 44.8
28 M	12 30 25	5 42 17	13 51 54	19 56 23	25 57.6	1♎17.6	20 45.4	4 47.3	17 18.5	26 11.7	10 02.8	23 44.7	28 18.3	20 44.0
29 Tu	12 34 22	6 41 10	26 03 01	2♊12 11	25 50.2	3 06.8	21 51.6	4 58.8	17 41.9	26 19.9	10 09.9	23 46.4	28 16.8	20 43.1
30 W	12 38 18	7 40 06	8♊24 15	14 39 39	25 45.5	4 55.3	22 57.6	5 09.5	18 05.5	26 28.0	10 16.9	23 47.9	28 15.3	20 42.3

LONGITUDE — October 2037

Day	Sid.Time	☉	0 hr ☽	Noon ☽	True ☊	☿	♀	♂	⚳	♃	♄	♅	♆	♇
1 Th	12 42 15	8♎39 05	20♊58 48	27♊22 12	25♋43.3	6♎43.1	24♏03.5	5♊19.5	18♏29.0	26♋35.9	10♍23.9	23♋49.5	28♈13.7	20♒41.5
2 F	12 46 11	9 38 05	3♋50 19	10♋23 38	25D42.8	8 30.2	25 09.1	5 28.7	18 52.7	26 43.7	10 30.9	23 51.0	28R12.1	20R40.7
3 Sa	12 50 08	10 37 08	17 02 36	23 47 37	25R43.0	10 16.5	26 14.7	5 37.2	19 16.4	26 51.4	10 37.9	23 52.4	28 10.6	20 39.9
4 Su	12 54 05	11 36 14	0♌39 00	7♌37 00	25 42.6	12 02.1	27 20.0	5 44.8	19 40.1	26 58.9	10 44.8	23 53.8	28 09.0	20 39.2
5 M	12 58 01	12 35 21	14 41 43	21 53 04	25 40.5	13 46.9	28 25.2	5 51.6	20 03.9	27 06.3	10 51.7	23 55.1	28 07.4	20 38.4
6 Tu	13 01 58	13 34 31	29 10 48	6♍34 27	25 35.8	15 30.8	29 30.1	5 57.6	20 27.7	27 13.5	10 58.5	23 56.4	28 05.8	20 37.7
7 W	13 05 54	14 33 43	14♍03 19	21 36 29	25 28.4	17 14.0	0♐34.9	6 02.8	20 51.6	27 20.6	11 05.3	23 57.6	28 04.2	20 37.0
8 Th	13 09 51	15 32 57	29 12 50	6♎51 05	25 18.6	18 56.4	1 39.4	6 07.1	21 15.6	27 27.6	11 12.0	23 58.8	28 02.5	20 36.4
9 F	13 13 47	16 32 14	14♎29 51	22 07 39	25 07.5	20 38.0	2 43.8	6 10.5	21 39.6	27 34.4	11 18.7	23 59.9	28 00.9	20 35.7
10 Sa	13 17 44	17 31 32	29 43 05	7♏14 48	24 56.3	22 18.8	3 47.9	6 13.1	22 03.6	27 41.0	11 25.4	24 01.0	27 59.2	20 35.1
11 Su	13 21 40	18 30 52	14♏41 37	22 02 31	24 46.4	23 58.8	4 51.8	6 14.9	22 27.7	27 47.5	11 32.0	24 02.0	27 57.6	20 34.5
12 M	13 25 37	19 30 14	29 16 46	6♐23 47	24 38.8	25 38.1	5 55.5	6R15.7	22 51.8	27 53.9	11 38.5	24 03.0	27 55.9	20 34.0
13 Tu	13 29 33	20 29 38	13♐23 19	20 15 16	24 33.8	27 16.7	6 58.9	6 15.7	23 15.9	28 00.1	11 45.1	24 03.9	27 54.3	20 33.4
14 W	13 33 30	21 29 04	26 59 44	3♑37 01	24 31.3	28 54.6	8 02.1	6 14.8	23 40.2	28 06.1	11 51.5	24 04.8	27 52.6	20 32.9
15 Th	13 37 27	22 28 32	10♑07 31	16 31 43	24 30.6	0♏31.7	9 05.0	6 13.0	24 04.4	28 12.0	11 57.9	24 05.6	27 50.9	20 32.4
16 F	13 41 23	23 28 01	22 50 14	29 03 41	24 30.5	2 08.2	10 07.6	6 10.3	24 28.7	28 17.7	12 04.3	24 06.3	27 49.3	20 32.0
17 Sa	13 45 20	24 27 32	5♒12 41	11♒17 56	24 29.9	3 44.0	11 10.0	6 06.7	24 53.0	28 23.2	12 10.6	24 07.0	27 47.6	20 31.5
18 Su	13 49 16	25 27 05	17 20 03	23 19 40	24 27.7	5 19.2	12 12.0	6 02.2	25 17.3	28 28.6	12 16.8	24 07.7	27 45.9	20 31.1
19 M	13 53 13	26 26 39	29 17 22	5♓13 43	24 23.1	6 53.7	13 13.7	5 56.9	25 41.7	28 33.9	12 23.0	24 08.3	27 44.2	20 30.7
20 Tu	13 57 09	27 26 15	11♓09 12	17 04 17	24 15.5	8 27.6	14 15.2	5 50.6	26 06.1	28 38.9	12 29.1	24 08.8	27 42.6	20 30.3
21 W	14 01 06	28 25 53	22 59 24	28 54 52	24 05.1	10 01.0	15 16.2	5 43.5	26 30.6	28 43.8	12 35.2	24 09.3	27 40.9	20 30.0
22 Th	14 05 02	29 25 33	4♈51 01	10♈48 06	23 52.3	11 33.7	16 17.0	5 35.5	26 55.0	28 48.5	12 41.2	24 09.8	27 39.2	20 29.7
23 F	14 08 59	0♏25 15	16 46 20	22 45 54	23 38.2	13 05.8	17 17.4	5 26.6	27 19.6	28 53.1	12 47.2	24 10.1	27 37.5	20 29.4
24 Sa	14 12 56	1 24 59	28 46 57	4♉49 35	23 23.8	14 37.4	18 17.4	5 16.9	27 44.1	28 57.5	12 53.1	24 10.5	27 35.8	20 29.1
25 Su	14 16 52	2 24 45	10♉53 56	17 00 05	23 10.3	16 08.4	19 17.1	5 06.3	28 08.7	29 01.7	12 58.9	24 10.7	27 34.2	20 28.9
26 M	14 20 49	3 24 32	23 08 09	29 18 16	22 58.8	17 38.9	20 16.3	4 54.9	28 33.3	29 05.7	13 04.7	24 11.0	27 32.5	20 28.6
27 Tu	14 24 45	4 24 22	5♊30 33	11♊45 10	22 50.1	19 08.8	21 15.2	4 42.6	28 57.9	29 09.5	13 10.4	24 11.1	27 30.8	20 28.4
28 W	14 28 42	5 24 14	18 02 20	24 22 16	22 44.4	20 38.1	22 13.6	4 29.5	29 22.5	29 13.2	13 16.0	24 11.2	27 29.2	20 28.3
29 Th	14 32 38	6 24 09	0♋45 15	7♋11 34	22 41.4	22 06.9	23 11.6	4 15.7	29 47.2	29 16.7	13 21.6	24R11.3	27 27.5	20 28.1
30 F	14 36 35	7 24 05	13 41 32	20 15 32	22D40.6	23 35.1	24 09.2	4 01.0	0♐11.9	29 20.0	13 27.1	24 11.3	27 25.8	20 28.0
31 Sa	14 40 31	8 24 04	26 53 53	3♌36 55	22R40.7	25 02.8	25 06.3	3 45.6	0 36.7	29 23.1	13 32.5	24 11.3	27 24.2	20 28.0

Astro Data

	Dy Hr Mn
♃☌♅	8 10:34
☽0S	11 8:12
♄∠♅	13 20:20
☉0S	22 16:13
☽0N	25 6:49
☿0S	29 18:42
☽0S	8 19:01
♃□♆	12 18:17
♂ R	12 23:10
♄⚼♆	22 5:38
☽0N	22 13:06
♅ R	30 2:00

Planet Ingress

		Dy Hr Mn
♀	♏	10 1:39
☿	♍	10 2:19
♂	♊	11 20:30
☉	♎	22 16:14
☿	♎	27 19:00
♀	♐	6 23:04
☿	♏	15 4:09
☉	♏	23 1:51
⚳	♐	30 0:25

Last Aspect / ☽ Ingress (September)

Last Aspect Dy Hr Mn			☽ Ingress	Dy Hr Mn
1 17:30	♂	☌	♊	2 1:31
4 7:30	♆	⚹	♋	4 9:37
6 11:53	♆	□	♌	6 13:55
8 12:55	♆	△	♍	8 14:55
10 13:27	♂	△	♎	10 14:12
12 11:45	♆	☍	♏	12 13:54
14 5:46	♃	△	♐	14 16:01
16 19:14	♆	△	♑	16 21:52
19 4:30	♆	□	♒	19 7:24
21 16:12	♆	⚹	♓	21 19:17
23 22:58	♃	△	♈	24 7:59
26 17:05	♆	☌	♉	26 20:24
29 0:25	♃	⚹	♊	29 7:43

Last Aspect / ☽ Ingress (October)

Last Aspect Dy Hr Mn			☽ Ingress	Dy Hr Mn
1 13:36	♆	⚹	♋	1 16:54
3 19:41	♆	□	♌	3 22:52
5 23:37	♀	□	♍	6 1:20
7 21:07	♃	⚹	♎	8 1:14
9 21:17	♆	☍	♏	10 0:27
11 21:35	♃	△	♐	12 1:12
14 2:15	☿	⚹	♑	14 5:25
16 10:30	♃	☍	♒	16 13:49
18 20:54	♆	⚹	♓	19 1:26
21 11:37	♃	△	♈	21 14:12
24 0:17	♃	□	♉	24 2:25
26 11:35	♃	⚹	♊	26 13:21
28 17:51	♆	⚹	♋	28 22:35
31 4:26	♃	☌	♌	31 5:34

☽ Phases & Eclipses

Dy Hr Mn		
2 22:04	☾	10♊46
9 18:27	●	17♍25
16 10:37	☽	23♐55
24 11:33	○	1♈46
2 10:30	☾	9♋34
9 2:36	●	16♎09
16 0:17	☽	22♑59
24 4:38	○	1♉07
31 21:08	☾	8♌47

Astro Data

1 September 2037
Julian Day # 50283
SVP 4♓44'16"
GC 27♐21.9 ⚴ 5♎34.5
Eris 28♈23.7R ⚵ 4♎00.8
⚷ 25♊22.9 ⚶ 11♉20.4
☽ Mean ☊ 26♋30.1

1 October 2037
Julian Day # 50313
SVP 4♓44'13"
GC 27♐22.0 ⚴ 18♎47.6
Eris 28♈09.2R ⚵ 14♎52.1
⚷ 26♊00.9 ⚶ 9♉20.8R
☽ Mean ☊ 24♋54.7

November 2037 LONGITUDE

Day	Sid.Time	☉	0 hr ☽	Noon ☽	True ☊	☿	♀	♂	⚳	♃	♄	♅	♆	♇
1 Su	14 44 28	9♏24 04	10♌24 58	17♌18 15	22♋40.5	26♏29.8	26♐02.9	3♊29.5	1♐01.4	29♋26.1	13♍37.9	24♋11.1	27♈22.6	20♒27.9
2 M	14 48 25	10 24 07	24 16 56	1♍21 05	22R 38.9	27 56.2	26 59.0	3R 12.7	1 26.2	29 28.8	13 43.2	24R 11.0	27R 20.9	20D 27.9
3 Tu	14 52 21	11 24 12	8♍30 38	15 45 19	22 35.0	29 22.0	27 54.6	2 55.2	1 51.0	29 31.4	13 48.4	24 10.8	27 19.3	20 27.9
4 W	14 56 18	12 24 19	23 04 45	0♎28 18	22 28.4	0♐47.1	28 49.7	2 37.0	2 15.8	29 33.8	13 53.5	24 10.5	27 17.7	20 27.9
5 Th	15 00 14	13 24 28	7♎55 11	15 24 28	22 19.5	2 11.5	29 44.2	2 18.3	2 40.7	29 35.9	13 58.6	24 10.2	27 16.1	20 27.9
6 F	15 04 11	14 24 40	22 55 03	0♏25 42	22 09.1	3 35.1	0♑38.2	1 59.0	3 05.6	29 37.9	14 03.6	24 09.8	27 14.5	20 28.0
7 Sa	15 08 07	15 24 53	7♏55 14	15 22 23	21 58.6	4 57.8	1 31.5	1 39.2	3 30.4	29 39.7	14 08.5	24 09.4	27 12.9	20 28.1
8 Su	15 12 04	16 25 07	22 45 59	0♐05 01	21 49.1	6 19.7	2 24.2	1 19.0	3 55.3	29 41.3	14 13.4	24 08.9	27 11.3	20 28.3
9 M	15 16 00	17 25 24	7♐18 36	14 26 01	21 41.6	7 40.6	3 16.2	0 58.3	4 20.3	29 42.7	14 18.1	24 08.3	27 09.8	20 28.4
10 Tu	15 19 57	18 25 42	21 26 47	28 20 36	21 36.8	9 00.3	4 07.6	0 37.3	4 45.2	29 43.9	14 22.8	24 07.8	27 08.2	20 28.6
11 W	15 23 54	19 26 02	5♑07 23	11♑47 12	21D 34.4	10 18.9	4 58.3	0 15.9	5 10.2	29 44.9	14 27.4	24 07.1	27 06.7	20 28.8
12 Th	15 27 50	20 26 23	18 20 16	24 46 59	21 34.0	11 36.1	5 48.2	29♉54.3	5 35.1	29 45.8	14 31.9	24 06.4	27 05.2	20 29.1
13 F	15 31 47	21 26 46	1♒07 46	7♒23 11	21 34.6	12 51.8	6 37.3	29 32.4	6 00.1	29 46.4	14 36.3	24 05.7	27 03.7	20 29.3
14 Sa	15 35 43	22 27 10	13 33 50	19 40 22	21R 35.3	14 05.8	7 25.6	29 10.4	6 25.1	29 46.8	14 40.7	24 04.9	27 02.2	20 29.6
15 Su	15 39 40	23 27 35	25 43 24	1♓43 38	21 34.9	15 17.9	8 13.1	28 48.3	6 50.1	29R 47.0	14 44.9	24 04.0	27 00.7	20 30.0
16 M	15 43 36	24 28 02	7♓41 42	13 38 14	21 32.7	16 27.9	8 59.6	28 26.2	7 15.1	29 47.0	14 49.1	24 03.1	26 59.3	20 30.3
17 Tu	15 47 33	25 28 29	19 33 52	25 29 08	21 28.2	17 35.5	9 45.3	28 04.0	7 40.1	29 46.8	14 53.1	24 02.1	26 57.8	20 30.7
18 W	15 51 29	26 28 59	1♈24 36	7♈20 44	21 21.4	18 40.4	10 30.0	27 41.8	8 05.2	29 46.5	14 57.1	24 01.1	26 56.4	20 31.1
19 Th	15 55 26	27 29 29	13 17 59	19 16 43	21 12.6	19 42.1	11 13.7	27 19.8	8 30.2	29 45.9	15 01.0	24 00.1	26 55.0	20 31.5
20 F	15 59 23	28 30 01	25 17 16	1♉19 54	21 02.6	20 40.4	11 56.3	26 57.9	8 55.2	29 45.1	15 04.8	23 59.0	26 53.6	20 32.0
21 Sa	16 03 19	29 30 34	7♉24 51	13 32 17	20 52.2	21 34.7	12 37.8	26 36.2	9 20.3	29 44.1	15 08.5	23 57.8	26 52.3	20 32.5
22 Su	16 07 16	0♐31 09	19 42 19	25 55 02	20 42.6	22 24.6	13 18.3	26 14.7	9 45.3	29 43.0	15 12.2	23 56.6	26 50.9	20 33.0
23 M	16 11 12	1 31 45	2♊10 29	8♊28 42	20 34.4	23 09.3	13 57.5	25 53.6	10 10.4	29 41.6	15 15.7	23 55.4	26 49.6	20 33.5
24 Tu	16 15 09	2 32 23	14 49 41	21 13 26	20 28.4	23 48.4	14 35.5	25 32.7	10 35.4	29 40.0	15 19.1	23 54.1	26 48.3	20 34.1
25 W	16 19 05	3 33 02	27 39 57	4♋09 14	20 24.7	24 21.0	15 12.2	25 12.2	11 00.5	29 38.3	15 22.5	23 52.7	26 47.0	20 34.7
26 Th	16 23 02	4 33 43	10♋41 21	17 16 18	20D 23.4	24 46.4	15 47.6	24 52.2	11 25.6	29 36.3	15 25.7	23 51.3	26 45.8	20 35.3
27 F	16 26 58	5 34 25	23 54 09	0♌35 00	20 23.7	25 03.9	16 21.7	24 32.6	11 50.6	29 34.2	15 28.9	23 49.9	26 44.5	20 35.9
28 Sa	16 30 55	6 35 09	7♌18 57	14 06 04	20 25.0	25R 12.6	16 54.2	24 13.5	12 15.7	29 31.8	15 31.9	23 48.4	26 43.3	20 36.6
29 Su	16 34 52	7 35 54	20 56 29	27 50 15	20R 26.3	25 11.8	17 25.3	23 54.9	12 40.8	29 29.3	15 34.9	23 46.9	26 42.2	20 37.3
30 M	16 38 48	8 36 41	4♍47 26	11♍48 00	20 26.6	25 00.7	17 54.9	23 36.8	13 05.9	29 26.5	15 37.7	23 45.3	26 41.0	20 38.0

December 2037 LONGITUDE

Day	Sid.Time	☉	0 hr ☽	Noon ☽	True ☊	☿	♀	♂	⚳	♃	♄	♅	♆	♇
1 Tu	16 42 45	9♐37 30	18♍51 54	25♍58 58	20♋25.4	24♐38.9	18♑22.8	23♉19.4	13♐30.9	29♋23.6	15♍40.5	23♋43.7	26♈39.9	20♒38.7
2 W	16 46 41	10 38 19	3♎08 56	10♎21 28	20R 22.3	24R 05.9	18 49.1	23R 02.6	13 56.0	29R 20.4	15 43.1	23R 42.1	26R 38.7	20 39.5
3 Th	16 50 38	11 39 11	17 36 05	24 52 11	20 17.6	23 21.9	19 13.7	22 46.5	14 21.0	29 17.1	15 45.7	23 40.4	26 37.7	20 40.3
4 F	16 54 34	12 40 03	2♏09 07	9♏26 07	20 11.9	22 27.3	19 36.5	22 31.0	14 46.1	29 13.6	15 48.1	23 38.6	26 36.6	20 41.1
5 Sa	16 58 31	13 40 57	16 42 22	23 57 03	20 05.8	21 23.0	19 57.4	22 16.3	15 11.2	29 09.9	15 50.4	23 36.8	26 35.6	20 42.0
6 Su	17 02 27	14 41 52	1♐09 18	8♐18 21	20 00.4	20 10.7	20 16.4	22 02.2	15 36.2	29 06.0	15 52.7	23 35.0	26 34.6	20 42.8
7 M	17 06 24	15 42 49	15 23 29	22 24 04	19 56.2	18 52.2	20 33.4	21 49.0	16 01.3	29 02.0	15 54.8	23 33.2	26 33.6	20 43.7
8 Tu	17 10 21	16 43 46	29 19 36	6♑09 42	19 53.6	17 30.1	20 48.3	21 36.5	16 26.3	28 57.7	15 56.8	23 31.3	26 32.6	20 44.6
9 W	17 14 17	17 44 44	12♑54 08	19 32 48	19D 52.8	16 07.2	21 01.2	21 24.8	16 51.3	28 53.3	15 58.7	23 29.3	26 31.7	20 45.6
10 Th	17 18 14	18 45 43	26 05 42	2♒33 00	19 53.4	14 46.2	21 11.8	21 14.0	17 16.3	28 48.7	16 00.6	23 27.4	26 30.8	20 46.6
11 F	17 22 10	19 46 42	8♒54 57	15 11 53	19 55.0	13 29.8	21 20.2	21 03.9	17 41.3	28 43.9	16 02.3	23 25.3	26 30.0	20 47.5
12 Sa	17 26 07	20 47 42	21 24 14	27 32 29	19 56.8	12 20.3	21 26.3	20 54.7	18 06.3	28 39.0	16 03.9	23 23.3	26 29.1	20 48.6
13 Su	17 30 03	21 48 43	3♓37 10	9♓38 53	19 58.3	11 19.7	21 30.0	20 46.3	18 31.3	28 33.9	16 05.3	23 21.2	26 28.3	20 49.6
14 M	17 34 00	22 49 44	15 38 12	21 35 46	19R 59.0	10 29.1	21R 31.3	20 38.7	18 56.3	28 28.6	16 06.7	23 19.1	26 27.6	20 50.6
15 Tu	17 37 57	23 50 46	27 32 11	3♈28 05	19 58.5	9 49.4	21 30.1	20 31.9	19 21.2	28 23.2	16 08.0	23 17.0	26 26.8	20 51.7
16 W	17 41 53	24 51 48	9♈24 03	15 20 41	19 56.8	9 20.9	21 26.5	20 26.0	19 46.1	28 17.6	16 09.1	23 14.8	26 26.1	20 52.8
17 Th	17 45 50	25 52 50	21 18 33	27 18 08	19 54.0	9 03.4	21 20.3	20 20.9	20 11.0	28 11.9	16 10.2	23 12.6	26 25.4	20 53.9
18 F	17 49 46	26 53 53	3♉19 56	9♉24 23	19 50.5	8D 56.5	21 11.7	20 16.7	20 35.9	28 06.0	16 11.1	23 10.4	26 24.8	20 55.1
19 Sa	17 53 43	27 54 57	15 31 51	21 42 40	19 46.7	8 59.7	21 00.5	20 13.3	21 00.8	27 59.9	16 11.9	23 08.1	26 24.2	20 56.3
20 Su	17 57 39	28 56 00	27 57 04	4♊15 16	19 43.2	9 12.1	20 46.9	20 10.6	21 25.7	27 53.8	16 12.7	23 05.8	26 23.6	20 57.4
21 M	18 01 36	29 57 05	10♊37 22	17 03 27	19 40.2	9 33.0	20 30.7	20 08.8	21 50.5	27 47.5	16 13.3	23 03.5	26 23.0	20 58.6
22 Tu	18 05 32	0♑58 10	23 33 30	0♋07 28	19 38.2	10 01.6	20 12.2	20D 07.8	22 15.3	27 41.0	16 13.8	23 01.2	26 22.5	20 59.9
23 W	18 09 29	1 59 15	6♋45 13	13 26 35	19D 37.3	10 37.1	19 51.3	20 07.6	22 40.1	27 34.5	16 14.1	22 58.8	26 22.0	21 01.1
24 Th	18 13 26	3 00 20	20 11 23	26 59 22	19 37.3	11 18.8	19 28.2	20 08.2	23 04.9	27 27.8	16 14.4	22 56.4	26 21.6	21 02.4
25 F	18 17 22	4 01 27	3♌50 18	10♌43 54	19 38.1	12 06.0	19 02.9	20 09.5	23 29.6	27 21.0	16R 14.6	22 54.0	26 21.1	21 03.7
26 Sa	18 21 19	5 02 33	17 39 53	24 38 01	19 39.3	12 58.0	18 35.6	20 11.6	23 54.3	27 14.0	16 14.6	22 51.6	26 20.8	21 05.0
27 Su	18 25 15	6 03 41	1♍37 59	8♍39 33	19 40.4	13 54.3	18 06.4	20 14.5	24 19.0	27 07.0	16 14.6	22 49.1	26 20.4	21 06.3
28 M	18 29 12	7 04 48	15 42 28	22 46 27	19 41.3	14 54.4	17 35.6	20 18.0	24 43.7	26 59.8	16 14.4	22 46.7	26 20.1	21 07.6
29 Tu	18 33 08	8 05 57	29 51 16	6♎56 41	19R 41.6	15 57.9	17 03.3	20 22.4	25 08.4	26 52.6	16 14.1	22 44.2	26 19.8	21 09.0
30 W	18 37 05	9 07 05	14♎02 24	21 08 11	19 41.4	17 04.3	16 29.6	20 27.4	25 33.0	26 45.2	16 13.7	22 41.7	26 19.5	21 10.4
31 Th	18 41 01	10 08 15	28 13 43	5♏18 42	19 40.7	18 13.4	15 54.9	20 33.1	25 57.6	26 37.8	16 13.2	22 39.2	26 19.3	21 11.8

Astro Data	Dy Hr Mn
♇ D	3 3:38
☽ 0S	5 5:46
♃∠♄	16 0:15
♃ R	16 2:18
☽ 0N	18 20:45
☿ R	28 22:03
☽ 0S	2 14:34
♀ R	14 12:48
☽ 0N	16 5:25
☿ D	18 16:14
♂ D	23 6:32
♄ R	26 11:37
☽ 0S	29 20:53

Planet Ingress	Dy Hr Mn
☿ ♐	3 22:41
♀ ♑	5 19:00
♂ ♉R	12 5:41
☉ ♐	21 23:40
☉ ♑	21 13:09

Last Aspect Dy Hr Mn		☽ Ingress	Dy Hr Mn
2 5:34	☿ □	♍	2 9:43
4 10:31	♃ ⚹	♎	4 11:14
6 10:43	♃ □	♏	6 11:19
8 11:21	♃ △	♐	8 11:52
10 9:54	♆ △	♑	10 14:55
12 21:25	♃ ☍	♒	12 21:51
15 6:19	♂ □	♓	15 8:32
17 20:42	♃ △	♈	17 21:09
20 8:52	♃ □	♉	20 9:22
22 19:17	♃ ⚹	♊	22 19:50
24 22:23	♆ ⚹	♋	25 4:20
27 10:11	♃ ☌	♌	27 10:57
29 10:02	♆ △	♍	29 15:45

Last Aspect Dy Hr Mn		☽ Ingress	Dy Hr Mn
1 17:42	♃ ⚹	♎	1 18:44
3 19:15	♃ □	♏	3 20:27
5 20:38	♃ △	♐	5 22:04
7 19:11	♆ △	♑	8 1:11
10 5:04	♃ ☍	♒	10 7:14
12 9:56	♆ ⚹	♓	12 16:50
15 1:48	♃ △	♈	15 4:59
17 13:46	♃ □	♉	17 17:23
19 24:00	♃ ⚹	♊	20 3:55
22 5:10	♆ ⚹	♋	22 11:46
24 12:49	♃ ☌	♌	24 17:17
26 14:56	♆ △	♍	26 21:12
28 19:06	♃ ⚹	♎	29 0:15
30 21:25	♃ □	♏	31 3:00

☽ Phases & Eclipses Dy Hr Mn	
7 12:04	● 15♏25
14 18:00	☽ 22♒42
22 21:36	○ 0♊55
30 6:08	☾ 8♍22
6 23:40	● 15♐11
14 14:43	☽ 22♓57
22 13:40	○ 1♋02
29 14:06	☾ 8♎11

Astro Data

1 November 2037
Julian Day # 50344
SVP 4♓44'10"
GC 27♐22.1 ⚴ 2♏35.0
Eris 27♈50.8R ⚵ 25♎59.7
⚷ 25♊29.5R ⚶ 2♉00.0R
☽ Mean ☊ 23♋16.2

1 December 2037
Julian Day # 50374
SVP 4♓44'06"
GC 27♐22.1 ⚴ 15♏45.3
Eris 27♈34.9R ⚵ 6♏14.2
⚷ 24♊01.8R ⚶ 26♈33.6R
☽ Mean ☊ 21♋40.9

LONGITUDE — January 2038

Day	Sid.Time	☉	0 hr ☽	Noon ☽	True ☊	☿	♀	♂	⚳	♃	♄	♅	♆	♇
1 F	18 44 58	11♑09 25	12♏22 49	19♏25 43	19♋39.7	19♐24.8	15♑19.3	20♉39.6	26♐22.1	26♋30.3	16♍12.6	22♋36.6	26♈19.1	21♒13.2
2 Sa	18 48 55	12 10 35	26 27 02	3♐26 24	19R38.7	20 38.3	14R43.2	20 46.7	26 46.7	26R22.7	16R11.9	22R34.1	26R19.0	21 14.6
3 Su	18 52 51	13 11 45	10♐23 27	17 17 48	19 37.9	21 53.6	14 06.7	20 54.5	27 11.2	26 15.0	16 11.1	22 31.5	26 18.9	21 16.1
4 M	18 56 48	14 12 56	24 09 07	0♑57 04	19 37.3	23 10.5	13 30.0	21 03.0	27 35.6	26 07.3	16 10.1	22 29.0	26 18.8	21 17.5
5 Tu	19 00 44	15 14 06	7♑41 21	14 21 45	19D37.1	24 28.9	12 53.5	21 12.1	28 00.1	25 59.5	16 09.1	22 26.4	26D18.8	21 19.0
6 W	19 04 41	16 15 17	20 58 05	27 30 13	19 37.1	25 48.6	12 17.4	21 21.9	28 24.5	25 51.6	16 07.9	22 23.8	26 18.7	21 20.5
7 Th	19 08 37	17 16 27	3♒58 05	10♒21 42	19 37.3	27 09.6	11 42.0	21 32.3	28 48.8	25 43.7	16 06.7	22 21.2	26 18.8	21 22.0
8 F	19 12 34	18 17 38	16 41 10	22 56 38	19 37.5	28 31.6	11 07.4	21 43.3	29 13.2	25 35.8	16 05.3	22 18.6	26 18.8	21 23.5
9 Sa	19 16 30	19 18 47	29 08 19	5♓16 29	19R37.6	29 54.6	10 34.0	21 55.0	29 37.4	25 27.8	16 03.8	22 16.0	26 18.9	21 25.1
10 Su	19 20 27	20 19 57	11♓21 31	17 23 48	19 37.5	1♑18.6	10 01.8	22 07.2	0♑01.7	25 19.8	16 02.2	22 13.4	26 19.1	21 26.6
11 M	19 24 24	21 21 05	23 23 47	29 21 57	19 37.4	2 43.3	9 31.2	22 20.0	0 25.9	25 11.7	16 00.5	22 10.8	26 19.2	21 28.2
12 Tu	19 28 20	22 22 14	5♈18 51	11♈15 00	19 37.2	4 08.9	9 02.2	22 33.3	0 50.0	25 03.6	15 58.7	22 08.2	26 19.4	21 29.8
13 W	19 32 17	23 23 21	17 11 00	23 07 26	19D37.2	5 35.3	8 35.2	22 47.2	1 14.2	24 55.6	15 56.8	22 05.6	26 19.7	21 31.3
14 Th	19 36 13	24 24 28	29 04 55	5♉04 00	19 37.3	7 02.3	8 10.1	23 01.7	1 38.2	24 47.5	15 54.8	22 03.0	26 19.9	21 32.9
15 F	19 40 10	25 25 35	11♉05 19	17 09 24	19 37.6	8 30.0	7 47.2	23 16.6	2 02.3	24 39.4	15 52.7	22 00.4	26 20.2	21 34.6
16 Sa	19 44 06	26 26 41	23 16 49	29 28 03	19 38.3	9 58.4	7 26.5	23 32.1	2 26.2	24 31.3	15 50.5	21 57.8	26 20.6	21 36.2
17 Su	19 48 03	27 27 46	5♊43 33	12♊03 43	19 39.1	11 27.4	7 08.1	23 48.1	2 50.2	24 23.3	15 48.2	21 55.2	26 21.0	21 37.8
18 M	19 51 59	28 28 50	18 28 53	24 59 16	19 39.9	12 57.0	6 52.1	24 04.6	3 14.0	24 15.2	15 45.8	21 52.6	26 21.4	21 39.5
19 Tu	19 55 56	29 29 54	1♋35 02	8♋16 14	19R40.5	14 27.2	6 38.6	24 21.5	3 37.9	24 07.2	15 43.4	21 50.0	26 21.8	21 41.1
20 W	19 59 53	0♒30 57	15 02 46	21 54 30	19 40.7	15 58.0	6 27.6	24 38.9	4 01.7	23 59.2	15 40.8	21 47.5	26 22.3	21 42.8
21 Th	20 03 49	1 31 59	28 51 07	5♌52 14	19 40.3	17 29.4	6 19.0	24 56.7	4 25.4	23 51.3	15 38.1	21 44.9	26 22.8	21 44.5
22 F	20 07 46	2 33 01	12♌57 20	20 05 52	19 39.2	19 01.4	6 13.0	25 15.0	4 49.1	23 43.4	15 35.3	21 42.4	26 23.4	21 46.1
23 Sa	20 11 42	3 34 02	27 17 08	4♍30 28	19 37.6	20 34.0	6D09.5	25 33.7	5 12.7	23 35.5	15 32.5	21 39.8	26 23.9	21 47.8
24 Su	20 15 39	4 35 02	11♍45 07	19 00 23	19 35.6	22 07.2	6 08.4	25 52.8	5 36.3	23 27.7	15 29.5	21 37.3	26 24.6	21 49.5
25 M	20 19 35	5 36 02	26 15 32	3♎29 57	19 33.7	23 41.0	6 09.8	26 12.3	5 59.8	23 19.9	15 26.5	21 34.8	26 25.2	21 51.2
26 Tu	20 23 32	6 37 01	10♎43 01	17 54 14	19 32.2	25 15.4	6 13.6	26 32.3	6 23.3	23 12.2	15 23.3	21 32.3	26 25.9	21 52.9
27 W	20 27 28	7 38 00	25 03 09	2♏09 26	19D31.4	26 50.5	6 19.7	26 52.5	6 46.7	23 04.6	15 20.1	21 29.8	26 26.6	21 54.7
28 Th	20 31 25	8 38 59	9♏12 50	16 13 08	19 31.4	28 26.2	6 28.2	27 13.2	7 10.0	22 57.0	15 16.8	21 27.3	26 27.3	21 56.4
29 F	20 35 22	9 39 56	23 10 14	0♐04 03	19 32.3	0♒02.5	6 38.9	27 34.2	7 33.3	22 49.6	15 13.5	21 24.9	26 28.1	21 58.1
30 Sa	20 39 18	10 40 53	6♐54 35	13 41 49	19 33.8	1 39.5	6 51.9	27 55.6	7 56.5	22 42.2	15 10.0	21 22.5	26 29.0	21 59.9
31 Su	20 43 15	11 41 50	20 25 48	27 06 33	19 35.3	3 17.1	7 06.9	28 17.4	8 19.7	22 34.9	15 06.5	21 20.1	26 29.8	22 01.6

LONGITUDE — February 2038

Day	Sid.Time	☉	0 hr ☽	Noon ☽	True ☊	☿	♀	♂	⚳	♃	♄	♅	♆	♇
1 M	20 47 11	12♒42 46	3♑44 08	10♑18 34	19♋36.4	4♒55.5	7♑24.0	28♉39.5	8♑42.8	22♋27.7	15♍02.9	21♋17.7	26♈30.7	22♒03.3
2 Tu	20 51 08	13 43 40	16 49 54	23 18 10	19R36.7	6 34.6	7 43.1	29 01.9	9 05.8	22R20.6	14R59.2	21R15.3	26 31.6	22 05.1
3 W	20 55 04	14 44 34	29 43 24	6♒05 38	19 35.6	8 14.3	8 04.1	29 24.7	9 28.8	22 13.7	14 55.4	21 13.0	26 32.6	22 06.9
4 Th	20 59 01	15 45 27	12♒24 53	18 41 13	19 33.2	9 54.8	8 27.0	29 47.8	9 51.7	22 06.8	14 51.6	21 10.7	26 33.5	22 08.6
5 F	21 02 57	16 46 18	24 54 40	1♓05 21	19 29.4	11 36.1	8 51.6	0♊11.2	10 14.6	22 00.0	14 47.7	21 08.4	26 34.5	22 10.4
6 Sa	21 06 54	17 47 09	7♓13 22	13 18 52	19 24.5	13 18.1	9 18.0	0 34.9	10 37.3	21 53.4	14 43.8	21 06.1	26 35.6	22 12.1
7 Su	21 10 51	18 47 58	19 22 02	25 23 06	19 19.1	15 00.8	9 46.1	0 58.9	11 00.0	21 46.9	14 39.7	21 03.9	26 36.7	22 13.9
8 M	21 14 47	19 48 45	1♈22 20	7♈20 04	19 13.7	16 44.4	10 15.7	1 23.2	11 22.6	21 40.5	14 35.6	21 01.7	26 37.8	22 15.7
9 Tu	21 18 44	20 49 31	13 16 40	19 12 32	19 09.0	18 28.7	10 46.8	1 47.8	11 45.1	21 34.3	14 31.5	20 59.5	26 38.9	22 17.4
10 W	21 22 40	21 50 16	25 08 08	1♉03 57	19 05.4	20 13.9	11 19.5	2 12.7	12 07.6	21 28.2	14 27.3	20 57.4	26 40.1	22 19.2
11 Th	21 26 37	22 50 59	7♉00 33	12 58 28	19D03.3	21 59.8	11 53.6	2 37.8	12 30.0	21 22.2	14 23.1	20 55.3	26 41.3	22 21.0
12 F	21 30 33	23 51 40	18 58 18	25 00 39	19 02.8	23 46.5	12 29.0	3 03.3	12 52.3	21 16.4	14 18.7	20 53.2	26 42.5	22 22.7
13 Sa	21 34 30	24 52 20	1♊06 09	7♊15 24	19 03.5	25 33.9	13 05.7	3 28.9	13 14.5	21 10.8	14 14.4	20 51.2	26 43.7	22 24.5
14 Su	21 38 26	25 52 58	13 29 00	19 47 31	19 05.0	27 22.2	13 43.7	3 54.8	13 36.6	21 05.3	14 10.0	20 49.1	26 45.0	22 26.3
15 M	21 42 23	26 53 35	26 11 30	2♋41 23	19 06.7	29 11.2	14 23.0	4 21.0	13 58.7	21 00.0	14 05.6	20 47.2	26 46.4	22 28.0
16 Tu	21 46 20	27 54 10	9♋17 35	16 00 20	19R07.6	1♓00.8	15 03.3	4 47.3	14 20.7	20 54.8	14 01.1	20 45.2	26 47.7	22 29.8
17 W	21 50 16	28 54 43	22 49 49	29 46 02	19 07.1	2 51.2	15 44.9	5 13.9	14 42.5	20 49.8	13 56.6	20 43.4	26 49.1	22 31.6
18 Th	21 54 13	29 55 14	6♌48 48	13♌57 48	19 04.8	4 42.1	16 27.5	5 40.8	15 04.3	20 44.9	13 52.0	20 41.5	26 50.5	22 33.3
19 F	21 58 09	0♓55 44	21 12 30	28 32 12	19 00.5	6 33.5	17 11.1	6 07.8	15 26.0	20 40.3	13 47.4	20 39.7	26 51.9	22 35.1
20 Sa	22 02 06	1 56 12	5♍56 02	13♍22 58	18 54.6	8 25.4	17 55.7	6 35.1	15 47.6	20 35.7	13 42.8	20 37.9	26 53.3	22 36.8
21 Su	22 06 02	2 56 39	20 51 55	28 21 43	18 47.7	10 17.5	18 41.3	7 02.5	16 09.2	20 31.4	13 38.1	20 36.2	26 54.8	22 38.6
22 M	22 09 59	3 57 04	5♎51 11	13♎19 13	18 40.8	12 09.8	19 27.9	7 30.2	16 30.6	20 27.2	13 33.4	20 34.5	26 56.3	22 40.3
23 Tu	22 13 55	4 57 28	20 44 45	28 06 53	18 34.8	14 02.1	20 15.3	7 58.0	16 51.9	20 23.3	13 28.7	20 32.8	26 57.9	22 42.1
24 W	22 17 52	5 57 51	5♏24 53	12♏38 11	18 30.4	15 54.1	21 03.6	8 26.0	17 13.2	20 19.5	13 24.0	20 31.2	26 59.4	22 43.8
25 Th	22 21 49	6 58 12	19 46 20	26 49 09	18D28.1	17 45.7	21 52.7	8 54.2	17 34.3	20 15.8	13 19.3	20 29.6	27 01.0	22 45.5
26 F	22 25 45	7 58 32	3♐46 30	10♐38 28	18 27.6	19 36.5	22 42.6	9 22.6	17 55.4	20 12.4	13 14.5	20 28.1	27 02.6	22 47.2
27 Sa	22 29 42	8 58 50	17 25 10	24 06 51	18 28.4	21 26.2	23 33.2	9 51.2	18 16.3	20 09.1	13 09.7	20 26.6	27 04.2	22 49.0
28 Su	22 33 38	9 59 07	0♑43 47	7♑16 20	18R29.5	23 14.4	24 24.6	10 20.0	18 37.2	20 06.1	13 04.9	20 25.2	27 05.9	22 50.7

Astro Data Dy Hr Mn	Planet Ingress Dy Hr Mn	Last Aspect Dy Hr Mn	☽ Ingress Dy Hr Mn	Last Aspect Dy Hr Mn	☽ Ingress Dy Hr Mn	☽ Phases & Eclipses Dy Hr Mn	Astro Data
♃□♆ 2 23:49	☿ ♑ 9 13:33	1 23:59 ♃ △	♐ 2 6:05	2 23:02 ♂ △	♒ 3 0:31	5 13:43 ● 15♑18	1 January 2038
♆D 6 5:34	⚳ ♑ 10 10:20	4 3:48 ♆ △	♑ 4 10:19	5 3:13 ♆ ⚹	♓ 5 9:53	5 13:47:12 ✔ A 03'18"	Julian Day # 50405
☽0N 12 13:58	☉ ♒ 19 23:50	6 9:48 ♆ □	♒ 6 16:37	7 4:52 ♃ △	♈ 7 21:15	13 12:35 ☽ 23♈25	SVP 4♓44'00"
♅⚻♇ 21 14:36	☿ ♒ 29 11:23	9 0:10 ☿ ⚹	♓ 9 1:41	10 3:05 ♆ ☌	♉ 10 9:51	21 4:01 ○ 1♌12	GC 27♐22.2 ⚴ 28♏44.8
♀D 24 10:21		11 3:42 ♃ △	♈ 11 13:17	12 9:31 ☉ □	♊ 12 21:50	21 3:50 • A 0.899	Eris 27♈25.5R ⚵ 15♏39.9
☽0S 26 2:24	♂ ♊ 5 0:34	13 18:28 ♆ ☌	♉ 14 1:51	15 4:30 ♆ ⚹	♋ 15 7:03	27 22:02 ☾ 8♏03	⚷ 22♊09.1R ⚶ 27♈29.0
	☿ ♓ 15 22:42	16 5:38 ☉ △	♊ 16 13:02	17 6:55 ♆ □	♌ 17 12:24		☽ Mean ☊ 20♋02.4
♃⚻♇ 4 6:52	☉ ♓ 18 13:53	18 14:30 ♆ ⚹	♋ 18 21:08	19 9:16 ♆ △	♍ 19 14:23	4 5:53 ● 15♒30	
☽0N 8 21:28		20 19:44 ♆ □	♌ 21 1:58	20 23:36 ♅ ⚹	♎ 21 14:37	12 9:31 ☽ 23♉45	1 February 2038
♃☌♅ 19 16:56		22 22:31 ♆ △	♍ 23 4:31	23 10:07 ♆ ☍	♏ 23 15:05	19 16:11 ○ 1♍06	Julian Day # 50436
☽0S 22 9:41		24 23:38 ♂ △	♎ 25 6:12	25 5:03 ♇ □	♐ 25 17:28	26 6:57 ☾ 7♐46	SVP 4♓43'55"
		27 2:20 ♆ ☍	♏ 27 8:21	27 17:21 ♆ △	♑ 27 22:40		GC 27♐22.3 ⚴ 10♐26.4
		29 7:32 ♂ ☍	♐ 29 11:53				Eris 27♈26.3 ⚵ 23♏00.6
		31 10:54 ♆ △	♑ 31 17:13				⚷ 20♊44.4R ⚶ 4♉02.6
							☽ Mean ☊ 18♋23.9

March 2038 — LONGITUDE

Day	Sid.Time	☉	0 hr ☽	Noon ☽	True ☊	☿	♀	♂	⚳	♃	♄	♅	♆	♇
1 M	22 37 35	10♓59 23	13♑44 48	20♑09 32	18♋30.0	25♓00.8	25♑16.6	10♊48.9	18♑57.9	20♋03.2	13♍00.1	20♋23.8	27♈07.6	22♒52.4
2 Tu	22 41 31	11 59 37	26 30 52	2♒49 07	18R 28.9	26 44.9	26 09.3	11 18.0	19 18.5	20R 00.5	12R 55.3	20R 22.4	27 09.3	22 54.1
3 W	22 45 28	12 59 49	9♒04 34	15 17 28	18 25.4	28 26.2	27 02.7	11 47.3	19 39.1	19 58.0	12 50.5	20 21.1	27 11.0	22 55.7
4 Th	22 49 24	14 00 00	21 28 01	27 36 26	18 19.3	0♈04.2	27 56.7	12 16.7	19 59.5	19 55.7	12 45.7	20 19.9	27 12.7	22 57.4
5 F	22 53 21	15 00 08	3♓42 52	9♓47 29	18 10.7	1 38.3	28 51.2	12 46.3	20 19.8	19 53.6	12 40.9	20 18.7	27 14.5	22 59.1
6 Sa	22 57 18	16 00 15	15 50 24	21 51 46	18 00.2	3 08.0	29 46.3	13 16.0	20 40.0	19 51.7	12 36.1	20 17.5	27 16.3	23 00.7
7 Su	23 01 14	17 00 21	27 51 43	3♈50 22	17 48.4	4 32.7	0♒42.0	13 45.9	21 00.0	19 50.0	12 31.3	20 16.4	27 18.1	23 02.4
8 M	23 05 11	18 00 24	9♈47 55	15 44 34	17 36.5	5 51.8	1 38.2	14 15.9	21 20.0	19 48.4	12 26.6	20 15.3	27 19.9	23 04.0
9 Tu	23 09 07	19 00 25	21 40 31	27 36 03	17 25.4	7 04.9	2 34.9	14 46.1	21 39.8	19 47.1	12 21.8	20 14.3	27 21.8	23 05.7
10 W	23 13 04	20 00 24	3♉31 29	9♉27 10	17 16.2	8 11.4	3 32.0	15 16.4	21 59.5	19 46.0	12 17.0	20 13.4	27 23.7	23 07.3
11 Th	23 17 00	21 00 21	15 23 30	21 20 57	17 09.4	9 10.8	4 29.6	15 46.9	22 19.1	19 45.1	12 12.3	20 12.5	27 25.6	23 08.9
12 F	23 20 57	22 00 16	27 20 00	3♊21 12	17 05.2	10 02.7	5 27.7	16 17.5	22 38.5	19 44.3	12 07.6	20 11.6	27 27.5	23 10.5
13 Sa	23 24 53	23 00 09	9♊25 07	15 32 22	17D 03.4	10 46.7	6 26.2	16 48.2	22 57.8	19 43.8	12 02.9	20 10.8	27 29.4	23 12.0
14 Su	23 28 50	24 00 00	21 43 33	27 59 18	17 03.2	11 22.7	7 25.1	17 19.0	23 17.0	19 43.4	11 58.3	20 10.0	27 31.4	23 13.6
15 M	23 32 47	24 59 48	4♋20 15	10♋46 59	17R 03.6	11 50.2	8 24.5	17 50.0	23 36.1	19D 43.3	11 53.7	20 09.3	27 33.3	23 15.2
16 Tu	23 36 43	25 59 34	17 20 03	23 59 56	17 03.6	12 09.3	9 24.2	18 21.1	23 55.0	19 43.3	11 49.1	20 08.7	27 35.3	23 16.7
17 W	23 40 40	26 59 18	0♌46 59	7♌41 27	17 01.9	12R 19.9	10 24.3	18 52.3	24 13.8	19 43.6	11 44.5	20 08.1	27 37.3	23 18.2
18 Th	23 44 36	27 59 00	14 43 25	21 52 45	16 57.9	12 22.0	11 24.7	19 23.6	24 32.5	19 44.0	11 40.0	20 07.6	27 39.3	23 19.8
19 F	23 48 33	28 58 39	29 09 07	6♍31 58	16 51.2	12 15.9	12 25.5	19 55.0	24 51.0	19 44.7	11 35.5	20 07.1	27 41.3	23 21.3
20 Sa	23 52 29	29 58 16	14♍00 30	21 33 40	16 42.1	12 01.9	13 26.7	20 26.5	25 09.3	19 45.5	11 31.1	20 06.6	27 43.4	23 22.7
21 Su	23 56 26	0♈57 51	29 10 16	6♎48 57	16 31.6	11 40.4	14 28.1	20 58.1	25 27.6	19 46.5	11 26.7	20 06.2	27 45.4	23 24.2
22 M	0 00 22	1 57 25	14♎28 15	22 06 44	16 20.9	11 12.0	15 29.9	21 29.8	25 45.6	19 47.7	11 22.4	20 05.9	27 47.5	23 25.7
23 Tu	0 04 19	2 56 56	29 42 58	7♏15 40	16 11.1	10 37.4	16 32.0	22 01.6	26 03.6	19 49.1	11 18.1	20 05.6	27 49.6	23 27.1
24 W	0 08 15	3 56 25	14♏43 43	22 06 14	16 03.5	9 57.4	17 34.5	22 33.6	26 21.4	19 50.7	11 13.8	20 05.4	27 51.7	23 28.5
25 Th	0 12 12	4 55 53	29 22 32	6♐32 10	15 58.5	9 13.0	18 37.2	23 05.6	26 39.0	19 52.4	11 09.6	20 05.2	27 53.8	23 29.9
26 F	0 16 09	5 55 19	13♐34 54	20 30 43	15 56.0	8 25.1	19 40.2	23 37.7	26 56.5	19 54.4	11 05.5	20 05.1	27 55.9	23 31.3
27 Sa	0 20 05	6 54 44	27 19 44	4♑02 14	15 55.4	7 34.9	20 43.4	24 09.9	27 13.8	19 56.5	11 01.4	20D 05.0	27 58.1	23 32.7
28 Su	0 24 02	7 54 06	10♑38 36	17 09 16	15 55.4	6 43.3	21 46.9	24 42.2	27 31.0	19 58.9	10 57.4	20 05.0	28 00.2	23 34.1
29 M	0 27 58	8 53 27	23 34 43	29 55 29	15 54.8	5 51.5	22 50.7	25 14.5	27 48.0	20 01.4	10 53.4	20 05.1	28 02.4	23 35.4
30 Tu	0 31 55	9 52 46	6♒12 05	12♒25 01	15 52.6	5 00.6	23 54.7	25 47.0	28 04.8	20 04.1	10 49.5	20 05.2	28 04.5	23 36.7
31 W	0 35 51	10 52 04	18 34 46	24 41 47	15 47.8	4 11.3	24 59.0	26 19.5	28 21.5	20 07.0	10 45.7	20 05.3	28 06.7	23 38.0

April 2038 — LONGITUDE

Day	Sid.Time	☉	0 hr ☽	Noon ☽	True ☊	☿	♀	♂	⚳	♃	♄	♅	♆	♇
1 Th	0 39 48	11♈51 19	0♓46 28	6♓49 12	15♋40.1	3♈24.7	26♒03.4	26♊52.2	28♑37.9	20♋10.0	10♍41.9	20♋05.5	28♈08.9	23♒39.3
2 F	0 43 44	12 50 32	12 50 17	18 50 02	15R 29.4	2R 41.5	27 08.1	27 24.9	28 54.3	20 13.3	10R 38.2	20 05.8	28 11.1	23 40.6
3 Sa	0 47 41	13 49 44	24 48 40	0♈46 24	15 16.4	2 02.3	28 13.0	27 57.7	29 10.4	20 16.7	10 34.6	20 06.1	28 13.3	23 41.8
4 Su	0 51 38	14 48 53	6♈43 27	12 39 57	15 01.9	1 27.6	29 18.1	28 30.6	29 26.3	20 20.3	10 31.0	20 06.5	28 15.5	23 43.1
5 M	0 55 34	15 48 01	18 36 05	24 32 00	14 47.2	0 57.9	0♓23.4	29 03.5	29 42.1	20 24.0	10 27.6	20 06.9	28 17.7	23 44.3
6 Tu	0 59 31	16 47 06	0♉27 53	6♉23 53	14 33.5	0 33.4	1 28.9	29 36.6	29 57.7	20 28.0	10 24.2	20 07.4	28 20.0	23 45.4
7 W	1 03 27	17 46 09	12 20 14	18 17 10	14 21.7	0 14.2	2 34.5	0♋09.7	0♒13.1	20 32.1	10 20.8	20 07.9	28 22.2	23 46.6
8 Th	1 07 24	18 45 11	24 14 57	0♊13 54	14 12.6	0 00.5	3 40.4	0 42.9	0 28.3	20 36.4	10 17.6	20 08.5	28 24.4	23 47.8
9 F	1 11 20	19 44 10	6♊14 23	12 16 48	14 06.6	29♓52.3	4 46.4	1 16.2	0 43.3	20 40.9	10 14.5	20 09.1	28 26.7	23 48.9
10 Sa	1 15 17	20 43 07	18 21 36	24 29 17	14 03.3	29D 49.6	5 52.5	1 49.5	0 58.1	20 45.5	10 11.4	20 09.8	28 28.9	23 50.0
11 Su	1 19 13	21 42 01	0♋40 21	6♋55 24	14D 02.1	29 52.2	6 58.9	2 22.9	1 12.8	20 50.3	10 08.4	20 10.5	28 31.2	23 51.1
12 M	1 23 10	22 40 54	13 14 57	19 39 37	14R 02.1	0♈00.0	8 05.3	2 56.3	1 27.2	20 55.3	10 05.5	20 11.3	28 33.4	23 52.1
13 Tu	1 27 07	23 39 44	26 09 55	2♌46 25	14 01.9	0 12.9	9 12.0	3 29.9	1 41.4	21 00.4	10 02.7	20 12.2	28 35.7	23 53.2
14 W	1 31 03	24 38 31	9♌29 31	16 19 37	14 00.4	0 30.7	10 18.7	4 03.5	1 55.4	21 05.7	10 00.0	20 13.1	28 37.9	23 54.2
15 Th	1 35 00	25 37 17	23 16 57	0♍21 35	13 56.8	0 53.1	11 25.7	4 37.1	2 09.2	21 11.1	9 57.3	20 14.0	28 40.2	23 55.2
16 F	1 38 56	26 36 00	7♍33 24	14 52 05	13 50.6	1 20.1	12 32.7	5 10.8	2 22.7	21 16.7	9 54.8	20 15.0	28 42.5	23 56.2
17 Sa	1 42 53	27 34 41	22 17 05	29 47 35	13 42.0	1 51.3	13 39.9	5 44.6	2 36.1	21 22.4	9 52.3	20 16.1	28 44.7	23 57.1
18 Su	1 46 49	28 33 20	7♎22 34	15♎00 49	13 31.9	2 26.6	14 47.2	6 18.4	2 49.2	21 28.4	9 50.0	20 17.2	28 47.0	23 58.1
19 M	1 50 46	29 31 56	22 40 57	0♏21 30	13 21.4	3 05.9	15 54.7	6 52.3	3 02.2	21 34.4	9 47.7	20 18.4	28 49.3	23 59.0
20 Tu	1 54 42	0♉30 31	8♏00 58	15 37 56	13 11.7	3 48.9	17 02.3	7 26.2	3 14.9	21 40.6	9 45.5	20 19.6	28 51.5	23 59.8
21 W	1 58 39	1 29 04	23 11 04	0♐39 13	13 04.1	4 35.5	18 10.0	8 00.2	3 27.3	21 47.0	9 43.5	20 20.8	28 53.8	24 00.7
22 Th	2 02 36	2 27 36	8♐01 28	15 17 06	12 58.9	5 25.5	19 17.8	8 34.2	3 39.6	21 53.5	9 41.5	20 22.1	28 56.0	24 01.5
23 F	2 06 32	3 26 06	22 25 39	29 26 53	12D 56.3	6 18.7	20 25.8	9 08.3	3 51.6	22 00.1	9 39.6	20 23.5	28 58.3	24 02.4
24 Sa	2 10 29	4 24 34	6♑20 44	13♑07 23	12 55.6	7 15.0	21 33.9	9 42.4	4 03.3	22 06.9	9 37.8	20 24.9	29 00.6	24 03.2
25 Su	2 14 25	5 23 01	19 47 05	26 20 13	12R 56.0	8 14.4	22 42.0	10 16.6	4 14.9	22 13.8	9 36.1	20 26.4	29 02.8	24 03.9
26 M	2 18 22	6 21 26	2♒47 18	9♒08 51	12 56.2	9 16.5	23 50.3	10 50.8	4 26.1	22 20.9	9 34.5	20 27.9	29 05.1	24 04.7
27 Tu	2 22 18	7 19 49	15 25 27	21 37 40	12 55.1	10 21.4	24 58.7	11 25.1	4 37.2	22 28.1	9 33.1	20 29.4	29 07.3	24 05.4
28 W	2 26 15	8 18 11	27 46 05	3♓51 17	12 52.0	11 28.9	26 07.2	11 59.5	4 47.9	22 35.4	9 31.7	20 31.0	29 09.6	24 06.1
29 Th	2 30 11	9 16 31	9♓53 47	15 54 06	12 46.5	12 39.0	27 15.8	12 33.9	4 58.4	22 42.9	9 30.4	20 32.7	29 11.8	24 06.7
30 F	2 34 08	10 14 49	21 52 42	27 50 02	12 38.5	13 51.5	28 24.5	13 08.3	5 08.7	22 50.5	9 29.2	20 34.4	29 14.1	24 07.4

Astro Data	Planet Ingress	Last Aspect	☽ Ingress	Last Aspect	☽ Ingress	☽ Phases & Eclipses
Dy Hr Mn	Dy Hr Mn	Dy Hr Mn	Dy Hr Mn	Dy Hr Mn	Dy Hr Mn	Dy Hr Mn
☿0N 3 22:45	☿ ♈ 4 10:57	2 1:11 ♆ □	♒ 2 6:37	3 6:04 ♂ □	♈ 3 10:27	5 23:16 ● 15♓28
☽0N 8 3:51	♀ ♒ 6 17:55	4 11:13 ♆ ⚹	♓ 4 16:42	5 21:36 ♂ ⚹	♉ 5 23:04	14 3:43 ☽ 23♊39
♄□♆ 9 11:58	☉ ♈ 20 12:42	6 8:52 ♅ △	♈ 7 4:17	7 23:04 ♇ □	♊ 8 11:32	21 2:11 ○ 0♎33
♃ D 15 17:53		9 11:31 ♆ ☌	♉ 9 16:52	10 22:23 ☿ □	♋ 10 22:42	27 17:37 ☾ 7♑09
☿ R 18 6:07	♀ ♓ 5 3:24	11 15:37 ♇ □	♊ 12 5:20	13 4:25 ♆ □	♌ 13 6:59	
☉0N 20 12:41	⚳ ♒ 6 15:33	14 11:07 ♆ ⚹	♋ 14 15:49	15 9:09 ♆ △	♍ 15 11:24	4 16:44 ● 15♈01
☽0S 21 19:34	♂ ♋ 7 4:58	16 18:23 ♆ □	♌ 16 22:38	16 22:27 ♃ ⚹	♎ 17 12:20	12 18:03 ☽ 22♋56
♅ D 28 4:28	☿ ♓R 8 13:09	18 21:34 ♆ △	♍ 19 1:23	19 10:37 ☉ ☍	♏ 19 11:26	19 10:37 ○ 29♎29
♃☌♅ 30 21:42	☿ ♈ 12 11:57	20 10:10 ♂ □	♎ 21 1:18	21 1:19 ♇ □	♐ 21 10:57	26 6:17 ☾ 6♒07
	☉ ♉ 19 23:30	22 20:59 ♆ ☍	♏ 23 0:27	23 11:11 ♆ △	♑ 23 12:57	
☽0N 4 9:50		24 14:15 ♇ □	♐ 25 1:02	25 17:02 ♆ □	♒ 25 18:47	
☿0S 9 7:39		27 1:06 ♆ △	♑ 27 4:45	28 2:42 ♆ ⚹	♓ 28 4:23	
☿ D 10 12:13		29 8:25 ♆ □	♒ 29 12:09	30 13:17 ♀ ☌	♈ 30 16:22	
☽0S 18 6:46		31 18:45 ♆ ⚹	♓ 31 22:28			
☿0N 22 15:09						

Astro Data

1 March 2038
Julian Day # 50464
SVP 4♓43'52"
GC 27♐22.3 ⚴ 18♐59.7
Eris 27♈35.7 ⚵ 26♏45.9
⚷ 20♊23.5 ⚶ 12♉56.5
☽ Mean ☊ 16♋55.0

1 April 2038
Julian Day # 50495
SVP 4♓43'49"
GC 27♐22.4 ⚴ 24♐40.4
Eris 27♈53.1 ⚵ 26♏22.8R
⚷ 21♊11.6 ⚶ 24♉38.4
☽ Mean ☊ 15♋16.5

LONGITUDE May 2038

Day	Sid.Time	☉	0 hr ☽	Noon ☽	True ☊	☿	♀	♂	⯰	♃	♄	♅	♆	♇
1 Sa	2 38 05	11♉13 06	3♈46 27	9♈42 18	12♋28.5	15♈06.4	29♓33.3	13♋42.8	5♒18.7	22♋58.2	9♍28.1	20♋36.1	29♈16.3	24♒08.0
2 Su	2 42 01	12 11 22	15 37 55	21 33 32	12R 17.2	16 23.7	0♈42.2	14 17.3	5 28.4	23 06.1	9R 27.2	20 37.9	29 18.5	24 08.6
3 M	2 45 58	13 09 35	27 29 25	3♉25 44	12 05.6	17 43.1	1 51.1	14 51.9	5 37.8	23 14.1	9 26.3	20 39.7	29 20.7	24 09.2
4 Tu	2 49 54	14 07 47	9♉22 43	15 20 32	11 54.8	19 04.8	3 00.2	15 26.5	5 47.0	23 22.2	9 25.5	20 41.6	29 22.9	24 09.7
5 W	2 53 51	15 05 58	21 19 21	27 19 21	11 45.6	20 28.7	4 09.3	16 01.2	5 55.9	23 30.4	9 24.9	20 43.6	29 25.1	24 10.2
6 Th	2 57 47	16 04 07	3♊20 43	9♊23 40	11 38.7	21 54.6	5 18.5	16 35.9	6 04.5	23 38.8	9 24.3	20 45.5	29 27.3	24 10.7
7 F	3 01 44	17 02 13	15 28 27	21 35 18	11 34.2	23 22.7	6 27.7	17 10.7	6 12.8	23 47.3	9 23.9	20 47.6	29 29.5	24 11.2
8 Sa	3 05 40	18 00 19	27 44 31	3♋56 26	11D 32.2	24 52.8	7 37.1	17 45.5	6 20.9	23 55.9	9 23.5	20 49.6	29 31.7	24 11.6
9 Su	3 09 37	18 58 22	10♋11 24	16 29 48	11 32.0	26 25.0	8 46.5	18 20.4	6 28.6	24 04.6	9 23.3	20 51.7	29 33.9	24 12.1
10 M	3 13 34	19 56 23	22 52 03	29 18 34	11 32.9	27 59.2	9 55.9	18 55.3	6 36.1	24 13.4	9D 23.1	20 53.9	29 36.0	24 12.4
11 Tu	3 17 30	20 54 23	5♌49 45	12♌26 02	11R 33.9	29 35.5	11 05.5	19 30.2	6 43.2	24 22.4	9 23.1	20 56.1	29 38.2	24 12.8
12 W	3 21 27	21 52 21	19 07 45	25 55 15	11 34.1	1♉13.8	12 15.1	20 05.2	6 50.1	24 31.4	9 23.2	20 58.3	29 40.3	24 13.1
13 Th	3 25 23	22 50 16	2♍48 44	9♍48 20	11 32.7	2 54.1	13 24.8	20 40.2	6 56.6	24 40.6	9 23.4	21 00.6	29 42.4	24 13.5
14 F	3 29 20	23 48 10	16 54 03	24 05 42	11 29.5	4 36.4	14 34.5	21 15.2	7 02.8	24 49.9	9 23.7	21 02.9	29 44.5	24 13.7
15 Sa	3 33 16	24 46 02	1♎22 57	8♎45 15	11 24.5	6 20.7	15 44.3	21 50.3	7 08.7	24 59.3	9 24.0	21 05.2	29 46.6	24 14.0
16 Su	3 37 13	25 43 53	16 11 54	23 42 00	11 18.3	8 07.1	16 54.1	22 25.4	7 14.3	25 08.7	9 24.5	21 07.6	29 48.7	24 14.2
17 M	3 41 09	26 41 42	1♏14 28	8♏48 09	11 11.6	9 55.5	18 04.1	23 00.5	7 19.6	25 18.3	9 25.1	21 10.1	29 50.8	24 14.4
18 Tu	3 45 06	27 39 29	16 21 47	23 54 09	11 05.4	11 45.9	19 14.0	23 35.7	7 24.6	25 28.0	9 25.8	21 12.5	29 52.9	24 14.6
19 W	3 49 02	28 37 15	1♐23 59	8♐50 12	11 00.6	13 38.3	20 24.1	24 10.9	7 29.3	25 37.8	9 26.6	21 15.0	29 54.9	24 14.8
20 Th	3 52 59	29 34 59	16 11 46	23 27 53	10 57.5	15 32.8	21 34.2	24 46.2	7 33.6	25 47.7	9 27.6	21 17.6	29 56.9	24 14.9
21 F	3 56 56	0♊32 43	0♑37 54	7♑41 22	10D 56.3	17 29.2	22 44.3	25 21.5	7 37.6	25 57.6	9 28.6	21 20.2	29 59.0	24 15.0
22 Sa	4 00 52	1 30 25	14 38 02	21 27 49	10 56.6	19 27.6	23 54.6	25 56.8	7 41.3	26 07.7	9 29.7	21 22.8	0♉01.0	24 15.1
23 Su	4 04 49	2 28 06	28 10 48	4♒47 11	10 57.9	21 27.8	25 04.9	26 32.1	7 44.6	26 17.9	9 30.9	21 25.4	0 03.0	24 15.2
24 M	4 08 45	3 25 46	11♒17 18	17 41 34	10 59.4	23 30.0	26 15.2	27 07.5	7 47.6	26 28.1	9 32.2	21 28.1	0 04.9	24R 15.2
25 Tu	4 12 42	4 23 25	24 00 28	0♓14 33	11R 00.3	25 33.9	27 25.6	27 42.9	7 50.2	26 38.5	9 33.7	21 30.9	0 06.9	24 15.2
26 W	4 16 38	5 21 04	6♓24 22	12 30 29	11 00.1	27 39.4	28 36.0	28 18.4	7 52.5	26 48.9	9 35.2	21 33.6	0 08.8	24 15.2
27 Th	4 20 35	6 18 41	18 33 30	24 33 59	10 58.5	29 46.5	29 46.5	28 53.9	7 54.5	26 59.4	9 36.8	21 36.4	0 10.7	24 15.1
28 F	4 24 32	7 16 17	0♈32 29	6♈29 33	10 55.4	1♊54.9	0♉57.1	29 29.4	7 56.1	27 10.0	9 38.5	21 39.2	0 12.7	24 15.0
29 Sa	4 28 28	8 13 52	12 25 41	18 21 20	10 51.0	4 04.5	2 07.7	0♌05.0	7 57.3	27 20.7	9 40.4	21 42.1	0 14.5	24 14.9
30 Su	4 32 25	9 11 26	24 16 58	0♉12 57	10 45.8	6 15.1	3 18.3	0 40.5	7 58.2	27 31.5	9 42.3	21 45.0	0 16.4	24 14.8
31 M	4 36 21	10 09 00	6♉09 40	12 07 25	10 40.3	8 26.5	4 29.0	1 16.2	7R 58.7	27 42.3	9 44.3	21 47.9	0 18.2	24 14.7

LONGITUDE June 2038

Day	Sid.Time	☉	0 hr ☽	Noon ☽	True ☊	☿	♀	♂	⯰	♃	♄	♅	♆	♇
1 Tu	4 40 18	11♊06 32	18♉06 31	24♉07 11	10♋35.2	10♊38.3	5♉39.7	1♌51.8	7♒58.9	27♋53.3	9♍46.4	21♋50.9	0♉20.1	24♒14.5
2 W	4 44 14	12 04 04	0♊09 40	6♊14 10	10R 30.9	12 50.4	6 50.5	2 27.5	7R 58.7	28 04.3	9 48.7	21 53.8	0 21.9	24R 14.3
3 Th	4 48 11	13 01 34	12 20 50	18 29 52	10 27.9	15 02.5	8 01.3	3 03.3	7 58.2	28 15.4	9 51.0	21 56.9	0 23.7	24 14.1
4 F	4 52 07	13 59 04	24 41 24	0♋55 34	10D 26.3	17 14.2	9 12.2	3 39.0	7 57.3	28 26.5	9 53.4	21 59.9	0 25.4	24 13.8
5 Sa	4 56 04	14 56 32	7♋12 33	13 32 28	10 26.0	19 25.4	10 23.1	4 14.8	7 56.0	28 37.8	9 55.9	22 03.0	0 27.2	24 13.5
6 Su	5 00 01	15 54 00	19 55 30	26 21 48	10 26.7	21 35.7	11 34.0	4 50.6	7 54.4	28 49.1	9 58.5	22 06.1	0 28.9	24 13.2
7 M	5 03 57	16 51 26	2♌51 33	9♌24 54	10 28.1	23 45.0	12 45.0	5 26.5	7 52.4	29 00.4	10 01.3	22 09.2	0 30.6	24 12.9
8 Tu	5 07 54	17 48 51	16 02 03	22 43 09	10 29.5	25 52.9	13 56.0	6 02.4	7 50.1	29 11.9	10 04.1	22 12.4	0 32.3	24 12.6
9 W	5 11 50	18 46 15	29 28 21	6♍17 45	10R 30.7	27 59.3	15 07.1	6 38.3	7 47.3	29 23.4	10 07.0	22 15.5	0 34.0	24 12.2
10 Th	5 15 47	19 43 38	13♍11 26	20 09 24	10 31.1	0♋04.0	16 18.2	7 14.2	7 44.3	29 35.0	10 09.9	22 18.7	0 35.6	24 11.8
11 F	5 19 43	20 41 00	27 11 35	4♎17 50	10 30.6	2 06.8	17 29.3	7 50.2	7 40.8	29 46.6	10 13.0	22 21.9	0 37.2	24 11.4
12 Sa	5 23 40	21 38 21	11♎27 55	18 41 27	10 29.2	4 07.7	18 40.5	8 26.2	7 37.0	29 58.3	10 16.2	22 25.2	0 38.8	24 10.9
13 Su	5 27 36	22 35 40	25 57 58	3♏16 52	10 27.3	6 06.5	19 51.7	9 02.2	7 32.9	0♌10.1	10 19.5	22 28.5	0 40.4	24 10.4
14 M	5 31 33	23 32 59	10♏37 30	17 59 05	10 25.2	8 03.1	21 02.9	9 38.3	7 28.4	0 21.9	10 22.8	22 31.8	0 41.9	24 09.9
15 Tu	5 35 30	24 30 17	25 20 46	2♐41 43	10 23.2	9 57.5	22 14.2	10 14.4	7 23.5	0 33.8	10 26.2	22 35.1	0 43.4	24 09.4
16 W	5 39 26	25 27 35	10♐01 01	17 17 50	10 21.8	11 49.6	23 25.5	10 50.5	7 18.3	0 45.7	10 29.8	22 38.4	0 44.9	24 08.9
17 Th	5 43 23	26 24 51	24 31 22	1♑40 54	10D 21.0	13 39.5	24 36.9	11 26.6	7 12.7	0 57.7	10 33.4	22 41.8	0 46.4	24 08.3
18 F	5 47 19	27 22 08	8♑45 50	15 45 39	10 20.9	15 26.9	25 48.3	12 02.8	7 06.8	1 09.8	10 37.1	22 45.2	0 47.8	24 07.7
19 Sa	5 51 16	28 19 23	22 39 59	29 28 35	10 21.4	17 12.0	26 59.7	12 39.0	7 00.6	1 21.9	10 40.9	22 48.5	0 49.2	24 07.1
20 Su	5 55 12	29 16 39	6♒11 22	12♒48 19	10 22.3	18 54.7	28 11.2	13 15.2	6 54.0	1 34.0	10 44.8	22 52.0	0 50.6	24 06.5
21 M	5 59 09	0♋13 54	19 19 34	25 45 20	10 23.2	20 35.0	29 22.7	13 51.4	6 47.1	1 46.2	10 48.7	22 55.4	0 52.0	24 05.8
22 Tu	6 03 05	1 11 08	2♓05 57	8♓21 47	10 24.1	22 13.0	0♊34.3	14 27.7	6 39.8	1 58.5	10 52.7	22 58.8	0 53.3	24 05.2
23 W	6 07 02	2 08 23	14 33 16	20 40 55	10 24.6	23 48.4	1 45.9	15 04.0	6 32.3	2 10.8	10 56.9	23 02.3	0 54.6	24 04.5
24 Th	6 10 59	3 05 37	26 45 15	2♈46 49	10R 24.8	25 21.5	2 57.6	15 40.4	6 24.4	2 23.1	11 01.1	23 05.8	0 55.9	24 03.8
25 F	6 14 55	4 02 52	8♈46 10	14 43 54	10 24.7	26 52.1	4 09.2	16 16.7	6 16.1	2 35.5	11 05.3	23 09.3	0 57.2	24 03.0
26 Sa	6 18 52	5 00 06	20 40 34	26 36 44	10 24.3	28 20.3	5 21.0	16 53.1	6 07.6	2 48.0	11 09.7	23 12.8	0 58.4	24 02.3
27 Su	6 22 48	5 57 20	2♉32 56	8♉29 41	10 23.8	29 46.0	6 32.7	17 29.6	5 58.7	3 00.4	11 14.1	23 16.3	0 59.6	24 01.5
28 M	6 26 45	6 54 34	14 27 30	20 26 48	10 23.3	1♌09.1	7 44.5	18 06.0	5 49.6	3 13.0	11 18.7	23 19.9	1 00.8	24 00.7
29 Tu	6 30 41	7 51 48	26 28 03	2♊31 36	10 22.9	2 29.7	8 56.4	18 42.5	5 40.2	3 25.5	11 23.3	23 23.4	1 01.9	23 59.9
30 W	6 34 38	8 49 03	8♊37 49	14 46 58	10 22.7	3 47.8	10 08.2	19 19.0	5 30.4	3 38.2	11 27.9	23 27.0	1 03.0	23 59.0

Astro Data	Planet Ingress	Last Aspect	☽ Ingress	Last Aspect	☽ Ingress	☽ Phases & Eclipses	Astro Data
Dy Hr Mn	Dy Hr Mn	Dy Hr Mn	Dy Hr Mn	Dy Hr Mn	Dy Hr Mn	Dy Hr Mn	1 May 2038
☽0N 1 16:11	♀ ♈ 1 21:19	3 3:43 ♆ ☌	♉ 3 5:04	1 19:36 ♃ ✶	♊ 1 23:41	4 9:21 ● 14♉01	Julian Day # 50525
♀0N 4 22:54	☿ ♉ 11 18:02	5 5:42 ♇ □	♊ 5 17:20	3 23:07 ♇ △	♋ 4 10:13	12 4:19 ☽ 21♌34	SVP 4♓43'46"
♃⚻♇ 10 9:12	☉ ♊ 20 22:24	8 3:27 ♆ ✶	♋ 8 4:23	6 16:37 ♃ ☌	♌ 6 18:44	18 18:25 ○ 27♏55	GC 27♐22.5 ⚳ 24♐15.8R
♄ D 11 6:23	♆ ♉ 22 0:18	10 12:32 ♆ □	♌ 10 13:17	8 18:41 ☿ ✶	♍ 9 0:56	25 20:45 ☾ 4♓44	Eris 28♈12.7 ✱ 21♏20.1R
♃∠♄ 11 13:56	☿ ♊ 27 14:32	12 18:34 ♆ △	♍ 12 19:07	11 4:16 ♃ ✶	♎ 11 4:45		⚷ 22♊58.9 ⚶ 6♊58.0
☽0S 15 17:10	♀ ♉ 27 16:35	14 13:14 ♃ ✶	♎ 14 21:44	12 21:04 ♇ △	♏ 13 6:37	3 0:25 ● 12♊34	☽ Mean ☊ 13♋41.1
♇ R 25 2:22	♂ ♌ 29 8:39	16 21:45 ♆ ☍	♏ 16 22:02	14 22:04 ♇ □	♐ 15 7:36	10 11:13 ☽ 19♍42	
☽0N 28 23:19		18 18:25 ☉ ☍	♐ 18 21:45	17 2:32 ☉ ☍	♑ 17 9:10	17 2:32 ○ 26♐02	1 June 2038
	☿ ♋ 10 11:14	20 22:53 ♆ △	♑ 20 22:56	19 7:11 ♀ △	♒ 19 12:56	17 2:45 ☍ A 0.442	Julian Day # 50556
⯰ R 1 11:54	♃ ♌ 12 15:27	22 20:25 ♃ ☍	♒ 23 3:17	21 19:33 ♀ □	♓ 21 20:01	24 12:41 ☾ 3♈07	SVP 4♓43'41"
☽0S 12 1:17	☉ ♋ 21 6:11	25 6:00 ♀ ✶	♓ 25 11:32	23 19:05 ☿ △	♈ 24 6:27		GC 27♐22.6 ⚳ 17♐09.3R
♃□♆ 16 10:09	♀ ♊ 22 0:30	27 21:09 ♂ △	♈ 27 22:55	26 15:58 ☿ □	♉ 26 18:51		Eris 28♈30.9 ✱ 14♏42.9R
☽0N 25 7:06	☿ ♌ 27 16:00	30 6:29 ♃ □	♉ 30 11:34	28 19:06 ♇ □	♊ 29 7:00		⚷ 25♊30.4 ⚶ 20♊12.9
							☽ Mean ☊ 12♋02.6

July 2038 LONGITUDE

Day	Sid.Time	☉	0 hr ☽	Noon ☽	True ☊	☿	♀	♂	⚳	♃	♄	♅	♆	♇
1 Th	6 38 34	9♋46 17	20♊59 20	27♊15 04	10♋22.6	5♌03.1	11♊20.1	19♌55.6	5♒20.4	3♌50.8	11♍32.7	23♋30.6	1♉04.1	23♒58.2
2 F	6 42 31	10 43 31	3♋34 22	9♋57 18	10R 22.6	6 15.8	12 32.1	20 32.2	5R 10.2	4 03.5	11 37.5	23 34.1	1 05.2	23R 57.3
3 Sa	6 46 28	11 40 45	16 23 56	22 54 18	10 22.6	7 25.7	13 44.1	21 08.8	4 59.7	4 16.2	11 42.4	23 37.7	1 06.2	23 56.4
4 Su	6 50 24	12 37 59	29 28 21	6♌06 02	10 22.5	8 32.8	14 56.1	21 45.4	4 48.9	4 29.0	11 47.4	23 41.3	1 07.2	23 55.5
5 M	6 54 21	13 35 13	12♌47 16	19 31 53	10 22.2	9 37.0	16 08.1	22 22.1	4 37.9	4 41.8	11 52.4	23 45.0	1 08.2	23 54.5
6 Tu	6 58 17	14 32 26	26 19 47	3♍10 48	10 21.8	10 38.2	17 20.2	22 58.8	4 26.7	4 54.6	11 57.5	23 48.6	1 09.1	23 53.6
7 W	7 02 14	15 29 39	10♍04 43	17 01 21	10 21.3	11 36.3	18 32.3	23 35.5	4 15.2	5 07.5	12 02.7	23 52.2	1 10.0	23 52.6
8 Th	7 06 10	16 26 52	24 00 29	1♎01 53	10 20.9	12 31.2	19 44.5	24 12.3	4 03.6	5 20.3	12 07.9	23 55.8	1 10.9	23 51.6
9 F	7 10 07	17 24 05	8♎05 20	15 10 32	10D 20.7	13 22.8	20 56.6	24 49.1	3 51.7	5 33.2	12 13.3	23 59.5	1 11.7	23 50.6
10 Sa	7 14 03	18 21 18	22 17 14	29 25 07	10 20.8	14 10.9	22 08.9	25 25.9	3 39.7	5 46.2	12 18.6	24 03.1	1 12.6	23 49.6
11 Su	7 18 00	19 18 30	6♏33 51	13♏43 05	10 21.3	14 55.5	23 21.1	26 02.7	3 27.5	5 59.1	12 24.1	24 06.8	1 13.3	23 48.6
12 M	7 21 57	20 15 43	20 52 27	28 01 31	10 22.1	15 36.4	24 33.4	26 39.6	3 15.2	6 12.1	12 29.6	24 10.4	1 14.1	23 47.5
13 Tu	7 25 53	21 12 55	5♐09 52	12♐17 02	10 22.9	16 13.5	25 45.7	27 16.5	3 02.7	6 25.1	12 35.2	24 14.1	1 14.8	23 46.5
14 W	7 29 50	22 10 08	19 22 35	26 26 02	10R 23.6	16 46.6	26 58.1	27 53.4	2 50.1	6 38.2	12 40.8	24 17.8	1 15.5	23 45.4
15 Th	7 33 46	23 07 21	3♑26 56	10♑24 51	10 23.9	17 15.5	28 10.5	28 30.4	2 37.3	6 51.2	12 46.5	24 21.4	1 16.2	23 44.3
16 F	7 37 43	24 04 34	17 19 22	24 10 08	10 23.5	17 40.2	29 22.9	29 07.3	2 24.5	7 04.3	12 52.3	24 25.1	1 16.8	23 43.2
17 Sa	7 41 39	25 01 47	0♒56 49	7♒39 11	10 22.5	18 00.5	0♋35.3	29 44.4	2 11.5	7 17.4	12 58.1	24 28.7	1 17.4	23 42.1
18 Su	7 45 36	25 59 01	14 17 03	20 50 19	10 20.8	18 16.3	1 47.8	0♍21.4	1 58.5	7 30.5	13 04.0	24 32.4	1 17.9	23 40.9
19 M	7 49 33	26 56 15	27 18 58	3♓43 02	10 18.5	18 27.4	3 00.4	0 58.4	1 45.4	7 43.7	13 09.9	24 36.1	1 18.5	23 39.8
20 Tu	7 53 29	27 53 30	10♓02 41	16 18 06	10 16.1	18R 33.7	4 13.0	1 35.5	1 32.3	7 56.8	13 15.9	24 39.7	1 19.0	23 38.6
21 W	7 57 26	28 50 45	22 29 35	28 37 28	10 13.7	18 35.1	5 25.6	2 12.7	1 19.1	8 10.0	13 21.9	24 43.4	1 19.4	23 37.5
22 Th	8 01 22	29 48 02	4♈42 09	10♈44 06	10 11.9	18 31.6	6 38.3	2 49.8	1 05.9	8 23.1	13 28.0	24 47.0	1 19.9	23 36.3
23 F	8 05 19	0♌45 19	16 43 49	22 41 49	10D 10.8	18 23.2	7 51.0	3 27.0	0 52.7	8 36.3	13 34.1	24 50.7	1 20.3	23 35.1
24 Sa	8 09 15	1 42 36	28 38 41	4♉34 59	10 10.6	18 09.8	9 03.7	4 04.2	0 39.5	8 49.5	13 40.4	24 54.3	1 20.6	23 33.9
25 Su	8 13 12	2 39 55	10♉31 18	16 28 15	10 11.2	17 51.6	10 16.5	4 41.5	0 26.3	9 02.7	13 46.6	24 58.0	1 21.0	23 32.7
26 M	8 17 08	3 37 15	22 26 24	28 26 20	10 12.5	17 28.8	11 29.3	5 18.7	0 13.1	9 15.9	13 52.9	25 01.6	1 21.3	23 31.4
27 Tu	8 21 05	4 34 35	4♊28 38	10♊33 48	10 14.1	17 01.4	12 42.1	5 56.1	29♑60.0	9 29.2	13 59.3	25 05.2	1 21.5	23 30.2
28 W	8 25 01	5 31 57	16 42 21	22 54 43	10 15.6	16 29.9	13 55.0	6 33.4	29 46.9	9 42.4	14 05.7	25 08.9	1 21.8	23 29.0
29 Th	8 28 58	6 29 19	29 11 17	5♋32 22	10R 16.5	15 54.6	15 08.0	7 10.8	29 33.9	9 55.7	14 12.1	25 12.5	1 22.0	23 27.7
30 F	8 32 55	7 26 43	11♋58 12	18 28 58	10 16.4	15 16.0	16 21.0	7 48.2	29 21.0	10 08.9	14 18.6	25 16.1	1 22.1	23 26.5
31 Sa	8 36 51	8 24 07	25 04 43	1♌45 25	10 14.9	14 34.6	17 34.0	8 25.7	29 08.1	10 22.2	14 25.2	25 19.7	1 22.3	23 25.2

August 2038 LONGITUDE

Day	Sid.Time	☉	0 hr ☽	Noon ☽	True ☊	☿	♀	♂	⚳	♃	♄	♅	♆	♇
1 Su	8 40 48	9♌21 32	8♌30 56	15♌21 03	10♋12.1	13♌51.1	18♋47.0	9♍03.1	28♑55.4	10♌35.4	14♍31.8	25♋23.3	1♉22.4	23♒23.9
2 M	8 44 44	10 18 58	22 15 24	29 13 37	10R 08.2	13R 06.1	20 00.1	9 40.6	28R 42.9	10 48.7	14 38.4	25 26.9	1 22.5	23R 22.6
3 Tu	8 48 41	11 16 24	6♍15 12	13♍19 36	10 03.7	12 20.5	21 13.2	10 18.2	28 30.4	11 01.9	14 45.1	25 30.4	1R 22.5	23 21.3
4 W	8 52 37	12 13 52	20 26 16	27 34 35	9 59.1	11 35.1	22 26.4	10 55.8	28 18.1	11 15.2	14 51.8	25 34.0	1 22.5	23 20.0
5 Th	8 56 34	13 11 19	4♎43 59	11♎53 53	9 55.3	10 50.7	23 39.5	11 33.4	28 06.0	11 28.4	14 58.5	25 37.5	1 22.5	23 18.7
6 F	9 00 30	14 08 48	19 03 47	26 13 11	9 52.6	10 08.1	24 52.8	12 11.0	27 54.1	11 41.7	15 05.3	25 41.0	1 22.4	23 17.4
7 Sa	9 04 27	15 06 17	3♏21 41	10♏28 57	9D 51.4	9 28.3	26 06.0	12 48.7	27 42.4	11 54.9	15 12.2	25 44.6	1 22.3	23 16.1
8 Su	9 08 24	16 03 48	17 34 40	24 38 37	9 51.6	8 51.9	27 19.3	13 26.4	27 30.8	12 08.2	15 19.0	25 48.1	1 22.2	23 14.8
9 M	9 12 20	17 01 18	1♐40 35	8♐40 28	9 52.7	8 19.7	28 32.6	14 04.1	27 19.5	12 21.4	15 25.9	25 51.5	1 22.0	23 13.5
10 Tu	9 16 17	17 58 50	15 38 06	22 33 24	9 54.1	7 52.4	29 46.0	14 41.9	27 08.4	12 34.6	15 32.9	25 55.0	1 21.8	23 12.2
11 W	9 20 13	18 56 23	29 26 17	6♑16 38	9R 55.0	7 30.7	0♌59.4	15 19.6	26 57.5	12 47.8	15 39.9	25 58.5	1 21.6	23 10.9
12 Th	9 24 10	19 53 56	13♑04 21	19 49 19	9 54.6	7 14.9	2 12.8	15 57.5	26 46.9	13 01.0	15 46.9	26 01.9	1 21.4	23 09.5
13 F	9 28 06	20 51 31	26 31 26	3♒10 34	9 52.5	7D 05.6	3 26.2	16 35.3	26 36.5	13 14.2	15 53.9	26 05.3	1 21.1	23 08.2
14 Sa	9 32 03	21 49 06	9♒46 35	16 19 22	9 48.4	7 03.0	4 39.7	17 13.2	26 26.4	13 27.4	16 01.0	26 08.7	1 20.7	23 06.9
15 Su	9 36 00	22 46 43	22 48 49	29 14 51	9 42.4	7 07.5	5 53.3	17 51.1	26 16.6	13 40.5	16 08.1	26 12.1	1 20.4	23 05.6
16 M	9 39 56	23 44 21	5♓37 25	11♓56 29	9 35.1	7 19.2	7 06.8	18 29.1	26 07.0	13 53.7	16 15.2	26 15.4	1 20.0	23 04.2
17 Tu	9 43 53	24 42 00	18 12 08	24 24 24	9 27.1	7 38.2	8 20.4	19 07.0	25 57.7	14 06.8	16 22.4	26 18.8	1 19.6	23 02.9
18 W	9 47 49	25 39 41	0♈33 28	6♈39 32	9 19.2	8 04.6	9 34.1	19 45.1	25 48.7	14 19.9	16 29.5	26 22.1	1 19.1	23 01.6
19 Th	9 51 46	26 37 23	12 42 52	18 43 46	9 12.2	8 38.3	10 47.7	20 23.1	25 40.0	14 33.0	16 36.8	26 25.4	1 18.7	23 00.2
20 F	9 55 42	27 35 06	24 42 39	0♉39 56	9 06.8	9 19.3	12 01.4	21 01.2	25 31.6	14 46.1	16 44.0	26 28.7	1 18.2	22 58.9
21 Sa	9 59 39	28 32 52	6♉36 07	12 31 43	9 03.3	10 07.4	13 15.2	21 39.3	25 23.6	14 59.1	16 51.2	26 31.9	1 17.6	22 57.6
22 Su	10 03 35	29 30 39	18 27 19	24 23 30	9D 01.8	11 02.5	14 29.0	22 17.5	25 15.8	15 12.2	16 58.5	26 35.1	1 17.0	22 56.3
23 M	10 07 32	0♍28 27	0♊20 54	6♊20 09	9 01.8	12 04.3	15 42.8	22 55.7	25 08.4	15 25.2	17 05.8	26 38.3	1 16.4	22 55.0
24 Tu	10 11 28	1 26 18	12 21 54	18 26 48	9 02.7	13 12.6	16 56.7	23 33.9	25 01.3	15 38.2	17 13.2	26 41.5	1 15.8	22 53.6
25 W	10 15 25	2 24 10	24 35 27	0♋48 27	9R 03.7	14 27.0	18 10.6	24 12.2	24 54.5	15 51.1	17 20.5	26 44.7	1 15.1	22 52.3
26 Th	10 19 22	3 22 04	7♋06 22	13 29 40	9 03.9	15 47.2	19 24.5	24 50.5	24 48.0	16 04.1	17 27.9	26 47.8	1 14.5	22 51.0
27 F	10 23 18	4 19 59	19 58 46	26 33 58	9 02.4	17 12.8	20 38.5	25 28.8	24 41.9	16 17.0	17 35.3	26 50.9	1 13.7	22 49.7
28 Sa	10 27 15	5 17 57	3♌15 26	10♌03 15	8 58.8	18 43.4	21 52.5	26 07.2	24 36.2	16 29.8	17 42.7	26 54.0	1 13.0	22 48.4
29 Su	10 31 11	6 15 56	16 57 18	23 57 18	8 52.8	20 18.6	23 06.5	26 45.6	24 30.8	16 42.7	17 50.1	26 57.0	1 12.2	22 47.2
30 M	10 35 08	7 13 56	1♍02 51	8♍13 20	8 44.9	21 57.7	24 20.6	27 24.1	24 25.7	16 55.5	17 57.5	27 00.0	1 11.4	22 45.9
31 Tu	10 39 04	8 11 58	15 28 02	22 46 06	8 35.8	23 40.5	25 34.7	28 02.5	24 21.0	17 08.3	18 04.9	27 03.0	1 10.6	22 44.6

Astro Data	Dy Hr Mn	Planet Ingress	Dy Hr Mn
♅⚻♇	7 14:08	♀ ♋	17 0:18
☽0S	9 7:08	♂ ♍	17 22:09
☿R	21 6:59	☉ ♌	22 17:01
☽0N	22 14:59	⚳ ♑R	27 11:55
♆R	4 1:58	♀ ♌	10 16:35
☽0S	5 12:20	☉ ♍	23 0:11
☿D	14 8:50		
♄⚼♆	17 3:14		
☽0N	18 22:27		

Last Aspect Dy Hr Mn		☽ Ingress Dy Hr Mn	
1 5:44	♇ △	♋	1 17:14
3 13:20	♅ ☌	♌	4 0:58
5 19:44	♇ ☍	♍	6 6:26
7 23:49	♅ ⚹	♎	8 10:14
10 5:00	♂ ⚹	♏	10 12:59
12 9:36	♂ □	♐	12 15:19
14 14:36	♂ △	♑	14 18:05
16 12:27	♅ ☍	♒	16 22:19
18 17:15	♇ ☌	♓	19 5:01
21 12:28	☉ △	♈	21 14:42
23 16:21	♅ □	♉	24 2:44
26 5:09	♅ ⚹	♊	26 15:07
28 13:06	♇ △	♋	29 1:33
31 0:24	♅ ☌	♌	31 8:51

Last Aspect Dy Hr Mn		☽ Ingress Dy Hr Mn	
2 1:57	♇ ☍	♍	2 13:19
4 8:37	♅ ⚹	♎	4 16:04
6 11:06	♅ □	♏	6 18:21
8 17:00	♀ △	♐	8 21:08
10 13:07	♇ ⚹	♑	11 0:59
12 23:10	♅ ☍	♒	13 6:16
15 0:32	♇ ☌	♓	15 13:25
17 15:44	♅ △	♈	17 22:54
20 5:14	☉ △	♉	20 10:39
22 23:13	☉ □	♊	22 23:18
24 22:33	♂ □	♋	25 10:27
27 12:31	♅ ☌	♌	27 18:11
29 10:25	♀ ☌	♍	29 22:14
31 21:01	♂ ☌	♎	31 23:49

☽ Phases & Eclipses Dy Hr Mn		Astro Data
2 13:33	● 10♋47	1 July 2038
2 13:32:55	● A 00'60"	Julian Day # 50586
9 16:02	☽ 17♎34	SVP 4♓43'36"
16 11:50	○ 24♑04	GC 27♐22.6 ⚴ 9♐10.4R
16 11:36	● A 0.500	Eris 28♈42.3 ⚵ 11♏33.7R
24 5:41	☾ 1♉28	⚷ 28♊12.1 ⚶ 3♋12.6
		☽ Mean ☊ 10♋27.3
1 0:42	● 8♌54	1 August 2038
7 20:23	☽ 15♏26	Julian Day # 50617
14 22:58	○ 22♒15	SVP 4♓43'31"
22 23:13	☾ 29♉58	GC 27♐22.7 ⚴ 6♐35.6
30 10:14	● 7♍10	Eris 28♈45.0R ⚵ 13♏10.9
		⚷ 0♋49.3 ⚶ 16♋33.3
		☽ Mean ☊ 8♋48.9

LONGITUDE — September 2038

Day	Sid.Time	☉	0 hr ☽	Noon ☽	True ☊	☿	♀	♂	⚳	♃	♄	♅	♆	♇
1 W	10 43 01	9♍10 02	0♎06 34	7♎28 28	8♋26.5	25♌26.3	26♌48.8	28♍41.1	24♑16.7	17♌21.0	18♍12.4	27♋06.0	1♉09.7	22♒43.3
2 Th	10 46 57	10 08 07	14 50 47	22 12 34	8R18.3	27 14.8	28 02.9	29 19.6	24R12.7	17 33.7	18 19.9	27 08.9	1R08.8	22R42.1
3 F	10 50 54	11 06 13	29 32 57	6♏51 07	8 12.0	29 05.4	29 17.1	29 58.2	24 09.1	17 46.4	18 27.3	27 11.8	1 07.9	22 40.8
4 Sa	10 54 51	12 04 21	14♏06 27	21 18 25	8 08.1	0♍57.8	0♍31.3	0♎36.9	24 05.9	17 59.1	18 34.8	27 14.6	1 06.9	22 39.6
5 Su	10 58 47	13 02 30	28 26 39	5♐30 56	8D06.4	2 51.4	1 45.5	1 15.5	24 03.0	18 11.6	18 42.3	27 17.4	1 05.9	22 38.3
6 M	11 02 44	14 00 41	12♐31 08	19 27 14	8 06.3	4 46.1	2 59.8	1 54.2	24 00.5	18 24.2	18 49.8	27 20.2	1 04.9	22 37.1
7 Tu	11 06 40	14 58 53	26 19 17	3♑07 26	8R06.7	6 41.3	4 14.1	2 33.0	23 58.3	18 36.7	18 57.3	27 23.0	1 03.9	22 35.9
8 W	11 10 37	15 57 07	9♑51 50	16 32 40	8 06.5	8 36.9	5 28.4	3 11.8	23 56.5	18 49.2	19 04.8	27 25.7	1 02.9	22 34.7
9 Th	11 14 33	16 55 22	23 10 06	29 44 20	8 04.6	10 32.6	6 42.8	3 50.6	23 55.1	19 01.6	19 12.4	27 28.4	1 01.8	22 33.5
10 F	11 18 30	17 53 39	6♒15 31	12♒43 46	8 00.2	12 28.1	7 57.1	4 29.4	23 54.0	19 14.0	19 19.9	27 31.0	1 00.7	22 32.3
11 Sa	11 22 26	18 51 57	19 09 13	25 31 56	7 53.0	14 23.3	9 11.5	5 08.3	23 53.3	19 26.3	19 27.4	27 33.7	0 59.6	22 31.2
12 Su	11 26 23	19 50 17	1♓51 58	8♓09 23	7 43.1	16 18.0	10 25.9	5 47.2	23D53.0	19 38.6	19 34.9	27 36.2	0 58.4	22 30.0
13 M	11 30 20	20 48 39	14 24 13	20 36 29	7 31.2	18 12.1	11 40.4	6 26.2	23 53.0	19 50.8	19 42.4	27 38.8	0 57.2	22 28.9
14 Tu	11 34 16	21 47 02	26 46 14	2♈53 33	7 18.2	20 05.4	12 54.8	7 05.2	23 53.3	20 03.0	19 49.9	27 41.3	0 56.0	22 27.7
15 W	11 38 13	22 45 28	8♈58 29	15 01 12	7 05.2	21 58.0	14 09.3	7 44.2	23 54.1	20 15.1	19 57.4	27 43.7	0 54.8	22 26.6
16 Th	11 42 09	23 43 55	21 01 50	27 00 37	6 53.3	23 49.7	15 23.8	8 23.3	23 55.1	20 27.1	20 05.0	27 46.2	0 53.6	22 25.5
17 F	11 46 06	24 42 25	2♉57 50	8♉53 46	6 43.5	25 40.4	16 38.4	9 02.4	23 56.5	20 39.2	20 12.5	27 48.5	0 52.3	22 24.4
18 Sa	11 50 02	25 40 56	14 48 49	20 43 24	6 36.2	27 30.2	17 53.0	9 41.5	23 58.3	20 51.1	20 20.0	27 50.9	0 51.0	22 23.4
19 Su	11 53 59	26 39 30	26 38 01	2♊33 11	6 31.7	29 19.1	19 07.6	10 20.7	24 00.4	21 03.0	20 27.5	27 53.2	0 49.7	22 22.3
20 M	11 57 55	27 38 06	8♊29 28	14 27 29	6 29.5	1♎06.9	20 22.2	11 00.0	24 02.9	21 14.8	20 34.9	27 55.5	0 48.4	22 21.3
21 Tu	12 01 52	28 36 44	20 27 53	26 31 20	6 28.9	2 53.8	21 36.8	11 39.2	24 05.6	21 26.6	20 42.4	27 57.7	0 47.0	22 20.2
22 W	12 05 49	29 35 24	2♋38 30	8♋50 03	6 28.9	4 39.7	22 51.5	12 18.6	24 08.8	21 38.3	20 49.9	27 59.9	0 45.7	22 19.2
23 Th	12 09 45	0♎34 07	15 06 39	21 28 54	6 28.3	6 24.5	24 06.2	12 57.9	24 12.3	21 50.0	20 57.4	28 02.0	0 44.3	22 18.2
24 F	12 13 42	1 32 52	27 57 23	4♌32 33	6 26.1	8 08.4	25 20.9	13 37.3	24 16.1	22 01.6	21 04.8	28 04.1	0 42.9	22 17.3
25 Sa	12 17 38	2 31 38	11♌14 47	18 04 17	6 21.5	9 51.3	26 35.7	14 16.8	24 20.2	22 13.1	21 12.2	28 06.1	0 41.4	22 16.3
26 Su	12 21 35	3 30 28	25 01 08	2♍05 11	6 14.2	11 33.3	27 50.4	14 56.3	24 24.7	22 24.6	21 19.7	28 08.1	0 40.0	22 15.4
27 M	12 25 31	4 29 19	9♍16 07	16 33 21	6 04.5	13 14.3	29 05.2	15 35.8	24 29.4	22 35.9	21 27.1	28 10.1	0 38.5	22 14.5
28 Tu	12 29 28	5 28 12	23 56 08	1♎23 28	5 53.2	14 54.4	0♎20.0	16 15.4	24 34.6	22 47.2	21 34.5	28 12.0	0 37.1	22 13.5
29 W	12 33 24	6 27 07	8♎54 15	16 27 12	5 41.7	16 33.6	1 34.9	16 55.0	24 40.0	22 58.5	21 41.8	28 13.9	0 35.6	22 12.7
30 Th	12 37 21	7 26 05	24 01 02	1♏34 25	5 31.3	18 11.9	2 49.7	17 34.6	24 45.7	23 09.6	21 49.2	28 15.7	0 34.1	22 11.8

LONGITUDE — October 2038

Day	Sid.Time	☉	0 hr ☽	Noon ☽	True ☊	☿	♀	♂	⚳	♃	♄	♅	♆	♇
1 F	12 41 17	8♎25 04	9♏06 07	16♏34 59	5♋23.0	19♎49.3	4♎04.6	18♎14.3	24♑51.8	23♌20.7	21♍56.5	28♋17.5	0♉32.5	22♒11.0
2 Sa	12 45 14	9 24 05	24 00 04	1♐20 34	5R17.5	21 25.8	5 19.4	18 54.0	24 58.2	23 31.7	22 03.8	28 19.2	0R31.0	22R10.1
3 Su	12 49 11	10 23 08	8♐35 54	15 45 40	5 14.7	23 01.5	6 34.3	19 33.8	25 04.9	23 42.6	22 11.1	28 20.9	0 29.5	22 09.3
4 M	12 53 07	11 22 12	22 49 40	29 47 51	5 13.8	24 36.4	7 49.2	20 13.6	25 11.9	23 53.4	22 18.4	28 22.5	0 27.9	22 08.6
5 Tu	12 57 04	12 21 19	6♑40 18	13♑27 14	5 13.8	26 10.5	9 04.1	20 53.5	25 19.2	24 04.2	22 25.6	28 24.1	0 26.3	22 07.8
6 W	13 01 00	13 20 27	20 08 54	26 45 40	5 13.3	27 43.7	10 19.1	21 33.4	25 26.8	24 14.9	22 32.8	28 25.6	0 24.7	22 07.1
7 Th	13 04 57	14 19 36	3♒17 53	9♒45 54	5 11.2	29 16.2	11 34.0	22 13.3	25 34.6	24 25.4	22 40.0	28 27.1	0 23.1	22 06.3
8 F	13 08 53	15 18 48	16 10 07	22 30 52	5 06.6	0♏47.9	12 49.0	22 53.3	25 42.8	24 35.9	22 47.2	28 28.5	0 21.5	22 05.6
9 Sa	13 12 50	16 18 01	28 48 29	5♓03 15	4 59.0	2 18.7	14 03.9	23 33.3	25 51.2	24 46.3	22 54.3	28 29.9	0 19.9	22 05.0
10 Su	13 16 46	17 17 16	11♓15 27	17 25 16	4 48.7	3 48.8	15 18.9	24 13.4	26 00.0	24 56.6	23 01.4	28 31.2	0 18.3	22 04.3
11 M	13 20 43	18 16 33	23 32 56	29 38 36	4 36.3	5 18.2	16 33.9	24 53.5	26 09.0	25 06.9	23 08.4	28 32.5	0 16.7	22 03.7
12 Tu	13 24 40	19 15 52	5♈42 25	11♈44 31	4 22.7	6 46.7	17 48.9	25 33.6	26 18.3	25 17.0	23 15.5	28 33.7	0 15.0	22 03.1
13 W	13 28 36	20 15 13	17 45 02	23 44 06	4 09.1	8 14.5	19 03.9	26 13.8	26 27.8	25 27.0	23 22.5	28 34.9	0 13.4	22 02.5
14 Th	13 32 33	21 14 36	29 41 51	5♉38 29	3 56.6	9 41.5	20 18.9	26 54.0	26 37.6	25 36.9	23 29.4	28 36.1	0 11.7	22 01.9
15 F	13 36 29	22 14 01	11♉34 10	17 29 08	3 46.1	11 07.7	21 34.0	27 34.3	26 47.7	25 46.8	23 36.4	28 37.1	0 10.1	22 01.4
16 Sa	13 40 26	23 13 29	23 23 40	29 18 04	3 38.3	12 33.0	22 49.0	28 14.6	26 58.0	25 56.5	23 43.3	28 38.2	0 08.4	22 00.9
17 Su	13 44 22	24 12 58	5♊12 43	11♊08 00	3 33.3	13 57.5	24 04.1	28 55.0	27 08.6	26 06.1	23 50.1	28 39.1	0 06.7	22 00.4
18 M	13 48 19	25 12 30	17 04 23	23 02 22	3D30.9	15 21.1	25 19.2	29 35.4	27 19.4	26 15.6	23 56.9	28 40.0	0 05.1	21 59.9
19 Tu	13 52 15	26 12 04	29 02 30	5♋05 23	3 30.4	16 43.8	26 34.3	0♏15.8	27 30.5	26 25.0	24 03.7	28 40.9	0 03.4	21 59.5
20 W	13 56 12	27 11 40	11♋11 36	17 21 47	3R30.8	18 05.6	27 49.4	0 56.3	27 41.8	26 34.4	24 10.5	28 41.7	0 01.7	21 59.1
21 Th	14 00 09	28 11 19	23 36 36	29 56 39	3 31.1	19 26.3	29 04.5	1 36.8	27 53.4	26 43.6	24 17.1	28 42.5	0 00.0	21 58.7
22 F	14 04 05	29 11 00	6♌22 34	12♌54 53	3 30.2	20 46.0	0♏19.6	2 17.4	28 05.2	26 52.6	24 23.8	28 43.2	29♈58.3	21 58.3
23 Sa	14 08 02	0♏10 43	19 34 05	26 20 32	3 27.3	22 04.6	1 34.7	2 58.1	28 17.2	27 01.6	24 30.4	28 43.8	29 56.7	21 58.0
24 Su	14 11 58	1 10 28	3♍14 30	10♍16 01	3 22.0	23 21.9	2 49.9	3 38.7	28 29.5	27 10.5	24 37.0	28 44.4	29 55.0	21 57.7
25 M	14 15 55	2 10 15	17 24 59	24 41 04	3 14.5	24 37.9	4 05.0	4 19.5	28 42.0	27 19.2	24 43.5	28 45.0	29 53.3	21 57.4
26 Tu	14 19 51	3 10 05	2♎03 41	9♎32 01	3 05.6	25 52.4	5 20.2	5 00.2	28 54.7	27 27.8	24 49.9	28 45.5	29 51.6	21 57.1
27 W	14 23 48	4 09 56	17 05 03	24 41 35	2 56.2	27 05.4	6 35.4	5 41.0	29 07.7	27 36.3	24 56.4	28 45.9	29 49.9	21 56.9
28 Th	14 27 44	5 09 50	2♏20 17	9♏59 42	2 47.6	28 16.7	7 50.5	6 21.9	29 20.8	27 44.7	25 02.7	28 46.3	29 48.2	21 56.7
29 F	14 31 41	6 09 46	17 38 25	25 15 03	2 40.8	29 26.1	9 05.7	7 02.8	29 34.2	27 52.9	25 09.0	28 46.6	29 46.6	21 56.5
30 Sa	14 35 38	7 09 43	2♐48 21	10♐17 13	2 36.4	0♐33.4	10 20.9	7 43.8	29 47.8	28 01.0	25 15.3	28 46.9	29 44.9	21 56.4
31 Su	14 39 34	8 09 43	17 40 47	24 58 20	2D34.4	1 38.5	11 36.1	8 24.8	0♒01.6	28 09.0	25 21.5	28 47.1	29 43.2	21 56.2

Astro Data

	Dy Hr Mn
☽0S	1 19:00
♂0S	6 2:23
♃⚺♄	11 17:31
⚳ D	12 23:42
☽0N	15 5:16
☿0S	21 9:48
☉0S	22 22:03
♃☍♇	25 18:12
☽0S	29 4:17
♀0S	30 19:59
♄⚻♇	3 6:45
☽0N	12 11:40
☽0S	26 15:25

Planet Ingress

		Dy Hr Mn
♂	♎	3 13:06
☿	♍	3 23:42
♀	♍	4 1:52
☿	♎	19 21:05
☉	♎	22 22:03
♀	♎	28 5:34
☿	♏	7 23:27
♂	♏	19 2:38
♆	♈R	21 12:21
♀	♏	22 5:44
☉	♏	23 7:42
☿	♐	29 23:59
⚳	♒	31 9:09

Last Aspect / ☽ Ingress (September)

Last Aspect Dy Hr Mn			☽ Ingress	Dy Hr Mn
2 22:25	♀	⚹	♏	3 0:44
4 22:00	♅	△	♐	5 2:38
6 17:30	♇	⚹	♑	7 6:29
9 7:50	♅	☍	♒	9 12:29
11 6:20	♇	☌	♓	11 20:27
14 1:46	♅	△	♈	14 6:19
16 13:32	♅	□	♉	16 18:01
19 4:16	☿	△	♊	19 6:50
21 16:28	☉	□	♋	21 18:50
24 0:10	♅	☌	♌	24 3:45
25 19:17	♃	☌	♍	26 8:29
28 6:52	♅	⚹	♎	28 9:46
30 6:44	♅	□	♏	30 9:30

Last Aspect / ☽ Ingress (October)

Last Aspect Dy Hr Mn			☽ Ingress	Dy Hr Mn
2 7:02	♅	△	♐	2 9:48
4 1:55	☿	⚹	♑	4 12:21
6 15:03	♅	☍	♒	6 17:56
8 16:01	♃	☍	♓	9 2:17
11 9:49	♅	△	♈	11 12:42
13 21:46	♅	□	♉	14 0:37
16 10:39	♅	⚹	♊	16 13:25
19 1:52	♂	△	♋	19 1:54
21 12:06	♆	□	♌	21 12:06
23 18:17	♆	△	♍	23 18:23
25 18:38	♅	⚹	♎	25 20:40
27 20:03	♆	☍	♏	27 20:20
29 19:10	☿	☌	♐	29 19:32
31 19:54	♆	△	♑	31 20:23

☽ Phases & Eclipses

Dy Hr Mn		
6 1:52	☽	13♐36
13 12:26	○	20♓50
21 16:28	☾	28♊48
28 18:59	●	5♎45
5 9:54	☽	12♑16
13 4:23	○	19♈56
21 8:25	☾	28♋02
28 3:54	●	4♏50

Astro Data

1 September 2038
Julian Day # 50648
SVP 4♓43'27"
GC 27♐22.8 ⚴ 10♐15.8
Eris 28♈37.9R ⚵ 18♏43.6
⚷ 2♋50.5 ⚶ 29♋31.6
☽ Mean ☊ 7♋10.3

1 October 2038
Julian Day # 50678
SVP 4♓43'25"
GC 27♐22.8 ⚴ 17♐41.2
Eris 28♈23.5R ⚵ 26♏33.6
⚷ 3♋51.1 ⚶ 11♌18.7
☽ Mean ☊ 5♋35.0

November 2038 LONGITUDE

Day	Sid.Time	☉	0 hr ☽	Noon ☽	True ☊	☿	♀	♂	⚳	♃	♄	♅	♆	♇
1 M	14 43 31	9♏09 44	2♑09 26	9♑13 49	2♋34.3	2♐40.9	12♏51.3	9♏05.8	0♒15.7	28♌16.9	25♍27.6	28♋47.3	29♈41.6	21♒56.1
2 Tu	14 47 27	10 09 46	16 11 25	23 02 19	2 35.3	3 40.5	14 06.5	9 46.9	0 29.9	28 24.6	25 33.7	28 47.4	29R 39.9	21R 56.1
3 W	14 51 24	11 09 50	29 46 44	6♒24 58	2R 36.1	4 37.0	15 21.7	10 28.0	0 44.3	28 32.2	25 39.8	28R 47.4	29 38.3	21 56.0
4 Th	14 55 20	12 09 56	12♒57 27	19 24 36	2 35.9	5 29.9	16 37.0	11 09.2	0 58.9	28 39.7	25 45.7	28 47.4	29 36.7	21D 56.0
5 F	14 59 17	13 10 03	25 46 53	2♓04 48	2 33.9	6 18.8	17 52.2	11 50.4	1 13.7	28 47.0	25 51.7	28 47.4	29 35.0	21 56.0
6 Sa	15 03 13	14 10 12	8♓18 49	14 29 23	2 29.8	7 03.3	19 07.4	12 31.6	1 28.7	28 54.1	25 57.5	28 47.2	29 33.4	21 56.0
7 Su	15 07 10	15 10 22	20 36 58	26 41 58	2 23.6	7 42.8	20 22.6	13 12.9	1 43.9	29 01.2	26 03.3	28 47.1	29 31.8	21 56.1
8 M	15 11 07	16 10 34	2♈44 45	8♈45 41	2 15.7	8 16.9	21 37.8	13 54.3	1 59.3	29 08.1	26 09.0	28 46.8	29 30.2	21 56.2
9 Tu	15 15 03	17 10 47	14 45 03	20 43 09	2 06.9	8 44.7	22 53.0	14 35.7	2 14.8	29 14.8	26 14.7	28 46.6	29 28.6	21 56.3
10 W	15 19 00	18 11 02	26 40 14	2♉36 31	1 58.0	9 05.8	24 08.2	15 17.1	2 30.5	29 21.4	26 20.3	28 46.2	29 27.0	21 56.4
11 Th	15 22 56	19 11 19	8♉32 15	14 27 37	1 49.8	9 19.5	25 23.5	15 58.6	2 46.4	29 27.9	26 25.8	28 45.8	29 25.5	21 56.6
12 F	15 26 53	20 11 37	20 22 49	26 18 04	1 43.2	9R 24.9	26 38.7	16 40.1	3 02.5	29 34.2	26 31.2	28 45.4	29 23.9	21 56.8
13 Sa	15 30 49	21 11 57	2♊13 35	8♊09 36	1 38.4	9 21.4	27 53.9	17 21.7	3 18.7	29 40.3	26 36.6	28 44.9	29 22.4	21 57.0
14 Su	15 34 46	22 12 19	14 06 22	20 04 11	1D 35.7	9 08.5	29 09.2	18 03.3	3 35.1	29 46.3	26 42.0	28 44.4	29 20.8	21 57.2
15 M	15 38 42	23 12 43	26 03 21	2♋04 13	1 34.9	8 45.6	0♐24.4	18 44.9	3 51.7	29 52.1	26 47.2	28 43.8	29 19.3	21 57.5
16 Tu	15 42 39	24 13 08	8♋07 11	14 12 38	1 35.6	8 12.4	1 39.6	19 26.7	4 08.4	29 57.8	26 52.4	28 43.1	29 17.8	21 57.8
17 W	15 46 36	25 13 36	20 21 03	26 32 52	1 37.2	7 28.9	2 54.9	20 08.4	4 25.3	0♍03.4	26 57.5	28 42.4	29 16.4	21 58.1
18 Th	15 50 32	26 14 05	2♌48 36	9♌08 45	1 38.9	6 35.5	4 10.1	20 50.2	4 42.3	0 08.7	27 02.5	28 41.7	29 14.9	21 58.5
19 F	15 54 29	27 14 35	15 33 49	22 04 16	1R 39.9	5 32.8	5 25.4	21 32.1	4 59.5	0 13.9	27 07.5	28 40.9	29 13.4	21 58.9
20 Sa	15 58 25	28 15 08	28 40 32	5♍23 00	1 39.8	4 22.3	6 40.6	22 14.0	5 16.8	0 19.0	27 12.4	28 40.0	29 12.0	21 59.3
21 Su	16 02 22	29 15 43	12♍11 59	19 07 39	1 38.3	3 05.7	7 55.9	22 55.9	5 34.3	0 23.8	27 17.2	28 39.1	29 10.6	21 59.7
22 M	16 06 18	0♐16 19	26 10 02	3♎19 04	1 35.3	1 45.2	9 11.2	23 37.9	5 52.0	0 28.5	27 21.9	28 38.1	29 09.2	22 00.2
23 Tu	16 10 15	1 16 57	10♎34 24	17 55 36	1 31.3	0 23.4	10 26.4	24 20.0	6 09.7	0 33.1	27 26.5	28 37.1	29 07.8	22 00.7
24 W	16 14 11	2 17 36	25 21 56	2♏52 34	1 26.9	29♏03.1	11 41.7	25 02.1	6 27.7	0 37.4	27 31.1	28 36.0	29 06.5	22 01.2
25 Th	16 18 08	3 18 17	10♏26 26	18 02 21	1 22.8	27 46.9	12 57.0	25 44.2	6 45.7	0 41.6	27 35.5	28 34.9	29 05.1	22 01.7
26 F	16 22 05	4 19 00	25 39 04	3♐15 17	1 19.6	26 37.2	14 12.2	26 26.4	7 03.9	0 45.6	27 39.9	28 33.8	29 03.8	22 02.3
27 Sa	16 26 01	5 19 44	10♐49 44	18 21 10	1D 17.7	25 36.1	15 27.5	27 08.6	7 22.3	0 49.4	27 44.2	28 32.6	29 02.5	22 02.9
28 Su	16 29 58	6 20 30	25 48 33	3♑10 54	1 17.2	24 45.1	16 42.8	27 50.9	7 40.7	0 53.1	27 48.5	28 31.3	29 01.3	22 03.5
29 M	16 33 54	7 21 16	10♑27 31	17 37 48	1 17.9	24 05.1	17 58.1	28 33.2	7 59.4	0 56.6	27 52.6	28 30.0	29 00.0	22 04.1
30 Tu	16 37 51	8 22 04	24 41 24	1♒38 07	1 19.3	23 36.7	19 13.4	29 15.6	8 18.1	0 59.9	27 56.7	28 28.6	28 58.8	22 04.8

December 2038 LONGITUDE

Day	Sid.Time	☉	0 hr ☽	Noon ☽	True ☊	☿	♀	♂	⚳	♃	♄	♅	♆	♇
1 W	16 41 47	9♐22 52	8♒27 56	15♒11 00	1♋20.9	23♏19.8	20♐28.6	29♏58.0	8♒36.9	1♍03.0	28♍00.6	28♋27.2	28♈57.6	22♒05.5
2 Th	16 45 44	10 23 42	21 47 31	28 17 51	1 22.1	23D 14.2	21 43.9	0♐40.5	8 55.9	1 05.9	28 04.5	28R 25.8	28R 56.4	22 06.2
3 F	16 49 40	11 24 32	4♓42 26	11♓01 44	1R 22.5	23 19.1	22 59.2	1 23.0	9 15.0	1 08.6	28 08.3	28 24.3	28 55.3	22 07.0
4 Sa	16 53 37	12 25 23	17 16 16	23 26 34	1 22.1	23 34.0	24 14.4	2 05.5	9 34.2	1 11.2	28 11.9	28 22.7	28 54.2	22 07.7
5 Su	16 57 34	13 26 15	29 33 11	5♈36 39	1 20.7	23 57.9	25 29.7	2 48.1	9 53.6	1 13.6	28 15.5	28 21.2	28 53.1	22 08.5
6 M	17 01 30	14 27 07	11♈37 31	17 36 16	1 18.7	24 30.0	26 44.9	3 30.7	10 13.0	1 15.8	28 19.0	28 19.5	28 52.0	22 09.4
7 Tu	17 05 27	15 28 01	23 33 23	29 29 21	1 16.2	25 09.4	28 00.2	4 13.4	10 32.6	1 17.7	28 22.4	28 17.9	28 50.9	22 10.2
8 W	17 09 23	16 28 55	5♉24 35	11♉19 28	1 13.7	25 55.3	29 15.4	4 56.1	10 52.2	1 19.6	28 25.7	28 16.1	28 49.9	22 11.1
9 Th	17 13 20	17 29 50	17 14 21	23 09 36	1 11.4	26 46.9	0♑30.6	5 38.9	11 12.0	1 21.2	28 29.0	28 14.4	28 48.9	22 12.0
10 F	17 17 16	18 30 47	29 05 29	5♊02 18	1 09.7	27 43.6	1 45.9	6 21.7	11 31.9	1 22.6	28 32.1	28 12.6	28 48.0	22 12.9
11 Sa	17 21 13	19 31 43	11♊00 17	16 59 42	1 08.6	28 44.7	3 01.1	7 04.6	11 51.9	1 23.8	28 35.1	28 10.8	28 47.0	22 13.8
12 Su	17 25 09	20 32 41	23 00 43	29 03 36	1D 08.2	29 49.7	4 16.3	7 47.5	12 12.0	1 24.9	28 38.0	28 08.9	28 46.1	22 14.8
13 M	17 29 06	21 33 40	5♋08 31	11♋15 42	1 08.3	0♐58.0	5 31.6	8 30.4	12 32.1	1 25.7	28 40.8	28 07.0	28 45.3	22 15.8
14 Tu	17 33 03	22 34 40	17 25 20	23 37 38	1 08.9	2 09.2	6 46.8	9 13.4	12 52.4	1 26.4	28 43.6	28 05.0	28 44.4	22 16.8
15 W	17 36 59	23 35 40	29 52 51	6♌11 12	1 09.7	3 22.9	8 02.0	9 56.5	13 12.8	1 26.8	28 46.2	28 03.1	28 43.6	22 17.8
16 Th	17 40 56	24 36 42	12♌32 55	18 58 15	1 10.5	4 38.9	9 17.2	10 39.6	13 33.3	1R 27.1	28 48.7	28 01.0	28 42.8	22 18.9
17 F	17 44 52	25 37 44	25 27 28	2♍00 48	1 11.1	5 56.8	10 32.4	11 22.7	13 53.8	1 27.2	28 51.1	27 59.0	28 42.1	22 20.0
18 Sa	17 48 49	26 38 47	8♍38 29	15 20 44	1R 11.4	7 16.3	11 47.6	12 05.9	14 14.5	1 27.1	28 53.5	27 56.9	28 41.3	22 21.1
19 Su	17 52 45	27 39 51	22 07 43	28 59 34	1 11.5	8 37.3	13 02.8	12 49.1	14 35.2	1 26.7	28 55.7	27 54.8	28 40.6	22 22.2
20 M	17 56 42	28 40 56	5♎56 20	12♎58 00	1 11.4	9 59.6	14 18.0	13 32.4	14 56.1	1 26.2	28 57.8	27 52.6	28 40.0	22 23.3
21 Tu	18 00 38	29 42 02	20 04 25	27 15 23	1 11.3	11 23.1	15 33.2	14 15.7	15 17.0	1 25.5	28 59.8	27 50.4	28 39.3	22 24.5
22 W	18 04 35	0♑43 09	4♏30 32	11♏49 22	1D 11.2	12 47.5	16 48.4	14 59.1	15 38.0	1 24.6	29 01.7	27 48.2	28 38.7	22 25.7
23 Th	18 08 32	1 44 16	19 11 17	26 35 34	1 11.2	14 12.8	18 03.6	15 42.5	15 59.1	1 23.5	29 03.5	27 46.0	28 38.2	22 26.9
24 F	18 12 28	2 45 24	4♐01 23	11♐27 49	1 11.3	15 38.9	19 18.8	16 26.0	16 20.3	1 22.2	29 05.2	27 43.7	28 37.6	22 28.1
25 Sa	18 16 25	3 46 33	18 53 54	26 18 40	1R 11.4	17 05.7	20 34.0	17 09.5	16 41.6	1 20.7	29 06.8	27 41.4	28 37.1	22 29.3
26 Su	18 20 21	4 47 42	3♑41 08	11♑00 22	1 11.3	18 33.1	21 49.2	17 53.1	17 02.9	1 19.0	29 08.2	27 39.1	28 36.6	22 30.6
27 M	18 24 18	5 48 52	18 15 33	25 25 57	1 11.1	20 01.1	23 04.3	18 36.7	17 24.3	1 17.1	29 09.6	27 36.8	28 36.2	22 31.9
28 Tu	18 28 14	6 50 01	2♒30 58	9♒30 09	1 10.5	21 29.6	24 19.5	19 20.3	17 45.8	1 15.0	29 10.9	27 34.4	28 35.8	22 33.2
29 W	18 32 11	7 51 11	16 23 10	23 09 52	1 09.7	22 58.6	25 34.6	20 04.0	18 07.4	1 12.7	29 12.0	27 32.0	28 35.4	22 34.5
30 Th	18 36 08	8 52 20	29 50 13	6♓24 20	1 08.8	24 28.0	26 49.8	20 47.7	18 29.0	1 10.3	29 13.0	27 29.6	28 35.1	22 35.9
31 F	18 40 04	9 53 30	12♓52 27	19 14 53	1 08.0	25 57.9	28 04.9	21 31.5	18 50.7	1 07.6	29 14.0	27 27.1	28 34.8	22 37.2

Astro Data Dy Hr Mn	Planet Ingress Dy Hr Mn	Last Aspect Dy Hr Mn	☽ Ingress Dy Hr Mn	Last Aspect Dy Hr Mn	☽ Ingress Dy Hr Mn	☽ Phases & Eclipses Dy Hr Mn
♅R 3 22:03	♀ ♐ 15 4:13	2 23:46 ♆ □	♒ 3 0:24	2 13:12 ♆ ✶	♓ 2 15:10	3 21:25 ☽ 11♒33
♇D 4 20:22	♃ ♍ 16 21:21	5 7:14 ♆ ✶	♓ 5 8:01	4 21:40 ♅ △	♈ 5 0:53	11 22:28 ○ 19♉38
♃⊻♅ 5 13:15	☉ ♐ 22 5:32	7 16:08 ♅ △	♈ 7 18:33	7 10:42 ♆ ☌	♉ 7 13:02	19 22:11 ☾ 27♌40
☽0N 8 18:02	☿ ♏R 23 18:55	10 5:38 ♆ ☌	♉ 10 6:44	9 22:49 ♄ △	♊ 10 1:50	26 13:48 ● 4♐24
♃△♆ 11 4:46		12 18:41 ♃ □	♊ 12 19:30	12 11:25 ♆ ✶	♋ 12 13:52	
☿R 12 14:58	♂ ♐ 1 13:07	15 7:35 ♃ ✶	♋ 15 7:53	14 21:50 ♄ ✶	♌ 15 0:14	3 12:47 ☽ 11♓27
☽0S 23 2:16	♀ ♑ 9 2:13	17 17:14 ♆ □	♌ 17 18:38	17 5:58 ♆ △	♍ 17 8:20	11 17:32 ○ 19♊46
	☿ ♐ 12 15:42	20 0:58 ♆ △	♍ 20 2:23	19 11:53 ♄ ☌	♎ 19 13:45	11 17:45 ☍ A 0.804
☿D 2 12:31	☉ ♑ 21 19:03	22 4:10 ♅ ✶	♎ 22 6:27	21 16:22 ☉ ✶	♏ 21 16:33	19 9:30 ☾ 27♍33
☽0N 6 0:51		24 6:00 ♆ ☍	♏ 24 7:25	23 16:00 ♄ ✶	♐ 23 17:30	26 1:03 ● 4♑20
♄✶♅ 6 14:21		26 4:36 ♅ △	♐ 26 6:52	25 16:34 ♄ □	♑ 25 18:00	26 1:00:09 ☌ T 02'19"
♄⚻♆ 14 17:50		28 5:13 ♆ △	♑ 28 6:48	27 18:18 ♄ △	♒ 27 19:43	
♃R 17 8:41		30 7:39 ♂ ✶	♒ 30 9:09	29 21:44 ♆ ✶	♓ 30 0:18	
☽0S 20 10:33						

Astro Data

1 November 2038
Julian Day # 50709
SVP 4♓43'21"
GC 27♐22.9 ⚴ 27♐37.7
Eris 28♈05.1R ⚵ 6♐14.5
⚷ 3♋40.2R ⚶ 21♌57.6
☽ Mean ☊ 3♋56.5

1 December 2038
Julian Day # 50739
SVP 4♓43'16"
GC 27♐23.0 ⚴ 8♑24.4
Eris 27♈49.1R ⚵ 16♐29.4
⚷ 2♋22.9R ⚶ 29♌31.8
☽ Mean ☊ 2♋21.2

LONGITUDE — January 2039

Day	Sid.Time	☉	0 hr ☽	Noon ☽	True ☊	☿	♀	♂	⚳	♃	♄	♅	♆	♇
1 Sa	18 44 01	10♑54 39	25♓32 02	1♈44 23	1♋07.4	27♐28.2	29♑20.0	22♐15.3	19♒12.5	1♍04.7	29♍14.8	27♋24.7	28♈34.5	22♒38.6
2 Su	18 47 57	11 55 48	7♈52 28	13 56 49	1D07.2	28 58.9	0♒35.1	22 59.1	19 34.4	1R01.7	29 15.5	27R22.2	28R34.3	22 40.0
3 M	18 51 54	12 56 57	19 58 03	25 56 45	1 07.6	0♑30.0	1 50.2	23 43.0	19 56.3	0 58.5	29 16.1	27 19.7	28 34.1	22 41.4
4 Tu	18 55 50	13 58 06	1♉53 32	7♉48 59	1 08.5	2 01.5	3 05.3	24 26.9	20 18.2	0 55.1	29 16.6	27 17.2	28 33.9	22 42.8
5 W	18 59 47	14 59 15	13 43 41	19 38 11	1 09.8	3 33.4	4 20.3	25 10.9	20 40.3	0 51.5	29 17.0	27 14.7	28 33.8	22 44.3
6 Th	19 03 43	16 00 23	25 33 02	1♊28 44	1 11.2	5 05.6	5 35.4	25 54.9	21 02.4	0 47.7	29 17.2	27 12.1	28 33.7	22 45.7
7 F	19 07 40	17 01 31	7♊25 44	13 24 28	1 12.5	6 38.2	6 50.4	26 39.0	21 24.5	0 43.8	29R17.4	27 09.6	28 33.6	22 47.2
8 Sa	19 11 37	18 02 39	19 25 19	25 28 36	1R13.2	8 11.3	8 05.4	27 23.1	21 46.7	0 39.7	29 17.5	27 07.0	28D33.6	22 48.7
9 Su	19 15 33	19 03 46	1♋34 38	7♋43 38	1 13.2	9 44.7	9 20.4	28 07.2	22 09.0	0 35.4	29 17.4	27 04.4	28 33.6	22 50.2
10 M	19 19 30	20 04 54	13 55 48	20 11 17	1 12.2	11 18.5	10 35.4	28 51.4	22 31.3	0 30.9	29 17.2	27 01.9	28 33.7	22 51.7
11 Tu	19 23 26	21 06 01	26 30 10	2♌52 30	1 10.1	12 52.8	11 50.3	29 35.6	22 53.7	0 26.3	29 17.0	26 59.3	28 33.8	22 53.2
12 W	19 27 23	22 07 08	9♌18 19	15 47 36	1 07.3	14 27.5	13 05.3	0♑19.9	23 16.1	0 21.5	29 16.6	26 56.7	28 33.9	22 54.8
13 Th	19 31 19	23 08 14	22 20 17	28 56 20	1 03.8	16 02.7	14 20.2	1 04.2	23 38.6	0 16.5	29 16.1	26 54.1	28 34.0	22 56.3
14 F	19 35 16	24 09 21	5♍35 38	12♍18 07	1 00.3	17 38.3	15 35.1	1 48.5	24 01.1	0 11.4	29 15.5	26 51.5	28 34.2	22 57.9
15 Sa	19 39 12	25 10 27	19 03 41	25 52 13	0 57.2	19 14.4	16 50.0	2 32.9	24 23.7	0 06.1	29 14.8	26 48.9	28 34.4	22 59.5
16 Su	19 43 09	26 11 33	2♎43 37	9♎37 48	0 55.1	20 50.9	18 04.8	3 17.4	24 46.4	0 00.7	29 14.0	26 46.3	28 34.7	23 01.1
17 M	19 47 06	27 12 39	16 34 37	23 34 00	0D54.1	22 28.0	19 19.7	4 01.8	25 09.0	29♌55.1	29 13.0	26 43.6	28 34.9	23 02.7
18 Tu	19 51 02	28 13 44	0♏35 47	7♏39 50	0 54.3	24 05.6	20 34.5	4 46.3	25 31.8	29 49.4	29 12.0	26 41.0	28 35.3	23 04.3
19 W	19 54 59	29 14 50	14 45 57	21 53 55	0 55.5	25 43.8	21 49.3	5 30.9	25 54.5	29 43.5	29 10.9	26 38.4	28 35.6	23 05.9
20 Th	19 58 55	0♒15 55	29 03 27	6♐14 15	0 57.1	27 22.5	23 04.1	6 15.5	26 17.3	29 37.5	29 09.6	26 35.8	28 36.0	23 07.6
21 F	20 02 52	1 17 00	13♐25 54	20 37 58	0R58.3	29 01.8	24 18.9	7 00.1	26 40.2	29 31.3	29 08.3	26 33.2	28 36.4	23 09.2
22 Sa	20 06 48	2 18 05	27 49 55	5♑01 13	0 58.6	0♒41.6	25 33.7	7 44.8	27 03.1	29 25.0	29 06.8	26 30.6	28 36.9	23 10.9
23 Su	20 10 45	3 19 09	12♑11 15	19 19 24	0 57.4	2 22.0	26 48.4	8 29.5	27 26.1	29 18.6	29 05.3	26 28.0	28 37.4	23 12.5
24 M	20 14 41	4 20 12	26 25 01	3♒27 30	0 54.4	4 03.1	28 03.1	9 14.3	27 49.0	29 12.1	29 03.6	26 25.4	28 37.9	23 14.2
25 Tu	20 18 38	5 21 15	10♒26 16	17 20 48	0 49.7	5 44.7	29 17.8	9 59.1	28 12.1	29 05.4	29 01.8	26 22.9	28 38.5	23 15.9
26 W	20 22 35	6 22 16	24 10 41	0♓55 34	0 43.8	7 26.9	0♓32.5	10 43.9	28 35.1	28 58.6	29 00.0	26 20.3	28 39.1	23 17.6
27 Th	20 26 31	7 23 17	7♓35 12	14 09 29	0 37.3	9 09.7	1 47.1	11 28.8	28 58.2	28 51.8	28 58.0	26 17.7	28 39.7	23 19.3
28 F	20 30 28	8 24 17	20 38 23	27 02 02	0 31.1	10 53.2	3 01.7	12 13.7	29 21.3	28 44.8	28 55.9	26 15.2	28 40.4	23 21.0
29 Sa	20 34 24	9 25 15	3♈20 37	9♈34 27	0 25.8	12 37.2	4 16.3	12 58.6	29 44.5	28 37.7	28 53.7	26 12.6	28 41.1	23 22.7
30 Su	20 38 21	10 26 12	15 43 54	21 49 27	0 22.1	14 21.8	5 30.8	13 43.6	0♓07.7	28 30.5	28 51.5	26 10.1	28 41.8	23 24.4
31 M	20 42 17	11 27 08	27 51 38	3♉50 59	0D20.1	16 06.9	6 45.3	14 28.6	0 30.9	28 23.2	28 49.1	26 07.6	28 42.6	23 26.1

LONGITUDE — February 2039

Day	Sid.Time	☉	0 hr ☽	Noon ☽	True ☊	☿	♀	♂	⚳	♃	♄	♅	♆	♇
1 Tu	20 46 14	12♒28 03	9♉48 09	15♉43 44	0♋19.8	17♒52.5	7♓59.8	15♑13.6	0♓54.1	28♌15.9	28♍46.7	26♋05.1	28♈43.4	23♒27.9
2 W	20 50 10	13 28 57	21 38 25	27 32 51	0 20.8	19 38.6	9 14.3	15 58.7	1 17.4	28R08.5	28R44.1	26R02.7	28 44.2	23 29.6
3 Th	20 54 07	14 29 49	3♊27 41	9♊23 34	0 22.4	21 25.1	10 28.7	16 43.8	1 40.7	28 01.0	28 41.5	26 00.2	28 45.1	23 31.3
4 F	20 58 04	15 30 40	15 21 07	21 20 55	0R23.7	23 11.9	11 43.0	17 29.0	2 04.0	27 53.4	28 38.7	25 57.8	28 46.0	23 33.1
5 Sa	21 02 00	16 31 30	27 23 33	3♋29 29	0 24.1	24 58.9	12 57.4	18 14.1	2 27.4	27 45.8	28 35.9	25 55.4	28 47.0	23 34.8
6 Su	21 05 57	17 32 19	9♋39 10	15 52 59	0 22.7	26 46.1	14 11.7	18 59.3	2 50.8	27 38.1	28 33.0	25 53.0	28 47.9	23 36.6
7 M	21 09 53	18 33 06	22 11 13	28 34 04	0 19.1	28 33.2	15 25.9	19 44.6	3 14.2	27 30.4	28 30.0	25 50.7	28 48.9	23 38.3
8 Tu	21 13 50	19 33 51	5♌01 40	11♌34 01	0 13.4	0♓20.2	16 40.1	20 29.8	3 37.6	27 22.6	28 26.9	25 48.3	28 49.9	23 40.1
9 W	21 17 46	20 34 36	18 11 03	24 52 36	0 05.7	2 06.7	17 54.3	21 15.1	4 01.0	27 14.8	28 23.8	25 46.0	28 51.0	23 41.8
10 Th	21 21 43	21 35 19	1♍38 22	8♍28 01	29♊56.7	3 52.6	19 08.4	22 00.5	4 24.5	27 06.9	28 20.5	25 43.7	28 52.1	23 43.6
11 F	21 25 39	22 36 01	15 21 09	22 17 18	29 47.6	5 37.6	20 22.5	22 45.9	4 47.9	26 59.0	28 17.2	25 41.5	28 53.2	23 45.3
12 Sa	21 29 36	23 36 41	29 15 58	6♎16 41	29 39.2	7 21.4	21 36.6	23 31.3	5 11.4	26 51.1	28 13.8	25 39.3	28 54.4	23 47.1
13 Su	21 33 33	24 37 21	13♎18 57	20 22 18	29 32.6	9 03.6	22 50.6	24 16.7	5 34.9	26 43.2	28 10.3	25 37.1	28 55.5	23 48.9
14 M	21 37 29	25 37 59	27 26 20	4♏30 43	29 28.2	10 43.8	24 04.5	25 02.2	5 58.5	26 35.3	28 06.8	25 34.9	28 56.7	23 50.6
15 Tu	21 41 26	26 38 37	11♏35 07	18 39 18	29D26.2	12 21.4	25 18.4	25 47.7	6 22.0	26 27.3	28 03.1	25 32.8	28 58.0	23 52.4
16 W	21 45 22	27 39 13	25 43 04	2♐46 17	29 26.0	13 56.1	26 32.3	26 33.2	6 45.5	26 19.4	27 59.4	25 30.6	28 59.3	23 54.1
17 Th	21 49 19	28 39 48	9♐48 49	16 50 35	29R26.7	15 27.2	27 46.1	27 18.8	7 09.1	26 11.5	27 55.7	25 28.6	29 00.6	23 55.9
18 F	21 53 15	29 40 22	23 51 27	0♑51 20	29 27.1	16 54.2	28 59.9	28 04.4	7 32.7	26 03.6	27 51.8	25 26.5	29 01.9	23 57.6
19 Sa	21 57 12	0♓40 55	7♑50 04	14 47 30	29 26.1	18 16.3	0♈13.7	28 50.0	7 56.3	25 55.7	27 47.9	25 24.5	29 03.2	23 59.4
20 Su	22 01 08	1 41 26	21 43 25	28 37 34	29 22.7	19 32.9	1 27.4	29 35.7	8 19.9	25 47.8	27 44.0	25 22.6	29 04.6	24 01.1
21 M	22 05 05	2 41 56	5♒29 39	12♒19 23	29 16.4	20 43.4	2 41.0	0♒21.4	8 43.5	25 39.9	27 40.0	25 20.6	29 06.0	24 02.9
22 Tu	22 09 02	3 42 25	19 06 24	25 50 24	29 07.5	21 47.1	3 54.6	1 07.1	9 07.2	25 32.1	27 35.9	25 18.7	29 07.5	24 04.6
23 W	22 12 58	4 42 51	2♓31 02	9♓08 01	28 56.5	22 43.3	5 08.2	1 52.8	9 30.8	25 24.3	27 31.7	25 16.9	29 08.9	24 06.3
24 Th	22 16 55	5 43 17	15 41 06	22 10 06	28 44.3	23 31.4	6 21.7	2 38.6	9 54.4	25 16.6	27 27.5	25 15.1	29 10.4	24 08.1
25 F	22 20 51	6 43 40	28 34 54	4♈55 27	28 32.2	24 10.9	7 35.1	3 24.3	10 18.1	25 08.9	27 23.3	25 13.3	29 12.0	24 09.8
26 Sa	22 24 48	7 44 01	11♈11 49	17 24 09	28 21.3	24 41.3	8 48.5	4 10.2	10 41.7	25 01.3	27 19.0	25 11.6	29 13.5	24 11.5
27 Su	22 28 44	8 44 21	23 32 38	29 37 36	28 12.5	25 02.3	10 01.8	4 56.0	11 05.4	24 53.8	27 14.7	25 09.9	29 15.1	24 13.2
28 M	22 32 41	9 44 39	5♉39 26	11♉38 34	28 06.3	25R13.7	11 15.1	5 41.8	11 29.0	24 46.3	27 10.3	25 08.2	29 16.7	24 14.9

Astro Data Dy Hr Mn	Planet Ingress Dy Hr Mn	Last Aspect Dy Hr Mn	☽ Ingress Dy Hr Mn	Last Aspect Dy Hr Mn	☽ Ingress Dy Hr Mn	☽ Phases & Eclipses Dy Hr Mn	Astro Data
☽0N 2 8:20	♀ ♒ 2 0:47	1 7:09 ♄ ☍	♈ 1 8:37	2 14:24 ♄ △	♊ 2 16:59	2 7:38 ☽ 11♈45	1 January 2039
♄R 8 11:56	☿ ♑ 3 4:06	3 17:17 ♆ ⚹	♉ 3 20:11	5 2:44 ♆ ⚹	♋ 5 5:09	10 11:47 ○ 20♋04	Julian Day # 50770
♆D 8 17:01	♂ ♑ 12 1:14	6 7:34 ♄ △	♊ 6 9:01	7 12:28 ♆ □	♌ 7 14:40	17 18:43 ☾ 27♎30	SVP 4♓43'11"
☽0S 16 16:04	♃ ♌R 16 14:57	8 19:31 ♄ □	♋ 8 20:54	9 19:04 ♆ △	♍ 9 21:06	24 13:37 ● 4♒24	GC 27♐23.0 ⚴ 20♑01.2
♃⚻♄ 26 5:37	☉ ♒ 20 5:45	11 5:15 ♄ ⚹	♌ 11 6:36	11 22:17 ♄ ☌	♎ 12 1:15		Eris 27♈39.5R ⚵ 27♐26.2
♃△♆ 29 1:31	☿ ♒ 22 2:01	13 11:20 ♆ △	♍ 13 13:55	14 2:33 ♆ ☍	♏ 14 4:21	1 4:46 ☽ 12♉10	⚷ 0♋26.7R ⚶ 2♍23.4R
☽0N 29 16:23	♀ ♓ 26 1:33	15 17:55 ♄ ☌	♎ 15 19:14	16 3:54 ♄ ⚹	♐ 16 7:17	9 3:40 ○ 20♌14	☽ Mean ☊ 0♋42.7
	⚳ ♓ 30 4:03	17 22:46 ♃ ⚹	♏ 17 22:59	18 9:49 ☉ ⚹	♑ 18 10:32	16 2:37 ☾ 27♏16	
♄⊼♆ 2 10:58		20 1:15 ☉ ⚹	♐ 20 1:35	20 13:47 ♂ ☌	♒ 20 14:24	23 3:19 ● 4♓21	1 February 2039
☽0S 12 21:06	☿ ♓ 8 7:28	22 2:43 ♃ △	♑ 22 3:37	22 17:54 ♆ ⚹	♓ 22 19:28		Julian Day # 50801
♀0N 21 1:45	☊ ♊R 10 3:26	24 4:30 ♄ △	♒ 24 6:06	24 21:50 ♄ ☍	♈ 25 2:40		SVP 4♓43'06"
♃⚻♅ 24 18:16	☉ ♓ 18 19:47	26 8:33 ♃ ☍	♓ 26 10:21	27 11:15 ♆ ☌	♉ 27 12:44		GC 27♐23.1 ⚴ 1♒32.7
☽0N 26 0:28	♀ ♈ 19 7:33	28 15:35 ♄ ☍	♈ 28 17:37				Eris 27♈40.1 ⚵ 8♑12.7
☿0N 26 13:40	♂ ♒ 21 0:47	31 1:41 ♆ ☌	♉ 31 4:17				⚷ 28♊46.7R ⚶ 28♌17.6R
							☽ Mean ☊ 29♊04.2

March 2039 LONGITUDE

Day	Sid.Time	☉	0 hr ☽	Noon ☽	True ☊	☿	♀	♂	⚳	♃	♄	♅	♆	♇
1 Tu	22 36 37	10♓44 55	17♉35 33	23♉30 55	28♊02.7	25♓15.4	12♈28.3	6♒27.7	11♓52.7	24♌38.9	27♍05.9	25♋06.6	29♈18.3	24♒16.6
2 W	22 40 34	11 45 09	29 25 19	5♊19 23	28D01.2	25R07.5	13 41.4	7 13.6	12 16.3	24R31.6	27R01.4	25R05.0	29 19.9	24 18.3
3 Th	22 44 31	12 45 20	11♊13 47	17 09 13	28R01.1	24 50.3	14 54.5	7 59.5	12 40.0	24 24.3	26 56.9	25 03.5	29 21.6	24 20.0
4 F	22 48 27	13 45 30	23 06 23	29 05 58	28 01.2	24 24.3	16 07.5	8 45.5	13 03.6	24 17.2	26 52.4	25 02.0	29 23.3	24 21.7
5 Sa	22 52 24	14 45 38	5♋08 40	11♋15 06	28 00.6	23 50.1	17 20.5	9 31.4	13 27.3	24 10.2	26 47.8	25 00.6	29 25.0	24 23.4
6 Su	22 56 20	15 45 44	17 25 53	23 41 33	27 58.1	23 08.7	18 33.4	10 17.4	13 50.9	24 03.2	26 43.2	24 59.2	29 26.7	24 25.0
7 M	23 00 17	16 45 47	0♌02 34	6♌29 18	27 53.0	22 21.0	19 46.2	11 03.4	14 14.5	23 56.4	26 38.6	24 57.9	29 28.5	24 26.7
8 Tu	23 04 13	17 45 49	13 02 00	19 40 47	27 45.2	21 28.3	20 58.9	11 49.4	14 38.2	23 49.6	26 33.9	24 56.6	29 30.3	24 28.3
9 W	23 08 10	18 45 48	26 25 39	3♍16 27	27 35.0	20 31.9	22 11.6	12 35.5	15 01.8	23 43.0	26 29.3	24 55.4	29 32.1	24 30.0
10 Th	23 12 06	19 45 46	10♍12 49	17 14 20	27 23.2	19 33.2	23 24.2	13 21.5	15 25.4	23 36.5	26 24.6	24 54.2	29 33.9	24 31.6
11 F	23 16 03	20 45 41	24 20 21	1♎30 10	27 10.9	18 33.5	24 36.7	14 07.6	15 49.0	23 30.1	26 19.9	24 53.0	29 35.7	24 33.2
12 Sa	23 20 00	21 45 35	8♎42 59	15 57 56	26 59.6	17 34.3	25 49.1	14 53.7	16 12.6	23 23.9	26 15.2	24 51.9	29 37.6	24 34.8
13 Su	23 23 56	22 45 26	23 14 08	0♏30 45	26 50.3	16 36.7	27 01.5	15 39.8	16 36.2	23 17.7	26 10.5	24 50.8	29 39.5	24 36.4
14 M	23 27 53	23 45 17	7♏46 58	15 02 07	26 43.7	15 41.9	28 13.8	16 25.9	16 59.8	23 11.7	26 05.7	24 49.8	29 41.4	24 38.0
15 Tu	23 31 49	24 45 05	22 15 34	29 26 51	26 40.0	14 50.9	29 26.0	17 12.1	17 23.3	23 05.9	26 01.0	24 48.9	29 43.3	24 39.5
16 W	23 35 46	25 44 52	6♐35 37	13♐41 35	26 38.6	14 04.5	0♉38.2	17 58.3	17 46.9	23 00.2	25 56.2	24 48.0	29 45.2	24 41.1
17 Th	23 39 42	26 44 37	20 44 37	27 44 38	26 38.4	13 23.3	1 50.2	18 44.4	18 10.5	22 54.6	25 51.5	24 47.1	29 47.2	24 42.6
18 F	23 43 39	27 44 21	4♑41 40	11♑35 44	26 38.1	12 47.8	3 02.2	19 30.6	18 34.0	22 49.1	25 46.8	24 46.3	29 49.2	24 44.2
19 Sa	23 47 35	28 44 03	18 26 54	25 15 16	26 36.4	12 18.3	4 14.1	20 16.9	18 57.5	22 43.9	25 42.0	24 45.6	29 51.1	24 45.7
20 Su	23 51 32	29 43 43	2♒00 52	8♒43 47	26 32.3	11 55.0	5 26.0	21 03.1	19 21.0	22 38.7	25 37.3	24 44.9	29 53.1	24 47.2
21 M	23 55 29	0♈43 21	15 24 02	22 01 36	26 25.1	11 37.9	6 37.7	21 49.3	19 44.5	22 33.8	25 32.6	24 44.3	29 55.2	24 48.7
22 Tu	23 59 25	1 42 58	28 36 28	5♓08 34	26 15.1	11 27.1	7 49.4	22 35.6	20 08.0	22 29.0	25 27.9	24 43.7	29 57.2	24 50.1
23 W	0 03 22	2 42 32	11♓37 49	18 04 09	26 02.8	11D22.3	9 00.9	23 21.9	20 31.5	22 24.3	25 23.2	24 43.1	29 59.3	24 51.6
24 Th	0 07 18	3 42 05	24 27 28	0♈47 41	25 49.1	11 23.4	10 12.4	24 08.1	20 54.9	22 19.8	25 18.5	24 42.6	0♉01.3	24 53.0
25 F	0 11 15	4 41 35	7♈04 45	13 18 40	25 35.5	11 30.2	11 23.8	24 54.4	21 18.3	22 15.5	25 13.8	24 42.2	0 03.4	24 54.5
26 Sa	0 15 11	5 41 03	19 29 27	25 37 11	25 23.0	11 42.5	12 35.2	25 40.7	21 41.7	22 11.3	25 09.2	24 41.8	0 05.5	24 55.9
27 Su	0 19 08	6 40 30	1♉41 59	7♉44 05	25 12.6	12 00.0	13 46.4	26 27.0	22 05.1	22 07.4	25 04.6	24 41.5	0 07.6	24 57.3
28 M	0 23 04	7 39 54	13 43 43	19 41 13	25 04.9	12 22.5	14 57.5	27 13.3	22 28.4	22 03.6	25 00.0	24 41.2	0 09.7	24 58.6
29 Tu	0 27 01	8 39 16	25 36 59	1♊31 27	25 00.1	12 49.7	16 08.5	27 59.6	22 51.8	21 59.9	24 55.5	24 41.0	0 11.8	25 00.0
30 W	0 30 57	9 38 36	7♊25 08	13 18 34	24D57.7	13 21.4	17 19.4	28 45.9	23 15.1	21 56.5	24 50.9	24 40.9	0 14.0	25 01.3
31 Th	0 34 54	10 37 53	19 12 23	25 07 11	24 57.2	13 57.2	18 30.3	29 32.2	23 38.3	21 53.2	24 46.5	24 40.7	0 16.1	25 02.7

April 2039 LONGITUDE

Day	Sid.Time	☉	0 hr ☽	Noon ☽	True ☊	☿	♀	♂	⚳	♃	♄	♅	♆	♇
1 F	0 38 51	11♈37 09	1♋03 38	7♋02 26	24♊57.4	14♓37.0	19♉41.0	0♓18.5	24♓01.6	21♌50.1	24♍42.0	24♋40.7	0♉18.3	25♒04.0
2 Sa	0 42 47	12 36 22	13 04 16	19 09 50	24R57.3	15 20.6	20 51.6	1 04.8	24 24.8	21R47.2	24R37.6	24D40.7	0 20.5	25 05.3
3 Su	0 46 44	13 35 32	25 19 47	1♌34 47	24 55.8	16 07.7	22 02.1	1 51.1	24 48.0	21 44.5	24 33.3	24 40.8	0 22.6	25 06.5
4 M	0 50 40	14 34 41	7♌55 25	14 22 10	24 52.2	16 58.2	23 12.5	2 37.5	25 11.2	21 42.0	24 28.9	24 40.9	0 24.8	25 07.8
5 Tu	0 54 37	15 33 47	20 55 30	27 35 41	24 46.2	17 51.9	24 22.7	3 23.8	25 34.3	21 39.6	24 24.7	24 41.0	0 27.0	25 09.0
6 W	0 58 33	16 32 50	4♍22 52	11♍17 04	24 37.9	18 48.6	25 32.9	4 10.1	25 57.4	21 37.5	24 20.5	24 41.2	0 29.2	25 10.2
7 Th	1 02 30	17 31 52	18 18 06	25 25 33	24 28.1	19 48.1	26 42.9	4 56.4	26 20.5	21 35.5	24 16.3	24 41.5	0 31.4	25 11.4
8 F	1 06 26	18 30 51	2♎38 53	9♎57 19	24 17.7	20 50.4	27 52.8	5 42.7	26 43.5	21 33.7	24 12.2	24 41.8	0 33.7	25 12.6
9 Sa	1 10 23	19 29 48	17 19 59	24 45 48	24 08.0	21 55.2	29 02.6	6 29.0	27 06.5	21 32.1	24 08.1	24 42.2	0 35.9	25 13.8
10 Su	1 14 20	20 28 43	2♏13 41	9♏42 29	24 00.0	23 02.5	0♊12.3	7 15.4	27 29.5	21 30.6	24 04.1	24 42.6	0 38.1	25 14.9
11 M	1 18 16	21 27 37	17 11 04	24 38 24	23 54.5	24 12.3	1 21.8	8 01.7	27 52.4	21 29.4	24 00.2	24 43.1	0 40.4	25 16.0
12 Tu	1 22 13	22 26 28	2♐03 29	9♐25 33	23D51.5	25 24.3	2 31.2	8 48.0	28 15.3	21 28.3	23 56.3	24 43.7	0 42.6	25 17.1
13 W	1 26 09	23 25 18	16 43 54	23 58 02	23 50.7	26 38.5	3 40.5	9 34.3	28 38.1	21 27.5	23 52.5	24 44.2	0 44.9	25 18.2
14 Th	1 30 06	24 24 06	1♑07 36	8♑12 24	23 51.2	27 54.8	4 49.7	10 20.6	29 01.0	21 26.8	23 48.7	24 44.9	0 47.1	25 19.2
15 F	1 34 02	25 22 53	15 12 20	22 07 27	23R51.8	29 13.3	5 58.7	11 06.9	29 23.8	21 26.3	23 45.0	24 45.6	0 49.4	25 20.3
16 Sa	1 37 59	26 21 38	28 57 50	5♒43 38	23 51.4	0♈33.7	7 07.6	11 53.2	29 46.5	21 26.0	23 41.4	24 46.3	0 51.6	25 21.3
17 Su	1 41 55	27 20 21	12♒25 05	19 02 22	23 49.2	1 56.0	8 16.3	12 39.5	0♈09.2	21D25.9	23 37.9	24 47.1	0 53.9	25 22.2
18 M	1 45 52	28 19 02	25 35 45	2♓05 27	23 44.7	3 20.3	9 24.9	13 25.8	0 31.9	21 26.0	23 34.4	24 48.0	0 56.1	25 23.2
19 Tu	1 49 49	29 17 42	8♓31 41	14 54 37	23 37.9	4 46.4	10 33.4	14 12.1	0 54.5	21 26.2	23 31.0	24 48.9	0 58.4	25 24.1
20 W	1 53 45	0♉16 20	21 14 28	27 31 23	23 29.3	6 14.4	11 41.7	14 58.4	1 17.1	21 26.7	23 27.7	24 49.9	1 00.7	25 25.1
21 Th	1 57 42	1 14 56	3♈45 30	9♈56 56	23 19.6	7 44.1	12 49.8	15 44.6	1 39.6	21 27.3	23 24.4	24 50.9	1 02.9	25 26.0
22 F	2 01 38	2 13 30	16 05 49	22 12 17	23 09.9	9 15.7	13 57.9	16 30.9	2 02.1	21 28.1	23 21.2	24 51.9	1 05.2	25 26.8
23 Sa	2 05 35	3 12 02	28 16 27	4♉18 26	23 00.9	10 49.0	15 05.7	17 17.1	2 24.6	21 29.1	23 18.2	24 53.0	1 07.5	25 27.7
24 Su	2 09 31	4 10 33	10♉18 26	16 16 37	22 53.6	12 24.1	16 13.4	18 03.3	2 47.0	21 30.3	23 15.1	24 54.2	1 09.7	25 28.5
25 M	2 13 28	5 09 01	22 13 12	28 08 28	22 48.3	14 00.9	17 21.0	18 49.5	3 09.3	21 31.7	23 12.2	24 55.4	1 12.0	25 29.3
26 Tu	2 17 24	6 07 28	4♊02 41	9♊56 12	22 45.3	15 39.5	18 28.3	19 35.7	3 31.6	21 33.2	23 09.4	24 56.7	1 14.2	25 30.1
27 W	2 21 21	7 05 53	15 49 25	21 42 44	22D44.3	17 19.8	19 35.5	20 21.9	3 53.8	21 35.0	23 06.6	24 58.0	1 16.5	25 30.8
28 Th	2 25 18	8 04 16	27 36 39	3♋31 39	22 44.8	19 01.9	20 42.5	21 08.0	4 16.0	21 36.9	23 04.0	24 59.4	1 18.8	25 31.6
29 F	2 29 14	9 02 36	9♋28 18	15 27 10	22 46.2	20 45.7	21 49.4	21 54.1	4 38.2	21 39.0	23 01.4	25 00.8	1 21.0	25 32.3
30 Sa	2 33 11	10 00 55	21 28 51	27 33 59	22 47.6	22 31.3	22 56.0	22 40.3	5 00.2	21 41.3	22 58.9	25 02.3	1 23.3	25 33.0

Astro Data	Dy Hr Mn
☿R	1 4:11
♃☍♇	3 23:43
☿0S	8 11:25
☽0S	12 4:17
♅⚻♇	19 11:09
☉0N	20 18:34
☿D	23 19:21
☽0N	25 7:58
♄⚻♇	28 17:30
♄⚹♅	1 19:12
♅D	1 23:34
☽0S	8 14:06
♃D	17 14:53
☿0N	20 10:54
☽0N	21 14:37

Planet Ingress	Dy Hr Mn
♀ ♉	15 23:18
☉ ♈	20 18:33
♆ ♉	23 20:42
♂ ♓	1 2:24
♀ ♊	10 7:46
☿ ♈	16 2:01
⚳ ♈	17 2:15
☉ ♉	20 5:19

Last Aspect Dy Hr Mn		☽ Ingress Dy Hr Mn
1 19:14	♄ △	♊ 2 1:11
4 12:35	♆ ⚹	♋ 4 13:48
6 22:54	♆ □	♌ 6 23:55
9 5:27	♆ △	♍ 9 6:17
11 3:24	♄ ☌	♎ 11 9:29
13 10:35	♆ ☍	♏ 13 11:09
15 6:18	♄ ⚹	♐ 15 12:55
17 15:32	♆ △	♑ 17 15:53
19 20:10	♆ □	♒ 19 20:25
22 2:26	♆ ⚹	♓ 22 2:33
24 1:40	♄ ☍	♈ 24 10:29
26 12:07	♂ ⚹	♉ 26 20:38
29 4:19	♂ □	♊ 29 8:54
31 21:33	♂ △	♋ 31 21:52

Last Aspect Dy Hr Mn		☽ Ingress Dy Hr Mn
2 22:44	♅ ☌	♌ 3 8:59
5 7:37	♇ ☍	♍ 5 16:17
7 14:21	♀ △	♎ 7 19:37
9 12:45	♇ △	♏ 9 20:25
11 13:01	♇ □	♐ 11 20:40
13 16:54	☿ □	♑ 13 22:06
16 1:49	☿ ⚹	♒ 16 1:50
18 4:27	☉ ⚹	♓ 18 8:07
20 6:50	♅ △	♈ 20 16:45
22 18:25	♇ ⚹	♉ 23 3:26
25 6:37	♇ □	♊ 25 15:47
27 19:45	♇ △	♋ 28 4:51
30 7:01	♅ ☌	♌ 30 16:46

☽ Phases & Eclipses Dy Hr Mn	
3 2:16	☽ 12♊21
10 16:36	○ 19♍57
17 10:09	☾ 26♐40
24 18:01	● 3♈57
1 21:56	☽ 12♋02
9 2:54	○ 19♎07
15 18:08	☾ 25♑38
23 9:36	● 3♉06

Astro Data

1 March 2039
Julian Day # 50829
SVP 4♓43'02"
GC 27♐23.2 ⚴ 11♒25.8
Eris 27♈49.4 ⚵ 17♑17.4
⚷ 28♊08.6R ⚶ 21♌11.3R
☽ Mean ☊ 27♊35.3

1 April 2039
Julian Day # 50860
SVP 4♓42'59"
GC 27♐23.3 ⚴ 21♒14.3
Eris 28♈06.8 ⚵ 25♑53.0
⚷ 28♊41.5 ⚶ 17♌14.9R
☽ Mean ☊ 25♊56.8

LONGITUDE — May 2039

Day	Sid.Time	☉	0 hr ☽	Noon ☽	True ☊	☿	♀	♂	⚳	♃	♄	♅	♆	♇
1 Su	2 37 07	10♉59 12	3♌43 11	9♌57 05	22♊48.3	24♈18.6	24♊02.5	23♓26.3	5♈22.3	21♌43.8	22♍56.5	25♋03.8	1♉25.5	25♒33.6
2 M	2 41 04	11 57 26	16 16 16	22 41 17	22R47.7	26 07.8	25 08.7	24 12.4	5 44.2	21 46.4	22R54.2	25 05.4	1 27.7	25 34.2
3 Tu	2 45 00	12 55 39	29 12 39	5♍50 45	22 45.4	27 58.7	26 14.7	24 58.4	6 06.1	21 49.2	22 52.0	25 07.0	1 30.0	25 34.8
4 W	2 48 57	13 53 49	12♍35 54	19 28 17	22 41.6	29 51.3	27 20.6	25 44.5	6 28.0	21 52.2	22 49.9	25 08.6	1 32.2	25 35.4
5 Th	2 52 53	14 51 57	26 27 53	3♎34 32	22 36.7	1♉45.8	28 26.2	26 30.4	6 49.8	21 55.3	22 47.9	25 10.3	1 34.4	25 36.0
6 F	2 56 50	15 50 04	10♎47 53	18 07 23	22 31.2	3 42.0	29 31.6	27 16.4	7 11.5	21 58.7	22 45.9	25 12.1	1 36.6	25 36.5
7 Sa	3 00 47	16 48 09	25 32 15	3♏01 35	22 25.9	5 39.9	0♋36.8	28 02.4	7 33.1	22 02.1	22 44.1	25 13.9	1 38.8	25 37.0
8 Su	3 04 43	17 46 12	10♏34 17	18 09 10	22 21.7	7 39.6	1 41.7	28 48.3	7 54.7	22 05.8	22 42.4	25 15.7	1 41.0	25 37.5
9 M	3 08 40	18 44 13	25 45 00	3♐20 31	22 18.9	9 41.0	2 46.4	29 34.2	8 16.3	22 09.6	22 40.7	25 17.6	1 43.2	25 38.0
10 Tu	3 12 36	19 42 13	10♐54 32	18 25 55	22D17.8	11 43.9	3 50.9	0♈20.1	8 37.7	22 13.6	22 39.2	25 19.6	1 45.4	25 38.4
11 W	3 16 33	20 40 11	25 53 41	3♑17 01	22 18.1	13 48.5	4 55.1	1 05.9	8 59.1	22 17.8	22 37.8	25 21.6	1 47.6	25 38.8
12 Th	3 20 29	21 38 09	10♑35 15	17 47 53	22 19.3	15 54.4	5 59.0	1 51.7	9 20.5	22 22.1	22 36.4	25 23.6	1 49.7	25 39.2
13 F	3 24 26	22 36 04	24 54 37	1♒55 16	22 20.8	18 01.7	7 02.7	2 37.5	9 41.8	22 26.6	22 35.2	25 25.7	1 51.9	25 39.5
14 Sa	3 28 22	23 33 59	8♒49 49	15 38 20	22R21.8	20 10.2	8 06.2	3 23.3	10 03.0	22 31.2	22 34.0	25 27.8	1 54.0	25 39.9
15 Su	3 32 19	24 31 52	22 21 02	28 58 09	22 22.0	22 19.7	9 09.3	4 09.1	10 24.1	22 36.0	22 33.0	25 29.9	1 56.2	25 40.2
16 M	3 36 16	25 29 44	5♓30 00	11♓56 56	22 21.0	24 30.0	10 12.2	4 54.8	10 45.1	22 41.0	22 32.1	25 32.1	1 58.3	25 40.5
17 Tu	3 40 12	26 27 35	18 19 18	24 37 30	22 18.7	26 41.0	11 14.8	5 40.4	11 06.1	22 46.1	22 31.2	25 34.4	2 00.4	25 40.7
18 W	3 44 09	27 25 25	0♈51 54	7♈02 52	22 15.5	28 52.2	12 17.1	6 26.1	11 27.0	22 51.3	22 30.5	25 36.6	2 02.5	25 40.9
19 Th	3 48 05	28 23 13	13 10 45	19 15 55	22 11.8	1♊03.6	13 19.1	7 11.7	11 47.9	22 56.8	22 29.8	25 39.0	2 04.6	25 41.1
20 F	3 52 02	29 21 00	25 18 39	1♉19 17	22 07.9	3 14.8	14 20.8	7 57.3	12 08.6	23 02.3	22 29.3	25 41.3	2 06.6	25 41.3
21 Sa	3 55 58	0♊18 46	7♉18 06	13 15 23	22 04.4	5 25.5	15 22.2	8 42.8	12 29.3	23 08.0	22 28.9	25 43.7	2 08.7	25 41.4
22 Su	3 59 55	1 16 31	19 11 22	25 06 21	22 01.7	7 35.4	16 23.2	9 28.3	12 49.9	23 13.9	22 28.6	25 46.2	2 10.7	25 41.6
23 M	4 03 51	2 14 14	1♊00 35	6♊54 19	21 59.9	9 44.4	17 23.9	10 13.7	13 10.4	23 19.9	22 28.3	25 48.7	2 12.8	25 41.7
24 Tu	4 07 48	3 11 57	12 47 50	18 41 26	21D59.1	11 52.1	18 24.3	10 59.2	13 30.8	23 26.1	22D28.2	25 51.2	2 14.8	25 41.7
25 W	4 11 45	4 09 37	24 35 24	0♋30 04	21 59.3	13 58.2	19 24.3	11 44.5	13 51.1	23 32.4	22 28.2	25 53.7	2 16.8	25 41.8
26 Th	4 15 41	5 07 17	6♋25 46	12 22 53	22 00.2	16 02.6	20 23.9	12 29.9	14 11.4	23 38.8	22 28.3	25 56.3	2 18.7	25R41.8
27 F	4 19 38	6 04 55	18 21 49	24 22 59	22 01.5	18 05.1	21 23.1	13 15.1	14 31.5	23 45.4	22 28.5	25 59.0	2 20.7	25 41.8
28 Sa	4 23 34	7 02 32	0♌26 49	6♌33 48	22 02.8	20 05.4	22 22.0	14 00.4	14 51.6	23 52.1	22 28.8	26 01.6	2 22.7	25 41.8
29 Su	4 27 31	8 00 07	12 44 25	18 59 08	22 03.9	22 03.5	23 20.4	14 45.6	15 11.6	23 59.0	22 29.2	26 04.3	2 24.6	25 41.7
30 M	4 31 27	8 57 41	25 18 26	1♍42 48	22R04.6	23 59.2	24 18.4	15 30.7	15 31.4	24 05.9	22 29.7	26 07.1	2 26.5	25 41.6
31 Tu	4 35 24	9 55 13	8♍12 41	14 48 27	22 04.6	25 52.4	25 15.9	16 15.8	15 51.2	24 13.1	22 30.3	26 09.8	2 28.4	25 41.5

LONGITUDE — June 2039

Day	Sid.Time	☉	0 hr ☽	Noon ☽	True ☊	☿	♀	♂	⚳	♃	♄	♅	♆	♇
1 W	4 39 20	10♊52 44	21♍30 27	28♍18 56	22♊04.1	27♊43.0	26♋13.0	17♈00.9	16♈10.9	24♌20.3	22♍31.0	26♋12.6	2♉30.3	25♒41.4
2 Th	4 43 17	11 50 14	5♎14 02	12♎15 45	22R03.3	29 31.0	27 09.6	17 45.9	16 30.5	24 27.7	22 31.8	26 15.5	2 32.1	25R41.2
3 F	4 47 14	12 47 42	19 23 58	26 38 23	22 02.2	1♋16.3	28 05.7	18 30.8	16 49.9	24 35.2	22 32.7	26 18.3	2 34.0	25 41.0
4 Sa	4 51 10	13 45 09	3♏58 32	11♏23 45	22 01.2	2 58.9	29 01.3	19 15.7	17 09.3	24 42.8	22 33.7	26 21.2	2 35.8	25 40.8
5 Su	4 55 07	14 42 35	18 53 15	26 26 04	22 00.5	4 38.8	29 56.3	20 00.5	17 28.6	24 50.6	22 34.8	26 24.2	2 37.6	25 40.6
6 M	4 59 03	15 40 00	4♐01 07	11♐37 15	22D00.1	6 15.8	0♌50.9	20 45.4	17 47.7	24 58.4	22 36.1	26 27.1	2 39.4	25 40.3
7 Tu	5 03 00	16 37 25	19 13 14	26 47 54	22 00.1	7 50.0	1 44.8	21 30.1	18 06.8	25 06.4	22 37.4	26 30.1	2 41.1	25 40.1
8 W	5 06 56	17 34 48	4♑20 05	11♑48 43	22 00.3	9 21.4	2 38.2	22 14.8	18 25.8	25 14.5	22 38.8	26 33.2	2 42.9	25 39.8
9 Th	5 10 53	18 32 11	19 12 52	26 31 46	22 00.6	10 49.9	3 31.0	22 59.5	18 44.6	25 22.8	22 40.3	26 36.2	2 44.6	25 39.4
10 F	5 14 49	19 29 33	3♒44 47	10♒51 28	22 00.8	12 15.5	4 23.1	23 44.1	19 03.4	25 31.1	22 41.9	26 39.3	2 46.3	25 39.1
11 Sa	5 18 46	20 26 54	17 51 33	24 44 56	22 01.0	13 38.2	5 14.6	24 28.6	19 22.0	25 39.5	22 43.6	26 42.4	2 47.9	25 38.7
12 Su	5 22 43	21 24 15	1♓31 36	8♓11 45	22R01.1	14 58.0	6 05.5	25 13.1	19 40.5	25 48.1	22 45.5	26 45.5	2 49.6	25 38.3
13 M	5 26 39	22 21 35	14 45 36	21 13 31	22D01.1	16 14.7	6 55.7	25 57.5	19 58.9	25 56.8	22 47.4	26 48.7	2 51.2	25 37.9
14 Tu	5 30 36	23 18 55	27 35 55	3♈53 14	22 01.1	17 28.4	7 45.1	26 41.9	20 17.1	26 05.6	22 49.4	26 51.9	2 52.8	25 37.4
15 W	5 34 32	24 16 14	10♈05 59	16 14 38	22 01.3	18 39.0	8 33.8	27 26.2	20 35.3	26 14.5	22 51.5	26 55.1	2 54.4	25 36.9
16 Th	5 38 29	25 13 34	22 19 45	28 21 47	22 01.5	19 46.4	9 21.8	28 10.5	20 53.3	26 23.5	22 53.7	26 58.3	2 55.9	25 36.4
17 F	5 42 25	26 10 52	4♉21 17	10♉18 42	22 01.9	20 50.6	10 09.0	28 54.7	21 11.2	26 32.6	22 56.0	27 01.6	2 57.5	25 35.9
18 Sa	5 46 22	27 08 11	16 14 29	22 09 07	22 02.4	21 51.5	10 55.3	29 38.8	21 29.0	26 41.8	22 58.4	27 04.9	2 59.0	25 35.4
19 Su	5 50 18	28 05 29	28 02 58	3♊56 26	22 02.9	22 49.0	11 40.8	0♉22.9	21 46.6	26 51.1	23 00.9	27 08.2	3 00.5	25 34.8
20 M	5 54 15	29 02 46	9♊49 52	15 43 37	22R03.3	23 43.1	12 25.5	1 06.9	22 04.1	27 00.5	23 03.4	27 11.5	3 01.9	25 34.2
21 Tu	5 58 12	0♋00 03	21 38 00	27 33 18	22 03.3	24 33.6	13 09.2	1 50.8	22 21.4	27 10.0	23 06.1	27 14.8	3 03.4	25 33.6
22 W	6 02 08	0 57 20	3♋29 48	9♋27 46	22 02.9	25 20.4	13 51.9	2 34.7	22 38.7	27 19.6	23 08.9	27 18.2	3 04.8	25 33.0
23 Th	6 06 05	1 54 37	15 27 28	21 29 09	22 02.0	26 03.4	14 33.7	3 18.5	22 55.8	27 29.3	23 11.8	27 21.6	3 06.1	25 32.3
24 F	6 10 01	2 51 52	27 33 05	3♌39 30	22 00.7	26 42.5	15 14.5	4 02.2	23 12.7	27 39.1	23 14.7	27 25.0	3 07.5	25 31.6
25 Sa	6 13 58	3 49 08	9♌48 40	16 00 51	21 59.1	27 17.6	15 54.1	4 45.8	23 29.5	27 49.0	23 17.8	27 28.4	3 08.8	25 30.9
26 Su	6 17 54	4 46 22	22 16 20	28 35 23	21 57.5	27 48.6	16 32.7	5 29.4	23 46.1	27 59.0	23 20.9	27 31.9	3 10.1	25 30.2
27 M	6 21 51	5 43 37	4♍58 17	11♍25 19	21 56.1	28 15.4	17 10.1	6 12.9	24 02.6	28 09.1	23 24.1	27 35.3	3 11.4	25 29.5
28 Tu	6 25 48	6 40 50	17 56 45	24 32 51	21D55.1	28 37.8	17 46.3	6 56.3	24 18.9	28 19.2	23 27.4	27 38.8	3 12.6	25 28.7
29 W	6 29 44	7 38 03	1♎13 51	7♎59 57	21 54.8	28 55.8	18 21.2	7 39.7	24 35.1	28 29.5	23 30.8	27 42.3	3 13.8	25 27.9
30 Th	6 33 41	8 35 16	14 51 16	21 47 55	21 55.1	29 09.2	18 54.9	8 23.0	24 51.1	28 39.8	23 34.3	27 45.8	3 15.0	25 27.1

Astro Data	Planet Ingress
Dy Hr Mn	Dy Hr Mn
☽0S 6 1:02	☿ ♉ 4 13:50
♂0N 14 7:42	♀ ♋ 6 22:27
♃⊻♄ 14 23:35	♂ ♈ 10 1:30
☽0N 18 20:43	☿ ♊ 19 0:23
♅⊼♇ 20 11:44	☉ ♊ 21 4:12
♄D 25 3:07	
♇R 26 19:21	☿ ♋ 2 18:32
	♀ ♌ 5 13:36
☽0S 2 10:53	♂ ♉ 18 23:32
♃☍♇ 11 9:41	☉ ♋ 21 11:59
☽0N 15 2:58	
♃⊻♅ 22 6:31	
⚳0N 24 5:55	
☽0S 29 18:16	

Last Aspect	☽ Ingress	Last Aspect	☽ Ingress
Dy Hr Mn	Dy Hr Mn	Dy Hr Mn	Dy Hr Mn
2 19:24 ☿ △	♍ 3 1:26	1 10:47 ☿ □	♎ 1 14:56
5 2:37 ♀ □	♎ 5 5:59	3 14:33 ♀ □	♏ 3 17:31
7 0:07 ♇ △	♏ 7 7:10	5 11:57 ♅ △	♐ 5 17:39
9 5:43 ♂ △	♐ 9 6:43	7 10:12 ♇ ⚹	♑ 7 17:05
10 23:36 ♇ ⚹	♑ 11 6:39	9 12:07 ♅ ☍	♒ 9 17:45
13 0:51 ♅ ☍	♒ 13 8:42	11 13:37 ♃ ☍	♓ 11 21:17
15 6:00 ♇ ☌	♓ 15 13:53	13 22:33 ♅ △	♈ 14 4:34
17 16:47 ☿ ⚹	♈ 17 22:20	16 11:36 ♂ ☌	♉ 16 15:16
20 0:45 ♇ ⚹	♉ 20 9:21	18 22:05 ♅ ⚹	♊ 19 3:58
22 13:21 ♅ ⚹	♊ 22 21:57	21 11:12 ♃ ⚹	♋ 21 16:57
25 2:15 ♇ △	♋ 25 10:59	23 23:41 ♅ ☌	♌ 24 4:49
27 15:11 ♅ ☌	♌ 27 23:07	26 10:50 ♃ ☌	♍ 26 14:40
30 0:44 ♇ ☍	♍ 30 8:48	28 19:32 ☿ ⚹	♎ 28 21:48

☽ Phases & Eclipses	Astro Data
Dy Hr Mn	
1 14:09 ☽ 11♌04	1 May 2039
8 11:21 ○ 17♏45	Julian Day # 50890
15 3:18 ☾ 24♒11	SVP 4♓42'56"
23 1:39 ● 1♊49	GC 27♐23.3 ⚴ 28♒53.0
31 2:26 ☽ 9♍32	Eris 28♈26.4 ⚵ 1♒42.0
	⚷ 0♋21.5 ⚶ 20♌16.4
	☽ Mean ☊ 24♊21.4
6 18:49 ○ 15♐56	
6 18:54 • P 0.885	1 June 2039
13 14:18 ☾ 22♓27	Julian Day # 50921
21 17:23 ● 0♋13	SVP 4♓42'51"
21 17:12:52 • A 04'05"	GC 27♐23.4 ⚴ 3♓46.4
29 11:18 ☽ 7♎36	Eris 28♈44.7 ⚵ 3♒33.9R
	⚷ 2♋54.1 ⚶ 28♌40.6
	☽ Mean ☊ 22♊42.9

July 2039 LONGITUDE

Day	Sid.Time	☉	0 hr ☽	Noon ☽	True ☊	☿	♀	♂	⚳	♃	♄	♅	♆	♇
1 F	6 37 37	9♋32 28	28♎49 52	5♏57 01	21♊56.1	29♋18.1	19♌27.1	9♉06.2	25♈07.0	28♌50.2	23♍37.9	27♋49.3	3♉16.2	25♒26.3
2 Sa	6 41 34	10 29 40	13♏09 08	20 25 54	21 57.3	29R 22.3	19 58.0	9 49.3	25 22.7	29 00.7	23 41.6	27 52.9	3 17.3	25R 25.4
3 Su	6 45 30	11 26 51	27 46 50	5♐11 18	21 58.3	29 21.9	20 27.4	10 32.3	25 38.2	29 11.3	23 45.3	27 56.4	3 18.4	25 24.6
4 M	6 49 27	12 24 02	12♐38 35	20 07 47	21R58.9	29 16.8	20 55.3	11 15.3	25 53.6	29 21.9	23 49.2	28 00.0	3 19.5	25 23.7
5 Tu	6 53 23	13 21 14	27 37 59	5♑08 08	21 58.5	29 07.2	21 21.6	11 58.2	26 08.8	29 32.7	23 53.1	28 03.6	3 20.5	25 22.8
6 W	6 57 20	14 18 25	12♑37 11	20 04 05	21 57.0	28 53.1	21 46.3	12 41.0	26 23.8	29 43.5	23 57.1	28 07.2	3 21.6	25 21.9
7 Th	7 01 17	15 15 36	27 27 48	4♒47 25	21 54.6	28 34.7	22 09.3	13 23.7	26 38.7	29 54.3	24 01.1	28 10.8	3 22.5	25 21.0
8 F	7 05 13	16 12 47	12♒02 07	19 11 13	21 51.4	28 12.2	22 30.5	14 06.4	26 53.3	0♍05.3	24 05.3	28 14.4	3 23.5	25 20.0
9 Sa	7 09 10	17 09 58	26 14 11	3♓10 41	21 48.0	27 45.9	22 50.0	14 48.9	27 07.8	0 16.3	24 09.5	28 18.0	3 24.4	25 19.1
10 Su	7 13 06	18 07 10	10♓00 31	16 43 37	21 44.8	27 16.2	23 07.6	15 31.4	27 22.1	0 27.4	24 13.8	28 21.6	3 25.3	25 18.1
11 M	7 17 03	19 04 22	23 20 07	29 50 13	21 42.4	26 43.5	23 23.3	16 13.8	27 36.2	0 38.6	24 18.2	28 25.2	3 26.2	25 17.1
12 Tu	7 20 59	20 01 35	6♈14 17	12♈32 43	21D41.0	26 08.2	23 37.0	16 56.1	27 50.2	0 49.8	24 22.7	28 28.9	3 27.0	25 16.1
13 W	7 24 56	20 58 48	18 46 02	24 54 47	21 40.8	25 30.9	23 48.7	17 38.4	28 03.9	1 01.1	24 27.2	28 32.5	3 27.8	25 15.0
14 Th	7 28 52	21 56 01	0♉59 32	7♉00 53	21 41.7	24 52.3	23 58.3	18 20.5	28 17.4	1 12.4	24 31.8	28 36.2	3 28.6	25 14.0
15 F	7 32 49	22 53 15	12 59 28	18 55 53	21 43.2	24 12.9	24 05.8	19 02.6	28 30.8	1 23.8	24 36.5	28 39.8	3 29.3	25 12.9
16 Sa	7 36 46	23 50 30	24 50 44	0♊44 35	21 44.9	23 33.4	24 11.1	19 44.5	28 43.9	1 35.3	24 41.3	28 43.5	3 30.0	25 11.8
17 Su	7 40 42	24 47 45	6♊38 00	12 31 31	21R46.2	22 54.5	24R14.2	20 26.4	28 56.8	1 46.9	24 46.1	28 47.2	3 30.7	25 10.7
18 M	7 44 39	25 45 01	18 25 36	24 20 42	21 46.6	22 16.9	24 15.0	21 08.2	29 09.5	1 58.5	24 51.1	28 50.8	3 31.3	25 09.6
19 Tu	7 48 35	26 42 17	0♋17 15	6♋15 35	21 45.5	21 41.3	24 13.6	21 49.8	29 22.0	2 10.2	24 56.0	28 54.5	3 31.9	25 08.5
20 W	7 52 32	27 39 34	12 16 02	18 18 53	21 42.8	21 08.3	24 09.7	22 31.4	29 34.3	2 21.9	25 01.1	28 58.2	3 32.5	25 07.4
21 Th	7 56 28	28 36 52	24 24 20	0♌32 37	21 38.4	20 38.5	24 03.5	23 12.9	29 46.3	2 33.7	25 06.2	29 01.9	3 33.1	25 06.2
22 F	8 00 25	29 34 10	6♌43 52	12 58 12	21 32.7	20 12.5	23 55.0	23 54.2	29 58.1	2 45.5	25 11.4	29 05.5	3 33.6	25 05.1
23 Sa	8 04 21	0♌31 28	19 15 42	25 36 26	21 26.1	19 50.8	23 44.0	24 35.5	0♉09.7	2 57.4	25 16.7	29 09.2	3 34.1	25 03.9
24 Su	8 08 18	1 28 47	2♍00 26	8♍27 46	21 19.4	19 33.9	23 30.7	25 16.7	0 21.1	3 09.3	25 22.0	29 12.9	3 34.5	25 02.7
25 M	8 12 15	2 26 06	14 58 26	21 32 27	21 13.4	19 22.0	23 15.0	25 57.7	0 32.2	3 21.3	25 27.4	29 16.6	3 34.9	25 01.5
26 Tu	8 16 11	3 23 25	28 09 51	4♎50 41	21 08.7	19D 15.6	22 57.0	26 38.7	0 43.1	3 33.4	25 32.8	29 20.3	3 35.3	25 00.3
27 W	8 20 08	4 20 45	11♎34 56	18 22 40	21 05.7	19 14.8	22 36.7	27 19.5	0 53.7	3 45.4	25 38.3	29 23.9	3 35.7	24 59.1
28 Th	8 24 04	5 18 06	25 13 54	2♏08 39	21D04.6	19 20.0	22 14.2	28 00.2	1 04.1	3 57.6	25 43.9	29 27.6	3 36.0	24 57.9
29 F	8 28 01	6 15 27	9♏06 54	16 08 38	21 04.9	19 31.1	21 49.6	28 40.8	1 14.2	4 09.8	25 49.5	29 31.2	3 36.3	24 56.7
30 Sa	8 31 57	7 12 48	23 13 44	0♐22 04	21 05.9	19 48.4	21 22.9	29 21.3	1 24.1	4 22.0	25 55.2	29 34.9	3 36.5	24 55.4
31 Su	8 35 54	8 10 10	7♐33 24	14 47 25	21R06.9	20 11.9	20 54.3	0♊01.7	1 33.7	4 34.3	26 01.0	29 38.6	3 36.7	24 54.2

August 2039 LONGITUDE

Day	Sid.Time	☉	0 hr ☽	Noon ☽	True ☊	☿	♀	♂	⚳	♃	♄	♅	♆	♇
1 M	8 39 50	9♌07 32	22♐03 44	29♐21 49	21♊06.8	20♋41.7	20♌23.9	0♊42.0	1♉43.1	4♍46.6	26♍06.8	29♋42.2	3♉36.9	24♒52.9
2 Tu	8 43 47	10 04 55	6♑41 04	14♑00 47	21R04.8	21 17.6	19R52.0	1 22.2	1 52.2	4 58.9	26 12.7	29 45.8	3 37.1	24R51.7
3 W	8 47 44	11 02 19	21 20 11	28 38 27	21 00.7	21 59.8	19 18.6	2 02.2	2 01.0	5 11.3	26 18.6	29 49.5	3 37.2	24 50.4
4 Th	8 51 40	11 59 44	5♒54 43	13♒08 09	20 54.5	22 48.0	18 43.9	2 42.1	2 09.5	5 23.7	26 24.6	29 53.1	3 37.3	24 49.1
5 F	8 55 37	12 57 09	20 17 56	27 23 21	20 46.7	23 42.3	18 08.3	3 22.0	2 17.8	5 36.2	26 30.6	29 56.7	3 37.4	24 47.8
6 Sa	8 59 33	13 54 35	4♓23 47	11♓18 42	20 38.2	24 42.6	17 31.8	4 01.7	2 25.8	5 48.7	26 36.7	0♌00.3	3R37.4	24 46.5
7 Su	9 03 30	14 52 03	18 07 45	24 50 44	20 30.0	25 48.6	16 54.8	4 41.2	2 33.5	6 01.2	26 42.8	0 03.9	3 37.4	24 45.2
8 M	9 07 26	15 49 32	1♈27 31	7♈58 13	20 22.9	27 00.3	16 17.4	5 20.7	2 41.0	6 13.8	26 49.0	0 07.5	3 37.3	24 43.9
9 Tu	9 11 23	16 47 02	14 23 00	20 42 12	20 17.6	28 17.5	15 40.0	6 00.0	2 48.1	6 26.4	26 55.3	0 11.0	3 37.3	24 42.6
10 W	9 15 19	17 44 33	26 56 12	3♉05 31	20 14.5	29 39.9	15 02.7	6 39.3	2 54.9	6 39.0	27 01.6	0 14.6	3 37.1	24 41.3
11 Th	9 19 16	18 42 06	9♉10 40	15 12 18	20D 13.2	1♌07.2	14 25.9	7 18.3	3 01.5	6 51.6	27 07.9	0 18.1	3 37.0	24 40.0
12 F	9 23 13	19 39 40	21 11 01	27 07 30	20 13.4	2 39.3	13 49.6	7 57.3	3 07.7	7 04.3	27 14.3	0 21.7	3 36.8	24 38.7
13 Sa	9 27 09	20 37 15	3♊02 25	8♊56 27	20R 14.2	4 15.9	13 14.2	8 36.1	3 13.6	7 17.0	27 20.7	0 25.2	3 36.6	24 37.4
14 Su	9 31 06	21 34 52	14 50 15	20 44 27	20 14.6	5 56.5	12 39.9	9 14.8	3 19.3	7 29.8	27 27.2	0 28.7	3 36.4	24 36.1
15 M	9 35 02	22 32 31	26 39 39	2♋36 28	20 13.8	7 40.8	12 06.9	9 53.4	3 24.6	7 42.6	27 33.7	0 32.2	3 36.1	24 34.7
16 Tu	9 38 59	23 30 11	8♋35 23	14 36 54	20 10.9	9 28.4	11 35.3	10 31.8	3 29.5	7 55.4	27 40.3	0 35.6	3 35.8	24 33.4
17 W	9 42 55	24 27 52	20 41 25	26 49 18	20 05.7	11 19.0	11 05.4	11 10.1	3 34.2	8 08.2	27 46.9	0 39.1	3 35.5	24 32.1
18 Th	9 46 52	25 25 35	3♌00 50	9♌16 13	19 57.9	13 12.1	10 37.3	11 48.2	3 38.5	8 21.0	27 53.5	0 42.5	3 35.1	24 30.8
19 F	9 50 48	26 23 19	15 35 33	21 58 56	19 48.0	15 07.3	10 11.0	12 26.2	3 42.5	8 33.9	28 00.2	0 45.9	3 34.7	24 29.5
20 Sa	9 54 45	27 21 04	28 26 18	4♍57 35	19 36.9	17 04.3	9 46.8	13 04.0	3 46.1	8 46.7	28 06.9	0 49.3	3 34.3	24 28.1
21 Su	9 58 42	28 18 51	11♍32 37	18 11 12	19 25.4	19 02.5	9 24.8	13 41.7	3 49.4	8 59.6	28 13.7	0 52.7	3 33.8	24 26.8
22 M	10 02 38	29 16 39	24 53 06	1♎38 03	19 14.9	21 01.7	9 04.9	14 19.2	3 52.4	9 12.6	28 20.5	0 56.0	3 33.3	24 25.5
23 Tu	10 06 35	0♍14 28	8♎25 46	15 16 00	19 06.3	23 01.6	8 47.3	14 56.6	3 55.0	9 25.5	28 27.3	0 59.4	3 32.8	24 24.2
24 W	10 10 31	1 12 18	22 08 29	29 02 59	19 00.2	25 01.7	8 32.1	15 33.8	3 57.3	9 38.4	28 34.2	1 02.7	3 32.2	24 22.9
25 Th	10 14 28	2 10 10	5♏59 20	12♏57 20	18 56.7	27 01.9	8 19.2	16 10.8	3 59.2	9 51.4	28 41.1	1 06.0	3 31.7	24 21.5
26 F	10 18 24	3 08 03	19 56 53	26 57 52	18D 55.5	29 01.9	8 08.6	16 47.7	4 00.8	10 04.4	28 48.1	1 09.2	3 31.0	24 20.2
27 Sa	10 22 21	4 05 57	4♐00 12	11♐03 45	18R 55.5	1♍01.5	8 00.5	17 24.4	4 02.0	10 17.3	28 55.0	1 12.5	3 30.4	24 18.9
28 Su	10 26 17	5 03 52	18 08 27	25 14 10	18 55.4	3 00.5	7 54.8	18 01.0	4 02.9	10 30.3	29 02.0	1 15.7	3 29.7	24 17.6
29 M	10 30 14	6 01 49	2♑20 41	9♑27 48	18 54.2	4 58.8	7D 51.4	18 37.4	4R 03.4	10 43.3	29 09.1	1 18.9	3 29.0	24 16.4
30 Tu	10 34 11	6 59 47	16 35 12	23 42 31	18 50.7	6 56.2	7 50.4	19 13.6	4 03.5	10 56.3	29 16.1	1 22.0	3 28.3	24 15.1
31 W	10 38 07	7 57 46	0♒49 19	7♒55 06	18 44.4	8 52.7	7 51.7	19 49.6	4 03.3	11 09.3	29 23.2	1 25.2	3 27.5	24 13.8

Astro Data

	Dy Hr Mn
☿ R	2 21:50
☽ 0N	12 9:58
♀ R	18 8:37
♄ ⚻ ♇	21 12:04
♃ △ ♆	26 16:01
☽ 0S	26 23:28
☿ D	27 3:07
♆ R	6 15:59
☽ 0N	8 17:52
☽ 0S	23 4:20
⚳ R	30 9:19
♀ D	30 10:16

Planet Ingress

		Dy Hr Mn
♃	♍	8 0:25
⚳	♉	22 15:51
☉	♌	22 22:49
♂	♊	31 10:59
♅	♌	6 10:01
☿	♌	10 17:39
☉	♍	23 6:00
☿	♍	26 23:39

Last Aspect / ☽ Ingress

Last Aspect Dy Hr Mn			☽ Ingress	Dy Hr Mn
1 0:42	☿	□	♏	1 1:59
3 2:36	☿	△	♐	3 3:36
5 2:57	♃	△	♑	5 3:47
7 2:02	☿	☍	♒	7 4:08
8 22:26	♇	☌	♓	9 6:29
11 9:22	♅	△	♈	11 12:18
13 19:11	♅	□	♉	13 22:02
16 7:52	♅	⚹	♊	16 10:29
18 13:39	♇	△	♋	18 23:25
21 9:02	♅	☌	♌	21 10:56
23 10:59	♇	☍	♍	23 20:15
26 2:04	♅	⚹	♎	26 3:18
28 7:20	♅	□	♏	28 8:17
30 10:41	♅	△	♐	30 11:23

Last Aspect / ☽ Ingress

Last Aspect Dy Hr Mn			☽ Ingress	Dy Hr Mn
1 6:38	♄	□	♑	1 13:03
3 13:57	♅	☍	♒	3 14:14
5 7:36	♇	☌	♓	5 16:27
7 15:24	♄	☍	♈	7 21:20
10 4:26	☿	□	♉	10 5:57
12 12:14	♄	△	♊	12 17:50
15 1:44	♄	□	♋	15 6:45
17 13:53	♄	⚹	♌	17 18:10
19 20:52	☉	☌	♍	20 2:53
22 6:06	♄	☌	♎	22 9:06
24 3:55	♇	△	♏	24 13:39
26 16:07	☿	□	♐	26 17:11
28 18:28	♄	□	♑	28 20:03
30 21:27	♄	△	♒	30 22:37

☽ Phases & Eclipses

Dy Hr Mn		
6 2:05	○	13♑55
13 3:39	☾	20♈39
21 7:55	●	28♋27
28 17:51	☽	5♏32
4 9:58	○	11♒55
11 19:37	☾	19♉00
19 20:52	●	26♌45
26 23:18	☽	3♐35

Astro Data

1 July 2039
Julian Day # 50951
SVP 4♓42'46"
GC 27♐23.5 ⚴ 4♓11.5R
Eris 28♈56.3 ⚵ 0♒08.6R
⚷ 5♋45.0 ⚶ 9♍56.7
☽ Mean ☊ 21♊07.6

1 August 2039
Julian Day # 50982
SVP 4♓42'40"
GC 27♐23.5 ⚴ 29♒18.9R
Eris 28♈59.1R ⚵ 23♑05.3R
⚷ 8♋39.1 ⚶ 23♍34.5
☽ Mean ☊ 19♊29.2

LONGITUDE September 2039

Day	Sid.Time	☉	0 hr ☽	Noon ☽	True ☊	☿	♀	♂	⚳	♃	♄	♅	♆	♇
1 Th	10 42 04	8♍55 47	14♒59 18	22♒01 21	18♊35.4	10♍48.1	7♌55.4	20♊25.5	4♉02.7	11♍22.3	29♍30.3	1♌28.3	3♉26.7	24♒12.5
2 F	10 46 00	9 53 49	29 00 40	5♓56 40	18R 24.3	12 42.5	8 01.2	21 01.2	4R 01.7	11 35.4	29 37.5	1 31.4	3R 25.9	24R 11.3
3 Sa	10 49 57	10 51 53	12♓48 49	19 36 39	18 12.2	14 35.7	8 09.4	21 36.7	4 00.4	11 48.4	29 44.6	1 34.4	3 25.0	24 10.0
4 Su	10 53 53	11 49 58	26 19 48	2♈57 58	18 00.2	16 27.8	8 19.6	22 12.1	3 58.7	12 01.4	29 51.8	1 37.4	3 24.2	24 08.7
5 M	10 57 50	12 48 06	9♈30 59	15 58 47	17 49.5	18 18.7	8 32.0	22 47.3	3 56.7	12 14.4	29 59.0	1 40.4	3 23.2	24 07.5
6 Tu	11 01 46	13 46 15	22 21 26	28 39 07	17 40.9	20 08.5	8 46.5	23 22.2	3 54.2	12 27.4	0♎06.2	1 43.4	3 22.3	24 06.3
7 W	11 05 43	14 44 26	4♉52 06	11♉00 45	17 35.0	21 57.0	9 02.9	23 57.0	3 51.4	12 40.5	0 13.5	1 46.3	3 21.4	24 05.0
8 Th	11 09 40	15 42 39	17 05 30	23 06 54	17 31.6	23 44.4	9 21.3	24 31.6	3 48.2	12 53.5	0 20.8	1 49.2	3 20.4	24 03.8
9 F	11 13 36	16 40 54	29 05 30	5♊01 57	17 30.2	25 30.6	9 41.6	25 06.0	3 44.7	13 06.5	0 28.1	1 52.1	3 19.3	24 02.6
10 Sa	11 17 33	17 39 11	10♊56 53	16 51 00	17 30.0	27 15.6	10 03.6	25 40.2	3 40.7	13 19.5	0 35.4	1 54.9	3 18.3	24 01.4
11 Su	11 21 29	18 37 30	22 44 58	28 39 31	17 29.9	28 59.5	10 27.5	26 14.2	3 36.4	13 32.5	0 42.7	1 57.7	3 17.2	24 00.2
12 M	11 25 26	19 35 52	4♋35 18	10♋33 01	17 28.7	0♎42.2	10 53.0	26 48.0	3 31.8	13 45.5	0 50.0	2 00.5	3 16.2	23 59.1
13 Tu	11 29 22	20 34 15	16 33 16	22 36 40	17 25.6	2 23.8	11 20.2	27 21.6	3 26.7	13 58.5	0 57.4	2 03.2	3 15.0	23 57.9
14 W	11 33 19	21 32 41	28 43 46	4♌55 01	17 20.0	4 04.4	11 49.0	27 54.9	3 21.3	14 11.5	1 04.7	2 05.9	3 13.9	23 56.8
15 Th	11 37 15	22 31 08	11♌10 49	17 31 29	17 11.6	5 43.8	12 19.3	28 28.1	3 15.5	14 24.4	1 12.1	2 08.6	3 12.7	23 55.6
16 F	11 41 12	23 29 38	23 57 14	0♍28 08	17 01.0	7 22.1	12 51.0	29 01.0	3 09.4	14 37.4	1 19.5	2 11.2	3 11.5	23 54.5
17 Sa	11 45 08	24 28 09	7♍04 11	13 45 14	16 48.9	8 59.4	13 24.2	29 33.6	3 02.8	14 50.3	1 26.9	2 13.8	3 10.3	23 53.4
18 Su	11 49 05	25 26 43	20 31 04	27 21 19	16 36.4	10 35.7	13 58.7	0♋06.1	2 56.0	15 03.3	1 34.3	2 16.4	3 09.1	23 52.3
19 M	11 53 02	26 25 18	4♎15 32	11♎13 13	16 24.8	12 10.9	14 34.5	0 38.3	2 48.7	15 16.2	1 41.7	2 18.9	3 07.8	23 51.2
20 Tu	11 56 58	27 23 55	18 13 49	25 16 45	16 15.3	13 45.1	15 11.6	1 10.2	2 41.2	15 29.1	1 49.2	2 21.3	3 06.6	23 50.2
21 W	12 00 55	28 22 34	2♏21 26	9♏27 19	16 08.5	15 18.3	15 49.9	1 41.9	2 33.2	15 41.9	1 56.6	2 23.8	3 05.3	23 49.1
22 Th	12 04 51	29 21 15	16 33 53	23 40 43	16 04.5	16 50.5	16 29.3	2 13.4	2 25.0	15 54.8	2 04.0	2 26.2	3 03.9	23 48.1
23 F	12 08 48	0♎19 57	0♐47 24	7♐53 38	16D 03.0	18 21.7	17 09.9	2 44.5	2 16.4	16 07.6	2 11.5	2 28.5	3 02.6	23 47.1
24 Sa	12 12 44	1 18 41	14 59 11	22 03 51	16R 02.9	19 51.9	17 51.6	3 15.5	2 07.5	16 20.4	2 18.9	2 30.8	3 01.2	23 46.1
25 Su	12 16 41	2 17 27	29 07 31	6♑10 03	16 02.9	21 21.1	18 34.3	3 46.1	1 58.2	16 33.2	2 26.3	2 33.1	2 59.9	23 45.1
26 M	12 20 37	3 16 15	13♑11 23	20 11 24	16 01.9	22 49.3	19 18.0	4 16.5	1 48.7	16 46.0	2 33.8	2 35.3	2 58.5	23 44.1
27 Tu	12 24 34	4 15 04	27 10 02	4♒07 09	15 58.8	24 16.5	20 02.7	4 46.6	1 38.8	16 58.7	2 41.2	2 37.5	2 57.0	23 43.2
28 W	12 28 31	5 13 55	11♒02 35	17 56 09	15 53.0	25 42.6	20 48.3	5 16.5	1 28.7	17 11.4	2 48.7	2 39.7	2 55.6	23 42.2
29 Th	12 32 27	6 12 47	24 47 37	1♓36 45	15 44.6	27 07.7	21 34.9	5 46.1	1 18.3	17 24.1	2 56.1	2 41.8	2 54.2	23 41.3
30 F	12 36 24	7 11 42	8♓23 15	15 06 51	15 34.2	28 31.8	22 22.3	6 15.3	1 07.6	17 36.7	3 03.5	2 43.8	2 52.7	23 40.4

LONGITUDE October 2039

Day	Sid.Time	☉	0 hr ☽	Noon ☽	True ☊	☿	♀	♂	⚳	♃	♄	♅	♆	♇
1 Sa	12 40 20	8♎10 38	21♓47 15	28♓24 12	15♊22.7	29♎54.8	23♌10.5	6♋44.3	0♉56.6	17♍49.3	3♎10.9	2♌45.8	2♉51.2	23♒39.6
2 Su	12 44 17	9 09 36	4♈57 28	11♈26 50	15R 11.3	1♏16.6	23 59.6	7 13.0	0R 45.4	18 01.9	3 18.3	2 47.8	2R 49.7	23R 38.7
3 M	12 48 13	10 08 36	17 52 13	24 13 32	15 01.1	2 37.3	24 49.5	7 41.4	0 33.9	18 14.4	3 25.8	2 49.7	2 48.2	23 37.9
4 Tu	12 52 10	11 07 39	0♉30 48	6♉44 06	14 52.8	3 56.8	25 40.2	8 09.4	0 22.2	18 26.9	3 33.2	2 51.6	2 46.7	23 37.1
5 W	12 56 06	12 06 43	12 53 37	18 59 36	14 47.1	5 15.1	26 31.6	8 37.2	0 10.2	18 39.4	3 40.5	2 53.4	2 45.1	23 36.3
6 Th	13 00 03	13 05 50	25 02 21	1♊02 17	14 43.9	6 32.0	27 23.7	9 04.6	29♈58.1	18 51.8	3 47.9	2 55.2	2 43.6	23 35.5
7 F	13 04 00	14 04 59	6♊59 51	12 55 34	14D 42.8	7 47.6	28 16.5	9 31.7	29 45.7	19 04.2	3 55.3	2 56.9	2 42.0	23 34.7
8 Sa	13 07 56	15 04 11	18 49 58	24 43 41	14 43.2	9 01.6	29 10.0	9 58.5	29 33.2	19 16.6	4 02.6	2 58.6	2 40.4	23 34.0
9 Su	13 11 53	16 03 24	0♋37 19	6♋31 34	14R 44.1	10 14.1	0♍04.1	10 24.9	29 20.4	19 28.9	4 10.0	3 00.2	2 38.8	23 33.3
10 M	13 15 49	17 02 40	12 27 04	18 24 32	14 44.5	11 25.0	0 58.9	10 51.0	29 07.5	19 41.2	4 17.3	3 01.8	2 37.2	23 32.6
11 Tu	13 19 46	18 01 58	24 24 37	0♌28 00	14 43.5	12 34.0	1 54.2	11 16.7	28 54.5	19 53.4	4 24.6	3 03.4	2 35.6	23 31.9
12 W	13 23 42	19 01 19	6♌35 17	12 47 05	14 40.6	13 41.0	2 50.1	11 42.0	28 41.3	20 05.6	4 31.9	3 04.9	2 34.0	23 31.3
13 Th	13 27 39	20 00 42	19 03 54	25 26 12	14 35.6	14 46.0	3 46.6	12 07.0	28 27.9	20 17.7	4 39.2	3 06.3	2 32.4	23 30.7
14 F	13 31 35	21 00 07	1♍54 21	8♍28 35	14 28.5	15 48.6	4 43.7	12 31.6	28 14.5	20 29.8	4 46.5	3 07.7	2 30.7	23 30.1
15 Sa	13 35 32	21 59 34	15 09 01	21 55 39	14 20.1	16 48.8	5 41.2	12 55.7	28 01.0	20 41.8	4 53.7	3 09.0	2 29.1	23 29.5
16 Su	13 39 29	22 59 04	28 48 18	5♎46 40	14 11.2	17 46.1	6 39.3	13 19.5	27 47.3	20 53.8	5 00.9	3 10.3	2 27.4	23 29.0
17 M	13 43 25	23 58 35	12♎50 17	19 58 32	14 03.0	18 40.5	7 37.8	13 42.9	27 33.7	21 05.7	5 08.1	3 11.5	2 25.8	23 28.4
18 Tu	13 47 22	24 58 09	27 10 45	4♏26 06	13 56.2	19 31.5	8 36.8	14 05.8	27 19.9	21 17.6	5 15.3	3 12.7	2 24.1	23 27.9
19 W	13 51 18	25 57 44	11♏43 46	19 02 51	13 51.5	20 18.9	9 36.3	14 28.3	27 06.2	21 29.4	5 22.4	3 13.8	2 22.4	23 27.4
20 Th	13 55 15	26 57 22	26 22 31	3♐41 57	13D 49.2	21 02.2	10 36.2	14 50.3	26 52.4	21 41.1	5 29.5	3 14.9	2 20.8	23 27.0
21 F	13 59 11	27 57 01	11♐00 24	18 17 14	13 48.9	21 41.1	11 36.6	15 12.0	26 38.6	21 52.8	5 36.6	3 15.9	2 19.1	23 26.6
22 Sa	14 03 08	28 56 43	25 31 54	2♑43 57	13 49.8	22 15.0	12 37.3	15 33.1	26 24.9	22 04.4	5 43.7	3 16.9	2 17.4	23 26.2
23 Su	14 07 04	29 56 25	9♑53 03	16 58 57	13R 51.0	22 43.6	13 38.5	15 53.8	26 11.2	22 16.0	5 50.7	3 17.8	2 15.7	23 25.8
24 M	14 11 01	0♏56 10	24 01 30	1♒00 36	13 51.6	23 06.2	14 40.0	16 14.0	25 57.5	22 27.5	5 57.7	3 18.7	2 14.0	23 25.4
25 Tu	14 14 58	1 55 56	7♒56 13	14 48 21	13 50.8	23 22.3	15 41.9	16 33.7	25 43.9	22 38.9	6 04.7	3 19.5	2 12.4	23 25.1
26 W	14 18 54	2 55 44	21 37 00	28 22 15	13 48.2	23R 31.2	16 44.2	16 53.0	25 30.4	22 50.3	6 11.6	3 20.3	2 10.7	23 24.8
27 Th	14 22 51	3 55 33	5♓04 06	11♓42 37	13 43.7	23 32.5	17 46.9	17 11.7	25 16.9	23 01.6	6 18.5	3 21.0	2 09.0	23 24.5
28 F	14 26 47	4 55 25	18 17 50	24 49 46	13 37.8	23 25.6	18 49.9	17 29.9	25 03.6	23 12.8	6 25.4	3 21.6	2 07.3	23 24.3
29 Sa	14 30 44	5 55 17	1♈18 28	7♈43 56	13 31.1	23 09.9	19 53.2	17 47.6	24 50.4	23 23.9	6 32.2	3 22.2	2 05.6	23 24.0
30 Su	14 34 40	6 55 12	14 06 11	20 25 15	13 24.5	22 45.0	20 56.9	18 04.8	24 37.3	23 35.0	6 39.0	3 22.8	2 03.9	23 23.8
31 M	14 38 37	7 55 08	26 41 11	2♉54 03	13 18.5	22 10.8	22 00.9	18 21.4	24 24.4	23 46.0	6 45.7	3 23.2	2 02.3	23 23.7

Astro Data

	Dy Hr Mn
☽0N	5 2:17
☿0S	13 1:44
☽0S	19 11:00
⚳0S	22 0:10
☉0S	23 3:51
♄✶♅	26 19:10
♄⚻♆	29 6:48
♃∠♅	1 4:07
♃Q♆	1 15:14
☽0N	2 10:26
♅□♆	3 1:23
♄0S	15 8:34
☽0S	16 20:18
☿ R	27 3:55
♃⚻♇	29 12:11

Planet Ingress

		Dy Hr Mn
♄	♎	5 15:16
☿	♎	12 2:06
♂	♋	18 7:30
☉	♎	23 3:51
☿	♏	1 13:31
⚳	♈R	6 8:14
♀	♍	9 10:11
☉	♏	23 13:26

☽0N29 17:36

Last Aspect / ☽ Ingress (September)

Last Aspect Dy Hr Mn			☽ Ingress	Dy Hr Mn
1 15:44	♇	☌	♓	2 1:42
4 6:19	♄	☍	♈	4 6:37
6 3:20	♇	✶	♉	6 14:35
8 13:54	♇	□	♊	9 1:50
11 12:47	☿	□	♋	11 14:43
13 7:37	☉	✶	♌	14 2:29
16 9:13	♂	✶	♍	16 11:09
18 8:24	☉	☌	♎	18 16:37
20 9:33	♇	△	♏	20 20:00
22 22:17	☉	✶	♐	22 22:40
24 14:53	♇	✶	♑	25 1:29
26 17:03	☿	□	♒	27 4:53
29 3:11	☿	△	♓	29 9:09

Last Aspect / ☽ Ingress (October)

Last Aspect Dy Hr Mn			☽ Ingress	Dy Hr Mn
30 16:33	♃	☍	♈	1 14:55
3 13:13	♀	△	♉	3 23:01
6 4:08	♀	□	♊	6 9:55
8 21:47	♀	✶	♋	8 22:44
10 14:36	♃	✶	♌	11 11:05
13 8:24	♇	☍	♍	13 20:29
15 9:48	♃	☌	♎	16 2:04
17 19:10	☉	☌	♏	18 4:40
19 19:13	♇	□	♐	20 5:56
22 5:13	☉	✶	♑	22 7:26
23 22:04	♃	✶	♒	24 10:16
26 3:18	☿	□	♓	26 14:55
28 9:27	☿	△	♈	28 21:34
30 17:41	♇	✶	♉	31 6:23

☽ Phases & Eclipses

Dy Hr Mn		
2 19:25	○	10♓12
10 13:47	☾	17♊44
18 8:24	●	25♍18
25 4:54	☽	2♑00
2 7:25	○	8♈58
10 9:01	☾	16♋55
17 19:10	●	24♎16
24 11:52	☽	0♒56
31 22:37	○	8♉22

Astro Data

1 September 2039
Julian Day # 51013
SVP 4♓42'36"
GC 27♐23.6 ⚴ 21♒35.8R
Eris 28♈52.1R ⚵ 18♑23.9R
⚷ 11♋03.8 ⚶ 8♎30.4
☽ Mean ☊ 17♊50.7

1 October 2039
Julian Day # 51043
SVP 4♓42'33"
GC 27♐23.7 ⚴ 16♒41.6R
Eris 28♈37.8R ⚵ 19♑31.9
⚷ 12♋31.0 ⚶ 23♎46.9
☽ Mean ☊ 16♊15.3

November 2039 LONGITUDE

Day	Sid.Time	☉	0 hr ☽	Noon☽	True☊	☿	♀	♂	⚳	♃	♄	♅	♆	♇
1 Tu	14 42 33	8♏55 07	9♉03 56	15♉10 57	13♊13.9	21♏27.2	23♍05.2	18♋37.5	24♈11.6	23♍56.9	6♎52.4	3♌23.7	2♉00.6	23♒23.5
2 W	14 46 30	9 55 07	21 15 15	27 17 03	13R10.9	20R34.6	24 09.8	18 53.0	23R59.1	24 07.8	6 59.1	3 24.1	1R58.9	23R23.4
3 Th	14 50 27	10 55 10	3♊16 34	9♊14 05	13D09.6	19 33.7	25 14.8	19 07.9	23 46.7	24 18.6	7 05.7	3 24.4	1 57.3	23 23.3
4 F	14 54 23	11 55 14	15 09 57	21 04 32	13 09.8	18 25.5	26 20.0	19 22.3	23 34.5	24 29.2	7 12.3	3 24.6	1 55.6	23 23.2
5 Sa	14 58 20	12 55 20	26 58 14	2♋51 32	13 11.1	17 11.7	27 25.5	19 36.0	23 22.5	24 39.8	7 18.8	3 24.9	1 54.0	23 23.2
6 Su	15 02 16	13 55 29	8♋44 56	14 38 57	13 12.9	15 54.1	28 31.2	19 49.1	23 10.8	24 50.4	7 25.3	3 25.0	1 52.3	23D23.2
7 M	15 06 13	14 55 39	20 34 10	26 31 11	13 14.7	14 35.1	29 37.3	20 01.6	22 59.3	25 00.8	7 31.7	3 25.1	1 50.7	23 23.2
8 Tu	15 10 09	15 55 51	2♌30 35	8♌33 01	13R15.9	13 17.2	0♎43.6	20 13.5	22 48.1	25 11.1	7 38.1	3R25.2	1 49.1	23 23.2
9 W	15 14 06	16 56 06	14 39 05	20 49 24	13 16.1	12 02.8	1 50.1	20 24.7	22 37.1	25 21.4	7 44.5	3 25.2	1 47.4	23 23.3
10 Th	15 18 02	17 56 22	27 04 33	3♍25 05	13 15.1	10 54.5	2 56.9	20 35.2	22 26.4	25 31.6	7 50.8	3 25.1	1 45.8	23 23.4
11 F	15 21 59	18 56 41	9♍51 30	16 24 11	13 13.0	9 54.2	4 04.0	20 45.0	22 16.0	25 41.6	7 57.0	3 25.0	1 44.2	23 23.5
12 Sa	15 25 56	19 57 01	23 03 28	29 49 33	13 10.0	9 03.5	5 11.2	20 54.2	22 05.8	25 51.6	8 03.2	3 24.8	1 42.6	23 23.6
13 Su	15 29 52	20 57 23	6♎42 28	13♎42 09	13 06.7	8 23.7	6 18.7	21 02.6	21 56.0	26 01.5	8 09.3	3 24.6	1 41.1	23 23.8
14 M	15 33 49	21 57 47	20 48 19	28 00 32	13 03.6	7 55.5	7 26.4	21 10.3	21 46.5	26 11.2	8 15.4	3 24.3	1 39.5	23 24.0
15 Tu	15 37 45	22 58 13	5♏18 13	12♏40 36	13 01.1	7D38.9	8 34.3	21 17.2	21 37.3	26 20.9	8 21.4	3 24.0	1 37.9	23 24.2
16 W	15 41 42	23 58 41	20 06 46	27 35 43	12 59.5	7 33.9	9 42.4	21 23.5	21 28.4	26 30.5	8 27.4	3 23.6	1 36.4	23 24.5
17 Th	15 45 38	24 59 10	5♐06 22	12♐37 38	12D59.0	7 39.9	10 50.7	21 28.9	21 19.9	26 40.0	8 33.3	3 23.1	1 34.9	23 24.7
18 F	15 49 35	25 59 41	20 08 24	27 37 38	12 59.4	7 56.4	11 59.2	21 33.6	21 11.7	26 49.3	8 39.2	3 22.6	1 33.4	23 25.1
19 Sa	15 53 31	27 00 14	5♑04 22	12♑27 47	13 00.4	8 22.5	13 07.9	21 37.5	21 03.9	26 58.6	8 44.9	3 22.1	1 31.9	23 25.4
20 Su	15 57 28	28 00 47	19 47 09	27 01 56	13 01.6	8 57.3	14 16.7	21 40.6	20 56.5	27 07.7	8 50.7	3 21.5	1 30.4	23 25.8
21 M	16 01 25	29 01 22	4♒11 42	11♒16 10	13 02.6	9 39.8	15 25.8	21 43.0	20 49.4	27 16.8	8 56.3	3 20.8	1 29.0	23 26.1
22 Tu	16 05 21	0♐01 58	18 15 11	25 08 45	13R03.1	10 29.4	16 35.0	21 44.5	20 42.6	27 25.7	9 01.9	3 20.1	1 27.5	23 26.6
23 W	16 09 18	1 02 35	1♓56 53	8♓39 45	13 03.1	11 25.0	17 44.3	21R45.2	20 36.3	27 34.5	9 07.4	3 19.3	1 26.1	23 27.0
24 Th	16 13 14	2 03 13	15 17 33	21 50 31	13 02.4	12 26.0	18 53.8	21 45.1	20 30.3	27 43.1	9 12.9	3 18.5	1 24.7	23 27.5
25 F	16 17 11	3 03 52	28 18 57	4♈43 08	13 01.4	13 31.6	20 03.5	21 44.2	20 24.7	27 51.7	9 18.3	3 17.6	1 23.3	23 27.9
26 Sa	16 21 07	4 04 32	11♈03 22	17 19 59	13 00.1	14 41.2	21 13.3	21 42.4	20 19.5	28 00.1	9 23.6	3 16.7	1 22.0	23 28.5
27 Su	16 25 04	5 05 14	23 33 15	29 43 28	12 58.9	15 54.2	22 23.3	21 39.8	20 14.7	28 08.5	9 28.9	3 15.7	1 20.6	23 29.0
28 M	16 29 00	6 05 56	5♉50 56	11♉55 53	12 57.9	17 10.3	23 33.4	21 36.3	20 10.2	28 16.7	9 34.0	3 14.7	1 19.3	23 29.6
29 Tu	16 32 57	7 06 40	17 58 35	23 59 18	12 57.2	18 28.8	24 43.7	21 32.0	20 06.2	28 24.7	9 39.1	3 13.6	1 18.0	23 30.2
30 W	16 36 54	8 07 25	29 58 16	5♊55 42	12D56.9	19 49.5	25 54.1	21 26.9	20 02.5	28 32.7	9 44.2	3 12.5	1 16.7	23 30.8

December 2039 LONGITUDE

Day	Sid.Time	☉	0 hr ☽	Noon☽	True☊	☿	♀	♂	⚳	♃	♄	♅	♆	♇
1 Th	16 40 50	9♐08 12	11♊51 53	17♊47 02	12♊56.9	21♏12.1	27♎04.6	21♋20.9	19♈59.2	28♍40.5	9♎49.1	3♌11.3	1♉15.5	23♒31.4
2 F	16 44 47	10 08 59	23 41 27	29 35 22	12 57.1	22 36.2	28 15.3	21R14.0	19R56.3	28 48.2	9 54.0	3R10.1	1R14.2	23 32.1
3 Sa	16 48 43	11 09 48	5♋29 06	11♋22 58	12 57.3	24 01.6	29 26.1	21 06.3	19 53.9	28 55.7	9 58.8	3 08.9	1 13.0	23 32.8
4 Su	16 52 40	12 10 38	17 17 18	23 12 29	12R57.4	25 28.2	0♏37.0	20 57.8	19 51.8	29 03.1	10 03.6	3 07.5	1 11.8	23 33.5
5 M	16 56 36	13 11 30	29 08 54	5♌06 59	12 57.5	26 55.7	1 48.1	20 48.3	19 50.0	29 10.4	10 08.2	3 06.2	1 10.7	23 34.3
6 Tu	17 00 33	14 12 22	11♌07 10	17 09 58	12 57.4	28 24.0	2 59.3	20 38.1	19 48.7	29 17.6	10 12.8	3 04.8	1 09.5	23 35.1
7 W	17 04 29	15 13 16	23 15 50	29 25 17	12 57.2	29 52.9	4 10.6	20 26.9	19 47.8	29 24.6	10 17.3	3 03.3	1 08.4	23 35.9
8 Th	17 08 26	16 14 11	5♍38 52	11♍57 03	12D57.1	1♐22.5	5 22.0	20 15.0	19D47.3	29 31.4	10 21.7	3 01.8	1 07.3	23 36.7
9 F	17 12 23	17 15 08	18 20 22	24 49 16	12 57.1	2 52.6	6 33.5	20 02.2	19 47.1	29 38.1	10 26.0	3 00.3	1 06.3	23 37.5
10 Sa	17 16 19	18 16 05	1♎24 11	8♎05 27	12 57.4	4 23.0	7 45.1	19 48.6	19 47.3	29 44.7	10 30.3	2 58.7	1 05.2	23 38.4
11 Su	17 20 16	19 17 04	14 53 21	21 48 03	12 57.9	5 53.9	8 56.8	19 34.2	19 48.0	29 51.1	10 34.4	2 57.0	1 04.2	23 39.3
12 M	17 24 12	20 18 04	28 49 35	5♏57 49	12 58.6	7 25.0	10 08.7	19 19.0	19 49.0	29 57.4	10 38.5	2 55.3	1 03.2	23 40.2
13 Tu	17 28 09	21 19 05	13♏12 27	20 33 03	12 59.2	8 56.4	11 20.6	19 03.0	19 50.4	0♎03.5	10 42.5	2 53.6	1 02.3	23 41.2
14 W	17 32 05	22 20 07	27 58 55	5♐29 16	12R59.7	10 28.1	12 32.6	18 46.3	19 52.1	0 09.5	10 46.4	2 51.9	1 01.4	23 42.1
15 Th	17 36 02	23 21 11	13♐03 06	20 39 16	12 59.7	12 00.0	13 44.7	18 28.9	19 54.3	0 15.3	10 50.2	2 50.1	1 00.5	23 43.1
16 F	17 39 58	24 22 14	28 16 35	5♑53 46	12 59.1	13 32.1	14 56.9	18 10.8	19 56.8	0 21.0	10 53.9	2 48.2	0 59.6	23 44.1
17 Sa	17 43 55	25 23 19	13♑29 34	21 02 45	12 57.9	15 04.3	16 09.1	17 52.0	19 59.7	0 26.5	10 57.5	2 46.3	0 58.8	23 45.2
18 Su	17 47 52	26 24 24	28 32 14	5♒57 01	12 56.3	16 36.8	17 21.5	17 32.6	20 03.0	0 31.8	11 01.0	2 44.4	0 58.0	23 46.2
19 M	17 51 48	27 25 29	13♒16 18	20 29 27	12 54.4	18 09.4	18 33.9	17 12.6	20 06.6	0 37.0	11 04.5	2 42.5	0 57.2	23 47.3
20 Tu	17 55 45	28 26 35	27 36 03	4♓35 50	12 52.8	19 42.2	19 46.4	16 52.0	20 10.7	0 42.0	11 07.8	2 40.5	0 56.5	23 48.4
21 W	17 59 41	29 27 41	11♓28 43	18 14 47	12D51.7	21 15.1	20 58.9	16 30.9	20 15.0	0 46.8	11 11.1	2 38.4	0 55.8	23 49.5
22 Th	18 03 38	0♑28 47	24 54 13	1♈27 22	12 51.4	22 48.3	22 11.5	16 09.4	20 19.8	0 51.5	11 14.2	2 36.4	0 55.1	23 50.7
23 F	18 07 34	1 29 53	7♈54 35	14 16 20	12 51.8	24 21.6	23 24.2	15 47.4	20 24.8	0 56.0	11 17.3	2 34.3	0 54.4	23 51.8
24 Sa	18 11 31	2 30 59	20 33 07	26 45 26	12 53.1	25 55.1	24 36.9	15 25.0	20 30.3	1 00.3	11 20.2	2 32.1	0 53.8	23 53.0
25 Su	18 15 27	3 32 06	2♉53 50	8♉58 50	12 54.7	27 28.8	25 49.8	15 02.3	20 36.0	1 04.5	11 23.1	2 30.0	0 53.2	23 54.2
26 M	18 19 24	4 33 13	15 00 55	21 00 36	12 56.4	29 02.8	27 02.6	14 39.3	20 42.2	1 08.5	11 25.9	2 27.8	0 52.7	23 55.4
27 Tu	18 23 21	5 34 20	26 58 20	2♊54 32	12R57.6	0♑37.0	28 15.6	14 16.0	20 48.6	1 12.3	11 28.5	2 25.5	0 52.2	23 56.7
28 W	18 27 17	6 35 27	8♊49 37	14 43 58	12 58.0	2 11.4	29 28.6	13 52.5	20 55.4	1 16.0	11 31.1	2 23.3	0 51.7	23 57.9
29 Th	18 31 14	7 36 34	20 37 53	26 31 43	12 57.2	3 46.1	0♐41.6	13 28.8	21 02.5	1 19.4	11 33.6	2 21.0	0 51.2	23 59.2
30 F	18 35 10	8 37 42	2♋25 43	8♋20 10	12 55.0	5 21.0	1 54.7	13 05.0	21 09.9	1 22.7	11 35.9	2 18.7	0 50.8	24 00.5
31 Sa	18 39 07	9 38 50	14 15 18	20 11 21	12 51.5	6 56.3	3 07.9	12 41.1	21 17.7	1 25.8	11 38.2	2 16.4	0 50.4	24 01.8

Astro Data	Dy Hr Mn
♇ D	6 13:57
♅ R	8 21:06
♀0S	10 17:14
☽0S	13 7:05
♄□♇	15 23:36
☿ D	16 10:39
♂ R	23 20:49
☽0N	25 23:40
⚳ D	9 9:29
☽0S	10 16:58
⚳0N	21 10:39
♃⊼♆	23 4:38
☽0N	23 5:32

Planet Ingress	Dy Hr Mn
♀ ♎	7 20:14
☉ ♐	22 11:13
♀ ♏	3 23:28
☿ ♐	7 13:54
♃ ♎	12 22:06
☉ ♑	22 0:42
☿ ♑	27 2:35
♀ ♐	28 22:20

Last Aspect Dy Hr Mn		☽ Ingress Dy Hr Mn
2 5:37	♃ △	♊ 2 17:26
4 23:48	♀ □	♋ 5 6:10
7 18:51	♀ ⚹	♌ 7 18:59
9 16:57	♇ ☍	♍ 10 5:33
12 4:54	♃ ☌	♎ 12 12:18
14 4:20	♇ △	♏ 14 15:17
16 10:14	♃ ⚹	♐ 16 15:51
18 10:42	♃ □	♑ 18 15:49
20 13:46	☉ ⚹	♒ 20 16:57
22 9:01	♇ ☌	♓ 22 20:33
24 23:01	♃ ☍	♈ 25 3:09
26 23:51	♇ ⚹	♉ 27 12:32
29 20:58	♃ △	♊ 30 0:04

Last Aspect Dy Hr Mn		☽ Ingress Dy Hr Mn
2 10:23	♃ □	♋ 2 12:50
4 23:56	♃ ⚹	♌ 5 1:43
7 13:01	☿ □	♍ 7 13:07
9 20:52	♃ ☌	♎ 9 21:27
11 15:11	♇ △	♏ 12 1:59
13 17:05	♇ □	♐ 14 3:14
15 16:50	♇ ⚹	♑ 16 2:43
17 7:03	♂ ☍	♒ 18 2:21
20 0:37	☉ ⚹	♓ 20 4:06
21 18:06	☿ □	♈ 22 9:19
24 10:08	☿ △	♉ 24 18:19
27 1:32	♀ ☍	♊ 27 6:07
29 6:49	♇ △	♋ 29 19:04

☽ Phases & Eclipses Dy Hr Mn	
9 3:47	☾ 16♌35
16 5:47	● 23♏43
22 21:18	☽ 0♓25
30 16:51	○ 8♊20
30 16:56	• P 0.943
8 20:46	☾ 16♍36
15 16:33	● 23♐33
15 16:23:44	• T 01'52"
22 10:03	☽ 0♈24
30 12:39	○ 8♋39

Astro Data

1 November 2039
Julian Day # 51074
SVP 4♓42'30"
GC 27♐23.7 ⚵ 16♒55.6
Eris 28♈19.3R ⚶ 25♑56.5
⚷ 12♋46.5R ⚴ 10♏06.6
☽ Mean ☊ 14♊36.8

1 December 2039
Julian Day # 51104
SVP 4♓42'25"
GC 27♐23.8 ⚵ 21♒29.2
Eris 28♈03.3R ⚶ 5♒39.5
⚷ 11♋46.0R ⚴ 26♏09.8
☽ Mean ☊ 13♊01.5

LONGITUDE — January 2040

Day	Sid.Time	☉	0 hr ☽	Noon☽	True☊	☿	♀	♂	⚳	♃	♄	♅	♆	♇
1 Su	18 43 03	10♑39 57	26♋08 32	2♌07 06	12♊46.8	8♑31.8	4♐21.1	12♋17.3	21♈25.8	1♎28.8	11♎40.3	2♌14.0	0♉50.1	24♒03.2
2 M	18 47 00	11 41 05	8♌07 15	14 09 14	12R41.5	10 07.7	5 34.4	11R53.4	21 34.2	1 31.5	11 42.4	2R11.6	0R49.8	24 04.5
3 Tu	18 50 57	12 42 14	20 13 18	26 19 42	12 36.2	11 43.9	6 47.7	11 29.6	21 42.8	1 34.1	11 44.3	2 09.2	0 49.5	24 05.9
4 W	18 54 53	13 43 22	2♍28 45	8♍40 44	12 31.3	13 20.5	8 01.1	11 05.9	21 51.8	1 36.5	11 46.2	2 06.8	0 49.2	24 07.3
5 Th	18 58 50	14 44 31	14 56 00	21 14 53	12 27.6	14 57.4	9 14.5	10 42.4	22 01.1	1 38.7	11 47.9	2 04.4	0 49.0	24 08.7
6 F	19 02 46	15 45 40	27 37 46	4♎05 01	12D25.3	16 34.7	10 28.0	10 19.1	22 10.7	1 40.7	11 49.6	2 01.9	0 48.8	24 10.1
7 Sa	19 06 43	16 46 49	10♎37 01	17 14 06	12 24.6	18 12.4	11 41.5	9 56.1	22 20.6	1 42.5	11 51.1	1 59.4	0 48.7	24 11.6
8 Su	19 10 39	17 47 58	23 56 36	0♏44 49	12 25.3	19 50.4	12 55.1	9 33.4	22 30.7	1 44.2	11 52.5	1 56.9	0 48.5	24 13.0
9 M	19 14 36	18 49 07	7♏38 58	14 39 08	12 26.7	21 28.9	14 08.7	9 11.0	22 41.2	1 45.6	11 53.9	1 54.4	0 48.5	24 14.5
10 Tu	19 18 32	19 50 17	21 45 23	28 57 32	12R28.1	23 07.8	15 22.3	8 49.0	22 51.9	1 46.9	11 55.1	1 51.9	0D48.4	24 16.0
11 W	19 22 29	20 51 26	6♐15 21	13♐38 20	12 28.7	24 47.1	16 36.0	8 27.4	23 02.9	1 48.0	11 56.2	1 49.3	0 48.4	24 17.5
12 Th	19 26 26	21 52 36	21 05 51	28 37 05	12 27.7	26 26.8	17 49.7	8 06.4	23 14.2	1 48.9	11 57.2	1 46.8	0 48.4	24 19.0
13 F	19 30 22	22 53 45	6♑11 03	13♑46 35	12 24.7	28 07.0	19 03.4	7 45.8	23 25.8	1 49.5	11 58.1	1 44.2	0 48.5	24 20.5
14 Sa	19 34 19	23 54 55	21 22 29	28 57 27	12 19.7	29 47.5	20 17.2	7 25.8	23 37.6	1 50.0	11 58.9	1 41.6	0 48.6	24 22.0
15 Su	19 38 15	24 56 03	6♒30 11	13♒59 27	12 13.2	1♒28.3	21 31.0	7 06.3	23 49.7	1 50.3	11 59.5	1 39.0	0 48.7	24 23.6
16 M	19 42 12	25 57 11	21 24 10	28 43 20	12 06.0	3 09.5	22 44.9	6 47.5	24 02.0	1R50.5	12 00.1	1 36.4	0 48.9	24 25.2
17 Tu	19 46 08	26 58 19	5♓56 11	13♓02 10	11 59.1	4 51.0	23 58.7	6 29.3	24 14.6	1 50.4	12 00.5	1 33.8	0 49.1	24 26.7
18 W	19 50 05	27 59 25	20 00 53	26 52 13	11 53.4	6 32.7	25 12.6	6 11.8	24 27.4	1 50.1	12 00.9	1 31.2	0 49.3	24 28.3
19 Th	19 54 01	29 00 31	3♈36 11	10♈12 58	11 49.5	8 14.6	26 26.5	5 55.0	24 40.5	1 49.6	12 01.1	1 28.6	0 49.6	24 29.9
20 F	19 57 58	0♒01 36	16 42 54	23 06 27	11D47.6	9 56.6	27 40.4	5 38.9	24 53.8	1 48.9	12R01.3	1 26.0	0 49.9	24 31.5
21 Sa	20 01 55	1 02 40	29 24 08	5♉36 33	11 47.5	11 38.7	28 54.4	5 23.6	25 07.4	1 48.1	12 01.3	1 23.4	0 50.3	24 33.1
22 Su	20 05 51	2 03 44	11♉44 19	17 48 07	11 48.5	13 20.6	0♑08.3	5 09.0	25 21.2	1 47.0	12 01.2	1 20.7	0 50.6	24 34.8
23 M	20 09 48	3 04 46	23 48 36	29 46 24	11 49.8	15 02.3	1 22.3	4 55.2	25 35.2	1 45.8	12 01.0	1 18.1	0 51.0	24 36.4
24 Tu	20 13 44	4 05 47	5♊42 09	11♊36 29	11R50.4	16 43.7	2 36.3	4 42.1	25 49.4	1 44.4	12 00.7	1 15.5	0 51.5	24 38.1
25 W	20 17 41	5 06 48	17 29 57	23 23 05	11 49.5	18 24.4	3 50.4	4 29.9	26 03.9	1 42.8	12 00.3	1 12.9	0 52.0	24 39.7
26 Th	20 21 37	6 07 47	29 16 22	5♋10 14	11 46.5	20 04.2	5 04.4	4 18.4	26 18.6	1 41.0	11 59.8	1 10.3	0 52.5	24 41.4
27 F	20 25 34	7 08 46	11♋05 04	17 01 12	11 40.9	21 43.0	6 18.5	4 07.7	26 33.5	1 39.0	11 59.1	1 07.7	0 53.0	24 43.1
28 Sa	20 29 30	8 09 43	22 58 57	28 58 31	11 32.9	23 20.3	7 32.6	3 57.9	26 48.6	1 36.8	11 58.4	1 05.1	0 53.6	24 44.8
29 Su	20 33 27	9 10 40	5♌00 08	11♌03 56	11 22.8	24 55.9	8 46.7	3 48.8	27 03.9	1 34.4	11 57.6	1 02.5	0 54.2	24 46.4
30 M	20 37 24	10 11 36	17 10 03	23 18 36	11 11.4	26 29.2	10 00.8	3 40.6	27 19.4	1 31.8	11 56.6	0 59.9	0 54.9	24 48.1
31 Tu	20 41 20	11 12 31	29 29 38	5♍43 14	10 59.7	27 59.8	11 15.0	3 33.1	27 35.1	1 29.1	11 55.6	0 57.4	0 55.6	24 49.8

LONGITUDE — February 2040

Day	Sid.Time	☉	0 hr ☽	Noon☽	True☊	☿	♀	♂	⚳	♃	♄	♅	♆	♇
1 W	20 45 17	12♒13 24	11♍59 28	18♍18 25	10♊48.8	29♒27.2	12♑29.1	3♋26.5	27♈51.0	1♎26.2	11♎54.4	0♌54.8	0♉56.3	24♒51.5
2 Th	20 49 13	13 14 17	24 40 10	1♎04 49	10R39.7	0♓50.7	13 43.3	3R20.6	28 07.1	1R23.1	11R53.2	0R52.3	0 57.0	24 53.3
3 F	20 53 10	14 15 10	7♎32 32	14 03 27	10 33.1	2 09.7	14 57.5	3 15.6	28 23.3	1 19.8	11 51.8	0 49.7	0 57.8	24 55.0
4 Sa	20 57 06	15 16 01	20 37 44	27 15 38	10 29.2	3 23.6	16 11.7	3 11.3	28 39.8	1 16.3	11 50.4	0 47.2	0 58.6	24 56.7
5 Su	21 01 03	16 16 51	3♏57 20	10♏43 03	10D27.7	4 31.4	17 25.9	3 07.8	28 56.4	1 12.7	11 48.8	0 44.7	0 59.5	24 58.4
6 M	21 04 59	17 17 41	17 33 01	24 27 23	10 27.7	5 32.6	18 40.2	3 05.1	29 13.3	1 08.9	11 47.1	0 42.2	1 00.4	25 00.2
7 Tu	21 08 56	18 18 30	1♐26 17	8♐29 46	10R28.1	6 26.2	19 54.4	3 03.2	29 30.3	1 04.9	11 45.4	0 39.7	1 01.3	25 01.9
8 W	21 12 53	19 19 18	15 37 47	22 50 11	10 27.6	7 11.6	21 08.7	3D02.1	29 47.5	1 00.7	11 43.5	0 37.3	1 02.2	25 03.6
9 Th	21 16 49	20 20 05	0♑06 39	7♑26 44	10 25.0	7 48.0	22 23.0	3 01.7	0♉04.8	0 56.4	11 41.5	0 34.9	1 03.2	25 05.4
10 F	21 20 46	21 20 51	14 49 49	22 15 08	10 19.7	8 14.8	23 37.3	3 02.1	0 22.4	0 51.9	11 39.5	0 32.5	1 04.2	25 07.1
11 Sa	21 24 42	22 21 36	29 41 45	7♒08 41	10 11.5	8 29.4	24 51.6	3 03.2	0 40.0	0 47.2	11 37.3	0 30.1	1 05.3	25 08.9
12 Su	21 28 39	23 22 20	14♒34 47	21 58 57	10 01.1	8R37.4	26 05.9	3 05.1	0 57.9	0 42.4	11 35.1	0 27.7	1 06.4	25 10.6
13 M	21 32 35	24 23 02	29 20 05	6♓37 09	9 49.4	8 32.8	27 20.2	3 07.7	1 15.9	0 37.4	11 32.7	0 25.4	1 07.5	25 12.4
14 Tu	21 36 32	25 23 43	13♓49 14	20 55 33	9 37.8	8 17.6	28 34.5	3 11.0	1 34.1	0 32.3	11 30.3	0 23.1	1 08.6	25 14.1
15 W	21 40 28	26 24 22	27 55 33	4♈48 49	9 27.6	7 52.0	29 48.8	3 15.0	1 52.4	0 27.0	11 27.7	0 20.8	1 09.8	25 15.9
16 Th	21 44 25	27 24 59	11♈35 10	18 14 33	9 19.6	7 16.7	1♒03.2	3 19.8	2 10.9	0 21.5	11 25.1	0 18.5	1 11.0	25 17.6
17 F	21 48 22	28 25 35	24 47 08	1♉13 13	9 14.4	6 32.6	2 17.5	3 25.2	2 29.5	0 16.0	11 22.4	0 16.3	1 12.2	25 19.3
18 Sa	21 52 18	29 26 09	7♉33 12	13 47 36	9 11.6	5 40.8	3 31.8	3 31.2	2 48.3	0 10.2	11 19.6	0 14.1	1 13.4	25 21.1
19 Su	21 56 15	0♓26 42	19 57 00	26 02 03	9D10.8	4 42.7	4 46.2	3 38.0	3 07.2	0 04.4	11 16.7	0 11.9	1 14.7	25 22.8
20 M	22 00 11	1 27 12	2♊03 26	8♊01 51	9R10.8	3 40.0	6 00.5	3 45.4	3 26.3	29♍58.4	11 13.7	0 09.8	1 16.0	25 24.6
21 Tu	22 04 08	2 27 41	13 58 01	19 52 36	9 10.4	2 34.2	7 14.8	3 53.4	3 45.5	29 52.3	11 10.6	0 07.7	1 17.4	25 26.3
22 W	22 08 04	3 28 08	25 46 19	1♋39 47	9 08.7	1 27.3	8 29.2	4 02.0	4 04.8	29 46.0	11 07.5	0 05.6	1 18.7	25 28.0
23 Th	22 12 01	4 28 33	7♋33 39	13 28 28	9 04.7	0 20.8	9 43.5	4 11.2	4 24.2	29 39.7	11 04.3	0 03.6	1 20.1	25 29.8
24 F	22 15 57	5 28 56	19 24 45	25 22 59	8 57.8	29♒16.4	10 57.8	4 21.1	4 43.8	29 33.2	11 01.0	0 01.6	1 21.6	25 31.5
25 Sa	22 19 54	6 29 18	1♌23 34	7♌26 50	8 48.2	28 15.3	12 12.2	4 31.5	5 03.6	29 26.6	10 57.6	29♋59.6	1 23.0	25 33.2
26 Su	22 23 51	7 29 37	13 33 03	19 42 25	8 36.0	27 19.0	13 26.5	4 42.4	5 23.4	29 19.9	10 54.2	29 57.7	1 24.5	25 34.9
27 M	22 27 47	8 29 55	25 55 04	2♍11 04	8 22.4	26 28.1	14 40.9	4 53.9	5 43.4	29 13.1	10 50.7	29 55.8	1 26.0	25 36.7
28 Tu	22 31 44	9 30 11	8♍30 26	14 53 07	8 08.3	25 43.5	15 55.2	5 06.0	6 03.4	29 06.2	10 47.1	29 54.0	1 27.5	25 38.4
29 W	22 35 40	10 30 25	21 19 02	27 48 05	7 55.2	25 05.7	17 09.6	5 18.6	6 23.6	28 59.2	10 43.4	29 52.2	1 29.1	25 40.1

Astro Data

Dy Hr Mn	
☽0S	7 0:07
♆D	11 5:09
♃⚹♅	11 21:11
♃R	16 13:19
☽0N	19 12:34
♄R	21 4:14
♅□♆	1 1:06
☽0S	3 4:59
♃⚻♅	8 4:56
♂D	9 11:49
☿R	12 13:40
☽0N	15 21:17
♃⚹♅	17 9:36

Planet Ingress

	Dy Hr Mn
☿ ♒	14 14:59
☉ ♒	20 11:22
♀ ♑	22 9:18
☿ ♓	1 21:17
⚳ ♉	9 5:21
♀ ♒	15 15:36
☉ ♓	19 1:25
♃ ♍R	20 5:37
☿ ♒R	23 19:38
♅ ♋R	25 7:40

Last Aspect / ☽ Ingress

Last Aspect Dy Hr Mn		☽ Ingress Dy Hr Mn	Last Aspect Dy Hr Mn		☽ Ingress Dy Hr Mn
30 21:19	♂ ☌	♌ 1 7:45	31 23:44	♀ △	♎ 2 9:59
3 7:37	♇ ☍	♍ 3 19:10	4 7:49	♇ △	♏ 4 16:55
4 22:33	☉ △	♎ 6 4:25	6 12:57	♇ □	♐ 6 21:32
8 0:28	♇ △	♏ 8 10:41	8 15:41	♇ ⚹	♑ 8 23:49
10 4:11	♇ □	♐ 10 13:43	10 14:25	♀ ☌	♒ 11 0:29
12 5:08	♇ ⚹	♑ 12 14:12	12 17:13	♇ ☌	♓ 13 1:05
14 13:29	☿ ☌	♒ 14 13:39	15 2:25	☿ ⚹	♈ 15 3:36
16 4:55	♇ ☌	♓ 16 14:07	17 6:19	☉ ⚹	♉ 17 9:43
18 14:09	☉ ⚹	♈ 18 17:33	19 10:42	♇ □	♊ 19 19:53
20 21:38	♀ △	♉ 21 1:09	22 8:10	♃ □	♋ 22 8:37
23 1:35	♇ □	♊ 23 12:27	24 20:16	♃ ⚹	♌ 24 21:14
25 14:37	♇ △	♋ 26 1:29	27 1:44	☿ ☍	♍ 27 7:50
27 1:50	♄ □	♌ 28 14:03	29 15:48	♅ ⚹	♎ 29 16:03
30 19:03	☿ ☍	♍ 31 0:59			

☽ Phases & Eclipses

Dy Hr Mn		
7 11:07	☾	16♎45
14 3:26	●	23♑33
21 2:22	☽	0♉38
29 7:56	○	9♌00
5 22:34	☾	16♏44
12 14:26	●	23♒28
19 21:35	☽	0♊51
28 1:01	○	9♍03

Astro Data

1 January 2040
Julian Day # 51135
SVP 4♓42'19"
GC 27♐23.9 ⚴ 29♒07.4
Eris 27♈53.6R ⚵ 18♒06.1
⚷ 9♋51.0R ⚶ 12♐41.6
☽ Mean ☊ 11♊23.1

1 February 2040
Julian Day # 51166
SVP 4♓42'14"
GC 27♐24.0 ⚴ 8♓31.6
Eris 27♈54.1 ⚵ 2♓11.0
⚷ 7♋56.1R ⚶ 28♐46.6
☽ Mean ☊ 9♊44.6

March 2040 LONGITUDE

Day	Sid.Time	☉	0 hr ☽	Noon ☽	True ☊	☿	♀	♂	⚳	♃	♄	♅	♆	♇
1 Th	22 39 37	11♓30 38	4♎20 07	10♎54 59	7♊44.0	24♒34.8	18♒23.9	5♋31.7	6♉43.9	28♍52.1	10♎39.7	29♋50.4	1♉30.7	25♒41.8
2 F	22 43 33	12 30 49	17 32 35	24 12 47	7R 35.6	24R 11.0	19 38.3	5 45.3	7 04.4	28R 45.0	10R 35.9	29R 48.7	1 32.3	25 43.4
3 Sa	22 47 30	13 30 58	0♏55 29	7♏40 39	7 30.3	23 54.3	20 52.6	5 59.4	7 24.9	28 37.7	10 32.0	29 47.0	1 33.9	25 45.1
4 Su	22 51 26	14 31 06	14 28 14	21 18 15	7 27.8	23D 44.5	22 07.0	6 13.9	7 45.6	28 30.4	10 28.1	29 45.3	1 35.6	25 46.8
5 M	22 55 23	15 31 12	28 10 44	5♐05 42	7 27.1	23 41.5	23 21.3	6 29.0	8 06.3	28 23.0	10 24.1	29 43.7	1 37.2	25 48.5
6 Tu	22 59 20	16 31 17	12♐03 12	19 03 16	7 27.1	23 44.8	24 35.7	6 44.5	8 27.2	28 15.6	10 20.1	29 42.2	1 38.9	25 50.1
7 W	23 03 16	17 31 20	26 05 52	3♑10 57	7 26.4	23 54.2	25 50.1	7 00.5	8 48.2	28 08.1	10 16.0	29 40.6	1 40.7	25 51.8
8 Th	23 07 13	18 31 22	10♑18 22	17 27 54	7 23.9	24 09.4	27 04.4	7 16.9	9 09.2	28 00.5	10 11.9	29 39.2	1 42.4	25 53.4
9 F	23 11 09	19 31 22	24 39 12	1♒51 50	7 18.7	24 30.1	28 18.8	7 33.7	9 30.4	27 52.9	10 07.7	29 37.7	1 44.2	25 55.1
10 Sa	23 15 06	20 31 21	9♒05 17	16 18 53	7 10.7	24 55.8	29 33.1	7 51.0	9 51.7	27 45.2	10 03.5	29 36.4	1 46.0	25 56.7
11 Su	23 19 02	21 31 18	23 31 55	0♓43 38	7 00.3	25 26.4	0♓47.5	8 08.7	10 13.1	27 37.5	9 59.2	29 35.0	1 47.8	25 58.3
12 M	23 22 59	22 31 12	7♓53 14	14 59 54	6 48.6	26 01.3	2 01.8	8 26.8	10 34.6	27 29.8	9 54.8	29 33.7	1 49.6	25 59.9
13 Tu	23 26 55	23 31 05	22 02 55	29 01 36	6 36.9	26 40.5	3 16.2	8 45.2	10 56.1	27 22.0	9 50.5	29 32.5	1 51.5	26 01.5
14 W	23 30 52	24 30 56	5♈55 24	12♈43 53	6 26.3	27 23.6	4 30.5	9 04.1	11 17.8	27 14.2	9 46.1	29 31.3	1 53.3	26 03.0
15 Th	23 34 49	25 30 45	19 26 43	26 03 45	6 17.9	28 10.3	5 44.9	9 23.4	11 39.5	27 06.5	9 41.6	29 30.2	1 55.2	26 04.6
16 F	23 38 45	26 30 32	2♉34 59	9♉00 31	6 12.1	29 00.4	6 59.2	9 43.0	12 01.4	26 58.7	9 37.1	29 29.1	1 57.1	26 06.2
17 Sa	23 42 42	27 30 16	15 20 34	21 35 31	6 08.9	29 53.7	8 13.5	10 03.0	12 23.3	26 50.9	9 32.6	29 28.0	1 59.1	26 07.7
18 Su	23 46 38	28 29 59	27 45 46	3♊51 52	6D 07.9	0♓50.0	9 27.8	10 23.4	12 45.3	26 43.1	9 28.1	29 27.0	2 01.0	26 09.2
19 M	23 50 35	29 29 39	9♊54 21	15 53 53	6 08.2	1 49.2	10 42.2	10 44.1	13 07.4	26 35.3	9 23.5	29 26.1	2 03.0	26 10.7
20 Tu	23 54 31	0♈29 17	21 51 05	27 46 40	6R 08.6	2 51.0	11 56.5	11 05.1	13 29.6	26 27.5	9 18.9	29 25.2	2 04.9	26 12.2
21 W	23 58 28	1 28 53	3♋41 17	9♋35 38	6 08.3	3 55.3	13 10.7	11 26.5	13 51.9	26 19.8	9 14.3	29 24.3	2 06.9	26 13.7
22 Th	0 02 24	2 28 26	15 30 23	21 26 12	6 06.3	5 02.1	14 25.0	11 48.2	14 14.2	26 12.0	9 09.7	29 23.6	2 08.9	26 15.2
23 F	0 06 21	3 27 57	27 23 40	3♌23 24	6 02.0	6 11.0	15 39.3	12 10.2	14 36.6	26 04.3	9 05.1	29 22.8	2 11.0	26 16.7
24 Sa	0 10 18	4 27 26	9♌25 54	15 31 38	5 55.4	7 22.2	16 53.6	12 32.5	14 59.1	25 56.7	9 00.4	29 22.1	2 13.0	26 18.1
25 Su	0 14 14	5 26 52	21 41 01	27 54 22	5 46.7	8 35.4	18 07.8	12 55.1	15 21.6	25 49.1	8 55.7	29 21.5	2 15.1	26 19.5
26 M	0 18 11	6 26 17	4♍11 56	10♍33 51	5 36.5	9 50.6	19 22.1	13 17.9	15 44.3	25 41.5	8 51.1	29 20.9	2 17.1	26 20.9
27 Tu	0 22 07	7 25 39	17 00 13	23 31 00	5 25.9	11 07.7	20 36.3	13 41.1	16 06.9	25 34.0	8 46.4	29 20.4	2 19.2	26 22.3
28 W	0 26 04	8 24 59	0♎06 05	6♎45 18	5 15.9	12 26.6	21 50.6	14 04.5	16 29.7	25 26.5	8 41.7	29 19.9	2 21.3	26 23.7
29 Th	0 30 00	9 24 17	13 28 23	20 15 01	5 07.5	13 47.3	23 04.8	14 28.2	16 52.5	25 19.1	8 37.0	29 19.5	2 23.4	26 25.1
30 F	0 33 57	10 23 33	27 04 53	3♏57 36	5 01.4	15 09.7	24 19.0	14 52.2	17 15.4	25 11.8	8 32.3	29 19.1	2 25.5	26 26.4
31 Sa	0 37 53	11 22 47	10♏52 48	17 50 06	4 57.8	16 33.9	25 33.2	15 16.4	17 38.4	25 04.5	8 27.7	29 18.8	2 27.7	26 27.7

April 2040 LONGITUDE

Day	Sid.Time	☉	0 hr ☽	Noon ☽	True ☊	☿	♀	♂	⚳	♃	♄	♅	♆	♇
1 Su	0 41 50	12♈21 59	24♏49 09	1♐49 39	4♊56.5	17♓59.6	26♓47.4	15♋40.9	18♉01.4	24♍57.4	8♎23.0	29♋18.5	2♉29.8	26♒29.1
2 M	0 45 46	13 21 10	8♐51 19	15 53 54	4D 56.8	19 27.0	28 01.6	16 05.6	18 24.5	24R 50.3	8R 18.3	29R 18.3	2 32.0	26 30.4
3 Tu	0 49 43	14 20 19	22 57 12	0♑01 00	4 57.8	20 56.0	29 15.8	16 30.6	18 47.7	24 43.2	8 13.7	29 18.2	2 34.1	26 31.6
4 W	0 53 40	15 19 26	7♑05 10	14 09 32	4R 58.5	22 26.6	0♈30.0	16 55.8	19 10.9	24 36.3	8 09.1	29 18.0	2 36.3	26 32.9
5 Th	0 57 36	16 18 31	21 13 56	28 18 12	4 57.8	23 58.7	1 44.2	17 21.2	19 34.2	24 29.5	8 04.4	29D 18.0	2 38.5	26 34.1
6 F	1 01 33	17 17 35	5♒22 06	12♒25 24	4 55.3	25 32.3	2 58.4	17 46.8	19 57.5	24 22.8	7 59.8	29 18.0	2 40.7	26 35.4
7 Sa	1 05 29	18 16 37	19 27 50	26 29 05	4 50.7	27 07.5	4 12.6	18 12.7	20 20.9	24 16.1	7 55.3	29 18.1	2 42.9	26 36.6
8 Su	1 09 26	19 15 37	3♓28 46	10♓26 32	4 44.4	28 44.1	5 26.8	18 38.8	20 44.3	24 09.6	7 50.7	29 18.2	2 45.1	26 37.7
9 M	1 13 22	20 14 35	17 21 58	24 14 40	4 37.0	0♈22.3	6 40.9	19 05.1	21 07.8	24 03.2	7 46.2	29 18.3	2 47.3	26 38.9
10 Tu	1 17 19	21 13 31	1♈04 14	7♈50 17	4 29.6	2 02.0	7 55.1	19 31.6	21 31.4	23 56.9	7 41.7	29 18.6	2 49.5	26 40.0
11 W	1 21 15	22 12 25	14 32 31	21 10 40	4 22.9	3 43.3	9 09.2	19 58.4	21 55.0	23 50.8	7 37.2	29 18.8	2 51.8	26 41.2
12 Th	1 25 12	23 11 17	27 44 31	4♉13 57	4 17.6	5 26.1	10 23.4	20 25.3	22 18.7	23 44.7	7 32.8	29 19.2	2 54.0	26 42.3
13 F	1 29 09	24 10 08	10♉38 55	16 59 29	4 14.2	7 10.4	11 37.5	20 52.4	22 42.4	23 38.8	7 28.4	29 19.5	2 56.2	26 43.3
14 Sa	1 33 05	25 08 56	23 15 45	29 27 58	4D 12.7	8 56.2	12 51.6	21 19.7	23 06.1	23 33.0	7 24.0	29 20.0	2 58.5	26 44.4
15 Su	1 37 02	26 07 42	5♊36 22	11♊41 21	4 12.9	10 43.6	14 05.7	21 47.2	23 29.9	23 27.4	7 19.7	29 20.5	3 00.7	26 45.4
16 M	1 40 58	27 06 26	17 43 19	23 42 45	4 14.1	12 32.6	15 19.8	22 14.9	23 53.8	23 21.9	7 15.4	29 21.0	3 03.0	26 46.4
17 Tu	1 44 55	28 05 08	29 40 10	5♋36 08	4 15.8	14 23.1	16 33.9	22 42.8	24 17.7	23 16.5	7 11.2	29 21.6	3 05.2	26 47.4
18 W	1 48 51	29 03 47	11♋31 13	17 26 03	4 17.3	16 15.2	17 48.0	23 10.9	24 41.6	23 11.3	7 07.0	29 22.3	3 07.5	26 48.4
19 Th	1 52 48	0♉02 25	23 21 16	29 17 29	4R 18.0	18 08.9	19 02.0	23 39.1	25 05.6	23 06.3	7 02.9	29 23.0	3 09.8	26 49.4
20 F	1 56 44	1 01 00	5♌15 21	11♌15 28	4 17.4	20 04.1	20 16.1	24 07.5	25 29.7	23 01.4	6 58.8	29 23.7	3 12.0	26 50.3
21 Sa	2 00 41	1 59 33	17 18 25	23 24 48	4 15.4	22 01.0	21 30.1	24 36.0	25 53.7	22 56.6	6 54.8	29 24.6	3 14.3	26 51.2
22 Su	2 04 38	2 58 04	29 35 06	5♍49 47	4 12.1	23 59.3	22 44.1	25 04.7	26 17.8	22 52.0	6 50.8	29 25.4	3 16.6	26 52.1
23 M	2 08 34	3 56 32	12♍09 15	18 33 48	4 07.9	25 59.2	23 58.2	25 33.6	26 42.0	22 47.6	6 46.9	29 26.3	3 18.8	26 52.9
24 Tu	2 12 31	4 54 59	25 03 41	1♎39 00	4 03.2	28 00.6	25 12.2	26 02.6	27 06.2	22 43.3	6 43.1	29 27.3	3 21.1	26 53.8
25 W	2 16 27	5 53 23	8♎19 47	15 05 55	3 58.7	0♉03.4	26 26.1	26 31.8	27 30.4	22 39.2	6 39.3	29 28.3	3 23.3	26 54.6
26 Th	2 20 24	6 51 46	21 57 13	28 53 21	3 55.0	2 07.6	27 40.1	27 01.1	27 54.6	22 35.2	6 35.6	29 29.4	3 25.6	26 55.4
27 F	2 24 20	7 50 06	5♏53 55	12♏58 24	3 52.5	4 13.0	28 54.1	27 30.5	28 18.9	22 31.4	6 31.9	29 30.5	3 27.9	26 56.1
28 Sa	2 28 17	8 48 25	20 06 13	27 16 46	3D 51.3	6 19.6	0♉08.1	28 00.1	28 43.2	22 27.8	6 28.3	29 31.7	3 30.1	26 56.9
29 Su	2 32 13	9 46 43	4♐29 23	11♐43 24	3 51.3	8 27.2	1 22.0	28 29.8	29 07.6	22 24.4	6 24.8	29 32.9	3 32.4	26 57.6
30 M	2 36 10	10 44 58	18 58 09	26 13 02	3 52.3	10 35.6	2 36.0	28 59.7	29 32.0	22 21.1	6 21.3	29 34.2	3 34.6	26 58.3

Astro Data

	Dy Hr Mn
♄⚼♇	1 2:50
☽0S	1 10:04
☿D	5 11:21
☽0N	14 6:46
☉0N	20 0:13
♃⚻♇	22 3:42
☽0S	28 17:20
♅D	5 21:45
♀0N	6 21:03
☽0N	10 15:26
☿0N	12 12:02
☽0S	25 2:40

Planet Ingress

	Dy Hr Mn
♀ ♓	10 20:40
☿ ♓	17 14:45
☉ ♈	20 0:13
♀ ♈	4 2:17
☿ ♈	9 6:35
☉ ♉	19 11:01
☿ ♉	25 11:20
♀ ♉	28 9:23

Last Aspect / ☽ Ingress (March)

Last Aspect Dy Hr Mn		☽ Ingress Dy Hr Mn
2 22:00	♅ □	♏ 2 22:21
5 2:43	♅ △	♐ 5 3:10
7 3:32	♃ □	♑ 7 6:37
9 8:17	♅ ☍	♒ 9 8:54
11 4:03	♇ ☌	♓ 11 10:47
13 12:53	♅ △	♈ 13 13:41
15 18:18	♅ □	♉ 15 19:14
18 3:19	♅ ⚹	♊ 18 4:23
20 9:21	♃ □	♋ 20 16:31
23 3:59	♅ ☌	♌ 23 5:14
25 8:57	♇ ☍	♍ 25 16:00
27 22:37	♅ ⚹	♎ 27 23:49
30 3:55	♅ □	♏ 30 5:06

Last Aspect / ☽ Ingress (April)

Last Aspect Dy Hr Mn		☽ Ingress Dy Hr Mn
1 7:42	♅ △	♐ 1 8:52
3 10:36	♀ □	♑ 3 11:58
5 13:42	♅ ☍	♒ 5 14:53
7 12:13	♇ ☌	♓ 7 18:01
9 20:53	♅ △	♈ 9 22:07
12 2:54	♅ □	♉ 12 4:10
14 11:45	♅ ⚹	♊ 14 13:02
16 19:27	☉ ⚹	♋ 17 0:40
19 12:11	♅ ☌	♌ 19 13:26
21 18:43	♇ ☍	♍ 22 0:48
24 8:01	♅ ⚹	♎ 24 9:01
26 13:02	♅ □	♏ 26 13:55
28 15:45	♅ △	♐ 28 16:32
30 13:15	♇ ⚹	♑ 30 18:16

☽ Phases & Eclipses

Dy Hr Mn		
6 7:20	☾	16♐20
13 1:47	●	23♓06
20 18:00	☽	0♋44
28 15:13	○	8♎33
4 14:07	☾	15♑25
11 14:01	●	22♈17
19 13:39	☽	0♌06
27 2:39	○	7♏27

Astro Data

1 March 2040
Julian Day # 51195
SVP 4♓42'10"
GC 27♐24.0 ⚵ 18♓11.2
Eris 28♈03.7 ⚶ 16♓22.8
⚷ 6♋57.3R ⚴ 12♑58.1
☽ Mean ☊ 8♊12.4

1 April 2040
Julian Day # 51226
SVP 4♓42'07"
GC 27♐24.1 ⚵ 28♓53.2
Eris 28♈21.1 ⚶ 2♈19.3
⚷ 7♋13.1 ⚴ 26♑32.7
☽ Mean ☊ 6♊33.9

LONGITUDE — May 2040

Day	Sid.Time	☉	0 hr ☽	Noon ☽	True ☊	☿	♀	♂	⚳	♃	♄	♅	♆	♇
1 Tu	2 40 07	11♉43 13	3♑27 28	10♑40 54	3♊53.6	12♉44.7	3♉49.9	29♋29.7	29♉56.4	22♍18.0	6♎17.9	29♋35.5	3♉36.9	26♒58.9
2 W	2 44 03	12 41 25	17 52 52	25 03 00	3 54.9	14 54.2	5 03.9	29 59.8	0♊20.9	22R 15.1	6R 14.6	29 36.9	3 39.1	26 59.6
3 Th	2 48 00	13 39 37	2♒10 55	9♒16 21	3R 55.6	17 03.9	6 17.8	0♌30.1	0 45.4	22 12.3	6 11.4	29 38.3	3 41.4	27 00.2
4 F	2 51 56	14 37 46	16 19 04	23 18 54	3 55.4	19 13.5	7 31.7	1 00.5	1 09.9	22 09.7	6 08.2	29 39.8	3 43.6	27 00.8
5 Sa	2 55 53	15 35 55	0♓15 40	7♓09 17	3 54.4	21 22.7	8 45.7	1 31.0	1 34.5	22 07.3	6 05.2	29 41.3	3 45.8	27 01.4
6 Su	2 59 49	16 34 01	13 59 39	20 46 41	3 52.7	23 31.3	9 59.6	2 01.6	1 59.0	22 05.1	6 02.2	29 42.9	3 48.0	27 01.9
7 M	3 03 46	17 32 07	27 30 20	4♈10 33	3 50.5	25 39.0	11 13.5	2 32.4	2 23.7	22 03.1	5 59.2	29 44.5	3 50.3	27 02.5
8 Tu	3 07 42	18 30 11	10♈47 18	17 20 35	3 48.3	27 45.4	12 27.4	3 03.2	2 48.3	22 01.2	5 56.4	29 46.2	3 52.5	27 02.9
9 W	3 11 39	19 28 13	23 50 22	0♉16 39	3 46.3	29 50.3	13 41.3	3 34.2	3 13.0	21 59.5	5 53.6	29 47.9	3 54.7	27 03.4
10 Th	3 15 36	20 26 14	6♉39 30	12 58 56	3 44.9	1♊53.4	14 55.2	4 05.4	3 37.6	21 58.0	5 51.0	29 49.6	3 56.9	27 03.9
11 F	3 19 32	21 24 14	19 15 03	25 27 56	3D 44.1	3 54.5	16 09.0	4 36.6	4 02.4	21 56.7	5 48.4	29 51.4	3 59.0	27 04.3
12 Sa	3 23 29	22 22 12	1♊37 45	7♊44 40	3 44.0	5 53.3	17 22.9	5 07.9	4 27.1	21 55.6	5 45.9	29 53.3	4 01.2	27 04.7
13 Su	3 27 25	23 20 08	13 48 55	19 50 43	3 44.5	7 49.6	18 36.8	5 39.4	4 51.9	21 54.6	5 43.5	29 55.2	4 03.4	27 05.0
14 M	3 31 22	24 18 03	25 50 24	1♋48 17	3 45.2	9 43.3	19 50.6	6 11.0	5 16.7	21 53.9	5 41.2	29 57.1	4 05.5	27 05.4
15 Tu	3 35 18	25 15 56	7♋44 45	13 40 13	3 46.1	11 34.2	21 04.5	6 42.6	5 41.5	21 53.3	5 38.9	29 59.1	4 07.7	27 05.7
16 W	3 39 15	26 13 47	19 35 07	25 29 56	3 47.0	13 22.1	22 18.3	7 14.4	6 06.3	21 52.9	5 36.8	0♌01.2	4 09.8	27 06.0
17 Th	3 43 11	27 11 37	1♌25 11	7♌21 24	3 47.6	15 07.1	23 32.2	7 46.3	6 31.2	21D 52.7	5 34.8	0 03.3	4 12.0	27 06.3
18 F	3 47 08	28 09 25	13 19 08	19 18 58	3R 48.0	16 48.9	24 46.0	8 18.3	6 56.0	21 52.7	5 32.8	0 05.4	4 14.1	27 06.5
19 Sa	3 51 05	29 07 12	25 21 26	1♍27 08	3 48.0	18 27.5	25 59.8	8 50.4	7 20.9	21 52.8	5 31.0	0 07.5	4 16.2	27 06.7
20 Su	3 55 01	0♊04 56	7♍36 38	13 50 27	3 47.9	20 02.8	27 13.6	9 22.5	7 45.8	21 53.1	5 29.2	0 09.7	4 18.3	27 06.9
21 M	3 58 58	1 02 39	20 09 05	26 33 00	3 47.7	21 34.9	28 27.4	9 54.8	8 10.7	21 53.7	5 27.6	0 12.0	4 20.3	27 07.1
22 Tu	4 02 54	2 00 21	3♎02 36	9♎38 10	3 47.4	23 03.6	29 41.2	10 27.2	8 35.6	21 54.4	5 26.0	0 14.3	4 22.4	27 07.2
23 W	4 06 51	2 58 00	16 19 55	23 07 59	3D 47.3	24 28.8	0♊55.0	10 59.6	9 00.6	21 55.2	5 24.5	0 16.6	4 24.4	27 07.3
24 Th	4 10 47	3 55 39	0♏02 19	7♏02 46	3 47.3	25 50.7	2 08.8	11 32.2	9 25.5	21 56.3	5 23.1	0 19.0	4 26.5	27 07.4
25 F	4 14 44	4 53 16	14 09 02	21 20 41	3R 47.3	27 09.0	3 22.5	12 04.8	9 50.5	21 57.5	5 21.9	0 21.4	4 28.5	27 07.5
26 Sa	4 18 40	5 50 52	28 37 06	5♐57 35	3 47.3	28 23.8	4 36.3	12 37.5	10 15.5	21 58.9	5 20.7	0 23.8	4 30.5	27 07.5
27 Su	4 22 37	6 48 26	13♐21 18	20 47 19	3 47.2	29 35.0	5 50.0	13 10.3	10 40.5	22 00.5	5 19.6	0 26.3	4 32.5	27R 07.5
28 M	4 26 34	7 46 00	28 14 40	5♑42 22	3 47.0	0♋42.6	7 03.8	13 43.2	11 05.5	22 02.3	5 18.6	0 28.9	4 34.5	27 07.5
29 Tu	4 30 30	8 43 33	13♑09 25	20 34 53	3 46.5	1 46.5	8 17.6	14 16.2	11 30.5	22 04.2	5 17.8	0 31.4	4 36.4	27 07.5
30 W	4 34 27	9 41 05	27 57 55	5♒17 44	3 46.0	2 46.6	9 31.3	14 49.2	11 55.6	22 06.3	5 17.0	0 34.0	4 38.4	27 07.4
31 Th	4 38 23	10 38 35	12♒33 42	19 45 18	3 45.4	3 42.9	10 45.1	15 22.4	12 20.6	22 08.6	5 16.3	0 36.7	4 40.3	27 07.3

LONGITUDE — June 2040

Day	Sid.Time	☉	0 hr ☽	Noon ☽	True ☊	☿	♀	♂	⚳	♃	♄	♅	♆	♇
1 F	4 42 20	11♊36 05	26♒52 10	3♓54 02	3♊45.1	4♋35.2	11♊58.8	15♌55.6	12♊45.7	22♍11.1	5♎15.7	0♌39.3	4♉42.2	27♒07.2
2 Sa	4 46 16	12 33 35	10♓50 45	17 42 18	3D 45.0	5 23.6	13 12.6	16 28.9	13 10.8	22 13.7	5R 15.2	0 42.0	4 44.1	27R 07.1
3 Su	4 50 13	13 31 03	24 28 44	1♈10 11	3 45.4	6 08.0	14 26.3	17 02.3	13 35.9	22 16.5	5 14.9	0 44.8	4 45.9	27 06.9
4 M	4 54 09	14 28 31	7♈46 49	14 18 54	3 46.1	6 48.1	15 40.0	17 35.7	14 00.9	22 19.5	5 14.6	0 47.6	4 47.8	27 06.7
5 Tu	4 58 06	15 25 58	20 46 40	27 10 24	3 47.1	7 24.1	16 53.8	18 09.3	14 26.0	22 22.6	5 14.4	0 50.4	4 49.6	27 06.5
6 W	5 02 03	16 23 24	3♉30 23	9♉46 54	3 48.2	7 55.8	18 07.5	18 42.9	14 51.1	22 25.9	5D 14.3	0 53.2	4 51.4	27 06.3
7 Th	5 05 59	17 20 50	16 00 13	22 10 37	3R 49.0	8 23.0	19 21.3	19 16.6	15 16.3	22 29.4	5 14.3	0 56.1	4 53.2	27 06.0
8 F	5 09 56	18 18 15	28 18 21	4♊23 41	3 49.3	8 45.8	20 35.0	19 50.4	15 41.4	22 33.0	5 14.5	0 59.0	4 55.0	27 05.7
9 Sa	5 13 52	19 15 39	10♊26 50	16 28 04	3 48.9	9 04.1	21 48.8	20 24.2	16 06.5	22 36.8	5 14.7	1 01.9	4 56.7	27 05.4
10 Su	5 17 49	20 13 03	22 27 37	28 25 42	3 47.6	9 17.9	23 02.5	20 58.2	16 31.6	22 40.8	5 15.0	1 04.9	4 58.5	27 05.1
11 M	5 21 45	21 10 26	4♋22 35	10♋18 31	3 45.6	9 27.1	24 16.2	21 32.2	16 56.8	22 44.9	5 15.5	1 07.9	5 00.2	27 04.7
12 Tu	5 25 42	22 07 47	16 13 46	22 08 37	3 42.9	9R 31.7	25 30.0	22 06.3	17 21.9	22 49.2	5 16.0	1 11.0	5 01.8	27 04.3
13 W	5 29 39	23 05 08	28 03 23	3♌58 25	3 39.9	9 31.7	26 43.7	22 40.4	17 47.1	22 53.6	5 16.6	1 14.0	5 03.5	27 03.9
14 Th	5 33 35	24 02 29	9♌54 05	15 50 45	3 36.9	9 27.3	27 57.4	23 14.7	18 12.2	22 58.2	5 17.4	1 17.1	5 05.1	27 03.5
15 F	5 37 32	24 59 48	21 48 51	27 48 40	3 34.3	9 18.6	29 11.1	23 49.0	18 37.3	23 03.0	5 18.2	1 20.2	5 06.8	27 03.0
16 Sa	5 41 28	25 57 06	3♍51 11	9♍56 23	3 32.4	9 05.6	0♋24.9	24 23.3	19 02.5	23 07.9	5 19.2	1 23.4	5 08.4	27 02.5
17 Su	5 45 25	26 54 24	16 04 56	22 17 23	3D 31.5	8 48.6	1 38.6	24 57.8	19 27.6	23 13.0	5 20.2	1 26.5	5 09.9	27 02.0
18 M	5 49 21	27 51 40	28 34 14	4♎55 59	3 31.6	8 27.9	2 52.3	25 32.3	19 52.7	23 18.2	5 21.3	1 29.7	5 11.5	27 01.5
19 Tu	5 53 18	28 48 56	11♎23 08	17 56 08	3 32.5	8 03.7	4 06.0	26 06.8	20 17.9	23 23.6	5 22.6	1 32.9	5 13.0	27 00.9
20 W	5 57 14	29 46 11	24 35 20	1♏21 03	3 34.0	7 36.5	5 19.7	26 41.5	20 43.0	23 29.1	5 23.9	1 36.2	5 14.5	27 00.4
21 Th	6 01 11	0♋43 25	8♏13 29	15 12 43	3 35.4	7 06.7	6 33.4	27 16.2	21 08.1	23 34.7	5 25.4	1 39.5	5 15.9	26 59.8
22 F	6 05 08	1 40 39	22 18 40	29 31 05	3R 36.2	6 34.7	7 47.1	27 50.9	21 33.2	23 40.5	5 26.9	1 42.8	5 17.4	26 59.2
23 Sa	6 09 04	2 37 53	6♐49 35	14♐13 32	3 35.9	6 01.1	9 00.8	28 25.8	21 58.4	23 46.5	5 28.5	1 46.1	5 18.8	26 58.5
24 Su	6 13 01	3 35 05	21 42 09	29 14 29	3 34.2	5 26.4	10 14.5	29 00.7	22 23.5	23 52.6	5 30.3	1 49.4	5 20.2	26 57.9
25 M	6 16 57	4 32 18	6♑49 26	14♑25 46	3 31.2	4 51.2	11 28.2	29 35.6	22 48.6	23 58.8	5 32.1	1 52.8	5 21.6	26 57.2
26 Tu	6 20 54	5 29 30	22 02 14	29 37 33	3 27.2	4 16.1	12 41.9	0♍10.6	23 13.7	24 05.1	5 34.0	1 56.1	5 22.9	26 56.5
27 W	6 24 50	6 26 42	7♒10 29	14♒39 55	3 22.6	3 41.8	13 55.6	0 45.7	23 38.8	24 11.6	5 36.0	1 59.5	5 24.2	26 55.8
28 Th	6 28 47	7 23 54	22 04 49	29 24 24	3 18.4	3 08.8	15 09.2	1 20.8	24 03.9	24 18.3	5 38.2	2 03.0	5 25.5	26 55.0
29 F	6 32 43	8 21 06	6♓38 00	13♓45 12	3 15.0	2 37.7	16 22.9	1 56.0	24 29.0	24 25.0	5 40.4	2 06.4	5 26.8	26 54.3
30 Sa	6 36 40	9 18 18	20 45 44	27 39 31	3D 12.9	2 09.0	17 36.6	2 31.3	24 54.0	24 31.9	5 42.7	2 09.8	5 28.0	26 53.5

Astro Data

	Dy Hr Mn
♄0N	5 14:51
☽0N	7 22:21
♃ D	18 3:59
☽0S	22 12:32
♇ R	27 13:26
☽0N	4 3:55
♄ D	6 17:56
☿ R	13 0:19
☽0S	18 21:07
♄0S	28 6:32

Planet Ingress

	Dy Hr Mn
⚳ ♊	1 15:30
♂ ♌	2 12:08
☿ ♊	9 13:52
♅ ♌	15 22:14
☉ ♊	20 9:57
♀ ♊	22 18:07
☿ ♋	27 20:43
♀ ♋	16 3:54
☉ ♋	20 17:48
♂ ♍	26 4:43

Last Aspect / ☽ Ingress

Last Aspect Dy Hr Mn		☽ Ingress Dy Hr Mn
2 19:41	♅ ☍	♒ 2 20:19
4 18:23	♇ ☌	♓ 4 23:33
7 4:00	♅ △	♈ 7 4:29
9 11:06	♅ □	♉ 9 11:29
11 20:34	♅ ⚹	♊ 11 20:49
14 2:30	♇ △	♋ 14 8:22
16 13:37	☉ ⚹	♌ 16 21:07
19 7:02	☉ □	♍ 19 9:09
21 15:55	♀ △	♎ 21 18:24
23 18:57	♇ △	♏ 23 23:56
25 21:33	♇ □	♐ 26 2:16
27 22:12	♇ ⚹	♑ 28 2:49
29 14:25	♃ △	♒ 30 3:19

Last Aspect / ☽ Ingress

Last Aspect Dy Hr Mn		☽ Ingress Dy Hr Mn
1 0:26	♇ ☌	♓ 1 5:20
2 20:01	♃ ☍	♈ 3 9:54
5 11:53	♇ ⚹	♉ 5 17:21
7 21:38	♇ □	♊ 8 3:20
10 9:18	♇ △	♋ 10 15:10
12 13:23	♃ ⚹	♌ 13 3:57
15 15:03	♀ ⚹	♍ 15 16:21
17 21:34	☉ □	♎ 18 2:43
20 9:00	☉ △	♏ 20 9:37
22 9:07	♂ □	♐ 22 12:48
24 11:37	♂ △	♑ 24 13:12
26 3:10	♃ △	♒ 26 12:36
28 7:55	♇ ☌	♓ 28 12:59
30 6:29	♃ ☍	♈ 30 16:07

☽ Phases & Eclipses

Dy Hr Mn	
3 20:01	☾ 13♒59
11 3:29	● 21♉04
11 3:43:03	● P 0.531
19 7:02	☽ 28♌55
26 11:48	○ 5♐50
26 11:46	● T 1.535
2 2:19	☾ 12♓10
9 18:04	● 19♊30
17 21:34	☽ 27♍17
24 19:20	○ 3♑53

Astro Data

1 May 2040
Julian Day # 51256
SVP 4♓42'04"
GC 27♐24.2 ⚴ 9♈11.1
Eris 28♈40.8 ⚵ 18♈16.9
⚷ 8♋43.9 ⚶ 7♒04.7
☽ Mean ☊ 4♊58.6

1 June 2040
Julian Day # 51287
SVP 4♓41'58"
GC 27♐24.2 ⚴ 19♈19.8
Eris 28♈59.0 ⚵ 5♉06.7
⚷ 11♋16.2 ⚶ 13♒29.5
☽ Mean ☊ 3♊20.1

July 2040 LONGITUDE

Day	Sid.Time	☉	0 hr ☽	Noon ☽	True ☊	☿	♀	♂	⚳	♃	♄	♅	♆	♇
1 Su	6 40 37	10♋15 30	4♈26 40	11♈07 21	3♊12.3	1♋43.2	18♋50.3	3♍06.6	25♊19.1	24♍39.0	5♎45.1	2♌13.3	5♉29.2	26♒52.7
2 M	6 44 33	11 12 43	17 41 54	24 10 42	3 13.0	1R 20.8	20 04.0	3 42.0	25 44.2	24 46.1	5 47.6	2 16.8	5 30.4	26R 51.8
3 Tu	6 48 30	12 09 55	0♉34 11	6♉52 52	3 14.4	1 02.3	21 17.7	4 17.5	26 09.2	24 53.4	5 50.1	2 20.3	5 31.5	26 51.0
4 W	6 52 26	13 07 08	13 07 13	19 17 45	3 15.8	0 47.8	22 31.4	4 53.0	26 34.3	25 00.8	5 52.8	2 23.8	5 32.6	26 50.1
5 Th	6 56 23	14 04 21	25 24 56	1♊29 16	3R 16.6	0 37.8	23 45.1	5 28.6	26 59.3	25 08.3	5 55.6	2 27.4	5 33.7	26 49.3
6 F	7 00 19	15 01 34	7♊31 10	13 31 04	3 16.0	0D 32.4	24 58.8	6 04.2	27 24.3	25 16.0	5 58.4	2 30.9	5 34.8	26 48.4
7 Sa	7 04 16	15 58 48	19 29 21	25 26 21	3 13.7	0 32.0	26 12.6	6 39.9	27 49.3	25 23.8	6 01.4	2 34.5	5 35.8	26 47.4
8 Su	7 08 12	16 56 02	1♋22 24	7♋17 47	3 09.3	0 36.5	27 26.3	7 15.7	28 14.3	25 31.7	6 04.4	2 38.1	5 36.8	26 46.5
9 M	7 12 09	17 53 16	13 12 46	19 07 35	3 02.9	0 46.1	28 40.0	7 51.5	28 39.3	25 39.7	6 07.6	2 41.7	5 37.8	26 45.6
10 Tu	7 16 06	18 50 29	25 02 29	0♌57 41	2 55.1	1 01.0	29 53.7	8 27.4	29 04.3	25 47.9	6 10.8	2 45.3	5 38.7	26 44.6
11 W	7 20 02	19 47 44	6♌53 23	12 49 50	2 46.4	1 21.1	1♌07.4	9 03.3	29 29.2	25 56.1	6 14.1	2 48.9	5 39.7	26 43.6
12 Th	7 23 59	20 44 58	18 47 15	24 45 53	2 37.6	1 46.4	2 21.1	9 39.3	29 54.2	26 04.5	6 17.5	2 52.5	5 40.5	26 42.6
13 F	7 27 55	21 42 12	0♍46 01	6♍47 57	2 29.6	2 17.0	3 34.8	10 15.4	0♋19.1	26 13.0	6 21.0	2 56.1	5 41.4	26 41.6
14 Sa	7 31 52	22 39 26	12 52 00	18 58 32	2 23.1	2 52.8	4 48.5	10 51.5	0 44.0	26 21.6	6 24.5	2 59.8	5 42.2	26 40.6
15 Su	7 35 48	23 36 40	25 07 56	1♎20 37	2 18.6	3 33.9	6 02.2	11 27.7	1 08.8	26 30.3	6 28.2	3 03.4	5 43.0	26 39.5
16 M	7 39 45	24 33 55	7♎37 03	13 57 39	2D 16.2	4 20.1	7 15.9	12 04.0	1 33.7	26 39.1	6 31.9	3 07.1	5 43.7	26 38.4
17 Tu	7 43 41	25 31 09	20 22 54	26 53 17	2 15.6	5 11.4	8 29.6	12 40.2	1 58.5	26 48.0	6 35.7	3 10.7	5 44.5	26 37.4
18 W	7 47 38	26 28 24	3♏29 13	10♏11 06	2 16.2	6 07.8	9 43.2	13 16.6	2 23.3	26 57.0	6 39.6	3 14.4	5 45.1	26 36.3
19 Th	7 51 35	27 25 39	16 59 18	23 54 02	2R 17.1	7 09.2	10 56.9	13 53.0	2 48.1	27 06.1	6 43.6	3 18.0	5 45.8	26 35.2
20 F	7 55 31	28 22 54	0♐55 27	8♐03 33	2 17.1	8 15.5	12 10.6	14 29.5	3 12.9	27 15.4	6 47.7	3 21.7	5 46.4	26 34.1
21 Sa	7 59 28	29 20 09	15 18 09	22 38 54	2 15.6	9 26.6	13 24.3	15 06.0	3 37.6	27 24.7	6 51.8	3 25.4	5 47.0	26 32.9
22 Su	8 03 24	0♌17 25	0♑05 13	7♑36 18	2 11.8	10 42.5	14 37.9	15 42.5	4 02.4	27 34.1	6 56.0	3 29.1	5 47.6	26 31.8
23 M	8 07 21	1 14 41	15 11 10	22 48 41	2 05.7	12 03.1	15 51.6	16 19.2	4 27.1	27 43.6	7 00.3	3 32.8	5 48.1	26 30.6
24 Tu	8 11 17	2 11 58	0♒27 31	8♒06 17	1 57.7	13 28.2	17 05.2	16 55.8	4 51.7	27 53.3	7 04.7	3 36.5	5 48.6	26 29.5
25 W	8 15 14	3 09 15	15 43 35	23 18 04	1 48.9	14 57.7	18 18.9	17 32.6	5 16.4	28 03.0	7 09.1	3 40.2	5 49.1	26 28.3
26 Th	8 19 11	4 06 33	0♓48 27	8♓13 38	1 40.2	16 31.4	19 32.5	18 09.4	5 41.0	28 12.8	7 13.7	3 43.8	5 49.5	26 27.1
27 F	8 23 07	5 03 52	15 32 45	22 45 06	1 32.7	18 09.2	20 46.2	18 46.2	6 05.6	28 22.6	7 18.2	3 47.5	5 49.9	26 25.9
28 Sa	8 27 04	6 01 12	29 50 13	6♈47 54	1 27.3	19 50.9	21 59.8	19 23.1	6 30.1	28 32.6	7 22.9	3 51.2	5 50.3	26 24.7
29 Su	8 31 00	6 58 33	13♈38 06	20 20 59	1 24.0	21 36.2	23 13.4	20 00.0	6 54.7	28 42.7	7 27.6	3 54.9	5 50.6	26 23.5
30 M	8 34 57	7 55 54	26 56 50	3♉26 05	1D 22.8	23 24.8	24 27.1	20 37.1	7 19.2	28 52.8	7 32.5	3 58.6	5 51.0	26 22.2
31 Tu	8 38 53	8 53 17	9♉49 14	16 06 51	1 22.8	25 16.6	25 40.7	21 14.1	7 43.7	29 03.1	7 37.3	4 02.3	5 51.2	26 21.0

August 2040 LONGITUDE

Day	Sid.Time	☉	0 hr ☽	Noon ☽	True ☊	☿	♀	♂	⚳	♃	♄	♅	♆	♇
1 W	8 42 50	9♌50 42	22♉19 33	28♉27 57	1♊23.2	27♋11.1	26♌54.3	21♍51.2	8♋08.1	29♍13.4	7♎42.3	4♌05.9	5♉51.5	26♒19.8
2 Th	8 46 46	10 48 07	4♊32 40	10♊34 20	1R 22.9	29 08.0	28 08.0	22 28.4	8 32.5	29 23.8	7 47.3	4 09.6	5 51.7	26R 18.5
3 F	8 50 43	11 45 33	16 33 33	22 30 50	1 20.9	1♌06.9	29 21.6	23 05.7	8 56.9	29 34.3	7 52.4	4 13.3	5 51.8	26 17.2
4 Sa	8 54 40	12 43 01	28 26 44	4♋21 43	1 16.5	3 07.6	0♍35.2	23 43.0	9 21.2	29 44.9	7 57.6	4 17.0	5 52.0	26 16.0
5 Su	8 58 36	13 40 29	10♋16 14	16 10 38	1 09.3	5 09.7	1 48.8	24 20.3	9 45.6	29 55.5	8 02.8	4 20.6	5 52.1	26 14.7
6 M	9 02 33	14 37 59	22 05 17	28 00 28	0 59.5	7 12.7	3 02.5	24 57.7	10 09.8	0♎06.2	8 08.1	4 24.3	5 52.2	26 13.4
7 Tu	9 06 29	15 35 30	3♌56 27	9♌53 26	0 47.6	9 16.4	4 16.1	25 35.2	10 34.1	0 17.0	8 13.4	4 27.9	5R 52.2	26 12.1
8 W	9 10 26	16 33 02	15 51 36	21 51 09	0 34.5	11 20.5	5 29.7	26 12.7	10 58.3	0 27.9	8 18.8	4 31.6	5 52.2	26 10.8
9 Th	9 14 22	17 30 35	27 52 12	3♍54 55	0 21.2	13 24.7	6 43.3	26 50.3	11 22.4	0 38.9	8 24.3	4 35.2	5 52.2	26 09.5
10 F	9 18 19	18 28 09	9♍59 25	16 05 54	0 08.9	15 28.6	7 56.8	27 27.9	11 46.5	0 49.9	8 29.9	4 38.8	5 52.1	26 08.2
11 Sa	9 22 15	19 25 43	22 14 29	28 25 24	29♉58.5	17 32.2	9 10.4	28 05.6	12 10.6	1 01.0	8 35.5	4 42.4	5 52.0	26 06.9
12 Su	9 26 12	20 23 19	4♎38 51	10♎55 07	29 50.8	19 35.1	10 24.0	28 43.4	12 34.6	1 12.1	8 41.1	4 46.0	5 51.9	26 05.6
13 M	9 30 08	21 20 56	17 14 27	23 37 11	29 45.9	21 37.2	11 37.6	29 21.2	12 58.6	1 23.4	8 46.8	4 49.6	5 51.8	26 04.3
14 Tu	9 34 05	22 18 34	0♏03 40	6♏34 16	29 43.5	23 38.4	12 51.1	29 59.0	13 22.5	1 34.7	8 52.6	4 53.1	5 51.6	26 03.0
15 W	9 38 02	23 16 12	13 09 21	19 49 17	29 42.8	25 38.6	14 04.6	0♎36.9	13 46.4	1 46.0	8 58.4	4 56.7	5 51.3	26 01.7
16 Th	9 41 58	24 13 52	26 34 24	3♐25 00	29 42.8	27 37.6	15 18.2	1 14.9	14 10.2	1 57.4	9 04.3	5 00.2	5 51.1	26 00.4
17 F	9 45 55	25 11 33	10♐21 19	17 23 27	29 42.2	29 35.4	16 31.7	1 52.9	14 34.0	2 08.9	9 10.3	5 03.8	5 50.8	25 59.1
18 Sa	9 49 51	26 09 15	24 31 25	1♑45 03	29 39.8	1♍31.9	17 45.2	2 31.0	14 57.8	2 20.5	9 16.3	5 07.3	5 50.5	25 57.7
19 Su	9 53 48	27 06 58	9♑04 02	16 27 48	29 34.9	3 27.1	18 58.7	3 09.1	15 21.5	2 32.1	9 22.3	5 10.8	5 50.1	25 56.4
20 M	9 57 44	28 04 42	23 55 40	1♒26 43	29 27.3	5 20.9	20 12.2	3 47.3	15 45.1	2 43.7	9 28.4	5 14.3	5 49.8	25 55.1
21 Tu	10 01 41	29 02 27	8♒59 51	16 33 52	29 17.5	7 13.4	21 25.6	4 25.5	16 08.7	2 55.5	9 34.6	5 17.7	5 49.3	25 53.8
22 W	10 05 38	0♍00 13	24 07 28	1♓39 21	29 06.5	9 04.6	22 39.1	5 03.8	16 32.2	3 07.2	9 40.8	5 21.2	5 48.9	25 52.5
23 Th	10 09 34	0 58 01	9♓08 14	16 32 57	28 55.6	10 54.3	23 52.5	5 42.1	16 55.7	3 19.0	9 47.0	5 24.6	5 48.4	25 51.2
24 F	10 13 31	1 55 50	23 52 28	1♈05 56	28 45.9	12 42.7	25 05.9	6 20.5	17 19.1	3 30.9	9 53.3	5 28.0	5 47.9	25 49.9
25 Sa	10 17 27	2 53 41	8♈12 43	15 12 26	28 38.5	14 29.8	26 19.3	6 58.9	17 42.4	3 42.8	9 59.6	5 31.4	5 47.4	25 48.6
26 Su	10 21 24	3 51 34	22 04 50	28 49 56	28 33.6	16 15.5	27 32.7	7 37.4	18 05.7	3 54.8	10 06.0	5 34.8	5 46.8	25 47.3
27 M	10 25 20	4 49 29	5♉27 54	11♉59 03	28 31.2	17 59.8	28 46.1	8 16.0	18 29.0	4 06.9	10 12.4	5 38.1	5 46.2	25 46.0
28 Tu	10 29 17	5 47 25	18 23 47	24 42 40	28 30.4	19 42.9	29 59.5	8 54.6	18 52.2	4 18.9	10 18.9	5 41.4	5 45.6	25 44.7
29 W	10 33 13	6 45 23	0♊56 16	7♊05 13	28 30.5	21 24.6	1♎12.9	9 33.2	19 15.3	4 31.1	10 25.4	5 44.7	5 44.9	25 43.4
30 Th	10 37 10	7 43 23	13 10 12	19 11 52	28 30.1	23 05.1	2 26.2	10 12.0	19 38.3	4 43.2	10 32.0	5 48.0	5 44.2	25 42.1
31 F	10 41 06	8 41 25	25 10 54	1♋07 56	28 28.2	24 44.3	3 39.6	10 50.7	20 01.3	4 55.4	10 38.6	5 51.3	5 43.5	25 40.8

Astro Data Dy Hr Mn	Planet Ingress Dy Hr Mn	Last Aspect Dy Hr Mn	☽ Ingress Dy Hr Mn	Last Aspect Dy Hr Mn	☽ Ingress Dy Hr Mn	☽ Phases & Eclipses Dy Hr Mn	Astro Data
☽0N 1 9:27	♀ ♌ 10 14:03	2 17:01 ♇ ✶	♉ 2 22:55	1 13:31 ♃ △	♊ 1 15:01	1 10:19 ☾ 10♈11	1 July 2040
☿D 7 2:21	⚳ ♋ 12 17:37	5 2:47 ♇ □	♊ 5 9:03	4 2:30 ♃ □	♋ 4 3:09	9 9:16 ● 17♋47	Julian Day # 51317
☽0S 16 3:32	☉ ♌ 22 4:42	7 14:44 ♇ △	♋ 7 21:13	6 5:29 ♂ ✶	♌ 6 16:02	17 9:17 ☽ 25♎25	SVP 4♓41'53"
♃⊼♇ 16 10:27		10 9:35 ♀ ☌	♌ 10 10:03	8 20:37 ♇ ☍	♍ 9 4:14	24 2:07 ○ 1♒48	GC 27♐24.3 ⚴ 28♉06.3
☽0N 28 16:23	☿ ♌ 2 22:33	12 15:53 ♇ ☍	♍ 12 22:28	11 11:20 ♂ ☌	♎ 11 15:03	30 21:07 ☾ 8♉18	Eris 29♈10.4 ⚵ 21♉29.2
	♀ ♍ 4 0:31	15 2:33 ♃ ☌	♎ 15 9:25	13 16:35 ♇ △	♏ 13 23:53		⚷ 14♋15.4 ⚶ 13♒12.6R
♆R 8 5:25	♃ ♎ 5 22:04	17 11:31 ♇ △	♏ 17 17:41	16 0:08 ☿ □	♐ 16 6:02	8 0:28 ● 16♌05	☽ Mean ☊ 1♊44.8
☽0S 12 8:25	☊ ♉R 11 8:15	19 18:29 ☉ △	♐ 19 22:26	18 2:25 ♇ ✶	♑ 18 9:06	15 18:37 ☽ 23♏32	
♂0S 16 15:02	♂ ♎ 14 12:37	21 19:47 ♃ □	♑ 21 23:52	19 16:25 ♀ △	♒ 20 9:42	22 9:11 ○ 29♒53	1 August 2040
♃0S 19 22:41	☿ ♍ 17 17:03	23 19:48 ♃ △	♒ 23 23:17	22 9:11 ☉ ☍	♓ 22 9:21	29 11:18 ☾ 6♊44	Julian Day # 51348
☽0N 25 1:10	☉ ♍ 22 11:54	25 17:03 ♇ ☌	♓ 25 22:42	24 1:06 ♀ ☍	♈ 24 10:10		SVP 4♓41'48"
♅□♆ 29 13:10	♀ ♎ 28 12:10	27 21:37 ♃ ☍	♈ 28 0:17	26 6:34 ♇ ✶	♉ 26 14:06		GC 27♐24.4 ⚴ 5♉07.1
♀0S 30 10:39		29 22:58 ♇ ✶	♉ 30 5:37	28 13:59 ♇ □	♊ 28 22:11		Eris 29♈13.1R ⚵ 8♊06.3
♄□♇ 31 18:48				31 1:01 ♇ △	♋ 31 9:43		⚷ 17♋26.4 ⚶ 6♒43.6R
							☽ Mean ☊ 0♊06.3

LONGITUDE — September 2040

Day	Sid.Time	☉	0 hr ☽	Noon ☽	True ☊	☿	♀	♂	⚳	♃	♄	♅	♆	♇
1 Sa	10 45 03	9♍39 29	7♋03 35	12♋58 27	28♉24.0	26♍22.2	4♎52.9	11♎29.6	20♋24.2	5♎07.7	10♎45.2	5♌54.5	5♉42.8	25♒39.5
2 Su	10 49 00	10 37 35	18 53 04	24 47 55	28R 17.2	27 58.9	6 06.2	12 08.5	20 47.1	5 20.0	10 51.9	5 57.7	5R 42.0	25R 38.3
3 M	10 52 56	11 35 43	0♌43 29	6♌40 07	28 07.8	29 34.4	7 19.6	12 47.4	21 09.9	5 32.4	10 58.6	6 00.9	5 41.2	25 37.0
4 Tu	10 56 53	12 33 52	12 38 10	18 37 56	27 56.2	1♎08.6	8 32.9	13 26.4	21 32.6	5 44.7	11 05.4	6 04.0	5 40.3	25 35.8
5 W	11 00 49	13 32 03	24 39 38	0♍43 27	27 43.2	2 41.6	9 46.1	14 05.5	21 55.2	5 57.2	11 12.1	6 07.1	5 39.5	25 34.5
6 Th	11 04 46	14 30 16	6♍49 32	12 58 00	27 30.1	4 13.4	10 59.4	14 44.6	22 17.8	6 09.6	11 19.0	6 10.2	5 38.6	25 33.3
7 F	11 08 42	15 28 31	19 08 53	25 22 17	27 17.9	5 43.9	12 12.7	15 23.8	22 40.2	6 22.1	11 25.8	6 13.3	5 37.6	25 32.1
8 Sa	11 12 39	16 26 47	1♎38 12	7♎56 43	27 07.7	7 13.3	13 25.9	16 03.0	23 02.6	6 34.7	11 32.7	6 16.3	5 36.7	25 30.8
9 Su	11 16 35	17 25 05	14 17 51	20 41 40	27 00.0	8 41.4	14 39.1	16 42.3	23 25.0	6 47.2	11 39.6	6 19.3	5 35.7	25 29.6
10 M	11 20 32	18 23 24	27 08 15	3♏37 44	26 55.3	10 08.3	15 52.3	17 21.7	23 47.2	6 59.8	11 46.6	6 22.3	5 34.7	25 28.4
11 Tu	11 24 29	19 21 46	10♏10 13	16 45 53	26D 53.0	11 33.9	17 05.5	18 01.1	24 09.3	7 12.4	11 53.5	6 25.3	5 33.7	25 27.2
12 W	11 28 25	20 20 09	23 24 55	0♐07 30	26 52.7	12 58.3	18 18.7	18 40.5	24 31.4	7 25.1	12 00.5	6 28.2	5 32.6	25 26.1
13 Th	11 32 22	21 18 33	6♐53 50	13 44 06	26R 53.1	14 21.3	19 31.9	19 20.0	24 53.3	7 37.8	12 07.6	6 31.1	5 31.5	25 24.9
14 F	11 36 18	22 16 59	20 38 27	27 36 58	26 53.1	15 43.0	20 45.0	19 59.6	25 15.2	7 50.5	12 14.6	6 33.9	5 30.4	25 23.8
15 Sa	11 40 15	23 15 27	4♑39 41	11♑46 32	26 51.7	17 03.4	21 58.1	20 39.2	25 37.0	8 03.2	12 21.7	6 36.7	5 29.3	25 22.6
16 Su	11 44 11	24 13 56	18 57 19	26 11 42	26 48.2	18 22.4	23 11.2	21 18.9	25 58.7	8 16.0	12 28.8	6 39.5	5 28.2	25 21.5
17 M	11 48 08	25 12 27	3♒29 13	10♒49 17	26 42.2	19 39.9	24 24.3	21 58.6	26 20.3	8 28.8	12 35.9	6 42.2	5 27.0	25 20.4
18 Tu	11 52 04	26 11 00	18 11 09	25 33 56	26 34.3	20 55.9	25 37.3	22 38.4	26 41.8	8 41.6	12 43.1	6 45.0	5 25.8	25 19.3
19 W	11 56 01	27 09 34	2♓56 42	10♓18 27	26 25.1	22 10.3	26 50.4	23 18.2	27 03.2	8 54.4	12 50.3	6 47.6	5 24.6	25 18.2
20 Th	11 59 58	28 08 10	17 38 10	24 54 51	26 16.0	23 23.0	28 03.4	23 58.1	27 24.5	9 07.2	12 57.4	6 50.3	5 23.3	25 17.1
21 F	12 03 54	29 06 48	2♈07 38	9♈15 41	26 07.8	24 34.0	29 16.3	24 38.1	27 45.7	9 20.1	13 04.6	6 52.9	5 22.1	25 16.1
22 Sa	12 07 51	0♎05 27	16 18 21	23 15 10	26 01.6	25 43.2	0♏29.3	25 18.1	28 06.7	9 33.0	13 11.9	6 55.4	5 20.8	25 15.0
23 Su	12 11 47	1 04 09	0♉05 46	6♉50 01	25 57.6	26 50.4	1 42.2	25 58.1	28 27.7	9 45.9	13 19.1	6 57.9	5 19.5	25 14.0
24 M	12 15 44	2 02 54	13 27 53	19 59 30	25D 55.8	27 55.5	2 55.1	26 38.3	28 48.6	9 58.8	13 26.4	7 00.4	5 18.1	25 13.0
25 Tu	12 19 40	3 01 40	26 25 10	2♊45 13	25 55.9	28 58.5	4 08.0	27 18.4	29 09.3	10 11.7	13 33.6	7 02.9	5 16.8	25 12.0
26 W	12 23 37	4 00 29	9♊00 07	15 10 25	25 56.9	29 59.0	5 20.9	27 58.7	29 30.0	10 24.7	13 40.9	7 05.3	5 15.4	25 11.0
27 Th	12 27 33	4 59 20	21 16 40	27 19 31	25R 57.9	0♏57.0	6 33.8	28 38.9	29 50.5	10 37.6	13 48.2	7 07.6	5 14.0	25 10.1
28 F	12 31 30	5 58 13	3♋19 36	9♋17 33	25 58.2	1 52.2	7 46.6	29 19.3	0♌10.9	10 50.6	13 55.5	7 10.0	5 12.6	25 09.1
29 Sa	12 35 27	6 57 08	15 14 02	21 09 40	25 56.9	2 44.4	8 59.4	29 59.7	0 31.2	11 03.5	14 02.8	7 12.2	5 11.2	25 08.2
30 Su	12 39 23	7 56 06	27 05 04	3♌00 50	25 53.6	3 33.3	10 12.2	0♏40.2	0 51.4	11 16.5	14 10.2	7 14.5	5 09.7	25 07.3

LONGITUDE — October 2040

Day	Sid.Time	☉	0 hr ☽	Noon ☽	True ☊	☿	♀	♂	⚳	♃	♄	♅	♆	♇
1 M	12 43 20	8♎55 06	8♌57 30	14♌55 35	25♉48.4	4♏18.7	11♏25.0	1♏20.7	1♌11.4	11♎29.5	14♎17.5	7♌16.7	5♉08.3	25♒06.4
2 Tu	12 47 16	9 54 08	20 55 33	26 57 47	25R 41.5	5 00.3	12 37.8	2 01.3	1 31.3	11 42.5	14 24.9	7 18.8	5R 06.8	25R 05.6
3 W	12 51 13	10 53 13	3♍02 38	9♍10 24	25 33.5	5 37.7	13 50.5	2 41.9	1 51.1	11 55.5	14 32.2	7 20.9	5 05.3	25 04.7
4 Th	12 55 09	11 52 19	15 21 18	21 35 30	25 25.2	6 10.6	15 03.2	3 22.6	2 10.7	12 08.5	14 39.6	7 23.0	5 03.8	25 03.9
5 F	12 59 06	12 51 28	27 53 07	4♎14 10	25 17.5	6 38.5	16 15.9	4 03.4	2 30.2	12 21.5	14 46.9	7 25.0	5 02.3	25 03.1
6 Sa	13 03 02	13 50 38	10♎38 40	17 06 35	25 11.2	7 01.0	17 28.6	4 44.2	2 49.6	12 34.5	14 54.3	7 27.0	5 00.7	25 02.3
7 Su	13 06 59	14 49 51	23 37 49	0♏12 16	25 06.6	7 17.7	18 41.2	5 25.0	3 08.8	12 47.5	15 01.6	7 28.9	4 59.2	25 01.5
8 M	13 10 55	15 49 06	6♏49 49	13 30 20	25D 04.2	7 28.1	19 53.9	6 06.0	3 27.8	13 00.5	15 09.0	7 30.8	4 57.6	25 00.8
9 Tu	13 14 52	16 48 23	20 13 41	26 59 45	25 03.6	7R 31.6	21 06.5	6 46.9	3 46.7	13 13.5	15 16.4	7 32.6	4 56.0	25 00.1
10 W	13 18 49	17 47 41	3♐48 25	10♐39 35	25 04.4	7 28.0	22 19.0	7 28.0	4 05.5	13 26.5	15 23.7	7 34.4	4 54.5	24 59.4
11 Th	13 22 45	18 47 02	17 33 11	24 29 06	25 05.8	7 16.6	23 31.6	8 09.1	4 24.1	13 39.5	15 31.1	7 36.1	4 52.9	24 58.7
12 F	13 26 42	19 46 24	1♑27 17	8♑27 37	25R 07.1	6 57.2	24 44.1	8 50.2	4 42.5	13 52.5	15 38.4	7 37.8	4 51.2	24 58.0
13 Sa	13 30 38	20 45 48	15 29 59	22 34 14	25 07.5	6 29.6	25 56.6	9 31.5	5 00.8	14 05.4	15 45.8	7 39.5	4 49.6	24 57.4
14 Su	13 34 35	21 45 14	29 40 12	6♒47 36	25 06.6	5 53.5	27 09.0	10 12.7	5 18.9	14 18.4	15 53.1	7 41.1	4 48.0	24 56.8
15 M	13 38 31	22 44 41	13♒56 10	21 05 29	25 04.2	5 09.1	28 21.4	10 54.0	5 36.8	14 31.3	16 00.5	7 42.6	4 46.4	24 56.2
16 Tu	13 42 28	23 44 10	28 15 09	5♓24 40	25 00.5	4 16.8	29 33.8	11 35.4	5 54.6	14 44.3	16 07.8	7 44.1	4 44.7	24 55.6
17 W	13 46 25	24 43 41	12♓33 29	19 41 01	24 56.1	3 17.3	0♐46.1	12 16.8	6 12.2	14 57.2	16 15.1	7 45.5	4 43.1	24 55.1
18 Th	13 50 21	25 43 13	26 46 40	3♈49 51	24 51.5	2 11.6	1 58.4	12 58.3	6 29.6	15 10.1	16 22.4	7 46.9	4 41.4	24 54.6
19 F	13 54 18	26 42 48	10♈49 59	17 46 34	24 47.5	1 01.0	3 10.7	13 39.9	6 46.8	15 23.0	16 29.7	7 48.3	4 39.8	24 54.1
20 Sa	13 58 14	27 42 24	24 39 06	1♉27 14	24 44.5	29♎47.3	4 22.9	14 21.5	7 03.8	15 35.8	16 37.0	7 49.6	4 38.1	24 53.6
21 Su	14 02 11	28 42 03	8♉10 39	14 49 10	24D 42.8	28 32.4	5 35.1	15 03.1	7 20.7	15 48.7	16 44.2	7 50.8	4 36.4	24 53.2
22 M	14 06 07	29 41 43	21 22 40	27 51 10	24 42.5	27 18.7	6 47.3	15 44.8	7 37.3	16 01.5	16 51.5	7 52.0	4 34.7	24 52.8
23 Tu	14 10 04	0♏41 26	4♊14 47	10♊33 42	24 43.3	26 08.2	7 59.4	16 26.6	7 53.8	16 14.3	16 58.7	7 53.1	4 33.1	24 52.4
24 W	14 14 00	1 41 11	16 48 10	22 58 35	24 44.8	25 03.2	9 11.5	17 08.4	8 10.1	16 27.1	17 05.9	7 54.2	4 31.4	24 52.0
25 Th	14 17 57	2 40 58	29 05 19	5♋08 52	24 46.5	24 05.6	10 23.6	17 50.3	8 26.2	16 39.9	17 13.1	7 55.2	4 29.7	24 51.6
26 F	14 21 54	3 40 48	11♋09 45	17 08 30	24 47.9	23 17.0	11 35.6	18 32.3	8 42.0	16 52.6	17 20.3	7 56.2	4 28.0	24 51.3
27 Sa	14 25 50	4 40 39	23 05 42	29 01 58	24R 48.8	22 38.7	12 47.5	19 14.3	8 57.7	17 05.3	17 27.4	7 57.1	4 26.3	24 51.0
28 Su	14 29 47	5 40 33	4♌57 52	10♌54 03	24 48.8	22 11.4	13 59.5	19 56.3	9 13.1	17 18.0	17 34.6	7 58.0	4 24.6	24 50.8
29 M	14 33 43	6 40 29	16 51 05	22 49 34	24 48.0	21D 55.6	15 11.4	20 38.4	9 28.3	17 30.7	17 41.7	7 58.8	4 23.0	24 50.5
30 Tu	14 37 40	7 40 27	28 50 03	4♍53 05	24 46.3	21 51.3	16 23.2	21 20.6	9 43.3	17 43.3	17 48.8	7 59.6	4 21.3	24 50.3
31 W	14 41 36	8 40 27	10♍59 09	17 08 42	24 44.2	21 58.2	17 35.0	22 02.9	9 58.0	17 55.9	17 55.8	8 00.3	4 19.6	24 50.1

Astro Data

	Dy Hr Mn
☿0S	3 23:54
♃⚻♆	4 4:00
♃✳♆	6 13:33
☽0S	8 13:30
☽0N	21 11:02
⊙0S	22 9:46
♃□♇	25 12:31
☽0S	5 20:20
☿R	9 12:06
☽0N	18 20:22
☿D	30 9:06
♃☌♄	31 11:48

Planet Ingress

	Dy Hr Mn
☿ ♎	3 18:30
♀ ♏	22 2:22
⊙ ♎	22 9:46
☿ ♏	26 12:24
⚳ ♌	27 23:08
♂ ♏	29 12:11
♀ ♐	16 20:41
☿ ♎R	20 7:54
⊙ ♏	22 19:21

Last Aspect / ☽ Ingress (September)

Last Aspect Dy Hr Mn		☽ Ingress Dy Hr Mn
2 19:27 ☿ ✳	♌	2 22:32
5 1:50 ♇ ☍	♍	5 10:34
6 15:15 ⊙ ☍	♎	7 20:52
9 20:56 ♇ △	♏	10 5:18
12 3:38 ♇ □	♐	12 11:47
14 8:12 ♇ ✳	♑	14 16:04
16 8:31 ⊙ △	♒	16 18:16
18 12:06 ♀ △	♓	18 19:13
20 17:44 ⊙ ☍	♈	20 20:27
22 16:42 ☿ ☍	♉	22 23:50
24 21:44 ♇ □	♊	25 6:46
27 14:48 ♂ △	♋	27 17:20
28 21:27 ♄ □	♌	30 5:54

Last Aspect / ☽ Ingress (October)

Last Aspect Dy Hr Mn		☽ Ingress Dy Hr Mn
2 8:18 ♇ ☍	♍	2 18:00
3 22:03 ♀ ✳	♎	5 4:00
7 2:34 ♇ △	♏	7 11:38
9 8:28 ♇ □	♐	9 17:18
11 12:51 ♇ ✳	♑	11 21:30
13 18:14 ♀ ✳	♒	14 0:33
16 1:18 ⊙ △	♓	16 2:56
16 22:54 ♂ △	♈	18 5:28
20 9:18 ☿ ☍	♉	20 9:25
22 6:28 ♇ □	♊	22 16:01
24 15:45 ☿ △	♋	25 1:48
26 23:42 ☿ □	♌	27 13:57
29 16:02 ♇ ☍	♍	30 2:19

☽ Phases & Eclipses

Dy Hr Mn		
6 15:15	●	14♍38
14 2:09	☽	21♐53
20 17:44	○	28♓22
28 4:43	☾	5♋40
6 5:27	●	13♎34
13 8:42	☽	20♑38
20 4:51	○	27♈25
28 0:28	☾	5♌12

Astro Data

1 September 2040
Julian Day # 51379
SVP 4♓41'44"
GC 27♐24.4 ⚴ 8♉16.3
Eris 29♈06.0R ⚵ 23♊43.1
⚷ 20♋15.3 ⚶ 1♒14.4R
☽ Mean ☊ 28♉27.8

1 October 2040
Julian Day # 51409
SVP 4♓41'41"
GC 27♐24.5 ⚴ 5♉19.0R
Eris 28♈51.5R ⚵ 6♋41.1
⚷ 22♋11.0 ⚶ 2♒25.2
☽ Mean ☊ 26♉52.5

November 2040 LONGITUDE

Day	Sid.Time	☉	0 hr ☽	Noon ☽	True ☊	☿	♀	♂	⚳	♃	♄	♅	♆	♇
1 Th	14 45 33	9♏40 29	23♍22 06	29♍39 41	24♉41.8	22♎15.7	18♐46.8	22♏45.2	10♌12.5	18♎08.4	18♎02.9	8♌00.9	4♉17.9	24♒49.9
2 F	14 49 29	10 40 33	6♎01 43	12♎28 21	24R 39.7	22 43.3	19 58.5	23 27.5	10 26.8	18 21.0	18 09.9	8 01.5	4R 16.2	24R 49.8
3 Sa	14 53 26	11 40 40	18 59 41	25 35 43	24 37.9	23 20.0	21 10.2	24 09.9	10 40.9	18 33.5	18 16.9	8 02.1	4 14.5	24 49.7
4 Su	14 57 22	12 40 48	2♏16 23	9♏01 31	24 36.9	24 05.0	22 21.8	24 52.4	10 54.6	18 45.9	18 23.8	8 02.5	4 12.9	24 49.6
5 M	15 01 19	13 40 58	15 50 53	22 44 09	24D 36.5	24 57.4	23 33.4	25 34.9	11 08.2	18 58.3	18 30.7	8 03.0	4 11.2	24 49.5
6 Tu	15 05 16	14 41 10	29 40 58	6♐40 54	24 36.7	25 56.4	24 45.0	26 17.5	11 21.4	19 10.7	18 37.6	8 03.3	4 09.6	24D 49.5
7 W	15 09 12	15 41 23	13♐43 31	20 48 18	24 37.3	27 01.2	25 56.5	27 00.1	11 34.5	19 23.0	18 44.5	8 03.7	4 07.9	24 49.5
8 Th	15 13 09	16 41 39	27 54 48	5♑02 31	24 38.0	28 10.9	27 07.9	27 42.8	11 47.2	19 35.3	18 51.3	8 03.9	4 06.3	24 49.5
9 F	15 17 05	17 41 56	12♑11 00	19 19 47	24 38.7	29 24.9	28 19.3	28 25.6	11 59.7	19 47.6	18 58.1	8 04.1	4 04.6	24 49.5
10 Sa	15 21 02	18 42 14	26 28 28	3♒36 40	24 39.2	0♏42.6	29 30.6	29 08.4	12 11.9	19 59.8	19 04.8	8 04.3	4 03.0	24 49.6
11 Su	15 24 58	19 42 33	10♒44 02	17 50 16	24R 39.3	2 03.4	0♑41.8	29 51.3	12 23.8	20 11.9	19 11.5	8 04.4	4 01.4	24 49.7
12 M	15 28 55	20 42 54	24 55 04	1♓58 12	24 39.3	3 26.8	1 53.0	0♐34.2	12 35.4	20 24.0	19 18.2	8R 04.4	3 59.8	24 49.8
13 Tu	15 32 52	21 43 16	8♓59 25	15 58 31	24 39.0	4 52.3	3 04.1	1 17.1	12 46.8	20 36.0	19 24.8	8 04.4	3 58.2	24 50.0
14 W	15 36 48	22 43 40	22 55 18	29 49 34	24 38.8	6 19.8	4 15.1	2 00.2	12 57.8	20 48.0	19 31.4	8 04.4	3 56.6	24 50.2
15 Th	15 40 45	23 44 05	6♈41 10	13♈29 54	24D 38.6	7 48.7	5 26.1	2 43.2	13 08.6	20 59.9	19 37.9	8 04.2	3 55.1	24 50.4
16 F	15 44 41	24 44 31	20 15 37	26 58 10	24 38.6	9 18.8	6 37.0	3 26.4	13 19.0	21 11.8	19 44.4	8 04.0	3 53.5	24 50.6
17 Sa	15 48 38	25 44 59	3♉37 26	10♉13 16	24 38.6	10 50.0	7 47.8	4 09.5	13 29.1	21 23.6	19 50.9	8 03.8	3 52.0	24 50.9
18 Su	15 52 34	26 45 28	16 45 37	23 14 23	24R 38.7	12 22.0	8 58.5	4 52.8	13 39.0	21 35.4	19 57.3	8 03.5	3 50.4	24 51.1
19 M	15 56 31	27 45 59	29 39 32	6♊01 07	24 38.6	13 54.6	10 09.1	5 36.1	13 48.5	21 47.1	20 03.6	8 03.2	3 48.9	24 51.4
20 Tu	16 00 27	28 46 32	12♊19 08	18 33 43	24 38.4	15 27.7	11 19.7	6 19.4	13 57.7	21 58.7	20 09.9	8 02.8	3 47.4	24 51.8
21 W	16 04 24	29 47 06	24 44 59	0♋53 09	24 37.8	17 01.3	12 30.2	7 02.8	14 06.6	22 10.3	20 16.2	8 02.3	3 45.9	24 52.2
22 Th	16 08 21	0♐47 42	6♋58 26	13 01 09	24 37.0	18 35.1	13 40.5	7 46.3	14 15.1	22 21.8	20 22.4	8 01.8	3 44.5	24 52.5
23 F	16 12 17	1 48 19	19 01 38	25 00 16	24 36.1	20 09.1	14 50.8	8 29.8	14 23.3	22 33.3	20 28.5	8 01.3	3 43.0	24 53.0
24 Sa	16 16 14	2 48 58	0♌57 28	6♌53 43	24 35.1	21 43.3	16 01.0	9 13.4	14 31.1	22 44.7	20 34.6	8 00.7	3 41.6	24 53.4
25 Su	16 20 10	3 49 38	12 49 31	18 45 24	24 34.3	23 17.6	17 11.1	9 57.0	14 38.7	22 56.0	20 40.7	8 00.0	3 40.2	24 53.9
26 M	16 24 07	4 50 20	24 41 56	0♍39 40	24D 33.9	24 51.9	18 21.1	10 40.7	14 45.8	23 07.2	20 46.7	7 59.3	3 38.8	24 54.4
27 Tu	16 28 03	5 51 04	6♍39 14	12 41 11	24 34.0	26 26.3	19 31.0	11 24.4	14 52.6	23 18.4	20 52.6	7 58.5	3 37.4	24 54.9
28 W	16 32 00	6 51 49	18 46 07	24 54 37	24 34.5	28 00.6	20 40.8	12 08.2	14 59.0	23 29.5	20 58.5	7 57.7	3 36.1	24 55.4
29 Th	16 35 56	7 52 36	1♎07 13	7♎24 25	24 35.6	29 35.0	21 50.5	12 52.0	15 05.1	23 40.5	21 04.3	7 56.8	3 34.7	24 56.0
30 F	16 39 53	8 53 24	13 46 42	20 14 27	24 36.9	1♐09.3	23 00.1	13 35.9	15 10.8	23 51.5	21 10.1	7 55.9	3 33.4	24 56.6

December 2040 LONGITUDE

Day	Sid.Time	☉	0 hr ☽	Noon ☽	True ☊	☿	♀	♂	⚳	♃	♄	♅	♆	♇
1 Sa	16 43 50	9♐54 13	26♎47 56	3♏27 25	24♉38.1	2♐43.6	24♑09.5	14♐19.9	15♌16.1	24♎02.3	21♎15.8	7♌54.9	3♉32.1	24♒57.2
2 Su	16 47 46	10 55 04	10♏12 57	17 04 31	24R 38.8	4 17.9	25 18.9	15 03.9	15 21.0	24 13.1	21 21.4	7R 53.9	3R 30.8	24 57.9
3 M	16 51 43	11 55 57	24 01 58	1♐04 58	24 38.9	5 52.1	26 28.1	15 48.0	15 25.5	24 23.8	21 27.0	7 52.8	3 29.6	24 58.6
4 Tu	16 55 39	12 56 50	8♐13 04	15 25 42	24 37.9	7 26.3	27 37.2	16 32.1	15 29.7	24 34.4	21 32.5	7 51.7	3 28.4	24 59.3
5 W	16 59 36	13 57 45	22 42 08	0♑01 34	24 36.1	9 00.5	28 46.2	17 16.3	15 33.4	24 45.0	21 37.9	7 50.5	3 27.2	25 00.0
6 Th	17 03 32	14 58 41	7♑23 06	14 45 48	24 33.4	10 34.6	29 55.0	18 00.5	15 36.7	24 55.4	21 43.3	7 49.2	3 26.0	25 00.8
7 F	17 07 29	15 59 37	22 08 43	29 30 57	24 30.5	12 08.7	1♒03.7	18 44.8	15 39.7	25 05.8	21 48.6	7 48.0	3 24.9	25 01.5
8 Sa	17 11 25	17 00 35	6♒51 39	14♒10 02	24 27.6	13 42.9	2 12.3	19 29.1	15 42.2	25 16.0	21 53.8	7 46.6	3 23.7	25 02.3
9 Su	17 15 22	18 01 32	21 25 27	28 37 21	24 25.5	15 17.0	3 20.6	20 13.4	15 44.3	25 26.2	21 59.0	7 45.3	3 22.6	25 03.2
10 M	17 19 19	19 02 31	5♓45 21	12♓49 09	24D 24.4	16 51.2	4 28.9	20 57.9	15 46.0	25 36.3	22 04.1	7 43.8	3 21.6	25 04.0
11 Tu	17 23 15	20 03 30	19 48 35	26 43 34	24 24.4	18 25.4	5 36.9	21 42.3	15 47.3	25 46.2	22 09.1	7 42.4	3 20.5	25 04.9
12 W	17 27 12	21 04 29	3♈34 09	10♈20 23	24 25.4	19 59.6	6 44.8	22 26.9	15 48.2	25 56.1	22 14.0	7 40.9	3 19.5	25 05.8
13 Th	17 31 08	22 05 29	17 02 26	23 40 28	24 27.0	21 33.9	7 52.5	23 11.4	15R 48.6	26 05.9	22 18.9	7 39.3	3 18.5	25 06.7
14 F	17 35 05	23 06 29	0♉14 42	6♉45 19	24 28.6	23 08.3	9 00.0	23 56.0	15 48.6	26 15.6	22 23.7	7 37.7	3 17.5	25 07.6
15 Sa	17 39 01	24 07 31	13 12 32	19 36 32	24R 29.6	24 42.8	10 07.3	24 40.7	15 48.2	26 25.1	22 28.4	7 36.0	3 16.6	25 08.6
16 Su	17 42 58	25 08 32	25 57 32	2♊15 41	24 29.5	26 17.5	11 14.4	25 25.4	15 47.4	26 34.6	22 33.0	7 34.4	3 15.7	25 09.6
17 M	17 46 54	26 09 35	8♊31 08	14 44 02	24 27.7	27 52.2	12 21.3	26 10.1	15 46.1	26 43.9	22 37.6	7 32.6	3 14.8	25 10.6
18 Tu	17 50 51	27 10 37	20 54 31	27 02 42	24 24.2	29 27.1	13 28.0	26 55.0	15 44.5	26 53.2	22 42.1	7 30.9	3 14.0	25 11.7
19 W	17 54 48	28 11 41	3♋08 44	9♋12 44	24 19.1	1♑02.2	14 34.5	27 39.8	15 42.4	27 02.3	22 46.5	7 29.0	3 13.2	25 12.7
20 Th	17 58 44	29 12 45	15 14 52	21 15 18	24 12.7	2 37.4	15 40.7	28 24.7	15 39.8	27 11.4	22 50.8	7 27.2	3 12.4	25 13.8
21 F	18 02 41	0♑13 50	27 14 13	3♌11 52	24 05.7	4 12.8	16 46.7	29 09.7	15 36.8	27 20.3	22 55.0	7 25.3	3 11.6	25 14.9
22 Sa	18 06 37	1 14 55	9♌08 30	15 04 26	23 58.8	5 48.4	17 52.5	29 54.7	15 33.4	27 29.1	22 59.2	7 23.4	3 10.9	25 16.0
23 Su	18 10 34	2 16 01	21 00 00	26 55 37	23 52.6	7 24.2	18 58.0	0♑39.7	15 29.6	27 37.8	23 03.2	7 21.4	3 10.2	25 17.2
24 M	18 14 30	3 17 07	2♍51 41	8♍48 41	23 47.9	9 00.2	20 03.3	1 24.8	15 25.3	27 46.3	23 07.2	7 19.4	3 09.5	25 18.3
25 Tu	18 18 27	4 18 14	14 47 08	20 47 34	23 44.8	10 36.4	21 08.3	2 09.9	15 20.6	27 54.8	23 11.1	7 17.4	3 08.9	25 19.5
26 W	18 22 23	5 19 22	26 50 35	2♎56 45	23D 43.7	12 12.8	22 13.0	2 55.1	15 15.5	28 03.1	23 14.9	7 15.3	3 08.3	25 20.7
27 Th	18 26 20	6 20 30	9♎06 41	15 21 00	23 44.0	13 49.4	23 17.4	3 40.4	15 10.0	28 11.3	23 18.6	7 13.2	3 07.7	25 21.9
28 F	18 30 17	7 21 39	21 40 17	28 05 06	23 45.3	15 26.2	24 21.6	4 25.6	15 04.0	28 19.4	23 22.2	7 11.0	3 07.2	25 23.2
29 Sa	18 34 13	8 22 49	4♏35 59	11♏13 21	23R 46.7	17 03.2	25 25.4	5 11.0	14 57.6	28 27.3	23 25.8	7 08.9	3 06.7	25 24.4
30 Su	18 38 10	9 23 58	17 57 34	24 48 52	23 47.3	18 40.3	26 28.9	5 56.3	14 50.8	28 35.2	23 29.2	7 06.7	3 06.2	25 25.7
31 M	18 42 06	10 25 09	1♐47 19	8♐52 50	23 46.3	20 17.5	27 32.2	6 41.8	14 43.6	28 42.8	23 32.6	7 04.4	3 05.8	25 27.0

Astro Data (Dy Hr Mn)

☽0S 2 5:08
♇D 7 6:04
♅R 12 17:55
☽0N 15 3:43
☽0S 29 14:36

♃△♇ 7 1:22
☽0N 12 9:06
⚳R 14 1:20
☽0S 26 22:51

Planet Ingress (Dy Hr Mn)

☿ ♏ 9 22:58
♀ ♑ 10 21:55
♂ ♐ 11 16:54
☉ ♐ 21 17:07
☿ ♐ 29 18:22

♀ ♒ 6 13:44
☿ ♑ 18 20:18
☉ ♑ 21 6:34
♂ ♑ 22 14:51

Last Aspect / ☽ Ingress

Last Aspect Dy Hr Mn		☽ Ingress Dy Hr Mn
31 22:02 ♂ ✶	♎	1 12:38
3 10:37 ♇ △	♏	3 19:56
5 17:12 ♂ ☌	♐	6 0:33
7 23:25 ☿ ✶	♑	8 3:31
10 4:05 ♂ ✶	♒	10 5:56
11 23:51 ♇ ☌	♓	12 8:39
13 22:42 ☉ △	♈	14 12:18
16 8:11 ♇ ✶	♉	16 17:27
18 19:07 ☉ ☍	♊	19 0:38
21 0:14 ♇ △	♋	21 10:16
23 7:00 ♃ □	♌	23 22:04
26 0:25 ♇ ☍	♍	26 10:40
28 18:53 ☿ ✶	♎	28 21:51

Last Aspect Dy Hr Mn		☽ Ingress Dy Hr Mn
30 20:38 ♇ △	♏	1 5:48
3 3:28 ♀ ✶	♐	3 10:10
5 3:46 ♇ ✶	♑	5 11:57
7 4:43 ♃ □	♒	7 12:47
9 6:37 ♃ △	♓	9 14:18
11 2:47 ♂ □	♈	11 17:44
13 16:28 ♃ ☍	♉	13 23:33
15 22:28 ♇ □	♊	16 7:41
18 17:26 ☿ ☍	♋	18 17:48
21 0:03 ♃ □	♌	21 5:33
23 13:26 ♃ ✶	♍	23 18:13
24 12:27 ☿ △	♎	26 6:13
28 12:27 ♃ ☌	♏	28 15:33
30 15:07 ♀ □	♐	30 20:57

☽ Phases & Eclipses (Dy Hr Mn)

4 18:57 ● 12♏58
4 19:09:03 ● P 0.808
11 15:25 ☽ 19♒51
18 19:07 ○ 27♉03
18 19:05 • T 1.398
26 21:09 ☾ 5♍13

4 7:34 ● 12♐46
10 23:31 ☽ 19♓32
18 12:17 ○ 27♊11
26 17:04 ☾ 5♎32

Astro Data

1 November 2040
Julian Day # 51440
SVP 4♓41'37"
GC 27♐24.6 ⚴ 26♈23.5R
Eris 28♈33.1R ⚵ 15♋43.1
⚷ 22♋56.8 ⚶ 9♒34.9
☽ Mean ☊ 25♉14.0

1 December 2040
Julian Day # 51470
SVP 4♓41'32"
GC 27♐24.7 ⚴ 19♈32.0R
Eris 28♈17.0R ⚵ 17♋17.8R
⚷ 22♋18.8R ⚶ 20♒04.4
☽ Mean ☊ 23♉38.7

LONGITUDE — January 2041

Day	Sid.Time	☉	0 hr ☽	Noon ☽	True ☊	☿	♀	♂	⚳	♃	♄	♅	♆	♇
1 Tu	18 46 03	11♑26 19	16♐05 07	23♐23 40	23♉43.0	21♑54.8	28♒35.0	7♑27.2	14♌35.9	28♎50.4	23♎35.8	7♌02.2	3♉05.4	25♒28.3
2 W	18 49 59	12 27 30	0♑47 47	8♑16 34	23R37.6	23 32.1	29 37.6	8 12.7	14R27.9	28 57.8	23 39.0	6R59.9	3R05.0	25 29.7
3 Th	18 53 56	13 28 41	15 48 55	23 23 37	23 30.3	25 09.4	0♓39.8	8 58.3	14 19.5	29 05.1	23 42.1	6 57.6	3 04.7	25 31.0
4 F	18 57 53	14 29 52	0♒59 21	8♒34 45	23 22.1	26 46.5	1 41.6	9 43.9	14 10.7	29 12.2	23 45.0	6 55.2	3 04.4	25 32.4
5 Sa	19 01 49	15 31 03	16 08 30	23 39 25	23 14.0	28 23.4	2 43.0	10 29.5	14 01.5	29 19.2	23 47.9	6 52.9	3 04.1	25 33.8
6 Su	19 05 46	16 32 13	1♓06 22	8♓28 29	23 07.1	29 60.0	3 44.0	11 15.2	13 52.0	29 26.1	23 50.7	6 50.5	3 03.9	25 35.2
7 M	19 09 42	17 33 23	15 45 03	22 55 34	23 02.1	1♒36.0	4 44.6	12 00.9	13 42.1	29 32.8	23 53.3	6 48.1	3 03.7	25 36.6
8 Tu	19 13 39	18 34 32	29 59 46	6♈57 31	22D59.5	3 11.5	5 44.8	12 46.7	13 31.9	29 39.3	23 55.9	6 45.6	3 03.5	25 38.0
9 W	19 17 35	19 35 41	13♈48 53	20 34 05	22 58.8	4 46.1	6 44.5	13 32.4	13 21.3	29 45.7	23 58.4	6 43.2	3 03.4	25 39.5
10 Th	19 21 32	20 36 49	27 13 23	3♉47 11	22 59.4	6 19.6	7 43.7	14 18.3	13 10.4	29 52.0	24 00.8	6 40.7	3 03.3	25 40.9
11 F	19 25 28	21 37 57	10♉15 55	16 40 01	23R00.2	7 51.7	8 42.4	15 04.1	12 59.2	29 58.1	24 03.1	6 38.2	3 03.2	25 42.4
12 Sa	19 29 25	22 39 04	22 59 58	29 16 13	23 00.2	9 22.2	9 40.7	15 50.0	12 47.7	0♏04.1	24 05.2	6 35.7	3D03.2	25 43.9
13 Su	19 33 22	23 40 11	5♊29 12	11♊39 20	22 58.3	10 50.6	10 38.4	16 36.0	12 35.9	0 09.9	24 07.3	6 33.2	3 03.2	25 45.4
14 M	19 37 18	24 41 17	17 47 00	23 52 32	22 53.8	12 16.5	11 35.5	17 21.9	12 23.9	0 15.5	24 09.3	6 30.6	3 03.2	25 46.9
15 Tu	19 41 15	25 42 23	29 56 13	5♋58 20	22 46.5	13 39.5	12 32.1	18 07.9	12 11.6	0 21.0	24 11.1	6 28.1	3 03.3	25 48.5
16 W	19 45 11	26 43 28	11♋59 05	17 58 41	22 36.5	14 58.9	13 28.1	18 54.0	11 59.1	0 26.3	24 12.9	6 25.5	3 03.4	25 50.0
17 Th	19 49 08	27 44 33	23 57 18	29 55 05	22 24.5	16 14.2	14 23.5	19 40.1	11 46.3	0 31.5	24 14.6	6 22.9	3 03.6	25 51.6
18 F	19 53 04	28 45 37	5♌52 12	11♌48 48	22 11.2	17 24.7	15 18.2	20 26.2	11 33.3	0 36.5	24 16.1	6 20.4	3 03.8	25 53.1
19 Sa	19 57 01	29 46 40	17 45 02	23 41 06	21 57.8	18 29.6	16 12.3	21 12.3	11 20.1	0 41.4	24 17.6	6 17.8	3 04.0	25 54.7
20 Su	20 00 57	0♒47 43	29 37 12	5♍33 33	21 45.5	19 28.0	17 05.7	21 58.5	11 06.8	0 46.1	24 18.9	6 15.2	3 04.2	25 56.3
21 M	20 04 54	1 48 45	11♍30 28	17 28 15	21 35.2	20 19.3	17 58.4	22 44.7	10 53.2	0 50.6	24 20.2	6 12.5	3 04.5	25 57.9
22 Tu	20 08 51	2 49 47	23 27 16	29 27 57	21 27.5	21 02.4	18 50.4	23 31.0	10 39.5	0 54.9	24 21.3	6 09.9	3 04.9	25 59.5
23 W	20 12 47	3 50 49	5♎30 43	11♎36 06	21 22.7	21 36.6	19 41.6	24 17.3	10 25.7	0 59.1	24 22.4	6 07.3	3 05.2	26 01.2
24 Th	20 16 44	4 51 50	17 44 37	23 56 51	21D20.4	22 01.0	20 32.0	25 03.6	10 11.8	1 03.1	24 23.3	6 04.7	3 05.6	26 02.8
25 F	20 20 40	5 52 50	0♏13 24	6♏34 50	21 19.9	22R14.9	21 21.6	25 50.0	9 57.8	1 06.9	24 24.1	6 02.1	3 06.0	26 04.4
26 Sa	20 24 37	6 53 50	13 01 46	19 34 45	21R20.1	22 17.9	22 10.3	26 36.4	9 43.7	1 10.6	24 24.8	5 59.4	3 06.5	26 06.1
27 Su	20 28 33	7 54 50	26 14 17	3♐00 48	21 19.6	22 09.4	22 58.2	27 22.8	9 29.5	1 14.1	24 25.4	5 56.8	3 07.0	26 07.7
28 M	20 32 30	8 55 49	9♐54 35	16 55 50	21 17.5	21 49.6	23 45.2	28 09.2	9 15.4	1 17.4	24 25.9	5 54.2	3 07.5	26 09.4
29 Tu	20 36 26	9 56 47	24 04 30	1♑20 22	21 12.7	21 18.5	24 31.2	28 55.7	9 01.1	1 20.5	24 26.3	5 51.6	3 08.1	26 11.1
30 W	20 40 23	10 57 45	8♑42 59	16 11 39	21 05.1	20 37.0	25 16.2	29 42.2	8 46.9	1 23.5	24 26.6	5 49.0	3 08.7	26 12.8
31 Th	20 44 20	11 58 42	23 45 23	1♒23 03	20 55.1	19 45.8	26 00.2	0♒28.8	8 32.7	1 26.3	24 26.8	5 46.4	3 09.3	26 14.5

LONGITUDE — February 2041

Day	Sid.Time	☉	0 hr ☽	Noon ☽	True ☊	☿	♀	♂	⚳	♃	♄	♅	♆	♇
1 F	20 48 16	12♒59 37	9♒03 17	16♒44 36	20♉43.6	18♒46.5	26♓43.1	1♒15.4	8♌18.6	1♏28.8	24♎26.9	5♌43.8	3♉10.0	26♒16.2
2 Sa	20 52 13	14 00 32	24 25 28	2♓04 23	20R32.0	17R40.8	27 24.9	2 02.0	8R04.5	1 31.2	24R26.8	5R41.2	3 10.7	26 17.9
3 Su	20 56 09	15 01 25	9♓39 55	17 10 50	20 21.7	16 30.4	28 05.6	2 48.6	7 50.5	1 33.5	24 26.7	5 38.6	3 11.4	26 19.6
4 M	21 00 06	16 02 18	24 36 03	1♈54 48	20 13.8	15 17.7	28 45.0	3 35.2	7 36.6	1 35.5	24 26.4	5 36.0	3 12.2	26 21.3
5 Tu	21 04 02	17 03 08	9♈06 28	16 10 47	20 08.7	14 04.5	29 23.1	4 21.9	7 22.8	1 37.3	24 26.1	5 33.5	3 13.0	26 23.0
6 W	21 07 59	18 03 57	23 07 37	29 57 04	20 06.2	12 53.0	29 60.0	5 08.6	7 09.1	1 39.0	24 25.6	5 30.9	3 13.8	26 24.7
7 Th	21 11 55	19 04 45	6♉39 23	13♉14 59	20 05.5	11 44.9	0♈35.5	5 55.3	6 55.6	1 40.5	24 25.1	5 28.4	3 14.7	26 26.4
8 F	21 15 52	20 05 32	19 44 19	26 07 56	20 05.4	10 41.8	1 09.5	6 42.0	6 42.3	1 41.8	24 24.4	5 25.8	3 15.6	26 28.2
9 Sa	21 19 49	21 06 16	2♊26 25	8♊40 23	20 04.7	9 44.8	1 42.1	7 28.8	6 29.1	1 42.9	24 23.6	5 23.3	3 16.5	26 29.9
10 Su	21 23 45	22 07 00	14 50 24	20 57 04	20 02.3	8 55.0	2 13.1	8 15.6	6 16.2	1 43.8	24 22.7	5 20.9	3 17.5	26 31.6
11 M	21 27 42	23 07 41	27 00 56	3♋02 30	19 57.1	8 12.7	2 42.6	9 02.4	6 03.5	1 44.5	24 21.7	5 18.4	3 18.5	26 33.3
12 Tu	21 31 38	24 08 21	9♋02 14	15 00 34	19 49.0	7 38.4	3 10.3	9 49.2	5 51.0	1 45.0	24 20.7	5 15.9	3 19.5	26 35.1
13 W	21 35 35	25 09 00	20 57 53	26 54 30	19 38.0	7 12.2	3 36.4	10 36.0	5 38.8	1 45.4	24 19.5	5 13.5	3 20.6	26 36.8
14 Th	21 39 31	26 09 37	2♌50 43	8♌46 45	19 24.7	6 53.9	4 00.6	11 22.8	5 26.8	1R45.6	24 18.2	5 11.1	3 21.7	26 38.6
15 F	21 43 28	27 10 13	14 42 50	20 39 09	19 10.0	6D43.4	4 23.0	12 09.7	5 15.1	1 45.5	24 16.8	5 08.7	3 22.8	26 40.3
16 Sa	21 47 24	28 10 46	26 35 51	2♍33 05	18 55.2	6 40.2	4 43.5	12 56.6	5 03.7	1 45.3	24 15.3	5 06.4	3 24.0	26 42.0
17 Su	21 51 21	29 11 19	8♍31 00	14 29 45	18 41.4	6 44.1	5 02.0	13 43.5	4 52.6	1 44.9	24 13.7	5 04.0	3 25.1	26 43.8
18 M	21 55 18	0♓11 50	20 29 30	26 30 26	18 29.8	6 54.6	5 18.4	14 30.4	4 41.8	1 44.3	24 12.0	5 01.7	3 26.3	26 45.5
19 Tu	21 59 14	1 12 19	2♎32 48	8♎36 48	18 20.9	7 11.3	5 32.8	15 17.4	4 31.3	1 43.5	24 10.2	4 59.4	3 27.6	26 47.2
20 W	22 03 11	2 12 48	14 42 47	20 51 03	18 15.1	7 33.8	5 45.0	16 04.3	4 21.2	1 42.5	24 08.3	4 57.2	3 28.8	26 48.9
21 Th	22 07 07	3 13 14	27 01 59	3♏16 00	18 12.1	8 01.6	5 55.0	16 51.3	4 11.4	1 41.4	24 06.3	4 55.0	3 30.1	26 50.7
22 F	22 11 04	4 13 40	9♏33 34	15 55 09	18D11.2	8 34.3	6 02.7	17 38.3	4 02.0	1 40.0	24 04.3	4 52.8	3 31.5	26 52.4
23 Sa	22 15 00	5 14 04	22 21 15	28 52 20	18R11.4	9 11.7	6 08.1	18 25.3	3 53.0	1 38.5	24 02.1	4 50.6	3 32.8	26 54.1
24 Su	22 18 57	6 14 27	5♐28 54	12♐11 22	18 11.3	9 53.2	6R11.1	19 12.3	3 44.3	1 36.8	23 59.8	4 48.5	3 34.2	26 55.8
25 M	22 22 53	7 14 49	19 00 07	25 55 23	18 10.0	10 38.7	6 11.7	19 59.3	3 36.0	1 34.9	23 57.5	4 46.4	3 35.6	26 57.6
26 Tu	22 26 50	8 15 09	2♑57 21	10♑05 58	18 06.4	11 27.8	6 09.9	20 46.4	3 28.1	1 32.8	23 55.0	4 44.3	3 37.1	26 59.3
27 W	22 30 47	9 15 28	17 21 02	24 42 08	18 00.2	12 20.2	6 05.6	21 33.4	3 20.6	1 30.5	23 52.5	4 42.3	3 38.5	27 01.0
28 Th	22 34 43	10 15 45	2♒08 38	9♒39 41	17 51.7	13 15.7	5 58.8	22 20.5	3 13.5	1 28.0	23 49.8	4 40.3	3 40.0	27 02.7

Astro Data

	Dy Hr Mn
☽0N	8 14:24
♆ D	12 16:37
☽0S	23 4:59
☿ R	26 6:14
♀0N	30 10:20
♄ R	1 16:02
☽0N	4 21:53
♃ R	14 20:23
☿ D	16 10:28
☽0S	19 10:00
♀ R	25 6:08

Planet Ingress

	Dy Hr Mn
♀ ♓	2 20:38
☿ ♒	6 12:01
♃ ♏	11 19:34
☉ ♒	19 17:14
♂ ♒	30 21:10
♀ ♈	6 12:00
☉ ♓	18 7:18

Last Aspect / ☽ Ingress (January)

Last Aspect Dy Hr Mn		☽ Ingress Dy Hr Mn
1 21:04 ♀ ⚹	♑	1 22:43
3 21:04 ♃ □	♒	3 22:26
5 21:11 ♃ △	♓	5 22:13
7 2:19 ☉ ⚹	♈	8 0:00
10 4:45 ♃ ☍	♉	10 5:03
12 5:12 ♇ □	♊	12 13:24
14 15:47 ♇ △	♋	15 0:07
17 7:13 ☉ ☍	♌	17 12:10
19 16:31 ♇ ☍	♍	20 0:46
21 23:18 ♂ △	♎	22 13:04
24 16:02 ♇ △	♏	24 23:35
27 1:26 ♂ ⚹	♐	27 6:41
29 3:29 ♇ ⚹	♑	29 9:48
31 3:07 ♀ ⚹	♒	31 9:50

Last Aspect / ☽ Ingress (February)

Last Aspect Dy Hr Mn		☽ Ingress Dy Hr Mn
2 2:55 ♇ ☌	♓	2 8:44
4 6:33 ♀ ☌	♈	4 8:51
6 5:44 ♇ ⚹	♉	6 12:05
8 12:38 ♇ □	♊	8 19:20
10 23:03 ♇ △	♋	11 5:56
13 6:47 ♄ □	♌	13 18:15
16 2:22 ☉ ☍	♍	16 6:52
16 13:43 ♆ △	♎	18 18:57
20 23:36 ♇ △	♏	21 5:43
23 8:23 ♇ □	♐	23 14:04
25 13:47 ♇ ⚹	♑	25 18:59
27 10:40 ♄ □	♒	27 20:33

☽ Phases & Eclipses

Dy Hr Mn	
2 19:09	● 12♑46
9 10:07	☽ 19♈31
17 7:13	○ 27♋32
25 10:34	☾ 5♏49
1 5:44	● 12♒44
7 23:41	☽ 19♉34
16 2:22	○ 27♌46
24 0:30	☾ 5♐46

Astro Data

1 January 2041
Julian Day # 51501
SVP 4♓41'26"
GC 27♐24.7 ⚴ 20♈34.7
Eris 28♈07.5R ⚵ 11♋15.6R
⚷ 20♋31.1R ⚶ 2♓58.7
☽ Mean ☊ 22♉00.2

1 February 2041
Julian Day # 51532
SVP 4♓41'20"
GC 27♐24.8 ⚴ 28♈54.4
Eris 28♈08.2 ⚵ 5♋54.7R
⚷ 18♋24.6R ⚶ 16♓59.1
☽ Mean ☊ 20♉21.8

March 2041 — LONGITUDE

Day	Sid.Time	☉	0 hr ☽	Noon ☽	True ☊	☿	♀	♂	⚳	♃	♄	♅	♆	♇
1 F	22 38 40	11♓16 00	17♒14 12	24♒50 58	17♉41.7	14♒14.2	5♈49.6	23♒07.6	3♌06.8	1♏25.4	23♎47.1	4♌38.3	3♉41.5	27♒04.4
2 Sa	22 42 36	12 16 14	2♓28 38	10♓05 46	17R31.5	15 15.3	5R37.8	23 54.6	3R00.5	1R22.5	23R44.3	4R36.4	3 43.1	27 06.1
3 Su	22 46 33	13 16 26	17 40 58	25 12 55	17 22.2	16 18.9	5 23.5	24 41.7	2 54.6	1 19.5	23 41.4	4 34.5	3 44.6	27 07.8
4 M	22 50 29	14 16 36	2♈40 24	10♈02 24	17 15.0	17 24.9	5 06.8	25 28.8	2 49.2	1 16.3	23 38.5	4 32.6	3 46.2	27 09.4
5 Tu	22 54 26	15 16 45	17 18 07	24 26 58	17 10.4	18 33.0	4 47.7	26 15.9	2 44.2	1 12.9	23 35.4	4 30.8	3 47.9	27 11.1
6 W	22 58 22	16 16 51	1♉28 36	8♉22 52	17D08.2	19 43.3	4 26.2	27 03.0	2 39.7	1 09.4	23 32.3	4 29.1	3 49.5	27 12.8
7 Th	23 02 19	17 16 55	15 09 50	21 49 41	17 07.9	20 55.5	4 02.5	27 50.1	2 35.5	1 05.7	23 29.1	4 27.3	3 51.2	27 14.4
8 F	23 06 16	18 16 57	28 22 46	4♊49 33	17 08.7	22 09.6	3 36.5	28 37.2	2 31.8	1 01.8	23 25.8	4 25.6	3 52.9	27 16.1
9 Sa	23 10 12	19 16 57	11♊10 33	17 26 21	17R09.3	23 25.5	3 08.6	29 24.3	2 28.6	0 57.8	23 22.4	4 24.0	3 54.6	27 17.7
10 Su	23 14 09	20 16 55	23 37 33	29 44 47	17 08.7	24 43.1	2 38.7	0♓11.4	2 25.8	0 53.5	23 19.0	4 22.4	3 56.3	27 19.3
11 M	23 18 05	21 16 50	5♋48 41	11♋49 51	17 06.3	26 02.3	2 07.1	0 58.5	2 23.4	0 49.2	23 15.5	4 20.8	3 58.1	27 20.9
12 Tu	23 22 02	22 16 44	17 48 51	23 46 15	17 01.6	27 23.1	1 33.9	1 45.6	2 21.5	0 44.6	23 11.9	4 19.3	3 59.8	27 22.5
13 W	23 25 58	23 16 35	29 42 34	5♌38 15	16 54.7	28 45.5	0 59.3	2 32.7	2 20.0	0 39.9	23 08.3	4 17.9	4 01.6	27 24.1
14 Th	23 29 55	24 16 24	11♌33 45	17 29 26	16 45.9	0♓09.3	0 23.6	3 19.8	2 18.9	0 35.1	23 04.6	4 16.4	4 03.5	27 25.7
15 F	23 33 51	25 16 11	23 25 39	29 22 40	16 36.0	1 34.5	29♓47.0	4 06.9	2D18.3	0 30.1	23 00.8	4 15.1	4 05.3	27 27.3
16 Sa	23 37 48	26 15 55	5♍20 46	11♍20 08	16 25.8	3 01.2	29 09.7	4 54.0	2 18.1	0 24.9	22 57.0	4 13.7	4 07.2	27 28.9
17 Su	23 41 45	27 15 38	17 20 59	23 23 27	16 16.4	4 29.2	28 32.0	5 41.1	2 18.3	0 19.6	22 53.1	4 12.5	4 09.0	27 30.4
18 M	23 45 41	28 15 19	29 27 42	5♎33 51	16 08.5	5 58.6	27 54.2	6 28.2	2 19.0	0 14.2	22 49.1	4 11.2	4 10.9	27 32.0
19 Tu	23 49 38	29 14 57	11♎42 02	17 52 23	16 02.8	7 29.3	27 16.4	7 15.3	2 20.1	0 08.6	22 45.1	4 10.0	4 12.8	27 33.5
20 W	23 53 34	0♈14 34	24 05 04	0♏20 13	15 59.3	9 01.4	26 39.0	8 02.4	2 21.6	0 02.9	22 41.1	4 08.9	4 14.8	27 35.0
21 Th	23 57 31	1 14 09	6♏38 03	12 58 46	15D57.9	10 34.8	26 02.2	8 49.4	2 23.5	29♎57.1	22 37.0	4 07.8	4 16.7	27 36.5
22 F	0 01 27	2 13 43	19 22 35	25 49 47	15 58.3	12 09.5	25 26.3	9 36.5	2 25.8	29 51.1	22 32.8	4 06.8	4 18.7	27 38.0
23 Sa	0 05 24	3 13 14	2♐20 37	8♐55 21	15 59.6	13 45.5	24 51.5	10 23.6	2 28.6	29 45.0	22 28.6	4 05.8	4 20.7	27 39.4
24 Su	0 09 20	4 12 44	15 34 18	22 17 42	16R00.9	15 22.9	24 18.0	11 10.6	2 31.8	29 38.8	22 24.4	4 04.8	4 22.7	27 40.9
25 M	0 13 17	5 12 12	29 05 46	5♑58 41	16 01.5	17 01.5	23 46.0	11 57.7	2 35.3	29 32.5	22 20.1	4 03.9	4 24.7	27 42.4
26 Tu	0 17 14	6 11 38	12♑56 33	19 59 23	16 00.6	18 41.5	23 15.7	12 44.7	2 39.3	29 26.0	22 15.8	4 03.1	4 26.7	27 43.8
27 W	0 21 10	7 11 03	27 07 02	4♒19 16	15 58.0	20 22.8	22 47.3	13 31.8	2 43.7	29 19.5	22 11.4	4 02.3	4 28.8	27 45.2
28 Th	0 25 07	8 10 26	11♒35 42	18 55 47	15 53.9	22 05.5	22 20.9	14 18.8	2 48.4	29 12.8	22 07.0	4 01.6	4 30.8	27 46.6
29 F	0 29 03	9 09 47	26 18 49	3♓43 58	15 48.7	23 49.5	21 56.5	15 05.8	2 53.6	29 06.1	22 02.6	4 00.9	4 32.9	27 48.0
30 Sa	0 33 00	10 09 06	11♓10 17	18 36 45	15 43.2	25 34.8	21 34.4	15 52.8	2 59.2	28 59.2	21 58.2	4 00.3	4 35.0	27 49.3
31 Su	0 36 56	11 08 23	26 02 19	3♈25 55	15 38.2	27 21.5	21 14.6	16 39.8	3 05.1	28 52.2	21 53.7	3 59.7	4 37.1	27 50.7

April 2041 — LONGITUDE

Day	Sid.Time	☉	0 hr ☽	Noon ☽	True ☊	☿	♀	♂	⚳	♃	♄	♅	♆	♇
1 M	0 40 53	12♈07 38	10♈46 31	18♈03 14	15♉34.4	29♓09.6	20♓57.1	17♓26.7	3♌11.4	28♎45.2	21♎49.2	3♌59.1	4♉39.2	27♒52.0
2 Tu	0 44 49	13 06 51	25 15 14	2♉21 51	15D32.1	0♈59.1	20R42.0	18 13.7	3 18.1	28R38.1	21R44.6	3R58.7	4 41.3	27 53.3
3 W	0 48 46	14 06 02	9♉22 37	16 17 11	15 31.4	2 50.0	20 29.4	19 00.6	3 25.2	28 30.9	21 40.1	3 58.2	4 43.5	27 54.6
4 Th	0 52 42	15 05 11	23 05 22	29 47 10	15 32.1	4 42.3	20 19.2	19 47.6	3 32.6	28 23.7	21 35.5	3 57.9	4 45.6	27 55.9
5 F	0 56 39	16 04 18	6♊22 41	12♊52 10	15 33.6	6 36.0	20 11.4	20 34.5	3 40.4	28 16.3	21 30.9	3 57.6	4 47.8	27 57.2
6 Sa	1 00 36	17 03 22	19 15 57	25 34 27	15 35.3	8 31.0	20 06.1	21 21.3	3 48.6	28 09.0	21 26.3	3 57.3	4 50.0	27 58.4
7 Su	1 04 32	18 02 24	1♋48 10	7♋57 38	15R36.5	10 27.5	20D03.2	22 08.2	3 57.1	28 01.5	21 21.7	3 57.1	4 52.1	27 59.7
8 M	1 08 29	19 01 24	14 03 24	20 06 05	15 37.0	12 25.4	20 02.7	22 55.0	4 05.9	27 54.0	21 17.1	3 57.0	4 54.3	28 00.9
9 Tu	1 12 25	20 00 22	26 06 15	2♌04 31	15 36.3	14 24.6	20 04.5	23 41.8	4 15.1	27 46.5	21 12.4	3 56.9	4 56.5	28 02.0
10 W	1 16 22	20 59 17	8♌01 28	13 57 38	15 34.4	16 25.1	20 08.7	24 28.6	4 24.6	27 38.9	21 07.8	3D56.8	4 58.7	28 03.2
11 Th	1 20 18	21 58 10	19 53 35	25 49 35	15 31.6	18 26.8	20 15.1	25 15.4	4 34.5	27 31.3	21 03.2	3 56.8	5 00.9	28 04.4
12 F	1 24 15	22 57 00	1♍46 48	7♍44 58	15 28.1	20 29.7	20 23.8	26 02.1	4 44.7	27 23.7	20 58.6	3 56.9	5 03.2	28 05.5
13 Sa	1 28 11	23 55 49	13 44 43	19 46 24	15 24.5	22 33.7	20 34.6	26 48.9	4 55.2	27 16.1	20 53.9	3 57.0	5 05.4	28 06.6
14 Su	1 32 08	24 54 35	25 50 19	1♎56 44	15 21.1	24 38.7	20 47.6	27 35.6	5 06.0	27 08.4	20 49.3	3 57.2	5 07.6	28 07.7
15 M	1 36 05	25 53 19	8♎05 52	14 17 53	15 18.4	26 44.4	21 02.5	28 22.2	5 17.1	27 00.7	20 44.7	3 57.4	5 09.8	28 08.7
16 Tu	1 40 01	26 52 02	20 32 56	26 51 07	15 16.5	28 50.9	21 19.5	29 08.9	5 28.5	26 53.0	20 40.1	3 57.7	5 12.1	28 09.8
17 W	1 43 58	27 50 42	3♏12 31	9♏37 09	15D15.7	0♉57.8	21 38.4	29 55.5	5 40.3	26 45.4	20 35.6	3 58.0	5 14.3	28 10.8
18 Th	1 47 54	28 49 20	16 05 04	22 36 17	15 15.7	3 04.9	21 59.2	0♈42.1	5 52.3	26 37.7	20 31.0	3 58.4	5 16.6	28 11.8
19 F	1 51 51	29 47 57	29 10 46	5♐48 31	15 16.5	5 12.0	22 21.8	1 28.7	6 04.6	26 30.0	20 26.5	3 58.9	5 18.8	28 12.8
20 Sa	1 55 47	0♉46 32	12♐29 31	19 13 45	15 17.6	7 18.9	22 46.1	2 15.2	6 17.2	26 22.4	20 22.0	3 59.3	5 21.1	28 13.7
21 Su	1 59 44	1 45 05	26 01 09	2♑51 42	15 18.7	9 25.2	23 12.1	3 01.7	6 30.1	26 14.7	20 17.5	3 59.9	5 23.3	28 14.7
22 M	2 03 40	2 43 37	9♑45 20	16 41 57	15 19.6	11 30.5	23 39.7	3 48.2	6 43.2	26 07.1	20 13.0	4 00.5	5 25.6	28 15.6
23 Tu	2 07 37	3 42 07	23 41 28	0♒43 42	15R20.0	13 34.7	24 08.9	4 34.7	6 56.7	25 59.5	20 08.6	4 01.2	5 27.9	28 16.5
24 W	2 11 34	4 40 36	7♒48 29	14 55 35	15 19.8	15 37.4	24 39.5	5 21.1	7 10.4	25 52.0	20 04.1	4 01.9	5 30.1	28 17.4
25 Th	2 15 30	5 39 03	22 04 40	29 15 23	15 19.2	17 38.2	25 11.7	6 07.5	7 24.3	25 44.5	19 59.8	4 02.6	5 32.4	28 18.2
26 F	2 19 27	6 37 28	6♓27 19	13♓39 58	15 18.4	19 36.8	25 45.1	6 53.9	7 38.5	25 37.0	19 55.4	4 03.4	5 34.7	28 19.0
27 Sa	2 23 23	7 35 51	20 52 49	28 05 16	15 17.4	21 33.0	26 20.0	7 40.2	7 53.0	25 29.6	19 51.1	4 04.3	5 36.9	28 19.8
28 Su	2 27 20	8 34 13	5♈16 42	12♈26 30	15 16.6	23 26.5	26 56.0	8 26.5	8 07.7	25 22.2	19 46.8	4 05.2	5 39.2	28 20.6
29 M	2 31 16	9 32 34	19 34 04	26 38 47	15 16.1	25 17.1	27 33.3	9 12.8	8 22.7	25 14.9	19 42.6	4 06.2	5 41.4	28 21.4
30 Tu	2 35 13	10 30 52	3♉40 07	10♉37 33	15D15.8	27 04.5	28 11.8	9 59.0	8 37.9	25 07.7	19 38.4	4 07.2	5 43.7	28 22.1

Astro Data

	Dy Hr Mn
☽0N	4 7:51
⚳D	16 11:01
♅□♆	18 14:13
☽0S	18 15:38
☉0N	20 6:08
☽0N	31 18:32
☿0N	4 9:31
♃△♇	7 17:10
♀D	8 5:09
♅D	10 19:07
♀0S	12 18:44
☽0S	14 22:46
♂0N	20 19:51
☽0N	28 3:43
♀0N	30 0:11

Planet Ingress

	Dy Hr Mn
♂ ♓	10 6:11
☿ ♓	14 9:22
♀ ♓R	15 3:32
☉ ♈	20 6:08
♃ ♎R	21 0:03
☿ ♈	1 23:05
☿ ♉	17 1:05
♂ ♈	17 14:19
☉ ♉	19 16:56

Last Aspect / ☽ Ingress

Last Aspect Dy Hr Mn		☽ Ingress Dy Hr Mn
1 15:30	♇ ☌	♓ 1 20:06
2 15:41	☉ ☌	♈ 3 19:41
5 16:39	♇ ⚹	♉ 5 21:28
7 23:42	♂ □	♊ 8 3:00
10 7:13	♇ △	♋ 10 12:30
12 10:51	♄ □	♌ 13 0:35
15 8:07	♇ ☍	♍ 15 13:15
17 21:40	♀ ☍	♎ 18 1:04
20 6:43	♇ △	♏ 20 11:21
22 15:20	♇ □	♐ 22 19:42
25 0:52	♃ ⚹	♑ 25 1:35
27 3:45	♃ □	♒ 27 4:49
29 4:34	♃ △	♓ 29 5:58
31 0:47	☿ ☌	♈ 31 6:25

Last Aspect Dy Hr Mn		☽ Ingress Dy Hr Mn
2 5:44	♃ ☍	♉ 2 8:00
4 8:39	♇ □	♊ 4 12:23
6 16:54	♃ △	♋ 6 20:31
9 3:27	♃ □	♌ 9 7:49
11 16:32	♇ ☍	♍ 11 20:25
14 2:52	♂ ☍	♎ 14 8:11
16 16:32	♂ ☍	♏ 16 17:57
18 22:14	♇ □	♐ 19 1:29
21 3:54	♇ ⚹	♑ 21 7:00
23 4:00	♃ □	♒ 23 10:46
25 10:24	♇ ☌	♓ 25 13:14
27 8:57	♀ ☌	♈ 27 15:11
29 14:55	♇ ⚹	♉ 29 17:43

☽ Phases & Eclipses

Dy Hr Mn	
2 15:41	● 12♓25
9 15:52	☽ 19♊27
17 20:20	○ 27♍36
25 10:33	☾ 5♑09
1 1:31	● 11♈42
8 9:40	☽ 18♋56
16 12:02	○ 26♎52
23 17:25	☾ 3♒55
30 11:48	● 10♉30
30 11:52:21	● T 01'51"

Astro Data

1 March 2041
Julian Day # 51560
SVP 4♓41'17"
GC 27♐24.9 ⚴ 10♉30.7
Eris 28♈17.5 ⚵ 7♋25.4
⚷ 17♋06.4R ⚶ 0♈03.1
☽ Mean ☊ 18♉52.8

1 April 2041
Julian Day # 51591
SVP 4♓41'14"
GC 27♐24.9 ⚴ 26♉10.3
Eris 28♈34.8 ⚵ 14♋49.9
⚷ 16♋56.9 ⚶ 14♈34.7
☽ Mean ☊ 17♉14.3

LONGITUDE — May 2041

Day	Sid.Time	☉	0 hr ☽	Noon☽	True☊	☿	♀	♂	⚳	♃	♄	♅	♆	♇
1 W	2 39 09	11♉29 09	17♉30 41	24♉19 10	15♉15.9	28♉48.5	28♓51.4	10♈45.2	8♌53.4	25♎00.6	19♎34.3	4♌08.3	5♉46.0	28♒22.8
2 Th	2 43 06	12 27 25	1♊02 47	7♊41 22	15 16.1	0♊29.0	29 32.1	11 31.4	9 09.1	24R53.5	19R30.2	4 09.4	5 48.2	28 23.5
3 F	2 47 03	13 25 38	14 14 52	20 43 21	15 16.3	2 05.9	0♈13.7	12 17.5	9 25.0	24 46.5	19 26.2	4 10.6	5 50.5	28 24.1
4 Sa	2 50 59	14 23 49	27 06 56	3♋25 52	15R16.4	3 38.9	0 56.4	13 03.6	9 41.2	24 39.6	19 22.2	4 11.8	5 52.7	28 24.8
5 Su	2 54 56	15 21 59	9♋40 26	15 50 59	15 16.5	5 08.1	1 40.1	13 49.7	9 57.6	24 32.8	19 18.3	4 13.1	5 54.9	28 25.4
6 M	2 58 52	16 20 06	21 57 58	28 01 50	15 16.4	6 33.3	2 24.6	14 35.7	10 14.2	24 26.0	19 14.4	4 14.5	5 57.2	28 26.0
7 Tu	3 02 49	17 18 12	4♌03 06	10♌02 19	15D16.4	7 54.4	3 10.0	15 21.6	10 31.0	24 19.4	19 10.6	4 15.8	5 59.4	28 26.5
8 W	3 06 45	18 16 16	16 00 02	21 56 49	15 16.3	9 11.3	3 56.3	16 07.6	10 48.0	24 12.9	19 06.9	4 17.3	6 01.6	28 27.1
9 Th	3 10 42	19 14 18	27 53 15	3♍49 56	15 16.5	10 24.1	4 43.4	16 53.4	11 05.3	24 06.5	19 03.2	4 18.7	6 03.9	28 27.6
10 F	3 14 38	20 12 17	9♍47 25	15 46 14	15 16.8	11 32.5	5 31.3	17 39.3	11 22.7	24 00.2	18 59.6	4 20.3	6 06.1	28 28.0
11 Sa	3 18 35	21 10 15	21 46 56	27 50 01	15 17.4	12 36.6	6 19.9	18 25.1	11 40.3	23 54.0	18 56.0	4 21.9	6 08.3	28 28.5
12 Su	3 22 32	22 08 12	3♎55 56	10♎05 06	15 18.0	13 36.3	7 09.3	19 10.8	11 58.2	23 47.9	18 52.5	4 23.5	6 10.5	28 28.9
13 M	3 26 28	23 06 06	16 17 53	22 34 36	15 18.7	14 31.6	7 59.3	19 56.5	12 16.2	23 42.0	18 49.1	4 25.1	6 12.7	28 29.3
14 Tu	3 30 25	24 03 59	28 55 28	5♏20 41	15R19.2	15 22.3	8 50.1	20 42.2	12 34.4	23 36.2	18 45.7	4 26.9	6 14.8	28 29.7
15 W	3 34 21	25 01 50	11♏50 21	18 24 30	15 19.3	16 08.3	9 41.4	21 27.8	12 52.8	23 30.5	18 42.5	4 28.6	6 17.0	28 30.1
16 Th	3 38 18	25 59 40	25 03 04	1♐45 57	15 18.9	16 49.8	10 33.5	22 13.4	13 11.4	23 24.9	18 39.3	4 30.4	6 19.2	28 30.4
17 F	3 42 14	26 57 29	8♐32 57	15 23 48	15 18.0	17 26.5	11 26.1	22 58.9	13 30.1	23 19.5	18 36.1	4 32.3	6 21.3	28 30.7
18 Sa	3 46 11	27 55 16	22 18 12	29 15 46	15 16.6	17 58.4	12 19.3	23 44.4	13 49.0	23 14.2	18 33.1	4 34.2	6 23.5	28 31.0
19 Su	3 50 07	28 53 02	6♑16 05	13♑18 45	15 15.0	18 25.6	13 13.1	24 29.8	14 08.1	23 09.1	18 30.1	4 36.2	6 25.6	28 31.3
20 M	3 54 04	29 50 47	20 23 18	27 29 18	15 13.3	18 47.9	14 07.4	25 15.2	14 27.4	23 04.1	18 27.2	4 38.2	6 27.7	28 31.5
21 Tu	3 58 01	0♊48 30	4♒36 19	11♒43 54	15 12.0	19 05.3	15 02.3	26 00.6	14 46.8	22 59.3	18 24.4	4 40.2	6 29.8	28 31.7
22 W	4 01 57	1 46 13	18 51 41	25 59 18	15D11.3	19 18.0	15 57.6	26 45.9	15 06.4	22 54.6	18 21.7	4 42.3	6 31.9	28 31.9
23 Th	4 05 54	2 43 54	3♓06 23	10♓12 40	15 11.4	19 25.8	16 53.5	27 31.2	15 26.2	22 50.0	18 19.0	4 44.4	6 34.0	28 32.1
24 F	4 09 50	3 41 35	17 17 50	24 21 39	15 12.1	19R28.8	17 49.8	28 16.4	15 46.1	22 45.6	18 16.5	4 46.6	6 36.1	28 32.2
25 Sa	4 13 47	4 39 14	1♈23 52	8♈24 14	15 13.3	19 27.2	18 46.6	29 01.6	16 06.2	22 41.4	18 14.0	4 48.8	6 38.1	28 32.3
26 Su	4 17 43	5 36 53	15 22 34	22 18 37	15 14.7	19 21.1	19 43.8	29 46.7	16 26.4	22 37.3	18 11.6	4 51.0	6 40.2	28 32.4
27 M	4 21 40	6 34 31	29 12 11	6♉03 04	15R15.6	19 10.6	20 41.4	0♉31.7	16 46.7	22 33.4	18 09.3	4 53.3	6 42.2	28 32.4
28 Tu	4 25 36	7 32 07	12♉51 03	19 35 56	15 15.8	18 56.1	21 39.4	1 16.7	17 07.3	22 29.6	18 07.1	4 55.7	6 44.2	28R32.4
29 W	4 29 33	8 29 43	26 17 33	2♊55 42	15 14.8	18 37.6	22 37.8	2 01.7	17 27.9	22 26.1	18 04.9	4 58.0	6 46.2	28 32.4
30 Th	4 33 30	9 27 17	9♊30 16	16 01 08	15 12.7	18 15.7	23 36.6	2 46.6	17 48.8	22 22.6	18 02.9	5 00.5	6 48.2	28 32.4
31 F	4 37 26	10 24 51	22 28 15	28 51 34	15 09.5	17 50.7	24 35.7	3 31.5	18 09.7	22 19.4	18 00.9	5 02.9	6 50.1	28 32.4

LONGITUDE — June 2041

Day	Sid.Time	☉	0 hr ☽	Noon☽	True☊	☿	♀	♂	⚳	♃	♄	♅	♆	♇
1 Sa	4 41 23	11♊22 23	5♋11 08	11♋27 03	15♉05.4	17♊22.9	25♈35.2	4♉16.3	18♌30.8	22♎16.3	17♎59.1	5♌05.4	6♉52.1	28♒32.3
2 Su	4 45 19	12 19 54	17 39 26	23 48 31	15R01.0	16R52.9	26 35.1	5 01.0	18 52.0	22R13.4	17R57.3	5 08.0	6 54.0	28R32.2
3 M	4 49 16	13 17 24	29 54 32	5♌57 50	14 56.8	16 21.2	27 35.2	5 45.7	19 13.4	22 10.7	17 55.7	5 10.5	6 55.9	28 32.1
4 Tu	4 53 12	14 14 52	11♌58 46	17 57 47	14 53.3	15 48.4	28 35.6	6 30.3	19 34.9	22 08.2	17 54.1	5 13.1	6 57.8	28 31.9
5 W	4 57 09	15 12 20	23 55 20	29 51 56	14 50.9	15 14.9	29 36.4	7 14.9	19 56.5	22 05.8	17 52.6	5 15.8	6 59.7	28 31.8
6 Th	5 01 06	16 09 46	5♍48 07	11♍44 28	14D49.7	14 41.4	0♉37.5	7 59.4	20 18.3	22 03.6	17 51.2	5 18.5	7 01.6	28 31.6
7 F	5 05 02	17 07 11	17 41 34	23 40 01	14 49.8	14 08.5	1 38.8	8 43.9	20 40.1	22 01.6	17 50.0	5 21.2	7 03.4	28 31.3
8 Sa	5 08 59	18 04 35	29 40 26	5♎43 25	14 50.9	13 36.6	2 40.4	9 28.3	21 02.1	21 59.7	17 48.8	5 23.9	7 05.2	28 31.1
9 Su	5 12 55	19 01 58	11♎49 33	17 59 24	14 52.5	13 06.4	3 42.3	10 12.6	21 24.2	21 58.1	17 47.7	5 26.7	7 07.0	28 30.8
10 M	5 16 52	19 59 19	24 13 30	0♏32 19	14 54.0	12 38.4	4 44.5	10 56.9	21 46.4	21 56.6	17 46.7	5 29.5	7 08.8	28 30.5
11 Tu	5 20 48	20 56 40	6♏56 15	13 25 39	14R54.7	12 13.0	5 46.9	11 41.1	22 08.7	21 55.3	17 45.8	5 32.4	7 10.6	28 30.2
12 W	5 24 45	21 54 00	20 00 45	26 41 40	14 54.2	11 50.7	6 49.5	12 25.3	22 31.2	21 54.2	17 45.0	5 35.3	7 12.3	28 29.9
13 Th	5 28 41	22 51 19	3♐28 25	10♐20 52	14 51.9	11 31.8	7 52.4	13 09.4	22 53.7	21 53.2	17 44.3	5 38.2	7 14.0	28 29.5
14 F	5 32 38	23 48 37	17 18 46	24 21 42	14 48.0	11 16.6	8 55.6	13 53.4	23 16.4	21 52.4	17 43.7	5 41.1	7 15.7	28 29.1
15 Sa	5 36 35	24 45 55	1♑29 09	8♑40 27	14 42.7	11 05.5	9 58.9	14 37.4	23 39.1	21 51.9	17 43.2	5 44.1	7 17.4	28 28.7
16 Su	5 40 31	25 43 12	15 54 51	23 11 34	14 36.6	10 58.5	11 02.5	15 21.3	24 02.0	21 51.5	17 42.8	5 47.1	7 19.0	28 28.2
17 M	5 44 28	26 40 29	0♒29 42	7♒48 24	14 30.6	10D56.0	12 06.4	16 05.2	24 25.0	21D51.2	17 42.5	5 50.2	7 20.7	28 27.8
18 Tu	5 48 24	27 37 45	15 06 51	22 24 16	14 25.5	10 57.9	13 10.4	16 49.0	24 48.0	21 51.2	17 42.3	5 53.2	7 22.3	28 27.3
19 W	5 52 21	28 35 01	29 39 57	6♓53 19	14 21.9	11 04.5	14 14.6	17 32.8	25 11.2	21 51.3	17D42.2	5 56.3	7 23.9	28 26.8
20 Th	5 56 17	29 32 17	14♓03 54	21 11 19	14D20.0	11 15.6	15 19.1	18 16.4	25 34.4	21 51.6	17 42.2	5 59.4	7 25.4	28 26.3
21 F	6 00 14	0♋29 33	28 15 19	5♈15 45	14 19.8	11 31.5	16 23.7	19 00.1	25 57.8	21 52.1	17 42.3	6 02.6	7 26.9	28 25.7
22 Sa	6 04 10	1 26 48	12♈12 33	19 05 43	14 20.6	11 52.0	17 28.6	19 43.6	26 21.2	21 52.8	17 42.5	6 05.8	7 28.5	28 25.1
23 Su	6 08 07	2 24 03	25 55 17	2♉41 22	14R21.8	12 17.2	18 33.6	20 27.1	26 44.8	21 53.6	17 42.8	6 09.0	7 29.9	28 24.5
24 M	6 12 04	3 21 18	9♉24 02	16 03 25	14 22.2	12 46.9	19 38.8	21 10.6	27 08.4	21 54.7	17 43.2	6 12.2	7 31.4	28 23.9
25 Tu	6 16 00	4 18 34	22 39 38	29 12 46	14 21.1	13 21.2	20 44.2	21 54.0	27 32.1	21 55.9	17 43.7	6 15.5	7 32.8	28 23.3
26 W	6 19 57	5 15 49	5♊42 53	12♊10 05	14 18.0	14 00.0	21 49.7	22 37.3	27 55.9	21 57.2	17 44.3	6 18.7	7 34.2	28 22.6
27 Th	6 23 53	6 13 04	18 34 24	24 55 53	14 12.5	14 43.2	22 55.4	23 20.5	28 19.8	21 58.8	17 45.0	6 22.0	7 35.6	28 21.9
28 F	6 27 50	7 10 18	1♋14 33	7♋30 26	14 04.8	15 30.8	24 01.3	24 03.7	28 43.8	22 00.6	17 45.8	6 25.4	7 37.0	28 21.2
29 Sa	6 31 46	8 07 33	13 43 35	19 54 04	13 55.5	16 22.8	25 07.3	24 46.8	29 07.9	22 02.5	17 46.7	6 28.7	7 38.3	28 20.5
30 Su	6 35 43	9 04 47	26 01 58	2♌07 25	13 45.4	17 18.9	26 13.5	25 29.9	29 32.0	22 04.6	17 47.7	6 32.1	7 39.6	28 19.7

Astro Data			Planet Ingress			Last Aspect			☽ Ingress		Last Aspect			☽ Ingress		☽ Phases & Eclipses		Astro Data
	Dy Hr Mn			Dy Hr Mn		Dy Hr Mn				Dy Hr Mn	Dy Hr Mn				Dy Hr Mn	Dy Hr Mn		1 May 2041
☽0S	12 6:59		☿ ♊	2 4:59		1 21:09	☿ ☌		♊	1 22:07	2 17:56	♀ □		♌	3 0:11	8 3:55	☽ 17♌57	Julian Day # 51621
☿R	24 15:39		♀ ♈	3 4:09		4 2:27	♇ △		♋	4 5:28	5 11:26	♀ △		♍	5 12:16	16 0:54	○ 25♏33	SVP 4♓41'10"
☽0N	25 10:23		☉ ♊	20 15:50		6 4:56	♃ □		♌	6 15:55	6 21:42	☉ □		♎	8 0:39	16 0:43	☍ P 0.064	GC 27♐25.0 ⚵ 13♊01.0
♇R	29 3:34		♂ ♉	26 19:06		9 1:09	♇ ☍		♍	9 4:16	10 8:10	♇ △		♏	10 10:59	22 22:27	☾ 2♓11	Eris 28♈54.5 ✱ 25♋08.9
						10 21:38	☉ △		♎	11 16:16	12 15:12	♇ □		♐	12 17:52	29 22:57	● 8♊56	⚷ 18♋11.0 ⚶ 28♈24.1
☽0S	8 15:13		♀ ♉	5 21:17		13 23:11	♇ △		♏	14 2:01	14 18:57	♇ ⚹		♑	14 21:30			☽ Mean ☊ 15♉39.0
☿D	17 13:43		☉ ♋	20 23:37		16 6:11	♇ □		♐	16 8:51	16 9:48	♃ □		♒	16 23:11	6 21:42	☽ 16♍33	
♃D	18 6:15					18 10:43	♇ ⚹		♑	18 13:16	18 21:59	♇ ☌		♓	19 0:33	14 11:00	○ 23♐46	1 June 2041
♄D	20 1:12					20 8:01	♂ □		♒	20 16:14	20 6:49	♂ ⚹		♈	21 2:59	21 3:13	☾ 0♈09	Julian Day # 51652
☽0N	21 15:21					22 16:17	♇ ☌		♓	22 18:46	23 4:24	♇ ⚹		♉	23 7:13	28 11:18	● 7♋09	SVP 4♓41'05"
						24 3:41	☿ □		♈	24 21:37	25 10:29	♇ □		♊	25 13:27			GC 27♐25.1 ⚵ 1♋16.1
						26 22:51	♇ ⚹		♉	27 1:24	27 18:31	♇ △		♋	27 21:38			Eris 29♈12.8 ✱ 7♌20.9
						29 4:03	♇ □		♊	29 6:41	29 23:13	♀ ⚹		♌	30 7:48			⚷ 20♋37.2 ⚶ 12♉09.9
						31 11:24	♇ △		♋	31 14:09								☽ Mean ☊ 14♉00.5

July 2041 — LONGITUDE

Day	Sid.Time	☉	0 hr ☽	Noon ☽	True ☊	☿	♀	♂	⚳	♃	♄	♅	♆	♇
1 M	6 39 40	10♋02 01	8♌10 33	14♌11 34	13♉35.4	18♊19.3	27♉19.8	26♉12.8	29♌56.3	22♎06.8	17♎48.8	6♌35.5	7♉40.9	28♒19.0
2 Tu	6 43 36	10 59 14	20 10 45	26 08 23	13R 26.5	19 23.8	28 26.3	26 55.7	0♍20.6	22 09.3	17 50.0	6 38.9	7 42.1	28R 18.2
3 W	6 47 33	11 56 28	2♍04 48	8♍00 26	13 19.3	20 32.4	29 32.9	27 38.6	0 45.0	22 11.9	17 51.2	6 42.3	7 43.4	28 17.4
4 Th	6 51 29	12 53 41	13 55 44	19 51 11	13 14.4	21 45.0	0♊39.7	28 21.3	1 09.4	22 14.6	17 52.6	6 45.8	7 44.5	28 16.6
5 F	6 55 26	13 50 53	25 47 20	1♎44 46	13 11.7	23 01.6	1 46.5	29 04.0	1 34.0	22 17.6	17 54.1	6 49.2	7 45.7	28 15.7
6 Sa	6 59 22	14 48 06	7♎44 04	13 45 54	13D 10.8	24 22.1	2 53.5	29 46.6	1 58.6	22 20.7	17 55.7	6 52.7	7 46.8	28 14.8
7 Su	7 03 19	15 45 18	19 50 53	25 59 40	13 11.2	25 46.5	4 00.7	0♊29.2	2 23.2	22 24.0	17 57.4	6 56.2	7 47.9	28 14.0
8 M	7 07 15	16 42 30	2♏12 54	8♏31 10	13R 11.8	27 14.6	5 08.0	1 11.7	2 48.0	22 27.4	17 59.2	6 59.7	7 49.0	28 13.1
9 Tu	7 11 12	17 39 42	14 55 03	21 25 03	13 11.6	28 46.6	6 15.3	1 54.1	3 12.8	22 31.0	18 01.0	7 03.2	7 50.1	28 12.1
10 W	7 15 08	18 36 54	28 01 33	4♐44 52	13 09.7	0♋22.2	7 22.9	2 36.4	3 37.7	22 34.8	18 03.0	7 06.8	7 51.1	28 11.2
11 Th	7 19 05	19 34 06	11♐35 10	18 32 25	13 05.5	2 01.4	8 30.5	3 18.7	4 02.6	22 38.8	18 05.1	7 10.4	7 52.1	28 10.3
12 F	7 23 02	20 31 18	25 36 28	2♑46 56	12 59.0	3 44.0	9 38.3	4 00.9	4 27.6	22 42.9	18 07.2	7 13.9	7 53.0	28 09.3
13 Sa	7 26 58	21 28 30	10♑03 13	17 24 34	12 50.3	5 30.0	10 46.2	4 43.0	4 52.7	22 47.1	18 09.5	7 17.5	7 54.0	28 08.3
14 Su	7 30 55	22 25 42	24 50 03	2♒18 34	12 40.5	7 19.2	11 54.2	5 25.0	5 17.8	22 51.5	18 11.8	7 21.1	7 54.8	28 07.3
15 M	7 34 51	23 22 55	9♒48 57	17 19 57	12 30.6	9 11.4	13 02.3	6 07.0	5 43.0	22 56.1	18 14.3	7 24.7	7 55.7	28 06.3
16 Tu	7 38 48	24 20 08	24 50 23	2♓19 04	12 21.9	11 06.3	14 10.5	6 48.9	6 08.2	23 00.8	18 16.8	7 28.3	7 56.6	28 05.3
17 W	7 42 44	25 17 22	9♓45 00	17 07 16	12 15.2	13 03.9	15 18.9	7 30.7	6 33.5	23 05.7	18 19.4	7 32.0	7 57.4	28 04.2
18 Th	7 46 41	26 14 36	24 25 11	1♈38 12	12 10.9	15 03.7	16 27.4	8 12.5	6 58.9	23 10.8	18 22.1	7 35.6	7 58.1	28 03.2
19 F	7 50 38	27 11 51	8♈45 58	15 48 18	12D 09.0	17 05.5	17 36.0	8 54.2	7 24.3	23 15.9	18 24.9	7 39.3	7 58.9	28 02.1
20 Sa	7 54 34	28 09 06	22 45 11	29 36 42	12R 08.6	19 09.1	18 44.6	9 35.8	7 49.8	23 21.3	18 27.8	7 42.9	7 59.6	28 01.0
21 Su	7 58 31	29 06 23	6♉23 01	13♉04 24	12 08.7	21 14.1	19 53.4	10 17.3	8 15.3	23 26.8	18 30.8	7 46.6	8 00.3	27 59.9
22 M	8 02 27	0♌03 40	19 41 10	26 13 39	12 08.1	23 20.1	21 02.4	10 58.8	8 40.9	23 32.4	18 33.9	7 50.3	8 00.9	27 58.8
23 Tu	8 06 24	1 00 58	2♊42 09	9♊07 03	12 05.7	25 26.9	22 11.4	11 40.2	9 06.5	23 38.2	18 37.0	7 53.9	8 01.5	27 57.6
24 W	8 10 20	1 58 17	15 28 37	21 47 08	12 00.7	27 34.1	23 20.5	12 21.5	9 32.2	23 44.1	18 40.3	7 57.6	8 02.1	27 56.5
25 Th	8 14 17	2 55 37	28 02 54	4♋16 05	11 52.9	29 41.5	24 29.7	13 02.8	9 58.0	23 50.2	18 43.6	8 01.3	8 02.7	27 55.3
26 F	8 18 13	3 52 58	10♋26 55	16 35 33	11 42.3	1♌48.8	25 39.0	13 43.9	10 23.8	23 56.4	18 47.0	8 05.0	8 03.2	27 54.2
27 Sa	8 22 10	4 50 19	22 42 07	28 46 46	11 29.7	3 55.7	26 48.4	14 25.0	10 49.6	24 02.7	18 50.5	8 08.7	8 03.7	27 53.0
28 Su	8 26 07	5 47 41	4♌49 36	10♌50 45	11 16.0	6 02.0	27 57.9	15 06.0	11 15.5	24 09.2	18 54.1	8 12.4	8 04.1	27 51.8
29 M	8 30 03	6 45 04	16 50 21	22 48 33	11 02.4	8 07.5	29 07.5	15 46.9	11 41.4	24 15.8	18 57.8	8 16.1	8 04.5	27 50.6
30 Tu	8 34 00	7 42 27	28 45 33	4♍41 32	10 50.0	10 12.1	0♋17.2	16 27.7	12 07.4	24 22.6	19 01.5	8 19.8	8 04.9	27 49.4
31 W	8 37 56	8 39 51	10♍36 47	16 31 35	10 39.6	12 15.5	1 26.9	17 08.4	12 33.5	24 29.5	19 05.3	8 23.5	8 05.3	27 48.2

August 2041 — LONGITUDE

Day	Sid.Time	☉	0 hr ☽	Noon ☽	True ☊	☿	♀	♂	⚳	♃	♄	♅	♆	♇
1 Th	8 41 53	9♌37 16	22♍26 17	28♍21 16	10♉31.9	14♌17.7	2♋36.8	17♊49.1	12♍59.5	24♎36.5	19♎09.2	8♌27.2	8♉05.6	27♒47.0
2 F	8 45 49	10 34 41	4♎16 59	10♎13 55	10R 27.0	16 18.5	3 46.7	18 29.7	13 25.7	24 43.7	19 13.2	8 30.9	8 05.9	27R 45.7
3 Sa	8 49 46	11 32 07	16 12 37	22 13 39	10 24.6	18 18.0	4 56.7	19 10.2	13 51.8	24 51.0	19 17.3	8 34.6	8 06.1	27 44.5
4 Su	8 53 42	12 29 33	28 17 36	4♏25 08	10 23.9	20 16.1	6 06.8	19 50.6	14 18.0	24 58.4	19 21.5	8 38.3	8 06.4	27 43.2
5 M	8 57 39	13 27 01	10♏36 53	16 53 29	10 23.8	22 12.6	7 17.0	20 30.9	14 44.2	25 06.0	19 25.7	8 42.0	8 06.6	27 42.0
6 Tu	9 01 36	14 24 29	23 15 35	29 43 45	10 23.3	24 07.6	8 27.3	21 11.1	15 10.5	25 13.6	19 30.0	8 45.7	8 06.7	27 40.7
7 W	9 05 32	15 21 58	6♐18 31	12♐00 19	10 21.3	26 01.1	9 37.7	21 51.3	15 36.8	25 21.4	19 34.4	8 49.4	8 06.8	27 39.4
8 Th	9 09 29	16 19 27	19 49 29	26 46 10	10 16.9	27 53.0	10 48.1	22 31.3	16 03.2	25 29.4	19 38.8	8 53.1	8 06.9	27 38.2
9 F	9 13 25	17 16 58	3♑50 23	11♑01 54	10 10.1	29 43.4	11 58.6	23 11.3	16 29.6	25 37.4	19 43.4	8 56.7	8 07.0	27 36.9
10 Sa	9 17 22	18 14 29	18 20 18	25 44 52	10 01.0	1♍32.3	13 09.2	23 51.2	16 56.0	25 45.6	19 48.0	9 00.4	8R 07.0	27 35.6
11 Su	9 21 18	19 12 02	3♒14 44	10♒48 47	9 50.6	3 19.6	14 19.9	24 31.0	17 22.4	25 53.8	19 52.6	9 04.1	8 07.0	27 34.3
12 M	9 25 15	20 09 35	18 25 44	26 04 13	9 40.0	5 05.3	15 30.7	25 10.7	17 48.9	26 02.2	19 57.4	9 07.7	8 07.0	27 33.0
13 Tu	9 29 11	21 07 09	3♓42 47	11♓20 02	9 30.5	6 49.6	16 41.6	25 50.3	18 15.5	26 10.7	20 02.2	9 11.4	8 06.9	27 31.7
14 W	9 33 08	22 04 45	18 54 39	26 25 27	9 23.0	8 32.3	17 52.5	26 29.9	18 42.0	26 19.3	20 07.1	9 15.0	8 06.8	27 30.4
15 Th	9 37 05	23 02 22	3♈51 26	11♈11 49	9 18.2	10 13.6	19 03.5	27 09.3	19 08.6	26 28.1	20 12.0	9 18.7	8 06.6	27 29.1
16 F	9 41 01	24 00 01	18 26 03	25 33 47	9D 15.9	11 53.4	20 14.6	27 48.7	19 35.2	26 36.9	20 17.0	9 22.3	8 06.5	27 27.8
17 Sa	9 44 58	24 57 41	2♉34 52	9♉29 19	9 15.3	13 31.7	21 25.8	28 27.9	20 01.8	26 45.8	20 22.1	9 25.9	8 06.3	27 26.5
18 Su	9 48 54	25 55 23	16 17 18	22 59 07	9R 15.5	15 08.6	22 37.1	29 07.1	20 28.5	26 54.9	20 27.3	9 29.5	8 06.0	27 25.2
19 M	9 52 51	26 53 07	29 35 06	6♊05 42	9 15.2	16 44.0	23 48.4	29 46.2	20 55.2	27 04.0	20 32.5	9 33.1	8 05.8	27 23.9
20 Tu	9 56 47	27 50 52	12♊31 21	18 52 38	9 13.4	18 17.9	24 59.9	0♋25.2	21 22.0	27 13.3	20 37.8	9 36.6	8 05.5	27 22.6
21 W	10 00 44	28 48 39	25 09 42	1♋23 20	9 09.2	19 50.5	26 11.4	1 04.1	21 48.7	27 22.7	20 43.1	9 40.2	8 05.1	27 21.3
22 Th	10 04 40	29 46 27	7♋33 49	13 41 34	9 02.4	21 21.5	27 23.0	1 42.9	22 15.5	27 32.1	20 48.5	9 43.7	8 04.8	27 20.0
23 F	10 08 37	0♍44 17	19 46 57	25 50 16	8 53.1	22 51.2	28 34.6	2 21.6	22 42.3	27 41.7	20 54.0	9 47.3	8 04.4	27 18.6
24 Sa	10 12 34	1 42 09	1♌51 49	7♌51 51	8 41.9	24 19.3	29 46.3	3 00.3	23 09.2	27 51.4	20 59.6	9 50.8	8 04.0	27 17.3
25 Su	10 16 30	2 40 02	13 50 37	19 48 17	8 29.6	25 46.0	0♌58.1	3 38.8	23 36.1	28 01.1	21 05.1	9 54.3	8 03.5	27 16.0
26 M	10 20 27	3 37 57	25 45 04	1♍41 09	8 17.3	27 11.2	2 10.0	4 17.2	24 03.0	28 11.0	21 10.8	9 57.7	8 03.0	27 14.7
27 Tu	10 24 23	4 35 53	7♍36 42	13 31 55	8 06.1	28 34.9	3 21.9	4 55.5	24 29.9	28 20.9	21 16.5	10 01.2	8 02.5	27 13.4
28 W	10 28 20	5 33 50	19 27 00	25 22 10	7 56.8	29 57.0	4 33.9	5 33.7	24 56.8	28 31.0	21 22.3	10 04.6	8 01.9	27 12.1
29 Th	10 32 16	6 31 49	1♎17 41	7♎13 51	7 49.9	1♎17.5	5 46.0	6 11.8	25 23.8	28 41.1	21 28.1	10 08.1	8 01.3	27 10.8
30 F	10 36 13	7 29 50	13 10 58	19 09 25	7 45.7	2 36.5	6 58.2	6 49.8	25 50.8	28 51.3	21 34.0	10 11.5	8 00.7	27 09.5
31 Sa	10 40 09	8 27 52	25 09 36	1♏11 59	7D 43.9	3 53.8	8 10.4	7 27.7	26 17.8	29 01.7	21 39.9	10 14.8	8 00.1	27 08.3

Astro Data

	Dy Hr Mn
☽ 0S	5 22:29
☽ 0N	18 20:38
♅□♆	25 22:12
☽ 0S	2 4:29
♆ R	10 19:57
☽ 0N	15 4:04
♃△♇	21 8:50
☿0S	27 11:40
☽ 0S	29 9:52

Planet Ingress

		Dy Hr Mn
⚳	♍	1 15:41
♀	♊	3 21:45
♂	♊	6 19:32
☿	♋	10 6:31
☉	♌	22 10:28
☿	♌	25 15:29
♀	♋	30 6:06
☿	♍	9 15:38
♂	♋	19 20:29
☉	♍	22 17:37
♀	♌	24 16:34
☿	♎	28 12:53

Last Aspect / ☽ Ingress (July)

Last Aspect Dy Hr Mn			☽ Ingress	Dy Hr Mn
2 17:07	♀	□	♍	2 19:48
5 6:16	♂	△	♎	5 8:29
7 16:20	♇	△	♏	7 19:45
10 0:18	♇	□	♐	10 3:33
12 4:17	♇	⚹	♑	12 7:22
13 20:44	♃	□	♒	14 8:18
16 5:13	♇	☌	♓	16 8:16
18 2:23	☉	△	♈	18 9:16
20 9:14	☉	□	♉	20 12:41
22 15:14	♇	□	♊	22 18:59
24 23:47	♇	△	♋	25 3:45
27 2:34	♃	□	♌	27 14:25
30 2:07	♀	⚹	♍	30 2:30

Last Aspect / ☽ Ingress (August)

Last Aspect Dy Hr Mn			☽ Ingress	Dy Hr Mn
31 13:19	♂	□	♎	1 15:20
3 22:54	♇	△	♏	4 3:21
6 8:13	♇	□	♐	6 12:30
8 14:12	☿	△	♑	8 17:31
10 12:01	♃	□	♒	10 18:49
12 14:19	♇	☌	♓	12 18:10
14 12:08	♂	□	♈	14 17:45
16 16:01	♂	⚹	♉	16 19:34
18 20:02	♇	□	♊	19 0:46
21 6:36	☉	⚹	♋	21 9:19
23 18:03	♀	☌	♌	23 20:17
26 4:49	♃	⚹	♍	26 8:35
27 0:53	♆	△	♎	28 21:23
31 7:38	♃	☌	♏	31 9:37

☽ Phases & Eclipses

Dy Hr Mn		
6 14:14	☽	14♎53
13 19:02	○	21♑45
20 9:14	☾	28♈03
28 1:04	●	5♌22
5 4:54	☽	13♏10
12 2:06	○	19♒46
18 17:44	☾	26♉09
26 16:17	●	3♍48

Astro Data

1 July 2041
Julian Day # 51682
SVP 4♓40'59"
GC 27♐25.1 ⚴ 19♋03.7
Eris 29♈24.4 ⚵ 19♌47.4
⚷ 23♋41.5 ⚶ 24♉40.4
☽ Mean ☊ 12♉25.2

1 August 2041
Julian Day # 51713
SVP 4♓40'54"
GC 27♐25.2 ⚴ 7♌02.7
Eris 29♈27.2R ⚵ 2♍49.5
⚷ 27♋08.6 ⚶ 6♊17.0
☽ Mean ☊ 10♉46.7

LONGITUDE — September 2041

Day	Sid.Time	☉	0 hr ☽	Noon ☽	True ☊	☿	♀	♂	⚳	♃	♄	♅	♆	♇
1 Su	10 44 06	9♍25 55	7♏17 02	13♏25 17	7♉43.8	5♎09.3	9♌22.6	8♋05.4	26♍44.8	29♎12.1	21♎45.9	10♌18.2	7♉59.4	27♒07.0
2 M	10 48 03	10 24 00	19 37 16	25 53 34	7 44.6	6 23.1	10 35.0	8 43.1	27 11.8	29 22.5	21 51.9	10 21.5	7R58.7	27R05.7
3 Tu	10 51 59	11 22 06	2♐14 44	8♐41 19	7R45.2	7 35.0	11 47.4	9 20.7	27 38.9	29 33.1	21 58.0	10 24.9	7 57.9	27 04.4
4 W	10 55 56	12 20 14	15 13 51	21 52 47	7 44.8	8 45.0	12 59.8	9 58.1	28 06.0	29 43.8	22 04.1	10 28.1	7 57.2	27 03.2
5 Th	10 59 52	13 18 23	28 38 32	5♑31 20	7 42.6	9 52.9	14 12.4	10 35.5	28 33.0	29 54.5	22 10.3	10 31.4	7 56.4	27 01.9
6 F	11 03 49	14 16 34	12♑31 20	19 38 31	7 38.4	10 58.7	15 25.0	11 12.7	29 00.1	0♏05.3	22 16.5	10 34.7	7 55.6	27 00.7
7 Sa	11 07 45	15 14 46	26 52 37	4♒13 12	7 32.3	12 02.3	16 37.6	11 49.8	29 27.3	0 16.2	22 22.8	10 37.9	7 54.7	26 59.5
8 Su	11 11 42	16 12 59	11♒39 37	19 10 57	7 25.0	13 03.5	17 50.3	12 26.8	29 54.4	0 27.2	22 29.1	10 41.1	7 53.8	26 58.2
9 M	11 15 38	17 11 15	26 46 09	4♓23 57	7 17.3	14 02.2	19 03.1	13 03.7	0♎21.5	0 38.2	22 35.5	10 44.2	7 52.9	26 57.0
10 Tu	11 19 35	18 09 31	12♓03 00	19 41 55	7 10.4	14 58.1	20 15.9	13 40.5	0 48.7	0 49.3	22 41.9	10 47.4	7 52.0	26 55.8
11 W	11 23 32	19 07 50	27 19 18	4♈53 50	7 05.1	15 51.2	21 28.8	14 17.2	1 15.8	1 00.5	22 48.3	10 50.5	7 51.0	26 54.6
12 Th	11 27 28	20 06 10	12♈24 20	19 49 49	7 01.9	16 41.3	22 41.8	14 53.7	1 43.0	1 11.7	22 54.8	10 53.5	7 50.0	26 53.4
13 F	11 31 25	21 04 33	27 09 28	4♉22 42	7D00.7	17 28.0	23 54.8	15 30.2	2 10.2	1 23.1	23 01.3	10 56.6	7 49.0	26 52.2
14 Sa	11 35 21	22 02 57	11♉29 06	18 28 31	7 01.1	18 11.3	25 07.9	16 06.5	2 37.4	1 34.5	23 07.9	10 59.6	7 48.0	26 51.1
15 Su	11 39 18	23 01 24	25 20 55	2♊06 27	7 02.3	18 50.8	26 21.1	16 42.7	3 04.6	1 45.9	23 14.5	11 02.6	7 46.9	26 49.9
16 M	11 43 14	23 59 53	8♊45 23	15 18 05	7R03.5	19 26.2	27 34.3	17 18.8	3 31.8	1 57.4	23 21.2	11 05.6	7 45.8	26 48.8
17 Tu	11 47 11	24 58 24	21 45 00	28 06 36	7 03.8	19 57.2	28 47.6	17 54.7	3 59.1	2 09.0	23 27.8	11 08.5	7 44.7	26 47.6
18 W	11 51 07	25 56 57	4♋23 25	10♋35 57	7 02.6	20 23.6	0♍00.9	18 30.6	4 26.3	2 20.7	23 34.6	11 11.4	7 43.6	26 46.5
19 Th	11 55 04	26 55 33	16 44 46	22 50 23	6 59.6	20 44.8	1 14.3	19 06.3	4 53.6	2 32.4	23 41.3	11 14.2	7 42.4	26 45.4
20 F	11 59 01	27 54 10	28 53 16	4♌53 54	6 54.9	21 00.7	2 27.8	19 41.8	5 20.8	2 44.2	23 48.1	11 17.1	7 41.2	26 44.3
21 Sa	12 02 57	28 52 50	10♌52 44	16 50 11	6 48.9	21 10.8	3 41.3	20 17.3	5 48.1	2 56.0	23 54.9	11 19.9	7 40.0	26 43.3
22 Su	12 06 54	29 51 32	22 46 35	28 42 19	6 42.1	21R14.8	4 54.8	20 52.6	6 15.3	3 07.9	24 01.8	11 22.6	7 38.8	26 42.2
23 M	12 10 50	0♎50 16	4♍37 40	10♍32 55	6 35.2	21 12.2	6 08.5	21 27.7	6 42.6	3 19.9	24 08.6	11 25.3	7 37.5	26 41.2
24 Tu	12 14 47	1 49 02	16 28 20	22 24 09	6 28.9	21 02.8	7 22.1	22 02.8	7 09.9	3 31.9	24 15.6	11 28.0	7 36.2	26 40.1
25 W	12 18 43	2 47 49	28 20 35	4♎17 52	6 23.9	20 46.3	8 35.8	22 37.7	7 37.2	3 44.0	24 22.5	11 30.7	7 34.9	26 39.1
26 Th	12 22 40	3 46 39	10♎16 12	16 15 49	6 20.4	20 22.4	9 49.6	23 12.4	8 04.4	3 56.1	24 29.5	11 33.3	7 33.6	26 38.1
27 F	12 26 36	4 45 31	22 16 56	28 19 48	6D18.6	19 51.2	11 03.4	23 47.0	8 31.7	4 08.2	24 36.4	11 35.8	7 32.3	26 37.1
28 Sa	12 30 33	5 44 25	4♏24 42	10♏31 54	6 18.4	19 12.6	12 17.3	24 21.4	8 59.0	4 20.5	24 43.5	11 38.4	7 30.9	26 36.2
29 Su	12 34 29	6 43 20	16 41 44	22 54 30	6 19.3	18 26.8	13 31.2	24 55.7	9 26.3	4 32.7	24 50.5	11 40.9	7 29.5	26 35.2
30 M	12 38 26	7 42 18	29 10 36	5♐30 22	6 20.9	17 34.5	14 45.1	25 29.9	9 53.6	4 45.0	24 57.6	11 43.3	7 28.1	26 34.3

LONGITUDE — October 2041

Day	Sid.Time	☉	0 hr ☽	Noon ☽	True ☊	☿	♀	♂	⚳	♃	♄	♅	♆	♇
1 Tu	12 42 23	8♎41 17	11♐54 12	18♐22 29	6♉22.6	16♎36.2	15♍59.1	26♋03.9	10♎20.8	4♏57.4	25♎04.6	11♌45.7	7♉26.7	26♒33.4
2 W	12 46 19	9 40 18	24 55 35	1♑33 51	6R23.6	15R33.0	17 13.2	26 37.7	10 48.1	5 09.8	25 11.8	11 48.1	7R25.3	26R32.5
3 Th	12 50 16	10 39 21	8♑17 35	15 07 00	6 23.8	14 26.1	18 27.3	27 11.4	11 15.4	5 22.3	25 18.9	11 50.4	7 23.8	26 31.6
4 F	12 54 12	11 38 26	22 02 15	29 03 23	6 22.8	13 17.2	19 41.4	27 44.9	11 42.6	5 34.8	25 26.0	11 52.7	7 22.4	26 30.8
5 Sa	12 58 09	12 37 32	6♒10 18	13♒22 47	6 20.8	12 07.8	20 55.5	28 18.3	12 09.9	5 47.3	25 33.2	11 55.0	7 20.9	26 29.9
6 Su	13 02 05	13 36 40	20 40 24	28 02 37	6 18.1	10 59.8	22 09.7	28 51.5	12 37.2	5 59.9	25 40.4	11 57.2	7 19.4	26 29.1
7 M	13 06 02	14 35 50	5♓28 41	12♓57 43	6 15.1	9 55.2	23 24.0	29 24.5	13 04.4	6 12.5	25 47.5	11 59.3	7 17.8	26 28.3
8 Tu	13 09 58	15 35 01	20 28 45	28 00 40	6 12.4	8 55.7	24 38.3	29 57.4	13 31.6	6 25.1	25 54.7	12 01.5	7 16.3	26 27.5
9 W	13 13 55	16 34 15	5♈32 19	13♈02 33	6 10.4	8 03.1	25 52.6	0♌30.1	13 58.9	6 37.8	26 02.0	12 03.5	7 14.8	26 26.8
10 Th	13 17 52	17 33 30	20 30 16	27 54 27	6D09.3	7 18.9	27 07.0	1 02.6	14 26.1	6 50.5	26 09.2	12 05.5	7 13.2	26 26.0
11 F	13 21 48	18 32 48	5♉14 10	12♉28 40	6 09.3	6 44.1	28 21.4	1 35.0	14 53.3	7 03.2	26 16.4	12 07.5	7 11.6	26 25.3
12 Sa	13 25 45	19 32 08	19 37 20	26 39 45	6 10.0	6 19.6	29 35.8	2 07.2	15 20.5	7 16.0	26 23.7	12 09.5	7 10.1	26 24.6
13 Su	13 29 41	20 31 30	3♊35 38	10♊24 54	6 11.1	6D05.9	0♎50.3	2 39.2	15 47.7	7 28.8	26 30.9	12 11.3	7 08.5	26 24.0
14 M	13 33 38	21 30 54	17 07 34	23 43 49	6 12.4	6 03.2	2 04.8	3 11.0	16 14.9	7 41.7	26 38.2	12 13.2	7 06.9	26 23.3
15 Tu	13 37 34	22 30 21	0♋13 55	6♋38 15	6 13.4	6 11.4	3 19.4	3 42.6	16 42.0	7 54.5	26 45.5	12 15.0	7 05.3	26 22.7
16 W	13 41 31	23 29 50	12 57 14	19 11 23	6R13.9	6 30.1	4 34.0	4 14.1	17 09.2	8 07.4	26 52.8	12 16.7	7 03.6	26 22.1
17 Th	13 45 27	24 29 21	25 21 13	1♌27 17	6 13.9	6 58.9	5 48.7	4 45.3	17 36.4	8 20.3	27 00.0	12 18.4	7 02.0	26 21.5
18 F	13 49 24	25 28 55	7♌30 10	13 30 24	6 13.2	7 37.1	7 03.3	5 16.4	18 03.5	8 33.3	27 07.3	12 20.1	7 00.4	26 21.0
19 Sa	13 53 21	26 28 31	19 28 35	25 25 14	6 12.2	8 23.9	8 18.0	5 47.3	18 30.6	8 46.3	27 14.6	12 21.7	6 58.7	26 20.4
20 Su	13 57 17	27 28 09	1♍20 51	7♍15 58	6 11.0	9 18.6	9 32.8	6 17.9	18 57.7	8 59.3	27 21.9	12 23.2	6 57.1	26 19.9
21 M	14 01 14	28 27 49	13 11 02	19 06 28	6 09.8	10 20.2	10 47.5	6 48.3	19 24.8	9 12.3	27 29.2	12 24.7	6 55.4	26 19.4
22 Tu	14 05 10	29 27 31	25 02 40	1♎00 00	6 08.8	11 28.0	12 02.4	7 18.6	19 51.9	9 25.3	27 36.5	12 26.2	6 53.7	26 19.0
23 W	14 09 07	0♏27 15	6♎58 47	12 59 20	6 08.1	12 41.2	13 17.2	7 48.6	20 19.0	9 38.4	27 43.8	12 27.6	6 52.0	26 18.5
24 Th	14 13 03	1 27 02	19 01 52	25 06 39	6D07.7	13 59.0	14 32.1	8 18.3	20 46.0	9 51.4	27 51.1	12 28.9	6 50.4	26 18.1
25 F	14 17 00	2 26 50	1♏13 52	7♏23 41	6 07.6	15 20.9	15 46.9	8 47.9	21 13.0	10 04.5	27 58.3	12 30.2	6 48.7	26 17.7
26 Sa	14 20 56	3 26 41	13 36 17	19 51 47	6 07.7	16 46.2	17 01.9	9 17.2	21 40.0	10 17.6	28 05.6	12 31.4	6 47.0	26 17.4
27 Su	14 24 53	4 26 33	26 10 18	2♐31 59	6 07.8	18 14.2	18 16.8	9 46.3	22 07.0	10 30.7	28 12.9	12 32.6	6 45.3	26 17.0
28 M	14 28 50	5 26 28	8♐56 55	15 25 13	6R08.0	19 44.7	19 31.8	10 15.1	22 34.0	10 43.9	28 20.1	12 33.8	6 43.6	26 16.7
29 Tu	14 32 46	6 26 24	21 56 59	28 32 19	6 08.0	21 17.0	20 46.8	10 43.7	23 00.9	10 57.0	28 27.4	12 34.8	6 41.9	26 16.4
30 W	14 36 43	7 26 21	5♑11 18	11♑54 01	6 07.9	22 50.9	22 01.8	11 12.1	23 27.8	11 10.1	28 34.6	12 35.9	6 40.3	26 16.2
31 Th	14 40 39	8 26 21	18 40 32	25 30 52	6D07.8	24 26.0	23 16.8	11 40.2	23 54.7	11 23.3	28 41.9	12 36.8	6 38.6	26 15.9

Astro Data

	Dy Hr Mn
☽0N	11 13:57
☿R	22 14:45
⊙0S	22 15:28
☽0S	25 15:34
☽0N	9 0:54
♃☍♆	12 2:04
♄△♇	12 14:55
☿D	14 5:51
⚳0S	15 2:50
♀0S	15 15:26
☽0S	22 22:17

Planet Ingress

	Dy Hr Mn
♃ ♏	6 0:13
⚳ ♎	8 16:58
♀ ♍	18 11:42
⊙ ♎	22 15:28
♂ ♌	8 13:55
♀ ♎	12 19:47
⊙ ♏	23 1:03

Last Aspect / ☽ Ingress

Last Aspect Dy Hr Mn		☽ Ingress Dy Hr Mn
2 14:17	♇ □	♐ 2 19:47
5 2:06	♃ ✶	♑ 5 2:23
6 16:25	♄ □	♒ 7 5:07
9 0:18	♇ ☌	♓ 9 5:05
10 9:25	⊙ ☍	♈ 11 4:14
12 23:33	♇ ✶	♉ 13 4:42
15 2:38	♇ □	♊ 15 13:51
17 13:26	♀ ✶	♋ 17 15:36
19 20:49	⊙ ✶	♌ 20 2:13
22 7:57	♇ ☍	♍ 22 14:37
24 11:15	♂ ✶	♎ 25 3:21
27 8:37	♇ △	♏ 27 15:18
29 19:03	♇ □	♐ 30 1:34

Last Aspect Dy Hr Mn		☽ Ingress Dy Hr Mn
2 2:57	♇ ✶	♑ 2 9:11
4 9:41	♂ ☍	♒ 4 13:36
6 9:28	♇ ☌	♓ 6 15:10
8 6:09	♀ ☍	♈ 8 15:10
10 9:36	♇ ✶	♉ 10 15:25
12 17:33	♀ △	♊ 12 17:45
14 17:24	♄ △	♋ 14 23:34
17 3:08	♄ □	♌ 17 9:08
19 15:44	♄ ✶	♍ 19 21:16
20 15:33	♃ ✶	♎ 22 9:59
24 17:26	♄ ☌	♏ 24 21:36
27 0:13	♇ □	♐ 27 7:14
29 11:51	♄ ✶	♑ 29 14:39
31 17:36	♄ □	♒ 31 19:49

☽ Phases & Eclipses

Dy Hr Mn	
3 17:20	☽ 11♐35
10 9:25	○ 18♓03
17 5:34	☾ 24♊43
25 8:42	● 2♎40
3 3:34	☽ 10♑19
9 18:04	○ 16♈49
16 21:06	☾ 23♋52
25 1:32	● 2♏01
25 1:36:22	● A 06'07"

Astro Data

1 September 2041
Julian Day # 51744
SVP 4♓40'50"
GC 27♐25.3 ⚴ 24♌13.9
Eris 29♈20.2R ⚵ 15♍44.2
⚷ 0♌23.9 ⚶ 15♊42.9
☽ Mean ☊ 9♉08.2

1 October 2041
Julian Day # 51774
SVP 4♓40'47"
GC 27♐25.3 ⚴ 9♍50.6
Eris 29♈05.8R ⚵ 27♍52.0
⚷ 2♌53.5 ⚶ 21♊22.1
☽ Mean ☊ 7♉32.9

November 2041 LONGITUDE

Day	Sid.Time	☉	0 hr ☽	Noon ☽	True☊	☿	♀	♂	⚳	♃	♄	♅	♆	♇
1 F	14 44 36	9♏26 22	2♒25 03	9♒23 01	6♉07.7	26♎02.1	24♎31.9	12♌08.0	24♎21.5	11♏36.5	28♎49.1	12♌37.8	6♉36.9	26♒15.7
2 Sa	14 48 32	10 26 24	16 24 42	23 29 56	6 07.8	27 38.9	25 46.9	12 35.6	24 48.4	11 49.6	28 56.3	12 38.6	6R 35.2	26R 15.5
3 Su	14 52 29	11 26 28	0♓38 30	7♓50 04	6 08.2	29 16.3	27 02.0	13 02.9	25 15.2	12 02.8	29 03.5	12 39.4	6 33.5	26 15.4
4 M	14 56 25	12 26 33	15 04 15	22 20 33	6 08.7	0♏54.0	28 17.1	13 30.0	25 41.9	12 15.9	29 10.6	12 40.2	6 31.8	26 15.3
5 Tu	15 00 22	13 26 40	29 38 26	6♈57 13	6 09.3	2 32.0	29 32.2	13 56.7	26 08.7	12 29.1	29 17.8	12 40.9	6 30.2	26 15.1
6 W	15 04 19	14 26 49	14♈16 13	21 34 40	6 09.8	4 10.0	0♏47.4	14 23.2	26 35.4	12 42.3	29 24.9	12 41.5	6 28.5	26 15.1
7 Th	15 08 15	15 26 59	28 51 49	6♉06 51	6R 10.0	5 48.1	2 02.5	14 49.4	27 02.0	12 55.4	29 32.0	12 42.1	6 26.8	26 15.0
8 F	15 12 12	16 27 11	13♉19 02	20 27 40	6 09.8	7 26.2	3 17.7	15 15.3	27 28.7	13 08.6	29 39.1	12 42.7	6 25.2	26D 15.0
9 Sa	15 16 08	17 27 25	27 32 07	4♊31 50	6 08.9	9 04.1	4 32.9	15 41.0	27 55.3	13 21.8	29 46.2	12 43.2	6 23.5	26 15.0
10 Su	15 20 05	18 27 41	11♊26 24	18 15 30	6 07.5	10 41.9	5 48.1	16 06.3	28 21.9	13 34.9	29 53.3	12 43.6	6 21.9	26 15.0
11 M	15 24 01	19 27 59	24 58 55	1♋36 35	6 05.7	12 19.6	7 03.4	16 31.3	28 48.4	13 48.1	0♏00.3	12 44.0	6 20.2	26 15.1
12 Tu	15 27 58	20 28 18	8♋08 33	14 34 58	6 03.8	13 57.0	8 18.6	16 56.0	29 14.9	14 01.2	0 07.3	12 44.3	6 18.6	26 15.1
13 W	15 31 54	21 28 40	20 56 05	27 12 13	6 02.0	15 34.2	9 33.9	17 20.4	29 41.4	14 14.4	0 14.3	12 44.6	6 17.0	26 15.2
14 Th	15 35 51	22 29 03	3♌23 49	9♌31 21	6 00.7	17 11.1	10 49.2	17 44.4	0♏07.8	14 27.5	0 21.2	12 44.8	6 15.4	26 15.4
15 F	15 39 48	23 29 28	15 35 19	21 36 19	6D 00.2	18 47.8	12 04.5	18 08.1	0 34.2	14 40.6	0 28.2	12 44.9	6 13.8	26 15.5
16 Sa	15 43 44	24 29 55	27 34 54	3♍31 42	6 00.4	20 24.2	13 19.8	18 31.5	1 00.6	14 53.7	0 35.0	12 45.0	6 12.2	26 15.7
17 Su	15 47 41	25 30 24	9♍27 19	15 22 23	6 01.5	22 00.4	14 35.1	18 54.5	1 26.9	15 06.8	0 41.9	12R 45.1	6 10.6	26 15.9
18 M	15 51 37	26 30 55	21 17 28	27 13 09	6 03.0	23 36.4	15 50.5	19 17.1	1 53.2	15 19.8	0 48.7	12 45.1	6 09.1	26 16.2
19 Tu	15 55 34	27 31 27	3♎10 01	9♎08 35	6 04.7	25 12.1	17 05.8	19 39.4	2 19.4	15 32.9	0 55.5	12 45.0	6 07.5	26 16.4
20 W	15 59 30	28 32 01	15 09 20	21 12 43	6 06.2	26 47.6	18 21.2	20 01.3	2 45.6	15 45.9	1 02.3	12 44.9	6 06.0	26 16.7
21 Th	16 03 27	29 32 37	27 19 06	3♏28 51	6R 06.9	28 22.8	19 36.6	20 22.8	3 11.8	15 59.0	1 09.0	12 44.7	6 04.4	26 17.0
22 F	16 07 23	0♐33 15	9♏42 14	15 59 27	6 06.6	29 57.9	20 52.0	20 43.9	3 37.9	16 12.0	1 15.7	12 44.4	6 02.9	26 17.4
23 Sa	16 11 20	1 33 54	22 20 39	28 45 54	6 04.9	1♐32.7	22 07.4	21 04.6	4 03.9	16 24.9	1 22.4	12 44.1	6 01.4	26 17.7
24 Su	16 15 17	2 34 34	5♐15 14	11♐48 33	6 01.9	3 07.4	23 22.8	21 24.9	4 29.9	16 37.9	1 29.0	12 43.8	6 00.0	26 18.1
25 M	16 19 13	3 35 16	18 25 46	25 06 42	5 57.9	4 41.9	24 38.2	21 44.8	4 55.9	16 50.8	1 35.6	12 43.4	5 58.5	26 18.6
26 Tu	16 23 10	4 35 59	1♑51 07	8♑38 47	5 53.3	6 16.3	25 53.7	22 04.2	5 21.8	17 03.7	1 42.1	12 42.9	5 57.1	26 19.0
27 W	16 27 06	5 36 44	15 29 23	22 22 40	5 48.7	7 50.5	27 09.1	22 23.2	5 47.7	17 16.6	1 48.6	12 42.4	5 55.6	26 19.5
28 Th	16 31 03	6 37 29	29 18 17	6♒15 59	5 44.7	9 24.6	28 24.6	22 41.8	6 13.5	17 29.4	1 55.1	12 41.9	5 54.2	26 20.0
29 F	16 34 59	7 38 15	13♒15 29	20 16 29	5 42.0	10 58.6	29 40.0	22 59.8	6 39.2	17 42.2	2 01.5	12 41.2	5 52.9	26 20.5
30 Sa	16 38 56	8 39 02	27 18 46	4♓22 06	5D 40.8	12 32.5	0♐55.5	23 17.5	7 04.9	17 55.0	2 07.8	12 40.6	5 51.5	26 21.1

December 2041 LONGITUDE

Day	Sid.Time	☉	0 hr ☽	Noon ☽	True☊	☿	♀	♂	⚳	♃	♄	♅	♆	♇
1 Su	16 42 53	9♐39 50	11♓26 16	18♓31 05	5♉41.0	14♐06.3	2♐10.9	23♌34.6	7♏30.5	18♏07.7	2♏14.1	12♌39.8	5♉50.1	26♒21.7
2 M	16 46 49	10 40 39	25 36 19	2♈41 47	5 42.3	15 40.1	3 26.4	23 51.3	7 56.1	18 20.4	2 20.4	12R 39.1	5R 48.8	26 22.3
3 Tu	16 50 46	11 41 29	9♈47 15	16 52 28	5 43.8	17 13.8	4 41.8	24 07.5	8 21.6	18 33.1	2 26.6	12 38.2	5 47.5	26 22.9
4 W	16 54 42	12 42 20	23 57 10	1♉01 00	5R 44.8	18 47.5	5 57.3	24 23.1	8 47.0	18 45.7	2 32.7	12 37.3	5 46.2	26 23.6
5 Th	16 58 39	13 43 11	8♉03 39	15 04 43	5 44.5	20 21.1	7 12.8	24 38.3	9 12.4	18 58.3	2 38.8	12 36.4	5 45.0	26 24.2
6 F	17 02 35	14 44 04	22 03 48	29 00 28	5 42.4	21 54.8	8 28.2	24 53.0	9 37.7	19 10.9	2 44.9	12 35.4	5 43.7	26 24.9
7 Sa	17 06 32	15 44 57	5♊54 19	12♊44 54	5 38.2	23 28.4	9 43.7	25 07.1	10 03.0	19 23.4	2 50.9	12 34.4	5 42.5	26 25.7
8 Su	17 10 28	16 45 52	19 31 51	26 14 49	5 32.1	25 02.0	10 59.2	25 20.6	10 28.2	19 35.8	2 56.8	12 33.3	5 41.4	26 26.4
9 M	17 14 25	17 46 47	2♋53 32	9♋27 47	5 24.7	26 35.6	12 14.7	25 33.7	10 53.3	19 48.3	3 02.7	12 32.2	5 40.2	26 27.2
10 Tu	17 18 22	18 47 44	15 57 27	22 22 28	5 16.7	28 09.2	13 30.2	25 46.1	11 18.4	20 00.6	3 08.6	12 31.0	5 39.1	26 28.0
11 W	17 22 18	19 48 41	28 42 55	4♌58 56	5 09.1	29 42.8	14 45.7	25 58.0	11 43.3	20 12.9	3 14.3	12 29.7	5 37.9	26 28.9
12 Th	17 26 15	20 49 40	11♌10 44	17 18 38	5 02.5	1♑16.3	16 01.2	26 09.3	12 08.3	20 25.2	3 20.1	12 28.5	5 36.9	26 29.7
13 F	17 30 11	21 50 40	23 23 03	29 24 25	4 57.6	2 49.9	17 16.7	26 19.9	12 33.1	20 37.4	3 25.7	12 27.1	5 35.8	26 30.6
14 Sa	17 34 08	22 51 40	5♍23 15	11♍20 07	4 54.8	4 23.3	18 32.2	26 30.0	12 57.9	20 49.6	3 31.3	12 25.7	5 34.8	26 31.5
15 Su	17 38 04	23 52 42	17 15 37	23 10 24	4D 53.8	5 56.7	19 47.7	26 39.4	13 22.6	21 01.7	3 36.8	12 24.3	5 33.8	26 32.4
16 M	17 42 01	24 53 44	29 05 07	5♎00 26	4 54.3	7 29.9	21 03.2	26 48.2	13 47.2	21 13.8	3 42.3	12 22.8	5 32.8	26 33.3
17 Tu	17 45 57	25 54 48	10♎57 00	16 55 31	4 55.6	9 03.0	22 18.7	26 56.3	14 11.8	21 25.8	3 47.7	12 21.3	5 31.8	26 34.3
18 W	17 49 54	26 55 52	22 56 36	29 00 51	4R 56.6	10 35.8	23 34.2	27 03.8	14 36.2	21 37.7	3 53.0	12 19.7	5 30.9	26 35.3
19 Th	17 53 51	27 56 57	5♏08 52	11♏21 09	4 56.6	12 08.3	24 49.8	27 10.6	15 00.6	21 49.6	3 58.3	12 18.1	5 30.0	26 36.3
20 F	17 57 47	28 58 03	17 38 08	24 00 11	4 54.6	13 40.5	26 05.3	27 16.7	15 24.9	22 01.4	4 03.5	12 16.5	5 29.1	26 37.3
21 Sa	18 01 44	29 59 10	0♐27 35	7♐00 28	4 50.3	15 12.1	27 20.8	27 22.1	15 49.1	22 13.2	4 08.6	12 14.8	5 28.3	26 38.4
22 Su	18 05 40	1♑00 18	13 38 52	20 22 43	4 43.4	16 43.2	28 36.4	27 26.8	16 13.3	22 24.9	4 13.7	12 13.0	5 27.5	26 39.5
23 M	18 09 37	2 01 26	27 11 46	4♑05 41	4 34.6	18 13.5	29 51.9	27 30.7	16 37.3	22 36.5	4 18.7	12 11.3	5 26.7	26 40.6
24 Tu	18 13 33	3 02 35	11♑04 00	18 06 10	4 24.5	19 42.8	1♑07.4	27 33.9	17 01.3	22 48.1	4 23.6	12 09.4	5 26.0	26 41.7
25 W	18 17 30	4 03 43	25 11 30	2♒19 20	4 14.3	21 11.0	2 23.0	27 36.4	17 25.1	22 59.6	4 28.4	12 07.6	5 25.3	26 42.9
26 Th	18 21 26	5 04 52	9♒28 56	16 39 35	4 05.2	22 37.9	3 38.5	27 38.1	17 48.9	23 11.0	4 33.2	12 05.7	5 24.6	26 44.0
27 F	18 25 23	6 06 01	23 50 35	1♓01 21	3 58.2	24 03.1	4 54.0	27R 39.1	18 12.6	23 22.3	4 37.8	12 03.7	5 24.0	26 45.2
28 Sa	18 29 20	7 07 10	8♓11 18	15 20 01	3 53.7	25 26.3	6 09.5	27 39.2	18 36.2	23 33.6	4 42.5	12 01.8	5 23.3	26 46.4
29 Su	18 33 16	8 08 19	22 27 08	29 32 24	3D 51.6	26 47.2	7 25.1	27 38.7	18 59.6	23 44.8	4 47.0	11 59.7	5 22.8	26 47.6
30 M	18 37 13	9 09 28	6♈35 36	13♈36 40	3 51.4	28 05.2	8 40.6	27 37.3	19 23.0	23 55.9	4 51.4	11 57.7	5 22.2	26 48.9
31 Tu	18 41 09	10 10 36	20 35 32	27 32 12	3R 51.9	29 20.0	9 56.1	27 35.1	19 46.3	24 06.9	4 55.8	11 55.6	5 21.7	26 50.1

Astro Data	Planet Ingress	Last Aspect	☽ Ingress	Last Aspect	☽ Ingress	☽ Phases & Eclipses	Astro Data
Dy Hr Mn	Dy Hr Mn	Dy Hr Mn	Dy Hr Mn	Dy Hr Mn	Dy Hr Mn	Dy Hr Mn	1 November 2041
☽0N 5 10:39	☿ ♏ 3 22:45	2 21:13 ♄ △	♓ 2 22:56	1 11:20 ♃ △	♈ 2 7:26	1 12:06 ☽ 9♒27	Julian Day # 51805
♃□♅ 6 10:37	♀ ♏ 5 20:52	3 19:06 ♃ △	♈ 5 0:35	4 4:08 ♇ ⚹	♉ 4 10:16	8 4:45 ○ 16♉09	SVP 4♓40'43"
♇ D 9 0:11	♄ ♏ 11 10:59	7 1:01 ♄ ☍	♉ 7 1:53	6 7:30 ♇ □	♊ 6 13:43	8 4:35 ☍ P 0.170	GC 27♐25.4 ⚵ 24♍37.8
♅ R 17 17:18	⚳ ♏ 14 4:53	8 21:49 ♇ □	♊ 9 4:13	8 12:21 ♇ △	♋ 8 18:46	15 16:08 ☾ 23♌40	Eris 28♈47.4R ⚴ 9♎41.9
☽0S 19 5:53	☉ ♐ 21 22:50	11 9:03 ♄ △	♋ 11 9:04	10 7:29 ♃ △	♌ 11 2:27	23 17:38 ● 1♐48	⚷ 4♌19.0 ⚶ 21♊31.4R
	☿ ♐ 22 12:33	13 0:05 ☉ △	♌ 13 17:24	13 6:13 ♇ ☍	♍ 13 13:11	30 19:50 ☽ 8♓59	☽ Mean ☊ 5♉54.4
☽0N 2 17:33	♀ ♐ 29 18:22	15 21:20 ♇ ☍	♍ 16 4:52	15 13:34 ☉ □	♎ 16 1:51		
☽0S 16 13:36		18 10:27 ☉ ⚹	♎ 18 17:37	18 8:07 ♂ ⚹	♏ 18 13:56	7 17:43 ○ 15♊59	1 December 2041
♂ R 28 5:40	☿ ♑ 11 16:25	20 21:58 ♇ △	♏ 21 5:14	20 18:09 ♂ □	♐ 20 23:09	15 13:34 ☾ 23♍57	Julian Day # 51835
☽0N 29 22:16	☉ ♑ 21 12:19	23 7:24 ♇ □	♐ 23 14:18	23 3:55 ♀ ☌	♑ 23 4:54	23 8:08 ● 1♑52	SVP 4♓40'38"
	♀ ♑ 23 14:34	25 14:08 ♇ ⚹	♑ 25 20:43	24 20:04 ♃ ⚹	♒ 25 8:06	30 3:47 ☽ 8♈49	GC 27♐25.5 ⚵ 7♎10.3
		27 21:06 ♀ ⚹	♒ 28 1:12	27 6:22 ♂ ☍	♓ 27 10:17		Eris 28♈31.3R ⚴ 20♎00.2
		29 22:21 ♇ ☌	♓ 30 4:34	29 6:51 ☿ ⚹	♈ 29 12:47		⚷ 4♌15.9R ⚶ 15♊34.0R
				31 15:25 ☿ □	♉ 31 16:16		☽ Mean ☊ 4♉19.1

LONGITUDE — January 2042

Day	Sid.Time	☉	0 hr ☽	Noon ☽	True ☊	☿	♀	♂	⚳	♃	♄	♅	♆	♇
1 W	18 45 06	11♑11 45	4♉26 39	11♉18 54	3♉51.8	0♒31.0	11♑11.6	27♌32.2	20♏09.4	24♏17.9	5♏00.1	11♌53.5	5♉21.2	26♒51.4
2 Th	18 49 02	12 12 53	18 08 58	24 56 50	3R 49.9	1 37.4	12 27.1	27R 28.4	20 32.5	24 28.7	5 04.3	11R 51.3	5R 20.8	26 52.7
3 F	18 52 59	13 14 01	1♊42 26	8♊25 41	3 45.4	2 38.7	13 42.6	27 23.9	20 55.4	24 39.5	5 08.4	11 49.2	5 20.3	26 54.0
4 Sa	18 56 55	14 15 09	15 06 30	21 44 43	3 37.9	3 34.0	14 58.0	27 18.5	21 18.3	24 50.2	5 12.4	11 47.0	5 20.0	26 55.4
5 Su	19 00 52	15 16 17	28 20 11	4♋52 44	3 27.6	4 22.5	16 13.5	27 12.3	21 41.0	25 00.8	5 16.4	11 44.7	5 19.6	26 56.7
6 M	19 04 49	16 17 25	11♋22 12	17 48 25	3 15.2	5 03.3	17 29.0	27 05.3	22 03.6	25 11.3	5 20.2	11 42.5	5 19.3	26 58.1
7 Tu	19 08 45	17 18 33	24 11 16	0♌30 41	3 01.7	5 35.4	18 44.5	26 57.6	22 26.2	25 21.7	5 24.0	11 40.2	5 19.0	26 59.5
8 W	19 12 42	18 19 40	6♌46 36	12 59 05	2 48.4	5 58.1	19 59.9	26 48.9	22 48.6	25 32.1	5 27.7	11 37.8	5 18.8	27 00.9
9 Th	19 16 38	19 20 48	19 08 12	25 14 07	2 36.4	6R 10.5	21 15.4	26 39.5	23 10.8	25 42.3	5 31.3	11 35.5	5 18.5	27 02.3
10 F	19 20 35	20 21 55	1♍17 05	7♍17 24	2 26.7	6 11.8	22 30.9	26 29.3	23 33.0	25 52.5	5 34.8	11 33.1	5 18.4	27 03.7
11 Sa	19 24 31	21 23 03	13 15 27	19 11 40	2 19.7	6 01.6	23 46.3	26 18.3	23 55.0	26 02.5	5 38.2	11 30.7	5 18.2	27 05.1
12 Su	19 28 28	22 24 10	25 06 33	1♎00 40	2 15.5	5 39.5	25 01.8	26 06.4	24 16.9	26 12.4	5 41.6	11 28.3	5 18.1	27 06.6
13 M	19 32 25	23 25 17	6♎54 38	12 49 03	2D 13.7	5 05.7	26 17.2	25 53.8	24 38.7	26 22.3	5 44.8	11 25.9	5 18.0	27 08.1
14 Tu	19 36 21	24 26 24	18 44 38	24 42 03	2R 13.3	4 20.7	27 32.7	25 40.4	25 00.4	26 32.0	5 48.0	11 23.4	5D 18.0	27 09.6
15 W	19 40 18	25 27 31	0♏42 00	6♏45 13	2 13.3	3 25.5	28 48.1	25 26.2	25 21.9	26 41.7	5 51.0	11 20.9	5 18.0	27 11.1
16 Th	19 44 14	26 28 38	12 52 22	19 04 06	2 12.5	2 21.5	0♒03.5	25 11.2	25 43.3	26 51.2	5 54.0	11 18.4	5 18.0	27 12.6
17 F	19 48 11	27 29 44	25 21 04	1♐43 46	2 09.7	1 10.6	1 19.0	24 55.5	26 04.5	27 00.6	5 56.8	11 15.9	5 18.0	27 14.1
18 Sa	19 52 07	28 30 51	8♐12 41	14 48 10	2 04.4	29♑55.0	2 34.4	24 39.1	26 25.7	27 09.9	5 59.6	11 13.4	5 18.1	27 15.6
19 Su	19 56 04	29 31 57	21 30 23	28 19 26	1 56.2	28 37.1	3 49.8	24 22.0	26 46.6	27 19.1	6 02.3	11 10.8	5 18.3	27 17.2
20 M	20 00 00	0♒33 02	5♑15 11	12♑17 19	1 45.5	27 19.3	5 05.2	24 04.2	27 07.5	27 28.2	6 04.8	11 08.3	5 18.4	27 18.8
21 Tu	20 03 57	1 34 08	19 25 21	26 38 36	1 33.3	26 03.9	6 20.7	23 45.7	27 28.2	27 37.2	6 07.3	11 05.7	5 18.7	27 20.4
22 W	20 07 54	2 35 12	3♒56 16	11♒17 21	1 20.8	24 53.0	7 36.1	23 26.6	27 48.7	27 46.0	6 09.7	11 03.1	5 18.9	27 21.9
23 Th	20 11 50	3 36 16	18 40 49	26 05 34	1 09.4	23 48.2	8 51.4	23 06.9	28 09.1	27 54.8	6 12.0	11 00.5	5 19.2	27 23.5
24 F	20 15 47	4 37 18	3♓30 30	10♓54 36	1 00.4	22 50.9	10 06.8	22 46.7	28 29.3	28 03.4	6 14.1	10 57.9	5 19.5	27 25.1
25 Sa	20 19 43	5 38 20	18 16 56	25 36 40	0 54.2	22 01.9	11 22.2	22 25.9	28 49.4	28 11.9	6 16.2	10 55.3	5 19.8	27 26.8
26 Su	20 23 40	6 39 21	2♈53 10	10♈05 56	0 50.9	21 21.7	12 37.6	22 04.6	29 09.3	28 20.2	6 18.2	10 52.7	5 20.2	27 28.4
27 M	20 27 36	7 40 20	17 14 37	24 19 02	0D 49.8	20 50.5	13 52.9	21 42.9	29 29.0	28 28.4	6 20.0	10 50.1	5 20.6	27 30.0
28 Tu	20 31 33	8 41 19	1♉19 05	8♉14 49	0R 49.8	20 28.3	15 08.2	21 20.7	29 48.6	28 36.6	6 21.8	10 47.4	5 21.0	27 31.7
29 W	20 35 29	9 42 16	15 06 21	21 53 50	0 49.4	20 14.9	16 23.5	20 58.2	0♐08.0	28 44.5	6 23.5	10 44.8	5 21.5	27 33.3
30 Th	20 39 26	10 43 12	28 37 28	5♊17 28	0 47.4	20D 09.7	17 38.8	20 35.3	0 27.2	28 52.4	6 25.0	10 42.2	5 22.0	27 35.0
31 F	20 43 23	11 44 07	11♊54 03	18 27 24	0 42.8	20 12.4	18 54.1	20 12.2	0 46.3	29 00.1	6 26.5	10 39.6	5 22.6	27 36.7

LONGITUDE — February 2042

Day	Sid.Time	☉	0 hr ☽	Noon ☽	True ☊	☿	♀	♂	⚳	♃	♄	♅	♆	♇
1 Sa	20 47 19	12♒45 00	24♊57 43	1♋25 07	0♉35.2	20♑22.4	20♒09.4	19♌48.8	1♐05.2	29♏07.7	6♏27.8	10♌36.9	5♉23.2	27♒38.3
2 Su	20 51 16	13 45 53	7♋49 44	14 11 39	0R 24.8	20 39.2	21 24.7	19R 25.2	1 23.9	29 15.1	6 29.1	10R 34.3	5 23.8	27 40.0
3 M	20 55 12	14 46 44	20 30 55	26 47 35	0 12.2	21 02.3	22 39.9	19 01.4	1 42.5	29 22.4	6 30.2	10 31.7	5 24.5	27 41.7
4 Tu	20 59 09	15 47 34	3♌01 40	9♌13 13	29♈58.5	21 31.1	23 55.1	18 37.5	2 00.8	29 29.6	6 31.3	10 29.1	5 25.1	27 43.4
5 W	21 03 05	16 48 23	15 22 15	21 28 49	29 44.9	22 05.2	25 10.4	18 13.5	2 19.0	29 36.6	6 32.2	10 26.5	5 25.9	27 45.1
6 Th	21 07 02	17 49 10	27 33 02	3♍34 59	29 32.5	22 44.1	26 25.6	17 49.5	2 37.0	29 43.5	6 33.1	10 23.9	5 26.6	27 46.8
7 F	21 10 58	18 49 57	9♍34 51	15 32 49	29 22.3	23 27.4	27 40.7	17 25.6	2 54.8	29 50.2	6 33.8	10 21.3	5 27.4	27 48.5
8 Sa	21 14 55	19 50 42	21 29 10	27 24 12	29 14.8	24 14.7	28 55.9	17 01.6	3 12.4	29 56.8	6 34.4	10 18.7	5 28.2	27 50.2
9 Su	21 18 52	20 51 26	3♎18 18	9♎11 52	29 10.2	25 05.7	0♓11.1	16 37.8	3 29.8	0♐03.2	6 34.9	10 16.1	5 29.1	27 51.9
10 M	21 22 48	21 52 09	15 05 24	20 59 25	29D 08.1	26 00.0	1 26.2	16 14.2	3 47.0	0 09.5	6 35.3	10 13.6	5 29.9	27 53.6
11 Tu	21 26 45	22 52 51	26 54 30	2♏51 14	29 07.8	26 57.4	2 41.3	15 50.7	4 04.0	0 15.7	6 35.7	10 11.0	5 30.9	27 55.3
12 W	21 30 41	23 53 32	8♏50 17	14 52 18	29R 08.4	27 57.7	3 56.4	15 27.5	4 20.8	0 21.7	6 35.9	10 08.5	5 31.8	27 57.1
13 Th	21 34 38	24 54 12	20 57 59	27 08 00	29 08.6	29 00.6	5 11.5	15 04.6	4 37.3	0 27.5	6R 36.0	10 05.9	5 32.8	27 58.8
14 F	21 38 34	25 54 51	3♐23 01	9♐43 40	29 07.6	0♒05.8	6 26.6	14 41.9	4 53.7	0 33.2	6 36.0	10 03.4	5 33.8	28 00.5
15 Sa	21 42 31	26 55 28	16 10 32	22 44 06	29 04.5	1 13.3	7 41.7	14 19.7	5 09.9	0 38.7	6 35.8	10 01.0	5 34.8	28 02.2
16 Su	21 46 27	27 56 05	29 24 46	6♑12 46	28 59.1	2 22.9	8 56.7	13 57.9	5 25.8	0 44.1	6 35.6	9 58.5	5 35.9	28 04.0
17 M	21 50 24	28 56 40	13♑08 14	20 11 03	28 51.5	3 34.4	10 11.8	13 36.5	5 41.5	0 49.3	6 35.3	9 56.0	5 37.0	28 05.7
18 Tu	21 54 21	29 57 14	27 20 56	4♒37 22	28 42.3	4 47.8	11 26.8	13 15.5	5 57.0	0 54.3	6 34.9	9 53.6	5 38.2	28 07.4
19 W	21 58 17	0♓57 47	11♒59 37	19 26 47	28 32.8	6 02.8	12 41.8	12 55.1	6 12.2	0 59.2	6 34.4	9 51.2	5 39.3	28 09.1
20 Th	22 02 14	1 58 18	26 57 45	4♓31 18	28 24.0	7 19.4	13 56.8	12 35.3	6 27.2	1 03.9	6 33.7	9 48.8	5 40.5	28 10.9
21 F	22 06 10	2 58 47	12♓06 09	19 41 00	28 16.9	8 37.6	15 11.7	12 16.0	6 41.9	1 08.4	6 33.0	9 46.5	5 41.7	28 12.6
22 Sa	22 10 07	3 59 15	27 14 34	4♈45 42	28 12.3	9 57.2	16 26.7	11 57.3	6 56.4	1 12.8	6 32.1	9 44.1	5 43.0	28 14.3
23 Su	22 14 03	4 59 41	12♈13 23	19 36 45	28D 10.1	11 18.2	17 41.6	11 39.3	7 10.7	1 17.0	6 31.2	9 41.8	5 44.3	28 16.0
24 M	22 18 00	6 00 05	26 55 10	4♉08 47	28 10.0	12 40.5	18 56.5	11 22.0	7 24.7	1 21.0	6 30.1	9 39.5	5 45.6	28 17.7
25 Tu	22 21 56	7 00 27	11♉15 20	18 16 41	28 10.9	14 04.1	20 11.4	11 05.3	7 38.4	1 24.8	6 29.0	9 37.3	5 46.9	28 19.5
26 W	22 25 53	8 00 47	25 12 09	2♊01 53	28R 11.8	15 28.9	21 26.2	10 49.4	7 51.9	1 28.5	6 27.7	9 35.0	5 48.3	28 21.2
27 Th	22 29 50	9 01 06	8♊46 05	15 25 02	28 11.7	16 55.0	22 41.0	10 34.1	8 05.2	1 32.0	6 26.4	9 32.8	5 49.7	28 22.9
28 F	22 33 46	10 01 22	21 59 04	28 28 31	28 09.9	18 22.3	23 55.8	10 19.6	8 18.1	1 35.3	6 24.9	9 30.7	5 51.1	28 24.6

Astro Data	Planet Ingress	Last Aspect	☽ Ingress	Last Aspect	☽ Ingress	☽ Phases & Eclipses	Astro Data
Dy Hr Mn	Dy Hr Mn	Dy Hr Mn	Dy Hr Mn	Dy Hr Mn	Dy Hr Mn	Dy Hr Mn	1 January 2042
♄☌♆ 6 6:27	☿ ♒ 1 1:21	2 16:27 ♂ □	♊ 2 20:58	1 4:57 ♇ △	♋ 1 9:21	6 8:55 ○ 16♋10	Julian Day # 51866
☿R 10 2:47	♀ ♒ 16 10:52	4 22:03 ♂ ⚹	♋ 5 3:03	3 17:00 ♃ △	♌ 3 18:10	14 11:26 ☾ 24♎25	SVP 4♓40'32"
☽0S 12 20:43	☿ ♑R 18 10:27	7 2:05 ♃ △	♌ 7 11:02	6 4:15 ♃ □	♍ 6 4:52	21 20:43 ● 1♒56	GC 27♐25.6 ⚵ 17♎23.2
♆D 15 6:20	☉ ♒ 19 23:01	9 15:34 ♇ ☍	♍ 9 21:27	8 17:13 ♃ ⚹	♎ 8 17:17	28 12:50 ☽ 8♉43	Eris 28♈21.6R ⚴ 28♎41.8
♃□♇ 19 5:56	⚳ ♐ 29 2:05	12 2:06 ♃ ⚹	♎ 12 9:57	11 2:02 ♇ △	♏ 11 6:15		⚷ 2♌47.9R ⚶ 8♊21.4R
☽0N 26 3:37		14 18:22 ♀ □	♏ 14 22:36	13 15:58 ☿ ⚹	♐ 13 17:31	5 1:59 ○ 16♌23	☽ Mean ☊ 2♉40.6
♆D 30 15:33	☊ ♈R 4 9:23	17 3:33 ♇ □	♐ 17 8:46	15 21:34 ♇ ⚹	♑ 16 1:03	13 7:18 ☾ 24♏42	
	♃ ♐ 8 23:53	19 10:11 ♇ ⚹	♑ 19 14:55	16 17:14 ♀ ⚹	♒ 18 4:24	20 7:40 ● 1♓47	1 February 2042
☽0S 9 3:07	♀ ♓ 9 8:28	21 13:38 ♃ ⚹	♒ 21 17:32	20 1:55 ♇ ☌	♓ 20 4:50	26 23:31 ☽ 8♊30	Julian Day # 51897
♄R 13 22:51	☿ ♒ 14 9:53	23 14:58 ♃ □	♓ 23 18:19	21 4:15 ♀ ☌	♈ 22 4:23		SVP 4♓40'26"
☽0N 22 11:56	☉ ♓ 18 13:06	25 16:18 ♃ △	♈ 25 19:14	24 2:15 ♇ ⚹	♉ 24 5:06		GC 27♐25.6 ⚵ 23♎05.4
		27 17:27 ♇ ⚹	♉ 27 21:44	26 5:30 ♇ □	♊ 26 8:25		Eris 28♈22.1 ⚴ 4♏10.4
		30 0:20 ♃ ☍	♊ 30 2:28	28 11:53 ♇ △	♋ 28 14:50		⚷ 0♌35.7R ⚶ 6♊51.4
							☽ Mean ☊ 1♉02.1

March 2042 LONGITUDE

Day	Sid.Time	☉	0 hr ☽	Noon ☽	True ☊	☿	♀	♂	⚳	♃	♄	♅	♆	♇
1 Sa	22 37 43	11♓01 36	4♋53 44	11♋15 06	28♈06.0	19♒50.7	25♓10.6	10♌05.9	8♐30.8	1♐38.5	6♏23.4	9♌28.6	5♉52.6	28♒26.3
2 Su	22 41 39	12 01 48	17 32 55	23 47 32	28R 00.0	21 20.2	26 25.3	9R 52.9	8 43.2	1 41.5	6R 21.8	9R 26.5	5 54.1	28 28.0
3 M	22 45 36	13 01 58	29 59 13	6♌08 16	27 52.4	22 50.9	27 40.0	9 40.7	8 55.4	1 44.3	6 20.0	9 24.4	5 55.6	28 29.6
4 Tu	22 49 32	14 02 07	12♌14 54	18 19 22	27 44.0	24 22.7	28 54.7	9 29.3	9 07.2	1 46.9	6 18.2	9 22.4	5 57.1	28 31.3
5 W	22 53 29	15 02 13	24 21 52	0♍22 35	27 35.6	25 55.6	0♈09.3	9 18.6	9 18.8	1 49.3	6 16.2	9 20.4	5 58.7	28 33.0
6 Th	22 57 25	16 02 17	6♍21 43	12 19 27	27 27.9	27 29.7	1 24.0	9 08.7	9 30.1	1 51.6	6 14.2	9 18.4	6 00.2	28 34.6
7 F	23 01 22	17 02 19	18 15 58	24 11 29	27 21.7	29 04.8	2 38.6	8 59.6	9 41.1	1 53.6	6 12.1	9 16.5	6 01.8	28 36.3
8 Sa	23 05 19	18 02 20	0♎06 13	6♎00 25	27 17.4	0♓41.0	3 53.1	8 51.3	9 51.8	1 55.5	6 09.9	9 14.6	6 03.5	28 37.9
9 Su	23 09 15	19 02 19	11 54 22	17 48 23	27D 15.1	2 18.4	5 07.7	8 43.8	10 02.2	1 57.2	6 07.6	9 12.7	6 05.1	28 39.6
10 M	23 13 12	20 02 16	23 42 48	29 38 00	27 14.6	3 56.9	6 22.2	8 37.0	10 12.3	1 58.8	6 05.2	9 10.9	6 06.8	28 41.2
11 Tu	23 17 08	21 02 11	5♏34 25	11♏32 31	27 15.5	5 36.5	7 36.7	8 31.1	10 22.1	2 00.1	6 02.7	9 09.2	6 08.5	28 42.8
12 W	23 21 05	22 02 05	17 32 46	23 35 43	27 17.2	7 17.3	8 51.1	8 25.9	10 31.6	2 01.2	6 00.2	9 07.4	6 10.2	28 44.4
13 Th	23 25 01	23 01 57	29 41 55	5♐51 54	27 18.8	8 59.3	10 05.5	8 21.5	10 40.8	2 02.2	5 57.5	9 05.8	6 11.9	28 46.1
14 F	23 28 58	24 01 47	12♐06 17	18 25 36	27R 19.9	10 42.4	11 19.9	8 17.8	10 49.6	2 03.0	5 54.8	9 04.1	6 13.7	28 47.6
15 Sa	23 32 54	25 01 36	24 50 25	1♑21 12	27 19.9	12 26.7	12 34.3	8 15.0	10 58.2	2 03.6	5 52.0	9 02.5	6 15.5	28 49.2
16 Su	23 36 51	26 01 23	7♑58 26	14 42 28	27 18.5	14 12.1	13 48.7	8 12.8	11 06.3	2 04.0	5 49.1	9 01.0	6 17.3	28 50.8
17 M	23 40 48	27 01 08	21 33 30	28 31 41	27 15.7	15 58.8	15 03.0	8 11.5	11 14.2	2R 04.2	5 46.1	8 59.4	6 19.1	28 52.4
18 Tu	23 44 44	28 00 52	5♒36 56	12♒49 02	27 12.0	17 46.8	16 17.3	8D 10.9	11 21.7	2 04.2	5 43.0	8 58.0	6 21.0	28 53.9
19 W	23 48 41	29 00 34	20 07 31	27 31 45	27 07.8	19 35.9	17 31.5	8 11.0	11 28.9	2 04.0	5 39.9	8 56.6	6 22.9	28 55.5
20 Th	23 52 37	0♈00 14	5♓00 55	12♓33 59	27 03.9	21 26.3	18 45.8	8 11.9	11 35.7	2 03.7	5 36.7	8 55.2	6 24.7	28 57.0
21 F	23 56 34	0 59 52	20 09 50	27 47 11	27 00.9	23 17.9	20 00.0	8 13.4	11 42.2	2 03.1	5 33.4	8 53.8	6 26.7	28 58.5
22 Sa	0 00 30	1 59 28	5♈24 45	13♈01 15	26D 59.0	25 10.7	21 14.1	8 15.7	11 48.3	2 02.4	5 30.0	8 52.6	6 28.6	29 00.0
23 Su	0 04 27	2 59 02	20 35 27	28 06 13	26 58.5	27 04.8	22 28.3	8 18.7	11 54.1	2 01.5	5 26.6	8 51.3	6 30.5	29 01.5
24 M	0 08 23	3 58 34	5♉32 35	12♉53 44	26 59.1	29 00.1	23 42.4	8 22.5	11 59.5	2 00.3	5 23.1	8 50.1	6 32.5	29 03.0
25 Tu	0 12 20	4 58 03	20 09 02	27 18 04	27 00.4	0♈56.6	24 56.4	8 26.8	12 04.6	1 59.0	5 19.5	8 49.0	6 34.5	29 04.4
26 W	0 16 17	5 57 31	4♊20 32	11♊16 22	27 01.8	2 54.3	26 10.4	8 31.9	12 09.2	1 57.6	5 15.9	8 47.9	6 36.5	29 05.9
27 Th	0 20 13	6 56 56	18 05 36	24 48 24	27R 02.9	4 53.1	27 24.4	8 37.6	12 13.6	1 55.9	5 12.2	8 46.9	6 38.5	29 07.3
28 F	0 24 10	7 56 19	1♋25 01	7♋55 49	27 03.3	6 52.9	28 38.4	8 44.0	12 17.5	1 54.0	5 08.4	8 45.9	6 40.5	29 08.7
29 Sa	0 28 06	8 55 39	14 21 11	20 41 35	27 02.9	8 53.8	29 52.3	8 51.0	12 21.1	1 52.0	5 04.6	8 45.0	6 42.5	29 10.1
30 Su	0 32 03	9 54 57	26 57 26	3♌09 14	27 01.6	10 55.5	1♉06.2	8 58.7	12 24.3	1 49.8	5 00.7	8 44.1	6 44.6	29 11.5
31 M	0 35 59	10 54 13	9♌17 27	15 22 33	26 59.7	12 58.0	2 20.0	9 06.9	12 27.1	1 47.4	4 56.8	8 43.2	6 46.7	29 12.9

April 2042 LONGITUDE

Day	Sid.Time	☉	0 hr ☽	Noon ☽	True ☊	☿	♀	♂	⚳	♃	♄	♅	♆	♇
1 Tu	0 39 56	11♈53 27	21♌24 57	27♌25 06	26♈57.4	15♈01.1	3♉33.8	9♌15.8	12♐29.5	1♐44.8	4♏52.8	8♌42.5	6♉48.7	29♒14.2
2 W	0 43 52	12 52 38	3♍23 22	9♍20 10	26R 55.1	17 04.7	4 47.5	9 25.2	12 31.6	1R 42.0	4R 48.8	8R 41.7	6 50.8	29 15.5
3 Th	0 47 49	13 51 47	15 15 50	21 10 41	26 53.1	19 08.5	6 01.3	9 35.2	12 33.2	1 39.1	4 44.7	8 41.0	6 52.9	29 16.9
4 F	0 51 45	14 50 54	27 05 02	2♎59 12	26 51.6	21 12.3	7 14.9	9 45.8	12 34.5	1 36.0	4 40.6	8 40.4	6 55.0	29 18.2
5 Sa	0 55 42	15 49 59	8♎53 26	14 48 00	26 50.7	23 15.8	8 28.6	9 56.9	12 35.4	1 32.7	4 36.4	8 39.8	6 57.2	29 19.4
6 Su	0 59 39	16 49 02	20 43 11	26 39 15	26D 50.4	25 18.8	9 42.1	10 08.5	12R 35.9	1 29.2	4 32.2	8 39.3	6 59.3	29 20.7
7 M	1 03 35	17 48 02	2♏36 27	8♏35 04	26 50.6	27 21.0	10 55.7	10 20.7	12 36.0	1 25.6	4 28.0	8 38.8	7 01.5	29 22.0
8 Tu	1 07 32	18 47 01	14 35 23	20 37 43	26 51.2	29 21.9	12 09.2	10 33.4	12 35.7	1 21.8	4 23.7	8 38.4	7 03.6	29 23.2
9 W	1 11 28	19 45 58	26 42 22	2♐49 40	26 51.9	1♉21.4	13 22.7	10 46.6	12 35.0	1 17.9	4 19.4	8 38.1	7 05.8	29 24.4
10 Th	1 15 25	20 44 54	8♐59 59	15 13 40	26 52.6	3 18.9	14 36.1	11 00.3	12 33.9	1 13.7	4 15.0	8 37.8	7 08.0	29 25.6
11 F	1 19 21	21 43 47	21 31 06	27 52 40	26 53.2	5 14.1	15 49.5	11 14.5	12 32.5	1 09.5	4 10.6	8 37.5	7 10.2	29 26.8
12 Sa	1 23 18	22 42 39	4♑18 43	10♑49 38	26R 53.5	7 06.7	17 02.8	11 29.1	12 30.6	1 05.0	4 06.2	8 37.3	7 12.4	29 27.9
13 Su	1 27 14	23 41 30	17 25 44	24 07 19	26 53.6	8 56.3	18 16.2	11 44.3	12 28.3	1 00.4	4 01.8	8 37.1	7 14.6	29 29.1
14 M	1 31 11	24 40 18	0♒54 37	7♒47 47	26 53.5	10 42.7	19 29.4	11 59.8	12 25.7	0 55.7	3 57.3	8 37.1	7 16.8	29 30.2
15 Tu	1 35 08	25 39 05	14 46 51	21 51 48	26 53.4	12 25.4	20 42.7	12 15.9	12 22.6	0 50.7	3 52.8	8D 37.0	7 19.0	29 31.3
16 W	1 39 04	26 37 50	29 02 24	6♓18 21	26D 53.3	14 04.3	21 55.8	12 32.3	12 19.1	0 45.7	3 48.3	8 37.0	7 21.2	29 32.3
17 Th	1 43 01	27 36 33	13♓39 10	21 04 10	26 53.4	15 39.1	23 09.0	12 49.2	12 15.3	0 40.5	3 43.8	8 37.1	7 23.5	29 33.4
18 F	1 46 57	28 35 14	28 32 37	6♈03 33	26 53.5	17 09.5	24 22.1	13 06.6	12 11.0	0 35.1	3 39.2	8 37.2	7 25.7	29 34.4
19 Sa	1 50 54	29 33 54	13♈35 59	21 08 48	26R 53.5	18 35.5	25 35.2	13 24.3	12 06.4	0 29.6	3 34.7	8 37.4	7 27.9	29 35.4
20 Su	1 54 50	0♉32 32	28 40 53	6♉11 07	26 53.5	19 56.7	26 48.2	13 42.4	12 01.4	0 24.0	3 30.1	8 37.6	7 30.2	29 36.4
21 M	1 58 47	1 31 08	13♉38 26	21 01 50	26 53.3	21 13.1	28 01.2	14 01.0	11 55.9	0 18.2	3 25.5	8 37.9	7 32.4	29 37.4
22 Tu	2 02 43	2 29 42	28 20 29	5♊33 40	26 52.8	22 24.5	29 14.1	14 19.9	11 50.1	0 12.3	3 21.0	8 38.2	7 34.7	29 38.3
23 W	2 06 40	3 28 14	12♊40 48	19 41 31	26 52.1	23 30.8	0♊27.0	14 39.2	11 44.0	0 06.3	3 16.4	8 38.6	7 37.0	29 39.2
24 Th	2 10 37	4 26 44	26 35 36	3♋22 57	26 51.3	24 31.9	1 39.8	14 58.9	11 37.4	0 00.2	3 11.8	8 39.1	7 39.2	29 40.2
25 F	2 14 33	5 25 11	10♋03 40	16 37 56	26 50.5	25 27.7	2 52.6	15 19.0	11 30.5	29♏53.9	3 07.2	8 39.6	7 41.5	29 41.0
26 Sa	2 18 30	6 23 37	23 06 03	29 28 25	26D 50.1	26 18.2	4 05.4	15 39.4	11 23.3	29 47.6	3 02.7	8 40.1	7 43.7	29 41.9
27 Su	2 22 26	7 22 00	5♌45 30	11♌57 46	26 50.1	27 03.2	5 18.1	16 00.2	11 15.7	29 41.1	2 58.1	8 40.7	7 46.0	29 42.7
28 M	2 26 23	8 20 22	18 05 48	24 10 09	26 50.5	27 42.8	6 30.7	16 21.3	11 07.7	29 34.5	2 53.6	8 41.4	7 48.3	29 43.5
29 Tu	2 30 19	9 18 41	0♍11 22	6♍10 02	26 51.4	28 16.8	7 43.3	16 42.7	10 59.4	29 27.9	2 49.0	8 42.1	7 50.5	29 44.3
30 W	2 34 16	10 16 58	12 06 43	18 01 55	26 52.6	28 45.3	8 55.8	17 04.4	10 50.8	29 21.1	2 44.5	8 42.9	7 52.8	29 45.1

Astro Data

	Dy Hr Mn
☿0N	7 14:28
☽0S	8 9:11
♄☍♆	10 2:45
♃ R	18 2:48
♂ D	18 19:52
☉0N	20 11:55
☽0N	21 22:45
☿0N	26 18:41
☽0S	4 15:20
⚳ R	7 6:31
♅ D	15 18:59
☽0N	18 9:44
♃□♇	27 6:42

Planet Ingress

		Dy Hr Mn
♀	♈	5 9:00
☿	♓	8 1:48
☉	♈	20 11:54
☿	♈	25 0:22
♀	♉	29 14:30
☿	♉	8 19:37
☉	♉	19 22:41
♀	♊	23 3:07
♃	♏R	24 12:42

Last Aspect / ☽ Ingress

Last Aspect Dy Hr Mn		☽ Ingress Dy Hr Mn
2 17:39	♀ △	♌ 3 0:02
5 8:20	♇ ☍	♍ 5 11:15
6 20:11	☉ ☍	♎ 7 23:47
10 10:05	♇ △	♏ 10 12:45
12 22:09	♇ □	♐ 13 0:35
15 7:21	♇ ⚹	♑ 15 9:31
17 9:13	☉ ⚹	♒ 17 14:31
19 14:15	♇ ☌	♓ 19 15:58
21 3:57	☿ ☌	♈ 21 15:29
23 13:29	♇ ⚹	♉ 23 15:03
25 15:01	♇ □	♊ 25 16:35
27 19:50	♇ △	♋ 27 21:25
28 12:01	☉ □	♌ 30 5:53

Last Aspect / ☽ Ingress

Last Aspect Dy Hr Mn		☽ Ingress Dy Hr Mn
1 15:39	♇ ☍	♍ 1 17:11
2 6:57	♆ △	♎ 4 5:56
6 17:26	♇ △	♏ 6 18:45
9 5:18	♇ □	♐ 9 6:28
11 14:57	♇ ⚹	♑ 11 15:58
13 11:10	☉ □	♒ 13 22:24
16 0:49	♇ ☌	♓ 16 1:36
17 15:39	♀ ⚹	♈ 18 2:20
20 1:28	♇ ⚹	♉ 20 2:06
22 2:08	♇ □	♊ 22 2:45
24 5:24	♇ △	♋ 24 6:00
26 12:36	♃ △	♌ 26 13:00
28 23:05	♇ ☍	♍ 28 23:37

☽ Phases & Eclipses

Dy Hr Mn		
6 20:11	○	16♍23
14 23:22	☾	24♐30
21 17:24	●	1♈13
28 12:01	☽	7♋56
5 14:17	○	15♎56
5 14:30	•	A 0.868
13 11:10	☾	23♑39
20 2:21	●	0♉09
20 2:17:30	•	T 04'51"
27 2:21	☽	6♌59

Astro Data

1 March 2042
Julian Day # 51925
SVP 4♓40'22"
GC 27♐25.7 ⚴ 22♎17.6R
Eris 28♈31.3 ⚵ 5♏01.8R
⚷ 28♋54.4R ⚶ 10♊58.8
☽ Mean ☊ 29♈33.2

1 April 2042
Julian Day # 51956
SVP 4♓40'19"
GC 27♐25.8 ⚴ 14♎30.0R
Eris 28♈48.6 ⚵ 0♏46.0R
⚷ 28♋13.4 ⚶ 19♊35.7
☽ Mean ☊ 27♈54.7

LONGITUDE May 2042

Day	Sid.Time	☉	0 hr ☽	Noon ☽	True ☊	☿	♀	♂	⚳	♃	♄	♅	♆	♇
1 Th	2 38 12	11♉15 13	23♍56 12	29♍50 01	26♈53.9	29♉08.2	10♊08.3	17♌26.5	10♐41.8	29♏14.2	2♏40.0	8♌43.7	7♉55.0	29♒45.8
2 F	2 42 09	12 13 26	5♎43 50	11♎38 06	26 54.9	29 25.5	11 20.7	17 48.9	10R 32.5	29R 07.3	2R 35.5	8 44.6	7 57.3	29 46.5
3 Sa	2 46 06	13 11 37	17 33 11	23 29 28	26R 55.5	29 37.4	12 33.1	18 11.5	10 22.9	29 00.3	2 31.1	8 45.5	7 59.6	29 47.2
4 Su	2 50 02	14 09 47	29 27 16	5♏26 52	26 55.3	29R 43.8	13 45.4	18 34.5	10 13.1	28 53.2	2 26.6	8 46.5	8 01.8	29 47.9
5 M	2 53 59	15 07 55	11♏28 32	17 32 30	26 54.3	29 45.0	14 57.7	18 57.7	10 02.9	28 46.0	2 22.2	8 47.5	8 04.1	29 48.5
6 Tu	2 57 55	16 06 01	23 38 59	29 48 09	26 52.3	29 41.0	16 09.9	19 21.3	9 52.4	28 38.8	2 17.8	8 48.6	8 06.3	29 49.2
7 W	3 01 52	17 04 05	6♐00 12	12♐15 14	26 49.6	29 32.0	17 22.0	19 45.1	9 41.7	28 31.5	2 13.5	8 49.7	8 08.5	29 49.8
8 Th	3 05 48	18 02 09	18 33 26	24 54 54	26 46.4	29 18.4	18 34.1	20 09.2	9 30.7	28 24.1	2 09.2	8 50.9	8 10.8	29 50.3
9 F	3 09 45	19 00 10	1♑19 47	7♑48 11	26 43.2	29 00.5	19 46.2	20 33.5	9 19.5	28 16.7	2 04.9	8 52.1	8 13.0	29 50.9
10 Sa	3 13 41	19 58 10	14 20 13	20 56 00	26 40.4	28 38.5	20 58.2	20 58.1	9 08.0	28 09.2	2 00.7	8 53.4	8 15.2	29 51.4
11 Su	3 17 38	20 56 09	27 35 38	4♒19 14	26 38.4	28 13.0	22 10.1	21 23.0	8 56.3	28 01.7	1 56.4	8 54.7	8 17.5	29 51.9
12 M	3 21 35	21 54 07	11♒06 52	17 58 34	26D 37.5	27 44.5	23 22.0	21 48.1	8 44.4	27 54.2	1 52.3	8 56.1	8 19.7	29 52.4
13 Tu	3 25 31	22 52 03	24 54 24	1♓54 18	26 37.7	27 13.3	24 33.8	22 13.5	8 32.3	27 46.6	1 48.2	8 57.5	8 21.9	29 52.8
14 W	3 29 28	23 49 58	8♓58 12	16 05 56	26 38.7	26 40.2	25 45.6	22 39.1	8 20.0	27 39.0	1 44.1	8 59.0	8 24.1	29 53.2
15 Th	3 33 24	24 47 52	23 17 16	0♈31 53	26 40.2	26 05.8	26 57.3	23 04.9	8 07.5	27 31.4	1 40.1	9 00.6	8 26.3	29 53.6
16 F	3 37 21	25 45 44	7♈49 21	15 09 07	26R 41.3	25 30.5	28 08.9	23 31.0	7 54.9	27 23.8	1 36.1	9 02.1	8 28.5	29 54.0
17 Sa	3 41 17	26 43 36	22 30 34	29 52 58	26 41.7	24 55.1	29 20.5	23 57.3	7 42.1	27 16.1	1 32.1	9 03.8	8 30.6	29 54.4
18 Su	3 45 14	27 41 26	7♉15 31	14♉37 22	26 40.6	24 20.2	0♋32.0	24 23.9	7 29.2	27 08.5	1 28.3	9 05.4	8 32.8	29 54.7
19 M	3 49 10	28 39 15	21 57 38	29 15 26	26 38.1	23 46.4	1 43.5	24 50.6	7 16.1	27 00.9	1 24.5	9 07.2	8 35.0	29 55.0
20 Tu	3 53 07	29 37 02	6♊29 55	13♊40 19	26 34.1	23 14.2	2 54.9	25 17.6	7 03.0	26 53.2	1 20.7	9 08.9	8 37.1	29 55.3
21 W	3 57 04	0♊34 48	20 45 57	27 46 14	26 29.1	22 44.2	4 06.3	25 44.8	6 49.8	26 45.6	1 17.0	9 10.8	8 39.3	29 55.5
22 Th	4 01 00	1 32 33	4♋40 45	11♋29 12	26 23.7	22 16.8	5 17.6	26 12.2	6 36.5	26 38.0	1 13.4	9 12.6	8 41.4	29 55.7
23 F	4 04 57	2 30 16	18 11 27	24 47 29	26 18.6	21 52.4	6 28.8	26 39.8	6 23.1	26 30.4	1 09.8	9 14.5	8 43.5	29 55.9
24 Sa	4 08 53	3 27 57	1♌17 25	7♌41 31	26 14.6	21 31.5	7 40.0	27 07.7	6 09.7	26 22.8	1 06.3	9 16.5	8 45.6	29 56.1
25 Su	4 12 50	4 25 37	14 00 06	20 13 38	26 11.9	21 14.3	8 51.0	27 35.7	5 56.3	26 15.3	1 02.8	9 18.5	8 47.7	29 56.2
26 M	4 16 46	5 23 16	26 22 36	2♍27 34	26D 10.8	21 01.1	10 02.0	28 03.9	5 42.9	26 07.8	0 59.5	9 20.5	8 49.8	29 56.4
27 Tu	4 20 43	6 20 52	8♍29 07	14 27 53	26 11.1	20 52.1	11 13.0	28 32.3	5 29.5	26 00.4	0 56.2	9 22.6	8 51.8	29 56.5
28 W	4 24 40	7 18 28	20 24 31	26 19 37	26 12.3	20D 47.4	12 23.8	29 00.9	5 16.1	25 53.0	0 52.9	9 24.7	8 53.9	29 56.5
29 Th	4 28 36	8 16 02	2♎13 51	8♎07 50	26 13.9	20 47.1	13 34.6	29 29.7	5 02.8	25 45.7	0 49.8	9 26.9	8 55.9	29 56.6
30 F	4 32 33	9 13 34	14 02 09	19 57 21	26R 15.0	20 51.3	14 45.3	29 58.6	4 49.5	25 38.4	0 46.7	9 29.1	8 57.9	29R 56.6
31 Sa	4 36 29	10 11 06	25 54 00	1♏52 34	26 15.1	21 00.0	15 55.9	0♍27.7	4 36.3	25 31.2	0 43.7	9 31.4	8 59.9	29 56.6

LONGITUDE June 2042

Day	Sid.Time	☉	0 hr ☽	Noon ☽	True ☊	☿	♀	♂	⚳	♃	♄	♅	♆	♇
1 Su	4 40 26	11♊08 36	7♏53 29	13♏57 09	26♈13.4	21♉13.2	17♋06.5	0♍57.0	4♐23.1	25♏24.0	0♏40.7	9♌33.7	9♉01.9	29♒56.5
2 M	4 44 22	12 06 05	20 03 52	26 13 56	26R 09.8	21 30.8	18 17.0	1 26.5	4R 10.1	25R 16.9	0R 37.9	9 36.0	9 03.9	29R 56.5
3 Tu	4 48 19	13 03 33	2♐27 32	8♐44 49	26 04.1	21 52.8	19 27.3	1 56.1	3 57.2	25 09.9	0 35.1	9 38.4	9 05.8	29 56.4
4 W	4 52 15	14 01 00	15 05 51	21 30 40	25 56.9	22 19.2	20 37.6	2 25.9	3 44.4	25 03.0	0 32.4	9 40.8	9 07.8	29 56.3
5 Th	4 56 12	14 58 26	27 59 14	4♑31 26	25 48.7	22 49.8	21 47.8	2 55.8	3 31.7	24 56.2	0 29.8	9 43.3	9 09.7	29 56.2
6 F	5 00 09	15 55 51	11♑07 10	17 46 17	25 40.4	23 24.5	22 58.0	3 25.9	3 19.2	24 49.5	0 27.3	9 45.8	9 11.6	29 56.0
7 Sa	5 04 05	16 53 15	24 28 35	1♒13 53	25 32.8	24 03.4	24 08.0	3 56.2	3 06.9	24 42.8	0 24.8	9 48.3	9 13.5	29 55.8
8 Su	5 08 02	17 50 39	8♒02 00	14 52 44	25 26.9	24 46.2	25 18.0	4 26.6	2 54.7	24 36.3	0 22.5	9 50.9	9 15.4	29 55.6
9 M	5 11 58	18 48 02	21 45 56	28 41 27	25 23.0	25 33.0	26 27.8	4 57.2	2 42.8	24 29.9	0 20.2	9 53.5	9 17.2	29 55.4
10 Tu	5 15 55	19 45 25	5♓39 08	12♓38 51	25D 21.3	26 23.5	27 37.6	5 27.9	2 31.0	24 23.5	0 18.0	9 56.2	9 19.0	29 55.2
11 W	5 19 51	20 42 47	19 40 30	26 43 57	25 21.2	27 17.8	28 47.3	5 58.8	2 19.4	24 17.3	0 15.9	9 58.9	9 20.9	29 54.9
12 Th	5 23 48	21 40 08	3♈49 04	10♈55 42	25 21.9	28 15.7	29 56.9	6 29.8	2 08.1	24 11.2	0 13.9	10 01.6	9 22.6	29 54.6
13 F	5 27 44	22 37 29	18 03 39	25 12 39	25R 22.4	29 17.1	1♌06.4	7 00.9	1 57.0	24 05.2	0 12.0	10 04.3	9 24.4	29 54.2
14 Sa	5 31 41	23 34 50	2♉22 25	9♉32 33	25 21.6	0♊22.1	2 15.8	7 32.2	1 46.2	23 59.3	0 10.1	10 07.1	9 26.2	29 53.9
15 Su	5 35 38	24 32 11	16 42 38	23 52 08	25 18.7	1 30.6	3 25.2	8 03.7	1 35.6	23 53.6	0 08.4	10 09.9	9 27.9	29 53.5
16 M	5 39 34	25 29 30	1♊00 31	8♊07 09	25 13.3	2 42.4	4 34.4	8 35.3	1 25.3	23 48.0	0 06.7	10 12.8	9 29.6	29 53.1
17 Tu	5 43 31	26 26 50	15 11 26	22 12 44	25 05.5	3 57.5	5 43.5	9 07.0	1 15.3	23 42.5	0 05.2	10 15.7	9 31.3	29 52.7
18 W	5 47 27	27 24 09	29 10 29	6♋04 08	24 56.0	5 16.0	6 52.5	9 38.9	1 05.5	23 37.2	0 03.7	10 18.6	9 33.0	29 52.3
19 Th	5 51 24	28 21 27	12♋53 13	19 37 22	24 45.6	6 37.7	8 01.4	10 10.9	0 56.1	23 32.0	0 02.4	10 21.6	9 34.6	29 51.8
20 F	5 55 20	29 18 45	26 16 21	2♌49 59	24 35.5	8 02.6	9 10.3	10 43.0	0 47.0	23 27.0	0 01.1	10 24.6	9 36.2	29 51.3
21 Sa	5 59 17	0♋16 02	9♌18 17	15 41 19	24 26.8	9 30.8	10 19.0	11 15.3	0 38.2	23 22.1	29♎59.9	10 27.6	9 37.8	29 50.8
22 Su	6 03 13	1 13 18	21 59 17	28 12 30	24 20.0	11 02.0	11 27.5	11 47.7	0 29.7	23 17.3	29 58.8	10 30.6	9 39.4	29 50.3
23 M	6 07 10	2 10 34	4♍21 21	10♍26 18	24 15.6	12 36.5	12 36.0	12 20.2	0 21.5	23 12.7	29 57.9	10 33.7	9 40.9	29 49.7
24 Tu	6 11 07	3 07 49	16 27 54	22 26 44	24D 13.4	14 14.0	13 44.3	12 52.8	0 13.7	23 08.3	29 57.0	10 36.8	9 42.5	29 49.1
25 W	6 15 03	4 05 03	28 23 25	4♎18 37	24 12.8	15 54.6	14 52.6	13 25.6	0 06.2	23 04.0	29 56.2	10 39.9	9 43.9	29 48.5
26 Th	6 19 00	5 02 17	10♎13 00	16 07 15	24R 13.1	17 38.2	16 00.7	13 58.5	29♏59.0	22 59.8	29 55.5	10 43.1	9 45.4	29 47.9
27 F	6 22 56	5 59 30	22 02 02	27 58 02	24 13.2	19 24.7	17 08.6	14 31.5	29 52.3	22 55.9	29 54.9	10 46.3	9 46.9	29 47.2
28 Sa	6 26 53	6 56 42	3♏55 52	9♏56 10	24 12.1	21 14.1	18 16.5	15 04.6	29 45.8	22 52.1	29 54.4	10 49.5	9 48.3	29 46.6
29 Su	6 30 49	7 53 55	15 59 28	22 06 18	24 09.1	23 06.3	19 24.1	15 37.8	29 39.7	22 48.4	29 54.0	10 52.7	9 49.7	29 45.9
30 M	6 34 46	8 51 07	28 17 05	4♐32 12	24 03.5	25 01.2	20 31.7	16 11.2	29 34.0	22 45.0	29 53.7	10 56.0	9 51.0	29 45.2

Astro Data Dy Hr Mn	Planet Ingress Dy Hr Mn	Last Aspect Dy Hr Mn	☽ Ingress Dy Hr Mn	Last Aspect Dy Hr Mn	☽ Ingress Dy Hr Mn	☽ Phases & Eclipses Dy Hr Mn	Astro Data
☽0S 1 21:46	♀ ♋ 18 1:15	1 10:48 ♃ ⚹	♎ 1 12:20	2 19:10 ♇ □	♐ 2 19:17	5 6:50 ○ 14♏55	1 May 2042
☿R 5 5:13	☉ ♊ 20 21:32	4 0:41 ♇ △	♏ 4 1:06	5 3:35 ♇ ⚹	♑ 5 3:42	12 19:19 ☾ 22♒12	Julian Day # 51986
☽0N 15 18:39	♂ ♍ 30 13:10	6 12:02 ♇ □	♐ 6 12:23	7 0:31 ♃ ⚹	♒ 7 9:49	19 10:56 ● 28♉37	SVP 4♓40'15"
☿D 29 1:32		8 21:14 ♇ ⚹	♑ 8 21:31	9 14:08 ♇ ☌	♓ 9 14:16	26 18:19 ☽ 5♍38	GC 27♐25.8 ⚵ 6♎25.6R
☽0S 29 4:31	♀ ♌ 12 13:04	11 1:28 ☿ △	♒ 11 4:18	11 15:48 ♀ △	♈ 11 17:32		Eris 29♈08.3 ⚶ 24♎02.5R
♇R 30 16:38	☿ ♊ 14 3:58	13 8:32 ♇ ☌	♓ 13 8:45	13 19:52 ♇ ⚹	♉ 13 20:02	3 20:49 ○ 13♐25	⚷ 29♋02.8 ⚴ 0♋19.9
	☉ ♋ 21 5:17	15 7:04 ♃ △	♈ 15 11:07	15 22:07 ♇ □	♊ 15 22:18	11 1:01 ☾ 20♓17	☽ Mean ☊ 26♈19.4
☽0N 12 0:45	♄ ♎R 21 10:28	17 12:02 ♇ ⚹	♉ 17 12:11	18 1:13 ♇ △	♋ 18 1:26	17 19:49 ● 26♊46	
☽0S 25 11:29	⚳ ♏R 26 8:44	19 13:05 ♇ □	♊ 19 13:14	19 19:00 ♃ △	♌ 20 6:48	25 11:30 ☽ 4♎04	1 June 2042
		21 15:44 ♇ △	♋ 21 15:51	22 15:27 ♄ ⚹	♍ 22 15:29		Julian Day # 52017
		23 15:07 ♃ △	♌ 23 21:36	24 13:23 ♃ ⚹	♎ 25 3:16		SVP 4♓40'10"
		26 7:01 ♇ ☍	♍ 26 7:08	27 15:55 ♄ ☌	♏ 27 16:06		GC 27♐25.9 ⚵ 4♎37.7
		28 11:06 ♃ ⚹	♎ 28 19:28	30 2:50 ♇ □	♐ 30 3:18		Eris 29♈26.7 ⚶ 19♎44.2R
		31 8:08 ♇ △	♏ 31 8:14				⚷ 1♌15.6 ⚴ 12♋51.5
							☽ Mean ☊ 24♈40.9

July 2042 — LONGITUDE

Day	Sid.Time	☉	0 hr ☽	Noon ☽	True ☊	☿	♀	♂	⚳	♃	♄	♅	♆	♇
1 Tu	6 38 42	9♋48 18	10♐51 55	17♐16 26	23♈55.5	26♊58.5	21♌39.1	16♍44.6	29♏28.7	22♏41.7	29♎53.5	10♌59.3	9♉52.4	29♒44.4
2 W	6 42 39	10 45 30	23 45 50	0♑20 05	23R45.3	28 58.3	22 46.4	17 18.2	29R23.7	22R38.5	29D53.4	11 02.6	9 53.7	29R43.7
3 Th	6 46 36	11 42 41	6♑59 05	13 42 36	23 33.8	1♋00.2	23 53.5	17 51.9	29 19.0	22 35.6	29 53.4	11 05.9	9 55.0	29 42.9
4 F	6 50 32	12 39 52	20 30 20	27 21 52	23 22.1	3 04.0	25 00.5	18 25.7	29 14.8	22 32.8	29 53.5	11 09.3	9 56.3	29 42.1
5 Sa	6 54 29	13 37 04	4♒16 45	11♒14 32	23 11.4	5 09.5	26 07.3	18 59.6	29 10.9	22 30.2	29 53.7	11 12.6	9 57.5	29 41.3
6 Su	6 58 25	14 34 15	18 14 39	25 16 38	23 02.7	7 16.5	27 13.9	19 33.6	29 07.4	22 27.7	29 54.0	11 16.0	9 58.7	29 40.5
7 M	7 02 22	15 31 26	2♓20 00	9♓24 17	22 56.6	9 24.6	28 20.4	20 07.7	29 04.2	22 25.5	29 54.4	11 19.5	9 59.9	29 39.7
8 Tu	7 06 18	16 28 38	16 29 07	23 34 09	22 53.2	11 33.6	29 26.7	20 41.9	29 01.4	22 23.4	29 54.9	11 22.9	10 01.0	29 38.8
9 W	7 10 15	17 25 50	0♈39 08	7♈43 50	22D51.9	13 43.2	0♍32.9	21 16.2	28 59.0	22 21.5	29 55.5	11 26.3	10 02.2	29 37.9
10 Th	7 14 12	18 23 03	14 48 05	21 51 46	22R51.7	15 53.0	1 38.9	21 50.6	28 57.0	22 19.7	29 56.2	11 29.8	10 03.2	29 37.0
11 F	7 18 08	19 20 16	28 54 46	5♉56 58	22 51.5	18 02.7	2 44.7	22 25.1	28 55.3	22 18.2	29 57.0	11 33.3	10 04.3	29 36.1
12 Sa	7 22 05	20 17 29	12♉58 16	19 58 32	22 49.8	20 12.3	3 50.3	22 59.8	28 54.0	22 16.8	29 57.8	11 36.8	10 05.3	29 35.1
13 Su	7 26 01	21 14 44	26 57 35	3♊55 14	22 45.8	22 21.2	4 55.8	23 34.5	28 53.1	22 15.6	29 58.8	11 40.3	10 06.4	29 34.2
14 M	7 29 58	22 11 58	10♊51 14	17 45 17	22 39.0	24 29.4	6 01.1	24 09.3	28 52.5	22 14.6	29 59.9	11 43.9	10 07.3	29 33.2
15 Tu	7 33 54	23 09 13	24 37 04	1♋26 14	22 29.6	26 36.7	7 06.2	24 44.3	28D52.3	22 13.8	0♏01.1	11 47.4	10 08.3	29 32.2
16 W	7 37 51	24 06 29	8♋12 28	14 55 24	22 18.0	28 42.8	8 11.1	25 19.3	28 52.5	22 13.1	0 02.4	11 51.0	10 09.2	29 31.2
17 Th	7 41 47	25 03 45	21 34 44	28 10 11	22 05.5	0♌47.7	9 15.8	25 54.5	28 53.0	22 12.7	0 03.7	11 54.6	10 10.1	29 30.2
18 F	7 45 44	26 01 01	4♌41 32	11♌08 38	21 53.1	2 51.2	10 20.3	26 29.7	28 54.0	22 12.4	0 05.2	11 58.2	10 10.9	29 29.2
19 Sa	7 49 41	26 58 18	17 31 27	23 49 57	21 42.1	4 53.2	11 24.6	27 05.0	28 55.2	22D12.3	0 06.8	12 01.8	10 11.7	29 28.1
20 Su	7 53 37	27 55 35	0♍04 17	6♍14 37	21 33.3	6 53.6	12 28.6	27 40.5	28 56.9	22 12.4	0 08.4	12 05.4	10 12.5	29 27.1
21 M	7 57 34	28 52 52	12 21 14	18 24 29	21 27.1	8 52.4	13 32.5	28 16.0	28 58.9	22 12.6	0 10.2	12 09.1	10 13.3	29 26.0
22 Tu	8 01 30	29 50 09	24 24 48	0♎22 41	21 23.5	10 49.5	14 36.1	28 51.6	29 01.2	22 13.1	0 12.0	12 12.7	10 14.0	29 24.9
23 W	8 05 27	0♌47 27	6♎18 39	12 13 19	21D22.0	12 44.9	15 39.4	29 27.4	29 03.9	22 13.7	0 14.0	12 16.3	10 14.7	29 23.8
24 Th	8 09 23	1 44 45	18 07 18	24 01 17	21R21.7	14 38.6	16 42.6	0♎03.2	29 07.0	22 14.5	0 16.0	12 20.0	10 15.4	29 22.7
25 F	8 13 20	2 42 03	29 55 55	5♏51 54	21 21.8	16 30.6	17 45.4	0 39.1	29 10.3	22 15.5	0 18.2	12 23.7	10 16.0	29 21.6
26 Sa	8 17 16	3 39 22	11♏49 55	17 50 39	21 21.0	18 20.9	18 48.0	1 15.1	29 14.1	22 16.7	0 20.4	12 27.4	10 16.6	29 20.4
27 Su	8 21 13	4 36 41	23 54 45	0♐02 48	21 18.5	20 09.4	19 50.3	1 51.2	29 18.2	22 18.1	0 22.7	12 31.0	10 17.2	29 19.3
28 M	8 25 10	5 34 01	6♐15 24	12 33 00	21 13.8	21 56.2	20 52.4	2 27.3	29 22.6	22 19.6	0 25.1	12 34.7	10 17.7	29 18.1
29 Tu	8 29 06	6 31 21	18 56 02	25 24 48	21 06.6	23 41.2	21 54.1	3 03.6	29 27.3	22 21.3	0 27.6	12 38.4	10 18.2	29 16.9
30 W	8 33 03	7 28 42	1♑59 30	8♑40 10	20 57.3	25 24.6	22 55.6	3 39.9	29 32.4	22 23.2	0 30.2	12 42.1	10 18.7	29 15.8
31 Th	8 36 59	8 26 04	15 26 45	22 19 01	20 46.6	27 06.2	23 56.7	4 16.4	29 37.8	22 25.3	0 32.9	12 45.8	10 19.1	29 14.6

August 2042 — LONGITUDE

Day	Sid.Time	☉	0 hr ☽	Noon ☽	True ☊	☿	♀	♂	⚳	♃	♄	♅	♆	♇
1 F	8 40 56	9♌23 26	29♑16 37	6♒19 01	20♈35.7	28♌46.1	24♍57.6	4♎52.9	29♏43.5	22♏27.5	0♏35.7	12♌49.5	10♉19.5	29♒13.4
2 Sa	8 44 52	10 20 49	13♒25 39	20 35 46	20R25.6	0♍24.4	25 58.1	5 29.5	29 49.6	22 30.0	0 38.6	12 53.2	10 19.9	29R12.1
3 Su	8 48 49	11 18 13	27 48 37	5♓03 22	20 17.5	2 00.9	26 58.3	6 06.2	29 55.9	22 32.5	0 41.5	12 57.0	10 20.3	29 10.9
4 M	8 52 45	12 15 38	12♓19 15	19 35 29	20 11.8	3 35.8	27 58.1	6 43.0	0♐02.5	22 35.3	0 44.6	13 00.7	10 20.6	29 09.7
5 Tu	8 56 42	13 13 04	26 51 20	4♈06 11	20 08.8	5 09.0	28 57.6	7 19.8	0 09.5	22 38.2	0 47.7	13 04.4	10 20.8	29 08.5
6 W	9 00 39	14 10 31	11♈19 30	18 30 51	20D07.9	6 40.5	29 56.7	7 56.8	0 16.7	22 41.3	0 50.9	13 08.1	10 21.1	29 07.2
7 Th	9 04 35	15 07 59	25 39 54	2♉46 23	20R08.1	8 10.3	0♎55.4	8 33.8	0 24.3	22 44.6	0 54.2	13 11.8	10 21.3	29 05.9
8 F	9 08 32	16 05 29	9♉50 10	16 51 08	20 08.5	9 38.4	1 53.8	9 10.9	0 32.1	22 48.1	0 57.6	13 15.5	10 21.5	29 04.7
9 Sa	9 12 28	17 03 00	23 49 13	0♊44 25	20 07.7	11 04.8	2 51.7	9 48.1	0 40.3	22 51.7	1 01.0	13 19.2	10 21.6	29 03.4
10 Su	9 16 25	18 00 33	7♊36 44	14 26 09	20 04.9	12 29.4	3 49.3	10 25.4	0 48.7	22 55.5	1 04.6	13 22.9	10 21.7	29 02.2
11 M	9 20 21	18 58 07	21 12 40	27 56 17	19 59.7	13 52.2	4 46.5	11 02.8	0 57.4	22 59.4	1 08.2	13 26.6	10 21.8	29 00.9
12 Tu	9 24 18	19 55 42	4♋36 57	11♋14 36	19 52.2	15 13.3	5 43.2	11 40.3	1 06.4	23 03.5	1 11.9	13 30.4	10R21.8	28 59.6
13 W	9 28 14	20 53 19	17 49 12	24 20 41	19 42.9	16 32.5	6 39.4	12 17.8	1 15.7	23 07.8	1 15.7	13 34.1	10 21.9	28 58.3
14 Th	9 32 11	21 50 57	0♌48 56	7♌13 55	19 32.8	17 49.8	7 35.2	12 55.4	1 25.2	23 12.3	1 19.6	13 37.7	10 21.8	28 57.0
15 F	9 36 08	22 48 36	13 35 35	19 53 54	19 22.7	19 05.2	8 30.6	13 33.2	1 35.0	23 16.9	1 23.6	13 41.4	10 21.8	28 55.7
16 Sa	9 40 04	23 46 17	26 08 53	2♍20 35	19 13.7	20 18.5	9 25.4	14 11.0	1 45.1	23 21.6	1 27.6	13 45.1	10 21.7	28 54.4
17 Su	9 44 01	24 43 58	8♍29 06	14 34 35	19 06.6	21 29.8	10 19.7	14 48.9	1 55.5	23 26.6	1 31.7	13 48.8	10 21.6	28 53.1
18 M	9 47 57	25 41 41	20 37 37	26 37 21	19 01.7	22 39.0	11 13.5	15 26.8	2 06.1	23 31.6	1 35.9	13 52.4	10 21.4	28 51.8
19 Tu	9 51 54	26 39 25	2♎35 13	8♎31 14	18D59.1	23 45.9	12 06.7	16 04.9	2 16.9	23 36.9	1 40.2	13 56.1	10 21.2	28 50.5
20 W	9 55 50	27 37 10	14 25 50	20 19 29	18 58.5	24 50.4	12 59.3	16 43.0	2 28.0	23 42.3	1 44.5	13 59.7	10 21.0	28 49.2
21 Th	9 59 47	28 34 56	26 12 43	2♏06 06	18 59.2	25 52.5	13 51.4	17 21.2	2 39.4	23 47.8	1 49.0	14 03.4	10 20.7	28 47.9
22 F	10 03 43	29 32 44	8♏00 14	13 55 44	19 00.4	26 52.1	14 42.8	17 59.5	2 51.0	23 53.5	1 53.4	14 07.0	10 20.5	28 46.6
23 Sa	10 07 40	0♍30 33	19 53 16	25 53 29	19R01.3	27 48.9	15 33.6	18 37.9	3 02.8	23 59.4	1 58.0	14 10.6	10 20.1	28 45.3
24 Su	10 11 37	1 28 22	1♐57 01	8♐04 33	19 01.2	28 42.9	16 23.7	19 16.3	3 14.9	24 05.4	2 02.7	14 14.2	10 19.8	28 44.0
25 M	10 15 33	2 26 14	14 16 41	20 33 59	18 59.4	29 33.9	17 13.1	19 54.8	3 27.2	24 11.5	2 07.4	14 17.8	10 19.4	28 42.7
26 Tu	10 19 30	3 24 06	26 56 59	3♑26 06	18 55.9	0♎21.7	18 01.8	20 33.5	3 39.8	24 17.8	2 12.2	14 21.3	10 19.0	28 41.4
27 W	10 23 26	4 22 00	10♑01 42	16 43 59	18 50.6	1 06.1	18 49.7	21 12.1	3 52.5	24 24.3	2 17.0	14 24.9	10 18.6	28 40.1
28 Th	10 27 23	5 19 55	23 33 02	0♒28 46	18 44.3	1 46.8	19 36.8	21 50.9	4 05.5	24 30.8	2 21.9	14 28.4	10 18.1	28 38.8
29 F	10 31 19	6 17 51	7♒30 58	14 39 11	18 37.6	2 23.8	20 23.1	22 29.7	4 18.7	24 37.6	2 26.9	14 32.0	10 17.6	28 37.5
30 Sa	10 35 16	7 15 48	21 52 53	29 11 17	18 31.3	2 56.7	21 08.6	23 08.6	4 32.1	24 44.4	2 32.0	14 35.5	10 17.1	28 36.2
31 Su	10 39 12	8 13 48	6♓33 33	13♓58 43	18 26.4	3 25.3	21 53.2	23 47.6	4 45.8	24 51.4	2 37.1	14 39.0	10 16.5	28 34.9

Astro Data Dy Hr Mn	Planet Ingress Dy Hr Mn	Last Aspect Dy Hr Mn	☽ Ingress Dy Hr Mn	Last Aspect Dy Hr Mn	☽ Ingress Dy Hr Mn	☽ Phases & Eclipses Dy Hr Mn	Astro Data
♄ D 2 23:49	☿ ♋ 3 0:12	2 11:12 ♄ ⚹	♑ 2 11:24	31 15:03 ♀ △	♒ 1 1:14	3 8:11 ○ 11♑34	1 July 2042
☽ 0N 9 5:21	♀ ♍ 9 0:04	4 16:24 ♄ □	♒ 4 16:35	3 2:17 ♇ ☌	♓ 3 3:38	10 5:39 ☾ 18♈08	Julian Day # 52047
⚳ D 15 12:17	♄ ♏ 14 14:00	6 19:52 ♄ △	♓ 6 20:02	5 2:51 ♀ ☍	♈ 5 5:12	17 5:53 ● 24♋49	SVP 4♓40'04"
♃ D 19 12:49	☿ ♌ 17 2:48	8 10:00 ♃ △	♈ 8 22:54	7 5:48 ♇ ⚹	♉ 7 7:19	25 5:03 ☽ 2♏25	GC 27♐26.0 ⚴ 9♎07.7
☽ 0S 22 18:28	☉ ♌ 22 16:07	11 1:45 ♄ ☍	♉ 11 1:51	9 9:05 ♇ □	♊ 9 10:43		Eris 29♈38.4 ⚵ 20♎23.9
♂ 0S 26 2:17	♂ ♎ 24 9:53	13 4:30 ♇ □	♊ 13 5:14	11 13:56 ♇ △	♋ 11 15:42	1 17:34 ○ 9♒37	⚷ 4♌19.8 ⚶ 25♋48.2
		15 8:39 ♇ △	♋ 15 9:28	13 9:45 ♃ △	♌ 13 22:29	8 10:36 ☾ 16♉02	☽ Mean ☊ 23♈05.6
♀ 0S 5 4:41	☿ ♍ 2 6:00	17 7:41 ♂ ⚹	♌ 17 15:21	16 5:21 ♇ ☍	♍ 16 7:27	15 18:03 ● 23♌03	
☽ 0N 5 10:49	⚳ ♐ 4 2:57	19 22:49 ♇ ☍	♍ 19 23:52	18 5:45 ♃ ⚹	♎ 18 18:47	23 21:57 ☽ 0♐55	1 August 2042
♆ R 13 9:11	♀ ♎ 6 13:21	22 10:49 ☉ ⚹	♎ 22 11:14	21 5:17 ♇ △	♏ 21 7:43	31 2:04 ○ 7♓50	Julian Day # 52078
☽ 0S 19 1:17	☉ ♍ 22 23:19	24 22:52 ♇ △	♏ 25 0:08	23 17:41 ♇ □	♐ 23 20:09		SVP 4♓39'59"
☿ 0S 21 8:54	☿ ♎ 26 0:55	27 10:35 ♇ □	♐ 27 11:55	26 3:15 ♇ ⚹	♑ 26 5:40		GC 27♐26.0 ⚴ 17♎50.5
		29 19:04 ♇ ⚹	♑ 29 20:23	28 1:36 ♃ ⚹	♒ 28 11:11		Eris 29♈41.4R ⚵ 25♎13.4
				30 11:03 ♇ ☌	♓ 30 13:20		⚷ 7♌59.6 ⚶ 9♌41.0
							☽ Mean ☊ 21♈27.1

LONGITUDE — September 2042

Day	Sid.Time	☉	0 hr ☽	Noon ☽	True ☊	☿	♀	♂	⚳	♃	♄	♅	♆	♇
1 M	10 43 09	9♍11 48	21♓25 44	28♓53 35	18♈23.2	3♎49.3	22♎36.8	24♎26.7	4♐59.6	24♏58.6	2♏42.2	14♌42.4	10♉15.9	28♒33.7
2 Tu	10 47 06	10 09 51	6♈21 13	13♈47 40	18D 21.8	4 08.4	23 19.6	25 05.8	5 13.6	25 05.8	2 47.5	14 45.9	10R 15.3	28R 32.4
3 W	10 51 02	11 07 55	21 12 04	28 33 39	18 22.1	4 22.3	24 01.3	25 45.0	5 27.8	25 13.2	2 52.8	14 49.3	10 14.6	28 31.1
4 Th	10 54 59	12 06 01	5♉51 46	13♉05 55	18 23.3	4R 30.9	24 42.0	26 24.3	5 42.3	25 20.8	2 58.2	14 52.7	10 13.9	28 29.8
5 F	10 58 55	13 04 10	20 15 44	27 20 58	18 24.6	4 33.6	25 21.7	27 03.7	5 56.9	25 28.4	3 03.6	14 56.1	10 13.2	28 28.6
6 Sa	11 02 52	14 02 20	4♊21 29	11♊17 14	18R 25.4	4 30.5	26 00.2	27 43.1	6 11.7	25 36.2	3 09.1	14 59.5	10 12.4	28 27.3
7 Su	11 06 48	15 00 32	18 08 15	24 54 37	18 25.0	4 21.1	26 37.7	28 22.6	6 26.7	25 44.1	3 14.6	15 02.8	10 11.7	28 26.1
8 M	11 10 45	15 58 47	1♋36 29	8♋14 02	18 23.2	4 05.3	27 13.9	29 02.2	6 41.9	25 52.2	3 20.2	15 06.2	10 10.9	28 24.9
9 Tu	11 14 41	16 57 03	14 47 25	21 16 51	18 19.9	3 43.0	27 49.0	29 41.9	6 57.3	26 00.4	3 25.9	15 09.5	10 10.0	28 23.6
10 W	11 18 38	17 55 22	27 42 33	4♌04 40	18 15.6	3 14.2	28 22.7	0♏21.7	7 12.9	26 08.7	3 31.6	15 12.8	10 09.2	28 22.4
11 Th	11 22 35	18 53 42	10♌23 26	16 39 01	18 10.6	2 38.9	28 55.1	1 01.5	7 28.6	26 17.1	3 37.4	15 16.0	10 08.3	28 21.2
12 F	11 26 31	19 52 05	22 51 34	29 01 18	18 05.7	1 57.5	29 26.2	1 41.4	7 44.5	26 25.6	3 43.2	15 19.3	10 07.3	28 20.0
13 Sa	11 30 28	20 50 29	5♍08 22	11♍12 57	18 01.4	1 10.3	29 55.8	2 21.4	8 00.6	26 34.3	3 49.1	15 22.5	10 06.4	28 18.8
14 Su	11 34 24	21 48 55	17 15 14	23 15 25	17 58.2	0 18.0	0♏23.9	3 01.5	8 16.9	26 43.1	3 55.1	15 25.6	10 05.4	28 17.6
15 M	11 38 21	22 47 23	29 13 43	5♎10 23	17 56.2	29♍21.2	0 50.5	3 41.6	8 33.3	26 52.0	4 01.1	15 28.8	10 04.4	28 16.5
16 Tu	11 42 17	23 45 53	11♎05 40	16 59 52	17D 55.5	28 21.0	1 15.4	4 21.9	8 49.9	27 01.0	4 07.1	15 31.9	10 03.4	28 15.3
17 W	11 46 14	24 44 24	22 53 19	28 46 22	17 55.9	27 18.6	1 38.7	5 02.1	9 06.6	27 10.1	4 13.2	15 35.0	10 02.3	28 14.1
18 Th	11 50 10	25 42 58	4♏39 26	10♏32 56	17 57.1	26 15.4	2 00.3	5 42.5	9 23.6	27 19.3	4 19.3	15 38.0	10 01.2	28 13.0
19 F	11 54 07	26 41 33	16 27 19	22 23 07	17 58.8	25 12.8	2 20.0	6 23.0	9 40.6	27 28.7	4 25.5	15 41.1	10 00.1	28 11.9
20 Sa	11 58 04	27 40 10	28 20 49	4♐20 59	18 00.4	24 12.3	2 37.9	7 03.5	9 57.9	27 38.1	4 31.7	15 44.1	9 59.0	28 10.8
21 Su	12 02 00	28 38 48	10♐24 12	16 31 00	18 01.5	23 15.6	2 53.9	7 44.1	10 15.2	27 47.7	4 38.0	15 47.1	9 57.9	28 09.7
22 M	12 05 57	29 37 28	22 42 00	28 57 44	18R 02.0	22 24.0	3 07.9	8 24.7	10 32.8	27 57.3	4 44.4	15 50.0	9 56.7	28 08.6
23 Tu	12 09 53	0♎36 10	5♑18 46	11♑45 34	18 01.6	21 38.9	3 19.8	9 05.5	10 50.4	28 07.1	4 50.7	15 52.9	9 55.5	28 07.5
24 W	12 13 50	1 34 54	18 18 36	24 58 13	18 00.5	21 01.6	3 29.7	9 46.3	11 08.2	28 17.0	4 57.1	15 55.8	9 54.3	28 06.5
25 Th	12 17 46	2 33 39	1♒44 39	8♒38 03	17 58.8	20 32.9	3 37.3	10 27.2	11 26.2	28 26.9	5 03.6	15 58.6	9 53.0	28 05.5
26 F	12 21 43	3 32 26	15 38 25	22 45 32	17 56.9	20 13.6	3 42.8	11 08.1	11 44.3	28 37.0	5 10.1	16 01.4	9 51.7	28 04.4
27 Sa	12 25 39	4 31 15	29 59 06	7♓18 33	17 55.2	20D 04.1	3R 45.9	11 49.1	12 02.5	28 47.2	5 16.6	16 04.2	9 50.5	28 03.4
28 Su	12 29 36	5 30 05	14♓43 11	22 12 09	17 53.9	20 04.9	3 46.8	12 30.2	12 20.9	28 57.4	5 23.2	16 06.9	9 49.1	28 02.4
29 M	12 33 32	6 28 58	29 44 26	7♈18 55	17D 53.1	20 15.7	3 45.3	13 11.4	12 39.4	29 07.8	5 29.8	16 09.6	9 47.8	28 01.5
30 Tu	12 37 29	7 27 52	14♈54 25	22 29 44	17 53.0	20 36.6	3 41.4	13 52.6	12 58.0	29 18.2	5 36.4	16 12.3	9 46.5	28 00.5

LONGITUDE — October 2042

Day	Sid.Time	☉	0 hr ☽	Noon ☽	True ☊	☿	♀	♂	⚳	♃	♄	♅	♆	♇
1 W	12 41 26	8♎26 49	0♉03 43	7♉35 14	17♈53.4	21♍07.2	3♏35.1	14♏33.9	13♐16.7	29♏28.8	5♏43.1	16♌14.9	9♉45.1	27♒59.6
2 Th	12 45 22	9 25 48	15 03 18	22 27 02	17 54.0	21 47.0	3R 26.5	15 15.3	13 35.6	29 39.4	5 49.8	16 17.5	9R 43.7	27R 58.7
3 F	12 49 19	10 24 49	29 45 44	6♊58 51	17 54.8	22 35.3	3 15.4	15 56.7	13 54.6	29 50.1	5 56.5	16 20.0	9 42.3	27 57.8
4 Sa	12 53 15	11 23 52	14♊06 00	21 06 58	17 55.3	23 31.7	3 01.9	16 38.2	14 13.7	0♐00.9	6 03.3	16 22.5	9 40.9	27 56.9
5 Su	12 57 12	12 22 58	28 01 39	4♋50 07	17R 55.6	24 35.3	2 46.1	17 19.8	14 32.9	0 11.8	6 10.1	16 25.0	9 39.4	27 56.0
6 M	13 01 08	13 22 06	11♋32 30	18 09 02	17 55.7	25 45.5	2 28.0	18 01.5	14 52.3	0 22.8	6 16.9	16 27.4	9 38.0	27 55.2
7 Tu	13 05 05	14 21 17	24 40 03	1♌05 54	17 55.5	27 01.4	2 07.6	18 43.2	15 11.8	0 33.8	6 23.8	16 29.8	9 36.5	27 54.3
8 W	13 09 02	15 20 30	7♌26 58	13 43 40	17 55.2	28 22.4	1 45.1	19 25.0	15 31.3	0 45.0	6 30.7	16 32.1	9 35.0	27 53.5
9 Th	13 12 58	16 19 45	19 56 24	26 05 36	17 55.0	29 47.9	1 20.4	20 06.9	15 51.0	0 56.2	6 37.6	16 34.4	9 33.5	27 52.7
10 F	13 16 55	17 19 02	2♍11 41	8♍15 01	17D 54.8	1♎17.0	0 53.8	20 48.9	16 10.8	1 07.5	6 44.5	16 36.7	9 31.9	27 52.0
11 Sa	13 20 51	18 18 21	14 15 59	20 14 57	17 54.8	2 49.3	0 25.4	21 30.9	16 30.8	1 18.8	6 51.5	16 38.9	9 30.4	27 51.2
12 Su	13 24 48	19 17 43	26 12 15	2♎08 11	17 54.9	4 24.3	29♎55.2	22 13.0	16 50.8	1 30.3	6 58.5	16 41.1	9 28.9	27 50.5
13 M	13 28 44	20 17 06	8♎03 05	13 57 14	17R 55.0	6 01.3	29 23.5	22 55.1	17 10.9	1 41.8	7 05.5	16 43.2	9 27.3	27 49.8
14 Tu	13 32 41	21 16 32	19 50 54	25 44 21	17 54.9	7 40.1	28 50.4	23 37.4	17 31.1	1 53.4	7 12.5	16 45.3	9 25.7	27 49.1
15 W	13 36 37	22 16 00	1♏37 53	7♏31 46	17 54.7	9 20.2	28 16.2	24 19.7	17 51.5	2 05.1	7 19.6	16 47.3	9 24.1	27 48.5
16 Th	13 40 34	23 15 29	13 26 17	19 21 44	17 54.2	11 01.4	27 41.1	25 02.1	18 11.9	2 16.8	7 26.6	16 49.3	9 22.5	27 47.8
17 F	13 44 30	24 15 01	25 18 25	1♐16 40	17 53.4	12 43.2	27 05.2	25 44.5	18 32.4	2 28.6	7 33.7	16 51.2	9 20.9	27 47.2
18 Sa	13 48 27	25 14 35	7♐16 50	13 19 17	17 52.4	14 25.6	26 28.8	26 27.0	18 53.1	2 40.5	7 40.9	16 53.1	9 19.3	27 46.6
19 Su	13 52 24	26 14 10	19 24 25	25 32 39	17 51.4	16 08.3	25 52.1	27 09.6	19 13.8	2 52.5	7 48.0	16 55.0	9 17.7	27 46.0
20 M	13 56 20	27 13 47	1♑44 23	8♑00 05	17 50.5	17 51.1	25 15.5	27 52.3	19 34.6	3 04.5	7 55.1	16 56.8	9 16.0	27 45.5
21 Tu	14 00 17	28 13 26	14 20 10	20 45 04	17D 50.0	19 33.9	24 39.1	28 35.0	19 55.5	3 16.5	8 02.3	16 58.5	9 14.4	27 45.0
22 W	14 04 13	29 13 07	27 15 12	3♒50 58	17 49.9	21 16.5	24 03.1	29 17.8	20 16.5	3 28.7	8 09.4	17 00.2	9 12.7	27 44.5
23 Th	14 08 10	0♏12 50	10♒32 40	17 20 36	17 50.4	22 59.0	23 27.9	0♐00.6	20 37.6	3 40.9	8 16.6	17 01.9	9 11.1	27 44.0
24 F	14 12 06	1 12 34	24 14 55	1♓15 42	17 51.3	24 41.1	22 53.7	0 43.6	20 58.7	3 53.1	8 23.8	17 03.5	9 09.4	27 43.6
25 Sa	14 16 03	2 12 19	8♓22 53	15 36 15	17 52.4	26 23.0	22 20.5	1 26.5	21 20.0	4 05.4	8 31.0	17 05.0	9 07.7	27 43.1
26 Su	14 19 59	3 12 07	22 55 25	0♈19 50	17 53.4	28 04.4	21 48.8	2 09.6	21 41.3	4 17.8	8 38.2	17 06.5	9 06.0	27 42.7
27 M	14 23 56	4 11 56	7♈48 47	15 21 23	17R 53.9	29 45.4	21 18.7	2 52.7	22 02.7	4 30.2	8 45.4	17 08.0	9 04.4	27 42.3
28 Tu	14 27 53	5 11 47	22 56 35	0♉33 15	17 53.6	1♏26.0	20 50.3	3 35.9	22 24.2	4 42.6	8 52.6	17 09.4	9 02.7	27 42.0
29 W	14 31 49	6 11 40	8♉10 09	15 46 01	17 52.4	3 06.1	20 23.8	4 19.1	22 45.8	4 55.2	8 59.8	17 10.7	9 01.0	27 41.7
30 Th	14 35 46	7 11 35	23 19 38	0♊49 51	17 50.2	4 45.8	19 59.4	5 02.4	23 07.4	5 07.7	9 07.0	17 12.0	8 59.3	27 41.4
31 F	14 39 42	8 11 32	8♊15 35	15 35 58	17 47.6	6 25.0	19 37.1	5 45.8	23 29.1	5 20.4	9 14.3	17 13.2	8 57.6	27 41.1

Astro Data

	Dy Hr Mn
☽0N	1 18:51
☿R	5 11:22
☽0S	15 7:49
☿0N	20 16:00
☉0S	22 21:12
♃□♇	23 12:58
☿D	27 22:22
♀R	28 8:43
☽0N	29 5:21
☽0S	12 14:01
☿0S	12 14:12
☽0N	26 16:29
♄☍♆	29 15:10

Planet Ingress

		Dy Hr Mn
♂	♏	9 22:55
♀	♏	13 15:32
☿	♍R	14 19:46
☉	♎	22 21:13
♃	♐	4 10:00
☿	♎	9 15:20
♀	♎R	12 8:16
☉	♏	23 6:51
♂	♐	23 11:38
☿	♏	27 15:28

Last Aspect / ☽ Ingress (September)

Last Aspect Dy Hr Mn			☽ Ingress	Dy Hr Mn
1 5:39	♃	△	♈	1 13:47
3 11:56	♇	⚹	♉	3 14:21
5 13:55	♇	□	♊	5 16:31
7 18:31	♂	△	♋	7 21:06
10 0:46	♀	□	♌	10 4:18
12 12:51	♀	⚹	♍	12 13:55
15 1:08	☿	☌	♎	15 1:33
17 10:54	♇	△	♏	17 14:30
19 23:41	♇	□	♐	20 3:19
22 13:22	☉	□	♑	22 13:58
24 17:58	♃	⚹	♒	24 20:56
26 21:51	♃	□	♓	27 0:01
28 22:53	♃	△	♈	29 0:25
30 20:44	♇	⚹	♉	30 23:54

Last Aspect / ☽ Ingress (October)

Last Aspect Dy Hr Mn			☽ Ingress	Dy Hr Mn
2 23:58	♃	☍	♊	3 0:24
4 23:51	♇	△	♋	5 3:27
7 3:32	☿	⚹	♌	7 9:56
9 15:30	♇	☍	♍	9 19:40
11 14:42	♂	⚹	♎	12 7:40
14 18:02	♀	☌	♏	14 20:41
17 5:00	♇	□	♐	17 9:26
19 16:19	♇	⚹	♑	19 20:39
22 3:16	♂	⚹	♒	22 5:01
24 5:58	♇	☌	♓	24 9:51
25 1:16	♆	⚹	♈	26 11:28
28 7:30	♇	⚹	♉	28 11:08
30 6:58	♇	□	♊	30 10:40

☽ Phases & Eclipses

Dy Hr Mn		
6 17:10	☾	14♊15
14 8:51	●	21♍41
22 13:22	☽	29♐41
29 10:36	○	6♈26
29 10:46	☍	A 0.953
6 2:36	☾	12♋59
14 2:04	●	20♎52
14 2:00:42	●	A 07'44"
22 2:54	☽	28♑51
28 19:50	○	5♉31

Astro Data

1 September 2042
Julian Day # 52109
SVP 4♓39'55"
GC 27♐26.1 ⚵ 28♎57.1
Eris 29♈34.5R ⚶ 2♏48.5
⚷ 11♌40.0 ⚴ 23♌49.2
☽ Mean ☊ 19♈48.6

1 October 2042
Julian Day # 52139
SVP 4♓39'52"
GC 27♐26.2 ⚵ 11♏01.0
Eris 29♈20.2R ⚶ 11♏45.0
⚷ 14♌44.9 ⚴ 7♍30.6
☽ Mean ☊ 18♈13.3

November 2042 LONGITUDE

Day	Sid.Time	☉	0 hr ☽	Noon ☽	True ☊	☿	♀	♂	⚳	♃	♄	♅	♆	♇
1 Sa	14 43 39	9♏11 31	22♊50 16	29♊57 57	17♈44.7	8♏03.7	19♎17.1	6♐29.2	23♐50.9	5♐33.0	9♏21.5	17♌14.4	8♉55.9	27♒40.8
2 Su	14 47 35	10 11 32	6♋58 40	13♋52 16	17R42.2	9 42.0	18R59.5	7 12.7	24 12.7	5 45.7	9 28.7	17 15.6	8R54.3	27R40.6
3 M	14 51 32	11 11 36	20 38 45	27 18 18	17 40.4	11 19.8	18 44.3	7 56.3	24 34.7	5 58.5	9 36.0	17 16.7	8 52.6	27 40.4
4 Tu	14 55 28	12 11 41	3♌51 11	10♌17 47	17D39.7	12 57.2	18 31.5	8 39.9	24 56.7	6 11.3	9 43.2	17 17.7	8 50.9	27 40.2
5 W	14 59 25	13 11 49	16 38 34	22 54 05	17 40.0	14 34.1	18 21.2	9 23.6	25 18.7	6 24.1	9 50.4	17 18.7	8 49.2	27 40.1
6 Th	15 03 22	14 11 59	29 04 52	5♍11 30	17 41.3	16 10.6	18 13.4	10 07.4	25 40.9	6 37.0	9 57.6	17 19.6	8 47.5	27 40.0
7 F	15 07 18	15 12 11	11♍14 35	17 14 41	17 43.0	17 46.7	18 08.0	10 51.2	26 03.1	6 50.0	10 04.8	17 20.5	8 45.8	27 39.8
8 Sa	15 11 15	16 12 24	23 12 23	29 08 12	17 44.8	19 22.4	18D05.2	11 35.1	26 25.3	7 02.9	10 12.1	17 21.3	8 44.2	27 39.8
9 Su	15 15 11	17 12 40	5♎02 41	10♎56 17	17R46.0	20 57.8	18 04.8	12 19.1	26 47.7	7 15.9	10 19.3	17 22.1	8 42.5	27 39.7
10 M	15 19 08	18 12 58	16 49 27	22 42 36	17 46.1	22 32.8	18 06.8	13 03.1	27 10.0	7 29.0	10 26.4	17 22.8	8 40.8	27D39.7
11 Tu	15 23 04	19 13 17	28 36 06	4♏30 17	17 44.7	24 07.4	18 11.1	13 47.2	27 32.5	7 42.1	10 33.6	17 23.4	8 39.2	27 39.7
12 W	15 27 01	20 13 38	10♏25 27	16 21 51	17 41.6	25 41.7	18 17.8	14 31.3	27 55.0	7 55.2	10 40.8	17 24.0	8 37.5	27 39.7
13 Th	15 30 57	21 14 01	22 19 44	28 19 18	17 36.9	27 15.8	18 26.8	15 15.5	28 17.6	8 08.3	10 48.0	17 24.5	8 35.9	27 39.8
14 F	15 34 54	22 14 26	4♐20 46	10♐24 18	17 30.9	28 49.5	18 38.0	15 59.8	28 40.2	8 21.5	10 55.1	17 25.0	8 34.2	27 39.9
15 Sa	15 38 51	23 14 52	16 30 04	22 38 15	17 24.2	0♐22.9	18 51.4	16 44.1	29 02.9	8 34.7	11 02.2	17 25.5	8 32.6	27 40.0
16 Su	15 42 47	24 15 20	28 49 01	5♑02 34	17 17.5	1 56.1	19 06.8	17 28.5	29 25.6	8 47.9	11 09.4	17 25.8	8 31.0	27 40.1
17 M	15 46 44	25 15 50	11♑19 05	17 38 47	17 11.6	3 29.0	19 24.3	18 13.0	29 48.4	9 01.2	11 16.5	17 26.2	8 29.4	27 40.3
18 Tu	15 50 40	26 16 20	24 01 55	0♒28 41	17 07.0	5 01.7	19 43.8	18 57.5	0♑11.3	9 14.5	11 23.5	17 26.4	8 27.8	27 40.5
19 W	15 54 37	27 16 52	6♒59 23	13 34 16	17 04.2	6 34.1	20 05.2	19 42.1	0 34.2	9 27.8	11 30.6	17 26.6	8 26.2	27 40.7
20 Th	15 58 33	28 17 25	20 13 35	26 57 36	17D03.2	8 06.3	20 28.5	20 26.7	0 57.1	9 41.1	11 37.6	17 26.8	8 24.7	27 41.0
21 F	16 02 30	29 17 59	3♓46 32	10♓40 33	17 03.7	9 38.3	20 53.5	21 11.4	1 20.1	9 54.4	11 44.7	17 26.9	8 23.1	27 41.2
22 Sa	16 06 26	0♐18 35	17 39 45	24 44 10	17 05.0	11 10.1	21 20.3	21 56.1	1 43.1	10 07.8	11 51.7	17R26.9	8 21.5	27 41.5
23 Su	16 10 23	1 19 11	1♈53 43	9♈08 11	17R06.1	12 41.6	21 48.8	22 40.9	2 06.2	10 21.2	11 58.6	17 26.9	8 20.0	27 41.9
24 M	16 14 20	2 19 49	16 27 12	23 50 17	17 06.2	14 12.9	22 18.8	23 25.8	2 29.3	10 34.6	12 05.6	17 26.8	8 18.5	27 42.2
25 Tu	16 18 16	3 20 28	1♉16 44	8♉45 44	17 04.3	15 44.0	22 50.5	24 10.7	2 52.5	10 48.0	12 12.5	17 26.7	8 17.0	27 42.6
26 W	16 22 13	4 21 08	16 16 19	23 47 24	17 00.3	17 14.8	23 23.7	24 55.6	3 15.7	11 01.4	12 19.4	17 26.5	8 15.5	27 43.0
27 Th	16 26 09	5 21 50	1♊17 50	8♊46 28	16 54.0	18 45.4	23 58.3	25 40.6	3 38.9	11 14.9	12 26.3	17 26.3	8 14.1	27 43.4
28 F	16 30 06	6 22 32	16 12 07	23 33 44	16 46.3	20 15.7	24 34.3	26 25.7	4 02.2	11 28.3	12 33.1	17 26.0	8 12.6	27 43.9
29 Sa	16 34 02	7 23 17	0♋50 21	8♋01 10	16 37.8	21 45.7	25 11.7	27 10.8	4 25.5	11 41.8	12 39.9	17 25.6	8 11.2	27 44.4
30 Su	16 37 59	8 24 03	15 05 32	22 03 04	16 29.8	23 15.4	25 50.4	27 56.0	4 48.9	11 55.3	12 46.7	17 25.2	8 09.8	27 44.9

December 2042 LONGITUDE

Day	Sid.Time	☉	0 hr ☽	Noon ☽	True ☊	☿	♀	♂	⚳	♃	♄	♅	♆	♇
1 M	16 41 56	9♐24 50	28♋53 29	5♌36 45	16♈23.2	24♐44.6	26♎30.4	28♐41.2	5♑12.3	12♐08.8	12♏53.4	17♌24.8	8♉08.4	27♒45.4
2 Tu	16 45 52	10 25 38	12♌12 59	18 42 27	16R18.5	26 13.5	27 11.5	29 26.5	5 35.7	12 22.3	13 00.1	17R24.2	8R07.0	27 46.0
3 W	16 49 49	11 26 28	25 05 32	1♍22 43	16D16.0	27 41.8	27 53.8	0♑11.8	5 59.2	12 35.8	13 06.8	17 23.7	8 05.6	27 46.6
4 Th	16 53 45	12 27 20	7♍34 36	13 41 46	16 15.4	29 09.6	28 37.2	0 57.2	6 22.7	12 49.3	13 13.4	17 23.0	8 04.3	27 47.2
5 F	16 57 42	13 28 12	19 44 54	25 44 40	16 16.0	0♑36.6	29 21.7	1 42.7	6 46.2	13 02.7	13 20.0	17 22.4	8 03.0	27 47.8
6 Sa	17 01 38	14 29 06	1♎41 46	7♎36 53	16R16.9	2 03.0	0♏07.3	2 28.2	7 09.8	13 16.3	13 26.6	17 21.6	8 01.7	27 48.5
7 Su	17 05 35	15 30 01	13 30 40	19 23 44	16 17.2	3 28.3	0 53.8	3 13.7	7 33.4	13 29.8	13 33.1	17 20.9	8 00.4	27 49.1
8 M	17 09 31	16 30 58	25 16 42	1♏10 08	16 15.9	4 52.7	1 41.2	3 59.3	7 57.0	13 43.3	13 39.6	17 20.0	7 59.2	27 49.8
9 Tu	17 13 28	17 31 56	7♏04 31	13 00 19	16 12.1	6 15.7	2 29.6	4 45.0	8 20.7	13 56.8	13 46.0	17 19.1	7 57.9	27 50.6
10 W	17 17 25	18 32 55	18 57 57	24 57 44	16 05.7	7 37.4	3 18.8	5 30.7	8 44.4	14 10.3	13 52.4	17 18.2	7 56.7	27 51.3
11 Th	17 21 21	19 33 54	0♐59 57	7♐04 51	15 56.7	8 57.3	4 08.9	6 16.4	9 08.1	14 23.8	13 58.8	17 17.2	7 55.6	27 52.1
12 F	17 25 18	20 34 55	13 12 35	19 23 15	15 45.4	10 15.2	4 59.7	7 02.2	9 31.8	14 37.3	14 05.1	17 16.2	7 54.4	27 52.9
13 Sa	17 29 14	21 35 57	25 36 57	1♑53 40	15 32.9	11 30.8	5 51.4	7 48.1	9 55.6	14 50.7	14 11.3	17 15.1	7 53.3	27 53.8
14 Su	17 33 11	22 37 00	8♑13 24	14 36 08	15 20.3	12 43.7	6 43.8	8 34.0	10 19.4	15 04.2	14 17.6	17 13.9	7 52.2	27 54.6
15 M	17 37 07	23 38 03	21 01 49	27 30 22	15 08.7	13 53.5	7 36.9	9 19.9	10 43.2	15 17.7	14 23.7	17 12.7	7 51.1	27 55.5
16 Tu	17 41 04	24 39 07	4♒01 47	10♒36 01	14 59.3	14 59.6	8 30.6	10 05.9	11 07.0	15 31.1	14 29.8	17 11.5	7 50.1	27 56.4
17 W	17 45 00	25 40 11	17 13 03	23 52 57	14 52.5	16 01.5	9 25.1	10 52.0	11 30.9	15 44.6	14 35.9	17 10.2	7 49.1	27 57.3
18 Th	17 48 57	26 41 15	0♓35 43	7♓21 28	14 48.6	16 58.5	10 20.1	11 38.0	11 54.8	15 58.0	14 41.9	17 08.8	7 48.1	27 58.3
19 F	17 52 54	27 42 20	14 10 16	21 02 13	14D47.1	17 50.0	11 15.8	12 24.1	12 18.6	16 11.4	14 47.8	17 07.4	7 47.1	27 59.3
20 Sa	17 56 50	28 43 25	27 57 26	4♈55 58	14R47.0	18 35.1	12 12.1	13 10.3	12 42.5	16 24.8	14 53.7	17 06.0	7 46.2	28 00.2
21 Su	18 00 47	29 44 30	11♈57 51	19 03 04	14 47.1	19 13.0	13 08.9	13 56.5	13 06.5	16 38.1	14 59.6	17 04.5	7 45.3	28 01.3
22 M	18 04 43	0♑45 36	26 11 30	3♉22 57	14 46.0	19 42.8	14 06.3	14 42.7	13 30.4	16 51.5	15 05.3	17 03.0	7 44.4	28 02.3
23 Tu	18 08 40	1 46 42	10♉37 04	17 53 24	14 42.5	20 03.7	15 04.3	15 29.0	13 54.3	17 04.8	15 11.1	17 01.4	7 43.5	28 03.4
24 W	18 12 36	2 47 48	25 11 23	2♊30 19	14 36.2	20R14.7	16 02.7	16 15.3	14 18.3	17 18.1	15 16.7	16 59.8	7 42.7	28 04.4
25 Th	18 16 33	3 48 54	9♊49 23	17 07 43	14 27.0	20 15.0	17 01.6	17 01.7	14 42.3	17 31.3	15 22.3	16 58.1	7 41.9	28 05.5
26 F	18 20 30	4 50 01	24 24 22	1♋38 26	14 15.6	20 04.0	18 01.1	17 48.1	15 06.2	17 44.6	15 27.9	16 56.4	7 41.2	28 06.7
27 Sa	18 24 26	5 51 08	8♋49 00	15 55 15	14 03.0	19 41.3	19 00.9	18 34.5	15 30.2	17 57.8	15 33.3	16 54.7	7 40.5	28 07.8
28 Su	18 28 23	6 52 15	22 56 28	29 52 05	13 50.8	19 06.7	20 01.3	19 21.0	15 54.2	18 11.0	15 38.8	16 52.9	7 39.8	28 09.0
29 M	18 32 19	7 53 23	6♌41 41	13♌25 01	13 40.0	18 20.6	21 02.1	20 07.5	16 18.2	18 24.1	15 44.1	16 51.1	7 39.1	28 10.2
30 Tu	18 36 16	8 54 31	20 01 59	26 32 38	13 31.7	17 23.9	22 03.2	20 54.0	16 42.3	18 37.3	15 49.4	16 49.2	7 38.5	28 11.4
31 W	18 40 12	9 55 39	2♍57 11	9♍15 59	13 26.1	16 17.8	23 04.8	21 40.6	17 06.3	18 50.4	15 54.6	16 47.3	7 37.9	28 12.6

Astro Data	Planet Ingress	Last Aspect	☽ Ingress	Last Aspect	☽ Ingress	☽ Phases & Eclipses	Astro Data
Dy Hr Mn	Dy Hr Mn	Dy Hr Mn	Dy Hr Mn	Dy Hr Mn	Dy Hr Mn	Dy Hr Mn	1 November 2042
☽0S 8 20:00	☿ ♐ 15 6:06	1 8:08 ♇ △	♋ 1 12:03	30 18:57 ♀ □	♌ 1 1:58	4 15:53 ☾ 12♌21	Julian Day # 52170
♀D 9 4:05	⚳ ♑ 18 0:09	2 20:53 ♀ □	♌ 3 16:55	3 5:06 ♇ ☍	♍ 3 9:21	12 20:30 ● 20♏35	SVP 4♓39'47"
♇D 10 19:23	☉ ♐ 22 4:39	5 21:15 ♇ ☍	♍ 6 1:48	4 11:04 ♄ ✶	♎ 5 20:34	20 14:33 ☽ 28♒24	GC 27♐26.3 ⚵ 24♏12.9
♃⚻♆ 15 8:39		7 13:14 ☿ ✶	♎ 8 13:45	8 5:12 ♇ △	♏ 8 9:37	27 6:07 ○ 5♊07	Eris 29♈01.8R ⚴ 21♏55.3
♅R 22 15:17	♂ ♑ 3 5:44	10 22:05 ♇ △	♏ 11 2:51	10 17:46 ♇ □	♐ 10 22:01		⚷ 16♌55.8 ⚶ 21♍19.8
☽0N 23 1:43	☿ ♑ 5 1:53	13 10:41 ♇ □	♐ 13 15:21	13 4:22 ♇ ✶	♑ 13 8:23	4 9:20 ☾ 12♍21	☽ Mean ☊ 16♈34.8
	♀ ♏ 6 8:12	15 21:46 ♇ ✶	♑ 16 2:17	15 11:25 ♄ ✶	♒ 15 16:36	12 14:31 ● 20♐41	
☽0S 6 2:10	☉ ♑ 21 18:05	18 3:31 ☉ ✶	♒ 18 11:07	17 19:18 ♇ ☌	♓ 17 22:56	20 0:29 ☽ 28♓14	1 December 2042
♃⚹♄ 7 23:28		20 14:33 ☉ □	♓ 20 17:22	20 0:29 ☉ □	♈ 20 3:31	26 17:44 ○ 5♋05	Julian Day # 52200
☽0N 20 7:48		22 7:00 ♂ □	♈ 22 20:50	22 3:05 ♇ ✶	♉ 22 6:22		SVP 4♓39'42"
♃△♅ 23 6:36		24 18:15 ♇ ✶	♉ 24 21:57	24 4:43 ♇ □	♊ 24 7:54		GC 27♐26.3 ⚵ 7♐14.0
☿R 25 0:43		26 18:17 ♇ □	♊ 26 21:55	26 6:08 ♇ △	♋ 26 9:16		Eris 28♈45.6R ⚴ 2♐08.1
		28 18:52 ♇ △	♋ 28 22:37	27 18:12 ☿ ☍	♌ 28 12:14		⚷ 17♌38.1R ⚶ 3♎52.5
				30 15:04 ♇ ☍	♍ 30 18:27		☽ Mean ☊ 14♈59.5

LONGITUDE — January 2043

Day	Sid.Time	☉	0 hr ☽	Noon ☽	True ☊	☿	♀	♂	⚳	♃	♄	♅	♆	♇
1 Th	18 44 09	10♑56 48	15♍29 26	21♍38 06	13♈23.2	15♑04.3	24♏06.8	22♑27.2	17♑30.3	19♐03.4	15♏59.7	16♌45.4	7♉37.3	28♒13.8
2 F	18 48 05	11 57 57	27 42 33	3♎43 26	13R 22.1	13R 45.7	25 09.2	23 13.9	17 54.3	19 16.4	16 04.8	16R 43.4	7R 36.8	28 15.1
3 Sa	18 52 02	12 59 06	9♎41 26	15 37 16	13 22.0	12 24.5	26 11.9	24 00.6	18 18.4	19 29.4	16 09.8	16 41.4	7 36.3	28 16.4
4 Su	18 55 59	14 00 15	21 31 38	27 25 15	13 21.7	11 03.4	27 15.0	24 47.3	18 42.4	19 42.4	16 14.8	16 39.3	7 35.8	28 17.6
5 M	18 59 55	15 01 25	3♏18 48	9♏12 58	13 19.9	9 45.1	28 18.4	25 34.1	19 06.5	19 55.3	16 19.6	16 37.2	7 35.4	28 19.0
6 Tu	19 03 52	16 02 35	15 08 22	21 05 37	13 15.9	8 31.8	29 22.1	26 20.9	19 30.5	20 08.2	16 24.4	16 35.1	7 35.0	28 20.3
7 W	19 07 48	17 03 46	27 05 14	3♐07 43	13 09.0	7 25.4	0♐26.1	27 07.7	19 54.6	20 21.0	16 29.1	16 32.9	7 34.6	28 21.6
8 Th	19 11 45	18 04 56	9♐13 28	15 22 49	12 59.2	6 27.4	1 30.5	27 54.6	20 18.6	20 33.8	16 33.8	16 30.7	7 34.3	28 23.0
9 F	19 15 41	19 06 07	21 36 01	27 53 15	12 47.1	5 38.7	2 35.1	28 41.4	20 42.7	20 46.5	16 38.3	16 28.5	7 34.0	28 24.4
10 Sa	19 19 38	20 07 17	4♑14 35	10♑40 02	12 33.5	4 59.8	3 40.0	29 28.4	21 06.7	20 59.2	16 42.8	16 26.3	7 33.7	28 25.8
11 Su	19 23 34	21 08 27	17 09 30	23 42 50	12 19.6	4 31.0	4 45.1	0♒15.3	21 30.8	21 11.8	16 47.2	16 24.0	7 33.5	28 27.2
12 M	19 27 31	22 09 37	0♒19 48	7♒00 10	12 06.7	4 11.9	5 50.6	1 02.3	21 54.8	21 24.4	16 51.6	16 21.7	7 33.3	28 28.6
13 Tu	19 31 28	23 10 46	13 43 36	20 29 49	11 56.1	4D 02.3	6 56.2	1 49.3	22 18.8	21 36.9	16 55.8	16 19.4	7 33.1	28 30.1
14 W	19 35 24	24 11 55	27 18 30	4♓09 21	11 48.4	4 01.6	8 02.1	2 36.3	22 42.8	21 49.4	17 00.0	16 17.0	7 33.0	28 31.5
15 Th	19 39 21	25 13 03	11♓02 06	17 56 33	11 43.8	4 09.3	9 08.3	3 23.4	23 06.9	22 01.8	17 04.0	16 14.6	7 32.9	28 33.0
16 F	19 43 17	26 14 11	24 52 29	1♈49 47	11D 41.8	4 24.6	10 14.6	4 10.5	23 30.9	22 14.2	17 08.0	16 12.2	7 32.8	28 34.5
17 Sa	19 47 14	27 15 17	8♈48 21	15 48 07	11R 41.6	4 46.9	11 21.2	4 57.6	23 54.9	22 26.5	17 11.9	16 09.8	7D 32.8	28 36.0
18 Su	19 51 10	28 16 23	22 49 01	29 51 00	11 41.7	5 15.6	12 28.0	5 44.7	24 18.8	22 38.8	17 15.8	16 07.3	7 32.8	28 37.5
19 M	19 55 07	29 17 28	6♉54 00	13♉57 56	11 40.9	5 50.1	13 35.0	6 31.8	24 42.8	22 50.9	17 19.5	16 04.9	7 32.9	28 39.0
20 Tu	19 59 03	0♒18 33	21 02 37	28 07 53	11 38.0	6 29.9	14 42.1	7 19.0	25 06.8	23 03.1	17 23.2	16 02.4	7 32.9	28 40.6
21 W	20 03 00	1 19 36	5♊13 26	12♊18 56	11 32.5	7 14.4	15 49.5	8 06.1	25 30.7	23 15.1	17 26.7	15 59.9	7 33.1	28 42.1
22 Th	20 06 57	2 20 39	19 23 57	26 28 00	11 24.2	8 03.1	16 57.1	8 53.3	25 54.6	23 27.1	17 30.2	15 57.4	7 33.2	28 43.7
23 F	20 10 53	3 21 40	3♋30 32	10♋31 01	11 13.9	8 55.7	18 04.8	9 40.6	26 18.5	23 39.0	17 33.6	15 54.8	7 33.4	28 45.2
24 Sa	20 14 50	4 22 41	17 28 50	24 23 27	11 02.3	9 51.8	19 12.7	10 27.8	26 42.4	23 50.9	17 36.9	15 52.3	7 33.6	28 46.8
25 Su	20 18 46	5 23 41	1♌14 20	8♌01 01	10 51.0	10 51.1	20 20.8	11 15.0	27 06.3	24 02.7	17 40.1	15 49.7	7 33.9	28 48.4
26 M	20 22 43	6 24 40	14 43 09	21 20 26	10 40.8	11 53.1	21 29.0	12 02.3	27 30.2	24 14.4	17 43.2	15 47.1	7 34.2	28 50.0
27 Tu	20 26 39	7 25 39	27 52 43	4♍19 55	10 32.9	12 57.8	22 37.4	12 49.6	27 54.0	24 26.0	17 46.2	15 44.6	7 34.5	28 51.6
28 W	20 30 36	8 26 36	10♍42 07	16 59 27	10 27.5	14 04.9	23 46.0	13 36.9	28 17.8	24 37.6	17 49.1	15 42.0	7 34.9	28 53.2
29 Th	20 34 32	9 27 33	23 12 12	29 20 44	10D 24.8	15 14.0	24 54.7	14 24.2	28 41.6	24 49.1	17 52.0	15 39.4	7 35.2	28 54.9
30 F	20 38 29	10 28 29	5♎25 27	11♎26 52	10 24.1	16 25.2	26 03.6	15 11.5	29 05.4	25 00.5	17 54.7	15 36.7	7 35.7	28 56.5
31 Sa	20 42 26	11 29 24	17 25 34	23 22 08	10 24.7	17 38.2	27 12.6	15 58.8	29 29.2	25 11.8	17 57.3	15 34.1	7 36.1	28 58.2

LONGITUDE — February 2043

Day	Sid.Time	☉	0 hr ☽	Noon ☽	True ☊	☿	♀	♂	⚳	♃	♄	♅	♆	♇
1 Su	20 46 22	12♒30 19	29♎17 12	5♏11 28	10♈25.6	18♑52.8	28♐21.8	16♒46.2	29♑52.9	25♐23.1	17♏59.9	15♌31.5	7♉36.6	28♒59.8
2 M	20 50 19	13 31 13	11♏05 36	17 00 16	10R 25.8	20 09.1	29 31.0	17 33.6	0♒16.6	25 34.2	18 02.3	15R 28.9	7 37.2	29 01.5
3 Tu	20 54 15	14 32 06	22 56 10	28 53 57	10 24.4	21 26.7	0♑40.4	18 20.9	0 40.3	25 45.3	18 04.7	15 26.2	7 37.7	29 03.1
4 W	20 58 12	15 32 58	4♐54 15	10♐57 41	10 21.0	22 45.8	1 50.0	19 08.3	1 04.0	25 56.3	18 06.9	15 23.6	7 38.3	29 04.8
5 Th	21 02 08	16 33 50	17 04 46	23 16 00	10 15.3	24 06.1	2 59.6	19 55.7	1 27.6	26 07.2	18 09.1	15 21.0	7 39.0	29 06.5
6 F	21 06 05	17 34 41	29 31 48	5♑52 29	10 07.6	25 27.6	4 09.4	20 43.1	1 51.2	26 18.1	18 11.1	15 18.4	7 39.6	29 08.2
7 Sa	21 10 01	18 35 30	12♑18 16	18 49 17	9 58.6	26 50.3	5 19.3	21 30.6	2 14.8	26 28.8	18 13.1	15 15.7	7 40.3	29 09.9
8 Su	21 13 58	19 36 19	25 25 32	2♒06 56	9 49.3	28 14.1	6 29.3	22 18.0	2 38.3	26 39.4	18 15.0	15 13.1	7 41.1	29 11.6
9 M	21 17 55	20 37 06	8♒53 14	15 44 09	9 40.6	29 38.9	7 39.3	23 05.4	3 01.9	26 50.0	18 16.7	15 10.5	7 41.8	29 13.3
10 Tu	21 21 51	21 37 52	22 39 14	29 38 02	9 33.4	1♒04.8	8 49.5	23 52.9	3 25.3	27 00.4	18 18.4	15 07.9	7 42.6	29 15.0
11 W	21 25 48	22 38 37	6♓39 58	13♓44 29	9 28.4	2 31.7	9 59.8	24 40.3	3 48.8	27 10.8	18 19.9	15 05.3	7 43.5	29 16.7
12 Th	21 29 44	23 39 20	20 50 59	27 58 52	9D 25.7	3 59.5	11 10.1	25 27.7	4 12.2	27 21.0	18 21.3	15 02.7	7 44.4	29 18.4
13 F	21 33 41	24 40 01	5♈07 37	12♈16 42	9 25.2	5 28.3	12 20.6	26 15.2	4 35.6	27 31.1	18 22.7	15 00.1	7 45.2	29 20.1
14 Sa	21 37 37	25 40 41	19 25 42	26 34 13	9 26.1	6 58.0	13 31.1	27 02.6	4 58.9	27 41.2	18 23.9	14 57.5	7 46.2	29 21.8
15 Su	21 41 34	26 41 19	3♉41 55	10♉48 32	9 27.4	8 28.6	14 41.7	27 50.1	5 22.2	27 51.1	18 25.1	14 54.9	7 47.1	29 23.5
16 M	21 45 30	27 41 56	17 53 51	24 57 41	9R 28.2	10 00.1	15 52.4	28 37.5	5 45.5	28 00.9	18 26.1	14 52.4	7 48.1	29 25.2
17 Tu	21 49 27	28 42 31	1♊59 52	9♊00 18	9 27.7	11 32.6	17 03.2	29 24.9	6 08.7	28 10.7	18 27.0	14 49.8	7 49.2	29 26.9
18 W	21 53 24	29 43 04	15 58 49	22 55 17	9 25.5	13 05.9	18 14.0	0♓12.4	6 31.9	28 20.3	18 27.9	14 47.3	7 50.2	29 28.7
19 Th	21 57 20	0♓43 35	29 49 35	6♋41 32	9 21.5	14 40.2	19 24.9	0 59.8	6 55.0	28 29.8	18 28.6	14 44.8	7 51.3	29 30.4
20 F	22 01 17	1 44 05	13♋30 58	20 17 42	9 16.0	16 15.4	20 35.9	1 47.2	7 18.1	28 39.1	18 29.2	14 42.3	7 52.5	29 32.1
21 Sa	22 05 13	2 44 32	27 01 34	3♌42 20	9 09.8	17 51.5	21 47.0	2 34.6	7 41.1	28 48.4	18 29.7	14 39.9	7 53.6	29 33.8
22 Su	22 09 10	3 44 58	10♌19 52	16 53 58	9 03.5	19 28.5	22 58.1	3 22.1	8 04.1	28 57.6	18 30.1	14 37.4	7 54.8	29 35.5
23 M	22 13 06	4 45 22	23 24 30	29 51 22	8 58.0	21 06.5	24 09.3	4 09.5	8 27.1	29 06.6	18 30.4	14 35.0	7 56.0	29 37.2
24 Tu	22 17 03	5 45 45	6♍14 32	12♍33 58	8 53.8	22 45.4	25 20.5	4 56.9	8 50.0	29 15.5	18 30.6	14 32.6	7 57.2	29 38.9
25 W	22 20 59	6 46 06	18 49 43	25 01 54	8 51.2	24 25.3	26 31.9	5 44.3	9 12.8	29 24.3	18R 30.8	14 30.2	7 58.5	29 40.6
26 Th	22 24 56	7 46 25	1♎10 41	7♎16 18	8D 50.2	26 06.1	27 43.2	6 31.6	9 35.6	29 33.0	18 30.8	14 27.8	7 59.8	29 42.3
27 F	22 28 53	8 46 42	13 19 01	19 19 12	8 50.7	27 48.0	28 54.7	7 19.0	9 58.4	29 41.5	18 30.6	14 25.5	8 01.1	29 44.0
28 Sa	22 32 49	9 46 58	25 17 15	1♏13 37	8 52.1	29 30.8	0♒06.2	8 06.4	10 21.1	29 50.0	18 30.4	14 23.2	8 02.5	29 45.7

Astro Data

	Dy Hr Mn
☽0S	2 9:03
♄□♅	8 1:20
☿D	14 1:50
☽0N	16 12:15
♆D	17 17:06
♃⚼♆	18 0:18
☽0S	29 16:47
☽0N	12 18:07
♄R	25 23:41
☽0S	26 0:42
♃⚼♅	26 0:45
♃✶♇	27 20:54

Planet Ingress

	Dy Hr Mn
♀ ♐	7 2:13
♂ ♒	11 4:10
☉ ♒	20 4:43
⚳ ♒	1 19:11
♀ ♑	2 22:01
☿ ♒	9 17:55
♂ ♓	18 5:44
☉ ♓	18 18:43
♀ ♒	28 9:56
☿ ♓	28 18:46

Last Aspect / ☽ Ingress (January)

Last Aspect Dy Hr Mn		☽ Ingress Dy Hr Mn
1 17:20 ♀ ✶	♎	2 4:33
4 13:47 ♇ △	♏	4 17:15
7 2:31 ♇ □	♐	7 5:48
9 12:59 ♇ ✶	♑	9 16:00
11 6:54 ☉ ☌	♒	11 23:24
14 2:07 ♇ ☌	♓	14 4:43
16 1:35 ☉ ✶	♈	16 8:51
18 9:54 ♇ ✶	♉	18 12:15
20 12:55 ♇ □	♊	20 15:10
22 15:51 ♇ △	♋	22 18:01
24 0:11 ♄ △	♌	24 21:49
27 1:48 ♇ ☍	♍	27 3:56
29 3:00 ♃ □	♎	29 13:17

Last Aspect / ☽ Ingress (February)

Last Aspect Dy Hr Mn		☽ Ingress Dy Hr Mn
31 23:23 ♇ △	♏	1 1:27
3 12:18 ♇ □	♐	3 14:12
5 23:13 ♇ ✶	♑	6 0:54
8 4:15 ☿ ☌	♒	8 8:13
10 11:20 ♇ ☌	♓	10 12:38
12 10:56 ♃ □	♈	12 15:24
14 16:43 ♇ ✶	♉	14 17:46
16 19:37 ♇ □	♊	16 20:35
18 23:25 ♇ △	♋	19 0:18
20 12:35 ♀ ☍	♌	21 5:20
23 11:34 ♇ ☍	♍	23 12:16
25 20:38 ♃ □	♎	25 21:42
28 9:28 ♀ □	♏	28 9:31

☽ Phases & Eclipses

Dy Hr Mn	
3 6:09	☾ 12♎44
11 6:54	● 20♑55
18 9:06	☽ 28♈09
25 6:58	○ 5♌11
2 4:16	☾ 13♏12
9 21:09	● 21♒00
16 17:01	☽ 27♉55
23 21:59	○ 5♍10

Astro Data

1 January 2043
Julian Day # 52231
SVP 4♓39'36"
GC 27♐26.4 ⚵ 20♐28.6
Eris 28♈35.8R ⚴ 12♐32.7
⚷ 16♌44.9R ⚶ 15♎03.3
☽ Mean ☊ 13♈21.0

1 February 2043
Julian Day # 52262
SVP 4♓39'31"
GC 27♐26.5 ⚵ 2♑58.4
Eris 28♈36.1 ⚴ 22♐11.6
⚷ 14♌40.0R ⚶ 22♎47.1
☽ Mean ☊ 11♈42.5

March 2043 LONGITUDE

Day	Sid.Time	☉	0 hr ☽	Noon ☽	True ☊	☿	♀	♂	⚳	♃	♄	♅	♆	♇
1 Su	22 36 46	10♓47 13	7♏08 46	13♏03 15	8♈54.0	1♓14.7	1♒17.7	8♓53.7	10♒43.7	29♐58.2	18♏30.1	14♌20.9	8♉03.9	29♒47.4
2 M	22 40 42	11 47 26	18 57 38	24 52 29	8 55.7	2 59.6	2 29.4	9 41.1	11 06.4	0♑06.4	18R 29.7	14R 18.6	8 05.3	29 49.1
3 Tu	22 44 39	12 47 37	0♐48 26	6♐46 06	8R 56.7	4 45.6	3 41.0	10 28.4	11 28.9	0 14.5	18 29.2	14 16.4	8 06.7	29 50.8
4 W	22 48 35	13 47 48	12 46 07	18 49 05	8 56.8	6 32.6	4 52.8	11 15.8	11 51.4	0 22.4	18 28.6	14 14.2	8 08.2	29 52.5
5 Th	22 52 32	14 47 56	24 55 36	1♑06 15	8 55.7	8 20.7	6 04.6	12 03.1	12 13.8	0 30.1	18 27.9	14 12.1	8 09.7	29 54.1
6 F	22 56 28	15 48 03	7♑21 34	13 42 01	8 53.6	10 09.9	7 16.4	12 50.4	12 36.2	0 37.8	18 27.1	14 09.9	8 11.2	29 55.8
7 Sa	23 00 25	16 48 08	20 07 59	26 39 50	8 50.7	12 00.1	8 28.3	13 37.7	12 58.5	0 45.3	18 26.1	14 07.8	8 12.7	29 57.5
8 Su	23 04 22	17 48 12	3♒17 43	10♒01 47	8 47.5	13 51.5	9 40.2	14 25.0	13 20.8	0 52.6	18 25.1	14 05.8	8 14.3	29 59.1
9 M	23 08 18	18 48 14	16 51 58	23 48 06	8 44.5	15 43.8	10 52.1	15 12.2	13 43.0	0 59.8	18 24.0	14 03.7	8 15.9	0♓00.8
10 Tu	23 12 15	19 48 14	0♓49 52	7♓56 51	8 42.0	17 37.3	12 04.1	15 59.5	14 05.1	1 06.9	18 22.8	14 01.7	8 17.5	0 02.4
11 W	23 16 11	20 48 13	15 08 27	22 23 59	8 40.5	19 31.7	13 16.2	16 46.7	14 27.2	1 13.8	18 21.4	13 59.8	8 19.1	0 04.0
12 Th	23 20 08	21 48 09	29 42 39	7♈03 39	8D 39.9	21 27.1	14 28.2	17 33.9	14 49.2	1 20.6	18 20.0	13 57.8	8 20.8	0 05.6
13 F	23 24 04	22 48 03	14♈26 03	21 49 01	8 40.2	23 23.4	15 40.4	18 21.1	15 11.1	1 27.2	18 18.5	13 56.0	8 22.5	0 07.3
14 Sa	23 28 01	23 47 55	29 11 39	6♉33 10	8 41.1	25 20.7	16 52.5	19 08.3	15 33.0	1 33.7	18 16.9	13 54.1	8 24.2	0 08.9
15 Su	23 31 57	24 47 46	13♉52 49	21 09 57	8 42.2	27 18.6	18 04.7	19 55.4	15 54.8	1 40.0	18 15.2	13 52.3	8 25.9	0 10.4
16 M	23 35 54	25 47 34	28 24 03	5♊34 39	8 43.2	29 17.3	19 16.9	20 42.5	16 16.5	1 46.2	18 13.4	13 50.5	8 27.7	0 12.0
17 Tu	23 39 51	26 47 19	12♊41 26	19 44 09	8R 43.8	1♈16.5	20 29.1	21 29.6	16 38.2	1 52.2	18 11.5	13 48.8	8 29.5	0 13.6
18 W	23 43 47	27 47 03	26 42 39	3♋36 51	8 43.8	3 16.1	21 41.3	22 16.7	16 59.7	1 58.0	18 09.5	13 47.1	8 31.3	0 15.2
19 Th	23 47 44	28 46 44	10♋26 45	17 12 25	8 43.3	5 15.9	22 53.6	23 03.8	17 21.2	2 03.7	18 07.4	13 45.5	8 33.1	0 16.7
20 F	23 51 40	29 46 23	23 53 53	0♌31 19	8 42.4	7 15.6	24 05.9	23 50.8	17 42.7	2 09.3	18 05.2	13 43.9	8 34.9	0 18.3
21 Sa	23 55 37	0♈45 59	7♌04 49	13 34 32	8 41.4	9 15.1	25 18.3	24 37.8	18 04.0	2 14.7	18 03.0	13 42.3	8 36.8	0 19.8
22 Su	23 59 33	1 45 34	20 00 39	26 23 17	8 40.4	11 14.1	26 30.6	25 24.7	18 25.3	2 19.9	18 00.6	13 40.8	8 38.7	0 21.3
23 M	0 03 30	2 45 06	2♍42 38	8♍58 50	8 39.6	13 12.1	27 43.0	26 11.7	18 46.5	2 24.9	17 58.2	13 39.4	8 40.5	0 22.8
24 Tu	0 07 26	3 44 35	15 12 03	21 22 28	8 39.1	15 09.0	28 55.4	26 58.6	19 07.5	2 29.8	17 55.7	13 38.0	8 42.5	0 24.3
25 W	0 11 23	4 44 03	27 30 15	3♎35 35	8D 38.9	17 04.2	0♓07.9	27 45.5	19 28.6	2 34.6	17 53.1	13 36.6	8 44.4	0 25.7
26 Th	0 15 20	5 43 29	9♎38 39	15 39 40	8 38.9	18 57.5	1 20.3	28 32.3	19 49.5	2 39.1	17 50.4	13 35.3	8 46.3	0 27.2
27 F	0 19 16	6 42 53	21 38 53	27 36 33	8 39.0	20 48.4	2 32.8	29 19.2	20 10.3	2 43.5	17 47.6	13 34.0	8 48.3	0 28.6
28 Sa	0 23 13	7 42 14	3♏32 56	9♏28 22	8R 39.2	22 36.4	3 45.4	0♈06.0	20 31.1	2 47.7	17 44.8	13 32.7	8 50.3	0 30.1
29 Su	0 27 09	8 41 34	15 23 10	21 17 44	8 39.2	24 21.2	4 57.9	0 52.7	20 51.8	2 51.8	17 41.8	13 31.6	8 52.3	0 31.5
30 M	0 31 06	9 40 53	27 12 27	3♐07 45	8 39.1	26 02.3	6 10.5	1 39.5	21 12.4	2 55.7	17 38.8	13 30.4	8 54.3	0 32.9
31 Tu	0 35 02	10 40 09	9♐04 07	15 02 02	8 39.0	27 39.4	7 23.1	2 26.2	21 32.9	2 59.4	17 35.7	13 29.3	8 56.3	0 34.3

April 2043 LONGITUDE

Day	Sid.Time	☉	0 hr ☽	Noon ☽	True ☊	☿	♀	♂	⚳	♃	♄	♅	♆	♇
1 W	0 38 59	11♈39 24	21♐02 00	27♐04 34	8♈38.8	29♈12.0	8♓35.7	3♈12.9	21♒53.3	3♑02.9	17♏32.6	13♌28.3	8♉58.4	0♓35.6
2 Th	0 42 55	12 38 36	3♑10 17	9♑19 41	8D 38.6	0♉39.9	9 48.3	3 59.5	22 13.6	3 06.3	17R 29.3	13R 27.3	9 00.4	0 37.0
3 F	0 46 52	13 37 47	15 33 19	21 51 42	8 38.7	2 02.7	11 01.0	4 46.1	22 33.8	3 09.5	17 26.0	13 26.4	9 02.5	0 38.3
4 Sa	0 50 49	14 36 57	28 15 21	4♒44 42	8 39.0	3 20.0	12 13.6	5 32.7	22 53.9	3 12.5	17 22.7	13 25.5	9 04.6	0 39.7
5 Su	0 54 45	15 36 04	11♒20 08	18 01 59	8 39.5	4 31.7	13 26.3	6 19.3	23 13.9	3 15.3	17 19.2	13 24.7	9 06.7	0 41.0
6 M	0 58 42	16 35 10	24 50 25	1♓45 32	8 40.2	5 37.6	14 39.0	7 05.8	23 33.8	3 17.9	17 15.7	13 23.9	9 08.8	0 42.3
7 Tu	1 02 38	17 34 14	8♓47 16	15 55 25	8 40.9	6 37.3	15 51.8	7 52.3	23 53.7	3 20.4	17 12.1	13 23.1	9 10.9	0 43.5
8 W	1 06 35	18 33 15	23 09 35	0♈29 14	8R 41.4	7 30.8	17 04.5	8 38.7	24 13.4	3 22.6	17 08.5	13 22.5	9 13.1	0 44.8
9 Th	1 10 31	19 32 15	7♈53 38	15 21 56	8 41.4	8 18.0	18 17.3	9 25.2	24 33.0	3 24.7	17 04.8	13 21.8	9 15.2	0 46.0
10 F	1 14 28	20 31 13	22 53 08	0♉26 07	8 40.9	8 58.7	19 30.0	10 11.5	24 52.4	3 26.6	17 01.0	13 21.3	9 17.4	0 47.2
11 Sa	1 18 24	21 30 09	7♉59 44	15 32 50	8 39.7	9 32.8	20 42.8	10 57.9	25 11.8	3 28.3	16 57.2	13 20.7	9 19.5	0 48.4
12 Su	1 22 21	22 29 03	23 04 14	0♊32 55	8 38.1	10 00.3	21 55.6	11 44.2	25 31.1	3 29.9	16 53.4	13 20.3	9 21.7	0 49.6
13 M	1 26 18	23 27 55	7♊57 54	15 18 22	8 36.3	10 21.3	23 08.4	12 30.4	25 50.2	3 31.2	16 49.4	13 19.8	9 23.9	0 50.8
14 Tu	1 30 14	24 26 44	22 33 41	29 43 20	8 34.8	10 35.7	24 21.2	13 16.7	26 09.3	3 32.4	16 45.5	13 19.5	9 26.1	0 51.9
15 W	1 34 11	25 25 32	6♋47 01	13♋44 34	8D 33.7	10R 43.7	25 34.0	14 02.8	26 28.2	3 33.3	16 41.4	13 19.2	9 28.3	0 53.0
16 Th	1 38 07	26 24 17	20 35 57	27 21 16	8 33.4	10 45.3	26 46.9	14 49.0	26 47.0	3 34.1	16 37.4	13 18.9	9 30.5	0 54.1
17 F	1 42 04	27 22 59	4♌00 43	10♌34 36	8 33.8	10 40.9	27 59.7	15 35.1	27 05.6	3 34.7	16 33.3	13 18.7	9 32.7	0 55.2
18 Sa	1 46 00	28 21 40	17 03 14	23 27 01	8 35.0	10 30.5	29 12.5	16 21.1	27 24.2	3 35.1	16 29.1	13 18.6	9 34.9	0 56.3
19 Su	1 49 57	29 20 18	29 46 22	6♍01 41	8 36.5	10 14.6	0♈25.4	17 07.1	27 42.6	3R 35.4	16 24.9	13 18.5	9 37.2	0 57.3
20 M	1 53 53	0♉18 54	12♍13 23	18 21 54	8 38.0	9 53.6	1 38.2	17 53.1	28 00.9	3 35.4	16 20.7	13D 18.5	9 39.4	0 58.3
21 Tu	1 57 50	1 17 27	24 27 37	0♎30 54	8R 39.0	9 28.0	2 51.1	18 39.0	28 19.0	3 35.2	16 16.4	13 18.5	9 41.6	0 59.3
22 W	2 01 47	2 15 59	6♎32 06	12 31 34	8 39.2	8 58.2	4 04.0	19 24.9	28 37.1	3 34.9	16 12.1	13 18.5	9 43.9	1 00.3
23 Th	2 05 43	3 14 29	18 29 35	24 26 27	8 38.2	8 24.9	5 16.8	20 10.7	28 55.0	3 34.4	16 07.8	13 18.7	9 46.1	1 01.2
24 F	2 09 40	4 12 57	0♏22 26	6♏17 48	8 35.9	7 48.7	6 29.7	20 56.5	29 12.7	3 33.6	16 03.4	13 18.8	9 48.4	1 02.2
25 Sa	2 13 36	5 11 23	12 12 46	18 07 37	8 32.4	7 10.4	7 42.6	21 42.2	29 30.4	3 32.7	15 59.0	13 19.1	9 50.6	1 03.1
26 Su	2 17 33	6 09 47	24 02 35	29 57 56	8 28.0	6 30.7	8 55.5	22 27.9	29 47.9	3 31.7	15 54.6	13 19.4	9 52.9	1 04.0
27 M	2 21 29	7 08 09	5♐53 54	11♐50 48	8 23.0	5 50.3	10 08.5	23 13.6	0♓05.2	3 30.4	15 50.2	13 19.7	9 55.1	1 04.8
28 Tu	2 25 26	8 06 30	17 48 55	23 48 36	8 18.0	5 10.0	11 21.4	23 59.2	0 22.4	3 28.9	15 45.7	13 20.1	9 57.4	1 05.7
29 W	2 29 22	9 04 50	29 50 11	5♑54 04	8 13.6	4 30.4	12 34.3	24 44.7	0 39.5	3 27.3	15 41.3	13 20.5	9 59.7	1 06.5
30 Th	2 33 19	10 03 07	12♑00 38	18 10 19	8 10.3	3 52.4	13 47.3	25 30.3	0 56.4	3 25.4	15 36.8	13 21.0	10 01.9	1 07.3

Astro Data Dy Hr Mn	Planet Ingress Dy Hr Mn	Last Aspect Dy Hr Mn	☽ Ingress Dy Hr Mn	Last Aspect Dy Hr Mn	☽ Ingress Dy Hr Mn	☽ Phases & Eclipses Dy Hr Mn	Astro Data
☽0N 12 2:57	♃ ♑ 1 17:07	2 22:02 ♇ □	♐ 2 22:22	1 16:47 ☿ △	♑ 1 17:46	4 1:09 ☾ 13♐21	1 March 2043
☿0N 17 23:04	♇ ♓ 9 0:46	5 9:40 ♇ ⚹	♑ 5 9:52	3 3:38 ♄ ⚹	♒ 4 3:15	11 9:10 ● 20♓41	Julian Day # 52290
☉0N 20 17:28	☿ ♈ 16 20:36	6 20:52 ♄ ⚹	♒ 7 18:04	5 10:44 ♄ □	♓ 6 8:58	18 1:04 ☽ 27♊20	SVP 4♓39'27"
☽0S 25 7:54	☉ ♈ 20 17:29	9 2:41 ♄ □	♓ 9 22:35	7 14:07 ♄ △	♈ 8 11:12	25 14:28 ○ 4♎50	GC 27♐26.5 ⚴ 13♑02.1
♃∠♄ 28 1:51	♀ ♓ 25 9:23	11 9:10 ☉ ☌	♈ 12 0:28	9 19:08 ☉ ☌	♉ 10 11:19	25 14:32 • T 1.114	Eris 28♈45.2 ⚵ 29♐35.1
♂0N 30 23:01	♂ ♈ 28 8:57	13 1:08 ♀ ⚹	♉ 14 1:19	11 20:57 ♀ ⚹	♊ 12 11:07		⚷ 12♌39.4R ⚶ 24♎43.6R
		15 23:48 ☿ ⚹	♊ 16 2:40	14 2:30 ☉ ⚹	♋ 14 12:28	2 18:57 ☾ 12♑56	☽ Mean ☊ 10♈13.6
☽0N 8 13:41	☿ ♉ 2 0:56	18 1:04 ☉ □	♋ 18 5:42	16 10:52 ♀ △	♌ 16 16:45	9 19:08 ● 19♈50	
☿R 16 6:18	♀ ♈ 19 3:39	20 10:32 ☉ △	♌ 20 11:03	18 22:06 ☉ △	♍ 19 0:26	9 18:57:49 • T non-C	1 April 2043
♃R 20 4:04	☉ ♉ 20 4:16	22 12:15 ♀ ☍	♍ 22 18:51	20 8:04 ♄ ⚹	♎ 21 10:59	16 10:10 ☽ 26♋20	Julian Day # 52321
♅D 20 17:50	⚳ ♓ 27 4:47	24 23:43 ♂ ☍	♎ 25 4:55	23 2:48 ♂ ☍	♏ 23 23:15	24 7:24 ○ 4♏02	SVP 4♓39'23"
☽0S 21 13:59		26 19:49 ☿ ☍	♏ 27 16:50	25 7:41 ♄ ☌	♐ 26 12:04		GC 27♐26.6 ⚴ 21♑53.9
♀0N 22 3:15		29 4:43 ♄ ☌	♐ 30 5:40	28 12:23 ♂ △	♑ 29 0:19		Eris 29♈02.4 ⚵ 5♑15.6
							⚷ 11♌21.7R ⚶ 19♎55.9R
							☽ Mean ☊ 8♈35.1

LONGITUDE — May 2043

Day	Sid.Time	☉	0 hr ☽	Noon ☽	True ☊	☿	♀	♂	⚳	♃	♄	♅	♆	♇
1 F	2 37 16	11♉01 23	24♑23 35	0♒40 53	8♈08.3	3♉16.4	15♈00.2	26♈15.7	1♓13.2	3♑23.4	15♏32.3	13♌21.6	10♉04.2	1♓08.1
2 Sa	2 41 12	11 59 38	7♒02 42	13 29 29	8D 07.8	2R 43.1	16 13.2	27 01.2	1 29.8	3R 21.2	15R 27.8	13 22.2	10 06.4	1 08.8
3 Su	2 45 09	12 57 51	20 01 40	26 39 40	8 08.5	2 12.9	17 26.2	27 46.6	1 46.2	3 18.9	15 23.3	13 22.9	10 08.7	1 09.5
4 M	2 49 05	13 56 03	3♓23 50	10♓14 27	8 09.9	1 46.3	18 39.2	28 31.9	2 02.5	3 16.3	15 18.7	13 23.6	10 11.0	1 10.2
5 Tu	2 53 02	14 54 13	17 11 40	24 15 32	8R 11.2	1 23.7	19 52.2	29 17.2	2 18.7	3 13.5	15 14.2	13 24.3	10 13.2	1 10.9
6 W	2 56 58	15 52 22	1♈25 57	8♈42 38	8 11.8	1 05.3	21 05.2	0♉02.4	2 34.6	3 10.6	15 09.7	13 25.1	10 15.5	1 11.6
7 Th	3 00 55	16 50 29	16 05 07	23 32 45	8 11.0	0 51.3	22 18.2	0 47.6	2 50.4	3 07.5	15 05.2	13 26.0	10 17.7	1 12.2
8 F	3 04 51	17 48 35	1♉04 39	8♉39 48	8 08.3	0 41.9	23 31.2	1 32.8	3 06.1	3 04.2	15 00.6	13 26.9	10 20.0	1 12.8
9 Sa	3 08 48	18 46 39	16 17 01	23 55 01	8 03.8	0D 37.2	24 44.2	2 17.9	3 21.5	3 00.8	14 56.1	13 27.9	10 22.2	1 13.4
10 Su	3 12 45	19 44 41	1♊32 28	9♊08 01	7 58.1	0 37.1	25 57.3	3 02.9	3 36.8	2 57.2	14 51.6	13 29.0	10 24.5	1 14.0
11 M	3 16 41	20 42 42	16 40 24	24 08 29	7 51.7	0 41.7	27 10.3	3 47.9	3 51.9	2 53.4	14 47.1	13 30.0	10 26.7	1 14.5
12 Tu	3 20 38	21 40 42	1♋31 15	8♋47 55	7 45.7	0 51.0	28 23.3	4 32.9	4 06.8	2 49.4	14 42.6	13 31.2	10 28.9	1 15.0
13 W	3 24 34	22 38 39	15 57 55	23 00 51	7 40.9	1 04.8	29 36.4	5 17.8	4 21.6	2 45.3	14 38.2	13 32.4	10 31.2	1 15.5
14 Th	3 28 31	23 36 35	29 56 33	6♌45 02	7 37.7	1 23.1	0♉49.4	6 02.6	4 36.2	2 41.0	14 33.7	13 33.6	10 33.4	1 16.0
15 F	3 32 27	24 34 28	13♌26 29	20 01 11	7D 36.3	1 45.9	2 02.4	6 47.4	4 50.5	2 36.6	14 29.3	13 34.9	10 35.6	1 16.4
16 Sa	3 36 24	25 32 20	26 29 34	2♍52 06	7 36.4	2 12.9	3 15.5	7 32.1	5 04.7	2 32.0	14 24.9	13 36.2	10 37.8	1 16.8
17 Su	3 40 20	26 30 10	9♍09 21	15 21 52	7 37.5	2 44.0	4 28.5	8 16.8	5 18.7	2 27.2	14 20.5	13 37.6	10 40.0	1 17.2
18 M	3 44 17	27 27 59	21 30 16	27 35 06	7R 38.7	3 19.2	5 41.6	9 01.4	5 32.5	2 22.3	14 16.1	13 39.0	10 42.2	1 17.6
19 Tu	3 48 14	28 25 45	3♎36 58	9♎36 25	7 39.1	3 58.2	6 54.6	9 46.0	5 46.1	2 17.2	14 11.8	13 40.5	10 44.3	1 17.9
20 W	3 52 10	29 23 30	15 33 57	21 30 03	7 37.9	4 41.1	8 07.7	10 30.5	5 59.4	2 12.0	14 07.5	13 42.1	10 46.5	1 18.2
21 Th	3 56 07	0♊21 14	27 25 12	3♏19 45	7 34.7	5 27.5	9 20.7	11 14.9	6 12.6	2 06.7	14 03.3	13 43.6	10 48.7	1 18.5
22 F	4 00 03	1 18 56	9♏14 06	15 08 34	7 29.2	6 17.6	10 33.8	11 59.3	6 25.6	2 01.2	13 59.0	13 45.3	10 50.8	1 18.8
23 Sa	4 04 00	2 16 37	21 03 27	26 58 58	7 21.4	7 11.0	11 46.9	12 43.7	6 38.4	1 55.6	13 54.8	13 46.9	10 53.0	1 19.0
24 Su	4 07 56	3 14 16	2♐55 23	8♐52 53	7 11.8	8 07.8	13 00.0	13 28.0	6 50.9	1 49.8	13 50.7	13 48.7	10 55.1	1 19.2
25 M	4 11 53	4 11 55	14 51 39	20 51 53	7 01.3	9 07.8	14 13.1	14 12.2	7 03.3	1 44.0	13 46.6	13 50.4	10 57.2	1 19.4
26 Tu	4 15 49	5 09 32	26 53 44	2♑57 25	6 50.6	10 11.0	15 26.2	14 56.4	7 15.4	1 38.0	13 42.5	13 52.3	10 59.3	1 19.6
27 W	4 19 46	6 07 08	9♑03 05	15 10 58	6 40.9	11 17.2	16 39.3	15 40.6	7 27.3	1 31.8	13 38.5	13 54.1	11 01.4	1 19.7
28 Th	4 23 43	7 04 43	21 21 18	27 34 21	6 32.9	12 26.3	17 52.4	16 24.7	7 39.0	1 25.6	13 34.6	13 56.0	11 03.5	1 19.8
29 F	4 27 39	8 02 17	3♒50 23	10♒09 44	6 27.1	13 38.4	19 05.5	17 08.7	7 50.4	1 19.2	13 30.6	13 58.0	11 05.6	1 19.9
30 Sa	4 31 36	8 59 50	16 32 44	22 59 45	6 23.8	14 53.4	20 18.7	17 52.7	8 01.6	1 12.8	13 26.8	14 00.0	11 07.6	1 20.0
31 Su	4 35 32	9 57 22	29 31 08	6♓07 17	6D 22.6	16 11.2	21 31.8	18 36.6	8 12.6	1 06.2	13 23.0	14 02.0	11 09.7	1R 20.0

LONGITUDE — June 2043

Day	Sid.Time	☉	0 hr ☽	Noon ☽	True ☊	☿	♀	♂	⚳	♃	♄	♅	♆	♇
1 M	4 39 29	10♊54 54	12♓48 33	19♓35 14	6♈22.7	17♉31.7	22♉45.0	19♉20.5	8♓23.3	0♑59.5	13♏19.2	14♌04.1	11♉11.7	1♓20.0
2 Tu	4 43 25	11 52 24	26 27 36	3♈25 52	6R 23.2	18 55.0	23 58.1	20 04.3	8 33.8	0R 52.7	13R 15.5	14 06.3	11 13.7	1R 20.0
3 W	4 47 22	12 49 54	10♈30 05	17 40 12	6 22.7	20 20.9	25 11.3	20 48.1	8 44.0	0 45.9	13 11.9	14 08.4	11 15.7	1 19.9
4 Th	4 51 18	13 47 23	24 55 59	2♉17 05	6 20.5	21 49.6	26 24.5	21 31.8	8 54.0	0 38.9	13 08.3	14 10.6	11 17.7	1 19.9
5 F	4 55 15	14 44 52	9♉42 52	17 12 35	6 15.7	23 20.9	27 37.7	22 15.4	9 03.7	0 31.9	13 04.8	14 12.9	11 19.6	1 19.8
6 Sa	4 59 12	15 42 19	24 45 15	2♊19 45	6 08.5	24 54.8	28 50.9	22 59.0	9 13.2	0 24.8	13 01.3	14 15.2	11 21.6	1 19.7
7 Su	5 03 08	16 39 47	9♊54 50	17 29 11	5 59.2	26 31.3	0♊04.1	23 42.6	9 22.4	0 17.6	12 57.9	14 17.6	11 23.5	1 19.5
8 M	5 07 05	17 37 13	25 01 31	2♋30 32	5 49.0	28 10.5	1 17.4	24 26.1	9 31.4	0 10.3	12 54.6	14 19.9	11 25.5	1 19.4
9 Tu	5 11 01	18 34 38	9♋55 05	17 14 11	5 39.0	29 52.3	2 30.6	25 09.5	9 40.0	0 03.0	12 51.3	14 22.4	11 27.4	1 19.2
10 W	5 14 58	19 32 02	24 27 02	1♌33 03	5 30.4	1♊36.6	3 43.8	25 52.9	9 48.4	29♐55.6	12 48.2	14 24.8	11 29.2	1 19.0
11 Th	5 18 54	20 29 25	8♌31 51	15 23 16	5 23.9	3 23.5	4 57.1	26 36.2	9 56.5	29 48.2	12 45.1	14 27.3	11 31.1	1 18.7
12 F	5 22 51	21 26 47	22 07 20	28 44 16	5 19.9	5 12.9	6 10.3	27 19.4	10 04.4	29 40.7	12 42.0	14 29.9	11 32.9	1 18.5
13 Sa	5 26 47	22 24 08	5♍14 24	11♍38 12	5D 18.1	7 04.8	7 23.6	28 02.6	10 11.9	29 33.2	12 39.1	14 32.5	11 34.8	1 18.2
14 Su	5 30 44	23 21 28	17 56 11	24 08 59	5R 17.7	8 59.1	8 36.9	28 45.7	10 19.2	29 25.6	12 36.2	14 35.1	11 36.6	1 17.9
15 M	5 34 41	24 18 47	0♎17 13	6♎21 34	5 17.8	10 55.8	9 50.1	29 28.8	10 26.2	29 18.0	12 33.4	14 37.7	11 38.3	1 17.5
16 Tu	5 38 37	25 16 05	12 22 41	18 21 13	5 17.2	12 54.7	11 03.4	0♊11.8	10 32.9	29 10.4	12 30.7	14 40.4	11 40.1	1 17.2
17 W	5 42 34	26 13 22	24 17 49	0♏13 05	5 15.0	14 55.8	12 16.7	0 54.8	10 39.3	29 02.8	12 28.0	14 43.1	11 41.8	1 16.8
18 Th	5 46 30	27 10 39	6♏07 34	12 01 48	5 10.5	16 58.9	13 30.0	1 37.7	10 45.3	28 55.1	12 25.4	14 45.9	11 43.5	1 16.4
19 F	5 50 27	28 07 54	17 56 16	23 51 22	5 03.2	19 03.9	14 43.3	2 20.5	10 51.1	28 47.5	12 23.0	14 48.7	11 45.2	1 16.0
20 Sa	5 54 23	29 05 10	29 47 30	5♐44 59	4 53.3	21 10.5	15 56.6	3 03.3	10 56.6	28 39.8	12 20.6	14 51.5	11 46.9	1 15.5
21 Su	5 58 20	0♋02 24	11♐44 05	17 45 01	4 41.3	23 18.5	17 10.0	3 46.0	11 01.8	28 32.1	12 18.3	14 54.4	11 48.6	1 15.0
22 M	6 02 17	0 59 38	23 47 58	29 53 05	4 28.0	25 27.8	18 23.3	4 28.7	11 06.7	28 24.5	12 16.0	14 57.3	11 50.2	1 14.5
23 Tu	6 06 13	1 56 52	6♑00 28	12♑10 12	4 14.7	27 38.0	19 36.7	5 11.3	11 11.2	28 16.8	12 13.9	15 00.2	11 51.8	1 14.0
24 W	6 10 10	2 54 05	18 22 22	24 37 01	4 02.3	29 48.9	20 50.1	5 53.8	11 15.5	28 09.2	12 11.8	15 03.2	11 53.4	1 13.5
25 Th	6 14 06	3 51 18	0♒54 15	7♒14 06	3 51.9	2♋00.2	22 03.5	6 36.3	11 19.4	28 01.6	12 09.9	15 06.2	11 55.0	1 12.9
26 F	6 18 03	4 48 31	13 36 42	20 02 09	3 44.2	4 11.6	23 16.9	7 18.8	11 23.0	27 54.0	12 08.0	15 09.2	11 56.5	1 12.3
27 Sa	6 21 59	5 45 44	26 30 36	3♓02 15	3 39.4	6 22.9	24 30.3	8 01.1	11 26.2	27 46.5	12 06.2	15 12.2	11 58.0	1 11.7
28 Su	6 25 56	6 42 56	9♓37 16	16 15 53	3 37.1	8 33.7	25 43.7	8 43.5	11 29.2	27 39.0	12 04.5	15 15.3	11 59.5	1 11.1
29 M	6 29 52	7 40 09	22 58 20	29 44 50	3 36.4	10 43.8	26 57.2	9 25.7	11 31.7	27 31.5	12 02.9	15 18.4	12 01.0	1 10.5
30 Tu	6 33 49	8 37 21	6♈35 36	13♈30 47	3 36.4	12 53.0	28 10.6	10 07.9	11 34.0	27 24.1	12 01.4	15 21.5	12 02.4	1 09.8

Astro Data

	Dy Hr Mn
☽0N	5 23:59
☿D	10 0:20
☽0S	18 19:25
♄□♅	24 20:18
♃✶♇	29 9:36
♇R	1 8:40
☽0N	2 7:59
♃□♅	13 13:40
☽0S	15 1:12
☽0N	29 13:31
♄☍♆	30 3:39

Planet Ingress

	Dy Hr Mn
♂ ♉	6 10:43
♀ ♉	13 19:46
☉ ♊	21 3:10
♀ ♊	7 10:39
☿ ♊	9 13:48
♃ ♐R	9 21:44
♂ ♊	16 5:24
☉ ♋	21 11:00
☿ ♋	24 14:01

Last Aspect / ☽ Ingress

Last Aspect Dy Hr Mn		☽ Ingress Dy Hr Mn
1 3:02 ♂□	♒	1 10:42
3 14:07 ♂✶	♓	3 17:58
4 20:43 ♄△	♈	5 21:37
7 9:50 ♀☌	♉	7 22:17
9 3:22 ☉☌	♊	9 21:34
11 17:21 ♀✶	♋	11 21:31
13 11:19 ☉✶	♌	14 0:06
15 21:06 ☉□	♍	16 6:35
18 11:45 ☉△	♎	18 16:48
19 20:12 ♅✶	♏	21 5:14
22 9:40 ♅☌	♐	23 18:06
24 21:55 ♅△	♑	26 6:09
27 15:11 ♀△	♒	28 16:40
30 6:30 ♀□	♓	31 0:53

Last Aspect / ☽ Ingress

Last Aspect Dy Hr Mn		☽ Ingress Dy Hr Mn
1 18:05 ♀✶	♈	2 6:07
3 6:06 ♅△	♉	4 8:17
6 6:00 ♀☌	♊	6 8:19
7 10:36 ☉☌	♋	8 7:58
10 1:53 ♂✶	♌	10 9:22
12 13:42 ♃△	♍	12 14:19
14 22:12 ♃□	♎	14 23:26
17 9:39 ♃✶	♏	17 11:33
18 17:35 ♅□	♐	20 0:25
22 9:07 ♃☌	♑	22 12:14
23 12:07 ♄△	♒	24 22:17
27 2:26 ♃✶	♓	27 6:26
29 8:07 ♃□	♈	29 12:27

☽ Phases & Eclipses

Dy Hr Mn		
2 9:00	☾	11♒52
9 3:22	●	18♉26
15 21:06	☽	24♌56
23 23:38	○	2♐45
31 19:26	☾	10♓15
7 10:36	●	16♊36
14 10:20	☽	23♍17
22 14:22	○	1♑05
30 2:54	☾	8♈16

Astro Data

1 May 2043
Julian Day # 52351
SVP 4♓39'19"
GC 27♐26.7 ⚴ 26♑49.7
Eris 29♈22.1 ⚵ 6♑53.2R
⚷ 11♌36.6 ⚶ 12♎58.2R
☽ Mean ☊ 6♈59.8

1 June 2043
Julian Day # 52382
SVP 4♓39'14"
GC 27♐26.7 ⚴ 26♑17.6R
Eris 29♈40.6 ⚵ 3♑30.0R
⚷ 13♌25.5 ⚶ 11♎28.7
☽ Mean ☊ 5♈21.3

July 2043 — LONGITUDE

Day	Sid.Time	☉	0 hr ☽	Noon ☽	True ☊	☿	♀	♂	⚳	♃	♄	♅	♆	♇
1 W	6 37 46	9♋34 34	20♈30 30	27♈34 47	3♈35.7	15♋01.2	29♊24.1	10♊50.1	11♓35.9	27♐16.7	12♏00.0	15♌24.7	12♉03.8	1♓09.1
2 Th	6 41 42	10 31 47	4♉43 32	11♉56 32	3R33.2	17 08.0	0♋37.6	11 32.2	11 37.5	27R09.4	11R58.6	15 27.9	12 05.2	1R08.4
3 F	6 45 39	11 29 01	19 13 25	26 33 41	3 28.2	19 13.5	1 51.1	12 14.2	11 38.7	27 02.2	11 57.4	15 31.1	12 06.5	1 07.6
4 Sa	6 49 35	12 26 14	3♊56 39	11♊21 30	3 20.5	21 17.3	3 04.7	12 56.2	11 39.6	26 55.0	11 56.2	15 34.4	12 07.9	1 06.9
5 Su	6 53 32	13 23 28	18 47 17	26 12 56	3 10.8	23 19.5	4 18.2	13 38.1	11R40.1	26 47.9	11 55.2	15 37.6	12 09.2	1 06.1
6 M	6 57 28	14 20 42	3♋37 24	10♋59 34	2 59.9	25 20.0	5 31.8	14 20.0	11 40.3	26 40.9	11 54.3	15 40.9	12 10.5	1 05.3
7 Tu	7 01 25	15 17 55	18 18 24	25 32 55	2 49.2	27 18.6	6 45.4	15 01.8	11 40.1	26 33.9	11 53.4	15 44.2	12 11.7	1 04.5
8 W	7 05 21	16 15 09	2♌42 18	9♌45 54	2 39.7	29 15.4	7 59.0	15 43.5	11 39.6	26 27.1	11 52.6	15 47.6	12 12.9	1 03.7
9 Th	7 09 18	17 12 23	16 43 13	23 33 57	2 32.5	1♌10.3	9 12.6	16 25.2	11 38.7	26 20.3	11 52.0	15 51.0	12 14.1	1 02.8
10 F	7 13 15	18 09 36	0♍17 58	6♍55 20	2 27.7	3 03.3	10 26.2	17 06.8	11 37.4	26 13.6	11 51.4	15 54.3	12 15.3	1 02.0
11 Sa	7 17 11	19 06 50	13 26 13	19 50 58	2 25.4	4 54.3	11 39.8	17 48.3	11 35.8	26 07.1	11 51.0	15 57.7	12 16.4	1 01.1
12 Su	7 21 08	20 04 03	26 09 59	2♎23 49	2D24.8	6 43.4	12 53.5	18 29.8	11 33.9	26 00.6	11 50.6	16 01.2	12 17.5	1 00.2
13 M	7 25 04	21 01 16	8♎33 01	14 38 14	2R25.0	8 30.6	14 07.1	19 11.3	11 31.5	25 54.3	11 50.3	16 04.6	12 18.6	0 59.3
14 Tu	7 29 01	21 58 29	20 40 07	26 39 19	2 25.0	10 15.8	15 20.8	19 52.6	11 28.9	25 48.0	11 50.1	16 08.1	12 19.7	0 58.3
15 W	7 32 57	22 55 43	2♏36 30	8♏32 21	2 23.8	11 59.1	16 34.5	20 33.9	11 25.8	25 41.9	11D50.1	16 11.5	12 20.7	0 57.4
16 Th	7 36 54	23 52 56	14 27 29	20 22 30	2 20.6	13 40.4	17 48.2	21 15.2	11 22.4	25 35.9	11 50.1	16 15.0	12 21.7	0 56.4
17 F	7 40 50	24 50 10	26 17 59	2♐14 27	2 15.1	15 19.8	19 01.9	21 56.3	11 18.7	25 30.1	11 50.2	16 18.6	12 22.6	0 55.4
18 Sa	7 44 47	25 47 23	8♐12 23	14 12 12	2 07.2	16 57.2	20 15.6	22 37.5	11 14.6	25 24.4	11 50.4	16 22.1	12 23.6	0 54.4
19 Su	7 48 44	26 44 37	20 14 16	26 18 54	1 57.3	18 32.7	21 29.4	23 18.5	11 10.1	25 18.8	11 50.8	16 25.6	12 24.5	0 53.4
20 M	7 52 40	27 41 52	2♑26 20	8♑36 45	1 46.3	20 06.3	22 43.2	23 59.5	11 05.3	25 13.3	11 51.2	16 29.2	12 25.3	0 52.4
21 Tu	7 56 37	28 39 06	14 50 17	21 06 59	1 35.1	21 37.9	23 56.9	24 40.5	11 00.2	25 08.0	11 51.7	16 32.8	12 26.2	0 51.3
22 W	8 00 33	29 36 21	27 26 55	3♒50 01	1 24.8	23 07.5	25 10.7	25 21.3	10 54.7	25 02.8	11 52.3	16 36.4	12 27.0	0 50.3
23 Th	8 04 30	0♌33 37	10♒16 16	16 45 36	1 16.2	24 35.2	26 24.5	26 02.2	10 48.8	24 57.8	11 53.0	16 40.0	12 27.8	0 49.2
24 F	8 08 26	1 30 53	23 17 55	29 53 08	1 09.9	26 00.8	27 38.4	26 42.9	10 42.6	24 52.9	11 53.8	16 43.6	12 28.5	0 48.1
25 Sa	8 12 23	2 28 10	6♓31 11	13♓12 00	1 06.2	27 24.5	28 52.2	27 23.6	10 36.1	24 48.2	11 54.7	16 47.2	12 29.2	0 47.0
26 Su	8 16 19	3 25 28	19 55 33	26 41 47	1D04.8	28 46.0	0♌06.1	28 04.3	10 29.2	24 43.6	11 55.7	16 50.9	12 29.9	0 45.9
27 M	8 20 16	4 22 46	3♈30 43	10♈22 21	1 05.0	0♍05.5	1 20.0	28 44.9	10 22.0	24 39.2	11 56.8	16 54.5	12 30.6	0 44.7
28 Tu	8 24 13	5 20 06	17 16 41	24 13 43	1R05.8	1 22.8	2 33.9	29 25.4	10 14.5	24 34.9	11 58.0	16 58.2	12 31.2	0 43.6
29 W	8 28 09	6 17 26	1♉13 27	8♉15 49	1 06.2	2 38.0	3 47.8	0♋05.8	10 06.7	24 30.8	11 59.3	17 01.8	12 31.8	0 42.5
30 Th	8 32 06	7 14 48	15 20 43	22 27 59	1 05.2	3 50.8	5 01.7	0 46.2	9 58.5	24 26.8	12 00.7	17 05.5	12 32.3	0 41.3
31 F	8 36 02	8 12 11	29 37 21	6♊48 28	1 02.2	5 01.4	6 15.7	1 26.6	9 50.0	24 23.1	12 02.1	17 09.2	12 32.8	0 40.1

August 2043 — LONGITUDE

Day	Sid.Time	☉	0 hr ☽	Noon ☽	True ☊	☿	♀	♂	⚳	♃	♄	♅	♆	♇
1 Sa	8 39 59	9♌09 35	14♊00 56	21♊14 12	0♈57.1	6♍09.6	7♌29.6	2♋06.9	9♓41.2	24♐19.5	12♏03.7	17♌12.9	12♉33.3	0♓38.9
2 Su	8 43 55	10 07 00	28 27 40	5♋40 39	0R50.4	7 15.3	8 43.6	2 47.1	9R32.1	24R16.0	12 05.4	17 16.6	12 33.8	0R37.8
3 M	8 47 52	11 04 26	12♋52 26	20 02 16	0 42.6	8 18.4	9 57.7	3 27.3	9 22.7	24 12.8	12 07.2	17 20.3	12 34.2	0 36.6
4 Tu	8 51 49	12 01 53	27 09 25	4♌13 11	0 34.9	9 18.8	11 11.7	4 07.4	9 13.0	24 09.7	12 09.0	17 24.0	12 34.6	0 35.3
5 W	8 55 45	12 59 21	11♌12 57	18 08 11	0 28.1	10 16.5	12 25.7	4 47.4	9 03.0	24 06.8	12 11.0	17 27.8	12 35.0	0 34.1
6 Th	8 59 42	13 56 50	24 58 26	1♍43 24	0 23.0	11 11.2	13 39.8	5 27.4	8 52.8	24 04.1	12 13.0	17 31.5	12 35.3	0 32.9
7 F	9 03 38	14 54 20	8♍22 54	14 56 52	0 19.9	12 02.9	14 53.9	6 07.3	8 42.3	24 01.5	12 15.2	17 35.2	12 35.6	0 31.7
8 Sa	9 07 35	15 51 50	21 25 21	27 48 33	0D18.7	12 51.3	16 07.9	6 47.1	8 31.6	23 59.1	12 17.4	17 38.9	12 35.9	0 30.4
9 Su	9 11 31	16 49 22	4♎06 44	10♎20 16	0 19.1	13 36.4	17 22.0	7 26.9	8 20.6	23 56.9	12 19.7	17 42.6	12 36.1	0 29.2
10 M	9 15 28	17 46 54	16 29 34	22 35 10	0 20.4	14 17.9	18 36.1	8 06.6	8 09.3	23 54.9	12 22.2	17 46.4	12 36.3	0 27.9
11 Tu	9 19 24	18 44 27	28 37 36	4♏37 28	0 21.8	14 55.7	19 50.3	8 46.3	7 57.9	23 53.1	12 24.7	17 50.1	12 36.4	0 26.6
12 W	9 23 21	19 42 01	10♏35 21	16 31 55	0R22.7	15 29.6	21 04.4	9 25.8	7 46.2	23 51.5	12 27.3	17 53.8	12 36.6	0 25.4
13 Th	9 27 17	20 39 36	22 27 45	28 23 31	0 22.4	15 59.3	22 18.5	10 05.4	7 34.4	23 50.0	12 30.0	17 57.5	12 36.7	0 24.1
14 F	9 31 14	21 37 12	4♐19 48	10♐17 13	0 20.6	16 24.7	23 32.7	10 44.8	7 22.3	23 48.8	12 32.7	18 01.3	12 36.7	0 22.8
15 Sa	9 35 11	22 34 49	16 16 19	22 17 37	0 17.1	16 45.5	24 46.9	11 24.2	7 10.1	23 47.7	12 35.6	18 05.0	12R36.7	0 21.5
16 Su	9 39 07	23 32 27	28 21 36	4♑28 42	0 12.3	17 01.5	26 01.1	12 03.5	6 57.7	23 46.8	12 38.6	18 08.7	12 36.7	0 20.2
17 M	9 43 04	24 30 06	10♑39 17	16 53 39	0 06.7	17 12.5	27 15.2	12 42.8	6 45.2	23 46.1	12 41.6	18 12.4	12 36.7	0 19.0
18 Tu	9 47 00	25 27 46	23 12 01	29 34 34	0 00.8	17R18.3	28 29.5	13 22.0	6 32.6	23 45.6	12 44.7	18 16.1	12 36.6	0 17.7
19 W	9 50 57	26 25 27	6♒01 22	12♒32 24	29♓55.3	17 18.6	29 43.7	14 01.1	6 19.8	23 45.3	12 48.0	18 19.8	12 36.5	0 16.4
20 Th	9 54 53	27 23 09	19 07 39	25 46 57	29 50.8	17 13.4	0♍57.9	14 40.2	6 06.9	23D45.1	12 51.3	18 23.5	12 36.4	0 15.1
21 F	9 58 50	28 20 53	2♓30 08	9♓16 56	29 47.8	17 02.5	2 12.1	15 19.2	5 53.8	23 45.2	12 54.6	18 27.2	12 36.2	0 13.8
22 Sa	10 02 47	29 18 38	16 07 05	23 00 16	29D46.4	16 45.8	3 26.4	15 58.1	5 40.8	23 45.4	12 58.1	18 30.9	12 36.0	0 12.5
23 Su	10 06 43	0♍16 25	29 56 10	6♈54 26	29 46.4	16 23.3	4 40.6	16 37.0	5 27.6	23 45.8	13 01.7	18 34.6	12 35.8	0 11.2
24 M	10 10 40	1 14 13	13♈54 46	20 56 49	29 47.4	15 55.1	5 54.9	17 15.8	5 14.3	23 46.4	13 05.3	18 38.2	12 35.5	0 09.9
25 Tu	10 14 36	2 12 03	28 00 17	5♉04 53	29 48.8	15 21.3	7 09.2	17 54.5	5 01.1	23 47.2	13 09.0	18 41.9	12 35.2	0 08.6
26 W	10 18 33	3 09 55	12♉10 18	19 16 18	29 50.1	14 42.4	8 23.5	18 33.2	4 47.7	23 48.2	13 12.8	18 45.5	12 34.9	0 07.3
27 Th	10 22 29	4 07 49	26 22 37	3♊28 57	29R50.7	13 58.6	9 37.8	19 11.8	4 34.4	23 49.3	13 16.7	18 49.2	12 34.5	0 06.0
28 F	10 26 26	5 05 44	10♊35 05	17 40 42	29 50.2	13 10.6	10 52.1	19 50.4	4 21.1	23 50.7	13 20.6	18 52.8	12 34.1	0 04.7
29 Sa	10 30 22	6 03 42	24 45 32	1♋49 17	29 48.6	12 19.1	12 06.5	20 28.9	4 07.7	23 52.2	13 24.6	18 56.4	12 33.7	0 03.4
30 Su	10 34 19	7 01 41	8♋51 36	15 52 11	29 46.1	11 24.9	13 20.8	21 07.3	3 54.4	23 53.9	13 28.8	19 00.0	12 33.3	0 02.1
31 M	10 38 16	7 59 42	22 50 40	29 46 42	29 43.1	10 29.0	14 35.2	21 45.7	3 41.2	23 55.8	13 33.0	19 03.6	12 32.8	0 00.8

Astro Data

	Dy Hr Mn
♃⚻♆	2 23:44
♃∠♄	4 6:59
⚳ R	6 11:54
☽ 0S	12 8:09
♄ D	15 18:08
☽ 0N	26 18:09
☽ 0S	8 16:16
♄☍♆	15 21:21
♆ R	15 21:58
☿ R	19 1:34
♃ D	20 18:36
☽ 0N	23 0:02

Planet Ingress

	Dy Hr Mn
♀ ♋	1 23:43
☿ ♌	8 21:16
☉ ♌	22 21:55
♀ ♌	26 10:02
☿ ♍	27 10:19
♂ ♋	29 8:32
☊ ♓R	18 15:10
♀ ♍	19 17:17
☉ ♍	23 5:11

Last Aspect / ☽ Ingress (July)

Last Aspect Dy Hr Mn		☽ Ingress Dy Hr Mn
1 15:22	♀ ⚹	♉ 1 16:05
2 22:00	☿ ⚹	♊ 3 17:36
5 12:56	♃ ☍	♋ 5 18:07
7 15:24	☿ ☌	♌ 7 19:27
9 16:53	♃ △	♍ 9 23:28
11 23:48	♃ □	♎ 12 7:22
14 10:18	♃ ⚹	♏ 14 18:44
16 19:44	☉ △	♐ 17 7:29
19 10:02	♃ ☌	♑ 19 19:14
22 3:25	☉ ☍	♒ 22 4:48
24 5:55	♂ △	♓ 24 12:12
26 14:33	♂ □	♈ 26 17:50
28 21:22	♂ ⚹	♉ 28 21:54
30 2:55	♅ □	♊ 31 0:38

Last Aspect / ☽ Ingress (August)

Last Aspect Dy Hr Mn		☽ Ingress Dy Hr Mn
1 17:06	♃ ☍	♋ 2 2:33
2 23:29	♆ ⚹	♌ 4 4:49
5 22:27	♃ △	♍ 6 8:55
8 4:49	♃ □	♎ 8 16:09
10 14:38	♃ ⚹	♏ 11 2:44
12 22:15	♀ □	♐ 13 15:15
15 17:30	♀ △	♑ 16 3:14
17 12:36	☿ △	♒ 18 12:48
20 15:06	☉ ☍	♓ 20 19:33
22 13:18	♃ □	♈ 23 0:07
24 16:49	♃ △	♉ 25 3:23
26 11:08	♅ □	♊ 27 6:07
28 22:28	♃ ☍	♋ 29 8:54
30 21:28	♂ ☌	♌ 31 12:23

☽ Phases & Eclipses

Dy Hr Mn	
6 17:52	● 14♋35
14 1:48	☽ 21♎34
22 3:25	○ 29♑16
29 8:24	☾ 6♉09
5 2:24	● 12♌36
12 18:58	☽ 19♏59
20 15:06	○ 27♒31
27 13:10	☾ 4♊11

Astro Data

1 July 2043
Julian Day # 52412
SVP 4♓39'09"
GC 27♐26.8 ⚴ 19♑55.3R
Eris 29♈52.4 ⚵ 26♐57.0R
⚷ 16♌20.9 ⚶ 16♎51.4
☽ Mean ☊ 3♈46.0

1 August 2043
Julian Day # 52443
SVP 4♓39'03"
GC 27♐26.9 ⚴ 11♑54.1R
Eris 29♈55.6R ⚵ 21♐54.7R
⚷ 20♌06.4 ⚶ 27♎09.4
☽ Mean ☊ 2♈07.5

LONGITUDE September 2043

Day	Sid.Time	☉	0 hr ☽	Noon ☽	True ☊	☿	♀	♂	⚳	♃	♄	♅	♆	♇
1 Tu	10 42 12	8♍57 45	6♌39 57	13♌30 06	29♓40.0	9♍32.5	15♍49.6	22♋24.0	3♓27.9	23♐57.9	13♏37.2	19♌07.2	12♉32.3	29♒59.6
2 W	10 46 09	9 55 49	20 16 51	26 59 55	29R 37.4	8R 36.6	17 03.9	23 02.2	3R 14.8	24 00.2	13 41.6	19 10.7	12R 31.7	29R 58.3
3 Th	10 50 05	10 53 55	3♍39 06	10♍14 13	29 35.6	7 42.6	18 18.3	23 40.3	3 01.7	24 02.6	13 46.0	19 14.2	12 31.1	29 57.0
4 F	10 54 02	11 52 03	16 45 11	23 11 57	29D 34.7	6 51.5	19 32.7	24 18.4	2 48.7	24 05.2	13 50.5	19 17.8	12 30.5	29 55.7
5 Sa	10 57 58	12 50 12	29 34 32	5♎53 03	29 34.7	6 04.7	20 47.1	24 56.4	2 35.8	24 08.1	13 55.0	19 21.3	12 29.9	29 54.5
6 Su	11 01 55	13 48 23	12♎07 38	18 18 31	29 35.4	5 23.3	22 01.5	25 34.3	2 23.1	24 11.0	13 59.6	19 24.8	12 29.2	29 53.2
7 M	11 05 51	14 46 36	24 26 00	0♏30 25	29 36.6	4 48.2	23 16.0	26 12.2	2 10.5	24 14.2	14 04.3	19 28.2	12 28.5	29 51.9
8 Tu	11 09 48	15 44 50	6♏32 10	12 31 41	29 37.9	4 20.2	24 30.4	26 49.9	1 58.0	24 17.6	14 09.1	19 31.7	12 27.7	29 50.7
9 W	11 13 44	16 43 06	18 29 28	24 26 02	29 39.0	4 00.3	25 44.8	27 27.6	1 45.7	24 21.1	14 14.0	19 35.1	12 27.0	29 49.5
10 Th	11 17 41	17 41 23	0♐21 55	6♐17 42	29 39.8	3D 48.7	26 59.3	28 05.3	1 33.6	24 24.8	14 18.9	19 38.5	12 26.2	29 48.2
11 F	11 21 38	18 39 42	12 13 57	18 11 15	29R 40.1	3 46.1	28 13.7	28 42.8	1 21.7	24 28.7	14 23.9	19 41.9	12 25.4	29 47.0
12 Sa	11 25 34	19 38 03	24 10 13	0♑11 25	29 39.9	3 52.5	29 28.1	29 20.3	1 10.0	24 32.7	14 28.9	19 45.2	12 24.5	29 45.8
13 Su	11 29 31	20 36 25	6♑15 24	12 22 42	29 39.2	4 08.1	0♎42.6	29 57.7	0 58.5	24 36.9	14 34.0	19 48.6	12 23.6	29 44.6
14 M	11 33 27	21 34 49	18 33 51	24 49 16	29 38.4	4 32.8	1 57.0	0♌35.1	0 47.2	24 41.3	14 39.2	19 51.9	12 22.7	29 43.4
15 Tu	11 37 24	22 33 14	1♒09 22	7♒34 28	29 37.4	5 06.4	3 11.5	1 12.3	0 36.1	24 45.9	14 44.4	19 55.2	12 21.8	29 42.2
16 W	11 41 20	23 31 41	14 04 49	20 40 34	29 36.6	5 48.6	4 25.9	1 49.5	0 25.3	24 50.6	14 49.7	19 58.5	12 20.8	29 41.1
17 Th	11 45 17	24 30 09	27 21 46	4♓08 23	29 36.0	6 39.0	5 40.4	2 26.6	0 14.7	24 55.5	14 55.1	20 01.7	12 19.9	29 39.9
18 F	11 49 13	25 28 39	11♓00 15	17 57 06	29D 35.7	7 37.1	6 54.8	3 03.7	0 04.4	25 00.6	15 00.5	20 04.9	12 18.8	29 38.8
19 Sa	11 53 10	26 27 12	24 58 33	2♈04 09	29 35.6	8 42.5	8 09.3	3 40.6	29♒54.4	25 05.8	15 06.0	20 08.1	12 17.8	29 37.6
20 Su	11 57 07	27 25 46	9♈13 18	16 25 25	29 35.7	9 54.5	9 23.7	4 17.5	29 44.6	25 11.2	15 11.5	20 11.3	12 16.7	29 36.5
21 M	12 01 03	28 24 22	23 39 46	0♉55 41	29 35.8	11 12.5	10 38.2	4 54.3	29 35.2	25 16.7	15 17.1	20 14.4	12 15.6	29 35.4
22 Tu	12 05 00	29 23 00	8♉12 25	15 29 17	29R 35.9	12 35.9	11 52.7	5 31.0	29 26.0	25 22.4	15 22.8	20 17.5	12 14.5	29 34.3
23 W	12 08 56	0♎21 41	22 45 35	0♊00 43	29 35.8	14 04.1	13 07.1	6 07.7	29 17.1	25 28.3	15 28.5	20 20.6	12 13.4	29 33.2
24 Th	12 12 53	1 20 24	7♊14 08	14 25 20	29 35.8	15 36.4	14 21.6	6 44.3	29 08.5	25 34.3	15 34.2	20 23.6	12 12.2	29 32.1
25 F	12 16 49	2 19 09	21 33 54	28 39 32	29D 35.7	17 12.2	15 36.1	7 20.8	29 00.3	25 40.4	15 40.1	20 26.6	12 11.0	29 31.1
26 Sa	12 20 46	3 17 56	5♋41 57	12♋40 59	29 35.7	18 51.0	16 50.6	7 57.2	28 52.4	25 46.8	15 45.9	20 29.6	12 09.8	29 30.0
27 Su	12 24 42	4 16 46	19 36 31	26 28 27	29 36.0	20 32.3	18 05.1	8 33.5	28 44.7	25 53.2	15 51.8	20 32.6	12 08.6	29 29.0
28 M	12 28 39	5 15 38	3♌16 45	10♌01 27	29 36.4	22 15.5	19 19.6	9 09.8	28 37.5	25 59.9	15 57.8	20 35.5	12 07.3	29 28.0
29 Tu	12 32 36	6 14 32	16 42 32	23 20 05	29 37.0	24 00.4	20 34.0	9 46.0	28 30.5	26 06.6	16 03.8	20 38.4	12 06.1	29 27.0
30 W	12 36 32	7 13 28	29 54 07	6♍24 43	29 37.7	25 46.4	21 48.5	10 22.0	28 23.9	26 13.6	16 09.9	20 41.2	12 04.7	29 26.0

LONGITUDE October 2043

Day	Sid.Time	☉	0 hr ☽	Noon ☽	True ☊	☿	♀	♂	⚳	♃	♄	♅	♆	♇
1 Th	12 40 29	8♎12 27	12♍51 57	19♍15 53	29♓38.2	27♍33.2	23♎03.0	10♌58.0	28♒17.7	26♐20.6	16♏16.0	20♌44.0	12♉03.4	29♒25.1
2 F	12 44 25	9 11 27	25 36 36	1♎54 12	29R 38.3	29 20.7	24 17.5	11 33.9	28R 11.8	26 27.8	16 22.2	20 46.8	12R 02.1	29R 24.1
3 Sa	12 48 22	10 10 30	8♎08 47	14 20 28	29 37.9	1♎08.4	25 32.0	12 09.8	28 06.2	26 35.2	16 28.4	20 49.6	12 00.7	29 23.2
4 Su	12 52 18	11 09 35	20 29 24	26 35 44	29 37.0	2 56.3	26 46.6	12 45.5	28 01.1	26 42.7	16 34.7	20 52.3	11 59.3	29 22.3
5 M	12 56 15	12 08 41	2♏39 40	8♏41 25	29 35.4	4 44.1	28 01.1	13 21.1	27 56.3	26 50.3	16 41.0	20 54.9	11 57.9	29 21.4
6 Tu	13 00 11	13 07 50	14 41 14	20 39 26	29 33.5	6 31.7	29 15.6	13 56.7	27 51.8	26 58.1	16 47.3	20 57.6	11 56.5	29 20.5
7 W	13 04 08	14 07 00	26 36 19	2♐32 16	29 31.3	8 18.9	0♏30.1	14 32.1	27 47.7	27 06.0	16 53.7	21 00.2	11 55.1	29 19.6
8 Th	13 08 05	15 06 13	8♐27 42	14 23 01	29 29.1	10 05.8	1 44.6	15 07.5	27 44.0	27 14.1	17 00.2	21 02.7	11 53.6	29 18.8
9 F	13 12 01	16 05 27	20 18 44	26 15 20	29 27.4	11 52.1	2 59.1	15 42.7	27 40.7	27 22.3	17 06.6	21 05.2	11 52.1	29 18.0
10 Sa	13 15 58	17 04 43	2♑13 22	8♑13 21	29D 26.4	13 37.9	4 13.6	16 17.9	27 37.7	27 30.6	17 13.1	21 07.7	11 50.7	29 17.2
11 Su	13 19 54	18 04 01	14 15 54	20 21 33	29 26.1	15 23.0	5 28.0	16 52.9	27 35.1	27 39.0	17 19.7	21 10.1	11 49.2	29 16.4
12 M	13 23 51	19 03 21	26 30 54	2♒44 30	29 26.7	17 07.6	6 42.5	17 27.9	27 32.9	27 47.6	17 26.3	21 12.5	11 47.6	29 15.7
13 Tu	13 27 47	20 02 42	9♒02 54	15 26 35	29 27.9	18 51.4	7 57.0	18 02.8	27 31.0	27 56.3	17 32.9	21 14.9	11 46.1	29 14.9
14 W	13 31 44	21 02 05	21 56 01	28 31 34	29 29.4	20 34.6	9 11.5	18 37.5	27 29.5	28 05.1	17 39.5	21 17.2	11 44.6	29 14.2
15 Th	13 35 40	22 01 30	5♓13 30	12♓01 59	29 30.8	22 17.1	10 26.0	19 12.2	27 28.4	28 14.1	17 46.2	21 19.4	11 43.0	29 13.5
16 F	13 39 37	23 00 57	18 57 04	25 58 38	29R 31.5	23 59.0	11 40.4	19 46.8	27 27.6	28 23.2	17 52.9	21 21.7	11 41.4	29 12.9
17 Sa	13 43 34	24 00 25	3♈06 24	10♈19 57	29 31.2	25 40.1	12 54.9	20 21.2	27D 27.3	28 32.4	17 59.7	21 23.8	11 39.8	29 12.2
18 Su	13 47 30	24 59 56	17 38 38	25 01 42	29 29.7	27 20.6	14 09.3	20 55.6	27 27.2	28 41.7	18 06.4	21 26.0	11 38.2	29 11.6
19 M	13 51 27	25 59 28	2♉28 15	9♉57 13	29 26.9	29 00.4	15 23.8	21 29.8	27 27.6	28 51.1	18 13.2	21 28.0	11 36.6	29 11.0
20 Tu	13 55 23	26 59 03	17 27 31	24 58 00	29 23.2	0♏39.6	16 38.2	22 04.0	27 28.3	29 00.6	18 20.1	21 30.1	11 35.0	29 10.4
21 W	13 59 20	27 58 40	2♊27 33	9♊55 06	29 19.2	2 18.1	17 52.7	22 38.0	27 29.3	29 10.3	18 26.9	21 32.1	11 33.4	29 09.8
22 Th	14 03 16	28 58 19	17 19 41	24 40 26	29 15.4	3 56.0	19 07.1	23 12.0	27 30.8	29 20.0	18 33.8	21 34.0	11 31.8	29 09.3
23 F	14 07 13	29 58 01	1♋56 42	9♋07 58	29 12.6	5 33.3	20 21.6	23 45.8	27 32.5	29 29.9	18 40.7	21 35.9	11 30.1	29 08.8
24 Sa	14 11 09	0♏57 44	16 13 50	23 14 08	29D 11.1	7 10.0	21 36.0	24 19.5	27 34.7	29 39.9	18 47.7	21 37.8	11 28.5	29 08.3
25 Su	14 15 06	1 57 30	0♌08 48	6♌57 54	29 10.9	8 46.2	22 50.5	24 53.1	27 37.1	29 50.0	18 54.6	21 39.6	11 26.8	29 07.8
26 M	14 19 03	2 57 19	13 41 35	20 20 07	29 11.9	10 21.8	24 04.9	25 26.6	27 40.0	0♑00.2	19 01.6	21 41.4	11 25.2	29 07.4
27 Tu	14 22 59	3 57 09	26 53 46	3♍22 52	29 13.5	11 56.9	25 19.4	26 00.0	27 43.1	0 10.5	19 08.6	21 43.1	11 23.5	29 07.0
28 W	14 26 56	4 57 02	9♍47 48	16 08 53	29 15.0	13 31.4	26 33.8	26 33.2	27 46.7	0 20.9	19 15.6	21 44.7	11 21.8	29 06.6
29 Th	14 30 52	5 56 56	22 26 30	28 40 58	29R 15.7	15 05.5	27 48.2	27 06.4	27 50.5	0 31.4	19 22.7	21 46.3	11 20.1	29 06.2
30 F	14 34 49	6 56 53	4♎52 35	11♎01 40	29 15.0	16 39.0	29 02.7	27 39.4	27 54.7	0 42.0	19 29.7	21 47.9	11 18.5	29 05.9
31 Sa	14 38 45	7 56 52	17 08 28	23 13 13	29 12.3	18 12.1	0♐17.1	28 12.2	27 59.3	0 52.7	19 36.8	21 49.4	11 16.8	29 05.5

Astro Data Dy Hr Mn	Planet Ingress Dy Hr Mn	Last Aspect Dy Hr Mn	☽ Ingress Dy Hr Mn	Last Aspect Dy Hr Mn	☽ Ingress Dy Hr Mn	☽ Phases & Eclipses Dy Hr Mn
☽0S 5 0:40	♇ ♒R 1 3:36	2 17:20 ♇ ☍	♍ 2 17:24	2 6:18 ☿ ☌	♎ 2 8:22	3 13:19 ● 10♍57
☿D 11 7:04	♀ ♎ 12 22:16	4 14:11 ♂ ⚹	♎ 5 0:48	4 17:29 ♇ △	♏ 4 18:44	11 13:02 ☽ 18♐42
♀0S 15 6:04	♂ ♌ 13 13:27	7 10:44 ♇ △	♏ 7 11:00	7 5:31 ♇ □	♐ 7 6:52	19 1:48 ○ 26♓02
☽0N 19 8:23	⚳ ♒R 18 22:30	9 22:53 ♇ □	♐ 9 23:16	9 18:07 ♇ ⚹	♑ 9 19:32	19 1:52 • T 1.255
☉0S 23 3:08	☉ ♎ 23 3:08	12 11:09 ♇ ⚹	♑ 12 11:37	11 7:06 ☉ □	♒ 12 6:44	25 18:42 ☾ 2♋36
		14 5:17 ☉ △	♒ 14 21:49	14 13:17 ♇ ☌	♓ 14 14:39	
☽0S 2 8:14	☿ ♎ 2 20:46	17 4:06 ♇ ☌	♓ 17 4:41	16 16:07 ♃ □	♈ 16 18:47	3 3:13 ● 9♎49
☿0S 5 2:58	♀ ♏ 7 2:19	19 1:48 ☉ ☍	♈ 19 8:31	18 18:43 ♇ ⚹	♉ 18 20:01	3 3:01:48 • A non-C
♃⚻♆ 6 7:50	☿ ♏ 20 2:24	21 9:48 ♇ ⚹	♉ 21 10:28	20 18:44 ♇ □	♊ 20 20:03	11 7:06 ☽ 17♑52
☽0N 16 18:39	☉ ♏ 23 12:48	23 11:14 ♇ □	♊ 23 11:59	22 19:46 ♃ ☍	♋ 22 20:47	18 11:57 ○ 25♈00
⚳D 18 1:32	♃ ♑ 26 11:31	25 13:27 ♇ △	♋ 25 14:17	24 8:55 ♀ △	♌ 24 23:45	25 2:29 ☾ 1♌34
♃⚹♇ 21 10:57	♀ ♐ 31 6:29	27 0:10 ☿ ⚹	♌ 27 18:12	27 4:06 ♇ ☍	♍ 27 5:44	
☽0S 29 14:18		29 23:09 ♇ ☍	♍ 30 0:11	29 10:07 ♀ ⚹	♎ 29 14:33	

Astro Data

1 September 2043
Julian Day # 52474
SVP 4♓38'58"
GC 27♐27.0 ⚴ 8♑36.7R
Eris 29♈48.9R ⚵ 22♐02.4
⚷ 24♌07.3 ⚶ 10♏19.0
☽ Mean ☊ 0♈29.0

1 October 2043
Julian Day # 52504
SVP 4♓38'55"
GC 27♐27.0 ⚴ 10♑57.6
Eris 29♈34.7R ⚵ 26♐48.1
⚷ 27♌45.5 ⚶ 24♏40.8
☽ Mean ☊ 28♓53.7

November 2043 — LONGITUDE

Day	Sid.Time	☉	0 hr ☽	Noon ☽	True ☊	☿	♀	♂	⚳	♃	♄	♅	♆	♇
1 Su	14 42 42	8♏56 53	29♎16 09	5♏17 27	29♓07.7	19♏44.7	1♐31.5	28♌45.0	28♒04.1	1♑03.5	19♏43.9	21♌50.9	11♉15.1	29♒05.2
2 M	14 46 38	9 56 56	11♏17 18	17 15 54	29R 01.2	21 16.9	2 46.0	29 17.6	28 09.4	1 14.5	19 51.0	21 52.3	11R 13.4	29R 05.0
3 Tu	14 50 35	10 57 01	23 13 26	29 10 04	28 53.3	22 48.6	4 00.4	29 50.0	28 14.9	1 25.5	19 58.1	21 53.6	11 11.7	29 04.7
4 W	14 54 32	11 57 07	5♐06 02	11♐01 33	28 44.7	24 19.9	5 14.8	0♍22.4	28 20.7	1 36.5	20 05.2	21 54.9	11 10.0	29 04.5
5 Th	14 58 28	12 57 15	16 56 52	22 52 18	28 36.2	25 50.8	6 29.2	0 54.6	28 26.9	1 47.7	20 12.4	21 56.2	11 08.3	29 04.3
6 F	15 02 25	13 57 25	28 48 08	4♑44 45	28 28.7	27 21.2	7 43.6	1 26.6	28 33.4	1 59.0	20 19.5	21 57.4	11 06.6	29 04.1
7 Sa	15 06 21	14 57 37	10♑42 33	16 41 58	28 22.9	28 51.2	8 58.0	1 58.5	28 40.2	2 10.4	20 26.7	21 58.5	11 05.0	29 04.0
8 Su	15 10 18	15 57 50	22 43 29	28 47 38	28 19.1	0♐20.7	10 12.4	2 30.3	28 47.4	2 21.8	20 33.8	21 59.6	11 03.3	29 03.9
9 M	15 14 14	16 58 05	4♒54 56	11♒05 57	28D 17.3	1 49.8	11 26.8	3 01.9	28 54.8	2 33.3	20 41.0	22 00.6	11 01.6	29 03.8
10 Tu	15 18 11	17 58 21	17 21 17	23 41 31	28 17.3	3 18.5	12 41.2	3 33.4	29 02.5	2 44.9	20 48.1	22 01.6	10 59.9	29 03.7
11 W	15 22 07	18 58 38	0♓07 11	6♓38 50	28 18.2	4 46.6	13 55.5	4 04.7	29 10.6	2 56.6	20 55.3	22 02.5	10 58.2	29D 03.7
12 Th	15 26 04	19 58 57	13 16 57	20 01 54	28R 19.3	6 14.3	15 09.9	4 35.9	29 18.9	3 08.4	21 02.5	22 03.4	10 56.6	29 03.7
13 F	15 30 01	20 59 17	26 54 01	3♈53 24	28 19.4	7 41.4	16 24.2	5 06.9	29 27.5	3 20.2	21 09.7	22 04.2	10 54.9	29 03.7
14 Sa	15 33 57	21 59 39	11♈00 05	18 13 49	28 17.7	9 08.0	17 38.5	5 37.7	29 36.4	3 32.1	21 16.8	22 05.0	10 53.3	29 03.7
15 Su	15 37 54	23 00 02	25 34 12	3♉00 34	28 13.7	10 33.9	18 52.9	6 08.4	29 45.6	3 44.1	21 24.0	22 05.7	10 51.6	29 03.8
16 M	15 41 50	24 00 27	10♉32 04	18 07 35	28 07.3	11 59.2	20 07.2	6 38.9	29 55.0	3 56.2	21 31.2	22 06.3	10 50.0	29 03.9
17 Tu	15 45 47	25 00 53	25 45 54	3♊25 36	27 59.0	13 23.8	21 21.5	7 09.3	0♓04.7	4 08.3	21 38.4	22 06.9	10 48.3	29 04.0
18 W	15 49 43	26 01 22	11♊05 15	18 43 25	27 49.9	14 47.6	22 35.8	7 39.5	0 14.7	4 20.6	21 45.5	22 07.5	10 46.7	29 04.2
19 Th	15 53 40	27 01 52	26 18 41	3♋49 51	27 41.1	16 10.5	23 50.0	8 09.5	0 25.0	4 32.8	21 52.7	22 08.0	10 45.1	29 04.3
20 F	15 57 36	28 02 23	11♋15 51	18 35 49	27 33.7	17 32.5	25 04.3	8 39.4	0 35.5	4 45.2	21 59.9	22 08.4	10 43.5	29 04.6
21 Sa	16 01 33	29 02 56	25 49 10	2♌55 29	27 28.5	18 53.3	26 18.6	9 09.1	0 46.3	4 57.6	22 07.0	22 08.8	10 41.9	29 04.8
22 Su	16 05 30	0♐03 32	9♌54 38	16 46 38	27 25.6	20 12.9	27 32.8	9 38.5	0 57.4	5 10.1	22 14.1	22 09.1	10 40.4	29 05.0
23 M	16 09 26	1 04 08	23 31 39	0♍10 02	27D 24.7	21 31.1	28 47.1	10 07.9	1 08.7	5 22.6	22 21.3	22 09.4	10 38.8	29 05.3
24 Tu	16 13 23	2 04 47	6♍42 11	13 08 37	27 25.1	22 47.6	0♑01.3	10 37.0	1 20.2	5 35.2	22 28.4	22 09.6	10 37.2	29 05.6
25 W	16 17 19	3 05 27	19 29 50	25 46 26	27R 25.5	24 02.4	1 15.5	11 05.9	1 32.0	5 47.9	22 35.5	22 09.7	10 35.7	29 05.9
26 Th	16 21 16	4 06 09	1♎58 56	8♎07 54	27 25.0	25 15.0	2 29.7	11 34.6	1 44.0	6 00.6	22 42.6	22 09.8	10 34.2	29 06.3
27 F	16 25 12	5 06 52	14 13 52	20 17 17	27 22.4	26 25.3	3 43.9	12 03.1	1 56.3	6 13.4	22 49.7	22R 09.8	10 32.7	29 06.7
28 Sa	16 29 09	6 07 37	26 18 39	2♏18 19	27 17.1	27 32.9	4 58.1	12 31.5	2 08.8	6 26.2	22 56.7	22 09.8	10 31.2	29 07.1
29 Su	16 33 05	7 08 23	8♏16 41	14 14 03	27 08.8	28 37.4	6 12.3	12 59.6	2 21.5	6 39.1	23 03.8	22 09.7	10 29.7	29 07.5
30 M	16 37 02	8 09 11	20 10 42	26 06 51	26 57.7	29 38.3	7 26.5	13 27.4	2 34.5	6 52.1	23 10.8	22 09.6	10 28.2	29 08.0

December 2043 — LONGITUDE

Day	Sid.Time	☉	0 hr ☽	Noon ☽	True ☊	☿	♀	♂	⚳	♃	♄	♅	♆	♇
1 Tu	16 40 59	9♐10 00	2♐02 44	7♐58 31	26♓44.6	0♑35.2	8♑40.6	13♍55.1	2♓47.7	7♑05.1	23♏17.8	22♌09.4	10♉26.8	29♒08.5
2 W	16 44 55	10 10 50	13 54 21	19 50 25	26R 30.2	1 27.5	9 54.8	14 22.5	3 01.1	7 18.1	23 24.8	22R 09.2	10R 25.4	29 09.0
3 Th	16 48 52	11 11 42	25 46 52	1♑43 52	26 16.0	2 14.5	11 08.9	14 49.7	3 14.8	7 31.2	23 31.8	22 08.9	10 24.0	29 09.5
4 F	16 52 48	12 12 34	7♑41 36	13 40 16	26 02.9	2 55.5	12 23.0	15 16.7	3 28.6	7 44.4	23 38.7	22 08.5	10 22.6	29 10.1
5 Sa	16 56 45	13 13 28	19 40 08	25 41 28	25 52.1	3 29.8	13 37.1	15 43.5	3 42.7	7 57.6	23 45.7	22 08.1	10 21.2	29 10.7
6 Su	17 00 41	14 14 22	1♒44 35	7♒49 52	25 44.1	3 56.6	14 51.2	16 09.9	3 57.0	8 10.8	23 52.6	22 07.7	10 19.9	29 11.3
7 M	17 04 38	15 15 18	13 57 43	20 08 36	25 39.1	4 15.0	16 05.2	16 36.2	4 11.5	8 24.1	23 59.4	22 07.1	10 18.5	29 11.9
8 Tu	17 08 34	16 16 13	26 22 59	2♓41 24	25 36.7	4R 24.1	17 19.2	17 02.2	4 26.1	8 37.4	24 06.3	22 06.6	10 17.2	29 12.6
9 W	17 12 31	17 17 10	9♓04 23	15 32 28	25 36.2	4 23.2	18 33.2	17 27.9	4 41.0	8 50.8	24 13.1	22 05.9	10 16.0	29 13.3
10 Th	17 16 28	18 18 07	22 06 11	28 46 00	25 36.2	4 11.6	19 47.2	17 53.4	4 56.1	9 04.2	24 19.9	22 05.3	10 14.7	29 14.0
11 F	17 20 24	19 19 05	5♈32 22	12♈25 36	25 35.4	3 48.7	21 01.2	18 18.6	5 11.4	9 17.6	24 26.6	22 04.5	10 13.5	29 14.7
12 Sa	17 24 21	20 20 04	19 25 55	26 33 22	25 32.8	3 14.3	22 15.1	18 43.5	5 26.8	9 31.1	24 33.3	22 03.7	10 12.3	29 15.5
13 Su	17 28 17	21 21 03	3♉47 48	11♉08 51	25 27.6	2 28.6	23 29.0	19 08.1	5 42.4	9 44.6	24 40.0	22 02.9	10 11.1	29 16.3
14 M	17 32 14	22 22 02	18 35 57	26 08 15	25 19.4	1 32.1	24 42.8	19 32.5	5 58.3	9 58.1	24 46.7	22 02.0	10 09.9	29 17.1
15 Tu	17 36 10	23 23 03	3♊44 41	11♊23 59	25 09.0	0 26.2	25 56.7	19 56.6	6 14.3	10 11.7	24 53.3	22 01.1	10 08.8	29 17.9
16 W	17 40 07	24 24 04	19 04 44	26 45 26	24 57.3	29♐12.3	27 10.5	20 20.4	6 30.4	10 25.3	24 59.9	22 00.1	10 07.7	29 18.8
17 Th	17 44 04	25 25 06	4♋24 34	12♋00 41	24 45.7	27 52.8	28 24.2	20 43.9	6 46.8	10 38.9	25 06.4	21 59.0	10 06.6	29 19.7
18 F	17 48 00	26 26 09	19 32 26	26 58 42	24 35.6	26 30.3	29 38.0	21 07.1	7 03.3	10 52.6	25 12.9	21 57.9	10 05.5	29 20.6
19 Sa	17 51 57	27 27 12	4♌18 34	11♌31 20	24 28.0	25 07.5	0♒51.7	21 30.0	7 20.0	11 06.3	25 19.4	21 56.8	10 04.5	29 21.5
20 Su	17 55 53	28 28 16	18 36 37	25 34 12	24 23.1	23 47.3	2 05.4	21 52.5	7 36.8	11 20.0	25 25.8	21 55.6	10 03.5	29 22.5
21 M	17 59 50	29 29 21	2♍24 07	9♍06 35	24 20.8	22 32.1	3 19.0	22 14.7	7 53.8	11 33.7	25 32.2	21 54.3	10 02.5	29 23.5
22 Tu	18 03 46	0♑30 27	15 41 55	22 10 37	24 20.3	21 24.2	4 32.6	22 36.6	8 11.0	11 47.5	25 38.5	21 53.0	10 01.6	29 24.4
23 W	18 07 43	1 31 33	28 33 14	4♎50 22	24 20.3	20 25.2	5 46.2	22 58.2	8 28.3	12 01.3	25 44.8	21 51.7	10 00.6	29 25.5
24 Th	18 11 39	2 32 40	11♎02 39	17 10 45	24 19.5	19 36.2	6 59.7	23 19.4	8 45.7	12 15.1	25 51.1	21 50.3	9 59.7	29 26.5
25 F	18 15 36	3 33 48	23 15 19	29 16 57	24 17.0	18 57.8	8 13.2	23 40.2	9 03.4	12 28.9	25 57.3	21 48.8	9 58.9	29 27.6
26 Sa	18 19 33	4 34 57	5♏16 15	11♏13 47	24 11.8	18 30.3	9 26.7	24 00.7	9 21.1	12 42.7	26 03.4	21 47.3	9 58.1	29 28.6
27 Su	18 23 29	5 36 06	17 10 05	23 05 34	24 03.7	18 13.3	10 40.1	24 20.8	9 39.1	12 56.7	26 09.5	21 45.8	9 57.2	29 29.7
28 M	18 27 26	6 37 16	29 00 41	4♐55 48	23 52.7	18D 06.5	11 53.5	24 40.5	9 57.1	13 10.4	26 15.6	21 44.2	9 56.5	29 30.9
29 Tu	18 31 22	7 38 26	10♐51 12	16 47 11	23 39.5	18 09.3	13 06.9	24 59.8	10 15.3	13 24.3	26 21.6	21 42.6	9 55.7	29 32.0
30 W	18 35 19	8 39 36	22 43 57	28 41 41	23 25.1	18 20.9	14 20.2	25 18.7	10 33.7	13 38.2	26 27.5	21 40.9	9 55.0	29 33.2
31 Th	18 39 15	9 40 47	4♑40 34	10♑40 42	23 10.6	18 40.7	15 33.5	25 37.2	10 52.2	13 52.1	26 33.4	21 39.2	9 54.3	29 34.4

Astro Data (Dy Hr Mn)

	Dy Hr Mn
♇ D	12 11:28
☽ 0N	13 4:51
♄□♅	21 18:15
☽ 0S	25 19:19
♅ R	27 15:40
♃⊡♅	1 19:53
☿ R	8 22:00
☽ 0N	10 12:52
♃∠♄	12 19:55
♃△♆	15 7:13
☽ 0S	23 0:56
☿ D	28 16:47

Planet Ingress

	Dy Hr Mn
♂ ♍	3 19:23
☿ ♐	8 6:26
⚳ ♓	17 0:23
☉ ♐	22 10:36
♀ ♑	24 11:35
☿ ♑	30 20:55
☿ ♐R	15 20:46
♀ ♒	18 19:10
☉ ♑	22 0:02

Last Aspect / ☽ Ingress

Last Aspect Dy Hr Mn		☽ Ingress Dy Hr Mn
31 23:39	♇ △	♏ 1 1:27
3 13:25	♂ □	♐ 3 13:41
6 0:33	♇ ⚹	♑ 6 2:25
7 19:33	♄ ⚹	♒ 8 14:22
10 22:02	♇ ☌	♓ 10 23:47
12 13:48	♄ △	♈ 13 5:21
15 5:39	♇ ⚹	♉ 15 7:10
17 5:10	♇ □	♊ 17 6:38
19 4:23	♇ △	♋ 19 5:52
21 4:56	☉ △	♌ 21 7:02
23 10:02	♇ ☍	♍ 23 11:42
25 8:18	☿ □	♎ 25 20:09
28 5:37	♇ △	♏ 28 7:23
30 18:07	♇ □	♐ 30 19:52

Last Aspect / ☽ Ingress

Last Aspect Dy Hr Mn		☽ Ingress Dy Hr Mn
3 6:49	♇ ⚹	♑ 3 8:31
5 8:07	♄ ⚹	♒ 5 20:33
8 5:23	♇ ☌	♓ 8 6:54
10 3:58	♄ △	♈ 10 14:12
12 16:30	♇ ⚹	♉ 12 17:44
14 16:59	♇ □	♊ 14 18:06
16 16:00	♇ △	♋ 16 17:05
18 16:43	♀ ☍	♌ 18 16:55
20 18:40	♇ ☍	♍ 20 19:45
22 18:33	♄ ⚹	♎ 23 2:45
25 12:21	♇ △	♏ 25 13:26
28 1:00	♇ □	♐ 28 2:00
30 13:44	♇ ⚹	♑ 30 14:37

☽ Phases & Eclipses

Dy Hr Mn		
1 19:59	●	9♏17
10 0:14	☽	17♒29
16 21:54	○	24♉25
23 13:47	☾	1♍09
1 14:38	●	9♐17
9 15:29	☽	17♓26
16 8:03	○	24♊14
23 5:06	☾	1♎14
31 9:49	●	9♑35

Astro Data

1 November 2043
Julian Day # 52535
SVP 4♓38'52"
GC 27♐27.1 ⚴ 17♑22.3
Eris 29♈16.2R ⚵ 5♑05.8
⚷ 0♍43.7 ⚶ 10♐32.1
☽ Mean ☊ 27♓15.2

1 December 2043
Julian Day # 52565
SVP 4♓38'47"
GC 27♐27.2 ⚴ 25♑52.1
Eris 29♈00.0R ⚵ 15♑16.4
⚷ 2♍19.5 ⚶ 26♐25.6
☽ Mean ☊ 25♓39.9

LONGITUDE — January 2044

Day	Sid.Time	☉	0 hr ☽	Noon ☽	True ☊	☿	♀	♂	⚳	♃	♄	♅	♆	♇
1 F	18 43 12	10♑41 58	16♑42 15	22♑45 17	22♓57.4	19♐07.8	16♒46.7	25♍55.2	11♓10.8	14♑06.0	26♏39.3	21♌37.5	9♉53.7	29♒35.6
2 Sa	18 47 08	11 43 09	28 49 58	4♒56 24	22R 46.3	19 41.5	17 59.8	26 12.9	11 29.6	14 20.0	26 45.1	21R 35.7	9R 53.1	29 36.8
3 Su	18 51 05	12 44 19	11♒04 46	17 15 15	22 38.1	20 21.2	19 12.9	26 30.1	11 48.4	14 33.9	26 50.8	21 33.9	9 52.5	29 38.0
4 M	18 55 02	13 45 30	23 28 04	29 43 29	22 32.9	21 06.2	20 26.0	26 46.8	12 07.5	14 47.8	26 56.5	21 32.0	9 52.0	29 39.3
5 Tu	18 58 58	14 46 40	6♓01 47	12♓23 19	22D 30.5	21 55.9	21 39.0	27 03.1	12 26.6	15 01.8	27 02.1	21 30.1	9 51.4	29 40.6
6 W	19 02 55	15 47 51	18 48 26	25 17 31	22 30.1	22 49.8	22 51.9	27 18.9	12 45.8	15 15.7	27 07.6	21 28.1	9 51.0	29 41.9
7 Th	19 06 51	16 49 00	1♈50 58	8♈29 10	22R 30.5	23 47.5	24 04.8	27 34.3	13 05.2	15 29.6	27 13.1	21 26.1	9 50.5	29 43.2
8 F	19 10 48	17 50 10	15 12 30	22 01 15	22 30.7	24 48.5	25 17.6	27 49.1	13 24.7	15 43.6	27 18.5	21 24.1	9 50.1	29 44.5
9 Sa	19 14 44	18 51 18	28 55 42	5♉55 58	22 29.3	25 52.5	26 30.4	28 03.5	13 44.3	15 57.5	27 23.9	21 22.0	9 49.7	29 45.8
10 Su	19 18 41	19 52 27	13♉02 06	20 13 55	22 25.8	26 59.2	27 43.1	28 17.4	14 04.0	16 11.4	27 29.2	21 19.9	9 49.3	29 47.2
11 M	19 22 37	20 53 35	27 31 08	4♊53 13	22 19.7	28 08.2	28 55.7	28 30.7	14 23.9	16 25.3	27 34.4	21 17.8	9 49.0	29 48.6
12 Tu	19 26 34	21 54 42	12♊19 29	19 49 02	22 11.6	29 19.4	0♓08.2	28 43.6	14 43.8	16 39.3	27 39.5	21 15.6	9 48.8	29 50.0
13 W	19 30 31	22 55 49	27 20 48	4♋53 37	22 02.2	0♑32.6	1 20.7	28 55.9	15 03.9	16 53.2	27 44.6	21 13.5	9 48.5	29 51.4
14 Th	19 34 27	23 56 56	12♋26 12	19 57 16	21 52.7	1 47.4	2 33.1	29 07.6	15 24.0	17 07.1	27 49.7	21 11.2	9 48.3	29 52.8
15 F	19 38 24	24 58 02	27 25 34	4♌49 56	21 44.4	3 03.9	3 45.4	29 18.8	15 44.3	17 20.9	27 54.6	21 09.0	9 48.1	29 54.3
16 Sa	19 42 20	25 59 08	12♌09 23	19 23 03	21 38.0	4 21.8	4 57.6	29 29.5	16 04.6	17 34.8	27 59.5	21 06.7	9 48.0	29 55.7
17 Su	19 46 17	27 00 13	26 30 18	3♍30 43	21 34.1	5 41.0	6 09.7	29 39.5	16 25.0	17 48.7	28 04.3	21 04.4	9 47.9	29 57.2
18 M	19 50 13	28 01 18	10♍24 03	17 10 16	21D 32.5	7 01.4	7 21.8	29 49.0	16 45.6	18 02.5	28 09.0	21 02.1	9 47.8	29 58.7
19 Tu	19 54 10	29 02 23	23 49 31	0♎22 03	21 32.8	8 22.9	8 33.8	29 57.9	17 06.2	18 16.4	28 13.7	20 59.7	9D 47.7	0♓00.2
20 W	19 58 07	0♒03 27	6♎48 15	13 08 37	21 33.9	9 45.5	9 45.6	0♎06.1	17 27.0	18 30.2	28 18.3	20 57.3	9 47.7	0 01.7
21 Th	20 02 03	1 04 31	19 23 43	25 34 07	21R 34.9	11 09.1	10 57.4	0 13.8	17 47.8	18 44.0	28 22.8	20 54.9	9 47.8	0 03.2
22 F	20 06 00	2 05 35	1♏40 29	7♏43 26	21 34.8	12 33.6	12 09.2	0 20.7	18 08.7	18 57.8	28 27.2	20 52.5	9 47.8	0 04.7
23 Sa	20 09 56	3 06 38	13 43 38	19 41 42	21 33.1	13 59.0	13 20.8	0 27.1	18 29.7	19 11.5	28 31.6	20 50.0	9 47.9	0 06.3
24 Su	20 13 53	4 07 41	25 38 15	1♐33 52	21 29.2	15 25.2	14 32.3	0 32.8	18 50.8	19 25.3	28 35.8	20 47.5	9 48.1	0 07.8
25 M	20 17 49	5 08 43	7♐29 05	13 24 24	21 23.3	16 52.2	15 43.7	0 37.7	19 12.0	19 39.0	28 40.0	20 45.1	9 48.2	0 09.4
26 Tu	20 21 46	6 09 45	19 20 17	25 17 08	21 15.7	18 20.0	16 55.0	0 42.1	19 33.2	19 52.7	28 44.2	20 42.5	9 48.4	0 11.0
27 W	20 25 42	7 10 47	1♑15 20	7♑15 09	21 07.1	19 48.6	18 06.3	0 45.7	19 54.6	20 06.4	28 48.2	20 40.0	9 48.7	0 12.5
28 Th	20 29 39	8 11 47	13 16 53	19 20 43	20 58.3	21 17.9	19 17.4	0 48.6	20 16.0	20 20.0	28 52.1	20 37.5	9 48.9	0 14.1
29 F	20 33 36	9 12 47	25 26 51	1♒35 23	20 50.3	22 47.9	20 28.4	0 50.8	20 37.5	20 33.6	28 56.0	20 34.9	9 49.3	0 15.7
30 Sa	20 37 32	10 13 45	7♒46 26	14 00 05	20 43.7	24 18.6	21 39.3	0 52.2	20 59.1	20 47.2	28 59.8	20 32.4	9 49.6	0 17.4
31 Su	20 41 29	11 14 43	20 16 23	26 35 23	20 39.0	25 50.1	22 50.1	0R 52.9	21 20.8	21 00.7	29 03.5	20 29.8	9 50.0	0 19.0

LONGITUDE — February 2044

Day	Sid.Time	☉	0 hr ☽	Noon ☽	True ☊	☿	♀	♂	⚳	♃	♄	♅	♆	♇
1 M	20 45 25	12♒15 40	2♓57 09	9♓21 42	20♓36.4	27♑22.2	24♓00.7	0♎52.9	21♓42.5	21♑14.3	29♏07.1	20♌27.2	9♉50.4	0♓20.6
2 Tu	20 49 22	13 16 35	15 49 08	22 19 31	20D 35.8	28 55.1	25 11.3	0R 52.1	22 04.3	21 27.7	29 10.6	20R 24.6	9 50.8	0 22.3
3 W	20 53 18	14 17 29	28 52 56	5♈29 31	20 36.6	0♒28.6	26 21.7	0 50.6	22 26.2	21 41.2	29 14.0	20 22.0	9 51.3	0 23.9
4 Th	20 57 15	15 18 22	12♈09 23	18 52 39	20 38.1	2 02.9	27 32.0	0 48.3	22 48.1	21 54.6	29 17.4	20 19.4	9 51.8	0 25.6
5 F	21 01 11	16 19 14	25 39 27	2♉29 53	20 39.6	3 37.9	28 42.1	0 45.2	23 10.1	22 07.9	29 20.6	20 16.7	9 52.4	0 27.2
6 Sa	21 05 08	17 20 04	9♉24 02	16 21 56	20R 40.3	5 13.7	29 52.1	0 41.4	23 32.2	22 21.3	29 23.8	20 14.1	9 53.0	0 28.9
7 Su	21 09 05	18 20 52	23 23 33	0♊28 46	20 39.7	6 50.2	1♈02.0	0 36.8	23 54.3	22 34.5	29 26.8	20 11.5	9 53.6	0 30.5
8 M	21 13 01	19 21 40	7♊37 22	14 49 04	20 37.6	8 27.4	2 11.7	0 31.4	24 16.5	22 47.8	29 29.8	20 08.8	9 54.2	0 32.2
9 Tu	21 16 58	20 22 25	22 03 26	29 19 55	20 34.2	10 05.4	3 21.2	0 25.2	24 38.8	23 01.0	29 32.7	20 06.2	9 54.9	0 33.9
10 W	21 20 54	21 23 09	6♋37 54	13♋56 39	20 30.0	11 44.2	4 30.6	0 18.3	25 01.1	23 14.1	29 35.5	20 03.6	9 55.7	0 35.6
11 Th	21 24 51	22 23 52	21 15 21	28 33 10	20 25.7	13 23.8	5 39.9	0 10.6	25 23.5	23 27.2	29 38.2	20 01.0	9 56.4	0 37.3
12 F	21 28 47	23 24 33	5♌49 14	13♌02 44	20 21.8	15 04.2	6 48.9	0 02.0	25 45.9	23 40.3	29 40.8	19 58.3	9 57.2	0 39.0
13 Sa	21 32 44	24 25 13	20 12 51	27 18 53	20 19.0	16 45.4	7 57.8	29♍52.8	26 08.4	23 53.3	29 43.3	19 55.7	9 58.0	0 40.7
14 Su	21 36 40	25 25 51	4♍20 15	11♍16 28	20D 17.5	18 27.5	9 06.5	29 42.7	26 31.0	24 06.2	29 45.7	19 53.1	9 58.9	0 42.4
15 M	21 40 37	26 26 28	18 07 09	24 52 08	20 17.3	20 10.4	10 15.1	29 31.8	26 53.5	24 19.1	29 48.0	19 50.5	9 59.8	0 44.1
16 Tu	21 44 34	27 27 03	1♎31 17	8♎04 40	20 18.2	21 54.2	11 23.4	29 20.2	27 16.2	24 31.9	29 50.2	19 47.9	10 00.7	0 45.8
17 W	21 48 30	28 27 38	14 32 27	20 54 52	20 19.6	23 38.9	12 31.6	29 07.8	27 38.9	24 44.7	29 52.3	19 45.3	10 01.6	0 47.5
18 Th	21 52 27	29 28 11	27 12 17	3♏25 07	20 21.3	25 24.5	13 39.6	28 54.7	28 01.6	24 57.5	29 54.4	19 42.7	10 02.6	0 49.2
19 F	21 56 23	0♓28 42	9♏33 51	15 39 01	20 22.6	27 11.0	14 47.4	28 40.8	28 24.4	25 10.1	29 56.3	19 40.1	10 03.6	0 50.9
20 Sa	22 00 20	1 29 13	21 41 10	27 40 53	20R 23.3	28 58.4	15 54.9	28 26.2	28 47.2	25 22.7	29 58.1	19 37.5	10 04.6	0 52.6
21 Su	22 04 16	2 29 42	3♐38 48	9♐35 29	20 23.2	0♓46.6	17 02.3	28 10.8	29 10.1	25 35.3	29 59.8	19 35.0	10 05.7	0 54.3
22 M	22 08 13	3 30 10	15 31 33	21 27 35	20 22.3	2 35.8	18 09.5	27 54.8	29 33.1	25 47.8	0♐01.5	19 32.4	10 06.8	0 56.0
23 Tu	22 12 09	4 30 37	27 24 08	3♑21 46	20 20.6	4 25.8	19 16.5	27 38.0	29 56.0	26 00.2	0 03.0	19 29.9	10 08.0	0 57.7
24 W	22 16 06	5 31 02	9♑20 58	15 22 12	20 18.5	6 16.7	20 23.2	27 20.6	0♈19.1	26 12.6	0 04.4	19 27.4	10 09.1	0 59.4
25 Th	22 20 03	6 31 26	21 25 54	27 32 25	20 16.3	8 08.4	21 29.7	27 02.6	0 42.1	26 24.8	0 05.7	19 24.9	10 10.3	1 01.1
26 F	22 23 59	7 31 48	3♒42 06	9♒55 11	20 14.2	10 00.9	22 36.0	26 43.9	1 05.2	26 37.1	0 07.0	19 22.4	10 11.6	1 02.8
27 Sa	22 27 56	8 32 09	16 11 52	22 32 20	20 12.7	11 54.1	23 42.1	26 24.6	1 28.4	26 49.2	0 08.1	19 20.0	10 12.8	1 04.5
28 Su	22 31 52	9 32 28	28 56 37	5♓24 47	20 11.7	13 48.0	24 47.9	26 04.8	1 51.5	27 01.3	0 09.1	19 17.6	10 14.1	1 06.2
29 M	22 35 49	10 32 45	11♓56 48	18 32 35	20D 11.4	15 42.3	25 53.4	25 44.5	2 14.8	27 13.3	0 10.0	19 15.1	10 15.4	1 07.9

Astro Data	Planet Ingress	Last Aspect	☽ Ingress	Last Aspect	☽ Ingress	☽ Phases & Eclipses	Astro Data
Dy Hr Mn	Dy Hr Mn	Dy Hr Mn	Dy Hr Mn	Dy Hr Mn	Dy Hr Mn	Dy Hr Mn	1 January 2044
♃∠♇ 3 19:49	♀ ♓ 12 9:17	1 19:46 ♄ ⚹	♒ 2 2:18	3 1:41 ☿ ⚹	♈ 3 2:02	8 4:03 ☽ 17♈30	Julian Day # 52596
☽0N 6 18:18	☿ ♑ 13 1:23	4 11:52 ♇ ☌	♓ 4 12:32	4 17:28 ♃ □	♉ 5 7:38	14 18:52 ○ 24♋14	SVP 4♓38'40"
☽0S 19 8:40	♇ ♓ 19 9:31	6 15:48 ♂ ☍	♈ 6 20:38	7 10:15 ♄ ☍	♊ 7 11:11	21 23:48 ☾ 1♏35	GC 27♐27.2 ⚴ 5♒54.7
♆ D 20 5:45	♂ ♎ 19 18:00	9 1:25 ♇ ⚹	♉ 9 1:51	8 20:49 ♅ ⚹	♋ 9 13:06	30 4:06 ● 9♒54	Eris 28♈50.0R ⚵ 27♑12.4
♃⚻♅ 29 13:57	☉ ♒ 20 10:39	11 3:44 ♇ □	♊ 11 4:03	11 13:47 ♄ △	♌ 11 14:23		⚷ 2♍17.3R ⚶ 13♑03.6
♂ R 31 23:12		13 3:59 ♇ △	♋ 13 4:13	13 16:07 ♄ □	♍ 13 16:34	6 13:47 ☽ 17♉25	☽ Mean ☊ 24♓01.4
	☿ ♒ 3 4:40	15 2:56 ♂ ⚹	♌ 15 4:09	15 20:54 ♄ ⚹	♎ 15 21:14	13 6:43 ○ 24♌12	
☽0N 2 23:05	♀ ♈ 6 14:42	17 5:52 ♇ ☍	♍ 17 5:58	18 3:41 ☉ △	♏ 18 5:23	20 20:21 ☾ 1♐50	1 February 2044
♀0N 7 7:39	♂ ♍R 12 17:27	19 11:15 ♂ ☌	♎ 19 11:19	20 16:36 ♄ ☌	♐ 20 16:39	28 20:14 ● 9♓53	Julian Day # 52627
☽0S 15 18:11	☉ ♓ 19 0:37	21 2:58 ♅ ⚹	♏ 21 20:42	23 0:44 ♂ □	♑ 23 5:14	28 20:24:38 ✔ A 02'27"	SVP 4♓38'35"
	☿ ♓ 21 1:41	24 5:57 ♄ ☌	♐ 24 8:50	25 11:03 ♂ △	♒ 25 16:48		GC 27♐27.3 ⚴ 16♒28.5
	♄ ♐ 21 14:21	26 2:48 ♅ △	♑ 26 21:29	27 14:24 ♀ ⚹	♓ 28 1:58		Eris 28♈50.2 ⚵ 10♒00.8
	⚳ ♈ 23 16:08	29 6:48 ♄ ⚹	♒ 29 8:54				⚷ 0♍39.3R ⚶ 29♑34.5
		31 16:41 ♄ □	♓ 31 18:27				☽ Mean ☊ 22♓23.0

March 2044 — LONGITUDE

Day	Sid.Time	☉	0 hr ☽	Noon ☽	True ☊	☿	♀	♂	⚳	♃	♄	♅	♆	♇
1 Tu	22 39 45	11♓33 00	25♓12 00	1♈54 55	20♓11.5	17♓37.2	26♈58.7	25♍23.6	2♈38.0	27♑25.2	0♐10.8	19♌12.8	10♉16.7	1♓09.6
2 W	22 43 42	12 33 14	8♈41 08	15 30 26	20 12.0	19 32.2	28 03.8	25R 02.3	3 01.3	27 37.1	0 11.5	19R 10.4	10 18.1	1 11.3
3 Th	22 47 38	13 33 25	22 22 35	29 17 21	20 12.7	21 27.4	29 08.5	24 40.6	3 24.6	27 48.8	0 12.1	19 08.1	10 19.5	1 12.9
4 F	22 51 35	14 33 35	6♉14 29	13♉13 44	20 13.3	23 22.5	0♉13.0	24 18.5	3 48.0	28 00.5	0 12.6	19 05.7	10 20.9	1 14.6
5 Sa	22 55 32	15 33 42	20 14 51	27 17 34	20 13.7	25 17.3	1 17.2	23 56.1	4 11.3	28 12.1	0 13.0	19 03.5	10 22.4	1 16.3
6 Su	22 59 28	16 33 47	4♊21 37	11♊26 46	20R 13.9	27 11.4	2 21.0	23 33.3	4 34.7	28 23.6	0 13.3	19 01.2	10 23.9	1 17.9
7 M	23 03 25	17 33 51	18 32 44	25 39 13	20 13.9	29 04.6	3 24.6	23 10.3	4 58.2	28 35.1	0 13.5	18 59.0	10 25.4	1 19.6
8 Tu	23 07 21	18 33 52	2♋45 56	9♋52 34	20 13.8	0♈56.6	4 27.8	22 47.1	5 21.6	28 46.4	0R 13.6	18 56.8	10 26.9	1 21.2
9 W	23 11 18	19 33 51	16 58 46	24 04 12	20D 13.7	2 46.8	5 30.7	22 23.8	5 45.1	28 57.7	0 13.6	18 54.6	10 28.4	1 22.9
10 Th	23 15 14	20 33 47	1♌08 29	8♌11 14	20 13.7	4 35.0	6 33.2	22 00.3	6 08.6	29 08.9	0 13.5	18 52.5	10 30.0	1 24.5
11 F	23 19 11	21 33 42	15 12 04	22 10 35	20 13.8	6 20.6	7 35.4	21 36.7	6 32.2	29 20.0	0 13.3	18 50.4	10 31.6	1 26.1
12 Sa	23 23 07	22 33 34	29 06 23	5♍59 08	20 13.9	8 03.2	8 37.2	21 13.1	6 55.7	29 30.9	0 13.0	18 48.3	10 33.3	1 27.7
13 Su	23 27 04	23 33 24	12♍48 29	19 34 09	20R 14.0	9 42.2	9 38.6	20 49.5	7 19.3	29 41.8	0 12.6	18 46.3	10 34.9	1 29.3
14 M	23 31 01	24 33 13	26 15 52	2♎53 28	20 13.9	11 17.2	10 39.6	20 25.9	7 42.9	29 52.6	0 12.0	18 44.3	10 36.6	1 30.9
15 Tu	23 34 57	25 32 59	9♎26 49	15 55 50	20 13.5	12 47.7	11 40.3	20 02.4	8 06.5	0♒03.3	0 11.4	18 42.4	10 38.3	1 32.5
16 W	23 38 54	26 32 43	22 20 34	28 41 04	20 12.8	14 13.1	12 40.5	19 39.1	8 30.2	0 14.0	0 10.7	18 40.4	10 40.0	1 34.1
17 Th	23 42 50	27 32 26	4♏57 30	11♏10 06	20 11.9	15 33.0	13 40.3	19 15.9	8 53.8	0 24.5	0 09.9	18 38.5	10 41.7	1 35.7
18 F	23 46 47	28 32 07	17 19 08	23 24 57	20 10.8	16 47.0	14 39.6	18 53.0	9 17.5	0 34.9	0 09.0	18 36.7	10 43.5	1 37.2
19 Sa	23 50 43	29 31 46	29 27 57	5♐28 35	20 09.8	17 54.6	15 38.5	18 30.3	9 41.2	0 45.2	0 08.0	18 34.9	10 45.3	1 38.8
20 Su	23 54 40	0♈31 24	11♐27 21	17 24 45	20 09.0	18 55.5	16 37.0	18 07.9	10 04.9	0 55.4	0 06.9	18 33.1	10 47.1	1 40.3
21 M	23 58 36	1 30 59	23 21 21	29 17 43	20D 08.6	19 49.4	17 34.9	17 45.8	10 28.6	1 05.5	0 05.7	18 31.4	10 48.9	1 41.8
22 Tu	0 02 33	2 30 33	5♑14 27	11♑12 07	20 08.8	20 35.9	18 32.4	17 24.2	10 52.4	1 15.5	0 04.4	18 29.7	10 50.8	1 43.3
23 W	0 06 30	3 30 05	17 11 19	23 12 38	20 09.5	21 15.0	19 29.3	17 02.9	11 16.1	1 25.3	0 03.0	18 28.1	10 52.6	1 44.8
24 Th	0 10 26	4 29 36	29 16 38	5♒23 50	20 10.6	21 46.3	20 25.7	16 42.1	11 39.9	1 35.1	0 01.5	18 26.5	10 54.5	1 46.3
25 F	0 14 23	5 29 04	11♒34 45	17 49 48	20 12.0	22 09.9	21 21.6	16 21.8	12 03.7	1 44.8	29♏59.9	18 24.9	10 56.4	1 47.8
26 Sa	0 18 19	6 28 31	24 09 24	0♓33 50	20 13.2	22 25.7	22 16.9	16 02.0	12 27.5	1 54.3	29 58.2	18 23.4	10 58.3	1 49.3
27 Su	0 22 16	7 27 56	7♓03 22	13 38 08	20R 13.9	22R 33.8	23 11.7	15 42.8	12 51.3	2 03.7	29 56.4	18 22.0	11 00.3	1 50.7
28 M	0 26 12	8 27 19	20 18 10	27 03 26	20 13.9	22 34.3	24 05.8	15 24.2	13 15.1	2 13.0	29 54.5	18 20.5	11 02.2	1 52.1
29 Tu	0 30 09	9 26 39	3♈53 44	10♈48 49	20 12.9	22 27.4	24 59.3	15 06.1	13 38.9	2 22.2	29 52.5	18 19.2	11 04.2	1 53.6
30 W	0 34 05	10 25 58	17 48 16	24 51 38	20 11.0	22 13.5	25 52.1	14 48.7	14 02.8	2 31.3	29 50.5	18 17.8	11 06.2	1 55.0
31 Th	0 38 02	11 25 15	1♉58 20	9♉07 45	20 08.3	21 53.0	26 44.3	14 32.0	14 26.6	2 40.2	29 48.3	18 16.5	11 08.2	1 56.3

April 2044 — LONGITUDE

Day	Sid.Time	☉	0 hr ☽	Noon ☽	True ☊	☿	♀	♂	⚳	♃	♄	♅	♆	♇
1 F	0 41 58	12♈24 29	16♉19 13	23♉32 02	20♓05.2	21♈26.4	27♉35.8	14♍16.0	14♈50.5	2♒49.0	29♏46.1	18♌15.3	11♉10.2	1♓57.7
2 Sa	0 45 55	13 23 42	0♊45 32	7♊59 02	20R 02.2	20R 54.4	28 26.5	14R 00.7	15 14.3	2 57.7	29R 43.8	18R 14.1	11 12.3	1 59.1
3 Su	0 49 52	14 22 52	15 11 56	22 23 40	19 59.9	20 17.7	29 16.5	13 46.1	15 38.2	3 06.3	29 41.4	18 13.0	11 14.3	2 00.4
4 M	0 53 48	15 22 00	29 33 47	6♋41 51	19D 58.6	19 37.0	0♊05.8	13 32.2	16 02.0	3 14.7	29 38.9	18 11.9	11 16.4	2 01.7
5 Tu	0 57 45	16 21 05	13♋47 35	20 50 42	19 58.4	18 53.2	0 54.1	13 19.1	16 25.9	3 23.0	29 36.3	18 10.9	11 18.5	2 03.1
6 W	1 01 41	17 20 08	27 51 02	4♌48 28	19 59.2	18 07.3	1 41.7	13 06.8	16 49.7	3 31.1	29 33.7	18 09.9	11 20.6	2 04.3
7 Th	1 05 38	18 19 09	11♌42 56	18 34 23	20 00.7	17 20.2	2 28.3	12 55.2	17 13.6	3 39.2	29 30.9	18 09.0	11 22.7	2 05.6
8 F	1 09 34	19 18 07	25 22 47	2♍08 09	20 02.2	16 32.8	3 14.1	12 44.4	17 37.4	3 47.1	29 28.1	18 08.1	11 24.8	2 06.9
9 Sa	1 13 31	20 17 03	8♍50 29	15 29 47	20R 03.1	15 46.0	3 58.9	12 34.4	18 01.3	3 54.8	29 25.2	18 07.3	11 26.9	2 08.1
10 Su	1 17 27	21 15 57	22 06 03	28 39 16	20 02.9	15 00.7	4 42.6	12 25.1	18 25.1	4 02.4	29 22.2	18 06.5	11 29.1	2 09.3
11 M	1 21 24	22 14 48	5♎09 26	11♎36 33	20 01.1	14 17.7	5 25.4	12 16.7	18 49.0	4 09.9	29 19.2	18 05.7	11 31.2	2 10.5
12 Tu	1 25 21	23 13 38	18 00 36	24 21 34	19 57.7	13 37.6	6 07.1	12 09.0	19 12.8	4 17.2	29 16.0	18 05.1	11 33.4	2 11.7
13 W	1 29 17	24 12 26	0♏39 31	6♏54 27	19 52.8	13 01.0	6 47.7	12 02.1	19 36.6	4 24.4	29 12.9	18 04.4	11 35.5	2 12.9
14 Th	1 33 14	25 11 12	13 06 27	19 15 39	19 46.7	12 28.6	7 27.1	11 56.0	20 00.5	4 31.5	29 09.6	18 03.9	11 37.7	2 14.0
15 F	1 37 10	26 09 55	25 22 11	1♐26 14	19 40.2	12 00.5	8 05.4	11 50.7	20 24.3	4 38.3	29 06.3	18 03.3	11 39.9	2 15.1
16 Sa	1 41 07	27 08 38	7♐28 04	13 27 57	19 33.8	11 37.3	8 42.4	11 46.1	20 48.1	4 45.1	29 02.9	18 02.9	11 42.1	2 16.2
17 Su	1 45 03	28 07 18	19 26 15	25 23 21	19 28.3	11 19.0	9 18.2	11 42.3	21 11.9	4 51.7	28 59.4	18 02.5	11 44.3	2 17.3
18 M	1 49 00	29 05 57	1♑19 40	7♑15 42	19 24.2	11 05.7	9 52.6	11 39.3	21 35.7	4 58.1	28 55.9	18 02.1	11 46.5	2 18.4
19 Tu	1 52 56	0♉04 34	13 11 59	19 09 02	19 21.8	10 57.7	10 25.6	11 37.1	21 59.5	5 04.4	28 52.3	18 01.8	11 48.7	2 19.4
20 W	1 56 53	1 03 09	25 07 28	1♒07 53	19D 21.0	10D 54.8	10 57.3	11 35.6	22 23.3	5 10.6	28 48.6	18 01.5	11 50.9	2 20.5
21 Th	2 00 50	2 01 43	7♒10 52	13 17 05	19 21.6	10 57.0	11 27.4	11D 34.9	22 47.1	5 16.6	28 44.9	18 01.3	11 53.2	2 21.5
22 F	2 04 46	3 00 15	19 27 06	25 41 33	19 23.0	11 04.2	11 56.0	11 34.9	23 10.9	5 22.4	28 41.1	18 01.2	11 55.4	2 22.5
23 Sa	2 08 43	3 58 45	2♓00 58	8♓25 51	19R 24.3	11 16.3	12 23.0	11 35.6	23 34.7	5 28.1	28 37.3	18 01.1	11 57.6	2 23.4
24 Su	2 12 39	4 57 13	14 56 39	21 33 41	19 24.7	11 33.2	12 48.4	11 37.1	23 58.4	5 33.6	28 33.4	18D 01.0	11 59.9	2 24.4
25 M	2 16 36	5 55 40	28 17 12	5♈07 16	19 23.5	11 54.7	13 12.1	11 39.3	24 22.1	5 38.9	28 29.5	18 01.1	12 02.1	2 25.3
26 Tu	2 20 32	6 54 05	12♈03 50	19 06 42	19 20.4	12 20.6	13 34.0	11 42.2	24 45.9	5 44.1	28 25.5	18 01.1	12 04.4	2 26.2
27 W	2 24 29	7 52 29	26 15 26	3♉29 28	19 15.1	12 50.8	13 54.1	11 45.9	25 09.6	5 49.1	28 21.5	18 01.2	12 06.6	2 27.0
28 Th	2 28 25	8 50 51	10♉48 05	18 10 21	19 08.2	13 25.0	14 12.3	11 50.2	25 33.3	5 53.9	28 17.4	18 01.4	12 08.9	2 27.9
29 F	2 32 22	9 49 11	25 35 18	3♊01 50	19 00.4	14 03.3	14 28.5	11 55.2	25 56.9	5 58.6	28 13.3	18 01.6	12 11.2	2 28.7
30 Sa	2 36 19	10 47 29	10♊28 51	17 55 16	18 52.8	14 45.2	14 42.7	12 00.9	26 20.6	6 03.1	28 09.2	18 01.9	12 13.4	2 29.5

Astro Data

	Dy Hr Mn
☽0N	1 5:31
☿0N	8 6:39
♄R	8 22:27
☽0S	14 3:39
♃∗♄	16 5:08
⊙0N	19 23:22
♃⚺♇	25 20:59
☿R	28 1:31
☽0N	28 14:11
⚳0N	6 5:28
☽0S	10 11:18
☿D	20 13:36
♂D	21 23:37
♅D	24 18:52
☽0N	24 23:49

Planet Ingress

		Dy Hr Mn
♀	♉	4 7:09
☿	♈	7 23:50
♃	♒	15 4:28
⊙	♈	19 23:22
♄	♏R	25 10:04
♀	♊	4 9:10
⊙	♉	19 10:08

Last Aspect / ☽ Ingress

Last Aspect Dy Hr Mn		☽ Ingress Dy Hr Mn
1 3:51	♃ ∗	♈ 1 8:35
3 11:43	♀ ☌	♉ 3 13:14
5 13:34	♃ △	♊ 5 16:36
7 18:39	♃ □	♋ 7 19:20
9 20:24	♃ ☍	♌ 9 22:04
11 6:16	♅ ☌	♍ 12 1:33
14 6:27	♃ △	♎ 14 6:45
15 17:10	♅ ∗	♏ 16 14:30
18 23:04	⊙ △	♐ 19 1:04
20 15:19	☿ △	♑ 21 13:25
23 7:54	☿ □	♒ 24 1:25
26 10:54	♄ □	♓ 26 10:57
28 17:01	♄ △	♈ 28 17:11
30 7:37	☿ ☌	♉ 30 20:41

Last Aspect Dy Hr Mn		☽ Ingress Dy Hr Mn
1 22:20	♄ ☍	♊ 1 22:44
3 8:39	☿ ∗	♋ 4 0:44
6 2:58	♄ △	♌ 6 3:42
8 7:16	♄ □	♍ 8 8:12
10 13:19	♄ ∗	♎ 10 14:29
12 9:40	⊙ ☍	♏ 12 22:44
15 7:24	♄ ☌	♐ 15 9:09
17 18:01	⊙ △	♑ 17 21:19
20 7:24	♄ ∗	♒ 20 9:45
22 17:40	♄ □	♓ 22 20:12
25 0:25	♄ △	♈ 25 3:02
26 10:09	♅ △	♉ 27 6:14
29 4:17	♄ ☍	♊ 29 7:07

☽ Phases & Eclipses

Dy Hr Mn	
6 21:18	☽ 16♊57
13 19:42	○ 23♍53
13 19:39	• T 1.203
21 16:54	☾ 1♑43
29 9:27	● 9♈20
5 3:46	☽ 16♋01
12 9:40	○ 23♎08
20 11:50	☾ 1♒03
27 19:43	● 8♉11

Astro Data

1 March 2044
Julian Day # 52656
SVP 4♓38'31"
GC 27♐27.4 ⚴ 26♒17.7
Eris 28♈59.6 ⚵ 22♒23.8
⚷ 28♌26.7R ⚶ 14♒37.4
☽ Mean ☊ 20♓50.8

1 April 2044
Julian Day # 52687
SVP 4♓38'28"
GC 27♐27.4 ⚴ 6♓12.2
Eris 29♈16.9 ⚵ 5♓43.2
⚷ 26♌34.3R ⚶ 29♒56.3
☽ Mean ☊ 19♓12.3

LONGITUDE May 2044

Day	Sid.Time	☉	0 hr ☽	Noon ☽	True ☊	☿	♀	♂	⚳	♃	♄	♅	♆	♇
1 Su	2 40 15	11♉45 45	25♊20 03	2♋42 16	18♓46.3	15♈30.8	14♊54.9	12♍07.3	26♈44.2	6♒07.4	28♏05.0	18♌02.3	12♉15.7	2♓30.3
2 M	2 44 12	12 43 59	10♋01 09	17 16 03	18R41.6	16 19.8	15 04.9	12 14.3	27 07.8	6 11.6	28R00.8	18 02.7	12 17.9	2 31.1
3 Tu	2 48 08	13 42 11	24 26 31	1♌32 13	18D39.0	17 12.2	15 12.7	12 22.0	27 31.4	6 15.5	27 56.5	18 03.1	12 20.2	2 31.8
4 W	2 52 05	14 40 21	8♌32 59	15 28 48	18 38.4	18 07.7	15 18.3	12 30.3	27 55.0	6 19.3	27 52.2	18 03.6	12 22.5	2 32.5
5 Th	2 56 01	15 38 29	22 19 42	29 05 53	18 38.9	19 06.3	15R21.5	12 39.2	28 18.6	6 23.0	27 47.9	18 04.2	12 24.7	2 33.2
6 F	2 59 58	16 36 35	5♍47 32	12♍24 55	18R39.7	20 07.9	15 22.4	12 48.8	28 42.1	6 26.4	27 43.6	18 04.8	12 27.0	2 33.9
7 Sa	3 03 54	17 34 39	18 58 19	25 28 01	18 39.6	21 12.3	15 20.9	12 58.9	29 05.6	6 29.7	27 39.2	18 05.4	12 29.2	2 34.5
8 Su	3 07 51	18 32 41	1♎54 17	8♎17 24	18 37.8	22 19.4	15 17.0	13 09.6	29 29.1	6 32.8	27 34.8	18 06.2	12 31.5	2 35.2
9 M	3 11 48	19 30 41	14 37 35	20 55 03	18 33.5	23 29.2	15 10.7	13 20.9	29 52.5	6 35.7	27 30.4	18 06.9	12 33.7	2 35.7
10 Tu	3 15 44	20 28 39	27 09 59	3♏22 32	18 26.7	24 41.6	15 01.8	13 32.7	0♉15.9	6 38.4	27 26.0	18 07.7	12 36.0	2 36.3
11 W	3 19 41	21 26 36	9♏32 51	15 41 02	18 17.4	25 56.6	14 50.6	13 45.1	0 39.3	6 41.0	27 21.5	18 08.6	12 38.2	2 36.9
12 Th	3 23 37	22 24 32	21 47 13	27 51 29	18 06.3	27 14.0	14 36.9	13 58.0	1 02.7	6 43.3	27 17.1	18 09.5	12 40.4	2 37.4
13 F	3 27 34	23 22 26	3♐53 59	9♐54 51	17 54.3	28 33.8	14 20.8	14 11.5	1 26.1	6 45.5	27 12.6	18 10.5	12 42.7	2 37.9
14 Sa	3 31 30	24 20 18	15 54 13	21 52 18	17 42.4	29 56.0	14 02.3	14 25.5	1 49.4	6 47.5	27 08.1	18 11.6	12 44.9	2 38.4
15 Su	3 35 27	25 18 09	27 49 18	3♑45 31	17 31.6	1♉20.5	13 41.5	14 39.9	2 12.7	6 49.3	27 03.7	18 12.6	12 47.1	2 38.8
16 M	3 39 23	26 15 59	9♑41 14	15 36 51	17 22.8	2 47.3	13 18.5	14 54.9	2 35.9	6 51.0	26 59.2	18 13.8	12 49.3	2 39.2
17 Tu	3 43 20	27 13 47	21 32 44	27 29 22	17 16.5	4 16.4	12 53.3	15 10.4	2 59.2	6 52.4	26 54.7	18 14.9	12 51.6	2 39.6
18 W	3 47 17	28 11 35	3♒27 14	9♒26 54	17 12.7	5 47.7	12 26.1	15 26.3	3 22.4	6 53.7	26 50.2	18 16.2	12 53.8	2 40.0
19 Th	3 51 13	29 09 21	15 28 55	21 33 56	17D11.1	7 21.3	11 57.0	15 42.7	3 45.5	6 54.7	26 45.7	18 17.5	12 55.9	2 40.4
20 F	3 55 10	0♊07 06	27 42 32	3♓55 22	17 10.9	8 57.0	11 26.2	15 59.6	4 08.7	6 55.6	26 41.2	18 18.8	12 58.1	2 40.7
21 Sa	3 59 06	1 04 50	10♓13 05	16 36 17	17R11.1	10 35.1	10 53.8	16 16.9	4 31.8	6 56.3	26 36.8	18 20.2	13 00.3	2 41.0
22 Su	4 03 03	2 02 32	23 05 30	29 41 16	17 10.6	12 15.3	10 20.0	16 34.7	4 54.8	6 56.8	26 32.3	18 21.6	13 02.5	2 41.3
23 M	4 06 59	3 00 14	6♈23 59	13♈13 54	17 08.3	13 57.7	9 45.1	16 52.9	5 17.9	6 57.1	26 27.9	18 23.1	13 04.6	2 41.5
24 Tu	4 10 56	3 57 55	20 11 11	27 15 45	17 03.7	15 42.4	9 09.1	17 11.5	5 40.8	6R57.2	26 23.4	18 24.6	13 06.8	2 41.8
25 W	4 14 52	4 55 34	4♉27 22	11♉45 32	16 56.4	17 29.3	8 32.4	17 30.6	6 03.8	6 57.1	26 19.0	18 26.2	13 08.9	2 42.0
26 Th	4 18 49	5 53 13	19 09 35	26 38 34	16 47.0	19 18.3	7 55.1	17 50.0	6 26.7	6 56.9	26 14.6	18 27.8	13 11.0	2 42.1
27 F	4 22 46	6 50 51	4♊11 24	11♊46 48	16 36.4	21 09.6	7 17.5	18 09.9	6 49.6	6 56.4	26 10.2	18 29.5	13 13.1	2 42.3
28 Sa	4 26 42	7 48 27	19 23 25	26 59 52	16 25.8	23 03.0	6 39.9	18 30.2	7 12.4	6 55.7	26 05.8	18 31.2	13 15.2	2 42.4
29 Su	4 30 39	8 46 02	4♋34 47	12♋06 55	16 16.4	24 58.5	6 02.5	18 50.8	7 35.2	6 54.9	26 01.5	18 33.0	13 17.3	2 42.5
30 M	4 34 35	9 43 36	19 35 08	26 58 31	16 09.3	26 56.1	5 25.4	19 11.9	7 58.0	6 53.9	25 57.2	18 34.8	13 19.4	2 42.6
31 Tu	4 38 32	10 41 09	4♌16 21	11♌28 08	16 04.8	28 55.8	4 49.1	19 33.3	8 20.7	6 52.6	25 52.9	18 36.7	13 21.5	2 42.6

LONGITUDE June 2044

Day	Sid.Time	☉	0 hr ☽	Noon ☽	True ☊	☿	♀	♂	⚳	♃	♄	♅	♆	♇
1 W	4 42 28	11♊38 40	18♌33 35	25♌32 35	16♓02.6	0♊57.4	4♊13.6	19♍55.1	8♉43.3	6♒51.2	25♏48.7	18♌38.6	13♉23.5	2♓42.7
2 Th	4 46 25	12 36 09	2♍25 12	9♍11 37	16R02.1	3 00.9	3R39.1	20 17.2	9 05.9	6R49.6	25R44.5	18 40.6	13 25.6	2R42.7
3 F	4 50 22	13 33 38	15 52 09	22 27 09	16 02.0	5 06.2	3 06.0	20 39.7	9 28.5	6 47.8	25 40.3	18 42.6	13 27.6	2 42.6
4 Sa	4 54 18	14 31 05	28 57 04	5♎22 19	16 01.2	7 13.0	2 34.3	21 02.5	9 51.0	6 45.9	25 36.2	18 44.6	13 29.6	2 42.6
5 Su	4 58 15	15 28 30	11♎43 23	18 00 42	15 58.6	9 21.3	2 04.3	21 25.7	10 13.4	6 43.7	25 32.1	18 46.7	13 31.6	2 42.5
6 M	5 02 11	16 25 55	24 14 42	0♏25 46	15 53.4	11 30.8	1 36.2	21 49.2	10 35.9	6 41.4	25 28.1	18 48.9	13 33.5	2 42.4
7 Tu	5 06 08	17 23 19	6♏34 17	12 40 34	15 45.4	13 41.3	1 09.9	22 13.0	10 58.2	6 38.8	25 24.1	18 51.0	13 35.5	2 42.3
8 W	5 10 04	18 20 41	18 44 54	24 47 33	15 34.7	15 52.6	0 45.8	22 37.1	11 20.5	6 36.1	25 20.1	18 53.2	13 37.4	2 42.1
9 Th	5 14 01	19 18 03	0♐48 44	6♐48 38	15 22.1	18 04.4	0 23.8	23 01.6	11 42.8	6 33.3	25 16.2	18 55.5	13 39.4	2 42.0
10 F	5 17 57	20 15 24	12 47 26	18 45 18	15 08.4	20 16.5	0 04.0	23 26.3	12 05.0	6 30.2	25 12.3	18 57.8	13 41.3	2 41.8
11 Sa	5 21 54	21 12 44	24 42 24	0♑38 54	14 54.7	22 28.5	29♉46.6	23 51.3	12 27.1	6 27.0	25 08.5	19 00.2	13 43.2	2 41.6
12 Su	5 25 51	22 10 04	6♑34 57	12 30 47	14 42.3	24 40.3	29 31.6	24 16.7	12 49.2	6 23.5	25 04.8	19 02.5	13 45.0	2 41.3
13 M	5 29 47	23 07 23	18 26 37	24 22 42	14 32.0	26 51.5	29 18.9	24 42.3	13 11.2	6 20.0	25 01.1	19 05.0	13 46.9	2 41.0
14 Tu	5 33 44	24 04 41	0♒19 21	6♒16 54	14 24.3	29 01.8	29 08.7	25 08.1	13 33.2	6 16.2	24 57.5	19 07.4	13 48.7	2 40.8
15 W	5 37 40	25 01 59	12 15 44	18 16 17	14 19.4	1♋11.1	29 00.9	25 34.3	13 55.1	6 12.3	24 53.9	19 09.9	13 50.5	2 40.4
16 Th	5 41 37	25 59 16	24 19 01	0♓24 27	14 16.9	3 19.2	28 55.5	26 00.7	14 17.0	6 08.2	24 50.4	19 12.5	13 52.3	2 40.1
17 F	5 45 33	26 56 33	6♓33 08	12 45 39	14D16.3	5 25.7	28D52.4	26 27.4	14 38.8	6 03.9	24 46.9	19 15.1	13 54.1	2 39.7
18 Sa	5 49 30	27 53 50	19 02 33	25 24 28	14R16.4	7 30.7	28 51.8	26 54.4	15 00.5	5 59.4	24 43.5	19 17.7	13 55.8	2 39.3
19 Su	5 53 26	28 51 06	1♈51 57	8♈25 31	14 16.1	9 33.9	28 53.5	27 21.6	15 22.2	5 54.8	24 40.2	19 20.3	13 57.6	2 38.9
20 M	5 57 23	29 48 22	15 05 41	21 52 47	14 14.4	11 35.3	28 57.4	27 49.0	15 43.8	5 50.1	24 36.9	19 23.0	13 59.3	2 38.5
21 Tu	6 01 20	0♋45 39	28 47 07	5♉48 46	14 10.6	13 34.7	29 03.6	28 16.7	16 05.3	5 45.2	24 33.7	19 25.7	14 01.0	2 38.0
22 W	6 05 16	1 42 55	12♉57 40	20 13 33	14 04.3	15 32.1	29 12.0	28 44.7	16 26.8	5 40.1	24 30.6	19 28.5	14 02.6	2 37.6
23 Th	6 09 13	2 40 10	27 35 52	5♊03 55	13 55.9	17 27.4	29 22.5	29 12.9	16 48.2	5 34.9	24 27.5	19 31.3	14 04.3	2 37.1
24 F	6 13 09	3 37 26	12♊36 42	20 13 05	13 46.2	19 20.6	29 35.1	29 41.4	17 09.5	5 29.5	24 24.6	19 34.1	14 05.9	2 36.5
25 Sa	6 17 06	4 34 42	27 51 43	5♋31 12	13 36.4	21 11.6	29 49.6	0♎10.1	17 30.8	5 24.0	24 21.7	19 37.0	14 07.5	2 36.0
26 Su	6 21 02	5 31 57	13♋10 05	20 46 56	13 27.7	23 00.4	0♊06.2	0 39.0	17 52.0	5 18.4	24 18.9	19 39.9	14 09.1	2 35.4
27 M	6 24 59	6 29 12	28 20 29	5♌49 33	13 21.0	24 47.1	0 24.5	1 08.1	18 13.1	5 12.6	24 16.1	19 42.8	14 10.6	2 34.8
28 Tu	6 28 55	7 26 26	13♌13 12	20 30 42	13 16.8	26 31.6	0 44.7	1 37.5	18 34.1	5 06.7	24 13.4	19 45.8	14 12.2	2 34.2
29 W	6 32 52	8 23 40	27 41 31	4♍45 23	13D14.9	28 13.8	1 06.6	2 07.1	18 55.0	5 00.6	24 10.9	19 48.8	14 13.7	2 33.6
30 Th	6 36 49	9 20 53	11♍42 13	18 32 04	13 14.7	29 53.8	1 30.3	2 36.9	19 15.9	4 54.4	24 08.3	19 51.8	14 15.1	2 32.9

Astro Data	Dy Hr Mn
♀ R	6 9:03
☽ 0S	7 16:51
☽ 0N	22 8:39
♃ R	24 14:04
♇ R	1 23:14
☽ 0S	3 21:36
♀ D	18 6:38
☽ 0N	18 15:38
♂ 0S	26 20:21

Planet Ingress	Dy Hr Mn
⚳ ♉	9 19:40
☿ ♉	14 13:10
☉ ♊	20 9:03
☿ ♊	1 0:43
♀ ♉R	10 17:16
☿ ♋	14 22:46
☉ ♋	20 16:52
♂ ♎	25 3:36
♀ ♊	26 3:22
☿ ♌	30 13:30

Last Aspect Dy Hr Mn		☽ Ingress	Dy Hr Mn
30 12:11	♅ ⚹	♋	1 7:35
3 5:56	♄ △	♌	3 9:23
5 9:42	♄ □	♍	5 13:37
7 16:02	♄ ⚹	♎	7 20:26
9 17:27	☿ ☍	♏	10 5:28
12 10:52	♄ ☌	♐	12 16:15
14 4:35	♅ △	♑	15 4:24
17 11:26	☉ △	♒	17 17:03
20 4:03	☉ □	♓	20 4:26
22 6:20	♄ △	♈	22 12:34
23 20:56	♅ △	♉	24 16:35
26 11:22	♄ ☍	♊	26 17:21
27 22:36	♅ ⚹	♋	28 16:45
30 11:56	☿ ⚹	♌	30 16:57

Last Aspect Dy Hr Mn		☽ Ingress	Dy Hr Mn
1 12:28	♄ □	♍	1 19:45
3 17:54	♄ ⚹	♎	4 1:57
5 13:28	♅ ⚹	♏	6 11:10
8 13:04	♄ ☌	♐	8 22:23
10 21:47	♂ □	♑	11 10:41
13 21:49	♀ △	♒	13 23:21
16 9:06	♀ □	♓	16 11:12
18 18:27	♀ ⚹	♈	18 20:33
20 7:36	♅ △	♉	21 2:05
23 2:45	♀ ☌	♊	23 3:53
25 3:21	♂ □	♋	25 3:21
26 17:35	♄ △	♌	27 2:39
28 18:10	♄ □	♍	29 3:54

☽ Phases & Eclipses Dy Hr Mn	
4 10:29	☽ 14♌37
12 0:18	○ 21♏56
20 4:03	☾ 29♒48
27 3:41	● 6♊31
2 18:35	☽ 12♍52
10 15:17	○ 20♐23
18 17:01	☾ 28♓06
25 10:26	● 4♋31

Astro Data

1 May 2044
Julian Day # 52717
SVP 4♓38'23"
GC 27♐27.5 ⚴ 14♓38.9
Eris 29♈36.7 ⚵ 18♓21.4
⚷ 26♌08.2 ⚶ 13♓35.0
☽ Mean ☊ 17♓37.0

1 June 2044
Julian Day # 52748
SVP 4♓38'18"
GC 27♐27.6 ⚴ 21♓22.9
Eris 29♈55.1 ⚵ 0♈41.9
⚷ 27♌22.5 ⚶ 25♓49.3
☽ Mean ☊ 15♓58.5

July 2044 LONGITUDE

Day	Sid.Time	☉	0 hr ☽	Noon ☽	True ☊	☿	♀	♂	⚳	♃	♄	♅	♆	♇
1 F	6 40 45	10♋18 06	25♍15 10	1♎51 51	13♓15.3	1♌31.6	1♊55.5	3♎06.9	19♉36.7	4♒48.1	24♏05.9	19♌54.9	14♉16.6	2♓32.3
2 Sa	6 44 42	11 15 18	8♎22 34	14 47 46	13R 15.4	3 07.2	2 22.3	3 37.2	19 57.4	4R 41.7	24R 03.6	19 58.0	14 18.0	2R 31.6
3 Su	6 48 38	12 12 30	21 07 59	27 23 44	13 14.2	4 40.5	2 50.7	4 07.6	20 18.0	4 35.2	24 01.3	20 01.1	14 19.4	2 30.8
4 M	6 52 35	13 09 42	3♏35 33	9♏43 59	13 11.0	6 11.6	3 20.5	4 38.2	20 38.5	4 28.6	23 59.2	20 04.2	14 20.8	2 30.1
5 Tu	6 56 31	14 06 54	15 49 29	21 52 33	13 05.4	7 40.4	3 51.8	5 09.1	20 59.0	4 21.8	23 57.1	20 07.4	14 22.1	2 29.3
6 W	7 00 28	15 04 05	27 53 36	3♐53 02	12 57.6	9 06.9	4 24.4	5 40.1	21 19.3	4 15.0	23 55.1	20 10.6	14 23.4	2 28.6
7 Th	7 04 24	16 01 17	9♐51 12	15 48 26	12 48.2	10 31.1	4 58.3	6 11.3	21 39.6	4 08.1	23 53.2	20 13.8	14 24.7	2 27.8
8 F	7 08 21	16 58 28	21 45 01	27 41 12	12 37.8	11 53.0	5 33.5	6 42.7	21 59.8	4 01.1	23 51.4	20 17.1	14 26.0	2 27.0
9 Sa	7 12 18	17 55 39	3♑37 13	9♑33 18	12 27.5	13 12.4	6 09.9	7 14.3	22 19.8	3 54.0	23 49.6	20 20.3	14 27.2	2 26.1
10 Su	7 16 14	18 52 51	15 29 38	21 26 24	12 18.1	14 29.5	6 47.5	7 46.1	22 39.8	3 46.8	23 48.0	20 23.6	14 28.5	2 25.3
11 M	7 20 11	19 50 02	27 23 50	3♒22 07	12 10.4	15 44.0	7 26.2	8 18.0	22 59.7	3 39.5	23 46.4	20 26.9	14 29.6	2 24.4
12 Tu	7 24 07	20 47 14	9♒21 29	15 22 10	12 04.9	16 56.0	8 06.1	8 50.1	23 19.5	3 32.2	23 45.0	20 30.3	14 30.8	2 23.5
13 W	7 28 04	21 44 27	21 24 26	27 28 36	12 01.6	18 05.4	8 46.9	9 22.4	23 39.2	3 24.8	23 43.6	20 33.7	14 31.9	2 22.6
14 Th	7 32 00	22 41 39	3♓34 59	9♓43 58	12D 00.5	19 12.1	9 28.8	9 54.9	23 58.8	3 17.4	23 42.3	20 37.0	14 33.0	2 21.7
15 F	7 35 57	23 38 52	15 55 55	22 11 17	12 00.8	20 16.0	10 11.7	10 27.5	24 18.3	3 09.8	23 41.1	20 40.4	14 34.1	2 20.8
16 Sa	7 39 54	24 36 06	28 30 30	4♈54 00	12 02.0	21 17.1	10 55.5	11 00.3	24 37.7	3 02.3	23 40.1	20 43.9	14 35.1	2 19.8
17 Su	7 43 50	25 33 20	11♈22 15	17 55 41	12R 03.1	22 15.2	11 40.2	11 33.3	24 56.9	2 54.7	23 39.1	20 47.3	14 36.1	2 18.8
18 M	7 47 47	26 30 35	24 34 42	1♉19 39	12 03.2	23 10.3	12 25.8	12 06.4	25 16.1	2 47.0	23 38.2	20 50.8	14 37.1	2 17.8
19 Tu	7 51 43	27 27 51	8♉10 46	15 08 14	12 01.8	24 02.1	13 12.2	12 39.7	25 35.2	2 39.3	23 37.4	20 54.3	14 38.1	2 16.8
20 W	7 55 40	28 25 07	22 12 04	29 22 07	11 58.7	24 50.7	13 59.5	13 13.2	25 54.1	2 31.6	23 36.6	20 57.8	14 39.0	2 15.8
21 Th	7 59 36	29 22 25	6♊38 04	13♊59 26	11 54.0	25 35.8	14 47.5	13 46.8	26 12.9	2 23.9	23 36.0	21 01.3	14 39.9	2 14.8
22 F	8 03 33	0♌19 43	21 25 30	28 55 24	11 48.2	26 17.3	15 36.2	14 20.6	26 31.6	2 16.2	23 35.5	21 04.9	14 40.7	2 13.7
23 Sa	8 07 29	1 17 02	6♋28 05	14♋02 24	11 42.3	26 55.0	16 25.7	14 54.6	26 50.2	2 08.4	23 35.1	21 08.4	14 41.6	2 12.7
24 Su	8 11 26	2 14 22	21 37 05	29 10 53	11 36.9	27 28.9	17 15.9	15 28.7	27 08.7	2 00.6	23 34.8	21 12.0	14 42.3	2 11.6
25 M	8 15 23	3 11 42	6♌42 33	14♌10 56	11 33.0	27 58.6	18 06.7	16 03.0	27 27.0	1 52.9	23D 34.6	21 15.6	14 43.1	2 10.5
26 Tu	8 19 19	4 09 03	21 34 59	28 53 51	11D 30.7	28 24.1	18 58.1	16 37.4	27 45.2	1 45.1	23D 34.4	21 19.2	14 43.8	2 09.4
27 W	8 23 16	5 06 24	6♍06 50	13♍13 26	11 30.1	28 45.2	19 50.2	17 12.0	28 03.3	1 37.3	23 34.4	21 22.8	14 44.5	2 08.3
28 Th	8 27 12	6 03 45	20 13 21	27 06 28	11 30.8	29 01.7	20 42.9	17 46.7	28 21.2	1 29.6	23 34.5	21 26.4	14 45.2	2 07.2
29 F	8 31 09	7 01 08	3♎52 47	10♎32 30	11 32.3	29 13.4	21 36.1	18 21.6	28 39.0	1 21.9	23 34.6	21 30.1	14 45.8	2 06.0
30 Sa	8 35 05	7 58 30	17 05 53	23 33 20	11 33.7	29R 20.2	22 29.9	18 56.6	28 56.7	1 14.2	23 34.9	21 33.7	14 46.4	2 04.9
31 Su	8 39 02	8 55 54	29 55 17	6♏12 15	11R 34.5	29 22.0	23 24.2	19 31.7	29 14.2	1 06.6	23 35.3	21 37.4	14 47.0	2 03.7

August 2044 LONGITUDE

Day	Sid.Time	☉	0 hr ☽	Noon ☽	True ☊	☿	♀	♂	⚳	♃	♄	♅	♆	♇
1 M	8 42 58	9♌53 18	12♏24 44	18♏33 19	11♓34.1	29♌18.6	24♊19.1	20♎07.0	29♉31.6	0♒59.0	23♏35.7	21♌41.0	14♉47.6	2♓02.5
2 Tu	8 46 55	10 50 42	24 38 33	0♐40 58	11R 32.4	29R 10.1	25 14.4	20 42.5	29 48.9	0R 51.4	23 36.3	21 44.7	14 48.1	2R 01.4
3 W	8 50 52	11 48 07	6♐41 07	12 39 30	11 29.5	28 56.3	26 10.2	21 18.0	0♊06.0	0 43.9	23 36.9	21 48.4	14 48.5	2 00.2
4 Th	8 54 48	12 45 33	18 36 37	24 32 54	11 25.5	28 37.4	27 06.6	21 53.7	0 22.9	0 36.4	23 37.7	21 52.1	14 49.0	1 59.0
5 F	8 58 45	13 43 00	0♑28 46	6♑25 18	11 20.9	28 13.4	28 03.4	22 29.6	0 39.7	0 29.1	23 38.5	21 55.8	14 49.4	1 57.8
6 Sa	9 02 41	14 40 27	12 20 50	18 17 42	11 16.3	27 44.5	29 00.6	23 05.5	0 56.3	0 21.7	23 39.5	21 59.5	14 49.8	1 56.6
7 Su	9 06 38	15 37 56	24 15 30	0♒14 31	11 12.1	27 11.0	29 58.2	23 41.6	1 12.8	0 14.5	23 40.5	22 03.2	14 50.1	1 55.3
8 M	9 10 34	16 35 25	6♒14 59	12 17 07	11 08.8	26 33.3	0♋56.3	24 17.8	1 29.1	0 07.3	23 41.7	22 07.0	14 50.4	1 54.1
9 Tu	9 14 31	17 32 55	18 21 07	24 27 10	11 06.6	25 51.9	1 54.8	24 54.2	1 45.3	0 00.2	23 42.9	22 10.7	14 50.7	1 52.9
10 W	9 18 27	18 30 26	0♓35 29	6♓46 13	11D 05.7	25 07.4	2 53.7	25 30.7	2 01.3	29♑53.2	23 44.2	22 14.4	14 51.0	1 51.6
11 Th	9 22 24	19 27 59	12 59 35	19 15 46	11 05.8	24 20.3	3 53.0	26 07.3	2 17.1	29 46.3	23 45.7	22 18.1	14 51.2	1 50.4
12 F	9 26 21	20 25 33	25 34 58	1♈57 24	11 06.8	23 31.6	4 52.7	26 44.0	2 32.8	29 39.5	23 47.2	22 21.9	14 51.3	1 49.1
13 Sa	9 30 17	21 23 08	8♈23 17	14 52 50	11 08.1	22 42.1	5 52.7	27 20.9	2 48.3	29 32.7	23 48.8	22 25.6	14 51.5	1 47.8
14 Su	9 34 14	22 20 44	21 26 16	28 03 49	11 09.5	21 52.7	6 53.1	27 57.8	3 03.6	29 26.1	23 50.5	22 29.3	14 51.6	1 46.6
15 M	9 38 10	23 18 23	4♉45 40	11♉31 58	11R 10.4	21 04.4	7 53.9	28 34.9	3 18.7	29 19.6	23 52.3	22 33.1	14 51.7	1 45.3
16 Tu	9 42 07	24 16 02	18 22 51	25 18 21	11 10.8	20 18.1	8 55.0	29 12.1	3 33.7	29 13.2	23 54.2	22 36.8	14 51.7	1 44.0
17 W	9 46 03	25 13 44	2♊18 29	9♊23 07	11 10.3	19 34.8	9 56.4	29 49.5	3 48.4	29 06.9	23 56.2	22 40.5	14R 51.8	1 42.7
18 Th	9 50 00	26 11 27	16 32 04	23 44 59	11 09.3	18 55.5	10 58.1	0♏27.0	4 03.0	29 00.8	23 58.3	22 44.3	14 51.7	1 41.4
19 F	9 53 56	27 09 11	1♋01 26	8♋20 50	11 07.7	18 20.9	12 00.2	1 04.6	4 17.4	28 54.8	24 00.4	22 48.0	14 51.7	1 40.2
20 Sa	9 57 53	28 06 58	15 42 33	23 05 46	11 06.1	17 51.8	13 02.5	1 42.3	4 31.5	28 48.9	24 02.7	22 51.8	14 51.6	1 38.9
21 Su	10 01 50	29 04 45	0♌29 39	7♌53 17	11 04.7	17 28.9	14 05.1	2 20.1	4 45.5	28 43.1	24 05.1	22 55.5	14 51.5	1 37.6
22 M	10 05 46	0♍02 35	15 15 44	22 36 07	11 03.7	17 12.7	15 08.0	2 58.0	4 59.3	28 37.5	24 07.5	22 59.2	14 51.3	1 36.3
23 Tu	10 09 43	1 00 25	29 53 32	7♍07 11	11D 03.3	17D 03.8	16 11.2	3 36.1	5 12.8	28 32.0	24 10.1	23 02.9	14 51.2	1 35.0
24 W	10 13 39	1 58 17	14♍16 24	21 20 35	11 03.4	17 02.5	17 14.7	4 14.3	5 26.2	28 26.7	24 12.7	23 06.6	14 50.9	1 33.7
25 Th	10 17 36	2 56 10	28 19 17	5♎12 12	11 03.9	17 08.9	18 18.4	4 52.6	5 39.3	28 21.5	24 15.4	23 10.3	14 50.7	1 32.4
26 F	10 21 32	3 54 05	11♎59 09	18 40 05	11 04.6	17 23.4	19 22.3	5 31.0	5 52.2	28 16.5	24 18.2	23 14.0	14 50.4	1 31.1
27 Sa	10 25 29	4 52 01	25 15 06	1♏44 22	11 05.2	17 45.8	20 26.5	6 09.5	6 04.9	28 11.6	24 21.1	23 17.7	14 50.1	1 29.8
28 Su	10 29 25	5 49 58	8♏08 10	14 26 52	11 05.7	18 16.3	21 31.0	6 48.2	6 17.3	28 06.9	24 24.1	23 21.4	14 49.7	1 28.5
29 M	10 33 22	6 47 57	20 40 55	26 50 46	11R 06.0	18 54.6	22 35.7	7 26.9	6 29.5	28 02.3	24 27.2	23 25.0	14 49.4	1 27.2
30 Tu	10 37 19	7 45 57	2♐56 56	9♐00 00	11 06.1	19 40.6	23 40.6	8 05.8	6 41.5	27 57.9	24 30.4	23 28.7	14 49.0	1 25.9
31 W	10 41 15	8 43 59	15 00 30	20 59 01	11 06.0	20 34.1	24 45.7	8 44.8	6 53.3	27 53.7	24 33.6	23 32.4	14 48.5	1 24.7

Astro Data

	Dy Hr Mn
☽0S	1 3:28
☽0N	15 21:01
♃⊻♇	22 20:38
♄ D	27 7:29
☽0S	28 11:30
☿ R	31 8:23
☽0N	12 2:10
♆ R	17 12:39
☿ D	24 4:12
☽0S	24 21:13

Planet Ingress

	Dy Hr Mn
☉ ♌	22 3:45
⚳ ♊	3 3:37
♀ ♋	7 12:44
♃ ♑R	9 12:44
♂ ♏	17 18:44
☉ ♍	22 10:56

Last Aspect / ☽ Ingress (July)

Last Aspect Dy Hr Mn		☽ Ingress Dy Hr Mn
30 21:58 ♄ ⚹	♎	1 8:36
2 21:49 ♅ ⚹	♏	3 17:02
5 16:07 ♄ ☌	♐	6 4:13
7 20:58 ♅ △	♑	8 16:41
10 16:45 ♄ ⚹	♒	11 5:14
13 4:36 ♄ □	♓	13 16:58
15 15:01 ☉ △	♈	16 2:49
18 2:48 ☉ □	♉	18 9:39
20 10:18 ☉ ⚹	♊	20 13:03
22 7:36 ☿ ⚹	♋	22 13:43
24 3:07 ♄ △	♌	24 13:18
26 11:10 ☿ ☌	♍	26 13:49
28 5:49 ♄ ⚹	♎	28 17:06
30 22:56 ☿ ⚹	♏	31 0:09

Last Aspect / ☽ Ingress (August)

Last Aspect Dy Hr Mn		☽ Ingress Dy Hr Mn
2 9:02 ☿ □	♐	2 10:38
4 20:00 ☿ △	♑	4 23:02
6 22:49 ♄ ⚹	♒	7 11:31
9 14:37 ☿ ☍	♓	9 22:51
12 7:43 ♃ ⚹	♈	12 8:20
14 14:27 ♃ □	♉	14 15:29
16 18:40 ♃ △	♊	16 20:04
18 16:19 ☉ ⚹	♋	18 22:19
20 21:13 ♃ ☍	♌	20 23:12
22 14:30 ♄ □	♍	23 0:11
25 0:08 ♃ △	♎	25 2:55
27 5:28 ♃ □	♏	27 8:46
29 14:19 ♃ ⚹	♐	29 18:11

☽ Phases & Eclipses

Dy Hr Mn	
2 4:50	☽ 10♎58
10 6:23	○ 18♑39
18 2:48	☾ 26♈09
24 17:12	● 2♌27
31 17:42	☽ 9♏10
8 21:15	○ 16♒58
16 10:04	☾ 24♉11
23 1:07	● 0♍34
23 1:17:00	● T 02'04"
30 9:20	☽ 7♐40

Astro Data

1 July 2044
Julian Day # 52778
SVP 4♓38'12"
GC 27♐27.7 ⚵ 24♓49.5
Eris 0♉06.8 ⚘ 11♈14.5
⚷ 29♌58.6 ⚶ 4♈49.5
☽ Mean ☊ 14♓23.2

1 August 2044
Julian Day # 52809
SVP 4♓38'07"
GC 27♐27.7 ⚵ 23♓42.5R
Eris 0♉09.8R ⚘ 19♈21.8
⚷ 3♍40.0 ⚶ 9♈24.0
☽ Mean ☊ 12♓44.7

LONGITUDE September 2044

Day	Sid.Time	☉	0 hr ☽	Noon☽	True☊	☿	♀	♂	⚳	♃	♄	♅	♆	♇
1 Th	10 45 12	9♍42 01	26♐56 07	2♑52 22	11♓05.9	21♌34.8	25♋51.1	9♏23.8	7♊04.8	27♑49.7	24♏36.9	23♌36.0	14♉48.0	1♓23.4
2 F	10 49 08	10 40 06	8♑48 17	14 44 24	11D05.8	22 42.2	26 56.7	10 03.0	7 16.0	27R45.8	24 40.4	23 39.6	14R47.5	1R22.1
3 Sa	10 53 05	11 38 11	20 41 14	26 39 12	11 05.8	23 56.1	28 02.5	10 42.3	7 27.0	27 42.1	24 43.9	23 43.2	14 47.0	1 20.8
4 Su	10 57 01	12 36 18	2♒38 47	8♒40 19	11 05.9	25 15.8	29 08.5	11 21.7	7 37.8	27 38.6	24 47.4	23 46.8	14 46.4	1 19.6
5 M	11 00 58	13 34 27	14 44 12	20 50 42	11 06.1	26 41.1	0♌14.7	12 01.2	7 48.3	27 35.2	24 51.1	23 50.4	14 45.8	1 18.3
6 Tu	11 04 54	14 32 37	27 00 06	3♓12 36	11R06.3	28 11.2	1 21.1	12 40.7	7 58.5	27 32.1	24 54.8	23 54.0	14 45.2	1 17.1
7 W	11 08 51	15 30 49	9♓28 23	15 47 35	11 06.3	29 45.8	2 27.7	13 20.4	8 08.5	27 29.1	24 58.7	23 57.5	14 44.6	1 15.8
8 Th	11 12 48	16 29 02	22 10 18	28 36 33	11 06.1	1♍24.2	3 34.5	14 00.2	8 18.2	27 26.3	25 02.6	24 01.0	14 43.9	1 14.6
9 F	11 16 44	17 27 18	5♈06 22	11♈39 43	11 05.6	3 06.0	4 41.5	14 40.1	8 27.6	27 23.7	25 06.5	24 04.6	14 43.1	1 13.3
10 Sa	11 20 41	18 25 35	18 16 35	24 56 51	11 04.8	4 50.7	5 48.7	15 20.1	8 36.8	27 21.2	25 10.6	24 08.0	14 42.4	1 12.1
11 Su	11 24 37	19 23 54	1♉40 28	8♉27 18	11 03.8	6 37.7	6 56.1	16 00.2	8 45.6	27 19.0	25 14.7	24 11.5	14 41.6	1 10.9
12 M	11 28 34	20 22 16	15 17 13	22 10 06	11 02.8	8 26.6	8 03.7	16 40.4	8 54.2	27 16.9	25 18.9	24 15.0	14 40.8	1 09.7
13 Tu	11 32 30	21 20 39	29 05 48	6♊04 07	11 02.1	10 16.9	9 11.4	17 20.7	9 02.5	27 15.1	25 23.2	24 18.4	14 40.0	1 08.5
14 W	11 36 27	22 19 05	13♊04 53	20 07 55	11D01.7	12 08.4	10 19.4	18 01.0	9 10.5	27 13.4	25 27.6	24 21.8	14 39.1	1 07.3
15 Th	11 40 23	23 17 33	27 12 58	4♋19 46	11 01.9	14 00.7	11 27.5	18 41.5	9 18.2	27 11.9	25 32.0	24 25.2	14 38.2	1 06.1
16 F	11 44 20	24 16 03	11♋28 04	18 37 30	11 02.6	15 53.3	12 35.7	19 22.1	9 25.6	27 10.6	25 36.5	24 28.6	14 37.3	1 04.9
17 Sa	11 48 17	25 14 35	25 47 44	2♌58 21	11 03.6	17 46.2	13 44.2	20 02.8	9 32.7	27 09.5	25 41.1	24 32.0	14 36.4	1 03.8
18 Su	11 52 13	26 13 10	10♌08 54	17 18 55	11 04.7	19 39.1	14 52.8	20 43.6	9 39.4	27 08.6	25 45.8	24 35.3	14 35.4	1 02.6
19 M	11 56 10	27 11 46	24 27 52	1♍35 16	11R05.5	21 31.8	16 01.5	21 24.5	9 45.9	27 07.9	25 50.5	24 38.6	14 34.4	1 01.5
20 Tu	12 00 06	28 10 24	8♍40 33	15 43 12	11 05.6	23 24.0	17 10.4	22 05.5	9 52.0	27 07.4	25 55.3	24 41.9	14 33.4	1 00.3
21 W	12 04 03	29 09 05	22 42 43	29 38 38	11 04.8	25 15.8	18 19.4	22 46.5	9 57.8	27 07.1	26 00.1	24 45.2	14 32.3	0 59.2
22 Th	12 07 59	0♎07 47	6♎30 31	13♎18 04	11 03.1	27 07.0	19 28.6	23 27.7	10 03.2	27D07.0	26 05.1	24 48.4	14 31.2	0 58.1
23 F	12 11 56	1 06 31	20 00 58	26 39 03	11 00.5	28 57.5	20 38.0	24 09.0	10 08.3	27 07.0	26 10.1	24 51.6	14 30.1	0 57.0
24 Sa	12 15 52	2 05 18	3♏12 13	9♏40 28	10 57.4	0♎47.2	21 47.4	24 50.3	10 13.1	27 07.3	26 15.1	24 54.8	14 29.0	0 55.9
25 Su	12 19 49	3 04 06	16 03 54	22 22 40	10 54.1	2 36.2	22 57.1	25 31.8	10 17.5	27 07.8	26 20.3	24 57.9	14 27.8	0 54.9
26 M	12 23 45	4 02 55	28 37 03	4♐47 22	10 51.1	4 24.3	24 06.8	26 13.3	10 21.6	27 08.4	26 25.5	25 01.0	14 26.7	0 53.8
27 Tu	12 27 42	5 01 47	10♐54 02	16 57 30	10 48.8	6 11.5	25 16.7	26 55.0	10 25.3	27 09.3	26 30.7	25 04.1	14 25.5	0 52.8
28 W	12 31 39	6 00 40	22 58 16	28 56 54	10D47.5	7 57.8	26 26.7	27 36.7	10 28.7	27 10.4	26 36.0	25 07.2	14 24.2	0 51.8
29 Th	12 35 35	6 59 36	4♑53 57	10♑50 02	10 47.4	9 43.3	27 36.8	28 18.5	10 31.7	27 11.6	26 41.4	25 10.2	14 23.0	0 50.8
30 F	12 39 32	7 58 32	16 45 45	22 41 44	10 48.2	11 27.9	28 47.1	29 00.4	10 34.4	27 13.1	26 46.9	25 13.2	14 21.7	0 49.8

LONGITUDE October 2044

Day	Sid.Time	☉	0 hr ☽	Noon☽	True☊	☿	♀	♂	⚳	♃	♄	♅	♆	♇
1 Sa	12 43 28	8♎57 31	28♑38 34	4♒36 51	10♓49.8	13♎11.6	29♌57.4	29♏42.4	10♊36.7	27♑14.7	26♏52.4	25♌16.1	14♉20.4	0♓48.8
2 Su	12 47 25	9 56 31	10♒37 10	16 40 04	10 51.5	14 54.4	1♍07.9	0♐24.5	10 38.6	27 16.5	26 57.9	25 19.1	14R19.1	0R47.9
3 M	12 51 21	10 55 33	22 46 03	28 55 36	10R53.0	16 36.3	2 18.6	1 06.6	10 40.2	27 18.6	27 03.5	25 22.0	14 17.8	0 46.9
4 Tu	12 55 18	11 54 37	5♓09 05	11♓26 51	10 53.5	18 17.4	3 29.3	1 48.9	10 41.3	27 20.8	27 09.2	25 24.8	14 16.4	0 46.0
5 W	12 59 14	12 53 43	17 49 10	24 16 13	10 52.7	19 57.7	4 40.2	2 31.2	10 42.1	27 23.2	27 14.9	25 27.6	14 15.1	0 45.1
6 Th	13 03 11	13 52 51	0♈48 05	7♈24 46	10 50.4	21 37.1	5 51.1	3 13.6	10R42.6	27 25.8	27 20.7	25 30.4	14 13.7	0 44.2
7 F	13 07 08	14 52 00	14 06 09	20 52 04	10 46.4	23 15.8	7 02.2	3 56.1	10 42.6	27 28.6	27 26.5	25 33.2	14 12.3	0 43.4
8 Sa	13 11 04	15 51 12	27 42 12	4♉36 11	10 41.3	24 53.6	8 13.4	4 38.7	10 42.3	27 31.5	27 32.4	25 35.9	14 10.8	0 42.5
9 Su	13 15 01	16 50 26	11♉33 37	18 33 58	10 35.6	26 30.7	9 24.8	5 21.3	10 41.6	27 34.7	27 38.3	25 38.6	14 09.4	0 41.7
10 M	13 18 57	17 49 43	25 36 45	2♊41 26	10 30.0	28 07.0	10 36.2	6 04.1	10 40.5	27 38.0	27 44.3	25 41.2	14 07.9	0 40.9
11 Tu	13 22 54	18 49 01	9♊47 27	16 54 19	10 25.3	29 42.6	11 47.7	6 46.9	10 39.0	27 41.5	27 50.3	25 43.8	14 06.5	0 40.1
12 W	13 26 50	19 48 22	24 01 34	1♋08 46	10 22.1	1♏17.5	12 59.4	7 29.8	10 37.1	27 45.3	27 56.4	25 46.4	14 05.0	0 39.3
13 Th	13 30 47	20 47 45	8♋15 33	15 21 37	10D20.6	2 51.7	14 11.1	8 12.8	10 34.8	27 49.1	28 02.5	25 48.9	14 03.5	0 38.6
14 F	13 34 43	21 47 11	22 26 42	29 30 36	10 20.7	4 25.2	15 23.0	8 55.8	10 32.1	27 53.2	28 08.7	25 51.4	14 01.9	0 37.9
15 Sa	13 38 40	22 46 39	6♌33 08	13♌34 09	10 21.8	5 58.0	16 34.9	9 39.0	10 29.1	27 57.5	28 14.9	25 53.8	14 00.4	0 37.2
16 Su	13 42 37	23 46 09	20 33 34	27 31 13	10R23.1	7 30.2	17 47.0	10 22.2	10 25.6	28 01.9	28 21.2	25 56.2	13 58.8	0 36.5
17 M	13 46 33	24 45 41	4♍27 00	11♍20 47	10 23.7	9 01.7	18 59.1	11 05.5	10 21.7	28 06.5	28 27.5	25 58.6	13 57.3	0 35.8
18 Tu	13 50 30	25 45 16	18 12 23	25 01 39	10 22.6	10 32.5	20 11.4	11 48.9	10 17.5	28 11.3	28 33.9	26 00.9	13 55.7	0 35.2
19 W	13 54 26	26 44 53	1♎48 22	8♎32 20	10 19.5	12 02.7	21 23.7	12 32.4	10 12.8	28 16.2	28 40.2	26 03.2	13 54.1	0 34.5
20 Th	13 58 23	27 44 32	15 13 20	21 51 10	10 14.0	13 32.3	22 36.1	13 15.9	10 07.7	28 21.4	28 46.7	26 05.4	13 52.5	0 34.0
21 F	14 02 19	28 44 13	28 25 37	4♏56 31	10 06.5	15 01.2	23 48.6	13 59.6	10 02.3	28 26.7	28 53.1	26 07.6	13 50.9	0 33.4
22 Sa	14 06 16	29 43 56	11♏23 44	17 47 11	9 57.5	16 29.5	25 01.2	14 43.3	9 56.5	28 32.2	28 59.7	26 09.7	13 49.3	0 32.8
23 Su	14 10 12	0♏43 40	24 06 50	0♐22 42	9 48.0	17 57.1	26 13.8	15 27.1	9 50.3	28 37.8	29 06.2	26 11.8	13 47.6	0 32.3
24 M	14 14 09	1 43 27	6♐34 55	12 43 39	9 38.8	19 24.0	27 26.6	16 10.9	9 43.7	28 43.6	29 12.8	26 13.9	13 46.0	0 31.8
25 Tu	14 18 06	2 43 16	18 49 08	24 51 42	9 30.9	20 50.2	28 39.4	16 54.9	9 36.7	28 49.6	29 19.4	26 15.9	13 44.3	0 31.3
26 W	14 22 02	3 43 06	0♑51 44	6♑49 40	9 24.9	22 15.7	29 52.3	17 38.9	9 29.4	28 55.8	29 26.0	26 17.8	13 42.7	0 30.9
27 Th	14 25 59	4 42 58	12 46 00	18 41 17	9 21.2	23 40.4	1♎05.3	18 22.9	9 21.6	29 02.1	29 32.7	26 19.8	13 41.0	0 30.4
28 F	14 29 55	5 42 52	24 36 07	0♒31 06	9D19.6	25 04.4	2 18.3	19 07.1	9 13.6	29 08.6	29 39.4	26 21.6	13 39.4	0 30.0
29 Sa	14 33 52	6 42 47	6♒26 55	12 24 12	9 19.6	26 27.5	3 31.4	19 51.3	9 05.1	29 15.2	29 46.2	26 23.4	13 37.7	0 29.6
30 Su	14 37 48	7 42 44	18 23 39	24 25 54	9 20.4	27 49.7	4 44.6	20 35.6	8 56.4	29 22.0	29 53.0	26 25.2	13 36.0	0 29.3
31 M	14 41 45	8 42 43	0♓31 38	6♓41 28	9R21.1	29 11.0	5 57.8	21 19.9	8 47.2	29 28.9	29 59.7	26 26.9	13 34.3	0 28.9

Astro Data (Dy Hr Mn)

☽0N 8 8:28
☽0S 21 6:56
⊙0S 22 8:49
♃D 22 14:54
☿0S 25 20:51

☽0N 5 16:30
⚳R 7 3:03
♃✶♄ 8 4:47
☽0S 18 14:53
♀0S 29 14:25

Planet Ingress (Dy Hr Mn)

♀ ♌ 5 6:41
☿ ♍ 7 15:31
⊙ ♎ 22 8:49
☿ ♎ 24 1:39

♀ ♍ 1 12:52
♂ ♐ 1 22:02
☿ ♏ 11 16:23
⊙ ♏ 22 18:27
♀ ♎ 26 14:32
♄ ♐ 31 12:53

Last Aspect Dy Hr Mn		☽ Ingress Dy Hr Mn
31 17:10	♅ △	♑ 1 6:11
3 15:04	♀ ☍	♒ 3 18:43
6 0:56	☿ ☍	♓ 6 5:49
8 9:50	♃ ✶	♈ 8 14:35
10 16:17	♃ □	♉ 10 21:01
12 20:51	♃ △	♊ 13 1:34
14 19:12	♅ ✶	♋ 15 4:42
17 2:17	♃ ☍	♌ 17 7:02
19 2:16	♄ □	♍ 19 9:19
21 11:05	⊙ ☌	♎ 21 12:37
23 12:51	♃ □	♏ 23 18:07
25 21:08	♃ ✶	♐ 26 2:41
28 6:25	♀ △	♑ 28 14:07

Last Aspect Dy Hr Mn		☽ Ingress Dy Hr Mn
1 1:32	♂ ✶	♒ 1 2:44
3 8:21	♄ □	♓ 3 14:05
5 17:46	♃ ✶	♈ 5 22:32
7 23:39	♃ □	♉ 8 4:00
10 3:33	♄ ☍	♊ 10 7:27
12 2:55	♅ ✶	♋ 12 10:04
14 9:40	♄ △	♌ 14 12:50
16 13:27	♄ □	♍ 16 16:17
18 18:18	♄ ✶	♎ 18 20:48
20 23:57	♃ □	♏ 21 2:53
23 9:32	♄ ☌	♐ 23 11:16
25 20:26	♀ □	♑ 25 22:16
28 10:14	♄ ✶	♒ 28 10:57
30 22:50	♄ □	♓ 30 22:58

☽ Phases & Eclipses (Dy Hr Mn)

7 11:26 ○ 15♓29
7 11:21 • T 1.045
14 15:59 ☾ 22♊29
21 11:05 ● 29♍07
29 3:32 ☽ 6♑39

7 0:31 ○ 14♈24
13 21:54 ☾ 21♋12
20 23:38 ● 28♎13
28 23:29 ☽ 6♒12

Astro Data

1 September 2044
Julian Day # 52840
SVP 4♓38'03"
GC 27♐27.8 ⚴ 17♓29.4R
Eris 0♉02.9R ⚵ 22♈21.9R
⚷ 7♍52.3 ⚶ 7♈09.3R
☽ Mean ☊ 11♓06.2

1 October 2044
Julian Day # 52870
SVP 4♓37'59"
GC 27♐27.9 ⚴ 10♓06.4R
Eris 29♈48.6R ⚵ 18♈32.1R
⚷ 11♍56.3 ⚶ 0♈00.8R
☽ Mean ☊ 9♓30.9

November 2044 LONGITUDE

Day	Sid.Time	☉	0 hr ☽	Noon ☽	True☊	☿	♀	♂	⚳	♃	♄	♅	♆	♇
1 Tu	14 45 41	9♏42 43	12♓55 57	19♓15 38	9♓20.6	0♐31.3	7♎11.1	22♐04.4	8♊37.8	29♑36.0	0♐06.6	26♌28.6	13♉32.6	0♓28.6
2 W	14 49 38	10 42 45	25 40 56	2♈12 12	9R18.2	1 50.5	8 24.5	22 48.8	8R28.0	29 43.3	0 13.4	26 30.2	13R31.0	0R28.4
3 Th	14 53 35	11 42 48	8♈49 39	15 33 22	9 13.3	3 08.4	9 37.9	23 33.4	8 17.9	29 50.7	0 20.3	26 31.7	13 29.3	0 28.1
4 F	14 57 31	12 42 53	22 23 19	29 19 16	9 05.8	4 25.0	10 51.4	24 18.0	8 07.5	29 58.2	0 27.2	26 33.2	13 27.6	0 27.9
5 Sa	15 01 28	13 43 00	6♉20 50	13♉27 30	8 56.4	5 40.2	12 05.0	25 02.7	7 56.8	0♒05.9	0 34.1	26 34.7	13 25.9	0 27.6
6 Su	15 05 24	14 43 09	20 38 34	27 53 14	8 45.8	6 53.8	13 18.6	25 47.4	7 45.8	0 13.8	0 41.0	26 36.1	13 24.2	0 27.5
7 M	15 09 21	15 43 20	5♊10 37	12♊29 46	8 35.3	8 05.6	14 32.3	26 32.3	7 34.5	0 21.8	0 48.0	26 37.5	13 22.5	0 27.3
8 Tu	15 13 17	16 43 33	19 49 43	27 09 32	8 26.2	9 15.4	15 46.1	27 17.1	7 22.9	0 29.9	0 55.0	26 38.8	13 20.8	0 27.2
9 W	15 17 14	17 43 48	4♋28 22	11♋45 27	8 19.2	10 22.9	16 59.9	28 02.1	7 11.1	0 38.2	1 02.0	26 40.0	13 19.1	0 27.1
10 Th	15 21 10	18 44 04	19 00 09	26 11 58	8 14.9	11 28.0	18 13.7	28 47.1	6 59.1	0 46.6	1 09.0	26 41.2	13 17.5	0 27.0
11 F	15 25 07	19 44 23	3♌20 30	10♌25 31	8D12.9	12 30.3	19 27.7	29 32.1	6 46.8	0 55.1	1 16.0	26 42.4	13 15.8	0 26.9
12 Sa	15 29 04	20 44 44	17 26 53	24 24 35	8 12.7	13 29.4	20 41.7	0♑17.3	6 34.2	1 03.8	1 23.1	26 43.5	13 14.1	0D26.9
13 Su	15 33 00	21 45 06	1♍18 39	8♍09 11	8R12.9	14 24.9	21 55.7	1 02.5	6 21.5	1 12.6	1 30.2	26 44.5	13 12.4	0 26.9
14 M	15 36 57	22 45 31	14 56 19	21 40 13	8 12.2	15 16.5	23 09.8	1 47.7	6 08.5	1 21.6	1 37.2	26 45.5	13 10.8	0 26.9
15 Tu	15 40 53	23 45 57	28 21 00	4♎58 50	8 09.6	16 03.6	24 23.9	2 33.0	5 55.4	1 30.7	1 44.3	26 46.4	13 09.1	0 27.0
16 W	15 44 50	24 46 25	11♎33 49	18 06 02	8 04.2	16 45.6	25 38.1	3 18.4	5 42.1	1 39.9	1 51.4	26 47.3	13 07.5	0 27.0
17 Th	15 48 46	25 46 56	24 35 33	1♏02 22	7 55.6	17 21.9	26 52.3	4 03.8	5 28.6	1 49.2	1 58.5	26 48.1	13 05.8	0 27.1
18 F	15 52 43	26 47 27	7♏26 29	13 47 54	7 44.3	17 51.9	28 06.6	4 49.3	5 15.0	1 58.7	2 05.6	26 48.9	13 04.2	0 27.3
19 Sa	15 56 39	27 48 01	20 06 35	26 22 30	7 30.8	18 14.8	29 20.9	5 34.9	5 01.3	2 08.3	2 12.8	26 49.6	13 02.6	0 27.4
20 Su	16 00 36	28 48 36	2♐35 38	8♐46 01	7 16.5	18 29.8	0♏35.3	6 20.5	4 47.5	2 18.0	2 19.9	26 50.3	13 00.9	0 27.6
21 M	16 04 33	29 49 12	14 53 41	20 58 44	7 02.4	18R36.3	1 49.7	7 06.2	4 33.6	2 27.8	2 27.0	26 50.9	12 59.3	0 27.8
22 Tu	16 08 29	0♐49 50	27 01 17	3♑01 32	6 49.8	18 33.4	3 04.1	7 51.9	4 19.6	2 37.8	2 34.2	26 51.4	12 57.7	0 28.1
23 W	16 12 26	1 50 29	8♑59 44	14 56 13	6 39.7	18 20.6	4 18.6	8 37.7	4 05.6	2 47.9	2 41.3	26 51.9	12 56.2	0 28.3
24 Th	16 16 22	2 51 09	20 51 19	26 45 30	6 32.4	17 57.2	5 33.1	9 23.5	3 51.5	2 58.0	2 48.4	26 52.3	12 54.6	0 28.6
25 F	16 20 19	3 51 51	2♒39 15	8♒33 05	6 28.0	17 23.0	6 47.6	10 09.4	3 37.4	3 08.4	2 55.6	26 52.7	12 53.0	0 28.9
26 Sa	16 24 15	4 52 33	14 27 37	20 23 22	6 26.0	16 38.1	8 02.2	10 55.3	3 23.3	3 18.8	3 02.7	26 53.0	12 51.5	0 29.3
27 Su	16 28 12	5 53 17	26 21 17	2♓21 46	6 25.5	15 42.9	9 16.8	11 41.3	3 09.2	3 29.3	3 09.9	26 53.3	12 50.0	0 29.6
28 M	16 32 09	6 54 02	8♓25 37	14 33 31	6 25.5	14 38.3	10 31.4	12 27.3	2 55.2	3 39.9	3 17.0	26 53.5	12 48.4	0 30.0
29 Tu	16 36 05	7 54 47	20 46 11	27 04 15	6 24.6	13 25.8	11 46.0	13 13.4	2 41.2	3 50.7	3 24.1	26 53.6	12 46.9	0 30.4
30 W	16 40 02	8 55 34	3♈28 18	9♈58 53	6 21.8	12 07.3	13 00.7	13 59.5	2 27.2	4 01.5	3 31.2	26 53.7	12 45.4	0 30.9

December 2044 LONGITUDE

Day	Sid.Time	☉	0 hr ☽	Noon ☽	True☊	☿	♀	♂	⚳	♃	♄	♅	♆	♇
1 Th	16 43 58	9♐56 21	16♈36 25	23♈21 11	6♓16.5	10♐45.4	14♏15.4	14♑45.7	2♊13.4	4♒12.4	3♐38.3	26♌53.7	12♉44.0	0♓31.3
2 F	16 47 55	10 57 10	0♉13 19	7♉12 47	6R08.4	9R22.7	15 30.2	15 31.9	1R59.6	4 23.5	3 45.4	26R53.7	12R42.5	0 31.8
3 Sa	16 51 51	11 57 59	14 19 18	21 32 27	5 58.0	8 02.1	16 44.9	16 18.1	1 46.0	4 34.6	3 52.5	26 53.6	12 41.1	0 32.3
4 Su	16 55 48	12 58 50	28 51 31	6♊15 38	5 46.3	6 46.2	17 59.7	17 04.4	1 32.5	4 45.9	3 59.6	26 53.5	12 39.7	0 32.9
5 M	16 59 44	13 59 42	13♊43 44	21 14 38	5 34.4	5 37.3	19 14.5	17 50.7	1 19.1	4 57.2	4 06.7	26 53.3	12 38.3	0 33.5
6 Tu	17 03 41	15 00 35	28 47 05	6♋19 45	5 23.9	4 37.4	20 29.4	18 37.1	1 05.9	5 08.6	4 13.8	26 53.1	12 36.9	0 34.1
7 W	17 07 38	16 01 29	13♋51 25	21 20 55	5 15.7	3 47.8	21 44.3	19 23.5	0 52.9	5 20.2	4 20.8	26 52.8	12 35.6	0 34.7
8 Th	17 11 34	17 02 24	28 47 14	6♌09 30	5 10.4	3 09.3	22 59.2	20 10.0	0 40.0	5 31.8	4 27.9	26 52.4	12 34.2	0 35.3
9 F	17 15 31	18 03 20	13♌27 06	20 39 32	5 07.8	2 42.1	24 14.1	20 56.5	0 27.4	5 43.5	4 34.9	26 52.0	12 32.9	0 36.0
10 Sa	17 19 27	19 04 17	27 46 32	4♍47 59	5D07.2	2D26.2	25 29.0	21 43.0	0 14.9	5 55.3	4 41.9	26 51.6	12 31.6	0 36.7
11 Su	17 23 24	20 05 16	11♍43 55	18 34 27	5R07.3	2 21.2	26 44.0	22 29.6	0 02.7	6 07.2	4 48.9	26 51.0	12 30.4	0 37.4
12 M	17 27 20	21 06 16	25 19 50	2♎00 20	5 06.9	2 26.4	27 59.0	23 16.2	29♉50.8	6 19.1	4 55.8	26 50.5	12 29.1	0 38.2
13 Tu	17 31 17	22 07 16	8♎36 16	15 08 00	5 04.7	2 41.0	29 14.0	24 02.9	29 39.1	6 31.2	5 02.8	26 49.8	12 27.9	0 38.9
14 W	17 35 13	23 08 18	21 35 51	28 00 09	4 59.9	3 04.3	0♐29.0	24 49.6	29 27.6	6 43.3	5 09.7	26 49.1	12 26.7	0 39.7
15 Th	17 39 10	24 09 21	4♏21 11	10♏39 14	4 52.2	3 35.4	1 44.1	25 36.3	29 16.5	6 55.5	5 16.6	26 48.4	12 25.5	0 40.5
16 F	17 43 07	25 10 25	16 54 32	23 07 17	4 41.8	4 13.4	2 59.1	26 23.1	29 05.6	7 07.8	5 23.5	26 47.6	12 24.4	0 41.4
17 Sa	17 47 03	26 11 30	29 17 40	5♐25 49	4 29.4	4 57.7	4 14.2	27 09.9	28 55.1	7 20.2	5 30.3	26 46.8	12 23.2	0 42.2
18 Su	17 51 00	27 12 35	11♐31 52	17 35 56	4 16.0	5 47.5	5 29.3	27 56.7	28 44.9	7 32.6	5 37.1	26 45.9	12 22.1	0 43.1
19 M	17 54 56	28 13 42	23 38 08	29 38 34	4 02.9	6 42.1	6 44.4	28 43.6	28 35.0	7 45.2	5 43.9	26 44.9	12 21.1	0 44.0
20 Tu	17 58 53	29 14 48	5♑37 23	11♑34 44	3 51.1	7 40.9	7 59.5	29 30.5	28 25.4	7 57.7	5 50.7	26 43.9	12 20.0	0 45.0
21 W	18 02 49	0♑15 56	17 30 47	23 25 47	3 41.5	8 43.5	9 14.7	0♒17.5	28 16.2	8 10.4	5 57.4	26 42.9	12 19.0	0 45.9
22 Th	18 06 46	1 17 03	29 19 58	5♒13 39	3 34.6	9 49.4	10 29.8	1 04.4	28 07.3	8 23.1	6 04.1	26 41.8	12 18.0	0 46.9
23 F	18 10 42	2 18 11	11♒07 11	17 01 00	3 30.5	10 58.2	11 45.0	1 51.4	27 58.8	8 35.9	6 10.8	26 40.6	12 17.1	0 47.9
24 Sa	18 14 39	3 19 19	22 55 31	28 51 15	3D28.9	12 09.5	13 00.1	2 38.4	27 50.7	8 48.8	6 17.5	26 39.4	12 16.1	0 48.9
25 Su	18 18 36	4 20 27	4♓48 45	10♓48 35	3 29.0	13 23.1	14 15.3	3 25.5	27 42.9	9 01.7	6 24.1	26 38.2	12 15.2	0 49.9
26 M	18 22 32	5 21 36	16 51 24	22 57 49	3 29.9	14 38.6	15 30.5	4 12.5	27 35.5	9 14.7	6 30.6	26 36.9	12 14.3	0 51.0
27 Tu	18 26 29	6 22 44	29 08 30	5♈24 05	3R30.5	15 55.9	16 45.7	4 59.6	27 28.5	9 27.8	6 37.2	26 35.5	12 13.5	0 52.1
28 W	18 30 25	7 23 52	11♈45 13	18 12 30	3 29.8	17 14.6	18 00.9	5 46.7	27 21.9	9 40.9	6 43.6	26 34.1	12 12.7	0 53.2
29 Th	18 34 22	8 25 00	24 46 27	1♉27 31	3 27.2	18 34.8	19 16.0	6 33.9	27 15.7	9 54.1	6 50.1	26 32.6	12 11.9	0 54.3
30 F	18 38 18	9 26 09	8♉16 01	15 12 07	3 22.4	19 56.2	20 31.2	7 21.0	27 09.9	10 07.3	6 56.5	26 31.2	12 11.1	0 55.5
31 Sa	18 42 15	10 27 17	22 15 49	29 26 55	3 15.6	21 18.6	21 46.5	8 08.2	27 04.5	10 20.6	7 02.9	26 29.6	12 10.4	0 56.6

Astro Data

	Dy Hr Mn
☽0N	2 1:33
♄□♇	4 14:15
♃⊻♇	8 4:08
♇D	13 4:09
☽0S	14 20:25
♃✶♄	21 4:58
☿R	21 16:53
☽0N	29 10:07
♅R	1 14:48
☿D	11 11:32
☽0S	12 0:57
☽0N	26 17:03

Planet Ingress

		Dy Hr Mn
☿	♐	1 2:36
♃	♒	4 17:34
♂	♑	12 2:49
♀	♏	20 0:37
☉	♐	21 16:16
⚳	♉R	11 17:26
♀	♐	14 2:43
♂	♒	21 3:04
☉	♑	21 5:45

Last Aspect / ☽ Ingress (November)

Last Aspect Dy Hr Mn			☽ Ingress	Dy Hr Mn
2 7:25	♃	✶	♈	2 7:58
4 13:07	♃	□	♉	4 13:10
6 9:52	♅	□	♊	6 15:29
8 12:13	♂	☍	♋	8 16:39
9 22:37	☉	△	♌	10 18:22
12 16:01	♅	☌	♍	12 21:43
14 14:06	☉	✶	♎	15 2:59
17 4:06	♅	✶	♏	17 10:04
19 14:59	☉	☌	♐	19 18:59
21 23:40	♅	△	♑	22 5:57
23 7:58	♆	△	♒	24 18:36
27 1:04	♅	☍	♓	27 7:18
28 12:08	☿	□	♈	29 17:31

Last Aspect / ☽ Ingress (December)

Last Aspect Dy Hr Mn			☽ Ingress	Dy Hr Mn
1 18:13	♅	△	♉	1 23:37
3 20:47	♅	□	♊	4 1:52
5 20:59	♅	✶	♋	6 1:56
7 12:41	♀	△	♌	8 1:58
9 22:27	♅	☌	♍	10 3:47
12 4:00	♀	✶	♎	12 8:23
14 9:47	♅	✶	♏	14 15:46
16 19:07	♅	□	♐	17 1:23
19 8:54	☉	☌	♑	19 12:43
20 13:31	♆	△	♒	22 1:21
24 7:34	♅	☍	♓	24 14:19
25 19:39	♀	□	♈	27 1:39
29 3:13	♅	△	♉	29 9:24
31 7:06	♅	□	♊	31 12:55

☽ Phases & Eclipses

Dy Hr Mn		
5 12:28	○	13♉44
12 5:11	☾	20♌28
19 14:59	●	27♏56
27 19:38	☽	6♓13
4 23:35	○	13♊28
11 14:54	☾	20♍13
19 8:54	●	28♐06
27 14:01	☽	6♈28

Astro Data

1 November 2044
Julian Day # 52901
SVP 4♓37'56"
GC 27♐27.9 ⚵ 6♓28.0R
Eris 29♈30.2R ✱ 11♈48.6R
⚷ 15♍36.1 ⚶ 24♓59.0R
☽ Mean ☊ 7♓52.4

1 December 2044
Julian Day # 52931
SVP 4♓37'51"
GC 27♐28.0 ⚵ 8♓20.1
Eris 29♈14.0R ✱ 11♈08.3
⚷ 18♍04.6 ⚶ 26♓37.2
☽ Mean ☊ 6♓17.1

LONGITUDE — January 2045

Day	Sid.Time	☉	0 hr ☽	Noon ☽	True ☊	☿	♀	♂	⚳	♃	♄	♅	♆	♇
1 Su	18 46 11	11♑28 25	6♊44 58	14♊09 19	3♓07.5	22♐42.1	23♐01.7	8♒55.4	26♉59.5	10♒33.9	7♐09.2	26♌28.0	12♉09.7	0♓57.8
2 M	18 50 08	12 29 33	21 39 05	29 13 10	2R59.2	24 06.4	24 16.9	9 42.6	26R55.0	10 47.3	7 15.5	26R26.4	12R09.1	0 59.0
3 Tu	18 54 05	13 30 41	6♋50 20	14♋29 12	2 51.6	25 31.6	25 32.1	10 29.8	26 50.8	11 00.7	7 21.7	26 24.7	12 08.4	1 00.2
4 W	18 58 01	14 31 49	22 08 24	29 46 30	2 45.9	26 57.5	26 47.3	11 17.1	26 47.0	11 14.2	7 27.9	26 23.0	12 07.8	1 01.5
5 Th	19 01 58	15 32 57	7♌22 12	14♌54 20	2 42.3	28 24.1	28 02.6	12 04.3	26 43.7	11 27.8	7 34.1	26 21.3	12 07.3	1 02.7
6 F	19 05 54	16 34 06	22 21 52	29 44 00	2D41.0	29 51.4	29 17.8	12 51.6	26 40.7	11 41.3	7 40.2	26 19.5	12 06.7	1 04.0
7 Sa	19 09 51	17 35 14	7♍00 07	14♍09 50	2 41.4	1♑19.3	0♑33.1	13 38.9	26 38.2	11 55.0	7 46.2	26 17.6	12 06.2	1 05.3
8 Su	19 13 47	18 36 22	21 12 55	28 09 22	2 42.7	2 47.7	1 48.3	14 26.2	26 36.0	12 08.6	7 52.2	26 15.8	12 05.8	1 06.6
9 M	19 17 44	19 37 30	4♎59 16	11♎42 51	2R43.9	4 16.8	3 03.6	15 13.5	26 34.3	12 22.3	7 58.2	26 13.8	12 05.3	1 07.9
10 Tu	19 21 41	20 38 39	18 20 25	24 52 22	2 44.1	5 46.3	4 18.9	16 00.8	26 33.0	12 36.1	8 04.1	26 11.9	12 04.9	1 09.3
11 W	19 25 37	21 39 47	1♏19 08	7♏41 08	2 42.6	7 16.4	5 34.1	16 48.2	26 32.1	12 49.9	8 09.9	26 09.9	12 04.6	1 10.6
12 Th	19 29 34	22 40 56	13 58 51	20 12 43	2 39.3	8 47.1	6 49.4	17 35.5	26D31.6	13 03.7	8 15.7	26 07.9	12 04.2	1 12.0
13 F	19 33 30	23 42 04	26 23 10	2♐30 38	2 34.1	10 18.2	8 04.7	18 22.9	26 31.6	13 17.6	8 21.4	26 05.8	12 03.9	1 13.4
14 Sa	19 37 27	24 43 13	8♐35 28	14 38 04	2 27.6	11 49.8	9 20.0	19 10.2	26 31.9	13 31.5	8 27.1	26 03.7	12 03.7	1 14.8
15 Su	19 41 23	25 44 21	20 38 43	26 37 44	2 20.4	13 22.0	10 35.3	19 57.6	26 32.6	13 45.4	8 32.7	26 01.6	12 03.4	1 16.3
16 M	19 45 20	26 45 29	2♑35 24	8♑31 57	2 13.2	14 54.6	11 50.6	20 45.0	26 33.8	13 59.4	8 38.2	25 59.4	12 03.3	1 17.7
17 Tu	19 49 16	27 46 36	14 27 37	20 22 38	2 06.8	16 27.8	13 05.8	21 32.4	26 35.3	14 13.4	8 43.7	25 57.2	12 03.1	1 19.1
18 W	19 53 13	28 47 43	26 17 12	2♒11 32	2 01.8	18 01.5	14 21.1	22 19.8	26 37.3	14 27.4	8 49.2	25 55.0	12 03.0	1 20.6
19 Th	19 57 10	29 48 49	8♒05 53	14 00 29	1 58.4	19 35.7	15 36.4	23 07.2	26 39.7	14 41.5	8 54.5	25 52.7	12 02.9	1 22.1
20 F	20 01 06	0♒49 55	19 55 34	25 51 27	1D56.8	21 10.4	16 51.7	23 54.6	26 42.4	14 55.6	8 59.8	25 50.4	12 02.8	1 23.6
21 Sa	20 05 03	1 51 00	1♓48 25	7♓46 50	1 56.7	22 45.7	18 07.0	24 42.0	26 45.5	15 09.7	9 05.1	25 48.1	12D02.8	1 25.1
22 Su	20 08 59	2 52 04	13 47 04	19 49 31	1 57.9	24 21.6	19 22.2	25 29.5	26 49.1	15 23.8	9 10.2	25 45.8	12 02.8	1 26.6
23 M	20 12 56	3 53 07	25 54 38	2♈02 53	1 59.6	25 58.0	20 37.5	26 16.9	26 53.0	15 38.0	9 15.3	25 43.4	12 02.8	1 28.1
24 Tu	20 16 52	4 54 09	8♈14 45	14 30 43	2 01.4	27 35.0	21 52.8	27 04.3	26 57.3	15 52.2	9 20.4	25 41.0	12 02.9	1 29.7
25 W	20 20 49	5 55 10	20 51 20	27 17 03	2R02.6	29 12.6	23 08.0	27 51.7	27 01.9	16 06.4	9 25.3	25 38.6	12 03.0	1 31.2
26 Th	20 24 45	6 56 10	3♉48 21	10♉25 40	2 02.8	0♒50.9	24 23.3	28 39.1	27 07.0	16 20.6	9 30.2	25 36.2	12 03.2	1 32.8
27 F	20 28 42	7 57 09	17 09 20	23 59 38	2 01.9	2 29.7	25 38.6	29 26.5	27 12.4	16 34.8	9 35.1	25 33.7	12 03.4	1 34.3
28 Sa	20 32 39	8 58 07	0♊56 43	8♊00 34	1 59.9	4 09.2	26 53.8	0♓13.9	27 18.2	16 49.1	9 39.8	25 31.2	12 03.6	1 35.9
29 Su	20 36 35	9 59 03	15 11 02	22 27 47	1 57.2	5 49.4	28 09.0	1 01.2	27 24.3	17 03.3	9 44.5	25 28.8	12 03.9	1 37.5
30 M	20 40 32	10 59 59	29 50 17	7♋17 49	1 54.2	7 30.3	29 24.3	1 48.6	27 30.8	17 17.6	9 49.1	25 26.2	12 04.2	1 39.1
31 Tu	20 44 28	12 00 53	14♋49 28	22 24 12	1 51.5	9 11.8	0♒39.5	2 36.0	27 37.7	17 31.9	9 53.6	25 23.7	12 04.5	1 40.7

LONGITUDE — February 2045

Day	Sid.Time	☉	0 hr ☽	Noon ☽	True ☊	☿	♀	♂	⚳	♃	♄	♅	♆	♇
1 W	20 48 25	13♒01 46	0♌00 48	7♌38 02	1♓49.5	10♒54.0	1♒54.7	3♓23.3	27♉44.9	17♒46.2	9♐58.1	25♌21.2	12♉04.9	1♓42.4
2 Th	20 52 21	14 02 38	15 14 36	22 49 16	1D48.4	12 37.0	3 10.0	4 10.7	27 52.4	18 00.5	10 02.5	25R18.6	12 05.3	1 44.0
3 F	20 56 18	15 03 29	0♍20 50	7♍48 15	1 48.3	14 20.6	4 25.2	4 58.0	28 00.2	18 14.8	10 06.7	25 16.1	12 05.7	1 45.6
4 Sa	21 00 14	16 04 19	15 10 36	22 27 10	1 49.0	16 05.0	5 40.4	5 45.3	28 08.4	18 29.1	10 11.0	25 13.5	12 06.2	1 47.2
5 Su	21 04 11	17 05 08	29 37 23	6♎40 55	1 50.1	17 50.1	6 55.6	6 32.7	28 17.0	18 43.4	10 15.1	25 10.9	12 06.6	1 48.9
6 M	21 08 08	18 05 56	13♎37 33	20 27 18	1 51.3	19 35.9	8 10.8	7 20.0	28 25.8	18 57.7	10 19.2	25 08.3	12 07.2	1 50.5
7 Tu	21 12 04	19 06 43	27 10 15	3♏46 40	1 52.2	21 22.3	9 26.0	8 07.2	28 35.0	19 12.0	10 23.1	25 05.7	12 07.7	1 52.2
8 W	21 16 01	20 07 29	10♏16 52	16 41 17	1R52.7	23 09.5	10 41.2	8 54.5	28 44.4	19 26.4	10 27.0	25 03.0	12 08.3	1 53.9
9 Th	21 19 57	21 08 14	23 00 22	29 14 38	1 52.6	24 57.3	11 56.4	9 41.8	28 54.2	19 40.7	10 30.8	25 00.4	12 09.0	1 55.5
10 F	21 23 54	22 08 59	5♐24 36	11♐30 50	1 52.0	26 45.6	13 11.6	10 29.1	29 04.3	19 55.0	10 34.6	24 57.8	12 09.7	1 57.2
11 Sa	21 27 50	23 09 42	17 33 51	23 34 11	1 51.0	28 34.6	14 26.7	11 16.3	29 14.7	20 09.3	10 38.2	24 55.2	12 10.4	1 58.9
12 Su	21 31 47	24 10 24	29 32 21	5♑28 48	1 49.9	0♓23.9	15 41.9	12 03.5	29 25.4	20 23.7	10 41.8	24 52.5	12 11.1	2 00.6
13 M	21 35 43	25 11 05	11♑24 02	17 18 27	1 48.8	2 13.7	16 57.1	12 50.7	29 36.4	20 38.0	10 45.2	24 49.9	12 11.9	2 02.3
14 Tu	21 39 40	26 11 45	23 12 28	29 06 27	1 48.0	4 03.7	18 12.3	13 37.9	29 47.7	20 52.3	10 48.6	24 47.3	12 12.7	2 03.9
15 W	21 43 37	27 12 23	5♒00 44	10♒55 37	1 47.4	5 53.9	19 27.4	14 25.1	29 59.3	21 06.6	10 51.9	24 44.6	12 13.5	2 05.6
16 Th	21 47 33	28 13 00	16 51 25	22 48 23	1D47.1	7 44.0	20 42.6	15 12.3	0♊11.2	21 20.9	10 55.1	24 42.0	12 14.4	2 07.3
17 F	21 51 30	29 13 35	28 46 47	4♓46 49	1 47.1	9 33.9	21 57.7	15 59.4	0 23.3	21 35.2	10 58.2	24 39.4	12 15.3	2 09.0
18 Sa	21 55 26	0♓14 09	10♓48 44	16 52 45	1 47.1	11 23.3	23 12.8	16 46.5	0 35.7	21 49.4	11 01.3	24 36.7	12 16.2	2 10.7
19 Su	21 59 23	1 14 41	22 59 06	29 07 59	1R47.2	13 12.1	24 27.9	17 33.6	0 48.4	22 03.7	11 04.2	24 34.1	12 17.2	2 12.4
20 M	22 03 19	2 15 12	5♈19 38	11♈34 19	1 47.2	14 59.7	25 43.0	18 20.7	1 01.3	22 17.9	11 07.0	24 31.5	12 18.2	2 14.1
21 Tu	22 07 16	3 15 40	17 52 14	24 13 40	1 47.1	16 46.0	26 58.1	19 07.7	1 14.5	22 32.1	11 09.8	24 28.9	12 19.2	2 15.8
22 W	22 11 12	4 16 07	0♉38 51	7♉08 04	1 46.9	18 30.5	28 13.2	19 54.7	1 28.0	22 46.3	11 12.4	24 26.3	12 20.2	2 17.5
23 Th	22 15 09	5 16 32	13 41 32	20 19 31	1 46.6	20 12.8	29 28.3	20 41.7	1 41.7	23 00.5	11 15.0	24 23.7	12 21.3	2 19.2
24 F	22 19 06	6 16 56	27 02 12	3♊49 46	1D46.5	21 52.3	0♓43.3	21 28.7	1 55.7	23 14.7	11 17.4	24 21.2	12 22.5	2 20.9
25 Sa	22 23 02	7 17 17	10♊42 19	17 39 55	1 46.6	23 28.6	1 58.4	22 15.7	2 09.9	23 28.8	11 19.8	24 18.6	12 23.6	2 22.6
26 Su	22 26 59	8 17 36	24 42 32	1♋50 01	1 47.0	25 01.1	3 13.4	23 02.6	2 24.3	23 42.9	11 22.1	24 16.1	12 24.8	2 24.3
27 M	22 30 55	9 17 54	9♋02 08	16 18 30	1 47.6	26 29.1	4 28.4	23 49.5	2 39.0	23 57.0	11 24.3	24 13.6	12 26.0	2 26.0
28 Tu	22 34 52	10 18 09	23 38 38	1♌01 53	1 48.3	27 52.2	5 43.4	24 36.3	2 53.9	24 11.1	11 26.3	24 11.1	12 27.3	2 27.6

Astro Data

Aspect	Dy Hr Mn
♃□♆	8 7:09
☽0S	8 7:12
⚳D	13 4:14
♆D	21 16:18
☽0N	22 22:37
☽0S	4 16:31
☽0N	19 4:13
☿0N	28 11:55
♃☍♅	28 11:57

Planet Ingress

Planet	Sign	Dy Hr Mn
☿	♑	6 14:22
♀	♑	7 1:27
☉	♒	19 16:23
☿	♒	25 23:35
♂	♓	28 4:59
♀	♒	30 23:24
☿	♓	12 6:45
⚳	♊	15 13:25
☉	♓	18 6:24
♀	♓	23 22:08

Last Aspect / ☽ Ingress (January)

Last Aspect Dy Hr Mn		☽ Ingress	Dy Hr Mn
2 7:37	♅ ⚹	♋	2 13:14
3 10:22	☉ ☍	♌	4 12:21
6 12:14	☿ △	♍	6 12:26
7 18:15	☉ △	♎	8 15:13
10 14:27	♅ ⚹	♏	10 21:32
12 23:28	♅ □	♐	13 7:04
15 10:48	♅ △	♑	15 18:47
18 4:27	☉ ☌	♒	18 7:33
20 11:58	♅ ☍	♓	20 20:22
22 22:18	☿ ⚹	♈	23 8:00
25 16:04	☿ □	♉	25 17:01
27 21:59	♂ □	♊	27 22:23
29 16:55	♅ ⚹	♋	30 0:16
30 19:37	♆ ⚹	♌	31 23:59

Last Aspect / ☽ Ingress (February)

Last Aspect Dy Hr Mn		☽ Ingress	Dy Hr Mn
2 15:57	♅ ☌	♍	2 23:27
3 18:58	♆ △	♎	5 0:38
6 20:19	♅ ⚹	♏	7 5:07
9 3:52	♅ □	♐	9 13:28
11 23:53	☿ ⚹	♑	12 0:56
13 2:17	♂ ⚹	♒	14 13:49
16 23:52	☉ ☌	♓	17 2:27
18 11:47	♂ ☌	♈	19 13:41
21 17:42	♀ ⚹	♉	21 22:48
23 19:16	♅ □	♊	24 5:15
25 23:17	♅ ⚹	♋	26 8:55
28 6:21	☿ △	♌	28 10:20

☽ Phases & Eclipses

Dy Hr Mn	Phase	Position
3 10:22	○	13♋27
10 3:33	☾	20♎17
18 4:27	●	28♑28
26 5:10	☽	6♉39
1 21:07	○	13♌25
8 19:05	☾	20♏25
16 23:52	●	28♒43
16 23:56:06	●	A 07'32"
24 16:38	☽	6♊29

Astro Data

1 January 2045
Julian Day # 52962
SVP 4♓37'45"
GC 27♐28.1 ⚴ 14♓35.0
Eris 29♈04.2R ⚵ 18♈23.6
⚷ 19♍01.4 ⚶ 3♈46.3
☽ Mean ☊ 4♓38.6

1 February 2045
Julian Day # 52993
SVP 4♓37'39"
GC 27♐28.1 ⚴ 23♓41.9
Eris 29♈04.5 ⚵ 1♉00.1
⚷ 18♍09.0R ⚶ 14♈14.7
☽ Mean ☊ 3♓00.2

March 2045 LONGITUDE

Day	Sid.Time	☉	0 hr ☽	Noon ☽	True ☊	☿	♀	♂	⚳	♃	♄	♅	♆	♇
1 W	22 38 48	11♓18 22	8♌27 33	15♌54 45	1♓48.9	29♓09.6	6♓58.4	25♓23.1	3♊09.0	24♒25.1	11♐28.3	24♌08.6	12♉28.5	2♓29.3
2 Th	22 42 45	12 18 33	23 22 34	0♍50 00	1R 49.2	0♈20.7	8 13.4	26 09.9	3 24.4	24 39.1	11 30.2	24R 06.1	12 29.8	2 31.0
3 F	22 46 41	13 18 43	8♍16 04	15 39 46	1 48.9	1 25.1	9 28.3	26 56.7	3 39.9	24 53.1	11 32.0	24 03.7	12 31.1	2 32.7
4 Sa	22 50 38	14 18 50	23 00 10	0♎16 23	1 48.0	2 22.1	10 43.3	27 43.4	3 55.7	25 07.1	11 33.7	24 01.2	12 32.5	2 34.3
5 Su	22 54 35	15 18 56	7♎27 42	14 33 30	1 46.5	3 11.3	11 58.2	28 30.1	4 11.7	25 21.0	11 35.3	23 58.8	12 33.9	2 36.0
6 M	22 58 31	16 19 00	21 33 18	28 26 47	1 44.6	3 52.3	13 13.1	29 16.8	4 27.9	25 34.9	11 36.7	23 56.4	12 35.3	2 37.7
7 Tu	23 02 28	17 19 03	5♏13 49	11♏54 21	1 42.5	4 24.6	14 28.0	0♈03.4	4 44.3	25 48.7	11 38.1	23 54.1	12 36.7	2 39.3
8 W	23 06 24	18 19 04	18 28 30	24 56 32	1 40.7	4 48.1	15 42.9	0 50.0	5 00.9	26 02.6	11 39.4	23 51.7	12 38.2	2 41.0
9 Th	23 10 21	19 19 03	1♐18 46	7♐35 36	1 39.5	5 02.6	16 57.8	1 36.6	5 17.7	26 16.3	11 40.6	23 49.4	12 39.7	2 42.6
10 F	23 14 17	20 19 01	13 47 34	19 55 10	1D 39.0	5R 08.1	18 12.7	2 23.1	5 34.7	26 30.1	11 41.7	23 47.1	12 41.2	2 44.2
11 Sa	23 18 14	21 18 57	25 59 00	1♑59 39	1 39.4	5 04.7	19 27.5	3 09.6	5 51.9	26 43.8	11 42.7	23 44.9	12 42.7	2 45.9
12 Su	23 22 10	22 18 52	7♑57 44	13 53 51	1 40.6	4 52.6	20 42.4	3 56.1	6 09.3	26 57.5	11 43.6	23 42.7	12 44.3	2 47.5
13 M	23 26 07	23 18 44	19 48 38	25 42 38	1 42.2	4 32.3	21 57.2	4 42.5	6 26.8	27 11.1	11 44.4	23 40.5	12 45.9	2 49.1
14 Tu	23 30 04	24 18 35	1♒36 26	7♒30 33	1 43.9	4 04.3	23 12.0	5 28.9	6 44.6	27 24.7	11 45.1	23 38.3	12 47.5	2 50.7
15 W	23 34 00	25 18 25	13 25 30	19 21 45	1 45.3	3 29.4	24 26.8	6 15.3	7 02.5	27 38.2	11 45.7	23 36.2	12 49.1	2 52.3
16 Th	23 37 57	26 18 12	25 19 43	1♓19 46	1R 45.9	2 48.3	25 41.6	7 01.6	7 20.6	27 51.7	11 46.2	23 34.1	12 50.8	2 53.9
17 F	23 41 53	27 17 57	7♓22 14	13 27 25	1 45.3	2 02.2	26 56.4	7 47.9	7 38.9	28 05.1	11 46.5	23 32.0	12 52.5	2 55.4
18 Sa	23 45 50	28 17 41	19 35 32	25 46 46	1 43.3	1 12.0	28 11.2	8 34.1	7 57.3	28 18.5	11 46.8	23 30.0	12 54.2	2 57.0
19 Su	23 49 46	29 17 22	2♈01 17	8♈19 09	1 40.1	0 19.0	29 25.9	9 20.4	8 15.9	28 31.8	11 47.0	23 28.0	12 55.9	2 58.6
20 M	23 53 43	0♈17 02	14 40 27	21 05 12	1 35.8	29♓24.3	0♈40.6	10 06.5	8 34.7	28 45.1	11R 47.1	23 26.0	12 57.7	3 00.1
21 Tu	23 57 39	1 16 39	27 33 23	4♉04 59	1 30.8	28 29.2	1 55.3	10 52.7	8 53.7	28 58.4	11 47.0	23 24.1	12 59.4	3 01.6
22 W	0 01 36	2 16 15	10♉39 57	17 18 14	1 25.9	27 34.7	3 10.0	11 38.8	9 12.8	29 11.5	11 46.9	23 22.2	13 01.2	3 03.2
23 Th	0 05 33	3 15 48	23 59 45	0♊44 27	1 21.7	26 42.1	4 24.7	12 24.8	9 32.0	29 24.7	11 46.7	23 20.4	13 03.1	3 04.7
24 F	0 09 29	4 15 19	7♊32 16	14 23 07	1 18.7	25 52.1	5 39.3	13 10.8	9 51.4	29 37.7	11 46.4	23 18.6	13 04.9	3 06.2
25 Sa	0 13 26	5 14 47	21 16 57	28 13 40	1D 17.1	25 05.7	6 54.0	13 56.8	10 11.0	29 50.7	11 45.9	23 16.8	13 06.8	3 07.7
26 Su	0 17 22	6 14 14	5♋13 12	12♋15 27	1 17.1	24 23.6	8 08.6	14 42.7	10 30.7	0♓03.7	11 45.4	23 15.1	13 08.6	3 09.1
27 M	0 21 19	7 13 37	19 20 15	26 27 27	1 18.1	23 46.3	9 23.2	15 28.6	10 50.5	0 16.6	11 44.8	23 13.4	13 10.5	3 10.6
28 Tu	0 25 15	8 12 59	3♌36 49	10♌48 02	1 19.6	23 14.2	10 37.7	16 14.4	11 10.5	0 29.4	11 44.1	23 11.8	13 12.4	3 12.0
29 W	0 29 12	9 12 18	18 00 47	25 14 36	1R 20.6	22 47.7	11 52.3	17 00.2	11 30.6	0 42.1	11 43.3	23 10.2	13 14.4	3 13.5
30 Th	0 33 08	10 11 35	2♍29 00	9♍43 24	1 20.5	22 26.8	13 06.8	17 46.0	11 50.9	0 54.8	11 42.3	23 08.6	13 16.3	3 14.9
31 F	0 37 05	11 10 49	16 57 10	24 09 39	1 18.5	22 11.8	14 21.3	18 31.6	12 11.3	1 07.4	11 41.3	23 07.1	13 18.3	3 16.3

April 2045 LONGITUDE

Day	Sid.Time	☉	0 hr ☽	Noon ☽	True ☊	☿	♀	♂	⚳	♃	♄	♅	♆	♇
1 Sa	0 41 02	12♈10 02	1♎20 07	8♎27 54	1♓14.7	22♓02.5	15♈35.8	19♈17.3	12♊31.8	1♓20.0	11♐40.2	23♌05.6	13♉20.3	3♓17.7
2 Su	0 44 58	13 09 12	15 32 20	22 32 46	1R 09.0	21D 58.9	16 50.3	20 02.9	12 52.5	1 32.5	11R 39.0	23R 04.2	13 22.3	3 19.0
3 M	0 48 55	14 08 20	29 28 41	6♏19 37	1 02.0	22 01.0	18 04.7	20 48.5	13 13.2	1 44.9	11 37.7	23 02.8	13 24.3	3 20.4
4 Tu	0 52 51	15 07 27	13♏05 15	19 45 20	0 54.5	22 08.4	19 19.1	21 34.0	13 34.1	1 57.2	11 36.3	23 01.5	13 26.3	3 21.7
5 W	0 56 48	16 06 32	26 19 48	2♐48 39	0 47.5	22 21.1	20 33.5	22 19.4	13 55.2	2 09.5	11 34.8	23 00.2	13 28.3	3 23.1
6 Th	1 00 44	17 05 35	9♐12 03	15 30 13	0 41.6	22 38.8	21 47.9	23 04.9	14 16.3	2 21.7	11 33.2	22 59.0	13 30.4	3 24.4
7 F	1 04 41	18 04 36	21 43 32	27 52 25	0 37.4	23 01.4	23 02.3	23 50.2	14 37.6	2 33.8	11 31.6	22 57.8	13 32.5	3 25.7
8 Sa	1 08 37	19 03 35	3♑57 21	9♑58 55	0D 35.1	23 28.5	24 16.7	24 35.6	14 58.9	2 45.8	11 29.8	22 56.7	13 34.5	3 27.0
9 Su	1 12 34	20 02 33	15 57 42	21 54 21	0 34.6	24 00.0	25 31.0	25 20.9	15 20.4	2 57.8	11 27.9	22 55.6	13 36.6	3 28.2
10 M	1 16 31	21 01 28	27 49 31	3♒43 51	0 35.3	24 35.6	26 45.3	26 06.1	15 42.1	3 09.7	11 26.0	22 54.6	13 38.8	3 29.5
11 Tu	1 20 27	22 00 22	9♒38 01	15 32 41	0 36.6	25 15.2	27 59.6	26 51.3	16 03.8	3 21.5	11 23.9	22 53.6	13 40.9	3 30.7
12 W	1 24 24	22 59 15	21 28 28	27 25 59	0R 37.4	25 58.5	29 13.9	27 36.5	16 25.6	3 33.2	11 21.8	22 52.6	13 43.0	3 31.9
13 Th	1 28 20	23 58 05	3♓25 48	9♓28 26	0 37.0	26 45.3	0♉28.2	28 21.6	16 47.5	3 44.8	11 19.6	22 51.8	13 45.2	3 33.1
14 F	1 32 17	24 56 54	15 34 22	21 43 59	0 34.7	27 35.6	1 42.4	29 06.6	17 09.6	3 56.3	11 17.3	22 50.9	13 47.3	3 34.2
15 Sa	1 36 13	25 55 40	27 57 38	4♈15 34	0 30.1	28 29.0	2 56.7	29 51.6	17 31.7	4 07.8	11 14.9	22 50.1	13 49.5	3 35.4
16 Su	1 40 10	26 54 25	10♈37 57	17 04 52	0 23.1	29 25.6	4 10.9	0♉36.6	17 54.0	4 19.2	11 12.4	22 49.4	13 51.6	3 36.5
17 M	1 44 06	27 53 08	23 36 17	0♉12 08	0 14.2	0♈25.0	5 25.1	1 21.5	18 16.3	4 30.4	11 09.8	22 48.7	13 53.8	3 37.6
18 Tu	1 48 03	28 51 49	6♉52 12	13 36 14	0 04.3	1 27.2	6 39.2	2 06.4	18 38.8	4 41.6	11 07.2	22 48.1	13 56.0	3 38.7
19 W	1 51 59	29 50 28	20 23 54	27 14 51	29♒54.2	2 32.1	7 53.4	2 51.2	19 01.3	4 52.7	11 04.5	22 47.5	13 58.2	3 39.8
20 Th	1 55 56	0♉49 05	4♊08 40	11♊04 55	29 45.3	3 39.5	9 07.5	3 35.9	19 24.0	5 03.6	11 01.7	22 47.0	14 00.4	3 40.9
21 F	1 59 53	1 47 40	18 03 13	25 03 10	29 38.2	4 49.4	10 21.6	4 20.6	19 46.7	5 14.5	10 58.8	22 46.5	14 02.6	3 41.9
22 Sa	2 03 49	2 46 13	2♋04 24	9♋06 37	29 33.6	6 01.7	11 35.7	5 05.3	20 09.5	5 25.3	10 55.9	22 46.1	14 04.9	3 42.9
23 Su	2 07 46	3 44 44	16 09 31	23 12 53	29D 31.4	7 16.3	12 49.8	5 49.9	20 32.4	5 36.0	10 52.8	22 45.8	14 07.1	3 43.9
24 M	2 11 42	4 43 12	0♌16 33	7♌20 20	29 31.0	8 33.0	14 03.8	6 34.5	20 55.4	5 46.6	10 49.7	22 45.4	14 09.3	3 44.9
25 Tu	2 15 39	5 41 38	14 24 07	21 27 47	29R 31.4	9 52.0	15 17.9	7 19.0	21 18.5	5 57.0	10 46.6	22 45.2	14 11.6	3 45.8
26 W	2 19 35	6 40 02	28 31 12	5♍34 11	29 31.4	11 13.0	16 31.8	8 03.4	21 41.7	6 07.4	10 43.3	22 45.0	14 13.8	3 46.7
27 Th	2 23 32	7 38 24	12♍36 35	19 38 10	29 29.9	12 36.2	17 45.8	8 47.8	22 04.9	6 17.6	10 40.0	22 44.8	14 16.0	3 47.6
28 F	2 27 28	8 36 44	26 38 40	3♎37 44	29 26.0	14 01.3	18 59.8	9 32.1	22 28.3	6 27.8	10 36.6	22 44.7	14 18.3	3 48.5
29 Sa	2 31 25	9 35 01	10♎35 03	17 30 13	29 19.3	15 28.4	20 13.7	10 16.4	22 51.7	6 37.8	10 33.2	22D 44.7	14 20.5	3 49.4
30 Su	2 35 22	10 33 17	24 22 48	1♏12 25	29 10.1	16 57.5	21 27.6	11 00.7	23 15.2	6 47.7	10 29.7	22 44.7	14 22.8	3 50.2

Astro Data Dy Hr Mn	Planet Ingress Dy Hr Mn	Last Aspect Dy Hr Mn	☽ Ingress Dy Hr Mn	Last Aspect Dy Hr Mn	☽ Ingress Dy Hr Mn	☽ Phases & Eclipses Dy Hr Mn
☽0S 4 3:32	☿ ♈ 2 4:46	2 1:54 ♃ ☍	♍ 2 10:39	2 12:54 ♅ ✱	♏ 3 0:55	3 7:54 ○ 13♍08
♂0N 9 12:18	♂ ♈ 7 10:15	4 7:32 ♂ ☍	♎ 4 11:33	4 17:56 ♅ □	♐ 5 6:46	3 7:43 • A 0.962
☿R 10 14:44	☿ ♓R 19 20:23	6 6:54 ♃ △	♏ 6 14:44	7 3:35 ♂ △	♑ 7 16:11	10 12:51 ☾ 20♐21
☽0N 18 10:50	♀ ♈ 19 22:57	8 14:06 ♃ □	♐ 8 21:31	9 20:10 ♀ □	♒ 10 4:25	18 17:16 ● 28♓31
☉0N 20 5:08	☉ ♈ 20 5:09	11 1:17 ♃ ✱	♑ 11 8:01	12 16:01 ♀ ✱	♓ 12 17:09	26 0:58 ☽ 5♋47
♄R 20 18:14	♃ ♓ 26 5:09	13 6:40 ☉ ✱	♒ 13 20:44	15 0:09 ☿ ☌	♈ 15 3:54	
♀0N 22 11:47		16 4:56 ♃ ☌	♓ 16 9:21	17 7:28 ☉ ☌	♉ 17 11:38	1 18:44 ○ 12♎27
☿0S 25 20:26	♀ ♉ 13 2:54	18 17:16 ☉ ☌	♈ 18 20:08	19 4:13 ♅ □	♊ 19 16:48	9 7:54 ☾ 19♑52
☽0S 31 13:40	♂ ♉ 15 16:28	21 2:27 ♃ ✱	♉ 21 4:30	21 8:06 ♅ ✱	♋ 21 20:28	17 7:28 ● 27♈42
☿D 2 15:11	☿ ♈ 17 2:03	23 9:36 ♃ □	♊ 23 10:41	22 20:29 ♆ ✱	♌ 23 23:32	24 7:13 ☽ 4♌32
♃☌♇ 12 9:02	☊ ♒R 18 22:05	25 14:50 ♃ △	♋ 25 15:03	25 14:12 ♅ ☌	♍ 26 2:31	
☽0N 14 18:29	☉ ♉ 19 15:54	27 7:39 ☿ △	♌ 27 17:57	27 8:29 ♀ △	♎ 28 5:46	
☿0N 22 16:47		29 8:34 ♅ ☌	♍ 29 19:53	29 21:08 ♅ ✱	♏ 30 9:52	
☽0S 27 21:07		31 8:46 ☿ ☍	♎ 31 21:46			
♅D 29 18:23						

Astro Data

1 March 2045
Julian Day # 53021
SVP 4♓37'35"
GC 27♐28.2 ⚴ 3♈30.3
Eris 29♈13.6 ⚵ 14♉55.1
⚷ 16♍12.7R ⚶ 25♈16.7
☽ Mean ☊ 1♓31.2

1 April 2045
Julian Day # 53052
SVP 4♓37'32"
GC 27♐28.3 ⚴ 15♈29.8
Eris 29♈30.9 ⚵ 1♊40.6
⚷ 13♍53.6R ⚶ 8♉23.5
☽ Mean ☊ 29♒52.7

LONGITUDE — May 2045

Day	Sid.Time	☉	0 hr ☽	Noon ☽	True ☊	☿	♀	♂	⚳	♃	♄	♅	♆	♇
1 M	2 39 18	11♉31 31	7♏58 39	14♏41 08	28♒58.9	18♈28.6	22♉41.5	11♉44.9	23♊38.7	6♓57.6	10♐26.1	22♌44.8	14♉25.0	3♓51.0
2 Tu	2 43 15	12 29 44	21 19 34	27 53 41	28R 46.9	20 01.5	23 55.3	12 29.0	24 02.4	7 07.3	10R 22.5	22 44.9	14 27.3	3 51.8
3 W	2 47 11	13 27 54	4♐23 19	10♐48 25	28 35.2	21 36.4	25 09.2	13 13.1	24 26.1	7 16.8	10 18.8	22 45.1	14 29.6	3 52.6
4 Th	2 51 08	14 26 04	17 08 57	23 25 04	28 24.9	23 13.2	26 23.0	13 57.1	24 49.9	7 26.3	10 15.1	22 45.3	14 31.8	3 53.3
5 F	2 55 04	15 24 11	29 36 58	5♑44 55	28 16.8	24 51.9	27 36.8	14 41.1	25 13.7	7 35.6	10 11.3	22 45.6	14 34.1	3 54.1
6 Sa	2 59 01	16 22 17	11♑49 18	17 50 33	28 11.2	26 32.5	28 50.6	15 25.0	25 37.6	7 44.9	10 07.5	22 45.9	14 36.3	3 54.8
7 Su	3 02 57	17 20 22	23 49 13	29 45 49	28 08.1	28 15.0	0♊04.3	16 08.9	26 01.6	7 54.0	10 03.6	22 46.3	14 38.6	3 55.4
8 M	3 06 54	18 18 25	5♒40 59	11♒35 22	28D 06.9	29 59.4	1 18.1	16 52.7	26 25.7	8 02.9	9 59.7	22 46.8	14 40.8	3 56.1
9 Tu	3 10 51	19 16 27	17 29 37	23 24 27	28R 06.8	1♉45.7	2 31.8	17 36.5	26 49.8	8 11.8	9 55.7	22 47.3	14 43.1	3 56.7
10 W	3 14 47	20 14 28	29 20 31	5♓18 32	28 06.7	3 34.0	3 45.5	18 20.2	27 14.0	8 20.5	9 51.6	22 47.8	14 45.4	3 57.3
11 Th	3 18 44	21 12 27	11♓19 09	17 23 01	28 05.6	5 24.1	4 59.2	19 03.9	27 38.3	8 29.1	9 47.6	22 48.4	14 47.6	3 57.9
12 F	3 22 40	22 10 24	23 30 43	29 42 48	28 02.4	7 16.2	6 12.9	19 47.5	28 02.6	8 37.6	9 43.4	22 49.1	14 49.8	3 58.5
13 Sa	3 26 37	23 08 21	5♈59 44	12♈21 54	27 56.8	9 10.2	7 26.5	20 31.1	28 27.0	8 45.9	9 39.3	22 49.8	14 52.1	3 59.0
14 Su	3 30 33	24 06 16	18 49 35	25 22 57	27 48.5	11 06.0	8 40.1	21 14.6	28 51.5	8 54.1	9 35.1	22 50.5	14 54.3	3 59.5
15 M	3 34 30	25 04 10	2♉02 03	8♉46 46	27 38.0	13 03.8	9 53.8	21 58.1	29 16.0	9 02.1	9 30.9	22 51.4	14 56.6	4 00.0
16 Tu	3 38 26	26 02 02	15 36 54	22 32 03	27 26.1	15 03.4	11 07.4	22 41.5	29 40.6	9 10.1	9 26.6	22 52.2	14 58.8	4 00.5
17 W	3 42 23	26 59 53	29 31 46	6♊35 26	27 14.1	17 04.7	12 20.9	23 24.9	0♋05.2	9 17.8	9 22.3	22 53.2	15 01.0	4 00.9
18 Th	3 46 20	27 57 43	13♊42 22	20 51 52	27 03.2	19 07.8	13 34.5	24 08.2	0 29.9	9 25.5	9 18.0	22 54.1	15 03.2	4 01.3
19 F	3 50 16	28 55 31	28 03 09	5♋15 30	26 54.5	21 12.5	14 48.0	24 51.5	0 54.7	9 33.0	9 13.7	22 55.2	15 05.5	4 01.7
20 Sa	3 54 13	29 53 18	12♋28 13	19 40 39	26 48.5	23 18.8	16 01.5	25 34.7	1 19.5	9 40.3	9 09.3	22 56.3	15 07.7	4 02.1
21 Su	3 58 09	0♊51 03	26 52 15	4♌02 33	26 45.3	25 26.4	17 15.0	26 17.8	1 44.3	9 47.5	9 05.0	22 57.4	15 09.9	4 02.4
22 M	4 02 06	1 48 46	11♌11 11	18 17 54	26D 44.1	27 35.3	18 28.5	27 00.9	2 09.2	9 54.5	9 00.6	22 58.6	15 12.0	4 02.7
23 Tu	4 06 02	2 46 27	25 22 30	2♍24 51	26R 44.1	29 45.2	19 42.0	27 44.0	2 34.2	10 01.4	8 56.1	22 59.8	15 14.2	4 03.0
24 W	4 09 59	3 44 07	9♍24 54	16 22 36	26 43.7	1♊56.0	20 55.4	28 27.0	2 59.2	10 08.2	8 51.7	23 01.1	15 16.4	4 03.3
25 Th	4 13 56	4 41 45	23 17 58	0♎10 57	26 41.9	4 07.4	22 08.8	29 09.9	3 24.3	10 14.8	8 47.3	23 02.4	15 18.5	4 03.5
26 F	4 17 52	5 39 22	7♎01 34	13 49 46	26 37.7	6 19.2	23 22.1	29 52.8	3 49.4	10 21.2	8 42.8	23 03.8	15 20.7	4 03.7
27 Sa	4 21 49	6 36 58	20 35 28	27 18 36	26 30.8	8 31.1	24 35.5	0♊35.6	4 14.5	10 27.5	8 38.4	23 05.2	15 22.8	4 03.9
28 Su	4 25 45	7 34 32	3♏59 03	10♏36 40	26 21.2	10 42.8	25 48.8	1 18.4	4 39.7	10 33.6	8 33.9	23 06.7	15 25.0	4 04.1
29 M	4 29 42	8 32 05	17 11 18	23 42 49	26 09.8	12 54.0	27 02.1	2 01.1	5 05.0	10 39.6	8 29.5	23 08.2	15 27.1	4 04.2
30 Tu	4 33 38	9 29 36	0♐11 04	6♐35 57	25 57.4	15 04.6	28 15.4	2 43.8	5 30.3	10 45.4	8 25.0	23 09.8	15 29.2	4 04.4
31 W	4 37 35	10 27 07	12 57 21	19 15 15	25 45.2	17 14.1	29 28.6	3 26.4	5 55.6	10 51.0	8 20.6	23 11.5	15 31.3	4 04.4

LONGITUDE — June 2045

Day	Sid.Time	☉	0 hr ☽	Noon ☽	True ☊	☿	♀	♂	⚳	♃	♄	♅	♆	♇
1 Th	4 41 31	11♊24 36	25♐29 40	1♑40 38	25♒34.4	19♊22.5	0♋41.9	4♊09.0	6♋21.0	10♓56.5	8♐16.1	23♌13.1	15♉33.4	4♓04.5
2 F	4 45 28	12 22 05	7♑48 20	13 52 56	25R 25.7	21 29.3	1 55.1	4 51.5	6 46.4	11 01.8	8R 11.7	23 14.9	15 35.4	4 04.6
3 Sa	4 49 25	13 19 33	19 54 43	25 54 01	25 19.5	23 34.6	3 08.3	5 34.0	7 11.9	11 07.0	8 07.2	23 16.6	15 37.5	4R 04.6
4 Su	4 53 21	14 17 00	1♒51 13	7♒46 46	25 16.0	25 37.9	4 21.4	6 16.4	7 37.4	11 12.0	8 02.8	23 18.5	15 39.5	4 04.6
5 M	4 57 18	15 14 26	13 41 12	19 35 04	25D 14.5	27 39.3	5 34.6	6 58.7	8 02.9	11 16.8	7 58.4	23 20.3	15 41.6	4 04.5
6 Tu	5 01 14	16 11 51	25 28 57	1♓23 29	25 14.5	29 38.6	6 47.7	7 41.1	8 28.5	11 21.4	7 54.0	23 22.2	15 43.6	4 04.5
7 W	5 05 11	17 09 16	7♓19 19	13 17 09	25R 14.9	1♋35.7	8 00.8	8 23.3	8 54.1	11 25.9	7 49.6	23 24.2	15 45.6	4 04.4
8 Th	5 09 07	18 06 40	19 17 38	25 21 27	25 14.7	3 30.4	9 13.9	9 05.5	9 19.8	11 30.2	7 45.3	23 26.2	15 47.6	4 04.3
9 F	5 13 04	19 04 03	1♈29 15	7♈41 40	25 13.1	5 22.8	10 27.0	9 47.7	9 45.5	11 34.3	7 40.9	23 28.2	15 49.5	4 04.2
10 Sa	5 17 00	20 01 26	13 59 17	20 22 34	25 09.3	7 12.8	11 40.0	10 29.8	10 11.2	11 38.3	7 36.6	23 30.3	15 51.5	4 04.0
11 Su	5 20 57	20 58 49	26 51 59	3♉27 48	25 03.3	9 00.3	12 53.0	11 11.9	10 37.0	11 42.0	7 32.3	23 32.4	15 53.4	4 03.8
12 M	5 24 54	21 56 11	10♉10 13	16 59 16	24 55.3	10 45.3	14 06.1	11 53.9	11 02.8	11 45.6	7 28.1	23 34.6	15 55.3	4 03.6
13 Tu	5 28 50	22 53 32	23 54 49	0♊56 34	24 46.0	12 27.8	15 19.0	12 35.9	11 28.7	11 49.0	7 23.8	23 36.8	15 57.2	4 03.4
14 W	5 32 47	23 50 53	8♊04 02	15 16 36	24 36.4	14 07.7	16 32.0	13 17.8	11 54.5	11 52.3	7 19.6	23 39.1	15 59.1	4 03.1
15 Th	5 36 43	24 48 14	22 33 28	29 53 47	24 27.7	15 45.1	17 44.9	13 59.6	12 20.5	11 55.3	7 15.5	23 41.4	16 01.0	4 02.9
16 F	5 40 40	25 45 33	7♋16 32	14♋40 44	24 20.8	17 19.9	18 57.9	14 41.5	12 46.4	11 58.2	7 11.4	23 43.8	16 02.8	4 02.6
17 Sa	5 44 36	26 42 52	22 05 23	29 29 30	24 16.2	18 52.1	20 10.8	15 23.2	13 12.4	12 00.8	7 07.3	23 46.1	16 04.6	4 02.2
18 Su	5 48 33	27 40 11	6♌52 12	14♌12 44	24D 14.0	20 21.7	21 23.6	16 04.9	13 38.4	12 03.3	7 03.3	23 48.6	16 06.5	4 01.9
19 M	5 52 29	28 37 28	21 30 26	28 44 47	24 13.7	21 48.7	22 36.5	16 46.6	14 04.4	12 05.6	6 59.3	23 51.0	16 08.2	4 01.5
20 Tu	5 56 26	29 34 45	5♍55 25	13♍02 03	24 14.4	23 13.0	23 49.3	17 28.2	14 30.5	12 07.7	6 55.3	23 53.5	16 10.0	4 01.1
21 W	6 00 23	0♋32 00	20 04 32	27 02 48	24R 15.1	24 34.6	25 02.1	18 09.8	14 56.6	12 09.6	6 51.4	23 56.1	16 11.7	4 00.7
22 Th	6 04 19	1 29 15	3♎56 54	10♎46 51	24 14.7	25 53.4	26 14.8	18 51.3	15 22.7	12 11.4	6 47.6	23 58.7	16 13.5	4 00.3
23 F	6 08 16	2 26 30	17 32 48	24 14 52	24 12.6	27 09.5	27 27.5	19 32.7	15 48.9	12 12.9	6 43.8	24 01.3	16 15.2	3 59.8
24 Sa	6 12 12	3 23 43	0♏53 10	7♏27 53	24 08.3	28 22.7	28 40.2	20 14.1	16 15.1	12 14.2	6 40.0	24 03.9	16 16.8	3 59.3
25 Su	6 16 09	4 20 56	13 59 07	20 27 00	24 02.1	29 33.1	29 52.9	20 55.4	16 41.2	12 15.4	6 36.3	24 06.6	16 18.5	3 58.8
26 M	6 20 05	5 18 09	26 51 39	3♐13 09	23 54.4	0♌40.4	1♌05.5	21 36.7	17 07.5	12 16.4	6 32.7	24 09.4	16 20.1	3 58.3
27 Tu	6 24 02	6 15 22	9♐31 37	15 47 07	23 46.0	1 44.8	2 18.1	22 18.0	17 33.7	12 17.1	6 29.1	24 12.1	16 21.7	3 57.7
28 W	6 27 59	7 12 34	21 59 46	28 09 38	23 37.7	2 46.0	3 30.7	22 59.2	18 00.0	12 17.7	6 25.6	24 14.9	16 23.3	3 57.1
29 Th	6 31 55	8 09 45	4♑16 51	10♑21 33	23 30.4	3 44.0	4 43.2	23 40.3	18 26.3	12 18.1	6 22.1	24 17.8	16 24.9	3 56.5
30 F	6 35 52	9 06 57	16 23 53	22 24 03	23 24.6	4 38.7	5 55.8	24 21.4	18 52.6	12R 18.3	6 18.8	24 20.6	16 26.4	3 55.9

Astro Data (Dy Hr Mn)

	Dy Hr Mn
☽0N	12 2:25
♃□♄	17 21:02
☽0S	25 2:10
♇R	3 16:38
☽0N	8 9:53
☽0S	21 6:54

Planet Ingress (Dy Hr Mn)

		Dy Hr Mn
♀	♊	7 10:35
☿	♉	8 12:08
⚳	♋	17 6:56
☉	♊	20 14:47
☿	♊	23 14:43
♂	♊	26 16:02
♀	♋	31 22:17
☿	♋	6 16:21
☉	♋	20 22:35
♀	♌	25 14:21
☿	♌	25 21:28

Last Aspect / ☽ Ingress (May)

Last Aspect Dy Hr Mn			☽ Ingress	Dy Hr Mn
2 3:59	♀	☍	♐	2 15:53
4 11:34	☿	△	♑	5 0:45
7 8:25	☿	□	♒	7 12:29
9 10:45	♅	☍	♓	10 1:20
11 20:09	☉	⚹	♈	12 12:33
14 7:22	♅	△	♉	14 20:21
16 18:28	☉	☌	♊	17 0:48
18 15:25	♅	⚹	♋	19 3:15
20 22:22	♂	⚹	♌	21 5:14
23 6:38	☿	□	♍	23 7:53
25 10:07	♂	△	♎	25 11:41
27 6:39	♀	△	♏	27 16:50
29 10:56	♅	□	♐	29 23:39

Last Aspect / ☽ Ingress (June)

Last Aspect Dy Hr Mn			☽ Ingress	Dy Hr Mn
31 19:34	♅	△	♑	1 8:44
2 15:24	♆	△	♒	3 20:15
6 7:45	☿	△	♓	6 9:11
7 20:24	☉	□	♈	8 21:06
10 17:49	♅	△	♉	11 5:43
12 23:27	♅	□	♊	13 10:24
15 3:06	☉	☌	♋	15 12:10
16 19:34	♀	☌	♌	17 12:50
19 11:47	☉	⚹	♍	19 14:05
21 8:12	♀	⚹	♎	21 17:07
23 18:22	♀	□	♏	23 22:23
25 18:52	♅	□	♐	26 5:55
28 4:21	♅	△	♑	28 15:36

☽ Phases & Eclipses (Dy Hr Mn)

Dy Hr Mn		
1 5:53	○	11♏17
9 2:52	☾	18♒54
16 18:28	●	26♉18
23 12:40	☽	2♍48
30 17:54	○	9♐44
7 20:24	☾	17♓29
15 3:06	●	24♊27
21 18:30	☽	0♎48
29 7:17	○	7♑59

Astro Data

1 May 2045
Julian Day # 53082
SVP 4♓37'28"
GC 27♐28.4 ⚴ 27♈52.6
Eris 29♈50.6 ⚵ 18♊22.0
⚷ 12♍38.1R ⚶ 21♉28.1
☽ Mean ☊ 28♒17.4

1 June 2045
Julian Day # 53113
SVP 4♓37'23"
GC 27♐28.4 ⚴ 11♉14.3
Eris 0♉09.1 ⚵ 5♋31.5
⚷ 13♍00.7 ⚶ 5♊01.6
☽ Mean ☊ 26♒38.9

July 2045

LONGITUDE

Day	Sid.Time	☉	0 hr ☽	Noon ☽	True ☊	☿	♀	♂	⚳	♃	♄	♅	♆	♇
1 Sa	6 39 48	10♋04 08	28♑22 17	4♒18 51	23♒20.8	5♌30.0	7♌08.2	25♊02.5	19♋18.9	12♓18.3	6♐15.4	24♌23.5	16♉27.9	3♓55.3
2 Su	6 43 45	11 01 20	10♒14 04	16 08 16	23D 18.9	6 17.8	8 20.7	25 43.5	19 45.3	12R 18.1	6R 12.2	24 26.5	16 29.4	3R 54.6
3 M	6 47 41	11 58 31	22 01 52	27 55 18	23 18.7	7 02.0	9 33.1	26 24.5	20 11.7	12 17.7	6 09.0	24 29.4	16 30.9	3 54.0
4 Tu	6 51 38	12 55 42	3♓49 02	9♓43 36	23 19.7	7 42.4	10 45.5	27 05.4	20 38.1	12 17.2	6 05.8	24 32.4	16 32.3	3 53.2
5 W	6 55 34	13 52 54	15 39 33	21 37 27	23 21.3	8 18.9	11 57.8	27 46.2	21 04.5	12 16.4	6 02.8	24 35.4	16 33.7	3 52.5
6 Th	6 59 31	14 50 06	27 37 54	3♈41 32	23R 22.7	8 51.4	13 10.2	28 27.1	21 31.0	12 15.4	5 59.8	24 38.5	16 35.1	3 51.8
7 F	7 03 28	15 47 18	9♈48 57	16 00 47	23 23.2	9 19.7	14 22.5	29 07.8	21 57.4	12 14.3	5 56.9	24 41.6	16 36.5	3 51.0
8 Sa	7 07 24	16 44 31	22 17 35	28 39 56	23 22.5	9 43.8	15 34.7	29 48.6	22 23.9	12 12.9	5 54.1	24 44.7	16 37.8	3 50.2
9 Su	7 11 21	17 41 44	5♉08 19	11♉43 08	23 20.3	10 03.5	16 47.0	0♋29.2	22 50.4	12 11.4	5 51.3	24 47.8	16 39.1	3 49.4
10 M	7 15 17	18 38 57	18 24 43	25 13 15	23 16.8	10 18.7	17 59.2	1 09.9	23 16.9	12 09.6	5 48.6	24 51.0	16 40.4	3 48.6
11 Tu	7 19 14	19 36 11	2♊08 47	9♊11 11	23 12.3	10 29.3	19 11.3	1 50.5	23 43.5	12 07.7	5 46.0	24 54.2	16 41.7	3 47.8
12 W	7 23 10	20 33 25	16 20 10	23 35 15	23 07.5	10R 35.1	20 23.5	2 31.0	24 10.0	12 05.6	5 43.5	24 57.4	16 42.9	3 46.9
13 Th	7 27 07	21 30 40	0♋55 47	8♋20 56	23 03.1	10 36.3	21 35.6	3 11.5	24 36.6	12 03.3	5 41.1	25 00.7	16 44.1	3 46.1
14 F	7 31 03	22 27 55	15 49 43	23 21 05	22 59.7	10 32.6	22 47.7	3 52.0	25 03.2	12 00.8	5 38.7	25 04.0	16 45.3	3 45.2
15 Sa	7 35 00	23 25 11	0♌53 52	8♌26 56	22D 57.6	10 24.2	23 59.7	4 32.4	25 29.8	11 58.1	5 36.4	25 07.3	16 46.4	3 44.3
16 Su	7 38 57	24 22 26	15 59 06	23 29 19	22 57.0	10 11.0	25 11.7	5 12.7	25 56.4	11 55.2	5 34.2	25 10.6	16 47.5	3 43.4
17 M	7 42 53	25 19 42	0♍56 38	8♍20 11	22 57.6	9 53.2	26 23.7	5 53.0	26 23.0	11 52.1	5 32.1	25 14.0	16 48.6	3 42.4
18 Tu	7 46 50	26 16 58	15 39 18	22 53 26	22 58.8	9 31.0	27 35.6	6 33.3	26 49.6	11 48.9	5 30.1	25 17.3	16 49.7	3 41.4
19 W	7 50 46	27 14 14	0♎02 14	7♎05 26	23 00.2	9 04.5	28 47.5	7 13.5	27 16.3	11 45.4	5 28.2	25 20.7	16 50.7	3 40.5
20 Th	7 54 43	28 11 30	14 02 58	20 54 48	23R 01.1	8 34.2	29 59.3	7 53.6	27 42.9	11 41.8	5 26.3	25 24.1	16 51.7	3 39.5
21 F	7 58 39	29 08 46	27 41 05	4♏21 58	23 01.2	8 00.3	1♍11.1	8 33.7	28 09.6	11 38.0	5 24.6	25 27.6	16 52.7	3 38.5
22 Sa	8 02 36	0♌06 03	10♏57 41	17 28 33	23 00.2	7 23.5	2 22.9	9 13.8	28 36.3	11 34.1	5 22.9	25 31.0	16 53.6	3 37.5
23 Su	8 06 32	1 03 20	23 54 50	0♐16 53	22 58.3	6 44.1	3 34.6	9 53.8	29 03.0	11 30.0	5 21.3	25 34.5	16 54.5	3 36.4
24 M	8 10 29	2 00 37	6♐35 01	12 49 33	22 55.6	6 02.8	4 46.2	10 33.8	29 29.6	11 25.6	5 19.9	25 38.0	16 55.4	3 35.4
25 Tu	8 14 26	2 57 55	19 00 48	25 09 05	22 52.6	5 20.3	5 57.8	11 13.7	29 56.3	11 21.2	5 18.5	25 41.5	16 56.2	3 34.3
26 W	8 18 22	3 55 13	1♑14 42	7♑17 56	22 49.6	4 37.4	7 09.4	11 53.6	0♌23.0	11 16.5	5 17.2	25 45.0	16 57.0	3 33.2
27 Th	8 22 19	4 52 32	13 19 02	19 18 17	22 47.0	3 54.7	8 20.9	12 33.4	0 49.8	11 11.7	5 16.0	25 48.6	16 57.8	3 32.2
28 F	8 26 15	5 49 51	25 15 57	1♒12 16	22 45.1	3 13.1	9 32.4	13 13.2	1 16.5	11 06.8	5 14.9	25 52.2	16 58.6	3 31.1
29 Sa	8 30 12	6 47 11	7♒07 31	13 01 58	22D 44.0	2 33.3	10 43.8	13 53.0	1 43.2	11 01.7	5 13.8	25 55.7	16 59.3	3 29.9
30 Su	8 34 08	7 44 32	18 55 53	24 49 34	22 43.8	1 56.1	11 55.2	14 32.7	2 09.9	10 56.4	5 12.9	25 59.3	17 00.0	3 28.8
31 M	8 38 05	8 41 54	0♓43 19	6♓37 29	22 44.2	1 22.1	13 06.5	15 12.3	2 36.6	10 51.0	5 12.1	26 02.9	17 00.6	3 27.7

August 2045

LONGITUDE

Day	Sid.Time	☉	0 hr ☽	Noon ☽	True ☊	☿	♀	♂	⚳	♃	♄	♅	♆	♇
1 Tu	8 42 01	9♌39 16	12♓32 25	18♓28 30	22♒45.1	0♌52.2	14♍17.8	15♋51.9	3♌03.4	10♓45.4	5♐11.4	26♌06.5	17♉01.2	3♓26.5
2 W	8 45 58	10 36 40	24 26 08	0♈25 45	22 46.3	0R 26.8	15 29.0	16 31.5	3 30.1	10R 39.7	5R 10.7	26 10.2	17 01.8	3R 25.4
3 Th	8 49 55	11 34 04	6♈27 49	12 32 47	22 47.4	0 06.5	16 40.1	17 11.0	3 56.8	10 33.8	5 10.2	26 13.8	17 02.4	3 24.2
4 F	8 53 51	12 31 30	18 41 09	24 53 25	22 48.2	29♋51.7	17 51.3	17 50.5	4 23.6	10 27.8	5 09.7	26 17.5	17 02.9	3 23.0
5 Sa	8 57 48	13 28 57	1♉10 05	7♉31 38	22R 48.6	29D 43.0	19 02.3	18 29.9	4 50.3	10 21.7	5 09.4	26 21.1	17 03.4	3 21.8
6 Su	9 01 44	14 26 26	13 58 32	20 31 11	22 48.6	29 40.4	20 13.3	19 09.3	5 17.1	10 15.4	5 09.1	26 24.8	17 03.9	3 20.6
7 M	9 05 41	15 23 55	27 09 57	3♊55 09	22 48.3	29 44.4	21 24.3	19 48.7	5 43.8	10 09.0	5 08.9	26 28.5	17 04.3	3 19.4
8 Tu	9 09 37	16 21 27	10♊46 55	17 45 22	22 47.7	29 55.0	22 35.2	20 28.0	6 10.6	10 02.5	5D 08.9	26 32.2	17 04.7	3 18.2
9 W	9 13 34	17 18 59	24 50 23	2♋01 46	22 47.1	0♌12.5	23 46.1	21 07.3	6 37.3	9 55.9	5 08.9	26 35.9	17 05.1	3 17.0
10 Th	9 17 30	18 16 33	9♋19 07	16 41 51	22 46.6	0 36.8	24 56.9	21 46.5	7 04.1	9 49.1	5 09.0	26 39.6	17 05.4	3 15.8
11 F	9 21 27	19 14 08	24 09 14	1♌40 23	22 46.2	1 07.9	26 07.6	22 25.7	7 30.8	9 42.3	5 09.3	26 43.4	17 05.7	3 14.5
12 Sa	9 25 24	20 11 44	9♌14 15	16 49 44	22D 46.1	1 45.9	27 18.3	23 04.8	7 57.6	9 35.3	5 09.6	26 47.1	17 06.0	3 13.3
13 Su	9 29 20	21 09 21	24 25 38	2♍00 44	22 46.1	2 30.6	28 29.0	23 43.9	8 24.3	9 28.2	5 10.0	26 50.8	17 06.2	3 12.0
14 M	9 33 17	22 07 00	9♍33 53	17 03 59	22R 46.1	3 22.0	29 39.5	24 23.0	8 51.1	9 21.1	5 10.6	26 54.5	17 06.4	3 10.8
15 Tu	9 37 13	23 04 39	24 30 03	1♎51 14	22 46.2	4 19.9	0♎50.0	25 02.0	9 17.8	9 13.8	5 11.2	26 58.3	17 06.6	3 09.5
16 W	9 41 10	24 02 19	9♎06 51	16 16 23	22 46.1	5 24.1	2 00.5	25 40.9	9 44.5	9 06.5	5 11.9	27 02.0	17 06.7	3 08.2
17 Th	9 45 06	25 00 01	23 19 30	0♏16 00	22 45.9	6 34.4	3 10.9	26 19.8	10 11.2	8 59.1	5 12.7	27 05.8	17 06.8	3 07.0
18 F	9 49 03	25 57 43	7♏05 52	13 49 12	22D 45.7	7 50.6	4 21.2	26 58.7	10 37.9	8 51.6	5 13.6	27 09.5	17 06.9	3 05.7
19 Sa	9 52 59	26 55 27	20 26 12	26 57 12	22 45.6	9 12.3	5 31.4	27 37.5	11 04.6	8 44.1	5 14.6	27 13.3	17R 06.9	3 04.4
20 Su	9 56 56	27 53 12	3♐22 34	9♐42 43	22 45.8	10 39.2	6 41.6	28 16.3	11 31.3	8 36.5	5 15.7	27 17.0	17 06.9	3 03.1
21 M	10 00 53	28 50 58	15 58 08	22 09 18	22 46.1	12 10.9	7 51.7	28 55.0	11 58.0	8 28.8	5 16.9	27 20.8	17 06.9	3 01.8
22 Tu	10 04 49	29 48 45	28 16 43	4♑20 52	22 46.8	13 47.1	9 01.7	29 33.7	12 24.7	8 21.1	5 18.2	27 24.5	17 06.8	3 00.6
23 W	10 08 46	0♍46 33	10♑22 14	16 21 18	22 47.6	15 27.4	10 11.7	0♌12.4	12 51.3	8 13.3	5 19.6	27 28.2	17 06.7	2 59.3
24 Th	10 12 42	1 44 23	22 18 30	28 14 17	22 48.4	17 11.2	11 21.5	0 51.0	13 18.0	8 05.5	5 21.1	27 32.0	17 06.6	2 58.0
25 F	10 16 39	2 42 13	4♒09 01	10♒03 06	22 49.0	18 58.3	12 31.3	1 29.5	13 44.6	7 57.7	5 22.7	27 35.7	17 06.4	2 56.7
26 Sa	10 20 35	3 40 05	15 56 53	21 50 41	22R 49.3	20 48.0	13 41.0	2 08.0	14 11.2	7 49.9	5 24.4	27 39.5	17 06.2	2 55.4
27 Su	10 24 32	4 37 59	27 44 49	3♓39 34	22 49.1	22 40.0	14 50.7	2 46.5	14 37.8	7 42.0	5 26.2	27 43.2	17 06.0	2 54.1
28 M	10 28 28	5 35 54	9♓35 13	15 32 01	22 48.2	24 33.9	16 00.2	3 24.9	15 04.4	7 34.1	5 28.0	27 46.9	17 05.7	2 52.8
29 Tu	10 32 25	6 33 50	21 30 16	27 30 11	22 46.7	26 29.2	17 09.7	4 03.3	15 31.0	7 26.2	5 30.0	27 50.6	17 05.4	2 51.5
30 W	10 36 22	7 31 49	3♈32 02	9♈36 06	22 44.7	28 25.6	18 19.0	4 41.7	15 57.6	7 18.3	5 32.0	27 54.3	17 05.1	2 50.3
31 Th	10 40 18	8 29 49	15 42 39	21 51 57	22 42.4	0♍22.8	19 28.3	5 20.0	16 24.1	7 10.3	5 34.2	27 58.0	17 04.7	2 49.0

Astro Data	Dy Hr Mn
♃ R	1 0:38
☽ 0N	5 16:31
☿ R	13 5:39
☽ 0S	18 13:29
☽ 0N	1 22:31
☿ D	6 9:29
♄ D	8 15:02
☽ 0S	14 22:41
♀0S	15 23:21
♆ R	20 0:18
☽ 0N	29 4:26

Planet Ingress	Dy Hr Mn
♂ ♋	8 18:45
♀ ♍	20 12:14
☉ ♌	22 9:28
⚳ ♌	25 15:17
☿ ♋R	3 21:27
☿ ♌	8 19:53
♀ ♎	14 18:58
☉ ♍	22 16:40
♂ ♌	23 4:19
☿ ♍	31 7:21

Last Aspect Dy Hr Mn		☽ Ingress Dy Hr Mn
30 0:04	♆ △	♒ 1 3:17
3 8:44	♂ △	♓ 3 16:14
6 1:01	♂ □	♈ 6 4:42
8 14:15	♂ ⚹	♉ 8 14:29
10 11:21	♅ □	♊ 10 20:18
12 14:15	♅ ⚹	♋ 12 22:29
14 10:30	☉ ☌	♌ 14 22:34
16 14:59	♀ ☌	♍ 16 22:29
18 18:05	☉ ⚹	♎ 18 23:56
21 1:54	☉ □	♏ 21 4:08
23 3:05	♅ □	♐ 23 11:28
25 13:04	♅ △	♑ 25 21:32
27 7:18	♆ △	♒ 28 9:34
30 14:23	♅ ☍	♓ 30 22:32

Last Aspect Dy Hr Mn		☽ Ingress Dy Hr Mn
1 9:04	♆ ⚹	♈ 2 11:09
4 21:23	☿ □	♉ 4 21:47
7 4:32	☿ ⚹	♊ 7 5:04
9 2:55	♅ ⚹	♋ 9 8:38
11 2:24	♀ ⚹	♌ 11 9:20
13 3:47	♅ ☌	♍ 13 8:49
15 0:21	♂ ⚹	♎ 15 8:58
17 6:28	♅ ⚹	♏ 17 11:32
19 13:19	♂ △	♐ 19 17:40
22 2:15	☉ △	♑ 22 3:24
23 13:31	♆ △	♒ 24 15:34
26 23:53	♅ ☍	♓ 27 4:35
28 15:08	♆ ⚹	♈ 29 16:59

☽ Phases & Eclipses Dy Hr Mn	
7 11:32	☾ 15♈46
14 10:30	● 22♋24
21 1:54	☽ 28♎45
28 22:12	○ 6♒14
5 23:58	☾ 13♉58
12 17:40	● 20♌25
12 17:42:39	● T 06'06"
19 11:57	☽ 26♏55
27 14:09	○ 4♓43
27 13:55	● A 0.682

Astro Data

1 July 2045
Julian Day # 53143
SVP 4♓37'17"
GC 27♐28.5 ⚴ 24♉33.1
Eris 0♉21.0 ⚵ 21♋42.7
⚷ 14♍59.3 ⚶ 17♊55.7
☽ Mean ☊ 25♒03.6

1 August 2045
Julian Day # 53174
SVP 4♓37'12"
GC 27♐28.6 ⚴ 8♊28.6
Eris 0♉24.2R ⚵ 7♌46.9
⚷ 18♍19.3 ⚶ 0♋44.7
☽ Mean ☊ 23♒25.1

LONGITUDE — September 2045

Day	Sid.Time	☉	0 hr ☽	Noon☽	True☊	☿	♀	♂	⚳	♃	♄	♅	♆	♇
1 F	10 44 15	9♍27 51	28♈04 18	4♉20 01	22♒40.1	2♍20.3	20♎37.5	5♌58.2	16♌50.6	7♓02.4	5♐36.4	28♌01.7	17♉04.3	2♓47.7
2 Sa	10 48 11	10 25 54	10♉39 23	17 02 45	22R38.2	4 17.9	21 46.6	6 36.4	17 17.2	6R54.5	5 38.7	28 05.4	17R03.9	2R46.4
3 Su	10 52 08	11 24 00	23 30 25	0♊02 42	22D37.0	6 15.5	22 55.6	7 14.6	17 43.7	6 46.7	5 41.2	28 09.1	17 03.4	2 45.1
4 M	10 56 04	12 22 08	6♊39 53	13 22 14	22 36.6	8 12.8	24 04.6	7 52.7	18 10.1	6 38.8	5 43.7	28 12.8	17 03.0	2 43.9
5 Tu	11 00 01	13 20 17	20 09 57	27 03 12	22 37.1	10 09.5	25 13.4	8 30.8	18 36.6	6 31.0	5 46.3	28 16.4	17 02.4	2 42.6
6 W	11 03 57	14 18 29	4♋02 03	11♋06 29	22 38.2	12 05.7	26 22.2	9 08.9	19 03.0	6 23.2	5 49.0	28 20.1	17 01.9	2 41.4
7 Th	11 07 54	15 16 43	18 16 21	25 31 23	22 39.6	14 01.1	27 30.8	9 46.9	19 29.5	6 15.5	5 51.7	28 23.7	17 01.3	2 40.1
8 F	11 11 51	16 14 59	2♌51 11	10♌15 11	22R40.7	15 55.6	28 39.4	10 24.9	19 55.9	6 07.8	5 54.6	28 27.3	17 00.7	2 38.9
9 Sa	11 15 47	17 13 16	17 42 39	25 12 45	22 41.1	17 49.3	29 47.8	11 02.8	20 22.2	6 00.1	5 57.6	28 31.0	17 00.1	2 37.6
10 Su	11 19 44	18 11 36	2♍44 30	10♍16 50	22 40.2	19 41.9	0♏56.2	11 40.7	20 48.6	5 52.5	6 00.6	28 34.6	16 59.4	2 36.4
11 M	11 23 40	19 09 57	17 48 38	25 18 46	22 38.1	21 33.6	2 04.4	12 18.5	21 14.9	5 45.0	6 03.7	28 38.1	16 58.7	2 35.1
12 Tu	11 27 37	20 08 20	2♎46 06	10♎09 38	22 34.8	23 24.1	3 12.6	12 56.3	21 41.2	5 37.6	6 07.0	28 41.7	16 58.0	2 33.9
13 W	11 31 33	21 06 45	17 28 24	24 41 39	22 30.8	25 13.7	4 20.6	13 34.0	22 07.5	5 30.2	6 10.3	28 45.2	16 57.2	2 32.7
14 Th	11 35 30	22 05 12	1♏48 45	8♏49 17	22 26.5	27 02.1	5 28.5	14 11.7	22 33.7	5 22.9	6 13.6	28 48.8	16 56.4	2 31.5
15 F	11 39 26	23 03 40	15 42 58	22 29 43	22 22.8	28 49.5	6 36.3	14 49.3	22 59.9	5 15.7	6 17.1	28 52.3	16 55.6	2 30.3
16 Sa	11 43 23	24 02 10	29 09 36	5♐42 50	22 20.0	0♎35.8	7 44.0	15 26.9	23 26.1	5 08.6	6 20.7	28 55.8	16 54.7	2 29.1
17 Su	11 47 20	25 00 41	12♐09 44	18 30 44	22D18.6	2 21.0	8 51.6	16 04.5	23 52.2	5 01.6	6 24.3	28 59.2	16 53.9	2 27.9
18 M	11 51 16	25 59 14	24 46 20	0♑57 03	22 18.5	4 05.1	9 59.0	16 42.0	24 18.3	4 54.7	6 28.0	29 02.7	16 53.0	2 26.8
19 Tu	11 55 13	26 57 49	7♑03 32	13 06 21	22 19.6	5 48.2	11 06.3	17 19.5	24 44.4	4 47.9	6 31.8	29 06.1	16 52.0	2 25.6
20 W	11 59 09	27 56 25	19 06 08	25 03 30	22 21.2	7 30.3	12 13.4	17 56.9	25 10.4	4 41.2	6 35.7	29 09.5	16 51.1	2 24.5
21 Th	12 03 06	28 55 03	0♒59 03	6♒53 22	22 22.9	9 11.3	13 20.4	18 34.2	25 36.4	4 34.7	6 39.7	29 12.9	16 50.1	2 23.4
22 F	12 07 02	29 53 43	12 47 01	18 40 29	22R23.9	10 51.4	14 27.3	19 11.6	26 02.4	4 28.2	6 43.7	29 16.3	16 49.1	2 22.2
23 Sa	12 10 59	0♎52 25	24 34 17	0♓28 50	22 23.6	12 30.4	15 34.0	19 48.8	26 28.3	4 21.9	6 47.8	29 19.6	16 48.0	2 21.1
24 Su	12 14 55	1 51 08	6♓24 33	12 21 46	22 21.5	14 08.5	16 40.5	20 26.0	26 54.2	4 15.7	6 52.0	29 22.9	16 47.0	2 20.0
25 M	12 18 52	2 49 53	18 20 48	24 21 56	22 17.6	15 45.7	17 46.9	21 03.2	27 20.1	4 09.7	6 56.3	29 26.2	16 45.9	2 18.9
26 Tu	12 22 49	3 48 40	0♈25 21	6♈31 17	22 11.9	17 21.9	18 53.1	21 40.3	27 45.9	4 03.8	7 00.6	29 29.5	16 44.7	2 17.9
27 W	12 26 45	4 47 29	12 39 50	18 51 10	22 04.7	18 57.1	19 59.2	22 17.4	28 11.6	3 58.0	7 05.0	29 32.7	16 43.6	2 16.8
28 Th	12 30 42	5 46 21	25 05 21	1♉22 29	21 56.8	20 31.5	21 05.0	22 54.5	28 37.4	3 52.4	7 09.5	29 35.9	16 42.4	2 15.8
29 F	12 34 38	6 45 14	7♉42 37	14 05 49	21 49.0	22 05.0	22 10.8	23 31.5	29 03.0	3 46.9	7 14.0	29 39.1	16 41.3	2 14.8
30 Sa	12 38 35	7 44 09	20 32 09	27 01 42	21 42.0	23 37.6	23 16.3	24 08.4	29 28.7	3 41.6	7 18.7	29 42.3	16 40.0	2 13.8

LONGITUDE — October 2045

Day	Sid.Time	☉	0 hr ☽	Noon☽	True☊	☿	♀	♂	⚳	♃	♄	♅	♆	♇
1 Su	12 42 31	8♎43 07	3♊34 32	10♊10 44	21♒36.7	25♎09.3	24♏21.6	24♌45.3	29♌54.3	3♓36.4	7♐23.4	29♌45.4	16♉38.8	2♓12.8
2 M	12 46 28	9 42 07	16 50 26	23 33 43	21R33.4	26 40.2	25 26.8	25 22.2	0♍19.8	3R31.4	7 28.1	29 48.5	16R37.6	2R11.8
3 Tu	12 50 24	10 41 10	0♋20 41	7♋11 29	21D32.1	28 10.2	26 31.8	25 59.0	0 45.3	3 26.6	7 33.0	29 51.6	16 36.3	2 10.8
4 W	12 54 21	11 40 15	14 06 09	21 04 46	21 32.3	29 39.3	27 36.5	26 35.8	1 10.8	3 21.9	7 37.9	29 54.6	16 35.0	2 09.8
5 Th	12 58 18	12 39 22	28 07 20	5♌13 45	21 33.3	1♏07.6	28 41.1	27 12.5	1 36.2	3 17.4	7 42.9	29 57.6	16 33.7	2 09.0
6 F	13 02 14	13 38 31	12♌23 54	19 37 30	21R34.0	2 35.0	29 45.5	27 49.1	2 01.5	3 13.1	7 47.9	0♍00.6	16 32.3	2 08.1
7 Sa	13 06 11	14 37 43	26 54 12	4♍13 30	21 33.4	4 01.5	0♐49.6	28 25.8	2 26.8	3 09.0	7 53.0	0 03.5	16 31.0	2 07.2
8 Su	13 10 07	15 36 57	11♍34 45	18 57 15	21 30.6	5 27.1	1 53.5	29 02.3	2 52.0	3 05.0	7 58.2	0 06.4	16 29.6	2 06.3
9 M	13 14 04	16 36 13	26 20 09	3♎42 32	21 25.4	6 51.8	2 57.2	29 38.8	3 17.2	3 01.2	8 03.4	0 09.3	16 28.2	2 05.4
10 Tu	13 18 00	17 35 31	11♎03 25	18 21 51	21 17.9	8 15.5	4 00.7	0♍15.3	3 42.3	2 57.6	8 08.7	0 12.1	16 26.7	2 04.6
11 W	13 21 57	18 34 51	25 36 53	2♏47 41	21 08.8	9 38.3	5 03.9	0 51.7	4 07.4	2 54.2	8 14.1	0 14.9	16 25.3	2 03.8
12 Th	13 25 53	19 34 13	9♏53 27	16 53 37	20 59.1	11 00.0	6 06.9	1 28.0	4 32.4	2 51.0	8 19.5	0 17.7	16 23.8	2 03.0
13 F	13 29 50	20 33 38	23 47 40	0♐35 21	20 49.9	12 20.7	7 09.6	2 04.3	4 57.3	2 47.9	8 25.0	0 20.4	16 22.4	2 02.2
14 Sa	13 33 46	21 33 04	7♐16 30	13 51 09	20 42.3	13 40.2	8 12.0	2 40.6	5 22.2	2 45.1	8 30.5	0 23.1	16 20.9	2 01.4
15 Su	13 37 43	22 32 32	20 19 29	26 41 47	20 36.8	14 58.6	9 14.1	3 16.8	5 47.0	2 42.4	8 36.1	0 25.8	16 19.4	2 00.7
16 M	13 41 40	23 32 01	2♑58 28	9♑10 03	20 33.6	16 15.7	10 15.9	3 52.9	6 11.7	2 40.0	8 41.8	0 28.4	16 17.9	2 00.0
17 Tu	13 45 36	24 31 33	15 17 05	21 20 11	20D32.4	17 31.5	11 17.5	4 29.0	6 36.4	2 37.7	8 47.5	0 31.0	16 16.3	1 59.3
18 W	13 49 33	25 31 06	27 20 02	3♒17 18	20 32.6	18 45.8	12 18.7	5 05.0	7 01.0	2 35.7	8 53.2	0 33.5	16 14.8	1 58.6
19 Th	13 53 29	26 30 40	9♒12 41	15 06 51	20R33.2	19 58.5	13 19.6	5 40.9	7 25.5	2 33.8	8 59.0	0 36.0	16 13.2	1 58.0
20 F	13 57 26	27 30 17	21 00 29	26 54 13	20 33.1	21 09.6	14 20.1	6 16.8	7 49.9	2 32.2	9 04.9	0 38.4	16 11.7	1 57.3
21 Sa	14 01 22	28 29 55	2♓48 42	8♓44 28	20 31.4	22 18.9	15 20.2	6 52.7	8 14.3	2 30.7	9 10.8	0 40.8	16 10.1	1 56.7
22 Su	14 05 19	29 29 35	14 42 03	20 41 57	20 27.3	23 26.1	16 20.0	7 28.5	8 38.6	2 29.5	9 16.8	0 43.2	16 08.5	1 56.1
23 M	14 09 15	0♏29 17	26 44 33	2♈50 13	20 20.6	24 31.1	17 19.4	8 04.2	9 02.8	2 28.4	9 22.8	0 45.5	16 06.9	1 55.6
24 Tu	14 13 12	1 29 01	8♈59 12	15 11 44	20 11.2	25 33.7	18 18.4	8 39.8	9 26.9	2 27.6	9 28.9	0 47.8	16 05.2	1 55.0
25 W	14 17 09	2 28 46	21 27 55	27 47 50	19 59.7	26 33.7	19 17.0	9 15.4	9 50.9	2 26.9	9 35.0	0 50.0	16 03.6	1 54.5
26 Th	14 21 05	3 28 34	4♉11 28	10♉38 43	19 47.1	27 30.7	20 15.2	9 51.0	10 14.9	2 26.5	9 41.1	0 52.2	16 02.0	1 54.0
27 F	14 25 02	4 28 23	17 09 30	23 43 37	19 34.4	28 24.4	21 12.9	10 26.5	10 38.8	2D26.2	9 47.3	0 54.4	16 00.3	1 53.6
28 Sa	14 28 58	5 28 15	0♊20 53	7♊01 06	19 23.0	29 14.5	22 10.2	11 01.9	11 02.6	2 26.2	9 53.6	0 56.5	15 58.7	1 53.1
29 Su	14 32 55	6 28 09	13 44 01	20 29 29	19 13.8	0♐00.5	23 06.9	11 37.3	11 26.3	2 26.4	9 59.9	0 58.5	15 57.0	1 52.7
30 M	14 36 51	7 28 05	27 17 17	4♋07 16	19 07.4	0 42.1	24 03.2	12 12.6	11 49.9	2 26.7	10 06.2	1 00.6	15 55.4	1 52.3
31 Tu	14 40 48	8 28 03	10♋59 20	17 53 23	19 03.8	1 18.7	24 59.0	12 47.9	12 13.4	2 27.3	10 12.6	1 02.5	15 53.7	1 51.9

Astro Data (Dy Hr Mn)

♃□♄ 9 17:46
☽0S 11 9:28
☿0S 17 11:34
☉0S 22 14:34
☽0N 25 10:47

☽0S 8 19:42
☽0N 22 17:45
♃ D 28 4:37

Planet Ingress (Dy Hr Mn)

♀ ♏ 9 16:16
☿ ♎ 16 3:54
☉ ♎ 22 14:34

⚳ ♍ 1 17:23
☿ ♏ 4 17:36
♅ ♍ 6 7:12
♀ ♐ 6 17:26
♂ ♍ 10 1:56
☉ ♏ 23 0:14
☿ ♐ 29 11:43

Last Aspect (Dy Hr Mn) — **☽ Ingress** (Dy Hr Mn)

31 23:51 ♅ △ — ♉ 1 3:42
3 8:31 ♅ □ — ♊ 3 11:55
5 14:07 ♅ ⚹ — ♋ 5 17:05
7 15:33 ♀ □ — ♌ 7 19:21
9 17:17 ♅ ☌ — ♍ 9 19:38
11 5:09 ☿ ☌ — ♎ 11 19:32
13 18:51 ♅ ⚹ — ♏ 13 20:56
16 1:10 ☿ ⚹ — ♐ 16 1:32
18 8:16 ♅ △ — ♑ 18 10:09
20 18:21 ☉ △ — ♒ 20 22:00
23 9:39 ♅ ☍ — ♓ 23 11:02
24 21:32 ♀ △ — ♈ 25 23:10
28 8:36 ♅ △ — ♉ 28 9:23
30 16:56 ♅ □ — ♊ 30 17:28

Last Aspect (Dy Hr Mn) — **☽ Ingress** (Dy Hr Mn)

2 23:06 ♅ ⚹ — ♋ 2 23:24
5 0:03 ♀ △ — ♌ 5 3:11
7 2:06 ♂ ☌ — ♍ 7 5:05
8 8:00 ♆ △ — ♎ 9 5:58
10 10:38 ☉ ☌ — ♏ 11 7:19
12 11:09 ♆ ☍ — ♐ 13 10:57
15 3:30 ☉ ⚹ — ♑ 15 18:18
17 18:57 ☉ □ — ♒ 18 5:22
20 13:20 ☉ △ — ♓ 20 18:18
22 17:59 ☿ △ — ♈ 23 6:26
24 18:29 ♀ △ — ♉ 25 16:09
27 21:04 ☿ ☍ — ♊ 27 23:22
29 16:59 ♀ ☍ — ♋ 30 4:46

☽ Phases & Eclipses (Dy Hr Mn)

4 10:05 ☾ 12♊17
11 1:29 ● 18♍44
18 1:31 ☽ 25♐34
26 6:13 ○ 3♈34

3 18:33 ☾ 10♋57
10 10:38 ● 17♎32
17 18:57 ☽ 24♑49
25 21:32 ○ 2♉53

Astro Data

1 September 2045
Julian Day # 53205
SVP 4♓37'08"
GC 27♐28.6 ⚴ 22♊06.4
Eris 0♉17.4R ⚵ 23♌00.3
⚷ 22♍28.4 ⚶ 12♋37.0
☽ Mean ☊ 21♒46.6

1 October 2045
Julian Day # 53235
SVP 4♓37'05"
GC 27♐28.7 ⚴ 4♋00.5
Eris 0♉03.2R ⚵ 6♍42.5
⚷ 26♍46.5 ⚶ 22♋31.2
☽ Mean ☊ 20♒11.3

November 2045 LONGITUDE

Day	Sid.Time	☉	0 hr ☽	Noon ☽	True ☊	☿	♀	♂	⚳	♃	♄	♅	♆	♇
1 W	14 44 44	9♏28 03	24♋49 22	1♌47 15	19♒02.5	1♐49.7	25♐54.2	13♍23.0	12♍36.8	2♓28.1	10♐19.0	1♍04.4	15♉52.0	1♓51.6
2 Th	14 48 41	10 28 06	8♌47 00	15 48 37	19R 02.4	2 14.7	26 48.9	13 58.2	13 00.2	2 29.0	10 25.4	1 06.3	15R 50.4	1R 51.3
3 F	14 52 38	11 28 10	22 52 01	29 57 08	19 02.2	2 32.9	27 43.1	14 33.2	13 23.4	2 30.2	10 31.9	1 08.1	15 48.7	1 51.0
4 Sa	14 56 34	12 28 17	7♍03 48	14♍11 49	19 00.5	2R 43.8	28 36.6	15 08.2	13 46.5	2 31.6	10 38.4	1 09.9	15 47.0	1 50.7
5 Su	15 00 31	13 28 25	21 20 52	28 30 35	18 56.3	2 46.7	29 29.5	15 43.1	14 09.5	2 33.2	10 45.0	1 11.6	15 45.3	1 50.4
6 M	15 04 27	14 28 36	5♎40 29	12♎50 00	18 49.2	2 40.8	0♑21.8	16 18.0	14 32.4	2 34.9	10 51.6	1 13.3	15 43.6	1 50.2
7 Tu	15 08 24	15 28 49	19 58 30	27 05 19	18 39.2	2 25.8	1 13.4	16 52.8	14 55.2	2 36.9	10 58.2	1 14.9	15 41.9	1 50.0
8 W	15 12 20	16 29 03	4♏09 45	11♏11 07	18 27.1	2 01.1	2 04.3	17 27.5	15 17.9	2 39.1	11 04.9	1 16.5	15 40.2	1 49.8
9 Th	15 16 17	17 29 20	18 08 45	25 02 06	18 14.1	1 26.6	2 54.5	18 02.1	15 40.5	2 41.5	11 11.6	1 18.0	15 38.5	1 49.7
10 F	15 20 13	18 29 38	1♐50 40	8♐34 03	18 01.6	0 42.1	3 44.0	18 36.7	16 03.0	2 44.1	11 18.3	1 19.5	15 36.8	1 49.5
11 Sa	15 24 10	19 29 58	15 12 01	21 44 27	17 50.7	29♏48.1	4 32.6	19 11.1	16 25.3	2 46.9	11 25.1	1 20.9	15 35.2	1 49.4
12 Su	15 28 07	20 30 19	28 11 21	4♑32 50	17 42.2	28 45.3	5 20.5	19 45.6	16 47.5	2 49.8	11 31.8	1 22.2	15 33.5	1 49.4
13 M	15 32 03	21 30 42	10♑49 11	17 00 44	17 36.6	27 35.0	6 07.5	20 19.9	17 09.6	2 53.0	11 38.7	1 23.6	15 31.8	1 49.3
14 Tu	15 36 00	22 31 06	23 07 56	29 11 18	17 33.6	26 19.0	6 53.5	20 54.1	17 31.6	2 56.4	11 45.5	1 24.8	15 30.1	1D 49.3
15 W	15 39 56	23 31 32	5♒11 26	11♒08 57	17D 32.6	24 59.3	7 38.7	21 28.3	17 53.4	2 59.9	11 52.4	1 26.0	15 28.4	1 49.3
16 Th	15 43 53	24 31 59	17 04 32	22 58 52	17R 32.6	23 38.5	8 22.9	22 02.4	18 15.1	3 03.7	11 59.2	1 27.2	15 26.8	1 49.4
17 F	15 47 49	25 32 27	28 52 40	4♓46 37	17 32.3	22 19.3	9 06.0	22 36.4	18 36.7	3 07.6	12 06.1	1 28.3	15 25.1	1 49.4
18 Sa	15 51 46	26 32 57	10♓41 26	16 37 46	17 30.8	21 04.2	9 48.1	23 10.3	18 58.1	3 11.8	12 13.1	1 29.3	15 23.5	1 49.5
19 Su	15 55 42	27 33 28	22 36 17	28 37 35	17 27.0	19 55.7	10 29.1	23 44.1	19 19.4	3 16.1	12 20.0	1 30.3	15 21.8	1 49.6
20 M	15 59 39	28 34 00	4♈42 12	10♈50 38	17 20.7	18 55.7	11 08.9	24 17.9	19 40.5	3 20.6	12 27.0	1 31.2	15 20.2	1 49.7
21 Tu	16 03 36	29 34 33	17 03 16	23 20 27	17 11.6	18 05.8	11 47.6	24 51.5	20 01.5	3 25.3	12 33.9	1 32.1	15 18.5	1 49.9
22 W	16 07 32	0♐35 08	29 42 25	6♉09 15	17 00.3	17 27.1	12 24.9	25 25.1	20 22.4	3 30.1	12 40.9	1 32.9	15 16.9	1 50.1
23 Th	16 11 29	1 35 44	12♉41 00	19 17 35	16 47.8	17 00.0	13 01.0	25 58.6	20 43.1	3 35.2	12 47.9	1 33.7	15 15.3	1 50.3
24 F	16 15 25	2 36 21	25 58 47	2♊44 19	16 35.1	16D 44.5	13 35.7	26 32.0	21 03.6	3 40.4	12 55.0	1 34.4	15 13.7	1 50.5
25 Sa	16 19 22	3 37 00	9♊33 49	16 26 50	16 23.6	16 40.4	14 09.0	27 05.3	21 24.0	3 45.8	13 02.0	1 35.0	15 12.1	1 50.8
26 Su	16 23 18	4 37 41	23 22 54	0♋21 28	16 14.3	16 47.0	14 40.8	27 38.6	21 44.3	3 51.4	13 09.1	1 35.6	15 10.5	1 51.1
27 M	16 27 15	5 38 22	7♋22 04	14 24 11	16 07.9	17 03.8	15 11.1	28 11.7	22 04.4	3 57.2	13 16.1	1 36.2	15 09.0	1 51.4
28 Tu	16 31 12	6 39 06	21 27 23	28 31 15	16 04.3	17 29.7	15 39.8	28 44.7	22 24.3	4 03.1	13 23.2	1 36.7	15 07.4	1 51.8
29 W	16 35 08	7 39 51	5♌35 27	12♌39 41	16D 03.1	18 03.9	16 06.9	29 17.7	22 44.0	4 09.2	13 30.3	1 37.1	15 05.9	1 52.2
30 Th	16 39 05	8 40 37	19 43 46	26 47 30	16R 03.3	18 45.6	16 32.3	29 50.5	23 03.6	4 15.5	13 37.4	1 37.5	15 04.4	1 52.5

December 2045 LONGITUDE

Day	Sid.Time	☉	0 hr ☽	Noon ☽	True ☊	☿	♀	♂	⚳	♃	♄	♅	♆	♇
1 F	16 43 01	9♐41 25	3♍50 45	10♍53 27	16♒03.6	19♏33.9	16♑55.9	0♎23.3	23♍23.0	4♓21.9	13♐44.5	1♍37.8	15♉02.9	1♓53.0
2 Sa	16 46 58	10 42 14	17 55 28	24 56 43	16R 02.7	20 27.9	17 17.7	0 55.9	23 42.2	4 28.5	13 51.6	1 38.1	15R 01.4	1 53.4
3 Su	16 50 54	11 43 05	1♎57 06	8♎56 27	15 59.7	21 27.1	17 37.6	1 28.5	24 01.2	4 35.3	13 58.7	1 38.3	14 59.9	1 53.9
4 M	16 54 51	12 43 57	15 54 36	22 51 18	15 54.0	22 30.6	17 55.6	2 00.9	24 20.1	4 42.2	14 05.8	1 38.4	14 58.4	1 54.4
5 Tu	16 58 47	13 44 50	29 46 19	6♏39 19	15 45.9	23 38.0	18 11.5	2 33.2	24 38.7	4 49.3	14 12.9	1 38.5	14 57.0	1 54.9
6 W	17 02 44	14 45 45	13♏29 59	20 17 58	15 35.8	24 48.7	18 25.4	3 05.4	24 57.2	4 56.6	14 20.0	1R 38.6	14 55.6	1 55.5
7 Th	17 06 41	15 46 41	27 02 55	3♐44 29	15 24.8	26 02.4	18 37.1	3 37.5	25 15.4	5 04.0	14 27.1	1 38.5	14 54.2	1 56.0
8 F	17 10 37	16 47 38	10♐22 23	16 56 22	15 14.1	27 18.4	18 46.6	4 09.5	25 33.5	5 11.6	14 34.2	1 38.5	14 52.8	1 56.6
9 Sa	17 14 34	17 48 36	23 26 13	29 51 49	15 04.7	28 36.6	18 53.9	4 41.4	25 51.3	5 19.3	14 41.3	1 38.3	14 51.4	1 57.3
10 Su	17 18 30	18 49 35	6♑13 09	12♑30 15	14 57.5	29 56.7	18 58.8	5 13.1	26 09.0	5 27.2	14 48.4	1 38.1	14 50.1	1 57.9
11 M	17 22 27	19 50 35	18 43 13	24 52 18	14 52.8	1♐18.4	19R 01.4	5 44.7	26 26.4	5 35.2	14 55.5	1 37.9	14 48.7	1 58.6
12 Tu	17 26 23	20 51 35	0♒57 47	7♒00 01	14D 50.5	2 41.4	19 01.5	6 16.2	26 43.6	5 43.4	15 02.6	1 37.6	14 47.4	1 59.3
13 W	17 30 20	21 52 36	12 59 27	18 56 35	14 50.2	4 05.6	18 59.2	6 47.6	27 00.6	5 51.7	15 09.7	1 37.2	14 46.2	2 00.0
14 Th	17 34 16	22 53 38	24 51 57	0♓46 09	14 51.2	5 30.8	18 54.4	7 18.8	27 17.3	6 00.2	15 16.8	1 36.8	14 44.9	2 00.8
15 F	17 38 13	23 54 40	6♓39 48	12 33 34	14 52.4	6 56.9	18 47.2	7 49.9	27 33.8	6 08.8	15 23.9	1 36.4	14 43.7	2 01.5
16 Sa	17 42 10	24 55 42	18 28 07	24 24 07	14R 53.1	8 23.8	18 37.4	8 20.9	27 50.1	6 17.6	15 30.9	1 35.8	14 42.5	2 02.3
17 Su	17 46 06	25 56 45	0♈22 16	6♈23 12	14 52.3	9 51.3	18 25.1	8 51.7	28 06.2	6 26.5	15 38.0	1 35.3	14 41.3	2 03.2
18 M	17 50 03	26 57 48	12 27 35	18 36 00	14 49.7	11 19.5	18 10.3	9 22.4	28 22.0	6 35.5	15 45.0	1 34.6	14 40.1	2 04.0
19 Tu	17 53 59	27 58 52	24 49 00	1♉07 04	14 45.1	12 48.2	17 53.0	9 53.0	28 37.5	6 44.7	15 52.0	1 33.9	14 39.0	2 04.9
20 W	17 57 56	28 59 56	7♉30 36	13 59 54	14 38.7	14 17.3	17 33.4	10 23.4	28 52.8	6 54.0	15 59.0	1 33.2	14 37.9	2 05.8
21 Th	18 01 52	0♑01 00	20 35 10	27 16 26	14 31.2	15 46.9	17 11.5	10 53.7	29 07.9	7 03.4	16 06.0	1 32.4	14 36.8	2 06.7
22 F	18 05 49	1 02 05	4♊03 39	10♊56 36	14 23.4	17 16.9	16 47.4	11 23.8	29 22.7	7 12.9	16 13.0	1 31.6	14 35.7	2 07.6
23 Sa	18 09 45	2 03 10	17 54 56	24 58 11	14 16.3	18 47.3	16 21.1	11 53.8	29 37.2	7 22.6	16 19.9	1 30.7	14 34.7	2 08.6
24 Su	18 13 42	3 04 16	2♋05 43	9♋16 53	14 10.6	20 17.9	15 52.9	12 23.6	29 51.5	7 32.5	16 26.8	1 29.7	14 33.7	2 09.5
25 M	18 17 39	4 05 22	16 30 54	23 46 59	14 06.9	21 49.0	15 22.9	12 53.3	0♎05.5	7 42.4	16 33.7	1 28.7	14 32.7	2 10.5
26 Tu	18 21 35	5 06 28	1♌04 19	8♌22 07	14D 05.3	23 20.3	14 51.3	13 22.8	0 19.2	7 52.5	16 40.6	1 27.7	14 31.8	2 11.6
27 W	18 25 32	6 07 35	15 39 40	22 56 16	14 05.4	24 51.9	14 18.3	13 52.2	0 32.6	8 02.6	16 47.5	1 26.6	14 30.9	2 12.6
28 Th	18 29 28	7 08 43	0♍11 21	7♍24 25	14 06.7	26 23.8	13 44.1	14 21.4	0 45.8	8 12.9	16 54.3	1 25.4	14 30.0	2 13.7
29 F	18 33 25	8 09 50	14 35 04	21 42 59	14 08.2	27 56.1	13 08.9	14 50.4	0 58.6	8 23.3	17 01.1	1 24.2	14 29.1	2 14.8
30 Sa	18 37 21	9 10 59	28 47 56	5♎49 47	14R 09.0	29 28.6	12 32.9	15 19.3	1 11.2	8 33.9	17 07.9	1 22.9	14 28.3	2 15.9
31 Su	18 41 18	10 12 08	12♎48 24	19 43 44	14 08.7	1♑01.4	11 56.5	15 47.9	1 23.4	8 44.5	17 14.7	1 21.6	14 27.5	2 17.0

Astro Data

	Dy Hr Mn
☽0S	5 3:27
☿R	5 8:08
♇D	14 17:35
☽0N	19 1:09
☿D	25 8:55
☽0S	2 8:34
♅R	6 16:04
♂0S	8 14:01
♄×♆	10 16:36
♀R	12 1:30
☽0N	16 8:31
☽0S	29 13:20

Planet Ingress

	Dy Hr Mn
♀ ♑	6 1:58
☿ ♏R	11 7:02
☉ ♐	21 22:05
♂ ♎	30 18:56
☿ ♐	10 12:59
☉ ♑	21 11:36
⚳ ♎	25 2:33
☿ ♑	30 20:08

Last Aspect / ☽ Ingress

Last Aspect Dy Hr Mn		☽ Ingress Dy Hr Mn
31 8:33	♆ ⚹	♌ 1 8:56
3 7:58	♀ △	♍ 3 12:05
5 13:45	♀ □	♎ 5 14:30
6 8:40	♄ ⚹	♏ 7 16:56
8 23:17	♂ ⚹	♐ 9 20:44
11 7:05	♂ □	♑ 12 3:24
14 6:51	♀ ⚹	♒ 14 13:37
16 15:27	☉ □	♓ 17 2:17
19 9:41	☉ △	♈ 19 14:43
20 15:09	♄ △	♉ 22 0:33
24 0:31	♂ △	♊ 24 7:09
26 7:09	♂ □	♋ 26 11:23
28 12:24	♂ ⚹	♌ 28 14:31
29 21:37	☿ □	♍ 30 17:27

Last Aspect Dy Hr Mn		☽ Ingress Dy Hr Mn
2 3:48	☿ ⚹	♎ 2 20:39
4 3:18	♀ □	♏ 5 0:24
6 20:48	☿ ☌	♐ 7 5:17
8 11:43	☉ ☌	♑ 9 12:15
11 0:33	♀ ☌	♒ 11 22:06
13 18:30	☉ ⚹	♓ 14 10:26
16 13:10	☉ □	♈ 16 23:15
19 5:31	☉ △	♉ 19 9:53
20 18:20	♀ △	♊ 21 16:50
23 0:14	☿ ☍	♋ 23 20:29
24 22:36	♀ ☍	♌ 25 22:14
27 15:34	☿ △	♍ 27 23:41
29 23:49	☿ □	♎ 30 2:03

☽ Phases & Eclipses

Dy Hr Mn		
2 2:11	☾	10♌04
8 21:50	●	16♏54
16 15:27	☽	24♒41
24 11:45	○	2♊36
1 9:48	☾	9♍36
8 11:43	●	16♐47
16 13:10	☽	24♓59
24 0:51	○	2♋36
30 18:13	☾	9♎27

Astro Data

1 November 2045
Julian Day # 53266
SVP 4♓37'00"
GC 27♐28.8 ⚴ 12♋39.8
Eris 29♈44.8R ⚵ 19♍25.0
⚷ 0♎58.8 ⚶ 29♋50.8
☽ Mean ☊ 18♒32.8

1 December 2045
Julian Day # 53296
SVP 4♓36'55"
GC 27♐28.8 ⚴ 13♋26.8R
Eris 29♈28.5R ⚵ 29♍39.3
⚷ 4♎16.1 ⚶ 2♌09.6R
☽ Mean ☊ 16♒57.5

LONGITUDE — January 2046

Day	Sid.Time	☉	0 hr ☽	Noon☽	True☊	☿	♀	♂	⚳	♃	♄	♅	♆	♇
1 M	18 45 14	11♑13 17	26♎35 45	3♏24 29	14♒06.8	2♑34.6	11♑19.9	16♎16.4	1♎35.4	8♓55.3	17♐21.4	1♍20.3	14♉26.7	2♓18.1
2 Tu	18 49 11	12 14 27	10♏09 54	16 52 01	14R 03.3	4 08.0	10R 43.3	16 44.8	1 47.0	9 06.1	17 28.1	1R 18.9	14R 26.0	2 19.3
3 W	18 53 08	13 15 37	23 30 52	0♐06 26	13 58.7	5 41.8	10 06.9	17 12.9	1 58.3	9 17.1	17 34.7	1 17.4	14 25.2	2 20.5
4 Th	18 57 04	14 16 47	6♐38 43	13 07 45	13 53.5	7 16.0	9 31.1	17 40.8	2 09.3	9 28.2	17 41.4	1 15.9	14 24.6	2 21.7
5 F	19 01 01	15 17 58	19 33 31	25 56 01	13 48.4	8 50.5	8 56.1	18 08.6	2 20.0	9 39.4	17 48.0	1 14.4	14 23.9	2 22.9
6 Sa	19 04 57	16 19 08	2♑15 18	8♑31 23	13 44.0	10 25.3	8 22.1	18 36.1	2 30.3	9 50.7	17 54.5	1 12.8	14 23.3	2 24.1
7 Su	19 08 54	17 20 19	14 44 21	20 54 16	13 40.7	12 00.5	7 49.3	19 03.4	2 40.3	10 02.0	18 01.1	1 11.2	14 22.7	2 25.4
8 M	19 12 50	18 21 29	27 01 18	3♒05 36	13D 38.9	13 36.2	7 18.0	19 30.5	2 49.9	10 13.5	18 07.6	1 09.5	14 22.2	2 26.7
9 Tu	19 16 47	19 22 39	9♒07 22	15 06 51	13 38.4	15 12.2	6 48.2	19 57.4	2 59.2	10 25.1	18 14.0	1 07.8	14 21.7	2 28.0
10 W	19 20 44	20 23 49	21 04 22	27 00 16	13 39.0	16 48.6	6 20.3	20 24.1	3 08.1	10 36.8	18 20.4	1 06.0	14 21.2	2 29.3
11 Th	19 24 40	21 24 58	2♓54 54	8♓48 44	13 40.5	18 25.5	5 54.2	20 50.5	3 16.7	10 48.6	18 26.8	1 04.2	14 20.7	2 30.6
12 F	19 28 37	22 26 07	14 42 14	20 35 54	13 42.3	20 02.8	5 30.3	21 16.8	3 24.9	11 00.4	18 33.1	1 02.4	14 20.3	2 32.0
13 Sa	19 32 33	23 27 15	26 30 17	2♈25 56	13 43.9	21 40.6	5 08.5	21 42.7	3 32.8	11 12.4	18 39.4	1 00.5	14 19.9	2 33.3
14 Su	19 36 30	24 28 22	8♈23 28	14 23 29	13R 45.1	23 18.9	4 49.0	22 08.5	3 40.2	11 24.4	18 45.6	0 58.6	14 19.6	2 34.7
15 M	19 40 26	25 29 29	20 26 35	26 33 24	13 45.4	24 57.6	4 31.9	22 34.0	3 47.3	11 36.6	18 51.8	0 56.6	14 19.3	2 36.1
16 Tu	19 44 23	26 30 36	2♉44 31	9♉00 29	13 44.9	26 36.9	4 17.1	22 59.3	3 54.0	11 48.8	18 57.9	0 54.6	14 19.0	2 37.5
17 W	19 48 19	27 31 41	15 21 51	21 49 04	13 43.6	28 16.7	4 04.9	23 24.3	4 00.4	12 01.1	19 04.0	0 52.6	14 18.7	2 38.9
18 Th	19 52 16	28 32 46	28 22 31	5♊02 30	13 41.8	29 56.9	3 55.1	23 49.0	4 06.3	12 13.5	19 10.1	0 50.5	14 18.5	2 40.3
19 F	19 56 13	29 33 50	11♊49 10	18 42 34	13 39.8	1♒37.7	3 47.7	24 13.5	4 11.8	12 25.9	19 16.1	0 48.4	14 18.4	2 41.8
20 Sa	20 00 09	0♒34 53	25 42 34	2♋48 55	13 38.0	3 19.1	3 42.9	24 37.8	4 17.0	12 38.5	19 22.0	0 46.3	14 18.2	2 43.2
21 Su	20 04 06	1 35 56	10♋01 10	17 18 42	13 36.6	5 00.9	3D 40.6	25 01.7	4 21.8	12 51.1	19 27.9	0 44.1	14 18.1	2 44.7
22 M	20 08 02	2 36 58	24 40 47	2♌06 32	13D 35.8	6 43.2	3 40.7	25 25.4	4 26.1	13 03.8	19 33.8	0 41.9	14 18.0	2 46.2
23 Tu	20 11 59	3 37 59	9♌34 58	17 05 01	13 35.6	8 26.0	3 43.2	25 48.8	4 30.0	13 16.5	19 39.6	0 39.7	14D 18.0	2 47.7
24 W	20 15 55	4 38 59	24 35 37	2♍05 41	13 36.0	10 09.3	3 48.1	26 11.9	4 33.6	13 29.3	19 45.3	0 37.4	14 18.0	2 49.2
25 Th	20 19 52	5 39 59	9♍34 13	17 00 16	13 36.6	11 53.1	3 55.4	26 34.7	4 36.7	13 42.2	19 51.0	0 35.2	14 18.0	2 50.7
26 F	20 23 48	6 40 58	24 22 59	1♎41 43	13 37.3	13 37.2	4 04.9	26 57.2	4 39.4	13 55.2	19 56.6	0 32.8	14 18.1	2 52.3
27 Sa	20 27 45	7 41 56	8♎55 51	16 05 01	13 37.8	15 21.6	4 16.7	27 19.4	4 41.6	14 08.2	20 02.1	0 30.5	14 18.2	2 53.8
28 Su	20 31 42	8 42 54	23 08 55	0♏07 23	13R 38.1	17 06.3	4 30.6	27 41.3	4 43.5	14 21.3	20 07.6	0 28.1	14 18.3	2 55.4
29 M	20 35 38	9 43 52	7♏00 25	13 48 03	13 38.2	18 51.2	4 46.7	28 02.9	4 44.9	14 34.5	20 13.1	0 25.7	14 18.5	2 56.9
30 Tu	20 39 35	10 44 49	20 30 25	27 07 45	13 38.0	20 36.2	5 04.8	28 24.1	4 45.8	14 47.7	20 18.5	0 23.3	14 18.7	2 58.5
31 W	20 43 31	11 45 45	3♐40 17	10♐08 17	13 37.8	22 21.1	5 24.8	28 45.0	4R 46.4	15 01.0	20 23.8	0 20.9	14 18.9	3 00.1

LONGITUDE — February 2046

Day	Sid.Time	☉	0 hr ☽	Noon☽	True☊	☿	♀	♂	⚳	♃	♄	♅	♆	♇
1 Th	20 47 28	12♒46 41	16♐32 05	22♐51 58	13♒37.7	24♒05.8	5♑46.8	29♎05.5	4♎46.5	15♓14.3	20♐29.0	0♍18.4	14♉19.2	3♓01.7
2 F	20 51 24	13 47 35	29 08 15	5♑21 14	13D 37.7	25 50.1	6 10.6	29 25.6	4R 46.1	15 27.8	20 34.2	0R 16.0	14 19.5	3 03.3
3 Sa	20 55 21	14 48 29	11♑31 13	17 38 28	13 37.7	27 33.8	6 36.1	29 45.4	4 45.3	15 41.2	20 39.3	0 13.5	14 19.9	3 04.9
4 Su	20 59 17	15 49 22	23 43 16	29 45 51	13 37.9	29 16.5	7 03.4	0♏04.9	4 44.1	15 54.7	20 44.4	0 11.0	14 20.3	3 06.5
5 M	21 03 14	16 50 14	5♒46 30	11♒45 26	13R 38.0	0♓58.1	7 32.3	0 23.9	4 42.4	16 08.3	20 49.4	0 08.4	14 20.7	3 08.2
6 Tu	21 07 11	17 51 04	17 42 53	23 39 07	13 37.9	2 38.1	8 02.8	0 42.5	4 40.3	16 21.9	20 54.3	0 05.9	14 21.1	3 09.8
7 W	21 11 07	18 51 54	29 34 22	5♓28 53	13 37.5	4 16.2	8 34.7	1 00.7	4 37.8	16 35.6	20 59.1	0 03.3	14 21.6	3 11.4
8 Th	21 15 04	19 52 42	11♓22 56	17 16 51	13 36.9	5 51.8	9 08.2	1 18.6	4 34.8	16 49.3	21 03.9	0 00.7	14 22.1	3 13.1
9 F	21 19 00	20 53 28	23 10 54	29 05 27	13 35.9	7 24.5	9 43.0	1 36.0	4 31.3	17 03.1	21 08.6	29♌58.2	14 22.7	3 14.7
10 Sa	21 22 57	21 54 13	5♈00 52	10♈57 33	13 34.7	8 53.8	10 19.1	1 52.9	4 27.4	17 16.9	21 13.2	29 55.6	14 23.2	3 16.4
11 Su	21 26 53	22 54 57	16 55 55	22 56 24	13 33.5	10 18.9	10 56.6	2 09.5	4 23.1	17 30.7	21 17.8	29 53.0	14 23.9	3 18.0
12 M	21 30 50	23 55 39	28 59 31	5♉05 44	13 32.5	11 39.2	11 35.3	2 25.5	4 18.4	17 44.6	21 22.3	29 50.3	14 24.5	3 19.7
13 Tu	21 34 46	24 56 20	11♉15 34	17 29 33	13D 31.9	12 54.1	12 15.1	2 41.2	4 13.2	17 58.6	21 26.7	29 47.7	14 25.2	3 21.4
14 W	21 38 43	25 56 59	23 48 10	0♊11 57	13 31.8	14 02.7	12 56.1	2 56.3	4 07.6	18 12.5	21 31.0	29 45.1	14 25.9	3 23.1
15 Th	21 42 40	26 57 36	6♊41 21	13 16 48	13 32.3	15 04.5	13 38.2	3 11.0	4 01.6	18 26.6	21 35.2	29 42.5	14 26.7	3 24.7
16 F	21 46 36	27 58 12	19 58 39	26 47 09	13 33.3	15 58.6	14 21.4	3 25.2	3 55.2	18 40.6	21 39.4	29 39.8	14 27.5	3 26.4
17 Sa	21 50 33	28 58 45	3♋42 30	10♋44 41	13 34.5	16 44.5	15 05.6	3 39.0	3 48.4	18 54.7	21 43.5	29 37.2	14 28.3	3 28.1
18 Su	21 54 29	29 59 18	17 53 37	25 08 58	13 35.6	17 21.4	15 50.7	3 52.2	3 41.1	19 08.8	21 47.5	29 34.6	14 29.1	3 29.8
19 M	21 58 26	0♓59 48	2♌30 16	9♌56 51	13R 36.2	17 49.0	16 36.8	4 04.9	3 33.5	19 23.0	21 51.4	29 32.0	14 30.0	3 31.5
20 Tu	22 02 22	2 00 17	17 27 53	25 02 21	13 36.0	18 06.7	17 23.8	4 17.1	3 25.5	19 37.1	21 55.2	29 29.3	14 30.9	3 33.1
21 W	22 06 19	3 00 43	2♍39 05	10♍16 52	13 34.7	18R 14.3	18 11.7	4 28.7	3 17.1	19 51.3	21 59.0	29 26.7	14 31.9	3 34.8
22 Th	22 10 15	4 01 09	17 54 24	25 30 24	13 32.5	18 11.8	19 00.3	4 39.8	3 08.3	20 05.6	22 02.7	29 24.1	14 32.9	3 36.5
23 F	22 14 12	5 01 33	3♎03 38	10♎33 00	13 29.7	17 59.2	19 49.9	4 50.4	2 59.2	20 19.8	22 06.3	29 21.4	14 33.9	3 38.2
24 Sa	22 18 09	6 01 55	17 57 29	25 16 19	13 26.6	17 37.0	20 40.1	5 00.4	2 49.7	20 34.1	22 09.8	29 18.8	14 34.9	3 39.9
25 Su	22 22 05	7 02 16	2♏28 53	9♏34 45	13 23.9	17 05.6	21 31.2	5 09.8	2 39.8	20 48.4	22 13.2	29 16.2	14 36.0	3 41.6
26 M	22 26 02	8 02 36	16 33 43	23 25 42	13 22.0	16 25.9	22 22.9	5 18.6	2 29.6	21 02.8	22 16.5	29 13.6	14 37.1	3 43.3
27 Tu	22 29 58	9 02 54	0♐10 50	6♐49 20	13D 21.2	15 38.9	23 15.3	5 26.8	2 19.1	21 17.1	22 19.8	29 11.0	14 38.2	3 44.9
28 W	22 33 55	10 03 11	13 21 33	19 47 53	13 21.6	14 45.9	24 08.4	5 34.4	2 08.3	21 31.5	22 22.9	29 08.5	14 39.4	3 46.6

Astro Data

	Dy Hr Mn
☽0N	12 15:35
♀D	21 22:59
♆D	24 3:38
☽0S	25 20:38
♃✶♆	28 6:27
⚳R	1 5:18
☽0N	8 22:15
☿R	21 18:03
☽0S	22 7:01

Planet Ingress

	Dy Hr Mn
☿ ♒	18 12:44
☉ ♒	19 22:17
♂ ♏	4 5:57
☿ ♓	4 22:14
♅ ♌R	8 18:54
☉ ♓	18 12:17

Last Aspect / ☽ Ingress (January)

Last Aspect Dy Hr Mn		☽ Ingress Dy Hr Mn
31 7:39 ♄ ✶	♏	1 5:59
2 7:38 ♆ ☍	♐	3 11:48
4 20:48 ♂ ✶	♑	5 19:42
7 8:15 ♂ □	♒	8 5:53
9 22:08 ♂ △	♓	10 18:05
12 16:05 ☉ ✶	♈	13 7:05
15 9:44 ☉ □	♉	15 18:42
18 1:32 ☿ △	♊	18 2:57
19 21:45 ♂ △	♋	20 7:16
22 0:55 ♂ □	♌	22 8:36
24 2:19 ♂ ✶	♍	24 8:39
25 16:39 ♄ □	♎	26 9:12
28 7:41 ♂ ☌	♏	28 11:47
29 22:23 ☿ □	♐	30 17:15

Last Aspect / ☽ Ingress (February)

Last Aspect Dy Hr Mn		☽ Ingress Dy Hr Mn
2 0:15 ♂ ✶	♑	2 1:40
3 8:05 ♃ ✶	♒	4 12:28
6 6:24 ♄ ✶	♓	7 0:52
8 19:45 ♄ □	♈	9 13:51
12 1:43 ♅ △	♉	12 1:59
14 11:10 ♅ □	♊	14 11:38
16 17:00 ♅ ✶	♋	16 17:36
18 1:55 ♃ △	♌	18 19:56
20 19:00 ♅ ☌	♍	20 19:50
22 6:30 ♅ □	♎	22 19:08
24 18:41 ♅ ✶	♏	24 19:51
26 22:16 ♅ □	♐	26 23:41

☽ Phases & Eclipses

Dy Hr Mn	
7 4:25	● 17♑01
15 9:44	☽ 25♈24
22 12:53	○ 2♌39
22 13:03	• P 0.053
29 4:13	☾ 9♏24
5 23:11	● 17♒19
5 23:06:27	• A 09'16"
14 3:22	☽ 25♉35
20 23:46	○ 2♍30
27 16:24	☾ 9♐14

Astro Data

1 January 2046
Julian Day # 53327
SVP 4♓36'50"
GC 27♐28.9 ⚴ 4♋50.4R
Eris 29♈18.5R ⚵ 6♋55.2
⚷ 6♎16.9 ⚶ 27♋53.2R
☽ Mean ☊ 15♒19.0

1 February 2046
Julian Day # 53358
SVP 4♓36'44"
GC 27♐29.0 ⚴ 28♊31.2R
Eris 29♈18.7 ⚵ 9♋03.6R
⚷ 6♎28.2R ⚶ 20♋04.7R
☽ Mean ☊ 13♒40.6

March 2046 — LONGITUDE

Day	Sid.Time	☉	0 hr ☽	Noon ☽	True ☊	☿	♀	♂	⚳	♃	♄	♅	♆	♇
1 Th	22 37 51	11♓03 27	26♐08 48	2♑24 50	13♒22.8	13♓48.2	25♑02.1	5♏41.4	1♎57.2	21♓45.9	22♐26.0	29♌05.9	14♉40.6	3♓48.3
2 F	22 41 48	12 03 41	8♑36 30	14 44 20	13 24.6	12R 47.3	25 56.5	5 47.7	1R 45.7	22 00.3	22 29.0	29R 03.3	14 41.8	3 50.0
3 Sa	22 45 44	13 03 53	20 48 52	26 50 36	13 26.3	11 44.7	26 51.4	5 53.4	1 34.0	22 14.8	22 31.9	29 00.8	14 43.1	3 51.6
4 Su	22 49 41	14 04 04	2♒50 00	8♒47 32	13R 27.3	10 42.0	27 46.8	5 58.4	1 22.1	22 29.2	22 34.7	28 58.3	14 44.4	3 53.3
5 M	22 53 38	15 04 13	14 43 38	20 38 40	13 27.2	9 40.6	28 42.8	6 02.7	1 09.8	22 43.7	22 37.4	28 55.8	14 45.7	3 55.0
6 Tu	22 57 34	16 04 20	26 32 59	2♓26 56	13 25.4	8 41.7	29 39.3	6 06.3	0 57.4	22 58.1	22 40.0	28 53.3	14 47.0	3 56.6
7 W	23 01 31	17 04 26	8♓20 47	14 14 49	13 21.9	7 46.6	0♒36.3	6 09.3	0 44.7	23 12.6	22 42.5	28 50.8	14 48.4	3 58.3
8 Th	23 05 27	18 04 30	20 09 16	26 04 23	13 16.8	6 56.1	1 33.8	6 11.5	0 31.9	23 27.1	22 44.9	28 48.3	14 49.8	3 59.9
9 F	23 09 24	19 04 31	2♈00 22	7♈57 26	13 10.4	6 11.1	2 31.8	6 13.0	0 18.8	23 41.6	22 47.2	28 45.9	14 51.2	4 01.6
10 Sa	23 13 20	20 04 31	13 55 50	19 55 46	13 03.4	5 31.9	3 30.1	6R 13.8	0 05.6	23 56.1	22 49.5	28 43.5	14 52.6	4 03.2
11 Su	23 17 17	21 04 29	25 57 30	2♉01 16	12 56.4	4 59.1	4 28.9	6 13.9	29♍52.3	24 10.7	22 51.6	28 41.1	14 54.1	4 04.8
12 M	23 21 13	22 04 25	8♉07 22	14 16 07	12 50.1	4 32.8	5 28.1	6 13.2	29 38.8	24 25.2	22 53.6	28 38.8	14 55.6	4 06.4
13 Tu	23 25 10	23 04 18	20 27 50	26 42 54	12 45.3	4 13.1	6 27.7	6 11.8	29 25.2	24 39.7	22 55.6	28 36.4	14 57.1	4 08.1
14 W	23 29 07	24 04 10	3♊01 40	9♊24 33	12 42.3	3 59.9	7 27.7	6 09.6	29 11.5	24 54.2	22 57.4	28 34.1	14 58.7	4 09.7
15 Th	23 33 03	25 03 59	15 51 56	22 24 15	12D 41.2	3D 53.1	8 28.0	6 06.7	28 57.7	25 08.8	22 59.2	28 31.8	15 00.3	4 11.3
16 F	23 37 00	26 03 46	29 01 52	5♋45 08	12 41.5	3 52.5	9 28.7	6 03.1	28 43.9	25 23.3	23 00.8	28 29.6	15 01.9	4 12.9
17 Sa	23 40 56	27 03 31	12♋34 21	19 29 44	12 42.7	3 57.9	10 29.8	5 58.6	28 30.1	25 37.8	23 02.4	28 27.4	15 03.5	4 14.4
18 Su	23 44 53	28 03 13	26 31 24	3♌39 21	12R 43.9	4 09.0	11 31.1	5 53.4	28 16.2	25 52.3	23 03.9	28 25.2	15 05.2	4 16.0
19 M	23 48 49	29 02 53	10♌53 26	18 13 17	12 44.0	4 25.6	12 32.8	5 47.5	28 02.4	26 06.8	23 05.2	28 23.0	15 06.8	4 17.6
20 Tu	23 52 46	0♈02 31	25 38 25	3♍08 05	12 42.4	4 47.3	13 34.8	5 40.8	27 48.5	26 21.4	23 06.5	28 20.9	15 08.5	4 19.1
21 W	23 56 42	1 02 07	10♍41 24	18 17 16	12 38.6	5 13.9	14 37.1	5 33.3	27 34.7	26 35.8	23 07.6	28 18.8	15 10.2	4 20.7
22 Th	0 00 39	2 01 41	25 54 29	3♎31 45	12 32.7	5 45.0	15 39.7	5 25.0	27 21.0	26 50.3	23 08.7	28 16.7	15 12.0	4 22.2
23 F	0 04 36	3 01 12	11♎07 41	18 41 00	12 25.2	6 20.5	16 42.6	5 16.0	27 07.3	27 04.8	23 09.6	28 14.7	15 13.7	4 23.7
24 Sa	0 08 32	4 00 42	26 10 27	3♏34 54	12 17.1	7 00.0	17 45.8	5 06.2	26 53.7	27 19.3	23 10.5	28 12.7	15 15.5	4 25.2
25 Su	0 12 29	5 00 10	10♏53 27	18 05 22	12 09.4	7 43.3	18 49.2	4 55.7	26 40.2	27 33.8	23 11.3	28 10.7	15 17.3	4 26.7
26 M	0 16 25	5 59 36	25 10 09	2♐07 30	12 03.1	8 30.2	19 52.9	4 44.4	26 26.8	27 48.2	23 11.9	28 08.8	15 19.2	4 28.2
27 Tu	0 20 22	6 59 00	8♐57 20	15 39 46	11 58.7	9 20.6	20 56.8	4 32.3	26 13.6	28 02.6	23 12.5	28 06.9	15 21.0	4 29.7
28 W	0 24 18	7 58 23	22 15 03	28 43 33	11D 56.5	10 14.1	22 01.0	4 19.5	26 00.6	28 17.1	23 13.0	28 05.1	15 22.9	4 31.1
29 Th	0 28 15	8 57 44	5♑05 47	11♑22 19	11 56.1	11 10.6	23 05.4	4 06.0	25 47.7	28 31.5	23 13.3	28 03.3	15 24.8	4 32.6
30 F	0 32 11	9 57 03	17 33 44	23 40 42	11 56.7	12 10.0	24 10.1	3 51.8	25 35.0	28 45.9	23 13.6	28 01.5	15 26.7	4 34.0
31 Sa	0 36 08	10 56 20	29 43 53	5♒43 55	11R 57.5	13 12.0	25 14.9	3 36.8	25 22.5	29 00.2	23 13.8	27 59.8	15 28.6	4 35.4

April 2046 — LONGITUDE

Day	Sid.Time	☉	0 hr ☽	Noon ☽	True ☊	☿	♀	♂	⚳	♃	♄	♅	♆	♇
1 Su	0 40 05	11♈55 36	11♒41 26	17♒37 04	11♒57.5	14♓16.7	26♒20.0	3♏21.2	25♍10.2	29♓14.6	23♐13.8	27♌58.1	15♉30.5	4♓36.8
2 M	0 44 01	12 54 49	23 31 23	29 24 55	11R 55.8	15 23.7	27 25.2	3R 04.9	24R 58.1	29 28.9	23R 13.8	27R 56.5	15 32.5	4 38.2
3 Tu	0 47 58	13 54 01	5♓18 11	11♓11 36	11 51.7	16 33.1	28 30.7	2 47.9	24 46.3	29 43.2	23 13.6	27 54.9	15 34.4	4 39.6
4 W	0 51 54	14 53 11	17 05 35	23 00 29	11 44.9	17 44.8	29 36.3	2 30.3	24 34.8	29 57.5	23 13.4	27 53.3	15 36.4	4 41.0
5 Th	0 55 51	15 52 18	28 56 37	4♈54 13	11 35.6	18 58.5	0♓42.2	2 12.2	24 23.6	0♈11.8	23 13.1	27 51.8	15 38.4	4 42.3
6 F	0 59 47	16 51 24	10♈53 31	16 54 40	11 24.3	20 14.4	1 48.1	1 53.4	24 12.6	0 26.0	23 12.6	27 50.3	15 40.4	4 43.6
7 Sa	1 03 44	17 50 28	22 57 51	29 03 11	11 11.9	21 32.2	2 54.3	1 34.1	24 01.9	0 40.2	23 12.1	27 48.9	15 42.5	4 44.9
8 Su	1 07 40	18 49 30	5♉10 45	11♉20 41	10 59.4	22 51.9	4 00.6	1 14.4	23 51.6	0 54.4	23 11.4	27 47.5	15 44.5	4 46.2
9 M	1 11 37	19 48 30	17 33 03	23 48 00	10 48.0	24 13.5	5 07.1	0 54.1	23 41.6	1 08.5	23 10.7	27 46.2	15 46.6	4 47.5
10 Tu	1 15 33	20 47 27	0♊05 37	6♊26 05	10 38.7	25 36.9	6 13.8	0 33.4	23 31.9	1 22.6	23 09.9	27 44.9	15 48.7	4 48.8
11 W	1 19 30	21 46 23	12 49 34	19 16 15	10 31.9	27 02.2	7 20.5	0 12.3	23 22.6	1 36.7	23 09.0	27 43.7	15 50.8	4 50.0
12 Th	1 23 27	22 45 16	25 46 23	2♋20 12	10 27.9	28 29.1	8 27.5	29♎50.9	23 13.6	1 50.8	23 07.9	27 42.5	15 52.9	4 51.3
13 F	1 27 23	23 44 07	8♋57 59	15 39 59	10D 26.3	29 57.8	9 34.5	29 29.2	23 05.0	2 04.8	23 06.8	27 41.4	15 55.0	4 52.5
14 Sa	1 31 20	24 42 55	22 26 29	29 17 41	10R 26.1	1♈28.1	10 41.7	29 07.2	22 56.8	2 18.7	23 05.6	27 40.3	15 57.1	4 53.7
15 Su	1 35 16	25 41 41	6♌13 47	13♌14 54	10 26.3	3 00.2	11 49.0	28 44.9	22 49.0	2 32.7	23 04.3	27 39.3	15 59.2	4 54.8
16 M	1 39 13	26 40 25	20 21 03	27 32 06	10 25.4	4 33.9	12 56.5	28 22.5	22 41.5	2 46.6	23 02.9	27 38.3	16 01.4	4 56.0
17 Tu	1 43 09	27 39 07	4♍47 50	12♍07 49	10 22.5	6 09.2	14 04.1	27 59.9	22 34.4	3 00.4	23 01.4	27 37.3	16 03.5	4 57.1
18 W	1 47 06	28 37 46	19 31 28	26 58 03	10 16.9	7 46.2	15 11.8	27 37.2	22 27.7	3 14.2	22 59.8	27 36.5	16 05.7	4 58.2
19 Th	1 51 02	29 36 24	4♎26 38	11♎56 11	10 08.6	9 24.9	16 19.6	27 14.5	22 21.5	3 28.0	22 58.1	27 35.6	16 07.9	4 59.3
20 F	1 54 59	0♉34 59	19 25 34	26 53 35	9 58.2	11 05.1	17 27.5	26 51.7	22 15.6	3 41.7	22 56.3	27 34.8	16 10.1	5 00.4
21 Sa	1 58 56	1 33 32	4♏19 03	11♏40 52	9 46.9	12 47.1	18 35.6	26 29.0	22 10.1	3 55.4	22 54.5	27 34.1	16 12.3	5 01.5
22 Su	2 02 52	2 32 04	18 58 01	26 09 36	9 35.8	14 30.7	19 43.7	26 06.3	22 05.0	4 09.0	22 52.5	27 33.4	16 14.5	5 02.5
23 M	2 06 49	3 30 34	3♐14 59	10♐13 39	9 26.3	16 16.0	20 52.0	25 43.8	22 00.4	4 22.6	22 50.5	27 32.8	16 16.7	5 03.5
24 Tu	2 10 45	4 29 02	17 05 18	23 49 52	9 19.1	18 02.9	22 00.4	25 21.4	21 56.1	4 36.2	22 48.4	27 32.2	16 18.9	5 04.5
25 W	2 14 42	5 27 28	0♑27 25	6♑58 12	9 14.4	19 51.5	23 08.9	24 59.2	21 52.3	4 49.7	22 46.2	27 31.7	16 21.1	5 05.5
26 Th	2 18 38	6 25 53	13 22 33	19 40 59	9 12.1	21 41.8	24 17.5	24 37.3	21 48.9	5 03.1	22 43.9	27 31.2	16 23.3	5 06.5
27 F	2 22 35	7 24 17	25 54 03	2♒02 22	9 11.5	23 33.8	25 26.2	24 15.6	21 45.9	5 16.5	22 41.5	27 30.8	16 25.6	5 07.4
28 Sa	2 26 31	8 22 38	8♒06 35	14 07 23	9 11.4	25 27.5	26 34.9	23 54.3	21 43.3	5 29.8	22 39.0	27 30.4	16 27.8	5 08.3
29 Su	2 30 28	9 20 58	20 05 29	26 01 33	9 10.9	27 22.9	27 43.8	23 33.3	21 41.2	5 43.1	22 36.5	27 30.1	16 30.1	5 09.2
30 M	2 34 25	10 19 17	1♓56 14	7♓50 13	9 08.7	29 20.0	28 52.8	23 12.7	21 39.4	5 56.3	22 33.9	27 29.9	16 32.3	5 10.1

Astro Data	Dy Hr Mn
♃□♄	4 23:11
☽0N	8 4:34
♂R	11 2:12
☿D	16 2:13
☉0N	20 10:59
☽0S	21 18:27
♃⚻♅	27 18:19
♄R	1 14:47
☽0N	4 10:40
♃∠♆	7 16:30
♃0N	15 4:44
☿0N	17 8:15
☽0S	18 4:20
♃⊻♇	26 18:28

Planet Ingress	Dy Hr Mn
♀ ♒	6 20:43
⚳ ♍R	10 22:07
☉ ♈	20 10:59
♃ ♈	4 16:12
♀ ♓	4 20:38
♂ ♎R	12 1:52
☿ ♈	13 12:36
☉ ♉	19 21:40
☿ ♉	30 20:08

Last Aspect Dy Hr Mn		☽ Ingress	Dy Hr Mn
1 5:39	♅ △	♑	1 7:22
3 12:02	♀ ☌	♒	3 18:19
6 4:47	♅ ☍	♓	6 7:01
8 6:35	♃ ☌	♈	8 19:57
11 5:26	♅ △	♉	11 8:00
13 15:36	♅ □	♊	13 18:16
15 23:04	♅ ⚹	♋	16 1:44
18 1:53	☉ △	♌	18 5:52
20 4:22	♅ ☌	♍	20 7:00
22 1:18	♃ ☍	♎	22 6:26
24 3:18	♅ ⚹	♏	24 6:11
26 5:08	♅ □	♐	26 8:19
28 11:10	♃ □	♑	28 14:23
30 22:17	♃ ⚹	♒	31 0:32

Last Aspect Dy Hr Mn		☽ Ingress	Dy Hr Mn
2 9:00	♅ ☍	♓	2 13:11
4 12:26	♄ □	♈	5 2:08
7 9:34	♅ △	♉	7 13:52
9 19:34	♅ □	♊	9 23:49
12 7:35	♂ △	♋	12 7:44
14 11:42	♂ □	♌	14 13:14
16 13:21	♂ ⚹	♍	16 16:05
18 5:37	♄ □	♎	18 16:52
20 13:06	♅ ⚹	♏	20 17:01
22 14:21	♅ □	♐	22 18:29
24 18:41	♅ △	♑	24 23:10
26 21:47	♀ ⚹	♒	27 8:00
29 15:17	☿ ⚹	♓	29 20:04

☽ Phases & Eclipses Dy Hr Mn	
7 18:17	● 17♓20
15 17:14	☽ 25♊17
22 9:28	○ 1♎55
29 6:59	☾ 8♑45
6 11:53	● 16♈51
14 3:23	☽ 24♋22
20 18:22	○ 0♏51
27 23:32	☾ 7♒52

Astro Data

1 March 2046
Julian Day # 53386
SVP 4♓36'40"
GC 27♐29.0 ⚴ 1♋39.0
Eris 29♈27.7 ⚵ 5♎34.6R
⚷ 5♎08.2R ⚶ 16♋36.1R
☽ Mean ☊ 12♒11.6

1 April 2046
Julian Day # 53417
SVP 4♓36'37"
GC 27♐29.1 ⚴ 11♋33.9
Eris 29♈44.9 ⚵ 28♍17.9R
⚷ 2♎46.2R ⚶ 19♋22.2
☽ Mean ☊ 10♒33.1

LONGITUDE — May 2046

Day	Sid.Time	☉	0 hr ☽	Noon ☽	True ☊	☿	♀	♂	⚳	♃	♄	♅	♆	♇
1 Tu	2 38 21	11♉17 34	13♓44 05	19♓38 23	9♒04.2	1♉18.7	0♈01.8	22♎52.6	21♍38.1	6♈09.5	22♐31.2	27♌29.7	16♉34.5	5♓10.9
2 W	2 42 18	12 15 49	25 33 40	1♈30 22	8R57.0	3 19.0	1 11.0	22R33.0	21R37.2	6 22.6	22R28.4	27R29.5	16 36.8	5 11.7
3 Th	2 46 14	13 14 03	7♈28 54	13 29 38	8 47.1	5 21.0	2 20.2	22 13.8	21D36.7	6 35.6	22 25.5	27 29.4	16 39.0	5 12.5
4 F	2 50 11	14 12 15	19 32 49	25 38 42	8 35.0	7 24.4	3 29.5	21 55.2	21 36.6	6 48.6	22 22.6	27D29.4	16 41.3	5 13.3
5 Sa	2 54 07	15 10 26	1♉47 27	7♉59 10	8 21.7	9 29.3	4 38.8	21 37.2	21 36.9	7 01.6	22 19.6	27 29.4	16 43.6	5 14.1
6 Su	2 58 04	16 08 35	14 13 54	20 31 41	8 08.3	11 35.5	5 48.3	21 19.9	21 37.7	7 14.4	22 16.5	27 29.4	16 45.8	5 14.8
7 M	3 02 00	17 06 42	26 52 29	3♊16 17	7 55.9	13 43.0	6 57.8	21 03.1	21 38.9	7 27.2	22 13.3	27 29.6	16 48.1	5 15.5
8 Tu	3 05 57	18 04 48	9♊43 00	16 12 36	7 45.7	15 51.5	8 07.4	20 47.0	21 40.4	7 39.9	22 10.1	27 29.7	16 50.3	5 16.2
9 W	3 09 54	19 02 51	22 45 01	29 20 13	7 38.3	18 00.9	9 17.0	20 31.7	21 42.4	7 52.6	22 06.8	27 30.0	16 52.6	5 16.9
10 Th	3 13 50	20 00 53	5♋58 12	12♋39 00	7 33.7	20 11.0	10 26.7	20 17.0	21 44.8	8 05.2	22 03.5	27 30.2	16 54.9	5 17.5
11 F	3 17 47	20 58 54	19 22 37	26 09 08	7D31.7	22 21.5	11 36.5	20 03.1	21 47.6	8 17.7	22 00.0	27 30.6	16 57.1	5 18.1
12 Sa	3 21 43	21 56 52	2♌58 39	9♌51 13	7R31.4	24 32.3	12 46.3	19 49.9	21 50.7	8 30.1	21 56.5	27 31.0	16 59.4	5 18.7
13 Su	3 25 40	22 54 48	16 46 55	23 45 50	7 31.5	26 43.0	13 56.2	19 37.4	21 54.3	8 42.5	21 53.0	27 31.4	17 01.6	5 19.3
14 M	3 29 36	23 52 43	0♍47 55	7♍53 10	7 30.9	28 53.3	15 06.1	19 25.8	21 58.2	8 54.8	21 49.4	27 31.9	17 03.9	5 19.8
15 Tu	3 33 33	24 50 36	15 01 23	22 12 22	7 28.4	1♊03.1	16 16.1	19 14.9	22 02.6	9 07.0	21 45.7	27 32.5	17 06.1	5 20.4
16 W	3 37 29	25 48 26	29 25 45	6♎41 04	7 23.5	3 11.9	17 26.1	19 04.8	22 07.3	9 19.1	21 42.0	27 33.1	17 08.3	5 20.9
17 Th	3 41 26	26 46 16	13♎57 43	21 15 01	7 16.1	5 19.6	18 36.3	18 55.5	22 12.4	9 31.1	21 38.2	27 33.7	17 10.6	5 21.3
18 F	3 45 23	27 44 03	28 32 11	5♏48 22	7 06.7	7 25.8	19 46.4	18 47.1	22 17.8	9 43.1	21 34.4	27 34.4	17 12.8	5 21.8
19 Sa	3 49 19	28 41 49	13♏02 43	20 14 20	6 56.3	9 30.4	20 56.6	18 39.4	22 23.6	9 55.0	21 30.6	27 35.2	17 15.0	5 22.2
20 Su	3 53 16	29 39 34	27 22 26	4♐26 16	6 46.2	11 33.0	22 06.9	18 32.5	22 29.8	10 06.8	21 26.6	27 36.0	17 17.3	5 22.6
21 M	3 57 12	0♊37 17	11♐25 12	18 18 43	6 37.3	13 33.5	23 17.2	18 26.4	22 36.3	10 18.5	21 22.7	27 36.9	17 19.5	5 23.0
22 Tu	4 01 09	1 35 00	25 06 30	1♑48 18	6 30.4	15 31.6	24 27.6	18 21.2	22 43.2	10 30.2	21 18.7	27 37.8	17 21.7	5 23.3
23 W	4 05 05	2 32 41	8♑24 06	14 53 57	6 26.0	17 27.4	25 38.1	18 16.7	22 50.4	10 41.7	21 14.6	27 38.8	17 23.9	5 23.7
24 Th	4 09 02	3 30 20	21 18 04	27 36 46	6D24.0	19 20.6	26 48.6	18 13.0	22 57.9	10 53.2	21 10.5	27 39.8	17 26.1	5 24.0
25 F	4 12 58	4 27 59	3♒50 29	9♒59 41	6 23.7	21 11.1	27 59.1	18 10.2	23 05.8	11 04.5	21 06.4	27 40.9	17 28.3	5 24.3
26 Sa	4 16 55	5 25 37	16 04 58	22 06 53	6 24.3	22 58.8	29 09.7	18 08.1	23 14.0	11 15.8	21 02.2	27 42.0	17 30.4	5 24.5
27 Su	4 20 52	6 23 14	28 06 07	4♓03 17	6R24.9	24 43.7	0♉20.4	18 06.8	23 22.6	11 27.0	20 58.0	27 43.2	17 32.6	5 24.7
28 M	4 24 48	7 20 49	9♓59 05	15 54 09	6 24.5	26 25.7	1 31.0	18D06.3	23 31.5	11 38.1	20 53.8	27 44.4	17 34.7	5 24.9
29 Tu	4 28 45	8 18 24	21 49 09	27 44 42	6 22.4	28 04.7	2 41.8	18 06.5	23 40.6	11 49.1	20 49.6	27 45.7	17 36.9	5 25.1
30 W	4 32 41	9 15 58	3♈41 24	9♈39 48	6 18.2	29 40.8	3 52.6	18 07.6	23 50.1	11 59.9	20 45.3	27 47.0	17 39.0	5 25.3
31 Th	4 36 38	10 13 31	15 40 26	21 43 45	6 11.8	1♋13.9	5 03.4	18 09.4	23 59.9	12 10.7	20 40.9	27 48.4	17 41.2	5 25.4

LONGITUDE — June 2046

Day	Sid.Time	☉	0 hr ☽	Noon ☽	True ☊	☿	♀	♂	⚳	♃	♄	♅	♆	♇
1 F	4 40 34	11♊11 03	27♈50 09	3♉59 57	6♒03.6	2♋43.9	6♉14.3	18♎12.0	24♍10.1	12♈21.4	20♐36.6	27♌49.8	17♉43.3	5♓25.5
2 Sa	4 44 31	12 08 35	10♉13 25	16 30 45	5R54.4	4 10.9	7 25.2	18 15.3	24 20.5	12 32.0	20R32.3	27 51.3	17 45.4	5 25.6
3 Su	4 48 27	13 06 05	22 52 03	29 17 22	5 44.9	5 34.8	8 36.2	18 19.4	24 31.2	12 42.5	20 27.9	27 52.8	17 47.5	5 25.6
4 M	4 52 24	14 03 35	5♊46 38	12♊19 48	5 36.3	6 55.5	9 47.2	18 24.2	24 42.2	12 52.9	20 23.5	27 54.4	17 49.5	5R25.7
5 Tu	4 56 21	15 01 04	18 56 41	25 37 05	5 29.2	8 13.0	10 58.2	18 29.8	24 53.5	13 03.1	20 19.1	27 56.0	17 51.6	5 25.7
6 W	5 00 17	15 58 31	2♋20 46	9♋07 30	5 24.2	9 27.3	12 09.3	18 36.1	25 05.1	13 13.3	20 14.7	27 57.7	17 53.7	5 25.7
7 Th	5 04 14	16 55 58	15 57 01	22 49 04	5D21.5	10 38.3	13 20.4	18 43.1	25 17.0	13 23.3	20 10.2	27 59.4	17 55.7	5 25.6
8 F	5 08 10	17 53 24	29 43 23	6♌39 44	5 20.8	11 45.9	14 31.5	18 50.8	25 29.1	13 33.2	20 05.8	28 01.2	17 57.7	5 25.6
9 Sa	5 12 07	18 50 48	13♌37 56	20 37 48	5 21.5	12 50.2	15 42.7	18 59.1	25 41.5	13 43.0	20 01.4	28 03.0	17 59.7	5 25.5
10 Su	5 16 03	19 48 11	27 39 08	4♍41 48	5 22.7	13 50.9	16 53.9	19 08.2	25 54.2	13 52.7	19 56.9	28 04.9	18 01.7	5 25.3
11 M	5 20 00	20 45 33	11♍45 38	18 50 27	5R23.4	14 48.1	18 05.2	19 17.9	26 07.1	14 02.3	19 52.5	28 06.8	18 03.7	5 25.2
12 Tu	5 23 57	21 42 54	25 56 04	3♎02 17	5 22.8	15 41.7	19 16.5	19 28.3	26 20.3	14 11.7	19 48.0	28 08.7	18 05.6	5 25.0
13 W	5 27 53	22 40 14	10♎08 49	17 15 23	5 20.6	16 31.5	20 27.8	19 39.3	26 33.7	14 21.1	19 43.6	28 10.7	18 07.6	5 24.8
14 Th	5 31 50	23 37 33	24 21 37	1♏27 07	5 16.6	17 17.5	21 39.2	19 51.0	26 47.4	14 30.3	19 39.2	28 12.8	18 09.5	5 24.6
15 F	5 35 46	24 34 52	8♏31 28	15 34 11	5 11.2	17 59.6	22 50.5	20 03.2	27 01.3	14 39.4	19 34.8	28 14.9	18 11.4	5 24.4
16 Sa	5 39 43	25 32 09	22 34 47	29 32 46	5 05.1	18 37.6	24 02.0	20 16.1	27 15.5	14 48.3	19 30.3	28 17.0	18 13.3	5 24.1
17 Su	5 43 39	26 29 26	6♐27 41	13♐19 04	4 59.0	19 11.6	25 13.4	20 29.6	27 29.9	14 57.2	19 26.0	28 19.2	18 15.2	5 23.8
18 M	5 47 36	27 26 42	20 06 34	26 49 51	4 53.8	19 41.3	26 24.9	20 43.6	27 44.5	15 05.9	19 21.6	28 21.4	18 17.0	5 23.5
19 Tu	5 51 32	28 23 57	3♑28 40	10♑02 51	4 49.9	20 06.7	27 36.5	20 58.2	27 59.4	15 14.4	19 17.2	28 23.7	18 18.9	5 23.2
20 W	5 55 29	29 21 12	16 32 20	22 57 09	4D47.6	20 27.7	28 48.1	21 13.4	28 14.4	15 22.9	19 12.9	28 26.0	18 20.7	5 22.9
21 Th	5 59 26	0♋18 27	29 17 24	5♒33 16	4 47.0	20 44.2	29 59.7	21 29.1	28 29.7	15 31.2	19 08.6	28 28.3	18 22.5	5 22.5
22 F	6 03 22	1 15 41	11♒45 03	17 53 05	4 47.6	20 56.2	1♊11.3	21 45.3	28 45.2	15 39.4	19 04.3	28 30.7	18 24.3	5 22.1
23 Sa	6 07 19	2 12 55	23 57 45	29 59 33	4 49.1	21 03.6	2 23.0	22 02.1	29 00.9	15 47.4	19 00.0	28 33.1	18 26.0	5 21.6
24 Su	6 11 15	3 10 09	5♓58 59	11♓56 35	4 50.8	21R06.5	3 34.8	22 19.4	29 16.8	15 55.3	18 55.7	28 35.6	18 27.7	5 21.2
25 M	6 15 12	4 07 23	17 52 56	23 48 37	4R52.2	21 04.8	4 46.5	22 37.2	29 32.9	16 03.0	18 51.5	28 38.1	18 29.5	5 20.7
26 Tu	6 19 08	5 04 36	29 44 16	5♈40 29	4 52.7	20 58.6	5 58.3	22 55.5	29 49.3	16 10.7	18 47.3	28 40.6	18 31.1	5 20.2
27 W	6 23 05	6 01 50	11♈37 53	17 37 03	4 52.0	20 47.9	7 10.2	23 14.3	0♎05.8	16 18.1	18 43.2	28 43.2	18 32.8	5 19.7
28 Th	6 27 01	6 59 04	23 38 34	29 42 59	4 50.1	20 33.1	8 22.1	23 33.5	0 22.5	16 25.4	18 39.1	28 45.8	18 34.5	5 19.2
29 F	6 30 58	7 56 17	5♉50 48	12♉02 28	4 47.2	20 14.1	9 34.0	23 53.3	0 39.4	16 32.6	18 35.0	28 48.5	18 36.1	5 18.6
30 Sa	6 34 55	8 53 31	18 18 24	24 38 53	4 43.6	19 51.4	10 46.0	24 13.5	0 56.5	16 39.6	18 31.0	28 51.2	18 37.7	5 18.0

Astro Data	Planet Ingress	Last Aspect	☽ Ingress	Last Aspect	☽ Ingress	☽ Phases & Eclipses	Astro Data
Dy Hr Mn	Dy Hr Mn	Dy Hr Mn	Dy Hr Mn	Dy Hr Mn	Dy Hr Mn	Dy Hr Mn	1 May 2046
☽0N 1 16:53	♀ ♈ 1 11:22	1 17:49 ♄ □	♈ 2 8:58	31 23:58 ♅ △	♉ 1 4:14	6 2:57 ● 15♉47	Julian Day # 53447
⚳D 4 4:28	☿ ♊ 15 0:19	4 15:37 ♅ △	♉ 4 20:31	3 9:22 ♅ □	♊ 3 13:19	13 10:26 ☽ 22♌51	SVP 4♓36'33"
♀0N 4 12:54	☉ ♊ 20 20:30	7 1:10 ♅ □	♊ 7 5:52	5 16:09 ♅ ⚹	♋ 5 19:50	20 3:17 ○ 29♏19	GC 27♐29.2 ⚴ 24♋07.3
♅D 4 19:53	♀ ♉ 27 5:05	9 8:40 ♅ ⚹	♋ 9 13:12	7 4:47 ♂ □	♌ 8 0:29	27 17:08 ☾ 6♓36	Eris 0♉04.6 ⚵ 23♍42.7R
☽0S 15 11:20	☿ ♋ 30 16:53	11 4:00 ☿ ⚹	♌ 11 18:47	10 0:42 ♅ ☌	♍ 10 4:00		⚷ 0♎48.7R ⚶ 26♋59.5
♂D 28 15:33		13 18:26 ♅ ☌	♍ 13 22:39	11 15:29 ☉ □	♎ 12 6:52	4 15:24 ● 14♊12	☽ Mean ☊ 8♒57.8
☽0N 28 23:33	☉ ♋ 21 4:16	15 16:42 ☉ △	♎ 16 0:57	14 6:30 ♅ ⚹	♏ 14 9:32	11 15:29 ☽ 20♍54	
	♀ ♊ 21 12:06	17 22:24 ♅ ⚹	♏ 18 2:25	16 9:49 ♅ □	♐ 16 12:47	18 13:11 ○ 27♐30	1 June 2046
♃⚼♅ 4 16:16	⚳ ♎ 27 3:38	20 3:17 ☉ ☍	♐ 20 4:27	18 14:45 ♅ △	♑ 18 17:42	26 10:41 ☾ 5♈01	Julian Day # 53478
♇R 5 7:27		22 4:29 ♅ △	♑ 22 8:45	21 0:14 ♀ △	♒ 21 1:21		SVP 4♓36'29"
☽0S 11 16:18		24 10:18 ♀ □	♒ 24 16:35	23 9:07 ♅ ☍	♓ 23 12:01		GC 27♐29.3 ⚴ 8♌17.4
☿R 24 14:59		27 3:41 ♀ ⚹	♓ 27 3:49	25 6:30 ♅ △	♈ 26 0:32		Eris 0♉23.2 ⚵ 24♍25.2
☽0N 25 6:46		29 12:47 ☿ □	♈ 29 16:33	28 10:07 ♅ △	♉ 28 12:33		⚷ 0♎11.0 ⚶ 7♌58.3
♄⚻♆ 29 7:27				30 19:54 ♅ □	♊ 30 22:01		☽ Mean ☊ 7♒19.3

July 2046 LONGITUDE

Day	Sid.Time	☉	0 hr ☽	Noon ☽	True ☊	☿	♀	♂	⚳	♃	♄	♅	♆	♇
1 Su	6 38 51	9♋50 45	1♊04 12	7♊34 31	4♒39.7	19♋25.1	11♊57.9	24♎34.2	1♎13.7	16♈46.5	18♐27.0	28♌53.9	18♉39.3	5♓17.4
2 M	6 42 48	10 47 59	14 09 52	20 50 15	4R36.1	18R55.7	13 10.0	24 55.3	1 31.2	16 53.2	18R23.0	28 56.7	18 40.8	5R16.8
3 Tu	6 46 44	11 45 12	27 35 32	4♋25 30	4 33.3	18 23.7	14 22.0	25 16.9	1 48.8	16 59.8	18 19.1	28 59.5	18 42.4	5 16.2
4 W	6 50 41	12 42 26	11♋19 51	18 18 11	4 31.5	17 49.5	15 34.1	25 38.9	2 06.6	17 06.2	18 15.3	29 02.3	18 43.9	5 15.5
5 Th	6 54 37	13 39 40	25 20 04	2♌25 00	4D30.8	17 13.6	16 46.3	26 01.3	2 24.6	17 12.4	18 11.5	29 05.2	18 45.3	5 14.8
6 F	6 58 34	14 36 54	9♌32 26	16 41 48	4 31.2	16 36.7	17 58.4	26 24.2	2 42.8	17 18.5	18 07.8	29 08.1	18 46.8	5 14.1
7 Sa	7 02 30	15 34 07	23 52 33	1♍04 08	4 32.1	15 59.3	19 10.6	26 47.5	3 01.1	17 24.4	18 04.1	29 11.0	18 48.2	5 13.4
8 Su	7 06 27	16 31 20	8♍16 02	15 27 44	4 33.4	15 22.2	20 22.9	27 11.1	3 19.6	17 30.2	18 00.4	29 14.0	18 49.6	5 12.6
9 M	7 10 24	17 28 33	22 38 48	29 48 49	4 34.4	14 45.8	21 35.1	27 35.2	3 38.2	17 35.8	17 56.8	29 17.0	18 51.0	5 11.9
10 Tu	7 14 20	18 25 46	6♎57 26	14♎04 18	4R35.0	14 11.0	22 47.4	27 59.7	3 57.0	17 41.2	17 53.3	29 20.0	18 52.3	5 11.1
11 W	7 18 17	19 22 58	21 09 09	28 11 44	4 34.9	13 38.2	23 59.7	28 24.5	4 16.0	17 46.5	17 49.9	29 23.0	18 53.7	5 10.3
12 Th	7 22 13	20 20 11	5♏11 49	12♏09 14	4 34.1	13 08.1	25 12.1	28 49.7	4 35.1	17 51.6	17 46.5	29 26.1	18 55.0	5 09.5
13 F	7 26 10	21 17 24	19 03 48	25 55 22	4 32.8	12 41.3	26 24.5	29 15.3	4 54.3	17 56.5	17 43.1	29 29.3	18 56.2	5 08.6
14 Sa	7 30 06	22 14 36	2♐43 48	9♐28 58	4 31.2	12 18.2	27 36.9	29 41.2	5 13.7	18 01.2	17 39.9	29 32.4	18 57.5	5 07.8
15 Su	7 34 03	23 11 49	16 10 46	22 49 07	4 29.7	11 59.2	28 49.3	0♏07.4	5 33.2	18 05.8	17 36.7	29 35.6	18 58.7	5 06.9
16 M	7 38 00	24 09 02	29 23 57	5♑55 12	4 28.5	11 44.8	0♋01.8	0 34.0	5 52.9	18 10.2	17 33.6	29 38.8	18 59.9	5 06.0
17 Tu	7 41 56	25 06 15	12♑22 52	18 46 57	4 27.7	11 35.2	1 14.4	1 01.0	6 12.7	18 14.4	17 30.5	29 42.0	19 01.0	5 05.1
18 W	7 45 53	26 03 28	25 07 30	1♒24 34	4D27.4	11D30.8	2 26.9	1 28.2	6 32.7	18 18.5	17 27.5	29 45.3	19 02.2	5 04.2
19 Th	7 49 49	27 00 42	7♒38 18	13 48 50	4 27.5	11 31.7	3 39.5	1 55.8	6 52.7	18 22.3	17 24.6	29 48.5	19 03.3	5 03.2
20 F	7 53 46	27 57 56	19 56 22	26 01 08	4 27.9	11 38.2	4 52.2	2 23.7	7 12.9	18 26.0	17 21.8	29 51.8	19 04.3	5 02.3
21 Sa	7 57 42	28 55 11	2♓03 26	8♓03 35	4 28.4	11 50.3	6 04.9	2 51.9	7 33.2	18 29.5	17 19.0	29 55.2	19 05.4	5 01.3
22 Su	8 01 39	29 52 27	14 01 57	19 58 57	4 29.0	12 08.1	7 17.6	3 20.4	7 53.7	18 32.9	17 16.3	29 58.5	19 06.4	5 00.3
23 M	8 05 35	0♌49 43	25 54 59	1♈50 34	4 29.4	12 31.7	8 30.3	3 49.2	8 14.3	18 36.0	17 13.7	0♍01.9	19 07.4	4 59.3
24 Tu	8 09 32	1 47 00	7♈46 11	13 42 22	4 29.7	13 01.2	9 43.1	4 18.3	8 35.0	18 38.9	17 11.2	0 05.3	19 08.3	4 58.3
25 W	8 13 29	2 44 18	19 39 39	25 38 36	4R29.8	13 36.4	10 56.0	4 47.7	8 55.8	18 41.7	17 08.7	0 08.7	19 09.2	4 57.2
26 Th	8 17 25	3 41 37	1♉39 48	7♉43 48	4D29.8	14 17.3	12 08.8	5 17.4	9 16.7	18 44.3	17 06.4	0 12.1	19 10.1	4 56.2
27 F	8 21 22	4 38 57	13 51 09	20 02 25	4 29.8	15 04.0	13 21.7	5 47.4	9 37.7	18 46.7	17 04.1	0 15.6	19 11.0	4 55.1
28 Sa	8 25 18	5 36 18	26 18 05	2♊38 38	4 29.9	15 56.3	14 34.7	6 17.6	9 58.9	18 48.9	17 01.9	0 19.1	19 11.8	4 54.0
29 Su	8 29 15	6 33 39	9♊04 28	15 35 55	4 30.0	16 54.2	15 47.7	6 48.1	10 20.2	18 50.9	16 59.8	0 22.6	19 12.6	4 53.0
30 M	8 33 11	7 31 02	22 13 14	28 56 35	4 30.3	17 57.6	17 00.7	7 18.9	10 41.6	18 52.7	16 57.7	0 26.1	19 13.4	4 51.9
31 Tu	8 37 08	8 28 26	5♋46 00	12♋41 23	4 30.6	19 06.4	18 13.8	7 50.0	11 03.1	18 54.3	16 55.8	0 29.6	19 14.1	4 50.7

August 2046 LONGITUDE

Day	Sid.Time	☉	0 hr ☽	Noon ☽	True ☊	☿	♀	♂	⚳	♃	♄	♅	♆	♇
1 W	8 41 04	9♌25 51	19♋42 31	26♋49 03	4♒30.8	20♋20.4	19♋26.9	8♏21.3	11♎24.7	18♈55.7	16♐53.9	0♍33.2	19♉14.9	4♓49.6
2 Th	8 45 01	10 23 16	4♌00 30	11♌16 12	4R30.8	21 39.5	20 40.0	8 52.9	11 46.4	18 56.9	16R52.2	0 36.8	19 15.5	4R48.5
3 F	8 48 58	11 20 43	18 35 28	25 57 27	4 30.5	23 03.6	21 53.2	9 24.7	12 08.2	18 58.0	16 50.5	0 40.4	19 16.2	4 47.3
4 Sa	8 52 54	12 18 10	3♍21 15	10♍45 57	4 29.9	24 32.4	23 06.4	9 56.8	12 30.1	18 58.8	16 48.9	0 44.0	19 16.8	4 46.2
5 Su	8 56 51	13 15 38	18 10 36	25 34 19	4 29.0	26 05.6	24 19.6	10 29.1	12 52.1	18 59.4	16 47.4	0 47.6	19 17.4	4 45.0
6 M	9 00 47	14 13 07	2♎56 15	10♎15 37	4 27.9	27 43.2	25 32.9	11 01.7	13 14.2	18 59.8	16 46.0	0 51.2	19 17.9	4 43.8
7 Tu	9 04 44	15 10 36	17 31 48	24 44 14	4 27.0	29 24.7	26 46.2	11 34.5	13 36.4	19R00.1	16 44.7	0 54.8	19 18.4	4 42.6
8 W	9 08 40	16 08 06	1♏52 30	8♏56 17	4D26.5	1♌09.9	27 59.5	12 07.6	13 58.7	19 00.1	16 43.5	0 58.5	19 18.9	4 41.4
9 Th	9 12 37	17 05 37	15 55 25	22 49 48	4 26.5	2 58.3	29 12.9	12 40.9	14 21.0	19 00.0	16 42.3	1 02.2	19 19.3	4 40.2
10 F	9 16 33	18 03 09	29 39 25	6♐24 22	4 27.0	4 49.8	0♌26.3	13 14.4	14 43.5	18 59.6	16 41.3	1 05.8	19 19.7	4 39.0
11 Sa	9 20 30	19 00 42	13♐04 46	19 40 48	4 28.0	6 43.9	1 39.7	13 48.1	15 06.1	18 59.0	16 40.4	1 09.5	19 20.1	4 37.8
12 Su	9 24 27	19 58 15	26 12 39	2♑40 33	4 29.2	8 40.1	2 53.2	14 22.0	15 28.7	18 58.3	16 39.5	1 13.2	19 20.5	4 36.6
13 M	9 28 23	20 55 49	9♑04 44	15 25 26	4 30.4	10 38.3	4 06.7	14 56.2	15 51.4	18 57.3	16 38.8	1 16.9	19 20.8	4 35.3
14 Tu	9 32 20	21 53 25	21 42 54	27 57 19	4R31.1	12 37.8	5 20.2	15 30.5	16 14.2	18 56.2	16 38.1	1 20.6	19 21.1	4 34.1
15 W	9 36 16	22 51 01	4♒08 57	10♒17 58	4 31.2	14 38.4	6 33.8	16 05.1	16 37.1	18 54.8	16 37.6	1 24.4	19 21.3	4 32.8
16 Th	9 40 13	23 48 39	16 24 37	22 29 04	4 30.2	16 39.8	7 47.4	16 39.9	17 00.1	18 53.3	16 37.1	1 28.1	19 21.5	4 31.6
17 F	9 44 09	24 46 18	28 31 33	4♓32 15	4 28.3	18 41.6	9 01.0	17 14.8	17 23.1	18 51.6	16 36.8	1 31.8	19 21.7	4 30.3
18 Sa	9 48 06	25 43 58	10♓31 25	16 29 16	4 25.5	20 43.6	10 14.7	17 50.0	17 46.2	18 49.6	16 36.5	1 35.5	19 21.9	4 29.1
19 Su	9 52 02	26 41 40	22 26 03	28 22 04	4 22.0	22 45.4	11 28.4	18 25.3	18 09.4	18 47.5	16 36.3	1 39.3	19 22.0	4 27.8
20 M	9 55 59	27 39 23	4♈17 36	10♈12 59	4 18.2	24 46.9	12 42.1	19 00.9	18 32.6	18 45.2	16D36.2	1 43.0	19 22.1	4 26.5
21 Tu	9 59 56	28 37 07	16 08 34	22 04 47	4 14.6	26 47.8	13 55.9	19 36.6	18 56.0	18 42.6	16 36.3	1 46.8	19 22.1	4 25.2
22 W	10 03 52	29 34 53	28 02 01	4♉00 45	4 11.6	28 48.0	15 09.7	20 12.5	19 19.4	18 39.9	16 36.4	1 50.5	19R22.1	4 24.0
23 Th	10 07 49	0♍32 41	10♉01 27	16 04 39	4 09.5	0♍47.3	16 23.6	20 48.6	19 42.8	18 37.0	16 36.6	1 54.3	19 22.1	4 22.7
24 F	10 11 45	1 30 31	22 10 51	28 20 36	4D08.6	2 45.7	17 37.5	21 24.9	20 06.4	18 33.9	16 36.9	1 58.0	19 22.0	4 21.4
25 Sa	10 15 42	2 28 22	4♊34 28	10♊52 58	4 08.8	4 43.1	18 51.4	22 01.4	20 30.0	18 30.7	16 37.3	2 01.8	19 22.0	4 20.1
26 Su	10 19 38	3 26 15	17 16 37	23 45 55	4 09.9	6 39.3	20 05.3	22 38.0	20 53.7	18 27.2	16 37.8	2 05.5	19 21.9	4 18.8
27 M	10 23 35	4 24 10	0♋21 16	7♋03 02	4 11.5	8 34.4	21 19.3	23 14.9	21 17.4	18 23.5	16 38.4	2 09.3	19 21.8	4 17.6
28 Tu	10 27 31	5 22 07	13 51 29	20 46 34	4R12.8	10 28.2	22 33.4	23 51.9	21 41.2	18 19.7	16 39.1	2 13.1	19 21.6	4 16.3
29 W	10 31 28	6 20 06	27 48 48	4♌57 29	4 13.3	12 20.8	23 47.4	24 29.0	22 05.1	18 15.7	16 39.9	2 16.8	19 21.4	4 15.0
30 Th	10 35 25	7 18 06	12♌12 28	19 33 11	4 12.5	14 12.2	25 01.5	25 06.4	22 29.1	18 11.5	16 40.8	2 20.6	19 21.1	4 13.7
31 F	10 39 21	8 16 08	26 58 55	4♍28 47	4 10.1	16 02.3	26 15.6	25 43.9	22 53.1	18 07.1	16 41.8	2 24.3	19 20.8	4 12.4

Astro Data	Planet Ingress	Last Aspect	☽ Ingress	Last Aspect	☽ Ingress	☽ Phases & Eclipses	Astro Data
Dy Hr Mn	Dy Hr Mn	Dy Hr Mn	Dy Hr Mn	Dy Hr Mn	Dy Hr Mn	Dy Hr Mn	1 July 2046
☽0S 8 21:27	♂ ♏ 15 5:14	3 2:26 ♅ ⚹	♋ 3 4:15	1 0:00 ☿ ☌	♌ 1 17:20	4 1:40 ● 12♋18	Julian Day # 53508
♃△♄ 11 21:31	♀ ♋ 16 11:23	5 0:52 ♂ □	♌ 5 7:55	3 1:06 ♆ □	♍ 3 18:34	10 19:55 ☽ 18♎45	SVP 4♓36'23"
☿D 18 19:53	☉ ♌ 22 15:10	7 8:51 ♅ ☌	♍ 7 10:13	5 12:57 ♅ ⚹	♎ 5 19:12	18 0:56 ○ 25♑37	GC 27♐29.3 ⚴ 22♌23.2
☽0N 22 14:13	♅ ♍ 22 22:31	8 20:58 ♀ □	♎ 9 12:19	7 15:43 ♀ □	♏ 7 20:50	18 1:06 • P 0.246	Eris 0♉35.2 ⚵ 29♍22.2
		11 14:02 ♅ ⚹	♏ 11 15:05	10 0:20 ♀ △	♐ 10 0:36	26 3:21 ☾ 3♉21	⚷ 1♎16.0 ⚶ 20♌25.5
☽0S 5 4:44	☿ ♌ 7 20:09	13 18:18 ♅ □	♐ 13 19:11	11 10:44 ♃ △	♑ 12 7:01		☽ Mean ☊ 5♒44.0
♃R 8 4:15	♀ ♌ 10 3:25	16 0:24 ♅ △	♑ 16 1:06	13 19:28 ♆ △	♒ 14 15:57	2 10:27 ● 10♌20	
⚳0S 12 15:41	☉ ♍ 22 22:26	18 0:56 ☉ ☍	♒ 18 9:18	16 14:51 ☉ ☍	♓ 17 2:56	2 10:21:14 • T 04'51"	1 August 2046
☽0N 18 21:24	☿ ♍ 23 2:27	20 19:40 ♅ ☍	♓ 20 19:54	18 17:48 ♆ ⚹	♈ 19 15:18	9 1:17 ☽ 16♏40	Julian Day # 53539
♄D 20 19:13		22 10:14 ♆ ⚹	♈ 23 8:16	22 2:20 ☉ △	♉ 22 3:57	16 14:51 ○ 23♒56	SVP 4♓36'17"
♆R 22 13:26		24 22:00 ♃ ☌	♉ 25 20:42	23 21:48 ♂ ☍	♊ 24 15:12	24 18:38 ☾ 1♊46	GC 27♐29.4 ⚴ 7♍00.9
		27 10:21 ♆ ☌	♊ 28 7:01	26 4:31 ♀ ⚹	♋ 26 23:22	31 18:27 ● 8♍32	Eris 0♉38.6R ⚵ 7♎14.2
		29 17:55 ♃ ⚹	♋ 30 13:52	28 17:32 ♂ △	♌ 29 3:42		⚷ 3♎56.1 ⚶ 4♍29.9
				30 21:39 ♀ ☌	♍ 31 4:51		☽ Mean ☊ 4♒05.5

LONGITUDE — September 2046

Day	Sid.Time	☉	0 hr ☽	Noon ☽	True ☊	☿	♀	♂	⚳	♃	♄	♅	♆	♇
1 Sa	10 43 18	9♍14 11	12♍01 41	19♍36 28	4♒06.2	17♍51.1	27♌29.8	26♏21.6	23♎17.1	18♈02.5	16♐42.9	2♍28.1	19♉20.5	4♓11.2
2 Su	10 47 14	10 12 16	27 11 51	4♎46 35	4R01.2	19 38.6	28 44.0	26 59.5	23 41.2	17R57.8	16 44.1	2 31.8	19R20.2	4R09.9
3 M	10 51 11	11 10 22	12♎19 25	19 49 11	3 55.9	21 25.0	29 58.2	27 37.5	24 05.4	17 52.9	16 45.4	2 35.5	19 19.8	4 08.6
4 Tu	10 55 07	12 08 30	27 14 53	4♏35 38	3 51.0	23 10.0	1♍12.4	28 15.7	24 29.6	17 47.8	16 46.8	2 39.2	19 19.4	4 07.3
5 W	10 59 04	13 06 40	11♏50 46	18 59 49	3 47.3	24 53.9	2 26.7	28 54.0	24 53.9	17 42.6	16 48.2	2 43.0	19 19.0	4 06.1
6 Th	11 03 00	14 04 51	26 02 29	2♐58 38	3D45.1	26 36.5	3 41.0	29 32.5	25 18.2	17 37.2	16 49.8	2 46.7	19 18.5	4 04.8
7 F	11 06 57	15 03 03	9♐48 21	16 31 48	3 44.5	28 17.9	4 55.3	0♐11.2	25 42.6	17 31.7	16 51.5	2 50.4	19 18.0	4 03.5
8 Sa	11 10 54	16 01 17	23 09 14	29 41 03	3 45.3	29 58.2	6 09.6	0 50.0	26 07.1	17 26.0	16 53.2	2 54.1	19 17.5	4 02.3
9 Su	11 14 50	16 59 32	6♑07 38	12♑29 28	3 46.6	1♎37.2	7 24.0	1 28.9	26 31.6	17 20.1	16 55.1	2 57.7	19 16.9	4 01.0
10 M	11 18 47	17 57 49	18 46 59	25 00 41	3R47.9	3 15.2	8 38.4	2 08.0	26 56.1	17 14.1	16 57.1	3 01.4	19 16.3	3 59.8
11 Tu	11 22 43	18 56 08	1♒11 01	7♒18 24	3 48.1	4 52.0	9 52.8	2 47.2	27 20.7	17 08.0	16 59.1	3 05.1	19 15.7	3 58.6
12 W	11 26 40	19 54 28	13 23 16	19 26 00	3 46.8	6 27.6	11 07.2	3 26.6	27 45.3	17 01.7	17 01.2	3 08.7	19 15.0	3 57.3
13 Th	11 30 36	20 52 49	25 26 55	1♓26 22	3 43.3	8 02.2	12 21.7	4 06.1	28 10.0	16 55.3	17 03.5	3 12.3	19 14.3	3 56.1
14 F	11 34 33	21 51 13	7♓24 36	13 21 54	3 37.6	9 35.6	13 36.1	4 45.8	28 34.7	16 48.8	17 05.8	3 16.0	19 13.6	3 54.9
15 Sa	11 38 29	22 49 38	19 18 29	25 14 35	3 29.9	11 08.0	14 50.7	5 25.5	28 59.4	16 42.1	17 08.2	3 19.6	19 12.9	3 53.7
16 Su	11 42 26	23 48 05	1♈10 22	7♈06 05	3 20.7	12 39.2	16 05.2	6 05.4	29 24.2	16 35.4	17 10.7	3 23.1	19 12.1	3 52.5
17 M	11 46 22	24 46 34	13 01 54	18 58 02	3 10.7	14 09.4	17 19.7	6 45.5	29 49.1	16 28.5	17 13.3	3 26.7	19 11.3	3 51.3
18 Tu	11 50 19	25 45 05	24 54 43	0♉52 13	3 01.0	15 38.5	18 34.3	7 25.6	0♏13.9	16 21.5	17 16.0	3 30.3	19 10.5	3 50.1
19 W	11 54 16	26 43 38	6♉50 47	12 50 46	2 52.3	17 06.4	19 48.9	8 06.0	0 38.8	16 14.4	17 18.8	3 33.8	19 09.6	3 49.0
20 Th	11 58 12	27 42 13	18 52 28	24 56 18	2 45.4	18 33.3	21 03.6	8 46.4	1 03.8	16 07.1	17 21.6	3 37.3	19 08.7	3 47.8
21 F	12 02 09	28 40 50	1♊02 40	7♊12 02	2 40.7	19 59.1	22 18.2	9 26.9	1 28.8	15 59.8	17 24.6	3 40.8	19 07.8	3 46.7
22 Sa	12 06 05	29 39 30	13 24 52	19 41 41	2D38.3	21 23.7	23 32.9	10 07.6	1 53.8	15 52.4	17 27.6	3 44.3	19 06.8	3 45.5
23 Su	12 10 02	0♎38 12	26 03 01	2♋29 21	2 37.8	22 47.1	24 47.6	10 48.4	2 18.9	15 44.9	17 30.7	3 47.8	19 05.9	3 44.4
24 M	12 13 58	1 36 56	9♋01 12	15 39 03	2 38.4	24 09.4	26 02.3	11 29.4	2 44.0	15 37.4	17 33.9	3 51.2	19 04.9	3 43.3
25 Tu	12 17 55	2 35 43	22 23 17	29 14 16	2R39.0	25 30.5	27 17.1	12 10.4	3 09.2	15 29.7	17 37.2	3 54.6	19 03.9	3 42.2
26 W	12 21 51	3 34 31	6♌10 10	13♌17 06	2 38.6	26 50.3	28 31.9	12 51.6	3 34.4	15 22.0	17 40.6	3 58.0	19 02.8	3 41.1
27 Th	12 25 48	4 33 22	20 28 55	27 47 22	2 36.2	28 08.8	29 46.6	13 32.9	3 59.6	15 14.2	17 44.1	4 01.4	19 01.7	3 40.0
28 F	12 29 45	5 32 15	5♍11 53	12♍41 46	2 31.4	29 25.9	1♎01.5	14 14.3	4 24.8	15 06.4	17 47.6	4 04.8	19 00.6	3 39.0
29 Sa	12 33 41	6 31 10	20 16 01	27 53 31	2 24.1	0♏41.6	2 16.3	14 55.9	4 50.1	14 58.5	17 51.2	4 08.1	18 59.5	3 37.9
30 Su	12 37 38	7 30 07	5♎32 54	13♎12 46	2 14.9	1 55.8	3 31.1	15 37.5	5 15.4	14 50.6	17 55.0	4 11.4	18 58.3	3 36.9

LONGITUDE — October 2046

Day	Sid.Time	☉	0 hr ☽	Noon ☽	True ☊	☿	♀	♂	⚳	♃	♄	♅	♆	♇
1 M	12 41 34	8♎29 07	20♎51 40	28♎28 10	2♒05.0	3♏08.4	4♎46.0	16♐19.3	5♏40.7	14♈42.6	17♐58.8	4♍14.7	18♉57.2	3♓35.9
2 Tu	12 45 31	9 28 08	6♏00 55	13♏28 45	1R55.5	4 19.3	6 00.9	17 01.2	6 06.1	14R34.6	18 02.6	4 17.9	18R56.0	3R34.9
3 W	12 49 27	10 27 11	20 50 43	28 06 02	1 47.6	5 28.4	7 15.8	17 43.2	6 31.5	14 26.5	18 06.6	4 21.2	18 54.7	3 33.9
4 Th	12 53 24	11 26 16	5♐14 14	12♐15 01	1 42.0	6 35.6	8 30.7	18 25.3	6 56.9	14 18.5	18 10.6	4 24.4	18 53.5	3 32.9
5 F	12 57 20	12 25 22	19 08 19	25 54 16	1 38.8	7 40.7	9 45.6	19 07.5	7 22.4	14 10.4	18 14.7	4 27.5	18 52.2	3 32.0
6 Sa	13 01 17	13 24 31	2♑33 09	9♑05 20	1D37.7	8 43.5	11 00.6	19 49.8	7 47.9	14 02.4	18 18.9	4 30.7	18 50.9	3 31.0
7 Su	13 05 14	14 23 41	15 31 21	21 51 45	1R37.8	9 43.9	12 15.5	20 32.3	8 13.3	13 54.3	18 23.2	4 33.8	18 49.6	3 30.1
8 M	13 09 10	15 22 53	28 07 07	4♒18 04	1 37.9	10 41.6	13 30.5	21 14.8	8 38.9	13 46.2	18 27.5	4 36.8	18 48.3	3 29.2
9 Tu	13 13 07	16 22 06	10♒25 14	16 29 11	1 37.0	11 36.5	14 45.4	21 57.4	9 04.4	13 38.1	18 32.0	4 39.9	18 46.9	3 28.4
10 W	13 17 03	17 21 21	22 30 31	28 29 46	1 34.0	12 28.2	16 00.4	22 40.1	9 30.0	13 30.1	18 36.4	4 42.9	18 45.6	3 27.5
11 Th	13 21 00	18 20 39	4♓27 26	10♓23 58	1 28.4	13 16.4	17 15.4	23 23.0	9 55.5	13 22.1	18 41.0	4 45.9	18 44.2	3 26.6
12 F	13 24 56	19 19 58	16 19 46	22 15 12	1 19.8	14 00.9	18 30.4	24 05.9	10 21.1	13 14.1	18 45.6	4 48.8	18 42.8	3 25.8
13 Sa	13 28 53	20 19 18	28 10 34	4♈06 09	1 08.5	14 41.2	19 45.4	24 48.9	10 46.7	13 06.1	18 50.3	4 51.7	18 41.3	3 25.0
14 Su	13 32 49	21 18 41	10♈02 11	15 58 52	0 55.2	15 17.0	21 00.4	25 32.0	11 12.4	12 58.2	18 55.1	4 54.6	18 39.9	3 24.2
15 M	13 36 46	22 18 06	21 56 21	27 54 48	0 41.0	15 47.8	22 15.5	26 15.2	11 38.0	12 50.3	18 59.9	4 57.5	18 38.4	3 23.5
16 Tu	13 40 43	23 17 33	3♉54 22	9♉55 12	0 26.8	16 13.1	23 30.5	26 58.4	12 03.7	12 42.5	19 04.8	5 00.3	18 36.9	3 22.7
17 W	13 44 39	24 17 02	15 57 26	22 01 14	0 14.0	16 32.5	24 45.6	27 41.8	12 29.4	12 34.8	19 09.8	5 03.0	18 35.4	3 22.0
18 Th	13 48 36	25 16 34	28 06 47	4♊14 19	0 03.4	16 45.4	26 00.6	28 25.3	12 55.1	12 27.1	19 14.9	5 05.8	18 33.9	3 21.3
19 F	13 52 32	26 16 07	10♊24 05	16 36 22	29♑55.7	16R51.3	27 15.7	29 08.8	13 20.8	12 19.5	19 20.0	5 08.5	18 32.4	3 20.6
20 Sa	13 56 29	27 15 43	22 51 31	29 09 52	29 51.0	16 49.6	28 30.8	29 52.4	13 46.5	12 11.9	19 25.1	5 11.1	18 30.9	3 19.9
21 Su	14 00 25	28 15 21	5♋31 51	11♋57 52	29 48.8	16 40.0	29 45.9	0♑36.2	14 12.3	12 04.5	19 30.4	5 13.8	18 29.3	3 19.3
22 M	14 04 22	29 15 01	18 28 21	25 03 45	29 48.3	16 21.8	1♏01.0	1 20.0	14 38.0	11 57.1	19 35.7	5 16.4	18 27.7	3 18.7
23 Tu	14 08 18	0♏14 44	1♌44 29	8♌30 55	29 48.2	15 54.8	2 16.2	2 03.9	15 03.8	11 49.8	19 41.0	5 18.9	18 26.2	3 18.1
24 W	14 12 15	1 14 29	15 23 22	22 22 01	29 47.3	15 18.9	3 31.3	2 47.8	15 29.6	11 42.6	19 46.5	5 21.4	18 24.6	3 17.5
25 Th	14 16 12	2 14 16	29 26 59	6♍38 10	29 44.4	14 34.1	4 46.4	3 31.9	15 55.4	11 35.5	19 51.9	5 23.9	18 23.0	3 16.9
26 F	14 20 08	3 14 05	13♍55 20	21 17 59	29 38.8	13 40.8	6 01.6	4 16.0	16 21.2	11 28.5	19 57.5	5 26.3	18 21.4	3 16.4
27 Sa	14 24 05	4 13 56	28 45 29	6♎16 54	29 30.5	12 39.7	7 16.7	5 00.2	16 47.0	11 21.7	20 03.1	5 28.7	18 19.7	3 15.9
28 Su	14 28 01	5 13 50	13♎51 12	21 27 06	29 20.0	11 32.0	8 31.9	5 44.5	17 12.8	11 14.9	20 08.7	5 31.0	18 18.1	3 15.4
29 M	14 31 58	6 13 46	29 03 16	6♏38 20	29 08.4	10 19.0	9 47.1	6 28.9	17 38.6	11 08.3	20 14.4	5 33.3	18 16.5	3 15.0
30 Tu	14 35 54	7 13 43	14♏10 54	21 39 41	28 57.1	9 02.8	11 02.3	7 13.3	18 04.4	11 01.8	20 20.2	5 35.5	18 14.8	3 14.5
31 W	14 39 51	8 13 43	29 03 34	6♐21 34	28 47.5	7 45.5	12 17.5	7 57.9	18 30.3	10 55.5	20 26.0	5 37.7	18 13.2	3 14.1

Astro Data

	Dy Hr Mn
☽0S	1 14:29
♃□♅	5 11:00
☿0S	9 5:23
♃△♄	12 13:21
☽0N	15 3:53
♅☍♇	22 18:19
☉0S	22 20:23
☽0S	29 1:26
♀0S	30 6:31
♄⊼♆	12 0:37
☽0N	12 9:41
☿ R	19 18:58
☽0S	26 11:22

Planet Ingress

		Dy Hr Mn
♀	♍	3 12:35
♂	♐	7 5:04
☿	♎	8 12:26
⚳	♏	17 22:34
☉	♎	22 20:23
♀	♎	27 16:17
☿	♏	28 22:45
☊	♑R	18 21:37
♂	♑	20 16:09
♀	♏	21 16:30
☉	♏	23 6:05

Last Aspect / ☽ Ingress (September)

Last Aspect Dy Hr Mn		☽ Ingress	Dy Hr Mn
1 23:08	♂ ⚹	♎	2 4:26
3 8:54	♃ ☍	♏	4 4:29
6 5:45	♂ ☌	♐	6 6:50
7 13:47	♃ △	♑	8 12:35
10 0:57	♆ △	♒	10 21:41
12 11:38	♆ □	♓	13 9:07
15 6:41	☉ ☍	♈	15 21:38
17 8:28	♄ △	♉	18 10:15
20 17:55	☉ △	♊	20 21:57
22 20:05	♀ □	♋	23 7:23
25 8:16	♀ ⚹	♌	25 13:19
27 12:38	☿ ⚹	♍	27 15:36
28 22:00	♆ △	♎	29 15:18

Last Aspect / ☽ Ingress (October)

Last Aspect Dy Hr Mn		☽ Ingress	Dy Hr Mn
30 19:24	♄ ⚹	♏	1 14:26
2 20:51	♆ ☍	♐	3 15:10
4 23:19	♂ ☌	♑	5 19:22
7 6:15	♆ △	♒	8 3:38
9 23:35	♂ ⚹	♓	10 15:01
12 15:59	♂ □	♈	13 3:42
15 8:27	♂ △	♉	15 16:11
17 5:14	♆ ☌	♊	18 3:42
20 13:26	♂ ☍	♋	20 13:35
22 20:09	☉ □	♌	22 20:53
24 7:32	♄ △	♍	25 0:55
26 9:49	♄ □	♎	27 1:59
28 9:56	♄ ⚹	♏	29 1:30
30 6:31	♆ ☍	♐	31 1:32

☽ Phases & Eclipses

Dy Hr Mn		
7 9:08	☽	14♐56
15 6:41	○	22♓37
23 8:17	☾	0♋29
30 2:27	●	7♎07
6 20:42	☽	13♑46
14 23:43	○	21♈48
22 20:09	☾	29♋35
29 11:18	●	6♏12

Astro Data

1 September 2046
Julian Day # 53570
SVP 4♓36'13"
GC 27♐29.5 ⚴ 21♍33.9
Eris 0♉32.0R ⚵ 16♎44.0
⚷ 7♎43.7 ⚶ 19♍23.7
☽ Mean ☊ 2♒27.0

1 October 2046
Julian Day # 53600
SVP 4♓36'10"
GC 27♐29.5 ⚴ 5♎28.3
Eris 0♉17.8R ⚵ 26♎45.8
⚷ 11♎58.8 ⚶ 4♎20.2
☽ Mean ☊ 0♒51.7

November 2046 — LONGITUDE

Day	Sid.Time	☉	0 hr ☽	Noon ☽	True ☊	☿	♀	♂	⚳	♃	♄	♅	♆	♇
1 Th	14 43 47	9♏13 44	13♐32 59	20♐37 18	28♑40.3	6♏29.5	13♏32.7	8♑42.5	18♏56.1	10♈49.3	20♐31.9	5♍39.9	18♉11.5	3♓13.7
2 F	14 47 44	10 13 47	27 34 13	4♑23 41	28R35.9	5R17.1	14 47.9	9 27.2	19 22.0	10R43.2	20 37.8	5 42.0	18R09.8	3R13.4
3 Sa	14 51 41	11 13 51	11♑05 49	17 40 52	28D33.9	4 10.7	16 03.1	10 11.9	19 47.8	10 37.3	20 43.8	5 44.1	18 08.2	3 13.0
4 Su	14 55 37	12 13 57	24 09 17	0♒31 33	28 33.5	3 12.3	17 18.3	10 56.7	20 13.7	10 31.6	20 49.8	5 46.1	18 06.5	3 12.7
5 M	14 59 34	13 14 05	6♒48 14	13 00 00	28R33.7	2 23.4	18 33.5	11 41.6	20 39.5	10 26.0	20 55.9	5 48.0	18 04.8	3 12.4
6 Tu	15 03 30	14 14 14	19 07 28	25 11 20	28 33.1	1 45.3	19 48.7	12 26.5	21 05.4	10 20.5	21 02.0	5 50.0	18 03.1	3 12.1
7 W	15 07 27	15 14 24	1♓12 15	7♓10 50	28 30.9	1 18.5	21 03.9	13 11.5	21 31.2	10 15.2	21 08.2	5 51.8	18 01.4	3 11.9
8 Th	15 11 23	16 14 36	13 07 44	19 03 31	28 26.2	1D03.4	22 19.1	13 56.6	21 57.0	10 10.1	21 14.4	5 53.7	17 59.7	3 11.7
9 F	15 15 20	17 14 50	24 58 43	0♈53 49	28 18.8	0 59.9	23 34.3	14 41.7	22 22.9	10 05.2	21 20.6	5 55.4	17 58.0	3 11.5
10 Sa	15 19 16	18 15 05	6♈49 15	12 45 25	28 08.8	1 07.5	24 49.5	15 26.9	22 48.7	10 00.4	21 26.9	5 57.2	17 56.4	3 11.3
11 Su	15 23 13	19 15 22	18 42 39	24 41 13	27 56.8	1 25.6	26 04.7	16 12.2	23 14.5	9 55.8	21 33.2	5 58.8	17 54.7	3 11.2
12 M	15 27 09	20 15 40	0♉41 21	6♉43 15	27 43.8	1 53.3	27 19.9	16 57.5	23 40.4	9 51.4	21 39.6	6 00.5	17 53.0	3 11.1
13 Tu	15 31 06	21 16 00	12 47 03	18 52 52	27 30.9	2 29.9	28 35.2	17 42.8	24 06.2	9 47.2	21 46.0	6 02.0	17 51.3	3 11.0
14 W	15 35 03	22 16 22	25 00 47	1♊10 53	27 19.2	3 14.5	29 50.4	18 28.2	24 32.0	9 43.1	21 52.5	6 03.5	17 49.6	3 10.9
15 Th	15 38 59	23 16 45	7♊23 14	13 37 54	27 09.6	4 06.1	1♐05.6	19 13.7	24 57.8	9 39.3	21 59.0	6 05.0	17 47.9	3D10.9
16 F	15 42 56	24 17 10	19 54 57	26 14 30	27 02.7	5 03.9	2 20.8	19 59.2	25 23.6	9 35.6	22 05.5	6 06.4	17 46.2	3 10.9
17 Sa	15 46 52	25 17 37	2♋36 40	9♋01 35	26 58.6	6 07.1	3 36.1	20 44.8	25 49.4	9 32.1	22 12.1	6 07.8	17 44.6	3 10.9
18 Su	15 50 49	26 18 06	15 29 28	22 00 30	26D57.0	7 15.0	4 51.3	21 30.4	26 15.2	9 28.8	22 18.7	6 09.1	17 42.9	3 10.9
19 M	15 54 45	27 18 37	28 34 55	5♌12 59	26 57.1	8 27.0	6 06.5	22 16.0	26 41.0	9 25.7	22 25.3	6 10.4	17 41.2	3 11.0
20 Tu	15 58 42	28 19 09	11♌54 56	18 41 00	26R57.9	9 42.4	7 21.8	23 01.7	27 06.7	9 22.8	22 31.9	6 11.6	17 39.6	3 11.1
21 W	16 02 39	29 19 43	25 31 26	2♍26 23	26 58.2	11 00.8	8 37.0	23 47.5	27 32.5	9 20.1	22 38.6	6 12.8	17 37.9	3 11.2
22 Th	16 06 35	0♐20 18	9♍25 56	16 30 05	26 56.9	12 21.7	9 52.2	24 33.3	27 58.2	9 17.6	22 45.4	6 13.9	17 36.3	3 11.4
23 F	16 10 32	1 20 56	23 38 43	0♎51 36	26 53.5	13 44.8	11 07.5	25 19.2	28 24.0	9 15.3	22 52.1	6 14.9	17 34.6	3 11.5
24 Sa	16 14 28	2 21 35	8♎08 18	15 28 17	26 47.8	15 09.6	12 22.7	26 05.1	28 49.7	9 13.2	22 58.9	6 15.9	17 33.0	3 11.7
25 Su	16 18 25	3 22 16	22 50 50	0♏15 05	26 40.3	16 35.9	13 38.0	26 51.0	29 15.4	9 11.4	23 05.7	6 16.8	17 31.4	3 11.9
26 M	16 22 21	4 22 58	7♏40 05	15 04 48	26 31.7	18 03.5	14 53.2	27 37.0	29 41.1	9 09.7	23 12.5	6 17.7	17 29.8	3 12.2
27 Tu	16 26 18	5 23 43	22 28 08	29 49 03	26 23.2	19 32.1	16 08.5	28 23.1	0♐06.8	9 08.2	23 19.4	6 18.5	17 28.2	3 12.5
28 W	16 30 14	6 24 28	7♐06 32	14♐19 40	26 15.9	21 01.5	17 23.8	29 09.2	0 32.4	9 06.9	23 26.3	6 19.3	17 26.6	3 12.8
29 Th	16 34 11	7 25 15	21 27 42	28 30 01	26 10.6	22 31.7	18 39.0	29 55.3	0 58.1	9 05.9	23 33.2	6 20.0	17 25.0	3 13.1
30 F	16 38 08	8 26 02	5♑26 10	12♑15 54	26 07.4	24 02.5	19 54.3	0♒41.5	1 23.7	9 05.0	23 40.1	6 20.7	17 23.5	3 13.5

December 2046 — LONGITUDE

Day	Sid.Time	☉	0 hr ☽	Noon ☽	True ☊	☿	♀	♂	⚳	♃	♄	♅	♆	♇
1 Sa	16 42 04	9♐26 51	18♑59 05	25♑35 49	26♑06.5	25♏33.7	21♐09.5	1♒27.7	1♐49.3	9♈04.4	23♐47.0	6♍21.3	17♉21.9	3♓13.8
2 Su	16 46 01	10 27 41	2♒06 17	8♒30 48	26D07.1	27 05.4	22 24.8	2 13.9	2 14.9	9R04.0	23 54.0	6 21.8	17R20.4	3 14.2
3 M	16 49 57	11 28 32	14 49 46	21 03 43	26 08.5	28 37.3	23 40.0	3 00.2	2 40.4	9D03.7	24 01.0	6 22.3	17 18.9	3 14.7
4 Tu	16 53 54	12 29 23	27 13 11	3♓18 46	26R09.8	0♐09.5	24 55.3	3 46.5	3 05.9	9 03.7	24 08.0	6 22.7	17 17.4	3 15.1
5 W	16 57 50	13 30 15	9♓21 07	15 20 51	26 10.3	1 42.0	26 10.5	4 32.8	3 31.4	9 03.9	24 15.0	6 23.1	17 15.9	3 15.6
6 Th	17 01 47	14 31 08	21 18 37	27 15 03	26 09.2	3 14.6	27 25.8	5 19.2	3 56.9	9 04.3	24 22.0	6 23.4	17 14.4	3 16.1
7 F	17 05 43	15 32 02	3♈10 46	9♈06 22	26 06.2	4 47.3	28 41.0	6 05.6	4 22.4	9 05.0	24 29.0	6 23.7	17 13.0	3 16.6
8 Sa	17 09 40	16 32 57	15 02 23	20 59 21	26 01.6	6 20.2	29 56.2	6 52.0	4 47.8	9 05.8	24 36.1	6 23.9	17 11.5	3 17.2
9 Su	17 13 37	17 33 52	26 57 44	2♉57 57	25 55.4	7 53.1	1♑11.4	7 38.4	5 13.2	9 06.8	24 43.1	6 24.1	17 10.1	3 17.8
10 M	17 17 33	18 34 48	9♉00 22	15 05 19	25 48.5	9 26.2	2 26.6	8 24.9	5 38.5	9 08.1	24 50.2	6 24.1	17 08.7	3 18.4
11 Tu	17 21 30	19 35 45	21 13 02	27 23 43	25 41.5	10 59.3	3 41.9	9 11.4	6 03.9	9 09.5	24 57.3	6R24.2	17 07.4	3 19.0
12 W	17 25 26	20 36 43	3♊37 32	9♊54 33	25 35.1	12 32.6	4 57.1	9 57.9	6 29.2	9 11.2	25 04.3	6 24.2	17 06.0	3 19.7
13 Th	17 29 23	21 37 42	16 14 50	22 38 23	25 30.0	14 05.9	6 12.3	10 44.4	6 54.5	9 13.0	25 11.4	6 24.1	17 04.7	3 20.4
14 F	17 33 19	22 38 41	29 05 10	5♋35 08	25 26.6	15 39.3	7 27.5	11 31.0	7 19.7	9 15.1	25 18.5	6 24.0	17 03.4	3 21.1
15 Sa	17 37 16	23 39 41	12♋08 12	18 44 18	25D25.0	17 12.8	8 42.7	12 17.5	7 44.9	9 17.3	25 25.6	6 23.8	17 02.1	3 21.8
16 Su	17 41 12	24 40 43	25 23 20	2♌05 13	25 25.0	18 46.4	9 57.9	13 04.1	8 10.1	9 19.8	25 32.7	6 23.5	17 00.8	3 22.6
17 M	17 45 09	25 41 44	8♌49 54	15 37 17	25 26.1	20 20.1	11 13.0	13 50.7	8 35.2	9 22.5	25 39.8	6 23.2	16 59.6	3 23.3
18 Tu	17 49 06	26 42 47	22 27 20	29 19 58	25 27.7	21 53.9	12 28.2	14 37.3	9 00.3	9 25.3	25 46.9	6 22.9	16 58.3	3 24.1
19 W	17 53 02	27 43 51	6♍15 09	13♍12 49	25 29.2	23 27.9	13 43.4	15 24.0	9 25.4	9 28.4	25 54.0	6 22.5	16 57.1	3 24.9
20 Th	17 56 59	28 44 55	20 12 53	27 15 13	25R29.9	25 02.0	14 58.6	16 10.6	9 50.4	9 31.6	26 01.1	6 22.0	16 56.0	3 25.8
21 F	18 00 55	29 46 01	4♎19 39	11♎26 00	25 29.4	26 36.3	16 13.7	16 57.3	10 15.4	9 35.1	26 08.2	6 21.5	16 54.8	3 26.7
22 Sa	18 04 52	0♑47 07	18 34 00	25 43 17	25 27.7	28 10.8	17 28.9	17 44.0	10 40.4	9 38.7	26 15.3	6 20.9	16 53.7	3 27.6
23 Su	18 08 48	1 48 14	2♏53 28	10♏04 04	25 25.0	29 45.4	18 44.1	18 30.7	11 05.3	9 42.6	26 22.3	6 20.3	16 52.6	3 28.5
24 M	18 12 45	2 49 22	17 14 34	24 24 22	25 21.7	1♑20.3	19 59.2	19 17.4	11 30.2	9 46.6	26 29.4	6 19.6	16 51.5	3 29.4
25 Tu	18 16 42	3 50 30	1♐32 54	8♐39 30	25 18.5	2 55.4	21 14.4	20 04.1	11 55.0	9 50.9	26 36.5	6 18.8	16 50.5	3 30.4
26 W	18 20 38	4 51 39	15 43 34	22 44 32	25 15.6	4 30.7	22 29.5	20 50.9	12 19.8	9 55.3	26 43.6	6 18.1	16 49.5	3 31.3
27 Th	18 24 35	5 52 49	29 41 50	6♑35 02	25 13.7	6 06.3	23 44.7	21 37.6	12 44.6	9 59.9	26 50.6	6 17.2	16 48.5	3 32.4
28 F	18 28 31	6 53 58	13♑23 43	20 07 37	25D12.8	7 42.2	24 59.8	22 24.4	13 09.3	10 04.7	26 57.6	6 16.3	16 47.5	3 33.4
29 Sa	18 32 28	7 55 08	26 46 32	3♒20 22	25 12.9	9 18.3	26 14.9	23 11.0	13 33.9	10 09.7	27 04.7	6 15.4	16 46.6	3 34.4
30 Su	18 36 24	8 56 18	9♒49 09	16 12 59	25 13.8	10 54.7	27 30.0	23 57.9	13 58.5	10 14.8	27 11.7	6 14.4	16 45.7	3 35.5
31 M	18 40 21	9 57 28	22 32 05	28 46 43	25 15.1	12 31.4	28 45.1	24 44.7	14 23.1	10 20.2	27 18.7	6 13.3	16 44.8	3 36.6

Astro Data Dy Hr Mn	Planet Ingress Dy Hr Mn
☽0N 8 15:24	♀ ♐ 14 15:04
☿D 9 7:27	☉ ♐ 22 3:57
♇D 16 8:49	⚳ ♐ 27 5:40
☽0S 22 18:41	♂ ♒ 29 14:27
♃D 4 1:09	☿ ♐ 4 9:31
☽0N 5 21:54	♀ ♑ 8 13:12
♅R 11 16:11	☉ ♑ 21 17:30
☽0S 19 23:47	☿ ♑ 23 15:41

Last Aspect Dy Hr Mn	☽ Ingress Dy Hr Mn	Last Aspect Dy Hr Mn	☽ Ingress Dy Hr Mn
1 11:51 ♄ ☌	♑ 2 4:15	1 11:56 ☿ ⚹	♒ 1 20:06
3 12:50 ♆ △	♒ 4 11:00	4 4:53 ☿ □	♓ 4 5:28
6 3:42 ♄ ⚹	♓ 6 21:35	6 12:24 ♀ □	♈ 6 17:34
8 19:23 ♀ △	♈ 9 10:11	8 19:20 ♄ △	♉ 9 6:05
11 5:40 ♄ △	♉ 11 22:37	10 16:02 ♆ ☌	♊ 11 17:02
14 9:06 ♀ ☍	♊ 14 9:42	13 16:48 ♄ ☍	♋ 14 1:42
16 4:04 ♄ ☍	♋ 16 19:05	15 8:55 ♆ ⚹	♌ 16 8:16
18 20:30 ☉ △	♌ 19 2:34	18 7:04 ☉ △	♍ 18 13:10
21 6:12 ☉ □	♍ 21 7:47	20 14:44 ☉ □	♎ 20 16:40
23 2:17 ♂ △	♎ 23 10:35	22 16:37 ☿ ⚹	♏ 22 19:10
25 6:11 ♂ □	♏ 25 11:36	24 3:53 ♀ ⚹	♐ 24 21:24
27 9:32 ♂ ⚹	♐ 27 12:18	26 18:55 ♄ ☌	♑ 27 0:31
29 3:29 ♄ ☌	♑ 29 14:35	28 21:41 ♀ ☌	♒ 29 5:53
		31 9:09 ♄ ⚹	♓ 31 14:22

☽ Phases & Eclipses Dy Hr Mn	
5 12:30	☽ 13♒15
13 17:06	○ 21♉29
21 6:12	☾ 29♌05
27 21:51	● 5♐49
5 7:58	☽ 13♓20
13 9:57	○ 21♊32
20 14:44	☾ 28♍52
27 10:40	● 5♑49

Astro Data

1 November 2046
Julian Day # 53631
SVP 4♓36'07"
GC 27♐29.6 ⚴ 19♎30.9
Eris 29♈59.4R ⚵ 7♏28.5
⚷ 16♎26.6 ⚶ 20♎04.3
☽ Mean ☊ 29♑13.2

1 December 2046
Julian Day # 53661
SVP 4♓36'02"
GC 27♐29.7 ⚴ 2♏31.7
Eris 29♈43.0R ⚵ 17♏42.9
⚷ 20♎17.7 ⚶ 5♏18.7
☽ Mean ☊ 27♑37.9

LONGITUDE January 2047

Day	Sid.Time	☉	0 hr ☽	Noon ☽	True ☊	☿	♀	♂	⚳	♃	♄	♅	♆	♇
1 Tu	18 44 17	10♑58 38	4♓57 16	11♓04 07	25♑16.5	14♑08.4	0♒00.2	25♒31.5	14♐47.6	10♈25.7	27♐25.7	6♍12.2	16♉44.0	3♓37.7
2 W	18 48 14	11 59 47	17 07 48	23 08 47	25 17.7	15 45.8	1 15.3	26 18.3	15 12.0	10 31.4	27 32.6	6R 11.0	16R 43.1	3 38.8
3 Th	18 52 11	13 00 57	29 07 39	5♈04 58	25R 18.4	17 23.4	2 30.3	27 05.0	15 36.4	10 37.3	27 39.6	6 09.8	16 42.4	3 40.0
4 F	18 56 07	14 02 06	11♈01 21	16 57 22	25 18.5	19 01.4	3 45.4	27 51.8	16 00.7	10 43.4	27 46.5	6 08.6	16 41.6	3 41.1
5 Sa	19 00 04	15 03 15	22 53 39	28 50 47	25 18.1	20 39.6	5 00.4	28 38.6	16 25.0	10 49.6	27 53.4	6 07.2	16 40.9	3 42.3
6 Su	19 04 00	16 04 23	4♉49 20	10♉49 52	25 17.3	22 18.2	6 15.4	29 25.3	16 49.2	10 56.0	28 00.3	6 05.9	16 40.2	3 43.5
7 M	19 07 57	17 05 32	16 52 54	22 58 55	25 16.2	23 57.1	7 30.4	0♓12.1	17 13.4	11 02.6	28 07.1	6 04.5	16 39.5	3 44.7
8 Tu	19 11 53	18 06 40	29 08 20	5♊21 33	25 15.2	25 36.2	8 45.4	0 58.9	17 37.5	11 09.3	28 13.9	6 03.0	16 38.9	3 46.0
9 W	19 15 50	19 07 47	11♊38 53	18 00 34	25 14.3	27 15.6	10 00.4	1 45.6	18 01.6	11 16.2	28 20.8	6 01.5	16 38.3	3 47.2
10 Th	19 19 46	20 08 55	24 26 46	0♋57 35	25 13.6	28 55.3	11 15.3	2 32.4	18 25.5	11 23.2	28 27.5	6 00.0	16 37.8	3 48.5
11 F	19 23 43	21 10 02	7♋33 02	14 13 02	25D 13.3	0♒35.0	12 30.2	3 19.1	18 49.5	11 30.5	28 34.3	5 58.4	16 37.2	3 49.8
12 Sa	19 27 40	22 11 09	20 57 26	27 46 00	25 13.2	2 14.9	13 45.1	4 05.8	19 13.3	11 37.8	28 41.0	5 56.8	16 36.7	3 51.1
13 Su	19 31 36	23 12 15	4♌38 27	11♌34 25	25 13.3	3 54.9	15 00.0	4 52.5	19 37.1	11 45.4	28 47.7	5 55.1	16 36.3	3 52.4
14 M	19 35 33	24 13 21	18 33 29	25 35 13	25 13.4	5 34.7	16 14.9	5 39.2	20 00.8	11 53.1	28 54.4	5 53.4	16 35.8	3 53.8
15 Tu	19 39 29	25 14 27	2♍39 09	9♍44 48	25R 13.5	7 14.5	17 29.7	6 25.9	20 24.5	12 00.9	29 01.0	5 51.6	16 35.4	3 55.1
16 W	19 43 26	26 15 33	16 51 42	23 59 24	25 13.4	8 53.9	18 44.6	7 12.6	20 48.1	12 08.9	29 07.6	5 49.8	16 35.1	3 56.5
17 Th	19 47 22	27 16 38	1♎07 27	8♎15 26	25 13.3	10 32.9	19 59.4	7 59.3	21 11.6	12 17.0	29 14.1	5 48.0	16 34.7	3 57.9
18 F	19 51 19	28 17 43	15 22 59	22 29 47	25D 13.2	12 11.2	21 14.2	8 45.9	21 35.1	12 25.3	29 20.7	5 46.1	16 34.4	3 59.3
19 Sa	19 55 15	29 18 48	29 35 30	6♏39 53	25 13.2	13 48.7	22 28.9	9 32.6	21 58.5	12 33.7	29 27.2	5 44.2	16 34.2	4 00.7
20 Su	19 59 12	0♒19 53	13♏42 40	20 43 39	25 13.5	15 25.1	23 43.7	10 19.2	22 21.8	12 42.3	29 33.6	5 42.2	16 33.9	4 02.1
21 M	20 03 09	1 20 58	27 42 38	4♐39 24	25 13.9	17 00.1	24 58.4	11 05.8	22 45.0	12 51.0	29 40.0	5 40.2	16 33.7	4 03.6
22 Tu	20 07 05	2 22 02	11♐33 48	18 25 39	25 14.6	18 33.3	26 13.1	11 52.4	23 08.2	12 59.9	29 46.4	5 38.2	16 33.6	4 05.1
23 W	20 11 02	3 23 06	25 14 45	2♑00 58	25 15.3	20 04.4	27 27.8	12 39.0	23 31.3	13 08.9	29 52.7	5 36.1	16 33.5	4 06.5
24 Th	20 14 58	4 24 09	8♑44 09	15 24 07	25R 15.9	21 32.8	28 42.5	13 25.6	23 54.3	13 18.0	29 59.0	5 34.0	16 33.4	4 08.0
25 F	20 18 55	5 25 12	22 00 45	28 33 57	25 16.0	22 58.0	29 57.1	14 12.2	24 17.2	13 27.3	0♑05.3	5 31.9	16 33.3	4 09.5
26 Sa	20 22 51	6 26 13	5♒03 37	11♒29 42	25 15.5	24 19.4	1♓11.7	14 58.7	24 40.0	13 36.7	0 11.5	5 29.7	16D 33.3	4 11.0
27 Su	20 26 48	7 27 14	17 52 12	24 11 07	25 14.4	25 36.4	2 26.3	15 45.2	25 02.8	13 46.2	0 17.6	5 27.5	16 33.3	4 12.5
28 M	20 30 44	8 28 14	0♓26 32	6♓38 36	25 12.7	26 48.3	3 40.9	16 31.7	25 25.4	13 55.9	0 23.7	5 25.3	16 33.3	4 14.1
29 Tu	20 34 41	9 29 13	12 47 28	18 53 23	25 10.5	27 54.3	4 55.4	17 18.2	25 48.0	14 05.7	0 29.8	5 23.0	16 33.4	4 15.6
30 W	20 38 38	10 30 11	24 56 38	0♈57 34	25 08.1	28 53.6	6 09.9	18 04.7	26 10.5	14 15.6	0 35.8	5 20.8	16 33.5	4 17.2
31 Th	20 42 34	11 31 07	6♈56 33	12 54 01	25 05.9	29 45.3	7 24.4	18 51.1	26 32.9	14 25.6	0 41.8	5 18.4	16 33.7	4 18.7

LONGITUDE February 2047

Day	Sid.Time	☉	0 hr ☽	Noon ☽	True ☊	☿	♀	♂	⚳	♃	♄	♅	♆	♇
1 F	20 46 31	12♒32 03	18♈50 28	24♈46 24	25♑04.2	0♓28.8	8♓38.8	19♓37.5	26♐55.2	14♈35.8	0♑47.7	5♍16.1	16♉33.9	4♓20.3
2 Sa	20 50 27	13 32 57	0♉42 21	6♉38 53	25D 03.2	1 03.1	9 53.2	20 23.9	27 17.4	14 46.0	0 53.5	5R 13.7	16 34.1	4 21.9
3 Su	20 54 24	14 33 50	12 36 37	18 36 07	25 03.1	1 27.5	11 07.5	21 10.2	27 39.5	14 56.4	0 59.3	5 11.3	16 34.4	4 23.5
4 M	20 58 20	15 34 41	24 38 01	0♊42 53	25 03.8	1R 41.6	12 21.9	21 56.6	28 01.5	15 06.9	1 05.1	5 08.9	16 34.7	4 25.1
5 Tu	21 02 17	16 35 31	6♊51 19	13 03 53	25 05.2	1 44.8	13 36.1	22 42.9	28 23.4	15 17.5	1 10.8	5 06.5	16 35.0	4 26.7
6 W	21 06 13	17 36 20	19 21 03	25 43 20	25 06.9	1 37.0	14 50.4	23 29.1	28 45.3	15 28.3	1 16.4	5 04.0	16 35.4	4 28.3
7 Th	21 10 10	18 37 08	2♋11 04	8♋44 36	25 08.3	1 18.2	16 04.6	24 15.4	29 07.0	15 39.1	1 22.0	5 01.6	16 35.8	4 29.9
8 F	21 14 07	19 37 54	15 24 07	22 09 41	25R 09.1	0 48.7	17 18.7	25 01.6	29 28.6	15 50.0	1 27.5	4 59.1	16 36.2	4 31.5
9 Sa	21 18 03	20 38 38	29 01 18	5♌58 46	25 08.7	0 09.2	18 32.8	25 47.8	29 50.1	16 01.1	1 32.9	4 56.6	16 36.7	4 33.2
10 Su	21 22 00	21 39 21	13♌01 44	20 09 45	25 07.0	29♒20.6	19 46.9	26 33.9	0♑11.5	16 12.2	1 38.3	4 54.0	16 37.2	4 34.8
11 M	21 25 56	22 40 03	27 22 13	4♍38 22	25 04.0	28 24.4	21 00.9	27 20.0	0 32.8	16 23.4	1 43.7	4 51.5	16 37.7	4 36.4
12 Tu	21 29 53	23 40 44	11♍57 24	19 18 24	25 00.0	27 22.0	22 14.9	28 06.1	0 54.0	16 34.8	1 48.9	4 48.9	16 38.3	4 38.1
13 W	21 33 49	24 41 23	26 40 25	4♎02 31	24 55.6	26 15.3	23 28.8	28 52.2	1 15.0	16 46.2	1 54.1	4 46.4	16 38.9	4 39.7
14 Th	21 37 46	25 42 01	11♎23 48	18 43 27	24 51.4	25 06.1	24 42.7	29 38.2	1 36.0	16 57.7	1 59.3	4 43.8	16 39.5	4 41.4
15 F	21 41 42	26 42 38	26 00 42	3♏14 56	24 48.2	23 56.3	25 56.6	0♈24.2	1 56.8	17 09.3	2 04.3	4 41.2	16 40.2	4 43.0
16 Sa	21 45 39	27 43 14	10♏25 40	17 32 32	24D 46.3	22 47.7	27 10.4	1 10.1	2 17.6	17 21.1	2 09.4	4 38.6	16 40.9	4 44.7
17 Su	21 49 36	28 43 49	24 35 16	1♐33 46	24 45.9	21 42.0	28 24.1	1 56.0	2 38.2	17 32.9	2 14.3	4 36.0	16 41.6	4 46.4
18 M	21 53 32	29 44 23	8♐27 58	15 17 56	24 46.7	20 40.6	29 37.8	2 41.9	2 58.7	17 44.8	2 19.2	4 33.4	16 42.4	4 48.1
19 Tu	21 57 29	0♓44 55	22 03 46	28 45 38	24 48.2	19 44.6	0♈51.5	3 27.8	3 19.1	17 56.8	2 24.0	4 30.7	16 43.2	4 49.7
20 W	22 01 25	1 45 26	5♑23 42	11♑58 10	24R 49.7	18 54.9	2 05.1	4 13.6	3 39.3	18 08.8	2 28.7	4 28.1	16 44.0	4 51.4
21 Th	22 05 22	2 45 56	18 29 13	24 57 03	24 50.4	18 12.2	3 18.7	4 59.4	3 59.4	18 21.0	2 33.4	4 25.5	16 44.9	4 53.1
22 F	22 09 18	3 46 24	1♒21 50	7♒43 43	24 49.5	17 36.8	4 32.2	5 45.1	4 19.4	18 33.2	2 37.9	4 22.8	16 45.8	4 54.8
23 Sa	22 13 15	4 46 51	14 02 50	20 19 18	24 46.7	17 08.9	5 45.6	6 30.9	4 39.3	18 45.5	2 42.5	4 20.2	16 46.7	4 56.4
24 Su	22 17 11	5 47 17	26 33 15	2♓44 44	24 41.7	16 48.5	6 59.0	7 16.5	4 59.0	18 57.9	2 46.9	4 17.6	16 47.7	4 58.1
25 M	22 21 08	6 47 40	8♓53 54	15 00 48	24 34.9	16 35.4	8 12.4	8 02.2	5 18.6	19 10.4	2 51.2	4 14.9	16 48.7	4 59.8
26 Tu	22 25 05	7 48 02	21 05 35	27 08 21	24 26.7	16D 29.4	9 25.7	8 47.8	5 38.0	19 22.9	2 55.5	4 12.3	16 49.7	5 01.5
27 W	22 29 01	8 48 22	3♈09 18	9♈08 37	24 17.9	16 30.2	10 38.9	9 33.4	5 57.3	19 35.6	2 59.7	4 09.7	16 50.8	5 03.1
28 Th	22 32 58	9 48 40	15 06 31	21 03 17	24 09.3	16 37.4	11 52.1	10 18.9	6 16.5	19 48.3	3 03.9	4 07.1	16 51.8	5 04.8

Astro Data	Planet Ingress	Last Aspect	☽ Ingress	Last Aspect	☽ Ingress	☽ Phases & Eclipses	Astro Data
Dy Hr Mn	Dy Hr Mn	Dy Hr Mn	Dy Hr Mn	Dy Hr Mn	Dy Hr Mn	Dy Hr Mn	1 January 2047
☽0N 2 5:42	♀ ♒ 1 11:56	2 20:54 ♄ □	♈ 3 1:45	31 15:08 ♃ ☌	♉ 1 22:34	4 5:32 ☽ 13♈46	Julian Day # 53692
☽0S 16 5:14	♂ ♓ 7 5:47	5 11:34 ♂ ⚹	♉ 5 14:19	3 17:28 ♂ ⚹	♊ 4 10:36	12 1:23 ○ 21♋44	SVP 4♓35'56"
♆D 26 14:54	☿ ♒ 11 3:35	7 14:12 ☿ △	♊ 8 1:40	6 7:32 ♂ □	♋ 6 19:58	12 1:26 • T 1.234	GC 27♐29.8 ⚵ 14♏54.0
☽0N 29 14:12	☉ ♒ 20 4:11	10 7:22 ♄ ☍	♋ 10 10:14	8 17:20 ♂ △	♌ 9 1:42	18 22:34 ☾ 28♎45	Eris 29♈32.9R ⚴ 27♏37.0
	♄ ♑ 24 15:42	12 1:23 ☉ ☍	♌ 12 15:55	11 2:22 ☿ ☍	♍ 11 4:21	26 1:45 ● 6♒00	⚷ 23♎11.9 ⚶ 20♏40.3
☿R 5 7:01	♀ ♓ 25 12:55	14 17:41 ♄ △	♍ 14 19:30	13 3:07 ♂ ☍	♎ 13 5:25	26 1:33:18 • P 0.891	☽ Mean ☊ 25♑59.4
♄⚼♆ 10 6:11	☿ ♓ 31 19:35	16 20:42 ♄ □	♎ 16 22:07	15 0:21 ☉ △	♏ 15 6:36		
☽0S 12 13:15		18 23:40 ♄ ⚹	♏ 19 0:41	17 6:44 ☉ □	♐ 17 9:18	3 3:10 ☽ 14♉11	1 February 2047
♃⊻♆ 12 19:45	☿ ♒R 9 16:52	20 17:39 ♀ □	♐ 21 3:57	18 20:54 ☿ ⚹	♑ 19 14:14	10 14:41 ○ 21♌46	Julian Day # 53723
♅☍♇ 15 1:27	⚳ ♑ 9 23:06	23 8:10 ♄ ☌	♑ 23 8:25	20 23:33 ♃ □	♒ 21 21:26	17 6:44 ☾ 28♏31	SVP 4♓35'51"
♂0N 16 14:34	♂ ♈ 14 23:24	24 14:05 ♆ △	♒ 25 14:38	23 8:57 ♃ ⚹	♓ 24 6:40	24 18:27 ● 6♓04	GC 27♐29.8 ⚵ 25♏18.9
♀0N 20 13:02	☉ ♓ 18 18:12	27 15:01 ☿ ☌	♓ 27 23:09	25 15:33 ♆ ⚹	♈ 26 17:42		Eris 29♈33.0 ⚴ 6♐04.8
♃⚼♅ 25 19:12	♀ ♈ 18 19:14	29 8:39 ♂ ☌	♈ 30 10:05				⚷ 24♎28.3 ⚶ 5♐02.6
☽0N 25 22:08							☽ Mean ☊ 24♑20.9
☿D 26 21:06							

March 2047 LONGITUDE

Day	Sid.Time	☉	0 hr ☽	Noon☽	True☊	☿	♀	♂	⚳	♃	♄	♅	♆	♇
1 F	22 36 54	10♓48 57	26♈59 15	2♉54 46	24♑01.8	16♒50.7	13♈05.2	11♈04.4	6♑35.5	20♈01.0	3♑07.9	4♍04.4	16♉53.0	5♓06.5
2 Sa	22 40 51	11 49 11	8♉50 15	14 46 10	23R 56.0	17 09.8	14 18.2	11 49.8	6 54.3	20 13.8	3 11.9	4R 01.8	16 54.1	5 08.1
3 Su	22 44 47	12 49 24	20 43 01	26 41 21	23 52.3	17 34.2	15 31.2	12 35.2	7 13.1	20 26.7	3 15.7	3 59.2	16 55.3	5 09.8
4 M	22 48 44	13 49 34	2♊41 43	8♊44 44	23D 50.7	18 03.6	16 44.1	13 20.6	7 31.6	20 39.7	3 19.5	3 56.6	16 56.5	5 11.5
5 Tu	22 52 40	14 49 42	14 51 01	21 01 13	23 50.7	18 37.6	17 57.0	14 05.9	7 50.0	20 52.7	3 23.3	3 54.1	16 57.7	5 13.1
6 W	22 56 37	15 49 49	27 15 55	3♋35 46	23 51.7	19 15.9	19 09.8	14 51.2	8 08.3	21 05.8	3 26.9	3 51.5	16 59.0	5 14.8
7 Th	23 00 34	16 49 53	10♋01 18	16 33 02	23R 52.8	19 58.3	20 22.5	15 36.4	8 26.4	21 19.0	3 30.4	3 49.0	17 00.3	5 16.4
8 F	23 04 30	17 49 55	23 11 25	29 56 45	23 52.8	20 44.4	21 35.1	16 21.6	8 44.3	21 32.2	3 33.9	3 46.4	17 01.6	5 18.1
9 Sa	23 08 27	18 49 55	6♌49 14	13♌48 53	23 51.0	21 34.0	22 47.7	17 06.8	9 02.1	21 45.4	3 37.3	3 43.9	17 03.0	5 19.7
10 Su	23 12 23	19 49 53	20 55 34	28 08 55	23 46.9	22 26.9	24 00.1	17 51.8	9 19.7	21 58.7	3 40.6	3 41.4	17 04.4	5 21.4
11 M	23 16 20	20 49 49	5♍28 23	12♍53 09	23 40.5	23 22.8	25 12.5	18 36.9	9 37.1	22 12.1	3 43.8	3 38.9	17 05.8	5 23.0
12 Tu	23 20 16	21 49 42	20 22 17	27 54 39	23 32.2	24 21.5	26 24.9	19 21.9	9 54.4	22 25.5	3 46.9	3 36.4	17 07.2	5 24.6
13 W	23 24 13	22 49 34	5♎28 58	13♎03 55	23 22.9	25 23.0	27 37.1	20 06.9	10 11.5	22 39.0	3 49.9	3 34.0	17 08.7	5 26.2
14 Th	23 28 09	23 49 24	20 38 11	28 10 29	23 13.9	26 26.9	28 49.3	20 51.8	10 28.4	22 52.5	3 52.8	3 31.6	17 10.1	5 27.8
15 F	23 32 06	24 49 13	5♏39 41	13♏04 44	23 06.3	27 33.2	0♉01.3	21 36.7	10 45.1	23 06.1	3 55.7	3 29.2	17 11.7	5 29.4
16 Sa	23 36 03	25 48 59	20 24 52	27 39 26	23 00.9	28 41.8	1 13.4	22 21.5	11 01.7	23 19.7	3 58.5	3 26.8	17 13.2	5 31.0
17 Su	23 39 59	26 48 44	4♐48 02	11♐50 28	22 57.8	29 52.5	2 25.3	23 06.3	11 18.0	23 33.4	4 01.1	3 24.4	17 14.8	5 32.6
18 M	23 43 56	27 48 28	18 46 40	25 36 46	22D 56.8	1♓05.3	3 37.1	23 51.0	11 34.2	23 47.1	4 03.7	3 22.1	17 16.4	5 34.2
19 Tu	23 47 52	28 48 10	2♑20 59	8♑59 37	22 57.0	2 19.9	4 48.9	24 35.7	11 50.2	24 00.8	4 06.2	3 19.8	17 18.0	5 35.8
20 W	23 51 49	29 47 50	15 33 03	22 01 43	22R 57.4	3 36.5	6 00.6	25 20.4	12 06.0	24 14.6	4 08.6	3 17.5	17 19.6	5 37.3
21 Th	23 55 45	0♈47 28	28 26 01	4♒46 25	22 56.8	4 54.8	7 12.1	26 05.0	12 21.6	24 28.5	4 10.9	3 15.3	17 21.3	5 38.9
22 F	23 59 42	1 47 04	11♒03 20	17 17 08	22 54.2	6 14.8	8 23.6	26 49.5	12 37.1	24 42.3	4 13.1	3 13.0	17 22.9	5 40.4
23 Sa	0 03 38	2 46 39	23 28 13	29 36 52	22 48.8	7 36.5	9 35.1	27 34.1	12 52.3	24 56.2	4 15.2	3 10.8	17 24.7	5 41.9
24 Su	0 07 35	3 46 12	5♓43 24	11♓48 03	22 40.5	8 59.8	10 46.4	28 18.5	13 07.3	25 10.2	4 17.2	3 08.7	17 26.4	5 43.5
25 M	0 11 32	4 45 42	17 51 02	23 52 34	22 29.6	10 24.7	11 57.6	29 03.0	13 22.0	25 24.2	4 19.1	3 06.5	17 28.1	5 45.0
26 Tu	0 15 28	5 45 11	29 52 46	5♈51 50	22 16.6	11 51.1	13 08.8	29 47.3	13 36.6	25 38.2	4 20.9	3 04.4	17 29.9	5 46.5
27 W	0 19 25	6 44 38	11♈49 53	17 47 05	22 02.7	13 19.0	14 19.8	0♉31.7	13 51.0	25 52.2	4 22.6	3 02.4	17 31.7	5 47.9
28 Th	0 23 21	7 44 02	23 43 34	29 39 32	21 48.9	14 48.4	15 30.7	1 16.0	14 05.1	26 06.3	4 24.3	3 00.3	17 33.5	5 49.4
29 F	0 27 18	8 43 25	5♉35 11	11♉30 45	21 36.4	16 19.3	16 41.6	2 00.2	14 19.0	26 20.4	4 25.8	2 58.3	17 35.3	5 50.9
30 Sa	0 31 14	9 42 45	17 26 32	23 22 50	21 26.2	17 51.6	17 52.3	2 44.4	14 32.7	26 34.6	4 27.2	2 56.4	17 37.2	5 52.3
31 Su	0 35 11	10 42 04	29 20 03	5♊18 34	21 18.7	19 25.3	19 03.0	3 28.5	14 46.2	26 48.7	4 28.5	2 54.5	17 39.1	5 53.7

April 2047 LONGITUDE

Day	Sid.Time	☉	0 hr ☽	Noon☽	True☊	☿	♀	♂	⚳	♃	♄	♅	♆	♇
1 M	0 39 07	11♈41 20	11♊18 52	17♊21 27	21♑14.1	21♓00.5	20♉13.5	4♉12.6	14♑59.4	27♈02.9	4♑29.8	2♍52.6	17♉41.0	5♓55.2
2 Tu	0 43 04	12 40 33	23 26 52	29 35 42	21R 12.0	22 37.1	21 23.9	4 56.7	15 12.4	27 17.1	4 30.9	2R 50.7	17 42.9	5 56.6
3 W	0 47 00	13 39 45	5♋48 33	12♋06 02	21 11.5	24 15.2	22 34.2	5 40.7	15 25.2	27 31.3	4 31.9	2 48.9	17 44.8	5 58.0
4 Th	0 50 57	14 38 54	18 28 46	24 57 20	21 11.5	25 54.6	23 44.4	6 24.6	15 37.7	27 45.6	4 32.9	2 47.2	17 46.7	5 59.3
5 F	0 54 54	15 38 01	1♌32 17	8♌14 04	21 10.8	27 35.5	24 54.4	7 08.5	15 50.0	27 59.9	4 33.7	2 45.4	17 48.7	6 00.7
6 Sa	0 58 50	16 37 05	15 03 05	21 59 34	21 08.3	29 17.8	26 04.4	7 52.4	16 02.0	28 14.2	4 34.4	2 43.8	17 50.7	6 02.0
7 Su	1 02 47	17 36 07	29 03 35	6♍15 00	21 03.2	1♈01.6	27 14.2	8 36.2	16 13.8	28 28.5	4 35.1	2 42.1	17 52.7	6 03.4
8 M	1 06 43	18 35 07	13♍33 28	20 58 24	20 55.5	2 46.8	28 23.9	9 19.9	16 25.3	28 42.8	4 35.6	2 40.5	17 54.7	6 04.7
9 Tu	1 10 40	19 34 04	28 28 59	6♎04 08	20 45.6	4 33.5	29 33.4	10 03.6	16 36.6	28 57.1	4 36.1	2 39.0	17 56.7	6 06.0
10 W	1 14 36	20 33 00	13♎42 37	21 23 00	20 34.5	6 21.7	0♊42.8	10 47.3	16 47.6	29 11.4	4 36.4	2 37.5	17 58.7	6 07.3
11 Th	1 18 33	21 31 54	29 03 49	6♏43 33	20 23.6	8 11.4	1 52.1	11 30.8	16 58.3	29 25.8	4 36.6	2 36.0	18 00.8	6 08.5
12 F	1 22 29	22 30 45	14♏20 46	21 54 09	20 14.0	10 02.6	3 01.3	12 14.4	17 08.8	29 40.2	4R 36.8	2 34.6	18 02.9	6 09.8
13 Sa	1 26 26	23 29 35	29 22 34	6♐45 06	20 06.7	11 55.2	4 10.3	12 57.9	17 19.0	29 54.6	4 36.8	2 33.2	18 05.0	6 11.0
14 Su	1 30 23	24 28 23	14♐01 06	21 10 06	20 02.2	13 49.4	5 19.2	13 41.3	17 28.9	0♉08.9	4 36.8	2 31.9	18 07.0	6 12.2
15 M	1 34 19	25 27 10	28 11 54	5♑06 29	20 00.1	15 45.1	6 27.9	14 24.7	17 38.6	0 23.3	4 36.6	2 30.6	18 09.2	6 13.4
16 Tu	1 38 16	26 25 55	11♑54 01	18 34 47	19 59.6	17 42.3	7 36.5	15 08.1	17 48.0	0 37.8	4 36.4	2 29.4	18 11.3	6 14.6
17 W	1 42 12	27 24 38	25 09 12	1♒37 44	19 59.6	19 41.0	8 45.0	15 51.4	17 57.1	0 52.2	4 36.0	2 28.2	18 13.4	6 15.8
18 Th	1 46 09	28 23 19	8♒00 55	14 19 18	19 58.8	21 41.1	9 53.3	16 34.7	18 05.9	1 06.6	4 35.6	2 27.0	18 15.5	6 16.9
19 F	1 50 05	29 21 59	20 33 25	26 43 50	19 56.2	23 42.6	11 01.4	17 17.9	18 14.4	1 21.0	4 35.0	2 26.0	18 17.7	6 18.0
20 Sa	1 54 02	0♉20 37	2♓51 05	8♓55 37	19 51.0	25 45.4	12 09.4	18 01.0	18 22.6	1 35.4	4 34.4	2 24.9	18 19.9	6 19.1
21 Su	1 57 58	1 19 13	14 57 56	20 58 24	19 43.0	27 49.5	13 17.2	18 44.2	18 30.5	1 49.8	4 33.7	2 23.9	18 22.0	6 20.2
22 M	2 01 55	2 17 47	26 57 25	2♈55 18	19 32.3	29 54.7	14 24.9	19 27.2	18 38.1	2 04.3	4 32.8	2 23.0	18 24.2	6 21.3
23 Tu	2 05 52	3 16 20	8♈52 20	14 48 46	19 19.6	2♉01.0	15 32.4	20 10.2	18 45.4	2 18.7	4 31.9	2 22.1	18 26.4	6 22.3
24 W	2 09 48	4 14 51	20 44 49	26 40 41	19 05.9	4 08.2	16 39.8	20 53.2	18 52.3	2 33.1	4 30.9	2 21.2	18 28.6	6 23.3
25 Th	2 13 45	5 13 20	2♉36 33	8♉32 34	18 52.4	6 16.1	17 47.0	21 36.2	18 59.0	2 47.5	4 29.7	2 20.5	18 30.8	6 24.3
26 F	2 17 41	6 11 47	14 28 56	20 25 49	18 40.0	8 24.5	18 54.0	22 19.0	19 05.3	3 01.9	4 28.5	2 19.7	18 33.0	6 25.3
27 Sa	2 21 38	7 10 12	26 23 24	2♊21 55	18 29.8	10 33.2	20 00.8	23 01.9	19 11.4	3 16.3	4 27.2	2 19.0	18 35.2	6 26.3
28 Su	2 25 34	8 08 35	8♊21 37	14 22 47	18 22.4	12 41.9	21 07.4	23 44.6	19 17.1	3 30.7	4 25.8	2 18.4	18 37.4	6 27.2
29 M	2 29 31	9 06 57	20 25 44	26 30 51	18 17.7	14 50.4	22 13.8	24 27.4	19 22.4	3 45.1	4 24.3	2 17.8	18 39.7	6 28.1
30 Tu	2 33 27	10 05 16	2♋38 31	8♋49 11	18D 15.6	16 58.4	23 20.1	25 10.1	19 27.5	3 59.5	4 22.7	2 17.3	18 41.9	6 29.0

Astro Data	Planet Ingress	Last Aspect	☽ Ingress	Last Aspect	☽ Ingress	☽ Phases & Eclipses	Astro Data
Dy Hr Mn	Dy Hr Mn	Dy Hr Mn	Dy Hr Mn	Dy Hr Mn	Dy Hr Mn	Dy Hr Mn	1 March 2047
♃∠♇ 1 23:46	♀ ♉ 15 11:33	28 9:26 ♃ ☌	♉ 1 6:06	2 7:25 ♃ ⚹	♋ 2 12:47	4 22:53 ☽ 14♊17	Julian Day # 53751
♄△♅ 10 15:29	☿ ♓ 17 14:30	2 16:59 ☿ □	♊ 3 18:37	4 17:14 ♃ □	♌ 4 21:13	12 1:38 ○ 21♍24	SVP 4♓35'47"
☽0S 11 23:39	☉ ♈ 20 16:54	5 11:43 ♃ ⚹	♋ 6 5:12	6 22:48 ♃ △	♍ 7 1:35	18 16:12 ☾ 27♐59	GC 27♐29.9 ⚴ 1♐48.6
☉0N 20 16:54	♂ ♉ 26 18:51	7 20:47 ♃ □	♌ 8 12:06	9 0:51 ♀ △	♎ 9 2:24	26 11:45 ● 5♈45	Eris 29♈41.8 ⚵ 11♐36.0
☽0N 25 4:35		10 4:30 ♀ △	♍ 10 15:03	11 0:24 ♃ ☍	♏ 11 1:28		⚷ 24♎00.8R ⚶ 16♐24.2
	☿ ♈ 6 21:48	12 1:38 ☉ ☍	♎ 12 15:19	12 5:51 ♆ ☍	♐ 13 1:01	3 15:12 ☽ 13♋48	☽ Mean ☊ 22♑52.0
☽0S 8 10:27	♀ ♊ 9 21:11	14 13:07 ♀ ☍	♏ 14 14:55	14 18:02 ☉ △	♑ 15 3:07	10 10:37 ○ 20♎30	
☿0N 9 18:47	♃ ♉ 13 21:05	16 13:53 ☿ □	♐ 16 15:55	17 3:31 ☉ □	♒ 17 8:58	17 3:31 ☾ 27♑04	1 April 2047
♄ R 13 11:48	☉ ♉ 20 3:34	18 16:12 ☉ □	♑ 18 19:48	19 17:36 ☉ ⚹	♓ 19 18:24	25 4:41 ● 4♉56	Julian Day # 53782
☽0N 21 9:50	☿ ♉ 22 13:00	20 18:34 ♂ □	♒ 21 2:57	21 7:14 ♂ ⚹	♈ 22 6:07		SVP 4♓35'44"
♃△♅ 23 17:22		23 7:44 ♂ ⚹	♓ 23 12:45	23 13:37 ♀ ⚹	♉ 24 18:43		GC 27♐30.0 ⚴ 3♐39.6R
		24 23:13 ♆ ⚹	♈ 26 0:14	26 16:03 ♂ ☌	♊ 27 7:15		Eris 29♈59.0 ⚵ 14♐02.9
		28 4:40 ♃ ☌	♉ 28 12:41	29 2:43 ♀ ☌	♋ 29 18:50		⚷ 22♎05.0R ⚶ 25♐47.3
		30 0:20 ♆ ☌	♊ 31 1:20				☽ Mean ☊ 21♑13.5

LONGITUDE — May 2047

Day	Sid.Time	☉	0 hr ☽	Noon ☽	True ☊	☿	♀	♂	⚳	♃	♄	♅	♆	♇
1 W	2 37 24	11♉03 34	15♋03 20	21♋21 28	18♑15.2	19♉05.6	24♊26.1	25♉52.7	19♑32.2	4♉13.8	4♑21.0	2♍16.8	18♉44.2	6♓29.9
2 Th	2 41 21	12 01 49	27 44 06	4♌11 44	18R 15.7	21 11.6	25 31.9	26 35.3	19 36.5	4 28.2	4R 19.2	2R 16.4	18 46.4	6 30.8
3 F	2 45 17	13 00 02	10♌44 52	17 23 59	18 15.8	23 16.2	26 37.5	27 17.8	19 40.5	4 42.5	4 17.4	2 16.1	18 48.6	6 31.6
4 Sa	2 49 14	13 58 14	24 09 27	1♍01 35	18 14.5	25 19.0	27 42.9	28 00.3	19 44.2	4 56.8	4 15.4	2 15.7	18 50.9	6 32.4
5 Su	2 53 10	14 56 23	8♍00 34	15 06 26	18 11.2	27 19.8	28 48.1	28 42.7	19 47.5	5 11.1	4 13.4	2 15.5	18 53.1	6 33.2
6 M	2 57 07	15 54 30	22 19 01	29 37 59	18 05.6	29 18.4	29 53.0	29 25.1	19 50.5	5 25.4	4 11.3	2 15.3	18 55.4	6 34.0
7 Tu	3 01 03	16 52 35	7♎02 44	14♎32 30	17 58.0	1♊14.5	0♋57.7	0♊07.5	19 53.2	5 39.6	4 09.1	2 15.1	18 57.6	6 34.7
8 W	3 05 00	17 50 38	22 06 16	29 42 52	17 49.3	3 07.8	2 02.1	0 49.7	19 55.4	5 53.9	4 06.8	2 15.0	18 59.9	6 35.4
9 Th	3 08 56	18 48 40	7♏20 58	14♏59 10	17 40.5	4 58.3	3 06.3	1 32.0	19 57.4	6 08.1	4 04.4	2D 15.0	19 02.2	6 36.1
10 F	3 12 53	19 46 40	22 36 06	0♐10 23	17 32.8	6 45.7	4 10.2	2 14.2	19 59.0	6 22.3	4 01.9	2 15.0	19 04.4	6 36.8
11 Sa	3 16 50	20 44 39	7♐40 48	15 06 15	17 27.0	8 29.9	5 13.9	2 56.3	20 00.2	6 36.5	3 59.4	2 15.0	19 06.7	6 37.4
12 Su	3 20 46	21 42 36	22 25 52	29 39 00	17 23.5	10 10.8	6 17.2	3 38.4	20 01.0	6 50.6	3 56.8	2 15.2	19 08.9	6 38.1
13 M	3 24 43	22 40 32	6♑45 11	13♑44 12	17D 22.2	11 48.3	7 20.3	4 20.5	20R 01.5	7 04.8	3 54.1	2 15.3	19 11.2	6 38.7
14 Tu	3 28 39	23 38 26	20 36 00	27 20 44	17 22.4	13 22.3	8 23.2	5 02.5	20 01.7	7 18.9	3 51.3	2 15.5	19 13.4	6 39.3
15 W	3 32 36	24 36 20	3♒58 38	10♒30 05	17 23.4	14 52.8	9 25.7	5 44.4	20 01.5	7 32.9	3 48.5	2 15.8	19 15.7	6 39.8
16 Th	3 36 32	25 34 12	16 55 34	23 15 36	17R 24.1	16 19.6	10 27.9	6 26.3	20 00.9	7 47.0	3 45.5	2 16.2	19 17.9	6 40.4
17 F	3 40 29	26 32 02	29 30 44	5♓41 32	17 23.7	17 42.8	11 29.8	7 08.2	19 59.9	8 01.0	3 42.5	2 16.5	19 20.2	6 40.9
18 Sa	3 44 25	27 29 52	11♓48 37	17 52 33	17 21.5	19 02.3	12 31.4	7 50.0	19 58.5	8 15.0	3 39.5	2 17.0	19 22.4	6 41.4
19 Su	3 48 22	28 27 40	23 53 52	29 53 06	17 17.2	20 17.9	13 32.7	8 31.8	19 56.8	8 28.9	3 36.3	2 17.5	19 24.7	6 41.8
20 M	3 52 19	29 25 27	5♈50 46	11♈47 18	17 11.0	21 29.8	14 33.7	9 13.5	19 54.7	8 42.9	3 33.1	2 18.0	19 26.9	6 42.3
21 Tu	3 56 15	0♊23 13	17 43 09	23 38 40	17 03.2	22 37.8	15 34.3	9 55.2	19 52.3	8 56.8	3 29.8	2 18.6	19 29.1	6 42.7
22 W	4 00 12	1 20 58	29 34 13	5♉30 05	16 54.7	23 41.8	16 34.5	10 36.9	19 49.5	9 10.6	3 26.5	2 19.2	19 31.3	6 43.1
23 Th	4 04 08	2 18 42	11♉26 33	17 23 51	16 46.1	24 41.8	17 34.4	11 18.5	19 46.3	9 24.4	3 23.1	2 20.0	19 33.6	6 43.4
24 F	4 08 05	3 16 24	23 22 12	29 21 48	16 38.4	25 37.7	18 33.9	12 00.1	19 42.7	9 38.2	3 19.6	2 20.7	19 35.8	6 43.8
25 Sa	4 12 01	4 14 05	5♊22 51	11♊25 31	16 32.2	26 29.5	19 33.0	12 41.6	19 38.8	9 51.9	3 16.1	2 21.5	19 38.0	6 44.1
26 Su	4 15 58	5 11 45	17 29 58	23 36 25	16 27.8	27 17.1	20 31.8	13 23.0	19 34.5	10 05.6	3 12.5	2 22.4	19 40.2	6 44.4
27 M	4 19 54	6 09 24	29 45 03	5♋56 05	16D 25.4	28 00.4	21 30.1	14 04.5	19 29.8	10 19.3	3 08.8	2 23.3	19 42.4	6 44.6
28 Tu	4 23 51	7 07 01	12♋09 46	18 26 21	16 24.9	28 39.4	22 27.9	14 45.9	19 24.8	10 32.9	3 05.1	2 24.3	19 44.5	6 44.9
29 W	4 27 48	8 04 37	24 46 07	1♌09 23	16 25.7	29 13.9	23 25.4	15 27.2	19 19.4	10 46.5	3 01.3	2 25.3	19 46.7	6 45.1
30 Th	4 31 44	9 02 11	7♌36 27	14 07 39	16 27.1	29 43.9	24 22.3	16 08.5	19 13.6	11 00.0	2 57.5	2 26.4	19 48.9	6 45.3
31 F	4 35 41	9 59 44	20 43 17	27 23 39	16R 28.5	0♋09.4	25 18.8	16 49.7	19 07.5	11 13.5	2 53.7	2 27.5	19 51.0	6 45.5

LONGITUDE — June 2047

Day	Sid.Time	☉	0 hr ☽	Noon ☽	True ☊	☿	♀	♂	⚳	♃	♄	♅	♆	♇
1 Sa	4 39 37	10♊57 16	4♍09 01	10♍59 35	16♑29.1	0♋30.2	26♋14.8	17♊30.9	19♑01.1	11♉26.9	2♑49.8	2♍28.7	19♉53.2	6♓45.6
2 Su	4 43 34	11 54 46	17 55 29	24 56 43	16R 28.4	0 46.4	27 10.3	18 12.1	18R 54.3	11 40.2	2R 45.8	2 29.9	19 55.3	6 45.7
3 M	4 47 30	12 52 15	2♎03 14	9♎14 48	16 26.2	0 58.0	28 05.2	18 53.2	18 47.2	11 53.6	2 41.8	2 31.2	19 57.4	6 45.8
4 Tu	4 51 27	13 49 43	16 31 02	23 51 25	16 22.8	1 04.9	28 59.6	19 34.3	18 39.8	12 06.8	2 37.8	2 32.5	19 59.5	6 45.9
5 W	4 55 23	14 47 09	1♏15 15	8♏41 43	16 18.7	1R 07.2	29 53.4	20 15.3	18 32.0	12 20.0	2 33.7	2 33.9	20 01.6	6 45.9
6 Th	4 59 20	15 44 35	16 09 53	23 38 42	16 14.3	1 05.0	0♌46.7	20 56.3	18 23.9	12 33.2	2 29.6	2 35.3	20 03.7	6R 45.9
7 F	5 03 17	16 41 59	1♐07 05	8♐33 57	16 10.6	0 58.3	1 39.3	21 37.2	18 15.5	12 46.3	2 25.4	2 36.8	20 05.8	6 45.9
8 Sa	5 07 13	17 39 23	15 58 13	23 18 56	16 07.8	0 47.4	2 31.3	22 18.1	18 06.8	12 59.4	2 21.2	2 38.3	20 07.8	6 45.9
9 Su	5 11 10	18 36 45	0♑35 14	7♑46 23	16D 06.4	0 32.4	3 22.6	22 58.9	17 57.8	13 12.3	2 17.0	2 39.9	20 09.9	6 45.8
10 M	5 15 06	19 34 07	14 51 49	21 51 08	16 06.3	0 13.6	4 13.2	23 39.8	17 48.5	13 25.3	2 12.8	2 41.5	20 11.9	6 45.8
11 Tu	5 19 03	20 31 28	28 44 06	5♒30 36	16 07.2	29♊51.4	5 03.2	24 20.5	17 38.9	13 38.1	2 08.5	2 43.2	20 13.9	6 45.7
12 W	5 22 59	21 28 49	12♒10 44	18 44 38	16 08.7	29 26.0	5 52.4	25 01.3	17 29.0	13 51.0	2 04.2	2 44.9	20 15.9	6 45.5
13 Th	5 26 56	22 26 09	25 12 37	1♓35 04	16 10.1	28 57.8	6 40.9	25 41.9	17 18.8	14 03.7	1 59.9	2 46.6	20 17.9	6 45.4
14 F	5 30 53	23 23 29	7♓52 24	14 05 08	16R 11.2	28 27.5	7 28.6	26 22.6	17 08.4	14 16.4	1 55.5	2 48.5	20 19.9	6 45.2
15 Sa	5 34 49	24 20 48	20 13 47	26 18 56	16 11.5	27 55.4	8 15.5	27 03.2	16 57.7	14 29.0	1 51.2	2 50.3	20 21.8	6 45.0
16 Su	5 38 46	25 18 06	2♈21 08	8♈20 58	16 10.9	27 22.1	9 01.5	27 43.8	16 46.8	14 41.6	1 46.8	2 52.2	20 23.7	6 44.8
17 M	5 42 42	26 15 25	14 19 00	20 15 46	16 09.3	26 48.1	9 46.7	28 24.3	16 35.6	14 54.0	1 42.4	2 54.2	20 25.7	6 44.5
18 Tu	5 46 39	27 12 43	26 11 48	2♉07 37	16 07.1	26 14.1	10 31.0	29 04.8	16 24.2	15 06.4	1 38.0	2 56.2	20 27.6	6 44.3
19 W	5 50 35	28 10 01	8♉03 40	14 00 24	16 04.4	25 40.6	11 14.4	29 45.3	16 12.6	15 18.8	1 33.6	2 58.2	20 29.4	6 44.0
20 Th	5 54 32	29 07 18	19 58 12	25 57 28	16 01.8	25 08.2	11 56.8	0♋25.7	16 00.8	15 31.1	1 29.2	3 00.3	20 31.3	6 43.7
21 F	5 58 28	0♋04 35	1♊58 29	8♊01 34	15 59.4	24 37.5	12 38.3	1 06.1	15 48.9	15 43.3	1 24.7	3 02.4	20 33.2	6 43.3
22 Sa	6 02 25	1 01 52	14 06 57	20 14 53	15 57.5	24 08.9	13 18.7	1 46.4	15 36.7	15 55.4	1 20.3	3 04.6	20 35.0	6 43.0
23 Su	6 06 22	1 59 08	26 25 30	2♋39 00	15 56.4	23 43.0	13 58.0	2 26.7	15 24.4	16 07.4	1 15.9	3 06.8	20 36.8	6 42.6
24 M	6 10 18	2 56 24	8♋55 30	15 15 07	15D 56.0	23 20.2	14 36.1	3 07.0	15 11.9	16 19.4	1 11.4	3 09.1	20 38.6	6 42.2
25 Tu	6 14 15	3 53 40	21 37 55	28 04 00	15 56.3	23 00.8	15 13.1	3 47.3	14 59.2	16 31.3	1 07.0	3 11.4	20 40.4	6 41.7
26 W	6 18 11	4 50 55	4♌33 26	11♌06 16	15 57.0	22 45.3	15 48.9	4 27.4	14 46.5	16 43.1	1 02.6	3 13.7	20 42.1	6 41.3
27 Th	6 22 08	5 48 10	17 42 33	24 22 19	15 57.9	22 34.0	16 23.5	5 07.6	14 33.6	16 54.8	0 58.2	3 16.1	20 43.8	6 40.8
28 F	6 26 04	6 45 24	1♍05 37	7♍52 27	15 58.7	22 27.0	16 56.7	5 47.7	14 20.7	17 06.4	0 53.8	3 18.5	20 45.5	6 40.3
29 Sa	6 30 01	7 42 37	14 42 48	21 36 40	15 59.3	22D 24.5	17 28.5	6 27.8	14 07.6	17 18.0	0 49.4	3 21.0	20 47.2	6 39.8
30 Su	6 33 57	8 39 50	28 33 57	5♎34 34	15R 59.6	22 26.8	17 58.9	7 07.8	13 54.5	17 29.4	0 45.0	3 23.5	20 48.9	6 39.2

Astro Data

Aspect	Dy Hr Mn
♃△♄	1 22:44
☽0S	5 19:34
♅ D	9 20:12
♄⚼♆	9 23:25
♃✶♇	11 13:43
⚳ R	14 8:54
☽0N	18 15:10
☽0S	2 2:16
♄△♅	5 11:13
☿ R	5 12:06
♇ R	6 20:53
☽0N	14 21:51
♃⚼♄	24 0:20
☽0S	29 7:33
☿ D	29 12:37

Planet Ingress

Planet	Sign	Dy Hr Mn
♀	♋	6 14:36
☿	♊	6 20:32
♂	♊	7 7:46
☉	♊	21 2:21
☿	♋	31 2:39
♀	♌	5 14:57
☿	♊R	11 3:06
♂	♋	19 20:44
☉	♋	21 10:05

Last Aspect / ☽ Ingress (May)

Last Aspect Dy Hr Mn		☽ Ingress	Dy Hr Mn
1 21:01	♂ ✶	♌	2 4:14
4 6:28	♂ □	♍	4 10:13
6 12:26	♀ □	♎	6 12:36
6 19:22	♄ □	♏	8 12:27
9 18:26	☉ ☍	♐	10 11:43
10 23:55	☿ ☍	♑	12 12:35
14 4:53	☉ △	♒	14 16:47
16 16:47	☉ □	♓	17 0:57
19 8:53	☉ ✶	♈	19 12:14
21 9:44	☿ ✶	♉	22 0:52
23 16:22	♆ ☌	♊	24 13:16
26 19:40	☿ ☌	♋	27 0:29
28 20:16	♀ ☌	♌	29 9:50
30 22:23	♆ □	♍	31 16:39

Last Aspect / ☽ Ingress (June)

Last Aspect Dy Hr Mn		☽ Ingress	Dy Hr Mn
2 16:02	♀ ✶	♎	2 20:33
4 20:53	♀ □	♏	4 21:58
6 6:14	♆ ☍	♐	6 22:12
8 10:15	♂ ☍	♑	8 23:02
10 9:08	♆ △	♒	11 2:14
13 7:14	☿ △	♓	13 9:00
15 15:03	☿ □	♈	15 19:19
18 5:28	♂ ✶	♉	18 7:42
20 1:05	♆ ☌	♊	20 20:04
22 19:19	☿ ☌	♋	23 6:54
24 22:10	♆ ✶	♌	25 15:35
27 8:48	☿ ✶	♍	27 22:03
29 13:23	☿ □	♎	30 2:28

☽ Phases & Eclipses

Dy Hr Mn	Phase	Position
3 3:28	☽	12♌39
9 18:26	○	19♏04
16 16:47	☾	25♒46
24 20:29	●	3♊37
1 11:56	☽	10♍57
8 2:06	○	17♐16
15 7:46	☾	24♓11
23 10:37	●	1♋56
23 10:52:25	●	P 0.313
30 17:38	☽	8♎53

Astro Data

1 May 2047
Julian Day # 53812
SVP 4♓35'40"
GC 27♐30.0 ⚵ 28♏27.4R
Eris 0♉18.7 ✱ 11♐38.3R
⚷ 19♎47.7R ⚶ 29♐33.6
☽ Mean ☊ 19♑38.1

1 June 2047
Julian Day # 53843
SVP 4♓35'35"
GC 27♐30.1 ⚵ 19♏28.3R
Eris 0♉37.4 ✱ 5♐16.3R
⚷ 18♎15.2R ⚶ 26♐09.6R
☽ Mean ☊ 17♑59.6

July 2047 — LONGITUDE

Day	Sid.Time	☉	0 hr ☽	Noon ☽	True ☊	☿	♀	♂	⚳	♃	♄	♅	♆	♇
1 M	6 37 54	9♋37 02	12♎38 21	19♎45 04	15♑59.5	22♊33.8	18♌27.9	7♋47.8	13♑41.4	17♉40.8	0♑40.6	3♍26.0	20♉50.5	6♓38.7
2 Tu	6 41 51	10 34 15	26 54 25	4♏06 04	15R59.2	22 45.8	18 55.3	8 27.8	13R28.2	17 52.1	0R36.3	3 28.6	20 52.1	6R38.1
3 W	6 45 47	11 31 26	11♏19 35	18 34 26	15 58.7	23 02.7	19 21.1	9 07.7	13 15.0	18 03.2	0 32.0	3 31.2	20 53.7	6 37.5
4 Th	6 49 44	12 28 38	25 50 04	3♐05 52	15 58.3	23 24.5	19 45.3	9 47.6	13 01.7	18 14.3	0 27.7	3 33.9	20 55.3	6 36.8
5 F	6 53 40	13 25 49	10♐21 10	17 35 16	15 58.1	23 51.3	20 07.7	10 27.5	12 48.5	18 25.3	0 23.4	3 36.6	20 56.8	6 36.2
6 Sa	6 57 37	14 23 00	24 47 30	1♑57 11	15D57.9	24 23.0	20 28.4	11 07.3	12 35.3	18 36.2	0 19.2	3 39.3	20 58.3	6 35.5
7 Su	7 01 33	15 20 11	9♑03 42	16 06 28	15R57.9	24 59.6	20 47.2	11 47.1	12 22.1	18 47.0	0 15.0	3 42.0	20 59.8	6 34.8
8 M	7 05 30	16 17 22	23 04 59	29 58 51	15 57.9	25 41.0	21 04.2	12 26.8	12 09.0	18 57.7	0 10.8	3 44.8	21 01.3	6 34.1
9 Tu	7 09 26	17 14 33	6♒47 45	13♒31 28	15 57.8	26 27.3	21 19.2	13 06.5	11 55.9	19 08.3	0 06.7	3 47.7	21 02.7	6 33.4
10 W	7 13 23	18 11 45	20 09 53	26 43 01	15 57.6	27 18.4	21 32.3	13 46.2	11 42.9	19 18.9	0 02.6	3 50.5	21 04.2	6 32.6
11 Th	7 17 20	19 08 56	3♓10 57	9♓33 52	15 57.3	28 14.1	21 43.2	14 25.9	11 29.9	19 29.2	29♐58.5	3 53.4	21 05.5	6 31.9
12 F	7 21 16	20 06 08	15 52 02	22 05 48	15 56.9	29 14.5	21 52.1	15 05.5	11 17.1	19 39.5	29 54.4	3 56.4	21 06.9	6 31.1
13 Sa	7 25 13	21 03 21	28 15 33	4♈21 46	15 56.5	0♋19.5	21 58.8	15 45.1	11 04.4	19 49.7	29 50.5	3 59.3	21 08.2	6 30.3
14 Su	7 29 09	22 00 33	10♈24 55	16 25 33	15D56.3	1 29.0	22 03.3	16 24.6	10 51.7	19 59.8	29 46.5	4 02.3	21 09.6	6 29.4
15 M	7 33 06	22 57 47	22 24 14	28 21 31	15 56.3	2 43.0	22R05.6	17 04.1	10 39.3	20 09.8	29 42.6	4 05.4	21 10.8	6 28.6
16 Tu	7 37 02	23 55 01	4♉17 59	10♉14 13	15 56.6	4 01.3	22 05.6	17 43.6	10 27.0	20 19.6	29 38.8	4 08.4	21 12.1	6 27.7
17 W	7 40 59	24 52 16	16 10 46	22 08 12	15 57.3	5 24.0	22 03.2	18 23.1	10 14.8	20 29.4	29 35.0	4 11.5	21 13.3	6 26.9
18 Th	7 44 55	25 49 31	28 07 03	4♊07 50	15 58.2	6 50.9	21 58.5	19 02.5	10 02.8	20 39.0	29 31.2	4 14.6	21 14.5	6 26.0
19 F	7 48 52	26 46 47	10♊10 59	16 16 58	15 59.2	8 21.9	21 51.5	19 41.9	9 51.0	20 48.5	29 27.5	4 17.8	21 15.7	6 25.0
20 Sa	7 52 49	27 44 04	22 26 08	28 38 50	16 00.0	9 56.9	21 42.1	20 21.3	9 39.4	20 57.9	29 23.9	4 21.0	21 16.9	6 24.1
21 Su	7 56 45	28 41 21	4♋55 21	11♋15 52	16R00.5	11 35.7	21 30.3	21 00.6	9 28.0	21 07.2	29 20.3	4 24.2	21 18.0	6 23.2
22 M	8 00 42	29 38 39	17 40 33	24 09 28	16 00.4	13 18.2	21 16.1	21 39.9	9 16.8	21 16.3	29 16.8	4 27.4	21 19.1	6 22.2
23 Tu	8 04 38	0♌35 57	0♌42 37	7♌19 58	15 59.6	15 04.3	20 59.6	22 19.2	9 05.9	21 25.4	29 13.3	4 30.6	21 20.1	6 21.2
24 W	8 08 35	1 33 16	14 01 23	20 46 42	15 58.2	16 53.6	20 40.8	22 58.5	8 55.2	21 34.3	29 09.9	4 33.9	21 21.2	6 20.2
25 Th	8 12 31	2 30 35	27 35 39	4♍27 57	15 56.2	18 45.9	20 19.8	23 37.7	8 44.8	21 43.0	29 06.6	4 37.2	21 22.2	6 19.2
26 F	8 16 28	3 27 54	11♍23 19	18 21 22	15 53.9	20 41.0	19 56.6	24 16.9	8 34.6	21 51.7	29 03.3	4 40.6	21 23.1	6 18.2
27 Sa	8 20 24	4 25 14	25 21 45	2♎24 06	15 51.7	22 38.5	19 31.3	24 56.0	8 24.7	22 00.2	29 00.1	4 43.9	21 24.1	6 17.2
28 Su	8 24 21	5 22 35	9♎28 03	16 33 13	15 50.1	24 38.2	19 04.0	25 35.1	8 15.0	22 08.5	28 57.0	4 47.3	21 25.0	6 16.1
29 M	8 28 18	6 19 56	23 39 16	0♏45 52	15D49.3	26 39.7	18 34.8	26 14.2	8 05.7	22 16.8	28 53.9	4 50.7	21 25.8	6 15.0
30 Tu	8 32 14	7 17 17	7♏52 42	14 59 28	15 49.4	28 42.7	18 04.0	26 53.3	7 56.6	22 24.9	28 50.9	4 54.1	21 26.7	6 14.0
31 W	8 36 11	8 14 39	22 05 53	29 11 40	15 50.2	0♌46.8	17 31.5	27 32.3	7 47.9	22 32.8	28 48.0	4 57.6	21 27.5	6 12.9

August 2047 — LONGITUDE

Day	Sid.Time	☉	0 hr ☽	Noon ☽	True ☊	☿	♀	♂	⚳	♃	♄	♅	♆	♇
1 Th	8 40 07	9♌12 02	6♐16 32	13♐20 14	15♑51.6	2♌51.7	16♌57.7	28♋11.3	7♑39.5	22♉40.7	28♐45.2	5♍01.0	21♉28.3	6♓11.8
2 F	8 44 04	10 09 25	20 22 27	27 22 57	15 52.9	4 57.1	16R22.7	28 50.2	7R31.3	22 48.4	28R42.4	5 04.5	21 29.1	6R10.7
3 Sa	8 48 00	11 06 49	4♑21 24	11♑17 32	15R53.7	7 02.7	15 46.8	29 29.2	7 23.5	22 55.9	28 39.7	5 08.0	21 29.8	6 09.5
4 Su	8 51 57	12 04 13	18 11 03	25 01 39	15 53.5	9 08.3	15 10.1	0♌08.1	7 16.1	23 03.3	28 37.1	5 11.5	21 30.5	6 08.4
5 M	8 55 54	13 01 38	1♒49 04	8♒33 02	15 52.0	11 13.4	14 32.9	0 47.0	7 08.9	23 10.5	28 34.6	5 15.1	21 31.1	6 07.3
6 Tu	8 59 50	13 59 04	15 13 19	21 49 45	15 49.1	13 18.0	13 55.5	1 25.8	7 02.1	23 17.7	28 32.1	5 18.6	21 31.8	6 06.1
7 W	9 03 47	14 56 31	28 22 11	4♓50 31	15 45.1	15 21.9	13 18.0	2 04.6	6 55.6	23 24.6	28 29.7	5 22.2	21 32.4	6 04.9
8 Th	9 07 43	15 54 00	11♓14 45	17 34 55	15 40.3	17 24.9	12 40.8	2 43.4	6 49.5	23 31.4	28 27.4	5 25.8	21 32.9	6 03.8
9 F	9 11 40	16 51 29	23 51 08	0♈03 34	15 35.3	19 26.8	12 04.0	3 22.2	6 43.7	23 38.1	28 25.2	5 29.4	21 33.4	6 02.6
10 Sa	9 15 36	17 48 59	6♈12 29	12 18 11	15 30.6	21 27.6	11 28.0	4 00.9	6 38.2	23 44.5	28 23.1	5 33.0	21 33.9	6 01.4
11 Su	9 19 33	18 46 31	18 21 02	24 21 28	15 26.9	23 27.1	10 52.8	4 39.7	6 33.1	23 50.9	28 21.1	5 36.6	21 34.4	6 00.2
12 M	9 23 29	19 44 05	0♉19 58	6♉17 03	15 24.4	25 25.3	10 18.9	5 18.4	6 28.4	23 57.1	28 19.1	5 40.3	21 34.8	5 58.9
13 Tu	9 27 26	20 41 39	12 13 17	18 09 13	15D23.4	27 22.2	9 46.2	5 57.0	6 24.0	24 03.1	28 17.3	5 43.9	21 35.2	5 57.7
14 W	9 31 22	21 39 16	24 05 28	0♊02 40	15 23.7	29 17.7	9 15.1	6 35.7	6 19.9	24 08.9	28 15.5	5 47.6	21 35.6	5 56.5
15 Th	9 35 19	22 36 53	6♊01 26	12 02 21	15 25.0	1♍11.8	8 45.7	7 14.3	6 16.3	24 14.6	28 13.8	5 51.3	21 35.9	5 55.3
16 F	9 39 16	23 34 33	18 06 03	24 13 06	15 26.6	3 04.4	8 18.2	7 52.9	6 12.9	24 20.2	28 12.2	5 55.0	21 36.3	5 54.0
17 Sa	9 43 12	24 32 13	0♋24 03	6♋39 22	15R27.9	4 55.6	7 52.6	8 31.5	6 10.0	24 25.5	28 10.7	5 58.7	21 36.5	5 52.8
18 Su	9 47 09	25 29 55	12 59 29	19 24 45	15 28.1	6 45.3	7 29.1	9 10.0	6 07.4	24 30.7	28 09.3	6 02.4	21 36.8	5 51.5
19 M	9 51 05	26 27 39	25 55 26	2♌31 41	15 26.8	8 33.6	7 07.7	9 48.6	6 05.1	24 35.7	28 08.0	6 06.1	21 37.0	5 50.3
20 Tu	9 55 02	27 25 24	9♌13 33	16 00 56	15 23.6	10 20.5	6 48.7	10 27.1	6 03.2	24 40.6	28 06.7	6 09.9	21 37.1	5 49.0
21 W	9 58 58	28 23 11	22 53 39	29 51 20	15 18.6	12 06.0	6 31.9	11 05.5	6 01.7	24 45.3	28 05.6	6 13.6	21 37.3	5 47.8
22 Th	10 02 55	29 20 58	6♍53 32	13♍59 41	15 12.2	13 50.1	6 17.5	11 44.0	6 00.6	24 49.7	28 04.6	6 17.3	21 37.4	5 46.5
23 F	10 06 51	0♍18 47	21 09 06	28 21 04	15 05.1	15 32.7	6 05.4	12 22.4	5 59.8	24 54.1	28 03.6	6 21.1	21 37.4	5 45.2
24 Sa	10 10 48	1 16 38	5♎34 48	12♎49 33	14 58.4	17 14.0	5 55.7	13 00.8	5D59.4	24 58.2	28 02.8	6 24.8	21R37.5	5 43.9
25 Su	10 14 45	2 14 29	20 04 32	27 19 03	14 52.8	18 53.9	5 48.4	13 39.2	5 59.3	25 02.1	28 02.0	6 28.6	21 37.5	5 42.7
26 M	10 18 41	3 12 22	4♏32 28	11♏44 15	14 48.9	20 32.5	5 43.5	14 17.5	5 59.6	25 05.9	28 01.4	6 32.3	21 37.4	5 41.4
27 Tu	10 22 38	4 10 16	18 53 57	26 01 13	14D47.0	22 09.7	5D41.0	14 55.8	6 00.2	25 09.5	28 00.8	6 36.1	21 37.4	5 40.1
28 W	10 26 34	5 08 12	3♐05 47	10♐07 30	14 46.8	23 45.6	5 40.7	15 34.1	6 01.2	25 12.9	28 00.3	6 39.9	21 37.3	5 38.8
29 Th	10 30 31	6 06 08	17 06 16	24 02 02	14 47.7	25 20.2	5 42.8	16 12.4	6 02.6	25 16.1	28 00.0	6 43.6	21 37.2	5 37.5
30 F	10 34 27	7 04 06	0♑54 48	7♑44 38	14R48.6	26 53.4	5 47.2	16 50.6	6 04.3	25 19.2	27 59.7	6 47.4	21 37.0	5 36.3
31 Sa	10 38 24	8 02 06	14 31 32	21 15 32	14 48.6	28 25.3	5 53.8	17 28.9	6 06.3	25 22.0	27 59.5	6 51.2	21 36.8	5 35.0

Astro Data

	Dy Hr Mn
☽ 0N	12 6:06
♀ R	15 23:48
♃☌♆	22 20:11
☽ 0S	26 13:16
☽ 0N	8 15:02
♅☍♇	16 7:20
☽ 0S	22 20:50
♆ R	25 1:17
⚳ D	25 4:40
♀ D	28 2:08

Planet Ingress

	Dy Hr Mn
♄ ♐R	11 3:01
☿ ♋	13 4:59
☉ ♌	22 20:57
☿ ♌	31 2:58
♂ ♌	4 7:00
☿ ♍	14 20:52
☉ ♍	23 4:12

Last Aspect / ☽ Ingress

Last Aspect Dy Hr Mn		☽ Ingress Dy Hr Mn
1 16:47 ☿ △	♏	2 5:10
3 15:51 ♆ ☍	♐	4 6:53
5 22:49 ☿ ☍	♑	6 8:43
7 20:25 ☿ △	♒	8 12:02
10 13:10 ☿ △	♓	10 18:04
13 3:15 ☿ □	♈	13 3:25
15 14:43 ♄ △	♉	15 15:19
17 17:58 ☉ ⚹	♊	18 3:46
20 13:26 ♄ ☍	♋	20 14:36
22 7:09 ♂ ☌	♌	22 22:42
25 2:42 ♄ △	♍	25 4:13
27 6:14 ♄ □	♎	27 7:55
29 8:52 ♄ ⚹	♏	29 10:43
31 9:04 ♂ △	♐	31 13:22

Last Aspect Dy Hr Mn		☽ Ingress Dy Hr Mn
2 14:16 ♄ ☌	♑	2 16:30
4 8:30 ♃ △	♒	4 20:47
7 0:16 ♄ ⚹	♓	7 3:01
9 8:50 ♄ □	♈	9 11:53
11 20:00 ♄ △	♉	11 23:20
14 10:12 ☿ □	♊	14 11:55
16 19:44 ♄ ☍	♋	16 23:14
18 21:28 ♃ ⚹	♌	19 7:26
21 9:17 ☉ ☌	♍	21 12:15
23 11:31 ♄ □	♎	23 14:44
25 13:11 ♄ ⚹	♏	25 16:27
27 10:32 ♃ ☍	♐	27 18:44
29 18:54 ♄ ☌	♑	29 22:24

☽ Phases & Eclipses

Dy Hr Mn	
7 10:35	○ 15♑17
7 10:36	• T 1.752
15 0:11	☾ 22♈30
22 22:51	● 0♌05
22 22:36:18	• P 0.361
29 22:04	☽ 6♏44
5 20:40	○ 13♒22
13 17:35	☾ 20♉55
21 9:17	● 28♌17
28 2:51	☽ 4♐46

Astro Data

1 July 2047
Julian Day # 53873
SVP 4♓35'30"
GC 27♐30.2 ⚴ 15♏04.1R
Eris 0♉49.5 ⚵ 29♏45.1R
⚷ 18♎18.0 ⚶ 19♐21.0R
☽ Mean ☊ 16♑24.3

1 August 2047
Julian Day # 53904
SVP 4♓35'25"
GC 27♐30.2 ⚴ 17♏22.9
Eris 0♉53.0R ⚵ 28♏32.4
⚷ 20♎02.3 ⚶ 16♐57.6
☽ Mean ☊ 14♑45.9

LONGITUDE — September 2047

Day	Sid.Time	⊙	0 hr ☽	Noon ☽	True ☊	☿	♀	♂	⚳	♃	♄	♅	♆	♇
1 Su	10 42 20	9♍00 06	27♑56 42	4♒35 02	14♑46.8	29♍55.9	6♌02.6	18♌07.1	6♑08.7	25♉24.7	27♐59.5	6♍54.9	21♉36.6	5♓33.7
2 M	10 46 17	9 58 08	11♒10 30	17 43 07	14R42.6	1♎25.2	6 13.5	18 45.2	6 11.4	25 27.1	27D59.5	6 58.7	21R36.3	5R32.4
3 Tu	10 50 14	10 56 12	24 12 50	0♓39 37	14 36.0	2 53.2	6 26.5	19 23.4	6 14.5	25 29.4	27 59.6	7 02.4	21 36.0	5 31.2
4 W	10 54 10	11 54 17	7♓03 24	13 24 09	14 27.3	4 19.8	6 41.6	20 01.5	6 17.9	25 31.5	27 59.8	7 06.2	21 35.7	5 29.9
5 Th	10 58 07	12 52 24	19 41 51	25 56 31	14 16.9	5 45.0	6 58.6	20 39.6	6 21.6	25 33.4	28 00.1	7 09.9	21 35.3	5 28.6
6 F	11 02 03	13 50 32	2♈08 12	8♈16 57	14 06.0	7 08.9	7 17.5	21 17.7	6 25.7	25 35.1	28 00.5	7 13.7	21 35.0	5 27.4
7 Sa	11 06 00	14 48 43	14 22 56	20 26 19	13 55.6	8 31.3	7 38.3	21 55.7	6 30.1	25 36.6	28 01.0	7 17.4	21 34.5	5 26.1
8 Su	11 09 56	15 46 55	26 27 21	2♉26 21	13 46.4	9 52.4	8 00.9	22 33.8	6 34.8	25 37.9	28 01.7	7 21.2	21 34.1	5 24.8
9 M	11 13 53	16 45 09	8♉23 39	14 19 42	13 39.3	11 11.9	8 25.2	23 11.8	6 39.8	25 39.0	28 02.4	7 24.9	21 33.6	5 23.6
10 Tu	11 17 49	17 43 26	20 14 56	26 09 54	13 34.6	12 30.0	8 51.2	23 49.8	6 45.2	25 39.9	28 03.2	7 28.6	21 33.1	5 22.3
11 W	11 21 46	18 41 44	2♊05 09	8♊01 16	13D32.2	13 46.4	9 18.9	24 27.8	6 50.8	25 40.6	28 04.1	7 32.3	21 32.5	5 21.1
12 Th	11 25 43	19 40 04	13 58 54	19 58 42	13 31.6	15 01.3	9 48.1	25 05.7	6 56.8	25 41.1	28 05.1	7 36.1	21 32.0	5 19.9
13 F	11 29 39	20 38 27	26 01 20	2♋07 28	13R31.9	16 14.4	10 18.8	25 43.7	7 03.1	25 41.4	28 06.1	7 39.8	21 31.3	5 18.6
14 Sa	11 33 36	21 36 52	8♋17 44	14 32 48	13 32.2	17 25.8	10 51.0	26 21.6	7 09.6	25R41.5	28 07.3	7 43.4	21 30.7	5 17.4
15 Su	11 37 32	22 35 19	20 53 13	27 19 31	13 31.4	18 35.3	11 24.5	26 59.5	7 16.5	25 41.4	28 08.6	7 47.1	21 30.0	5 16.2
16 M	11 41 29	23 33 48	3♌52 08	10♌31 23	13 28.6	19 42.9	11 59.4	27 37.4	7 23.7	25 41.1	28 10.0	7 50.8	21 29.3	5 15.0
17 Tu	11 45 25	24 32 19	17 17 28	24 10 25	13 23.3	20 48.3	12 35.6	28 15.2	7 31.2	25 40.6	28 11.5	7 54.5	21 28.6	5 13.8
18 W	11 49 22	25 30 51	1♍10 05	8♍16 08	13 15.4	21 51.6	13 13.1	28 53.1	7 38.9	25 39.9	28 13.1	7 58.1	21 27.9	5 12.6
19 Th	11 53 18	26 29 26	15 28 04	22 45 10	13 05.5	22 52.5	13 51.7	29 30.9	7 47.0	25 39.0	28 14.7	8 01.7	21 27.1	5 11.4
20 F	11 57 15	27 28 03	0♎06 33	7♎31 13	12 54.6	23 50.8	14 31.5	0♍08.7	7 55.3	25 37.9	28 16.5	8 05.3	21 26.2	5 10.2
21 Sa	12 01 12	28 26 42	14 58 03	22 25 53	12 43.9	24 46.5	15 12.5	0 46.4	8 03.9	25 36.6	28 18.4	8 08.9	21 25.4	5 09.1
22 Su	12 05 08	29 25 23	29 53 35	7♏20 02	12 34.7	25 39.2	15 54.4	1 24.2	8 12.8	25 35.0	28 20.3	8 12.5	21 24.5	5 07.9
23 M	12 09 05	0♎24 05	14♏44 15	22 05 23	12 27.8	26 28.8	16 37.5	2 01.9	8 22.0	25 33.3	28 22.4	8 16.1	21 23.6	5 06.8
24 Tu	12 13 01	1 22 49	29 22 44	6♐35 47	12 23.6	27 15.1	17 21.5	2 39.6	8 31.4	25 31.4	28 24.5	8 19.6	21 22.7	5 05.7
25 W	12 16 58	2 21 35	13♐44 09	20 47 40	12D21.8	27 57.6	18 06.4	3 17.3	8 41.1	25 29.3	28 26.8	8 23.2	21 21.7	5 04.6
26 Th	12 20 54	3 20 23	27 46 15	4♑39 58	12R21.5	28 36.2	18 52.3	3 54.9	8 51.1	25 27.0	28 29.1	8 26.7	21 20.7	5 03.5
27 F	12 24 51	4 19 12	11♑28 58	18 13 27	12 21.5	29 10.4	19 39.1	4 32.5	9 01.3	25 24.5	28 31.5	8 30.2	21 19.7	5 02.4
28 Sa	12 28 47	5 18 03	24 53 40	1♒29 54	12 20.5	29 40.0	20 26.7	5 10.2	9 11.8	25 21.8	28 34.0	8 33.7	21 18.7	5 01.3
29 Su	12 32 44	6 16 56	8♒02 25	14 31 31	12 17.4	0♏04.6	21 15.2	5 47.7	9 22.5	25 18.9	28 36.7	8 37.1	21 17.6	5 00.2
30 M	12 36 41	7 15 50	20 57 25	27 20 20	12 11.5	0 23.7	22 04.4	6 25.3	9 33.5	25 15.8	28 39.3	8 40.5	21 16.5	4 59.2

LONGITUDE — October 2047

Day	Sid.Time	⊙	0 hr ☽	Noon ☽	True ☊	☿	♀	♂	⚳	♃	♄	♅	♆	♇
1 Tu	12 40 37	8♎14 46	3♓40 29	9♓58 00	12♑02.6	0♏36.9	22♌54.5	7♍02.8	9♑44.7	25♉12.5	28♐42.1	8♍43.9	21♉15.4	4♓58.1
2 W	12 44 34	9 13 44	16 13 01	22 25 39	11R51.1	0R43.9	23 45.3	7 40.3	9 56.2	25R09.0	28 45.0	8 47.3	21R14.3	4R57.1
3 Th	12 48 30	10 12 44	28 35 59	4♈44 05	11 37.7	0 44.1	24 36.8	8 17.8	10 07.9	25 05.4	28 48.0	8 50.7	21 13.1	4 56.1
4 F	12 52 27	11 11 46	10♈50 02	16 53 56	11 23.4	0 37.2	25 29.1	8 55.3	10 19.8	25 01.5	28 51.0	8 54.0	21 11.9	4 55.1
5 Sa	12 56 23	12 10 51	22 55 52	28 55 59	11 09.6	0 22.8	26 22.0	9 32.8	10 31.9	24 57.5	28 54.2	8 57.3	21 10.7	4 54.1
6 Su	13 00 20	13 09 57	4♉54 27	10♉51 27	10 57.3	0 00.6	27 15.6	10 10.2	10 44.3	24 53.3	28 57.4	9 00.6	21 09.5	4 53.2
7 M	13 04 16	14 09 05	16 47 15	22 42 10	10 47.3	29♎30.5	28 09.8	10 47.6	10 56.9	24 48.9	29 00.7	9 03.9	21 08.2	4 52.2
8 Tu	13 08 13	15 08 16	28 36 32	4♊30 46	10 40.2	28 52.4	29 04.7	11 25.0	11 09.7	24 44.3	29 04.1	9 07.1	21 06.9	4 51.3
9 W	13 12 09	16 07 29	10♊25 19	16 20 42	10 35.9	28 06.6	0♍00.1	12 02.4	11 22.8	24 39.6	29 07.6	9 10.3	21 05.6	4 50.4
10 Th	13 16 06	17 06 44	22 17 28	28 16 13	10 34.0	27 13.5	0 56.1	12 39.7	11 36.0	24 34.7	29 11.1	9 13.5	21 04.3	4 49.5
11 F	13 20 03	18 06 02	4♋17 34	10♋22 12	10 33.6	26 13.8	1 52.7	13 17.1	11 49.5	24 29.6	29 14.8	9 16.6	21 03.0	4 48.7
12 Sa	13 23 59	19 05 22	16 30 45	22 43 55	10 33.6	25 08.6	2 49.8	13 54.4	12 03.2	24 24.3	29 18.5	9 19.8	21 01.6	4 47.8
13 Su	13 27 56	20 04 44	29 02 21	5♌26 39	10 32.8	23 59.1	3 47.5	14 31.7	12 17.0	24 18.9	29 22.3	9 22.9	21 00.2	4 47.0
14 M	13 31 52	21 04 08	11♌57 25	18 35 06	10 30.3	22 47.2	4 45.6	15 09.0	12 31.1	24 13.3	29 26.2	9 25.9	20 58.8	4 46.2
15 Tu	13 35 49	22 03 35	25 20 04	2♍12 34	10 25.3	21 34.6	5 44.2	15 46.2	12 45.4	24 07.6	29 30.2	9 28.9	20 57.4	4 45.4
16 W	13 39 45	23 03 04	9♍12 38	16 20 08	10 17.7	20 23.4	6 43.4	16 23.4	12 59.8	24 01.7	29 34.2	9 31.9	20 56.0	4 44.6
17 Th	13 43 42	24 02 35	23 34 40	0♎55 40	10 08.0	19 15.8	7 42.9	17 00.6	13 14.5	23 55.6	29 38.4	9 34.9	20 54.5	4 43.8
18 F	13 47 38	25 02 08	8♎22 17	15 53 29	9 57.0	18 13.7	8 42.9	17 37.8	13 29.3	23 49.4	29 42.6	9 37.8	20 53.0	4 43.1
19 Sa	13 51 35	26 01 44	23 28 04	1♏04 41	9 46.1	17 18.9	9 43.3	18 15.0	13 44.4	23 43.1	29 46.8	9 40.7	20 51.5	4 42.4
20 Su	13 55 32	27 01 21	8♏41 57	16 18 29	9 36.6	16 33.0	10 44.2	18 52.1	13 59.6	23 36.6	29 51.2	9 43.6	20 50.0	4 41.7
21 M	13 59 28	28 01 01	23 52 57	1♐24 09	9 29.5	15 57.1	11 45.4	19 29.2	14 15.0	23 30.0	29 55.6	9 46.4	20 48.5	4 41.0
22 Tu	14 03 25	29 00 42	8♐51 05	16 12 56	9 25.1	15 32.0	12 47.0	20 06.3	14 30.6	23 23.2	0♑00.2	9 49.2	20 47.0	4 40.3
23 W	14 07 21	0♏00 25	23 29 03	0♑39 05	9D23.2	15D18.2	13 49.0	20 43.4	14 46.4	23 16.4	0 04.7	9 51.9	20 45.4	4 39.7
24 Th	14 11 18	1 00 10	7♑42 48	14 40 10	9 23.0	15 15.7	14 51.4	21 20.4	15 02.3	23 09.4	0 09.4	9 54.6	20 43.9	4 39.1
25 F	14 15 14	1 59 57	21 31 19	28 16 28	9R23.4	15 24.3	15 54.1	21 57.4	15 18.4	23 02.3	0 14.1	9 57.3	20 42.3	4 38.5
26 Sa	14 19 11	2 59 45	4♒55 56	11♒30 05	9 23.1	15 43.4	16 57.1	22 34.4	15 34.7	22 55.1	0 18.9	9 59.9	20 40.7	4 37.9
27 Su	14 23 07	3 59 34	17 59 21	24 24 08	9 21.1	16 12.6	18 00.5	23 11.4	15 51.1	22 47.8	0 23.8	10 02.5	20 39.1	4 37.4
28 M	14 27 04	4 59 26	0♓44 53	7♓01 59	9 16.7	16 50.9	19 04.2	23 48.3	16 07.7	22 40.4	0 28.7	10 05.1	20 37.5	4 36.9
29 Tu	14 31 01	5 59 19	13 15 51	19 26 50	9 09.6	17 37.6	20 08.2	24 25.2	16 24.5	22 32.9	0 33.7	10 07.6	20 35.9	4 36.4
30 W	14 34 57	6 59 14	25 35 15	1♈41 25	9 00.2	18 31.8	21 12.6	25 02.1	16 41.4	22 25.3	0 38.8	10 10.0	20 34.3	4 35.9
31 Th	14 38 54	7 59 10	7♈45 33	13 47 55	8 49.0	19 32.7	22 17.2	25 38.9	16 58.4	22 17.7	0 43.9	10 12.5	20 32.6	4 35.5

Astro Data	Planet Ingress	Last Aspect	☽ Ingress	Last Aspect	☽ Ingress	☽ Phases & Eclipses	Astro Data
Dy Hr Mn	Dy Hr Mn	Dy Hr Mn	Dy Hr Mn	Dy Hr Mn	Dy Hr Mn	Dy Hr Mn	1 September 2047
☿0S 1 8:03	☿ ♎ 1 13:05	1 2:31 ☿ △	♒ 1 3:42	3 0:21 ♄ □	♈ 3 2:44	4 8:55 ○ 11♓47	Julian Day # 53935
♄D 1 18:31	♂ ♍ 20 6:30	3 7:01 ♄ ⚹	♓ 3 10:46	5 11:56 ♄ △	♉ 5 14:08	12 11:20 ☾ 19♊38	SVP 4♓35'20"
☽0N 4 23:17	⊙ ♎ 23 2:09	5 15:59 ♄ □	♈ 5 19:51	8 0:01 ♀ □	♊ 8 2:50	19 18:33 ● 26♍45	GC 27♐30.3 ⚴ 24♏35.4
♃R 14 12:38	☿ ♏ 29 7:05	8 3:08 ♄ △	♉ 8 7:06	10 13:50 ♄ ☍	♋ 10 15:27	26 9:30 ☽ 3♑14	Eris 0♉46.6R ⚵ 2♐06.7
☽0S 19 6:20		10 10:59 ♃ ☌	♊ 10 19:47	12 16:14 ☿ □	♌ 13 1:49		⚷ 23♎10.4 ⚶ 21♐42.1
⊙0S 23 2:09	☿ ♎R 6 12:32	13 4:06 ♄ ☍	♋ 13 7:50	15 7:17 ♄ △	♍ 15 8:10	3 23:43 ○ 10♈42	☽ Mean ☊ 13♑07.4
	♀ ♍ 9 11:57	15 8:58 ♃ ⚹	♌ 15 16:56	17 9:54 ♄ □	♎ 17 10:30	12 4:23 ☾ 18♋47	
☽0N 2 5:53	♄ ♑ 22 11:10	17 19:21 ♂ ☌	♍ 17 22:01	19 9:57 ♄ ⚹	♏ 19 10:18	19 3:29 ● 25♎41	1 October 2047
☿R 3 0:46	⊙ ♏ 23 11:50	19 20:59 ♄ □	♎ 19 23:49	20 23:29 ♃ ☍	♐ 21 9:45	25 19:14 ☽ 2♒18	Julian Day # 53965
☽0S 16 16:35		21 21:28 ♄ ⚹	♏ 22 0:10	23 10:50 ⊙ ⚹	♑ 23 10:54		SVP 4♓35'18"
☿D 24 5:20		23 17:41 ♃ ☍	♐ 24 1:02	25 2:46 ♃ △	♒ 25 15:06		GC 27♐30.4 ⚴ 4♐15.7
☽0N 29 11:02		26 1:12 ♄ ☌	♑ 26 3:52	27 9:01 ♃ □	♓ 27 22:35		Eris 0♉32.5R ⚵ 8♐52.2
		28 8:32 ☿ □	♒ 28 9:16	29 22:14 ♂ ☍	♈ 30 8:40		⚷ 27♎04.6 ⚶ 1♑03.2
		30 14:30 ♄ ⚹	♓ 30 17:02				☽ Mean ☊ 11♑32.0

November 2047 LONGITUDE

Day	Sid.Time	☉	0 hr ☽	Noon ☽	True ☊	☿	♀	♂	⚳	♃	♄	♅	♆	♇
1 F	14 42 50	8♏59 08	19♈48 43	25♈48 06	8♑37.1	20♎39.4	23♍22.1	26♍15.8	17♑15.6	22♉09.9	0♑49.1	10♍14.8	20♉31.0	4♓35.0
2 Sa	14 46 47	9 59 09	1♉46 17	7♉43 24	8R 25.5	21 51.2	24 27.3	26 52.6	17 33.0	22R 02.1	0 54.4	10 17.2	20R 29.3	4R 34.6
3 Su	14 50 43	10 59 11	13 39 37	19 35 09	8 15.2	23 07.4	25 32.8	27 29.4	17 50.5	21 54.3	0 59.7	10 19.5	20 27.7	4 34.3
4 M	14 54 40	11 59 15	25 30 11	1♊24 55	8 06.9	24 27.3	26 38.6	28 06.1	18 08.1	21 46.3	1 05.1	10 21.7	20 26.0	4 33.9
5 Tu	14 58 36	12 59 21	7♊19 38	13 14 38	8 01.2	25 50.3	27 44.7	28 42.8	18 25.9	21 38.4	1 10.5	10 23.9	20 24.3	4 33.6
6 W	15 02 33	13 59 29	19 10 13	25 06 46	7 57.9	27 16.0	28 51.0	29 19.6	18 43.8	21 30.3	1 16.0	10 26.1	20 22.7	4 33.3
7 Th	15 06 30	14 59 39	1♋04 43	7♋04 31	7D 56.9	28 43.9	29 57.5	29 56.2	19 01.9	21 22.3	1 21.6	10 28.2	20 21.0	4 33.0
8 F	15 10 26	15 59 50	13 06 40	19 11 41	7 57.4	0♏13.6	1♎04.3	0♎32.9	19 20.1	21 14.2	1 27.2	10 30.3	20 19.3	4 32.7
9 Sa	15 14 23	17 00 04	25 20 09	1♌32 38	7 58.6	1 44.8	2 11.3	1 09.5	19 38.4	21 06.1	1 32.9	10 32.3	20 17.6	4 32.5
10 Su	15 18 19	18 00 20	7♌49 44	14 12 03	7R 59.5	3 17.2	3 18.6	1 46.1	19 56.8	20 57.9	1 38.6	10 34.3	20 15.9	4 32.3
11 M	15 22 16	19 00 38	20 40 06	27 14 26	7 59.2	4 50.5	4 26.1	2 22.7	20 15.4	20 49.7	1 44.4	10 36.2	20 14.2	4 32.1
12 Tu	15 26 12	20 00 58	3♍55 29	10♍43 35	7 57.2	6 24.6	5 33.8	2 59.3	20 34.1	20 41.6	1 50.2	10 38.1	20 12.5	4 32.0
13 W	15 30 09	21 01 20	17 38 57	24 41 38	7 53.1	7 59.3	6 41.7	3 35.8	20 52.9	20 33.4	1 56.1	10 39.9	20 10.8	4 31.8
14 Th	15 34 05	22 01 44	1♎51 32	9♎08 17	7 47.3	9 34.4	7 49.9	4 12.3	21 11.9	20 25.2	2 02.1	10 41.7	20 09.2	4 31.7
15 F	15 38 02	23 02 09	16 31 20	23 59 54	7 40.5	11 09.8	8 58.2	4 48.8	21 31.0	20 17.0	2 08.1	10 43.4	20 07.5	4 31.6
16 Sa	15 41 59	24 02 37	1♏33 00	9♏09 29	7 33.5	12 45.4	10 06.7	5 25.2	21 50.1	20 08.9	2 14.1	10 45.1	20 05.8	4 31.6
17 Su	15 45 55	25 03 06	16 48 02	24 27 15	7 27.3	14 21.2	11 15.4	6 01.6	22 09.5	20 00.7	2 20.2	10 46.8	20 04.1	4D 31.6
18 M	15 49 52	26 03 37	2♐05 46	9♐42 13	7 22.8	15 57.0	12 24.3	6 38.0	22 28.9	19 52.6	2 26.3	10 48.3	20 02.4	4 31.6
19 Tu	15 53 48	27 04 10	17 15 21	24 44 04	7D 20.2	17 32.8	13 33.3	7 14.3	22 48.4	19 44.6	2 32.5	10 49.9	20 00.7	4 31.6
20 W	15 57 45	28 04 43	2♑07 28	9♑24 50	7 19.6	19 08.5	14 42.6	7 50.6	23 08.1	19 36.6	2 38.8	10 51.3	19 59.1	4 31.6
21 Th	16 01 41	29 05 19	16 35 41	23 39 42	7 20.4	20 44.2	15 51.9	8 26.9	23 27.8	19 28.6	2 45.0	10 52.8	19 57.4	4 31.7
22 F	16 05 38	0♐05 55	0♒36 47	7♒26 59	7 21.9	22 19.8	17 01.5	9 03.1	23 47.7	19 20.7	2 51.3	10 54.1	19 55.7	4 31.8
23 Sa	16 09 34	1 06 32	14 10 30	20 47 38	7R 23.3	23 55.3	18 11.2	9 39.3	24 07.6	19 12.8	2 57.7	10 55.5	19 54.1	4 31.9
24 Su	16 13 31	2 07 11	27 18 45	3♓44 19	7 23.7	25 30.7	19 21.0	10 15.5	24 27.7	19 05.1	3 04.1	10 56.7	19 52.4	4 32.1
25 M	16 17 28	3 07 50	10♓04 49	16 20 44	7 22.8	27 05.9	20 31.0	10 51.6	24 47.9	18 57.4	3 10.5	10 57.9	19 50.8	4 32.3
26 Tu	16 21 24	4 08 31	22 32 36	28 40 55	7 20.2	28 41.0	21 41.1	11 27.7	25 08.1	18 49.7	3 17.0	10 59.1	19 49.1	4 32.5
27 W	16 25 21	5 09 13	4♈46 10	10♈48 49	7 16.2	0♐15.9	22 51.4	12 03.8	25 28.5	18 42.2	3 23.5	11 00.2	19 47.5	4 32.7
28 Th	16 29 17	6 09 56	16 49 19	22 48 05	7 11.1	1 50.7	24 01.8	12 39.8	25 48.9	18 34.7	3 30.1	11 01.2	19 45.9	4 33.0
29 F	16 33 14	7 10 40	28 45 28	4♉41 50	7 05.4	3 25.5	25 12.4	13 15.8	26 09.5	18 27.4	3 36.6	11 02.2	19 44.3	4 33.2
30 Sa	16 37 10	8 11 25	10♉37 30	16 32 45	6 59.9	5 00.1	26 23.0	13 51.7	26 30.1	18 20.1	3 43.3	11 03.2	19 42.7	4 33.6

December 2047 LONGITUDE

Day	Sid.Time	☉	0 hr ☽	Noon ☽	True ☊	☿	♀	♂	⚳	♃	♄	♅	♆	♇
1 Su	16 41 07	9♐12 11	22♉27 51	28♉23 02	6♑55.0	6♐34.6	27♎33.9	14♎27.6	26♑50.8	18♉13.0	3♑49.9	11♍04.0	19♉41.1	4♓33.9
2 M	16 45 03	10 12 59	4♊18 34	10♊14 38	6R 51.3	8 09.0	28 44.8	15 03.5	27 11.6	18R 06.0	3 56.6	11 04.9	19R 39.6	4 34.3
3 Tu	16 49 00	11 13 48	16 11 29	22 09 21	6 49.0	9 43.3	29 55.8	15 39.4	27 32.5	17 59.0	4 03.3	11 05.6	19 38.0	4 34.6
4 W	16 52 57	12 14 38	28 08 27	4♋09 02	6D 48.0	11 17.6	1♏07.0	16 15.2	27 53.5	17 52.3	4 10.0	11 06.4	19 36.5	4 35.1
5 Th	16 56 53	13 15 29	10♋11 23	16 15 46	6 48.3	12 51.9	2 18.3	16 50.9	28 14.5	17 45.6	4 16.8	11 07.0	19 35.0	4 35.5
6 F	17 00 50	14 16 21	22 22 31	28 31 57	6 49.5	14 26.1	3 29.7	17 26.7	28 35.6	17 39.1	4 23.6	11 07.6	19 33.5	4 36.0
7 Sa	17 04 46	15 17 15	4♌44 26	11♌00 22	6 51.2	16 00.3	4 41.2	18 02.3	28 56.9	17 32.7	4 30.4	11 08.2	19 32.0	4 36.4
8 Su	17 08 43	16 18 09	17 20 06	23 44 04	6 52.8	17 34.5	5 52.9	18 38.0	29 18.1	17 26.4	4 37.3	11 08.7	19 30.5	4 37.0
9 M	17 12 39	17 19 05	0♍12 38	6♍46 11	6R 53.8	19 08.7	7 04.6	19 13.6	29 39.5	17 20.3	4 44.1	11 09.1	19 29.0	4 37.5
10 Tu	17 16 36	18 20 03	13 25 05	20 09 36	6 54.2	20 43.0	8 16.4	19 49.2	0♒01.0	17 14.3	4 51.0	11 09.5	19 27.6	4 38.1
11 W	17 20 32	19 21 01	26 59 58	3♎56 18	6 53.6	22 17.3	9 28.4	20 24.7	0 22.5	17 08.5	4 57.9	11 09.8	19 26.2	4 38.6
12 Th	17 24 29	20 22 01	10♎58 38	18 06 50	6 52.3	23 51.7	10 40.4	21 00.2	0 44.1	17 02.9	5 04.9	11 10.1	19 24.7	4 39.2
13 F	17 28 26	21 23 01	25 20 37	2♏39 35	6 50.4	25 26.1	11 52.5	21 35.6	1 05.7	16 57.4	5 11.8	11 10.3	19 23.4	4 39.9
14 Sa	17 32 22	22 24 03	10♏03 06	17 30 25	6 48.5	27 00.7	13 04.7	22 11.0	1 27.5	16 52.1	5 18.8	11 10.4	19 22.0	4 40.5
15 Su	17 36 19	23 25 06	25 00 37	2♐32 41	6 46.7	28 35.3	14 17.0	22 46.4	1 49.3	16 46.9	5 25.8	11 10.5	19 20.7	4 41.2
16 M	17 40 15	24 26 10	10♐05 29	17 37 51	6 45.6	0♑10.0	15 29.4	23 21.7	2 11.1	16 41.9	5 32.8	11R 10.6	19 19.3	4 41.9
17 Tu	17 44 12	25 27 15	25 08 38	2♑36 44	6D 45.1	1 44.9	16 41.8	23 56.9	2 33.1	16 37.1	5 39.8	11 10.6	19 18.0	4 42.7
18 W	17 48 08	26 28 20	10♑01 05	17 20 50	6 45.2	3 19.9	17 54.3	24 32.1	2 55.1	16 32.5	5 46.8	11 10.5	19 16.8	4 43.4
19 Th	17 52 05	27 29 26	24 35 11	1♒43 34	6 45.8	4 54.9	19 06.9	25 07.2	3 17.1	16 28.1	5 53.9	11 10.4	19 15.5	4 44.2
20 F	17 56 02	28 30 32	8♒45 33	15 40 55	6 46.6	6 30.1	20 19.6	25 42.3	3 39.2	16 23.8	6 00.9	11 10.2	19 14.3	4 45.0
21 Sa	17 59 58	29 31 38	22 29 33	29 11 31	6 47.4	8 05.4	21 32.3	26 17.3	4 01.4	16 19.7	6 08.0	11 09.9	19 13.0	4 45.9
22 Su	18 03 55	0♑32 45	5♓47 01	12♓16 20	6 47.9	9 40.8	22 45.1	26 52.3	4 23.7	16 15.9	6 15.1	11 09.6	19 11.9	4 46.7
23 M	18 07 51	1 33 51	18 39 51	24 58 02	6R 48.2	11 16.2	23 57.9	27 27.2	4 45.9	16 12.2	6 22.2	11 09.3	19 10.7	4 47.6
24 Tu	18 11 48	2 34 58	1♈11 23	7♈20 26	6 48.3	12 51.7	25 10.8	28 02.1	5 08.3	16 08.7	6 29.2	11 08.9	19 09.6	4 48.5
25 W	18 15 44	3 36 05	13 25 45	19 27 55	6 48.1	14 27.2	26 23.8	28 36.9	5 30.7	16 05.4	6 36.3	11 08.4	19 08.5	4 49.4
26 Th	18 19 41	4 37 12	25 27 30	1♉25 02	6 47.9	16 02.7	27 36.8	29 11.7	5 53.1	16 02.3	6 43.4	11 07.9	19 07.4	4 50.3
27 F	18 23 37	5 38 20	7♉21 05	13 16 10	6 47.7	17 38.2	28 49.9	29 46.3	6 15.6	15 59.4	6 50.5	11 07.3	19 06.3	4 51.3
28 Sa	18 27 34	6 39 27	19 10 46	25 05 21	6D 47.6	19 13.4	0♐03.0	0♏21.0	6 38.2	15 56.7	6 57.6	11 06.6	19 05.3	4 52.3
29 Su	18 31 31	7 40 35	1♊00 21	6♊56 08	6 47.6	20 48.5	1 16.2	0 55.6	7 00.8	15 54.2	7 04.7	11 06.0	19 04.3	4 53.3
30 M	18 35 27	8 41 42	12 53 04	18 51 29	6 47.8	22 23.3	2 29.5	1 30.1	7 23.4	15 51.9	7 11.8	11 05.2	19 03.3	4 54.3
31 Tu	18 39 24	9 42 50	24 51 40	0♋53 52	6R 47.9	23 57.6	3 42.8	2 04.5	7 46.1	15 49.8	7 18.9	11 04.4	19 02.4	4 55.4

Astro Data Dy Hr Mn	Planet Ingress Dy Hr Mn	Last Aspect Dy Hr Mn	☽ Ingress Dy Hr Mn	Last Aspect Dy Hr Mn	☽ Ingress Dy Hr Mn	☽ Phases & Eclipses Dy Hr Mn	Astro Data
♀0S 10 10:20	♀ ♎ 7 12:54	1 0:37 ☿ ☍	♉ 1 20:26	30 18:24 ♆ ☌	♊ 1 15:16	2 16:59 ○ 10♉12	1 November 2047
♂0S 12 17:21	♂ ♎ 7 14:28	4 4:54 ♂ △	♊ 4 9:08	2 22:14 ♂ △	♋ 4 3:43	10 19:41 ☾ 18♌20	Julian Day # 53996
☽0S 13 1:47	☿ ♏ 8 8:23	6 20:56 ♂ □	♋ 6 21:50	5 18:31 ♆ ⚹	♌ 6 14:51	17 13:00 ● 25♏06	SVP 4♓35'14"
♃☌♆ 16 23:33	☉ ♐ 22 9:39	8 15:58 ♃ ⚹	♌ 9 9:02	8 4:06 ♆ □	♍ 8 23:37	24 8:42 ☽ 1♓59	GC 27♐30.4 ⚴ 15♐46.5
♇ D 17 23:58	☿ ♐ 27 7:58	11 0:25 ♃ □	♍ 11 16:59	10 13:07 ☿ □	♎ 11 5:13		Eris 0♉14.0R ⚵ 18♐04.4
☽0N 25 16:13		13 5:17 ☉ ⚹	♎ 13 20:54	12 22:43 ☿ ⚹	♏ 13 7:39	2 11:56 ○ 10♊13	⚷ 1♏29.3 ⚶ 13♑36.1
♃⚼♄ 28 20:02	♀ ♏ 3 13:24	14 9:41 ♀ ☌	♏ 15 21:33	14 14:58 ♆ ☍	♐ 15 7:57	10 8:30 ☾ 18♍11	☽ Mean ☊ 9♑53.5
	⚳ ♒ 10 10:56	17 13:00 ☉ ☌	♐ 17 20:42	16 23:39 ☉ ☌	♑ 17 7:48	16 23:39 ● 24♐56	
♄⚼♆ 7 16:28	☿ ♑ 16 9:28	18 16:38 ♀ ⚹	♑ 19 20:32	19 0:25 ♂ □	♒ 19 9:05	16 23:50:09 ● P 0.882	1 December 2047
♄⚹♇ 8 10:51	☉ ♑ 21 23:08	21 22:05 ☉ ⚹	♒ 21 22:56	21 12:39 ☉ ⚹	♓ 21 13:28	24 1:52 ☽ 2♈09	Julian Day # 54026
☽0S 10 8:48	♂ ♏ 27 21:27	23 18:32 ☿ □	♓ 24 5:00	23 9:53 ♀ △	♈ 23 21:42		SVP 4♓35'10"
♅ R 16 17:23	♀ ♐ 28 11:00	26 12:00 ☿ △	♈ 26 14:35	26 7:17 ♂ ☍	♉ 26 9:08		GC 27♐30.5 ⚴ 27♐37.7
☽0N 22 23:19		28 14:45 ♀ ☍	♉ 29 2:30	27 23:50 ♆ ☌	♊ 28 21:58		Eris 29♈57.6R ⚵ 28♐19.3
				29 20:24 ♅ □	♋ 31 10:13		⚷ 5♏35.7 ⚶ 27♑20.4
							☽ Mean ☊ 8♑18.2

LONGITUDE January 2048

Day	Sid.Time	☉	0 hr ☽	Noon☽	True☊	☿	♀	♂	⚳	♃	♄	♅	♆	♇
1 W	18 43 20	10♑43 58	6♋58 18	13♋05 11	6♑47.9	25♑31.5	4♐56.1	2♏38.9	8♒08.8	15♉47.9	7♑26.0	11♍03.6	19♉01.4	4♓56.4
2 Th	18 47 17	11 45 06	19 14 40	25 26 55	6R47.6	27 04.6	6 09.5	3 13.3	8 31.6	15R46.3	7 33.1	11R02.7	19R00.6	4 57.5
3 F	18 51 13	12 46 14	1♌42 05	8♌00 15	6 47.1	28 36.8	7 23.0	3 47.5	8 54.4	15 44.8	7 40.2	11 01.7	18 59.7	4 58.6
4 Sa	18 55 10	13 47 22	14 21 34	20 46 08	6 46.2	0♒07.8	8 36.4	4 21.7	9 17.3	15 43.5	7 47.3	11 00.7	18 58.9	4 59.8
5 Su	18 59 06	14 48 31	27 14 04	3♍45 27	6 45.2	1 37.5	9 50.0	4 55.9	9 40.2	15 42.5	7 54.3	10 59.7	18 58.1	5 00.9
6 M	19 03 03	15 49 39	10♍20 25	16 59 01	6 44.2	3 05.5	11 03.6	5 30.0	10 03.1	15 41.6	8 01.4	10 58.6	18 57.3	5 02.1
7 Tu	19 07 00	16 50 48	23 41 22	0♎27 32	6 43.3	4 31.5	12 17.2	6 04.0	10 26.1	15 41.0	8 08.4	10 57.4	18 56.6	5 03.3
8 W	19 10 56	17 51 57	7♎17 34	14 11 30	6D42.9	5 55.0	13 30.8	6 37.9	10 49.1	15 40.5	8 15.5	10 56.2	18 55.9	5 04.5
9 Th	19 14 53	18 53 06	21 09 17	28 10 53	6 43.0	7 15.5	14 44.5	7 11.8	11 12.1	15D40.3	8 22.5	10 55.0	18 55.2	5 05.7
10 F	19 18 49	19 54 15	5♏16 07	12♏24 49	6 43.7	8 32.6	15 58.3	7 45.6	11 35.2	15 40.3	8 29.5	10 53.6	18 54.5	5 06.9
11 Sa	19 22 46	20 55 24	19 36 41	26 51 18	6 44.8	9 45.7	17 12.1	8 19.3	11 58.3	15 40.5	8 36.5	10 52.3	18 53.9	5 08.2
12 Su	19 26 42	21 56 33	4♐08 14	11♐26 53	6 45.9	10 53.9	18 25.9	8 52.9	12 21.5	15 40.9	8 43.5	10 50.9	18 53.3	5 09.5
13 M	19 30 39	22 57 43	18 46 37	26 06 43	6R46.8	11 56.7	19 39.7	9 26.5	12 44.7	15 41.5	8 50.5	10 49.4	18 52.8	5 10.8
14 Tu	19 34 35	23 58 52	3♑26 23	10♑44 48	6 47.0	12 53.2	20 53.6	10 00.0	13 07.9	15 42.3	8 57.4	10 48.0	18 52.3	5 12.1
15 W	19 38 32	25 00 01	18 01 10	25 14 40	6 46.2	13 42.5	22 07.5	10 33.3	13 31.1	15 43.3	9 04.4	10 46.4	18 51.8	5 13.4
16 Th	19 42 29	26 01 09	2♒24 34	9♒30 11	6 44.4	14 23.8	23 21.4	11 06.7	13 54.4	15 44.5	9 11.3	10 44.8	18 51.4	5 14.7
17 F	19 46 25	27 02 16	16 30 56	23 26 22	6 41.8	14 56.1	24 35.4	11 39.9	14 17.7	15 46.0	9 18.2	10 43.2	18 50.9	5 16.1
18 Sa	19 50 22	28 03 23	0♓16 07	7♓00 00	6 38.5	15 18.6	25 49.4	12 13.0	14 41.0	15 47.6	9 25.0	10 41.5	18 50.6	5 17.5
19 Su	19 54 18	29 04 30	13 37 55	20 09 56	6 35.1	15R30.6	27 03.4	12 46.0	15 04.4	15 49.5	9 31.9	10 39.8	18 50.2	5 18.8
20 M	19 58 15	0♒05 35	26 36 13	2♈57 02	6 32.1	15 31.5	28 17.4	13 19.0	15 27.8	15 51.5	9 38.7	10 38.0	18 49.9	5 20.2
21 Tu	20 02 11	1 06 40	9♈12 44	15 23 47	6 29.9	15 20.8	29 31.4	13 51.8	15 51.1	15 53.8	9 45.5	10 36.2	18 49.6	5 21.7
22 W	20 06 08	2 07 43	21 30 40	27 33 56	6D28.9	14 58.4	0♑45.5	14 24.6	16 14.6	15 56.2	9 52.3	10 34.4	18 49.4	5 23.1
23 Th	20 10 04	3 08 46	3♉34 12	9♉32 04	6 29.0	14 24.6	1 59.5	14 57.2	16 38.0	15 58.9	9 59.0	10 32.5	18 49.2	5 24.5
24 F	20 14 01	4 09 48	15 28 10	21 23 07	6 30.1	13 40.1	3 13.6	15 29.8	17 01.4	16 01.7	10 05.7	10 30.6	18 49.0	5 26.0
25 Sa	20 17 58	5 10 49	27 17 33	3♊12 06	6 31.9	12 45.8	4 27.7	16 02.2	17 24.9	16 04.7	10 12.4	10 28.6	18 48.8	5 27.5
26 Su	20 21 54	6 11 49	9♊07 19	15 03 48	6 33.7	11 43.2	5 41.9	16 34.6	17 48.4	16 08.0	10 19.0	10 26.6	18 48.7	5 28.9
27 M	20 25 51	7 12 48	21 02 02	27 02 33	6R35.1	10 34.3	6 56.0	17 06.9	18 11.9	16 11.4	10 25.6	10 24.6	18 48.7	5 30.4
28 Tu	20 29 47	8 13 45	3♋05 45	9♋12 01	6 35.5	9 21.0	8 10.2	17 39.0	18 35.4	16 15.1	10 32.2	10 22.5	18D48.6	5 31.9
29 W	20 33 44	9 14 42	15 21 41	21 34 59	6 34.4	8 05.6	9 24.4	18 11.1	18 58.9	16 18.9	10 38.7	10 20.4	18 48.6	5 33.5
30 Th	20 37 40	10 15 38	27 52 09	4♌13 16	6 31.6	6 50.3	10 38.6	18 43.0	19 22.4	16 22.9	10 45.3	10 18.3	18 48.7	5 35.0
31 F	20 41 37	11 16 33	10♌38 24	17 07 31	6 27.2	5 37.3	11 52.8	19 14.8	19 46.0	16 27.1	10 51.7	10 16.1	18 48.7	5 36.5

LONGITUDE February 2048

Day	Sid.Time	☉	0 hr ☽	Noon☽	True☊	☿	♀	♂	⚳	♃	♄	♅	♆	♇
1 Sa	20 45 34	12♒17 27	23♌40 34	0♍17 23	6♑21.5	4♒28.5	13♑07.0	19♏46.6	20♒09.5	16♉31.4	10♑58.1	10♍13.9	18♉48.8	5♓38.1
2 Su	20 49 30	13 18 19	6♍57 48	13 41 36	6R15.1	3R25.3	14 21.2	20 18.2	20 33.1	16 36.0	11 04.5	10R11.7	18 49.0	5 39.6
3 M	20 53 27	14 19 11	20 28 30	27 18 14	6 08.8	2 29.0	15 35.5	20 49.6	20 56.7	16 40.7	11 10.9	10 09.4	18 49.1	5 41.2
4 Tu	20 57 23	15 20 02	4♎10 32	11♎05 08	6 03.4	1 40.4	16 49.7	21 21.0	21 20.3	16 45.6	11 17.2	10 07.2	18 49.3	5 42.8
5 W	21 01 20	16 20 52	18 01 45	25 00 10	5 59.6	1 00.1	18 04.0	21 52.3	21 43.9	16 50.7	11 23.4	10 04.8	18 49.6	5 44.3
6 Th	21 05 16	17 21 42	2♏00 10	9♏01 32	5D57.6	0 28.2	19 18.3	22 23.4	22 07.5	16 56.0	11 29.7	10 02.5	18 49.8	5 45.9
7 F	21 09 13	18 22 30	16 04 06	23 07 42	5 57.4	0 04.8	20 32.6	22 54.4	22 31.1	17 01.5	11 35.8	10 00.1	18 50.1	5 47.5
8 Sa	21 13 09	19 23 18	0♐12 10	7♐17 20	5 58.4	29♑49.7	21 47.0	23 25.3	22 54.7	17 07.1	11 42.0	9 57.8	18 50.5	5 49.1
9 Su	21 17 06	20 24 05	14 23 02	21 29 01	5 59.7	29D42.5	23 01.3	23 56.0	23 18.3	17 12.9	11 48.1	9 55.3	18 50.9	5 50.7
10 M	21 21 03	21 24 50	28 35 03	5♑40 51	6R00.4	29 42.8	24 15.7	24 26.6	23 41.9	17 18.9	11 54.1	9 52.9	18 51.3	5 52.4
11 Tu	21 24 59	22 25 35	12♑46 02	19 50 13	5 59.5	29 50.3	25 30.0	24 57.1	24 05.6	17 25.0	12 00.1	9 50.5	18 51.7	5 54.0
12 W	21 28 56	23 26 19	26 52 59	3♒53 50	5 56.4	0♒04.4	26 44.4	25 27.4	24 29.2	17 31.3	12 06.0	9 48.0	18 52.2	5 55.6
13 Th	21 32 52	24 27 01	10♒52 17	17 47 51	5 51.0	0 24.6	27 58.8	25 57.5	24 52.8	17 37.8	12 11.9	9 45.5	18 52.7	5 57.3
14 F	21 36 49	25 27 42	24 40 04	1♓28 28	5 43.4	0 50.6	29 13.1	26 27.5	25 16.4	17 44.4	12 17.7	9 43.0	18 53.3	5 58.9
15 Sa	21 40 45	26 28 21	8♓12 41	14 52 24	5 34.4	1 21.8	0♒27.5	26 57.4	25 40.1	17 51.2	12 23.5	9 40.4	18 53.9	6 00.6
16 Su	21 44 42	27 28 59	21 27 24	27 57 32	5 24.8	1 57.8	1 41.9	27 27.1	26 03.7	17 58.2	12 29.2	9 37.9	18 54.5	6 02.2
17 M	21 48 38	28 29 35	4♈22 47	10♈43 14	5 15.7	2 38.2	2 56.3	27 56.6	26 27.3	18 05.3	12 34.9	9 35.3	18 55.1	6 03.9
18 Tu	21 52 35	29 30 09	16 59 02	23 10 29	5 08.0	3 22.8	4 10.7	28 25.9	26 50.9	18 12.5	12 40.5	9 32.8	18 55.8	6 05.5
19 W	21 56 31	0♓30 42	29 17 54	5♉21 44	5 02.4	4 11.1	5 25.0	28 55.1	27 14.5	18 20.0	12 46.0	9 30.2	18 56.5	6 07.2
20 Th	22 00 28	1 31 13	11♉22 28	17 20 41	4 59.0	5 02.8	6 39.4	29 24.2	27 38.1	18 27.5	12 51.5	9 27.6	18 57.3	6 08.8
21 F	22 04 25	2 31 42	23 16 57	29 11 56	4D57.7	5 57.8	7 53.8	29 53.0	28 01.7	18 35.3	12 56.9	9 25.0	18 58.1	6 10.5
22 Sa	22 08 21	3 32 10	5♊06 17	11♊00 41	4 57.9	6 55.7	9 08.2	0♐21.7	28 25.2	18 43.1	13 02.3	9 22.4	18 58.9	6 12.2
23 Su	22 12 18	4 32 35	16 55 47	22 52 18	4 58.7	7 56.3	10 22.6	0 50.2	28 48.8	18 51.1	13 07.6	9 19.8	18 59.8	6 13.8
24 M	22 16 14	5 32 59	28 50 53	4♋52 10	4R59.2	8 59.5	11 37.0	1 18.5	29 12.3	18 59.3	13 12.8	9 17.2	19 00.6	6 15.5
25 Tu	22 20 11	6 33 21	10♋56 44	17 05 09	4 58.4	10 05.0	12 51.4	1 46.6	29 35.9	19 07.6	13 18.0	9 14.5	19 01.6	6 17.2
26 W	22 24 07	7 33 41	23 17 53	29 35 22	4 55.5	11 12.8	14 05.8	2 14.5	29 59.4	19 16.0	13 23.1	9 11.9	19 02.5	6 18.8
27 Th	22 28 04	8 33 59	5♌57 54	12♌25 43	4 50.1	12 22.6	15 20.1	2 42.2	0♓22.9	19 24.6	13 28.2	9 09.3	19 03.5	6 20.5
28 F	22 32 00	9 34 15	18 58 54	25 37 28	4 42.1	13 34.4	16 34.5	3 09.8	0 46.4	19 33.3	13 33.1	9 06.7	19 04.5	6 22.2
29 Sa	22 35 57	10 34 29	2♍21 16	9♍10 02	4 32.1	14 48.1	17 48.9	3 37.1	1 09.9	19 42.1	13 38.0	9 04.0	19 05.5	6 23.8

Astro Data

	Dy Hr Mn
☽0S	6 14:24
♃D	10 2:19
☽0N	19 8:43
☿R	20 1:46
♄△♅	27 9:07
♆D	29 1:26
☽0S	2 20:33
☿D	9 22:47
☽0N	15 18:49
♃☌♆	24 16:25

Planet Ingress

		Dy Hr Mn
☿	♒	4 9:55
☉	♒	20 9:48
♀	♑	21 21:16
☿	♑R	7 18:22
☿	♒	12 5:35
♀	♒	15 3:07
☉	♓	18 23:50
♂	♐	21 17:51
⚳	♓	26 12:37

Last Aspect / ☽ Ingress (January)

Last Aspect Dy Hr Mn		☽ Ingress	Dy Hr Mn
2 15:34	☿ ☍	♌	2 20:45
4 8:40	♆ □	♍	5 5:06
6 15:32	♆ △	♎	7 11:11
8 18:51	☉ □	♏	9 15:05
11 1:26	☉ ⚹	♐	11 17:11
13 0:29	♀ ☌	♑	13 18:22
15 11:34	☉ ☌	♒	15 19:57
17 14:13	♀ ⚹	♓	17 23:31
20 6:06	☉ ⚹	♈	20 6:24
21 11:54	☿ ⚹	♉	22 16:51
24 6:47	♆ ☌	♊	25 5:30
26 5:49	☿ △	♋	27 17:52
29 6:40	♆ ⚹	♌	30 4:02

Last Aspect / ☽ Ingress (February)

Last Aspect Dy Hr Mn		☽ Ingress	Dy Hr Mn
31 16:04	♂ □	♍	1 11:29
3 0:10	♂ ⚹	♎	3 16:43
4 22:54	♀ □	♏	5 20:34
7 23:33	☿ ⚹	♐	7 23:39
9 10:02	☉ ⚹	♑	10 2:24
12 5:19	☿ ☌	♒	12 5:20
14 2:49	♂ □	♓	14 9:23
16 11:01	♂ △	♈	16 15:48
17 15:35	♄ □	♉	19 1:23
21 13:27	♂ ☍	♊	21 13:38
22 8:41	♅ □	♋	24 2:18
25 16:00	♃ ⚹	♌	26 12:47
28 0:55	♃ □	♍	28 19:49

☽ Phases & Eclipses

Dy Hr Mn	
1 6:58	○ 10♋31
1 6:54	☍ T 1.128
8 18:51	☾ 18♎09
15 11:34	● 24♑59
22 21:57	☽ 2♉33
31 0:16	○ 10♌47
7 3:18	☾ 18♏00
14 0:33	● 24♒59
21 19:24	☽ 2♊50
29 14:39	○ 10♍41

Astro Data

1 January 2048
Julian Day # 54057
SVP 4♓35'04"
GC 27♐30.6 ⚴ 10♑01.8
Eris 29♈47.4R ⚵ 9♑40.8
⚷ 9♏05.5 ⚶ 12♒25.0
☽ Mean ☊ 6♑39.8

1 February 2048
Julian Day # 54088
SVP 4♓34'58"
GC 27♐30.7 ⚴ 22♑04.2
Eris 29♈47.2 ⚵ 21♑18.2
⚷ 11♏14.9 ⚶ 27♒52.1
☽ Mean ☊ 5♑01.3

March 2048 — LONGITUDE

Day	Sid.Time	☉	0 hr ☽	Noon ☽	True ☊	☿	♀	♂	⚳	♃	♄	♅	♆	♇
1 Su	22 39 54	11♓34 42	16♍03 25	23♍00 54	4♑20.9	16♒03.4	19♒03.3	4♐04.2	1♓33.3	19♉51.1	13♑42.9	9♍01.4	19♉06.6	6♓25.5
2 M	22 43 50	12 34 52	0♎01 57	7♎05 56	4R 09.8	17 20.5	20 17.7	4 31.1	1 56.8	20 00.2	13 47.6	8R 58.8	19 07.7	6 27.1
3 Tu	22 47 47	13 35 01	14 12 10	21 20 01	4 00.0	18 39.1	21 32.1	4 57.8	2 20.2	20 09.4	13 52.3	8 56.1	19 08.8	6 28.8
4 W	22 51 43	14 35 09	28 28 48	5♏37 55	3 52.3	19 59.3	22 46.5	5 24.3	2 43.6	20 18.7	13 57.0	8 53.5	19 10.0	6 30.4
5 Th	22 55 40	15 35 15	12♏46 51	19 55 08	3 47.4	21 20.9	24 00.9	5 50.5	3 07.0	20 28.2	14 01.5	8 50.9	19 11.2	6 32.1
6 F	22 59 36	16 35 20	27 02 23	4♐08 19	3D 45.0	22 44.0	25 15.3	6 16.5	3 30.4	20 37.8	14 06.0	8 48.3	19 12.4	6 33.8
7 Sa	23 03 33	17 35 23	11♐12 43	18 15 28	3 44.5	24 08.5	26 29.7	6 42.3	3 53.7	20 47.5	14 10.4	8 45.7	19 13.7	6 35.4
8 Su	23 07 29	18 35 24	25 16 27	2♑15 39	3R 44.7	25 34.3	27 44.0	7 07.8	4 17.0	20 57.3	14 14.7	8 43.1	19 15.0	6 37.0
9 M	23 11 26	19 35 24	9♑13 02	16 08 33	3 44.2	27 01.4	28 58.4	7 33.1	4 40.3	21 07.3	14 19.0	8 40.6	19 16.3	6 38.7
10 Tu	23 15 23	20 35 22	23 02 12	29 53 54	3 41.9	28 29.8	0♓12.8	7 58.1	5 03.6	21 17.3	14 23.2	8 38.0	19 17.6	6 40.3
11 W	23 19 19	21 35 19	6♒43 35	13♒31 07	3 36.9	29 59.4	1 27.2	8 22.8	5 26.9	21 27.5	14 27.3	8 35.5	19 19.0	6 41.9
12 Th	23 23 16	22 35 13	20 16 21	26 59 05	3 28.8	1♓30.3	2 41.6	8 47.3	5 50.1	21 37.8	14 31.3	8 32.9	19 20.4	6 43.5
13 F	23 27 12	23 35 06	3♓39 07	10♓16 13	3 18.0	3 02.5	3 56.0	9 11.5	6 13.3	21 48.2	14 35.2	8 30.4	19 21.8	6 45.2
14 Sa	23 31 09	24 34 57	16 50 11	23 20 47	3 05.2	4 35.9	5 10.4	9 35.4	6 36.5	21 58.7	14 39.1	8 27.9	19 23.2	6 46.8
15 Su	23 35 05	25 34 46	29 47 52	6♈11 18	2 51.5	6 10.5	6 24.7	9 59.0	6 59.6	22 09.3	14 42.8	8 25.4	19 24.7	6 48.4
16 M	23 39 02	26 34 33	12♈31 00	18 46 58	2 38.3	7 46.3	7 39.1	10 22.3	7 22.7	22 20.0	14 46.5	8 22.9	19 26.2	6 49.9
17 Tu	23 42 58	27 34 18	24 59 14	1♉07 58	2 26.6	9 23.3	8 53.5	10 45.2	7 45.8	22 30.8	14 50.1	8 20.5	19 27.7	6 51.5
18 W	23 46 55	28 34 01	7♉13 23	13 15 45	2 17.3	11 01.6	10 07.8	11 07.9	8 08.9	22 41.7	14 53.6	8 18.1	19 29.3	6 53.1
19 Th	23 50 52	29 33 42	19 15 26	25 12 52	2 10.8	12 41.1	11 22.2	11 30.3	8 31.9	22 52.7	14 57.1	8 15.6	19 30.8	6 54.7
20 F	23 54 48	0♈33 20	1♊08 32	7♊03 00	2 07.1	14 21.9	12 36.5	11 52.3	8 54.9	23 03.8	15 00.4	8 13.3	19 32.5	6 56.2
21 Sa	23 58 45	1 32 56	12 56 51	18 50 43	2 05.5	16 03.9	13 50.8	12 14.0	9 17.8	23 15.0	15 03.7	8 10.9	19 34.1	6 57.8
22 Su	0 02 41	2 32 30	24 45 17	0♋41 12	2 05.2	17 47.1	15 05.1	12 35.3	9 40.7	23 26.2	15 06.9	8 08.6	19 35.7	6 59.3
23 M	0 06 38	3 32 02	6♋39 12	12 39 58	2 05.1	19 31.7	16 19.4	12 56.3	10 03.6	23 37.6	15 09.9	8 06.3	19 37.4	7 00.8
24 Tu	0 10 34	4 31 31	18 44 12	24 52 34	2 04.0	21 17.5	17 33.7	13 17.0	10 26.4	23 49.1	15 12.9	8 04.0	19 39.1	7 02.3
25 W	0 14 31	5 30 59	1♌05 40	7♌24 05	2 01.0	23 04.6	18 48.0	13 37.3	10 49.2	24 00.6	15 15.9	8 01.8	19 40.8	7 03.8
26 Th	0 18 27	6 30 23	13 48 17	20 18 39	1 55.4	24 53.1	20 02.3	13 57.2	11 11.9	24 12.2	15 18.7	7 59.5	19 42.5	7 05.3
27 F	0 22 24	7 29 46	26 55 28	3♍38 51	1 47.2	26 42.8	21 16.6	14 16.7	11 34.6	24 23.9	15 21.4	7 57.3	19 44.3	7 06.8
28 Sa	0 26 21	8 29 06	10♍28 47	17 25 02	1 36.8	28 33.9	22 30.8	14 35.9	11 57.3	24 35.7	15 24.0	7 55.2	19 46.1	7 08.3
29 Su	0 30 17	9 28 24	24 27 16	1♎34 56	1 25.1	0♈26.3	23 45.1	14 54.6	12 19.9	24 47.6	15 26.6	7 53.0	19 47.9	7 09.7
30 M	0 34 14	10 27 40	8♎47 20	16 03 39	1 13.3	2 20.0	24 59.3	15 13.0	12 42.5	24 59.5	15 29.0	7 51.0	19 49.7	7 11.2
31 Tu	0 38 10	11 26 54	23 22 56	0♏44 13	1 02.8	4 15.1	26 13.6	15 30.9	13 05.0	25 11.6	15 31.4	7 48.9	19 51.5	7 12.6

April 2048 — LONGITUDE

Day	Sid.Time	☉	0 hr ☽	Noon ☽	True ☊	☿	♀	♂	⚳	♃	♄	♅	♆	♇
1 W	0 42 07	12♈26 06	8♏06 28	15♏28 44	0♑54.5	6♈11.5	27♓27.8	15♐48.5	13♓27.5	25♉23.7	15♑33.7	7♍46.9	19♉53.4	7♓14.0
2 Th	0 46 03	13 25 17	22 50 06	0♐09 46	0R 49.0	8 09.2	28 42.0	16 05.6	13 49.9	25 35.8	15 35.9	7R 44.9	19 55.3	7 15.4
3 F	0 50 00	14 24 26	7♐27 01	14 41 19	0 46.2	10 08.2	29 56.3	16 22.2	14 12.3	25 48.1	15 37.9	7 42.9	19 57.2	7 16.8
4 Sa	0 53 56	15 23 32	21 52 16	28 59 34	0D 45.4	12 08.3	1♈10.5	16 38.4	14 34.7	26 00.4	15 39.9	7 41.0	19 59.1	7 18.2
5 Su	0 57 53	16 22 38	6♑03 03	13♑02 41	0R 45.6	14 09.7	2 24.7	16 54.1	14 57.0	26 12.8	15 41.8	7 39.1	20 01.0	7 19.6
6 M	1 01 50	17 21 41	19 58 27	26 50 26	0 45.3	16 12.1	3 38.9	17 09.4	15 19.2	26 25.2	15 43.6	7 37.3	20 03.0	7 20.9
7 Tu	1 05 46	18 20 43	3♒38 46	10♒23 35	0 43.5	18 15.5	4 53.1	17 24.1	15 41.4	26 37.7	15 45.3	7 35.5	20 05.0	7 22.2
8 W	1 09 43	19 19 42	17 05 01	23 43 12	0 39.2	20 19.7	6 07.3	17 38.3	16 03.6	26 50.3	15 46.9	7 33.7	20 06.9	7 23.6
9 Th	1 13 39	20 18 40	0♓18 15	6♓50 16	0 32.2	22 24.6	7 21.5	17 52.1	16 25.6	27 03.0	15 48.5	7 32.0	20 08.9	7 24.9
10 F	1 17 36	21 17 37	13 19 19	19 45 27	0 22.6	24 30.1	8 35.6	18 05.3	16 47.7	27 15.7	15 49.9	7 30.3	20 11.0	7 26.1
11 Sa	1 21 32	22 16 31	26 08 42	2♈29 04	0 11.2	26 35.9	9 49.8	18 17.9	17 09.6	27 28.4	15 51.2	7 28.6	20 13.0	7 27.4
12 Su	1 25 29	23 15 23	8♈46 34	15 01 14	29♐58.9	28 41.8	11 04.0	18 30.0	17 31.6	27 41.2	15 52.4	7 27.0	20 15.0	7 28.7
13 M	1 29 25	24 14 14	21 13 04	27 22 08	29 46.9	0♉47.4	12 18.1	18 41.6	17 53.4	27 54.1	15 53.5	7 25.5	20 17.1	7 29.9
14 Tu	1 33 22	25 13 02	3♉28 30	9♉32 19	29 36.3	2 52.7	13 32.3	18 52.5	18 15.2	28 07.1	15 54.5	7 24.0	20 19.2	7 31.1
15 W	1 37 18	26 11 49	15 33 42	21 32 54	29 27.8	4 57.1	14 46.4	19 02.9	18 36.9	28 20.0	15 55.5	7 22.5	20 21.2	7 32.3
16 Th	1 41 15	27 10 33	27 30 10	3♊25 50	29 21.9	7 00.5	16 00.5	19 12.7	18 58.6	28 33.1	15 56.3	7 21.1	20 23.3	7 33.5
17 F	1 45 12	28 09 16	9♊20 14	15 13 50	29 18.6	9 02.4	17 14.6	19 21.9	19 20.2	28 46.2	15 57.0	7 19.7	20 25.5	7 34.7
18 Sa	1 49 08	29 07 56	21 07 05	27 00 31	29D 17.5	11 02.6	18 28.7	19 30.5	19 41.8	28 59.3	15 57.6	7 18.4	20 27.6	7 35.8
19 Su	1 53 05	0♉06 34	2♋54 42	8♋50 13	29 17.8	13 00.6	19 42.8	19 38.5	20 03.2	29 12.5	15 58.2	7 17.1	20 29.7	7 36.9
20 M	1 57 01	1 05 10	14 47 44	20 47 53	29R 18.7	14 56.3	20 56.9	19 45.8	20 24.6	29 25.8	15 58.6	7 15.9	20 31.9	7 38.0
21 Tu	2 00 58	2 03 44	26 51 21	2♌58 46	29 19.1	16 49.1	22 10.9	19 52.5	20 46.0	29 39.0	15 58.9	7 14.7	20 34.0	7 39.1
22 W	2 04 54	3 02 15	9♌10 49	15 28 08	29 18.2	18 39.0	23 25.0	19 58.6	21 07.2	29 52.4	15 59.1	7 13.5	20 36.2	7 40.2
23 Th	2 08 51	4 00 44	21 51 15	28 20 43	29 15.4	20 25.6	24 39.0	20 03.9	21 28.4	0♊05.7	15R 59.3	7 12.5	20 38.4	7 41.2
24 F	2 12 47	4 59 11	4♍56 55	11♍40 09	29 10.6	22 08.7	25 53.0	20 08.7	21 49.5	0 19.1	15 59.3	7 11.4	20 40.5	7 42.3
25 Sa	2 16 44	5 57 36	18 30 34	25 28 08	29 03.9	23 48.1	27 07.0	20 12.7	22 10.5	0 32.6	15 59.2	7 10.4	20 42.7	7 43.3
26 Su	2 20 41	6 55 59	2♎32 41	9♎43 48	28 56.0	25 23.6	28 21.0	20 16.0	22 31.5	0 46.0	15 59.1	7 09.5	20 44.9	7 44.3
27 M	2 24 37	7 54 20	17 00 54	24 23 12	28 48.0	26 55.1	29 35.0	20 18.7	22 52.4	0 59.6	15 58.8	7 08.6	20 47.1	7 45.2
28 Tu	2 28 34	8 52 39	1♏49 45	9♏19 28	28 40.7	28 22.4	0♉49.0	20 20.7	23 13.2	1 13.1	15 58.5	7 07.7	20 49.3	7 46.2
29 W	2 32 30	9 50 57	16 51 13	24 23 46	28 35.1	29 45.4	2 03.0	20 21.9	23 33.9	1 26.7	15 58.0	7 07.0	20 51.6	7 47.1
30 Th	2 36 27	10 49 13	1♐55 56	9♐26 36	28 31.6	1♊03.9	3 16.9	20R 22.4	23 54.6	1 40.3	15 57.5	7 06.2	20 53.8	7 48.0

Astro Data (Dy Hr Mn)

☽0S 1 4:34
☽0N 14 3:27
☉0N 19 22:35
☽0S 28 14:04
☿0N 31 9:59

♀0N 6 7:49
☽0N 10 9:41
♅☍♇ 11 22:18
♄ R 24 7:55
☽0S 24 23:38
♃⚼♄ 27 10:43
♂ R 30 16:54

Planet Ingress (Dy Hr Mn)

♀ ♓ 10 7:51
☿ ♓ 11 12:09
☉ ♈ 19 22:35
☿ ♈ 29 6:25

♀ ♈ 3 13:12
☊ ♐R 12 9:52
☿ ♉ 13 2:56
☉ ♉ 19 9:19
♃ ♊ 23 1:45
♀ ♉ 27 20:06
☿ ♊ 29 16:22

Last Aspect / ☽ Ingress (March)

Last Aspect Dy Hr Mn			☽ Ingress Dy Hr Mn	
1 6:30	♃	△	♎	1 23:57
3 12:22	♀	△	♏	4 2:33
5 19:33	♀	□	♐	6 5:00
8 3:28	♀	✶	♑	8 8:07
9 20:46	♃	△	♒	10 12:11
12 2:18	♃	□	♓	12 17:25
14 14:29	☉	☌	♈	15 0:23
16 4:16	♄	□	♉	17 9:47
19 21:36	☉	✶	♊	19 21:41
21 5:23	☿	□	♋	22 10:37
24 9:55	♃	✶	♌	24 21:54
26 19:12	♃	□	♍	27 5:31
29 0:25	♃	△	♎	29 9:21
30 11:03	♄	□	♏	31 10:48

Last Aspect / ☽ Ingress (April)

Last Aspect Dy Hr Mn			☽ Ingress Dy Hr Mn	
2 9:23	♀	△	♐	2 11:44
3 14:51	♂	☌	♑	4 13:42
6 11:15	♃	△	♒	6 17:33
8 17:46	♃	□	♓	8 23:27
11 2:21	♃	✶	♈	11 7:17
13 5:21	☉	☌	♉	13 17:10
16 1:56	♃	☌	♊	16 5:03
18 16:43	☉	✶	♋	18 18:05
21 5:22	♃	✶	♌	21 6:11
23 4:29	♀	△	♍	23 15:02
25 8:46	☿	△	♎	25 19:42
27 5:22	♂	✶	♏	27 21:04
29 6:22	♆	☍	♐	29 20:55

☽ Phases & Eclipses (Dy Hr Mn)

7 10:46 ☾ 17♐32
14 14:29 ● 24♓41
22 16:05 ☽ 2♋43
30 2:06 ○ 10♎03

5 18:12 ☾ 16♑38
13 5:21 ● 23♈58
21 10:03 ☽ 1♌59
28 11:14 ○ 8♏51

Astro Data

1 March 2048
Julian Day # 54117
SVP 4♓34'55"
GC 27♐30.7 ⚳ 2♒30.8
Eris 29♈56.4 ⚵ 1♒58.1
⚷ 11♏40.8R ⚶ 12♓18.8
☽ Mean ☊ 3♑29.1

1 April 2048
Julian Day # 54148
SVP 4♓34'52"
GC 27♐30.8 ⚳ 12♒09.2
Eris 0♉13.6 ⚵ 12♒36.6
⚷ 10♏27.9R ⚶ 27♓26.4
☽ Mean ☊ 1♑50.6

LONGITUDE May 2048

Day	Sid.Time	☉	0 hr ☽	Noon ☽	True ☊	☿	♀	♂	⚳	♃	♄	♅	♆	♇
1 F	2 40 23	11♉47 27	16♐54 45	24♐19 28	28♐30.2	2♊18.0	4♉30.9	20♐22.2	24♓15.1	1♊54.0	15♑56.8	7♍05.5	20♉56.0	7♓48.9
2 Sa	2 44 20	12 45 39	1♑40 03	8♑55 56	28D30.4	3 27.5	5 44.8	20R21.2	24 35.6	2 07.6	15R56.1	7R04.9	20 58.2	7 49.8
3 Su	2 48 16	13 43 50	16 06 43	23 12 09	28 31.6	4 32.4	6 58.8	20 19.5	24 56.0	2 21.4	15 55.2	7 04.3	21 00.5	7 50.6
4 M	2 52 13	14 42 00	0♒12 08	7♒06 40	28R32.6	5 32.5	8 12.7	20 17.0	25 16.4	2 35.1	15 54.3	7 03.8	21 02.7	7 51.4
5 Tu	2 56 10	15 40 08	13 55 51	20 39 52	28 32.8	6 27.8	9 26.7	20 13.8	25 36.6	2 48.9	15 53.3	7 03.3	21 05.0	7 52.2
6 W	3 00 06	16 38 15	27 18 56	3♓53 21	28 31.3	7 18.3	10 40.6	20 09.8	25 56.7	3 02.7	15 52.2	7 02.9	21 07.2	7 53.0
7 Th	3 04 03	17 36 20	10♓23 22	16 49 17	28 28.1	8 03.9	11 54.5	20 05.0	26 16.8	3 16.5	15 50.9	7 02.5	21 09.5	7 53.7
8 F	3 07 59	18 34 24	23 11 23	29 29 58	28 23.1	8 44.4	13 08.4	19 59.5	26 36.7	3 30.3	15 49.6	7 02.2	21 11.7	7 54.5
9 Sa	3 11 56	19 32 27	5♈45 18	11♈57 36	28 16.9	9 20.0	14 22.3	19 53.2	26 56.6	3 44.2	15 48.2	7 01.9	21 14.0	7 55.2
10 Su	3 15 52	20 30 28	18 07 08	24 14 05	28 10.1	9 50.5	15 36.2	19 46.1	27 16.4	3 58.1	15 46.7	7 01.7	21 16.2	7 55.9
11 M	3 19 49	21 28 28	0♉18 42	6♉21 09	28 03.4	10 16.0	16 50.1	19 38.2	27 36.0	4 12.0	15 45.1	7 01.5	21 18.5	7 56.5
12 Tu	3 23 45	22 26 26	12 21 39	18 20 24	27 57.5	10 36.3	18 04.0	19 29.6	27 55.6	4 25.9	15 43.4	7 01.4	21 20.7	7 57.2
13 W	3 27 42	23 24 23	24 17 35	0♊13 28	27 53.0	10 51.5	19 17.9	19 20.3	28 15.1	4 39.8	15 41.7	7D01.4	21 23.0	7 57.8
14 Th	3 31 39	24 22 18	6♊08 16	12 02 15	27 50.0	11 01.7	20 31.7	19 10.2	28 34.5	4 53.8	15 39.8	7 01.4	21 25.3	7 58.4
15 F	3 35 35	25 20 11	17 55 44	23 49 01	27D48.8	11R07.0	21 45.6	18 59.4	28 53.7	5 07.8	15 37.9	7 01.4	21 27.5	7 58.9
16 Sa	3 39 32	26 18 03	29 42 30	5♋36 32	27 49.0	11 07.3	22 59.5	18 47.8	29 12.9	5 21.8	15 35.8	7 01.6	21 29.8	7 59.5
17 Su	3 43 28	27 15 54	11♋31 35	17 28 07	27 50.2	11 02.8	24 13.3	18 35.6	29 31.9	5 35.8	15 33.7	7 01.7	21 32.0	8 00.0
18 M	3 47 25	28 13 43	23 26 36	29 27 36	27 51.9	10 53.8	25 27.1	18 22.7	29 50.8	5 49.8	15 31.5	7 01.9	21 34.3	8 00.5
19 Tu	3 51 21	29 11 30	5♌31 38	11♌39 16	27 53.5	10 40.5	26 41.0	18 09.1	0♈09.7	6 03.8	15 29.2	7 02.2	21 36.5	8 01.0
20 W	3 55 18	0♊09 15	17 51 05	24 07 38	27R54.5	10 23.0	27 54.8	17 54.9	0 28.4	6 17.8	15 26.8	7 02.5	21 38.7	8 01.4
21 Th	3 59 14	1 06 59	0♍29 29	6♍57 06	27 54.5	10 01.9	29 08.6	17 40.1	0 47.0	6 31.8	15 24.4	7 02.9	21 41.0	8 01.8
22 F	4 03 11	2 04 41	13 30 58	20 11 27	27 53.4	9 37.4	0♊22.4	17 24.7	1 05.4	6 45.9	15 21.8	7 03.4	21 43.2	8 02.2
23 Sa	4 07 08	3 02 21	26 58 49	3♎53 12	27 51.2	9 09.9	1 36.2	17 08.7	1 23.8	6 59.9	15 19.2	7 03.8	21 45.4	8 02.6
24 Su	4 11 04	4 00 00	10♎54 37	18 02 53	27 48.4	8 40.1	2 50.0	16 52.2	1 42.0	7 14.0	15 16.5	7 04.4	21 47.6	8 03.0
25 M	4 15 01	4 57 38	25 17 40	2♏38 25	27 45.3	8 08.4	4 03.8	16 35.2	2 00.1	7 28.0	15 13.7	7 05.0	21 49.9	8 03.3
26 Tu	4 18 57	5 55 14	10♏04 25	17 34 45	27 42.4	7 35.3	5 17.5	16 17.7	2 18.1	7 42.1	15 10.9	7 05.6	21 52.1	8 03.6
27 W	4 22 54	6 52 49	25 08 22	2♐44 08	27 40.3	7 01.5	6 31.3	15 59.8	2 36.0	7 56.1	15 08.0	7 06.3	21 54.3	8 03.9
28 Th	4 26 50	7 50 23	10♐20 50	17 57 11	27D39.2	6 27.5	7 45.1	15 41.4	2 53.7	8 10.2	15 05.0	7 07.1	21 56.5	8 04.1
29 F	4 30 47	8 47 56	25 32 01	3♑04 10	27 39.1	5 54.0	8 58.8	15 22.7	3 11.3	8 24.2	15 01.9	7 07.9	21 58.6	8 04.3
30 Sa	4 34 43	9 45 27	10♑32 37	17 56 31	27 39.7	5 21.5	10 12.6	15 03.7	3 28.8	8 38.3	14 58.8	7 08.7	22 00.8	8 04.6
31 Su	4 38 40	10 42 58	25 15 08	2♒27 57	27 40.9	4 50.5	11 26.3	14 44.3	3 46.1	8 52.3	14 55.6	7 09.6	22 03.0	8 04.7

LONGITUDE June 2048

Day	Sid.Time	☉	0 hr ☽	Noon ☽	True ☊	☿	♀	♂	⚳	♃	♄	♅	♆	♇
1 M	4 42 37	11♊40 28	9♒34 34	16♒34 47	27♐42.0	4♊21.6	12♊40.1	14♐24.6	4♈03.3	9♊06.3	14♑52.3	7♍10.6	22♉05.1	8♓04.9
2 Tu	4 46 33	12 37 57	23 28 34	0♓15 58	27 42.9	3R55.2	13 53.8	14R04.8	4 20.4	9 20.4	14R49.0	7 11.6	22 07.3	8 05.0
3 W	4 50 30	13 35 26	6♓57 09	13 32 24	27R43.2	3 31.9	15 07.6	13 44.7	4 37.3	9 34.4	14 45.6	7 12.7	22 09.4	8 05.1
4 Th	4 54 26	14 32 53	20 02 03	26 26 28	27 42.9	3 11.8	16 21.3	13 24.5	4 54.1	9 48.4	14 42.1	7 13.8	22 11.5	8 05.2
5 F	4 58 23	15 30 20	2♈46 04	9♈01 17	27 42.0	2 55.5	17 35.1	13 04.2	5 10.7	10 02.4	14 38.6	7 15.0	22 13.7	8 05.3
6 Sa	5 02 19	16 27 47	15 12 34	21 20 21	27 40.8	2 43.0	18 48.8	12 43.9	5 27.2	10 16.4	14 35.0	7 16.2	22 15.8	8R05.3
7 Su	5 06 16	17 25 12	27 25 04	3♉27 07	27 39.3	2 34.7	20 02.5	12 23.6	5 43.5	10 30.4	14 31.3	7 17.4	22 17.8	8 05.3
8 M	5 10 12	18 22 37	9♉26 55	15 24 50	27 38.0	2D30.7	21 16.3	12 03.3	5 59.7	10 44.4	14 27.6	7 18.8	22 19.9	8 05.3
9 Tu	5 14 09	19 20 02	21 21 14	27 16 26	27 36.8	2 31.0	22 30.0	11 43.1	6 15.7	10 58.4	14 23.9	7 20.1	22 22.0	8 05.3
10 W	5 18 06	20 17 25	3♊10 47	9♊04 35	27 36.1	2 35.9	23 43.8	11 23.1	6 31.5	11 12.3	14 20.1	7 21.6	22 24.0	8 05.2
11 Th	5 22 02	21 14 48	14 58 08	20 51 42	27D35.7	2 45.3	24 57.5	11 03.2	6 47.2	11 26.3	14 16.2	7 23.0	22 26.1	8 05.1
12 F	5 25 59	22 12 10	26 45 35	2♋40 04	27 35.7	2 59.2	26 11.2	10 43.6	7 02.7	11 40.2	14 12.3	7 24.6	22 28.1	8 05.0
13 Sa	5 29 55	23 09 32	8♋35 26	14 32 00	27 35.9	3 17.6	27 25.0	10 24.3	7 18.1	11 54.1	14 08.4	7 26.1	22 30.1	8 04.9
14 Su	5 33 52	24 06 53	20 30 03	26 29 55	27 36.2	3 40.6	28 38.7	10 05.4	7 33.3	12 07.9	14 04.4	7 27.7	22 32.1	8 04.7
15 M	5 37 48	25 04 12	2♌31 56	8♌36 28	27 36.6	4 07.9	29 52.4	9 46.8	7 48.3	12 21.8	14 00.3	7 29.4	22 34.1	8 04.5
16 Tu	5 41 45	26 01 31	14 43 53	20 54 33	27 36.8	4 39.7	1♋06.1	9 28.6	8 03.1	12 35.6	13 56.3	7 31.1	22 36.0	8 04.3
17 W	5 45 42	26 58 50	27 08 53	3♍27 17	27R36.9	5 15.7	2 19.8	9 10.9	8 17.8	12 49.4	13 52.2	7 32.9	22 38.0	8 04.1
18 Th	5 49 38	27 56 07	9♍50 08	16 17 50	27D36.9	5 56.0	3 33.6	8 53.7	8 32.2	13 03.2	13 48.0	7 34.7	22 39.9	8 03.8
19 F	5 53 35	28 53 23	22 50 44	29 29 10	27 36.9	6 40.5	4 47.3	8 37.0	8 46.5	13 17.0	13 43.8	7 36.5	22 41.8	8 03.5
20 Sa	5 57 31	29 50 39	6♎13 24	13♎03 38	27 37.0	7 29.1	6 01.0	8 20.9	9 00.6	13 30.7	13 39.6	7 38.4	22 43.7	8 03.2
21 Su	6 01 28	0♋47 54	19 59 58	27 02 24	27 37.2	8 21.7	7 14.7	8 05.4	9 14.5	13 44.4	13 35.4	7 40.4	22 45.6	8 02.9
22 M	6 05 24	1 45 08	4♏10 49	11♏24 56	27 37.5	9 18.3	8 28.4	7 50.6	9 28.3	13 58.1	13 31.1	7 42.4	22 47.4	8 02.5
23 Tu	6 09 21	2 42 22	18 44 20	26 08 25	27 37.9	10 18.8	9 42.1	7 36.4	9 41.8	14 11.7	13 26.8	7 44.4	22 49.3	8 02.2
24 W	6 13 17	3 39 35	3♐36 28	11♐07 35	27 38.3	11 23.1	10 55.7	7 22.8	9 55.1	14 25.4	13 22.5	7 46.5	22 51.1	8 01.8
25 Th	6 17 14	4 36 48	18 40 48	26 15 00	27R38.4	12 31.2	12 09.4	7 10.0	10 08.2	14 38.9	13 18.1	7 48.6	22 52.9	8 01.4
26 F	6 21 11	5 34 00	3♑49 04	11♑21 51	27 38.3	13 43.1	13 23.1	6 57.9	10 21.1	14 52.5	13 13.8	7 50.8	22 54.7	8 00.9
27 Sa	6 25 07	6 31 12	18 52 12	26 19 06	27 37.7	14 58.7	14 36.8	6 46.5	10 33.9	15 06.0	13 09.4	7 53.0	22 56.4	8 00.5
28 Su	6 29 04	7 28 24	3♒41 35	10♒58 51	27 36.8	16 17.9	15 50.5	6 35.9	10 46.4	15 19.5	13 05.0	7 55.2	22 58.2	8 00.0
29 M	6 33 00	8 25 36	18 10 16	25 15 21	27 35.6	17 40.8	17 04.2	6 26.0	10 58.6	15 32.9	13 00.6	7 57.5	22 59.9	7 59.5
30 Tu	6 36 57	9 22 48	2♓13 46	9♓05 25	27 34.3	19 07.2	18 17.8	6 16.9	11 10.7	15 46.3	12 56.2	7 59.9	23 01.6	7 58.9

Astro Data	Dy Hr Mn
☽ 0N	7 14:30
♅ D	13 22:39
☿ R	16 1:32
☽ 0S	22 8:00
♃□♅	23 18:57
♃□♇	28 1:28
☽ 0N	3 19:59
♇ R	7 8:21
☿ D	8 21:59
☽ 0S	18 14:49
♃⚻♄	20 23:52
♅☍♇	30 4:12

Planet Ingress		Dy Hr Mn
⚳	♈	18 23:39
☉	♊	20 8:09
♀	♊	22 4:43
♀	♋	15 14:28
☉	♋	20 15:55

Last Aspect Dy Hr Mn			☽ Ingress	Dy Hr Mn
1 5:35	♂	☌	♑	1 21:16
3 8:16	♆	△	♒	3 23:39
5 12:45	♆	□	♓	6 4:53
7 20:11	♆	⚹	♈	8 12:57
10 3:19	♂	△	♉	10 23:23
12 20:59	☉	☌	♊	13 11:33
15 2:19	♂	☍	♋	16 0:36
18 9:20	☉	⚹	♌	18 13:04
20 19:55	♀	□	♍	20 23:05
22 14:44	♆	△	♎	23 5:16
24 10:04	♂	⚹	♏	25 7:42
26 18:50	♆	☍	♐	27 7:41
28 8:30	♂	☌	♑	29 7:06
30 18:41	♆	△	♒	31 7:53

Last Aspect Dy Hr Mn			☽ Ingress	Dy Hr Mn
1 21:35	♆	□	♓	2 11:32
4 4:00	♆	⚹	♈	4 18:44
6 6:29	♀	⚹	♉	7 5:08
9 2:01	♆	☌	♊	9 17:32
11 21:18	♀	☌	♋	12 6:35
14 4:03	♆	⚹	♌	14 18:58
16 22:40	☉	⚹	♍	17 5:27
19 10:51	☉	□	♎	19 12:55
20 13:02	♄	□	♏	21 17:00
23 6:37	♆	☍	♐	23 18:13
24 17:19	♃	☍	♑	25 17:57
27 6:32	♆	△	♒	27 17:58
29 8:09	♆	□	♓	29 20:09

☽ Phases & Eclipses Dy Hr Mn		
5 2:24	☾	15♒17
12 20:59	●	22♉48
21 0:17	☽	0♍39
27 18:58	○	7♐10
3 12:06	☾	13♓36
11 12:51	●	21♊17
11 12:58:51	●	A 04'58"
19 10:51	☽	28♍51
26 2:09	○	5♑11
26 2:02	●	P 0.639

Astro Data

1 May 2048
Julian Day # 54178
SVP 4♓34'49"
GC 27♐30.9 ⚵ 19♒06.0
Eris 0♉33.4 ⚶ 21♒26.7
⚷ 8♏17.6R ⚴ 11♈29.7
☽ Mean ☊ 0♑15.3

1 June 2048
Julian Day # 54209
SVP 4♓34'44"
GC 27♐30.9 ⚵ 22♒27.8
Eris 0♉52.0 ⚶ 27♒54.4
⚷ 6♏12.2R ⚴ 25♈05.0
☽ Mean ☊ 28♐36.8

July 2048 LONGITUDE

Day	Sid.Time	☉	0 hr ☽	Noon ☽	True ☊	☿	♀	♂	⚳	♃	♄	♅	♆	♇
1 W	6 40 53	10♋20 00	15♓50 16	22♓28 28	27♐33.3	20♊37.1	19♋31.5	6♐08.6	11♈22.6	15♊59.7	12♑51.8	8♍02.3	23♉03.2	7♓58.4
2 Th	6 44 50	11 17 12	29 00 17	5♈26 04	27D32.7	22 10.5	20 45.2	6R01.1	11 34.2	16 13.0	12R47.3	8 04.7	23 04.9	7R57.8
3 F	6 48 46	12 14 24	11♈46 14	18 01 17	27 32.7	23 47.4	21 58.9	5 54.5	11 45.6	16 26.3	12 42.9	8 07.1	23 06.5	7 57.2
4 Sa	6 52 43	13 11 37	24 11 44	0♉18 09	27 33.3	25 27.6	23 12.6	5 48.6	11 56.8	16 39.5	12 38.5	8 09.6	23 08.1	7 56.6
5 Su	6 56 40	14 08 49	6♉21 04	12 21 05	27 34.4	27 11.0	24 26.3	5 43.6	12 07.7	16 52.7	12 34.0	8 12.2	23 09.7	7 56.0
6 M	7 00 36	15 06 02	18 18 43	24 14 32	27 35.9	28 57.6	25 39.9	5 39.4	12 18.4	17 05.9	12 29.6	8 14.7	23 11.3	7 55.3
7 Tu	7 04 33	16 03 16	0♊09 03	6♊02 44	27 37.3	0♋47.3	26 53.6	5 36.1	12 28.8	17 19.0	12 25.2	8 17.3	23 12.8	7 54.6
8 W	7 08 29	17 00 29	11 56 04	17 49 29	27R38.3	2 39.9	28 07.3	5 33.6	12 39.0	17 32.1	12 20.8	8 20.0	23 14.3	7 53.9
9 Th	7 12 26	17 57 43	23 43 22	29 38 05	27 38.6	4 35.2	29 21.0	5 31.9	12 49.0	17 45.1	12 16.4	8 22.7	23 15.8	7 53.2
10 F	7 16 22	18 54 57	5♋33 59	11♋31 21	27 37.9	6 33.0	0♌34.7	5D31.1	12 58.7	17 58.0	12 12.0	8 25.4	23 17.2	7 52.5
11 Sa	7 20 19	19 52 11	17 30 28	23 31 34	27 36.1	8 33.2	1 48.4	5 31.2	13 08.1	18 10.9	12 07.6	8 28.2	23 18.7	7 51.7
12 Su	7 24 15	20 49 26	29 34 54	5♌40 40	27 33.4	10 35.4	3 02.1	5 32.1	13 17.3	18 23.8	12 03.2	8 31.0	23 20.1	7 51.0
13 M	7 28 12	21 46 40	11♌49 03	18 00 14	27 29.8	12 39.5	4 15.8	5 33.8	13 26.2	18 36.6	11 58.9	8 33.8	23 21.5	7 50.2
14 Tu	7 32 09	22 43 55	24 14 24	0♍31 43	27 25.9	14 45.0	5 29.4	5 36.4	13 34.8	18 49.3	11 54.5	8 36.7	23 22.8	7 49.3
15 W	7 36 05	23 41 09	6♍52 20	13 16 26	27 22.0	16 51.7	6 43.1	5 39.8	13 43.1	19 02.0	11 50.2	8 39.6	23 24.1	7 48.5
16 Th	7 40 02	24 38 24	19 44 12	26 15 48	27 18.8	18 59.4	7 56.8	5 44.0	13 51.2	19 14.6	11 46.0	8 42.5	23 25.4	7 47.7
17 F	7 43 58	25 35 39	2♎51 23	9♎31 08	27 16.6	21 07.6	9 10.5	5 49.0	13 59.0	19 27.2	11 41.7	8 45.5	23 26.7	7 46.8
18 Sa	7 47 55	26 32 54	16 15 12	23 03 41	27D15.6	23 16.1	10 24.1	5 54.9	14 06.5	19 39.7	11 37.5	8 48.5	23 28.0	7 45.9
19 Su	7 51 51	27 30 10	29 56 42	6♏54 17	27 15.9	25 24.5	11 37.8	6 01.5	14 13.8	19 52.2	11 33.3	8 51.5	23 29.2	7 45.0
20 M	7 55 48	28 27 25	13♏56 24	21 02 58	27 17.0	27 32.8	12 51.4	6 08.9	14 20.7	20 04.5	11 29.2	8 54.6	23 30.4	7 44.1
21 Tu	7 59 44	29 24 41	28 13 47	5♐28 34	27 18.4	29 40.5	14 05.1	6 17.1	14 27.4	20 16.9	11 25.0	8 57.6	23 31.5	7 43.2
22 W	8 03 41	0♌21 57	12♐46 54	20 08 15	27R19.4	1♌47.5	15 18.7	6 26.0	14 33.7	20 29.1	11 21.0	9 00.8	23 32.7	7 42.2
23 Th	8 07 38	1 19 13	27 31 59	4♑57 20	27 19.4	3 53.5	16 32.3	6 35.7	14 39.8	20 41.3	11 16.9	9 03.9	23 33.8	7 41.3
24 F	8 11 34	2 16 30	12♑23 27	19 49 23	27 17.8	5 58.5	17 46.0	6 46.2	14 45.5	20 53.4	11 13.0	9 07.1	23 34.8	7 40.3
25 Sa	8 15 31	3 13 47	27 14 11	4♒36 51	27 14.6	8 02.3	18 59.6	6 57.3	14 51.0	21 05.4	11 09.0	9 10.3	23 35.9	7 39.3
26 Su	8 19 27	4 11 05	11♒56 27	19 12 04	27 09.9	10 04.7	20 13.2	7 09.1	14 56.1	21 17.4	11 05.1	9 13.5	23 36.9	7 38.3
27 M	8 23 24	5 08 24	26 22 56	3♓28 23	27 04.3	12 05.8	21 26.8	7 21.7	15 00.9	21 29.3	11 01.2	9 16.8	23 37.9	7 37.2
28 Tu	8 27 20	6 05 43	10♓27 52	17 21 04	26 58.4	14 05.3	22 40.4	7 34.9	15 05.4	21 41.1	10 57.4	9 20.1	23 38.8	7 36.2
29 W	8 31 17	7 03 03	24 07 45	0♈47 52	26 53.1	16 03.4	23 54.0	7 48.8	15 09.6	21 52.9	10 53.7	9 23.4	23 39.8	7 35.1
30 Th	8 35 13	8 00 25	7♈21 32	13 48 58	26 49.0	17 59.8	25 07.6	8 03.3	15 13.4	22 04.5	10 50.0	9 26.7	23 40.7	7 34.1
31 F	8 39 10	8 57 47	20 10 30	26 26 34	26 46.5	19 54.7	26 21.2	8 18.5	15 17.0	22 16.1	10 46.3	9 30.0	23 41.5	7 33.0

August 2048 LONGITUDE

Day	Sid.Time	☉	0 hr ☽	Noon ☽	True ☊	☿	♀	♂	⚳	♃	♄	♅	♆	♇
1 Sa	8 43 07	9♌55 10	2♉37 42	8♉44 26	26♐45.6	21♌47.9	27♌34.8	8♐34.4	15♈20.1	22♊27.6	10♑42.7	9♍33.4	23♉42.4	7♓31.9
2 Su	8 47 03	10 52 35	14 47 22	20 47 10	26D46.0	23 39.5	28 48.4	8 50.8	15 23.0	22 39.1	10R39.2	9 36.8	23 43.2	7R30.8
3 M	8 51 00	11 50 01	26 44 28	2♊39 53	26 47.3	25 29.6	0♍01.9	9 07.9	15 25.5	22 50.4	10 35.7	9 40.2	23 43.9	7 29.7
4 Tu	8 54 56	12 47 28	8♊34 06	14 27 42	26 48.7	27 18.0	1 15.5	9 25.6	15 27.7	23 01.7	10 32.3	9 43.7	23 44.7	7 28.6
5 W	8 58 53	13 44 56	20 21 18	26 15 27	26R49.4	29 04.7	2 29.1	9 43.9	15 29.5	23 12.9	10 29.0	9 47.2	23 45.4	7 27.4
6 Th	9 02 49	14 42 26	2♋10 41	8♋07 28	26 48.6	0♍49.9	3 42.7	10 02.8	15 31.0	23 24.0	10 25.7	9 50.6	23 46.1	7 26.3
7 F	9 06 46	15 39 56	14 06 15	20 07 24	26 45.9	2 33.5	4 56.2	10 22.3	15 32.1	23 35.0	10 22.5	9 54.2	23 46.7	7 25.1
8 Sa	9 10 42	16 37 28	26 11 15	2♌18 04	26 41.1	4 15.5	6 09.8	10 42.4	15 32.9	23 45.9	10 19.3	9 57.7	23 47.3	7 24.0
9 Su	9 14 39	17 35 00	8♌28 04	14 41 23	26 34.2	5 56.0	7 23.3	11 03.0	15R33.3	23 56.7	10 16.3	10 01.2	23 47.9	7 22.8
10 M	9 18 36	18 32 34	20 58 07	27 18 19	26 25.7	7 34.8	8 36.9	11 24.1	15 33.3	24 07.4	10 13.3	10 04.8	23 48.5	7 21.6
11 Tu	9 22 32	19 30 09	3♍42 00	10♍09 06	26 16.4	9 12.1	9 50.4	11 45.8	15 33.0	24 18.0	10 10.3	10 08.4	23 49.0	7 20.4
12 W	9 26 29	20 27 45	16 39 34	23 13 18	26 07.3	10 47.9	11 03.9	12 08.0	15 32.4	24 28.6	10 07.5	10 11.9	23 49.5	7 19.2
13 Th	9 30 25	21 25 22	29 50 13	6♎30 12	25 59.2	12 22.1	12 17.4	12 30.8	15 31.3	24 39.0	10 04.7	10 15.6	23 49.9	7 18.0
14 F	9 34 22	22 23 00	13♎13 08	19 58 58	25 53.1	13 54.8	13 30.9	12 54.0	15 29.9	24 49.3	10 02.0	10 19.2	23 50.3	7 16.7
15 Sa	9 38 18	23 20 39	26 47 36	3♏38 58	25 49.2	15 25.9	14 44.4	13 17.8	15 28.2	24 59.5	9 59.4	10 22.8	23 50.7	7 15.5
16 Su	9 42 15	24 18 18	10♏33 03	17 29 46	25D47.5	16 55.5	15 57.9	13 42.0	15 26.0	25 09.6	9 56.8	10 26.5	23 51.1	7 14.3
17 M	9 46 11	25 15 59	24 29 07	1♐31 01	25 47.4	18 23.4	17 11.4	14 06.7	15 23.5	25 19.6	9 54.4	10 30.1	23 51.4	7 13.0
18 Tu	9 50 08	26 13 41	8♐35 24	15 42 07	25R48.0	19 49.8	18 24.8	14 31.9	15 20.7	25 29.5	9 52.0	10 33.8	23 51.7	7 11.8
19 W	9 54 05	27 11 24	22 51 01	0♑01 50	25 48.2	21 14.6	19 38.3	14 57.5	15 17.5	25 39.3	9 49.7	10 37.5	23 51.9	7 10.6
20 Th	9 58 01	28 09 08	7♑14 13	14 27 47	25 46.9	22 37.8	20 51.7	15 23.6	15 13.9	25 49.0	9 47.5	10 41.2	23 52.2	7 09.3
21 F	10 01 58	29 06 54	21 41 59	28 56 15	25 43.3	23 59.3	22 05.1	15 50.1	15 10.0	25 58.6	9 45.4	10 44.9	23 52.3	7 08.1
22 Sa	10 05 54	0♍04 40	6♒09 54	13♒22 13	25 37.1	25 19.0	23 18.5	16 17.0	15 05.7	26 08.0	9 43.3	10 48.6	23 52.5	7 06.8
23 Su	10 09 51	1 02 28	20 32 27	27 39 52	25 28.5	26 37.1	24 31.9	16 44.3	15 01.0	26 17.4	9 41.4	10 52.3	23 52.6	7 05.5
24 M	10 13 47	2 00 17	4♓43 45	11♓43 26	25 18.3	27 53.4	25 45.2	17 12.1	14 56.0	26 26.6	9 39.5	10 56.1	23 52.7	7 04.3
25 Tu	10 17 44	2 58 07	18 38 22	25 28 05	25 07.6	29 07.8	26 58.6	17 40.2	14 50.6	26 35.7	9 37.7	10 59.8	23 52.8	7 03.0
26 W	10 21 40	3 55 59	2♈12 15	8♈50 40	24 57.4	0♎20.3	28 11.9	18 08.7	14 44.8	26 44.7	9 36.1	11 03.5	23R52.8	7 01.7
27 Th	10 25 37	4 53 53	15 23 18	21 50 11	24 48.8	1 30.8	29 25.3	18 37.6	14 38.8	26 53.6	9 34.5	11 07.3	23 52.8	7 00.4
28 F	10 29 34	5 51 49	28 11 33	4♉27 40	24 42.4	2 39.2	0♎38.6	19 06.8	14 32.3	27 02.3	9 32.9	11 11.1	23 52.7	6 59.2
29 Sa	10 33 30	6 49 46	10♉38 58	16 45 55	24 38.5	3 45.5	1 51.9	19 36.4	14 25.5	27 10.9	9 31.5	11 14.8	23 52.6	6 57.9
30 Su	10 37 27	7 47 45	22 49 05	28 49 04	24D36.7	4 49.5	3 05.1	20 06.4	14 18.4	27 19.4	9 30.2	11 18.6	23 52.5	6 56.6
31 M	10 41 23	8 45 46	4♊46 31	10♊42 06	24 36.3	5 51.1	4 18.4	20 36.7	14 10.9	27 27.8	9 29.0	11 22.3	23 52.4	6 55.3

Astro Data (Dy Hr Mn)	Planet Ingress (Dy Hr Mn)	Last Aspect (Dy Hr Mn)	☽ Ingress (Dy Hr Mn)	Last Aspect (Dy Hr Mn)	☽ Ingress (Dy Hr Mn)	☽ Phases & Eclipses (Dy Hr Mn)
☽0N 1 3:38	☿ ♋ 7 1:44	1 13:04 ♆ ⚹	♈ 2 1:51	3 6:03 ♀ □	♊ 3 6:36	2 23:59 ☾ 11♈46
♂D 10 22:40	♀ ♌ 10 0:42	4 0:57 ☿ ⚹	♉ 4 11:24	5 18:43 ♆ ⚹	♋ 5 19:35	11 4:05 ● 19♋33
☽0S 15 20:44	☿ ♌ 21 15:41	6 15:13 ♀ ⚹	♊ 6 23:42	7 19:15 ♆ ⚹	♌ 8 7:30	18 18:33 ☽ 26♎49
☽0N 28 13:17	☉ ♌ 22 2:48	8 11:24 ♃ ☌	♋ 9 12:44	10 5:54 ♃ ⚹	♍ 10 17:04	25 9:35 ○ 3♒08
		11 11:34 ♆ ⚹	♌ 12 0:50	12 14:19 ♃ □	♎ 13 0:18	
♃⊻♆ 8 15:26	♀ ♍ 3 11:22	13 22:20 ♆ □	♍ 14 11:00	14 20:39 ♃ △	♏ 15 5:37	1 14:32 ☾ 10♉01
⚳R 10 3:22	☿ ♍ 6 0:34	16 8:48 ☉ ⚹	♎ 16 18:49	17 0:33 ☉ □	♐ 17 9:25	9 18:00 ● 17♌49
♄△♅ 11 19:21	☉ ♍ 22 10:04	18 18:33 ☉ □	♏ 19 0:06	19 6:55 ☉ △	♑ 19 11:57	17 0:33 ☽ 24♏48
☽0S 12 2:54	☿ ♎ 26 5:14	21 1:15 ☉ △	♐ 21 2:56	21 3:36 ♆ △	♒ 21 13:46	23 18:08 ○ 1♓17
☿0S 24 5:54	♀ ♎ 27 23:23	22 12:34 ♃ ☍	♑ 23 4:00	23 9:39 ♃ △	♓ 23 15:57	31 7:43 ☾ 8♊35
☽0N 24 23:27		24 18:05 ♆ △	♒ 25 4:29	25 19:09 ☿ ☍	♈ 25 20:03	
♆R 26 15:01		26 19:22 ♆ □	♓ 27 6:06	27 21:39 ♃ ⚹	♉ 28 3:27	
♀0S 29 21:34		28 23:09 ♆ ⚹	♈ 29 10:33	30 2:07 ♆ ☌	♊ 30 14:23	
		31 11:49 ♀ △	♉ 31 18:53			

Astro Data

1 July 2048
Julian Day # 54239
SVP 4♓34'39"
GC 27♐31.0 ⚴ 20♒35.3R
Eris 1♉04.0 ⚵ 29♒54.6R
⚷ 5♏20.3R ⚶ 6♉52.5
☽ Mean ☊ 27♐01.5

1 August 2048
Julian Day # 54270
SVP 4♓34'34"
GC 27♐31.1 ⚴ 13♒41.1R
Eris 1♉07.4R ⚵ 26♒06.7R
⚷ 6♏05.3 ⚶ 16♉51.8
☽ Mean ☊ 25♐23.0

LONGITUDE — September 2048

Day	Sid.Time	☉	0 hr ☽	Noon ☽	True ☊	☿	♀	♂	⚳	♃	♄	♅	♆	♇
1 Tu	10 45 20	9♍43 49	16♊36 30	22♊30 24	24♐36.5	6♎50.2	5♎31.7	21♐07.4	14♈03.1	27♊36.0	9♑27.8	11♍26.1	23♉52.2	6♓54.1
2 W	10 49 16	10 41 54	28 24 30	4♋19 27	24R36.2	7 46.7	6 44.9	21 38.4	13R54.9	27 44.1	9R26.8	11 29.9	23R52.0	6R52.8
3 Th	10 53 13	11 40 01	10♋15 54	16 14 27	24 34.3	8 40.2	7 58.2	22 09.7	13 46.5	27 52.0	9 25.9	11 33.7	23 51.8	6 51.5
4 F	10 57 09	12 38 10	22 15 38	28 19 58	24 30.2	9 30.8	9 11.4	22 41.4	13 37.7	27 59.8	9 25.0	11 37.4	23 51.5	6 50.3
5 Sa	11 01 06	13 36 21	4♌27 54	10♌39 45	24 23.4	10 18.2	10 24.6	23 13.4	13 28.5	28 07.5	9 24.3	11 41.2	23 51.2	6 49.0
6 Su	11 05 03	14 34 33	16 55 50	23 16 19	24 13.9	11 02.1	11 37.8	23 45.7	13 19.1	28 15.1	9 23.6	11 45.0	23 50.9	6 47.7
7 M	11 08 59	15 32 47	29 41 18	6♍10 47	24 02.5	11 42.4	12 51.0	24 18.3	13 09.4	28 22.5	9 23.0	11 48.7	23 50.5	6 46.5
8 Tu	11 12 56	16 31 03	12♍44 42	19 22 50	23 49.9	12 18.8	14 04.1	24 51.2	12 59.4	28 29.7	9 22.6	11 52.5	23 50.1	6 45.2
9 W	11 16 52	17 29 21	26 04 57	2♎50 43	23 37.4	12 50.9	15 17.3	25 24.5	12 49.1	28 36.8	9 22.2	11 56.3	23 49.6	6 44.0
10 Th	11 20 49	18 27 41	9♎39 47	16 31 45	23 26.3	13 18.6	16 30.4	25 58.0	12 38.5	28 43.8	9 21.9	12 00.0	23 49.2	6 42.7
11 F	11 24 45	19 26 02	23 26 12	0♏22 44	23 17.5	13 41.4	17 43.5	26 31.8	12 27.6	28 50.6	9 21.8	12 03.8	23 48.7	6 41.5
12 Sa	11 28 42	20 24 25	7♏20 59	14 20 36	23 11.5	13 59.1	18 56.6	27 05.8	12 16.6	28 57.2	9D21.7	12 07.5	23 48.1	6 40.2
13 Su	11 32 38	21 22 49	21 21 17	28 22 49	23 08.3	14 11.4	20 09.7	27 40.2	12 05.2	29 03.7	9 21.7	12 11.3	23 47.6	6 39.0
14 M	11 36 35	22 21 15	5♐24 59	12♐27 38	23 07.2	14R17.8	21 22.8	28 14.8	11 53.6	29 10.0	9 21.9	12 15.0	23 47.0	6 37.8
15 Tu	11 40 32	23 19 43	19 30 39	26 33 56	23 07.1	14 18.1	22 35.8	28 49.7	11 41.9	29 16.2	9 22.1	12 18.7	23 46.4	6 36.6
16 W	11 44 28	24 18 12	3♑37 23	10♑40 53	23 06.7	14 11.9	23 48.8	29 24.8	11 29.9	29 22.2	9 22.4	12 22.5	23 45.7	6 35.4
17 Th	11 48 25	25 16 43	17 44 18	24 47 28	23 04.7	13 59.1	25 01.8	0♑00.2	11 17.7	29 28.1	9 22.8	12 26.2	23 45.0	6 34.2
18 F	11 52 21	26 15 15	1♒50 09	8♒52 04	23 00.2	13 39.3	26 14.8	0 35.8	11 05.3	29 33.8	9 23.4	12 29.9	23 44.3	6 33.0
19 Sa	11 56 18	27 13 49	15 52 54	22 52 15	22 52.8	13 12.6	27 27.7	1 11.7	10 52.7	29 39.3	9 24.0	12 33.5	23 43.6	6 31.8
20 Su	12 00 14	28 12 25	29 49 41	6♓44 45	22 42.8	12 38.8	28 40.6	1 47.8	10 40.0	29 44.7	9 24.7	12 37.2	23 42.8	6 30.6
21 M	12 04 11	29 11 03	13♓36 59	20 25 57	22 30.9	11 58.1	29 53.5	2 24.1	10 27.1	29 49.9	9 25.5	12 40.9	23 42.0	6 29.5
22 Tu	12 08 07	0♎09 42	27 11 13	3♈52 25	22 18.3	11 10.9	1♏06.4	3 00.6	10 14.1	29 54.9	9 26.4	12 44.5	23 41.1	6 28.3
23 W	12 12 04	1 08 24	10♈29 16	17 01 31	22 06.3	10 17.8	2 19.2	3 37.3	10 01.0	29 59.8	9 27.4	12 48.2	23 40.3	6 27.2
24 Th	12 16 00	2 07 07	23 29 05	29 51 56	21 55.8	9 19.5	3 32.1	4 14.3	9 47.8	0♋04.5	9 28.5	12 51.8	23 39.4	6 26.0
25 F	12 19 57	3 05 53	6♉10 09	12♉23 53	21 47.8	8 17.0	4 44.9	4 51.4	9 34.5	0 09.0	9 29.7	12 55.4	23 38.5	6 24.9
26 Sa	12 23 54	4 04 40	18 33 27	24 39 10	21 42.4	7 11.6	5 57.6	5 28.8	9 21.0	0 13.4	9 31.0	12 59.0	23 37.5	6 23.8
27 Su	12 27 50	5 03 31	0♊41 29	6♊40 54	21 39.6	6 04.8	7 10.4	6 06.4	9 07.6	0 17.5	9 32.4	13 02.6	23 36.6	6 22.7
28 M	12 31 47	6 02 23	12 37 59	18 33 19	21D38.7	4 58.2	8 23.1	6 44.1	8 54.0	0 21.5	9 33.9	13 06.1	23 35.6	6 21.6
29 Tu	12 35 43	7 01 17	24 27 34	0♋21 23	21R38.8	3 53.5	9 35.8	7 22.0	8 40.5	0 25.3	9 35.5	13 09.7	23 34.5	6 20.6
30 W	12 39 40	8 00 14	6♋15 28	12 10 31	21 38.8	2 52.5	10 48.5	8 00.2	8 26.9	0 29.0	9 37.2	13 13.2	23 33.5	6 19.5

LONGITUDE — October 2048

Day	Sid.Time	☉	0 hr ☽	Noon ☽	True ☊	☿	♀	♂	⚳	♃	♄	♅	♆	♇
1 Th	12 43 36	8♎59 13	18♋07 12	24♋06 13	21♐37.7	1♎56.9	12♏01.2	8♑38.5	8♈13.3	0♋32.4	9♑39.0	13♍16.7	23♉32.4	6♓18.5
2 F	12 47 33	9 58 15	0♌08 12	6♌13 46	21R34.7	1R08.1	13 13.9	9 17.0	7R59.7	0 35.7	9 40.9	13 20.2	23R31.3	6R17.4
3 Sa	12 51 29	10 57 18	12 23 29	18 37 50	21 29.3	0 27.5	14 26.5	9 55.7	7 46.1	0 38.7	9 42.9	13 23.6	23 30.2	6 16.4
4 Su	12 55 26	11 56 24	24 57 13	1♍21 59	21 21.3	29♍56.2	15 39.1	10 34.5	7 32.5	0 41.6	9 44.9	13 27.1	23 29.0	6 15.4
5 M	12 59 23	12 55 32	7♍52 18	14 28 17	21 11.4	29 34.8	16 51.7	11 13.6	7 19.1	0 44.3	9 47.1	13 30.5	23 27.9	6 14.4
6 Tu	13 03 19	13 54 43	21 09 53	27 56 56	21 00.2	29D23.9	18 04.2	11 52.8	7 05.6	0 46.8	9 49.4	13 33.9	23 26.7	6 13.5
7 W	13 07 16	14 53 55	4♎49 07	11♎46 01	20 49.1	29 23.7	19 16.7	12 32.1	6 52.3	0 49.1	9 51.7	13 37.3	23 25.4	6 12.5
8 Th	13 11 12	15 53 09	18 47 07	25 51 47	20 39.2	29 34.0	20 29.2	13 11.7	6 39.0	0 51.2	9 54.2	13 40.6	23 24.2	6 11.6
9 F	13 15 09	16 52 26	2♏59 21	10♏09 07	20 31.3	29 54.7	21 41.7	13 51.4	6 25.9	0 53.1	9 56.7	13 43.9	23 22.9	6 10.7
10 Sa	13 19 05	17 51 44	17 20 22	24 32 24	20 26.2	0♎25.3	22 54.2	14 31.2	6 12.9	0 54.9	9 59.3	13 47.2	23 21.6	6 09.8
11 Su	13 23 02	18 51 05	1♐44 37	8♐56 27	20D23.6	1 05.1	24 06.6	15 11.2	6 00.1	0 56.4	10 02.1	13 50.5	23 20.3	6 08.9
12 M	13 26 58	19 50 27	16 07 23	23 17 03	20 23.1	1 53.6	25 19.0	15 51.4	5 47.4	0 57.7	10 04.9	13 53.7	23 19.0	6 08.0
13 Tu	13 30 55	20 49 51	0♑25 07	7♑31 21	20 23.7	2 49.8	26 31.4	16 31.7	5 34.8	0 58.9	10 07.8	13 57.0	23 17.6	6 07.2
14 W	13 34 52	21 49 16	14 35 34	21 37 40	20R24.2	3 53.1	27 43.7	17 12.1	5 22.5	0 59.8	10 10.8	14 00.2	23 16.2	6 06.4
15 Th	13 38 48	22 48 44	28 37 34	5♒35 10	20 23.4	5 02.6	28 56.0	17 52.7	5 10.3	1 00.5	10 13.9	14 03.3	23 14.9	6 05.6
16 F	13 42 45	23 48 13	12♒30 28	19 23 22	20 20.6	6 17.6	0♐08.2	18 33.4	4 58.4	1 01.1	10 17.0	14 06.4	23 13.4	6 04.8
17 Sa	13 46 41	24 47 43	26 13 48	3♓01 42	20 15.5	7 37.4	1 20.4	19 14.3	4 46.7	1 01.4	10 20.3	14 09.5	23 12.0	6 04.0
18 Su	13 50 38	25 47 16	9♓46 58	16 29 26	20 08.1	9 01.3	2 32.6	19 55.2	4 35.2	1R01.5	10 23.6	14 12.6	23 10.6	6 03.3
19 M	13 54 34	26 46 50	23 09 00	29 45 30	19 59.2	10 28.6	3 44.8	20 36.3	4 24.0	1 01.5	10 27.1	14 15.6	23 09.1	6 02.5
20 Tu	13 58 31	27 46 26	6♈18 47	12♈48 43	19 49.6	11 58.8	4 56.9	21 17.5	4 13.0	1 01.2	10 30.6	14 18.6	23 07.6	6 01.8
21 W	14 02 27	28 46 04	19 15 12	25 38 09	19 40.4	13 31.4	6 08.9	21 58.8	4 02.2	1 00.7	10 34.2	14 21.6	23 06.1	6 01.1
22 Th	14 06 24	29 45 45	1♉57 30	8♉13 17	19 32.5	15 06.0	7 20.9	22 40.3	3 51.8	1 00.1	10 37.9	14 24.5	23 04.6	6 00.5
23 F	14 10 21	0♏45 27	14 25 34	20 34 27	19 26.5	16 42.1	8 32.9	23 21.8	3 41.6	0 59.2	10 41.6	14 27.4	23 03.1	5 59.8
24 Sa	14 14 17	1 45 11	26 40 08	2♊42 51	19 22.7	18 19.5	9 44.8	24 03.4	3 31.7	0 58.1	10 45.5	14 30.3	23 01.5	5 59.2
25 Su	14 18 14	2 44 58	8♊42 56	14 40 44	19D21.0	19 57.8	10 56.7	24 45.2	3 22.1	0 56.9	10 49.4	14 33.1	23 00.0	5 58.6
26 M	14 22 10	3 44 46	20 36 40	26 31 14	19 21.2	21 36.8	12 08.6	25 27.1	3 12.9	0 55.4	10 53.4	14 35.9	22 58.4	5 58.0
27 Tu	14 26 07	4 44 37	2♋24 55	8♋18 19	19 22.4	23 16.3	13 20.4	26 09.0	3 03.9	0 53.7	10 57.5	14 38.7	22 56.8	5 57.5
28 W	14 30 03	5 44 30	14 12 01	20 06 39	19 24.0	24 56.2	14 32.2	26 51.1	2 55.3	0 51.8	11 01.6	14 41.4	22 55.2	5 57.0
29 Th	14 34 00	6 44 25	26 02 51	2♌01 16	19R25.0	26 36.2	15 43.9	27 33.2	2 47.0	0 49.8	11 05.9	14 44.1	22 53.6	5 56.4
30 F	14 37 56	7 44 22	8♌02 34	14 07 25	19 24.9	28 16.2	16 55.6	28 15.5	2 39.0	0 47.5	11 10.2	14 46.7	22 52.0	5 56.0
31 Sa	14 41 53	8 44 22	20 16 25	26 30 10	19 23.2	29 56.2	18 07.2	28 57.8	2 31.3	0 45.0	11 14.6	14 49.3	22 50.4	5 55.5

Astro Data Dy Hr Mn	Planet Ingress Dy Hr Mn
☽0S 8 10:12	♂ ♑ 17 11:51
♄D 12 16:58	♀ ♏ 21 14:08
☿R 15 1:10	☉ ♎ 22 8:02
☽0N 21 8:21	♃ ♋ 23 12:58
⊙0S 22 8:02	
	☿ ♍R 4 8:37
☿0N 5 8:28	☿ ♎ 9 16:44
☽0S 5 18:48	♀ ♐ 16 9:16
☿D 7 0:28	☉ ♏ 22 17:44
☿0S 14 17:35	☿ ♏ 31 12:55
☽0N 18 14:56	
♃R 18 15:59	

Last Aspect Dy Hr Mn	☽ Ingress Dy Hr Mn
1 22:29 ♃ ☌	♋ 2 3:14
4 3:10 ♆ ⚹	♌ 4 15:16
6 21:25 ♃ ⚹	♍ 7 0:35
9 4:26 ♃ □	♎ 9 6:58
11 9:20 ♃ △	♏ 11 11:21
13 4:10 ♆ ☍	♐ 13 14:46
15 16:38 ♃ ☍	♑ 15 17:50
17 12:53 ☉ △	♒ 17 20:52
19 23:47 ♃ △	♓ 20 0:18
22 4:50 ♃ □	♈ 22 5:02
23 0:27 ☿ ☍	♉ 24 12:15
26 9:58 ♆ ☌	♊ 26 22:37
28 0:54 ♅ □	♋ 29 11:16

Last Aspect Dy Hr Mn	☽ Ingress Dy Hr Mn
1 10:53 ♆ ⚹	♌ 1 23:44
3 21:15 ♆ □	♍ 4 9:27
6 14:32 ☿ ☌	♎ 6 15:36
7 17:46 ☉ ☌	♏ 8 18:58
10 10:02 ♆ ☍	♐ 10 21:06
12 5:48 ☉ ⚹	♑ 12 23:18
14 23:27 ♀ ⚹	♒ 15 2:22
16 20:20 ☉ △	♓ 17 6:39
19 0:02 ♆ ⚹	♈ 19 12:26
21 18:26 ☉ ☍	♉ 21 20:16
23 17:49 ♂ △	♊ 24 6:36
26 0:25 ☿ △	♋ 26 19:05
29 2:28 ♂ ☍	♌ 29 7:57
31 4:59 ♆ □	♍ 31 18:40

☽ Phases & Eclipses Dy Hr Mn	
8 6:26	● 16♍18
15 6:05	☽ 23♐05
22 4:48	○ 29♓52
30 2:47	☾ 7♋38
7 17:46	● 15♎08
14 12:21	☽ 21♑50
21 18:26	○ 29♈02
29 22:16	☾ 7♌10

Astro Data

1 September 2048
Julian Day # 54301
SVP 4♓34'30"
GC 27♐31.1 ⚴ 6♒27.8R
Eris 1♉00.7R ⚵ 18♒49.1R
⚷ 8♏24.2 ⚶ 23♉12.3
☽ Mean ☊ 23♐44.5

1 October 2048
Julian Day # 54331
SVP 4♓34'27"
GC 27♐31.2 ⚴ 3♒55.5
Eris 0♉46.6R ⚵ 15♒05.1R
⚷ 11♏44.9 ⚶ 23♉53.1R
☽ Mean ☊ 22♐09.2

November 2048 LONGITUDE

Day	Sid.Time	☉	0 hr ☽	Noon ☽	True ☊	☿	♀	♂	⚳	♃	♄	♅	♆	♇
1 Su	14 45 50	9♏44 23	2♍49 13	9♍14 00	19♐19.8	1♏36.1	19♐18.8	29♑40.3	2♈24.1	0♋42.4	11♑19.1	14♍51.9	22♉48.8	5♓55.1
2 M	14 49 46	10 44 27	15 44 56	22 22 15	19R 14.8	3 15.8	20 30.4	0♒22.8	2R 17.1	0R 39.5	11 23.6	14 54.4	22R 47.1	5R 54.6
3 Tu	14 53 43	11 44 32	29 06 06	5♎56 30	19 08.9	4 55.2	21 41.9	1 05.4	2 10.5	0 36.4	11 28.2	14 56.8	22 45.5	5 54.2
4 W	14 57 39	12 44 40	12♎53 18	19 56 09	19 02.8	6 34.4	22 53.3	1 48.1	2 04.3	0 33.2	11 32.9	14 59.3	22 43.8	5 53.9
5 Th	15 01 36	13 44 50	27 04 37	4♏18 03	18 57.3	8 13.3	24 04.7	2 30.9	1 58.5	0 29.7	11 37.7	15 01.7	22 42.1	5 53.5
6 F	15 05 32	14 45 02	11♏35 42	18 56 43	18 53.0	9 51.8	25 16.1	3 13.8	1 53.0	0 26.1	11 42.5	15 04.0	22 40.5	5 53.2
7 Sa	15 09 29	15 45 15	26 20 08	3♐45 00	18 50.5	11 30.0	26 27.4	3 56.8	1 47.9	0 22.3	11 47.4	15 06.3	22 38.8	5 52.9
8 Su	15 13 25	16 45 30	11♐10 19	18 35 10	18D 49.7	13 07.9	27 38.6	4 39.8	1 43.2	0 18.3	11 52.4	15 08.6	22 37.1	5 52.6
9 M	15 17 22	17 45 47	25 58 40	3♑20 02	18 50.3	14 45.4	28 49.8	5 22.9	1 38.9	0 14.1	11 57.4	15 10.8	22 35.4	5 52.4
10 Tu	15 21 19	18 46 06	10♑38 36	17 53 48	18 51.7	16 22.6	0♑00.9	6 06.1	1 34.9	0 09.7	12 02.5	15 13.0	22 33.8	5 52.2
11 W	15 25 15	19 46 25	25 05 14	2♒12 35	18 53.2	17 59.4	1 11.9	6 49.4	1 31.4	0 05.2	12 07.7	15 15.1	22 32.1	5 52.0
12 Th	15 29 12	20 46 46	9♒15 37	16 14 15	18R 54.1	19 35.9	2 22.9	7 32.7	1 28.2	0 00.4	12 13.0	15 17.2	22 30.4	5 51.8
13 F	15 33 08	21 47 09	23 08 27	29 58 15	18 53.9	21 12.1	3 33.8	8 16.1	1 25.4	29♊55.5	12 18.3	15 19.2	22 28.7	5 51.7
14 Sa	15 37 05	22 47 33	6♓43 43	13♓25 00	18 52.4	22 48.0	4 44.6	8 59.6	1 23.0	29 50.5	12 23.6	15 21.2	22 27.0	5 51.5
15 Su	15 41 01	23 47 58	20 02 13	26 35 32	18 49.8	24 23.5	5 55.3	9 43.1	1 21.0	29 45.2	12 29.0	15 23.1	22 25.3	5 51.5
16 M	15 44 58	24 48 24	3♈05 06	9♈31 05	18 46.3	25 58.8	7 06.0	10 26.7	1 19.3	29 39.8	12 34.5	15 25.0	22 23.6	5 51.4
17 Tu	15 48 54	25 48 52	15 53 39	22 12 57	18 42.4	27 33.8	8 16.5	11 10.3	1 18.1	29 34.2	12 40.1	15 26.8	22 21.9	5 51.3
18 W	15 52 51	26 49 21	28 29 07	4♉42 19	18 38.7	29 08.5	9 27.0	11 54.0	1 17.2	29 28.5	12 45.7	15 28.6	22 20.2	5D 51.3
19 Th	15 56 47	27 49 52	10♉52 42	17 00 24	18 35.6	0♐43.0	10 37.4	12 37.7	1D 16.7	29 22.7	12 51.3	15 30.3	22 18.5	5 51.3
20 F	16 00 44	28 50 24	23 05 36	29 08 28	18 33.4	2 17.3	11 47.7	13 21.5	1 16.6	29 16.6	12 57.0	15 32.0	22 16.9	5 51.4
21 Sa	16 04 41	29 50 58	5♊09 12	11♊08 01	18D 32.3	3 51.4	12 57.9	14 05.3	1 16.8	29 10.5	13 02.8	15 33.7	22 15.2	5 51.4
22 Su	16 08 37	0♐51 33	17 05 09	23 00 53	18 32.2	5 25.3	14 08.0	14 49.1	1 17.5	29 04.2	13 08.6	15 35.3	22 13.5	5 51.5
23 M	16 12 34	1 52 10	28 55 30	4♋49 22	18 32.9	6 59.0	15 18.1	15 33.1	1 18.5	28 57.7	13 14.5	15 36.8	22 11.8	5 51.6
24 Tu	16 16 30	2 52 49	10♋42 50	16 36 19	18 34.1	8 32.6	16 28.0	16 17.0	1 19.9	28 51.2	13 20.4	15 38.3	22 10.2	5 51.8
25 W	16 20 27	3 53 29	22 30 16	28 25 09	18 35.6	10 06.0	17 37.8	17 01.0	1 21.6	28 44.5	13 26.4	15 39.7	22 08.5	5 51.9
26 Th	16 24 23	4 54 10	4♌21 29	10♌19 47	18 36.9	11 39.3	18 47.5	17 45.0	1 23.8	28 37.6	13 32.5	15 41.1	22 06.9	5 52.1
27 F	16 28 20	5 54 53	16 20 37	22 24 33	18 37.9	13 12.4	19 57.1	18 29.1	1 26.3	28 30.7	13 38.5	15 42.4	22 05.2	5 52.3
28 Sa	16 32 17	6 55 38	28 32 10	4♍44 03	18R 38.3	14 45.5	21 06.5	19 13.2	1 29.1	28 23.6	13 44.7	15 43.7	22 03.6	5 52.6
29 Su	16 36 13	7 56 24	11♍00 44	17 22 46	18 38.1	16 18.5	22 15.9	19 57.4	1 32.3	28 16.4	13 50.8	15 44.9	22 02.0	5 52.8
30 M	16 40 10	8 57 12	23 50 38	0♎24 45	18 37.5	17 51.3	23 25.1	20 41.6	1 35.9	28 09.1	13 57.1	15 46.1	22 00.4	5 53.1

December 2048 LONGITUDE

Day	Sid.Time	☉	0 hr ☽	Noon ☽	True ☊	☿	♀	♂	⚳	♃	♄	♅	♆	♇
1 Tu	16 44 06	9♐58 01	7♎05 27	13♎52 58	18♐36.6	19♐24.1	24♑34.3	21♒25.8	1♈39.8	28♊01.8	14♑03.3	15♍47.2	21♉58.8	5♓53.4
2 W	16 48 03	10 58 51	20 47 25	27 48 44	18R 35.6	20 56.7	25 43.2	22 10.0	1 44.1	27R 54.3	14 09.6	15 48.2	21R 57.2	5 53.8
3 Th	16 51 59	11 59 43	4♏56 43	12♏10 59	18 34.7	22 29.3	26 52.1	22 54.3	1 48.7	27 46.7	14 16.0	15 49.2	21 55.6	5 54.1
4 F	16 55 56	13 00 37	19 30 59	26 55 59	18 34.1	24 01.8	28 00.8	23 38.7	1 53.7	27 39.1	14 22.4	15 50.2	21 54.1	5 54.5
5 Sa	16 59 52	14 01 31	4♐25 06	11♐57 17	18D 33.9	25 34.1	29 09.4	24 23.0	1 59.0	27 31.3	14 28.8	15 51.0	21 52.5	5 55.0
6 Su	17 03 49	15 02 27	19 31 27	27 06 22	18 33.9	27 06.4	0♒17.9	25 07.4	2 04.7	27 23.5	14 35.3	15 51.9	21 51.0	5 55.4
7 M	17 07 46	16 03 24	4♑40 53	12♑13 49	18 34.0	28 38.4	1 26.2	25 51.8	2 10.7	27 15.7	14 41.8	15 52.7	21 49.5	5 55.9
8 Tu	17 11 42	17 04 21	19 44 06	27 10 44	18 34.2	0♑10.3	2 34.3	26 36.3	2 17.0	27 07.8	14 48.3	15 53.4	21 48.0	5 56.4
9 W	17 15 39	18 05 20	4♒32 54	11♒49 54	18R 34.3	1 41.9	3 42.3	27 20.7	2 23.7	26 59.8	14 54.9	15 54.0	21 46.5	5 56.9
10 Th	17 19 35	19 06 18	19 01 16	26 06 37	18 34.4	3 13.3	4 50.1	28 05.2	2 30.7	26 51.8	15 01.6	15 54.6	21 45.0	5 57.4
11 F	17 23 32	20 07 18	3♓05 47	9♓58 43	18D 34.3	4 44.4	5 57.7	28 49.7	2 38.0	26 43.7	15 08.2	15 55.2	21 43.6	5 58.0
12 Sa	17 27 28	21 08 17	16 45 30	23 25 44	18 34.3	6 15.0	7 05.1	29 34.2	2 45.6	26 35.6	15 14.9	15 55.7	21 42.1	5 58.6
13 Su	17 31 25	22 09 18	0♈01 24	6♈31 08	18 34.4	7 45.2	8 12.3	0♓18.8	2 53.5	26 27.5	15 21.6	15 56.1	21 40.7	5 59.2
14 M	17 35 21	23 10 19	12 55 50	19 15 57	18 34.7	9 14.8	9 19.4	1 03.3	3 01.8	26 19.3	15 28.3	15 56.5	21 39.3	5 59.9
15 Tu	17 39 18	24 11 20	25 31 52	1♉44 01	18 35.3	10 43.7	10 26.2	1 47.9	3 10.3	26 11.2	15 35.1	15 56.8	21 37.9	6 00.5
16 W	17 43 15	25 12 22	7♉52 48	13 58 37	18 36.0	12 11.7	11 32.8	2 32.5	3 19.2	26 03.0	15 41.9	15 57.1	21 36.6	6 01.2
17 Th	17 47 11	26 13 25	20 01 52	26 02 53	18 36.7	13 38.7	12 39.2	3 17.0	3 28.3	25 54.9	15 48.7	15 57.3	21 35.3	6 01.9
18 F	17 51 08	27 14 28	2♊02 02	7♊59 38	18R 37.2	15 04.6	13 45.3	4 01.6	3 37.7	25 46.7	15 55.6	15 57.5	21 33.9	6 02.7
19 Sa	17 55 04	28 15 31	13 55 58	19 51 20	18 37.4	16 29.0	14 51.2	4 46.2	3 47.4	25 38.5	16 02.5	15 57.6	21 32.7	6 03.4
20 Su	17 59 01	29 16 35	25 45 59	1♋40 13	18 37.1	17 51.7	15 56.9	5 30.8	3 57.4	25 30.4	16 09.4	15R 57.6	21 31.4	6 04.2
21 M	18 02 57	0♑17 40	7♋34 15	13 28 21	18 36.1	19 12.3	17 02.3	6 15.4	4 07.7	25 22.3	16 16.3	15 57.6	21 30.1	6 05.0
22 Tu	18 06 54	1 18 45	19 22 48	25 17 51	18 34.6	20 30.6	18 07.5	7 00.0	4 18.3	25 14.2	16 23.2	15 57.5	21 28.9	6 05.9
23 W	18 10 50	2 19 51	1♌13 47	7♌10 54	18 32.5	21 46.2	19 12.3	7 44.6	4 29.1	25 06.2	16 30.2	15 57.4	21 27.7	6 06.7
24 Th	18 14 47	3 20 57	13 09 33	19 10 03	18 30.2	22 58.4	20 16.9	8 29.2	4 40.2	24 58.1	16 37.1	15 57.2	21 26.6	6 07.6
25 F	18 18 44	4 22 04	25 12 46	1♍18 07	18 27.9	24 06.8	21 21.2	9 13.8	4 51.5	24 50.2	16 44.1	15 57.0	21 25.4	6 08.5
26 Sa	18 22 40	5 23 11	7♍26 31	13 38 22	18 26.0	25 10.9	22 25.3	9 58.4	5 03.1	24 42.3	16 51.1	15 56.7	21 24.3	6 09.4
27 Su	18 26 37	6 24 19	19 54 09	26 14 18	18D 24.8	26 09.7	23 29.0	10 43.0	5 15.0	24 34.4	16 58.2	15 56.3	21 23.2	6 10.4
28 M	18 30 33	7 25 28	2♎39 17	9♎09 31	18 24.4	27 02.8	24 32.3	11 27.6	5 27.1	24 26.6	17 05.2	15 55.9	21 22.1	6 11.3
29 Tu	18 34 30	8 26 37	15 45 26	22 27 21	18 25.0	27 49.1	25 35.4	12 12.2	5 39.5	24 18.9	17 12.3	15 55.4	21 21.1	6 12.3
30 W	18 38 26	9 27 46	29 15 34	6♏10 17	18 26.2	28 27.8	26 38.1	12 56.8	5 52.1	24 11.2	17 19.3	15 54.9	21 20.0	6 13.3
31 Th	18 42 23	10 28 56	13♏11 35	20 19 24	18 27.7	28 58.1	27 40.5	13 41.5	6 04.9	24 03.7	17 26.4	15 54.3	21 19.1	6 14.4

Astro Data	Planet Ingress	Last Aspect	☽ Ingress	Last Aspect	☽ Ingress	☽ Phases & Eclipses	Astro Data
Dy Hr Mn	Dy Hr Mn	Dy Hr Mn	Dy Hr Mn	Dy Hr Mn	Dy Hr Mn	Dy Hr Mn	
☽0S 2 3:57	♂ ♒ 1 23:09	2 12:44 ♆ △	♎ 3 1:35	2 12:09 ♃ △	♏ 2 15:42	6 4:40 ● 14♏27	1 November 2048
☽0N 14 19:55	♀ ♑ 10 11:42	4 17:26 ♀ ⚹	♏ 5 4:52	4 13:53 ♀ ⚹	♐ 4 16:56	12 20:30 ☽ 21♒08	Julian Day # 54362
♇ D 18 16:56	♃ ♊R 12 14:08	6 18:03 ♆ ☍	♐ 7 5:56	6 12:27 ♃ ☍	♑ 6 16:35	20 11:21 ○ 28♉49	SVP 4♓34'24"
⚳ D 20 7:08	☿ ♐ 19 1:04	9 4:00 ♀ ☌	♑ 9 6:33	8 3:20 ♆ △	♒ 8 16:35	28 16:35 ☾ 7♍07	GC 27♐31.3 ⚵ 6♒30.0
☽0S 29 12:31	☉ ♐ 21 15:35	10 19:46 ♆ △	♒ 11 8:16	10 15:34 ♂ ☌	♓ 10 18:40		Eris 0♉28.1R ⚴ 18♒00.6
		13 11:55 ♃ △	♓ 13 12:03	12 17:40 ♃ □	♈ 12 23:57	5 15:31 ● 14♐10	⚷ 15♏51.0 ⚶ 18♉07.5R
☽0N 12 1:34	♀ ♒ 6 5:44	15 17:47 ♃ □	♈ 15 18:17	15 1:23 ♃ ⚹	♉ 15 8:38	5 15:35:26 ● T 03'28"	☽ Mean ☊ 20♐30.7
♄△♅ 18 18:40	☿ ♑ 8 9:18	18 1:59 ♃ ⚹	♉ 18 2:55	17 3:07 ♆ ☌	♊ 17 19:55	12 7:30 ☽ 20♓57	
♅ R 20 17:44	♂ ♓ 13 1:53	20 11:21 ☉ ☍	♊ 20 13:43	20 6:40 ☉ ☍	♋ 20 8:36	20 6:40 ○ 29♊03	1 December 2048
☽0S 26 19:49	☉ ♑ 21 5:04	23 0:11 ♃ ☌	♋ 23 2:11	22 4:17 ♆ ⚹	♌ 22 21:31	20 6:28 ● A 0.962	Julian Day # 54392
		24 23:18 ♆ ⚹	♌ 25 15:12	24 23:24 ♃ ⚹	♍ 25 9:27	28 8:33 ☾ 7♎17	SVP 4♓34'19"
		27 23:50 ♃ ⚹	♍ 28 2:51	27 11:51 ☿ △	♎ 27 19:03		GC 27♐31.4 ⚵ 12♒33.8
		30 7:56 ♃ □	♎ 30 11:15	29 21:58 ☿ □	♏ 30 1:18		Eris 0♉11.7R ⚴ 26♒15.3
							⚷ 19♏55.5 ⚶ 11♉00.5R
							☽ Mean ☊ 18♐55.4

LONGITUDE — January 2049

Day	Sid.Time	☉	0 hr ☽	Noon ☽	True ☊	☿	♀	♂	⚳	♃	♄	♅	♆	♇
1 F	18 46 19	11♑30 07	27♏33 32	4♐53 36	18♐28.9	29♑18.9	28♒42.5	14♓26.1	6♈18.0	23♊56.2	17♑33.5	15♍53.7	21♉18.1	6♓15.4
2 Sa	18 50 16	12 31 18	12♐19 01	19 49 01	18R29.4	29R29.6	29 44.2	15 10.7	6 31.3	23R48.8	17 40.6	15R53.0	21R17.2	6 16.5
3 Su	18 54 13	13 32 29	27 22 42	4♑58 57	18 28.6	29 29.2	0♓45.4	15 55.3	6 44.9	23 41.6	17 47.7	15 52.3	21 16.3	6 17.6
4 M	18 58 09	14 33 40	12♑36 35	20 14 17	18 26.5	29 17.3	1 46.3	16 39.9	6 58.7	23 34.4	17 54.8	15 51.5	21 15.4	6 18.7
5 Tu	19 02 06	15 34 50	27 50 46	5♒24 44	18 23.1	28 53.5	2 46.7	17 24.4	7 12.7	23 27.3	18 01.9	15 50.6	21 14.5	6 19.8
6 W	19 06 02	16 36 01	12♒55 01	20 20 31	18 19.0	28 17.9	3 46.7	18 09.0	7 26.9	23 20.4	18 09.0	15 49.7	21 13.7	6 21.0
7 Th	19 09 59	17 37 11	27 40 21	4♓53 50	18 14.7	27 31.0	4 46.3	18 53.6	7 41.4	23 13.5	18 16.2	15 48.8	21 12.9	6 22.1
8 F	19 13 55	18 38 21	12♓00 26	18 59 52	18 10.9	26 33.8	5 45.3	19 38.1	7 56.0	23 06.8	18 23.2	15 47.8	21 12.2	6 23.3
9 Sa	19 17 52	19 39 31	25 52 02	2♈36 59	18 08.2	25 27.7	6 43.9	20 22.7	8 10.9	23 00.3	18 30.4	15 46.7	21 11.5	6 24.5
10 Su	19 21 49	20 40 40	9♈14 57	15 46 15	18D06.9	24 14.7	7 42.0	21 07.2	8 26.0	22 53.8	18 37.5	15 45.6	21 10.8	6 25.8
11 M	19 25 45	21 41 48	22 11 21	28 30 44	18 07.0	22 57.2	8 39.5	21 51.7	8 41.2	22 47.5	18 44.6	15 44.5	21 10.1	6 27.0
12 Tu	19 29 42	22 42 56	4♉44 58	10♉54 39	18 08.2	21 37.5	9 36.5	22 36.2	8 56.7	22 41.4	18 51.7	15 43.3	21 09.5	6 28.2
13 W	19 33 38	23 44 03	17 00 21	23 02 42	18 10.0	20 18.3	10 32.9	23 20.7	9 12.4	22 35.4	18 58.8	15 42.0	21 08.9	6 29.5
14 Th	19 37 35	24 45 10	29 02 16	4♊59 37	18 11.7	19 01.9	11 28.7	24 05.2	9 28.2	22 29.5	19 05.9	15 40.7	21 08.3	6 30.8
15 F	19 41 31	25 46 16	10♊55 16	16 49 45	18R12.5	17 50.5	12 23.9	24 49.6	9 44.3	22 23.8	19 13.0	15 39.3	21 07.8	6 32.1
16 Sa	19 45 28	26 47 21	22 43 31	28 36 58	18 11.8	16 45.8	13 18.5	25 34.1	10 00.5	22 18.3	19 20.1	15 37.9	21 07.3	6 33.5
17 Su	19 49 24	27 48 26	4♋30 30	10♋24 28	18 09.3	15 49.1	14 12.4	26 18.5	10 16.9	22 12.9	19 27.1	15 36.5	21 06.8	6 34.8
18 M	19 53 21	28 49 30	16 19 09	22 14 49	18 04.7	15 01.3	15 05.6	27 02.8	10 33.5	22 07.7	19 34.2	15 35.0	21 06.4	6 36.2
19 Tu	19 57 18	29 50 34	28 11 43	4♌10 03	17 58.2	14 22.9	15 58.0	27 47.2	10 50.2	22 02.7	19 41.2	15 33.5	21 06.0	6 37.5
20 W	20 01 14	0♒51 37	10♌10 00	16 11 45	17 50.3	13 53.8	16 49.7	28 31.5	11 07.2	21 57.8	19 48.3	15 31.9	21 05.6	6 38.9
21 Th	20 05 11	1 52 40	22 15 26	28 21 15	17 41.6	13 34.1	17 40.7	29 15.9	11 24.3	21 53.1	19 55.3	15 30.2	21 05.3	6 40.3
22 F	20 09 07	2 53 41	4♍29 21	10♍39 54	17 33.0	13D23.4	18 30.8	0♈00.1	11 41.5	21 48.6	20 02.3	15 28.6	21 05.0	6 41.7
23 Sa	20 13 04	3 54 43	16 53 06	23 09 10	17 25.4	13 21.2	19 20.1	0 44.4	11 59.0	21 44.2	20 09.3	15 26.9	21 04.8	6 43.1
24 Su	20 17 00	4 55 43	29 28 21	5♎50 52	17 19.5	13 27.0	20 08.5	1 28.6	12 16.5	21 40.0	20 16.3	15 25.1	21 04.5	6 44.6
25 M	20 20 57	5 56 44	12♎17 03	18 47 09	17 15.7	13 40.2	20 56.1	2 12.9	12 34.3	21 36.1	20 23.2	15 23.3	21 04.3	6 46.0
26 Tu	20 24 53	6 57 43	25 21 30	2♏00 24	17D14.1	14 00.3	21 42.7	2 57.1	12 52.2	21 32.3	20 30.2	15 21.5	21 04.2	6 47.5
27 W	20 28 50	7 58 43	8♏44 09	15 32 59	17 14.2	14 26.6	22 28.3	3 41.2	13 10.2	21 28.7	20 37.1	15 19.6	21 04.0	6 49.0
28 Th	20 32 47	8 59 41	22 27 09	29 26 46	17 15.2	14 58.6	23 12.9	4 25.4	13 28.4	21 25.3	20 44.0	15 17.7	21 03.9	6 50.5
29 F	20 36 43	10 00 39	6♐31 52	13♐42 23	17R16.0	15 35.8	23 56.5	5 09.5	13 46.8	21 22.0	20 50.8	15 15.7	21 03.9	6 52.0
30 Sa	20 40 40	11 01 37	20 58 05	28 18 36	17 15.6	16 17.7	24 39.0	5 53.6	14 05.3	21 19.0	20 57.7	15 13.7	21D03.9	6 53.5
31 Su	20 44 36	12 02 34	5♑43 20	13♑11 35	17 13.0	17 03.9	25 20.4	6 37.7	14 23.9	21 16.2	21 04.5	15 11.7	21 03.9	6 55.0

LONGITUDE — February 2049

Day	Sid.Time	☉	0 hr ☽	Noon ☽	True ☊	☿	♀	♂	⚳	♃	♄	♅	♆	♇
1 M	20 48 33	13♒03 30	20♑42 25	28♑14 47	17♐07.8	17♑54.0	26♓00.6	7♈21.8	14♈42.7	21♊13.5	21♑11.3	15♍09.6	21♉03.9	6♓56.5
2 Tu	20 52 29	14 04 24	5♒47 31	13♒19 23	17R00.3	18 47.6	26 39.6	8 05.8	15 01.7	21R11.1	21 18.1	15R07.5	21 04.0	6 58.1
3 W	20 56 26	15 05 18	20 49 09	28 15 35	16 51.1	19 44.4	27 17.3	8 49.8	15 20.7	21 08.9	21 24.8	15 05.4	21 04.1	6 59.6
4 Th	21 00 22	16 06 11	5♓37 36	12♓54 13	16 41.3	20 44.2	27 53.6	9 33.8	15 39.9	21 06.8	21 31.5	15 03.2	21 04.3	7 01.2
5 F	21 04 19	17 07 02	20 04 40	27 08 21	16 32.1	21 46.7	28 28.6	10 17.7	15 59.2	21 05.0	21 38.2	15 01.0	21 04.5	7 02.8
6 Sa	21 08 16	18 07 51	4♈04 54	10♈54 08	16 24.4	22 51.6	29 02.2	11 01.6	16 18.7	21 03.4	21 44.8	14 58.8	21 04.7	7 04.3
7 Su	21 12 12	19 08 40	17 36 05	24 10 55	16 19.1	23 58.8	29 34.2	11 45.5	16 38.3	21 01.9	21 51.4	14 56.5	21 05.0	7 05.9
8 M	21 16 09	20 09 27	0♉38 57	7♉00 40	16 16.1	25 08.1	0♈04.7	12 29.4	16 58.0	21 00.7	21 58.0	14 54.2	21 05.3	7 07.5
9 Tu	21 20 05	21 10 12	13 16 36	19 27 20	16D15.2	26 19.3	0 33.6	13 13.2	17 17.8	20 59.7	22 04.5	14 51.9	21 05.6	7 09.1
10 W	21 24 02	22 10 56	25 33 33	1♊35 54	16 15.5	27 32.4	1 00.8	13 57.0	17 37.7	20 58.9	22 11.0	14 49.6	21 05.9	7 10.7
11 Th	21 27 58	23 11 38	7♊35 06	13 31 50	16R16.0	28 47.1	1 26.2	14 40.7	17 57.8	20 58.3	22 17.5	14 47.2	21 06.3	7 12.3
12 F	21 31 55	24 12 19	19 26 46	25 20 33	16 15.6	0♒03.4	1 49.9	15 24.4	18 17.9	20 57.9	22 23.9	14 44.9	21 06.8	7 14.0
13 Sa	21 35 51	25 12 58	1♋13 48	7♋07 04	16 13.3	1 21.2	2 11.6	16 08.1	18 38.2	20D57.7	22 30.3	14 42.4	21 07.2	7 15.6
14 Su	21 39 48	26 13 35	13 00 53	18 55 44	16 08.6	2 40.4	2 31.4	16 51.8	18 58.6	20 57.6	22 36.6	14 40.0	21 07.7	7 17.2
15 M	21 43 45	27 14 11	24 52 01	0♌50 07	16 01.0	4 00.9	2 49.2	17 35.4	19 19.1	20 57.8	22 42.9	14 37.6	21 08.3	7 18.8
16 Tu	21 47 41	28 14 45	6♌50 19	12 52 52	15 50.7	5 22.8	3 05.0	18 19.0	19 39.7	20 58.2	22 49.2	14 35.1	21 08.8	7 20.5
17 W	21 51 38	29 15 18	18 57 58	25 05 44	15 38.3	6 45.8	3 18.6	19 02.5	20 00.4	20 58.8	22 55.4	14 32.6	21 09.4	7 22.1
18 Th	21 55 34	0♓15 49	1♍16 16	7♍29 37	15 24.8	8 10.0	3 30.0	19 46.0	20 21.2	20 59.6	23 01.6	14 30.1	21 10.1	7 23.8
19 F	21 59 31	1 16 19	13 45 49	20 04 50	15 11.3	9 35.4	3 39.1	20 29.5	20 42.1	21 00.6	23 07.7	14 27.6	21 10.7	7 25.4
20 Sa	22 03 27	2 16 47	26 26 39	2♎51 17	14 59.2	11 01.9	3 46.0	21 12.9	21 03.1	21 01.8	23 13.7	14 25.0	21 11.4	7 27.1
21 Su	22 07 24	3 17 13	9♎18 41	15 48 53	14 49.2	12 29.5	3 50.5	21 56.3	21 24.2	21 03.2	23 19.8	14 22.5	21 12.2	7 28.7
22 M	22 11 20	4 17 39	22 21 30	28 57 47	14 42.2	13 58.2	3R52.6	22 39.7	21 45.3	21 04.8	23 25.7	14 19.9	21 12.9	7 30.4
23 Tu	22 15 17	5 18 03	5♏36 37	12♏18 32	14 38.1	15 27.9	3 52.2	23 23.0	22 06.6	21 06.6	23 31.7	14 17.3	21 13.7	7 32.0
24 W	22 19 13	6 18 25	19 03 40	25 52 08	14D36.4	16 58.7	3 49.4	24 06.3	22 28.0	21 08.6	23 37.5	14 14.8	21 14.6	7 33.7
25 Th	22 23 10	7 18 46	2♐44 06	9♐39 41	14R36.1	18 30.5	3 44.1	24 49.5	22 49.4	21 10.8	23 43.3	14 12.2	21 15.4	7 35.3
26 F	22 27 07	8 19 06	16 38 59	23 42 01	14 36.0	20 03.4	3 36.4	25 32.7	23 11.0	21 13.1	23 49.1	14 09.6	21 16.3	7 37.0
27 Sa	22 31 03	9 19 25	0♑48 45	7♑59 00	14 34.7	21 37.3	3 26.1	26 15.9	23 32.6	21 15.7	23 54.8	14 06.9	21 17.3	7 38.7
28 Su	22 35 00	10 19 42	15 12 32	22 28 55	14 31.0	23 12.2	3 13.3	26 59.1	23 54.3	21 18.4	24 00.5	14 04.3	21 18.2	7 40.3

Astro Data

	Dy Hr Mn
☿R	2 23:17
☽0N	8 9:58
☽0S	23 2:12
☿D	23 6:20
♂0N	23 16:28
♆D	30 13:25
♀0N	30 13:58
♄△♆	31 9:50
♃⊼♄	1 17:47
☽0N	4 20:48
♃⊻♆	5 18:28
⚳0N	6 1:37
♄∠♇	10 10:29
♃D	14 0:26
☽0S	19 8:42

Planet Ingress

	Dy Hr Mn
♀ ♓	2 18:11
☉ ♒	19 15:42
♂ ♈	22 11:55
♀ ♈	8 8:11
☿ ♒	12 10:56
☉ ♓	18 5:44
♀ R	22 20:44
♃⊻⊻	28 9:28

Last Aspect / ☽ Ingress (January)

Last Aspect Dy Hr Mn		☽ Ingress	Dy Hr Mn
1 2:42	☿ ✶	♐	1 4:01
2 18:18	♃ ☍	♑	3 4:09
5 1:57	☿ ☌	♒	5 3:24
6 16:51	♃ △	♓	7 3:51
9 0:16	☿ ✶	♈	9 7:19
11 2:26	☿ □	♉	11 14:51
13 13:30	☉ △	♊	14 1:56
16 5:22	♂ □	♋	16 14:49
19 2:30	☉ ☍	♌	19 3:38
20 23:21	♃ ✶	♍	21 15:14
23 9:19	♃ □	♎	24 1:00
25 17:08	♃ △	♏	26 8:24
28 0:43	♀ △	♐	28 12:57
30 5:44	♀ □	♑	30 14:45

Last Aspect / ☽ Ingress (February)

Last Aspect Dy Hr Mn		☽ Ingress	Dy Hr Mn
1 8:17	♀ ✶	♒	1 14:47
3 0:33	♃ △	♓	3 14:49
5 14:24	♀ ☌	♈	5 16:55
7 11:36	☿ □	♉	7 22:47
10 3:01	☿ △	♊	10 8:49
12 9:28	☉ △	♋	12 21:30
14 19:31	♃ ☍	♌	15 10:19
17 20:49	☉ ☍	♍	17 21:32
19 17:48	♄ △	♎	20 6:40
22 1:52	♄ □	♏	22 13:53
24 8:02	♄ ✶	♐	24 19:14
26 15:17	♂ △	♑	26 22:38

☽ Phases & Eclipses

Dy Hr Mn		
4 2:26	●	14♑09
10 21:57	☽	21♈06
19 2:30	○	29♋26
26 21:34	☾	7♏22
2 13:17	●	14♒08
9 15:40	☽	21♉19
17 20:49	○	29♌38
25 7:38	☾	7♐08

Astro Data

1 January 2049
Julian Day # 54423
SVP 4♓34'14"
GC 27♐31.4 ⚴ 21♒04.2
Eris 0♉01.6R ⚵ 8♓30.0
⚷ 23♏40.8 ⚶ 9♉01.4
☽ Mean ☊ 17♐16.9

1 February 2049
Julian Day # 54454
SVP 4♓34'08"
GC 27♐31.5 ⚴ 0♓49.4
Eris 0♉01.6 ⚵ 23♓13.2
⚷ 26♏23.5 ⚶ 13♉28.5
☽ Mean ☊ 15♐38.4

March 2049 LONGITUDE

Day	Sid.Time	☉	0 hr ☽	Noon ☽	True ☊	☿	♀	♂	⚳	♃	♄	♅	♆	♇
1 M	22 38 56	11♓19 57	29♑47 37	7♒07 57	14♐24.4	24♒48.1	2♈58.1	27♈42.2	24♈16.1	21♊21.4	24♑06.1	14♍01.7	21♉19.2	7♓42.0
2 Tu	22 42 53	12 20 11	14♒29 07	21 50 14	14R 15.0	26 25.1	2R 40.4	28 25.3	24 38.0	21 24.5	24 11.6	13R 59.1	21 20.3	7 43.6
3 W	22 46 49	13 20 23	29 10 17	6♓28 19	14 03.5	28 03.1	2 20.4	29 08.3	25 00.0	21 27.8	24 17.1	13 56.5	21 21.3	7 45.3
4 Th	22 50 46	14 20 34	13♓43 20	20 54 25	13 51.1	29 42.1	1 58.1	29 51.3	25 22.0	21 31.3	24 22.5	13 53.8	21 22.4	7 46.9
5 F	22 54 42	15 20 42	28 00 46	5♈01 41	13 39.1	1♓22.3	1 33.5	0♉34.3	25 44.1	21 35.0	24 27.8	13 51.2	21 23.5	7 48.6
6 Sa	22 58 39	16 20 49	11♈56 41	18 45 22	13 28.8	3 03.5	1 06.8	1 17.2	26 06.3	21 38.9	24 33.1	13 48.6	21 24.7	7 50.2
7 Su	23 02 36	17 20 53	25 27 34	2♉03 17	13 21.0	4 45.7	0 38.2	2 00.1	26 28.6	21 43.0	24 38.4	13 45.9	21 25.8	7 51.9
8 M	23 06 32	18 20 56	8♉32 39	14 55 56	13 16.0	6 29.1	0 07.7	2 43.0	26 50.9	21 47.2	24 43.5	13 43.3	21 27.1	7 53.5
9 Tu	23 10 29	19 20 56	21 13 32	27 25 56	13 13.5	8 13.6	29♓35.5	3 25.8	27 13.3	21 51.6	24 48.6	13 40.7	21 28.3	7 55.1
10 W	23 14 25	20 20 55	3♊33 42	9♊37 28	13 12.7	9 59.2	29 01.8	4 08.6	27 35.8	21 56.2	24 53.6	13 38.1	21 29.6	7 56.8
11 Th	23 18 22	21 20 51	15 37 53	21 35 38	13 12.7	11 46.0	28 26.9	4 51.3	27 58.3	22 01.0	24 58.6	13 35.5	21 30.9	7 58.4
12 F	23 22 18	22 20 45	27 31 27	3♋26 00	13 12.3	13 33.9	27 50.9	5 34.0	28 20.9	22 05.9	25 03.5	13 32.9	21 32.2	8 00.0
13 Sa	23 26 15	23 20 36	9♋19 59	15 14 04	13 10.4	15 22.9	27 14.1	6 16.6	28 43.6	22 11.0	25 08.3	13 30.3	21 33.5	8 01.6
14 Su	23 30 11	24 20 26	21 08 52	27 04 59	13 06.2	17 13.2	26 36.7	6 59.3	29 06.3	22 16.3	25 13.1	13 27.8	21 34.9	8 03.2
15 M	23 34 08	25 20 13	3♌02 59	9♌03 19	12 59.4	19 04.5	25 58.9	7 41.8	29 29.1	22 21.7	25 17.8	13 25.2	21 36.3	8 04.8
16 Tu	23 38 05	26 19 58	15 06 26	21 12 41	12 49.9	20 57.1	25 21.1	8 24.4	29 52.0	22 27.3	25 22.4	13 22.7	21 37.7	8 06.4
17 W	23 42 01	27 19 41	27 22 22	3♍35 40	12 38.3	22 50.8	24 43.5	9 06.8	0♉14.9	22 33.1	25 26.9	13 20.1	21 39.2	8 08.0
18 Th	23 45 58	28 19 22	9♍52 45	16 13 38	12 25.5	24 45.7	24 06.3	9 49.3	0 37.8	22 39.0	25 31.4	13 17.6	21 40.7	8 09.6
19 F	23 49 54	29 19 01	22 38 19	29 06 44	12 12.7	26 41.6	23 29.8	10 31.7	1 00.8	22 45.1	25 35.8	13 15.1	21 42.2	8 11.1
20 Sa	23 53 51	0♈18 38	5♎38 44	12♎14 08	12 01.1	28 38.7	22 54.3	11 14.0	1 23.9	22 51.4	25 40.1	13 12.6	21 43.7	8 12.7
21 Su	23 57 47	1 18 13	18 52 43	25 34 16	11 51.6	0♈36.7	22 19.9	11 56.4	1 47.0	22 57.8	25 44.3	13 10.2	21 45.3	8 14.2
22 M	0 01 44	2 17 46	2♏18 32	9♏05 18	11 44.9	2 35.8	21 47.0	12 38.6	2 10.2	23 04.3	25 48.5	13 07.7	21 46.9	8 15.8
23 Tu	0 05 40	3 17 17	15 54 22	22 45 34	11 41.1	4 35.7	21 15.6	13 20.9	2 33.4	23 11.0	25 52.5	13 05.3	21 48.5	8 17.3
24 W	0 09 37	4 16 47	29 38 44	6♐33 46	11D 39.7	6 36.4	20 45.9	14 03.1	2 56.7	23 17.9	25 56.5	13 02.9	21 50.1	8 18.8
25 Th	0 13 34	5 16 14	13♐30 34	20 29 06	11 39.8	8 37.7	20 18.2	14 45.2	3 20.0	23 24.9	26 00.5	13 00.5	21 51.8	8 20.3
26 F	0 17 30	6 15 40	27 29 18	4♑31 07	11R 40.2	10 39.5	19 52.6	15 27.4	3 43.4	23 32.0	26 04.3	12 58.2	21 53.4	8 21.9
27 Sa	0 21 27	7 15 05	11♑34 27	18 39 13	11 39.7	12 41.7	19 29.1	16 09.5	4 06.8	23 39.3	26 08.1	12 55.8	21 55.2	8 23.3
28 Su	0 25 23	8 14 27	25 45 13	2♒52 15	11 37.3	14 43.9	19 07.9	16 51.5	4 30.3	23 46.8	26 11.8	12 53.5	21 56.9	8 24.8
29 M	0 29 20	9 13 48	10♒00 01	17 08 07	11 32.4	16 45.9	18 49.0	17 33.5	4 53.8	23 54.3	26 15.4	12 51.3	21 58.6	8 26.3
30 Tu	0 33 16	10 13 07	24 16 07	1♓23 29	11 25.2	18 47.5	18 32.5	18 15.5	5 17.4	24 02.1	26 18.9	12 49.0	22 00.4	8 27.7
31 W	0 37 13	11 12 24	8♓29 40	15 34 01	11 16.1	20 48.3	18 18.4	18 57.4	5 41.0	24 09.9	26 22.3	12 46.8	22 02.2	8 29.2

April 2049 LONGITUDE

Day	Sid.Time	☉	0 hr ☽	Noon ☽	True ☊	☿	♀	♂	⚳	♃	♄	♅	♆	♇
1 Th	0 41 09	12♈11 39	22♓35 56	29♓34 48	11♐06.1	22♈48.1	18♓06.8	19♉39.3	6♉04.6	24♊17.9	26♑25.6	12♍44.6	22♉04.0	8♓30.6
2 F	0 45 06	13 10 53	6♈30 03	13♈21 11	10R 56.4	24 46.4	17R 57.7	20 21.2	6 28.3	24 26.0	26 28.9	12R 42.4	22 05.8	8 32.0
3 Sa	0 49 02	14 10 04	20 07 45	26 49 26	10 48.0	26 42.9	17 51.0	21 03.0	6 52.0	24 34.3	26 32.1	12 40.3	22 07.7	8 33.4
4 Su	0 52 59	15 09 13	3♉26 02	9♉57 26	10 41.6	28 37.2	17 46.7	21 44.8	7 15.8	24 42.7	26 35.1	12 38.2	22 09.5	8 34.8
5 M	0 56 56	16 08 20	16 23 39	22 44 48	10 37.6	0♉28.9	17D 44.9	22 26.5	7 39.6	24 51.2	26 38.1	12 36.1	22 11.4	8 36.2
6 Tu	1 00 52	17 07 25	29 01 09	5♊12 58	10D 35.9	2 17.6	17 45.4	23 08.2	8 03.4	24 59.8	26 41.0	12 34.1	22 13.3	8 37.6
7 W	1 04 49	18 06 27	11♊20 42	17 24 49	10 36.0	4 02.9	17 48.2	23 49.9	8 27.3	25 08.6	26 43.9	12 32.1	22 15.3	8 38.9
8 Th	1 08 45	19 05 28	23 25 51	29 24 22	10 37.0	5 44.6	17 53.4	24 31.5	8 51.2	25 17.5	26 46.6	12 30.2	22 17.2	8 40.3
9 F	1 12 42	20 04 26	5♋21 00	11♋16 22	10R 38.2	7 22.3	18 00.8	25 13.1	9 15.2	25 26.5	26 49.2	12 28.2	22 19.2	8 41.6
10 Sa	1 16 38	21 03 22	17 11 10	23 06 02	10 38.5	8 55.7	18 10.4	25 54.6	9 39.1	25 35.6	26 51.8	12 26.4	22 21.1	8 42.9
11 Su	1 20 35	22 02 15	29 01 37	4♌58 34	10 37.4	10 24.5	18 22.1	26 36.1	10 03.1	25 44.9	26 54.2	12 24.5	22 23.1	8 44.2
12 M	1 24 31	23 01 06	10♌57 30	16 59 00	10 34.5	11 48.4	18 36.0	27 17.6	10 27.2	25 54.3	26 56.6	12 22.7	22 25.1	8 45.4
13 Tu	1 28 28	23 59 55	23 03 36	29 11 48	10 29.6	13 07.4	18 51.8	27 59.0	10 51.2	26 03.7	26 58.8	12 20.9	22 27.2	8 46.7
14 W	1 32 25	24 58 42	5♍24 01	11♍40 35	10 23.1	14 21.1	19 09.6	28 40.4	11 15.3	26 13.3	27 01.0	12 19.2	22 29.2	8 47.9
15 Th	1 36 21	25 57 27	18 01 46	24 27 45	10 15.7	15 29.4	19 29.2	29 21.7	11 39.4	26 23.0	27 03.1	12 17.5	22 31.2	8 49.1
16 F	1 40 18	26 56 09	0♎58 37	7♎34 21	10 08.0	16 32.2	19 50.8	0♊03.0	12 03.5	26 32.8	27 05.0	12 15.9	22 33.3	8 50.3
17 Sa	1 44 14	27 54 50	14 14 50	20 59 52	10 01.1	17 29.4	20 14.0	0 44.3	12 27.7	26 42.7	27 06.9	12 14.3	22 35.4	8 51.5
18 Su	1 48 11	28 53 28	27 49 09	4♏42 19	9 55.5	18 20.8	20 39.1	1 25.5	12 51.9	26 52.7	27 08.7	12 12.7	22 37.5	8 52.7
19 M	1 52 07	29 52 05	11♏38 58	18 38 38	9 51.8	19 06.4	21 05.7	2 06.7	13 16.1	27 02.8	27 10.4	12 11.2	22 39.6	8 53.8
20 Tu	1 56 04	0♉50 39	25 40 49	2♐45 03	9D 50.1	19 46.0	21 34.0	2 47.8	13 40.3	27 13.0	27 12.0	12 09.8	22 41.7	8 55.0
21 W	2 00 00	1 49 13	9♐50 50	16 57 44	9 50.1	20 19.8	22 03.7	3 28.9	14 04.6	27 23.3	27 13.5	12 08.3	22 43.8	8 56.1
22 Th	2 03 57	2 47 44	24 05 18	1♑13 09	9 51.1	20 47.6	22 35.0	4 10.0	14 28.9	27 33.7	27 14.9	12 07.0	22 45.9	8 57.2
23 F	2 07 54	3 46 14	8♑20 56	15 28 22	9 52.6	21 09.4	23 07.7	4 51.0	14 53.2	27 44.2	27 16.3	12 05.6	22 48.1	8 58.2
24 Sa	2 11 50	4 44 42	22 35 10	29 41 05	9R 53.5	21 25.3	23 41.8	5 32.0	15 17.5	27 54.8	27 17.5	12 04.3	22 50.3	8 59.3
25 Su	2 15 47	5 43 09	6♒45 53	13♒49 22	9 53.4	21 35.4	24 17.1	6 12.9	15 41.8	28 05.5	27 18.6	12 03.1	22 52.4	9 00.3
26 M	2 19 43	6 41 34	20 51 20	27 51 35	9 51.8	21R 39.7	24 53.7	6 53.8	16 06.2	28 16.2	27 19.6	12 01.9	22 54.6	9 01.3
27 Tu	2 23 40	7 39 57	4♓49 52	11♓45 59	9 48.7	21 38.4	25 31.6	7 34.7	16 30.6	28 27.1	27 20.5	12 00.8	22 56.8	9 02.3
28 W	2 27 36	8 38 19	18 39 42	25 30 47	9 44.5	21 31.7	26 10.6	8 15.6	16 55.0	28 38.0	27 21.4	11 59.7	22 59.0	9 03.3
29 Th	2 31 33	9 36 39	2♈19 00	9♈04 05	9 39.8	21 19.9	26 50.6	8 56.4	17 19.4	28 49.1	27 22.1	11 58.6	23 01.2	9 04.3
30 F	2 35 29	10 34 58	15 45 52	22 24 07	9 35.1	21 03.2	27 31.8	9 37.2	17 43.8	29 00.2	27 22.7	11 57.6	23 03.4	9 05.2

Astro Data	Dy Hr Mn
☽0N	4 7:46
☽0S	18 16:02
☉0N	20 4:30
☿0N	22 16:25
☽0N	31 16:38
♀D	5 18:38
♀0S	6 3:04
☽0S	15 0:12
♄Q♅	19 18:10
♃⚻♄	20 9:20
☿R	26 18:22
☽0N	27 22:51

Planet Ingress		Dy Hr Mn
☿	♓	4 16:18
♂	♉	4 16:51
♀	♓R	8 17:49
⚳	♉	16 20:25
☉	♈	20 4:30
☿	♈	21 4:33
☿	♉	5 5:44
♂	♊	16 10:15
☉	♉	19 15:15

Last Aspect Dy Hr Mn		☽ Ingress	Dy Hr Mn
28 19:47	♂ □	♒	1 0:20
2 23:19	♂ ⚹	♓	3 1:22
4 17:53	♄ ⚹	♈	5 3:23
6 22:26	♄ □	♉	7 8:14
9 16:02	♀ ⚹	♊	9 17:01
12 1:12	♀ □	♋	12 5:01
14 11:06	♀ △	♌	14 17:53
16 14:27	♃ ⚹	♍	17 5:05
19 12:25	☉ ☍	♎	19 13:38
21 12:18	♄ □	♏	21 19:54
23 17:28	♄ ⚹	♐	24 0:37
25 17:04	♃ ☍	♑	26 4:18
28 0:42	♄ ☌	♒	28 7:10
29 23:30	♃ △	♓	30 9:39

Last Aspect Dy Hr Mn		☽ Ingress	Dy Hr Mn
1 6:33	♄ ⚹	♈	1 12:43
3 11:46	☿ ☌	♉	3 17:45
5 19:27	♄ △	♊	6 1:53
8 3:38	♃ ☌	♋	8 13:12
10 19:39	♄ ☍	♌	11 1:58
13 9:30	♂ □	♍	13 13:34
15 21:32	♂ △	♎	15 22:13
18 1:06	☉ ☍	♏	18 3:49
20 2:34	♄ ⚹	♐	20 7:20
22 5:46	♃ ☍	♑	22 9:57
24 7:57	♄ ☌	♒	24 12:32
26 12:43	♃ △	♓	26 15:41
28 17:34	♃ □	♈	28 19:54

☽ Phases & Eclipses Dy Hr Mn	
4 0:13	● 13♓51
11 11:27	☽ 21♊19
19 12:25	○ 29♍20
26 15:11	☾ 6♑24
2 11:41	● 13♈10
10 7:29	☽ 20♋52
18 1:06	○ 28♎27
24 21:12	☾ 5♒07

Astro Data

1 March 2049
Julian Day # 54482
SVP 4♓34'05"
GC 27♐31.6 ⚴ 10♓05.9
Eris 0♉10.5 ⚵ 7♈56.2
⚷ 27♏31.7 ⚶ 21♉13.0
☽ Mean ☊ 14♐09.4

1 April 2049
Julian Day # 54513
SVP 4♓34'02"
GC 27♐31.6 ⚴ 20♓22.0
Eris 0♉27.6 ⚵ 25♈17.2
⚷ 27♏08.2R ⚶ 2♊10.4
☽ Mean ☊ 12♐30.9

LONGITUDE — May 2049

Day	Sid.Time	☉	0 hr ☽	Noon ☽	True ☊	☿	♀	♂	⚳	♃	♄	♅	♆	♇
1 Sa	2 39 26	11♉33 15	28♈58 41	5♉29 26	9♐31.2	20♉42.1	28♓14.0	10♊17.9	18♉08.3	29♊11.4	27♑23.3	11♍56.7	23♉05.6	9♓06.1
2 Su	2 43 23	12 31 30	11♉56 19	18 19 17	9R 28.3	20R 17.1	28 57.1	10 58.6	18 32.7	29 22.7	27 23.7	11R 55.8	23 07.8	9 07.0
3 M	2 47 19	13 29 44	24 38 23	0♊53 42	9D 26.8	19 48.4	29 41.2	11 39.3	18 57.2	29 34.0	27 24.0	11 54.9	23 10.0	9 07.9
4 Tu	2 51 16	14 27 56	7♊05 24	13 13 41	9 26.6	19 16.9	0♈26.2	12 19.9	19 21.7	29 45.5	27 24.3	11 54.1	23 12.3	9 08.7
5 W	2 55 12	15 26 06	19 18 51	25 21 12	9 27.4	18 42.9	1 12.1	13 00.5	19 46.2	29 57.0	27R 24.4	11 53.4	23 14.5	9 09.5
6 Th	2 59 09	16 24 14	1♋21 08	7♋19 05	9 28.9	18 07.2	1 58.7	13 41.1	20 10.7	0♋08.6	27 24.4	11 52.7	23 16.7	9 10.3
7 F	3 03 05	17 22 20	13 15 31	19 10 57	9 30.5	17 30.4	2 46.2	14 21.6	20 35.3	0 20.3	27 24.4	11 52.1	23 19.0	9 11.1
8 Sa	3 07 02	18 20 24	25 05 55	1♌01 00	9 32.0	16 53.2	3 34.5	15 02.1	20 59.8	0 32.0	27 24.2	11 51.5	23 21.2	9 11.9
9 Su	3 10 58	19 18 27	6♌56 46	12 53 50	9R 32.9	16 16.2	4 23.5	15 42.6	21 24.3	0 43.8	27 24.0	11 51.0	23 23.5	9 12.6
10 M	3 14 55	20 16 27	18 52 48	24 54 15	9 32.9	15 40.1	5 13.2	16 23.0	21 48.9	0 55.7	27 23.6	11 50.5	23 25.7	9 13.3
11 Tu	3 18 52	21 14 26	0♍58 47	7♍06 58	9 32.2	15 05.5	6 03.6	17 03.4	22 13.4	1 07.6	27 23.1	11 50.0	23 28.0	9 14.0
12 W	3 22 48	22 12 23	13 19 18	19 36 16	9 30.6	14 32.9	6 54.6	17 43.7	22 38.0	1 19.6	27 22.6	11 49.7	23 30.2	9 14.7
13 Th	3 26 45	23 10 18	25 58 17	2♎25 42	9 28.6	14 02.9	7 46.3	18 24.0	23 02.5	1 31.7	27 21.9	11 49.3	23 32.5	9 15.3
14 F	3 30 41	24 08 11	8♎58 47	15 37 39	9 26.5	13 35.9	8 38.6	19 04.3	23 27.1	1 43.8	27 21.2	11 49.1	23 34.7	9 16.0
15 Sa	3 34 38	25 06 03	22 22 23	29 12 53	9 24.6	13 12.4	9 31.5	19 44.6	23 51.7	1 56.0	27 20.4	11 48.9	23 37.0	9 16.6
16 Su	3 38 34	26 03 53	6♏08 58	13♏10 19	9 23.1	12 52.6	10 25.0	20 24.8	24 16.2	2 08.2	27 19.4	11 48.7	23 39.3	9 17.1
17 M	3 42 31	27 01 41	20 16 28	27 26 53	9D 22.2	12 36.9	11 19.0	21 04.9	24 40.8	2 20.5	27 18.4	11 48.6	23 41.5	9 17.7
18 Tu	3 46 27	27 59 29	4♐40 56	11♐57 51	9 22.0	12 25.3	12 13.5	21 45.1	25 05.4	2 32.9	27 17.3	11D 48.5	23 43.8	9 18.2
19 W	3 50 24	28 57 14	19 16 54	26 37 15	9 22.4	12 18.2	13 08.6	22 25.2	25 30.0	2 45.3	27 16.1	11 48.5	23 46.0	9 18.7
20 Th	3 54 21	29 54 59	3♑58 06	11♑18 39	9 23.0	12D 15.6	14 04.2	23 05.2	25 54.6	2 57.8	27 14.8	11 48.6	23 48.3	9 19.2
21 F	3 58 17	0♊52 43	18 38 11	25 56 01	9 23.8	12 17.5	15 00.3	23 45.3	26 19.2	3 10.3	27 13.4	11 48.7	23 50.5	9 19.7
22 Sa	4 02 14	1 50 25	3♒11 32	10♒24 15	9 24.4	12 23.9	15 56.8	24 25.3	26 43.7	3 22.8	27 11.9	11 48.8	23 52.7	9 20.1
23 Su	4 06 10	2 48 06	17 33 44	24 39 39	9R 24.8	12 34.9	16 53.8	25 05.3	27 08.3	3 35.5	27 10.3	11 49.0	23 55.0	9 20.5
24 M	4 10 07	3 45 47	1♓41 46	8♓39 54	9 24.8	12 50.4	17 51.2	25 45.2	27 32.9	3 48.1	27 08.7	11 49.3	23 57.2	9 20.9
25 Tu	4 14 03	4 43 26	15 33 57	22 23 55	9 24.6	13 10.3	18 49.0	26 25.1	27 57.5	4 00.8	27 06.9	11 49.6	23 59.4	9 21.3
26 W	4 18 00	5 41 04	29 09 47	5♈51 36	9 24.3	13 34.6	19 47.2	27 05.0	28 22.1	4 13.6	27 05.0	11 50.0	24 01.7	9 21.6
27 Th	4 21 56	6 38 42	12♈29 27	19 03 27	9 23.9	14 03.1	20 45.8	27 44.9	28 46.7	4 26.4	27 03.1	11 50.4	24 03.9	9 21.9
28 F	4 25 53	7 36 18	25 33 42	2♉00 20	9 23.7	14 35.7	21 44.8	28 24.7	29 11.3	4 39.3	27 01.1	11 50.9	24 06.1	9 22.2
29 Sa	4 29 50	8 33 54	8♉23 28	14 43 17	9D 23.5	15 12.4	22 44.1	29 04.5	29 35.8	4 52.2	26 59.0	11 51.4	24 08.3	9 22.5
30 Su	4 33 46	9 31 29	20 59 53	27 13 27	9R 23.5	15 53.0	23 43.8	29 44.3	0♊00.4	5 05.1	26 56.8	11 52.0	24 10.5	9 22.7
31 M	4 37 43	10 29 02	3♊24 08	9♊32 07	9 23.5	16 37.4	24 43.8	0♋24.1	0 25.0	5 18.1	26 54.5	11 52.6	24 12.7	9 22.9

LONGITUDE — June 2049

Day	Sid.Time	☉	0 hr ☽	Noon ☽	True ☊	☿	♀	♂	⚳	♃	♄	♅	♆	♇
1 Tu	4 41 39	11♊26 35	15♊37 34	21♊40 43	9♐23.5	17♉25.5	25♈44.2	1♋03.8	0♊49.5	5♋31.1	26♑52.1	11♍53.3	24♉14.8	9♓23.1
2 W	4 45 36	12 24 06	27 41 47	3♋41 01	9R 23.3	18 17.3	26 44.8	1 43.5	1 14.1	5 44.2	26R 49.6	11 54.1	24 17.0	9 23.3
3 Th	4 49 32	13 21 36	9♋38 41	15 35 07	9 22.9	19 12.6	27 45.7	2 23.1	1 38.6	5 57.2	26 47.1	11 54.9	24 19.2	9 23.4
4 F	4 53 29	14 19 06	21 30 37	27 25 35	9 22.3	20 11.3	28 47.0	3 02.8	2 03.2	6 10.4	26 44.5	11 55.7	24 21.3	9 23.6
5 Sa	4 57 25	15 16 34	3♌20 23	9♌15 29	9 21.6	21 13.4	29 48.5	3 42.4	2 27.7	6 23.5	26 41.8	11 56.6	24 23.5	9 23.7
6 Su	5 01 22	16 14 00	15 11 18	21 08 21	9 20.9	22 18.7	0♉50.3	4 21.9	2 52.2	6 36.7	26 39.0	11 57.6	24 25.6	9 23.7
7 M	5 05 19	17 11 26	27 07 09	3♍08 11	9 20.3	23 27.3	1 52.3	5 01.5	3 16.7	6 49.9	26 36.2	11 58.6	24 27.7	9 23.8
8 Tu	5 09 15	18 08 51	9♍12 02	15 19 14	9D 20.0	24 39.1	2 54.6	5 41.0	3 41.2	7 03.2	26 33.3	11 59.7	24 29.8	9R 23.8
9 W	5 13 12	19 06 14	21 30 20	27 45 52	9 20.1	25 53.9	3 57.1	6 20.5	4 05.7	7 16.4	26 30.3	12 00.8	24 31.9	9 23.8
10 Th	5 17 08	20 03 36	4♎06 20	10♎32 11	9 20.7	27 11.9	4 59.9	6 59.9	4 30.1	7 29.7	26 27.2	12 01.9	24 34.0	9 23.8
11 F	5 21 05	21 00 58	17 03 52	23 41 43	9 21.5	28 32.8	6 03.0	7 39.4	4 54.6	7 43.1	26 24.1	12 03.1	24 36.1	9 23.7
12 Sa	5 25 01	21 58 18	0♏25 58	7♏16 46	9 22.5	29 56.8	7 06.2	8 18.8	5 19.0	7 56.4	26 20.9	12 04.4	24 38.1	9 23.6
13 Su	5 28 58	22 55 38	14 14 08	21 17 57	9 23.4	1♊23.7	8 09.7	8 58.1	5 43.4	8 09.8	26 17.6	12 05.7	24 40.2	9 23.5
14 M	5 32 54	23 52 56	28 27 54	5♐43 33	9R 23.9	2 53.6	9 13.4	9 37.5	6 07.8	8 23.2	26 14.3	12 07.1	24 42.2	9 23.4
15 Tu	5 36 51	24 50 14	13♐04 17	20 29 20	9 23.7	4 26.4	10 17.3	10 16.8	6 32.2	8 36.6	26 10.9	12 08.5	24 44.2	9 23.3
16 W	5 40 48	25 47 31	27 57 47	5♑28 37	9 22.8	6 02.1	11 21.4	10 56.1	6 56.6	8 50.0	26 07.4	12 10.0	24 46.2	9 23.1
17 Th	5 44 44	26 44 48	13♑00 44	20 33 00	9 21.1	7 40.6	12 25.8	11 35.4	7 20.9	9 03.5	26 03.9	12 11.5	24 48.2	9 22.9
18 F	5 48 41	27 42 04	28 04 16	5♒33 28	9 18.9	9 22.1	13 30.3	12 14.6	7 45.2	9 16.9	26 00.3	12 13.0	24 50.2	9 22.7
19 Sa	5 52 37	28 39 20	12♒59 37	20 21 50	9 16.6	11 06.3	14 35.0	12 53.8	8 09.6	9 30.4	25 56.7	12 14.7	24 52.1	9 22.4
20 Su	5 56 34	29 36 36	27 39 24	4♓51 45	9 14.6	12 53.4	15 40.0	13 33.0	8 33.8	9 43.9	25 53.0	12 16.3	24 54.1	9 22.2
21 M	6 00 30	0♋33 51	11♓58 30	18 59 23	9D 13.3	14 43.1	16 45.1	14 12.2	8 58.1	9 57.4	25 49.2	12 18.0	24 56.0	9 21.9
22 Tu	6 04 27	1 31 06	25 54 19	2♈43 19	9 13.0	16 35.5	17 50.4	14 51.3	9 22.4	10 11.0	25 45.4	12 19.8	24 57.9	9 21.6
23 W	6 08 23	2 28 21	9♈26 32	16 04 12	9 13.5	18 30.5	18 55.8	15 30.5	9 46.6	10 24.5	25 41.6	12 21.6	24 59.8	9 21.2
24 Th	6 12 20	3 25 36	22 36 36	29 04 04	9 14.7	20 28.0	20 01.4	16 09.6	10 10.8	10 38.1	25 37.7	12 23.4	25 01.6	9 20.9
25 F	6 16 17	4 22 51	5♉27 00	11♉45 46	9 16.3	22 27.7	21 07.2	16 48.7	10 35.0	10 51.6	25 33.7	12 25.3	25 03.5	9 20.5
26 Sa	6 20 13	5 20 06	18 00 45	24 12 22	9 17.7	24 29.6	22 13.2	17 27.7	10 59.2	11 05.2	25 29.7	12 27.2	25 05.3	9 20.1
27 Su	6 24 10	6 17 21	0♊20 58	6♊26 54	9R 18.5	26 33.5	23 19.3	18 06.8	11 23.3	11 18.8	25 25.7	12 29.2	25 07.1	9 19.7
28 M	6 28 06	7 14 36	12 30 31	18 32 07	9 18.1	28 39.2	24 25.6	18 45.8	11 47.4	11 32.4	25 21.6	12 31.2	25 08.9	9 19.2
29 Tu	6 32 03	8 11 50	24 32 00	0♋30 26	9 16.4	0♋46.3	25 32.0	19 24.8	12 11.5	11 46.0	25 17.5	12 33.3	25 10.7	9 18.8
30 W	6 35 59	9 09 05	6♋27 40	12 23 58	9 13.3	2 54.7	26 38.5	20 03.8	12 35.6	11 59.6	25 13.4	12 35.4	25 12.4	9 18.3

Astro Data	Planet Ingress	Last Aspect	☽ Ingress	Last Aspect	☽ Ingress	☽ Phases & Eclipses	Astro Data
Dy Hr Mn	Dy Hr Mn	Dy Hr Mn	Dy Hr Mn	Dy Hr Mn	Dy Hr Mn	Dy Hr Mn	1 May 2049
♀0N 2 17:35	♀ ♈ 3 22:05	1 0:13 ♃ ⚹	♉ 1 1:53	1 20:49 ♀ ⚹	♋ 2 4:37	2 0:12 ● 12♉03	Julian Day # 54543
♄R 6 9:13	♃ ♋ 5 18:14	3 9:32 ♀ ⚹	♊ 3 10:17	4 15:01 ♀ □	♌ 4 17:13	10 1:59 ☽ 19♌52	SVP 4♓33'59"
☽0S 12 8:41	☉ ♊ 20 14:05	4 10:08 ♂ ☌	♋ 5 21:17	6 18:37 ♆ □	♍ 7 5:45	17 11:15 ○ 27♏00	GC 27♐31.7 ⚴ 29♓50.4
♅D 19 0:48	⚳ ♊ 30 11:36	8 4:41 ♄ ☍	♌ 8 9:56	9 9:36 ♄ △	♎ 9 16:15	17 11:27 ☍ A 0.764	Eris 0♉47.4 ⚵ 12♉44.5
☿D 20 13:59	♂ ♋ 30 21:28	10 9:04 ♆ □	♍ 10 22:04	11 16:49 ♄ □	♏ 11 23:14	24 2:55 ☾ 3♓24	⚷ 25♏24.6R ⚶ 14♊07.3
☽0N 25 3:55		13 2:37 ♄ △	♎ 13 7:30	13 20:21 ♄ ⚹	♐ 14 2:33	31 14:01 ● 10♊34	☽ Mean ☊ 10♐55.6
	♀ ♉ 5 16:29	15 8:44 ♄ □	♏ 15 13:22	15 19:28 ☉ ☍	♑ 16 3:15	31 13:59:59 ☌ A 04'45"	
♄⚼♅ 1 2:23	☿ ♊ 12 12:54	17 11:46 ♄ ⚹	♐ 17 16:15	17 20:46 ♄ ☌	♒ 18 3:05		1 June 2049
☽0S 8 16:51	☉ ♋ 20 21:49	19 4:48 ♂ ☍	♑ 19 17:31	20 2:37 ☉ △	♓ 20 3:53	8 17:58 ☽ 18♍23	Julian Day # 54574
♇R 8 19:17	☿ ♋ 29 3:17	21 14:07 ♄ ☌	♒ 21 18:43	21 23:48 ♄ ⚹	♈ 22 7:11	15 19:28 ○ 25♐08	SVP 4♓33'55"
♃△♇ 18 22:04		23 12:46 ♂ △	♓ 23 21:06	24 5:37 ♄ □	♉ 24 13:45	15 19:14 ☍ A 0.251	GC 27♐31.8 ⚴ 8♈34.7
♃∠♆ 21 8:58		25 20:20 ♄ ⚹	♈ 26 1:30	26 14:30 ♄ △	♊ 26 23:19	22 9:43 ☾ 1♈26	Eris 1♉06.1 ⚵ 1♊05.7
☽0N 21 10:07		28 4:56 ♂ ⚹	♉ 28 8:15	27 23:59 ♅ □	♋ 29 10:59	30 4:52 ● 8♋52	⚷ 23♏09.1R ⚶ 27♊12.7
♄△♆ 30 15:47		30 11:28 ♄ △	♊ 30 17:23				☽ Mean ☊ 9♐17.1

July 2049 — LONGITUDE

Day	Sid.Time	☉	0 hr ☽	Noon ☽	True ☊	☿	♀	♂	⚳	♃	♄	♅	♆	♇
1 Th	6 39 56	10♋06 19	18♋19 33	24♋14 41	9♐08.8	5♋04.1	27♉45.2	20♋42.7	12♊59.6	12♋13.2	25♑09.2	12♍37.6	25♉14.1	9♓17.7
2 F	6 43 53	11 03 33	0♌09 36	6♌04 32	9R 03.5	7 14.2	28 52.0	21 21.7	13 23.6	12 26.8	25R 04.9	12 39.8	25 15.9	9R 17.2
3 Sa	6 47 49	12 00 47	11 59 48	17 55 39	8 57.7	9 24.7	29 59.0	22 00.6	13 47.6	12 40.4	25 00.7	12 42.1	25 17.5	9 16.6
4 Su	6 51 46	12 58 01	23 52 25	29 50 26	8 52.1	11 35.4	1♊06.1	22 39.5	14 11.6	12 53.9	24 56.4	12 44.4	25 19.2	9 16.1
5 M	6 55 42	13 55 14	5♍50 04	11♍51 44	8 47.3	13 45.8	2 13.3	23 18.4	14 35.5	13 07.6	24 52.1	12 46.7	25 20.8	9 15.5
6 Tu	6 59 39	14 52 27	17 55 51	24 02 52	8 43.8	15 55.9	3 20.6	23 57.2	14 59.3	13 21.2	24 47.8	12 49.1	25 22.4	9 14.8
7 W	7 03 35	15 49 40	0♎13 17	6♎27 34	8D 41.9	18 05.3	4 28.1	24 36.1	15 23.2	13 34.8	24 43.4	12 51.5	25 24.0	9 14.2
8 Th	7 07 32	16 46 52	12 46 13	19 09 45	8 41.5	20 13.8	5 35.7	25 14.9	15 47.0	13 48.3	24 39.0	12 53.9	25 25.6	9 13.5
9 F	7 11 28	17 44 05	25 38 39	2♏13 21	8 42.2	22 21.2	6 43.3	25 53.7	16 10.7	14 01.9	24 34.7	12 56.4	25 27.2	9 12.8
10 Sa	7 15 25	18 41 17	8♏54 15	15 41 42	8 43.6	24 27.4	7 51.2	26 32.4	16 34.5	14 15.5	24 30.3	12 58.9	25 28.7	9 12.1
11 Su	7 19 22	19 38 30	22 35 53	29 36 55	8R 44.7	26 32.3	8 59.1	27 11.2	16 58.2	14 29.1	24 25.8	13 01.5	25 30.2	9 11.4
12 M	7 23 18	20 35 42	6♐44 46	13♐59 12	8 44.9	28 35.6	10 07.1	27 49.9	17 21.8	14 42.6	24 21.4	13 04.1	25 31.6	9 10.7
13 Tu	7 27 15	21 32 54	21 19 48	28 45 57	8 43.5	0♌37.3	11 15.3	28 28.6	17 45.4	14 56.1	24 17.0	13 06.8	25 33.1	9 09.9
14 W	7 31 11	22 30 07	6♑16 51	13♑51 29	8 40.1	2 37.4	12 23.6	29 07.3	18 09.0	15 09.7	24 12.6	13 09.5	25 34.5	9 09.1
15 Th	7 35 08	23 27 20	21 28 42	29 07 11	8 35.0	4 35.8	13 31.9	29 46.0	18 32.6	15 23.2	24 08.1	13 12.2	25 35.9	9 08.3
16 F	7 39 04	24 24 33	6♒45 36	14♒22 34	8 28.6	6 32.4	14 40.4	0♌24.7	18 56.0	15 36.7	24 03.7	13 14.9	25 37.3	9 07.5
17 Sa	7 43 01	25 21 46	21 56 48	29 27 04	8 21.9	8 27.3	15 49.0	1 03.3	19 19.5	15 50.2	23 59.2	13 17.7	25 38.6	9 06.7
18 Su	7 46 57	26 19 00	6♓52 20	14♓11 44	8 15.6	10 20.3	16 57.7	1 41.9	19 42.9	16 03.7	23 54.8	13 20.6	25 39.9	9 05.8
19 M	7 50 54	27 16 15	21 24 39	28 30 37	8 10.7	12 11.5	18 06.5	2 20.6	20 06.3	16 17.1	23 50.4	13 23.4	25 41.2	9 05.0
20 Tu	7 54 51	28 13 30	5♈29 26	12♈21 05	8 07.7	14 00.9	19 15.5	2 59.2	20 29.6	16 30.5	23 45.9	13 26.3	25 42.5	9 04.1
21 W	7 58 47	29 10 46	19 05 41	25 43 30	8D 06.4	15 48.5	20 24.5	3 37.7	20 52.9	16 44.0	23 41.5	13 29.2	25 43.7	9 03.2
22 Th	8 02 44	0♌08 03	2♉14 56	8♉40 26	8 06.6	17 34.3	21 33.6	4 16.3	21 16.1	16 57.4	23 37.1	13 32.2	25 44.9	9 02.3
23 F	8 06 40	1 05 21	15 00 32	21 15 47	8 07.6	19 18.3	22 42.8	4 54.9	21 39.3	17 10.7	23 32.7	13 35.2	25 46.1	9 01.3
24 Sa	8 10 37	2 02 40	27 26 44	3♊33 59	8R 08.5	21 00.5	23 52.2	5 33.4	22 02.4	17 24.1	23 28.3	13 38.2	25 47.3	9 00.4
25 Su	8 14 33	2 59 59	9♊38 03	15 39 29	8 08.3	22 40.9	25 01.6	6 11.9	22 25.5	17 37.4	23 24.0	13 41.3	25 48.4	8 59.4
26 M	8 18 30	3 57 20	21 38 47	27 36 24	8 06.2	24 19.5	26 11.1	6 50.5	22 48.6	17 50.7	23 19.6	13 44.4	25 49.5	8 58.4
27 Tu	8 22 26	4 54 41	3♋32 45	9♋28 14	8 01.9	25 56.3	27 20.7	7 29.0	23 11.5	18 04.0	23 15.3	13 47.5	25 50.5	8 57.4
28 W	8 26 23	5 52 03	15 23 11	21 17 55	7 55.1	27 31.3	28 30.4	8 07.5	23 34.5	18 17.3	23 11.0	13 50.6	25 51.6	8 56.4
29 Th	8 30 20	6 49 26	27 12 41	3♌07 44	7 46.0	29 04.5	29 40.2	8 46.0	23 57.3	18 30.5	23 06.8	13 53.8	25 52.6	8 55.4
30 F	8 34 16	7 46 49	9♌03 17	14 59 32	7 35.4	0♍36.0	0♋50.1	9 24.4	24 20.1	18 43.7	23 02.5	13 57.0	25 53.5	8 54.3
31 Sa	8 38 13	8 44 13	20 56 41	26 54 55	7 23.9	2 05.6	2 00.0	10 02.9	24 42.9	18 56.8	22 58.3	14 00.2	25 54.5	8 53.3

August 2049 — LONGITUDE

Day	Sid.Time	☉	0 hr ☽	Noon ☽	True ☊	☿	♀	♂	⚳	♃	♄	♅	♆	♇
1 Su	8 42 09	9♌41 38	2♍54 24	8♍55 22	7♐12.7	3♍33.4	3♋10.1	10♌41.3	25♊05.6	19♋09.9	22♑54.1	14♍03.5	25♉55.4	8♓52.2
2 M	8 46 06	10 39 04	14 58 01	21 02 37	7R 02.7	4 59.4	4 20.2	11 19.8	25 28.2	19 23.0	22R 50.0	14 06.8	25 56.3	8R 51.1
3 Tu	8 50 02	11 36 30	27 09 26	3♎18 46	6 54.7	6 23.5	5 30.4	11 58.2	25 50.8	19 36.1	22 45.9	14 10.1	25 57.1	8 50.0
4 W	8 53 59	12 33 57	9♎30 57	15 46 23	6 49.1	7 45.7	6 40.7	12 36.6	26 13.3	19 49.1	22 41.9	14 13.4	25 57.9	8 48.9
5 Th	8 57 55	13 31 25	22 05 26	28 28 32	6 46.1	9 05.9	7 51.0	13 15.0	26 35.7	20 02.1	22 37.8	14 16.8	25 58.7	8 47.8
6 F	9 01 52	14 28 54	4♏56 07	11♏28 38	6D 45.1	10 24.2	9 01.5	13 53.3	26 58.1	20 15.0	22 33.9	14 20.2	25 59.5	8 46.7
7 Sa	9 05 49	15 26 23	18 06 29	24 50 04	6R 45.2	11 40.4	10 12.0	14 31.7	27 20.4	20 27.9	22 30.0	14 23.6	26 00.2	8 45.5
8 Su	9 09 45	16 23 53	1♐39 43	8♐35 40	6 45.5	12 54.6	11 22.6	15 10.0	27 42.6	20 40.8	22 26.1	14 27.0	26 00.9	8 44.4
9 M	9 13 42	17 21 24	15 38 04	22 46 54	6 44.6	14 06.6	12 33.3	15 48.4	28 04.8	20 53.6	22 22.3	14 30.4	26 01.6	8 43.2
10 Tu	9 17 38	18 18 55	0♑01 58	7♑22 57	6 41.7	15 16.4	13 44.1	16 26.7	28 26.8	21 06.4	22 18.5	14 33.9	26 02.2	8 42.1
11 W	9 21 35	19 16 28	14 49 13	22 20 01	6 36.2	16 23.9	14 54.9	17 05.0	28 48.9	21 19.1	22 14.8	14 37.4	26 02.8	8 40.9
12 Th	9 25 31	20 14 01	29 54 22	7♒31 03	6 28.3	17 29.0	16 05.8	17 43.3	29 10.8	21 31.8	22 11.1	14 40.9	26 03.4	8 39.7
13 F	9 29 28	21 11 36	15♒08 49	22 46 16	6 18.6	18 31.6	17 16.8	18 21.6	29 32.7	21 44.4	22 07.5	14 44.4	26 03.9	8 38.5
14 Sa	9 33 24	22 09 11	0♓21 59	7♓54 38	6 08.1	19 31.6	18 27.9	18 59.9	29 54.4	21 57.0	22 04.0	14 48.0	26 04.4	8 37.3
15 Su	9 37 21	23 06 48	15 22 59	22 45 56	5 58.2	20 28.9	19 39.1	19 38.2	0♋16.1	22 09.5	22 00.5	14 51.5	26 04.9	8 36.1
16 M	9 41 18	24 04 27	0♈02 39	7♈12 28	5 49.9	21 23.3	20 50.3	20 16.5	0 37.8	22 22.0	21 57.1	14 55.1	26 05.3	8 34.9
17 Tu	9 45 14	25 02 06	14 14 57	21 09 56	5 43.9	22 14.7	22 01.6	20 54.7	0 59.3	22 34.4	21 53.7	14 58.7	26 05.7	8 33.6
18 W	9 49 11	25 59 48	27 57 25	4♉37 34	5 40.4	23 02.9	23 13.0	21 33.0	1 20.8	22 46.8	21 50.4	15 02.3	26 06.1	8 32.4
19 Th	9 53 07	26 57 31	11♉10 44	17 37 21	5D 38.9	23 47.7	24 24.5	22 11.2	1 42.2	22 59.1	21 47.2	15 05.9	26 06.4	8 31.2
20 F	9 57 04	27 55 15	23 57 58	0♊13 10	5R 38.7	24 29.0	25 36.0	22 49.5	2 03.5	23 11.4	21 44.0	15 09.6	26 06.7	8 29.9
21 Sa	10 01 00	28 53 01	6♊23 35	12 29 54	5 38.7	25 06.6	26 47.7	23 27.7	2 24.7	23 23.6	21 40.9	15 13.2	26 07.0	8 28.7
22 Su	10 04 57	29 50 49	18 32 45	24 32 46	5 37.6	25 40.1	27 59.4	24 06.0	2 45.8	23 35.7	21 37.9	15 16.9	26 07.2	8 27.4
23 M	10 08 53	0♍48 39	0♋30 35	6♋26 47	5 34.6	26 09.5	29 11.1	24 44.2	3 06.8	23 47.8	21 35.0	15 20.6	26 07.5	8 26.2
24 Tu	10 12 50	1 46 30	12 21 55	18 16 29	5 28.9	26 34.4	0♌23.0	25 22.4	3 27.7	23 59.9	21 32.1	15 24.3	26 07.6	8 24.9
25 W	10 16 47	2 44 23	24 10 57	0♌05 41	5 20.5	26 54.6	1 34.9	26 00.6	3 48.6	24 11.8	21 29.3	15 28.0	26 07.8	8 23.7
26 Th	10 20 43	3 42 17	6♌01 05	11 57 25	5 09.4	27 09.9	2 46.9	26 38.8	4 09.3	24 23.7	21 26.6	15 31.7	26 07.9	8 22.4
27 F	10 24 40	4 40 13	17 54 58	23 53 56	4 56.3	27 19.9	3 58.9	27 17.0	4 29.9	24 35.5	21 24.0	15 35.4	26 07.9	8 21.1
28 Sa	10 28 36	5 38 11	29 54 29	5♍56 47	4 42.3	27R 24.5	5 11.0	27 55.2	4 50.4	24 47.3	21 21.4	15 39.1	26R 08.0	8 19.9
29 Su	10 32 33	6 36 10	12♍00 57	18 07 06	4 28.6	27 23.4	6 23.2	28 33.4	5 10.9	24 59.0	21 18.9	15 42.9	26 08.0	8 18.6
30 M	10 36 29	7 34 11	24 15 19	0♎25 42	4 16.2	27 16.4	7 35.5	29 11.6	5 31.2	25 10.6	21 16.5	15 46.6	26 08.0	8 17.3
31 Tu	10 40 26	8 32 13	6♎38 23	12 53 29	4 06.1	27 03.3	8 47.8	29 49.8	5 51.4	25 22.1	21 14.2	15 50.3	26 07.9	8 16.0

Astro Data Dy Hr Mn	Planet Ingress Dy Hr Mn	Last Aspect Dy Hr Mn	☽ Ingress Dy Hr Mn	Last Aspect Dy Hr Mn	☽ Ingress Dy Hr Mn	☽ Phases & Eclipses Dy Hr Mn	Astro Data
♃⚹♅ 3 15:32	♀ ♊ 3 12:22	1 19:51 ♀ ⚹	♌ 1 23:41	2 21:37 ♆ △	♎ 3 5:33	8 7:11 ☽ 16♎35	1 July 2049
☽0S 6 0:16	☿ ♌ 13 4:36	4 2:54 ♆ □	♍ 4 12:19	5 1:05 ♄ □	♏ 5 14:51	15 2:31 ○ 23♑05	Julian Day # 54604
♄∠♇ 15 10:32	♂ ♌ 15 20:41	6 14:36 ♆ △	♎ 6 23:34	7 14:04 ♆ ☍	♐ 7 21:06	21 18:50 ☾ 29♈27	SVP 4♓33'49"
☽0N 18 18:40	☉ ♌ 22 8:38	8 23:52 ♂ □	♏ 9 7:58	9 2:15 ☉ △	♑ 9 23:57	29 20:08 ● 7♌09	GC 27♐31.8 ⚴ 15♈13.1
	♀ ♋ 29 18:48	11 7:40 ♂ △	♐ 11 12:39	11 17:54 ♆ △	♒ 12 0:09		Eris 1♉18.3 ⚵ 18♊48.6
☽0S 2 6:54	☿ ♍ 30 2:30	12 10:29 ♅ □	♑ 13 13:59	13 17:12 ♆ □	♓ 13 23:25	6 17:53 ☽ 14♏43	⚷ 21♏35.2R ⚶ 10♋13.9
♃☍♄ 14 22:26		15 13:04 ♂ ☍	♒ 15 13:23	15 17:27 ♆ ⚹	♈ 15 23:56	13 9:21 ○ 21♒05	☽ Mean ☊ 7♐41.8
☽0N 15 5:11	⚳ ♋ 14 18:08	17 5:53 ♆ □	♓ 17 12:53	17 19:20 ☉ △	♉ 18 3:39	20 7:12 ☾ 27♉44	
☿0S 19 13:44	☉ ♍ 22 15:49	19 9:44 ☉ △	♈ 19 14:33	20 7:12 ☉ □	♊ 20 11:35	28 11:20 ● 5♍37	1 August 2049
♃□♇ 21 21:07	♀ ♌ 24 4:20	21 18:50 ☉ □	♉ 21 19:51	22 14:21 ♆ ☌	♋ 22 22:58		Julian Day # 54635
☿R 28 19:23	♂ ♍ 31 18:25	23 20:45 ♆ ☌	♊ 24 5:00	25 5:22 ♆ ⚹	♌ 25 11:48		SVP 4♓33'45"
♆R 29 3:13		26 8:49 ♀ ☌	♋ 26 16:50	27 19:09 ♂ ☌	♍ 28 0:11		GC 27♐31.9 ⚴ 18♈51.3
☽0S 29 13:11		28 21:16 ♆ ⚹	♌ 29 5:39	30 5:57 ♆ ☌	♎ 30 11:10		Eris 1♉21.8R ⚵ 6♋39.5
		31 9:59 ♆ □	♍ 31 18:11				⚷ 21♏22.4 ⚶ 23♋46.6
							☽ Mean ☊ 6♐03.3

LONGITUDE — September 2049

Day	Sid.Time	☉	0 hr ☽	Noon☽	True☊	☿	♀	♂	⚳	♃	♄	♅	♆	♇
1 W	10 44 22	9♍30 16	19♎11 11	25♎31 40	3♐58.8	26♍44.0	10♌00.2	0♍28.0	6♋11.4	25♋33.6	21♑12.0	15♍54.1	26♉07.8	8♓14.8
2 Th	10 48 19	10 28 21	1♏55 08	8♏21 51	3R54.5	26R18.5	11 12.6	1 06.1	6 31.4	25 45.0	21R09.9	15 57.9	26R07.7	8R13.5
3 F	10 52 15	11 26 28	14 52 07	21 26 12	3D52.6	25 46.9	12 25.1	1 44.3	6 51.3	25 56.3	21 07.8	16 01.6	26 07.5	8 12.2
4 Sa	10 56 12	12 24 35	28 04 25	4♐47 06	3R52.2	25 09.4	13 37.7	2 22.5	7 11.0	26 07.6	21 05.8	16 05.4	26 07.3	8 11.0
5 Su	11 00 09	13 22 45	11♐34 31	18 26 54	3 52.2	24 26.3	14 50.3	3 00.6	7 30.6	26 18.7	21 04.0	16 09.2	26 07.1	8 09.7
6 M	11 04 05	14 20 56	25 24 25	2♑27 11	3 51.3	23 38.0	16 03.0	3 38.8	7 50.1	26 29.8	21 02.2	16 13.0	26 06.8	8 08.4
7 Tu	11 08 02	15 19 08	9♑35 07	16 48 04	3 48.4	22 45.3	17 15.7	4 16.9	8 09.4	26 40.8	21 00.5	16 16.7	26 06.6	8 07.2
8 W	11 11 58	16 17 21	24 05 41	1♒27 27	3 43.0	21 49.0	18 28.5	4 55.0	8 28.7	26 51.7	20 58.9	16 20.5	26 06.2	8 05.9
9 Th	11 15 55	17 15 36	8♒52 39	16 20 26	3 35.0	20 50.2	19 41.4	5 33.2	8 47.8	27 02.5	20 57.4	16 24.3	26 05.9	8 04.7
10 F	11 19 51	18 13 53	23 49 47	1♓19 34	3 25.2	19 49.9	20 54.3	6 11.3	9 06.7	27 13.2	20 56.0	16 28.1	26 05.5	8 03.4
11 Sa	11 23 48	19 12 11	8♓48 36	16 15 40	3 14.4	18 49.6	22 07.3	6 49.4	9 25.6	27 23.8	20 54.7	16 31.8	26 05.1	8 02.2
12 Su	11 27 44	20 10 31	23 39 37	0♈59 23	3 04.1	17 50.5	23 20.4	7 27.5	9 44.3	27 34.4	20 53.4	16 35.6	26 04.6	8 00.9
13 M	11 31 41	21 08 53	8♈14 02	15 22 49	2 55.3	16 54.1	24 33.5	8 05.6	10 02.8	27 44.8	20 52.3	16 39.4	26 04.1	7 59.7
14 Tu	11 35 38	22 07 17	22 25 10	29 20 43	2 48.9	16 01.8	25 46.6	8 43.7	10 21.3	27 55.2	20 51.3	16 43.1	26 03.6	7 58.5
15 W	11 39 34	23 05 43	6♉09 18	12♉50 55	2 45.0	15 14.9	26 59.9	9 21.9	10 39.5	28 05.5	20 50.3	16 46.9	26 03.1	7 57.2
16 Th	11 43 31	24 04 11	19 25 44	25 54 04	2D43.4	14 34.5	28 13.1	10 00.0	10 57.7	28 15.6	20 49.5	16 50.7	26 02.5	7 56.0
17 F	11 47 27	25 02 42	2♊16 21	8♊33 04	2 43.3	14 01.8	29 26.5	10 38.1	11 15.6	28 25.7	20 48.7	16 54.4	26 01.9	7 54.8
18 Sa	11 51 24	26 01 14	14 44 50	20 52 14	2R43.7	13 37.5	0♍39.9	11 16.2	11 33.4	28 35.7	20 48.1	16 58.2	26 01.3	7 53.6
19 Su	11 55 20	26 59 49	26 55 57	2♋56 37	2 43.7	13 22.2	1 53.4	11 54.3	11 51.1	28 45.6	20 47.5	17 01.9	26 00.6	7 52.4
20 M	11 59 17	27 58 26	8♋54 56	14 51 32	2 42.1	13D16.5	3 06.9	12 32.4	12 08.6	28 55.3	20 47.1	17 05.7	25 59.9	7 51.3
21 Tu	12 03 13	28 57 05	20 47 03	26 42 05	2 38.4	13 20.5	4 20.5	13 10.5	12 26.0	29 05.0	20 46.7	17 09.4	25 59.2	7 50.1
22 W	12 07 10	29 55 46	2♌37 10	8♌32 51	2 32.2	13 34.3	5 34.1	13 48.7	12 43.1	29 14.5	20 46.4	17 13.1	25 58.4	7 48.9
23 Th	12 11 07	0♎54 29	14 29 35	20 27 46	2 23.7	13 57.7	6 47.8	14 26.8	13 00.1	29 24.0	20 46.3	17 16.8	25 57.6	7 47.8
24 F	12 15 03	1 53 15	26 27 47	2♍29 56	2 13.5	14 30.4	8 01.5	15 04.9	13 16.9	29 33.3	20D46.2	17 20.5	25 56.8	7 46.6
25 Sa	12 19 00	2 52 02	8♍34 27	14 41 31	2 02.3	15 12.1	9 15.3	15 43.0	13 33.6	29 42.5	20 46.2	17 24.2	25 55.9	7 45.5
26 Su	12 22 56	3 50 52	20 51 18	27 03 52	1 51.3	16 02.2	10 29.1	16 21.1	13 50.0	29 51.6	20 46.4	17 27.9	25 55.1	7 44.4
27 M	12 26 53	4 49 43	3♎19 17	9♎37 34	1 41.3	17 00.2	11 43.0	16 59.2	14 06.3	0♌00.6	20 46.6	17 31.5	25 54.2	7 43.2
28 Tu	12 30 49	5 48 37	15 58 43	22 22 44	1 33.3	18 05.3	12 56.9	17 37.3	14 22.4	0 09.4	20 47.0	17 35.2	25 53.2	7 42.1
29 W	12 34 46	6 47 32	28 49 35	5♏19 15	1 27.8	19 17.0	14 10.8	18 15.4	14 38.3	0 18.2	20 47.4	17 38.8	25 52.3	7 41.1
30 Th	12 38 42	7 46 29	11♏51 44	18 27 03	1D24.8	20 34.5	15 24.9	18 53.5	14 54.0	0 26.8	20 47.9	17 42.4	25 51.3	7 40.0

LONGITUDE — October 2049

Day	Sid.Time	☉	0 hr ☽	Noon☽	True☊	☿	♀	♂	⚳	♃	♄	♅	♆	♇
1 F	12 42 39	8♎45 29	25♏05 14	1♐46 21	1♐24.0	21♍57.2	16♍38.9	19♍31.6	15♋09.5	0♌35.3	20♑48.6	17♍46.0	25♉50.3	7♓38.9
2 Sa	12 46 36	9 44 30	8♐30 28	15 17 40	1 24.6	23 24.4	17 53.0	20 09.7	15 24.8	0 43.6	20 49.3	17 49.6	25R49.2	7R37.9
3 Su	12 50 32	10 43 33	22 08 03	29 01 40	1R25.7	24 55.3	19 07.1	20 47.8	15 39.9	0 51.8	20 50.1	17 53.2	25 48.2	7 36.8
4 M	12 54 29	11 42 37	5♑58 34	12♑58 47	1 26.1	26 29.6	20 21.3	21 25.9	15 54.7	0 59.9	20 51.1	17 56.7	25 47.1	7 35.8
5 Tu	12 58 25	12 41 43	20 02 14	27 08 47	1 25.1	28 06.5	21 35.5	22 04.0	16 09.4	1 07.9	20 52.1	18 00.2	25 46.0	7 34.8
6 W	13 02 22	13 40 51	4♒18 14	11♒30 15	1 22.2	29 45.6	22 49.8	22 42.1	16 23.8	1 15.8	20 53.2	18 03.8	25 44.8	7 33.8
7 Th	13 06 18	14 40 01	18 44 23	26 00 05	1 17.4	1♎26.5	24 04.1	23 20.2	16 38.0	1 23.5	20 54.5	18 07.2	25 43.7	7 32.9
8 F	13 10 15	15 39 12	3♓16 42	10♓33 31	1 11.0	3 08.8	25 18.4	23 58.3	16 52.0	1 31.0	20 55.8	18 10.7	25 42.5	7 31.9
9 Sa	13 14 11	16 38 25	17 49 43	25 04 29	1 03.8	4 52.1	26 32.8	24 36.4	17 05.8	1 38.4	20 57.2	18 14.2	25 41.2	7 31.0
10 Su	13 18 08	17 37 41	2♈16 58	9♈26 23	0 56.9	6 36.2	27 47.2	25 14.5	17 19.3	1 45.7	20 58.8	18 17.6	25 40.0	7 30.1
11 M	13 22 04	18 36 58	16 31 59	23 33 08	0 51.1	8 20.7	29 01.6	25 52.6	17 32.6	1 52.9	21 00.4	18 21.0	25 38.8	7 29.1
12 Tu	13 26 01	19 36 17	0♉29 18	7♉20 05	0 46.9	10 05.5	0♎16.1	26 30.7	17 45.7	1 59.9	21 02.1	18 24.4	25 37.5	7 28.3
13 W	13 29 58	20 35 38	14 05 12	20 44 33	0D44.7	11 50.5	1 30.6	27 08.8	17 58.5	2 06.7	21 03.9	18 27.7	25 36.2	7 27.4
14 Th	13 33 54	21 35 02	27 18 06	3♊46 01	0 44.2	13 35.3	2 45.2	27 46.9	18 11.1	2 13.4	21 05.8	18 31.0	25 34.8	7 26.5
15 F	13 37 51	22 34 28	10♊08 30	16 25 55	0 45.1	15 20.0	3 59.8	28 25.0	18 23.4	2 20.0	21 07.8	18 34.3	25 33.5	7 25.7
16 Sa	13 41 47	23 33 56	22 38 40	28 47 14	0 46.8	17 04.4	5 14.4	29 03.1	18 35.4	2 26.4	21 09.9	18 37.6	25 32.1	7 24.9
17 Su	13 45 44	24 33 26	4♋52 10	10♋54 02	0 48.3	18 48.5	6 29.1	29 41.3	18 47.2	2 32.7	21 12.1	18 40.9	25 30.8	7 24.1
18 M	13 49 40	25 32 59	16 53 27	22 51 01	0R49.2	20 32.1	7 43.8	0♎19.4	18 58.7	2 38.8	21 14.4	18 44.1	25 29.4	7 23.3
19 Tu	13 53 37	26 32 34	28 47 24	4♌43 11	0 48.9	22 15.3	8 58.5	0 57.5	19 09.9	2 44.7	21 16.8	18 47.3	25 27.9	7 22.6
20 W	13 57 33	27 32 11	10♌39 01	16 35 28	0 47.1	23 58.0	10 13.3	1 35.6	19 20.9	2 50.5	21 19.3	18 50.5	25 26.5	7 21.8
21 Th	14 01 30	28 31 50	22 33 06	28 32 28	0 43.8	25 40.1	11 28.1	2 13.8	19 31.6	2 56.1	21 21.9	18 53.6	25 25.0	7 21.1
22 F	14 05 27	29 31 32	4♍34 03	10♍38 17	0 39.3	27 21.8	12 42.9	2 51.9	19 42.0	3 01.6	21 24.5	18 56.7	25 23.6	7 20.4
23 Sa	14 09 23	0♏31 16	16 45 32	22 56 09	0 34.2	29 02.8	13 57.8	3 30.0	19 52.0	3 06.9	21 27.3	18 59.8	25 22.1	7 19.7
24 Su	14 13 20	1 31 02	29 10 23	5♎28 26	0 29.0	0♏43.3	15 12.6	4 08.2	20 01.8	3 12.0	21 30.1	19 02.8	25 20.6	7 19.1
25 M	14 17 16	2 30 49	11♎50 24	18 16 22	0 24.4	2 23.2	16 27.6	4 46.3	20 11.3	3 16.9	21 33.1	19 05.8	25 19.0	7 18.4
26 Tu	14 21 13	3 30 40	24 46 19	1♏20 10	0 20.8	4 02.6	17 42.5	5 24.4	20 20.5	3 21.7	21 36.1	19 08.8	25 17.5	7 17.8
27 W	14 25 09	4 30 32	7♏57 48	14 39 03	0 18.5	5 41.5	18 57.5	6 02.6	20 29.4	3 26.3	21 39.2	19 11.7	25 15.9	7 17.2
28 Th	14 29 06	5 30 26	21 23 42	28 11 31	0D17.7	7 19.8	20 12.5	6 40.7	20 37.9	3 30.8	21 42.4	19 14.7	25 14.4	7 16.7
29 F	14 33 02	6 30 21	5♐02 14	11♐55 37	0 18.0	8 57.5	21 27.5	7 18.9	20 46.1	3 35.1	21 45.7	19 17.5	25 12.8	7 16.1
30 Sa	14 36 59	7 30 19	18 51 22	25 49 15	0 19.2	10 34.8	22 42.5	7 57.0	20 54.0	3 39.1	21 49.1	19 20.4	25 11.2	7 15.6
31 Su	14 40 56	8 30 18	2♑48 59	9♑50 20	0 20.7	12 11.6	23 57.6	8 35.1	21 01.6	3 43.1	21 52.6	19 23.2	25 09.6	7 15.1

Astro Data

	Dy Hr Mn
♃✶♆	4 11:31
☿0N	9 9:31
☽0N	11 16:00
☿ D	20 14:11
☉0S	22 13:43
♄ D	24 15:36
☽0S	25 19:49
☽0N	9 1:16
☿0S	9 5:38
♀0S	15 2:17
♂0S	21 23:31
☽0S	23 3:19

Planet Ingress

		Dy Hr Mn
♀	♍	17 22:57
☉	♎	22 13:44
♃	♌	27 10:30
☿	♎	6 15:26
♀	♎	12 6:49
♂	♎	17 23:48
☉	♏	22 23:26
☿	♏	24 1:39

Last Aspect / ☽ Ingress (September)

Last Aspect Dy Hr Mn			☽ Ingress	Dy Hr Mn
1 12:04	♃	□	♏	1 20:24
3 20:29	♆	☍	♐	4 3:27
5 21:47	☿	□	♑	6 7:50
8 4:26	♃	☍	♒	8 9:38
10 3:37	♆	□	♓	10 9:53
12 6:19	♃	△	♈	12 10:22
14 9:29	♃	□	♉	14 13:09
16 16:48	♀	□	♊	16 19:42
18 23:05	☉	□	♋	19 6:07
21 16:58	☉	✶	♌	21 18:41
23 22:59	♆	□	♍	24 7:02
26 17:26	♃	✶	♎	26 17:38
28 9:01	♄	□	♏	29 2:11

Last Aspect / ☽ Ingress (October)

Last Aspect Dy Hr Mn			☽ Ingress	Dy Hr Mn
1 1:22	♆	☍	♐	1 8:50
3 3:58	☿	□	♑	3 13:41
5 13:50	☿	△	♒	5 16:48
7 11:33	♆	□	♓	7 18:36
9 14:40	♀	☍	♈	9 20:11
11 7:37	♄	□	♉	11 23:09
14 0:19	♂	△	♊	14 4:59
16 12:33	♂	□	♋	16 14:23
18 17:57	☉	□	♌	19 2:27
21 11:59	☉	✶	♍	21 14:55
23 16:41	♆	△	♎	24 1:35
25 18:05	♄	□	♏	26 9:34
28 6:49	♆	☍	♐	28 15:11
30 6:07	♀	✶	♑	30 19:10

☽ Phases & Eclipses

Dy Hr Mn		
5 2:29	☽	13♐00
11 17:06	○	19♓25
18 23:05	☾	26♊28
27 2:06	●	4♎25
4 9:40	☽	11♑37
11 2:55	○	18♈15
18 17:57	☾	25♋48
26 16:16	●	3♏41

Astro Data

1 September 2049
Julian Day # 54666
SVP 4♓33'41"
GC 27♐32.0 ⚵ 17♈20.0R
Eris 1♉15.3R ⚵ 23♋34.0
⚷ 22♏45.7 ⚶ 7♌09.3
☽ Mean ☊ 4♐24.8

1 October 2049
Julian Day # 54696
SVP 4♓33'39"
GC 27♐32.1 ⚵ 10♈24.9R
Eris 1♉01.2R ⚵ 8♌26.2
⚷ 25♏23.5 ⚶ 19♌36.2
☽ Mean ☊ 2♐49.5

November 2049 LONGITUDE

Day	Sid.Time	☉	0 hr ☽	Noon ☽	True ☊	☿	♀	♂	⚳	♃	♄	♅	♆	♇
1 M	14 44 52	9♏30 19	16♑53 04	23♑56 57	0♐21.9	13♏47.8	25♎12.6	9♎13.3	21♋08.8	3♌46.8	21♑56.2	19♍25.9	25♉08.0	7♓14.6
2 Tu	14 48 49	10 30 22	1♒01 45	8♒07 13	0R 22.5	15 23.7	26 27.7	9 51.4	21 15.7	3 50.3	21 59.8	19 28.6	25R 06.4	7R 14.2
3 W	14 52 45	11 30 25	15 13 06	22 19 08	0 22.2	16 59.0	27 42.8	10 29.6	21 22.2	3 53.7	22 03.5	19 31.3	25 04.8	7 13.8
4 Th	14 56 42	12 30 31	29 25 03	6♓30 30	0 21.1	18 33.9	28 58.0	11 07.7	21 28.4	3 56.9	22 07.4	19 34.0	25 03.1	7 13.4
5 F	15 00 38	13 30 38	13♓35 10	20 38 40	0 19.2	20 08.5	0♏13.1	11 45.8	21 34.2	3 59.9	22 11.2	19 36.6	25 01.5	7 13.0
6 Sa	15 04 35	14 30 46	27 40 39	4♈40 42	0 17.0	21 42.6	1 28.2	12 24.0	21 39.7	4 02.7	22 15.2	19 39.1	24 59.8	7 12.6
7 Su	15 08 31	15 30 56	11♈38 25	18 33 25	0 14.9	23 16.3	2 43.4	13 02.1	21 44.8	4 05.3	22 19.3	19 41.7	24 58.2	7 12.3
8 M	15 12 28	16 31 08	25 25 20	2♉13 49	0 13.2	24 49.6	3 58.6	13 40.3	21 49.5	4 07.8	22 23.4	19 44.1	24 56.5	7 12.0
9 Tu	15 16 25	17 31 21	8♉58 34	15 39 21	0 12.1	26 22.6	5 13.8	14 18.4	21 53.9	4 10.0	22 27.6	19 46.6	24 54.8	7 11.7
10 W	15 20 21	18 31 37	22 15 58	28 48 17	0D 11.7	27 55.3	6 29.0	14 56.6	21 57.9	4 12.1	22 31.9	19 49.0	24 53.1	7 11.4
11 Th	15 24 18	19 31 54	5♊16 17	11♊39 57	0 12.0	29 27.6	7 44.3	15 34.7	22 01.5	4 14.0	22 36.3	19 51.3	24 51.5	7 11.2
12 F	15 28 14	20 32 13	17 59 24	24 14 48	0 12.6	0♐59.6	8 59.5	16 12.9	22 04.7	4 15.7	22 40.7	19 53.6	24 49.8	7 11.0
13 Sa	15 32 11	21 32 33	0♋26 23	6♋34 26	0 13.5	2 31.3	10 14.8	16 51.1	22 07.6	4 17.1	22 45.2	19 55.9	24 48.1	7 10.8
14 Su	15 36 07	22 32 56	12 39 20	18 41 29	0 14.4	4 02.7	11 30.1	17 29.2	22 10.0	4 18.4	22 49.8	19 58.1	24 46.4	7 10.6
15 M	15 40 04	23 33 20	24 41 20	0♌39 23	0 15.2	5 33.8	12 45.4	18 07.4	22 12.1	4 19.5	22 54.5	20 00.3	24 44.7	7 10.5
16 Tu	15 44 00	24 33 46	6♌36 11	12 32 16	0 15.6	7 04.5	14 00.7	18 45.6	22 13.7	4 20.4	22 59.2	20 02.4	24 43.0	7 10.4
17 W	15 47 57	25 34 14	18 28 13	24 24 38	0R 15.8	8 35.0	15 16.1	19 23.8	22 15.0	4 21.1	23 04.1	20 04.5	24 41.3	7 10.3
18 Th	15 51 54	26 34 44	0♍22 06	6♍21 14	0 15.7	10 05.1	16 31.4	20 01.9	22 15.8	4 21.6	23 08.9	20 06.6	24 39.6	7 10.2
19 F	15 55 50	27 35 16	12 22 34	18 26 43	0 15.5	11 34.9	17 46.8	20 40.1	22R 16.3	4 21.9	23 13.9	20 08.5	24 37.9	7D 10.2
20 Sa	15 59 47	28 35 49	24 34 10	0♎45 26	0 15.3	13 04.4	19 02.2	21 18.3	22 16.3	4R 22.1	23 18.9	20 10.5	24 36.2	7 10.2
21 Su	16 03 43	29 36 24	7♎00 58	13 21 07	0D 15.2	14 33.5	20 17.6	21 56.5	22 15.9	4 22.0	23 24.0	20 12.4	24 34.5	7 10.2
22 M	16 07 40	0♐37 01	19 46 13	26 16 30	0 15.1	16 02.2	21 33.0	22 34.7	22 15.1	4 21.7	23 29.1	20 14.2	24 32.9	7 10.3
23 Tu	16 11 36	1 37 40	2♏52 05	9♏33 00	0 15.2	17 30.4	22 48.4	23 12.9	22 13.8	4 21.2	23 34.4	20 16.0	24 31.2	7 10.3
24 W	16 15 33	2 38 20	16 19 12	23 10 30	0R 15.3	18 58.2	24 03.8	23 51.1	22 12.2	4 20.5	23 39.7	20 17.7	24 29.5	7 10.4
25 Th	16 19 29	3 39 02	0♐06 36	7♐07 08	0 15.3	20 25.4	25 19.2	24 29.3	22 10.1	4 19.6	23 45.0	20 19.4	24 27.8	7 10.5
26 F	16 23 26	4 39 45	14 11 35	21 19 25	0 15.1	21 52.1	26 34.7	25 07.5	22 07.6	4 18.5	23 50.4	20 21.1	24 26.2	7 10.7
27 Sa	16 27 23	5 40 29	28 30 00	5♑42 40	0 14.6	23 18.0	27 50.1	25 45.7	22 04.6	4 17.2	23 55.9	20 22.7	24 24.5	7 10.9
28 Su	16 31 19	6 41 14	12♑56 43	20 11 27	0 13.9	24 43.2	29 05.6	26 23.9	22 01.3	4 15.7	24 01.5	20 24.2	24 22.9	7 11.1
29 M	16 35 16	7 42 01	27 26 12	4♒40 21	0 13.1	26 07.5	0♐21.0	27 02.1	21 57.5	4 14.0	24 07.0	20 25.7	24 21.2	7 11.3
30 Tu	16 39 12	8 42 48	11♒53 19	19 04 36	0 12.4	27 30.8	1 36.5	27 40.3	21 53.3	4 12.1	24 12.7	20 27.1	24 19.6	7 11.5

December 2049 LONGITUDE

Day	Sid.Time	☉	0 hr ☽	Noon ☽	True ☊	☿	♀	♂	⚳	♃	♄	♅	♆	♇
1 W	16 43 09	9♐43 36	26♒13 45	3♓20 26	0♐12.0	28♐53.0	2♐51.9	28♎18.4	21♋48.7	4♌10.0	24♑18.4	20♍28.5	24♉18.0	7♓11.8
2 Th	16 47 05	10 44 25	10♓24 22	17 25 20	0D 12.0	0♑13.8	4 07.4	28 56.6	21R 43.7	4R 07.8	24 24.2	20 29.8	24R 16.3	7 12.1
3 F	16 51 02	11 45 15	24 23 10	1♈17 48	0 12.5	1 33.0	5 22.9	29 34.8	21 38.2	4 05.3	24 30.0	20 31.1	24 14.7	7 12.4
4 Sa	16 54 58	12 46 06	8♈09 09	14 57 12	0 13.5	2 50.5	6 38.3	0♏13.0	21 32.4	4 02.6	24 35.9	20 32.3	24 13.1	7 12.8
5 Su	16 58 55	13 46 57	21 41 57	28 23 26	0 14.6	4 05.9	7 53.8	0 51.2	21 26.1	3 59.7	24 41.8	20 33.5	24 11.6	7 13.2
6 M	17 02 52	14 47 50	5♉01 38	11♉36 36	0 15.7	5 18.9	9 09.3	1 29.4	21 19.5	3 56.7	24 47.8	20 34.6	24 10.0	7 13.6
7 Tu	17 06 48	15 48 43	18 08 22	24 36 56	0R 16.4	6 29.2	10 24.8	2 07.5	21 12.4	3 53.5	24 53.8	20 35.6	24 08.4	7 14.0
8 W	17 10 45	16 49 37	1♊02 22	7♊24 42	0 16.3	7 36.3	11 40.2	2 45.7	21 05.0	3 50.0	24 59.9	20 36.6	24 06.9	7 14.4
9 Th	17 14 41	17 50 33	13 43 57	20 00 13	0 15.4	8 39.7	12 55.7	3 23.9	20 57.1	3 46.4	25 06.0	20 37.6	24 05.4	7 14.9
10 F	17 18 38	18 51 29	26 13 33	2♋24 04	0 13.4	9 39.0	14 11.2	4 02.1	20 48.9	3 42.6	25 12.2	20 38.5	24 03.9	7 15.4
11 Sa	17 22 34	19 52 26	8♋31 53	14 37 12	0 10.5	10 33.4	15 26.7	4 40.3	20 40.3	3 38.6	25 18.4	20 39.3	24 02.4	7 16.0
12 Su	17 26 31	20 53 24	20 40 11	26 41 05	0 07.1	11 22.3	16 42.2	5 18.5	20 31.4	3 34.5	25 24.7	20 40.1	24 00.9	7 16.5
13 M	17 30 27	21 54 23	2♌40 12	8♌37 51	0 03.4	12 05.0	17 57.7	5 56.7	20 22.0	3 30.2	25 31.0	20 40.8	23 59.4	7 17.1
14 Tu	17 34 24	22 55 23	14 34 23	20 30 15	29♏59.9	12 40.6	19 13.2	6 34.9	20 12.4	3 25.6	25 37.4	20 41.5	23 58.0	7 17.7
15 W	17 38 21	23 56 24	26 25 54	2♍21 47	29 57.2	13 08.2	20 28.7	7 13.0	20 02.3	3 21.0	25 43.8	20 42.1	23 56.6	7 18.3
16 Th	17 42 17	24 57 26	8♍18 28	14 16 30	29D 55.4	13 27.0	21 44.2	7 51.2	19 52.0	3 16.1	25 50.2	20 42.6	23 55.2	7 19.0
17 F	17 46 14	25 58 29	20 16 26	26 18 53	29 54.9	13R 36.1	22 59.7	8 29.4	19 41.3	3 11.1	25 56.7	20 43.1	23 53.8	7 19.6
18 Sa	17 50 10	26 59 33	2♎24 27	8♎33 43	29 55.4	13 34.8	24 15.3	9 07.6	19 30.2	3 05.9	26 03.2	20 43.6	23 52.4	7 20.3
19 Su	17 54 07	28 00 37	14 47 17	21 05 42	29 56.8	13 22.2	25 30.8	9 45.8	19 18.9	3 00.5	26 09.8	20 44.0	23 51.1	7 21.0
20 M	17 58 03	29 01 43	27 29 29	3♏59 05	29 58.6	12 58.1	26 46.3	10 24.0	19 07.3	2 55.0	26 16.4	20 44.3	23 49.7	7 21.8
21 Tu	18 02 00	0♑02 50	10♏34 53	17 17 09	0♐00.0	12 22.3	28 01.8	11 02.2	18 55.4	2 49.4	26 23.0	20 44.6	23 48.4	7 22.6
22 W	18 05 56	1 03 57	24 06 03	1♐01 34	0R 00.6	11 35.0	29 17.4	11 40.4	18 43.2	2 43.5	26 29.7	20 44.8	23 47.2	7 23.4
23 Th	18 09 53	2 05 05	8♐03 34	15 11 45	29♏59.7	10 37.2	0♑32.9	12 18.5	18 30.8	2 37.6	26 36.4	20 44.9	23 45.9	7 24.2
24 F	18 13 50	3 06 13	22 25 36	29 44 27	29 57.1	9 30.0	1 48.4	12 56.7	18 18.1	2 31.5	26 43.1	20 45.0	23 44.7	7 25.0
25 Sa	18 17 46	4 07 22	7♑07 29	14♑33 44	29 53.0	8 15.5	3 04.0	13 34.9	18 05.2	2 25.2	26 49.9	20R 45.1	23 43.5	7 25.9
26 Su	18 21 43	5 08 31	22 02 06	29 31 29	29 47.7	6 55.8	4 19.5	14 13.1	17 52.1	2 18.8	26 56.6	20 45.1	23 42.3	7 26.8
27 M	18 25 39	6 09 40	7♒00 42	14♒28 41	29 42.1	5 33.7	5 35.0	14 51.2	17 38.8	2 12.3	27 03.5	20 45.0	23 41.1	7 27.7
28 Tu	18 29 36	7 10 50	21 54 21	29 16 49	29 36.9	4 12.0	6 50.5	15 29.4	17 25.4	2 05.7	27 10.3	20 44.9	23 40.0	7 28.6
29 W	18 33 32	8 11 59	6♓35 18	13♓49 11	29 32.9	2 53.1	8 06.1	16 07.5	17 11.7	1 58.9	27 17.2	20 44.7	23 38.9	7 29.5
30 Th	18 37 29	9 13 08	20 58 03	28 01 37	29D 30.6	1 39.7	9 21.6	16 45.7	16 58.0	1 52.0	27 24.1	20 44.4	23 37.8	7 30.5
31 F	18 41 26	10 14 17	4♈59 45	11♈52 28	29 30.0	0 33.5	10 37.1	17 23.8	16 44.1	1 45.0	27 31.0	20 44.1	23 36.7	7 31.5

Astro Data	Dy Hr Mn
☽ 0N	5 8:06
♄∠♇	5 21:37
☽ 0S	19 11:41
⚳ R	20 0:56
♇ D	20 9:40
♃ R	20 12:42
♄△♆	1 10:28
☽ 0N	2 13:31
☽ 0S	16 20:20
☿ R	17 21:02
♅ R	25 18:13
☽ 0N	29 20:01

Planet Ingress		Dy Hr Mn
♀	♏	5 7:49
☿	♐	11 20:26
☉	♐	21 21:21
♀	♐	29 5:19
☿	♑	2 7:53
♂	♏	4 3:50
☊	♏R	14 11:36
☉	♑	21 10:53
☊	♐	21 11:23
♀	♑	23 1:33
☊	♏R	23 7:04

Last Aspect Dy Hr Mn		☽ Ingress	Dy Hr Mn
1 14:21	♀ □	♒	1 22:15
3 22:00	♀ △	♓	4 0:59
5 19:27	♆ ⚹	♈	6 3:58
7 18:36	♄ □	♉	8 8:03
10 10:09	☿ ☍	♊	10 14:12
12 3:37	♅ □	♋	12 23:09
15 0:08	♆ ⚹	♌	15 10:41
17 14:33	☉ □	♍	17 23:16
20 7:27	☉ ⚹	♎	20 10:32
22 6:50	♄ □	♏	22 18:48
24 14:17	♆ ☍	♐	24 23:49
26 18:40	♂ ⚹	♑	27 2:30
29 4:09	♀ ⚹	♒	29 4:15

Last Aspect Dy Hr Mn		☽ Ingress	Dy Hr Mn
1 3:40	☿ ⚹	♓	1 6:21
3 0:07	♄ ⚹	♈	3 9:44
5 5:19	♄ □	♉	5 14:54
7 12:32	♄ △	♊	7 22:03
9 13:12	♅ □	♋	10 7:19
12 9:26	♄ ☍	♌	12 18:38
14 19:00	♆ □	♍	15 7:13
17 11:16	☉ □	♎	17 19:16
20 2:05	☉ ⚹	♏	20 4:39
22 4:06	♄ ⚹	♐	22 10:14
23 21:14	♅ □	♑	24 12:25
26 7:50	♄ ☌	♒	26 12:46
28 2:52	♆ □	♓	28 13:11
30 10:55	♄ ⚹	♈	30 15:23

☽ Phases & Eclipses Dy Hr Mn	
2 16:20	☽ 10♒41
9 15:39	○ 17♉41
9 15:52	• A 0.681
17 14:33	☾ 25♌41
25 5:37	● 3♐23
25 5:33:48	• AT00'38"
1 23:41	☽ 10♓13
9 7:29	○ 17♊39
17 11:16	☾ 25♍57
24 17:53	● 3♑21
31 8:54	☽ 10♈06

Astro Data

1 November 2049
Julian Day # 54727
SVP 4♓33'35"
GC 27♐32.1 ⚴ 2♈19.7R
Eris 0♉42.6R ⚵ 21♌20.5
⚷ 28♏59.8 ⚶ 1♍22.8
☽ Mean ☊ 1♐11.0

1 December 2049
Julian Day # 54757
SVP 4♓33'31"
GC 27♐32.2 ⚴ 29♓47.7
Eris 0♉26.2R ⚵ 29♌59.7
⚷ 2♐50.7 ⚶ 10♍45.2
☽ Mean ☊ 29♏35.6

LONGITUDE — January 2050

Day	Sid.Time	☉	0 hr ☽	Noon ☽	True ☊	☿	♀	♂	⚳	♃	♄	♅	♆	♇
1 Sa	18 45 22	11♑15 26	18♈39 53	25♈22 13	29♏30.8	29♐36.1	11♑52.6	18♏01.9	16♋30.1	1♌37.9	27♑37.9	20♍43.8	23♉35.7	7♓32.5
2 Su	18 49 19	12 16 34	1♉59 43	8♉32 43	29 32.3	28R 48.4	13 08.1	18 40.0	16R 16.0	1R 30.7	27 44.9	20R 43.4	23R 34.7	7 33.5
3 M	18 53 15	13 17 43	15 01 32	21 26 31	29R 33.5	28 11.0	14 23.6	19 18.1	16 01.9	1 23.5	27 51.9	20 42.9	23 33.7	7 34.6
4 Tu	18 57 12	14 18 51	27 48 00	4♊06 18	29 33.7	27 43.9	15 39.0	19 56.3	15 47.7	1 16.1	27 58.9	20 42.4	23 32.8	7 35.7
5 W	19 01 08	15 19 59	10♊21 43	16 34 30	29 32.1	27 27.0	16 54.5	20 34.4	15 33.5	1 08.6	28 05.9	20 41.8	23 31.8	7 36.8
6 Th	19 05 05	16 21 07	22 44 55	28 53 10	29 28.2	27D 19.7	18 10.0	21 12.5	15 19.2	1 01.1	28 12.9	20 41.2	23 31.0	7 37.9
7 F	19 09 01	17 22 15	4♋59 26	11♋03 53	29 21.9	27 21.6	19 25.5	21 50.6	15 05.0	0 53.4	28 20.0	20 40.5	23 30.1	7 39.0
8 Sa	19 12 58	18 23 23	17 06 40	23 07 57	29 13.5	27 31.9	20 40.9	22 28.6	14 50.8	0 45.8	28 27.0	20 39.8	23 29.3	7 40.2
9 Su	19 16 55	19 24 30	29 07 51	5♌06 32	29 03.6	27 50.0	21 56.4	23 06.7	14 36.6	0 38.0	28 34.1	20 39.0	23 28.5	7 41.3
10 M	19 20 51	20 25 37	11♌04 11	17 00 58	28 53.1	28 15.2	23 11.9	23 44.8	14 22.5	0 30.2	28 41.2	20 38.1	23 27.7	7 42.5
11 Tu	19 24 48	21 26 45	22 57 06	28 52 53	28 42.8	28 46.8	24 27.3	24 22.9	14 08.4	0 22.3	28 48.3	20 37.2	23 27.0	7 43.7
12 W	19 28 44	22 27 52	4♍48 34	10♍44 30	28 33.8	29 24.2	25 42.8	25 00.9	13 54.5	0 14.4	28 55.4	20 36.3	23 26.3	7 45.0
13 Th	19 32 41	23 28 58	16 41 05	22 38 45	28 26.8	0♑06.8	26 58.2	25 39.0	13 40.6	0 06.5	29 02.5	20 35.3	23 25.6	7 46.2
14 F	19 36 37	24 30 05	28 37 56	4♎39 12	28 22.1	0 54.1	28 13.6	26 17.1	13 26.9	29♋58.5	29 09.6	20 34.2	23 24.9	7 47.5
15 Sa	19 40 34	25 31 12	10♎43 03	16 50 07	28D 19.8	1 45.5	29 29.1	26 55.1	13 13.3	29 50.5	29 16.8	20 33.1	23 24.3	7 48.7
16 Su	19 44 30	26 32 18	23 00 58	29 16 13	28 19.4	2 40.8	0♒44.5	27 33.2	12 59.9	29 42.4	29 23.9	20 32.0	23 23.7	7 50.0
17 M	19 48 27	27 33 24	5♏36 30	12♏02 23	28 20.0	3 39.4	1 59.9	28 11.2	12 46.7	29 34.4	29 31.0	20 30.8	23 23.2	7 51.3
18 Tu	19 52 24	28 34 30	18 34 26	25 13 08	28R 20.7	4 41.0	3 15.3	28 49.2	12 33.6	29 26.3	29 38.2	20 29.5	23 22.7	7 52.6
19 W	19 56 20	29 35 36	1♐58 52	8♐51 54	28 20.2	5 45.4	4 30.8	29 27.2	12 20.8	29 18.2	29 45.3	20 28.2	23 22.2	7 54.0
20 Th	20 00 17	0♒36 42	15 52 23	23 00 13	28 17.7	6 52.2	5 46.2	0♐05.2	12 08.2	29 10.2	29 52.5	20 26.9	23 21.8	7 55.3
21 F	20 04 13	1 37 47	0♑15 09	7♑36 41	28 12.7	8 01.3	7 01.6	0 43.2	11 55.8	29 02.1	29 59.6	20 25.5	23 21.3	7 56.7
22 Sa	20 08 10	2 38 51	15 04 04	22 36 22	28 05.0	9 12.4	8 17.0	1 21.2	11 43.7	28 54.1	0♒06.8	20 24.0	23 21.0	7 58.1
23 Su	20 12 06	3 39 55	0♒12 23	7♒50 48	27 55.4	10 25.4	9 32.4	1 59.2	11 31.9	28 46.0	0 13.9	20 22.5	23 20.6	7 59.5
24 M	20 16 03	4 40 59	15 30 12	23 09 07	27 44.9	11 40.0	10 47.7	2 37.1	11 20.4	28 38.0	0 21.0	20 21.0	23 20.3	8 00.9
25 Tu	20 19 59	5 42 01	0♓46 05	8♓19 47	27 34.8	12 56.2	12 03.1	3 15.1	11 09.1	28 30.1	0 28.2	20 19.4	23 20.0	8 02.3
26 W	20 23 56	6 43 02	15 49 03	23 12 53	27 26.5	14 13.8	13 18.5	3 53.0	10 58.2	28 22.1	0 35.3	20 17.8	23 19.8	8 03.8
27 Th	20 27 53	7 44 02	0♈30 34	7♈41 34	27 20.5	15 32.8	14 33.8	4 30.9	10 47.6	28 14.2	0 42.4	20 16.1	23 19.6	8 05.2
28 F	20 31 49	8 45 01	14 45 36	21 42 36	27 17.2	16 53.0	15 49.1	5 08.8	10 37.3	28 06.4	0 49.5	20 14.4	23 19.4	8 06.7
29 Sa	20 35 46	9 45 59	28 32 39	5♉16 00	27D 16.0	18 14.4	17 04.4	5 46.6	10 27.4	27 58.6	0 56.6	20 12.6	23 19.2	8 08.2
30 Su	20 39 42	10 46 55	11♉53 02	18 24 10	27R 16.0	19 36.9	18 19.7	6 24.5	10 17.9	27 50.9	1 03.7	20 10.8	23 19.1	8 09.7
31 M	20 43 39	11 47 51	24 49 54	1♊10 48	27 16.1	21 00.4	19 35.0	7 02.3	10 08.7	27 43.3	1 10.8	20 09.0	23 19.1	8 11.1

LONGITUDE — February 2050

Day	Sid.Time	☉	0 hr ☽	Noon ☽	True ☊	☿	♀	♂	⚳	♃	♄	♅	♆	♇
1 Tu	20 47 35	12♒48 45	7♊27 22	13♊40 09	27♏15.0	22♑24.9	20♒50.3	7♐40.2	9♋59.9	27♋35.7	1♒17.8	20♍07.1	23♉19.0	8♓12.7
2 W	20 51 32	13 49 38	19 49 40	25 56 23	27R 11.7	23 50.4	22 05.6	8 18.0	9R 51.4	27R 28.2	1 24.9	20R 05.2	23D 19.0	8 14.2
3 Th	20 55 28	14 50 29	2♋00 45	8♋03 10	27 05.5	25 16.8	23 20.8	8 55.8	9 43.4	27 20.9	1 31.9	20 03.2	23 19.1	8 15.7
4 F	20 59 25	15 51 20	14 03 59	20 03 30	26 56.2	26 44.1	24 36.0	9 33.5	9 35.7	27 13.5	1 38.9	20 01.3	23 19.1	8 17.2
5 Sa	21 03 22	16 52 09	26 01 59	1♌59 42	26 44.2	28 12.2	25 51.2	10 11.3	9 28.5	27 06.3	1 45.9	19 59.2	23 19.2	8 18.8
6 Su	21 07 18	17 52 57	7♌56 48	13 53 30	26 30.2	29 41.3	27 06.4	10 49.0	9 21.6	26 59.2	1 52.9	19 57.2	23 19.4	8 20.3
7 M	21 11 15	18 53 43	19 49 56	25 46 15	26 15.2	1♒11.1	28 21.6	11 26.8	9 15.2	26 52.2	1 59.8	19 55.1	23 19.5	8 21.9
8 Tu	21 15 11	19 54 29	1♍42 37	7♍39 11	26 00.6	2 41.9	29 36.7	12 04.5	9 09.2	26 45.3	2 06.8	19 52.9	23 19.7	8 23.5
9 W	21 19 08	20 55 13	13 36 08	19 33 39	25 47.3	4 13.4	0♓51.9	12 42.2	9 03.6	26 38.5	2 13.7	19 50.8	23 20.0	8 25.1
10 Th	21 23 04	21 55 56	25 32 01	1♎31 28	25 36.5	5 45.8	2 07.0	13 19.9	8 58.4	26 31.8	2 20.5	19 48.6	23 20.2	8 26.6
11 F	21 27 01	22 56 38	7♎32 20	13 35 00	25 28.6	7 19.0	3 22.1	13 57.5	8 53.7	26 25.3	2 27.4	19 46.4	23 20.5	8 28.2
12 Sa	21 30 57	23 57 18	19 39 52	25 47 22	25 23.8	8 53.0	4 37.2	14 35.2	8 49.3	26 18.9	2 34.2	19 44.1	23 20.9	8 29.8
13 Su	21 34 54	24 57 58	1♏58 02	8♏12 23	25 21.5	10 27.8	5 52.3	15 12.8	8 45.4	26 12.6	2 41.0	19 41.8	23 21.3	8 31.4
14 M	21 38 51	25 58 37	14 30 57	20 54 20	25 20.9	12 03.6	7 07.4	15 50.4	8 42.0	26 06.4	2 47.8	19 39.5	23 21.7	8 33.1
15 Tu	21 42 47	26 59 14	27 23 04	3♐57 41	25 20.9	13 40.1	8 22.4	16 28.0	8 38.9	26 00.4	2 54.6	19 37.2	23 22.1	8 34.7
16 W	21 46 44	27 59 50	10♐38 41	17 26 28	25 20.0	15 17.5	9 37.5	17 05.6	8 36.3	25 54.6	3 01.3	19 34.8	23 22.6	8 36.3
17 Th	21 50 40	29 00 26	24 21 20	1♑23 27	25 17.2	16 55.8	10 52.5	17 43.1	8 34.1	25 48.8	3 08.0	19 32.5	23 23.1	8 37.9
18 F	21 54 37	0♓01 00	8♑32 47	15 49 06	25 11.8	18 35.0	12 07.5	18 20.6	8 32.4	25 43.3	3 14.6	19 30.0	23 23.7	8 39.6
19 Sa	21 58 33	1 01 32	23 11 58	0♒40 40	25 03.6	20 15.1	13 22.5	18 58.1	8 31.1	25 37.9	3 21.3	19 27.6	23 24.3	8 41.2
20 Su	22 02 30	2 02 04	8♒14 16	15 51 38	24 53.2	21 56.1	14 37.4	19 35.6	8 30.2	25 32.6	3 27.9	19 25.2	23 24.9	8 42.8
21 M	22 06 26	3 02 33	23 31 24	1♓12 07	24 41.7	23 38.0	15 52.4	20 13.0	8D 29.8	25 27.5	3 34.4	19 22.7	23 25.5	8 44.5
22 Tu	22 10 23	4 03 01	8♓52 17	16 30 24	24 30.5	25 20.9	17 07.3	20 50.4	8 29.8	25 22.6	3 40.9	19 20.2	23 26.2	8 46.1
23 W	22 14 20	5 03 28	24 05 03	1♈35 00	24 20.8	27 04.7	18 22.2	21 27.8	8 30.2	25 17.8	3 47.4	19 17.7	23 26.9	8 47.8
24 Th	22 18 16	6 03 52	8♈59 13	16 16 53	24 13.7	28 49.5	19 37.1	22 05.1	8 31.1	25 13.2	3 53.8	19 15.2	23 27.7	8 49.4
25 F	22 22 13	7 04 15	23 27 26	0♉30 34	24 09.3	0♓35.2	20 51.9	22 42.4	8 32.4	25 08.8	4 00.2	19 12.6	23 28.5	8 51.1
26 Sa	22 26 09	8 04 36	7♉26 09	14 14 18	24D 07.4	2 22.0	22 06.7	23 19.7	8 34.1	25 04.5	4 06.6	19 10.1	23 29.3	8 52.7
27 Su	22 30 06	9 04 55	20 55 15	27 29 24	24R 07.2	4 09.7	23 21.5	23 56.9	8 36.2	25 00.5	4 12.9	19 07.5	23 30.1	8 54.4
28 M	22 34 02	10 05 12	3♊57 14	10♊19 18	24 07.3	5 58.4	24 36.3	24 34.1	8 38.8	24 56.6	4 19.2	19 05.0	23 31.0	8 56.0

Astro Data Dy Hr Mn	Planet Ingress Dy Hr Mn	Last Aspect Dy Hr Mn	☽ Ingress Dy Hr Mn	Last Aspect Dy Hr Mn	☽ Ingress Dy Hr Mn	☽ Phases & Eclipses Dy Hr Mn
☿ D 6 18:54	☿ ♐R 1 1:31	1 19:11 ☿ △	♉ 1 20:22	2 3:34 ♀ △	♋ 2 20:01	8 1:40 ○ 17♋57
☽ 0S 13 4:26	☿ ♑ 13 8:21	4 0:14 ♄ △	♊ 4 4:11	5 3:17 ☿ ☍	♌ 5 7:59	16 6:19 ☾ 26♎18
♃☍♄ 17 17:15	♃ ♋R 14 7:26	6 8:58 ☿ ☍	♋ 6 14:11	7 17:51 ♀ ☍	♍ 7 20:33	23 4:58 ● 3♒22
☽ 0N 26 5:17	♀ ♒ 15 21:51	8 22:45 ♄ ☍	♌ 9 1:45	10 2:06 ♃ ⚹	♎ 10 8:57	29 20:49 ☽ 10♉08
	☉ ♒ 19 21:35	11 11:47 ☿ △	♍ 11 14:16	12 13:01 ♃ □	♏ 12 20:11	
♆ D 2 1:14	♂ ♐ 20 8:42	14 0:57 ♄ △	♎ 14 2:44	14 22:12 ☉ □	♐ 15 4:48	6 20:49 ○ 18♌15
☽ 0S 9 11:34	♄ ♒ 21 13:16	16 12:49 ♃ □	♏ 16 13:23	17 7:39 ☉ ⚹	♑ 17 9:39	14 22:12 ☾ 26♏24
⚳ D 21 23:41		18 19:56 ♄ ⚹	♐ 18 20:30	19 3:58 ♃ ☍	♒ 19 10:55	21 15:05 ● 3♓10
☽ 0N 22 16:37	☿ ♒ 6 17:01	20 7:44 ♅ □	♑ 20 23:35	20 23:50 ♆ □	♓ 21 10:07	28 11:31 ☽ 10♊04
♄⚼♅ 26 21:30	♀ ♓ 8 19:26	22 21:51 ♃ ☍	♒ 22 23:41	23 1:59 ♃ △	♈ 23 9:27	
	☉ ♓ 18 11:36	24 12:18 ♆ □	♓ 24 22:47	25 2:54 ♃ □	♉ 25 11:08	
	☿ ♓ 25 4:02	26 20:23 ♃ △	♈ 26 23:09	27 7:28 ♃ ⚹	♊ 27 16:38	
		28 23:07 ♃ □	♉ 29 2:35			
		31 5:31 ♃ ⚹	♊ 31 9:46			

Astro Data

1 January 2050
Julian Day # 54788
SVP 4♓33'26"
GC 27♐32.3 ⚴ 3♈49.5
Eris 0♉15.9R ⚵ 2♍43.4R
⚷ 6♐38.6 ⚶ 16♍34.8
☽ Mean ☊ 27♏57.2

1 February 2050
Julian Day # 54819
SVP 4♓33'21"
GC 27♐32.3 ⚴ 12♈47.7
Eris 0♉15.8 ⚵ 27♌52.9R
⚷ 9♐41.5 ⚶ 16♍02.5R
☽ Mean ☊ 26♏18.7

March 2050 — LONGITUDE

Day	Sid.Time	☉	0 hr ☽	Noon ☽	True ☊	☿	♀	♂	⚳	♃	♄	♅	♆	♇
1 Tu	22 37 59	11♓05 27	16♊36 11	22♊48 31	24♏06.7	7♓48.2	25♓51.1	25♐11.3	8♋41.7	24♋52.9	4♒25.4	19♍02.4	23♉31.9	8♓57.6
2 W	22 41 55	12 05 39	28 56 54	5♋01 56	24R 04.3	9 38.9	27 05.8	25 48.4	8 45.1	24R 49.4	4 31.6	18R 59.8	23 32.9	8 59.3
3 Th	22 45 52	13 05 50	11♋04 13	17 04 18	23 59.4	11 30.6	28 20.5	26 25.5	8 48.9	24 46.0	4 37.7	18 57.2	23 33.9	9 00.9
4 F	22 49 49	14 05 59	23 02 39	28 59 47	23 51.7	13 23.2	29 35.1	27 02.6	8 53.0	24 42.9	4 43.8	18 54.6	23 34.9	9 02.6
5 Sa	22 53 45	15 06 06	4♌56 04	10♌51 54	23 41.5	15 16.8	0♈49.8	27 39.6	8 57.6	24 39.9	4 49.8	18 52.0	23 35.9	9 04.2
6 Su	22 57 42	16 06 10	16 47 37	22 43 28	23 29.4	17 11.2	2 04.4	28 16.6	9 02.6	24 37.2	4 55.8	18 49.4	23 37.0	9 05.9
7 M	23 01 38	17 06 13	28 39 42	4♍36 33	23 16.4	19 06.5	3 18.9	28 53.6	9 07.9	24 34.6	5 01.7	18 46.7	23 38.1	9 07.5
8 Tu	23 05 35	18 06 14	10♍34 10	16 32 43	23 03.6	21 02.5	4 33.5	29 30.5	9 13.6	24 32.2	5 07.6	18 44.1	23 39.2	9 09.1
9 W	23 09 31	19 06 13	22 32 22	28 33 16	22 52.0	22 59.2	5 48.0	0♑07.4	9 19.8	24 30.0	5 13.4	18 41.5	23 40.4	9 10.8
10 Th	23 13 28	20 06 10	4♎35 32	10♎39 21	22 42.6	24 56.4	7 02.5	0 44.3	9 26.2	24 28.0	5 19.2	18 38.9	23 41.6	9 12.4
11 F	23 17 24	21 06 05	16 44 55	22 52 26	22 35.8	26 54.0	8 16.9	1 21.1	9 33.1	24 26.1	5 24.9	18 36.2	23 42.8	9 14.0
12 Sa	23 21 21	22 05 59	29 02 08	5♏14 18	22 31.8	28 51.8	9 31.3	1 57.9	9 40.3	24 24.5	5 30.5	18 33.6	23 44.0	9 15.6
13 Su	23 25 17	23 05 51	11♏29 15	17 47 19	22D 30.3	0♈49.7	10 45.7	2 34.6	9 47.9	24 23.1	5 36.1	18 31.0	23 45.3	9 17.2
14 M	23 29 14	24 05 41	24 08 54	0♐34 23	22 30.4	2 47.3	12 00.1	3 11.3	9 55.8	24 21.8	5 41.7	18 28.4	23 46.6	9 18.8
15 Tu	23 33 11	25 05 29	7♐04 10	13 38 41	22R 31.2	4 44.5	13 14.4	3 48.0	10 04.1	24 20.8	5 47.2	18 25.8	23 47.9	9 20.4
16 W	23 37 07	26 05 16	20 18 18	27 03 21	22 31.7	6 40.9	14 28.8	4 24.6	10 12.7	24 20.0	5 52.6	18 23.2	23 49.3	9 22.0
17 Th	23 41 04	27 05 01	3♑54 09	10♑50 53	22 30.8	8 36.2	15 43.0	5 01.2	10 21.7	24 19.3	5 57.9	18 20.6	23 50.7	9 23.6
18 F	23 45 00	28 04 45	17 53 36	25 02 15	22 27.8	10 30.0	16 57.3	5 37.7	10 31.0	24 18.8	6 03.2	18 18.0	23 52.1	9 25.2
19 Sa	23 48 57	29 04 26	2♒16 36	9♒36 13	22 22.7	12 21.9	18 11.5	6 14.2	10 40.6	24D 18.6	6 08.5	18 15.5	23 53.6	9 26.8
20 Su	23 52 53	0♈04 06	17 00 30	24 28 37	22 15.8	14 11.4	19 25.7	6 50.6	10 50.6	24 18.5	6 13.7	18 12.9	23 55.0	9 28.3
21 M	23 56 50	1 03 45	1♓59 37	9♓32 21	22 07.9	15 58.2	20 39.8	7 26.9	11 00.9	24 18.6	6 18.8	18 10.4	23 56.5	9 29.9
22 Tu	0 00 46	2 03 21	17 05 36	24 38 06	21 59.9	17 41.8	21 54.0	8 03.2	11 11.5	24 18.9	6 23.8	18 07.8	23 58.0	9 31.4
23 W	0 04 43	3 02 55	2♈08 35	9♈35 52	21 53.1	19 21.7	23 08.1	8 39.4	11 22.4	24 19.4	6 28.8	18 05.3	23 59.6	9 33.0
24 Th	0 08 40	4 02 27	16 58 52	24 16 39	21 48.1	20 57.5	24 22.1	9 15.6	11 33.7	24 20.1	6 33.7	18 02.8	24 01.2	9 34.5
25 F	0 12 36	5 01 57	1♉28 29	8♉33 50	21D 45.3	22 28.7	25 36.1	9 51.7	11 45.2	24 21.0	6 38.5	18 00.3	24 02.8	9 36.0
26 Sa	0 16 33	6 01 25	15 32 22	22 23 56	21 44.5	23 54.9	26 50.1	10 27.8	11 57.1	24 22.1	6 43.3	17 57.9	24 04.4	9 37.5
27 Su	0 20 29	7 00 51	29 08 33	5♊46 23	21 45.2	25 15.8	28 04.1	11 03.8	12 09.2	24 23.4	6 48.0	17 55.4	24 06.0	9 39.0
28 M	0 24 26	8 00 14	12♊17 46	18 43 05	21 46.6	26 31.0	29 18.0	11 39.7	12 21.6	24 24.9	6 52.6	17 53.0	24 07.7	9 40.5
29 Tu	0 28 22	8 59 35	25 02 51	1♋17 34	21R 47.8	27 40.2	0♉31.9	12 15.5	12 34.4	24 26.5	6 57.1	17 50.6	24 09.4	9 42.0
30 W	0 32 19	9 58 54	7♋27 51	13 34 18	21 48.0	28 43.1	1 45.7	12 51.3	12 47.4	24 28.4	7 01.6	17 48.2	24 11.1	9 43.5
31 Th	0 36 15	10 58 11	19 37 31	25 38 06	21 46.7	29 39.5	2 59.5	13 27.0	13 00.7	24 30.4	7 06.0	17 45.9	24 12.8	9 44.9

April 2050 — LONGITUDE

Day	Sid.Time	☉	0 hr ☽	Noon ☽	True ☊	☿	♀	♂	⚳	♃	♄	♅	♆	♇
1 F	0 40 12	11♈57 25	1♌36 39	7♌33 44	21♏43.6	0♉29.1	4♉13.2	14♑02.7	13♋14.2	24♋32.6	7♒10.3	17♍43.6	24♉14.6	9♓46.4
2 Sa	0 44 09	12 56 37	13 29 52	19 25 35	21R 38.9	1 11.9	5 26.9	14 38.2	13 28.0	24 35.1	7 14.6	17R 41.3	24 16.4	9 47.8
3 Su	0 48 05	13 55 46	25 21 18	1♍17 28	21 32.8	1 47.6	6 40.6	15 13.8	13 42.1	24 37.6	7 18.7	17 39.0	24 18.2	9 49.2
4 M	0 52 02	14 54 54	7♍14 28	13 12 36	21 26.1	2 16.3	7 54.2	15 49.2	13 56.4	24 40.4	7 22.8	17 36.7	24 20.0	9 50.6
5 Tu	0 55 58	15 53 59	19 12 11	25 13 29	21 19.4	2 37.9	9 07.8	16 24.5	14 11.0	24 43.4	7 26.8	17 34.5	24 21.8	9 52.0
6 W	0 59 55	16 53 02	1♎16 41	7♎21 59	21 13.3	2 52.4	10 21.3	16 59.8	14 25.9	24 46.5	7 30.8	17 32.3	24 23.7	9 53.4
7 Th	1 03 51	17 52 03	13 29 32	19 39 29	21 08.6	2R 59.9	11 34.8	17 35.0	14 40.9	24 49.8	7 34.6	17 30.2	24 25.5	9 54.7
8 F	1 07 48	18 51 02	25 51 56	2♏07 00	21 05.4	3 00.6	12 48.3	18 10.2	14 56.3	24 53.3	7 38.4	17 28.0	24 27.4	9 56.1
9 Sa	1 11 44	19 49 59	8♏24 47	14 45 25	21D 03.9	2 54.7	14 01.7	18 45.2	15 11.8	24 56.9	7 42.1	17 25.9	24 29.3	9 57.4
10 Su	1 15 41	20 48 54	21 08 59	27 35 38	21 03.9	2 42.5	15 15.1	19 20.2	15 27.6	25 00.7	7 45.7	17 23.9	24 31.3	9 58.7
11 M	1 19 37	21 47 47	4♐05 29	10♐38 40	21 04.9	2 24.4	16 28.4	19 55.0	15 43.6	25 04.7	7 49.2	17 21.9	24 33.2	10 00.0
12 Tu	1 23 34	22 46 39	17 15 21	23 55 41	21 06.5	2 00.8	17 41.7	20 29.8	15 59.8	25 08.9	7 52.7	17 19.9	24 35.2	10 01.3
13 W	1 27 31	23 45 29	0♑39 47	7♑27 47	21 08.0	1 32.3	18 54.9	21 04.5	16 16.3	25 13.2	7 56.0	17 17.9	24 37.2	10 02.6
14 Th	1 31 27	24 44 17	14 19 47	21 15 49	21R 08.7	0 59.5	20 08.1	21 39.1	16 33.0	25 17.8	7 59.3	17 16.0	24 39.2	10 03.9
15 F	1 35 24	25 43 03	28 15 52	5♒19 49	21 08.5	0 23.0	21 21.3	22 13.6	16 49.9	25 22.4	8 02.5	17 14.1	24 41.2	10 05.1
16 Sa	1 39 20	26 41 48	12♒27 31	19 38 39	21 07.1	29♈43.7	22 34.4	22 48.0	17 07.0	25 27.3	8 05.6	17 12.3	24 43.2	10 06.3
17 Su	1 43 17	27 40 31	26 52 50	4♓09 34	21 04.7	29 02.3	23 47.5	23 22.3	17 24.3	25 32.2	8 08.6	17 10.5	24 45.3	10 07.5
18 M	1 47 13	28 39 13	11♓28 13	18 48 04	21 01.8	28 19.6	25 00.5	23 56.5	17 41.8	25 37.4	8 11.5	17 08.7	24 47.3	10 08.7
19 Tu	1 51 10	29 37 52	26 08 22	3♈28 14	20 58.8	27 36.4	26 13.5	24 30.6	17 59.5	25 42.7	8 14.3	17 07.0	24 49.4	10 09.9
20 W	1 55 06	0♉36 30	10♈46 50	18 03 17	20 56.2	26 53.5	27 26.5	25 04.6	18 17.4	25 48.2	8 17.1	17 05.3	24 51.5	10 11.0
21 Th	1 59 03	1 35 06	25 16 48	2♉26 36	20 54.5	26 11.8	28 39.4	25 38.4	18 35.5	25 53.8	8 19.7	17 03.6	24 53.6	10 12.2
22 F	2 03 00	2 33 40	9♉32 03	16 32 36	20D 53.7	25 31.8	29 52.2	26 12.1	18 53.8	25 59.6	8 22.3	17 02.0	24 55.7	10 13.3
23 Sa	2 06 56	3 32 12	23 27 50	0♊17 27	20 53.9	24 54.3	1♊05.0	26 45.7	19 12.3	26 05.6	8 24.7	17 00.5	24 57.8	10 14.4
24 Su	2 10 53	4 30 43	7♊01 17	13 39 20	20 54.7	24 19.8	2 17.8	27 19.1	19 30.9	26 11.6	8 27.1	16 58.9	24 59.9	10 15.5
25 M	2 14 49	5 29 11	20 11 40	26 38 28	20 56.0	23 48.9	3 30.5	27 52.5	19 49.8	26 17.9	8 29.4	16 57.5	25 02.1	10 16.5
26 Tu	2 18 46	6 27 37	3♋00 02	9♋16 45	20 57.2	23 21.9	4 43.2	28 25.7	20 08.8	26 24.3	8 31.6	16 56.1	25 04.2	10 17.6
27 W	2 22 42	7 26 01	15 29 01	21 37 21	20 58.2	22 59.1	5 55.8	28 58.7	20 28.0	26 30.8	8 33.7	16 54.7	25 06.4	10 18.6
28 Th	2 26 39	8 24 23	27 42 15	3♌44 18	20R 58.8	22 40.9	7 08.3	29 31.6	20 47.4	26 37.5	8 35.7	16 53.3	25 08.5	10 19.6
29 F	2 30 35	9 22 42	9♌44 02	15 42 04	20 58.7	22 27.4	8 20.8	0♒04.4	21 06.9	26 44.3	8 37.6	16 52.1	25 10.7	10 20.6
30 Sa	2 34 32	10 21 00	21 38 57	27 35 16	20 58.2	22 18.6	9 33.3	0 37.0	21 26.6	26 51.3	8 39.4	16 50.8	25 12.9	10 21.5

Astro Data

	Dy Hr Mn
♀0N	7 1:16
☽0S	8 17:57
☿0N	13 21:04
♃□♇	15 15:25
♃ D	20 9:08
☉0N	20 10:20
☽0N	22 3:45
☽0S	5 0:21
☿ R	8 2:28
♃□♇	9 16:58
☽0N	18 12:45

Planet Ingress

	Dy Hr Mn
♀ ♈	4 20:00
♂ ♑	9 7:09
☿ ♈	13 1:53
☉ ♈	20 10:21
♀ ♉	29 1:39
☿ ♉	31 21:31
☿ ♈R	16 2:15
☉ ♉	19 21:03
♀ ♊	22 14:34
♂ ♒	29 8:46

Last Aspect / ☽ Ingress (March)

Last Aspect Dy Hr Mn		☽ Ingress Dy Hr Mn
1 18:36	♀ □	♋ 2 2:04
4 13:20	♀ △	♌ 4 14:02
6 23:50	♂ △	♍ 7 2:42
9 3:56	♃ ⚹	♎ 9 14:53
11 15:03	♃ □	♏ 12 1:52
14 0:25	♃ △	♐ 14 10:56
16 10:09	☉ □	♑ 16 17:11
18 17:26	☉ ⚹	♒ 18 20:15
20 11:06	♆ □	♓ 20 20:49
22 11:29	♃ △	♈ 22 20:34
24 12:10	♀ ☌	♉ 24 21:32
26 15:29	♃ ⚹	♊ 27 1:32
29 4:20	☿ ⚹	♋ 29 9:30
31 20:42	☿ □	♌ 31 20:46

Last Aspect / ☽ Ingress (April)

Last Aspect Dy Hr Mn		☽ Ingress Dy Hr Mn
2 21:50	♆ □	♍ 3 9:24
5 11:00	♃ ⚹	♎ 5 21:28
7 22:03	♃ □	♏ 8 7:57
10 7:11	♃ △	♐ 10 16:27
12 9:47	☉ △	♑ 12 22:49
14 18:58	♃ ☍	♒ 15 2:57
17 3:57	☿ ⚹	♓ 17 5:09
18 23:13	♃ △	♈ 19 6:19
21 2:00	☿ ☌	♉ 21 7:54
23 5:31	♂ △	♊ 23 11:29
25 6:55	☿ ⚹	♋ 25 18:19
28 3:13	♂ ☍	♌ 28 4:33
30 7:11	♆ □	♍ 30 16:53

☽ Phases & Eclipses

Dy Hr Mn	
8 15:24	○ 18♍15
16 10:09	☾ 26♐01
23 0:42	● 2♈35
30 4:19	☽ 9♋40
7 8:13	○ 17♎43
14 18:25	☾ 25♑00
21 10:27	● 1♉31
28 22:10	☽ 8♌49

Astro Data

1 March 2050
Julian Day # 54847
SVP 4♓33'17"
GC 27♐32.4 ⚴ 23♈44.3
Eris 0♉24.5 ⚵ 21♌00.2R
⚷ 11♐21.5 ⚶ 9♍56.3R
☽ Mean ☊ 24♏49.7

1 April 2050
Julian Day # 54878
SVP 4♓33'15"
GC 27♐32.5 ⚴ 8♉02.9
Eris 0♉41.6 ⚵ 17♌57.0
⚷ 11♐41.2R ⚶ 3♍20.1R
☽ Mean ☊ 23♏11.2

LONGITUDE May 2050

Day	Sid.Time	☉	0 hr ☽	Noon ☽	True ☊	☿	♀	♂	⚳	♃	♄	♅	♆	♇
1 Su	2 38 29	11♉19 16	3♍31 35	9♍28 26	20♏57.2	22♈14.8	10♊45.7	1♒09.5	21♋46.5	26♋58.4	8♒41.1	16♍49.6	25♉15.1	10♓22.4
2 M	2 42 25	12 17 29	15 26 18	21 25 41	20R 56.1	22D 15.7	11 58.0	1 41.8	22 06.5	27 05.6	8 42.7	16R 48.5	25 17.3	10 23.4
3 Tu	2 46 22	13 15 41	27 27 01	3♎30 41	20 55.0	22 21.5	13 10.3	2 14.0	22 26.6	27 13.0	8 44.2	16 47.4	25 19.5	10 24.3
4 W	2 50 18	14 13 51	9♎37 04	15 46 26	20 54.0	22 32.1	14 22.5	2 46.0	22 46.9	27 20.4	8 45.7	16 46.3	25 21.7	10 25.1
5 Th	2 54 15	15 11 59	21 59 04	28 15 09	20 53.4	22 47.2	15 34.7	3 17.9	23 07.4	27 28.1	8 47.0	16 45.3	25 23.9	10 26.0
6 F	2 58 11	16 10 05	4♏34 51	10♏58 15	20D 53.0	23 07.0	16 46.8	3 49.6	23 28.0	27 35.8	8 48.2	16 44.4	25 26.2	10 26.8
7 Sa	3 02 08	17 08 09	17 25 26	23 56 22	20 53.0	23 31.1	17 58.9	4 21.1	23 48.8	27 43.7	8 49.4	16 43.5	25 28.4	10 27.6
8 Su	3 06 04	18 06 12	0♐31 02	7♐09 20	20 53.1	23 59.5	19 10.9	4 52.5	24 09.7	27 51.7	8 50.4	16 42.6	25 30.6	10 28.4
9 M	3 10 01	19 04 14	13 51 10	20 36 24	20 53.3	24 32.1	20 22.8	5 23.6	24 30.7	27 59.8	8 51.4	16 41.8	25 32.9	10 29.2
10 Tu	3 13 58	20 02 14	27 24 50	4♑16 18	20R 53.4	25 08.6	21 34.7	5 54.6	24 51.9	28 08.1	8 52.2	16 41.1	25 35.1	10 29.9
11 W	3 17 54	21 00 13	11♑10 35	18 07 27	20 53.5	25 49.0	22 46.5	6 25.4	25 13.2	28 16.5	8 52.9	16 40.4	25 37.4	10 30.7
12 Th	3 21 51	21 58 10	25 06 42	2♒08 04	20 53.4	26 33.1	23 58.3	6 56.1	25 34.6	28 25.0	8 53.6	16 39.8	25 39.6	10 31.4
13 F	3 25 47	22 56 06	9♒11 17	16 16 07	20D 53.4	27 20.8	25 10.0	7 26.5	25 56.2	28 33.6	8 54.2	16 39.2	25 41.9	10 32.0
14 Sa	3 29 44	23 54 01	23 22 15	0♓29 25	20 53.4	28 11.9	26 21.6	7 56.7	26 17.8	28 42.3	8 54.6	16 38.6	25 44.1	10 32.7
15 Su	3 33 40	24 51 54	7♓37 16	14 45 30	20 53.5	29 06.3	27 33.2	8 26.6	26 39.7	28 51.1	8 55.0	16 38.1	25 46.4	10 33.3
16 M	3 37 37	25 49 46	21 53 45	29 01 37	20 53.9	0♉03.9	28 44.7	8 56.4	27 01.6	29 00.1	8 55.2	16 37.7	25 48.6	10 33.9
17 Tu	3 41 33	26 47 37	6♈08 44	13♈14 39	20 54.4	1 04.6	29 56.2	9 25.9	27 23.7	29 09.1	8 55.4	16 37.3	25 50.9	10 34.5
18 W	3 45 30	27 45 27	20 18 58	27 21 14	20 54.9	2 08.3	1♋07.6	9 55.2	27 45.8	29 18.3	8R 55.4	16 37.0	25 53.1	10 35.1
19 Th	3 49 27	28 43 16	4♉21 03	11♉17 59	20R 55.3	3 15.0	2 18.9	10 24.2	28 08.1	29 27.6	8 55.4	16 36.7	25 55.4	10 35.6
20 F	3 53 23	29 41 03	18 11 40	25 01 45	20 55.4	4 24.4	3 30.2	10 53.0	28 30.6	29 37.0	8 55.3	16 36.5	25 57.6	10 36.1
21 Sa	3 57 20	0♊38 50	1♊47 56	8♊29 58	20 55.0	5 36.6	4 41.4	11 21.6	28 53.1	29 46.5	8 55.0	16 36.3	25 59.9	10 36.6
22 Su	4 01 16	1 36 34	15 07 41	21 40 58	20 54.1	6 51.6	5 52.6	11 49.8	29 15.7	29 56.0	8 54.7	16 36.2	26 02.1	10 37.1
23 M	4 05 13	2 34 18	28 09 46	4♋34 09	20 52.7	8 09.1	7 03.6	12 17.8	29 38.5	0♌05.7	8 54.3	16D 36.1	26 04.4	10 37.6
24 Tu	4 09 09	3 32 00	10♋54 11	17 10 06	20 51.0	9 29.3	8 14.7	12 45.6	0♌01.4	0 15.5	8 53.7	16 36.1	26 06.6	10 38.0
25 W	4 13 06	4 29 40	23 22 08	29 30 36	20 49.2	10 52.0	9 25.6	13 13.0	0 24.3	0 25.4	8 53.1	16 36.1	26 08.8	10 38.4
26 Th	4 17 02	5 27 19	5♌35 52	11♌38 23	20 47.7	12 17.2	10 36.4	13 40.1	0 47.4	0 35.4	8 52.4	16 36.2	26 11.1	10 38.8
27 F	4 20 59	6 24 56	17 38 37	23 37 04	20 46.5	13 44.9	11 47.2	14 07.0	1 10.6	0 45.5	8 51.6	16 36.4	26 13.3	10 39.1
28 Sa	4 24 56	7 22 32	29 34 17	5♍30 50	20D 46.0	15 15.1	12 57.9	14 33.6	1 33.8	0 55.6	8 50.7	16 36.6	26 15.5	10 39.4
29 Su	4 28 52	8 20 07	11♍27 18	17 24 15	20 46.3	16 47.7	14 08.6	14 59.8	1 57.2	1 05.9	8 49.6	16 36.9	26 17.7	10 39.7
30 M	4 32 49	9 17 40	23 22 17	29 21 59	20 47.2	18 22.8	15 19.1	15 25.7	2 20.6	1 16.2	8 48.5	16 37.2	26 20.0	10 40.0
31 Tu	4 36 45	10 15 12	5♎23 54	11♎28 35	20 48.6	20 00.3	16 29.6	15 51.4	2 44.2	1 26.7	8 47.3	16 37.5	26 22.2	10 40.3

LONGITUDE June 2050

Day	Sid.Time	☉	0 hr ☽	Noon ☽	True ☊	☿	♀	♂	⚳	♃	♄	♅	♆	♇
1 W	4 40 42	11♊12 42	17♎36 33	23♎48 15	20♏50.1	21♉40.3	17♋40.0	16♒16.6	3♌07.8	1♌37.2	8♒46.1	16♍37.9	26♉24.4	10♓40.5
2 Th	4 44 38	12 10 12	0♏04 07	6♏24 28	20 51.3	23 22.6	18 50.3	16 41.6	3 31.6	1 47.8	8R 44.7	16 38.4	26 26.5	10 40.7
3 F	4 48 35	13 07 40	12 49 35	19 19 42	20R 51.9	25 07.4	20 00.5	17 06.2	3 55.4	1 58.5	8 43.2	16 38.9	26 28.7	10 40.9
4 Sa	4 52 31	14 05 07	25 54 52	2♐35 09	20 51.5	26 54.6	21 10.6	17 30.5	4 19.3	2 09.2	8 41.6	16 39.5	26 30.9	10 41.0
5 Su	4 56 28	15 02 33	9♐20 25	16 10 29	20 49.9	28 44.2	22 20.6	17 54.3	4 43.3	2 20.1	8 40.0	16 40.2	26 33.1	10 41.2
6 M	5 00 25	15 59 58	23 05 03	0♑03 44	20 47.3	0♊36.1	23 30.6	18 17.9	5 07.4	2 31.0	8 38.2	16 40.8	26 35.2	10 41.3
7 Tu	5 04 21	16 57 22	7♑06 04	14 11 30	20 43.8	2 30.3	24 40.4	18 41.0	5 31.5	2 42.0	8 36.4	16 41.6	26 37.4	10 41.3
8 W	5 08 18	17 54 46	21 19 25	28 29 14	20 40.1	4 26.8	25 50.2	19 03.8	5 55.8	2 53.1	8 34.5	16 42.4	26 39.5	10 41.4
9 Th	5 12 14	18 52 09	5♒40 17	12♒51 57	20 36.6	6 25.5	26 59.8	19 26.1	6 20.1	3 04.2	8 32.5	16 43.2	26 41.6	10R 41.4
10 F	5 16 11	19 49 31	20 03 39	27 14 51	20 33.9	8 26.3	28 09.4	19 48.0	6 44.5	3 15.4	8 30.4	16 44.1	26 43.7	10 41.5
11 Sa	5 20 07	20 46 53	4♓25 02	11♓33 49	20D 32.3	10 29.1	29 18.9	20 09.5	7 09.0	3 26.7	8 28.2	16 45.0	26 45.8	10 41.4
12 Su	5 24 04	21 44 14	18 40 51	25 45 49	20 32.1	12 33.7	0♌28.2	20 30.6	7 33.5	3 38.1	8 25.9	16 46.0	26 47.9	10 41.4
13 M	5 28 00	22 41 35	2♈48 32	9♈48 49	20 32.9	14 40.0	1 37.5	20 51.2	7 58.1	3 49.5	8 23.6	16 47.1	26 50.0	10 41.3
14 Tu	5 31 57	23 38 55	16 46 32	23 41 37	20 34.3	16 47.9	2 46.7	21 11.3	8 22.8	4 01.0	8 21.1	16 48.2	26 52.1	10 41.2
15 W	5 35 54	24 36 16	0♉33 57	7♉23 31	20R 35.7	18 57.1	3 55.8	21 30.9	8 47.6	4 12.5	8 18.6	16 49.3	26 54.1	10 41.1
16 Th	5 39 50	25 33 35	14 10 15	20 54 04	20 36.2	21 07.3	5 04.8	21 50.1	9 12.5	4 24.2	8 16.0	16 50.5	26 56.2	10 41.0
17 F	5 43 47	26 30 55	27 34 56	4♊12 47	20 35.4	23 18.3	6 13.6	22 08.7	9 37.4	4 35.9	8 13.3	16 51.8	26 58.2	10 40.8
18 Sa	5 47 43	27 28 13	10♊47 32	17 19 07	20 32.9	25 29.9	7 22.4	22 26.9	10 02.4	4 47.6	8 10.6	16 53.1	27 00.2	10 40.7
19 Su	5 51 40	28 25 32	23 47 29	0♋12 35	20 28.6	27 41.7	8 31.1	22 44.5	10 27.4	4 59.4	8 07.8	16 54.5	27 02.2	10 40.5
20 M	5 55 36	29 22 50	6♋34 23	12 52 54	20 22.8	29 53.5	9 39.6	23 01.5	10 52.6	5 11.3	8 04.9	16 55.9	27 04.2	10 40.2
21 Tu	5 59 33	0♋20 07	19 08 10	25 20 16	20 15.9	2♋05.0	10 48.0	23 18.0	11 17.7	5 23.2	8 01.9	16 57.3	27 06.1	10 40.0
22 W	6 03 29	1 17 24	1♌29 20	7♌35 33	20 08.7	4 15.9	11 56.4	23 34.0	11 43.0	5 35.2	7 58.8	16 58.8	27 08.1	10 39.7
23 Th	6 07 26	2 14 40	13 39 09	19 40 26	20 01.9	6 26.1	13 04.5	23 49.4	12 08.3	5 47.2	7 55.7	17 00.4	27 10.0	10 39.4
24 F	6 11 23	3 11 55	25 39 43	1♍37 25	19 56.2	8 35.2	14 12.6	24 04.2	12 33.7	5 59.3	7 52.5	17 02.0	27 11.9	10 39.1
25 Sa	6 15 19	4 09 10	7♍33 59	13 29 54	19 52.2	10 43.1	15 20.5	24 18.4	12 59.1	6 11.5	7 49.2	17 03.6	27 13.8	10 38.7
26 Su	6 19 16	5 06 25	19 25 41	25 21 55	19D 49.9	12 49.6	16 28.3	24 32.0	13 24.6	6 23.7	7 45.9	17 05.3	27 15.7	10 38.4
27 M	6 23 12	6 03 38	1♎19 11	7♎18 06	19 49.4	14 54.5	17 36.0	24 45.0	13 50.2	6 35.9	7 42.5	17 07.1	27 17.5	10 38.0
28 Tu	6 27 09	7 00 51	13 19 17	19 23 23	19 50.1	16 57.8	18 43.5	24 57.4	14 15.8	6 48.2	7 39.0	17 08.9	27 19.4	10 37.6
29 W	6 31 05	7 58 04	25 31 00	1♏42 44	19 51.3	18 59.3	19 50.9	25 09.1	14 41.4	7 00.5	7 35.5	17 10.7	27 21.2	10 37.1
30 Th	6 35 02	8 55 17	7♏59 10	14 20 49	19R 52.3	20 59.0	20 58.1	25 20.2	15 07.2	7 12.9	7 31.9	17 12.6	27 23.0	10 36.7

Astro Data

	Dy Hr Mn
☿ D	1 19:12
☽ 0S	2 7:31
☽ 0N	15 19:25
♄ R	18 14:30
♅ D	24 4:15
☽ 0S	29 15:41
♃∠♅	1 13:49
♇ R	10 10:01
☽ 0N	12 1:10
☽ 0S	26 0:20

Planet Ingress

	Dy Hr Mn
☿ ♉	16 10:25
♀ ♋	17 13:17
☉ ♊	20 19:52
♃ ♌	22 21:49
⚳ ♌	24 10:35
☿ ♊	6 4:19
♀ ♌	12 2:14
☿ ♋	20 13:11
☉ ♋	21 3:34

Last Aspect / ☽ Ingress (May)

Last Aspect Dy Hr Mn		☽ Ingress Dy Hr Mn
2 23:24 ♃ ⚹	♎	3 5:03
5 10:29 ♃ □	♏	5 15:20
7 19:00 ♃ △	♐	7 23:04
9 19:15 ☿ △	♑	10 4:32
12 5:35 ♃ ☍	♒	12 8:22
14 7:53 ☿ ⚹	♓	14 11:10
16 11:57 ♃ △	♈	16 13:38
18 15:23 ♃ □	♉	18 16:32
20 20:13 ♃ ⚹	♊	20 20:48
22 2:41 ♅ □	♋	23 3:26
25 5:24 ☿ ⚹	♌	25 12:58
27 17:16 ♆ □	♍	28 0:52
30 5:55 ♆ △	♎	30 13:16

Last Aspect / ☽ Ingress (June)

Last Aspect Dy Hr Mn		☽ Ingress Dy Hr Mn
31 22:52 ♀ □	♏	1 23:52
4 1:03 ♆ ☍	♐	4 7:22
5 15:06 ♂ ⚹	♑	6 11:54
8 8:56 ☿ △	♒	8 14:32
10 11:08 ♆ □	♓	10 16:36
12 13:46 ♆ ⚹	♈	12 19:12
14 11:55 ☉ ⚹	♉	14 23:01
16 22:52 ♆ ☌	♊	17 4:22
19 8:23 ☉ ☌	♋	19 11:36
21 15:27 ♆ ⚹	♌	21 21:05
24 3:04 ♆ □	♍	24 8:44
26 15:50 ♆ △	♎	26 21:21
28 23:05 ♂ △	♏	29 8:42

☽ Phases & Eclipses

Dy Hr Mn	
6 22:27	○ 16♏35
6 22:32	• T 1.077
14 0:05	☾ 23♒25
20 20:52	● 0♊02
20 20:42:51	● AT00'21"
28 16:06	☽ 7♍32
5 9:52	○ 14♐57
12 4:41	☾ 21♓27
19 8:23	● 28♊17
27 9:18	☽ 5♎57

Astro Data

1 May 2050
Julian Day # 54908
SVP 4♓33'12"
GC 27♐32.5 ⚴ 23♉31.5
Eris 1♉01.4 ⚵ 21♌00.6
⚷ 10♐32.2R ⚶ 3♍18.9
☽ Mean ☊ 21♏35.9

1 June 2050
Julian Day # 54939
SVP 4♓33'08"
GC 27♐32.6 ⚴ 10♊46.5
Eris 1♉20.1 ⚵ 28♌19.0
⚷ 8♐26.6R ⚶ 9♍44.5
☽ Mean ☊ 19♏57.4

July 2050 LONGITUDE

Day	Sid.Time	☉	0 hr ☽	Noon ☽	True ☊	☿	♀	♂	⚳	♃	♄	♅	♆	♇
1 F	6 38 58	9♋52 29	20♏48 07	27♏21 25	19♏52.1	22♋56.7	22♌05.2	25♒30.7	15♌32.9	7♌25.3	7♒28.3	17♍14.5	27♉24.8	10♓36.2
2 Sa	6 42 55	10 49 40	4♐01 00	10♐46 59	19R 50.2	24 52.5	23 12.1	25 40.5	15 58.8	7 37.8	7R 24.6	17 16.5	27 26.5	10R 35.7
3 Su	6 46 52	11 46 52	17 39 20	24 37 55	19 46.2	26 46.2	24 18.9	25 49.6	16 24.6	7 50.3	7 20.8	17 18.5	27 28.3	10 35.2
4 M	6 50 48	12 44 03	1♑42 22	8♑52 11	19 40.2	28 38.0	25 25.5	25 58.0	16 50.5	8 02.8	7 17.0	17 20.6	27 30.0	10 34.6
5 Tu	6 54 45	13 41 14	16 06 43	23 25 09	19 32.6	0♌27.7	26 31.9	26 05.8	17 16.5	8 15.4	7 13.2	17 22.7	27 31.7	10 34.1
6 W	6 58 41	14 38 26	0♒46 33	8♒09 57	19 24.4	2 15.4	27 38.2	26 12.8	17 42.5	8 28.0	7 09.3	17 24.9	27 33.3	10 33.5
7 Th	7 02 38	15 35 37	15 34 17	22 58 32	19 16.4	4 01.0	28 44.3	26 19.1	18 08.6	8 40.7	7 05.3	17 27.1	27 35.0	10 32.9
8 F	7 06 34	16 32 49	0♓21 43	7♓42 57	19 09.9	5 44.6	29 50.2	26 24.7	18 34.7	8 53.4	7 01.3	17 29.3	27 36.6	10 32.2
9 Sa	7 10 31	17 30 01	15 01 27	22 16 35	19 05.2	7 26.2	0♍55.9	26 29.5	19 00.9	9 06.1	6 57.3	17 31.6	27 38.2	10 31.6
10 Su	7 14 27	18 27 13	29 27 53	6♈35 00	19D 02.8	9 05.7	2 01.5	26 33.6	19 27.1	9 18.9	6 53.2	17 33.9	27 39.8	10 30.9
11 M	7 18 24	19 24 26	13♈37 42	20 35 57	19 02.2	10 43.1	3 06.8	26 36.9	19 53.3	9 31.7	6 49.1	17 36.3	27 41.4	10 30.2
12 Tu	7 22 21	20 21 39	27 29 43	4♉19 09	19 02.7	12 18.5	4 12.0	26 39.4	20 19.6	9 44.5	6 44.9	17 38.7	27 42.9	10 29.5
13 W	7 26 17	21 18 53	11♉04 22	17 45 36	19R 03.2	13 51.8	5 17.0	26 41.2	20 45.9	9 57.4	6 40.7	17 41.1	27 44.4	10 28.8
14 Th	7 30 14	22 16 07	24 23 03	0♊56 56	19 02.6	15 23.1	6 21.8	26R 42.2	21 12.3	10 10.2	6 36.5	17 43.6	27 45.9	10 28.0
15 F	7 34 10	23 13 22	7♊27 28	13 54 52	19 00.0	16 52.2	7 26.4	26 42.4	21 38.8	10 23.2	6 32.2	17 46.1	27 47.4	10 27.3
16 Sa	7 38 07	24 10 38	20 19 16	26 40 52	18 54.8	18 19.3	8 30.8	26 41.8	22 05.2	10 36.1	6 28.0	17 48.7	27 48.8	10 26.5
17 Su	7 42 03	25 07 54	2♋59 45	9♋16 03	18 47.0	19 44.3	9 35.0	26 40.4	22 31.7	10 49.1	6 23.6	17 51.3	27 50.2	10 25.7
18 M	7 46 00	26 05 10	15 29 49	21 41 10	18 36.8	21 07.1	10 38.9	26 38.3	22 58.3	11 02.1	6 19.3	17 53.9	27 51.6	10 24.9
19 Tu	7 49 57	27 02 27	27 50 10	3♌56 53	18 25.0	22 27.6	11 42.7	26 35.3	23 24.9	11 15.1	6 14.9	17 56.6	27 53.0	10 24.0
20 W	7 53 53	27 59 44	10♌01 25	16 03 55	18 12.6	23 46.0	12 46.2	26 31.6	23 51.5	11 28.1	6 10.5	17 59.3	27 54.3	10 23.2
21 Th	7 57 50	28 57 02	22 04 31	28 03 24	18 00.6	25 02.1	13 49.4	26 27.2	24 18.1	11 41.2	6 06.1	18 02.1	27 55.6	10 22.3
22 F	8 01 46	29 54 19	4♍00 49	9♍57 04	17 50.1	26 15.8	14 52.4	26 21.9	24 44.8	11 54.2	6 01.7	18 04.9	27 56.9	10 21.4
23 Sa	8 05 43	0♌51 38	15 52 27	21 47 22	17 41.8	27 27.1	15 55.2	26 16.0	25 11.6	12 07.3	5 57.3	18 07.7	27 58.1	10 20.5
24 Su	8 09 39	1 48 56	27 42 15	3♎37 35	17 36.0	28 35.9	16 57.7	26 09.3	25 38.3	12 20.4	5 52.8	18 10.6	27 59.3	10 19.6
25 M	8 13 36	2 46 15	9♎33 54	15 31 46	17 32.8	29 42.2	17 59.9	26 01.9	26 05.1	12 33.6	5 48.4	18 13.5	28 00.5	10 18.6
26 Tu	8 17 32	3 43 34	21 31 47	27 34 35	17D 31.6	0♍45.9	19 01.8	25 53.8	26 31.9	12 46.7	5 43.9	18 16.4	28 01.7	10 17.7
27 W	8 21 29	4 40 54	3♏40 50	9♏51 09	17R 31.5	1 46.7	20 03.4	25 45.0	26 58.8	12 59.8	5 39.4	18 19.3	28 02.8	10 16.7
28 Th	8 25 25	5 38 15	16 06 14	22 26 40	17 31.5	2 44.7	21 04.8	25 35.6	27 25.7	13 13.0	5 35.0	18 22.3	28 03.9	10 15.7
29 F	8 29 22	6 35 35	28 53 04	5♐25 55	17 30.5	3 39.8	22 05.8	25 25.5	27 52.6	13 26.2	5 30.5	18 25.4	28 05.0	10 14.7
30 Sa	8 33 19	7 32 57	12♐05 38	18 52 33	17 27.6	4 31.7	23 06.5	25 14.9	28 19.5	13 39.4	5 26.1	18 28.4	28 06.1	10 13.7
31 Su	8 37 15	8 30 18	25 46 47	2♑48 20	17 22.2	5 20.4	24 06.9	25 03.6	28 46.5	13 52.5	5 21.6	18 31.5	28 07.1	10 12.6

August 2050 LONGITUDE

Day	Sid.Time	☉	0 hr ☽	Noon ☽	True ☊	☿	♀	♂	⚳	♃	♄	♅	♆	♇
1 M	8 41 12	9♌27 41	9♑56 58	17♑12 15	17♏14.2	6♍05.7	25♍06.9	24♒51.8	29♌13.5	14♌05.7	5♒17.2	18♍34.6	28♉08.1	10♓11.6
2 Tu	8 45 08	10 25 04	24 33 31	1♒59 55	17R 04.4	6 47.4	26 06.6	24R 39.5	29 40.5	14 18.9	5R 12.7	18 37.7	28 09.0	10R 10.6
3 W	8 49 05	11 22 28	9♒30 23	17 03 42	16 53.5	7 25.4	27 05.9	24 26.7	0♍07.6	14 32.2	5 08.3	18 40.9	28 10.0	10 09.5
4 Th	8 53 01	12 19 53	24 38 34	2♓13 38	16 43.0	7 59.5	28 04.9	24 13.4	0 34.6	14 45.4	5 03.9	18 44.1	28 10.9	10 08.4
5 F	8 56 58	13 17 18	9♓47 37	17 19 14	16 34.0	8 29.5	29 03.4	23 59.7	1 01.7	14 58.6	4 59.5	18 47.3	28 11.7	10 07.3
6 Sa	9 00 55	14 14 45	24 47 26	2♈11 15	16 27.4	8 55.2	0♎01.6	23 45.5	1 28.9	15 11.8	4 55.1	18 50.6	28 12.6	10 06.2
7 Su	9 04 51	15 12 13	9♈30 00	16 43 09	16 23.4	9 16.4	0 59.3	23 31.0	1 56.0	15 25.0	4 50.7	18 53.9	28 13.4	10 05.1
8 M	9 08 48	16 09 43	23 50 22	0♉51 31	16 21.6	9 32.9	1 56.7	23 16.2	2 23.2	15 38.2	4 46.4	18 57.2	28 14.1	10 03.9
9 Tu	9 12 44	17 07 14	7♉46 37	14 35 49	16 21.3	9 44.6	2 53.6	23 01.1	2 50.4	15 51.4	4 42.1	19 00.5	28 14.9	10 02.8
10 W	9 16 41	18 04 46	21 19 23	27 57 36	16 21.2	9R 51.2	3 50.1	22 45.7	3 17.6	16 04.7	4 37.8	19 03.9	28 15.6	10 01.7
11 Th	9 20 37	19 02 20	4♊30 53	10♊59 36	16 20.0	9 52.6	4 46.1	22 30.1	3 44.8	16 17.9	4 33.5	19 07.2	28 16.3	10 00.5
12 F	9 24 34	19 59 55	17 24 09	23 44 57	16 16.8	9 48.7	5 41.6	22 14.3	4 12.1	16 31.1	4 29.3	19 10.6	28 16.9	9 59.3
13 Sa	9 28 30	20 57 31	0♋02 22	6♋16 44	16 10.9	9 39.3	6 36.7	21 58.5	4 39.4	16 44.3	4 25.1	19 14.1	28 17.6	9 58.2
14 Su	9 32 27	21 55 09	12 28 23	18 37 36	16 02.1	9 24.4	7 31.2	21 42.5	5 06.7	16 57.5	4 20.9	19 17.5	28 18.1	9 57.0
15 M	9 36 24	22 52 48	24 44 36	0♌49 38	15 50.8	9 04.0	8 25.3	21 26.6	5 34.0	17 10.7	4 16.8	19 21.0	28 18.7	9 55.8
16 Tu	9 40 20	23 50 29	6♌52 51	12 54 27	15 37.7	8 38.1	9 18.8	21 10.7	6 01.3	17 23.9	4 12.7	19 24.5	28 19.2	9 54.6
17 W	9 44 17	24 48 10	18 54 33	24 53 20	15 23.9	8 07.0	10 11.7	20 54.9	6 28.7	17 37.0	4 08.7	19 28.0	28 19.7	9 53.4
18 Th	9 48 13	25 45 53	0♍50 57	6♍47 32	15 10.5	7 31.0	11 04.0	20 39.2	6 56.1	17 50.2	4 04.7	19 31.5	28 20.2	9 52.1
19 F	9 52 10	26 43 37	12 43 18	18 38 27	14 58.6	6 50.3	11 55.8	20 23.7	7 23.5	18 03.3	4 00.7	19 35.0	28 20.6	9 50.9
20 Sa	9 56 06	27 41 23	24 33 13	0♎27 53	14 49.1	6 05.6	12 46.9	20 08.4	7 50.9	18 16.5	3 56.8	19 38.6	28 21.0	9 49.7
21 Su	10 00 03	28 39 10	6♎22 48	12 18 19	14 42.3	5 17.4	13 37.3	19 53.4	8 18.3	18 29.6	3 52.9	19 42.2	28 21.3	9 48.5
22 M	10 03 59	29 36 57	18 14 52	24 12 55	14 38.2	4 26.6	14 27.1	19 38.7	8 45.7	18 42.7	3 49.1	19 45.8	28 21.6	9 47.2
23 Tu	10 07 56	0♍34 47	0♏12 57	6♏15 32	14D 36.5	3 33.9	15 16.2	19 24.4	9 13.1	18 55.7	3 45.4	19 49.4	28 21.9	9 46.0
24 W	10 11 52	1 32 37	12 21 15	18 30 43	14 36.3	2 40.4	16 04.5	19 10.6	9 40.6	19 08.8	3 41.7	19 53.0	28 22.2	9 44.7
25 Th	10 15 49	2 30 28	24 44 32	1♐03 21	14R 36.5	1 47.1	16 52.1	18 57.1	10 08.1	19 21.8	3 38.1	19 56.7	28 22.4	9 43.5
26 F	10 19 46	3 28 21	7♐27 44	13 58 17	14 36.1	0 55.2	17 38.8	18 44.2	10 35.5	19 34.9	3 34.5	20 00.3	28 22.6	9 42.2
27 Sa	10 23 42	4 26 15	20 35 30	27 19 48	14 34.1	0 05.7	18 24.8	18 31.8	11 03.0	19 47.8	3 31.0	20 04.0	28 22.7	9 41.0
28 Su	10 27 39	5 24 10	4♑11 29	11♑10 40	14 29.8	29♌19.7	19 09.8	18 19.9	11 30.5	20 00.8	3 27.5	20 07.7	28 22.9	9 39.7
29 M	10 31 35	6 22 07	18 17 21	25 31 16	14 23.2	28 38.3	19 54.0	18 08.6	11 58.0	20 13.8	3 24.2	20 11.4	28 23.0	9 38.4
30 Tu	10 35 32	7 20 05	2♒51 56	10♒18 40	14 14.7	28 02.5	20 37.3	17 57.9	12 25.5	20 26.7	3 20.8	20 15.1	28 23.0	9 37.2
31 W	10 39 28	8 18 04	17 50 31	25 26 20	14 05.1	27 33.0	21 19.5	17 47.9	12 53.1	20 39.6	3 17.6	20 18.8	28R 23.0	9 35.9

Astro Data	Dy Hr Mn
♃☍♄	1 16:25
☽0N	9 7:56
♂R	15 6:03
♃⚻♇	15 19:12
☽0S	23 8:36
♀0S	4 22:01
☽0N	5 16:47
☿R	11 6:23
♄⚼♅	14 22:46
☽0S	19 15:48
♃⚺♅	29 5:48
♆R	31 16:37

Planet Ingress	Dy Hr Mn
☿ ♌	5 5:54
♀ ♍	8 15:35
☉ ♌	22 14:23
☿ ♍	25 18:36
⚳ ♍	3 5:17
♀ ♎	6 11:21
☉ ♍	22 21:34
☿ ♌R	27 14:52

Last Aspect Dy Hr Mn		☽ Ingress	Dy Hr Mn
1 12:06	♆ ☍	♐	1 16:47
3 14:03	♂ ⚹	♑	3 21:07
5 18:43	♆ △	♒	5 22:44
7 22:07	♀ ☍	♓	7 23:25
9 20:57	♆ ⚹	♈	10 0:54
11 22:30	♂ ⚹	♉	12 4:23
14 6:09	♆ ☌	♊	14 10:16
16 12:02	♂ △	♋	16 18:18
19 0:04	♆ ⚹	♌	19 4:14
21 11:44	♆ □	♍	21 15:55
24 0:33	♆ △	♎	24 4:39
26 8:43	♂ △	♏	26 16:47
28 22:30	♆ ☍	♐	29 2:04
30 22:56	♂ ⚹	♑	31 7:14

Last Aspect Dy Hr Mn		☽ Ingress	Dy Hr Mn
2 5:48	♆ △	♒	2 8:47
4 5:35	♆ □	♓	4 8:28
6 8:14	♀ ☍	♈	6 8:26
7 23:15	♂ ⚹	♉	8 10:31
10 12:33	♆ ☌	♊	10 15:43
12 9:12	♂ △	♋	12 23:55
15 7:02	♆ ⚹	♌	15 10:22
17 18:55	♆ □	♍	17 22:17
20 7:42	♆ △	♎	20 11:03
22 3:00	♂ △	♏	22 23:34
25 6:55	♆ ☍	♐	25 10:00
27 16:36	☿ △	♑	27 16:42
29 16:42	♆ △	♒	29 19:20
31 16:38	♆ □	♓	31 19:10

☽ Phases & Eclipses Dy Hr Mn	
4 18:52	○ 13♑00
11 9:47	☾ 19♈19
18 21:18	● 26♋27
27 1:07	☽ 4♏15
3 2:22	○ 10♒59
9 16:50	☾ 17♉19
17 11:49	● 24♌48
25 14:58	☽ 2♐38

Astro Data

1 July 2050
Julian Day # 54969
SVP 4♓33'03"
GC 27♐32.7 ⚴ 28♊17.6
Eris 1♉32.4 ⚵ 7♍37.1
⚷ 6♐30.7R ⚶ 19♍59.6
☽ Mean ☊ 18♏22.1

1 August 2050
Julian Day # 55000
SVP 4♓32'57"
GC 27♐32.8 ⚴ 16♋44.7
Eris 1♉36.1R ⚵ 18♍26.3
⚷ 5♐32.7R ⚶ 3♎05.8
☽ Mean ☊ 16♏43.6

LONGITUDE — September 2050

Day	Sid.Time	☉	0 hr ☽	Noon ☽	True ☊	☿	♀	♂	⚳	♃	♄	♅	♆	♇
1 Th	10 43 25	9♍16 05	3♓04 50	10♓44 36	13♏55.7	27♌10.6	22♎00.8	17♒38.5	13♍20.6	20♌52.4	3♒14.4	20♍22.5	28♉23.0	9♓34.6
2 F	10 47 21	10 14 07	18 24 12	26 02 11	13R 47.6	26R 55.9	22 41.0	17R 29.8	13 48.1	21 05.2	3R 11.3	20 26.2	28R 23.0	9R 33.4
3 Sa	10 51 18	11 12 11	3♈37 15	11♈08 12	13 41.7	26D 49.3	23 20.2	17 21.7	14 15.6	21 18.0	3 08.3	20 30.0	28 22.9	9 32.1
4 Su	10 55 15	12 10 17	18 34 04	25 54 03	13 38.3	26 51.2	23 58.2	17 14.4	14 43.2	21 30.8	3 05.3	20 33.7	28 22.8	9 30.8
5 M	10 59 11	13 08 25	3♉07 37	10♉14 24	13D 37.0	27 01.7	24 35.0	17 07.8	15 10.7	21 43.5	3 02.4	20 37.5	28 22.7	9 29.6
6 Tu	11 03 08	14 06 35	17 14 18	24 07 19	13 37.3	27 20.9	25 10.7	17 02.0	15 38.3	21 56.2	2 59.6	20 41.2	28 22.5	9 28.3
7 W	11 07 04	15 04 46	0♊53 38	7♊33 33	13R 38.0	27 48.8	25 45.0	16 56.8	16 05.8	22 08.9	2 56.9	20 45.0	28 22.3	9 27.0
8 Th	11 11 01	16 03 00	14 07 27	20 35 47	13 38.1	28 25.2	26 18.1	16 52.5	16 33.4	22 21.5	2 54.2	20 48.8	28 22.0	9 25.8
9 F	11 14 57	17 01 16	26 59 00	3♋17 38	13 36.7	29 09.7	26 49.8	16 48.9	17 01.0	22 34.1	2 51.6	20 52.5	28 21.8	9 24.5
10 Sa	11 18 54	17 59 34	9♋32 10	15 43 06	13 33.1	0♍02.2	27 20.2	16 46.2	17 28.5	22 46.7	2 49.1	20 56.3	28 21.5	9 23.3
11 Su	11 22 50	18 57 54	21 50 53	27 55 58	13 27.3	1 02.2	27 49.0	16 44.2	17 56.1	22 59.2	2 46.7	21 00.1	28 21.1	9 22.0
12 M	11 26 47	19 56 16	3♌58 45	9♌59 37	13 19.3	2 09.2	28 16.4	16D 43.0	18 23.7	23 11.6	2 44.4	21 03.9	28 20.8	9 20.8
13 Tu	11 30 44	20 54 40	15 58 54	21 56 54	13 09.9	3 22.7	28 42.2	16 42.6	18 51.2	23 24.1	2 42.2	21 07.7	28 20.4	9 19.6
14 W	11 34 40	21 53 06	27 53 53	3♍50 07	12 59.9	4 42.1	29 06.3	16 43.1	19 18.8	23 36.4	2 40.0	21 11.4	28 19.9	9 18.3
15 Th	11 38 37	22 51 34	9♍45 48	15 41 10	12 50.1	6 07.0	29 28.8	16 44.3	19 46.4	23 48.8	2 37.9	21 15.2	28 19.5	9 17.1
16 F	11 42 33	23 50 04	21 36 25	27 31 44	12 41.5	7 36.6	29 49.5	16 46.4	20 13.9	24 01.0	2 36.0	21 19.0	28 19.0	9 15.9
17 Sa	11 46 30	24 48 35	3♎27 21	9♎23 29	12 34.7	9 10.4	0♏08.4	16 49.3	20 41.5	24 13.3	2 34.1	21 22.8	28 18.4	9 14.6
18 Su	11 50 26	25 47 09	15 20 22	21 18 17	12 30.2	10 47.8	0 25.4	16 53.0	21 09.0	24 25.5	2 32.3	21 26.6	28 17.9	9 13.4
19 M	11 54 23	26 45 44	27 17 30	3♏18 23	12D 27.8	12 28.4	0 40.5	16 57.4	21 36.6	24 37.6	2 30.6	21 30.3	28 17.3	9 12.2
20 Tu	11 58 19	27 44 21	9♏21 16	15 26 34	12 27.4	14 11.5	0 53.5	17 02.7	22 04.1	24 49.6	2 29.0	21 34.1	28 16.6	9 11.0
21 W	12 02 16	28 43 00	21 34 42	27 46 09	12 28.3	15 56.6	1 04.5	17 08.8	22 31.7	25 01.7	2 27.4	21 37.9	28 16.0	9 09.9
22 Th	12 06 12	29 41 40	4♐01 22	10♐20 53	12 29.7	17 43.4	1 13.4	17 15.7	22 59.2	25 13.6	2 26.0	21 41.6	28 15.3	9 08.7
23 F	12 10 09	0♎40 22	16 45 10	23 14 43	12R 30.8	19 31.5	1 20.1	17 23.4	23 26.7	25 25.5	2 24.7	21 45.4	28 14.6	9 07.5
24 Sa	12 14 06	1 39 06	29 49 59	6♑31 21	12 31.0	21 20.5	1 24.6	17 31.8	23 54.2	25 37.4	2 23.5	21 49.2	28 13.8	9 06.4
25 Su	12 18 02	2 37 52	13♑19 09	20 13 36	12 29.6	23 10.0	1R 26.7	17 41.0	24 21.7	25 49.1	2 22.3	21 52.9	28 13.1	9 05.2
26 M	12 21 59	3 36 39	27 14 46	4♒22 37	12 26.5	24 59.9	1 26.6	17 50.9	24 49.2	26 00.9	2 21.3	21 56.6	28 12.3	9 04.1
27 Tu	12 25 55	4 35 28	11♒36 51	18 51 04	12 22.1	26 49.9	1 24.0	18 01.5	25 16.7	26 12.5	2 20.3	22 00.3	28 11.4	9 03.0
28 W	12 29 52	5 34 18	26 22 35	3♓52 35	12 16.8	28 39.8	1 19.1	18 12.9	25 44.2	26 24.1	2 19.5	22 04.1	28 10.6	9 01.8
29 Th	12 33 48	6 33 10	11♓26 02	19 01 47	12 11.5	0♎29.5	1 11.8	18 25.0	26 11.6	26 35.6	2 18.7	22 07.8	28 09.7	9 00.7
30 F	12 37 45	7 32 05	26 38 33	4♈15 02	12 06.9	2 18.8	1 02.0	18 37.7	26 39.1	26 47.0	2 18.1	22 11.4	28 08.8	8 59.7

LONGITUDE — October 2050

Day	Sid.Time	☉	0 hr ☽	Noon ☽	True ☊	☿	♀	♂	⚳	♃	♄	♅	♆	♇
1 Sa	12 41 41	8♎31 01	11♈49 56	19♈22 01	12♏03.7	4♎07.6	0♏49.8	18♒51.1	27♍06.5	26♌58.4	2♒17.5	22♍15.1	28♉07.8	8♓58.6
2 Su	12 45 38	9 29 59	26 50 10	4♉13 26	12D 02.1	5 55.9	0R 35.3	19 05.2	27 33.9	27 09.7	2R 17.1	22 18.8	28R 06.8	8R 57.5
3 M	12 49 35	10 29 00	11♉31 00	18 42 19	12 02.0	7 43.5	0 18.4	19 19.9	28 01.3	27 21.0	2 16.7	22 22.4	28 05.8	8 56.5
4 Tu	12 53 31	11 28 03	25 46 57	2♊44 42	12 03.1	9 30.5	29♎59.2	19 35.3	28 28.7	27 32.1	2 16.5	22 26.1	28 04.8	8 55.4
5 W	12 57 28	12 27 08	9♊35 32	16 19 33	12 04.7	11 16.8	29 37.7	19 51.3	28 56.0	27 43.2	2 16.3	22 29.7	28 03.8	8 54.4
6 Th	13 01 24	13 26 15	22 57 00	29 28 12	12 06.1	13 02.3	29 14.2	20 07.9	29 23.4	27 54.2	2D 16.3	22 33.3	28 02.7	8 53.4
7 F	13 05 21	14 25 25	5♋53 36	12♋13 39	12R 06.8	14 47.1	28 48.6	20 25.0	29 50.7	28 05.2	2 16.3	22 36.9	28 01.6	8 52.4
8 Sa	13 09 17	15 24 37	18 28 52	24 39 48	12 06.5	16 31.1	28 21.0	20 42.8	0♎18.1	28 16.0	2 16.5	22 40.5	28 00.5	8 51.4
9 Su	13 13 14	16 23 51	0♌46 59	6♌50 59	12 04.9	18 14.3	27 51.7	21 01.2	0 45.3	28 26.8	2 16.7	22 44.0	27 59.3	8 50.5
10 M	13 17 10	17 23 08	12 52 18	18 51 28	12 02.2	19 56.8	27 20.8	21 20.1	1 12.6	28 37.5	2 17.1	22 47.6	27 58.1	8 49.5
11 Tu	13 21 07	18 22 26	24 48 58	0♍45 15	11 58.7	21 38.5	26 48.4	21 39.6	1 39.9	28 48.1	2 17.5	22 51.1	27 56.9	8 48.6
12 W	13 25 04	19 21 47	6♍40 45	12 35 52	11 54.8	23 19.5	26 14.7	21 59.6	2 07.1	28 58.6	2 18.1	22 54.6	27 55.7	8 47.7
13 Th	13 29 00	20 21 10	18 30 57	24 26 20	11 50.9	24 59.7	25 40.0	22 20.2	2 34.3	29 09.0	2 18.7	22 58.1	27 54.4	8 46.8
14 F	13 32 57	21 20 36	0♎22 20	6♎19 11	11 47.7	26 39.2	25 04.5	22 41.3	3 01.5	29 19.3	2 19.5	23 01.5	27 53.2	8 45.9
15 Sa	13 36 53	22 20 03	12 17 10	18 16 30	11 45.2	28 18.0	24 28.3	23 02.9	3 28.7	29 29.5	2 20.3	23 04.9	27 51.9	8 45.0
16 Su	13 40 50	23 19 33	24 17 25	0♏20 07	11D 43.8	29 56.1	23 51.8	23 25.0	3 55.8	29 39.7	2 21.3	23 08.4	27 50.6	8 44.2
17 M	13 44 46	24 19 04	6♏24 48	12 31 41	11 43.4	1♏33.5	23 15.2	23 47.6	4 22.9	29 49.7	2 22.3	23 11.7	27 49.2	8 43.4
18 Tu	13 48 43	25 18 38	18 40 58	24 52 53	11 43.8	3 10.3	22 38.6	24 10.7	4 50.0	29 59.7	2 23.5	23 15.1	27 47.9	8 42.6
19 W	13 52 39	26 18 13	1♐07 39	7♐25 32	11 44.9	4 46.4	22 02.4	24 34.3	5 17.1	0♍09.5	2 24.7	23 18.4	27 46.5	8 41.8
20 Th	13 56 36	27 17 50	13 46 45	20 11 36	11 46.1	6 21.9	21 26.8	24 58.3	5 44.1	0 19.3	2 26.1	23 21.8	27 45.1	8 41.0
21 F	14 00 33	28 17 29	26 40 19	3♑13 10	11 47.3	7 56.8	20 52.0	25 22.8	6 11.1	0 28.9	2 27.5	23 25.0	27 43.7	8 40.3
22 Sa	14 04 29	29 17 10	9♑50 25	16 32 16	11 48.2	9 31.0	20 18.2	25 47.7	6 38.0	0 38.5	2 29.1	23 28.3	27 42.3	8 39.5
23 Su	14 08 26	0♏16 52	23 18 56	0♒10 32	11R 48.5	11 04.7	19 45.7	26 13.0	7 04.9	0 47.9	2 30.8	23 31.5	27 40.8	8 38.8
24 M	14 12 22	1 16 36	7♒07 07	14 08 41	11 48.2	12 37.9	19 14.7	26 38.7	7 31.8	0 57.2	2 32.5	23 34.7	27 39.3	8 38.2
25 Tu	14 16 19	2 16 22	21 15 06	28 26 07	11 47.5	14 10.4	18 45.3	27 04.9	7 58.7	1 06.4	2 34.4	23 37.9	27 37.9	8 37.5
26 W	14 20 15	3 16 09	5♓41 23	13♓00 23	11 46.6	15 42.5	18 17.7	27 31.4	8 25.5	1 15.5	2 36.3	23 41.0	27 36.4	8 36.8
27 Th	14 24 12	4 15 58	20 22 30	27 47 00	11 45.6	17 14.0	17 52.0	27 58.3	8 52.3	1 24.5	2 38.4	23 44.1	27 34.8	8 36.2
28 F	14 28 08	5 15 49	5♈13 01	12♈39 37	11 44.9	18 44.9	17 28.4	28 25.6	9 19.0	1 33.4	2 40.5	23 47.2	27 33.3	8 35.6
29 Sa	14 32 05	6 15 42	20 05 51	27 30 42	11D 44.4	20 15.3	17 07.0	28 53.2	9 45.7	1 42.1	2 42.7	23 50.3	27 31.8	8 35.0
30 Su	14 36 01	7 15 36	4♉53 12	12♉12 28	11 44.3	21 45.2	16 47.9	29 21.2	10 12.4	1 50.7	2 45.1	23 53.3	27 30.2	8 34.5
31 M	14 39 58	8 15 33	19 27 39	26 38 02	11 44.4	23 14.6	16 31.2	29 49.5	10 39.0	1 59.3	2 47.5	23 56.3	27 28.6	8 34.0

Astro Data

	Dy Hr Mn
☽0N	2 3:24
☿D	3 18:44
♂D	13 11:03
☽0S	15 22:00
☉0S	22 19:30
♀R	25 22:22
☽0N	29 14:23
☿0S	1 7:02
♄D	6 12:45
♃□♆	7 4:53
☽0S	13 3:59
☽0N	27 0:03

Planet Ingress

		Dy Hr Mn
☿	♍	10 11:03
♀	♏	17 1:05
☉	♎	22 19:30
☿	♎	29 5:32
♀	♎R	4 11:02
⚳	♎	7 20:08
☿	♏	16 12:58
♃	♍	18 12:47
☉	♏	23 5:13
♂	♓	31 20:51

Last Aspect / ☽ Ingress (September)

Last Aspect Dy Hr Mn			☽ Ingress	Dy Hr Mn
2 15:42	♆	⚹	♈	2 18:16
4 13:35	☿	△	♉	4 18:47
6 19:31	♆	☌	♊	6 22:24
9 3:36	☿	⚹	♋	9 5:43
11 12:50	♆	⚹	♌	11 16:06
14 2:07	♀	⚹	♍	14 4:15
16 13:36	♆	△	♎	16 17:00
18 18:22	♃	⚹	♏	19 5:25
21 13:59	☉	⚹	♐	21 16:18
23 16:03	♃	△	♑	24 0:18
26 1:38	♆	△	♒	26 4:39
28 2:54	♆	□	♓	28 5:49
30 2:23	♆	⚹	♈	30 5:18

Last Aspect / ☽ Ingress (October)

Last Aspect Dy Hr Mn			☽ Ingress	Dy Hr Mn
2 0:23	♃	△	♉	2 5:07
4 3:57	♆	☌	♊	4 7:15
6 11:35	♀	△	♋	6 12:59
8 18:57	♀	□	♌	8 22:27
11 7:59	♃	☌	♍	11 10:28
13 19:00	♆	△	♎	13 23:15
16 11:05	☿	☌	♏	16 11:20
18 17:36	♆	☍	♐	18 21:50
21 2:14	☉	⚹	♑	21 6:07
23 7:40	♆	△	♒	23 11:42
25 10:40	♆	□	♓	25 14:36
27 11:40	♆	⚹	♈	27 15:35
29 14:18	♂	⚹	♉	29 16:02
31 17:34	♂	□	♊	31 17:41

☽ Phases & Eclipses

Dy Hr Mn		
1 9:32	○	9♓10
8 2:52	☾	15♊41
16 3:51	●	23♍30
24 2:35	☽	1♑16
30 17:33	○	7♈46
7 16:33	☾	14♋37
15 20:50	●	22♎42
23 12:12	☽	0♒17
30 3:17	○	6♉54
30 3:22	☍	T 1.054

Astro Data

1 September 2050
Julian Day # 55031
SVP 4♓32'54"
GC 27♐32.8 ⚵ 4♌56.1
Eris 1♉29.7R ⚴ 29♍50.6
⚷ 6♐04.5 ⚶ 17♎47.8
☽ Mean ☊ 15♏05.1

1 October 2050
Julian Day # 55061
SVP 4♓32'52"
GC 27♐32.9 ⚵ 21♌36.7
Eris 1♉15.7R ⚴ 11♎01.5
⚷ 7♐57.6 ⚶ 3♏00.2
☽ Mean ☊ 13♏29.7

November 2050 LONGITUDE

Day	Sid.Time	☉	0 hr ☽	Noon ☽	True ☊	☿	♀	♂	⚳	♃	♄	♅	♆	♇
1 Tu	14 43 55	9♏15 31	3♊43 02	10♊42 13	11♏44.6	24♏43.5	16♎16.9	0♓18.1	11♎05.6	2♍07.6	2♒50.0	23♍59.2	27♉27.1	8♓33.5
2 W	14 47 51	10 15 32	17 35 18	24 22 07	11 44.8	26 11.8	16R 05.1	0 47.1	11 32.1	2 15.9	2 52.6	24 02.1	27R 25.5	8R 33.0
3 Th	14 51 48	11 15 34	1♋02 39	7♋37 02	11R 45.0	27 39.5	15 55.7	1 16.3	11 58.6	2 24.1	2 55.3	24 05.0	27 23.9	8 32.5
4 F	14 55 44	12 15 39	14 05 28	20 28 17	11 45.0	29 06.7	15 48.8	1 45.9	12 25.1	2 32.1	2 58.1	24 07.8	27 22.2	8 32.1
5 Sa	14 59 41	13 15 46	26 45 53	2♌58 44	11D 44.9	0♐33.3	15 44.5	2 15.7	12 51.5	2 40.0	3 01.0	24 10.6	27 20.6	8 31.6
6 Su	15 03 37	14 15 55	9♌07 21	15 12 17	11 44.9	1 59.3	15D 42.5	2 45.9	13 17.8	2 47.7	3 04.0	24 13.4	27 19.0	8 31.2
7 M	15 07 34	15 16 06	21 14 05	27 13 22	11 45.0	3 24.6	15 43.1	3 16.3	13 44.1	2 55.3	3 07.1	24 16.1	27 17.3	8 30.9
8 Tu	15 11 30	16 16 19	3♍10 42	9♍06 40	11 45.3	4 49.2	15 46.0	3 47.0	14 10.4	3 02.8	3 10.2	24 18.8	27 15.7	8 30.5
9 W	15 15 27	17 16 34	15 01 51	20 56 46	11 45.8	6 13.1	15 51.3	4 18.0	14 36.6	3 10.2	3 13.5	24 21.5	27 14.0	8 30.2
10 Th	15 19 24	18 16 50	26 51 58	2♎47 55	11 46.5	7 36.1	15 58.9	4 49.2	15 02.8	3 17.4	3 16.8	24 24.1	27 12.3	8 29.9
11 F	15 23 20	19 17 09	8♎45 05	14 43 53	11 47.3	8 58.3	16 08.8	5 20.7	15 28.9	3 24.5	3 20.3	24 26.7	27 10.7	8 29.6
12 Sa	15 27 17	20 17 30	20 44 42	26 47 50	11 47.9	10 19.5	16 20.9	5 52.5	15 55.0	3 31.4	3 23.8	24 29.2	27 09.0	8 29.4
13 Su	15 31 13	21 17 52	2♏53 36	9♏02 15	11R 48.2	11 39.6	16 35.1	6 24.5	16 21.0	3 38.2	3 27.4	24 31.7	27 07.3	8 29.2
14 M	15 35 10	22 18 17	15 13 57	21 28 52	11 48.1	12 58.4	16 51.4	6 56.7	16 46.9	3 44.8	3 31.1	24 34.1	27 05.6	8 29.0
15 Tu	15 39 06	23 18 43	27 47 07	4♐08 47	11 47.3	14 16.0	17 09.8	7 29.2	17 12.8	3 51.3	3 34.9	24 36.5	27 03.9	8 28.8
16 W	15 43 03	24 19 10	10♐33 54	17 02 27	11 46.0	15 32.0	17 30.0	8 01.9	17 38.6	3 57.6	3 38.7	24 38.9	27 02.2	8 28.6
17 Th	15 46 59	25 19 39	23 34 27	0♑09 50	11 44.2	16 46.4	17 52.2	8 34.8	18 04.4	4 03.8	3 42.7	24 41.2	27 00.5	8 28.5
18 F	15 50 56	26 20 10	6♑48 34	13 30 35	11 42.1	17 58.8	18 16.2	9 08.0	18 30.1	4 09.8	3 46.7	24 43.5	26 58.9	8 28.4
19 Sa	15 54 53	27 20 42	20 15 46	27 04 04	11 40.2	19 09.0	18 42.0	9 41.3	18 55.7	4 15.7	3 50.8	24 45.7	26 57.2	8 28.3
20 Su	15 58 49	28 21 15	3♒55 23	10♒49 37	11 38.8	20 16.8	19 09.5	10 14.9	19 21.3	4 21.4	3 55.0	24 47.9	26 55.5	8 28.3
21 M	16 02 46	29 21 49	17 46 38	24 46 19	11D 38.0	21 21.8	19 38.6	10 48.6	19 46.8	4 26.9	3 59.3	24 50.0	26 53.8	8D 28.3
22 Tu	16 06 42	0♐22 24	1♓48 31	8♓53 03	11 38.2	22 23.6	20 09.3	11 22.6	20 12.2	4 32.3	4 03.6	24 52.1	26 52.1	8 28.3
23 W	16 10 39	1 23 01	15 59 42	23 08 13	11 39.1	23 21.9	20 41.6	11 56.7	20 37.6	4 37.6	4 08.1	24 54.1	26 50.4	8 28.3
24 Th	16 14 35	2 23 38	0♈18 18	7♈29 34	11 40.4	24 16.0	21 15.3	12 31.0	21 02.8	4 42.6	4 12.6	24 56.1	26 48.7	8 28.3
25 F	16 18 32	3 24 17	14 41 37	21 53 58	11 41.8	25 05.5	21 50.4	13 05.5	21 28.1	4 47.5	4 17.1	24 58.1	26 47.0	8 28.4
26 Sa	16 22 28	4 24 57	29 06 06	6♉17 27	11R 42.6	25 49.8	22 27.0	13 40.2	21 53.2	4 52.2	4 21.8	25 00.0	26 45.3	8 28.5
27 Su	16 26 25	5 25 38	13♉27 26	20 35 25	11 42.5	26 28.2	23 04.8	14 15.0	22 18.3	4 56.8	4 26.5	25 01.8	26 43.7	8 28.7
28 M	16 30 22	6 26 21	27 40 48	4♊43 00	11 41.0	26 59.9	23 43.9	14 49.9	22 43.2	5 01.2	4 31.3	25 03.6	26 42.0	8 28.8
29 Tu	16 34 18	7 27 04	11♊41 29	18 35 44	11 38.3	27 24.2	24 24.3	15 25.1	23 08.2	5 05.4	4 36.2	25 05.3	26 40.3	8 29.0
30 W	16 38 15	8 27 49	25 25 23	2♋10 05	11 34.4	27 40.2	25 05.9	16 00.3	23 33.0	5 09.5	4 41.1	25 07.0	26 38.7	8 29.2

December 2050 LONGITUDE

Day	Sid.Time	☉	0 hr ☽	Noon ☽	True ☊	☿	♀	♂	⚳	♃	♄	♅	♆	♇
1 Th	16 42 11	9♐28 36	8♋49 39	15♋23 56	11♏29.8	27♐47.2	25♎48.6	16♓35.7	23♎57.8	5♍13.3	4♒46.1	25♍08.7	26♉37.0	8♓29.4
2 F	16 46 08	10 29 24	21 52 58	28 16 51	11R 25.1	27R 44.4	26 32.4	17 11.3	24 22.4	5 17.0	4 51.2	25 10.3	26R 35.4	8 29.7
3 Sa	16 50 04	11 30 13	4♌35 45	10♌49 59	11 20.9	27 31.1	27 17.2	17 46.9	24 47.0	5 20.6	4 56.4	25 11.8	26 33.8	8 30.0
4 Su	16 54 01	12 31 03	16 59 56	23 06 00	11 17.7	27 06.7	28 03.1	18 22.7	25 11.5	5 23.9	5 01.6	25 13.3	26 32.1	8 30.3
5 M	16 57 58	13 31 55	29 08 44	5♍08 39	11D 15.9	26 31.2	28 49.9	18 58.7	25 35.9	5 27.1	5 06.9	25 14.7	26 30.5	8 30.6
6 Tu	17 01 54	14 32 48	11♍06 22	17 02 28	11 15.5	25 44.6	29 37.7	19 34.7	26 00.3	5 30.0	5 12.2	25 16.1	26 28.9	8 31.0
7 W	17 05 51	15 33 43	22 57 37	28 52 26	11 16.4	24 47.5	0♏26.4	20 10.9	26 24.5	5 32.8	5 17.6	25 17.5	26 27.3	8 31.4
8 Th	17 09 47	16 34 38	4♎47 34	10♎43 39	11 18.0	23 41.0	1 15.9	20 47.2	26 48.6	5 35.4	5 23.1	25 18.7	26 25.8	8 31.8
9 F	17 13 44	17 35 35	16 41 17	22 41 04	11 19.8	22 26.9	2 06.3	21 23.7	27 12.7	5 37.9	5 28.6	25 20.0	26 24.2	8 32.2
10 Sa	17 17 40	18 36 33	28 43 33	4♏49 13	11R 21.1	21 07.2	2 57.5	22 00.2	27 36.6	5 40.1	5 34.2	25 21.1	26 22.7	8 32.7
11 Su	17 21 37	19 37 33	10♏58 31	17 11 50	11 21.1	19 44.6	3 49.4	22 36.8	28 00.5	5 42.1	5 39.9	25 22.2	26 21.1	8 33.2
12 M	17 25 33	20 38 33	23 29 28	29 51 40	11 19.4	18 21.8	4 42.1	23 13.6	28 24.2	5 44.0	5 45.6	25 23.3	26 19.6	8 33.7
13 Tu	17 29 30	21 39 34	6♐18 32	12♐50 08	11 15.7	17 01.7	5 35.5	23 50.5	28 47.9	5 45.6	5 51.4	25 24.3	26 18.1	8 34.2
14 W	17 33 27	22 40 37	19 26 25	26 07 13	11 10.1	15 46.8	6 29.5	24 27.5	29 11.4	5 47.1	5 57.2	25 25.3	26 16.6	8 34.8
15 Th	17 37 23	23 41 40	2♑52 19	9♑41 22	11 03.1	14 39.4	7 24.2	25 04.6	29 34.8	5 48.4	6 03.1	25 26.1	26 15.1	8 35.4
16 F	17 41 20	24 42 43	16 34 02	23 29 49	10 55.4	13 41.1	8 19.6	25 41.7	29 58.2	5 49.5	6 09.0	25 27.0	26 13.7	8 36.0
17 Sa	17 45 16	25 43 47	0♒28 17	7♒28 55	10 48.1	12 53.1	9 15.5	26 19.0	0♏21.4	5 50.4	6 15.0	25 27.8	26 12.3	8 36.6
18 Su	17 49 13	26 44 52	14 31 15	21 34 48	10 42.0	12 15.9	10 12.0	26 56.4	0 44.5	5 51.1	6 21.1	25 28.5	26 10.8	8 37.3
19 M	17 53 09	27 45 57	28 39 08	5♓43 53	10 37.7	11 49.8	11 09.1	27 33.8	1 07.4	5 51.6	6 27.1	25 29.2	26 09.4	8 37.9
20 Tu	17 57 06	28 47 02	12♓48 43	19 53 20	10D 35.5	11D 34.6	12 06.7	28 11.4	1 30.3	5 51.9	6 33.3	25 29.8	26 08.1	8 38.6
21 W	18 01 02	29 48 07	26 57 32	4♈01 07	10 35.2	11 29.8	13 04.9	28 49.0	1 53.0	5R 52.0	6 39.5	25 30.3	26 06.7	8 39.4
22 Th	18 04 59	0♑49 13	11♈03 57	18 05 54	10 36.1	11 34.8	14 03.5	29 26.7	2 15.6	5 51.9	6 45.7	25 30.8	26 05.4	8 40.1
23 F	18 08 56	1 50 19	25 06 51	2♉06 42	10R 37.1	11 48.7	15 02.6	0♈04.5	2 38.1	5 51.6	6 52.0	25 31.2	26 04.1	8 40.9
24 Sa	18 12 52	2 51 25	9♉05 18	16 02 29	10 37.3	12 10.9	16 02.2	0 42.3	3 00.5	5 51.1	6 58.3	25 31.6	26 02.8	8 41.7
25 Su	18 16 49	3 52 31	22 58 04	29 51 50	10 35.5	12 40.5	17 02.3	1 20.2	3 22.7	5 50.5	7 04.7	25 32.0	26 01.5	8 42.5
26 M	18 20 45	4 53 37	6♊43 32	13♊32 51	10 31.3	13 16.8	18 02.8	1 58.2	3 44.8	5 49.6	7 11.1	25 32.2	26 00.3	8 43.4
27 Tu	18 24 42	5 54 44	20 19 31	27 03 13	10 24.5	13 59.1	19 03.7	2 36.3	4 06.8	5 48.5	7 17.6	25 32.4	25 59.0	8 44.2
28 W	18 28 38	6 55 51	3♋43 39	10♋20 33	10 15.4	14 46.7	20 05.0	3 14.3	4 28.6	5 47.3	7 24.1	25 32.6	25 57.8	8 45.1
29 Th	18 32 35	7 56 58	16 53 41	23 22 51	10 04.7	15 39.0	21 06.8	3 52.5	4 50.3	5 45.8	7 30.6	25 32.7	25 56.7	8 46.0
30 F	18 36 31	8 58 06	29 47 56	6♌08 54	9 53.6	16 35.5	22 08.9	4 30.7	5 11.9	5 44.2	7 37.2	25R 32.8	25 55.5	8 47.0
31 Sa	18 40 28	9 59 14	12♌25 47	18 38 41	9 43.0	17 35.7	23 11.4	5 09.0	5 33.3	5 42.4	7 43.8	25 32.7	25 54.4	8 47.9

Astro Data (Dy Hr Mn)

	Dy Hr Mn
♀ D	6 18:46
☽ 0S	9 10:52
♃⚻♄	10 8:31
⚳ 0S	20 0:07
♇ D	21 22:13
☽ 0N	23 7:31
☿ R	1 17:21
☽ 0S	6 19:16
♃⚻♄	12 2:17
☽ 0N	20 13:41
☿ D	21 11:33
♃ R	21 13:18
♂ 0N	24 10:24
♅ R	30 18:45

Planet Ingress (Dy Hr Mn)

	Dy Hr Mn
☿ ♐	5 2:45
☉ ♐	22 3:08
♀ ♏	6 23:03
⚳ ♏	16 13:53
☉ ♑	21 16:40
♂ ♈	23 9:10

Last Aspect / ☽ Ingress (November)

Last Aspect Dy Hr Mn		☽ Ingress Dy Hr Mn
2 11:24	♅ □	♋ 2 22:07
5 1:08	♆ ⚹	♌ 5 6:14
7 12:08	♆ □	♍ 7 17:35
10 0:43	♆ △	♎ 10 6:21
11 14:52	♀ ☌	♏ 12 18:19
14 22:40	♆ ☍	♐ 15 4:11
17 2:00	♅ □	♑ 17 11:42
19 12:32	☉ ⚹	♒ 19 17:09
21 20:27	☉ □	♓ 21 20:55
23 18:11	♆ ⚹	♈ 23 23:29
25 17:37	☿ △	♉ 26 1:30
27 22:22	♆ ☌	♊ 28 3:57
30 3:51	☿ ☍	♋ 30 8:08

Last Aspect / ☽ Ingress (December)

Last Aspect Dy Hr Mn		☽ Ingress Dy Hr Mn
2 8:49	♆ ⚹	♌ 2 15:15
4 22:30	♀ ⚹	♍ 5 1:42
7 7:06	♆ △	♎ 7 14:17
9 11:34	☿ ⚹	♏ 10 2:31
12 5:22	♆ ☍	♐ 12 12:16
14 10:45	♅ □	♑ 14 18:55
16 16:42	♆ △	♒ 16 23:11
18 21:27	☉ ⚹	♓ 19 2:17
21 4:16	☉ □	♈ 21 5:10
22 0:47	☿ △	♉ 23 8:23
25 5:19	♆ ☌	♊ 25 12:14
27 9:18	♅ □	♋ 27 17:17
29 16:46	♆ ⚹	♌ 30 0:23

☽ Phases & Eclipses (Dy Hr Mn)

Dy Hr Mn	
6 9:58	☾ 14♌11
14 13:43	● 22♏23
14 13:30:53	• P 0.887
21 20:27	☽ 29♒43
28 15:11	○ 6♊34
6 6:29	☾ 14♍19
14 5:19	● 22♐24
21 4:16	☽ 29♓28
28 5:17	○ 6♋39

Astro Data

1 November 2050
Julian Day # 55092
SVP 4♓32'49"
GC 27♐33.0 ⚴ 7♍04.8
Eris 0♉57.2R ⚵ 22♎21.0
⚷ 10♐58.6 ⚶ 19♏21.6
☽ Mean ☊ 11♏51.2

1 December 2050
Julian Day # 55122
SVP 4♓32'44"
GC 27♐33.0 ⚴ 19♍18.2
Eris 0♉40.6R ⚵ 2♏39.2
⚷ 14♐28.4 ⚶ 5♐30.7
☽ Mean ☊ 10♏15.9

About Neil F. Michelsen

May 11, 1931—May 15, 1990

Neil F. Michelsen was born and raised in Chicago, Illinois. His birth time is 5:34 am CST. A *magna cum laude* graduate in mathematics from University of Miami, he joined IBM in 1959, and was later transferred to the White Plains headquarters. An iconoclast who was always interested in new ideas, he attended a 1970 astrology workshop by Zipporah Dobyns, Ph.D. and was inspired to program the hand calculations to compute a natal chart on an IBM 1130 computer. This was the beginning that ultimately led to his founding of Astro Computing Services in 1973. The new business, at first operated from his home in Pelham, NY, and later in San Diego, CA, quickly became popular with astrologers everywhere, who could now get charts and many other complex calculations easily and quickly .

In 1976 Neil began ACS Publications by publishing ***The American Ephemeris 1931-1980***, the first in his series of computer generated ephemerides that are his most enduring legacy. As a primary pioneer of computer technology for astrology, Neil set the standards for accuracy. Although he never practiced as an astrologer himself, he became one of the most influential forces in the development of modern astrology by providing the tools that facilitated the work of astrologers worldwide. Highly active in the astrological community, Neil served 12 years as Chairman of National Council for Geocosmic Research, and was a prime mover in bringing about the first United Astrology Congress in 1986.

About Rique Pottenger

Rique Pottenger was born September 16, 1949, in Tucson, Arizona at 6:18 AM. He has a B.S. in Math and Astronomy from the University of Arizona and an M.S. in Computer Science from UCLA. Though never formally trained in astrology, he has absorbed quite a bit of it over the years as he is the eldest son of Zipporah Dobyns, and Maritha Pottenger is his sister. Rique had intended to become a mathematician until he discovered computer programming, and he has now been a programmer for more than 30 years. He has written programs for machines from 8 to 32-bits, running under many different operating systems. From 1984 to 2004, Rique was employed at Astro Computing Services and ACS Publications where he programmed some of the company's most popular interpreted reports. After the death of founder Neil F. Michelsen in 1990, Rique became responsible for maintaining and improving Astro's production programs. This included his taking the major role of implementing Michelsen's wishes to switch from mainframe computers to a modern and faster Windows-based PC network. After designing and programming the new system and recommending new equipment, Rique then trained the staff in how to use the new system. Later, Rique programmed the company's *Electronic Astrologer* software series. He also assumed responsibility for maintaining and improving the ACS Atlas database.

Now semi-retired, Rique continues to do astrological programming for a small list of clients. He lives in Opelika, Alabama with his beloved wife, Zowie Wharton, and their two cats. In their spare time, they work at home-improvement projects (both have lots of Virgo), play computer games on their home network, and do puzzles together.

Books by Neil F. Michelsen

The American Ephemeris 1931-1980
& Book of Tables
The American Ephemeris 1901-1930
The American Ephemeris 1941-1950
The American Ephemeris 1951-1960
The American Ephemeris 1971-1980
The American Ephemeris 1981-1990
The American Ephemeris 1991-2000
The American Ephemeris for the 20th Century
1900 to 2000 at Midnight
The American Ephemeris for the 20th Century
1900 to 2000 at Noon
The American Ephemeris for the 21th Century
1900 to 2050 at Midnight
The American Ephemeris for the 21th Century
1900 to 2050 at Noon
The American Sidereal Ephemeris 1976-2000
*The American Sidereal Ephemeris 2001-2025**
The American Heliocentric Ephemeris 1901-2000
*The American Heliocentric Ephemeris 2001-2050**
The American Midpoint Ephemeris 1986-1990
The American Midpoint Ephemeris 1990-1995
*The American Midpoint Ephemeris 1996-2000**
The American Book of Tables
The Koch Book of Tables
The Uranian Transneptune Ephemeris 1850-2050
Comet Halley Ephemeris 1901-1996
Search for the Christmas Star
(with Maria Kay Simms)
The Asteroid Ephemeris
(with Zip Dobyns and Rique Pottenger)
*Tables of Planetary Phenomena**

* includes posthumous publication

Books by Rique Pottenger

The New American Ephemeris for the 21st Century, 2000-2100 at Midnight:
Michelsen Memorial Edition
The New American Ephemeris 2007-2020: Longitude, Declination, Latitude and Daily Aspectarian
The New American Midpoint Ephemeris 2006-2020
The Asteroid Ephemeris 1900-2050 with Chiron and the Black Moon
(with Zipporah Dobyns, Ph.D. and Neil F. Michelsen)
The American Ephemeris 2001-2010
The International Atlas, Expanded Sixth Edition (with Thomas C. Shanks)
The New American Ephemeris for the 20th Century, 1900-2000 at Midnight
The New American Ephemeris for the 20th Century, 1900-2000 at Noon

and Revisions to:
The American Ephemeris for the 20th Century, Revised 5th Edition
The American Ephemeris for the 21st Century, 2000-2050, at Midnight, Expanded Second Edition
The American Ephemeris for the 21st Century, 2000-2050, at Noon, Revised Second Edition
The Michelsen Book of Tables

CPSIA information can be obtained
at www.ICGtesting.com
Printed in the USA
LVHW101552160919
631227LV00008B/382/P

9 781934 976142